The USER'S™ WEBSTER *Dictionary*

A unique dictionary for home, school, and office that defines words in their typical contexts and provides examples of idiomatic usage

by

THOMAS M. PAIKEDAY

Chief Editor,
𝕿𝖍𝖊 𝕹𝖊𝖜 𝖄𝖔𝖗𝖐 𝕿𝖎𝖒𝖊𝖘 *Everyday Dictionary*,
The Penguin Canadian Dictionary, etc.

LEXICOGRAPHY, INC.
Toronto & New York

Copyright © 2000, Thomas M. Paikeday

Published by
Lexicography, Inc.
P.O. Box 91054
Toronto, Canada
M9C 2X0
Telephone: (905)371-2065

U.S. Address:
Lexicography, Inc.
2735 Princess Street
North Bellmore, NY 11710

All Rights Reserved. No part of this book may be reproduced in any form or by any electronic or mechanical means, including information storage and retrieval systems, without permission in writing from the publisher, except by reviewers who may quote brief passages in their reviews.

LIBRARY OF CONGRESS CATALOG CARD NUMBER: 98-67088

CANADIAN CATALOGUING IN PUBLICATION DATA
Main entry under title:
The User's™ Webster: a unique dictionary for home, school, and office that defines words in their typical contexts and provides examples of idiomatic usage

ISBN 0-920865-03-8 (pbk.)   ISBN 0-920865-02-X (bound)

1. English language – Dictionaries. I. Paikeday, Thomas M.

PE1628.U83 1998   423   C98-932440-8

Manufactured in Canada
10 9 8 7 6 5 4 3 2 1

THE USER'S™ WEBSTER

The experts say ...

"Here, at last, is a dictionary that is up to date, easy to use, and fun to read." – John Robert Colombo, author / editor of over 100 reference books.

"Your decades of experience, combined with your strong sense that a dictionary should be above all useful, have paid off . . . I almost wish I could do another dictionary, so as to steal your innovations." – Professor Emeritus Robert L. Chapman, Drew University, lexicographer since 1960.

"Its unique emphasis on collocations makes this dictionary particularly useful to new learners of English." – David B. Guralnik, Editor-in-Chief Emeritus, *Webster's New World* dictionaries, Simon & Schuster, Cleveland, OH.

"This works! And, it is a dictionary that will offer home, school, and professional readers and writers accurate definitions in context good for years to come." – Professor William R. Martin, Dept. of Education, George Mason University, Fairfax, VA.

THOMAS M. PAIKEDAY has been a full-time lexicographer of American and Canadian dictionaries since 1964. His important works include **The Winston Dictionaries of Canadian English** (Intermediate edition, 1969; Compact edition, 1970; Elementary edition, 1975), **The New York Times Everyday Dictionary**, 1982 (CD-ROM edition, Toronto, 1990), and **The Penguin Canadian Dictionary**, 1990. Paikeday pioneered the use of microcomputers for collecting and analyzing lexicographical data. He is also the author of **The Native Speaker Is Dead!** (Toronto & New York, 1985; Japanese edition, Tokyo, 1990), a discussion with Noam Chomsky and 40 other linguists, philosophers, psychologists, and lexicographers. He has written numerous articles on lexicography and has been a regular columnist on new words and meanings for the quarterly **English Today**, Cambridge, England.

✢

*This work is dedicated
to the memory of
my parents,
the first English experts in my life.*

✢

ACKNOWLEDGMENTS

I wish to thank Zac J. Zacharias for acting as my American collaborator since 1985.

Special thanks are due to John Robert Colombo for his editorial advice and help.

Thanks are also due to the following persons for helping in various ways: (1) commenting on the dictionary's original and revised manuscripts; (2) professional advice based on experience in book manufacturing, publishing, and marketing; (3) help with the computer, desk-top publishing software, and databases; (4) providing lexicographically useful insights into socio-linguistic behavior; (5) other kinds of personal and professional service that had a generally edifying influence and which enabled this lexicographer to cope with life and preserve his "mens sana in corpore sano."

Dennis Ablett ... John Bailey, Esq. ... Sister Jessica A. Bell, SSA ... Helen J. Brown ... G. Fred Browning ... Robert L. Chapman ... Nimmy & George Chavara ... Mary V. Chemparathy ... Sarah Cherian ... Rev. James Cherickal ... Paul Christophersen ... Anne & Ivan Chruszcz ... Maureen Clarke ... Donald Clement ... Ruth Colombo ... Stephen Conland ... Laura Cowan ... Dale Daniels ... Thomas David ... Brenda, Peter & Judith Desa ... Elizabeth Doktor ... Peter van Dorsser ... Robert Eagan ... Patricia Edlund ... Rev. Douglas Gordon, SJ ... Ruth Green ... David B. Guralnik ... Marion Hebb, Esq.... Rev. Hilario Fernandez ... M. V. George & Leelamma ... Jacquie Hunt ... Gita & Balu Iyer ... Rev. Thomas Kalarathil ... Rakesh Kalra ... Lissie & Thomas Kannarkat ... Marlene & Milan Karadza ... Marie Koprich ... Chandrika & Gopi Kumar ... Cathy & Michael Kuo ... Elsie & Kunju Kuriakose ... Joan & Sunny Kuriakose ... Jessie & Siby Kurian ... Suja & Sabu Kurian ... E. Lahnsteiner, MD ... Frank Liu ... William R. Martin ... Kathleen McAuley ... Wendy McCully ... Achamma & Delina Manjooran ... Sabina & C. V. Manuel ... Irene & Yasuhiro Matsumoto ... Frank M. McCormick ... G. Wesley McCullough ... Rev. L. D. Murphy, SJ ... John Nause ... Santha & Sunny Nallengara ... Mary Nambiaparambil ... Nurses of Holy Spirit Hospital, Bombay ... Santosh Pachikara ... Rev. Alexander Paikada, CMI ... Anne-Marie Paikeday ... Cecily & Cynthia Paikeday ... Mary Paikeday ... Maya & Mathai Paikeday ... Nancy & Tony Paikeday ... Gilbert Papali ... Paresh Parikh ... N. Parker-Jervis ... Rev. L. Patrick, OCD ... Rajan S. Prabhu, MD ... K. & A. Prasad ... Akshay Purohit ... Sister Reji, SMS ... Louie Rosario ... Mary Lynn & Marilyn Scott ... Brian Scrivo ... Gracy & Thomas Sebastian ... Eleanor Sese ... Heather Shiffman ... Laila & P. J. Simon ... Rev. T. N. Siqueira, SJ ... Bryan Sutherland ... Robert L. Thallukolly ... A. Thomas, MD ... Grace Thomas-Rajan ... Nick Phomasone ... John Townshend, CMA ... A. J. Varghese ... Leena & Reggie Varghese ... Ajit, Angie & Asha Vargis ... Murray G. Wanamaker ... Lynn Watt ... William J. Young ... Arthur M. Zsabo, Esq.

PREFACE

The User's™ Webster is a relatively new concept in lexicography. Its linguistic principles were enunciated at length in our Preface to *The Penguin Canadian Dictionary* (Toronto, 1990) and professionally reviewed in the 1990 *Dictionaries,* Journal of The Dictionary Society of North America. It was gratifying to see some of those principles, especially the role of abstract definitions, adopted in the 1995 *Cambridge International Dictionary of English.*

What is new to *The User's™ Webster* is the entering of the most common collocations of the language as lexical items, inventoried like words, phrases, pronunciations, derivatives, idioms, etc. Hence the plenitude of illustrative material, which may surprise those who are used to seeing only one phrase or sentence per definition.

This new dimension of the dictionary is based on the linguistic fact that, in the normal and natural course, people acquire languages mainly by listening and imitation. Children, as they grow older, understand, without the benefit of formal definitions, words heard in context and use them in grammatical sentences of their own with the appropriate parts of speech and inflectional forms.

The *User's™* dictionary formalizes this knowledge and, within its limited scope, offers a representative sample of the typical combinations of words and structures heard in everyday discourse. All careful users of the language, learners as well as learned, resort to dictionaries for guidance on matters of usage besides the more common uses of checking spelling and meaning.

Speaking of learners and learned, as Professor Claire Kramsch of UCLA recently stated in her guest column headed "The privilege of the nonnative speaker" (*PMLA,* May 1997), "Originally ... those who were born into a language were considered its native speakers, with grammatical intuitions that nonnative speakers did not have .... In the last ten years, linguists have started to examine [the native speaker] construct critically, beginning with Thomas Paikeday in his 1985 book *The Native Speaker Is Dead!"* (end of what may sound like blowing one's horn).

The User's™ Webster is based on the principle of mainstreaming the "linguistically challenged" with those considered normal. We think the native-speaker / foreign-learner distinction is somewhat invidious and therefore unnecessary.

Briefly, the following are the new features of this dictionary:

1. DECODING (finding the meaning): To help the user determine which definition each word being looked up falls under, especially when context is lacking, the common collocations of the defined word are given. For example, in the usages of **Georgian,** as in *a Georgian country house, drawl, four-poster, mansion; Georgian independence, nationalism; the Georgian period, style,* the dictionary helps the user determine which ones refer to the State of Georgia, the country of Georgia, and Georges of England. In the usages of **global** (*a global change, command, effect, epidemic, scale, strategy, view, war; global implications, issues, strategies*), which ones mean "worldwide" and which "all-inclusive"? Is a **live-in** *maid* necessarily in a *live-in relationship?*

2. ENCODING (using a word or meaning idiomatically): The listing of accepted combinations of a word should help the user use the word idiomatically, as **blue** (meaning "off-color"), which is used in *blue jokes, language, movies; "blue drama, prose, verse"* would not make sense. The same goes for **electric** *battery, current, guitar, heating, lighting, power,* etc. as distinguished from **electrical** *activity, appliance, discharge, engineer, equipment, industries,* etc.

3. SYNONYM DISCRIMINATION: To help the user use synonyms idiomatically, pairs like **frail** and **fragile** are defined and then distinguished by showing how they are used instead of giving supplementary synonym notes. Thus, we say: *a* **fragile** *condition, environment, toy, truce; fragile happiness,* but *a* **frail** *beauty, constitution, excuse, flower, smile, voice; frail hands, hopes, humanity; in frail health.* Similarly, triplets like **nutritional, nutritious,** and **nutritive:** *nutritional aspects, claims, data, deficiency, needs, value,* but *delicious and* **nutritious** *dishes; Spinach is very nutritious; a nutritious breakfast, diet, food, meal,* and **nutritive** *functions, plasma; the nutritive process.* See also **primeval, primitive,** and **primordial.**

4. ADJECTIVES, ATTRIBUTIVE AND PREDICATIVE: As clearly laid out in *A Comprehensive Grammar of the English Language* (Randolph Quirk, et al., Longman, 1985), criteria for adjectives are: (a) attributive use; (b) predicative use with copula *seem;* (c) pre-modification by *very;* (d) comparability. We have labeled *adj.* only adjectives that meet the first two criteria; these (which we call true adjectives) form the vast majority.

However, an adjective like **possessed** in the sense of "having" as in *a woman possessed of initiative,* or "controlled" as in *possessed with fury* and *possessed by missionary zeal* cannot be used attributively, as in *a possessed person.* In *a possessed person* or *She is possessed,* the word is used as an *adj.* meaning "controlled by an evil spirit." We have tried to distinguish such usages by labeling predicative adjectives (the first two of the above examples) *adjp.* The *adja.* (attributive adjective) label is used for adjectives like **piecemeal** as in *piecemeal changes, operations, reforms; a piecemeal approach, expansion, process; in a piecemeal fashion.*

Language being a changing entity, an adjective that is attributive today may gain predicative use tomorrow, as **fraught** in the senses of "very tense" and "worrisome." Since the late sixties (cf. *The Oxford English Dictionary,* Second Edition), usages such as *a controversy that is passionate and fraught; a fraught atmosphere, issue, situation* have become acceptable English.

5. COLLOCATIONS AND STRUCTURES: (a) What modifier to use, as before a noun such as **comeback** ("recovery"), as in *a big, major, quick, strong comeback.* (b) What nouns it may modify, as in *comeback kid, plan, trail.* (c) What verbs to use with this noun, as *to make, plan, stage a comeback,* etc. Often a user may know that **differences** (in the sense of "disagreements") may be *settled,* but wants to know what alternative words are available. The thesaurus gives *conclude, confirm, decide, determine,* and *judge* as synonyms for **settle,** but verbs that may be idiomatically used with **differences** are *compose, reconcile, resolve, set aside,* and *thrash out.* (d) The various structures in which **cinch** ("something easy to do") or **cold turkey** ("abruptly") is used. (e) What prepositions to use with a word such as **gloom,** as in *gloom about* or *over the future of the environment.*

6. DEADWOOD: As in avoiding abstract definitions, we eschew entries for words that do not exist in current English; e.g., **sophisticate** as a verb. Only the noun **sophisticate** and adjective **sophisticated** are used in current English; we have tried to do justice to those uses; the same for **straiten.**

7. USABLE PRONUNCIATIONS: We use a pronunciation system that is based on common English spellings that the user is familiar with (without using unnecessary and un-English respellings like "rayj" for **rage** and "stohr" for **store**) instead of an abstract system of diacritical marks or the International Phonetic Alphabet which require a key for decoding. (A full explanation of

this spelling-based pronunciation system is given in the author's "Who Needs IPA?" in *English Today*, January 1993, Cambridge, U.K.).

8. VOCABULARY: *The User's™ Webster* is a revised and expanded edition of our *New York Times Everyday Dictionary* (New York, 1982). The vocabulary we have added has been drawn from a CD-ROM database of hundreds of contemporary books and journals published in the U.S. in the 1990s, supplemented by a smaller selection of Canadian and British publications. The dictionary should not need revision for at least another decade, when minimal changes will be required. (More about this in our "O Corpora!", *Lexicographica*, Tübingen, August 1992).

Occasionally we have gone out of our way to satisfy special interests, as in including four-letter words. With all due respect, in a professional job done for our friend Bob Ilson, editor of the Oxford *International Journal of Lexicography* at the time, one positive comment that his reviewer of *The Penguin Canadian Dictionary* had to make was the elevation of her "cunt-fuck-shit" trinity as the touchstone of a 75,000-entry dictionary meant for schools (*IJL*, Autumn 1994). Kathy Rooney of Bloomsbury Publishing will not miss those and similar taboo words in this work meant for a wider audience. However, user discretion is advised.

In this connection, users may want to compare *The User's™ Webster* with so-called learner's dictionaries and dictionaries of word combinations in regard to practical value and usefulness.

The User's™ Webster should come in handy for all the uses that may be reasonably expected of dictionaries of this size and price range by a variety of users. We earnestly hope this will be found to be a truly user-friendly dictionary. The streaks of humor appearing in it (as at **disposal, last word,** and **wink,** though tastes may differ) merely show that the English-speaking people are not a humorless lot.

The User's™ Webster caps a 35-year career devoted to North American lexicography. Researching, compiling, and producing this dictionary has been a true labor of love.

Thomas M. Paikeday

USER'S GUIDE

The User's™ Webster is designed for use without explanatory notes, pronunciation keys, and such aids. The user should be able to pick up the dictionary cold and find the desired information if it is within the scope of the book. However, a few tips on some of the main features of this dictionary are offered below.

I. WHAT ENTRIES TO FIND

Most commonly used generic words and phrases are entered in this dictionary.

All entries are shown in boldface type. Entries include main entries, or headwords, in **sans serif** boldface and subentries in both **regular** and *italic* boldface, as illustrated below. Subentries are phrases, idioms, undefined derivatives, and different parts of speech of the main entry. Examples:

Main entries or headwords: **green, greenback, greenbean, greenbelt,** etc.

An example of seven boldfaced subentries under **green** *n.*:

adj. green(s) fees ...**3** something green: *salad* **greens**.... —*adj.* **1** of the color of greenery: ... *The* **green card** *is proof*.... —*v.* make or become green ... *n.: the greening of deserts..* —**green.ness** *n.*

II. HOW TO FIND AN ENTRY

(a) First check the word or phrase you are looking up as a main entry in its strict alphabetical place; e.g., **limited** between **limit** and **limo; maid of honor** between **maid-in-waiting** and **maidservant; spell checker** between **spellbind** and **spelling.**

(b) If a phrase is not found as above, check for it among the boldfaced items included under its first component as main entry; e.g., **last laugh** under the main entry **last, married quarters** under **married,** and **toast of the town** under **toast.**

(c) If a phrase is still not found, check it under other suspected headwords; e.g., **no way, shape, or form** under **shape** rather than **no** or **way.** Such multi-word idioms may also be found as illustrative material under its other keywords. Thus a variant such as **any manner, shape, or form** may be found under **form.** Again, **on the spur of the moment,** which is defined under **spur,** is further illustrated in italics under **moment.**

III. SPELLINGS & VARIANTS

American spelling is normally used in *The User's™ Webster.*

Canadian spellings are shown as variants, followed by the label *Cdn.*; e.g., **centre, colour, defence, hydro, equalled, equalling.**

Peculiarly British words and spellings are shown with the label *Brit.;* e.g., **analyse, bonny, brolly, jewellery, tyre.**

IV. SYLLABICATION

Syllabication is shown for a word at its first entry as a headword. The syllabication of hyphenated words like **capital-intensive** and open compounds like **capital city** should be looked up under their component words.

Syllable division in spellings uses a different system from that used in pronunciations, as in the second pronunciation of **at.ta.ché** (at.uh.SHAY, uh.TASH.ay). This is explained in the next section.

V. PRONUNCIATION SYSTEM

(a) SYLLABLE DIVISION: As a general rule, a syllable division is made: (1) after the vowel if the vowel is long, diphthongized, or unstressed, the resulting syllable being called an "open" syllable; (2) after the consonant if the vowel is short and carries a stress, which results in a "closed" syllable. Examples: a.*back*, *ab*.a.cus, *ab*.ra.ca.*dab*.ra ... ze.ro, Zo.ro.*as*.tri.an, in which the underlined syllables are closed, the others being open. This is only the most general of the rules of syllabication, but it is useful to know it explicitly.

(b) The user is assumed to have acquired a familiarity with the basic sound-spelling patterns of English, as in the most common words of the language. No pronunciation is indicated for sounds whose spelling is such that only one pronunciation is normally possible. Such are:

VOWELS:

The vowel sounds of: *at, sail, lake, air; bed, day; big, deep, deer, hide, bye, fire; on, cause, law, more; bone, oh, how, our, boy, oil; ah, but, poor, cure; uh, burn.*

Vowel sounds in certain phonetic contexts or positions: (1) words ending in *-oal, -oat, -old, -olk, -olt,* etc. have the long "o" or diphthong; (2) words and syllables ending in *-ete, -ew, -ool, -oon, -oop, -oose, -ooth, -ude, -uke, -ume, -ute,* etc. have long vowels, with the exception of *wool;* (3) words and syllables ending in *-ee, -o,* and *-oo* are long or diphthongized.

CONSONANTS: The initial consonant sounds of: *bad, can, chair, dog, fat, go, ghost, guess, guy, hat, just, keep, lake, make, name, page, quick, red, same, take, the, thin, very, wait, what, yes, zoo.*

These and other rules of English pronunciation are taken as implicitly known to users who have attained the primary-school (Grade 8) level of proficiency in reading and speaking.

However, some pronunciations are made more explicit by additional helps, as in (awl.THOH, "TH" as in "the"), (ES.theet, "th" as in "thin"), (uh.LOOF, long "OO"), (buh.BOOSH.kuh, short or long "OO"), and (uh.DUCE, *rhyme:* produce).

(c) ACCENTUATION

Several levels of stress may be noted in English words when they are studied in isolation.

Thus, **com.mu.ni.ty** could be analyzed as having its stresses distributed on the basis of relative force in this order of syllables: 3-1-4-2. In actual use, however, one rarely hears the main stress placed on the second syllable. In **com.mu.ni.ca.tion,** the main stress is supposed to be on the fourth syllable, but it is frequently placed on the second. Sentence stress partly explains this variation between what is correct when words are studied in isolation and how words are pronounced in actual, continuous speech.

Most dictionaries routinely indicate a primary and a secondary stress for words of three syllables or more, as in **ac.cen.tu.ate** which is shown with a primary stress on the second syllable and a secondary stress on the last.

The User's™ *Webster* uses a more simplified system of accentuation, as explained below.

(d) TO READ OFF THE PRONUNCIATIONS

1. A stressed syllable is shown in capitals.

2. A word of two syllables is assumed to have its stress on the first syllable if it is left unmarked for stress, as **milk.shake** (MILK.shake) whose accentuation and pronunciation are taken as self-explanatory.

3. In multisyllabic words, only the main stress is normally indicated, secondary stresses being considered variable, as explained above.

4. A second stress, however, is indicated using capitals when there are more than two syllables preceding the main stress and the syllable with the greater stress may be in doubt.

Thus, **u.til.i.tar.i.an** (yoo.TIL.uh.TAIR.ee.un) is shown with the second syllable in capitals as well as the fourth. This kind of double stressing is normally not required when all but one of the syllables have neutral vowels, as in **et.y.mo.log.i.cal** (et.uh.muh.LOJ.uh.cul), in which only the first syllable has a full vowel and which, therefore, is the only other syllable besides the fourth that may be pronounced with a stress. The fullness of the vowel should give the syllable any stress that is required for good enunciation.

5. The letter group (uh) always stands for the unstressed neutral vowel, also called schwa, as in the first syllable of **a.bove** (uh.BUV), the middle syllable of **syl.la.ble** (SIL.uh.bul), and the last syllable of **i.de.a** (eye.DEE.uh).

6. Letter groups with (u) plus another consonant, as in **ob.tain** (ub.TAIN), **ran.dom** (RAN.dum), **rang.er** (RAIN.jur), **ray.ment** (RAY.munt), etc. are also normally pronounced with a neutral vowel if they are not shown stressed. Exceptions would be when a syllable becomes more prominent or gets a secondary stress because of its existence as a separate word.

Thus, "-nut," the second syllable of **do.nut** (DOH.nut), could be pronounced either with a neutral sound or as if it rhymed with **nut**. But the second syllable of **rib.bon** (RIB.un) cannot rhyme with **bun** because "-bon" is not a word or word element. See also **asset, convent, despot, product, shogun, slogan,** and **surplus.**

7. The letter group (zh) is used for the sound of the "s" in *measure, usual, vision,* etc.; the sound of "g" in *beige, regime,* etc.; the sound of "j" in *jabot, joual,* etc.; and the sound of "z" in *azure, seizure,* etc.

8. All other pronunciations should be read using the most common English sounds of the syllables used in the respelling. Thus, **live.long** (LIV.long), **live.ly** (LIVE.lee), **rind** (RINED), etc.

9. When an alternative pronunciation or the pronunciation of a derivative is shown in abbreviated form, as in **mil.i.tar.i.ly** (-TAIR.uh.lee), the full pronunciation should be read as (mil.uh.TAIR.uh.lee) based on the previous word **mil.i.tar.y** (MIL.uh.tair.ee). As explained above, the relative force between the stresses of the first and third syllables of a word like **mil.i.tar.i.ly** is of mainly academic importance to the dictionary user.

VI. MEANING
KINDS OF DEFINITIONS

The User's™ Webster has five kinds of definitions.

1. Formal definitions. Most of the formal definitions are of the following type:

ice cream *n.* a frozen dessert of sweetened and flavored cream.

2. Informal definitions. Note how **classmate** and **classroom** are included in the fourth definition of class:

class . . . 4 a group of students, or **classmates,** instructed together, usu. in the same room, or **classroom.**

3. Meaning in context. Sometimes an entry is defined in the context provided by an illustrative phrase or sentence, as in the definition of **fun:**

fun *n.* amusement or what provides amusement; sport: *Skating is fun; We had a lot of fun skating; Children throw snowballs **for fun** or **in fun**; Guy likes to **poke fun at** or **make fun of** Cora's walk; The rain spoiled the fun; Life is not all **fun and games**.*

Note how **for fun, in fun, poke fun at, make fun of,** and **fun and games** have been defined in actual contexts of usage.

4. Meaning by paraphrase. Sometimes a paraphrase is given in parentheses right where a word may call for explanation of its precise meaning, as in the definition of **whirl**:

—*v.* swing round and round rapidly and continuously, as leaves caught in the wind or a car gone out of control: *Dancing couples whirled about the room; He whirled her away in his new sports car; Her head whirled* (= She felt dizzy), *and she passed out.*

5. Meaning by illustration. After a word has been formally defined and illustrated in one part of speech, it is often redundant to give a formal definition of the same meaning in a different part of speech. Note how the *adja.* subentry **round-trip** follows the noun definition:

round trip *n.* a trip to and back from a place; *adv.: We drove 884 miles round trip from Atlanta to Orlando; adja.: a **round-trip** fare, flight, ticket.*

VII. GRAMMAR & USAGE
(a) SYNTAX

The syntax of the words entered in *The User's*™ *Webster* can be studied almost exhaustively by examining the illustrative material given in italics under each entry. Since the natural process of learning a language is by listening and imitation, no attempt is made to set out the grammar of words in formal terms except for the labeling of categories of words and brief notes about their idiomatic usage enclosed within parentheses.

Those interested in formal grammar, however, can find the information they want by examining the illustrative examples. Thus, the examples given under **consider** should yield the grammatical information about the word, as given in parentheses below:

They considered her application [transitive use] ... *took time to consider* [intransitive] ... *They considered it briefly, carefully, favorably, religiously, seriously* [five modifying adverbs] ... *considered her intelligent, qualified, a genius* [object of verb may be an adjective, participial adjective, or a noun with definite article] ... *They had considered him (to be) not promotable* [noun/pronoun plus adjective as object, with optional "to be"] ... *They considered her for his job* [object: noun/pronoun plus prepositional phrase] ... *considered her as his replacement* [object: noun/pronoun plus noun phrase with "as"] ... *He considered resigning, his alternatives, where to go* [three kinds of verb objects: "-ing" form, noun, "where" clause] ... *They said he had done a good job, **all things considered*** [idiom and how it is used] ... *He had done a good job, **considering*** [another verbal idiom, used with implied object] ... *an especially good job considering his inexperience, considering that he was inexperienced* [how the idiom is used followed by noun or noun clause] ... *That was their **considered** opinion* [a fixed form of the headword used as participipial adjective].

(b) PARTS OF SPEECH

The part of speech of each entry is given using the abbreviations listed following this Guide.

Two new part-of-speech labels show distinctions in the use of adjectives.

(1) *adja.* stands for "attributive adjective," as **crying** in *a crying fit, jag, room, shame, spell, towel.* Such adjectives may only be used as modifiers before nouns.

(2) *adjp.* stands for "predicative adjective," as **bound** in *They're bound for home; morally bound; bound by marriage vows; It's bound to rain today; homeward bound,* etc. Such adjectives may only be used following a linking verb such as *is* or *seem.*

The above labels are normally used in cases judged significant or when more than one example is given.

The label *adj.* is used only for true adjectives that can be used as both *adja.* and *adjp.* These form the vast majority of adjectives.

(c) HOW TO USE WORDS & MEANINGS

Suppose you are not sure how to use the word "root" referring to someone having settled down in a country. At the entry **root**, you see these sentences: *Plants strike* or *take root in the soil; We have struck root* or *roots* (= settled down) *in Florida.* This should tell you that *strike* (not *put down, send, take,* etc.) is the word that goes with "root" in the usage you have in mind and that either "root" or "roots" would be correct. You only have to pattern your sentence after the one given in the dictionary.

(d) CONTRASTIVE EXAMPLES OF USAGE

Note the following sets of illustrative examples:

notwithstanding *prep.:* ... *The party went on notwithstanding the lateness of the hour.* —**conj.:** *The party went on notwithstanding the hour was late.* —**adv.:** *The lateness of the hour notwithstanding, the party went on.*

sake *n.* ... : *For our children's sake, please stop arguing;* **For the sake of** *our children, please stop arguing; Please stop arguing,* **for goodness sake;** [for added force] **For Heaven's sake,** *please stop arguing. I'm saying this for both our sakes, for your sake and mine. Let's not* **argue for arguing's sake** (= because we like to argue). *Let's suppose,* **for argument's sake** (= as a starting point), *that life does exist on Mars.*

taboo *adj.* ... : *To Muslims, food is taboo before sunset during Ramadan.* —**n.:** ... *Eating before sunset is under a rigid taboo.* —**v.:** ... *Eating before sunset is tabooed.*

It may look as though the dictionary is repeating itself. But the purpose is to illustrate various parts of speech and usages of the same word using sentences with minimal change of meaning so as to bring out grammatical and usage differences contrastively.

VIII. MISCELLANEOUS MECHANICS

(a) PARENTHESES

Besides obvious purposes like enclosing pronunciation respellings, parentheses are used in special ways as listed below:

1. To give brief definitions within illustrative examples, as in the definition of **dollar for dollar** below. Sometimes the brief definition is preceded by a label such as *Slang for* and *Informal for* as in the second sentence below:

dol.lar (DOLL.ur) *n.* **1** the basic money unit in the U.S., Canada, Australia, and other countries: ... *to feel, look, smell like a million dollars* (*Informal for* splendid); ***Dollar for dollar*** (= *proportionately to the money involved*) *this car is second to none.*

Sometimes a brief definition or explanation in italics is run on with the rest of the sentence in italics if it can be done without a break in the syntax, as in the examples below:

*An **educated guess** (based on some knowledge of the facts) is likely to be right.*

*Marsupials are **pouched** animals (that have an external pouch for carrying their young).*

The parentheses are not dispensed with because, strictly speaking, what is in parentheses is redundant when you consider the meaning of **educated guess** and **pouched** respectively.

2. To telescope two definitions into one, as in the following:

East Asian *n. & adj.* (a person) of or from the region comprising E. China, Japan, North and South Korea, Taiwan, and nearby islands.

Here the noun definition should be read as "a person of or from...." and the adjective definition is the part outside the parentheses: "of or from...."

run *v.* (cause) to move at a pace faster than walking.

The above should be read as two definitions: "cause to move at a pace faster than walking" and "move at a pace faster than walking." The two definitions have been telescoped into one to save space.

3. To show alternative structures, as in the following:

de.sir.ous (di.ZYE.rus) *adj.* desiring or wishing: *A mother is desirous of her children's good; She is desirous that they (should) do well in life.*

In the second sentence, *should* is placed in parentheses to show that both "She is desirous that they do well in life" and "She is desirous that they should do well in life" are correct.

Other examples:

Boys ganged (up) together at the corner.

in (or **out of**) **gear** connected (or not connected) to the motor; hence working (or not working) properly.

gift of (the) gab

lead someone (on) a merry chase.

4. To enclose short grammar and usage notes and other explanations. Square brackets are used for this purpose, as in the following entries:

a.bed (uh.BED) *adj. & adv.* [literary use] in bed: *to lie abed of a Sunday morning.*

a.ghast (uh.GAST) *adjp.* [used after its noun] horrified: *She was aghast; Everyone stood aghast at the sight.*

em.cee (EM.see) *n. Informal* [short form] master of ceremonies.

(b) PREPOSITIONS IN ITALICS

Giving prepositions in italics, as in the following examples, is another space-saving device. The definition itself shows how to use the headword, so no illustrative sentence is necessary. Thus **evict,** as shown below, should be used in a sentence like "to evict someone from his house," not "out of his house."

evict *v.* oust or discharge a tenant *from* a house or land by legal process.

moon *v.* spend time or wander *about* or *around* idly.

mull *v.* ponder *over* a problem, proposal, etc.

sally *v.* go *forth* or set *out,* as if to attack.

scuffle *v.* to struggle *with* someone at close quarters.

(c) SMALL CAPITALS

Small capitals indicate cross-references which should be looked up for a formal definition or for more information. Thus:

apices See APEX.
holloware ... cf. FLATWARE.
—kind of *Informal.* same as SORT OF.
should *pt.* of SHALL.

(d) QUOTED WORDS

Occasionally, you may find a word or phrase given in quotes instead of boldface as you might expect. Such quotes are used to show that the quoted word or phrase is outside the scope of this dictionary to be entered and defined fully. However, the word or phrase is being used to explain a meaning because of its relevance in the particular context in which it appears. Thus:

HIV ... "human immunodeficiency virus," the cause of AIDS.

monosodium glutamate ... also called "MSG."

mullet ... an edible fish of warm waters, esp. the "gray" and "red" mullets.

nelson ... a wrestling hold in which leverage is applied with one arm ("half nelson") or both ("full nelson") passed from behind....

(e) ROMAN "OR"

The roman "or" is used between italicized words and phrases that may be used as alternatives, as in:

alley ... *Stamp-collecting is not up* or *down my alley.*

impotent ... *that would make* or *render nuclear weapons impotent....*

net ... *to cast* or *spread a net for fish.*

--------- ☺ ---------

$100 PRIZE
FOR FEEDBACK

The Publisher will pay US$100 to the user who sends in the most useful comments on *The User's™ Webster*. Comments must be received at the address given below by Dec. 31, 2000. Everyone who writes in enclosing a self-addressed envelope (a stamped envelope if from the U.S. or Canada) will be informed of the results of the contest. Topics on which comments are invited: (1) Where did you purchase the dictionary and what did you pay? (2) What was your main consideration in choosing *The User's™ Webster* – price, number of pages, typography, display of information, the information itself? (3) What features of *The User's™ Webster* do you find particularly useful? (4) What other dictionaries have you used? (5) Is English your first language? (6) Did you notice any errors or omissions in the dictionary? (7) Do you have any suggestions for making *The User's™ Webster* more useful? Please write to:

**Lexicography, Inc.
P.O. Box 91054
Toronto, Canada
M9C 2X0**

Comments and questions about the dictionary may also be sent directly to the lexicographer by e-mail:

t.paikeday@sympatico.ca
tpaikeday@hotmail.com

ABBREVIATIONS
USED IN THE DICTIONARY

adj. adjective
adja. attributive adjective
adjp. predicative adjective
adv. adverb
art. article
Brit. British
C. Central
Cdn. Canadian
comb.form. combining form
comp. comparative
conj. conjunction
cpd. compound
def. definition
esp. especially
fem. feminine
indef. indefinite
indic. indicative
interj. interjection
masc. masculine
n. noun
neut. neuter
part. participle
pers. person
pl. plural
pp. past participle
pres. present
pron. pronoun
pt. past tense
Scot. Scottish
sing. singular
superl. superlative
usu. usually
v. verb
viz. namely
superl. superlative
usu. usually
v. verb
viz. namely

A or **a** (AY) *n.* **A's** or **a's** **1** the first letter of the English alphabet. **2** [used to indicate the first, highest, or best of a group]: *He got an A on the test; grade A eggs; an A1 student; a company with a triple-A credit rating.* —***comb.form.*** shaped like an A: *an A-frame house; an A-line skirt; an A-tent.*

a (AY, uh) *indef.art.* **1** a single thing but not a particular one: *a bird, book, boy.* **2** [used with "a," to refer to a single group]: *a lot of books; a few boys.* **3** [used with "many" before singular nouns for plural meaning]: *many a book* (= many books). **4** [used with "of"]: *birds of a feather* (= of the same kind). —***prep.*** each: *twice a week.*

a- *prefix.* **1** on: *afire, ashore; The house is a-building* (= being built); *The times are a-changing* (= undergoing change). **2** not: *amoral, asexual, asocial.*

aard.vark (ARD.vark) *n.* a S. African anteater.

ab- *prefix.* away; from: *abduct, aberrant, abnormal.*

a.back (uh.BAC) *adv.*: *I was **taken aback*** (= startled) *by the announcement; Her answer took him aback.*

ab.a.cus (AB.uh.cus) *n.* **-cus.es** or **-ci** (-sye) a frame of parallel rods holding beads, used for calculating.

a.baft (uh.BAFT) *adv.* at or toward the back part of a ship. —***prep.*** behind.

ab.a.lo.ne (ab.uh.LOH.nee) *n.* a large, edible shellfish whose ear-shaped shell is used for making ornaments.

a.ban.don (uh.BAN.dun) *v.* give up or desert: *the order to abandon ship; He abandoned his car in the snow; He abandoned it to its fate; She abandoned her naval career for one in the army; to abandon oneself to despair, grief, pleasure;* ***adj.***: *an **abandoned** car, claim, goal, mine, project, quarry, site, well; The orphans felt abandoned.* —*n.* carefree manner: *She sang with abandon; to spend money with gay, gleeful, joyous, merry, mindless, wild abandon; He drove with reckless abandon.* —**a.ban.don.ment** *n.*

a.base (uh.BACE) *v.* **a.bas.es, a.based, a.bas.ing** lower or humble: *He abased himself before the king;* ***adj.***: *She felt humiliated and **abased**.* —**a.base.ment** *n.*

a.bashed (uh.BASHT) *adj.* ashamed: *He looked slightly abashed.*

a.bate (uh.BATE) *v.* **a.bates, a.bat.ed, a.bat.ing** make or become less: *The storm has abated; drugs to abate pain.* —**a.bate.ment** *n.*: *a tax abatement.*

ab.at.toir (AB.ut.war) *n.* a place where animals are killed for market.

ab.ba.cy (AB.uh.see) *n.* **-cies** (the term of) office of an abbot.

ab.bé (AB.ay) *n.* a French priest, originally only an abbot.

ab.bess (AB.is) *n.* the head, or Mother Superior, of a convent or group of nuns.

ab.bey (AB.ee) *n.* **ab.beys** a monastery or convent or its church.

ab.bot (AB.ut) *n.* the head, or Father Superior, of a group of monks, usu. living in an abbey.

ab.bre.vi.ate (uh.BREE.vee.ate) *v.* **-ates, -at.ed, -at.ing** shorten: *to abbreviate a career, program, phrase, story, visit; "Professor" is abbreviated to "Prof.";* ***adj.***: *an **abbreviated** edition, list, skirt.* —**ab.bre.vi.a.tion** (-AY.shun) *n.*

ABC *n.* **ABC's** or **ABCs** **1** the alphabet: *as easy* or *simple as ABC.* **2** basics or fundamentals: *the ABC's of driving a car.*

ab.di.cate (AB.duh.cate) *v.* **-cates, -cat.ed, -cat.ing** give up a position, power, right, etc.: *King Edward VIII abdicated in 1936; He abdicated the throne; to abdicate one's responsibilities.* —**ab.di.ca.tion** (-CAY.shun) *n.*

ab.do.men (AB.duh.mun, ab.DOH.mun) *n.* **1** the human belly. **2** the last segment of an insect's body. —**ab.dom.i.nal** (ab.DOM.uh.nul) *adj.*: *abdominal pain.* —**abdominals** *n.pl.* abdominal muscles.

ab.duct (ab.DUCT) *v.* take away someone by force; kidnap: *The infant was abducted from its home.* —**ab.duc.tion** *n.* —**ab.duc.tor** *n.*

a.beam (uh.BEEM) *adv.* by the side (of a ship); abreast: *abeam of us.*

a.bed (uh.BED) *adjp. & adv.* [literary] in bed: *to lie abed of a Sunday morning.*

ab.er.rant (ab.ER.unt) *adj.* not normal in behavior; deviant.

ab.er.ra.tion (ab.uh.RAY.shun) *n.* **1** deviation: *a mental aberration.* **2** distortion: *Optical aberrations cause bad focusing.*

a.bet (uh.BET) *v.* **a.bets, a.bet.ted, a.bet.ting** encourage in doing wrong: *to aid and abet a thief; The rumors were aided and abetted by leaks from confidential sources.* —**a.bet.tor** or **a.bet.ter** *n.*

a.bey.ance (uh.BAY.unce) *n.* suspension: *a law held in abeyance; a rule that has fallen into abeyance* (= disuse).

ab.hor (ub.HOR) *v.* **ab.hors, ab.horred, ab.hor.ring** to hate intensely: *He abhors getting drunk; abhors drunkenness; "Nature abhors a vacuum"* (= An absolute vacuum cannot exist in nature). —**ab.hor.rence** *n.*: *People hold drug dealers in abhorrence.* —**ab.hor.rent** *adj.*:

abide / abort

Child abuse is abhorrent to human nature.
a.bide (uh.BIDE) *v.* **a.bides,** *pt. & pp.* **a.bode** or **a.bid.ed, a.bid.ing** **1** put up with a person or thing: *He's so nasty no one can abide him; People like Mother Teresa can't abide human misery.* **2** observe or obey: *You can rely on him to* **abide by** *the rules; to abide by an agreement, commitment, decision, demand, requirement, the truth, one's promises, someone's advice, wishes; adj.: a* **law-abiding** *citizen.* **3** *pt.* **abode** stay: *"Abide with me"; adj.: an* **abiding** (= lasting) *belief, commitment, concern, faith, interest, love; abiding happiness, optimism, pride.*

a.bil.i.ty (uh.BIL.i.tee) *n.* **-ties** power or skill: *the human being's ability to think; a woman of great ability; He did the job* **to the best of his ability** (= as well as he could); *to appreciate, demonstrate, display, recognize, show ability; creative, exceptional, innate, natural, outstanding, remarkable ability.*

ab.ject (AB.ject) *adj.* low or degrading: *to make an abject apology; to live in abject poverty; abject submission;* **ab.ject.ly** *adv.*

ab.jure (ab.JOOR) *v.* **-jures, -jured, -jur.ing** solemnly give up: *to abjure one's faith, an ideal, terrorism.* —**ab.jur.er** *n.* —**ab.jur.a.tor.y** (-tor.ee) *adj.* —**ab.ju.ra.tion** (ab.juh.RAY.shun) *n.*

ab.late (ab.LATE) *v.* **-lates, -lat.ed, -lat.ing** remove; carry or wear away; **ab.la.tion** *n.*

ab.la.tive (AB.luh.tiv) *n.* a grammatical form in some languages meaning "from, by, away from" something: *In "ab ovo"* (= from the egg), *ovo is ablative; adj.: in the ablative case.*

a.blaze (uh.BLAZE) *adjp.* on fire: *a house set ablaze; He was* **ablaze with** (= very excited with) *fury.*

a.ble (AY.bul) *adj.* **a.bler, a.blest** **1** having the means or power: *The child is able to walk by itself; She's able and willing to work.* **2** skilful or talented: *an able lawyer, leader, ruler.* —**a.bly** (-blee) *adv.*

-able *adj. suffix.* that can be done, as specified: *applicable, avoidable, bearable, bendable, readable.*

able-bodied *adj.* having a healthy body: *an able-bodied citizen, man, woman, worker; An* **able-bodied** (or **able**) *seaman* ranks above an ordinary seaman.

a.bloom (uh.BLOOM, long "OO") *adjp.* in flower: *Trees are abloom in early spring.*

ab.lu.tions (ab.LOO.shuns) *n.pl.* ceremonial washing or bathing.

ably See ABLE.

ab.ne.gate (AB.nuh.gate) *v.* **-gates, -gat.ed, -gat.ing** deny to oneself; surrender. —**ab.ne.ga.tion** (-GAY.shun) *n.*

ab.nor.mal (ab.NOR.mul) *adj.* not normal: *abnormal behavior, circumstances, weather; Snow at this time of year is abnormal; an abnormal condition, growth, response.* —**ab.nor.mal.ly** *adv.* —**ab.nor.mal.i.ty** (ab.nor.MAL.i.tee) *n.: congenital abnormalities.*

a.board (uh.BORD) *adv. & prep.* on, onto, or in a ship, train, plane, etc.: *All aboard! Come aboard! to climb, go aboard; to be aboard a bus, flight, jet, ship, train; Welcome aboard! She was brought aboard* (= appointed) *as anchor for the evening news.*

a.bode (uh.BODE) *pt. & pp.* OF ABIDE. —*n.* where one lives; dwelling: *Al took up his abode here in the 1920s; the eternal, heavenly abode of the souls of the dead; a man of no fixed abode* (= address).

a.bol.ish (uh.BOL.ish) *v.* do away with a custom, practice, or institution: *to abolish censorship, the death penalty, laws, monopolies, rights, rules, slavery, taxes.*

ab.o.li.tion (ab.uh.LISH.un) *n.* an abolishing: *the abolition of atomic weapons, capital punishment, slavery.* —**a.bol.ish.ment** *n.* abolishing: *the abolishment of controls, duties, restrictions.* —**ab.o.li.tion.ist** *n. & adj.*

A-bomb *n.* an atomic bomb.

a.bom.i.na.ble (uh.BOM.uh.nuh.bul) *adj.* loathsome or disgusting: *an abominable crime; The* **Abominable Snowman** *is said to be a humanoid, hairy beast that lives in the Himalayas;* **a.bom.i.na.bly** *adv.*

a.bom.i.nate (uh.BOM.uh.nate) *v.* **-nates, -nat.ed, -nat.ing** hate intensely. —**a.bom.i.na.tion** (-NAY.shun) *n.: He thinks TV dinners that pack little meat and sell for high prices are an abomination.*

ab.o.rig.i.nal (ab.uh.RIJ.uh.nul) *adj.* **1** having existed first in a place: *aboriginal art, languages, people, plants, rocks, titles.* **2** having to do with aboriginals: *aboriginal claims, culture, issues, rights.* —*n.* a member of an aboriginal people; also **ab.o.rig.i.ne** (-uh.nee): *the Australian aborigines.*

a.born.ing (uh.BORN.ing) *adv.* [literary] while being born or produced: *an independence movement that died aborning.*

a.bort (uh.BORT) *v.* end a plan or process before completion: *to abort a flight on takeoff; to abort a child, coup, fetus, mission, plan, pregnancy; a woman who has aborted; The revolution aborted*

abortion / absentee

(= ended) *in a few days.*

a.bor.tion (uh.BOR.shun) *n.* termination of a pregnancy: *to get, have, induce an abortion; to do* or *perform an abortion on a woman; a therapeutic abortion; legalized abortion; women wanting abortion on demand; spontaneous abortion* (= miscarriage); **adj***a.*: *an abortion clinic, drug, lobby, pill; the abortion issue, question; abortion-rights activists.*

a.bor.tion.ist *n.* [unfavorable use] one who favors or effects the abortion of unwanted fetuses.

a.bor.tive (uh.BOR.tiv) *adj.* that fails to succeed: *an abortive attempt, coup, effort.*

a.bound (uh.BOWND) *v.* have or exist in large numbers: *Fish abound in this lake; The lake abounds in* or *with fish.*

a.bout (uh.BOWT) *prep. & adv.* **1** near or nearly; around: *I saw him about here; We are about 2 km from the river; It is about time; The guests were seated about* (on the lawn); *It was late when she set about* (= started) *getting dinner ready.* **2** concerning: *Tell me about her; How about that? What's it all about? Let's be quick about it* (= Let's do it quickly). **—adj***p.* **1** active: *He is up and about at 6 a.m. every day.* **2** ready: *She was about to leave; He's* **not about to** (= is very unwilling to) *resign.*

about-face *n.* a reversal, esp. of attitude: *The politician did an about-face after the election.* **—***v.* **-fac.es, -faced, -fac.ing** turn to face the opposite way.

a.bove (uh.BUV) *prep.* higher, earlier, or more than: *We are flying above the clouds; We value honor above wealth;* **Above all,** *we try to be honest.* **—adv.**: *See page 10 above; a kite flying above.* **—***adj.*: *the above words; The words above are to be deleted; It's 40 degrees above* (= above zero). **—***n.*: *The orders came from above* (= from the superiors); *none of the above* (= above-mentioned words, items, etc.).

a.bove.board (uh.buv.BORD) *adj. & adv.* without dishonesty: *She's always quite open and aboveboard in her dealings.*

ab.ra.ca.dab.ra (AB.ruh.cuh.DAB.ruh) *n.* a word or speech supposed to have magical effect; also, jargon; gibberish: *I've no use for all the abracadabra he conjures up.*

a.brade (uh.BRAID) *v.* **a.brades, a.brad.ed, a.brad.ing** rub away: *The forger had abraded the signature panel on the credit card.*

a.bra.sion (uh.BRAY.zhun) *n.* **1** a rubbing away. **2** a scraped part or area, as on the skin.

a.bra.sive (uh.BRAY.siv) *adj.* **1** that grinds and polishes: *an abrasive material like sand;* **n.**: *Diamonds are used as abrasives.* **2** rough or irritating: *a fellow with an abrasive manner; He's an abrasive personality.*

a.breast (uh.BREST) *adjp. & adv.* side by side: *We marched two abreast; TV helps him* **keep abreast of** (= stay informed about) *current events.*

a.bridge (uh.BRIJ) *v.* **a.bridg.es, a.bridged, a.bridg.ing** make less: to abridge a right, one's freedom; **adj.**: *an* **abridged** (= shortened) *edition or version of a book.* **—a.bridg.ment** or **a.bridge.ment** *n.*

a.broad (uh.BRAWD) *adjp. & adv.* **1** out of one's country: *our sales abroad; to study abroad; We invest in businesses both at home and abroad; He has been abroad 10 years; went abroad as a reporter; He's now returning* **from abroad.** **2** widespread: *A rumor is abroad that he is missing.*

ab.ro.gate (AB.ruh.gate) *v.* **-gates, -gat.ed, -gat.ing** repeal or abolish: *to abrogate a contract, law, responsibility, right, treaty.* **—ab.ro.ga.tion** (-GAY.shun) *n.*

a.brupt (uh.BRUPT) *adj.* sharp, not slow or smooth: *an abrupt turn in the road; an abrupt change, departure, decision, end, halt, transition; his abrupt manner of taking leave.* **—a.brupt.ly** *adv.*; **a.brupt.ness** *n.*

ab.scess (AB.ses) *n.* a collection of pus in a body tissue: *an abscess of the gums;* **adj.**: *an* **abscessed** *tooth.*

ab.scond (ab.SCOND) *v.* sneak off and hide: *He absconded with the money; absconded from the country;* **adj.**: *the* **absconding** *thief.* **—ab.scond.er** *n.*

ab.sence (AB.sunce) *n.* a being absent: *It happened during his absence; an unexplained absence; He's noted for his frequent absences from work; But his absence doesn't make the boss's heart grow fonder.*

ab.sent (AB.sunt) *adj.* not present: *to be absent without leave; He was absent (from school) on Monday; the absent student.* **—prep.** [legal use] without: *Absent proof of purchase, a refund is impossible.* **—***v.* (ab.SENT) be absent: *He absented himself from duty for many days.* **—ab.sent.ly** (AB.sunt.lee) *adv.*

ab.sen.tee (ab.sun.TEE) *n.* one who is absent: *No absentees today;* **adj.***a.*: *absentee ownership, an absentee ballot, landlord, owner, parent, voter; An absentee rate of 4.6% is considered unacceptable; Voters who are unable to come to the polls vote by

absenteeism / abuse

absentee ballot (by mail).
ab.sen.tee.ism (ab.sun.TEE.iz.um) *n.* habitual or customary absence: *school absenteeism; Three percent is considered normal absenteeism in business.*
absent-minded (ab.sunt.MINE.did) *adj.* inattentive or forgetful; **absent-mindedly** *adv.;* **absent-mindedness** *n.*
ab.sinthe (AB.sinth) *n.* a strong green licorice-flavored liqueur.
ab.so.lute (AB.suh.loot, long "oo") *adj.* complete or perfect: *the absolute truth; absolute proof, trust; The accused was given an* **absolute discharge** *(with no criminal record) because of new evidence; the absolute* or *unlimited power exercised by an absolute* (= despotic) *ruler.*
—**ab.so.lut.ism** *n.*
ab.so.lute.ly (AB.suh.loot.lee) *adv.* completely or entirely: *He's absolutely mistaken.* —**interj.** (-LOOT.lee) certainly!
absolute zero *n.* the lowest temperature possible, −273.16˚C.
ab.so.lu.tion (ab.suh.LOO.shun) *n.* remission of sin through a church sacrament: *A priest pronounces absolution at the end of a confession.*
ab.so.lut.ism (AB.suh.loo.tiz.um) *n.* government with unlimited power; despotism.
ab.solve (ab.ZOLV) *v.* **ab.solves, ab.solved, ab.solv.ing** to free: *to absolve someone from blame, guilt, obligations, promises, sins.*
ab.sorb (ab.ZORB) *v.* take in, as a sponge does a liquid: *Paper absorbs moisture; Rugs absorb sound; Baking soda absorbs odors; Canada absorbs thousands of immigrants each year; The small companies were absorbed into a large conglomerate; Chess absorbs his attention;* **adj.:** *He finds chess quite* **absorbing** (= taking up all his attention); *an absorbing tale.* —**absorbed** *adj.* with attention completely taken up: *a philosopher found absorbed in thought; completely, deeply, thoroughly, totally absorbed; She's quite absorbed in her homework; especially absorbed with* or *by math problems; her absorbed and lifelong interest in math; too self-absorbed to notice what's going on.* —**ab.sorb.en.cy** *n.*
—**ab.sorb.ent** *adj. & cpd.:* absorbent pads, paper towels; **absorbent cotton** (for surgical and cosmetic uses); *shock-absorbent shoe soles; sound-absorbent carpeting.*
—**ab.sorp.tion** *n.;* **ab.sorp.tive** *adj.*
ab.stain (ab.STAIN) *v.* keep away from something on principle, as in self-denial: *to abstain from alcohol, meat, sex, smoking, voting.* —**ab.stain.er** *n.*
ab.ste.mi.ous (ab.STEE.mee.us) *adj.*

moderate in eating, drinking, etc.; **ab.ste.mi.ous.ly** *adv.;* **ab.ste.mi.ous.ness** *n.*
ab.sten.tion (ab.STEN.shun) *n.* an act of abstaining, as from voting: *10 in favor, 7 against, and 3 abstentions.*
ab.sti.nence (AB.stuh.nunce) *n.* the act of abstaining in self-denial: *He practices complete* or *total abstinence from liquor, meat, tobacco, etc.; a period of abstinence.* —**ab.sti.nent** (-nunt) *adj.*
ab.stract (ab.STRACT) *v.* take out or remove something from a mass or body: *to abstract iron from ore; A pickpocket abstracts* (= steals) *money from a purse; The idea of greenness is abstracted* (= taken by the mind) *from green objects; to abstract* (= summarize) *an essay in 100 words;* **adj.: abstracted** *analyses, information; The philosopher wore an abstracted* (= lost in thought) *expression, look;* **ab.stract.ed.ly** *adv.;* **ab.strac.tion** *n.* —**adj.** (AB.stract) existing only in the mind, removed from reality; not concrete: *Greenness is an abstract idea* or *concept; abstract principles, thinking, theories;* **Abstract art** *does not represent real objects; abstract canvases, forms, paintings, patterns.* —**n.** (AB.stract) **1** summary: *a 100-word abstract of a thesis.* **2** something that is abstract or theoretical: *to talk* **in the abstract** (= in theoretical terms) *without giving concrete examples.*
—**ab.stract.ly** *adv.;* **ab.stract.ness** *n.*
ab.struse (ab.STROOSE) *adj.* difficult for the lay person to understand: *an abstruse discipline such as higher mathematics; an abstruse artist, poet.*
ab.surd (ab.ZURD) *adj.* not sensible; ridiculous: *It's absurd to ask for such a big raise; patently, simply, totally absurd.*
—**ab.sur.di.ty** (-di.tee) *n.: to pursue a theory to the point of absurdity; the height of absurdity.* —**ab.surd.ly** *adv.*
ab.sur.dism (ab.ZURD.iz.um) *n.* a philosophy that considers the world as meaningless and irrational. —**ab.sur.dist** *adj.: an absurdist approach, ending, play, story; absurdist comedy, drama, humor.*
a.bun.dance (uh.BUN.dunce) *n.* plenty: *a life of abundance; There's food in abundance after a harvest; an abundance of food; such great, overflowing abundance.*
a.bun.dant (uh.BUN.dunt) *adj.* plentiful: *Food is abundant after a harvest; a country abundant in raw materials; There's abundant evidence for pressing charges.* —**a.bun.dant.ly** *adv.*
a.buse (uh.BYOOZ) *v.* **a.bus.es, a.bused, a.bus.ing 1** use or treat badly: *No tool lasts long if abused; to abuse*

an animal by beating it; *Employees abuse a trust by stealing.* **2** insult: *He got drunk and abused his boss.* —***n.*** (uh.BYOOSE) **1** wrong or improper use: *an old car that has taken a lot of abuse; alcohol, drug, substance abuse; abuse of credit, language, power, privileges, trust; human rights abuses.* **2** bad treatment: *child abuse; emotional, physical, sexual, verbal abuse.* **3** insult: *a term of abuse; words of abuse; a torrent of abuse; She heaped, hurled, showered abuse (= insults) on him.* —**a.bu.sive** (-siv) *adj.*; **a.bu.sive.ly** *adv.*; **a.bu.sive.ness** *n.*

a.but (uh.BUT) *v.* **a.buts, a.but.ted, a.but.ting** have a common border or end with something: *His garage abuts on* or *upon my lot.* —**a.but.ment** *n.* a structure supporting an arch, bridge, etc.

a.but.tals (uh.BUT.tuls) *n.pl.* land boundaries common with other properties.

a.buzz (uh.BUZ) *adj.* buzzing: *The company is abuzz with rumors of a takeover; The media set the world abuzz.*

a.bys.mal (uh.BIZ.mul) *adj.* extremely bad: *His record is abysmal; an abysmal failure; his abysmal ignorance.* —**a.bys.mal.ly** *adv.*: *abysmally poor.*

a.byss (uh.BIS) *n.* a hole that is too deep to measure: *a gaping, yawning abyss; on the edge of an abyss; into the abyss (= depth) of ignorance, shame, sin.* —**a.bys.sal** (-sul) *adj.*

a.ca.cia (uh.CAY.shuh) *n.* a thorny tree of warm regions that yields a gum.

ac.a.deme (AC.uh.deem) *n.* the world of scholars, esp. at the university level: *the groves* or *halls of academe* (= the world of universities). Also **ac.a.de.mi.a** (-DEE.mee.uh) *n.*

ac.a.dem.ic (ac.uh.DEM.ic) *adj.* **1** having only theoretical value: *How he managed to pass is now academic; academic issues.* **2** having to do with teaching and studying: *academic achievements, careers, circles, discipline, exercises, institutions, journals, life, performance, qualifications, societies, standards; the academic community, world; the **academic freedom** of professors who can say what they think without fear; The **academic year** usually starts in September; academic (= not technical or commercial) courses, subjects.* —*n.* **1** a professor. **2 academics** *pl.* scholarly activities: *She shines in both academics and sports.* —**ac.a.dem.i.cal.ly** *adv.*

a.cad.e.mi.cian (ac.uh.duh.MISH.un) *n.* a member of an academy (def. 1).

a.cad.e.my (uh.CAD.uh.mee) *n.* **-mies 1** a society of learned people: *an academy of science; the French Academy.* **2** a school for special studies: *military, naval, police, riding academies; We studied together at the academy; a girls' academy.*

Academy Award *n.* an annual award of the Academy of Motion Picture Arts and Sciences of Hollywood for outstanding achievements in film making; an Oscar.

A.ca.di.an (uh.CAY.dee.un) *n. & adj.* (a person) of or from **Acadia,** the French-speaking region of New Brunswick and Nova Scotia: *The Cajuns of Louisiana are descendants of Acadians deported from Acadia in 1755 and 1758; Acadian French.*

a.can.thus (uh.CAN.thus, "th" as in "thin") *n.* **-thus.es** or **-thi** (-thye) **1** an architectural representation of the leaves of a Mediterranean plant. **2** this plant.

a cap.pel.la (ah.cuh.PEL.uh) *adj. & adv. Music.* without instrumental accompaniment.

ac.cede (ac.SEED) *v.* **-cedes, -ced.ed, -ced.ing 1** agree, esp. under pressure: *She acceded to the blackmailer's demands; to accede to a treaty, to someone's wishes.* **2** assume: *to accede to an office, to a position, to the throne.* —**ac.ces.sion** (ac.SESH.un) *n.*

ac.cel.er.an.do (ac.SEL.uh.RAHN.doh) *adv. & adj. Music.* gradually faster in tempo.

ac.cel.er.ate (ac.SEL.uh.rate) *v.* **-ates, -at.ed, -at.ing** speed up: *The car can accelerate from zero to 60 km/h in 8 seconds; to accelerate an engine, development, movement, process, trend; to accelerate changes, growth.* —**ac.cel.er.a.tion** (-RAY.shun) *n.*

ac.cel.er.a.tor (ac.SEL.uh.ray.tur) *n.* **1** the gas pedal of an automobile: *to step on* or *depress* or *press the accelerator; to ease up on* or *let up on* or *release the accelerator; the accelerator pedal.* **2** a machine that increases the speed and energy of atomic particles or nuclei; atom smasher; also called "particle accelerator."

ac.cent (AC.sent) *n.* **1** a style of speaking a language, esp. one that is different from one's own: *the various accents heard in the English-speaking world; When the Texan Lyndon Johnson became U.S. president, Texans said at last they had a president who could speak English without an accent; to speak with a heavy, middling, neutral, slight, strong, thick ac-*

accentuate / accident

cent; *He affects, assumes, cultivates, imitates, puts on a British accent when traveling in the U.K.* **2** emphasis placed on a syllable in speaking or a mark placed on a written word: *Most English words have their accent on the first syllable; French words have acute, grave, and circumflex accents* (= accent marks); *"Rôle" is often written with a circumflex accent.* **3** artistic emphasis in fashion and design: *The accent was on the layered look in women's fashions; to add a decorative accent to furniture; an overcoat with a London accent;* **adj.:** *an accent* (= emphasizing) *color, texture, tone; accent furniture and accessories; accent rugs and pillows; accent pieces.* —*v.* (also ac.-SENT) emphasize: *Makeup accents her good looks; a product that accents the flavor of good food;* **adj.:** *The* **accented** *syllable of "accord" is the second; He speaks a heavily accented English* (= with a heavy foreign accent).

ac.cen.tu.ate (ac.SEN.choo.ate) *v.* **-ates, -at.ed, -at.ing** to emphasize: *to accentuate the positive; to accentuate an aspect, atmosphere, a detail, feature, figure, look, problem, tendency, trend.*
—**ac.cen.tu.a.tion** (-AY.shun) *n.*

ac.cept (ac.SEPT) *v.* **1** approve of and receive something: *to accept an application, bribe, gift, offer, position, proposal, ride, responsibility, settlement, situation; to accept defeat, reality; to accept something blindly, fully, readily; to be accepted* (as a member) *in high society; to be accepted by a society, into a circle, community, group; a machine that accepts bills but not coins.* **2** agree: *I accept that I made a mistake.* —**adj.:** *to feel* **accepted** *or rejected; an* **accepted** (= a generally agreed-on) *fact, opinion, truth; to be* **accepting** *of liberal views;* **cpd.:** *a blindly-accepted dogma; widely-accepted myths.*

ac.cep.ta.ble (ac.SEP.tuh.bul) *adj.* **1** that can be accepted; agreeable: *Is this acceptable to you? The terms of a contract have to be mutually acceptable to the parties concerned; completely, fully acceptable.* **2** endurable: *pollen count that is considered acceptable; within acceptable limits; an acceptable level of emission from a factory.* —**ac.cep.ta.bly** (-blee) *adv.*
—**ac.cep.ta.bil.i.ty** (-BIL.i.tee) *n.*

ac.cep.tance (ac.SEP.tunce) *n.* an act of accepting or being accepted: *three refusals and no acceptances yet; a belief that has gained wide acceptance; a theory that has found universal acceptance; the blind acceptance of a dogma; the growing, increasing, rapid, strong, wide-spread acceptance of a new trend; consumer acceptance;* **adj.:** *the acceptance rate for applications from foreign countries; a winner's acceptance speech.*

ac.cep.ta.tion (ac.sep.TAY.shun) *n.* accepted meaning: *the usual acceptation of a word.*

ac.cess (AC.ses) *n.* a going to or reaching a place: *a password for gaining or getting access to computer data; He was denied access; to block, give, grant, offer, provide, restrict access to private property; Everyone has access to elementary education; direct, easy, free, limited, random, unlimited access; The stairs are the only access to* (= means of reaching) *those rooms; The rooms are not easy of access* (= not easy to reach); **adj.:** *an access point; the* **access time** *between requesting and receiving data from a computer storage medium such as a disk.* —*v.* gain access to something: *to access computer data.*

ac.ces.si.ble (ac.SES.uh.bul) *adj.* within reach: *A hospital should be easily accessible to all; an island that is accessible only by air; accessible entrances, information, markets, prices; an area that is wheelchair-accessible; an accessible* (= approachable) *leader.* —**ac.ces.si.bly** (-blee) *adv.*
—**ac.ces.si.bil.i.ty** (-BIL.i.tee) *n.*

ac.ces.sion (ac.SESH.un) *n.* **1** an acceding, assuming, or attaining: *an heir's accession to the throne; accession to an office, to a position, to power, to leadership; a nation's accession to independence, to a human rights convention.* **2** something added: *a library's new accessions* (= additions, esp. books); *the* **accession number** (under which a file is entered in a database).

ac.ces.so.ry (ac.SES.uh.ree) *n.* **-ries 1** an item added to complement or complete an outfit: *Tires are not auto accessories, but power steering, power windows, sunroof, and tape decks are; The shop sells pins, rings, bracelets, and other accessories; bath, clothing, decorative, dress, fur, fashion, hair, kitchen, matching, men's accessories;* **adj.:** *an accessory store; an* **accessories** *department, designer, line, market.* **2** helper: *an accessory to a crime; An* **accessory before** *or* **after the fact** *is not involved in the actual commission of the crime.*

ac.ci.dence (AC.si.dunce) *n.* the grammar of word inflections, such as case forms.

ac.ci.dent (AC.si.dunt) *n.* **1** a mishap that causes hurt or damage: *He met with* or *had an accident; car, fatal, traffic accidents; The accident occurred* or *happened* or *took place on the highway; He was* (involved) *in a hit-and-run accident;*

how to prevent automobile accidents; bad, dreadful, fatal, frightful, horrible, nasty, serious, terrible, unfortunate accidents. **2** chance: *It was (by) pure accident, not by design, that I found the loot; I met her* **by accident;** *It is* **no accident** *that I happen to love this woman who has the same tastes as I.* —**ac.ci.den.tal** (-DEN.tul) *adj.* Also *n.* a change in a musical key, as a sharp or flat note. —**ac.ci.den.tal.ly** *adv.*

ac.claim (uh.CLAIM) *v.* applaud or hail: *They acclaimed him leader; acclaimed his resolve to reduce taxes; He was acclaimed (as) a hero for saving the child's life; adj.: the most* **acclaimed** *player of the year; an acclaimed writer; acclaimed for his bravery.* —*n.* praise: *The book received wide critical acclaim; It brought her popular acclaim; to earn, gain, win acclaim; great, high, international, universal, widespread acclaim.*

ac.cla.ma.tion (ac.luh.MAY.shun) *n.* an act of acclaiming: *She won or was elected* **by acclamation** (= unopposed; without a vote).

ac.cli.mate (AC.luh.mate) *v.* **-mates, -mat.ed, -mat.ing** same as ACCLIMATIZE. —**ac.cli.ma.tion** (-MAY.shun) *n.*

ac.cli.ma.tize (uh.CLYE.muh.tize) *v.* **-tiz.es, -tized, -tiz.ing** to accustom: *to acclimatize ourselves to new surroundings;* **adj.**: *We become* or *get* **acclimatized** *to a new climate, environment, situation.* —**ac.cli.ma.ti.za.tion** (-tuh.ZAY.shun, -tye-) *n.*

ac.cliv.i.ty (uh.CLIV.uh.tee) *n.* **-ties** an uphill slope.

ac.co.lade (AC.uh.lade) *n.* great appreciation or praise: *to deserve, draw, earn, get, receive, win an accolade; the accolades accorded to or bestowed on or conferred on or given to our hero; Is the Nobel Prize the world's highest accolade?*

ac.com.mo.date (uh.COM.uh.date) *v.* **-dates, -dat.ed, -dat.ing 1** have room for: *This hotel can accommodate 400 people; a car that can accommodate five passengers.* **2** adjust or adapt: *to accommodate (oneself) to new surroundings.* **3** provide for: *special arrangements to accommodate the needs of the disabled; to accommodate attitudes, changes, differences, growth, interests, wishes; a menu that accommodates vegetarians; He accommodated her with a loan;* **adj.**: *a very* **accommodating** *neighbor.*

ac.com.mo.da.tion (uh.com.uh.DAY.shun) *n.* **1** lodging and related services: *Hotel accommodation was scarce during the Olympics; bed-and-breakfast, first-class, luxury, overnight, public, tourist, travel accommodations; a hotel with accommodations for 300 people; She found the* **accommodations** (= lodging) *pleasant.* **2** favor: *He did it as an accommodation for a friend.* **3** settlement: *to come to, find, make, reach, seek, work out an accommodation with the opposite party.* **4** an adaptation or adjustment: *an accommodation to wartime conditions.*

ac.com.pa.ni.ment (uh.CUM.pun.i.munt) *n.* something that accompanies: *a piano accompaniment to a song; vocal and instrumental accompaniment; They danced to the accompaniment of drums; Chest pain is often an accompaniment to anxiety; a cup of sauce that makes four accompaniment servings.* —**ac.com.pa.nist** *n.* one who plays a musical accompaniment.

ac.com.pa.ny (uh.CUM.puh.nee) *v.* **-nies, -nied, -ny.ing 1** go along with: *The child's mother accompanied her; pain accompanied by fever; steaks accompanied by string beans and carrots.* **2** to play or sing supporting a solo part: *to accompany a singer on the piano.*

ac.com.plice (uh.COM.plis) *n.* a companion in wrongdoing: *an unwilling accomplice; an accomplice in or to a crime.*

ac.com.plish (uh.COM.plish) **1** *v.* succeed in doing; achieve: *to accomplish a mission, objective, task; What can we accomplish in half an hour? Landing on the moon is now an* **accomplished** *fact.* **2 accomplished** *adj.* talented: *an accomplished actor; accomplished at acting and singing.*

ac.com.plish.ment (uh.COM.plish.munt) *n.* **1** skill acquired by great effort: *It's no mean accomplishment to be able to play the piano; sewing, cooking, and such accomplishments.* **2** achievement: *a major accomplishment; the accomplishment of one's goals, objectives; a feeling, record, sense of accomplishment; her accomplishments of the past year.*

ac.cord (uh.CORD) *v.* **1** give or grant: *We accorded him a hero's welcome.* **2** agree: *His actions do not accord with his words.* —*n.* agreement: *to reach an accord with our neighbor on arms control; a peace accord between two countries; a free-trade accord; to act in accord with our wishes; to live in perfect accord* (= harmony); *He signed the agreement* **of his own accord** (= without outside influence); *The motion was passed* **with one accord** (= unanimously).

ac.cord.ance (uh.COR.dunce) *n.* agreement: *The goods were shipped* **in accordance** *with your wishes.*

ac.cord.ing *adj.* agreeing: *You'll be pun-*

accordion / accumulate

ished **according as** (= depending on how or whether) *you sin.* —**according to 1** in agreement with: *Everything went according to plan.* **2** as stated by an authority: *the creation according to the Bible; It's 8:25 according to this watch.* **3** on the basis of something: *shoes classified according to size.* —**according to Hoyle** according to the rules; the way it is usu. done.
—**ac.cord.ing.ly** *adv.* in agreement: *These are the rules, act accordingly.*
ac.cor.di.on (uh.COR.dee.un) *n.* a musical instrument worked with a boxlike bellows and a keyboard at each end: *a skirt with accordion pleats (like an accordion's bellows).*
—**ac.cor.di.on.ist** *n.*
ac.cost (uh.COST) *v.* approach uninvited: *to be accosted by beggars; A police officer accosted the demonstrators and told them to move on.*
ac.count (uh.COWNT) *v.* consider or reckon: *An accused is accounted innocent until proven guilty; Account yourself lucky you were not killed in the accident; Someone has to* **account for** (= explain) *the missing money.* —*n.* **1** a report: *a press account; to give* or *render an account to one's superiors; accurate, biased, detailed, eyewitness, running, true, vivid accounts; an account of what happened; a newspaper account of the incident; a great man* **by all accounts**. **2** a transaction: *to settle an account by paying up; I have an account* (= dispute) *to settle with him.* **3** consideration: *When you* **take account of everything** or **when you take everything into account,** *there's nothing to be sorry about; He was late* **on account of** (= because of) *rain; No one will be excused* **on any account** (= for any reason); *The bank president was held* **to account** (= was accountable) *for an embezzlement by a loan officer; a journey undertaken on the company's account* (= behalf); *Don't be late on my account* (= for my sake). **4** a business arrangement: *to keep,* **open** *a savings account at a bank; a checking account; All receipts are paid into our current account; active, dormant, e-mail, inactive, retirement accounts; a businessman on an expense account.* **5** business that a client brings or the client itself: *an advertising account; account management (by a team of managers); an* **account executive** *(in charge of a client's business).* **6 accounts** *pl.* record of money transactions; books: *to keep accounts;* **accounts receivable** (= moneys due on sales), **accounts payable** (= moneys to be paid for purchases); *He's good at* **accounts** (= keeping accounting records). **7 accounts** *pl.* differences: *the settling of accounts and vendettas; to square accounts.*

ac.count.a.ble (uh.COWN.tuh.bul) *adj.* responsible or answerable: *I am accountable to my superiors for my actions; They will be held accountable for my actions.* —**ac.count.a.bil.i.ty** (-BIL.i.tee) *n.*

ac.count.an.cy (uh.COWN.tun.see) *n.* the systematic keeping of business records.

ac.count.ant (uh.COWN.tunt) *n.* one trained in keeping business records or money accounts; bookkeeper: *A certified public accountant in the U.S. is the equivalent of a chartered accountant in the British Commonwealth countries.*

account executive See ACCOUNT, *n.* 5.
accounting (uh.COWN.ting) *n.* **1** the system of bookkeeping used by accountants or their work: *cost accounting;* **adja.:** *accounting firms, offices, practices, systems, terminals; the accounting profession.* **2** explanation: *The boss wants an accounting of the missing money.*

ac.cou.ter.ments (uh.COO.tur.munts) *n.pl.* a soldier's military trappings. Also **ac.cou.tre.ments** *Cdn.*

ac.cred.it (uh.CRED.it) *v.* **1** depute or send out officially: *an envoy accredited to the Vatican.* **2** attribute or credit: *a discovery accredited to Newton.*

ac.cred.it.ed (uh.CRED.i.tid) *adj.* officially recognized: *an accredited authority on the subject; an accredited institution, laboratory, university; the accredited value of a stock; an accredited Australian wine (guaranteed to be of good quality).*
—**ac.cred.i.ta.tion** (-uh.TAY.shun) *n.*
ac.cre.tion (uh.CREE.shun) *n.* a growth or increase by gradual addition.
—**ac.cre.tive** (-tiv) *adj.*
ac.crue (uh.CROO) *v.* **ac.crues, ac.crued, ac.cru.ing** add on gradually: *Interest accrues to an account from savings deposits; to accrue advantages, benefits, charges, debts, funds, leave, liabilities, losses, profits, rewards;* **adj.:** *the interest* **accrued** *on the remaining balance of a loan; accrued expenses, interest, pension, wages.*
—**ac.cru.al** (uh.CROO.ul) *n.*
ac.cul.tu.rate (uh.CUL.chuh.rate) *v.* **-rates, -rat.ed, -rat.ing** adapt to or adopt another culture. —**ac.cul.tu.ra.tion** (-RAY.shun) *n.*
ac.cu.mu.late (uh.CUE.myuh.late) *v.* **-lates, -lat.ed, -lat.ing** pile or heap up: *Snow accumulates in the winter; Data, debts, deposits, dust, evidence, funds, money, pollutants, writings may accumulate; to*

accuracy / achromatic

ac.cu.mu.la.tion (-LAY.shun) *n.* accumulate capital, fat, fortunes, interest, knowledge, power, riches, wealth, wisdom. —**ac.cu.mu.la.tion** (-LAY.shun) *n.*

ac.cu.ra.cy (AC.yuh.ruh.see) *n.* the quality of being accurate: *the accuracy of your figures; an 85% accuracy rate; to improve accuracy; the degree, level of accuracy; complete, deadly, great, high, precise, scientific, uncanny accuracy.*

ac.cu.rate (AC.yuh.rit) *adj.* having no errors: *an accurate source of information; The report is accurate in every detail; 95% accurate is accurate (to) within 5%; highly, quite accurate; Is it accurate to say that 365 days make a year? an accurate aim, assessment, clock, description, figure, forecast, report, picture, thermometer; an accurate* (= careful and exact) *typist, accurate in his work.* —**ac.cu.rate.ly** *adv.*

ac.cursed (uh.CURST) *adj.* hated or hateful: *the accursed custom of slavery.* Also **ac.curst.**

ac.cu.sa.tion (ac.yoo.ZAY.shun) *n.* a charge of wrongdoing: *to bring or make an accusation of murder against someone; an accusation that he committed murder; damaging, false, grave, groundless, sweeping accusations.*

ac.cu.sa.tive (uh.CUE.zuh.tiv) *n. & adj.* (a grammatical case) indicating object: *"Me" is the accusative (case) of "I."*

ac.cu.sa.to.ry (uh.CUE.zuh.tor.ee) *adj.* accusing: *his accusatory looks; She spoke in an accusatory tone; to point an accusatory finger at someone.*

ac.cuse (uh.KYOOZ) *v.* **-cus.es, -cused, -cus.ing** charge with an offense: *He is accused of murder;* **adj.**: *He stands* **accused***; an accused person;* **n.**: *He is the* **accused** (= accused person) *in the murder case; She is another of the* **accused** (= accused people). —**ac.cus.er** *n.*

ac.cus.tom (uh.CUS.tum) *v.* make or become used to something: *He accustomed himself to the cold.* —**accustomed 1** *adjp.* used: *He has grown or become or is accustomed to the cold; She is accustomed to working late.* **2** *adja.* usual: *He's out for his accustomed walk.*

ace *n.* **1** the highest of a set of playing cards: *the ace of spades; an ace card.* **2** in tennis and handball, a serve that is not touched by the receiver: *He dealt his opponent 19 aces during the game; He fired and scored many aces.* **3** an expert: *He's an ace at flying; a bullpen ace; a flying ace; a relief ace; a tennis ace;* **adja.**: *an ace pilot; our ace (baseball) pitcher, reliever.* —**ace in the hole** *Informal.* a hidden advantage: *When oil became scarce, some nations turned to coal as their ace in the hole.* —**ace up one's sleeve** a hidden and tricky advantage. —*v.* **ac.es, aced, ac.ing 1** in tennis, etc., win a point against one's opponent. **2** *Informal.* win, as with an A grade: *The new car aced the test drive; She aced it* (= did it very well).

a.cer.bic (uh.SUR.bic) *adj.* acidic or sharp-tasting: *an acerbic critic, style, writer; acerbic comments, humor, wit;* **a.cer.bi.cal.ly** *adv.* —**a.cer.bi.ty** (-bi.tee) *n.* **-ties:** *No one can stand the acerbity of his wit; We are tired of his acerbities.*

a.ce.ta.min.o.phen (uh.see.tuh.MIN.uh. fun) *n.* a drug used to relieve pain and reduce fever.

ac.e.tate (AS.i.tate) *n.* a fiber, plastic film, or fabric made from cellulose and acetic acid.

a.ce.tic acid (uh.SEE.tic-) *n.* a colorless acid found in vinegar; hence **acetic** *adj.*

ac.e.tone (AS.i.tone) *n.* a colorless, volatile, flammable liquid solvent.

a.cet.y.lene (uh.SET.uh.leen) *n.* a colorless flammable gas used in welding and cutting.

ac.e.tyl.sal.i.cyl.ic acid (uh.SEE.tul.sal. i.SIL.ic-) same as ASPIRIN.

ache (AKE) *n.* a dull continuous pain: *the ache of hunger; a dull ache; He suffers from* **aches and pains.** —*comb.form:* *backache, headache, stomachache.* —*v.* **aches, ached ach.ing** have an ache: *My back aches; He is aching* (*Informal* for wanting very much) *to go home; aching over his wife's death; aching for his loved ones, for understanding; Ache no more;* **adj.**: *They waited with* **aching** *hearts; her aching back, bones, eyes, feet, joints, muscles.*

a.chieve (uh.CHEEV) *v.* **a.chieves, a.chieved, a.chiev.ing** gain by overcoming difficulties: *to achieve fame, an aim, an effect, a goal, an objective, a result, success in life.* —**a.chieve.ment** *n.*: *brilliant, crowning, dazzling, great, high, major, notable, outstanding, signal, striking, superb achievements; achievements in science; women of achievement.*
—**a.chiev.a.ble** *adj.* —**a.chiev.er** *n.*: *high, top achievers.*

A.chil.les' heel (uh.KIL.eez-) *n.* a mortal weakness or weak point, like the heel of **Achilles,** the legendary Greek hero of the "Iliad."

Achilles' tendon *n.* the tendon linking the calf muscles and the heel.

ach.ro.mat.ic (ac.ruh.MAT.ic) *adj.* **1** *Music.* diatonic. **2** free of color separation in light refraction: *an achromatic*

lens. —**ach.ro.mat.i.cal.ly** adv.
ach.y (AY.kee) adj. painful: *an achy feeling; achy feet, muscles, pains.*
ac.id (AS.id) n. **1** a sour substance with a biting quality: *Corrosive acids eat into metal;* **adja. & cpd:** *The lime is an acid fruit; acid soil; Books are printed on acid-free paper for minimal deterioration; an acid-green pool table; acid-laden fog.* **2** *Slang.* LSD; **adja.:** *an acid freak, house, pad, trip.* **3** sharp: *She has an acid tongue; an acid wit.* —**ac.id.ly** adv.
ac.id.head (AS.id.hed) n. *Informal.* an LSD user.
a.cid.ic (uh.SID.ic) adj. acid-containing: *acidic compounds, foods, ingredients, solutions, waters, wines; Coffee and carbonated drinks are very acidic.* —**a.cid.i.ty** (-i.tee) n.
a.cid.i.fy (uh.SID.uh.fye) v. **-fies, -fied, -fy.ing** make or become sour or acid.
acid rain (or **precipitation**) n. rain or snow containing acids formed in the atmosphere by industrial pollutants such as sulfur dioxide.
acid rock n. rock music with drugs as theme.
acid test n. a decisive test, as for gold which acids do not attack.
a.cid.u.late (uh.SIJ.oo.late) v. **-lates, -lat.ed, -lat.ing** make slightly acid or sour-tasting. —**a.cid.u.lous** (-lus) adj. —**a.cid.u.la.tion** (-LAY.shun) n.
acid wash n. a washing method using acid, esp. for giving the faded look to blue denim; **adja.:** *acid-wash denim, jeans; the acid-wash process.*
ac.knowl.edge (ak.NOL.ij) v. **-edg.es, -edged, -edg.ing 1** admit as true: *He acknowledged defeat; acknowledged that he had been beaten; acknowledged me to be the winner; She gratefully acknowledged receipt of the letter; She acknowledged* (= admitted receiving) *the letter.* **2** recognize someone: *He acknowledged me in the crowd; She acknowledged me as the winner;* **adj.:** *the* **acknowledged** *winner.* —**ac.knowl.edg.ment** n.: *He made a public acknowledgment of his mistake; a receipt issued in acknowledgment of a payment.* Also **ac.knowl.edge.ment** *Cdn.*
ac.me (AC.mee) n. the highest point: *to attain* or *reach the acme of her career as a dancer.*
ac.ne (AC.nee) n. a skin disease that causes pimples.
ac.o.lyte (AC.uh.lite) n. **1** a helper, as at a church service. **2** a follower.
ac.o.nite (AC.uh.nite) n. **1** any of several poisonous plants, esp. the monkshood. **2** a drug made from one of them.

a.corn (AY.corn) n. the nut of an oak tree: *"Giant oaks from little acorns grow."*
a.cous.tic (uh.COO.stic) or **a.cous.ti.cal** (-sti.cul) adj. **1** relating to sound or hearing: *the acoustic nerve; Acoustic tiles absorb sound; the acoustical difference between an empty theater and a full one; acoustic design, output, padding, properties, qualities, shortcomings; acoustical consultants, research, societies; an* **acoustic coupler** *for connecting a telephone handset to a computer.* **2** not electrically amplified: *an acoustic guitar; acoustic and electric pianos; acoustic jazz.*
—**a.cous.tics** n.pl. **1** [takes *sing.* v.] the science of sound: *Acoustics is taught here.* **2** [takes *pl.* v.] sound qualities of enclosed spaces: *The acoustics of this auditorium are good.* —**a.cous.ti.cal.ly** adv.
ac.quaint (uh.QUAINT) v. make familiar: *She's new here and has to acquaint herself thoroughly with her job; to acquaint students with the basics of computers.*
ac.quaint.ance (uh.QUAIN.tunce) n. **1** personal knowledge or familiarity: *to keep up, renew, strike up an acquaintance with someone; to acquire, have an acquaintance with someone; a nodding, passing, personal, slight acquaintance; after only a few hours' acquaintance; a lawyer's close acquaintance with law; He's someone* **of my acquaintance** (= someone known to me); *I'd like to* **make her acquaintance** (= to meet her). **2** a person one has met but does not know well: *She's an acquaintance of mine, not a friend or relative; casual acquaintances; We have many mutual business and social acquaintances; a trusted old acquaintance charged with* **acquaintance rape.** —**ac.quaint.ance.ship** n.
acquainted adjp. **1** known to someone: *They have to get acquainted (with each other); a get-acquainted meeting; to be casually, closely, intimately, well acquainted with one's fellow workers.* **2** familiar: *to become acquainted with a business.*
ac.qui.esce (ak.wee.ES) v. **-esc.es, -esced, -esc.ing** agree passively: *He found it hard to acquiesce meekly in* or *to the umpire's ruling.* —**ac.qui.es.cence** (-unce) n. —**ac.qui.es.cent** (-unt) adj.
ac.quire (uh.QUIRE) v. **-quires, -quired, -quir.ing** get by effort: *to acquire assets, businesses, companies, learning, property, rights, tastes, territory, wealth, weapons.* —**acquired** adj.: *Speech is an acquired, not inborn skill; an acquired, not inherited character* or *characteristic.* —**ac.quire.ment** n.

ac.qui.si.tion (ac.wuh.ZISH.un) *n.* the act of acquiring or something acquired: *the acquisition of knowledge; Our museum's latest acquisition is a Picasso; company acquisitions and mergers.*

ac.quis.i.tive (uh.QUIZ.uh.tiv) *adj.* eager to get and keep things: *A chipmunk is acquisitive by nature; Jan is acquisitive of lands and wealth; a greedy and acquisitive businessman.* —**ac.quis.i.tive.ness** *n.*

ac.quit (uh.QUIT) *v.* **-quits, -quit.ted, -quit.ting 1** to free someone of a charge: *The accused was acquitted; He was acquitted of murder; acquitted on all counts.* **2** to conduct: *He acquitted himself well at the interview; acquitted herself like a pro.*

ac.quit.tal (uh.QUIT.ul) *n.* an act or instance of being acquitted of a charge: *A jury brings in an acquittal; He was convicted on one charge but won acquittals on the others.*

a.cre (AY.cur) *n.* **1** a unit of land area equal to 43,560 sq. ft. (4047 sq. meters): *The estate covers many acres; acres of land, forest, grapes, timber, vineyards, wheat, wilderness.* **2 acres** *pl.* lands: *to clear a forest for cultivable acres; green, irrigated, rich, wooded acres.*

a.cre.age (AY.cur.ij) *n.* area in acres; hence, amount of land: *total acreage; riverfront acreages.*

ac.rid (AC.rid) *adj.* **1** sharp and biting to the taste or smell: *acrid air, fumes, smell, smoke.* **2** sharp and bitter in tone: *acrid words.* —**ac.rid.ly** *adv.* —**ac.rid.ness** or **ac.rid.i.ty** (ac.RID.i.tee) *n.*

ac.ri.mo.ni.ous (ac.ruh.MOH.nee.us) *adj.* characterized by acrimony: *an acrimonious battle, debate, divorce, exchange, fight.* —**ac.ri.mo.ni.ous.ly** *adv.*

ac.ri.mo.ny (AC.ruh.moh.nee) *n.* bitterness of language or tone: *acrimony and distrust; the acrimony between rival factions.*

acro- *comb.form.* height, summit, etc.: *acrobat, acrophobia, acropolis.*

ac.ro.bat (AC.ruh.bat) *n.* one who performs on a tightrope, trapeze, etc., as at a circus: *a verbal acrobat.*

—**ac.ro.bat.ic** (-BAT.ic) *adj.*: *a trapeze artist's acrobatic flips, routines, skills.*

acrobatics *n.pl.* **1** [takes *sing. v.*] the skill of an acrobat: *Her acrobatics is of Olympic standard.* **2** [takes *pl. v.*] the feats of an acrobat: *Some of her acrobatics are scary; intellectual acrobatics.*

ac.ro.nym (AC.ruh.nim) *n.* a pronounceable word formed by joining the first letters of a phrase: *NATO is an acronym for North Atlantic Treaty Organization.*

ac.ro.pho.bi.a (ac.ruh.FOH.bee.uh) *n.* an abnormal fear of high places.

a.crop.o.lis (uh.CROP.uh.lis) *n.* the fortified crowning part of an ancient Greek city, esp. the **Acropolis** of Athens.

a.cross (uh.CROS) *prep. & adv.* from one side to the other: *Let's walk across (the street); He lives across (= on the opposite side of) the street; The street is 100 feet across; She lives across (the street) from (= opposite) us; He went across the border to the States; He works across the border in Detroit; Detroit is across the border (= in the U.S.); our neighbors across the border (= in the other country); The news was flashed across the nation; People from across (= from all over) the country flocked to the capital; Honesty is the best policy, but it is difficult to **get it across to** people (= make them appreciate it); I ran or **came across** (= met) an old friend yesterday.* —**across the board** equally for all categories: *Pay scales were raised across the board;* **adja.**: *an **across-the-board** pay raise, price increase, tax hike.*

a.cros.tic (uh.CROS.tic) *n.* a geometric arrangement of words from which a new word can be read, as NEWS from North, East, West, and South arranged in a column.

a.cryl.ic (uh.CRIL.ic) *n.* **1** a synthetic substance in the form of paints, textile fibers such as Acrilan and Orlon, and transparent resins such as Lucite and Plexiglas; *adj.*: *acrylic acid; an acrylic fiber, finish, plastic, paint, painting, resin, substance, sweater.* **2** a picture painted in acrylic: *an exhibition of watercolors, oils, and acrylics.*

act *n.* **1** something done: *an act of faith, folly, heroism, love, mercy, vengeance, war, will; a kind act; an act (= law) of Parliament; caught in the act (= action) of stealing; to get into the act (= participate).* **2** a performance: *a circus act; a disappearing act; a nightclub act; a drama in five acts (= parts); The child is **putting on an act** (Informal for putting on a show) to get sympathy; He was told to **clean up his act** (Informal for act properly) or resign; Let's **get our act together** (= get organized).* —*v.* **1** do something: *We acted quickly to put out the fire; Lawyers act **for** (= represent) their clients; She acts (= does what is needed) on their advice; She acts (= behaves) politely toward her competitors; Some people act (= take action) out of fear; They act as if it was the end of the world; Lou is acting as (= tem-*

porarily filling the position of) *principal*; **adja.**: *She is the **acting** (= temporary) principal.* **2** perform as an actor: *to act out a story; to act in a play; He's acting* (= performing as) *the clown; Act your age* (= Behave more maturely)! **adja**: *an **acting** career, coach, role; acting lessons*; **n.**: *play acting.* —**act up** *Informal.* behave badly: *The child acts up when his parents are away; My arthritis acts up* (= gives trouble) *in cold weather; It acts up on me now and then.*

ac.ti.nide (AC.tuh.nide) *n.* any of a series of radioactive chemical elements, from **actinium** through Lawrencium in the periodic table.

ac.tion (AC.shun) *n.* **1** the act or process of doing; also, what is done: *the corrosive action of acid on metal; Watch the action on the stage; The action takes place in 1990; The action has been dragging so far, but it is beginning to pick up; to institute* or *take action in a court of law; legal action; Firefighters **go into action*** (= start work) *at a moment's notice; They put a plan into action; The police **take action** against smugglers; take action to stop smuggling; Good examples spur us into action; "Actions speak louder than words"; soldiers killed or missing **in action*** (= in battle); *enemy action; He saw action* (= took part in the fighting) *during World War II; A car is **out of action*** (= useless) *without fuel; affirmative action; a concerted, decisive, delaying, direct, disciplinary, drastic, emergency, hasty, immediate, job, joint, military, police, prompt, rearguard, remedial, reflex, vigorous action; a course of action; Go where **the action*** (*Informal* for activity) *is.* **2** a lawsuit: *to bring an action against the defaulter; A judge may dismiss an action; an action for divorce; civil, class, criminal, libel actions.*

ac.tion.a.ble (AC.shuh.nuh.bul) *adj.* giving cause for a legal action: *actionable behavior; an actionable offense, procedure.*

ac.ti.vate (AC.tuh.vate) *v.* **-vates, -vated, -vat.ing** make active, as by an outside agent: *Smoke activates the alarm; Heat activates chemical processes; a voice-activated recorder;* **Activated charcoal** (*treated with steam and air*) *is used in filters as a purifying agent.* —**ac.ti.va.tion** (-VAY.shun) *n.*

ac.tive (AC.tiv) *adj.* having life and motion: *a very active child; He continues to lead an active life at 65; still physically and mentally active; active in many fields; active on many fronts; She takes an active interest in sports; an active effort, listener, lifestyle, market, player, role; active consideration, involvement, participation; An active volcano erupts from time to time; Tennis is an active sport; casual and* **active** *sportswear (such as for running, fitness, and bicycling); an active* (= not dormant) *business account; an active* (= not silent) *partner; a soldier on* **active duty** (= not on reserve or retired status). —**ac.tive.ly** *adv.*

active voice *n.* a form of sentence in which the doer is the subject of the verb, as "Students write exams" as opposed to "Exams are written by students" (PASSIVE VOICE).

ac.tiv.ist (AC.tuh.vist) *n.* one who resorts to direct action to achieve something for the common good: *animal rights, environmental, farm, peace, student, union activists.* —**ac.tiv.ism** *n.*

ac.tiv.i.ty (ac.TIV.i.tee) *n.* **-ties** the state of doing or something done: *There was a burst of activity just before the Christmas party; a school buzzing* or *humming with activity; to break off* or *terminate a prohibited activity; Terrorist activity has been curbed; Business activity is paralyzed by the strike; There's political and subversive activity going on behind the scenes; creative, intellectual, mental, military, physical, scientific activity; Running is an activity that requires effort; We engage in, participate in, take part in cultural activities at school; leisure, outdoor, outside, recreational, social activities; He's too busy studying to engage in extracurricular activities.*

act of God *n.* an unforeseeable accident that is beyond human control, as an earthquake, flood, or tornado: *The insurance company considered the broken water main an act of God and refused to pay for the damage.*

ac.tor (AC.tur) *n.* one who plays a role, as in a play or movie: *a famous actor of Hamlet; to cast an actor in the role of Hamlet; a character actor; child actor; movie actor; The prime minister was a key* or *leading* or *major actor in the independence movement.* —**ac.tress** (-tris) *fem.*

ac.tu.al (AC.choo.ul) *adj.* real and existing, not imagined, estimated, etc.: *The actual cost was less than the estimate; its actual worth; an actual happening; actual and potential sales.* —**ac.tu.al.ly** *adv.* —**ac.tu.al.i.ty** (-AL.i.tee) *n.* **-ties**: *ideals and actualities; In actuality, only a few lives were lost.*

ac.tu.al.ize (AC.choo.uh.lize) *v.* **-iz.es, -ized, -iz.ing** make actual; bring into being: *to actualize dreams, plans, potentials, visions; People actualize* (= fulfill) *themselves through their work.*

ac.tu.ar.y (AC.choo.air.ee) *n.* **-ar.ies** a statistician who calculates insurance risks, premiums, annuities, etc. —**ac.tu.ar.i.al** (-AIR.ee.ul) *adj.*

ac.tu.ate (AC.choo.ate) *v.* **-ates, -at.ed, -at.ing** **1** motivate for action: *to be actuated by compassion, greed, malice, self-interest.* **2** put in operation: *the pressure that actuates a brake system;* ***adj.* & *cpd.:*** *an **actuating** device; a foot-actuated parking brake.* —**ac.tu.a.tion** (-AY.shun) *n.*

ac.tu.a.tor (AC.choo.ay.tur) *n.* one that puts something in operation: *Control actuators keep an aircraft level; a brake actuator; valve actuators.*

a.cu.i.ty (uh.CUE.i.tee) *n.* sharpness or keenness, esp. of perception: *mental acuity; visual acuity; acuity of hearing.*

a.cu.men (uh.CUE.mun) *n.* keenness of insight and judgment: *to demonstrate, display, show good business acumen; a lawyer's legal acumen; financial, intellectual, political acumen.*

ac.u.punc.ture (AC.yoo.punk.chur) *n.* a method of treating disease and pain by inserting needles at specific points on the body, traditionally used by the Chinese. —**ac.u.punc.tur.ist** *n.*

a.cute (uh.CUTE) *adj.* **1** critical or severe: *an acute crisis, problem, shortage of water; acute ill-health, pain, hardship, poverty.* **2** of diseases, likely to come to a crisis, but of short duration; not chronic: *acute gastritis, indigestion; an **acute-care** hospital (providing emergency and other short-term services).* **3** keen or sharp: *a dog's acute sense of hearing; an acute analysis, insight, thinker; the **acute accent** (= accent mark slanting left to right, as in blasé); an **acute angle** (of less than 90 degrees).* —**a.cute.ly** *adv.*

ad *n. Informal.* an advertisement: *"Teachers Wanted" is a want ad for teachers; a help-wanted ad; a classified, not display ad.*

ad- *prefix.* to; toward: *adjoin, administer, advert.*

ad.age (AD.ij) *n.* a popular saying in long use; proverb; maxim: *"Look before you leap" is an old adage.*

a.da.gio (uh.DAH.joh) *adj. & adv. Music.* in slow time. —*n.* **1** an adagio movement. **2** a slow ballet duet.

Ad.am (AD.um) *n.* in the Bible, the name of the first man: *I would **not know him from Adam** (= would not be able to recognize him).*

ad.a.mant (AD.uh.munt) *adj.* unchanging in behavior; unyielding: *He won't change his mind, he's quite adamant; adamant about his views on the subject; He's adamant that the proposal be dropped; an adamant defense, opponent, refusal; adamant opposition.* —**ad.a.mant.ly** *adv.:* *He's adamantly against or opposed to abortion.*

Adam's apple *n.* a projection in the front of the neck, seen esp. in men.

a.dapt (uh.DAPT) *v.* modify something or oneself to suit a different situation: *He found it hard to adapt (himself) to the new climate;* ***adj.:*** *a story **adapted** for TV; a screenplay adapted from a novel; Cactuses are adapted to life in the desert.*
—**a.dap.ta.ble** (-tuh.bul) *adj.*
—**a.dapt.a.bil.i.ty** (-tuh.BIL.i.tee) *n.*
—**ad.ap.ta.tion** (ad.up.TAY.shun) *n.:* *an adaptation of a novel for TV.*
—**a.dapt.er** or **a.dap.tor** (uh.DAP.tur) *n.* —**a.dap.tive** (-tiv) *adj.*

add *v.* join something to another: *He added sugar to my coffee; It added to (= increased) the taste; He added (= also said) that no cream was available; You get 6 if you add 1, 2, and 3; He can add (= do sums) and subtract; We **add on** new wings to our main building as business expands; We **add to** (= increase) our staff; His stories don't **add up** (= make sense); Those smiles **add up to** (= amount to) mischief.* —**add fuel to the fire** or **flame** *Informal.* make a problem, situation, etc. worse. —**add insult to injury** make matters even worse, as by taunting after hurting.

ad.dend (AD.end) *n.* a number to be added, as 3 in 3 + 2 = 5.

ad.den.dum (uh.DEN.dum) *n., pl.* **-da** something to be added, esp. to a book; appendix.

ad.der *n.* **1** a poisonous Old World viper. **2** a poisonous snake such as the "puff adder" of Africa and the "death adder" of Australia. **3** a harmless North American snake, also called "blowing adder."

ad.dict (AD.ict) *n.* one who does something habitually and compulsively, esp. one who uses narcotics: *a confirmed addict; a drug addict;* ***adj.:*** *a patient who is chronically, hopelessly **addicted** to drugs.*
—**ad.dic.tion** (uh.DIC.shun) *n.:* *addiction to drugs; Physical dependence produces addiction.* —**ad.dic.tive** (-tiv) *adj.:* *Cocaine, heroine, tobacco, etc. are addictive; addictive substances.*

ad.di.tion (uh.DISH.un) *n.* **1** the process or an act of adding: *to do an addition.* **2** a person or thing added: *The new addition to our family is a girl; He gets a salary and a bonus **in addition**; a bonus **in addition to** (= as well as) his salary.*
—**ad.di.tion.al** *adj.;* **ad.di.tion.al.ly** *adv.*

additive / adjudicate

ad.di.tive (AD.uh.tiv) *n.* an added substance: *Color is often an additive in foods; an additive ingredient.*

ad.dle (AD.ul) *v.* **ad.dles, ad.dled, ad.dling** 1 of eggs, make or become rotten; *adj.: an addled egg.* 2 make or become confused: *Alcohol addles rather than clarifies the mind.*

addle-brained *adj.* confused or muddled: *an addle-brained agitator.* Also **ad.dle.head.ed** or **ad.dle.pat.ed.**

ad.dress (uh.DRES) *v.* 1 speak to someone: *to address an audience; People address important officials respectfully; We address the French teacher as "Madam."* 2 write the destination on something being sent: *to address envelopes, mail.* 3 apply oneself to a question, problem, etc.: *The speaker addressed himself to the problem of unemployment; to address (= deal with) a problem.* —*n.* 1 an elaborate speech: *to deliver or give a presidential address; an eloquent, keynote, inaugural, moving, stirring address; an address about social reform.* 2 (also AD.res) the location of a person or business: *Our address is 1776 Madison Avenue; Did you leave a forwarding address when you changed your address? I couldn't find you at the old address; Write your return address on the top left corner of the envelope; a business address; home, permanent, temporary addresses.* 3 the location of information in a computer memory. —**ad.dress.a.ble** *adj.*

ad.dress.ee (ad.res.EE) *n.* one to whom something such as a letter is addressed.

ad.duce (uh.DUCE, *rhyme:* produce) *v.* **ad.duc.es, ad.duced, ad.duc.ing** give as an example or as evidence.

ad.e.noids (AD.uh.noids) *n.pl.* lymphoid tissue growths in the throat behind the nose. —**ad.e.noi.dal** (-NOY.dul) *adj.*

a.dept (uh.DEPT) *adj.* skilled or expert: *Guy is adept at billiards; the adept touch of the artist; an adept hand, merchant.* —*n.* (AD.ept) one who is adept; skilled person. —**a.dept.ly** (uh.DEPT.lee) *adv.*; **a.dept.ness** *n.*

ad.e.quate (AD.uh.quit) *adj.* sufficient to satisfy a need: *remuneration adequate for the work done; supplies that are barely adequate to the need.* —**ad.e.quate.ly** *adv.* —**ad.e.quate.ness** or **ad.e.qua.cy** (-kwuh.see) *n.*

ad.here (ad.HERE) *v.* **-heres, -hered, -her.ing** 1 stick firmly: *Glue helps things to adhere to each other.* 2 stick; hence, be devoted to: *to adhere to a plan, policy; to adhere closely, strictly, stubbornly.* —**ad.he.sion** (ad.HEE.zhun) *n.*

ad.her.ent (ad.HEER.unt) *n.* close follower and supporter: *an adherent of the civil rights movement.* —**ad.her.ence** (-unce) *n.*

ad.he.sive (ad.HEE.siv) *n.* a sticky substance: *Gum is an adhesive; Patriotism serves as an adhesive (= something that sticks parts together) for national unity.* —*adj.* sticking, sticky, or stuck: *Adhesive paper is used for labels and stickers; adhesive paste used in bookbinding; Paperbacks come with adhesive (= not stitched but "perfect") binding; a bandage kept in place with adhesive tape.* —**ad.he.sive.ness** *n.*

ad hoc *adj.* for a particular purpose: *an ad hoc committee to study street lighting; an ad hoc measure, policy, solution; The plan is experimental and ad hoc.*

ad ho.mi.nem (ad.HOM.uh.num) *adj.* attacking the person rather than addressing the issue: *to use an ad hominem approach, argument; an ad hominem attack, style; to resort to ad hominem measures; adv.: You're arguing ad hominem.*

a.dieu (uh.DEW) *n. & interj.* **a.dieus** or **a.dieux** (-DEWS) farewell: *We bade him adieu; We said adieu.*

ad in.fi.ni.tum (AD.in.fuh.NYE.tum) *adv. Latin.* without limit; endlessly: *You can count 1, 2, 3, 4, and so on ad infinitum.*

a.di.os (ad.ee.OSE) *interj.* good-bye.

ad.i.pose (AD.uh.pose) *adj.* having to do with fat: *adipose tissue.* —**ad.i.pos.i.ty** (-POS.i.tee) *n.*

ad.ja.cent (uh.JAY.sunt) *adj.* near or next: *the house adjacent to ours;* **ad.ja.cent.ly** *adv.* —**ad.ja.cen.cy** *n.*

ad.jec.tive (AJ.ic.tiv) *n.* a word that qualifies a noun, as "good" in "the good book" or "The book is good." —**ad.jec.ti.val** (-TYE.vul) *adj.*

ad.join (uh.JOIN) *v.* be next to and touching something: *My property adjoins his; Adjoining the kitchen is our dining room; adj.: an adjoining building, room, space, wall.*

ad.journ (uh.JURN) *v.* 1 suspend a meeting or session: *We adjourned for lunch; The committee adjourned for a week.* 2 *Informal.* move to another place: *Shall we adjourn to the living room?* —**ad.journ.ment** *n.*

ad.judge (uh.JUJ) *v.* **ad.judg.es, ad.judged, ad.judg.ing** 1 award by law, as by a judge: *The house was adjudged to his ex-wife.* 2 judge: *Jim was adjudged (to be) the winner of the debate.*

ad.ju.di.cate (uh.JOO.duh.cate) *v.* **-cates, -cat.ed, -cat.ing** 1 settle a claim

adjunct / admit

judicially: *to adjudicate a dispute.*
2 serve as a judge or referee: *to adjudicate on a case; to adjudicate a debate, a music festival.* —**ad.ju.di.ca.tion** (-CAY.shun) *n.* —**ad.ju.di.ca.tor** (-cay.tur) *n.*
ad.junct (AJ.unct) *adj.* attached to something without forming a part of it: *an adjunct professor (not a faculty member).* —*n.* an addition: *an adjunct to* or *of something.*
ad.jure (uh.JOOR) *v.* **-jures, -jured, -jur.ing** urge earnestly or solemnly: *The minister adjured the young offender to think of his future.* —**ad.ju.ra.tion** (aj.uh.RAY.shun) *n.*
ad.just (uh.JUST) *v.* **1** change slightly so as to suit a new condition: *The eyes adjust (themselves) to light; Sound volume should be adjusted to the size of the audience; Do not adjust your (TV) set; Please adjust the dial to "Low"; to adjust* (= adapt oneself) *to a new climate;* *adj.*: *He is well adjusted to his new environment.* **2** settle: *An insurance adjuster adjusts claims after adjusting* (= determining the amount of) *the losses.* —**ad.just.a.ble** *adj.* —**ad.just.er** or **ad.jus.tor** *n.*; **ad.just.ment** *n.*
ad.ju.tant (AJ.uh.tunt) *n.* **1** an officer who helps a commander as an administrative assistant. **2** a large stork of Asia and Africa.
ad lib *adv. Informal.* in a free style, without using a script or musical score.
ad-lib (ad.LIB) *adj.* free-style: *an ad-lib comment, joke, performance.* —*v.* **-libs, -libbed, -lib.bing** deliver lines or a speech spontaneously. —*n.* a free-style comment or remark. —**ad-lib.ber** *n.*
ad.mail *n.* the direct-mail component of the postal service; junk mail.
ad.man *n.* **-men** a man in the advertising business.
ad.mass (AD.mas) *n.* **1** the section of a population that is easily influenced by mass advertising. **2** a mass-marketing system.
ad.min.is.ter (ad.MIN.is.tur) *v.* **1** direct the taking of something: *to administer a medicine, an oath of allegiance.* **2** manage: *to administer a department;* to **administer to** (= help with) *the needs of a community.* —**ad.min.is.tra.ble** (-truh.bul) *adj.*
ad.min.is.trate (ad.MIN.is.trate) *v.* administer: *Wine is administrated by the department of agriculture.*
ad.min.is.tra.tion (ad.MIN.is.TRAY.shun) *n.* **1** an administering: *the administration of justice by the courts; a course in business administration; public administration of resources.* **2** government: *a civilian administration; military administrations; the Nixon administration.*
ad.min.is.tra.tive (ad.MIN.is.truh.tiv) *adj.* having to do with administration: *administrative duties, reform, red tape, responsibility.* —**ad.min.is.tra.tor** (-tray.tur) *n.* one who administers or manages: *the administrator of an estate; school administrators.*
ad.mi.ra.ble (AD.muh.ruh.bul) *adj.* that deserves to be admired: *an admirable performance;* **ad.mi.ra.bly** *adv.*
ad.mi.ral (AD.muh.rul) *n.* a naval officer ranking above a captain or commodore.
ad.mi.ral.ty (AD.muh.rul.tee) *n.* **-ties** a court having jurisdiction in maritime cases: *admiralty laws.*
ad.mi.ra.tion (ad.muh.RAY.shun) *n.* **1** an act of admiring or being admired; a feeling of wonder, esteem, or approval: *to arouse, command, express, win admiration; to feel admiration for someone; He looks at her with admiration; He looks up to her in admiration; He's filled with admiration for her; Admiration can be blind, deep, grudging, mutual, sincere, strong, undying.* **2** one who is admired: *She is the admiration of her friends.*
ad.mire (ad.MIRE) *v.* **-mires, -mired, -mir.ing** regard with wonder, esteem, or approval: *She admires him greatly; admires his family; admires him for his many achievements; admires his being so successful in his profession;* **ad.mir.er** *n.* —**ad.mir.ing.ly** *adv.*
ad.mis.si.ble (ad.MIS.uh.bul) *adj.* worthy of being allowed, esp. in court: *admissible evidence.* —**ad.mis.si.bil.i.ty** (-BIL.i.tee) *n.*
ad.mis.sion (ad.MISH.un) *n.* **1** entrance with rights, privileges, etc.: *to apply for* or *seek admission to a school; to be denied, granted, refused admission; Admission to the army is restricted and selective, not open or free; He gained admission by fair means.* **2** entrance fee: *The admission to the show is $65; The general admission (for unreserved seats) is $45.* **3** acknowledgment or confession: *to make an admission of guilt; a damaging admission; an admission that he had helped in the crime; He was guilty by* or *on his own admission.*
ad.mit (ad.MIT) *v.* **-mits, -mit.ted, -mit.ting 1** allow: *Latecomers will not be admitted to the show; This rule does not* **admit of** (*Formal for* allow or tolerate)

exceptions. **2** acknowledge: *The accused readily admitted to the police that he had taken part in the burglary; He* **admitted to** *(Formal for* confessed*) his complicity in the crime; admitted to his stealing the money; admitted (to) doing it.*

ad.mit.tance (ad.MIT.unce) *n. Formal.* physical entrance to a place: *He tried to gain admittance to the show; was denied admittance.*

ad.mit.ted.ly (ad.MIT.id.lee) *adv.* as admitted: *Boys and girls, admittedly, are different from each other.*

ad.mix (ad.MIX) *v.* mix together; mix in. —**ad.mix.ture** (-chur) *n.*

ad.mon.ish (ad.MON.ish) *v. Formal.* warn someone mildly but seriously: *The principal admonished the students for being lazy; admonished them to be more diligent.* —**ad.mon.i.tor.y** (-uh.tor.ee) *adj.* —**ad.mon.i.tion** (ad.muh.NISH.un) *n.*

ad nau.se.am (ad.NAW.zee.um) *adv.* to a sickening degree: *He keeps repeating his jokes ad nauseam.*

a.do (uh.DOO) *n.* fuss or bother: *The child made much ado about* or *over being ignored; Without further* or *more ado, he left the scene.*

a.do.be (uh.DOH.bee) *n.* a structure of sun-dried bricks; *adja.: an adobe house, wall.*

ad.o.les.cence (ad.uh.LES.unce) *n.* the period between childhood and maturity. —**ad.o.les.cent** *n.: Teenagers are adolescents;* **adj.***: her adolescent shyness.*

A.don.is (uh.DON.is) *n.* in Greek myth, a beautiful youth.

a.dopt (uh.DOPT) *v.* **1** take as one's own child: *The childless couple adopted an orphan girl; adopted her as their own;* **adj.***: an* **adopted** *child.* **2** take up and use as one's own: *to adopt a foreign costume, custom, language.* **3** agree to; accept: *A meeting adopts a resolution.*
—**a.dop.tion** *n.: Disowned children are put up for adoption; an adoption agency.*
—**a.dop.tive** (uh.DOP.tiv) *adja.: Guy's* **adoptive** (= not natural) *parents; their* **adoptive** (= adopted) *child Guy.*

a.dore (uh.DOR) *v.* **-dores, -dored, -dor.ing** **1** worship: *"We adore thee, O Lord!"* **2** *Informal.* be extremely fond of a person or thing: *A mother adores her baby; She adores singing in public; He adores the couple for their devotion to the cause.* —**a.dor.a.ble** *adj.;* **a.dor.a.bly** (-blee) *adv.* —**ad.o.ra.tion** (ad.uh.RAY.shun) *n.*

a.dorn (uh.DORN) *v.* decorate: *She adorns herself with jewels.*
—**a.dorn.ment** *n.*

ad.re.nal (uh.DREE.nul) *adj.* relating to two glands, one above each kidney: *an adrenal secretion.*

ad.ren.al.in or **ad.ren.al.ine** (uh.DREN.uh.lin) *n.* a hormone made by the **adrenal glands** and secreted into the blood during anger, fear, etc., preparing the body for quick action: *a shot of adrenalin; Watching hockey gets his adrenalin flowing* or *going* or *pumping.*
—**Adrenalin** *Trademark.*

a.drift (uh.DRIFT) *adjp. & adv.* drifting without aim or guidance: *a boat found adrift on the lake; It was cast adrift by someone; Crowds of demonstrators were turned adrift on the streets.*

a.droit (uh.DROIT) *adj.* skillful: *an adroit politician; an admirer adroit at* or *in flattery.*

ad.sorb (ad.SORB, -ZORB) *v.* take up and hold a substance such as a gas, steam, etc. on the surface, as charcoal does. —**ad.sor.bent** *n. & adj.*
—**ad.sorp.tion** *n.* —**ad.sorp.tive** (-tiv) *adj.*

ad.u.la.tion (aj.uh.LAY.shun) *n.* servile praise; flattery: *the adulation of followers.* —**ad.u.la.tor** *n.* —**ad.u.la.to.ry** (-luh.tor.ee) *adj.*

a.dult (uh.DULT, AD.ult) *n.* a mature living being, esp. a person of legal age: *Consenting adults may enter into an agreement to do anything that is not illegal.*
—*adj.: She's not very adult in her behavior; an adult butterfly (past the pupa stage); adult* or *continuing education (offered to adults who want to improve their knowledge or skills); an adult movie (to which children are not admitted).*
—**a.dult.hood** (short "oo") *n.*

a.dul.ter.ant (uh.DUL.tuh.runt) *n.* something that adulterates: *Water may be an adulterant in wine.*

a.dul.ter.ate (uh.DUL.tuh.rate) *v.* **-ates, -at.ed, -at.ing** make impure by adding something inferior or foreign: *The wine was adulterated with water;* **a.dul.ter.a.tor** *n.* —**a.dul.ter.a.tion** (-RAY.shun) *n.*

a.dul.ter.ous *adj.* having to do with adultery: *an adulterous husband, relationship, wife.* —**a.dul.ter.ous.ly** *adv.*

a.dul.ter.y (uh.DUL.tuh.ree) *n.* **-ter.ies** a married person's sexual relationship with someone other than the legal spouse: *to commit adultery with someone.*
—**a.dul.ter.er** *n.;* **a.dul.ter.ess** *fem.*

ad.um.brate (AD.um.brate) *v.* **-brates, -brat.ed, -brat.ing** suggest in advance or in an incomplete way. —**ad.um.bra.tion** (-BRAY.shun) *n.*

ad va.lor.em (ad.vuh.LOR.um) *adj.* according to the value: *an ad valorem levy, tax, (customs) duty.*

ad.vance (ad.VANCE) *v.* **-vanc.es, -vanced, -vanc.ing 1** come or go forward: *The army is advancing; It advances against the enemy; advances to or toward the country's borders; advances into enemy territory; Prices advance* (= increase) *with inflation.* **2** put forward: *to advance an opinion unasked; She was advanced* (= promoted) *to a higher pay bracket; We advanced* (= lent) *him $100 till payday; The date of publication has been advanced (to an earlier date).* **—n. 1** an advancing or something advanced: *an advance of $100; an advance paid to an author against royalties; Our army made an advance* (= forward movement) *against the enemy; It pressed the advance to or toward the country's borders and into enemy territory.* **2** progress: *the advance of high technology; the* **advances** (= developments) *made in microcomputers.* **3 advances** *pl.* overtures: *The management made advances to the union; The union rebuffed or rejected the advances; She resisted his advances* (= acts of wooing). **—in advance** before due time: *A month's rent was paid in advance; royalties paid in advance* (= ahead of sales or publication). **—adj.** ahead of time; prior: *The police had advance information of the plot; an advance copy, notice, party, payment; advance publicity.*

advanced (ad.VANST) *adj.* being ahead: *an advanced level of achievement; advanced English; an advanced student; advanced studies; the industrially advanced countries of Europe; A man of 90 is rather advanced in years* (= rather old).

advance man *n.* one who prepares a tour ahead of a political candidate.

ad.vance.ment (ad.VANCE.munt) *n.* a moving forward: *the advancement of peace; rapid, slow advancement; to block, further, speed one's professional advancement.*

ad.van.tage (ad.VAN.tij) *n.* superiority or what results from it: *Education is an advantage when applying for a job; The educated have an advantage over the uneducated; the advantages of education; a clear, decided, mutual, obvious, unfair advantage; He used his public office to personal advantage* (= gain); *He wouldn't* **take advantage of** (= exploit) *her youth; Disadvantages outweigh advantages; His education worked to his advantage in getting promoted; He was at an advantage because of his education; He used his education to good advantage; In tennis, a server says, "Advantage in!"* (= a chance to score the next point and the game); *Advantage Jones* (= Jones is in the winning position)! **—ad.van.ta.geous** (ad.vun.TAY.jus) *adj.*: *A change of wind will be advantageous to us; It would be advantageous to wait a little;* **ad.van.ta.geous.ly** *adv.*

ad.vent (AD.vent) *n.* the coming or arrival of a person or thing that changes a situation or condition: *the advent of spring; the advent of space travel; The season of* **Advent**, *a period before Christmas, commemorates the coming of Christ.*

ad.ven.ti.tious (ad.ven.TISH.us) *adj.* added externally; acquired: *adventitious blessings, odors, roots (of the banyan tree).*

ad.ven.ture (ad.VEN.chur) *n.* a risky, exciting, or challenging experience: *the adventures of Ulysses; an explorer's spirit of adventure; People have or meet with adventures; bold, breathtaking, exciting, thrilling adventures; a sailor in search of high adventure; It's an adventure to sail or sailing the high seas.* **—v. -tures, -tured, -tur.ing** dare to go *into a place, on an undertaking.*

ad.ven.tur.er (ad.VEN.chur.ur) *n.* **1** one who undertakes adventures: *a dauntless, intrepid adventurer.* **2** one who seeks his fortune by soldiering or unscrupulous means.

ad.ven.ture.some (ad.VEN.chur.sum) *adj.* risky or daring: *adventuresome investors, spirit, tastes.*

ad.ven.tur.ess (ad.VEN.chur.us) *n.* **1** a woman who schemes to obtain wealth and rank: *a bold adventuress.* **2** a woman who undertakes adventures.

ad.ven.tur.ous (ad.VEN.chur.us) *adj.* **1** full of adventure: *an adventurous expedition, life.* **2** daring: *an adventurous explorer;* also **ad.ven.ture.some.**

ad.verb (AD.vurb) *n.* a word modifying a verb, adjective, or another adverb, as "very" and "slowly" in "She's very good" and "He speaks very slowly." **—ad.ver.bi.al** (ad.VUR.bee.ul) *adj.*

ad.ver.sa.ri.al (ad.vur.SAIR.ee.ul) *adj.* adversary or opposing: *an adversarial relationship.*

ad.ver.sa.ry (AD.vur.sair.ee) *n.* **-ries** an opponent: *a bold, formidable, worthy adversary.* **—adj.** opposing or antagonistic: *the adversary climate in labor relations; divorce and such adversary proceedings; in an adversary role; the adversary system of union-management relations.*

ad.verse (AD.vurce, ad.VURCE) *adj.* opposing or unfavorable: *an adverse decision; adverse winds, working condi-*

adversity / aerobatic

tions; conditions that are adverse to our interests. —**ad.verse.ly** adv.
ad.ver.si.ty (ad.VUR.si.tee) n. -ties misfortune: patience in adversity; to face, overcome adversity; the **adversities** (= hardships) of life, of old age.
ad.vert (AD.vurt) v. **1** direct one's attention to something. **2** [short form] advertise. —n. [short form] advertisement.
ad.ver.tise (AD.vur.tize) v. -tis.es, -tised, -tis.ing announce something by a paid notice in a journal, on TV, radio, etc.: to advertise a job, position, vacancy; to advertise that a vacancy exists; advertise for an editor; adj.: an **advertised** policy, price, product. —**ad.ver.tis.er** n.
ad.ver.tise.ment (ad.vur.TIZE.munt) n. a notice advertising something; ad: to place, publish, run, take out an advertisement for an editor.
advertising n. **1** advertisements: a paper that carries no advertising; outdoor advertising using billboards; word-of-mouth advertising. **2** the preparation and publishing of advertisements; adja.: the advertising manager of a newspaper; an advertising agency, brochure, campaign, department, firm, slogan; advertising material, revenue, standards.
ad.ver.to.ri.al (ad.vur.TOR.ee.ul) n. advertising published like editorial material, esp. in print: Newspapers run advertorials; a 60-second video advertorial; adja.: an advertorial idea, insert, material, package, page, program, section.
ad.vice (ad.VICE) n. **1** opinion given by a person on what to do in a given situation: Seek advice when you need help; A father gives or offers advice to his son; a bit or piece or words of advice; professional advice on a legal matter; She acted on or upon, not against her lawyer's advice; She refused to deal with him **on advice of** counsel; to disregard, follow, refuse, take, turn a deaf ear to advice; friendly, good, misleading, parting, sage, sensible, sound, unasked-for, unsolicited advice; Our advice to you is to see another lawyer. **2** a notice or information, as about a delivery to be expected: a remittance advice; shipping advices from our exporters.
ad.vis.a.ble (ad.VYE.zuh.bul) adj. recommended: Rest is advisable when you are tired; It is advisable to rest a little.
—**ad.vis.a.bil.i.ty** (-BIL.i.tee) n.
ad.vise (ad.VIZE) v. -vis.es, -vised, -vis.ing **1** give advice: The doctor advised her to take rest; He advised (= recommended) rest; cpd: an **ill-advised** move; a **well-advised** rest. **2** give notice: We will advise you when it arrives; adjp.: We will keep you **advised** (= informed).
—**ad.vis.er** or **ad.vi.sor** n.: an adviser to the government on security matters.
ad.vis.ed.ly (ad.VYE.zid.lee) adv. after consideration: a word used advisedly.
ad.vise.ment (ad.VIZE.munt) n. [legal use] careful consideration: The court agreed to take the matter under advisement.
ad.vi.so.ry (ad.VYE.zuh.ree) adj. giving advice: an advisory body, committee, council, opinion; to act in an advisory capacity, role. —n. a warning report: A weather advisory has been issued.
ad.vo.ca.cy (AD.vuh.cuh.see) n. the advocating of something: the advocacy of better day care; adja.: a citizen advocacy group for lowering taxes; advocacy advertising, as about butter being better than margarine; **advocacy journalism** (with much personal involvement by the reporter).
ad.vo.cate (AD.vuh.kit) n. one who defends or supports a person or cause, as a lawyer: Gandhi was a strong advocate of nonviolence. —v. (AD.vuh.cate) -cates, -cat.ed, -cat.ing defend or support: He advocated nonviolence; advocated disobeying unjust laws.
ae.gis (EE.jis) n. auspices or protection: The nations of the world meet under the aegis of the U.N.
ae.o.li.an (ee.OH.lee.un) adj. having to do with the wind: The **aeolian harp** is a stringed box that produces musical sounds when a current of air blows over it.
ae.on (EE.on) same as EON.
aer.ate (AIR.ate) v. -ates, -at.ed, -at.ing infuse with a gas, as soda water with carbon dioxide: Blood is aerated with oxygen in the lungs; aerated water.
—**aer.a.tor** n. —**aer.a.tion** (air.AY.shun) n.
aer.i.al (AIR.ee.ul) adj. of, in, or by air: an aerial attack, battle, survey; a firefighter's aerial ladder; aerial photography.
—n. a TV or radio antenna.
—**aer.i.al.ly** adv.
aer.i.al.ist (AIR.ee.uh.list) n. one who performs on a trapeze, tightrope, etc. in a circus.
aer.ie (AIR.ee) same as EYRIE.
aero (AIR.oh) **1** adj. aerodynamic or aerodynamically designed: the aero look; aero styling; aero helmets. **2** comb. form. having to do with the air, with gases, or with aircraft: aerobic, aerodrome, aeronaut.
aer.o.bat.ic (air.oh.BAT.ic) **1** adj. having to do with feats performed with

an airplane: *an aerobatic display.* **2 aerobatics** *n.pl.* [takes *sing. v.*] aerobatic feats.

aer.o.bic (air.OH.bic) **1** *adj.* having to do with improving the body's use of oxygen: *her aerobic capacity; aerobic exercises.* **2 aerobics** *n.pl.* [takes *sing. v.*] aerobic exercises or their performance: *Aerobics is good for you.*

aer.o.drome (AIR.uh.drome) *n. Brit.* airfield.

aer.o.dy.nam.ic (AIR.oh.dye.NAM.ic) *adj.* having to do with the forces exerted by gases in motion: *aerodynamic design, drag, efficiency, forces, looks, styling of sports cars.*

aer.o.gram (AIR.oh.gram) *n.* an air letter.

aer.o.naut (AIR.uh.nawt) *n.* one who operates an airship, balloon, etc. —**aer.o.nau.tic** (-NAW.tic) *adj.*

aer.o.nau.tics (air.uh.NAW.tics) *n.pl.* [takes *sing. v.*] the science of the design, manufacture, and operation of aircraft.

aer.o.pause (AIR.uh.paws) *n.* the altitude above the earth at which the air is too thin for airplanes to fly.

aer.o.plane (AIR.uh.plane) *n. Brit.* airplane.

aer.o.sol (AIR.oh.sol) *n.* a container for spraying a liquid under pressure; *adja.: an aerosol deodorant; a product sold in aerosol form; an aerosol insecticide, spray; an **aerosol bomb*** (= can).

aer.o.space (AIR.oh.space) *n.* the part of space in which airplanes, rockets, etc. travel; *adja.: aerospace industries, medicine, research.*

aer.y (AIR.ee) *adj.* ethereal. —*n.* same as EYRIE.

aes.thete (ES.theet, "th" as in "thin") *n.* one who appreciates artistic beauty. —**aes.thet.ic** (es.THET.ic) or **aes.thet.i.cal** *adj.* —**aes.thet.i.cal.ly** *adv.*

aes.thet.ics (es.THET.ics) *n.pl.* [takes *sing. v.*] the philosophy of artistic beauty.

aether same as ETHER.

a.far (uh.FAR) *adv.* far away: *Explorers went afar in search of new lands; People came from afar to attend the convention.*

af.fa.ble (AF.uh.bul) *adj.* pleasant to talk to: *an affable person; his affable* (= friendly) *smile;* **af.fa.bly** (-blee) *adv.* —**af.fa.bil.i.ty** (-BIL.i.tee) *n.*

af.fair (uh.FAIR) *n.* **1** a temporary love relationship: *He is having or carrying on an affair with his colleague; casual, clandestine, illicit, love, romantic, secret, tempestuous affairs.* **2** a business or event: *A wedding is a social affair; Our wedding was a private affair; delicate, dull, formal, gala, informal, shabby, sinister, sordid, ugly affairs; to cover up, hush up, investigate an affair; an **affair of honor*** (= duel); *That's his affair* (= concern), *not yours.* **3 affairs** *pl.* matters of general interest: *current affairs; to conduct affairs of state; to arrange, manage, settle, straighten out one's affairs; cultural affairs; the Minister of External or Foreign Affairs; an expert in international affairs; national affairs; the Minister of Veterans Affairs.*

af.fect (uh.FECT) *v.* **1** have an influence on a person or thing: *Smoking affects your health; Metals are affected by heat and cold; The tragedy affected everyone deeply, profoundly, strongly; Everyone was much affected by it;* **adj.**: *a badly affected area, community, economy; The tragedy was a very **affecting*** (= moving) *experience;* **adv.**: *She spoke to us **affectingly*** (= feelingly) *about it.* **2** pretend: *He affects ignorance of what happened; She affected an air of innocence; She affected not to hear;* **adj.**: *an **affected*** (= artificial) *Oxford accent.* —**af.fec.ted.ly** *adv.*

af.fec.ta.tion (af.ek.TAY.shun) *n.* behavior or attitude that is assumed or put on for show: *His Oxford accent is a mere affectation.*

af.fec.tion (uh.FEK.shun) *n.* **1** feeling of love for someone: *to demonstrate, display, return, show affection; to feel affection for someone; to gain or win someone's affection; a deep, strong, warm affection; to alienate a spouse's affections and cause a separation.* **2** disease: *TB is an affection of the lungs.* —**af.fec.tion.ate** (-shun.it) *adj.: She is very affectionate to or toward her friends.* —**af.fec.tion.ate.ly** *adv.*

af.fer.ent (AF.ur.unt) *adj.* bringing to a central organ: *afferent nerves leading to the brain; afferent impulses, pathways.*

af.fi.ance (uh.FYE.unce) *v.* **-anc.es, -anced, -anc.ing** pledge to marry: *His daughter was affianced to a lawyer;* **adj.**: *a newly **affianced** couple.*

af.fi.da.vit (af.uh.DAY.vit) *n.* a written statement made on oath: *Lawyers file affidavits on behalf of clients.*

af.fil.i.ate (uh.FIL.ee.ate) *v.***-ates, -at.ed, -at.ing** connect as a member or branch: *The parent company affiliated a new store; A left-wing organization would be unlikely to affiliate itself with a right-wing movement;* **adj.**: *The two stores are **affiliated**; They are affiliated to or with a national chain.* —*n.*(-ee.it) a

affinity / afraid

member or branch: *The new store is an affiliate of the national chain; the broadcasting affiliate of a media giant.*
—**af.fil.i.a.tion** (-AY.shun) *n.*: *schools in affiliation with a university; party, political, religious affiliations.*

af.fin.i.ty (uh.FIN.i.tee) *n.* **-ties 1** connection based on kinship or common interests: *There are relatives by birth and by affinity (= marriage); In-laws are tied by bonds of affinity, not by blood; the close affinity of Canadian English with American; the many affinities between Canadian and American English in pronunciation, vocabulary, etc.; An* **affinity card** *is a credit card issued to an* **affinity group** *such as a trade or professional organization, school alumni, or customers of an airline.* **2** attraction based on kinship: *to feel, have, show an affinity to one's relatives; the strong affinity of European languages for American words.*

af.firm (uh.FURM) *v.* say firmly: *She affirmed her innocence; affirmed that she was innocent.* —**af.fir.ma.tion** (af.ur.MAY.shun) *n.*

af.fir.ma.tive (uh.FIR.muh.tiv) *adj.* saying "yes"; positive: *an affirmative response; a program of* **affirmative action** *to give women and minorities equal opportunity with the majority in employment, school admissions, etc. by favoring them over other candidates.* —*n.* the "yes" form of answer: *He replied* **in the affirmative;** *The* **affirmative** (= the ayes or "yes" side) *won the debate.*
—**af.fir.ma.tive.ly** *adv.*

af.fix (uh.FIX) *v.* attach or add: *to affix a signature to a document.* —*n.* (AF.ix) a prefix or suffix.

af.fla.tus (uh.FLAY.tus) *n.* inspiration; creative impulse.

af.flict (uh.FLICT) *v.* cause suffering to someone: *He is afflicted with gout.*
—**af.flic.tion** (-FLIC.shun) *n.*: *Gout is an affliction of the joints; We sympathize with him in his affliction.*

af.flu.ent (AF.loo.unt) *adj.* increasingly prosperous; well-to-do: *our affluent relatives; an affluent family, society, suburb; We live in affluent times; He is affluent in worldly goods.* —**af.flu.ence** *n.*

af.ford (uh.FORD) *v.* **1** be able to spare the time, money, etc. for something: *Can we afford two cars? I can't afford* (= am unable) *to miss work; I could ill afford to go on leave without pay.* **2** give or furnish: *Music affords us pleasure.*
—**af.for.da.ble** *adj.*: *The homeless are looking for affordable housing at affordable prices.*

af.for.est.a.tion (uh.for.is.TAY.shun) *n.* the conversion of land into forest.
—**af.for.est** *v.*

af.fray (uh.FRAY) *v.* a noisy fight; brawl; fray.

af.front (uh.FRUNT) *v.* offend openly or knowingly. —*n.* an open or intentional expression of disrespect: *She took it as an affront; an affront to her dignity; Her dignity suffered an affront; a shocking affront; It was indeed an affront to common decency.*

Af.ghan (AF.gun) *n.* **1** a person of or from **Afghanistan**, a C. Asian country, or the language spoken there; also *adj.* **2** afghan a woven, knitted, or crocheted shawl or coverlet with a geometric pattern. **3** also **Afghan hound,** a hunting dog with a long head, large ears, and thick silky coat.

a.fi.cio.na.do (uh.fish.uh.NAH.doh) *n., pl.* **-dos** a devotee, enthusiast, or fan: *an aficionado of the theater.*

a.field (uh.FEELD) *adjp. & adv.* away from home: *He wandered* **far afield** *and got lost.*

a.fire (uh.FIRE) *adjp. & adv.* on fire: *The house was set afire or aflame; politicians* **afire with** (= consumed by) *patriotic love.* Also **a.flame** (uh.FLAME).

a.float (uh.FLOTE) *adjp. & adv.* floating: *to set a leaking boat afloat again; to keep a company afloat* (= save it from bankruptcy); *There are rumors afloat* (= going around) *that the company is about to go under.*

a.flut.ter (uh.FLUT.ur) *adjp.* excited: *John was all aflutter over the approaching examinations; aflutter with nervousness.*

a.foot (uh.FOOT) *adjp.* under way: *A scheme is afoot to raise funds for a new university.*

a.fore.men.tioned (uh.FOR.men.shund) *adja.* mentioned before.

a.fore.said (uh.FOR.sed) *adja.* referred to above.

a.fore.thought (uh.FOR.thawt) *adjp.* premeditated: *murder, with malice aforethought.*

a for.ti.or.i (AY.for.tee.OR.ee) *Latin.* with even greater reason.

a.foul (uh.FOWL) *adjp. & adv.* entangled. —**run** or **fall afoul of** be in conflict or collision with something: *It ran afoul of the other ship in the dark; to run afoul of the law.*

a.fraid (uh.FRAID) *adjp.* **1** fearful: *He's deathly, terribly afraid of water; afraid to swim; afraid that he might drown; Are you afraid of being late?* **2** sorry that something is, was, or will be as specified: *I'm afraid we are late; I'm afraid so; Will* he survive? *I'm afraid not.*

A-frame *adj.* of a building, having steep roofs overhanging the sides and meeting in a steep A-like point: *an A-frame cottage, house.* —*n.* an A-shaped structure.

a.fresh (uh.FRESH) *adv.* anew or again: *to start afresh after each failure.*

Af.ri.can (AF.ruh.cun) *n.* a person of or from Africa. —*adj.*: *He's African by birth; Swahili is an African language; an* **African American** (= Black American).

African violet *n.* a house plant of African origin with velvety leaves and usu. purple flowers.

Af.ri.kaans (af.ruh.KAHNS) *n.* a Dutch-derived language that is one of South Africa's official languages. —*adj.* having to do with Afrikaans or Afrikaners.

Af.ri.ka.ner (af.ruh.KAH.nur) *n.* a South African of European descent, esp. one speaking Afrikaans.

Af.ro (AF.roh) *n.* a style of doing the hair in a dense bushy mass. —*adj.* of Africa, Afros, etc.: *an Afro haircut.*

Afro-American *n. & adj.* Black or African American: *a school of Afro-American studies.*

aft *adj. & adv.* to, at, or near the rear of a craft: *an aft mast, sail; Let's go aft; the lavatories aft (of the airplane).*

af.ter (AF.tur) *prep.* following: *Jill comes after Jack; Jack is named after* (= same as) *his father, but he takes after* (= is like) *his mother; a woman after* (= according to) *my own heart; The police are after* (= pursuing) *him; This happens day after day* (= daily) *in city after city* (= in every city); *You were expected here at 10 and now it is 20 after* (= 10:20); *We're human after all* (= in spite of everything). —*adja.* later or following: *In after years, he regretted his actions; after-sales service;* **adv.**: *Jack fell ill first, Jill came after; Both recovered shortly after;* **conj.**: *He stayed long after the others had left.*

af.ter.birth (AF.tur.birth) *n.* the placenta and fetal membranes expelled from the uterus after a birth.

af.ter.burn.er (AF.tur.bur.nur) *n.* an auxiliary burner in a jet engine for increasing the plane's thrust.

af.ter.care (AF.tur.care) *n.* treatment following discharge from hospital or prison.

af.ter.ef.fect (AF.tur.i.fect) *n.* a secondary or later effect: *a drug with no after-effects or side effects.*

af.ter.glow (AF.tur.gloh) *n.* **1** the glow seen in the sky after a sunset. **2** a pleasant feeling remaining after an experience: *in the afterglow of victory.*

after hours *adv.* past the regular closing time, as after school or work: *to call, meet, work after hours; a convenience store that is open after hours;* **adja.**: *an after-hours bar, club, job; after-hours activities, attractions, business, work.*

af.ter.im.age (AF.tur.im.ij) *n.* a visual sensation that continues after its object has passed.

af.ter.life (AF.tur.life) *n.* life after death.

af.ter.math (AF.tur.math) *n.* **1** a second crop, esp. of hay. **2** an outcome or result: *famine and disease as the aftermath of war; In the aftermath of the famine, people began to emigrate.*

af.ter.noon (af.tur.NOON) *n.* the time between noon and evening: *We started work at one o'clock in the afternoon; on Saturday afternoon; We worked all afternoon; We never work afternoons on Saturdays.* —*adja.* (AF.tur.noon): *an afternoon conference, nap, tea.*

after-shave *n.* a scented lotion to dab on the face after shaving.

af.ter.taste (AF.tur.taist) *n.* **1** a taste remaining in the mouth, as after eating or drinking something: *Mouthwashes leave an aftertaste; nice, pleasant, unpleasant aftertastes.* **2** a lingering feeling of a previous experience: *a bitter aftertaste; an aftertaste of last night's outburst.*

af.ter.tax (AF.tur.tax) *adja.* after taxes are deducted: *aftertax profits.*

af.ter.thought (AF.tur.thought) *n.* something that comes to mind after the occasion has passed.

af.ter.ward (AF.tur.wurd) *adv.* after that; later: *He fell ill and died shortly afterward.* Also **af.ter.wards.**

a.gain (uh.GAIN) *adv.* more times: *You can say that again; Not again, dear; I've told you* **again and again** or **time and time again** (= repeatedly) *not to do it; She might say yes,* **and again** or **and then again** (= on the other hand) *she might not; I got $200 – first $100, and then* **as much again** (= an equal amount) *as bonus;* **Now and again** (= sometimes) *our neighbors offer to cut our grass.*

a.gainst (uh.GENST, "G" as in "go") *prep.* opposing: *to swim against the current; I'm against a picnic today; Don't lean against the wall; Two against one is unfair; Take an umbrella against* (= in preparation for) *the chance of rain; two houses* **over against** (= facing) *each other.*

¹**a.gape** (uh.GAPE) *adjp.* with mouth

wide open: *The children were agape with astonishment; with eyes popping and mouth agape.*

²**ag.a.pe** (AG.uh.pay) *n.* **1** selfless Christian love. **2** a communal meal in token of this; love feast.

a.gar (AH.gar) *n.* a jellylike substance derived from seaweed and used as a bacterial growth medium ("nutrient agar"), in cooking, and as a laxative; also **agar-agar.**

ag.ate (AG.it, "G" as in "go") *n.* a semiprecious stone colored in patches or bands.

a.ga.ve (uh.GAH.vee) *n.* a tropical plant with thick fleshy leaves and a long flower stalk.

age *n.* **1** a period or length of life: *He's 15 years of age; At age 15, he hopes to live to a ripe old age; an advanced, early, tender, young age; in middle age when you are 40 to 65 years old; You don't* **look your age** (= You seem younger than you are); *children of school age; retirement age; to reach the venerable age of 90; an old woman bent with age; people of all ages; to* **act** or **be one's age** (= to behave reasonably); *It seems* **ages** (*Informal* for a long time) *since we met; 15 is below the* **age of consent** *for marriage; She has reached the* **age of discretion** (= of legal responsibility); *At 18 one is* **of age** (= legally an adult) *in many countries; You're supposed to have* **come of age** *at 18; There are attempts to reduce the* **age of majority** (= of legal independence) *from 18; He has to produce an age-of-majority card before buying liquor; An old man is* **over age** *for military service; At 15, you are* **under age** (= too young) *to drive.* **2** a historical or cultural stage: *the Stone Age of civilization; the Victorian Age; the Age of Mammals; World War II ushered in the nuclear age; the age of automation; the progress of civilization through* **the ages** (= the centuries; history). —*v.* **ag.es, aged, ag.ing** or **age.ing** grow or make old: *Some age faster than others; Wine is aged in storage casks after fermentation to develop its flavor.*

aged *adj.* **1** (AIJD) *adjp.* having age as specified: *a pensioner aged 90.* **2** (AY.jid) advanced in age: *an aged pensioner; a home for the aged; the sick and* **the aged** (= old people). **3** (AIJD) matured: *aged cheese, beef, wine.*

age.ism (AY.jiz.um) *n.* discrimination based on age: *to eliminate racism, sexism, and ageism.* Also **ag.ism.**

age.less *adj.* **1** always young: *an ageless beauty.* **2** eternal: *the ageless genius of Shakespeare.*

age-long *adj.* lasting a very long time: *the end of an age-long tyranny.*

a.gen.cy (AY.jun.see) *n.* **-cies 1** an office or service: *advertising, law-enforcement, news, regulatory, ticket, travel agencies; He works at an employment agency; an intelligence agency for gathering information secretly.* **2** means of doing something: *Miracles are beyond human agency.*

a.gen.da (uh.JEN.duh) *n.* **-das 1** a list of things to be done, as on a program: *to draw up* or *make up an agenda; to put something on the agenda; What's the next item on the agenda?* **2** plan: *ambitious agendas; a hidden agenda; politicians advancing* or *pushing their own agendas.*

a.gent (AY.junt) *n.* one who acts for another: *an enemy agent; He was not a free agent in the negotiations; A literary agent helps authors deal with publishers; a real-estate agent; a press agent; shipping agent; A secret agent spies for his government; The spy was a double agent; Catalysts are chemical agents; a cleaning agent* (= substance) *such as soap.*

agent pro.vo.ca.teur (-proh.VOC.uh.TUR) *n., pl.* **a.gents pro.vo.ca.teurs** (-TUR) one sent to infiltrate a suspected group and provoke them to illegal actions.

age of consent, age of discretion, age of majority See AGE.

age-old *adj.* existing for a very long time: *an age-old custom, institution, question; age-old problems, rivalries, values.*

ag.glom.er.ate (uh.GLOM.uh.rit) *adj.* formed into a rounded mass: *an agglomerate flower head.* —*n.* such a mass: *an agglomerate of volcanic rock;* also **ag.glom.er.a.tion** (-RAY.shun) *n.: a vast agglomeration of primeval matter; urban agglomerations of buildings.*

ag.glu.ti.nate (uh.GLOO.tuh.nate) *v.* **-nates, -nat.ed, -nat.ing** cause to adhere or clump together, as bacteria or blood cells. —**ag.glu.ti.na.tion** (-NAY.shun) *n.*

ag.gran.dize (uh.GRAN.dize) *v.* **-diz.es, -dized, -diz.ing** make *oneself* greater in power, wealth, or position.

—**ag.gran.dize.ment** (uh.GRAN.diz.munt) *n.: personal aggrandizement at public expense; territorial aggrandizement of the superpowers.*

ag.gra.vate (AG.ruh.vate) *v.* **-vates, -vat.ed, -vat.ing** make worse or more serious: *His excuses only aggravated the quarrel; to aggravate a condition, crisis, problem, situation; to aggravate misery,* tensions; *adj.*: *The new arrangements left the people **aggravated**; charged with **aggravated assault** using a deadly weapon*; *adj.*: *his **aggravating** (= annoying) behavior, manner; aggravating circumstances.* —**ag.gra.va.tion** (-VAY.shun) *n.*

ag.gre.gate (AG.ruh.gate) *v.* **-gates, -gat.ed, -gat.ing** collect together in a mass or cluster. —*adj.* (-git) forming a collection or cluster: *The blackberry and the raspberry are aggregate fruits; aggregate marks, sales.* —**in the aggregate** collectively; as a whole. —**ag.gre.ga.tion** (-GAY.shun) *n.* collection: *an aggregation of museum exhibits.*

ag.gres.sion (uh.GRESH.un) *n.* **1** an act of attacking first: *They vowed never to commit (an act of) aggression against a neutral nation; armed, naked, outright, unprovoked aggression.* **2** aggressiveness: *Aggression is manifested in overt and covert ways by destruction, greed, ambition, etc.*

ag.gres.sive (uh.GRES.iv) *adj.* **1** tending to attack: *the aggressive instinct; an aggressive nation; an aggressive weapon (made for use in attack).* **2** forceful or energetic: *an aggressive approach, campaign, sales rep, style; aggressive leadership.* —**ag.gres.sive.ly** *adv.*; **ag.gres.sive.ness** *n.*

ag.gres.sor (uh.GRES.ur) *n.* one who commits aggression: *The Nazis were branded the aggressors in World War II.*

ag.grieved (uh.GREEVD) *adj.* having suffered grief or hurt: *Jane felt aggrieved she didn't get a raise; felt aggrieved about not getting a raise; She's the aggrieved party.*

a.ghast (uh.GAST) *adjp.* horrified: *She was aghast; Everyone stood aghast at the sight.*

ag.ile (AJ.ul, -ile) *adj.* quick and nimble: *a leopard's agile movements; her agile wit;* **ag.ile.ly** *adv.* —**a.gil.i.ty** (uh.JIL.i.tee) *n.*

ag.ism (AY.jiz.um) same as AGEISM.

ag.i.tate (AJ.uh.tate) *v.* **-tates, -tat.ed, -tat.ing** disturb or stir up: *the sea agitated by a storm;* **to agitate** (= arouse public opinion) *strongly for or against a piece of legislation;* *adj.*: *She seemed agitated by the delay.* —**ag.i.ta.tion** (-TAY.shun) *n.* —**ag.i.ta.tor** (-tay.tur) *n.* one that stirs: *Our washer needs a new agitator; a political agitator (who stirs up people).*

a.gleam (uh.GLEEM) *adjp.* gleaming.
a.glit.ter (uh.GLIT.ur) *adjp.* glittering.
a.glow (uh.GLOH) *adjp.* glowing: *Her face was aglow with joy.*

ag.nos.tic (ag.NOS.tic) *n.* one who asserts that the existence of God and the supernatural are unknowable: *He's not an atheist, just an agnostic; adj.*: *his agnostic position, views.* —**ag.nos.ti.cism** (-tuh.siz.um) *n.*

a.go (uh.GO) *adv.* [used after a verb in the past tense] back in time: *I saw him 50 years ago; That was long ago; It was long ago that this happened.*

a.gog (uh.GOG) *adjp.* excited: *The town was all agog (with excitement); The announcement left the town agog; The town was agog over the victory.*

ag.o.nize (AG.uh.nize) *v.* **-niz.es, -nized, -niz.ing** be in agony: *Tim is agonizing over his homework; adj.*: *He has an **agonized** (= distressed) look; They had an **agonizing** (= distressing) time in a hijacked plane; adv.*: *Service is **agonizingly** (= distressingly) slow here.*

ag.o.ny (AG.uh.nee) *n.* **-nies** intense pain or suffering in body or mind: *the agony of suspense; The accident victim spent hours in mortal agony before dying; We are in great agony to learn the worst; Why prolong the agony when we can open the envelope and get it over with?*

ag.o.ra (AG.uh.ruh) *n.* in ancient Greece, a marketplace as a place of popular assembly.

a.grar.i.an (uh.GRAIR.ee.un) *adj.* having to do with land ownership, farms, etc.: *an agrarian party serving agrarian interests;* **a.grar.i.an.ism** *n.*

a.gree (uh.GREE) *v.* **a.grees, a.greed, a.gree.ing 1** say yes; concur: *I agree with you completely, entirely, fully, readily, wholeheartedly about reaching a settlement; I couldn't agree (with you) more; I agree on or to a compromise; I agree that it is a good deal; We agreed on the terms of the deal; We agreed to sign the deal; adjp.*: *We are **agreed** (= satisfied) it is a good deal.* **2** be in harmony: *John's account agrees with Jane's; In "He go," the verb doesn't agree with the subject; Sea food and this climate don't agree with me (= suit my well-being).*

a.gree.a.ble (uh.GREE.uh.bul) *adj.* **1** ready to agree: *an agreeable negotiator, I'm agreeable to the idea.* **2** pleasing: *an agreeable smile, voice; The idea is agreeable to me (= I like the idea).* —**a.gree.a.ble.ness** or **a.gree.a.bil.i.ty** (-BIL.i.tee) *n.* —**a.gree.a.bly** *adv.*

a.gree.ment (uh.GREE.munt) *n.* **1** the act of agreeing: *We are in full agreement on the question; to settle all disputes by mutual agreement.* **2** accord, treaty, or contract: *to carry out, come to, conclude, enter into, reach, sign, work out an* agreement; to break, denounce, violate an agreement; binding, contractual, gentleman's, iron-clad, tacit, tentative agreements; an agreement between two parties; an agreement on or about a disputed matter; an agreement to pay a monthly rent; an agreement that the rent would be paid on the first of each month. **3** grammatical concord: "She do his own hair" lacks agreement in number and gender; It should read "She does her own hair."

ag.ri.busi.ness (AG.ruh.biz.nis) *n.* the farming industry, including equipment, fertilizers, and related services.

ag.ri.cul.ture (AG.ruh.cul.chur) *n.* **1** farming or husbandry. **2** the science of farming. —**ag.ri.cul.tur.al** (-CUL.chur.ul) *adj.*; **ag.ri.cul.tur.al.ly** *adv.* —**ag.ri.cul.tur.ist** or **ag.ri.cul.tur.al.ist** *n.*

a.grol.o.gy (uh.GROL.uh.jee) *n.* a branch of agriculture dealing with soils. —**a.grol.o.gist** *n.*

a.gron.o.my (uh.GRON.uh.mee) *n.* the science of land management and production of crops. Also **ag.ro.nom.ics** (ag.ruh.NOM.ics) *n.pl.* [used with *sing. v.*]. —**a.gron.o.mist** (uh.GRON.uh.mist) *n.*

a.ground (uh.GROUND) *adv.* of a craft, touching the bottom in shallow water: *The ship ran aground.*

a.gue (AIG.yoo) *n.* a usu. malarial fever with periodic chills and sweating.

ah or **a.ha** (ah.HAH) *interj.* indicating surprise, triumph, pain, etc.: *Ah, yes, I remember; Aha! I've caught you red-handed.*

a.head (uh.HED) *adjp. & adv.* forward: *Look straight ahead when driving; We are far ahead of everyone else; Watch the road ahead of you; Go ahead and tell us; We're trying to get ahead* (= succeed) *in life; My watch is ahead by a couple of minutes; We'll be ahead of time when we get there; You're* **ahead of the times** (= very modern); *to* **get ahead of** (= outdo) *the competition and stay ahead; She always seems to get* **ahead of the game** (= to have an advantage); *The captain ordered* **full speed ahead** (= to go at full speed).

a.hem (uh.HEM) *interj.* [like a clearing of the throat] used to attract attention.

-aholic *comb.form* [forming *n.* or *adj.* like "alcoholic"] addicted to what is specified: *sleepaholic, spendaholic, workaholic.*

a.hoy (uh.HOY) *interj.* used by sailors to warn or hail: *Ship ahoy!*

aid *n.* help: *He went to her aid; He was charged with giving aid and comfort to the enemy; to cut off, extend, give, offer, provide, render aid to poor nations; economic, financial, and foreign aid; to withdraw aid; TV is an audio-visual aid; a hearing aid; rhymes, mnemonics, and such memory aids; teaching aids such as chalkboards and wall maps; a benefit performance* **in aid of** *the Red Cross.* —*v.* help: *They aided her with money; aided him in his work; a publication that was* **aided and abetted** (= helped and encouraged) *by her friends.*

aide (AID) *n.* helper or assistant: *a nurse's aide; teacher's aides; He works as an aide to the president.*

aide-de-camp (AID.duh.camp) *n., pl.* **aides-de-camp** (AID.duh-) a military officer who is an assistant to a senior officer.

aid.man *n.* **-men** a medical aide in a field unit.

AIDS *n.* "acquired immune deficiency syndrome," an often fatal disorder causing severe damage to the body's defenses against disease.

ail *v.* be ill: *What ails her* (= is making her ill)? *adj.: an* **ailing** *child, economy, society.*

ai.le.ron (AY.luh.ron) *n.* a movable section of the rear edge of an airplane's wing that helps it to turn left or right.

ail.ment (AIL.munt) *n.* illness: *a common ailment; minor ailments.*

aim *v.* direct an object, remark, or action: *Aim your dart at the target; Aim for the bull's-eye; The remark was aimed at the whole group; She is aiming to be a lawyer; aiming for success.* —*n.* **1** an aiming: *Keep a steady aim at the target;* **Take aim** *carefully before shooting.* **2** purpose: *people with no aim in life; His long-range aim was to become a teacher, the immediate aim to get a degree; Our final aim should be to be happy; Idealistic and lofty aims are hard to achieve.* —**aim.less** *adj.: an aimless existence, life; aimless wandering.* —**aim.less.ly** *adv.;* **aim.less.ness** *n.*

ain't *Informal.* am not; are not; is not; has not; have not: *I ain't gonna do it; Egalitarian it ain't; You ain't seen nothin' yet.* —**Ain't I?** *Informal.* Am I not?

air *n.* **1** atmosphere, esp. the mixture of gases surrounding the Earth: *We need air to breathe; We inhale air and exhale carbon dioxide; Open the windows for a breath of fresh air; balmy, bracing, brisk, crisp, dry, foul, humid, polluted, refreshing, stale air; A blast of hot air hit me as I opened the furnace; Birds fly in the air; to travel* **by air** (= in an airplane); *There is a rumor* **in the air** (= going around); *Our plans disappeared* **into thin air** (= completely) *when our money was stolen; A program is either* **on** *or* **off the air** (= being or not being broadcast); *She likes to* **take the air** (= go out for fresh air) *after dinner; The result of the election is* **up in the air** (= uncertain); *She will be* **walking on air** (= elated) *if she wins*. **2** a manner: *There's an air of dignity about her; a detached, nonchalant, superior, triumphant air; He* **puts on airs** (= unnatural ways of behavior) *to impress people*. **3** a tune or melody: *The band played a martial air*. —*v*. expose to the air: *A stuffy room needs to be aired; to* **air** (= go public with) *a grievance; The new show airs* (= starts being broadcast) *tomorrow; n.: The grievances got a good* **airing** (= discussion) *at the meeting.*

air.bag *n*. a protective bag designed to inflate in front of an automobile passenger in a crash.

air base *n*. an operating headquarters for military aircraft.

air bladder *n*. in most fishes, a sac containing air that helps to maintain buoyancy and aid respiration.

air.borne (AIR.born) *adj*. carried by air; flying: *airborne invasions, pollens, seeds; an airborne warning and control system; Drinks are served only after the airplane becomes airborne* (= when it is up in the air).

air.brain same as AIRHEAD.

air brake *n*. a brake worked by compressed air.

air.brush (AIR.brush) *n*. a compressed-air device for touching up artwork. —*v*. apply the airbrush to artwork: *Blemishes on a photo can be airbrushed away.*

air.bus *n*. a wide-bodied passenger jet aircraft.

air cleaner same as AIR FILTER.

air-condition *v*. control humidity, temperature, etc. using a refrigerating device called an air-conditioner; *adj*.: *an* **air-conditioned** *building, car, room; He works in air-conditioned comfort; n.: central air-conditioning for the whole building*. —**air-conditioner** *n*.

air.craft (AIR.craft) *n. sing. & pl.* an airplane or other air vehicle including helicopters and balloons: *enemy aircraft; an unidentified aircraft; Many aircraft were shot down in the battle.*

aircraft carrier *n*. a warship with a deck for aircraft to land and take off.

air cushion vehicle *n*. a vehicle that travels on a cushion of air by means of jets or fans blowing downward and raising it a few meters above the ground or water.

air.drop (AIR.drop) *v.* **-drops, -dropped, -drop.ping** deliver cargo or personnel by parachute. —*n*. such a delivery.

air express *n*. the shipping of parcels by air; **Air Express** *Service mark.*

air.fare *n*. fare for an airplane trip.

air.field *n*. a field where airplanes land and take off.

air filter *n*. a device for filtering out dust, pollen, etc. from an engine, air-conditioner, etc.

air.foil *n*. a controlling part of an airplane such as a wing, rudder, or aileron.

air force *n*. the air arm of a nation's armed forces.

air gun *n*. a gun that is worked by compressed air or a gas and uses BB shot or pellets.

air.head *n*. *Informal*. one who is silly or stupid.

air hole *n*. a hole for passing or getting air, esp. a breathing hole for water animals, as in the ice covering a pond or river.

air hostess *n*. a female flight attendant.

air lane *n*. a path regularly used by airplanes.

air.less *adj*. without movement of air: *an airless room*.

air letter *n*. a letter mailed by air that consists of a sheet of paper folded, sealed, and addressed without an envelope.

air.lift *n*. the transporting of people and supplies by air. —*v.: Supplies were airlifted to the disaster area.*

air.line *n*. a regular passenger service by air: *commuter, domestic, feeder, international, national airlines.*

air.lin.er (AIR.lye.nur) *n*. an airline's passenger plane.

air.lock *n*. **1** a blockage caused by air, as in a water pipe. **2** an airtight chamber, as in a caisson.

air.mail *n*. the transporting of mail by air: *a letter sent via* or *by airmail to Japan*. —*v.: to airmail a letter.*

air.man (AIR.mun) *n*. **-men 1** a member of an air force, esp. one in the lower ranks. **2** an aviator.

air mattress *n*. a pad that is inflated for use as a mattress.

air mile same as NAUTICAL MILE.

air.mo.bile (AIR.moh.bil) *adj*. of ground troops, that are moved to combat areas by air, as by helicopter.

air piracy / alabaster

air piracy *n.* aircraft hijacking. —**air pirate** *n.*

air pistol *n.* a handgun that is worked by compressed air or a gas and uses BB shot or pellets.

air.plane *n.* a heavier-than-air machine with fixed wings that is powered by a propeller or jet: *to board, bring down or shoot down, land, ditch, fly, hijack, navigate an airplane; Airplanes may crash, cruise at a certain altitude, gain altitude as they go up, land* or *touch down at airports, level off after reaching an altitude, lose altitude when there is flight trouble, taxi along the runway before taking off.*

air plant *n.* a plant that grows on another plant, drawing nourishment from air and rain, as mosses.

air.play *n.* the playing of a song or musical composition by a radio station.

air pocket *n.* **1** a partial vacuum or other atmospheric condition that makes an aircraft lose altitude while in flight: *to hit an air pocket.* **2** trapped air: *Pack it carefully to press out air pockets.*

air pollution *n.* contamination of the air by industrial gases, automobile exhausts, etc.

air.port *n.* a place with established facilities for planes, passengers, and cargo: *to land at an airport.*

air pump *n.* a piece of equipment for compressing or removing air.

air raid *n.* an attack by armed aircraft on a ground target: *to carry out* or *conduct an air raid; an air raid alert.*

air rifle *n.* a rifle that is worked by compressed air or a gas and uses BB shot or pellets.

air.ship *n.* a lighter-than-air craft equipped with power for propulsion and steering; dirigible.

air show *n.* **1** a display of aircraft and their maneuvers: *to put on* or *stage an air show.* **2** an exhibition of aircraft and the aerospace industry.

air.sick *adj.* nauseated from the movements of an aircraft. —**air.sick.ness** *n.*

air.space *n.* the space above a country over which it has jurisdiction.

air.speed *n.* the speed of an aircraft relative to the air through which it flies.

air strike *n.* an attack from the air.

air strip *n.* a strip of ground used as an airfield; landing strip.

air terminal *n.* a building with arrival and departure facilities for airline passengers.

air.tight *adj.* **1** too tight for air to get in or out: *airtight buildings, containers;* *adv.:* Store (it) airtight at room temperature; to wrap a cake airtight. **2** flawless: *an airtight alibi, argument, confession.*

air.time *n.* **1** broadcast time, as on TV or radio: *airtime sales; blocks of airtime; commercial airtime; The Good Samaritan was awarded two hours of free airtime.* **2** the time when a broadcast begins: *with only a minute to airtime; the 7 o'clock airtime for evening news.* **3** flight time: *The airtime between New York and Toronto is less than an hour.*

air-to-air *adj.* directed from an aircraft to a target in the air: *air-to-air combat, missiles.*

air-to-ground *adj.* directed from an aircraft to a ground target.

air waves *n.pl.* the medium of transmission of radio and TV: *the newest star of the national air waves.*

air.way *n.* **1** a route used by airplanes; air lane. **2** air passageway to the lungs, to a mine, etc.

air.wom.an (AIR.woom.un) *n.* **-wom.en** a woman aviator or member of an air force.

air.wor.thy (AIR.wur.thee) *adj.* of airplanes, fit to be flown. —**air.wor.thi.ness** *n.*

air.y (AIR.ee) *adj.* **air.i.er, -i.est 1** having plenty of air circulating in it: *an airy ambiance, cabin, room; bright and airy; light and airy fabrics; an open, airy feeling.* **2** light-hearted or breezy: *an airy greeting, wave; airy promises.* —**air.i.ly** *adv.;* **air.i.ness** *n.*

aisle (ILE) *n.* a passageway between two rows of seats, shelves, etc. as in an auditorium or supermarket: *to clear the aisles; to walk up the aisle to the altar; Nuts and candy are in Aisle (= row) 7B.* —**aisled** *adj.*

a.jar (uh.JAR) *adjp.* of a door, hinged window, etc., partly open: *The door is ajar.*

a.kim.bo (uh.KIM.boh) *adv.* with the hands on the hips and the elbows pointing outward: *He stood with arms akimbo barring her way.*

a.kin (uh.KIN) *adjp.* related; of the same stock: *"Three" is* **akin to** *the German "drei."*

à la or **a la** (AH.lah) *prep.* in the style or after the manner of a person or thing: *tragedy à la Shakespeare.*

al.a.bas.ter (AL.uh.bas.tur) *n.* a soft, white stone that resembles marble. —**adj***a.* made of or like alabaster: *an alabaster vase; her alabaster skin.*

à la carte (ah.luh.CART) *adj. & adv.* ordered from a menu item by item, not as a complete meal: *an à la carte dinner.*

a.lac.ri.ty (uh.LAC.ri.tee) *n.* eager readiness: *The trustees acted with alacrity to vote themselves a raise.*

à la king (al.uh.KING) *adj.* diced and served in a cream sauce with chopped peppers, mushrooms, etc.: *chicken à la king.*

à la mode (al.uh.MODE) *adj.* in the fashion: *"Apple pie à la mode" is served with ice cream.*

a.larm (uh.LARM) *n.* **1** sudden fear: *The news caused alarm; People expressed, felt great alarm at what was happening.* **2** warning: *Sound the fire alarm; The alarm was set to go off at 6 a.m.; to activate, deactivate, give, raise, set off, sound, turn off an alarm; burglar, false, smoke alarms; Leave the building when the alarm goes off* or *rings* or *sounds; the alarm (signal) of an* **alarm clock.** —*cpd.:* A **three-alarm fire** *has three companies of firefighters and vehicles responding; a* **four-alarm** *(Informal for very hot) Indian curry.* —*v.* frighten: *We didn't mean to alarm you;* **adj.:** *Don't be* **alarmed;** *an* **alarming** *state of affairs.*

a.larm.ist (uh.LARM.ist) *n.* one who raises alarms needlessly; **adj.:** *alarmist views on the nuclear threat.*

a.las (uh.LAS) *interj.* indicating regret, anxiety, sorrow, etc.

A.las.kan (uh.LAS.kun) *n. & adj.* (a person) of or from the state of Alaska.

alb (ALB) *n.* a long, white robe of linen worn by a priest during ceremonies.

al.ba.core (AL.buh.core) *n.* any of several fishes of the tuna group.

Al.ba.ni.an (al.BAY.nee.un) **1** *n. & adj.* (a person) of or from **Albania**, a Balkan country. **2** *n.* the Albanian language.

al.ba.tross (AL.buh.tros) *n.* **-tross.es** a large-winged sea bird related to the petrel: *The charge of accepting a bribe proved an albatross around his neck* (= something that impaired his effectiveness).

al.be.it (awl.BEE.it) *conj. Formal.* although; admittedly: *There's still a chance, albeit slim.*

al.bi.nism (AL.buh.niz.um) *n.* lack of skin coloration that results in very pale skin, white hair, and pink eyes from birth.

al.bi.no (al.BYE.noh) *n.* a human or animal born with albinism.

al.bum (AL.bum) *n.* **1** a book in which stamps, photographs, or other objects are kept as a collection. **2** a record of several pieces of music or a set of such records.

al.bu.men (al.BYOO.mun) *n.* **1** the white of an egg. **2** the protein substance which forms egg white, found also in many plant and animal tissues and juices, better known as **albumin.**

al.che.my (AL.cuh.mee) *n.* miraculous change of the ordinary into something precious, like the turning of base metals into gold, as attempted by medieval chemists. —**al.chem.ist** *n.*

al.co.hol (AL.cuh.hol) *n.* **1** a liquid forming the intoxicating element of drinks such as beer, wine, and whiskey, also called "ethyl alcohol": *to distill, make alcohol; pure, unadulterated alcohol; grain alcohol.* **2** such a drink: *to abstain from alcohol; The tavern reeked of alcohol.* **3** any chemical compound similar to alcohol: *methyl* or *wood alcohol; rubbing alcohol.*

al.co.hol.ic (al.cuh.HOL.ic) *adj.* containing alcohol: *an alcoholic drink.* —*n.* one who suffers from excessive use of alcohol: *a chronic alcoholic.*
—**al.co.hol.ism** (AL.cuh.hol.iz.um) *n.*

al.cove (AL.cohv) *n.* **1** a nook or recessed room, as in a library. **2** a sheltered area in a garden.

al den.te (ahl.DEN.tay) *adj. Italian.* firm to the teeth when cooked; not soft: *Cook the spaghetti until tender but al dente.*

al.der (ALL.dur) *n.* a tree or shrub of the birch family.

al.der.man (AWL.dur.mun) *n.* **-men** a member of a municipal council.

ale *n.* a beerlike liquor brewed from malt and hops.

a.le.a.to.ry (AIL.ee.uh.tor.ee) *adj.* **1** depending on chance. **2** of music, random and improvised.

a.lem.bic (uh.LEM.bic) *n.* a device formerly used for distilling; hence, something which purifies.

a.lert (uh.LURT) *adj.* watchful and ready to act, as a sentinel on duty: *an alert security guard; alert in answering the door; Be always alert to danger.* —*v.* warn: *The siren alerted us to the danger of an air raid.* —*n.* **1** a warning signal: *to call, call off, cancel an alert; to place* or *put the army on alert; a full alert; red alert; in a state of alert; during an air raid alert* (= during the period of the warning); *Be* **on the alert** (= on the lookout) *for pickpockets.* —**a.lert.ly** *adv.;* **a.lert.ness** *n.*

Aleut / alkali

A.leut (uh.LOOT) *n.* **1** an aboriginal of the **Aleutian Islands,** a chain of islands W. of Alaska. **2** the language of the Aleuts. Also **A.leu.tian** (uh.LOO.shun) *n. & adj.*

ale.wife *n.* **-wives** a herringlike fish used for food, fertilizer, etc.

Al.ex.an.dri.an (al.ig.ZAN.dree.un) *adj.* having to do with **Alexander** the Great (King of Macedonia, 4th c. B.C.), **Alexandria** (a city of Egypt), or Hellenistic Greece.

al.ex.an.drine (al.ig.ZAN.drin) *n.* an iambic hexameter verse; also *adj.*

a.lex.i.a (uh.LEX.ee.uh) *n.* reading inability caused by brain damage.

al.fal.fa (al.FAL.fuh) *n.* a cloverlike plant used as fodder.

al.fres.co (al.FRES.coh) *adv.* in the open air: *to dine alfresco;* **adja.:** *an alfresco breakfast on the patio.*

al.ga (AL.guh) *n., pl.* **-gae** (-jee) a primitive form of aquatic plant life such as seaweed or pond scum. —**al.gal** (-gul) *adj.*

al.ge.bra (AL.juh.bruh) *n.* a branch of mathematics that uses symbols in place of quantities. —**al.ge.bra.ic** (-BRAY.ic) or **al.ge.bra.i.cal** *adj.*

Al.ge.ri.an (al.JEER.ee.un) *n. & adj.* (a person) of or from **Algeria,** a country of N. Africa.

Al.gon.qui.an (al.GONG.kee.un) *n.* **1** a large family of Amerindian languages. **2** an Indian of an Algonquian tribe. Also **Al.gon.ki.an.**

Al.gon.quin (al.GONG.quin) *n.* **1** (a member of) any of certain Amerindian tribes that lived in the Ottawa River valley. **2** their Algonquian language.

al.go.rithm (AL.guh.rith.um, "th" as in "the") *n.* a set of rules in a mathematical operation for solving a problem.

a.li.as (AY.lee.us) *adv.* also known as: *Jones, alias Johnson.* —*n.* an assumed name: *a criminal with many aliases, checking in at hotels under a new alias each time.*

al.i.bi (AL.uh.bye) *n.* an accused person's plea of being elsewhere when the crime was committed: *His alibi wouldn't hold up; to break* or *disprove an alibi; to confirm someone's alibi; to establish an alibi; an airtight, foolproof, unassailable alibi; He provided no alibis* (*Informal* for excuses) *for his absence.*

al.ien (AY.lee.un) *n.* foreigner: *an enemy alien; illegal aliens coming in across the border; registration of aliens; a visit by aliens* (= extraterrestrial beings) *from Mars.* —*adj.* foreign: *a naturalized citizen of alien origin; a way of life that is alien to our culture.*

al.ien.ate (AY.lee.uh.nate) *v.* **-ates, -at.ed, -at.ing** cause to be withdrawn, estranged, or separated: *Salespeople try not to alienate potential customers;* **adj.:** *youth feeling alienated from society.*

al.ien.a.tion (AY.lee.uh.NAY.shun) *n.* an estrangement or withdrawal: *He suffered alienation from his associates; A third party is sued for alienation of affection between* (= transference of love away from) *spouses.*

a.light (uh.LITE) *v.* **a.lights,** *pt. & pp.* **a.light.ed** or **a.lit** (uh.LIT), **a.light.ing** descend: *to alight from a cab; The bird alighted on a branch.* —*adjp.* **1** on fire: *to set a house alight.* **2** lit or bright: *a cloudless night alight with stars; faces alight with joy.*

a.lign (uh.LINE) *v.* arrange properly, as in a line: *The front wheels need aligning; He aligned himself* (= formed an alliance) *with the leftists.* Also **a.line, a.lines, a.lined, a.lin.ing.** —**a.lign.ment** or **a.line.ment** *n.: The wheels are either in or out of alignment.*

a.like (uh.LIKE) *adjp.* similar: *Identical twins always look alike.* —*adv.* similarly: *The law treats everyone alike.* —**a.like.ness** *n.*

al.i.ment (AL.uh.munt) *n.* food to keep the body functioning.

al.i.men.ta.ry (al.uh.MEN.tuh.ree) *adj.* having to do with nourishment: *The alimentary canal* (or **tract**) *extends from the mouth to the anus; The alimentary system consists of the intestines, digestive glands, etc.*

al.i.mo.ny (AL.uh.moh.nee) *n.* **-nies** an allowance paid by one spouse to the other on separation or divorce: *The courts usually award alimony to an unemployed spouse.*

aline, alinement See ALIGN.

A-line *adj.* of garments, in the shape of an "A," esp. with a flared bottom: *an A-line skirt.*

alit a *pt.* or *pp.* of ALIGHT.

a.live (uh.LIVE) *adjp.* living: *Is the snake dead or alive? The abortion issue is very much alive* (= not dead); *A claim must be kept alive* (= active) *in order to be valid; He's not only breathing but quite alive to* (= conscious of) *what is happening around him; The sleepy town is alive with* (= full of) *tourists in the summer.* —**alive and kicking** or **alive and well** *Informal.* quite well and healthy.

al.ka.li (AL.kuh.lye) *n.* **-lis** or **-lies** a substance such as caustic soda that combines with acids to form salts. —**al.ka.line** *adj.* —**al.ka.lin.i.ty** (-LIN.i.tee) *n.*

al.ka.loid (AL.kuh.loid) *n.* a bitter, nitrogenous organic compound of vegetable origin, such as morphine or quinine. —**al.ka.loid.al** (-LOID.ul) *adj.*

al.kyd (AL.kid) *n.* a synthetic resin used in protective coatings such as paints and lacquers.

all (AWL) *adja.* the whole number, amount, extent, etc. of a group or class: *It rained all day; We are all mortal; The ambulance came with all speed; Ito, of all people, would never do such a thing; It's sunny all year round in the tropics.* —**pron.** [takes *pl. v.* when used as *pl.* subject] the whole number, amount, etc.: *All are mortal; All is not lost;* [used with "of" before a personal pron. or to express limited meaning] *All of them work hard; I mean all the women; all of the women who are employed here; He's a child* **after all** (= in spite of everything); *Anyone* **at all** (= in any way) *for tennis? There are 200* **in all** (= altogether). —*n.* everything: *You must give your all for this cause; In his will, Joe left his all to his wife.* —*adv.* wholly: *a child left all by himself; I'm all in favor of the idea; He came with all possible speed; I told you* **all along** (= all the time) *to be careful; The job is* **all but** (= almost) *done; I'm* **all in** (Informal for tired); **All in all** (= as a whole), *it was a fair deal; a small country whose army numbers* **all of** (= at least) *500; They went* **all out** (= with full effort) *to help the refugees; She has traveled* **all over** (= everywhere in) *the world; That's Dad* **all over** (= behavior typical of Dad); *Are you* **all right** (= safe, well, etc.)?; *He didn't do much work,* **all the same** (= anyhow; nevertheless) *he got paid; I feel* **all the worse** (= so much the worse) *for the medication; The trip cost me $300* **all told** (= altogether). —**all quiet on the Western front** *Informal.* It's calm and peaceful (at the place mentioned).
—**all the time:** *Some people complain all the time* (= habitually); *Lou was driving around without a license and I knew it all the time* (= throughout that period).

Al.lah (AL.uh, AH.luh) *n.* in Islam, the supreme being; God.

all-American *adj.* **1** wholly American: *an all-American team.* **2** the best American: *an all-American quarterback.*

all-around same as ALL-ROUND.

al.lay (uh.LAY) *v.* make less: *to allay one's anger, apprehensions, doubts, fears, pain, trouble.*

all-clear *n.* a signal indicating the end of an air raid or other threat.

al.le.ga.tion (al.luh.GAY.shun) *n.* an alleging or what is alleged: *a false, serious, unsubstantiated, vague allegation about someone; an allegation of theft against Jon; an allegation that Jon has stolen $200; to deny, drop, make, refute, retract, withdraw an allegation.*

al.lege (uh.LEJ) *v.* **al.leg.es, al.leged, al.leg.ing** put forward a claim, accusation, excuse, etc. without proof: *He alleged that she stole the money; $200 is alleged to have been stolen; Poverty has been alleged (as reason) for the theft;* **adja.:** *an alleged crime; the alleged thief.*
—**al.leg.ed.ly** (-id.lee) *adv.*

al.le.giance (uh.LEE.junce) *n.* loyalty owed to one's country, a government, cause, leader, etc.: *an oath of allegiance; They pledged or swore allegiance to the flag; true, unfailing, unswerving allegiance; to disavow or forsake one's allegiance to a cause.*

al.le.go.ry (AL.uh.gor.ee) *n.* **-ries** a story with characters, places, and events representing abstractions such as patience, purity, truth, and justice: *George Orwell's "Animal Farm" is an allegory.* —**al.le.gor.ic** (-GOR.ic) or **al.le.gor.i.cal** *adj.*

al.le.gro (uh.LEG.roh) *adj. & adv. Music.* in quick time. —*n.* a musical passage played in quick time.

al.le.lu.ia (al.uh.LOO.yuh) same as HALLELUJAH.

Allen wrench (AL.un-) *n.* an L-shaped wrench with hexagonal ends to fit into bolt and screw sockets.

al.ler.gen (AL.ur.jun) *n.* something that causes an allergy. —**al.ler.gen.ic** (-JEN.ic) *adj.*

al.ler.gic (uh.LUR.jic) *adj.* sensitive to particular things: *He's allergic to milk; an allergic reaction; She's quite allergic (Informal for disinclined) to math.*

al.ler.gist (AL.ur.jist) *n.* an allergy specialist.

al.ler.gy (AL.ur.jee) *n.* **-gies** an abnormal sensitivity to particular things such as foods, smoke, dust, pollen, or insect venom: *to acquire, develop an allergy.*

al.le.vi.ate (uh.LEE.vee.ate) *v.* **-ates, -at.ed, -at.ing** make more bearable; lessen: *to alleviate misery, pain, suffering.*
—**al.le.vi.a.tion** (-AY.shun) *n.*

al.ley (AL.ee) *n.* **al.leys** a narrow passageway, as between rows of buildings: *the stray cat in our back alley; a blind alley* (= road closed at one end); *The ball rolled down the alley* (= bowling lane) *and knocked down the pins; Stamp-collecting is not **up** or **down my alley*** (*Informal for* not my area of interest).

alley cat *n.* a stray cat.

all-fired *adj.* extreme or extremely: *His all-fired nerve!* —*adv.* [used before what it modifies]: *He's so all-fired arrogant.*

All Fools' Day *n.* April 1; April Fools' Day.

all fours *n.pl.* **1** all four legs. **2** a person's arms and legs or hands and knees: *to scrounge around **on all fours**.*

All.hal.lows (all.HAL.oze) same as ALL SAINTS' DAY.

al.li.ance (uh.LYE.unce) *n.* a union, association, or relationship: *We entered into or formed an alliance with our neighbors against a burglar; an alliance to watch for prowlers; a military alliance; an unholy political alliance between opposition parties; to dissolve an alliance.*

allied, allies See ALLY.

al.li.ga.tor (AL.uh.gay.tur) *n.* a reptile similar to the crocodile but with a broader snout.

all-important *adj.* of the greatest importance.

all-inclusive *adj.* inclusive of everything: *an all-inclusive price.*

al.lit.er.ate (uh.LIT.uh.rate) *v.* **-ates, -at.ed, -at.ing** have or use the same initial sound in successive words, as "Cossack commanders cannonading came." —**al.lit.er.a.tive** (-ruh.tiv) *adj.:* alliterative verse. —**al.lit.er.a.tion** (al.uh.tuh.RAY.shun) *n.*

all-night.er *n.* a party, session, etc. lasting all night: *to pull all-nighters in preparation for exams.*

al.lo.cate (AL.uh.cate) *v.* **-cates, -cat.ed, -cat.ing** give funds, space, duties, etc. to someone or for a specific purpose: *to allocate funds for education; money allocated to charities.*
—**al.lo.ca.tion** (-CAY.shun) *n.: to make an allocation; allocations to charities; the allocation of funds for health care.*

al.lo.cu.tion (al.uh.CUE.shun) *n.* a formal authoritative address, as of the Pope.

al.lot (uh.LOT) *v.* **al.lots, al.lot.ted, al.lot.ting** assign or distribute: *the time allotted to each speaker; A fixed time is allotted for each question.* —**al.lot.ment** *n.*

all-out *adj.* using all resources: *an all-out campaign, effort, struggle; all-out war.*

all.o.ver (ALL.oh.vur) *adj.* covering the whole surface: *an allover design, pattern, sort of feeling.*

al.low (uh.LOW, *rhyme:* HOW) *v.* **1** let have or do: *He allows his son $10 a week; allows him to play on the street; She allows herself no luxuries; No smoking is allowed; An hour is allowed for lunch.* **2** agree: *The judge allowed that the claim was reasonable; He allowed* (= agreed to) *the claim; The judge did not **allow for** *(= take into consideration) *his age in sentencing him; a rule that **allows of*** (= admits of) *no exception.*
—**al.low.a.ble** *adj.;* **al.low.ed.ly** (-id.lee) *adv.*

al.low.ance (uh.LOW.unce) *n.* **1** a granting or conceding: *the allowance of a claim; to **make allowances for*** (= excuse) *human error.* **2** a sum granted: *His son gets a weekly allowance of $10; She gets a cost-of-living allowance in addition to wages; a trade-in allowance deducted from the price of a new car; a sales rep's travel allowance.*

al.loy (AL.oy, uh.LOY) *n.* a combination of one metal with another of lower quality, as brass (copper with zinc or tin) and steel (iron with carbon).
—*v.* mix, as a metal, with something of lower quality; hence, debase.

all-points bulletin *n.* a police advisory issued in all directions, as when a fugitive is being sought.

all right *adj.p. & adv.* **1** in good order; satisfactory: *I was feeling sick, but I'm all right now; She's doing all right in school.* **2** yes; certainly: *All right, you may go to the movie; That's my dog, all right.* —**all-right** *adj.* *Informal.* passably good: *an all-right fellow.*

all-round *adj.* accomplished in every way: *an all-round candidate, student.*

All Saints' Day *n.* November 1, a day to commemorate Christian saints; Allhallows.

All Souls' Day *n.* November 2, a day of prayer for the dead.

all.spice *n.* a spice obtained from the berry of a West Indian shrub.

all-terrain vehicle *n.* a motor vehicle that has large, balloonlike tires, designed for use on rough, marshy, or sandy ground, as on farms.

all-time *adj.* *Informal.* **1** of record level: *an all-time favorite, high, low, record.* **2** that takes up all one's time: *an all-time job.*

al.lude (uh.LOOD, long "OO") *v.* **al.ludes, al.lud.ed, al.lud.ing** refer, usu. indirectly: *The speaker alluded to them in passing (without mentioning*

al.lure (uh.LOOR) v. **al.lures, al.lured, al.lur.ing** attract by something that offers pleasure, reward, etc.: *Beauty allures men and women*; *adj.*: *an alluring* (= tempting) *sight*. —*n.* attraction: *the allure of riches*; also **al.lure.ment**.

al.lu.sion (uh.LOO.zhun) n. an alluding: *to make an allusion to the past*. —**al.lu.sive** (uh.LOO.siv) *adj.*; **al.lu.sive.ly** adv.; **al.lu.sive.ness** n.

al.lu.vi.um (uh.LOO.vee.um) n. a deposit of sand or mud left by flowing water, as on a river bed. —**al.lu.vi.al** adj.: *alluvial deposits, soils*.

al.ly (uh.LYE, AL.eye) v. **al.lies, al.lied, al.ly.ing** unite by some relationship or bond: *The U.S. allied (itself) with the British in World War II against the Axis powers*; *adj.*: *Dutch and English are **allied*** (= related) *languages*; *I am allied to them by marriage*; *to lobby for allied interests*. —*n.*, *pl.* **al.lies** one united to another: *a faithful, staunch friend and ally*; *The U.S. and Britain were the chief **Allies** in World War II*.

al.ma ma.ter (AL.muh.MAY.tur) n. an institution in which one was educated.

al.ma.nac (AWL.muh.nac) n. a calendar-based annual publication giving information about the sun, moon, and tides and miscellaneous other useful data.

al.might.y (awl.MYE.tee) adj. all-powerful: *an almighty being*; *God Almighty*; *fear of the **Almighty*** (= God); *the almighty dollar*.

al.mond (AH.mund, AL-) n. an edible nut that is oval-shaped with pointed ends or the tree bearing it; *adj.*: *an **almond-eyed*** (= Oriental-looking) *child*.

al.most (AWL.mohst) adv. very nearly: *I am almost finished*; *She said almost nothing of importance in her lecture*.

alms (AHMS) n.pl. money, clothes, food, etc. given to the poor as charity: *to dispense alms for the needy*.

alms.house n. a home for poor people.

al.oe (AL.oh) n. **al.oes 1** a fleshy African plant of the lily family with sharp-pointed spiny leaves: *The century plant, called also the "American aloe," is an agave*. **2 aloes** [with *sing. v.*] a purgative prepared from aloe juice. **3 aloe vera** (-VEER.uh) a yuccalike aloe whose leaves yield a gelatinous substance used as an emollient for the hair and skin.

a.loft (uh.LOFT) adv. high up in the air: *flags flying aloft*; *to soar aloft like a kite*.

a.lo.ha (uh.LOH.huh) interj. Hawaiian greeting or farewell.

a.lone (uh.LONE) adjp. & adv. **1** by oneself: *He likes to eat alone*; *She was left alone with no one to talk to*; *You can find her alone reading in a corner of the library*; *all, almost, always, quite, really, very much alone*; *The child is home alone*. **2** only: *He lives for money alone*; *God alone knows what happened*. —**let alone** not to mention: *He can't even afford a car, let alone a house*. —**let** or **leave alone** not interfere with a person or thing: *Let her alone*. —**let well enough alone** leave things as they are.

a.long (uh.LONG) adv. & prep. **1** from one end to the other: *cars parked along the street*. **2** onward: *We were driving along (the highway)*; *Bring your friends along with you*; *Bring them along*; *I knew about her **all along*** (= all the time); *It happened **along about*** (Informal for near) *noon*; *Tell them I'll **be along*** (Informal for be there).

a.long.shore (uh.LONG.shore) adv. by the shore.

a.long.side (uh.LONG.side) adv. & prep. side by side: *a bike driven alongside (of) a car*; *He was driving alongside when hit*.

a.loof (uh.LOOF, long "OO") **1** adv. at a distance: *He holds* or *keeps (himself) aloof in company*; *He remains* or *stands aloof from others*. **2** adj. reserved or withdrawn: *his aloof expression, manner*; *He's an aloof character*; *a bit aloof after his wife's death*. —**a.loof.ly** adv.; **a.loof.ness** n.

a.loud (uh.LOWD) adv. **1** so as to be heard: *Please read aloud*. **2** loudly: *He called aloud for help*.

alp n. a high mountain.

al.pac.a (al.PAC.uh) n. **1** a South American animal of the camel family that yields wool. **2** its wool or the soft and resilient cloth made from it.

al.pha (AL.fuh) n. the first letter of the Greek alphabet [A, α]. —**alpha and omega** the beginning and the end.

al.pha.bet (AL.fuh.bet) n. the letters used to write a language; the ABC: *The English alphabet is phonetic and symbolic*; *the Arabic, Greek, Hebrew, Roman alphabets*.

al.pha.bet.ic (al.fuh.BET.ic) or **al.pha.bet.i.cal** (-BET.i.cul) adj. **1** using an alphabet: *Most languages have alphabetic systems of writing*; *Chinese characters are pictographic, not alphabetic*. **2** in the order of the letters of the alphabet: *words in alphabetical order*. —**al.pha.bet.i.cal.ly** adv.

alphabetize / altogether

al.pha.bet.ize (AL.fuh.buh.tize) *v.* **-iz.es, -ized, -iz.ing** put in alphabetical order. —**al.pha.bet.i.za.tion** (-tuh.ZAY.shun, -tye-) *n.*

al.pha.nu.mer.ic (AL.fuh.new.MER.ic) *adj.* with letters and numbers combined: *L4W 2C3 is an alphanumeric postal code.*

alpha rhythm *n.* the relaxed rhythmic activity of the brain as observable on an electroencephalograph, normally between 8 and 13 cycles per second; slow brain wave: *Biofeedback teaches you to generate alpha rhythms.* Also **alpha wave.**

Al.pine or **al.pine** (AL.pine) *adj.* having to do with high mountains: *an alpine glacier, hut, plant, pond, rose, tent, wilderness;* **Alpine skiing** *includes downhill and slalom events; the Teutonic, Mediterranean, and the shorter, darker, and broad-headed alpine racial types; the alpine (= very high) increase in fat consumption.*

al.pin.ism (AL.puh.niz.um) *n.* mountain-climbing, esp. in the **Alps,** a European mountain system; **al.pin.ist** *n.*

al.read.y (all.RED.ee) *adv.* **1** by the time specified: *The train had already left when I reached the station.* **2** even before the specified time: *Have you finished already?*

al.right (awl.RITE) *adjp. & adv.* [nonstandard] ALL RIGHT.

al.so (AWL.soh) *adv.* as well: *She also was there; Not only Jim but also his wife saw her.*

also-ran *n. Informal.* a defeated candidate, contestant, etc.

al.tar (AWL.tur) *n.* a raised structure or table used in divine worship: *to kneel at an altar; to* **lead her to the altar** (= marry her, esp. in a church).

altar boy or **altar girl** *n.* a boy or girl who assists a priest at religious ceremonies.

al.tar.piece (AWL.tur.peece) *n.* a painting or other work of art at the back of an altar.

al.ter (AWL.tur) *v.* change partially; modify: *to alter clothes to suit a fashion; A ship alters course, direction; He has altered; His whole outlook has altered since returning from abroad; Circumstances alter cases* (= change the situation); *adj.:* **altered** *states of consciousness attained by clairvoyance, telepathy, whirling, etc.* —**al.ter.a.ble** *adj.* —**al.ter.a.tion** (-RAY.shun) *n.: to make major, minor, slight alterations in a story.*

al.ter.ca.tion (awl.tur.CAY.shun) *n.* a noisy argument; quarrel: *He had an altercation with his neighbor about* or *over the location of a fence; altercations between spouses.*

alter ego *n.* **1** one's second self. **2** an intimate friend.

al.ter.nate (AWL.tur.nate) *v.* **-nates, -nat.ed, -nat.ing** occur, arrange, or do by turns: *Jack and I alternate in doing the dishes; We alternate between cooking and washing; We alternate one job with another; Farmers alternate* (= rotate) *crops to save the soil;* **n.:** *The direction of* **alternating current** *changes at regular intervals.* —**adja. 1** following each other by turns: *Jack and I do the dishes on alternate days.* **2** substitute; alternative: *We went by an alternate route; alternate sources of energy such as the sun, wind, and water.* —*n.* (-nit) a substitute: *convention delegates and their alternates; Have meat or some meat alternate in your diet.*

al.ter.nate.ly (AWL.tur.nate.lee) *adv.* by turns: *She laughed and cried alternately as she told the story of the ups and downs of her life.*

al.ter.na.tive (awl.TUR.nuh.tiv) *n.* a choice between two or more possibilities: *Facing dismissal, he has no alternative but to resign; Resignation is the only alternative to being fired; Can you propose or suggest another alternative? At this time, changing jobs is not a viable alternative; His boss has various alternatives.* —**adja. 1** substitute: *an alternative plan of escape.* **2** offering something different from the established, conventional, traditional, etc.: *an alternative life style; an alternative school offering alternative education using a nontraditional curriculum; tapping* **alternative energy** *sources such as the wind and the sun for protecting the environment.* —**al.ter.na.tive.ly** *adv.*

al.ter.na.tor (AWL.tur.nay.tur) *n.* a generator that produces alternating current.

al.though (awl.THOH, "TH" as in "the") *conj.* in spite of the fact that: *Al is able to walk although he's very ill.*

al.tim.e.ter (al.TIM.i.tur) *n.* a barometer for showing altitude.

al.ti.tude (AL.tuh.tude) *n.* height above sea level: *to reach an altitude of 9,000 m; a high altitude; Airplanes cruise at that altitude; They lose altitude in bad weather; Nothing grows at those altitudes.*

al.to (AL.toh) *n.* **-tos 1** the lowest female voice. **2** a singer or instrument in this range of voice.

al.to.geth.er (awl.tuh.GETH.ur, "TH" as in "the") *adv.* on the whole: *The* expenses came to $500 altogether; Things are not altogether bad. —**in the altogether** Informal. in the nude.

al.tru.ism (AL.troo.iz.um) n. selfless concern for the welfare of others; opposed to EGOISM. —**al.tru.ist** n. —**al.tru.is.tic** (-IS.tic) adj.

¹**al.um** (AL.um) n. a colorless crystalline compound of aluminum used medically and in manufacturing.

²**a.lum** (uh.LUM) n. Informal. alumnus or alumna.

a.lu.mi.num (uh.LOO.muh.num) n. a light white metal. —**al.u.min.i.um** (al.yoo.MIN.yum) Brit.

a.lum.na (uh.LUM.nuh) n., pl. **-nae** (-nee) a former female student of a particular school: the Nurses Alumnae Association.

a.lum.nus (uh.LUM.nus) n., pl. **-ni** (-nye) a former male student of a particular school.

al.ve.o.lar (al.VEE.uh.lur) adj. having to do with a small cavity or hollow, esp. a tooth socket, or **alveolus**: "T," "d," and "s" are alveolar sounds.

al.ways (AWL.waze, -wiz) adv. at all times: He is always punctual; She is always (= repeatedly) asking to go to the movies.

Alz.hei.mer's disease (ALTS.hye.murs-) n. a degenerative disease of the brain cells.

am first person sing. pres. indicative of BE.

a.main (uh.MAIN) adv. [old use] at full speed; hastily; with full strength.

a.mal.gam (uh.MAL.gum) n. **1** a mercury alloy, as used in teeth fillings. **2** a blending or union, esp. of organizations.

a.mal.ga.mate (uh.MAL.guh.mate) v. **-mates, -mat.ed, -mat.ing** unite or combine without loss of identity, as labor unions: Municipalities often amalgamate with others into regional governments; The companies amalgamated to form a national chain; Our town is amalgamated with Metro; adj.: an **amalgamated** labor union. —**a.mal.ga.ma.tion** (-MAY.shun) n.

am.a.ranth (AM.uh.ranth) n. Poetic. a flower that never fades. —**am.a.ranth.ine** (-RANTH.in) adj.

am.a.ret.to (am.uh.RET.oh) n., pl. **-ret.tos** an almond-flavored liqueur.

am.a.ryl.lis (am.uh.RIL.is) n. a bulbous plant with red or pink lilylike flowers.

a.mass (uh.MAS) v. heap up or accumulate: He quickly amassed a fortune by trading in stocks; **a.mass.ment** n.

am.a.teur (AM.uh.tur, -choor) n. **1** one who engages in a hobby, sport, or other activity without accepting payment; nonprofessional: Some amateurs turn professional after acquiring some skill and experience. **2** an inexperienced practitioner of an art or skill: a rank amateur. —**adj.** nonprofessional: an amateur athletic association, competition, painter; amateur hockey, radio, sports. —**am.a.teur.ism** n.

am.a.teur.ish (am.uh.TUR.ish, -CHOOR.ish) adj. unskilled or inexperienced.

am.a.to.ry (AM.uh.tor.ee) adj. having to do with sexual love: amatory verses.

a.maze (uh.MAZE) v. **a.maz.es, a.mazed, a.maz.ing** bewilder or be bewildered or confused: Their decision amazes me; adj.: I'm **amazed** to hear you didn't get the job; I'm amazed that you have been bypassed; quite amazed at their decision; It's **amazing** that she can refuse such a good job. —**a.maze.ment** n.: To my complete, total, utter amazement, she refused the job; We stared in amazement at each other; I expressed my amazement at or with her refusal. —**a.maz.ing.ly** adv.

am.a.zon (AM.uh.zon) n. a strong aggressive woman, like the **Amazons,** a warriorlike race of women of Greek myth. —**am.a.zo.ni.an** (-ZOH.nee.un) adj.

am.bas.sa.dor (am.BAS.uh.dur) n. the official representative of a foreign government: the U.S. ambassador to India; An ambassador is sometimes recalled for consultations at home; an ambassador-at-large; a goodwill ambassador; a roving ambassador; **am.bas.sa.dor.ship** n. —**am.bas.sa.dor.i.al** (-DOR.ee.ul) adj.

am.ber (AM.bur) n. a yellowish-brown fossil resin used in jewelry. —**adj.** of the color of amber: The traffic light goes amber for a few seconds before turning red.

am.ber.gris (AM.bur.gris) n. a waxy substance from the intestines of sperm whales that is used as a fixative in perfume-making.

am.bi.ance (AM.bee.unce) n. surrounding atmosphere or environment: a restaurant famous for its ambiance and good food; also **am.bi.ence.**

am.bi.dex.trous (am.bi.DEX.trus) adj. **1** able to use both hands equally well. **2** skillful or versatile. **3** deceitful or double-dealing.

am.bi.ence same as AMBIANCE.

am.bi.ent (AM.bee.unt) adj. surrounding: a mountain peak concealed by ambient clouds; Ambient tobacco smoke in the workplace is hurtful to nonsmokers; The blind can locate themselves by an ambient vision that works subconsciously.

am.big.u.i.ty (am.big.YOO.i.tee) *n.* **-ties** the state of being ambiguous or something ambiguous: *to avoid ambiguity; an ambiguity about* or *concerning his position; to clear up* or *remove an ambiguity.*

am.big.u.ous (am.BIG.yoo.us) *adj.* having more than one meaning: *an ambiguous position, response, term, wording.* —**am.big.u.ous.ly** *adv.*

am.bit *n.* a sphere of influence or authority; bounds or scope: *within the ambit of his power.*

am.bi.tion (am.BISH.un) *n.* a strong desire to achieve a goal: *men and women of ambition; the many ambitions of our younger days; to achieve, attain, fulfill, realize, restrain one's ambition; The Nobel Prize spurred* or *stirred his ambition to become a scientist; It was his greatest ambition* (= goal); *an aggressor's territorial ambitions; his boundless, overweening, unbridled ambition and greed.*

am.bi.tious (am.BISH.us) *adj.* having ambition: *an ambitious youth; She is ambitious to win an Olympic gold; an ambitious attempt, plan, undertaking; a program that is too ambitious for our budget.*

am.biv.a.lent (am.BIV.uh.lunt) *adj.* having conflicting feelings about the same object or person: *ambivalent attitudes, feelings, reactions; The government seems ambivalent about its policy toward refugees.* —**am.biv.a.lence** *n.*

am.ble (AM.bul) *n.* an easy, leisurely gait, as of a horse. —*v.* **-bles, -bled, -bling** move at an amble: *He ambled along while we stopped for a chat.* —**am.bler** *n.*

am.bro.sia (am.BROH.zhuh) *n.* **1** in classical myths, the food of the gods. **2** anything considered very delicious. —**am.bro.sial** *adj.*

am.bu.lance (AMB.yuh.lunce) *n.* a vehicle for taking the sick and wounded to hospital.

ambulance chaser *n. Informal.* a lawyer who goes after accident victims urging them to sue for damages, etc.

am.bu.la.to.ry (AMB.yuh.luh.tor.ee) *adj.* having to do with walking: *Ambulatory medical care is given in emergency and outpatient departments; ambulatory patients.*

am.bus.cade (AM.bus.cade) same as AMBUSH.

am.bush (AM.bush) *n.* **1** a lying in wait to attack by surprise; also, such a trap or the attackers: *to attack an enemy from ambush; to lie in ambush for them; to lay* or *set an ambush* (= trap) *for the enemy; to draw them into the ambush; The enemy ran into the ambush; They had been trapped by ambush.* **2** such an attack: *The enemy was greeted with an ambush of automatic weapons fire.* —*v.* **am.bush.es, am.bushed, am.bush.ing** attack from ambush: *The enemy was ambushed and defeated.*

a.me.ba (uh.MEE.buh), etc. same as AMOEBA, etc.

a.mel.io.rate (uh.MEEL.yuh.rate) *v.* **-rates, -rat.ed, -rat.ing** to make a condition, plight, situation, etc. better or more tolerable: *to ameliorate the condition of the poor; The situation did not ameliorate* (= improve). —**a.mel.io.ra.tion** (-RAY.shun) *n.* —**a.mel.io.ra.tive** (-ray.tiv) *adj.*

a.men or **A.men** (ay.MEN, ah.MEN) *interj.* expressing agreement, as to a prayer: *The Lord help us, Amen! I'll say amen to that.* —*n.:* *They responded with a chorus of amens.*

a.me.na.ble (uh.MEE.nuh.bul, uh.MEN.uh-) *adj.* responsive: *a child who is amenable to reason; We are amenable to compromise.* —**a.me.na.bly** *adv.* —**a.me.na.ble.ness** or **a.me.na.bil.i.ty** (-BIL.i.tee) *n.*

amen corner *n.* the part of a church congregation that leads the others in saying "Amen."

a.mend (uh.MEND) *v.* change in order to improve: *to amend one's life; to amend a constitution, resolution, the wording of a law.* —**a.mend.ment** *n.*

a.mends *n.pl.* [takes *sing.* or *pl. v.*] reparation for a harm or hurt: *Al made amends for his past misdeeds.*

a.men.i.ty (uh.MEN.i.tee, uh.MEEN-) *n.* **-ties 1** a feature that makes a place or facility more comfortable: *a hotel with amenities such as sauna and color TV; They offer amenities for relaxation and enjoyment.* **2 amenities** *pl.:* *to exchange amenities* (= greetings); *to observe the amenities* (= courtesies) *of diplomacy.*

Am.er.a.sian (am.uh.RAY.zhun) *n. & adj.* (a person) of mixed Asian and American parentage.

A.mer.i.can (uh.MER.uh.cun) *n.* **1** a person of or from North or South America, esp. a U.S. national. **2** English as used in the U.S.: *General American;* also **American English.** —*adj.* having to do with North and/or South America or their peoples or cultures, esp. the U.S.: *as American as apple pie; the* **American dream** *of prosperity and* happiness with some peace.

A.mer.i.can.a (uh.mer.i.CAN.uh) *n.pl.* things of American cultural interest, as art, books, furniture, etc.; *adja.:* Americana collections, museums, pieces.

American Indian *n.* a member of any of the aboriginal peoples of North America, excepting the Inuit.

A.mer.i.can.ism (uh.MER.uh.cuh.niz.um) *n.* **1** a word, usage, cultural trait, etc. that is typical of the United States: *In spite of their Americanisms, the hostages escaped from Iran passing as Canadians.* **2** devotion to things American. —**A.mer.i.can.ist** *n.*

A.mer.i.can.ize (uh.MER.uh.cuh.nize) *v.* **-iz.es, -ized, -iz.ing** make American. —**A.mer.i.can.i.za.tion** (-nuh.ZAY.shun, -nye-) *n.*

American plan *n.* a hotel charging rate that includes room and meals; cf. EUROPEAN PLAN.

American Sign Language *n.* a system of manual signs used by the deaf in North America. Also **ASL.**

am.er.ic.i.um (am.uh.RISH.ee.um) *n.* a white radioactive metallic element.

Am.er.ind (AM.uh.rind) or **Am.er.ind.i.an** (-RIN.dee.un) *n. & adj.* American Indian; Native American.

am.e.thyst (AM.uh.thist, "th" as in "thin") *n.* **1** a gem of a purple or violet color. **2** its color.

a.mi.a.ble (AY.mee.uh.bul) *adj.* friendly and good-natured: *an amiable leader, personality, tone of voice; He lectured us in a relaxed and amiable fashion; a bunch of amiable eccentrics;* **a.mi.a.bly** *adv.* —**a.mi.a.ble.ness** or **a.mi.a.bil.i.ty** (-BIL.i.tee) *n.*

am.i.ca.ble (AM.uh.cuh.bul) *adj.* showing goodwill and love of peace: *amicable coexistence, negotiations; an amicable agreement, departure, parting of the ways; an amicable meeting between labor and management; the amicable settlement of a dispute; an amicable separation; She spoke to the rioters in an amicable tone.* —**am.i.ca.bly** *adv.*

a.mid (uh.MID) or **a.midst** (uh.MIDST) *prep.* in the midst of something: *The child got lost amid the confusion of the fair.*

a.mid.ships (uh.MID.ships) *adv.* toward the middle of a craft, as between a ship's bow and stern: *The aircraft was broken amidships, with the cockpit landing in one place and the tail section in another.*

a.midst same as AMID.

a.mi.go (uh.MEE.goh) *n.* **-gos** (-goze) Spanish. a friend.

A.mish (AH.mish, AM.ish) *n.pl.* a Mennonite sect founded in the 17th century by the Swiss Jacob Ammann.

a.miss (uh.MIS) *adjp. & adv.* wrong or wrongly: *Something went amiss with the arrangements; Is something amiss? Don't take my words amiss.*

am.i.ty (AM.i.tee) *n.* **-ties** friendly relations: *to live in amity like good neighbors.*

am.me.ter (AM.ee.tur) *n.* an instrument for measuring an electric current.

am.mo (AM.oh) *n. Informal.* ammunition.

am.mo.ni.a (uh.MONE.yuh) *n.* a strong-smelling gas used in refrigeration, fertilizers, and as a liquid cleaning agent.

am.mu.ni.tion (am.yuh.NISH.un) *n.* objects for firing, as bullets, shells, grenades, and rockets, with their fuses, charges, etc.: *live ammunition; The scandal provided ammunition* (= firing materials) *for press attacks against the government.*

am.ne.sia (am.NEE.zhuh) *n.* loss of memory, often temporary. —**am.ne.si.ac** (-zee.ac) or **am.ne.sic** (-zic) *n. & adj.*

am.nes.ty (AM.nus.tee) *n.* **-ties** a general pardon granted by a government, esp. to political offenders: *to declare an amnesty for political prisoners; The U.S. granted amnesty posthumously to General Lee in 1975; an* **amnesty act** *offering a pardon for those who took part in the rebellion; an* **amnesty day** *for returning overdue books without paying fines; an* **amnesty program** *for illegal immigrants to legalize their status within a certain period.* —*v.* **-ties** (-tees), **-tied** (-teed), **-ty.ing** (-tee.ing) pardon, esp. a group.

am.ni.o.cen.te.sis (AM.nee.oh.sen.TEE.sis) *n.* a test for detecting abnormalities of a fetus by drawing and examining a sample of the amniotic fluid.

am.ni.ot.ic fluid (am.nee.OT.ic-) *n.* fluid from a membranous sac enclosing the fetus in the womb.

a.moe.ba (uh.MEE.buh) *n.* **-bas** or **-bae** (-bee) a microscopic one-celled organism found in soil and water that multiplies by splitting into two independent cells. —**a.moe.bic** *adj.*: *amoebic dysentery.*

a.mok (uh.MUK, -MOK) *adv.* **run amok** rush about wildly in a murderous frenzy.

a.mong (uh.MUNG) *prep.* **1** in the middle of a group: *a town nestled among the hills; Einstein is among* (= one of) *the greatest men of science.* **2** to, with, by,

amontillado / amusement park

etc. a group: *how to share $100 among seven people; Discuss it among yourselves.* Also **amongst.**

a.mon.til.la.do (uh.mon.tuh.LAH.doh) *n.* **-dos** a pale dry sherry.

a.mor.al (ay.MOR.ul) *adj.* neither moral nor immoral: *an infant's amoral (= innocent) behavior.* —**a.mor.al.ly** *adv.*

am.o.rous (AM.uh.rus) *adj.* related to love, esp. sexual: *amorous advances, glances, inclinations, love, novels, verse, women;* **am.o.rous.ly** *adv.*

a.mor.phous (uh.MOR.fus) *adj.* **1** having no definite shape or form: *an amorphous mass of clay; a writer's amorphous style.* **2** not crystalline: *amorphous glass, minerals.*

a.mor.tize (AM.ur.tize, uh.MOR.tize) *n.* **-tiz.es, -tized, -tiz.ing** pay off a mortgage, debt, etc. by installment payments. —**am.or.ti.za.tion** (-fuh.ZAY.shun, -tye-) *n.*

a.mount (uh.MOWNT) *n.* a quantity, esp. as a mass: *a large amount of money; the full amount asked for; considerable, enormous, huge, moderate, negligible, small, substantial amounts; No amount of discussion will help.* —*v.* add up: *His debts amount to $10,000; disloyalty amounting to treason; He never amounted to anything as a mayor.*

a.mour (uh.MOOR) *n.* a love affair, esp. one that is illicit.

amp *n.* [short form] **1** ampere or amperage: *a 7.5-amp motor; amps, watts, and horsepower ratings.* **2** amplifier: *power amps; amps and speakers.* **3** amputation; amputee: *war amps.*

am.pere (AM.peer) *n.* a unit of electric current, equal to one coulomb per second.

am.per.age (AM.puh.rij) *n.* the strength of an electric current in amperes.

am.per.sand (AM.pur.sand) *n.* the symbol "&" meaning "and."

am.phet.a.mine (am.FET.uh.meen, -min) *n.* a compound drug used as a nasal decongestant and as a stimulant.

am.phib.i.an (am.FIB.ee.un) *n.* **1** an animal such as a frog or seal that can live in water and on land. **2** a vehicle such as an aircraft, tank, or truck that can operate on land and water.

am.phib.i.ous (am.FIB.ee.us) *adj.* **1** adapted for land and water: *amphibious troops.* **2** carried out on land and water: *an amphibious attack.* —**am.phib.i.ous.ly** *adv.;* **am.phib.i.ous.ness** *n.*

am.phi.the.a.ter (AM.fuh.thee.uh.tur, "th" as in "thin") *n.* a building with an arena or stage in the middle and rows of seats rising around it. Also **am.phi.the.a.tre** *Cdn.*

am.ple (AM.pul) *adj.* **-pler, -plest** more than adequate in size, capacity, or amount: *a car with ample room for four passengers; an income that is ample for all his needs; a man of ample means.* —**am.ple.ness** *n.*

am.pli.fi.er (AM.pluh.fye.ur) *n.* an amplifying device: *an electronic amplifier for strengthening sound and picture signals.*

am.pli.fy (AM.pluh.fye) *v.* **-fies, -fied, -fy.ing** make larger or fuller: *to amplify a narrative with details; a device to amplify (= strengthen) a voice or electric current.* —**am.pli.fi.ca.tion** (-fuh.CAY.shun) *n.*

am.pli.tude (AM.pluh.tude) *n.* fullness or largeness, as the extent to which a pendulum or wave oscillates: *radio signals based on amplitude or frequency modulation.*

am.ply (AM.plee) *adv.* in an ample manner: *amply clear, demonstrated, deserved, justified, satisfied.*

am.pule (AM.pule) *n.* a small glass sealed glass vessel that holds a hypodermic injection solution.

am.pu.tate (AMP.yuh.tate) *v.* **-tates, -tat.ed, -tat.ing** cut off a limb by surgery. —**am.pu.ta.tion** (-TAY.shun) *n.*

am.pu.tee (AMP.yuh.tee) *n.* one who has had a limb cut off by surgery.

a.muck (uh.MUK) same as AMOK.

am.u.let (AM.yuh.lit) *n.* something worn on one's person as protection against evil; charm; talisman.

a.muse (uh.MUZE) *v.* **a.mus.es, a.mused, a.mus.ing** to interest lightly; engage the attention humorously: *He kept the children amused by telling them stories; Your jokes don't amuse me very much; It amuses me that he would use such a ploy; to amuse oneself by playing solitaire; She amused the audience with little tricks; adj.: We were **amused** at or by her tricks; We were greatly, highly, thoroughly, very much amused by what we saw; We found it very **amusing**; It was amusing to all of us.* —**a.muse.ment** *n.: a party to provide amusement for the company; Much to our amusement, no one appeared at the party; People found amusement in all sorts of diversions.*

amusement park *n.* a place of outdoor entertainment equipped with rides, booths for games, snack bars, etc. Also **amusement center.**

an (AN, 'n) *indef.art.* the form of "a" used when a vowel sound follows: *an event; an honor; an M.A.*

an.a.bol.ic (an.uh.BOL.ic) *adj.* having to do with the biological process by which food is converted into living tissue: *An* **anabolic steroid** *is a synthetic derivative of testosterone.*

a.nach.ro.nism (uh.NAC.ruh.niz.um) *n.* a person or thing that is out of its proper time: *Horse-drawn vehicles may seem an anachronism on our streets today.* —**a.nach.ro.nis.tic** (-NIS.tic) *adj.*

an.a.con.da (an.uh.CON.duh) *n.* a large South American tropical snake that crushes its prey in its coils.

a.nae.mi.a (uh.NEE.mee.uh) same as ANEMIA.

an.aer.obe (AN.uh.robe) *n.* an organism that can survive without oxygen, as bacteria. —**an.aer.o.bic** (-ROH.bic) *adj.*

an.aes.the.sia (an.is.THEE.zhuh, "TH" as in "thin"), etc. same as ANESTHESIA, etc.

an.a.gram (AN.uh.gram) *n.* a word or group of words formed by rearranging the letters of another word or phrase: *"Agitator" is an anagram for "I got a rat."*

a.nal (AY.nul) *adj.* having to do with the anus; **a.nal.ly** *adv.*

an.al.ge.si.a (an.ul.JEE.zhuh) *n.* absence of the sense of pain.

an.al.ge.sic (an.ul.JEE.zic) *n.* a pain-killing drug or ointment. —*adj.* pain-killing: *Heating pads, warm baths, etc. have an analgesic effect.*

an.a.log (AN.uh.log) same as ANALOGUE.

analog computer (AN.uh.log-) *n.* a calculating device in which numbers correspond proportionally to quantities such as weights or lengths, as on a ruler.

a.nal.o.gous (uh.NAL.uh.gus) *adj.* similar or comparable: *The fin of a fish is analogous to a wing in its function; The two processes are not analogous (with each other).*

an.a.logue (AN.uh.log) *n.* something similar or parallel to something else in properties or functions: *The gill of a fish is the analogue of a lung; a meat analogue made from soya beans.*

a.nal.o.gy (uh.NAL.uh.jee) *n.* **-gies** **1** likeness or similarity between things that are unlike each other; extended comparison: *He drew or made an analogy between a watch and the universe; an analogy based on their orderly movement; a close, not superficial analogy; the analogy of the universe to* or *with a watch.* **2** a process of reasoning or comparison based on similarity: *He argued* or *reasoned by false analogy that since one of the twins likes popcorn the other must too; It was by analogy that "cows" came to replace the old form "kine"; "Cows" was formed on the analogy of other plurals.* —**an.a.log.i.cal** (an.uh.LOJ.i.cul) *adj.;* **an.a.log.i.cal.ly** *adv.*

anal retentive (AY.nul.ri.TEN.tiv) *n.* [contemptuous use] one who is meticulous and exacting, not lax or uninhibited: *Some anal retentive wants me to use more commas;* **anal-retentive** *adj.:* this anal-retentive editor, lawyer.

analyse *Brit.* ANALYZE.

a.nal.y.sis (uh.NAL.uh.sis) *n., pl.* **-ses** (-seez) **1** the separation of something into its parts: *to make chemical analyses of substances into their constituent elements.* **2** an examination of the parts of anything or a statement of the result of such a study: *Your analysis of the poem is very penetrating; a careful, in-depth, painstaking, thorough analysis; On further analysis, the scheme was found to be a fraud; In the last, final, ultimate analysis, most of life's joys are transitory.* **3** psychoanalysis: *to undergo analysis on a therapist's couch.*

an.a.lyst (AN.uh.list) *n.* one who makes analyses, as a psychoanalyst or chemist: *a financial analyst; systems analyst.*

an.a.lyt.i.cal (an.uh.LIT.i.cul) or **an.a.lyt.ic** *adj.* having to do with analysis: *the analytical method; an analytical mind; analytical chemistry, psychology, skills; an analytic framework, instrument, tool;* **analytical geometry** *(using coordinates); English is more of an* **analytic(al) language** *than a synthetic one; cf.* SYNTHETIC. —**an.a.lyt.i.cal.ly** *adv.*

an.a.lyze (AN.uh.lize) *v.* **-lyz.es, -lyzed, -lyz.ing** make an analysis: *to analyze a substance for carbon; to analyze a sentence into its parts; to analyze causes, motives, people.* —**an.a.lyz.er** *n.* Also **an.a.lyse; an.a.lys.er** *Brit.*

an.a.pest (AN.uh.pest) *n.* **1** a foot of verse made up of two short or unaccented syllables followed by a long or accented one, as in "I am lord of the fowl and the brute." **2** a line of such verse. —**an.a.pest.ic** (-PEST.ic) *adj.*

an.ar.chy (AN.ur.kee) *n.* **-chies** lawlessness or disorder caused by absence of government or control: *Anarchy reigned during the riot; complete, total, utter anarchy.* —**an.ar.chism** (-kiz.um) *n.;* **an.ar.chist** (-kist) *n.* —**a.nar.chic** (uh.NAR.kic) or **a.nar.chi.cal** *adj.*

a.nath.e.ma (uh.NATH.uh.muh, "TH" as in "thin") *n.* **1** a curse invoking damnation: *The church used to declare or pronounce anathemas on nonconformists such as heretics and schismatics; An anathema could be lifted from a sinner after he had done penance.* **2** a hated person or thing: *Liquor is anathema to her.*

a.nath.e.ma.tize (uh.NATH.uh.muh.tize) *v.* **-tiz.es, -tized, -tiz.ing** curse or excommunicate.

an.a.tom.i.cal (an.uh.TOM.i.cul) *adj.* having to do with anatomy; also **an.a.tom.i.c.** —**an.a.tom.i.cal.ly** *adv.*

a.nat.o.mist (uh.NAT.uh.mist) *n.* an expert in anatomy.

a.nat.o.mize (uh.NAT.uh.mize) *v.* **-miz.es, -mized, -miz.ing** examine the structure of something, as by dissecting it.

a.nat.o.my (uh.NAT.uh.mee) *n.* **-mies 1** the science of the structure of bodies and their parts: *comparative anatomy of different animals.* **2** a structure or analysis: *the anatomy of a frog, murder, poem.*

-ance or **-ence** *n.* suffix indicating action, state, quality, or amount: *abundance, dependence, resistance.* Also **-ancy** or **-ency:** *consistency, truancy.*

an.ces.tor (AN.ses.tur) *n.* a person from whom one is descended; forebear: *our remote ancestors; Worship of ancestors is common in many cultures.* —**an.ces.tral** (an.SES.trul) *adj.*

an.ces.try (AN.ses.tree) *n.* **-tries** a line of ancestors; lineage: *Most white people are of European ancestry; Public schools admit children of all ancestries and religions; North American blacks trace their ancestry to Africa.*

an.chor (ANK.ur) *n.* **1** a heavy object lowered by cable from a ship to hold it in place: *A ship casts* or *drops anchor in a harbor; It* **rides at anchor** *while anchored; It* **weighs anchor** (= takes up the anchor) *and sails away.* **2** a team leader, as the coordinator of a telecast; also **an.chor.man, anchor person, an.chor.wom.an.** **3** a person in a responsible or sensitive position, as the one finishing a relay race or at the end of a tug-of-war team.
—*v.* **1** secure or moor, as a ship or balloon: *We anchored our boat in a bay; securely anchored; The posts are firmly anchored in the ground.* **2** act as anchor: *the guy who anchors the evening news; A supermarket will anchor the new shopping mall (as its main retail store).*

an.chor.age (ANK.ur.ij) *n.* a place to anchor, as a bay or harbor.

an.cho.vy (AN.choh.vee) *n.* **-vies** a small herringlike fish.

an.cien re.gime (ahn.SYAHN.ray.ZHEEM) *n.* French. the old order, as in France before the Revolution.

an.cient (AYN.shunt) *adj.* belonging to olden days: *an ancient monument; tales of ancient Rome; That's ancient history!* —*n.* an aged person: *according to the ancients* (= people of olden days). —**an.cient.ly** *adv.*; **an.cient.ness** *n.*

an.cil.lar.y (AN.suh.lair.ee) *adj.* in a helping role: *Logic is ancillary to philosophy; an ancillary subject; ancillary equipment, industries, markets, products, services.*

-ancy See -ANCE.

and *conj.* **1** [used to join words, phrases, sentences, etc.]: *Jack, Jon, and Jill; Tom, Dick, Harry and his wife.* **2** referring to the second of a pair: *ham and* (= and eggs). —**and how!** *interj.* expressing emphatic agreement: *Did she win? And how!*

an.dan.te (ahn.DAHN.tay) *adj. & adv.* Music. in moderately slow time. —*n.* a musical passage in such time.

An.de.an (AN.dee.un) *adj.* having to do with the region of the **Andes,** a mountain range of W. South America: *Andean countries, governments, highlands, Incas.*

and.i.ron (AN.dye.urn) *n.* one of a pair of metal holders for keeping logs in a fireplace.

and/or *conj.* [used when "and" or "or" may be read as the connective]: *You can have coffee with cream and/or sugar* (= with cream and sugar, with cream, or with sugar).

an.dro.gen (AN.druh.jun) *n.* a hormone that induces masculine characteristics. —**an.dro.gen.ic** (-.JEN.ic) *adj.*

an.drog.e.nous (an.DROJ.uh.nus) *adj.* producing male offspring.

an.drog.y.nous (an.DROJ.uh.nus) *adj.* having male and female characteristics.

an.droid (AN.droid) *n.* a creature such as an automaton or a robot having human form; also *adj.*

an.drol.o.gy (an.DROL.uh.jee) *n.* the medical specialty concerned with the male reproductive tract and its diseases.

an.ec.dote (AN.ic.dote) *n.* a short, often humorous or instructive account of an incident in a person's life: *to narrate, relate, tell an anecdote of one's childhood; funny, witty anecdotes.*

—**an.ec.dot.al** (-DOH.tul) *adj*.: *anecdotal accounts, evidence, reports (of a nonscientific nature).*

a.ne.mi.a (uh.NEE.mee.uh) *n*. weakness or paleness from lack of red cells in the blood: *pernicious anemia; sickle-cell anemia.* —**a.ne.mic** *adj*.

an.e.mom.e.ter (an.uh.MOM.uh.tur) *n*. an instrument for measuring the force and speed of winds.

a.nem.o.ne (uh.NEM.uh.nee) *n*. a plant of the buttercup family, having showy, usu. white flowers: *The sea anemone is a marine animal.*

an.er.oid (AN.uh.roid) *adj*. not using fluid: *An aneroid barometer indicates air pressure by means of an elastic metal disk connected to a needle.*

an.es.the.sia (an.is.THEE.zhuh, "TH" as in "thin") *n*. loss of the sense of pain, cold, touch, etc., as by use of an anesthetic: *Local anesthesia in a part of the body, as when teeth are extracted, wears off after a time; General anesthesia puts a person to sleep during surgery; Deep hypnosis can produce or induce anesthesia in a subject.*

an.es.the.si.ol.o.gy (AN.is.thee.zee.OL.uh.jee) *n*. the science of administering anesthetics; **an.es.the.si.ol.o.gist** *n*.

an.es.thet.ic (an.is.THET.ic) *adj*. causing anesthesia. —*n*. an anesthetic agent such as ether: *to administer or give an anesthetic to a patient; to have or take an anesthetic; He was operated on while under (an) anesthetic.*
—**an.es.thet.i.cal.ly** *adv*.

an.es.thet.ist (uh.NES.thuh.tist) *n*. a physician who administers anesthetics.

an.es.the.tize (uh.NES.thuh.tize) *v*. -tiz.es, -tized, -tiz.ing render insensible, as by anesthesia.
—**an.es.the.ti.za.tion** (-tuh.ZAY.shun, -tye-) *n*.

an.eu.rysm or **an.eu.rism** (AN.yuh.riz.um) *n*. an abnormal dilation of the wall of an artery.

a.new (uh.NEW) *adv*. again or afresh: *After a short cease-fire, fighting broke out anew.*

an.gel (AIN.jul) *n*. **1** a spiritual being, usu. in the role of a heavenly messenger: *a guardian angel; The nurse was like a ministering angel to him.* **2** one regarded as good and lovely: *You're an angel!* —**an.gel.ic** (an.JEL.ic) or **an.gel.i.cal** (-i.cul) *adj*.
—**an.gel.i.cal.ly** *adv*.

angel (food) cake *n*. a white fluffy cake made with egg whites.

angel dust *n*. *Informal*. **1** the tranquilizer "PCP" sniffed or smoked as a narcotic. **2** a synthetic heroin.

An.ge.le.no (an.juh.LEE.noh) *n*. **-nos** a person of or from Los Angeles.

angel money *n*. venture capital put up by a private investor.

an.ger (ANG.gur) *n*. a strong feeling of hurt or displeasure; ire: *to arouse, express, show, stir up anger; to allay, appease, calm, swallow one's anger; He used to vent his anger on his family; He felt a blind, burning, deep-seated, seething, unbridled anger at being fired from his job; anger toward society; burning with anger; In a blaze or fit of anger, he yelled at his boss; He struck in anger; an outburst of repressed anger.* —*v*. **an.gers, an.gered, an.ger.ing** make or be angry: *Foul play angers him; It angers him to think that people can get away with murder.*

an.gi.na (an.JYE.nuh) *n*. any illness characterized by spasmodic pain, esp. **angina pectoris,** a heart ailment accompanied by sudden bursts of chest pain. —**an.gi.nal** (-nul) *adj*.

angio- *comb.form*. having to do with a vessel, esp. blood vessel: *angiogram; angiology; angioplasty.*

an.gi.o.gram (AN.gee.uh.gram) *n*. an X-ray picture of blood vessels.

an.gi.ol.o.gy (an.jee.OL.uh.jee) *n*. the study of blood and lymph vessels.

an.gi.o.plas.ty (AN.jee.oh.PLAS.tee) *n*. repair of blood vessels: *balloon angioplasty (by inserting a balloon-tipped catheter into a blood vessel to unclog it); coronary angioplasty.*

an.gi.o.sperm (AN.jee.uh.spurm) *n*. a plant such as the orchid or the rose that bears seeds in a closed ovary; cf. GYMNOSPERM.

an.gle (ANG.gul) *n*. **1** the space between two lines or surfaces that meet: *An obtuse angle of 120 degrees is complementary to an acute angle of 60 degrees; the angle of a roof; a right angle (of 90 degrees).* **2** a deviation from a straight line: *The leaning tower of Pisa stands at a slight angle; a hat set at a rakish angle.* **3** a point of view; aspect: *two accounts from different angles; Look at it from various angles; When something is offered free, you suspect an angle (Informal for motive) or a gimmick somewhere.*
—*v*. **-gles, -gled, -gling 1** to fish with a hook or try to get as with a fishhook: *to angle for trout, for an invitation, for compliments.* **2** to slant or bias; *adj*.: *an angled account of the incident.* —**an.gler** *n*.

an.gle.worm (ANG.gul.wurm) *n*. an

earthworm used as a bait; dew worm.

An.gli.can (ANG.gli.cun) *n.* a member of the Church of England or a related church; *adj.*: *The U.S. Episcopal Church is in the Anglican Communion.*
—**An.gli.can.ism** (-cuh.niz.um) *n.*

An.gli.ci.sm (ANG.gluh.siz.um) *n.* a typically English expression, trait, etc.; Briticism.

an.gli.cize (ANG.gluh.size) *v.* **-ciz.es, -cized, -ciz.ing** make something English. —**an.gli.ci.za.tion** (-suh.ZAY.shun, -sye-) *n.* Also **an.gli.fy, -fies, -fied, -fy.ing.**

An.glo (ANG.gloh) *n.* **-glos** a white English-speaking North American.

Anglo- *comb.form.* English: *Anglo-Canadian, Anglo-Catholic, Anglo-French, Anglo-Saxon.*

An.glo.phile (ANG.gluh.file) *n.* an admirer of English and things English.

An.glo.phobe (ANG.gluh.fobe) *n.* one who hates or fears England and things English.

An.glo.phone or **an.glo.phone** (ANG.gluh.fone) *n.* in a multilingual nation, one whose first language is English. —*adj.* English-speaking: *Canada's Anglophone population.*

Anglo-Saxon *n.* **1** a member or descendant of the Angles, Saxons, and Jutes who settled in Britain in the 5th and 6th centuries. **2** the Old English language. —*adj.* having to do with the Anglo-Saxons: *Anglo-Saxon countries; people of Anglo-Saxon descent; the Anglo-Saxon establishment, mind, world; four-letter Anglo-Saxon words consisting of plain and simple, sometimes unrefined, words.*

an.go.ra (an.GOR.uh) *n.* **1** wool or cloth made from a goat, rabbit, or cat with long, silky hair; mohair. **2** such a goat, rabbit, or cat.

an.gry (ANG.gree) *adj.* **-gri.er, -gri.est 1** full of anger: *The boss got or became angry at or with us for being late; He's always angry about something or other; She's never angry at being pestered by kids; She was angry to find out what happened; angry that her child had stolen something; an angry look; the angry (= stormy) sea.* **2** inflamed; red: *an angry wound.* —**an.gri.ly** *adv.*

angst *n.* anxiety and related feelings: *middle-age angst; our angst-ridden times.*

ang.strom (ANG.strum) *n.* a unit of length equal to one ten-billionth of a meter.

an.guish (ANG.gwish) *n.* intense pain, esp. of the mind: *The child's disappearance caused much anguish in the community; The parents were in deep mental anguish at or over what might have happened.* —*v.* be in pain: *He anguishes over trifles; adj.: She wears an **anguished** (= pained) expression.*

an.gu.lar (ANG.yuh.lur) *adj.* **1** having an angle or angles; sharp-cornered: *an angular structure.* **2** bony or stiff-looking: *an angular face; angular features.* **3** measured by an angle: *the angular distance; an angular measure; angular velocity.* —**an.gu.lar.ly** (-lur.lee) *adv.* —**an.gu.lar.i.ty** (-LAIR.i.tee) *n.*

An.gus (ANG.gus) *n.* a Scottish breed of black hornless cattle.

an.hy.dride (an.HYE.dride) *n.* a chemical compound from which water has been removed.

an.hy.drous (an.HYE.drus) *adj.* without water, esp. "water of crystallization."

an.i.line (AN.i.lin) *n.* a colorless, poisonous, oily liquid obtained from benzene, used in making dyes, drugs, explosives, etc.

an.i.mad.vert (an.uh.mad.VURT) *v.* make adverse comments *on* or *upon* a subject. —**an.i.mad.ver.sion** (-VUR.zhun) *n.*

an.i.mal (AN.uh.mul) *n.* a living being that has sensation and can move about: *Both beasts and humans are animals; Some of us are party animals, others are political animals, but we are all rational animals; They are mostly wild animals; draft animals such as the horse and camel; Wolves are pack animals; Ants are social animals; caged, carnivorous, flesh-eating, predatory animals; to train an animal to do tricks; People butcher, domesticate, hunt, neuter, slaughter, skin, stuff, trap animals; He's a mere animal (= brute) in his eating habits; There's something of **the animal** (= animal nature) in all of us; There's **no such animal** (= no person or thing) as the average American.* —*adj.* having to do with animals: *Lard and butter are animal fats; **animal husbandry** (= care of domestic animals for milk and meat); the animal kingdom as opposed to the vegetable; Food is one of our animal (= physical) needs; an animal (= sensual) appetite; our animal (= brutish) desires, instincts.*

an.i.mal.ism (AN.uh.muh.liz.um) *n.* the belief in and practice of sensuality as a way of life; **an.i.mal.ist** *n.*
—**an.i.mal.is.tic** (-LIS.tic) *adj.*
—**an.i.mal.i.ty** (-MAL.i.tee) *n.*

an.i.mal.ize (AN.uh.muh.lize) *v.* **-iz.es, -ized, -iz.ing** cause to become like an animal. —**an.i.mal.i.za.tion**

(-luh.ZAY.shun, -lye-) n.
animal rights activist n. one who campaigns for humane treatment of animals.
animal spirits n.pl. overflow of liveliness.
an.i.mate (AN.uh.mit) adj. living; active: *Plants are part of animate nature.* —v. (AN.uh.mate) **-mates, -mat.ed, -mat.ing 1** give life, vigor, or interest to something: *a debate animated by lively wit;* adj.: *an* **animated** *discussion, expression, face;* **an.i.mat.ed.ly** adv. **2** make a moving picture using drawings: *to animate a story; An* **animated cartoon** *is a series of drawings photographed like a moving picture.* —**an.i.ma.tion** (-MAY.shun) n.: *a dead body in suspended animation; the animation of a story by a cartoonist.*
an.i.ma.tor (AN.uh.may.tur) n. one who makes an animated cartoon.
an.i.mism (AN.uh.miz.um) n. the belief that inanimate things such as rocks, winds, and rivers have souls; **an.i.mist** n. —**an.i.mis.tic** (-MIS.tic) adj.
an.i.mos.i.ty (an.uh.MOS.i.tee) n. **-ties** intense dislike bordering on hostility: *to arouse* or *stir up animosity in the community; racial and religious animosities; It's natural to feel animosity against* or *to* or *toward the favored few; the animosity between religious sects; a burning, deep-seated, seething, violent animosity.*
an.i.mus (AN.uh.mus) n. dislike based on ill will or prejudice.
an.i.on (AN.eye.un) n. a negatively charged ion. —**an.i.on.ic** (-ON.ic) adj.
an.ise (AN.is) n. an herb of the parsley family with sweet-smelling seeds called **aniseed** that are used in medicine and flavoring.
ankh (ANGK) n. an ancient Egyptian emblem of life in the shape of a cross with a loop for its upper vertical arm.
an.kle (ANK.ul) n. the part of a leg that links the foot to the calf: *to sprain* or *twist one's ankle; the ballerina's well-turned* (= shapely) *ankles;* **cpd**: *The child stood* **ankle-deep** *in mud; an* **ankle-length** *skirt.*
an.klet (ANK.lit) n. **1** an ankle ornament, as a band or chain. **2** a short sock.
an.nals (AN.uls) n.pl. historical records: *The trade pact opened a new chapter in the annals of Canadian-American relations.* —**an.nal.ist** (AN.uh.list) n.
an.neal (uh.NEEL) v. toughen and temper glass, metal, etc. by slow cooling and heating.
an.ne.lid (AN.uh.lid) n. an animal such as earthworms and leeches that have bodies composed of ringlike segments: *an annelid worm.*
an.nex (uh.NEX) v. take and attach, usu. a territory, to itself: *A city sometimes annexes a suburb.* —n. (AN.ex) something attached, as an addition to a building: *a hospital annex for outpatients; a clause added as an annex to the treaty.* —**an.nex.a.tion** (-AY.shun) n.
an.ni.hi.late (uh.NYE.uh.late) v. **-lates, -lat.ed, -lat.ing** destroy completely: *to annihilate an army, city, plan.* —**an.ni.hi.la.tion** (-LAY.shun) n.
an.ni.ver.sa.ry (an.uh.VUR.suh.ree) n. **-ries** the yearly recurring date of an event: *1987 marked the 20th anniversary of her arrival in Canada; to celebrate, commemorate an anniversary; golden, silver, wedding anniversaries; It takes 65 years to reach one's diamond anniversary; what to do on the next anniversary;* **adja.**: *an anniversary celebration, dinner.*
an.no Dom.i.ni (an.oh.DOM.uh.nee, -nye) adv. Latin. [usu. abbreviated as A.D.] in the year of the Lord (following Christ's birth): *in A.D. 1867.*
an.no.tate (AN.uh.tate) v. **-tates, -tat.ed, -tat.ing** provide a text with notes: *to annotate a text;* adj.: *an* **annotated** *edition of Shakespeare.* —**an.no.ta.tor** n. —**an.no.ta.tion** (-TAY.shun) n.: *to make marginal annotations on a manuscript; a text edited with copious annotations.*
an.nounce (uh.NOWNCE) v. **an.nounc.es, an.nounced, an.nounc.ing 1** make known publicly: *to announce a wedding date; They announced that they would wed on January 4; It was announced to the press; He announces* (= reads, describes, or comments on) *news, sports, and weather on radio.* **2** state the name of a person, flight, etc. on arrival: *The butler announced the guests; Flight 401 has just been announced.* —**an.nounce.ment** n.
an.nounc.er (uh.NOWN.sur) n. one who announces programs, reads news, etc. on radio or TV.
an.noy (uh.NOY) v. irritate or disturb: *Phone calls annoy her;* adj.: *She is* **annoyed** *at* or *with him for making too many calls; She is annoyed that he often calls in the middle of the night; Phone calls can be very* **annoying***; Callers are annoying to people who wish to be left alone; It's annoying that people try to sell things by phone.* —**an.noy.ing.ly** adv.
an.noy.ance (uh.NOY.unce) n. **1** the

feeling of being annoyed: *To her great annoyance, he arrived very late; Much to his own annoyance, she had left the scene; She felt and showed annoyance at or over or with his behavior; She expressed her annoyance that he always kept her waiting.* **2** one that annoys; nuisance: *Boarders proved to be an annoyance to the family.*

an.nu.al (AN.yoo.ul) *adj.* **1** yearly: *your annual income; Marigolds and zinnias are annual plants (that complete the life cycle in one year).* **2** happening every year: *Birthdays are annual events; an annual meeting; Cross-sections of tree trunks show* **annual rings** *indicating each year's growth.* —*n.* **1** annual plant. **2** yearbook. —**an.nu.al.ly** *adv.*

an.nu.i.tant (uh.NEW.uh.tunt) *n.* one who receives an annuity.

an.nu.i.ty (uh.NEW.i.tee) *n.* **-ties** a fixed sum of money paid yearly on an investment.

an.nul (uh.NUL) *v.* **an.nuls, an.nulled, an.nul.ling** cancel or make a marriage, law, etc. void. —**an.nul.ment** *n.: The Pope grants marriage annulments.*

an.nu.lar (AN.yoo.lur) *adj.* ringlike: *An annular eclipse shows the rim of the heavenly body like a ring.*

an.nu.lus (AN.yuh.lus) *n.* **-lus.es** or **-li** (-lye) a ringlike part, marking, or formation.

an.nun.ci.a.tion (uh.nun.see.AY.shun) *n.* an announcing, esp. **the Annunciation** of the motherhood of the Virgin Mary by the angel Gabriel or the commemoration of it on March 25. —**an.nun.ci.a.to.ry** (uh.NUN.see.uh.tor.ee) *adj.*

an.ode *n.* the positively charge electrode of an electrolytic cell or electron tube or the negative terminal of a primary cell.

an.o.dyne (AN.uh.dine) *n.* a drug that relieves pain, as codeine: *Time is the anodyne of sorrow.*

a.noint (uh.NOINT) *v.* **1** apply oil or ointment to someone, esp. as a religious rite: *the Roman Catholic sacrament* **Anointing of the sick**, *formerly called "extreme unction."* **2** consecrate: *to anoint a queen; Elizabeth II was anointed queen in 1953.*

a.nom.a.ly (uh.NOM.uh.lee) *n.* **-lies** (-leez) something irregular or abnormal, as stairs that lead nowhere: *the anomaly of time in the movie "Back to the Future"; the anomaly of large houses lying vacant while more and more people live on the streets.* —**a.nom.a.lous** (-lus) *adj.: the anomalous situation of an unknown French play becoming a huge hit in its English version.*

an.o.mie (AN.uh.mee) *n.* loss of faith in human nature and social values. Also **an.o.my.**

a.non (uh.NON) *adv.* soon: *But more of that anon.* —**ever and anon** now and then.

a.non.y.mous (uh.NON.uh.mus) *adj.* with no name given: *an anonymous author, call, caller, letter;* **a.non.y.mous.ly** *adv.* —**a.no.nym.i.ty** (an.uh.NIM.i.tee) *n.*

a.noph.e.les (uh.NOF.uh.leez) *n. sing. & pl.* a malaria-carrying mosquito.

an.o.rak (AN.uh.rak) *n.* a hooded pullover jacket, originally one made of fur for use in the Arctic.

an.o.rex.i.a (an.uh.REX.ee.uh) *n.* an eating disorder, esp. of young women, characterized by loss of appetite and resulting starvation from anxiety to control weight; in full "anorexia nervosa." —**an.o.rex.ic** (-REX.ic) *n. & adj.* (a patient) having anorexia.

an.oth.er (uh.NUTH.ur, "TH" as in "the") *pron. & adj.* an additional, different, or similar one: *This cup is broken, get me another; Have another drink; She's a brilliant physicist, another Einstein.*

an.swer (AN.sur) *n.* a reply to a question: *to give, offer, provide an answer to a question; The answer is No; I have nothing more to say in answer to your question; appropriate, blunt, curt, civil, evasive, glib, negative, positive, ready, straight, vague, witty answers; the right answer; the wrong answer; Even doctors don't have or know all the answers to your health problems; Dieting may be the answer* (= solution) *to his weight problem; The CN Tower is Canada's answer* (= matching response) *to the world's tallest structures.* —*v.* say or act in answer: *to answer a question; Please answer the phone; I'll* **answer the door** (= see who is there); *A stick will answer* (= suit) *my purpose very well; Don't* **answer back** (= reply rudely) *to your father, mother, and older sisters; You will have to* **answer for** (= be responsible for) *the broken china;* **n.**: *An* **answering service** *handles phone calls for clients.* —**answer to 1** explain to: *You'll have to answer to the manager.* **2** correspond: *This one answers to the description of the missing dog.* **3** respond: *He answers to the name "Tiger."*

an.swer.a.ble (AN.sur.uh.bul) *adj.* responsible: *We are answerable to our superiors for carrying out our duties.*

ant *n.* any of a family of small social insects related to bees: *a colony of ants; army ants; He's got **ants in his pants*** (*Informal for* He's very restless or anxious).
ant- same as ANTI-.
ant.ac.id (an.TAS.id) *n.* a chemical that neutralizes acidity, as baking soda.
an.tag.o.nism (an.TAG.uh.niz.um) *n.* opposition or hostility between persons: *to arouse, stir up antagonism between friends; People feel a strong antagonism to or toward anyone seen as a threat to their livelihood.*
an.tag.o.nist (an.TAG.uh.nist) *n.* adversary or opponent: *a formidable antagonist.* —**an.tag.o.nis.tic** (-NIS.tic) *adj.*
an.tag.o.nize (an.TAG.uh.nize) *v.* **-iz.es, -ized, -iz.ing** make someone hostile: *He antagonized the rest of the group by giving special consideration to a few.*
Ant.arc.tic (ant.ARC.tic, -AR.tic) *adj.* of the south polar region of the Earth: *the Antarctic region; The **Antarctic Circle**, the parallel at 66° 33' S, encloses the South Frigid Zone; the Antarctic Ocean.*
ant bear *n.* a large anteater of South America; great anteater; also called "giant anteater."
an.te (AN.tee) *n.* a stake put up by a poker player. —**raise the ante** raise the price. —*v.* **-tes,** *pt. & pp.* **-ted** or **-teed, -te.ing** put up an ante. —**ante up** *Informal.* pay one's due share in a joint venture.
ante- *prefix. & v. prefix.* before; prior: *antechamber, antedate, antenatal.*
ant.eat.er (ANT.eet.ur) *n.* a long-snouted mammal that feeds on ants, as the aardvark or the ant bear.
an.te.bel.lum (an.ti.BEL.um) *adj.* of the period before the U.S. Civil War.
an.te.ce.dent (an.tuh.SEE.dunt) *n.* a person or thing going before, as a word or phrase to which a pronoun refers: *In the sentence "When I borrow a book I return it," "book" is the antecedent of "it"; a nonentity with no **antecedents** (= known ancestors).* —*adj.* preceding: *antecedent circumstances.*
—**an.te.ce.dent.ly** *adv.*
—**an.te.ce.dence** (-dunce) *n.*
an.te.cham.ber (AN.tee.chame.bur) *n.* a side room leading into a larger room.
an.te.date (AN.tee.date) *v.* **-dates, -dat.ed, -dat.ing 1** date a document, check, etc. earlier than the actual date. **2** happen earlier than another event.
an.te.di.lu.vi.an (AN.tee.duh.LOO.vee.un) *adj.* very ancient, antiquated, or obsolete: *an antediluvian custom.*
—*n.* one who is antediluvian: *He's an antediluvian in his attitude to TV.*
an.te.lope (AN.tuh.lope) *n.* a deerlike animal such as the chamois, gazelle, and pronghorn.
ante me.rid.i.em (-muh.RID.ee.um) *adj.* Latin. in the forenoon; a.m.
an.te.na.tal (an.tee.NAY.tul) *adj.* before-birth; prenatal.
an.ten.na (an.TEN.uh) *n.* **1** a wire, rod, or dish used in sending or receiving TV and radio signals; aerial: *a loop antenna; a TV antenna.* **2** *pl.* also **an.ten.nae** (-ee) a hornlike feeler on the head of an insect.
an.te.ri.or (an.TEER.ee.ur) *adj.* coming before in position or time.
an.te.room (AN.tee.room) *n.* a small room opening into one larger; waiting room.
an.them (ANTH.um) *n.* a hymn of praise, devotion, or triumph: *our national anthem; the college anthem; A band strikes up or plays an anthem.*
ant.hill *n.* a pile of earth thrown up by ants at the entrance to their nest.
an.thol.o.gy (an.THOL.uh.jee) *n.* **-gies** (-jeez) a collection of writings, usu. on one theme by many authors.
—**an.thol.o.gist** *n.*
an.thra.cite (AN.thruh.cite) *n.* a hard coal that is mostly carbon and burns with great heat and little smoke.
an.thrax *n.* an infectious, often fatal disease of cattle and sheep, caused by a bacillus.
an.thro.po.cen.tric (an.thruh.poh.CEN.tric) *adj.* human-centered or based on human values.
an.thro.poid (AN.thruh.poid) *adj.* humanlike: *the anthropoid apes.*
—*n.* an ape such as the chimpanzee, gibbon, or gorilla.
an.thro.pol.o.gy (an.thruh.POL.uh.jee) *n.* the study of human origins, characteristics, and cultural development.
—**an.thro.pol.o.gist** *n.*
—**an.thro.po.log.i.cal** (-puh.LOJ.i.cul) *adj.*
an.thro.po.mor.phic (anth.ruh.puh.MOR.fic) *adj.* attributing human characteristics to gods, animals, etc.
anti- *prefix* [indicating opposition]: *antacid, anti-American, anticapitalist.*
an.ti (AN.tye, -tee) *n.* **-tis** *Informal.* one who opposes something: *The vote was three pros and two antis;* **prep.***: She is*

antiaircraft / antipathy

anti everything foreign.

an.ti.air.craft (an.tee.AIR.craft, an.tye-) *adj.* for use against aircraft: *an antiaircraft gun.*

an.ti.bac.te.ri.al (AN.tee.bac.TEER.ee.ul, AN.tye-) *adj.* that checks or protects from bacteria: *an antibacterial agent.*

an.ti.bal.lis.tic missile (AN.ti.buh.LIS.tic-) *n.* a missile for destroying a ballistic missile in flight.

an.ti.bi.ot.ic (AN.tee.bye.OT.ic, AN.tye-) *n.* a substance such as penicillin that can destroy or prevent the growth of harmful microorganisms.

an.ti.bod.y (AN.tee.bod.ee) *n.* **-bod.ies** a substance produced in the blood to fight disease germs, poisons, etc.

an.tic (AN.tic) *n.* a clownish act; caper. —*adj.* ludicrous; odd: *antic characters, comedies, humor.* —*v.* **-tics, -ticked, -tick.ing** cut capers: *a buffoon anticking on the stage.*

an.tic.i.pate (an.TIS.uh.pate) *v.* **-pates, -pat.ed, -pat.ing** foresee something and act accordingly: *We anticipated trouble during the strike; anticipated missing our mail; Anticipating rain, we took an umbrella;* **an.tic.i.pa.to.ry** (-puh.tor.ee) *adj.* —**an.tic.i.pa.tion** (-PAY.shun) *n.*: *We look forward to your visit with eager* or *keen anticipation; We took an umbrella in anticipation of rain.*

an.ti.cli.max (an.tee.CLY.max, AN.tye-) *n.* a sudden descent from the serious to the trivial in a series of events or in what is said or done: *The rain was an anticlimax to the victory parade.* —**an.ti.cli.mac.tic** (-clye.MAC.tic) *adj.*

an.ti.clock.wise (an.tee.CLOCK.wize) *adj. & adv.* in the direction opposite to the movement of a clock's hands.

an.ti.co.ag.u.lant (AN.tee.coh.AG.yuh.lunt) *n. & adj.* (a substance, esp. a medicine) that prevents the clotting of blood.

an.ti.cy.clone (an.tee.SYE.clone, AN.tye-) *n.* a rotating system of winds originating from a center of high pressure. —**an.ti.cy.clon.ic** (-sye.CLON.ic) *adj.*

an.ti.de.pres.sant (AN.tee.duh.PRES.unt, AN.tye-) *adj.* tending to prevent emotional depression. —*n.* an antidepressant drug; also called "energizer."

an.ti.dote (AN.tuh.dote) *n.* a remedy against poison, evil, or other harm: *There are specific antidotes for* or *against* or *to various poisons.* —**an.ti.do.tal** (-DOH.tul) *adj.*

an.ti.fit (AN.tee.fit) *adj.* baggy: *antifit jeans.*

an.ti.freeze (AN.tee.freez) *n.* a substance added to gasoline, radiator coolant, etc. to prevent freezing.

an.ti.gen (AN.tuh.jun) *n.* a foreign substance such as a virus or pollen that produces antibodies when it enters the body. —**an.ti.gen.ic** (an.tuh.JEN.ic) *adj.*

an.ti.he.ro (AN.tee.heer.oh, AN.tye-) *n.* **-roes** the protagonist in a novel or play who lacks the traditional virtues of a heroic character.

an.ti.his.ta.mine (an.tee.HIS.tuh.meen, an.tye-) *n.* a medicine for colds and allergies.

an.ti.knock (an.tee.NOCK, an.tye-) *n.* a fuel additive that reduces the noise of too rapid combustion in an engine.

an.ti.lock (AN.ti.lock) *adj.* nonlocking: *antilock brakes, braking systems.* —**antilocks** *n.pl.*

an.ti.mag.net.ic (AN.tee.mag.NET.ic, AN.tye-) *adj.* esp. of a watch, made with nonmagnetic metals to ensure constant movement of parts.

an.ti.mat.ter (AN.ti.mat.ur) *n.* a theoretical form of matter composed of antiparticles.

an.ti.mo.ny (AN.ti.moh.nee) *n.* a silver-white metallic element used in alloys to make them harder.

an.ti.neu.tri.no (AN.ti.new.TREE.noh) *n.* the antiparticle of the neutrino.

an.ti.neu.tron (an.ti.NEW.tron) *n.* the antiparticle of the neutron.

an.ti.nu.cle.ar (an.tee.NEW.clee.ur, an.tye-) *adj.* opposed to the use of nuclear energy for any purpose.

an.ti.no.mi.an (an.tuh.NOH.mee.un) *n.* one who believes that faith alone, without adherence to moral laws, is necessary for salvation. Also *adj.*: *antinomian behavior.*

an.tin.o.my (an.TIN.uh.mee) *n.* **-mies** a contradiction inherent in the same law or between laws.

an.ti.ox.i.dant (an.tee.OX.uh.dunt) *n.* a substance that inhibits oxidation and thus deterioration: *Vitamin C is an antioxidant in the blood.*

anti-nuke (an.tee.NUKE, an.tye-) *n. & adj. Informal.* (one) opposed to nuclear arms, nuclear energy, etc.

an.ti.par.ti.cle (an.tee.PAR.ti.cul) *n.* an elementary atomic particle identical in mass with, but opposite in electric charge and magnetic properties to an ordinary atomic particle: *A positron is the antiparticle of an electron.*

an.ti.pas.to (an.ti.PAS.toh) *n.* **-tos** an hors d'oeuvre.

an.tip.a.thy (an.TIP.uh.thee, "th" as in

"thin") *n.* **-thies** deep dislike or an object of it: *the antipathy of cats to water; Lotteries were a lifelong antipathy of his.*
an.ti.per.son.nel (AN.tee.pur.suh.NEL) *adj.* in war, designed for use against humans rather than materials: *an antipersonnel bomb.*
an.ti.per.spi.rant (an.tee.PUR.spuh.runt) *n.* a cosmetic preparation for checking perspiration.
an.ti.phon (AN.tuh.fon) *n.* a psalm or chant sung responsively or in alternate parts. —**an.tiph.o.nal** (an.TIF.uh.nul) *adj.*
an.tip.o.de (an.TIP.uh.dee) *n.* **1 Antipodes** *pl.* a diametrically opposite place or region of the earth, esp. Australia and New Zealand: *Canberra is in the Antipodes.* **2** something that is contrary to another: *Thrift and prodigality are antipodes; Violence is the antipode of peace.* —**an.tip.o.de.an** (-DEE.un) *adj.*
an.ti.pol.lu.tion (AN.tee.puh.LOO.shun, AN.tye-) *adja.* designed to counteract or prevent pollution: *antipollution devices, measures.*
an.ti.quar.i.an (an.tuh.QUAIR.ee.un) **1** *adj.* antique in interest: *a vast antiquarian collection.* **2** *n.* same as ANTIQUARY.
an.ti.quar.y (AN.tuh.quair.ee) *n.* **-quar.ies** one who collects or studies antiquities.
an.ti.quat.ed (AN.tuh.quay.tid) *adj.* out of date or old-fashioned: *a man of antiquated ideas.*
an.tique (an.TEEK) *n.* a once useful object that is now of mostly cultural value, as a century-old piece of furniture, pottery, or costume. —*adja.* **1** having to do with antiques: *an antique dealer, shop; antique furniture.* **2** ancient: *an antique city; antique heroes.* —*v.* **-tiques, -tiqued, -ti.quing** make something look like an antique; *adj.*: *an* **antiqued** *effect, finish; painted and antiqued steel.*
an.tiq.ui.ty (an.TIK.wi.tee) *n.* **-ties 1** great age: *discarded because of its antiquity.* **2** former times: *great men and women of antiquity.* **3 antiquities** *pl.* ancient remains. *Greek and Roman antiquities.*
anti-Semite (an.tee.SEM.ite, an.tye-) *n.* one who hates Jews. —**anti-Semitic** (AN.tee.suh.MIT.ic, AN.tye-) *adj.*; **anti-Semitism** *n.*
an.ti.sep.tic (an.tuh.SEP.tic) *adj.* **1** destroying disease germs: *Carbolic acid and alcohol are antiseptic agents; an antiseptic lotion, mouthwash, smell.* **2** lifeless or sterile, being extremely clean: *antiseptic visions of nuclear warfare.* —*n.* an antiseptic agent.
an.ti.se.rum (AN.tuh.seer.um) *n.* a serum effective against a specific substance.
an.ti.so.cial (an.tee.SOH.shul, an.tye-) *adj.* **1** not sociable: *an antisocial activity, fellow, life.* **2** against the good of society: *Stealing is antisocial.*
an.tith.e.sis (an.TITH.uh.sis, "TH" as in "thin") *n., pl.* **-ses** (-seez) **1** a contrasting idea or expression, as "Give me liberty or give me death!" **2** something that is contrasting: *Private ownership is the very antithesis of communism; the antithesis between good and evil.* —**an.ti.thet.i.cal** (an.ti.THET.i.cul) *adj.*
an.ti.tox.in (an.tee.TOX.in) *n.* an antibody or serum injected against a disease.
an.ti.trades (AN.tee.trades) *n.pl.* winds blowing in an opposite direction to the trade winds.
an.ti.trust (AN.tee.trust, AN.tye-) *adja.* having to do with laws against business monopolies: *antitrust legislation, policies; an antitrust suit, violation.*
an.ti.ven.in (an.tee.VEN.in) *n.* a serum for use against snake venom.
ant.ler (ANT.lur) *n.* a branched horn of an animal of the deer family: *Deer lock antlers in a fight; They shed their antlers each winter and grow new ones in the spring.* —**ant.lered** (ANT.lurd) *adj.* having antlers: *antlered animals, game.*
ant lion *n.* an insect resembling a dragonfly whose larva, the doodle bug, feeds on ants trapped in a conical pit in which it awaits its prey.
an.to.nym (AN.tuh.nim) *n.* a word that means the opposite of another: *"Black" is the antonym of "white."*
ants.y *adj.* **ants.i.er, ants.i.est** *Informal.* nervous or fidgety: *to be, feel, get antsy.*
an.u.re.sis (an.yoo.REE.sis) *n.* inability to urinate; failure in the secretion of urine from the kidneys.
a.nus (AY.nus) *n.* the opening at the end of the alimentary canal.
an.vil (AN.vil) *n.* a heavy block on which to hammer metals into shape.
anx.i.e.ty (ang.ZYE.uh.tee) *n.* **1** fear in thinking of what may happen: *a mother's anxiety for her child's safety; to relieve her anxiety; deep, grave, great, high anxiety; In his anxiety about the trip, he forgot to pay his rent.* **2** *pl.* **-ties** an instance of such fear: *the anxieties of unemployment.* **3** eagerness: *a pupil's anxiety to please his teacher.*
anx.ious (ANK.shus) *adj.* **1** worried or troubled: *She spent many anxious hours*

waiting for her child; She was anxious for the child's safety; anxious about what might happen. **2** very eager: Neighbors were anxious to help; They were anxious that she shouldn't worry. —**anx.ious.ly** adv.

an.y (EN.ee) adja. one out of many or some out of much of something [in positive statements and in questions when an affirmative answer is expected]: Do we have any oranges? Any old hat will do; Just any of them will suffice; as any child could tell you; [with implied negative] There's hardly any time left; He spoke without any hesitation. —**pron.** some: I have no money – have you any? —**adv.** to some degree: Has her luck improved any? Is she any better today? Is the book any good at all? —**at any rate** in whatever case; at least. —**in any case** or **event** whatever happens.

an.y.bod.y (EN.ee.bod.ee) pron. **1** any person; anyone: Anybody home? Do you have anybody to mind the baby? It's **anybody's guess** (= a question no one can answer). **2** any person of importance: Is she anybody here?

an.y.how (EN.ee.how) adv. anyway; nevertheless.

an.y.more (EN.ee.more) adv. any longer.

an.y.one (EN.ee.wun) pron. any person; anybody.

an.y.place (EN.ee.place) adv. anywhere.

an.y.thing (EN.ee.thing) n., pron. & adv. any one thing or something: You don't see anything in the dark; He will do anything for money; Fay is **anything but** (= not at all) fat; He cried **like anything** (Informal for a great deal).

an.y.time (EN.ee.time) adv. at any time: He may call anytime now.

an.y.way (EN.ee.way) adv. in any way.

an.y.where (EN.ee.where) adv. & pron. in or to any place.

an.y.wise (EN.ee.wise) adv. in any manner.

A-OK adj. & adv. Informal. quite all right.

A1 or **A one** adj. Informal. excellent.

a.or.ta (ay.OR.tuh) n. the main artery carrying blood from the heart to the rest of the body. —**a.or.tic** adj.: aortic aneurysms, deposits, swellings.

a.pace (uh.PACE) adv. [used after its verb] quickly: to continue or proceed apace.

A.pach.e (uh.PACH.ee) n. a member of an Indian tribe of S.W. United States and Mexico.

a.part (uh.PART) adjp. & adv. away from each other: two houses three miles apart; they are far apart; I took him apart (= aside) for a private chat; Don't tear the thing apart (= into parts); Handle it carefully or it will **fall apart** (= go to pieces); Twins are difficult to **tell apart** (= distinguish); Joking apart (= excepted), we want to go to the moon; The apes are **a class apart** (= separate) from other animals; They are **worlds apart** (= very different) from humans; **Apart from** (= besides) errors, the book is also out of date.

a.part.heid (uh.PAR.tate, -tide) n. the political policy of racial segregation.

a.part.ment (uh.PART.munt) n. a suite of rooms for living in; flat: bachelor, duplex, efficiency, high-rise, penthouse, studio apartments.

apartment block (or **building** or **house**) n. a building containing many apartments.

apartment complex n. **1** a group of apartment buildings. **2** an apartment building with adjoining amenities.

apartment hotel n. a hotel containing apartments with housekeeping facilities for guests on a temporary or permanent basis.

ap.a.thet.ic (ap.uh.THET.ic, "TH" as in "thin") adj. showing apathy: He is apathetic to or toward the poor; quite apathetic about their condition.

ap.a.thy (AP.uh.thee, "th" as in "thin") n. lack of feeling or interest; indifference: He feels apathy toward the poor; to show apathy; to cast off or shed or throw off one's apathy and do something.

ap.a.tite (AP.uh.tite) n. a crystalline mineral containing calcium phosphate.

ape n. **1** a large tailless monkey such as the chimpanzee, gibbon, or gorilla; one of the "great apes" or "higher apes." **2** any monkey. **3** one who mimics another's behavior like an ape. **4** a clumsy person. —**go ape** Informal. **1** go crazy. **2** go crazy over an object of admiration. —v. **apes, aped, ap.ing** imitate someone or someone's behavior in a silly way.

a.pe.ri.tif (ah.per.i.TEEF) n. an alcoholic drink taken before a meal.

ap.er.ture (AP.ur.chur) n. an opening or hole, as of a camera.

a.pex (AY.pex) n. **a.pex.es** or **ap.i.ces** (AP.uh.seez) the highest point or climax: at the apex of her fortunes. —**ap.i.cal** (AP.i.cul) adj.

a.pha.sia (uh.FAY.zhuh) n. loss of the ability to use or understand language, resulting from brain damage.

—**a.pha.si.ac** (-zee.ac) or **a.pha.sic** (-zic) *n. & adj.*
a.phe.li.on (uh.FEE.lee.un) *n., pl.* **-li.a** (-lee.uh) the point in a solar orbit that is farthest from the sun.
a.phid (AY.fid) or **a.phis** (AY.fis) *n.* **a.phids** or **a.phi.des** (-fuh.deez) a small insect that lives on the juice of plants.
aph.o.rism (AF.uh.riz.um) *n.* a pithy expression of a general truth, as the saying "The dog is man's best friend." —**aph.o.ris.tic** (af.uh.RIS.tic) *adj.*
aph.ro.dis.i.ac (af.ruh.DIZ.ee.ac) *n.* a food, drug, etc. that excites sexual desire: *Oysters are supposed to be aphrodisiacs; adj*.: *aphrodisiac charms, effects, power;* also **aph.ro.di.si.a.cal** (AF.ruh.di.ZYE.uh.cul) *adj.*
a.pi.ar.i.an (ay.pee.AIR.ee.un) *adj.* having to do with beekeeping. —*n.* beekeeper; also **a.pi.a.rist** (AY.pee.uh.rist)
a.pi.ar.y (AY.pee.air.ee) *n.* **-ar.ies** a box for keeping bees in hives.
apical, apices See APEX.
a.pi.cul.ture (AY.puh.cul.chur) *n.* beekeeping.
a.piece (uh.PEECE) *adv.* to or for each: *They cost $5 apiece.*
a.plen.ty (uh.PLEN.tee) *adjp. & adv.* in plenty: *challenge, evidence, fireworks, reasons aplenty; It cost aplenty.*
a.plomb (uh.PLOM) *n.* poise or self-confidence in bearing or behavior: *She spoke with the aplomb typical of a professional who knows her job.*
ap.ne.a (AP.nee.uh) *n.* stoppage of breathing for a minute or two: *Sleep apnea has been blamed in infant crib deaths.*
a.poc.a.lypse (uh.POC.uh.lips) *n.* a revelation or prophecy of something final and conclusive, as in the **Apocalypse**, or the "Book of Revelation," the last book of the Bible: *Are we facing a nuclear apocalypse* (= end)? —**a.poc.a.lyp.tic** (-LIP.tic) or **a.poc.a.lyp.ti.cal** (-ti.cul) *adj.*
a.poc.ry.pha (uh.POC.ruh.fuh) *n.pl.* writings from a dubious source connected with something authentic, like the **Apocrypha** attached to the Bible. —**a.poc.ry.phal** (-ful) *adj.* unauthentic: *an apocryphal account, anecdote, book; The story is purely apocryphal.*
ap.o.gee (AP.uh.jee) *n.* **1** the point in an orbit (as of a satellite) or trajectory (as of a rocket) that is farthest from the earth: *There is a difference of over 50,000 km between the moon's apogee and perigee.* **2** the highest point; apex: *to reach the apogee of one's career.*
a.po.lit.i.cal (ay.puh.LIT.i.cul) *adj.* not related to politics.
a.pol.lo (uh.POL.oh) *n.* a handsome youth, like the Greek god **Apollo.**
a.pol.o.get.ic (uh.pol.uh.JET.ic) *adj.* making an apology: *an apologetic smile; He was apologetic about his absence.* —**a.pol.o.get.i.cal.ly** *adv.*
ap.o.lo.gi.a (ap.uh.LOH.jee.uh) *n.* a formal defense of one's position.
a.pol.o.gist (uh.POL.uh.jist) *n.* one who speaks or writes in defense of a cause: *an apologist for the cause.*
a.pol.o.gize (uh.POL.uh.jize) *v.* **-giz.es, -gized, -giz.ing** make an apology: *He apologized to them for his rudeness.*
a.pol.o.gy (uh.POL.uh.jee) *n.* **-gies 1** an expression of regret for an offense: *He made* or *offered no apology for his rude remarks; my apologies for what happened; They demanded an apology; an abject, humble, public, sincere apology.* **2** a poor specimen or substitute: *a mere apology for the real thing.*
ap.o.plec.tic (ap.uh.PLEC.tic) *adj.* showing symptoms of apoplexy: *an apoplectic attack, stroke; an apoplectic* (= paralyzing) *fit, fury, rage.*
ap.o.plex.y (AP.uh.plex.ee) *n.* a stroke resulting in partial paralysis.
a.pos.ta.sy (uh.POS.tuh.see) *n.* **-sies** an abandoning of one's religious faith, political party, or other allegiance: *his apostasy from the priesthood.*
a.pos.tate (uh.POS.tate, -tit) *n.* one guilty of apostasy: *an apostate from the faith; an apostate priest.*
a pos.te.ri.o.ri (AY.poh.steer.ee.OH.rye, -ree) *adja. & adv.* of reasoning, proceeding from effect to cause, not a priori.
a.pos.tle (uh.POS.ul) *n.* **1** one of Christ's twelve disciples. **2** a first missionary: *the apostle to the Indies.* **3** leader of a movement: *an apostle of women's rights.*
a.pos.to.late (uh.POS.tuh.lit, -late) *n.* the work of an apostle: *Mother Teresa's apostolate of mercy; lay apostolates such as the Christian Family Movement.*
a.pos.tol.ic (ap.uh.STOL.ic) *adj.* **1** having to do with Christ's disciples: *the apostolic church established by Peter; in apostolic times.* **2** papal: *the apostolic blessing; an apostolic delegate.*
a.pos.tro.phe (uh.POS.truh.fee) *n.* **1** a punctuation mark indicating possession (*John's*), plural (*3 A's*), or contraction (*isn't*). **2** a rhetorical passage addressed to an imaginary or absent

apothecary / appellate   Page 48, *User's*™ *Webster*, © 2000, T. M. Paikeday

person or a personified object, as "Milton! thou shouldst be living at this hour."

a.poth.e.car.y (uh.POTH.uh.cair.ee, "TH" as in "thin") *n.* **-car.ies** a pharmacist; druggist.

ap.o.thegm (AP.uh.them, "th" as in "thin") *n.* a short, pithy saying or maxim such as "Honesty is the best policy."

a.poth.e.o.sis (uh.poth.ee.OH.sis, "th" as in "thin") *n., pl.* **-ses** (-seez) glorification or idealization: *He was the apotheosis of chivalry.*

Ap.pa.la.chian (ap.uh.LAY.chun) *adj.* having to do with a chain of mountains of E. North America, extending from Quebec south to Alabama.

ap.pall (uh.POL) *v.* **ap.palls, ap.palled, ap.pal.ling** fill with shock and dismay: *We are appalled at or by the misery of the poor; We are appalled to see the misery around us; appalled that such conditions could exist among us; adj.: the **appalling** condition of the slums.* Also **ap.pal** *Cdn.*

Ap.pa.loo.sa (ap.uh.LOO.suh) *n.* a hardy Western breed of saddle horse, distinguished by a spotted rump.

ap.pa.rat.chik (ah.puh.RAH.chik) *n.* [contemptuous use] a functionary or bureaucrat working for a Communist party; flunky.

ap.pa.ra.tus (ap.uh.RAT.us, -RAY.tus) *n.* **-tus** or **-tus.es** equipment for a specific task: *a gym apparatus; laboratory apparatus; a party's election apparatus* (= organization).

ap.par.el (uh.PAIR.ul) *n.* clothing or attire: *intimate apparel* (= women's underclothing). —*v.* **-els, -eled, -el.ing** clothe; *adjp.: The children were brightly **appareled** for the festival; Nature seemed appareled* (= adorned) *in celestial light.* Also **ap.par.elled, ap.par.el.ling** *Cdn.*

ap.par.ent (uh.PAIR.unt) *adj.* **1** visible; evident: *His limp is quite apparent; It soon became clearly, increasingly apparent who was lying; It was apparent to all that Jon was telling the truth.* **2** seeming: *an apparent advantage, contradiction, failure.* —**ap.par.ent.ly** *adv.*

ap.par.i.tion (ap.uh.RISH.un) *n.* a supernatural vision; ghost; specter: *a strange apparition in the middle of the night.*

ap.peal (uh.PEEL) *n.* **1** an earnest call for help: *an appeal to the public; He made an appeal for funds, mercy; a desperate, final, last, ringing, stirring appeal; an eloquent, emotional, irresistible appeal.* **2** a sending of a case to a higher court for a new hearing or an application for it: *to deny, dismiss, file, lodge, lose, reject, throw out, win an appeal; an appeal against a decision; an appeal from a lower court; He took the appeal to the Supreme Court; There was no appeal from their decision.* **3** interest or attraction: *a show that has lost its appeal; box-office appeal; sales, sex, snob appeal.* —*v.* **1** request earnestly: *The convict appealed to the King for clemency; appealed to him to be merciful.* **2** refer to a higher authority: *They appealed against the lower court's decision; The decision was appealed to the Supreme Court.* **3** interest or attract: *a movie appealing to the young; adj.: A picture is more **appealing** than words.* —**ap.peal.ing.ly** *adv.*

ap.pear (uh.PEER) *v.* **1** become visible: *The sun appears on a clear day.* **2** arrive: *The boss hadn't appeared by 11 a.m.; Police appeared on the scene (of the crime); They appeared at the door; They appeared unannounced; The president appeared in person.* **3** seem: *She appeared dejected; She appeared to have suffered much; It appeared (to us) that the case was lost.* **4** to be published: *A book appears on the market; An essay appears in print; Stories appear in the papers.* **5** present oneself: *He was ordered to appear in court on a charge of speeding; to appear before a committee; Actors appear on stage.* **6** act as a lawyer: *She appeared for the prosecution; appeared against the accused.*

ap.pear.ance (uh.PEER.unce) *n.* **1** an appearing: *the timely appearance of the police; The lawyer was making her first appearance in court; At first appearance, he makes a good impression; a guest appearance on a TV show; a cameo appearance; personal appearance; Our boss **puts in an appearance*** (= appears for a short while) *at work every day.* **2** outward impression: *He gives an appearance of honesty; From or To all appearances, he is honest; One cannot judge by appearances alone; A candidate has to be neat in appearance; the immaculate appearance of her home; a disheveled, shabby, unkempt, untidy appearance; Although broke, he tries to **keep up appearances*** (= tries to appear to be all right).

ap.pease (uh.PEEZ) *v.* **ap.peas.es, ap.peased, ap.peas.ing** pacify by satisfying: *to appease his hunger; It's useless to try to appease an aggressor.* —**ap.pease.ment** *n.*

ap.pel.lant (uh.PEL.unt) *n.* one who appeals to a higher court.

ap.pel.late (uh.PEL.ut) *adja.* having

appellation / appliqué

power to hear appeals: *an appellate court, judge, jurisdiction.*

ap.pel.la.tion (ap.uh.LAY.shun) *n.* **1** the act of naming. **2** a designation, as "Her Majesty, the Queen."

ap.pend (uh.PEND) *v.* add at the end of a document; affix: *a chart appended to a statement.*

ap.pend.age (uh.PEN.dij) *n.* **1** an added part: *Frills are decorative appendages to costumes.* **2** a body part such as an arm, tail, or fin: *The appendix is an appendage of the large intestine.*

ap.pen.dec.to.my (ap.un.DEC.tuh.mee) *n.* **-mies** surgical removal of the appendix.

ap.pen.di.ci.tis (uh.pen.duh.SYE.tis) *n.* inflammation of the appendix.

ap.pen.dix (ap.PEN.dix) *n.* **-dix.es** or **-di.ces** (-duh.seez) **1** section added at the end of a book or document: *There are two appendixes to the book.* **2** a short tubelike appendage of the large intestine: *The appendix may burst or rupture when it is inflamed.*

ap.per.tain (AP.ur.tain) *v.* belong rightfully: *duties that appertain to his office.*

ap.pe.tite (AP.uh.tite) *n.* a natural desire of the body, esp. for food: *to curb, satisfy, spoil, take away, whet one's appetite; to work up an appetite for dinner; sexual appetite; a healthy, hearty, insatiable, ravenous, voracious appetite; Good appetite!*

ap.pe.tiz.er (AP.uh.tye.zur) *n.* a food or drink meant to stimulate the appetite.

ap.pe.tiz.ing (AP.uh.tye.zing) *adj.* stimulating the appetite: *What's that appetizing smell from the kitchen?*
—**ap.pe.tiz.ing.ly** *adv.*

ap.plaud (uh.PLAWD) *v.* express approval, as by clapping hands: *The audience applauded heartily, loudly; His election was applauded (= praised) by everyone.*

ap.plause (uh.PLAWS) *n.* an applauding: *Loud applause greeted the winner; She spoke to the prolonged, thunderous applause of her admirers; a burst, ripple, round of applause; Her speech drew, got, won applause (= praise) for her party.*

ap.ple (AP.ul) *n.* a round fleshy fruit with a core of seeds; also, the tree bearing it: *cooking apples such as Rome Beauty; Delicious and McIntosh are eating apples; baked apples; candied apples; a real slick apple (Informal for guy).*

ap.ple.cart (AP.ul.cart) *n.* esp. **upset one's** or **the applecart,** upset a system, undertaking, plan, or situation;

disprove a theory, etc.

ap.ple.jack (AP.ul.jack) *n.* a liquor distilled from cider.

apple of discord *n.* cause of rivalry and contention, like the golden apple inscribed "For the most beautiful" which caused rivalry among Aphrodite, Athena, and Hera of Greek myth.

apple of one's eye *n.* a very dear one.

apple pie *n.* the commonest of fruit pies which is made with apples.
—**apple-pie** *adja.* having to do with traditional North American values: *apple-pie wholesomeness; a motherhood-and-apple-pie issue; I found everything in apple-pie order* (= neat and orderly arrangement).

apple-polish *v. Informal.* curry favor with someone.

ap.ple.sauce (AP.ul.sauce) *n.* **1** stewed apples in pulp form. **2** *Informal.* nonsense.

ap.pli.ance (uh.PLY.unce) *n.* a piece of equipment: *electric kettles, irons, and such small appliances; a major appliance such as a dishwasher or refrigerator; kitchen appliances.*

ap.pli.ca.ble (AP.luh.cuh.bul, uh.PLIC.uh.bul) *adj.* that applies: *a law applicable to the situation;*
ap.pli.ca.bly *adv.* —**ap.pli.ca.bil.i.ty** (-BIL.i.tee) *n.*

ap.pli.cant (AP.luh.kunt) *n.* one who applies for a job, loan, etc.

ap.pli.ca.tion (ap.luh.CAY.shun) *n.* **1** a request: *His job application is on file; a formal, written application; to file, fill in or fill out, make, put in, reject, send in, screen, submit, turn down, withdraw an application; something available to the public on or by application; an application form.* **2** a putting on: *two applications of the ointment.* **3** a putting into practice: *the application of a method; the application of theory to practice; (computer) software applications such as word processing.* **4** bearing or reference: *a discovery with many applications in daily life.* **5** attention: *with close application to detail, to one's studies.*

application program *n.* a program written for external uses, as distinguished from a system program that helps run the computer.

ap.pli.ca.tor (AP.luh.cay.tur) *n.* an applying device.

applied (uh.PLIDE) *adj.* put to practical use: *applied arts, chemistry, mathematics, research, sciences.*

ap.pli.qué (ap.luh.KAY) *n.* a decorative design or ornament cut out for attaching to something. —*v.* **-quées,**

apply / apprentice

-quéed, -quée.ing; *adj.*: *an appliquéed floral design.*

ap.ply (uh.PLY) *v.* **ap.plies, ap.plied, ap.ply.ing 1** make a request: *to apply for a job; He applied to the bank for a loan; Students apply* (= seek admission) *to universities; They apply to be admitted.* **2** put on: *to apply two coats of paint to a wall; Apply the brakes to stop the car.* **3** put in practice: *to apply a rule.* **4** have a bearing on a person or thing: *This rule applies in all cases; It applies to you.* **5** devote to some end: *to apply oneself to studies.* —**ap.pli.er** *n.*

ap.point (uh.POINT) *v.* **1** set or fix a time or place; *adj.*: *We met at the appointed time and place.* **2** assign to a position: *Jim was appointed to the vacancy; was appointed to serve as manager; was appointed (as) manager; adj. & cpd: an appointed,* not elected *senate; a newly appointed member; a court-appointed trustee; a self-appointed guardian.* **3 appointed** *adj.* furnished or equipped: *a luxuriously appointed cabin; a well-appointed office.*

ap.poin.tee (uh.poin.TEE) *n.* one who is appointed.

ap.poin.tive (uh.POIN.tiv) *adj.* having to do with appointment: *appointive powers; an appointive* (= not elected) *office.*

ap.point.ment (uh.POINT.munt) *n.* **1** an agreement to meet: *to break, cancel, fix, keep, make an appointment with a doctor; an appointment to see the doctor; visits by appointment only.* **2** an assignment to a position: *a letter of appointment following a job offer; She received an appointment as manager of the company and held it for three years; a temporary appointment, not a permanent one.* **3 appointments** *pl.* furnishings: *a car's interior appointments and exterior design.* **4** [used on product labels] **by appointment to** approved by Her Majesty the Queen, etc.

ap.por.tion (uh.POR.shun) *v.* allot as a share or portion: *The judge apportioned blame for the accident equally between the parties; liability apportioned among those responsible.* —**ap.por.tion.ment** *n.*

ap.po.site (AP.uh.zit) *adj.* relevant and suitable: *an apposite answer, comparison, quotation, remark, suggestion; a proposal apposite to the occasion.*

ap.po.si.tion (ap.uh.ZISH.un) *n.* the placing of a noun next to another noun as an explanation: *In "Jack the giant-killer," "the giant-killer" is in apposition to or with "Jack."* —**ap.po.si.tion.al** *adj.*

ap.prais.al (uh.PRAY.zul) *n.* an appraising; estimate of worth: *to give or make an appraisal; an objective appraisal of the facts.*

ap.praise (uh.PRAIZ) *v.* **ap.prais.es, ap.praised, ap.prais.ing** estimate the worth or value of a gem, house, situation, etc. as an expert: *a painting appraised at $1 million.* —**ap.prais.er** *n.*

ap.pre.ci.a.ble (uh.PREE.shuh.bul) *adj.* capable of being measured or perceived: *an appreciable rise in temperature; an appreciable improvement.* —**ap.pre.ci.a.bly** *adv.*

ap.pre.ci.ate (uh.PREE.shee.ate) *v.* **-ates, -at.ed, -at.ing 1** understand the meaning or value of something: *I fully appreciate the risks involved; Not everyone appreciates poetry; Everyone likes to be appreciated; We deeply, greatly, highly, sincerely appreciate your help; We appreciate your helping us; We appreciate the fact that you went out of your way to help us; I would appreciate* (= like to have) *your help.* **2** rise in value: *House prices appreciate in the spring.* —**ap.pre.ci.a.tion** (-AY.shun) *n.*: *to demonstrate, display, express, show our appreciation for your services; The honorary degree was given in appreciation of her services to the country.* —**ap.pre.ci.a.tive** (-shee.uh.tiv) *adj.*: *an appreciative gesture, glance, letter; We are deeply appreciative of your help;* **ap.pre.ci.a.tive.ly** *adv.*

ap.pre.hend (ap.ruh.HEND) *v.* **1** arrest: *to apprehend a burglar.* **2** anticipate with fear: *to apprehend danger in the dark.*

ap.pre.hen.sion (ap.ruh.HEN.shun) *n.* **1** fear or foreboding: *The mother felt grave apprehension for her child's safety; Everyone tried to allay her apprehensions and to reassure her.* **2** conception: *He was under a wrong apprehension; He had no clear apprehension of the situation.* **3** a seizing or arrest: *the apprehension of stolen goods; the apprehension of the thief.*

ap.pre.hen.sive (ap.ruh.HEN.siv) *adj.* fearful: *He was apprehensive about or for or of what might happen; He was apprehensive that the child might get lost.* —**ap.pre.hen.sive.ly** *adv.*

ap.pren.tice (uh.PREN.tis) *n.* a learner in a trade or profession: *law apprentices; an apprentice to an electrician; An apprentice graduates as a journeyman.* —*v.* **-tic.es, -ticed, -tic.ing** place someone as an apprentice: *He apprenticed his son to a tailor.* —**ap.pren.tice.ship** *n.*: *an apprenticeship in carpentry; to fill an apprenticeship (position); to serve an apprenticeship* (term).

ap.prise (uh.PRIZE) v. **ap.pris.es, ap.prised, ap.pris.ing** Formal. advise or inform: *Apprised of danger, he fled the country.*

ap.proach (uh.PROHCH) v. **1** move near or nearer to a person or thing: *Night was fast approaching; as we approached London; The pilot was directed to approach the airport from the east.* **2** go to someone with a specific aim: *to approach the bank for a loan; to approach the boss about a raise; to approach the manager with a suggestion.* —**n.** an approaching: *to find a means of approach to the snowbound airport; to make an approach for a bank loan; A pilot makes his approach with the landing gear down and the flaps lowered; He took the unusual approach of calling on the manager at his home; It was not a judicious approach to the problem; a forthright, pragmatic, rational, scholarly, scientific approach; They fled at our approach; With the approach of Christmas, business booms; an approach from a sales rep; She spurned his approaches* (= advances); *The police sealed all approaches* (= means of approach) *to the city.*

ap.proach.a.ble (uh.PROH.chuh.bul) adj. that can be approached: *a quite approachable* (= friendly) *boss.*
—**ap.proach.a.bil.i.ty** (-BIL.i.tee) n.

ap.pro.ba.tion (ap.ruh.BAY.shun) n. approval with pleasure.

ap.pro.pri.ate (uh.PROH.pree.ate) v. **-ates, -at.ed, -at.ing 1** make one's own: *He tends to appropriate what he borrows.* **2** assign to a specific purpose: *the funds appropriated by government for education.* —**adj.** (-pree.it) proper or suitable: *It's not appropriate to wear casual clothes to a formal banquet; Wear something appropriate to the occasion; What is appropriate for me may not be appropriate for you; It is appropriate that everyone be suitably attired;* **appropriate technology** *that is appropriate to the economic conditions of the country or region where it is to be used;*
ap.pro.pri.ate.ly adv.
—**ap.pro.pri.a.tor** (-ay.tur) n.

ap.pro.pri.a.tion (uh.PROH.pree. AY.shun) n. money allotted for a purpose in a budget: *The government makes appropriations for various departments; an appropriation bill.*

ap.prov.al (uh.PROO.vul) n. act of approving: *Her project met with or received my approval; received his stamp of approval; a seal of approval; He gave his approval for the project; approval to carry on with it; his complete, tacit, unqualified approval; The goods were shipped* **on approval** (= to be returned if not acceptable).

ap.prove (uh.PROOV) v. **ap.proves, ap.proved, ap.prov.ing 1** accept as satisfactory: *She examined his plan and approved it wholeheartedly.* **2** view favorably: *She* **approved** *of his plan.*
—**ap.prov.ing.ly** adv.

ap.prox.i.mate (uh.PROX.uh.mit) adj. nearly accurate or exact: *her approximate age; our approximate time of arrival.*
—v. (-mate) **-mates, -mat.ed, -mat.ing** come near to something; approach: *John's record approximates the champion's; a figure approximated* (= brought near) *to the nearest million.* —**ap.prox.i.mate. ly** (-mit.lee) adv. —**ap.prox.i.ma.tion** (-MAY.shun) n.

ap.pur.te.nance (uh.PUR.tuh.nunce) n. an appendage, accessory, or adjunct: *a company car, expense account, and such appurtenances of his office.*

a.pres-ski (ah.pray.SKEE) n. the relaxation period after skiing; **adja.**: *apres-ski activities, boots, clothes, parties.*

ap.ri.cot (AP.ruh.cot, AY.pruh-) n. an orange-colored oval fruit similar to the peach.

A.pril (AY.prul) n. the fourth month of the calendar, having 30 days.

April fool n. a victim of a practical joke on April 1, **April Fool's Day.**

a pri.o.ri (ah.pree.OR.ee, ay.pry.OR.eye) adja. & adv. of reasoning, proceeding from cause to effect, not a posteriori.

a.pron (AY.prun) n. **1** a garment worn in front and tied behind to protect clothes while working: *a man tied to his wife's* **apron strings** (= overly dependent on his wife). **2** a front part, as of a stage.

ap.ro.pos (ap.ruh.POH) adj. & adv. relevant and timely: *Your remark is quite apropos;* **apropos of** (= with reference to) *what you said yesterday.*

apse (APS) n. a recessed and vaulted part of a building, esp. one at the end of a church.

apt adj. **1** appropriate: *an apt observation.* **2** likely or inclined: *Students are apt to work too hard on the eve of examinations.* **3** naturally suited: *She's apt at solving problems.* —**apt.ly** adv.; **apt.ness** n.

ap.ti.tude (AP.tuh.tude) n. natural ability or capacity: *a leader with a special aptitude for solving problems; to demonstrate or show a natural aptitude for music; a mechanical aptitude; a* **scholastic**

aptitude test for determining a candidate's areas of special fitness.

aq.ua (AK.wuh) *n., pl.* **-uae** (-wee) or **-uas** water. —*adj.* [short form] aquamarine.

aq.ua.cul.ture (AK.wuh.cul.chur) *n.* **1** the cultivation of fish and water plants, usu. in an artificial stream, pond, etc. **2** same as HYDROPONICS. —**aq.ua.cul.tur.al** (-CUL.chuh.rul) *adj.* —**aq.ua.cul.tur.ist** *n.*

aq.ua.farm (AK.wuh.farm) *n.* an artificial pond or other body of water used in aquaculture.

aqua-lung (AK.wuh.lung) *n.* an underwater breathing apparatus; scuba; **Aqua-Lung** *Trademark.*

aq.ua.ma.rine (ak.wuh.muh.REEN) *n.* a bluish-green beryl. —*adj.* bluish-green.

aq.ua.plane (AK.wuh.plane) *n.* a board pulled by a motorboat, which one rides on water standing up.

a.quar.i.um (uh.QUAIR.ee.um) *n.* **-i.ums** or **-i.a** **1** container for displaying water animals and plants. **2** an establishment housing many such displays.

A.quar.i.us (uh.QUAIR.ee.us) *n.* **1** a southern constellation and the 11th sign of the zodiac. **2** a person born under this sign.

a.quat.ic (uh.KWOT.ic, -KWAT.ic) **1** *adj.* having to do with water: *The water lily is an aquatic plant; aquatic animals; aquatic sports such as swimming and sailing.* **2 aquatics** *n.pl.* water sports.

aq.ua.vit (AK.wuh.vit) *n.* a Scandinavian liquor flavored with caraway seed.

aqua vi.tae (-VYE.tee) *n.* alcohol or a strong liquor.

aq.ue.duct (AK.wuh.duct) *n.* **1** an elevated channel for bringing water from a distance. **2** a structure supporting such a channel.

a.que.ous (AY.quee.us, AK.wee.us) *adj.* dissolved in water; watery: *an aqueous solution of a medication.*

aq.ui.cul.ture (AK.wuh.cul.chur) same as AQUACULTURE.

aq.ui.fer (AK.wuh.fur) *n.* a water-containing layer of porous rock, sand, or gravel.

aq.ui.line (AK.wuh.line) *adj.* like an eagle: *an **aquiline** nose* (shaped like an eagle's beak).

Ar.ab (AIR.ub) *n.* a person of or from an Arabic-speaking country. —*adj.* having to do with the Arabs: *Arab countries, culture, customs; The name sounds Arab.*

ar.a.besque (air.uh.BESK) *n.* **1** an architectural design with intertwining flowers, foliage, and geometric figures; *adj.:* an arabesque design, style. **2** a ballet pose in which one leg is extended horizontally behind the dancer with the foot pointed and the knee straight. **3** in music, a florid melodic figure or a composition based on one.

A.ra.bi.an (uh.RAY.bee.un) *n.* a person of or from **Arabia,** the peninsula between the Red Sea and the Persian Gulf. —*adj.* having to do with Arabia or the Arabs: *the Arabian camel, Desert, horse, Peninsula, Sea.*

Ar.a.bic (AIR.uh.bic) *n.* a Semitic language spoken in Arabia, Jordan, Syria, Iraq, and N. Africa. —*adj.* having to do with the language and culture of the Arabs: *the Arabic alphabet, language; Arabic poetry.*

Arabic numeral *n.* any of the symbols 0, 1, etc. to 9.

Ar.a.bist (AIR.uh.bist) *n.* an expert in Arab culture or language.

ar.a.ble (AIR.uh.bul) *adj.* suitable for cultivation: *arable land.*

a.rach.nid (uh.RAC.nid) *n.* an eight-legged insect of the group that includes spiders, scorpions, mites, and ticks.

Ar.a.ma.ic (air.uh.MAY.ic) *n.* a N.W. Semitic language that was widely spoken over S.W. Asia between 300 B.C. and A.D. 650.

ar.bi.ter (AR.buh.tur) *n.* one recognized as the authority on a disputed matter: *The dictionary is the arbiter of correct usage for most people.*

ar.bi.tra.ble (AR.buh.truh.bul) *adj.* capable of being arbitrated.

ar.bi.trage (AR.buh.trij) *n.* the buying and selling of currency, stocks, commodities, etc. in different markets at the same time to profit from price differences. —**ar.bi.trag.er** or **ar.bi.tra.geur** (-zhur) *n.*

ar.bi.trar.y (AR.buh.trair.ee) *adj.* **1** not based on reason: *an arbitrary decision.* **2** despotic: *a dictator's arbitrary powers, rule.* —**ar.bi.trar.i.ly** *adv.*

ar.bi.trate (AR.buh.trate) *v.* **-trates, -trat.ed, -trat.ing** **1** judge between disputing parties: *someone to arbitrate between the parties.* **2** settle by arbitration: *When talks failed, they arbitrated the dispute.* —**ar.bi.tra.tor** (-tray.tur) *n.*

ar.bi.tra.tion (ar.buh.TRAY.shun) *n.* the settlement of a dispute by judge or arbiter: *to go to, resort to arbitration; The parties had to agree to binding arbi-*

tration because the dispute affected the public interest; compulsory arbitration.
ar.bor (AR.bur) *n.* a shady corner formed by overhanging vegetation. Also **ar.bour** *Cdn.*
ar.bo.real (ar.BOR.ee.ul) *adj.* having to do with trees: *arboreal existence, habitats, vegetation; Monkeys are arboreal (= tree-dwelling) animals.*
ar.bo.re.tum (ar.buh.REE.tum) *n.* **-tums** or **-ta** a place where trees and shrubs are grown and displayed.
ar.bor.ite (AR.buh.rite) *n.* a plastic covering material: *cabinets made of arborite and formica; arborite countertops;* **Arborite** *Trademark.*
ar.bor.vi.tae (ar.bur.VYE.tee) *n.* any of various trees of the pine family that have scalelike leaves.
ar.bour *Cdn.* ARBOR.
ar.bu.tus (ar.BYOO.tus) *n.* **1** a plant of the heath family with fragrant pink or white flowers and red berries. **2** the mayflower, also called "trailing arbutus."
arc *n.* anything curved like a bow, as a segment of a circle. —*v.* **arcs, arced** or **arcked, arc.ing** or **arck.ing** form or move in an arc, as an electrical discharge across two points.
ar.cade (ar.CADE) *n.* **1** a covered passageway lined with shops. **2** an amusement center: *pinball, video-game arcades; coin-operated arcade games.* **3** a series of arches with columns supporting them.
Ar.ca.di.a (ar.CAY.dee.uh) *n.* a region of quiet contentment, like a district of ancient Greece of the same name.
—**Ar.ca.di.an** *n. & adj.*: *Arcadian beauty, innocence, simplicity.*
ar.cane (ar.CANE) *adj.* hidden or mysterious: *arcane issues, knowledge, language, matters, references, subjects.*
arch *n.* a curved structure built over a passage, as in gateways and bridges; also, anything similar: *a triumphal arch; the twin golden arches of a fast-food chain; the superior arch of his eyebrows; the arch of the foot.* —*v.* curve like an arch: *A rainbow arched over the field;* *adj.:* *with eyebrows arched in amazement; an arched roof.* —*adj.* **1** saucy or roguish in a playful manner: *"Rhymes with rich," said the arch heading of the story about a rich but spiteful woman.* **2** adja. chief: *the arch enemy, rival, villain.*
—**arch.ly** *adv.;* **arch.ness** *n.*
ar.chae.ol.o.gy (ar.kee.OL.uh.jee) *n.* the study of human history as seen in fossils, tombs, artifacts, etc.
—**ar.chae.o.log.i.cal** (-uh.LOJ.i.cul)

adj.: *to dig at an archaeological site.*
ar.cha.ic (ar.CAY.ic) *adj.* of an earlier period: *the archaic language of the Bible; archaic laws, vocabulary.*
ar.cha.ism (AR.kee.iz.um) *n.* an archaic word: *"Forsooth" is an archaism for "truly."*
arch.an.gel (ARK.ain.jul) *n.* an angel of the highest order.
arch.bish.op (ARCH.bish.up) *n.* a bishop of the highest rank.
arch.bish.op.ric (arch.BISH.up.ric) *n.* an archbishop's jurisdiction or position.
arch.di.o.cese (arch.DYE.uh.sis) *n.* the diocese of an archbishop.
arch.duch.y (arch.DUCH.ee) *n.* **-duch.ies** the territory of an archduke.
arch.duke (ARCH.duke) *n.* a prince of the former royal family of Austria; **arch.duch.ess** (arch.DUCH.is) *fem.*
—**arch.du.cal** (arch.DEW.cul) *adj.*
arch.en.e.my (arch.EN.uh.mee) *n.* **-mies** chief enemy, esp. Satan.
ar.che.ol.o.gy (ar.kee.OL.uh.jee) same as ARCHAEOLOGY.
arch.er (ARCH.ur) *n.* one who uses a bow and arrows.
arch.er.y (ARCH.uh.ree) *n.* the art of shooting with a bow and arrows.
ar.che.type (AR.ki.type) *n.* the original model or pattern on which things of the same type are based; prototype.
—**ar.che.typ.al** (-TYE.pul) or **ar.che.typ.i.cal** (-TIP.i.cul) *adj.*
arch.fiend (arch.FEEND) *n.* chief fiend, esp. Satan.
ar.chi.e.pis.co.pal (AR.kee.i.PIS.cuh.pul) *adj.* having to do with an archbishop.
ar.chi.pel.a.go (ar.cuh.PEL.uh.go) *n.* **-gos** or **-goes** a group of islands: *the Philippine archipelago.*
ar.chi.tect (AR.cuh.tect) *n.* one who designs buildings and supervises their construction.
ar.chi.tec.ton.ic (AR.cuh.tec.TON.ic) **1** *adj.* having to do with architectural principles. **2 architectonics** *n.pl.* [with *sing.* or *pl. v.*] the science of architecture, also, the design of a building.
ar.chi.tec.ture (AR.cuh.tec.chur) *n.* **1** the art or science of building: *Byzantine, Colonial, Gothic, Greek, Modern, Roman architecture.* **2** building design: *the architecture of a church.* **3** the manner in which the components of a computer system are put together.
—**ar.chi.tec.tur.al** (ar.cuh.TEC.chur.ul) *adj.*: *an architectural beauty, disaster, marvel;* **ar.chi.tec.tur.al.ly** *adv.*

ar.chive (AR.kive) *n.* **1** a historical document or public record: *a valuable archive of information and opinions.* **2 archives,** *pl.* [with *sing. v.*] an institution that keeps archives: *The National Archives is closed for repairs.* —**ar.chi.val** (-kye.vul) *adj.* —**ar.chi.vist** (AR.cuh.vist) *n.*

arch.way (ARCH.way) *n.* a passageway with an arch over it.

arc.tic or **Arc.tic** (ARC.tic, AR-) **1** *adj.* usu. **Arctic,** having to do with the **Arctic,** the north polar region: *The Arctic Circle, the parallel at 66° 33' N, encloses the North Frigid Zone; the Arctic char* (= variety of salmon); *an Arctic plant; the Arctic winter.* **2** *adj.* usu. **arctic,** bitterly cold: *arctic air, weather; an arctic* (= frigid) *disposition.*

ar.dent (AR.dunt) *adj.* intensely devoted, enthusiastic, or zealous: *an ardent lover; his ardent desire for freedom; an ardent champion of the feminists.* —**ar.dent.ly** *adv.*

ar.dor (AR.dur) *n.* intensity of feeling: *to cool* or *dampen one's ardor; his patriotic ardor; the public's ardor for the new government; the **ardors*** (= passions) *of youth.* Also **ar.dour** *Cdn.*

ar.du.ous (AR.joo.us) *adj.* requiring much energy and effort: *an arduous climb uphill.* —**ar.du.ous.ly** *adv.*; **ar.du.ous.ness** *n.*

are 1 (AR) the form of BE used with *you, we, they.* **2** (AIR) *n.* a metric unit of area equal to 100 sq. meters.

ar.e.a (AIR.ee.uh) *n.* **1** the extent of a surface: *a vast area of desert; an area of three hectares.* **2** a specific kind of area: *a built-up area; the catchment area of a river; an economically depressed area; desert, disaster, drainage, high-pressure, low-pressure, metropolitan areas; a penalty area in soccer; play, residential, rural, service areas; the slum area of a city; a staging area for the military; rural and urban areas; Toronto and area* (= suburbs); **adja.:** *students from area schools* (= schools of the area). **3** a specific portion of an area: *to close off, rope off an area; an **area rug*** (covering part of a floor). **4** a sphere of knowledge or activity: *an area of knowledge; his area of specialty.* —**ar.e.al** *adj.*

area code *n.* a usu. three-digit number designating a telephone area.

ar.e.a.way (AIR.ee.uh.way) *n.* a small sunken area for light and air or for access to a basement.

a.re.na (uh.REE.nuh) *n.* **1** an enclosed area used for a show or sports activity; also, a building housing one: *a sports arena.* **2** a sphere of activity, esp. one involving struggle or competition: *in the political arena.*

arena theater *n.* a theater with the stage in the center; "theater-in-the-round."

aren't (ARNT) are not: *They aren't here yet; I'm a bit late, aren't I?* (*Informal for* am I not?).

ar.gent (AR.junt) *n.* & *adj.* [old or rare] silver.

Ar.gen.tine (AR.jun.teen) or **Ar.gen.tin.e.an** (-TIN.ee.un) *n.* & *adj.* (a person) of or from **Argentina,** a South American country.

ar.gon (AR.gon) *n.* an inert gaseous element found in the atmosphere and used as a filler for electric bulbs.

ar.go.sy (AR.guh.see) *n.* **-sies 1** a fleet of merchant ships. **2** rich cargo.

ar.got (AR.gut, AR.goh) *n.* the private language of a particular group, esp. that of the underworld.

ar.gu.a.ble (ARG.yoo.uh.bul) *adj.* **1** questionable or doubtful: *That there is life on other planets is arguable; an arguable issue.* **2** that can be supported by reasoning: *It is arguable that life could exist on other planets;* **ar.gu.a.bly** (-blee) *adv.*: *Einstein is arguably the greatest scientist of the twentieth century.*

ar.gue (ARG.yoo) *v.* **-gues, -gued, -gu.ing 1** give reasons in order to persuade, attack, or defend: *People argued for and against capital punishment; We argue with our children; We argue about* or *over their grades; Lawyers argue cases; Some argue ably; to argue that all are equal; to argue calmly, logically, heatedly, vehemently; She argued me into buying a new house; I argued her out of selling our old car; The children have stopped arguing* (= quarreling). **2** indicate or show: *a tough decision that argues a lot of maturity.*

ar.gu.ment (ARG.yoo.munt) *n.* **1** a giving of reasons for or against something: *cogent, compelling, convincing, persuasive, telling, valid, weak arguments; to drive home, present, press, put forward, refute an argument; his argument that the death penalty should be restored; The judge heard the closing arguments of plaintiff and defendant.* **2** dispute or quarrel: *An argument breaks out between neighbors; an argument about* or *over repairing a fence; to get into* or *have an argument with the neighbors; a bitter, heated, loud, violent argument; The police settled the argument; The rain clinched the argument about where to hold the picnic.*

ar.gu.men.ta.tion (ARG.yuh.men.TAY.

shun) *n.* the process of reasoning.
ar.gu.men.ta.tive (arg.yuh.MEN.tuh.tiv) *adj.* fond of arguing or disputing.
ar.gyle (AR.guile) *n.* **1** a varicolored knitting pattern composed of diamonds: *Argyles are hot this season; adj.: an argyle border; argyle-patterned sweaters; argyle sweaters.* **2** a sock having this pattern: *a computer-designed argyle with welt details in navy; thick wools and argyles* (= argyle socks). Also **argyll.**
a.ri.a (AR.ee.uh) *n.* a vocal solo with accompaniment during an opera or oratorio.
ar.id (AIR.id) *adj.* **1** dry or parched: *an arid desert.* **2** dull: *an arid discourse.*
—**a.rid.i.ty** (uh.RID.i.tee) *n.*
Ar.i.es (AIR.eez) *n.* **1** a N. constellation and the first sign of the zodiac; also called "Ram." **2** a person born under this sign.
a.right (uh.RITE) *adv.* rightly; all right.
a.rise (uh.RIZE) *v.* **a.ris.es, a.rose, a.ris.en** (uh.RIZ.un), **a.ris.ing 1** come to be: *If the need arises, phone for help; Do superstitions arise* (= result) *from ignorance?* **2** [old use] rise: *Arise and go home.*
ar.is.toc.ra.cy (air.is.TOC.ruh.see) *n.* **-cies 1** the nobility: *the British aristocracy.* **2** an elite group or a government by the elite.
ar.is.to.crat (uh.RIS.tuh.crat) *n.* a member of an elite group. —**a.ris.to.crat.ic** (-CRAT.ic) *adj.*
Ar.is.to.te.lian (air.is.toh.TEEL.yun) *n.* a follower of **Aristotle,** Greek philosopher, 384-322 B.C., or of his philosophy; *adj.: Aristotelian concepts, logic, philosophers, thought.*
a.rith.met.ic (uh.RITH.met.ic) *n.* **1** computation with numbers, using addition, subtraction, multiplication, and division. **2** what something involves or results in: *the arithmetic of house-hunting; The collapse of Communism changed* **the arithmetic of** (= the resulting condition of) *world politics.* —**ar.ith.met.ic** (air.ith.MET.ic) or **ar.ith.met.i.cal** (-i.cul) *adj.* —**a.rith.me.ti.cian** (uh.rith.muh.TISH.un) *n.*
-arium *n. suffix.* denoting place or relationship: *aquarium, herbarium, honorarium, sanitarium.*
ark *n.* **1** a chest or box: *The Israelites kept the two tablets containing the Ten Commandments in the* **Ark of the Covenant;** *The scrolls of the Torah are kept in an ark in synagogues.* **2** a huge boat like the one in which Noah and his family were preserved during the Flood.
arm *n.* **1** either of one's two upper limbs: *to cross, fold, raise, swing, wave one's arms; to twist arms* (= use pressure); *She threw her arms around the child and hugged her; to stand with arms akimbo; We saw Dick walking* **arm in arm** (= with arms linked) *with Jane; She was received* **with open arms** (= warmly); *It won't cost you* **an arm and a leg** (= a lot of money) *to eat at that restaurant; to be kept at* **arm's length** (= at a distance). **2** something resembling an arm: *the arms of a chair, shirt; the tone arm or pickup of a record player; The Gulf of California is an arm of the North Pacific; The army and navy are arms* (= branches) *of the military; One should be afraid of* **the long arm of the law** (*that has power to seize, control, etc.*). **3 arms** *pl.* weapons: *the right to bear arms; the call to arms when a war breaks out; to* **lay down one's arms** (= surrender); *to* **present arms** *in salute;* **royal arms** (= coat of arms); **small arms** (= guns); *They decided to* **take up arms** (= fight) *against drunken drivers; soldiers who are* **under arms** (= armed) *at all times; The people were* **up in arms** (= ready to fight) *over the new taxes; to accelerate, curb, step up the* **arms race** *between the superpowers.*
—*v.* **1** equip with weapons: *an ordinance to arm the citizenry against the enemy; They armed themselves to meet the attack.* See also ARMED. **2** get ready for action: *to arm a missile before firing; The alarm will go off only if armed.*
ar.ma.da (ar.MAH.duh) *n.* **1** a fleet of warships. **2** a flotilla.
ar.ma.dil.lo (ar.muh.DIL.oh) *n.* **-los** a small burrowing animal with a protective shell of bony plates.
Ar.ma.ged.don (ar.muh.GED.un, "G" as in "go") *n.* the final conflict between good and evil, as foretold in the Bible.
ar.ma.ment (AR.muh.munt) *n.* **1** weapons and supplies: *armaments of war; adja.: the armaments industry.* **2** the process of arming for war.
ar.ma.ture (AR.muh.chur) *n.* **1** the rotating part of a dynamo or motor, in which current is produced. **2** a protective covering.
arm.chair (ARM.chair) *n.* a chair with armrests. —**adja.** theoretical or unrealistic: *armchair critics, generals, philosophers, quarterbacks, strategy, theorizing, travelers.*
armed *adj.* equipped, as with weapons: *an armed camp; armed robbery of a bank; Take care, he's armed and dangerous; She came armed with a letter from the president; The terrorists were* **armed to the**

teeth (= heavily armed); **armed neutrality** (= state of readiness to fight while remaining neutral); *the armed services* or *forces* (= army, navy, air force, etc.).
Ar.me.ni.an (ar.MEE.nee.un) *n. & adj.* (a person) of or from a region including **Armenia**, a country of S.E. Europe, and parts of Turkey and Iran: *the Armenian church, language.*
arm.ful *n.* **-fuls** as much as can be held in one arm or in both together.
arm.hole *n.* an opening in a garment for the wearer's arm.
ar.mi.stice (AR.muh.stis) *n.* an agreement to stop fighting, as after a war: *to agree on, declare, make, sign, suspend, violate, work out an armistice.*
arm.let (ARM.lit) *n.* a band worn on an arm around the sleeve.
arm.lock same as HAMMERLOCK.
ar.mor (AR.mur) *n.* **1** a usu. metal protective covering, as the steel platings of ships and tanks: *a medieval soldier's suit of armor; heavy and light armor; a police officer wearing soft body armor; Bullets couldn't pierce the armor; You think a knight in shining armor will protect you; I see a* **chink in his armor** (= a weak point in an apparently strong position); *an armor-plated vehicle.* **2** armored cars, tanks, etc.: *The city was ringed by troops, armor, and artillery.* Also **ar.mour** *Cdn.*
ar.mored (AR.murd) *adj.* **1** covered or protected with armor: *an* **armored car** (= closed truck for carrying money). **2** equipped with armor-covered vehicles, guns, etc.: *an armored column, corps, division.* Also **ar.moured** *Cdn.*
ar.mor.i.al (ar.MOR.ee.ul) *adj.* pertaining to heraldry: *The* **armorial bearings** (= coat of arms) *of Canada have a sprig of maple on a silver shield and the royal arms of England, Scotland, Ireland, and France.*
ar.mor.y (AR.muh.ree) *n.* **ar.mor.ies** a place for making or storing arms; arsenal. Also **ar.mour.y** *Cdn.*
armour, armoured, etc. *Cdn.* ARMOR, etc.
arm.pit *n.* the hollow under the arm where it joins the body.
arm.rest *n.* support for the arm or elbow.
arm's-length *adja.* distant: *the difference between an arm's-length relationship between strangers and a family relationship; an arm's-length policy, transaction.*
arm-twisting *n.* pressure to force someone to do something. —**arm-twister** *n.*
arm wrestling *n.* a trial of strength between two who sit across a table, rest their elbows on it, grip each other's hand, and try to force each other's arm down.
ar.my (AR.mee) *n.* **-mies 1** a trained and organized group, esp. military: *to command, deploy, drill, equip, field, mobilize, overrun, raise, rout an army; to join the army; to put an army to flight; rebel, regular, standing, volunteer armies.* **2** any similar group: *the Salvation Army; an army of workers; an army of ants.*
a.ro.ma (uh.ROH.muh) *n.* the penetrating and usu. pleasant odor of foods, wines, spices, etc.: *aromas wafting from the kitchen; coffee with a fine aroma; a delicate, fragrant, pleasant aroma; a perfume with a woodsy aroma; the dungy aromas* (= smells) *around a zoo.*
ar.o.mat.ic (air.uh.MAT.ic) *adj.* fragrant: *an aromatic bark, tobacco; an aromatic ad for a perfume.*
arose *pt.* of ARISE.
a.round (uh.ROUND) *adv. & prep.* **1** in a circle: *to drive around (the block); He measures 70 cm around (the waist); a patient who needs watching* **around the clock** (= 24 hours). **2** here and there in a place: *to browse around (in a library); Stick around (here).* **3** *Informal.* near or nearly: *a car costing around $50,000.* **4** on the other side: *He went around the corner.* **5** in the opposite way: *Turn around!* —**be around** *Informal.* be active, seen, well-known, etc.: *She has been around for some time and is listed in the Who's Who; Is that famous singer still around?* —**first** (or **second** etc.) **time around** on the first (or second, etc.) occasion: *We hope to win the next time around.* —**get around** *Informal.* find time to do something: *I never got around to answering that letter.*
a.rouse (uh.ROWZE) *v.* **a.rous.es, a.roused, a.rous.ing 1** awaken: *He was aroused from sleep.* **2** evoke: *to arouse pity; behavior that arouses suspicion.* —**a.rous.al** *n.*
ar.peg.gi.o (ar.PEJ.ee.oh) *n.* **-os** in music, a chord whose notes are to be played in rapid succession.
aroused *adj.* excited: *The patient gets violent when aroused; He is in an aroused state; to be emotionally, highly, sexually aroused.*
ar.raign (uh.RAIN) *v.* call before a court to be charged: *He was arraigned on a charge of spreading malicious reports.* —**ar.raign.ment** *n.*
ar.range (uh.RAINJ) *v.* **-rang.es, -ranged, -rang.ing** set up in a certain way: *She arranged the flowers tastefully in*

vases; books neatly arranged on shelves; to arrange for a loan; Ask the bank manager to arrange a loan for a client; to arrange a meeting for 8 p.m.; to arrange that we should meet at 8 p.m.; He has arranged to meet with us at 8 p.m.; a composition arranged (= adapted) for the piano; *adj.*: an **arranged** loan, marriage, meeting, summit.

ar.range.ment (uh.RANGE.munt) *n.*
1 an arranging: *to make* or *work out an arrangement for our next meeting; a meeting by special arrangement; under an arrangement with the Minister concerned; to complete the **arrangements*** (= preparations) *for us to meet in New York.*
2 something arranged: *floral, flower, seating, working arrangements.*

ar.rant (AIR.unt) *adj.* downright; utter: *What arrant nonsense!*

ar.ras (AIR.us) *n. sing. & pl.* tapestry, esp. as a wall hanging or screen.

ar.ray (uh.RAY) *n.* **1** a splendid or imposing arrangement or display: *an army in battle array; an array of jewelry; beautiful in her bridal array; an array of facts and figures.* **2** an arrangement of elements forming a unit: *a radio antenna array; an array of solar cells.*
—*v.*: *Troops array* (= position) *themselves for battle; adj.: They are **arrayed** against the enemy; She was arrayed* (= dressed) *like a queen.*

ar.rears (uh.REERS) *n.pl.* overdue debts or other unfulfilled obligations: *arrears of rent, work; He is **in arrears with*** (= owing) *his rent; His rent is **in arrears*** (= being owed).

ar.rest (uh.REST) *v.* **1** to capture and hold legally: *Police arrested the suspect; a ship arrested after an oil spill; adj.: an **arresting*** (= attention-capturing) *view of the lake.* **2** stop growth, development, etc.: *a drug to arrest the growth of the AIDS virus.* —*n.* **1** legal detention: *The police make arrests saying "You are **under arrest"**; He was placed* or *put under arrest; He tried to resist arrest; charged the police with wrongful arrest; The arrest was made for murder; an arrest made on a murder charge; She made a citizen's arrest and handed over the thief to the police; a house arrest; to issue an arrest warrant.* **2** stoppage: *cardiac arrest; a case of respiratory arrest after receiving muscle-relaxing drugs.*

ar.rhyth.mi.a (uh.RITH.mee.uh) *n.* irregularity of heart beat; **ar.rhyth.mic** *adj.*

ar.rière-pen.sée (AR.ee.air.pahn.SAY) *n. French.* ulterior motive.

ar.ri.val (uh.RYE.vul) *n.* an arriving: *The crowd awaited the hero's arrival; arrival at the airport, in town, from abroad; the baby's arrival* (= birth); *early and late arrivals* (= people who come early and late); *adj.:* the arrival lounge on the arrival level of an airport; arrival time.

ar.rive (uh.RIVE) *v.* **ar.rives, ar.rived, ar.riv.ing** reach, esp. a place: *We arrived in London safe and sound; To arrive on time is better than arriving early or late; A baby arrives* (= is born); *The wedding day arrived* (= came) *at last; Votes showed that the young politician had arrived* (= attained recognition); *to **arrive at*** (= reach) *an agreement, conclusion, decision.*

ar.ri.ve.der.ci (AR.ee.veh.DER.chee) *interj. Italian.* till we meet again; goodbye.

ar.ro.gance (AIR.uh.gunce) *n.* a haughty manner or attitude: *the arrogance of power; his insufferable arrogance; the arrogance of the newly rich; He had the arrogance to ask for a 50% raise.*

ar.ro.gant (AIR.uh.gunt) *adj.* excessively or unpleasantly sure of oneself: *He's arrogant toward the poor; an arrogant demand.* —**ar.ro.gant.ly** *adv.*

ar.ro.gate (AIR.uh.gate) *v.* **-gates, -gat.ed, -gat.ing** take or claim without right: *He arrogated too much authority to himself.* —**ar.ro.ga.tion** (-GAY.shun) *n.*

ar.row (AIR.oh) *n.* **1** slender, pointed shaft used as a missile shot from a bow: *straight as an arrow; a poisoned arrow; a spent arrow.* **2** an arrowlike figure [⇒] used to point, as on a sign or a map.

ar.row.head (AIR.oh.hed) *n.* the pointed tip of an arrow.

ar.row.root (AIR.oh.root) *n.* **1** a starch made from the roots of a tropical American plant. **2** the plant.

ar.roy.o (uh.ROY.oh) *n.* **-os 1** in S.W. United States, a channel cut by an intermittent flow of water; gully. **2** a flowing rivulet.

arse (ARS) same as ASS (buttocks).

ar.se.nal (AR.suh.nul) *n.* a place where arms and ammunition are made or stored: *The dictionary is an arsenal* (= storehouse) *of words.*

ar.sen.ic (AR.suh.nic) *n.* a poisonous chemical element used in insecticides, weed-killers, etc.

ar.son (AR.sun) *n.* the wrongful burning of property: *to commit arson; Arson is suspected in the fire.*

ar.son.ist (AR.suh.nist) *n.* one who commits arson.

art *n.* **1** the creation or expression of beauty: *works of art such as paintings*

and sculptures; the fine arts of painting and sculpture; abstract, commercial, folk, modern, pop, primitive art; arts and crafts; **adja.**: the art community; an arts festival, school, student. **2** skilled activity: to practice the art of writing; the occult art; the applied, decorative, graphic, industrial, language, martial, performing, plastic, visual arts; There's an art to it (= a knack of doing it). **3** usu. **arts** pl. the humanities, as distinguished from science: a Bachelor of Arts; the liberal arts. **4** artfulness or cunning; also, tricks: His wily arts didn't fool her.
—v. [old use] the form of BE used with thou.

art dec.o (art.DEC.oh) n. a style of design characterized by geometric forms, used in architecture, fashions, and furnishings; also **Art Deco**.

ar.te.fact same as ARTIFACT.

ar.te.ri.al (ar.TEER.ee.ul) adj. of or like an artery: arterial blood, railroads, roads.
—n. a through street or expressway.

ar.te.ri.ole (ar.TEER.ee.ole) n. any of an artery's branches leading to capillaries.

ar.te.ri.o.scle.ro.sis (ar.TEER.ee.oh. skluh.ROH.sis) n. a chronic disease in which hardening of the arteries impairs blood circulation.

ar.ter.y (AR.tuh.ree) n. **-ter.ies 1** any of the tubular vessels that carry blood from the heart to every part of the body: a blocked or occluded coronary artery; a ruptured artery; hardening of the arteries due to cholesterol build-up. **2** a main route of transportation or communication: a major artery; traffic arteries.

ar.te.sian well (ar.TEE.zhun-) n. a well bored deep to a source of water that gushes up because of its pressure.

art.ful adj. **1** showing art or skill: her artful handiwork; artful persuasion. **2** crafty; cunning: an artful dodger, guy, response; an artful blend of truth and falsehood. —**art.ful.ly** adv.; **art.ful.ness** n.

art gallery n. **1** a permanent exhibition of paintings and other works of art, less comprehensive than an **art museum** which may also contain displays of science, history, etc. **2** a private establishment for the marketing of art.

ar.thrit.ic (ar.THRIT.ic, "TH" as in "thin") adj. having to do with arthritis.
—n. an arthritic patient.

ar.thri.tis (ar.THRYE.tis) n. inflammation of the body joints.

ar.thro.pod (AR.thruh.pod) n. a backboneless animal such as insects, spiders, and crabs that have segmented bodies and jointed antennae and limbs.

Ar.thu.ri.an (ar.THOO.ree.un) adj. having to do with King **Arthur** of 6th century Britain: Arthurian legends, romances.

ar.ti.choke (AR.ti.choke) n. a tall thistlelike herb with a large flower head that is used as a vegetable.

ar.ti.cle (AR.ti.cul) n. **1** a particular thing, item, or object: an article of clothing, food, furniture; secondhand articles; toilet articles like soap and cologne; **the genuine article** (= real thing); Little Lee is quite an article (Informal for quite cute or clever). **2** a section or clause of a document: the articles of a constitution; an **article of faith** (= a basic belief); They filed **articles of association** (= bylaws) governing the day-to-day running of the company. **3** a nonfiction essay or story: a magazine article. **4** same as DEFINITE ARTICLE or INDEFINITE ARTICLE: the grammatical articles.
—v. **-cles, -cled, -cling** bind by a contract or serve as a law apprentice, accounting student, etc.: She was articled to the firm of Smith & Smith; **adja.**: an **articled** clerk; an **articling** law student.

ar.tic.u.lar (ar.TIK.yuh.lur) adj. having to do with body joints: articular cartilages, membranes, pain.

ar.tic.u.late (ar.TIK.yuh.lit) adj. **1** of speech, clear and distinct. **2** of a person, able to express thoughts clearly: So excited, he was barely articulate. —v. (-late) **-lates, -lat.ed, -lat.ing** express or speak distinctly. —**articulated** adj. joined together: An articulated bus is preferred to a double-decker; articulated railroad cars. —**ar.tic.u.late.ly** (-lit.lee) adv. —**ar.tic.u.la.tion** (-LAY.shun) n.

ar.ti.fact (AR.tuh.fact) n. a product of human hands, esp. an item of archaeological interest: Bits of charcoal, stone tools, and other artifacts 16,000 years old were found at the dig; the artifacts recovered from the Titanic; The book is a mere literary artifact with no artistic value.

ar.ti.fice (AR.tuh.fis) n. **1** skill used to trick or deceive: Some sales people are masters of artifice. **2** an inventive trick or expedient: the various artifices used in displaying merchandise.

ar.ti.fic.er (AR.TIF.uh.sur) n. a skilled craftsman.

ar.ti.fi.cial (ar.tuh.FISH.ul) adj. **1** made by human skill, not natural: an artificial gene, limb, lung, sweetener; artificial blood, light, silk; an artificial (earth) satellite; **artificial insemination** (of a female);

artificial intelligence (programmed into a computer); **artificial respiration** (by mechanical or manual methods such as mouth-to-mouth resuscitation) used on a person whose lungs are not working. **2** affected, not natural: *an artificial smile.* —**ar.ti.fi.cial.ly** (-uh.lee) *adv.* —**ar.ti.fi.ci.al.i.ty** (AR.tuh.fish.ee.AL.i.tee) *n.*

ar.til.ler.y (ar.TIL.uh.ree) *n.* **1** mounted guns of large caliber: *field artillery; heavy artillery.* **2** a branch of an army equipped with such guns.

artily, artiness See ARTY.

ar.ti.san (AR.tuh.zun, -zan) *n.* a manually skilled worker, as a tailor or carpenter.

ar.tist *n.* **1** one who practices a fine art, as a painter or sculptor: *gifted, struggling, talented artists; a sidewalk artist.* **2** one who practices a skilled activity, sometimes of a shady nature: *a con artist; escape artist; makeup artist; ripoff artist; trapeze artists.* —**ar.tis.tic** (ar.TIS.tic) *adj.* —**ar.tis.ti.cal.ly** *adv.*

ar.tiste (ar.TEEST) *n.* a professional entertainer, esp. a singer, actor, or dancer.

art.ist.ry (AR.tis.tree) *n.* artistic skill or quality: *the brilliant artistry of a fireworks display.*

art.less *adj.* **1** free from cunning: *a child's artless questions.* **2** natural, not artificial: *the artless grace of the gazelle.* **3** lacking artistry: *an artless contraption.* —**art.less.ly** *adv.;* **art.less.ness** *n.*

art.mo.bile (ART.muh.beel) *n.* an art exhibit in a trailer.

art museum See ART GALLERY.

arts.y *adj.* **arts.i.er, -i.est** same as ARTY.

art.work *n.* **1** the work of a painter, sculptor, etc.: *Inuit artwork on display.* **2** the graphic portions of a printed text. **3** typeset and graphic matter assembled for printing.

art.y (AR.tee) *adj.* **art.i.er, -i.est** *Informal.* artistic in a showy or pretentious way. —**art.i.ly** *adv.;* **art.i.ness** *n.*

ar.um (AIR.um) *n.* a plant with large leaves and tiny flowers on a fleshy spike enveloped in a white hoodlike spathe, as the jack-in-the-pulpit.

Ar.y.an (AIR.ee.un) *n.* **1** a member of a prehistoric people from whom most of the peoples of Europe, India, and Iran are descended. **2** their family of languages. **3** [in racist use] white Caucasian, often non-Jewish.

as (AZ) *adv.* **1** in or to the same degree: *See that oak – our flagpole has to be as tall.* **2** for instance: *felines, as lions and leopards.* —**conj. 1** in the same way as: *tall as an oak; He did as promised; The papers report everything as it happens.* **2** while: *He wept as he told the story.* **3** because: *He stopped work as he was tired.* **4** though: *(As) tall as John is, he's shorter than Jim.* **5** with the result that: *I wasn't so worried as to lose sleep over it.* —**prep. 1** in the character or position of someone: *Speaking as a lawyer, I am against it.* **2** like: *cool as a cucumber.* —**as ... as** [indicating sameness]: *He's as busy as a bee; as far as the North Pole; She's as good as gold; I'll be as happy as a lark.* —**as far as** *Informal.* as for: *As far as getting a gold medal, I believe she will.* —**as for** [used in the beginning of a sentence or clause] as regards: *As for me, I don't work on Sunday.* —**as from** as of: *You are hired as from Monday.* —**as if** or **as though**: *It looks as though it might rain* (= as it usu. looks when it is going to rain). —**as is** unchanged: *a scratched chair sold as is at a reduced price.* —**as of** [indicating starting time]: *As of now, there are 30 of us; As of last week he was all right.* —**as to** as regards: *As to me, I don't work on Sunday; My pal is indifferent as to* (= about) *when he is asked to work.*

as.a.fet.i.da (as.uh.FET.i.duh) *n.* a strong-smelling gum obtained from an Asiatic plant, used in medicine and as a seasoning.

as.bes.tos (as.BES.tus) *n.* a nonburning fibrous mineral used for fireproofing.

as.cend (uh.SEND) *v.* go higher up: *to ascend a mountain, river; mist ascending from a valley.* **adj.**: *the ascending part of the aorta, colon, etc.; ascending tones in music.* —**ascend the throne** become king or queen.

as.cend.an.cy (uh.SEN.dun.see) *n.* dominance: *to attain or gain ascendancy over a rival.* Also **as.cend.en.cy.**

as.cend.ant (uh.SEN.dunt) *n. & adj.* (position) of rising influence or power: *His star is in the ascendant* (position). Also **as.cen.dent.**

as.cend.er (uh.SEN.dur) *n.* one that ascends, as the part of an "l" or "f" that is above the body of the letter.

as.cen.sion (uh.SEN.shun) *n.* the act of ascending: *one's ascension to power, the presidency, stardom, the throne; Christ's Ascension* (= the Christian belief of Christ's going bodily into Heaven).

as.cent (uh.SENT) *n.* a climbing upward: *their victorious ascent of Everest; They made the ascent in many stages; The first part was a gradual, not a steep ascent* (= way going up); *their slow ascent* (= climb) *uphill; an ascent* (= slope) *of*

15 degrees; *the theory of the ascent* (= *rise*) *of humans from the apes.*
as.cer.tain (as.ur.TAIN) *v.* find out with certainty: *to ascertain the facts of a story, someone's qualifications, the truth; to ascertain that he is still alive.*
—**as.cer.tain.a.ble** (-nuh.bul) *adj.*
as.cet.ic (uh.SET.ic) *adj.* self-denying in regard to life's comforts, esp. with a religious motive. Also **as.cet.i.cal** (-i.cul). —*n.* one who leads an ascetic life: *an ascetic's regimen of life; an ascetic who fasts on Fridays.* —**as.cet.i.cism** *n.*
ASCII (AS.kee) *n.* "American Standard Code for Information Interchange," a computer coding method for representing letters, numbers, etc. up to a total of 128 characters and symbols.
a.scor.bic acid (uh.SCOR.bic-) *n.* Vitamin C, used against scurvy.
as.cot (AS.cut, -cot) *n.* a neck scarf for men, worn looped under the chin, with the ends overlapping and lying flat.
as.cribe (uh.SCRIBE) *v.* **as.cribes, as.cribed, as.crib.ing** attribute a cause or quality to something as typical of it: *Many errors can be ascribed to ignorance; He ascribes his successes to luck; an artifact ascribed* (= *attributed*) *to the Stone Age.* —**as.crip.tion** *n.*
a.sep.sis (uh.SEP.sis) *n.* the condition of wounds, dressings, etc. being free from germs. —**a.sep.tic** *adj.*: *aseptic conditions, containers, packaging.*
a.sex.u.al (ay.SEK.shoo.ul) *adj.* without sexual activity; sexless: *Budding and cell division are forms of asexual reproduction.*
ash *n.* **1** a tree with compound leaves and tough wood; also, the wood. **2** the soft, gray, powdery substance left after burning: *The place was covered with volcanic ash; dust, ash, and cinders.* **3 ashes** *pl.*: *The wood was burned to ashes; to rake the ashes after a fire; a town reduced to ashes; the ashes of a cremated person; to spread the ashes to the winds; A phoenix is believed to rise from its ashes.*
a.shamed (uh.SHAMED) *adjp.* feeling shame: *He's ashamed to go on welfare; ashamed that he can't find a job; thoroughly ashamed of himself.*
—**a.sham.ed.ly** (-mid.lee) *adv.*
ash can *n.* **1** a can for trash. **2** a garbage can.
ash.en (ASH.un) *adj.* **1** pale like the color of ashes: *Her face was ashen with fear.* **2** made of ash wood.
a.shore (uh.SHORE) *adv.* to or on the shore: *The refugees were put or set ashore by an unknown ship; They went ashore without being caught; came ashore yesterday; They are now ashore in police custody.*
ash.ram (ASH.rum) *n.* **1** a Hindu hermitage. **2** a religious retreat.
ash.tray *n.* a small dish for tobacco ash, cigar butts, etc.
Ash Wednesday *n.* the first day of Lent.
ash.y *adj.* **ash.i.er, -i.est** like ashes: *an ashy deposit.*
A.sian (AY.zhun, -shun) *adj.* having to do with Asia: *Asian affairs, countries, cultures, markets; the Asian flu; the Asian Games; an Asian-American immigrant.*
—*n.* a person of or from Asia: *the* **Central Asians** *of Tibet, Mongolia, and Sinkiang (China);* **North Asians** *of Russia, from the Urals to the Pacific;* **Southwest Asians** *of Afghanistan, the Arabian Peninsula, Cyprus, Iran, Iraq, Jordan, Lebanon, Sinai, Syria, and Turkey.* See also EAST ASIAN, SOUTH ASIAN, SOUTHEAST ASIAN.
A.si.at.ic (ay.shee.AT.ic) *n.* [old use, now derogatory in reference to persons] same as ASIAN; *adj.*: *the Asiatic elephant; an Asiatic plant.*
a.side (uh.SIDE) *adv.* [used after its verb] to one side: *to push, put, shove, take a person or thing aside; to stand aside; The high court set aside* (= *rejected*) *the lower court's decision; Joking aside* (= *apart*), *I remain firm in my view; Only adults were present,* **aside from** (= *except for*) *a few infants.* —*n.* **1** an actor's words that other actors are not supposed to hear. **2** digression: *He told the story as an aside to the class.*
as.i.nine (AS.uh.nine) *adj.* utterly stupid: *a silly and asinine excuse; an asinine joke, policy; asinine behavior.*
—**as.i.nin.i.ty** (-NIN.i.tee) *n.*
ask *v.* **1** call for an answer: *to ask a question; She asked him point-blank how old he was; Ask me another!* (*Informal for* I don't know the answer). **2** request: *She asked him his name; He asked her to wait; He asked his friend for a loan; asked a favor of his friend; She asked to be excused; He asked that the matter be kept secret; Guests ask leave of their hosts before leaving; We ask advice of friends; He asked help from his buddy; He asked for help; She asked for or asked to see the boss; He was asking too much or asking for the moon; Please ask* (= *invite*) *him in; He was hoping she would ask him out* (= *ask for a date*); *She never asked him back* (= *invited him in return*); *You* **asked for it** (*Informal for provoked it*); *He was* **asking for** (= *inviting*) *trouble;*

n.: *A free sample is yours* **for the asking** (*Informal for* You can get it merely by asking). **3** inquire: *Jim asks after you; He asks about your health; We had to ask our way around the town.*

a.skance (uh.SKANCE) *adv.: He looked askance* (= with disapproval or suspicion) *at my suggestion.*

a.skew (uh.SKEW) *adj. & adv.* [used after its noun or verb] **1** leaning to one side: *Your hat is a bit askew; a picture hung askew on the wall.* **2** amiss: *when things go askew.*

asking price *n.* the maximum price desired by a seller.

a.sleep (uh.SLEEP) *adjp. & adv.* in or into a state of sleep: *He's fast asleep; sound asleep; He fell asleep at his desk; My foot is asleep* (= numb). **—asleep at the switch** *Informal.* negligent in one's duty; not vigilant.

asp *n.* a small venomous snake.

as.par.a.gus (uh.SPAIR.uh.gus) *n.* **1** a plant of the lily family whose tender shoots are used as a vegetable. **2** the shoots.

as.par.tame (AS.pur.tame) *n.* a low-calorie sugar substitute.

as.pect (AS.pect) *n.* appearance, as from one point of view: *to study a question in all its aspects; a house with a southern aspect* (= exposure); *a man of solemn aspect* (= look); *a frightening, grim, humorous aspect.* **—as.pec.tu.al** (as.PECK.choo.ul) *adj.*

as.pen (AS.pun) *n.* a poplar with leaves that flutter in the slightest wind: *the quaking aspen.*

as.per.i.ty (as.PER.i.tee) *n.* **-ties** the roughness of a surface or harshness of temper, tone, weather, etc.; also, an instance of it: *the asperities of life in the Arctic.*

as.perse (uh.SPURSE) *v.* **-pers.es, -persed, -pers.ing** slander: *He was aspersed with damaging allegations.*
—**as.per.sion** (as.PUR.shun) *n.: The story cast aspersions on his good name.*

as.phalt (AS.fault) *n.* a mixture of sand or gravel with a brownish black bituminous substance that is used in paving streets —*v.* pave with asphalt: *to asphalt a street.*

asphalt jungle *n.* a crowded city viewed as a place hard to survive in.

as.pho.del (AS.fuh.del) *n.* a plant of the lily family with white or yellow flowers.

as.phyx.i.a (as.FIX.ee.uh) *n.* suffocation caused by lack of oxygen.

as.phyx.i.ate (as.FIX.ee.ate) *v.* **-ates, -at.ed, -at.ing** suffocate or be suffocated by carbon monoxide poisoning, electric shock, strangulation, etc. —**as.phyx.i.a.tion** (-ee.AY.shun) *n.*

as.pic (AS.pic) *n.* **1** a jelly made with fish or meat stock. **2** [old use] asp.

as.pi.rant (AS.puh.runt) *n.* one who aspires: *an aspirant to the ministry; aspirants for a position.*

as.pi.rate (AS.puh.rate) *v.* **-rates, -rat.ed, -rat.ing 1** utter with an "h" sound: *He has a tendency to aspirate his "it" into "hit."* **2** draw in, as by suction: *Liquid aspirated down the windpipe could cause suffocation.* **—adj.** (-rit) aspirated: *The "h" is not aspirate in "honor" and "hour."*

as.pi.ra.tion (as.puh.RAY.shun) *n.* **1** desire to attain a goal or an instance of it: *lofty, noble aspirations; a subject people's aspirations to independence; Priesthood was one of his early aspirations.* **2** the pronouncing of an "h" sound as in "hit." **3** a drawing in, out, up, etc. by suction, as into the lungs or windpipe: *The mucus was removed from the patient's windpipe by aspiration.* **—as.pi.ra.tion.al** *adj.* having to do with higher values or tastes: *an aspirational attitude, brand, influence.*

as.pi.ra.tor (AS.puh.ray.tur) *n.* a suction device for removing fluids from a space or cavity.

as.pire (uh.SPIRE) *v.* **-pires, -pired, -pir.ing** have a desire to attain a goal: *to aspire for fame, freedom, knowledge; He aspires to become a doctor; She aspires to the highest office of the land; adja.: an aspiring actor, scholar, singer.*

as.pir.in (AS.puh.rin, -prin) *n.* a white crystalline drug for relieving pain and fever; also, a tablet of it: *The doctor told her to take two aspirin or aspirins and call him in the morning; buffered aspirin to protect your stomach; an aspirin tablet.*

ass *n.* **1** a braying animal related to the horse but smaller; donkey. **2** stupid person: *Don't make an ass of yourself; a pompous ass; "The law is an ass"* (= The law needs to be changed). **3** [vulgar slang] the buttocks: *Get off your ass; He's a pain in the ass; She's up to her ass in work.*

as.sail (uh.SAIL) *v.* attack violently, as with repeated blows: *Relentless winds assailed the coast; He was assailed bitterly by his foes; assailed with doubts, insults, questions;* **as.sail.a.ble** *adj.* **—as.sail.ant** (-unt) *n.* attacker.

as.sas.sin (uh.SAS.in) *n.* a murderer of a prominent person, esp. a hired killer.

assassinate / assiduous

as.sas.si.nate (uh.SAS.uh.nate) *v.* -nates, -nat.ed, -nat.ing kill as an assassin. —**as.sas.si.na.tion** (-NAY.shun) *n.*: *political assassinations; an assassination carried out by a hired killer; character assassination (by slander).*

as.sault (uh.SAULT) *n.* **1** an attack, esp. a violent and sudden one: *They carried out, led, made an assault against the fortress; an assault on enemy positions; The fortress was taken by assault; an all-out, armed, military assault; the final assault on Mount Everest; She considers rock music an assault on her ears;* **adj.**: *assault forces, pilots, rifles, squads, troops, weapons.* **2** [legal use] a physical threat: *If you strike at someone and miss, that constitutes only assault; If you hit, you commit* **assault and battery** (= threat with actual use of force). **3** [legal use] an attack: *aggravated assault such as assault with a deadly weapon; He was charged with attempted rape and indecent assault; sexual assault* (= rape). —*v.* attack: *He was assaulted in the street.* —**as.sault.er** *n.*

as.say (AS.ay, as.AY) *n.* a test or analysis of a precious metal, ore, drug, etc. to determine quality or composition: *a biological assay* or *bioassay.* —*v.* **1** analyze or test: *a theme that she assays in her novels.* **2** attempt or try: *Many have assayed to conquer Everest.*

as.sem.blage (uh.SEM.blij) *n.* **1** the act or process of assembling; assembly. **2** an assembled group. **3** (also ah.sahm.BLAZH) an artistic composition using odds and ends; **as.sem.blag.ist** *n.*

as.sem.ble (uh.SEM.bul) *v.* -bles, -bled, -bling **1** gather together: *We assembled in the auditorium;* **adj.**: *the assembled press, staff, workers.* **2** put together: *to assemble a computer system;* **adj.**: *an assembled automobile.*

as.sem.bler (uh.SEM.blur) *n.* **1** one that assembles. **2** a computer program for automatically converting assembly-language instructions into machine language. **3** an assembly language.

as.sem.bly (uh.SEM.blee) *n.* -blies **1** an assembling: *the daily assembly before school begins; the freedom of peaceful assembly; an unlawful assembly of picketers; a gear assembly (of transmission parts); some assembly (of the parts) required.* **2** a legislative body: *to convene an assembly; a legislative assembly.*

assembly language *n.* a programming language in which several elementary operations are grouped together in each command, the commands being directly convertible to machine language.

assembly line *n.* a factory system in which each worker does a specific operation in assembling a product: *to work on an assembly line.*

as.sem.bly.man (uh.SEM.blee.mun) *n.* -men a member of a legislative body. —**as.sem.bly.wom.an** *n.* -wom.en.

as.sent (uh.SENT) *v.* express acceptance or adherence: *to assent to an opinion, proposal.* —*n.* agreement: *a nod of assent; They withheld their assent to the proposal; A bill is given royal assent* (= acceptance) *after passage through both houses of parliament.*

as.sert (uh.SURT) *v.* claim or say forcefully: *He asserted his innocence; asserted that he was innocent.* —**assert oneself** insist on one's rights.

as.ser.tion (uh.SUR.shun) *n.* an asserting: *to make a bold, sweeping, unfounded assertion against someone; to deny, refute an assertion; her assertion of innocence; her assertion that she is innocent.*

as.ser.tive (uh.SUR.tiv) *adj.* that asserts oneself or itself: *an assertive young woman; an assertive check design.* —**as.ser.tive.ly** *adv.*; **as.ser.tive.ness** *n.*

assertiveness training *n.* training to help one act with self-confidence and get positive results.

as.sess (uh.SES) *v.* **1** determine a payment as damages, a fine, levy, or tax or impose it: *Each member was assessed $300 as fee.* **2** estimate property, income, etc. for taxation: *The house was assessed at $250,000.* **3** evaluate: *to assess the merit of a thesis; to assess a situation.* —**as.sess.ment** *n.* —**as.ses.sor** (-sur) *n.*

as.set (AS.et) *n.* **1** a person or thing that is considered valuable or useful: *Experience is a valuable asset in a job applicant; She is an asset to the firm.* **2 assets** *pl.* property that may be used to pay one's debts, as cash, merchandise, accounts receivable, real estate, securities, trademarks, and good will: *to realize, unfreeze (financial) assets; current, family, financial, frozen, hidden, intangible, liquid, personal assets.*

as.sev.er.ate (uh.SEV.uh.rate) *v.* -ates, -at.ed, -at.ing declare solemnly. —**as.sev.er.a.tion** (-RAY.shun) *n.*: *an asseveration of faith.*

as.sid.u.ous (uh.SIJ.oo.us) *adj.* diligent and unremitting in one's effort: *She was assiduous in her efforts to get top marks; She studied with assiduous application; a most assiduous critic;*

as.sid.u.ous.ly *adv.* —**as.sid.u.i.ty** (as.uh.DEW.i.tee) *n.*

as.sign (uh.SINE) *v.* **1** give out as someone's share: *A teacher assigns work; He assigned us an easy task.* **2** appoint to a post or duty: *A reporter is assigned to a story.* **3** name or specify: *to assign an hour for a ceremony; to assign a motive for a murder; to assign* (= ascribe) *an artifact to a certain culture.* **4** [legal use] transfer ownership: *to assign a book's copyright.* —*n.* same as ASSIGNEE. —**as.sign.a.ble** *adj.* —**as.sign.er** or **as.sign.or** *n.*

as.sign.ee (uh.sye.NEE) *n.* one to whom an ownership or right is legally assigned.

as.sign.ment (uh.SINE.munt) *n.* **1** task or duty assigned: *The teacher gave us a math assignment* (= homework); *That was one tough assignment she handed out; Most of us did the assignment; Some were late to hand in the assignment.* **2** task or mission: *a reporter sent on a special assignment; He was* **on assignment** *in Mexico for a month; an assignment to report on the earthquake; He carried out his assignment brilliantly; dangerous, difficult, easy, overseas, rough, tough assignments; an assignment* (= appointment) *to a foreign embassy.* **3** an act of assigning, esp. a transfer of ownership.

as.sim.i.late (uh.SIM.uh.late) *v.* **-lates, -lat.ed, -lat.ing 1** take something in and make it similar to itself: *The body assimilates food by digestion; The mind assimilates* (= absorbs) *knowledge.* **2** make or become similar to something: *The "p" sound in "cupboard"* (CUB.urd) *is assimilated to "b"; North America has assimilated millions of people from all over the world; Immigrants try to assimilate into or to a community; They assimilate with the rest of the population.* —**as.sim.i.la.tion** (-LAY.shun) *n.*

as.sist (uh.SIST) *v. Formal.* to help; aid: *to assist at an operation, in taking pictures, with the staging of a play.* —*n.* in a game, an instance of helping a teammate, as to make a putout or score a goal: *She made three baskets and two assists during the game; He could get out of the car only with an assist* (*Informal for* a helping hand) *from his wife.* —**as.sis.tance** (-tunce) *n.*: *to give, offer, provide, render assistance to someone; clerical assistance; Phone 411 for directory assistance; She was of great assistance to us during the emergency; considerable, economic, financial, legal, material, technical assistance.*

as.sis.tant (uh.SIS.tunt) *n.* one who helps: *marketing, office, research, teaching assistants; an assistant to the president;* —*adj.*: *an assistant editor, manager, professor.*

as.size (uh.SIZE) *n.* **1** an inquest by judge and jury. **2 assizes** *pl.* periodic sessions of a law court.

as.so.ci.ate (uh.SOH.shee.ate, -see.ate) *v.* **-ates, -at.ed, -at.ing 1** join or be connected: *to associate with bad characters;* **adj.**: *Jones and Smith are associated in a law firm; The Associated Press is an association of newspapers.* **2** to link in the mind: *Children associate birthdays with gifts.* —*n.* (*also* -shee.it, -see.it) companion or colleague. —**adj.** associated in function, but not fully in regard to privileges and responsibilities: *an associate editor, judge, member; Some colleges award an* **associate degree** *after two years of study; An* **associate professor** *ranks below a full professor but above an assistant professor.*

as.so.ci.a.tion (uh.soh.see.AY.shun) *n.* **1** the act of associating: *articles of association* (= incorporation); *the association* (= linking) *of ideas in the mind.* **2** connection: *He has ended his association with that company; He has started a new business in close association with his brothers.* **3** a group or union: *to form an association; The Commonwealth of Nations is a free association of countries with British connections; a bar association* (= lawyers' association).

as.so.ci.a.tive (uh.SOH.see.ay.tiv, -uh.tiv) *adj.* **1** depending on association: *an associative idea, image; associative learning by the linking of ideas.* **2** in mathematics, not dependent on order of grouping: *Addition and multiplication are associative operations.*

as.so.nance (AS.uh.nunce) *n.* resemblance of vowel sounds that gives the effect of a partial rhyme, as in "seen-feel"; **as.so.nant** *adj.*

as.sort.ed (uh.SOR.tid) *adj.* of various kinds; miscellaneous: *a box of assorted candies, greeting cards; cats, dogs, and assorted other pets; an* **ill-assorted** (= badly matched) *pair.* —**as.sort.ment** *n.*: *We carry a wide assortment of greeting cards.*

as.suage (uh.SWAGE) *v.* **as.suag.es, as.suaged, as.suag.ing** lessen or pacify feelings, desires, etc. that need satisfaction: *to assuage one's fears, feelings, guilt, pain, sorrow.*

as.sume (uh.SUME, "YOO" or "OO") *v.* **as.sumes, as.sumed, as.sum.ing 1** suppose: *Let's assume there's life on Mars; Never assume too much when dealing with a stranger; Everyone is assumed* to be innocent until proven guilty. **2** take on a responsibility, right, etc. as one's own: *to assume the role of a mediator; The junta assumed dictatorial powers; She assumes her new duties on Monday; The problem assumed awesome proportions;* **adj.:** *a very **assuming*** (= presumptuous) *young man.* **3** put on: *to assume an air of indifference; to assume a posture; Proteus could assume any form;* **adj.:** *under an **assumed** name.*

as.sump.tion (uh.SUM.shun) *n.* **1** an assuming or something assumed: *He made an assumption that proved to be erroneous; a false assumption; not a reasonable, safe, or valid assumption; an assumption about something he had no proof of; an assumption of guilt; He proceeded on the assumption that the money had been stolen.* **2** a taking up: *No date has been set for the assumption of office by the new mayor; the **Assumption*** (= taking up into Heaven) *of the Virgin Mary.*
—**as.sump.tive** *adj.*

as.sur.ance (uh.SHOOR.unce) *n.* an assuring or being assured: *He had given us every assurance that we would get the contract; He gave us assurances of a quick decision; assurances that the decision would be made before the end of the week; He spoke with assurance* (= confidence).

as.sure (uh.SHOOR) *v.* **as.sures, as.sured, as.sur.ing** make someone certain of something; guarantee: *The car is quite safe, I can assure you; I can assure you of its roadworthiness.*
—**as.sur.er** *n.*

assured (uh.SHOORD) *adj.* sure or secure: *Her future is assured, thanks to the inheritance; There is an assured demand for newer and better computers; Rest assured* (= confident) *your child will recover.* —*n.* a person in whose favor an insurance policy is issued; an insured.
—**as.sur.ed.ly** (-rid.lee) *adv.*
—**as.sur.ed.ness** *n.*

As.syr.i.an (uh.SEER.ee.un) *adj. & n.* (a person) of or from **Assyria**, an ancient empire that extended from the Nile to the Caspian Sea.

as.ta.tine (AS.tuh.teen) *n.* a very unstable radioactive chemical element.

as.ter (AS.tur) *n.* a plant of the composite family, bearing daisylike flowers of varying color.

as.ter.isk (AS.tuh.risk) *n.* **1** a star-shaped figure [*] used as a reference mark; **adj.:** *an **asterisked*** (= indicated by asterisk) *footnote.* **2** a mere footnote; hence, an insignifiicant person or thing: *an event relegated to the asterisk of history; an asterisk of antiquity.*

a.stern (uh.STURN) *adj. & adv.* at or toward the rear of a ship; behind: *The boat came up astern of the ship.*

as.ter.oid (AS.tuh.roid) *n.* any of the many small planets orbiting around the sun between Mars and Jupiter.
—**as.ter.oi.dal** (-ROY.dul) *adj.*

asth.ma (AZ.muh) *n.* a chest disease marked by coughing, wheezing, and other breathing difficulties.

asth.mat.ic (az.MAT.ic) *n.* an asthma patient; **adj.:** *an asthmatic attack* (= attack of asthma).

a.stig.ma.tism (uh.STIG.muh.tiz.um) *n.* a focusing defect in a lens, esp. of the eye, which results in blurred vision.
—**as.tig.mat.ic** (as.tig.MAT.ic) *n. & adj.*

a.stir (uh.STUR) *adjp. & adv.* **1** in an excited state: *a town astir with the news of victory.* **2** out of bed; awake.

as.ton.ish (uh.STON.ish) *v.* surprise so greatly as to seem unbelievable: *I was astonished to hear of your successes; I was astonished at your behavior; Your acrobatic feats astonish me;* **adj.:** *an **astonished** spectator; I am astonished that you can do such things.* —**astonishing** *adj.:* *The acrobat can perform some really astonishing feats; They are astonishing to watch.*
—**as.ton.ish.ing.ly** *adv.*
—**as.ton.ish.ment** *n.:* *To our astonishment, she succeeded in every one of them; Everyone stared in astonishment at her performance; They expressed astonishment at her skills.*

as.tound (uh.STOWND) *v.* strike with sudden surprise: *The news of the tragedy astounded us;* **adj.:** *We were **astounded** at or by the news; astounded that such a thing could happen.* —**astounding** *adj.:* *It was astounding to hear that she had broken the previous record; an astounding feat.* —**as.tound.ing.ly** *adv.*

a.strad.dle (uh.STRAD.ul) *adv.* [used after its verb] astride: *She rides astraddle.* —**prep.:** *seated astraddle her horse.*

as.tra.khan (AS.truh.can) *n.* the curly fur made from the young lambs of a breed of Asian sheep from **Astrakhan**, a city in the U.S.S.R.; karakul: *an astrakhan cap.*

as.tral (AS.trul) *adj.* pertaining to the stars; stellar: *astral influences.*

a.stray (uh.STRAY) *adv.* [used after its verb] away from the right course: *How did he go astray? He was led astray by bad companions.*

a.stride (uh.STRIDE) *adj. & adv.* with legs on either side: *She likes to ride her horse astride; Astride riding seems safer.*
—**prep.:** *He came sliding down astride a*

banister; The city grew astride (= on both sides of) *the river.*

as.trin.gent (uh.STRIN.junt) *adj.* tending to contract blood vessels, tissues, etc. —*n.* an astringent substance: *Shaving lotions contain astringents.*

as.trol.o.gy (uh.STROL.uh.jee) *n.* the study of the influence of stars on human affairs. —**as.trol.o.ger** *n.*
—**as.tro.log.i.cal** (as.truh.LOJ.i.cul) *adj.*

as.tro.naut (AS.truh.nawt) *n.* a person trained for space flights.
—**as.tro.naut.ic** (-NAW.tic) or **as.tro.naut.i.cal** (-ti.cul) *adj.*

astronautics *n.pl.* [takes *sing. v.*] the science of making and operating spacecraft.

as.tro.nom.i.cal (as.truh.NOM.i.cul) *adj.* **1** having to do with astronomy. **2** extraordinarily large: *an astronomical price, sum.*

as.tron.o.my (uh.STRON.uh.mee) *n.* -mies the study of heavenly bodies.
—**as.tron.o.mer** *n.*

as.tro.phys.ics (as.troh.FIZ.ics) *n.pl.* [takes *sing. v.*] the science of the physical properties and chemical composition of heavenly bodies.
—**as.tro.phys.i.cal** *adj.;* **as.tro.phys.i.cist** *n.*

as.tute (uh.STUTE) *adj.* shrewd and sagacious, esp. in aiming for advantage: *an astute lawyer, politician, remark; She is very astute at persuading people.*
—**as.tute.ly** *adv.;* **as.tute.ness** *n.*

a.sun.der (uh.SUN.dur) *adv.* [used after its verb] separated into parts: *families torn asunder by war; driven, forced, rent asunder.*

a.sy.lum (uh.SYE.lum) *n.* **1** protection or sanctuary: *Refugees seek political asylum; Asylum is not denied in genuine cases; Most receive* or *are granted asylum.*
2 [former use] refuge or hospital: *lunatic* or *mental asylums.*

a.sym.me.try (ay.SIM.uh.tree) *n.* lack of symmetry: *the asymmetry of a winding staircase.* —**a.sym.met.ri.c** (ay.suh.MET.ric) or **a.sym.met.ri.cal** (-ri.cul) *adj.: an asymmetrical dress.*
—**a.sym.met.ri.cal.ly** *adv.*

at *prep.* [indicating] **1** position in time, place, etc.: *I met her at noon; I'll see you at school.* **2** direction, movement, rate, degree, etc.: *Aim at the target; to drive at top speed; men at work; nations at war; He's at it* (Informal for busy with it) *again.* **3** manner, condition, state, etc.: *a body at rest; goods sold at auction; We're happy at his victory.*

at.a.vism (AT.uh.viz.um) *n.* reappearance of a hereditary characteristic after a gap of several generations: *resurgent ethnic atavism.* —**at.a.vis.tic** (-VIS.tic) *adj: atavistic hostilities, resentments, terror;* **at.a.vis.ti.cal.ly** *adv.*

ate *pt.* of EAT.

at.el.ier (AT.ul.yay) *n.* a workshop or studio, esp. an artist's.

A-tent *n.* an A-shaped tent with no vertical wall.

Ath.a.bas.can or **Ath.a.pas.kan** (ath.uh.BAS.cun, -PAS.cun, "th" as in "thin") *n.* **1** an Amerindian language family of western U.S. and Canada. **2** (a member of) a people speaking an Athabascan language.

a.the.ism (AY.thee.iz.um, "th" as in "thin") *n.* the denial of God's existence; **a.the.ist** *n.* —**a.the.is.tic** (-IS.tic) or **a.the.is.ti.cal** (-IS.ti.cul) *adj.*

ath.e.ne.um (ath.uh.NEE.um, "th" as in "thin") *n.* **1** an institution of learning. **2** a literary or scientific club. Also **ath.e.nae.um.**

A.the.ni.an (uh.THEE.nee.un) *n. & adj.* (a person) of or from **Athens,** capital of Greece.

ath.er.o.scle.ro.sis (ath.uh.ruh.skluh.ROH.sis, "th" as in "thin") *n.* thickening of arterial walls because of fatty accumulations inside them.
—**ath.er.o.scle.rot.ic** (-ROT.ic) *adj.*

a.thirst (uh.THIRST) *adjp.* longing: *She's athirst for adventure, freedom, glory, news.*

ath.lete (ATH.leet, "TH" as in "thin") *n.* one trained to compete in athletics: *an all-round, amateur, world-class athlete; professional athletes.*

athlete's foot *n.* a contagious skin disease of the feet.

ath.let.ic (ath.LET.ic) **1** athletics *n.pl.* [takes *sing. v.*] physical exercises, sports, and games: *intercollegiate athletics.* **2** *adj.* having to do with athletics: *an athletic event; a man of athletic build; his athletic prowess; An* **athletic support** (= elastic belt and pouch for the genitals) *is worn by men during athletics.*

at home *n.* a reception held at one's home. —**at-home** *adja.: at-home entertaining, parties; an at-home dress (suitable for home wear).*

-athon *comb.form.* an activity that is like a marathon in duration: *bikeathon, skiathon, telethon, walkathon, workathon.*

a.thwart (uh.THWORT) *adv. & prep.* from side to side of something: *riding athwart the path of an army.*

a.tilt (uh.TILT) *adj. & adv.* in a tilted position.

At.lan.tic (at.LAN.tic) *adja.* having to do

with the **Atlantic Ocean** lying between the Americas in the west and Europe and Africa in the east.

at.las (AT.lus) *n.* a book of maps.

at.mos.phere (AT.mus.feer) *n.* **1** the air surrounding the Earth or a similar gaseous envelope around any heavenly body: *a polluted atmosphere; rarefied atmosphere; the upper atmosphere.* **2** the environment of any place: *We met in a friendly atmosphere; formal, informal, relaxed, stifling, tense atmosphere; This restaurant is crowded, but it has atmosphere* (= a distinctive ambiance).

at.mos.pher.ic (at.mus.FEER.ic, -FER.ic) **1** *adj.* of the atmosphere: *an atmospheric disturbance; atmospheric pressure.* **2 atmospherics** *n.pl.* disturbances caused in radio reception by natural phenomena, as during a storm.

at.oll (AT.ol) *n.* a ring of coral reefs and islands enclosing a lagoon.

at.om (AT.um) *n.* **1** the smallest particle of an element that may be involved in chemical reactions: *the splitting of the atom; to harness the atom* (= atomic energy). **2** a tiny bit; jot: *There's not an atom of truth in what he says.*

atom bomb *n.* a very destructive weapon that uses the energy, or **atomic energy,** released by the splitting of atomic nuclei. Also **atomic bomb.**

a.tom.ic (uh.TOM.ic) *adja.* having to do with atomic energy; nuclear: *the atomic age; atomic energy, physics, warfare, warheads; a very precise **atomic clock**; the **atomic club*** (= nations possessing nuclear weapons); *an **atomic pile** or **atomic reactor*** (= a device or vessel used for chemical reaction that releases atomic energy). —**a.tom.i.cal.ly** *adv.*

atomic weight *n.* the weight of an atom of an element as compared with that of an atom of carbon.

at.om.ism (AT.uh.miz.um) *n.* the philosophical theory that the universe is ultimately composed of indestructible atoms; **at.o.mist** *n.* —**at.o.mis.tic** (-MIS.tic) *adj.*

at.o.mize (AT.uh.mize) *v.* **-iz.es, -ized, -iz.ing** reduce a liquid, esp. a medicine or perfume, into a fine spray using a device called an atomizer; **at.o.miz.er** *n.* —**at.om.i.za.tion** (-muh.ZAY.shun, -mye-) *n.*

atom smasher *n. Informal.* same as ACCELERATOR, 2.

a.ton.al (ay.TOH.nul) *adj.* of music, not based on a key; **a.ton.al.ly** *adv.* —**a.to.nal.i.ty** (ay.toh.NAL.i.tee) *n.*

a.tone (uh.TONE) *v.* **a.tones, a.toned,**

a.ton.ing make up for a wrong: *He atoned for past misdeeds by philanthropy.*

a.tone.ment (uh.TONE.munt) *n.* satisfaction for wrongdoing; amends: *in atonement for his sins; to make atonement for her misdeeds.*

a.top (uh.TOP) *prep. & adv.* on top: *The balloon landed atop a building; a bird perched atop of a tower.*

a.tri.um (AY.tree.um) *n.* **a.tri.a** (-uh) or **a.tri.ums 1** the main room or entrance hall of an ancient Roman house. **2** an entrance chamber or cavity of a body part, as the auricles of the heart and the cavity behind the eardrum.

a.tro.cious (uh.TROH.shus) *adj.* **1** wicked or horrifying. **2** *Informal.* very bad: *Her manners are atrocious; an atrocious necktie.*

a.troc.i.ty (uh.TROS.i.tee) *n.* **-ties** something atrocious: *death-camp atrocities; the horrible atrocities committed by the Nazis;* [informal] *the atrocities of bad spellers.*

at.ro.phy (AT.ruh.fee) *n.* the wasting away or stop in growth of a body part or tissue, as in polio. —*v.* **-phies, -phied, -phy.ing** affect with atrophy: *Skills atrophy from lack of practice;* **adj.**: *an **atrophied** limb, muscle.*

at.ro.pine (AT.ruh.peen) *n.* a belladonna extract used to control spasms and to dilate the pupil of the eye for examination.

atta- *comb.form.* that's the; that's a: *attaboy, attagirl; Attaway, baby!*

at.ta.boy (AT.uh.boy) *interj.* expressing encouragement to a boy; way to go!: *Attaboy, Bob!*

at.tach (uh.TACH) *v.* **1** unite one to another by a bond or tie so as to keep them together: *to attach a label to a parcel; I attach my signature to a petition; The school is attached to a university; a garage attached to a house;* **adj.**: *an **attached** garage; two friends deeply attached to each other); He's strongly attached to his family.* **2** attribute or be attributed: *Do you attach any political significance to the mayor's speech? No blame attaches to his spouse for John's conduct; What's the use of attaching blame without suggesting a cure?* **3** take away by legal writ: *A debtor's property may be attached.* —**at.tach.ment** *n.*: *to feel a close, strong attachment to one's family; It was no mere sentimental attachment; He formed some lasting attachments* (= friendships) *while at college; A vacuum cleaner comes with several attachments* (= devices).

at.ta.ché (at.uh.SHAY, uh.TASH.ay) *n.*

attack / attenuate

1 a diplomatic official: *cultural, military, naval, press attachés.* **2** a thin suitcase for carrying papers; also **attaché case.**

at.tack (uh.TAK) *n.* **1** an offensive action against a person or thing: *The French launched* or *mounted an attack on England; England* **came** or **was under attack;** *They launched an attack against enemy forces; "Attack is the best form of defense"; to blunt, carry out, lead, make, press, provoke, repel, repulse, spearhead an attack; air, all-out, concerted, enemy, frontal, mock, pre-emptive, sneak, surprise attacks; An attack may fail, fizzle out, succeed.* **2** an aggressive speech or writing: *a newspaper attack on Government policies; a bitter, blistering, scurrilous, vicious, wanton attack.* **3** an affliction: *to have an attack of measles; He died of a heart attack; fatal, recurrent, slight, sudden attacks.* **4** the start of an activity: *to make a fresh attack on a problem.*
—*v.* make an attack: *to attack the enemy; A disease attacks the body; Who attacked first? She was attacked viciously in the media.* —**at.tack.er** *n.*

at.ta.girl (AT.uh.girl) *interj.* expressing encouragement to a girl; way to go!: *Attagirl, Annie!*

at.tain (uh.TAIN) *v.* **1** reach a state, position, goal, etc.: *to attain the age of 21; to attain success by hard work.* **2 attain to** succeed in reaching: *to attain to great power and glory; to attain to man's estate.* —**at.tain.a.ble** *adj.*

at.tain.ment *n.* the act of attaining or something attained, esp. something distinguished; accomplishment: *a position difficult of attainment; a woman of great cultural attainments.*

at.tar (AT.ur) *n.* a fragrant oil obtained from flowers: *Roses yield* **attar of roses.**

at.tempt (uh.TEMT) **1** *v.* make an effort to do something; try: *Many failed in attempting (to climb) Everest; He attempted the same exam three times;* **adj.:** *an* **attempted** *assassination, coup, coverup, invasion, takeover.* **2** *n.* an effort or try: *an attempt at the Olympic gold; an attempt at being funny; an attempt to be funny; to make an attempt* (= attack) *on the premier's life; The attempt was foiled* or *thwarted; abortive, all-out, bold, concerted, deliberate, feeble, first, fruitless, futile, half-hearted, last-ditch, premature, successful attempts; He gave up after repeated attempts.*

at.tend (uh.TEND) *v.* **1** be present at a place or function: *to attend church, meetings, school; a speech attended* (= accompanied) *by shouts from the audience; the* **attending** *physician; adj.: The meeting was well* **attended.** **2** pay attention to a person or thing: *Let's attend to our duties; Sales clerks attend to* (= help) *customers; Nurses attend* (= care for) *the sick; Students are supposed to attend* (= listen to what is being taught) *in class; Waiters* **attend on** (= serve) *customers.*

at.ten.dance (uh.TEN.dunce) *n.* a being present: *No doctor is in attendance on Sundays; Attendance is compulsory at school; average, low, poor attendance; Attendance falls* or *goes down, goes up; Attendance is checked daily; Attendance* (= count of people attending) *is taken in the morning; a boss who expects his employees to* **dance attendance on** (= be servile to) *him.*

at.ten.dant (uh.TEN.dunt) **1** *adj.* attending: *the attendant* (= on duty) *nurse; evils* **attendant on** (= connected with) *wars.* **2** *n.* a person in a specified service: *a flight attendant; parking-lot attendant; wedding attendant; She worked as an attendant to the princess.*

at.ten.tion (uh.TEN.shun) *n.* the act of listening or caring: *for your attention; a note for the boss's attention; The wound requires immediate attention; Please bring it to the nurse's attention; to attract, capture, catch, command, distract, divert, draw, hold, retain, rivet someone's attention; to devote, escape, focus one's attention; one's undivided attention; close, meticulous, personal, rapt attention; with great attention to detail; The soldiers have been called to attention; They come to* or *snap to attention; to stand* **at attention** (= in an erect posture), *not at ease; Students should* **pay attention** (= listen carefully) *to what is taught; The youngster liked the* **attentions** (= courtesies) *he received; Young children have a very short* **attention span** (= period during which they can concentrate on one thing).

at.ten.tive (uh.TEN.tiv) *adj.* paying attention: *Teachers like attentive pupils; Be attentive* (= considerate) *to her needs.*
—**at.ten.tive.ly** *adv.;* **at.ten.tive.ness** *n.*

at.ten.u.ate (un.TEN.yoo.ate) *v.* **-ates, -at.ed, -at.ing** make or become thin or weak, less dense, harmful, etc.: *Wire is attenuated by being drawn out; a body attenuated by lack of nourishment; to attenuate the amplitude of a signal; adj.: a drug prepared in an* **attenuated** *form for medicinal use.* —**at.ten.u.a.tion** (-AY.shun) *n.* lessening: *The high green walls along the highway are for the attenuation of noise; wave attenuation.*
—**at.ten.u.a.tor** *n.*

at.test (uh.TEST) *v.* bear witness to the truth or genuineness of something: *a signature attested by two witnesses; They attest (to) its genuineness.* —**at.tes.ta.tion** (at.uh.STAY.shun) *n.*

at.tic (AT.ic) *n.* a room or space just under a roof.

Attic *n. & adj.* (having to do with) Athens or Athenians; hence, classical: *Attic architecture.*

at.tire (uh.TIRE) *n.* dress or clothes: *casual, civilian, formal attire.* —*v.* **at.tires, at.tired, at.tir.ing** array; *adj.*: *He came attired in regal splendor.*

at.ti.tude (AT.uh.tude) *n.* **1** the way one feels or thinks about something: *a cooperative attitude; to assume* or *take an attitude of defiance; his attitude toward his superiors; belligerent, cavalier, condescending, defiant, firm, hands-off, holier-than-thou, liberal, negative, positive, reverent, scornful, selfish attitudes; the attitude that his needs always come first.* **2** a pose, position, or posture: *She stood in the doorway in a threatening attitude* (= posture); *A signal was sent to shift the attitude* (= position in the sky) *of a space station veering out of control; arabesques and attitudes* (= ballet poses). —**strike an attitude** assume a posture. —**at.ti.tu.di.nal** (-TUE.dun.ul) *adj.*

at.ti.tu.di.nize (at.uh.TUE.dun.ize) *v.* **-niz.es, -nized, -niz.ing** take an affected attitude: *Is this philosopher merely attitudinizing in his writings?*

at.tor.ney (uh.TUR.nee) *n.* **-neys 1** person with legal authority to act for another; lawyer: *to hire, retain an attorney; defense, district, prosecuting attorneys.* **2** legal authority: *a power of attorney appointing someone to act for the signer.*

attorney general *n.* **attorney generals** or **attorneys general 1** the chief law officer of a country, province, or state. **2** a minister of justice in some countries.

at.tract (uh.TRACT) *v.* draw toward one: *Honey attracts bees; The goings-on attracted everyone's attention; adj.: Joe felt attracted to Jane; to be, become, remain attracted.*

at.trac.tant (uh.TRAC.tunt) *n.* something that attracts: *a sex attractant; attractants and repellents; an attractant scent.*

at.trac.tion (uh.TRAC.shun) *n.* **1** an attracting: *magnetic attraction and repulsion.* **2** charm: *Joe feels a strong attraction to Jane; an irresistible attraction; sexual attraction?* **3** something that attracts: *a country's scenic, tourist attractions; The movie was a great box-office attraction; today's "extra added" attraction.*

at.trac.tive (uh.TRAC.tiv) *adj.* that attracts: *a beautiful and attractive child; a sexually attractive figure; an attractive bargain; an offer that sounds very attractive to everyone; at.trac.tive.ly adv.; at.trac.tive.ness n.* —**at.trac.tor** or **at.tract.er** *n.*

at.trib.ute (uh.TRIB.yoot) *v.* **-utes, -ut.ed, -ut.ing** consider as belonging to a person or thing: *He attributes his successes to luck; a play attributed to Bacon; The tax department says income from money loaned to your wife will be attributed to you.* —**at.trib.u.ta.ble** (-tuh.bul) *adj.* —*n.* (AT.ruh.bute) an inherent characteristic: *Being all-powerful is an attribute of God.* —**at.tri.bu.tion** (-BYOO.shun) *n.*: *The politician wouldn't say it for attribution* (= wouldn't be quoted).

at.trib.u.tive (uh.TRIB.yuh.tiv) *adj.* of a word, coming before and modifying, as in "Bible story" and "good book." —*n.* an attributive word: *In "The book is good," "good" is a predicate adjective, not an attributive adjective as in "the good book."* —**at.trib.u.tive.ly** *adv.*

at.tri.tion (uh.TRISH.un) *n.* **1** a wearing away; gradual weakening: *A war of attrition could destroy both sides.* **2** reduction in numbers through resignations, retirements, and deaths: *the high rate of attrition in our senior staff; $300,000 was saved by attrition and $1 million by cutbacks.*

at.tune (uh.TUNE) *v.* **at.tunes, at.tuned, at.tun.ing** tune: *an experience to attune students to the rules of ecology; adj.: A mother's ears are attuned to her children's voices.*

a.twit.ter (uh.TWIT.ur) *adj. & adv.* [used after what it modifies] *Informal.* twittering; excited.

a.typ.i.cal (ay.TIP.i.cul) *adj.* not typical; unusual: *behavior that is atypical of children.*

au.burn (AW.burn) *n.* reddish brown: *His hair is a shiny auburn; adj.: her auburn hair.*

au cou.rant (oh.coo.RAHN) *adj.* French. modern or up to date: *Everyone likes to be au courant; to be au courant with fashion changes; an au courant fashion, style.*

auc.tion (AWK.shun) *n.* sale by bidding: *The house was put up for auction; sold at* or *by auction; I bought it at an auction; an auction held in New York; The auction took place last year.* —*v.* **auction off** sell at auction. —**auc.tion.a.ble** *adj.* —**auc.tion.eer** (awk.shuh.NEER) *n.*

auc.to.ri.al (awk.TOR.ee.ul) *adj.* having to do with an author.

au.da.cious (aw.DAY.shus) *adj.* bold in an impudent or daring manner: *It was audacious of him to ask his teacher for a date; an audacious act.* —**au.dac.i.ty** (aw.DAS.i.tee) *n.*: sheer audacity; *He had the audacity to reject the hand held out by her.*

au.di.ble (AW.duh.bul) *adj.* loud enough to be heard: *in an audible voice;* **au.di.bly** (-blee) *adv.*
—**au.di.bil.i.ty** (-BIL.i.tee) *n.*

au.di.ence (AW.dee.unce) *n.* **1** a group of listeners or spectators, as in an auditorium or theater: *The meeting attracted* or *drew a large audience; an appreciative, enthusiastic audience; capacity, captive, live, passive, responsive, select, standing-room-only, sympathetic audiences.* **2** those reached by books and media: *a TV audience; a novelist with a large audience* (= readership); *high audience ratings.* **3** a formal interview: *to seek an audience with the Pope; I was at a papal audience; The Queen received us in audience; to give* or *grant an audience to someone.* **4** an opportunity to be heard: *If once given audience, some complaints only get worse.*

au.di.o (AW.dee.oh) **1** *n.* the sound portion of a telecast or film, distinguished from the video; *adja.*: *an audio component, frequency, tape; audio equipment.* **2** *comb.form.* having to do with hearing: *audiocassette, audiophile, audiovisual.*

au.di.ol.o.gy (aw.dee.OL.uh.jee) *n.* the science of hearing; **au.di.ol.o.gist** (-jist) *n.*

au.di.o.phile (AW.dee.uh.file) *n.* one who is fond of hi-fi equipment and sound reproduction as a hobby: *High-quality audiophile records sell at premium prices.*

au.di.o.tex or **au.di.o.text** *n.* auditory information services such as voice mail, chat lines, and talking yellow pages.

au.di.o.vis.u.al (AW.dee.oh.VIZH.oo.ul) **1** *adj.* having to do with both audio and visual communication: *audiovisual aids;* **Audiovisual education** *uses films, record players, and slides; audiovisual teaching materials.* **2 audiovisuals** *n.pl.* audiovisual aids used in education.

au.dit (AW.dit) *n.* **1** an official checking and verification of business accounts: *to carry out* or *conduct an annual audit; Cheaters live in fear of a tax audit.* **2** a report of such a checking.
—*v.* **1** officially examine a business ac-count. **2** attend a course of study, but not for credit.

au.di.tion (aw.DISH.un) *n.* a trial given to an actor, singer, etc. before hiring: *The recruiter holds auditions at his hotel.*
—*v.* **1** give an audition to someone: *The director was auditioning actors yesterday.* **2** perform for trial: *Three girls auditioned for* or *to play the leading role.*

au.di.tor (AW.duh.tur) *n.* **1** one who audits. **2** listener.

au.di.to.ri.um (aw.duh.TOR.ee.um) *n.* **-ri.ums** or **-ri.a** (-ree.uh) **1** a hall or theater for seating audiences. **2** a building containing one.

au.di.to.ry (AW.duh.tor.ee) *adj.* having to do with hearing: *Auditory nerves connect the ear to the brain; auditory voices.*

audit trail *n.* a record of transactions that can be traced from a computer output back to the original document.

auf Wie.der.se.hen (owf.VEE.dur.zay.un) *interj.* German. farewell!

au.ger (AW.gur) *n.* any of various tools for boring holes in wood, in the earth, etc.

aught (AWT) *n.* **1** a cipher; zero; ought. **2** anything: *for aught I know.*

aug.ment (awg.MENT) *v.* make or become larger: *to augment one's income with a sideline; a stream augmented by rains.* —**aug.men.ta.tion** (-TAY.shun) *n.*

au gra.tin (oh.GRAH.tin) *adj.* French. of dishes, with a light crust of bread crumbs or grated cheese: *potato au gratin; an au gratin dish, pan.*

au.gur (AW.gur) *n.* one who foretells the future; soothsayer. —*v.* **1** foretell, esp. from signs and omens. **2** be a sign of something; bode: *A long drought does not augur well for a good harvest; It augurs ill for everyone.*

au.gu.ry (AUG.yuh.ree) *n.* **-ries 1** divination. **2** a sign or omen.

au.gust (aw.GUST) *adj.* majestic: *an august personage.* —**au.gust.ly** *adv.;* **au.gust.ness** *n.*

Au.gust (AW.gust) *n.* the 8th month of the year, having 31 days: *the August sun.*

au jus (oh.ZHOO) *adj.* French. of cooked meat, served with its own juices.

auk (AWK) *n.* an oceanic bird such as the puffin: *the flightless "great auk" extinct since 1844.*

auld *adj.* Scottish. old, as in **auld lang syne** (awld.lang.zyne), the good old days.

au na.tu.rel (OH.nah.too.REL) *adj.*

French. **1** in the natural state; nude: *to pose au naturel.* **2** of food, plainly cooked: *You'll enjoy it au naturel rather than flavored.*

aunt (ANT, AHNT) *n.* one's father's or mother's sister; also **aun.tie, aun.ty** *Informal.*

au pair (oh.PAIR) **1** *adja.* having to do with a domestic arrangement for exchange of services, as a foreign student living in a French home doing light housework while going to school: *an au pair girl, program, placement agency, student.* **2** *n.* a young person in such an arrangement: *Most au pairs find the experience rewarding.*

au.ra (AW.ruh) *n.* **-ras** or **-rae** (-ree) **1** a distinctive atmosphere or quality, esp. about a person: *an aura of credibility, holiness, melancholy, mystery, permanence, power, quality.* **2** a ring or circle of light or other emission: *a glittering aura; the electrical aura around a hydroelectric station.*

au.ral (AW.rul) *adj.* of the ear: *aural comprehension, memory; an aural surgeon.* **—au.ral.ly** *adv.*

au.re.ole (AW.ree.ole) *n.* a circle of light; halo or aura.

au re.voir (oh.ruv.WAR) *n. & interj. French.* good-bye.

au.ri.cle (AW.ri.cul) *n.* **1** the external ear. **2** the earlike part of any other organ, as the upper chambers of the heart. **—au.ric.u.lar** (aw.RIK.yoo.lur) *adj.* having to do with the ear.

au.ro.ra (uh.ROR.uh) *n.* **-ras** or **-rae** (-ree) flashes of light seen in the night sky, esp. near the poles. **—au.ro.ral** (-rul) *adj.*

aurora aus.tra.lis (-aw.STRAY.lis) *n.* the aurora seen in southern regions.

aurora bo.re.al.is (-bor.ee.AL.is) *n.* the aurora of northern skies.

aus.cul.ta.tion (aw.skul.TAY.shun) *n.* a listening, esp. with a stethoscope, to the sounds of the internal organs to determine their condition.

aus.pice (AWS.pis) *n.* usu. **auspices** *pl.* patronage: *a meeting held under the auspices of the Y.M.C.A.*

aus.pi.cious (aw.SPISH.us) *adj.* having good omens; propitious: *an auspicious day for starting on a journey; an auspicious moment, occasion, sign, start; auspicious beginnings, conditions.* **—aus.pi.cious.ly** *adv.*

Aus.sie (AW.see) *n. & adj. Informal.* Australian.

aus.tere (aw.STEER) *adj.* strict and self-disciplined in manner or style: *an austere monk; an austere, unadorned style;*

aus.tere.ly *adv.* **—aus.ter.i.ty** (aw.STER.i.tee) *n.: to practice austerity.*

aus.tral (AW.strul) **1** *adj.* southern. **2** *n.* the basic money unit of Argentina.

Aus.tra.li.an (aw.STRAY.lee.un) *n. & adj.* (a person) of or from **Australia,** an island continent to the S.E. of Asia.

Aus.tri.an (AW.stree.un) *n. & adj.* (a person) of or from **Austria,** a country of C. Europe.

au.tar.chy (AW.tar.kee) *n.* **-chies** absolute sovereignty. **—au.tar.chic** (aw.TAR.kic) *adj.*

au.tar.ky (AW.tar.kee) *n.* **-kies** economic self-sufficiency. **—au.tar.kic** (aw.TAR.kic) *adj.*

au.teur (oh.TUR) *n.* the creative force behind an artistic production: *The film director, not the author of the screenplay, is seen as the real auteur of a film.*

au.then.tic (aw.THEN.tic, "TH" as in "thin") *adj.* reliable, as true to the original; genuine: *an authentic signature.* **—au.then.ti.cal.ly** *adv.*

au.then.ti.cate (au.THEN.tuh.cate) *v.* **-cates, -cat.ed, -cat.ing** prove or determine to be authentic: *a painting authenticated as genuine; adj.: an* **authenticated** *Picasso.* **—au.then.ti.ca.tion** (-CAY.shun) *n.*

au.then.tic.i.ty (au.then.TIS.i.tee) *n.* the state of being authentic: *to doubt, establish, prove, question, vouch for the authenticity of a signature.*

au.thor (AW.thur, "th" as in "thin") *n.* one who makes or originates something, esp. something written: *anonymous, classical, contemporary authors; a noted author; a prolific author of romances; a Latin author; to translate a Latin author* (= author's book); *the author of a plot.* **—***v.* be the author of something: *Shakespeare authored many plays.* **—au.thor.i.al** (aw.THOR.ee.ul) *adj.: authorial comments, responsibility, rights, tone, voice.* **—au.thor.ship** *n.*

authoring *n.* the creation of computer programs, databases, and other applications; *adja.: authoring languages, software, systems.*

au.thor.i.tar.i.an (aw.THOR.uh. TAIR.ee.un) *adj.* demanding submission to authority without regard to individual freedom: *an authoritarian government.* **—au.thor.i.tar.i.an.ism** *n.*

au.thor.i.ta.tive (aw.THOR.uh.tay.tiv) *adj.* having authority: *an authoritative source of information; an authoritative text.* **—au.thor.i.ta.tive.ly** *adv.*

au.thor.i.ty (aw.THOR.i.tee) *n.* **-ties** **1** the power or right to do something: *an order issued under the authority of a*

authorization / automaton

judge; the authority to arrest a suspect; A president speaks with authority; She is a woman of authority; Luc never abuses or oversteps his authority; to assume, defy, deny, invoke, reject, undermine, wield authority; absolute, full, legal, ministerial, parental, royal, supreme authority; to delegate authority for day-to-day government; to exercise authority over a department; The department is under her authority; Orders are issued on or by her authority; She is **in authority** (= charge) there. **2 the authorities** *pl.* government officials: Crimes have to be reported to the authorities; the civil, government, local authorities. **3** a person, institution, etc. having expert knowledge: He is the greatest living authority on the subject; He cited or invoked the dictionary as authority for his usage of the term; invoked the authority of his dictionary; a competent, irrefutable, leading, outstanding, reliable, respected, unimpeachable authority; I can tell you on good authority that he is still alive; I can assure you on the highest authority that it is so.

au.thor.i.za.tion (AW.thuh.ruh.ZAY.shun, -rye-) *n.* official permission: to give, grant, receive, revoke authorization to begin work on a project; authorization for the work to begin.

au.thor.ize (AW.thuh.rize) *v.* **-iz.es, -ized, -iz.ing** permit or allow officially: The minister has authorized the expenditure; He has authorized us to spend the money; *adj.:* We are **authorized** to do it; authorized parking; King James I's **Authorized Version** of the Bible.

au.tism (AW.tiz.um) *n.* a mental disorder of children that is characterized by daydreaming and other signs of withdrawal from reality. —**au.tis.tic** (aw.TIS.tic) *adj.:* Autistic children are often mute; autistic savants with outstanding skills.

auto- *comb.form.* **1** of or by oneself: autocrat, autograph. **2** automatic: autodialer, autofocus, autopilot. **3** having to do with automobiles: automaker, automotive, automan.

au.to (AW.toh) *n.* **-tos** an automobile; *adja.:* the auto industry; auto parts.

au.to.bahn (AW.toh.bahn) *n.* a German expressway.

au.to.bi.og.ra.phy (AW.toh.bye.OG.ruh.fee) *n.* **-phies** an author's own life history. —**au.to.bi.og.ra.pher** (-ruh.fur) *n.* —**au.to.bi.o.graph.i.cal** (-bye.uh.GRAF.i.cul) *adj.*

au.toch.tho.nous (aw.TOK.thuh.nus, "th" as in "thin") *adj.* of flora, fauna, minerals, etc., indigenous.

au.toc.ra.cy (aw.TOC.ruh.see) *n.* **-cies** government by an autocrat.

au.to.crat (AW.tuh.crat) *n.* one who has absolute power. —**au.to.crat.ic** (-CRAT.ic) *adj.*

au.to.graph (AW.tuh.graf) *n.* a person's signature given for its sentimental value. —*v.* put an autograph on something: Authors autograph their books for buyers; *adj.:* a movie star's **autographed** portrait.

au.to.im.mune (AW.toh.im.yoon) *adj.* having to do with the manufacture of antibodies that destroy an organism's own tissues: an autoimmune disorder, reaction, response; an autoimmune disease such as multiple sclerosis or rheumatoid arthritis. —**au.to.im.mu.ni.ty** (-YOO.ni.tee) *n.*

au.to.in.tox.i.ca.tion (AW.toh.in.tox.i.CAY.shun) *n.* poisoning by toxins produced in one's body.

au.tol.o.gous (aw.TOL.uh.gus) *adj.* derived from the same organism: autologous blood donations, transfusions, bone marrow transplants.

au.to.mak.er (AW.toh.may.kur) *n.* an automobile manufacturer; also

au.to.man (AW.toh.man).

au.to.mate (AW.tuh.mate) *v.* **-mates, -mat.ed, -mat.ing** operate or control a process, equipment, or system automatically, esp. by use of computers and robots; *adj.:* an **automated** factory, teller machine, vehicle, workplace.

au.to.mat.ic (aw.toh.MAT.ic) *adj.* **1** self-acting, as machines under set conditions: a fully automatic camera; a radio receiver with automatic frequency control; a car's automatic gearshift, transmission; an **automatic pilot** (= autopilot); an **automatic rifle** (= machine gun); a bank's **automatic teller machine** for customers to make cash withdrawals, deposits, etc. **2** machinelike in action: an automatic (= routine) annual pay raise; an automatic (= unconscious) response. —**au.to.mat.i.cal.ly** (-uh.cuh.lee) *adv.*

au.to.ma.tion (aw.tuh.MAY.shun) *n.* the automatic control and operation of a process, as by use of computers or robots: Automation replaces much unskilled labor.

au.tom.a.tism (aw.TOM.uh.tiz.um) *n.* involuntary activity, as in sleepwalking, digestion, etc.

au.tom.a.tize (aw.TOM.uh.tize) *v.* **-tiz.es, -tized, -tiz.ing** make automatic. —**au.tom.a.ti.za.tion** (-tuh.ZAY.shun, -tye-) *n.*

au.tom.a.ton (aw.TOM.uh.tun) *n.* **-tons** or **-ta** (-tuh) a robot or similar

automobile / average

self-acting mechanism.
au.to.mo.bile (aw.tuh.moh.BEEL) *n.* a self-propelled, usu. four-wheeled passenger vehicle: *to drive, operate, ride in, park an automobile;* **adj.**: *the automobile industry; automobile insurance, production, repairs, safety, sales; an automobile association, dealer, engine, policy.*
au.to.mo.tive (aw.tuh.MOH.tiv) *adj.* having to do with automobiles: *an automotive engine, part, worker; the automotive industry.*
au.to.nom.ic (aw.tuh.NOM.ic) *adj.* governing involuntary actions: *the autonomic nervous system.*
au.ton.o.my (aw.TON.uh.mee) *n.* **-mies** self-government: *to grant, seek autonomy.* —**au.ton.o.mous** (-mus) *adj.*
au.to.pi.lot (AW.toh.pye.lut) *n.* a device for automatically piloting an airplane; automatic pilot.
au.top.sy (AW.top.see) *n.* **-sies** the examination of a corpse to determine cause of death; post-mortem: *to do an autopsy on an accident victim.* —*v.* **-sies, -sied, -sy.ing** perform an autopsy on a body: *Those dead of unknown causes are usually autopsied.*
au.to.route (AW.toh.root) *n.* a French expressway.
au.to.stra.da (aw.toh.STRAH.duh) *n.* an Italian expressway.
au.to.sug.ges.tion (aw.toh.suh.JES.chun) *n.* mental suggestion to oneself; self-hypnosis.
au.tumn (AW.tum) *n.* the season between summer and winter; fall. —**au.tum.nal** (aw.TUM.nul) *adj.*
aux.il.ia.ry (awg.ZIL.yuh.ree) *adj.* having a helping, subordinate, or supplementary function: *an auxiliary organization, police force, power plant; An* **auxiliary verb** *such as "is" or "can" is used with another verb, as in "is gone" or "can go."* —*n., pl.* **-ries** an auxiliary person, institution, etc.: *an auxiliary* (= bishop) *assisting a diocesan bishop; a nursing auxiliary* (= member of a nursing group); *a women's auxiliary* (= organization of women helpers).
aux.in *n.* a plant hormone affecting growth.
a.vail (uh.VAIL) *v.* be of use or advantage; profit: *A last-minute effort will avail us nothing; It won't avail against the heavy odds we face; He bought a house to* **avail himself of** (= make use of) *a tax deduction.* —*n.* **avails** *pl.* profits: *a pimp charged with living off the avails (of prostitution).* —**to no avail, of no avail, to little avail,** or **of little avail** of no help: *The strike was of no avail in forc-*

Page 72, *User's™ Webster,* © 2000, T. M. Paikeday

ing a settlement.
a.vail.a.ble (uh.VAY.luh.bul) *adj.* obtainable: *Front row seats are not easily available to the general public; Balcony seats are readily available; He was too busy to be available* (= free) *for an interview; He couldn't make himself available* (to be interviewed). —**a.vail.a.bil.i.ty** (-BIL.i.tee) *n.*
av.a.lanche (AV.uh.lanch) *n.* a massive descent of loose earth, snow, or rock from a mountain: *The skiers were buried under an avalanche; an avalanche of mail from an enthusiastic public.* —*v.* overwhelm or bombard: *The Minister was avalanched with questions from reporters.*
a.vant-garde (ah.vahnt.GARD) *n.* the front line or vanguard of a movement, esp. in the arts: *the German avant-garde;* **adj.**: *an avant-garde art form, idea, painter.* Also **a.vant.garde.** —**a.vant-gar.dist** or **a.vant.gar.dist** *n.*
av.a.rice (AV.uh.ris) *n.* greed for money combined with miserliness: *the avarice of a usurer.* —**av.a.ri.cious** (-RISH.us) *adj.*: *an avaricious moneylender.*
a.vast (uh.VAST) *interj.* [nautical use] away!
av.a.tar (AV.uh.tar) *n.* in Hinduism, a god's incarnation in human or animal form: *Eve is an avatar of honesty.*
a.vaunt (uh.VAWNT) *interj. Archaic.* away!
Ave Maria (AH.vay.muh.REE.uh) *n.* the Hail Mary.
a.venge (uh.VENJ) *v.* **a.veng.es, a.venged, a.veng.ing** take revenge for a wrong or on behalf of the wronged one: *Hamlet wanted to avenge his father's murder; to avenge his father;* to avenge himself on or upon Claudius; **adj.**: *God's avenging angel; an avenging force.* —**a.ven.ger** *n.*
av.e.nue (AV.uh.new) *n.* **1** a street, usu. a wide one: *a tree-lined avenue; He lives on Bernard Avenue.* **2** an approach: *to explore every avenue or all avenues to a peaceful settlement.*
a.ver (uh.VUR) *v.* **a.vers, a.verred, a.verr.ing** *Formal.* assert confidently.
av.er.age (AV.uh.rij) *n.* the arithmetic mean: *To calculate* or *work out the average of three numbers, you add them up and divide the sum by 3; 4 is the average of 1, 3, and 8; She is well* **above average** (= above the ordinary level of achievement) *in her class; She has an A average in all subjects; Our car uses 7L of gas per 100 km* **on the** or **on an average** (= normally). —*adj.* common or ordinary: *The average student gets a pass*

mark; *She has an above-average IQ.* —*v.* **-ag.es, -aged, -ag.ing** do, get, or come to an average: *Her pay averages $800 a week; She averages 30 hours on the job each week; Losses and gains* **average out** (= even out) *to a small profit each year.*

a.verse (uh.VURCE) *adj.* disinclined or opposed to something because of distaste or repugnance: *an austere man averse to any kind of self-indulgence.*

a.ver.sion (uh.VUR.zhun) *n.* the state of being averse; dislike: *Some people have a built-in aversion to smoking; Some take an aversion to smoking; a deep, distinct, marked aversion to certain things; TV is one of his pet aversions* (= objects of aversion).

aversion therapy *n.* a method of treatment that makes a bad habit or behavior repugnant to the patient.

a.vert (uh.VURT) *v.* **1** turn away: *The child averted her eyes from the scary picture.* **2** prevent a danger or misfortune: *A strike was averted at the last moment.*

A.ves.tan (uh.VES.tun) **1** *adj.* having to do with **Avesta,** the Zoroastrian scriptures. **2** *n. & adj.* (having to do with) the Old Iranian language of the Avesta.

a.vi.an (AY.vee.un) *adj.* of birds: *avian flight; an avian enthusiast, paradise.*

a.vi.ar.y (AY.vee.air.ee) *n.* **-ries 1** a bird cage. **2** a house for birds, as in a zoo.

a.vi.a.tion (ay.vee.AY.shun) *n.* flying as an art, science, or industry: *civil, military aviation;* **Aviation medicine** *deals with illnesses peculiar to flyers and astronauts.*

a.vi.a.tor (AY.vee.ay.tur) *n.* an airplane pilot; *adj.: green wraparound aviator sunglasses; aviator jackets.* —**a.vi.a.trix** (-AY.trix), **-tri.ces** *fem.*

av.id (AV.id) *adj.* eager to have and enjoy more and more of something: *an avid golfer; an avid reader of romances; Midas was avid* (= greedy) *for gold.* —**av.id.ly** *adv.* —**a.vid.i.ty** (uh.VID.i.tee) *n.*

a.vi.on.ics (ay.vee.ON.ics) *n.pl.* [takes *sing. v.*] electronics applied to aviation and astronautics. —**a.vi.on.ic** *adj.*

av.o.ca.do (av.uh.CAD.oh) *n.* **-dos** or **does** a greenish, pear-shaped tropical fruit, its color, or the tree bearing it.

av.o.ca.tion (av.uh.CAY.shun) *n.* a side occupation or hobby pursued with dedication. —**av.o.ca.tion.al** *adj.*

a.void (uh.VOID) *v.* keep away from something harmful or undesirable: *Drive on the right to avoid collisions; to avoid colliding with oncoming traffic;* *There are loopholes for avoiding taxes without having to evade them; She avoids fatty foods* **like the plague** (*Informal for* totally). —**a.void.a.ble** *adj.*; **a.void.a.bly** *adv.* —**a.void.ance** (-unce) *n.*

av.oir.du.pois (av.ur.duh.POIZ) *n.* **1** the weight system based on pounds and ounces; *adj.: avoirdupois pounds; 500 pounds avoirdupois.* **2** *Informal.* one's weight: *a man of great moral avoirdupois.*

a.vouch (uh.VOWCH) *v.* vouch for.

a.vow (uh.VOW) *v.* acknowledge openly; admit with assurance in the face of hostility: *He avows himself (to be) an animal rights activist;* **adja.:** *He's an* **avowed** *animal rights activist; his avowed admiration, commitment, goal, intention, purpose.* —**a.vow.al** (-ul) *n.* —**a.vow.ed.ly** (-id.lee) *adv.*

a.vun.cu.lar (uh.VUNK.yuh.lur) *adj.* characteristic of an uncle: *his avuncular manner.*

aw *interj.* expressing disappointment, regret, etc.: *Aw, come on! Aw shucks!*

a.wait (uh.WAIT) *v.* wait for a person or thing: *I await your reply;* *adj. & cpd: an eagerly* **awaited** *announcement; one of the most keenly awaited trials; the much-awaited publication; a long-awaited wedding.*

a.wake (uh.WAKE) *adj.* **1** roused from sleep: *He's fully awake; wide awake.* **2** alert or aware: *a new recruit who is awake to his duties; the alpha rhythm of the awake brain.* —*v.* **a.wakes,** *pt.* **a.woke** or **a.waked,** *pp.* **a.waked, a.woke** or **a.wok.en,** *pres.part.* **a.wak.ing** wake up; be roused: *I awoke at 6 yesterday; awoke from a sound sleep; awoke to the sound of the radio; I awoke to find everyone gone.*

a.wak.en (uh.WAY.kun) *v. pt. & pp.* **a.wak.ened** awake; wake up: *I was awakened by the alarm; My fears were awakened.*

awakening *n.* a waking up: *a rude, sudden awakening; a bugle's awakening call; the new awakening* (= awareness) *about animal rights.*

a.ward (uh.WORED) *v.* give officially on the basis of merit, as a decoration, prize, or ruling: *They award scholarships to needy students; The judge awarded custody of the children to their father.* —*n.* something awarded: *She received an award made annually by the city council; a money award; Some awards are granted on the basis of need; The fastest horse was given the highest award; Who presented the awards? an arbitration* *award* (= ruling).

a.ware (uh.WARE) **1** *adj.* conscious or having knowledge of something: *I am aware of my rights; Are you aware that you were late for work all last week? I have recently become aware of a new trend; I'm keenly, painfully, very much aware of my shortcomings.* **2** *adj.* informed: *a politically aware student; These youths are aware, well-adjusted people.*
—**a.ware.ness** *n.*

a.wash (uh.WOSH) *adjp. & adv.* being washed; flooded: *The dish was just bits of meat and vegetables awash in murky gravy; a speech awash* (= flowing) *with self-pity.*

a.way (uh.WAY) *adv.* [used after its verb] **1** at a distance from the speaker or from a place, person, etc. referred to: *Get away from the fire; Please go away;* [in exclamations] *Away with the nuisance!* **2** far: *She's away down on the list; away back in 1926.* Also **way** *Informal.* **3** on: *Time is ticking away; He's grinding away at his task.* —**adj. 1** *adjp.* distant: *Our school is only 2 km away; Lee is far away in Taiwan; The boss is away* (= gone) *on business.* **2** *adja.* away from home: *There are special football trains to away games* (played at the opponent's place, not a "home game"); *the away team.* —**do away with** get rid of; kill. —**far and away** or **out and away** very much. —**right away** or **straight away** at once: *Go home right away!*

awe (AW) *n.* a mixed emotion of fear, respect, wonder, reverence, etc., esp. as felt toward something supernatural: *The heavens inspire awe in us; Our boss is held* **in awe by** *everyone at work; The subjects stand* **in awe of** *Her Majesty.*
—*v.* **awes, awed, aw.ing** fill with awe: *a poet awed by nature's wonders; The tourists seemed awed into silence.*

a.weigh (uh.WAY) *adjp.* suspended: *With anchors aweigh, the boat put out to sea.*

awe.some (AW.sum) *adj.* **1** *Informal.* quite impressive: *His achievements are awesome.* **2** causing awe: *an awesome sight.*

awe.strick.en (AW.strick.un) or **awe.struck** *adj.* filled with awe.

aw.ful (AW.ful) *adj. Informal.* **1** terrible: *an awful crime.* **2** very bad: *his awful manners; It was an awful mistake; We feel awful about it; It's awful that we had to go through with it.* **3** very great: *an awful lot of waiting; I don't know an awful lot about computers.* —*adv. Informal.* very: *It's awful hot in here!*

aw.ful.ly (AW.fuh.lee) *adv. Informal.* very: *95°F is awfully hot; You're awfully nice.*

a.while (uh.WHILE) *adv.* for some time: *Stay awhile and have a coffee.*

a.whirl (uh.WURL) *adj. & adv.* in a whirl: *The news set the whole school awhirl with rumors.*

awk.ward (AWK.wurd) *adj.* **1** clumsy; graceless: *awkward movements; He is awkward with mechanical tools.* **2** uncomfortable or embarrassing: *an awkward posture; an awkward moment, silence; a lawyer dealing with awkward facts; found herself in an awkward position; She felt awkward dealing with that client.*
—**awk.ward.ly** *adv.;* **awk.ward.ness** *n.*

awl *n.* a pointed tool for piercing holes in leather, wood, etc.

awn *n.* bristle or bristles on the head of a grass or cereal grain; beard: *Barley, oats, etc. have awns; adj.: Some fruits and leaf-tips are also* **awned** (= having bristles).

awn.ing *n.* an overhanging shelter, often of canvas, above a door or window.

awoke, awoken a *pt. & pp.* of AWAKE.

A.WOL (AY.wall) **1** *adj.* absent without official leave, esp. from the military: *to go AWOL; an AWOL marine.* **2** **awol** *n.* one who goes AWOL.

a.wry (uh.RYE) *adjp. & adv.* askew; amiss: *Her life was awry; schemes that go awry.*

ax *n., pl.* **ax.es** (AK.siz) a tool with a heavy cutting blade fitted parallel to the handle: *He came out swinging an ax; A lumberjack wields an ax.* —**get the ax** *Informal.* be terminated: *The employees and the project got the ax.* —**have an ax to grind** *Informal.* have a private, selfish motive. —*v.* **ax.es, axed, ax.ing** cut, get rid of, etc. with an ax: *The lumberjack axed down the tree; Many TV shows have been axed* (= canceled) *because of poor ratings.* Also **axe.**

ax.el (AK.sul) *n.* in figure skating, a jump executed with 1½ turns in the air: *double axels; triple axels.*

axes *pl.* of AX, AXE, or AXIS.

ax.i.al (AK.see.ul) *adj.* having to do with an axis: *axial symmetry; an* **axial skeleton** (of the head and trunk alone); **ax.i.al.ly** *adv.*

ax.i.om (AK.see.um) *n.* a self-evident truth or principle: *Everyone accepts the axiom that the whole equals the sum of its parts; Change is an axiom of the fashion world.* —**ax.i.o.mat.ic** (-uh.MAT.ic) *adj.*

ax.is (AK.sis) *n., pl.* **ax.es** (AK.seez) **1** a straight line around which an object

rotates or is symmetrical: *The Earth rotates on its axis.* **2** a reference line: *the x and y axes of a graph.*
ax.le (AK.sul) *n.* **1** a shaft that turns with a wheel or wheels attached to it. **2** a fixed shaft with bearings at either end for wheels: *an automobile's axis; the axle tree* (= shaft with wheels at either end) *of a wagon or carriage.*
a.ya.tol.lah (ah.yuh.TOL.luh) *n.* **1** a title for a distinguished Muslim clergyman. **2** a powerful leader.
ay (EYE) *adv. & n.* same as AYE.
aye *adv.* **1** (AY) *Poetic.* forever. **2** (EYE) yes: *Aye, aye, sir!* —**n.** (EYE) a yes vote or voter: *The ayes have it.*
a.zal.ea (uh.ZAIL.yuh) *n.* any of a group of flowering shrubs of the heath family.
az.i.muth (AZ.uh.muth) *n.* the distance in degrees from due north or south to an object, usu. measured clockwise along the horizon. —**az.i.muth.al** (-MUTH.ul) *adj.*
Az.tec (AZ.tek) *n.* (a member of) a highly advanced people in Mexico before the Spanish invasion; also, their language; *adj.: Aztec culture, embroidery, emperors, gods, myths, temples; the Aztec language.* —**Az.tec.an** *adj.*
az.ure (AZH.ur) *n.* sky-blue: *the azure sky.*

.... **B, b** ....

B or **b** (BEE) *n.* **B's** or **b's 1** the second letter of the English Alphabet. **2** second in a series, esp. second highest or best: *He received a B (grade) in math.*
B.A. *n.* **B.A.'s** the degree of Bachelor of Arts or one holding it: *He took a history B.A.; She's a B.A. in music.*
baa (BAH) *v.* **baas, baaed** (BAHD), **baa.ing** bleat, as a sheep does.
—*n.* the bleating of a sheep.
bab.ble (BAB.ul) *v.* **bab.bles, bab.bled, bab.bling 1** talk very freely, foolishly, or indistinctly: *to babble a secret.* **2** murmur, as a baby does: *He babbled something in her ear; adj.: a babbling brook.*
—*n.* such talk or murmur: *a baby's babble; a confused babble; the incessant babble heard at a bazaar.* —**bab.bler** *n.*
babe *n.* **1** a baby: *a babe in arms.* **2** *Slang* [intimate male use] a girl or woman as a sex object. —**babe in the woods** an innocent or helpless person.
ba.bel (BAY.bul, BAB.ul) *n.* a noisy confusion: *He tried to make himself heard above the babel of voices; a babel of dialects.*
ba.boon (ba.BOON) *n.* a big monkey with a muzzle like a dog's.

ba.bush.ka (buh.BOOSH.kuh, short or long "OO") *n.* **1** a usu. triangular head scarf that is tied under the chin. **2** in Russia, an elderly grandmother.
ba.by (BAY.bee) *n.* **-bies 1** an infant: *Only women can have babies; A pregnant woman normally carries a baby to term or carries a baby for nine months; A premature baby is not a full-term baby; Doctors and midwives deliver babies; a new-born baby; Mothers nurse babies, but anyone may change them* (= change their diapers); *Babies are weaned from breast to bottle in the first few months; She sang "Rock-a-bye baby!" and lulled him to sleep in the cradle; Babies babble, burp, coo, crawl, creep, drool, teethe; Some babies are stillborn; Test-tube babies are the latest.* **2** the youngest of a group: *the baby of the family.* **3** a childish person: *You're some baby!* **4** [used in a familiar way to address or to refer to someone] *Slang.* a person: *You've come a long way, baby!* **5** *Slang* [often offensive] sex object; babe. **6** an object of special care or concern: *The dictionary project is my baby.* —**adj. 1** having to do with babies: *baby clothes, shoes.* **2** very young or small: *a baby bird, monkey, seal.*
—*v.* treat with excessive care: *to baby a new car.* —**ba.by.hood** (BAY.bee.hood, short "oo") *n.* —**ba.by.ish** *adj.*
baby beef *n.* beef from a one- or two-year-old calf.
baby bonding *n.* emotional union between mother and baby that is believed to begin soon after birth.
baby boom *n.* the sudden increase in the birth rate experienced in the late 1940s as a result of veterans rejoining their families after World War II.
baby boomer *n.* a member of a social and economic group composed of those born during the baby boom and noted for their materialistic lifestyles and habits in the 1980s, with yuppies forming the upper crust.
baby buggy (or **carriage**) *n.* a buggy for pushing infants in.
baby bust *n.* the decline in the birth rate experienced in the 1970s because of changing social attitudes and economic conditions.
baby face *n.* a face like a baby's.
baby grand piano *n.* the smallest grand piano, only five to six feet (1.5 to 1.8 m) long.
Bab.y.lo.ni.an (bab.ee.LOH.nee.un) *adj.* of or like **Babylon,** the wealthy and luxurious capital of the ancient Mesopotamian empire: *Babylonian splendor.*
ba.by.sit (BAY.bee.sit) *v.* **-sits, -sat,**

-sit.ting look after a child while its parents are away: *Eve babysits for Mrs. Smith; babysits her two children;* **ba.by.sit.ter** *n.* Also **baby-sit, baby-sit.ter.**

baby walker *n.* a device to help a baby to walk.

bac.ca.lau.re.ate (bac.uh.LOR.ee.it) *n.* the bachelor's degree.

bac.ca.rat (BAC.uh.rah) *n.* a card game used for gambling.

bac.cha.nal (bac.uh.NAL) *n.* 1 a drunken revel, originally in honor of **Bacchus,** Greek wine god; also **bac.cha.na.li.a** (-NAY.lee.uh) *n.pl.* 2 a reveler. —**bac.cha.na.li.an** (-NAY.lee.un) *adj.*: *bacchanalian orgies.*

bach *n. Informal.* a bachelor. —*v.* **bach it** live a single life during one's spouse's absence.

bach.e.lor (BACH.uh.lur) *n.* 1 an unmarried man: *a confirmed bachelor; eligible bachelors.* 2 one who has received an undergraduate degree: *Bachelor of Arts; Bachelor of Engineering; She's working on her bachelor's (degree).* 3 an apartment in which the living room doubles as the bedroom; also **bachelor apartment.** —**bach.e.lor.hood** (short "oo") *n.*

bach.e.lor.ette (bach.uh.luh.RET) *n.* 1 a smaller-size bachelor apartment. 2 an unmarried young woman living by herself.

bachelor girl *n. Informal* [offensive to women] an independent single young woman; career woman.

bachelor pad *n. Informal.* a bachelor's living quarters.

bachelor party *n.* a party for a bridegroom to mark the end of his bachelorhood.

ba.cil.lus (buh.SIL.us) *n., pl.* **-cil.li** (-SIL.eye) a bacterium, esp. one that is rod-shaped or causes disease. —**ba.cil.la.ry** (BAS.i.lair.ee) *adj.*

back *n.* 1 the rear part of the human body or the corresponding part in animals: *my aching back; seated on a horse's back; a stab in the back; She was lying on her back; At the end of February we say we have broken the back of* (= been through most of) *the winter; He broke his back* (= worked very hard) *to finish writing the book on time.* 2 anything that supports or covers the back: *the back of a chair, dress, picture frame.* 3 a part that is behind the front: *the back of the head; the back of a book, newspaper, postcard, spoon; a room at the back of the house; He was seated in the back* (= back seat) *of the car; I know it like the back of my hand* (= thoroughly). 4 a player stationed in the backfield. —**(in the) back of** *Informal.* behind: *Stand back of the line; a tennis court in the back of the house; The experience remained in the back of my mind* (= in the subconscious). —**behind one's back** in one's absence or without one's knowledge. —**be on one's back** harass one: *He complains that the boss is on his back all day.* —**get off one's back** stop harassing one: *Get off my back, will you?* —**get** (or **put**) **one's back up** make (or become) uncooperative or angry. —**have one's back to the wall** be in a desperate situation. —**on one's back** sick in bed. —*adj.* 1 in, at, or toward the rear: *a back alley, fence, flip, room, shed; back country.* 2 of the past: *a periodical's back issues* (that are no longer on sale); *back pay, rent* (that is owing). —*adv.* 1 at or toward the rear: *Stand back!* 2 in reserve or restraint: *Hold back your best card.* 3 in, at, or toward an earlier time, state, or position: *Bring the book back; It happened back in 1926; way back in 1910; Things are back to normal after the strike* (= as they were before the strike). 4 in return: *to pay back a loan.* —**back and forth** to and fro: *to drive, fly, go, shuttle, travel back and forth;* *n.*: *There's going to be a lot of back and forth on this project;* *adja.*: *a back-and-forth dialog, flow of ideas.* —**go back on one's promise** or **word** fail to keep one's promise. —*v.* 1 move backward or to the rear: *to back (a car) into a parking space; to back a car out of a garage.* 2 bet on; support: *to back a candidate; to back the right horse.* 3 form the back of or provide backing for something: *High cliffs backed the beach.* 4 have the back lying opposite to a place: *Our house backs onto a park.* —**back and fill** 1 of automobiles, go back and forth in an effort to get out when bogged down in snow or mud. 2 *Informal.* be changing one's mind; be undecided. —**back away** (or **off**) withdraw: *They backed away without starting a fight; "Back off," she shouted to her attacker; He decided to back off from his initial demands.* —**back down** withdraw from a stand one has taken. —**back east** in or to the eastern part of the country, as viewed from the West. —**back out** withdraw: *to back out of a commitment.* —**back up** 1 support: *Jim backed up her story; He backed her up.* 2 accumulate and clog: *The drain is backed up.* 3 move in reverse: *He backed up to the* loading dock; *The teacher backed up and repeated the earlier part of the lesson.* **4** make a backup copy: *to back up a disk, file, program.*

back.ache *n.* a dull pain in the lower back: *a nagging, persistent backache.*

back bench *n.* one of the seats in a parliament for members who are not in the front benches occupied by the cabinet or shadow cabinet: *a career on the back benches; applause from the back benches;* **adj***.: a* **back-bench** *M.P.* —**back-bencher** *n.*

back.bite *v.* **-bites, -bit, -bit.ten, -bit.ing** speak ill of someone who is absent. —**back.bit.er** *n.*

back.board *n.* in basketball, the upright rebound board behind the basket.

back.bone *n.* **1** the spinal column. **2** courage or resolution: *to have the backbone to stand up to a bully.* **3** main support: *Customers are the backbone of a business.*

back.breaking (BACK.bray.king) *adj.* of work, very tiring.

back burner *n.* usu. **on the back burner,** in a position of low priority.

back.check.ing (BAC.chek.ing) *n.* in hockey and lacrosse, the harrying of an advancing opposing player by a forward while backing away to defend the goal.

back country *n.* unsettled area behind a settled one.

back.date *v.* **-dates, -dat.ed, -dat.ing** put a date on a document that is earlier than the actual date: *The contract was backdated to January 1;* **adj***.: a* **backdated** *check.*

back door *n.* a rear entrance: *an open back door; to get in by* or *through the back door (using unfair influence).* —**back-door** *adj.* **1** by the rear of a building: *a back-door exit.* **2** indirect, devious, or dishonest: *back-door businesses, deals, influence.*

back.drop *n.* **1** a usu. painted cloth hung at the back of a stage. **2** background: *Recent events provide a backdrop for the present situation; the present situation seen against the backdrop of recent events.*

back.er *n.* a supporter of a candidate, horse in a race, project, etc.: *the financial backer of a project.*

back.field *n.* the football players or their positions behind the line of scrimmage.

back.fire *n.* **1** a fire set to check a forest or prairie fire by burning off its fuel. **2** an improperly timed fuel explosion, as in an automobile engine.

—*v.* **-fires, -fired, -fir.ing** happen in a way opposite to what is intended: *a plan that backfired.*

back flip *n.* a backward somersault or dive.

back.gam.mon (BAC.gam.un) *n.* a board game with counters moved according to throws of the dice.

back.ground *n.* **1** ground or setting behind something, as distant scenery in a painting or music for a movie: *music to serve as an appropriate background for the performance; a leader who likes to stay* **in the background** (= in a less visible or important place); *The politician was speaking to reporters* **on background** (= for information only, not to be quoted);* **adj***.: background knowledge, information, music, noise.* **2** conditions that influence something: *She has a good family background; academic, broad, cultural, educational, historical, political, religious backgrounds; He has no background* (= experience) *for the job; the background of* (= conditions existing before) *the war.*

back.ground.er (BAC.ground.ur) *n.* a report or briefing for giving background information.

back.hand *adj.* with the hand in the position opposite to the usual one: *a backhand stroke in tennis (with the back of the hand forward); backhand writing (slanting to the left);* **adv***.: He returned the ball backhand; She hit him backhand across the face.* —*n.* a backhand stroke or writing: *a tennis player with a devastating two-handed backhand.*

back.hand.ed (BACK.han.did) *adj. & adv.* **1** backhand. **2** having an opposite intent; sarcastic: *a backhanded apology, compliment.*

back.hoe *n.* an excavating machine consisting of a tractor with a bucket attached in front that is drawn toward the machine.

backing *n.* **1** support or strengthening. **2** material used for this.

back.lash *n.* hostile reaction: *the backlash against the new taxes.*

back.log *n.* a piling up of something that should have been attended to, as work: *to accumulate, build up, reduce a backlog; a growing backlog of orders waiting to be filled.* —*v.* **-logs, -logged, -log.ging** accumulate.

back number *n. Informal.* a person or thing that is out of date, as an old issue of a periodical.

back order *n.* a purchase order waiting to be filled. —**back-order** *v.*

back.pack *n.* a knapsack, esp. on a

backpedal / bad

metal frame. —*v.* hike with or carry in a backpack; **back.pack.er** *n.*
back.ped.al (BACK.ped.ul) *v.* **1** pedal backward. **2** retreat: *to backpedal on a promise.*
back.seat *n.* a secondary position, as a seat in the back of a vehicle: *a distinguished Canadian who won't take a backseat to anyone else in the world.*
backseat driver *n.* a passenger who offers unwanted advice to the driver.
back.side *n.* **1** the buttocks: *a kick in the backside; Get off your backside.* **2** the back or rear: *the backside of the building.*
back.slap.per (BACK.slap.ur) *n.* an effusively friendly person.
back.slash *n.* a short stroke [\] slanted in the direction opposite that of a slash, used in computer commands.
back.slide *v.* **-slides,** *pp.* **-slid** or **-slid.den, -slid.ing** fall back into lax ways, esp. morally. —**back.slid.er** *n.*
back.space *v.* **-spac.es, -spaced, -spac.ing** move one space backward on a typewriter or computer display.
back.spin *n.* a spin that makes a ball slow down or bounce backward.
back-stabbing *n.* discrediting a person by underhand means; also **back stabbing.**
back.stage *adv.* **1** in or to the area behind the stage, not seen by the audience: *He went backstage to congratulate the actors.* **2** in private; behind the scenes: *What goes on backstage is anybody's guess.*
back.stairs *adj.a.* sordid and secret: *backstairs intrigue.*
back.stop *n. Sports.* a fence or screen to stop balls from getting away.
back.stretch *n.* the racetrack straightaway opposite the homestretch.
back.stroke *n.* a style of swimming on one's back: *to do* or *swim the backstroke.*
back talk *n.* an impudent retort.
back-to-back *adj. & adv.* **1** with the backs against each other: *Before a duel, the opponents stand back-to-back; to photocopy back-to-back* (= on both sides of the paper). **2** *Informal.* one after another: *We had ten wins back-to-back; exhausted from back-to-back interviews with job applicants.*
back.track *v.* **1** go back the way one came. **2** retreat; back down.
back.up *n.* **1** a backing up of a flow: *a backup of sewage, traffic.* **2** support or substitute: *extra equipment as backup in case of a breakdown; She used to sing backup for him;* **adj.:** *a backup airplane, computer, copy, disk, plan, power supply.*
back.ward (BACK.wurd) *adv.* **1** to the back or past; with the rear leading. **2** in the wrong way; to a worse condition: *He bends* or *leans over backward* (= tries extraordinarily hard) *to please his customers.* Also **back.wards.** —*adj.* **1** turned toward the back in time or space: *a backward flow, glance, journey, look, step.* **2** slow in development: *a backward region, student; He is backward in his studies but not backward* (= shy or diffident) *in speaking his mind.* —**backwards and forwards** to and fro.
—**back.ward.ness** *n.*
back.wash *n.* **1** air or water thrown back, as by a propeller or oars. **2** a resulting situation; aftermath.
back.wa.ter (BACK.wot.ur) *n.* **1** a body of water without a current or flow, as a lagoon or inlet. **2** an unprogressive area: *a cultural backwater of civilization.*
back.woods *n.pl.* **1** thinly populated forest land. **2** a remote and backward area. —**back.woods.man** *n.* **-men.**
back.yard *n.* an area at the back of one's house.
ba.con (BAY.cun) *n.* cured and smoked hog flesh: *crisp, lean, smoked bacon; a rasher of bacon; bacon and eggs for breakfast.* —**bring home the bacon** *Informal.* **1** provide for one's family. **2** win the prize; succeed. —**save one's bacon** *Informal.* escape danger or trouble.
bac.te.ri.a (bac.TEER.ee.uh) *n.pl.* microscopic organisms that cause disease, fermentation, etc.; **bac.te.ri.al** (-ee.ul) *adj.*: *a bacterial canker.*
—**bac.te.ri.um** *sing.*
bac.te.ri.ol.o.gy (bac.TEER.ee.OL. uh.jee) *n.* the study of bacteria; **bac.te.ri.ol.o.gist** *n.* —**bac.te.ri.o.log.ic** (-ee.uh.LOJ.ic) or **bac.te.ri.o.log.i.cal** *adj.*
bac.te.ri.o.phage (bac.TEER.ee.uh.faij) *n.* a virus that kills bacteria.
bad *adj.* **1** *comp.* **worse** (WURSE), *superl.* **worst** (WURST) not good; having undesirable qualities: *bad language, news; bad plumbing (that leaks); Smoking is bad* (= unhealthy); *an egg gone bad* (= rotten); *He looks bad* (= sick); *I feel bad* (= sorry) *about it; Too bad* (= unfortunate) *you lost; a bad* (= severe) *cold; a* **bad boy** (= boy who misbehaves); *a* **bad check** *(that bounces); a* **bad debt** *(that cannot be collected);* **bad ice** *(that is thin or melting).* **2** (pronounced with lengthened vowel) **bad.der, bad.dest** *Slang.* excellent: *the baddest man on earth.* —**not bad** *Informal.* not unsatisfactory; fairly good; also **not half bad** or **not so bad.**

—*adv.* [nonstandard] badly: *He wasn't hurt that bad in the accident.* —*n.* **the bad** what is bad: *to take the bad with the good.* —**go from bad to worse** get worse from day to day. —**in bad** *Informal.* in disfavor with someone. —**to the bad** *Informal.* to or in a bad condition: *a good man who went to the bad; He was put to the bad* (= put in debt) *by his generosity toward friends; He was about $1 million to the bad* (= in debt). —**bad.ness** *n.*
bad blood *n.* ill will.
bad.die or **bad.dy** (BAD.ee) *n.* **bad.dies** *Informal.* a really bad guy; villain.
bade (BAD) a *pt.* of BID.
badge (BAJ) *n.* an emblem or device worn to show one's membership or rank: *a police officer's badge; a badge* (= symbol) *of slavery such as the language of the conqueror.*
badg.er (BAJ.ur) *n.* a digging animal of the weasel family with white markings on its head. —*v.* pester or torment without ceasing: *She was badgered with questions by reporters; He was badgered into joining the party.*
bad.i.nage (bad.i.NAZH) *n.* banter.
bad.lands *n.pl.* dry barren land eroded into strange shapes: *the badlands of South Dakota.*
bad.ly (BAD.lee) *adv.* **1** in an undesirable manner: *He behaved badly.* **2** very much: *a badly needed book.* **3** [nonstandard] bad: *I feel badly about it.*
bad.min.ton (BAD.min.tun) *n.* a racket game in which a shuttlecock or "birdie" is hit back and forth over a net.
bad-mouth *v. Informal.* speak badly of a person or thing.
bad news *n. Informal.* a person, situation, event, etc. that is unpleasant or unwelcome.
Bae.de.ker (BAY.duh.kur) *n.* a guidebook for travelers.
baf.fle (BAF.ul) *v.* **baf.fles, baf.fled, baf.fling** frustrate by confusing or puzzling: *a mystery that completely baffles me; adj.: a baffling illness, question, spectacle; something of a baffling nature.* —*n.* a device for slowing or redirecting the flow of air, water, etc. —**baf.fle.ment** *n.*
baf.fle.gab (BAF.ul.gab) *n. Informal.* jargon used by bureaucrats, academics, etc., as when a nanny paid by the government was described as "a member of the staff who interfaces with the children in a habitual way."
bag *n.* **1** a container of paper, cloth, etc., usu. one that can be opened and closed: *a bag of sugar; a brown-bag or brown-paper bag; duffel, kit, flight, garment, grab, grocery bags; overnight, paper, plastic, shopping, sleeping, tea, tote bags; She uses a punching bag for working out her frustrations; He packed his bags* (= suitcases, etc.) *and left; He was told to clear out bag and baggage* (= with all his possessions); *Check your bags* (= luggage) *at the check-in counter.* **2** the amount of game shot or caught. —**in the bag** *Informal.* assured of success; sewed up. —*v.* **bags, bagged, bag.ging** **1** put into a bag or bags. **2** shoot or catch game. —**bag.ger** *n.*
bag.a.telle (bag.uh.TEL) *n.* **1** a trifle, esp. a short musical composition. **2** a board game played with a cue and balls.
ba.gel (BAY.gul) *n.* a hard, leavened, ring-shaped roll.
bag.gage (BAG.ij) *n.* **1** suitcases, personal effects, etc. that one travels with; luggage: *to check baggage before boarding; carry-on baggage; excess baggage.* **2** burden or impediment: *a speech loaded with patronizing baggage; the psychological baggage of preconceived ideas.*
bag.gy (BAG.ee) *adj.* **bag.gi.er, bag.gi.est** sagging or bulging like a bag: *baggy jeans, trousers; a bit baggy in the seat.* —*n.* **baggies** a small bag.
bag lady *n.* a homeless, usu. elderly woman who carries her possessions in a shopping bag.
bag.man (BAG.mun) *n.* **-men 1** a traveling salesman or fund-raiser. **2** *Informal.* a racketeer who collects money, pays out bribes, etc.
bagn.io (BAN.yoh) *n.* a brothel.
bag.pipe *n.* usu. **bag.pipes,** *pl.* a wind instrument consisting of a bag with pipes attached to it: *to play the bagpipes.* —**bag.pip.er** *n.*
ba.guette (ba.GET) *n.* a gem cut into a long rectangle.
bah *interj.* expressing contempt, disgust, etc.
Ba.ha.mi.an (buh.HAY.mee.un) *n. & adj.* (a person) of or from the **Bahamas,** a Commonwealth country of islands S.E. of Florida.
bail *n.* **1** a scoop, bucket, etc. for bailing water out of a boat. **2** the semicircular handle of a kettle or pail. **3** a security of money posted to free someone from jail until trial: *Carl was granted bail; The bail was set at $50,000; He was set free on a $50,000 bail; was freed or released on bail; Friends had put up* or *posted* or *provided* or *stood bail for him; Others were denied bail; They had*

trouble making or raising bail; No one would go bail for them; However, Carl jumped or skipped bail and failed to appear in court; He forfeited bail. —v. **1** grant bail to someone. **2** release on bail. —**bail out 1** get someone released on bail. **2** clear a boat of water by dipping: *They bailed the water out of the boat.* **3** parachute from an airplane: *The pilot bailed out of the plane before it crashed.* —**bail.a.ble** (-luh.bul) *adj.*: *a bailable offense, person.*

bail.ee (bay.LEE) *n.* a person to whom property is entrusted as bail.

bail.iff (BAY.lif) *n.* **1** an official who assists in a courtroom. **2** a sheriff's assistant.

bail.i.wick (BAY.lee.wick) *n.* **1** a bailiff's jurisdiction. **2** one's area of expertise or activity: *She doesn't accept work that is outside her bailiwick.*

bail.or *n.* a person who puts up property or money as bail.

bail.out *n.* financial aid provided to save a person, organization, or country from bankruptcy.

bails.man *n.* -**men** a bondsman.

bait *n.* a lure or enticement, as food placed in a trap or on a hook to catch animals or fish: *a tempting bait;* to hold out, nibble at, offer, put out, set out bait; to rise to the bait; to swallow or take the bait. —v. **1** put bait in or on something: *to bait a hook, trap.* **2** torment mercilessly for fun, as in "bearbaiting." —**bait.er** *n.*

bait and switch *n.* a sales tactic of attracting customers with a low-priced item in the hope of selling higher-priced goods.

bake *v.* **bakes, baked, bak.ing** cook, dry, or harden by dry heat, as in an oven or kiln: *to bake a cake for the party; bricks baked in the sun; a can of (Boston) baked beans* (= baked white dry beans with salt pork in tomato sauce). —*n.* a social event at which baked food is usu. served, as a clambake.

bak.er (BAY.kur) *n.* one who bakes and sells bread, rolls, cakes, etc.

baker's dozen *n.* a dozen plus one.

bak.er.y (BAY.kuh.ree) *n.* -**ries** where baked goods are made or sold; also **bake.shop.**

baking powder *n.* a leavening agent containing baking soda, starch, and acid.

baking soda *n.* a sodium compound used as a leavening agent.

bal.a.lai.ka (bal.uh.LYE.kuh) *n.* a guitarlike Russian three-stringed instrument with a triangular body.

bal.ance (BAL.unce) *n.* **1** a weighing instrument, usu. one supported in the center with pans hanging on either side: *His future hangs* **in the balance** (= is uncertain). **2** a state in which both sides are equal: *The rider tried to keep his balance; He lost his balance and fell; He was thrown off balance; He couldn't recover his balance before falling;* to strike a balance between being harsh and lenient; *Why disturb or upset the delicate balance that exists in the community? The books are* **in balance** (= Debit equals credit); *a system of checks and balances* (= controls) *for the even distribution of power.* **3** harmony or proportion: *a picture with a good balance of weights and colors.* **4** remainder or difference: *I paid $55 of the $100 due and she paid the balance* (= $45); *The last line of the statement shows your bank balance; a country's foreign-trade balance* or *balance of trade.* —**off balance** unsteady: *The boat got off balance and turned over; He was caught off balance* (= unprepared) *and failed the test.* —**on balance** all in all: *On balance, it was a fair deal.* —v. **-anc.es, -anced, -anc.ing** make, come, or be in a state of equilibrium: *He balanced the cup on his knee; to balance a budget so that there is neither surplus nor deficit; to balance the pros and cons* (= weigh the relative merits) *of an issue; The gains balance* (= equal) *the losses;* **adj.**: *a more balanced view of things; A* **balanced diet** *has the right kinds and quantities of foods; a well-balanced meal; the* **balancing act** *of finding more money without raising taxes.*

balance beam *n.* a horizontal beam on upright posts on which gymnasts perform.

balance of power *n.* power to upset a balance: *In a minority government, a third party may hold the balance of power by aligning itself with one or the other of the two leading parties; the strategic balance of power in the Middle East; The* **balance of terror** *between East and West because of the atomic threat helped keep the peace.*

balance of trade or **trade balance** *n.* the difference of value between imports and exports: *The trade balance is favorable if exports exceed imports.*

balance sheet *n.* a financial statement showing assets, liabilities, and net worth.

balance wheel *n.* a wheel that regulates the movement of a clock or watch.

bal.co.ny (BAL.cuh.nee) *n*. **-nies 1** an overhanging gallery in a theater, auditorium, etc.; *adj*.: *a balconied library.* **2** an outside projecting platform with a railing around it; *adj.*: *a balconied apartment.*

bald (BAWLD) *adj*. **1** without the usual covering, esp. of hair on the head or something resembling it: *I'm bald under my hat; A bald tire has no tread left; A bald cypress tree is a conifer that loses its leaves unlike other conifers that are evergreens; The bald eagle has a white head; the treeless bald prairie.* **2** plain or blunt: *a bald statement, style of writing.* —**bald.ly** *adv*.; **bald.ness** *n*.

bal.der.dash (BAWL.dur.dash) *n*. nonsense.

balding *adj*. becoming bald: *He's 25 and balding; the balding head of a balding man; n.: a treatment to reverse balding.*

bale *n*. a large package of goods or material, compressed and bound: *a bale of cotton, hay.* —*v*. **bales, baled, bal.ing** make cotton, hay, newspaper, etc. into bales. —**bal.er** *n*.

ba.leen (buh.LEEN) *n*. whalebone.

bale.ful *adj*. threatening evil; ominous: *a baleful glance, influence, look, stare.* —**bale.ful.ly** *adv*.

Ba.li.nese (bal.uh.NEEZ) *n*., *sing. & pl.* a person of or from **Bali**, an island in Indonesia. Also *adj*.

balk (BAWK) *v*. **1** refuse to proceed: *Some horses balk at the slightest obstacle; When it was time to do as promised, she balked; He balked at the idea of a pay cut.* **2** frustrate by putting obstacles in the way: *The police balked the efforts of the gang.* —*n*. in baseball, an illegal hesitation by the pitcher.

Bal.kan (BAWL.kun) *adj*. having to do with **the Balkans**, the countries in the Balkan Peninsula in S.E. Europe comprising Bulgaria, Greece, Albania, Yugoslavia, etc.

balk.y *adj*. **balk.i.er, -i.est** that tends to balk; reluctant: *a balky banker, horse, mule; balky brakes, engines, pedals.*

ball (BAWL) *n*. **1** a usu. round object, esp. one used in sports: *a golf ball; tennis ball; a cue ball used in billiards; When in danger, the hedgehog curls up in a ball; a sterile absorbent cotton ball; a fortune-teller's crystal ball; to bat, bounce, catch, drop, fumble a ball; A ball is dead when it has ceased to bounce; a ball of string; the ball (= sole) of the foot.* **2** a game played with a ball, esp. baseball; *adj*.: *a ball boy (fielding tennis balls); ball games such as football and tennis; a ball park, player.* **3** in baseball, a batted or pitched ball: *foul ball; fast ball; low ball.* **4** a formal dancing party: *costume, fancy-dress, inaugural, masked balls; I met her at a ball.* **5** *Informal*. a good time: *We had a ball.* —**be** or **get** or **have on the ball** *Informal*. efficient or alert: *She's really on the ball in her job; Her boss doesn't have to tell her to get on the ball; It didn't take the boss long to find out what she had on the ball* (= how good she was). —**play ball** cooperate with someone. —**start the ball rolling** begin an activity. —*v*. form into a ball. —**ball up** *Informal*. **1** ruin or spoil something organized, as a plan, project, etc. **2** confuse: *Your explanation has me all balled up.*

bal.lad (BAL.ud) *n*. **1** a narrative song in stanzas, esp. a folk song. **2** a popular love song. —**bal.lad.eer** (bal.uh.DEER) *n*. —**bal.lad.ry** *n*.

ball-and-socket joint *n*. a joint, as of the hip or shoulder, having a knoblike part fitting into a hollow.

bal.last (BAL.ust) *n*. **1** heavy material carried to stabilize a ship, aircraft, etc.: *to drop, take on ballast.* **2** crushed stone used in making concrete or to hold railroad ties in place. —*v*. load with ballast.

ball bearing *n*. **1** a bearing with small steel balls turning to reduce friction. **2** such a ball.

bal.le.ri.na (bal.uh.REE.nuh) *n*. a female ballet dancer.

bal.let (BAL.ay) *n*. an elaborate, graceful, stylized form of dance: *to dance, perform, stage a ballet; classical, folk, water ballet.* —**bal.let.ic** (ba.LET.ic) *adj*.

bal.let.o.mane (ba.LET.uh.mane) *n*. a ballet enthusiast. —**bal.let.o.ma.ni.a** (-MAY.nee.uh) *n*.

ball game *n*. a game played with a ball: *It's a (whole) new ball game (Informal for a new or different situation).*

bal.lis.tic (buh.LIS.tic) **1** *adj*. having to do with the flight of a projectile: *A ballistic missile is powered only while ascending, reaching its target in free flight.* **2 ballistics** *n.pl.* [takes *sing. v.*] the study of the motion and behavior of bullets, rockets, bombs, etc.; *adj*.: *a ballistics expert, laboratory, test.* —**go ballistic** get excited or become irrational.

ball of wax *n*. *Slang*. affair or business: *the whole ball of wax* (= everything related or essential).

bal.loon (buh.LOON) *n*. an airtight bag filled with helium, hot air, etc. and often used to lift loads into the atmosphere: *to blow up, deflate, fly, inflate a* *balloon; a trial balloon; weather balloons.* **—bal.loon.ist** *n.*

bal.lot (BAL.ut) *n.* **1** a piece of paper used in secret voting containing a list of candidates: *Cast your ballot; an absentee ballot; Spoiled ballots are invalidated; void ballots.* **2** the act, method, or right of voting: *They voted by secret ballot, not open ballot; a straw ballot* (= straw poll). **3** the votes cast or the result: *ballots for and against a proposal; The ballot was against the death penalty.* **—v.** vote or decide by ballot: *They were balloting for a new leader;* **n.:** *The balloting went on till 6 a.m.*

ballot box *n.* a box into which ballots are put by voters: *to* **stuff the ballot boxes** (= put fraudulent votes in a ballot box). **—ballot stuffing** *n.*

ball.park *n.* a baseball field: *A* **ballpark figure** (= a figure that is a reasonable estimate) *for that project is $500,000; It may cost around $500,000, in that ballpark* (= range).

ball-point pen *n.* a pen with a ball bearing for a point, which rolls ink from a cartridge onto the paper.

ball.room *n.* a large hall for social dancing.

ball.sy (BALL.zee) *adj. Slang.* cocky and aggressive: *a ballsy fellow.*

bal.ly.hoo (BAL.ee.hoo) *n.* extravagant and noisy advertising. **—v. -hooes, -hooed, -hoo.ing** praise or publicize with ballyhoo.

balm (BAHM) *n.* **1** an aromatic medicinal ointment or lotion: *a healing balm.* **2** something soothing: *the balm of friendship and understanding.*

balm.y (BAH.mee) *adj.* **balm.i.er, -i.est** mild and soothing, not hot or cold: *the balmy beaches of Bermuda; a balmy breeze, climate; a balmy region of steady sunshine; a balmy temperature of 5°C; balmy weather.* **—balm.i.ness** *n.*

ba.lo.ney (buh.LOH.nee) *n.* **1** bologna sausage. **2** *Slang.* false and worthless talk; bunk.

bal.sa (BAWL.suh) *n.* the lighter-than-cork wood of a tropical American tree.

bal.sam (BAWL.sum) *n.* the fragrant resin of several trees, used esp. in medicines.

balsam fir *n.* a North American evergreen valued for its pulpwood and as a Christmas tree.

Bal.tic (BAWL.tic) *adj.* having to do with the **Baltic Sea** between Sweden and the U.S.S.R. or to the **Baltic States** made up of Estonia, Lithuania, and Latvia. **—n.** the Baltic Sea.

bal.us.ter (BAL.us.tur) *n.* a post supporting a railing.

bal.us.trade (BAL.us.trade) *n.* a row of posts with a rail on top of them.

bam.boo (bam.BOO) *n.* a tall, woody, often hollow-stemmed grass used for fishing poles, making huts, etc.; *adja.: bamboo huts, shoots.*

bam.boo.zle (bam.BOO.zul) *v.* **-zles, -zled, -zling** *Informal.* cheat or deceive: *He bamboozled her into buying an old encyclopedia, saying it would help to improve her child's grades; The old man was bamboozled out of his savings.* **—n.:** *a monumental bamboozle* (= deception). **—bam.boo.zler** *n.*

ban *v.* **bans, banned, ban.ning** officially disapprove of and prohibit a show, book, organization, person, or activity: *The troublemakers were banned from entering the school; Ban the bomb!* **adj.:** *a book banned in Boston; a banned film; a banned list* (of banned items). **—n.** an official prohibition: *the nuclear test ban; They put* or *placed a ban on smoking in the office; a movie under a ban imposed by the government; The ban was later lifted.*

ba.nal (buh.NAL, BAY.nul) *adj.* commonplace or dull: *banal compliments, humor, remarks.* **—ba.nal.i.ty** (buh.NAL.i.tee) *n.* **-ties.**

ba.na.na (buh.NAN.uh) *n.* **1** a long, curved tropical fruit with a yellowish peel. **2** *Slang.* a person playing a role: *the top banana* (= leading comic); *second banana; They are two tough bananas.* **3 bananas** *pl. Informal.* crazy: *She'll go bananas with boredom; Your music is driving me bananas.* **4 bananas** *interj.* nonsense.

banana republic *n.* any small Latin American country whose economy depends mostly on fruits, esp. one ruled by a despot.

banana seat *n.* an elongated bicycle seat.

banana split *n.* a dessert of ice cream with split banana.

band *n.* **1** a thin strip of flexible material used around something: *a hat band; a rubber band; the gold band around the rim of a cup; a wedding band* (= metal ring). **2** a range of radio frequencies: *a citizens' band; a short-wave band; a broadband radio antenna.* **3** a group of musicians playing on brass, woodwind, and percussion instruments: *a band playing in the park; five-piece, jazz, marching, military, school, steel, string bands; Strike up the band! The band struck up and played the national anthem; Everyone got up and start-*

ed shouting to **beat the band** (*Informal* for with much noise). **4** a united group of people or animals: *a band of deer; a roving band* (= gang) *of marauders, outlaws, robbers, thieves.* **5 bands** *pl.* a pair of strips hung from the front of the collar in academic, clerical, and legal costumes. **7 bands** *pl.* braces for the teeth. —*v.* **1** put or have a band around: *Birds are banded, released, and captured again for studying their travel routes; adj.: the naturally **banded*** (= striped) *rattlesnake; banded glassware, patterns.* **2** get together for a common purpose: *They banded together for protection; The students banded together to vote against a fee increase.*

band.age (BAN.dij) *n.* a strip of gauze or cloth used to bind or cover an injured part of the body: *to apply, put on, remove a bandage.* —*v.* **-ag.es, -aged, -ag.ing** put a bandage on a body part, wound, etc.

band-aid *n.* **1** a small adhesive gauze bandage used to cover cuts. **2** something temporary or stopgap: *It's just a million-dollar band-aid.* —*adj.*: *a band-aid approach, measure; a mere band-aid solution to a perennial problem; to give band-aid treatment when major surgery is called for.* —**Band-Aid** *Trademark.*

ban.dan.a or **ban.dan.na** (ban.DAN.uh) *n.* a large brightly colored handkerchief or scarf.

band.box *n.* a light, round or oval box for holding hats or collars.

ban.deau (BAN.doh) *n.* **1** a narrow band tied around the forehead. **2** a narrow brassiere: *a bandeau bra.*

ban.di.coot (BAN.di.coot) *n.* **1** a ratlike marsupial of Australia. **2** a large destructive rat of India and Sri Lanka.

ban.dit (BAN.dit) *n.* **-dits** or **-dit.ti** (ban.DIT.ee) an outlaw, esp. one of a band of robbers: *a masked bandit; a **one-arm bandit** (Informal* for slot machine). —**ban.dit.ry** (BAN.dit.ree) *n.*

ban.do.leer or **ban.do.lier** (ban.duh.LEER) *n.* a cartridge belt worn across the chest and over one shoulder.

band saw *n.* a power saw whose cutting edge is a toothed endless steel belt.

band.stand *n.* a raised platform for a musical band, usu. a roofed one outdoors.

band.wag.on (BAND.wag.un) *n.* a large, decorated wagon used to carry a band in a parade. —**climb** or **hop** or **jump on the bandwagon** support a cause when it is winning, esp. in a political campaign.

ban.dy (BAN.dee) *v.* **-dies, -died, -dy.ing** knock back and forth; exchange gossip, insults, etc., esp. frivolously or in anger: *All they did was bandy words about; They bandied words with their opponents instead of debating the issues.* —*adj.* curved outward: *bandy legs.*

bandy-legged (BAN.dee.leg.id, -legd) same as BOWLEGGED.

bane 1 *n.* a cause of death or woe: *the bane of one's existence; Alcohol proved to be the bane of his life.* **2** *comb.form.* poison: *fleabane, flybane, ratsbane, wolfsbane.*

bane.ful (BANE.ful) *adj.* evil: *the baneful influence of drugs on society.*

bang *v.* **1** strike hard or with a loud noise: *She banged on the door; She accidentally banged her head against the door; Don't let the door bang behind you; She banged into him* (= met him by accident) *on her way back; He was banging away* (= working hard) *at his old typewriter.* **2** handle roughly or noisily: *He was pretty **banged up** at the initiation ceremony; a **banged-up** automobile.* **3** cut hair in bangs. —*n.* **1** a sudden loud noise: *He slammed the door with a bang; the "big bang" theory of the origin of the universe.* **2** a noisy blow. **3** *Informal.* a thrill: *You'll get a bang out of this; how to get the most bang for your buck.* **4** usu. **bangs** *pl.* a fringe of hair cut squarely across the forehead: *to cut* or *trim one's bangs.* —*adv. Informal.* directly or exactly: *He ran bang into the wall; to stay bang up to date; Prices go up and bang go savings; He arrived bang on the hour; That's **bang on*** (= exactly right).

ban.gle (BANG.gul) *n.* **1** a rigid bracelet worn on the wrist or ankle. **2** an ornament hanging from this.

bang-up *adj.* first-rate: *a bang-up business, finish, job, story.*

ban.ish *v.* **1** expel from a country: *Convicts used to be banished instead of being hanged; He was banished from England; banished to Australia.* **2** send away, esp. from the mind: *how to banish care and woe.* —**ban.ish.ment** (BAN.ish.munt) *n.*

ban.is.ter (BAN.is.tur) *n.* the railing along a set of stairs: *to slide down the banister.* Also **ban.nis.ter.**

ban.jo (BAN.joh) *n.* **-jos** a usu. five-stringed musical instrument with a long neck and a round, hollow, skin-covered body. —**ban.jo.ist** *n.*

bank *n.* **1** a pile or heap: *a bank of snow; a bank of clouds.* **2** usu. **banks** *pl.* a shallow area under water; shoal.

3 the edge of a body of water: *the two banks of a river; standing on the opposite bank; a rugged bank.* **4** the inward tilt of a vehicle, esp. an aircraft, as it turns: *The pilot put the plane into a steep bank.* **5** the slant in a road or course at a curve. **6** a row or tier, as of oars, organ keys, etc.: *film crews with their banks of floodlights; a bank (= set) of elevators.* **7** a business establishment that deals in money deposits, loans, etc.: *central, chartered, national, savings banks; Banks may close, collapse, fail.* **8** a reserve or supply for drawing from: *a blood bank; data banks full of information; eye banks; food banks for the hungry; a memory bank; how to enjoy a good vacation without* **breaking the bank** (= *a vacation you can afford*). —*v.* **1** pile up; also, heap fuel, ashes, etc. on a fire to slow its burning: *The camper banked the fire and went to sleep.* **2** tilt; *adj.*: *This turn is too steeply* **banked** *for the average driver.* **3** put money in a bank: *She banks her savings.* **4** do business at a bank: *Where do you bank?* —**bank on** rely on: *We banked on her support; She was banking on having more money to spend.* —**bank.a.ble** *adj.*

bank.book *n.* a bank customer's record of deposits and withdrawals.

bank card *n.* a card issued by a bank for electronic banking or as a credit card.

bank.er *n.* one who owns or manages a bank: **Banker's hours** *used to be from 10 to 3.*

bank.ing *n.* the work or occupation of a banker.

bank note *n.* a note issued by a bank guaranteeing payment of a stated sum to bearer.

bank rate *n.* the interest rate set by a country's national bank.

bank.roll (BANK.role) *n.* Informal. a supply of ready money. —*v.* finance: *a new project bankrolled by some bold investors.*

bank.rupt *n.* **1** a person or business legally declared unable to pay creditors fully. **2** one totally lacking in a specified quality: *a moral bankrupt.* —*v.* make bankrupt: *Farmers complain of being bankrupted by quotas, levies, etc.* —*adj.* unable to pay debts or meet obligations: *Companies go bankrupt; a bankrupt corporation; a government bankrupt* (= *devoid*) *of leadership.*

bank.rupt.cy (BANK.rup.see) *n.* -**cies** bankrupt condition: *The struggling businessman declared or filed for or petitioned for or went into personal bankruptcy to get rid of his debts; companies driven to bankruptcy by the recession.*

ban.ner (BAN.ur) *n.* **1** a flag or standard, esp. a large strip of cloth bearing a slogan: *to carry, unfurl a banner; banners waving or fluttering in the wind; The U.S. national flag is the Star-Spangled Banner; Campaign banners were stretched across the streets of Rome; People gathered under the banner* (= rallying point) *of the U.N.; a* **banner headline** (*running across a newspaper page*). **2** a banner headline: *The banner read, "Make love, not war."* —*adj.* outstanding: *We're expecting a banner sales year; It was a banner year for the school's swimming team.*

bannister same as BANISTER.

banns *n.pl.* the announcement in church of an intended marriage: *Banns are usually published* or *announced on three successive Sundays.*

ban.quet (BANK.wit) *n.* an elaborate feast, usu. in honor of a person or event: *to arrange, cater, give, hold a banquet; farewell, formal, lavish, state, sumptuous, wedding banquets; I met him at the banquet for the new mayor.* —**ban.quet.er** *n.*

ban.quette (bang.KET) *n.* **1** a platform for gunners behind a parapet or inside a trench wall. **2** an upholstered bench along a wall.

ban.shee *n.* in Irish and Scottish folklore, a female spirit whose wail foretells a death in the house: *screaming like a banshee; a raving banshee.*

ban.tam (BAN.tum) *n.* **1** a dwarfish but aggressive breed of domestic fowl. **2** a small aggressive person. **3** also **bantamweight,** a boxer weighing between 113 and 118 lb. (52 and 54 kg for Olympics). —*adj.* aggressive though small: *a bantam battalion, league; her bantam spirit; a bantam hockey team.*

ban.ter (BAN.tur) *n.* playful teasing: *good-natured, light, witty banter; to exchange banter with friends.* —*v.* **1** tease good-humoredly. **2** joke playfully *with* someone.

Ban.tu (BAN.too) *n. & adj.* (having to do with) a Negroid people of C. and S. Africa or their language.

ban.yan (BAN.yun) *n.* a fig tree of India with aerial shoots that grow into the soil forming new trunks.

ban.zai (bahn.ZYE) *interj.* a Japanese cheer or battle cry.

banzai attack *n.* a usu. suicidal mass attack.

ba.o.bab (BAY.oh.bab) *n.* a tropical tree with a thick trunk, large edible fruit, and medicinally useful bark and leaves.

bap.tism (BAP.tiz.um) *n.* **1** a baptizing: *to administer, receive, undergo baptism.* **2** an initiation: *a soldier's **baptism of fire*** (= first experience of combat). —**bap.tis.mal** (bap.TIZ.mul) *adj.*: *a baptismal font, name, rite; baptismal vows, water.*

Bap.tist (BAP.tist) *n.* a member of a Protestant church that baptizes mature believers by immersion.

bap.tis.ter.y (BAP.tis.tree) *n.* **-ter.ies** a place or a tank of water for baptizing; also **bap.tis.try** *n.* **-tries.**

bap.tize (bap.TIZE, BAP.tize) *v.* **-tiz.es, -tized, -tiz.ing** **1** admit a person to a church by a rite using water. **2** give a first name to someone; christen: *He was baptized John; They baptized him John.* **3** initiate or inaugurate: *a party thrown to baptize a new barbecue.*

bar *n.* **1** a regular oblong piece of wood, metal, etc.: *an iron bar; a bar of soap; candy bars.* **2** a bar used to block a passage or fasten a door: *a window bar; a bar to progress; a color bar between whites and blacks.* **3** something made of a bar: *a wrecking bar; the horizontal and parallel bars for gymnasts; the torsion bar of an automobile's suspension; ballerinas warming up at the bar* (= barre); *a keyboard's space bar* (= lever). **4** a band, as of color or sunlight. **5** a sales counter, as one serving drinks: *a cash bar at a convention; cosmetics, salad, snack bars.* **6** a room or pub where drinks are sold: *a singles bar; Joe's bar and grill; Tim drinks at the bar every evening; He drops into the bar on his way home; He met his wife in the bar.* **7 the bar** a law court or tribunal: *the prisoner at the bar; before the bar of conscience; the bar of public opinion.* **8 the bar** the legal profession: *Law students read for the bar; They are called* or *admitted to the bar; Judges are normally chosen from the bar.* **9** a vertical line dividing a staff of music into measures; also, a portion so divided: *He played a few bars of the national anthem.* —**behind bars** in prison. —*v.* **bars, barred, bar.ring** **1** fasten with a bar: *Bar the door; adj.: a barred window* (protected with bars). **2** exclude: *The heckler was barred from future meetings; They barred* (= forbade) *his attending the meetings.* —*prep.* excepting: *bar none; bar one.* Also **barring:** *Everyone, barring Tim, was present; Barring* (= except in case of) *a miracle, the sun should rise tomorrow.*

barb *n.* **1** a backward-turned point, as on a fishhook or arrow. **2** something sharp or cutting, as criticism or sarcasm: *her barbs of wit; to endure barbs; to sling barbs of ridicule at a poet.*

bar.bar.i.an (bar.BAIR.ee.un) *n.* **1** a member of a primitive or relatively less developed culture: *Greeks spoke of the barbarians from the north.* **2** an uncultured person or brute. —*adja.* having to do with barbarians: *barbarian customs, hordes, invasions, peoples.*

bar.bar.ic (bar.BAIR.ic) *adj.* wild, uncivilized, or exotic: *barbaric customs, ornaments, people; the barbaric splendor of a temple's interior.*

bar.ba.rism (BAR.buh.riz.um) *n.* **1** a primitive level of civilization: *to live in barbarism.* **2** a cruel or savage act or trait. **3** a nonstandard usage such as "irregardless."

bar.bar.i.ty (bar.BAIR.i.tee) *n.* **-ties** **1** a cruel or savage act or custom: *the barbarities of warfare.* **2** a primitive or uncultured condition: *living in barbarity; Nazism was a regression to barbarity.*

bar.ba.rous (BAR.buh.rus) *adj.* **1** savage; brutal; uncivilized. **2** of words and expressions, nonstandard. —**bar.ba.rous.ly** *adv.*

bar.be.cue (BAR.buh.cue) *n.* **1** an outdoor pit, fireplace, or portable grill for roasting meats. **2** a party at which such food is served: *We have barbecues in the summer.* —*v.* **-cues, -cued, -cu.ing** **1** cook on a barbecue. **2** cook with a seasoned sauce, or **barbecue sauce,** made with tomatoes and vinegar.

barbed *adj.* having barbs: *a barbed* (= sarcastic) *comment.*

barbed wire *n.* wire with sharp points along it, used for fences or barricades: *Barbed wire was strung around the compound.*

bar.bell *n.* a metal rod or bar with variable weights on both ends, lifted for exercise.

bar.ber (BAR.bur) *n.* one who cuts hair, shaves beards, etc. as a trade.

bar.ber.ry (BAR.ber.ee) *n.* **-ber.ries** a low thorny shrub with red berries.

bar.ber.shop (BAR.bur.shop) *n.* a barber's place of business.

barbershop quartet *n.* a group of four male harmonized voices singing popular songs.

bar.bi.can (BAR.bi.cun) *n.* a fortified approach to a city, esp. a tower over a gate.

Bar.bie doll (BAR.bee-) *n.* **1** a popular brand of miniature adult blond blue-eyed doll; **Barbie Doll** *Trademark.*

barbiturate / bark

2 *Informal*. a mindless person.
bar.bi.tu.rate (bar.BICH.ur.it) *n*. a sedative or sleep-inducing drug that is potentially addictive.
barb.wire same as BARBED WIRE.
bar.ca.rolle (BAR.cuh.role) *n*. **1** a Venetian gondolier's song. **2** a similar piece of music with a beat suggestive of the rhythm of rowing.
bar chart *n*. a chart showing comparative figures using parallel bars of varying lengths; also **bar graph**.
bar code *n*. a code of bars and numbers printed on products for use in computerized checkout and inventory systems, esp. the universal product code.
bard *n*. a tribal poet or minstrel: *"the Bard of Avon"* (= Shakespeare).
bare *adj*. **bar.er, bar.est 1** without its natural or usual covering, as shoes for the feet: *bare feet; a bare head; He uprooted the tree with his bare hands; the bare* (= unadorned) *facts; bare walls; a bare* (= empty) *cupboard; a hillside bare of vegetation; to lay bare* (= expose) *the facts, secrets, the truth of a story*. **2** mere: *the bare necessities of life; a budget cut to the bare bones* (= essentials); *They won with a bare* (= scanty) *majority; the bare* (= stark) *truth*. —*v*. **bares, bared, bar.ing** lay bare or reveal: *The dog growled and bared its teeth*.
bare.back or **bare.backed** *adj. & adv*. without a saddle: *bareback riding*.
bare-boned *adj*. having no frills; unadorned: *bare-boned facts; no-frills, bare-boned prices*.
bare-bones *adja*. having only the bare essentials: *a bare-bones budget, operation, style of writing*.
bare.faced *adj*. shameless: *a barefaced liar, lie*.
bare.foot *adv*. without shoes: *to run barefoot in the park; adja.: barefoot children; a barefoot dance; the barefoot doctors* (= medical auxiliaries) *of China's rural areas*. Also **bare.foot.ed**.
bar graph same as BAR CHART.
bare.hand.ed (BARE.han.did) *adj. & adv*. with empty hands, as without a tool or weapon.
bare.head.ed (BARE.hed.id) *adj. & adv*. with head exposed; hatless.
bare-knuckle *adj*. **1** without boxing gloves: *a bare-knuckle prizefight*. **2** fierce in fighting: *a bare-knuckle approach, competition, contest, style*. Also **adv**.
bare.leg.ged (BARE.leg.id, -legd) *adj. & adv*. with no leg-covering: *barelegged children shivering on street corners*.
bare.ly *adv*. **1** scantily: *a barely furnished room*. **2** scarcely: *She had barely met him when he proposed; He barely survived the fire*. —**bare.ness** *n*.
bar.fly *n*. **-flies** *Informal*. one who regularly drinks in bars.
bar.gain (BARG.in) *n*. **1** an agreement or deal to buy, sell, etc.: *to make* or *seal* or *strike a bargain with someone; a sales rep who drives a hard bargain; But he always meets his end of the bargain* or *keeps his side of the bargain* (= carries out what he has agreed to do); *She tried to make the best of a bad bargain* (= do her best in the difficult situation). **2** something bought at a low price: *People shop for bargains; trying to find or get good bargains; It's a real bargain at that price*. —**in** or **into the bargain** in addition. —*v*. negotiate terms, as of a deal or contract: *to bargain with a sales rep for a used car; to bargain over the terms of a lease; n.: collective bargaining; plea bargaining*. —**bargain on** or **for** expect or anticipate: *He met with trouble he hadn't bargained for*.
—**bar.gain.er** *n*.
bargain-basement *adja*. cheap or inexpensive: *The new airline started bargain-basement flights across the Atlantic; a bargain-basement deal, fare, figure, price*.
bargaining chip *n*. something used in negotiations to gain an advantage or concession from the opposite party: *The question of overtime pay was used as a bargaining chip during the final negotiations*.
barge (BARJ) *n*. **1** a big flat-bottomed freight boat used on canals, rivers, etc. **2** a finely decorated ceremonial boat: *Cleopatra's barge on the Nile*.
—*v*. **barg.es, barged, barg.ing 1** transport by barge. **2** move or intrude clumsily or rudely: *He has a way of barging into a room; He barges in without knocking; barging in on people's conversations*.
bar.i.tone (BAIR.uh.tone) *n*. a male singing voice lower than tenor and higher than bass: *He sings baritone; He's a baritone (singer)*.
bar.i.um (BAIR.ee.um) *n*. a soft, silver-white metallic chemical element: *A fluid mixture of barium is given rectally as barium enema for taking a barium X ray of the intestinal tract*.
bark *n*. **1** a short gruff sound typically made by a dog; "bow-wow": *a loud bark; an angry bark; "His bark is worse than his bite"* (= He is frightening but harmless). **2** the tough outer covering of woody stems and roots: *to peel the bark off trees*. **3** See BARQUE. —*v*. **1** ut-

ter a bark: *Dogs bark; They bark at strangers, especially letter carriers.* **2** speak sharply or hoarsely: *an officer who barks orders.* **3** take the bark off a tree. **4** *Informal.* scrape the skin of a body part: *He fell and barked his shin.*
—**bark up the wrong tree** have one's efforts, criticisms, etc. misdirected; be on the wrong track.

bar.keep.er (BAR.kee.pur) *n.* **1** a bartender. **2** owner of a bar serving liquor. Also **bar.keep.**

bark.er *n.* one who loudly calls out to attract people, esp. to a sideshow or sale.

bar.ley (BAR.lee) *n.* a grain used for food and in making beer and whiskey.

bar.maid *n.* a woman who serves drinks in a bar.

bar.man *n.* **-men** a bartender.

bar mitz.vah (bar.MITS.vuh) *n.* **1** a Jewish ceremony for a 13-year-old boy to mark his taking on of religious responsibility. **2** such a boy.

barm.y *adj.* **barm.i.er, -i.est** crazy or foolish: *They have gone totally barmy to join in the gold rush.*

barn *n.* **1** a large building for sheltering farm equipment, animals, crops and feed, etc.: *It's no use locking the barn door after the horse has escaped.* **2** a similar building for buses, trucks, etc.

bar.na.cle (BAR.nuh.cul) *n.* a marine shellfish that fastens itself firmly to rocks, timbers, ship hulls, etc.: *clinging barnacles.*

barn burner *n. Informal.* something sensational or exciting: *Her speech was a barn burner.*

barn.storm *v.* tour the countryside giving plays, speeches, or exhibitions of stunt flying.

barn.yard *n.* a yard near a barn.
—*adj.* earthy: *low barnyard humor.*

ba.rom.e.ter (buh.ROM.uh.tur) *n.* **1** an instrument for measuring atmospheric pressure: *A barometer falls, rises, is steady.* **2** an indicator of change: *Polls are a barometer of public opinion.*
—**bar.o.met.ric** (bair.uh.MET.ric) *adj.*

bar.on (BAIR.un) *n.* **1** a peer of the lowest inherited rank; **bar.on.ess** *fem.* **2** a magnate: *beef, cattle, coal, mining, oil barons; the barons of the board room.*
—**bar.on.age** (BAIR.uh.nij) *n.*

bar.on.et (BAIR.uh.net) *n.* a member of a titled order ranking below baron; **bar.on.et.cy** *n.* **-cies.**

ba.ro.ni.al (buh.ROH.nee.ul) *adj.* **1** of a baron: *baronial privileges.* **2** large or ample: *baronial rooms; a house of baronial dimensions.*

baron of beef *n.* two sirloins joined at the backbone.

ba.roque (buh.ROKE) *adj.* in a 17th century style noted for florid ornamentation, bordering on the grotesque: *baroque architecture, furniture, music, opera, poetry, sculpture; a baroque garden with canals, cascades, and fountains; a baroque pearl (of irregular shape).*

barque (BARK) *n.* a sailing ship with the furthest aft mast rigged fore-and-aft and the others rigged square; also **bark.**

bar.racks (BAIR.uks) *n.pl.* [takes *sing.* or *pl. v.*] a building housing soldiers: *a school built like a barracks; refugee barracks.*

bar.ra.cu.da (bair.uh.COO.duh) *n.* a thin-bodied, fierce fish of tropical seas.

bar.rage (buh.RAHZH) *n.* **1** a heavy, sustained burst of artillery fire. **2** a continuous stream: *a barrage of abuse, complaints, goals, questions; a barrage of balloons sent up by protestors.* —*v.*
bar.rag.es, bar.raged, bar.rag.ing hit with a barrage: *The speaker was barraged with questions.*

barrage balloon *n.* a balloon flown anchored to the ground with a cable to obstruct enemy aircraft.

barre (BAR) *n.* a horizontal rod attached to a wall that ballet dancers use for balance when practicing: *Ballet training begins at the barre.*

barred *pt. & pp.* of BAR: *a barred window.*

bar.rel (BAIR.ul) *n.* **1** a round cask with bulging sides; drum: *Petroleum products are measured in barrels of 159L; barrels of oil, beer, brew, wine.* **2** a cylindrical part of an apparatus or machine, esp. the firing tube of a gun. **3** *Informal.* a great amount: *a barrel of fun, knowledge, laughs, resources.* —**over a barrel** *Informal.* at someone's mercy.
—*v.* **bar.rels, bar.reled, bar.rel.ing** **1** pack in a barrel. **2** *Informal.* travel at high speed: *stopped by police while barreling along the highway.* Also **bar.elled, bar.rel.ling** *Cdn.*

barrel-chested *adj.* having a broad chest.

barrel organ *n.* a street musician's hand organ that is worked by cranking a cylinder in a box containing pipes.

barrel roll *n.* a complete longitudinal revolution of an aircraft in flight.

bar.ren (BAIR.un) *adj.* **1** not bearing fruit; unproductive: *a barren desert, region; a barren (= sterile) woman.* **2** de-

barrette / baseman

void: *Animals are not barren of intelligence; an attempt that was barren of results.* —*n.* usu. **barrens** *pl.* a barren region. —**bar.ren.ness** *n.*

bar.rette (bah.RET) *n.* a small hair clasp.

bar.ri.cade (BAIR.uh.cade) *n.* a hastily built rampart or barrier, esp. one blocking a street: *to place* or *set up a barricade; to remove* or *take down a barricade; a barbed-wire barricade; Man the barricades, citizens!* —*v.* **-cades, -cad.ed, -cad.ing** block, obstruct, or protect, esp. with a barricade.

bar.ri.er (BAIR.ee.ur) *n.* something that blocks, hinders, or separates, esp. a fence or wall: *to erect, overcome, place, remove, set up barriers; Do not cross a police barrier; Watch how easily the horse takes the barrier; cultural, language, social, sound barriers; to break down the barriers between the races; barriers to progress.*

barrier reef *n.* a coral reef parallel to and separated by a channel from a coast.

barring (BAR.ing) See BAR.

bar.ri.o (BAH.ree.oh) *n.* **-os** a Spanish-speaking part of an American city.

bar.ris.ter (BAIR.is.tur) *n.* a lawyer, traditionally one who argues cases.

bar.room *n.* a room with a bar for selling liquor.

bar.row (BAIR.oh) *n.* **1** a mound over an ancient grave site. **2** a wheelbarrow or handcart.

bar.stool *n.* a high stool used at a bar.

bar.ten.der (BAR.ten.dur) *n.* one who serves liquor at a bar.

bar.ter *v.* to trade without using money: *The trapper bartered his furs for a rifle.* —*n.* the practice of bartering goods and services: *The pioneers engaged in barter with the natives; Barter precedes a money economy; People form barter clubs for making cashless trades and evading taxes.* —**bar.ter.er** *n.*

bas.al (BAY.sul) *adj.* having to do with the base or basis: *a basal reader (textbook); basal* (= very light) *anesthesia.*

basal metabolism *n.* the minimal amount of energy used by an organism for cell activity, respiration, and circulation, as when at rest.

ba.salt (buh.SAWLT, BAY.sawlt) *n.* a dark, hard, often glassy volcanic rock. —**ba.sal.tic** (-SAWL.tic) *adj.*

base *adj.* **1** greedy and selfish; ignoble: *base cowardice.* **2** of metals, not precious: *a base coin made with an alloy; brass, lead, zinc, and such base* (= not noble) *metals.* —**base.ly** *adv.*; **base.ness**

n. —*n.* **1** the lower or supporting part of a statue, figure, etc.: *the base of a triangle.* **2** the number on which a numbering system is built: *10 is the base of the decimal system.* **3** a camp or town supplying food, equipment, etc. for a military or other undertaking: *to set up a base of operations; a forward base; army, military, missile, naval bases; The power base of the party is among the peasantry; the base camp of the mountain climbers.* **4** the main ingredient: *a paint with an oil base.* **5** a substance that reacts with an acid to form a salt: *Strong bases are called alkalis.* **6** the part of a word to which affixes are added; stem: *The base of "mistakenly" is "take."* **7** in baseball, one of the four points to be touched for a run to count: *to* **touch base** (= be in contact) *with someone; The speaker* **touched all bases** (= points to be considered) *in his keynote address.* —**base on balls** a baseball batter's advance to first base after being pitched four balls. —**get to first base with** *Informal.* begin to have any success with someone. —**off base** *Informal.* mistaken or unprepared: *completely, way off base.*
—*v.* **bas.es, based, bas.ing 1** place at a base: *where to base nuclear missiles; a journalist based in Bombay;* **cpd:** *land-based aircraft; a Paris-based organization; a California-based firm.* **2** have or provide a foundation for something: *She bases her conclusions on surveys; something to base a case, claim, decision, estimate on;* **adj. & cpd:** *a story* **based** *upon facts; a movie based on a novel; a broad-based regional plan; an oil-based paint.*

base.ball *n.* **1** a game played by two teams of nine players each on a diamond-shaped field with a bat and ball. **2** the ball.

base.board *n.* a molding at the base of a wall.

base.born *adj.* of low or illegitimate birth; ignoble.

base.coat *n.* a first coat of paint or plaster given before the finishing coat.

base hit *n.* in baseball, a hit allowing a batter to get on base without the help of an opponent's error or the forcing out of a teammate.

base.less (BAIS.lis) *adj.* without foundation: *a baseless allegation.*

base.line *n.* **1** in baseball, one of the four lanes connecting the bases. **2** the line at either end of a tennis court. **3** a line serving as a base, esp. in surveying. Also **base line.**

base.man (BASE.mun) *n.* **-men** an infielder playing at first, second, or third base.

base.ment (BAIS.munt) *n.* **1** the foundation of a building. **2** the lowest story, at least partly underground: *a finished basement with a kitchen and recreation room; the bargain basement of a department store.* —*adj.: a basement apartment, kitchen, office; a* **basement bargain** (= cheap bargain).

base on balls *n.* a baseball batter's advance to first base after being pitched four balls.

base pay *n.* pay exclusive of overtime and other additions.

base runner *n.* a baseball player on the team at bat who has reached or is trying to reach a base.

bases *pl.* of BASE or BASIS.

bash *v. Informal.* hit very hard; smash: *He bashed his head against the wall;* **n.**: *union* **bashing** *by management.* —**n.** *Informal.* a party: *a birthday bash; the bash for her 21st birthday.*

bash.ful *adj.* shy, as a child or youth; sensitive and timid. —**bash.ful.ly** *adv.;* **bash.ful.ness** *n.*

bas.ic (BAY.sic) *adj.* **1** fundamental: *a basic outline of the course; life's basic necessities; students who commit errors in basic English; The three R's are basic to education; to take basic training in life-saving; basic monetary units such as the dollar and pound.* **2** in chemistry, having to do with a base. —**n. 1** something basic; usu. **basics** *pl.*: *The negotiators got down to basics; the basics of algebra.* **2 Basic** or **BASIC** a computer language that uses common English terms. —**bas.i.cal.ly** (-sic.lee) *adv.*

bas.il (BAZ.ul) *n.* an aromatic cooking herb of the mint family.

ba.sil.i.ca (buh.SIL.i.cuh) *n.* **1** a rectangular building with an apse and side aisles used as a church, esp. by early Christians. **2** a Roman Catholic church with certain ceremonial rights.

bas.i.lisk (BAS.uh.lisk) *n.* a mythical lizard with a fatal breath and glance.

ba.sin (BAY.sin) *n.* **1** an open, shallow, rounded vessel for water; also, a sink. **2** a usu. enclosed body of water, as a harbor or pond: *a tidal basin.* **3** the area passed through by a river: *the Amazon basin.* **4** a broad, rounded depression in a land mass.

ba.sis (BAY.sis) *n., pl.* **ba.ses** (-seez) foundation: *a case with a firm or solid basis on evidence; the scientific basis of a theory; a complaint without any basis; It rests on a shaky basis; The new president put the company on a sound economic basis; Common interests are or form or provide a good basis* (= common ground) *for friendship; friends on a first-name basis* (= footing); *He is paid on a monthly basis* (= arrangement); *He was hired on the basis of* (= relying on) *recommendations.*

bask *v.* enjoy being exposed to warmth, love, admiration, etc.: *See the people basking on the beach; They like to bask in the sunshine; to bask in glory.*

bas.ket (BAS.kit) *n.* **1** a container usu. made of interwoven strips of wood, cane, fiber, etc.: *to weave a basket; a laundry basket made of plastic; picnic baskets; wastepaper baskets; a basket of apples* (= apples in a basket); *an interlaced* **basket weave** *pattern used in textile design.* **2** a round hoop fitted with an open, hanging net that forms the goal in basketball. **3** a throw of the ball through a basketball hoop that counts as a score: *to make, miss, score, shoot, sink a basket.*

bas.ket.ball (BAS.kit.ball) *n.* **1** a game played with an inflated round ball by two teams of five players each. **2** the ball.

basket case *n.* a totally incapacitated person or entity: *Some poor countries are true basket cases; to bring corporate basket cases* (= bankrupt companies) *back to health.*

bas.ket.ful (BAS.kit.ful) *n.* the contents of a basket.

bas mitz.vah (bahs.MITS.vuh) same as BATH MITZVAH.

Basque (BASK) *n.* **1** a member of an ethnically unique people of the Pyrenees; *adj.: the Basque country; the Basque provinces of northern Spain; Basque separatists.* **2** their language.

bas-relief (bah.ri.LEEF) *n.* a form of sculpture in which figures stand out slightly from their flat background.

bass (BAYCE) *adj.* of the lowest pitch of male voice: *a bass drum, instrument, section, player, singer, voice.* —**n. 1** a male singer or an instrument with a bass range: *a double bass; accompaniment on bass and percussion.* **2** the lowest part in harmonic arrangements: *He sings a deep bass.* **3** (BASS) any of a group of spiny finned game fishes of lakes and seas: *striped bass; bass fishing.*

bas.set hound or **basset** (BAS.it) *n.* a short-legged, long-eared breed of dog.

bas.si.net (bas.uh.NET) *n.* a hooded, basketlike baby's bed.

bas.so (BAS.oh) *n.* **bas.sos** a singer with a bass voice.

bas.soon (buh.SOON) *n.* a double-reed

wind instrument with a bass range.
bass viol (BAYCE-) same as DOUBLE BASS.
bass.wood *n.* the North American linden tree.
bast *n.* a bark fiber used to make rope, matting, etc.
bas.tard (BAS.turd) *n.* **1** *Informal* [abusive] an offensive person: *That greedy bastard!* **2** *Informal* [jocular]: *You little bastard!* **3** an illegitimate child. **—adj**. **1** illegitimate: *a bastard child; bastard birth, offspring*. **2** inferior: *bastard mahogany*. **—bas.tard.ly** *adj.* base or vicious: *a bastardly trick*.
bas.tard.ize (BAS.tur.dize) *v.* **-iz.es, -ized, -iz.ing 1** make or declare bastard. **2** corrupt or debase; *adj.: a Basque who speaks good Spanish and a **bastardized** French*.
baste *v.* **bastes, bast.ed, bast.ing 1** fasten with large stitches: *The tailor basted the hem of the skirt before stitching it*. **2** beat or scold soundly; *n.: a good, sound, thorough **basting** for using foul language*. **3** pour drippings, sauce, etc. over meat or fish while it is cooking; *adj.: basted turkey*.
bas.tille (bas.TEEL) *n.* a tyrannically run prison, like **the Bastille** which fell during the French Revolution.
bas.tion (BAS.chun) *n.* **1** a fortified projection of a wall or rampart. **2** a strong position: *a club that was the last bastion of male chauvinists*.
bat *n.* **1** a stick or paddle for hitting the ball in baseball, cricket, etc.: *He swung his bat to hit the ball*. **2** a type of nocturnal animal, including the vampire and the "flying fox," that has wings of membrane: *blind as a bat*. **3** a blow. **—at bat** taking one's turn as a hitter in baseball. **—off the bat** *Informal.* without any delay; right away: *right off the bat*. **—v. bats, bat.ted, bat.ting 1** hit with a bat. **2** flutter eyelids: *She didn't **bat an eye*** (= showed no surprise) *at the news*. **—go to bat for** (or **against**) defend (or oppose) someone.
batch *n.* a group of things or people processed at one time: *a fresh batch of bread, dough, loaves; a batch of pea soup; a new batch of problems, trainees; **batch** **processing** of many transactions together on a computer*.
ba.teau (ba.TOH) *n., pl.* **ba.teaux** (-TOZE) a flat-bottomed light boat, usu. with narrow bow and stern.
bated (BAY.tid) *adj.* usu. **with bated breath,** holding the breath in excitement, expectation, fear, etc.: *She awaited his arrival with bated breath* (= in suspense).
bath *n.* **1** a washing of the body in water: *to take a bath in the morning; Stockholders **took a bath*** (*Informal* for suffered a financial loss) *when the market crashed*. **2** the water, tub, or room used for bathing: *to draw a bath; Run the bath till the tub is half full; A sauna is a steam bath; whirlpool baths; an apartment with a bedroom, kitchen, and bath; one and a half baths* (= one four-piece bathroom and a two-piece washroom). **3 baths** *pl.* a building with bathing pools and rooms: *Roman baths; Turkish baths*.
bathe ("th" as in "the") *v.* **bathes, bathed, bath.ing 1** take or subject to a bath: *to bathe a child; We bathe in warm water*. **2** go swimming: *to bathe in the sea; adj.: a **bathing** beach, beauty, cap, costume; bathing trunks*. **3** soak: *Bathe your foot in warm water; We bathe in the sun; adj.: He was all **bathed*** (= wet) *with sweat; The meadows were **bathed in*** (= covered with) *sunlight*. **—bath.er** *n*.
ba.thet.ic (ba.THET.ic, "TH" as in "thin") *adj.* characterized by bathos.
bath.house *n.* **1** a building for bathing. **2** a building for swimmers to change clothes in.
bathing suit *n.* a swimsuit.
bath mitz.vah (baht.MITS.vuh) *n.* a ceremony for a girl similar to the bar mitzvah.
ba.thos (BAY.thos, "th" as in "thin") *n.* **1** a sudden transition from the sublime to the trivial. **2** overdone or insincere pathos.
bath.robe *n.* a loose robe worn when going to and from a bath, for lounging, etc.
bath.room *n.* **1** a room for taking baths, usu. one with a toilet, washbasin, and bathtub or shower. **2** a washroom or lavatory.
bath.tub *n.* a tub for bathing.
ba.tik (buh.TEEK, BAT.ik) *n.* a technique for dyeing cloth by coating with wax the parts to remain uncolored.
ba.tiste (buh.TEEST) *n.* a soft, lightweight cloth of wool, cotton, or rayon.
bat.mitz.vah (baht.MITS.vuh) same as BATH MITZVAH.
ba.ton (buh.TON, *rhyme:* ON) *n.* **1** a light stick used by the conductor to direct an orchestra: *a great performance under the baton of Seiji Ozawa*. **2** any similar rod or staff, as one carried as a symbol of authority: *A drum majorette leads a parade twirling a baton in display; In a relay race, each runner of a team

carries a baton and hands or *passes it to the next runner; a field marshal's baton; The police made a baton (= truncheon) charge to disperse the mob.*
bats.man (BATS.mun) *n.* **-men** a batter in baseball or cricket: *the lead-off batsman.*
batt (BAT) *n.* a batting of cotton, wool, or other material: *friction-fit batts of fiberglass for insulation.*
bat.tal.ion (buh.TAL.yun) *n.* **1** a military unit made up of two or more companies, batteries, etc.: *Hitler's big battalions.* **2** a large organized group: *battalions of census takers.*
bat.ten (BAT.un) *n.* a long thin board used for flooring or to fasten other boards in place. —*v.* **1 batten down the hatches** secure a ship's hatch covers, esp. before a storm. **2** thrive or grow fat: *He leads a life of ease battening on the generosity of relatives.*
bat.ter *n.* **1** in baseball, one whose turn it is to bat. **2** a beaten mixture of flour, milk, eggs, etc. that can be poured for cooking or used as a coating: *pancake batter.* —*v.* strike or pound heavily or repeatedly: *to batter away at a door; The police had to batter down the door; The storm battered the coast for several days; n.: The dollar took a battering in foreign exchange markets yesterday.*
battered *adj.* **1** beaten up; physically abused: *a home for battered women.* **2** worn, as from rough use: *a battered old car, house, sailboat.* **3** weakened: *a battered competition, economy, foreign currency, plan.*
battering ram *n.* a heavy, metal-tipped log used to batter down walls, doors, etc.
bat.ter.y (BAT.uh.ree) *n.* **bat.ter.ies 1** a device for storing or generating electricity: *to charge the storage battery of an automobile; Most flashlight batteries cannot be recharged; A car battery charges itself as the engine runs; When a battery discharges or runs down, it is a dead battery.* **2** a set of similar things used together, as an array of guns: *a missile battery; He had to face a battery of press cameras; a battery of questions, searchlights, tests and X rays.* **3** an artillery unit of guns and soldiers: *A battalion is composed of two or more batteries.* **4** [legal use] the unlawful use of force by one person against another, esp. an attack: *He was charged with assault and battery; Even touching a person in a hostile way could constitute battery; Surgery without informed consent was ruled battery upon*

the patient. **5** in baseball, the pitcher and catcher.
batting *n.* flat wads of the fibers of cotton, wool, etc. as used in furniture stuffing: *Cotton batting is used in bandages.*
batting average *n.* a person's level of success or achievement, as of a baseball player at bat: *a legislator with a low batting average with his constituents.*
bat.tle (BAT.ul) *n.* a conflict or struggle, esp. a large armed combat: *the Battle of Trafalgar; wounds received in battle; soldiers killed in battle; a battle for supremacy; a battle of wits, words; "The first blow is half the battle"; We lost a few battles but won the war; to do battle; to join battle with the enemy; to fight, terminate, wage a battle; bloody, decisive, fierce, losing, naval, pitched, raging, running battles; The will led to a long battle among or between the family members for or over possession of the house; the continuing battle against inflation; the* **battle line** *along which opposing forces meet; to take up one's* **battle station.** —*v.* **bat.tles, bat.tled, bat.tling** to fight: *to battle against or with someone for or over something.*
battle-ax or **battle-axe** *n.* **-ax.es 1** a heavy ax used as a weapon. **2** *Informal.* an aggressive domineering woman.
battle cry *n.* a slogan or cry used as encouragement in a conflict.
battle fatigue same as SHELL SHOCK.
bat.tle.field (BAT.ul.feeld) *n.* the site of a battle: *on the battlefields of Normandy; a bloody battlefield;* **adja.:** *battlefield areas, casualties, dress, trails.*
bat.tle.front (BAT.ul.frunt) *n.* where a battle is being fought: *the green-line battlefront dividing the eastern and western parts of the city; along, at, from, on the battlefront.*
bat.tle.ground (BAT.ul.ground) *n.* a battlefield, esp. an area of conflict: *The island became a major battleground for logging companies and environmentalists.*
bat.tle.ment (BAT.ul.munt) *n.* a parapet or top of a defensive wall.
battle of the bulge *n. Informal.* the struggle to get rid of body fat.
battle royal *n., pl.* **battles royal** a fight involving more than two combatants; free fight.
bat.tle.ship (BAT.ul.ship) *n.* a warship of the most heavily armed class.
bat.ty (BAT.ee) *adj.* **bat.ti.er, bat.ti.est** *Informal.* crazy or eccentric.: *He's gone batty from the strain; the bored and batty*

who watch TV all day.

bau.ble (BAW.bul) *n.* a worthless, showy trinket.

baud *n.* a data transmission speed of one bit per second: *an old 1,200-baud modem.*

baulk, baulky same as BALK, BALKY.

baux.ite *n.* the claylike ore of aluminum.

Ba.var.i.an (buh.VAIR.ee.un) *n. & adj.* (a person) of or from **Bavaria,** a southern German state.

bawd.y *adj.* **bawd.i.er, -i.est** obscene or indecent in a humorous way: *bawdy jokes, songs;* charged with keeping a common **bawdy house** (= brothel).
—*n.:* Chaucer's bawdy (= coarse language and humor). —**baw.di.ly** *adv.;* **baw.di.ness** *n.*

bawl *v.* shout, cry, or weep loudly: *to bawl like a baby; The boss* **bawled him out** (*Informal* for scolded him vigorously) *for sleeping on the job.*

bay *n.* **1** a deep, continuous barking, esp. of hunting dogs. **2** the position of someone who is cornered or checked: *The sniper kept* or *held the police* **at bay**; *a wild boar* **brought to bay** *by hounds.* **3** a separate compartment: *a bomb bay in an aircraft; service bays of a repair shop;* the sick bay (= infirmary) *of a ship.* **4** a recess in an outer wall, esp. one with a window, or **bay window. 5** a body of water extending into the land, usu. smaller than a gulf, sometimes an estuary: *the Bay of Bengal.* **6** a kind of laurel whose leaves (**bay leaves**) are used dried in cooking and to weave garlands. **7 bays** *pl.* fame and honor.
—*adj.* reddish-brown: *a bay horse.*
—*v.* give repeated prolonged barks: *a dog baying at the moon.*

bay.ber.ry (BAY.ber.ee) *n.* **-ber.ries 1** a tropical American tree whose oil-bearing leaves are used in bay rum. **2** any of several shrubs, as the wax myrtle.

bay.o.net (BAY.uh.net) *n.* a heavy knife made to be attached to a rifle barrel for hand-to-hand combat: *The soldiers advanced with bayonets fixed; They were ordered to lie down at bayonet point; a bayonet thrust.* —*v.* **-nets, -net.ed, -net.ing** stab with a bayonet. Also **-net.ted, -net.ting.**

bay.ou (BY.oh, -oo) *n.* in Louisiana, Mississippi, and Texas, a shallow, usu. sluggish channel, tributary, or offshoot of a body of water.

bay rum *n.* a fragrant liquid used in soothing skin lotions.

bay window See BAY, 4.

ba.zaar (buh.ZAR) *n.* **1** a marketplace, as in Middle Eastern countries: *It happened in a bazaar in Cairo; In some villages, public life centers around the bazaar; I purchased some curios at the village bazaar.* **2** a sale of assorted goods, usu. for a charity: *I met her at the bazaar; a church bazaar.* Also **ba.zar.**

ba.zoo.ka (buh.ZOO.kuh) *n.* a portable firing tube for launching armor-piercing rockets.

BB *n.* shot of 0.4572 cm (0.18 in) diameter, as used in an air gun, or **BB gun.**

be (BEE) *auxiliary v.* (I) **am;** (you, we, they) **are;** (he, she, it) **is;** *pt.* (I, he, she, it) **was,** (you, we, they) **were;** *pp.* **been** (BIN); **be.ing 1** [used to show existence]: *Is there life on Mars? Old Pete is no more; Dick and Jane were here; That was a week ago; They will be here tomorrow; Let "l" be the speed of light;* **Be that as it may** (= in spite of that), *everyone is expected to attend the wedding; If I am to be punished for telling the truth,* **so be it** (= let it be so). **2** [used to join subject and predicate]: *To work is to pray; This is my hat; The sky is blue; The dog is a mammal.* **3** [used with a present participle to show continued action]: *He is sitting on the fence.* **4** [used with a past participle to form the passive voice]: *They were hit by a car.* **5** [used with "to" to show futurity, expectation, duty, etc.]: *She hopes to be a lawyer some day; The missing man was to have come to last night's party.*

beach (BEECH) *n.* a shallowly sloping shore usu. covered with sand or small stones: *a private beach belonging to a cottage; a cottage situated on* or *at the beach; Hawaiian beaches; a sandy beach; the tidal beaches of the Bay of Fundy;* **adja.:** *a million-dollar beach house; beach umbrellas.*
—*v.* bring or force onto a beach: *to beach a boat, whale;* **adj.:** *a beached* (*Informal* for unemployed) *fisherman.*

beach ball *n.* an inflated ball for playing on the beach.

beach bum *n. Informal.* one who spends a lot of time on beaches, esp. a surfer.

beach.comb.er (BEECH.coh.mur) *n.* a person who lives on what may be picked up along the beach.

beach.head (BEECH.hed) *n.* a fortified advance position on a beach held by invading forces: *to establish and secure a beachhead.*

beach.wear *n.* clothes to wear on the beach.

bea.con (BEE.cun) *n.* a fire, lighthouse, buoy, radio signal, or other device used to guide or warn ships, aircraft, etc.: *Aeronautical beacons mark the route to an airport; Radio beacons are of great help to ships in foggy weather; Her shining example should serve as a beacon* (= guiding light) *to all of us.*

bead (BEED) *n.* a small globular object of glass, wood, etc. pierced for stringing together: *prayer beads; beads* (= droplets) *of dew, perspiration, sweat.* —**draw a bead on** take aim at someone. —**say** or **count** or **tell one's beads** say prayers, as with a rosary. —*v.* ornament with beads: *Drops of sweat beaded* (= formed into beads) *on his brow; adj.: a beaded dress (decorated with beads).*

bea.dle (BEE.dul) *n.* a parish official keeping order in church.

bead.y (BEE.dee) *adj.* **bead.i.er, -i.est** small, round, and shiny: *beady eyes.*

bea.gle (BEE.gul) *n.* a small hound with a smooth coat and drooping ears.

beak (BEEK) *n.* **1** a hard, sharp, often hooked mouth structure, esp. a bird's bill. **2** *Informal.* the human nose. —**beaked** *adj.*

beak.er (BEE.kur) *n.* **1** a broad-mouthed vessel with a pouring lip and no handle, used in laboratories. **2** a goblet.

be-all and end-all *n.* the whole: *Her kids are the be-all and end-all of her existence.*

beam (BEEM) *n.* **1** a long, heavy piece of wood, steel, etc. used in building: *The beams and girders supporting a building are laid horizontally, with the columns carrying their load.* **2** the crosspiece of a ship, balance, balance beam, etc. **3** a stream of rays, waves, particles, etc.: *the high beam and low beam of an automobile's headlight; a radio beam guiding aircraft; a beam of hope; A beam weapon can fire laser beams against enemy missiles.* —**on** or **off the beam** *Informal.* on or off the right track. —*v.* **1** send in a beam: *a TV program beamed to North America via satellite from Europe; propaganda beamed at enemy nations.* **2** smile radiantly: *She was beaming with joy.*

bean (BEEN) *n.* **1** an edible, usu. kidney-shaped seed of a pod-bearing plant or the seed of the coffee shrub: *broad, kidney, lima, navy, pinto, string beans; snap* or *wax beans; Green beans are used without shelling; canned beans.* **2** *Informal.* the head. —*v.* to hit on the head. —**full of beans** *Informal.* **1** very lively. **2** quite mistaken. —**spill the beans** *Informal.* reveal a secret.

bean.bag *n.* a cushionlike seat used on the floor, consisting of a cloth bag filled with beans or polystyrene beads. Also **beanbag chair.**

bean.ball *n.* a baseball pitched at a batter's head.

bean counter *n. Informal.* an accountant or statistician for whom numbers are everything.

bean curd same as TOFU.

bean.ie (BEE.nee) *n.* a small skullcap.

bean.stalk *n.* the stem of a bean plant.

bear (BAIR) *n.* **1** a large, thick-furred, short-tailed mammal: *black, brown, grizzly, kodiak, polar, wild bears; a stuffed teddy bear.* **2** a gruff or clumsy person. —*v.* **bears, bore, borne, bear.ing 1** carry: *Mules bear loads; The right to bear arms was crucial in pioneer days; She can bear herself with dignity under the most malicious attacks; "Beware of people who come bearing gifts"; Do not bear* (= give) *false witness; He has to bear* (= take) *the blame for this; Let's bear that in mind* (= remember it); *She bears them no grudge* (= feels no grudge toward them) *for the defeat she suffered.* **2** suffer or endure without being broken: *He can't bear the pain; She can't bear to look at him suffering; He just can't bear the sight of blood; She can't bear being alone at night; People used to be branded and made to bear the mark of slavery all their lives; Can this theory bear* (= stand) *examination? a case that bears* (= is worth) *looking into; a strong witness who can bear up* (= remain strong) *under any cross-examination; Please bear with* (= be patient with) *me for another minute while I finish the story.* **3** [See BORN for adjectival usage] give birth to offspring: *Women bear children; She has borne two sons; a child borne by a poor woman; Trees bear* (= yield) *fruit.* **4** lean or press: *Guilt bears heavily on a killer's mind; Remember to bear* (= go toward) *right* or *to the right at the next lights; Watch that truck bearing down* (= coming threateningly) *on you from behind; Here are some facts bearing on* (= relating to) *the case; Facts will bear out* (= confirm) *the truth; The rich sometimes bring their influence to bear* (= exert influence) *on people in power.* —**bear.er** *n.*

bear.a.ble (BAIR.uh.bul) *adj.* that can be endured: *The pain is bearable.*

beard (BEERD) *n.* **1** the hair on a man's face: *to grow a beard; to shave off, stroke, trim one's beard; bushy, light, neat, thick, trim beards.* **2** a similar bristly growth on a plant or animal, as in the **bearded seal** of the Arctic. —*v.* **beard**

bearing / Beaujolais

the lion in his den face a person boldly on his own ground.
bear·ing (BAIR.ing) *n.* **1** how one comports oneself: *a man of noble bearing; dignified, military, regal, royal bearing.* **2** a part supporting a machine's moving part: *a ball bearing; roller bearings; The bearing has burned out.* **3** relation: *This story has no direct bearing on the case.* **4** direction: *to take a bearing on the tower with a compass; The fog was so thick we lost our* **bearings** (= sense of direction or position).
bear·ish (BAIR.ish) *adj.* negative in direction or attitude: *The stock market is bearish on corn prices and friendly to bullish for soybeans; He's somewhat bearish on our hopes of winning.*
bear·skin (BAIR.skin) *n.* a rug, blanket, or tall fur cap made from a bear's skin or similar fur.
beast (BEEST) *n.* **1** an animal, esp. a four-legged one: *a wild beast; The camel is a* **beast of burden** (= animal used for carrying loads). **2** a cruel or coarse person: *He behaves like a beast; The beast* (= beastlike nature) *in him acts up now and then.* —**beast·ly** *adj.* **-li·er, -li·est** very bad: *I'm suffering from a beastly cold; beastly manners, savagery;* **adv.**: *It's beastly* (= extremely) *cold outside.* —**beast·li·ness** *n.*
beat (BEET) *v.* **beats,** *pt.* **beat,** *pp.* **beat** or **beat·en, beat·ing** **1** strike repeatedly: *He was robbed and beaten by thugs; was beaten brutally, mercilessly, severely, viciously; to beat the drum; to beat eggs in a cup; gold beaten into leaves; Watch the rain beating against the window; An adult's heart beats about 72 times a minute; to beat a person into submission; He was beaten unconscious; was found beaten to death; to beat* (= mark) *time with the foot; to* **beat swords into plowshares** (= go from war to peace); *People will* **beat a path to your door** (= come and see you) *if you do something remarkable.* **2** defeat or outdo: *I can beat him at chess; He beat me out in the math test; She beat him to the corner* (by getting there first); *He was beaten* (Informal for tricked) *for $5; Bicycling beats* (= is preferable to) *walking.* **3** pulsate regularly, as the heart, a flying bird's wings, etc. **4** travel with difficulty, repeatedly, or to find something: *hunters beating the woods for game.* —**beat a retreat** withdraw or retreat quickly.
—**beat about** or **around the bush** avoid coming to the point. —**beat down 1** descend mercilessly: *The sun beat down on the parched earth all summer.* **2** reduce or make someone reduce a price: *to beat the price down to $100; He haggled and beat me down to $100.* —**beat it** *Informal.* leave quickly.
—**beats me** *Informal.* puzzles me: *It beats me how she does it; How she does it beats me; How does she do it? Beats me.*
—**beat up** *Informal.* thrash soundly: *to beat someone up* or *beat up on someone.*
—*n.* **1** a time unit or accent in music. **2** regular or rhythmic striking: *People danced to the beat of the drum; a steady, rhythmic beat; the beat of the heart; an irregular beat; In a shock, one feels the heart stopping or skipping a beat;* **Without skipping** or **missing a beat** (= calmly or without any interruption) *she listened till the end.* **3** a path traveled or job done regularly: *a police officer walking her beat.* —*adj.* **1** *Informal.* tired; exhausted: *I'm dead beat.* **2** having to do with beatniks: *the beat generation; beat poetry.*
beat·en (BEET.un) a *pp.* of BEAT.
—*adj.* & *cpd.*: *beaten egg whites; We ate at a restaurant* **off the beaten track** or **path** (= out of the accustomed route); *a weather-beaten face, jacket, look, house; beaten-down prices.*
be·a·tif·ic (bee.uh.TIF.ic) *adj.* blissful: *a beatific expression, smile; the beatific vision* (of God).
be·at·i·fy (bee.AT.uh.fye) *v.* **-fies, -fied, -fy·ing** **1** make blissful. **2** in the Roman Catholic church, officially declare a dead person to be in Heaven.
—**be·at·i·fi·ca·tion** (-fuh.CAY.shun) *n.*
beat·ing *n.* an act of striking repeatedly or its effect: *a brutal, severe, vicious beating at the hands of thugs; Our team got* or *took a merciless beating* (= lost badly) *in the finals.*
be·at·i·tude (bee.AT.uh.tude) *n.* **1** supreme joy or blessedness. **2** **Beatitude** one of Christ's declarations beginning "Blessed are...."
beat·nik *n.* a member of the social rebels of the 1950s who expressed themselves in distinctive speech, clothing, music, and literature.
beat-up *adj. Informal.* battered or damaged: *a beat-up old car.*
beau (BOH) *n.* **beaus** or **beaux** (BOZE) **1** a fine-looking dandy. **2** a woman's escort or suitor: *a steady beau of hers.*
beau geste (-ZHEST) *n., pl.* **beaux gestes** or **beau gestes** (-ZHEST) a noble or generous gesture.
beau i·de·al (-eye.DEE.ul) *n., pl.* **beau ideals** the perfect model of its type.
Beau·jo·lais (boh.zhoh.LAY) *n.* a French red wine.

beau monde (-MOND) *n.*, *pl.* **beaux mondes** or **beau mondes** (boh.MOND) fashionable society.

beaut (BYOOT) *n. Informal* [often ironic] something of superlative quality: *Your hat's a real beaut!*

beau.te.ous (BYOO.tee.us) *adj.* [literary] beautiful.

beau.ti.cian (byoo.TISH.un) *n.* one who cuts or styles hair and provides other beauty treatments such as manicures and facials.

beau.ti.ful (BYOO.tuh.ful) *adj.* having beauty; pleasing to the mind or senses: *a beautiful child, day, girl, scene, song; The ballet was beautiful to watch; the **beautiful people*** (= people of wealth and fashion). —**beau.ti.ful.ly** *adv.*

beau.ti.fy (BYOO.tuh.fye) *v.* **-fies, -fied, -fy.ing** make or become beautiful. —**beau.ti.fi.ca.tion** (-fuh.CAY.shun) *n.*

beau.ty (BYOO.tee) *n.* **-ties 1** a combination of pleasing qualities: *Does make-up really enhance your beauty?* **2** a person or thing having attractive qualities, usu. a woman: *a dazzling, raving, striking, wholesome beauty; Dad is a bathing beauty in his new swimming trunks;* **adja.**: *Feminists frown upon **beauty contests** and beauty queens as exploitation of women.*

beauty shop (or **parlor** or **salon**) *n.* a business establishment giving cosmetic care to women's hair, hands, and face.

beaux arts (boh.ZAR) *n.pl.* the fine arts.

bea.ver (BEE.vur) *n.* a large rodent with flat tail and strong incisors noted for its activity: *a large colony of beavers; He's busy as a beaver; She works like a beaver* (= is very industrious); *an eager beaver* (= very zealous) *reporter; a **beaver dam*** (built by beavers); *the **beaver pelt** tag of authenticity of a piece of native art or craft.*

be.bop (BEE.bop) *n.* early modern jazz characterized by dissonant chords, eccentric rhythms, and fast tempos: *the world of bebop;* **adja.**: *the bebop era, generation, movement, school; bebop art, harmony, qualities; a bebop trumpet.* Also **bop.** —**be.bop.per** *n.*

be.calmed (bi.CAHMD) *adj.* made motionless by lack of wind: *a ship becalmed in the South Seas.*

became *pt.* of BECOME.

be.cause (bi.CAWZ, -CUZ) *conj.* for the reason that: *I like the hat because it fits me; I like it **because of*** (= on account of) *its fit.*

beck *n.* a summoning gesture: *A slave had to be at his master's **beck and call*** (= ready to obey on command) *all day.*

beck.on (BECK.un) *v.* summon, esp. with a gesture of the hand or head: *He beckoned to her; beckoned her to follow him to the office.*

be.come (bi.CUM) *v.* **-comes, -came, -come, -com.ing 1** come or grow to be: *Children become adults; She wants to become a doctor; He wants to become rich and famous; What **became of*** (= happened to) *your old car?* **2** suit: *It ill becomes one to swear in public.*

becoming *adj.* suitable and attractive: *She came dressed in a very becoming fashion for the interview; The hat is very becoming to you;* **be.com.ing.ly** *adv.*

bed *n.* **1** a piece of furniture for sleeping: *bunk, double, king-size, queen-size, roll-away, single, sofa, twin beds; a trundle bed; water beds; a feather bed* (= mattress); *We **go to bed*** (= retire to sleep) *at 11; The kids are put to bed at 9; We try to get out of bed at 6; She likes to lie or stay late in bed on holidays; Maids make or make up beds* (= arrange beds) *in hotel rooms; I had to take to my bed* (= remain in bed) *with a fever all last week; She pays for her **bed and board*** (= food and lodging); *a **bed-and-breakfast** establishment* (= inn or guesthouse offering lodging and breakfast). **2** a place where something lies: *miners working on a bed of coal; the bed of a river, of the ocean; a house built on a bed* (= foundation) *of concrete.* **3** a piece of ground for planting: *a flower bed.* —**get up on the wrong side of the bed** *Informal.* wake up in a bad mood. —**go to bed with** *Informal.* have sex with someone. —**make the bed** arrange a bed for use. —*v.* **beds, bed.ded, bed.ding 1** put or go to bed: *We had to **bed down** on the floor.* **2** plant, as in a bed; *n.*: *plants ready for **bedding;** adj.*: *posts bedded* (= embedded) *in concrete.* **3** lay out in a bed: *to bed out the plants.*

be.daub (bi.DAWB) *v.* smear or smudge: *The wall was bedaubed with mud.*

be.daz.zle (bi.DAZ.ul) *v.* **-daz.zles, -daz.zled, -daz.zling 1** blind with brightness. **2** dazzle or confuse.

bed.bug *n.* a bloodsucking insect often infesting beds.

bed chesterfield *n.* a sofa bed.

bed.clothes *n.pl.* sheets and blankets for a bed.

bedding (BED.ing) *n.* **1** bedclothes or material to sleep on. **2** a building foundation.

be.deck (bi.DEK) *v.* to ornament or adorn.

be.dev.il (bi.DEV.ul) *v.* **-ils, -iled, -il.ing** plague or confuse: *The use of nuclear power is an issue that bedevils humanity.* Also **be.dev.illed, be.dev.il.ling** *Cdn.* —**be.dev.il.ment** *n.*

be.dew (bi.DEW) *v.* wet or sprinkle, as with dew: *a face bedewed with tears.*

bed.fel.low (BED.fel.oh) *n.* one sharing a bed: *Politics makes strange bedfellows* (= makes very different people come together).

be.dim (bi.DIM) *v.* **-dims, -dimmed, -dim.ming** make dim.

bed.lam (BED.lum) *n.* uproar and confusion.

bed of roses *n.* a luxurious existence.

Bed.ou.in (BED.oo.in) *n.* an Arab who leads a nomadic life.

bed.pan *n.* a pan used in bed or at bedside as a toilet.

bed.post *n.* one of the corner supports on an old-fashioned bed such as a four-poster: *This is **between you and me and the bedpost** (Informal for This is confidential).*

be.drag.gled (bi.DRAG.uld) *adj.* wet, limp, and dirty: *her bedraggled appearance, clothes, hair.*

bed.rid.den (BED.rid.un) *adj.* confined to bed by age or illness.

bed.rock *n.* solid rock under soil, loose rock, etc.: *Philosophers consider morality the bedrock* (= basis or foundation) *of civilization.* —**adj.** fundamental or crucial: *a bedrock decision, quality, question.*

bed.roll *n.* a roll of portable bedding, as a sleeping bag, for camping out.

bed.room *n.* a room for sleeping: *Mom and Dad use the master bedroom; We've a spare bedroom for guests;* **adj.**: *a bedroom group* or *set (of furniture); a bedroom suite (of rooms);* a **bedroom city** or **community** or **suburb** *from which people commute to work in a crowded metropolis.*

bed.side *n.* the area close to a bed, as of a sick person: *We were at her bedside during her last moments;* **adj.**: *a bedside lamp; the doc's fine bedside manner; a book for bedside reading.*

bed.sore *n.* a sore caused by being bedridden.

bed.spread *n.* a decorative cover for the bedclothes.

bed.stead (BED.sted) *n.* a frame for the springs and mattress of a bed.

bed.time *n.* the time one usu. goes to bed: *It's past your bedtime.*

bee *n.* **1** a small four-winged stinging insect that gathers nectar from flowers: *a colony of queen bees, worker bees, and drones; as busy as a bee; He keeps bees as a hobby; a swarm of bees flying away to form a new colony.* **2** a busy gathering or activity: *knitting, quilting, sewing, spelling, spinning bees.* —**bee in one's bonnet** *Informal.* a notion or idea that is a preoccupation or obsession: *She's got a bee in her bonnet about eating only vegetables.*

beech *n.* a hardwood tree with silvery gray bark and edible nuts.

beef *n.* **1** *pl.* **beeves** (BEEVS) the meat of full-grown cattle: *Prime beef is the meat of steers and young cows; Bull and cow are other classes of beef; Choice, good, and utility are various grades of beef; cuts of beef such as brisket, chuck, and round; Beef may be braised, broiled, roasted, stewed; corned beef (cured by salting); ground beef (minced by grinding); a herd of good beef* (= beef cattle); *Texas beeves.* **2** brawn or strength: *The singer needs to put more beef in her voice.* **3** *pl.* **beefs** *Informal.* a complaint: *to have a beef.* —*v.* **1** *Informal.* complain: *What's he beefing about?* **2 beef up** strengthen: *to beef up a police force; to beef up security for the royal visit.*

beef.cake *n. Informal.* a pictorial display of muscles on the male body.

beef.steak (BEEF.stake) *n.* a thick slice of beef for broiling, frying, etc.

beef.y *adj.* strong-looking: *a beefy bodyguard, bouncer.*

bee.hive *n.* **1** a hive of bees or one made for them. **2** a busy place: *a beehive of activity.*

bee.keep.er (BEE.kee.pur) *n.* one who tends domesticated bees for their honey. —**bee.keep.ing** *n.*

bee.line *n.* shortest route: *They made a beeline for the cafeteria when the bell rang.*

Be.el.ze.bub (bee.EL.zi.bub) *n.* Satan.

been *pt.* of BE: *I've **been to*** (= visited) *Europe.*

beep *n.* a short high-pitched tone given as a signal. —*v.* give or make a beep: *She beeped* (= sounded) *her horn to warn the bicyclist.*

beep.er *n.* a beeping device, esp. a radio receiver carried on one's person for receiving signals to phone customers, patients, etc.

beer *n.* **1** an alcoholic drink made from malted barley and hops: *a bottle, can, glass, mug, stein of beer; light beer with less alcohol; near beer with low alcohol content.* **2** a soft drink made from extracts of roots, bark, etc.: *ginger beer; root beer.* —**adj.**: *beer bottles, kegs; a*

beery / begot

beer belly (*Informal* for potbelly or a man with one); *a zoo with a* **beer garden** (where beer is sold); *a* **beer joint** (*Slang* for beer tavern).
beer.y *adj.* **beer.i.er, -i.est** having to do with beer: *a beery flavor, lunch, tavern.*
beet *n.* a plant with edible red or white roots: *as red as a beet.*
bee.tle *n.* an insect with hard forewings covering the flying wings when at rest: *Some well-known beetles are the June bug, the ladybug, and the firefly.* —*v.* **bee.tles, bee.tled, bee.tling** 1 overhang; *adj.:* **beetling** *cliffs.* 2 to scurry. —*adj*a. overhanging or projecting: *a hairy man with beetle brows.* —**beetle-browed** or **beetling** *adj.*
beeves a *pl.* of BEEF.
be.fall (bi.FAWL) *v.* **be.falls, be.fell, be.fall.en, be.fall.ing** happen to someone: *No one knows what strange fate befell him.*
be.fit (bi.FIT) *v.* **-fits, -fit.ted, -fit.ting** be appropriate to a person or thing: *He came dressed* **as befits** *someone of his rank; in clothes befitting a prince; adj.: dressed in* **befitting** (= appropriate) *style.*
be.fog (bi.FOG) *v.* **-fogs, -fogged, -fog.ging** cover with fog; confuse: *obscure wits befogged with drink.*
be.fore (bi.FOR) *adv.* earlier or formerly: *This has happened before; same as before; Before, we used to get up at 6, but now it's 9.* —**before long** soon. —*prep.* 1 earlier than: *the day before yesterday; on or before October 11.* 2 ahead of: *She puts honor before everything else.* 3 in front of: *He knelt before the queen; a case before* (= being considered by) *the court.* —*conj.* sooner than: *He would beg or borrow before he would steal.*
be.fore.hand (bi.FOR.hand) *adj. & adv.* in advance; ahead of time: *Let me know beforehand; It's wise to be ready beforehand in case of trouble.*
be.foul (bi.FOWL) *v.* make dirty; foul: *a stream befouled by city wastes.*
be.friend (bi.FREND) *v.* 1 act as a friend to someone: *to befriend the needy.* 2 make a friend of someone: *She befriended the new girl in school.*
be.fud.dle (bi.FUD.ul) *v.* **-fud.dles, -fud.dled, -fud.dling** confuse, as with drink. —**be.fud.dle.ment** *n.*
beg *v.* **begs, begged, beg.ging** 1 ask for handouts: *He begs for a living or He lives by begging; He is so desperate he would beg, borrow, or steal; He begs his bread* (as charity). 2 ask formally: *I beg to differ.* 3 ask earnestly: *I humbly beg your forgiveness; I must beg a favor of you; I beg (of) you to forgive me; I beg for mercy; I beg your pardon; I beg pardon of you.* —**beg off** ask to be released from an obligation. —**beg the question** assume the truth of what is to be proved. —**go begging** have few buyers: *Houses go begging during a depression.*
be.gan *pt.* of BEGIN.
be.get (bi.GET) *v.* **-gets,** *pt.* **-got,** *pp.* **-got.ten** or **-got, -get.ting** 1 be the father of someone: *Abraham begot Isaac.* 2 cause: *Does poverty beget crime?*
beg.gar (BEG.ur) *n.* one who begs for a living: *"Beggars can't be choosers"* (= One shouldn't criticize what is received free). —*v. Formal.* make poor: *He was beggared by the loss of his job; The sight of Everest* **beggars description** (= is too great for words to describe).
beg.gar.ly (BEG.ur.lee) *adj.* very poor: *long hours and beggarly wages.*
beg.gar.y (BEG.uh.ree) *n.* great poverty.
be.gin (bi.GIN, "G" in "go") *v.* **-gins, -gan, -gun, -gin.ning** start to do or exist: *The alphabet begins with ABC; ABC begins the alphabet; Let's begin to read or begin reading; Let's begin the lesson; We'll begin by singing the national anthem; Please begin at* (= start from) *the beginning; We begin on* (= start work on) *a new project today; We are beginning to see the light* (= understand it); *When did life begin* (= come into being) *on Earth? The pile-up on the highway was so bad the police* **couldn't begin to** (= come near to) *sort it out; You have to be interested in the book* **to begin with** (= as the first step). —**be.gin.ner** *n.: We are all beginners when we learn something new; He's a mere beginner* (= one lacking in skill and experience).
beginning *n.* a start or starting: *In or At the beginning we had no idea of what to do; We made a good beginning; Today marks the beginning of a new era; a new beginning after many failures; the beginning of the end of the war; Start at the beginning; from the beginning of the poem; the very beginning; Can you recite the poem from* **beginning to end?** *a millionaire who rose from humble* **beginnings** (= origins); *We see the* **beginnings** (= early stages) *of a settlement of the dispute.* —*adj*a. basic or elementary: *a beginning course, dictionary, student.*
be.gone (bi.GON) *interj. Poetic.* Go away: *"Begone, dull care!"*
be.gon.ia (bi.GOHN.yuh) *n.* any of a group of decorative plants with attractive leaves and flowers.
begot, begotten See BEGET.

be.grime (bi.GRIME) v. **-grimes, -grimed, -grim.ing** to make dirty: *a mechanic with hands begrimed with grease and dirt.*
be.grudge (bi.GRUJ) v. **-grudg.es, -grudged, -grudg.ing** envy or resent: *Let's not begrudge him his good fortune.* —**be.grudg.ing.ly** adv.
be.guile (bi.GUILE) v. **-guiles, -guiled, -guil.ing 1** deceive by charm and persuasion: *He was beguiled into betraying his plans; He was beguiled out of all his savings; a pretty tale to beguile* (= entertain) *fools (with).* **2** pass time pleasantly: *She reads to beguile her leisure hours.* —**be.guile.ment** n. —**be.guil.er** n.
begun pp. of BEGIN.
be.half (bi.HAF) n. interest or benefit: *a lawyer acting in her client's behalf.* —**on** or **in behalf of** in the interest of someone: *A lawyer acts on* or *in behalf of his client; She spoke on behalf of* (= representing) *all of us.*
be.have (bi.HAIV) v. **-haves, -haved, -hav.ing 1** conduct oneself according to a standard: *Children are taught to behave (well); to behave respectfully toward teachers; Billy, behave yourself* (= behave properly)*! how to behave in public; to behave like civilized people.* **2** perform or act: *The machine behaved well during the tests; How do acids behave in the presence of alkalis?*
be.hav.ior (bi.HAIV.yur) n. a way of behaving or acting: *The drugged man showed strange behavior; animal behavior; social behavior; to study the behavior of animals under varying conditions; abnormal, criminal, disciplined, disruptive, infantile, irrational, modest, normal, obsequious, scandalous, sullen, ungentlemanly, unorthodox, unruly behavior; to engage in high-risk behaviors; behaviors exhibited by patients; compulsive behaviors; His sentence was reduced for good behavior (in prison); Be on your best behavior* (= Behave properly); **adja.**: *a behavior pattern; behavior modification, therapy.* —**be.hav.ior.al** adj.: *a behavioral problem; Psychology and sociology are* **behavioral sciences.** Also **be.hav.iour, be.hav.iour.al** Cdn.
be.hav.ior.ism (bi.HAIV.yur.iz.um) n. a branch of psychology based solely on the observation and analysis of objective behavior. —**be.hav.ior.ism** n.; **be.hav.ior.ist** n. & adj.
—**be.hav.ior.is.tic** (-yuh.RIS.tic) adj. Also **be.hav.iour.ism, be.hav.iour.ist, be.hav.iour.is.tic** Cdn.
be.head (bi.HED) v. cut off the head of someone: *Traitors used to be beheaded.*
beheld pt. & pp. of BEHOLD.
be.he.moth (bi.HEE.muth) n. a large, monstrously powerful beast or thing.
be.hest (bi.HEST) n. a command or urgent request: *We act at your behest; at the behest of friends and relatives.*
be.hind (bi.HINED) adv. in, to, or at the rear, a previous place or time, etc.: *We were seated behind, not in front of her; the child he left behind in Vietnam; to remain* or *stay behind when everyone is gone; a pupil falling* or *lagging behind in school* (= slow at learning); *He's behind* (= in arrears) *in* or *with his rent; He's behind by $900.* —**prep. 1** later than: *He finished behind the others.* **2** in or to the rear of a person or thing: *He is behind you; What is behind* (= hidden by) *this clever scheme? Jimmy does naughty things* **behind his mother's back** (= unknown to her); *activity going on* **behind the scenes** (= in secret); **adja.**: *a behind-the-scenes activity.* **3** supporting: *We are solidly behind you all the way.* —**n.** Informal. buttocks: *He fell on his behind.*
be.hind.hand (bi.HINED.hand) adv. in arrears or backward: *Your dues are behindhand this month; You're behindhand with the rent; You're also behindhand with* or *in your homework; You're never behindhand in offering help when we have a party.*
be.hold (bi.HOLED) v. **-holds, -held, -hold.ing** gaze upon something: *Lo and behold, the rabbit is gone! Open your eyes and behold the wonders of nature!* —**be.hold.er** n.: *"Beauty is in the eye of the beholder."*
be.hold.en (bi.HOLE.dun) adj. [sometimes ironical] obliged: *I'm not beholden to anyone for the wealth I have accumulated; She's truly beholden to you for your kindness.*
be.hoove (bi.HOOV) v. **-hooves, -hooved, -hoov.ing** be necessary or proper for someone: *It behooves us to be modest.*
beige (BAIZH) n. & adj. yellowish brown.
being (BEE.ing) See BE. —**n. 1** existence; life: *the question of being as opposed to becoming; brought into being by peculiar circumstances; How did the universe come into being?* **2** one that exists or is thought to exist: *an extraterrestrial being; human beings; a mortal being; We are rational beings; Ghosts are supernatural beings.* **3** one's nature: *He loved her with his whole being.* —**for the time being** for the present; for now.

be.jew.eled (bi.JEW.uld) *adj.* adorned with jewels: *bejeweled young goddesses.* Also **be.jew.elled** *Cdn.*

be.la.bor (bi.LAY.bur) *v.* **1** attack with blows or words. **2** dwell too long on a subject; labor: *The lecturer belabored the point for a whole hour.* Also **be.la.bour** *Cdn.*

be.lat.ed (bi.LAY.tid) *adj.* delayed: *Happy New Year and a belated Merry Christmas!* **—be.lat.ed.ly** *adv.*

be.lay (bi.LAY) *v.* **-lays, -layed, -lay.ing** **1** secure a rope around a cleat or pin, called **belaying pin** on a ship. **2** secure a mountain climber by a rope. **3** [nautical use] stop: *Belay there!*

belch *v.* let out something noisily or violently, esp. stomach gas: *Babies are said to "burp," not belch; The chimneys belched smoke.* **—n.** an act of belching or what is belched: *Someone let out a belch which disturbed the speaker; The volcano released* or *emitted a great belch of fire.*

be.lea.guer (bi.LEE.gur) *v.* **-guers, -guered, -guer.ing** besiege or harass; *adj.: a beleaguered town; the beleaguered diplomats in a troubled country.*

bel.fry (BEL.free) *n.* **-fries** **1** a chamber in a bell tower in which bells are hung; also, the bell tower. **—have bats in one's belfry** *Informal.* be eccentric or crazy.

Bel.gian (BEL.jun) *n. & adj.* (a person) of or from **Belgium,** a monarchy in W. Europe.

be.lie (bi.LYE) *v.* **-lies, -lied, -ly.ing** prove false: *Facts belied her story; His face belied (= gave a false idea of) his true feelings; Fate belied (= disappointed) our hopes.*

be.lief (bi.LEEF) *n.* the act of believing or something believed: *Nothing could shake her belief in God; They tried their best to make her give up* or *relinquish her beliefs; the religious beliefs expressed in her writings; superstitious beliefs held by the people; He did it in the belief that he was right; erroneous, false, mistaken beliefs; It is my firm belief (= opinion) that he was telling the truth; Some of the reports about him are **beyond belief** (= impossible to believe).*

be.lieve (bi.LEEV) *v.* **-lieves, -lieved, -liev.ing** **1** accept as true: *I believe his story; to believe firmly, mistakenly, sincerely, strongly; a story about him that is hard to believe; I cannot believe it of him; We all know and believe that we will die some day.* **2** have faith: *He believes in ghosts; That's the truth, believe me; Do you believe in exercise (= consider it as worth any-*

thing)? **3** suppose: *I believe you trust him; I believe so; Do you think he did it? I believe not.* **—be.liev.a.ble** *adj.: a believable story.* **—be.liev.er** *n.: the fellowship of true believers; a firm, sincere, strong believer in life after death.*

be.lit.tle (bi.LIT.ul) *v.* **-lit.tles, -lit.tled, -lit.tling** make seem small: *Don't belittle her merits; adj.: a belittling (= disparaging) remark.*

bell *n.* **1** a hollow, usu. metallic object that makes a ringing sound when struck: *church bells; I didn't hear the door bell (= the striking of the bell); I hear wedding bells (= I think they are going to get married); Bells chime, peal, ring, sound, toll; to ring* or *sound a bell; The boxer was **saved by the bell** (because the round ended before he was counted out by the referee).* **2** something with the typical bell's flared shape: *the bell of a flower; a diving bell.* **3** a measure of time (half an hour) at sea: *Call the watch at six bells.* **—v.** flare like a bell; *adj.: a belled skirt.*

bel.la.don.na (bel.uh.DON.uh) *n.* **1** a bushy plant of the nightshade family yielding a poisonous drug. **2** this drug; atropine.

bell-bottom *adja.* flaring at the bottom of the leg: *bell-bottom pants* or *trousers,* or **bell-bottoms** *n.pl.* Also **bell-bottom** *n.*

bell.boy or **bell.hop** *n.* a club or hotel employee who carries luggage, runs errands, etc.

bell captain *n.* one who is in charge of bellboys.

belle (BEL) *n.* a popular and handsome woman: *a Southern belle.* **—the belle of the ball** the favorite woman of the party.

belles-let.tres (bel.LET.ruh) *n.pl.* [takes sing. v.] literature as one of the fine arts. **—bel.let.rist** (-LET.rist) *n.* **—bel.le.tris.tic** (bel.let.RIS.tic) *adj.*

bellhop same as BELLBOY.

bel.li.cose (BEL.uh.cose) *adj.* disposed to start a fight: *a bellicose mood, nation, people; to live in bellicose estrangement.* **—bel.li.cos.i.ty** (-COS.i.tee) *n.*

bel.lig.er.ent (buh.LIJ.uh.runt) *adj.* **1** engaged in war or hostile activities: *the belligerent powers of the Middle East; a country that is belligerent toward its neighbor.* **2** aggressive by nature: *a belligerent, swaggering bully.* **—n.** a belligerent person or state: *The U.N. condemned the belligerents.* **—bel.lig.er.ent.ly** *adv.* **—bel.lig.er.ence** (-runce) *n.*

bell.man *n.* **-men** a bellhop.

bel.low (BEL.oh) *v.* make a deep roar, as a bull, or shout in this way: *He bellowed with pain; He bellows out orders to his men.* —*n.* a bellowing roar or shout.

bel.lows (BEL.oze) *n. sing. & pl.* **1** a usu. hand-operated device for blowing air, as to fan a fire: *Let me show you how to use* or *operate a bellows; See how the bellows works.* **2** something resembling a bellows, as the pleated part of an accordion.

bell.pull *n.* a handle attached to a cord to ring a bell with.

bells *n.pl. Informal.* bell-bottoms.

bells and whistles *n.pl. Informal.* accessories or frills, as of a computer system.

bell.weth.er (BELL.weth.ur, "th" as in "the") *n.* a person or thing considered as the indicator of a trend: *The Dow Jones industrial average is a bellwether of economic change.*

bel.ly (BEL.ee) *n.* **bel.lies 1** the cavity of the body that includes the stomach and bowels, esp. when bulging: *He has pain in his belly; Les Halles, which housed the world's biggest food market, was called "the belly of Paris"; He has always been a slave to his belly* (= a glutton); *Many companies* **went belly up** (*Informal for* collapsed or failed) *during the last recession.* **2** the inside of an animal, aircraft, etc.: *in the belly of a whale; the belly of a ship; the price of live hogs and frozen* **pork bellies** (= sides of pork for making bacon) *on the Chicago Mercantile Exchange.* —*v.* **bel.lies, bel.lied, bel.ly.ing** swell out: *a sail bellying in the wind.*

bel.ly.ache (BEL.ee.ake) *n.* an abdominal pain. —*v.* **-aches, -ached, -ach.ing** *Slang.* complain in a grumbling manner: *What are you bellyaching about? Quit your bellyaching.*

bel.ly.but.ton (BEL.ee.but.un) *n. Informal.* the navel.

belly dance *n.* an erotic Middle Eastern dance performed by a woman. —**belly dancer** *n.*

belly flop *n.* a dive with the swimmer hitting the water stomach first: *to do a belly flop.*

bel.ly.ful (BEL.ee.ful) *n. Informal.* all that one wants or can take: *That country has had its bellyful of war and famine.*

belly laugh *n.* a deep, hearty laugh.

be.long (bi.LONG) *v.* **1** be related to another as owned: *The dog belongs to Jim; Jim* **belongs to** (= is a member of) *the Rotary Club;* **n.:** *a community in which you feel a sense of* **belonging** (= closeness). **2** have one's proper place: *Home is where you belong; The chair belongs in the corner; All these words belong under "B".*

belongings *n.pl.* movable possessions: *our earthly belongings; your personal belongings.*

Be.la.ru.sian (bel.uh.ROO.see.un) *adj.* having to do with the people or the language of **Belarus,** a country of E. Europe, formerly part of the Soviet Union. —*n.* **1** a person of or from Belarus. **2** the Slavic language of Belarus.

Be.lo.rus.sian (BEL.oh.rush.un) same as BYELORUSSIAN and BELORUSIAN.

be.lov.ed (bi.LUV.id, -LUVD) *adj.* very much loved: *She was beloved by* or *of all who came to know her; her beloved husband.* —*n.* a beloved one: *Dearly beloved!*

be.low (bi.LOH) *prep.* lower than: *It's 10 below zero (temperature); She went below deck; The Dead Sea is below sea level; He is below* (= under) *21; A major is below a colonel in rank.* —*adv.* in, to, or at a lower position: *It is 10 below* (= 10° below zero) *right now; See page 85 below* (= further on). —**down below** in the lower part of a house, ship, etc. —**here below** on earth.

belt *n.* **1** a band of material worn around the waist: *the belt of her dress; to buckle, loosen, undo one's belt; Fasten your seat belts; a cartridge belt; life belt; money belt; safety belt; shoulder belt; She is a black belt in judo; Jim holds a brown belt in karate; It's not fair to hit one* **below the belt;** *She has years of experience* **under her belt** (= to her credit); *We* **tighten our belts** (= consume less) *in hard times;* **adj.:** *We stop eating out as a* **belt-tightening** *measure.* **2** an endless strap used to move or drive something: *a conveyor belt; the fan belt of an engine; a belt conveyor system.* **3** an area distinct in some way: *a belt of trees; corn, cotton, farm, fruit belts; the prairie grain belt; a green belt (of parkland); the nickel belt around Sudbury, Ontario; a parkway belt.* **4** *Slang.* a whack. **5** *Slang.* a swallow of drink: *No belt for the road, please!* —**adj.** encircling or ringing: *a* **belt highway** *bypassing an urban area; a* **belt line** *service of ferries touching the islands.* —*v.* **1** encircle with a belt. **2** *Informal.* beat, as with a belt: *She belted him one.* **3** *Slang.* gulp or guzzle: *to belt down one cola after another.* —**belt out** sing something forcefully.

belt.way *n.* a highway bypassing a city.

be.lu.ga (buh.LOO.guh) *n.* a white stur-

geon whose roe is used for caviar.
bel.ve.dere (BEL.vuh.deer) *n.* a structure providing a fine view, as an open gallery or a summerhouse.
be.moan (be.MOHN) *v.* mourn over something: *to bemoan a loss.*
be.muse (bi.MYOOZ) *v.* **-mus.es, -mused, -mus.ing** have one confused or lost in thought: *The retired politician was bemused by the fact that he received no job offers;* *adj.:* *her bemused approach; a bemused smile; They seemed more bemused than amused by the elaborate arrangements.*
bench *n.* **1** a long seat for two or more people: *a park bench.* **2** a long, sturdy work table: *a work bench.* **3** the office of a judge: *a lawyer appointed to the bench; a ruling from the bench; the bar and* **the bench** (= judges collectively). **4 benches** *pl.* places in a legislature: *There was much shouting from the opposition benches; He spent two terms on the back benches before joining the cabinet.* —**on the bench 1** sitting as a judge. **2** not playing in the game: *He got two minutes on the bench (as penalty in ice hockey).* —*v.* put or keep someone on a bench, as unable to play: *He was benched for two minutes for using a profanity; benched by the umpire.*
bench.er *n.* **1** a judge or magistrate. **2** a member of a governing body of the legal profession such as the Law Society of Upper Canada.
bench.mark or **bench mark** *n.* **1** a reference point in surveying. **2** a measuring standard: *a court decision that will serve as a benchmark in future cases; a benchmark decision.*
bench press *n.* a weightlifting exercise in which the lifter lies on a bench and raises a barbell up and down above the chest.
bench seat *n.* a seat that extends the full width of an automobile.
bench warrant *n.* a court order to have someone arrested: *to issue a bench warrant.*
bend *v.* **bends, bent, bend.ing 1** make, be, or become crooked or curved: *Bend down and touch your toes; Try to bend this bar; a wire bent into a coat hanger; Trees bend in the wind; The highway bends to the right after the bridge.* **2** submit or cause to submit: *She refused to bend to his will.* **3** direct or turn: *to bend one's efforts to a task; a lobby group that is* **bending the legislators' ears** (*Informal* for pressuring them) *about auto insurance rates; a session that really bent (Informal* for made a powerful impact on) *her mind; They* **bend over backward** (= try very hard) *to please customers.* —*n.* **1** a crooked or curved form or part: *a sharp bend in the road.* **2 the bends** same as DECOMPRESSION SICKNESS.
bend.er *n. Slang.* a drinking spree: *to go off* **on a bender.**
be.neath (bi.NEETH, "TH" as in "thin") *prep.* **1** below: *the valley beneath the mountain; adv.:* *She looked down at the valley beneath.* **2** unworthy of someone: *Is manual work beneath you? behavior that is* **beneath** (= unworthy of even) **contempt.**
ben.e.dic.tion (ben.uh.DIC.shun) *n.* a blessing, esp. one at the end of a church service.
ben.e.fac.tion (ben.uh.FAC.shun) *n.* a charitable gift, as given by a benefactor.
ben.e.fac.tor (ben.uh.FAC.tur) *n.* one who helps another, esp. by donations; **ben.e.fac.tress** *fem.*
ben.e.fice (BEN.uh.fis) *n.* a church position, as of a vicar, or the income that goes with it.
be.nef.i.cent (buh.NEF.uh.sunt) *adj.* doing good, esp. charitable works. —**be.nef.i.cence** *n.*
ben.e.fi.cial (ben.uh.FISH.ul) *adj.* helpful or favorable: *Fresh air is beneficial to health; It's especially beneficial for office workers; He finds it beneficial to exercise regularly.* —**ben.e.fi.cial.ly** *adv.*
ben.e.fi.ci.ar.y (ben.uh.FISH.ee.air.ee) *n.* **-aries** one who receives a benefit, as from an insurance policy, trust, or will: *His wife was named as the beneficiary of his insurance policy.*
ben.e.fit (BEN.uh.fit) *n.* **1** something that does good; advantage: *Is nuclear power a benefit to humanity? It has to be properly used to be of benefit to anyone; Use it to humanity's benefit rather than for destruction; the benefits of dieting; We derive, get, reap many benefits from good habits; Because of insufficient evidence, the accused was given* **the benefit of the doubt** *and acquitted.* **2** financial help or payment: *a death benefit; Most companies provide fringe benefits such as sick leave and a dental plan; a tax benefit; retirement benefits; She collected disability, maternity, sickness, strike, unemployment, and other benefits during her long career.* **3** a performance, sale, etc. to help a person or cause: *to have or hold a benefit; The play was staged as a benefit; a benefit performance.* —*v.* **1** do good to someone: *Wars benefit no one.* **2** derive good: *Everyone benefits by experience;*

Only the lucky few **benefit from** (= get) windfalls.

be.nev.o.lence (buh.NEV.uh.lunce) *n.* desire to do charitable deeds: *acts of benevolence.* —**be.nev.o.lent** *adj.*: *She was benevolent to* or *toward the poor;* **be.nev.o.lent.ly** *adv.*

be.night.ed (bi.NYE.tid) *adj.* unenlightened: *his benighted ideas on immigration.* —**be.night.ed.ly** *adv.*

be.nign (bi.NINE) *adj.* **1** kind and gracious: *a benign old man; a benign smile; a benign* (= mild) *climate; The armed forces complain of* **benign neglect** (= indifference) *on the part of the government in regard to manpower and resources.* **2** not harmful or malignant: *a benign tumor;* also **be.nig.nant** (bi.NIG.nunt): *a benignant, not cancerous growth.* —**be.nig.ni.ty** (bi.NIG.ni.tee) *n.* **-ties.**

ben.i.son (BEN.uh.sun) *n.* [old use] a blessing.

bent *pt.* of BEND. —*adj.* **1** curved or crooked: *a bent bicycle rim.* **2** determined: *She's* **bent on** *becoming a lawyer; youths bent on winning.* —**bent out of shape** *Informal.* **1** drunk. **2** extremely upset. —*n.* a natural inclination: *her artistic bent; his bent for mischief; She followed her bent and became a lawyer.*

ben.ton.ite (BEN.tuh.nite) *n.* an absorbent clay used in paints, medicines, etc. —**ben.ton.it.ic** (-NIT.ic) *adj.*

bent.wood *adj.* of furniture, made of wood bent into shape: *a bentwood chair.*

be.numb (bi.NUM) *v.* deaden the feelings; *adj.:* *hands benumbed by cold; the benumbing effect of sorrow.*

ben.zene (BEN.zeen) *n.* an aromatic, colorless liquid hydrocarbon used in making solvents, dyes, etc., whose carbon atoms are arranged in a closed hexagon, or **benzene ring.**

ben.zine (BEN.zeen) *n.* a volatile, colorless liquid used as a cleaning solvent and as a motor fuel.

be.queath (bi.QUEETH, "TH" as in "thin") *v.* hand down or leave money, possessions, etc., esp. in a will, *to* someone after one's death.

be.quest (bi.QUEST) *n.* **1** an act of bequeathing: *to make a bequest to one's favorite charity.* **2** something bequeathed.

be.rate (bi.RATE) *v.* **-rates, -rat.ed, -rat.ing** scold severely: *The security guard was berated for sleeping on the job.*

be.reave (bi.REEV) *v.* **-reaves, -reaved, -reav.ing** deprive by death. —*adj.:* *a dead man's* **bereaved** *family; The bereaved husband wept by his wife's coffin.* —*n.pl.:* *The bereaved* (relatives) *stood around the grave.* —**be.reave.ment** *n.*

be.reft (bi.REFT) *adjp.* deprived: *a refugee bereft of kin; a life bereft of joy; a future bereft of all hope.*

be.ret (buh.RAY) *n.* a flat, round cloth or felt cap.

berg *n.* an iceberg.

ber.i.ber.i (BER.ee.ber.ee) *n.* a disease caused by a lack of thiamine, leading to muscular stiffness or paralysis and great weakness.

be.rib.boned (bi.RIB.und) *adj.* decorated with ribbons: *a beribboned window.*

Ber.ke.li.um (bur.KEE.lee.um) *n.* a synthetic radioactive element.

Ber.lin.er (bur.LIN.ur) *n.* a person of or from **Berlin,** the capital of Germany.

berm *n.* **1** a ridge or other barrierlike formation: *The building is surrounded by a* **berm** (= high mound of earth) *which protects it from street noise.* **2** a shoulder, as of a road, or shoulderlike formation or ledge.

Ber.mu.da shorts (bur.MEW.duh-) or **Ber.mu.das** *n.pl.* knee-length shorts.

ber.ry (BER.ee) *n.* **ber.ries 1** a usu. small, fleshy fruit with many seeds, as a blueberry or strawberry: *to pick berries; Botanically, a tomato is a berry although it looks like a fruit and is used as a vegetable.* **2** a dried seed: *coffee berries.*

ber.serk (bur.SURK) *adv.* in or into a destructive frenzy: *The soccer fans went berserk and caused some destruction; adj.:* *The women were not berserk except for one berserk youngster.*

berth *n.* **1** a sleeping place in a ship, railroad car, etc. **2** an anchoring place for a ship. —**give a wide berth to** keep a safe distance from someone. —*v.* put into or occupy a berth.

ber.yl (BER.ul) *n.* a hard, lustrous mineral of various colors used as a gem, as emerald and aquamarine.

be.ryl.li.um (buh.RIL.ee.um) *n.* a hard, rare, metallic element used in alloys.

be.seech (bi.SEECH) *v.* **-seech.es,** *pt. & pp.* **-seeched** or **-sought** (-SAWT), **-seech.ing** *Formal.* beg earnestly: *Mercy, I beseech you! I beseech you to show mercy.*

be.set (bi.SET) *v.* **-sets, -set, -set.ting** attack on all sides: *a traveler beset by robbers; a mind beset with fears; adja.:* *a* **besetting** (= predominant) *problem; Pride was the king's besetting sin.*

be.side (bi.SIDE) *prep.* at or near the side of a person or thing: *The garage is beside the house, not attached to it.* —**beside oneself** distraught or agitated *with* despair, fear, grief, joy, rage, etc.: *She was beside herself* (= very angry)

when she found out the truth. —**beside the point** irrelevant.
besides (bi.SIDES) *prep. & adv.* in addition to: *Besides being smart, he's hardworking; He owns a house and a cottage besides; He owns a cottage besides his house.*
be.siege (bi.SEEJ) *v.* **-sieg.es, -sieged, -sieg.ing** lay siege to a person or thing; surround: *Enemy troops besieged the city; Employment agencies were besieged* (= crowded around) *by the jobless; Employers were besieged* (= pressed) *with applications; adj.: a besieged bank, city, manager.*
be.smear (bi.SMEER) *v.* smear or sully: *The wall was besmeared with paint; adj.: a besmeared reputation.*
be.smirch (bi.SMURCH) *v.* harm a reputation: *His writings besmirched her good name; adj.: her besmirched reputation.*
be.som (BEE.zum) *n.* a broom, as used in the game of curling.
be.sot.ted (be.SOT.id) *adj.* intoxicated: *a besotted lover; He was besotted with her charms.*
besought a *pt. & pp.* of BESEECH.
be.span.gle (bi.SPANG.gul) *v.* **-gles, -gled, -gling** decorate with spangles; *adj.: a bejeweled and bespangled actress; a star-bespangled sky.*
be.spat.ter (bi.SPAT.ur) *v.* spatter or soil with dirt, calumny, etc.
be.speak (bi.SPEEK) *v.* **-speaks, -spoke, -spok.en, -speak.ing** be a sign of something: *an omen that bespeaks good fortune.*
bespoke (bi.SPOKE) *adj*a. custom-made: *a bespoke jacket, suit; a bespoke* (= custom) *tailor.*
be.sprin.kle (bi.SPRING.kul) *v.* **-kles, -kled, -kling** sprinkle: *a lawn besprinkled with dew.*
best *adj. superl.* of GOOD: *May the best man win; It's best that we remain silent on the subject; The dog is man's best friend; She thought it best to ignore the man.*
—*n.* something that is best: *For the idealist, the best is not good enough; The best is yet to come; He tried his very* or *level best to do a good job; He did his best on the job, gave his best to the company; He was not in the best of health; It was too much to hope for at the best of times; The weather is at its best in the spring; Jan is the best in her class; Jon is the next best* or *second best;* **To the best of my knowledge** (= as far as I know), *he has never been married; Please give my best* (Informal for best wishes) *to the family; All the best!*
—*adv. superl.* of WELL: *Luc came out best; She does best in math.* —**as best one can** as well as possible. —**at best** under the most favorable conditions. —**for the best** good or well: *It's all for the best, don't worry.* —**get the best of** defeat; outwit. —**had best** ought to: *I'd best stay in school.* —**make the best of** do as well as possible despite something unfavorable: *to make the best of a bad bargain.* —**the best of both worlds** the good aspects of two different situations without any of their disadvantages. —**the best part of** almost all of something: *He was absent for the best part of the day.* —**with the best (of them)** as well as any.
—*v.* outdo: *The boxer was bested in a fair fight.*
best-before date *n.* a date by which a perishable item of food should be consumed.
bes.tial (BES.tee.ul, BES.chul) *adj.* of or like beasts; savage: *bestial cruelty;* **bes.tial.ly** *adv.* —**bes.ti.al.i.ty** (-tee.AL.i.tee) *n.*
be.stir (bi.STUR) *v.* **-stirs, -stirred, -stir.ring** *Formal.* make active: *It's morning, let's bestir ourselves!*
best man *n.* a bridegroom's male attendant.
be.stow (bi.STOH) *v.* give as an honor or gift: *They bestowed a doctorate on* or *upon him.* —**be.stow.al** (-ul) *n.*
be.stride (bi.STRIDE) *v.* **-strides, -strode, -strid.den, -strid.ing** sit, stand, or get astride: *The knight bestrode his horse.*
best.sell.er (BEST.SEL.ur) *n.* a book, record, etc. that sells better than others of its kind: *Dictionaries are perennial bestsellers.* —**best.sell.ing** *adj*a.
bet *n.* 1 an agreement that the one who is wrong about an outcome will give something, usu. a sum of money, to the one who is right; wager: *We made a $100 bet that we would win the election; They accepted the bet; A bookmaker is taking bets on who will form the next government; She wouldn't have done it except on a bet; He hedges his bets* (= protects himself) *by placing bets on more than one horse; If there's an earthquake, then* **all bets are off** (= everything is uncertain). 2 that on which a bet is made: *His team is a safe bet (to win); a sure bet; In this weather, your best bet* (= safest alternative) *is to take the train.*
—*v.* **bets,** *pt. & pp.* **bet** or **bet.ted, bet.ting** 1 make a bet; wager, usu. money: *We bet (him) $50 that he would lose the vote; He bets only on horses; n.: off-track betting.* 2 claim as though betting: *I bet she'll win.* —**you bet!** *Infor-*

mal. certainly!

be.ta (BAY.tuh, BEE.tuh) **1** *n.* the second letter of the Greek alphabet [Β, β]. **2** *adja.* having to do with the testing of new or updated software, hardware, or a similar product prior to its release: *a beta copy, release, test, test site, version.*

be.take (bi.TAKE) *v.* **-takes, -took, -tak.en, -tak.ing** cause *oneself* to go: *They betook themselves to the air waves in a propaganda blitz.*

beta particle *n.* an electron or positron emitted by a radioactive substance, a stream of which is called a **beta ray.**

be.tel (BEE.tul) *n.* a tropical vine whose leaf is chewed as a stimulant with lime and **betel nuts** (from the "betel palm" tree) by people of S. Asia.

bête noire (BAIT.nwar) *n., pl.* **bêtes noires** (BAIT.nwars) a person or thing that one abhors.

be.think (bi.THINK) *v.* **-thinks, -thought, -think.ing** make oneself recall or reconsider: *Bethink yourself of your patriotic duty.*

be.tide (bi.TIDE) *v.* befall: *Woe betide you if you fail this test!*

be.times (bi.TIMES) *adv.* in good time; early in the day, year, etc.

be.to.ken (bi.TOH.kun) *v.* be a sign of: *preparations betokening war.*

betook *pt.* of BETAKE.

be.tray (bi.TRAY) *v.* **1** be disloyal by breach of faith: *He betrayed his best friend to his enemies; to betray one's country, a trust;* **adj.:** *He felt* **betrayed** (= forsaken) *when his family ignored him in his time of need; a betrayed friend.* **2** reveal on purpose: *to betray a confidence, secret.* **3** show, esp. unwittingly: *His shaking hands betrayed his nervousness.*
 —**be.tray.al** (bi.TRAY.ul) *n.*

be.troth.al (bi.TROH.thul, bi.TROTH.ul, "th" as in "thin") *n.* engagement to be married.

be.trothed (bi.TROTHED, bi.TROTHT) *n. & adj.* (one) engaged to be married.

bet.ter (BET.ur) *adj., comp.* of GOOD: *Is he any better today? a better man; He's much better than he was last week; It's better to give than to receive; It's better that we give rather than take from others; He's better at chess than at tennis; Mom kissed the sore spot and made it* **all better.**
 —*adv. comp.* of WELL: *You better believe it* (Informal for You're absolutely right).
 —**better half** *Informal.* one's spouse.
 —**better off** in a better condition.
 —**for better or (for) worse** whatever happens: *He is your spouse for better or for worse.* —**get the better of** outdo or overcome someone. —**had better ought to.** —**the better part of** more than half of something: *He was absent for the better part of the day.* —**think better of** reconsider something.
 —*n.* **1** one that is better: *the better of the two; a change* **for the better** (= an improvement); *Events took a turn for the better;* $5,000 **or better** (= more); *Listen to your elders and* **betters** (= superiors). **2** same as BETTOR. —*v.* improve: *He bettered himself by training; was able to better* (= outdo) *his previous record.*

bet.ter.ment (BET.ur.munt) *n.* improvement, esp. of society: *She devoted her life to the betterment of humanity.*

bet.tor (BET.ur) *n.* one who bets. Also **bet.ter.**

be.tween (bi.TWEEN) *prep.* indicating **1** [a midway position, place, time, degree, etc.]: *the road between here and Jerusalem; some time between 7 and 8 p.m.; a position between two extremes.* **2** [joint or related ownership, action, connection, etc.]: *We own 100 hectares between the two of us;* **Between them,** *the three women have over 100 years of experience on this job; just* **between you and me** (= confidentially). **3** [choice involving two or more]: *I can't choose between the two ties; a race between chuckwagons; the main differences between the three of us.*
 —**between you and I** [overcorrect form of "between you and me"]
 —*adv.*: *He eats only breakfast and supper, with snacks* **in between;** *Her visits have become* **few and far between** (= very rare).

be.twixt (bi.TWIXT) *prep. & adv.* between: *The peacemaker was caught* **betwixt and between** (the two parties).

bev.el (BEV.ul) *n.* an angle other than 90°, as of a sloping surface, edge, etc.
 —*v.* **bev.els, bev.eled, bev.el.ing** cut to, set at, or have a bevel; *adj.: a beveled mirror.* Also **bev.elled, bev.el.ling** *Cdn.*

bev.er.age (BEV.rij) *n.* a drink other than water: *to order a beverage with one's meal; alcoholic beverages; carbonated beverages.*

bev.y (BEV.ee) *n.* **bev.ies** group: *a bevy of deer, girls, larks, phone calls, projects, quails, roes.*

be.wail (bi.WAIL) *v.* lament: *to bewail one's fate, misfortune.*

be.ware (bi.WARE) *v.* be careful or cautious: *(Let the) buyer beware; Beware of the dog.*

be.whisk.ered (bi.WHIS.kurd) *adj.* bearded.

bewigged / bicycle

bewigged (bi.WIGD) *adj.* wearing a wig.
be.wil.der (bi.WIL.dur) *v.* puzzle and confuse: *He was bewildered by everything that had happened that night;* ***adj.****: a **bewildered** look; a **bewildering** array of artifacts for sale.* —**be.wil.der.ment** *n.*
be.witch (bi.WICH) *v.* **1** cast a magic spell on someone, esp. with evil intent: *He's easily bewitched by flattery.* **2** charm: *Macbeth was bewitched into contemplating murder;* ***adj.****: a **bewitching** beauty, smile.* —**be.witch.ment** *n.*
be.yond (bi.YOND) *prep.* **1** on the other side: *You can't see beyond the horizon; She was told not to stay beyond midnight; How time never ends is **beyond me*** (= more than I can understand). **2** outside the limits: *to live beyond one's means and go broke; He was found guilty of murder beyond a reasonable doubt; It has been proven beyond the shadow of a doubt; a beautiful scene that is beyond words to describe; She was grateful **beyond measure*** (= more than can be measured) *for the kindness shown to her husband; a subject that is really **beyond my depth*** (= beyond my understanding); *behavior that is **beyond the pale*** (= unacceptable). —***adv.*** farther on: *The view stretches to the horizon and beyond.* —*n.* **the back of beyond** *Informal.* beyond the farthest limit; **the (great) beyond** the afterlife.
bez.el (BEZ.ul) *n.* **1** a sloping surface, as the edge of a chisel or a side on a cut gem. **2** a grooved rim holding a watch crystal or a gem in its place.
bi.an.nu.al (bye.AN.yoo.ul) *adj.* occurring twice a year; semiannual. —**bi.an.nu.al.ly** *adv.*
bi.as (BYE.us) *n.* **bi.as.es 1** an inclination for or against something; prejudice: *a hiring policy that shows strong bias against women and minorities; a deep-rooted bias; Some companies have a bias toward or for or in favor of younger personnel.* **2** a slanting line across the weave of a fabric: *cloth that is cut **on the bias*** (= diagonally); ***adja.****: a bias seam; a radial, not bias (ply) tire.* —*v.* **bi.as.es, bi.ased, bi.as.ing** prejudice: *His experience biased him against bureaucrats;* ***adj.****: The juror was rejected because he seemed very **biased**; The report was biased against the elderly; It seemed biased toward younger people.* Also **bi.assed, bi.as.sing** *Cdn.*
bi.ath.lon (bye.ATH.lon) *n.* a sport or skill combining skiing and rifle-shooting.
bib *n.* **1** a cloth tied under a child's chin at meals: *He appeared in his **best bib and tucker*** (*Informal* for best clothes) *for his mom's graduation.* **2** the top part of an apron or overalls. —*v.* drink excessively: *a brawling, beer-bibbing heavyweight;* ***n.****: a wine **bibber**.*
bi.be.lot (BEE.buh.loh) *n.* a small but valued object; trinket.
Bi.ble (BYE.bul) *n.* **1** the sacred scriptures, esp. of the Christians: *The Koran is the Bible of the Muslims.* **2 bible** an authoritative book of reference: *the bible of the trade.* —**Bib.li.cal** or **bib.li.cal** (BIB.li.cul) *adj.*
Bible Belt *n.* a region of fundamentalist believers in the Bible.
bib.li.og.ra.phy (bib.lee.OG.ruh.fee) *n.* **-phies 1** a list of books and articles on a topic or by one author: *an annotated bibliography.* **2** the study of editions, history, etc. of published works. —**Bib.li.o.graph.ic** (-uh.GRAF.ic) or **bib.li.o.graph.i.cal** (-i.cul) *adj.*
bib.li.o.phile (BIB.lee.uh.file) *n.* a lover or collector of books.
bib.u.lous (BIB.yoo.lus) *adj.* given to alcoholic drink.
bi.cam.er.al (bye.CAM.uh.rul) *adj.* having two houses of legislature: *the bicameral system.*
bi.car.bon.ate (bye.CAR.buh.nit) *n.* an acid salt of carbonic acid.
bicarbonate of soda same as SODIUM BICARBONATE.
bi.cen.ten.ni.al (bye.sen.TEN.ee.ul) *n.* a 200th anniversary or its celebration: *to celebrate, mark, observe a bicentennial;* ***adja.****: a bicentennial celebration, project, year.* Also **bi.cen.te.nar.y** (-TEN.uh.ree, -TEE.nuh.ree).
bi.ceps (BYE.seps) *n. sing. & pl.* the muscle at the front of the upper arm: *flexing his biceps like a wrestler.*
bick.er (BICK.ur) *v.* quarrel pettily: *to bicker with a salesclerk about* or *over the price of a small article;* ***n.****: the constant **bickering** going on between the children.*
bi.con.cave (bye.con.CAVE) *adj.* concave on both sides: *a biconcave lens.*
bi.con.vex (bye.con.VEX) *adj.* convex on both sides.
bi.cul.tur.al (bye.CUL.chur.ul) *adj.* having to do with two cultures: *a bicultural nation;* **bi.cul.tur.al.ism** *n.*
bi.cus.pid (bye.CUS.pid) *n.* a tooth having two points: *We have eight bicuspids, or premolars; bicuspid teeth.*
bi.cy.cle (BYE.suh.cul) *n.* a two-wheeled vehicle, usu. driven by pedals, with a seat and handlebars: *to get on* or *mount a bicycle; An exercise bicycle is a stationary*

bid / bigotry

bicycle. —*v.* **-cles, -cled, -cling** ride a bicycle: *He was bicycling along the highway; bicycling home at night.* —**bi.cy.clist** *n.*

bid *v.* **bids,** *pt.* **bid,** *pp.* **bid** or **bid.den, bid.ding 1** *pt.* **bade** (BAD) tell: *They bade him be silent; She bids us farewell today.* **2** offer a price at an auction: *She bid $50 for the chair.* **3** in bridge, declare the trump suit and how many points or tricks one will make: *His partner had bid three hearts.* **4** try to get, win, etc.: *Six firms bid on the work contract; Everyone wanted to bid for the painting; The new stadium* **bids fair to** (= seems likely to) *become a world attraction.* —*n.* **1** an act of bidding or offering: *to call for, enter, file, invite, make, submit bids; to raise one's bids; an opening bid; sealed bids; Three hearts could be a bad bid; The work contract was* **up for bids**; *Six firms* **put in bids** (= offers) *for the contract.* **2** an attempt to get, win, etc.: *a bid for popular support; He made a desperate bid to regain his lost influence.* —**bid.der** *n.*

bid.da.ble (BID.uh.bul) *adj.* **1** *Informal.* ready to obey. **2** worth bidding on: *a biddable hand in bridge.*

bidding *n.* **1** offering of bids: *The bidding opened at $100,000.* **2** command: *His secretary is not supposed to make coffee at his bidding; He would like someone to* **do his bidding** (= do what he commands) *at all times.*

bid.dy (BID.ee) *n.* **bid.dies 1** a hen, esp. a young one. **2** a gossipy or shrewish old woman.

bide *v.* **bides,** *pt.* **bode** or **bid.ed,** *pp.* **bid.ed, bid.ing** [old use] wait or remain. —**bide one's time** await one's opportunity.

bi.det (bi.DAY) *n.* a low basin for washing the genitals and anal area.

bi.en.ni.al (bye.EN.ee.ul) *adja.* **1** occurring every two years: *a biennial convention.* **2** lasting two years: *a biennial plant;* *n.:* *The beet and carrot are biennials.* —**bi.en.ni.al.ly** *adv.*

bier (BEER) *n.* a movable stand for a coffin or corpse.

bi.fo.cal (bye.FOH.cul) **1** *adj.* having two focal lengths: *a bifocal lens.* **2** **bifocals** *n.pl.* spectacles with divided lenses for distant and close vision.

bi.fur.cate (BY.fur.cate) *v.* **-cates, -cat.ed, -cat.ing** divide into two branches. —**bi.fur.ca.tion** (-CAY.shun) *n.*

big *adj.* **big.ger, big.gest 1** large in regard to size, weight, or bulk; not small: *a big box; a store that carries special sizes of clothes for big* (= large or fat) *and tall men; a woman big* (= pregnant) *with child; the Big Apple* (= New York). **2** important or powerful: *He's a big man on campus; big business, government; a big fish* or *gun* or *shot (Informal for* important person). **3** full-grown; older: *You're a big boy now; your big brother, sister.* **4** generous: *a big benefactor with a big heart; It's big of him to apologize.* **5** boastful: *big talk; What's the* **big idea** (= Why are you so boastful or aggressive)? —**big on** *Informal.* enthusiastic about something: *He's big on parties for all occasions.* —**big with** *Informal.* **1** popular with: *Miniskirts are* or *count big with the younger set.* **2** successful with: *Miniskirts don't go over* or *hit (it)* or *make it* or *score* or *win big with older folks.* —**too big for one's boots** or **breeches** too cocky or self-important. —*adv. Informal.* **1** on a grand scale: *Think big.* **2** boastfully: *He talks big but achieves little.* —**big.ness** *n.*

big.a.my (BIG.uh.mee) *n.* the crime of being married to two people where the law allows marriage to only one person at a time: *to commit, practice bigamy.* —**big.a.mist** —**big.a.mous** *adj.*

big bang *n.* a primeval explosion of cosmogonic matter supposed to have caused our present universe.

big blue *n.* **1** a blue-chip corporation. **2** a conservative political party.

Big Brother *n.* **1** a layman who volunteers to befriend a fatherless boy. **2** the all-powerful leader of an authoritarian state: *Big Brother is watching you.* —**Big Broth.er.ism** *n.*

big deal *n. Informal* [usu. ironical] something of importance: *So you got a Cadillac – big deal! Don't make such a big deal about* or *of* or *out of your Cadillac; Getting a Cadillac is no big deal these days.*

Big.foot See SASQUATCH.

big.horn *n.* a large-horned wild sheep of the Rocky Mountains.

bight *n.* **1** a gently curving bay. **2** the slack or looped part of a rope.

big leagues *n.pl. Informal.* the major leagues in baseball.

big name *n. Informal.* a well-known, popular person, esp. an entertainer; *adja.: a big-name actor.*

big.ot (BIG.ut) *n.* an intolerant, blindly prejudiced person: *a fanatical, narrow-minded bigot.* —**big.ot.ed** *adj.: a bigoted attitude; He's bigoted against minorities.*

big.ot.ry (BIG.uh.tree) *n.* **-tries** bigoted attitude or behavior: *to stir up or*

arouse bigotry; religious bigotry.
big shot n. Informal. an important person.
big stick n. the threat of coercive action: waving America's big stick; a boss who carries a big stick; **adj**.: **big-stick** diplomacy.
big-ticket adj. high-priced: a big-ticket item; big-ticket decisions, expenses, losses, programs, purchases, sales, weapons; big-ticket business, electronics.
big time n. Informal. the top level of a field such as entertainment: The singer hit or made the big time. —**big-time** adj.: big-time crime; a big-time gambler, outfit, spender; a big-time operator (= wheeler-dealer).
big top n. Informal. the main tent of a circus: life under the big top (= life in the circus).
big.wig n. Informal. an important person.
bike n. Informal. a bicycle or motorcycle: to ride a bike. —v. **bikes, biked, bik.ing.** —**bik.er** n.
bi.ki.ni (bi.KEE.nee) n. a woman's scanty two-piece bathing suit.
bi.lat.er.al (bye.LAT.uh.rul) adj. made by or affecting both sides equally: a bilateral agreement, policy, treaty; An animal's body has **bilateral symmetry,** but a potato doesn't. —**bi.lat.er.al.ly** adv.
bile n. 1 a greenish-yellow fluid produced in the liver. 2 bad temper.
bilge (BILJ) n. 1 water that collects in the bottom of a ship. 2 Informal. nonsense; also **bilge water.**
bi.lin.gual (bye.LING.gwul) adj. having to do with two languages: a bilingual country, document, person, school, service; U.S. schools provide **bilingual education** in native languages other than English.
bi.lin.gual.ism (bye.LING.gwuh.liz.um) n. the use of two languages, esp. the policy of using them on an equal footing.
bil.ious (BIL.yus) adj. 1 having to do with the bile: a bilious attack; The color is a bilious yellow. 2 ill-tempered: a bilious old man. —**bil.i.ous.ness** n.
bilk v. cheat, esp. by taking money: He bilked the poor widow out of her savings. —**bilk.er** n.
bilk joint n. Slang. a shop that cheats its customers; gyp joint.
bill n. 1 a list of payments due: Guests settle their hotel bills before checking out; We ran up a huge bill for phone calls last month. 2 a list of items, as on a menu, theater program, etc.: a bill of fare. 3 a poster: Post no bills (here)! 4 a piece of paper money: to change or break a $100 bill; He tried to pass a counterfeit $20 bill; Marked bills are used by police to catch thieves. 5 a proposed law: to draft, introduce, oppose, pass, propose, reject, shelve, support, veto, vote down a bill; The bill was railroaded through the House. 6 a certificate or similar document: a bill of exchange, health, lading, rights, sale. 7 the hard mouth parts of a bird; beak. —**fill** or **fit the bill** Informal. meet the requirements. —**foot the bill** Informal. settle the bill; make the payment: He footed the bill for the whole party. —v. 1 present with a bill: Please bill us at the end of the month; to bill for services rendered. 2 advertise with bills: Ali was billed as the world's greatest; Jim was billed to appear as Macbeth. —**bill and coo** kiss and caress.
bill.board n. a signboard for posters, notices, etc.; **adj**.: billboard advertising, campaigns, signs, space.
bil.let (BIL.it) n. 1 a soldier's lodging in a civilian's house: an officer's billet. 2 a lodging assigned to someone as a guest in a private home. —v. to quarter troops by billet: The platoon was billeted in our village.
bill.fold n. a wallet.
bil.liards (BIL.yurds) n. a game played by striking hard balls with a cue on a rectangular, cloth-covered table. —**billiard** adj.: a billiard ball, player, room, table.
billing n. a display of performers' names according to their importance: a British actor who gets top billing in New York.
bil.lings.gate (BIL.ings.gate) n. vulgar abuse.
bil.lion (BIL.yun) n. 1 a thousand million; 1,000,000,000: Ten billion dollars; billions of dollars. 2 [British use] a million million; 1,000,000,000,000. —**bil.lionth** (BIL.yunth) n. & adj.
bil.lion.aire (bil.yuh.NAIR) n. one whose wealth amounts to at least a billion dollars, francs, etc.
bill of exchange n. a document requiring the payment of a sum to a named person; draft.
bill of fare n. a menu.
bill of goods n. a shipment of merchandise to sell: We have been **sold a bill of goods** (Informal for cheated).
bill of health n. a certificate of good health: to get or receive a clean bill of health; The auditors gave the company a clean bill of health.
bill of lading n. a document listing goods received for shipment.
bill of rights n. a declaration of the ba-

sic rights of a people, as in a country's constitution.

bill of sale *n.* a document showing the price, date, etc. of something sold by one to another.

bil.low (BIL.oh) *n.* a swelling or surging mass, as a large wave of water. —*v.* rise, swell, or roll in billows: *Smoke billowed from the burning oil well.* —**bil.low.y** *adj.* swelling: *the billowy ocean; an airy billowy dress for summer wear.*

bil.ly (BIL.ee) *n.* **bil.lies** *Informal.* a small club carried by a police officer; nightstick; truncheon; also called "billy club."

billy goat *n.* a male goat.

bim.bo (BIM.boh) *n. Slang.* **-bos** a dumb or insignificant person.

bi.met.al.lic (bye.muh.TAL.ic) *adj.* 1 made of two metals: *a bimetallic can, coil, strip, thermostat;* also **bi.metal.** 2 pertaining to bimetallism.

bi.met.al.lism (bye.MET.ul.ism) *n.* the simultaneous use of gold and silver as monetary standards; **bi.met.al.list** *n.*

bi.month.ly (bye.MUNTH.lee) *adj.* 1 occurring once in two months. 2 [loosely] occurring twice a month; semimonthly. —*n., pl.* **-lies** a bimonthly publication.

bin *n.* a large box or container: *coal, grain, laundry, recycling, storage, utility bins; a bargain bin (of discounted goods).*

bi.na.ry (BYE.nuh.ree) *adj.* having two parts, elements, etc.: *Orange and green are* **binary colors** *composed of two primary colors; The* **binary digits** *are 0 and 1; a* **binary star** (= *two stars revolving around each other*); *The number 9 is written as 1001 in the* **binary system** *or code or notation (that uses only 0 and 1);* **binary cell** See CELL.

bind (BINED) *v.* **binds, bound** (BOWND), **bind.ing** 1 to tie: *She binds her hair with ribbons; Reapers bind sheaves of wheat; The suspect was bound to a post until the police arrived.* 2 bandage: *A nurse bound up his wounds.* 3 obligate or constrain: *an apprentice bound to serve for three years; The contract binds you to deliver on time; He was* **bound over** (= *made to promise in court*) *to keep the peace.* 4 stick together or cause to cohere: *Cement binds gravel well.* 5 strengthen or decorate an edge with braid, tape, etc. 6 fasten a book's pages together or inside a cover, as done in a bindery: *a book bound in leather.* —*n. Informal.* a difficult situation: *The loss of his job put him in a financial bind; She found herself in the dou-* ble bind of being sick and jobless.

bind.er (BINE.dur) *n.* 1 a folder that holds paper together: *a loose-leaf binder; ring binders.* 2 one that binds: *a book binder; Cut grain has been tied with* **binder twine** *instead of binder wire since the 1880s.* 3 a binding clause of a contract specifying a condition, as in an insurance agreement.

bind.er.y (BINE.duh.ree) *n.* **-ries** a place where books are bound.

binding (BINE.ding) 1 *n.* something that binds, as a book's cover, the boot fastenings on skis, etc.: *cloth, leather binding; to sew on a binding* (= strip of fabric). 2 *adj.* obligatory: *A contract is binding on* or *upon the parties concerned.*

binge (BINJ) *n. Informal.* a spree: *to go on a shopping binge; a scoring binge in hockey; a binge of borrowing and spending; a binge drinker.* —*v.* **bing.es, binged, binge.ing:** *You can get a headache if you go without food for several hours and then binge; bingeing on junk food; alcohol bingeing.*

bin.go (BING.go) *n.* **-gos** a gambling game played on cards with numbered squares. —*interj.* expressing suddenness: *Bingo! said the winner of the game; When the lunch bell goes, bingo! They drop everything and leave.*

bin.na.cle (BIN.uh.cul) *n.* 1 a case or stand for a ship's compass. 2 a recessed frame for instruments on the dash of an automobile.

bin.oc.ul.ar (buh.NOK.yuh.lur, bye-) 1 *adj.* using or for use by both eyes at once: *a binocular microscope; binocular vision.* 2 **binoculars** *n.pl.* an optical instrument like a telescope with lens tubes for both eyes, as opera glasses or field glasses: *a pair of binoculars; She trained her binoculars on her favorite horse.*

bi.no.mi.al (bye.NOH.mee.ul) *n.* 1 a mathematical expression consisting of two terms linked by a + or − sign, as "3x − 4xy." 2 a two-word scientific name indicating genus and species, as "Equus caballus" (horse) and "Equus asinus" (ass). —*adj.:* *a binomial equation, expression, series, system; binomial nomenclature; the binomial theorem.*

bio (BYE.oh) 1 *n.* [short form] biography, esp. a short one. 2 *comb.form.* having to do with life or living things: *bioassay, biochemistry, bioethics, biohazard.*

bi.o.chem.is.try (bye.oh.KEM.is.tree) *n.* a branch of chemistry dealing with living organisms and their chemical processes. —**bi.o.chem.i.cal** *adj.*
—**bi.o.chem.ist** *n.*

bi.o.cide (BYE.uh.cide) *n.* **1** a substance that can destroy life, as chlorine. **2** the destruction of life.
bi.o.clean (BYE.uh.cleen) *adj.* free from microorganisms, esp. harmful ones.
bi.o.de.grad.a.ble (BYE.oh.di.GRAY.duh.bul) *adj.* able to be broken down by biological agents, esp. bacteria: *Plastics are not biodegradable; biodegradable paper.*
bi.o.di.ver.si.ty (BYE.oh.di.VUR.si.tee) *n.* the great variety of plants and animals seen in a biological environment: *conservation of biodiversity.*
bi.o.eth.ics (bye.oh.ETH.ics) *n.pl.* [takes *sing. v.*] the ethics of biological research and its application to medicine, as in artificial insemination, genetic engineering, and organ transplants.
bi.o.feed.back (bye.oh.FEED.back) *n.* the technique of mental control of the body's unconscious processes, as by using a machine that monitors brain waves.
bi.o.flick (BYE.oh.flick) *n. Slang.* a TV show or movie based on a person's life story.
bi.o.gas (BYE.oh.gas) *n.* a gas produced by decaying organic matter, esp. methane used as a fuel.
bi.og.ra.phy (bye.OG.ruh.fee) *n.* **-phies** the story of a person's life as written by another; **bi.og.ra.pher** *n.* —**bi.o.graph.ic** (bye.uh.GRAF.ic) or **bi.o.graph.i.cal** (-i.cul) *adj.*
bi.o.haz.ard (bye.oh.HAZ.urd) *n.* a hazard resulting from a biological agent such as a virus or a dangerous environmental condition.
bi.o.log.i.cal (bye.uh.LOJ.i.cul) *adj.* having to do with living organisms: *a biological agent, pesticide, science, system; biological wastes;* a **biological parent** (= birth parent).
biological clock *n.* a built-in timing system controlling cyclical behavior in organisms, as sleeping patterns, bird migrations, and the blossoming of flowers.
biological warfare *n.* warfare using poisonous germs, insects, etc. to destroy plant, animal, and human life.
bi.ol.o.gy (bye.OL.uh.jee) *n.* the science of living organisms and life processes. —**bi.ol.o.gist** *n.*
bi.o.mass (BYE.oh.mas) *n.* vegetable and animal waste materials used as a source of energy; *adj.*: *biomass energy; a biomass reactor; Wood, garbage, and other biological wastes form* **biomass fuels** *that produce renewable energy.*
bi.ome (BYE.ohm) *n.* a typical community of plants and animals based on a particular climate: *grassland, tropical forest, tundra biomes.*
bi.o.med.i.cine (bye.oh.MED.uh.sin) *n.* the medical study of reactions to abnormal environments, esp. in space travel. —**bi.o.med.i.cal** *adj.*
bi.o.morph (BYE.oh.morf) *n.* an artistically created form or design that is suggestive of a living organism. —**bi.o.mor.phic** (-MOR.fic) *adj.*: *biomorphic shapes.*
bi.on.ics (bye.ON.ics) *n.pl.* the study and design of electronic devices modeled on living things. —**bi.on.ic** *adj.*: *a child with a bionic arm.*
bi.o.phy.sics (bye.oh.FIZ.ics) *n.* the study of life processes using the principles and methods of physics; **bi.o.phys.i.cal** *adj.*; **bi.o.phys.i.cist** *n.*
bi.op.sy (bye.OP.see) *n.* **-sies** the removal and diagnostic examination of fluid or tissue from a living body.
bi.o.rhythm (BYE.oh.rith.um) *n.* the rhythm of cyclical behavior in organisms, as in sleeping and waking.
bi.o.sphere (BYE.us.feer) *n.* that part of the earth and the atmosphere in which life is found.
bi.o.tech.nol.o.gy (BYE.oh.tek.NOL.uh.jee) *n.* the industrial use of living things such as microorganisms, bacteria, etc., as in waste recycling, genetic engineering, etc.
bi.ot.ic (bye.OT.ic) *adj.* caused by or having to do with living things: *the biotic environment.*
bi.par.ti.san (bye.PAR.tuh.zun) *adj.* having to do with two sides or parties: *a bipartisan committee.* —**bi.par.ti.san.ship** *n.*
bi.par.tite (bye.PAR.tite) *adj.* divided into two parts: *a bipartite agreement; bipartite leaves.*
bi.ped (BYE.ped) *adj.* two-footed: *Humans are biped animals;* **n.**: *We are all bipeds, including those in wheelchairs.*
bi.plane (BYE.plane) *n.* an airplane with two main wings one above the other.
bi.po.lar (bye.POH.lur) *adj.* **1** having two opposing forces or tendencies: *the bipolar depression of manic-depressives; bipolar devices, output, transistors; a bipolar world.* **2** of or living in the two polar regions: *a bipolar species.* —**bi.po.lar.i.ty** (-poh.LAIR.i.tee) *n.*
bi.ra.cial (bye.RAY.shul) *adj.* having to do with two races: *a biracial society.* —**bi.ra.cial.ism** *n.*
birch *n.* **1** a hardwood tree whose smooth bark peels off in layers. **2** a

bunch of birch twigs used to give a whipping. —*v.* whip: *Criminals used to be birched as punishment.*

Birch.er *n.* a member of the **John Birch Society,** an extreme right-wing group.

bird *n.* **1** a two-legged, feathered, winged animal: *as free as a bird; Birds build nests, sing, soar, twitter, warble; game, migratory, wading, water birds; "A bird in the hand* (= something one already has) *is worth two in the bush"; "Birds of a feather* (= people of the same kind) *flock together."* **2** *Informal.* a person: *He's a rare bird at these meetings; clever, literary, strange birds; a wise old bird; a funny* (= eccentric) *bird.* **3** *Informal.* a shuttlecock, clay pigeon, missile, satellite, etc. that flies or seems to: *The first commercial communications satellite called "Early Bird" was launched in 1965.* **4** *Slang* [derogatory] a young woman; chick. —**for the birds** *Informal.* worthless: *Al says economics is strictly for the birds.* —**the birds and the bees** *Informal.* the basic facts about sex: *She learned about the birds and the bees in Family Studies class.*

bird.brain *n.* a stupid person. —**bird.brained** *adj.*

bird call *n.* the cry of a bird: *to imitate bird calls.*

bird dog *n.* **1** a sporting dog such as a pointer or retriever that smells the air and locates game birds shot down by the hunter. **2** *Informal.* a talent scout, detective, chaperon, or other person or instrument that works like a bird dog. —**bird-dog** *v.* **-dogs, -dogged, -dog.ging:** *He was assigned to bird-dog* (= tail) *the suspect around town.*

bird.er *n.* a birdwatcher.

bird.ie (BUR.dee) *n.* **1** in golf, a one-under-par score on a hole. **2** a little bird.

birding same as BIRDWATCHING.

bird of paradise *n.* a beautifully plumed bird of New Guinea.

bird of passage *n.* **1** a migratory bird. **2** *Informal.* one who moves or travels about constantly.

bird of prey *n.* a bird such as the eagle or hawk that kills other animals for food.

bird.seed *n.* an assorted mixture of seeds for feeding birds.

bird's-eye *adja.* **1** quick or general: *a bird's-eye-view* (= quick survey) *of American literature.* **2** with markings like a bird's eye: *the bird's-eye maple used esp. for veneers; a bird's-eye pattern.*

bird.strike *n.* the crashing of a bird into an aircraft.

bird.watch.ing (BIRD.woch.ing) *n.* the study of birds in their natural surroundings. —**bird.watch.er** *n.*

bi.ret.ta (buh.RET.uh) *n.* a square clerical cap.

birth *n.* a being born or coming into existence: *He weighed only six pounds at birth; He is British by birth; You have one* **birth date,** *or date of birth, but many birthdays; She* **gave birth to** (= brought forth) *triplets; It was a difficult birth* (= act of giving birth); *breech, multiple, premature births; a man of noble birth* (= parentage); *Today marks the birth* (= beginning) *of a new era; a* **birth defect** *such as a birthmark, cleft palate, or color blindness; The project was aborted after enduring or suffering many* **birth pangs.**

birth control *n.* the use of a device or method to prevent pregnancy: *People like to practice birth control under the name "family planning."*

birth.day *n.* the anniversary of a birth: *to celebrate, mark, reach a birthday; on her 90th birthday; Happy birthday (to you)!* **adja.:** *a birthday boy, card, girl, party, present.*

birthday suit *n. Informal.* the state of nudity, as when an infant is born.

birth.ing *n.* the act of giving birth; **adja.:** *a birthing center, room.*

birth.mark *n.* a mark on the skin that is present from birth.

birth mother *n.* the woman who gives birth to a child.

birth parent *n.* the birth mother or the man who fathers a child; a natural or biological, not adoptive parent of a child.

birth.place *n.* one's place of birth.

birth.rate *n.* the ratio of births to total population in an area: *the falling birthrate; a rising birthrate.*

birth.right *n.* a right to an inheritance, citizenship, etc. based on when or where one is born.

birth.stone *n.* a gemstone symbolizing the month of one's birth, as garnet (January), amethyst (February), etc.

bis.cuit (BIS.kit) *n.* **1** a small bread or roll leavened without yeast: *soda biscuits; tea biscuits.* **2** *Brit.* a cracker or cookie: *a cream biscuit; sweet biscuits.*

bi.sect (bye.SECT) *v.* **1** divide into two usu. equal parts. **2** bifurcate. —**bi.sec.tion** *n.*: *the bisection of an angle.* —**bi.sec.tor** *n.*

bi.sex.u.al (bye.SEK.shoo.ul) *adj.* having to do with both sexes: *Bisexual people are sexually attracted to members of both sexes; Earthworms are bisexual* (= have both male and female organs). **—n.** a bisexual person, animal, or plant. **—bi.sex.u.al.i.ty** (-AL.i.tee) *n.*

bish.op (BISH.up) *n.* **1** a clergyman who usu. heads a diocese and has authority over other clergy. **2** a chess piece that moves diagonally.

bish.op.ric (BISH.up.ric) *n.* a bishop's rank, office, or jurisdiction.

bis.muth (BIZ.muth) *n.* a brittle, whitish metallic element used in drugs and alloys.

bi.son (BYE.sun) *n. sing. & pl.* a wild, oxlike bovine with large shaggy head and a hump at the shoulders: *a herd of bison; The European bison and the North American buffalo are related species.*

bisque (BISK) *n.* a creamy thick soup often made with shellfish.

bis.tro (BIS.troh) *n.* **-tros** a small restaurant, bar, or nightclub.

bit *n.* **1** a small portion, amount, interval, etc.: *a bit of paper; a tiny bit; bits and pieces of information gathered from hearsay; Wait a bit* (= little while); *He tried to do his bit* (= fair share); *She's every bit* (= quite) *like her father and every bit* (= just) *as talented as her brother; He's **a bit of a** (= somewhat of a) comic; You can do the whole thing **bit by bit** (= little by little); The shelf is **a bit** (= slightly) too high for me; She's **not the least bit** (= not at all) worried; He admits to cheating **a little bit**; That's quite **a bit** (= more than a little) to admit.* **2** the cutting edge of a tool, esp. one for boring and drilling: *a brace and bit; drill bits.* **3** the part of a bridle held in a horse's mouth: *He has a tendency to **take the bit in his mouth*** (= take charge) *and do things his own way.* **4** in entertainment, a short act or routine; *adj*.: *a bit part in a play; a bit player.* **5** *Informal.* a stereotyped act, behavior, speech, etc.: *Her husband did the jealousy bit.* **6** in computers, a binary digit representing the smallest unit of information, as a 0 or 1: *A byte is eight bits long in the oldest microprocessors; The first modems used to receive and transmit data at 300 bits per second; the third-generation 32 bit microprocessor;* *adj.*: *In **bit-mapped** graphics, a bit in the computer memory controls each pixel of the display.*

bitch *n.* **1** *Slang.* a woman looked on with scorn. **2** *Slang.* anything that causes one to complain: *Money is such a bitch; this bitch of a toothache!* [used as intensifier] *a or **one bitch of a** (Slang for a very bad) job.* **3** *Slang.* something admirable; lulu: *a or **one bitch of an album**; It's a bitch;* *adj*.: *a bitching* (= very) *good single.* **4** [technical use] the adult female of a dog or other canine. **—v.** *Slang.* **1** complain: *He's always bitching about something or other.* **2** botch or bungle: *The project was bitched up by incompetent workers.*

bitch.y (BICH.ee) *adj.* **bitch.i.er, -i.est** *Slang.* spiteful or ill-tempered.

bite *v.* **bites,** *pt.* **bit,** *pp.* **bit.ten** or **bit, bit.ing** seize, pierce, or cut with or as if with the teeth, as a dog, snake, or mosquito: *Some dogs bite letter carriers; Fish bite at baits, but they aren't biting today; She likes to bite into* or *on an apple; She bit off a large piece; Snow tires bite into snow; fingers bitten by frost; He would never **bite the hand that fed him*** (= be ungrateful). **—bite one's tongue** restrain oneself from saying something. **—bite the bullet** suffer something painful without complaining. **—bite the dust** be utterly defeated. **—n.** **1** an act of biting: *dog, insect, mosquito, snake bites; a dog with a powerful bite* (= biting ability). **2** what is bitten off: *He took a big bite out of my apple; There's just enough time to grab* or *have a quick bite* (Informal for light meal); *The new taxes take a big bite* (= deduction) *from* or *out of our earnings.* **—put the bite on** *Informal.* press someone for money or favors.

bite-size or **bite-sized** *adj.* small and easy to use: *Dice the sausage into bite-size pieces; a newspaper featuring bite-size stories.*

biting (BYE.ting) *adj.* sharp or stinging: *a biting odor, wind; biting criticism, sarcasm.* **—bit.ing.ly** *adv.*

bit-mapped See BIT.

bit.ter *adj.* **1** having a sharp, unpleasant taste: *bitter medicine; a **bitter pill to swallow*** (=an unpleasant fact). **2** harsh or unpleasant: *That was bitter news to hear; bitter winter weather; Early frost means a bitter* (= bad) *harvest; to fight to the **bitter end*** (= the very end, even if unpleasant). **3** expressing sorrow or resentment: *She is bitter about the defeat; a bitter disappointment; He shed bitter tears.* **4** full of hatred: *a bitter dispute, enemy.* **—n.** **1** something bitter: *He soon learned to **take the bitter with the sweet**.* **2 bitters** *n.pl.* a usu. alcoholic bitter liquid used as a tonic or cocktail flavoring. **—bit.ter.ly** *adv.* **—bit.ter.ness** *n.*: *There's a touch of bitterness in her poetry; He feels bitterness toward his former employers; He gave vent to his bitterness about* or *over their exploiting him.*

bit.tern (BIT.urn) *n.* a heronlike marsh bird with a booming cry.

bit.ter.sweet (BIT.ur.sweet) *adj.* painful though pleasant: *a bittersweet memory; those bittersweet jokes about the loss of his job.* —*n.* **1** a climbing vine with orange seed pods. **2** a climbing vine with poisonous berries.

bi.tu.men (bi.TUE.mun) *n.* asphalt, tar, or other viscous substance used to surface roads. —**bi.tu.mi.nous** (-muh.nus) *adj.* soft: *bituminous coal, crude oil, molasses.*

bi.valve (BYE.valv) *n.* any mollusk with two hinged shells, as a clam. —*adj.* having two movable parts, like a clamshell: *The pea has a bivalve pod.*

biv.ou.ac (BIV.uh.wac) *n.* a temporary camp in the open, esp. for soldiers: *They are on bivouac; gone on bivouac; They set up a bivouac in the mountains.* —*v.* **-acs, -acked, -ack.ing:** *The platoon bivouacked in the woods; They bivouacked at a former army barracks.*

bi.week.ly (bye.WEEK.lee) *adj. & adv.* **1** once every two weeks. **2** [loosely] twice a week; semiweekly. —*n., pl.* **-lies** a biweekly publication.

bi.year.ly (bye.YEER.lee) *adj. & adv.* **1** once every two years. **2** loosely, twice a year; semiyearly.

biz *n.* [short form] business: *show biz; Banking biz is big biz; the biz world.*

bi.zarre (buh.ZAR) *adj.* strikingly odd, eccentric, or fantastic: *a bizarre appearance; bizarre behavior; a bizarre series of events; He led a bizarre life.*

blab *v.* **blabs, blabbed, blab.bing** *Informal.* talk foolishly, as by revealing a secret or something confidential. —*n.* **1** one who blabs. **2** a blab's chatter.

blab.ber (BLAB.ur) **1** *v.* **blab.bers, blab.bered, blab.ber.ing** to talk or communicate foolishly or indiscreetly. **2** *n.* one who blabs.

blab.ber.mouth (BLAB.ur.mouth) *n. Informal.* one who blabbers: *the blabbermouths who give away secrets.*

black *n.* **1** the color that is opposed to white: *basic black; jet black;* **Put it down in black and white** (= in writing); *a company operating* **in the black** (= making a profit, not in the red). **2** a pigment, clothing, etc. of black: *The widow wore black (in mourning); Black is beautiful; black tie.* **3** also **Black,** a person of African origin: *Congress of Black Women of Canada.* —*v.* make or become black; blacken: *A shoeshine boy blacks shoes.* —**black out 1** to faint. **2** cover or darken: *All lights had to be blacked out during the war; A power failure blacked out much of the city during a storm last year; The censor blacked out certain parts of the story.* —*adj.* **1** very dark; of the color black: *a black flag;* **black gold** (= petroleum). **2** dirty: *hands black with grease.* **3** bad in some way: *a black* (= gloomy) *future, night; a black* (= morbid) *depression; a black* (= angry) *look; the* **Black Death** (from bubonic plague) of the 1300s; Two disastrous **Black Fridays** left many U.S. investors bankrupt in 1869 and 1873; The same thing happened on **Black Monday,** 19 October 1987. **4** also **Black,** having to do with the black people: *a black family, ghetto, leader, neighborhood; black culture, history, politics, power, studies; a black Hebrew sect; the black Jews of Ethiopia; a* **Black English** *dialect.*

black-and-blue *adj.* darkly bruised, as from a beating.

black-and-white *adj.* **1** not in color: *a black-and-white drawing, movie.* **2** clearcut; not gray: *It's not a black-and-white issue; He thinks of morals in black-and-white terms.*

black art *n.* witchcraft.

black.ball *n.* a negative vote, esp. against a prospective member or employee. —*v.* keep out or exclude: *Women and minorities are sometimes blackballed from management jobs; n.: After much* **blackballing** *by France, Britain was allowed to join the Common Market in 1973.*

black belt *n.* **1** the highest rating in judo or karate. **2** a person thus rated.

black.ber.ry (BLAK.ber.ee) *n.* **-ber.ries** the fleshy but seedy fruit of a bramble bush.

black.bird *n.* any of various North American birds whose males are black.

black.board *n.* a dark, smooth board for writing on with chalk: *to erase a blackboard; to write on the blackboard.*

black box *n.* **1** the flight recorder of an aircraft. **2** any complex electronic device whose mode of operation is unknown to the user.

black.en (BLACK.un) *v.* to darken or sully: *a face blackened with soot; to blacken someone's image, name, reputation; adj.: He came out of the fight with a* **blackened** *eye.*

black eye *n. Informal.* **1** a dark bruise around the eye: *to get a black eye.* **2** a bad reputation: *The rumors gave him a black eye.*

black.guard (BLAG.urd) *n.* a villainous or foul-mouthed person.

black.head *n.* a dark clog of oil and dirt in a skin pore.

black hole *n.* **1** a region in outer space

of such great density and gravity that even light cannot escape from it. **2** something that continually wastes resources: *Government spending is sometimes a black hole; a financial black hole.* **3** an empty space or void: *During the war, thousands of people disappeared into the black hole of memory.* **4** a dungeon or similar place: *the Black Hole of Calcutta.*

black humor *n.* comedy stressing the morbid and the absurd.

blacking *n.* a substance for blackening something, esp. shoes.

black.jack *n.* **1** a short leather-covered club with a flexible handle. **2** a card game, also called "twenty-one." —*v.* **1** hit with a blackjack. **2** force someone by threatening, as if with a blackjack.

black light *n.* ultraviolet or infrared light that is invisible.

black.list *n.* a list of people who are disapproved of. —*v.* to put someone on such a list.

black lung *n.* a lung disease caused by breathing coal dust.

black magic *n.* witchcraft.

black.mail *n.* **1** payment extorted, esp. by a threat of discreditable exposure: *to pay blackmail.* **2** such extortion: *to commit blackmail.* —*v.* subject someone to blackmail: *She was blackmailed into submission.* —**black.mail.er** *n.*

black market *n.* the buying and selling of goods and exchanging money in violation of government regulations: *It's available on the black market;* **adja.**: *Tourists are warned against* **black-market** *dealings in foreign countries.* —**black marketer** or **marketeer** *n.*
—**black-marketing** or **black-marketeering** *n.*

Black Muslim *n.* a member of a black Islamic group called "Nation of Islam" advocating the separation of blacks and whites.

black nationalism *n.* a movement urging a separate black nation; **black nationalist.**

black.out *n.* a blacking out, as in the absence of light, consciousness, etc.: *Blackouts are imposed* or *ordered in wartime; The news blackout was lifted when the emergency was over.*

Black Panther *n.* a militant group of American blacks of the 1960s and 1970s.

black sheep *n.* a person considered disgraceful by the rest of a group: *the black sheep of the family.*

black.smith *n.* one who works with iron, esp. one who shoes horses.

black tie *n.* a tuxedo or the black bow tie that is worn with it. —**black-tie** *adja.* requiring semiformal costume: *The banquet was a black-tie affair.*

black.top *n.* asphalt or similar material for surfacing roads: *a blacktop sealer; a scenic stretch of blacktop* (= paved road). —*v.* **-tops, -topped, -top.ping;** *adj.*: *a freshly* **blacktopped** *driveway.*

blad.der (BLAD.ur) *n.* **1** a bag of membrane that collects urine from the kidneys: *a full bladder; to empty one's bladder* (= urinate). **2** any similar object, as the air bag inside a football.

blade *n.* **1** the thin, flat cutting part of a sword, knife, ax, skate runner, etc.: *blunt, dull, sharp blades; a razor blade;* the rotary blade of a mower. **2** a similar part on a propeller, oar, paddle, etc. **3** the long flat leaf of a grass or cereal. **4** a spirited young man.

blah *n. Informal.* **1** baloney or bunk: *all the blah you hear about freedom and democracy.* **2** boredom: *a case of the February* **blahs** *at the end of winter;* **adja.**: *a blah* (= bored) *attitude; a blah* (= boring) *performance.*

blame *v.* **blames, blamed, blam.ing** consider someone responsible for something bad: *They blamed the pitcher for the loss; Don't blame it on me; I'm not* **to blame** (= responsible) *for it.* —*n.* responsibility for something bad: *It was hard to fix the blame for the broken window; The blame seemed to fall on Guy; Everyone put the blame on him; They laid the blame at his door; Guy tried to shift the blame to someone else; Matt took the blame in the end.* —**blam.a.ble** (BLAY.muh.bul) *adj.*

blame.wor.thy (BLAME.wur.thee) *adj.* deserving blame.

blanch *v.* make or become pale or white: *His face blanched with fear; He blanched at the gruesome sight; Fruit, vegetables, etc. are blanched* (= boiled briefly) *before being frozen;* **adj.**: *blanched almonds* (with skin removed).

blanc.mange (bluh.MAHNZH) *n.* a sweet, jellylike dessert made with milk, starch, etc.

bland *adj.* **1** pleasing or soothing, not irritating: *a bland diet, smile.* **2** dull: *a bland character, leader, personality, report.* —**bland.ly** *adv.*; **bland.ness** *n.*

blan.dish (BLAN.dish) *v.* persuade using flattery; cajole; **blan.dish.ment** *n.*

blank *adj.* having nothing on or in it; empty: *a blank expression, look, page, sheet of paper, space, stare; a blank cartridge* (with no bullet); *a blank window* (with no decoration); *Suddenly my mind went blank* (= I couldn't recall anything); *It was blank* (= absolute) *terror; The police have run into a* **blank wall** (= having no leads) *in their investigation.* —*n.* something blank or empty: *Fill in the blanks; Keys are cut from blanks; A starter pistol fires only blanks; Our investigations* **drew a blank** (*Informal for* were unsuccessful). —*v.* reduce to nothing: *They blanked the Bruins 2-0* (= the Bruins scored nothing); *He* **blanked out** (= deleted) *the offending words; Suddenly my mind* **blanked out** (= I couldn't remember anything).

blank check *n.* 1 a signed check with the amount to be filled in by the recipient. 2 freedom of action: *He was given a blank check to negotiate a contract.*

blan.ket (BLANK.it) *n.* 1 a large cloth covering used for warmth, esp. on a bed: *a woolen blanket.* 2 a covering: *a blanket of snow.* —*v.* cover like a blanket: *A fog blanketed the coast.* —*adj.* covering all cases: *a blanket amnesty, authorization, condemnation, pardon, refusal, rule, veto.*

blank verse *n.* unrhymed iambic pentameter, as used in Shakespeare's plays.

blare *v.* **blares, blared, blar.ing** sound or call out loudly and brashly: *The radio blared out the news.*

blar.ney (BLAR.nee) *n.* flattery or coaxing: *That's sheer blarney!* —**kiss the Blarney Stone** get skill in coaxing and flattering.

bla.sé (blah.ZAY) *adj.* bored by too much of something: *TV viewers are blasé about all the sex and violence they watch.*

blas.pheme (blas.FEEM) *v.* **-phemes, -phemed, -phem.ing** speak impiously about God or something sacred: *to blaspheme (against) God; He is prone to blaspheme when tipsy;* **blas.phem.er** *n.* —**blas.phe.mous** (BLAS.fuh.mus) *adj.;* **blas.phe.mous.ly** *adv.*

blas.phe.my (BLAS.fuh.mee) *n.* **-mies** 1 contemptuous treatment, esp. in words, of anything considered divine: *to commit blasphemy.* 2 an instance of it: *to utter blasphemies against Allah.*

blast *n.* 1 a powerful gust of air, gases, etc.: *The spark set off a blast; a blast of hot air; the trumpet's blast* (= loud sound); *They worked away* **at full blast** (*Informal for* at maximum capacity). 2 an explosion or the shock wave from it: *a bomb blast.* 3 a critical or abusive attack: *an icy blast; a vicious blast; a withering blast against the Opposition.* 4 a blight that withers plants. 5 *Informal.* a wild good time; ball.
—*v.* 1 explode: *Danger, blasting! Rockets* **blast off** (= take off with an explosion) *from the launch pad.* 2 criticize violently: *editorials blasting the government.* 3 wither; *adj.:* **blasted** *flowers; the blasted* (= blighted or darned) *imbecile!*

blast furnace *n.* a furnace that uses blasts of air to improve combustion for smelting.

blast.off *n.* the takeoff of a rocket, missile, etc.

blat *v. Informal.* 1 bleat. 2 speak loudly.

bla.tant (BLAY.tunt) *adj.* openly offensive; flagrant: *a blatant falsehood; He acted in blatant disregard of the rules of decency.* —**bla.tant.ly** *adv.*

blath.er (BLATH.ur, "TH" as in "the") *v.* talk foolishly and without making sense: *to blather about truth and justice.* —*n.* such talk: *sheer blather;* also **blath.er.skite.**

blaze *n.* 1 the sudden shooting up of a flame: *The fire burst into a blaze; They tried to extinguish* or *put out the blaze.* 2 something similar to a blaze: *the blaze of the tropical sun; in the full blaze of publicity; a blaze* (= outburst) *of fury; the blaze* (= brilliant display) *of fall colors.* —*v.* **blaz.es, blazed, blaz.ing** burn furiously: *He was blazing with anger; adj.: a blazing inferno.* —**blaze a trail** mark out a path, as through the woods: *Amelia Earhart blazed a trail for women pilots.* —**blaze away** keep shooting *at* someone.

blaz.er (BLAY.zur) *n.* a light sports jacket, often blue with metal buttons.

bla.zon (BLAY.zun) *n.* 1 a coat of arms. 2 a showy display. —*v.* 1 publicize widely: *a billboard blazoning forth the virtues of the new soft drink.* 2 display or adorn: *The title was blazoned across the book's cover.*

bleach (BLEECH) *v.* make or become pale or white: *She bleached her hair blond; adj. & cpd:* **bleached** *fiber, hair, paper; chlorine-bleached wood pulp; sun-bleached bones.* —*n.* a bleaching agent: *laundry bleach; liquid bleach.*

bleach.ers (BLEE.churs) *n.pl.* tiers of usu. roofless seats for spectators.

bleak (BLEEK) *adj.* 1 barren and windswept: *bleak cliffs.* 2 cold and raw: *a bleak wind.* 3 gloomy: *The company faces a bleak future.* —**bleak.ly** *adv.;* **bleak.ness** *n.*

blear.y (BLEER.ee) *adj.* esp. of eyes, blurred or unclear from fatigue, tears, etc. —**bleary-eyed** *adj.* —**blear.i.ly** *adv.*

bleat (BLEET) *v. & n.* (make) the cry of a calf, goat, or sheep.

bleed v. **bleeds, bled, bleed.ing 1** shed blood: *He lay there bleeding profusely from his wounds; He bled to death; My heart bleeds* (= feels sympathy) *for him; The injured tree is bleeding* (= losing its sap); *n.: internal bleeding from the stomach.* **2** draw blood, etc. from someone: *The thugs bled him white* (= took all his money). **3** extend or run from its regular position: *Some colors bleed* (= run) *when wet; Allow tire pressure to bleed off* (= be released) *by slightly opening the valve;* **adj.:** *a bleeding check pattern; a bleeding illustration (that goes to the edge of the page); the bleeding madras.*
bleed.er n. a hemophiliac.
bleeding heart n. **1** a person overly sympathetic to the disadvantaged. **2** a perennial plant with heart-shaped pink, white, or rosy-red flowers.
bleep adj. *Slang.* taboo or vulgar: *a bleep job.* —**n. 1** a beep: *the bleeps of a Geiger counter; A bleep sound replaces coarse language on TV meant for family viewing.* **2** what a beep stands for, esp. a vulgar expletive: *That's a pile of bleep* (= something vulgar); *He's been called a meddler, fascist, and a bleep* (= "four-letter word").
blem.ish n. a surface imperfection or flaw, as a stain or spot: *a beautiful skin marred by blemishes; She was acquitted without the least blemish on her character.* —v. to spoil or taint, as by a blemish.
blench v. flinch or draw back: *He blenched as the light suddenly shone on him; He blenched at the dazzling light.*
blend v. mix or combine into one: *The ingredients should be blended rather than beaten; architecture that blends with the environment; A chameleon blends into its surroundings; voices blending (together) in harmony; She blended in with the crowd; Blended whiskey is composed of several whiskeys or other spirits.* —**n.** something blended: *a blend of teas;* "Smog" *is a blend of* "smoke" *and* "fog." —**blend.er** n.
bless v. **bless.es,** pt. & pp. **blessed** or **blest, bless.ing 1** make holy, happy, good, etc.: *(May) God bless you! God bless!* **2** ask divine favor for a person or thing: *The minister blessed his congregation.*
bless.ed (BLES.id) adj. **1** holy: *the blessed martyrs; It's more blessed to give than to receive.* **2** fortunate: *Blessed are the merciful; blessed events, relief, times.* **3** (BLEST) favored: *She is blessed with good health; They felt blessed when the child was born; the oil-blessed Arabs.*
—**bless.ed.ly** adv.; **bless.ed.ness** n.

blessing n. **1** a prayer for divine favor, as grace said at a meal: *to bestow a blessing on someone; a priestly blessing; Who will ask the blessing* (= say grace)? **2** a grant of divine favor; happy event: *It was a blessing that I missed the ill-fated flight; When you feel like complaining, count* (= remember) *your blessings; My missing the flight turned out to be a blessing in disguise because the plane was forced to land.* **3** approval: *He did it with his wife's blessing; She gave her blessing to the project.*
blest a pp. of BLESS.
blew pt. of BLOW.
blight n. **1** a disease that causes plants to wither or die: *a potato blight.* **2** decay or the resulting ugliness: *Slums are a blight on the landscape; Childhood misery cast a blight on or upon her future; urban blight.* —v. affect with blight; **adj.:** *a blighted apple tree; her blighted hopes; blighted neighborhoods.*
blimp n. **1** a nonrigid airship. **2** *Slang.* a fat person.
blind (BLINED) adj. **1** unable to see: *He's blind as a bat; He turned a blind eye to* (= pretended not to notice) *what was going on.* **2** not using vision: *We made a blind landing because of fog;* **adv.:** *a pilot flying blind in a storm.* **3** wanting in perception, reason, judgment, forethought, etc.: *blind to his fate; blind with fury; blind chance, faith, love.* **4** hidden: *a blind intersection, spot; the blind* (= windowless) *side of a house.* **5** involving the unknown: *a blind date, purchase.* —v. make blind: *Paul was blinded by the light; rushed with blinding speed; blinded by fury; Love blinded her to his faults.* —n. something to shut out light: *Venetian blinds; to adjust, draw, lower, raise the blinds.* —**blind.ly** adv.; **blind.ness** n.
blind alley n. **1** a road closed at one end: *to go down or up a blind alley.* **2** a mistaken course of action: *They felt boxed into a blind alley.*
blind date n. **1** a date between people who have never met. **2** either partner.
blind.er n. one of a pair of flaps blocking a horse's sideways vision.
blind.fold v. tie a cloth over the eyes of someone. —n. a cloth so used.
blind.side v. hit unexpectedly, as a car from a side that the driver cannot see.
blind spot n. **1** a place one cannot see. **2** a weakness or failing, esp. one the subject is unaware of: *an all-round scholar with but one blind spot.*
blind trust n. an arrangement for one's financial affairs to be handled by an-

other person without one's own involvement so as to avoid conflict of interest when holding public office.

blink *v.* **1** shut and open the eyes quickly, as when dazzled by light: *He listened to the charge without once blinking* (= showing any surprise); *They blinked first* (= showed lack of determination); *Teachers sometimes* **blink at** (= ignore) *mischievous behavior; The child tried to* **blink away** *or* **blink back** (= repress) *her tears.* **2** to flicker or flash lights on and off; *adja.: the blinking cursor on a computer screen.* —*n.* an act of blinking; glimmer. —**on the blink** *Informal.* out of order.

blink.er *n.* **1** a flashing light. **2** a blinder.

blintz *or* **blin.tze** (BLINT.suh) *n.* a thin pancake rolled around a usu. cheese filling.

blip *n.* a dot of light on a radar screen. —*v.* **blips, blipped, blip.ping** to erase electronically and substitute a bleep: *A censor may blip words or lines from a sequence.*

bliss *n.* complete, serene happiness: *heavenly, marital, pure, wedded bliss;* "*Ignorance is bliss*" *(when you don't know the worst); It was bliss to be without TV for a few days.* —*v.* **bliss out** *Informal.* go into a state of ecstacy, as under the influence of a guru. —**bliss.ful** *adj.: a blissful existence, life, state; in blissful ignorance;* **bliss.ful.ly** *adv.;* **bliss.ful.ness** *n.*

blis.ter (BLIS.tur) *n.* **1** a patch of skin raised and filled with fluid, as from a rubbing or burn: *Blisters burst, form.* **2** a similar bulging, as on paint or metal. —*v.* form blisters: *The new shoes blistered her heel; His hands blister easily; The paint is blistering off.*

blistering *adja.* very hot or angry: *the blistering heat of the midday sun; in the blistering sun; a blistering attack, look, tongue; blistering words;* *adv.*: *It's blistering hot in here.*

blister pack *n.* a packaging using transparent material on a stiff backing; bubble pack: *Some tablets come in a blister pack of clear plastic bubbles on a cardboard strip.*

blithe ("th" as in "the") *adj.* cheerful and carefree: *blithe spirits.* —**blithe.ly** *adv.;* **blithe.some** *adj.*

blith.er.ing (BLITH.uh.ring, "TH" as in "the") *adj.* *Informal.* foolish: *the blithering imbecile! his blithering innocence.*

blitz *n.* **1** a lightning-fast military attack. **2** an intensive campaign: *a public relations blitz.* —*v.* overwhelm: *Video games have blitzed the science toys market; The Japanese blitzed* (= beat) *the Russians 7-1.*

bliz.zard (BLIZ.urd) *n.* **1** a severe snowstorm driven by high winds: *A blizzard struck in March and raged through the weekend.* **2** an enormous amount: *a blizzard of bills, greeting cards, paperwork, streamers and confetti.*

bloat *v.* swell, as with fat, gas, vanity, etc.: *Her abdomen was bloated with fluid;* *adj.: a* **bloated** *belly, carcass; He suffers from a bloated ego; a bloated budget, bureaucracy; bloated figures on a financial statement; He has a bloated head* (= high opinion of himself).

blob *n.* a shapeless mass; also, a spot of color: *a blob of grease, paint.*

bloc *n.* a usu. political grouping of nations, parties, etc. for a common purpose: *the NATO bloc; a voting bloc; the former Soviet bloc nations.*

block *n.* **1** a solid mass of wood, stone, metal, etc., usu. with at least one flat side: *a concrete block for building; a chopping block; an engine block containing the cylinders; Children play with building blocks of wood, plastic, etc.; a runner's starting block.* **2** a hindrance: *He has a mental block about anything alcoholic; He proved a stumbling block in our efforts to raise money.* **3** a building with many units: *an apartment block; office blocks.* **4** an urban area with streets on all four sides: *a building that occupies an entire city block; neighbors who live in the same block; I went around the block in search of the child, then walked ten blocks* (= block lengths) *to the school; the* **new kid on the block** (*Informal* for newcomer). **5** a number of company shares, seats close together, lines of type, etc.: *to delete, exchange, move blocks* (= sections) *of text on the video display.* **6** an auction platform: *The painting goes* **on the block** (= up for sale by bidding) *tomorrow.* **7** *Informal.* the head. —*v.* **1** hinder or obstruct: *A fallen tree blocked the road; players trying to block one another's moves; a blocked-up nose.* **2** support with a block: *It's safer to block up the other wheels before changing a tire.* —**block off** close or seal off: *The firefighters had to block off the street for safety's sake.* —**block out 1** make a sketch or plan in outline: *The artist blocked out a sketch of his painting;* also **block in.** **2** cover part of a picture or view. —**block.age** (-ij) *n.*

block.ade (block.ADE) *n.* a blocking off of the access to a city, harbor, etc.: *the blockade of Cuba during the 1962 missile* *crisis; to break, impose, lift, maintain a blockade; Ships trying to run the blockade* (= to slip through) *were fired at.* —*v.* to impose a blockade.

block.bust.er (BLOCK.bus.tur) *n. Informal.* **1** a very powerful bomb. **2** something with a very powerful impact: *The show was a blockbuster.*

block.head (BLOCK.hed) *n.* a stupid person.

block house *n.* a reinforced building for observation or protection in a dangerous operation.

block letter *n.* a capital letter: *a headline in big block letters.*

bloke *n. Brit. Informal.* a fellow or guy.

blond *adj.* **1** yellowish or light-colored: *blond complexion; blond hair and blue eyes; blond furniture, lace, silk, skin, wood.* **2** having blond hair: *a blond child with blond parents; an actress described as a* **blond bombshell** (= strikingly attractive blonde). —*n.* a blond person, esp. male: *Though her parents are blonds, she is a brunette.*

blonde (BLOND) *n.* a blond woman or girl: *There are not many natural platinum blondes (with very light hair); It's silly to typecast anyone as a dumb blonde.* —*adj a.* esp. of women, having blond hair: *the blonde lady over there.*

blood (BLUD) *n.* **1** the red fluid in veins and arteries: *Blood coagulates, clots, congeals, curdles, flows; Blood spurts from a wound; to donate blood to a blood bank; to draw, let, lose blood; to shed or spill blood by killing; Blood is typed or grouped as A, AB, B, and O; pure blood; whole blood.* **2** life or vigor: *The younger employees inject fresh* or *new blood into a company; old blood* (= personnel); *The book was written at the cost of a lot of* **blood, sweat, and tears;** *tired blood* (Informal for rundown condition of body). **3** passion or feeling: *There's bad blood* (= ill feeling) *between the two brothers; Abel was murdered* **in cold blood** (= cruelly and without feeling); *She's careful never to respond* **in hot blood** (= a temper). **4** family or descent: *The two are related by blood; "Blood is thicker than water"; a horse of good blood; a woman of royal blood; Poetry* **runs in their blood** (= They have been poets for generations); *They are your own flesh and blood* (= relatives); *We're all blood* (= blood brothers); *It's* **too rich for our blood** (= too expensive). —**make someone's blood boil** (or **run cold** or **freeze**) make someone angry (or frightened).

blood and thunder *n.* violent melodrama.

blood bank *n.* a place where blood is stored for use in transfusions.

blood.bath *n.* a massacre.

blood brother *n.* **1** one's brother by birth. **2** one's brother or kin by a ceremony of mixing blood from one's body with that of another. **3** a fellow black.

blood cell *n.* a red or white corpuscle of the blood.

blood count *n.* the number of red and white cells in an amount of blood.

blood.cur.dling (BLUD.curd.ling) *adj.* terrifying.

blood doping *n.* injection of an athlete with his or her own blood to improve performance.

blood.ed 1 *adj.* of fine pedigree: *blooded horses.* **2** *comb.form.* having the specified kind of blood: *cold-blooded, full-blooded, hot-blooded, red-blooded, warm-blooded.*

blood feud *n.* a feud arising from a violent crime.

blood group *n.* any of the types into which human blood is grouped for transfusion purposes on the basis of antigen compatibility; blood type.

blood.hound *n.* a large, long-eared, keen-scented tracking dog.

blood.less *adj.* **1** without violence or bloodshed: *a bloodless coup, revolution.* **2** lacking vigor or feeling: *a cerebral, bloodless style of verse.*

blood.let.ting (BLUD.let.ing) *n.* **1** therapeutic bleeding. **2** bloodshed.

blood.line *n.* a line of direct descent.

blood.mo.bile (BLUD.moh.beel) *n.* a truck, van, etc. outfitted for collecting blood donations.

blood poisoning *n.* any blood disease caused by toxins, infections, etc.

blood pressure *n.* the pressure of the blood on the blood-vessel walls: *High* or *elevated blood pressure and low blood pressure are bad symptoms.*

blood relative *n.* a relative related by birth, not marriage.

blood.shed *n.* the violent shedding of blood; killing.

blood.shot *adj.* red from inflammation: *bloodshot eyes.*

blood sport *n.* a sport such as foxhunting that involves shedding blood.

blood.stain *n.* a dark stain made by blood. —**blood.stained** *adj.*

blood stream *n.* the flow of blood in the arteries, veins, capillaries, etc.

blood.suck.er (BLUD.suck.ur) *n.* a leech or other creature that sucks blood; **blood.suck.ing** *adj.*

blood test *n.* the clinical testing of a

blood sample.
blood.thirst.y (BLUD.thurs.tee) *adj.* eager to kill.
blood type same as BLOOD GROUP.
blood.y (BLUD.ee) *adj.* **blood.i.er, -i.est** 1 of, containing, or stained with blood; bleeding: *a bloody nose, sword.* 2 having to do with bloodshed: *a bloody persecution, tyrant.* 3 *Slang.* damned: *a bloody miracle, nuisance, shame;* *adv.:* *We may bloody well get out of here; Writing a book is bloody hard work.* —**scream** or **cry** or **yell bloody murder** or **blue murder** *Informal.* make an outcry; complain loudly.
Bloody Mary *n.* a vodka-and-tomato-juice cocktail.
bloody-minded *adj.* 1 bloodthirsty. 2 tiresome or cantankerous.
—**bloody-mindedness** *n.*
bloom (long "oo") *n.* 1 a flower of the flowering state: *Lay out your garden carefully to ensure bloom from spring to fall; Our trees are in bloom or in full bloom* (= full of flowers) *in May.* 2 a flourishing condition: *He died in the (full) bloom of youth; The bloom may fade, as the company is heading for bankruptcy; Soon, the bloom was off their romance.* —*v.* 1 of plants and trees, have flowers: *blooming geraniums.* 2 flourish; glow with health; *adj.:* *You look positively blooming; a blooming business; a late-blooming genius.*
bloom.er *n.* 1 one that flowers. 2 *Informal.* blooper.
bloomers *n.pl.* 1 baggy women's trousers gathered at the knee. 2 women's underpants of this style.
blooming *adja. Informal.* darned: *a blooming disaster.* See also BLOOM.
bloop.er (BLOO.pur) *n. Informal.* a stupid mistake.
blos.som (BLOS.um) *n.* a flower, esp. of a fruit tree: *cherry blossoms; when apples are in blossom* (= flowering). —*v.* to flower or develop: *Youth blossom into the leaders of tomorrow; a chance meeting that blossomed into a romance.* —**blos.som.y** *adj.*
blot *n.* a stain, as of spilled ink: *The incident left a blot on his good name.* —*v.* **blots, blot.ted, blot.ting** 1 put a blot on something; stain. 2 absorb, esp. spilled ink, with absorbent paper. —**blot out** 1 cover over: *The smoke and dust blotted out the sun.* 2 destroy: *to blot out the memories of the war; to blot it out of one's memory, mind.*
blotch *n.* an irregular discoloration or stain, esp. a skin blemish. —**blotch.y** *adj.* **blotch.i.er, -i.est:** *a blotchy complex-*

ion, effect, skin.
blot.ter *n.* 1 a sheet of blotting paper. 2 a daily record sheet: *the police blotter of arrests, charges, etc.*
blotting paper *n.* a soft paper used to dry ink after writing.
blot.to (BLOT.oh) *adjp. Slang.* in a drunk state: *He was blotto and couldn't remember a thing afterward.*
blouse (*rhyme:* house) *n.* 1 a loose shirtlike garment, esp. for women: *a full blouse; a peasant blouse.* 2 a kind of smock or shirt, as worn by artists, peasants, sailors, etc. —*v.* **blous.es, bloused, blous.ing** fall in a fold *above* or *over a hip, boot, etc.: a dress bloused below a collar of antique lace; bloused at the waist.*
blou.son (BLOW.son, BLOO.son, "OW" as in "HOW," *rhyme:* on) *n.* a blouse or dress with material blousing over the waistband: *a blouson of soft fabric with striped borders; a blouson top.*
blow (BLOH) *v.* **blows, blew** (BLOO), **blown, blow.ing** 1 of air, be in motion: *The wind is blowing hard.* 2 make a stream of air with the mouth or nose: *He blew her a kiss; When the tea is hot, he blows on it; to blow one's nose* (to clear it); *She came in puffing and blowing* (= panting) *after jogging; to blow out* (= extinguish) *a candle;* **There she blows** (= There is the whale spouting air and water)! 3 move or be moved by wind: *A leaf blew down from the tree.* 4 make or do by blowing: *a child blowing bubbles; to blow* (= sound) *a bugle, horn, trumpet, whistle.* 5 burst, as a fuse, tire, etc.; explode: *She will* **blow her top** (*Informal* for lose her temper or explode) *when she finds out.* 6 *Informal.* spend extravagantly: *Charlie blew $1,000 at the races.* 7 *Informal.* bungle: *The actor blew his lines.* —**blow in** or **into** *Informal.* arrive unexpectedly: *He blew into town with a new show.* —**blow it** *Informal.* ruin one's chances. —**blow one's horn** or **trumpet** brag or boast. —**blow someone's mind** *Slang.* evoke feelings of admiration, awe, etc. or overwhelm: *Your new car will blow his mind.* —**blow one's top** or **lid** or **stack** *Slang.* lose one's temper. Also **blow a gasket** or **fuse.** —**blow over** pass over or be finished: *Wait till the storm blows over; Let the controversy blow over.*
—**blow the lid off** *Informal.* uncover: *He threatened to blow the lid off the whole scandal.* —**blow the whistle** *Informal.* report *on* someone or something to the authorities. —**blow up 1** explode: *a bridge blown up by terrorists.* 2 *Infor-*

mal. get very angry. **3** make larger; enlarge or inflate. —*n.* **1** a hard stroke: *He dealt or delivered or struck him a crushing blow; a knockout blow; The crowd heaped or rained blows on him; She's still reeling under the blows received; He took a blow to or on his chin; a blow to his hopes; Her speech struck a blow for reform; a blow against tyranny; to cushion, deflect, dodge, parry, ward off a blow; decisive, glancing, hard, heavy, mortal, resounding, severe, staggering, telling blows; It was a low blow* (= was unfair) *to question his motives; They* **come to blows** or *start* **exchanging blows** (= begin fighting) *as soon as they start arguing; Tell me what happened* **blow by blow** (= in detail); *adj.: a* **blow-by-blow** (= detailed) *account, chronicle, description.* **2** a blowing, as of the nose. **3** a heavy storm.

blow-dry *v.* to dry hair using a blow dryer.

blow dryer *n.* an electric blower for drying the hair.

blow.fly *n.* **-flies** a blue or green fly that lays its eggs in dead meat or living tissue and spreads disease germs.

blow.gun *n.* a tube for shooting a dart by blowing.

blow.out *n.* **1** a bursting of a tire; flat tire: *to have a blowout; fix a blowout.* **2** an uncontrollable flow of oil or gas from a well. **3** *Informal.* something overwhelming or out of the ordinary: *The 38-16 score was the second blowout in a row in the Superbowl; The record sale was clearly a blowout; the annual Mardi Gras blowout* (= noisy celebration); *adj.: a great blowout party, weekend.* **4** *Informal.* a clearance sale at deep discount prices.

blow.pipe *n.* a tube for forcing in air, as to fan a fire, blow glass, launch a missile, etc.

blow.sy (BLOW.zee, "OW" as in "how") *adj.* **-si.er, -si.est** untidy and coarse: *She played the blowsy and boozy Lady Hamilton.* Also **blow.zy.**

blow.torch *n.* a portable torch for shooting a gasoline flame under pressure.

blow.up *n.* **1** an explosion. **2** an enlarged photograph. **3** a fit of anger.

blow.y *adj.* **blow.i.er, -i.est** windy: *a cold, blowy day.*

blowzy same as BLOWSY.

BLT *n.* **BLTs** *Informal.* a sandwich of bacon, lettuce, and tomato.

blub.ber *n.* fat, esp. of whales, seals, etc. —*v.* weep noisily; **blub.ber.er** *n.* —**blub.ber.y** *adj.*

blub.ber.head (BLUB.ur.hed) *n. Slang.* stupid person; fathead.

blu.cher (BLOO.cur, -chur) *n.* a style of shoe in which the vamp is one piece with the tongue.

bludg.eon (BLUJ.un) *n.* a short heavy club. —*v.* beat with a bludgeon: *The baby seals were bludgeoned to death; She was bludgeoned* (= coerced) *into joining them.*

blue (BLOO) *n.* **1** the color of a cloudless daytime sky: *a patch of blue; The color is a light blue.* **2** something in this color, as clothing or a dye: *She was decked in blue; clothes washed in blue.* **3 the blue:** *The UFO disappeared into the blue* (= blue sky); *out in the blue* (= blue ocean); *The news came as a bolt from the blue* (= as a shock); *The principal appeared* **out of the blue** (= unexpectedly). —**blues** *pl.* **1** [with *pl. v.*] a melancholy mood: *to sing the blues* (*Informal* for to complain); *the blue-collar blues* (= boredom and depression) *of assembly-line workers; the Monday morning blues.* **2** [with *sing. v.*] a slow, sad style of jazz, characterized by so-called "blue" notes sung or played a half-tone flat. —*adj.* **blu.er, blu.est** **1** of the color blue: *a face blue with cold; blue eyes and blond hair.* **2** gloomy: *He's feeling somewhat blue today; He's developed* **blue flu** (*Informal* for He's calling in sick). **3** *adj.* puritanical: *Sunday blue laws.* **4** *adj.* noble or aristocratic: *born of blue blood.* **5** conservative: *a true-blue Canadian; He's more of a red Tory than a blue or even pink one.* **6** *Informal.* off-color; risqué: *blue jokes, language, movies.* —**blue around the gills** *Informal.* looking or feeling sick. —**once in a blue moon** very rarely. —**blu.ish** *adj.*

blue baby *n.* a baby born with a bluish skin from a heart defect.

blue.bell *n.* a plant with blue, bell-shaped flowers.

blue.ber.ry (BLOO.ber.ee) *n.* **-ber.ries** the small, edible, dark-blue fruit of a wild or cultivated shrub.

blue.bird *n.* a small, North American songbird whose male is bright blue.

blue.blood *n.* aristocrat: *The zoo board was a group of bluebloods.*

blue-blooded *adj.* of aristocratic birth.

blue.bon.net (BLOO.bon.it) *n.* a blue wild flower of the S.W. United States.

blue book *n.* an official publication: *a blue book* (= listing) *of socially prominent people; a 2,000-page blue book of the government's spending estimates.*

blue.bot.tle (BLOO.bot.ul) *n.* any of several flies with blue bodies.

blue box *n.* **1** an electronic device for bypassing telephone circuits and making illegal toll-free calls. **2** a box for putting out recyclable waste such as cans and bottles.

blue cheese *n.* a creamy white cheese with veins of bluish mold.

blue chip *n.* an expensive, secure investment stock: *The original $50 investment is a blue chip today; The rally on the stock exchange was led by established blue chips.* —**blue-chip** *adj.* highly valued: *a blue-chip client, corporation, investment, visitors' list.*

blue-collar *adj.* having to do with manual or industrial workers: *a blue-collar family, job, neighborhood, stronghold; the blue-collar trades; tensions between white-collar and unionized blue-collar workers;* ***adjp.:*** *a job that is typically* **blue collar.**

blue flu See BLUE, *adj.* 2.

blue.grass *n.* **1** a grass with bluish stems, common in Kentucky. **2** Southern country music played on string instruments; ***adj.:*** *a bluegrass musical festival; the bluegrass style of music.*

blue.ing same as BLUING.

blue jay *n.* a bold and loud bird of E. North America with a crested head and blue and white feathers.

blue jeans *n.* jeans of heavy blue denim.

blue.nose *n.* a puritan. —**blue.nosed** *adj.* puritanical: *those bluenosed censors.*

blue pages *n.pl.* a section of the telephone directory printed on blue paper, in which government agencies are listed.

blue-pencil *v.* -cils, -ciled, -cil.ing delete or edit out. Also **blue-pencilled, blue-pencilling** *Cdn.*

blue.print *n.* **1** a kind of photographic reproduction of building plans, maps, etc.: *to draw up* or *make up a blueprint.* **2** a detailed plan: *a blueprint for peace, progress, reform; the blueprint stage of a plan; v.: to blueprint a plan, program.*

blue ribbon *n.* an award of excellence. —**blue-ribbon** *adj.* composed of specially qualified or distinguished members: *a blue-ribbon audience, committee, jury, panel.*

blue-sky *adj.* having no practical value or application: *a blue-sky estimate, figure; blue-sky thinking; blue-sky* (= worthless) *stock; a* **blue-sky law** *designed to protect investors from fraudulent stockbrokers.*

blue.stock.ing (BLOO.stock.ing) *n.* a woman having literary or intellectual interests.

blue streak *n.* a rapid stream of words: *The child was chattering* or *talking a blue streak about learning to write his name at school that day.*

blues.y (BLOO.see) *adj.* **blues.i.er, -i.est** having to do with the blues: *a bluesy swinging beat; bluesy rock numbers, settings, shuffles.*

bluff *v.* mislead or intimidate by a false show of confidence or strength: *He was only bluffing, didn't really mean it; tried to bluff me into lending him money.* —*n.* **1** an attempt to threaten or mislead: *I didn't fall for his bluff; He backed down when she* **called his bluff** (= challenged him). **2** a steep, flat-fronted cliff or bank: *on a high bluff overlooking the lake.* **3** a grove of trees. —*adj.* **1** steep and flat-fronted: *a bluff shoreline.* **2** blunt and good-natured: *his bluff refusal.*

blu.ing or **blue.ing** (BLOO.ing) *n.* a blue laundering additive.

blun.der *n.* a mistake made from ignorance or stupidity: *He committed a costly blunder; a grave, stupid, terrible blunder; It was a tactical blunder not to consult her.* —*v.* **1** move clumsily: *He blundered through the jungle.* **2** make a foolish mistake: *He blundered; She* **blundered upon** *the solution to the puzzle* (= found it by mistake).

blun.der.buss (BLUN.dur.bus) *n.* **1** a wide-muzzled old-fashioned gun. **2** one who blunders.

blunt *adj.* **1** without a sharp edge; dull: *a blunt knife, object, pencil.* **2** plain-spoken: *Forgive my being blunt; I'm a blunt person.* —*v.* make or become blunt: *He blunted his ax on the rock; Alcohol blunts your senses.* —**blunt.ly** *adv.;* **blunt.ness** *n.*

blur *v.* **blurs, blurred, blur.ring** make or become indistinct or dim: *Memories blur and fade away; to blur a distinction; adj.: His motives are too* **blurred**; *blurred features, images, vision.* —*n.* something indistinct: *The cars raced past in a blur; You can see it only as a blur in the picture.* —**blur.ry** *adj.: a blurry distinction, photograph; blurry vision.*

blurb *n.* a publisher's write-up of a book, printed on its dust jacket.

blurt *v.* say without thinking: *The child blurted out the secret.*

blush *v.* turn red in the face from shame, modesty, etc.: *She blushes readily; He blushed for* or *with shame; He blushes at the mere mention of the subject.* —*n.* **1** a reddening of the face: *The story brought a deep blush to his cheeks.* **2** appearance: *the blush of dawn in the* morning sky; *the first blush of youth; The plan may seem harmless* **at first blush** (= on first examination). —**blush.ful** *adj.*

blush.er *n.* face rouge that is pink; also **blush** or **blush-on**.

blus.ter (BLUS.tur) *v.* **1** blow in heavy gusts. **2** speak or act in noisy threats or boasts. —*n.* such behavior: *a bully's empty bluster.* —**blus.ter.er** *n.*

blus.ter.y (BLUS.tuh.ree) *adj.* blowing or windy: *a blustery day; blustery weather.*

B'nai B'rith (buh.NAY.BRITH) *n.* an international Jewish service organization.

B.O. or **BO** (BEE.oh) *n. Informal.* body odor.

bo.a (BOH.uh) *n.* **1** a tropical snake, esp. the **boa constrictor,** which crushes and swallows its prey. **2** a long scarf of feathers or fluffy fur.

boar (BOR) *n.* **1** a male pig. **2** a fierce Old World wild pig.

board (BORD) *n.* **1** a long, thin, rectangular piece of wood: *boards for a boardwalk.* **2** a flat piece of material for a special use: *bulletin, chess, cutting, dart, diving, drawing, ironing, sounding boards; adj.: a board fence; a book's* **board covers** *(made of stiff material).* **3** a table for serving food: *room and board* (= meals). **4** an official council: *to serve on a board of directors; the chairman of the board; boards of education, health, studies, trade; editorial, parole, school boards.* **5** same as CIRCUIT BOARD. —**the boards** *n.pl.* **1** in hockey and lacrosse, the board fence enclosing the rink or field. **2** the stage: *An actor is said to tread the boards; She was off the boards for a year because of illness.* —**above board** open and honest. —**across the board** affecting every member of the group: *a pay raise of 5% across the board;* **adj.:** *an across-the-board pay raise.* —**go by the board** become forgotten, abandoned, lost, etc.; fail completely. —**on board** **1** aboard a ship, train, etc.: *the people on board a bus.* **2** into a working relationship: *Come on board* (= Join us)! Also **aboard.** —*v.* **1** cover or shut with boards: *The windows were boarded up before the storm.* **2** get on a ship, bus, train, etc.: *It's time to board (the flight); Flight 181 is now boarding* (= being boarded); **adj.:** *a* **boarding** *card or pass, lounge, passenger, ticket, zone.* **3** provide with meals and usu. lodging for regular payment: *Our landlady boards 10 students; I boarded my horse* (= arranged with a stable for its lodging and feed) *when I went on holidays;* **adj.:** *a* **boarding** *house, kennel, school.* **4** in hockey and box lacrosse, to

bodycheck an opponent into the boards.

board.er *n.* one who pays for meals and often a room, as at a **boarding house:** *She takes in boarders.*

boarding *n.* in hockey and box lacrosse, an illegal bodychecking of an opponent; also **board-checking.**

board.room *n.* the conference room in which a governing body such as a school board or board of directors meets.

board.sail.ing (BORD.say.ling) same as SAILBOARDING.

board.walk *n.* a sidewalk or beach promenade built of boards.

boast (BOHST) *v.* **1** speak of one's abilities, deeds, etc. with too much pride: *He likes to boast about* or *of his wealth; to boast that he is wealthy.* **2** be proud to have: *The town boasts a new concert hall.* —*n.* a boasting or the subject of it: *Some of his claims are just empty boasts; to make an idle, vain, proud boast.* —**boast.ful** *adj.;* **boast.ful.ly** *adv.;* **boast.ful.ness** *n.*

boat (BOHT) *n.* **1** a vessel for water travel, esp. a small open one: *to launch, row, sail, swamp, upset a boat; a patrol boat; We crossed the Channel by boat; A boat heaves, pitches, rolls, sails.* **2** a dish for serving sauces: *a gravy boat.* —**in the same boat** in the same circumstances. —**miss the boat** miss one's opportunity. —**rock the boat** *Informal.* cause problems by disturbing the way things are. —*v.* **1** travel in a boat: *to go boating; Anne boated down the river.* **2** take in a boat: *He boated the 1,000-pounder (fish) in 30 minutes.*

boat.er *n.* **1** one who boats. **2** a flat-topped hard straw hat.

boat.man (BOHT.mun) *n.* -**men** a man who operates, works with, or deals in boats.

boat people *n.pl.* refugees fleeing or arriving by boat.

boat.swain (BOH.sun) *n.* a ship's petty officer in charge of the deck, hull, anchor, etc.

bob *v.* **bobs, bobbed, bob.bing 1** move up and down, as a cork on water. **2** come up or come in suddenly: *He bobbed into the room.* **3** cut short; *adj.: a horse with a* **bobbed** *tail.* —*n.* **1** a rapid up-and-down movement: *a bob of the head.* **2** a float for a fishing line. **3** a woman's short hair style. **4** a small weight, as on a plumb line.

bob.by *n.* **bob.bies** *Brit. Informal.* a policeman

bobby pin *n.* a small ridged hair clip.

bobby-soxer (BOB.ee.sox.ur) *n. Informal.* a teen-aged girl of the 1940s, esp. one who wore ankle-high **bobby socks** (or **sox**) folded over the shoes.

bob.cat *n.* a spotted, tan or reddish brown North American wildcat.

bob.sled *n.* **1** a joined pair of short sleds. **2** a heavy racing sled with two sets of runners, a steering wheel, and brakes. —*v.* **-sleds, -sled.ded, -sled.ding.**

bob.white *n.* any of several North American quails.

boc.cie, boc.ce or **boc.ci** (BOCH.ee) *n.* an Italian form of lawn bowling.

bock or **bock beer** *n.* a dark, sweetish beer.

bod *n. Slang.* body: *Most people have neither the bods nor the boodle to dress in fashion; Thousands of sweaty bods* (= people) *packed the stadium.*

bode 1 *pt.* of BIDE. **2** *v.* **bodes, bod.ed, bod.ing** be a sign of something to happen: *A long drought does not bode well for a good harvest; It bodes ill for a good harvest; It bodes us no good.*

bod.ice (BOD.is) *n.* the fitted upper portion of a woman's dress.

bod.ied (BOD.eed) *comb.form.* having a body as specified: *an able-bodied sailor; a full-bodied wine; wide-bodied jets.*

bod.i.less (BOD.ee.lis) *adj.* not having a body; disembodied.

bod.i.ly (BOD.uh.lee) *adja.* of the body, not of the mind: *charged with assault causing bodily harm; a bodily ailment, fluid, function, hygiene, illness, injury, need, organ; bodily aches, activities, changes, integrity, well-being.* —*adv.* **1** in person, not in spirit: *A spirit cannot be bodily present.* **2** as a whole: *The group walked out bodily; He was lifted bodily and thrown out of the bar.*

bod.kin *n.* **1** a pointed instrument such as a kind of awl or an ornamental hairpin. **2** a needle for pulling tape or ribbon through something.

bod.y *n.* **bod.ies 1** the physical structure of an organism, esp. of a human: *a sound mind in a healthy body; the body beautiful;* **Over my dead body** (= It can't be done while I'm alive)! *We need two warm bodies* (Informal for persons) *for the moving job; The body* (= corpse) *of the President will lie in state; She loved him* **body and soul** (= totally). **2** a physical object: *a solid body; dust particles and such foreign bodies in the eye; The moon is a celestial* or *heavenly body.* **3** the trunk or main part: *the body of the essay; an automobile body (exclusive of chassis and engine).* **4** a large mass: *A lake is a body of water; a body of evidence, information, knowledge.* **5** a group or unit: *an advisory, deliberative, governing body; the body politic; the student body; The workers walked out* **in a body** (= all together). **6** a bodylike quality, esp. thickness: *Her hair has body; This paint has body; a wine with body* (= richness).

body bag *n.* a plastic or rubber bag used for removing corpses.

body blow *n.* a severe setback or defeat, as a hard blow between neck and waistline in boxing: *The new legislation administered* or *dealt a body blow to the insurance industry.*

body.check *n.* in hockey and lacrosse, a checking of an opposing player by hitting from the front or side and above the knees with one's hip or shoulder. Also *v.*

body English *n.* body movements reflecting a player's desire to control a ball after throwing it.

bod.y.guard (BOD.ee.gard) *n.* one or more guards protecting a person.

body language *n.* postures, gestures, etc. as expressing feelings, thoughts, or attitudes: *Leo can read both Italian and Italian body language.*

body pack *n.* a wireless device secretly worn on the person, as of an undercover police officer, for transmitting and recording conversations.

body politic *n.* the people as a political unit under a government.

body rub *n.* a nonmedical massage, as given in a massage parlor; *adj.*: *a* **body-rub** *parlor, studio.*

body shirt *n.* a close-fitting shirt-and-panty combination that is sewn or snapped at the crotch.

body snatcher *n.* one who illegally digs up corpses, esp. for dissection.

body stocking *n.* a close-fitting light garment covering the trunk and often the legs and arms.

Boer (BOHR, BOOR) *n.* a South African of Dutch descent;

bof.fin (BOF.un) *n. Informal.* a technical expert: *a computer boffin.*

bof.fo (BOF.oh) *adj. Informal.* successful, as a box-office hit: *a boffo Kung Fu movie.* —*adv.* well: *It did boffo at the box office.*

bog *n.* an area of wet marshy ground: *a peat bog.* —*v.* **bogs, bogged, bog.ging** get stuck in or as if in a bog; mire: *The talks (got) bogged down on the question of overtime; a student* **bogged down** *in* or *with homework.*

bo.gey (BOH.gee, "g" as in "go") *n.* **-geys 1** a frightening spirit or something feared: *The final examinations were his bogey;* also **bo.gy** or **bo.gie,** *pl.* **-gies. 2** in golf, one stroke over par on a hole. —*v.* make this score.

bog.gle (BOG.ul) *v.* **bog.gles, bog.gled, bog.gling** be bewildered: *The mind boggles at the idea of limitless space and time; Space and time boggle* (= bewilder) *the mind.*

bo.gus (BOH.gus) *adj.* fake: *a bogus 20-dollar bill; a bogus issue; Their system is bogus and corrupt.*

bogy See BOGEY.

Bo.he.mi.an or **bo.he.mi.an** (boh.HEE.mee.un) *n.* one, esp. an artist, who lives in an unconventional manner; *adj.: a Bohemian lifestyle.*

boil *v.* **1** cause a liquid to bubble and vaporize by heating to the temperature at which it changes to gas: *Let's boil some water in the kettle; adj.: We have a **boiling** kettle (of water).* **2** cook or sterilize in boiling water: *to boil an egg.* **3** be very hot: *I'm boiling in here; She's boiling* (= seething) *with rage; adja.: a kettle of boiling water; the boiling* (= churning or swirling) *rapids of the Niagara River; adv.: a boiling hot day; She's boiling mad.* —**boil down** condense by boiling: *Your essay is too long – boil it down to 500 words; It all boils down* (= amounts) *to greed.* —*n.* **1** the state of boiling: *to bring the water to a boil; Water comes to a boil at 100°C; Keep it at a gentle boil for 10 minutes.* **2** a swollen and pus-filled skin infection: *A boil comes to a head and bursts when ripe.*

boil.er *n.* a tank, pot, etc. in which water is boiled, as for steam power or cooking.

boil.er.plate (BOY.lur.plate) *n.* **1** steel plate for making boilers. **2** *Informal.* standardized material, as syndicated news and features supplied to small newspapers by metropolitan dailies in stereotyped form on plates. **3** standardized material. —*adja.* standardized: *boilerplate contracts, language, paragraphs, text.*

boiler room *n.* **1** a room in which boilers are located. **2** *Informal.* a high-pressure sales operation conducted from a back room full of solicitors using telephones and prepared sales pitches. Also **boiler shop, bucket shop.**

boiling point *n.* the temperature at which a liquid begins to boil: *Water reaches the boiling point at 100°C.*

bo.ing (BOH.ing) [like the sound of a plucked string] *interj.* expressing ecstasy or vibrations: *When the baton landed on the twirler's head, the boys went boing.*

bois.ter.ous (BOIS.tur.us) *adj.* noisily exuberant: *his boisterous good humor; a boisterous* (= rowdy) *party.*
—**bois.ter.ous.ly** *adv.;*
bois.ter.ous.ness *n.*

bo.la (BOH.luh) *n.* a weapon thrown at animals to entangle and catch them, consisting of weighted balls on the end of long cords; also **bo.las** (-lus).

bold *adj.* **1** courageous; daring: *a bold adventurer; He felt a bit nervous, but put on a bold front; He **made bold** to ask her age; If I may be so bold as to ask your age, madam?* **2** impudent: *a bold youth.* **3** distinctly visible: *The hills stood out against the sky in bold outline; He painted it with a few bold strokes of the brush.* **4** steep: *a bold cliff.* —**bold.ly** *adv.;*
bold.ness *n.*

bold.face *n.* a heavy, dark style of type, as **this.**

bold.faced *adj.* **1** in boldface: *boldfaced entries, type.* **2** impudent: *the boldfaced youth.*

bole *n.* a tree trunk.

bo.le.ro (buh.LAIR.oh) *n.* **1** a short, open-fronted jacket with or without sleeves and collar. **2** a Spanish dance in 3/4 time.

bol.i.var (BOL.uh.var) *n.* the basic unit of currency in Venezuela.

Bo.liv.i.an (buh.LIV.ee.un) *n. & adj.* (a person) of or from **Bolivia,** a South American republic.

boll (BOLE) *n.* a round seed pod, as of cotton, flax, etc.

bo.lo.gna (buh.LOH.nee) *n.* a large sausage of smoked mixed meats; also **bologna sausage.**

bo.lo tie (BOH.loh-) *n.* a necktie of thin cord with an ornamental clasp instead of a knot.

Bol.she.vik (BOLE.shuh.vik) *adj.* Communist; also, extremely radical.
—**Bol.she.vism** *n.* —**Bol.she.vist** *n. & adj.*

bol.ster (BOLE.stur) *n.* **1** a long, thin, firm pillow, cushion, etc. used as a support. **2** a support. —*v.* prop up: *a pep talk to bolster their sagging spirits.*

bolt *n.* **1** a rod or bar used to fasten a door, window, etc. **2** a metal fastener made of a rod or pin with threads on one end and a head at the other: *nuts and bolts.* **3** a roll of cloth: *We buy denim by the bolt; bolt ends of fabrics.* **4** a blast of lightning: *Her resignation came as **a bolt from the blue*** (= as a shock). **5** a dash, as if to escape: *The dog made a bolt for the door.* —**have shot one's bolt** exhausted oneself, as in old age:

bolus / bone

It's tragic that some young people have shot their bolt by age 20. —**sit bolt upright** sit stiffly erect. —*v.* **1** fasten the bolt on something: *Shut the door and bolt it; It bolts* (= is bolted) *at the bottom.* **2** run away, as if scared: *The horse bolted from the barn; His supporters suddenly bolted; They bolted the Liberals and joined the Tories.* **3** swallow food rapidly: *Don't bolt (down) your lunch.* **4** sift using a sieve, etc.: *to bolt flour, grain.*

bo.lus (BOH.lus) *n.* a round lump to be swallowed, as a ball of chewed food or a large pill.

bomb (BOM) *n.* **1** a projectile filled with explosives, gas, incendiary material, etc.: *to deactivate, defuse, detonate, drop, explode, set off a bomb; A bomb explodes* or *goes off; atom, atomic, clean, hydrogen, incendiary, letter, stink, time bombs; a smart* (= guided) *bomb; Ban **the Bomb*** (= the atomic bomb)! **2** an aerosol spray can. **3** *Slang.* a total failure: *The book was a bomb.* —*v.* **1** destroy or attack with bombs: *to bomb a city;* ***adj.***: *a bombing attack, raid, run.* **2** *Slang.* be a total failure: *The show bombed.*

bom.bard (bom.BARD) *v.* attack with or as if with heavy guns: *Warships bombarded the coast; The prime minister was bombarded with letters and telegrams.* —**bom.bard.ment** *n.*

bom.bar.dier (bom.buh.DEER) *n.* a crew member of a bomber who aims and releases the bombs.

bom.bast (BOM.bast) *n.* pretentious and lofty writing or speech. —**bom.bas.tic** (bom.BAS.tic) *adj.*

bomb bay *n.* a compartment on the underside of a bomber from which bombs are released.

bombed (BOMD) *adj. Slang.* intoxicated: *Some of those drivers are anywhere from tipsy to flat-out bombed; He's bombed* or *bombed out on drugs.*

bomb.er (BOM.ur) *n.* an airplane designed to drop bombs: *a fighter bomber; long-range bombers.*

bomber jacket *n.* a short jacket, usu. leather, of the kind worn by air crew.

bomb.proof *adj.* able to resist a bomb explosion: *a bombproof basement.*

bomb.shell *n.* **1** a bomb. **2** someone or something that creates a sensation: *He dropped a bombshell when he announced the winner; a blonde bombshell.*

bomb.sight *n.* a bomb-aiming device used in aircraft.

bo.na fi.de (BOH.nuh.fide, -FYE.dee) *adja.* without intent to deceive; genuine: *a bona fide offer to purchase; Parking for bona fide hotel guests only; bona fide reasons for delay.*

bo.nan.za (buh.NAN.zuh) *n.* something very profitable or rewarding: *The movie proved a box-office bonanza.*

bon.bon (BON.bon) *n.* a candy, esp. with a soft center and chocolate coating.

bond *n.* **1** something that unites, ties, obliges, etc.: *We are united in the bond of matrimony; They strengthened their bond by signing a contract; a bond of friendship with someone; to break the bonds* (= fetters) *of slavery; The slaves cast off their bonds and became free; Mortar makes a good bond* (= cement or adhesive) *between bricks.* **2** a pledge or guarantee, as an insurance agreement to pay an employer for loss caused by an employee: *a fidelity bond* or *surety bond; bail bonds; fiduciary bonds; He furnished* or *posted a bond for $100,000; He forfeited the bond by not delivering as promised.* **3** a pledge by a government or corporation to repay a loan with interest on a specified date: *savings bonds; I cashed in* or *redeemed my bonds before they matured.* **4** a strong, superior kind of paper; also called "bond paper." —**in bond** of imported goods, in storage in a bonded warehouse awaiting payment of taxes: *whiskey (that was) bottled in bond.* —*v.* **1** join or unite: *two boards bonded (together) by glue; A newborn is ready to bond to anyone, but an older child takes longer;* ***adj.***: *Are women more **bonded** to each other than men are? a fire hose with a covering of **bonded fabric** (composed of several materials).* **2** guarantee with a bond: *He has bonded himself to collect and pay all duties;* ***adj.***: *a **bonded** contractor, employee, housemaid, winery.* **3** place goods in a bonded warehouse till tariffs are paid; ***adj.***: ***bonded** goods, storage, whiskey.*

bond.age (BOND.ij) *n.* slavery or serfdom: *He lived all his life in bondage to his creditors.*

bonded warehouse *n.* a warehouse for the storage of dutiable goods, the operator of it being bonded to secure the payment before goods are released.

bond.hold.er (BOND.hold.ur) *n.* a holder of a bond issued by a government or corporation.

bonds.man (BONDS.mun) *n.* **-men** one who provides bail; surety.

bone *n.* the hard substance of vertebrate skeletons or a piece of it: *He fell and broke a bone; A doctor set the fractured bone; Broken bones knit; I have **a bone to pick with** (Informal for a com-*

plaint against) *you*; *Services have been cut to the bone* (= drastically reduced) *because of budget cuts*; *I knew* or *could feel in my bones* (= had a deep-seated feeling) *this was going to happen*; *He makes no bones about* (= does not feel bothered by) *telling everyone he dropped out of school*; *The frightened child stood there chilled* or *frozen to the bone.*
—*v.* **bones, boned, bon.ing** take the bones out of something: *to bone a fish.*
—**bone up** study hard: *He's boning up on his math*; *boning up for his finals.*
bone china *n.* a fine china made of white clay mixed with bone ash.
bone-dry *adj.* very dry.
bone.head *n. Slang.* a stupid person.
—*adj.*: *a bonehead* (= stupid) *statement*; *bonehead English* (= basic composition) *for people who can't write*; *adj.*: *a bone-headed remark.*
bone marrow *n.* See MARROW, def. 1.
bone.meal *n.* crushed bone used as feed for fertilizer.
bone of contention *n.* a subject of dispute: *Language is often a bone of contention in bilingual societies.*
bon.er (BOH.nur) *n. Slang.* a blooper.
bon.fire (BON.fire) *n.* a large fire built outdoors, as for a celebration: *They built a bonfire and sat around it.*
bon.go (BONG.go) *n.* -**gos** 1 either of a pair of small drums, called **bongo drums**, joined together for playing with the hands. 2 an African antelope with narrow white stripes.
bon.ho.mie (bon.uh.MEE) *n.* good-natured amiability; also **bon.hom.mie.**
bo.ni.to (buh.NEE.toh) *n., pl.* -**tos** or -**toes** a tunalike ocean fish.
bon.kers (BONK.urs) *adj. Slang.* nuts or crazy: *He went bonkers in that movie*; *He seems even more bonkers in this movie than in previous ones*; *offbeat, bizarre, a little bonkers.*
bon mot (bohn.MOH) *n., pl.* **bons mots** (-MOZE), a witty remark, as "Students of the world arise; you've nothing to lose but your marks!"
bon.net (BON.it) *n.* 1 a head covering for women and children that is tied under the chin. 2 any hood or covering.
bon.ny or **bon.nie** *adj.* **bon.ni.er, bon.ni.est** *Scots. & Brit.* healthy and good-looking: *a bonny lass, prince.*
bon.sai (bon.SYE) *n. sing. & pl.* 1 an ornamental dwarf tree: *the bonsai gardens of Japan.* 2 the art of growing bonsai.
bo.nus (BOH.nus) *n.* -**nus.es** something paid or given as an extra: *Everyone received a Christmas bonus of $500*; *a bonus shot* (= extra free throw) *in basketball.*
bon vi.vant (bon.vi.VAHNT) *n.* one who likes good food and drink and other pleasures of life.
bon voy.age (bon.voy.AZH) *n.* farewell; (Have a) pleasant trip!
bon.y (BOH.nee) *adj.* **bon.i.er, -i.est** 1 having to do with bones: *a bony fish* (full of bones); *a bony growth* (like a bone). 2 having prominent bones: *bony faces, features, hands, knees.*
bon.zo (BON.zoh) *adjp. Slang.* nuts or crazy.
boo *interj. & n., pl.* **boos** 1 a sustained "boo" sound made to show disapproval. 2 a sound made abruptly to startle someone: *He sneaked up behind her and said "Boo!"* —*v.* **boos, booed, boo.ing** make a "boo" at someone: *They booed him*; *He was booed off the stage.*
boob (long "oo") *n. Slang.* 1 a dolt. 2 booboo: *a report that is replete with financial boobs.* 3 a woman's breast.
boo.boo *n.* -**boos** *Slang.* a blunder: *to make a booboo.*
boob tube *n. Slang.* TV or a TV set.
boo.by (BOO.bee) *n.* -**bies** 1 a doltish person. 2 a swimming sea bird that lights on ships and easily allows itself to be caught.
booby hatch *n. Slang.* a mental institution.
booby prize *n.* a prize given to a loser in fun.
booby trap *n.* a deceptive object that explodes or injures when touched: *to set a booby trap.* —**booby-trap** *v.* -**traps, -trapped, -trapping:** *Terrorists booby-trapped the car and it exploded.*
boo.dle (BOO.dul) *n. Slang.* 1 a large amount; caboodle. 2 money, esp. as a bribe or loot from corrupt practices.
boo.gie or **boo.gy** (BOOG.ee, short or long "OO") *n.* rock music for dancing. —*v.* **boo.gies, boo.gied, boo.gy.ing** to dance to rock music. Also **boo.gey.**
boogieman See BOGEYMAN.
book *n.* 1 a set of paper or similar sheets bound along one edge; *to bind a book*; *a book bound in leather.* 2 a literary, historical, etc. composition of some length: *to ban a book*; *to charge or check a book out of a library*; *to bring out, copyright, dedicate, edit, pirate, publish, put out, review, revise, write a book*; *to typeset a book* or *set a book in type*; *Books appear* or *come out* or *are published*; *A book goes out of print when it is sold out and is not reprinted*; *a coffee-table book*; *library book*; *picture book*; *rare book*; *a*

book translated from Arabic; The Bible is often called **the (Good) Book**; *A phone book is a reference book; a book on carpentry.* **3** a main division of such a work: *Genesis is the first book of the Bible.* **4 books** *pl.* financial and such records: *Accountants keep books; Auditors audit or go over* or *inspect the books; New members are entered on the books; Is he in the* **good or bad books** *of* (= in or out of favor with) *the president?* **5** something packaged in booklike form: *a book of coupons, matches, tickets; check books.* —**by the book** correctly or properly, according to the rules: *Let's go or play by the book.* —**make book** make or take bets. —**throw the book at someone** punish someone severely by making all possible charges and giving the maximum penalties.
—*v.* **1** engage in advance: *to book a room in a hotel; to book seats on a flight; a night club tour booked by a travel agent; Area hotels are booked up solid* (= no more rooms available); *n.: A* **booking** (= engagement or reservation) *was made, then canceled.* **2** make a charge against someone: *He was booked for theft.* **3** declare: *Employees sometimes book off sick as a job action; Hospitals book off* or *out of service due to shortage of beds.*
book.case *n.* a piece of furniture having bookshelves.
book club *n.* a company that sells books at a discount to members.
book.end *n.* something used to keep a row of books upright: *a pair of bookends; people from the bookends of the continent* (= from coast to coast).
book.ie (BOOK.ee) *n.* Informal. bookmaker.
book.ish *adj.* based on books, not practical: *the bookish views of a bookish scholar; a bookish* (= pedantic or affected) *style of writing.*
book jacket same as DUST JACKET.
book.keep.er (BOOK.kee.pur) *n.* one who keeps business records and accounts.
book.keep.ing *n.* accountancy; also, the work: *Who does the bookkeeping for your company?*
book learning *n.* knowledge gained from books; theoretical knowledge.
book.let *n.* a thin, usu. paperbound book.
book.mak.er (BOOK.may.kur) *n.* one who accepts bets, usu. on races.
book.mak.ing (BOOK.may.king) *n.* the business of taking bets, as on horses.
book.man (BOOK.mun) *n.* **-men 1** one who loves books. **2** a bookseller or book publisher.
book.mark *n.* **1** something put in a book to mark a place. **2** an electronic reference mark, as a tag or character, placed in a text or at an Internet site.
book match *n.* one of the matches forming a matchbook.
book.mo.bile (BOOK.moh.beel) *n.* a truck equipped as a mobile library or bookstore.
book.sell.er (BOOK.sel.ur) *n.* one who runs a bookstore.
book.shelf *n.* **-shelves** a shelf to keep books on.
book.shop or **book.store** *n.* a place where books are sold.
book.stack *n.* usu. **book.stacks**, collection of books in a library; stacks.
book value *n.* **1** in accounting, a firm's assets minus its liabilities. **2** an asset's depreciated value.
book.worm *n.* **1** an insect that eats into books. **2** an avid reader or student.
Bool.e.an (BOO.lee.un) *adj.* having to do with a binary logical system using the operators "and," "or," and "not" for retrieving information from a computer database: *Boolean algebra, logic, operators.*
boom (long "oo") *n.* **1** a long horizontal pole, as one used to hold out the bottom edge of a sail, support a load on a derrick, hold a microphone, etc. **2** a barrier: *A boom of connected logs is used to contain floating timber; An ice boom builds up in the Niagara River at Lake Erie during the winter; Sandbags filled with absorbent material were placed as booms along the channel to prevent the oil spill from entering the river.* **3** a deep, loud sound: *a sonic boom.* **4** a sudden increase: *the postwar baby boom; The boom has passed its peak;* the **boom-and-bust** *cycle (of prosperity and depression).* —**lower the boom** *Informal.* crack down *on* someone.
—*v.* **1** make or utter with a deep resonant sound: *Guns boomed in the distance; Tchaikovsky's 1812 Overture, complete with cannons booming on cue.* **2** become suddenly prosperous, famous, active, etc.: *Business is booming; Industry boomed after World War II; Compact disk sales boomed in the late 1980s.*
boom.box *n.* a large portable radio, usu. combined with cassette player
boom.er same as BABY BOOMER.
boom.er.ang (BOO.muh.rang) *n.* **1** a curved stick thrown as a weapon that returns to the thrower. **2** something that rebounds to its author's disadvantage: *The politician had thrown a boomer-*

ang by his dirty tricks. —*v.*: *His dirty tricks boomeranged on him.*
boom.let (BOOM.lit) *n.* a small boom or increase: *a boomlet of popularity.*
boom town *n.* a suddenly prosperous town.
boon *n.* a great blessing or benefit: *Insulin has been a boon to diabetics; Grant me one boon* (= favor).
boon companion *n.* close friend.
boon.docks *n.pl. Informal.* a rural or backwoods area: *She lives somewhere out in the boondocks.*
boon.dog.gle (BOON.dog.ul, long "OO") *n. Informal.* waste of public funds: *The Commission was a massive financial boondoggle with $15 million gone down the drain.*
boor (rhyme: poor) *n.* a rude or coarse person, esp. a rustic: *He's just a boor, not a gentleman.* —**boor.ish** *adj.*: *boorish manners.*
boost (long "oo") *v.* raise: *a pep talk to boost his morale; to boost prices, production, sales; Ads are used to boost* (= promote) *a product.* —*n.* a raising or increase: *Give me a boost up the tree; a boost in salary; The promotion was a big boost to his ego.*
boost.er *n.* one that boosts: *Civic boosters try to attract conventions to their cities; a morale booster.* —**adja.**: *Jumper cables* or **booster cables** *are used for jump-starting a car by connecting its dead battery to the live battery of another; a* **booster rocket** *for launching a spacecraft.*
booster shot *n.* a supplementary dose of vaccine or antigen.
boot (long "oo") *n.* 1 heavy footwear covering part of the leg: *rubber boots; work boots.* 2 kick: *He got* **the boot** (= got fired) *after only a week on the job.* —**lick someone's boots** behave like a slave toward someone. —**to boot** as well: *a good student and a soccer player to boot.* —*v.* 1 kick. 2 **boot out** *Informal.* dismiss, esp. from a job. 3 start a computer: *I used to* **boot up** *my old computer by turning on the power, popping the DOS disk in Drive 0, and pressing the "on" button.*
boot.black *n.* one who cleans and shines shoes and boots.
boot camp *n.* in the U.S., a basic training center for new recruits to the coast guard, navy, etc.
boot.ee or **boot.ie** (BOO.tee) *n.* a baby's shoe made of soft cloth.
booth (long "oo") *n.* a small enclosed area, esp. a private stall or compartment: *a phone booth; the projection booth in a movie theater; voting booth; a restau-*

rant booth with a table and two bench seats.
boot.leg *v.* **-legs, -legged, -leg.ging** make, buy, or sell liquor or something similar illegally: *Saccharin-sweetened soft drinks were being bootlegged* (= sold) *in some stores even after the ban;* **adj.**: *a bootlegging operation.* —*n.*: *He bought some bootleg; bootleg gin.* —**boot.leg.ger** *n.*
bootleg turn *n.* an abrupt turning around of an automobile using the emergency brake.
boot.strap *n.* 1 a strap at the top of a boot for pulling it on: *She has pulled herself up* **by her own bootstraps** (= risen from poverty or depression by her own efforts without outside help). 2 a short routine of instructions for loading a program into a computer.
boot.y *n.* **boot.ies** goods seized jointly by pirates, soldiers in a war, etc.
booze *n. Informal.* alcoholic drink. —*v.* **booz.es, boozed, booz.ing** drink to excess; **booz.er** *n.* —**booz.y** *adj.*: *boozy drivers.*
bop *n.* 1 same as BEBOP: *jazz of the bop variety.* 2 *Informal.* hit: *a bop on the head.* —*v.* **bops, bopped, bop.ping** dance to bop music: *She's bopping to a Sixties beat; She used to bop with the best of them.* —**bop.per** *n.*
bo.rac.ic acid (buh.RAS.ic-) same as BORIC ACID.
bo.rax (BOR.ax) *n.* a white powder that is a compound of sodium and boric acid, used in cleaning, medicines, enamels, etc.
Bor.deaux (bor.DOH) *n.* a wine from the Bordeaux region in S.W. France.
bor.del.lo (bor.DEL.oh) *n.* a brothel.
bor.der (BOR.dur) *n.* 1 an edge or boundary, esp. between two states, countries, etc.: *The goods were smuggled across* or *over the border from Mexico; Detroit is close to the Canadian border; Niagara Falls is at* or *on the border; It is warmer south of the border; Anyone may travel as far as* or *up to the national border; to cross, draw, establish, fix, patrol a border; to slip across a border; closed, common, disputed, recognized, unguarded borders.* 2 a strip outlining an edge: *a lace border on a cuff.* —*v.* provide with a border: *Trees bordered the grounds; His actions* **border on** (= are close to) *the insane.*
bor.der.land (BOR.dur.land) *n.* land near a border; fringe area: *the borderland* (= intermediate condition) *between waking and sleeping.*

bor.der.line (BOR.dur.line) *n.* a line marking a border: *on the borderline between passing and failing.* —*adj.* marginal: *He's not quite insane, but a borderline case; a borderline pass in a test.*

bore *pt.* of BEAR. —*v.* **bores, bored, bor.ing 1** make a usu. long, narrow hole, esp. by drilling or digging: *to bore a tunnel; to bore a hole through concrete.* **2** make tired by repeating, being dull, etc.: *I won't bore you with the details; We were bored to death;* **adj.**: *We were* **bored** *having nothing to do;* **bored stiff** (= very bored); *It was* **boring** *to be in that city.* —*n.* **1** a bored hole: *the bore* (= hollow) *of a pipe, gun; a large-bore engine.* **2** a boring person or thing: *a frightful, insufferable, utter bore.* **3** a tidal wave with a steep front.

bo.re.al (BOR.ee.ul) *adj.* having to do with the North: *boreal forests full of needleleaf trees; a boreal bog, chickadee, owl.*

bore.dom (BOR.dum) *n.* the condition of being bored: *He fell asleep out of utter boredom; It was sheer boredom watching that movie.*

bo.ric acid *n.* a white, water-soluble compound of boron used as an antiseptic, in glass-making, and to produce borax.

born *adj.* [no degrees of comparison] **1** brought forth by birth: *A child is born (to its parents); The baby was born in 1987; born into a good family; In that year, of every ten born, only two survived to adulthood; Our baby was born at midnight; born in or at Bombay; We are born free; Meeting his long-lost mother was like being* **born again***; a child* **born of** *a poor woman; a hope born of desperation; He was* **born and bred** (= born and raised) *a Muslim; a woman* **born to** *lead; Not everyone is* **born with a silver spoon in his mouth** (= born wealthy); *She was* **not born yesterday** (= is experienced); *cpd:* *an Asian-born child; the first-born of each family; the poor and the well-born.* **2** natural: *a born genius, leader, loser; Poets are said to be born* (= are so by nature), *not made.*

born-again *adja.* reborn mentally or emotionally: *a born-again Baptist, idealism, love of big cars.*

borne a *pp.* of BEAR. —**comb.form.** carried: *air-borne dust and dirt; blood-borne infections; food-borne illnesses, organisms; river-borne sediments; water-borne contamination.*

bo.ron (BOR.on) *n.* a nonmetallic element used in alloys and to control nuclear reactions.

bor.ough (BUR.oh) *n.* **1** a municipality within a metropolitan area: *the five boroughs of New York City.* **2** in various countries, an incorporated town, village, or county.

bor.row (BOR.oh) *v.* **1** get something from another to use for a time: *Can I borrow $50 (from you) till payday? books borrowed from the library; adj.:* **borrowed** *books, funds, money; a patient living on* **borrowed time** (= living beyond the expected period). **2** take and use: *Did you borrow $5 from my wallet? "Pizza" was borrowed from Italian into English; n.: "En masse" is a* **borrowing** *from French* (= word adopted from French). —**bor.row.er** *n.*

borscht (BORSHT) *n.* a kind of Russian beet soup.

bor.zoi (BOR.zoy) *n.* a tall, lean, spotted Russian wolfhound.

bosh *n. Informal.* nonsense!

bosk or **bos.ket** (BOS.kit) *n.* a thicket or small grove.

bosk.y *adj.* **bosk.i.er, -i.est** wooded; shaded: *bosky hills.*

bos'n or **bo's'n** See BOSUN.

bos.om (BOOZ.um, long or short "OO") *n.* **1** the chest or breasts: *She held the baby to her bosom; a matronly woman with an ample bosom; Under the jacket, he wore a shirt with a bosom* (= front) *and no back.* **2** close relationship: *He was received into the bosom of the church; in the bosom of one's family;* **adja.**: *his bosom* (= very close) *buddy, friend.* —**bos.om.y** *adj.* ample-breasted.

boss *n.* one who gives orders, as an employer or foreman: *She is the absolute or undisputed boss around here; He's only a straw boss (with very little power); party bosses of politics.* —*v.* act like a boss toward someone: *His older brother likes to boss him around.* —**boss.y** *adj.*

bo.sun (BOH.sun) *n.* boatswain. Also **bos'n, bo's'n, bo'sun.**

bo.tan.i.cal (buh.TAN.i.cul) **1** *adj.* having to do with plants: *a botanical garden, print, specimen, theme.* **2** *n.* a product or design based on plants: *a printed botanical; the trend in botanicals; herbs and botanicals.*

bot.a.ny (BOT.uh.nee) *n.* the science of plants. —**bot.a.nist** *n.*

botch *v.* bungle a job: *Joe was told to fix the car, but he botched it (up); adj.: a* **botched** *job.*

both (BOHTH, "th" as in "thin") *adj.* the one as well as the other: *I met both boys; I spoke to both the boys; Jane and Mary both were there; both Jane and Mary; You can't have it both ways, only* one way or the other. —**pron.**: *I met both (= the two) of the boys.* —**adv.**: *Jon is both older and taller; Tim can both sing and dance.*

both.er (BOTH.ur, "TH" as in "the") *v.* disturb or trouble: *He bothers me when I am busy; bothers me about a loan; bothers everyone with his problems; It bothers me (to hear) that he is dishonest; He never bothers* (= takes the trouble) *to ask for what he wants; Please don't* **bother yourself** (= trouble yourself) *about fixing me lunch; Don't* **bother with** *it.* —*n.* trouble or concern: *It is a bother to have to hire relatives; Relatives are sometimes a bother* (= source of concern) *to employers;* also **both.er.a.tion** (-uh.RAY.shun) *n.*

bot.tle (BOT.ul) *n.* **1** a usu. narrow-necked container for liquids: *a wine bottle; a bottle of wine* (= traditionally 25 oz / 710 ml); *a bottle of pop; Give the baby her bottle* (= nursing bottle); *a baby bottle or nursing bottle; a hot-water bottle; disposable, no-deposit, no-return, returnable bottles.* **2 the bottle** *Informal.* use of alcohol, esp. in excess: *The poor fellow took to the bottle to drown his grief; He would hit the bottle every night.* —*v.* **bot.tles, bot.tled, bot.tling** put something in a bottle: *It's not healthy to* **bottle up** (= repress) *your emotions;* **adj.:** *bottled beer, beverages, water.*

bot.tle.neck (BOT.ul.nek) *n.* something that hinders progress or causes a slowdown, as a narrow spot in a busy road: *We were caught or trapped in a bottleneck; to eliminate a bottleneck; a bottleneck in the production line.*

bot.tom (BOT.um) *n.* **1** the part that is underneath or lowest: *the bottom of the ocean, ship, stairs, well; It sank to the bottom; a suitcase with a false bottom (for hiding things); New recruits start at the bottom and work their way up; Let's get to the bottom* (= clear up the mystery) *of this affair; The bottom fell out of the coffee market* (= Coffee prices collapsed); **At bottom** (= Basically) *he's a good fellow; She loved him* **from the bottom of her heart** (= most sincerely). **2** *Informal.* buttocks: *The baby fell on her bottom.* —**bottoms up!** [a drinking toast]. —**adja.** lowest or last: *That's my bottom offer; You can* **bet your bottom dollar** (*Informal for everything you have*) *I won't lose.* —*v.* of prices, etc. that vary over time, reach the lowest level before going up again: *The recession seems to be bottoming out.*

bot.tom.less (BOT.um.lis) *adj.* (as if) having no bottom: *It seemed a bottomless pit; the bottomless depths of the ocean; a bottomless mystery.*

bottom line *n. Informal.* the result that counts, as the final figure in a financial statement, showing a profit or loss: *a store trying to improve its bottom line; The bottom line is to keep working hard toward your goal.* —**bottom-line** *adja.* **1** concerned with profits: *a bottom-line executive; The president has to be a bottom-line person; bottom-line publishing.* **2** realistic: *a bottom-line approach.*

bot.u.lism (BOCH.uh.liz.um) *n.* a kind of food poisoning caused by a bacterial toxin, esp. in improperly canned foods.

bou.doir (BOOD.war, long "OO") *n.* a woman's private room.

bouf.fant (boo.FAHNT) *adj.* puffed out or full: *a bouffant coiffure, hairdo, skirt, sleeve.*

bou.gain.vil.le.a (boo.gun.VIL.ee.uh) *n.* a shrub or climber of warm climates bearing small flowers within large red or purple flowerlike leaves.

bough (rhyme: how) *n.* a main branch of a tree.

bought *pt. & pp.* of BUY.

bouil.la.baisse (bool.yuh.BACE) *n.* a chowder containing many kinds of fish and shellfish: *He's a bouillabaisse of emotions; a bouillabaisse of taxes.*

bouil.lon (BOOL.yon) *n.* a clear broth.

boul.der (BOLE.dur) *n.* a large, usu. rounded stone.

boule (BOOL) *n.* a pear-shaped synthetic gem.

boul.e.vard (BOO.luh.vard) *n.* **1** a broad, often tree-lined street; [as a name] *Lake Shore Boulevard.* **2** the grassy strip between a sidewalk and the street. **3** a median dividing a highway.

bounce *v.* **bounc.es, bounced, bounc.ing 1** move up and down elastically: *a child bouncing a ball; The ball bounced off the wall; it bounced down the road; He bounced* (= jumped) *to his feet; He bounced out into the street;* **adja.:** *a bouncing* (= strong and healthy) *baby boy.* **2** *Informal.* of a check, be returned because of insufficient funds: *Checks that bounce are known as "rubber checks."* **3** *Informal.* eject for rowdy behavior, as a bouncer. —**bounce back** *Informal.* start again with new vigor, as after a defeat. —*n.* **1** a bouncing: *I missed the ball on the first bounce.* **2** vigor or enthusiasm: *There's a bounce to his stride.* **3 the bounce** *Informal.* a dismissal; the bum's rush. —**bounc.er** *n.*

bounc.y *adj.* **bounc.i.er, -i.est** having

bounce or vigor: *a bouncy mattress, step, style, swing, walk.*

bound (BOWND) *pt. & pp.* of BIND: *The body was found bound and gagged.* —*adjp.* **1** tied or obligated: *He's morally bound to inform the police; Spouses are bound by marriage vows.* **2** certain: *It is bound to rain today.* **3** going to a place: *homeward bound; They're bound for home; east-bound traffic.* —**bound up with** or **in** closely connected with something: *a question bound up with what is right and wrong; a devoted husband whose interests are bound up in family matters.* —*comb.form.* confined or restricted by: *He felt duty-bound to support his boss; house-bound because of illness; an ice-bound expressway; No take-offs from a snow-bound airport.* —*v.* **1** leap, spring, jump, etc.: *kangaroos bounding across the plain.* **2** form the boundary of a place: *The U.S. bounds Mexico in the north.* —*n.* **1** a bounding: *He cleared the fence in a single bound.* **2** usu. **bounds,** a limit, border, or boundary: *Who sets the bounds for outside activities? He acted beyond the bounds of reason; Her joy knew no bounds; She kicked the ball out of bounds; Bars and nightclubs are* **out of bounds** (= forbidden) *to children.*

bound.a.ry (BOWN.duh.ree) *n.* **-ries** a line, plane, point, etc. that forms a limit or border: *Mexico has a common boundary with the U.S.; The 49th parallel forms much of the northern boundary between the U.S. and Canada.*

bound.en (BOWN.dun) *adja.* obligatory: *It's our bounden duty to help the poor.*

bound.less *adj.* having no limits: *boundless enthusiasm;* **bound.less.ly** *adv.*

boun.ti.ful (BOWN.tuh.ful) or **boun.te.ous** (-tee.us) *adj.* plentiful; also, liberal: *blessed with a bountiful harvest; Nature's bountiful gifts; Lady Bountiful.* —**boun.ti.ful.ly** or **boun.te.ous.ly** *adv.*

boun.ty (BOWN.tee) *n.* **-ties 1** generous giving; liberality: *The farmer's market looked like a display of the earth's bounty; silos full of the field's bounty; the endless bounty of TV.* **2** a reward or grant offered by a government: *a cash bounty offered for wolf pelts; The government used to pay a bounty on wolves; Two* **bounty hunters** *kidnaped the Canadian and took him back to the U.S. to face charges.*

bou.quet *n.* **1** (boh.KAY, boo.KAY) a bunch of cut flowers: *brickbats and bouquets* (= compliments). **2** (boo.KAY) an aroma, as of wine, brandy, etc.: *a wine with an elegant bouquet.*

bour.bon (BUR.bun) *n.* a whiskey distilled from a mash of corn, malt, and rye.

bour.geois (boorzh.WAH) **1** *n. sing. & pl.* a member of the middle class, esp. a property owner, shopkeeper, etc.; capitalist. **2** *adj.* capitalistic in outlook: *Bourgeois attitudes undermine the arts.*

bout *n.* **1** a period of an activity or experience: *bouts of anger, depression, despair, melancholy, nausea; a bout of (the) flu; a severe bout of diarrhea; drinking bouts.* **2** a contest: *a wrestling bout; her bouts with the bottle.*

bour.geoi.sie (boor.zhwah.ZEE) *n.* the bourgeois or capitalist class.

bourse (BOORS) *n.* a money market or stock exchange, esp. in Europe.

bou.tique (boo.TEEK) *n.* a small fashionable shop.

bou.ton.niere (boo.tun.EER) *n.* a flower to be worn in a buttonhole.

bo.vine (BOH.vine) *adj.* **1** of or like an ox or cow: *The antelope is a bovine animal; bovine malaria.* **2** slow and dull: *his bovine laziness.* —*n.* a bovine animal.

¹**bow** (rhyme: how) *v.* bend the head or body, esp. as a sign of respect, submission, etc.: *They bow before the altar; We bow to* (= accept) *the inevitable; to* **bow down to** (= submit to) *a dictatorship; He's too self-respecting to* **bow and scrape** (= behave slavishly); *She decided to* **bow out** (= get out) *of her job; to* **bow to** (= agree to) *his mother's wishes; adj.: an old man* **bowed** (= bent) *with age; a widow* **bowed down** (= weighed down) *with grief.* —*n.* **1** a bending of the head or body: *He made a low bow; The ballerina* **took a bow** (= came back on stage to receive applause) *at the end of the recital.* **2** the front part of a ship; opposed to STERN: *The speech was interpreted as a* **shot across the bow** of (= warning to) *the medical fraternity.*

²**bow** (BOH) *n.* **1** a weapon for shooting arrows: *He drew his bow and shot an arrow.* **2** a light stick strung with horsehair for playing a violin, viola, etc. **3** a knot with loops: *Tie a bow in her hair.* **4** something curved, esp. a rainbow. —*v.* **1** bend or curve. **2** play with a bow: *to bow a fiddle.*

bowd.ler.ize (BOWD.luh.rize, "OW" as in "HOW") *v.* **-iz.es, -ized, -iz.ing** revise a book, play, etc. so as to remove portions considered improper; expurgate: *Shakespeare was bowdlerized by Thomas Bowdler; adj.: a* **bowdlerized** *edition of the Bible.*

bow.el (BOW.ul, *rhyme:* vowel) *n.* **1** an

intestine: *He has pain in his bowels; loose* **bowels** (= feces); **adja.**: *a bowel movement* (= emptying of the bowels). 2 **bowels** *pl.* deep interior: *down in the bowels of the coal mine.*

bow.er (BOW.ur, rhyme: OUR) *n.* a recess shaded by trees or vines; arbor.

bow.er.y (BOW.uh.ree, "OW" as in "HOW") *n.* the part of a city inhabited by the poor and homeless.

bowl (BOLE) *n.* 1 a deep, rounded dish: *finger, punch, salad, sugar bowls; a bowl of rice or soup* (= rice or soup in a bowl); *the bowl* (= bowl-shaped part) *of a smoking pipe.* 2 a heavy ball used in games such as bowling. 3 a throw of such a ball. —*v.* 1 play at bowling: *He goes bowling on weekends.* 2 roll a ball or hoop. —**bowl along** move quickly along. —**bowl over** fall or roll over: *The car bowled over and caught fire; She came round the corner and nearly bowled me over; I was bowled over* (= stunned or overwhelmed) *by the announcement.*

bowl.der (BOLE.dur) same as BOULDER.

bow.legs (BOH.legs) *n.pl.* legs curved outward. —**bow.leg.ged** (-leg.id, -legd) *adj.*

bow.ler (BOH.lur) *n.* a stiff round hat with a narrow brim; derby.

bowling (BOH.ling) *n.* a game in which a ball is rolled down a wooden lane to knock over wooden pins; **adja.**: *a bowling ball, lane, pin.*

bowling alley *n.* a building with many bowling lanes.

bowling green *n.* a grass plot used for the game of lawn bowling.

bow.man (BOH.mun) *n.* **-men** an archer.

bow.sprit (BOW.sprit, BOH-) *n.* a spar projecting from a sailing ship's bow.

bow.string (BOH.string) *n.* a cord for an archer's bow.

bow tie (BOH.tie) *n.* a necktie that is worn knotted into a bow.

box *n.* 1 a usu. rectangular receptacle or container, often with a lid: *a shoe box; a box of candy* (= candy in a box); *You can rent a post office box for receiving your mail; a safety deposit box* (in a bunk); *a suggestion box; What's on* **the box** (Informal for TV) *tonight?* 2 a marked-off or enclosed area: *a jury box; a lacrosse box; witness box; Nobles used to have special boxes at the opera; a penalty box* (in hockey); *a press box (for journalists); a news item printed in a box* (= rectangular area marked like a box). 3 a booth or small shelter: *a sentry box.* 4 a blow with the open hand: *a box on the ear.* 5 an evergreen shrub or tree with a close-grained wood; boxwood. —*v.* 1 put into a box: *His clothes were boxed and mailed home;* **adj.**: *Pizza comes boxed; boxed candy, goods; a boxed set of CDs; The apartment is so small she feels boxed in* (= confined); *a boxed-off area;* **n.**: *gift boxing.* 2 strike with the open hand: *to box someone's ears.* 3 engage in boxing.

box.car *n.* an enclosed freight car.

box.er *n.* 1 one who boxes; pugilist. 2 a sturdy, deep-chested dog with a short coat.

boxer shorts *n.pl.* undershorts like a prizefighter's shorts.

box.ing *n.* the sport of fighting with one's fists.

Boxing Day *n.* a holiday following Christmas Day.

box lunch *n.* a lunch packed in a box.

box office *n.* 1 the ticket office at a theater. 2 money taken at a box office: *Studios use the weekend box office to calculate how well a movie is doing; Many new movies helped last year's box office.* 3 a financial success or successful show: *"Star Wars" was good box office.* —**box-office** **adja.** 1 having to do with the box office: *That movie was the biggest box-office draw of the season; The box-office gross* or *take is determined by the number of tickets a movie sells over the weekend; box-office hits, records, sales.* 2 successful: *the star's box-office performance.*

box score *n.* a tabulated summary of the plays of a baseball game, as usu. given in a box in a newspaper.

box spring *n.* a mattress base made of coil springs in a box.

box.wood same as BOX, *n.* 5.

boy *n.* 1 a male child: *That's a good boy! delivery, newspaper, shoeshine boys; That's my boy* (= well done)! *a boy wonder* (who arouses admiration). 2 *Informal.* a member of a team: *She's trying to be one of the boys; out drinking with the boys.* 3 [offensive] a male servant. —**interj.** expressing admiration: *Boy, is she hitting it! Oh boy!* —**boy.hood** *n.* —**boy.ish** *adj.*; **boy.ish.ly** *adv.*; **boy.ish.ness** *n.*

boy.cott (BOY.cot) *v.* refuse to have anything to do with a person, product, place, function, etc. —*n.* such a measure: *They imposed a boycott of* or *on nonunion products.*

boy.friend *n. Informal.* a male friend, esp. a girl's steady escort.

Boy Scout *n.* a member of the **Boy Scouts,** an international club for boys aged 11 to 17 that stresses outdoor life and helpfulness to others.

boy.sen.ber.ry (BOY.zun.ber.ee) *n.* **-ber.ries** a blackish-red berry, a cross between the loganberry, blackberry, and raspberry.

bo.zo (BOH.zoh) *n. Slang.* one with little brains, like "Bozo the Clown."

bra (BRAH) *n.* [short form] a brassiere.

brace *n.* **1** something used to support, clamp, hold things in place, etc.: *He wears a brace to support his weak leg; back, knee, neck, rib braces; a brace supporting the east wall.* **2** either of the signs {} used to enclose linked words, numbers, etc. **3** a crank-shaped handle for holding and turning a drilling bit: *a brace and bit.* **4** *sing. & pl.* a pair of a kind taken together: *several brace of partridges, quail; a brace of columns, M.P.s, pistols.* —*v.* **brac.es, braced, brac.ing 1** strengthen or support, esp. with a brace. **2** prepare: *Brace yourself for some bad news; to brace up to the inevitable.* **3** invigorate: *A cold shower will brace you up in the morning; adj.: the bracing mountain air.*

brace.let (BRACE.lit) *n.* an ornament worn around the arm or wrist: *a charm bracelet.*

bra.ce.ro (bruh.SAIR.oh) *n.* a Mexican allowed to work temporarily in the U.S.

braces *n.pl.* **1** a wire device worn on the teeth for straightening them. **2** suspenders for holding up trousers.

brack.en (BRAK.un) *n.* a large common fern with a tough stem.

brack.et (BRACK.it) *n.* **1** a usu. L-shaped device to support a shelf or balcony, wall lamp, etc. **2** a shelf so supported. **3** either of the signs ( ) used to enclose words, numbers, etc.: *a list of names with ages shown in brackets; round brackets.* **4** one of a pair of parentheses or braces { }: *square brackets [ ]; angle brackets ‹ ›.* **5** a range or group: *Teens are in the 13-19 age bracket; A higher income bracket means a higher tax bracket.* —*v.* **1** support with a bracket. **2** enclose, link, or set aside with or as if with brackets; *adj.: a bracketed phrase.*

brack.ish *adj.* slightly salty: *brackish water from a lake.*

bract *n.* a modified leaf on the stalk or at the base of a flower.

brad *n.* a thin, small-headed nail: *flooring brads.*

brae (BRAY) *n. Scot.* a sloping bank or hillside.

brag *v.* **brags, bragged, brag.ging** speak of one's abilities, deeds, etc. with too much pride; boast: *He brags about his clothes; That is nothing to brag about; He brags that he is the world's greatest boxer.* —**brag.ger** or **brag.gart** (BRAG.urt) *n.*

brag.ga.do.ci.o (brag.uh.DOH.shee.oh) *n.* **-os 1** a braggart. **2** boasting or cockiness: *the political braggadocio of the ruling party.*

Brah.ma (BRAH.muh) or **Brah.man** (-mun) *n.* **1** in Hinduism, the creator. **2** a hump-backed breed of cattle related to the Indian zebu: *The white Brahma bull is also known as "Brahmany bull."*

Brah.min (BRAH.mun) *n.* **1** an upper-class member of the Establishment, esp. in New England: *the Boston Brahmins.* **2** also **Brah.man,** a Hindu of the highest caste.

braid *n.* an interwoven or plaited cord of three or more strands: *her braids of hair; gold or silver braid* (= ornamental trim). —*v.* do into braids: *to braid one's hair; adj.: hair braided into pigtails.*

braille or **Braille** (BRAIL) *n.* a writing system for the blind that uses raised dots for characters which are read by touching.

brain *n.* **1** the center of a vertebrate's nervous system and thought processes, located in the head: *The brain consists of two hemispheres that control opposite sides of the body; Analytical, rational thinking is done with the left brain; The right brain is the creative or intuitive side; a boy who has computers on the brain* (*Informal* for constantly on his mind); *The poor fellow blew his brains out* (= shot himself through the head); *adja.: brain activity, cells, damage, death; a brain injury, scan, surgeon, tumor, wave.* **2** mind or intelligence: *She has a good brain for math; no brains for rocketry; a product of the fertile brains of undergraduates; brain power, work; a student with brains; lack of brains.* **3** an intelligent person: *some of the best brains in physics.* —**pick someone's brain** or **brains** get and use someone's ideas. —**rack** or **beat** or **cudgel one's brains** think hard over a problem.

brain.child *n. Informal.* someone's new idea or invention.

brain death *n.* death as determined by the permanent cessation of brain activity and shown by a flat EEG (electroencephalograph output).

brain drain *n.* the emigration of scientists, professionals, etc. from a country: *the brain drain from Third World countries to Europe and North America; to* plug the brain drain.

brain.storm *n.* a sudden inspired idea: *to have a brainstorm; A **brainstorming** session is held by a problem-solving group to pool their ideas.*

brains trust or **brain trust** *n.* a group of unofficial advisers.

brain.wash *v.* force a person *into* accepting a radically new set of beliefs.

brain wave *n.* **1** a rhythmic electric impulse in the brain. **2** a brainstorm.

brain.y *adj.* **brain.i.er, -i.est** having a good intellect: *brainy kids, students, youth; the brainiest supercomputers on the market.*

braise (BRAIZ) *v.* **brais.es, braised, brais.ing** to brown and simmer slowly: *pork chops braised in a skillet; **braised** beef.*

brake *n.* **1** a device for stopping a vehicle: *to apply* or *put on* or *step on the brakes; The car may skid if you jam on* or *slam on the brakes; an emergency brake; a car with power steering and power brakes; Brakes jam, lock, fail, hold, screech; He decided to put a brake on too rapid expansion of the business.* **2** bracken. **3** a thicket, as of cane plants. —*v.* use a brake: *The car may skid if you brake suddenly; The bus braked* (= stopped) *abruptly before a red light;* **adj.:** *the **braking** capability, equipment, system of a vehicle.*

brake fluid *n.* the liquid used in a hydraulic brake.

brake.man (BRAKE.mun) *n.* **-men** an assistant to a train conductor or engineer.

brake shoe *n.* a curved block that presses against and slows down a wheel when the brake is applied.

bram.ble *n.* a prickly shrub or vine such as the blackberry or loganberry. —**bram.bly** *adj.*: *a brambly hedge.*

bran *n.* the coarse seed covering of cereals that is separated by sifting: *oat bran; wheat bran.*

branch *n.* a part, division, or extension that is separate from the main body: *to trim the branches of a tree; the branch of a river; the various branches of medicine; a chartered bank with a network of branches;* **adj.:** *a branch manager, office.* —*v.* put out or separate into branches: *Latin, Greek, etc.* **branched off** *in prehistoric times; A newspaper **branches out** into book publishing;* **adj.:** *a **branched** arrangement, shape, structure.*

branch plant *n.* a business that is the subsidiary of an outside or foreign company.

brand *n.* **1** a label or mark identifying a particular product: *Colas are sold under many brands; two popular brands* (= varieties) *of cola; He drinks only name brand colas* (= well-known brands); *"Cola" itself was originally a **brand name*** (= registered trademark). **2** a piece of burned or burning wood; hence, an iron (**branding iron**) used red-hot to mark cattle, criminals, etc. **3** a mark made by a branding iron. **4** a stigma: *the brand of Cain, i.e., of "murderer."* —*v.* **1** to mark, as with a brand; **adjp.:** *an experience forever **branded** on his memory.* **2** stigmatize: *The spy was branded (as) a traitor.*

bran.dish *v.* wave around or display, as if to threaten: *to brandish a sword.*

brand-new *adj.* absolutely new and unused.

bran.dy *n.* **-dies** a liquor distilled from wine, as cognac, or from fermented fruit juices: *peach brandy.* —*v.* **-dies, -died, -dy.ing** treat or preserve with brandy; *adj.:* **brandied** *cherries.*

brash *adj.* impudently self-assertive: *a brash young man.* —**brash.ly** *adv.*; **brash.ness** *n.*

brass *n.* **1** an alloy of copper and either zinc or tin. **2** an object or things made of brass: *a shop specializing in brass; brasses such as fittings and ornaments; the strings and brass* or *brasses* (= brass instruments) *of an orchestra.* **3** *Informal.* brazen impudence: *He had the brass to ask me again for a loan.* **4** high-ranking officers, executives, etc. as a group: *army brass; the top brass of the industry.* —**get down to brass tacks** get down to specific details. —**adja.** made of brass: *a brass doorknob; a hoodlum wearing brass knuckles.*

bras.se.rie (bras.uh.REE) *n.* a restaurant serving food and beer.

brass hat *n. Slang.* a high-ranking officer.

bras.siere (bruh.ZEER) *n.* a woman's undergarment to support the breasts.

brass instrument same as BRASSWIND.

brass-tacks *adja.* basic or fundamental: *brass-tacks details, guidance, work.*

brass.ware *n.* things made of brass.

brass.wind *n.* a musical wind instrument made of brass, as the cornet, French horn, and trombone.

brass.y *adj.* **brass.i.er, -i.est 1** of or like brass. **2** harsh and blaring: *a brassy hairdo, voice.*

brat *n.* a bad-mannered child: *a spoiled brat.* —**brat.ty** *adj.*

brat.wurst *n.* a sausage made of pork: *beer and bratwurst.*

bra.va.do (bruh.VAH.doh) *n.* a false

and swaggering courage.
brave *adj.* courageous: *It was brave of him to attempt the rescue.* —*n.* an American Indian warrior: *braves on the warpath.* —*v.* **braves, braved, brav.ing** challenge or endure with courage: *It was going to be rough, but he decided to brave it out.* —**brave.ly** *adv.*
brav.er.y (BRAY.vuh.ree) *n.* the quality of being brave: *to demonstrate, display, show bravery.*
bra.vo (BRAH.voh) *interj. & n.* **-vos** a shout of approval.
bra.vu.ra (bruh.VIEW.ruh) *n.* a display of bravery or brilliance, esp. outstanding musical technique.
brawl *n.* a noisy, disorderly fight or quarrel: *a barroom brawl; a drunken brawl.* —*v.*: *to brawl in barrooms.* —**brawl.er** *n.*
brawn *n.* **1** big powerful muscles: *The bully was all brawn and no brains.* **2** pickled pork. —**brawn.y** *adj.*
bray *n.* the noisy, harsh call of a donkey; *v.*: *Stop braying like an ass.*
bra.zen (BRAY.zun) *adj.* **1** of or like brass: *brazen candlesticks.* **2** of sounds, blaring; brassy. **3** shameless or impudent: *brazen aggression, lies; a crook trying to be more brazen than the competition; a brazen-faced liar.* —**bra.zen.ly** *adv.*; **bra.zen.ness** *n.*
bra.zier (BRAY.zhur) *n.* **1** a brassworker. **2** a metal container holding live coals, as for grilling meat.
Bra.zil.ian (bruh.ZIL.yun) *n. & adj.* (a person) of or from **Brazil,** a South American country.
Brazil nut *n.* the three-sided edible nut of a tropical South American tree.
breach (BREECH) *n.* **1** a violation: *He committed a breach of etiquette; charged with breach of contract; She charged him with* **breach of promise** (to marry) *and sued for damages; a* **breach of the peace** (= public disturbance). **2** a break, gap, or rift: *a breach in the castle wall; to close a breach.* **3** a cessation of friendship: *to cause a breach; Other friends tried to heal the breach but to no avail.* —*v.* make a breach in something; break.
bread (BRED) *n.* **1** a basic item of food made of baked flour: *a loaf of bread; sliced bread; unleavened bread; white bread; whole-wheat bread; bread and butter; to put bread* (= food) *on the table; She would* **break bread** (= share a meal) *with people of any race or creed.* **2** livelihood: *to beg, earn one's bread; He works hard for his daily bread; A dishonorable discharge would have* **taken the bread out of his mouth** (= made it impossible for him to earn a living). **3** *Slang.* money; dough. —*v.* coat with breadcrumbs; *adj.*: *breaded veal cutlets.*
bread and butter *n.* one's chief source of income: *Writing stories is her bread and butter, not a hobby.* —**bread-and-butter** *adj a.* **1** of basic importance: *a bread-and-butter course, issue, matter; a retailer's bread-and-butter merchandise (that provides a regular income); a bread-and-butter customer* (on whom a business depends for its main income). **2** thanking for hospitality: *a bread-and-butter letter.*
bread.bas.ket (BRED.bas.kit) *n.* **1** a basket for bread or rolls. **2** a grain-growing area: *The Prairies are the breadbasket of this country.*
bread.board *n.* **1** a board to knead or cut bread on. **2** a board for laying out experimental electric circuits.
bread.crumb (BRED.crum) *n.* a tiny piece of bread broken off from a loaf or slice.
bread.fruit *n.* the round, starchy fruit of a tropical tree, which resembles bread when baked.
bread line *n.* a line of people waiting for food given as charity.
bread.stuff *n.* grain, flour, etc. for making bread.
breadth (BREDTH) *n.* **1** width: *It is 10 cm in breadth; has a breadth of 10 cm.* **2** scope or range: *breadth of culture, interests, learning; He shows great breadth of mind about religion; He claims to have traveled (through)* **the length and breadth** *of Mexico* (= from coast to coast).
bread.win.ner (BRED.win.ur) *n.* one whose earnings support a family.
break (BRAKE) *v.* **breaks, broke, bro.ken, break.ing 1** separate into two or more pieces, esp. by force: *The baseball broke the window; to break off* (= detach) *a small piece of dough.* **2** burst: *A blister breaks; Waves break on the beach.* **3** make or become inoperative: *The toilet is broken; it won't flush.* **4** disturb the order, continuity, etc. of something: *Soldiers break step while marching on a bridge; a scrape that breaks the skin.* **5** pause; interrupt: *We break for lunch at noon.* **6** reduce the force of something: *The shrubs broke his fall from the window.* **7** make submissive: *to break a wild horse; Suffering broke his spirit; was tortured until he broke* (= became submissive). **8** violate: *People break the law, their promises, speed limits; Supersonic planes break the sound barrier; She*

broke (= exceeded) *all records*; *n*.: *He was charged with* **breaking and entering** (= burglary). **9** make a sudden move or change: *They broke for cover when the rain came.* **10** come out suddenly: *Prisoners broke loose during the riot; Dawn breaks; A boy's voice breaks* (= changes suddenly) *during puberty; Who will break* (= disclose) *the news to the poor widow?* *adj*.*a*.: *a reporter sent to cover a* **breaking** (= developing) *news story*. —**break away** get away: *The hostages broke away from their captors.* —**break down 1** become inoperative or fail: *The car broke down; Marriages break down; Our negotiations broke down; He broke down* (= lost control) *and wept.* **2** separate into parts: *to break down a compound into its parts.* **3** overcome: *to break down social barriers.* —**break even** of a business, have income equaling expenses. —**break in 1** enter by force: *How did the burglars break in? Carla broke in on our conversation.* **2** prepare a person or thing for new duties, use, etc.: *to break in a new recruit; A new car has to be broken in gradually.* **3** interrupt: *At the height of the drama, the announcer broke in with a bulletin.* —**break into 1** enter by force: *Burglars broke into our house.* **2** get into or begin a new activity, state, etc.: *to break into journalism; to break into print* (= have something published); *to break into song* (= begin singing), *to break into* (= begin to use) *one's savings; to break into* (= have) *a cold sweat because of fear.* —**break off 1** stop abruptly: *She broke off her engagement; The lecturer broke off in mid-sentence; to break off diplomatic relations.* **2** separate: *a splinter group that broke off from the party.* —**break out 1** begin suddenly: *A war breaks out; He broke out in* (= developed) *a rash; She broke (out) into tears.* **2** get out: *Convicts break out of prison during a riot; A country breaks out of a recession.* **3** take out for distribution or consumption: *Let's break out the champagne and celebrate.* —**break up 1** disperse: *Break it up* (= Stop fighting)! *The radicals broke up* (= separated) *into splinter groups.* **2** end, esp. a relationship: *Children suffer most when a family breaks up; Pat broke up with Sue.* **3** Informal. (make) erupt into laughter: *The joke broke up the audience.* **4** of ice on lakes, rivers, roads, etc., to thaw in the spring; *n*.: *the* **breaking** *up of winter roads.* —*n*. **1** a breaking or something broken: *I see a break in the glass.* **2** a pause or change from what is going on: *Let's take a break; waiting for a break in the (bad) weather; Give me a break! a lucky break* (= piece of good luck). **3** a dash: *The hostages made a break for it when the lights went out.* —**break.a.ble** *adj*.

break.age (BRAY.kij) *n*. a breaking, the extent of it, or the loss caused.

break.a.way (BRAY.kuh.way) *n*. **1** a breaking away, as from a group. **2** in hockey, lacrosse, etc., an offensive move or run by a player that leaves defenders far behind. —*adj*. **1** that has broken away: *a breakaway group, sect.* **2** made to break easily, as for stage use: *a breakaway chair.*

break.danc.ing (BRAKE.dan.sing) *n*. an acrobatic dance of teenage youths characterized by writhings, tumblings, and shows of balance; also **breaking**. —**break.dance** *v*.

break.down *n*. **1** failure: *a breakdown of machinery.* **2** collapse: *a nervous breakdown.* **3** analysis: *a breakdown of population figures by area.*

break.er *n*. **1** one that breaks: *a circuit breaker.* **2** a wave that breaks into foam on a beach, reef, etc.

break.fast (BREK.fust) *n*. the morning meal: *He has breakfast in bed; a continental, hurried, not substantial breakfast; Cereals are used as breakfast foods; v*.: *to breakfast on ham and eggs.*

break.front *n*. a piece of furniture having a front with a projecting center portion; *adj*.*a*: *a breakfront bookcase, cabinet.*

break-in *n*. an act of entering by force: *a break-in by burglars.*

breaking same as BREAKDANCING.

break.neck *adj*. dangerous: *to drive at breakneck speeds; at a breakneck pace.*

break.out *n*. an escape, as out of prison.

break.through *n*. a sudden advance, as through obstacles: *diplomatic, medical, scientific breakthroughs.*

break.up *n*. **1** a breaking up: *the breakup of a marriage.* **2** the breaking up of ice on water in the spring: *spring breakup.*

break.wa.ter (BRAKE.wot.ur) *n*. a structure shielding a harbor, shore, etc. from heavy waves.

bream (BREEM, BRIM) *n*. **1** a carplike European fish. **2** a freshwater sunfish.

breast (BREST) *n*. **1** a mammary gland, esp. in a human: *an infant at its mother's breast.* **2** the front of an upper human torso or the similar part in animals: *He beat his breast* (= chest) *in sorrow; A child with a pigeon or chicken breast* (= protruding chest) *could use vi-*

tamin D; *a breast of chicken, fowl, lamb* (= specified meat with bone and muscle); *cpd: a three-button single-breasted jacket; a six-button double-breasted coat; the red-breasted robin.* **3** the seat of emotions: *Anger rose in his breast; You will feel better if you **make a clean breast of*** (= confess) *the affair.*

breast.bone *n.* a bone down the front of the chest to which the ribs are attached; sternum.

breast.feed *v.* **-feeds, -fed, -feed.ing** feed a baby at the breast, not from a bottle.

breast.plate *n.* a piece of armor or cloth covering the breast.

breast.stroke *n.* a swimming stroke done with the arms sweeping to the sides and back to the breast.

breast.plate *n.* a piece of armor covering the breast.

breast.work *n.* a low temporary wall for defense.

breath (BRETH, "TH" as in "thin") *n.* **1** the act or power of breathing: *Keep quiet and don't waste your breath; to draw or take a deep breath; Save your breath* (= Don't waste your time talking); *He fought for his beliefs to his **last breath*** (= till death); *He was so evasive he seemed to say yes and no **in the same breath*** (= at the same time); ***Don't hold your breath*** (= Don't wait too eagerly); *The scene is so beautiful it **takes your breath away*** (= it is thrilling); *He stopped to regain his breath when he was **out of breath*** (= breathing very hard from exertion); *He spoke **under** or **below his breath*** (= in a whisper). **2** a slight breeze: *a breath of fresh air; There's a breath* (= hint) *of spring in the air.* —**breath.less** *adj.: The finalists stood breathless with expectation.*
—**breath.less.ly** *adv.*

breath.a.lyz.er (BRETH.uh.lye.zur) *n.* a device for measuring the alcohol in a person's blood by analyzing a breath sample. —**Breathalyzer** *Trademark.*

breathe (BREETH, "TH" as in "the") *v.* **breathes, breathed, breath.ing 1** take in and expel air: *a jogger breathing heavily;* We breathe in (= take in air) and breathe out (= expel air) *all the time; a wine left to breathe* (= develop flavor by exposure to air); *Ask me while I yet breathe* (= while I am alive). **2** utter: *Don't breathe a word of this to anyone.* **3** blow or exhale: *Dragons breathe fire and smoke; He **breathed his last*** (= died). **4** inspire: *The money breathed new life into the project.* **5** say softly or in a whisper: *"I love you," she breathed.*

—**breathe down someone's neck** *Informal.* be annoyingly close behind someone. —**breathe easy** *Informal.* relax.

breath.er (BREE.thur, "th" as in "the") *n.* **1** *Informal.* one who breathes heavily, esp. one making an obscene phone call. **2** *Informal.* a short rest: *Take a breather.*

breathing space *n.* time to do something at one's ease: *We got some or a bit of or a little or a breathing space from our creditors to get organized; to allow, gain, have, need, seek breathing space; I want to give her some breathing space before she says Yes or No.* Also **breathing room** or **spell**.

breath mint *n.* a mint chewed for freshening one's breath.

breath.tak.ing (BRETH.tay.king) *adj.* thrilling: *a breathtaking view.*

breath test *n.* a breathalyzer test.

breath.y (BRETH.ee) *adj.* **breath.i.er, -i.est** breathlike in sound: *Sam's sexy, breathy, buttery voice; a great speech but for his breathy delivery.*

brec.ci.a (BRECH.ee.uh) *n.* a rock made up of sharp fragments bound together in a matrix.

bred *pt. & pp.* of BREED.

breech *n.* **1** buttocks. **2** the part of a gun behind the bore or barrel. **3 breeches** (BRICH.iz) *pl.* trousers, esp. knee-length ones: *riding breeches.*
—*adj.a. & adv.* with the buttocks or feet first: *a breech baby, birth, delivery, position, presentation; A fetus that is or presents breech usually changes to headdown or head-first position by delivery time.*

breed *v.* **breeds, bred, breed.ing 1** produce offspring: *Rabbits breed fast.* **2** cause or originate: *Does poverty breed crime? Disease breeds in unsanitary conditions; n.: Unsanitary conditions are the **breeding ground** of disease.* **3** raise; rear: *He was born and bred in this country; "What is bred in the bone will not go out of the flesh"* (= Hereditary characteristics are hard to get rid of); *n.: a woman of (good) **breeding*** (= upbringing); *cpd: farm-bred salmon; an ill-bred cad; her well-bred manners.* **4** produce animals by controlled mating: *Williams breeds hunting dogs.* —*n.* a kind, sort, etc. produced by or as if by breeding: *a new breed of horse; a new breed of media magnates; a rare breed of politicians.*

breed.er *n.* one that breeds: *a horse breeder; a breeder* (= causer) *of trouble; A **breeder reactor** produces more fissionable material than it consumes.*

breeze / brief

breeze n. a light wind: *A cool breeze blows; a gentle breeze; That job is a breeze* (Informal *for easy task*); **to shoot the breeze** (Informal *for* chat). —v. **breez.es, breezed, breez.ing** go quickly and easily: *She breezed into the room.*

breeze.way n. a covered, usu. open-sided connecting passage, as between a house and garage.

breez.y adj. with breezes blowing: *a breezy day; a gossip columnist's breezy* (= light and easy) *style.*

breth.ren [old & formal use] pl. of BROTHER.

Bret.on (BRET.un) n. & adj. **1** (a person) of or from Brittany, France: *Breton cuisine.* **2** (having to do with) the Celtic language of Brittany.

bre.vet (bri.VET) n. a commission to a higher rank without an increase in pay.

bre.vi.ar.y (BREE.vee.air.ee) n. **-ar.ies** in the Christian church, a book containing the required daily prayers, hymns, etc. for clerics.

brev.i.ty (BREV.i.tee) n. the quality of being brief or short: *"Brevity is the soul of wit."*

brew v. prepare tea, beer, etc. by steeping, boiling, etc.: *freshly brewed coffee; Trouble is brewing* (= forming). —n. something brewed, esp. beer: *a very tasty brew.* —**brew.er** n.

brew.er.y (BROO.uh.ree) n. **-er.ies** a place where beer or ale is brewed.

bri.ar (BRY.ur) same as BRIER.

bribe n. a gift, esp. of money, given to influence someone's conduct improperly. —v. **bribes, bribed, brib.ing** corrupt or influence someone with a bribe: *The babysitter bribed the children with promises of candy.* —**brib.er.y** (BRY.buh.ree) n.

bric-a-brac (BRIC.uh.brac) n. small ornamental knickknacks.

brick n. **1** a rectangular building block of baked clay: *Bricks are laid in rows to cover a wall; bricks and mortar; to hit the bricks* (Informal *for* be out on the streets); *arrested for throwing bricks* (= brickbats) *at the police; You dropped a brick* (Informal *for* committed a gaffe); *The criticism hit him* **like a ton of bricks.** **2** something resembling a brick: *a brick of ice cream; gold bricks; a brick* (= kilogram pack) *of marijuana.* —v. pave or construct with bricks: *It's better to brick up the old doorway.*

brick.bat n. a piece of brick used as a missile: *The speech received both bouquets and brickbats* (= insults).

brick.lay.er (BRICK.lay.ur) n. one who builds with bricks. —**brick.lay.ing** n.

brid.al (BRY.dul) adj. having to do with brides: *a bridal bouquet, fashion, gown, shower, veil.*

bridal registry n. a retail service for brides and wedding guests by which the brides' preferences in regard to gifts and wedding accessories are recorded for coordinated marketing.

bridal suite n. a suite of rooms for newly married couples, as in a hotel.

bride n. a woman about to be or recently married. —**bride.groom** masc.

brides.maid n. a bride's female attendant.

bridge n. **1** a structure providing passage across a depression, esp. a waterway: *a bridge built across a river; The bridge collapsed; "We will* **cross that bridge** (= deal with it) *when we come to it."* **2** something similar to a bridge: *The bridge connecting a pair of glasses rests on the bridge of the nose; a removable dental bridge (of artificial teeth attached to one's natural teeth); Faith is the bridge from despair to salvation.* **3** a raised platform on a ship, from which commands are given. **4** a four-handed card game, esp. "contract bridge" or "auction bridge." —**burn one's bridges (behind one)** leave oneself no way back. —v. **bridg.es, bridged, bridg.ing** be a bridge, join with a bridge, or build a bridge over something: *to bridge the gap.* —**bridge.a.ble** adj.

bridge.head n. a fortified advance position established to protect troops as they cross, land on, or invade enemy territory.

bridge.work n. one or more dental bridges.

bri.dle (BRY.dul) n. **1** on a horse's head, the harness to which the reins are attached; hence, a control or curb: *the bridle* (= loop) *of a snowshoe.* **2** a holding or controlling device: *the bridle of a kite, waterskiing towline.* —v. **-dles, -dled, -dling 1** put a bridle on an animal: *to bridle a pony; Bridle* (= control) *your temper.* **2** raise the head with the chin tucked in, as a sign of scorn, anger, etc.: *She bridles at the suggestion that she cheated.*

bridle path n. a path for horseback riding.

brief (BREEF) adj. **1** short in length or duration: *a brief visit.* **2** short and concise: *a brief letter, memorandum, reply.* —n. **1** a condensed summary, esp. of a legal case: *to file, present, submit a brief; He* **holds no brief for** (= does not argue for) *feminists but believes in the* *equality of the sexes;* **In brief** (= in a few words), *we won the case.* **2 briefs** *pl.* short, close-fitting underpants. —*v.* give essential information or instructions to someone: *to brief a lawyer on a case;* **brief.ing** *n.* —**brief.ly** *adv.*

brief.case *n.* a rectangular case, often of leather, for books, papers, etc.

brier (BRY.ur) *n.* a plant such as the blackberry and the wild rose having a thorny, woody stem: *Brer Rabbit hid in the brier patch.* Also **briar.**

brig *n.* **1** a square-rigged ship with two masts. **2** a ship's prison.

bri.gade (brig.ADE) *n.* **1** a military unit of two or more battalions or regiments. **2** a group with special tasks or duties: *the fire brigade; work brigades.*

brig.a.dier (brig.uh.DEER) *n.* an army officer ranking just above a colonel.

brig.and (BRIG.und) *n.* a member of a band of outlaws or robbers; **brig.and.age** *n.*

brig.an.tine (BRIG.un.teen) *n.* a ship with square-rigged foremast and fore-and-aft-rigged mainmast.

bright *adj.* shining with much light: *a bright light, star; bright colors; a bright* (= brightly colored) *green hat; a bright* (= cheerful) *prospect; a bright* (= intelligent) *young girl.* —*adv.*: *The stars shone bright* (= brightly). —**bright and early** quite early. —**bright.ly** *adv.;* **bright.ness** *n.*

bright.en (BRY.tun) *v.* make or become bright: *The sun brightens the landscape; Her face brightened at the prospect of going to Paris.* —**bright.en.er** *n.*

bril.liant (BRIL.yunt) *adj.* **1** exceptionally bright: *brilliant fall colors; brilliant sunshine; a brilliant red; a brilliant star.* **2** exceptionally good in some respect: *a brilliant* (= clever) *maneuver; a brilliant* (= splendid) *prospect; a brilliant* (= intelligent and resourceful) *young composer, student.* —**bril.liant.ly** *adv.* —**bril.liance** (-yunce) or **bril.lian.cy** *n.*

bril.lian.tine (BRIL.yun.teen) *n.* an oily hair dressing.

brim *n.* the edge or rim of a cup, bowl, etc.: *Fill it to the brim; a hat with a wide brim* (= projecting rim). —*v.* **brims, brimmed, brim.ming** be full to the brim: *a glass so full it's brimming over; She was brimming* (over) *with joy.* —**brim.ful** *adj.*

brim.stone *n.* sulfur: *The preacher called down* **fire and brimstone** *on sinners* (= threatened them with punishment).

brin.dle or **brin.dled** *adj.* tawny or gray with darker markings: *a brindled lion.*

brine *n.* **1** salt-saturated water. **2** the salty sea water; hence, the ocean.

bring *v.* **brings, brought** (BRAWT), **bring.ing 1** cause to come along with one: *She brought a friend to the party; I'll take the books to the library if you will bring them to me.* **2** cause a person or thing to come to a certain place, be in a certain condition, etc.: *Parents bring children into the world; The sun brings warmth; He was brought to grief by fate; The plaintiff brings a charge* (before a court); *He couldn't bring himself to do it.* **3** sell for: *What will it bring on the open market?* —**bring about** cause: *Moral decay can bring about the fall of a civilization.* —**bring around** persuade someone: *It's difficult to bring her around to our point of view.* —**bring down 1** present officially: *to bring down a budget.* **2 bring down the house** score a great success, as when the whole audience applauds. —**bring forth** give birth to young, not hatch: *Mammals bring forth their young.* —**bring home the bacon** *Informal.* **1** earn enough to support the family. **2** be successful. —**bring off** do successfully: *He can bring off the most difficult feats when you least expect it.* —**bring out** reveal: *Nothing like a couple of drinks to bring out the beast in him; The publishers will bring out* (= publish) *her new book in the fall.* —**bring to** or **around** revive from unconsciousness. —**bring up** raise: *Jim brought up the subject of money; Parents try to bring up their children as good citizens; He gulped it down but brought it up* (= vomited it) *in no time.*

brink *n.* the edge of a steep drop: *You may look down but be careful not to go over the brink; a company on the brink* (= verge) *of bankruptcy.*

brink.man.ship (BRINK.mun.ship) *n.* the strategy of pushing a risky situation to the crisis point.

bri.o (BREE.oh) *n.* vigor; liveliness.

bri.oche (bree.OHSH) *n.* a rich, round, yeast-leavened roll.

bri.quet or **bri.quette** (bri.KET) *n.* a small block of compressed coal dust, sawdust, etc. used as fuel, kindling, etc.: *charcoal briquets.*

brisk *adj.* quick-moving: *proceeded at a brisk pace; a brisk sale, shower, walk, wind; The air was brisk; Trading was brisk on the stock exchange; brisk growth.* —**brisk.ly** *adv.;* **brisk.ness** *n.*

bris.ket (BRIS.kit) *n.* the meat from an animal's breast.

bris.ling *n.* a sprat, esp. one canned as a sardine.

bris.tle (BRIS.ul) *n.* a short, stiff hair,

as on an animal, a brush, etc.
—*v*. **-tles, -tled, -tling** raise the bristles: *Fido's hair bristles when he is angry; The dog bristles at the sight of cats; She bristled with* (= showed) *indignation; The plan bristles* (= is thick) *with objections.*

Brit *n. & adj. Informal.* Briton; British; Britisher.

Bri.tan.nic (bri.TAN.ic) *adj.* British: *Her Britannic Majesty.*

Brit.i.cism (BRIT.uh.siz.um) *n.* a characteristically British word or idiom, as *lorry* for *truck.*

Brit.ish *adj.* having to do with **Britain** (= England, Scotland, and Wales) or its people: *the former British empire; British English; the British Isles* (= Britain, Ireland, and nearby islands). —*n.* **1 the British** the people of Britain. **2** also **British English**, the English language as spoken in Britain; also called "English English."

Brit.ish.er (BRIT.ish.ur) *n. Informal.* a Briton.

Brit.on (BRIT.un) *n.* **1** a person of or from Britain. **2** one of the pre-Anglo-Saxon people of Great Britain.

brit.tle (BRIT.ul) *adj.* hard but very easily broken: *brittle bones, glass, hair, nails; a tense and brittle* (= fragile) *manner.* —*n.* a brittle candy with nuts: *peanut brittle.* —**brit.tle.ness** *n.*

broach (BROHCH) *v.* bring up: *Now is the time to broach the subject of a raise with the boss.*

broad (BRAWD) *adj.* **1** wide from side to side: *a broad avenue; It's 100 meters broad.* **2** wide in scope; general: *a broad rule; in the broadest sense of the word; the broad outlines of a subject.* **3** clear or expansive: *the broad ocean; in broad daylight; a broad grin, smile.* **4** obvious: *a broad accent, hint.* **5** ribald: *noted for his broad humor; broad comedy.* **6** liberal and tolerant: *He has broad views on religion.* —*n.* Slang [offensive] a woman. —**broad.ly** *adv.*

broad.band *adj.* having a wide range of frequencies; hence, general: *broadband channels, radio systems, services, video; broadband objectives.*

broad.brush *adj.* rough or general: *broadbrush estimates; a broadbrush indictment.*

broad.cast *v.* **-casts,** *pt. & pp.* **-cast** or **-cast.ed, -cast.ing 1** transmit widely, esp. by radio or television: *The program was broadcast live from the studio; They broadcast it live.* **2** scatter seed widely. —*n.* a broadcasting or something broadcast: *a live broadcast; We in-*terrupt this broadcast for a special announcement; a broadcast beamed to Cuba; **adj**.: *broadcast journalism* (= radio and TV); *broadcast satellites* (that transmit TV signals); *broadcast* (= wide) *sowing;* **adv.**: *seed sown broadcast* (= widely).

broad.cloth *n.* a smooth, closely woven cloth, usu. of cotton or wool, originally in double width, used for shirts, pajamas, etc.

broad.en (BRAW.dun) *v.* make or become broad or broader: *The river broadens here; Reading broadens the mind.*

broad jump same as LONG JUMP.

broad.leaf *adj.* having broad, flat leaves and hard wood: *The beech, maple, oak, etc. are broadleaf, not needleleaf trees, which lose their leaves in the fall.*

broad.loom *n.* wide carpeting: *wall-to-wall broadloom; a piece of broadloom; broadloom carpeting;* **adj**.: *a broadloomed office.*

broad-minded *adj.* tolerant or liberal; not narrow-minded.

broad.sheet *n.* a full-size newspaper, not a tabloid.

broad.side *n.* **1** the side of a ship or similar vehicle; **adv**.: *The car was hit broadside* (= sideways) *by the truck;* **adj**.: *a broadside hit.* **2** a firing of all the guns on one side of a ship: *They fired a broadside at the enemy; He delivered a broadside* (= barrage of criticism or abuse) *against the opposition.* **3** a large sheet of paper printed usu. across its central fold, as for advertising, political tracts, etc.; also **broad.sheet.**

broad-spectrum *adj.* applicable to a wide variety of cases: *a broad-spectrum antibiotic* (for treating many diseases); *a broad-spectrum skin-care product; his broad-spectrum social activities.*

broad.sword *n.* a wide-bladed slashing sword.

broad.tail *n.* the shiny, rippled pelt of a kind of Asian lamb, esp. of one prematurely born.

Broad.way *n.* commercial theater in the U.S.: *She started performing on Broadway at age 9;* **adj.**: *a Broadway hit, musical, production, success.*

bro.cade (broh.CADE) *n.* a rich fabric with a raised design, as of gold or silver; **adj.**: *a brocaded fabric, sari, silk, vest.*

broc.co.li (BROC.uh.lee) *n.* a vegetable related to the cauliflower, having many small flower heads.

bro.chette (broh.SHET) *n.* a skewer for roasting or broiling.

bro.chure (broh.SURE) *n.* a pamphlet: *an advertising brochure.*

brogue (BROHG) *n.* **1** an Irish or Scottish accent: *She speaks with a soft Irish brogue; He asked me in a heavy brogue where I was from; a faint, rich, thick, brogue; Scottish brogue.* **2** a stout oxford shoe with a perforated pattern; wingtip.

broil *v.* cook by direct exposure to flame or great heat: *Meat may be broiled in a range or on a grill.* —**broiled** *adj.*: *broiled fish, steaks, tomatoes.*

broil.er *n.* **1** a pan or grill for broiling. **2** a young chicken suitable for broiling.

broke *pt.* of BREAK. —**adjp.** *Informal.* having no money: *The business went broke last year; He was flat broke at the end of the month.* —**go for broke** make a big try, staking everything.

bro.ken (BROH.kun) *pp.* of BREAK. —*adj.* **1** uneven: *broken ground.* **2** crushed or beaten: *His pride was broken by the defeat; a broken heart.* **3** disunited, esp. by divorce: *children from broken homes; a broken family, marriage.* **4** incorrectly spoken: *He answered in broken French.* —**bro.ken.ly** *adv.*; **bro.ken.ness** *n.*

broken-down *adj.* worn out; useless: *a broken-down car in a junkyard.*

broken-hearted *adj.* overcome by grief: *a sad and broken-hearted parent.*

bro.ker (BROH.kur) *n.* an agent for buying, selling, making contracts, etc.: *a customs broker; marriage brokers; a power broker of the underworld; We need an honest broker* (= mediator) *to mediate the dispute.*

bro.ker.age (BROH.kuh.rij) *n.* **1** a broker's fee. **2** the business of a broker.

brol.ly (BROL.ee) *n.* **brol.lies** *Brit. Informal.* umbrella.

bro.mide (BROH.mide) *n.* **1** a potassium compound used as a drug to calm the nerves. **2** a dull, obvious remark or idea. **3** its author.

bro.mine (BROH.meen) *n.* a liquid element used esp. in antiknock gasoline.

bronchi *pl.* of BRONCHUS.

bron.chi.al (BRONG.kee.ul) *adj.* having to do with the bronchi: *bronchial airways, asthma, pneumonia, tubes.* —**bron.chi.al.ly** *adv.*

bron.chi.tis (brong.KYE.tis) *n.* inflammation of the lining of the bronchi.

bron.chus (BRONG.kus) *n., pl.* **-chi** (-kye, -kee) either of the two branches of the trachea that lead to the lungs.

bron.co (BRONG.coh) *n.* **-cos** in the West, a wild or half-tamed horse: *the bucking bronco; bronco busting* (= taming).

bron.to.saur (BRON.tuh.sor) or **bron.to.sau.rus** (-SOR.us) *n.* **-saurs, -sau.rus.es** or **-sau.ri** (-rye) an herbivorous dinosaur up to 80 ft. (24.38 m) long.

Bronx cheer *n.* a noise of disapproval; raspberry.

bronze (BRONZ) *n.* **1** an alloy of copper and tin. **2** a work of art made of bronze. **3** the yellowish or reddish brown color of bronze. —*v.* **bron.zes, bronzed, bronz.ing 1** give a bronze color to a person or thing: *a beachcomber bronzed by the sun; Some people bronze* (= cast in bronze) *baby shoes and other keepsakes.* —**adja.** having to do with bronze: *Bronze tools and weapons mark the* **Bronze Age** *of civilization.*

brooch (BROHCH, BROOCH) *n.* an ornamental pin worn on a woman's dress.

brood (long "oo") *n.* the offspring in one family, as baby birds hatched at one time: *the Smiths and their noisy brood* (= children). —*v.* **1** hatch eggs by sitting on them. **2** ponder or worry: *He tends to brood about his losses; It's no use brooding over your past.* **3** look over from a close or commanding position: *From the top of the tower, I could brood over the whole city.* —**adja.** meant for breeding or hatching: *a brood mare; a brood range for waterfowl breeding; a brood stock of salmon.*

brood.er (BROO.dur) *n.* **1** one that broods or worries. **2** a bird that hatches eggs. **3** a heated enclosure for raising chicks without a hen.

brooding *adj.* **1** threatening: *the brooding eyes of a bull; a sheer brooding cliff.* **2** intense or keen: *a brooding drama, painting, woodcut; the brooding emotional intensity of the music.*

brood.y *adj.* ready or inclined to brood: *a broody hen; a broody poetic soul.*

brook (short "oo") *n.* a small stream: *babbling brooks.* —*v.* put up with something: *a dictator who would brook no differences of opinion.*

broom (short or long "oo") *n.* a brush-like tool with a long handle, used for sweeping: *"A new broom sweeps clean"* (= A new administration will make drastic changes).

broom.stick *n.* a broom's long handle: *Witches are supposed to ride on broomsticks.*

broth (*rhyme:* cloth) *n.* a clear stock left after boiling meat or vegetables in water: *beef broth; clear broth.*

broth.el (BROTH.ul, "TH" as in "thin") *n.* a prostitute's place of business; whorehouse.

broth.er (BRUTH.ur, "TH" as in "the") *n.* **1** a son of the same parents: *Cain and Abel were brothers.* **2** a fellow member of a particular group: *They became blood brothers by mixing each other's blood in a ceremony; A black man refers to his fellows as soul brothers; Brother John is a lay brother* (= not priest) *of a religious order.*

broth.er.hood (BRUTH.ur.hood, short "oo") *n.* **1** brotherly bond or feeling: *the brotherhood of nations; the brotherhood of man; universal brotherhood; to live in peace and brotherhood.* **2** an organization of people who share a belief, occupation, etc.: *the Brotherhood of Indian Nations; the Brotherhood of Locomotive Engineers.*

brother-in-law *n.* **brothers-in-law 1** a brother of one's spouse. **2** the husband of one's spouse's sister. **3** the husband of one's sister.

broth.er.ly (BRUTH.ur.lee) *adj.* of or like a brother: *a brotherly feeling; brotherly love.*

brougham (BROME, BROOM, BROO.um, long "OO") *n.* an early type of limousine with an open driver's seat.

brought *pt. & pp.* OF BRING.

brou.ha.ha (broo.HAH.hah) *n.* an uproar or fuss: *a brouhaha over a silly question of protocol.*

brow (rhyme: how) *n.* **1** the ridge over the eyes; eyebrow: *He knit his brows in a frown.* **2** the forehead: *a wrinkled brow.*

brow.beat *v.* **-beats, -beat, -beat.en, -beat.ing** intimidate, esp. by stern looks or speech: *He was browbeaten into withdrawing his remark;* **adj.**: *a browbeaten clerk.*

brown ("ow" as in "how") *adj.* of the color of chocolate: *his dark brown hair; a brown bear such as the grizzly; brown coal* (= lignite); *brown* (= unpolished) *rice;* **n.**: *the dark brown of her hair.* —*v.* make or become brown, esp. by cooking. —**browned off** *Informal.* bored; also, angry. —**brown.ish** *adj.*

brown-bag *v.* **-bags, -bagged, -bag.ging** *Informal.* carry one's own food or liquor to a restaurant, club, etc. or carry a lunch to work or school, esp. in a brown paper bag: *to brown-bag a lunch.* —**brown-bagger** *n.* —**brown-bagging** *n.*

brown belt *n.* **1** a rank in karate or judo below the black belt. **2** a person holding this rank.

brown goods *n.pl.* household goods which, unlike white goods, traditionally come in brown casings, as radios and TVs.

brown.ie (BROW.nee) *n.* **1** a helpful little elf. **2 Brownie** a junior member of the Girl Scouts or Girl Guides, usu. aged seven to nine. **3** a flat, rich, usu. chocolate cake with nuts.

Brownie points *n.pl. Informal.* credit or approval, like a Brownie earning her badges.

brown.nose *v.* **-nos.es, -nosed, -nos.ing** *Slang.* curry favor with or fawn over someone.

brown.out *n.* a partial reduction of lighting during a power shortage: *There are brownouts and occasional blackouts in our town.*

brown.stone *n.* **1** a reddish-brown sandstone. **2** a building faced with this.

browse (BROWZ) *v.* **brows.es, browsed, brows.ing 1** go through or examine books, merchandise, etc. in a casual way: *"Come in and browse," the sign said; Feel free to browse through the store.* **2** nibble on grass, young shoots, etc.: *Cows browse in the field; They browse on grass, shrubs, twigs; to browse off young trees.* —*n.* a browsing or what is browsed: *Tender shoots, shrubs, and twigs are good browse for cattle; a book good only for a browse; The Art Gallery is holding a browse tonight.*

browser *n.* a program that allows a computer user to navigate through large interconnected bodies of information organized using hypertext.

bru.cel.lo.sis (broo.suh.LOH.sis) *n.* a bacterial infection that causes spontaneous abortion in animals and fever in humans.

bru.in (BROO.in) *n.* a bear.

bruise (BROOZ) *n.* an injury that discolors the skin without breaking it: *cuts and bruises.* —*v.* **bruis.es, bruised, bruis.ing 1** inflict or suffer a bruise: *He fell off the bike and bruised his knee;* **adj.**: *a bruised apple (with its skin broken); a bruising experience, fight, struggle.* **2** hurt the feelings of someone; *adj.*: *his bruised ego.*

bruis.er (BROO.zur) *n. Informal.* a big, strong, pugnacious man.

bruit (BROOT, long "OO") *v.* spread or circulate a rumor, story, etc.: *the names being bruited about on campus for the post of president.*

brunch *n.* a late-morning meal combining breakfast and lunch: *a Sunday brunch.*

bru.net (broo.NET) **1** *adj.* brown in color; having dark hair and complexion: *Both her parents happen to be brunet.* **2** *n.* a man or boy with dark hair; **bru.nette** (broo.NET) *fem.*

brunt *n.* the hardest or greatest part: *They bore the brunt of the attack.*

brush *n.* **1** an area covered with low, rough shrubs and small trees: *He walked through thick brush.* **2** broken or cut branches; brushwood; *adj.:* *a **brush** fence, fire.* **3** a utensil made of bristles fastened in a handle, for applying paint, shaving cream, etc. or for cleaning teeth, clothing, hair, floors, etc.; *cpd:* brush-stroke; brushwork. **4** a light touch, encounter, or skirmish: *Her last illness was a close brush with death; He had a brush with the police.* —*v.* **1** clean, arrange, or spread with a brush: *to brush the hair, teeth; to brush a coat clean; He brushed the dust off the book; She knows how to **brush off** (= get rid of) unwelcome offers; You had better **brush up** or **brush up on** your (= refresh your knowledge of) math.* **2** touch lightly; graze: *The bullet only brushed his head; She brushed past me in the crowd without noticing.*

brush.off *n. Informal.* an abrupt cold rejection: *He got a swift brushoff when he tried his sales pitch on her.*

brush.wood *n.* **1** a thicket. **2** cut or broken branches of trees.

brusque (BRUSK) *adj.* impolitely abrupt; curt: *his brusque manner.* —**brusque.ly** *adv.;* **brusque.ness** *n.*

Brussels sprouts *n.* the small, cabbagelike heads that grow on the erect stalk of a vegetable of the mustard family.

bru.tal (BROO.tul) *adj.* **1** cruel or savage: *a brutal attack, lie, manner, murder, slaying; brutal violence; this brutal winter weather; It was brutal of her to refuse his apology.* **2** harsh but true: *the brutal facts, realities, truth.* —**bru.tal.ly** *adv.*

bru.tal.i.ty (broo.TAL.i.tee) *n.* **-ties** a brutal act or condition: *They suffered many brutalities such as being beaten and kicked; police brutality; the brutality of war.*

bru.tal.ize (BROO.tul.ize) *v.* **1** make brutal: *He was brutalized by hard work and poverty.* **2** treat brutally: *The kidnappers brutalized their victim.*

brute (BROOT, long "OO") *n.* **1** an irrational animal. **2** a coarse, cruel, or unthinking person: *Alcohol brings out the brute in him; They arrested the drunken brute.* —*adj.* **1** unthinking, not rational: *a brute animal, beast; He won by sheer brute strength; brute energy; the use of brute force.* **2** harsh but true: *the brute facts of the case; brute materialism.* **3** savage or stupid: *his brute manners, mentality; Some kill out of brute spite.*

bru.tish (BROO.tish) *adj.* savage: *the primitive's brutish condition.*

brux.ism (BRUX.iz.um) *n.* teeth grinding in sleep.

bub *n. Slang* [unfriendly use] fellow: *When Big Brother asks questions, bub, you answer.*

bub.ble (BUB.ul) *n.* **1** a roundish, enclosed, usu. hollow object: *She blows bubbles for fun; soap bubbles; A bubble bursts when pricked; He's so allergic to the air he lives in a plastic bubble.* **2** an unrealistic or delusive idea or scheme: *The real estate bubble burst after a few months of high profits.* **3** something bubble-shaped, as a kind of woman's hairdo or a car (**bubble car**) with a transparent dome top (**bubbletop**). —*v.* **bub.bles, bub.bled, bub.bling** make or sound like bubbles: *She was bubbling with enthusiasm; a child bubbling over with excitement.*

bubble brain same as BUBBLEHEAD.

bubble gum *n.* chewing gum that can be blown into bubbles: *the **bubble-gum set** (Informal for preteens).*

bub.ble.head (BUB.ul.hed) *n. Slang.* a stupid person. —**bubb.ble.head.ed** *adj. Slang.* silly or light-headed.

bubble memory *n.* data storage by means of bubbles formed on magnetic silica film, each bubble or its absence representing a binary digit.

bubble pack (or **wrap**) same as BLISTER PACK.

bub.bly (BUB.lee) *adj.* **1** having or like bubbles: *the bubbly champagne.* **2** spirited or enthusiastic: *in a bubbly mood; a bubbly personality; in bubbly spirits.* —*n.*, *pl.* **bub.blies** *Informal.* champagne: *Let's break out the bubbly!*

bu.bo (BEW.boh) *n.* **-boes** a swollen lymph gland in the groin or armpit, as in the bubonic plague.

bu.bon.ic plague (bew.BON.ic-) *n.* an often fatal disease transmitted by fleas and characterized by high fever and formation of buboes.

buc.ca.neer (buck.uh.NEER) *n.* a pirate or freebooter.

buck *n.* **1** *Informal.* dollar or money: *how to make a buck in these hard times; You're talking **big bucks** (= a great deal of money); She looks like **a million bucks** (= She's gorgeous).* **2** a full-grown male animal, esp. a deer: *There are bucks, bulls, stags, and harts of the antlered kind; a buck rabbit.* **3** a vigorous young man: *the young buck you see on that motorbike.* **4** a bucking. —*v.* **1** leap and plunge, as a horse trying to throw the rider off: *The raft bucked and heaved in the stormy sea; adja.: a bucking bronco.* **2** resist: *to buck a trend; You can't buck the system.* —**buck for** *Informal.* strive hard for something: *to buck for a promotion.* —**buck up** cheer up. —**pass the buck** *Informal.* pass on blame or responsibility to someone: *Let's pass the buck to the other department; The buck stops here* (= No passing the buck to anyone higher)! —*adv. Informal.* completely: *buck naked.*

buck.a.roo (BUCK.uh.roo) *n., pl.* **-roos** *Informal.* cowboy.

buck.board *n.* a four-wheeled buggy on a light plank body.

buck.et (BUCK.it) *n.* **1** a pail; also, the amount it holds, or **bucketful.** **2** the scoop of a dredge, steam shovel, etc. **3 the bucket** *Slang.* jail; cooler. —**kick the bucket** *Slang.* die.

bucket seat *n.* a car seat with a rounded back, for one passenger.

bucket shop same as BOILER ROOM.

buck.eye *n.* a kind of horse chestnut.

buck fever *n. Informal.* the nervousness of a new hunter seeing game for the first time.

buck.le (BUCK.ul) *n.* **1** a device for fastening a strap or belt: *to undo a buckle; belt buckles.* **2** a fold, wrinkle, bend, etc. —*v.* **-les, -led, -ling** **1** secure with a buckle: *to buckle a belt; The knight buckled on his sword; Please buckle up (your seat belt).* **2** collapse or give way, esp. under heat or pressure: *The pavement buckled in the hot sun; The landing gear buckled as the plane landed; The boxer buckled the champ's knees* (= made them bend) *with a straight right.* —**buckle down** start working very hard: *It's time to buckle down and get the job done.* —**buckle under** yield: *She won't buckle under to pressure from anyone.*

buck.ler *n.* a small round shield.

buck-passer *n.* one who passes the buck. —**buck-passing** *n.*

buck.ram (BUCK.rum) *n.* a heavy, sometimes two-ply fabric, stiffened with starch or glue, used in clothing and bookbinding.

buck.saw *n.* a two-handed wood saw set in a frame.

buck.shot *n.* a large size of lead shot: *Some people file lawsuits like scattering* *buckshot; The madman peppered the crowd with buckshot.*

buck.skin *n.* a soft, strong, yellowish-gray leather: *buckskin leggings.*

buck.thorn *n.* any of several related small trees or shrubs.

buck.tooth *n.* a projecting front tooth; **buck.toothed** *adj.*

buck.wheat *n.* a plant with heart-shaped leaves, grown for its three-sided seeds which are used as grain.

bu.col.ic (bew.COL.ic) *adj.* having to do with shepherds or pastoral life: *bucolic pleasures, poetry; a bucolic landscape, retreat, scene, setting, view.*

bud *n.* **1** a partly opened flower: *rose buds.* **2** a sprouting plant part containing immature leaves, flowers, etc. **3** something at its beginning stage. —*v.* **buds, bud.ded, bud.ding** **1** put out buds. **2** begin to develop; *adja.: a budding artist, crisis, friendship, poet.* —**nip in the bud** stop something at an early stage.

Bud.dhist (BOOD.ist, short or long "OO") *n.* a follower of **Buddhism,** a religion founded in India by the **Buddha** in the fifth century B.C. —*adj.: a Buddhist monastery, monk.*

bud.dy (BUD.ee) *n.* **bud.dies** *Informal.* a companion or pal: *his bosom buddy; an army buddy; an old buddy of mine; the **buddy system** of pairing together for protection, appointing friends to jobs, not charging fellow police officers, etc.;* [hostile use] *What's eating you, buddy?* —**buddy up** to get very close to or get chummy with someone.

buddy-buddy *adj. Informal.* very friendly or familiar: *It doesn't look good for teachers to act too buddy-buddy with their students.*

budge *v.* **budg.es, budged, budg.ing** move the slightest bit: *Stay here and don't budge! The stubborn mule couldn't be budged.*

budg.er.i.gar (BUJ.uh.ree.gar) *n.* an Australian parakeet with green, yellow, and blue feathers.

budg.et (BUJ.it) *n.* **1** a statement of expected expenditure and income: *our annual budget; balanced, federal, household, itemized budgets; to draw up a budget; adj.: a budget cut, deficit, item; the Finance Minister's **budget speech** in the legislature.* **2** an allocated sum: *We have a budget of only $1,000 for new books.* **3** a limited amount of money to spend: *I can't afford luxuries, I'm on a budget.* —*adja.* inexpensive: *budget meals at budget prices; a budget store.* —*v.* **1** allocate: *We've budgeted $1,000 for new books;* **adj.:** *the* **budgeted** *amount.* **2** provide for in anticipation: *We are budgeting an increase in business; a project budgeted at $4 million; A busy woman must budget her time, budget every minute of her day* (= plan in detail how her time is spent). —**bud.get.ar.y** (BUJ.uh.tair.ee) **adj.:** *budgetary austerity, decisions, imbalance, outlay, policy, pressures, principles, resources.* —**bud.get.er** or **bud.get.eer** (-TEER) *n.*

budg.ie (BUJ.ee) *n. Informal.* budgerigar.

buff *n.* **1** a block or wheel covered with soft leather, velvet, etc. that is used for polishing. **2** a brownish yellow. **3** *Informal.* bare skin: *a beach for sunning yourself* **in the buff.** **4** *Informal.* a fan or enthusiast: *car, history, jazz, word buffs.* —**adj.** of the color buff: *a buff jacket.* —*v.* polish, esp. with a buff: *He waxed and buffed the wooden floor.*

buf.fa.lo (BUFF.uh.loh) *n.* **-lo** or **-los** a kind of wild ox such as the North American bison, the **Cape buffalo** of Africa, and the domesticated **water buffalo** of India: *a place where a dwindling herd of wild buffalo still roam.* —**adj.:** *Indians used to eat* **buffalo berry** *with* **buffalo meat;** *to light a fire with* **buffalo chips** *(made of dried dung); A* **buffalo jump** *is where buffalo used to be stampeded over a cliff for killing.* —*v.* **-loes, -loed, -lo.ing** *Slang.* confuse: *We're totally buffaloed by the statement from headquarters.*

buff.er *n.* **1** one that buffs. **2** something that lessens the effect of an impact, shock, etc.: *He acted as a buffer between the warring parties; an alkaline buffer to neutralize the acid reaction of aspirin in the stomach;* hence **buffered aspirin. 3** a temporary storage device in a computer; memory: *Clear the buffer.*

buffer state *n.* a neutral country between two rival powers.

buffer zone *n.* an area separating two armies.

¹**buf.fet** (BUF.it) *v.* blow or toss about: *an airplane buffeted by heavy winds; a tragic character buffeted by fate.* —*n.* a blow, esp. with the hand.

²**buf.fet** (buh.FAY) *n.* **1** a sideboard: *a hutch and buffet for the dining room.* **2** a meal with food set out on a table or sideboard for guests to serve themselves: *an all-you-can-eat buffet; seated buffets; a buffet of retail services;* **adja.:** *a buffet dinner, restaurant, table; to entertain buffet style; a* **buffet line** *(of foods on the table).*

buf.foon (buh.FOON, long "OO") *n.* a clown or habitual joker: *He likes to play the buffoon at parties.* —**buf.foon.er.y** *n.*

bug *n.* **1** any insect or insectlike animal, esp. a pest: *bed bugs; June bugs.* **2** *Informal.* a disease-causing germ or virus: *There's a flu bug going around; Mom was bitten by the hula-hoop bug* (= craze). **3** *Informal.* an enthusiast: *a ham radio bug.* **4** *Informal.* a fault or problem in a machine or process: *He's working the bugs out of his robot; to get the bugs out of a computer program.* **5** a hidden listening device: *a bug installed in a telephone; Bugs had been planted even in flowerpots.* —*v.* **bugs, bugged, bug.ging 1** *Informal.* pester or annoy: *Something seems to be bugging him.* **2** hide a microphone in something: *They bugged the spy's telephone line.* **3** tap a conversation, speaker, etc. unknown to the speaker; **adj.:** *a* **bugged** *embassy, room, telephone; an illegally bugged conversation (monitored by an unauthorized party).* —**bug off** *Slang.* get lost. —**bug out** *Slang.* evade: *to bug out of a responsibility.*

bug.a.boo (BUG.uh.boo) *n. Informal.* a bogey or frightening spirit; hence, bugbear.

bug.bear *n.* **1** a source of persistent annoyance: *Little brothers can be the bugbear of a teenager's life.* **2** a bogey or bugaboo.

bug-eyed *adj.* with eyes sticking out: *He was bug-eyed with astonishment.*

bug.ger (BUG.ur) *n. Slang.* **1** one who bugs or plants bugs. **2** [in familiar conversation] bastard: *You little bugger!* —**bug.ger.y** *n.*

bug.gy (BUG.ee) *n.* **bug.gies** a light, usu. four-wheeled carriage: *a baby buggy; dune buggies; luggage buggies at an airport; a shopping buggy; the horse and buggy* (= carriage).

bu.gle (BEW.gul) *n.* a small, trumpetlike brass instrument: *Boy Scouts play the bugle at ceremonies; Military life is marked by bugle calls.* —**bu.gler** *n*

build (BILD) *v.* **builds, built, build.ing 1** construct barns, bridges, dwellings, houses, etc.: *Birds build nests; a novel built around one central character; shelves built into a wall; a statue built out of clay; a relationship built* (= based) *on trust.* **2** develop: *There's a crowd building outside; We're building* (= expanding) *for the future.* —**build up 1** increase or accumulate: *to build up a supply of cash; to build up hope, muscles, strength.* **2** develop with buildings. **3** promote: *ads to build up a new product.* —*n.* figure or physique: *a man of heavy build; husky build.* —**build.er** *n.*

build-down *n.* a slowing down instead of building up, as of weaponry.

building *n.* **1** a structure with walls and a roof, as a house, barn, factory, etc.: *to build, demolish, erect, put up, renovate a building; a building gutted by fire; an apartment building; dilapidated, ramshackle, tumbledown buildings.* **2** the act or trade of building: *prefabricated building; road building; adja.: building codes, construction, materials, permits, stones, trades; the building industry; Children play with **building blocks**; a **building machine** such as a crane, bulldozer, or concrete mixer.*

build-up *n.* an increase: *a military build-up on a country's border; She received a big build-up (= boost) in the media; traffic build-up (= congestion) during rush hour.*

built-in *adj.* forming an integral part: *walls with built-in bookshelves; a built-in closet; a built-in, not detached garage; a plan with a built-in drive for profits.*

built-up *adj.* developed with buildings: *the heavily built-up downtown area.*

bulb *n.* **1** something with a rounded, bulging end: *an electric light bulb; the rubber bulb of a syringe.* **2** a roundish underground bud from which a plant such as a tulip or onion grows. **3** such a plant.

bul.bous (BUL.bus) *adj.* having bulbs or shaped like a bulb: *a bulbous nose.*

Bul.gar.i.an (bul.GAIR.ee.un) *n. & adj.* (a person) of or from **Bulgaria**, a country in S.E. Europe.

bulge (BULJ) *n.* an outward swelling: *bulges of fat on the body; The post-war baby boom showed a bulge (= temporary rise) in the population curve.*
—*v.* **bulg.es, bulged, bulg.ing** swell: *Santa carries a sack bulging with toys.*

bul.gur *n.* parboiled, cracked, and dried wheat. Also **bul.ghur.**

bu.lim.i.a (byoo.LIM.ee.uh, boo-) *n.* an eating disorder in which the patient goes on an eating binge followed by fasting, using laxatives, vomiting, etc.

bulk *n.* **1** volume, quantity, mass, etc., esp. if great: *The elephant raised its bulk and stood up; a lumbering bulk of a beast; The bulk (= greater part) of an iceberg is under water; groceries sold in bulk (= in quantity) rather than in packages; adj.: bulk foods, purchases, sales, wine; Quantities of the same material are sent through the mails as **bulk mail** at special bulk rates.* **2** food material that is not digested: *Fiber adds bulk to diet to stimu-*

late bowel movement; also **bulk.age** (-ij).
—*v.* make or become larger: *She seems to be bulking up instead of slimming down; It's unwise to bulk up a debt instead of paying it off; For a satisfactory meal, bulk out fish with starches and vegetables; Capital costs **bulk large** (= stand out) in this year's budget; adja.: a **bulking** agent such as fiber.*

bulk.head *n.* a vertical partition in a ship, airplane, etc.: *a fireproof bulkhead; the bulkhead separating an automobile engine from the body.*

bulk.y *adj.* **bulk.i.er, -i.est** having bulk: *a bulky package; a bulky (= large and clumsy) person; a bulky (= relatively heavy) sweater; A bulky vegetable adds fiber to the diet; a bulky food such as bran.*

bull (short "oo") *n.* **1** an adult male of the ox family or of large animals such as the elephant, moose, seal, walrus, and whale. **2** an investor who buys stocks expecting prices to rise. **3** a papal document: *a papal bull; bulls of excommunication.* **4** *Slang.* nonsense.
—**bull in a china shop** one who is clumsy or tactless. —**shoot the bull** *Slang.* talk idly. —**take the bull by the horns** deal boldly with a difficult situation. —*adja.* **1** male: *a bull calf, moose.* **2** characterized by rising prices: *a bull market.*

bull.dog *n.* a short-haired dog with a pug nose and strong jaws. —*v.* attack like a bulldog, as in bulldogging.

bull.dog.ging (BULL.dog.ing) *n.* in rodeos, the stunt of plunging from horseback to the neck of a steer to wrestle it to the ground; steer wrestling.

bull.doze *v.* **-doz.es, -dozed, -doz.ing** **1** push, clear, gouge, etc. using a bulldozer: *They bulldozed a path through the jungle.* **2** force: *He bulldozed his way through the crowd; People were bulldozed (= intimidated or forced) into signing the petition.*

bull.doz.er (BULL.doh.zur) *n.* a heavy tractor with a wide frontal blade for digging, pushing earth, grading, etc.

bul.let (BULL.it, short "oo") *n.* **1** a small metal projectile shot from a gun: *to fire a bullet; He died in a hail of bullets; bullet holes.* **2** a heavy dot used as a display device in the beginning of a paragraph; *adj.: a bulleted paragraph.*

bul.le.tin (BULL.uh.tin, short "oo") *n.* **1** an announcement, esp. of news: *a late news bulletin about the earthquake.* **2** a periodical report, esp. for a society, group, etc.

bulletin board *n.* **1** a board to post notices on. **2** a privately operated information network that is accessed using a modem; also **bulletin-board system** or **BBS**.

bul.let.proof or **bullet-proof** *adj.* safe from bullets: *bulletproof glass, vehicles, vests; No business is bulletproof in hard economic times.*

bullet train *n.* a high-speed passenger train: *The bullet trains of Japan reach speeds of up to 200 km/h.*

bull.fight *n.* a spectator sport in which a matador, or **bullfighter**, provokes and then kills a fierce bull. —**bull.fight.ing** *n.*

bull.finch *n.* an Old World songbird with a heavy bill and black head.

bull.frog *n.* a large frog whose male has a deep croak.

bull.head.ed (BULL.hed.id) *adj.* unthinkingly stubborn.

bull.horn *n.* a small battery-powered megaphone, as used by police when dealing with a crowd.

bul.lion (BULL.yun, short "oo") *n.* gold or silver, esp. in bars.

bull.ish *adj.* **1** bull-like. **2** expecting, having, or causing a price rise: *the bullish growth of a computer giant; a bullish market; bullish speculators.* **3** *Informal.* enthusiastic or hopeful: *I'm bullish on or about home computers; a bullish outlook.* —**bull.ish.ness** *n.*

bull.ock (BULL.uk, short "oo") *n.* a castrated bull.

bull.pen *n.* **1** a pen for bulls. **2** a special enclosure in a jail. **3** in baseball, a warming-up area for relief pitchers.

bull session *n.* an informal, unstructured discussion.

bull's-eye *n.* a circle marking the center of a target: *He hit the bull's-eye; She scored a bull's-eye (hit).*

bull.shit *n.* [vulgar slang] nonsense.

bull.whip *n.* a whip with a short handle and a long lash.

bul.ly (BULL.ee, short "oo") *n.* **bul.lies** one who threatens or is cruel to a weaker person: *big, neighborhood, schoolyard, street, town bullies;* **adja.:** *this bully boy; bully mentality; bully ragging; People in high places sometimes use the* **bully pulpit** *of their position to cajole and coerce people below them.* —*v.* **bul.lies, bul.lied, bul.ly.ing** be a bully to someone: *He bullies the younger children during recess; She was bullied (= threatened) into agreeing.* —*adj. & interj.* splendid!

bul.rush (BULL.rush) *n.* a tall sedge or reed that grows in marshes.

bul.wark (BULL.wurk, short "oo") *n.* **1** a defensive wall or rampart. **2** usu. **bulwarks** *pl.* an extension of the ship's side above the deck to provide protection for people and objects on deck. **3** a protection or defense: *Freedom of expression is a bulwark of democracy; a bulwark against tyranny.*

bum *n.* **1** a loafer, vagrant, or hobo: *a beach bum; ski bum; welfare bum.* **2** *Informal.* a buttock. —**on the bum** *Informal.* **1** living as a bum. **2** malfunctioning. —**the bum's rush** *Slang.* ejection by force; instant dismissal: *He was given the bum's rush when he became abusive.* —*v.* **bums, bummed, bum.ming** *Slang.* **1** live by begging; loaf: *to bum around.* **2** beg; cadge: *He bummed a cigarette off her.* —*adj. Slang.* bad: *bum advice; an athlete with a bum knee; the victim of a* **bum rap** (= false charge); *a* **bum steer** (= bad direction or tip).

bum.ber.shoot (BUM.bur.shoot) *n. Informal.* umbrella.

bum.ble.bee (BUM.bul.bee) *n.* a large, hairy, black-and-yellow bee.

bum.mer (BUM.ur) *n. Slang.* a bad experience: *The trip was really a bummer.*

bump *v.* **1** collide with or knock forcibly: *She bumped against a chair; I bumped into her in the dark; bumped into* (*Informal* for chanced to meet) *an old friend at the convention.* **2** *Informal.* displace: *He was bumped from the overbooked flight; The gangsters decided to* **bump off** (*Slang* for kill) *the informer.* —*n.* **1** a blow or collision. **2** a bulge or hump: *a bump on his head.*

bump.er *n.* **1** a metal bar protecting either end of an automobile: *We were crawling bumper to bumper on the busy highway;* **adja.:** *The* **bumper-to-bumper** *traffic crawled to a halt; a* **bumper sticker** *with a slogan on it.* **2** a brimful cup of drink; hence, something exceptionally large; **adja.:** *a bumper crop, harvest; a bumper issue (of a journal).*

bump.kin *n.* an awkward or naive person: *city slickers and country bumpkins.*

bump.tious (BUMP.shus) *adj.* arrogantly self-assertive. —**bump.tious.ly** *adv.*

bump.y *adj.* **bump.i.er, -i.est** having or marked by bumps: *a bumpy growth, ride, road, start, transition; a bumpy flight in bumpy weather.*

bun *n.* **1** a roll: *a hamburger bun; hot cross buns; cheese, cinnamon, onion buns.* **2** a coil of hair at the back of the head: *A ballerina wears her hair in a bun.* **3** usu. **buns** *pl.* buttocks: *the baby's bare buns.*

bunch *n.* **1** a number of similar things growing or fastened together: *a bunch* of bananas, flowers, keys; *Some grasses grow in bunches* (= tufts). **2** *Informal.* group: *a bunch of fellow workers, boys; She is the best of the bunch.* —*v.* gather together: *Let's bunch up before the fire; a dress bunched up at the back.* —**bunch.y** *adj.*

bun.co (BUNK.oh) *n. Informal.* a confidence scheme. —*v.* **-cos, -coed, -co.ing** swindle.

bun.combe (BUNK.um) same as BUNKUM.

bun.dle (BUN.dul) *n.* **1** a number of things tied together or wrapped up; package: *a bundle of clothes for the cleaners; a bundle of sticks; a **bundle of joy*** (= newborn infant); *She's a **bundle of nerves*** (= very nervous) *at exam time.* **2** *Informal.* a great amount of money: *He made a bundle on the stock market.* —*v.* **bun.dles, bun.dled, bun.dling 1** tie or pack into a bundle: *We'll bundle up the newspapers for pickup; Let's **bundle up*** (= dress warmly) *and go for a walk; She bundled up her child against the cold.* **2** dispatch quickly: *to bundle the children off to school in the morning.*

bung *n.* a stopper used to plug a bunghole: *barrel bungs.*

bun.ga.low (BUNG.guh.loh) *n.* a house of one or one-and-one-half stories: *back-split, modest, small, three-bedroom bungalows.*

bun.gee jumping (BUN.jee-) *n.* the sport of leaping from a great height with an elastic cord attached to one's feet. Also **bungee diving.**

bung.hole *n.* a hole in the side of a barrel or cask through which it is filled or emptied.

bun.gle (BUN.gul) *v.* **-gles, -gled, -gling** do or work clumsily or improperly; botch: *He bungled the job; **n.**: It was a technological bungle; bureaucratic bungling.* —**bun.gler** *n.*

bun.ion (BUN.yun) *n.* a swollen, painful deformity of the first joint of the big toe.

bunk *n.* **1** a sleeping place, esp. a narrow bed or berth. **2** *Slang.* meaningless talk. —*v.* sleep in or provide with a bed, often a makeshift one: *We bunked in the old cabin.*

bunk bed *n.* one of a pair of beds set one above the other.

bunk.er *n.* **1** a storage area for fuel oil, coal, etc. on a ship. **2** a fortified, often underground shelter: *a defensive **bunker mentality**.* **3** in golf, a hazard, as a sandy hollow or mound of earth.

bunk.house *n.* a simple roughly built house equipped with sleeping bunks, as for cowhands on a ranch.

bun.kum (BUNK.um) *n. Slang.* nonsense; bunk.

bun.ny *n.* **bun.nies** *Informal.* **1** a rabbit. **2** an attractive, scantily clad nightclub waitress. **3** *Slang.* a woman attractive as a sexual playmate: *Playboy bunnies; beach bunnies.*

Bun.sen burner (BUN.sun-) *n.* a laboratory gas burner producing a very hot flame.

bunt *v.* hit a baseball a short distance with a half swing; *n.*: *The batter reached first base on a bunt.*

bunt.ing *n.* **1** a light cloth for flags, streamers, etc. **2** a hooded, baglike outdoor garment for an infant. **3** a short-billed bird of the finch family.

buoy (BOO.ee, BOY) *n.* **1** a floating marker anchored to indicate a channel, hidden hazard, etc.: *A bell buoy rings when tossed by the waves.* **2** a ring-shaped device for keeping a person afloat; lifebuoy. —*v.* (BOY) **1** mark with buoys. **2** keep afloat: *a barrel buoyed up by water; a balloon buoyed up by air; The good news buoyed up* (= cheered) *her spirits.*

buoy.an.cy (BOY.un.see) *n.* the ability to float: *A bladder provides buoyancy for fish; The buoyancy of water (to keep objects floating on it) increases with density.*

buoy.ant (BOY.unt) *adj.* able to float or keep something afloat: *Cork is naturally buoyant.* **2** cheerful: *He seemed in buoyant good spirits; Real estate enjoys a buoyant* (= resilient) *market in the spring.* —**buoy.ant.ly** *adv.*

bur or **burr** *n.* **1** the prickly seedcase or fruit of some plants. **2** such a plant. **3** a person or thing that sticks to one like a bur. —**bur.ry** *adj.*

bur.ble (BUR.bul) *v.* make a bubbling noise: *The percolator started burbling; She burbled* (= said or spoke) *excitedly.* —*n.*: *a burble of laughter.*

bur.bot (BUR.but) *n.* a freshwater fish of the cod family.

'burbs *n.pl. Informal.* suburbs: *to escape to the 'burbs.*

bur.den (BUR.dun) *n.* **1** something carried, as a ship's cargo; load: *The camel is a beast of burden; Distribute the burden by shifting weights.* **2** a responsibility, task, or worry: *He was a heavy burden to everyone in his final days; His age placed a big burden on his relatives; Jane bore the burden of caring for him all by herself; But he was not a financial burden; The burden was relieved only by his death; The **burden of proof*** (= obligation to prove one's point) *rests with the* *accuser.* **3** the central idea or theme: *the burden of the argument; the burden of her song.* —*v.* load: *Let's not burden him with our problems;* **adj.** *a heavily burdened horse.* —**bur.den.some** *adj.*

bur.dock *n.* a coarse, hairy weed with large leaves and prickly flower heads.

bu.reau (BYOOR.oh) *n.* **-reaus** or **-reaux** (-oze) **1** a chest of drawers; dresser. **2** an office: *a better business bureau; credit, news, tourist, travel, weather bureaus.*

bu.reau.cra.cy (byoo.ROC.ruh.see) *n.* **-cies 1** a graded organization of nonelected public officials. **2** an administrative system bound by fixed rules and red tape: *an aging, faceless, incompetent, overgrown, swollen bureaucracy.*

bu.reau.crat (BYOOR.uh.crat) *n.* an official working in a bureaucracy. —**bu.reau.crat.ic** (-CRAT.ic) *adj.*: *a tale of bureaucratic bungling.*

bu.ret or **bu.rette** (byoo.RET) *n.* a graduated glass cylinder with a tap near the bottom, for measuring a gas or liquid.

burg *n. Informal.* a small city or town.

bur.geon (BUR.jun) *v.* **1** to sprout leaves or buds. **2** expand or develop rapidly: *a company that burgeons into a conglomerate;* **adja.**: *the burgeoning electronics industry; burgeoning growth, markets, opportunities.*

bur.ger (BUR.gur) *n. Informal.* a hamburger. —*comb.form.* **1** a patty in a bun: *eggburger; fishburger.* **2** a hamburger: *a cheeseburger* (= hamburger with cheese); *soyaburger* (= hamburger with soya protein).

bur.gess (BUR.jis) *n.* **1** a citizen of a borough. **2** a property owner or ratepayer.

burgh (BURG) *n.* an incorporated Scottish town; borough.

burgh.er (BUR.gur) *n.* a solid citizen, as of a burgh or town.

bur.glar (BURG.lur) *n.* one who commits burglary: *A burglar alarm warns us about burglars.*

bur.glar.ize (BUR.gluh.rize) *v.* **-iz.es, -ized, -iz.ing** *Informal.* break into a house as a thief; *adj.*: *They found their home burglarized and vandalized when they returned from Florida.*

bur.gla.ry (BUR.gluh.ree) *n.* **-ries** the breaking and entering of a building to commit a crime, esp. robbery.

bur.gle (BUR.gul) *v.* **-gles, -gled, -gling** same as BURGLARIZE.

Bur.gun.dy (BUR.gun.dee) *n.* **-dies 1** a usu. red table wine, esp. one made in Burgundy, France. **2** a dark reddish brown color.

bur.i.al (BER.ee.ul) *n.* an act of burying, esp. a body: *The burial took place at sea; He was at the burial; The lottery system was given a decent burial; garbage burial;* **adja.**: *a burial ground, mound, plot, service, site; burial rites.*

burl *n.* a roundish outgrowth on a tree.

bur.lap *n.* a coarse, open-weave fiber cloth used esp. for bags.

bur.lesque (bur.LESK) *n.* **1** an entertainment featuring striptease acts, coarse humor, etc.; also **bur.lesk. 2** a travesty or parody. —*v.* **-lesques, -lesqued, -lesqu.ing** imitate satirically or humorously.

bur.ly (BUR.lee) *adj.* **-li.er, -li.est** big and strong; husky: *a big burly fellow.*

Bur.mese (bur.MEEZ) *n. & adj.* (a person) of or from **Burma,** former name of Myanmar, a S. Asian country.

burn *v.* **burns,** *pt. & pp.* **burned** or **burnt, burn.ing 1** be or set on fire and suffer its effects: *The house is burning; It'll burn to the ground, burn to ashes; He burned his hand in the oven; The meat was burned to a crisp; Joan of Arc was burned at the stake; She was burned to death; was burned alive; Fire burns* (= gives off great heat). **2** suffer the burning effects of acid, radiation, or electricity. **3** consume as fuel: *Our furnace burns gas; The first stage of the rocket burns for two minutes.* **4** feel or make feel hot: *He was burning with desire; her cheeks burning with shame; I held on to the rope although it burned* (= the skin came off) *my hands as I slid down; ears burning* (= very eager) *to hear about the scandal; It burns me up* (Informal for makes me angry) *that I wasn't given a chance;* **adja.**: *She had burning ears from the cold; burning eyes; a burning anger, desire, resentment; the burning sands of the desert; a burning* (= hotly discussed) *issue, question.* **5** spend freely: *I don't have money to burn.* **6** *Informal.* cause damage to someone: *He decided to quit the business after getting burned* (= suffering losses or becoming disillusioned). —**burn one's boats** or **bridges** *Informal.* leave oneself no means of escape or return. —**burn out** to become exhausted after a time and unable to carry on, as in some lines of work: *a burned-out teacher.*

—*n.* **1** a burning or an injury or mark made by burning: *A first-degree burn only reddens the skin; a slow burn* (= rising fury) *leading to a blowup.* **2** a firing of a rocket engine.

burn.er *n.* something that burns, heats, or emits flame, esp. a heating element or a stove: *a gas burner; The less urgent business is put on the back burner* (= position of low priority), *others on the front burner* (= position of high priority).

bur.nish *v.* polish: *The metal has been burnished to a high gloss; to burnish one's image;* **adj.:** *a burnished mahogany table; burnished steel;* **bur.nish.er** *n.* —*n.* luster or gloss.

bur.noose (bur.NOOS) *n.* a loose, hooded cloak worn esp. by Arabs.

burn.out *n.* 1 the cessation of firing of a rocket or jet engine. 2 exhaustion: *Some people suffer burnout after a time in a strenuous job; career burnout.*

burnt a *pt. & pp.* of BURN.

burnt offering *n.* a sacrificial offering made to a deity which is burned at the altar.

burp *n.* a soft belch: *The baby let out a burp.* —*v.* belch or cause to belch: *to burp a baby after feeding.*

burp gun *n.* an automatic pistol or light machine gun.

burr *n.* 1 a rough edge left by cutting, drilling, etc. 2 a roughly trilled "r" sound: *the Scottish burr.* 3 a whirring sound. 4 same as BUR. —**bur.ry** (BUR.ee) *adj.*

bur.ri.to (buh.REE.toh) *n.* a rolled tortilla with a filling of beef, beans, or cheese: *Mexican burritos.*

bur.ro (BUR.oh) *n.* a small donkey.

bur.row (BUR.oh) *n.* a tunnel or hole dug by a rabbit, mole, etc. —*v.* 1 dig a burrow: *Muskrats burrow into the banks of streams; a burrowing animal.* 2 search, move, or progress as if by digging a burrow: *He's burrowing through books and papers in search of evidence.*

bur.sa (BUR.suh) *n.* -**sas** or -**sae** (-see) a fluid-filled sac easing friction at a joint.

bur.sar (BUR.sur) *n.* the treasurer of a college or university.

bur.sa.ry (BUR.suh.ree) *n.* -**ries** 1 the treasury of a college or university. 2 a small scholarship: *Students receive bursaries.*

bur.si.tis (bur.SYE.tis) *n.* the swollen inflammation of a bursa.

burst *v.* **bursts, burst, burst.ing** 1 explode; break, esp. from internal pressure: *A bomb bursts; The creek burst its banks; He burst out laughing; The police burst into the house; She burst into tears; She burst out of the house crying; Don't burst in on* or **upon** (= interrupt) *us when we are busy.* 2 be very full: *Granaries are bursting with grain; The child was bursting to tell us the news; The room is so crowded it seems to* **burst at the seams.** —*n.* 1 a bursting: *a burst* (= series of shots) *of machine-gun fire; The sentry fired a burst at the escaping convicts.* 2 an outbreak, spurt, or effort: *a burst of applause, energy, speed.*

bur.y (BER.ee) *v.* **bur.ies, bur.ied, bur.y.ing** 1 put a corpse in the ground, underwater, etc., esp. with funeral rites: *to bury a body; He was buried alive in the landslide; He tried to forget his sorrow by burying* (= occupying) *himself in work; Let's* **bury the hatchet** (= make peace) *and be friends.* 2 hide: *The child buried her face in the pillow;* **adj.:** *where the soldiers lie* **buried;** *buried* (= hidden) *treasure.*

bus *n.* **bus.es** or **bus.ses** 1 a large public conveyance usu. having a fixed route and stopping points: *The children came by bus; They caught a bus; boarded the bus; Those who* **miss the bus** (*Informal for* lose the opportunity) *this time may not get another chance.* 2 a computer circuit for moving data to and from its central processing unit. —*v.* **bus.es** or **bus.ses, bused** or **bussed, bus.ing** or **bus.sing** 1 travel by bus: *We bus to school; We are bused* (= transported) *back at 3:30 p.m.* 2 act as a busboy or busgirl.

bus.boy *n.* a waiter's helper who sets and clears tables. —**bus.girl** *n.*

bus.by (BUZ.bee) *n.* -**bies** a formal military fur hat.

bush (short "oo") *n.* 1 a small woody plant with many branches but no central stem, as the lilac or the rose; shrub. 2 *Cdn.* wild, uninhabited land, esp. if forested: *to stay in the bush; bush country.* 3 grove: *a maple bush; sugar bush.* —**beat around** or **about the bush** approach or discuss a topic without coming to the point. —*v.* be thick like a bush. —**adj.** 1 amateur; hence, second-rate: *a bush league, performance.* 2 *Cdn.* of the bush: *a bush fire; an impassable bush* (= rural) *road.* —**bush.y** *adj.* **bush.i.er, -i.est:** *a bushy beard; a fox's bushy tail.*

bushed *adj. Informal.* 1 exhausted. 2 lonely and depressed.

bush.el (BUSH.ul, short "OO") *n.* a measure for bulky articles: *We sell apples by the bushel; A bushel of corn weighs 25.4 kg.*

bush.ing (short "oo") *n.* a cylindrical metal sleeve used to guide a shaft or reduce friction.

bush league *n.* a minor league, consid-

ered second-rate. **—bush-league** *adj.* second-rate: *to improve the bush-league status of their hockey team; a bush-league speech.*
bush line *n. Cdn.* an airline serving sparsely populated areas.
bush lot *n.* a wooded part of a farm.
Bush.man (BUSH.mun, short "oo") *n.* **-men** a member of a nomadic people of S.W. Africa, properly called "the San"; formerly **bushman, -men.**
bush pilot *n.* a pilot who services the bush country.
bush telegraph *n.* 1 any primitive form of communication. 2 the grapevine.
bush.whack (BUSH.whack, short "oo") *v.* 1 live in the bush, esp. in hiding. 2 make one's way through the bush. 3 ambush or raid. **—bush.whack.er** *n.*
busi.ness (BIZ.nis) *n.* 1 work or occupation: *Sales people travel on business; to mix business with pleasure; Each one minds his own business; That's none of her business* (= rightful concern); *Waiting in line is tiresome business* (= activity); *I mean business* (= I am in earnest); *a business card* bearing a company's name; *The business end of a tool, weapon, etc. is the end with which the action is performed, as the muzzle of a gun.* 2 a commercial undertaking such as a store or factory: *He gave up his job and went into business (for himself); Many businesses went out of business or closed down during the recession.* 3 commerce or trade: *She is in show business; Business is picking up after the recession; Business is booming; They are trying to drum up business for the new agency; We want your business; We'd like to do business with you.*
busi.ness.like (BIZ.nis.like) *adj.* efficient or purposeful: *Let's be businesslike and not waste any time.*
busi.ness.man (BIZ.nis.mun) *n.* **-men** one engaged in business, esp. as an owner or boss. **—busi.ness.wom.an** *n.* **-wom.en.**
busk.er (BUS.kur) *n.* a street musician or entertainer.
bus.kin *n.* a thick-soled, high-laced boot, as worn formerly by actors.
busman's holiday *n.* a vacation spent in activity similar to one's usual work.
buss *n. & v. Informal.* kiss.
bus stop *n.* a stopping point on a bus route.
bust *n.* 1 a sculpture of a person's head and upper chest. 2 a woman's bosom. 3 *Informal.* a police arrest or raid. 4 a failure or collapse: *the cycle of boom and bust; California or bust!* 5 punch.
—v. *Informal.* 1 burst, break, punch, tame, etc.: *He busted my toy! She busted his nose; The trees are busting into bloom; a bronco-busting cowboy.* 2 of police, to arrest: *He was busted for peddling drugs; They busted* (= raided) *the joint.* 3 demote: *He was busted to private.* 4 make or become penniless: *busted until payday.*
bust.er *n. Informal.* 1 one that busts or breaks: *a bronco buster; fuzz buster* (= speedtrap beater); *ghost busters.* 2 [hostile use] fellow: *Relax, buster!*
bus.tier (BUST.ee.yay) *n.* a woman's close-fitting, usu. strapless bodice or top.
bus.tle (BUS.ul) *n.* 1 busy activity: *the hustle and bustle of trading on the stock exchange; The bustle subsides when the bell rings.* 2 formerly, a cushion that makes a woman's skirt stick out at the back: *a maid in a bustle, apron, and lace cap.* **—v.** **-tles, -tled, -tling** move or work busily and fussily: *She bustles the children off to school at 8 everyday; It bustles with activity;* ***adj.:*** *the bustling stock exchange.*
bust.y *adj. Informal.* big-breasted.
bus.y (BIZ.ee) *adj.* **bus.i.er, -i.est** 1 active: *busy as a bee; a busy airport, lifestyle, schedule, secretary; Mom had a busy day at work; Bibi is busy with her homework; Homework keeps her busy; Dad is busy cooking; The phone is busy* (= in use, as you can tell by the **busy signal** (= tone). 2 of a design, having too many distracting details. **—v.** **bus.ies, bus.ied, bus.y.ing** make busy or active: *He busies himself with hobbies on weekends.* **—bus.i.ly** *adv.;* **bus.y.ness** *n.*
bus.y.bod.y (BIZ.ee.bod.ee) *n.* **-bod.ies** a nosey or meddlesome person.
bus.y.work (BIZ.ee.wurk) *n.* useless work to keep one occupied.
but *conj.* 1 yet; however; on the contrary: *She is short but thin; He visited, but could not stay long.* 2 if not; other than: *He would have come but that he was too busy.* **—prep.** except: *Everyone but he or him had left the scene; He wouldn't be alive today but for the operation; It happened on the last day but one* (= second day) *before the wedding.* **—adv.** [formal use] only: *There was but one survivor.* **—n.** an exception, condition, etc.: *no buts about it; no ands, ifs, or buts.*
bu.tane (BYOO.tane) *n.* a colorless, flammable gas used as a fuel.
butch (short "oo") *n. Slang.* an aggressively masculine person.
butch.er (BOOCH.ur, short "OO") *n.* 1 one who kills or dresses meat for

sale or consumption. **2** a brutal mass killer. **3** one who botches a job; bungler.
—*v.* slaughter: *They butcher cattle, hogs, and sheep; Thousands were butchered in the war; He butchered (= bungled) the job.* —**butch.er.y** (-uh.ree) *n.* **-er.ies.**

but.ler *n.* a chief male house-servant.

butt *n.* **1** a large cask. **2** the larger or handle end: *the butt of a pistol, rifle.* **3** a remaining or broken end: *a cigarette butt.* **4** an object of ridicule: *Bob is the butt of her jokes.* **5** a butting: *a head butt.* **6** *Informal.* buttocks: *a kick in the butt; He's a pain in the butt; Will you please get off your butt and do something? She's working her butt off for her kids; Her dad busted his butt to put her through school; I've half a mind to go in and **kick butt** (= do something effectively).*
—*v.* strike or push with the head or horns, as a goat does: *to butt against a wall; to butt heads with the competition.*
—**butt in** *Informal.* interfere: *She doesn't like to butt in when they're talking privately; never butts in on their conversation.* —**butt out** *Informal.* **1** stop interfering. **2** give up smoking. **3** stop smoking.

butte (BYOOT, long "OO") *n.* an isolated, flat-topped hill with steep sides, as in Montana and S. Alberta.

but.ter (BUT.ur) *n.* **1** a thick, rich food product made by churning cream: *a pat of butter; a whole stick of butter; fresh butter; rancid butter; sweet (= unsalted) butter; Fry it in butter.* **2** a similar product: *apple butter; peanut butter.*
—*v.* spread butter on something: *to butter a toast; He knows how to **butter up** or **up to** (= flatter) his boss to get a raise.*
—**but.ter.y** *adj.*

but.ter.cup (BUT.ur.cup) *n.* a shiny yellow wildflower: *a bright buttercup yellow.*

but.ter.fat (BUT.ur.fat) *n.* the fatty part of milk that is churned into butter.

but.ter.fin.gers (BUT.ur.fing.gurs) *n.* Informal. one who is clumsy and drops things: *a regular butterfingers;* **but.ter.fin.gered** *adj.*

but.ter.fly (BUT.ur.fly) *n.* **-flies** a slender, often colorful, four-winged insect that flies by day, flitting from flower to flower: *the monarch butterfly; a social butterfly who has time only for parties; He has **butterflies** or **butterflies in his stomach** (= a nervous feeling) just before an exam; adj.: a **butterfly** leg of lamb (prepared like a butterfly's spread wings).*

but.ter.milk (BUT.ur.milk) *n.* the milky liquid left after cream is churned for butter, made commercially by fermenting skim milk.

but.ter.nut (BUT.ur.nut) *n.* the oblong, edible, oily nut of a North American walnut tree.

but.ter.scotch (BUT.ur.scotch) *n.* a syrup, candy, or flavoring made with butter and brown sugar.

but.tock (BUT.uck) *n.* **1** either of the two fleshy rounded parts at the back of the hips. **2 buttocks** *pl.* the seat or rump.

but.ton (BUT.un) *n.* **1** a disk or knob used to fasten or ornament clothing. **2** a similar object: *Push* or *press the button for help; He pushed the panic button (= panicked); He's wearing a campaign button (= badge) on his lapel; She always arrives at 9 **on the button** (= exactly).* —*v.* fasten with a button: *Button (up) your shirt.* —**button up** or **button one's lip** *Informal.* be quiet.

buttoned-down or **button-down** *adj.* **1** having a buttoned-down collar: *the classic oxford button-down shirt.* **2** *Informal.* conventional or conservative: *our corporation's button-down image;* *adv.*: *She played him very buttoned-down.*

buttoned-up *adj. Informal.* prim and serious-minded.

but.ton.hole (BUT.un.hole) *n.* a slit or loop through which a button is passed. —*v.* **-holes, -holed, -hol.ing** stop and force someone to listen.

but.tress (BUT.ris) *n.* an external support built against a wall; hence, any support. —*v.* support: *to buttress a wall; a poor thesis buttressed with a long bibliography.*

bux.om (BUX.um) *adj.* plump and attractive: *a buxom young matron.*

buy *v.* **buys, bought** (BAWT), **buy.ing** acquire by payment in cash or kind: *He will buy me a car from a dealer; Dealers buy wholesale and sell retail; a temptation for impulse buying; panic buying of stocks; Our freedom was bought with their lives; He tried to buy his way into the club; The lawyer was accused of trying to buy (= bribe) the jury; No one will buy (Informal for believe) that story.* —**buy into** purchase shares in a company.
—**buy out** buy someone's shares or controlling interest in a business.
—**buy time** *Informal.* to stall so as to gain time. —**buy up** buy as much as one can of something.
—*n. Informal.* purchase: *a good buy; a great buy (= bargain) at such a low price.*
—**buy.er** *n.*: *It's a **buyer's market** when prices are low.*

buzz *v.* **1** make a vibrating, prolonged, z-like sound: *bees buzzing in the field; a* market buzzing with activity; Buzz (= telephone) for room service; When he became a nuisance, she told him to **buzz off** or **along** (Informal for go away). **2** fly an airplane low over something: *They buzzed the enemy ship.* —*n.* a buzzing sound: *the buzz of bees, rumor; the buzz of a saw; He appeared promptly at my buzz* (= when I pressed the buzzer); *Give me a buzz* (Informal for phone call) *when you are free.*

buz.zard (BUZ.urd) *n.* a bird of the vulture family: *The "turkey buzzard" is a New World vulture.*

buz.zer (BUZ.ur) *n.* a signaling device that makes a buzzing sound.

buzz word *n.* a high-sounding bit of jargon: *a computer buff who uses buzz words like "telecommute" and "wetware."*

by *prep.* **1** beside; near; at: *It's over by the door; I stopped by her house* (= visited her) *on my way back.* **2** through the agency of: *a book by Atwood; trapped by a snowstorm.* **3** during: *He works by night; The payment is due by* (= on or before) *May 31.* **4** according or in relation to: *Play by the rules; a lawyer by profession; He swears by the Bible.* **5** past: *She went by us at full speed; to Paris by way of* (= via) *London.* **6** to the extent of: *He missed the bus by 15 minutes.* **7** in the amount, lot, or unit of: *apples by the bushel; You pay by the hour; People came by the thousands.* **8** [used to indicate multiplication, division, linking of dimensions, etc.]: *Multiply 2 by 7 to get 14; Divide 14 by 2 to get 7; two by four* (= 2" x 4"). —*adv.*: *Keep close by* (= near) *in case of trouble; Don't lay it by* (= aside) *just yet; Stop by* (= visit) *on your way home; She drove by* (= past) *just now.* —**by and by** eventually. —**by and large** on the whole. —**by oneself** without others. —**by the by** or **by the way** incidentally.

bye *n.* an advance to the next round of a tournament because there is no other contestant with whom one can be paired: *Smith drew a bye; a bye to the semifinals.* —*interj. Informal.* good-bye: *Bye now!*

by-election *n.* a special election to fill a vacant seat between regular elections.

Bye.lo.rus.sian (byel.uh.RUSH.un) *n. & adj.* (a person) of or from Byelorussia or **Belarus**, a country of E. Europe.

by.gone (BY.gon) *adj*a. past: *in bygone days; a bygone age, era.* —*n.*: *"Let bygones be bygones"* (= Forgive and forget).

by.law *n.* a rule or regulation passed by a company, city, etc. to regulate its own affairs.

by.line or **by-line** *n.* the writer's name printed at the head of a newspaper story.

by.pass *n.* a road or passage around something: *Take the bypass to avoid city traffic; a coronary bypass* (around the blocked portion of an artery). —*v.* go around: *The canal bypasses the rapids.*

by.path *n.* a secondary or rarely used path or road.

by-product *n.* something produced incidentally to the chief product: *Molasses and syrup are by-products of sugar manufacture.*

by-road *n.* a side road.

by.stand.er (BY.stan.dur) *n.* a nonparticipating onlooker: *An innocent bystander was hit by the runaway car.*

byte *n.* a unit of computer data usu. consisting of 8 bits.

by.way *n.* **1** a bypath: *highways and byways.* **2** a less known topic or area: *in the byways of history.*

by.word *n.* **1** a proverbial saying. **2** a person or thing that is typical of a quality: *The newspapers are not all bywords for accuracy.* **3** watchword or guiding principle: *Efficiency is the byword for kitchen designers.*

By.zan.tine (BIZ.un.teen) *adj.* **1** having to do with the Byzantine Empire (A.D. 395-1453) and its culture, esp. its architecture. **2** characterized by intrigue: *a Byzantine struggle for power; the Byzantine world of big corporations linked to political parties.*

.... **C, c** ....

C or **c** (SEE) *n.* **C's** or **c's 1** the third letter of the English alphabet. **2** the third in a series; third highest: *a grade of C.*

cab *n.* **1** a taxicab: *to call for, go in, hail, hire, take a cab.* **2** the driver's compartment of a truck, crane, locomotive, etc.

ca.bal (cuh.BAL) *n.* a group of conspirators or plotters; a conspiracy. —*v.* **-bals, -balled, -bal.ling** join or form a cabal.

cab.a.la (CAB.uh.luh) *n.* **1** a mystic Jewish theosophy of the Middle Ages. **2** any esoteric system of beliefs; also **cab.a.lism; cab.a.list.** —**cab.a.lis.tic** (-LIS.tic) *adj.*

cab.al.le.ro (cab.ul.YAIR.oh) *n.* **-ros** a Spanish gentleman.

ca.ba.na (cuh.BAN.uh) *n.* a shelter used as a bathhouse near a beach or swimming pool.

cab.a.ret (cab.uh.RAY) *n.* **1** a restau-

rant providing liquor and light entertainment. **2** the entertainment itself.
cab.bage (CAB.ij) *n.* a vegetable with a dense round head of thick leaves: *heads of cabbage; a dish of corned beef and cabbage.*
cab.by or **cab.bie** (CAB.ee) *n.pl.* **cab.bies** *Informal.* one who drives a taxicab; also **cab.driv.er.**
Ca.ber.net (cab.ur.NAY) *n.* a dry red wine made from a variety of premium red grape.
cab.in *n.* **1** a small, rough dwelling of one story: *Pioneers lived in log cabins.* **2** a room on a ship or boat: *a first-class cabin; a **cabin boy** (= servant boy on a ship); **cabin class** (= accommodation intermediate between tourist class and first class).* **3** an enclosed space in an airplane for crew, cargo, or passengers.
cabin cruiser *n.* a small powered craft with built-in living facilities.
cab.i.net (CAB.uh.nit) *n.* **1** a cupboard-like structure for housing or displaying objects or equipment: *a china cabinet; the cabinet of a console TV; a filing cabinet for the office; a kitchen cabinet; a **cabinetmaker** (who makes woodwork and furniture); **cabinetwork.*** **2** the advisory council of a head of government: *a coalition cabinet; the shadow cabinet (of the opposition party); a decision taken **in cabinet** (= at a cabinet meeting); a cabinet minister, reshuffle.*
cab.i.net.ry (CAB.uh.ni.tree) *n.* a cabinetmaker's work; cabinetwork.
ca.ble (CAY.bul) *n.* **1** a rope of large diameter, usu. of steel or fiber. **2** the anchor cable of a ship: *The cable broke and our ship began to drift.* **3** a unit of length equal to 100 or 120 fathoms; also **cable length.** **4** a bundle of insulated electrical conductors. **5** also **ca.ble.gram,** a telegram transmitted by submarine cable: *He sent us a cable from Europe.* —*v.* **ca.bles, ca.bled, ca.bling 1** send a cablegram to someone: *He cabled us; cabled for money; cabled that he was broke.* **2** equip with cable TV: *to cable a neighborhood; adj.: the most heavily cabled areas, communities, countries; cabled homes; adja.: a **cabling** system; cabling power; n.: the cabling of America.* —**ca.bler** *n.*
cable car *n.* a car drawn by a moving cable, as on a hill or across a canyon.
ca.ble.cast (CAY.bul.cast) *v.* **-casts, -cast** or **-cast.ed, -cast.ing** to broadcast via cable: *to cablecast games, movies.* —*n.* such a broadcast: *a live cablecast; adj.: cablecast programs.*

—**ca.ble.cast.er** *n.*
cable-knit *adj.* knitted with a design resembling twisted rope: *a cable-knit sweater (or fishermen's sweater).*
cable TV *n.* television using a central antenna that serves a whole community.
cab.man (CAB.mun) *n.* **-men** a male cabby.
ca.bo.chon (CAB.uh.shon) *n.* a precious stone cut and polished with a rounded face but no facets.
ca.boo.dle (cuh.BOO.dul) *n. Slang.* **the whole (kit and) caboodle** the whole lot.
ca.boose (cuh.BOOSE) *n.* the car at the end of a freight train with sleeping and kitchen facilities for the train crew.
cab.ri.o.let (CAB.ree.uh.LAY) *n.* **1** a horse-drawn, two-wheeled, covered carriage. **2** a kind of convertible coupe.
cab.stand *n.* a parking place for taxicabs waiting for passengers.
ca.ca.o (cuh.COW) *n.* **-os** a small tropical American tree that yields seeds, called **cacao (beans),** from which cocoa and chocolate are made.
cac.ci.a.to.re (cah.chuh.TOR.ee) *adjp.* cooked with tomatoes, onions, and herbs: *veal cacciatore; chicken cacciatore.*
cache (CASH) *n.* **1** a hiding place, originally for food and supplies for future use. **2** goods hidden in a cache. —*v.* **cach.es, cached, cach.ing** hide: *The explorers cached their provisions in a cave.*
cache memory *n.* in a computer system, a high-speed buffer-type memory into which instructions and programs are loaded from the main memory.
cache.pot *n.* an ornamental container for a flowerpot.
ca.chet (cash.AY) *n.* **1** a mark or seal as an indication of official approval on a letter or document. **2** a mark of excellence or authenticity. **3** a design or advertisement stamped or printed on mail.
cack.le (CACK.ul) *v.* **1** make the shrill cry of a hen or goose. **2** laugh in such a way: *to cackle with glee.* —*n.* a hen's cry; also, speech or laughter like it: *Cut the cackle (Informal for* Stop the pointless chatter).
ca.coph.o.ny (cuh.COF.uh.nee) *n.* **-nies** unpleasant or discordant sound. —**ca.coph.o.nous** *adj.*
cac.tus (CAC.tus) *n., pl.* **-tus.es** or **-ti** (-tye) a leafless, spiny desert plant with fleshy stems.

cad *n.* an ungentlemanly ill-mannered person: *ill-bred cads.* —**cad.dish** *adj.*

CAD *n.* [acronym] computer-aided design; **adja.**: *CAD drawings, software, systems.*

ca.dav.er (cuh.DAV.ur) *n.* a dead body, esp. a corpse for dissection.

ca.dav.er.ous (cuh.DAV.uh.rus) *adj.* corpselike; pale and gaunt.

CAD/CAM *n.* computer-aided design and manufacture.

cad.dy (CAD.ee) *n.* **cad.dies** 1 also **cad.die,** one hired to assist a golfer to carry clubs. 2 a carrying device: *book, luggage, shopping, trailer, trash bag caddies.* 3 a holder or container: *a shower caddy (for shampoos, etc.); tea caddies.*
—*v.* **cad.dies, cad.died, cad.dy.ing** act as a caddie.

ca.dence (CAY.dunce) *n.* 1 a rhythm or flow of sound. 2 a timed measure, as for a march or dance. 3 modulation of pitch and volume of the voice; hence, the general character of the voice: *the pleasant cadence of her speech.* 4 a musical progression toward an harmonic conclusion. —**ca.denced** *adj.*

ca.den.za (cuh.DEN.zuh) *n.* a parenthetic ornamental flourish, either vocal or instrumental, just before the end of a work of music.

ca.det (cuh.DET) *n.* 1 a student in a military academy or one receiving military training, as a member of a "cadet corps": *army, military, naval, police cadets; a space cadet* (= a spaced-out person). 2 a 16- to 21-year-old Girl Guide: *In the U.S.,* **Cadette** *Girl Scouts are 12 to 14 years old.*

cadge *v.* **cadg.es, cadged, cadg.ing** *Informal.* get by begging: *trying to cadge cigarettes from passers-by.* —**cadg.er** *n.*

Cad.il.lac (CAD.uh.lac) *n.* something considered as the most outstanding of its kind: *the Cadillac of copying machines;* **adja.**: *a Cadillac plan, service;* **Cadillac** *Trademark.*

cad.mi.um (CAD.mee.um) *n.* a metallic element used in alloys, esp. for plating metals.

cad.re (CAD.ree) *n.* 1 a trained group, esp. military or political, forming the core of a larger organization: *A cadre of revolutionaries operated in each village.* 2 a revolutionary group or a member of one: *A high-ranking cadre arrived at the local meeting in a chauffeured car.*

ca.du.ce.us (cuh.DEW.see.us) *n., pl.* **-ce.i** (-see.eye) the winged staff of Mercury, now used as the emblem of the medical profession.

Cae.sar or **cae.sar** (SEE.zur) *n.* an absolute ruler, like the emperors of ancient Rome; **Cae.sar.ism** (-riz.um) *n.*

cae.sar.e.an or **Cae.sar.e.an** (si.ZAIR.ee.un) same as CESARIAN.

Caesar salad *n.* a tossed salad of greens, eggs, and anchovies with olive oil, lemon juice, and seasonings.

Cae.si.um same as CESIUM.

cae.su.ra (si.ZHOOR.uh) *n.* **-ras** or **-rae** (-ree) in poetry, a slight pause or break in the middle of a line of verse.

ca.fé (ca.FAY, cuh.FAY) *n.* a small restaurant or bar. Also **ca.fe.**

caf.e.te.ri.a (caf.uh.TEER.ee.uh) *n.* a restaurant where customers serve themselves at a counter and carry food to the tables: *a school cafeteria;* **adja.**: *a cafeteria selection of courses; The* **cafeteria plan** *(or* **cafeteria approach** *to or* **cafeteria concept of compensation***) allows employees to pick and choose their benefits.*

caf.fein.at.ed (CAF.uh.nay.tid) *adj.* caffeine-containing: *caffeinated beverages, drinks, coffee.*

caf.feine (ca.FEEN) *n.* a stimulant drug found in tea, coffee, chocolate, and colas. Also **caf.fein.**

caf.fe lat.te (CAF.ay.LAT.ay) *n.* espresso made with hot or steamed milk.

caf.tan (CAF.tan, -tun) *n.* 1 a long-sleeved Middle Eastern men's tunic reaching to the ankles and worn with a sash. 2 a caftanlike shirt or dress worn in Western countries as casual wear.

cage *n.* 1 an enclosure for animals, consisting of an open structure of metal or wooden bars or wire. 2 a similar structure or enclosure: *the batting cage of baseball players in training; an elevator cage; a bank teller's cage; the rib cage of the chest.* 3 [in news headings] basketball; **adja.**: *a cage coach, title.* —*v.* **cag.es, caged, cag.ing** put or keep in a cage.

cag.er (CAY.jur) *n.* [in news headings] a basketball player.

cag.ey (CAY.jee) *adj.* **cag.i.er, -i.est** *Informal.* 1 cunning: *the cagey fox.* 2 cautious: *The politician was cagey about committing himself.* —**cag.i.ly** *adv.;* **cag.i.ness** *n.*

ca.hoots (cuh.HOOTS, long "OO") *n. Slang.* **in cahoots (with)** in partnership, usu. of an improper nature.

cai.man (CAY.mun) *n.* a tropical American reptile closely related to the crocodile.

Cain *n.* a murderer, like the son of Adam and Eve in the Bible who killed his brother Abel: *the mark* or *brand of*

Cain. —**raise Cain** *Slang.* make a big commotion.

cairn *n.* a pile of stones set up as a monument.

cais.son (CAY.son, *rhyme:* on) *n.* **1** formerly, a horse-drawn, usu. two-wheeled ammunition wagon. **2** a watertight chamber filled with air under high pressure, used for underwater construction.

ca.jole (cuh.JOLE) *v.* **-joles, -joled, -jol.ing** persuade or coax, esp. with flattery; wheedle: *The child was cajoled into the dentist's chair.* —**ca.jol.er.y** *n.*

Ca.jun (CAY.jun) *n.* in Louisiana, a person descended from French immigrants exiled from Acadia in the 18th century; *adja.*: *Cajun cooking, country, traditions.*

cake *n.* **1** a sweet loaf, baked and often iced, usu. in a thick disk shape: *a piece or slice of cake; a birthday cake; layer cake; wedding cake.* **2** something made into a round type of shape: *fish cake; barley cakes; a cake of soap.* —**a piece of cake** *Informal.* something very easy to accomplish. —**have one's cake and eat it too** want to enjoy the advantages without accepting the disadvantages of a deal. —**take the cake** *Informal.* deserve a prize: *This takes the cake for the dullest novel of the year.*

cake.walk *n.* **1** a show dance characterized by an elaborate walk with a high prance. **2** *Informal.* a piece of cake; breeze.

cal.a.bash (CAL.uh.bash) *n.* **1** a tropical American tree bearing a fruit gourd. **2** the gourd. **3** a bottle, bowl, pipe, etc. made from this gourd.

cal.a.mine (CAL.uh.mine) *n.* a pinkish mixture of zinc and iron oxides used in skin lotions, ointments, etc.

ca.lam.i.ty (cuh.LAM.i.tee) *n.* **-ties** a grave misfortune that befalls a person or people: *The marriage proved to be the greatest calamity of his life; A collision with a kangaroo was the only calamity of our Australian tour.* —**ca.lam.i.tous** (-tus) *adj.*

ca.lash (cuh.LASH) *n.* **1** a four-passenger carriage with a folding top. **2** the folding top of a carriage. **3** formerly, a woman's folding hood or bonnet.

cal.car.e.ous (cal.CARE.ee.us) *adj.* resembling, containing, or composed of calcium, calcium carbonate, or lime; chalky.

cal.ced.o.ny (cal.SED.uh.nee) same as CHALCEDONY.

cal.cic (CAL.sic) *adj.* having to do with calcium or lime.

cal.cif.er.ous (cal.SIF.uh.rus) *adj.* yielding or containing calcium or calcium carbonate.

cal.ci.fi.ca.tion (cal.suh.fuh.CAY.shun) *n.* hardening by calcium formation: *Bones are formed by calcification; In old age, calcification of joints may set in.*

cal.ci.fy (CAL.suh.fye) *v.* **-fies, -fied, -fy.ing** harden by accumulation of calcium.

cal.ci.mine (CAL.suh.mine) *n.* a white or pale-colored wash or paint for plaster surfaces. —*v.* **-mines, -mined, -min.ing** paint with calcimine.

cal.cine (CAL.sine) *v.* **-cines, -cined, -cin.ing** reduce to quicklime or similar dry powder by heating but not melting. —**cal.ci.na.tion** (-suh.NAY.shun) *n.*

cal.ci.um (CAL.see.um) *n.* a soft, whitish, metallic element found in combination in limestone, chalk, marble, bone, etc.

cal.cu.late (CAL.kyuh.late) *v.* **-lates, -lat.ed, -lat.ing 1** compute mathematically or scientifically: *Actuaries calculate insurance premiums.* **2** evaluate or predict by common sense: *to calculate the consequences of an action.* —**cal.cu.la.ble** (-luh.bul) *adj.*; **cal.cu.la.bly** *adv.*

calculated *adj.* deliberate: *a calculated attempt, insult; a plan calculated (= designed) to cause delay; to take a **calculated risk** (with chances of failure already estimated).*

calculating *adj.* shrewd or clever in a selfish way: *a cold and calculating villain.*

cal.cu.la.tion (cal.kyuh.LAY.shun) *n.* **1** the process or result of calculating. **2** shrewd deliberation.

cal.cu.la.tor (CAL.kyuh.lay.tur) *n.* one that calculates, esp. an electronic machine that does arithmetic computations: *a pocket calculator.*

cal.cu.lus (CAL.kyuh.lus) *n.* **-lus.es 1** a system of computing using algebraic symbols: *differential and integral calculus.* **2** standard of judgment: *the moral calculus of war and peace; the cold-blooded calculus of terrorism.* **3** *pl.* **-li** (-lye) an abnormal stonelike growth in the body: *urinary calculi* (= kidney stones).

cal.de.ra (cal.DARE.uh) *n.* a large basin-shaped volcanic crater.

cal.dron (CAWL.drun) same as CAULDRON.

cal.en.dar (CAL.un.dur) *n.* **1** a system for determining the days, weeks, and months of a year; also, a table or chart showing this: *the Chinese, Gregorian, Julian calendar; a perpetual calen-*

calender / calla

dar *(useful for many years)*; *The* **calendar year** *runs from January to December.* **2** an ordered list; schedule: *a school calendar; a calendar of events; That's not on my calendar this week.* —*v.* record on a calendar or schedule.

cal.en.der (CAL.un.dur) *n.* a finishing machine used to give a gloss to cloth, paper, etc. —*v.* give such a finish; *n.: machine* **calendering**; *adja.: the* **calendering** *process, temperature; calendering equipment, systems; adj.: calendered chintz cloth, fibers, films.*

calf (CAF) *n.* **calves** (CAVZ) **1** the thick, fleshy back part of the lower leg. **2** the young of cattle and other large mammals such as the elephant, moose, porpoise, and whale: *Veal is calf meat; A cow is said to be* **in calf** (= pregnant). **3** calfskin.

calf love same as PUPPY LOVE.

calf.skin or **calf** *n.* leather made from calf hides.

cal.i.ber (CAL.i.bur) *n.* **1** the diameter of a bullet or other projectile: *A .20 [pronounced "twenty"] caliber bullet is 20/200 in. (5.08 mm) in diameter.* **2** the inside diameter of a tube or the barrel of a gun: *Smooth-bore guns use bullets of the same caliber as the bore.* **3** quality or excellence: *work of high caliber; A woman of her caliber is hard to find.* Also **cal.i.bre** *Cdn.*

cal.i.brate (CAL.uh.brate) *v.* **-brates, -brat.ed, -brat.ing 1** fix or adjust the graduations of a measuring instrument; *adj.: a well* **calibrated** *thermometer.* **2** find the caliber of a tube.
—**cal.i.bra.tion** (-BRAY.shun) *n.*
—**cal.i.bra.tor** (-bray.tur) *n.*

cal.i.co (CAL.i.coh) *n.* **-cos** or **-coes** a rough cotton cloth with a printed pattern: *a calico cat* (= spotted cat).

Cal.i.for.ni.an (cal.uh.FOR.nee.un) *n. & adj.* (a person) of or from **California**, a W. state of the U.S.

cal.i.for.ni.um (cal.uh.FOR.nee.um) *n.* a synthetic, metallic, radioactive element.

cal.i.per (CAL.uh.pur) *n.* **1** usu. **calipers** *pl.* an instrument with two curved legs, for measuring thicknesses or the diameters of tubes. **2** either of two plates that press against a rotating part, as the wheel of a bicycle or the disc of a car's wheel, to act as a brake: *caliper brakes.* Also **cal.li.per.**

ca.liph (CAY.lif, CAL-) *n.* the head of Islam; the title of Mohammed's successors. —**ca.liph.ate** (-ate, -it) *n.* the rule or jurisdiction of a caliph.

cal.is.then.ics (cal.us.THEN.ics, "TH" as in "thin") *n.pl.* simple physical exercises designed to develop grace and strength. —**cal.is.then.ic** *adj.*

calk (CAWK) same as CAULK.

call *v.* **1** summon; ask to come: *Did you call me? She felt called to the service of the poor.* **2** visit in person: *The plumber will be calling soon; Please call again; to call at a place.* **3** to telephone: *Tell her to call home; Our doctor will be calling soon; Many employees have called in sick today.* **4** deem or consider: *We'll call it even and go home.* **5** name: *Let's call the baby Jacques; The media called her a hero.* **6** to shout or cry: *Please call for help; a bird calling for its mate.* **7** require or demand, as a loan to be paid, cards to be shown in a game, etc.: *The bank has called the loan; This calls for an explanation.* **8** end: *The game was called because of rain.* **9** say or read out aloud: *to call the roll.* —**call in 1** summon as help: *to call in a consultant.* **2** withdraw from circulation, as old currency. **3** to report: *Someone just called in a bomb threat.* —**call into question** (make someone) doubt something. —**call off 1** cancel: *to call off an investigation.* **2** read out aloud; also **call out.** —**call on** pay a short visit to someone. —**call someone's bluff** *Informal.* challenge a pretentious claim. —**call someone on the carpet** *Informal.* summon for or give a rebuke. —**call the shots** *Informal.* be in charge. —**call up 1** (cause to) recollect. **2** to telephone. **3** bring or summon to an active state: *Young people are called up for military service; to call up images, text, etc. on a computer screen.*
—*n.* **1** a summoning: *a strike call; a call to battle; a divine call to the ministry; a bugle call* (= signal); *Doctors are* **on call** (= available) *in an emergency; a close call* (= narrow escape). **2** a visit: *Few doctors make house calls any more.* **3** an act of telephoning: *collect calls; A local call is not a long-distance call; station-to-station calls; We placed* or *made an operator-assisted person-to-person call to Jim; The operator put my call through to Baffin Island; a toll call; Will someone take that call, please?* **4** decision or ruling: *a bad call by an umpire in baseball.* **5** a cry or shout: *a call for help; a bird's mating call; a roll call* (= reading aloud of the roll); *Please stay* **within call** (= close enough to hear being called). **6** a demand: *There are too many calls on my time; a loan to be repaid on call.* **7** in card games, a bid. —**call.er** *n.*

cal.la or **calla lily** (CAL.uh-) *n.* a deco-

callback / camber

rative plant of the arum family.
call.back *n.* a manufacturer's notice to consumers to return a defective product; recall.
call-board *n.* a bulletin board for notices or schedules, as for theater rehearsals or train times.
call girl *n.* a prostitute available by telephone.
cal.lig.ra.phy (cuh.LIG.ruh.fee) *n.* penmanship; fine handwriting; **cal.lig.ra.pher** *n.* —**cal.lig.ra.phic** (cal.uh.GRAF.ic) *adj.*
call-in same as PHONE-IN.
calling *n.* a profession, occupation, or religious vocation.
calling card *n.* 1 also **visiting card**, a card bearing a person's name and address: *to leave one's calling card.* 2 a trace or identifying mark: *Independence is the calling card for companies selling franchises.* 3 a telephone charge card.
calliper same as CALIPER.
callisthenics same as CALISTHENICS.
call number *n.* a set of letters and numbers identifying a library book and its place on the shelves.
call of duty *n.* duty that is required by one's job: *an award for service above and beyond the call of duty.*
call of nature *n.* the need to urinate or defecate.
cal.los.i.ty (cal.OS.i.tee) *n.* **-ties 1** callousness. **2** a callus.
cal.lous (CAL.us) *adj.* **1** toughened: *A callus is an area of skin become callous by constant pressure or friction.* **2** insensitive: *He showed callous disregard for her condition; He seems callous to suffering; It was callous of him to ignore her.* —**cal.lous.ly** *adv.;* **cal.lous.ness** *n.*
cal.low (CAL.oh) *adj.* youthful and inexperienced: *a callow lad, youth.* —**cal.low.ness** *n.*
call-up *n.* a summons to military service.
cal.lus (CAL.us) *n.* **cal.lus.es** a tough, thickened area of skin or bark: *If you wear tight shoes, calluses may appear on the soles of your feet.* —*v.* form a callus on the skin: *Hard physical labor callused his hands;* *adj.: Soak the **callused** area in warm water.*
calm (CAHM) *n.* **1** a state of peacefulness; serenity: *Nothing could disturb the calm of her repose.* **2** at sea, a time or condition of no wind; doldrums: *the calm before the storm.* —*adj.* peaceful: *a calm and cool reaction.* —*v.* make or become quiet: *We tried to calm her; to calm her fears; Will you **calm down** and stop screaming?* —**calm.ly** *adv.;* **calm.ness** *n.*
cal.o.mel (CAL.uh.mel) *n.* mercurous chloride, a tasteless, white powder used as a purgative.
ca.lor.ic (cuh.LOR.ic) *adj.* energy-producing: *the caloric value of foods.*
cal.o.rie (CAL.uh.ree) *n.* **-ries 1** a unit for measuring heat energy. **2** the amount of energy produced by a food when used up by the body: *food calories; A workman needs up to 6,000 calories a day; A boiled egg supplies about 80 calories; She **counts calories** (of everything she eats); Junk food is high in calories but they are empty calories with little nutritive value.*
cal.o.rif.ic (cal.uh.RIF.ic) *adj.* productive of heat: *the calorific value of a fuel.*
cal.o.rim.e.ter (cal.uh.RIM.uh.tur) *n.* a device for measuring heat; **cal.o.ri.met.ric** (-ruh.MET.ric) *adj.* —**cal.o.rim.e.try** (-RIM.muh.tree) *n.* the measuring of heat.
cal.u.met (CAL.yuh.met) *n.* an ornamented, ceremonial pipe of the American Indians; also called "peace pipe."
ca.lum.ni.ate (cuh.LUM.nee.ate) *v.* **-ates, -at.ed, -at.ing** slander; malign; **ca.lum.ni.a.tion** (-AY.shun) *n.;* **ca.lum.ni.a.tor** (-ay.tur) *n.*
cal.um.ny (CAL.um.nee) *n.* **-nies** a malicious falsehood or accusation: *They heaped calumny on him.* —**ca.lum.ni.ous** (cuh.LUM.nee.us) *adj.;* **ca.lum.ni.ous.ly** *adv.*
calve (CAV) *v.* **calves, calved, calv.ing** bear a calf. —**calves** *pl.* of CALF.
Cal.vin.ism (CAL.vuh.niz.um) *n.* the doctrines of **John Calvin,** a French theologian, esp. predestination and salvation by grace. —**Cal.vin.ist** *n. & adj.* —**Cal.vin.is.tic** (-NIS.tic) *adj.*
calyces a *pl.* of CALYX.
ca.lyp.so (cuh.LIP.soh) *n.* **-sos** a type of West Indian folk song: *They danced to calypso rhythms.*
ca.lyx (CAY.lix, CAL.ix) *n.* **-lyx.es** or **-ly.ces** (-luh.seez) the outer ring of usu. green, leaflike sepals covering a flower bud.
cam *n.* a noncircular wheel used to give an up-and-down or eccentric motion to a connected part.
ca.ma.ra.de.rie (cam.uh.RAD.uh.ree) *n.* fellowship and loyalty among friends or comrades.
cam.ber (CAM.bur) *n.* **1** a slight upward arching, as of a road surface in the middle. **2** the adjustment of automobile wheels to make them closer together at the bottom. —*v.* to arch upward slightly.

cam.bi.um (CAM.bee.um) *n.* **-bi.ums** or **-bi.a** (-bee.uh) the layer of growing cells between the wood and bark of woody plants.

Cam.bo.di.an (cam.BOH.dee.un) *n. & adj.* (a person) of or from the Southeast Asian country of **Cambodia**.

Cam.bri.an (CAM.bree.un) *n.* the earliest period of the Paleozoic era of the earth beginning about 600 million years ago; *adj.*: *Cambrian rocks and fossils.*

cam.bric (CAME.bric) *n.* a delicate white linen or cotton fabric.

cam.cord.er (CAM.cor.dur) *n.* a camera-equipped videotape recorder for taking pictures and viewing them immediately afterward.

came *pt.* of COME.

cam.el (CAM.ul) *n.* a domestic, cud-chewing beast of burden with a humped back and long neck: *the two-humped Bactrian camel; an Arabian camel.*

cam.el.back (CAM.ul.back) *n.* **1** the back of a camel: *We crossed the desert on camelback.* **2** a rubber compound used in retreading tires.

ca.mel.li.a (cuh.MEEL.yuh) *n.* **1** a shrub of the tea family from Asia, esp. japonica. **2** its roselike flower.

ca.mel.o.pard (cuh.MEL.uh.pard) *n. Archaic.* the giraffe.

Cam.e.lot (CAM.uh.lot) *n.* an idyllic place of happiness, like the legendary King Arthur's court.

camel's hair *n.* a fabric made with camel's hair or a substitute: *The artist's camel's-hair brush is made of squirrel's-tail hair.*

Cam.em.bert (CAM.um.bare) *n.* a creamy, rich cheese of French origin.

cam.e.o (CAM.ee.oh) *n.* **-os 1** a small carving raised above its background, as on a layered gem, shell, medallion, etc. **2** in drama, television, or films, a brief appearance by a famous person: *a cameo role.* —*v.* **-os, -oed, -o.ing** portray or present in cameo.

cam.er.a (CAM.uh.ruh) *n.* an apparatus for taking photographs or motion pictures: *a TV camera; video camera; She refused to be interviewed on camera* (= live); *an off-camera interview;* **camera-ready** *copy prepared for photographic reproduction, as in printing.* —**in camera** in privacy.

cam.er.a.man (CAM.uh.ruh.man, -mun) *n.* **-men** a TV or movie camera operator.

cam.i.sole (CAM.uh.sole) *n.* a woman's sleeveless waist-length undergarment.

cam.o.mile (CAM.uh.mile) same as CHAMOMILE.

cam.ou.flage (CAM.uh.flahzh) *n.* **1** an appearance or disguise that imitates the surroundings. **2** materials for such a disguise. **3** any deceptive concealment. —*v.* **-flag.es, -flaged, -flag.ing** to conceal by camouflage: *tanks camouflaged with saplings.*

camp *n.* **1** a group of rough and temporary shelters, esp. military or recreational, usu. in the country; also, the members or location of such a group: *to pitch a camp; an army camp; an armed camp (of rioters); fishing camps; mining camps; a summer camp for children; trailer camp; We'll* **break camp** (= pack up) *and leave at dawn;* **adj.**: *a camp bed, chair, meeting; camp experiences; a woman's short-sleeved* **camp shirt** *with a notched collar and two breast pockets.* **2** a side in a debate or fight: *He belongs to the opposite camp.* **3** something so exaggerated, unnatural, or outlandish as to be considered amusing: *high camp; low camp.* —*adj.* outlandish or oversentimental in appeal: *camp art, clothes, fashions; dresses and oversized camp shirts.* —*v.* make, shelter in, or live in a camp; also **camp out**.

cam.paign (cam.PAIN) *n.* an organized activity aimed at a specific goal: *an election campaign; fund-raising campaign; whispering campaign (of spreading slander); to organize, mount or launch, conduct or wage a campaign.* —*v.* to conduct a campaign: *The candidate campaigned from door to door, for freedom, and against censorship.* —**cam.paign.er** *n.*

cam.pa.ni.le (cam.puh.NEE.lee) *n.* **-les** or **-li** (-lee) a bell tower, usu. one built as a separate structure.

cam.per (CAM.pur) *n.* **1** one who lives in a camp, esp. a recreational camp. **2** a vehicle adapted for camping: *a camper truck.*

camp.fire *n.* **1** an open fire at a camp. **2** the gathering or meeting held around it.

camp follower *n.* an unofficial member of a party; hanger-on.

camp.ground *n.* a camping area, often public, with facilities provided.

cam.phor (CAM.fur) *n.* an aromatic, medicinal gum obtained from an evergreen tree of the laurel family.

cam.phor.at.ed (CAM.fuh.ray.tid) *adj.* treated with camphor: *camphorated oil.*

camp meeting *n.* an evangelistic meeting held outdoors and lasting several days.

camp.o.ree (cam.puh.REE) *n.* a regional assembly or outing of Scouts or Guides; cf. JAMBOREE.

camp.site *n.* a place fit or prepared for a camp.

camp.stool *n.* a portable, folding stool.

cam.pus (CAM.pus) *n.* **-pus.es** the land and buildings of an educational institution: *the university campus; students living on campus; off-campus activities.*

camp.y *adj.* **camp.i.er, -i.est** interesting because exaggerated or unusual: *campy acting, fun; campy pink flamingo statues.*

cam.shaft *n.* the shaft on which a cam is mounted.

¹**can** *auxiliary v., pt.* **could** (COOD, short "OO") [indicating] **1** ability: *He can swim; He can be nasty at times.* **2** likelihood: *What could have happened to him?* **3** capacity or permission; may: *I can not accept that check; You can go now.*

²**can** *n.* **1** a metal container or what it contains: *garbage can; milk can; tin can; a can of peas.* **2** *Slang.* jail. **3** *Slang.* toilet. —*v.* **cans, canned, can.ning 1** preserve in cans or jars: *We can tomatoes;* adj.: *a jar of canned preserves.* **2** *Slang.* fire someone from a job. **3** *Informal.* stop: *Can that chatter!*

Ca.naan (CAY.nun) *n.* a promised land, as the biblical Palestine promised by God to the Israelites. —**Ca.naan.ite** *n.*

Canada goose (CAN.uh.duh-) *n.* a wild goose with a black head and neck, seen migrating south from Canada for the winter. Also **Canada**: *a flock of Canadas going south.*

Ca.na.di.an (cuh.NAY.dee.un) *n. & adj.* (a person) of or from Canada: *a Canadian by birth; Lee is a **New Canadian** who has recently come to Canada as a landed immigrant.* —**Ca.na.di.an.ness** *n.*

Ca.na.di.a.na (cuh.NAY.dee.AN.uh) *n.pl.* things of Canadian cultural interest, as art, books, furniture, etc.; *adja.: a Canadiana collection, museum.*

Canadian football *n.* the Canadian version of North American football with 12 players on each side instead of 11 and played on a field of different size from American football.

Canadian French *n.* the French language as used in Quebec and elsewhere in Canada.

Ca.na.di.an.ism (cuh.NAY.dee.uh.niz.um) *n.* **1** a word, pronunciation, usage, or custom distinctive of Canada or Canadians, as using "Eh?" at the end of a sentence. **2** devotion to Canada and its customs, traditions, etc.; also, the state of being distinctively Canadian: *Canadianism is tied to national unity.* —**Ca.na.di.an.ist** *n.*

Ca.na.di.an.ize (cuh.NAY.dee.uh.nize) *v.* **-iz.es, -ized, -iz.ing** make Canadian in character, customs, ownership, etc.: *to Canadianize industries.*

Ca.na.di.en (cuh.nay.dee.EN) *n.* a French Canadian; **Ca.na.di.enne** (cuh.nay.dee.EN), *fem.*

ca.naille (cuh.NAIL) *n.* riffraff; rabble: *the dirty canaille of the streets.*

ca.nal (cuh.NAL) *n.* **1** an artificial waterway: *a shipping canal; an irrigation canal.* **2** a duct or passage in the body: *the alimentary canal; the birth canal.*

ca.nal.boat (cuh.NAL.boat) *n.* a barge for use on canals.

ca.nal.ize (CAN.ul.ize, cuh.NAL.ize) *v.* **-iz.es, -ized, -iz.ing 1** build a canal or canals through an area. **2** direct something into or provide with a channel or outlet: *to canalize activities, energies, feelings.* —**ca.nal.i.za.tion** (can.ul.uh.ZAY.shun, -lye-) *n.*

ca.na.pé (CAN.uh.pee) *n.* a cracker or piece of toast, with a tasty topping, forming an appetizer: *anchovy canapés.*

ca.nard (cuh.NARD) *n.* a false rumor spread purposely; hoax.

ca.nar.y (cuh.NAIR.ee) *n.* **-nar.ies 1** a small, bright yellow songbird of the finch family. **2** a bright yellow; *adj.: a canary dress.*

ca.nas.ta (cuh.NAS.tuh) *n.* a card game developed from rummy played with two decks of cards.

can.can *n.* a lively French show dance characterized by high kicking.

can.cel (CAN.sul) *v.* **-cels, -celed, -cel.ing 1** cross out or delete: *to cancel a word; to cancel a postage stamp (to prevent re-use); to cancel a check (to make it invalid).* **2** annul or withdraw: *to cancel an appointment, game, meeting, order, reservation, show, subscription, trip.* **3** in arithmetic, to remove a common element from both parts of an equation or fraction. **4** neutralize or counterbalance: *The two arguments **cancel** (each other) **out**.* —*n.* a crossing out, annulment, or something canceled. —**can.cel.la.tion** (-suh.LAY.shun) *n.: The cancellation made the check nonnegotiable;* also **can.cel.a.tion**. Also **can.celled, can.cel.ling** *Cdn.*

can.cer (CAN.sur) *n.* **1** a malignant growth in a body part or the disease that causes it: *Smoking may lead to cancer of the lungs; One may develop lung cancer; She has breast cancer; inoperable*

cancer; terminal cancer; Electoral corruption is a cancer (= growing evil) *in the body politic.* **2 Cancer** *a* N. constellation and the fourth sign of the zodiac. **3** a person born under this sign.
—**can.cer.ous** *adj.*: *a cancerous growth.*
can.de.la.brum (can.duh.LAH.brum) *n.* a usu. ornamental candlestick with several branches; also **can.de.la.bra** (-bruh), **-bras.**
can.did *adj.* **1** truthful and sincere: *He was candid with me; candid about what he knew of the case; People don't always appreciate candid criticism.* **2** informal; unposed: *a few candid shots; The candid camera* (used for quick informal pictures) *never lies.* —**can.did.ly** *adv.*
can.di.da.cy (CAN.duh.duh.see) *n.* the act or condition of being a candidate: *He announced his candidacy; She withdrew her candidacy; His candidacy was unopposed.*
can.di.date (CAN.duh.date, -dit) *n.* **1** one who competes for a position: *an electoral candidate; a candidate for mayor.* **2** one who is eligible: *a Ph.D. candidate; a candidate for admission to the school.* **3** one that is suited for something: *Newsprint is a prime candidate for recycling.*
can.died (CAN.deed) *adj.* encrusted or cooked with sugar: *candied apples, dates, fruit; candied* (= sweet or flattering) *words.*
can.dle (CAN.dul) *n.* a usu. cylindrical mass of tallow, wax, etc. with a wick of fiber through it, which is burned for the light of its flame: *A candle is lit.* —**burn the candle at both ends** work too hard without getting enough rest.
can.dle.light (CAN.dul.lite) *n.* light shed by a candle: *to dine by candlelight.*
can.dle.lit (CAN.dul.lit) *adj.* lighted by candles: *a candlelit dinner.*
can.dle.pow.er (CAN.dul.pow.ur) *n.* light intensity, as measured by a standard unit called a "candle."
can.dle.stick (CAN.dul.stick) *n.* a holder for a single candle.
can.dle.wick (CAN.dul.wick) *n.* cotton yarn used for wicks and for embroidery.
can-do (CAN.doo) *adj. Informal.* willing and able to carry out a task: *a can-do attitude, image, person, spirit, style.*
can.dor (CAN.dur) *n.* the quality of being candid: *the candor of a child's expression; She spoke with complete candor; Her candor was disarming.* Also **can.dour** *Cdn.*
can.dy (CAN.dee) *n.* **-dies** (-dees) a sweet food made in various shapes with fruit, nuts, flavoring, etc.
—*v.* **-dies, -died, -dy.ing** encrust with sugar: *a recipe for candying apples;* **adj.**: *candied apples; candied dates; candied* (= sweet or flattering) *words.*
candy cane *n.* a red-striped Christmastime peppermint candy in the shape of a walking stick with a curved handle.
candy floss same as COTTON CANDY.
candy-striped *adj.* with thin, bright-colored stripes on a plain, usu. white background.
candy striper *n.* a young volunteer nursing assistant.
cane *n.* **1** a thin, woody, usu. flexible stem of a grass like sugar cane or bamboo, of certain palms, or of plants like the raspberry. **2** such a plant itself. **3** material for weaving into chairs, baskets, etc. **4** a walking stick. **5** a rod for flogging. —*v.* **canes, caned, can.ing 1** make or repair with cane. **2** flog.
cane.brake *n.* a dense growth of cane plants.
cane sugar *n.* sugar made from sugar cane.
can.ine (CAY.nine) *adj.* having to do with the group of animals that includes dogs, jackals, wolves, and foxes: *the canine devotion of a pet dog.*
—*n.* **1** a dog. **2** one of the four sharp teeth between the incisors and pre-molars; also **canine tooth.**
can.is.ter (CAN.is.tur) *n.* **1** light container of metal, plastic, etc. with a lid, used for storing tea, flour, crackers, etc. **2** a cylindrical projectile containing shot, tear gas, etc. **3** the boxlike tank or container of a vacuum cleaner; also, a vacuum cleaner equipped with one. **4** the boxlike filtering part of a gas mask.
can.ker (CANK.ur) *n.* **1** a disease that eats away tissue, as a rot or rust in plants. **2** a small sore in the mouth, or **canker sore. 3** a plant-eating insect larva, or **can.ker.worm.** —**can.ker.ous** *adj.*
can.na (CAN.uh) *n.* a tropical plant grown for its large leaves and bright, irregular flowers.
can.na.bis (CAN.uh.bis) *n.* **1** the dried flowering tops of the female hemp plant, the source of marijuana and hashish. **2** marijuana. **3** the plant itself.
canned *pt. & pp.* of CAN: *canned beef, food, fruit, goods.* —*adj.* recorded for reproduction: *canned applause, laughter,*

music; *a newspaper with many cartoons, crossword puzzles, and such canned* (= stock) *features*.
can.ner (CAN.ur) *n.* one that cans: *home canners; a pressure canner*.
can.ner.y (CAN.uh.ree) *n.* **can.ner.ies** a canning factory.
can.ni.bal (CAN.uh.bul) *n.* **1** one who eats human flesh: *a tribe of cannibals*. **2** an animal, as a spider, that feeds on its own kind. **3** a brutal savage. —**can.ni.bal.ism** *n.* —**can.ni.bal.is.tic** (-buh.LIS.tic) *adj.*
can.ni.bal.ize (CAN.uh.buh.lize) *v.* **-iz.es, -ized, -iz.ing** tear up old equipment, machines, etc. for parts to repair other equipment with: *He cannibalized a lawn mower and a motorbike to build his go-cart*.
can.nis.ter (CAN.is.tur) same as CANISTER.
can.non (CAN.un) *n.* **-nons** or **-non** a large, heavy gun mounted on a platform or carriage which fires a heavy metal shot: *to load and fire a cannon*.
can.non.ade (can.uh.NADE) *n.* a prolonged volley of cannon fire. Also *v.* **-ades, -ad.ed, -ad.ing**.
can.non.ball (CAN.un.ball) *n.* a heavy metal ball used as a cannon shot. —*v. Informal*. move quickly and with great force.
can.non.eer (can.uh.NEER) *n.* one who tends and fires cannon.
cannon fodder *n.* soldiers considered merely as expendable war materiel.
can.not (CAN.ot, cuh.NOT) [the commoner and less emphatic form of "can not"] can not: *I cannot sing; I cannot but* (= must) *admire his singing*.
can.nu.la (CAN.yuh.luh) *n.* **-las** or **-lae** (-lee) a narrow, surgical drainage tube inserted into a cavity, tumor, duct, etc. in the body.
can.ny (CAN.ee) *adj.* **can.ni.er, can.ni.est 1** shrewd or cunning: *a canny businessman, politician, trader*. **2** thrifty: *a canny landlord*. —**can.ni.ly** *adv.*
ca.noe (cuh.NOO) *n.* **-noes** a slender boat with pointed ends, usu. moved by paddles: *a birchbark canoe*. —*v.* **-noes, -noed, noe.ing** travel or transport in a canoe: *He canoed the load across the bay*.
ca.noe.ist (cuh.NOO.ist) *n.* one who paddles a canoe.
can of worms *n. Informal*. a source of trouble; Pandora's box.
ca.no.la (cuh.NOH.luh) *n.* **1** a variety of the rape plant, used as fodder and for its oil; formerly, rape, rapeseed. **2** the oil or meal prepared from it.

can.on (CAN.un) *n.* **1** a principle or rule of behavior: *This goes against the canons of good taste, decency*. **2** a law or rule of the church: *Nearly 1,800 canons comprise the Code of Canon Law*. **3** a list of items accepted as genuine and essential to a body of works: *to establish the canon of Shakespeare's works; books that are outside the canon of the Bible; the Confucian canon*. **4** a cleric serving in a cathedral. **5** a form of music, as a round, involving two or more parts or voices.
ca.ñon (CAN.yun) same as CANYON.
ca.non.i.cal (cuh.NON.i.cul) *adj.* **1** accepted or authoritative: *the canonical books of the Bible*. **2** according to canon law. —**ca.non.i.cal.ly** *adv.*
can.on.ize (CAN.uh.nize) *v.* **-iz.es, -ized, -iz.ing** in the Catholic Church, declare officially as a saint in Heaven. —**can.on.iz.a.tion** (-nuh.ZAY.shun) *n.*
canon law *n.* a body of laws and regulations of the Catholic Church.
can.o.py (CAN.uh.pee) *n.* **-pies** (-pees) an overhanging cover, esp. for ornamentation or protection: *A canopy is used over a four-poster bed; a canopy of trees; the canopy* (= cockpit cover) *of an airplane*. —*v.* **-pies, -pied, -py.ing** cover with a canopy; *adj.*: *a canopied entrance*.
canst [old use] the form of CAN used with "thou."
cant *n.* **1** language that is peculiar or exclusive: *thieves' cant* (= argot); *lawyer's cant* (= jargon). **2** empty, hypocritical, conventional speech: *all this cant about virtue*; *v.*: *They will cant about charity but won't give a penny*. **3** a sloping or angled surface, edge, or position; slant.
can't (CANT) cannot.
can.ta.bi.le (cahn.TAH.bi.lay) *adj. & adv. Music*. in a fluid, songlike style.
can.ta.loupe (CAN.tuh.lope) *n.* a small, orange-fleshed muskmelon with a hard, ribbed rind. Also **can.ta.loup**.
can.tan.ker.ous (can.TANK.uh.rus) *adj.* quarrelsome or bad-tempered: *a cantankerous old man*.
can.ta.ta (cuh.TAH.tah) *n.* a piece of choral music with solos and accompaniment, usu. dramatic, though not acted.
can.teen (can.TEEN) *n.* **1** a place that sells refreshments and small provisions: *a factory canteen*. **2** a recreation center, esp. at a military base. **3** a small metal flask for liquids, usu. canvas-covered.
can.ter (CAN.tur) *n.* a gentle gallop: *He*

rode at a canter. —*v.*: *The horse cantered along.*

can.ti.cle (CAN.ti.cul) *n.* a song or chant, usu. from the Bible, used in a church service.

can.ti.le.ver (CAN.tuh.lee.vur) *n.* a projecting structure or support fastened only at one end, as under a balcony or at either end of a bridge.

can.to (CAN.toh) *n.* **-tos** a major division of a long poem.

can.ton (CAN.tun) *n.* **1** an administrative division, as in France, Quebec, etc. **2** a territorial division, esp. a state in Switzerland. —*v.* **1** divide or apportion. **2** quarter troops in lodgings. —**can.ton.al** *adj.*: *a cantonal election.*

Can.ton.ese (can.tuh.NEEZ) *n.* **1** *sing. & pl.* a person of or from Canton, China. **2** the regional language of Canton. —*adj.*: *the Cantonese dialect; a Cantonese restaurant.*

can.ton.ment (can.TONE.munt, can.TON.munt, "TON" rhymes with "ON") *n.* **1** the billeting of troops. **2** a temporary housing for troops.

can.tor (CAN.tur) *n.* a solo or lead singer in a church or synagogue.

Ca.nuck (cuh.NUCK) *adj. Slang.* Canadian: *my Canuck friend*; *n.*: *a cute young Canuck; "Johnny Canuck" is supposed to personify Canada.*

can.vas (CAN.vus) *n.* **1** a strong, coarsely woven cloth used for sails, tents, etc.: *canvas deck shoes.* **2** something made using canvas, as an oil painting on canvas. —**under canvas 1** with sails spread. **2** in tents. —*v.* **-vas.es, -vased, -vas.ing** cover with canvas.

can.vas.back (CAN.vus.back) *n.* a North American wild duck with a gray back and reddish head and neck.

can.vass (CAN.vus) *v.* **1** go about asking for something; solicit: *to canvass donations, opinions, orders, votes; She's canvassing for the Heart Fund; He has canvassed everyone in sight and every house on this street.* **2** examine thoroughly or consider in detail: *to canvass ballots after votes are cast.* —*n.* **1** a soliciting: *a door-to-door canvass for the election candidate.* **2** examination: *a complete canvass of the proposal.* —**can.vass.er** *n.*

can.yon (CAN.yun) *n.* a deep narrow valley with high, sheer walls; gorge.

caou.tchouc (COW.chook) *n.* rubber in crude form.

cap *n.* **1** a soft, light head-covering: *a baseball cap; bathing cap; nurse's cap; skull cap; The graduates came to the ceremonies in cap* (= mortarboard) *and gown; She put on her thinking cap* (= started thinking); *He came to us **cap in hand*** (= humbly). **2** any covering, lid, or topmost part: *bottle caps; mushroom caps; The budget places a cap* (= upper limit) *on expenditures.* **3** percussion cap, esp. a small explosive charge in a paper capsule for use in a toy gun called a **cap pistol** or **cap gun**. —*v.* **caps, capped, cap.ping 1** place a cap on something; cover. **2** improve on something; outdo: *He can cap that trick.*

ca.pa.bil.i.ty (cay.puh.BIL.i.tee) *n.* **-ties** ability or potential: *She demonstrated her capabilities on the very first day; the capability to do a good job; a job that is within and not beyond her capabilities; the nuclear capability of the superpowers.*

ca.pa.ble (CAY.puh.bul) *adj.* competent: *a capable manager; He's quite capable; He did a capable job.* —**capable of** with the potential for something: *He is quite capable of winning the scholarship; a problem that is capable of solution.* —**ca.pa.bly** *adv.*

ca.pa.cious (cuh.PAY.shus) *adj.* able to hold a great deal: *a capacious dining room.* —**ca.pa.cious.ly** *adv.*; **ca.pa.cious.ness** *n.*

ca.pac.i.tance (cuh.PAS.i.tunce) *n.* an electric nonconductor's ability to store energy, measured as the ratio of charge on either of two opposite surfaces of the nonconductor to the potential between them. —**ca.pac.i.tive** *adj.*: *capacitive coupling, reactance.*

ca.pac.i.tate (cuh.PAS.i.tate) *v.* **-tates, -tat.ed, -tat.ing** make fit, able, or ready.

ca.pac.i.tor (cuh.PAS.i.tur) *n.* an electrical device for holding a stored charge in a circuit; formerly called condenser.

ca.pac.i.ty (cuh.PAS.i.tee) *n.* **-ties 1** the ability to do something: *your earning capacity; a woman of great mental capacity; her capacity for learning; a theater with a large seating capacity; a storage capacity of 30 tons.* **2** maximum ability: *a factory operating or running or working **at capacity**; at below, full, maximum, near, 90-percent, partial, peak, rated, reduced capacity; The theater was filled **to capacity*** (= to the limit); *A **capacity crowd** filled the theater.* **3** position or role: *He was acting in his official capacity; in an advisory capacity; in his capacity as president.*

cap-a-pie (cap.uh.PEE) *adv.* from head to foot: *armed cap-a-pie.*

ca.par.i.son (cuh.PAIR.uh.sun) *n.* a decorative covering for a horse and its harness; rich finery. —*v.* cover with rich finery: *The trees were caparisoned in autumn gold.*

cape *n.* **1** a full, sleeveless outer garment hanging from the shoulders. **2** a point of land projecting into a sea, lake, river, etc.: *the Cape of Good Hope.*

Cape buffalo See BUFFALO.

Cape Cod cottage *n.* a compact bungalow, usu. single-storied, with a central chimney and gabled roof.

ca.peesh (cuh.PEESH) *Slang.* **1** do you understand? **2** I understand.

cape.let (CAPE.lit) *n.* a short cape.

cape.lin (CAPE.lin) *n.* a small fish of the smelt family.

ca.per (CAY.pur) *n.* **1** a light playful jump. **2** a prank or trick: *a childish caper; the 1980 Canadian caper of rescuing Americans trapped in Iran.* **3** *Informal.* a crime. —**cut a caper** or **cut capers** to frolic about; also, play a prank: *Clowns like to cut capers before a crowd.* —*v.* leap about or frolic: *a lamb capering across the meadow.*

cap.ful *n.* the amount that a bottle cap can hold.

cap gun See CAP, *n.* 3.

cap.il.lar.i.ty (cap.uh.LAIR.i.tee) *n.* **-ties** the interaction of a solid and liquid surface that results in attraction or repulsion of the liquid.

cap.il.lar.y (CAP.uh.lair.ee, cuh.PIL.uh.ree) *adj.* **1** having a small bore; hairlike: *a capillary tube.* **2** having to do with capillarity: *capillary action, or attraction, of a liquid on the walls of a tube.* —*n., pl.* **-il.lar.ies** a capillary tube, esp. any of the tiny blood vessels linking the arteries to the veins.

cap.i.tal (CAP.uh.tul) *adj.* **1** most important or serious: *an act of capital folly.* **2** excellent: *a capital meal; a capital young lady.* **3** having to do with long-term assets: *capital costs, equipment, expenditures, improvements, investments, resources, spending.* —*n.* **1** capital city: *municipal, national, provincial capitals; a world capital such as Tokyo or London; the crime capital* (= main center of crime) *of North America?* **2** a capital letter. **3** the often ornate top of a pilaster or column. **4** material or financial assets engaged in or available for business expenditure: *to invest, raise, tie up, withdraw capital; The Republicans made political capital* (= gain) *out of the scandal involving the Democrats; the working capital (for running a business).* **5** capitalists or investors collectively: *Much capital left the country during the last recession.* —**cap.i.tal.ly** *adv.*

capital city *n.* chief city, esp. a governmental center.

capital gain *n.* profit made from the sale of real estate, bonds, and such assets: *a capital gains tax.*

capital goods *n.pl.* goods such as machinery and equipment used in the production of other goods.

capital-intensive *adj.* requiring the investment of capital more than of labor: *Atomic power plants are capital-intensive whereas coal-burning plants are labor-intensive.*

cap.i.tal.ism (CAP.uh.tuh.liz.um) *n.* an economic system with free markets and private ownership of capital.

cap.i.tal.ist (CAP.uh.tuh.list) *n.* **1** a person who owns invested capital. **2** one who supports capitalism. —**cap.i.tal.is.tic** (-LIS.tic) *adj.*

cap.i.tal.ize (CAP.uh.tuh.lize) *v.* **-iz.es, -ized, -iz.ing 1** write with or as a capital letter: *Names are capitalized.* **2** take advantage of or profit from something: *to capitalize on someone else's bad luck.* **3** supply capital for something: *to capitalize a business venture.*

capital letter *n.* an uppercase letter, as A, B, or C.

capital offense *n.* an offense punishable by death.

capital punishment *n.* the death penalty: *to impose capital punishment.*

capital ship *n.* a warship of the highest rank.

capital stock *n.* the total amount of capital invested in a corporation issued as shares.

cap.i.ta.tion (cap.uh.TAY.shun) *n.* a per-capita tax or levy: *capitation fees.*

cap.i.tol (CAP.uh.tul) *n.* a legislature building in the U.S.

ca.pit.u.late (cuh.PICH.uh.late) *v.* **-lates, -lat.ed, -lat.ing** surrender or yield: *He finally capitulated to their demands.* —**cap.i.tu.la.tion** (-LAY.shun) *n.*

cap.let (CAP.lit) *n.* a coated medicine tablet that is oval-shaped like a capsule.

cap.lin (CAP.lin) same as CAPELIN.

ca.pon (CAY.pon, *rhyme:* on) *n.* a rooster, castrated and fattened for eating.

cap.o.ral (CAP.uh.rul) *n.* a kind of tobacco.

ca.pote (cuh.POTE) *n.* a hooded cloak or cape

cap pistol See CAP, *n.* 3.

cap.puc.ci.no (cap.oo.CHEE.noh) *n.* -nos a hot beverage made of espresso coffee and steamed milk, topped with whipped cream.

ca.pric.cio (cuh.PREE.chee.oh) *n.* -pric.cios or -pric.ci (-chee) *Music.* an imaginative instrumental piece with a spirited tempo and free form

ca.price (cuh.PREECE) *n.* a change of mind without any apparent reason; whim; fickleness: *He did it merely out of caprice; It was pure caprice on his part.* —**ca.pri.ci.ous** (cuh.PRISH.us) *adj.*: *a capricious lover; capricious weather.* —**ca.pri.ci.ous.ly** *adv.*; **ca.pri.ci.ous.ness** *n.*

Cap.ri.corn (CAP.ri.corn) *n.* 1 a S. constellation and the 10th sign of the zodiac. Also **Cap.ri.corn.us.** 2 a person born under this sign.

cap.si.cum (CAP.suh.cum) *n.* a small shrubby plant of the nightshade family, varieties of which bear hot and sweet peppers.

cap.size (CAP.size) *v.* **-siz.es, -sized, -siz.ing** overturn or upset: *The canoe capsized in the storm.*

cap.stan (CAP.stun) *n.* 1 an upright rotating cylinder on which a cable, as in lifting weights, is wound. 2 a similar spindle that moves the tape in a tape recorder at a constant speed.

cap.su.lar (CAP.suh.lur) *adj.* in, of, or like a capsule.

cap.sul.ate (CAP.suh.late) or **cap.sul.at.ed** (-lay.tid) *adj.* enclosed in a capsule.

cap.sule (CAP.sul, -sule) *n.* 1 an enclosed protective covering, as for seeds, spores, oral doses of medicine, etc. 2 a separable enclosure for people, instruments, etc. in an airplane or rocket: *The space capsule almost burned on re-entry.* —*v.* **-sules, -suled, -sul.ing** capsulize. —*adj.* brief and concise: *a capsule account, biography, course, history, news report.*

cap.sul.ize (CAP.suh.lize) *v.* **-iz.es, -ized, -iz.ing** 1 put into a capsule. 2 express concisely; *adj.*: *capsulized history, news.*

cap.tain (CAP.tun) *n.* 1 a leader: *the captain of the baseball team; a bell captain; captains* (= outstanding people) *of industry.* 2 a military officer ranking just below major. 3 a naval officer ranking just below commodore or rear admiral. 4 the commander of a ship, fortress, garrison, etc. 5 the chief pilot of an airliner. —*v.* lead: *He captained the squad all season.* —**cap.tain.cy** (-see) *n.* **-cies.**

—**cap.tain.ship** *n.*

cap.tion (CAP.shun) *n.* 1 a brief legend under a picture or cartoon. 2 a subtitle in a movie. 3 a heading or title. —*v.* put a caption on something: *The artist captions his own cartoons.*

cap.tious (CAP.shus) *adj.* 1 overly critical; carping. 2 designed to confuse and trap; sophistical: *captious questions.* —**cap.tious.ly** *adv.*; **cap.tious.ness** *n.*

cap.ti.vate (CAP.tuh.vate) *v.* **-vates, -vat.ed, -vat.ing** enthrall or charm: *He was captivated by her beauty.* —**cap.ti.va.tion** (-VAY.shun) *n.* —**cap.ti.va.tor** (-vay.tur) *n.*

cap.tive (CAP.tiv) *n.* 1 one who is confined against his will, esp. a prisoner of war. 2 one who is captivated. —*adj.* 1 captured and confined: *a captive bird; The prisoner hated his captive condition; They were taken and held captive* (= prisoner) *for many years.* 2 forced, as by circumstances: *the captive audience of a classroom; a captive clientele, market, resource; captive prison labour; to become, fall, remain captive to outdated practices.* —**cap.tiv.i.ty** (cap.TIV.i.tee) *n.*

cap.tor (CAP.tur) *n.* one who captures: *the captor and his captives.*

cap.ture (CAP.chur) *v.* **-tures, -tured, -tur.ing** 1 seize by force or other means: *Spiders trap and then capture insects; Her performance captured our attention; adj.*: *a captured city, prisoner, soldier.* 2 record: *the capturing of computer data by keyboarding, scanning, etc.; His face has been captured on film.* —*n.* the act of capturing or one that has been captured.

Cap.u.chin (CAP.yoo.chin) *n.* 1 a Franciscan friar distinguished by a special hood. 2 **capuchin** a type of South American monkey with hair on its crown resembling a monk's hood.

car *n.* 1 an automobile: *getaway, police, sports cars; to jack up, road-test, tune up a car.* 2 a wheeled vehicle on rails: *cattle, dining, railroad cars.* 3 a compartment for passengers, freight, etc. in an elevator, dirigible, etc.

ca.ra.bao (cah.ruh.BOW) *n.* **-baos** a water buffalo.

car.a.bi.neer or **car.a.bi.nier** (cair.uh.bi.NEER) *n.* a soldier equipped with a carbine.

car.a.cole (CAIR.uh.cole) *n.* in riding, a horse's half turn to either side. Also *v.* **-coles, -coled, -col.ing.**

ca.rafe (cuh.RAF) *n.* a bottle for serving wine, water, coffee, etc.

car.a.mel (CAIR.uh.mul) *n.* 1 syrupy

burnt sugar that is dark and bitter, used for coloring and flavoring. **2** a rich, chewy candy. —**car.a.mel.ize** *v.* **-iz.es, -ized, -iz.ing** turn to caramel or like caramel in color: *to caramelize sugar for glazes;* **adj.:** *caramelized* (= browned) *apples, bacon, onions.*

car.a.pace (CAIR.uh.pace) *n.* a bony protective shell, as of a turtle, lobster, etc.

car.at (CAIR.ut) *n.* **1** same as KARAT. **2** a unit of weight of gems, equal to 200 mg.

car.a.van (CAIR.uh.van) *n.* **1** a party of traders, pilgrims, etc. traveling together for safety; hence, a line of vehicles: *a circus caravan.* **2** a van.

car.a.van.sa.ry (cair.uh.VAN.suh.ree) *n.* **-ries** an inn for caravans; also **car.a.van.se.rai** (-rye, -ray), **-rais.**

car.a.vel (CAIR.uh.vel) *n.* a small sailing ship of the 15th and 16th centuries with a high stern and broad bow.

car.a.way (CAIR.uh.way) *n.* the aromatic seeds of a parsleylike herb used for seasoning; also, the herb.

car bed *n.* a small bed for an infant used in a car.

car.bide *n.* a compound of carbon and another element or metal; **adja.:** *carbide cutting tools, drill bits.*

car.bine (CAR.been, -bine) *n.* a light rifle with a short barrel. —**car.bi.neer** same as CARABINEER.

car.bo.hy.drate (car.boh.HYE.drate) *n.* a compound of carbon, oxygen, and hydrogen, as cellulose, starch, and sugar, that provides body energy.

car.bol.ic acid (car.BOL.ic-) *n.* a caustic compound with antiseptic and anesthetic properties.

car bomb *n.* a bomb planted in a car by a terrorist.

car.bon (CAR.bun) *n.* **1** the common element of all organic compounds, esp. coal, petroleum, and other fuels: *Diamond is pure carbon.* **2** a carbon paper or a carbon copy.

car.bo.na.ceous (car.buh.NAY.shus) *adj.* yielding, made of, or pertaining to carbon: *carbonaceous fuels, materials, plant debris, ores, shale.*

car.bon.ate (CAR.buh.nate) *v.* **-ates, -at.ed, -at.ing** mix with carbon dioxide; **adj.:** *Club soda is* **carbonated** *water; carbonated beverages.* —**car.bon.a.tion** (-NAY.shun) *n.*

carbon black *n.* a fine powdered carbon used as a pigment in ink.

carbon copy *n.* **1** a copy of a document made using carbon paper. **2** something very similar to its original: *a mere carbon copy of the foreign edition;* **carbon-copy** *v.*

carbon dating *n.* a technique for dating carboniferous artifacts, which measures their content of **carbon 14,** a radioactive isotope of carbon.

carbon dioxide *n.* a heavy, odorless, colorless, incombustible gas produced by fermentation, combustion, and respiration.

car.bon.i.fer.ous (car.buh.NIF.uh.rus) *adj.* **1** containing or yielding a form of carbon. **2 Carboniferous** of or from a period of the Paleozoic era of the earth beginning about 345 million years ago when much coal was formed; *n.* the period itself.

carbon monoxide *n.* a light, odorless, colorless, combustible, very poisonous gas, as produced by automobile engines.

carbon paper *n.* a thin sheet coated on one side with a carbon-based pigment and inserted between sheets of paper for copying what is being written or typed.

car.bo.run.dum (car.buh.RUN.dum) *n.* an abrasive made of silicon carbide. —**Carborundum** *Trademark.*

car.boy *n.* a large bottle, usu. for dangerous liquids, protected by a wicker basket or a box.

car.bun.cle (CAR.bunk.ul) *n.* **1** a painful inflammation under the skin which produces pus. **2** a red garnet. —**car.bun.cu.lar** (car.BUNK.yuh.lur) *adj.*

car.bu.ret.ed (CAR.buh.ray.tid) *adj.* equipped with a carburetor: *a carbureted, not fuel-injected engine.*

car.bu.re.tion (car.buh.RAY.shun) *n.* the process of mixing air and a vaporized hydrocarbon (as gasoline) for exploding in an engine.

car.bu.ret.or (CAR.buh.ray.tur) *n.* in internal combustion engines, a device which combines air and fuel for proper burning.

car.cass (CAR.cus) *n.* **1** an animal corpse, esp. one dressed for use as meat. **2** *Informal.* the human body. **3** useless remains: *the carcass of a wrecked car.*

car.cin.o.gen (car.SIN.uh.jun) *n.* a cancer-causing substance. —**car.ci.no.gen.ic** (CAR.sin.oh.JEN.ic) *adj.*

car.ci.no.ma (car.suh.NOH.muh) *n.* an epithelial cancer. —**car.ci.nom.a.tous** (-NOM.uh.tus) *adj.*

car.coat *n.* a hip-length jacket or coat.

card *n.* **1** a small, usu. stiff rectangular

piece of paper used for many purposes: *a business card; a calling card or visiting card; a plastic credit card for charging purchases to an account; a get-well card; a greeting card for a birthday or Christmas; an identity card; index cards for a card file; a membership card; playing cards; a report card showing a pupil's progress at school; score cards.* **2 cards** *pl.* any game using playing cards: *We **played cards** all evening; She **played her cards right** (= did well) at the job interview; A politician playing the race* or *racial **card** is playing on racial feelings; It was a game in which we **held all the cards** (= we had the advantage); A promotion is not **in** or **on the cards** (= not likely) for you this year; to **put** or **lay one's cards on the table** (= be open and straightforward).* **3** a program at an event, esp. sports. **4** *Informal.* a witty or eccentric person. **5** a computer's internal plug-in circuit board. **6** a wire brush for combing and cleaning unspun cotton or wool; *v.: to card wool;* **card.er** *n.*

card.board *n.* a thick board made of several layers of paper pulp; **adj.**: *a cardboard box; a cardboard* (= stereotyped) *character.*

card-carrying *adj.* **1** officially registered: *a card-carrying Communist.* **2** *Informal.* identifiable as such: *a card-carrying Nazi, neurotic, pacifist.*

card catalog *n.* a file usu. made on index cards and arranged in alphabetical order, esp. one for books; also **card file.**

card.hold.er (CARD.hole.dur) *n.* one who carries a bank card, credit card, or membership card.

car.di.ac (CAR.dee.ac) *adj.* having to do with the heart or heart disease: *a cardiac arrest, condition, disease, shock, surgeon, unit.*

car.di.gan (CAR.duh.gun) *n.* a sweater or knitted jacket that opens down the front.

car.di.nal (CAR.dun.ul) *n.* **1** a dignitary of the Roman Catholic Church ranking next below the pope. **2** a crested red finch of North America. **3** a bright red. —**adj.** principal: *a cardinal fact, goal, principle, rule, sign; a matter of cardinal importance; the four cardinal directions;* a **cardinal number** (= 1, 2, 3, etc. as opposed to the ordinals, 1st, 2nd, 3rd, etc.); *North, South, East, and West are the four **cardinal points** of the compass; The four **cardinal virtues** are fortitude, justice, prudence, and temperance.*

card index same as CARD CATALOG.

car.di.o.gram (CAR.dee.uh.gram) same as ELECTROCARDIOGRAM.

car.di.o.lo.gy (car.dee.OL.uh.jee) *n.* the study of the heart, its diseases, and their treatment. —**car.di.ol.o.gist** *n.*

car.di.o.pul.mo.nar.y (CAR.dee.oh.PUL.muh.nair.ee) *adj.* having to do with the heart and lungs: *A heart-attack victim is given **cardiopulmonary resuscitation** (CPR) to restore breathing and circulation.*

car.di.o.vas.cu.lar (CAR.dee.oh.VAS.kyuh.lur) *adj.* having to do with the heart and blood vessels.

card shark, card.sharp or **card.sharp.er** (CARD.sharp.ur) *n.* *Informal.* one skilled in winning card games by cheating.

care *n.* **1** worry or anxiety: *to be free from care.* **2** supervision: *patients under a doctor's care; the tender loving care of parents; children left in our care; entrusted to the care of foster parents; child care; children in need of day care; extended care for the elderly; a hospital's intensive care unit;* **cpd.**: *a health-care center, provider, worker; a long-term-care facility; personal-care and primary-care physicians; pharmacare* (= drug insurance). **3** attention or caution: *to exercise care; Handle with care; with the utmost care;* **Take care** *to fasten your seat belt.* —*v.* **cares, cared, car.ing 1** feel anxiety, interest, or liking: *Who cares? I care about the future;* **adj.**: *a warm and* **caring** *person.* **2** be concerned: *I could* or **couldn't care less** (= I don't care); *You can do what you like,* **for all I care** (= I don't care). —**care for 1** take care of someone: *Nurses care for the sick.* **2** desire: *Do you care for some coffee?* **3** like or want: *I don't care for it at all.* —**(in) care of** at the address of someone. —**take care of** look after someone: *Parents take care of children; Take care of yourself;* **Take care** (= Be careful)!

ca.reen (cuh.REEN) *v.* **1** tip a ship to one side, esp. for cleaning; tilt or lean. **2** rush headlong unsteadily: *The car careened downhill and hit a tree.*

ca.reer (cuh.REER) *n.* **1** the course of one's working life: *your business career; school career; He retired at 65 after a brilliant, distinguished, successful career in the army; She had a checkered career; a career as a diplomat; a program for teachers in mid career; She retired after a full career in the same company; The racing car broke down* **in full career** (= while going at full speed); *a career*

woman *(who continues in her profession after marriage).* **2** a special period of one's working life: *a career in business; He made or carved out a career for himself in the army; a* **career decision** *(that may affect one's career); a* **career diplomat** *(= a diplomat all through his or her career).* —*v.* move swiftly; hurtle.

care.free *adj.* without care or worry: *She leads a carefree life.*

care.ful *adj.* using care: *Be careful near the fire; Be careful not to touch it; He did a careful job; She's very careful about details; Be extremely careful with explosives.* —**care.ful.ly** *adv.*; **care.ful.ness** *n.*

care.giv.er (CARE.giv.ur) *n.* one who looks after a child or adult in need of care.

care.less (CARE.lis) *adj.* **1** showing lack of care: *a careless error, observation, worker; He was quite rash and careless about consequences; It was careless of him to drive without buckling up.* **2** carefree or effortless: *an easy, careless grace.* —**care.less.ly** *adv.*; **care.less.ness** *n.*

ca.ress (cuh.RES) *n.* **1** a loving touch, stroke, kiss, or hug. **2** a light touch: *the caress of a gentle breeze.* —*v.* touch lovingly or lightly: *They caressed each other; A warm breeze caressed her cheek.* —**ca.ress.ing.ly** *adv.*

car.et (CAIR.ut) *n.* the mark [ʌ] used to show where something is to be inserted in written or printed matter.

care.tak.er (CAIR.tay.kur) *n.* one hired to oversee and maintain property, buildings, etc., often in the owner's absence; **adja.:** *a caretaker (= temporary) government, prime minister.*

care.worn *adj.* marked by grief or anxiety: *a haggard, careworn face.*

car.fare *n.* the price of a bus or streetcar ride.

car.go *n.* **-gos** or **-goes** the goods loaded in a ship, airplane, truck, etc.; *to carry, haul, load, take on cargo;* **adja.:** *a cargo liner, plane, ship.*

car.goed (CAR.gode) *adj.* loaded: *ships cargoed with gold.*

car.hop *n.* one who waits on cars at a drive-in restaurant.

Car.ib (CAIR.ib) *adj.* [short form] Caribbean.

Car.ib.be.an (cair.uh.BEE.un) *adj.* having to do with the region between the West Indies and Central and South America: *Caribbean countries; the Caribbean Sea; a Caribbean vacation (on one of the Caribbean islands).* —*n.* **1** the Caribbean Sea: *hurricanes from the Caribbean.* **2** the Caribbean region: the Spanish-speaking Caribbean. **3** a person of or from the Caribbean region.

car.i.bou (CAIR.uh.boo) *n.* a large North American deer similar to the reindeer.

car.i.ca.ture (CAIR.uh.cuh.choor, -chur) *n.* an exaggerated or distorted picture or writing that makes fun of one's peculiarities: *"Don Quixote" is a caricature of the romantic hero.* —*v.* **-tures, -tured, -tur.ing** represent in caricature: *The politician was caricatured in the paper as a clown.* —**car.i.ca.tur.ist** (CAIR.uh.cuh.CHOOR.ist, -chuh.rist) *n.*

car.ies (CAIR.eez) *n.* decay affecting bones or teeth.

car.il.lon (CAIR.uh.lon, *rhyme:* on) *n.* **1** a set of tuned bells played by means of a keyboard. **2** the music played. —**car.il.lon.er** (-luh.nur) or **car.il.lon.neur** (-luh.NUR) *n.*

car.jack.ing (CAR.jack.ing) *n.* the forcible taking of another person's vehicle. —**car.jack.er** *n.*

car.load *n.* in shipping by rail, the amount that a freight car can hold.

car.min.a.tive (car.MIN.uh.tiv) *n.* a medicine used for purging gas from the digestive tract; *adj.: carminative action.*

car.mine (CAR.min, -mine) *n.* a deep red pigment produced from the cochineal insect; also, the color; also *adj.*

car.nage (CAR.nij) *n.* massive killing.

car.nal (CAR.nul) *adj.* **1** sensual or fleshly: *Lust is carnal; carnal desires; He was charged with having* **carnal knowledge** *of (= sex with) a minor.* **2** worldly: *carnal pleasure, pursuits.* —**car.nal.ly** *adv.* —**car.nal.i.ty** (car.NAL.i.tee) *n.*

car.na.tion (car.NAY.shun) *n.* **1** a cultivated herb with many-petaled red, purple, pink, yellow, or white flowers: *red carnations.* **2** the flower or its medium-red color.

car.nel.ian (car.NEEL.yun) *n.* a clear reddish chalcedony, used as a gemstone.

carney or **carnie** same as CARNY.

car.ni.val (CAR.nuh.vul) *n.* **1** the pre-Lent season of merrymaking or revelry; **adja.:** *a carnival atmosphere, dance; the carnival season, spirit; a charity ball with a carnival theme; Mardi Gras is carnival time in New Orleans; a carnival-style winter festival.* **2** a festival: *a carnival weekend get-together at a ski resort; a winter carnival complete with a carnival queen; The show is a carnival on ice; The Food Fair is a culinary carnival.*

3 a traveling outfit providing rides, games, etc. in public places.

car.ni.vore (CAR.nuh.vore) *n.* **1** a flesh-eating mammal, as a cat, dog, bear, or seal. **2** a plant that feeds on insects.

car.niv.or.ous (car.NIV.uh.rus) *adj.* flesh- or insect-eating: *a carnivorous animal, plant.*

car.ny, car.nie or **car.ney** (CAR.nee) *n.* **-nies** or **-neys** *Informal.* **1** a carnival or fair; *adj.: a carny midway, salesman, ride.* **2** a carnival worker. **3** a carney's argot or jargon: *The barker is talking carny.* —*adja.: popcorn, candied apples, and such carny food.*

car.ol (CAIR.ul) *n.* a joyous song, often devotional or laudatory: *Christmas carols.* —*v.* **car.ols, car.oled, car.ol.ing** **1** sing carols: *We used to go caroling on Christmas eve.* **2** sing joyously: *We could hear robins caroling to the spring.* Also **car.olled, car.ol.ling** *Cdn.*

car.om (CAIR.um) *n.* **1** a hit and rebound. **2** in billiards, a shot where the cue ball rebounds from one ball to strike another. —*v.* hit and rebound: *The truck caromed off the wall.*

car.o.tene (CAIR.uh.teen) *n.* a hydrocarbon, orangish-yellow to red, found in many plants, esp. carrots, and a source of Vitamin A for animals; also **car.o.tin.**

ca.rot.id (cuh.ROT.id) *adja.* having to do with the two large arteries that carry blood via the neck to the head. —*n.* either of these arteries, one on each side of the neck.

ca.rous.al (cuh.ROW.zul, "OW" as in "HOW") *n.* a noisy drinking party or spree; carouse.

ca.rouse (cuh.ROWZE) *v.* **-rous.es, -roused, -rous.ing** revel and drink heavily. —*n.* a rowdy drinking party.

car.ou.sel (cair.uh.SEL) *n.* a merry-go-round or a similar revolving device: *the baggage carousel at the arrivals level of an airport; a five-disc carousel player; a CD carousel changer.*

carp *n.* an edible, large-scaled fish found in quiet, fresh waters. —*v.* find fault pettily or captiously: *He's always carping at something or other; adja.: a carping critic with a carping tongue.*

car.pal (CAR.pul) *adj.* having to do with the wrist: *carpal bones, joints; The carpal tunnel syndrome characterized by tingling, numbness, and weakening of the hands afflicts keyboarders working under pressure.* See also REPETITIVE. —*n.* a wrist bone.

car.pe di.em (car.pee.DEE.em) *n. Latin.* the philosophy of making the most of present circumstances.

car.pel (CAR.pul) *n.* a leaflike, female, seed-producing part of a flower; a simple pistil.

car.pen.ter (CAR.pun.tur) *n.* a workman who builds and repairs wooden objects, as houses, ships, etc.; *adj.: a well carpentered house.* —**car.pen.try** (-tree) *n.*

car.pet (CAR.pit) *n.* thick, heavy covering for floors and stairs; also, a piece of it: *The boss called him on the carpet* (= reprimanded him) *for his negligence; a carpet of grass, leaves, snow.* —*v.* cover with carpet: *a room carpeted with broadloom.*

car.pet.bag.ger (CAR.pit.bag.ur) *n.* a person from the northern states exploiting unsettled conditions in the South during Reconstruction.

car.pet.ing (CAR.pit.ing) *n.* carpet material; also, carpets collectively: *wall-to-wall carpeting* (= floor covering).

car pool *n.* a cooperative of automobile commuters who take turns driving the others in his or her own car.

car.port *n.* an automobile shelter, usu. under an extension of a house's roof.

car.ra.geen.an or **car.ra.geen.in** (CAIR.uh.jee.nun) *n.* the extract from an edible, dark red, branching seaweed called **carrageen** or **carrageen moss.**

car.rel (CAIR.ul) *n.* an individual study space in a library, usu. enclosed.

car.riage (CAIR.ij) *n.* **1** a wheeled passenger vehicle: *a baby carriage; horse-drawn carriages.* **2** the transport of goods. **3** posture or bearing: *an erect, proud carriage.* **4** a movable support: *a gun carriage; typewriter carriage.*

carriage trade *n.* the wealthy, esp. their patronage.

car.ri.er (CAIR.ee.ur) *n.* **1** one that carries: *an aircraft carrier; letter carrier; a paper carrier doing a carrier route; A mosquito is the carrier of malaria; A carrier remains unaffected while infecting others.* **2** a commercial transporter: *a common carrier; public carriers.* **3** a box or basket on a vehicle, esp. a bicycle.

carrier pigeon *n.* a message-carrying pigeon.

carrier wave *n.* an electromagnetic wave carrying a signal, as sound or a picture.

car.rion (CAIR.ee.un) *n.* dead, rotting flesh. —*adja.* carrion-eating: *the carrion beetle, crow.*

car.rom (CAIR.um) same as CAROM.

car.rot (CAIR.ut) *n.* **1** the edible, orange root of a vegetable. **2** an inducement: *the carrot and the stick; a bunch of financial carrots to attract buyers.* —**car.rot.y** *adj.* red.

carrot-and-stick *adja.* alternately rewarding and punishing: *the carrot-and-stick approach, policy, technique.*

car.rou.sel same as CAROUSEL.

car.ry (CAIR.ee) *v.* **car.ries, car.ried, car.ry.ing 1** hold and convey; bear: *a donkey carrying a load; She carries herself with dignity; She is carrying* (= is pregnant with) *her second child; Her views carry a lot of weight* (*Informal for* are highly valued) *around here.* **2** transport: *a pipe carrying water.* **3** travel: *Voices carry over the water.* **4** hold: *Carry your head high.* **5** take: *They carried the joke a bit too far.* **6** win: *The motion carried; The ayes carried the day.* **7** entail: *Any job carries some responsibility.* **8** support a debtor, an enterprise, etc.: *He carried the firm through hard times.* **9** have for sale: *We don't carry that line of goods.* **10** publish or broadcast: *Stories carried by the morning papers are also carried on the evening news.* —**carry away** be unduly influenced: *He tends to get a little carried away sometimes; He was carried away by anger.* —**carry on 1** continue: *to carry on a conversation; He was carrying on with it past midnight; Let's carry on in spite of the weather.* **2** have an affair with someone: *He was carrying on with his neighbor's wife.* —**carry out** fulfill or perform: *to carry out a duty, plan, promise, threat.* —**carry over** move forward, as in bookkeeping. —*n., pl.* **car.ries 1** the act or manner of carrying: *the fireman's carry.* **2** the range of a projectile. **3** a portage.

car.ry.all (CAIR.ee.all) *n.* any very spacious carriage, automobile, shopping bag, etc.

carrying charge *n.* the interest charged for paying in installments.

carrying-on *n.* **carryings-on** improper behavior between two persons.

carry-on *n.* a piece of luggage small enough to fit under an airplane seat, which a passenger is allowed to carry on board: *a passenger with two carry-ons; adja.: carry-on and checked bags; carry-on baggage, items; carry-on and cargo-hold luggage.*

car.ry.out (CAIR.ee.out) same as TAKEOUT.

car.ry.o.ver (CAIR.ee.oh.vur) *n.* what is left over or carried over, as in bookkeeping: *a carryover of thirteen days' unfinished business.*

car.seat *n.* a removable seat for a child to ride safely in an automobile.

car.sick *adj.* nauseated, esp. while traveling in a car, train, etc. —**car.sick.ness** *n.*

cart *n.* **1** a sturdy, two-wheeled utility vehicle usu. drawn by horses, oxen, etc. **2** any light, wheeled vehicle: *a golf cart; grocery cart; shopping cart.* —**put the cart before the horse** reverse the right order of things. —*v.* transport or convey: *to cart produce to market; Despite their protests, the children were carted off to bed.*

cart.age (CAR.tij) *n.* transport by cart or truck; also, carting charge.

carte blanche (CART.blahnsh) *n., pl.* **cartes blanches** (CART.blahnsh) a free hand; full discretionary power: *It was as if industries had been given carte blanche to pollute the air and water.*

car.tel (car.TEL) *n.* a monopolistic group of commercial interests: *a closed cartel of medical specialists; to break up a cartel; Cartels tend to force prices up.*

cart.er *n.* one engaged in cartage.

Car.te.sian (car.TEE.zhun) *adj.* having to do with the French philosopher and mathematician René Descartes: *a Cartesian coordinate, plane, product.*

car.ti.lage (CAR.tul.ij) *n.* a flexible, tough tissue related to the bone; gristle: *a torn cartilage.* —**car.ti.lag.i.nous** (-tuh.LAJ.uh.nus) *adj.*

car.tog.ra.phy (car.TOG.ruh.fee) *n.* the science of making maps and charts; **car.tog.ra.pher** *n.* —**car.to.graph.ic** (-tuh.GRAF.ic) *adj.*

car.ton (CAR.tun) *n.* **1** a cardboard box. **2** a container in which milk, cigarettes, or other articles are sold; also, its contents.

car.toon (car.TOON) *n.* **1** a humorous or satirical drawing. **2** a comic strip. **3** an animated cartoon. —**car.toon.ist** *n.*

car.tridge (CAR.trij) *n.* **1** a case or capsule of material, as film, ink, and tape, for use in an apparatus: *a video-game cartridge.* **2** a usu. cylindrical case containing the explosive charge and primer for a gun: *a blank cartridge; spent cartridges.*

cart.wheel *n.* a sideways handspring: *to turn cartwheels for fun.*

carve (CARV) *v.* **carves, carved, carv.ing 1** cut out or form artistically; sculpture: *figurines carved in wood; a figure carved out of stone; adj.: carved woodwork.* **2** divide: *to carve up the meat into pieces; to carve* (= slice and serve) *a*

turkey; n.: *a carving knife.* —**carv.er** *n.*
carving *n.* a carved object or the act or occupation of making such objects: *an ivory carving; wood carvings; Wood carving is her hobby.*
car wash or **car.wash** *n.* a place equipped for washing automobiles.
car.y.at.id (cair.ee.AT.id) *n.* a sculptured female figure used for a column.
ca.sa.ba (cuh.SAH.buh) *n.* a sweet, white-fleshed winter melon with a thick, yellow rind.
Cas.a.no.va (cas.uh.NOH.vuh) *n.* a man who has many love affairs with women.
cas.cade (cas.CADE) *n.* a steep waterfall or series of waterfalls or something resembling it: *a window adorned with cascades of lace.* —*v.* **-cades, -cad.ed, -cad.ing** fall like or in a cascade: *The stream cascades over a cliff.*
cas.car.a sa.gra.da (cas.CAIR.uh.suh.GRAY.duh) *n.* **1** the bark of the California buckthorn used as a laxative. **2** the tree itself. **3** the laxative.
case *n.* **1** a situation or an instance of it: *a clear case of fraud; The doctor saw three cases of measles today; Luc is not an isolated case; a terminal case of cancer; If that's the case, you're in trouble! a basket case (that is quite helpless); Please get off my case (Slang for* stop bothering me*); a **case in point** (= relevant instance); a **case study** (= analysis of a case history).* **2** a situation as a matter of litigation: *Lawyers argue cases; A case goes to trial; Courts hear* or *try cases; The defense rests (its case)* (= has finished its presentation); *"Case dismissed," said the judge; You don't have a case (that is strong); He lost the case; The case was settled out of court; Case closed; the detective who finally cracked the case* (= solved the crime). **3** a container or its contents: *an attaché case; a glass display case; packing case; A case of pop contains 24 cans.* **4** a cover: *a pillow case; watch case.* **5** the frame for a door or window. **6** a grammatical variation of a noun, pronoun, or adjective: *"They," "them," and "their" are in the nominative, objective, and possessive cases respectively.* —**in any case** anyhow.
—**in case** in the event: *In case of emergency dial zero; Take your umbrella in case it rains; just in case it rains; Take your umbrella **just in case***. —*v.* **cas.es, cased, cas.ing 1** *Informal.* inspect in preparation for theft: *Burglars case a bank first; He had cased the joint before breaking in.* **2** put in a case: *to case a window.*
case history *n.* the facts about a subject's past and present that are useful for a medical or social study.
ca.se.in (cay.SEEN) *n.* a protein obtained from milk, used in foods, plastics, paints, and cheese.
case law *n.* law as established by decisions in court cases, not by statutes.
case.load *n.* the number of cases handled by a court, social worker, etc.
case.ment (CASE.munt) *n.* **1** a window sash opening on hinges. **2** the window itself, or **casement window.**
case.work *n.* social work involving individual cases; **case.work.er** *n.*
cash *n.* ready money or its equivalent as payment: *We always pay (in) cash for groceries; Pay cash either in currency or by check; Cold cash and no checks, please; I ran out of cash and charged my purchases to a credit card; We carry only petty cash for daily expenses; The terms were strictly cash on delivery; a **cash advance** (= loan charged to a bank card).*
—*v.* exchange for cash: *to cash a check, money order.* —**cash in 1** turn into cash, as bonds or gambling chips, and withdraw. **2** *Informal.* die: *It was time for him to cash in (his chips).* —**cash in on** exploit fully; profit from something: *He cashed in on his sudden fame; to cash in on a favorable market.*
cash-and-carry *n.* a purchasing system of paying cash and taking delivery of goods.
cash bar *n.* a bar set up at a reception where guests may buy drinks.
cash card *n.* a plastic card in which one's bank balance is stored for easy electronic funds transfer.
cash cow *n. Informal.* a dependable source of income or profit.
cash crop *n.* a crop that is grown for sale, not for consumption on the farm.
cash discount *n.* discount allowed to customers who pay in cash or within a certain period.
cash.ew (CASH.oo) *n.* **1** the edible kidney-shaped nut of a tropical tree. **2** the tree itself.
cash flow *n.* the after-tax net income of a business.
cash.ier (ca.SHEER) *n.* **1** one who receives the payments from customers: *a cashier at a supermarket checkout.* **2** a financial officer of a bank or company.
—*v.* dismiss, esp. in disgrace: *The clerk was cashiered for embezzlement.*
cashier's check *n.* a check issued by a

bank, drawn on its own funds, as given to borrowers.

cash.less *adj.* without cash: *a **cashless** society* in which all transactions are carried out by electronic funds transfer.

cash.mere (CAZH.meer) *n.* **1** a soft fabric originally made from the wool of goats from Tibet and northern India. **2** such wool or a garment made with it.

cash register *n.* a machine, with a drawer for cash, that records sales, totals bills, etc.

casing (CAY.sing) *n.* what encloses something, as the airtight inner liner of a car tire, the skin of a sausage, the covering of a rifle cartridge, the interior frame of a door or window opening, or the steel lining of an oil well.

ca.si.no (cuh.SEE.noh) *n.* **-nos** a public establishment for amusements, esp. gambling: *a gambling casino.*

cask *n.* a barrel for liquids or the amount it holds.

cas.ket (CAS.kit) *n.* **1** a coffin. **2** a small box for valuables.

casque (CASK) *n.* a military helmet.

Cas.san.dra (cuh.SAN.druh) *n.* a prophet of doom whose warnings, though true, go unheeded.

cas.sa.va (cuh.SAH.vuh) *n.* **1** the starchy root of a tropical plant used for tapioca, bread, etc. **2** the plant itself.

cas.se.role (CAS.uh.role) *n.* **1** a deep, usu. covered dish for baking and serving food. **2** food cooked in a casserole: *to bake a casserole; a meat casserole; lima bean casserole.*

cas.sette (cuh.SET) *n.* a cartridge for photographic film or magnetic tape for use in a camera, tape player, etc.

cas.sia (CASH.uh) *n.* **1** the bark of a S.E. Asian tree, used for cinnamon. **2** the tree. **3** an E. Indian plant that yields senna.

cas.si.no (cuh.SEE.noh) *n.* a card game.

cas.sit.er.ite (cuh.SIT.uh.rite) *n.* a dark, heavy, tin-bearing ore.

cas.sock (CAS.uk) *n.* a usu. black, ankle-length garment worn by clergymen, choir singers, etc.

cas.so.war.y (CAS.uh.wair.ee) *n.* **-war.ies** a flightless bird of Australia and New Guinea, related to the emu.

cast *v.* **casts, cast, cast.ing 1** throw: *An angler casts a line; Fishermen cast nets; A snake casts* (= discards) *its skin; Voters cast* (= deposit) *ballots; actions that cast doubts on his competence; His remarks* **cast aspersions on** (= slandered) *her good name; He left the Liberals and **cast in his lot*** (= joined) *with the Tories.* **2** form in a mold: *to cast a bronze statue.* **3** assign an actor to a role: *Burton was cast as Caesar; He was cast in the hero's role.* **4** calculate: *to cast a horoscope.*
—**cast about** search: *Hounds cast about for a scent; a prisoner casting about for* (= seeking) *a means of escape.* —**cast off** free a ship from a dock. —*n.* **1** a throw: *a cast of the dice.* **2** something thrown or discarded: *a worm cast* (= excrement). **3** something molded, esp. a rigid plaster-of-Paris dressing for a broken limb: *Her leg is in a (plaster) cast.* **4** the actors in a play: *a cast of characters; a star-studded cast; supporting cast.* **5** color or quality: *a ruddy cast; a noble cast of mind.*

cas.ta.nets (cas.tuh.NETS) *n.pl.* a pair of small, hollowed-out pieces of wood, ivory, etc. held in the hand and clicked together for rhythm, used esp. in Spanish dancing.

cast.a.way (CAST.uh.way) *adj.* thrown away; set adrift: *a castaway sailor; n.: The castaways landed on the beach.*

caste (CAST) *n.* **1** a usu. hereditary social class defined by rigid barriers, as in traditional Hinduism. **2** status or prestige: *He was afraid of losing caste.*

cas.tel.lat.ed (CAS.tuh.lay.tid) *adj.* having turrets and battlements like a castle.

cast.er or **cas.tor** (CAS.tur) *n.* **1** a ball or swiveling wheel fitted to the legs of furniture, machines, etc. to make moving easier. **2** a small container for salt, relish, vinegar, etc. for use at the table.

cas.ti.gate (CAS.tuh.gate) *v.* **-gates, -gat.ed, -gat.ing** reprove strongly; punish; **cas.ti.ga.tor** (-gay.tur) *n.*
—**cas.ti.ga.tion** (-GAY.shun) *n.*

Cas.til.ian (cas.TIL.yun) *n.* **1** a citizen or native of Castile, Spain. **2** its dialect, now the dominant form of European Spanish; *adj.: the Castilian accent.*

casting *n.* **1** something molded or cast: *a brass casting.* **2** the excrement of earthworms. **3** a snake's discarded skin.

casting vote *n.* a chairperson's vote used to break a tie.

cast iron *n.* a hard, nonmalleable iron-carbon alloy made by casting.
—**cast-iron** *adj.* made or as if made of cast iron: *a cast-iron rod; a cast-iron* (= hardy) *constitution; a cast-iron* (= rigid) *policy, rule; a cast-iron* (= strong) *stomach, will.*

cas.tle (CAS.ul) *n.* **1** a large fortified dwelling or group of buildings, esp. one built in the Middle Ages; stronghold: *"A man's home is his castle"*; *a visionary who spends a lot of time* **building castles in the air** or **in Spain** (= daydreaming). **2** in chess, a rook.

cast-off or **cast.off** *adja.* discarded: *cast-off clothes, skin.* —*n.* someone or something discarded: *dressed in his brother's castoffs.*

cas.tor (CAS.tur) *n.* **1** same as CASTER. **2** a beaver hat.

castor oil *n.* a thick yellow oil obtained from the beans of a tropical plant and used as a purgative, lubricant, etc.

cas.trate (CAS.trate) *v.* **-trates, -trat.ed, -trat.ing** remove the testicles of a human or animal: *Farmers castrate hogs to fatten them for market.* —**cas.tra.tion** (cas.TRAY.shun) *n.*

cas.u.al (CAZH.oo.ul) *adj.* **1** accidental; chance: *a casual meeting.* **2** informal: *He comes to work in casual clothes; He adopts a casual attitude to work; He sounded quite casual* (= indifferent) *about losing his job.* **3** occasional: *We hire casual labor for seasonal work.* —**cas.u.al.ly** *adv.*; **cas.u.al.ness** *n.*

cas.u.al.ty (CAZH.ul.tee) *n.* **-ties 1** a victim (wounded, missing, or killed) of an accident or military action: *a traffic casualty; heavy casualties inflicted on the enemy; They suffered many casualties.* **2** a victim: *Automation claims many casualties among manual labor; He was a casualty of the electronic revolution.*

cas.u.ist.ry (CAZH.oo.is.tree) *n.* **-tries 1** subtle reasoning about right and wrong. **2** a clever but false rationalization; sophistry. —**cas.u.ist** *n.* —**cas.u.is.tic** (-IS.tic) *adj.*

ca.sus bel.li (CAIS.us.BEL.eye) *n. Latin.* a cause of or pretext for a war.

cat *n.* **1** a mammal of the same family as the lion, lynx, leopard, and panther, esp. a small domesticated species kept as a pet or to catch mice: *A cat meows; Cats purr when at ease; an alley cat; stray cats; a* **cat-and-mouse** *game (of constant escapes and captures).* **2** *Informal.* a malicious gossipy woman. *Informal.* a caterpillar tractor. —**let the cat out of the bag** reveal a secret.

ca.tab.o.lism (cuh.TAB.uh.liz.um) *n.* the breakdown of living tissue in plants and animals into simpler substances or waste products; destructive metabolism. —**cat.a.bol.ic** (cat.uh.BOL.ic) *adj.*

cat.a.clysm (CAT.uh.cliz.um) *n.* a sudden, destructive change, as a great flood or war. —**cat.a.clys.mic** (-CLIZ.mic) *adj.*

cat.a.combs (CAT.uh.cohms) *n.pl.* underground burial places connected by tunnels and chambers.

cat.a.falque (CAT.uh.falc) *n.* a decorated platform for a coffin at a funeral.

cat.a.log (CAT.uh.log) *n.* a complete, organized, often descriptive list, as of merchandise, library books, art exhibits, etc.: *a college catalog listing course offerings.* —*v.* **-logs, -loged, -log.ing** make a catalog of something: *He has his stamp collection all neatly cataloged.* Also **-logue, -logues, -logued, -logu.ing.** —**cat.a.log.er** or **cat.a.logu.er** *n.*

cat.a.lep.sy (CAT.uh.lep.see) *n.* an abnormal state of rigid physical immobility and unconsciousness. —**cat.a.lep.tic** (-LEP.tic) *n. & adj.*

ca.tal.pa (cuh.TAL.puh) *n.* a North American or Asiatic tree with broad leaves and long, thin pods.

ca.tal.y.sis (cuh.TAL.uh.sis) *n., pl.* **-ses** (-seez) the process of change induced in a chemical reaction by a catalyst.

cat.a.lyst (CAT.uh.list) *n.* **1** an agent that induces or speeds up a change without itself undergoing change: *Enzymes act as catalysts in digestion.* **2** one that is considered an instrument of change: *She was a catalyst of the feminist movement; a catalyst for change.* —**cat.a.lyt.ic** (-LIT.ic) *adj.*

catalytic converter *n.* an antipollution device used in automobiles to render exhaust gases harmless.

cat.a.lyze (CAT.uh.lize) *v.* **-lyz.es, -lyzed, -lyz.ing** act on or change, as a catalyst does: *The discovery of the New World catalyzed world exploration.*

cat.a.mar.an (cat.uh.muh.RAN) *n.* a slender raft of logs, usu. propelled by a paddle. **2** a twin-hulled sailboat.

cat.a.mount (CAT.uh.mount) *n.* any of the wildcats, as the puma, cougar, or lynx.

cat.a.pult (CAT.uh.pult) *n.* **1** a device for launching or hurling objects, as airplanes from a ship, pilots from an airplane, or missiles and stones in ancient warfare. **2** slingshot. —*v.* throw by or as if by a catapult: *He was catapulted to fame by his marriage to the princess; He catapults out of bed at five each morning.*

cat.a.ract (CAT.uh.ract) *n.* **1** a great rush or flood of water, esp. a steep waterfall. **2** blurred vision resulting from a clouding of the eye's lens: *Elderly people develop cataracts; an* *operation to remove a cataract.*

ca.tarrh (cuh.TAR) *n.* inflammation of and discharge from a mucous membrane.

ca.tas.tro.phe (cuh.TAS.truh.fee) *n.* something that ends as a great disaster: *A bank failure is a catastrophe affecting millions of people.* —**cat.a.stroph.ic** (cat.uh.STROF.ic) *adj.: a disaster of catastrophic proportions; catastrophic illness;* **cat.a.stroph.i.cal.ly** *adv.*

cat.a.ton.ic (cat.uh.TON.ic) *adj.* in the trancelike state of a patient who does not react, move, or talk: *people brainwashed into a state of catatonic approval of everything they are told; so catatonic I can't even think; catatonic confusion, silence, stupor.*

cat.bird *n.* a gray North American songbird with a mewing call. —**in the catbird seat** *Informal.* in an advantageous position.

cat.boat *n.* a boat with a single mast and sail set well forward.

cat burglar *n.* a burglar who breaks into buildings by climbing in from the outside.

cat.call *n.* a loud, rude noise expressing disapproval of a speaker, performer, etc.; *v.: The singer was booed and catcalled off the stage.*

catch *v.* **catch.es, caught** (CAWT), **catch.ing 1** take and hold: *to catch a ball; a barrel to catch rain in.* **2** get or grasp: *to catch sight of him; trying to catch her meaning.* **3** overtake or intercept: *Catch him before he leaves; He was at the station to catch the last train; There isn't enough time to catch a movie.* **4** apprehend: *You never catch him sleeping on the job; to catch a culprit red-handed.* **5** get or be tangled, stuck, etc.: *a finger caught in the door.* **6** be affected by something: *to catch (a) cold; A house catches fire.* **7** take hold: *flames catching on wood.* **8** act as a catcher. —**catch at** reach out to grasp; seize on: *"A drowning man will catch at a straw."* —**catch it** *Informal.* be scolded. —**catch on** become well-known or popular: *Slogans tend to catch on.* —**catch on to** come to understand: *The child soon caught on to what the adults were saying.* —**catch one's breath** to rest: *After running for a while, I stopped to catch my breath.* —**catch up** come up from behind and reach a person or thing: *A police cruiser catches up with a speeding car; He takes catnaps to catch up on lost sleep; n.: He has a lot of catching up to do in math.* —**caught up in** involved in something: *a premier caught up in a scandal; teens caught up in (= carried away by) the latest fads.* —*n.* **1** the act of catching; also, a simple ball game. **2** what is caught: *a small catch of fish; a good catch; the day's catch; His wife is a real catch (= good find).* **3** a latch; fastener: *a safety catch.* **4** a small fragment or piece; snatch: *Catches of songs could be heard.* **5** a break in the voice, as caused by fear or anxiety. **6** an unforeseen or hidden complication or problem: *What's the catch? It sounds so good there must be a catch to it.*

catch.all *n.* one that applies to many different things: *"Flu" is a catchall term for many illnesses.*

catch-as-catch-can *adj.* haphazard or random: *catch-as-catch-can wrestling; a hurried catch-as-catch-can news report.*

catch.er *n.* in baseball, one who receives the pitcher's throw behind home plate.

catching *adj.* **1** contagious. **2** catchy or easily remembered.

catch.ment area (or **basin**) *n.* the region from which a river collects its water.

catch.pen.ny (CATCH.pen.ee) *n.* **-pen.nies** an article making cheap money. —*adj.:* cheap and trashy: *a store packed with catchpenny goods.*

catch.phrase *n.* a catchy phrase: *"According to a recent survey" is a popular catchphrase in commercials.*

Catch-22 (CACH.twen.tee.TOO) *n.* a situation in which one is victimized either way, as when an applicant is refused jobs because he lacks job experience and lacks experience because he is refused jobs.

catch.up same as KETCHUP.

catch-up *n.* a coming up from being behind; recovery: *Their wages had slipped so far behind the rest of the industry, the union demanded a 35% raise for catch-up; Playing catch-up is sometimes a losing game.*

catch.word *n.* **1** a word or phrase that is merely catchy: *His speech was full of catchwords like "challenge" and "commitment."* **2** a guide word, as at the top of this page.

catch.y *adj.* **catch.i.er, -i.est 1** that catches one's attention and stays in the mind: *a catchy song, title, tune.* **2** tricky: *a catchy question.*

cat.e.chism (CAT.uh.kiz.um) *n.* **1** a set of questions and answers used for instruction, esp. in religion. **2** oral instruction or examination by question and answer. —**cat.e.chist** *n.*

cat.e.chize (CAT.uh.kize) *v.* **-chiz.es,**

-chized, -chiz.ing question closely or instruct by questioning: *The teacher catechized him in geography.*

cat.e.chu.men (cat.uh.CUE.mun) *n.* one being instructed in religion prior to baptism.

cat.e.gor.i.cal (cat.uh.GOR.i.cul) *adj.* unqualified or unconditional: *a categorical denial, rejection, statement.*

cat.e.go.rize (CAT.uh.guh.rize) *v.* **-riz.es, -rized, -riz.ing 1** classify: *people categorized by age, sex, and education; She categorized the group as tall, medium, and short.* **2** label: *a phenomenon categorized as supernatural.* —**cat.e.go.ri.za.tion** (-ruh.ZAY.shun, -rye-) *n.*

cat.e.go.ry (CAT.uh.gor.ee) *n.* **-go.ries** a basic division or class, esp. in logic or philosophy: *Parts of speech are categories of words; He's too great a guy to fit into any category of genius.*

ca.ter (CAY.tur) *v.* **1** furnish a reception, party, etc. with food, entertainment, or other service: *We cater for all occasions; We will cater the banquet.* **2** gratify: *He caters to her every whim.* —**ca.ter.er** *n.*

cater-corner (CAT.i.cor.nur) *adj.p.* diagonal; kitty-corner: *two gas stations cater-corner to each other at an intersection; The store is cater-corner from the hotel; adv.: a sofa set cater-corner across the room.* Also **cater-cornered**.

cat.er.pil.lar (CAT.ur.pil.ur) *n.* **1** a usu. hairy, wormlike larva of a butterfly, moth, etc. **2** a vehicle moved by two endless metal tracks instead of wheels: *a caterpillar tractor;* **Caterpillar** *Trademark.*

cat.er.waul (CAT.ur.wall) *v.* howl or screech like a cat; also *n.*

cat.fish *n.* a scaleless fish with a big head and whiskers like a cat's.

cat.gut *n.* a tough string made of the intestines of sheep, horses, etc. and used for sutures, stringing rackets, etc.

ca.thar.sis (cuh.THAR.sis, "TH" as in "thin") *n., pl.* **-ses** (-seez) a purification or release, esp. of the emotions, by witnessing tragic drama or by some other outlet or expression.

ca.thar.tic (cuh.THAR.tic) *adj.* purifying or purging. —*n.* a strong laxative.

ca.the.dral (cuh.THEE.drul, "TH" as in "thin") *n.* the principal church of a diocese: *A* **cathedral ceiling** *has exposed beams and often a skylight.*

cath.e.ter (CATH.uh.tur, "TH" as in "thin") *n.* a long, flexible tube inserted into a canal or cavity in the body, usu. to remove fluid, as urine from the bladder. —**cath.e.ter.i.za.tion** (-ruh.ZAY.shun, -rye-) *n.*

cath.ode (CATH.ode) *n.* the negatively charged electrode of an electrolytic cell or electron tube or the positive terminal of a primary cell; opposed to ANODE. —**ca.thod.ic** (cuh.THOD.ic) *adj.*

cathode-ray tube *n.* a vacuum tube in which a beam of electrons emitted from its cathode, or **cathode rays,** throws images on to a screen, as in radar and TV.

cath.o.lic (CATH.uh.lic) *adj.* **1** wide or general in appeal, interest, etc.: *a person of very catholic tastes; a movie of catholic appeal;* **cath.o.lic.i.ty** (-LIS.i.tee) *n.* **2 Catholic** having to do with the Roman Catholic Church: *a Catholic priest.* —*n.* a member of the Roman Catholic Church: *Protestants and Catholics.* —**Ca.thol.i.cism** (cuh.THOL.uh.siz.um) *n.*

cat.i.on (CAT.eye.un) *n.* a positively charged ion. —**cat.i.on.ic** (-ON.ic) *adj.*

cat.kin *n.* a long, drooping cluster of flowers, as on the birch or willow.

cat.like *adj.* like a cat; silent: *catlike footsteps.*

cat.nap *n.* a brief, light sleep. Also *v.* **-naps, -napped, -nap.ping.**

cat.nip *n.* a fragrant mint much liked by cats.

cat-o'-nine-tails (cat.uh.NINE.tails) *n. sing. & pl.* a whip with usu. nine knotted lashes fastened to a handle.

CAT scan same as CT SCAN.

cat's cradle *n.* a game in which a string, looped through the fingers in intricate but symmetrical designs, is transferred from player to player.

cat's-eye *n.* **-eyes** a gem, marble, etc. that reflects light with a distinctive gleam.

cat's-paw *n.* one used by another to do something risky or disreputable.

cat.suit *n.* a close-fitting, one-piece neck-to-ankle garment for women.

cat.sup same as KETCHUP.

cat.tail *n.* a marsh plant with a cylindrical, brown, furry flower spike on a tall stem.

cat.tle (CAT.ul) *n.pl.* cows, bulls, and other domestic bovines collectively: *a herd of cattle; to brand, drive, round up cattle; The refugees were herded like cattle into the camp.*

cat.tle.man (CAT.ul.mun) *n.* **-men** a rancher or cowboy.

cattle range *n.* an area used for grazing cattle.

cat.ty *adj.* **cat.ti.er, cat.ti.est** *Informal.*

slyly spiteful: *a catty child; She was somewhat catty about giving her rival due credit.* —**cat.ti.ly** *adv.;* **cat.ti.ness** *n.*
catty-corner(ed) same as CATER-CORNER(ED).
cat.walk *n.* **1** a narrow, usu. elevated walkway, as along a bridge. **2** the runway used by models in a fashion show.
Cau.ca.sian (caw.CAY.zhun) *n.* a person of the racial group to which most white people belong.
Cau.ca.soid (CAW.cuh.soid) *adj.* [former use] having to do with the races that are mostly white, including the light-skinned peoples of N. Africa, S.W. Asia, and the Indian subcontinent. Also *n.*
cau.cus (CAW.cus) *n.* a political party's meeting to debate policy, select candidates, etc. —*v.* **-cus.es, -cused, -cus.ing** hold a caucus: *They caucused all night.*
cau.dal (CAW.dul) *adj.* having to do with the tail or hind parts, as of a fish: *the caudal fin.* —**cau.dal.ly** *adv.*
cau.dil.lo (cow.THEEL.yoh, "TH" as in "the") *n.* **-dil.los** a military dictator, esp. in a Spanish-speaking country.
caught *pt. & pp.* of CATCH.
caul (CAWL) *n.* a membrane sometimes covering a baby's head at birth.
caul.dron (CAWL.drun) *n.* a large vat or pot for boiling: *a witch's cauldron.*
cau.li.flow.er (CAW.lee.flow.er) *n.* **1** the large white flower head of a kind of cabbage. **2** the plant itself.
cauliflower ear *n.* an ear misshapen and scarred by blows received in boxing.
caulk (CAWK) *v.* seal or make tight seams in a boat, pipe joints, cracks, etc., usu. with a filler; **caulk.er** *n.*
caus.al (CAW.zul) *adj.* having to do with a cause: *There seems no causal connection between her death and his disappearance.* **cau.sal.ly** *adv.* —**cau.sal.i.ty** (caw.ZAL.i.tee) *n.*
cau.sa.tion (caw.ZAY.shun) *n.* **1** the act of causing. **2** cause-and-effect relation. **3** cause.
cau.sa.tive (CAW.zuh.tiv) *adj.* acting as a cause: *the causative agent; a causative force.*
'cause *Informal.* because.
cause (CAWZ) *n.* **1** one that produces or is responsible for an effect, change, etc.: *The cause of the fire is unknown; She died of natural causes.* **2** grounds; reason: *He was fired from his job for cause; a court order to show cause why a judgment should not be executed; There's no cause for alarm; There's good cause to celebrate.* **3** a goal actively pursued or strongly supported: *to advance the cause of justice; a just cause; The money is for a worthy cause; You are fighting for a lost cause; He made common cause with the enemy.* **4** a legal case. —*v.* **caus.es, caused, caus.ing** bring about; make happen: *What caused the accident? He caused us a lot of trouble.*
cause cé.lè.bre (CAWZ.suh.LEB.ruh) *n., pl.* **causes cé.lè.bres** (CAWZ.suh.LEB.ruh) a famous case or controversy: *The abdication of King Edward VIII became a cause célèbre.*
cau.se.rie (COH.zuh.ree) *n.* a light, informal bit of writing or discussion.
cause.way *n.* a raised road or path across water or marshy ground.
caus.tic (CAW.stic) *adj.* **1** able to destroy or eat into (esp. flesh) chemically; corrosive: *the caustic action of soda.* **2** sharp or biting: *a caustic remark; his caustic wit.* —*n.* a caustic agent. —**caus.tic.i.ty** (caw.STIS.i.tee) *n.*
caustic soda *n.* a corrosive alkali used in bleaching, making soap, etc.
cau.ter.ize (CAW.tuh.rize) *v.* **-iz.es, -ized, -iz.ing** burn abnormal or injured tissue with a hot iron, caustic, or laser beam to kill infection, remove diseased tissue, etc. —**cau.ter.i.za.tion** (-ruh.ZAY.shun, -rye-) *n.*
cau.tion (CAW.shun) *n.* **1** regard for safety; wariness: *Drive with caution on icy roads; Proceed with caution; a word of caution; Exercise caution when walking on wet floors; Use extreme caution while handling explosives; He threw caution to the winds and jumped into the current.* **2** a mild warning or advice: *the judge's caution against repeating the offense; Caution! Wet Floor; Here are a few cautions; a caution flag.* —*v.* warn or admonish: *He cautioned her against driving too fast; cautioned her not to drive so fast; cautioned her about the dangers.*
cau.tion.ar.y (CAW.shuh.nair.ee) *adj.* warning of danger: *cautionary advice; a cautionary sign, tale.*
cau.tious (CAW.shus) *adj.* careful or wary: *She is cautious of strangers; cautious about traveling at night; cautious in the use of drugs; cautious with firearms; a cautious investor.* —**cau.tious.ly** *adv.;* **cau.tious.ness** *n.*
cav.al.cade (CAV.ul.cade) *n.* **1** a parade or procession, as of horses. **2** a progression: *a cavalcade of historical events.*
cav.a.lier (cav.uh.LEER) *n.* **1** an armed

rider. **2** a gallant; lady's escort.
—*adj.* casual or off-hand: *a cavalier attitude, manner; cavalier treatment; He acts with cavalier indifference to the rights of others; She's a bit cavalier about other people's comforts;* **cav.a.lier.ly** *adv.*

cav.al.ry (CAV.ul.ree) *n.* **-ries 1** mobile troops on horseback or in armored vehicles: *a cavalry unit of tanks and armored personnel carriers.* **2** horses and riders collectively; *adj*a.: *a cavalry charge, officer, regiment; to* **call in the cavalry** (= call for rescuers).
—**cav.al.ry.man** *n.* **-men.**

cave *n.* an underground cavity with an opening, usu. on a cliff or hillside: *to explore a cave.* —*v.* **caves, caved, cav.ing** esp. **cave in 1** collapse inward: *The old tunnel caved in.* **2** give in or yield: *Don't cave in to pressure.*

ca.ve.at (CAY.vee.ut) *n. Formal.* a caution.

caveat emp.tor (-EMP.tor) *Latin.* "Let the buyer beware," i.e. Make sure of a product's quality before buying it.

cave-in *n.* the occurrence or site of a collapse in a mine, tunnel, etc.

cave.man *n.* **1** a cave dweller of prehistoric times. **2** *Informal.* a strong but crude man.

cav.ern (CAV.urn) *n.* a huge or vast cave.

cav.ern.ous (CAV.ur.nus) *adj.* **1** full of caverns: *a cavernous mountain.* **2** of or like a cavern: *a cavernous* (= large and hollow) *structure; cavernous* (= deep-set) *eyes; a cavernous* (= resonant) *voice; the cavernous* (= large and spacious) *Grand Hotel.*

cav.i.ar (CAV.ee.ar) *n.* the salted eggs of salmon and other fishes eaten as an appetizer. Also **cav.i.are.**

cav.il (CAV.ul) *v.* **-ils, -iled, -il.ing** needlessly criticize or object to something; carp: *to cavil at little delays; This is no time to cavil about trivialities.*
—**cav.il.er** *n.* Also **cav.illed, cav.il.ling; cav.il.ler** *Cdn.*

cav.i.ty (CAV.i.tee) *n.* **-ties** a hollow place in a solid body: *the abdominal cavity; Dentists fill cavities (in teeth); the oral cavity (of the mouth).*

ca.vort (cuh.VORT) *v.* prance; caper: *See the horse cavorting in the field; young bucks cavorting on the dance floor.*

ca.vy (CAY.vee) *n.* **-vies** a South American rodent such as the guinea pig.

caw *n.* the harsh call of a crow, raven, etc. —*v.: Rooks cawed from the treetops.*

cay (CAY, KEE) *n.* a sandy or coral reef off a coast; key.

cay.enne (kye.EN) or **cayenne pepper** *n.* a spicy, red pepper made from capsicum fruits.

cay.man (CAY.mun) *n.* **-mans** same as CAIMAN.

Ca.yu.ga (kye.YOO.guh) *n.* **1** (a member of) a native Iroquoian Indian tribe, formerly living in central New York state. **2** the language of this tribe.

cay.use (KYE.yoose) *n.* **-us.es** a small Western range horse, originally bred by the Cayuse Indians of Oregon.

CB *n.* a range of radio frequencies meant for two-way communication between private parties; citizens band: *In CB slang, "chicken coop" means "weigh scales for trucks."*

CB.er (SEE.bee.ur) *n. Informal.* one who uses a CB radio.

CD-ROM (SEE.dee.ROM) *n.* a compact disc carrying a large volume of recorded text, often with graphics and sound.

cease (SEECE) *v.* **ceas.es, ceased, ceas.ing** come to an end or discontinue: *The music faded and then ceased; Extinct animals are those that have ceased to exist; The rebels were ordered to cease fire; an order to* **cease and desist** (from something illegal); *It snowed without ceasing all January.* —*n.: It snowed* **without cease** (= without end or pause) *all January.*

cease-fire *n.* a pause in open warfare: *to declare, observe, work out, sign a cease-fire; The cease-fire was broken soon after it went into effect; a cease-fire order from the U.N.; the* **cease-fire line** (= boundary) *between two warring nations.*

cease.less *adj.* endless; continual: *ceaseless activity, enmity, noise, rivalry, tumult.*
—**cease.less.ly** *adv.*

ce.cum (SEE.cum) *n., pl.* **ce.ca** (-cuh) a pouchlike formation at the beginning of the large intestine; **ce.cal** *adj.*

ce.dar (SEE.dur) *n.* **1** an evergreen coniferous tree with reddish, hardy, fragrant wood. **2** the wood; *adj*a.: *a cedar chest, fence; a cedar-lined closet.*

cede (SEED) *v.* **cedes, ced.ed, ced.ing** surrender a property, claim, right, etc. esp. by treaty: *Some land was ceded to the Crown by the Indians.*

ce.dil.la (si.DIL.uh) *n.* a mark put below a "c" (ç) to indicate an "s" sound.

ceil.ing (SEE.ling) *n.* **1** the interior, overhead covering of a room. **2** an upper limit, as on prices and wages, visibility, operable altitude for an airplane, etc.: *to put or set a ceiling on* *rents; They lifted the ceiling after a year.* —**hit the ceiling** or **roof** *Slang.* lose one's temper.

cel.an.dine (SEL.un.dine) *n.* **1** a biennial herb with yellow flowers, related to the poppy. **2** a perennial European plant called "lesser celandine," related to the buttercup.

ce.leb (suh.LEB) *n. Informal.* a celebrity or famous person.

cel.e.brant (SEL.uh.brunt) *n.* **1** a priest officiating at a ceremony. **2** a celebrator: *New Year's Eve celebrants.*

cel.e.brate (SEL.uh.brate) *v.* **-brates, -brat.ed, -brat.ing 1** hold festivities, rites, etc. in honor of an event: *He celebrated the victory with champagne; Most Christians celebrate Christmas on December 25.* **2** praise publicly; make known: *to celebrate the memory of the war heroes;* **adj.**: *France is celebrated* (= famous) *for its wines; celebrated as a producer of fine wines; a celebrated piano, poet, trial.* **3** perform solemnly: *to celebrate a marriage, Mass.* —**cel.e.bra.tion** (-BRAY.shun) *n.* —**cel.e.bra.tor** (-bray.tur) *n.;* **cel.e.bra.to.ry** (-bruh.tor.ee) *adj.*

ce.leb.ri.ty (suh.LEB.ri.tee) *n.* **-ties 1** renown or fame. **2** a famous person: *a Hollywood celebrity; local celebrities.*

ce.ler.i.ty (suh.LER.i.tee) *n.* rapidity.

cel.e.ry (SEL.uh.ree) *n.* a plant of the parsley family, grown for its crisp, edible stem: *a bunch of celery; a stick of celery.*

ce.les.ta (suh.LES.tuh) *n.* a keyboard instrument producing light, bell-like tones; also **ce.les.te.**

ce.les.tial (suh.LES.chul) *adj.* **1** having to do with the sky or the heavens: *The sun, moon, and stars are celestial bodies; The celestial equator runs through the sky directly above the earth's equator.* **2** heavenly or divine: *a goddess's celestial beauty.* —**ce.les.tial.ly** *adv.*

celestial navigation *n.* the determination of one's position and course by observing heavenly bodies.

celestial sphere *n.* the sphere centered around the earth, on which stars, planets, etc. seem to turn.

ce.li.ac (SEE.lee.ac) *adj.* abdominal.

cel.i.bate (SEL.uh.bit) *n.* one who stays unmarried, esp. by religious vow. —**adj.**: *a celibate life, nun, priest.* —**cel.i.ba.cy** (-buh.see) *n.*

cell *n.* **1** a small, separate space, as in a honeycomb. **2** a similar room to accommodate a monk, prisoner, etc.: *a prison cell.* **3** a basic unit of a larger structure: *a blood cell* (= the smallest independent unit of living tissue); *a dry cell* (= the basic component of an electric battery); *a binary cell* (= the basic storage unit of a computer memory).

cel.lar (SEL.ur) *n.* **1** a usu. underground storage room; also, its contents, esp. a store of wine. **2** basement. —**in the cellar** *Informal.* in last place in a sports league.

cel.lar.age (SEL.uh.rij) *n.* **1** a fee for storage in a cellar. **2** cellars collectively; storage room.

cel.lar.et (sel.uh.RET) *n.* a cabinet for liquor, wine, glasses, etc.; also **cel.lar.ette.**

cell.block *n.* a unit of a prison house: *the HIV cellblock.*

-celled *comb.form.* having a cell as specified: *one-celled algae; single-celled organisms.*

cel.lo (CHEL.oh) *n.* **cel.los** a large bass instrument of the violin family. —**cel.list** *n.*

cel.lo.phane (SEL.uh.fane) *n.* a thin, transparent moisture-proof wrapping material made of viscose used to keep foods fresh.

cell.phone *n.* a portable telephone that is part of a CELLULAR PHONE system.

cel.lu.lar (SEL.yuh.lur) *adj.* **1** cell-like; porous: *cellular rubber.* **2** having to do with cellphones: *cellular communications, radio, service.*

cellular phone *n.* a radiotelephone system for vehicles, in which a chain of transmitting stations, or cells, each serving a small area, relays the messages. Also **cellular telephone.**

cel.lu.lite (SEL.yuh.lite, -leet) *n.* fat or a fatty substance that accumulates under the skin, said to be the cause of bulges on thighs, hips, and buttocks.

cel.lu.loid (SEL.yuh.loid) *n.* **1** a flammable, colorless material used for toys, combs, photographic film, etc. **2** movie film; hence, the movie world. —**adj.** having to do with films; hence, artificial or unreal: *celluloid characters; the celluloid world of the movies.* —**Celluloid** *Trademark.*

cel.lu.lose (SEL.yuh.lohs) *n.* the basic substance of plant tissues, found esp. in wood pulp, cotton, etc. —**cel.lu.los.ic** (-LOH.sic) *n. & adj.*

Cel.si.us (SEL.see.us) *adj.* having to do with the temperature scale that has 0 and 100 degrees as the freezing and boiling points of water respectively.

Celt (KELT, SELT) *n.* **1** a member of a group of ancient European peoples, including the Britons and Gauls. **2** a

speaker of a Celtic language or a descendant of one.
Cel.tic (KEL.tic, SEL-) *adj.* of a group of languages that include Gaelic, Welsh, Breton, and Cornish.
cem.ba.lo (CHEM.buh.loh) *n., pl.* **-los** a harpsichord; **cem.ba.list** *n.*
ce.ment (suh.MENT) *n.* **1** a substance, esp. a powder of clay and lime, pastelike when mixed with water but hardening to a stony mass and used to bind building materials, make concrete, etc.: *Cement is poured into forms; then it sets as concrete; This floor is (made of) cement;* **Paper cement** and **rubber cement** are adhesives; *adja.: a cement (= concrete) mixer, sidewalk; a* **cement truck** *(carrying a cement mixer).* **2** a hard crust covering the roots of a tooth. —*v.* bind or cover with cement: *He cemented over the crack in the wall; Shared experiences help to cement (= join firmly) a friendship.*
ce.men.tum (suh.MEN.tum) same as CEMENT, *n.* 2.
cem.e.ter.y (SEM.uh.tair.ee) *n.* **-ter.ies** a burial ground.
cen.a.cle (SEN.uh.cul) *n.* a place where a group meets for communing together.
cen.o.bite (SEN.uh.bite) *n.* a member of a monastic community, as distinguished from a hermit. —**cen.o.bit.ic** (-BIT.ic) or **cen.o.bit.i.cal** *adj.*
cen.o.taph (SEN.uh.taf) *n.* a monument to a person buried elsewhere: *a cenotaph of the Unknown Soldier.*
Ce.no.zo.ic (see.nuh.ZOH.ic) *n.* the most recent era of geological time, beginning about 65 million years ago, when mammals, birds, etc. evolved; *adj.: Cenozoic rock formations.*
cen.ser (SEN.sur) *n.* a vessel for burning incense during religious ceremonies.
cen.sor (SEN.sur) *n.* **1** one authorized to prohibit or edit movies, news, books, etc. to make them conform to standards of morality, security requirements, etc.: *The censor cut 10 minutes from the film.* **2** one of two officials of ancient Rome who conducted the census and supervised public morals. —*v.* subject to censorship: *Mail from the troops was censored; Ten minutes were censored (= cut) from the film.* —**cen.sor.ship** *n.*
cen.so.ri.al (sen.SOR.ee.ul) *adj.* having to do with a censor: *censorial powers.*
cen.so.ri.ous (sen.SOR.ee.us) *adj.* fault-finding: *a censorious mentality.* —**cen.so.ri.ous.ly** *adv.*

cen.sure (SEN.shur) *n.* **1** harsh criticism or disapproval, esp. of an authoritative or official nature: *the censure of the church; a* **censure motion** *against the government.* **2** censorship. —*v.* **-sures, -sured, -sur.ing** subject to censure: *The professor and his teachings were censured by the authorities.* —**cen.sur.a.ble** (-ruh.bul) *adj.*
cen.sus (SEN.sus) *n.* an official count of the population, usu. including a record of age, sex, occupation, etc.
cent *n.* a unit or piece of money equal to 1/100 of the dollar; penny.
cen.taur (SEN.tor) *n.* a monster of Greek myths that is half man and half horse.
cen.ta.vo (sen.TAH.voh) *n.* **-vos** a unit or piece of money equal to 1/100th of the Cuban or Mexican peso, Brazilian cruzeiro, Portuguese escudo, etc.
cen.te.nar.i.an (sen.tuh.NAIR.ee.un) *n.* one who is at least 100 years old.
cen.te.nar.y (sen.TEE.nuh.ree) *n.* **-nar.ies** centennial: *1981 marked the centenary of Picasso's birth; Over 100,000 visitors are expected here during the centenary; adja.: a centenary celebration, year.*
cen.ten.ni.al (sen.TEN.ee.ul) *n.* a 100th anniversary or its celebration: *to honor Mrs. Smith on her centennial;* *adja.: a centennial celebration, program, souvenir, survey, year.*
cen.ter (SEN.tur) *n.* **1** the point equally distant from a figure's outermost edges: *the center of a circle; She hit the target right in the center* or *hit the target dead center; adja.: the center spot, zone.* **2** a focus of activity: *amusement, civic, community, crisis, cultural, day-care, health, immigration, nerve, shopping centers; Paris is a center for fashion; An active person is said to be at the center of things; The astronaut was the center of attention all evening.* **3** a player stationed in the middle: *The center passes the ball to the quarterback.* **4 Center** political moderates or their position.
—*v.* **1** put or be at the center: *to center a heading on the page; The children centered around the storyteller.* **2** concentrate or focus: *The story centers on a kidnap attempt; The student's efforts were centered on winning a scholarship.* Also **cen.tre** Cdn.
cen.ter.fold (SEN.tur.fold) *n.* a picture spread across the stapled or stitched center of a magazine, often on a foldout, usu. associated with nudity. Also **cen.tre.fold** Cdn.
center ice *n.* the neutral center zone of a hockey rink.

center of gravity *n.* the point at or on which a body will balance.

cen.ter.piece (SEN.tur.piece) *n.* a decorative object that is placed in a central position. Also **cen.tre.piece** *Cdn.*

cen.tes.i.mo (sen.TES.i.moh) *n.* **-mos** a unit or piece of money equal to 1/100th of the lira, peso, escudo, etc.

Cen.ti.grade (SEN.tuh.grade) former term for CELSIUS.

cen.ti.gram (SEN.tuh.gram) *n.* 1/100 of a gram; also **cen.ti.gramme** *Brit.*

cen.ti.li.ter (SEN.tuh.lee.tur) *n.* 1/100th of a liter; also **cen.ti.li.tre** *Cdn.*

cen.time (SAHN.teem) *n.* a unit or piece of money equal to 1/100th of a franc, Algerian dinar, etc.

cen.ti.me.ter (SEN.tuh.mee.tur) *n.* 1/100th of a meter; also **cen.ti.me.tre** *Cdn.*

cen.ti.pede (SEN.tuh.peed) *n.* a worm-shaped, insectlike creature with a pair of legs on each of its many body segments.

cen.tral (SEN.trul) *adj.* **1** at or near the center: *a central area, place, position; A hospital has to have a central* (= easy-to-reach) *location; the* **central city** (= core of a metropolitan area); *The countries south of Mexico and north of South America make up* **Central America.** **2** main or dominant: *a central library and its branches; the central government in a country's capital; a central authority, issue, truth; Freedom is* **central** *to* (= essential to) *our way of life.* **3** *adja.* operated from one main location: *a house with central air-conditioning, heating, and vacuum; central planning.* —*n.* a main telephone exchange or one of its operators. —**cen.tral.ly** *adv.*

cen.tral.ize (SEN.truh.lize) *v.* **-iz.es, -ized, -iz.ing 1** bring to a center: *Business is centralized in the downtown area.* **2** put government, offices, etc. under one main control: *Certain functions are centralized in the Federal Government.* —**cen.tral.i.za.tion** (-luh.ZAY.shun, -lye-) *n.*

central nervous system *n.* the part of the nervous system containing the brain and spinal cord.

central processing unit *n.* the main component of a computer system in which data is processed and instructions are executed.

centre, centrefold, centrepiece See CENTER, etc.

cen.trif.u.gal (sen.TRIF.yoo.gul) *adj.* tending to move away from the center: *On a merry-go round, the* **centrifugal force** *tends to pull a rider away from the center.*

cen.tri.fuge (SEN.truh.fyooj) *n.* a centrifugal machine, as one used to separate substances of differing densities such as cream and milk: *High-speed centrifuges are used to enrich uranium for weapons-grade material.*

cen.trip.e.tal (sen.TRIP.uh.tul) *adj.* tending to move toward the center: *On a merry-go-round, the* **centripetal force** *keeps you moving in a circular path.*

cen.trist (SEN.trist) *n.* a member of a moderate political party: *a centrist position* (between Right and Left). —**cen.trism** *n.*

cen.tro.some (SEN.truh.sohm) *n.* a protoplasmic body that is the dividing center in a cell.

cen.tu.rion (sen.CHOOR.ee.un, -TOOR.ee.un) *n.* the commander of a body of about 100 troops in the ancient Roman army.

cen.tu.ry (SEN.chuh.ree) *n.* **-ries 1** a period of 100 years: *The 21st century A.D. runs from 2001 through 2100; People have become more and more civilized over* or *through* **the centuries**. **2** any group or series of 100 similar things: *A cricket batsman scores a century* (=100 runs).

century plant *n.* an American agave that blooms once after a long life, then dies.

ceph.a.lo.pod (SEF.uh.luh.pod) *n.* a highly developed mollusk such as the squid, octopus, etc. with tentacles and a beaked mouth.

ce.ram.al (suh.RAM.ul) same as CERMET.

ce.ram.ic (suh.RAM.ic) *n.* **1 ceramics** *pl.* [takes *sing. v.*] the art of making earthenware, porcelain, etc. by firing clay or a similar material. **2** a product of ceramics: *Ceramics include bricks, cement, pottery, and sewer products;* *adj.*: *ceramic industries, tiles.* —**ce.ram.ist** or **ce.ram.i.cist** *n.*

ce.re.al (SEER.ee.ul) *n.* **1** a grass producing an edible grain, as wheat, oats, and rice; also, such a grain; *adj:* *cereal crops, grasses, grains, products.* **2** food made from a cereal grain: *ready-to-eat breakfast cereals such as cornflakes (cold cereal); a hot cereal such as oatmeal.*

cer.e.bel.lum (ser.uh.BEL.um) *n.* the part of the brain that controls muscular coordination.

ce.re.bral (suh.REE.brul, SER.uh.brul) *adj.* **1** having to do with the brain: *cerebral cortex, palsy.* **2** intellectual: *a hard cerebral style of verse.* —**ce.re.bral.ly** *adv.*

cerebral cortex *n.* the gray matter that controls the most complex nervous activities.

cerebral palsy *n.* a nervous disorder manifested in a lack of muscular co-ordination.

cer.e.brate (SER.uh.brate) *v.* **-brates, -brat.ed, -brat.ing** use the brain; cogitate; think. —**cer.e.bra.tion** (-BRAY.shun) *n.*

cer.e.brum (SER.uh.brum, suh.REE.brum) *n.* the most important and, in humans, largest part of the brain.

cere.cloth (SEER.cloth) *n.* a wax-coated cloth formerly used to shroud the dead.

cere.ment (SEER.munt) *n.* a shroud for the dead, esp. a cerecloth.

cer.e.mo.ni.al (ser.uh.MOH.nee.ul) *adj.* accompanied by or associated with ceremony: *The priest made a ceremonial offering; He donned ceremonial robes for the occasion.* —*n.* a ceremony or ritual; **cer.e.mo.ni.al.ly** *adv.*

cer.e.mo.ni.ous (ser.uh.MOH.nee.us) *adj.* full of or fond of ceremony: *A coronation is not a simple but a ceremonious affair; ceremonious courtesy, devotion, greetings; a ceremonious bow, occasion, procession, religion, welcome.* —**cer.e.mo.ni.ous.ly** *adv.*; **cer.e.mo.ni.ous.ness** *n.*

cer.e.mo.ny (SER.uh.moh.nee) *n.* **-nies** 1 a set of prescribed formal acts appropriate to a function such as a wedding or religious rite; also, the function itself: *to perform a religious ceremony; a flag-raising ceremony; funeral ceremony; marriage ceremony.* 2 formality: *The burial was conducted with appropriate ceremony; Everyone joined in the celebrations* **without ceremony**; *There's no need to* **stand on ceremony** (= be formal) *among friends.*

ce.rise (suh.REECE) *adj.* clear, bright red, or cherrylike in color; *n.* such a color.

ce.ri.um (SEER.ee.um) *n.* a soft, iron-gray metallic element.

cer.met (SUR.met) *n.* a strong, highly heat-resistant material, made of a ceramic bonded with a metal; ceramal.

cer.tain (SUR.tun) *adj.* 1 limited: *He received a certain portion of the profits; I trust him to a certain extent.* 2 particular but not specified: *I met a certain Mr. Smith; A certain amount of money was paid as a bribe; The play has a certain appeal;* **pron.***:* **Certain** *of his friends deserted him.* 3 assured: *He is facing certain death; There's no certain remedy for this ailment.* 4 *adjp.* completely sure: sure and certain; *We are certain to win; We are certain about winning; quite certain of the outcome; He made certain she would accept before he proposed; It is quite certain* (= sure as proven) *that the earth is round; I know* **for certain** (= without doubt) *it rained yesterday.* —**cer.tain.ly** *adv.*

cer.tain.ty (SUR.tun.tee) *n.* **-ties** 1 sureness of mind: *We can state with certainty that it will not rain today; Our certainty has been shaken by the darkening skies; There is no certainty of our winning in a lottery.* 2 a definite or proven fact or belief: *It's a physical certainty that the sun will rise tomorrow; That 2 + 2 is 4 is a mathematical certainty; It is a moral certainty* (= generally true) *that mothers love their offspring; We know this* **for a certainty** (= without a doubt).

cer.ti.fi.a.ble (sur.tuh.FYE.uh.bul) *adj.* 1 that can be certified: *a certifiable candidate, result.* 2 so ill mentally that the authorities have to be notified: *a certifiable lunatic.* —**cer.ti.fi.a.bly** *adv.*: *The patient seems certifiably dead; Hughes was certifiably insane.*

cer.tif.i.cate (sur.TIF.uh.kit) *n.* a usu. official document testifying to a qualification, fact, etc.: *birth, death, gift, marriage, teaching certificates; He cashed (in) his savings certificate; to issue a certificate of deposit, ownership, vaccination.* —**cer.ti.fi.ca.tion** (SUR.tuh.fuh.CAY.shun) *n.*

cer.ti.fy (SUR.tuh.fye) *v.* **-fies, -fied, -fy.ing** 1 declare, endorse, guarantee, etc., usu. by a certificate: *The mechanic has certified the car is roadworthy; a car certified to be roadworthy; certified (as) roadworthy; A* **certified check** *cannot be returned because the money is being held by the bank; Users of* **certified mail** *get a receipt signed by the addressee;* **Certified milk** *has to meet official standards; A* **certified public accountant** *is one qualified to practice under state law.* 2 declare to be insane: *A certified (mental) case is normally hospitalized.* —**cer.ti.fi.er** *n.*

cer.ti.tude (SUR.tuh.tude) *n. Formal.* sureness; certainty: *There's no absolute certitude about life after death; We cannot assert this with the certitude of mathematical truths.*

ce.ru.le.an (suh.ROO.lee.un) *adj.* sky-blue.

ce.ru.men (suh.ROO.mun) *n.* earwax.

cer.vix (SUR.vix) *n., pl.* **-vic.es** (-vi.seez) or **-vix.es** the neck-shaped lower end of the uterus. —**cer.vi.cal** *adj.*: *cervical cancer; a cervical* (= neck) *collar.*

ce.sar.e.an or **Ce.sar.e.an** (si.ZAIR.ee.un) *n.* the delivery of a fetus by surgical incision into the uterus: *The baby was delivered by cesarean; A cesarean had to be performed;* also **caesarean section, Caesarean section, C-section.**

ce.si.um (SEE.zee.um) *n.* a soft, silver-white metallic element used in photoelectric cells.

ces.sa.tion (ses.AY.shun) *n.* a ceasing: *a brief cessation of pain.*

ces.sion (SESH.un) *n.* a ceding or something ceded, as territory.

cess.pool (SES.pool) *n.* a covered pit or buried tank for sewage.

ce.ta.ce.an (si.TAY.shun) *n.* an aquatic mammal of a group that includes whales, dolphins, and porpoises. —*adj.* also **ce.ta.ceous** (-shus).

Cha.blis (shab.LEE, SHAB.lee) *n.* a dry white wine.

cha-cha (CHAH.chah) *n.* **1** a ballroom dance of Latin American origin. **2** the music for it. Also **cha-cha-cha.** —*v.* **-chas, -chaed, -cha.ing** dance the cha-cha.

cha.dor (CHUD.or) *n.* a long, usu. black garment traditionally worn by Muslim women draped around the body from head to foot.

chafe *v.* **chafes, chafed, chaf.ing 1** be irritated or impatient: *students chafing at restrictions; workers chafing under heavy loads.* **2** rub so as to warm hands, skin, etc. **3** wear away by rubbing action: *a sore caused by a chafing harness;* **n.:** *Friction from clothing can cause* **chafing** *of the skin.*

chaf.er (CHAY.fur) *n.* a beetle such as the cockchafer or june beetle.

chaff *n.* **1** the husks of grain and other matter discarded in threshing: *to separate the wheat from the chaff* (= trivial or worthless material). **2** light teasing; banter. —*v.* tease jovially: *to chaff a guy about his girlfriends.* —**chaff.er** *n.*

chaf.finch *n.* a small European songbird.

chaff.y (CHAF.ee) *adj.* **chaff.i.er, -i.est 1** like chaff; worthless. **2** full of chaff.

chaf.ing dish (CHAY.fing-) *n.* a dish with a heating device for cooking or warming food at the table.

cha.grin (shuh.GRIN) *n.* distress or irritation at failure, embarrassment, etc.: *To his great chagrin, his younger brother got the job.* —*v.* **-grins, -grined, -grin.ing** cause chagrin to someone: *It chagrined him to see that he was losing business;* **adj.:** *He was* **chagrined** *to learn that a rival got the job; felt chagrined at being rejected for the job; was chagrined*

that he didn't get the job.

chain *n.* **1** a flexible series of connected metal links used for binding, transmitting power, etc. **2 chains** *pl.* fetters or bonds: *the chains of love.* **3** a unit of linear measure: *The "surveyor's chain" is 66 ft. (20.12 m); The "engineer's chain" is 100 ft. (30.48 m).* **4** a series of usu. similar, connected things: *a chain of events; the chain of military command.* **5** same as CHAIN STORE: *a coast-to-coast supermarket chain.* —**in chains** in an enslaved condition. —*v.* bind, connect, or confine by or as if by chains: *a dog chained to a post.*

chain gang *n.* a group of prisoners chained together for outdoor labor.

chain letter *n.* a letter asking the recipient to send copies of it to others who are to do the same.

chain mail *n.* flexible body armor made of meshed metal links.

chain reaction *n.* a usu. self-sustaining series of events, esp. chemical or nuclear reactions, each of which causes the next one in the series.

chain saw *n.* a portable power saw with the teeth driven on an endless chain.

chain-smoke *v.* **-smokes, -smoked, -smok.ing** smoke a continuous series of cigarettes. —**chain-smoker** *n.*

chain store *n.* one of a chain of retail stores owned by one company; also **chain.**

chair *n.* **1** a seat with a back support: *a deck chair; easy chair; rocking chair; swivel chair; a dentist's chair; a dentist with a great chairside manner.* **2** a position of dignity, authority, etc., as a professorship: *to endow, establish a chair in linguistics; Mrs. Chen was appointed to the chair; We need someone to* **take the chair** (= to preside) *in the absence of the president.* **3** a chairman; chairperson: *Address all questions to the chair, please; Wait for the chair to recognize you; A new chair is to be elected.* **4** the electric chair for executing criminals: *He was sent to the chair.* —*v.* preside: *to chair a meeting.*

chair car *n.* a railroad car with reclining seats; parlor car.

chair lift *n.* a ski lift with chairs to ride in.

chair.man (CHAIR.mun) *n.* **-men 1** the person presiding at a meeting; president. **2** the head of a board, committee, etc.: *the department chairman; the chairman of the board.* —**chair.man.ship** *n.*

chair.per.son (CHAIR.pur.sun) *n.* one who presides over a meeting or heads a group such as a committee.

chair.wo.man (CHAIR.woom.un) *n.* **-men** a woman chairperson.

chaise (SHAYS) *n.* a light, two- or four-wheeled pleasure carriage.

chaise longue (SHAYS.long) *n., pl.* **chaise longues** (-longs) or **chaises longues** (SHAYS.longs) a chair with the seat extended to support the legs. Also **chaise lounge** (-lownj).

chal.ced.o.ny (cal.SED.uh.nee) *n.* **-nies** a pale, waxy, translucent quartz, including carnelian, onyx, etc.

cha.let (sha.LAY) *n.* **1** a Swiss dwelling with balconies and large projecting eaves. **2** a house, cottage, etc. in similar style. **3** an Alpine herdsman's hut.

chal.ice (CHAL.is) *n.* **1** a goblet, esp. a cup for Eucharistic wine. **2** the cup-shaped part of a flower.

chalk (CHAWK) *n.* **1** a soft, white limestone. **2** prepared chalk or a substitute used to write on chalkboards: *to write with chalk; a piece of chalk.* —*v.* rub, treat, write, etc. with chalk. —**chalk up 1** record or score: *He chalked up three wins against one defeat.* **2** attribute: *He chalked up his mistakes to youth and inexperience.*

chalk.board (CHAWK.board) *n.* a usu. black or green board prepared for writing on with chalk and used as a visual aid.

chalk.y *adj.* **chalk.i.er, -i.est** having the qualities of chalk: *a chalky deposit, fog, powder; chalky soil.*

chal.lenge (CHAL.unj) *v.* **chal.leng.es, chal.lenged, chal.leng.ing 1** demand identification: *Give the password when challenged by the sentry.* **2** invite to take part in a duel, game, etc.; dare: *She challenged him to a game of tennis; challenged him to fight.* **3** excite to effort, courage, etc.; *adj.*: *to feel* **challenged**; *physically challenged* (= handicapped) *youth; a very* **challenging** *career, environment, issue, problem, task.* **4** question the truth of something; dispute: *to challenge a claim, conclusion, will; to challenge* (= object to) *a prospective juror.* —*n.* **1** demand: *The sentry gave the challenge, "Who goes there?"* **2** a dare: *The boxer issued a challenge to all comers; There was no one to take up or accept or respond to the challenge; a formidable challenge; a challenge to human dignity.* **3** a situation calling for one's best efforts: *Journalism offers many challenges to a resourceful writer; It was a challenge just to keep breathing while waiting for help.* **4** objection: *The challenge was upheld and the juror was dropped.*

—**chal.lenge.a.ble** *adj.* —**chal.leng.er** *n.*

chal.lis (SHAL.ee) *n.* a light, fine clothing fabric of cotton, wool, etc. Also **chal.lie.**

cham.ber (CHAIM.bur) *n.* **1** a hall for assemblies, receptions, etc.: *an audience chamber; reception chamber.* **2** a council, board, legislative body, etc.: *The upper and lower houses are the two chambers of a bicameral legislature.* **3** any enclosed space: *the upper and lower chambers of the heart; A charge or cartridge is held in the chamber of a firearm; combustion, gas, torture chambers; a lady's chamber* (= bedroom). **4 chambers** *pl.* a judge's office: *I'll see you in chambers.*

cham.ber.lain (CHAIM.bur.lin) *n.* a high official at court, as a treasurer or the steward of a lord or monarch.

cham.ber.maid (CHAIM.bur.maid) *n.* a maid who makes beds and cleans rooms.

chamber music *n.* music written for small groups to perform, as in a string quartet.

chamber of commerce *n.* an association of local businesses promoting a community's commercial interests.

chamber pot *n.* a vessel used as a toilet in a bedroom.

cham.bray (SHAM.bray) *n.* a light, usu. cotton fabric for clothing, woven with white threads across a colored warp.

cha.me.le.on (cuh.MEEL.yun) *n.* **1** a lizard that changes color to match its surroundings. **2** a changeable person.

cham.fer (CHAM.fur) *n.* a beveled edge or corner; groove or flute. —*v.* cut or shape a chamfer in wood, stone, etc.

cham.ois (SHAM.ee) *n. sing. & pl.* **1** a soft leather used esp. as a polishing cloth. **2** (*also* sham.WAH) a goatlike mountain antelope of Europe and western Asia.

cham.o.mile (CAM.uh.mile) *n.* a daisylike, fragrant herb whose bitter dried flowers are used in a medicinal tea.

champ *v.* chew or bite vigorously; gnash the teeth. —**champ (at) the bit** show impatience or restlessness to begin something. —*n. Informal.* a champion.

cham.pagne (sham.PAIN) *n.* a sparkling wine, usu. white: *Let's break out the champagne and celebrate; pink champagne.*

cham.paign (sham.PAIN) *n.* an expanse of level, open land.

cham.pi.on (CHAM.pee.un) *v.* fight for a cause, person, etc.; defend. —*n.* **1** a valiant defender: *a champion of freedom.* **2** one holding first place or winning first prize, esp. in sports: *the defending champion of the world heavyweight title;* **adj**a.: *a champion athlete, boxer, poodle.* —**cham.pion.ship** *n.*

chance *n.* **1** an apparently uncaused event; luck: *It was by pure* or *sheer chance that we met in Moscow;* **adj**.: *a chance discovery, encounter, meeting.* **2** risk: *He is not taking any chances; He's afraid to take a chance on someone he doesn't know well; Should I take the chance?* **3** opportunity: *a chance for success; a chance to compete in the Olympics; He let his chance slip by; missed his chance; He hasn't got a chance; doesn't have* **a ghost of a chance.** **4** possibility: *There's only a slight* or *slim chance he'll win now; There's little* or *small chance of his winning; the chances of being a winner; (The) chances are he may lose; Jane stands a good chance of winning; He doesn't* **stand a chance** *against such heavy odds; He has entered anyhow* **on the off chance** (= on the remote possibility) *of his rival's dropping out.* —*v.* **chanc.es, chanced, chanc.ing 1** meet, come, happen, etc. accidentally: *He chanced on the discovery; He chanced to be there when it happened.* **2** hazard or risk: *It's too dangerous; don't chance it!*

chan.cel (CHAN.sul) *n.* the altar area of a church, used by the choir and clergy.

chan.cel.ler.y (CHAN.suh.luh.ree) *n.* **-cel.ler.ies 1** the rank or office of a chancellor. **2** the offices of a consulate or embassy.

chan.cel.lor (CHAN.suh.lur) *n.* a high official, as the heads of some European governments, the titular heads of some universities, church officials in charge of diocesan business, and judges in courts of equity: *Britain's* **chancellor of the exchequer** (= finance minister). —**chan.cel.lor.ship** *n.*

chan.cer.y (CHAN.suh.ree) *n.* **-cer.ies 1** the office or rank of a chancellor. **2** an office of public archives; record office. **3** a court of equity.

chan.cre (SHANG.cur) *n.* a hard, red sore which is the first symptom of syphilis. —**chan.crous** (-crus) *adj.*

chan.croid (SHANG.croid) *n.* a soft venereal ulcer, nonsyphilitic and caused by a bacterium. —**chan.croi.dal** (shang.CROY.dul) *adj.*

chanc.y (CHAN.see) *adj.* **chanc.i.er, -i.est** *Informal.* risky: *accidents caused by chancy driving; Fortune-telling is a chancy occupation.*

chan.de.lier (shan.duh.LEER) *n.* a many-branched hanging light fixture: *crystal chandeliers.*

chan.dler (CHAND.lur) *n.* **1** a retailer of provisions: *a ship's chandler.* **2** a candle maker or seller. —**chan.dler.y** *n.*

change *v.* **chang.es, changed, chang.ing 1** make or become different: *Jack changed his name; changed it from Smith to Jones; His beliefs have changed radically; One experience changed his life; He changes color when you mention it; Can you change a dollar (for quarters, dimes, etc.)?* **2** exchange: *I changed seats with her; We changed seats; to change dollars for francs.* **3** enter, put, take, etc. something in place of something else: *We change trains at the next stop; Let's change into beachwear; Later we'll change for dinner; Don't forget to change the baby* (= baby's diaper). —**change the channel** *Informal.* change the topic of conversation. —**change hands** pass from one owner to another. —**change one's tune** alter one's story or attitude. —*n.* **1** an alteration or difference: *the change of seasons from summer to fall; a refreshing, welcome change in the weather; There's a marked, striking change in his appearance with the hairpiece on; The new posting brought about* or *effected a drastic change in our lifestyle; Sweeping changes in government are taking place; The new government is a change for the better; People go away on weekends for a change of pace from the hectic life of the city; Let's eat out* **for a change** (= for variety). **2** something to be substituted: *Bring just one change of clothes; The doctor ordered a change of diet; a change of address.* **3** money returned from an overpayment: *The waiter brought back change.* **4** money in smaller units, esp. coins: *Let the waiter keep the change; Do you have change for a dollar? the loose change jingling in his pocket; small change; $10.15 is $10* **and change;** *a* **change purse** *for keeping change.* **4** a pattern or sequence for ringing bells. —**ring the changes** ring bells through all possible variations. *In his book, he rings all the changes on East versus West.* —**chang.er** *n.;* **change.ful** *adj.;* **change.less** *adj.*

change.a.ble (CHAIN.juh.bul) *adj.* capable of change: *a changeable temperament; changeable as the weather.*

change.house *n.* a building for bathers to change clothes in.

change.ling *n.* a child substituted for one that is stolen.

change of heart *n.* a change in thinking or attitude: *She had a change of heart at the last moment.*

change of life *n.* menopause.

change.o.ver (CHANGE.oh.vur) *n.* a complete conversion from one system, activity, etc. to another: *the changeover from the imperial to the metric system.*

chan.nel (CHAN.ul) *n.* **1** a long, narrow, usu. deep course or way, as a groove, duct, stream bed, the navigable part of a waterway (*a shipping channel*), or a large strait (*the English Channel*). **2** any path of transmission, communication, or activity, as a frequency range for one radio or TV signal: *Let's change the channel for a better program.* **3 channels** *pl.* official lines of communication: *diplomatic, military channels; a petition sent through the proper channels.* —*v.* **-nels, -neled, -nel.ing** make a channel for or in something: *He channels his money into profitable ventures; channels his profits to worthy causes;* also **chan.nelled, chan.nel.ling** *Cdn.* Also **chan.nel.ize** (CHAN.ul.ize) *v.* **-iz.es, -ized, -iz.ing.**

chan.son (SHAN.song, -sun) *n.* a song.

chant *n.* **1** a melody in which many words are sung to one note, esp. a religious song: *Gregorian chant.* **2** a rhythmic and repetitive utterance: *the chant of the mob outside the embassy.* —*v.* **1** sing or speak in a chant: *The demonstrators chanted slogans as they marched down the street.* **2** sing about a subject: *a poet chanting his love's virtues.* —**chant.er** *n.*

chan.teuse (shan.TOOZ) *n.* a female singer, esp. in a nightclub.

chan.tey (SHAN.tee) *n.* **-teys** or **-ties** a sailor's work song.

chan.ti.cleer (CHAN.tuh.cleer) *n.* a rooster.

chan.try (CHAN.tree) *n.* **-tries 1** an endowment for the singing of Masses for a deceased. **2** a chapel endowed for this purpose.

chan.ty (CHAN.tee) same as CHANTEY.

Cha.nu.kah (KAH.nuh.kuh) same as HANUKKAH.

cha.os (KAY.os) *n.* total disorganization: *to bring order out of chaos.* —**cha.ot.ic** (kay.OT.ic) *adj.*

chap *v.* **chaps, chapped, chap.ping** to dry, roughen, or crack because of cold, wind, etc.: *Too much dishwashing had chapped his hands;* **adj.:** *chapped lips.* —*n.* **1** *Informal.* a fellow; guy. **2 chaps** (also SHAPS) *pl.* protective leggings worn by cowboys over their trousers.

chap.ar.ral (shap.uh.RAL) *n.* in S.W. United States, an area of thick shrubs.

chap.book *n.* a popular pamphlet containing tracts, ballads, romances, etc., as once sold by chapmen.

cha.peau (sha.POH) *n.* **-peaus** or **-peaux** (-POZE) a hat.

chap.el (CHAP.ul) *n.* **1** a small church. **2** a small room for worship in a large church or cathedral. **3** a place of worship in a home, school, prison, etc. **4** a religious service held in a school: *to go to chapel; She's never late for chapel.*

chap.er.on (SHAP.uh.rone) *n.* a mature person who escorts a single young woman or supervises a social gathering of young people: *Teachers help out as chaperons at school dances.* Also **chap.er.one.** —*v.* **-ons** or **-ones, -oned, -on.ing:** *Teachers and parents chaperon school dances.* —**chap.er.on.age** (-roh.nij) *n.*

chap.fall.en (CHAP.foll.un) *adj.* downcast; crestfallen.

chap.lain (CHAP.lin) *n.* a clergyman serving in a public institution such as a club, hospital, prison, school, etc. or with the military. —**chap.lain.cy** *n.* **-cies.**

chap.let (CHAP.lit) *n.* **1** a garland of flowers, jewels, etc. for the head. **2** a string of beads, esp. one used in reciting prayers. —**chap.let.ed** *adj.*

chap.man (CHAP.mun) *n.* **-men** formerly in Britain, a traveling salesman; peddler.

chap.ter (CHAP.tur) *n.* **1** a major division of a book: *an introductory chapter; Chapter 3, verse 42 of the Koran says, "Oh Mary, Lo Allah has chosen thee and made thee pure and hath preferred thee above [all] the women of creation"; The novel closes with a chapter on the wedding; School was an exciting chapter* (= *period*) *of her youth.* **2** a local branch of a society: *the local chapter of the National Association of Chefs.* **3** a meeting of canons, monks, etc. —**chapter and verse 1** exact authority: *Can you cite or give or put down or quote chapter and verse for what you say?* **2** thoroughly: *I know the whole story chapter and verse.*

Chapter 11 *n.* a provision in U.S. law for a business to reorganize itself while facing bankruptcy: *The firm has filed for protection from creditors under Chapter 11 (of the U.S. Bankruptcy Code).*

char *n.* **1** one of several trouts including the brook trout. **2** *Brit.* a charwoman. **3** charcoal. —*v.* **chars,**

charred, char.ring 1 work as a charwoman. 2 burn to charcoal; scorch and blacken.

char.ac.ter (CAIR.uc.tur) *n.* 1 the distinctive personality of a person, group, etc.: *a man of fine character; Suffering builds character* (= moral strength); **adj.**: *character formation, traits; character assassination* (= slandering); *A **character witness** gives evidence in a legal action about the character of a person.* 2 a person in a story, drama, etc.: *"Hamlet," unlike "Julius Caesar," is a fictitious character; the leading character in a novel;* **adj.**: *a character actor, part, sketch.* 3 a distinguishing property; nature: *Each one has a character of his own; a directive of an official character.* 4 [usu. derogatory] a person: *He's quite a character* (= an eccentric); *dangerous, obnoxious, shady, suspicious, unpleasant characters; the most unforgettable* (= impressive) *character I have met.* 5 a symbol, as a letter or ideogram, or a unit of computer data representing one: *Roman characters; special characters such as mathematical symbols; italic characters* (= characters in italic style); *ASCII is a **character set**.* —**in** (or **out of**) **character** true (or false) to one's nature or role: *An actor should always be in character.*

char.ac.ter.is.tic (care.uc.tuh.RIS.tic) *n.* an identifying or distinctive property: *Stripes are a distinguishing characteristic of the zebra.* —**adj.** identifying or distinctive: *the characteristic odor of chlorine gas; Hospitality is characteristic of most cultures.* —**char.ac.ter.is.ti.cal.ly** *adv.*

char.ac.ter.ize (CAIR.uc.tuh.rize) *v.* **-iz.es, -ized, -iz.ing** 1 portray or describe as being of a certain kind: *equipment to analyze and characterize materials; Iago is characterized as a villain.* 2 be characteristic of or give a characteristic to something: *Thoroughness characterizes her work; He characterized the report as malicious; The zebra is characterized by its stripes.*
—**char.ac.ter.i.za.tion** (-ruh.ZAY.shun, -rye-) *n.*

cha.rade (shuh.RAID) *n.* 1 a pretense or false show: *The discussion proved to be a mere charade.* 2 **charades** *pl.* [takes *sing. v.*] a game in which each participant acts out words and phrases that have to be guessed.

char.broiled *adj.* broiled over a charcoal fire: *charbroiled steaks.*

char.coal *n.* 1 a dark gray, light, porous material made by partially burning wood, bone, etc. and used as fuel, in filters, etc. 2 a crayon or pencil made of this substance. 3 a sketch done with it.

chard *n.* the greens of a kind of beet used as a vegetable.

char.don.nay (shar.duh.NAY) *n.* a dry white wine.

charge *v.* **charg.es, charged, charg.ing** 1 fill, load, or saturate: *We have to charge our battery; The mechanic charges it up;* **adj.**: *The air was **charged** with excitement.* 2 impose on, as a task, responsibility, instruction, etc.: *He charged her with the task of reorganizing the office.* 3 ask (so much) in payment: *We will have to charge (you) for it; We can't charge less than $500; We charge by the minute* (= for each minute). 4 accuse, esp. officially: *The police charged her with speeding; They charged that she was driving 25 km over the limit.* 5 rush forward: *She charged into the store when the doors opened, but charged out again to get her purse from the car; The bull charged at us.* 6 record an item as an obligation or debt: *He went shopping and charged a lot of clothes; Books are charged out of a library by patrons.*
—*n.* 1 a load, as a quantity of explosive, electricity, etc.: *a positive or negative charge of electricity; a depth charge used against submarines; A charge explodes when set off.* 2 duty, custody, command, responsibility, etc.; also, a subject of it: *the judge's charge* (= instruction) *to the jury; babies placed in a sitter's charge* (= custody); *a babysitter's little charges; A sitter is put **in charge** of* (= responsible for) *a baby; Is she still in charge? Will someone please **take charge**?* 3 a price or cost: *an admission charge; There's a basic cover charge (for your place at the table) besides the charge for food and drink; The operator announcing the collect call asked, "Will you accept charges?" Will that be cash or charge* (= charge to your account)? 4 an accusation: *a baseless, false, frivolous, trumped-up charge; to bring, face, level, withdraw a charge; whether to drop or press **charges**; The police laid a charge of reckless driving against her; She denied the charge; The judge threw out the charge; She was arrested on another charge.* 5 an attack: *a fierce cavalry charge; to fight off a charge; the charge of the Light Brigade.* 6 *Informal.* a thrill: *an emotional charge; He got a real charge out of it.*
—**charge.a.ble** (CHAR.juh.bul) *adj.*

charge account *n.* an arrangement for buying on credit.

charge card *n.* a card issued by a firm to customers for charging purchases to an account, usu. up to a maximum limit; credit card.

char.gé d'af.faires (shar.ZHAY.duh.FAIR) *n.*, *pl.* **char.gés** (-ZHAY, -ZHAYZ) **d'af.faires** (-FAIR) a subordinate diplomatic official in charge of an embassy, delegation, etc.

charg.er *n.* **1** person or thing that charges: *a battery charger.* **2** a war horse.

charge sheet *n.* an indictment.

char.i.ot (CHAIR.ee.ut) *n.* a light, horse-drawn, two-wheeled cart, used formerly in racing, war, parades, etc. —**char.i.o.teer** (-uh.TEER) *n.*

cha.ris.ma (cuh.RIZ.muh) *n.* **1** divine grace or healing power. **2** a magical quality of arousing the devotion of one's followers: *a leader with charisma.*

char.is.mat.ic (cair.iz.MAT.ic) *adj.* **1** having to do with divine healing power: *a charismatic church, movement.* **2** arousing devotion: *a charismatic leader, personality.*

char.i.ta.ble (CHAIR.i.tuh.bul) *adj.* **1** kind, forgiving, etc.: *a charitable attitude, deed, purpose, spirit, view.* **2** helping the needy or having to do with it: *a charitable agency, cause, contribution, (tax) deduction, donation, foundation, gift, organization.* —**char.i.ta.bly** *adv.*

char.i.ty (CHAIR.i.tee) *n.* **1** love of fellow humans: *St. Paul urged faith, hope, and charity; "Charity begins at home."* **2** a forgiving attitude: *He treated his enemies with charity; They pleaded for charity.* **3** *pl.* **-ties** aid to the poor and needy; almsgiving: *to dispense, distribute, give charity; charity for widows and orphans.* **4** *pl.* **-ties** a charitable institution: *Give to your favorite charity; charities such as the Salvation Army.*

cha.ri.va.ri (shiv.uh.REE) same as SHIVAREE.

char.la.tan (SHAR.luh.tun) *n.* one claiming skills or knowledge that he does not have; phony; quack. —**char.la.tan.ism** *n.*

Charles.ton (CHARL.stun) *n.* a lively dance in 4/4 time, popular in the 1920's.

char.ley horse (CHAR.lee-) *n.* a muscular soreness or stiffness caused by strain or a blow.

charm *n.* **1** an attractive or pleasing personal quality: *the charm of youth; She turns on her charm when she wants something from her dad; A woman of irresistible charm; She exudes charm; Her presence lends charm to any gathering.* **2** a magic formula, ritual, object, etc.: *He wears a charm to ward off the evil eye.* —**work like a charm** function exactly as desired; succeed completely. —*v.* attract, please, win over, etc. by charm; *adj.:* *We would be charmed to accept your invitation; We are charmed by the prospect of meeting her; She seems to lead a charmed life (safe from dangers and difficulties); No one likes to break into his charmed (= exclusive) circle of friends.* —**charm.er** *n.*

char.meuse (shar.MOOZ) *n.* a fine semilustrous silk or synthetic crepe with a satin face.

charming *adj.* attractive or pleasing: *It's charming to watch children perform; a charming personality; She is charming to everyone;* **charm.ing.ly** *adv.*

char.nel house (CHAR.nul-) *n.* a building or vault for bones and corpses.

chart *n.* **1** a sheet or display showing special information with graphics, tables, etc.: *a weather chart; a patient's clinical chart; a flow chart (= diagram) showing the systems or operations of a computer.* **2** a map, esp. one for sea navigation. **3 charts** *pl.* the listings of sales by rank, esp. of songs: *Her album was number one on the charts; It topped the charts.* —*v.* map out using a chart; plan in detail: *to chart the position of a ship; to chart out a sales campaign.*

chart.er *n.* **1** a written authorization founding or giving rights to a corporation, university, etc.: *to apply for a charter; to grant a charter to trade in a territory; to charter (= original) member of a society.* **2** a constitution or manifesto of political principles: *the U.N. Charter.* **3** a travel arrangement in which a group hires a bus, ship, airplane, etc.: *tours and charters; scheduled and charter flights.* —*v.* **1** give a charter to an institution: *The Canadian government charters banks to do business in Canada.* **2** hire or lease: *to charter a bus for a trip to the zoo; to charter a flight to Britain.* —**chartered** *adj.* given rights by government charter: *a chartered accountant, bank, life underwriter.*

char.treuse (shar.TROOZ) *n.* a bright greenish yellow.

char.wom.an (CHAR.woom.un) *n.* **-wom.en** a hired cleaning woman.

char.y (CHAIR.ee) *adj.* **char.i.er, -i.est** **1** cautious: *She is chary about throwing away money; chary of being too generous.* **2** sparing: *a curmudgeon who is chary of kind words.* —**char.i.ly** *adv.;* **char.i.ness** *n.*

chase (CHACE) *v.* **chas.es, chased,**

chas.ing 1 pursue: *to chase after name and fame.* 2 drive away: *Chase that dog off the lawn.* 3 *Informal.* rush: *The boys went chasing down the street.* 4 engrave or emboss metal; *adj.*: *a chased silver teapot.* —*n.* 1 pursuit: *The police caught the robbers after a short chase; the thrill of the chase* (= hunting). 2 that which is hunted. 3 a groove, slot, etc. —**give chase** pursue. —**lead someone (on) a merry chase** make someone work hard toward a goal but in vain.
chas.er (CHAY.sur) *n.* 1 *Informal.* a light drink following hard liquor: *whiskey with a beer chaser.* 2 a person or thing that chases: *an ambulance chaser; a skirt* or *woman chaser.*
chasm (CAZ.um) *n.* 1 a deep gap: *a yawning chasm.* 2 a rift, as between former friends.
chas.sis (SHAS.ee, CHAS.ee) *n., pl.* **chas.sis** (-eez) 1 a supporting framework, as of a car, truck, radio, or TV set. 2 the landing-gear assembly of an airplane.
chaste *adj.* 1 free from improper sexual relations: *a chaste life, woman; a chaste* (= celibate) *priest.* 2 simple in style, plain, unadorned, etc.: *her chaste diction, prose, wit.* —**chaste.ly** *adv.*; **chaste.ness** *n.*
chas.ten (CHAY.sun) *v.* correct by punishing; purify; *adj.*: *The defeat had a chastening influence on his behavior.* —**chas.ten.er** *n.*
chas.tise (chas.TIZE) *v.* **-tis.es, -tised, -tis.ing** punish by a beating or severe reprimand. —**chas.tise.ment** (CHAS.tiz.munt, chas.TIZE-) *n.*
chas.ti.ty (CHAS.ti.tee) *n.* the state of abstaining from sexual relations: *the religious vows of poverty, chastity, and obedience.*
chas.u.ble (CHAZ.yuh.bul) *n.* the sleeveless outer vestment worn by a priest at Mass.
chat *v.* **chats, chat.ted, chat.ting** 1 talk in a light, easy manner: *In London, he goes to parties to meet and chat up* (= try to make friends with) *bureaucrats.* 2 exchange messages on a computer network in real time. —*n.* a chatting: *a chat about old times; a chat between friends; Franklin Roosevelt's famous fireside chats on radio.*
cha.teau or **châ.teau** (sha.TOH) *n.* **-teaus** or **-teaux** (-TOZE) a French castle; manor-house.
chat.e.laine (SHAT.ul.ain) *n.* the mistress of a chateau, castle, or large household.
chat.tel (CHAT.ul) *n.* an article of personal property that can be moved from place to place, unlike real estate such as land and houses: *a chattel mortgage (taken out on personal property).*
chat.ter (CHAT.ur) *n.* 1 a rapid series of brief, meaningless or mechanical sounds, as of a squirrel, birds, monkeys, the sound of typewriter keys, teeth clicking from cold, etc. 2 fast, idle conversation: *endless, idle, incessant chatter.* —*v.* 1 rattle: *teeth chattering from the cold.* 2 indulge in chatter; *n.*: *No chattering in class, please!* **chat.ter.er** *n.*
chat.ter.box (CHAT.ur.box) *n. Informal.* one who talks idly and without stopping.
chat.ty (CHAT.ee) *adj.* **chat.ti.er, chat.ti.est** 1 inclined to chat. 2 informal: *a chatty account, letter, news report.* —**chat.ti.ly** *adv.*; **chat.ti.ness** *n.*
chauf.feur (SHOH.fur) *n.* one employed as the driver of a car. —*v.* drive as a chauffeur: *He chauffeured his boss around town; adj.*: *a chauffeured limousine.*
chau.vin.ism (SHOH.vuh.niz.um) *n.* a blind, unreasonable, often aggressive loyalty to one's nation, race, sex, etc.: *male chauvinism;* **chau.vin.ist** *n.* —**chau.vin.is.tic** (-NIS.tic) *adj.*
cheap (CHEEP) *adj.* 1 costing comparatively little money, effort, etc.: *The car is cheap at that price; It's cheaper to live in the suburbs than in the city.* 2 selling goods at a low price: *a cheap store.* 3 of low quality: *a cheap hotel; cheap shoes; a cheap threat, trick.* 4 *Informal.* ashamed: *He felt cheap after cheating his friend.* 5 *Informal.* stingy. —*adv. Informal.* at a cheap price: *to buy cheap and sell dear.* —**cheap.ly** *adv.*; **cheap.ness** *n.*
cheap.en (CHEE.pun) *v.* make or become cheap; *adj.*: *goods cheapened by a shrinking market.*
cheap.ie (CHEE.pee) or **cheap.o** (-poh) *n. Informal.* 1 a stingy person. 2 a cheap article; *adja.*: *a cheapie film; cheapo parties.*
cheap shot *n.* an unfair statement or attack.
cheap.skate *n. Slang.* a stingy person.
cheat (CHEET) *v.* 1 take from someone by dishonesty or deceit: *An impostor cheated her out* (= deprived her) *of her money; Jim doesn't like to cheat on* (= be unfaithful to) *his wife.* 2 act or play dishonestly: *Jim cheats at cards.* 3 deprive of something: *An illness cheated him of his hopes.* 4 elude or escape from something: *He cheated death while the other passengers were killed in*

check / cheddar

the crash. —*n.* **1** an act of cheating; also, a trick or deception. **2** one that cheats. —**cheat.er** *n.*

check *n.* **1** a control: *Keep your horse in check; Your (chess) king is in check* (= in a threatened position). **2** an examination or verification; hence, a check or tick [✓] showing that a check has been made: *The police made a spot check of all cars that came by; They ran a check for prior convictions; A background check is made of all applicants.* **3** a token for reclaiming one's hat, baggage, etc.: *a hat check; a rain check for making a later claim or purchase.* **4** a small square or a regular pattern of squares: *red and white checks on the tablecloth.* **5** a bill in a restaurant, bar, etc. **6** a signed authorization for a bank to pay money from one's account: *We always pay by check; We issue, make out, write out checks in favor of people; Checks are drawn on the bank against our account; People present checks to a bank; They cash or deposit checks; Bad or N.S.F. checks bounce; Our checks are covered (with sufficient money in the account) so they will clear instead of bouncing; Most people will honor a travel or traveler's check purchased from a bank, exactly like a cashier's check or certified check; A (signed) blank check (that may be used to withdraw an indefinite amount of money) is given only to the most trustworthy;* also **cheque** *Cdn.*
—*v.* **1** stop: *He checked his urge to talk back.* **2** in chess, to threaten the king. **3** examine, inspect for accuracy, proper condition, etc.: *Please check my figures; If you're in doubt, check it out! The police checked into his story and checked through his files.* **4** tick with a check mark: *Please check in this box.* **5** correspond or refer to a list, original copy, authority, etc.: *His version checks with mine; It checks out* (= It's true); *I'll have to check with* (= speak to) *the boss on this.* **6** process something for another to have, use, store, etc.: *Cashiers check out groceries; The airline checked our baggage through* (= accepted it for shipment) *to London; Patrons check* (= borrow) *books out of libraries; Library clerks check* (= give) *them out.*
—**check in** (**at**) or **check into** formally enter a hotel, factory, etc.; sign in: *We'll check into some hotel; Let's check in at the Hilton.* —**check up on** or **check on** find out more about a person or thing: *The police checked up on his background.* —**check out** (**of**) formally leave an establishment after paying dues, etc.: *Let us check out of this hotel;*
Now is the time to check out.

check.book *n.* a book of blank checks. Also **cheque.book** *Cdn.*

checkbook journalism *n.* the practice of paying news sources for exclusive rights to a story.

checked *adj.* **1** having a pattern of squares: *a checked pattern, shirt, tablecloth.* **2** processed: *checked baggage, files, items.*

check.er *n.* **1** a piece used in the game of checkers. **2** one that checks: *a checker at the supermarket counter; a spelling* or *spell checker* (= computer program that checks spelling).

check.er.board (CHEK.ur.bord) *n.* a board used for playing checkers, with 64 squares in two alternate colours; *adj.a.: a black-and-white checkerboard floor; a checkerboard design, dress, pattern.* Also **cheq.uer.board** *Brit.*

check.ered (CHECK.urd) *adj.* **1** having a pattern of squares: *a red-and-white checkered dress; cars heading for the checkered flag; a checkered kaffiyeh, tablecloth.* **2** having many ups and downs: *a checkered career, history, past.* **3** having a pattern of alternating dark and light colors: *the checkered beetle, lily.* Also **cheq.uered** *Brit.*

check.ers *n.* a game played by two with 12 pieces each on a checkerboard.

check-in *n.* a checking in or where it is done: *baggage check-in at an airport; a hotel's automated credit-card check-in; adj.a.: a check-in area, counter, line, service, system.*

checking account *n.* a bank account against which checks may be drawn.

check.list *n.* a list of items to be referred to and verified.

check.mate *n.* in chess, a position of check which cannot be escaped; hence, total defeat. Also *v.* **-mates, -mat.ed, -mat.ing.**

check.off *n.* the automatic deduction of union dues from a pay check.

check.out or **check-out** *n.* a checking out or where it is done: *a supermarket checkout; at the express checkout; adj.a.: a checkout cashier, counter, girl, line, station; a hotel's checkout time for guests.*

check.point *n.* a place on a route where an inspection is made: *border, immigration, military checkpoints.*

check.room *n.* a room where hats, coats, etc. may be checked.

checks and balances *n.pl.* controls built into an administration for the even distribution of power.

check.up *n.* **1** an inspection. **2** a medical examination.

ched.dar (CHED.ur) *n.* a firm, smooth,

white-to-yellow cheese, ranging from sharp to mild in flavor.
cheek *n.* **1** the part on either side of the face below the eyes: *dimpled, rosy, ruddy cheeks; a starving man with hollow, sunken cheeks; couples dancing* **cheek to cheek;** *to* **turn the other cheek** (= patiently suffer injury instead of retaliating). **2** something like a cheek, esp. a buttock. **3** *Informal.* impudence: *He owes me money and had the cheek to phone me collect.* —**cheek by jowl** close together.
cheek.bone *n.* the bone just under the eye.
cheek.y *adj.* **cheek.i.er, -i.est** impudent: *a cheeky youth; her cheeky chutzpah;* **cheek.i.ly** *adv.;* **cheek.i.ness** *n.*
cheep *n.* a weak, high-pitched cry, as of a young bird.
cheer *n.* **1** a shout of enthusiasm or encouragement: *loud and prolonged cheers; Three cheers for democracy!* **2** joyous mood; hopeful state of mind: *Be of good cheer.* **3** hospitality; hence, food and drink: *Christmas cheer.* —**cheers** *interj.* used as a drinking toast.
—*v.* **1** make or become glad; hearten: *Let's cheer up; things will improve.* **2** shout a cheer; support: *Let's all cheer for the home team; cheer them on to victory.*
cheer.ful (CHEER.ful) *adj.* **1** having or causing cheer: *a bright and cheerful day.* **2** willing: *a cheerful helper.*
—**cheer.ful.ly** *adv.;* **cheer.ful.ness** *n.*
cheer.i.o (CHEER.ee.oh) *interj. & n.* **-os** *Informal.* **1** good-bye. **2** cheers!
cheer.lead.er (CHEER.lee.dur) *n.* the leader of a group cheering, esp. at a game or rally.
cheer.y *adj.* **cheer.i.er, -i.est** marked by or causing cheerfulness: *a cheery greeting, welcome; on a cheerier note.*
—**cheer.i.ly** *adv.;* **cheer.i.ness** *n.*
cheese (CHEEZ) *n.* a protein-rich food made from pressed milk curd.
—*v.* **cheese it!** *Slang.* scram! depart!
—**cheesed off** *Slang.* disgusted.
cheese.bur.ger (CHEEZ.bur.gur) *n.* a hamburger with a layer of cheese over the meat.
cheese.cake *n.* **1** a cake made of cottage or cream cheese in a crust of sweet crumbs. **2** *Informal.* pictorial display of attractive, scantily clad women; also, such attractiveness: *Not just cheesecake!* *adj.:* *cheesecake pictures, magazines, shots, videos.*
cheese.cloth *n.* a light, porous cotton gauze.
cheese.par.ing (CHEEZ.pair.ing) *n.*

cheek / Cherokee

1 stinginess. **2** a trifle saved by a miser; *adj.:* *petty, cheeseparing economies.*
chees.y *adj.* **chees.i.er, -i.est** **1** like cheese. **2** *Slang.* inferior; tawdry: *a dingy room with cheesy furnishings.*
—**chees.i.ness** *n.*
chee.tah (CHEE.tuh) *n.* a swift wild cat of Africa and S. Asia with a tawny, black-spotted coat, sometimes trained to hunt.
chef *n.* a cook, esp. a head cook.
che.la (KEE.luh) *n.* **-lae** (-lee) the grabbing claw of a crab, scorpion, etc.
chem.i.cal (KEM.i.cul) *adj.* having to do with chemistry: *a chemical bomb, burn, change, compound, experiment, formula, process, reaction;* *chemical apparatus, engineering;* **chemical warfare** *using poisonous gases.* —*n.* a chemical substance. —**chem.i.cal.ly** *adv.*
che.mise (shuh.MEEZ) *n.* **1** a woman's shirtlike undergarment. **2** a loose, waistless dress; shift.
chem.ist (KEM.ist) *n.* **1** a chemistry specialist. **2** *Brit.* a pharmacist or druggist.
chem.is.try (KEM.is.tree) *n.* **-tries** **1** the science of the composition, combination, and reactions of substances and their elements: *analytical, inorganic, physical chemistry; the chemistry of copper.* **2** how various elements work in combination: *your body chemistry; the odd chemistry* (= workings) *of mob hysteria; There's a special chemistry* (= bond of sympathy) *at work between Mario and Gerda.*
chem.o.ther.a.py (kee.moh.THER.uh.pee, kem.oh-) *n.* treatment of disease using chemicals.
chem.ur.gy (KEM.ur.jee) *n.* the utilization of organic materials, esp. farm products or by-products, in chemical industries. —**chem.ur.gic** (cuh.MUR.jic) *adj.*
che.nille (shi.NEEL) *n.* **1** a cord having a fuzzy pile, used in trim and embroidery. **2** a cloth made with this cord.
cheque *Cdn.* CHECK, *n.* 6.
cher.ish (CHER.ish) *v.* **1** to love and care for: *Good parents cherish their families; a promise to cherish each other in sickness and in health; a noble cause embraced and cherished by the masses;* *adj.:* *a* **cherished** *heirloom, possession.* **2** keep in mind with attachment or affection: *We had cherished hopes of his return; adj.: a* **cherished** *dream, memory, promise, tradition; one the most cherished of our freedoms; a* **long-cherished** *goal, ideal, vision.*
Cher.o.kee (CHER.uh.kee) *n.* **1** (a

member of) a tribe of American Indians now concentrated in Tennessee and Oklahoma. 2 their Iroquoian language; *adj.: the Cherokee alphabet.*

che.root (shuh.ROOT) *n.* a cigar with both ends cut square.

cher.ry (CHER.ee) *n.* **cher.ries 1** a firm, small, fleshy red fruit of a tree of the rose family. **2** the tree itself or its wood. **3** bright red color.

cherry-pick *v.* pick selectively from a group, as when shopping for bargains.

chert *n.* a kind of quartz that resembles flint.

cher.ub (CHER.ub) *n.* **1** a chubby, rosy-faced child. **2** *pl.* **-ub.im** an angel.

che.rub.ic (chuh.ROO.bic) *adj.* angelic: *a cherubic face.*

cher.vil (CHUR.vil) *n.* an herb whose leaves are used to flavor salads, soups, etc.

chess *n.* a game played on a checkerboard, or **chessboard**, by two people, each using 16 pieces called **chessmen**, *sing.* **chessman.** —*adja.: a chess master, move, piece, set, table.*

chest *n.* **1** the front of the body, from the bottom of the ribs to the neck: *a man's hairy chest; the barrel chest (of a lung patient); You'll feel much better if you get it off your chest (by telling someone); cpd: big-chested, broad-chested, flat-chested.* **2** a storage or shipping box with a lid: *a tool chest; medicine chest (= cabinet).* **3** a treasury or fund: *the community chest; a war chest for use in a strike or other aggressive action.* **4** a piece of furniture with drawers for clothes; also **chest of drawers.**

ches.ter.bed (CHES.tur.bed) *n.* a chesterfield or sofa that can be opened out into a bed.

ches.ter.field (CHES.tur.field) *n.* a sofa with a well-padded back and upright arm-rests.

chest.nut *n.* **1** the edible nut, enclosed in a prickly case, of a tree of the beech family: *We roast chestnuts for eating.* **2** the tree itself or its wood. **3** a reddish brown: *a chestnut horse.* **4** a stale joke, story, theme, etc.: *to do a chestnut; a new movie based on the old chestnut about identical twins getting mixed up.*

che.val glass (shuh.VAL-) *n.* a full-length mirror mounted between supports so as to be tilted.

chev.a.lier (shev.uh.LEER) *n.* a member of an order of merit, as the French Legion of Honor.

chev.i.ot (SHEV.ee.ut) *n.* **1** a sturdy, wool cloth for coats and suits. **2** a soft, strong cotton shirting.

chev.ron (SHEV.run) *n.* a badge of V-shaped stripes on a uniform sleeve, showing military rank.

chew (CHOO) *v.* grind or mash with the teeth; masticate: *It's good to chew our food well; He likes to chew on mints after dinner.* —**chew out** *Slang.* scold severely. —**chew over** *Slang.* ponder or discuss thoroughly. —**chew the rag** or **fat** *Slang.* talk casually; chat: *The two old friends chewed the rag for over an hour.* —*n.* **1** an act of chewing: *Give it a good chew.* **2** something chewed, esp. *a quid of tobacco.*

chewing gum *n.* a sticky substance such as the solidified latex of certain trees sweetened and flavored for chewing: *a piece* or *stick of chewing gum.*

chew.y *adj.* **chew.i.er, -i.est** thick and requiring some chewing: *cookies that are chewy rather than crisp.*

Chey.enne (shy.AN, -EN) *n.* **1** (a member of) an American Indian people now living in Montana, South Dakota, and Oklahoma; *adj.: a Cheyenne saddle.* **2** their Algonquian language.

Chi.an.ti (kee.AHN.tee) *n.* a dry red wine.

chi.a.ro.scu.ro (kee.AR.uh.SKYOOR.oh) *n.* **-ros 1** a style or technique of painting using light-and-shade effects. **2** a painting in this style. **3** the treatment of light and shade in a painting.

chic (SHEEK) *adj.* elegant and fashionable: *a chic dress, hat, lady; She thinks it's chic to be thin.* —*n.* sophistication; stylishness: *feminine chic; radical chic (= left-wing politics considered fashionable); Texas chic (= style featuring Western boots, hats, etc.)*

chi.can.er.y (shi.CAY.nuh.ree) *n.* **-er.ies 1** artful or sophistic trickery. **2** a deception or trick.

Chi.ca.no (chi.CAH.noh) *n.* **-nos** an American of Mexican origin; *adj.: Chicano Americans; the Chicano community.*

chi.chi (SHEE.shee) *adj.* very refined or elegant, often to excess: *a chichi fashion designer, outfit; It's kind of chichi.* —*n.* a person, thing, or quality that is chichi.

chick *n.* **1** a young domestic fowl: *a hen and its chicks.* **2** [slang term of familiarity] a young woman.

chick.a.dee (CHICK.uh.dee) *n.* **1** a small, gray, black-capped North American bird. **2** *Informal.* darling: *My little chickadee!*

Chick.a.saw (CHICK.uh.saw) *n.* **1** (a

member of) an American Indian tribe now concentrated in Oklahoma. **2** their language; also *adj.*

chick.en (CHICK.un) *n.* **1** the common barnyard fowl, raised for its flesh and eggs: *the clucking chicken; a brood of chickens; It's not wise to **count one's chickens before they are hatched*** (= act on the basis of premature hopes); *fried chicken* (= fried chicken flesh). **2** *Slang.* a coward: *When it comes to fighting, he's a chicken;* **to play chicken** (= exchange challenges in hopes that the other will back down before the actual showdown). —*adj. Slang.* **1** cowardly: *He's chicken; a chicken fellow;* also **chicken-hearted** and **chicken-livered**. **2** adhering to petty details or rules: *a chicken attitude; chicken regulations.* —**chicken out** withdraw because of fear.

chicken feed *n. Slang.* a paltry sum of money; pittance.

chicken pox *n.* a contagious, usu. childhood disease, causing fever and a blistering rash. Also **chick.en.pox**.

chicken wire *n.* a light wire mesh, usu. six-sided, used for fencing.

chick.let or **chic.let** (CHICK.lit) *n.* a small piece of candied chewing gum.

chick.pea (CHICK.pee) *n.* **1** a leguminous plant bearing edible seeds. **2** the seeds.

chick.weed *n.* a low, spreading plant with white flowers.

chic.le (CHICK.ul) *n.* the tasteless, gumlike, solidified latex of the sapodilla, and the basic ingredient in chewing gum.

chic.o.ry (CHIC.uh.ree) *n.* **-ries** a perennial herb with blue, daisylike flowers, whose leaves are used in salads and whose roasted roots are often added to ground coffee; *adj.:* a cup of *chicoried* (= chicory-flavored) *coffee.*

chide *v.* **chides;** *pt.* **chid** or **chid.ed;** *pp.* **chid, chid.ed** or **chid.den; chi.ding** scold mildly: *She chided her daughter for being late.*

chief *n.* the leader of a group, organization, etc.: *an Indian chief; our fire chief; the police chief; Hey Chief!* —*adja.* **1** highest ranking: *the chief executive officer of a company;* the **Chief Justice** of the Supreme Court; the **Chief Executive** (= U.S. President). **2** main: *my chief worry; one of the chief causes of cancer.*

chief.ly *adv.* **1** first of all; especially: *His diet is meant chiefly to reduce weight; Chiefly, he has to avoid fat.* **2** mainly or mostly: *His diet consists chiefly of nonfat foods.*

chief of staff *n.* a senior military officer or a head physician.

chief of state *n.* a constitutional head, as the U.S. president or the British sovereign in Canada.

chief.tain (CHEEF.tun) *n.* a chief, esp. of a tribe, clan, band, etc.: *a Scottish chieftain.* —**chief.tain.cy** *n.* **-cies.**

chif.fon (shi.FON) *n.* a light, diaphanous fabric of silk, nylon, etc., as used for wedding dresses. —*adja.* **1** made of chiffon: *a chiffon gown.* **2** light and fluffy: *a pineapple chiffon pie.* —**chif.fon.y** (SHIF.uh.nee) *adj.:* a *chiffony silk scarf.*

chif.fo.nier (shif.uh.NEER) *n.* a tall chest of drawers.

chig.ger *n.* **1** a blood-sucking mite larva that causes severe irritation. **2** a tropical flea that burrows under the skin of humans and animals.

chi.gnon (SHEEN.yon) *n.* a coil of hair worn at the nape of the neck or back of the head.

chig.oe same as CHIGGER, 2.

Chi.hua.hua (chi.WAH.wuh) *n.* a small, short-haired Mexican dog with large ears.

chil.blains (CHIL.blains) *n.* an itchy, red swelling of the fingers, toes, ears, or nose caused by exposure to cold: *to catch chilblains.*

child (CHILED) *n., pl.* **chil.dren** (CHIL.drun) **1** baby; infant: *A mother conceives a child; She carries a child for nine months, when she is **with child*** (= pregnant); *She gives birth to* or *has a child; She nurses her child till she goes back to work; a child at a day-care center.* **2** one who is growing up: *to adopt, feed, indulge, pamper, spoil a child; bright, gifted, happy, intelligent, loving, mischievous, obedient, precocious, sensitive, young children; delinquent children; neglected, problem, stubborn, underprivileged, unruly, wayward children; Legally, you are still a child at 16; adja.:* child *care, guidance, labor, psychology, welfare.* **3** offspring: *the only child of her parents; Our children have married and left;* adult *children;* the children (= descendants) of Adam; *the children of Israel* (= Jews). **4** a product of a particular period or influence: *a child of his times; a child of the 1990s.*

child.bear.ing (CHILD.bair.ing) *n.* childbirth: *pregnancy and childbearing; adja.:* a woman of childbearing age; *Childbearing years are normally between the ages of 25 and 44.*

child.bed *n.* the state of a woman in childbirth.

child.birth *n.* the act of giving birth.
child.hood *n.* the state or period of being a child: *a happy childhood.*
child.ish *adj.* foolish and immature: *It's childish of him to act like that; a childish prank.* —**child.ish.ly** *adv.;* **child.ish.ness** *n.* —**child.less** *adj.: a childless couple.*
child.like *adj.* like a child, esp. innocent, naive, etc.: *She spoke with childlike candor.*
child.mind.er (CHILD.mind.ur) *n.* Brit. babysitter.
child-proof *adj.* that children cannot open, damage, etc.: *a child-proof bottle, cap, lock.*
children's aid society *n.* a private social service agency funded by government to look after the needs of children lacking parental care.
child's play *n.* an easy or trivial job: *Assembling computers is child's play to him.*
Chil.e.an (CHIL.ee.un. chuh.LAY.un) *n. & adj.* (a person) of or from **Chile**, a South American country.
chil.i (CHIL.ee) *n.* **chil.ies** 1 the pod of a tropical American capsicum, dried to make a pungent pepper, often ground to make **chili powder** seasoning. 2 the plant. 3 a hot dish made with chili, meat, beans, etc.; also **chili con car.ne** (CHIL.ee.cun.CAR.nee).
chili sauce *n.* a sauce made with chilies or sweet peppers and tomatoes.
chill *n.* 1 a feeling of coldness: *The ghost story sent chills up her spine; The death cast a chill over the proceedings; She put the glass near the fire to take the chill off the drink; It's easy to catch a chill* (= cold) *in that draft; libel chill* (= fear of being unfairly sued for libel). 2 cool weather: *the chill of a fall day; He walked out into the chill of the night.* —*adj.* uncomfortably cool: *a chill December wind; The night is chill; She silenced him with a chill* (= cold) *stare.* —*v.* 1 make or get cold: *Chill the wine before serving; adj.: The skiers were chilled to the bone; a chilling wind.* 2 discourage; dampen: *to chill someone's friendliness, spirits; His negative attitude chilled our plans; adj.: a chilling effect; a chilling* (= frightening) *drama, observation, reminder, tale, truth.*
chill.er *n.* one that chills: *Meat is transported in special chillers; a chiller* (= scary book or movie) *called "Thirteen Ghosts."*
chill factor same as WINDCHILL.
chil.li same as CHILI (pepper).
chill.y (CHILL.ee) *adj.* **chill.i.er, -i.est** cold: *a chilly wind; chilly temperatures;* *weather; a chilly greeting, reception; chilly conditions, news, relations.* —**chill.i.ly** *adv.;* **chill.i.ness** *n.*
chimaera same as CHIMERA.
chime *n.* 1 a bell, as in a clock. 2 usu. **chimes** *pl.* a set of bells rung in melody: *We have chimes instead of a doorbell; Chimes sounded in the distance.* —*v.* **chimes, chimed, chim.ing** 1 ring or sound, esp. in harmony: *The clock chimed three.* 2 agree: *Your idea chimes with my own.* —**chime in** join in a conversation, song, etc. with agreement or harmony: *"So do I," she chimed in.*
chi.me.ra (kye.MEER.uh) *n.* 1 a monster of Greek myth with a lion's head, goat's body, and serpent's tail. 2 a terrible or bizarre fantasy; something unrealistic or illusory. Also **chi.mae.ra.**
chi.mer.i.cal (kye.MER.i.cul) *adj.* illusory or impractical: *a chimerical plan for reform; a vision of prosperity built on chimerical foundations.*
chim.ney (CHIM.nee) *n.* **-neys** 1 a vertical vent for the smoke and gases from a factory, fireplace, furnace, stove, etc.: *He smokes like a chimney; Santa Claus is supposed to come down the chimney; a chimney that is black with soot; Have it cleaned by a **chimney sweep**.* 2 a glass tube shielding a lamp flame.
chimp *n. Informal.* chimpanzee.
chim.pan.zee (chim.pan.ZEE, -PAN.zee) *n.* an intelligent, middle-sized African ape.
chin *n.* the part of the lower jaw below the lower lip: *a portly gentleman with a double chin.* —*v.* **chins, chinned, chin.ning** pull *oneself* up, as from a bar while hanging by the hands until the chin is level with or above the hands. —**keep one's chin up** not to get discouraged. —**take it on the chin** suffer courageously.
chi.na (CHYE.nuh) *n.* porcelain, esp. tableware of porcelain: *fine china; a set of china; adja.: china cups, dinnerware, dolls.*
Chi.na.man (CHYE.nuh.man) *n.* [offensive] a Chinese; **a Chinaman's chance** (= no chance at all).
Chi.na.town (CHYE.nuh.town) *n.* the Chinese quarter of a large city outside China.
chinch bug *n.* a white-winged insect that attacks grain crops.
chin.chil.la (chin.CHIL.uh) *n.* 1 a small South American rodent with a prized soft gray fur; also, its fur. 2 a deep-napped heavy wool cloth used for coats.
Chin.ese (chye.NEEZ) *n. sing. & pl.* 1 a

native of China or a descendant of one. **2** one of a group of related languages of China, esp. Mandarin.
—*adj.* pertaining to the nation, people, culture, or language of China: *Chinese food, silk; a Chinese laundry, puzzle, restaurant;* a set of **Chinese boxes** (*in a nested arrangement*).

Chinese checkers *n.* a game somewhat like checkers, played with marbles on a star-shaped board.

Chinese lantern *n.* a brightly-colored, collapsible paper lantern.

chink *n.* **1** a small crack: *a chink in his armor* (= weak point). **2** a sharp, metallic click. —*v.* **1** fill in cracks: *The pioneers chinked their log cabins with clay and straw, moss, etc. before winter.* **2** make a clicking sound: *You could hear coins chinking in his pocket.*

chin.less *adj.* lacking strength of character: *Our chinless wonders haven't won a game all season.*

chi.no (CHEE.noh) *n.* **1** a usu. khaki-colored cotton cloth. **2 chinos** *pl.* casual trousers made of this cloth.

chi.noi.se.rie (sheen.WAH.zuh.ree) *n.* a style of ornamentation suggestive of Chinese patterns and motifs.

Chi.nook (shuh.NOOK, long or short "OO") *n.* **1** (a member of) any of a group of American Indian tribes of northwestern U.S. **2** the language of a Chinook tribe, as **Chinookan**. **3 chinook** a warm Pacific wind that blows across the Rockies into the eastern plains.

Chinook Jargon *n.* a trade language of western North America based on Chinook.

chintz (CHINTS) *n.* a brightly patterned cotton cloth, usu. with a glossy finish.

chintz.y (CHINT.see) *adj.* **chintz.i.er, -i.est 1** of or decorated with chintz. **2** cheap and tacky: *a chintzy approach, bargain, job, publicity stunt.* **3** stingy.

chin-up *n.* the exercise of chinning oneself.

chip *n.* **1** a small cut or broken piece: *Wood chips littered the carpenter's shop; chocolate chips; cow chips* (= dried dung). **2** a flaw showing where a chip has been made: *a chip in the glass.* **3** a gambling token: *poker chips; He* **cashed in his chips** (*Slang for* died); **Let the chips fall where they may** (= Let actions take their natural course); **when the chips are down** (= in bad times). **4** a thin, crispy snack: *banana, corn, potato, tortilla chips.* **5** a small strip of something edible: *fish and chips*

(= french fries). **6** a semiconductor on which an integrated circuit is mounted: *computer, logic, memory, silicon chips.*
—**chip off the old block** one just like his father. —**chip on one's shoulder** a grievance: *He has a chip on his shoulder about being passed up for promotion.* —**in the chips** *Slang.* having much money. —*v.* **chips, chipped, chip.ping 1** cut or shape by chipping. **2** knock a chip from something: *Some cups and plates chip; He fell and chipped a tooth.* —**chip in** contribute.

chip.munk *n.* a small striped ground-dwelling North American squirrel.

chipped beef *n.* thin slices of smoked or dried beef.

Chip.pen.dale (CHIP.un.dale) *adj.* in the high-quality style of Thomas Chippendale, an 18th-century English furniture designer: *a Chippendale chair.*

chip.per *n.* a person or machine that chips. —*adj. Informal.* cheerful; vigorous; lively: *chipper as a sparrow; a chipper attitude.* —*v.* **chipper up** cheer up.

Chip.pe.wa (CHIP.uh.waw) same as OJIBWA.

chip.py 1 *n.* **chip.pies** *Slang.* a prostitute; also, a promiscuous young woman. **2** *adj. Slang.* rough or aggressive: *a chippy game, player.*

chip shot *n.* in golf, a short lobbed shot onto the green.

chi.rog.ra.phy (kye.ROG.ruh.fee) *n.* handwriting; also, calligraphy;
 chi.rog.ra.pher *n.* —**chi.ro.graph.ic** (-ruh.GRAF.ic) or **chi.ro.graph.i.cal** *adj.*

chi.ro.man.cy (KYE.ruh.man.see) *n.* palmistry.

chi.rop.o.dy (kuh.ROP.uh.dee) *n.* podiatry; **chi.rop.o.dist** *n.*

chi.ro.prac.tic (kye.ruh.PRAC.tic) *n.* the treatment of disease by the manipulation of the spine or other parts of the body: *Doctor of Chiropractic.*

chi.ro.prac.tor (KYE.ruh.prac.tur) *n.* a chiropractic doctor.

chirp *v.* utter a high, short sound, as small birds and insects such as crickets and grasshoppers do. —*n.* a tweet; peep.

chir.rup (CHUR.up) *v.* **1** chirp repeatedly. **2** make a similar noise, esp. by sucking, as in urging a horse forward; *n.: the chirrup of bullets whizzing by.*

chis.el (CHIZ.ul) *n.* a metal tool with a sloped cutting edge used to shape or cut wood, stone, or metal. —*v.* **-els, -eled, -el.ing 1** shape or work with a chisel: *to chisel a groove in a plank; adj.:*

a finely **chiseled** figure. **2** *Informal.* cheat or get by cheating: *The crook chiseled us out of $100.* Also **chis.elled, chis.el.ling** *Cdn.*
chis.el.er (CHIZ.uh.lur) *n. Slang.* a cheat or swindler. Also **chis.el.ler** *Cdn.*
chit *n.* **1** a short note. **2** a voucher for food, drink, merchandise, etc.: *meal chits.* **3** *Informal.* a child.
chit.chat *n.* small talk; chat.
chi.tin (KYE.tin) *n.* a hard, colorless, horny substance forming the outer covering of insects, crabs, etc. —**chi.tin.ous** *adj.*
chit.ter.lings (CHIT.lins, -lings) *n.pl.* the small intestines of hogs cooked, usu. fried, for food; also **chit.lins, chit.lings**.
chi.val.ric (shi.VAL.ric) *adj.* having to do with chivalry: *the chivalric code; chivalric rites.*
chiv.al.rous (SHIV.ul.rus) *adj.* having or showing chivalry: *his chivalrous manner; a chivalrous gentleman of the old school with chivalrous notions.* —**chiv.al.rous.ly** *adv.;* **chiv.al.rous.ness** *n.*
chiv.al.ry (SHIV.ul.ree) *n.* **1** the qualities of a perfect knight, such as courage, courtesy, and honor: *Is chivalry dead?* **2** the system of medieval knighthood: *the age of chivalry* (= Middle Ages).
chives *n.pl.* [takes *sing.* or *pl. v.*] a seasoning for soups, salads, etc. made from the long, narrow leaves of the **chive**, a plant related to the onion.
chlo.ral (CLOR.ul) *n.* a thin, colorless liquid made from alcohol and chlorine, used to make **chloral hydrate**, a strong sedative.
chlor.ide *n.* a compound of chlorine and another element or radical: *Sodium chloride is table salt.*
chlo.ri.nate (CLOR.uh.nate) *v.* **-nates, -nat.ed, -nat.ing** treat with chlorine or a compound of it, usu. to purify, esp. water. —**chlo.ri.na.tion** (-NAY.shun) *n.* —**chlo.ri.na.tor** (-nay.tur) *n.*
chlo.rine (CLOR.een) *n.* a greenish-yellow, poisonous, foul-smelling gas used to disinfect, bleach, etc.
chlo.ro.flu.o.ro.car.bon (clor.uh.FLOR.uh.car.bun) *n.* a gaseous compound containing chlorine, fluorine, and carbon that is used as aerosol propellants, refrigerants, and solvents and threatens the earth's protective ozone layer.
chlo.ro.form (CLOR.uh.form) *n.* a volatile, pleasant-smelling liquid, used as an anesthetic, in refrigerators, etc.
—*v.* **1** anesthetize with chloroform. **2** kill using chloroform.
chlo.ro.phyll (CLOR.uh.fil) *n.* the green coloring in plant cells which is necessary for photosynthesis. Also **chlo.ro.phyl**.
chock *n.* a block or wedge used to support or keep a barrel, wheel, boat hull, etc. from moving. —*v.* block with a chock or chocks: *We chocked the rear wheels before jacking up the car.*
—*adv.* as close, tight, etc. as possible: *a chair placed chock up against the door.*
chock-a-block (CHOCK.uh.bloc) *adjp.* closely packed: *The tenements are chock-a-block with people;* **adv.**: *families crammed chock-a-block into tenements; They are chock-a-block full of immigrants.*
chockbore same as CHOKEBORE.
chock-full *adjp.* as full as possible: *a room chock-full of books and papers.*
choc.o.late (CHOCK.lit) *n.* **1** a powder, syrup, solid, etc. made from roasted and processed seeds of the "cacao" tree. **2** a food made with chocolate: *a cup of hot chocolate (drink); a bar of milk chocolate;* **adja.**: *a chocolate bar, cake, candy, drink, flavor, ice cream; chocolate-chip cookies.* **3** a deep reddish brown color: *chocolate color.*
choc.o.lat.y or **choc.o.lat.ey** (CHOCK.luh.tee) *adj.* like chocolate: *She likes everything sweet and chocolaty; It's a chocolaty brown.*
Choc.taw *n.* **1** (a member of) an American Indian tribe now concentrated in Oklahoma. **2** their language. Also *adj.*
choice *n.* **1** the act or power of choosing: *a matter of choice; The choice is difficult; She did it of her own choice; He remains a bachelor* **by choice**. **2** something chosen; selection: *the people's choice; a poor choice of words; bad, first, good, happy, intelligent, judicious, random, wise choices; the choice of* or *among many possibilities; Take your choice (from the lot); Aluminum is the material* **of choice** (= the preferred one) *for a lightweight plane.* **3** an alternative: *the choice between marriage and the single life; Your reasons are so compelling, I have no choice but to agree.* **4** the best: *the choice of the lot.* **5** a variety to choose from; selection: *We offer a wide choice of colors.*
—*adja.* **choic.er, choic.est** very good in quality or kind: *the choicest cuts of meat; a choice portion of the turkey; a* **choice morsel** (= something tasty or pleasing).
choir (QUIRE) *n.* **1** a group of singers, esp. in a church: *to sing in a choir.* **2** a section of an orchestra with instru-

choirmaster / chordate

ments of the same type: *the brass choir.* **3** the part of a church used by the choir. —**choir.boy** *n.*; **choir.girl** *n.*

choir.mas.ter (QUIRE.mas.tur) *n.* the conductor of a choir.

choke *v.* **chokes, choked, chok.ing 1** have or cause difficulty in breathing: *The heavy smoke choked us up; Pollution is choking our lakes and rivers; a baseball team that is choking* (Slang for collapsing); *He choked on a piece of meat;* **n.***:* *It was death by* **choking. 2** limit the flow of air, water, etc.; clog: *He* **choked back** *his tears; Parliament decided to* **choke off** (= end) *the debate;* **adj.***: a* **choked** *voice; a pipe choked with mud; Our flower bed is choked with weeds; Al was too* **choked up** (= overcome with emotion) *to go on with his speech.* **3** grip a bat, golf club, etc. closer to the hitting end: *The six-footer choked up on the bat two inches.* —**n. 1** the action or sound of choking. **2** the air valve in a carburetor. **3** a narrowing of the bore of a gun near the muzzle; also **choke.bore.**

chok.er (CHOH.kur) *n. Informal.* something worn around the neck, as a short, close-fitting necklace.

chol.er (COLL.ur) *n.* anger; grouchiness.

chol.er.a (COLL.uh.ruh) *n.* a severe contagious disease of the digestive system which often results in death.

chol.er.ic (COLL.uh.ric, cuh.LER.ic) *adj.* hot-tempered: *He is choleric by temperament; He's of a choleric disposition.*

cho.les.ter.ol (cuh.LES.tuh.rol) *n.* a fatty substance in body tissues: *Fatty meats, butter, and eggs are high in cholesterol; Cutting down on cholesterol helps prevent hardening of the arteries; good cholesterol ("HDL") and bad ("LDL").*

chomp *v.* chew hard; champ: *Please don't chomp on your cigar when you speak to me.*

choose (CHOOZ) *v.* **choos.es, chose** (CHOZE), **cho.sen** (CHOH.zun), **choos.ing 1** pick according to one's judgment; select: *He chooses his partners carefully; We choose at random when all are equally good; We can also choose by lot or by tossing a coin; to choose from many applicants for a job; The judges found it difficult to choose between the two finalists; One was chosen as the winner; He was chosen to fill the vacancy;* **n.***: a candidate of her own* **choosing.** See also CHOSEN. **2** decide by oneself: *I chose to live in this country; I will do as I choose.*

choos.y (CHOO.zee) *adj.* **choos.i.er, -i.est** *Informal.* fussy in choosing; picky: *She's very choosy about what she wears.* —**choos.i.ness** *n.*

chop *v.* **chops, chopped, chop.ping 1** cut with a heavy blade, as an ax, cleaver, etc.: *He chopped down the tree; chopped up the logs into firewood;* **adj.***: finely* **chopped** *onions* (= cut into small pieces). **2** hit with a short, sharp stroke: *He chopped the ball.* —**n. 1** a chopping blow: *He cut the cable with one chop; She splits wood with karate chops.* **2** a piece chopped off, esp. a small cut of meat and bone: *lamb, mutton, pork, veal chops.* **3** an official permit or stamp of quality: **first-chop** *goods* (= goods of top quality). **4** a short, jerky motion, as of waves. **5 chops** *pl.* the jaws and surrounding flesh: *Fido licks his chops after a meal.*

chop.house *n.* a restaurant, esp. a steak house.

chop.per *n.* **1** a person or thing that chops: *a food chopper; meat chopper.* **2** *Informal.* a helicopter. **3** *Slang.* a motorcycle with its front modified, as one without fenders; customized motorcycle.

chop.py (CHOP.ee) *adj.* **chop.pi.er, chop.pi.est** irregular or changeable: *a choppy mood, ride, sea, wind; choppy waters; her choppy style of playing the piano.* —**chop.pi.ly** *adv.*; **chop.pi.ness** *n.*

chop.stick *n.* one of a pair of slender sticks held in one hand and used as an eating utensil in Oriental style.

chop su.ey (-SOO.ee) *n.* a Chinese-American dish of meat, bean sprouts, and other assorted vegetables in a sauce, with rice.

cho.ral (COR.ul) *adja.* having to do with a choir or chorus: *a choral arrangement, group, society; a three-part* **choral** *ode between the episodes of a Greek tragedy;* **choral music** *sung by a chorus as part of an opera;* **choral reading** *and* **choral speaking** *by many in unison.* —**chor.al.ly** *adv.*

cho.rale (cuh.RAL) *n.* **1** a simple choral hymn, esp. in a Lutheran church service. **2** its melody as set in harmony for voices or instruments: *a Bach chorale.* **3** a choir.

chord (CORD) *n.* **1** a set of three or more musical notes sounded together in harmony. **2** a line linking two points on a curve or circle. **3** an emotional response or reaction: *Her sad story struck a sympathetic chord in the audience.* —*v.* harmonize: *to chord a guitar.* —**chord.al** *adj.*

chor.date (COR.date) *n. & adj.* (an animal) of the group including verte-

chore / chromatic

brates that has a stiff cordlike structure running down its back.
chore *n.* a tiresome job, esp. a routine task: *The job was quite a chore; John does his chores before breakfast; the daily chore of taking out the garbage.*
cho.re.a (cuh.REE.uh) *n.* a nervous disorder causing irregular and uncontrolled muscular twitching, as St. Vitus's dance.
chor.e.o.graph (COR.ee.uh.graf) *v.* create the choreography for a dance; *adj.: a well choreographed show.* —**chor.e.o.graph.er** (-ee.OG.ruh.fur) *n.*
chor.e.og.ra.phy (cor.ee.OG.ruh.fee) *n.* the art of designing dances or ballets; also, the dancing. —**chor.e.o.graph.ic** (-uh.GRAF.ic) *adj.*
cho.rine (COR.een) *n. Informal.* a chorus girl.
chor.is.ter (COR.is.tur) *n.* **1** a member of a choir, esp. a choirboy. **2** a choir leader.
chor.tle (CHOR.tul) *v.* **-tles, -tled, -tling** give a gleeful, throaty chuckle: *She chortled in triumph.* —*n.: a chortle of delight.*
cho.rus (COR.us) *n.* **1** a choir: *a chorus of angels.* **2** any group of people who sing, dance, recite, etc. together, esp. the supporting players in a musical drama: *a male chorus.* **3** the part performed by a chorus; also, a piece of harmonic music written for a chorus: *the "Hallelujah" chorus.* **4** something said or sung in unison: *a chorus of praise; the anti-abortion chorus; "Absolutely," they said in chorus* (= all together). **5** a repeated part of a song or tune; refrain. —*v.* **-rus.es, -rused, -rus.ing** utter in unison.
chorus boy (or **girl**) *n.* a young man or young woman who sings and dances in the chorus of a musical show or revue.
chose, chosen See CHOOSE. —**cho.sen** (CHOH.zun) *adj.* selected or preferred: *the chosen few; a chosen corner, group, people, topic.*
chow (rhyme: how) *n. Informal.* food. —*v.* **chow down** eat.
chow.chow *n.* a relish made of pickled chopped vegetables.
chow.der (CHOW.dur) *n.* **1** a thick stewlike soup, usu. of seafood with a milk base: *clam, fish chowder.* **2** a similar dish: *corn chowder.*
chow mein (-MANE) *n.* a Chinese-American dish of fried noodles served with a thick stew of chopped meat and vegetables.

Page 196, *User's*™ *Webster*, © 2000, T. M. Paikeday

chrism (CRIZ.um) *n.* consecrated oil used in church sacraments.
chris.ten (CRIS.un) *v.* **1** baptize: *I christen* (= name) *you Margaret.* **2** name and dedicate formally, as a ship.
Chris.ten.dom (CRIS.un.dum) *n.* **1** Christians collectively: *news that struck terror into the heart of Christendom.* **2** the Christian world: *the holiest shrine of Christendom.*
Chris.tian (CRIS.chun) *adj.* having to do with Christ, his teachings, the religion based on them, or its followers: *Christian charity, churches, concern for others; Christian countries, ethics, piety; the Christian era* (starting with the birth of Christ). —*n.* a believer in Christ or Christianity.
Chris.ti.an.i.ty (cris.chee.AN.i.tee) *n.* **1** a religion based on Christ's teachings. **2** the state of being Christian: *No one doubts his Christianity; His Christianity doesn't go so far as turning the other cheek.*
Chris.tian.ize (CRIS.chuh.nize) *v.* **-iz.es, -ized, -iz.ing** make Christian in belief or character.
Christian name *n.* name given at baptism; a Christian's first name.
Christian Scientist *n.* a follower of **Christian Science,** a Scripture-based religious system that stresses spiritual healing.
chris.tie or **chris.ty** (CRIS.tee) *n.* **-ties** a turn in downhill skiing, also used to slow down or stop, made with a sideways skid.
Christ.like (CRY-) *adj.* like Christ; exhibiting patience, purity, and other virtues.
Christ.mas (CRIS.mus) *n.* a Christian festival celebrating the birth of Christ observed on December 25 (or January 7 in Eastern churches): *We wish you a Merry Christmas; I'm hoping for a white Christmas (with snowfall).* —*adj.: a Christmas card, carol, Day, Eve, gift, greeting, seal; Christmas cheer.*
—**Christ.mas.sy** or **Christ.mas.y** (-muh.see) *adj.*
Christ.mas.tide (CRIS.mus.tide) *n.* the Christmas festival season, esp. December 24 to January 6.
Christ.mas.time (CRIS.mus.time) *n.* the time of year around Christmas.
Christmas tree *n.* a usu. evergreen tree decorated and set up at Christmas: *to trim* (= decorate) *a Christmas tree.*
christy same as CHRISTIE.
chro.mat.ic (croh.MAT.ic) *adj.* **1** having to do with color: *Nature's chromatic splendor.* **2** in music, having to do with

the **chromatic scale** which proceeds by half tones: *a chromatic harmonica.* —**chro.mat.i.cal.ly** *adv.*

chro.mat.o.graph (croh.MAT.uh.graf) *n.* an instrument used in chromatography.

chro.ma.tog.ra.phy (croh.muh.TOG.ruh.fee) *n.* separation of the components of a mixture based on their different rates of adsorption when passed over a substance. —**chro.ma.to.graph.ic** (-toh.GRAF.ic) *adj.*

chrome (CROME) *n.* **1** chromium-plated trim, as of an automobile. **2** chromium; also, an alloy or pigment made with it; *adj.*: *chrome steel, yellow;* **chrome green** (= permanent green color used in printing textiles); **Chrome leather** *(tanned using a chromium solution) is used for shoe uppers, handbags, etc.* —**chro.mic** (CROH.mic) *adj.*

chro.mi.um (CROH.mee.um) *n.* a hard gray metal used in alloys, pigments, corrosion-resistant plating, etc.

chro.mo.some (CROH.muh.sohm) *n.* any of the gene-bearing bodies in a cell's nucleus. —**chro.mo.so.mal** (-SOH.mul) *adj.*

chron.ic (CRON.ic) *adj.* constant and long-lasting: *a chronic complainer, complaint, condition, disease, head cold, indigestion, patient, rebellion, sufferer, worry;* *adj.*: *a chronic-care facility, patient.* —**chron.i.cal.ly** *adv.*

chron.i.cle (CRON.i.cul) *n.* a bare historical record of events; account: *He kept a daily chronicle of his time in captivity.* —*v.* **-cles, -cled, -cling** narrate or record as in a chronicle: *He chronicled the election campaign from start to finish; He has chronicled the history of the Roman Empire.* —**chron.i.cler** *n.*

chron.o.graph (CRON.uh.graf) *n.* any device for precisely measuring time, as a stopwatch. —**chron.o.graph.ic** (-GRAF.ic) *adj.*

chron.o.log.i.cal (cron.uh.LOJ.i.cul) *adj.* **1** according to chronology: *Tell us what happened in* **chronological order** *(= earliest happenings first).* **2** measured by time: *He has a low mental age compared to his chronological (= actual) age.* —**chron.o.log.i.cal.ly** *adv.*

chro.nol.o.gy (cruh.NOL.uh.jee) *n.* **-gies** **1** the determination or arrangement of the dates and sequence of events: *The chronology of prehistory is still uncertain.* **2** a list or table showing this: *the chronology of the war.* —**chro.nol.o.gist** *n.*

chro.nom.e.ter (cruh.NOM.uh.tur) *n.* a precise watch or clock.

chrys.a.lis (CRIS.uh.lis) *n.* **1** the pupa of an insect; also, its firm cocoon. **2** something immature but developing; also, a cocoonlike protection: *youth emerging from the chrysalis of naivety.*

chry.san.the.mum (cri.SANTH.uh.mum) *n.* a colorful, fall-blooming perennial, composite flower.

chrys.o.lite (CRIS.uh.lite) same as OLIVINE.

chub *n.* a carplike freshwater fish.

chub.by (CHUB.ee) *adj.* **chub.bi.er, chub.bi.est** plump or fleshy: *chubby cheeks; the chubby faces of children.* —**chub.bi.ness** *n.*

chuck *v.* **1** tap or pinch lightly, esp. under the chin. **2** *Informal.* toss easily; throw: *She chucked the ball to him.* **3** *Informal.* throw away; dismiss: *to chuck out old shoes; Chuck it, it's hopeless now.* —*n.* **1** a tap or pinch: *a loving chuck.* **2** a throwing: *a quick chuck to the outfield.* **3** a device for holding a tool, bit, or piece of work in a drill, lathe, etc. **4** a cut of beef from the neck to the shoulder blade: *ground chuck; a chuck steak.*

chuck.hole *n.* a rough hole in a road.

chuck.le (CHUCK.ul) *v.* **-les, -led, -ling** laugh gently or to oneself: *She chuckled quietly and left the room; What was she chuckling about? was chuckling with glee at his blooper.* —*n.* a chuckling: *They had a good chuckle over what happened; She let out a hearty chuckle; a satisfied chuckle; a chuckle of mirth.*

chuck wagon or **chuck.wag.on** (CHUCK.wag.un) *n.* a wagon carrying food and kitchen equipment for feeding loggers, cowboys, etc.

chug *n.* a short, heavy, dull sound, as of a laboring engine. —*v.* **chugs, chugged, chug.ging** make such a sound or move while doing so: *an old car chugging up the hill; The train chugged along.*

chuk.ka (CHUCK.uh) *n.* **1** a playing period in polo; also **chuk.kar** (-ur); **chuk.ker.** **2** an ankle-length boot; also **chukka boot.**

chum *n.* **1** *Informal.* a close friend; buddy: *We were chums at school; We're old chums.* **2** a variety of Pacific salmon found along the E. coast of North America; also **chum salmon.** —*v.* **chums, chummed, chum.ming** make friends: *The two seem to be chumming up well; my son chumming up with yours.*

chum.my *adj.* **chum.mi.er, chum.mi.est**

Informal. friendly: *He was very chummy with her; was acting too chummy for a total stranger.* —**chum.mi.ly** *adv.;* **chum.mi.ness** *n.*

chump *n. Informal.* a dupe; fool.

chunk *n.* a thick, heavy piece: *a chunk of wood; You're asking for a big chunk (= large amount) of my time.*

chunk.y *adj.* **chunk.i.er, -i.est** **1** stocky or thickset: *a man of chunky build; a chunky volume; The puffin is a chunky bird.* **2** having chunks in it: *a thick, chunky soup.* —**chunk.i.ly** *adv.;* **chunk.i.ness** *n.*

church *n.* **1** a building for public, usu. Christian worship: *to consecrate* or *dedicate a church.* **2** a religious service: *They go to* or *attend church on Sundays; We were late for church; I saw her in church (= during the service); We met at church; We went home after church.* **3** [descriptive or generic use] Christians as a body: *the Catholic church; the universal church; Christian, evangelical, fundamentalist churches.* **4 Church** an organized group or a denomination within this body: *as the Church teaches; the Anglican, Baptist, Catholic, Episcopal, Established, Lutheran, Mennonite, Methodist, Mormon, Orthodox, Presbyterian, Protestant, United Church; the Church of England.* **5** religious as opposed to secular power: *separation of church and state.* **6** the clergy or clerical profession: *She entered the church at 25.* —*adj.: a church assembly, burial, school, service, wedding.*

church calendar *n.* a calendar indicating Christian feasts and festivals.

church.go.er (CHURCH.go.ur) *n.* a regular attender of church. —**church.go.ing** *n. & adj.*

church.man (CHURCH.mun) *n.* **-men** a clergyman: *a leading Anglican churchman.*

church.war.den (CHURCH.war.dun) *n.* an elected lay official of an Anglican or Episcopal church.

church.wom.an (CHURCH.woom.un) *n.* **-wom.en** an active woman member of a church.

church.yard *n.* the grounds of a church, esp. as a burial place.

church year *n.* the year according to the church calendar.

churl *n.* an ill-bred, bad-tempered person; boor. —**churl.ish** *adj.: churlish manners;* **churl.ish.ly** *adv.;* **churl.ish.ness** *n.*

churn *n.* a container for agitating milk or cream to make butter. —*v.* **1** make butter in a churn. **2** produce or suffer violent agitation: *A motor boat churns the water; The car churned (= moved with churning effect) through the snowbank; the* **churning** *waters of the rapids.* —**churn out** produce rapidly and mechanically: *He churns out one trashy novel after another.*

chute (SHOOT, long "OO") *n.* **1** a waterfall or rapids. **2** a passage or channel for shooting or sliding things down: *a mail chute; the emergency escape chute of an airliner; the discharge chute of a lawn mower.* **3** *Informal.* a parachute.

chut.ney (CHUT.nee) *n.* **-neys** a spicy, hot relish of fruits, herbs, chilies, etc.

chutz.pa or **chutz.pah** (HOOT.spuh, short "OO") *n. Informal.* **1** boldness or aggressiveness: *a woman of hope and chutzpa; a healthy blend of drive and chutzpah.* **2** gall or nerve: *the chutzpah of a snake-oil salesman.*

ciao (CHOW) *interj. Informal.* greetings; goodbye.

ci.ca.da (si.CAY.duh) *n.* a large insect with transparent wings, the males of which produce a high, droning sound.

cic.a.trix (SIC.uh.trix) *n., pl.* **-tri.ces** (-TRY.seez) scar tissue on an animal or plant.

ci.ce.ro.ne (sis.uh.ROH.nee) *n.* **-nes** or **-ni** (-nee) a sightseeing guide.

ci.der (SYE.dur) *n.* the pressed juice of apples, used as a beverage, either unfermented (**sweet cider**) or fermented (**hard cider**).

ci.gar (suh.GAR) *n.* a cylindrical roll of tobacco for smoking: *He kept puffing on his cigar as he talked.*

cig.a.rette (sig.uh.RET) *n.* a roll of finely cut tobacco covered with thin paper; also **cig.a.ret.**

cig.a.ril.lo (sig.uh.RIL.oh) *n.* **-ril.los** a small slender cigar.

cil.i.a (SIL.ee.uh) *n.pl.* **1** hairlike projections forming a fringe, esp. on a cell. **2** eyelashes.

cinch *n.* **1** the belt used to fasten a saddle or pack on a horse. **2** *Slang.* something easy to do or guaranteed: *The job is a cinch; It's a cinch that he'll win; He'll win – that's a cinch; He's a cinch to win; It'll be a cinch to beat them.* —*v.* **1** tighten a belt or cinch: *Don't cinch it too tight;* *adj.: a jacket* **cinched** *at the waist; cinched waists.* **2** *Slang.* make sure of something: *They cinched the game in the last quarter;* *adjp.: They had it* **cinched.**

cin.cho.na (sing.COH.nuh) *n.* a South American evergreen tree or its bark which yields quinine and related alkaloids.

cinc.ture (SINK.chur) *n.* the act of encircling; hence, a girdle or belt. Also *v.* **-tures, -tured, -tur.ing**.

cin.der (SIN.dur) *n.* **1** a piece of hard, solid residue of burning coal or wood: *The room is lined with* **cinder block;** *adj*: *a* **cinder-block** *building, bunker, vault; The walls are cinder-block*. **2** glowing coals; embers. **3 cinders** *pl*. ashes: *It was reduced to cinders*. —**cin.der.y** *adj*.

Cin.der.el.la (sin.duh.REL.uh) *n.* a person or thing that is neglected or unrecognized like the fairy-tale character of that name: *Libraries sometimes become the Cinderellas of educational budgeting;* **adj.:** *a Cinderella* (= neglected) *resource*.

cin.e.ma (SIN.uh.muh) *n.* **1** the art, industry, or medium of motion-picture films; also, films collectively: *the influence of American cinema on French culture*. **2** *Brit*. a movie or movie theater. —**cin.e.mat.ic** (-MAT.ic) *adj*.

cin.e.ma.theque (sin.uh.muh.TEK) *n.* a small theater for innovative and experimental films.

cin.e.ma.tog.ra.phy (sin.uh.muh.TOG.ruh.fee) *n.* the art of making movies, esp. its photographic aspects.
—**cin.e.ma.tog.ra.pher** *n*.
—**cin.e.mat.o.graph.ic** (SIN.uh.mat.uh.GRAF.ic) *adj*.

cinema ve.ri.té (-ver.uh.TAY) *n.* filmmaking in a style suggesting documentary realism; also, such a film.

cin.e.rar.i.um (sin.uh.RAIR.ee.um) *n., pl.* **-i.a** (-ee.uh) a depository for the ashes of cremated bodies.

cin.na.bar (SIN.uh.bar) *n.* **1** the principal ore of mercury. **2** its bright red color.

cin.na.mon (SIN.uh.mun) *n.* **1** a spice produced from the fragrant bark of a group of E. Asian trees of the laurel family. **2** the bark or the tree. **3** a yellowish brown.

cinque.foil (SINK.foil) *n.* a plant of the rose family having five-lobed leaves.

ci.on (SYE.un) same as SCION, 1.

ci.pher (SYE.fur) *n.* **1** zero (0) as indicating no quantity; hence, a nonentity: *a mere cipher*. **2** a coding system for concealing the meaning of a text; also, a coded message: *messages in cipher; spies trying to break a cipher without its key*. **3** any Arabic numeral.
—*v.* **1** solve or calculate arithmetically. **2** express information in a code.

cir.ca (SUR.cuh) *prep*. about: *born circa 1920*.

cir.ca.di.an (sur.CAY.dee.un) *adj*. in biology, acting or occurring in roughly 24-hour cycles: *the circadian rhythm of our eating and sleeping patterns*. —**cir.ca.di.an.ly** *adv*.

cir.cle (SUR.cul) *n.* **1** a closed round plane curve or the area bounded by it: *A compass is used to draw circles; Satellites describe circles around their planets; They joined hands and formed a circle around the pole; The Arctic and Antarctic Circles are polar circles; a traffic circle around a traffic island*. **2** something resembling a circle: *a circle of admirers; jobseekers caught in a vicious circle of lack of experience and consequent unemployment; People move in academic, business, close, diplomatic, exclusive, family, financial, inner, intimate, political, professional circles; the circle* (= cycle) *of the seasons; to go around* or *talk* **in circles** *without getting anywhere*. —**come full circle** or **cycle** return to the starting point after a sojourn.
—*v.* **-cles, -cled, -cling** enclose or move in a circle: *The teacher circled six errors; The jet circled* (above) *the airport*.

cir.clet (SUR.clit) *n.* a small circle, esp. as an ornament: *the gold circlet around her neck*.

cir.cuit (SUR.kit) *n.* **1** the path, distance, or journey around something: *A fence marks the circuit of the estate; the circuit of the moon around the earth*. **2** a regular course traveled by a sales rep, preacher (**circuit rider**), judge (**circuit judge**), entertainer, athletic competitor, etc.: *the professional golf circuit; the lecture circuit; a band playing the nightclub circuit; the cocktail party circuit*. **3** the path of an electric current, with its wiring and other equipment: *Current flows when the circuit is closed; If the current stops, there's a break in the circuit somewhere; A dangerous short circuit results when the main circuit is bypassed*.

circuit board *n.* a flat piece of material on which an array of computer chips is mounted.

circuit breaker *n.* a device for stopping the flow of electricity under special conditions such as overload: *The current stops when a circuit breaker is tripped*.

circuit court *n.* a court which sits in more than one place within a jurisdiction.

circuit judge See CIRCUIT.

cir.cu.i.tous (sir.CUE.uh.tus) *adj*. lengthy and indirect; roundabout: *They took a circuitous route to avoid reporters*. —**cir.cu.i.tous.ly** *adv*.

circuit rider See CIRCUIT.

cir.cuit.ry (SIR.cuh.tree) *n.* **-ries 1** the design or components of an electrical circuit. **2** such circuits collectively.

cir.cu.lar (SIRK.yuh.lur) *adj.* **1** having to do with the circle: *A quadrant is a unit of circular measure; a circular (= round) saw; the* **circular file** *(= round file); a circular letter, notice (distributed to many).* **2** circuitous or roundabout: *a circular explanation; circular reasoning.* —*n.* an advertisement, leaflet, etc. for mass distribution: *We send out circulars to the public; to distribute circulars from door to door.* —**cir.cu.lar.i.ty** (-LAIR.i.tee) *n.*

cir.cu.lar.ize (SIRK.yuh.luh.rize) *v.* **-iz.es, -ized, -iz.ing** publicize or poll with circulars. —**cir.cu.lar.i.za.tion** (-ruh.ZAY.shun, -rye-) *n.*

cir.cu.late (SIRK.yuh.late) *v.* **-lates, -lat.ed, -lat.ing** move, often in a circuit, from place to place, person to person, etc.: *A fan circulates air in a room; Please circulate this memo; Blood circulates in the body; A host is supposed to circulate among the guests; adj.: a widely* **circulated** *magazine.*

cir.cu.la.tion (sirk.yuh.LAY.shun) *n.* **1** the act of circulating, esp. of blood in the body: *Exercise helps improve circulation if you suffer from poor circulation; The government puts money into circulation; Bills are withdrawn from circulation as they get old; They cease to be in circulation.* **2** the distribution or total sales of a periodical: *a paper with a limited or small circulation; The Times enjoys a wide, national circulation; an enormous circulation of two million.*

cir.cu.la.to.ry (SIRK.yuh.luh.tor.ee) *adj.* having to do with the circulation of the blood: *He died of circulatory failure; The* **circulatory system** *contains the heart, blood vessels, and lymphatic vessels.*

cir.cum.cise (SUR.cum.size) *v.* **-cis.es, -cised, -cis.ing** cut off the foreskin of a male or clitoris of a female. —**cir.cum.cis.ion** (-SIZH.un) *n.*

cir.cum.fer.ence (sur.CUM.fuh.runce) *n.* **1** the perimeter of a circle or other figure: *It's three kilometers in circumference.* **2** outer boundary; periphery.

cir.cum.flex (SUR.cum.flex) *n.* a mark written above a vowel (as in â or ă) to show its quality, pitch, etc.

cir.cum.lo.cu.tion (SUR.cum.loh.CUE.shun) *n. Formal.* an indirect, evasive expression using too many words.

cir.cum.nav.i.gate (sur.cum.NAV.uh.gate) *v.* sail all the way around, esp. the world: *Magellan was the first to circumnavigate the world.* —**cir.cum.nav.i.ga.tion** (-GAY.shun) *n.*

cir.cum.scribe (SUR.cum.scribe) *v.* **-scribes, -scribed, -scrib.ing 1** draw a line around something. **2** restrict, limit in scope, etc.; *adj.: a narrowly* **circumscribed** *field of specialization.*

cir.cum.spect (SUR.cum.spect) *adj.* aware of possible consequences; cautious and prudent: *She is naturally very circumspect when dealing with strangers; circumspect moneylenders.* —**cir.cum.spec.tion** (-SPEC.shun) *n.*

cir.cum.stance (SUR.cum.stance, -stunce) *n.* **1** a fact or occurrence associated with a person or event; a condition or situation: *It was snowing heavily, the roads were slippery, the driver was exhausted, and such circumstances of the accident; In the present circumstance, there's no excuse; This cannot be allowed in any circumstance; a combination of circumstances pointing to the accused's guilt; He was absent without warning because of unforeseen circumstances; Acts of God are circumstances beyond our control; Use of force is justified in certain circumstances such as to defend oneself; She pleaded extenuating circumstances; He lived in straitened* **circumstances** *(= financial hardship);* **In** *or* **Under** *no circumstances (= never) would he tell a lie;* **In** *or* **Under the circumstances,** *the judge had to show mercy.* **2** chance: *She was a victim of circumstance.* **3** ceremony: *an emperor's life of pomp and circumstance.*

cir.cum.stan.tial (sur.cum.STAN.shul) *adj.* **1** having to do with or determined by circumstances; incidental: *We have strong, first-hand circumstantial evidence of the crime; But it's highly circumstantial evidence with no direct proof; Your case is purely circumstantial.* **2** with full details of the circumstances of time and place: *a circumstantial account, report; The most circumstantial picture would be a video.* —**cir.cum.stan.tial.ly** *adv.*

cir.cum.vent (sur.cum.VENT) *v.* **1** overcome by craft: *The plan was discovered and circumvented by the enemy.* **2** get around; avoid: *a plan to circumvent the rules.* **3** encircle: *circumvented by perils.* —**cir.cum.ven.tion** *n.*

cir.cus (SUR.cus) *n.* **-cus.es 1** a usu. traveling entertainment consisting of trained animals, acrobats, clowns, etc. performing in a tent: *a three-ring circus.* **2** *Informal.* an uproarious display or entertainment: *The show was too much of a circus for one man to handle; a media circus.*

cirque (SIRK) *n.* a semicircular, steep-walled hollow in a mountain, often at

cirrhosis / civil

the head of a valley.
cir.rho.sis (suh.ROH.sis) *n.*, *pl.* **-ses** (-seez) a severe, chronic disease of the liver. —**cir.rho.tic** (-ROT.ic) *adj.*
cir.rus (SEER.us) *n.*, *pl.* **cir.ri** (SEER.eye) a usu. white, high, thin, cloud.
cir.ro.cu.mu.lus (seer.oh.CUE.myuh.lus) *n.* a regular formation of small, puffy clouds at a great height.
cir.ro.stra.tus (seer.oh.STRAY.tus, -STRAT.us) *n.* a layer of high, thin, hazy clouds.
cis.at.lan.tic (sis.ut.LAN.tic) *adj.* on this (i.e. speaker's) side of the Atlantic.
cis.lu.nar (sis.LOO.nur) *adj.* between the earth and the moon's orbit.
cis.tern (SIS.turn) *n.* a storage tank for water, esp. rainwater.
cit.a.del (SIT.uh.dul) *n.* **1** a fortress: *the citadel overlooking Quebec City.* **2** a stronghold or refuge: *a citadel of democracy, freedom, power.*
ci.ta.tion (sye.TAY.shun) *n.* **1** a summons: *He was issued a citation for contempt of court; a citation to appear in court; traffic citations.* **2** commendation: *She received a citation for bravery.* **3** quotation: *He has citations to prove his point; a citation* (= passage) *from the Bible.*
cite *v.* **cites, cit.ed, cit.ing** **1** call to appear in court: *She was cited for a traffic violation.* **3** commend for bravery, dedication, etc. **3** quote; also, list, refer to, or bring forward as proof, example, etc.: *He likes to cite passages from the Koran; Job is often cited as a model of patience.*
cit.i.fy (SIT.uh.fye) *v.* **-fies, -fied, -fy.ing** make refined; urbanize; *adj.*: *There's a citified air about him.*
cit.i.zen (SIT.uh.zun) *n.* **1** a member of a state, owing allegiance to it and having full rights in it: *a citizen by birth; A permanent resident can become a naturalized citizen; She is considered a citizen of the world with a cosmopolitan outlook.* **2** one who lives in or was born in a specified city: *the citizens of Athens.* **3** a civilian: *law-abiding, leading, prominent, solid citizens; our senior citizens; Women and minorities often complain of being treated as second-class citizens; He made a citizen's arrest and held the burglar till the police arrived.* —**cit.i.zen.ly** *adj.*: *citizenly virtues.*
cit.i.zen.ry (SIT.uh.zun.ree) *n.* citizens collectively: *an informed citizenry; the citizenry of Rome.*
citizens band *n.* a short-wave radio frequency used for private transmissions.
cit.i.zen.ship (SIT.uh.zun.ship) *n.* the status of being a citizen: *to acquire, give up, grant, receive, renounce, revoke a citizenship; a certificate of citizenship; dual citizenship* (= citizenship of two countries).
cit.ric acid *n.* an acid usu. derived from lime or lemon juice, used in flavorings and in making **citrates,** salts or esters of this acid.
cit.ron (SIT.run) *n.* **1** a fragrant, lemonlike fruit with a thick rind. **2** the tree it grows on, native to Asia. **3** a melon having a thick, hard rind. **4** the preserved or candied rind of either citron fruit.
cit.ron.el.la (sit.ruh.NEL.uh) *n.* **1** a pale yellow, fragrant oil used in perfumes and insect repellents. **2** the Asiatic grass it is made from.
cit.rus (SIT.rus) *n.* **1** a thorny, evergreen tree bearing acid fruit, as the orange, grapefruit, lemon, and lime. **2** such a fruit. —**adj**.: *citrus colors, flavors, fruits, peel, shades;* also **cit.rous.** —**cit.rus.y** *adj.*: *a citrusy scent.*
cit.y (SIT.ee) *n.* **cit.ies** a large or important town, esp. one that is incorporated: *Canberra is a capital city; a densely populated city; People working in the city tend to live in the suburbs; satellite cities around a metropolitan area; Overcrowding, poverty, and crime are some of the problems of the inner* (= central) *city.* —**adj**.: *city driving, living, streets; A city council has legislative and administrative powers over a city; a city editor* (= local news editor); *the city fathers* (= city administrators); *the city state of Singapore.*
city hall or **City Hall** *n.* **1** a municipal government building. **2** a bureaucratic administration: *"You can't fight city hall"* (because it is futile).
city limits *n.pl.* city boundaries.
city slicker *n.* a sophisticated and wily person with city manners.
civ.et (SIV.it) *n.* **1** a strong-smelling, yellowish-brown substance used in perfumes and obtained from the **civet cat,** a catlike, carnivorous mammal of Africa. **2** the fur of this animal.
civ.ic (SIV.ic) **1** *adj*. having to do with a city, citizenship, etc.: *your civic duties; our civic pride; Our civic center contains the municipal headquarters and facilities for games and other community activities.* **2 civics** *n.pl.* [takes *sing. v.*] the study of the rights and duties of citizenship in relation to government.
civ.ies same as CIVVIES.
civ.il (SIV.ul) *adj.* **1** pertaining to the citizens in their relationship to the

state: *the civil and criminal codes of law; our* **civil liberties** *and rights as guaranteed by the Constitution; to bring a civil action against someone in a* **civil court** *(not criminal court).* **2** pertaining to the people as distinguished from the military or religious: *civil aviation; The civil name of Pope John Paul II was Karol Wojtyla; the civil (= government) service; a civil (= not religious) marriage.* **3** civilized: *At least be civil if you can't be polite or courteous; It was civil of her to invite him to her wedding after what happened; civil language; We live in a civil society; Keep a civil tongue in your head.* —**civ.il.ly** *adv.*

civil defense *n.* a system of warning, defense, and emergency aid for the people in case of war, natural disasters, etc.

civil disobedience *n.* disobedience against the government, as by boycotts and nonpayment of taxes.

civil engineering *n.* a branch of engineering that deals with roads, tunnels, and other public works.

ci.vil.i.an (suh.VIL.yun) *n.* a member of the general public, not a member of the military, police, etc.; **adj.**: *a civilian award; a soldier's return to civilian life; a return to civilian rule after a military dictatorship.*

ci.vil.i.ty (suh.VIL.i.tee) *n.* **-ties** politeness or a polite act.

civ.i.li.za.tion (siv.uh.luh.ZAY.shun, -lye-) *n.* **1** a high degree of cultural, social, and technological development: *to introduce, spread civilization.* **2** the culture of a time, place, people, etc.: *the rise and fall of civilizations since prehistoric times; Many ancient civilizations have been stamped out or destroyed or wiped out by invaders; the decay and collapse of the Aztec civilization; Western civilization has its roots in Greek and Roman culture.* **3** the act of civilizing: *the civilization of conquered nations.* **4** the comforts of modern society: *It took us many days to get back to civilization after getting lost in the jungle.*

civ.i.lize (SIV.uh.lize) *v.* **-liz.es, -lized, -liz.ing** bring to a higher degree of civilization: *Conquerors would try to civilize the conquered.*

civilized *adj.* refined or cultured: *civilized behavior, manners; a civilized country, dialogue, home, society; the civilized world that we live in; a civilized afternoon of ballet, dining, and some TV.*

civil libertarian *n.* one who advocates civil liberties.

civil rights *n.* a person's rights as a citizen, esp. the right to equal treatment regardless of sex, race, religion, etc.

civil servant *n.* a member of the **civil service,** the administrative branch of a government.

civil war *n.* a war waged by factions within a nation: *the* **Civil War** *between the N. and S. states of the Union (1861-65).*

civ.vies (SIV.eez) *n.pl. Informal.* civilian or regular attire as distinguished from a uniform.

clack *v.* **1** make a short, hard sound: *She clacked down the stairs in her clogs.* **2** chatter; **adj.:** *clacking* tongues. Also *n.* —**clack.er** *n.*

clad *adj.* clothed or covered: *a warmly clad hunter; a scantily clad bather; partially, lightly, fully clad bodies; an emperor clad in rags; a* **clad coin** *containing two outer layers of a copper-nickel alloy bonded to a core of pure copper;* **cpd:** *an iron-clad guarantee; the ivy-clad towers of our university;* **n.:** *stone* **cladding** *(= facing or covering) for the exterior walls of your home.*

claim *v.* **1** assert as a fact or right: *He claimed the crown (as his); claimed that the crown was his; claims to get more mileage with his new car; Let's claim (= ask for and get) our bags.* **2** take: *The fire claimed three lives.* —*n.* **1** a demand, request, or assertion of something, esp. as a right: *to enter, file, put forward, put in, submit a claim; A claim for compensation or damages against the offending party was settled out of court; The prospector staked (out) his claim to the territory (by marking it off with stakes); Family, colleagues, and friends make too many claims on my time for me to do any community work; His claim to fame is based on his scientific discoveries; to* **lay claim to** *an inheritance.* **2** something claimed, esp. land: *A rival prospector* **jumped his claim** *(= took it illegally).*

claim.ant (CLAY.munt) *n.* one who claims: *a claimant to the throne.*

clair.voy.ance (clair.VOY.unce) *n.* the ability to perceive what is beyond the senses; also, sharp intuition. —**clair.voy.ant** *n. & adj.;* **clair.voy.ant.ly** *adv.*

clam *n.* **1** a bivalve mollusk often used for food. **2** *Informal.* one who doesn't talk much. —*v.* **clams, clammed, clam.ming 1** dig for clams. **2 clam up** stop talking.

clam.bake *n.* **1** an outdoor party at which clams are steamed or baked. **2** any large, lively social gathering.

clam.ber (CLAM.bur) *v.* climb awk-

clammy / class

wardly, usu. with both hands and feet: *He clambered up the hill; clambered over the fence; clambered into a bus.*
clam.my (CLAM.ee) *adj.* **clam.mi.er, clam.mi.est** unpleasantly moist, cool, and sticky: *clammy hands, skin.* —**clam.mi.ly** *adv.;* **clam.mi.ness** *n.*
clam.or (CLAM.ur) *n.* a loud noise or shouting; a violent protest, demand, etc.: *a public clamor for reform; a clamor against the new bill.* —*v.* make a clamor: *children clamoring for attention; a crowd of demonstrators clamoring to see the minister.* —**clam.or.ous** *adj.;* **clam.or.ous.ly** *adv.* Also **clam.our** *Cdn.*
clamp *n.* **1** a band, vise, etc. for holding objects together. **2** a firm grip. —*v.* **1** fasten or hold firmly, as in a clamp. **2** impose: *to clamp controls on rising prices; to clamp on a curfew.* —**clamp down** *Informal.* impose restrictions: *The authorities are finally clamping down; They're clamping down on tax evaders.* —**clamp.down** *n.*
clam.shell *n.* **1** the shell of a clam. **2** a dredging bucket hinged like such a shell.
clan *n.* **1** a group of families, as among Indian tribes or Scottish highlanders, based on descent from a common ancestor: *a gathering of the clans.* **2** a group of associates or relatives; clique: *a Mafia clan; a clan of poets, power brokers, writers.*
clan.des.tine (clan.DES.tin) *adj.* secret or underhand: *a clandestine effort, life, love affair, meeting, policy.* —**clan.des.tine.ly** *adv.*
clang *n.* a loud ringing metallic sound: *the clang of steel.* —*v.: The dinner bell clanged at 6:00.*
clan.gor (CLANG.ur, -gur) *n.* a prolonged clang; clanging din. Also **clan.gour** *Cdn.*
clank *n.* an abrupt, loud, metallic sound; *v.: chains clanking in the dungeon; The door clanked shut.*
clan.nish *adj.* forming a group that excludes outsiders: *People become less clannish as they get more educated; their clannish loyalties.* —**clan.nish.ly** *adv.;* **clan.nish.ness** *n.*
clans.man (CLANS.mun) *n.* **-men** a member of a clan. —**clans.wom.an** *n.* **-wom.en.**
clap *n.* **1** a loud, flat noise, as of the palms of two hands struck sharply together. **2** applause. **3** a loud explosive noise: *a clap of thunder.* **4** a blow or slap. —*v.* **claps, clapped, clap.ping 1** strike the palms together; make a clapping noise; applaud: *to clap hands with joy;* *n.: The* **clapping** *went on for five minutes after the speech.* **2** slap: *to clap someone on the back.* **3** move, put, do, etc. suddenly and roughly: *They clapped him in irons; He was clapped in jail; A 10% duty was clapped on imports.*
clap.board (CLAB.urd, CLAP.bord) *n.* a long, narrow board with one edge thicker than the other, used as siding on houses. —*v.* cover with clapboards.
clap.per *n.* the tongue of a bell.
clap.trap *n.* cheap rhetoric used in speech, writing, etc. merely to win applause: *mere claptrap; cant and claptrap sentiment.*
claque (CLAK) *n.* a group hired to applaud in a theater.
clar.et (CLAIR.ut) *n.* **1** a dry red table wine. **2** its purplish red color.
clar.i.fy (CLAIR.uh.fye) *v.* **-fies, -fied, -fy.ing** make or become clear: *The situation will clarify as events develop; Clarify your meaning, position, views; adj.:* **clarified** *consomme; clarified* (= purified) *butter.* —**clar.i.fi.ca.tion** (-fuh.CAY.shun) *n.*
clar.i.net (clair.uh.NET) *n.* a single-reed woodwind instrument with finger holes and keys. —**clar.i.net.ist** or **clar.i.net.tist** *n.*
clar.i.on (CLAIR.ee.un) *n.* a medieval type of trumpet. —**adj.** clear and ringing: *the bugle's clarion call.*
clar.i.ty (CLAIR.i.tee) *n.* clearness: *His arguments came through with forceful clarity; clarity of the atmosphere; the clarity of a diamond; clarity of expression, thinking, speech, vision.*
clash *n.* **1** a conflict or disagreement: *a bloody, violent clash; the clash of or between opposing armies, interests, personalities; a clash with the neighbors.* **2** a loud, confused, usu. metallic sound of colliding: *the clash of cymbals, weapons.* —*v.* **1** to conflict: *Our troops clashed with the enemy; The two factions clashed* (= argued) *over the seating arrangements; Red and green clash in the picture.* **2** collide: *oil drums clashing together.*
clasp *n.* **1** a fastener, as a pin, hook, buckle, etc.: *a tie clasp.* **2** a firm grip or embrace. —*v.* **1** fasten with or as with a clasp; *adj.: a sweater that is* **clasped** *at the neck.* **2** grip with the hand; embrace: *He clasped the picture to his breast.*
class *n.* **1** a distinctive group with a common characteristic and name: *Apes, bears, mice, etc. form the class of mammals.* **2** a social division based on status, economic function, etc.: *educated, leisure, middle, privileged, ruling,*

underprivileged, upper, working classes; **adj.:** *a class conflict, distinction, struggle, war; class bias, consciousness, differences, hatred, superiority, warfare.* **3** a group defined by quality, level, condition, etc.: *cabin, economy, tourist classes; She usually travels first-class; He passed with first-class honors; a second-class citizen; She is in a class of her own* (= has no equal). **4** a group of students, or **classmates,** instructed together, usu. in the same room, or **classroom;** also, a lesson: *to attend, call off, cancel, conduct, cut, dismiss, hold, give, go to, miss, schedule, sit in on a class; the freshman, senior, sophomore classes; The class of 93 graduated in the year 1993; She was at the top of her class.* **5** *Informal.* style, high quality, etc.: *a woman with class; Kay doesn't have much class.*
—*v.* put in a class; classify; *She is classed as a genius.*

class act *n. Informal.* a person or thing of outstanding quality.

class action *n.* a law suit brought on behalf of all parties affected by an alleged injustice.

clas.sic (CLASS.ic) *adj.* **1** of traditionally recognized importance, value, excellence, etc.; classical: *the classic style of Milton; a classic epic, tragedy; a "classic car" built between 1925 and 1942; classic old movies.* **2** considered the greatest of its kind: *a classic collection, design, meal, work; classic cutlery, rock music; classic looks, shapes, styles, tunes.* **3** standard or typical: *a classic example of mismanagement; classic oriental features; a classic case of tuberculosis; the classic symptoms of smallpox; a classic nerd, response, situation, tale of broken promises.* —*n.* **1** an author, artist, or work considered as classic: *The Ramayana is a Hindu classic; the Louvre's treasured classics; such classics as "The Catcher in the Rye"; modern classics; a professor of* **classics** (= Greek and Roman literature). **2** something considered the greatest of its kind: *This salad is a culinary classic; film classics; a golf classic* (= great golf tournament).

clas.si.cal (CLASS.i.cul) *adj.* **1** having to do with ancient Greek or Roman culture or its qualities of simplicity, form, purity, etc.: *classical and modern architecture, education, languages, literature, mythology, scholars, studies, times; the classical world; classical grace and elegance; a hero in the classical mode.* **2** having to do with late 18th-century European music: *the classical music of Mozart; classical composers.* **3** traditional in form or content: *written in classical style; classical and modern ballet; classical economics, Marxism, oratory, physics.*
—**clas.si.cal.ly** *adv.*

clas.si.cism (CLASS.uh.siz.um) *n.* adherence to the stylistic standards of ancient Greece and Rome, as clarity, form, restraint, and grace.
—**clas.si.cist** *n.*

classified (CLASS.uh.fied) *adj.* **1** designated as secret: *classified information; a classified report on nuclear weapons.* **2** arranged by topic: *classified advertising; classified ads.* —*n.* a classified ad: *real estate classifieds.*

clas.si.fy (CLASS.uh.fy) *v.* **-fies, -fied, -fy.ing** put in groups according to type, topic, etc. —**clas.si.fi.a.ble** (-fye.uh.bul) *adj.* —**clas.si.fi.ca.tion** (-fuh.CAY.shun) *n.*

classmate, classroom See CLASS.

class.y *adj.* **class.i.er, -i.est** *Informal.* having class: *a very classy car, dress, hotel, look, style.*

clas.tic (CLAS.tic) *adj.* **1** formed from pieces of older rock: *a clastic sandstone.* **2** that can be taken apart: *a clastic anatomical model.*

clat.ter (CLAT.ur) *v.* move with or make a loud rattling sound: *Pots and pans clattered out of the cabinet.* —*n.* rattling noise: *the clatter of pots and pans.*

clause (CLAWS) *n.* **1** a part of a sentence having its own subject and verb: *main and subordinate* or *dependent clauses.* **2** a section of a document: *escalator, grandfather, penalty clauses.*

claus.tro.pho.bi.a (claw.struh.FOH.bee.uh) *n.* an abnormal fear of closed spaces such as elevators. —**claus.tro.pho.bic** *adj.*

clav.i.chord (CLAV.i.cord) *n.* a keyboard instrument used before the piano was invented.

clav.i.cle (CLAV.i.cul) *n.* the collarbone, connecting the shoulder blade and the breastbone.

cla.vier (cluh.VEER) *n.* **1** any stringed keyboard instrument. **2** a keyboard.

claw *n.* **1** a usu. sharp, curving nail on the foot of a bird, lizard, cat, etc. **2** the pincer of a lobster, some insects, etc.: *Cats can retract their claws.* **3** anything shaped like a claw, as the curved, split head of a hammer (**clawhammer**) used for pulling nails.
—*v.* grasp, scratch, dig, or move using or as if using claws: *a dog clawing at a locked door.*

clay *n.* **1** a fine-grained kind of earth, soft when wet, used for molding, brick-making, and ceramics: *potter's* clay; *modeling clay.* **2** wet ground or mud. **3** the human body: *this mortal clay.*

clay.ey (CLAY.ee) *adj.* **clay.i.er, -i.est** containing clay: *clayey soil.*

clay.more *n.* **1** a large Highland broadsword. **2** a kind of land mine.

clay pigeon *n.* a disk tossed as a target in trapshooting.

clean (CLEEN) *adj.* **1** free from dirt: *a clean shirt; an immaculately clean home; a spotlessly clean house.* **2** free from anything undesirable, as obscenity (*a clean joke; good clean fun*), pollution (*a clean blast, bomb; the Clean Air Act*), dishonesty (*a clean game*), complications (*the clean lines of a work of art*), illegal drugs (*an addict trying to stay clean*), etc. **3** complete or thorough: *a clean break with the past; a clean sweep of the polls; a clean profit of $100,000.* —**come clean** *Informal.* confess: *They were forced to come clean under interrogation.* —**adv.** **1** in a clean manner: *Let's play it clean.* **2** completely: *We're clean out of provisions; Stay clean out of sight.* —**v.** make or become clean: *to clean the kitchen; He doesn't mind cleaning up after his sister; In baseball, a cleaner is supposed to* **clean** (or **clear**) **the bases** (= hit a home run with players on bases). —**clean out** empty: *Please clean out your desk before leaving; The burglars cleaned out the shop; The shop was cleaned out of its inventory.* —**clean up** *Informal.* make a large profit; make a killing: *They cleaned up on the business deal; The book is just out and cleaning up.* —**clean up one's act** *Informal.* behave properly. —**clean.ness** *n.*

clean-cut *adj.* **1** having distinct outlines: *a clean-cut analysis of the problem; a clean-cut unambiguous statement; It's pretty clean-cut that he is not telling the whole truth.* **2** neat and wholesome: *a clean-cut young man; our clean-cut image as a political party.*

clean.er *n.* a person or thing that cleans: *street cleaners; dry cleaners; drain, floor, vacuum cleaners; She was taken* **to the cleaners** (= defrauded of all her money).

cleaning *n.* an act of cleaning: *Give it a thorough cleaning; Only dry cleaning will remove those spots; our annual spring cleaning of the house.* —**clean.ness** *n.*

clean.ly 1 (CLEEN.lee) *adv.* in a clean manner; without making a mess: *Watch the knife going cleanly into the cheese.* **2** (CLEN.lee) *adj.* **-li.er, -li.est** habitually clean and tidy: *the cat's reputation as a cleanly animal;*

clean.li.ness *n.*: *personal cleanliness; "Cleanliness is next to godliness."*

clean room *n.* an area free of dust, germs, etc., used for assembling precision equipment, laboratory experiments, etc.

cleanse (CLENZ) *v.* **cleans.es, cleansed, cleans.ing** clean and purify: *to cleanse a wound; to cleanse the air; to cleanse your heart of sin;* **adja.:** *a cleansing cream for your skin.*

cleans.er (CLEN.zur) *n.* a solvent or detergent for cleaning: *a kitchen cleanser.*

clean-shaven *adj.* of men, with facial hair shaved off.

clean.up *n.* **1** a thorough cleaning. **2** a large profit.

clear (CLEER) *adj.* **1** free from darkness or dimness, as a cloudless sky: *on a clear day; clear glass.* **2** free from anything unwanted or obscuring, as blurring (*a clear outline, tone, vision*), debt or deduction (*a clear profit, title*), obstruction (*clear sailing ahead*), contents (*a ship clear of cargo*), flaws or blemishes (*a clear complexion*), guilt (*a clear conscience*), or contact (*to stand clear of the machinery*). **3** free from doubt; obvious to the mind: *Is that clear to you? Are you clear about it? I'd like to make this crystal clear; It is clear that we have lost; It's as clear as day.* **4** keen or perceptive: *She has a clear head for math.*

—*n.* **in the clear** *Informal.* free of suspicion, danger, or obstructions: *The dropping of all charges left the suspect in the clear.* —*adv.* **1** in a clear manner: *I read you loud and clear* (= understand you perfectly). **2** completely: *It flew clear across the lake.* —*v.* **1** make or become clear: *The sky is clearing; to clear up a difficulty, misunderstanding; They cleared the snow from the driveway; cleared the land of trees; He was cleared of the murder charge; The rash will take time to* **clear up** (= heal). **2** make money as net profit: *We cleared $1 million last year.* **3** pass through checking procedures; get or give approval: *The motion cleared the committee; A flight is cleared for takeoff; an article cleared for publication; It has been cleared with the censors; We were cleared to land.* **4** go over, under, past, etc. without touching: *Watch the horse clear the fence.* —**clear out** *Informal.* **1** go away; leave: *He cleared out before he was thrown out.* **2** clean out: *He's clearing out his desk before leaving.* —**clear the air** resolve differences or tensions. —**clear.ly** *adv.;* **clear.ness** *n.*

clear.ance (CLEER.unce) *n.* **1** the distance at which something is removed from another; clearing space: *a bridge with enough clearance for trucks to pass under.* **2** a permission or authorization: *customs clearance; A pilot receives clearance to land; a security clearance; clearance papers.* **3** a clearing: *slum clearance; a warehouse clearance; a **clearance sale** (at reduced prices).*

clear-cut or **clear.cut 1** *adj.* distinctly outlined; hence, plain: *a clear-cut case of fraud; a clear-cut answer, definition, guarantee, issue, rule, victory.* **2** *n.* an area completely cleared of trees: *regrowth of trees in clearcuts.* **3** *n.* such clearing, or clearcutting: *the environmental aspects of clearcutting.*

clear-eyed *adj.* clearly thought-out; discerning: *a good, well-acted, clear-eyed production.*

clear-headed *adj.* sensible; mentally clear.

clearing (CLEER.ing) *n.* an area in the woods that is free of trees.

clear.ing.house (CLEER.ing.house) *n.* a central office, as for clearing checks between banks: *a clearinghouse for information; a publishers' clearinghouse (for selling publications at a discount).*

clear-sighted *adj.* clear-eyed.

cleat (CLEET) *n.* **1** a projection, as on the sole of a shoe to get a grip. **2** a two-horned projection around which a rope may be wound, as on boats.

cleav.age (CLEE.vij) *n.* a splitting or division: *the direction of cleavage in a gem; the sharp cleavages existing in society; a neckline cut low on a dress to show cleavage (suggesting the wearer's breasts).*

cleave (CLEEV) *v.* **1 cleaves, cleaved, cleav.ing** cling: *Traditional societies tend to cleave to age-old customs.* **2 cleaves;** *pt.* **cleft, cleaved** or **clove** (CLOHV); *pp.* **cleft, cleaved** or **clo.ven** (CLOH.vun); **cleav.ing** split or divide: *to cleave a piece of wood, a stick;* ***adj.:*** *The devil is often pictured with **cloven** feet; cattle, deer, pigs and such animals with **cloven** hoofs.*

cleav.er (CLEE.vur) *n.* a butcher's heavy, broad-bladed chopping tool: *a meat cleaver.*

clef *n.* a symbol on a musical staff indicating the pitch of the notes: *alto, bass, treble clefs.*

cleft a *pt. & pp.* of CLEAVE. —*adj.* split: *a cleft stick.* —*n.* a fissure or split: *a cleft in the rock.*

cleft palate *n.* a fissure in the roof of the mouth occurring as a congenital defect.

clem.a.tis (CLEM.uh.tis) *n.* a colorfully flowering vine of the buttercup family.

clem.en.cy (CLEM.un.see) *n.* mercy, as of a judge toward an offender: *a plea for clemency; to beg for, deny, seek, show clemency.*

clem.ent (CLEM.unt) *adj.* **1** mild, not harsh: *clement weather.* **2** lenient or forgiving: *a clement judge.*

clench *v.* close, grip, or fasten tightly: *to clench one's hand, jaw, teeth;* ***adj.:*** *a **clenched** fist, grip; clenched teeth.* —*n.* a tight grip.

clere.sto.ry (CLEER.stor.ee) *n.* **-ries** **1** in buildings, a windowed wall rising above an adjoining roof. **2** a similar structure, as for ventilation in railroad cars.

cler.gy (CLUR.jee) *n.* **-gies** [usu. takes *pl. v.*] a body of people in religious service, as monks, priests, rabbis, or nuns: *The clergy are distinguished from the laity.* —**cler.gy.man** *n.* **-men**. —**cler.gy.wom.an** *n.* **-wom.en**.

cler.ic *n.* a member of the clergy.

cler.i.cal (CLER.i.cul) *adj.* **1** having to do with clerks, office work, etc.: *typing and such clerical skills; a clerical error.* **2** having to do with the clergy: *a clerical collar.* —**cler.i.cal.ism** *n.* clerical power in government or politics.

clerk (CLURK) *n.* **1** an office worker, as one who types, files, etc. **2** an official in charge of records and regular business: *city, county, court clerks; the clerk (= chief administrative officer) of the legislature.* **3** a person in a sales or service function: *a desk clerk; room clerks in a hotel; sales clerks.* **4** a cleric: *a clerk in holy orders.* —*v.* work as a clerk: *Karen clerks in her father's store; She will start her law career clerking for a judge.* —**clerk.ship** *n.*

clev.er (CLEV.ur) *adj.* **1** showing quickness of mind, even if not deep or thorough: *a clever answer, child, reply, student.* **2** original or inventive: *a clever book, idea, trick.* **3** deft: *She is clever with her hands; clever at arranging flowers.* —**clev.er.ly** *adv.;* **clev.er.ness** *n.*

cli.ché (clee.SHAY) *n.* an expression, image, sentiment, situation, or theme considered hackneyed or overused among a group or at a particular time: *"Winds of change" was popular in the 1960s but has now become a cliché; A feminist who has toppled quite a few clichés; They think of Canada in clichés of Mounties, polar bears, and snow.*

cli.chéd (clee.SHADE) *adj.* that has become a cliché: *"Last but not least" is a* clichéd expression; a clichéd phrase, sentiment.

click *n.* **1** a short, sharp metallic sound, as of cocking a gun. **2** a sucking sound. —*v.* **1** make a click: *A soldier clicks his heels when he comes to attention; She clicked her tongue in delight; He clicks his teeth impatiently; The camera clicked when we were not looking; Before he could finish the sentence, the receiver was clicked off* (= the phone connection was cut off with a click); *Something clicked* (= flashed in the mind) *and I knew we had the right answer*. **2** *Informal*. to be a success: *The two seem to have clicked with each other; The new show clicked instantly with the prime-time audience*. **3** rapidly press and release the button of a computer mouse to control the cursor.

cli.ent (CLYE.unt) *n.* one who receives the services of a professional in a dependent relationship: *an accountant's, agent's, lawyer's, prostitute's clients; a welfare client* (= recipient); *adja.: a client* (= dependent) *state*.

cli.en.tele (clye.un.TEL) *n.* clients collectively.

cliff *n.* a high, steep-faced rocky prominence: *rugged, sheer, steep cliffs; to scale a cliff using ropes*.

cliff.hang.er (CLIFF.hang.ur) *n.* **1** a serialized adventure story or movie whose episodes end in suspense. **2** a suspenseful situation: *The game was a cliffhanger till the last play*.

cli.mac.ter.ic (clye.MAC.tuh.ric, -mac.TER.ic) *n.* a period of major change, esp. the menopause.

cli.mac.tic (clye.MAC.tic) *adj.* forming a climax: *the climactic final assault on Berlin*.

cli.mate (CLYE.mit) *n.* **1** the average weather of a region: *Alaska's cold climate; a damp, dry, hot, humid, invigorating, mild, temperate, tropical, warm, wet climate*. **2** a region considered in regard to its weather: *We live in a cold climate; Many birds move to warmer climates in the winter*. **3** the temper or condition of a place or time: *the political climate of Portugal*. —**cli.mat.ic** (clye.MAT.ic) *adj.: climatic changes; the climatic variations of the seasons*.

climate-control *n.* heating and air-conditoning, as in an automobile; *adja.: climate-control functions, push-buttons, systems; adj.: a climate-controlled building, walkway, warehouse*.

cli.ma.tol.o.gy (cly.muh.TOL.uh.jee) *n.* the science that studies climate; **cli.ma.tol.o.gist** *n.* —**cli.ma.to.log.i.cal** (-tuh.LOJ.i.cul) *adj.*

cli.max (CLYE.max) *n.* **1** the most important or significant, often final part or event; culmination: *a dramatic climax; The revelations bring the story to a thrilling climax; to mark, reach, work up to a climax*. **2** orgasm. —*v.* **-max.es, -maxed, -max.ing** attain or bring to a climax: *The Olympic win climaxed her efforts*.

climb (CLIME) *v.* **1** ascend; go up: *to climb a hill, mountain; to climb to the top; The moon climbed the night sky; Our stock is climbing*. **2** move along, up, down, etc. by using the hands and feet: *Any baby can climb out of that crib; Jack fell while climbing a tree; The infant climbed onto her mother's knees; It was easier to climb down the mountain; to climb aboard a wagon*. —*n.* a climbing: *The pilot put the plane into a steep climb; It was a hard, rough, tortuous climb up the mountain; a gradual climb to the top of the hill*.
—**climb.er** *n.: a mountain climber; social climbers*.

clime *n.* [usu. poetic] region; also, climate: *cold, distant, warmer climes*.

clinch *v.* **1** fasten firmly; hence, make certain or final: *The salesman clinched the deal; Our team clinched the victory in the final moments of the game; We also clinched the championship*. **2** in boxing, hold tight; *n.: The boxers went into a clinch*.

clinch.er *n.* a deciding or conclusive argument, element, event, etc.

cling *v.* **clings, clung, cling.ing** hang on to something as if attached to it: *Children cling to their mothers; children clinging together in the cold; A cooking odor may cling to the kitchen; to cling to a hope*.

clinging vine *n. Informal*. one who is too dependent on others.

cling.stone *n.* a kind of peach whose flesh adheres to the pit.

clin.ic *n.* **1** a medical treatment facility for outpatients: *a health clinic*. **2** such a facility run cooperatively by many specialists: *abortion, dental, family-planning clinics*. **3** any center for instruction, counseling, or a similar service: *a legal-aid clinic; a storefront clinic that gives financial advice; shoe clinic* (= repair shop); *a writers' clinic* (= short course of instruction).

clin.i.cal (CLIN.i.cul) *adj.* **1** having to do with treatment of illness: *a clinical examination, thermometer, trial; a doctor's clinical training, experience; the tests used in clinical psychology*; **Clinical medicine** *is the examination and treatment of patients*. **2** coldly analytical: *a clinical*

evaluation, interest, tone; *a psychologist's clinical attitude to a marriage breakup.*
—**clin.i.cal.ly** *adv.*

cli.ni.cian (cli.NISH.un) *n.* one who practices clinical medicine, psychiatry, etc.

clink *v.* make a short, sharp, ringing sound: *They clinked glasses in a toast.* —*n.* **1** a clinking sound: *the clink of cash, silverware.* **2** *Slang.* jail.

clink.er *n.* **1** a piece of fused, incombustible residue left when coal is burned; slag. **2** *Slang.* anything bad, as a flaw or failure, a blooper, lemon, or turkey: *a clinker of a play.* **3** *Slang.* jail: *He was tossed into the clinker.*

cli.o.met.rics (clee.oh.MET.riks) *n.pl.* the statistical study of historical data.

clip *v.* **clips, clipped, clip.ping 1** cut off, cut out, or cut short, as with shears, scissors, etc.: *to clip pictures from magazines; The plane clipped a sea wall and disintegrated on impact; adj.: a terse, clipped style of speech; hair clipped short; "Flu" is the clipped (= shortened) form of "influenza."* **2** hold tightly, esp. fasten with a clip: *He clipped his card to the memo.* **3** *Informal.* hit with a short, quick blow. **4** *Slang.* cheat, esp. by overcharging. —*n.* **1** a device for fastening or holding things together: *a paper clip; tie clips; a cartridge clip* (= feeding mechanism); *There were four bullets in the clip but none in the chamber.* **2** speed: *We were moving along at a fast clip.* **3** a piece of something clipped: *a clip from a movie; film clips; clips from her speeches;* also **clipping:** *nail clippings; press clippings.*

clip.board *n.* a small writing board having a clip to hold paper with.

clip joint *n.* an establishment, esp. a night club, that cheats customers.

clip.per (CLIP.ur) *n.* **1** often **clippers** *pl.* a tool for clipping, esp. shears for hair, wool, etc. **2** a long, narrow sailing ship; hence, any fast means of travel.

clique (CLEEK) *n.* a small exclusive group, usu. social or political. —**cli.quish** (-kish) *adj.:* serving narrow, cliquish interests.

clit.o.ris *n.* (CLIT.uh.ris) *n.* a sensitive erectile structure at the upper end of the vulva. —**clit.o.ral** *adj.*

cloak (CLOKE) *n.* **1** a loose, usu. sleeveless outer garment. **2** a concealment or disguise intended to deceive: *under the cloak of darkness; the cloak of friendship; attacking under the cloak of anonymity.* —*v.* cover with a cloak for the purpose of deceiving: *hospitality that cloaks treachery; adj.: a cloaked figure; plans cloaked in secrecy.*

cloak-and-dagger *adja.* having to do with spies: *James Bond's cloak-and-dagger adventures.*

cloak.room *n.* a room where coats, hats, etc. may be left for a time.

clob.ber (CLOB.ur) *v. Informal.* strike hard and repeatedly; defeat soundly; trounce: *They got clobbered in the finals.*

cloche (CLOHSH) *n.* a woman's close, bell-shaped hat.

clock *n.* a device for measuring or indicating time: *the hands of a clock; to stop the clock; cuckoo clocks; Workers check in and out of the factory by punching the time clock; a time bomb with a clock ticking inside; an alarm clock set to go off at 6 a.m.; when the clock strikes six; A watch is a clock made to be worn; to set the clock forward for daylight saving time; The new government's outdated policies will* **set** or **turn the clock back** *10 to 20 years; It was a race* **against the clock** *to catch the flight before it took off; He watched at his sick child's bedside* **around the clock** (= day and night); *adja.: a clock mechanism, pendulum, radio, tower.* —*v.* check with a clock or other device: *The police clocked the speeder at 120 km/h.*

clock speed *n.* the speed at which a computer can carry out commands, expressed in megahertz.

clock watcher *n.* one who is too eager to quit work at closing time.

clock.wise *adj. & adv.* in the same direction a clock's hands move in.

clock.work *n.* the mechanism of a clock; also, any similar machinery: *Everything went* **like clockwork** (= smoothly and precisely) *at the reception.*

clod *n.* **1** a lump of earth, mud, etc. **2** a dolt, lout, or boor. —**clod.dish** *adj.: his cloddish manners.*

clod.hop.per (CLOD.hop.ur) *n.* **1** a rustic, clumsy, or stupid person. **2** a heavy thick-soled shoe or boot.

clog *n.* **1** a heavy, wooden or wooden-soled shoe or boot. **2** a block of wood, as tied to the leg of an animal to prevent it from wandering; hence, an encumbrance. —*v.* **clogs, clogged, clog.ging** fill up and block or slow down: *Rush-hour traffic clogs the highways; adj.: a drain* **clogged** *with grease; clogged arteries.* —**clog.gy** (CLOG.ee) *adj.*

cloi.son.né (cloy.zuh.NAY) *n.* a kind of enamelwork decoration separated into compartments by metal strips; *adja.: cloisonné jewelry, patterns, techniques.*

clois.ter (CLOY.stur) *n.* **1** a covered

clomp / closure

walk with an open colonnade facing usu. on a quadrangle. **2** a place secluded for religious life; monastery or convent. —*v.* to be secluded from the world; *adj.*: *an order of* ***cloistered*** *nuns.*

clomp *v.* walk heavily; clump: *The child clomped down the stairs in her new boots;* *n.*: *the clomps of the horses's hooves.*

clone *n.* **1** an exact copy of its parent, as a plant variety multiplied from rooted cuttings. **2** an imitation of a commercial product, as of a computer. —*v.* **clones, cloned, clon.ing** produce as a clone. —**clon.al** (CLOH.nul) *adj.*

clonk *v. & n.* (make) a dull, hollow thump.

clop *n. & v.* **clops, clopped, clop.ping** (make) the sharp, hollow sound of a horse's hoof on pavement.

close (CLOZE) *v.* **clos.es, closed, clos.ing 1** stop up an opening or passage; shut: *The border has been closed off; Please close the door; close it tight; You can't close your eyes to the truth; They have closed the carwash for repairs;* *adj.*: *a* ***closed*** *border, door, meeting, mind, society.* **2** to conclude or end: *Let us close our meeting; We'll close with the national anthem; Our stocks closed strong (on the exchange); to close (= finalize) a deal with someone; to close a sale (= finish the transactions on it);* *adj.*: *The matter is closed; a* ***closed*** *issue, question.* **3** make or become close with no space between parts: *Close your hand into a fist; The order was given to close (= join) ranks; The troops* ***closed with*** *(= engaged) the enemy; as night closed around us; Police* ***closed on*** *the escaped convict (= made his escape impossible);* *adj.*: *a* ***closed*** *fist.* —**close down** stop entirely: *a factory closed down by a strike.* —**close in** encircle and advance upon: *The hunters closed in on the fox; closed in for a kill.* —**close out** sell all of a store's goods; sell a business. —*n.* a conclusion: *The sunset marks the close of day; to bring our talks to a close; as the meeting draws to a close; "Yours truly" is a complimentary close to a letter.* —*adj. & adv.* (rhyme: dose) **clos.er, clos.est 1** with little space between parts or elements; densely packed: *a close weave; soldiers in close ranks; precise, close reasoning.* **2** very near: *She lives close to work; Don't get too close to the cage; a close copy of the original; Your answer is close but not quite correct; a patient under close observation; He was close to tears; an attack at close range; Stay close by; The bullet hit close to the mark; two close (= intimate)* *friends who are close to each other; Ray's relationship with Mrs. Smith is getting* ***too close for comfort;*** *Has anyone seen Bigfoot* ***at close quarters?*** **3** nearly equal: *a close contest, decision, election, finish, match; The race is too close to call; a close score of 6-5; The vote was close.* **4** closed in; cramped: *a prisoner in close confinement; a period of close (= restricted) credit; Open a window, it's close (= hot and humid) in here.* **5** concealed; secretive: *as close as an oyster; He's close (= stingy) with his money.* —**play close to the chest** *or* **vest** be secretive. —**close.ly** *adv.*; **close.ness** *n.*

close call (or **shave**) *n. Informal.* a narrow escape.

closed book *n.* **1** a person or thing that is difficult to get acquainted with. **2** an investigation that is finished.

closed caption *n.* a TV subtitle that is invisible except on receivers equipped with a decoder, as used by the hearing-impaired. —**closed-captioned** *adj.*; **closed-captioning** *n.*

closed chapter *n.* something to be forgotten: *Her previous marriage is a closed chapter in her life.*

closed circuit *n.* **1** an unbroken circuit. **2** radio or TV transmission by wire, not broadcasting: *He watched the show from his hospital bed by closed circuit.*

closed shop *n.* an establishment in which only members of a labor union are hired.

close.fist.ed (CLOSE.fis.tid) *adj.* stingy; miserly.

close-knit *adj.* strongly united: *a close-knit group.*

close.mouthed *adj.* cautious in speaking; secretive: *She's closemouthed about his past.*

close.out *n.* a clearance sale at heavily reduced prices: *closeouts and markdowns;* *adja.*: *closeout goods, merchandise, models, sales, specials, stores.*

clos.et (CLOZ.it) *n.* **1** a small room or cabinet for storage of clothes, household goods, etc.: *broom, china, linen closets; a bedroom with a walk-in closet; to come out of* ***the closet*** *(= out of concealment).* **2** a room for private meetings, study, prayer, etc. —*adja.* secret or covert: *a closet addict, racist; closet loyalties.* —*v.* be alone with another in private conference: *He was closeted with his advisors for an hour.*

close-up *n.* a picture taken at close range: *a close-up of a butterfly's wing; a close-up look at moon craters; a revealing close-up (= detailed study).*

clo.sure (CLOH.zhur) *n.* **1** an act of

closing: *plant closures*. **2** a device for closing: *hook-and-loop, Velcro, zipper closures; tight closures*. **3** the closing off of a legislative debate by taking a vote: *to apply, invoke closure*. **4** a conclusion: *to bring closure to a traumatic experience*.
clot *n.* a mass of thickened liquid, esp. blood: *A clot forms to prevent loss of blood from a cut or wound*.
—*v.* **clots, clot.ted, clot.ting** thicken or coagulate, as blood.
cloth ("TH" as in "thin") *n.* **1** a woven, knitted, or felted fabric of natural or synthetic fibers: *strips of cloth*. **2** a piece of this for a specific purpose, as a tablecloth: *a loin cloth*. **3** **the cloth** the clergy: *a man of the cloth*.
clothe ("TH" as in "the") *v.* **clothes,** *pt. & pp.* **clothed** or **clad, cloth.ing** dress; *adj.*: *a partially clothed body; clothed in silk; villainies clothed* (= covered) *in fine words*.
clothes (CLOTHES, CLOZE) *n.pl.* garments; coverings: *to change, put on, strip off, take off, wash, wear clothes; civilian, night, old, plain, shabby, summer, Sunday, swaddling, tailor-made, trendy, winter clothes*; **"The emperor has no clothes"** (= What has long been accepted as true turns out to be false, as in the story of "The Emperor's New Clothes").
clothes.horse *n.* **1** a frame to hang clothes on; also **clothes hanger. 2** an affectedly fine dresser.
clothes.line *n.* a stretched cord for hanging out washed clothes to dry.
clothes.pin *n.* a clip for holding clothes on a clothesline.
clothes.press *n.* a receptacle for clothes, as a closet, wardrobe, chest.
clothes tree *n.* a post with hooks near the top for hanging coats, hats, etc.
cloth.ier (CLOH.thee.ur, "th" as in "the") *n.* **1** one who makes or sells clothing. **2** a cloth dealer.
cloth.ing (CLOH.thing, "th" as in "the") *n.* clothes: *an article of clothing; to model, put on, wear clothing; custom-made, heavy, light, outer, protective, summer, used, warm, winter clothing*.
clo.ture (CLOH.chur) *n.* the ending of a legislative debate by taking a vote.
cloud *n.* **1** a distinct, visible mass of water vapor hanging high in the air: *Rain clouds form in the sky; Threatening clouds gather on the horizon; the gathering clouds; Clouds scud across the sky; Clouds are dispersed by the wind; dark, heavy, scattered, storm, thick clouds; to seed clouds for producing rain*. **2** any light or puffy visible mass in the air: *a cloud of dust, mist, smoke, snow, steam; the mushroom cloud following an atomic explosion*. **3** swarm: *a cloud of locusts, horsemen*.
4 something seen as a carrier or harbinger: *a cloud on the horizon; a cloud of confusion, controversy, despair, doubt, uncertainty; clouds of change, gloom, glory; the darkening clouds of war*; "Every cloud has a silver lining" (= There is always a brighter side to a gloomy situation). —**in the clouds** in a fanciful dream; also, impractical. —**on cloud nine** *Informal.* joyfully elated. —**under a cloud 1** depressed. **2** in disgrace: *He left under a cloud when he quit his job*.
—*v.* cover or become covered with or as if with clouds: *The sky is clouding over; Anger clouded his face; adj.*: *to suffer from clouded vision; a clouded crystal ball, future, judgment, outlook, picture, reputation, situation*. —**cloud.less** *adj.*
cloud.ber.ry (CLOUD.ber.ee) *n.* -**ber.ries** a wild raspberry of northern regions; bakeapple.
cloud.burst *n.* a sudden downpour.
cloud-cuckoo-land *n.* the world of fantasy.
cloud seeding *n.* the scattering of chemicals in clouds to cause rainfall.
cloud.y (CLOW.dee) *adj.* **cloud.i.er, -i.est 1** covered with clouds: *Partly cloudy skies are forecast*. **2** not clear: *a cloudy day; cloudy notions*. —**cloud.i.ly** *adv.*; **cloud.i.ness** *n.*
clout (rhyme: out) *v. Informal.* **1** hit hard with the hand. **2** in baseball, hit a ball far. —*n. Informal.* **1** a heavy blow: *a clout on the snoot*. **2** influence, esp. political: *a senator who has or wields clout in Washington; Lou has a lot of clout with the prime minister*.
clove (CLOHV) *n.* **1** the dried flower bud of an Asiatic evergreen tree used as a spice called **cloves. 2** one of the segments of a compound bulb: *a clove of garlic*. —*v.* a *pt.* of CLEAVE.
clo.ven (CLOH.vun) a *pp.* of CLEAVE. —*adj.* split: *Cattle and sheep have cloven hoofs; the cloven foot* (= Satan).
cloven-hoofed or **cloven-footed** *adj.* **1** having split hoofs, as cattle and sheep. **2** satanic.
clo.ver (CLOH.vur) *n.* a plant with thick purple, pink, or white flower heads, used for pasturage: *A four-leaf clover is a sign of good luck; Since winning the lottery, he has been living* **in (the) clover** (= in luxury).
clo.ver.leaf (CLOH.vur.leef) *n.* -**leafs** or -**leaves** (-leevs) a highway interchange having ramps forming the shape of a

four-leaf clover.
clown (*rhyme:* down) *n.* **1** a professional jester or buffoon, esp. in a circus or parade. **2** an awkward, ill-mannered person. **3** one who constantly jokes or acts silly: *He likes to act* or *play the clown when others are talking seriously.* —*v.* act as or like a clown; play jokes or act silly: *He likes to clown around when others are talking seriously.* —**clown.ish** *adj.;* **clown.ish.ly** *adv.;* **clown.ish.ness** *n.*

cloy *v.* satiate, esp. with something sweet or rich; sate; surfeit: *Too much candy can be cloying;* **cloy.ing.ly** *adv.*

club *n.* **1** a thick, heavy, usu. tapered piece of wood used as a weapon. **2** a stick for striking the ball in various sports: *a golf club.* **3** a playing card marked with a stylized black clover leaf; also, the marking: ***Clubs*** (= the suit so marked) *is* or *are trumps.* **4** a group of people united for a social, sporting, charitable, or similar purpose; also, their meeting place: *book, country, fan, glee, tennis, yachting clubs; to break up, disband, form, organize a club; China joined the nuclear club in 1964; Welcome to the club (of people with similar interests)!* —*v.* **clubs, clubbed, club.bing 1** beat with or as with a club: *The baby seals were clubbed to death for their fur.* **2** join: *The children clubbed together to buy their teacher a present.*
—**club.ba.ble** *adj.* sociable; fit for a club: *a clubbable disposition, mood.*

club.by (CLUB.ee) *adj.* **club.bi.er, club.bi.est** sociable in an exclusive or clannish way.

club.foot *n.* **1** a usu. congenital malformation of the foot. **2** a foot so malformed. —**club.foot.ed** *adj.*

club.house *n.* a building occupied by a club.

club sandwich *n.* a sandwich of three slices of toast, various meats, dressing, lettuce, etc.

club soda *n.* carbonated water used as a mix for other drinks.

club steak *n.* a small beefsteak cut from the end of the loin.

cluck *v.* **1** make the sound of a hen calling her chicks. **2** make a similar sound with the tongue, as to coax a horse, express interest or concern, etc. —*n.* **1** a clucking sound: *a cluck of approval.* **2** *Slang.* a dull or incompetent person.

clue (CLOO) *n.* a word, thing, or idea that suggests the solution to a puzzle, mystery, crime, etc.: *The police have uncovered some vital clues to the murderer's identity; to discover, find, furnish, supply a clue; Crossword puzzles provide you with clues across and clues down; He does **not have a clue*** (Informal for does not know) *what we are talking about.* —*v.* **clues, clued, clu.ing** or **clue.ing** give a clue to someone: *Please clue me in on what happened.*

clump *n.* **1** a mass or lump: *clumps of hair, snow, tissue.* **2** a group of trees, plants, etc. standing or growing together: *large clumps of grasses; clumps of oaks and bushes.* **3** the sound of tramping feet. —*v.* **1** walk heavily: *the sound of boots clumping over the floor above.* **2** group into clumps: *the clumping of matter into galaxies.* —**clump.y** *adj.*

clum.sy (CLUM.zee) *adj.* **-si.er, -si.est 1** awkward; unwieldy; uncoordinated: *a clumsy amateur, weapon; It was so clumsy of him to drop the vase; He's a bit clumsy with his hands; She's rather clumsy at knitting.* **2** inept: *a clumsy apology.* —**clum.si.ly** *adv.;* **clum.si.ness** *n.*

clung *pt. & pp.* of CLING.

clunk *n.* the heavy, flat sound of metal being struck.

clunk.er *n. Informal.* **1** a noisy old machine in poor repair, esp. a car. **2** a clumsy person; duffer. **3** a flop or failure.

clunk.y *adj.* clumsy or ungraceful: *clunky shoes.*

clus.ter *n.* a group of similar objects or people situated together: *a cluster of grapes, houses, scientists; a cluster of galaxies; A **cluster bomb** contains smaller bombs that scatter hundreds of steel shards over a wide area; A **cluster headache** attacks in a series over several hours.*
—*v.* be, gather, or place in a cluster: *The people clustered in small groups; Some clustered around the speaker; They were clustered on street corners.*

clutch *v.* **1** grasp or hold suddenly or tightly, esp. with hands or claws; make a grab: *"A drowning man will clutch at a straw"; She clutched her child to her breast.* **2** operate a clutch mechanism. —*n.* **1** the act of clutching; also, a tight hold: *in the **clutches*** (= power) *of the devil, of the enemy.* **2** a device for engaging and disengaging a drive mechanism from the motor, as in a standard-shift automobile: *Depress the clutch to the floor when changing gears; Release the clutch after use; Riding the clutch (with the foot on it) causes needless wear on the clutch.* **3** *Informal.* a critical or dangerous situation: *a friend you can count on **in the clutch**.* **4** a nest of eggs or the chicks hatched from them.

5 a group of similar individuals: *A clutch of graduates formed the end of the procession.*

clut.ter (CLUT.ur) *n.* a disordered state; jumble; also, things in a disorganized state: *the clutter on his desk; to keep it clear of clutter; how to eliminate, reduce clutter; Advertising clutter in magazines is more bearable than on TV.* —*v.* litter with a disorganized mass of objects: *His desk is always cluttered up;* *adj.*: *a cluttered attic, landscape, look, office, workshop.*

c'mon (cuh.MON) *Informal.* come on: *C'mon in, Jane; Aw, C'mon off it! C'mon fellows!*

co- *prefix.* joint or jointly: *coauthor, co-heir, cooperate.*

coach *n.* **1** an enclosed passenger vehicle, as a bus, railroad car, or four-wheeled carriage: *a stage coach.* **2** a class of airline or train travel lower than first class. **3** one who trains or instructs others, esp. athletes, students, and singers: *baseball, drama, voice coaches.* —*v.* train or tutor: *Bill had to be coached for his finals; was coached in French and math.*

coach.man *n.* **-men** the driver of a carriage or coach.

co.ad.ju.tor (coh.uh.JOO.tur, coh.AJ.uh.tur) *n.* an assistant, esp. one designated to help and succeed a bishop.

co.ag.u.lant (coh.AG.yuh.lunt) *n.* a substance causing coagulation.

co.ag.u.late (coh.AG.yuh.late) *v.* **-lates, -lat.ed, -lat.ing** of a liquid, change or become changed to a solid or semisolid state; clot; set: *The white of the egg coagulates when boiled.* —**co.ag.u.la.tion** (-LAY.shun) *n.*

coal (COLE) *n.* **1** an organic, black or brown, combustible rock used as a fuel; also, a piece of this for burning: *to shovel coal into a furnace; a coal-fired furnace;* *adj.*: *coal beds, mines, seams; a coal plant (using coal as fuel).* **2** a piece of glowing wood, coal, etc.; ember: *a live, glowing coal; The yogi can walk a bed of (live) coals; We cooked it over hot coals.* —**rake** or **haul over the coals** reprimand severely. —*v.* provide with or take on a supply of coal.

co.a.lesce (coh.uh.LES) *v.* **-les.ces, -lesced, -les.cing** grow together or unite, as the edges of a wound when healing: *The parties coalesced into one.* —**co.a.les.cence** *n.*; **co.a.les.cent** *adj.*

coal field *n.* a region rich in coal.

coal gas *n.* a gas made from coal, used for heating, lighting, etc.

co.a.li.tion (coh.uh.LISH.un) *n.* a usu. temporary union of people, political parties, states, etc. for a common purpose: *They formed a coalition; a coalition of or between the Liberals and Conservatives; The coalition fell apart; The coalition dissolved or broke up for the election; a rainbow coalition (of members of various ethnic groups).* —**co.a.li.tion.ist** *n.*

coal tar *n.* a thick, black liquid by-product obtained from soft coal.

coarse (CORSE) *adj.* **coars.er, coars.est** **1** ordinary; inferior; hence, vulgar; unrefined; offensive: *coarse food, grain, language, manners, people.* **2** consisting of large, rough particles; having a rough texture or appearance: *a coarse grind, meal; coarse crumbs, bread, salt, sand; coarse-grained wood; almonds chopped coarse.* —**coarse.ly** *adv.*; **coarse.ness** *n.*

coars.en (COR.sun) *v.* make or become coarse.

coast (COHST) *n.* **1** the land along the sea: *The boat sank off the coast of Newfoundland; People live along the coast; a town located on the coast; She campaigned* **(from) coast to coast** *(= across the nation); He thought the* **coast was clear** *(= it was safe) when everyone had left.* **2** a slope for sledding or tobogganing. **3** the act of coasting. —*v.* **1** sail along a seacoast. **2** move without acceleration or effort, as sledding down a hill, gliding on a bicycle without pedaling, etc. —**coast.al** *adj.*: *coastal regions, shipping, villages, waters.*

coast.er *n.* a pad or disk used under a glass to protect the surface it rests on.

coaster brake *n.* a bicycle brake in the rear hub applied by pedaling backwards.

coast guard *n.* the military and police force which patrols a nation's seacoast and territorial waters.
—**coast.guards.man** (-mun) *n.* **-men.**

coast.line *n.* the outline or boundary of a coast: *along the California coastline; Follow the coastline to Davenport; jagged, rugged coastlines; coastlines blighted by oil spills.*

coat *n.* **1** a sleeved outer garment reaching at least to the waist: *She had a coat on; She took off her coat; all-weather, mink, fur, winter coats.* **2** a natural outer covering, as an animal's fur or feathers: *the silky coat of a cocker spaniel.* **3** a thin layer covering something, as paint on a wall: *We put on* or *applied a second coat; an outer, protective coat* or *coating of wax.* —*v.* apply or be a coat on something: *Frost coated the window; a floor coated with wax.*

coated *adj.*: *coated aspirin; a camera with a coated lens to eliminate reflections; smooth, coated paper used for artwork.*
coat hanger *n.* a hanger for a coat, dress, etc. that is made of wire, wood, or plastic in the shape of a person's shoulders with a hook at the top for hanging in a closet.
coat of arms *n.* the heraldic insignia of a person, family, institution, etc.
coat of mail *n.* a garment of chain mail worn as armor.
coat.tail *adja.* dependent or derivative: *a protective coattail provision in the law; coattail power, prestige.* —**coattails** *n.pl.* 1 the back flaps of a coat. 2 a politician's popularity that is strong enough to carry a follower to victory: *He rode to victory on the coattails of the prime minister.*
co.au.thor (coh.AW.thur) *n.* a collaborating author; *v.: A husband-and-wife team coauthored the report.*
coax (COHX) *v.* use persistent kindness, flattery, or effort to persuade or to produce a desired effect: *He coaxed his mother into agreeing; He had to coax the old car up the hill.* —**coax.ing.ly** *adv.*
co.ax.i.al (coh.AK.see.ul) *adj.* having a common axis. —**co.ax.i.al.ly** *adv.*
coaxial cable (or **line**) *n.* a line for transmitting television, telephone, and telegraph signals, made of a conducting core insulated from an outer conducting tube.
cob *n.* 1 the woody core of an ear of corn: *corn on the cob.* 2 a male swan. 3 a thickset horse with short legs.
co.balt (COH.bault) *n.* 1 a hard, gray metallic element used in alloys, pigments, etc. 2 a deep-to-greenish blue color: *a tulip print in red, teal, and cobalt; a cobalt blue tumbler.*
cob.ble (COB.ul) *v.* **cob.bles, cob.bled, cob.bling** 1 pave with cobblestones; *adj.: the cobbled streets of Spain.* 2 make or repair, esp. footwear. 3 make roughly and quickly: *It was cobbled up or together in a hurry.*
—*n.* same as COBBLESTONE.
cob.bler *n.* 1 one who repairs shoes. 2 a deep fruit pie with a thick crust only on top: *cherry cobbler; peach cobbler.*
cob.ble.stone (COB.ul.stone) *n.* a rounded stone of medium size, as used for paving.
co.bra (COH.bruh) *n.* a poisonous snake of Asia and Africa that can spread its neck skin into a hood.
cob.web *n.* 1 a web or a fine thread spun by a spider. 2 something flimsy but ensnaring: *cobwebs of suspicion.*
co.ca (COH.cuh) *n.* a South American shrub whose dried leaves are the source of cocaine.
co.caine (coh.CAIN) *n.* a drug made from the dried leaves of the coca, and used as a local anesthetic, stimulant, or addictive narcotic. Also **co.cain.**
coc.cus (COC.us) *n., pl.* **coc.ci** (COC.sye) a spherical bacterium; *comb.form:* streptococcus, gonococcus.
coc.cyx (COC.six) *n., pl.* **-cy.ges** (coc.SYE.jeez) the triangular bone at the base of the spine.
coch.i.neal insect (COCH.uh.neel-) *n.* a North American insect, the dried body of which is used to make **cochineal**, a deep red pigment.
coch.le.a (COC.lee.uh) *n., pl.* **-le.ae** (-lee.ee) or **-le.as** (-lee.us) the spiral tube of the inner ear, which is essential for hearing. —**coch.le.ar** (-ur) *adj.*
cock *n.* 1 the adult male of common barnyard fowl; also, any male bird: *a cock robin.* 2 a valve for controlling liquid or gas flow; faucet: *the drain cock of a boiler; the fuel cock of an engine.* 3 the hammer of a gun; also, its raised position, when ready for firing. 4 a small, cone-shaped pile, usu. of hay. —**the cock of the walk** a domineering or overbearing person.
—*v.* 1 turn up or to one side: *The horse cocked its ear; He cocked a quizzical eye; adj.: He wears his hat cocked.* 2 put in a position of readiness to fire or hit, as by drawing back: *to cock a gun; to cock a fist or arm.*
cock.ade (co.CADE) *n.* a knot of ribbon worn as a badge on the hat.
cock-a-doodle-doo (COCK.uh.doo.dul.DOO) *n.* the crowing of a cock.
cock.a.ma.mie or **cock.a.ma.my** (cock.uh.MAY.mee) *adj. Slang.* nonsensical; silly.
cock-and-bull story *n.* an improbable story or excuse.
cock.a.tiel (coc.uh.TEEL) *n.* a small crested parrot with gray and yellow feathers.
cock.a.too (COCK.uh.too) *n.* **-toos** a large crested parrot with feathers of white, red, orange, etc.
cock.a.trice (COC.uh.tris) *n.* a mythical serpent able to kill with its glance.
cock.cha.fer (COC.chay.fur) *n.* a large European beetle destructive to plants.
cock.crow *n.* sunrise; dawn.
cocked hat *n.* a hat with its brim turned up so as to form three cor-

ners. —**knock into a cocked hat** *Informal.* beat competition, plans, etc. thoroughly.

cock.er.el (COK.uh.rul) *n.* a rooster less than a year old.

cock.er spaniel or **cocker** *n.* a small breed of spaniel with long ears, silky coat, and a square muzzle.

cock.eye *n.* a squinting eye.

cock.eyed *adj.* 1 cross-eyed; askew. 2 *Slang.* absurd or foolish: *a cockeyed decision, idea, notion, scheme, theory.*

cock.fight *n.* a fight between roosters specially bred for the purpose; **cock.fight.ing** *n.*

cock.le (COCK.ul) *n.* 1 a weed that grows in grainfields. 2 an edible shellfish. —**warm the cockles of one's heart** make one feel pleased and happy.

cock.le.shell (COCK.ul.shell) *n.* 1 the heart-shaped shell of a cockle. 2 a light boat.

Cock.ney or **cock.ney** (COCK.nee) *n.* -neys 1 a native of London, esp. its East End. 2 the distinctive dialect of London's East End: *the Cockney accent.*

cock.pit *n.* 1 an enclosed area for cockfights. 2 the room in an airplane for the pilot and, in the larger planes, for the pilot and crew: *In the smallest planes, the pilot shares the cockpit with a passenger.* 3 a similar place for the pilot of a boat or the driver of a racing car.

cock.roach (COCK.rohch) *n.* a nocturnal insect pest found esp. in houses.

cocks.comb *n.* 1 the red, fleshy, comblike crest on a rooster's head. 2 coxcomb.

cock.sure *adj.* arrogantly self-confident.

cock.tail *n.* 1 a mixed, usu. iced alcoholic drink such as a martini: *a shaker for mixing cocktails*; **adja.:** *a cocktail dress, party, reception; a hotel's* **cocktail lounge** (= bar); *the bell-shaped and stemmed* **cocktail glass;** *the* **cocktail hour** *before dinner; a* **cocktail table** (= coffee table). 2 an appetizer course of a meal: *fruit, juice, shrimp cocktails; a* **cocktail sauce** (= mixture of lemon juice, ketchup, and horseradish) *served with a seafood appetizer.* 3 a mixture of dubious value: *We are mixing ourselves a deadly cocktail of poisons by too much use of farm pesticides.*

cock.y *adj.* **cock.i.er, -i.est** jauntily conceited; cocksure. —**cock.i.ly** *adv.;* **cock.i.ness** *n.*

co.co (COH.coh) *n.* -cos the coconut palm or a coconut.

co.coa (COH.coh) *n.* 1 chocolate in powder form. 2 a beverage made with this. 3 a light reddish brown.

cocoa butter *n.* a whitish-yellow fat obtained from cacao seeds and used in cosmetics, soap, etc.

co.co.nut (COH.cuh.nut) *n.* the large fruit of a tropical palm, or **coconut palm,** which is a husk-covered, hard-shelled seed containing a milky fluid, or **coconut milk,** and lined with an edible white meat that yields an oil, or **coconut oil,** used in soaps, foods, etc. Also **co.coa.nut.**

co.coon (cuh.COON, long "OO") *n.* 1 the fibrous covering spun by some insect larvae as a case for the pupa. 2 the egg case spun by spiders and other insects: *A nation emerges from its political cocoon when it gains independence.*

co.coon.ing (cuh.COO.ning) *n.* living isolated from society: *the cocooning trend.*

cod *n.* a fish of northern waters valuable for food.

co.da (COH.duh) *n.* a formally separate, concluding passage of a piece of music.

cod.der (COD.ur) *n.* a cod fisherman or cod fishing boat.

cod.dle (COD.ul) *v.* **cod.dles, cod.dled, cod.dling** 1 pamper. 2 cook in water just below the boiling point; *adj.:* **coddled** *eggs.*

code *n.* 1 a systematic collection of laws or regulations: *a code of conduct, ethics, honor, manners, silence; a dress code for students; building, civil, criminal, human rights, moral, motor vehicle, penal, tax codes; an unwritten code.* 2 a set of usu. arbitrary symbols that carry meaning; language: *the Morse code of dots and dashes; They established a telephone code for identification of callers — one ring, then hang up and dial again; the computer's binary* **machine code** *of zeros and ones; a spy trying to break or crack or decipher the enemy's code; a message sent in code; the three-digit telephone area code; the American zip code; the Canadian postal code; DNA contains the genetic code that determines our inherited characteristics.* —*v.* **codes, cod.ed, cod.ing** put into a code; *adj.:* a **coded** *message.*

co.deine or **co.dein** (COH.deen) *n.* a mild narcotic derived from opium, used esp. as a sedative and a cough suppressant.

code name *n.* a name used to disguise the identity of a secret agent or operation.

code word *n.* a word with a disguised

or hidden meaning, as given by parents to children for use as a password for identifying an authorized stranger.
co.dex (COH.dex) *n., pl.* **-di.ces** (-di.seez) a manuscript volume, esp. of an ancient text.
cod.fish same as COD.
codg.er (COJ.ur) *n. Informal.* an aging and somewhat odd fellow: *a shrewd old codger like Grandpa.*
codices *pl.* of CODEX.
cod.i.cil (COD.uh.sil) *n.* a supplement to a will, usu. modifying it.
cod.i.fy (COD.uh.fye, COH.duh-) *v.* **-fies, -fied, -fy.ing** collect and systematize laws, regulations, etc. into a code. —**cod.i.fi.ca.tion** (-fuh.CAY.shun) *n.: the codification of unwritten laws into statutes.* —**cod.i.fi.er** *n.*
cod.ling *n.* **1** a young cod; also, a hake. **2** a kind of green cooking apple.
co.ed (COH.ed) *n. Informal.* a female student at a coeducational school. —*adj. Informal.* **1** coeducational: *a coed dorm, school; The camp is not coed.* **2** having to do with coeds: *coed fashions.*
co.ed.u.ca.tion (COH.ej.uh.CAY.shun) *n.* the education of males and females together in the same school or class. —**co.ed.u.ca.tion.al** *adj.*
co.ef.fi.cient (coh.uh.FISH.unt) *n.* a number that is the measure of a property or characteristic: *Each material has a different coefficient of expansion; The treatment of women and minorities is a co-efficient* (= measure or yardstick) *of our culture.*
coe.len.ter.ate (si.LENT.uh.rate) *n.* a simple aquatic animal having a single body cavity, including corals and jellyfishes.
co.e.qual (coh.EEK.wul) *adj.* mutually equal, esp. in age or rank; also *n.;* **co.e.qual.ly** (-wuh.lee) *adv.* —**co.e.qual.i.ty** (-KWOL.i.tee) *n.*
co.erce (coh.URSE) *v.* **-erc.es, -erced, -erc.ing 1** compel or restrain by fear, violence, etc.: *a pacifist coerced into joining the army.* **2** gain or effect by force; *adj.: a coerced, not voluntary confession, signature; If you feel coerced, don't sign it.* —**co.er.cion** (-shun) *n.* —**co.er.cive** (-siv) *adj.*
co.e.val (coh.EE.vul) *adj.* of the same time period: *developments in Europe co-eval with events in Africa.* —**co.e.val.ly** *adv.*
co.ex.ist (coh.ig.ZIST) *v.* exist at the same place and time: *Nations have to coexist with one another) in peace and amity.* —**co.ex.is.tence** (-tunce) *n.: the peaceful coexistence of Arabs and Jews.*
cof.fee (COF.ee) *n.* **1** a caffeine-containing beverage made from the roasted and ground seeds, or **coffee beans**, of a small tropical tree: *to make, percolate, stir, strain coffee; black, decaffeinated, fresh, instant, strong, weak coffee; a cup of coffee; to take a* **coffee break** (at work). **2** the tree or its seeds: *to brew, grind, grow coffee.*
coffee cake *n.* a sweet cake often with nuts, raisins, icing, etc.
cof.fee.house (COF.ee.house) *n.* a restaurant serving coffee and light refreshments, often acting as a social gathering place.
coffee klatch same as KAFFEE-KLATSCH.
coffee pot *n.* a pot for making and serving coffee; also **cof.fee.mak.er.**
coffee shop *n.* a café, as in a hotel.
coffee table *n.* a low table used in front of a sofa.
coffee table book *n.* a large illustrated book for display on a coffee table.
cof.fer (COF.ur) *n.* **1 coffers** *pl.* fund or treasury: *the municipal coffers.* **2** a strongbox or vault for storing valuables. **3** a square or octagonal sunken panel of a ceiling; *adj.: a coffered ceiling, dome, vault.*
cof.fer.dam (COF.ur.dam) *n.* a temporary, watertight enclosure used to keep a submerged area dry for construction of piers, bridges, etc.
cof.fin (COF.in) *n.* a usu. oblong box used to bury the dead in: *The coffin was lowered into the grave.* —*adj.* oblong: *a coffin case; a coffin freezer, not an upright.*
cog *n.* **1** a tooth or projection, usu. on a gear or wheel used to transmit motion, as in a bicycle; also, a cogwheel: *a cog railway.* **2** a person or thing seen as an unimportant though necessary part of a large, impersonal operation.
co.gent (COH.junt) *adj.* powerfully convincing, as by its logic and rigor: *cogent arguments, reasons, writing;* **co.gent.ly** *adv.* —**co.gen.cy** (COH.jun.see) *n.*
cogged (COGD) *adj.* fitted with cogs: *the cogged rails of a cog railway.*
cog.i.tate (COJ.uh.tate) *v.* **-tates, -tat.ed, -tat.ing** think intently about something; ponder: *She cogitated over or on or about her next move.* —**cog.i.ta.tion** (-TAY.shun) *n.*
cog.nac (CONE.yak) *n.* a fine brandy.
cog.nate (COG.nate) *adj.* related by common origin: *English and Hindi are cognate languages.*

cog.ni.tion (cog.NISH.un) *n.* **1** the process of knowing, including perceiving and thinking. **2** the result of this; perception or thought. —**cog.ni.tive** (COG.nuh.tiv) *adj.*

cog.ni.zance (COG.nuh.zunce) *n.* conscious knowledge of something; awareness: *The accused had no cognizance of the events that followed; The court took cognizance of* (= recognized) *extenuating circumstances in sentencing the accused.* —**cog.ni.zant** (-zunt) *adjp.*: *He was fully cognizant of the seriousness of the charge.*

cog.no.men (cog.NOH.mun) *n.* -**no.mens** or -**nom.i.na** (-NOM.i.nuh) **1** a surname, esp. an ancient Roman family name, as "Caesar." **2** any name, esp. a nickname.

co.gno.scen.te (cone.yoh.SHEN.tay) *n., pl.* -**ti** (-tee) one with special knowledge; connoisseur: *a new literary style in vogue with the cognoscenti.*

cog railway *n.* a railroad on which a locomotive pulls itself up a steep incline by means of a cogwheel meshing with a cogged rail.

cog.wheel *n.* a wheel with cogs around the edge.

co.hab.it (COH.hab.it) *v.* live together like husband and wife without being married: *Dick cohabited with Jane before marrying; They were cohabiting.* —**co.hab.i.ta.tion** (coh.HAB.uh.TAY.shun) *n.*

co.heir (coh.AIR) *n.* a joint heir: *The brothers were coheirs to the estate.*

co.here (coh.HEER) *v.* -**heres, -hered, -her.ing** stick together as one mass; hence, connect logically: *Your arguments don't cohere; The first part of the essay doesn't cohere with the last.* —**co.her.ence** (-unce) *n.*

co.her.ent (coh.HEER.unt) *adj.* holding together or connected: *coherent ideas, reasoning, thought; coherent* (= intelligible) *speech.* —**co.her.ent.ly** *adv.*

co.he.sion (coh.HEE.zhun) *n.* a sticking together of parts: *Unity within a party depends on cohesion among the membership; Solids are more difficult to separate than liquids or gases because of the greater cohesion between molecules.* —**co.he.sive** (-siv, -ziv) *adj.*; **co.he.sive.ly** *adv.*; **co.he.sive.ness** *n.*

co.ho (COE.ho) *n.* a small salmon of the N. Pacific.

co.hort (COE.hort) *n.* **1** originally, a division of soldiers in a Roman legion; hence, a group. **2** associate or companion: *The burglar and his cohorts were caught red-handed.*

coif *n.* **1** a tight-fitting cap. **2** a hair style.

coif.feur (cwah.FUR) *n.* a male hairdresser; **coif.feuse** (cwah.FURZ) *fem.*

coif.fure (cwah.FYOOR) *n.* a hair style; coif.

coil *v.* to wind or move in a spiral or round shape; loop: *A snake coils around its prey; Coil the rope and hang it up; String is coiled into balls.* —*n.* **1** a series of connected loops or circles: *a radiator coil.* **2** one loop of this: *a coil of hair.* **3** a length of conducting wire wound spirally around a nonconducting core; also, a device using this: *an induction coil; the ignition coil of an automobile engine.*

coin *n.* **1** a piece of metal money: *He collects coins as a hobby; Drop a coin into the slot; We flip* or *throw* or *toss a coin to decide between alternatives; counterfeit, gold, rare, valuable coins; She returned the insult in his own coin* or *in the same coin* (= insulted him back); *the other side of the coin* (= the opposite side of the issue). **2** coins collectively: *He insisted on payment with* or *in coin* (= in cash). **3** *Informal.* money. —*v.* **1** to mint coins from metal. **2** create a new word, phrase, etc.: *Did Churchill coin "iron curtain"?* —**coin money** make a big profit. —**coin.er** *n.*

coin.age (COIN.ij) *n.* **1** the act of minting coins. **2** the coins minted. **3** an invented word or phrase: *"Canola" is a Canadian coinage for use instead of "rapeseed."*

co.in.cide (coh.in.SIDE) *v.* -**cides, -cid.ed, -cid.ing** **1** occupy or occur at the same point in space or time: *Her graduation coincided with her birthday.* **2** be identical; agree: *Our tastes in music coincide.*

co.in.ci.dence (coh.IN.suh.dunce) *n.* **1** a coinciding. **2** a remarkable and seemingly accidental instance of events happening together: *What a coincidence that both of you came today! It happened by a happy, odd, remarkable, strange coincidence; by mere, pure, sheer coincidence.* —**co.in.ci.den.tal** (-DEN.tul) *adj.*

coin machine *n.* a coin-operated vending machine; slot machine.

co.i.tus (COE.it.us) *n.* sexual intercourse; also **co.i.tion** (coe.ISH.un). —**co.i.tal** *adj.*

coke *n.* **1** a clean, hot-burning fuel used esp. in metal industries, made by removing gases from bituminous coal, or **coking coal**. **2** *Informal.* cocaine: *a coke peddler, sniffer.* **3 Coke** *Trademark.*

the soft drink "Coca-Cola."
co.la (COH.luh) *n.* **1** an African tree that bears caffeine-containing nuts, or **cola nuts,** used as a flavoring and in medicines. **2** the extract of this nut. **3** a carbonated drink flavored with cola extract. **4** a *pl.* of COLON. **5 COLA** cost-of-living adjustment to wages, benefits, etc.

col.an.der (CULL.un.dur) *n.* a bowllike perforated utensil for draining foods.

cold *adj.* **1** of a low temperature as compared to a norm, esp. body temperature: *a cold day; I feel cold; cold hands; cold to the touch.* **2** lacking in sympathy, encouragement, feeling, etc.: *a cold personality; She's cold toward her in-laws; His words were cold comfort; His appeals left him cold* (= did not impress or excite him); *cold* (= depressing) *facts; They asked for payment in cold or hard cash* (= money that you can feel). **3** clear or objective: *in the cold light of reality; the cold logic of her argument.* **4** *Informal.* unconscious: *The accident knocked him cold; He was out cold on the floor.* —**in cold blood** without emotion: *a cockatoo killed in cold blood.*
—**throw** or **pour cold water on something** discourage a plan, hopes, etc.
—*adv.* **1** *Informal.* absolutely; perfectly: *He turned me down cold when I asked for a raise; She knew the family law cold and could cite chapter and verse from memory.* **2** *Informal.* without preparation, warning, warm-up, etc.: *He went into the examination cold; She came to the job cold with no previous experience; You should be able to pick up a dictionary cold and use it without having to read any explanatory notes.* —*n.* **1** a condition of cold, esp. cold weather: *He went out into the cold without a coat; No one should be left out in the cold; biting, bitter, extreme, intense, severe cold;* to **come in from the cold** (= come back into favor). **2** a viral infection that causes a stuffed or runny nose: *You'll catch (a) cold if you sit in that draft; the common cold; to come down with, contract, fight off, have, nurse, shake off, throw off a cold; bad, lingering, severe, slight colds; chest and head colds.* —**cold.ly** *adv.;* **cold.ness** *n.*

cold-blooded *adj.* **1** without feeling; ruthless: *a cold-blooded approach, killer, murder.* **2** having a body temperature that varies with the environment: *cold-blooded animals such as fishes and reptiles.*

cold call *n.* a call made without prior warning or introduction to a prospective customer, employer, etc.

cold cream *n.* a cleansing and softening cream for the skin.

cold cuts *n.pl.* slices of cold meats and cheeses: *a plate of cold cuts;* **adja.: cold-cut** *platters.*

cold-eyed *adj.* unemotional; dispassionate.

cold feet *n.* a lack of courage or self-confidence: *He got cold feet and withdrew his application.*

cold front *n.* an advancing mass of cold air.

cold shoulder *n. Informal.* deliberate indifference; a snub: *He was given the cold shoulder when he applied to join the club.* —**cold-shoulder** *v.: Let's not cold-shoulder an old friend.*

cold snap *n.* a sudden period of cold weather.

cold sore *n.* a blister on the lips, usu. accompanying a cold or fever.

cold storage *n.* **1** refrigerated storage for preserving food, fur coats, etc. **2** the putting away of an idea, plan, etc. until needed: *It's in* or *gone into* or *put into cold storage.*

cold turkey *Informal.* **1** *n.* behavior or procedure that is abrupt, as sudden withdrawal from an addictive drug. **2** *adv.* abruptly: *to take kids off cocaine cold turkey; He quit smoking cold turkey; Do it cold turkey; He went cold turkey and quit smoking; She quit (drugs) cold turkey.*
—**cold-turkey** *adja.: a cold-turkey approach; a week of cold-turkey withdrawal from TV.*

cold war *n.* a state of suppressed, non-military hostility, as between nations opposed to each other.

cole.slaw (COLE.slaw) *n.* finely shredded raw cabbage as a salad; also **cole slaw.**

col.ic (COLL.ic) *n.* severe abdominal pain. —**col.ick.y** *adj.: a colicky infant.*

col.i.se.um (col.uh.SEE.um) *n.* a large multipurpose stadium for sports or other public entertainment.

co.li.tis (cuh.LYE.tis) *n.* an inflammation or dysfunction of the colon.

col.lab.o.rate (cuh.LAB.uh.rate) *v.* **-rates, -rat.ed, -rat.ing 1** work together: *He collaborated with her on the project; They collaborated.* **2** cooperate with an invading or occupying force: *He was accused of collaborating with the Nazis.* —**col.lab.o.ra.tion** (-RAY.shun) *n.;* **col.lab.o.ra.tion.ist** *n.* & *adj.: a collaborationist government, policy, role.*
—**col.lab.o.ra.tive** (-ray.tiv) *adj.*
—**col.lab.o.ra.tor** (-ray.tur) *n.: a war-time collaborator; The collaborator was*

convicted of treason.
col.lage (cuh.LAHZH) *n.* an artistic composition using diverse items; bits of paper, wood, cloth, etc. glued onto a board: *an essay that is a mere collage of quotations.* **—col.lag.ist** *n.*
col.lapse (cuh.LAPS) *v.* **-laps.es, -lapsed, -laps.ing 1** fall down or break down: *The bridge collapsed during the flood; collapsed from the force of the water; collapsed under its weight; The plot collapsed* (= failed completely). **2** fall helpless or become unable to function: *He collapsed under the strain; collapsed from mental fatigue.* **—n.** a breakdown or failure: *the collapse of a roof during a storm; the collapse of a business venture; an economic, emotional, mental, total collapse.* **—col.lap.si.ble** *adj.* that can be folded for storage: *a collapsible bed, chair.*
col.lar (COLL.ur) *n.* **1** something that encircles the neck, esp. the part of a garment that does so, the leather band around a dog's neck, or the similar part of a harness: *button-down, Roman, stiff, turndown collars; People get* **hot under the collar** (= angry). **2** something resembling a collar, as on a pipe. **—v. 1** put a collar on something. **2** seize; detain; arrest. **—col.lar.less** *adj.*
col.lar.bone (COLL.ur.bone) *n.* the clavicle.
col.lard (COLL.urd) *n.* usu. **collards** *pl.* the coarse edible leaves of a kind of cabbage that does not form a head.
col.late (cuh.LATE) *v.* **-lates, -lat.ed, -lat.ing 1** compare closely and note variants: *a scholar collating ancient texts; to collate one text with another.* **2** assemble pages in proper order, as after photocopying. **—col.la.tion** (-LAY.shun) *n.* **—col.la.tor** (-LAY.tur) *n.*
col.lat.er.al (cuh.LAT.uh.rul) *adj.* **1** from the same ancestors by a different line of descent; not lineal: *Brothers, uncles, etc. are collateral relations, not like parents and children; a collateral branch of the family.* **2** parallel: *bombing of military targets with minimal collateral damage to civilians.* **3** supporting: *collateral evidence.* **4** secured by a guarantee of repayment: *The bank manager offered us a* **collateral loan***; She asked for collateral* (= guaranteeing) *funds, security.*
—n. property pledged as security for a loan or obligation: *to put up collateral for a loan.*
col.league (COLL.eeg) *n.* an associate, esp. a fellow member of a profession.
col.lect (cuh.LECT) *v.* **1** bring or come together into a group or mass: *People collected on street corners; They collected around the speaker; He collects coins as a hobby.* **2** get control of oneself, one's thoughts, etc.; *adj.*: *a calm and* **collected** (= not distracted) *manner.* **3** ask for and receive payment, taxes, and such dues: *The paper boy comes collecting on Fridays; to collect benefits, bills, debts, pensions; He collected on his insurance.* **4** pick up: *to collect a parcel at the post office; to collect one's date.* **—adv.** paid for by the receiver: *Children phone home collect;* ***n.****: to make a* **collect call***.*
col.lect.i.ble (cuh.LEC.tuh.bul) *n.* an object fancied for its aesthetic appeal or nostalgic value: *License plates, fountain pens, and such collectibles are not fancied by collectors of art, coins, stamps, etc.* Also **col.lect.a.ble.**
col.lec.tion (cuh.LEC.shun) *n.* the act of collecting or what is collected: *art, butterfly, coin, private, stamp collections; She passed her hat round to take up a collection for the homeless;* **adja.***: a collection agency, letter; a* **collection plate** *to receive money offerings.*
col.lec.tive (cuh.LEC.tiv) *adja.* having to do with a group or unit: *collective action, consciousness, knowledge, wisdom; a collective decision, sense, sigh of relief; NATO is an agency of collective security; the collective ownership of property* (= ownership in common); *a* **collective agreement** *between labor and management; In* **collective bargaining***, employees negotiate wages, working conditions, etc. with their employer; a* **collective farm** *worked and managed by a group; a* **collective noun** *such as "class" or "flock" denoting a group.* **—n.** a collective organization: *an editorial collective (of journalists); a worker's collective.*
—col.lec.tive.ly *adv.*
col.lec.tiv.ism (cuh.LEC.tuh.viz.um) *n.* a system of collective ownership and control of the economy; **col.lec.tiv.ist** *n. & adj.*
col.lec.tiv.ize (cuh.LEC.tuh.vize) *v.* **-iz.es, -ized, -iz.ing** organize according to collectivist principles.
col.lec.tor (cuh.LEC.tur) *n.* one who collects: *art, garbage, stamp, tax, trash collectors; an avid collector of rare books; a book that has become a* **collector's item.**
col.leen (COLL.een) *n.* an Irish girl.
col.lege (COLL.ij) *n.* **1** an institution of higher education: *to go to college after high school; to graduate from college; She tried to put him through college* (= pay for it); *He dropped out of college; She flunked out of college; business, commu-*

nity, junior, military colleges; colleges of dentistry, education, pharmacy; She's away at college; made friends in college; back from college after graduation; out of college looking for work. **2** a group of people with common duties: *an electoral college; the College of Cardinals; a college of physicians and surgeons.*

col.le.gial (cuh.LEE.jul) *adj.* characterized by interaction among colleagues: *a collegial approach, atmosphere, body; collegial decision-making, relations.* —**col.le.gi.al.i.ty** (-jee.AL.i.tee) *n.*

col.le.gian (cuh.LEE.jun) *n.* a college student.

col.le.giate (cuh.LEE.jut) *adj.* having to do with a college or colleges: *a collegiate church, education, institution, library, student, textbook; collegiate level, life, sports, standards, types.*

col.le.gi.um (cuh.LEE.jee.um) *n., pl.* **-gi.a** (-jee.uh) or **-gi.ums** an executive body whose members have equal rank and power, as in the former Soviet Union.

col.lide (cuh.LIDE) *v.* **col.lides, col.lid.ed, col.lid.ing 1** come into violent contact: *The car collided head-on with a truck; They collided on the highway.* **2** come directly in conflict; clash: *The Government and the Opposition collide constantly during question period.*

col.lie (COLL.ee) *n.* a large long-haired dog originally bred in Scotland to herd sheep.

col.lier (COLL.yur) *n. Brit.* **1** a coal miner. **2** a coal ship.

col.lier.y (COLL.yuh.ree) *n.* **col.lier.ies** a coal mine with its equipment and buildings.

col.li.mate (COLL.uh.mate) *v.* **-mates, -mat.ed, -mat.ing** make light rays parallel; adjust the line of sight of a telescope, surveyor's level, etc.

col.li.sion (cuh.LIZH.un) *n.* a colliding: *head-on, midair, near collisions; a collision between two planes; one plane in collision with another; The government is on a **collision course** with the labor unions unless they drop the new bill.*

col.lo.cate (COLL.uh.cate) *v.* **-cates, -cat.ed, -cat.ing** exist side by side or close together: *"Door" collocates with "ajar," "back," "front," "close," "lock," "open," "shut," etc. in numerous idioms and structures.*

col.lo.cation (col.uh.CAY.shun) *n.* a collocating: *the collocation of "open" and "door" in a phrase like "open-door policy."*

col.lo.di.on (cuh.LOH.dee.un) *n.* a pale, flammable, viscous, quick-drying solution used in photographic plates, to protect wounds, etc.

col.loid (COLL.oid) *n.* a suspension of very fine, insoluble particles in a gaseous, liquid, or solid medium, as gelatin, foam rubber, or fog: *Silica gel is in colloid form.* —**col.loid.al** (cuh.LOY.dul) *adj.*

col.lo.qui.al (cuh.LOH.quee.ul) *adj.* characteristic of informal conversation: *a colloquial expression, as "forty winks" for "a short nap."* —**col.lo.qui.al.ly** *adv.*

col.lo.qui.al.ism (cuh.LOH.quee.uh.liz.um) *n.* a colloquial word or phrase; an informal expression: *"Fly off the handle" is a colloquialism for "lose one's temper."*

col.lo.qui.um (cuh.LOH.quee.um) *n., pl.* **-qui.a** (-uh) or **-qui.ums** a conference or seminar.

col.lo.quy (COLL.uk.wee) *n.* **-quies 1** a usu. formal dialogue or conversation. **2** a work written in this form.

col.lude (cuh.LOOD, long "OO") *v.* **-ludes, -lud.ed, -lud.ing** secretly collaborate *with* someone for an improper or fraudulent purpose. —**col.lu.sion** (-zhun) *n.: a spy working in collusion with the enemy; There was collusion between them.* —**col.lu.sive** (-siv) *adj.: collusive behavior.*

col.lu.vi.um (cuh.LOO.vee.um) *n., pl.* **-vi.a** or **-vi.ums** rubble and rock debris at the foot of a slope or cliff.

co.logne (cuh.LONE) *n.* a perfumed liquid made of fragrant oils in an alcohol base.

Co.lom.bi.an (cuh.LUM.bee.un) *n. & adj.* (a person) of or from **Colombia**, a South American country.

co.lon (COH.lun) *n.* **1** a punctuation mark [:] used to introduce a list, example, quotation, etc. **2** *pl.* **-lons** or **-la** (-luh), the lower part of the large intestine leading to the rectum.

colo.nel (CUR.nul) *n.* a military officer ranking above a lieutenant colonel and below a brigadier general, usu. in command of a regiment.

co.lo.ni.al (cuh.LOH.nee.ul) *adj.* **1** [often derogatory] having to do with a colony or colonies: *colonial oppression, possessions, power, status.* **2 Colonial** having to do with the period of U.S. history before independence: *colonial architecture, furniture.* —**co.lo.ni.al.ly** *adv.*

co.lo.ni.al.ism (cuh.LOH.nee.uh.liz.um) *n.* the policy and practice of acquiring and maintaining foreign colonies, especially for economic exploitation; **co.lo.ni.al.ist** *n.*

col.o.nist (COLL.uh.nist) *n.* one who lives in a colony, esp. a first settler.

col.o.nize (COLL.uh.nize) *v.* **-niz.es, -nized, -niz.ing** settle in a place or establish a colony: *North America was colonized by the Dutch, French, and British;* **col.o.niz.er** *n.* —**col.o.ni.za.tion** (-nuh.ZAY.shun, -nye-) *n.*

col.on.nade (coll.uh.NADE) *n.* a row of evenly spaced columns usu. supporting one side of the roof of a large building; *adj.*: *a colonnaded building, town hall.*

col.o.ny (COLL.uh.nee) *n.* **-nies 1** a dependency in a distant land controlled and settled from the mother country: *Thirteen former British colonies first made up the U.S.; the end of Hong Kong as a crown colony in 1997.* **2** a group of individuals of the same kind or calling living in one area: *artists', leper, nudist, penal colonies; a colony of ants.*

col.o.phon (COLL.uh.fon) *n.* **1** an inscription in a book giving particulars of its publisher, date, typefaces and paper used, etc. **2** a publisher's trademark.

col.or (CULL.ur) *n.* **1** the quality of things as they appear in light: *the bright colors of the rainbow; Red, blue, and yellow are the primary colors; attractive, brilliant, dark, dull, gaudy, rich, strong colors; the soft or subdued, not loud or harsh, colors of an evening scene; the vivid, warm colors of a painting; painted in natural color; Colors should match or blend, not clash; a movie in living color! Our garden is a riot of color; He described her performance in glowing colors;* **adj**.: *a color film, painting; color harmony, photography, printing, television.* **2** skin color, esp. as indicating health or embarrassment: *She lost color while in hospital; Rest and recuperation brought color back to her cheeks; He changes color whenever the subject is mentioned; a person* **of color** (= nonwhite). **3** the **colors** a flag, emblem, etc. of a nation, military unit, etc.: *the ceremony of trooping the colors; to serve with* **the colors** (= military); *She passed the test* **with flying colors** (= victoriously). **4** a lively or interesting quality: *Writers use dialect to add or lend local color to a story.* **5** appearance: *greed under the color of frugality; a new twist that gives a false color to what happened; You see him in his true color or colors* (= nature); *false evidence that gives or lends color* (= the appearance of truth) *to the charges.*

—*v.* **1** change the color of something; hence, paint or dye: *She colored her hair brown; Color it your way; Color* (= consider) *me happy.* **2** alter or misrepresent: *a story colored by the reporter's prejudices.* **3** change color; blush: *He colors at the very mention of the subject.* Also **col.our** *Cdn.*

col.or.ant (CULL.ur.unt) *n.* a coloring agent like dye, ink, or paint. Also **col.our.ant** *Cdn.*

col.or.a.tion (cull.uh.RAY.shun) *n.* the state or manner of being colored.

col.or.a.tu.ra (cull.uh.ruh.TOOR.uh) *n.* **1** elaborate or ornamental passages in music. **2** a soprano specializing in such music.

color bar *n.* restrictions imposed on nonwhites, as in voting rights, eating in restaurants, and use of beaches.

col.or.blind (CULL.ur.blined) *adj.* **1** unable to perceive or distinguish certain colors. **2** indifferent as to skin color. —**col.or.blind.ness** *n.* Also **col.our.blind, col.our.blind.ness** *Cdn.*

col.or.cast (CULL.ur.cast) *v.* telecast in color; *n.*: *a colorcast of the Santa Claus parade.* Also **col.our.cast** *Cdn.*

col.ored (CULL.urd) *adj.* **1** having color: *colored glasses.* **2** distorted; biased: *a highly colored account of what happened.* **3** [offensive] non-Caucasian, esp. Black: *Is he colored or white?* —*n., pl.* **coloreds** a racially mixed person: *the coloreds of the old South Africa.* Also **col.oured** *Cdn.*

col.or.fast (CULL.ur.fast) *adj.* having colors that will not fade or run: *colorfast cotton.* Also **col.our.fast** *Cdn.*

col.or.ful (CULL.ur.full) *adj.* **1** having strong or attractive colors: *a colorful costume, scene.* **2** lively or interesting: *a colorful character.* —**col.or.ful.ly** *adv.* Also **col.our.ful, col.our.ful.ly** *Cdn.*

col.or.ing (CUL.ur.ing) *n.* **1** appearance in regard to color: *her facial coloring; His hair has the same coloring as her mother; the natural coloring of flowers.* **2** coloring substance: *fabric, food, hair colorings.* **3** application of color; *adj*.: *a coloring agent, book, contest, kit.* Also **col.our.ing** *Cdn.*

color line same as COLOR BAR.

color scheme *n.* an arrangement of colors, as in interior design.

co.los.sal (cuh.LOSS.ul) *adj.* of human creations, huge like a colossus: *a colossal dam on the Nile; a colossal structure; a colossal achievement, failure, misunderstanding, task; losses on a colossal scale; his colossal greed, pride, stupidity; What a colossal waste!* —**co.los.sal.ly** *adv.*

co.los.sus (cuh.LOSS.us) *n., pl.* **-los.si** (-los.eye) or **-los.sus.es** something of huge size, like a statue of Apollo in ancient Rhodes: *Our phone company is a colossus of North American industry.*

colour, colourant, etc. *Cdn.* COLOR, COLORANT, etc.

col.por.teur (COLL.por.tur) *n.* a peddler or distributor of religious books.

colt *n.* **1** a young horse, donkey, etc., esp. a male. **2** an inexperienced youth.

colt.ish *adj.* frisky; lively: *coltish escapades.* —**colt.ish.ly** *adv.*

col.um.bine (COLL.um.bine) *n.* a plant of the buttercup family with spurred, five-petaled flowers of various colors.

col.umn (COLL.um) *n.* **1** a pillar, with its base and capital, usu. supporting a roof or upper story. **2** something resembling this: *the spinal column; vertebral column; the steering column of an automobile; a column of figures to be added; a column of smoke rising from a chimney; This page has two columns (of print).* **3** a file or row: *a tank column; a column of soldiers.* **4** a regular feature in a newspaper or magazine: *correspondence, gossip, obituary, sports columns; a syndicated column.* —**col.umned** *adj. a marbled and columned rotunda; the columned homes of the rich.* —**col.um.nar** (cuh.LUM.nur) *adj.: a columnar display of numeric data; a columnar glass case.*

col.um.nist (COLL.um.ist, -um.nist) *n.* one who contributes regularly to a newspaper or broadcast: *a gossip columnist; political columnists; the Channel 5 science columnist.*

com- *prefix.* together: *compact, compatriot, compress.*

co.ma (COH.muh) *n.* a prolonged period of deep unconsciousness, esp. as caused by injury, poison, or disease: *She is* or *lies in a deep coma; to fall* or *go* or *lapse* or *slip into a coma; an irreversible, permanent, vegetative coma; to come out of* or *emerge from* or *wake up from a coma.*

Co.man.che (cuh.MAN.chee) *n.* **1** (a member of) an American Indian tribe now living in Oklahoma; *adj.: a Comanche pony.* **2** their language.

co.ma.tose (COH.uh.tose, *rhyme:* dose) *adj.* having to do with coma: *a comatose patient, state; a comatose economy, market.*

comb (COHM) *n.* **1** a toothed instrument for arranging and sometimes holding the hair in place: *a tortoiseshell comb; We examined the records with a fine-tooth comb* (= very carefully). **2** the fleshy, usu. red crest on a rooster's head. **3** the crest of a wave. —*v.* **1** arrange, clean, etc. with a comb. **2** search thoroughly: *The police combed the house for clues.*

com.bat (cum.BAT) *v.* **-bats, -bat.ted** or **-bat.ed, -bat.ting** or **-bat.ing** fight or oppose: *Help combat heart disease; how to combat terrorism.* —*n.* (COM.bat) a fight between two people or armies: *to engage in* or *to go into combat; a close, deadly, hand-to-hand, military combat; two people locked in mortal combat; single combat (between two people); adja.: a combat mission, team; a combat unit wearing combat boots.*

com.bat.ant (cum.BAT.unt) *n.* a person engaged in combat.

combat fatigue same as SHELL SHOCK.

com.bat.ive (cum.BAT.iv) *adj.* ready or eager to fight: *He's in a combative mood; She did it in a combative spirit; a combative tone of voice.*

combat zone *n.* an area in which fighting is going on.

comb.er (COH.mur) same as BREAKER, 2.

com.bi.na.tion (com.buh.NAY.shun) *n.* **1** the act or state of combining or being combined: *Drinking and driving make a dangerous combination; a fabric made of Lycra in combination with other fibers.* **2** a united entity or group: *a free, rare, strange combination; a number-password combination for accessing a database.* **3** the series of letters and numbers that, when turned on a dial, will open a lock, or **combination lock**, as on a bank vault.

com.bine (cum.BINE) *v.* **-bines, -bined, -bin.ing** come or bring together; unite: *Let's combine our efforts; We'll combine business with pleasure; Husbands and wives often combine as partners in business.* —*n.* (COM.bine) **1** a mobile machine that both cuts and threshes grain. **2** a combination, esp. of business interests, sometimes unethical: *a business combine; dairy combines.*

comb.ings (COH.mings) *n.pl.* loose hair, wool, etc. removed by combing.

combining form *n.* a word form that is used only in combination with other words or combining forms; e.g.; *auto-, counter-, -crat, demo-, multi-, -pede.*

com.bo (COM.boh) *n. Informal.* combination: *a skirt-blouse-jacket combo; a beef-broccoli combo; a jazz combo* (= small group of musicians).

com.bus.ti.ble (cum.BUS.tuh.bul) *adj.* capable of burning: *combustible liquids such as gasoline and cooking oil; Paper, cloth, and wood are combustible materials; n.: All these are combustibles.*
—**com.bus.ti.bil.i.ty** (-BIL.i.tee) *n.*

com.bus.tion (cum.BUS.chun) *n.* a chemical reaction in a gaseous medium with release of heat; burning: *spontaneous combustion of rags soaked with oil; the internal combustion engine of an automobile.* —**com.bus.tive** (cum.BUS.tiv) *adj.*: *the combustive action of heat.*

come (CUM) *v.* **comes, came, come, com.ing** **1** move toward a position, condition, or state thought of as near the speaker: *Please come to our house; He's coming down the street; He came at me with a big smile; Water comes to a boil at 100°C; a jacket that looks great* **coming and going** (= in all situations); see also COMING. **2** occur; happen: *A birthday comes once a year; F comes before G in the alphabet; Z comes last; She will be a year older,* **come** *February* (= when February arrives). **3** originate: *He comes of good stock; She comes from Colombia; Chicks come from eggs; I know where you're* **coming from** (*Informal* for I know what you mean). —**come across 1** appear: *In his books, he comes across as a radical.* **2** also **come upon,** find or meet unexpectedly: *I came across or upon an old friend at the party.* —**come along** make an appearance: *We wanted to hail the first cab that came along; Then along comes this nearly empty bus.* —**come around 1** recover: *She has come around quickly after her recent illness.* **2** change to a different opinion or stand. —**come away** leave: *Each came away with a different impression of the show.* —**come back** return, esp. to fame, power, status, etc. —**come between** cause trouble between two people. —**come by** acquire or get: *Good editors are hard to come by these days.* —**come clean** *Informal.* tell the whole truth; confess. —**come down:** *an heirloom that has come down* (= that originated) *from our ancestors; The teacher came down hard on the students* (= punished them severely); *This talk about more money – it all comes down* (= amounts) *to greed; He came down* (= became afflicted) *with measles.* —**come in for** be subjected to something: *The new play came in for some harsh comment.* —**come into** receive, esp. by inheritance: *She will come into $500,000 on her aunt's death.* —**come off 1** become detached. **2** happen; succeed; fare. —**come off it!** or **come on!** *Informal.* stop behaving like that! —**come on** present oneself aggressively: *She's coming on a bit too strong for me; He comes on* (= comes across or appears) *rather dumb.* —**come out:** *Young women used to come out* (= debut) *at 18; She came out* (= turned out) *in her best outfit; They come out with* (= publish) *a dozen books each month.* —**come through** give or do what is required: *It takes time for them to come through with a contract offer.* —**come to 1** amount to: *That comes to $51.95 including taxes.* **2** (-TOO) regain consciousness: *The boxer came to within moments of the knockout.* —**come up roses** happen as desired. —**come up with** *Informal.* produce: *Try to come up with a better idea.* —**come what may** no matter what happens. —**how come?** *Informal.* why?

come.back *n.* **1** a return to power or status; recovery: *Some old fashions are making a comeback; to plan, stage a comeback; a big, major, quick, strong comeback;* **adj.***a.*: *a comeback plan; politicians on the comeback trail.* **2** a retort. **3** a cause for complaint.

co.me.di.an (cuh.MEE.dee.un) *n.* **1** one who acts in a comedy. **2** an amusing person, esp. a professional entertainer: *nightclub, stand-up, TV comedians.* —**co.me.di.enne** (-dee.EN) *fem.*

come.down *n.* a coming down in power or position.

com.e.dy (COM.uh.dee) *n.* **-dies 1** a play with a light, amusing tone: *a musical comedy; situation comedies.* **2** a dramatic piece with a happy ending; hence, this type, as opposed to tragedy. **3** humor: *popular comedy; slapstick comedy; the comedy of the situation; In nightclubs he does mostly comedy; high, low comedy;* **adj.***a.*: *a comedy act, hit, routine, team.* —**co.me.dic** (cuh.MEE.dic) *adj.*: *He had a long comedic career; her comedic flair, talents, wit.*

come-hither *adj.* sexually enticing or attractive: *Kay's come-hither appeal, charm, looks.*

come.ly (CUM.lee) *adj.* **-li.er, -li.est** attractive or good-looking: *a comely appearance; comely ladies, youth.* —**come.li.ness** *n.*

come-on *n. Informal.* an allurement; inducement: *Pens are being handed out as come-ons to attract customers.*

com.er (CUM.ur) *n. Informal.* **1** one who comes; *cpd.: a first-comer; latecomers; newcomers.* **2** a promising or rapidly advancing person: *He is ready to take on all comers; an up-and-comer.*

co.mes.ti.ble (cuh.MES.tuh.bul) *adj.* edible. —*n.* a basket of comestibles.

com.et (COM.it) *n.* a celestial body, esp. one orbiting the sun, with a small, bright center, a glowing "head" around it, and often a long glowing "tail."

come.up.pance (cum.UP.unce) *n. Informal.* just retribution; deserts: *In the end, the hero gets his comeuppance by losing everything he had.*

com.fit (CUM.fit) *n.* a confection, esp. a candied nut, fruit, etc.

com.fort (CUM.furt) *v.* soothe or console: *to comfort them in their hour of sorrow.* —*n.* **1** consolation: *a source of joy and comfort;* to **take comfort** in or from *recent improvements in our performance.* **2** a person or thing that gives consolation: *Your letter was a great comfort; The company's offer to help her find another job was* **cold comfort** to or *for the woman who was fired without warning.* **3** ease or well-being; also, something that causes this: *to live in comfort; a resort with all the comforts of home; Three in the front seat is too* **close for comfort.**

com.fort.a.ble (CUM.fur.tuh.bul) *adj.* being in a state of or giving comfort: *He's quite comfortable in bed; a comfortable chair, pew; She enjoys a comfortable income.* —**com.fort.a.ble.ness** *n.;* **com.fort.a.bly** *adv.*

com.fort.er (CUM.fur.tur) *n.* **1** a warm quilt. **2** a soft, woolen scarf.

comfort station *n.* a public toilet.

com.fy (CUM.fee) *adj.* **-fi.er, -fi.est** *Informal.* comfortable: *a comfy chair for grandma; a nice comfy pillow; comfy and cozy.*

com.ic (COM.ic) *adja.* **1** having to do with comedy or cartoons: *a comic actor, character, section of a newspaper.* **2** humorous or amusing in a thoughtful way: *a comic effect, sense; comic spirit.* —*n.* **1** a humorous person, esp. a professional comedian: *a standup comic.* **2** *Informal.* a comic book. **3** **comics** *pl.* a comics section, as of a newspaper; funnies: *full-color comics.*

com.i.cal (COM.i.cul) *adj.* provoking laughter; hilariously funny: *a comical air, outfit, performance, scene; She is trying to look comical in that hat.* —**com.i.cal.ly** *adv.*

comic book *n.* a booklet of comic strips telling adventurous or humorous stories.

comic strip *n.* a series of drawings telling a humorous or adventurous story.

coming *adj.* **1** approaching: *in the coming weeks; the coming attractions.* **2** *Informal.* showing promise of success: *the coming thing in neckwear.* —*n.* advent: *the coming of winter; The* **comings and goings** (= movements or activities) *of the new neighbors amused everyone; Chris-*
tians await the **Second Coming** *of the Messiah.*

com.i.ty (COM.i.tee) *n.* **-ties 1** civility or courtesy. **2** community: *our place in the comity of nations.*

com.ma (COM.uh) *n.* a punctuation mark [,] showing a slight separation or pause within a sentence or clause.

com.mand (cuh.MAND) *v.* **1** order with authority: *He commanded them to cease fire; He commanded that they cease fire;* adja.: *the* **commanding officer** (= the one in authority). **2** receive as one's due: *Knowledge commands respect; She commands a six-figure salary.* **3** have in one's control; also, overlook in a controlling manner: *The fort commands the valley;* adja.: *a fort built on* **commanding** *heights; a commanding* (= dominant) *position; She speaks in a commanding* (= authoritative) *voice.* —*n.* **1** an order or the giving of it: *to carry out, execute, give, issue, obey commands; At whose command did you open fire? a computer command or signal* (as by a keystroke) *to carry out a specific task.* **2** authority or ability to give commands: *Who is in command? the chain of command from the Chief of Staff down; to assume, exercise, place in, put in, relinquish, take over command; He was in firm command of or over the regiment till the end.* **3** a military force or similar organization: *the armed forces under a unified command; a decision made by the military high command* (= top commanders). **4** control: *She has a good, fluent command of Spanish.*

com.man.dant (COM.un.dant) *n.* a commanding officer.

com.man.deer (com.un.DEER) *v.* seize by force, esp. by military order.

com.mand.er (cuh.MAN.dur) *n.* one who commands, esp. a commanding officer: *the commander of a unit.*

commander in chief *n.* **commanders in chief** the supreme commander of all of the armed forces of a nation.

com.mand.ment (cuh.MAND.munt) *n.* a command or precept, esp. **Commandment,** one of the ten laws given by God to Moses: *to keep the commandments; the Ten Commandments.*

command module *n.* the section of a spacecraft containing astronauts and main controls and designed for reentry.

com.man.do (cuh.MAN.doh) *n.* **-dos** or **-does** (-doze) **1** a member of a small military force trained for quick raids into enemy territory. **2** the force itself.

command performance *n.* **1** an entertainment given at the request of a rul-

er or head of state. **2** an inspired or engineered action or show.
command post *n*. the field headquarters of a fighting unit.
com.mem.o.rate (cuh.MEM.uh.rate) *v*. **-rates, -rat.ed, -rat.ing 1** honor or observe the memory of a person or event. **2** be a memorial to a person or event: *a plaque commemorating war dead.* —**com.mem.o.ra.tion** (-RAY.shun) *n*. —**com.mem.o.ra.tive** (-ruh.tiv) *adj*.: *a commemorative stamp.*
com.mence (cuh.MENCE) *v*. **com.men.ces, com.menced, com.menc.ing** *Formal*. begin or start: *Let the games commence; The ceremonies commenced at noon.*
com.mence.ment (cuh.MENCE.munt) *n*. **1** a beginning: *the commencement of the ceremony.* **2** a ceremony for the granting of degrees or diplomas: *We'll see you at the commencement on May 23*; *adj*.: *a commencement address, speaker, speech; a commencement ceremony* or **commencement exercises.**
com.mend (cuh.MEND) *v*. **1** praise; recommend: *She was highly commended for her work.* **2** entrust to another's care: *In his will, he commended his children to his sister's care.* —**com.men.da.to.ry** (-duh.tor.ee) *adj*.: *commendatory comments, verses.* —**com.men.da.tion** (com.un.DAY.shun) *n*.
com.men.da.ble (cuh.MEN.duh.bul) *adj*. praiseworthy: *a commendable action; his highly commendable bravery.* —**com.men.da.bly** *adv*.
com.men.su.ra.ble (cuh.MEN.shuh.ruh.bul) *adj*. measurable by the same standard, as numbers evenly divisible by the same whole number: *21 and 28 are commensurable* (= divisible by 7). —**com.men.su.ra.bly** *adv*.
com.men.su.rate (cuh.MEN.shuh.rit) *adj*. proportionate: *He was paid a salary commensurate to his worth; Pay has to be commensurate with work performed; commensurate authority, costs, increases, pay.* —**com.men.su.rate.ly** *adv*.
com.ment (COM.ent) *n*. an explanatory or critical note, remark, or reaction: *critical, cryptic, fitting, nasty, off-the-record, passing comments; The incident aroused* or *caused* or *evoked* or *provoked considerable comment in the press; "No comment," the politician replied; Comments made about* or *on the incident are off the record.* —*v*. make a comment: *He commented that everyone seemed happy; refused to comment on* or *about the incident.*
com.men.tar.y (COM.un.tair.ee) *n*. -tar.ies **1** usu. **commentaries,** memoirs or a simple narrative. **2** a systematic series of comments, as on a text or a sports event: *He wrote a commentary on the Koran; a running commentary on a game.* **3** something that illustrates or reflects on a subject: *Pollution is a sad commentary on civilization.*
com.men.ta.tor (COM.un.tay.tur) *n*. one who reports and comments on news and politics on radio or TV.
com.merce (COM.urse) *n*. **1** trade: *to carry on, develop, engage in, expand commerce with other countries; overseas commerce; the commerce between the U.S. and Canada.* **2** dealings: *no commerce with the enemy; Latin used to be the language of commerce in Vatican circles.*
com.mer.cial (cuh.MUR.shul) *adj*. **1** having to do with commerce: *a commercial agent, attaché, bank, bureau, center, development, undertaking; commercial art, courses, education, grade, law, photography, programs, transport, treaties.* **2** oriented to profit-making: *Commercial television relies on advertising; academic and commercial publishers.* —*n*. a radio or TV advertisement: *a commercial sponsored by a bank.* —**com.mer.cial.ly** *adv*.
com.mer.cial.ism (cuh.MUR.shul.iz.um) *n*. excessive emphasis on profit-making.
com.mer.cial.ize (cuh.MUR.shul.ize) *v*. **-iz.es, -ized, -iz.ing** make commercial; put something on a commercial basis; *adj*.: *the highly* **commercialized** *North American Christmas (with a lot of buying and selling); a commercialized culture.* —**com.mer.cial.i.za.tion** (-luh.ZAY.shun, -lye-) *n*.
Com.mie (COM.ee) *n. & adj*. *Informal*. communist; also **Com.my, com.mie,** *pl*. **Com.mies, com.mies.**
com.mi.na.tion (com.uh.NAY.shun) *n*. threat; denunciation; **com.min.a.to.ry** (COM.i.nuh.tor.ee) *adj*.
com.min.gle (cuh.MING.gul) *v*. **-gles, -gled, -gling** mingle or mix together.
com.mis.er.ate (cuh.MIZ.uh.rate) *v*. **-ates, -at.ed, -at.ing** sympathize: *to commiserate with the unemployed; They commiserated over their misfortunes and found themselves falling in love.* —**com.mis.er.a.tion** (-RAY.shun) *n*.
com.mis.sar (COM.uh.sar) *n*. a communist party official who would watch over army officers and others to ensure their conformity to the wishes of the party: *a political commissar.*
com.mis.sar.i.at (com.i.SAIR.ee.ut) *n*. **1** a military body that supplies and

transports an army's provisions. **2** until 1946, a ministry in the Soviet government, presided over by a commissar.

com.mis.sar.y (COM.uh.sair.ee) *n.* **-sar.ies 1** a store selling food and other provisions at a temporary site or work camp. **2** a lunchroom, esp. in a movie studio.

com.mis.sion (cuh.MISH.un) *n.* **1** an act of committing: *the commission of a crime; sins of omission and commission.* **2** the granting of certain military ranks or the rank itself: *to award, confer, earn, grant, win a commission.* **3** a task entrusted to someone: *She received a commission from City Hall to paint a mural; to execute a commission.* **4** a group entrusted with a task, often as a government agency: *to appoint or establish a fact-finding, investigating, planning commission; a Royal Commission on the status of women; The commission was disbanded after it reported.* **5** a sales rep's fee, usu. a percentage of the sale price: *a 10% commission on all sales.* **—in** (or **out of**) **commission** in (or out of) working order or active service: *The plant has been in commission since 1980; It was put out of commission by a fire for a few days.* —*v.* give a commission: *The king commissioned him to explore the West; a painting commissioned by the city; He was commissioned an officer cadet;* **adj.:** *A lieutenant is a commissioned officer, not an enlisted man or woman.*

com.mis.sion.aire (cuh.mish.uh.NAIR) *n. Cdn.* a uniformed attendant or guard on duty at the entrance to a hotel, club, large shop, office, etc.

com.mis.sion.er (cuh.MISH.un.ur) *n.* **1** a member of a commission: *a police commissioner.* **2** the head of a usu. governmental agency: *the commissioner of education; the UN High Commissioner for Refugees.* **3** an administrative head: *a Salvation Army commissioner; a baseball commissioner.*

com.mit (cuh.MIT) *v.* **-mits, -mit.ted, -mit.ting 1** do something wrong or bad: *to commit aggression, atrocities, blackmail, blunders, crimes, mistakes, suicide.* **2** put in a special place: *to commit a person to prison, to a mental hospital; to commit a poem to memory; He never committed his thoughts to paper.* **3** pledge or promise oneself or resources to an action or use: *to commit funds to a project; He won't commit himself* (= say anything definite or binding) *on that issue;* **adj.:** *She is committed* (= devoted) *to helping the poor, to her principles; a committed Christian; a committed* (= assured) *rate of interest.*

com.mit.ment (cuh.MIT.munt) *n.* **1** a pledge or promise: *He gave* or *made a firm commitment to invest in our firm; a commitment that he would invest in our firm; He was unable to meet such heavy financial commitments.* **2** devotion: *a deep, total commitment to helping the poor.*

com.mit.tal (cuh.MIT.ul) *n.* a committing to a special place, as a body to a grave: *a committal* (= burial) *service.*

com.mit.tee (cuh.MIT.ee) *n.* an appointed or elected group that considers, acts on, promotes, or reports on particular matters: *to appoint, establish, form, organize, set up a committee; ad-hoc advisory, finance, select, standing, steering committees; a committee for economic development; a committee on inner-city schools; to sit on a committee (as a member); a* **committee of the whole** (= of all members of a legislative body).
—com.mit.tee.man (-mun) *n.* **-men;**
com.mit.tee.wom.an *n.* **-wom.en.**

com.mode (cuh.MODE) *n.* **1** a chest of drawers. **2** a portable washstand in a cupboard. **3** a low chair enclosing a chamber pot.

com.mod.i.ous (cuh.MOH.dee.us) *adj.* suitably spacious: *a commodious car trunk, closet.*

com.mod.i.ty (cuh.MOD.i.tee) *n.* **-ties** an article of use, esp. one transported and traded, as farm and mining products, textiles, and lumber: *a marketable commodity; to trade in commodities on the* **commodity exchange** or **commodity market.**

com.mo.dore (COM.uh.dor) *n.* **1** a wartime navy officer ranking just below a rear admiral. **2** the head of a yacht club, fleet, etc.

com.mon (COM.un) *adj.* **1** having to do with more than one: *Laws serve the common good; common interests; English is the common language of the British Commonwealth; Falling asleep is a weakness* **common to** *all of us.* **2** frequent; usual; general: *Cows are a common sight on the rural landscape, quite common; a matter of common knowledge; a common experience, occurrence; in common parlance; words in common use.* **3** ordinary; without distinction of quality or rank: *a common criminal, flower, lawyer, sailor, soldier; the common cat, people; common courtesy, decency; common salt; a* **common or garden** (= ordinary) **variety** *of an article.* **4** having no quality; inferior: *the common speech of the uneducated;* com-

mon manners; She looks rather common in that hairdo. —*n.* **1** a piece of land owned by and open to the public: *cows grazing on the village common; property held in common with* (= shared by) *the rest of the family.* **2 commons** *pl.* the common people. **3 Commons** the House of Commons, the lower house of a parliament. —**com.mon.ly** *adv.;* **com.mon.ness** *n.*

com.mon.al.i.ty (com.uh.NAL.i.tee) *n.* **1** the state or quality of having features or characteristics in common with others; also, such a feature or characteristic: *goods with commonality in terms of price and style; Women and minorities recognize their commonality; commonality of aspirations, disabilities, expectations, hopes, interests; commonalities such as being denied jobs.* **2** same as COMMONALTY.

com.mon.al.ty (COM.un.ul.tee) *n.* **-ties** the common people.

common carrier *n.* a commercial concern for carrying goods, people, or messages nationwide, as a telephone company.

common coin *n.* something widely used in a group: *words that are the common coin of our language.*

common denominator *n.* a number evenly divisible by the denominator of two or more fractions, as 14 for 3/7 and ½.

com.mon.er (COM.un.ur) *n.* one without noble rank.

common factor (or **divisor**) *n.* a number that divides evenly into two or more numbers: *A common factor of 16 and 24 is 8.*

common ground *n.* shared opinions or interests: *to meet on common ground (acceptable to the parties concerned).*

common law *n.* the uncodified body of law based on custom and court decisions. —**common-law** *adja.: a common-law husband, wife;* a **common-law marriage** *(based on cohabitation and valid by common law); adv.: They lived common-law for many years.*

common market *n.* an economic union of nations, usu. for lowering mutual trade barriers, esp., the (European) Common Market, or the European Union.

common multiple *n.* a multiple of two or more numbers: *18 is the least common multiple for 2, 3, 6, and 9.*

com.mon.place (COM.un.place) *n.* **1** a frequent thing: *In the 1890s, the automobile was more of a novelty than a commonplace.* **2** a trite or obvious remark or topic; platitude: *You've just stated a commonplace; It's a commonplace to say families are breaking up.* —*adj.* ordinary or usual: *a movie with a commonplace theme; It's becoming commonplace for people to own computers.*

common property *n.* **1** property held in common; also, public property, as a public park. **2** a matter of common knowledge.

common salt *n.* sodium chloride.

common sense *n.* ordinary practical judgment that is not based on sophistication: *He had the common sense not to contradict the boss; to show or use good, plain common sense.* Also **commonsense.** —**commonsense** or **common-sense** *adja.: a commonsense answer, approach, decision, notion, remedy, rule, suggestion, view, way.*

com.mon.sen.si.cal or **com.mon.sen. si.cal** (com.un.SEN.si.cul) *adj.* characterized by common sense: *a commonsensical answer, step, suggestion; That sounds very commonsensical.*

common stock *n.* an ordinary share in a corporation that is not a preferred stock.

common touch *n.* the gift of communicating with the common people: *an old senator who has lost the common touch.*

common wall *n.* a shared wall, as one separating two apartments.

com.mon.weal (COM.un.weel) *n.* the public good.

com.mon.wealth (COM.un.welth) *n.* **1** the body of citizens in a state. **2** a nation or state: *the Commonwealth of Australia; the Commonwealth of Massachusetts.* **3** an association of sovereign states, as the **Commonwealth of Nations** made up of Britain and its former colonies.

com.mo.tion (cuh.MOH.shun) *n.* noisy confusion; tumult: *The announcement caused, created, raised a commotion in the audience; The commotion soon subsided.*

com.mu.nal (cuh.MEW.nul, COM. yuh.nul) *adj.* **1** having to do with a commune or a system of common property; shared: *a communal farm, kitchen, meal, spirit, table; communal activity, bathhouses, life, living, ownership, property, sharing, wastes.* **2** having to do with a community or ethnic group: *communal feelings, harmony, hatreds, riots, solidarity, strife, tension, trouble, violence, war.* —**com.mu.nal.ism** *n.* strong attachment to one's own group or sect rather than to society as a whole. —**com.mu.nal.ly** *adv.*

com.mu.nal.ize (cuh.MEW.nuh.lize) *v.*

commune / commute

-iz.es, -ized, -iz.ing make common property: *the communalizing of natural resources.*

com.mune (cum.YOON) *v.* **-munes, -muned, -mun.ing** converse, esp. mentally: *Poets commune with Nature.* —*n.* (COM.yoon) **1** a group of people living and working together; community: *a hippie commune; a Friends of the Earth commune.* **2** the smallest division of government in some European countries, esp. France, resembling a township. **3** a communal unit or settlement: *Chinese communes.*

com.mu.ni.ca.ble (cuh.MEW.nuh.cuh.bul) *adj.* that can be easily communicated; contagious or infectious: *Mumps is a communicable disease.* —**com.mu.ni.ca.bil.i.ty** (-BIL.i.tee) *n.*

com.mu.ni.cant (cuh.MEW.nuh.kunt) *n.* one who does or may receive Communion.

com.mu.ni.cate (cuh.MEW.nuh.cate) *v.* **-cates, -cat.ed, -cat.ing** **1** pass on to or share with another: *to communicate diseases, information, feelings, thoughts; We were not allowed to communicate by letter or telephone with the outside world; adj.: two communicating computers; a communicating system.* **2** allow passage between; *adj.: two communicating rooms.* **3** administer or receive Holy Communion. —**com.mu.ni.ca.tor** *n.*

com.mu.ni.ca.tion (cuh.mew.nuh.CAY.shun) *n.* **1** the act or means of communicating: *to cut off communications; to establish communication with the trapped miners; stay in communication with the outside world; adj..: the communications guru Marshall McLuhan; Keep communication lines open; the communications media, technology; a communications satellite; Computers need **communications software** to send and receive data.* **2** a message: *The outpost received a communication from headquarters; to address, direct, send communications to headquarters; a direct, official, personal, private communication; a privileged communication between priest and penitent.*

com.mu.ni.ca.tive (cuh.MEW.nuh.cay.tiv, cuh.tiv) *adj.* willing to talk; not secretive: *a child who is not very communicative; a communicative disposition.*

com.mu.nion (cum.YOON.yun) *n.* **1** a sharing: *a communion of interests.* **2** fellowship; a group of people connected by religion: *the communion of saints; the Anglican Communion.* **3** intimate communication: *to hold communion with oneself.* **4 Communion** Holy Communion or the Lord's Supper: *to administer, receive, take Communion.*

com.mu.ni.qué (cuh.MEW.nuh.cay) *n.* an official announcement, esp. to the press; bulletin: *They issued a joint communiqué after the summit meeting; a communiqué on or about what they had discussed.*

com.mu.nism (COM.yuh.niz.um) *n.* **1** a social system based on the collective ownership of wealth and the absence of social class. **2 Communism** the revolutionary communist system, as practiced esp. in the former Soviet Union, based on the theories of Marx and Lenin and controlled by the **Communist Party.** —**com.mu.nist** or **Com.mu.nist** *n. & adj.* —**com.mu.nis.tic** (-NIS.tic) *adj.*

com.mu.ni.ty (cuh.MEW.ni.tee) *n.* **-ties 1** a group of people living in one place, esp. the population of a town, region, etc.: *a leader who has the support of the whole community; a close-knit community;* **community antenna television** (= cable TV); *a* **community chest** (= fund for charitable purposes); *a community* (= not teaching) *hospital.* **2** a group of people with similar interests: *academic, business, ethnic, Jewish, religious, scientific communities; Washington's diplomatic community.* **3** identity: *a community of interests and views.*

community college *n.* **1** a post-secondary educational institution for training in occupations and skills. **2** a junior college serving and supported by a regional community.

community property *n.* property jointly held by husband and wife.

com.mu.nize (COM.yuh.nize) *v.* **-niz.es, -nized, -niz.ing 1** make communistic. **2** make something the property of the community.

com.mu.ta.tion (com.yuh.TAY.shun) *n.* a commuting: *the commutation of a death sentence* (to life in prison); *a commutation ticket* (for commuters, usually at a reduced rate).

com.mu.ta.tive (COM.yuh.tay.tiv, cum.YOO.tuh.tiv) *adj. Math.* giving the same result regardless of the order in which the steps are taken: *Simple addition is commutative.*

com.mu.ta.tor (COM.yuh.tay.tur) *n.* a device for reversing the direction of electric current flow, used in direct current generators and electric motors.

com.mute (cum.YOOT) *v.* **-mutes, -mut.ed, -mut.ing 1** change or substitute, esp. reduce the severity of a penalty: *The death sentence was commuted to life imprisonment.* **2** travel regularly between home and place of work: *People commute to work by car, rail, and bus; They commute between city and suburb; People commute daily from the suburbs to the city.* —**n.** trip: *It's a two-hour commute to work.* —**com.mu.ter** *n.*

Commy same as COMMIE.

com.pact (COM.pact, cum.PACT) *adj.* **1** densely packed; solid: *a compact mass.* **2** condensed: *a compact style of writing.* **3** occupying a small space: *a compact volume.* —*n.* (COM.pact) **1** a small car. **2** an agreement: *to make a trade compact with the U.S.; a compact between labor and management.* **3** a small case for face powder. —*v.* (cum.PACT) pack tightly together; make compact: *cartons that can be compacted for disposal.* *adj.: compacted gravel; tightly compacted landfills; a compacted schedule; a compacting system.*
—**com.pac.tion** *n.*: *soil, waste compaction; compaction of sediments in the earth.*
—**com.pact.ly** *adv.*; **com.pact.ness** *n.*

compact disk (COM.pact-) *n.* a diskette containing music, data, or images in digital form to be read by an optical laser.

com.pac.tor (cum.PAC.tur) *n.* a machine for compacting earth to a firm density or one for compacting trash into small bundles.

com.pan.ion (cum.PAN.yun) *n.* one that accompanies another; close associate: *boon, close, faithful, inseparable, life, traveling companions; hired as a companion for an elderly lady; a **companion volume** containing the index to the encyclopedia.*

com.pan.ion.a.ble (cum.PAN.yun. uh.bul) *adj.* easy to associate with; sociable: *a leader who has made politics and humanity companionable; a companionable atmosphere, smile.* —**com.pan.ion.a.bly** (-blee) *adv.*

com.pan.ion.ship (cum.PAN.yun.ship) *n.* association or fellowship: *She used to enjoy his companionship; They lived in close companionship for many years.*

com.pan.ion.way (cum.PAN.yun.way) *n.* a staircase leading below deck on a ship.

com.pa.ny (CUM.puh.nee) *n.* **-nies** **1** a group of people who work or play together, as a musical or theatrical troupe, the officers and personnel of a ship, or a military unit smaller than a battalion. **2** a business organization: *to establish, form a company; finance, holding, insurance, investment, joint-stock, limited, shipping companies; The company failed, went bankrupt; a **company doctor** (retained by a company to care for its employees).* **3** guest(s): *We're having company for supper.* **4** one's associates or companions: *"A man is known by the company he keeps"; mixed company (including men and women); present company* (= those present). **5** companionship; fellowship: *the pleasure of your company at supper; He sought the company of the learned; They proved good company; He drinks only **in company*** (= socially); *He drinks **in company with*** (= together with) *friends; He had to **part company** with* (= leave) *them on Monday morning.* —**keep company** **1** associate: *a man and a woman keeping company; He is known to keep company with shady characters.* **2** accompany: *Keep her company.*

com.pa.ra.ble (COM.puh.ruh.bul, cum.PAIR.uh-) *adj.* able or worthy to be compared: *Apples and pears are not comparable in many respects; goods of comparable value.* —**com.pa.ra.bly** *adv.*

com.par.a.tive (cum.PAIR.uh.tiv) **1** *adj.* compared to another of the same kind; relative: *a comparative advantage, stranger, unknown.* **2** *adj.* having to do with comparison: *comparative advertising, anatomy, literature, philosophy, study; a **comparative adjective** such as "more" and "greater," as in "much-more-most" and "great-greater-greatest."*
—*n.:* "Better" *is the comparative of* "good." —**com.par.a.tive.ly** *adv.*

com.pare (cum.PARE) *v.* **1** examine to note differences and similarities: *to compare apples and* or *with oranges; They compare* (= may be compared) *advantageously, favorably; Compared to* or *with oranges, apples are generally sweeter.* **2** liken to a person or thing: *Apples cannot be compared to oranges in all respects.* **3** be equally good when compared: *Fast food can't compare with home-cooked meals.*

com.par.i.son (cum.PAIR.uh.sun) *n.* a comparing: *to draw* or *make a comparison between two things; Some things are beyond comparison; the many points of comparison* (= similarity) *between the two.*
—**in** or **by comparison with** or **to** when or if compared with: *One suffers in comparison to* or *with the other; One seems a bargain by comparison with* [rarely *to*] *the other.*

comparison-shop *v.* to shop for the best value by comparing prices and brands of competing items at various stores.

com.part.ment (cum.PART.munt) *n.* a division of a space, structure, etc.; separate room or area: *a first-class compartment; watertight compartments; glove, luggage, storage compartments.*

com.part.men.tal.ize (cum.part.MEN.tuh.lize) *v.* **-iz.es, -ized, -iz.ing** put into compartments: *Science gets compartmentalized as it becomes more specialized.*

com.pass (CUM.pus) *n.* **1** a device for indicating direction, esp. one with a magnetic needle that points north: *a mariner's compass; the 32 points* (= directions) *of the compass.* **2** usu. **compasses** *pl.* a V-shaped device with two hinged legs for drawing circles, measuring distances, etc. **3** extent; boundary: *Some things are beyond the compass of our imagination; so much in so small a compass.* —*v.* same as ENCOMPASS.

com.pas.sion (cum.PASH.un) *n.* sorrow or sympathy for another's sufferings, with desire to help: *to arouse, display, show, feel compassion for the poor; to act out of compassion; a deep, profound, strong sense of compassion.*

com.pas.sion.ate (cum.PASH.uh.nit) *adj.* having compassion: *a tender, compassionate heart; compassionate treatment of prisoners.* —**com.pas.sion.ate.ly** *adv.*

com.pat.i.ble (cum.PAT.uh.bul) *adj.* **1** able to live, function, or get along together: *a compatible blood donor, companion, pair; One is compatible with the other.* **2** of computer software and hardware, able to run on or work with a specified device or system; also *n.*: *PC compatibles.* —**com.pat.i.bil.i.ty** (-BIL.i.tee) *n.*

com.pa.tri.ot (cum.PAY.tree.ut) *n.* **1** a fellow citizen. **2** a colleague.

com.peer (cum.PEER, COM.peer) *n.* a person of equal rank; peer; also, a comrade: *They were compeers at a military training camp.*

com.pel (cum.PEL) *v.* **-pels, -pelled, -pel.ling 1** force: *Famine compelled him to steal.* **2** get by force, pressure, etc.: *The troops compelled submission from the people.*

compelling (cum.PEL.ing) *adj.* causing respect, interest, belief, etc.; forceful: *a compelling line of argument; a compelling tale; compelling evidence.*

com.pen.di.um (cum.PEN.dee.um) *n.*, *pl.* **-di.a** (-dee.uh) or **-di.ums** a short but comprehensive summary.

com.pen.sate (COM.pun.sate) *v.* **-sates, -sat.ed, -sat.ing 1** pay someone in order to make up for something: *to compensate a worker for injury suffered at work.* **2** make up for a defect or variation: *He drove faster to compensate for the time lost; His boldness only compensates for an inner timidity.*

com.pen.sa.tion (com.pun.SAY.shun) *n.* equivalent payment: *to make, offer, pay adequate, appropriate compensation; compensation for injury suffered.*

com.pen.sa.to.ry (cum.PEN.suh.tor.ee) *adv.* that compensates or makes up: *She was awarded compensatory damages of $6,000 for the damaged car; compensatory education for disadvantaged children.*

com.pete (cum.PEET) *v.* **-petes, -pet.ed, -pet.ing 1** vie for or as if for a prize; strive: *to compete in sports; to compete with one's rivals; They are competing for the gold medal.* **2** be as good as: *The corner store cannot compete with the supermarket.*

com.pe.tence (COM.puh.tunce) *n.* ability or fitness: *The court questioned the competence of the witness; his competence to give evidence; his competence in the language; to acquire, gain the necessary competence for a teaching position; It was beyond, not within the competence of the court to try the case.*

com.pe.tent (COM.puh.tunt) *adj.* quite able, qualified, etc.: *a highly competent judge of character; a competent scholar; She is competent in her subject; competent as a classicist; competent to teach the subject; She could do a competent job (that is satisfactory in all respects).*
—**com.pe.tent.ly** *adv.*

com.pe.ti.tion (com.puh.TISH.un) *n.* **1** opposition or rivalry: *He faces bitter, cutthroat, healthy, keen, stiff, strong competition; There's free competition among or between rivals; competition for control of the market; Each one is in competition with the others.* **2** a contest or match: *literary, music, sports competitions; an open competition for a prize.* **3** one's rivals: *He's trying to undercut or undersell the competition; The competition is hard to beat.*

com.pet.i.tive (cum.PET.uh.tiv) *adj.* liking or ready to compete: *a fiercely, keenly competitive spirit; competitive sports; We are competitive with* (= as good as) *our rivals.*

com.pet.i.tor (cum.PET.uh.tur) *n.* one who competes: *formidable, strong, unscrupulous competitors.*

com.pile (cum.PILE) *v.* **-piles, -piled, -pil.ing 1** collect information from different sources and prepare a volume: *to compile a dictionary, encyclopedia, list, volume of ballads.* **2** translate a computer program in a high-level lan-

guage into machine language using another program called a **compiler**.
—**com.pi.la.tion** (com.puh.LAY.shun) n.

com.pla.cen.cy (cum.PLAY.sun.see) n. the state of being complacent: *a smug complacency about the future.* Also **com.pla.cence** (-sunce).

com.pla.cent (cum.PLAY.sunt) *adj.* self-satisfied; unconcerned: *He's quite complacent about the future; an air of complacent superiority.* —**com.pla.cent.ly** *adv.*

com.plain (cum.PLAIN) *v.* express or describe one's dissatisfaction, discomfort, annoyance, etc.: *He complains of an aching back; complains about the neighbor's dog; complains to his wife; complains bitterly, constantly, loudly.*

com.plain.ant (cum.PLAIN.unt) *n.* [legal use] one who makes a complaint.

com.plaint (cum.PLAINT) *n.* **1** an act of complaining; also, an accusation or grievance: *A neighbor's behavior brought complaints from the public; Jon made or registered a complaint against his neighbors; filed or lodged a complaint with the police; bitter, legitimate, loud complaints; He had grounds or cause for complaint; They did not disregard, ignore, or reject his complaint; They responded to his complaint but did not act on it.* **2** a cause for complaining, esp. an illness: *a stomach complaint.*

com.plai.sant (cum.PLAY.zunt, -sunt) *adj.* eager to please; obliging: *a complaisant attitude;* **com.plai.sant.ly** *adv.* —**com.plai.sance** (-sunce) *n.*

com.pleat (cum.PLEET) *adj.* [old spelling of "complete," now used for effect] proficient or expert: *"The Compleat Angler" by Izaak Walton; the compleat family man, politician, showman.*

com.plect.ed (cum.PLEC.tid) *adj.* Regional. complexioned.

com.ple.ment (COM.pluh.munt) *n.* **1** something that completes: *Fine wine is a complement to good food.* **2** a word or words completing a predicate, as "fine" in "I feel fine." **3** a complete set or number: *a full complement of 32 teeth; a ship with its complement (= crew) of men.* —*v.* (com.pluh.MENT) complete: *The couple complement each other; The hairdo complements her good looks.*

com.ple.men.ta.ry (com.pluh.MEN.tuh.ree) *adj.* that completes: *Green is complementary to red;* **Complementary colors,** as red and green, combine in light to form white; **Complementary angles** add up to a right angle.

com.plete (cum.PLEET) *adj.* **1** having all of its parts; entire: *a complete deck of cards; a dinner complete with cake and coffee; a more complete set of instructions.* **2** perfect; thorough: *complete happiness; a complete fool, stranger, waste; an almost complete absence, breakdown, isolation, silence; for a more complete control of the market.* **3** concluded; finished: *The job is not quite complete; almost, nearly complete; 98% complete.* —*v.* **-pletes, -plet.ed, -plet.ing 1** make complete or entire: *to complete a circle, collection, set.* **2** finish doing: *to complete a contract, job, mission, task;* **adj.**: *a completed exercise, lesson, manuscript.* —**com.plete.ly** *adv.;* **com.plete.ness** *n.* —**com.ple.tion** (-PLEE.shun) *n.*: *Our work is nearing completion; We get paid on completion of work.*

com.plex (cum.PLEX, COM.plex) *adj.* **1** composed of distinct but connected parts; not simple: *a complex machine, system; A* **complex sentence** *has a main clause and subordinate clauses; a* **complex fraction** *such as 1½ / 4 or 2 / 3¼.* **2** complicated: *a problem too complex for a ten-year-old; a complex network, situation, web.* —*n.* (COM.plex) **1** a combination of related things, as buildings: *an industrial complex; a village-sized apartment complex; vitamin B complex.* **2** any obsessive fear, belief, etc.: *People suffer from complexes; the Electra, inferiority, Oedipus, superiority complexes.* —**com.plex.i.ty** (cum.PLEX.i.tee) *n.* **-ties.**

com.plex.ion (cum.PLEK.shun) *n.* **1** the natural color and texture of the skin, esp. of the face: *clear, dark, fair, pale, ruddy, sallow complexions.* **2** character or aspect: *Nuclear bombs have altered the complexion of modern warfare.* —**com.plex.ioned** (-shund) *comb.form:* dark-, fair-, light-complexioned.

com.pli.ance (cum.PLY.unce) *n.* the act of complying or obeying: *a delivery made* **in compliance with** *a customer's wishes; compliance with rules and regulations;* **adja.**: *a compliance department, officer.*

com.pli.ant (cum.PLY.unt) *adj.* tending to comply, give in, or yield: *compliant behavior; a missile system that is fully compliant with the ABM treaty;* **com.pli.ant.ly** *adv.*

com.pli.cate (COM.pluh.cate) *v.* **-cates, -cat.ed, -cat.ing** make complex, involved, or difficult: *Why complicate matters? adj.:* a **complicated** (= hard to analyze, solve, or understand) *issue, plot, problem, relationship, situation.*

com.pli.ca.tion (com.pluh.CAY.shun) *n.* a complicated condition: *to avoid com-*

plications; *Complications may arise* or *set in during an illness.*

com.plic.i.ty (cum.PLIS.i.tee) *n.* association in guilt: *He is suspected of complicity in the plot; complicity between law enforcement officials and drug pushers.*

com.pli.ment (COM.pluh.munt) *n.* **1** an expression of praise, admiration, or politeness: *She paid her secretary a compliment; a compliment on his good work; Children fish for compliments; He lavished* or *showered compliments on his wife; Please give* or *convey our sincere compliments to the chef; a back-handed compliment.* **2 compliments** *pl.* usu. formal greetings: *a book presented with the author's compliments; We received it (with the) compliments of the author; The author presents her compliments; conveys* or *sends her compliments.* —*v.* (-ment) pay a compliment to someone: *We complimented the cook on his fine cooking.*

com.pli.men.ta.ry (com.pluh.MEN.tuh.ree) *adj.* **1** expressing a compliment: *the complimentary close of a letter, as "Yours truly"; a complimentary remark.* **2** gratis or free: *Coffee is complimentary; a complimentary copy of our book.*

com.ply (cum.PLY) *v.* **-plies, -plied, -ply.ing** act in accordance with something: *They swore never to comply with terrorists' demands.*

com.po.nent (cum.POH.nunt) *n.* one of the parts of a complex object or group: *Copper and tin are the main components of bronze; Speakers are essential components of a stereo system.* —*adja.* constituent: *a component element, part.*

com.po.nen.try (cum.POH.nun.tree) *n.* components of a system collectively: *componentry of an automobile chassis; computer componentry.*

com.port (cum.PORT) *v.* **1** be in agreement with or suitable to something: *Poor manners do not comport with high ideals.* **2** behave: *He comported himself well, with dignity;* **com.port.ment** *n.*

com.pose (cum.POZE) *v.* **-pos.es, -posed, -pos.ing 1** make up or constitute, as out of parts or elements: *Air is mainly composed of oxygen and nitrogen.* **2** create, esp. a work of music or literature: *to compose an ode, opera, poem, song, speech; He sings as well as composes* (= writes music). **3** set type, as a compositor. **4** settle: *Let's compose our differences.* **5** gain control of oneself: *to compose oneself, one's feelings, thoughts;* *adj.*: *She remained* **composed** (= in control of herself) *throughout the cross-examination;* **com.pos.ed.ly** (-zid.lee) *adv.*

com.pos.er (cum.POH.zur) *n.* one who writes music or songs: *a popular composer; a major composer such as Mozart.*

com.pos.ite (COM.puh.zit, cum.POZ.it) *adja.* **1** made up of distinct separate parts: *a composite photograph, portrait, print; a composite sketch of a suspect prepared by a police artist.* **2** belonging to a large family of plants having compound flower heads: *The daisy and the dandelion are composite flowers.* —*n.* something that is composite: *His character was a composite of instinct and education.*

com.po.si.tion (com.puh.ZISH.un) *n.* **1** the act, art, or result of composing: *to perform, play a (musical) composition; to write a composition* (= essay); *All our composition* (= typesetting) *is done by computer.* **2** the arrangement of parts or elements: *a photographer with a good sense of composition; the ethnic composition* (= makeup) *of our community.*

com.pos.i.tor (cum.POZ.uh.tur) *n.* a typesetter.

com.post (COM.post, *rhyme:* most) *n.* a combination of decayed plant matter, garbage, and manure, used as a fertilizer: *Send dirty diapers to the compost; adj.*: *a compost bin, heap, pile.* —*v.* make compost: *to compost waste; adj.*: **composted** *chicken manure, grass clippings; n.*: *backyard* **composting***; adja.*: *composting kits, plants, projects, sites, technology.* —**com.post.a.ble** (cum.POST.uh.bul) *adj.*: *compostable diapers.*

com.po.sure (cum.POH.zhur) *n.* calmness: *She kept her composure in spite of provocations; to lose, regain, retain one's composure.*

com.pote (COM.pote) *n.* **1** fruit stewed or preserved in a syrup. **2** a shallow, stemmed dish for serving fruit, nuts, etc.

com.pound (COM.pound) *n.* **1** the area enclosing a group of buildings, as of a factory, prison, or residences. **2** something made by the union of two or more parts or elements, as a word such as "spaceship" or a substance such as water (hydrogen and oxygen). —*adj.* having many parts: *a compound leaf, number, sentence; The* **compound eye** *of an insect has many light-sensitive units.* —*v.* (cum.POUND) **1** mix together or produce by combining: *A pharmacist sometimes compounds drugs as prescribed; Water is compounded of hydrogen and oxygen.* **2** calculate compound interest: *Interest on your savings is compounded quarterly.* **3** make greater: *to compound*

compound / computerize

an error; *The huge waves compounded the problem for the survivors in the lifeboat.*
compound fracture *n.* a broken bone causing an open wound in the skin.
compound interest *n.* interest charged on the principal of the debt and the accumulated interest.
com.pre.hend (com.pri.HEND) *v.* **1** grasp mentally; understand: *Do you comprehend the endlessness of time?* **2** include in its scope: *The humanities comprehend a whole range of subjects.*
com.pre.hen.si.ble (com.pri.HEN.suh.bul) *adj.* understandable: *The theory of relativity is not comprehensible to the lay person;*
 com.pre.hen.si.bly (-suh.blee) *adv.*
 —**com.pre.hen.si.bil.i.ty** (-suh.BIL.i.tee) *n.*
com.pre.hen.sion (com.pri.HEN.shun) *n.* understanding: *A theory that is beyond the lay person's comprehension; It defies, eludes comprehension;* *adj.:* *comprehension levels, tests.*
com.pre.hen.sive (com.pri.HEN.siv) *adj.* inclusive of everything: *a comprehensive examination, insurance coverage, survey; a comprehensive piece of legislation.*
 —**com.pre.hen.sive.ly** *adv.*
 —**com.pre.hen.sive.ness** *n.*
com.press (cum.PRES) *v.* **-press.es, -pressed, -press.ing** pack or squeeze into a smaller space; condense: *We could compress this essay into a paragraph;* *adj.:* *Tires contain* **compressed** *air (under more than atmospheric pressure); compressed computer data; a compressed style of writing; a compressed three-day work week.* —*n.* (COM.press) a pad of gauze or cloth used to apply moisture, heat, cold, or pressure to the body, as to stop bleeding or relieve pain.
 —**com.pres.sion** (cum.PRESH.un) *n.:* *the extreme compression of his style; the compression chamber of an auto engine.*
 —**com.pres.sor** *n.*
com.prise (cum.PRIZE) *v.* **-pris.es, -prised, -pris.ing 1** be made up of; contain: *Our team comprises 18 players.* **2** *Informal.* make up; compose: *18 players comprise our team; Our team is comprised of 18 players.*
com.pro.mise (COM.pruh.mize) *n.* **1** the settlement of a difference or disagreement by concessions on both sides: *to work out an acceptable, fair, reasonable compromise with the opposite party; They agreed on or came to or reached a compromise after much negotiation; a compromise between labor and management; The new stadium is a compromise between* (= combination of) *a football field and a baseball park.* **2** a concession of something bad or wrong: *We can't agree to a compromise of principles.* —*v.* **-mis.es, -mised, -mis.ing 1** settle by or make a compromise: *Labor compromised with the management; They compromised on several key issues; a compromising approach.* **2** to damage something: *We cannot compromise principles; Let's do it without compromising the quality of our work; Dick compromised his reputation by accepting a bribe;* *adj.:* *He has been in many* **compromising** (= dishonorable) *positions, situations; compromising documents, letters; Here's a compromising photograph of the poor fellow.*
comp.trol.ler (cun.TROH.lur) same as CONTROLLER.
com.pul.sion (cum.PUL.shun) *n.* **1** an act of compelling or the state of being compelled: *He lied under compulsion; She felt a moral compulsion to tell the truth.* **2** an obsessive urge: *a neurotic compulsion; She felt a compulsion to diet and then to go on an eating binge.*
 —**com.pul.sive** (-siv) *adj.:* *a compulsive liar, neurosis, smoker.*
com.pul.so.ry (cum.PUL.suh.ree) *adj.* required by law or regulation: *Primary school attendance is compulsory for children; compulsory arbitration, auto insurance, military service.*
com.punc.tion (cum.PUNK.shun) *n.* a feeling of guilt, regret, or remorse: *He cheats without the slightest compunction; He feels no compunction about cheating.*
com.pute (cum.PYOOT) *v.* **-putes, -put.ed, -put.ing** calculate mathematically or with a computer. —**com.pu.ta.tion** (comp.yoo.TAY.shun) *n.;* **com.pu.ta.tion.al** *adj.:* *computational errors, power, software.*
com.put.er (cum.PEW.tur) *n.* an electronic machine that stores, manipulates, and analyzes information, and performs mathematical calculations: *analog, desktop, digital, general-purpose, home, mainframe, personal computers; to program a computer; The bank's computer is down* (= not functioning).
 —**com.put.er.ist** *n.*
com.put.er.ize (cum.PEW.tuh.rize) *v.* **-iz.es, -ized, -iz.ing** prepare, make more efficient, or produce by means of a computer: *to computerize an accounting system, business;* *adj.:* **computerized** *bookkeeping, data, factories, jobs, typesetting, traffic signals.*
 —**com.put.er.i.za.tion** (-ruh.ZAY.shun, -rye-) *n.*

computer literate *n.* one who is able to use a computer.

com.rade (COM.rad, -rid) *n.* **1** an associate or pal: *a comrade in arms* (= fellow fighter). **2 Comrade** a member of a left-wing group, esp. a communist. —**com.rade.ly** *adj.* —**com.rade.ship** *n.*

con *adv., prep. & n.* See PRO AND CON. —*n. Slang.* a convict. —*v.* **cons, conned, con.ning 1** *Slang.* swindle; cheat: *She was conned into signing the contract; a scheme for conning people out of their savings; adja.: a con artist, game, man.* **2** [old use] study something carefully in order to learn it: *to con one's lessons.*

con bri.o (con.BREE.oh) *adv. Music.* with vigor or liveliness.

con.cat.e.na.tion (con.CAT.uh.NAY.shun) *n.* a connected group of events or things: *a concatenation of misfortunes.* —**con.cat.e.nat.ed** (-nay.tid) *adj.*

con.cave (con.CAVE) *adj.* curved inward like the inside surface of a ball. —**con.cav.i.ty** (-CAV.i.tee) *n.* **-ties.**

con.ceal (cun.SEEL) *v.* keep secret or out of sight; hide; *adj.: The guerrilla leader always carried a* **concealed** *weapon.* —**con.ceal.ment** *n.*

con.cede (cun.SEED) *v.* **-cedes, -ced.ed, -ced.ing 1** admit as true or valid; acknowledge: *He conceded our point; conceded that he had lost the election.* **2** yield; give up: *They conceded the game after five innings; In the final stages of a vote count, the runner-up often concedes the election to the leading candidate.*

con.ceit (cun.SEET) *n.* a too high estimation of one's own worth: *a pompous chap, full of conceit.* —**con.ceit.ed** *adj.*

con.ceive (cun.SEEV) *v.* **-ceives, -ceived, -ceiv.ing 1** become pregnant with a child: *A woman conceives a child; Sterile women can't conceive.* **2** form an idea or notion; imagine: *the "average American" as conceived by statisticians; Can you conceive of a unicorn in our zoo? They have conceived a great dislike for him.* —**con.ceiv.a.ble** (-vuh.bul) *adj.;* **con.ceiv.a.bly** (-vuh.blee) *adv.*

con.cel.e.brant (cun.SEL.uh.brunt) *n.* one of two or more priests who concelebrate.

con.cel.e.brate (cun.SEL.uh.brate) *v.* **-brates, -brat.ed, -brat.ing** celebrate Communion or a mass jointly. —**con.cel.e.bra.tion** (-BRAY.shun) *n.*

con.cen.trate (CON.sun.trate) *v.* **-trates, -trat.ed, -trat.ing 1** focus or fix one's attentions, efforts, etc.: *to concentrate our energies on the task in hand; I'm trying to concentrate (on what I am doing); adj.: to make a* **concentrated** *effort.* **2** exist, come, or bring together in one place: *The company is concentrating its manufacturing in the Far East; He has concentrated power in the hands of his followers; Troops are concentrating along the border; adj.: Populations are found* **concentrated** *in urban centers; Industrial areas are the most concentrated sources of air pollution; wealth concentrated in the hands of a few.* **3** make a solution stronger; *adj.: frozen* **concentrated** *orange juice; a concentrated acid solution; in concentrated form.* —*n.* a concentrated food product: *Vitamin C concentrate; Dilute the concentrate to make soup.*

con.cen.tra.tion (con.sun.TRAY.shun) *n.* **1** the act or state of concentrating: *Noises tend to disturb our concentration; She is lost in deep concentration.* **2** something concentrated: *troop concentrations at the border; a concentration* (= broad study) *in physical sciences.* **3** strength: *the concentration of a sugar solution.*

concentration camp *n.* a prison camp for prisoners of war, political prisoners, and other internees.

con.cen.tric (con.SEN.tric) *adj.* having a common center or axis: *Tree trunks show concentric annual rings; the concentric circles of a target;* **con.cen.tri.cal.ly** *adv.* —**con.cen.tric.i.ty** (-sun.TRIS.i.tee) *n.*

con.cept (CON.sept) *n.* a usu. general idea or notion of a class or thing: *The concept of tallness is formed from tall objects; to formulate, frame a concept; clear, vague, valid concepts; the old concept of the earth as being flat; a bold, new concept in engineering; The* **concept car** *at the auto show may become a reality if consumers like it; A* **concept shop** *or* **shop concept** *is a specialty store within a department store.*

con.cep.tion (cun.SEP.shun) *n.* **1** the act or process of conceiving: *the conception of a child in the womb; Does life begin at conception? the conception of new ideas in the mind.* **2** concept or idea: *He has no conception of what she's talking about; the popular conception of the sun as going around the earth.*

con.cep.tu.al (cun.SEP.choo.ul) *adj.* having to do with concepts or their formation: *at the conceptual stage; the visual, audible, and conceptual forms of a word;* **con.cep.tu.al.ly** *adv.*

con.cep.tu.al.ize (cun.SEP.choo.uh.lize) *v.* **-liz.es, -lized, -liz.ing** form a concept of an object: *It's hard to conceptualize the infinity of space; Language helps us conceptualize.*

con.cern (cun.SURN) *v.* **1** be the business of someone: *Does that concern you? a letter addressed "To Whom It May Concern";* **prep.:** *a memo concerning* (= regarding) *absentees.* **2** interest or involve oneself: *People should concern themselves with the running of their country;* **adj.:** *a concerned citizen; Courts are concerned with justice; As far as I am concerned, all days are equally good.* **3** cause worry or anxiety to someone; **adj.:** *a concerned parent; She is concerned that her child may get lost; She has reason to be concerned when her child is late from school; She is concerned about* or *over* or *for her child's safety.* —*n.* **1** something that involves or concerns someone: *This is no concern of mine.* **2** regard or anxiety: *a question that arouses, causes, gives us concern; We expressed, felt, showed, voiced our concern about* or *over the matter; our concern that she might die of the illness; We did it out of concern for her health; Crime is an object of considerable, grave, growing, particular, public, serious concern; Her illness is a cause of deep concern to us.* **3** a business: *a mining concern; a going* (= successful) *concern; a paying* (= profitable) *concern.*
con.cert (CON.surt) *n.* **1** a program of public musical entertainment: *band, pop, rock concerts; A concert is canceled, given, held, staged; people at a concert.* **2** unity in action, opinion, etc.: *the concert of Europe against Napoleonic France.* —**in concert** in harmony: *acting, working in concert with others; voices raised in concert against the new bill.*
con.cert.ed (cun.SUR.tid) *adja.* mutually planned or accomplished; combined: *The Opposition made concerted efforts to topple the Government; concerted action, attacks;* **con.cert.ed.ly** *adv.*
con.cer.ti.na (con.sur.TEE.nuh) *n.* a small, accordionlike musical instrument: *high prison fences topped with concertinas* (= coils) *of barbed wire.*
con.cer.ti.no (con.chur.TEE.noh) *n.* a short concerto.
con.cert.mas.ter (CON.surt.mas.tur) *n.* the first violinist and usu. assistant conductor of an orchestra.
con.cer.to (cun.CHAIR.toh) *n.* **-tos** a piece of music for one or more solo instruments and orchestra: *to perform, play a concerto; a piano concerto; a violin concerto.*
con.ces.sion (cun.SESH.un) *n.* **1** the act of conceding or something conceded: *a concession to public demand.* **2** a piece of land or a privilege granted by a government or business, esp. to operate an industry or other business: *a food concession at a fair; mining, oil, parking concessions.* —**con.ces.sion.ar.y** (-uh.nair.ee) *adj.: concessionary tariffs.*
con.ces.sion.naire (cun.SESH.uh.NAIR) *n.* one holding an industrial or commercial concession.
con.ces.sive (cun.SES.iv) *adj.* having to do with conceding something: *"Although he left" is a concessive clause.*
conch (CONK, CONCH) *n.* **conchs** (CONKS) or **conch.es** (CON.chiz) **1** a large sea mollusk. **2** its spiral shell.
con.ci.erge (con.see.AIRZH) *n.* **1** the doorkeeper and usu. custodian of a building, esp. an apartment building. **2** a hotel official who caters to the special needs of guests.
con.cil.i.ate (cun.SIL.ee.ate) *v.* **-ates, -at.ed, -at.ing** win the goodwill of someone; placate.
con.cil.i.a.tion (cun.SIL.ee.AY.shun) *n.* the act or state of conciliating, esp. the settlement of a dispute by negotiation and compromise; **con.cil.i.a.tor** (-ee.ay.tur) *n.* —**con.cil.i.a.to.ry** (-ee.uh.tor.ee) *adj.: a conciliatory approach, gesture, message, speech, tone.*
con.cise (cun.SICE) *adj.* brief but expressing much; terse: *a concise expression, report, style;* **con.cise.ly** *adv.;* **con.cise.ness** *n.* —**con.ci.sion** (cuh.SIZH.un) *n.: the concision of her style.*
con.clave (CON.clave) *n.* a private or secret assembly, esp. of cardinals to elect a new pope: *budget conclaves; a party conclave.*
con.clude (cun.CLOOD, long "OO") *v.* **-cludes, -clud.ed, -clud.ing 1** end or finish: *The fair concluded on Friday; We concluded the meeting at 9 p.m.* **2** decide on the basis of evidence: *The court concluded that he was guilty.* **3** agree on or settle something: *to conclude a business deal with Japan.*
con.clu.sion (cun.CLOO.zhun) *n.* **1** end: *at the conclusion of the meeting;* **In conclusion** (= In ending), *I would like to thank everyone concerned.* **2** inference or judgment: *to arrive at, bring to, come to, draw, jump to a conclusion; erroneous, inevitable, reasonable, valid conclusions; The jury reached the conclusion that the accused was guilty; It was not a foregone* (= predetermined) *conclusion.*
con.clu.sive (cun.CLOO.siv) *adj.* decisive or final for ending doubt: *conclusive evidence, proof, studies.* —**con.clu.sive.ly** *adv.*
con.coct (cun.COCT) *v.* **1** prepare, often crudely, by mixing ingredients to-

gether: *a soup concocted from leftovers.* 2 invent: *a story concocted for the press;* **adj.:** *a concocted excuse, plot, scheme, story.* —**con.coc.tion** *n.*: *a new concoction whipped up for the occasion.*

con.com.i.tant (cun.COM.uh.tunt) *adj.* happening along with something else; accompanying: *circumstances concomitant with an event;* **n.:** *Disease is often a concomitant of poverty.*

con.cord (CON.cord) *n.* harmony or agreement, as in music, grammar (i.e. case, number, gender, or person), or between people: *an era of peace and concord between England and France; when France lived in concord with England.*

con.cor.dance (cun.COR.dunce) *n.* a listing of each word of a text in its context: *to compile a Shakespeare concordance.*

con.cor.dant (cun.COR.dunt) *adj.* agreeing; harmonious: *actions that are concordant with our principles; concordant musical notes.*

con.cor.dat (cun.COR.dat) *n.* an official agreement, esp. one between a pope and a state.

con.course (CON.corse) *n.* 1 a large space milling with people, as the main hall of a railroad terminal or a broad thoroughfare: *the vast concourse of Union Station; the main concourse of an airport; an underground shopping concourse.* 2 a coming together; hence, a great crowd: *a concourse of circumstances, events, people.*

con.cres.cence (con.CRES.unce) *n.* a growing together, as of cells or flower petals.

con.crete (CON.creet) *adj.* 1 existing in real experience of the senses, not abstract: *concrete evidence, examples, facts, figures, proof; a concrete noun such as "book," "flower," "girl"; A beautiful flower is beauty* **in the concrete.** 2 specific or definite, not vague or general: *concrete ideas, plans, proposals, terms; concrete thoughts that we can act upon.* 3 made of concrete: *concrete masonry; a concrete building block, mix, road surface, shelter, slab, walkway, wall;* a **concrete mixer** (that mixes concrete for pouring); *cement mixer); a* **concrete jungle** *full of skyscrapers.* —**n.** a hard building material made of sand, small stones, and cement: *to pour concrete into forms for hardening; pre-stressed, ready-mix, reinforced concrete; precast concrete used for pipes, beams, and girders.*
—*v.* (con.CREET) **-cretes, -cret.ed, -cret.ing** pave or coat with concrete;

adj.: *a concreted sidewalk.*

con.cre.tion (con.CREE.shun) *n.* 1 a hardening or solidifying. 2 something solidified, as minerals in rock or stones in the kidney.

con.cu.bine (CONK.yuh.bine) *n.* a woman kept by a man as his mistress or secondary wife. —**con.cu.bi.nage** (con.KEW.buh.nij) *n.*

con.cu.pis.cence (cun.KYOO.pi.sunce) *n.* a strong, usu. sensual desire, esp. lust; **con.cu.pis.cent** *adj.*

con.cur (cun.CUR) *v.* **-curs, -curred, -cur.ring** Formal. agree: *I concur fully, completely with you; I concur with your opinion; We concur that the building should be torn down; They concur in supporting abolition of capital punishment; They concur on almost everything;* **adja.:** *a concurring opinion.*

con.cur.rence (cun.CUR.unce) *n.* agreement: *The Liberals were in full concurrence with the Conservatives; The bill was passed with the concurrence of all parties.*

con.cur.rent (cun.CUR.unt) *adj.* 1 taking place at the same time: *two concurrent three-year sentences; a* **concurrent resolution** *(passed by both houses of a legislature).* 2 meeting or tending to meet at a point: *concurrent forces, lines.* —**con.cur.rent.ly** *adv.*

con.cus.sion (cun.CUSH.un, "USH" as in "rush") *n.* a severe shock or injury to the brain, as by a fall or blow on the head: *to receive, suffer a concussion; severe, simple, slight concussions.*

con.demn (cun.DEM) *v.* 1 utter strong criticism of a person or thing: *atrocities condemned by humanity.* 2 declare guilty: *He was condemned as a traitor; condemned for selling secrets to the enemy.* 3 to sentence or doom: *A murderer used to be condemned to death; He was condemned to 10 years in jail; condemned to live the rest of his life in disgrace;* **adj.:** *a* **condemned** *criminal.* 4 declare unfit for use; **adj.:** *a* **condemned** *bridge, building, property.* —**con.dem.na.to.ry** (-nuh.tor.ee) *adj.* —**con.dem.na.tion** (con.dum.NAY.shun) *n.*

con.dense (cun.DENSE) *v.* **-dens.es, -densed, -dens.ing** 1 make or become more dense or concentrated: *Water vapor condenses as dew; to condense light rays with a lens;* **adj.:** *Dew is* **condensed** *moisture; condensed (= evaporated and sweetened) milk, soup; condensed (= less wide), not expanded type.* 2 express in fewer words: *to condense an essay into a paragraph; to condense it to half its length;* **adj.:** *a story in* **condensed** *form; a condensed account, book, version.*

condenser / conduit

—**con.den.sa.tion** (con.den.SAY.shun) *n.*
con.dens.er (cun.DEN.sur) *n.* **1** See CAPACITOR. **2** any device for condensing, esp. light rays or vapors.
con.de.scend (con.di.SEND) *v.* be gracious enough to do something that is beneath one's dignity: *He condescended to meet with the servants;* **adj.**: *His manner was somewhat* **condescending** (= superior); **con.de.scend.ing.ly** *adv.*
—**con.de.scen.sion** (-SEN.shun) *n.*
con.dign (cun.DINE) *adj. Formal.* deserved, though harsh: *condign punishment.*
con.di.ment (CON.duh.munt) *n.* a food seasoning, as relish, mustard, or spices.
con.di.tion (cun.DISH.un) *n.* **1 conditions** *pl.* circumstances: *Under normal conditions it doesn't snow here in July; weather conditions; unsanitary working conditions; abnormal, difficult, ideal, squalid conditions; economic conditions; market conditions.* **2** a state of being, fitness, or health, seen as changeable: *a motor in good running condition; in bad, excellent, operating, poor, terrible condition; a patient in critical, fair, good, satisfactory, serious, stable condition; He's either* **in** *or* **out of condition** (= physically fit or unfit) *for a marathon.* **3** what something depends on for its being or happening; requirement: *the terms and conditions of an offer; a condition of the offer; the essential conditions for survival; to fulfill, impose, meet, satisfy, set, stipulate a condition; a bail condition; He spoke* **on condition that** *he not be identified;* **on condition of** *anonymity.* **4** a disease: *to have a heart condition; a skin condition such as acne.*
—*v.* **1** make conditional: *She led a life conditioned by her mother's whims.* **2** put into good condition: *Exercise conditions your body;* **n.**: *aerobic* **conditioning**; *a conditioning program.* **3** accustom or train: *Pavlov conditioned dogs to expect food every time a bell rang;* **adj.**: *a conditioned reflex, response.* —**con.di.tion.al** *adj.*; **con.di.tion.al.ly** *adv.*
con.di.tion.er (cun.DISH.nur) *n.* a cosmetic or other substance added to something to improve its quality: *hair, skin, water conditioners.*
con.do (CON.doh) *n.* **-dos** *Informal.* a condominium building or unit.
con.dole (cun.DOLE) *v.* **-doles, -doled, -dol.ing** feel or express sympathy: *They condoled with her on her husband's death.*
con.do.lence (cun.DOH.lunce) *n.* (expression of) sympathy: *We conveyed, expressed, offered our heartfelt, sincere condolences to the widow; a letter of condolence; Our condolences on the death of your husband.*
con.dom (CON.dum) *n.* a thin rubber sheath for the penis, for use in sexual intercourse to prevent infection and as a contraceptive.
con.do.min.i.um (con.duh.MIN.ee.um) *n.* **1** a residential building or complex in which single units are owned individually and the common property is owned and maintained jointly; also, a unit in this. **2** a territory controlled by two or more states: *the former Anglo-Egyptian condominium in the Sudan.*
con.done (cun.DOHN) *v.* **-dones, -doned, -don.ing** overlook or implicitly forgive misbehavior: *She would condone sloppiness, but not skipping school.*
—**con.do.na.tion** (con.duh.NAY.shun) *n.*
con.dor (CON.dur) *n.* a large vulture.
con.duce (cun.DUCE, *rhyme:* produce) *v.* **-duc.es, -duced, -duc.ing** tend to lead: *an atmosphere that conduces to study.* —**con.du.cive** (-DEW.siv) *adj.*: *an atmosphere that is conducive to study; a conducive climate, environment.*
con.duct (CON.duct) *n.* **1** behavior: *He was charged with disorderly conduct; conduct unbecoming an officer; early parole for good conduct.* **2** management: *the conduct of foreign affairs.*
—*v.* (cun.DUCT) **1** lead or guide: *A guide conducts a tour; She conducts tourists through the museum; He conducts them into and out of the building.* **2** manage: *the officer conducting the company's financial affairs.* **3** behave: *She conducts herself like a professional; He conducts himself with dignity.* **4** transmit: *The ability to conduct heat or electricity is one of the physical properties of matter.*
con.duc.tance (cun.DUC.tunce) *n.* the ability of something to conduct electricity.
con.duc.tion (cun.DUC.shun) *n.* transmission of heat or electricity by contact.
con.duc.tive (cun.DUC.tiv) *adj.* able to conduct heat, electricity, etc. —**con.duc.tiv.i.ty** (con.duc.TIV.i.tee) *n.*
con.duc.tor (cun.DUC.tur) *n.* **1** the leader or director of an orchestra or choir. **2** the person in charge of a bus, passenger train, etc. **3** something that enables heat, electricity, or sound to pass through: *a lightning conductor.*
con.duit (CON.dit, -doo.it) *n.* a pipe, channel, or tubing for carrying liq-

condyle / confide

uids, enclosing electric wires, etc.: *The secretary acted as a conduit (of information) to the minister.*

con.dyle (CON.dile) *n.* a rounded projection at the end of a bone which forms part of a joint. —**con.dy.lar** (-duh.lur) *adj.*

cone *n.* 1 a three-dimensional surface or solid with a usu. circular base, tapering to a point. 2 anything in this shape: *an ice-cream cone; the cone of a volcano; a pine cone* (= the dry, scaly fruit of a pine).

con.es.to.ga (con.is.TOH.guh) *n.* a sturdy covered wagon used esp. by prairie pioneers. Also **Conestoga wagon.**

co.ney (COH.nee) *n.* **-neys** or **-nies** same as CONY.

con.fab *v.* **-fabs, -fabbed, -fab.bing** *Informal.* confabulate; *n.* confabulation.

con.fab.u.late (cun.FAB.yuh.late) *v.* **-lates, -lat.ed, -lat.ing** talk together informally; confer; chat. —**con.fab.u.la.tion** (-LAY.shun) *n.*

con.fec.tion (cun.FEC.shun) *n.* a sweet treat, as candy, pastry, or ice cream; sweet delicacy. —**con.fec.tion.er** *n.*

con.fec.tion.er.y (cun.FEC.shuh.nair.ee) *n.* **-er.ies** 1 confections collectively. 2 a confectioner's shop.

con.fed.er.a.cy (cun.FED.uh.ruh.see) *n.* **-cies** an alliance of countries or states: *They formed a confederacy among the states; A Confederacy of 11 southern U.S. states broke away from the Union in 1860-61.*

con.fed.er.ate (cun.FED.uh.rate) *v.* **-ates, -at.ed, -at.ing** join or form into an alliance of people, organizations, states, etc. —*n.* (-rit) 1 an ally or accomplice. 2 a supporter of the U.S. Confederacy; *adj*a.: *a confederate army, dollar, government; the 11 Confederate States of America.*

con.fed.er.a.tion (cun.FED.uh.RAY.shun) *n.* 1 the act of confederating. 2 an alliance or union, esp. of states or countries: *The 13 colonies called their confederation the United States of America; the Articles of Confederation; the Confederation of National Trade Unions.* 3 **Confederation** the federal union of the Canadian provinces in 1867: *Newfoundland joined Confederation in 1949, as the tenth province.*

con.fer (cun.FUR) *v.* **-fers, -ferred, -fer.ring** 1 consult; exchange views: *Let's confer with the president on or about the new budget.* 2 grant or bestow: *to confer an honorary degree on the ambassador.* —**con.fer.ment** *n.*

con.fer.ee (con.fuh.REE) *n.* 1 one on whom something is conferred. 2 one taking part in a conference.

con.fer.ence (CON.fuh.runce) *n.* 1 a conferring or consulting: *I had a conference with my son's teacher; news, press, staff conferences; a conference between the two parties; a conference of teachers; a conference on teaching methods; The boss is in conference.* 2 a league of sports teams, schools, etc. —*v.* confer: *Teachers conference with parents.*

conference call *n.* a telephone call for talking with different people in different places at the same time.

con.fess (cun.FES) *v.* 1 acknowledge or admit, usu. a crime or fault: *I confess that I was mistaken; I confess my mistake; I confess to being mistaken; He confessed to everything he was charged with; He confessed to the police.* 2 tell one's sins to a priest to seek God's forgiveness: *I confess my sins; I confess to having sinned.* 3 of a priest, absolve someone from sins. —**con.fes.sed.ly** (-id.lee) *adv.*

con.fes.sion (cun.FESH.un) *n.* 1 the act or result of confessing, esp. a written statement or the telling of one's sins: *I have a confession to make; The "people's court" forced him to sign a confession; The confession was extorted from him; a forced, full, public confession; The accused repudiated, took back, withdrew her confession when she was set free; He made a voluntary deathbed confession that he was the real culprit; Priests hear confessions and forgive sins; to go to confession during Lent.* 2 a declaration of religious beliefs: *a confession of faith.* 3 a Christian denomination; communion: *the various confessions within Christianity.*

con.fes.sion.al (cun.FESH.uh.nul) *n.* an enclosure for private confession.

con.fes.sor (cun.FES.ur) *n.* 1 one who confesses. 2 a priest who hears confessions.

con.fet.ti (cun.FET.ee) *n.pl.* [takes *sing. v.*] little pieces of colored paper for throwing about in celebrations, esp. at weddings.

con.fi.dant (CON.fuh.dant) *n.* a person trusted with personal secrets; **con.fi.dante** (con.fuh.DANT, CON.fuh.dant) *fem.*

con.fide (cun.FIDE) *v.* **-fides, -fid.ed, -fid.ing** 1 tell or give to another in secrecy or trust; entrust: *the folly of confiding secrets to strangers; The child was confided to a neighbor's care.* 2 trust: *She confides in her parents;* **con.fid.ing** *adj.;* **con.fid.ing.ly** *adv.*

con.fi.dence (CON.fuh.dunce) *n.*
1 trust; reliance: *I place or put no confidence in his promises; He enjoyed, gained, had, won our confidence; She inspires, instills confidence in her followers; to have absolute, every, perfect confidence in someone's ability; Our confidence was shaken by his behavior.* **2** a feeling of assurance in oneself: *to face the future with confidence; He lacked the confidence to invest in the project.* **3** a trusting secrecy: *They told us everything in (the) strictest confidence; She took her brother into her confidence.* **4** a secret: *They used to exchange confidences; would never betray a confidence; He was accused of violating a confidence.* —*adja.* swindling; con: *a confidence game, man, trick.*
con.fi.dent (CON.fuh.dunt) *adj.* sure of oneself; certain: *a confident and aggressive sales rep; She is confident of the outcome of the trial; confident that she will win.* —**con.fi.dent.ly** *adv.*
con.fi.den.tial (con.fuh.DEN.shul) **1** *adj.* secret: *a strictly personal and confidential letter; confidential information, papers; a confidential* (= trusting) *tone of voice.* **2** *adja.* trusted with private affairs: *a confidential assistant, secretary, servant.*
—**con.fi.den.tial.ly** *adv.*
—**con.fi.den.ti.al.i.ty** (CON.fuh.den.shee.AL.i.tee) *n.*
con.fig.u.ra.tion (cun.FIG.yuh.RAY.shun) *n.* **1** a particular arrangement of parts or components: *the configuration of atoms in a molecule; the configuration of hardware and software working together as a system.* **2** outline or shape: *a planetary configuration; the configuration of the ocean floor.*
con.fig.ure (cun.FIG.yur) *v.* **-ures, -ured, -ur.ing** adapt or arrange the parts of a system to suit a particular purpose: *We configure computers to make the best use of the funds available.*
con.fine (cun.FINE) *v.* **-fines, -fined, -fin.ing** keep within limits or barriers; restrict: *His social life was confined to weekends; a soldier confined to quarters; Avoid arguments and confine yourself to the facts.*
con.fine.ment (cun.FINE.munt) *n.* a being confined: *He was put in solitary confinement; It happened during her confinement in hospital.*
con.fines (CON.fines) *n.pl.* limits: *Stay within the confines of your home.*
con.firm (cun.FURM) *v.* **1** strengthen: *Adversity only confirmed him in his resolve.* **2** verify: *The rumor was confirmed by later developments.* **3** make firm or definite: *to confirm an airline reservation; The decision has to be confirmed by the president; The children were confirmed* (as members by a religious rite) *at 13.*
—**con.firm.a.to.ry** (-muh.tor.ee) *adj.*
—**con.fir.ma.tion** (con.fur.MAY.shun) *n.*
con.firmed (cun.FURMD) *adja.* settled or unchanging: *a confirmed alcoholic, bachelor, invalid.*
con.fis.cate (CON.fis.cate) *v.* **-cates, -cat.ed, -cat.ing** seize property by public authority: *The heroin was confiscated by the police;* **con.fis.ca.tor** *n.;* **con.fis.ca.tion** (-CAY.shun) *n.*
—**con.fis.ca.tor.y** (cun.FIS.cuh.tor.ee) *adj.*
con.fla.gra.tion (con.fluh.GRAY.shun) *n.* a very destructive fire.
con.flate (con.FLATE) *v.* **-flates, -flat.ed, -flat.ing** combine or merge into one: *His history is often conflated with myths and legends.*
con.flict (CON.flict) *n.* **1** a fight; struggle: *an armed, direct conflict between two nations; a conflict about or over territorial rights; a conflict among the neighbors; Neighbors come into conflict with each other; to provoke, resolve a conflict; two parties who are always* **in conflict***; conflict resolution.* **2** a clash of opposing interests or viewpoints: *the unending conflict between religion and politics; a* **conflict of interest***, as between an official's public duty and private interest; His version of the accident is* **in conflict** (= disagreement) *with yours.* —*v.* (cun.FLICT) be in opposition; clash: *My interests conflict with yours;* *adj.:* *He feels unsure, somewhat* **conflicted** *about which offer to accept; conflicted emotions, relationships; People are torn by* **conflicting** *desires; conflicting claims, emotions, goals, views.*
con.flu.ence (CON.floo.unce) *n.* **1** a flowing together, as of two rivers. **2** a coming together, as of a crowd. Also **con.flux.** —**con.flu.ent** *adj.:* *confluent streams.*
con.form (cun.FORM) *v.* **1** correspond to or be like a pattern: *a pillow that conforms to the contours of the head and neck; A building should conform to the architect's specifications.* **2** comply with: *In some schools, students have to conform to a dress code; to conform to guidelines, norms, regulations, requirements, tenets.* **3** behave like others according to established norms: *No problem as long as you conform.* —**con.form.a.ble** *adj.* agreeable: *Her demands were not conformable to reason.* —**con.form.ance** *n.*
—**con.form.ist** *n.*

con.for.ma.tion (con.fur.MAY.shun) *n.* 1 a formation or structure. 2 the build of a racehorse.

con.form.i.ty (cun.FOR.mi.tee) *n.* agreement: *His actions were in conformity with his beliefs; We acted in conformity with her wishes; conformity with the dictates of reason, with the law, with orders; full, strict, total conformity; in conformity to local customs, demands, ideals, rules, standards.*

con.found (cun.FOUND) *v.* 1 confuse by surprising: *The weather confounded the forecasters; to confound one's critics, foes, opponents.* 2 mix up: *They had confounded fact with fancy.* —**con.found.ed** *adja. Informal.* damned: *those confounded communists!*

con.fra.ter.ni.ty (con.fruh.TUR.ni.tee) *n.* -ties 1 a brotherhood or association of confreres. 2 a religious or charitable group.

con.frere (CON.frair) *n.* 1 a fellow member of a religious community. 2 *Informal.* colleague.

con.front (cun.FRUNT) *v.* come or bring face to face with; meet and challenge: *The two armies confronted each other along the border; He had nothing to say when confronted with the facts.*

con.fron.ta.tion (con.frun.TAY.shun) *n.* active face-to-face opposition: *an atmosphere of confrontation; It provoked a direct confrontation with the police; civil rights confrontations; Question period in the House of Commons is a time of confrontation between Government and Opposition.* —**con.fron.ta.tion.al** *adj.*

Con.fu.cian (cun.FEW.shun) *n.* a follower of **Confucius**, a Chinese moral philosopher of the 6th c. B.C.: *a dedicated Confucian; adj.: Confucian teachings.* —**Con.fu.cian.ism** *n.*

con.fuse (cun.FUZE) *v.* **-fus.es, -fused, -fus.ing** 1 bewilder or perplex: *Too many brand names confuse the consumer; adj.: I'm quite **confused** by the conflicting versions of the incident; I find it very **confusing**.* 2 fail to distinguish: *Let's not confuse the issues; People confuse Tim and Tom or with his twin brother Tom.* —**con.fus.ed.ly** (-zid.lee) *adv.: to refer confusedly to the wrong twin;* **con.fus.ing.ly** *adv.: Twins are confusingly similar.*

con.fu.sion (cun.FEW.zhun) *n.* 1 a mixing up: *the confusion of tongues at the Tower of Babel.* 2 disorder: *It caused, created, was a scene of utter confusion; Complete confusion reigned; Arrangements were thrown into confusion by a last-minute change of plans.*

con.fute (cun.FYOOT) *v.* **-futes, -fut.ed, -fut.ing** prove a person, statement, etc. wrong. —**con.fu.ta.tion** (conf.yuh.TAY.shun) *n.*

con.ga (CONG.guh) *n.* 1 an Afro-Cuban dance performed by several dancers moving in single file. 2 a tall, thin, hand-beaten drum.

con.geal (cun.JEEL) *v.* thicken or solidify, as by freezing; coagulate or clot; *adj.: congealed blood, fat;* **con.geal.ment** *n.* —**con.ge.la.tion** (con.juh.LAY.shun) *n.*

con.ge.ner (CON.juh.nur) *n.* a person or thing of the same class or genus, as butter and margarine, lion and other cats, etc.

con.gen.ial (cun.JEEN.yul) *adj.* 1 of similar tastes and character: *congenial companions.* 2 agreeable or pleasing: *work that is congenial to his temperament; a congenial atmosphere, climate, weather.* —**con.gen.ial.ly** *adv.* —**con.ge.ni.al.i.ty** (-nee.AL.i.tee) *n.*

con.gen.i.tal (cun.JEN.uh.tul) *adj.* 1 present from birth: *a congenital abnormality, defect; congenital blindness, brain damage, heart disease; He has a congenital aversion to math.* 2 born: *a congenital latecomer, shoplifter; her congenital altruism.* —**con.gen.i.tal.ly** *adv.*

con.ger eel (CONG.gur-) *n.* a marine eel with coarse edible flesh.

con.ge.ries (CON.juh.reez) *n. sing. & pl.* a collection; pile: *an ill-assorted congeries of buildings.*

con.gest (cun.JEST) *v.* be or make too full, esp. parts of the body, with blood; clog. —**con.ges.tive** (-tiv) *adj.*

con.gest.ed (cun.JES.tid) *adj.* too full or clogged: *downtown streets congested with traffic; a congested airport, area, schedule, slum; congested lungs (clogged by blood).* —**con.ges.tion** (-chun) *n.: to relieve traffic congestion during the rush hour; nasal congestion; congestion of the lungs.*

con.glom.er.ate (cun.GLOM.uh.rit) *n.* 1 a composite mixture: *Canada is a conglomerate of world cultures.* 2 a corporation with widely diversified enterprises and interests. —**con.glom.er.a.tion** (-RAY.shun) *n.*

con.grat.u.late (cun.GRACH.uh.late) *v.* **-lates, -lat.ed, -lat.ing** express pleasure at another's success or good luck: *a message congratulating her on her graduation.* —**con.grat.u.la.tion** (-LAY.shun) *n.: We extend, offer our deep, hearty, sincere, warmest congratulations on or upon your graduation.* —**con.grat.u.la.to.ry** (-luh.tor.ee) *adj.: a congratulatory message.*

con.gre.gate (CONG.gruh.gate) *v.* **-gates, -gat.ed, -gat.ing** gather togeth-

er: *where kids tend to congregate.*
con.gre.ga.tion (cong.gruh.GAY.shun) *n.* **1** a gathering. **2** people attending a place of worship, esp. those present at a service.
con.gre.ga.tion.al (cong.gruh.GAY.shun.ul) *adj.* **1** having to do with a congregation. **2 Congregational** pertaining to the union of Protestant churches that practice **Congregationalism,** the self-government of local congregations; **Con.gre.ga.tion.al.ist** *n.*
con.gress (CONG.gris) *n.* **1** a meeting or convention: *to convene, hold a congress; a party congress.* **2** a national legislature: *the U.S. Congress.*
Con.gres.sion.al (con.GRESH.uh.nul) *adj.* having to do with the U.S. Congress: *a Congressional hearing; a **Congressional district** (each electing a representative); **Congressional Record** (= official report of proceedings of Congress).*
con.gress.man (CONG.gris.mun) *n.* **-men** a member of the U.S. House of Representatives. —**con.gress.wom.an** *n.* **-wom.en.**
con.gru.ent (CONG.roo.unt) *adj.* corresponding or agreeing: *Iraq and Iran have congruent interests in the Gulf; Their interests may not be congruent with those of Western nations;* **con.gru.ent.ly** *adv.* —**con.gru.ence** or **con.gru.i.ty** (cong.GROO.i.tee) *n.* Also **con.gru.ous** (-us) *adj.;* **con.gru.ous.ly** *adv.*
con.ic (CON.ic) or **con.i.cal** (-i.cul) *adj.* shaped like or pertaining to a cone: *a clown's conical cap; The parabola and ellipse are conic sections; a **conic** or **conical projection** (= map with radiating meridians and concentric parallels).*
con.i.fer (CON.uh.fur) *n.* a cone-bearing, usu. evergreen tree or bush, as the pine, spruce, and fir.
—**co.ni.fer.ous** (coh.NIF.uh.rus) *adj.: coniferous forests, trees, woods.*
con.jec.ture (cun.JEK.chur) *v.* **-tures, -tured, -tur.ing** guess because of insufficient evidence: *We can only conjecture that no lives have been lost in the accident;* *adj.:* **a conjectured** *estimate, figure.* —*n.:* *a report based on mere conjecture.* —**con.jec.tur.al** (-chuh.rul) *adj.: Fashion forecasting is more conjectural than weather forecasting; conjectural estimates, variations.*
con.join (cun.JOIN) *v.* join together: *Siamese twins conjoined at the back.*
—**con.joint** *adj.: individual and conjoint marital counseling;* **con.joint.ly** *adv.*
con.ju.gal (CON.juh.gul) *adj. Formal.* having to do with marriage: *the conjugal bliss of honeymooners; conjugal life, love, rights.* —**con.ju.gal.ly** *adv.*
con.ju.gate (CON.juh.gate) *v.* **-gates, -gat.ed, -gat.ing 1** give the inflected forms of a verb. **2** join together, as in marriage. —**con.ju.ga.tion** (-GAY.shun) *n.:* "Take-took-taken" is a **strong conjugation;** "Call," "move," and "add" belong to **weak conjugations** *that use "-ed" for the past tense and past participle.* —**con.ju.ga.tion.al** *adj.*
con.junc.tion (cun.JUNK.shun) *n.* **1** union or alignment: *The storm was caused by a rare conjunction of the Earth, Sun, and Moon; a note to be read in conjunction with the report.* **2** a connecting word: *"But," "and," "or," etc. are conjunctions used to link words, phrases, and clauses.*
con.junc.ti.va (con.junc.TYE.vuh) *n.* **-vas** or **-vae** (-vee) the mucous membrane that covers the eyeball and lines the inside of the eyelids.
con.junc.tive (cun.JUNK.tiv) *adj.* **1** conjoining; also, conjoined. **2** serving as a conjunction: *"But" is a conjunctive word.*
con.junc.ti.vi.tis (cun.JUNK.tuh.VYE.tis) *n.* the inflammation of the conjunctiva.
con.junc.ture (cun.JUNK.chur) *n.* a crucial combination of circumstances.
con.jure *v.* **-jures, -jured, -jur.ing 1** (CUN.jur, CON.jur) summon spirits, the devil, etc. by magic or a spell: *Magicians conjure rabbits out of their hats; The music* **conjured up** (= brought to mind) *visions of the Orient; John Smith is not exactly* **a name to conjure with** (= not a powerful or important name). **2** (cun.JOOR) *Formal.* appeal to, esp. by an oath: *I conjure you by all that's holy to hear my plea.* —**con.jur.er** or **con.jur.or** (CUN.jur.ur, CON-) *n.*
conk *v. Informal.* hit over the head.
—**conk out** *Informal.* **1** stop functioning suddenly: *Our motor conked out.* **2** collapse with fatigue; lose consciousness: *Father just conked out after a hard day.* **3** die: *Quit smoking before you conk out.*
con.nect (cuh.NECT) *v.* **1** link, join, or be joined: *My telephone line is connected to the rest of the system; The operator can connect me with anyone who has a phone; Our house was connected up only yesterday; I didn't connect you* (= link you mentally) *with the person who called yesterday;* *adj.:* *You are* **connected** *to your in-laws by marriage; You have been connected with them since your marriage; closely, intimately, loosely connected; We*

catch a **connecting** *flight out of Kansas.* **2** in sports, hit, shoot, throw, etc. successfully: *connected for a line drive.* —**con.nec.ted.ly** *adv.* —**con.nect.er** or **con.nec.tor** *n.*

con.nec.tion (cuh.NEC.shun) *n.* **1** a link or linkage: *There must be a loose connection in the wiring somewhere; Please speak up, we seem to have a bad connection; to establish a connection between smoking and cancer; to break* or *sever our connection with that party; to make a connection; a close, intimate connection; a tenuous connection; a company with many foreign, international connections* (= ties); *an executive with many business, professional, and social connections* (= acquaintances); *I missed my connection* (= connecting flight) *in Paris.* **2** an influential person: *He got the job through connections on his wife's side.* —**in connection with** in relation to: *They mentioned his previous job in connection with the present one.* —**in this** or **that** or **what connection** in relation to this or that or what: *In what connection did he mention my name?*

con.nec.tive (cuh.NEC.tiv) *adj.* connecting: *connective tissue.* —*n.* a word that connects, as a relative pronoun or conjunction.

conning tower *n.* the observation tower on top of a submarine.

con.nip.tion (cuh.NIP.shun) *n. Informal.* a fit of violent rage, alarm, excitement, etc.: *Grandma will have conniptions* or *a conniption if she finds out.* Also **conniption fit.**

con.nive (cuh.NIVE) *v.* **con.nives, con.nived, con.niv.ing 1** intentionally ignore wrongdoing: *Some officials connived at the use of drugs by athletes.* **2** secretly cooperate or conspire to do something wrong or unlawful: *He is known to be conniving with underworld figures to traffic in heroin.*
—**con.niv.ance** *n.*

con.nois.seur (con.uh.SUR) *n.* an expert in an area of artistic taste: *a connoisseur of art, furniture, wines.*

con.no.ta.tion (con.uh.TAY.shun) *n.* what a word means besides its strict or denotative meaning: *the unpleasant connotations of "capitalist."* —**con.no.ta.tive** (CON.uh.tay.tiv) *adj.: connotative meaning; the connotative values of words.*

con.note (cuh.NOTE) *v.* **con.notes, con.not.ed, con.not.ing** of words, convey as a meaning secondary to the strict meaning or denotation: *"Foreign" may connote hostility, but "imported" connotes distinctiveness.*

con.nu.bial (cuh.NEW.bee.ul) *adj.* of marriage; conjugal: *connubial bliss.*

con.quer (CONK.ur) *v.* gain mastery of a person or thing: *to conquer a country, one's fears, bad habits; to conquer a people (by defeating them); to conquer a mountain (by climbing it); Love conquers all; adj.: a conquered fortress, people, territory; adja.: a conquering army, hero, power.*
—**con.quer.or** *n.*

con.quest (CONK.west) *n.* the act of conquering or something conquered: *the Norman Conquest (of England); Alexander consolidated his conquests as he extended them eastward; the conquest of Mt. Everest; a final conquest; world conquests; Don Juan made the conquest of his lady's heart; Mexico was a Spanish conquest* (= conquered territory).

con.quis.ta.dor (con.QUIS.tuh.dor, cong.KEES-) *n.* **-dors** or **-dor.es** (-dor.eez, -dor.aze) a 16th-century Spanish conqueror in Central or South America.

con.san.guin.e.ous (con.san.GWIN.ee.us) *adj.* related by blood.

con.san.guin.i.ty (con.sang.GWIN.i.tee) *n.* relationship by blood: *Marriage is traditionally prohibited within certain degrees of consanguinity.*

con.science (CON.shunce) *n.* the awareness of right and wrong that prompts one to do good and avoid evil: *a cold-blooded murderer whose conscience never bothers him; She appealed to their conscience to release the innocent prisoner; a prisoner of conscience (in jail because of political or religious beliefs); He stole something and had it on his conscience all week; had a guilty conscience; He returned it as a matter of conscience; He could say with a clear conscience that he hadn't stolen anything; He had to return what he had taken* **in all conscience** (= in truth or fairness); **conscience money** (*paid to ease one's conscience*).

con.sci.en.tious (con.shee.EN.shus) *adj.* **1** ruled by or according to one's moral convictions: *a conscientious decision; A* **conscientious objector** *refuses to go to war.* **2** scrupulous and painstaking: *She's very conscientious about her duties.*
—**con.sci.en.tious.ly** *adv.*

con.scious (CON.shus) *adj.* **1** aware of or alert to: *He is fully conscious of the risks involved; quite conscious that there are risks involved.* **2** awake or mentally active: *The patient became conscious and started moving.* **3** aware of oneself, one's thoughts, and one's actions; deliberate: *Breathing is not a conscious activity; He made a conscious effort to im-*

prove; *a conscious artist, choice, omission.* —**con.scious.ly** *adv.*

con.scious.ness (CON.shus.nis) *n.* **1** the state of being conscious: *He was struck on the head and lost consciousness; It was hours before he recovered* or *regained consciousness.* **2** awareness: *He tried to raise the consciousness of the community to the danger of an epidemic; class, political, social consciousness.*

con.script (cun.SCRIPT) *v.* to compel by law into military service: *Canadians were conscripted into the army in 1917.* —*n.* (CON.script) one conscripted or drafted; draftee. —**con.scrip.tion** (cun.SCRIP.shun) *n.*

con.se.crate (CON.suh.crate) *v.* **-crates, -crat.ed, -crat.ing** make sacred or set aside as sacred, hallowed, or for religious use: *Bread and wine are consecrated during Mass; He consecrated* (= dedicated) *his life to helping the homeless.* —**con.se.cra.tion** (-CRAY.shun) *n.*: *the consecration of a new chapel.*

con.sec.u.tive (con.SEK.yuh.tiv) *adj.* following one after the other; successive: *He missed three consecutive days of school; absent for the fourth consecutive day.* —**con.sec.u.tive.ly** *adv.*

con.sen.sus (cun.SEN.sus) *n.* general agreement: *They could not reach a consensus on capital punishment or its abolition; There was a consensus that a vote on the question be postponed;* **consensus politics** *(based on finding agreement).*

con.sent (cun.SENT) *v.* give approval; agree: *He consented to be operated on; consented to the operation;* **adj.**: *He did it as a* **consenting** *adult.* —*n.* agreement: *to give, refuse, withhold one's consent; a plan adopted by common consent; general, mutual, parental, tacit consent; A patient's informed consent is required for an operation.*

con.se.quence (CON.suh.quence) *n.* **1** a result or effect: *We have to take the consequences of our actions; far-reaching, grave, inevitable, unforeseen consequences; He ignored repeated warnings and* **in consequence** *he was fired.* **2** importance: *a matter of little or no consequence; a woman of some consequence in her firm.*

con.se.quent (CON.suh.quent) *adj.* following logically or resulting as a consequence: *a major fire with a consequent loss of lives; The position was declared vacant consequent on* or *upon his resignation.* —**con.se.quent.ly** *adv.*

con.se.quen.tial (con.suh.QUEN.shul) *adj.* **1** following as a result: *consequential damages.* **2** of importance: *consequential changes in taxation; a consequen-* *tial appointment, decision, role.* **3** self-important: *His consequential manner doesn't impress anyone.*

con.ser.van.cy (cun.SUR.vun.see) *n.* **-cies** an organization dedicated to the conservation of natural resources: *a nature conservancy.*

con.ser.va.tion (con.sur.VAY.shun) *n.* the preservation or careful and controlled use, esp. of natural resources: *energy, forest, fuel, soil, water, wildlife conservation; conservation officers; a* **conservation road** *(giving access to a conservation area).* —**con.ser.va.tion.ist** *n.*

con.ser.va.tism (cun.SUR.vuh.tiz.um) *n.* a tendency to keep things as they are and resist social or political change.

con.ser.va.tive (cun.SUR.vuh.tiv) *adj.* **1** conforming to moderate or traditional tastes, views, etc.: *He wears conservative clothes; a conservative* (= reasonably low) *estimate; a conservative* (= solid or safe) *investment portfolio.* **2** given to conservatism: *conservative and progressive forces; conservative governments, parties, politics.* —*n.* **1** a conservative person: *a dyed-in-the-wool conservative; a political conservative; a small "c" conservative.* **2** **Conservative** a member or supporter of a conservative party; Tory. —**con.ser.va.tive.ly** *adv.*

con.ser.va.tor (CON.sur.vay.tur) *n.* a protector or guardian, esp. for one legally incompetent.

con.ser.va.to.ry (cun.SUR.vuh.tor.ee) *n.* **-ries 1** a school of music, drama, etc. **2** a glass-covered building or room for growing plants and flowers.

con.serve (cun.SURV) *v.* **-serves, -served, -serv.ing 1** keep in unchanged condition, without waste or destruction, for later use: *to conserve one's energy, resources, strength; to conserve capital, electricity, soils.* **2** preserve fruit by stewing with sugar. —*n.* (also CON.surv): *a strawberry conserve.*

con.serv.er (cun.SUR.vur) *n.* one that conserves: *Our survival depends on changing from a consumer society to a* **conserver society.**

con.sid.er (cun.SID.ur) *v.* think about with a purpose: *They considered her application; took time to consider; They considered it briefly, carefully, favorably, religiously, seriously; considered* (= believed or judged) *her qualified, intelligent, a genius; They had considered him (to be) not promotable; They considered her (as a candidate) for his job; considered her as his replacement; He considered* (= contemplated) *resigning, his alternatives, where*

to go; *They said he had done a good job,* **all things considered** (= everything being taken into account); *He had done a good job,* **considering**; *an especially good job* **considering** (= taking into account) *his inexperience, considering that he was inexperienced;* **adj.a.:** *That was their* **con.sid.ered** (= studied) *opinion.*
con.sid.er.a.ble (cun.SID.uh.ruh.bul) *adj.* important enough to be considered; great or large: *a woman of considerable influence; a considerable amount, sum, weight; She went to considerable trouble to help us; a man of considerable means* (= wealthy man). —**con.sid.er.a.bly** *adv.*
con.sid.er.ate (cun.SID.uh.rit) *adj.* thoughtful of others: *a kind and considerate boss; very considerate of the needs of others; considerate to* or *toward everyone.*
con.sid.er.a.tion (cun.SID.uh.RAY.shun) *n.* **1** careful thought: *His considerations on mortality give one food for thought; But have some consideration for her feelings; The award was made in consideration of her services to the community; The application is submitted for your consideration; We will take everything into consideration; Nothing will be left out of consideration; It is under consideration; They voted after lengthy consideration; On careful consideration, we have decided to reject it;* **On no consideration** (= in no case) *can we make an exception to the rules.* **2** something to consider: *Location is an important consideration in buying a house; an overriding consideration; Money is of no consideration* (= importance) *when we are looking for the best; He sold everything for $1 plus other considerations* (= benefits); *He will assign you a better seat, for a consideration* (= payment).
con.sign (cun.SIGN) *v.* **1** give over: *an orphan consigned to the state's custody; to consign papers to the fire.* **2** send goods, esp. to an agent for sale.
—**con.sign.or** or **con.sign.er** —**con.sign.ee** (CON.suh.nee, con.sye.NEE) *n.*
con.sign.ment (cun.SIGN.munt) *n.* a shipment of goods to a dealer: *It was shipped* **on consignment** (= to be paid for if and when sold).
con.sist (cun.SIST) *v.* **1** be made up or composed: *The team consists of six players.* **2** have as basis: *Loyalty consists in devotion to a person or cause.*
con.sis.ten.cy (cun.SIS.tun.see) *n.* **-cies** **1** degree of thickness or solidity of a thick liquid: *soil of gummy consistency; the consistency of molasses, syrup.* **2** conformity to previous actions, principles, etc.
con.sis.tent (cun.SIS.tunt) *adj.* conforming, not contradictory: *He followed a consistent policy throughout his career; a report that is not consistent with the facts; He has been a consistent* (= regular) *loser.* —**con.sis.tent.ly** *adv.*
con.sis.to.ry (cun.SIS.tuh.ree) *n.* **-ries** a solemn council, as of a church.
con.so.la.tion (con.suh.LAY.shun) *n.* comfort in sorrow or disappointment: *Her children were a consolation to the widow in her sorrow; They afforded consolation; Friends offered consolation; letters of consolation; It was a consolation to know* or *consolation knowing that the children were safe, a consolation that no one was hurt; a $100,000 grand prize and a $2,000* **consolation prize** (for coming close to winning).
con.sole (CON.sole) *n.* **1** a cabinet for a TV, radio, etc. that sits on the floor; **adj.a.:** *a console model, TV, unit.* **2** a control panel, as of a washing machine or stove: *a car with a gear-shift console on the driver's right; A computer operator sits at a console* (= desklike control unit). **3** the part of an organ having the stops, keys, etc.
—*v.* (cun.SOLE) **-soles, -soled, -sol.ing** comfort: *to console a widower on his wife's death; They consoled themselves with thoughts of a better future.*
con.sol.i.date (cun.SOL.uh.date) *v.* **-dates, -dat.ed, -dat.ing** **1** form or combine into one mass or organization; **adj.a.:** *a* **consolidated** (= central) *school in a rural area; a consolidated* (= unified) *school district; consolidated assets, revenues, sales.* **2** make secure or firm; strengthen: *to consolidate the company's position; Studying for an exam consolidates what you have learned.*
—**con.sol.i.da.tion** (-DAY.shun) *n.*
—**con.sol.i.da.tor** (-day.tur) *n.*
con.som.mé (CON.suh.may, con.suh.MAY) *n.* a clear soup made from meat or vegetables.
con.so.nance (CON.suh.nunce) *n.* **1** agreement; harmony, esp. of musical notes. **2** a rhymelike agreement of similar consonants but not vowels, as in *pull* and *will.*
con.so.nant (CON.suh.nunt) *adj.p.* in harmony or agreement: *a statement not consonant with his previous policies.*
—*n.* a sound or letter other than the vowels *a, e, i, o,* and *u.*
—**con.so.nan.tal** (-NAN.tul) *adj.:* *consonantal sounds.*
con.sort (CON.sort) *n.* a ruling mon-

consortium / constitutive

arch's spouse: *the prince who is the Queen's consort; the queen consort* (= king's wife). —*v.* (cun.SORT) **1** associate: *He's known to consort with drug pushers.* **2** agree: *Their actions do not consort with their principles.*

con.sor.ti.um (cun.SOR.shee.um, -SOR.tee.um) *n., pl.* **-ti.a** (-shee.uh) a combination of companies for a large-scale investment or other activity: *an oil-pipeline consortium; a consortium for the study of artificial intelligence.*

con.spec.tus (cun.SPEC.tus) *n.* a summary of something under consideration for an overall view.

con.spic.u.ous (cun.SPIC.yoo.us) *adj.* noticeable; remarkable: *He has been conspicuous for his charitable works; The president was **conspicuous by her absence** (because she was expected to be present); the **conspicuous consumption** of luxuries by the newly rich.*
—**con.spic.u.ous.ly** *adv.;* **con.spic.u.ous.ness** *n.*

con.spir.a.cy (cun.SPEER.ruh.see) *n.* **-cies** a secret planning, esp. by a group to act jointly to do something wrong; also, the plan or plot: *The rebellion began as a conspiracy; a conspiracy with the army to take over a government; a criminal conspiracy to commit arson, murder; to crush, foil a conspiracy; to hatch, organize a conspiracy against the leadership; a **conspiracy of silence** by witnesses unwilling to testify.*
—**con.spir.a.tor** (-tur) *n.*
—**con.spir.a.tor.i.al** (-TOR.ee.ul) *adj.*

con.spire (cun.SPIRE) *v.* **-spires, -spir.ed, -spir.ing** **1** plot together secretly: *They were accused of conspiring to overthrow the government.* **2** work together: *Many events conspired to spoil their plans.* —**con.spir.er** *n*

con.sta.ble (CON.stuh.bul) *n.* a police officer of the lowest rank.

con.stab.u.lar.y (cun.STAB.yuh.lair.ee) *n.* **-ries** **1** a police force. **2** an armed paramilitary force: *the Irish constabulary.*

con.stant (CON.stunt) **1** *adja.* continual or continuous: *There's a constant flow of water from the spring; the constant round of parties; constant change, pain, use, vigilance.* **2** *adj.* fixed: *a constant velocity, voltage, pressure; The jobless rate seems to remain constant.* **3** *adja.* faithful or true: *a constant companion, friend, supporter.* —*n.* an unchanging factor or quantity, not a variable: *The speed of light is a constant; Fear is a constant in criminal groups.* —**con.stant.ly** *adv*
—**con.stan.cy** *n.*

con.stel.la.tion (con.stuh.LAY.shun) *n.* a group of stars, as the Great Bear, Gemini, etc.: *a constellation of movie stars.*

con.ster.na.tion (con.stur.NAY.shun) *n.* shock or dismay that bewilders or confuses: *The announcement caused consternation in the audience; People looked for the exit in consternation; To their consternation, the doors were found locked.*

con.sti.pate (CON.stuh.pate) *v.* **-pates, -pat.ed, -pat.ing** cause constipation.

con.sti.pa.tion (con.stuh.PAY.shun) *n.* difficulty in emptying the bowels.

con.stit.u.en.cy (cun.STICH.oo.un.see) *n.* **-cies** **1** an electoral district represented by a member of a legislature. **2** a body of voters, supporters, or clients.

con.stit.u.ent (cun.STICH.oo.unt) *n.* **1** a member of a constituency: *The legislator writes to her constituents regularly.* **2** a part or component: *Fat is one of the constituents of milk.* —**adja.** **1** having to do with voters: *constituent affairs, complaints, pressure.* **2** component: *Fat is a constituent part of milk; a constituent element.* **3** empowered to write or change a constitution: *a constituent assembly.*

con.sti.tute (CON.stuh.tute) *v.* **-tutes, -tut.ed, -tut.ing** **1** be the parts of something; form or make up: *Twelve people normally constitute a jury.* **2** be regarded as: *an action that constitutes fraud; What constitutes greatness?* **3** set up or appoint: *to constitute an assembly;* *adj.*: *a duly **constituted** representative.*

con.sti.tu.tion (con.stuh.TUE.shun) *n.* **1** the makeup of anything, esp. a person's physical condition: *an iron, not weak constitution; Exercise is good for your constitution.* **2** the basic rules or laws of a state, nation, corporation, club, etc.: *to adopt, amend, draft, promulgate, uphold, write a constitution.*

con.sti.tu.tion.al (con.stuh.TUE. shuh.nul) *adj.* **1** physical: *a constitutional tendency to gain weight; a constitutional inability to tell a lie.* **2** having to do with a legal constitution: *Is this law constitutional? a constitutional amendment, convention, lawyer; The United Kingdom is a **constitutional monarchy**, the monarch having only limited power.* —*n.* Informal. a walk taken for one's health: *She's out taking her constitutional.*
—**con.sti.tu.tion.al.i.ty** (-NAL.i.tee) *n.*

con.sti.tu.tive (CON.sti.tue.tiv) *adj.* **1** that constitutes; hence, essential: *The constitutive elements of water are oxygen and hydrogen.* **2** that has power or authority: *a constitutive committee with con-*

stitutive powers.

con.strain (cun.STRAIN) v. restrain or confine: *He was constrained in iron chains; Clothes that constrain you may affect the safety of your driving.*

con.strained (cun.STRAINED) 1 adjp. forced or obliged: *The judge said she felt constrained to impose a long jail sentence.* 2 adja. strained or artificial: *a constrained laugh, silence, smile.*

con.straint (cun.STRAINT) n. 1 compulsion: *The prisoner obeyed only* **under constraint.** 2 restriction: *the constraints of military discipline; legal constraints; to place or put, to impose constraints on or upon trade between countries.*

con.strict (cun.STRICT) v. make smaller or tighter, as by tension: *to constrict arteries, blood vessels, tissues.*
—**con.stric.tion** n.; **con.stric.tive** (-tiv) adj.

con.stric.tor (cun.STRIC.tur) n. 1 a muscle that compresses, as those of the throat used in swallowing. 2 a snake that kills its prey by squeezing, as a boa or python.

con.struct (cun.STRUCT) v. build skillfully by putting parts together: *to construct an argument, bridge, model airplane; Students of geometry construct triangles.* —**con.struc.tor** n.

con.struc.tion (cun.STRUCK.shun) n. 1 the act of building, a building, or the building industry: *Our new house is under construction* (= being built); *commercial, modular, residential construction; a shoddy construction* (= building); *He is in construction* (= the building industry); **adja.**: *the construction business, boom; a construction engineer, firm; Everyone wears a helmet on a construction site.* 2 interpretation: *She put the wrong construction on what I said.* 3 arrangement of words: *the construction of a sentence; an idiomatic construction* (= phrase or sentence).

con.struc.tion.ist (cun.STRUC.shuh.nist) n. one who interprets laws, the Constitution, etc. in a specified way: *a strict constructionist.*

con.struc.tive (cun.STRUC.tiv) adj. useful: *Do something constructive; constructive criticism; a constructive policy, role, suggestion.* —**con.struc.tive.ly** adv.

con.strue (cun.STROO) v. **-strues, -strued, -stru.ing** 1 interpret: *The meaning of a sentence sometimes depends on how you construe it; He construed her words as a snub rather than as a compliment.* 2 analyze grammatically: *Long and involved sentences are hard to construe.* —**con.stru.al** n.

con.sul (CON.sul) n. an official appointed to protect a country's citizens and business interests in a foreign city.
—**con.su.lar** (-lur) adj. —**con.sul.ship** n.

con.sul.ate (CON.suh.lit) n. the position, residence, or offices of a consul.

con.sult (cun.SULT) v. 1 ask or refer to for advice or information: *He's gone to consult his lawyer about the case; She frequently consults her dictionary while studying; He consults* (= confers) *with his wife before making any decision; Our company consulted for* (= gave advice to) *the Royal Commission;* **n.**: *A* **consulting engineer** *gives expert advice.* 2 consider: *We have to consult our own best interests first.*

con.sult.ant (cun.SUL.tunt) n. one who can give expert advice on a specific subject: *business, educational, legal, medical, tax consultants; He works as a consultant for an engineering firm; a consultant to the minister on tax reform; a consultant in linguistics, a consultant* (= medical specialist) *in children's diseases.*
—**con.sul.tan.cy** n. **-cies.**

con.sul.ta.tion (con.sul.TAY.shun) n. the act of consulting: *She holds consultations with her staff about or on all important matters; It's better not to disturb her when she is in consultation.*

con.sul.ta.tive (cun.SUL.tuh.tiv) adj. advisory: *a consultative assembly, committee, council; The lawyer advised her in his consultative capacity.*

con.sum.a.ble (cun.SOO.muh.bul) n. something that can be consumed or used up: *food, fuel, and other consumables; office consumables such as pads and pencils.* —**adj.**: *consumable goods, items, supplies; a* **consumable book** (= a workbook that is discarded after use).

con.sume (cun.SOOM, long "OO") v. **-sumes, -sumed, -sum.ing** 1 eat or drink; also, get and use for oneself: *Moviegoers consume a lot of popcorn; Industrialized nations with 30% of the world's population consume 70% of its resources.* 2 destroy: *The house was consumed by fire.* 3 take up completely; engross: *Physics consumes all her time and energy;* **adja.**: *It's her* **consuming** *interest; a consuming passion.*

con.sum.er (cun.SOO.mur) n. a user of goods and services, as opposed to producer: *a consumers' association;* **adja.**: *a consumer cooperative; consumer appeal, awareness, credit, demand, education, protection, research, resistance.*

consumer goods n.pl. goods such as food, appliances, and automobiles that are produced for the use of the general public.

con.sum.er.ism (cun.SOO.muh.riz.um) n. a movement for protecting consumers from false advertising, unsafe products, etc. —**con.sum.er.ist** n.

consumer price index same as COST-OF-LIVING INDEX.

consumer society n. a society that consumes products and services unnecessarily.

con.sum.mate (CON.sum.it, cun.SUM.it) adja. complete or perfect, esp. skilled: *a consummate artist, liar, politician, virtuoso.*
—v. (CON.suh.mate) **-sum.mates, -sum.mat.ed, -sum.mat.ing** to complete or fulfill: *to consummate a deal, merger, sale; to consummate a marriage (with an act of sexual intercourse).*
—**con.sum.ma.tion** (-MAY.shun) n.

con.sump.tion (cun.SUMP.shun) n. **1** a consuming or being consumed: *the consumption of food; consumption by fire; an engine's fuel consumption* (= amount used up). **2** tuberculosis of the lungs.

con.sump.tive (cun.SUMP.tiv) adj. **1** having to do with consuming: *the consumptive needs of society; oil for consumptive use on a farm.* **2** [old use] having to do with tuberculosis: *a consumptive cough.* —n. a tuberculosis patient.

con.tact (CON.tact) n. **1** the touching of two objects; also, the state of being in touch or having a communications link: *to come in(to), establish, make, maintain, stay in, bring into, break off, lose contact with someone; to have body, close, cultural, intimate, direct, eye, face-to-face, personal, physical, social contact; at the point of contact; The bomb exploded on contact with the ground; She has not been in contact* (= in touch) *for some time.* **2** an electrical connection: *a device for breaking contact.* **3** an acquaintance: *business, international, professional, social contacts.* —v. to place, come, or get in contact with someone: *Let us contact headquarters first.* —**adja.**: *contact cement, men, periods, persons, printing; contact transmission of diseases;* **contact flying** *by observing landmarks.*

contact lens n. a light corrective lens placed over the pupil of the eye.

contact sport n. a sport such as football or hockey that involves body contact.

con.ta.gion (cun.TAY.jun) n. **1** the passing of a disease from one person to another by contact. **2** a disease so passed on or its cause. **3** the general spread of a bad influence: *Steps have to be taken before the contagion spreads among the student population.*

con.ta.gious (cun.TAY.jus) adj. **1** spreading by contact: *Plague is extremely, highly contagious; Strictly speaking, malaria is not contagious but infectious.* **2** loosely, infectious: *a contagious viral disease.* **3** catching: *Her enthusiasm is contagious; contagious laughter.*
—**con.ta.gious.ly** adv.; **con.ta.gious.ness** n.

con.tain (cun.TAIN) v. **1** hold within oneself or itself: *My purse contains just 75 cents; This bottle contains* (= has a capacity of) *two liters; 6 contains* (= is divisible exactly by) *2 and 3.* **2** hold in check; hold back: *They tried to contain the enemy on the left flank; to contain a fire; to contain an oil spill using booms; Green belts of parkland are used to contain urban sprawl; She can't contain herself for joy; He can't contain his enthusiasm.*

con.tain.er (cun.TAY.nur) n. **1** one that contains: *airtight, covered, glass, storage, trash, used containers.* **2** a large shipping receptacle of usu. standard size that can be carried easily on a **container ship,** or on a specially designed railroad car, or **container car.**

con.tain.er.ize (cun.TAIN.uh.rize) v. **-iz.es, -ized, -iz.ing** pack and ship freight in containers. —**con.tain.er.i.za.tion** (-ruh.ZAY.shun, -rye-) n.

con.tain.ment (cun.TAIN.munt) n. a containing or checking: *the containment of rising insurance rates.*

con.tam.i.nant (cun.TAM.uh.nunt) n. something that contaminates: *radioactive contaminants in the water.*

con.tam.i.nate (cun.TAM.uh.nate) v. **-nates, -nat.ed, -nat.ing** to dirty, infect, or taint by contact: *Pesticides can contaminate the water supply.*
—**con.tam.i.na.tion** (-NAY.shun) n.

con.temn (cun.TEM) v. treat or regard with contempt.

con.tem.plate (CON.tum.plate) v. **-plates, -plat.ed, -plat.ing** think about or look at thoughtfully: *to contemplate the view from the hilltop; He says he never contemplated quitting the team.*
—**con.tem.pla.tor** (-play.tur) n.

con.tem.pla.tion (con.tum.PLAY.shun) n. thoughtful consideration: *the contemplation of beauty.*

con.tem.pla.tive (cun.TEM.pluh.tiv) adj. given to contemplation: *a contemplative life, monk, religious order.* —n. one who lives a life of contemplation.

con.tem.po.ra.ne.ous (cun.TEM.puh.RAY.nee.us) adj. occurring at the same period as another: *two contempo-*

contemporary / continence

raneous events; **con.tem.po.ra.ne.ous.ly** adv. —**con.tem.po.ra.ne.i.ty** (-ruh.NEE.i.tee) n.
con.tem.po.rar.y (cun.TEM.puh.rair.ee) adj. **1** existing at the same period as another: *Laurier's life was contemporary with Queen Victoria's reign.* **2** modern; present-day: *contemporary English, events, furniture, styles, trends.*
—*n., pl.* **-ries** a person of the same period as another: *Laurier was a contemporary of Queen Victoria; Jo and I were contemporaries in school.*
con.tem.po.rize (cun.TEM.puh.rize) v. **-riz.es, -rized, -riz.ing** modernize: *the marketing need to contemporize old lines of goods.*
con.tempt (cun.TEMPT) n. **1** a regarding or being regarded as base, negligible, worthless, etc.; scorn: *Cowards deserve contempt; They should be treated with contempt; deep, profound, total, utter contempt; The bikers demonstrated, displayed, showed contempt for the law.* **2** a challenging of the authority or dignity of a judge or legislature: *He was held in contempt of court for disobeying a court order;* **civil contempt** (= disobedience of a decree issued by a court); **criminal contempt** (= flouting of a judge's authority in court). —**con.temp.ti.ble** adj.: *contemptible behavior; It was contemptible* (= deserving contempt) *of him to spit in front of her.* —**con.temp.ti.bly** adv.
con.temp.tu.ous (cun.TEM.choo.us) adj. full of or showing contempt; scornful: *a contemptuous look, sneer; a biker who is contemptuous of all authority; It was contemptuous of him* (= showing contempt) *to spit in front of her.*
con.tend (cun.TEND) v. **1** compete, as in combat or debate, *for* a prize, position, etc. *with* a person, situation, etc.: *The pioneers had to contend with the elements.* **2** claim or maintain: *He contends that you misled him.* —**con.tend.er** n.: *the leading contender; a likely contender for the leadership of the party.*
con.tent (CON.tent) n. **1 contents** pl. what is contained: *the contents of a box; a book's table of contents; the contents of a confidential letter.* **2** substance: *All objects have form and content; a book with no intellectual content; the content analysis of a book, film, etc.* **3** amount contained: *The salt content of butter is about 3%.* **4** (cun.TENT) satisfaction: *He ate to his heart's content.* —v. (cun.TENT) satisfy or please: *a modest man who contents himself with what he has achieved;* adj.: *a contented life, look, smile.*

—*adj.* (cun.TENT) satisfied: *He is content with his lot in life; content to remain as a clerk.*
con.ten.tion (cun.TEN.shun) n. **1** disagreement or rivalry that shows itself in fighting and controversy: *a bone of contention between the two parties; two advertisers appearing in contention* (= competition) *with each other.* **2** a disputed statement: *to rebut, refute a contention; It is his contention that you misled him.*
con.ten.tious (cun.TEN.shus) adj. **1** causing rivalry or dissent: *a contentious argument that never ends; a contentious claim that is hard to settle.* **2** having a fighting attitude: *a contentious and argumentative fellow; his contentious nature.* —**con.ten.tious.ly** adv.; **con.ten.tious.ness** n.
con.tent.ment (cun.TENT.munt) n. a satisfied state: *a life of peace and contentment.*
content sale n. the sale of everything in a house.
content word n. a word that refers to a thing or action, as nouns and verbs, not grammatical functions, as articles, prepositions, and pronouns.
con.ter.mi.nous (cun.TUR.muh.nus) adj. having the same or a common boundary; **conterminous United States** the continental U.S. minus Alaska.
con.test (CON.test) n. **1** competition: *baby, beauty, oratorical contests; to enter, hold, judge, stage a contest; a contest among friends; a contest between teams; a contest for a prize.* **2** a fight or dispute: *bitter, hard-fought, close, one-sided contests.* —v. (cun.TEST) **1** compete for something: *to contest a seat in an election.* **2** fight or argue over something: *He always contests his traffic tickets in court.* —**con.test.a.ble** adj. —**con.test.ant** n.
con.text (CON.text) n. the surrounding words that determine a word's meaning: *to be unfairly quoted out of context; a display showing key words in their contexts; a keyword-in-context* (= KWIC) *display; a dangerous admission to make in the context* (= circumstances) *of the trial.* —**con.tex.tu.al** (-TEX.choo.ul) adj.
con.tig.u.ous (cun.TIG.yoo.us) adj. touching along all or most of one side; next in space or time: *Canada is contiguous with or to the U.S.; the 48 contiguous states (excluding Alaska and Hawaii); A movie is made up of contiguous still pictures.* —**con.ti.gu.i.ty** (con.tig.YOO.i.tee) n.
con.ti.nence (CON.tuh.nunce) n. self-

restraint, esp. the ability to control a bodily need or function such as sex, urination, or evacuation.

con.ti.nent (CON.tuh.nunt) *adj.* having to do with or showing continence: *helping patients to become continent again; a continent patient.* —*n.* **1** one of the seven large continuous land masses, i.e., Africa, Antarctica, Asia, Australia, Europe, and North and South America: *Britain is in the continent of Europe.* **2 the Continent** mainland Europe in relation to Britain: *Britons like to holiday on the Continent.*

con.ti.nen.tal (con.tuh.NEN.tul) *adja.* having to do with a continent: *The Antarctic is one continental glacier; Hawaii is outside the continental U.S.; a* **continental breakfast** *of coffee and rolls (in European style); the* **Continental Divide** (= the high ground formed by the Rocky Mountains separating rivers flowing to the Atlantic from those flowing to the Pacific); *the* **continental drift** *theory of the movement of continents;* A **continental shelf** (= sloping sea bed) *contains continental deposits washed down by rivers.* —*n.* a person from mainland Europe.

con.tin.gen.cy (cun.TIN.jun.see) *n.* **-cies** a possibility that depends on chance or uncertain conditions: *An unforeseen contingency may arise; Be prepared for all contingencies; To provide for every contingency is impossible.* —**adja.**: *a contingency plan; a* **contingency fee** *(chargeable only if specified conditions are met); a* **contingency fund** *(to cover unexpected losses).*

con.tin.gent (cun.TIN.junt) **1** *adjp.* dependent: *His arrival is contingent on or upon the weather.* **2** *adja.* possible but uncertain: *a contingent agreement, plan; contingent sales charges.* —*n.* a number of people or things forming part of a larger group: *a contingent of cavalry, ships, troops; a campus with large contingents of overseas students.*

con.tin.u.al (cun.TIN.yoo.ul) *adj.* repeated frequently; periodic but unceasing: *a beach eroded by the continual action of the waves; Her sleep was disturbed by the continual barking of a dog.* —**con.tin.u.al.ly** *adv.*

con.tin.u.ance (cun.TIN.yoo.unce) *n.* a continuation or its duration: *his continuance in office; the continuance of a crisis.*

con.tin.ue (cun.TIN.yoo) *v.* **-ues, -ued, -u.ing** **1** go on being or doing something; carry on: *The strike continues; He wants to continue in his job; to continue as a clerk; to continue at the factory; to continue for another year; to continue on his career, journey; to continue with his work; She continues making or to make mistakes; The trains continue to be late; The nuisance continues unabated; It may continue all summer; The lecture continued after lunch; He takes night courses at a school of* **continuing education** (= adult education). **2** resume: *Dr. Smith continued the lecture after lunch.* **3** extend: *The mandate was continued for another year.* **4** adjourn: *The hearing was continued for a week.* —**con.tin.u.a.tion** (-AY.shun) *n.*

con.tin.u.i.ty (con.tuh.NEW.i.tee) *n.* **1** a continuous quality: *Chapter 3 breaks the continuity of the story.* **2** the working script showing the scenario for a movie, TV, or radio production, not the shooting script. **3** linking material for a TV or radio program.

con.tin.u.ous (cun.TIN.yoo.us) *adj.* without a break in space or time: *a continuous line of cars; the continuous passage of time.* —**con.tin.u.ous.ly** *adv.*

con.tin.u.um (cun.TIN.yoo.um) *n.* a continuous extent or series: *Time and space are continuums; Car prices vary along a continuum.*

con.tort (cun.TORT) *v.* twist out of shape; deform: *a face contorted by rage.* —**con.tor.tion** *n.*

con.tor.tion.ist (cun.TOR.shuh.nist) *n.* a performer who can put his body in strange postures.

con.tour (CON.toor) *n.* the outline of a surface of varying dimensions: *We flew low hugging the contours of the ground to elude enemy radar; the smooth, sweeping contours of a car's aerodynamic design; clothes that outline the contours of the body.* —**adja.** following the contours: *a contour chair;* **Contour lines** *connect points of equal elevation, as shown on a* **contour map.**

con.tra (CON.trah) *n.* a member of a right-wing guerrilla group in Nicaragua.

con.tra.band (CON.truh.band) *n.* illegally imported goods: *goods smuggled into the country as contraband; to import contraband;* **adja.**: *contraband liquor, trade.*

con.tra.cep.tion (con.truh.SEP.shun) *n.* the prevention of conception: *to practice, use contraception; oral contraception* (= use of the pill).

con.tra.cep.tive (con.truh.SEP.tiv) *n.* an agent used to prevent conception: *chemical, herbal, oral, vaginal contraceptives;* **adja.**: *a contraceptive measure; the variety of contraceptive devices, drugs, methods, techniques.*

con.tract (CON.tract) *n.* **1** an agree-

ment, esp. if legally binding: *legal, marriage, valid, void contracts; a secretly arranged sweetheart contract* or *deal* (= secret deal); *to assign, award, breach, break, cancel, carry out, conclude, draw up, enter into, execute, negotiate, ratify, repudiate, violate a contract; There's a* **contract out for** *Caputo* (Informal for Someone has been hired to kill Caputo); *the contract on Caputo.* **2** the final bid in a hand of **contract bridge** in which one scores toward the game only the points one has bid.
—*v.* (cun.TRACT) **1** agree in a contract: *They contracted to supply steel for the railroad; The railroad contracted with the company for steel supplies; They usually* **contract out** *the job of supplying steel.* **2** acquire something unwanted: *to contract debts, bad habits, diseases, obligations; a marriage contracted* (= entered into) *for unworthy reasons.* **3** make or become smaller, as by drawing in: *Cold contracts metals; The triceps muscle contracts as the arm is straightened; to contract* (= wrinkle) *one's brow in a frown; adj.: "I'm" is the* **contracted** (= shortened) *form of "I am."*
—**con.trac.tion** *n.: "It's" is the contraction for "It is"; Call the doctor when the contractions (of the uterus) are less than ten minutes apart and last for half a minute.* —**con.trac.tor** *n.: building, electrical, plumbing contractors.*
—**con.trac.tu.al** (-choo.ul) *adj.;* **con.trac.tu.al.ly** *adv.*

con.trac.tile (cun.TRAC.tul, -tile) *adj.* having to do with contracting or compressing: *the heart's contractile function.* —**con.trac.til.i.ty** (con.trac.TIL.i.tee) *n.*

con.tra.dict (con.truh.DICT) *v.* state the opposite or deny the truth or correctness of something: *One can't contradict facts; Facts may contradict your claims; The two stories contradict each other; He's always contradicting his superiors; Stop contradicting!*
con.tra.dic.tion (con.truh.DIC.shun) *n.* a contradicting: *apparent, basic, clear, glaring, inherent, internal contradictions; a story full of discrepancies and contradictions; His practice is in sharp contradiction with or to his principles; "Square circle" seems a* **contradiction in terms.**
—**con.tra.dic.to.ry** (-tuh.ree) *adj.: two contradictory versions of the same incident, one contradictory to the other.*

con.tra.dis.tinc.tion (con.truh.dis.TINK.shun) *n.* a contrasting distinction: *Humans, in contradistinction to animals, can talk.*

con.trail *n.* the visible trail of condensed water or ice particles behind a high-flying aircraft; condensation trail; vapor trail.
con.tra.in.di.cate (con.truh.IN.duh.cate) *v.* **-cates, -cat.ed, -cat.ing** of symptoms, make a treatment undesirable or unsafe; **con.tra.in.di.ca.tion** (-CAY.shun) *n.*
con.tral.to (cun.TRAL.toh) *n.* **-tos** the lowest female singing voice.
con.trap.tion (cun.TRAP.shun) *n. Informal.* a gadget: *to build, put together, slap together a contraption; a new-fangled contraption for polishing shoes.*
con.tra.pun.tal (con.truh.PUN.tul) *adj.* having to do with counterpoint: *a contrapuntal style.*
con.tra.ri.an (cun.TRAIR.ee.un) *n.* one who is opposed to the majority opinion: *a long-term contrarian; adj.: a contrarian approach, position, stance, strategy, theory, viewpoint.*
con.tra.ri.wise (con.TRAIR.ee.wize) *adv.* in a contrary manner.
con.tra.ry (CON.trair.ee) *adj.* **1** opposed: *His actions were contrary to company policies; two contrary* (= contrasting) *examples; two contrary* (= incompatible) *statements; a ship tossed by contrary* (= adverse) *winds.* **2** (*also* cun.TRAIR.ee) temperamentally opposed to obedience: *Mary is quite contrary; a contrary child.* —*n., pl.* **-ries** something opposite: *He was said to be cruel;* **On the contrary,** *he was very kind; He seemed very kind despite all reports* **to the contrary.** —**con.tra.ri.ly** *adv.;* **con.tra.ri.ness** *n.* —**con.tra.ri.e.ty** (con.truh.RYE.uh.tee) *n.*
con.trast (con.TRAST) *v.* **1** set in opposition to show differences: *Compare and contrast their behavior.* **2** exhibit differences when placed, seen, etc. together: *Her behavior contrasts sharply with his.* —*n.* (CON.trast) **1** comparison: *In contrast to* or *By contrast with Toronto, Washington is mild in winter.* **2** difference in comparison: *California is* or *presents a harsh, sharp, startling contrast to Colorado; The contrast between the two states is striking in winter; a TV picture that lacks contrast (between light and dark tones).* —**con.tras.tive** (con.TRAS.tiv) *adj.*
con.tra.vene (CON.truh.veen) *v.* **-venes, -vened, -ven.ing** go against or conflict with something: *a structure that contravenes the building code.* —**con.tra.ven.tion** (-VEN.shun) *n.: It's been built in contravention of the building code.*
con.tre.temps (con.truh.TAHNG) *n.*

sing. & pl. an unfortunate or awkward occurrence.

con.trib.ute (cun.TRIB.yoot, long "oo") *v.* **-utes, -ut.ed, -ut.ing** give jointly with others: *We contributed clothing, money, time, etc. for the refugees; We regularly contribute to charity; to contribute ideas, knowledge, etc. to a project; to contribute an article, poem, story, etc. to a magazine; Many things* **contributed to** (= jointly brought about) *his downfall.*
—**con.tri.bu.tion** (con.truh.BYOO.shun) *n.: She made or sent in a (charitable) contribution; generous, monetary, token, voluntary contributions to charity; He made many brilliant, key, major, notable, original, outstanding, remarkable, valuable contributions to knowledge; His contribution* (= article) *was accepted by the editor.*
—**con.trib.u.tor** (cun.TRIB.yuh.tur) *n.: a generous, regular contributor to charity; a prolific contributor to popular journals.*

con.trib.u.to.ry (cun.TRIB.yuh.tor.ee) *adj.* contributing: *a contributory cause of the accident; the accident victim's* **contributory negligence** *in not watching the traffic.*

con.trite (CON.trite) *adj.* sorrowful about having done wrong, with a firm purpose of amendment: *He prayed for forgiveness with a humble and contrite heart; a contrite sinner; He shed contrite tears.* —**con.trite.ness** *n.*

con.tri.tion (cun.TRISH.un) *n.* sorrow for having done wrong: *an act of contrition; He expressed, felt, showed contrition for his sins.*

con.triv.ance (cun.TRY.vunce) *n.* something contrived: *a new contrivance for peeling potatoes.*

con.trive (cun.TRIVE) *v.* **-trives, -trived, -triv.ing** plan and accomplish something cleverly or ingeniously: *The burglar contrived a way to break into the house; contrived to break in by an air vent; She escaped from the fire by a rope ladder contrived out of bed sheets;* ***adj.:* a contrived** (= labored or artificial) *alibi, excuse, gaiety.*

con.trol (cun.TROLE) *v.* **-trols, -trolled, -trol.ling** direct or restrain in order to keep within limits or on a course: *He can control his horse, but not his temper; The car is controlled by radio;* ***adj.:* a controlling** *factor in his life; a controlling interest in the company; a controlling majority.* —*n.* **1** power of directing or restraining; also, an act of controlling: *to* **assume** or **take control of** *a situation; to establish, exercise, exert control over the people working for you;; The car went out of control; He lost control of the car and landed in a ditch; absolute, close, full, lax, loose, parental, remote, strict control; birth, cost, damage, emission, fire, government, flight, flood, gun, mission, pest, quality, rent, stress, thought control; She wrested control of the plane from the hijacker; Now you are* **in control;** *Don't let the situation get* **out of control;** *They finally* **brought** or got the fire **under control.**
2 controls, *pl.* controlling mechanism: *The pilot took over the controls after freeing himself; He remained at the controls for the rest of the flight.* **3 controls** *pl.* restrictions: *to impose wage and price controls; to introduce rent controls; The government tightened controls on liquor sales; The controls were lifted or removed after a time.* **4** a standard used for comparison: *The first group got much better than the controls* (= members of the "control group") *who were given only a placebo, not the drug.* —*adj.: a control center, panel, tower, unit; a* **control freak** *who doesn't like to delegate; a* **control rod** *of a nuclear reactor; the* **control stick** *of an airplane.* —**con.trolled** (cun.TROLED) *adja.: a controlled celebration, economy, manner, voice; a freeway with* **controlled access** (having interchanges for exits and entrances); *a magazine with* **controlled circulation** (distributed free in select areas); *A* **controlled experiment** (using a standard for comparison) *has to be carried out under controlled conditions; a* **controlled substance** (= drug whose use is restricted by law). —**con.trol.la.ble** (-luh.bul) *adj.*

con.trol.ler (cun.TROH.lur) *n.* **1** one that directs or regulates: *an air-traffic controller; the flight controllers of a spacecraft; a floppy disc drive controller; CD-controllers.* **2** one who supervises finances and spending; comptroller.

con.tro.ver.sial (con.truh.VUR.shul) *adj.* **1** arousing controversy: *Abortion is a bitterly, highly controversial issue; a controversial author, claim, theory, view.* **2** fond of controversy: *a controversial philosopher.* —**con.tro.ver.sial.ly** *adv.*

con.tro.ver.sy (CON.truh.vur.see) *n.* **-sies** a conflict of opinion; dispute: *the bitter, furious, heated, lively, public, spirited controversy over* or *about abortion; the controversy between pro-life and pro-choice groups; Abortion arouses, causes, fuels, stirs up much controversy; a controversy that is hard to settle; He got into a controversy with the administration.*

con.tro.vert (CON.truh.vurt) *v.* argue against or about something; ***adj.:* a**

much **controverted** issue. —**con.tro.ver.ti.ble** adj.
con.tu.ma.cy (CON.tue.muh.see, cun.TUE.muh-) n. -cies headstrong resistance to authority. —**con.tu.ma.cious** (con.tue.MAY.shus) adj.; **con.tu.ma.cious.ly** adv.
con.tu.me.ly (cun.TUE.muh.lee, CON.tue-) n. -lies overbearing and humiliating words or action; insult. —**con.tu.me.li.ous** (-MEE.lee.us) adj.: contumelious treatment; **con.tu.me.li.ous.ly** adv.
con.tuse (cun.TUSE) v. -tus.es, -tused, -tus.ing bruise. —**con.tu.sion** n.
co.nun.drum (cuh.NUN.drum) n. Formal. **1** a riddle involving a pun; e.g. "When is a dress like a chair? Answer: When it is sat-in." **2** a hard-to-solve, confusing problem: the conundrum of balancing the budget without raising taxes.
con.ur.ba.tion (con.ur.BAY.shun) n. a group of continuous urban areas: the Greater London conurbation.
con.va.lesce (con.vuh.LES) v. -lesc.es, -lesced, -lesc.ing recover after an illness or injury; get better: She is convalescing from her recent illness. —**con.va.les.cence** (-unce) n.: during her convalescence. —**con.va.les.cent** (-unt) n. & adj.: convalescent care; A **convalescent home** is a house for convalescents.
con.vec.tion (con.VEC.shun) n. internal movement in a liquid or gas, caused esp. by variation in heating: Heating takes place by conduction, convection, and radiation; **adj.**: A space heater sets up convection currents; A **convection oven** blows and circulates hot air uniformly around the food; the sun's **convection zone** just below its surface. —**con.vec.tion.al** adj.: Equatorial forests thrive on convectional rains.
con.vec.tor (cun.VEC.tur) n. a room heating unit, as in a steam or hot-water system.
con.vene (cun.VEEN) v. -venes, -vened, -ven.ing come or bring together in a body: The mayor convened the town council; The meeting convenes at 3 p.m. —**con.ve.nor** or **con.ven.er** n.
con.ven.ience (cun.VEEN.yunce) n. **1** the quality of being convenient: the convenience of shopping by telephone; comfort and convenience. **2** ease or personal comfort: We will see you **at your convenience**; words arranged in alphabetical order **for your convenience**. **3** something that helps ease or comfort: It's a great convenience to live or living near the rapid transit; the microwave oven, electric kettle, and such modern conveniences; Is there a powder room, washroom, or convenience (= toilet) here?
convenience food n. prepackaged, easy-to-prepare food, as a TV dinner.
convenience store n. a small store carrying basic food items and other necessities that is open long hours.
con.ven.ient (cun.VEEN.yunt) adj. adapted for one's ease or comfort: five convenient locations to shop; a convenient illness during exam week; Is next week convenient for you? It's very convenient living or to live near the rapid transit; It's very convenient that you can take the subway to work. —**con.ven.ient.ly** adv.
convenor See CONVENE.
con.vent (CON.vent, -vunt) n. a community of nuns or where they live.
con.ven.ti.cle (cun.VEN.ti.cul) n. a meeting, esp. a secret religious assembly.
con.ven.tion (cun.VEN.shun) n. **1** a meeting, esp. of delegates: to hold a convention; annual, constitutional, national, party, political, sales conventions; a convention center. **2** an international agreement: a copyright convention; the Geneva conventions providing for the humane treatment of war prisoners and wounded. **3** accepted custom or usage; also, a practice so sanctioned: Whether you kiss or rub noses is a matter of convention; a mere convention; a social convention; not a rigid convention; the conventions of art, communication, games, language, parliamentary practice, religion, warfare.
con.ven.tion.al (cun.VEN.shuh.nul) adj. **1** customary: It is conventional to shake hands over a deal; a conventional greeting; The fleur-de-lis is a conventional representation of the lily; conventional as opposed to nuclear warfare; **conventional wisdom** (= a belief or set of commonly held beliefs). **2** ordinary: a conventional lifestyle, product, view; clothes that are too conventional for special occasions. —**con.ven.tion.al.ly** adv.
con.ven.tion.eer (cun.VEN.shuh.NEER) n. one attending a convention.
con.verge (cun.VURGE) v. -verg.es, -verged, -verg.ing move toward a common point or goal: The demonstrators converged on the Capitol; Converging lines meet. —**con.ver.gence** n. —**con.ver.gent** adj.
con.ver.sant (cun.VUR.sunt, CON.vur.sunt) adj. having knowledge or familiarity: a lawyer thoroughly conversant with contract law.

con.ver.sa.tion (con.vur.SAY.shun) *n.* a talk between two or more people: *the fine art of conversation; to begin, break off, bug, carry on, have, hold, interrupt, monitor, monopolize, stimulate, strike up, tap, tape, terminate a conversation; She tried hard to make conversation but the other party was not interested; animated, intimate, light, lively, private, serious, telephone conversation; I couldn't help overhearing fragments* or *scraps of their conversations; He had a conversation about cats with Joan; He was in conversation with Joan for two hours; Collectibles make great* **conversation pieces** (= items having curiosity or novelty value).
—**con.ver.sa.tion.al** *adj.*;
con.ver.sa.tion.al.ly *adv.*
—**con.ver.sa.tion.al.ist** *n.*: *a skilled and witty conversationalist.*

con.verse 1 (cun.VERSE) *v.* **-vers.es, -versed, -vers.ing** talk informally: *He can converse fluently about Germany in German with fellow students.* **2** (CON.verse) *n.* something opposed: *Her generosity is the converse of his stinginess;* **adj**.: *a converse proposition, situation, theorem.*

con.verse.ly (cun.VERSE.lee) *adv.* in the opposite way: *Our summer is New Zealand's winter, and conversely* (= Our winter is New Zealand's summer).

con.ver.sion (cun.VUR.zhun, -shun) *n.* **1** a converting or being converted; change: *the conversion of rooming houses to apartments; conversion of data to machine-readable form; a table for metric conversion; methods of conversion* (= refining) *of crude oil to make gasoline; He underwent a sudden conversion* (= religious change) *from Christianity to Islam; He also made some conversions* (= converts) *among his friends.* **2** illegal use of another's property: *The bailiff was charged with theft by conversion of $500* (= illegal use of property worth $500).

con.vert (cun.VURT) *v.* **1** change or adapt to a different form, use, etc.: *Alchemists wanted to convert base metals like lead to gold; We had to convert a lot of dollars to rupees for a vacation in India; to convert a barn into a restaurant; They will convert to production of the new model in July; She converted to Islam; Canada converted to the metric system long ago;* **adj**.: *His office is a* **converted** *barn; converted warehouses;* **Converted rice** *has been processed to preserve its mineral and vitamin content.* **2** persuade someone or be persuaded to adopt new principles, esp. as a religion: *He converted from Islam to Buddhism; He converted voluntarily;* **adj**.: *He's a* **converted** *Buddhist; It doesn't make sense* **to preach to the converted**. **3** illegally use another's property as one's own.
—*n.* (CON.vurt) one who has been converted: *a convert to Christianity; how to gain, make, win converts.*

con.vert.er (cun.VUR.tur) *n.* a converting device: *a pocket metric converter; an electrical converter for changing AC to DC; a catalytic converter; a hand-held cable-TV converter for viewing many channels.*

con.vert.i.ble (cun.VUR.tuh.bul) *adj.* that can be converted: *a bond that is convertible to stock; Dollars are freely convertible into other currencies; a convertible sofa that opens out into a bed.* —*n.* a car with a folding roof.

con.ver.tor (cun.VUR.tur) same as CONVERTER.

con.vex (CON.vex) *adj.* rounded outward, as the outer surface of a ball: *a convex lens.* —**con.vex.i.ty** (cun.VEX.i.tee) *n.* **-ties.**

con.vey (cun.VAY) *v.* **1** carry from place to place; conduct: *a pipe to convey water.* **2** pass on; communicate: *I conveyed my sympathies to the bereaved.* **3** transfer ownership of a property: *The title to the land was conveyed from the school to the church; The property was conveyed to the church.*

con.vey.ance (cun.VAY.unce) *n.* **1** a conveying; moving or transferring: *the conveyance of freight; the conveyance of an estate; a deed of conveyance.* **2** a means of conveying; vehicle: *a public conveyance.*

conveyor or **conveyor belt** *n.* an endless belt, chain, etc. for moving objects, as on an assembly line or at a supermarket checkout.

con.vict (cun.VICT) *v.* declare or prove guilty: *He was convicted of theft;* **adj**.: *He stands* **convicted**; *a convicted criminal, killer, prisoner.* —*n.* (CON.vict) one serving a prison term.

con.vic.tion (cun.VIC.shun) *n.* **1** a convicting: *Jon received a conviction for petty theft; That is just one of the many convictions the prosecutor got last year; The conviction was overturned on appeal.* **2** firm belief: *a burning, deep, firm, life-long, strong conviction that truth will win; He's a pacifist by conviction; He has the courage of his convictions to refuse to go to war; a story that carries conviction* (= that is convincing).

con.vince (cun.VINCE) *v.* **-vinc.es, -vinced, -vinc.ing** persuade; bring to a firm belief: *He convinced me that he is*

innocent; He convinced (*Informal* for persuaded) *me to tell it to the judge*; *adj.*: *I am* **convinced** (= persuaded) *of his innocence*; *absolutely, completely, firmly, thoroughly convinced that he is innocent; His arguments are very* **convincing** (= persuasive). —**con.vin.cing.ly** *adv.*: *He argues convincingly.*
con.viv.i.al (cun.VIV.ee.ul) *adj.* fond of, suited to, or having good company, good food, and good drink: *a convivial host; We had a convivial time at the party*; **con.viv.i.al.ly** *adv.* —**con.viv.i.al.i.ty** (-ee.AL.i.tee) *n.*
con.vo.ca.tion (con.vuh.CAY.shun) *n.* an assembly of churchmen, members of a university, etc.: *A convocation is held when degrees are to be conferred.*
con.voke (cun.VOKE) *v.* **-vokes, -voked, -vok.ing** *Formal.* summon for a deliberative or legislative purpose: *to convoke an assembly, congress, parliament.*
con.vo.lut.ed (CON.vuh.loo.tid) *adj.* coiled, esp. intricately; hence, complicated: *the brain's convoluted folds; long, convoluted sentences; a convoluted design, story, tangle of streets.*
con.vo.lu.tion (con.vuh.LOO.shun) *n.* something folded, twisted, or coiled together, esp. intricately: *the convolutions of the surface of the brain.*
con.voy (CON.voy) *v.* accompany as protection on a journey: *Aircraft convoyed the tankers.* —*n.* **1** an armed escort, as for ships: *The goods were shipped* **under convoy. 2** a group traveling together for safe or orderly transport: *a convoy of merchant ships; All shipping moved* **in convoy** *during World War II.*
con.vulse (cun.VULSE) *v.* **-vuls.es, -vulsed, -vuls.ing** throw into a convulsion or spasm; shake violently: *She was convulsed with laughter; when Yugoslavia was convulsed in civil war.*
con.vul.sion (cun.VUL.shun) *n.* **1** an involuntary, powerful muscular contraction; fit or seizure: *Epileptics go into convulsions.* **2** a powerful sudden or spasmodic action, as a revolution, earthquake, etc.: *convulsions of nature; The audience was thrown into convulsions of laughter; There were convulsions of panic during the stock market crash.* —**con.vul.sive** (-siv) *adj.*; **con.vul.sive.ly** *adv.*
co.ny (COH.nee) *n.* **-nies 1** a rabbit or rabbitlike mammal. **2** rabbit fur.
coo *n.* **1** the low, gentle murmuring of doves. **2** any similar sound. —*v.* **coos, cooed, coo.ing**: *the billing and cooing heard from park benches.*

convivial / cool

cook (short "oo") *v.* **1** prepare for eating by boiling, baking, frying, etc.: *We need someone to cook a meal for us; to cook us a meal; Who will cook supper? The eggs are cooking* (= being cooked) *now*; *n.*: *He does all our* **cooking**; *good home* **cooking. 2** treat with heat: *Uncover and cook five minutes longer.*
3 *Informal.* happen: *What's cooking?*
4 *Informal.* falsify; also, botch: *The embezzler cooked the (account) books.* **5** *Informal.* do or feel the right thing: *Now you're cooking!* —**cook one's goose** *Informal.* ruin oneself completely.
—**cook up** *Informal.* concoct or invent: *to cook up an excuse, plan, plot, pretext, story, tale.* —*n.* one who cooks: *the head cook; a short-order cook.*
cook.book *n.* a book of recipes.
cook.ie or **cook.y** (COOK.ee, short "OO") *n.* **cook.ies 1** a small, usu. flat cake made from a stiff, sweet dough: *chocolate chip cookie; caught with his hand in the* **cookie jar** (= caught accepting bribes); *That's how* or *the way* **the cookie crumbles** (= how the matter resolves itself). **2** *Slang.* person; guy: *a tough cookie.*
cookie cutter *n.* a device for cutting dough into shaped forms such as stars, circles, and hearts for making cookies. —**cookie-cutter** *adj.* having the same shape or form; stereotyped: *a cookie-cutter approach, concept, creation, design, formula, image, look, method, mold, sameness, solution; in a cookie-cutter fashion.*
cook.out *n.* a meal prepared and eaten outdoors, as on an outing: *to have a cookout; backyard, beachside, summer cookouts.*
Cook's tour *n.* a rapid guided tour of points of interest.
cool (long "oo") *adj.* **1** somewhat cold: *a cool breeze, summer, valley.* **2** protecting or relieving from heat: *a cool drink, summer jacket, suit.* **3** unemotional: *Keep a cool head; Keep, remain, stay cool* (= calm); *She is cool as a cucumber* (= unexcited); *cool* (= restrained) *jazz*; *He was cool* (= unfriendly) *toward us; was cool to* (= unreceptive of) *the new idea; According to McLuhan, radio is a hot medium, involving more listener participation to complete its communication than such cool media as films and TV.* **4** *Slang.* excellent; admirable: *It isn't cool to be jealous; It's cool not to take drugs; The Olympic Games cost a cool $1 billion.*
—**play it cool** *Slang.* be casual and impassive. —*n.* **1** something cool: *the cool of a summer night.* **2** *Slang.* compo-

coolant / cope

sure: *He blew his cool; He lost his cool and yelled at her; She kept her cool and just walked away.* —*v.* make or become cool: *Leave him to* **cool off** *or* **cool down,** *he'll come back; Tell him to* **cool it** (Slang for relax); **cpd:** *an air-cooled engine; a fan-cooled stereo; water-cooled turbos;* the **cooling-off period** *during which you may cancel a sales contract.* —**cool one's heels** *Informal.* be forced to wait. —**cool.ly** *adv.;* **cool.ness** *n.*

cool.ant (COO.lunt) *n.* a fluid used, as in an engine, to remove excess heat: *to add coolant to a radiator.*

cool.er (COO.lur) *n.* **1** one that cools or a cooling container or room. **2** a cool drink, esp. one that is slightly alcoholic. **3 the cooler** *Slang.* jail; slammer.

cool.ie (COO.lee) *n.* an unskilled, often exploited Oriental laborer.

coon (long "oo") *n. Informal.* raccoon: *I haven't seen him in a* **coon's age** (= for a long time); *a* **coon cap** *(made of a coon's skin)*

coon.skin *n.* the pelt of a raccoon or a cap made of it.

coop (long "oo") *n.* **1** a cage, pen etc., esp. for poultry: *a chicken coop.* **2** *Slang.* a jail: *The convict* **flew the coop** (= escaped). —*v.* confine: *The jury was cooped up in a hotel during the trial.*

co-op (COH.op) *n. & adj.a.* cooperative: *We do all our shopping at the co-op (store); a co-op housing project.*

coop.er *n.* one who makes or mends barrels, tubs, casks, etc.

co.op.er.ate (coh.OP.uh.rate) *v.* **-ates, -at.ed, -at.ing** work with others, esp. for a common goal: *to cooperate on a project with neighbors; They cooperated in building a fence.* —**co.op.er.a.tion** (-RAY.shun) *n.: We had the close, complete, whole-hearted cooperation of the teaching community; We appreciate your cooperation with us in this enterprise; This dictionary was prepared in cooperation with teachers.* —**co.op.er.a.tor** *n.* Also **co-operate, co-operation, co-operator.**

co.op.er.a.tive (coh.OP.ur.uh.tiv) **1** *adj.* having to do with cooperation: *cooperative behavior; in a cooperative mood.* **2** *adj.a.* having to do with an enterprise owned and usu. operated by members for their own benefit: *a cooperative apartment house, film club, health facility, savings-and-loan institution.* —*n.* a cooperative enterprise, esp. a store: *consumers', farmers', producers', workers' cooperatives.* —**co.op.er.a.tive.ly** *adv.* Also **co-operative, co-operatively.**

co-opt (coh.OPT) *v.* **1** choose as a partner or colleague: *A committee may co-opt more members.* **2** absorb into a culture, organization, etc.; also, take over: *a revolutionary co-opted by the system.*

co.or.di.nate (coh.OR.duh.nit) *adj.* of equal importance or rank; parallel: *the coordinate clauses of a compound sentence.* —*n.* **1** something that is coordinate: *a shirt-pant-sweater coordinate* (= matching set) *in navy blue;* **adj.a.:** *a coordinate* (= matching) *vest.* **2** a letter or number used as a reference in precisely locating something: *the X and Y coordinates of a graph; "L-7" gives the coordinates of Chalkdene Grove on the map.* —*v.* (-nate) **-ates, -at.ed, -at.ing 1** make or become coordinate: *She's looking for tops that coordinate with her jeans and shorts; "And," "but," "hence," etc. are* **coordinating conjunctions. 2** work or cause to work harmoniously together: *to coordinate police work on an escaped convict; a* **coordinating editor.** —*adj.:* **a coordinated** *assault on the fortress; in a coordinated manner, way; a coordinated presentation, response, strategy; a color-coordinated outfit.* —**co.or.di.nate.ly** (-nit.lee) *adv.;* **co.or.di.na.tor** (-nay.tur) *n.* Also **co-ordinate, co-ordinately, co-ordinator.**

co.or.di.na.tion (coh.OR.duh.NAY.shun) *n.* **1** a coordinating. **2** the harmonious functioning of various muscles in a complex action: *Brain injury may cause poor coordination, as in cerebral palsy.* Also **co-ordination.**

coot (long "oo") *n.* **1** any of several ducklike water birds: *bald as a coot; silly or stupid as a coot.* **2** *Informal.* a silly, usu. old man or woman: *crazy as a coot.*

coot.ie (COO.tee) *n. Slang.* a body louse.

cop *v.* **cops, copped, cop.ping** *Slang.* capture, seize, or steal: *The bird had been copped from his coop.* —**cop a plea** plead guilty to a lesser charge in order to avoid being tried on a more serious one. —**cop out** *Informal.* withdraw from or avoid commitment; back out: *He copped out of or on his obligation to pay back the loan.* —*n. Informal.* a police officer.

cope *n.* **1** an outer, enveloping cloak worn by clergy during ceremonies. **2** anything that covers like a cope; canopy. **3** a top part: *the cope* (= top half) *of a mold enclosing a pattern to be cast.* —*v.* **copes, coped, cop.ing** contend, usu. successfully; come to grips: *troubled teenagers trying to cope with life; Some just can't cope.*

Co.per.ni.can (coh.PUR.ni.cun) *adj.* having to do with **Copernicus,** a 15th century astronomer: *The Copernican system presents the earth as going around the sun (not the other way around); A Copernican revolution in our thinking seems called for.*

cope.stone *n.* topping or capping stone.

cop.i.er (COP.ee.ur) *n.* one that copies, esp. a duplicating machine.

co.pi.lot (COH.pye.lut) *n.* an assistant pilot.

cop.ing (COH.ping) *n.* the rooflike topping of a stone or brick wall.

co.pi.ous (COH.pee.us) *adj.* plentiful in quantity: *a copious discharge of steam; a text provided with copious notes.*
— **co.pi.ous.ly** *adv.;* **co.pi.ous.ness** *n.*

cop-out or **cop.out** *n. Informal.* a copping or backing out: *Resignation is an easy cop-out; He thought his easy life was a real cop-out and no challenge; Your answer is a cop-out.*

cop.per (COP.ur) *n.* **1** a reddish-brown metal or its color; **adj.:** *copper bracelets, mining, ore, tan, wire.* **2** *Brit.* a penny. **3** *Slang.* a police officer; cop.
— **cop.per.y** *adj.: coppery hair, tan.*

cop.per.as (COP.uh.rus) *n.* a greenish iron compound used in making ink and fertilizers.

cop.per.head (COP.ur.hed) *n.* a poisonous North American viper.

cop.pi.ce (COP.is) same as COPSE.

co.pra (COH.pruh, COP-) *n.* dried coconut meat from which oil is extracted.

copse (COPS) *n.* a thicket of shrubs or small trees.

Copt *n.* **1** one of a people descended from the ancient Egyptians. **2** a member of the Coptic Church.

cop.ter (COP.tur) *n. Informal.* helicopter.

Cop.tic *n. & adj.* (having to do with) the Afro-Asiatic liturgical language of the native Christian church, or the **Coptic Church,** of Egypt and Ethiopia.

cop.u.la (COP.yuh.luh) *n.* a linking verb connecting subject and predicate, as in "Man *is* mortal," "Jane *will be* here," "He *seems* happy."

cop.u.late (COP.yuh.late) *v.* **-lates, -lat.ed, -lat.ing** engage in coitus with someone; **cop.u.la.tive** *adj.*
— **cop.u.la.tion** (-LAY.shun) *n.*

cop.y (COP.ee) *n.* **cop.ies** **1** a close imitation or duplication of an original: *a copy of the Mona Lisa; fair and rough copies of a manuscript; a certified true copy of the document; a carbon copy of a letter; Make me a clean Xerox copy; Save the master copy; Run off 500 copies for me; Keep an extra copy as backup copy.* **2** a single specimen of a printed text, photograph, etc.: *a first printing of 100,000 copies; Authors autograph copies of their books for friends; leather-bound presentation copies; advance copies sent to reviewers; the hard copy printout from a computer; back copies (= issues) of a periodical.* **3** draft material to be typeset; manuscript; hence, the words of an advertisement: *the layout of copy and illustrations; Editors check copy produced by writers; newspaper copy; Scandals make good copy (= material) for the papers.*
—*v.* **cop.ies, cop.ied, cop.y.ing** reproduce closely or imitate: *He likes to copy from friends; He slavishly copies what the others do; Children tend to copy their parents; Text copies better (=gives better photocopies) than pictures.*

cop.y.book (COP.ee.book) *n.* a book containing samples of proper handwriting.

copy boy *n.* a boy who helps in a newspaper office doing errands, delivering copy, etc.

cop.y.cat (COP.ee.cat) *n. Informal.* a slavish imitator of others; **adj.:** *copycat crimes, marketing, products, services.*

copy desk *n.* a desk where newspaper copy is edited before typesetting.

copy-edit *v.* edit a manuscript for publication.

copy-editor *n.* one who edits copy, as for a book publisher or newspaper.

copying machine *n.* a photocopier.

cop.y.ist (COP.ee.ist) *n.* one who makes written copies.

cop.y.read.er (COP.ee.ree.dur) *n.* one who reads and corrects copy, as for a newspaper.

cop.y.right (COP.ee.rite) *n.* the legal right to reproduce, sell, or publish a work of art, literature, music, etc.: *Authors and publishers apply for, claim, hold, secure copyrights in or on their works; the government agency that registers or grants copyrights; You will infringe (a) copyright if you copy a book that is under copyright.*
—*v.:* to copyright a *play, story, work;*
adj.: a *copyrighted poem.*

cop.y.writ.er (COP.ee.rye.tur) *n.* one who writes advertising copy.

co.quet (coh.KET) *v.* **-quets, -quet.ted, -quet.ting** flirt with someone.

co.quet.ry (COH.kuh.tree) *n.* **-tries** a flirting act or attitude.

co.quette (coh.KET) *n.* a woman who frivolously seeks men's attentions.
— **co.quet.tish** *adj.*

cor.a.cle (COR.uh.cul) *n.* a light, roundish boat made of waterproof material stretched over a frame of wood, wicker, etc.

cor.al (COR.ul) *n.* **1** a stonelike substance formed from the skeletons of marine polyps; also, such a polyp; *adja.: a coral atoll, island, reef.* **2** a deep or yellowish pink or red; *adj.: her coral lips, lipstick.*

coral snake *n.* a brightly banded poisonous snake of tropical America and southern U.S.

cor.bel (COR.bul) *n.* a usu. wooden or stone projection from a wall that supports a weight above it.

cord *n.* **1** a thin rope of several strands or fibers; hence, something similar: *an extension cord for a lamp; our vocal cords; the umbilical cord of a fetus; the spinal cord of nerve tissue; the cords (= ribs) on corduroy cloth;* **Cords** (= corduroy pants) *are not allowed by our dress code.* **2** a measure of cut wood piled 4 ft. x 4 ft. x 8 ft. (approximately 1.2m x 1.2m x 2.4m). —*v.* **1** tie or provide with a cord or cords. **2** to pile wood in a cord.

cord.age (COR.dij) *n.* **1** cords and ropes collectively, esp. the ropes of a ship's rigging. **2** an amount of wood measured in cords.

cor.dial (COR.jul) *adj.* warm and hearty: *She was cordial to or toward us; He sent us cordial greetings; a cordial letter, welcome.* —*n.* a liqueur; also, a stimulant. —**cor.dial.ly** *adv.* —**cor.di.al.i.ty** (cor.dee.AL.i.tee) *n.* -ties.

cor.dil.le.ra (cor.dul.YAIR.uh, -DIL.uh.ruh) *n.* a chain or system of mountain ranges. —**cor.dil.le.ran** *adj.*

cord.ite *n.* a smokeless explosive produced in cord form.

cord.less (CORD.lis) *adj.* operating without cord, i.e., by battery power: *a cordless electric shaver, telephone.*

cor.don (COR.dun) *n.* **1** a line of police, soldiers, or forts guarding or isolating an area: *They formed a cordon to keep back the crowds; The police threw a cordon around the area.* **2** a decorative cord worn as a sign of honor. —*v.* put a protective cordon around something: *The police cordoned off the area.*

cor.do.van (COR.duh.vun) *n.* a fine, colored leather, used esp. for shoes.

cor.du.roy (COR.duh.roy) *n.* **1** a stout-ribbed fabric. **2 corduroys** *pl.* trousers made of this.

core *n.* **1** the center of something, as the hard, seed-containing part in fruits: *an apple core; the core of the earth, sun; the core of a nuclear reactor; the center core of a multi-lane highway; the downtown core; a 3% hard core of unemployable people; Explicit sex distinguishes hard-core from soft-core pornography.* **2** essence: *the core of the argument; the common core of meaning in the usages of a word; Prejudice is at the core of the problem.* —**to the core** completely: *conservative, good, honest, rotten to the core.* —*adja.* central: *a core factor to be borne in mind; the core values of our society; the* **core competencies** *that distinguish a company from its competition; a program of interdisciplinary* **core courses;** *a* **core curriculum** *of basic subjects; the random-access* **core memory** *of a computer using magnetic storage techniques; the* **core period,** *as 9:30 to 3:30, of a flexible-hours system when all personnel must be on the job; the* **core vocabulary** *of a reading program.* —*v.* remove the core of a fruit. —**cor.er** *n.*

core city *n.* the center of a large urban area; inner city; central city.

co.re.spon.dent (coh.ri.SPON.dunt) *n.* a person charged in a divorce action with having committed adultery with the sued spouse.

co.ri.an.der (COR.ee.an.dur) *n.* a Mediterranean herb whose seeds are used as a flavoring.

cork *n.* **1** the thick outer bark of a Mediterranean oak (**cork oak**) used for bottle stoppers, insulation, floats, etc. **2** a stopper for a bottle, esp. one made of cork: *to pop* or *remove a cork.*

corked (CORKT) *adj.* fouled by a bad cork: *corked wine.*

cork.screw *n.* a pointed metal spiral with a handle, used for pulling corks from bottles.

corm *n.* a bulblike, scaleless underground stem that can produce new plants.

cor.mo.rant (COR.muh.runt) *n.* a large, hook-billed diving bird that catches fish; hence, a glutton.

corn *n.* **1** a cultivated cereal grass bearing kernels on large ears; maize; also, the kernels or ears of this: *to grow, raise, husk corn; hybrid, Indian, sweet, young corn; an ear of corn; corn on the cob.* **2** any cereal grass or its seeds, esp. the dominant grain of an area. **3** *Slang.* something outdated or oversentimental. **4** a thickening of the skin at a point of friction or pressure, esp. on the feet.

corn borer *n.* a moth larva that feeds on the stalks and ears of corn.

corn bread *n.* a bread made with cornmeal.

corn.cob *n.* the woody core of an ear of corn: *A **corncob pipe** for smoking tobacco has a bowl made from a corncob.*

corn.crib *n.* a ventilated drying bin for corn.

cor.ne.a (COR.nee.uh) *n.* the transparent covering over the pupil and iris of the eye. —**cor.ne.al** *adj.: a corneal transplant.*

corn ear.worm *n.* a moth larva that feeds esp. on corn ears.

corned beef *n.* beef cured by salting: *corned beef on rye.*

cor.ner (COR.nur) *n.* **1** the intersection of two lines, planes, or streets: *It's in the corner of the room; a figure with four square corners; meet me at or on the corner of Main and Front streets; the upper right corner of a page; He hit his head on the corner of the cupboard; The phone booth is around the corner; You'll see it when you turn* or *round the corner (with your car).* **2** an area or region, esp. a quiet or remote place: *a quiet corner of the library; thoughts passing through the dark corners of the mind; a blind corner (that you cannot see); I could see what was going on out of the corner of my eye; People came from the (four) corners of the earth* or *globe; from all corners of the world; The news was flashed to every corner of the earth; I'm **in your corner*** (*Informal* for I'm your supporter). **3** a difficult position to escape from: *He found himself backed into a corner; He had painted himself into a corner; a tight corner; The patient has **turned the corner** (= improved) after being on the critical list.* **4** sufficient control of a commodity to force a price rise: *We have a corner on wheat* (= control of the wheat market). —**around the corner** very near: *They live around the corner; Christmas is just around the corner.* —**cut corners** economize. —*v.* **1** turn a corner; *n.:* Slow down for **cornering**. **2** drive into a corner: *a fugitive cornered by police.* **3** gain control of something: *to corner the market on wheat.*

cor.ner.stone (COR.nur.stone) *n.* **1** a stone joining walls at a corner, often one ceremonially laid in a building's foundation: *The mayor will lay the cornerstone of the new city hall.* **2** basic foundation: *Free elections are the cornerstone of democracy.*

cor.net (cor.NET) *n.* a trumpetlike instrument having three valves.

—**cor.net.ist** or **cor.net.tist** *n.*

corn flour *n.* **1** flour made from corn.
2 *Brit.* CORNSTARCH.

corn.flow.er (CORN.flow.er) *n.* a garden plant with showy composite flowers of blue, pink, or white.

cor.nice (COR.nis) *n.* a usu. projecting decorative molding along the top of a wall, room, or building.

corn.meal *n.* meal coarsely ground from corn.

corn.row (CORN.roh) *n.* a style of arranging hair in braided rows placed flat on the scalp.

corn snow *n.* coarse-grained snow resulting from melting and refreezing.

corn.stalk *n.* a stem of the corn plant.

corn.starch *n.* a refined corn flour used to thicken sauces and in making **corn sugar**, or dextrose, and **corn syrup** which contains glucose.

cor.nu.co.pi.a (cor.nuh.COH.pee.uh) *n.* **1** a horn of plenty, shown overflowing with fruits. **2** an abundance: *a cornucopia of fringe benefits.*

corn.y (COR.nee) *adj.* **corn.i.er, -i.est** *Informal.* rustic; old-fashioned; hackneyed; oversentimental: *a corny joke; corny old love songs.*

co.rol.la (cuh.ROL.uh, -ROH.luh) *n.* the petals around a flower.

cor.ol.lar.y (cuh.ROL.uh.ree, COR.uh.lair.ee) *n.* **-ol.lar.ies** a logical consequence; result; accompanying fact: *Good health comes as a corollary to good eating habits; a logical corollary.*

co.ro.na (cuh.ROH.nuh) *n.* **-nas** or **-nae** (-nee) something crownlike, as a glowing ring around the sun, moon, etc. or the upper part of a tooth or skull.

cor.o.nar.y (COR.uh.nair.ee) *adj.* having to do with the arteries that conduct blood to the heart muscle: *coronary arteries, attacks, heart disease; a coronary care unit for heart patients.*
—*n., pl.* **-nar.ies** a blockage in a coronary artery in the heart caused by a blood clot; coronary occlusion; also **coronary thrombosis**.

cor.o.na.tion (cor.uh.NAY.shun) *n.* the crowning of a king, queen, pope, etc.: *to hold a coronation.*

cor.o.ner (COR.uh.nur) *n.* a public official who investigates deaths that may not be from natural causes.

cor.o.net (cor.uh.NET) *n.* **1** a jeweled headband; ornamental garland. **2** a smaller crown worn by nonsovereign nobility or royalty.

corpora *pl.* of CORPUS.

cor.po.ral (COR.puh.rul) *n.* a noncommissioned officer below sergeant in the army, marines, or a police force. —*adj.* physical: *corporal punish-*

ment by whipping, beating, etc.
cor.po.rate (COR.puh.rit) *adj.* **1** of, like, or shared by a united group: *corporate action, effort, endeavor, responsibility.* **2** having to do with a corporation: *a corporate body, bond, chain, crime, elite, headquarters, image, sponsor; corporate greed, income tax, law, property, structure; A company's distinctive policies and behavior styles constitute its* **corporate culture.** —**cor.po.rate.ly** *adv.*
cor.po.ra.tion (cor.puh.RAY.shun) *n.* a group such as a business firm or municipality that is authorized to act as one legal entity: *commercial, foreign-owned, multinational, municipal corporations; to dissolve, establish* or *set up* or *form, manage, run a corporation; a charitable* or *nonprofit corporation such as the Red Cross.*
cor.po.re.al (cor.POR.ee.ul) *adj.* having to do with the body; hence, tangible or material; **cor.po.re.al.ly** *adv.* —**cor.po.re.al.i.ty** (-ee.AL.i.tee) *n.*
corps (COR) *n. sing. & pl.* **1** an organized group of people following the same occupation: *the diplomatic corps in Washington; the press corps; a volunteer corps.* **2** a branch of the armed forces providing a special service: *a medical corps; the Signal Corps; the U.S. Marine Corps; the Corps of Engineers.* **3** an army unit made up of more than one division: *an air, army corps; a corps of marines.*
corpse (CORPS) *n.* a dead, usu. human body: *to lay out a corpse for burial; to bury, dig up a corpse; to exhume a corpse for an autopsy.*
corps.man (COR.mun) *n.* **-men** same as AIDMAN.
cor.pu.lent (CORP.yuh.lunt) *adj.* obese; having a fat body. —**cor.pu.lence** (-lunce) or **cor.pu.len.cy** *n.*
cor.pus (COR.pus) *n., pl.* **-por.a** (-puh.ruh) **1** a body of writings or texts: *the corpus of Shakespeare's works; to collect* or *gather a corpus of texts for compiling a dictionary.* **2** the main part of a bodily organ or structure.
cor.pus.cle (COR.puh.sul) *n.* **1** a small, free-floating blood or lymph cell: *red and white corpuscles.* **2** a tiny particle, as in early theories of electricity and light propagation. —**cor.pus.cu.lar** (cor.PUSK.yuh.lur) *adj.: the corpuscular theory of light.*
corpus de.lic.ti (-di.LIC.tye) *n.* the factual evidence of a crime; hence, loosely, the body of a murder victim.
cor.ral (cuh.RAL) *n.* **1** a pen for horses or cattle. **2** a defensive circle of vehicles, as wagons. —*v.* **cor.rals, cor.ralled, cor.ral.ling** *Informal.* surround and catch: *Cowboys corral wild horses; Police corral drug dealers; A party whip corrals* (= gathers) *votes.*
cor.rect (cuh.RECT) *v.* **1** set right what is wrong: *to correct abuses, errors, excesses, mistakes; Eyeglasses correct vision.* **2** point out errors in a person or thing: *to correct exam papers; Correct me if I am wrong; Parents have to correct* (= discipline) *their children.* —*adj.* **1** free from fault or error, often according to a standard: *the correct information; a correct answer, translation; Is it correct that he was fired? She's correct in thinking he was fired, but he claims it is more correct to say he resigned.* **2** proper: *correct behavior, costumes, manners; a correct young man.* —**cor.rect.a.ble** *adj.* —**cor.rect.ly** *adv.;* **cor.rect.ness** *n.*
cor.rec.tion (cuh.REC.shun) *n.* **1** the act of correcting: *correction of faults; vision correction.* **2** an instance of correcting: *if I may make a correction; Your clock needs a correction of two minutes; to check, mark corrections in a text; to issue, print, publish, seek a correction;* **adj.:** *a correction fluid, procedure, system; a newspaper's corrections column.* **3** the treatment of offenders: *The correction of criminals outside the prison is usually by putting them on probation; a department of corrections.* —**cor.rec.tion.al** *adj.: correctional standards; a* **correctional center** *or* **facility** (= jail); *correctional institutions; a* **correctional officer** (= prison guard).
cor.rec.tive (cuh.REC.tiv) *adj.* meant to correct; remedial: *corrective justice, lenses, surgery, training; a corrective measure; n.: Glasses are a corrective for faulty vision.*
cor.re.late (COR.uh.late) *v.* **-lates, -lat.ed, -lat.ing** stand in or bring into a mutual or systematic relationship: *We correlate lower speed limits with greater safety.* —*n.* a correlated factor: *The diameter of a circle is a correlate of its circumference.* —**cor.re.la.tion** (-LAY.shun) *n.: the correlation between lower speed limits and greater safety.*
cor.rel.a.tive (cuh.REL.uh.tiv) *adj.* corresponding: *strikes and the correlative loss of productivity.*
cor.res.pond (cor.uh.SPOND) *v.* **1** agree: *Actual costs do not correspond with budget estimates.* **2** be parallel or similar: *The Latin "pater" corresponds to the English "father"; The upper house of a legislature corresponds to the British House of Lords; the* **corresponding** *period of the last financial year.* **3** communicate by

correspondence / coryza

mail: *They corresponded (with each other) for many years before meeting; a **corresponding member** of a society (who lives far away and keeps in touch by mail).*
 —**cor.re.spond.ing.ly** *adv.*: *Inflation causes a correspondingly high increase in wages.*

cor.re.spond.ence (cor.uh.SPOND.unce) *n.* **1** conformity or agreement: *His actions have no close correspondence with his promises; There is no one-to-one correspondence between sounds and letters, as "c" sounds as (s) in "nice" and (k) in "cat"; the correspondence between theory and practice; the correspondences* (= similarities) *between the two jobs.* **2** communication by letter: *to break off, carry on or conduct a correspondence; business, commercial, personal correspondence; to be in, enter into correspondence with someone; the correspondence between them; to take a* **correspondence course** *(by mail) in a subject.*

cor.re.spond.ent (cor.uh.SPOND.unt) *adj.* corresponding: *inflation and correspondent wage increases.* —*n.* one who communicates by mail, esp. a newspaper reporter: *our London correspondent; foreign, special, war correspondents.*

cor.ri.dor (COR.uh.dor) *n.* **1** a long passageway or hall: *Room 233 is down the corridor; Room 204 is across the corridor from 201; You walk through a long, narrow, winding corridor to reach her office; the* **corridors of power** (= places of influence) *reserved to the elite.* **2** a narrow path for access or transportation: *a high-speed rail corridor to downtown; Highway 401 is in the crowded commuter corridor north of the city; land acquired for a transportation corridor.*

cor.ri.gen.dum (cor.uh.JEN.dum) *n., pl.* **-da** something to be corrected in a printed text, often listed on a separate sheet: *Check the corrigenda before reading a book.*

cor.ri.gi.ble (COR.i.juh.bul) *adj.* able to be corrected.

cor.rob.o.rate (cuh.ROB.uh.rate) *v.* **-rates, -rat.ed, -rat.ing** support someone's evidence, a theory, etc.: *An independent witness corroborated her story.*
 —**cor.rob.o.ra.tion** (-RAY.shun) *n.*

cor.rode (cuh.RODE) *v.* **cor.rodes, cor.rod.ed, cor.rod.ing** eat away, destroy, or deteriorate slowly, as by chemical action; *adj.*: *a badly corroded battery terminal.* —**cor.ro.sion** (-ROH.zhun) *n.*

cor.ro.sive (cuh.ROH.siv) *adj.* that corrodes: *the corrosive action of salt water; a corrosive agent, effect; corrosive substances* such as acid, cleaning fluid, and drain cleaner. —*n.* a corrosive substance.

cor.ru.gate (COR.uh.gate) *v.* **-gates, -gat.ed, -gat.ing** form into parallel ridges and furrows; *adj.*: **corrugated** iron roofing; *corrugated paper; a corrugated* (= furrowed) *brow.*
 —**cor.ru.ga.tion** (-GAY.shun) *n.*

cor.rupt (cuh.RUPT) *adj.* **1** no longer pure; made evil, tainted, or immoral: *children made corrupt by the bad example of their elders; corrupt desires; a corrupt life; the corrupt* (= changed by usage) *form of a word.* **2** dishonest: *a corrupt customs official, judge, politician; corrupt practices such as bribery and ballot-box stuffing.* —*v.* make corrupt: *The choirmaster was charged with corrupting youth; Power corrupts; Bodies corrupt* (= decay); *Malayalam "adal" was corrupted* (= changed by usage) *to English "atoll."*
 —**cor.rupt.er** or **cor.rup.tor** *n.*
 —**cor.rup.tion** *n.*: *political corruption; bribery and corruption; "Atoll" is actually a corruption* (= changed form) *of Malayalam "adal."* —**cor.rupt.ly** *adv.*

cor.sage (cor.SAHZH) *n.* a small bouquet worn by a woman on the shoulder, waist, or wrist.

cor.sair *n.* a pirate or pirate ship: *Barbary corsairs.*

cor.set (COR.sit) *n.* a tight, often laced, woman's undergarment for shaping the figure.

cor.tege or **cor.tège** (cor.TEZH) *n.* a following of attendants; also, a procession: *a funeral cortege.*

cor.tex (COR.tex) *n., pl.* **-ti.ces** (-tuh.seez) or **-tex.es** an outer layer of covering tissue on an organ or plant part: *adrenal, cerebral cortex; The cortex, or middle layer of bark, contains chlorophyll.*

cor.ti.cal (COR.ti.cul) *adj.* of a cortex, esp. of the brain cortex.

cor.ti.co.ster.oid (cor.ti.coh.STEER.oid, -STER.oid) *n.* a steroid found in the adrenal cortex and made synthetically.

cor.ti.sone (COR.tuh.sone) *n.* a hormone from the adrenal cortex used to treat various disorders.

co.run.dum (cuh.RUN.dum) *n.* the second-hardest mineral, used for cutting, polishing, and as a gem.

cor.us.cate (COR.us.cate) *v.* **-cates, -cat.ed, -cat.ing** flash; glitter; *adj.*: *a coruscating light; her coruscating wit.*
 —**cor.us.ca.tion** (-CAY.shun) *n.*

cor.vette (cor.VET) *n.* a light, fast warship.

co.ry.za (cuh.RYE.zuh) *n.* a head cold; the common cold.

cos lettuce same as ROMAINE.
Co.sa Nos.tra (COH.zuh.NOSE.truh) *n.* the U.S. Mafia.
co.sign (COH.sine) *v.* sign a document along with another signer.
cosily, cosiness See COSY.
cos.met.ic (coz.MET.ic) *n.* **1** a substance, as lipstick, face powder, eye shadow, etc. for beautifying the skin, hair, nails, etc.: *to apply, put on, use cosmetics.* **2** anything that superficially covers up defects. —*adj.* serving to improve appearance: *a cosmetic cream, preparation; a name that has only cosmetic appeal; a merely cosmetic antipoverty program; cosmetic surgery.*
—**cos.met.i.cal.ly** *adv.*
cos.me.ti.cian (coz.mi.TISH.un) *n.* one trained in the use of cosmetics; cosmetologist.
cos.met.ize (COZ.mi.tize) *v.* **-iz.es, -ized, -iz.ing** improve something merely in appearance. Also **cos.met.i.cize** (coz.MET.uh.size).
cos.me.tol.o.gy (coz.mi.TOL.uh.jee) *n.* the work or art of applying cosmetics. —**cos.me.tol.o.gist** *n.*
cos.mic (COZ.mic) *adj.* **1** having to do with the cosmos: *cosmic forces, harmony, realms;* **Cosmic dust** forms clouds of fine particles of matter in outer space; **Cosmic rays** enter our atmosphere from outer space. **2** great in extent, intensity, or scope: *a cosmic approach, crisis; cosmic issues like cancer and AIDS; from the subatomic to the cosmic; in cosmic terms; its cosmic vastness; the cosmic proportions of our universe.* —**cos.mi.cal.ly** *adv.*
cos.mog.o.ny (coz.MOG.uh.nee) *n.* **-nies** the origin of the universe; also, an account of this: *mythical cosmogonies.*
cos.mol.o.gy (coz.MOL.uh.jee) *n.* **-gies** the philosophy or science of the universe as an ordered physical entity; **cos.mol.o.gist** *n.* —**cos.mo.log.i.cal** (-muh.LOJ.i.cul) *adj.*
cos.mo.naut (COZ.muh.nawt) *n.* a Russian astronaut.
cos.mo.pol.i.tan (coz.muh.POL.uh.tun) *adj.* **1** representing the whole world: *a cosmopolitan background, center, clientele, community, metropolis, population, society; a cosmopolitan bird (that is found throughout the world).* **2** not narrow or regional in outlook: *the cosmopolitan world of art; The cosmopolitan person is at home in any part of the world; a cosmopolitan atmosphere, charm, lifestyle, taste, vision.*
—*n.* one who is cosmopolitan: *a cosmopolitan and a famous world traveler.*
—**cos.mo.pol.i.tan.ism** *n.*
cos.mos (COZ.mus, -mos) *n.* **1** the universe as an ordered whole; hence, any complex, harmonious system. **2** *pl.* **cosmos** a colorful, composite tropical flower.
Cos.sack (COS.uk, -ak) *n.* one of a S. Russian people known as mounted warriors; *adj.:* Cossack horsemen.
cos.set (COS.it) *v.* **cos.sets, cos.set.ed, cos.et.ing** pamper or indulge: *The youngest child is often cosseted by the parents; adj.: a hotel that makes guests feel cosseted and coddled.*
cost *n.* **1** the price of something: *the high cost of housing; The average cost of a home goes up each spring; a cost that is hard to bear; We estimated the unit cost (= what each copy would cost) of the publication; We put or set the cost at $25; She decided to fight the election* **at all costs** or **at any cost** *without stopping to* **count the cost;** *He won the election at the cost of his health, home, and family; It was a terrible cost to pay; a service provided at no cost to the taxpayer.* **2** expenses: *We are trying to cut or reduce heating costs; His parents spared no cost to put him through college; He was fined $500 and* **costs** *(= expenses of the lawsuit); They paid his court costs; There are direct, fixed, indirect, overhead costs to be considered; A* **cost accounting** *system analyzes the costs of producing goods.*
—*v.* **1 costs, cost, cost.ing** require or entail as a payment or loss: *Houses cost too much; How much did it cost? It cost (us) $500,000; His mistake cost him dearly; It cost him his job.* **2 costs, cost.ed, cost.ing** determine the cost of something: *We costed out the book to determine if it was publishable.*
co-star *n.* a star of equal rank.
—*v.* **-stars, -starred, -star.ring:** *Vivien Leigh co-starred with Clark Gable in "Gone With the Wind"; She co-starred in the movie.*
Cos.ta Ri.can (cos.tuh.REE.cun) *n.* & *adj.* (a person) of or from **Costa Rica**, a country in S. Central America.
cost-effective *adj.* beneficial in proportion to the cost: *Computerization is cost-effective; cost-effective measures; a cost-effective system.*
cos.tive (COS.tiv) *adj.* slow-moving, as if constipated or constipating.
cost.ly *adj.* **-li.er, -li.est** that costs a great deal: *costly furs and jewels; a costly production delay; a costly victory; It's costly to replace the stolen furs.* —**cost.li.ness** *n.*
cost of living *n.* the average cost of food, shelter, clothing, and other necessities: *The cost of living has gone up*

twofold during the last 10 years; The strikers' demands included a better **cost-of-living allowance** or **COLA**; The **cost-of-living index** is a measure of how the cost of living changes periodically.

cos.tume (COS.toom, -tyoom, long "oo") *n.* a set of clothes: *academic, ballet, bathing, ethnic, folk, Halloween, Indian, national, native, peasant, stage costumes.* —*v.* **-tumes, -tumed, -tum.ing** dress; *adj.:* an actress *costumed* in Elizabethan style. —**cos.tum.er** (cos.TUE.mur) or **cos.tum.i.er** (-mee.ur) *n.*

costume jewelry *n.* inexpensive artificial ornaments made of glass, plastics, wood, leather, etc.

co.sy (COH.zee) *adj.* **co.si.er, co.si.est** same as COZY. —*n., pl.* **-sies** a covering for a teapot to keep it warm: *a tea cosy.* —**co.si.ly** *adv.;* **co.si.ness** *n.*

cot *n.* **1** a narrow bed of canvas over a usu. collapsible frame. **2** also **cote** (COHT), a shelter or shed, esp. for animals: *a dove cote.*

cot death same as CRIB DEATH.

co.te.rie (COH.tuh.ree) *n.* a usu. exclusive circle of people with a shared interest: *a literary coterie.*

co.ter.mi.nous (coh.TUR.muh.nus) same as CONTERMINOUS.

co.til.lion (coh.TIL.yun) *n.* **1** a lively dance with complex steps. **2** a formal ball.

cot.tage (COT.ij) *n.* a small, usu. rural house; also, a summer house: *We drive to the cottage on weekends.* —**cot.tag.er** *n.*

cottage cheese *n.* a soft, mild cheese made from soured skim milk.

cottage industry *n.* a small-scale manufacturing activity carried on as from home.

cot.ter or **cotter pin** *n.* a split pin used to hold parts in place, inserted through a hole and fastened by spreading the tips.

cot.ton (COT.un) *n.* **1** thread or cloth made from the white, fluffy seed hairs of a bushy plant: *absorbent cotton.* **2** the seed hairs or the plant itself: *to pick cotton; a bale of cotton.* —**cotton on to** *Informal.* understand. —**cotton to** take a liking to someone. —**cot.ton.y** *adj.:* The wind *carries* the feathered, cottony dandelion seeds far and wide.

Cotton Belt *n.* the region of southern U.S. where cotton is grown.

cotton candy *n.* a fluffy candy spun from melted sugar.

cotton gin *n.* a machine for cleaning seeds from cotton fibers.

cot.ton.mouth (COT.un.mouth) same as WATER MOCCASIN.

cotton-picking *adja. Informal.* darned: Politicians should keep their *cotton-picking* hands out of the private lives of people.

cot.ton.seed (COT.un.seed) *n.* the seed of the cotton plant, which yields **cottonseed oil** used in margarine, soap, linoleum, etc. and **cottonseed meal** used in feed and fertilizer.

cot.ton.tail (COT.un.tail) *n.* a small, white-tailed North American rabbit.

cot.ton.wood (COT.un.wood) *n.* a poplar having fluff around the seeds.

cot.y.le.don (cot.ul.EED.un) *n.* the first leaf sprouting from a seed.

couch (COWCH) *n.* a piece of furniture for sitting or lying down; sofa: *to lie, lounge, sit on a couch; the psychoanalyst's couch; a studio couch.* —*v.* **1** lay or lie on or as on a couch: Ambushers *couched* in the bushes. **2** to phrase; *adj.:* a request *couched* in diplomatic language.

couch.ant (COWCH.unt) *adj.* of animals in coats-of-arms, lying with raised head: *a lion couchant.*

cou.chette (coo.SHET) *n.* a train compartment that converts to provide sleeping berths.

couch potato *n.* one who spends too much time watching TV.

cou.gar (COO.gur) *n.* a large, light-brown wildcat.

cough (CAWF) *v.* **1** emit air forcefully and noisily from the lung: She *coughed* nervously when he mentioned the date; The engine *coughed*, sputtered, and died on us; *n.:* a fit of *coughing*. **2** utter or expel by coughing: He *coughed* up the fishbone that was choking him; Sam had no problem **coughing up** (*Informal* for producing) the cash they demanded. —*n.:* a cold with a bad *cough;* a hacking, heavy, persistent *cough;* a **cough drop** or lozenge to relieve a *cough;* a **cough syrup** (= syrupy medication to relieve a *cough*).

could (COOD, short "OO") *pt.* of CAN [also used to express possibility, condition, permission, etc.]: *Could* I see you for a minute? It *could* happen here; It *could* be serious if help doesn't arrive fast.

could.n't (COOD.unt, short "OO") could not.

cou.lee (COO.lee) *n.* **1** a stream bed or gully that is dry in summer. **2** a stream of lava.

cou.lomb (COO.lom, -lome) *n.* the amount of electricity transferred by one ampere in one second.

coun.cil (COWN.sul) *n.* a body or assembly chosen to discuss, advise, administer, or legislate: *an executive council; student councils; The U.N. Security*

Council; The mayor convened the town council. —**coun.ci.lor** or **coun.cil.lor** *n.* a council member.

coun.sel (COWN.sul) *v.* **-sels, -seled, -sel.ing** give advice to someone: *The lawyer counseled her client about his problem; She counseled him against acting rashly; counseled him to be patient; She counseled (= urged) patience; The client felt good about having* **counseled with** (= consulted) *her.* —*n.* **1** advice: *to give, offer counsel; sage, wise counsel; Let us* **take counsel together** (= discuss this together), *then* **take counsel with** (= get advice from) *our lawyer; I don't like to* **keep my own counsel** (= keep my plans secret). **2** *sing. & pl.* legal adviser(s); lawyer(s): *legal counsel; counsel for the defense, for the prosecution.* Also **coun.selled, coun.sel.ling** *Cdn.*

counseling (COWN.suh.ling) *n.* the giving of advice: *career, family, guidance, marriage, vocational counseling.* Also **counselling** *Cdn.*

coun.se.lor (COWN.suh.lur) *n.* **1** adviser: *a career counselor at our high school; a guidance counselor; a counselor to the ambassador; a counselor in the State Department.* **2** a lawyer. Also **coun.sel.lor** *Cdn.*

count *v.* **1** recite numbers in order: *Children learn to count (in ascending order); Can you count (from one) to ten in French? Before a rocket lifts off, they say, "T minus 30 seconds and counting"* (down to zero); *to* **count down** (in reverse order) *to zero.* **2** match a series of objects to such a series of numbers; total up: *Count your change; Let's* **count heads** or **noses** *to see how many are here.* **3** consider: *Count yourself lucky to be alive; They'll count an 80% mark as an A; It counts* (= is considered) *as an A; If you count Jim* (= take him into consideration), *there are six of us; Please* **count me in** (= include me) *as a member; If it's something illegal, you can* **count me out** (= leave me out); *A boxer is* **counted out** (= loses) *if he doesn't get up in ten seconds after being knocked down.* **4** depend or rely: *Never* **count on** *the weather; You can* **count (up)on** *us for help, to support you; You can* **count on** *winning* (= expect to win). **5** be of significant value: *Nowadays connections in high places don't* **count for** *much; Your marks count; They* **count toward** *qualifying for admission to college; One low mark won't* **count against** *you.* —*n.* **1** a counting or the resulting number: *Someone please* **keep count** *of the guests; Let's make or take an accurate, correct, exact body count;* *He got it right on the third count; What's the count* (= total) *now? The count stands at 237; It's 239 by my count; We've now* **lost count** *of them because of newcomers.* **2** a charge in an indictment: *five counts of robbery; He was found guilty on all counts.* **3** a European noble whose rank is analogous to that of an earl. —**count.a.ble** *adj.*

count.down *n.* a counting backward to the zero hour: *The countdown began at 16:00 hours; the final countdown for the moon flight; The countdown continues, "3, 2, 1, lift off!"*

coun.te.nance (COWN.tun.unce) *n.* **1** a person's face, esp. as expressing feelings: *an angry, happy, hideous, pleasant countenance.* **2** approval: *As vegetarians, we cannot give* or *lend countenance to killing in any form.* **3** composure; self-control: *Her icy stare put him* **out of countenance**; *The joke was so funny she could not* **keep her countenance** (= could not help laughing).
—*v.* **-nan.ces, -nanced, -nanc.ing** approve or tolerate: *We cannot countenance killing in any form.*

count.er *n.* **1** one that counts: *a calorie counter's guide to dieting.* **2** a token, chip, etc. used for counting or in games. **3** a long table, board, or other flat surface for displaying wares, conducting business, serving or preparing food, etc.: *bargain, jewelry, kitchen, lunch counters; Sometimes payments, sales, etc. are made* **under the counter** (= illicitly); *Drugs sold* **over the counter** *don't need a prescription.* **4** the opposite; a checking action: *an effective counter to the attack.* —*adv.* contrary: *Sorry, but your ideas go or run counter to accepted theories.* —*v.* act or speak in opposition to a person or thing; strike or answer back; offset: *efforts to counter inflationary losses; Her opponent countered that the question was irrelevant; The boxer countered (the blow) with a left hook.*
—*comb.form.* contrariety or opposition to: *counterclaim, countersuit.* **2** correspondence to: *counterpart, countersign.*

coun.ter.act (cown.tur.ACT) *v.* oppose or offset: *a drug to counteract the poison.*

coun.ter.at.tack (COWN.tur.uh.TACK) *n. & v.* attack in response: *They lost the battle, but counterattacked the next day; to launch, make a counterattack against the enemy.*

coun.ter.bal.ance (cown.tur.BAL.unce) *v.* **-anc.es, -anced, -anc.ing** oppose with equal weight; offset. —*n.* (COWN.tur.bal.unce) a weight or force that balances or offsets another:

He boasts many strengths as a counterbalance to his one weakness.

coun.ter.claim (COWN.tur.claim) *n.* an opposing claim, as in law against a plaintiff: *to bring, enter, make, plead a counterclaim against the plaintiff.* —*v.*: *The defendant counterclaimed $2 million.*

coun.ter.clock.wise (cown.tur.CLOCK.wize) *adj. & adv.* opposite in direction to the turning of a clock's hands.

coun.ter.cul.ture (COWN.tur.cul.chur) *n.* a culture with values opposed to the rest of society, as among youth: *The new counterculture is more into vegetables than drugs.* —**coun.ter.cul.tur.al** (-CUL.chuh.rul) *adj.*

coun.ter.es.pi.on.age (cown.tur.ES.pee.uh.nazh) *n.* secret activity to thwart enemy spying.

coun.ter.feit (COWN.tur.fit) *v.* make an imitation or replica, as of currency, so as to deceive or cheat: *They went to jail for counterfeiting (bills); He only counterfeited grief when she died.* —*n.*: *This $20 bill seems a counterfeit; a counterfeit twenty.*

coun.ter.in.sur.gen.cy (COWN.tur.in.SUR.jun.see) *n.* action to suppress insurgent rebels, esp. guerrillas; **coun.ter.in.sur.gent** *n. & adj.*

coun.ter.in.tel.li.gence (COWN.tur.in.TEL.uh.junce) *n.* action to thwart or mislead enemy spies or saboteurs: *to conduct counterintelligence.*

coun.ter.mand (COWN.tur.mand) *v.* revoke or call back an order with an opposite order.

coun.ter.mea.sure (COWN.tur.mezh.ur) *n.* opposing measure: *to take countermeasures against foreign tariffs.*

coun.ter.of.fen.sive (COWN.tur.uh.fen.siv) *n.* an offensive in anticipation of an attack: *to launch or undertake a counteroffensive against the invaders.*

coun.ter.pane (COWN.tur.pane) *n.* a bedspread.

coun.ter.part (COWN.tur.part) *n.* one that is similar or analogous: *The Secretary of State met her Russian counterpart; Our prime minister has a counterpart in the Russian premier; He is the counterpart of or to our prime minister*

coun.ter.point (COWN.tur.point) *n.* **1** a melody in contrasting harmony to the main melody; also, music having this. **2** a foil or contrast for something: *The funeral was a sad counterpoint to springtime.*

coun.ter.poise (COWN.tur.poiz) *n.* counterbalance; equilibrium. Also *v.* **-pois.es, -poised, -pois.ing.**

coun.ter.pro.duc.tive (COWN.tur.pruh.DUC.tiv) *adj.* having results opposite to those desired: *The punishment was so severe it proved to be counterproductive.*

coun.ter.rev.o.lu.tion (COWN.tur.rev.uh.LOO.shun) *n.* a movement to reverse the result of an earlier revolution; **coun.ter.rev.o.lu.tion.ar.y** *n. & adj.* **-ar.ies.**

coun.ter.sign (COWN.tur.sign) *v.* sign an already signed document to authenticate it. —*n.* such a signature; also **coun.ter.sig.na.ture** (-SIG.nuh.chur).

coun.ter.sink (COWN.tur.sink) *v.* **-sinks, -sunk, -sink.ing** widen a drilled hole near a surface so that a screw or bolt head will sit flush. —*n.* such a widening or a tool for making it.

coun.ter.spy (COWN.tur.spy) *n.* **-spies** one doing counterespionage.

coun.ter.ten.or (COWN.tur.ten.ur) *n.* the highest male singing voice, above a tenor.

coun.ter.vail (COWN.tur.vail) *n.* compensation or equalization: *to seek countervails against inequalities;* **adj.**: *countervail actions, cases, duties, inquiries, investigations, rulings, tariffs.*

countervailing *adj.* **1** counteracting: *a countervailing pressure to take action; countervailing advice, forces, military strength.* **2** compensating: *countervailing duties, tendencies, tariffs.*

coun.ter.weight (COWN.tur.wait) *n.* a counterbalance.

count.ess (COWN.tis) *n.* an earl's or count's wife or widow.

count.less (COWNT.lis) *adj.* too numerous to be counted: *countless hordes of insects; countless numbers of people; a countless number of inquiries.*

coun.tri.fied (CUN.truh.fide) *adj.* rustic or rural: *a countrified design, setting, version.*

coun.try (CUN.tree) *n.* **-tries 1** a nation or its territory: *to govern or rule or run a country; civilized, developing, host, neighboring, Third-World countries.* **2** a district or region: *mountainous country; wine country.* **3** a rural area: *living out in the country, back, open, rough, rugged country.* —**adj. 1** rural: *country gardens, homes, houses, roads, style, warmth.* **2** rustic: *country bumpkins, manners.* **3** having to do with country music: *a country hit, rocker, singer; country blues.*

country club *n.* a suburban social club, usu. having a golf course and other sports facilities.

country cousin *n.* a relative from the country who is new to city ways.

country-dance *n.* a native English folk dance in which dancers are arranged in two facing lines, a square, or a circle.

coun.try.man (CUN.tree.mun) *n.* **-men 1** a man from one's own country; compatriot. **2** (*also* -man) a rustic.

country mile *n. Informal.* long distance: *to walk a country mile; the best politician within a country mile of the Capitol.*

country music *n.* a modernization of the rural folk music of S. and W. United States.

coun.try.side (CUN.tree.side) *n.* a rural area: *Let's visit the countryside; The whole countryside* (= rural population) *is behind the farmers.*

coun.try.wom.an (CUN.tree.woom.un) *n.* **-wom.en 1** a woman from one's own country; compatriot: *She led her countrywomen in a 15-year campaign for equal rights.* **2** a rustic woman.

coun.ty (COWN.tee) *n.* **-ties** the major administrative division of a state or country.

coup (COO) *n.* **coups** (COOZ) **1** a sudden, strikingly successful action: *Smith scored a big coup over his rivals by being first.* **2** a sudden, usu. violent change in government: *to carry out, stage a coup; a bloodless coup; a bloody coup by the army; a military coup;* also **coup d'é.tat** (-day.TAH).

coup de grâce (COO.duh.GRAHS) *n.* a merciful deathblow to a sufferer.

coupe (COOP) *n.* a closed, two-door car smaller than a sedan: *a hatchback coupe.*

cou.pé (coo.PAY) *n.* **1** a closed carriage that seats two people inside and the driver outside. **2** a coupe.

cou.ple (CUP.ul) *v.* **-ples, -pled, -pling** join or link together; unite: *A locomotive is coupled to a train.* —*n.* **1** two similar things: *a couple of old boots that don't match as a pair.* **2** *Informal.* a few: *a couple of days back.* **3** two people, esp. a man and a woman considered as partners or mates: *a married couple; unmarried couples; couples swirling on the dance floor.* **4** a link or fastener.

cou.pler (CUP.lur) *n.* one that couples: *a railroad car with a coupler at each end.*

cou.plet (CUP.lit) *n.* two consecutive, usu. rhyming lines of verse in the same meter, as: *"Those who in quarrels interpose / Must often wipe a bloody nose."*

cou.pon (COO.pon, CUE-) *n.* **1** a ticket, part of a package or advertisement, etc. entitling the bearer to a discount, refund, etc.: *clip, detach, redeem coupons; discount, gift, ration coupons; coupon books.* **2** a form to be filled out for ordering something by mail, as included in an ad: *order coupons.* **3** a detachable interest certificate on a bond: *to clip coupons.*

cour.age (CUR.ij) *n.* the ability to persevere in the face of danger or hardship; bravery: *to demonstrate or display or show courage; to get up or muster or summon up courage; a woman of great courage; He lacks the courage to stand up for his rights; It takes courage to do it; the dauntless or indomitable courage of our pioneers; grim, moral, physical courage; He has the **courage of his convictions** to do what he thinks is right.*
—**cou.ra.geous** (cuh.RAY.jus) *adj.*;
cou.ra.geous.ly *adv.*

cou.ri.er (COOR.ee.ur, CUR-) *n.* one who carries messages, official papers, goods, etc.: *to dispatch a courier to the head office; We'll send it to you by courier; a diplomatic courier;* **adja.:** *courier delivery, services, traffic.*

course (CORSE) *n.* **1** a progression in space or time: *the course of events; the winding course of a river.* **2** the normal order, development, or duration: *the course of true love; The disease has run its course* (= is over); *He does favors for friends* **as a matter of course** (= as something normal or natural); *You will receive a reply* **in due course** (= when it is time); *They lost $5 million* **in the course of** (= during) *a month.* **3** route; direction: *What course are we sailing? to chalk out a course of action; Your only course may be to flee; to stay* (= persevere in) *the course; to steer* (= pursue) *the course; a plane that went* **off course** *and was lost; Our plane is* **on course** *for Vancouver.* **4** a study program: *They conduct or give or offer or teach courses in many areas; a course in calculus; a course on family planning; They cancel, introduce, organize, plan courses; Students may audit or sit in on courses; to complete, drop, drop out of, enroll for, fail, pass, register for, sign up for, take, withdraw from courses; advanced, beginning, correspondence, demanding, difficult, easy, elective, elementary, extension, graduate, gut, intensive, intermediate, introductory, laboratory, lecture, makeup, noncredit, refresher, required, rigorous, survey, undergraduate courses; Courses cover, deal with, treat subjects.* **5** an ordered series: *a course of lectures, studies; to undergo a course of treatment; a six-course dinner; a course* (= layer) *of bricks.* —**of course 1** certainly: *Of course, she's right.* **2** as one would expect: *Everyone, of course, has to* pay a fee. —v. **cours.es, coursed, cours.ing 1** move, run, or flow swiftly: *Blood courses through the veins.* **2** hunt, esp. deer or rabbits, with hounds.

course.ware (CORS.ware) *n.* software for teaching purposes.

course.work *n.* work done by a student for fulfilling academic requirements.

court (CORT) *n.* **1** a judge or judges who try legal cases; also, the place where this is done: *to take a person to court; to testify in court; in open court; A court adjourns; to hold court; Too many cases clog the courts; appellate, circuit, county, criminal, district, family, federal, high, juvenile, moot, municipal, night, probate, small claims, superior, supreme, traffic, trial courts; Order in the court! a court of appeals, chancery, common pleas, equity, law;* **adja.:** *a court appearance, battle, decision, hearing, order, ruling; court papers, proceedings, records.* **2** an open area with one or more buildings around it; courtyard. **3** an open area for playing a game such as tennis or basketball. **4** a king, queen, etc. with his or her family, retinue, advisers, and ministers; an assembly of this; also, a royal palace: *The royal family holds court; Visitors are presented at court; at the Court of St. James or at St. James's* (= at the British royal court); **adja.:** *a court jester; court life.* —v. **1** try to gain the favor or love of someone; woo: *He courted her with gifts and flowers.* **2** risk: *Those who drink and drive are courting disaster; to court arrest, danger, defeat, disappointment, failure.* —**out of court 1** without a trial: *a case settled out of court.* **2** unworthy of being given a hearing: *His wild schemes are quite out of court; They will be laughed out of court* (= dismissed as ridiculous). —**pay court to someone** *Formal.* try to please or woo someone.

cour.te.ous (CUR.tee.us) *adj.* gracious and considerate in manner; **cour.te.ous.ly** *adv.*

cour.te.san (COR.tuh.zun) *n.* a prostitute with a wealthy or high-ranking clientele; also **cour.te.zan.**

cour.te.sy (CUR.tuh.see) *n.* **-sies** (an instance of) polite, considerate, well-mannered behavior: *He showed us every courtesy; her professional, unfailing courtesy; as a courtesy to or toward new customers; He didn't have the courtesy to answer our letters; He did us the courtesy of not interrupting our conversation; as common courtesy dictates; Coffee and donuts are courtesy of* (= offered with the compliments of) *the management.*

court.house *n.* a building housing law courts.

cour.ti.er (COR.tee.ur) *n.* a member of a royal court.

court.ly (CORT.lee) *adj.* **-li.er, -li.est** polite and dignified; refined: *courtly love, manners; the courtly Mr. Smith.* —**court.li.ness** *n.*

court-martial *n.* **courts-martial** or **court-martials 1** a military court that tries offenders against military law. **2** such a trial: *to hold a court-martial; general, special, summary court-martials.* —v. **-tials, -tialed, -tial.ing:** *He was court-martialed for disobeying orders.* Also **court-martialled, court-martialling** *Cdn.*

court.room *n.* a room in which a law court sits; **adja.:** *a courtroom battle, drama, scene.*

court.ship *n.* a wooing.

court.yard *n.* an open area surrounded by buildings or such an area inside a large building.

cous.in (CUZ.in) *n.* **1** a child of one's aunt or uncle; also called "first cousin": *a first cousin once removed* (= first cousin's child). **2** relative: *a distant cousin; kissing cousins* (= close relatives); *Words are cousin* (= related) *to the deed.*

couth (COOTH, long "OO") *n.* refinement or polish: *Our cook has more couth than your maitre d'.*

cou.ture (coo.TOOR) *n.* the work of a couturier.

cou.tu.ri.er (coo.TOOR.ee.ur) *n.* one who designs and makes high-fashion clothes for women. —**cou.tu.ri.ère** or **cou.tu.ri.ere** (-ee.ur), *fem.*

cove (COHV) *n.* a small usu. sheltered bay.

cov.en (CUV.un, COH.vun) *n.* a group of assembled witches.

cov.e.nant (CUV.uh.nunt) *n.* **1** a formal and serious agreement: *God's covenant with Noah; the UN Covenant on Economic, Social, and Cultural Rights; a death covenant signed by lovers.* **2** a provision, as in a deed: *a covenant between real estate developers and home buyers restricting rooftop TV antennas; to ease restrictive covenants on homes.* —v. make an agreement: *They covenanted to deliver the steel on August 18 for a sum of $7,500.*

cov.er (CUV.ur) *v.* **1** to be or place something in front of, on top of, etc., esp. so as to conceal or protect; hence, lie or extend over something: *Snow covered the mountain; He covered his* tracks to avoid detection; Will you **cover for** me (= take my place) while I'm away? a war hero covered with glory; a politician accused of **covering up** (= concealing the truth) corruption; **n.:** floor, wall, window **coverings** (= tiles, drapes, etc.); **adj.:** a tightly **covered** container; a covered bridge, dish, terrace. **2** deal with something: This book covers the whole subject; a reporter covering (= reporting on) the coronation live; I can't cover (= travel over) more than 900 km a day; money to cover (= pay for) all expenses. **3** protect: The house and contents are covered by this insurance policy; It covers you against all perils; The shortstop shifted to cover third base; Bill covered (= accepted) my bet; Cover me (by shooting at the enemy) while I run for help; **adj.:** Keep him **covered** (by pointing your gun) so he won't escape. —**n. 1** something that covers, hides, or protects: Put the cover on the box; cloud, dust, mattress, pillow covers; a book with a torn cover; The cassette is being mailed **under separate cover** (= in another envelope); He read the book from **cover to cover**; They sought cover (during the attack); to provide air cover (= protection) for an advancing army; a sniper firing from cover; When the shooting starts, **take cover**; His business is just a cover (= pretense) for his spying. **2** a place setting for one person at a table: Covers were laid for 10. —**under cover** in concealment: to work under cover as a spy; He came here under cover of darkness; State budgets are kept under cover till the last minute.

cov.er.age (CUV.ur.ij) n. **1** a covering by insurance: to provide coverage; comprehensive or full coverage. **2** a reporting: the coverage of an election; live TV coverage; The election received complete, extensive, full, wide coverage in the media.

cov.er.alls (CUV.ur.awls) n.pl. a one-piece suit of protective work clothes.

cover charge n. a fixed additional charge in a restaurant, night club, etc.

cover crop n. a crop grown to enrich soil and prevent erosion, as clover, vetch, and rye.

covered wagon n. a pioneer wagon with an arched roof of canvas.

cover girl n. a glamorous young woman, as one who appears on a magazine cover.

cov.er.let (CUV.ur.lit) n. a bedspread.

cover letter n. a letter that explains or supports something enclosed; also **covering letter.**

cover story n. **1** the leading story in a magazine as pictured on its cover. **2** a story made up to hide something.

cov.ert (COH.vurt, CUV.urt) **1** adj. hidden or disguised, esp. illegal and protected: the Intelligence Agency's covert actions, operations. **2** n. a hiding place, esp. for game. —**cov.ert.ly** adv.

cov.er.up (CUV.ur.up) n. **1** a device or attempt to hide something: the coverup of a political scandal. **2** a loose outer garment. Also **cover-up.**

cov.et (CUV.it) v. strongly desire what is another's: She coveted Jane's car and constantly borrowed it. —**cov.et.ous** (-us) adj.: She is envious of Jane's good looks and covetous of her car; **cov.et.ous.ly** adv.; **cov.et.ous.ness** n.

cov.ey (CUV.ee) n. **-eys** a brood or small group of birds: a covey of quail, animal-rights activists, reporters.

cow n. **1** an adult female bovine: Holy cow! You can argue, complain, sit there, wait **till the cows come home** (= forever), but nothing will happen. **2** an adult female walrus, elephant, dolphin, moose, etc. **3 cows** [in cowboy use] cattle. —v. intimidate: They were cowed into submission.

cow.ard (COW.urd) n. one shamefully lacking in courage: an abject, dastardly, dirty coward. —**adj.:** his coward (= cowardly) cries, deceit; a coward deed. See also COWARDLY.

cow.ard.ice (COW.ur.dis) n. lack of courage: to show cowardice; abject, moral, rank cowardice; the streak of cowardice in his makeup.

cow.ard.ly (COW.urd.lee) adj. lacking courage: a cowardly deed, excuse, lion. —**cow.ard.li.ness** n.

cow.bird n. a kind of blackbird that lays eggs in other birds' nests.

cow.boy n. one who tends cattle on a ranch; also **cow.hand.**

cow.catch.er (COW.catch.ur) n. a projecting metal device on the front of a train to push obstacles off the tracks.

cow chip n. a dried piece of cattle dung used as a fuel.

cow.er (COW.ur) v. huddle or cringe in fear: a child cowering in a corner.

cow.girl n. a woman who tends cattle on a ranch.

cow.hand n. a cowboy.

cow.hide n. **1** leather made from a cow's hide; **adj**a.: a cowhide jacket, skirt, vest. **2** a whip of braided rawhide or leather.

cowl (rhyme: howl) n. a hood on a monk's habit; also, the habit.

cow.lick n. a tuft of hair that stubbornly sticks up.

cow.man n. **-men** a cattle rancher.

co-worker *n.* a fellow worker.
cow-poke or **cow.punch.er** (COW.punch.ur) *n. Informal.* a cowboy.
cow pony *n.* a horse ridden while tending cattle.
cow.pox *n.* a mild, smallpoxlike disease caused by a virus that provides humans with a temporary immunity to smallpox.
cow.rie (COW.ree) *n.* **-ries** a highly polished and brightly colored seashell, used as money and ornament.
cow.slip *n.* any of four plants with yellow flowers, esp. the marsh marigold.
cox *n. Informal.* coxswain.
cox.comb *n.* a foolish, conceited fop.
cox.swain *n.* one who commands a ship's boat or a racing shell.
coy *adj.* 1 bashful: *a coy manner, smile, suggestion.* 2 pretending to be shy; also, teasing: *a coy reply; He was coy about his plans to run for mayor.* —**coy.ly** *adv.;* **coy.ness** *n.*
coy.o.te (kye.OH.tee, KYE.ote) *n.* a small W. North American wolf.
coy.pu (COY.poo) *n.* a beaverlike South American animal valued for its fur; nutria.
coz.en (CUZ.un) *v.* deceive; cheat with a petty trick. —**coz.en.age** (-ij) *n.*
co.zy (COH.zee) *adj.* **co.zi.er, co.zi.est** 1 snug and comfortable: *Keep it cozy! the cat sleeping in a cozy corner of the sofa; a cozy place.* 2 *Informal.* comfortable and beneficial: *a cozy little deal; a cozy arrangement, business, cartel, consensus.* 3 *Informal.* friendly and intimate: *a cozy atmosphere, relationship, setup; Kay got too cozy with clients and was fired.* —*v.* **-zies, -zied, -zy.ing** become too friendly with someone: *The Canadian government was accused of cozying up to the Republicans.* —**co.zi.ly** *adv.;* **co.zi.ness** *n.*
crab *n.* 1 a ten-legged, broad-shelled aquatic animal. 2 a louse that infests the armpits, chest, pubic area, etc. of a patient: *a patient with crabs.* 3 a crab apple. 4 an ill-tempered grumbler.
—*v.* **crabs, crabbed, crab.bing** *Informal.* 1 complain ill temperedly: *He keeps on crabbing that the winter is too long.* 2 ruin by meddling: *Don't crab my act.*
crab apple *n.* a small, tart apple or the tree it grows on.
crab.bed (CRAB.id) *adj.* 1 crabby. 2 barely legible because cramped: *crabbed handwriting, notes.*
crab.by (CRAB.ee) *adj.* **crab.bi.er, crab.bi.est** ill-tempered or complaining. —**crab.bi.ly** *adv.;* **crab.bi.ness** *n.*
crab.grass *n.* an annual grass regarded as a weed in lawns.
crab louse same as CRAB, *n.* 2.
crack *v.* 1 make or cause to make a short, sharp noise: *to crack a whip; thunder cracking in the distance; He's good at cracking* (= telling) *jokes.* 2 break without separating into pieces: *The glass cracked in the heat; People crack under pressure.* 3 break into pieces: *to crack ice, nuts, wheat.* 4 *Informal.* open: *a student who didn't crack one book all year; She tried to make him crack a smile; They were nabbed by police before they could crack the brew; The dawn cracked early.* 5 open and get into: *to crack a safe, vault; to crack a business, market.* 6 change suddenly to a higher or a hoarse sound: *Her voice cracked with emotion; A boy's voice cracks at puberty.* 7 distill petroleum into its component chemicals. 8 *Informal.* solve: *Detective Brown cracked the case.* 9 hit sharply: *She cracked her head on the door as she entered.* —**crack down** become more strict: *Police crack down on drunk drivers at Christmas.* —**crack up** 1 especially of a car or plane, crash: *The airliner cracked up because of metal fatigue; The Soviet Union cracked up overnight.* 2 break down laughing. 3 *Informal.* break down mentally. 4 **cracked up** reputed: *not quite what it is cracked up to be.* —**get cracking** *Informal.* get moving or working fast: *Better get cracking if you want to finish on time.*
—*n.* 1 a sudden sharp sound, as of a whip, rifle fire, or thunder: *the crack of the (baseball) bat; the crack of sonic booms; cracks of gunfire.* 2 a narrow split or gap: *He looked through a crack in the wall.* 3 a cracking: *a crack in his voice.* 4 break: *We set out at the crack of dawn.* 5 a sharp blow: *a crack of the whip; She likes to make cracks* (= quips or wisecracks) *about his bald head.* 6 *Informal.* attempt or try: *I'll have a crack at it; You'll get the first crack at selling it.* 7 also **crack cocaine,** a very pure form of cocaine for smoking; *adja.: a crack addict; a **crack baby** (born to a crack-addicted mother).* —*adja.* excellent: *a crack performance, player, regiment, shot; crack troops..*
crack.down *n.* imposition of strict measures: *The police launch a crackdown on drunken driving at Christmas.*
cracked *adj.* 1 having cracks: *a cracked cup, egg, mirror.* 2 broken into pieces: *cracked ice;* **cracked wheat** (that has been

broken into coarse particles). **3** *Informal.* crazy.

crack.er *n.* **1** a thin, dry biscuit: *graham, soda, salted crackers.* **2** a firecracker. **3** a party favor that opens with a snapping noise.

cracker-barrel *adj. Informal.* plain and down-to-earth: *a cracker-barrel discussion; her cracker-barrel humor, philosophy.*

crack.er.jack (CRACK.ur.jack) *adj. Informal.* first-rate: *a crackerjack lawyer, outfit, salesman, team.*

crack.house *n.* a place where crack cocaine is made and sold.

crack.le (CRACK.ul) *v.* **-les, -led, -ling** make small cracking noises; *adj.:* a **crackling** *fire; a crackling* (= bubbly) *wine.* —*n.* **1** crackling noise: *the crackle of small-arms fire.* **2** many small cracks on china or porcelain; hence **crack.le.ware** *n.*

crack of doom *n.* the end of the world.

crack.pot *n. Informal.* eccentric: *There are some crackpots among the experts; adja.: some crackpot idea, notion, scheme, theory.*

cra.dle (CRAY.dul) *n.* **1** a baby's bed on rockers: *to rock a cradle.* **2** a frame to support something, esp. a telephone handset: *She tapped the cradle buttons to alert the operator but got cut off.* **3** birthplace: *The Mediterranean region is believed to be the cradle of Western civilization.* —**from the cradle to the grave** all one's life. —**rob the cradle** have a much younger spouse or sweetheart. —*v.* **-dles, -dled, -dling** place in or rock as if in a cradle: *She cradled his head in her lap.*

cra.dle.song (CRAY.dul.song) *n.* a lullaby.

craft *n.* **1** *sing. & pl.* a vessel or aircraft: *a landing craft; Small craft were swamped in the storm.* **2** *pl.* **crafts** a skill or skilled trade: *to learn, master, ply or practice a craft; arts and crafts; the people in a craft* (= occupation); *a craft union.* **3** sly cunning; skill in deceiving.

crafts.man (CRAFTS.mun) *n.* **-men** a skilled worker; artisan: *a master craftsman.* —**crafts.man.ship** *n.*

craft.y (CRAF.tee) *adj.* **craft.i.er, -i.est** showing craft; sly: *a crafty fox, leader, look.* —**craft.i.ly** *adv.;* **craft.i.ness** *n.*

crag *n.* a rugged, steeply projecting mass of rock. —**crag.gy** *adj.* **crag.gi.er, crag.gi.est** rugged and prominent: *craggy mountain peaks; his craggy features.* —**crag.gi.ness** *n.*

cram *v.* **crams, crammed, cram.ming** **1** fill too full or too fast; jam: *He crammed his books into the locker; a suitcase crammed full of* or *with clothes.* **2** feed or eat too much or too fast. **3** study hard at the last minute: *He's cramming for the test; n.: a desperate cram on the eve of the exam.* —**cram.mer** *n.*

cramp *n.* a sharp and painful muscle contraction: *He got a cramp in his leg while swimming; Bad eating habits may cause* **cramps** (= abdominal pain); *writer's cramp* (= stiffness of hand muscle). —*v.* **1** suffer a cramp: *My leg cramped while I was sleeping.* **2** restrict or place in a small space: *The laborers were cramped ten to a room; A heavy meal could* **cramp your style** (= spoil ease of performance); *adj.: We are somewhat* **cramped** *for space; cramped* (= congested) *accommodation; a cramped feeling, setting, life.* **3** turn a vehicle's wheels sharply.

cran.ber.ry (CRAN.ber.ee) *n.* **-ber.ries** a small red berry, used esp. for jelly and juice: **Cranberry sauce** *is stewed fruit.*

crane *n.* **1** a long-legged, long-necked wading bird similar to a heron or stork. **2** a hoisting machine having a projecting arm or a horizontal track: *to operate a crane.* —*v.* **cranes, craned, cran.ing** stretch one's neck for a better view.

crane fly *n.* a long-legged mosquitolike fly.

cra.ni.um (CRAY.nee.um) *n.* **-ni.ums** or **-ni.a** (-nee.uh) the skull, esp. the part enclosing the brain. —**cra.ni.al** *adj.: Cranial nerves connect the sense organs of the head with the brain.*

crank *n.* **1** a handle or rod bent at right angles to a rotating shaft: *Turn the crank to work the grinder.* **2** *Informal.* an eccentric and mischievous person; *adj.: a crank letter; crank (phone) calls.* —*v.* start or operate with a crank. —**crank out** churn out: *a novelist who cranks out three romances a year.* —**crank up** *Informal.* start up, as early auto engines: *politicians cranking up their election machinery.*

crank.case *n.* the housing of the crankshaft of an auto engine.

crank.shaft *n.* a shaft turned by or having a crank.

crank.y *adj.* **crank.i.er, -i.est 1** irritable; eccentric. **2** working badly or fitfully.

cran.ny (CRAN.ee) *n.* **cran.nies** a small corner or crevice: *He looked in every nook and cranny of the house for the lost diamond.*

crap *n.* [vulgar slang] excrement; something worthless: *That's a pile of crap!*

He never expected to get or to have to take that kind of crap (= nonsense).

crap.pie (CRAP.ee) *n.* a North American freshwater game fish related to the bass.

crap.py *adj.* **crap.pi.er, crap.pi.est** *Slang.* very bad or worthless.

craps *n.pl.* [takes *sing. v.*] a gambling game played with two dice; *adja.:* a *crap* game, shoot, table.

crap.shoot.er (CRAP.shoo.tur) *n.* a craps player.

crash *v.* 1 collide, break, fall, land, etc. with a great noise or much damage: *The car crashed through a store window; It crashed into a wall; China crashed to the floor; The plane crashed in flames.* 2 fail completely: *The stock market crashed* (= collapsed) *on October 19, 1987; Our hard drive has crashed* (= suddenly become inoperable). 3 *Informal.* enter without permission or invitation: *to crash a party.* 4 *Slang.* sleep in a place without having to pay: *The poor guy used to crash with friends when he was broke.* —*n.* 1 a crashing sound: *a loud or resounding crash; the crash of sheet metal, of waves on the shore.* 2 a crashing, esp. a collision or collapse: *a plane crash; the stock market crash of 1987.* —*adja.* 1 done in the least possible time: *a crash course, diet, program, project; a submarine's crash* (= fast) *dive.* 2 having to do with crashing: *a **crash helmet** worn by motorcyclists for protection; A **crash landing** is a forced landing of an aircraft that damages it; a foam **crash mat** for gym use.*

crash pad *n. Slang.* a place for nonpaying, temporary guests.

crash truck *n.* a specially equipped truck used for aid at a **crash site**, the scene of a plane crash.

crass *adj.* grossly stupid: *crass avarice, behavior, commercialism, ignorance, incompetence, stupidity; It was crass of him to offer her money for a labor of love.*

crate *n.* a storage or shipping case, esp. one made of wooden slats.
—*v.* **crates, crat.ed, crat.ing** put in a crate: *The movers crated our piano.*

cra.ter (CRAY.tur) *n.* a funnel- or bowl-shaped hollow: *bomb, impact, meteorite, volcanic craters; the craters on the moon.* —*v.* develop craters or deteriorate: *The junk bond market started cratering;* *n.:* *chemical breakdowns and cratering;* *adj.:* *the cratered surface of the moon; our cratered highways; a cratered* (= pock-marked) *complexion.*

cra.vat (cruh.VAT) *n.* a scarflike cloth worn loosely as a necktie.

crave *v.* **craves, craved, crav.ing** 1 ask for; beg: *to crave for forgiveness, mercy.* 2 desire strongly to satisfy a physical or emotional need: *to crave (for) admiration, freedom, intimacy, solitude; to crave (after) affection; to crave (for) a drink;* *n.:* *He feels or has a powerful or strong **craving** for a smoke even after quitting.*

cra.ven (CRAY.vun) *adja.* absolutely lacking in courage; cowardly: *a craven fear; a craven ambition, character, desire.*
—*n.* coward: *a base craven.*
—**cra.ven.ly** *adv.*

craw *n.* a bird's crop or animal's stomach. —**stick in the** or **one's craw** be unacceptable to one: *The partisan appointments really stick in our craw.*

craw.fish same as CRAYFISH.

crawl *v.* 1 move by pulling the body along the ground like a snake or worm; hence, move slowly; creep: *A baby crawls on the floor till it can walk; Traffic crawled along at 15 km/h; to crawl out from under the table; to crawl into somebody's favor* (by being overly nice); *She's too self-respecting to crawl* (= degrade herself) *for a favor;* *adja.:* *a **crawling** insect, position; creeping and crawling things.* 2 swim a crawl. 3 be covered with crawling things: *The kitchen floor was crawling with ants; a scary movie that makes your flesh crawl* (= feel as if covered with crawling things). —*n.* 1 a crawling movement; slow pace: *Rush-hour traffic slowed to a crawl; a backsplit house with **crawl space** beneath the first floor.* 2 a fast swimming stroke with alternate overarm movements, done lying prone with face in the water. —**crawl.er** *n.*

crawl space *n.* space under a floor with only enough room for a person to crawl through to inspect ducts, etc.

craw.ly *adj.* creepy.

cray.fish *n.* a small, freshwater crustacean resembling a lobster.

cray.on (CRAY.on, -un) *n.* 1 a drawing stick of charcoal, colored wax, or chalk: *colored crayons.* 2 a drawing made with this. —**crayoned** *adj.* done with a crayon: *a crayoned drawing, message, sketch.*

craze *v.* **craz.es, crazed, craz.ing** make or become crazy; *adj.:* *a **crazed** man; He was crazed with fear.* —*n.* a short-lived fad or mania: *the current, latest, newest craze that is sweeping North America.*

cra.zy (CRAY.zee) *adj.* **-zi.er, -zi.est** *Informal.* 1 insane: *He's crazy as a loon; He drives me crazy; She's dieting like*

crazy (= wildly). **2** extremely fond: *She's crazy about* or *for* or *over him.* **3** foolish or eccentric: *a crazy idea, scheme; It was crazy of him to do that.* —*n., pl.* **-zies** a crazy person. —**craz.i.ly** *adv.;* **craz.i.ness** *n.*
crazy quilt *n.* a quilt of multi-colored, irregular pieces.
creak (CREEK) *v.* make a harsh, squeaking sound like that of unoiled door hinges; *n.: a terrible creak in the bedroom floor; creaks and groans; the creak of leather.* —**creak.i.ly** *adv.;* **creak.i.ness** *n.* —**creak.y** *adj.*
creak.i.er, -i.est 1 full of creaks: *creaky old stairs.* **2** rundown: *a creaky old building; a creaky old man; the company's creaky image.*
cream (CREEM) *n.* **1** the yellowish, fatty content of milk from which butter is made: *Coffee cream* or *cereal cream has 18-20% butterfat; whipped cream.* **2** a food made with cream: *cream of tomato soup.* **3** something with a thick, smooth consistency, as a cosmetic or liqueur: *to apply cleansing, cold, facial, hand, shaving, skin, vanishing creams; "Irish Cream" (liqueur); cream sherry.* **4** a light, yellowish white color. **5** the best part: *These kids are the cream of the crop.* —*v.* **1** work to a creamy consistency; also, add cream to something. **2** remove the best of something: *Recruiters creamed off the best of us.* **3** *Slang.* hit hard and decisively: *They got creamed; He'll cream the ball on one shot.* —**cream.y** *adj.* **cream.i.er, -i.est:** *whipped to a creamy consistency.*
cream cheese *n.* a soft, smooth cheese made with cream.
cream.er *n.* **1** a pitcher for cream. **2** an artificial coffee whitener for use instead of cream.
cream.er.y (CREE.muh.ree) *n.* **-er.ies** a place for the processing or sale of dairy products.
cream puff *n.* **1** a pastry made with cream. **2** *Slang.* one who is out of condition; sissy: *He's bright and athletic and no cream puff.*
crease (CREECE) *n.* a line or wrinkle made usu. by folding or pressing, as the fold down the front and back of trousers: *creases in the pants; to iron out or remove the creases from a dress; skin creases.* —*v.* **creas.es, creased, creas.ing 1** make creases in something: *Permanent press clothes don't crease easily; a forehead creased with concern.* **2** graze with a bullet.
cre.ate (CREE.ate) *v.* **-ates, -at.ed, -at.ing 1** cause to exist: *The Bible says God created heaven and earth; Laurence Olivier* **created the part** (= was first to act the role). **2** cause: *The news created a lot of confusion, enthusiasm, excitement; The judgment created a disturbance, precedent, sensation.* **3** raise to a rank or title: *The pope creates cardinals.*
cre.a.tion (cree.AY.shun) *n.* **1** a creating; something created: *Do you believe in creation, evolution, or both? That piece of marble is one of Henry Moore's best creations.* **2** the world: *He looked all over creation for the fountain of youth.*
cre.a.tive (cree.AY.tiv) *adj.* that creates: *the creative arts, imagination, impulse; his creative efforts, genius, powers; her creative talents as an artist; Novels, plays, and poems are creative* (= imaginative) *writing.* —**cre.a.tiv.i.ty** (-ay.TIV.i.tee) *n.*
cre.a.tor (cree.AY.tur) *n.* one who creates: *Henry Moore is the creator* (= sculptor) *of "The Archer"; God* **the Creator.**
crea.ture (CREE.chur) *n.* one that has been created, esp. an animal or other being considered as dependent on a creator: *a poor creature; "all creatures great and small"; Martian creatures; Are human beings creatures of circumstances or circumstances the creatures of humans? The UFO is a creature of his imagination.*
creature comforts *n.pl.* physical comforts, as good food and shelter.
crèche (CRESH, CRAISH) *n.* **1** a scene representing Christ born in a stable. **2** a day-care center.
cre.dence (CREE.dunce) *n.* belief: *The rumors did not gain much credence; Few attach* or *give* or *lend credence to rumors.*
cre.den.tial (cri.DEN.shul) *n.* usu. **credentials** *pl.* a document stating one's right or ability to fill an office, do a job, etc.: *Ambassadors present their credentials at a ceremony; The school board examined his credentials as a teacher; Her only credential is a teaching diploma.*
cre.den.za (cri.DEN.zuh) *n.* a usu. legless sideboard or bookcase.
cred.i.bil.i.ty (cred.uh.BIL.i.tee) *n.* the quality of being credible: *The legislators who performed as they promised established their credibility; others lost their credibility; Their words lack, strain credibility;* **adja.:** *Those who don't tell the truth will face a credibility crisis or develop a* **credibility gap** (= lack of trust).
cred.i.ble (CRED.uh.bul) *adj.* believable: *a credible alternative, job, performance, story, threat;* **cred.i.bly** *adv.*
cred.it (CRED.it) *v.* **1** believe: *a story that is hard to credit.* **2** attribute: *a fable*

credited to Aesop; We credit him with inventiveness. **3** enter as a payment into an account: *$500,000 has been credited to your account.* —*n.* **1** belief: *a theory that has gained credit in recent times; New data have lent credit to the theory.* **2** recognition or honor: *Give credit where credit is due; She deserves credit; Her work does credit to her intelligence, reflects credit on her school; Her teachers can take credit for her work; They get some credit for being learned; It is to their credit that she graduated; With all due credit to those who helped her, she is a credit* (= source of recognition) *to her family;* the **credits** (= acknowledgments) *at the beginning or end of a show.* **3** financial reliability; also, the amount of money that may be borrowed or the time allowed for repayment: *Stores allow* or *extend* or *give* or *offer credit to customers; Some are denied* or *refused credit; consumer credit; to buy goods* **on credit** (= to be paid for later). —*adj.*: *a credit check followed by a redit report; your credit record.*

cred.it.a.ble (CRED.i.tuh.bul) *adj.* worthy of praise: *a creditable history, job, performance;* **cred.i.ta.bly** *adv.*

credit addict *n.* one who is addicted to buying on credit.

credit bureau *n.* an agency that investigates and keeps records of people's creditworthiness.

credit card *n.* a charge card issued to people for buying on credit up to a maximum line of credit or **credit line**.

cred.i.tor (CRED.i.tur) *n.* a person to whom one owes money: *to pay off one's creditors.*

credit union *n.* a cooperative savings-and-loan institution.

cre.do (CREE.doh, CRAY-) *n.* -dos a belief, esp. religious, or its statement; creed: *Equal pay for work of equal value is part of our credo.*

cre.du.li.ty (cruh.DEW.li.tee) *n.* readiness to believe easily: *a story that strains credulity.*

cred.u.lous (CREJ.uh.lus) *adj.* too willing to believe: *He is credulous, but her story didn't sound very credible.* —**cred.u.lous.ly** *adv.*; **cred.u.lous.ness** *n.*

Cree *n.* **1** (a member of) an Amerindian tribe of Canada. **2** their Algonquian language.

creed *n.* credo: *the Apostles' Creed; the Boy Scout Creed; to adhere to a business, national, political, religious creed; people of all creeds* (= religions) *and colors.*

creek (CREEK, CRIK) *n.* **1** a small stream. **2 Creek** an Amerindian confederacy whose members are now concentrated in Oklahoma; also, their language. —**up the creek (without a paddle)** *Informal.* in trouble.

creel *n.* a wicker basket used to carry a fisherman's catch.

creep *v.* **creeps, crept, creep.ing 1** move gradually or stealthily, close to the ground: *A cat creeps slowly toward a mouse; Vines creep along the ground and up trees and walls.* **2** appear unnoticed: *Errors creep into our work; Old age creeps up on us; adj.*: *a creeping vine; the creeping* (= slowly advancing) *materialism of our times; a creeping suspicion.* **3** feel as if something is creeping over one: *The noise made my flesh creep.* —*n.* **1** *Informal.* creepy feeling: *a spooky old house that gives me* **the creeps**. **2** *Slang.* a petty or very unpleasant person. —**creep.er** *n.*

creep.y *adj.* **creep.i.er, -i.est** feeling or causing fear or disgust: *a creepy fantasy, feeling; creepy music.* —**creep.i.ly** *adv.*; **creep.i.ness** *n.* Also **creepy-crawly**.

cre.mate (CREE.mate) *v.* **-mates, -mat.ed, -mat.ing** burn up a dead body. —**cre.ma.tion** (cri.MAY.shun) *n.*; *adj.*: *cremation caskets, grounds, remains.*

cre.ma.to.ry (CREE.muh.tor.ee) *n.* **-ries** a furnace or building for cremating. Also **cre.ma.to.ri.um** (-TOR.ee.um) *n.*

crème (CREM, CREEM) *n.* a sweet, creamy liqueur, as chocolate-flavored **crème de cacao** (CREEM.duh.COH.coh, CREEM.duh.cuh.CAH.oh) or mint-flavored **crème de menthe** (CREEM.duh.MAHNT, -MENTH).

cren.el.ate (CREN.ul.ate) *v.* **-el.ates, -el.at.ed, -el.at.ing** provide with battlements. Also **cren.el.late** *Cdn.* —**cren.el.a.tion** or **cren.el.la.tion** (-LAY.shun) *n.*

Cre.ole (CREE.ole) *n.* **1** a descendant of a French or Spanish settler. **2** the composite native language of a community dominated by a foreign language: *Haitian Creole is derived from French.* —**cre.ole** *adj.* **1** having to do with Creole culture: *Creole cooking, sauce, seasoning.* **2** served or cooked with tomatoes, onions, peppers, and spices: *shrimp creole; creole crabs.*

cre.o.sote (CREE.uh.sote) *n.* a pungent liquid used to preserve wood, distilled from wood or coal tar.

crepe or **crêpe** (CRAPE) *n.* **1** a thin fabric with a crinkled surface. **2** a thin, crepelike paper; also **crepe paper**.

crept *pt. & pp.* of CREEP.

cre.pus.cu.lar (cri.PUSK.yuh.lur) *adj.*

having to do with twilight: *crepuscular insects, light.*
cre.scen.do (cri.SHEN.doh) *adj. & adv.* gradually growing in volume. —*n.*: *The symphony ended with a deafening crescendo; The complaints rose to or reached a crescendo; a crescendo of complaints.*
cres.cent (CRES.unt) *n.* the shape of the moon when less than half of it is visible, having one convex and one concave edge: *the Cross and the Crescent* (= Islamic symbol); *He lives on Chalkdene Crescent* (= curved side street whose ends open on to a busier street); *adj*.: *a machine that makes pieces of crescent ice in crescent shape; the crescent moon; a crescent roll* (*pastry*).
cress *n.* a plant with pungent leaves that are used in salads or as a garnish.
crest *n.* **1** a tuft, comb, etc. on top of an animal's head: *a bird with a yellow crest;* *adj*.: *a crested bird.* **2** top: *the crest of a hill, movement, trend, wave.* **3** a coat of arms or other heraldic device; *adj*.: *a crested blazer, helmet.* —*v.* come to or form a crest or high: *The river crested 12 feet above flood level.*
crest.fal.len (CREST.fawl.un) *adj.* dejected or disappointed: *She was crestfallen to hear that she had lost; a crestfallen expression, face, look.*
cre.ta.ceous (cri.TAY.shus) *adj.* having to do with the geological period beginning about 130 million years ago, marked by the dying out of dinosaurs and the thriving of mammals.
cre.tin (CREE.tin, CRET.in) *n.* **1** one afflicted with cretinism. **2** an idiot. —**cre.ti.nous** *adj.*
cre.tin.ism (CREE.tin.iz.um, CRET-) *n.* deformity and mental retardation caused by a congenital thyroid deficiency.
cre.tonne (CREE.ton, "on" as in "don") *n.* a heavy, printed cotton fabric used for drapery and upholstery.
cre.vasse (cri.VAS) *n.* a deep crack in a glacier or an embankment.
crev.ice (CREV.is) *n.* a narrow opening; fissure.
crew 1 *n.* a group that works together: *the crew of an airplane; The ground crew services the airplanes; the crew of a ship, racing shell; camera, repair, stage crews; The whole crew* (*Informal* for group or crowd) *was present.* **2** *pt.* of CROW.
crew cut *n.* a man's very short haircut.
crew.el (CREW.ul) *n.* a loosely twisted, two-stranded yarn used in embroidery. —**crew.el.work** *n.*
crew neck *n.* a neckline that fits closely at the base of the throat, as of some sweaters.
crib *n.* **1** a high-sided baby's bed. **2** a manger. **3** a bin or small building for grain storage. **4** *Informal.* a translation or other aid used dishonestly by a student; pony. **5** an extra hand for the dealer in cribbage.
—*v.* **cribs, cribbed, crib.bing 1** shut up or confine. **2** *Informal.* cheat on an exam; use a crib. —**crib.ber** *n.*
crib.bage (CRIB.ij) *n.* a card game in which scores are kept using pegs on a board, or **cribbage board**.
crib death *n.* the sudden death of infants in their sleep because of breathing disturbances. Also **cot death, SIDS, sudden infant death syndrome.**
crick *n.* a painful muscular cramp, esp, in the neck.
crick.et (CRICK.it) *n.* **1** a grasshopper-like insect whose male chirps by rubbing his wings together. **2** a British game played between teams of 11 using a ball, bat, and two wickets: *Cheating is not cricket* (= sportsmanlike behavior). —**crick.et.er** *n.*
cried *pt. & pp.* of CRY.
cri.er (CRY.ur) *n.* one who cries out, shouting announcements, sales pitches, etc.: *the town crier shouting "Oyez, Oyez!"*
crime *n.* **1** a major illegal act; felony or misdemeanor: *to commit or perpetrate a crime; to investigate, prevent, report a crime; an atrocious, brutal, daring, heinous, horrible, infamous, outrageous, vicious, violent crime; a major or serious crime; a minor or petty crime; a crime of passion; a crime against humanity, society; a victimless crime such as gambling; war crimes; a white-collar crime such as fraud or embezzlement.* **2** criminal behavior; law-breaking: *to deter, eradicate or stamp out or wipe out crime; organized crime; adj*.: *crime detection, prevention, rates, syndicates.* **3** a disgraceful or regrettable condition or act: *It's a crime that there are homeless people dying in the winter.*
crim.i.nal (CRIM.uh.nul) *adj.* **1** having to do with crime: *a criminal act, case, charge, investigation, offense; criminal activity, behavior, conduct, wrongdoing; A* **criminal lawyer** *specializes in* **criminal law***; judged guilty of* **criminal negligence** (= reckless disregard of others' safety); *Kay has no* **criminal record** (*of having been convicted of a crime*). **2** guilty of a crime: *a criminal gang, offender.* **3** immoral or outrageous: *She has done nothing criminal; a criminal waste; It's*

criminal the way some people consume while others starve. —**n.** one guilty of a crime: *to apprehend* or *arrest a criminal; to pardon, parole, release, rehabilitate criminals; a common, habitual, hardened, infamous, notorious criminal; a band* or *gang of criminals; war criminals.*
—**crim.i.nal.ly** *adv.* —**crim.i.nal.i.ty** (-NAL.i.tee) *n.*
crim.i.nol.o.gy (crim.uh.NOL.uh.jee) *n.* the study of crime, criminals, and punishment; **crim.i.nol.o.gist** *n.*
crimp *v.* **1** make wavy, corrugated, bent, etc. **2** pinch, as the edges of a pie crust, to seal together. **3** inhibit or restrict: *Changes in taste have crimped demand for certain goods.* —**n.** a crimping or restraint: *Police raids have* **put a crimp in** (= hindered) *the gambling business.*
crim.son (CRIM.zun) **1** *n.* a purplish red; *adj.*: *a crimson rose; the crimson snows of the Arctic reddened by an alga.* **2** *v.* make crimson.
cringe *v.* **cring.es, cringed, cring.ing** **1** crouch, draw back, or cower in fear: *an animal so abused it cringes when it sees a whip; It cringes at the thought of being whipped; cringes when spanking is mentioned; cringes with fear.* **2** fawn servilely; *adj.*: *a* **cringing** *coward; obsequious and cringing behavior.*
crin.kle (CRINK.ul) *v.* **-kles, -kled, -kling 1** (cause to) wrinkle or crease, esp. a surface: *He crinkled his nose in disapproval; adj.: How did this note get* **crinkled** *up?* **2** rustle. —*n.* wrinkle: *Crinkles form around his eyes when he smiles.*
crin.kly (CRINK.lee) *adj.* **-kli.er, -kli.est 1** wrinkled: *crinkly hair.* **2** rustling: *crinkly silk.*
crin.o.line (CRIN.uh.lin) *n.* **1** a stiff fabric used to line garments. **2** a petticoat of this.
cripe *interj.* [used as an expletive]: *Cripes! The cops are here; Holy cripe!*
crip.ple (CRIP.ul) *n.* [offensive when used of humans] a physically disabled person or animal. —*v.* **crip.ples, crip.pled, crip.pling** disable physically; hence, weaken or damage: *Storms* **crippled** *rescue efforts; adj.: a hospital for* **crippled** *children; a crippled economy, industry, presidency; Arthritis is a* **crippling** *disease; a crippling debt burden, effect, impact, labor strike.*
—**crip.pler** *n.*
cri.sis (CRY.sis) *n., pl.* **-ses** (-seez) a critical or crucial situation, as when a patient may either live or die: *to aggravate, avert, cause, defuse, forestall,*

overcome, precipitate, provoke, ride out, settle, stir up a crisis; a grave, serious, impending, mounting crisis; a cabinet crisis; an economic or *financial crisis; energy, environmental, food, housing, identity, mid-life, monetary, political, population crises; The government faced a crisis over the scandal; the crisis in housing; a* **crisis center** (where people can phone for advice in a personal crisis); *a* **crisis management** *plan, team, technique.*
crisp *adj.* **1** firm and easy to break: *crisp bacon, carrots, crackers, lettuce.* **2** quite new: *a crisp 50-dollar bill; clean, crisp uniforms.* **3** clear and well-defined: *a crisp architectural design, illustration, reply, speech; a nice crisp blue.* **4** bracing: *the crisp morning air.*
—*v.* make crisp: *Use the microwave for crisping; well-crisped bacon.* —*n.* something crisp: *onion, potato, tortilla crisps; The toast was burned* **to a crisp.**
—**crisp.ly** *adv.*; **crisp.ness** *n.*
crisp.er *n.* a compartment in a refrigerator for keeping fruits and vegetables fresh.
crisp.y *adj.* **crisp.i.er, -i.est** of foods, crisp: *the crispy noodles served with Chinese food; crispy French fries.*
criss.cross *v.* **1** make crossing lines on something. **2** move back and forth over: *Searchlights crisscrossed the night sky.* —*n.* a set of crossing lines; *adj.*: *a crisscross design, pattern; crisscross sandals.* —*adv.* **1** in a crisscross manner: *sticks lying crisscross on the floor.* **2** awry: *plans that went crisscross.*
cri.te.ri.on (cry.TEER.ee.un) *n., pl.* **-ri.a** or **-ri.ons** a standard of judgment: *Wealth is no criterion of worth; to meet* or *satisfy the criteria for party leader.*
cri.te.ri.um (cry.TEER.ee.um) *n.* a bicycle race with many laps over a short course as opposed to a city-to-city road race.
crit.ic (CRIT.ic) *n.* **1** one who criticizes: *The senator answered his critics.* **2** one who discusses and judges esp. works of art: *a newspaper's art, drama, literary, music critics; a social critic; a harsh, severe, unkind critic; an impartial critic.*
crit.i.cal (CRIT.i.cul) *adj.* **1** crucial: *a patient in serious but not critical condition; Oxygen is critical to our survival; It is critical that we have enough air to breathe; a critical moment, question, role, stage, time.* **2** faultfinding: *a highly critical account; He is somewhat critical of her scholarship.* **3** of critics or criticism; evaluative: *a critical review of the book; a critical essay, reading, study, theory; critical writings.* —**crit.i.cal.ly** *adv.*

critical mass *n.* a condition that is necessary for maintaining a state or producing a result, as the minimum mass of fissionable material required to maintain a nuclear reaction: *to have, reach critical mass.*

criticise *Brit.* CRITICIZE.

crit.i.cism (CRIT.uh.siz.um) *n.* **1** the judgment of art, literature, etc. by a critic: *constructive, fair, sober, valid criticism; literary criticism; textual criticism.* **2** disapproval; faultfinding; also, an expression of this: *barbs of criticism; to arouse, express, offer, provoke, stir up, take criticism; to level criticism at someone; to subject someone to criticism; He tempers his criticism with wit; adverse, biting, damaging, devastating, mild, nitpicking, petty, scathing, severe, sharp, sweeping, unsparing, withering criticism.*

crit.i.cize (CRIT.uh.size) *v.* **-ciz.es, -cized, -ciz.ing 1** find fault with a person or thing: *He always criticizes her; criticizes her for being lazy; to criticize harshly, severely, sharply.* **2** evaluate critically: *to criticize a painting, performance, recital; to criticize fairly; to criticize her style, works.* Also **criticise** *Brit.*

cri.tique (cri.TEEK) *n.* a critical review, discussion, or analysis: *to give or present a critique.* —*v.*: *to critique a book, essay, proposal.*

crit.ter (CRIT.ur) *n. Informal.* creature: *Inflation is a hungry critter that has eaten away 45 cents of every dollar in just 25 years.*

croak (CROKE) *n.* the low, rough sound made by a frog. —*v.* **1** make a croak; utter with such a sound: *a crabby old fellow croaking his orders.* **2** *Slang.* kill or die. —**croak.er** *n.*

Cro.a.tian (croh.AY.shun) *n. & adj.* (a person) of or from **Croatia**, a Balkan nation.

cro.chet (croh.SHAY) *n.* a heavy lace made with one hooked needle. —*v.* **-chets, -cheted, -chet.ing:** *a crocheted sweater.* —**cro.chet.er** (-SHAY.ur) *n.*

crock *n.* **1** a pot, jar, etc. of earthenware: *They struck a crock of gold with the bestseller; That's baloney, a real* **crock of it** (*Slang* for potful of something disgusting). **2** *Slang.* one that is disliked, esp. one who is old, drunk, etc.

crock.er.y (CROCK.uh.ree) *n.* earthenware or crocks collectively.

croc.o.dile (CROC.uh.dile) *n.* a large, swimming reptile with a long tail and strong jaws coming to a sharper point than an alligator's: *to shed crocodile tears* (= to pretend sorrow).

cro.cus (CROH.cus) *n.* **-cus.es** or **-ci** (-sye) a flower related to the iris, with yellow, purple, or white blooms.

crois.sant (cruh.SAHNT) *n.* a crescent-shaped roll of rich pastry.

crone *n.* a witchlike, scrawny old woman.

cro.ny (CROH.nee) *n.* **-nies** a partisan friend: *a government crony; political cronies; cronies of the ruling party.*

crook (short "oo") *n.* **1** *Informal.* a thief or swindler: *"I'm not a crook," he said when arrested.* **2** a hooked stick, tool, or part, esp. a shepherd's staff.
—*v.* bend: *He goes whenever she crooks her little finger* (to summon her).
—**crook.ed** (-id) *adj.* **1** bent or curving: *crooked alleyways.* **2** dishonest: *crooked politicians.* —**crook.ed.ly** *adv.;* **crook.ed.ness** *n.*

croon (long "oo") *v.* **1** sing or hum softly. **2** sing a song in a soft voice: *to croon a lullaby.*

croon.er (CROO.nur) *n.* a professional singer of popular songs who uses a soft, smooth voice.

crop *n.* **1** an agricultural product: *a good crop of corn; our potato crop; a maple syrup crop; a crop of wool; to gather or harvest or reap a crop; Trees bear or yield crops; Farmers dust or spray crops; a bountiful or bumper crop; a cash, poor, record, staple crop;* **adja.:** *crop insurance, rotation, surpluses.* **2** a gathered group: *a new crop of apprentices, recruits, trainees.* **3** a pouchlike part in a bird's gullet. **4** a whip handle; also, a short riding whip. **5** a close haircut: *crop marks* (for indicating where a picture is to be cropped). —*v.* **crops, cropped, crop.ping 1** cut off short; cut the ends off something: *to crop a hedge, a horse's tail or ear, the edges of a book or photograph; She cropped my hair short;* **adj.:** *closely cropped hair.* **2** plant a crop on land: *to crop a few hectares with corn.* —**crop up** arise, turn up, or occur without warning: *the problems that crop up at work.*

crop-dusting *n.* the spraying of pesticides on crops from an aircraft.

crop.land *n.* land used for planting crops.

crop.per (CROP.ur) *n.* one that crops; sharecropper. —**come a cropper** fail; come to grief: *The prosecutor came a cropper himself for padding his payroll.*

cro.quet (croh.CAY) *n.* a lawn game in which wooden balls are knocked through hoops with wooden mallets.

cro.quette (croh.KET) *n.* a small mass of minced food coated with bread crumbs, then deep-fried.

cro.sier (CROH.zhur) *n.* a staff with a hooked end, carried by a bishop or abbot.

cross *n.* **1** a vertical post or beam with a horizontal piece near the top, like the **Cross** on which Christ was crucified: *Christians make the sign of the cross.* **2** a burden or affliction: *We all have our crosses to bear.* **3** an X-like mark: *As he couldn't write, he made or marked his cross on the deed.* **4** a hybrid: *The mule is a cross between a horse and a donkey.* **5** in boxing, a hook thrown over the head of an opponent. —*v.* **1** go or reach from one side to the other: *to cross the street; to cross from one side to the other; to cross over to the other side; She never omits to* **cross her t's and dot her i's** (= is very careful about detail). **2** draw a line or cross through writing to cancel something: *to* **cross out** *an error.* **3** meet and pass by something: *Other unionized workers refused to cross their picket line; Main Street crosses* (= intersects) *Front Street; She used to* **cross my path** *in the office; It never did* **cross my mind** (= occur to me) *to ask her out; I must have got my* **wires crossed** (= made some mistake). **4** place across one another: *People cross their fingers for good luck.* **5** make the sign of the cross on or over oneself: *Christians cross themselves in prayer.* **6** oppose or thwart: *He never crossed a guy for doing what he thought was right.* **7** cause to breed with a different species of animal or variety of plant: *You get a mule if you cross a donkey with a horse.* —**cross my heart** *Informal.* I swear I am telling the truth. —*adja.* **1** going across or intersecting: *the cross street at the next traffic lights; cross traffic, ventilation;* **cpd.***:* the **crossbar** *of a goalpost, bicycle frame; the* **crossbeam** *of a cross; Americans go* **cross-border** *shopping in Mexico and Canada; to sit* **cross-legged** *on the floor; the* **crosspiece** *of a crutch.* **2** contrary; opposing: *a cross wind.* **3** *adj.* angry: *She's cross at or with me for being late.* —**cross.ly** *adv.;* **cross.ness** *n.*

cross-action *n.* a countersuit brought by a defendant.

cross.bones *n.pl.* two thighbones laid across one another: *A "skull and crossbones" is a symbol of death.*

cross.bow *n.* a powerful bow mounted on a stock grooved to guide the arrow.

cross.breed *v.* -**breeds**, -**bred**, -**breeding** breed or cause to breed with a different species, variety, etc.: *sheep that have been crossbred.* —*n.* a crossbred plant or animal: *The mule is a crossbreed.*

cross-country *adj.* **1** across open country: *a cross-country event, marathon, resort; cross-country skiing, trails;* **adv.***:* *to run cross-country.* **2** across a nation: *a cross-country manhunt, poll, tour; cross-country hearings.*

cross.cur.rent (CROS.cur.unt) *n.* a current or tendency running counter to another.

cross.cut *v.* -**cuts**, -**cut**, -**cut.ting** cut across a wood grain, course, etc. —*adja.* **1** made for crosscutting: *a crosscut saw.* **2** sawed or cut across the grain. —*n.* a shortcut: *a crosscut through the schoolyard.*

cross-dresser *n.* one who dresses like the opposite sex.

cross-examine *v.* -**ines**, -**ined**, -**in.ing** question someone closely to check statements made. —**cross-examination** *n.*

cross-eye *n.* an eye turned inward toward the nose. —**cross-eyed** *adj.*: *We're all going cross-eyed reading reports that don't tell us anything.*

cross-fertilize *v.* -**liz.es**, -**lized**, -**liz.ing** **1** of a plant or flower, cause or undergo pollination by another plant or flower. **2** interact, influence, or enrich by or with ideas, cultures, etc. from different sources. —**cross-fertilization** *n.*

cross.fire *n.* intersecting lines of gunfire: *bystanders caught in a crossfire.*

cross hairs *n.pl.* fine lines on an optical eyepiece to assist sight or alignment.

cross.hatch *v.* mark with obliquely intersecting parallel lines.

crossing *n.* **1** an intersection: *a grade or level crossing; railroad crossings.* **2** an act of crossing: *We had a rough, not smooth, Atlantic crossing; We made the border crossing at Niagara Falls.* **3** a place for crossing a street, river, etc.: *deer, pedestrian, school crossings; There is a border crossing in Niagara Falls; A* **crossing guard** *helps children cross a street.*

cross.o.ver (CROS.oh.vur) *n.* a crossing, esp. a short track for switching a train to another line.

cross.piece *n.* a transverse piece.

cross-pollinate *v.* -**nates**, -**nat.ed**, -**nat.ing** fertilize a plant or flower with pollen from another. —**cross-pollination** (-NAY.shun) *n.*

cross-purpose *n.* an opposed though unintended purpose: *Tom and Tam work* **at cross-purposes** *with no benefit to the company.*

cross-question same as CROSS-EXAMINE.

cross-reference *n.* a reference to another part of the same book, list, etc.

cross.road *n.* an intersecting or connecting road. —**crossroads** *pl.* [takes *sing.* or *pl. v.*] **1** a meeting point for roads, travelers, etc.: *Look for signs at the next crossroads.* **2** a point where one must choose or decide: *She is at the crossroads of her career.*

cross section *n.* **1** a place or piece cut at right angles to the axis of something. **2** a sample representation of the whole: *a poll based on a cross section of the population.*

cross talk *n.* **1** contrary or opposing talk: *cross talk between siblings.* **2** garbled sounds intruding from another telephone, radio, or tape channel.

cross.walk *n.* a pedestrian crossing marked on a street.

cross.ways *adj. & adv.* across; diagonally: *The child lay crossways on the bed.* Also **cross.wise.**

cross.wind *n.* a wind at 90 degrees to one's course.

cross.wise same as CROSSWAYS.

cross.word puzzle or **cross.word** *n.* a game in which clues are given for words to be written in interlocking patterns of numbered squares.

crotch *n.* the point where two tree branches fork or where the legs diverge at the human pelvis: *the crotch of a pair of pants.*

crotch.et (CROCH.it) *n.* a stubborn or eccentric whim.

crotch.et.y (CROCH.i.tee) *adj.* eccentric and ill-tempered: *a crotchety old fellow.*

crouch (CROWCH) **1** *v.* lower the body with legs bent and limbs tucked in, as in cringing or preparing to run or leap. **2** *n.* such a position.

croup (CROOP) *n.* an inflammation of the larynx, as by infection, causing a deep, barking cough and wheezing.

crou.pi.er (CROO.pee.ur) *n.* one in charge of a gaming table, as at roulette.

crou.ton (CROO.ton, "on" as in "don") *n.* a cube of toasted bread served in salads, soups, etc.

crow (CROH) *n.* **1** a common black bird with a harsh call. **2** a crowing: *We'll start at cock's crow* (= dawn).
—*v.* **1** *pt.* also **crew,** utter a rooster's shrill cry. **2** feel or express triumph; exult: *The track star says his new record is nothing to crow about.* **3** make happy sounds as a baby does. —**as the crow flies** in a straight line: *New York to Washington is 240 miles but much shorter as the crow flies.* —**eat crow** be humiliated: *The minister had to eat crow and apologize to the press.*

crow.bar *n.* a steel or iron bar used for prying or as a lever.

crowd *n.* **1** a large group of people forming a mass; also, the masses: *He likes to be one of the crowd, to go along with the crowd, not stand out from the crowd.* **2** a group with a shared interest: *Last night we joined the theater crowd.* —*v.* **1** gather in a crowd: *People crowded into the room; They crowded around the speaker.* **2** fill or cram to excess: *The children crowded the hallways.* **3** press, shove, stand close to, etc.: *They crowded the shoppers out of their way; Don't crowd the driver; Don't crowd* (= pressure) *me! He is crowding* (= close to) *50 and still a bachelor.* —**crowd (on) sail** spread more sail to increase speed.

crow.foot (CROH.foot) *n.* **-foots** a buttercup or any other plant having leaves or flowers shaped like a bird's foot.

crown *n.* **1** a garland or wreath for the head, esp. as a victory emblem or award: *a laurel crown; He has earned his crown; a crown of thorns; the martyr's crown* (= honor); *the world heavyweight crown* (= title). **2** a jeweled headdress, diadem, etc. **3** *usu.* **Crown** a monarch or government: *territories ceded to* **the Crown** (= the monarch); *adj.: a Crown* (= government) *attorney; a crown colony* (= British overseas possession); *Crown* (= government) *lands;* **crown jewels** (= crown, scepter, etc. used by royalty on official occasions); *a crown prince or princess* (= heir apparent). **4** the top or a crownlike part of something, esp. of a tree, tooth, or head.
—*v.* **1** put a crown on someone; also, honor as someone: *Elizabeth II was crowned Queen; adj.: a newly crowned Mrs. Universe; two crowned heads of Europe.* **2** be or put at the top or best point: *a marble monument crowned by a golden dome; Her career was crowned with a Nobel prize; adja.: Winning the Nobel was her crowning achievement; a crowning glory, moment, tribute.* **3** cap a tooth with an artificial crown. **4** *Informal.* hit over the head.

crow's-foot *n., pl.* **-feet** a fine wrinkle at the outside corner of the eye.

crow's-nest *n.* an elevated, partly enclosed lookout platform, as on a ship's mast.

cro.zier (CROH.zhur) same as CROSIER.

cru.ces (CROO.seez) a *pl.* of CRUX.

cru.cial (CROO.shul) *adj.* decisive for the future: *a crucial decision; a decision that is crucial to or for our future; a crucial moment, operation, point, question, test; It's crucial that you take this test.* —**cru.cial.ly** *adv.*

cru.ci.ble (CROO.suh.bul) *n.* a heat-resistant pot or container for heating esp. metals to a very high temperature.

cru.ci.fix (CROO.suh.fix) *n.* a representation of Christ on the Cross; a cross.

cru.ci.fix.ion (croo.suh.FIK.shun) *n.* the crucifying of Christ; also **Crucifixion**.

cru.ci.form (CROO.suh.form) *adj.* cross-shaped.

cru.ci.fy (CROO.suh.fye) *v.* **-fies, -fied, -fy.ing** execute by nailing or tying to a cross; hence, persecute or torment in punishment.

crud *n. Slang.* **1** a deposit of dirt or filth. **2** one that is worthless or disgusting. —**crud.dy** *adj.*

crude *adj.* **1** raw or unprocessed: *crude oil, ore, rubber.* **2** unrefined or insensitive: *his crude behavior, life; crude habits, people, remarks.* **3** rough or unfinished: *crude ideas, log cabins, methods, paintings, schemes, shelters, workmanship.* —*n.* crude petroleum: *the price of domestic crude.* —**crude.ly** *adv.* —**crude.ness** or **cru.di.ty** *n.*

cru.el (CROO.ul) *adj.* causing grief or pain; inhumane; harsh: *a cruel and unusual punishment; a cruel blow, disease, predicament, remark, taskmaster, treatment, tyrant, wind; He can be cruel to animals; It was cruel of him to let the cat out in the cold.* —**cru.el.ly** *adv.*

cru.el.ty (CROO.ul.tee) *n.* **-ties** the quality of being cruel or cruel action: *His actions demonstrate or display or exhibit cruelty; deliberate, wanton cruelty to animals; the cruelty of neglecting children, of trapping wild animals; the cruelties of war.*

cru.et (CROO.it) *n.* a small glass bottle for serving vinegar, oil, etc.

cruise (CROOZ) *v.* **cruis.es, cruised, cruis.ing 1** sail, drive, or fly in an unhurried way or with no particular goal, as for pleasure, to patrol an area, etc.: *He cruised around the world in pursuit of pleasure; a taxi cruising for a fare; to cruise a street looking for pick-ups; John is **cruising for a bruising** (Informal for looking for trouble).* **2** operate at optimum speed and efficiency: *Our plane cruises at an altitude of 30,000 ft.; n.: The high gear is for **cruising**; The **cruising speed** is not the maximum speed.* —*n.* voyage: *to go on or take a cruise in the Mediterranean; a Caribbean cruise; a shakedown cruise; world cruises; a car equipped with **cruise control** (to automatically maintain a constant cruising speed).*

cruise missile *n.* a small, pilotless, long-range jet-powered missile that flies low to elude enemy radar.

cruis.er (CROO.zur) *n.* **1** a cabin cruiser. **2** a police patrol car. **3** a light, fast warship smaller than a battleship.

crul.ler *n.* a deep-fried sweet cake shaped like a stretched and twisted doughnut.

crumb (CRUM) *n.* **1** a scrap or small fragment, as of bread. **2** *Slang.* a contemptible person. —*v.* break something into crumbs or cover with crumbs.

crum.ble (CRUM.bul) *v.* **-bles, -bled, -bling 1** break into small pieces: *He crumbled the cookie; It crumbled easily.* **2** collapse or disintegrate: *The building crumbled into ruins; Their marriage crumbled.*

crum.my (CRUM.ee) *adj.* **crum.mi.er, crum.mi.est** *Slang.* miserable or wretched: *He felt crummy in the morning; had the crummy idea of calling in sick; read a crummy book; had a crummy lunch; got a crummy deal.*

crum.pet (CRUM.pit) *n.* a small, round, unsweetened griddle cake similar to a muffin.

crum.ple (CRUM.pul) *v.* **-ples, -pled, -pling 1** crush or become crushed into wrinkles: *She crumpled the letter and threw it away; adj.: a **crumpled** fender, heap of clothes, note.* **2** collapse or break down: *The accused crumpled under questioning and admitted his guilt; She crumpled in a faint; adj.: lay **crumpled** on the floor; a crumpled heap.*

crunch *v.* **1** chew, grind, crush, etc. with a loud noise; hence, make such a noise: *to crunch potato chips; Snow crunches underfoot in subzero weather.* **2** to process: *Computers crunch numbers besides performing logical operations.* —*n.* **1** a crunching. **2** a difficult situation; pinch: *True friends don't desert us in a crunch; when it comes to the crunch; an energy crunch (= shortage); adj.: crunch (= critical) negotiations; crunch time.* —**crunch.y** *adj.*: *crunchy cereals, corn chips, snow.*

cru.sade (croo.SADE) *n.* a zealous battle for a cause: *to conduct, embark on, engage in, go on, join, launch a crusade; the crusade against abortion; the crusade for women's rights.* —*v.* **-sades, -sad.ed, -sad.ing** *Some crusade against, others for, abortion on demand; adj.: a crusad-*

ing *feminist, journalist, knight.*
—**cru.sad.er** *n.*: a human rights crusader.

cruse (CROOZ, CROOS) *n.* a small earthen vessel for liquids.

crush *n.* **1** press or squeeze so as to break or damage: *She was crushed into the corner by the mob; You crushed my new suit.* **2** grind or break into small pieces; *adj.*: *crackers crushed fine; crushed ice, pepper, stone.* **3** overcome or destroy: *to crush a rebellion, uprising; adj.*: *She felt crushed and humiliated; adja.*: *a crushing blow, defeat, victory; the crushing heat of a summer day.* —*n.* **1** a crushing; also, a dense crowd of people: *the crush of people at a fair; A poor kitten was trampled in the crush.* **2** *Informal.* a strong temporary attraction; infatuation: *He had a youthful crush on his arts teacher.* **3** a fruit-juice drink: *lemon, orange crush.* —**crush.er** *n.*

crust *n.* **1** the hard surface of a loaf of bread; also, an end piece made mostly of this. **2** a pastry shell: *pie crust.* **3** any hard outer layer, as of the Earth: *A crust forms on snow when it freezes again after beginning to melt; v.*: *The snow crusted over during the night.* **4** *Informal.* impudence: *He had the crust to ask me for another loan.* —*v.* cover or become covered with a crust: *The snow has crusted over; adjp.*: *catfish crusted with pecans and bran.*

crus.ta.cean (crus.TAY.shun) *n.* a usu. aquatic arthropod having a hard shell, as clams, lobsters, and shrimps.
—*adj.*: *crustacean life;* also **crus.ta.ceous** (-shus).

crus.tal (CRUS.tul) *adj.* having to do with crust: *crustal rocks of the moon's surface.*

crust.y *adj.* **1** having a thick crust: *crusty French bread; a crusty snow cover.* **2** bad-tempered: *a crusty old major, veteran; his crusty humor.*

crutch *n.* a prop or aid, esp. a stick with a padded crosspiece that rests in the armpit, used as a support for walking: *to walk on* or *with crutches; The injured skier was on crutches for many weeks.*

crux *n.* **crux.es** or **cru.ces** (CROO.seez) the essential or crucial point: *the crux of the argument, controversy, negotiations, problem.*

cru.zei.ro (croo.ZAY.roh) *n.* **-ros** the basic unit of money in Brazil.

cry *v.* **cries, cried, cry.ing** **1** sob and weep; shed tears: *He cried with genuine sorrow; No use crying over spilled milk; She cried for joy on hearing the good news; She never goes crying* (= complaining) *to the media; But she cried her heart out when Jim lost; then cried herself to sleep; He spent all day **crying in his beer*** (*Informal* for feeling sorry for himself). **2** shout; call out: *to cry for help; to cry out in agony; to cry foul at the least injustice; They're ready to **cry havoc*** (= warn of disaster) *at the least suspicion of wrongdoing.* **3** announce or proclaim: *a peddler crying his wares.* **4** utter a characteristic call, as birds, hounds, etc. —**cry out** appeal: *The plight of the homeless cries out for attention; a heinous crime that cries out to heaven for vengeance; People always cry out* (= protest) *against injustices.* —**for crying out loud** *Slang.* for heaven's sake; for Pete's sake. —*n.*, *pl.* **cries 1** a bout of weeping: *Flo felt better after a good cry.* **2** a shout: *a cry for help; to give, raise, utter a cry; an anguished, heart-rending, loud, lusty, piercing, plaintive cry; a battle cry* or *war cry; a rallying cry.* **3** a characteristic call: *the cries of infants; the cry of the wolf.* —**a far cry** something quite different: *Fast food is a far cry from home-cooked meals.*

cry.ba.by (CRY.bay.bee) *n.* **-bies** one who cries or complains too much; *adja.*: *a crybaby act, attitude, plea.*

crying *adja.* **1** demanding attention: *a crying need; a crying* (= scandalous) *shame.* **2** having to do with crying: *a crying fit, jag, room, spell, room, towel.*

cry.o.gen.ics (cry.oh.JEN.ics) *n.pl.* [takes *sing. v.*] the study of very low temperatures and of processes using them; **cry.o.gen.ic** *adj.*; **cry.o.gen.i.cal.ly** *adv.*

cry.on.ic (cry.ON.ic) **1** *adj.* having to do with the freezing of bodies for later revival: *Cryonic societies keep freshly dead bodies in cryonic suspension to prevent deterioration, hoping to revive them.* **2** **cry-onics** *n.pl.* [takes *sing. v.*] the preservation of bodies by freezing.

cry.o.sur.ger.y (cry.oh.SUR.juh.ree) *n.* destruction of tissue using extreme cold.

crypt (CRIPT) *n.* an underground burial vault.

crypt.a.nal.y.sis (crip.tuh.NAL.uh.sis) *n.* the solving or breaking of secret codes.

cryp.tic (CRIP.tic) *adj.* secret or mystifying: *a cryptic comment, message, note, remark; the Mona Lisa's cryptic smile.*
—**cryp.ti.cal.ly** *adv.*

crypto- *comb.form.* **1** secret: *crypto-communist; crypto-Klansmen; cryptonym.* **2** coded: *cryptogram; cryptography.*

cryp.to.gram (CRIP.toh.gram) *n.* a message in code.
cryp.tog.ra.phy (crip.TOG.ruh.fee) *n.* the art of using or breaking codes; **cryp.tog.ra.pher** *n.*
cryp.to.nym (CRIP.tuh.nim) *n.* a secret name.
crys.tal (CRIS.tul) *n.* **1** colorless transparent quartz: *She tells fortunes by gazing into a* **crystal ball;** *People engage in* **crystal-gazing** (= speculation) *when they don't have evidence on which to base a judgment.* **2** high-quality glass used for tableware: *Why, it's clear as crystal! fine crystal goblets; Let me make our views* **crystal clear.** **3** a clear cover over a watch face. **4** a naturally formed three-dimensional structure of the molecules of a substance as it passes to the solid state: *ice, salt, sugar crystals.*
crys.tal.line (CRIS.tul.ine, -in) *adj.* having to do with crystals: *the crystalline structure of some gems; crystalline clarity, salt.*
crys.tal.lize (CRIS.tul.ize) *v.* **-tal.liz.es, -tal.lized, -tal.liz.ing** **1** form into crystals; take on crystalline structure. **2** impart or take on a fixed, definite form: *vague ideas that crystallized into a theory; to crystallize fears, feelings, thoughts, trends.* —*adj.*: *a* **crystallized** *vision; crystallized traditions; crystallized fruit, ginger, lemon peel (coated with sugar crystals).* —**crys.tal.li.za.tion** (-luh.ZAY.shun, -lye-) *n.*
C-section same as CESARIAN SECTION.
CT scan *n.* a picture produced by a computerized X-ray machine that produces three-dimensional pictures by scanning the images of a series of cross sections; also **CAT scan.** —**CT scanner** *n.*
cub *n.* **1** a young bear, lion, fox, etc.: *a panda cub.* **2** a novice: *a cub (reporter).* **3** a Boy Scout aged 8 to 10: *Cub Scouts.*
Cu.ban (CUE.bun) *n. & adj.* (a person) of or from **Cuba,** an island republic in the Caribbean.
cub.by.hole (CUB.ee.hole) *n.* a small space, compartment, or room.
cube *n.* **1** a solid shape bounded by six equal squares or something in such a shape: *bread, ice, sugar cubes.* **2** the product of a number multiplied by itself twice: *The cube of 2* (= 2 x 2 x 2) *is 8; The* **cube root** *of 8 is 2; to find or extract the cube root of 8.* —*v.* **cubes, cubed, cub.ing** **1** multiply by itself twice: *2 cubed is 8.* **2** shape or cut into cubes; *adj.*: **cubed** *ice, melon, steaks.*
cu.bic (CUE.bic) *adj.* **1** also **cu.bi.cal,** cube-shaped: *a cubic figure; cubical boxes.* **2** *adja.* extended in three dimensions: *One cubic meter is the volume of a cube one meter long, one meter wide, and one meter deep; Cubic content is expressed in cubic units; cubic space.* **3** raised to or relating to the third degree: *a cubic equation.*
cu.bi.cle (CUE.bi.cul) *n.* a small room or compartment: *a dormitory cubicle; a separate cubicle for each keyboarder.*
cubic measure *n.* measure of volume.
cub.ism (CUE.biz.um) *n.* a style of art employing abstract geometrical forms. —**cub.ist** *n. & adj.*
cu.bit (CUE.bit) *n.* an old-fashioned measure of length; 18-22 inches; 45-56 cm.
Cub Scout *n.* a member of the junior branch (ages 8-10) of the Boy Scouts.
cuck.old (CUCK.uld) *n.* a man with an unfaithful wife. —*v.* make someone a cuckold; *adj.*: *a* **cuckolded** *husband.* —**cuck.old.ry** *n.*
cuck.oo (COO.coo) *n.* **1** a bird with a distinctive call that lays its eggs in other birds' nests. **2** *Informal.* a foolish or silly person. —*adj.* crazy or silly: *He was nearly cuckoo with fear; a head full of cuckoo notions.*
cu.cum.ber (CUE.cum.bur) *n.* **1** a long, thin, green vegetable with a white flesh. **2** the vine it grows on: *She stays* **cool as a cucumber** *under provocation.*
cud *n.* a mouthful of food that animals such as cattle, deer, and camels bring up from their stomachs for rechewing. —**chew the cud** ponder or ruminate.
cud.dle (CUD.ul) *v.* **cud.dles, cud.dled, cud.dling** hold or nestle close; hug: *People cuddle up for greater warmth; They cuddle up with their children; Children cuddle up to their parents for the warmth of affection.*
cud.dly (CUD.lee) *adj.* good for cuddling: *It looks so cute and cuddly; a cuddly baby, infant, kitten.* Also **cud.dle.some** (CUD.ul.sum).
cudg.el (CUJ.ul) *n.* a stout club: *Lou's the only one around to* **take up the cudgels for** (= go to the defense of) *the underdog.* —*v.* **-els, -eled, -el.ing** beat with a cudgel: *The victim was cudgeled to death; Hard as I* **cudgeled my brains** (= Though I thought hard), *I couldn't solve the problem.* Also **cudg.elled, cudg.el.ling** *Cdn.*
cue *n.* **1** a signal indicating when the next speech, action, etc. should occur in a play; hence, a hint or indication: *to give the cue; They* **take their cue** *from*

their bosses; *The postal workers walked out on cue from headquarters.* **2** a long tapered stick used to strike the ball (**cue ball**) in billiards and similar games. —*v.* **cues, cued, cu.ing 1** hit a billiard ball, etc. with a cue stick. **2** give a cue or indication to help a person or thing at a specific point: *to cue an actor on his lines* (= prompt him); *Let's cue her in to* (= explain to her) *what happened; to cue* (= insert) *a few songs into the script.*

cue card *n.* **1** a large piece of cardboard with writing on it, held by a stagehand to prompt a television performer. **2** a small card held in the hand as a memory aid.

cues.ta (QUES.tuh) *n.* a hill or ridge with a cliff on one side and a slope on the other.

cuff *n.* a band or folded piece of cloth on the end of a shirt sleeve or pant leg; *adj.*: *pleated and cuffed pants.* —*v.* strike, usu. lightly with an open hand: *a bear cub cuffed into line by its mother.* —**off the cuff** impromptu: *Raj spoke off the cuff; adj.*: *an off-the-cuff remark.* —**on the cuff** on credit: *Ed buys his groceries on the cuff.*

cui.sine (kwi.ZEEN) *n.* a style of cooking; also, food so cooked: *Breton cuisine.*

cuke *n. Informal.* a cucumber.

cul-de-sac (cul.di.SAC) *n.* a dead-end street; blind alley.

cu.li.nar.y (CUE.luh.nair.ee, CULL.uh-) *adj.* having to do with cooking: *the culinary arts; a culinary delight, treat; his culinary expertise, skills, talents.*

cull *v.* select or gather: *to cull flowers from the garden; quotations culled from Keats; to cull* (= go over) *a field for grain; n.*: *the annual culling of seals; the culling* (= reducing) *of fleets for consolidating the navy.* —*n.* **1** a culling: *the cull of gray seals.* **2** something discarded: *As the culls are thrown out, 100 lb. of carrots shrinks to 60.*

cul.mi.nate (CULL.muh.nate) *v.* **-nates, -nat.ed, -nat.ing** reach its climax or best point: *The growing discontent culminated in a full-scale riot.* —**cul.mi.na.tion** (-NAY.shun) *n.*: *The award she won was the culmination of years of hard work.*

cu.lotte (cue.LOT) *n.* usu. **culottes** *pl.* a trouserlike divided skirt: *a culotte dress.*

cul.pa.ble (CUL.puh.bul) *adj.* deserving blame because of something done or omitted: *His attitude was blameworthy and his actions culpable; culpable homicide, negligence, stupidity; culpable but not guilty;* **cul.pa.bly** *adv.* —**cul.pa.bil.i.ty** (-BIL.i.tee) *n.*

cul.prit *n.* an accused or guilty person.

cult *n.* **1** a faddish or abnormal devotion to a person, thing, or idea: *the cult of old movies; fertility, personality, religious, satanic cults; adj.*: *a cult festival, figure, following, image, leader, member, object; cult indoctrination.* **2** a system of religious worship: *the cult of saints, of the Virgin Mary, of Zeus.* —**cult.ism** *n.*

cult.ist *n.* one who practices a cult: *a field dominated by kooks, cultists, and quasi-religious fanatics.*

cul.ti.vate (CULL.tuh.vate) *v.* **-vates, -vat.ed, -vat.ing 1** prepare soil and grow plants, trees, etc.: *to cultivate crops, gardens, the land, plantations, the soil, trees.* **2** grow or foster: *to cultivate an atmosphere of goodwill, a good image, an interest in music; to cultivate friendships, opportunities, relationships, tastes, values.* **3** to seek the goodwill of someone: *Political aspirants cultivate politicians; Politicians cultivate the electorate.* —**cultivated** *adj.* refined or improved: *wild and cultivated roses; We like to appear cultivated; a cultivated accent, air of sophistication, style, taste.* —**cul.ti.va.ble** (-vuh.bul) *adj.* —**cul.ti.va.tion** (-VAY.shun) *n.* —**cul.ti.va.tor** (-vay.tur) *n.*

cul.tur.al (CULL.chuh.rul) *adj.* having to do with culture: *a cultural attaché; cultural deprivation, exchange, history, inheritance, interests, mosaics, nationalism, revolution, societies; In a changing world, societies and institutions that are slow to adapt to change are said to suffer from* **cultural** or **culture lag.** —**cul.tur.al.ly** *adv.*

cul.ture (CULL.chur) *n.* **1** intellectual and emotional refinement; enlightenment: *a man of little culture; a woman of great culture; centers of culture and civilization; to bring culture to the people; to develop, disseminate, foster, spread culture.* **2** the result of such refinement; the arts, beliefs, customs, etc. of a group as a whole: *Aztec, Chinese, Greek culture; ancient, corporate, ethnic, human, mass, material, modern, tribal culture; Canada is a mosaic of cultures.* **3** growth or development: *the culture of the mind; beauty culture; physical culture.* **4** something grown, as in a laboratory: *bacterial cultures; the culture for making cheese; clones produced by tissue culture; a yogurt culture grown in Bulgaria.*

cultured (CULL.churd) *adj.* **1** refined: *a cultured gentleman; her cultured voice; cultured behavior.* **2** artificially cultivat-

culture shock / curd

ed: *a cultured variety of rose; cultured cells, pearls, tissues, yeasts.*
culture shock *n.* the shock of being thrust suddenly into a different society.
culture vulture *n. Informal.* a somewhat pretentious devotee of the arts.
cul.vert (CULL.vurt) *n.* a drainage passage under a railroad, highway, etc.
cum *prep.* plus: *an apartment cum workshop.*
cum.ber.some (CUM.bur.sum) *adj.* awkward or unwieldy: *a cumbersome device, operation, process; a cumbersome bureaucracy.* Also **cum.brous** (-brus).
cum.in (CUM.in) *n.* a seedlike, aromatic fruit of an herb used as a flavoring.
cum lau.de (coom.LOUD.uh, -dee, short "oo") *Latin.* with honors.
cum.mer.bund (CUM.ur.bund) *n.* a wide sash or waistband in men's formal dress.
cu.mu.la.tive (CYOOM.yuh.luh.tiv) *adj.* increasing by accumulation or continued addition: *the cumulative effect of exposure to radiation;* **cumulative interest** *(added to the principal sum and earning more interest).* —**cu.mu.la.tive.ly** *adv.*
cu.mu.lo.nim.bus (cyoom.yuh.loh.NIM.bus) *n.* a very high cumulus cloud with a spreading top, often linked with thunderstorms; thunderhead or thundercloud.
cu.mu.lus (CYOOM.yuh.lus) *n., pl.* **-li** (-lye) a cloud with a flat bottom and high rounded peaks on top.
cu.ne.i.form (cue.NEE.uh.form) *adj.* wedge-shaped: *cuneiform characters used in Assyrian and Persian writing.* —*n.* this system of writing.
cun.ni.lin.gus (cun.i.LING.gus) *n.* oral stimulation of the female genitals.
cun.ning (CUN.ing) *adj.* **1** cleverly deceptive: *a cunning fox, scheme, trick.* **2** skillfully made or done: *a cunning piece of workmanship.* **3** cute: *a cunning little girl; a cunning red dress.*
—*n.* **1** skill in deception; craftiness: *the cunning of a cat burglar; political cunning.* **2** skill or dexterity: *The wood carving shows cunning; He manipulates the market with cunning and precision.* —**cun.ning.ly** *adv.*
cunt *n.* [vulgar slang] the female genitals.
cup *n.* **1** a small, bowllike container, usu. with a handle: *a cup and saucer; coffee, drinking, paper, plastic cups; He drained the cup to the dregs; a bra with cups in sizes A, B, C, D, and DD (for 31 to 54 bust sizes).* **2** a cupful; an 8 oz. (236.59 ml) measure of capacity: *half a cup of coffee.* **3** prize or trophy, usu. a loving cup: *a challenge cup; the Grey Cup; Stanley Cup; We lost, they won the cup.* —**in one's cups** drunk; intoxicated. —*v.* **cups, cupped, cup.ping** shape or put into a cup: *He cupped his hand under his chin; She cupped the child's chin and kissed her;* *adj.*: *She sat with chin* **cupped** *in hand; cupped hands; a cupped handful of water.* —**cup.ful** *n.*
cup.board (CUB.urd) *n.* a small cabinet or closet: *a kitchen with built-in cupboards; The cupboard is bare* (= Nothing is available) *at our local employment office.*
cup.cake *n.* an individual cake baked in a cup-shaped container.
cu.pid (CUE.pid) *n.* a small, winged boy representing the Roman god of love: *She likes to play cupid making matches.*
cup of tea *n.* what interests one; one's own thing: *Skiing is not my cup of tea; It's a different cup of tea* (= different thing) *from skating.*
cu.po.la (CUE.puh.luh) *n.* a small dome on a roof.
cur *n.* a mongrel; a worthless dog.
cur.a.ble (KYOOR.uh.bul) *adj.* that can be cured: *a curable disease; 90% curable.*
cu.ra.çao (kyoor.uh.SOH) *n.* a sweet liqueur flavored with orange peel.
cu.rate (KYOOR.it) *n.* a clergyman who is assistant to a parish priest. —**cu.ra.cy** *n.*
curate's egg *n.* something with both good and bad qualities.
cur.a.tive (KYOOR.uh.tiv) *adj.* able to cure: *curative care, effects, measures, powers, properties, treatments, value; Is it curative or merely palliative? n.*: *a curative for fever.*
cu.ra.tor (cue.RAY.tur, CURE.uh.tur) *n.* one who administers a museum, art gallery, etc. —**cu.ra.tor.i.al** (cue.ruh.TOR.ee.ul) *adj.*
curb *n.* **1** a check or restraint: *a curb on drunk driving.* **2** a strap or chain used with a bit to check a horse. **3** a raised border for a street or driveway.
—*v.* control abruptly: *to curb one's curiosity, dog, enthusiasm, temper.*
curb crawling *n. Informal.* going around in one's car looking for pickups.
curb service *n.* service at the curb, as of customers in parked cars.
curb.side *n.* the area at or near a curb: *Leave your recyclables at curbside; curbside garbage pickup.*
curd *n.* **1** the coagulated solid part of milk: *small curds of soured milk; curds and whey; a bowl of curds.* **2** something similar to curds in consistency: *Soft*

curds form when eggs are cooked in a skillet; prepared lemon curd; orange curd; bean curd.

cur.dle (CUR.dul) *v.* **-dles, -dled, -dling** 1 thicken milk into curd. 2 seem to thicken: *The scream in the middle of the night curdled their blood with fear.*

cure (KYOOR) *n.* 1 a healing: *to effect, provide, work a cure; a complete, sure, miraculous cure.* 2 a drug or therapy that heals: *a cure for the common cold; a rest cure; water cure.* —*v.* **cures, cured, cur.ing** 1 heal; make better: *to cure people of their ills; a plan to cure the world's problems.* 2 preserve bacon, fish, etc. by salting, smoking, etc.: *Tobacco is cured by drying.* —**cur.a.ble** *adj.*

cu.ré (cue.RAY, KYOOR.ay) *n.* a French parish priest.

cure-all *n.* a supposedly universal cure; panacea.

cu.ret.tage (cure.uh.TAHZH) *n.* the medical scraping of a body cavity such as the uterus.

cur.few *n.* an evening hour at which one must be off the streets: *to impose, lift, violate a curfew; a midnight curfew; a curfew of 8 p.m. for children under 15.*

Cu.ri.a (KYOOR.ee.uh) *n., pl.* **-ae** (-ee) the judicial and administrative organization through which the Pope rules the Church.

cu.rie (KYOOR.ee) *n.* a basic unit of radioactivity, i.e. 3.7 x 10^{10} disintegrations per second.

cu.ri.o (CUE.ree.oh) *n.* **-os** a novel or unusual object; curiosity.

cu.ri.os.i.ty (cue.ree.OS.i.tee) *n.* **-ties** 1 a being curious: *to arouse, engage, excite, pique, satisfy, stir, whet one's curiosity; to provoke, spawn curiosity; a healthy, idle, insatiable, intellectual, natural, unquenchable curiosity; She did it out of mere curiosity; curiosity about the goings-on.* 2 a novel or unusual object: *the curiosities sold at a souvenir shop; Our library is an architectural curiosity.*

cu.ri.ous (KYOOR.ee.us) *adj.* 1 eager to know: *She is curious to know what happened; I'm curious about her background; He's just curious.* 2 too eager to know; inquisitive: *He's so curious; curious eyes, neighbors, questions.* 3 peculiar: *a curious state of affairs; Isn't it curious that he left without a word? What a curious thing to say!* —**cu.ri.ous.ly** *adv.*

cu.ri.um (KYOOR.ee.um) *n.* a highly radioactive artificial element.

curl *n.* something with a curved shape, esp. a ringlet of hair: *Her hair falls in curls; loose, soft, spiral, tight, wispy curls; a curl of smoke; the curl of a wave about to break; Scrape across the surface of a block of chocolate to make chocolate curls; cheese curls.* —*v.* 1 give a curl to something: *She helped Mary curl her hair; But her fees will **curl your hair** (Informal for will shock you).* 2 form in a curl or curls: *Smoke curls from the chimney; He's curled up in front of the TV; The cat curls up into a ball.*

curl.er *n.* a device for curling hair.

cur.lew *n.* a wading bird with a long narrow bill that curves downward.

curl.i.cue (CUR.li.cue) *n.* an ornate curl, as a flourish on a letter.

curl.ing *n.* a game in which round stones are slid toward a target across ice by two teams of four each.

curling iron *n.* a rodlike metal instrument that is heated and used for curling hair which is wound around it.

curl.y *adj.* **curl.i.er, -i.est** having or being in curls: *naturally curly hair; his curly head (with curly hair); a curly-headed child.*

cur.mudg.eon (cur.MUJ.un) *n.* a cantankerous old person. —**cur.mudg.eon.ly** *adv.*

cur.rant (CUR.unt) *n.* 1 a small, round, smooth berry with a tart flavor or the shrub it grows on: *black currants;* **adja.**: *red currant jelly; currant wine.* 2 a small seedless dried grape used esp. in puddings, cakes, and buns.

cur.ren.cy (CUR.un.see) *n.* **-cies** 1 the state or duration of being current; general use: *a coin that is no more in currency; It went out of currency; The rumor gained, had, enjoyed currency; wide currency.* 2 money circulating as legal tender: *to call in, issue, print, withdraw currency; hard, foreign, paper, soft, stable, weak currencies; currency exchange rates.*

cur.rent (CUR.unt) *adj.* 1 circulating: *a current coin.* 2 **adja.** now occurring; of the present: *Read the papers for current events; a current affairs TV program dealing with current issues; Money kept in a **current account** may be withdrawn on demand; **Current assets** are readily convertible to cash.* 3 generally accepted; prevalent: *current theories of the universe; the current usage of a word; current English.* —*n.* 1 something flowing in a path, as air, water, or electricity: *air currents; the flow of electric current; alternating and direct currents; an underwater current; The Gulf Stream is a warm current.* 2 a course or tendency: *It's easier to swim with, not against the current; the current of 20th-century liberalism; the current of unrest that is sweeping the nation.*

cur.rent.ly (CUR.unt.lee) *adv.* at pres-

ent: *legislation currently under review.*
cur.ric.u.lum (cuh.RICK.yuh.lum) *n.*, *pl.* **-la** (-luh) or **-lums** a school's program of studies: *Music is on the school curriculum; a basic or core curriculum; to draw up or design a curriculum; a curriculum (= set of courses) in math.*
—**cur.ri.cu.lar** (-lur) *adj.*: *curricular changes, issues, reform.*
curriculum vi.tae (-VYE.tee) *n.* a résumé; vita.
cur.ry (CUR.ee) *n.* **cur.ries** a sauce or dish seasoned with **curry powder,** a spicy mixture of turmeric and other spices: *a hot curry; mild curries; chicken, fish, vegetable curries.* —*v.* **cur.ries, cur.ried, cur.ry.ing** **1** prepare with curry; *adj.*: *curried chicken, sauce, shrimp.* **2** brush or rub down a horse using a brush with metal teeth, or **currycomb** (-cohm). —**curry favor** try to gain favor: *He would like to curry favor by flattery; She gives gifts to curry favor with the principal.*
curse *n.* **1** a calling down of evil on someone or something: *to pronounce or put a curse (up)on someone; to lift a curse; under the curse of their ancestors.* **2** an oath, esp. one using a sacred name: *to utter a curse against someone.* **3** a bane or scourge: *Scurvy was the curse of old-time sailors.* —*v.* **curs.es,** *pt. & pp.* **cursed** or **curst, curs.ing** **1** swear at someone: *She cursed her attacker for what he did to her.* **2** afflict: *He was cursed with poverty in old age; a nation cursed by a history it cannot escape.*
cur.sed (CUR.sid, CURST) *adj.* hated: *a cursed generation, land, nuisance.*
cur.sive (CUR.siv) *adj.* of printing or writing, with letters connected to each other: *cursive script.*
cur.sor (CUR.sur) *n.* on a video display, a manually controllable pointer of flashing light used as a position indicator.
cur.so.ry (CUR.suh.ree) *adj.* quick or hurried: *a cursory examination, glance, inspection, interest, look, reading of a book.* —**cur.so.ri.ly** (-ruh.lee) *adv.*
curt *adj.* short or brusque; nearly rude: *a curt response to a complaint;* **curt.ly** *adv.*
cur.tail (cur.TAIL) *v.* cut short; reduce: *to curtail expenditure.* —**cur.tail.ment** *n.*
cur.tain (CUR.tun) *n.* a piece of fabric hung before a stage, window, etc. to veil or shut off view: *to close, draw, hang, lower, open, put up, raise a curtain; to pull the curtains (shut); shower, stage, theater curtains; to raise, ring up, ring down the curtain on a performance; The curtain goes up or rises on a scene; The curtain comes down or drops or falls on a scene; His first show proved to be* **curtains** *(Informal for the end) for him.*
—*v.* furnish or conceal with a curtain: *One end of the cabin was* **curtained off** *for the ladies.*
curtain call *n.* a performer's return to the stage in answer to prolonged applause: *to take curtain calls.*
curt.sy (CURT.see) *n.* **-sies** a bow of respect by women made by bending the knees: *Mia made or bobbed or dropped a graceful curtsy to the audience.* —*v.* **-sies, -sied, -sy.ing:** *She curtsied to the Queen.* Also **curt.sey, -seys, -seyed, -sey.ing.**
cur.va.ceous (cur.VAY.shus) *adj.* having a full and rounded figure: *a curvaceous young woman.*
cur.va.ture (CUR.vuh.chur) *n.* a curving or curved part: *the curvature of space, of the earth; a deformity called "curvature of the spine."*
curve *n.* **1** a line, shape, or outline that bends with no straight portion: *a sharp curve in the road; The road describes or makes a curve to the east; a hairpin or horseshoe curve; the alluring curves of her figure; to plot a curve (= graph) using coordinates; your learning curve (as on a graph).* **2** a baseball pitched so as to swerve near the batter: *He threw me a curve (= tried to trick me) but to no avail; a* **curveball** *(= tricky move) that came close to cheating.*
—*v.* **curves, curved, curv.ing** bend: *The road curves quite sharply to the east.*
cur.vet (cur.VET) *n.* a horse's prancing leap.
cush.ion (COOSH.un, short "OO") *n.* **1** a pillow or pad for sitting, lying, or kneeling on. **2** something that absorbs shock or protects from a blow or shock: *An air cushion vehicle such as a Hovercraft rides on a cushion of air; A savings account will be a cushion to fall back on when you lose your job; a cushion against business losses.* —*v.* protect from or absorb the shock of something: *Wear protective shoulder pads to cushion falls; to cushion the impact; a youth cushioned from the realities of life by his protective parents.* —**cush.ion.y** *adj.*
cush.y (COOSH.ee, short "OO") *adj.* **cush.i.er, -i.est** easy or comfortable: *a cushy job, life, post.*
cusp *n.* **1** a pointed end, as of a leaf or tooth: *molar cusps; the cusps of the crescent moon.* **2** a turning point; verge: *on the cusp of change; a business on the cusp between profit and loss (= breaking even); goals on the cusp of being*

(= about to be) *realized; the cusp* (= end) *of the 1990s.*

cus.pid (CUS.pid) *n.* a single-pointed or canine tooth.

cus.pi.dor (CUS.pi.dor) *n.* a spittoon.

cuss *v. Informal* [same as CURSE but milder in tone]: *The punks started hollering and cussing at us;.*

cus.sed (CUS.id) *adj. Informal.* cursed; also, stubborn.

cuss word *n. Informal.* an oath or obscenity; swearword.

cus.tard (CUS.turd) *n.* a dessert made with a milk-and-egg mixture.

cus.to.dial (cus.TOH.dee.ul) *adj.* having to do with custody: *custodial accounts, care, parents, staff, workers;* **custodial assistance** (= help with grooming, dressing, etc.); *a* **custodial sentence** (= jail term).

cus.to.di.an (cus.TOH.dee.un) *n.* one who has custody, esp. of a property; caretaker or janitor.

cus.to.dy (CUS.tuh.dee) *n.* **-dies 1** safekeeping; guardianship: *The divorced couple fought for custody of the child; The mother was awarded or granted custody; She received, took custody of her child; joint custody (shared by both parents); a custody dispute.* **2** legal detention: *The drunk was held overnight in protective custody; police custody; Suspects are* **taken into** or **put in** *custody.*

cus.tom (CUS.tum) *n.* **1** a long-established practice: *to cherish, establish, observe* or *practice customs; ancient, local, old, pagan, quaint, tribal customs; It's our custom to bury the dead rather than cremate them; It is my custom* (= habit) *to go for a walk after supper.* **2 customs** *pl.* duty on imported goods: *We paid $100 in customs on the camera imported from Europe.* **3 customs** *pl.* [takes *sing. v.*] the department that levies this or a post manned by it: *Customs never closes; We had nothing to declare at customs; had no problem getting our baggage through customs; We cleared* or *got through* or *passed through* or *went through customs quickly.* **—adj a.** making or made to order: *Custom tailors make custom clothes;* **cpd:** *a custom-built house; custom-fitted covers; custom-made suits; custom-tailored clothes; to live in custom-tailored comfort.*

cus.tom.ar.y (CUS.tuh.mair.ee) *adj.* conventional: *It's customary among us to bury the dead; It's customary* (= usual) *for me to go for a walk daily; my customary* (= regular or habitual) *walk.*

—cus.tom.ar.i.ly *adv.*

cus.tom.er (CUS.tuh.mur) *n.* **1** one who purchases something, esp. regularly: *They offer gifts to attract customers; a cash customer who has no use for credit; prospective, satisfied, steady customers.* **2** a person; fellow: *shrewd, tough customers; an* **ugly customer** (= violent person).

cus.tom.house (CUS.tum.house) *n.* an office at which customs are paid.

cus.tom.ize (CUS.tuh.mize) *v.* **-miz.es, -mized, -miz.ing** build or alter something to specifications.

cut *v.* **cuts, cut, cut.ting 1** pierce or separate something with a sharp edge or object: *She cut the apple in two; to cut a loaf into slices; He cut* (= pierced) *his leg on the barbed wire.* **2** make or do something by or as if by cutting: *to cut diamonds, glass; to cut a road through the mountains; to cut a slice from a loaf; to cut* (= record and produce) *a phonograph record; He cuts his hair* (= gets a haircut) *every month; a farmer cutting* (= harvesting) *wheat; She cut* (= struck) *the horse with her whip; a cold wind that cuts you to the bone; The baby has cut her first tooth* (= Her first tooth has pierced the gum); *She cut her teeth* (= had her early training) *as a journalist on "The Times"; to cut* (*Informal* for make) *a deal.* **3** reduce or shorten: *We cut the work week to 30 hours; She has cut her hair; Censors cut movies; to cut short a career, program, speech, vacation;* "Shush," she said to **cut him short** (= reduce him to silence); *His sarcastic wit really cut* (= hurt) *her; She was cut to the quick* (= deeply hurt). **4** absent oneself from somewhere without leave: *He cut class to go to the movie.* **5** intersect: *where Sixth Avenue cuts Second Street; to cut* (= go directly) *across a field; Another driver* **cut me off** (= got in my way without warning), *then suddenly cut* (= changed direction) *to the right lane.* **6** divide a deck of cards. **7** yield to cutting: *This cheese is so soft it cuts easily.* **8** dilute: *to cut a drink with water.* **9** remove: *Ammonia cuts grease and dirt; She was* **cut out of** (= excluded from) *his will.* **—cut a figure** make an impression: *He cut a sorry figure with his humor.* **—cut and run** run away quickly. **—cut back** reduce: *to cut back* (= prune) *the shrubbery; She has cut back on her smoking.* **—cut both ways** have good and bad effects. **—cut down** reduce: *She has cut down on smoking; She* **cut him down to size** (= made him feel less important; deflated him). **—cut ice with someone** have influence; make an impression: *His wild claims cut no ice with me.* **—cut in** intrude, as move in front of another car; interrupt: *He cut in on our conversation; Ed cut in when Joe and Kay had just started dancing.* —**cut it 1** *Informal.* succeed; hack it: *He just couldn't cut it.* **2** look at it: *It's good business no matter how you cut it.* —**cut off** deprive of something: *They cut off our heat; We got lost and were cut off from civilization for a while.* —**cut out 1** *Informal.* stop: *Cut out that noise; Time to cut out* (= leave quickly). **2** suited: *He's not cut out to be a lawyer; not cut out for a legal career.* **3** planned and ready: *The astronauts have their work cut out for them.* —**cut up** *Informal.* **1** criticize harshly. **2** play pranks, clown around, etc. **3** upset: *He's really cut up about the loss.* —*n.* **1** a cutting or its result: *a cut on the chin from shaving; a superficial, not deep cut; cuts made in a story by the censors; a choice cut of beef; The road ran through a cut in the mountain; a crew cut; a stylish cut of hair, clothes; Everyone took a 20% cut* (= reduction) *in pay last year; a budget cut; tax cuts; a cut in expenditure; staff cuts; Each got a 20% cut* (*Informal* for share) *of the profits; Cadillacs are* **a cut above** (= superior to) *other cars.* **2** a printed picture: *a write-up illustrated with cuts.*

cut-and-dried *adj.* already prepared, as by formula; routine: *a cut-and-dried answer, plan, solution.* Also **cut-and-dry.**

cu.ta.ne.ous (cue.TAY.nee.us) *adj.* on or of the skin: *a cutaneous disorder, infection, ulcer.*

cut.a.way (CUT.uh.way) *n.* a tailcoat.

cut.back *n.* a reduction: *a budgetary cutback; a cutback in benefits, expenditure, services; staff cutbacks.*

cute *adj.* **cut.er, cut.est 1** pretty; dainty: *Babies are cute; a cute little hat.* **2** affectedly pleasing; artificial: *a cute act.* **3** *Informal.* frivolous or disrespectful: *He tried to be cute with her.* **4** *Informal.* sly or tricky. —**cute.ly** *adv.*; **cute.ness** *n.*

cute.sy or **cute.sie** (CUTE.see) *adj.* cute in a mannered or deliberate way.

cut glass *n.* glassware that is ornamented by having patterns cut into it.

cut.i.cle (CUE.ti.cul) *n.* **1** the tough skin at the edge of a nail. **2** the surface layer of skin. —**cu.tic.u.lar** (cue.TIC.yuh.lur) *adj.*

cu.tie or **cu.tey** (CUE.tee) *n. Informal.* a charming and inoffensive young person.

cut.lass (CUT.lus) *n.* a short, curved slashing sword.

cut.ler *n.* one who sells or makes knives and other cutting tools.

cut.ler.y (CUT.luh.ree) *n.* tableware such as spoons, forks, and knives; also, scissors, etc.

cut.let (CUT.lit) *n.* a small leg or rib cut of meat: *beef, chicken, veal cutlets.*

cut.line *n.* a caption to a printed picture.

cut.off *n.* a cutting off or what results from it: *cutoffs of funds, loans; aid, arms cutoffs; She wears cutoffs* (= jeans cut short) *in the summer; cutoffs* (= shortcuts) *built to eliminate winding roads; the Main Street cutoff* (= highway exit). —*adj.*: *a cutoff device, period, point, valve.*

cutoff date *n.* **1** date when an arrangement ends. **2** a deadline.

cut.out *n.* a pattern, picture, part (as the back of a dress), etc. designed to be or that has been cut out.

cut-rate *adj.* having to do with reduced prices: *cut-rate airlines, fares, fees, financing, gasoline, methods, offers, prices, stores.*

cut.ter *n.* **1** one that cuts. **2** a small, fast boat or sleigh.

cut.throat *n.* a murderer. —*adj.* merciless: *cutthroat ambition, competition, pricing; Competition is more cutthroat in large urban centers.*

cutting *n.* **1** a short slip for propagation of a plant. **2** the act of one that cuts or what is cut: *ribbon cutting* (= opening ceremony); *grass cuttings; press cuttings* (= clippings); *adj.*: *a cutting board, instrument; cutting* (= sharp) *pain; cutting* (= hurtful) *remarks; a* **cutting room** (for editing film).

cutting edge *n.* the forefront of something developing: *a company that is at* or *on the cutting edge of computer technology.*

cut.tle.fish (CUT.ul.fish) *n.* a squidlike mollusk that secretes an inky fluid.

cut.up *n.* one who plays pranks, clowns around, etc.

cut.work *n.* embroidery or needlework in which spaces are cut and either left open or filled with inserts.

cy.an (SYE.un) *n.* a greenish blue.

cy.a.nide (SYE.uh.nide) *n.* a poisonous chemical compound.

cyber- *comb.form.* having to do with computers and cyberspace: *cyberphobe, cyberpunk, cybertalk, cyberthon.*

cy.ber.na.tion (sye.bur.NAY.shun) *n.* the use of computers to control machines.

cy.ber.net.ics (sye.bur.NET.ics) *n.pl.* [takes *sing. v.*] the comparative study of information flow and control processes in humans and machines. —**cy.ber.net.ic** *adj.*

cy.ber.space (SY.bur.space) *n.* **1** the

world of computer networks, information exchange, and other activities. 2 the fantasy world of virtual reality.
cy.borg (SYE.borg) *n.* a human being who depends on mechanical parts for the carrying out of bodily functions.
cy.cla.mate (SYE.cluh.mate) *n.* an artificial salt of sodium or calcium used as a sugar substitute.
cy.cla.men (SYE.cluh.mun) *n.* a plant related to the primrose, having white, pink, or purple flowers.
cy.cle (SYE.cul) *n.* 1 a periodic action or event or the time taken for it: *the cycle of the seasons; Alternating current reverses direction at 60 cycles per second; the four stages in the life cycle of the butterfly; business, economic, menstrual cycles.* 2 circle: *The earth completes its cycle around the sun in one year;* to **come full cycle** See CIRCLE. 3 a bicycle, tricycle, or motorcycle. —*v.* **-cles, -cled, -cling** ride a cycle. —**cy.clist** *n.*
cy.cli.cal (SYE.clic.ul) *adj.* occurring in a cycle; regularly repeating: *the cyclical swings of the real-estate market; the cyclical nature of the hotel industry; a cyclical pattern.* Also **cy.clic.**
cy.clom.e.ter (sye.CLOM.i.tur) *n.* an instrument for measuring the distance traveled by a rotating wheel.
cy.clone (SYE.clone) *n.* a spiraling wind formation that includes hurricanes and tornados. —**cy.clon.ic** (sye.CLON.ic) *adj.*
cy.clo.ram.a (sye.cluh.RAM.uh) *n.* a large picture painted on a circular wall.
cy.clo.tron (SYE.cluh.tron) *n.* a high-speed particle accelerator using alternating electric fields.
cyl.in.der (SIL.un.dur) *n.* the round solid or hollow shape of a pencil, tin can, water pipe, etc. —**cy.lin.dri.cal** (suh.LIN.dri.cul) *adj.*
cym.bal (SIM.bul) *n.* a slightly concave brass disk used as a percussion instrument. —**cym.bal.ist** *n.*
cyn.ic (SIN.ic) *n.* one who sneers at the goodness of human nature and actions, attributing everything to self-interest. —**cyn.i.cal** (-i.cul) *adj.*: *She is cynical about his idealism.* —**cyn.i.cism** (-uh.siz.um) *n.*
cy.no.sure (SYE.nuh.sure) *n.* something that attracts attention, admiration, etc.: *The returning war hero was the cynosure of all eyes.*
cy.press (SYE.press) *n.* an evergreen tree of the pine family with scalelike leaves.
Cyp.ri.ot (SIP.ree.ut) *n. & adj.* (a person) of or from **Cyprus,** an island republic in the E. Mediterranean.
Cy.ril.lic (si.RIL.ic) *n.* a script derived from Greek, used in writing Slavic languages; *adj.*: *the Cyrillic alphabet, script.*
cyst (SIST) *n.* an abnormal sac in the body containing fluid. —**cys.tic** *adj.*
cystic fibrosis *n.* a hereditary disease affecting the pancreas, mucous membranes, and respiratory system.
cy.tol.o.gy (sye.TOL.uh.jee) *n.* the scientific study of cells; **cy.tol.o.gist** *n.* —**cy.to.log.ic** (-tuh.LOJ.ic) or **cy.to.log.i.cal** *adj.*
cy.to.plasm (SYE.tuh.plaz.um) *n.* the protoplasm of a cell outside the nucleus. —**cy.to.plas.mic** (-PLAZ.mic) *adj.*
cy.to.sine (SYE.tuh.seen) *n.* one of the basic coding chemicals in DNA and RNA.
czar or **tsar** (ZAR) *n.* 1 a baron; also, an autocrat: *energy, oil, financial, gambling czars.* 2 a Russian emperor (until 1917); **cza.ri.na** or **tsa.ri.na** (zah.REE.nuh) *fem.* —**czar.ist** or **tsar.ist** *n. & adj.*
Czech (CHEK) *n. & adj.* 1 (a person) of or from the **Czech Republic,** a country of C. Europe. 2 (having to do with) the Slavic language of the Czechs.

.... **D, d** ....

D or **d** (DEE) *n.* **D's** or **d's** the fourth letter of the English alphabet.
dab *v.* **dabs, dabbed, dab.bing** put on, touch, or strike with a light, quick, usu. soft stroke: *a child dabbing paste on paper; He dabbed at his eyes with a handkerchief; He dabbed his eyes.* —*n.*: *A quick dab removed the smudge; Put a little dab of butter on the toast.*
dab.ble (DAB.ul) *v.* **dab.bles, dab.bled, dab.bling** 1 spatter with water; splash. 2 play splashing in the water: *Ducks dabbled in the pond.* 3 work or do something amateurishly: *an amateur who dabbles in science; a banker who likes to dabble at gardening; One of the kids was caught dabbling with drugs.* —**dab.bler** *n.*
da.cha (DAH.chuh) *n.* a country house in Russia.
dachs.hund (DAHKS.hoond, short "oo") *n.* a breed of dog with a long, low body, a pointed snout, and drooping ears.
Da.cron (DAY.cron, DAC.ron) *adj.a. Trademark.* a synthetic fiber or a wrinkle-free cloth made from it. Also

da.cron.
dac.tyl (DAC.tul) *n.* a metrical foot having a long or stressed syllable followed by two short or unstressed syllables. —**dac.tyl.ic** (dac.TIL.ic) *adj.*: *dactylic hexameter.*
dad *n. Informal.* father.
Da.da or **da.da** (DAH.dah) *n.* an artistic and literary movement started in 1916 as a violent break with tradition. —**Da.da.ism** *n.*; **Da.da.ist** *n. & adj.*
dad.dy (DAD.ee) *n.* **dad.dies** 1 [child's word] father. 2 *Informal.* most respected member of a group; dean: *the daddy of all living presidents; the grand daddy of them all.*
daddy long.legs *n. sing. & pl.* 1 a spiderlike arachnid with long, thin legs. 2 *Brit.* a crane fly.
dae.mon (DEE.mun) same as DEMON.
daf.fo.dil (DAF.uh.dil) *n.* a yellow flower with long stems and narrow leaves that blooms in early spring.
daf.fy (DAF.ee) *adj.* **daf.fi.er, daf.fi.est** *Informal.* crazy or daft: *a daffy idea; Lu shows a talent for daffy comedy.*
—**daf.fi.ness** *n.*
daft *adj. Informal.* silly or foolish: *The speech was a bit daft.*
dag.ger (DAG.ur) *n.* 1 a pointed, two-edged knife used for stabbing. 2 a mark (†) used for reference. —**at daggers drawn** in open hostility *with* some. —**look daggers at** stare at someone with hate or fury.
da.guerre.o.type (duh.GAIR.uh.type) *n.* an early process for making photographs involving long exposure of a sensitized plate; also, such a photograph.
dahl.ia (DAL.yuh) *n.* a perennial plant with tuberous roots and showy composite flowers.
dai.ly (DAY.lee) *adja.* of, for, done, or occurring every day: *our daily habits, life, newspaper; on a daily basis; in daily use; He was paid a daily rate of $500.*
—*adv.*: *Take two pills thrice daily.*
—*n., pl.* **-lies** a newspaper put out every weekday.
daily double *n.* a bet on the winners in two races.
daily dozen *n.* a set of routine daily exercises.
dain.ty (DAIN.tee) *adj.* **-ti.er, -ti.est** 1 delicate and pleasing: *a dainty centerpiece for the table; a dainty dance step, dress.* 2 fussy; fastidious: *a dainty eater.* —*n., pl.* **-ties** a delicacy. —**dain.ti.ly** *adv.*; **dain.ti.ness** *n.*
dai.qui.ri (DYE.kuh.ree, DAK-) *n.* a cocktail of rum, sugar, and lime or lemon juice.
dair.y (DAIR.ee) *n.* **dair.ies** 1 also **dairy farm**, a farm specializing in milk production; *adja.*: *a dairy breed of cattle; dairy cattle, products.* 2 a place where milk and milk products are kept, processed, or sold. —**dair.y.maid** *n.* —**dair.y.man** *n.* **-men; dair.y.wom.an** *n.* **-wo.men.**
da.is (DAY.is) *n.* an elevated platform for a speaker, special guest, etc.
dai.sy (DAY.zee) *n.* **-sies** a composite flower with white rays and a yellow center; also, any similar flower: *fresh as a daisy;* to pick off the daisy petals one by one to determine whether or not something is going to happen; *The dead are supposed to* **push up daisies** *from their graves; The apartment flip was a* **daisy chain** (= linked series) *of deals that drove up the price at each sale.*
Da.ko.ta (duh.COH.tuh) *n.* 1 (a member of) an Amerindian tribe of North and South Dakota, Montana, and Minnesota. 2 their Siouan language.
—**Da.ko.tan** *n. & adj.*
dale *n.* a valley: *through hill and dale.*
dal.li.ance (DAL.ee.unce) *n.* a dallying or flirtation: *a brief dalliance with a young actress.*
dal.ly (DAL.ee) *v.* **dal.lies, dal.lied, dal.ly.ing** 1 waste time; dawdle: *a child dallying over a meal.* 2 trifle or play: *He dallied with the idea till it was too late; She was merely dallying with his affections* (= flirting).
Dal.ma.tian (dal.MAY.shun) *n.* a breed of white dog with black spots and a short, thick coat.
dam *n.* 1 an obstacle built across a watercourse to hold back the flow: *to build, construct, erect a dam; a storage dam; A dam bursts and floods a valley.* 2 a mother, esp. of a four-legged animal: *a thoroughbred horse with registered sire and dam.* —*v.* **dams, dammed, dam.ming:** *They dammed the creek to make a duck pond; It is unhealthy to* **dam up** (= bottle up) *your anger.*
dam.age (DAM.ij) *n.* 1 injury or hurt, esp. one resulting in loss: *to cause or do damage to something; inflict damage on someone; to repair or undo a damage; His car suffered or sustained a $2,000 damage in the accident; The damage from the fire was extensive; a damage set at $50,000; a grave damage to her reputation; a great, irreparable, serious, severe damage; irreversible damage to the brain from interruption of oxygen supply; Lasting or permanent damage was done; light or slight damage; fire, flood, material,*

property, structural, widespread damage.
2 damages *pl.* money as a recompense for loss or impairment: *to award, claim, pay, receive, recover damages for defamation of character; Compensatory, exemplary, nominal, punitive damages are awarded by courts.* —*v.* **-ag.es, -aged, -ag.ing** cause or suffer damage: *She damaged her toy; Smaller cars damage more easily;* **adj.:** *a badly* **damaged** *building; an easily damaged* (= easy to damage) *car; How cruel to describe a raped youth as* **damaged goods;** *a* **damaging** *effect, example, report.*

dam.a.scene (DAM.uh.seen) *v.* **-scenes, -scened, -scen.ing** decorate, esp. steel, with wavy lines or inlaid gold and silver, as is done to **Damascus steel,** a strong steel for sword blades.

dam.ask (DAM.usk) *n.* **1** a rich fabric with a woven-in pattern, used esp. for table linen; **adj.:** *damask linens, napkins, tablecloths.* **2** Damascus steel.

damask rose *n.* an Asiatic rose that is the source of attar of roses.

dame *n.* **1** lady: *Dame Fortune.* **2 Dame** a British title for women corresponding to knight. **3** *Informal* [used by men] a woman.

damn (DAM) *v.* **1** condemn: *a play damned by the critics;* **adj.:** *the* **damned** *and the saved.* **2** curse or swear saying "damn": *I'll be damned if I know; Damn it all!* —**damn with faint praise** praise so slightly as to imply fault.
—*n. Slang.* a damning: *He doesn't* **give or care a damn** (= doesn't care at all); *It's* **not worth a damn** (= is worthless); *People want answers and* **by damn** (= damn it!) *they're going to get them.*
—**damn** *Slang.* [intensifier] **1** *adj.:* *a damn fool; one damn thing after another.* **2** *adv.:* *You damn well know it; A damn fine mess we're in now; a damn good reason; Give it to anyone you damn like.*
—**dam.na.ble** (DAM.nuh.bul) *adj.*

dam.na.tion (dam.NAY.shun) *n.* a damning or being damned: *souls sent to eternal damnation.*

damned *adj.* & *adv.* same as DAMN.

damned.est (DAM.dist) *adj. Slang.* **1** worst: *the damnedest mess under the sun.* **2** utmost: *We'll do or try our damnedest to get out of it.*

damp *adj.* moderately wet, having absorbed moisture: *shoes damp from the rain;* *v.:* *An automatic washer fills itself, washes, rinses, and* **damp-dries** *clothes* (= dries them partially) *before shutting off.* —*n.* **1** a moderate wetness. **2** a harmful gas, as in coal mines.
—*v.* **1** make damp. **2** reduce enthusiasm, force, or power: *The defeat didn't damp his spirit.* Also **damp.en.**
—**damp.ness** *n.*

damp.er *n.* something that reduces or damps, as a plate for checking the draft in a flue, or a felt pad for stopping a piano string's vibration: *The news of the tragedy put a damper on the party.*

dam.sel (DAM.zul) *n.* [old use] a maiden: *Knights used to rescue damsels in distress.*

dam.sel.fly (DAM.sul.fly) *n.* **-flies** a small, slender kind of dragonfly.

dam.son (DAM.zun) *n.* a small, dark plum.

dance *v.* **danc.es, danced, danc.ing** **1** move the body and feet rhythmically, usu. to music; also, perform a particular dance step: *He's dancing in the rain; to dance the cha-cha; She's not the girl to* **dance to someone's tune** (= to be in someone else's power) *or* **dance attendance** *on anyone* (= follow anyone attending to their wishes). **2** move lightly, esp. up and down: *a boxer dancing around the ring.*
—*n.* **1** an act of dancing or a type of it, as the tango or waltz; also, music for it: *to do or perform a dance; a dance with the bride; a circle or round dance; a barn, belly, classical, folk, formal, modern, square, sword, tap, war dance; May I have this dance* (= this turn of dancing)? *a school of dance* (= dancing). **2** a party given for dancing: *She went to the school dance; made new friends at the dance; He sat out the whole dance because of a sprained ankle.* —**danc.er** *n.*
—**dancing** *n.:* *aerobic, ballroom, social, belly, break, folk, tap dancing.*

dan.de.lion (DAN.duh.lye.un) *n.* a bright-yellow composite flower having edible, jagged leaves; **adj.a.:** *dandelion blossoms, greens, salad, wine.*

dan.der (DAN.dur) *n. Informal.* **get one's dander up** make or become angry.

dan.di.fy (DAN.duh.fye) *v.* **-fies, -fied, -fy.ing** make resemble a dandy.

dan.dle (DAN.dul) *v.* **-dles, -dled, -dling** bounce a child up and down, as on one's knee or in one's arms.

dan.druff (DAN.druf) *n.* whitish flakes of dead skin from the scalp.

dan.dy (DAN.dee) *n.* **-dies 1** a man who is overly stylish and careful in dress; fop. **2** *Informal.* something excellent of its type: *That's a dandy.*
—*adj.* **-di.er, -di.est** excellent: *That is fine and dandy by me!*

Dane *n.* a person of or from **Denmark,**

a kingdom in N. Europe.

dan.ger (DAIN.jur) *n.* exposure to or risk of harm; also, a source of this: *An open manhole constitutes, creates, represents a danger to people; a clear and present danger; People are exposed to, face, run the danger of falling in; There's a danger that they may fall in; a deadly or grave or mortal danger of breaking one's neck; an imminent or impending danger; She sensed the danger; The danger was averted; He fell into the lake and was in danger of his life; was out of danger after a few days;* **adj**a.: *danger money, pay, signs, spots; a patient on the* **danger list.**

dan.ger.ous (DAIN.juh.rus) *adj.* liable to cause harm or loss unless dealt with carefully: *It's dangerous to play with fire; Firefighting is a dangerous occupation; The escaped convict is armed and dangerous; a dangerous person, place, thing.* **—dan.ger.ous.ly** *adv.*

dan.gle (DANG.gul) *v.* **-gles, -gled, -gling** (make) hang loosely and swing: *Fish dangled from a hook; He dangled it before or in front of his cat.*

Dan.iel (DAN.yul) *n.* a wise judge, esp. if youthful: *"a Daniel come to judgment."*

Dan.ish (DAY.nish) *adj.* having to do with Danes or Denmark: *Danish blue cheese.* **—n.** 1 the Danish language. 2 also **Danish pastry,** a rich pastry, usu. with filling and icing.

dank *adj.* injuriously or unpleasantly damp: *a dank dungeon, mist, prison cell.* **—dank.ly** *adv.;* **dank.ness** *n.*

dan.seur (dahn.SUR) *n.* a ballet dancer; **dan.seuse** (-SOOZ) *fem.*

dap.per (DAP.ur) *adj.* of men of small build, trim or smartly dressed: *a dapper fellow, youth; He looks quite dapper in his new suit; looks a bit too dapper for manual work.*

dap.ple (DAP.ul) *v.* **dap.ples, dap.pled, dap.pling** mark with spots. **—dap.ple** or **dap.pled** *adj.*: *a horse with a dappled rump; a sun-dappled porch.*

dare *v.* **dares** [or **dare** if followed by verb without "to"], **dared, dar.ing** 1 challenge: *She dared him to dive after her.* 2 have the boldness to do something: *if he dares to dive after her or if he dare dive after her; He dared not dive after her or didn't dare to dive after her; How dare he defy her?* 3 face boldly: *Brave men dare great dangers.* **—n.** a challenge: *He did it on a dare; He took the dare.* **—dar.er** *n.*

dare.dev.il (DARE.dev.il) *n.* one who acts with reckless courage; **adj.**: *a daredevil driver, skier, stunt.*

dare.say *v.* [used in pres. tense, first person sing.] venture to say: *I daresay it is freezing outside; You're right, I daresay.*

daring (DAIR.ing) *n.* bravery or boldness: *an act, man, woman, work of great daring.* **—adj.** brave or bold: *a daring action, crime, dress, effort, hero, idea, movie, plan, robbery, thing.* **—dar.ing.ly** *adv.*

dark *adj.* 1 lacking in light; not bright or light: *a dark and stormy night; It was pitch dark; a dark* (= overcast) *day; dark blue; dark hair; a deep dark* (= mysterious) *secret.* 2 unenlightened: *the* **Dark Ages** *of early medieval Europe; Africa was once known as the* **Dark Continent** (= unexplored continent). 3 gloomy; also, evil or angry: *a dark look; dark predictions.* **—n.** darkness: *Ed visited us in the dark of night; Some birds come out after dark* (= nightfall); *She kept him* **in the dark** (= in ignorance) *about her plans.* **—dark.ly** *adv.* **—dark.ness** *n.*: *complete or pitch or total darkness; when darkness falls.*

dark.en (DARK.un) *v.* dim or obscure: *Clouds darkened the sky; Her face darkened with rage; She told him never to* **darken her door** (= visit her) *again.*

dark glasses *n.pl.* sunglasses.

dark horse *n.* a contestant whose strength is still unknown; **adj.**: *a* **dark-horse** *candidate, contender; dark-horse odds.*

dark.room *n.* a room made dark for photographic developing.

dar.ling *n.* a dearly loved person or thing: *Is that you, darling? grandma's little darling; the darling of the film industry.* **—adj.**: *a darling child, dog; my darling Mimi; What a darling* (Informal for charming) *purse!*

darn 1 *v.* repair a hole, garment, etc. by interlacing yarn or thread: *to darn old socks.* 2 a hole thus repaired. 3 *n., v., adj. & adv. Informal.* damn: *Darn it! I don't give a darn; I heard no such darn thing; a darn good excuse.*

darned *adj. & adv. Informal.* same as DARN, 3. **—darned.est** *n. & adj.* utmost: *He did* or *tried his darnedest to find the lost key.*

dar.nel (DAR.nul) *n.* any of a group of weed grasses.

darning needle *n.* 1 a large needle for darning. 2 a dragonfly.

dart *n.* 1 a pointed missile that is thrown, blown by a blowgun, etc.: *The game of* **darts** *is played by aiming darts at a target on a board.* 2 a sudden, fast movement.

darter / date

—*v.* throw or move with sudden speed: *The frog darts out its tongue to catch a fly; She darted a glance at him; See the rabbits darting across the road.*

dart.er *n.* a small freshwater fish of the perch family.

Dar.win.i.an (dar.WIN.ee.uhn) *n. & adj.* (a follower) of Charles **Darwin**, a 19th-century English naturalist whose theory **Darwinism** holds that evolution took place by natural selection.

dash *v.* **1** move, throw, or strike with violent speed: *The winner dashed* (= ran) *across the finish line; As the bombs fell, people dashed for cover; In his fury, he dashed* (= threw) *the cup to the floor; Her hopes were dashed* (= destroyed); *She revived when he dashed* (= splashed) *water on her face; Five minutes is all it takes to* **dash off** (= write hastily) *a letter.* **2** mix with a bit of another substance: *water dashed with vinegar.* —**dash it (all)!** *Informal.* damn it (all)! —*n.* **1** a fast move, throw, or strike: *People made a quick dash for cover; a 100-m dash* (= race or sprint); *A dash* (= splashing) *of water on the face revived her.* **2** a small amount added or mixed in: *Add a dash of vanilla extract; a dash of color, salt, whiskey.* **3** vigorous, spirited action: *She plays with dash and vigor.* **4** a punctuation mark [–] that is longer than a hyphen. **5** dashboard: *She always carries a flashlight and road maps under the dash.*

dash.board *n.* an instrument panel below a vehicle's windshield.

dash.er *n.* **1** a plunger with paddles for agitating cream in a churn. **2** the ledge along the top of the boards of a hockey rink.

da.shi.ki (dah.SHEE.kee) *n.* a loose, brightly colored shirt or tunic.

dashing *adj.* **1** spirited: *a dashing young lieutenant.* **2** stylish: *the store's dashing image.*

das.tard.ly (DAS.turd.lee) *adj.* cowardly: *a dastardly betrayal, deed.*

da.ta (DAY.tuh, DAT.uh) *n.pl.* [used with *sing.* or *pl. v.* depending on sentence structure] basic information; facts as a basis for analysis: *biographical, scientific, statistical data; to cite, evaluate, gather, keyboard, punch in, retrieve, store, transmit data; Raw data is* [*not are*] *fed into the computer for processing; Great masses of data are* [*not is*] *confusing even to a computer; Census figures, school records, and such kind of data is* or *are called "derived data."* —*adj.:* **data conversion, files, search, transmission.**

data bank *n.* a large collection of computerized information: *data banks as a threat to privacy.*

da.ta.base (DAY.tuh.base) *n.* **1** an organized collection or file of information stored in a computer in the form of "records" subdivided into "fields." **2** the software for this.

dat.a.ble or **date.a.ble** (DAY.tuh.bul) *adj.* that can be dated: *a datable piece of pottery.*

data entry *n.* the keyboarding of data; also **data capture.**

data field *n.* an element of a database record, as name, address, phone number, etc. of a person.

data processing *n.* operations to convert, store, analyze, and retrieve data in usable form. —**data processor** *n.*

date *n.* **1** the time at which something exists, happens, is made, etc., esp. the day, month, and year: *to fix* or *set a date for our meeting; 1492 is a significant date in American history; Today's date is August 26; a target date for completion; at a certain date; at a later date; on a future date; one's* **date of birth**; *a* **closing date** (= deadline) *for applications.* **2** *Informal.* a social meeting, as between a male and female; also, a person with whom one has a date: *to have, make a date for lunch; Dick is Jane's date; They are out on a date; a blind date; double date; He broke* (= did not keep) *his date with Jan; a date with destiny* (= something that may change one's future). **3** the sweet oblong fruit of a palm tree. —**out of date** old-fashioned; obsolete: *Daily papers go* or *get* or *become out of date every day.* —**to date** until now: *We have 125 replies to date since the ad appeared.* —**up to date** using or knowing current information or methods: *We have to bring the boss up to date on what happened while he was away; to bring* or *make a publication up to date for a new edition; to keep up to date with something; to keep oneself up to date on something; to keep oneself* or *something up to date;* **adj.**: *an up-to-date edition.*

—*v.* **dates, dat.ed, dat.ing 1** record or mark the date on something: *a postcard dated 31 March.* **2** determine or show the date or age of a person or thing: *Carbon 14 is used to date artifacts; That expression dates you, Grandpa* (= shows you to be of an earlier generation). **3** have or make a date with someone: *Is your sister old enough to date (boys)?* **n.**: *She's into computer dating* (= dating via computer). —**date back to** or **date from** be in existence since: *Thanksgiving dates back to pioneer* days; *The November observance dates from 1939.*

dateable same as DATABLE.

dated (DAY.tid) *adj.* outmoded; out-of-date.

date.less *adj.* 1 undated. 2 timeless; also, too old to be datable. 3 undying: *dateless fame.*

date.line *n.* the place and date of origin of a document or story, as "New York, July 8."

date rape *n.* rape committed on one's partner during a date. Also **acquaintance rape.**

dating bar *n.* a bar for single people to find dates in.

da.tum (DAY.tum, DAT.um) *n., pl.* **-ta** or **-tums** [used technically; see DATA for *pl.* use] an item of information; a given fact: *a sense datum; a datum of consciousness, experience.*

daub *v.* 1 smear or coat, as with grease, clay, plaster, etc.: *to daub plaster on a wall; His hands were daubed* (= soiled) *with ink.* 2 paint crudely or rapidly: *a wall daubed with graffiti.* —*n.* 1 material for daubing: *a hut made of wattle and daub* (= mud or clay). 2 a daubing; smear or stain; also, a crude painting. —**daub.er** *n.*

daugh.ter (DAW.tur) *n.* 1 a female offspring: *an adopted daughter; foster daughters; She is like a daughter to me,* says her neighbor. 2 a descendant or product thought of as female: *Italian, French, Spanish, etc. are daughters of Latin; Radon daughters are the harmful radioactive decay products of radon gas;* **adja.**: *the daughter languages of Latin; a daughter cell, product.* —**daugh.ter.ly** *adj.*: *She cared for the elderly with daughterly devotion.*

daughter-in-law *n.* **daughters-in-law** the wife of one's son.

daunt *v.* frighten or discourage; *adj.*: *The prospect was rather daunting; a daunting array, challenge, task; She went ahead, nothing daunted* (= frightened by nothing). —**daunt.less** *adj.*: *her dauntless courage; a dauntless hero;* **daunt.less.ly** *adv.*

dau.phin (DAW.fin) *n.* till 1830, the title of the eldest son of the king of France.

dav.en.port (DAV.un.port) *n.* a large couch, often a day bed.

dav.it *n.* one of a pair of cranes for holding or raising and lowering a ship's small boat from the side.

daw.dle (DAW.dul) *v.* **-dles, -dled, -dling** waste time; idle: *to dawdle over breakfast; Stop dawdling, says Mom; Don't dawdle your summer away.* —**daw.dler** *n.*

dawn *n.* 1 the first light of day; daybreak: *We'll start at dawn; at the crack or break of dawn; Dawn breaks in the east.* 2 beginning: *at the dawn of civilization, of history; the dawn of hope, of a new era.* —*v.* become light at sunrise; hence, begin to develop, be clear, etc.: *The day dawns bright on a clear day; when the day dawns* (= when the sun rises); *An idea* **dawns on** or **upon** *you* (gradually); *It dawned on her that she was free at last.*

day *n.* 1 the period from sunrise to sunset: *a cool, cold, hot, sultry, sunny, warm day; an eventful, memorable, red-letter, wedding day; the opening day* (of an event); *New Year's Day;* **The day** (= The important day) *finally arrived; Paris by day* (= daytime sightseeing in Montreal) *is less exciting than Paris by night; Most people work* **days** (= during the day) *and sleep nights.* 2 the 24-hour period from midnight to midnight: *the seven days of the week; What time of day is it?* 3 the part of a day one works: *Our day starts at 9; We work an 8-hour day; She did the job in a day; She took the day off on Friday; She is off* **for the day** (= the rest of the day); *Some are paid* **by the day** or **on a day-to-day** *basis.* 4 a period or stage of existence; age or era: *in days of yore; in days to come; in Columbus's day; back in the old days; during the good old days in Europe; the halcyon days of our youth; It happened just the other day; the dog days of summer; You'll rue the day you do such a thing;* **one of these days** (= in the near future); *In this day and age no one should have to sleep in parks; His* **days are numbered** (= has only a limited time left). 5 a period of success, opportunity, power, etc.: *"Every dog has his day"; a retired politician who has had his day.* 6 success in a contest: *We've carried or won the day; The day is ours; They lost the day.* —**all in a day's work** the normal thing to happen. —**call it a day** consider it the end of the day; cease working. —**day after day** or **day in, day out** or **day in and day out** every day, always. —**day and night** continually. —**day in court** a chance to be heard before being judged. —**make one's day** make one quite happy: *"You made my day,"* said the woman when told she had won the contract.

day bed *n.* a couch that may be converted to a bed.

day.book *n.* a diary or journal.

day.break same as DAWN.

day care n. care of children outside of home and school, usu. while the parents are at work, as provided at a **day-care center** or **day nursery**.

day.dream n. a reverie; an unrealistic, pleasant thought; v.: *She daydreams about lottery wins.* —**day.dream.ing** n.

day.light n. **1** sunlight; daytime: *Rani likes to read by daylight; The bank was robbed in broad daylight.* **2** understanding, like reaching the end of a long journey in the dark: *We're longing to see daylight on this issue.* **3 daylights** insides or wits: *The boxer had the daylights whipped or beaten or walloped out of him; He scared the (living) daylights out of her with his scream.*

day nursery See DAY CARE.

day one or **Day One** n. the beginning of an enterprise or activity: *The business has been a success from day one.*

day school n. a private school without facilities to board students.

day student n. a college student living off campus.

day.time same as DAY, 1: *your daytime phone number; a daytime drama* or *daytime TV* (= soap opera).

daze v. **daz.es, dazed, daz.ing** bewilder or confuse by something sudden and excessive: *He was dazed by the tragedy;* adj.: *The tragedy left him dazed; a dazed expression, look, smile;* n.: *He was in a daze for hours after being hit on the head.*

daz.zle (DAZ.ul) v. **daz.zles, daz.zled, daz.zling** dim the vision of someone or overpower, as by bright light or brilliance: *High beams dazzle drivers in the opposing lane; She dazzles me by her wit;* adj.: *a dazzling beauty, display, effect, performance.* —n.: *the dazzle of diamonds, gold, headlights.* —**daz.zler** n.

D-day n. the starting date for a military or other operation, as 6 June 1944, when the Allies invaded Europe: *D-day minus two* (= two days before D-day).

dea.con (DEE.cun) n. an assistant to a minister or a clergyman ranking next to a priest; fem. **dea.con.ess.**

de.ac.ti.vate (dee.AC.tuh.vate) v. **-vates, -vat.ed, -vat.ing** make inactive or nonfunctional: *He deactivated the time bomb before it could go off.* —**de.ac.ti.va.tion** (DEE.ac.tuh.VAY.shun) n.

dead (DED) adj. **1** no longer alive: *Jon was left there for dead; He wasn't playing dead; was dead as a dodo or doornail; He had been shot dead; He is now dead and buried; He's dead and gone; She would not be caught dead dealing (Informal for would never deal) with a thug* again. **2** like death or being dead: *He collapsed in a dead faint; dead with fatigue; a criminal who is dead to* (= insensible of) *all shame; ears dead* (= numb) *with the cold; a dead* (= lifeless) *party; a dead* (= out of play) *ball; a dead* (= chargeless) *battery; The telephone line is dead; It has gone dead* (= There's no dial tone); *dead* (= infertile) *soil; The ship fell into a dead* (= complete) *calm.* **3** exact or unerring: *I hit it dead center; with dead accuracy; He's a dead shot with a rifle; It's a dead certainty; Your smile is a dead giveaway* (= sure sign). —**dead to the world** *Informal.* drunk, fast asleep, or unconscious.
—adv. quite: *Are you dead certain? Medicine is dead last in his career choices; It's dead perfect; We are dead set against dealing with terrorists; He's dead tired; dead wrong; It's dead* (= directly) *ahead; He stopped dead* (= as if dead) *in his tracks; He's **dead beat** (Informal for quite exhausted) and dead broke (Informal for penniless); Her words hit us **dead on*** (= right on target).
—n. **1** dead people: *the quick* or *living and the dead; Lazarus rose from (among) the dead.* **2** a state resembling death: *the dead* (= quietest part) *of the night; in the dead* (= coldest part) *of winter.*

dead.beat n. *Informal.* one who does not pay his debts or fair share.

dead.bolt n. a bolt that locks a door by being turned manually instead of by spring action.

dead duck n. *Informal.* one sure to be finished with or killed: *One wrong move and you are a dead duck.*

dead.en (DED.un) v. **1** deprive of sensation: *a soul deadened by the blows of fate.* **2** dull or weaken: *pain deadened by drugs.* **3** to sound-proof.

dead end n. **1** a street, hall, alley, etc. closed at the other end. **2** something with no chance for progress.

dead-end adj. closed at the other end: *a dead-end street; a dead-end job with no possibility of advancement; dead-end kids (of the slums) fighting for survival.*

dead.head v. *Informal.* of pilots, take a flight between assignments: *He's deadheading home to Toronto after the London-New York flight.* —n. **1** a freeloader, klutz, bore, etc. **2** a commercial vehicle without its usual payload. **3** a faded flower head.

dead heat n. a race or contest between two, as in an election, that ends in a tie.

dead letter n. **1** a letter that cannot be delivered or returned, as because of an illegible address. **2** a rule or law no longer enforced though not yet repealed.

dead.line *n.* the time by which something must be done: *to establish, extend, meet, miss, set a deadline; to work against a deadline* (= work to meet the deadline).

dead.lock *n.* a standstill resulting from two unrelenting forces: *to break a deadlock; reach a deadlock; v.: Union and management deadlocked over wage increases.*

dead.ly (DED.lee) *adj.* **-li.er, -li.est 1** likely to cause death: *assault with a deadly weapon; to use deadly force in self-defense; deadly machine-gun fire; a deadly disease, duel, poison; a **deadly cocktail** (of poisons); the seven **deadly sins** supposed to cause spiritual death.* **2** deathlike: *a deadly silence; in a low deadly voice.* **3** *adj a.* extreme; absolute: *in deadly earnest.* **4** unerring: *a deadly aim; with deadly accuracy; deadly efficiency.* —*adv.* very: *a deadly dull speech; deadly afraid, dangerous, earnest, serious.*

dead-on *adj.* precisely on time or target: *You're dead-on; his dead-on aim, judgment, timing.*

dead.pan 1 *adj.* without expression or emotion: *a deadpan comedian, face; his deadpan humor.* **2** *n.* a deadpan expression; poker face: *A shy smile split her deadpan.* **3** *v.* **-pans, -panned, -pan.ning** say in a deadpan style: *"All men are created equal," she deadpanned.*

dead reckoning *n.* the determination of a ship's location by using a compass and logbook but not astronomical observations.

dead ringer *n. Slang.* one who looks exactly like another; look-alike: *He's a dead ringer for Elvis Presley.*

dead weight *n.* the weight of anything that is heavy and motionless; hence, a heavy burden.

dead.wood *n.* **1** wood that is dead on a tree. **2** something useless and burdensome, as redundant personnel.

deaf (DEF) *adj.* unable to hear: *He's deaf as a post; stone deaf; She was deaf* (= unwilling to pay heed) *to his pleas; She turned a deaf ear; the blind and the deaf* (= deaf people). —**deaf.ness** *n.*

deaf.en (DEF.un) *v.* make deaf; *adj.: The applause was deafening; a deafening crash, noise, silence; the deafening roar of machinery.*

deaf-mute *n. & adj.* (one) who is deaf and dumb.

deal (DEEL) *v.* **deals, dealt** (DELT), **deal.ing 1** give out; distribute, esp. cards to players: *to deal someone four aces; The decree dealt a blow to free speech.* **2** do business: *Realtors deal in real estate.* —**deal with** treat: *how to deal with the public; The book deals with* (= is about) *slavery.*
—*n.* **1** a quantity or amount: *a good deal of money; The twins look a good deal alike; Lu spent a great deal of time on the job.* **2** a turn to deal: *Is it my deal now?* **3** a business arrangement: *Let's do or make a deal; to strike a deal, to cut* (Informal for make) *a deal with someone; a package deal; Our sales reps close or wrap up deals; It turned out to be a bad deal.* **4** treatment: *He wanted a fair deal; He got a rough or rotten or raw deal.* **5** bargain: *We have a great deal on carpets; He got a square deal* (= fair bargain); *The reforms promised a new deal* (= greater social justice) *for the poor;* [used ironically] *Big deal* (= something impressive)! **6** fir or pine wood cut into planks; also, a plank of this.

deal.er *n.* **1** one who deals: *The dealer also shuffles the cards.* **2** one who deals in goods or wares: *art, book, car, junk dealers; a dealer in used cars.*

deal.er.ship (DEE.lur.ship) *n.* a franchised sales agency: *a hardware dealership; a dealership covering California.*

dealing *n.* business: *I have no dealings with liars; He's capable of crooked dealing* (= behavior).

dean (DEEN) *n.* **1** the head of a faculty or other division in a university: *Dean of Humanities; Dean of Men; The **dean's list** recognizes students with very high marks.* **2** a senior or most respected member of a group: *the dean of U.S. historians.* **3** the head of a body of canons, as in a cathedral. —**dean.ship** *n.*

dear (DEER) *adj.* **1** beloved: *a child who is dear to her heart; She holds her dear; her dearest daughter; one of my dearest possessions; your dear ones; the nearest and dearest to my heart; the dear departed; She ran from the scene **for dear life*** (= as if trying to save her life); *n.: Come, my dear; Not tonight, dear; You're a real dear! what to do with the poor dear.* **2** *adj a.* warmly regarded: *a dear old buddy; Dear Diary; Dear Mr. Smith.* **3** expensive: *It's dear at the price; I repaid my loan in dearer dollars.* **4** sincere: *His dearest hope was for peace.*
—*adv.: We buy cheap and sell dear to make a profit; Not paying bills on time will cost you dear; ancient customs that we **hold dear*** (= cherish) —*interj.: Oh dear! Dear, dear, what's wrong? Dear me!*
—**dear.ly** *adv.;* **dear.ness** *n.*

Dear John or **Dear John letter** *n.* a letter from a wife or girlfriend, esp. to a soldier away from home, breaking off a relationship.

dearth (DURTH) *n.* a scarcity, as of food: *in time of dearth and famine; a crippling dearth of raw materials.*

death (DETH) *n.* the act of dying or the state of being dead; also, a cause of this: *He loved her till death; "Till death do us part," as they vowed at marriage; Riel was dignified in death as in life; to cause, face, feign death; the painful, lingering death of the terminally ill; a slow death; It was living death; He died a natural death; a sudden, untimely death in a crash; the crib death of infants; death by drowning, fire, hanging, lethal injection; He was beaten, burnt, shot, starved to death; He met a violent death at the hands of terrorists; She's mourning her brother's death; He was sent to death without a trial; sentenced to death; was put to death by firing squad; Arms dealers are called "merchants of death"; Death to fascism!*
—**at the point of death** or **at death's door** near death, as from illness. —**be the death of** cause the death of someone: *That job will be the death of her.* —**catch** or **take one's death of** suddenly become seriously ill with something. —**death on** devastation to: *a collection agency that is death on defaulters.* —**to death** too much: *bored to death; I've studied the problem to death; Let's not work ourselves to death.*

death.bed *n.* 1 the bed one is dying on. 2 one's last hours of life; *adja.:* a *deathbed confession, repentance, scene.*

death.blow *n.* a blow that kills; anything destructive: *The sudden withdrawal of grant money dealt a deathblow to the project.*

death.less *adj.* immortal: *poetry of deathless beauty.*

death.like *adj.* resembling death: *a deathlike pallor.*

death.ly *adj.* resembling or causing death: *a deathly silence, stillness, wound; adv.:* It was *deathly quiet outside; deathly afraid, sick.*

death mask See MASK.

death rattle *n.* a gurgle in the throat made by a dying person.

death row *n.* a section of prison housing those awaiting execution: *to be on death row.*

death's-head *n.* a skull symbolizing death.

death trap *n.* a place or situation that could pose a risk to life: *The tunnel could became a death trap in case of fire;* also **death.trap.**

death warrant *n.* 1 an order authorizing an execution. 2 *Informal.* doom: *You'll be signing your own death warrant if you do that.*

death.watch *n.* a vigil kept over the dying or dead.

death wish *n.* a wish for oneself or another to be dead.

deb *n. Informal.* a debutante.

de.ba.cle (di.BAH.cul) *n.* a sudden rout, disaster, or collapse.

de.bar (di.BAR) *v.* **-bars, -barred, -bar.ring** shut out, as from a right or privilege; prevent: *He was debarred from the meetings; The lawyer was convicted of fraud and debarred (from practicing law).* —**de.bar.ment** *n.*

de.base (di.BACE) *v.* **-bas.es, -based, -bas.ing** lower in position, character, or value; *adj.:* debased *coinage, morals, standards.* —**de.base.ment** *n.*

de.bate (di.BATE) *v.* **-bates, -bat.ed, -bat.ing** 1 discuss or consider an issue from both sides: *I debated for a long time whether to join or not.* 2 participate in a formal contest of argument: *to debate heatedly* or *hotly with the opposition; adj.:* a debating *club, team; good debating style.* —*n.* a debating: *to conduct, hold, moderate a debate; an acrimonious, bitter, heated, lively, spirited debate; a parliamentary debate; a debate in parliament; the ongoing debate about capital punishment.* —**de.bat.a.ble** *adj.* —**de.bat.er** *n.*

de.bauch (di.BAWCH) *v.* deprave; also, engage in sexual indulgence.

de.bau.chee (di.baw.CHEE) *n.* one who debauches.

de.bauch.er.y (di.BAW.chuh.ree) *n.* **-er.ies** sexual indulgence: *drunken debaucheries.*

de.ben.ture (di.BEN.chur) *n.* a bond guaranteed only by the general credit of the issuer.

de.bil.i.tate (di.BIL.uh.tate) *v.* **-tates, -tat.ed, -tat.ing** make weak or feeble; *adj.:* a debilitating *disease, effect, foreign debt, illness, injury.* —**de.bil.i.ty** *n.*

deb.it (DEB.it) *n.* 1 a sum owed, as recorded in an account. 2 a drawback or disadvantage. —*v.* charge: *Please debit the purchase to* or *against my account; Debit my account with the entire amount.*

debit card *n.* a card for effecting electronic funds transfer from buyer's bank account to seller's.

deb.o.nair (deb.uh.NAIR) *adj.* jaunty or dashing. Also **deb.o.naire.** —**deb.o.nair.ly** *adv.*

de.bouch (di.BOOSH) *v.* emerge or

make emerge into an open area: *infantry debouching onto the plain.*

de.brief (di.BREEF) *v.* question a diplomat, astronaut, etc. at the end of a mission to obtain information. —**de.brief.ing** *n.*

de.bris or **dé.bris** (duh.BREE, DAY.bree) *n.* broken remains; rubble: *to clear the debris of an earthquake.*

debt (DET) *n.* **1** what one owes another, esp. money: *I had a $5,000 debt; I owe her a debt of gratitude; to cancel, contract, discharge, get into, go into, incur, pay, pay off, recover, run up, settle, wipe out a debt; The creditor wrote off the unpaid debt; the national debt.* **2** the condition of owing: *Everyone tries to stay out of debt; He was deeply in debt from borrowing money to start a business.*

debt of honor *n.* a debt based on one's sense of honor for its repayment, as in betting.

debt.or (DET.ur) *n.* one who owes a debt, as opposed to creditor; *adja.*: *a debtor company, country, nation.*

de.bug (dee.BUG) *v.* **-bugs, -bugged, -bug.ging** remove the bugs from a machine, process, or environment: *to debug a computer program; The room was searched for hidden microphones and thoroughly debugged.*

de.bunk (dee.BUNK) *v. Informal.* show the falsity of something: *The survey debunked the myths about everyone being able to read and write; to debunk a claim, notion, theory, view.*

de.but (di.BYOO, DAY.byoo) *n.* **1** a first performance or appearance: *She didn't wait till 21 to make her debut* (= formal appearance in society); *She made her debut as a child actor at age five.* **2** the formal introduction of a young woman to society.

deb.u.tante (DEB.yoo.tahnt) *n.* a young woman making her debut.

dec.ade (DEC.ade) *n.* a ten-year period or set: *The decade of the 1990s runs from 1990 to 1999.*

dec.a.dence (DEC.uh.dunce) *n.* a decline or decay in standards, esp. in art or morals: *Educational decadence contributes to the high level of illiteracy; the decadence of Byzantine art.* —**dec.a.dent** *adj.* **1** low in artistic or moral standard: *decadent art, civilizations, culture, movements; For some people, it's trendy to be decadent.* **2** self-indulgently enjoyable: *Las Vegas at its decadent best; a very elegant and decadent $500 silk overcoat; a deliciously decadent dessert.*

de.caf (DEE.caf) *n.* [short form]
decaffeinated coffee.

de.caf.fein.ate (DEE.caf.uh.nate) *v.* **-ates, -at.ed, -at.ing** remove the caffeine, esp. from coffee; *adj.*: *decaffeinated beverages, coffee, cola.*

de.cal (di.CAL, DEE.cal) *n.* a design transferred onto a surface from specially prepared paper.

de.cal.co.ma.ni.a (di.CAL.cuh.MAY.nee.uh) *n.* **1** the process of making a decal. **2** a decal or its paper backing.

Dec.a.log (DEC.uh.log) *n.* the Ten Commandments; also **dec.a.log, Dec.a.logue, dec.a.logue.**

de.camp (di.CAMP) *v.* **1** break camp and leave. **2** run away, usu. secretly: *The club's treasurer decamped with $10,000.*

de.cant (di.CANT) *v.* pour a liquid gently, so as not to stir up the sediment: *The wine was decanted into smaller bottles.*

de.cant.er (di.CAN.tur) *n.* an ornamental bottle for serving wine, sherry, etc.

de.cap.i.tate (di.CAP.uh.tate) *v.* **-tates, -tat.ed, -tat.ing** cut off the head of someone; behead. —**de.cap.i.ta.tion** (-uh.TAY.shun) *n.*: *decapitation by guillotine.*

de.cath.lete (di.CATH.leet) *n.* one who competes in a decathlon.

de.cath.lon (di.CATH.lon, *rhyme:* on) *n.* a contest consisting of ten track-and-field events, as in the Olympics.

de.cay (di.CAY) *v.* **1** lose power, health, beauty, etc.: *Everything on earth decays; The magnetism of even permanent magnets decays in time; When the orbit of a satellite decays, it loses speed and altitude and falls to Earth.* **2** decompose or disintegrate: *Meat decays if left outside the refrigerator; Some radioactive substances decay* (= lose atomic particles) *faster than others.* —*n.* **1** loss of health, beauty, power, etc.: *the decay of the patient's mental faculties; a once-booming town now fallen into decay.* **2** decomposition or disintegration: *how to prevent tooth decay; the moral decay of our time; the slow decay of radium.*

de.cease (di.SEECE) *n.* [formal use with reference to people recently dead] death or demise. —**de.ceased** *adj.* dead: *her deceased husband; He is now deceased; n.*: *to pay our respects to the deceased.*

de.ced.ent (di.SEE.dunt) *n. Law.* a dead person.

de.ceit (di.SEET) *n.* **1** dishonesty: *behavior full of deceit; practiced deceit.*

2 a trick: *the con man's various deceits.* **—de.ceit.ful** *adj.*: *a deceitful ad campaign; deceitful conduct, schemes, statistics.*

de.ceive (di.SEEV) *v.* **-ceives, -ceived, -ceiv.ing** mislead deliberately, as by lying, trickery, or cheating: *The company was deceived into hiring the escaped convict.*

de.cel.er.ate (dee.SEL.uh.rate) *v.* **-ates, -at.ed, -at.ing** go or cause to go more slowly: *A driver decelerates the engine by taking the foot off the gas pedal or by applying the brakes; A spacecraft decelerates by reversing the thrust of the engines; Business activity decelerates as the economy slows down.* **—de.cel.er.a.tion** (-RAY.shun) *n.*

De.cem.ber (di.SEM.bur) *n.* the 12th month of the calendar year, with 31 days.

de.cen.cy (DEE.sun.see) *n.* 1 the quality of being decent; also, a propriety: *Observe the decencies when in good company.* 2 kindness, courtesy, or sense of obligation: *He doesn't have a spark of decency; We should have the decency to call and cancel a date we cannot keep; Common decency demands it.*

de.cen.ni.al (di.SEN.ee.ul) *adj.* 1 of or lasting 10 years. 2 occurring every 10 years: *the decennial census.* **—n.** a tenth anniversary.

de.cent (DEE.sunt) *adj.* 1 conforming to social conventions in regard to behavior: *decent and respectable people; a decent chap, man, student, woman; It was decent of her to pay for our meal; Don't come in yet, I'm not decent* (= dressed). 2 *Informal.* quite good: *a decent burial, job, meal, offer.* **—de.cent.ly** *adv.*

de.cen.tral.ize (dee.SEN.truh.lize) *v.* **-iz.es, -ized, -iz.ing** distribute something concentrated, as power, population, or industry, over a wider area: *to decentralize the federal bureaucracy; Good managers decentralize and delegate.* **—de.cen.tral.i.za.tion** (-luh.ZAY.shun, -lye-) *n.*

de.cep.tion (di.SEP.shun) *n.* 1 a deceiving or being deceived; deceit: *to practice deception.* 2 a trick, lie, etc.: *a magician's deceptions; a cruel, deliberate deception.* **—de.cep.tive** (-tiv) *adj.*: *deceptive advertising.* **—de.cep.tive.ly** *adv.*: *a deceptively simple question.*

dec.i.bel (DES.uh.bel) *n.* the unit of intensity of sound: *A whisper measures 20 decibels, an automobile horn up to 90; Teachers try to keep the **decibel level** (= noise level) down in their classrooms.*

de.cide (di.SIDE) *v.* **-cides, -cid.ed, -cid.ing** 1 settle or resolve: *The issue was decided by flipping a coin; The court case was decided in favor of Mr. Smith; The jury decided for* (= in favor of) *the defendant.* 2 make up one's mind: *I couldn't decide what to do with the money; to decide whether I wanted a cat or a dog; I found it difficult to decide between them; Finally I decided against having a pet; I decided to buy a new TV; We also decided on a vacation; We decided that we would go to the Bahamas.* 3 cause to decide: *A sense of fair play decided me on the question.*

decided *adj.* 1 definite: *a decided advantage, difference, opinion, success, victory; a man of decided views; decided in his opinions.* 2 determined or adamant: *He's quite decided about what to do; a decided approach; a very decided young man.* **—decidedly** *adv.* definitely: *decidedly different, easy, fewer, modern, ordinary, reckless.*

deciding *adj.* that settles a controversy or contest: *a deciding factor; the deciding game, run, vote.*

de.cid.u.ous (di.SIJ.oo.us) *adj.* of leaves, antlers, etc., falling off or out at a certain stage or periodically: *Baby teeth are deciduous; A deciduous forest is made up of deciduous trees (whose leaves fall off when it gets cold); Fame and glory are often deciduous* (= passing quickly).

dec.i.mal (DES.uh.mul) *adj.* having to do with units of ten or tenths: *decimal coinage, currency; the decimal system of weights and measures.* **—n.** 1 a fraction such as 0.05 that is expressed by a dot, or **decimal point,** followed by the numerator; also **decimal fraction.** 2 a decimal point: *one decimal five* (= 1.5).

dec.i.mate (DES.uh.mate) *v.* **-mates, -mat.ed, -mat.ing** destroy a large portion of a group: *cities decimated by plague; to decimate the enemy forces, buffalo herds.*

de.ci.pher (di.SYE.fur) *v.* interpret something written despite illegibility or a code; decode: *a pharmacist who has no problem deciphering a doctor's prescriptions.* **—de.ci.pher.a.ble** *adj.*

de.ci.sion (di.SIZH.un) *n.* 1 a deciding or resolution; also, a statement of this: *The judge's decision was appealed to a higher court; to arrive at, hand down, make, overrule, reach, render, reverse a decision; arbitrary, just, final, landmark, momentous, rash decisions; a decision to go ahead with the plan; a split* (= not unanimous) *decision.* 2 the ability to decide; also, determined firmness: *Lu lacks decision; His wife is a woman of decision.*

de.ci.sive (di.SYE.siv) *adj.* 1 determining or deciding: *the decisive moment of the war; a decisive advantage, influence, victory.* **2** determined or firm: *a leader of decisive judgment: She's very decisive in making her moves.* —**de.ci.sive.ly** *adv.*; **de.ci.sive.ness** *n.*

deck *n.* **1** a floor of a ship, esp. the main one: *to swab the deck; the main deck; promenade deck; the flight deck of an aircraft where the pilot sits; The flight deck of an aircraft carrier is used for landings and takeoffs; the upper* or *top deck of a double-decker (bus);* **Hit the deck** (Informal for lie low) *when shooting starts; A* **deck chair** *is a folding chair used on a ship's deck; A* **deck hand** *is a common sailor who works on deck.* **2** a platform or other surface similar to a ship's deck: *a pool deck with a jacuzzi; the rear deck (behind a car's back seat); sun decks.* **3** a pack of cards: *to cut, shuffle, stack a deck.* **4** a tape deck.
—**clear the decks** make ready. —**on deck** present and ready: *The next batter is on deck; If I were on deck, this wouldn't have happened.* —*v.* **1** provide or cover with a deck. **2** adorn or decorate: *Deck the halls; a bride decked out in all her finery.* **3** *Slang.* knock down to the floor, esp. with the fist: *The Twins decked* (= beat) *the Cardinals in the World Series.*

deck.le or **deckle edge** *n.* a ragged untrimmed edge on paper.
—**deckle-edged** *adj.*

de.claim (di.CLAIM) *v.* **1** recite or speak dramatically. **2** attack verbally: *to declaim against inflation and unemployment without doing anything about it.*
—**dec.la.ma.tion** (dec.luh.MAY.shun) *n.* —**de.clam.a.to.ry** (di.CLAM.uh.tor.ee) *adj.*

dec.la.ra.tion (dec.luh.RAY.shun) *n.* an announcement or statement: *Jack made a false declaration to customs; The accused issued a solemn declaration of innocence; In 1959, the U.N. adopted the Declaration of the Rights of the Child.*

de.clar.a.to.ry (di.CLAIR.uh.tor.ee) or **de.clar.a.tive** (-uh.tiv) *adj.* making a statement: *a declaratory sentence such as "I love you."*

de.clare (di.CLAIR) *v.* **-clares, -clared, -clar.ing 1** state or make known formally; announce: *The judges declared Jim the winner; declared Jim elected; declared Jim to have won the election; Iraq declared war on Iran; Iran declared that it would fight to the finish; Do you have anything to declare (that is dutiable)? adj.: a declared candidate, pacifist; his declared intention.* **2** state definitely: *Ed declared his love for Jane; declared that he loved her; They declared themselves (to be) in favor of marriage, (to be) against* or *opposed to divorce; Well, I declare!* (= I am surprised). **3** in bridge, name a trump suit or "no-trump." —**dec.lar.er** *n.*

de.clas.si.fy (dee.CLAS.uh.fye) *v.* **-fies, -fied, -fy.ing** make secret papers public or no longer classified.

de.clen.sion (di.CLEN.shun) *n.* a declining (def. 3).

de.cline (di.CLINE) *v.* **-clines, -clined, -clin.ing 1** slope or move downwards: *At the village, the land declines rapidly to the valley below; Her health, influence, power is declining* (= going from a better to a worse condition); *adja.: the declining birthrate; She is in her declining years* (= last part of life). **2** say no or refuse politely: *She declined his kind offer of a ride.* **3** give the grammatical cases, numbers, and genders of a noun, pronoun, or adjective.
—*n.* a going down or moving from a better to a worse position: *the decline and fall of the Roman Empire; a sharp decline in prices caused by an oversupply; The patient suffered* or *went into a gradual, steady decline; Interest in large cars was* **on the decline** (= going down) *when gas prices were going up.*
—**dec.li.na.tion** (dec.luh.NAY.shun) *n.*

de.cliv.i.ty (di.CLIV.i.tee) *n.* **-ties** a downhill slope.

de.code (dee.CODE) *v.* **-codes, -cod.ed, -cod.ing** translate out of code: *to decode a message in cipher; to decode genes, signals, symbols.* —**de.cod.er** *n.* an electronic decoding device: *Decoders are used to unscramble TV transmissions.*

dé.colle.tage (day.col.TAZH) *n.* **1** a low, revealing neckline: *deep décolletages.* **2** a garment having one.

dé.colle.té (day.col.TAY) *adj.* **1** of garments, having a low, revealing neckline: *a décolleté maillot.* **2** wearing such a dress.

de.col.o.nize (dee.COL.uh.nize) *v.* **-niz.es, -nized, -niz.ing** make a colony independent. —**de.col.o.ni.za.tion** (-nuh.ZAY.shun, -nye-) *n.*

de.com.mis.sion (dee.cuh.MISH.un) *v.* take out of service; *adj.: a decommissioned aircraft carrier.*

de.com.pose (dee.cum.POZE) *v.* **-pos.es, -posed, -pos.ing** break down into component parts; rot.
—**de.com.po.si.tion** (DEE.com.puh.ZISH.un) *n.*

de.com.press (dee.cum.PRESS) *v.* reduce the pressure in something.

de.com.pres.sion (dee.cum.PRESH.un)

decongestant / dedicated

n. the releasing of pressure: *The hostages were taken to a hospital for decompression after their release by the terrorists; The quickest way to put out a fire on an aircraft is decompression* (= getting rid of the oxygen); **Decompression sickness** *is caused by a too rapid release from pressure, as when deep-sea divers or caisson workers surface too quickly.*

de.con.ges.tant (dee.cun.JES.tunt) *n.* something that relieves congestion: *nasal decongestants; a decongestant spray.*

de.con.struct (dee.cun.STRUCT) *v.* to subject a literary text to deconstruction; hence, analyze or break it down.

de.con.struc.tion (dee.cun.STRUC.shun) *n.* the breaking down of a text for making various interpretations. —**de.con.struc.tion.ist** *n.*

de.con.tam.i.nate (dee.cun.TAM.uh.nate) *v.* -**nates, -nat.ed, -nat.ing** free from contaminants, esp. radioactivity or poison gas. —**de.con.tam.i.na.tion** (-NAY.shun) *n.*

de.con.trol (dee.cun.TROLE) *v.* -**trols, -trolled, -trol.ling** remove government controls from commodities, prices, gold coins, etc.: *to decontrol the economy.*

dé.cor or **de.cor** (day.COR) *n.* the style of decoration of a room or the layout of what is displayed in it: *a Scandinavian décor; bathroom, office, wall decor.*

dec.o.rate (DEC.uh.rate) *v.* -**ates, -at.ed, -at.ing 1** beautify what is plain by adding color or ornament: *We have to decorate the basement for the party.* **2** make a place suitable for living in: *The landlord is supposed to decorate the apartment by painting, wallpapering, etc. before we move in.* **3** honor with an award, medal, etc.: *a soldier decorated for heroism.* —**dec.o.ra.tive** *adj.*: *the decorative arts; decorative accessories, fabrics, pillows.* —**dec.o.ra.tor** (-ray.tur) *n.*: *an interior decorator.* —**dec.or.a.tion** (-RAY.shun) *n.*: *A decoration for bravery was awarded to the police officer; In December, it's time to put up Christmas decorations.*

de.co.rum (di.COR.um) *n.* seemliness or propriety in speech, action, appearance, etc.: *Strict decorum is observed during a state visit.* —**dec.o.rous** (DEC.uh.rus, di.COR.us) *adj.*

de.cou.page or **dé.cou.page** (day.coo.PAZH) *n.* the decoration of surfaces with usu. paper cutouts covered by layers of varnish or lacquer.

de.coy (di.COY) *n.* something used to draw others into danger, as a wooden bird to lure real birds within range of a hunter. —*v.* trick or lure into a trap.

de.crease (di.CREECE) *v.* -**creas.es, -creased, -creas.ing** grow or cause to grow smaller, less, etc.: *to decrease defense capability; Will you please decrease the volume (Informal for lower the volume or speak less loudly)?* —*n.* (DEE.creece): *A 25% decrease in car insurance rates is unlikely; There has been a gradual, steady decrease in industrial accidents; Traffic deaths seem to be* **on the decrease.** —**de.creas.ing.ly** *adv.*

de.cree (di.CREE) *n.* **1** an official order, as of a ruler: *to enact, enforce, issue, rescind, revoke a decree; to rule by presidential decree; a parliament dissolved by royal decree.* **2** a judgment, as of a court of law: *a divorce decree.* —*v.* -**crees, -creed, -cree.ing 1** to order by a decree: *Parliament decreed that the death penalty be abolished.* **2** bring into being by decree: *The government decreed a day of public mourning in honor of the dead hero; to decree amnesties, expenditures, policies.*

dec.re.ment (DEC.ruh.munt) *n.* a decrease, esp. if gradual; also, the amount of it.

de.crep.it (di.CREP.it) *adj.* worn-out or broken-down, esp. by long use: *a vehicle in a decrepit condition.* —**de.crep.i.tude** *n.*

de.cre.scen.do (day.cruh.SHEN.doh) *adj. & adv. Music.* decreasing in loudness. —*n., pl.* -**dos**: *a symphony closing with a gentle decrescendo.*

de.crim.i.nal.ize (dee.CRIM.uh.nuh.lize) *v.* -**iz.es, -ized, -iz.ing** make an action such as the possession of marijuana not criminal. —**de.crim.i.nal.i.za.tion** (-luh.ZAY.shun, -lye-) *n.*

de.cry (di.CRY) *v.* -**cries, -cried, -cry.ing** criticize openly and strongly: *The Opposition decried the Government's feeble efforts at reform.*

ded.i.cate (DED.uh.cate) *v.* -**cates, -cat.ed, -cat.ing 1** devote or commit, as to a sacred use, to a cause, etc.: *institutions dedicated to the preservation of freedom; to dedicate a chapel; a humanitarian who has dedicated himself to helping others.* **2** set apart: *a store that dedicates shelf space for environmentally friendly products; She dedicates her Sundays to shopping.* **3** address a book, song, etc. to someone as a mark of honor: *He dedicated the book to his wife.* —**ded.i.ca.to.ry** (-cuh.tor.ee) *adj.*: *dedicatory verses.* —**ded.i.ca.tion** (-CAY.shun) *n.*

dedicated 1 *adj.* devoted to a cause: *a*

dedicated dieter, parent, teacher, worker. **2** *adja.* set apart for a special use: *a dedicated machine, network, channel, phone line, program, system.*

de.duce (di.DUCE, *rhyme:* produce) *v.* **-duc.es, -duced, -duc.ing** infer by reasoning: *If A equals B and B equals C, then we deduce that A equals C.* —**de.duc.i.ble** (-suh.bul) *adj.*

de.duct (di.DUCT) *v.* take away or subtract: *Tuition fees may be deducted from income on tax returns.* —**de.duc.ti.ble** *n. & adj.*

de.duc.tion (di.DUC.shun) *n.* **1** a deducing or conclusion: *a logical deduction; a deduction that the death was a suicide.* **2** a deducting: *Allowable deductions from income include charitable donations; We try to claim as many deductions as possible to reduce the amount of tax to be paid.*

de.duc.tive (di.DUC.tiv) *adj.* of or characterized by inference from premises to conclusions: *deductive and inductive logic.* —**de.duc.tive.ly** *adv.*

deed *n.* **1** something done; action: *the brave deeds done* or *performed by heroes; chivalrous, daring, heroic, noble, wicked deeds; a friend who is faithful in word and deed.* **2** a signed legal document, esp. one conferring ownership of property: *Who holds the deed* (= title) *to this land?* —*v.* convey by deed: *The property had been deeded to him by his late wife.*

dee.jay (DEE.jay) *n. Informal.* a disk jockey.

deem *v. Formal.* believe or consider: *The scout deemed it unwise to light a fire in that area; She threatens to do as she deems fit.*

de-emphasize *v.* **-siz.es, -sized, -siz.ing** reduce the emphasis on something.

deep *adj.* **1** being or extending far down or in something: *the deep blue sea; The rocket was lost deep in space; He seems deep* (= immersed) *in thought; Sam is very deep* (= involved) *in debt; a deep* (= large) *discount, price cut; the deep* (= underlying meaning, not surface) *structure of a sentence.* **2** from front to back: *The sofa is 85 in wide and 36 in deep; The crowd that lined the street was ten deep in places along the route.* **3** from a depth: *Take a deep breath.* **4** of sound, low in pitch: *a deep voice.* **5** of color, rich or dark: *a deep red.* **6** profound or thorough: *deep emotions; a deep sleep; a deep silence; a deep, scholarly study; He found himself* **in deep water(s)** (= in difficulty) *in calculus.* **7** mysterious: *a deep secret.* **8** very serious or grave: *He was in deep trouble for skipping school.* —**go off the deep end** *Informal.* yield to anger or excitement. —*adv.* in a deep manner: *We dug deep in the earth; The children were lost deep in the woods; He works deep into the night; "Still waters run deep."* —*n.* depth: *in the deep of the night; denizens of the deep* (= ocean). —**deep.ly** *adv.*

deep.en (DEE.pun) *v.* become or make deeper: *The war deepened the recession; A youth's voice deepens as he grows into manhood;* **adja.:** *the deepening gloom, recession, rift.*

deep.freeze *n.* **1** a freezer for freezing food quickly. **2** condition of cold storage; hence, suspension of action: *November's deepfreeze damaged crops; We had to put the plan in (the) deepfreeze because of lack of funds.* Also *v.* **deep.freez.es,** *pt.* **-froze** or **-freezed,** *pp.* **-froz.en** or **-freezed, -freez.ing.**

deep-fry *v.* **-fries, -fried, -fry.ing** fry potatoes, onions, etc. immersed in oil or fat: *French fries are deep-fried;* **adja.:** *deep-fried fish, foods, potatoes; a deep-fry thermometer.*

deep pocket *n. Informal.* wealth: *Lawyers think accountants are the ones with the deep pocket.*

deep-rooted *adj.* firmly implanted, as a plant with deep roots: *a deep-rooted dislike, dissatisfaction; deep-rooted anxieties, fears, frustrations, prejudices, problems, traditions.*

deep-sea *adja.* having to do with the deep parts of the sea: *deep-sea divers, diving, exploration.*

deep-seated *adj.* **1** well below the surface: *a deep-seated illness.* **2** same as DEEP-ROOTED.

deep-set *adj.* deeply set: *deep-set eyes.*

Deep South *n.* an area of southern U.S. dominated by the culture and traditions of Alabama, Georgia, Louisiana, Mississippi, South Carolina, and related regions.

deep six *n. Slang.* the grave. —**give something the deep six** discard it. —**deep-six** *v.* throw overboard; discard.

deep space *n.* space beyond the moon or the solar system.

deer *n. sing. & pl.* any of a group of ruminant animals having cloven hooves, including moose, elk, white-tailed deer, and caribou: *a herd of deer; the fawn* (= young one) *of a deer; a female deer* (= doe); *a male deer* (= buck or stag); **adja.:** *deer crossings; deer hide; deer meat* (= venison); *the deer season* (for hunting deer).

deer.skin n. & adj. (a leather or garment) made of deer hide.

de-es.ca.late v. -lates, -lat.ed, -lat.ing decrease the scope or intensity of something: *to de-escalate a war.* —**de-es.ca.la.tion** n.

de.face (di.FACE) v. -fac.es, -faced, -fac.ing disfigure the surface of something: *He was arrested for defacing the War Memorial; to deface a building, flag, wall.* —**de.face.ment** n.

de fac.to (di.FAC.toh) adj. & adv. in actual fact; actual or actually: *De facto slavery still exists in some countries although de jure it has been abolished.*

de.fal.cate (di.FAL.cate) v. -cates, -cat.ed, -cat.ing misappropriate money entrusted to one. —**de.fal.ca.tion** (dee.fal.CAY.shun) n.

de.fame (di.FAME) v. -fames, -famed, -fam.ing injure someone or someone's reputation by libel or slander. —**de.fam.er** n. —**def.a.ma.tion** (def.uh.MAY.shun) n. —**de.fam.a.to.ry** (di.FAM.uh.tor.ee) adj.

de.fault (di.FAULT) v. 1 fail to do something, as appear in court, repay a loan, or enter a contest: *He defaulted on his debt and lost his credit rating.* 2 of a variable in a computer system, return to its preset value: *If a margin width is not specified by the user, the word processor defaults to the 12-space setting.* —n. 1 a failure to do what is expected of one: *The plaintiff lost his case by default; She went ahead as planned in default of* (= lacking) *instructions to the contrary.* 2 a particular value to which a variable is set in a computer system: *By default* (= Unless instructed otherwise), *all text is printed out with a 12-space left margin; Twelve spaces is the default margin.*

de.feat (di.FEET) v. 1 frustrate or thwart: *to defeat a bill in parliament; To talk to people about how you use your home security is to defeat its very purpose.* 2 beat: *to defeat the enemy in battle; The Yankees were defeated 2 to 1; soundly defeated;* **adj.**: *a defeated army, candidate, enemy, MP, nation.* —n. a defeating: *the defeat of the Yankees; They met* or *suffered defeat at the hands of the Blue Jays; to admit, concede, face, invite defeat; a crushing, humiliating, narrow, shameful, total defeat.*

de.feat.ism (di.FEE.tiz.um) n. a too ready acceptance or expectation of defeat. —**de.feat.ist** adj.: *a defeatist attitude, mentality.*

def.e.cate (DEF.uh.cate) v. -cates, -cat.ed, -cat.ing empty the bowels. —**def.e.ca.tion** (-CAY.shun) n.

de.fect (di.FECT) n. a lack, fault, or imperfection: *to correct speech defects such as lisping and stuttering; a glaring defect; birth, congenital, hearing, mental, physical, structural defects.* —v. to desert to another cause, party, country, etc.: *East European athletes used to defect to the West; They defected from communist countries.* —**de.fec.tion** n. —**de.fec.tor** n.

de.fec.tive (di.FEC.tiv) adj. having a defect: *She returned the defective appliance to the store;* A **defective verb** *such as "ought" lacks some of the usual forms as in "take-took-taken-taking."* —n. a subnormal person: *Mental defectives are not accepted for military training.*

defence Cdn. DEFENSE.

de.fend (di.FEND) v. 1 fight for a person or cause; also, argue in defense of something: *to defend yourself against an attacker; I defend your right to speak; to defend a proposal under attack.* 2 to maintain a position by fighting: *to defend a claim, one's actions, the world heavyweight title.* 3 speak in a law court for a defendant.

de.fend.ant (di.FEN.dunt) n. a person accused or sued in a court of law.

de.fend.er (di.FEN.dur) n. one who defends: *a staunch defender of the underprivileged; the challenger and the defender* (= holder) *of a title; a public defender.*

de.fense (di.FENCE) n. an act or means of defending: *civil defense; a defense of his position on disarmament; to conduct, organize, put up a defense; a heroic, military, national, strong defense; She spoke in defense of freedom and democracy; Is offense the best form of defense? a mutual defense pact.* Also **de.fence** Cdn.

defense mechanism n. an unconscious mental process or reaction of protection against unpleasant truths or feelings.

de.fen.si.ble (di.FEN.suh.bul) adj. that can be defended: *a defensible claim.*

de.fen.sive (di.FEN.siv) adj. 1 defending: *a defensive play, position, weapon; defensive driving.* 2 acting as though under attack: *He is rather defensive about his views; a defensive battery of tests ordered out of fear of being sued for malpractice; a defensive, negative, and poorly motivated group of employees.* —**on the defensive** 1 defending oneself: *Their aggressiveness kept us on the defensive.* 2 acting as though under attack: *Mention of the subject puts him on the defensive; He goes on the defensive when the subject is mentioned.*

de.fer (di.FUR) v. **-fers, -ferred, -fer.ring** 1 put off until later; postpone: *The judge deferred sentencing the convicted man;* adj.: *People buy on credit with a down payment followed by equal amounts of deferred payments; a deferred annuity, compensation plan, tax.* 2 yield to another's opinion or judgment, esp. as a courtesy: *I defer to your greater knowledge and experience in the matter.*

def.er.ence (DEF.uh.runce) n. courteous respect: *in deference to the feelings of others.* —**def.er.en.tial** (-REN.shul) adj.

de.fer.ment (di.FUR.munt) n. a delaying of induction into the military: *draft deferment for a student who is at college.* Also **de.fer.ral** (di.FUR.ul).

de.fi.ance (di.FYE.unce) n. 1 a challenge: *explorers bidding defiance to nature.* 2 bold refusal to obey: *defiance of authority; flagrant, open defiance; "Over my dead body," he said in defiance; He acted in defiance of* (= defying) *public opinion.* —**de.fi.ant** (-unt) adj.: *a defiant young hoodlum;* **de.fi.ant.ly** adv.

de.fi.cien.cy (di.FISH.un.see) n. the lack of something necessary or its amount: *a severe mental deficiency; to suffer from iron deficiency; a deficiency of $200 in the account; mineral deficiencies in the diet; nutritional deficiencies; vitamin deficiencies; Scurvy is a deficiency disease* (= one caused by lack of essential nutrients, esp. vitamins or minerals).

de.fi.cient (di.FISH.unt) adj. 1 lacking something necessary: *a diet that is deficient in vitamin C.* 2 insufficient: *a deficient supply of nutrients; deficient funds, logic, operations, skills.*

def.i.cit (DEF.uh.sit) n. the amount by which a sum is too small: *huge budgetary deficits; an operating deficit; trade deficits; The 1976 Olympics chalked up a $1 billion deficit;* **deficit spending** (using borrowed money for expenditures).

de.file (di.FILE) v. 1 **-files, -filed, -fil.ing** make dirty or impure; desecrate or dishonor: *a murderer's hands defiled with blood.* 2 (also DEE.file) n. a narrow pass or valley.

de.fine (di.FINE) v. **-fines, -fined, -fin.ing** 1 state the meaning of a word: *Please define your terms; "Square" may be defined as "a plane figure with four equal sides and angles."* 2 set the limits of something; specify: *a law defining the powers of the police; A position paper defines or outlines one's position or views on a subject; The height of the first hill defines the roller coaster and its momentum to do the whole track without mechanical help.* 3 show the edges or shape of something; adj.: *a clearly defined shape; a sharply defined TV picture.* —**de.fin.a.ble** (-nuh.bul) adj. —**de.fin.er** n.

def.i.nite (DEF.uh.nit) adj. 1 adja. well defined; clear and distinct: *A plan should have a definite goal in view; Tall players have a definite advantage over others in basketball.* 2 certain: *It's not definite yet that anyone will be here on Monday morning; I want a definite answer from you before Friday evening; Let us be definite about it.* —**def.i.nite.ly** adv. certainly: *My answer is, most definitely (yes)! No, definitely not! That is definitely* (= clearly) *untrue.* —**def.i.nite.ness** n.

definite article n. the word "the."

def.i.ni.tion (def.uh.NISH.un) n. 1 a defining or determining, esp. a statement of a word's meaning: *the dictionary definition of a word; to formulate, provide, write a definition;* **By definition** (= As the very term suggests), *a delta is a triangular piece of land.* 2 distinctness or clarity: *a picture with good definition; High-definition TV gives clearer and brighter pictures; Eyebrow pencils give definition to brows, mustaches, and beards.*

de.fin.i.tive (di.FIN.uh.tiv) adj. 1 conclusive: *a definitive yes-or-no reply; a definitive agreement, answer, decision, order of the highest court.* 2 the most complete and authentic to date: *a definitive study; the definitive text of Shakespeare.* 3 explicitly defining: *the definitive nature of boundaries; a country with no definitive borders.* —**de.fin.i.tive.ly** adv.

de.flate (di.FLATE) v. **-flates, -flat.ed, -flat.ing** 1 let the air or gas out of something inflated: *to deflate a tire.* 2 reduce the self-esteem of someone thought to be conceited: *to deflate his ego.* 3 reduce prices or the money supply in the economy; adj.: *a deflated economy; deflated expectations, markets, prices.* —**de.fla.tion** (-FLAY.shun) n.

de.flect (di.FLECT) v. turn aside or from a straight course: *Light rays are deflected by a prism; to deflect from the straight and narrow path.* —**de.flec.tion** n. —**de.flec.tor** n.

de.flow.er (di.FLOW.ur, rhyme: our) v. 1 take away the virginity of a woman. 2 strip of flowers; hence, ravage. —**def.lo.ra.tion** (def.luh.RAY.shun) n.

de.fog (di.FOG) v. **-fogs, -fogged, -fog.ging** remove fog or condensation. —**de.fog.ger** (di.FOG.ur) n.

de.fo.li.ant (di.FOH.lee.unt) n. a chemical defoliating agent.

defoliate / degree

de.fo.li.ate (di.FOH.lee.ate) *v.* **-ates, -at.ed, -at.ing** cause the leaves to fall from trees: *jungles defoliated in Vietnam.* —**de.fo.li.a.tion** (-AY.shun) *n.*

de.for.est (dee.FOR.ist) *v.* clear of trees: *The whole hillside was deforested; adj.: the most deforested areas in the Amazon; deforested lands.* —**de.for.est.a.tion** (-TAY.shun) *n.*

de.form (di.FORM) *v.* destroy the natural form of something; disfigure; also, become deformed: *Thalidomide deformed fetuses in the wombs of mothers who took the drug; a face deformed by anger and hate;* **adj.:** *the badly* **deformed** (= misshapen) *limbs of children of mothers who had taken the drug; Babies of drug addicts are sometimes born severely deformed.* —**de.for.ma.tion** (dee.for.MAY.shun) *n.*

de.form.i.ty (di.FOR.mi.tee) *n.* **-ties** a physical or moral flaw; disfigurement: *Clubfoot is a congenital deformity of the foot.*

de.fraud (di.FRAUD) *v.* deprive someone of something by fraud; swindle: *The bank was defrauded of $1 million.*

de.fray (di.FRAY) *v.* pay for costs or expenses: *a collection to defray the costs of the convention.*

de.frost (di.FROST) *v.* **1** thaw: *to defrost frozen meat.* **2** free or make free of ice or frost: *The older refrigerators had to be defrosted when ice built up in the freezer section; Automobiles have a windshield defrosting system.* —**de.frost.er** *n.*

deft *adj.* skillful, quick, and facile: *the deft fingers of a surgeon or pianist; a deft hand, performance, portrayal; the deft touches of an artist's brush; She's deft in handling a crisis.*

de.funct (di.FUNCT) *adj.* no longer existing; dead: *a defunct committee, idea, species; the now-defunct Soviet Union.*

de.fuse (dee.FUZE) *v.* **-fus.es, -fused, -fus.ing 1** remove the fuse of an explosive: *to defuse a bomb.* **2** make less dangerous or tense: *to defuse a dangerous crisis, an explosive issue, a volatile situation; to defuse anger, pressure, tension.*

de.fy (di.FYE) *v.* **-fies, -fied, -fy.ing 1** dare or challenge, esp. with mocking contempt: *She defied him to take the lie detector test; Those who defy the law get arrested.* **2** to exceed the power of something; resist: *beauty that defies description; too fat to defy gravity; a problem that defies solution; His feats seemed to defy even death.*

de.gas (dee.GAS) *v.* **-gas.ses, -gassed, -gas.sing** free of unwanted gas: *to degas a mine;* **adj.:** **degassed** *wood.*

de.gauss (dee.GOUSE) *v.* neutralize the magnetic properties of something: *to degauss a ship to protect it from mines; the degaussing button on a computer monitor.*

de.gen.er.ate (di.JEN.uh.rate) *v.* **-ates, -at.ed, -at.ing** decline to a worse condition: *The debate degenerated into a brawl.* —**adj.** (-uh.rit) degraded, as from normality: *a degenerate people, society; degenerate art forms;* **n.:** *a drunken degenerate.* —**de.gen.er.a.cy** *n.* —**de.gen.er.a.tion** (-uh.RAY.shun) *n.: Accumulation of fat around the heart, liver, etc. causes fatty degeneration interfering with their proper functioning.* —**de.gen.er.a.tive** (-ruh.tiv) *adj.: Arthritis is a degenerative disease; the degenerative nature of drug addiction.*

de.grad.a.ble (di.GRAY.duh.bul) *adj.* that can break down chemically: *Biologically degradable materials do not pollute the environment; degradable detergents, diapers, plastics.* —**de.grad.a.bil.i.ty** (-BIL.i.tee) *n.*

deg.ra.da.tion (deg.ruh.DAY.shun) *n.* a degrading: *moral degradation; public degradation; a life of misery and hopeless degradation.*

de.grade (di.GRADE) *v.* **-grades, -grad.ed, -grad.ing 1** decrease in rank, quality, or moral character; corrupt or disgrace: *Abuse of children degrades society; A man degrades himself by abusing children;* **adj.:** *It is* **degrading** *to human nature; a degrading portrayal of women.* **2** break down chemically.

de.gree (di.GREE) *n.* **1** a level or stage in a progression or series: *We have students at every degree of proficiency; people of all degrees and conditions in life; It's true to a great or large degree; a man who was wealthy to the highest or last degree; "Less" and "greater" are in the comparative degree of "little" and "great"; First-degree murder is the most serious murder.* **2** a relative amount or manner: *Everyone can tolerate pain to a or to a certain or to some degree; I don't mind the cold in the slightest degree; The patient's health is improving* **by degrees** (= step by step). **3** a unit of measurement, as for temperature or angles: *The freezing point of water is 32 degrees Fahrenheit or 0 degree Celsius; a 90-degree* (= right) *angle.* **4** a rank or title awarded by a college or university: *She's working for a degree in economics; She will receive or take her degree after four years of study; a bachelor's, master's, doctoral or doctor's degree; An honorary degree* (= not an earned one) *was*

dehorn / deliberate

bestowed or *conferred on our mayor.*
de.horn (dee.HORN) *v.* remove the horns: *to dehorn cattle.*
de.hu.man.ize (dee.HEW.muh.nize) *v.* **-iz.es, -ized, -iz.ing** make machinelike or inhuman: *movies that degrade and dehumanize women;* ***adj.:** the **dehumanizing** aspects of solitary confinement; a **dehumanized** assembly-line job.* —**de.hu.man.i.za.tion** (-nuh.ZAY.shun, -nye-) *n.*
de.hu.mid.i.fy (dee.hew.MID.uh.fye) *v.* **-fies, -fied, -fy.ing** reduce the moisture content of something, esp. air; **de.hu.mid.i.fi.er** *n.* —**de.hu.mid.i.fi.ca.tion** (-fuh.CAY.shun) *n.*
de.hy.drate (dee.HYE.drate) *v.* **-drates, -drat.ed, -drat.ing** dry, esp. foods to preserve them; ***adj.:** Instant coffee is **dehydrated** coffee; She felt weak and dehydrated* (= dried out by loss of body fluids). —**de.hy.dra.tion** (-hye.DRAY.shun) *n.* drying of the body: *High fever, heavy perspiration, etc. may cause dehydration.*
de.hy.dro.gen.ate (dee.hye.DROJ.uh.nate) *v.* **-ates, -at.ed, -at.ing** remove hydrogen from a compound: *dehydrogenated alcohol.* —**de.hy.dro.gen.a.tion** (-NAY.shun) *n.*
de.ice (DEE.ice) *v.* **-ic.es, -iced, -ic.ing** make or keep free of ice: *In freezing weather, airplanes have to be deiced before takeoff.* —**de.ic.er** *n.: an electric windshield deicer.*
de.i.fy (DEE.uh.fye) *v.* **-fies, -fied, -fy.ing** make into a god; also, regard or worship as a god: *to deify an emperor.* —**de.i.fi.ca.tion** (-fuh.CAY.shun) *n.*
deign (DAIN) *v.* of God and people in high station, be gracious and kind enough to do something: *The king deigned to visit us.*
de.ism (DEE.iz.um) *n.* a belief in God founded on reason, usu. holding that God created the world but does not control or affect it; **de.ist** *n.* —**de.is.tic** (dee.IS.tic) or **de.is.ti.cal** *adj.*
de.i.ty (DEE.uh.tee) *n.* **-ties 1** a divine being or divinity. **2 the Deity** God.
de.ja vu or **dé.jà vu** (day.zhah.VEW) *n.* a feeling of having previously experienced a novel situation: *a profound sense of deja vu; an impression of deja vu; a story with an element of deja vu.*
de.ject.ed (di.JEC.tid) *adj.* sad and downcast: *She seemed tired and dejected; a dejected and helpless look.* —**de.jec.tion** *n.: the gloomy dejection of a disappointed man.*
de ju.re (dee.JOOR.ee) *adj. & adv.* by right; legal: *A de jure government in exile does not have de facto power.*
de.lay (di.LAY) *v.* **1** put off until a later time; make late: *A snowstorm delayed our train; It delayed our arrival; delayed it until 2 a.m.;* ***adj. & cpd.:** a **delayed** marriage, penalty in hockey; a delayed reaction, response, start, trip; A delayed-action bomb was defused by the army; a long-delayed bill; rain-delayed sport events.* **2** linger; be late: *Don't delay!* —*n.* a delaying or being delayed: *Please reply without delay; This is a matter that brooks no delay; There was a two-hour delay before the flight took off.*
de.lec.ta.ble (di.LEC.tuh.bul) *adj.* pleasing and delicious: *a delectable dessert, fruit, treat, wine; a delectable combination of flavors;* ***n.:** the many delectables at a food fair.*
de.lec.ta.tion (dee.lec.TAY.shun) *n.* delight and entertainment: *a juggling act presented for your delectation.*
del.e.gate (DEL.uh.gate) *v.* **-gates, -gat.ed, -gat.ing 1** select as a representative: *He was delegated to represent his nation at the conference.* **2** entrust to someone as an agent: *A leader must know how to delegate authority; She doesn't like to delegate.* —*n.* (-git) one selected as a representative: *convention delegates.*
del.e.ga.tion (del.uh.GAY.shun) *n.* **1** a delegating: *the delegation of powers.* **2** a group of delegates: *to head a delegation; a delegation from the Vatican; to send a delegation to the U.N.*
de.lete (di.LEET) *v.* **-letes, -let.ed, -let.ing** strike out or omit: *to delete a word, a name from a list;* ***adj.:** a **deleted** passage, record, reference.* —**de.le.tion** (-LEE.shun) *n.*
del.e.ter.i.ous (del.uh.TEER.ee.us) *adj.* harmful, esp. to health: *Smoking is deleterious to health; its deleterious effects; deleterious consequences, influences.*
delft or **delft.ware** *n.* a pottery having a blue design painted on a white glaze.
del.i (DEL.ee) *n.* **-is** *Informal.* a delicatessen; ***adj.a.:** a deli counter; deli food, meats.*
do.lib.or.ate (di.LIB.uh.rate) *v.* **-ates, -at.ed, -at.ing** consider carefully; take counsel: *to deliberate about a move, on a subject, over a decision.* —***adj.** (-rit)* **1** intentional; well thought out: *a deliberate act, attempt, decision, effort, misuse of words, overdose; deliberate cruelty.* **2** slow and careful: *He's precise and deliberate in his enunciation; She took a deliberate step forward.* **de.lib.er.ate.ly** *adv.;* **de.lib.er.ate.ness** *n.*

de.lib.er.a.tion (di.LIB.uh.RAY.shun) *n.* **1** careful pondering: *the judge's lengthy deliberations.* **2** deliberateness: *the deliberation with which the murder was committed.* —**de.lib.er.a.tive** (-tiv) *adja.*: *A legislature is a deliberative assembly, body; the deliberative process.*

del.i.ca.cy (DEL.uh.cuh.see) *n.* -**cies 1** delicateness: *Proposing marriage is a matter of extreme, great delicacy; the delicacy of her health.* **2** a dainty or choice food: *We specialize in delicacies such as escargots; We also have other delicacies of the palate.*

del.i.cate (DEL.uh.kit) **1** *adja.* pleasing; fine, as because of lightness, softness, intricacy, subtlety, etc.: *a delicate fabric; a delicate shade of pink; a delicate weave.* **2** *adj.* needing care and tact or great skill and sensitivity: *the delicate question of her divorce; a delicate choice, situation, subject, surgical operation; a delicate* (= easily damaged) *lace dress.* **3** *adja.* having refined sensitivity, skill, tact, sensory discrimination, etc.: *She has a delicate ear for music; a delicate sense of smell; in delicate health; a delicate* (= frail) *child.* **4** *adjp.* modest: *very delicate in his approach to nudity.* —**del.i.cate.ly** *adv.*; **del.i.cate.ness** *n.*

del.i.ca.tes.sen (del.uh.cuh.TES.un) *n.* **1** a shop selling ready-to-eat food such as smoked meats, cheeses, salads, etc. **2** [takes *pl. v.*] such food.

de.li.cious (di.LISH.us) *adj.* **1** very pleasing, esp. to the taste or smell: *What is that delicious smell from the kitchen? Your cooking is delicious; a delicious flavor, fragrance, taste.* **2** delightful: *a delicious thought; the delicious irony of it all.* —**de.li.cious.ly** *adv.*; **de.li.cious.ness** *n.*

de.light (di.LITE) *v.* to take great pleasure or cause someone great pleasure: *a hunter who delights in the chase; The new toy delighted Billy.* **adj.**: *Billy seemed delighted with the new toy; We're delighted to meet you; We're delighted that you are in town.* —*n.* great pleasure: *Watching her dance was sheer delight; She plays pranks on boys with intense delight; She takes great delight in tormenting her kid brother; We enjoyed the delights of his well-furnished table; a garden of earthly delights.* —**de.light.ful** *adj.*: *an absolutely delightful book;* **de.light.ful.ly** *adv.*

De.li.lah (di.LYE.luh) *n.* the treacherous mistress of Samson; hence, a temptress.

de.lim.it (di.LIM.it) *v.* set out the limits or bounds of something. —**de.lim.i.ta.tion** (-i.TAY.shun) *n.*

de.lin.e.ate (di.LIN.ee.ate) *v.* -**ates, -at.ed, -at.ing** sketch or portray; hence, outline in words: *to delineate boundaries, details, features, objectives, patterns; to delineate a character, life, plan, role.* —**de.lin.e.a.tion** (-AY.shun) *n.*

de.lin.quen.cy (di.LINK.wun.see) *n.* behavior that is contrary to accepted norms: *acts of juvenile delinquency; mortgage delinquencies.*

de.lin.quent (di.LINK.wunt) *adj.* **1** overdue or unpaid: *a delinquent account; delinquent debts, payments, taxes.* **2** guilty by acting against or by neglect of duty or rules: *He has been delinquent in paying his dues; delinquent behavior, youths.* —*n.* a delinquent person: *a juvenile delinquent; tax delinquents.*

del.i.quesce (del.i.QUES) *v.* -**quesc.es, -quesced, -quesc.ing** liquefy by taking moisture from the air; also, melt away; **del.i.ques.cence** *n.* —**del.i.ques.cent** *adj.*: *Calcium chloride is deliquescent.*

de.lir.i.ous (di.LEER.ee.us) *adj.* excited, as with an attack of delirium: *a child delirious with high fever; She was delirious with joy.* —**de.lir.i.ous.ly** *adv.*: *deliriously happy.*

de.lir.i.um (di.LEER.ee.um) *n.* -**i.ums** *or* -**i.a 1** a short mental disturbance characterized by excited activity, disordered speech, confusion, etc.: *The child was in a delirium with high fever.* **2** a frenzied excitement: *She went into a delirium of joy on learning the good news.*

de.liv.er (di.LIV.ur) *v.* **1** set free; rescue: *to deliver the hostages from the terrorists.* **2** send to a target, terminal, audience, or other receiving end: *Letter carriers deliver* (= hand over or convey) *mail to people's homes; They used to deliver six days a week; The boxer can deliver* (= send) *a hard punch; to deliver a lecture, sermon; She delivered* (= read or said) *her speech well; She is so popular she could also deliver* (= get) *votes; She always delivers on* (= performs) *her promises.* **3** help to give birth: *Midwives and obstetricians deliver babies; Who delivered your wife* (= assisted at her delivery)? *She felt relieved when she had delivered herself of* (= produced or expressed) *her views on the subject.* —**de.liver (the goods)** perform as expected or required: *Can he deliver?*
—**de.liv.er.ance** (-uh.runce) *n.*
—**de.liv.er.er** *n.*

de.liv.er.y (di.LIV.uh.ree) *n.* -**er.ies 1** a delivering or the manner of delivering: *You accept* or *take delivery of the parcel sent "cash on delivery" after paying for it; Payment is collected on delivery of the parcel; general, rural, special delivery (of mail); the delivery of health care; an emergency, next-day, overnight, prompt delivery;* **adj.**: *a delivery boy, man, truck, van; a weapons delivery system for quick retaliation in case of a surprise attack.* **2** manner of speaking: *an orator with effective delivery; fast or slow delivery.* **3** childbirth: *She had an easy, normal vaginal delivery, not a Cesarian delivery or a breech delivery; the* **delivery room** *of a hospital.*

dell *n.* a small, usu. wooded glen: *the cottage in the dell.*

de.louse (dee.LOWSE) *v.* **-lous.es, -loused, -lous.ing** clean the lice from a head.

del.phin.i.um (del.FIN.ee.um) *n.* a plant bearing spikes of colorful flowers on tall stalks.

del.ta (DEL.tuh) *n.* **1** the fourth letter of the Greek alphabet [Δ, δ]. **2** a usually triangular area of silt or sand formed at a river mouth: *the delta of the Nile;* **adj.**: *the Delta region of the Mississippi; the triangular swept-back delta wing of an airplane.*

Delta ray *n.* a low-energy electron released from matter by alpha or other cosmic rays passing through it.

Delta wave *n.* any of the slow brain waves of deepest sleep.

de.lude (di.LOOD, long "OO") *v.* **-ludes, -lud.ed, -lud.ing** mislead into believing something false: *Election candidates often delude voters with promises; They are deluded into thinking the promises will be carried out; Let us not delude ourselves;* **adj.**: *a* **deluded** *admirer, believer, electorate.*

del.uge (DEL.yooj, long "oo") *n.* a flood, downpour, etc.: *a deluge of demands, phone calls, orders, publicity.* —*v.* **-ug.es, -uged, -ug.ing** flood: *a movie star deluged with fan mail.*

de.lu.sion (di.LOO.zhun) *n.* a deluding, esp. a persistent false belief in something unreal: *His offer is a snare and a delusion; He suffers from delusions of grandeur such as thinking he is the Savior; He cherishes, clings to, is under, or labors under the delusion that he is God incarnate.* —**de.lu.sion.al** *adj.*: *a delusional belief, disorder, patient; the delusional world;* also **de.lu.sion.ar.y.**

—**de.lu.sive** (-siv) *adj.*: *a delusive notion, quality.*

de.luxe (di.LUX, di.LOOKS, long or short "OO") *adj.* outstandingly good: *a hotel rated "triple A, deluxe, superior accommodation"; a deluxe facility, hotel, model, size, suite, unit, version; deluxe features; Their amenities are deluxe.*

delve *v.* **delves, delved, delv.ing** dig deeply, as in study: *to delve into old land deeds.*

de.mag.net.ize (dee.MAG.nuh.tize) *v.* **-iz.es, -ized, -iz.ing** take away the magnetic properties of something: *to demagnetize an iron bar.* —**de.mag.net.i.za.tion** (-tuh.ZAY.shun, -tye-) *n.*

dem.a.gogue (DEM.uh.gog) *n.* a leader who manipulates the people's passions. Also **dem.a.gog.** —**dem.a.gog.ic** (-GOJ.ic) *adj.* —**dem.a.gog.uer.y** (-gog.uh.ree) or **dem.a.go.gy** (-goh.jee) *n.*

de.mand (di.MAND) *v.* **1** ask for vehemently or as a right: *We demand justice; She demands an apology from you; He demands to be satisfied; He demands that she resign her job;* **adj.**: *Her job is more* **demanding** *than her husband's; It is very demanding of her energies.* **2** require: *a situation that demands tactful handling.* —*n.* **1** a demanding or being demanded: *The lady refused to yield to his demands; to drop, give in to, make, meet, reject, satisfy a demand; a demand for compensation; He makes too many demands on her time and patience; Dictionaries are always very much* **in demand** (= needed); **adj.**: *a demand bill, note (payable on presentation); a* **demand deposit** *(that the depositor may withdraw without notice);* **demand feeding** *of an infant (whenever it is hungry, instead of on a schedule); A* **demand loan** *is repayable* **on demand** (= when asked for). **2** the readiness and ability to buy a product: *the law of supply and demand; As the demand increases, the supply decreases and scarcity results; Can advertising create a demand? There's a brisk, great, strong demand for certain goods.*

de.mar.cate (di.MAR.cate) *v.* **-cates, -cat.ed, -cat.ing** mark the boundaries of; separate: *Pope Alexander VI tried to demarcate the New World between Spain and Portugal along the 48-degree-west line of longitude.* —**de.mar.ca.tion** (dee.mar.CAY.shun) *n.*: *The line of demarcation was ignored by the French, English, and the Dutch.*

dé.marche (day.MARSH) *n.* a maneuver or initiative, esp. in diplomacy.

de.mean (di.MEEN) *v.* degrade or debase: *People demean themselves by dishonesty; Manual work ennobles rather than demeans us; Pornography demeans women;* **adj.**: *Some consider manual work very* **demeaning**; *a demeaning experience.*

de.mean.or (di.MEE.nur) *n.* outward behavior as expressing attitude toward others: *She spends hours practicing the demeanor of a lawyer in court.* Also **de.mean.our** *Cdn.*

de.ment.ed (di.MEN.tid) *adj.* insane.

de.mer.it (dee.MER.it) *n.* 1 a fault or offense. 2 a score against one for this: *a student with three demerits for being late; The driver received three **demerit points** for disobeying a traffic signal.*

de.mesne (di.MAIN) *n.* 1 *Law.* possession and use of land by the owner: *to hold an estate in demesne.* 2 the land attached to a mansion; also, a region, domain, etc.: *the royal demesne.*

dem.i.god (DEM.i.god) *n.* 1 a hero born of a god and a mortal. 2 any godlike person.

dem.i.john (DEM.i.jon) *n.* a large bottle with a narrow neck, enclosed in wickerwork.

de.mil.i.ta.rize (dee.MIL.uh.tuh.rize) *v.* **-riz.es, -rized, -riz.ing** keep free of military equipment and troops; *adj.:* a **demilitarized** neutral zone between two warring nations.

dem.i.mon.daine (DEM.i.mon.DAIN) *n.* a woman on the borderline of respectability, as a rich man's mistress.

dem.i.monde (DEM.i.mond) *n.* demimondaines as a class.

de.mise (di.MIZE) *n. Formal.* decease; death: *Upon her uncle's demise, she gained title to the property.*

dem.i.tasse (DEM.i.tas) *n.* a small cup for serving strong black coffee.

de.mi.urge (DEE.mee.urj) *n.* a supernatural creative force.

dem.o (DEM.oh) *n. Informal.* 1 a demonstration, esp. a record or tape as a sample of someone's talent. 2 an automobile, program diskette, tape, etc. used as a demonstrator. 3 a political demonstration.

de.mo.bi.lize (di.MOH.buh.lize) *v.* **-iz.es, -ized, -iz.ing** free from military service: *to demobilize an army after a war.* —**de.mo.bi.li.za.tion** (-luh.ZAY.shun, -lye-) *n.*

de.moc.ra.cy (di.MOC.ruh.see) *n.* **-cies** 1 government by the people. 2 a political system of government by the people, either directly or through representatives: *the foundations of our democracy; constitutional, parliamentary, representative democracy.*

dem.o.crat (DEM.uh.crat) *n.* 1 one who believes in government by the people. 2 **Democrat** a member of the U.S. Democratic Party. —**dem.o.crat.ic** (-CRAT.ic) *adj.*

de.moc.ra.tize (di.MOC.ruh.tize) *v.* **-tiz.es, -tized, -tiz.ing** make or become democratic: *to democratize a nation, organization, political system.*

de.mo.dé (day.moh.DAY) *adj.* out-of-fashion.

de.mod.u.late (dee.MOJ.uh.late) *v.* **-lates, -lat.ed, -lat.ing** restore a modulated signal to its original form; **de.mod.u.la.tor** *n.* —**de.mod.u.la.tion** (-LAY.shun) *n.*

de.mog.ra.phy (di.MOG.ruh.fee) *n.* the statistical study of population data relating to age, income, education, marriages, etc.; **de.mog.ra.pher** *n.* —**de.mo.graph.ic** (dem.uh.GRAF.ic) *adj.;* **de.mo.graph.i.cal.ly** *adv.*

dem.oi.selle (dem.wuh.ZEL) *n.* a young woman.

de.mol.ish (di.MOL.ish) *v.* wreck totally; tear down: *The old hotel has been demolished; His arguments were demolished by the evidence produced in court.* —**dem.o.li.tion** (dem.uh.LISH.un) *n.:* *a historical site saved from demolition by developers; It was targeted or slated for demolition;* **adj.:** *a demolition crew, squad; a **demolition bomb** for wrecking buildings; the **demolition derby** of ramming cars together till only one is running; He was hit by a brick at a **demolition site** (where a building was being demolished).*

de.mon (DEE.mun) *n.* 1 a devil or evil spirit. 2 a person or thing considered evil: *to swear off the demon rum; Demon Vanity; a spelling demon (= hard-to-spell word).* 3 one who acts with great zeal or skill: *He's a demon for homework; His teacher is a demon for punctuality.* —**de.mon.ic** (di.MON.ic) *adj.*

de.mon.e.tize (dee.MON.i.tize) *v.* **-tiz.es, -tized, -tiz.ing** stop using the specified metal as money: *to demonetize silver.* —**de.mon.e.ti.za.tion** (-tuh.ZAY.shun, -tye-) *n.*

de.mo.ni.ac (di.MOH.nee.ac) or **de.mo.ni.a.cal** (dee.muh.NYE.uh.cul) *adj.* 1 of or like a demon. 2 possessed by the devil.

de.mo.nize (DEE.muh.nize) *v.* **-iz.es, -ized, -iz.ing** make demonlike: *to demonize drugs, enemies, the opposition.*

de.mon.stra.ble (di.MON.struh.bul) *adj.* that can be demonstrated or proved: *That the earth is round is a demonstrable fact.* —**de.mon.stra.bly** *adv.:* *The flat-earth theory is demonstrably absurd.*

dem.on.strate (DEM.un.strate) *v.* **-strates, -strat.ed, -strat.ing** 1 show or prove, as by examples or reasoning: *to demonstrate the fallacy of an argument; Please demonstrate that this gadget works;*

demonstrate also how it works; Now please demonstrate the gadget to my wife (= show her how it works). 2 display one's views, feelings, etc. by parading, shouting, etc.: *Children demonstrate their affection by hugging and kissing; Pacifists demonstrate against the war; They demonstrate for peace.* —**dem.on.stra.tion** (-STRAY.shun) *n.* —**dem.on.stra.tor** (-stray.tur) *n.*

de.mon.stra.tive (di.MON.struh.tiv) *adj.* 1 displaying one's feelings openly: *demonstrative actions, affection, behavior, persons.* 2 that demonstrates; giving proof: *evidence that is demonstrative of the truth.* —**de.mon.stra.tive.ly** *adv.*

de.mor.al.ize (di.MOR.uh.lize) *v.* **-iz.es, -ized, -iz.ing** weaken the morals, morale, or discipline of someone: *Drugs demoralize and weaken society; a young girl demoralized by a bad home environment;* **adj.:** *The army was quite demoralized by the defeat; a demoralized army, nation, society; a demoralizing effect, experience.* —**de.mor.al.i.za.tion** (-luh.ZAY.shun, -lye-) *n.*

de.mote (di.MOTE) *v.* **-motes, -mot.ed, -mot.ing** to lower in rank or station: *He was demoted because he was lazy; He was demoted to work on the assembly line.* —**de.mo.tion** (di.MOH.shun) *n.*

de.mot.ic (di.MOT.ic) *adj.* of the common people: *writing Egyptian in the demotic script; demotic Greek.*

de.mul.cent (di.MUL.sunt) *adj.* soothing; relieving irritation. —*n.* an oily or sticky medicine for soothing esp. mucous membranes.

de.mur (di.MUR) *v.* **-murs, -murred, -mur.ring** *Formal.* object or take exception: *He demurred at my offer;* **n.:** *She accepted it without demur.* —**de.mur.rer** *n.*

de.mure (di.MURE) *adj.* **-mur.er, -mur.est** reserved and modest: *Raquel appeared demure in a high-necked blouse tied with a bow at the throat; She struck a demure pose for the photographer.* —**de.mure.ly** *adv.*

de.mur.rage (di.MUR.ij) *n.* 1 the delay of a cargo conveyance beyond the time for loading or unloading. 2 a compensation for this delay: *to pay demurrage to shipping companies and railroads.*

den *n.* 1 a quiet, cozy room, such as a study. 2 a wild animal's lair: *a lion's den.* 3 a squalid or hidden dwelling: *crack, gambling, opium dens; a den of iniquity; a den of thieves.*

de.na.ture (dee.NAY.chur) *v.* **-tures, -tured, -tur.ing** 1 alter the natural qualities, esp. of alcohol, tea, etc. so that it is made unfit for consumption. 2 of fissionable matter, make unusable in nuclear weapons.

den.drite *n.* a branching extension of a nerve cell that receives impulses.

den.drol.o.gy (den.DROL.uh.jee) *n.* the science of trees. —**den.drol.o.gist** *n.*

den.gue (DENG.gee, -gay, "g" as in "go") *n.* a mosquito-transmitted fever causing great weakness, pain, esp. in the joints, and skin eruptions.

de.ni.al (di.NYE.ul) *n.* a denying or a statement of it: *the denial of a charge, of justice, of a child (as one's own); the denial that the child is one's own; a flat, outright, strong denial.*

de.nier (DEN.yur) *n.* a unit of weight indicating the fineness of yarns: *20-denier nylon stockings.*

den.i.grate (DEN.uh.grate) *v.* **-grates, -grat.ed, -grat.ing** blacken, esp. someone's name; also, belittle: *He was accused of denigrating her character and motives.* —**den.i.gra.tion** (-GRAY.shun) *n.*

den.im (DEN.um) *n.* 1 a heavy, twilled cotton cloth: *jeans of blue denim.* 2 something made of denim: *Normally denims* (= denim-made clothes) *are for casual wear;* **adj.a.:** *denim jackets, jeans, looks.*

den.i.zen (DEN.uh.zun) *n.* a plant or animal that has made a certain place its home: *the denizens of the forest; the finny denizens* (= fishes, etc.) *of the deep.*

de.nom.i.nate (di.NOM.uh.nate) *v.* **-nates, -nat.ed, -nat.ing** to name or indicate: *Democracy denominates a form of government.*

de.nom.i.na.tion (duh.nom.uh.NAY.shun) *n.* 1 a naming or designating. 2 a name, esp. of a class, group, etc.: *coins of small denominations* (= dimes, nickels, etc.). 3 a particular sect or group: *religious denominations; Protestants of various denominations.* —**de.nom.i.na.tion.al** (-shuh.nul) *adj.:* *a denominational school run by the Seventh Day Adventists.*

de.nom.i.na.tor (duh.NOM.uh.nay.tur) *n.* the number below the line in a fraction; divisor: *¼ and ¾ have the same denominator; They have a common denominator; The **lowest** or **least common denominator** of ½, ¼, and ¾ is 8.*

de.no.ta.tion (dee.noh.TAY.shun) *n.* the strict meaning of a word or what is referred to by it: *A logician considers a word's denotation, but a writer has to weigh also its connotations.* —**de.no.ta.tive** (DEE.noh.tay.tiv, di.NOH.tuh.tiv) *adj.:* *denotative meanings.*

de.note (di.NOTE) *v.* **-notes, -not.ed, -not.ing** mean or indicate; be the symbol for something: *A skull and crossbones denotes death or danger.*

de.noue.ment (day.noo.MAHNG) *n.* the conclusion or untangling of a complicated dramatic plot.

de.nounce (di.NOUNCE) *v.* **-nounc.es, -nounced, -nounc.ing 1** repudiate or reject: *The new government denounced the old treaty as a mere scrap of paper; Smith denounces* (= condemns publicly) *drug abuse and drug pushers roundly in his speeches.* See DENUNCIATION. **2** accuse or inform against someone: *Smith denounced his neighbor to the police as a drug pusher;* **de.nounce.ment** (-munt) *n.*

de no.vo (dee.NOH.voh) *Latin.* once more; anew.

dense (DENCE) *adj.* **dens.er, dens.est 1** having a great deal in a small space; compact; thick: *a dense cloud of smoke; a dense atmosphere, colony, crowd, jungle, neighborhood, population, texture, thicket, undergrowth; dense concentration, fog, traffic; a moist dense chocolate cake.* **2** *Informal.* hard to penetrate or understand: *dense arguments, prose; a dense dissertation on the afterlife; dense with jargon; His book is pretty dense stuff; 500 dense pages.* **3** *Informal.* thick-headed: *Our managers are so dense it is difficult to make them understand anything.*
—**dense.ly** *adv.;* **dense.ness** *n.*

den.si.ty (DEN.si.tee) *n.* **-ties 1** concentration: *the high density of population in urban areas; Traffic density reaches its peak during the rush hour.* **2** compactness of substance; relative weight: *Because of its lower density, ice floats in water.*

dent *n.* an impression made by hitting or pressing in: *a dent in the fender; to hammer out a dent; After two days he had hardly* **made a dent in** (= made any appreciable start on) *the work that had accumulated;* **to put a dent in** (= noticeably affect) *something.*
—*v.* make a dent in something: *A tin can is easily dented.*

den.tal (DEN.tul) *adja.* having to do with teeth or dentistry: *dental care, decay, hygiene; a dental appointment, record, surgeon, technician; dental consonants such as "t" and "d".*

dental floss *n.* a strong, flat thread for cleaning between teeth.

dental hygienist *n.* one who assists a dentist, esp. by cleaning teeth.

dental plate *n.* a denture.

den.ti.care (DEN.tuh.care) *n.* a dental insurance program sponsored by government.

den.ti.frice (DEN.tuh.fris) *n.* a powder, paste, etc. for cleaning teeth; toothpaste.

den.tin (DEN.tin) or **den.tine** (-teen) *n.* the hard, dense body of a tooth under the enamel.

den.tist (DEN.tist) *n.* one professionally trained to care for teeth: *the dentist's chair.*

den.tis.try (DEN.tis.tree) *n.* a dentist's art or profession.

den.ti.tion (den.TISH.un) *n.* the number, arrangement, and kind of teeth: *the characteristic dentition of ruminants.*

den.ture (DEN.chur) *n.* a set of false teeth: *full and partial dentures; A* **denture therapist** *makes dentures.*

den.tur.ist (DEN.chur.ist) *n.* one who makes and fits dentures; denture therapist.

de.nu.cle.ar.ize (dee.NEW.clee.uh.rize) *v.* **-iz.es, -ized, -iz.ing** make or keep free of nuclear weapons; *adj.: Some regions have been declared* **denuclearized** *zones.*

de.nude (di.NUDE) *v.* **-nudes, -nud.ed, -nud.ing** make bare: *hillsides denuded of trees by excessive logging.* —**de.nu.da.tion** (dee.new.DAY.shun) *n.*

de.nun.ci.a.tion (di.NUN.see.AY.shun) *n.* a denouncing or condemnation: *to issue, make a denunciation; a bitter, scathing, sweeping, vehement denunciation of government policy.*

de.ny (di.NYE) *v.* **-nies, -nied, -ny.ing 1** refuse to accept, recognize, etc.: *He denied the charge; denied that he was guilty; He denied knowing anything about it; to deny categorically, flatly, strongly, vehemently; Normally, a mother will not deny* (= disown) *her own children.* **2** refuse to give; say no to something: *All appeals were denied; She was denied admittance, bail, her civil rights; It takes an ascetic to* **deny oneself** (= manage without the things one needs).

de.o.dar (DEE.uh.dar) *n.* a Himalayan cedar grown ornamentally and for timber.

de.o.dor.ant (dee.OH.duh.runt) *n.* a deodorizer for the body: *to apply, put on, use, wear a deodorant; roll-on, spray, stick, underarm deodorants;* **adja.***: a deodorant commercial, soap, spray.*

de.o.dor.ize (dee.OH.duh.rize) *v.* **-iz.es, -ized, -iz.ing** remove or mask the unpleasant odor of something: *to deodorize a room.* —**de.o.dor.iz.er** *n.*

de.ox.i.dize (dee.OX.uh.dize) *v.* **-diz.es, -dized, -diz.ing** take oxygen, esp. out

of a compound.
de.ox.y.ri.bo.nu.cle.ic acid (dee.OX.i.RYE.boh.new.CLEE.ic-) *n.* a nucleic acid found in all living cells that transmits genetic information; DNA.
de.part (di.PART) *v. Formal.* leave: *Trains depart for various destinations from Grand Central; Bogus refugees may be told to depart the country; Queen Victoria departed this life* (= died) *in 1901.*
—**depart from** deviate or stray: *to depart from the path of virtue; to depart from the subject; to depart from the truth and tell a falsehood; to depart from the usual custom.* —**departed** *adj.* dead: *our departed brethren; n.: the dear departed; the souls of the departed.*
de.part.ment (di.PART.munt) *n.* **1** a division of a larger organization: *the editorial department of a newspaper; the linguistics department of the School of Arts and Science; the Department* (= Ministry) *of Labor; France is divided into departments instead of provinces or states.* **2** an area of interest or knowledge: *Sorry, not my department! In the weather department, the forecast calls for a snowy day.*
—**de.part.ment.al** (dee.part.MEN.tul) *adj.*
de.part.ment.al.ize (dee.part.MEN.tuh.lize) *v.* **-iz.es, -ized, -iz.ing** divide into departments; *adj.: a departmentalized store.*
department store *n.* a large store divided into departments selling different kinds of goods.
de.par.ture (di.PAR.chur) *n.* a departing: *This procedure marks a departure from (established) routine; His departure for Europe was sudden and unannounced; adj.: the departure date, gate; The departure level of the airport terminal has a departure lounge for passengers waiting for flights to be called.*
de.pend (di.PEND) *v.* **1** rely trustingly: *You can depend on* or *upon her to get things done.* **2** be contingent on or determined by something: *Will we have a picnic tomorrow? It depends; It depends on the weather.*
de.pend.a.ble (di.PEN.duh.bul) *adj.* trustworthy; *a dependable worker.*
—**de.pend.a.bil.i.ty** (-BIL.i.tee) *n.*
de.pend.ence (di.PEN.dunce) *n.* a depending: *drug dependence; a youth suffering from a dependence on* or *upon drugs.* Also **de.pend.ance.**
de.pend.en.cy (di.PEN.dun.see) *n.* **-cies** dependence; also, something dependent, as a region ruled by but not forming part of another country: *Those islands are a British dependency;*
colonial dependencies.
de.pend.ent (di.PEN.dunt) **1** *adj.* relying on another, esp. for food, shelter, etc.: *Children are dependent on their parents; There's a tax deduction for each dependent child.* **2** *adjp.* affected by something: *to be dependent on drugs.* **3** *adjp.* decided by something: *Your promotion is dependent on (your) passing the test.* **4** *adja.* subordinate: *a dependent clause, nation, territory.* —*n.: the parents and six dependents* (= children, seniors, etc.). Also **de.pend.ant.**
de.pict (di.PICT) *v.* portray in a picture or in words: *a rural landscape depicted in watercolors; It is depicted in great detail; It depicts sheep grazing in a meadow; It depicts sheep as part of the landscape.*
—**de.pic.tion** *n.*
de.pil.a.to.ry (di.PIL.uh.tor.ee) *adj.* having to do with removing body hair: *depilatory treatment.* —*n.* a depilatory substance.
de.plane (di.PLANE) *v.* **-planes, -planed, -plan.ing** get off an airplane: *to deplane at an airport.*
de.ple.ta.ble (di.PLEE.tuh.bul) *adj.* that can be used up: *Coal is a depletable, not renewable resource.*
de.plete (di.PLEET) *v.* **-pletes, -plet.ed, -plet.ing** empty out or exhaust: *Overspending has depleted our resources; We have been depleted of our funds, riches, stores, wealth; Now we have to deplete a massive debt.* —**de.ple.tion** (-shun) *n.: the rapid depletion of our natural resources.*
de.plor.a.ble (di.PLOR.uh.bul) *adj.* regrettable or lamentable: *a deplorable incident; a deplorable lack of cleanliness.*
—**de.plor.a.bly** *adv.*
de.plore (di.PLORE) *v.* **-plores, -plored, -plor.ing** feel deep regret about something: *We deplore the condition of the poor; Everyone deplores corruption.*
de.ploy (di.PLOY) *v.* arrange strategically: *The government deployed troops at the site of the demonstration.*
—**de.ploy.ment** *n.*
de.po.lar.ize (dee.POH.luh.rize) *v.* **-iz.es, -iz.ed, -iz.ing** make unpolarized; *adj.: depolarized light.*
—**de.po.lar.iz.er** *n.: A depolarizer is added to some batteries to ensure a steady current.* —**de.po.lar.i.za.tion** (-ruh.ZAY.shun, -rye-) *n.*
de.po.lit.i.cize (dee.puh.LIT.uh.size) *v.* **-ciz.es, -cized, -ciz.ing** remove from the realm of politics: *efforts to depoliticize the Olympics.*
de.pon.ent (di.POH.nunt) *n.* one who

gives a deposition for use in court.
de.pop.u.late (dee.POP.yuh.late) v. **-lates, -lat.ed, -lat.ing** reduce the population of a place greatly or totally: *The Black Death once depopulated Europe.* —**de.pop.u.la.tion** (-LAY.shun) n.

de.port (di.PORT) v. **1** expel an alien or criminal from a country: *Convicts used to be deported from England to Australia; The government deports bogus refugees;* **de.por.ta.tion** (dee.por.TAY.shun) n. **2** conduct oneself: *She deports herself with dignity.*

de.por.tee (di.por.TEE) n. a deported person.

de.port.ment (di.PORT.munt) n. one's cultivated behavior or conduct: *a woman of fine bearing and deportment.*

de.pose (di.POZE) v. **-pos.es, -posed, -pos.ing 1** remove from power or office: *an emperor deposed by the army.* **2** testify under oath, usu. in writing.

de.pos.it (di.POZ.it) v. **1** put money or valuables for safekeeping, as a security, etc.: *She deposits $100 each week in a savings account;* **adj.**: *deposit insurance, slips.* **2** leave or lay down: *gravel deposited by receding glaciers.* —**n.** what is deposited: *She tries to keep money on deposit to cover her checks; She makes a deposit at the beginning of each month; You leave a small deposit on returnable pop bottles; You forfeit your deposit if you don't return the bottles; deposits* (= masses or accumulations) *of coal, gas, iron, minerals, oil, sediment.* —**de.pos.i.tor** n.

dep.o.si.tion (dep.uh.ZISH.un) n. written testimony taken under oath: *He made a sworn deposition before a judge that he had witnessed what had happened that night.*

de.pos.i.to.ry (di.POZ.uh.tor.ee) n. **-ries** a place for depositing things: *a depository for secret government documents; a school board's textbook depository; a safe depository for your savings;* **adj.**: *a depository collection; a depository library* (officially designated to receive publications).

de.pot (DEE.poh) n. **1** a place for storing and distributing things, esp. military supplies: *an ammunition depot.* **2** a bus or railroad station.

de.prave (di.PRAVE) v. **-praves, -praved, -prav.ing** make wicked or perverted; corrupt: *youth depraved by bad influences;* **adj.**: *a depraved criminal, mind, youth.* —**de.prav.i.ty** (di.PRAV.i.tee) n. **-ties.**

dep.re.cate (DEP.ruh.cate) v. **-cates, -cat.ed, -cat.ing 1** disapprove of or plead against something: *a banker deprecating plans for monetary reform.* **2** belittle: *She modestly tries to deprecate her role in the firm's achievements.* —**dep.re.ca.tion** (-CAY.shun) n. —**dep.re.ca.to.ry** (-cuh.tor.ee) adj.

de.pre.ci.ate (di.PREE.shee.ate) v. **-ates, -at.ed, -at.ing 1** fall in value: *In our neighborhood, land doesn't depreciate; it appreciates in value; Once it is out of the showroom, a car begins to depreciate; A six-year-old car will be depreciated* (= reduced in price) *over six years when you trade it in;* **adj.**: *the depreciated value of a six-year-old car; A car is a fast depreciating asset.* **2** disparage. —**de.pre.ci.a.tion** (-AY.shun) n.

dep.re.da.tion (dep.ruh.DAY.shun) n. a plundering or laying waste: *the harsh depredations of estate taxes.*

de.press (di.PRESS) v. **1** press or push down: *to depress a lever, pedal.* **2** make sad: *The bad news depressed his spirits; It depressed him that his wife was ill;* **adj.**: *to be, feel, get depressed; He was depressed to learn of his wife's illness; He found the news from the hospital depressing.* **3** make poor economically: *Unemployment, business failures, etc. tend to depress the economy;* **adj.**: *an economically depressed area with poverty and high unemployment; a depressed economy, market.*

de.pres.sant (di.PRES.unt) n. one that depresses: *a depressant to calm the nerves;* **adj.**: *a depressant drug for a heart condition.*

de.pres.sion (di.PRESH.un) n. **1** a period of severe reduction in economic activity: *What causes a depression? an economic, major, minor depression; the Great Depression of the 1930s.* **2** a state of extreme sadness; dejection: *chronic, deep, severe depression.* **3** an area lower than its surroundings: *The meteorite caused a depression that is a mile wide.* —**de.pres.sive** (-PRES.iv) adj.

de.pres.sor (di.PRES.ur) n. one that depresses: *a tongue depressor used by a physician;* **adj.**: *a depressor muscle; a depressor nerve* (that lowers arterial blood pressure).

dep.ri.va.tion (dep.ruh.VAY.shun) n. the state of being deprived: *a child raised in hunger and deprivation* (of the necessities of life); *the many deprivations* (= lacks or wants) *suffered by poor children.*

de.prive (di.PRIVE) v. **-prives, -prived, -priv.ing** take or keep something away from someone: *a political prisoner deprived of his civil rights;* **adj.**: *Some grow up culturally deprived; A deprived child*

deprogram / derive

grows up without parental affection, a normal home life, etc.

de.pro.gram (dee.PROH.gram) v. **-grams, -grammed, -gram.ming** bring a religious convert back to his former way of life by attacking his beliefs in closed-door sessions; **de.pro.gram.mer** n. Also **-gramed, -gram.ing, -gram.er.**

depth n. **1** the quality or degree of deepness: *The lake is 600 ft in depth; a submarine cruising at a depth of 300 ft; She shows great depth of learning; The study lacks depth* (= is superficial). **2** a deep thing or place: *in the depths of outer space; the depths of the Great Depression; the depths of despair; fish that live in the ocean depths; at depths of up to 600 ft; I'm grateful from the depths of my heart;* **adja.:** *a depth finder; to drop a* **depth bomb** or **depth charge** *to destroy a submarine;* **Depth psychology** deals with unconscious mental processes. —**in depth** thoroughly and with penetration: *She studied it in depth;* **adja.:** *an* **in-depth** (= thorough) *news report.* —**out of** or **beyond one's depth** more than one is competent to do: *You may get lost if you venture too far beyond your depth in mathematics.*

dep.u.ta.tion (dep.yuh.TAY.shun) n. a person or group appointed to represent and act on behalf of others; delegation.

de.pute (di.PYOOT, long "OO") v. **-putes, -put.ed, -put.ing 1** appoint someone to act for one: *Prime Ministers deputed senior ministers to act as their deputies.* **2** assign a job, one's authority or power, etc. to someone; delegate: *Prime Ministers deputed their authority to senior ministers.*

dep.u.tize (DEP.yuh.tize) v. **-tiz.es, -tized, -tiz.ing** appoint someone as deputy.

dep.u.ty (DEP.yuh.tee) n. **-ties 1** one appointed to act officially for another: *My deputy* (= assistant) *will run things while I'm away;* **adja.:** *a deputy minister, secretary, sheriff.* **2** a people's representative: *a deputy of the French legislature; A Chamber of Deputies and a Senate form the Italian parliament.*

de.rail (di.RAIL) v. **1** run or cause to run off the rails: *The train derailed; Who derailed it?* **2** cause to fail: *to derail an agreement, attempt, deal, plan, process, program, treaty; to derail careers, legislation, negotiations.* —**de.rail.ment** n.

de.rail.leur (di.RAY.lur) n. a device for shifting a bicycle chain from one gear to another.

de.range (di.RAINJ) v. **-rang.es,** **-ranged, -rang.ing** make disturbed, disordered, or insane; **adj.:** *a* **deranged** *killer; a mentally deranged patient.* —**de.range.ment** n.

der.by (DUR.bee, *Brit.* DAR.bee) n. **-bies 1** a hat with a rounded crown and a thin, rolled brim. **2 Derby** any of several annual horse races: *the Kentucky Derby; Epsom's Derby at Surrey, England.* **3** an open race or contest: *a dog derby* (= dog-team race); *a soapbox derby* (= coasting race for small engineless cars made of wooden boxes); *demolition derby.*

de.reg.u.la.tion (DEE.reg.yuh.LAY.shun) n. the removal of unnecessary government regulations and restrictions in trade and industry.

der.e.lict (DER.uh.lict) adj. **1** neglectful: *He was found derelict in his duty.* **2** abandoned: *a derelict building; derelict cars rusting in a field; his derelict condition.* —n. one that is abandoned, as a ship at sea or a vagrant cast out by society.

der.e.lic.tion (der.uh.LIC.shun) n. an abandoning or a neglecting, as of duty.

de.ride (di.RIDE) v. **-rides, -rid.ed, -rid.ing** laugh at with contempt; ridicule.

de ri.gueur (duh.ree.GUR) adjp. required by fashion or social convention: *Black tie is de rigueur for men at a formal dinner dance.*

de.ri.sion (di.RIZH.un) n. a deriding or ridiculing: *an object of derision; He aroused* or *provoked derision wherever he went selling snake oil.* —**de.ri.sive** (di.RYE.siv) adj.: *derisive jeers, laughter, nicknames, publicity, references, remarks; He's derisive about democracy in the banana republics; a derisive* (= trivial or laughable) *sum.* Also **de.ri.so.ry** (-suh.ree) adj.: *a derisory amount, figure; a derisory $9.75.* —**de.ri.sive.ly** adv.

de.riv.a.tive (di.RIV.uh.tiv) adj. derived from another source: *derivative work; His poetry is very derivative* (= based on or borrowed from other sources). —n. something derived: *The word "Classify" is a derivative of "class"; Polystyrene and such plastics are made from petroleum derivatives such as ethylene.*

de.rive (di.RIVE) v. **-rives, -rived, -riv.ing 1** receive from a source: *He derives great satisfaction from his work; "Word" is derived from Old English; a conclusion derived* (= inferred or deduced) *from wrong premises.* **2** come from a source: *Much of our vocabulary derives from Anglo-Saxon; problems deriv-*

ing from social changes. **3** trace the origin of something, esp. a word: *Etymologists derive words.* —**der.i.va.tion** (der.uh.VAY.shun) *n.*

der.ma.ti.tis (dur.muh.TYE.tis) *n.* a skin inflammation.

der.ma.tol.o.gy (dur.muh.TOL.uh.jee) *n.* a branch of medicine specializing in the disorders of the skin; **der.ma.tol.o.gist** *n.*

der.o.gate (DER.uh.gate) *v.* **-gates, -gat.ed, -gat.ing** **1** take away: *not wanting to derogate from the colonel's authority.* **2** disparage. —**der.o.ga.tion** (-GAY.shun) *n.*

de.rog.a.to.ry (di.ROG.uh.tor.ee) *adj.* disparaging or insulting: *a derogatory remark; The remark was deleted as derogatory of* or *to* or *toward a section of the community.* —**de.rog.a.to.ri.ly** *adv.*

der.rick (DER.ic) *n.* a hoisting apparatus that can be assembled or disassembled on a work site.

der.ri.ère (der.ee.AIR) *n.* the buttocks.

der.ring-do (der.ing.DOO) *n.* bold deeds; reckless bravery: *a desperate deed of derring-do.*

der.rin.ger (DER.in.jur) *n.* a large-caliber, short-barreled pistol.

der.vish (DUR.vish) *n.* a member of any of the ascetic Islamic religious orders, some of which do a whirling dance.

de.sal.i.nate (dee.SAL.uh.nate) *v.* **-nates, -nat.ed, -nat.ing** same as DE-SALT. Also **de.sal.i.nize** *v.* **-niz.es, -nized, -niz.ing.** —**de.sal.i.na.tion** (-NAY.shun) *n.*: *the desalination of sea water for irrigation.*

de.salt (dee.SAWLT) *v.* remove salts from sea water, footwear, etc.

des.cant (DES.cant) *n.* a sung or played harmony to a simple melody; any song: *the nightingale's amorous descant.* —*v.* (des.CANT) sing; also, comment at length: *a physicist descanting on the theme of solar energy.*

de.scend (di.SEND) *v.* **1** move or extend downward; go down on or along something: *a hillside descending to the sea; We descend a staircase to reach the basement.* **2** sink in character or stoop: *She would never descend to name-calling and such tactics.* **3** come from ancestors: *He is descended from a royal family; Are the higher animals descended from lower forms of life? an heirloom that has descended* (= been passed by inheritance) *in the Ito family.* **4** attack suddenly; swoop or pounce: *The police descended on the convict's hideout.*

de.scend.ant (di.SEN.dunt) *n.* one in relation to one's grandparents or ancestors: *children, grandchildren, and later descendants; direct* (= lineal) *and collateral descendants; The Prince of Wales is a descendant of the family of Windsor.*

de.scent (di.SENT) *n.* **1** a descending: *The plane made a rapid descent from 15,000 ft; the descent* (= attack) *of pirates on the coast.* **2** a downward slope: *a gradual, not steep descent.* **3** ancestry or lineage: *Pedro is of Mexican descent; to trace one's descent.*

de.scram.ble (dee.SCRAM.bul) *v.* **-bles, -bled, -bling** same as UNSCRAMBLE.

de.scribe (di.SCRIBE) *v.* **-scribes, -scribed, -scrib.ing** **1** write or tell about a person or thing, esp. with graphic detail: *Describe the house you live in; Please describe it to us; describe it in detail, minutely, vividly; Describe how it is kept; Would you describe it as palatial?* **2** outline: *a set of compasses used to describe an arc.* —**de.scri.ba.ble** (-buh.bul) *adj.*

de.scrip.tion (di.SCRIP.shun) *n.* **1** a describing, esp. a picture of a person or thing in words: *a job description; to give, provide a description of the scene; an accurate, blow-by-blow, detailed, exact, lively, matter-of-fact, objective, picturesque, vivid description; a suspect who fits the description; who answers to the description given by the police; It's so grand that it beggars* or *defies description* (= so grand it cannot be described in words). **2** kind or type: *They carry merchandise of every description; a swindler of the worst description; Someone of that description cannot be trusted.* —**de.scrip.tive** (-tiv) *adj.*: *descriptive accounts, language, writing.* —**de.scrip.tive.ly** *adv.*

de.scrip.tor (di.SCRIP.tur) *n.* an index term in an information retrieval system.

de.scry (di.SCRY) *v.* **-scries, -scried, -scry.ing** catch sight of something: *The lookout descried a ship on the horizon.*

des.e.crate (DES.uh.crate) *v.* **-crates, -crat.ed, -crat.ing** violate a holy place; treat sacrilegiously. —**des.e.cra.tion** (-CRAY.shun) *n.*

de.seg.re.gate (dee.SEG.ruh.gate) *v.* **-gates, -gat.ed, -gat.ing** eliminate racial segregation in a place: *to desegregate beaches, churches, schools.* —**de.seg.re.ga.tion** (-GAY.shun) *n.*

de.se.lect (dee.si.LECT) *v.* dismiss while still in training: *a deselected Peace Corps volunteer.*

de.sen.si.tize (dee.SEN.suh.tize) *v.* **-tiz.es, -tized, -tiz.ing** make insensitive or less sensitive to irritants such as allergens, suffering, etc.

—**de.sen.si.ti.za.tion** (-tuh.ZAY.shun, -tye-) n.

¹**des.ert** (DEZ.urt) n. a region barren of plant life because of limited rainfall: *an arid, trackless desert; the Sahara Desert;* **adj**a.: *desert colors, conditions, storms; a desert* (= uninhabited) *island; the desert* (= very hot) *sun*.

²**de.sert** (di.ZURT) v. leave from a place of duty without permission: *He deserted his wife and children; He deserted them to join the army; When his courage deserted him* (= failed), *he deserted* (= went over) *to the enemy*. —**deserts** n.pl. something deserved; reward or punishment: *a villain who got his just deserts*. —**de.ser.tion** (di.ZUR.shun) n.

de.ser.ti.fi.ca.tion (di.ZUR.tuh.fi.CAY.shun) n. the process of a cultivated region becoming a desert because of drought and mismanagement.

de.serve (di.ZURV) v. **-serves, -served, -serv.ing** be worthy of something: *She deserved better (treatment) than that; She deserved well of them for her services; She deserved to be rewarded; He deserved what he got;* **adj**.: *a punishment that was richly, well deserved; a deserved fate; a well-deserved reputation; an allowance given to deserving candidates; to those who are deserving of help*. —**de.ser.ved.ly** (-vid.lee) adv.

des.ic.cate (DES.i.cate) v. **-ic.cates, -ic.cat.ed, -ic.cat.ing** dry, esp. to preserve: *desiccated vegetables*. —**des.ic.ca.tor** n. —**des.ic.ca.tion** (-CAY.shun) n.

de.sid.er.a.ta (di.SID.uh.RAY.tuh) n.pl. things that are needed and longed for, as in a given situation. —**de.sid.er.a.tum** sing.

de.sign (di.ZINE) n. **1** the combination of color, shape, parts, etc. in something: *We need a mural with good design for the reception area;* **adj**a.: *design elements; a design scheme*. **2** also **design.ing**, the art of making something: *a school of fashion design*. **3** a plan, blueprint, outline, or pattern: *designs for a new school; a dress with a paisley design; a design engineer*. **4** an intention, esp. evil: *He had sinister designs against or on or upon his nephew's inheritance; His answers were vague by design* (= deliberately). —v. **1** intend or plan; **adj**.: *a job designed to lead to promotion; designed as a stepping stone to a career; designed for ambitious youth*. **2** make a design for something: *They design airplanes for the military*.

des.ig.nate (DEZ.ig.nate) v. **-nates, -nat.ed, -nat.ing 1** specify or indicate: *The region was designated (as) a disaster area to qualify for aid; Striking is not allowed in services designated as essential; powers designated as being under state jurisdiction;* **adj**.: *a designated area, slot, task*. **2** select for an office, task, etc.: *They designated her to lead the delegation;* **adj**a.: *a designated successor; The designated driver* (of a group stays sober for driving the group back after drinks); *A designated hitter* bats for the pitcher during a baseball game. —**adj**. [follows its noun] picked out but not yet holding office: *The president designate takes office on January 1*. —**des.ig.na.tion** (-NAY.shun) n.

de.sign.er (di.ZYE.nur) n. one who designs: *a fashion designer; an interior designer*. —**adj**. made by a noted designer; hence, high-quality: *designer clothes with designer labels; designer fashions, jeans, wallpaper; a genius with designer brains*.

designer drug n. a synthesized narcotic such as crack that is more potent than the natural variety.

designing (di.ZYE.ning) **1** n. the art or work of creating designs: *kitchen designing;* **adj**a.: *a designing career, service*. **2** adj. cunningly scheming: *a designing fellow, woman*.

de.sire (di.ZIRE) v. **-sires, -sired, -sir.ing 1** wish or long for something: *to desire to be happy; Everyone desires health, wealth, and happiness*. **2** request: *The Queen desired an audience with the Pope*. —n. a desiring or something desired: *He looked at the car with great desire; to arouse, create, express, feel, satisfy, stifle, suppress, whet a desire; an ardent, blind, burning, fervent, growing, intense, keen, passionate, strong, unfulfilled desire; the desire for fame and glory; a desire to excel in everything*. —**de.sir.a.ble** adj.; **de.sir.a.bly** adv. —**de.sir.a.bil.i.ty** (-ruh.BIL.i.tee) n.

de.sir.ous (di.ZIRE.us) adjp. desiring or wishing: *A mother is desirous of her children's good; She is desirous that they (should) do well in life*.

de.sist (di.ZIST) v. Formal. stop: *a court order to cease and desist (from an illegal action)*.

desk n. **1** a flat-topped piece of furniture for writing: *Be at your desk at 9; He cleared his desk and quit his job; Files sat on his desk;* **adj**.: *a desk calendar, diary, drawer, job; a single-volume desk dictionary; A telephone doesn't occupy much desk space*. **2** a counter, stand, etc. for doing business: *The receptionist sits at the reception desk; Hotel guests reg-*

ister at the front desk; *The desk clerk will help you.* **3** a department: *a newspaper's city desk; a library's circulation desk; the reference desk.*

desk-top or **desk.top** *adj*. suitable for use on a desk: *a desk-top calculator, computer, copier;* **Desk-top publishing** *uses a microcomputer and laser printer.* —*n*. **1** the top of a desk. **2** a desk-top computer.

des.o.late (DES.uh.lit) *adj.* **1** not fit for habitation, esp. barren, deserted, ravaged, etc.: *a desolate Arctic plain; the desolate desert landscape.* **2** cheerless; lonely; abandoned: *a desolate existence, life, old dwelling.* —*v*. (-late) **-lates, -lat.ed, -lat.ing** make desolate: *farmlands desolated by a tornado.*
—**des.o.la.tion** (-LAY.shun) *n.*: *The fire left desolation in its wake; the complete, utter desolation of the landscape; The loner lived in desolation and misery.*

de.spair (di.SPAIR) *v.* lose all hope: *Don't despair; Columbus never despaired of reaching India.* —*n.* loss of hope: *He struggled hard to overcome despair; He gave up his efforts in despair; He jumped into a lake out of sheer, total, utter despair; The earthquake was the despair* (= cause of the feeling of loss) *of all his hopes.*

des.patch (di.SPATCH) same as DISPATCH.

des.per.a.do (des.puh.RAH.doh) *n., pl.* **-dos** or **-does** a reckless criminal or outlaw.

des.per.ate (DES.puh.rit) *adj.* ready to do anything because of despair: *a desperate criminal; a last desperate effort, move; a desperate crime (committed in despair); The refugees are desperate* (= in great need) *for help; They are in desperate* (= grave) *need.* —**des.per.ate.ly** *adv.;* **des.per.ate.ness** *n.*

des.per.a.tion (des.puh.RAY.shun) *n.* the state of being desperate: *He acted out of desperation; He jumped into the sea in desperation; She led a life of quiet desperation unable to achieve her ambition; a national policy directed against hunger, poverty, desperation, and chaos.*

des.pi.ca.ble (di.SPIC.uh.bul, DES.pic.uh.bul) *adj.* that deserves to be despised; utterly worthless and contemptible: *a despicable act, crime, tyrant; despicable behavior.* —**des.pi.ca.bly** *adv.*

de.spise (di.SPIZE) *v.* **-spis.es, -spised, -spis.ing** have utter contempt or disdain for a person or thing: *People are despised for their cowardice;* **adj.**: *Lepers were once the most* **despised** *and rejected of people; a despised dictator.*

de.spite (di.SPITE) *prep.* in spite of: *The child got hurt despite attempts to protect him;* [old use] *She stayed out late* **in despite of** *her parents' warning.*

de.spoil (di.SPOIL) *v.* rob or plunder: *She fell into evil company and was soon despoiled of her innocence.*

de.spo.li.a.tion (di.SPOH.lee.AY.shun) *n.* robbery or pillaging: *Bandits were responsible for the despoliation of the village.*

de.spond (di.SPOND) *v.* lose hope and lose heart. —*n.*: *the slough of despond.*

de.spond.en.cy (di.SPON.dun.see) *n.* a feeling of utter hopelessness and discouragement: *sheer despondency.*

de.spond.ent (di.SPON.dunt) *adj.* sad and hopeless: *a despondent lover; quite despondent about* or *over his rejection.*

des.pot (DES.pot, DESP.ut) *n.* a ruler with unlimited power, often cruel and unjust; tyrant: *He owned the company and ruled over it like a despot.*
—**des.pot.ic** (des.POT.ic) *adj.;*
des.pot.i.cal.ly *adv.* —**des.pot.ism** (DES.puh.tiz.um) *n.*

des.sert (di.ZURT) *n.* a course of fruit, pie, sweet foods, etc. at the end of a meal.

de.sta.bi.lize (dee.STAY.buh.lize) *v.* **-liz.es, -lized, -liz.ing** make less or not stable: *The secret service was accused of attempting to destabilize foreign governments.*

des.ti.na.tion (des.tuh.NAY.shun) *n.* the place something or someone is going to: *your place of departure and destination; a traveler's (city or country of) destination; to arrive at a destination; to reach one's final, ultimate destination; the destination of a letter, parcel, ship.*

des.tine (DES.tin) *v.* **-tines, -tined, -tin.ing** have as destination, goal, or purpose: *Our mortality destines us for death.*

destined *adjp.* bound: *Some of us are destined to be great; travelers destined for the Bahamas; students destined to enter college* or *destined for college; Princess Elizabeth was* **destined to** (= later did) *become queen.*

des.ti.ny (DES.tuh.nee) *n.* **-tin.ies** a course or end that seems determined in advance, esp. something great or noble: *to achieve, decide, fulfill, shape one's destiny; It was her destiny to win a Nobel Prize.*

des.ti.tute (*rhyme:* substitute) **1** *adj.* needy or penniless: *He died leaving his family destitute.* **2** *adjp.* devoid: *a boulevard destitute of trees.*

des.ti.tu.tion (des.tuh.TUE.shun) *n.* extreme poverty: *He lived in destitution all* his life; chronic, total destitution..

de.stroy (di.STROY) *v.* demolish or undo: *a hotel destroyed by fire; a king destroyed by pride; His efforts at reform were destroyed by the Depression; Rabid dogs are routinely destroyed* (= killed).

de.stroy.er (di.STROY.ur) *n.* **1** one that destroys. **2** a small, fast warship.

de.struct (di.STRUCT) *n.* the deliberate destroying of a missile in flight; *adja.: a destruct sequence, signal.*
—**de.struct.i.bil.i.ty** (-tuh.BIL.i.tee) *n.*
—**de.struct.i.ble** (-tuh.bul) *adj.*
—**de.struc.tor** *n.*

de.struct.ion (di.STRUC.shun) *n.* a destroying: *the complete, total destruction caused by a tornado; the willful and wanton destruction of property carried out by vandals; The preacher called down death and destruction on sinners; Drugs proved to be his destruction* (= cause or means of destruction).

de.struct.ive (di.STRUC.tiv) *adj.* that destroys: *a very destructive storm; destructive criticism; Criticism can be destructive of creativity; his destructive tendencies.*

des.ue.tude (DES.wi.tude) *n.* disuse: *Legislatures repeal laws that fall into desuetude.*

des.ul.to.ry (DES.ul.tor.ee) *adj.* not thorough or well organized; fitful or disconnected: *He carries out his duties in a desultory fashion, manner, way; desultory efforts, research.*

de.tach (di.TACH) *v.* separate or disengage: *to detach a coupon from the book; A number of men were detached and sent to scout ahead.*

detached (di.TACHT) *adj.* **1** not connected; separate: *A detached house stands by itself; A semi-detached house shares a wall with another house; a detached garage.* **2** impartial: *a detached manner, observer, tone, view; She seems detached and disinterested.*
—**de.tach.ed.ly** (-id.lee) *adv.*

de.tach.ment (di.TACH.munt) *n.* **1** lack of prejudice; impartiality. **2** a body of people, ships, etc. detached for special service: *an RCMP detachment.*

de.tail (di.TAIL, DEE.tail) *n.* **1** a particular or small item or part; also, such particulars in general or their treatment: *graphic, gruesome, lurid, sordid, microscopic, minor, minute, technical details; to treat a subject in great detail; a painter devoting great attention to detail; I won't bore you with the details of what happened; I will fill in or furnish the details later; I won't* **go into** *details or any detail; She has given an account of the in-* cident **in (great) detail.** **2** a group assigned to a specific task or duty: *a fatigue detail (on fatigue duty); a platoon on guard detail; to form a work detail.*
—*v.* **1** list or tell in detail: *to detail the new taxes.* **2** detach for a specific task; assign: *Two corporals were detailed to guard the prisoner; a unit detailed for a duty.* —**de.tailed** *adj.*: *a detailed account, analysis, plan, proposal, report, study.*

de.tain (di.TAIN) *v.* **1** hold back; delay: *We were detained at customs for two hours.* **2** keep in custody.

de.tain.ee (di.TAY.nee) *n.* a person in detention; prisoner: *political detainees.*

de.tect (di.TECT) *v.* find out or discover: *a machine to detect the presence of radioactive matter; She detected three adding errors in the bill.* —**de.tec.ta.ble** or **de.tec.ti.ble** (di.TEC.tuh.bul) *adj.*
—**de.tec.tion** (-shun) *n.*

de.tec.tive (di.TEC.tiv) *n.* one who investigates crimes, finds criminals, etc.: *private detectives; a police detective;* *adja.: a detective agency, novel, story; detective fiction.*

de.tec.tor (di.TEC.tur) *n.* one that detects: *traffic signals triggered by detectors placed on the roadway; metal, mine, smoke detectors; to take a lie-detector test.*

dé.tente or **de.tente** (day.TAHNT) *n.* a lessening of strain or hostility, as between nations: *the policy of détente.*

de.ten.tion (di.TEN.shun) *n.* a detaining: *He was held in detention as a preventive measure; a house of detention* (= jail); *a* **detention center** *or* **detention home** *(for young offenders).*

de.ter (di.TUR) *v.* **-ters, -terred, -ter.ring** hinder or discourage: *Does the threat of counter-attack deter nations from building nuclear bombs? to deter accidents, aggression, drug use, fraud, war.*
—**de.ter.ment** *n.*

de.ter.gent (di.TUR.junt) *n.* a cleaning agent, esp. a synthetic soap substitute: *dish, laundry, liquid detergents;* *adja.: the detergent action of gasoline additives in cleaning off engine deposits caused by the burning of fuel; a detergent powder, rash, shampoo.*

do.to.ri.o.rato (di.TEER.ee.uh.rate) *v.* **-rates, -rat.ed, -rat.ing** make or become weaker, worse, etc.: *Polio causes muscles to deteriorate; The strike situation is deteriorating.* —**de.te.ri.o.ra.tion** (-RAY.shun) *n.*

de.ter.mi.nant (di.TUR.muh.nunt) *n. Formal.* something that determines: *Interactions between sea and air are the main determinants of weather conditions; a determinant factor.*

de.ter.mi.nate (di.TUR.muh.nit) *adj.* having definite limits: *a determinate number, as "3," not a variable, as "x."* —**de.ter.mi.na.cy** *n.*

de.ter.mi.na.tion (di.TUR.muh.NAY.shun) *n.* **1** a determining or being determined: *the determination of the speed of light; The court took several days to come to a final determination of* (= decision on) *the case.* **2** firm intention: *She showed dogged, firm, iron, unyielding determination in prosecuting the case; his determination to succeed.*

de.ter.mine (di.TUR.min) *v.* **-mines, -mined, -min.ing** **1** decide: *He determined to change his life;* **adj.**: *He is quite* ***determined*** (= decided or resolved) *to change his life; a very determined* (= resolute) *approach, attempt, effort, look, teenager.* **2** fix beforehand; cause: *Is intelligence determined solely by heredity?* **3** settle: *The courts determine questions of guilt and innocence; They determine who is guilty and who is innocent.* **4** ascertain or find out: *to determine the position of a ship by radar; a committee to determine next year's budget needs; to determine where the next Olympics will be held; to determine that a child is in need of protection; an investigation to determine whether a charge should be laid.*

de.ter.min.ism (di.TUR.muh.niz.um) *n.* the doctrine that all actions are controlled by prior causes not subject to human will; **de.ter.min.ist** *n. & adj.*

de.ter.rence (di.TUR.unce, di.TER-) *n.* the act or a means of deterring. —**de.ter.rent** *n.* something that deters: *a nuclear deterrent; the ultimate deterrent; The H-bomb is a great deterrent to or against another world war;* **adj.**: *a deterrent effect, impact, measure, value, weapon.*

de.test (di.TEST) *v.* hate intensely; abhor: *She detests any kind of dishonesty.* —**de.test.a.ble** (-uh.bul) *adj.*

de.throne (di.THRONE) *v.* **-thrones, -throned, -thron.ing** remove from a throne or other position of power; **adja.**: *a dethroned emperor.* —**de.throne.ment** *n.*

det.o.nate (DET.uh.nate) *v.* **-nates, -nat.ed, -nat.ing** (cause to) explode: *to detonate a bomb, charge, explosive device; to detonate dynamite; The bomb was timed to detonate at midnight.* —**det.o.na.tion** (-NAY.shun) *n.* —**det.o.na.tor** (-nay.tur) *n.*: *A detonator is used to set off a charge.*

de.tour (DEE.toor) *n.* **1** a roundabout or secondary route used when the main road is closed: *The police set up a detour around the troubled area.* **2** any roundabout way. —*v.* make a detour: *to detour around bureaucratic obstacles.*

de.tox (DEE.tox) *v. Informal* [short form] detoxify: *to detox an addict.* —*n.* detoxification: *Some alcoholics go through detox many times;* **adj.**: *a detox center for sobering up; detox clinics, programs.*

de.tox.i.fy (dee.TOX.uh.fye) *v.* **-fies, -fied, -fy.ing** remove a poison or its effect from a body, system, etc. —**de.tox.i.fi.ca.tion** (-uh.fuh.CAY.shun) *n.*

de.tract (di.TRACT) *v.* take away; diminish: *a scar that detracts from his good looks.* —**de.trac.tion** *n.;* **de.trac.tor** (-tur) *n.*

de.train (dee.TRAIN) *v.* get or put off a train: *Everyone detrained for the river crossing.* —**de.train.ment** *n.*

det.ri.ment (DET.ruh.munt) *n.* harm or damage: *He stayed in his high-pressure job to the detriment of his health.* —**det.ri.men.tal** (-MEN.tul) *adj.*: *a policy detrimental to our interests; a detrimental effect; Is jogging more beneficial than detrimental?*

de.tri.tus (di.TRY.tus) *n.* material remaining after disintegration or breakdown: *a room littered with pop bottles, plastic cups, and such detritus of a late-night party.*

deuce (DEWCE) *n.* **1** a two in the game of cards or dice. **2** a tie score in tennis. **3** *Informal* [used as intensifier] devil: *What* ***the deuce*** *are you doing here?*

deu.te.ri.um (dew.TEER.ee.um) *n.* a heavy isotope of hydrogen, used in atomic reactors and bombs.

deut.sche mark (DOY.chuh-) *n.* the basic unit of money in West Germany, equal to 100 pfennigs. Also **deut.sche.mark.**

de.val.ue (dee.VAL.yoo) *v.* **-values, -valued, -valu.ing** reduce the value of currency in international trade: *to devalue the dollar.* —**de.val.u.a.tion** (-yoo.AY.shun) *n.*

dev.as.tate (DEV.uh.state) *v.* **-tates, -tat.ed, -tat.ing** **1** destroy totally; lay waste: *The invading army devastated the town.* **2** overwhelm: *We were devastated by the news of the tragedy.* —**devastating** *adj.* very destructive, effective, stunning, etc.: *a devastating analysis, argument, beauty, bore, dinner, fire, flood, tornado, war; her devastating humor, wit.* —**dev.as.ta.tion** (-uh.STAY.shun) *n.*: *Flood and earthquakes caused complete, total devastation* (= destruction).

de.vel.op (di.VEL.up) *v.* **1** grow or cause to grow larger, better, more mature, more complex, etc.: *Caterpillars develop from eggs; They develop into adult butterflies; Reading develops the mind; It takes time for flavor to develop after cooking; Trouble sometimes develops after the honeymoon; to develop a business, plan, policy, relationship, strategy, theory; Farmland is being developed* (= built on) *for new housing and industry; adj.: a fully developed plan; prosperous and (industrially) developed nations like Canada and the U.S.; a child's developing body; aid to developing* (= less-developed) *countries*. **2** make or become visible, active, usable, clear, etc.: *Film is developed by treating it with chemicals (so that the picture can be seen)*. **3** acquire gradually: *She developed an interest in politics; to develop diabetes, cancer, diseases, symptoms, tumors; to develop a reputation for being tough*. —**de.vel.op.er** *n.: Real-estate developers buy land to build on and sell; database, product, software developers*.
de.vel.op.ment (di.VEL.up.munt) *n.* a developing or something developed, esp. an occurrence or new state of affairs: *the development of the butterfly through its various stages; A dwarf is a case of arrested development; recent developments in international trade; a new housing development* (= group of buildings). —**de.vel.op.men.tal** (-up.MEN.tul) *adj*.
de.vi.ant (DEE.vee.unt) *adj.* that deviates: *Only a minority of physicians are deviant in regard to medical ethics; deviant behavior such as vandalism; n.: to be intolerant of the deviant* (= deviant people); *a sexual deviant; deviants and criminals*. —**de.vi.ance** (-unce) *n*.
de.vi.ate (DEE.vee.ate) *v.* **-ates, -at.ed, -at.ing** turn away, esp. from a standard or norm: *to deviate from what is customary, from a plan, from the truth; His later beliefs deviate sharply from his earlier views*. —**de.vi.a.tion** (-AY.shun) *n*.
de.vice (di.VICE) *n.* **1** something devised, as a scheme or plan: *a clever device for fooling the competition; a mnemonic device for remembering a list of names*. **2** a usu. mechanical invention: *a labor-saving device like the electric toothbrush; A bug is a listening device; a new device for catching mice; a useless intra-uterine device (for birth control)*. **3** a design or emblem, as on a coat of arms: *a heraldic device*. —**leave to one's own devices** allow one to do what one will or can.

dev.il (DEV.ul) *n.* **1** a demon: *That's the devil in me acting up; the economic devil of rampant inflation;* [as a mild oath] *It's a devil of a* (= extremely bad instance of *a*) *job to fix that car; What the devil did he mean?* **2** a wicked or reckless person: *a she devil*. **3** *Informal.* a person in regard to luck: *a lucky devil; the poor devil*. **4** a printer's helper: *pranks of the printer's devil* (= printing errors). —**the Devil** the supreme evil spirit. —**between the devil and the deep (blue) sea** in an unpleasant dilemma. —**the devil to pay** much trouble. —**give the devil his due** be fair or honest about a bad or disliked person. —**go to the devil 1** get lost! **2** be ruined, esp. morally. —**play the devil with** upset or ruin. —**speak of the devil (and he appears)** [said when one who is being referred to comes along]. —*v.* **-ils, -iled, -il.ing 1** badger or torment. **2** prepare, esp. ham or eggs, with hot seasonings: *deviled eggs*. Also **dev.illed, dev.il.ling** *Cdn*.
dev.il.ish (DEV.uh.lish) **1** *adj.* like the devil, esp. mischievous. **2** *adv. Informal.* extremely: *He was devilish lucky*. —**dev.il.ment** or **dev.il.ry** (-ree), **-ries** or **dev.il.try** (-tree), **-tries** *n.* mischief: *street kids who are always up to some deviltry or other*.
devil-may-care *adja.* not caring; reckless: *a devil-may-care attitude, flying ace, person*.
devil's advocate *n.* one who presents the opposite side of an argument: *to play the devil's advocate*.
de.vi.ous (DEE.vee.us) *adj.* **1** not straight: *The stream followed a devious path through the wood*. **2** underhand; not straightforward: *He made his fortune by devious means*.
de.vise (di.VIZE) *v.* **-vis.es, -vised, -vis.ing 1** contrive or invent: *We devised a siphon to bring water into the house*. **2** plot: *They devised the murder of the king*.
de.vi.tal.ize (dee.VYE.tul.ize) *v.* **-iz.es, -ized, -iz.ing** lessen or destroy the vitality of something.
de.void (di.VOID) *adj.* having none of or totally without something: *a tyrant devoid of any human feelings*.
de.voirs (duv.WARS) *n.pl.* respects or courtesies: *to pay devoirs to one's lord*.
dev.o.lu.tion (dev.uh.LOO.shun) *n.* a devolving: *They agitated for the devolution of power from London to a Scottish parliament*.
de.volve (di.VOLV) *v.* **-volves, -volved, -volv.ing** pass on authority, power,

etc. to someone else: *The new responsibilities devolved on or upon the oldest son.*

De.vo.ni.an (di.VOH.nee.un) *n. & adj.* (of) a geological period of the Paleozoic era, beginning about 405 million years ago.

de.vote (di.VOTE) *v.* **-votes, -vot.ed, -vot.ing** set apart or dedicate for a special purpose: *to devote one's life to politics; He devotes a lot of his spare time to his hobby; She has devoted herself entirely to the service of her community.*

devoted (di.VOH.tid) *adj.* very dedicated, faithful, or loving: *a devoted companion, helper, husband, mother, wife; a devoted student of music; Two parents who are completely, entirely devoted to their family.*

dev.o.tee (dev.uh.TEE) *n.* a devoted worshiper, follower, supporter, etc.: *the devotees of Zeus; a devotee of baseball.*

de.vo.tion (di.VOH.shun) *n.* **1** a devoting or being devoted, esp. great love or loyalty: *a soldier's unswerving devotion to duty; a child's blind devotion to its parents; a dog's slavish devotion to its master; her absolute, complete, deep, thorough, undying devotion to the cause of freedom.* **2** religious or spiritual dedication: *She practices yoga with great devotion; It's better not to disturb her when she is at her* **devotions** (= prayers or worship). —**de.vo.tion.al** *adj.*: *devotional music (used in a religious service).*

de.vour (di.VOUR, *rhyme:* OUR) *v.* **1** eat greedily: *The monster ravenously devoured everything in sight.* **2** consume: *a house devoured by flames; to be devoured by curiosity, hunger, jealousy.* **3** read, look at, listen to, etc. greedily: *He devours whodunits at the rate of two a week.*

de.vout (di.VOWT) *adj.* **1** very pious: *a devout follower of the Buddha; a devout attitude, supporter, worshiper; The devout (people) were assembled in the temple.* **2** earnest or heartfelt: *She spent her last moments in devout prayer; It's my devout wish that you will succeed.* —**de.vout.ly** *adv.;* **de.vout.ness** *n.*

dew *n.* moisture that condenses on cool bodies at night.

dew.ber.ry (DEW.ber.ee) *n.* **-ber.ries** a ground-trailing blackberry.

dew.claw *n.* a toe or hoof, as in deer, dogs, pigs, etc., which does not touch the ground.

dew.drop *n.* a drop of dew.

dew.lap *n.* a flap of loose skin hanging from an animal's throat.

dew point *n.* the air temperature at which dew forms.

dew worm *n. Regional.* the common earthworm.

dew.y (DEW.ee) *adj.* **dew.i.er, -i.est** wet (as) with dew: *a dewy freshness, glow, rose; Dora's dewy eyes; her* **dewy-eyed** (= naive or sentimental) *innocence.*

dex.ter.i.ty (dex.TER.i.tee) *n.* **1** skill in using the hands: *Some manual dexterity is required to thread a needle.* **2** clever skill: *Lawyers have the dexterity to get a witness to say what they want to hear.*

dex.ter.ous (DEX.tuh.rus) *adj.* **1** skillful with one's hands: *You need dexterous fingers to untie a knot; Sam is very dexterous with knitting needles.* **2** mentally quick or clever: *a dexterous lawyer, manager.* **3** done with dexterity: *a dexterous high-wire act; her dexterous handling of people.*

dex.trin *n.* a sticky substance made from starch and used in glues, for sizing, and in syrups. Also **dex.trine** (-trin).

dex.trose (DEX.trose, *rhyme:* dose) *n.* a pure form of sugar found in grapes, honey, and animal body fluids and used in jams, canning fruits, and in candy.

dex.trous (DEX.trus) same as DEXTEROUS.

dhar.ma (DAR.muh, DUR-) *n.* in Eastern religions, moral or religious law; also, truth.

dhow (DOW) *n.* a single-masted, lateen-rigged Arabian ship.

di.a.be.tes (dye.uh.BEE.teez, -tus) *n.* a disease in which a deficiency of natural insulin causes excess sugar in the blood and urine. —**di.a.bet.ic** (dye.uh.BET.ic) *n.*: *He's a diabetic; adj.*: *a diabetic patient.*

di.a.bol.ic (dye.uh.BOL.ic) or **di.a.bol.i.cal** (-i.cul) *adj.* devilish; evil or cruel: *a diabolical plan to kidnap a child.*

di.a.crit.ic (dye.uh.CRIT.ic) or **di.a.crit.i.cal** (-i.cul) *adj.* indicating a distinction: *a* **diacritical mark** (= diacritic). —*n.* a mark used with a letter, as in â, é, ö, or ç, to show a modification of its sound.

di.a.dem (DYE.uh.dem) *n.* a crown, wreath, etc. worn by a sovereign.

di.aer.e.sis same as DIERESIS.

di.ag.nose (dye.ug.NOSE, *rhyme:* DOSE) *v.* **-nos.es, -nosed, -nos.ing** identify, as a disease, from symptoms: *The doctor diagnosed measles; The mechanic diagnosed the problem as a clogged carburetor.*

di.ag.no.sis (dye.ug.NOH.sis) *n., pl.* **-ses** (-seez) the identification of a disease, problem, the nature of something, etc.: *The doctor's diagnosis was measles; A*

second opinion confirmed the diagnosis that it was a case of measles; The diagnosis of measles proved to be correct; a diagnosis of current economic problems.
—**di.a.gnos.tic** (-NOS.tic) *adja.* having to do with diagnosis: *a diagnostic test; diagnostic equipment, skills.*
—**di.a.gnos.ti.cian** (-nos.TISH.un) *n.*
di.ag.o.nal (dye.AG.uh.nul) *adj.* **1** running from one corner to the opposite in a figure of at least four sides: *diagonal angles.* **2** oblique: *a diagonal line, slash, slice, stripe, weave.* —*n.* **1** a diagonal line, as a virgule. **2** a cloth with a slanting weave; twill. —**di.ag.o.nal.ly** *adv.*
di.a.gram (DYE.uh.gram) *n.* a sketch or line drawing used to show the structure, functioning, etc. of something. —*v.* **-grams, -gramed** or **-grammed, -gram.ing** or **-grammed** make a diagram of something: *The statistician diagramed the results of his survey.*
—**di.a.gram.mat.ic** (-gruh.MAT.ic) *adj.*
di.al (DYE.ul) *n.* **1** a circular surface used to indicate measures of time, temperature, etc.: *the dial of a wrist watch; a barometer dial.* **2** a disk that can be turned to select, adjust, etc. an apparatus: *Tune in to a radio station or TV channel by using a knoblike dial; Modern telephones have push-buttons instead of a dial for making calls.* —*v.* **-als, -aled, -al.ing** use a dial; also, operate, select, etc. by using a dial: *She dialed the correct code to open the safe; We dial 411 for information; We can dial many places around the globe direct* (= without operator assistance). Also **di.alled, di.al.ling** *Cdn.* —**di.al.er** *n.*
dial-a- *comb.form* [used to indicate a service available by telephone]: *dial-a-bus, -date, -doctor, -joke, -pizza, -prayer, -thought.*
di.a.lect (DYE.uh.lect) *n.* a regionally or socially distinct form of a language, esp. if nonstandard: *In Southern Georgian dialect, "I wouldn't" becomes "Ah woon."* —**di.a.lec.tal** (-LEC.tul) *adj.*
di.a.lec.tic (dye.uh.LEC.tic) *n.* reasoned discussion; logic: *the dialectic of capitalism.* *adj.* also **dialectical**: *dialectical materialism.*
di.a.logue or **di.a.log** (DYE.uh.log) *n.* **1** a conversation; hence, a literary work representing a conversation or the conversational element in a literary work: *the Socratic dialogues of Plato; a play with a fast-paced dialogue.* **2** constructive discussion: *the ongoing dialogue between Protestants and Catholics; efforts to have a meaningful dialogue with the militants.* —*v.* discuss in order to exchange opinions and reach a consensus: *World leaders dialogue at a summit meeting.*

dialog box *n.* a window on a computer screen to help a user make menu selections, as in word processing.

dial tone *n.* the buzzing sound indicating that a telephone line is open for use.

di.al.y.sis (dye.AL.uh.sis) *n., pl.* **-ses** (-seez) the separation of different substances in a solution by passing it across a semipermeable membrane, as is done to cleanse the blood in an artificial-kidney machine, or "dialysis machine."

di.am.e.ter (dye.AM.uh.tur) *n.* the greatest width of a figure, esp. a line through the center of a circle, sphere, cylinder, etc.: *The ball is 15 inches in diameter.*

di.a.met.ri.cal (dye.uh.MET.ri.cul) *adj.* **1** of or on a diameter. **2** totally opposite: *diametrical viewpoints.* Also **di.a.met.ric.** —**di.a.met.ri.cal.ly** (-cuh.lee) *adv.*: *two ideologies diametrically opposed to each other.*

di.a.mond (DYE.mund, DYE.uh.-) *n.* **1** a gem that is a crystalline form of nearly pure carbon and the hardest naturally occurring mineral: *A diamond is cut, ground, polished, and set in a ring or crown; cut, flawless, perfect, sparkling diamonds; adja.: a diamond ear-ring, necklace, ring.* **2** a figure [♦] having four equal sides and two pairs of equal angles, one of which is acute. **3** something so shaped, as a playing card marked with this shape in red or a baseball field, esp. the infield.

diamond anniversary (or **jubilee**) *n.* a 60th or 75th year.

di.a.mond.back (DYE.mund.bak, DYE.uh.-) *n.* a large, poisonous rattlesnake of southern U.S.

diamond in the rough *n.* a good person with unpolished manners.

di.a.pa.son (dye.uh.PAIZ.un) *n.* **1** the full range of a musical instrument: *love, sorrow, anger, and the whole diapason of human emotion.* **2** the stop of an organ extending through its whole range.

di.a.per (DYE.pur, DYE.uh.pur) *n.* an absorbent cloth folded around a baby like underpants: *to change diapers; disposable diapers; a toddler clad only in his diaper; a new government still in diapers* (= in its infancy); *adja.: diaper pins, rash, service.* —*v.* put a diaper on someone: *how to diaper a baby.*

di.aph.a.nous (dye.AF.uh.nus) *adj.* of fabrics, fine and able to be seen through: *a diaphanous blouse; diaphanous material.*

di.a.pho.ret.ic (dye.uh.fuh.RET.ic) *n.* a medicine that increases perspiration; *adj.*: *a diaphoretic treatment.*

di.a.phragm (DYE.uh.fram) *n.* **1** a dome-shaped muscle separating the abdominal and chest cavities. **2** a thin disk or cone that vibrates to produce sound. **3** a disk with an opening used to regulate light entering a camera. **4** a cap placed as a contraceptive over the opening to the uterus. **—di.a.phrag.mat.ic** (-frag.MAT.ic) *adj.*

di.ar.rhe.a (dye.uh.REE.uh) *n.* too frequent and watery bowel movements: *an attack of diarrhea; No one can stand his verbal diarrhea* (Informal for talkativeness). Also **di.ar.rhoe.a.**

di.ar.y (DYE.uh.ree) *n.* **-ar.ies** a day-by-day record of one's thoughts, experiences, etc.: *Lu keeps a diary; He writes in his diary every night at bedtime; Dear Diary.* **—di.a.rist** *n.*

Di.as.po.ra (dye.AS.puh.ruh) *n.* **1** the Jews living outside Israel. **2** also **diaspora**, a scattering of a people: *Palestinians living in the diaspora in Lebanon, Kuwait, Jordan, etc.; the Irish diaspora in North America.*

di.as.tol.e (dye.AS.tuh.lee) *n.* the regularly recurring expansion of the heart following a systole. **—di.a.stol.ic** (dye.uh.STOL.ic) *adj.*: *diastolic blood pressure* (= the lower of the two numbers expressing blood pressure, as 80 in 120/80).

di.a.ther.my (DYE.uh.thur.mee) *n.* the heating of body tissues with high-frequency electricity as a medical treatment.

di.a.tom (DYE.uh.tum, -tom) *n.* a single-celled alga with a cell wall of mostly silica.

di.a.tom.ic (dye.uh.TOM.ic) *adj.* of a molecule, having two atoms.

di.a.ton.ic scale (dye.uh.TON.ic-) *n.* the standard eight-tone musical scale.

di.a.tribe (DYE.uh.tribe) *n.* a violent criticism: *a bitter diatribe against union leaders; a diatribe on gasoline prices.*

di.az.e.pam (dye.AZ.uh.pam) *n.* a mild tranquilizer.

dib *n.* a small marble. **—dibs** *pl.* **1** a game played with marbles. **2** *Informal.* money or dollars.

dib.ble (DIB.ul) *n.* a pointed gardener's tool for making holes, as for bulbs, seeds, and slips.

dice *n.pl., sing.* **dice** or **die 1** small cube(s) having one to six spots on its respective sides, used in games and gambling: *to roll, throw the dice; a roll of the dice; Beware of loaded dice!* **2** [takes *sing. v.*] a game played with dice. **—no dice** *Informal.* no luck; nothing doing. **—v. dic.es, diced, dic.ing 1** play with dice. **2** chop into small cubes: *to dice carrots.*

dic.ey (DYE.see) *adj.* **dic.i.er, -i.est** *Informal.* risky or uncertain: *His chances of getting a summer job are a bit dicey.*

di.chot.o.my (dye.COT.uh.mee) *n.* **-mies** division into two, usu. opposed parts: *the dichotomy between black and white, of theory and practice, of East versus West.* **—di.chot.o.mous** (-uh.mus) *adj.*

dick.ens (DICK.uns) *n.* [used as an intensifier] deuce; devil: *People are mad as the dickens; How the dickens did this happen? What the dickens are you doing? Where the dickens is your dad?*

dick.er *v.* bargain or haggle: *to dicker with a car dealer; to dicker for bargains; to dicker over the exchange value of the dollar.*

dick.ey (DICK.ee) *n.* **-eys 1** a detachable false shirt or blouse front worn under a jacket or sweater. **2** a little bird; also **dickey bird.** Also **dick.y,** *pl.* **dick.ies.**

di.cot.y.le.don (DYE.cot.ul.EE.dun) *n.* a plant having two cotyledons. **—di.cot.y.le.don.ous** (-LEE.dun.us) *adj.*

dic.ta (DIC.tuh) a *pl.* of DICTUM.

dic.ta.phone (DIC.tuh.fone) *n.* a machine that records speech for later transcription. **—Dictaphone** Trademark.

dic.tate (DIC.tate) *v.* **-tates, -tat.ed, -tat.ing 1** read or say something for someone else to write down: *an executive dictating a letter to his secretary.* **2** command with authority; give orders: *Don't let your kid brother dictate to you; Victors dictate the terms of surrender.* **—n.** an order or command: *the dictates of conscience.* **—dic.ta.tion** (dic.TAY.shun) *n.*: *Some give dictation and others take (down) dictation.*

dic.ta.tor (DIC.tay.tur, dic.TAY.tur) *n.* one who dictates, esp. an absolute, usu. unconstitutional ruler; tyrant: *a benevolent dictator; a military dictator;* **dic.ta.tor.ship** *n.* **—dic.ta.tor.i.al** (dic.tuh.TOR.ee.ul) *adj.*

dic.tion (DIC.shun) *n.* **1** choice of words for expressing ideas: *poor diction.* **2** the way one pronounces words: *a singer with clear diction.*

dic.tion.ar.y (DIC.shuh.nair.ee) *n.*

-ar.ies 1 a book listing words in alphabetical order, with pronunciation, meaning, and other information on them: *to compile, consult, refer to a dictionary; desk, college, etymological, pocket, pronouncing, unabridged dictionaries; Look it up in your dictionary.* 2 a book that translates words of one language into another: *a Russian-English dictionary.* 3 a reference list of words stored in a word-processing system for checking spelling.

dic.tum (DIC.tum) *n.* **-tums** or **-ta** a formal pronouncement of one's opinion.

did *pt.* of DO.

di.dac.tic (dye.DAC.tic) *adj.* intended to teach; moralizing: *didactic poetry, writers; a didactic manner, style.*
—**di.dac.ti.cism** *n.*

did.dle (DID.ul) *v.* **did.dles, did.dled, did.dling** *Informal.* 1 cheat: *People get tired of being diddled; He got diddled out of his reserved seat.* 2 waste time with trivialities: *He diddled away a month on useless research.* 3 juggle or handle carelessly: *Stop diddling with the china.*

did.dler *n. Informal.* a sex offender.

did.n't (DID.unt) did not.

di.do (DYE.doh) *n.* **-dos** or **-does** *Informal.* mischievous trick; caper.

die (DYE) *n.* 1 *sing.* OF DICE. 2 *pl.* **dies** a hard metal device used to shape material, as by stamping coins or medals, by cutting threads on a screw, or by extrusion, as wire. —**the die is cast** the step is taken and there is no going back. —*v.* **dies, died, dy.ing** 1 stop living, existing, or functioning: *People die by the sword,* **die by their own hands** (= kill themselves), *die for their beliefs,* **die in action** (= in battle); *The engine just died on us; The "right to bear arms" is a tradition that dies hard; People were* **dying off** *one by one from the plague; The passenger pigeon* **died out** (= became extinct) *years ago; Pete didn't like to retire because he wanted to* **die in harness** (= die while still actively working); *a gunfighter who* **died with his boots on** (= while still active). 2 lose power, vigor, or force: *We waited for the wind to die down or die away before sailing.* 3 *Informal.* desire very much: *Lou is dying to go to the dance; Jo still dies for a cigarette now and then.*

die.hard *n.* one who stubbornly refuses to give in or change; *adj.*: *diehard conservatives, hockey fans, leftists, traditionalists.*

di.er.e.sis (dye.ER.uh.sis) *n., pl.* **-ses** (-seez) two dots over a vowel to show that it is in a separate syllable, as in *naïve* (nah.EEV).

die.sel (DEE.zul) *n.* 1 also **diesel engine**, an internal-combustion engine without spark plugs that burns oil by the heat of air compression; *adj.*: *diesel fuel, motors, oil.* 2 a truck, locomotive, etc. driven by such an engine.

dieseling *n.* an internal combustion engine's continuing to run after the ignition is turned off.

di.et (DYE.ut) *n.* 1 one's regular food and drink: *He lives on a diet of French fries and cola; Everyone needs a balanced, nutritious diet; poor people on a starvation diet; Al is on a steady diet of cheap westerns.* 2 a special regimen: *He went on a low-fat diet to lose weight; crash, high-calorie, high-fiber, high-protein, low-fat, low-cholesterol diets; She's on a salt-free diet; adj.*: *a diet book, cola, drink, pop, soda.* 3 an assembly or parliament: *The Japanese Diet consists of two houses; The Diet of Worms, Germany, declared Martin Luther a heretic in 1521.*
—*v.* eat or drink according to rules: *He lost 10 lb by dieting for a few months.*

di.e.ta.ry (DYE.uh.tair.ee) *adj.* having to do with diet: *Jewish dietary laws;* **dietary fiber** (= roughage).

di.e.tet.ic (dye.uh.TET.ic) 1 *adj.* having to do with restricted diets: *high-priced dietetic foods; low-sodium foods from the dietetic section of the supermarket; dietetic soft drinks; dietetic use of table wines.* 2 **dietetics** *n.pl.* the study of healthy diets.

di.e.ti.tian (dye.uh.TISH.un) *n.* one trained to plan meals for a hospital, restaurant, school cafeteria, etc. Also **di.e.ti.cian**.

dif.fer (DIF.ur) *v.* 1 be different: *Tom and I differ widely; We differ in many respects; I differ from him in my attitude to food.* 2 disagree: *We differ about or on or over almost everything; He differs with me on what to eat; We* **beg to differ** (= disagree), *he says; After much arguing, we are hungry and* **agree to differ** or *disagree.*

dif.fer.ence (DIF.ur.unce) *n.* 1 something that distinguishes: *There's no difference between our viewpoints; Whether we stay or go makes no difference to me; a slight difference of opinion; The only difference between the cars is their color; Can you tell the difference?* *marked, striking, irreconcilable, minor, subtle, superficial differences.* 2 the amount by which things differ: *The difference between 18 and 6 is 12.* 3 a disagreement: *to compose, reconcile, resolve, set aside, settle, thrash out differences between parties; dif-*

ferences among friends. —**make a difference** be important; matter. —**split the difference** divide the difference equally; hence, compromise: *The negotiators split the difference for a 7% raise (halfway between 5% and 9%).*

dif.fer.ent (DIF.uh.runt) *adj.* not the same; dissimilar: *Her opinions are very different from his; much more different than he imagined; quite different to what her mother-in-law thought; as different as night and day; How do you like my new tie? Well, it's different* (= unusual); *I called seven different* (= separate or distinct) *times; Order a different* (= another) *meal if they're out of fish.*
—**different strokes for different folks** People and their ways differ.
—**dif.fer.ent.ly** *adv.*

dif.fer.en.tial (dif.uh.REN.shul) *adj* a. having to do with a difference or distinction: *a differential fee for foreign students; a differential price for foreign and domestic buyers of petroleum; She complained of getting differential* (= discriminatory) *treatment at work;* **Differential calculus** deals with the rate of change of known quantities; **Differential gears** make it possible for one rear wheel of a vehicle to turn faster that the other when cornering. —*n.* an absolute or percentage difference: *the price differential between wool and synthetic fibers; There's a 15% wage differential between the two job classifications.*

dif.fer.en.ti.ate (dif.uh.REN.shee.ate) *v.* -**ates, -at.ed, -at.ing** be, make, have, or recognize a difference: *One who is color-blind can't differentiate between colors; can't differentiate red from green; The two varieties are differentiated by color.*
—**dif.fer.en.ti.a.tion** (DIF.uh.ren.shee.AY.shun) *n.*

dif.fi.cult (DIF.uh.cult) *adj.* **1** requiring effort, strength, skill, patience, etc.; not easy: *It is difficult to get through medical school; I have a difficult problem for homework.* **2** hard to please, manage, get along with, etc.: *a difficult child who has been spoiled by his parents.*

dif.fi.cul.ty (DIF.uh.cul.tee) *n.* -**ties** **1** the fact or quality of being hard or troublesome: *a task of extraordinary difficulty; He reads German with some difficulty; She's in serious difficulty; She has difficulty paying for her groceries.* **2** something that is difficult; trouble or problem: *to be faced with, to come across, encounter, experience, face, meet difficulties; One has to clear up, overcome, resolve, surmount difficulties to achieve anything; to run into difficulties; when diffi-* *culties arise; The businessman found himself in financial difficulties.*

dif.fi.dent (DIF.uh.dunt) *adj.* not self-confident; timid: *He declined the offer with a diffident smile; Don't be shy or diffident;* **dif.fi.dent.ly** *adv.*
—**dif.fi.dence** *n.*

dif.fract (di.FRACT) *v.* break up light rays into bands of light and dark or of different colors, as when passing around the edge of an object or through a small slit, a hole, or a grating. —**dif.frac.tion** *n.* —**dif.frac.tive** *adj.*

dif.fuse (dif.YOOZE) *v.* **dif.fus.es, dif.fused, dif.fus.ing 1** spread widely: *The smell of perfume diffused through the room; to diffuse energy, knowledge, light; adj.:* soft **diffused** *light; a diffused effect.* **2** scatter; hence, break up: *to diffuse anger, crises, impacts, issues, radiation.*
—*adj.* (-YOOSE) spread out: *Diffuse or reflected light produces no glare; a rather diffuse, not focused concern; a diffuse* (= verbose), *rambling report.*
—**dif.fuse.ly** *adv.;* **dif.fuse.ness** *n.*
—**dif.fus.er** *n.*

dif.fu.sion (di.FEW.zhun) *n.* a diffusing or spreading: *the diffusion of gases in the air; the diffusion of knowledge through books and schools.* —**dif.fu.sive** (-siv) *adj.: the diffusive power of gases.*

dig *v.* **digs, dug, dig.ging 1** break up or scoop out earth, esp. for making or getting things: *Gardeners dig in the garden* (to prepare it for planting); *to dig a grave, hole; to dig potatoes* (out of the ground). **2** poke: *She dug me in the ribs with her umbrella; Her umbrella was digging into my ribs; She never stopped digging at* (= harassing and teasing) *me the whole afternoon.* **3** *Slang.* notice; like; understand: *Dig that car! He doesn't dig abstract art.* **4** search and explore: *to dig into the literature on UFOs; You have to dig long and hard to get anything out of him; She digs deep into her pockets to give* (= She gives generously) *to charity; n.: That's easy* **digging** (= an easy thing to do). —**dig in 1** *Informal.* begin to eat or work: *She brought out the sandwiches and told us to dig in.* **2** take a firm position; dig oneself a trench: *He prepared for battle and* **dug in his heels***.*
—**dig out** or **dig up** find (out) by much looking or research: *a reporter trying to dig up some information.*
—*n.* **1** a poke; hence, a pointed remark: *She likes to take a dig at me now and then.* **2** an archaeological excavation or its site: *The class has gone on a dig to look for Indian artifacts.* **3 digs** *pl.*

Informal. lodgings; quarters.

di.gest (DYE.jest) *n.* a short compilation or summary, esp. from diverse sources: *a legal digest; a weekly news digest.* —*v.* (di.JEST) **1** summarize and arrange. **2** break down food for absorption into the blood stream, as in the digestive system. **3** assimilate mentally: *I have read the report but have not digested everything.* —**di.gest.i.ble** (di.JES.tuh.bul) *adj.*

di.ges.tion (di.JES.chun) *n.* the system for digesting or the ability to digest food: *a man with a delicate digestion.* —**di.ges.tive** (-tiv) *adj.* having to do with digestion: *Saliva and bile are digestive juices; The food canal and the accessory glands make up the digestive system; digestive trouble.*

dig.ger (DIG.ur) *n.* a person who digs or a tool for digging.

diggings (DIG.ings) *n.pl.* **1** what is dug out. **2** a place where digging is being done. **3** *Informal.* a place to live. Also **digs.**

dig.it (DIJ.it) *n.* **1** a finger, thumb, or toe. **2** an Arabic numeral: *Inflation is in double digits (= more than 9%); five-digit figures (from 10,000 to 99,999).*

dig.i.tal (DIJ.uh.tul) *adj.* **1** having to do with numbers: *a digital clock radio; A digital watch does not have hands.* **2** binary-coded: *A digital (as opposed to an analog) computer calculates using binary numbers; Digital recording of sound eliminates wow and flutter; digital audio tape, disks.* **3** having to do with a finger: *a digital examination of the prostate; a digital joint.* —**dig.i.tal.ly** *adv.*

dig.i.tal.is (dij.i.TAL.is) *n.* a strong drug for heart ailments, derived from the purple foxglove.

dig.i.tize (DIJ.uh.tize) or **dig.i.tal.ize** (DIJ.uh.tul.ize) *v.* **-iz.es, -ized, -iz.ing** convert data, images, or sounds to digital or computer-readable form; **dig.i.tiz.er** *n.* —**dig.i.ti.za.tion** (-tuh.ZAY.shun, -tye-) *n.*

dig.ni.fied (DIG.nuh.fide) *adj.* having dignity: *a dignified air, answer, exit, manner, style; He was dignified in death (= died with dignity).*

dig.ni.fy (DIG.nuh.fye) *v.* **-fies, -fied, -fy.ing** give dignity to a person or thing: *The mayor dignified the school fair with her presence.*

dig.ni.tar.y (DIG.nuh.tair.ee) *n.* **-tar.ies** a person in a high rank or office: *a foreign dignitary; visiting dignitaries.*

dig.ni.ty (DIG.ni.tee) *n.* **-ties 1** intrinsic worth or value: *the dignity of human suffering.* **2** respect owed to one: *They were treated with great dignity.* **3** a calm, stately manner: *She lived and died in dignity; She never lost her dignity; She maintained her dignity under provocation.* **4** a high rank or office: *the dignity of her office.*

dig.ox.in (di.JOX.in) *n.* a form of digitalis used in treating congestive heart failure.

di.graph (DYE.graf) *n.* a pair of letters standing for one sound, as *ph* (= f) or *ea* (= e), as in *head.*

di.gress (dye.GRES) *v.* stray from the main subject. —**di.gres.sion** (-GRESH.un) *n.*: *The historian included a digression on tribal customs; a digression from the main theme.* —**di.gres.sive** (-siv) *adj.*: *a loose, digressive style of storytelling.*

dike *n.* a bank or levee to prevent flooding of low ground.

di.lap.i.dat.ed (duh.LAP.uh.day.tid) *adj.* falling to pieces; broken-down: *a dilapidated condition, house, truck.* —**di.lap.i.da.tion** (-DAY.shun) *n.*

dil.a.ta.tion (dil.uh.TAY.shun) *n.* an enlarging or stretching: *dilatation and curettage of the uterus.*

di.late (dye.LATE) *v.* **-lates, -lat.ed, -lat.ing 1** make wider or bigger: *eye drops to dilate the pupils for a checkup.* **2** write or speak at length: *The lecturer dilated on or upon his favorite subject.* —**di.la.tion** (-LAY.shun) *n.*

dil.a.tor.y (DIL.uh.tor.ee) *adj.* causing or inclined to delay or slow down: *a dilatory approach to homework; dilatory proceedings in committee; Filibuster is a dilatory tactic.* —**dil.a.tor.i.ly** *adv.;* **dil.a.tor.i.ness** *n.*

di.lem.ma (duh.LEM.uh) *n.* **1** a situation in which one is faced with competing alternatives: *Tim was in a dilemma when by mistake he arranged two dates for the same evening; He was on the horns of a dilemma.* **2** any difficult or problematic situation: *This poses a dilemma; We are faced with a dilemma; a moral dilemma; how to solve a dilemma.*

dil.et.tante (dil.uh.TAHNT, -TAHN.tee) *n.* **-tantes** or **-tan.ti** (-tee) one who merely dabbles in the arts. —**dil.et.tant.ish** *adj.*

dil.i.gent (DIL.uh.junt) *adj.* hard-working or painstaking: *a diligent pupil; diligent in his work.* —**dil.i.gent.ly** *adv.* —**dil.i.gence** *n.*

dill *n.* an herb used in pickling.

dill pickle *n.* a cucumber pickled with dill.

dil.ly (DIL.ee) *n.* **dil.lies** *Slang.* something remarkable: *The snowfall in June was a dilly.*

dil.ly.dal.ly (DIL.ee.DAL.ee) *v.* **-dal.lies, -dal.lied, -dal.ly.ing** waste time, esp. by hesitating or loitering.

di.lute (dye.LOOT, di.LOOT, long "OO") *v.* **-lutes, -lut.ed, -lut.ing** weaken by adding something else: *to dilute wine with water; to dilute* (= water down) *one's arguments, efforts, plans, policies, power, standards;* **adja.:** *dilute hydrochloric acid.* —**di.lu.tion** (-LOO.shun) *n.*

dim *adj.* **dim.mer, dim.mest 1** not bright or clear: *dim lighting; a dim chance, future, hope, image, memory, outlook, prospect, recollection.* **2** not seeing clearly: *Her eyes were dim and she couldn't see.* —**take a dim view of** regard something with disapproval or skepticism. —*v.* **dims, dimmed, dim.ming** make or become dim. —**dims** *n.pl.* an automobile's parking lights. —**dim.ly** *adv.;* **dim.ness** *n.*

dime *n.* a ten-cent coin: *Computers are a **dime a dozen*** (= cheap or easy to get) *these days.*

di.men.sion (di.MEN.shun) *n.* **1** a measurable magnitude, as length, width, and depth: *Time is often thought of as a fourth dimension.* **2** size; also, importance or range: *a disaster of great dimensions; The tragedy assumed serious dimensions as the bodies were uncovered.* —**di.men.sion.al** *adj.: a deeply dimensional portrayal; We live in a three-dimensional world; a multi-dimensional approach.* —**di.men.sion.al.ly** *adv.*

dime store same as FIVE-AND-DIME.

di.min.ish (di.MIN.ish) *v.* make or become smaller, less strong, etc.: *The force of the wind gradually diminished;* **adj.:** *She felt **diminished** by their cruel remarks; an enterprise affected by the law of **diminishing returns*** (= profit becoming proportionately less as effort is increased beyond a certain point). —**di.mi.nu.tion** (dim.uh.NEW.shun) *n.*

di.min.u.en.do (di.MIN.yoo.EN.doh) *adj. & adv. Music.* with gradually decreasing loudness.

di.min.u.tive (di.MIN.yuh.tiv) *adj.* very small in size: *the diminutive Mr. Smith; his diminutive figure, size, stature.* —*n.* a suffix denoting smallness, as *-ie, -let,* or *-kin* or a word formed with one, as *birdie, bracelet,* and *catkin.*

dim.i.ty (DIM.i.tee) *n.* **-ties** a light, strong cotton fabric.

dim.mer (DIM.ur) *n.* **1** a switch for dimming an electric light. **2 dimmers** *pl.* the low-beam headlights of an automobile; also, parking lights.

dim.ple (DIM.pul) *n.* a small depression, esp. in a body part, as on the cheeks or chin: *the dimples on a golf ball.* —*v.* **-ples, -pled, -pling** make or form dimples in something: *Her cheeks dimple when she laughs.* —**dim.ply** *adj.*

dim.wit *n. Informal.* a simpleton. —**dim.wit.ted** (DIM.wit.id) *adj.*

din *n.* a continuous, confused loud noise: *Her voice could be heard above the din; The crowd was making such a din she had to shout at the top of her voice.* —*v.* **dins, dinned, din.ning** force with a din; tell repeatedly: *Industriousness was dinned into him as a child.*

di.nar (di.NAR) *n.* **1** the basic unit of money in several Arab countries and in Yugoslavia. **2** 1/100 of the Iranian rial.

dine *v.* **dines, dined, din.ing** eat dinner: *We dine at home most of the time; We dine on whatever is in the fridge; We usually **dine out*** (= eat at a restaurant) *once a week.*

din.er (DYE.nur) *n.* **1** one who is dining: *Busboys are not supposed to speak to the diners.* **2** a restaurant car on a train. **3** a restaurant built like one: *We had ham and eggs at Pete's diner.*

di.nette (dye.NET) *n.* a nook or alcove for eating in: *a **dinette set*** (= table and chairs) *for your apartment.*

ding *n.* **1** also **dingdong**, the sound of a bell. **2** *Informal.* a tiny dent; *v.: Some clumsy driver dinged our car.*

ding-a-ling *n. Slang.* a crazy person.

ding.bat *n. Informal.* a stupid person.

ding.dong *n.* **1** a bell or its sound. **2** *Slang.* an eccentric person; nut.

din.ghy (DING.ee, -ghee) *n.* **-ghies 1** a small rowboat. **2** an inflatable raft for emergency use.

din.gle *n.* a small wooded valley.

din.go (DING.go) *n.* **-goes** an often tawny, medium-sized wild dog of Australia.

ding.us (DING.us) *n. Informal.* a gadget; something whose name does not come to mind.

din.gy (DIN.jee) *adj.* **ding.i.er, -i.est** dark and dirty; shabby: *a dingy coal-mining town; a dingy room in a cheap hotel.* —**din.gi.ly** *adv.;* **ding.i.ness** *n.*

dining *n.* eating, esp. dinner: *a restaurant for fine dining; dining and dancing;* **adja.:** *a dining area, hall, room, table; a railroad **dining car** or **lounge car*** (= diner); *a **dining chair*** (with upright back); *an outdoor five-piece dining collection or a five-piece indoor **dining set*** (both consisting of a table and four chairs); *a **dining spot*** (= restaurant).

dining lounge *n.* a dining room licensed to serve liquor with meals.

din.ky (DINK.ee) *adj. Informal.* **-ki.er, -ki.est** small and insignificant: *dinky toys; a dinky restaurant.*

din.ner (DIN.ur) *n.* **1** the main meal of the day, at noon or in the evening: *to eat, have, make, prepare dinner; What are we having for dinner? a chicken dinner; We were at dinner when he called; It happened during dinner.* **2** a formal meal; banquet.

dinner jacket *n.* a tuxedo.

dinner theater *n.* a restaurant in which a play is presented after dinner.

din.ner.ware (DIN.ur.ware) *n.* plates, bowls, cups, etc. for serving dinner.

di.no.saur (DYE.nuh.sor) *n.* **1** any of the often large, now extinct reptiles found in fossils. **2** something that is out of date or obsolete.

dint *n.* a dent. **—by dint of** by the effort or force of something: *He got rich by dint of hard work.*

di.o.cese (DYE.uh.sis, -seece) *n.* the area under a bishop's care. **—di.oc.e.san** (dye.OS.i.sun) *adj.: discussions at the diocesan synod.*

di.ode (DYE.ode) *n.* a two-electrode vacuum tube or semiconductor, esp. a rectifier.

di.o.ram.a (dye.oh.RAM.uh) *n.* a three-dimensional exhibit of a scene with modeled figures arranged in front of a painted background.

di.ox.in (dye.OX.un) *n.* a most poisonous chemical which occurs as a by-product in manufacturing pesticides.

dip *v.* **dips, dipped, dip.ping 1** immerse briefly in a liquid: *A fabric is dipped into a vat of dye; to dip pen in ink.* **2** ladle or scoop out; hence, reach down and take out: *Dip water from the bucket with a cup; Hard times forced them to dip into their life savings to pay the rent.* **3** go down: *The moon dipped behind the trees; Prices dipped at the end of the year.* **4** go down and up again; also, make to do so: *to dip a flag in salute.* **5** read or study superficially: *We dipped into Russian history.* **—n. 1** a dipping, esp. a brief swim: *to take a quick dip in the pool.* **2** something to dip finger food in: *a cheese dip; an onion-and-garlic dip for potato chips.* **3** a downward slope, depression, or course: *a dip in the road.*

diph.the.ri.a (dif.THEER.ee.uh, dip-) *n.* a dangerous contagious disease spread by a bacillus and characterized by a membrane clogging the throat.

diph.thong (DIF.thong, DIP-) *n.* a sound composed of two vowel sounds uttered together, as in *boil, pain,* and *cold.*

dip.loid *adj.* having twice the number of chromosomes found in a normal reproductive cell: *a diploid cell.*

di.plo.ma (di.PLOH.muh) *n.* a certificate of educational accomplishment: *Your degree is awarded on a diploma; Diplomas are awarded* or *conferred* or *given out* or *presented at convocations and graduation ceremonies; a high-school diploma; A teacher has to have a degree, diploma, or a certificate in education.*

di.plo.ma.cy (di.PLOH.muh.see) *n.* the art of a diplomat; skill in conducting relations between countries or people; tact: *the elaborate etiquette of international diplomacy; dollar, gunboat, quiet, shuttle, street diplomacy; Our manager relies on* or *uses* or *resorts to diplomacy rather than force to solve inter-personal problems.*

diploma mill *n.* an institution granting degrees of dubious value.

dip.lo.mat (DIP.luh.mat) *n.* **1** one empowered to represent a government in dealing with another government: *a career diplomat who has been long in the Federal Service.* **2** one who is tactful and skillful in dealing with people.

dip.lo.mat.ic (dip.luh.MAT.ic) *adj.* **1** tactful in dealing with delicate situations: *a diplomatic supervisor skilled at settling disputes.* **2** having to do with ambassadors: *diplomatic duties, representatives, service; A nation's **diplomatic corps*** or ***mission** working in the capital of a foreign country includes the ambassador or high commissioner, ministers, counselors, consuls, attachés, clerks, etc.; to enjoy, grant, have, withdraw **diplomatic immunity*** (= freedom from arrest, search, seizure, taxes, etc.).

di.plo.ma.tist (di.PLOH.muh.tist) *n.* a person with the qualities of a diplomat.

di.pole (DYE.pole) *n.* a radio or TV antenna consisting of a metal rod or wire split and separated in the center.

dip.per *n.* **1** something that dips, as a diving bird. **2** a long-handled cup or scoop. **3** same as BIG DIPPER or LITTLE DIPPER.

dip.so.ma.ni.a (dip.soh.AY.nee.uh) *n.* an uncontrollable craving for liquor.

dip.stick *n.* a stick dipped in a liquid, as engine oil, to measure its depth.

dip.sy-do (dip.see.DOO) *n. Slang.* a complicated or tricky act, as a hard-to-hit curveball.

dipsy-doodle *n. Slang.* **1** *dipsy-do: She did a dipsy-doodle with her hand to show how she felt about him.* **2** a deception or deceiver. —*v.* **-dles, -dled, -dling** move around in a deceptive manner: *The politician dipsy-doodled around the question instead of facing it.*

dip.ter.ous (DIP.tuh.rus) *adj.* two-winged, as mosquitoes and other insects.

dire *adj.* **dir.er, dir.est 1** terrible; disastrous: *dire consequences, predictions, threats.* **2** extreme; very difficult: *in dire need, poverty, straits.*

di.rect (di.RECT, dye-) *v.* **1** send or address: *Please direct your reply to him, c/o Mrs. Smith; remarks directed to or at his employees; The criticism was directed* (= pointed) *at or against the media; Better direct* (= aim) *your efforts to or toward something constructive; Can you direct* (= guide) *me to the library?* **2** give orders or guidance to someone; control or regulate: *She directs the children's department in the library; He's on the set directing a movie; The manager directed her staff to remain calm; Police direct traffic.* —*adj.* **1** *adj.* straight; unswerving; not stopping, interrupted, etc.: *in a direct line from A to B; a direct course, flight, hit, route.* **2** with nothing intervening or mediating: *in direct contact, sunlight; a direct connection, link, result; a direct* (= unbroken) *line of descent.* **3** blunt; straightforward; candid: *direct answers.* **4** *adj.* diametrical: *Hate is the direct antithesis of love; a direct opposite.* —*adv.* in a straight manner: *We flew from New York to Paris direct; They appealed direct to the voters.*

direct current *n.* electricity flowing in one direction only; cf. ALTERNATING CURRENT.

direct discourse same as DIRECT SPEECH.

di.rec.tion (di.REC.shun) *n.* **1** management: *He works under the direction of experts; We need a plan to give direction to our work.* **2** often **directions** *pl.* instructions on how to use or do something, get somewhere, etc.: *to follow, give, issue detailed directions for using the lawn mower; She had left directions with her husband in case the parcel arrived.* **3** where something is facing or going, as North, South, left, up, etc.; way: *Which direction did he go? in the opposite, right, wrong direction; The wind blew the papers in all directions; Al has a poor sense of direction; he often gets lost; new directions in literary criticism.*

di.rec.tion.al (di.REC.shuh.nul) *adj.* having to do with direction: *a directional radio antenna* (for signals from a particular direction); *an automobile's right and left directional* (= turn) *signals.*

di.rec.tive (di.REC.tiv) *n.* an order or rule: *The Minister has issued directives on hiring minority citizens; a directive that men and women (must) be given equal opportunity.*

di.rect.ly (di.RECT.lee) *adv.* **1** in a direct or straightforward manner: *smiling directly at us; She reports directly to the president; directly responsible.* **2** immediately: *We'll leave directly after work.* —**di.rect.ness** *n.*

direct mail *n.* advertising matter mailed to people on a list, as by a mail-order house.

di.rec.tor (di.REC.tur) *n.* one who directs: *an editorial director; funeral, managing, movie, program directors; a director of the company* (= member of the board of directors). —**di.rec.tor.ate** *n.* —**di.rec.tor.ship** *n.*

di.rec.to.ry (di.REC.tor.ee) *n.* **-ries 1** an alphabetical list of names along with addresses, phone numbers, etc.: *a city directory; telephone directory; a mall directory with map.* **2** a set of computer files forming a division of a larger set in a hierarchical structure, as on a disk.

direct speech *n.* reporting of dialog using the spoken words within quotation marks.

direct tax *n.* a tax such as income tax or sales tax that is paid by the person on whom it is levied.

dirge (DIRJ) *n.* a song or poem lamenting someone's death: *a funeral dirge.*

dir.i.gi.ble (DEER.uh.juh.bul, duh.RIJ.uh.bul) *n.* an airship. —*adj.* steerable.

dirk *n.* a straight-bladed dagger.

dirn.dl (DURN.dul) *n.* **1** a full skirt gathered at the waist. **2** a dress having this and a tight bodice.

dirt *n.* **1** soil or earth: *Children like to play in the dirt; Everyone* **hit the dirt** (Informal for fell to the ground) *when the firing started; adj.: a dirt floor, trail;* **dirt bike** (= trail bike); **dirt farmer** (who farms by himself); **dirt road** (= unpaved road); *a* **dirt track** *for bikes.* **2** grime or filth: *Detergents help wash dirt off clothes; He treats his men* **like dirt** (Informal for with utter contempt). **3** corruption or obscenity; pornography: *There's less dirt on TV during prime time; a campaign to get dirt off the newsstands; I just heard some dirt* (= slanderous gossip) *about the Joneses.* —**dirt cheap** *Informal.* very cheap: *You can buy it dirt cheap; adj.: at* **dirt-cheap**

dirty / disapprove

prices. —**dirt poor** so poor as to be without most of the essentials of life.
—**eat dirt** *Informal.* accept humiliating treatment; retract a statement.

dirt.y (DUR.tee) *adj.* **dirt.i.er, -i.est** 1 soiled; unclean: *dirty clothes, dishes, hands.* 2 unfair; low; base: *a dirty job, trick; political dirty tricks; dirty work.* 3 immoral; taboo; smutty: *a dirty book, movie, word; dirty language; the stereotype of "the dirty* (= *lecherous*) *old man."* 4 stormy or hostile: *dirty weather; He gave us a dirty look.* —*adv.* in a dirty way: *to fight dirty; talk dirty.*
—*v.* **dirt.ies, dirt.ied, dirt.y.ing** make dirty: *The children were told not to **dirty their hands** (= shame themselves) by stealing and lying.* —**dirt.i.ly** *adv.*
—**dirt.i.ness** *n.*

dirty linen *n.* private affairs of an embarrassing nature: *The Smiths never air or wash or hang out their dirty linen in public.* Also **dirty laundry.**

dirty pool *n. Informal.* unfair play.

dis *v.* **dis.ses, dissed, dis.sing** *Slang.* show disrespect to someone.

dis.a.bil.i.ty (dis.uh.BIL.i.tee) *n.* **-ties** the state of being disabled: *Blindness is a physical disability; Dyslexia is a learning or reading disability* (= *disorder*); *Some disabilities are caused by illness, others by injury; the disabilities of illiterate adults;* **adj.***:* *disability benefits, insurance; a disability pension for a wounded veteran.*

dis.a.ble (dis.AY.bul) *v.* **-bles, -bled, -bling** make unable, unfit, unqualified, etc., as by wounding: *a tank disabled by a land mine; to disable an alarm, powerline, system; Marriage disabled* (= *disqualified*) *her from inheriting;* **adj.***:* *a **disabling** disease, injury, stroke.*

disabled *adj.* 1 made unfit or inoperable: *a disabled car left on the road shoulder.* 2 handicapped: *a disabled veteran; the dead and the disabled; Children who are learning disabled and physically disabled are given special help; the mentally disabled* (= *mentally ill or retarded people*).

dis.a.buse (dis.uh.BYOOZE) *v.* **-bus.es, -bused, -bus.ing** free of mistaken ideas: *to disabuse a person of his errors.*

dis.ad.van.tage (dis.ud.VAN.tij) *n.* something that harms, works against, hinders, etc.; drawback: *Those who hadn't helped out in the kitchen were clearly at a disadvantage in the cooking contest; Everything seemed to work to our disadvantage; We all have certain aptitudes that outweigh or offset our disadvantages; Not knowing how to read is a decided disadvantage when applying for a job.*

disadvantaged (dis.ud.VAN.tijd) *adj.* lacking an acceptable basic standard of living, educational opportunities, civil rights, etc.: *an economically disadvantaged neighborhood; a disadvantaged sector of our society; a disadvantaged youngster.* —**dis.ad.van.ta.geous** (dis.AD.vun.TAY.jus) *adj.*

dis.af.fect (dis.uh.FECT) *v.* cause to be unfriendly, disloyal, or rebellious: *adj.:* *the **disaffected** masses of the unemployed; They became disaffected by the company's hiring policies.*
—**dis.af.fec.tion** *n.*

dis.a.gree (dis.uh.GREE) *v.* **-grees, -greed, -gree.ing** 1 fail to agree; differ: *People disagree on or about or over many things; Often we disagree sharply with our best friends; Sometimes we **agree to disagree** (on matters of opinion), but not when the bank balance disagrees with the checkbook register.* 2 cause distress or upset: *Sea food disagrees with some.*
—**dis.a.gree.ment** *n.*

dis.a.gree.a.ble (dis.uh.GREE.uh.bul) *adj.* 1 ill-tempered: *a disagreeable old grouch.* 2 unpleasant: *a disagreeable experience, habit, mood, task; Sea food is disagreeable to some.* —**dis.a.gree.a.ble.ness** *n.*; **dis.a.gree.a.bly** *adv.*

dis.al.low (dis.uh.LOW, *rhyme:* HOW) *v.* refuse to allow or accept officially: *The review board disallowed his claim; to disallow an appeal.*

dis.ap.pear (dis.uh.PEER) *v.* cease to be seen: *The magician made the rabbit disappear; Then he disappeared from view himself; Whales are disappearing* (= *dying out*) *because of excessive hunting.*
—**dis.ap.pear.ance** (-unce) *n.*

dis.ap.point (dis.uh.POINT) *v.* let someone down: *It disappointed us that we lost the America Cup; Our team disappointed us;* **adj.***:* *We were deeply **disappointed**; We were disappointed at or with his grades; not really disappointed in him; He too was disappointed to learn that he had failed; the **disappointing** turnout at our annual picnic; It's disappointing that so few turned up.* —**dis.ap.point.ment** (-munt) *n.*: *The picnic was a bit of a disappointment; We felt and expressed our disappointment at or about or over the poor turnout; a bitter, deep, keen, profound disappointment; To our great disappointment, the picnic had to be canceled.*

dis.ap.pro.ba.tion (DIS.ap.ruh.BAY.shun) *n. Formal.* disapproval.

dis.ap.prove (dis.uh.PROOV) *v.* **-ap.proves, -ap.proved, -ap.prov.ing** not accept or approve; have or express a bad opinion: *Father disapproves* of long hair. **—dis.ap.prov.al** (-PROO.vul) n.

dis.arm (dis.ARM) v. **1** take weapons away from someone; also, reduce or do away with military strength: *The police disarmed the robber; Germany and Japan were disarmed after World War II.* **2** make less hostile; make favorably inclined: *to disarm opposition; Her confession disarmed their suspicions;* adj.: *He won over the audience with a* **disarming** *smile.* **—dis.ar.ma.ment** (-muh.munt) n.: *nuclear disarmament.*

dis.ar.range (dis.uh.RAINJ) v. **-rang.es, -ranged, -rang.ing** disturb the order or arrangement: *clothes disarranged by being slept in; disarranged hair.* **—dis.ar.range.ment** n.

dis.ar.ray (dis.uh.RAY) n. disorganized condition; disorder: *Her clothes were in disarray; As the rain fell, the procession broke up in total disarray.* —v.: *papers disarrayed by the wind.*

dis.as.sem.ble (dis.uh.SEM.bul) v. **-bles, -bled, -bling** take or come apart: *to disassemble a bicycle for shipping.*

dis.as.so.ci.ate (dis.uh.SOH.shee.ate) v. **-ates, -at.ed, -at.ing** end or break off an association with a person or thing: *She disassociated (= dissociated) herself from their activities.*

dis.as.ter (diz.AS.tur) n. **1** a great misfortune causing much death or damage: *It was a major disaster for the nation and a personal calamity for the minister responsible; He was courting disaster when he made that decision; The disaster could have been averted; Another disaster or near disaster is impending; The hurricane-stricken town was declared a* **disaster area** *by the government (to qualify for emergency relief); A* **disaster film** *or* **movie** *capitalizes on fires, crashes, etc.* **2** a total failure: *The Edsel was a disaster of the car industry.* **—dis.as.trous** (diz.AS.trus) adj.: *There was a disastrous drought last year; It would be disastrous to wait and see what happens instead of doing something about it.* **—dis.as.trous.ly** adv.

dis.a.vow (dis.uh.VOW) v. Formal. to claim that one does not know about, does not approve of, or is not associated with something: *She disavowed the incriminating evidence; to disavow an intention, policy, responsibility.* **—dis.a.vow.al** (-ul) n.

dis.band (dis.BAND) v. break up an organization: *to disband a committee, company, organization, regiment; The group disbanded after a few months.*

dis.bar (dis.BAR) v. **-bars, -barred,** **-bar.ring** expel as a lawyer: *to be disbarred from practice.* **—dis.bar.ment** n.

dis.be.lief (dis.bi.LEEF) n. refusal to believe: *They stood aghast in utter disbelief; The story aroused widespread disbelief and suspicion.*

dis.be.lieve (dis.bi.LEEV) v. **-lieves, -lieved, -liev.ing** refuse or fail to believe. **—dis.be.liev.er** n.

dis.bur.den (dis.BUR.dun) v. rid of or eliminate a burden: *Confession helps to disburden ourselves of what is bothering us.*

dis.burse (dis.BURCE) v. **-burs.es, -bursed, -burs.ing** pay out or distribute: *The government disbursed the authorized funds to the school boards.* **—dis.burse.ment** n.: *a treasurer in charge of disbursements of research grants; a lawyer's bill of fees, charges, and disbursements.* **—dis.bur.sal** (-sul) n.

disc n. a phonograph record: *to cut (= make) a disc.* See also **disk.**

disc brake n. an automobile brake operated by the pressure applied to the sides of a disc locked on to the moving wheel.

dis.card (dis.CARD) v. get rid of something; throw away, as a used carton; adj.: **discarded** *clothes, newspapers, tires; a discarded policy, position, view.* —n. (DIS.card) something discarded, as a card or cards, an old library book, etc.: *Many old values have been thrown* **into the discard** *since World War II.*

disc drive n. a computer device for reading and writing data on discs.

dis.cern (di.SURN, -ZURN) v. perceive or distinguish: *We were able to discern mountains in the distance;* adj.: *an astute and* **discerning** *judge of character; the discerning eye; a discerning audience.* **—dis.cern.i.ble** adj.; **dis.cern.ment** n.

dis.charge (dis.CHARJ) v. **-charg.es, -charged, -charg.ing** **1** send forth or unload the contents of something: *The bus discharged its passengers; to discharge waste into rivers and lakes; to discharge a ship of its cargo; to discharge the cargo; The Niagara River discharges into Lake Ontario; Batteries discharge electricity; The pistol discharged accidentally; The battery is discharged (= dead); Discharge (= fire) your rifle in the air.* **2** be free of an obligation: *We discharge our duties (by doing them); Jim has discharged his debts (= paid them).* **3** let go of someone or something: *A prisoner is discharged early on parole; a clerk discharged (= dismissed) for theft; He had been discharged dishonorably from the Navy.* —n. (also DIS.charge) **1** a sending forth or emptying: *the discharge of the cargo from the ship's hold; a discharge of pus and blood from a wound; The patient continued to improve after his discharge from the hospital; an electrical discharge such as a spark across a gap.* **2** the fulfilling of an obligation: *the discharge of his legal responsibilities as a husband.* **3** dismissal: *He received an honorable discharge; The discharge (papers) came in the mail.*

dis.ci.ple (di.SYE.pul) *n.* a student or follower, esp. one of Christ's 12 apostles.

dis.ci.pli.nar.i.an (dis.uh.pluh.NAY.ree.un) *n.* one who believes in and enforces strict discipline: *a strict disciplinarian and a good principal.* —**dis.ci.pli.nar.y** (DIS.uh.pluh.nair.ee) *adja.: disciplinary action; a disciplinary body, committee, hearing, measure, problem.*

dis.ci.pline (DIS.uh.plin) *n.* **1** an area of learning: *medicine and affiliated disciplines such as nursing and pharmacy; Nadia won all four disciplines (= balance beam, uneven bars, vault, and floor exercises) for the gymnastic title.* **2** training to produce self-control, obedience, proper conduct, etc.; also, the results of this: *Principals try to establish and maintain discipline in their schools; They crack down on violations of discipline; Conduct that undermines discipline is not tolerated; firm, harsh, lax, loose, slack, stern, strict discipline; iron discipline; Military discipline means automatic unquestioning obedience; He lives in monastic discipline under the vows of poverty, chastity, and obedience; Where's your party discipline?* **3** corrective punishment: *the discipline committee of the Teachers' Federation.*
—*v.* -plines, -plined, -plin.ing **1** subject to corrective punishment: *Children used to be disciplined by being spanked.* **2** correct and train: *Children are best disciplined while young.*

disciplined *adj.* marked by discipline: *a disciplined writer; well disciplined kids; highly disciplined troops; It takes a disciplined (= organized and trained) mind to compile a dictionary.*

disc jockey *n.* a host of a program featuring recorded music.

dis.claim (dis.CLAIM) *v.* claim that one has no knowledge of or connection with something: *He disclaimed complicity in the plot.*

dis.claim.er (dis.CLAY.mur) *n.* a statement that disclaims something.

dis.close (dis.CLOZE) *v.* -clos.es, -closed, -clos.ing make visible or known; reveal: *The convict disclosed the names of his accomplices; He disclosed that he had been in jail before;* **n.:** *A **disclosing agent** or **tablet** shows where brushing is required by staining the plaque around teeth.*

dis.clo.sure (dis.CLOH.zhur) *n.* a disclosing or something disclosed: *The public, sensational, startling disclosures made in the media shocked the nation.*

dis.co (DIS.coh) *n.* **-cos** *Informal.* a discotheque or discotheque music; **adja.:** *disco dancing, music, sounds; the disco craze, scene; a disco bar, hit, star, tape.*
—*v.* **-coes, -coed, -co.ing** dance to disco music: *They discoed all night; discoed to the beat of the nineties.*

dis.col.or (dis.CULL.ur) *v.* change or spoil in color, as by fading, stains, or running of the dye. —**dis.col.or.a.tion** (DIS.cull.uh.RAY.shun) *n.* Also **dis.col.our** *Cdn.*

dis.com.bob.u.late (dis.cum.BOB.yuh.late) *v.* **-lates, -lat.ed, -lat.ing** *Informal.* upset or confuse: *He discombobulates his older colleagues by appearing at work casually dressed.*

dis.com.fit (dis.CUM.fit) *v.* defeat and confuse or disconcert: *an incident that's likely to discomfit the president;* **adj.:** *She felt utterly **discomfited** by his disappearance just when he was most wanted.*
—**dis.com.fi.ture** (-fuh.chur) *n.*

dis.com.fort (dis.CUM.furt) *n.* lack of comfort, bodily or mental; unease; also, an instance or cause of this: *Braces on teeth cause discomfort; to put up with the discomforts of travel; to bear small physical discomforts without complaining.*
—*v.:* *He is discomforted by his tight shoes.*

dis.com.mode (dis.cuh.MODE) *v.* **-com.modes, -com.mod.ed, -com.mod.ing** *Formal.* cause inconvenience or trouble to someone.

dis.com.pose (dis.cum.POZE) *v.* **-pos.es, -posed, -pos.ing** upset composure or poise; **adj.:** *He seemed a bit **discomposed** by the sudden bad news.*
—**dis.com.po.sure** (-POH.zhur) *n.*

dis.con.cert (dis.cun.SURT) *v.* ruin the calm self-control of someone; perturb: *He was disconcerted to find his hairpiece missing;* **adj.:** *Her criticism was quite **disconcerting**; a profoundly disconcerting experience; It was deeply disconcerting to hear that there would be no pay raises this year.*

dis.con.nect (dis.cuh.NECT) *v.* break the connection of something: *to disconnect one freight car from another; to disconnect (= unplug) a toaster.*

disconnected (dis.cuh.NEC.tid) *adj.*
1 not well linked; not coherent: *a*

disconsolate / discredit

disconnected narrative; disconnected thoughts. **2** not connected: *disconnected power, telephone, TV.*
dis.con.so.late (dis.CON.suh.lit) *adj.* sad; downcast; inconsolable; **dis.con.so.late.ly** *adv.*
dis.con.tent (dis.cun.TENT) *n.* a lack of contentment or satisfaction: *They tried to stir up discontent among the employees; Soon there was widespread discontent about vacations, discontent at low wage scales, discontent with the whole working environment; adj.: She is **discontented** with her job; the discontented masses.*
dis.con.tin.ue (dis.cun.TIN.yoo) *v.* **-ues, -ued, -u.ing** cease or cause to cease; break off: *She discontinued paying rent until the leak was fixed.*
—**dis.con.tin.u.ance** (-yoo.unce) or **dis.con.tin.u.a.tion** (DIS.cun.tin.yoo.AY.shun) *n.*
dis.con.ti.nu.i.ty (DIS.con.tuh.NEW.i.tee) *n.* **-ties** a gap or break.
dis.con.tin.u.ous (dis.cun.TIN.yoo.us) *adj.* not continuous; having breaks and interruptions; **dis.con.tin.u.ous.ly** *adv.*
dis.cord (DIS.cord) *n.* **1** disagreement or dispute: *to stir up discord in a community; discord between parents; discord among family members; Domestic or family discord sometimes leads to broken homes.* **2** disharmony in music; a harsh dissonance; din. —**dis.cor.dant** (-dunt) *adj.*
dis.co.theque (DIS.cuh.tek) *n.* a club for dancing to recorded music.
dis.count (DIS.count) *n.* an amount deducted from the regular price: *A 5% discount is given on cash purchases; a cash discount; Slightly soiled goods are sold **at a discount**.* —*v.* **1** reduce the price of something; deduct an amount from the price: *We discount all goods in the warehouse; We discount 5% from the regular price.* **2** allow for or anticipate bias, exaggeration, etc.; also, disregard as unreliable: *We tend to discount the rumors heard through the grapevine and the sensational stories in the press.*
—**dis.count.a.ble** *adj.: discountable merchandise.* —**dis.count.er** *n.*
dis.coun.te.nance (dis.COWN.tuh.nunce) *v.* **-nanc.es, -nanced, -nanc.ing** Formal. **1** disconcert; *adj.: She seemed a little **discountenanced** at being kept waiting.* **2** disapprove: *a disciplinarian who discountenances habitual tardiness.*
discount house (or **store**) *n.* a shop that sells goods at reduced prices.
dis.cour.age (dis.CUR.ij) *v.* **-ag.es, -aged, -ag.ing** **1** make less confident, hopeful, or courageous; dishearten: *The troops were discouraged by the early defeats; discouraged from further fighting; adj.: to become, feel, get **discouraged**; They sat there discouraged at or about or over what had happened; discouraged and demoralized workers; It was **discouraging** to see their efforts wasted.* **2** deter: *Heavy seas discouraged the rescuers from jumping into the water; It discouraged rescue efforts.* —**dis.cour.age.ment** *n.*
dis.course (DIS.corse) *n.* **1** a formal speech; treatise: *a philosophical discourse.* **2** verbal communication: *terms used in ordinary discourse; direct and indirect discourse.* —*v.* **-cours.es, -coursed, -cours.ing** **1** speak or write at length: *He discourses on or upon many matters in his book.* **2** converse: *Teachers don't like students discoursing too much about unrelated topics in class.*
dis.cour.te.ous (dis.CUR.tee.us) *adj.* rude and ill-mannered: *He was fired for being discourteous to customers.* —**dis.cour.te.ous.ly** *adv.*
dis.cour.te.sy (dis.CUR.tuh.see) *n.* **-sies** rudeness: *He apologized for his discourtesies; a grave discourtesy; She can't stand the discourtesy of being kept waiting.*
dis.cov.er (dis.CUV.ur) *v.* **1** get knowledge of something: *Police discovered several clues to the mystery; The body was finally discovered in the bushes; Children go to museums to discover how things work.* **2** be first to learn of, see, etc. a person or thing: *Did the Vikings discover North America?* —**dis.cov.er.er** *n.*
dis.cov.er.y (dis.CUV.uh.ree) *n.* **-er.ies** a discovering or what has been discovered: *the revolutionary discovery that the Earth goes around the Sun; the dramatic, exciting, startling, world-shaking discovery of the New World; The corpse was a grisly, horrible, shocking discovery; Banting and Best made the discovery of insulin; a medical, scientific discovery; the discovery of new talent for the stage; the recent discoveries in space.*
dis.cred.it (dis.CRED.it) *v.* **1** damage the believability of a person or thing: *The revelations were meant to discredit the opposition; The flat-earth theory has long been discredited.* **2** disbelieve: *One tends to discredit many of the rumors dished up in the papers.* —*n.* loss of good name or its cause: *The fact that he lied will be remembered to his discredit by future generations; He is a discredit to his school; Lying brings discredit to or on any self-respecting person; It throws discredit (= disbelief) on everything he has ever said.* —**dis.cred.i.ta.ble** (dis.CRED.i.tuh.bul) *adj.: discreditable conduct, behavior.*

dis.creet (dis.CREET) *adj.* **1** having or showing discretion and good judgment, esp. in speech: *She is very discreet in talking to the media; She keeps a discreet distance from them; Often she keeps a discreet silence or says, "Sorry, no comment!"* **2** tastefully modest: *She is known for her discreet charm; Her office is the picture of discreet elegance.*
—**dis.creet.ly** *adv.*
dis.crep.an.cy (dis.CREP.un.see) *n.* **-cies** a disagreement; conflict: *a glaring discrepancy; There are numerous, serious, wide discrepancies between the two versions of the incident.* —**dis.crep.ant** (-unt) *adj.*: *two widely discrepant versions of the same incident.*
dis.crete (dis.CREET) *adj.* distinct and individual; separate: *a stereo set made up of four discrete component units.*
dis.cre.tion (dis.CRESH.un) *n.* **1** discernment; judgment: *He backed out saying, "Discretion is the better part of valor"* (= Why take an unnecessary risk). **2** freedom to choose or act as one wishes: *I leave this to your discretion; broad, enormous, sole, wide discretion; One may not marry before the age of discretion; He has been authorized to incur expenses* **at (his) discretion.**
—**dis.cre.tion.ar.y** (-uh.nair.ee) *adj.*: *the discretionary* (= judgmental) *powers of a judge; discretionary funds for* **discretionary spending** (= spending as one wishes).
discretionary income *n.* money left after paying for life's necessities, taxes, etc. which one may save or spend on luxuries.
dis.crim.i.nate (dis.CRIM.uh.nate) *v.* **-nates, -nat.ed, -nat.ing 1** make or see a distinction, esp. in an intelligent way: *to discriminate between good and bad poetry; to discriminate good poetry from bad; to discriminate among many equally good options;* ***adj.***: *a man of* **discriminating** *taste in clothes; Banks have to be discriminating about their borrowers.* **2** act differently toward someone as a result of prejudice: *a club that discriminates against women (by excluding them).*
dis.crim.i.na.tion (dis.CRIM.uh.NAY.shun) *n.* **1** the ability to discriminate: *He doesn't show much discrimination in his choice of clothes.* **2** prejudice: *to practice discrimination; discrimination against minorities in housing; Minority groups are subjected to discrimination in various ways; age, racial, religious, sex discrimination.*
dis.crim.i.na.to.ry (dis.CRIM.uh.nuh.tor.ee) *adj.* that discriminates: *Discriminatory tariffs promote trade with some nations and discourage it with others; discriminatory* (= biased) *hiring, laws, policies, practices.*
dis.cur.sive (dis.CUR.siv) *adj.* **1** moving from topic to topic freely: *a discursive letter.* **2** logical, not intuitive: *discursive reasoning.* —**dis.cur.sive.ly** *adv.*; **dis.cur.sive.ness** *n.*
dis.cus *n.* **-cus.es 1** a heavy, round, flattish disk thrown for distance as a contest. **2** this contest, or **discus throw.**
dis.cuss (dis.CUS) *v.* talk about or consider a topic in all its aspects in speech or writing: *Let's discuss it with our friends; We discussed how we might put the money to good use.*
dis.cus.sant (dis.CUS.unt) *n.* one who discusses or comments, as at a seminar, panel discussion, etc.
dis.cus.sion (dis.CUSH.un, "USH" as in "rush") *n.* a discussing or its presentation; discourse: *to have, lead, provoke a discussion; to bring up a subject for discussion; A subject comes up for discussion; It is presently under discussion; an animated, frank, heated, lively, open, quiet, spirited discussion; a panel discussion.*
dis.dain (dis.DAIN) *v.* consider or reject as unworthy: *He disdained to accept the award because he thought he deserved something better.* —*n.* haughty contempt: *the look of proud disdain on his face.* —**dis.dain.ful** *adj.*: *He's disdainful of peers who have come up from the ranks; a disdainful silence.*
—**dis.dain.ful.ly** *adv.*
dis.ease (di.ZEEZ) *n.* a deviation of a plant or animal body from its healthy state; illness: *how the body fights disease; heart disease; the causes and symptoms of diseases; the breakout of a disease; the cure for a disease; the spread of a disease; to contract* or *come down with a disease; acute, chronic, communicable, congenital, contagious, deadly, fatal, infectious, incurable, occupational, rare, social, tropical, venereal diseases; Air pollution is a disease of industrial societies.*
—**diseased** (-ZEEZD) *adj.*: *diseased crops, a diseased liver; Some of the animals were dangerously diseased.*
dis.em.bark (dis.em.BARK) *v.* go or put ashore from a ship.
dis.em.bod.y (dis.em.BOD.ee) *v.* **-bod.ies, -bod.ied, -bod.y.ing** release from a body; ***adj.***: *a disembodied spirit, voice.* —**dis.em.bod.i.ment** *n.*
dis.em.bow.el (dis.em.BOW.ul, *rhyme*: VOWEL) *v.* **-els, -eled, -el.ing** remove the bowels from a body: *To clean a*

chicken for cooking means to disembowel it.
—**dis.em.bow.el.ment** n. Also **dis.em.bow.elled, dis.em.bow.el.ling** Cdn.

dis.en.chant (dis.en.CHANT) v. set free from mistaken belief or enchantment; *adj.*: *He was becoming* or *growing* **disenchanted** *with the life of an actor; a disenchanted public;* **dis.en.chant.ment** n.

dis.en.cum.ber (dis.en.CUM.bur) v. *Formal.* release from a burden or hindrance: *disencumbered of his responsibilities as mayor.*

dis.en.fran.chise (dis.en.FRAN.chise) same as DISFRANCHISE.

dis.en.gage (dis.en.GAGE) v. **-gag.es, -gaged, -gag.ing** free from being engaged, involved, or committed: *Depressing the clutch pedal disengages the clutch and disconnects the engine from the transmission; Troops were disengaged from the border confrontation.*
—**dis.en.gage.ment** n.

dis.en.tan.gle (dis.en.TANG.gul) v. **-gles, -gled, -gling 1** free from something that tangles or ties up: *He's trying to disentangle his hair from the comb.* **2** untangle: *to disentangle a snarled ball of wool.*

dis.es.tab.lish (dis.uh.STAB.lish) v. end the established state, esp. of a state church: *The Catholic Church was disestablished during the French Revolution.*
—**dis.es.tab.lish.ment** n.

dis.es.teem (dis.uh.STEEM) n. the condition of being little esteemed. Also v.

dis.fa.vor (dis.FAY.vur) n. the state of being disapproved of or being out of favor: *He looks upon* or *regards* or *views foreigners with disfavor; He fell into disfavor with his boss.* —v. *Formal.* not favor: *a plan disfavored by the board of directors.* Also **dis.fa.vour** Cdn.

dis.fig.ure (dis.FIG.yur) v. **-ures, -ured, -ur.ing** mar the appearance: *a child disfigured by a burn; The scar disfigures her face; adj.*: *a badly* **disfigured** *body.*
—**dis.fig.ure.ment** n.

dis.fran.chise (dis.FRAN.chize) v. **-chis.es, -chised, -chis.ing** deprive someone of a right, esp. citizenship rights or the right to vote.

dis.gorge (dis.GORJ) v. **-gorg.es, -gorged, -gorg.ing** spew forth, esp. something swallowed; hence, discharge: *a dragon disgorging smoke and flame; a river disgorging into the ocean; The bus disgorged its human cargo at the school.*

dis.grace (dis.GRACE) n. a loss of favor, good name, or honor; also, a cause of this: *Being poor is no disgrace but the condition of the poor is a disgrace to our civilization; Soldier, you've brought disgrace on your regiment; He had to leave his position* **in disgrace**; *He* **fallen into disgrace** *with his superiors.*
—v. **-grac.es, -graced, -grac.ing** bring disgrace on someone: *He disgraced himself by his behavior; He was publicly disgraced by being removed from office; adj.*: *a* **disgraced** *dictator.* —**dis.grace.ful** adj. shameful: *disgraceful behavior.*

dis.grun.tled (dis.GRUN.tuld) adj. displeased and dissatisfied: *The fisher folk became disgruntled at* or *over* or *with the rainy weather; They are a disgruntled lot; a disgruntled population; disgruntled investors, shoppers, taxpayers.*

dis.guise (dis.GUYS) v. **-guis.es, -guised, -guis.ing 1** change the appearance of a person or thing so as to conceal identity: *The warship was disguised to look like a merchant vessel; a robber disguised as a police officer.* **2** cover up; hide: *We can't disguise the fact that many people who have been through high school are still illiterate; to disguise one's feelings.* —n. **1** a disguising or disguised condition: *He went to the party* **in disguise**. **2** a means of disguise such as a wig, mask, or clothes: *a clever disguise; He put on a disguise and went to the Halloween party; He shed* or *threw off that disguise and assumed the disguise of a policeman; He made no disguise of* (= did not hide) *his intentions.*

dis.gust (dis.GUST) n. a feeling of sickened distaste, repugnance, or offense: *He discovered to his utter disgust that the vegetable dish contained meat; He felt, expressed disgust at what had happened.*
—v. cause disgust to someone: *His drunken behavior thoroughly disgusted her; adj.*: *When he sobered up, he said he was* **disgusted** *at* or *by* or *with it himself; Everyone thought it was quite* **disgusting** *to watch.* —**dis.gust.ing.ly** adv.

dish n. **1** a shallow, concave container for food. **2** a serving of food; also, food prepared in some way. **3** *Slang.* a good-looking person. **4** *Slang.* what meets one's taste; one's cup of tea. **5** same as EARTH STATION. **6 dishes** pl. plates, cups, bowls, etc. collectively, as left after meals: *Who'll do the dishes? We used to wash dishes to earn pocket money; The dishes are soaking now; You have to wash, rinse, and stack the dishes; She got a* **set of dishes** (= food containers) *for her bridal shower.* —v. put in a dish: *It's Dad's turn to dish the dinner; Dish it up, Dad!* —**dish out** or **up 1** put food into a dish. **2** *Informal.* give out, esp. freely: *Teachers dish out homework to students; It's easier to* **dish it out** (= give blame or punishment) *than to take it.*

dis.ha.bille (dis.uh.BEEL) *n.* the state of being partly or carelessly dressed, as in a robe or negligee: *Mom keeps telling Dad never to answer the door in dishabille.*

dis.har.mo.ny (dis.HAR.muh.nee) *n.* absence of harmony or agreement. —**dis.har.mo.ni.ous** (dis.har.MOH.nee.us) *adj.*

dish.cloth *n.* a cloth to wash dishes with.

dis.heart.en (dis.HAR.tun) *v.* discourage; dismay: *The defeat disheartened us all; adj.: We all felt disheartened; a disheartened group; It was quite disheartening to lose the very first game; a disheartening experience.*

dished (DISHT) *adj.* concave like a dish: *a dished face, steering wheel, top.*

di.shev.el (duh.SHEV.ul) *v.* **-els, -eled, -el.ing** disorder, muss, or rumple hair or clothing; also, do so to a person: *The wind disheveled his hair; adj.: Children return from play all disheveled; his disheveled appearance; a disheveled youngster.* —**di.shev.el.ment** *n.* Also **di.shev.elled, di.shev.el.ling** *Cdn.*

dis.hon.est (dis.ON.ist) *adj.* not truthful or honest: *It's dishonest to lie, cheat, steal, and break promises; dishonest profits* (made dishonestly, as from smuggled goods). —**dis.hon.est.ly** *adv.*

dis.hon.es.ty (dis.ON.is.tee) *n.* **-ties** 1 lack of honesty. 2 a dishonest act: *petty dishonesties.*

dis.hon.or (dis.ON.ur) *n.* a lack or loss of respect, honor, etc.; shame; also, a cause of this: *"Death before dishonor" went the battle cry as they refused to yield to the enemy.* —*v.* 1 show disrespect to a person or thing: *Let's not dishonor our noble traditions.* 2 refuse to honor: to dishonor an agreement, bill, check, commitment, credit card, lawful strike. —**dis.hon.or.a.ble** (-ur.uh.bul) *adj.*: *a dishonorable discharge from the military; dishonorable conduct;* **dis.hon.or.a.bly** *adv.* Also **dis.hon.our, dis.hon.our.a.ble; dis.hon.our.a.bly** *Cdn.*

dish.rag *n.* a dishcloth.

dish.tow.el (DISH.tow.ul) *n.* a towel for drying dishes.

dish.ware *n.* tableware.

dish.wash.er (DISH.wosh.ur) *n.* a person or machine that washes dishes: *to load* or *stack a dishwasher.*

dish.wa.ter (DISH.wot.ur) *n.* water to wash dishes and cooking utensils in; also, water that has been so used.

dish.y (DISH.ee) *adj. Slang.* attractive: *a dishy singer.*

dis.il.lu.sion (dis.i.LOO.zhun) *v.* to free someone of illusions or misconceptions: *He was living in a world of fantasy, but no one tried to disillusion him; adj.: He ended up a very disillusioned* (= disappointed and embittered) *man.* —**dis.il.lu.sion.ment** *n.*

dis.in.cen.tive (dis.in.SEN.tiv) *n.* deterrent: *welfare payments as a financial disincentive to work.*

dis.in.cline (dis.in.CLINE) *v.* **-clines, -clined, -clin.ing** be or make unwilling; *adjp.: People seem disinclined to work on Monday mornings.* —**dis.in.cli.na.tion** (dis.IN.cluh.NAY.shun) *n.*

dis.in.fect (dis.in.FECT) *v.* make free of disease germs: *to disinfect a room; Drinking water is disinfected with chlorine.*

dis.in.fect.ant (dis.in.FEC.tunt) *n. & adj.* (something) that disinfects.

dis.in.for.ma.tion (dis.IN.fur.MAY.shun) *n.* malicious propaganda, as by spreading false rumors: *a disinformation campaign.*

dis.in.gen.u.ous (dis.in.JEN.yoo.us) *adj.* not honest, open, or sincere: *It's disingenuous to say there is nothing to the rumor in order to divert attention; a disingenuous reply.*

dis.in.her.it (dis.in.HER.it) *v.* bar from inheriting: *She was disinherited for marrying against her father's will.*

dis.in.te.grate (dis.IN.tuh.grate) *v.* **-grates, -grat.ed, -grat.ing** break up into smaller or component parts: *Most meteoroids disintegrate and burn up in the atmosphere.* —**dis.in.te.gra.tion** (-tuh.GRAY.shun) *n.*

dis.in.ter (dis.in.TUR) *v.* **-ters, -terred, -ter.ring** dig up from the earth or a grave; exhume; **dis.in.ter.ment** *n.*

dis.in.ter.est.ed (dis.IN.tris.tid, -tuh.res.tid) *adj.* 1 unselfish or impartial: *a disinterested observer, offer, generosity, service.* 2 uninterested or indifferent: *He looked bored and disinterested; disinterested and uninformed clerks.*

dis.joint.ed (dis.JOIN.tid) *adj.* 1 broken at the joints. *a disjointed turkey.* 2 badly connected or incoherent: *a rambling and disjointed account, narrative; disjointed images, sentence structure, thoughts; the disjointed society we live in!*

disk *n.* 1 a computer storage device in a thin, flat, round shape for recording and reading back data using a drive mechanism: *a 5¼- or 3½-inch floppy disk; a hard or rigid disk; optical disks read by laser beams; to format a disk; copy* something on to a disk; make a backup disk. **2** a cartilage pad between vertebrae: *Al slipped* (= dislocated or ruptured) *a disk while playing football.* **3** a round, flat part or plate: *a kit including a buffer, adapter, and six sanding disks; the sun's disk* (= disklike figure). See also DISC.

disk drive *n.* a rotating device connected with a computer for recording and reading off data.

disk.ette (dis.KET) *n.* a 5¼- or 3½-inch computer storage disk.

disk pack *n.* a stack of computer storage disks forming a unit.

dis.like (dis.LIKE) *v.* **-likes, -liked, -lik.ing** not like: *Joe dislikes spinach; Jane dislikes playing with dolls.*
—*n.* a not liking; *a feeling of dislike; a cordial, deep, hearty, violent dislike; a dislike for or of dogs; Our dog has taken a strong dislike to the neighbor's cat; But the cat shows no dislike for Fido; The roommates don't know each other's likes and dislikes yet.*

dis.lo.cate (DIS.loh.cate, dis.LOH.cate) *v.* **-cates, -cat.ed, -cat.ing** move, as a bone of the body, from its proper position: *She dislocated her shoulder in the accident; Broken homes tend to dislocate people; workers dislocated by layoffs;* **adj.:** *a dislocated finger, hip, shoulder, worker; dislocated people such as the homeless; a dislocated economy.* —**dis.lo.ca.tion** (-loh.CAY.shun) *n.*

dis.lodge (dis.LOJ) *v.* **-lodg.es, -lodged, -lodg.ing** move forcibly from a position: *Artillery fire dislodged the enemy's infantry; The blow dislodged the filling from the tooth.*

dis.loy.al (dis.LOY.ul) *adj.* not loyal; unfaithful: *Troops disloyal to the government attacked the president's palace; a disloyal employee.* —**dis.loy.al.ly** *adv.*
—**dis.loy.al.ty** *n.* **-ties.**

dis.mal (DIZ.mul) *adj.* gloomy or depressing: *orphans facing a dismal future; a dismal failure, outlook, performance, record, showing; dismal weather.*
—**dis.mal.ly** *adv.*

dis.man.tle (dis.MAN.tul) *v.* **-tles, -tled, -tling 1** to strip something of covering, equipment, weapons, etc.; **adja.:** *the **dismantled** hulk of an abandoned bus.* **2** take apart: *a large desk dismantled for shipping; to dismantle a bureaucracy, military structure, pricing system; to dismantle trade barriers.*
—**dis.man.tle.ment** *n.*

dis.may (dis.MAY) *v.* dishearten, make afraid, or daunt, esp. about a problem to be resolved: *The students were dis-*mayed at the teachers' strike; dismayed to think they might fail the exam.
—*n.*: *The results of the exam filled us with dismay; We felt and expressed dismay at the number of failures; To our dismay, even the best student had failed.*
—**dis.may.ing.ly** *adv.*

dis.mem.ber (dis.MEM.bur) *v.* **1** cut or tear the limbs from a body; **adj.:** *a dismembered corpse.* **2** divide or tear into pieces: *Yugoslavia was dismembered by the civil war.* —**dis.mem.ber.ment** *n.*

dis.miss (dis.MIS) *v.* **1** allow or cause to leave; send away: *Class dismissed!* **2** release from a job, service, etc.: *He dismissed his chauffeur for reckless driving; was dismissed from his job.* **3** put out of one's mind; also, reject in court: *He dismissed the rumors as nonsense; "Case dismissed," said the judge.*

dis.miss.al (dis.MIS.ul) *n.* a being dismissed or sent away: *a curt dismissal; early dismissal because of snow.*

dis.mount (dis.MOUNT) *v.* **1** get down or cause to get off from a horse, vehicle, etc.: *Bicyclists are supposed to dismount and walk at a pedestrian crossing; The knight was dismounted by his opponent in a joust.* **2** remove something from its mounting: *to dismount a cannon from its carriage.* —*n.* an act of dismounting: *The gymnast dislocated an ankle on his dismount from the high bar.*

dis.o.be.dience (dis.uh.BEE.dee.unce) *n.* refusal to obey: *a soldier courtmartialed for disobedience; civil disobedience; willful disobedience.*
—**dis.o.be.di.ent** (dis.uh.BEE.dee.unt) *adj.: a disobedient child; disobedient to his parents.*

dis.o.bey (dis.uh.BAY) *v.* refuse or fail to obey: *dismissed for disobeying orders.*

dis.o.blige (dis.uh.BLIGE) *v.* **-blig.es, -bliged, -blig.ing 1** fail or refuse to oblige someone, as by not granting a request. **2** offend; inconvenience.

dis.or.der (dis.OR.dur) *n.* **1** a lack of orderly arrangement; disarray: *He leaves his room in disorder; The army retreated in disorder.* **2** a disturbance in functioning; mild disease: *bowel, brain, intestinal, mental, personality, respiratory, stomach disorders.* **3** an upset to the public peace: *to restore order where there is disorder; social disorders; Violent disorders* (= riots) *broke out in the country.*

dis.or.dered (dis.OR.durd) *adja.* marked by disorder: *He left the office in a disordered condition; a badly disordered desk; a disordered* (= sick) *mind.*

dis.or.der.ly (dis.OR.dur.lee) *adj*. **1** disorganized or disarrayed: *a disorderly pile of junk*. **2** unruly or riotous: *arrested for being drunk and disorderly; disorderly conduct (such as fighting in public)*. —**dis.or.der.li.ness** *n*.

dis.or.gan.ize (dis.OR.guh.nize) *v*. **-iz.es, -ized, -iz.ing** break up the orderly or systematic organization of a schedule, service, system, timetable, etc.: *Firing the department head disorganized operations; adj.: The department is now a **disorganized** mess; Everything is very disorganized.* —**dis.or.gan.i.za.tion** (-nuh.ZAY.shun, -nye-) *n*.

dis.o.ri.ent (dis.OR.ee.ent) *v*. cause to be lost or confused by taking someone out of familiar surroundings; *adj.: People become **disoriented** if shut up in a dungeon for some time; the disoriented* (= aimless) *youth of today*. —**dis.o.ri.en.ta.tion** (-TAY.shun) *n*.

dis.own (dis.OWN) *v*. deny that one owns, knows, or is connected with a person or thing; reject: *children disowned by their parents*.

dis.par.age (dis.PAIR.ij) *v*. **-ag.es, -aged, -ag.ing** *Formal*. cause to be less well thought of; also, treat or talk about a person or thing slightingly; *adj.: a **disparaging** remark, tone, word; adv.: He talks **disparagingly** about his rivals*.

dis.pa.rate (DIS.puh.rit, dis.PAIR.it) *adj*. fundamentally unlike: *Apples and oranges are not so disparate as chalk and cheese*. —**dis.par.i.ty** (dis.PAIR.i.tee) *n*. **-ties**: *the wide disparity in incomes; the great disparity between pay scales for men and women*.

dis.pas.sion.ate (dis.PASH.uh.nit) *adj*. calmly impartial; unemotional: *a cool dispassionate examination of the problem; a dispassionate analysis, observer, view; His manner throughout was cold and dispassionate.* —**dis.pas.sion.ate.ly** *adv*.

dis.patch (dis.PATCH) *v*. **1** send with directness or great speed: *Ambulances were dispatched to the scene of the accident; adj.: **radio-dispatched** delivery*. **2** deal with or finish quickly: *He dispatches the morning's business before lunch; The bull was dispatched* (= killed) *at the end of the bullfight*. —*n*. **1** a dispatching: *efficient, hasty, speedy dispatch; adj.: a dispatch bay, center, depot, service, system*. **2** fast efficiency: *She moved, worked with great dispatch to stop the trouble before it spread; diligence and dispatch*. **3** a message, report, etc., as for a government, a news service, or the military: *to file, send a dispatch; He was **mentioned in dispatches*** (for bravery in battle). Also **des.patch**.

dis.patch.er (dis.PATCH.ur) *n*. one who sends out trains, buses, taxis, etc. on schedule or as needed.

dis.pel (dis.PEL) *v*. **-pels, -pelled, -pel.ling** get rid of something by scattering or driving off: *The sun dispelled the early morning fog; The new evidence dispelled all doubts; to dispel fears, gloom, hopes, illusions, myths, notions, rumors, suggestions; The light that the book shed on the subject dispelled the mists of ignorance*.

dis.pen.sa.ry (dis.PEN.suh.ree) *n*. **-ries** a place where medicines are prepared and given out in a school, factory, hospital, etc.

dis.pen.sa.tion (dis.pen.SAY.shun) *n*. **1** a dispensing: *the dispensation of the laws*. **2** an exemption from a rule of law: *a papal dispensation allowing remarriage; No dispensation can be granted from divine law*. **3** an ordering of events; also, a resulting system or rule: *to live under the Christian dispensation; the new dispensation in Russia after Communist rule*.

dis.pense (dis.PENCE) *v*. **-pens.es, -pensed, -pens.ing** distribute or give out: *to dispense alms to the poor, food to the hungry; Courts dispense justice; Pharmacists dispense* (= prepare and give out) *medicines; Shall we **dispense with*** (= do without) *the formalities?* —**dis.pen.sa.ble** *adj*.

dis.pen.ser (dis.PEN.sur) *n*. one that dispenses, esp. a device for the convenient dispensing of something: *the ice dispenser of a fridge; cash, soap, tape, towel dispensers*.

dis.per.sal (dis.PUR.sul) *n*. a dispersing or scattering: *the natural dispersal of seeds; the dispersal of a crowd*.

dis.perse (dis.PURCE) *v*. **-pers.es, -persed, -pers.ing** **1** break up and distribute: *The crowd dispersed when the riot police appeared; new chemicals to disperse oil slicks in the harbor; In an emulsion, one liquid is dispersed or suspended in another, as oil in water*. **2** spread widely: *Seeds are dispersed in various ways by the wind, water, people, and animals; adj.: Maples are found widely **dispersed** in Canada*. —**dis.per.sion** (-PUR.shun) *n*.

dis.pir.it (di.SPEER.it) *v*. make sad, downcast, or discouraged: *The players were dispirited by repeated failures*.

dis.place (dis.PLACE) *v*. **-plac.es, -placed, -plac.ing** move from its proper place: *a ship that displaces 12,000 tons (of water); After World War II many* *displaced persons* (= those uprooted by war and political unrest) *came to the U.S.*

dis.place.ment (dis.PLACE.munt) *n.* a displacing or what is displaced: *the displacement of Jon as the club's treasurer; Naval ships are rated according to their displacement (of water equal to their weight in long tons).*

dis.play (dis.PLAY) *v.* expose clearly to the view; show or exhibit: *A store window is used to display merchandise; He thought to display his learning at the convention, but only succeeded in displaying his ignorance.* —*n.* **1** a displaying or what is displayed: *a dazzling, impressive, lavish, ostentatious, spectacular display of new fashions; Select the one you like from the display; a display of courage; a graphic display presented on the VDT; a modest display of one's talents; Private matters are not for public display; to make, put on a vulgar display of one's wealth; window displays;* **adja.:** *a display cabinet, case, window.* **2** the visual output of an electronic device or the output device used, as a monitor screen: *a liquid crystal display; video displays;* **adja.:** *a display screen, terminal, unit.*

dis.please (dis.PLEEZ) *v.* **-pleas.es, -pleased, -pleas.ing** be unpleasing to someone; annoy: *She's easily displeased by anything that doesn't suit her whims;* **adj.:** *Sam is very displeased with you; She's displeased that you haven't spoken to her all week; Your silence is displeasing to her.*

dis.pleas.ure (dis.PLEZH.ur) *n.* the feeling one has when displeased: *to incur the displeasure of the queen; He showed his displeasure with the day's happenings.*

dis.port (dis.PORT) *v.* esp. **disport oneself** Formal. frolic; play.

dis.pos.a.ble (dis.POH.zuh.bul) *adj.* **1** available to be used: *disposable dollars, funds, wealth; your disposable income* (= take-home pay). **2** to be used and then thrown away: *a disposable can, diaper, pop bottle; a disposable* (= dispensable) *relationship; our disposable society* (that throws things away instead of reusing them); *n.*: *the convenience of disposables; Disposables add to the garbage.* —**dis.pos.a.bil.i.ty** (-BIL.i.tee) *n.*

dis.pos.al (dis.POH.zul) *n.* **1** a disposition or arrangement: *the disposal of chessmen on a board.* **2** a getting rid of something: *garbage, sewage, waste disposal; the disposal* (= sale) *of the family farm; the disposal* (= giving away) *of grandpa's property according to his will.* **3** a device, usu. fitted in the kitchen sink, for shredding garbage which is then flushed down the drain; disposer. —**at one's disposal** to be used as one desires: *I'm at your disposal but she is not; She has placed her chauffeur at your disposal.*

dis.pose (dis.POZE) *v.* **-pos.es, -posed, -pos.ing 1** make ready or inclined: *to dispose the mind for receiving new ideas; Do TV shows dispose children to violent behavior?* **adjp.:** *She is not disposed* (= not in the mood) *to receive visitors today; The government is either well or ill disposed to grant your request; She's favorably disposed* (= inclined) *toward your proposal; The government is either well or ill disposed to grant your request.* **2** set in order; arrange: *"Man proposes, God disposes"; troops disposed in battle array.* —**dispose of 1** get rid of something unwanted: *the dangers of disposing of nuclear wastes; to dispose of assets, corpses, incriminating evidence, inventory, property.* **2** deal with successfully: *to dispose of complaints, problems, questions, tasks; The new champion disposed of* (= defeated) *the titleholder in no time; a mobster well known for disposing of* (= killing off) *his rivals.*

dis.pos.er (dis.POH.zur) same as DISPOSAL, 3.

dis.po.si.tion (dis.puh.ZISH.un) *n.* **1** a disposing of something; also, the power to dispose or use: *The heirs have disposition of the land; disposition of property by sale or gift; the final disposition.* **2** the way something is disposed; arrangement: *an elegant disposition of furniture; disposition of troops.* **3** one's general or natural tendency: *a woman of a pleasant disposition; a buoyant, genial, sunny, mild disposition; A disposition to fat or to get fat is usually inherited; a natural disposition to help people in trouble.*

dis.pos.sess (dis.puh.ZES) *v.* deprive someone of possession, esp. of land; evict: *They were dispossessed of their land;* **adj.:** *a dispossessed dirt farmer.* —**dis.pos.ses.sion** *n.*

dis.praise (dis.PRAIZ) *v.* **-prais.es, -praised, -prais.ing** speak in disapproval; disparage. Also *n.*

dis.proof (dis.PROOF) *n.* a disproving.

dis.pro.por.tion (dis.pruh.POR.shun) *n.* an absence of proportion.

dis.pro.por.tion.ate (dis.pruh.POR.shuh.nit) *adj.* out of proportion to something: *Your pay is disproportionate* (= low compared) *to the work involved; A disproportionate* (= too large) *amount*

of time is being spent on coffee breaks.
dis.prove (dis.PROOVE) v. **-proves, -proved, -prov.ing** prove wrong or false: *Creationists and evolutionists try to disprove each other's theories.*
dis.pu.ta.tion (dis.pew.TAY.shun) n. a debate or dispute, esp. the oral defense of an academic thesis.
dis.pu.ta.tious (dis.pew.TAY.shus) adj. given to arguing: *a disputatious committee; He is of a disputatious turn of mind.*
dis.pute (dis.PYOOT, long "OO") v. **-putes, -put.ed, -put.ing 1** argue or debate about something: *The speaker offered to dispute (the issue) with all comers; I do not dispute that the earth is round; The brothers are always disputing (= quarrelling).* **2** argue against the rightness or truth of something: *to dispute a claim, decision, election, statement, will.* **3** oppose or fight for in defense of something: *We'll dispute every inch of ground before yielding.* —n. an argument or quarrel, esp. one that is heated: *The argument led to a dispute; an acrimonious, bitter, sharp dispute; Religious disputes have led to bloodshed; to arbitrate, resolve, settle a dispute; Her claim to first prize is **beyond dispute** (= cannot be disputed); The contract settlement is still **in dispute** (= being disputed).* —**dis.pu.ta.ble** (-tuh.bul) adj. —**dis.put.er** or **dis.pu.tant** (DIS.pew.tunt, dis.PEW.tunt) n.
dis.qual.i.fy (dis.QUAL.uh.fye) v. **-fies, -fied, -fy.ing** make or declare unfit, ineligible, or unentitled: *The racehorse was disqualified because it was drugged.* —**dis.qual.i.fi.ca.tion** (-fuh.CAY.shun) n.
dis.quiet (dis.KWY.ut) v. upset the peace of mind or disturb the security of someone: *People are disquieted by news of friction between the superpowers;* adj.: *a very disquieting report.* —n. worry or anxiety: *a feeling of disquiet; We endured months of disquiet during the trial;* also **dis.qui.e.tude** n.
dis.qui.si.tion (dis.kwuh.ZISH.un) n. a lengthy discussion or inquiry; treatise.
dis.re.gard (dis.ruh.GARD) v. pay no attention or respect to something: *Please disregard this notice if you have already paid; Let's not disregard the advice of older and wiser people.* —n. lack of attention or respect: *Willful disregard of rules could land you in trouble; his disregard for his elders.* —**dis.re.gard.ful** adj.
dis.re.pair (dis.ri.PAIR) n. the state of being neglected and needing repairs: *a bridge that is in disrepair.*
dis.rep.u.ta.ble (dis.REP.yuh.tuh.bul) adj. having a bad reputation: *a disreputable businessman; his disreputable past; a disreputable part of town.*
dis.re.pute (dis.rip.YOOT, long "YOO") n. a state of ill repute; disgrace: *The theater fell into disrepute when it was taken over by the new management; It has been held in disrepute ever since.*
dis.res.pect (dis.ris.PECT) n. lack of respect: *without disrespect to our seniors; with no disrespect to our traditions; No disrespect was intended or meant.* —**dis.res.pect.ful** adj.: *a disrespectful remark.*
dis.robe (DIS.robe) v. **-robes, -robed, -rob.ing** take off clothing, esp. outer robes: *As everyone watched, Sam disrobed and dived into the pool.*
dis.rupt (dis.RUPT) v. break apart; hence, disturb or disorder: *attempts to disrupt debate in Congress.* —**dis.rup.tion** n.: *the total disruption of service caused by a strike; temporary disruptions in TV transmission.* —**dis.rup.tive** (-tiv) adj.: *disruptive activity, behavior, influences, strikers; The new policy proved disruptive of peace and harmony.*
dis.sat.is.fac.tion (DIS.sat.is.FAC.shun) n. the state of being dissatisfied: *The strikers expressed deep, keen, widespread dissatisfaction about or with working conditions.*
dis.sat.is.fied (dis.SAT.is.fide) adj. not satisfied; discontented: *He's dissatisfied at not getting a raise; a dissatisfied worker; He is dissatisfied with his pay.*
dis.sat.is.fy (dis.SAT.is.fye) v. **-fies, -fied, -fy.ing** fall short of satisfying.
dis.sect (dis.SECT) v. **1** cut into pieces for anatomical study: *to dissect a frog in biology class.* **2** analyze very finely. —**dis.sec.tion** n.: *a dissection (= analysis) of the causes of the revolution.*
dis.sem.ble (di.SEM.bul) v. **-bles, -bled, -bling 1** hide under a false guise: *He dissembled his emotions.* **2** feign or pretend: *He was merely dissembling sympathy.* —**dis.sem.bler** n. —**dis.sem.blance** (-blunce) n.
dis.sem.i.nate (di.SEM.uh.nate) v. **-ates, -at.ed, -at.ing** spread widely or to many people. —**dis.sem.i.na.tion** (-NAY.shun) n.: *the wide dissemination of knowledge through radio and TV.*
dis.sen.sion (di.SEN.shun) n. disagreement, esp. one causing hostility; quarrel: *They tried to sow dissension among the workers; to stir up dissension between rival groups.*
dis.sent (di.SENT) v. not agree; hold a different opinion: *One of the justices*

dissented from the views of the others; **adj**.: a **dissenting** judge, member, opinion, view, voice, vote.
—**n.** disagreement, as nonacceptance of the teachings of a church: *a matter that brooks no dissent; Some churches tolerate no dissent from traditional doctrines.* —**dis.sent.er** (di.SEN.tur) *n.*

dis.ser.ta.tion (dis.ur.TAY.shun) *n.* a long essay, esp. a doctoral thesis: *a dissertation on or about the novels of Jane Austen.*

dis.ser.vice (dis.SUR.vis) *n.* a harmful or injurious action: *Doing the children's homework is not only doing them a disservice but also a disservice to the great cause of education.*

dis.sev.er (dis.SEV.ur) *v.* separate; divide into parts.

dis.si.dence (DIS.uh.dunce) *n.* disagreement or dissent. —**dis.si.dent** *adj.*: *a dissident group; the expulsion of dissident trade unionists;* ***n.***: *persecution of political dissidents.*

dis.sim.i.lar (dis.SIM.uh.lur) *adj.* not similar; unlike: *Cats are not dissimilar to lions and leopards; comparison of dissimilar jobs for giving equal pay.*
—**dis.sim.i.lar.i.ty** (dis.suh.muh.LAIR.i.tee) *n.* **-ties.**

dis.si.mil.i.tude (dis.i.MIL.i.tude) *n.* lack of resemblance.

dis.sim.u.late (dis.SIM.yuh.late) *v.* **-lates, -lat.ed, -lat.ing** hide the truth; dissemble: *The job applicant dissimulated about his university degrees.*
—**dis.sim.u.la.tion** (-LAY.shun) *n.*
—**dis.sim.u.la.tor** (-lay.tur) *n.*

dis.si.pate (DIS.uh.pate) *v.* **-pates, -pat.ed, -pat.ing** **1** disperse; also, vanish or fade away, or cause to do so: *The sun dissipates the morning fog; The demonstrators waited for the tear gas to dissipate; Anger, energy, heat, myths, passions, vapors dissipate; to dissipate excess calories.* **2** waste foolishly; engage in wasteful, excessive pleasures: *a fortune dissipated by bad investments; a rich young man who dissipates his wealth by gambling in casinos.* —**dis.si.pa.tion** (-PAY.shun) *n.*: *a life of drunken dissipation.*

dis.so.ci.ate (di.SOH.shee.ate) *v.* **-ates, -at.ed, -at.ing** separate from association; cut off: *The Minister dissociated herself from the views expressed by her colleagues.* —**dis.so.ci.a.tion** (-AY.shun) *n.*

dis.so.lute (DIS.uh.loot) *adj.* profligate, immoral, and dissipated. —**dis.so.lute.ly** *adv.*; **dis.so.lute.ness** *n.*

dis.solve (di.ZOLV) *v.* **-solves, -solved, -solv.ing** **1** (make) go into solution: *Sugar dissolves in coffee; You dissolve it by stirring; Coffee dissolves sugar (= takes it in solution).* **2** lose identity and change or disappear: *On the screen, one scene dissolves into the next; Under cross-examination, the accusers dissolved into (= became) accused; The charges dissolved into thin air;* ***n.***: *The scenes changed in a series of dissolves.* **3** bring or come to an end: *to dissolve a marriage, parliament, partnership; Parliament dissolves at the end of a session;* ***adj.***: *a* ***dissolved*** *bond, marriage, party.* **4** break down: *The audience dissolved in laughter; The child dissolved in tears when his toy was crushed; Many marriages dissolve in divorce; Businesses dissolve during a depression; how to dissolve stress.*
—**dis.sol.va.ble** (-vuh.bul) *adj.*
dis.sol.u.ble (di.SOL.yuh.bul) *adj.* that can be dissolved; dissolvable.

dis.so.nance (DIS.uh.nunce) *n.* lack of harmony or agreement; discord: *a poet seeking harmony "from life's dissonance."*
—**dis.so.nant** *adj.*

dis.suade (di.SWADE) *v.* **dis.suades, dis.suad.ed, dis.suad.ing** advise or persuade not to do something: *We dissuaded her from quitting her job.*
—**dis.sua.sion** (-SWAY.zhun) *n.*
—**dis.sua.sive** (-siv) *adj.*

dis.taff (DIS.taff) *n.* **1** a stick for holding wool or flax for use in spinning. **2** women collectively; also, womanly occupations.
—**adj.** female: *distaff executives; He's related to the Silvas on the* ***distaff*** *side.*

dis.tal (DIS.tul) *adj.* far from a point of origin or attachment: *the distal (= outer) end of a leaf;* **dis.tal.ly** *adv.*

dis.tance (DIS.tunce) *n.* separation in space or time or its measure: *the distance between London and Paris; the distance from London to Paris; at a distance of a few kilometers; to cover, run, walk a distance; Let's keep a safe distance behind the car in front; Don't close the distance between our car and theirs; a braking, short, shouting, stopping, striking, walking distance; in the remote distances of history when the English language didn't exist; We have traveled quite a distance (= a long way) to come here; We can see the sea in the distance (= far away).*
—**go** or **last the distance** stay in or last till the end of something that requires sustained effort. —**keep one's distance** remain aloof or detached. —**keep someone at a distance** prevent someone from becoming friendly. —**v.** **-tanc.es, -tanced, -tanc.ing** place or keep at a distance: *We distanced ourselves from the*

policies of the new leaders.

dis.tant (DIS.tunt) *adj.* not close; far; away: *on the distant horizon; in the not too distant future; a distant relative; The school is two kilometers distant from our house; He acknowledged us with a rather distant* (= cold and aloof) *smile.*
—**dis.tant.ly** *adv.*

dis.taste (dis.TAIST) *n.* dislike or aversion: *She shows a strong distaste for romantic novels.* —**dis.taste.ful** *adj.*

dis.tem.per (dis.TEM.pur) *n.* a disease or disorder, esp. an infectious viral disease of young dogs and cats, often fatal.

dis.tend (dis.TEND) *v.* swell, as from internal pressure; *adj.*: *the distended tummies and skeletal frames of starving children.* —**dis.ten.tion** or **dis.ten.sion** *n.*

dis.tich (DIS.tik) *n.* a couplet.

dis.till (dis.TIL) *v.* **-tills, -tilled, -til.ling** 1 fall or cause to fall in drops, as by the condensation of vapor: *Salt is distilled from* or *out of sea water; Sometimes water distills through rocks and wets their surface; Flowers distil nectar; adj.: If you distil salt water you get pure **distilled** water.* 2 extract or emerge as the essential element; *adj.*: *a book that is the **distilled** wisdom of the ancients.* 3 produce or purify by distillation: *Malted barley is distilled to make whiskey; A license is required for distilling liquors; adj.: Whiskey, gin, rum, etc. are **distilled** liquors* or *spirits; adja.: a **distilling** company; the **distilling** industry.*
—**dis.til.la.tion** (dis.tuh.LAY.shun) *n.*

dis.til.late (DIS.til.it) *n.* a liquid resulting from distillation, as gasoline or whiskey.

dis.till.er (dis.TIL.ur) *n.* one who distills, esp. a producer of distilled alcoholic beverages.

dis.till.er.y (dis.TIL.uh.ree) *n.* **-er.ies** a place where alcoholic liquor is made.

dis.tinct (dis.TINCT) *adj.* 1 well-defined: *The Basques are a distinct group within Spanish society; a distinct accent, area, entity, minority, society, sound; The Maltese, Manx, Persian, and Siamese are four distinct breeds of cat; They are **distinct** (= different) from one another.* 2 definite: *Tall players have a distinct advantage in basketball; the distinct profile of a woman; There's a distinct hint of fall in the air; a distinct difference, edge, impression, possibility.* —**dis.tinct.ly** *adv.*; **dis.tinct.ness** *n.*

dis.tinc.tion (dis.TINK.shun) *n.* 1 a distinguishing or making a difference, as in treatment: *We pay our employees without distinction of sex.* 2 a difference; also, a trait, characteristic, etc. that makes a difference: *a philosopher who can draw* or *make a subtle distinction between being and becoming; to blur a distinction; clear-cut, fine, nice distinctions.* 3 excellence; also, something in recognition of this: *She passed the examination with distinction; She won many academic distinctions; a statesman of distinction; He enjoys* or *has* or *holds the dubious distinction of being the world's fattest man.*

dis.tinc.tive (dis.TINK.tiv) *adj.* marking the distinctness of something; characteristic: *the distinctive aroma of coffee; The aroma is distinctive of that type of coffee.* —**dis.tinc.tive.ly** *adv.*; **dis.tinc.tive.ness** *n.*

dis.tin.guish (dis.TING.gwish) *v.* 1 mark as different: *Speech distinguishes people from animals.* 2 perceive a difference; discriminate: *to distinguish between good and bad art.* 3 perceive or make out: *We were barely able to distinguish the hills in the distance.* 4 make famous, respected, etc.: *to distinguish oneself by gallantry in battle.*
—**dis.tin.guish.a.ble** (-gwish.uh.bul) *adj.*

distinguished *adj.* 1 famous or eminent: *a distinguished author; an award for distinguished service.* 2 having a dignified and superior manner: *a distinguished accent, gentleman, lady.*

dis.tort (dis.TORT) *v.* 1 twist out of its normal shape or condition. 2 alter or twist the truth, a story, etc.
—**dis.tor.tion** (-TOR.shun) *n.*: *The government claimed that the newspaper story was a gross distortion of the truth.*

dis.tract (dis.TRACT) *v.* draw one's attention away from something: *Don't distract me when I am trying to concentrate; A phone call distracted her from her homework; adj.: a distracting thought.*
—**distracted** *adj.* 1 with one's attention diverted: *He's easily distracted; Try not to become* or *get distracted.* 2 upset emotionally; bewildered by conflicting thoughts: *She wore a distracted look; to be distracted by* or *with anxiety, fear, grief.*

dis.trac.tion (dis.TRAC.shun) *n.* the state of being distracted or something that draws away one's attention: *She doesn't like distractions when trying to concentrate on her work; On weekends she looks for any distractions* (= amusements) *available in town; She was once driven to distraction* (= mental confusion) *by loneliness.*

dis.trait (dis.TRAY) *adj.* absent-minded;

inattentive.

dis.traught (dis.TRAWT) *adj.* mentally agitated or upset: *She was distraught with fear and pain; Hamlet was distraught* (= mad).

dis.tress (dis.TRESS) *n.* great danger or suffering of a temporary nature that calls for relief: *Wars bring distress and misery; to alleviate the distress of famine in Africa; economic, financial distress; He suffered great distress of body and mind; She felt deep distress at or over being unable to help; gastric distress* (= trouble). —*adj*.: *distress merchandise sold at a loss; Their houses were seized and sold at distress prices; a distress sale; the distress slaughter of cattle for lack of fodder;* "Mayday" and "SOS" are **distress signals** *used by airplanes and ships.* —*v.* cause distress to someone: *Your bad luck distresses me;* **adj.**: *We're* **distressed** *to hear you are ill; distressed at your plight; a distressed market; a **distressed area** with high unemployment, poverty, etc.; a tabletop with a distressed* (= marred to look like an antique) *finish; jeans with the distressed look;* **adj.**: *a **distressing** report about the famine in Africa; a distressing situation; It's distressing to think of so many children starving to death.* —**dis.tress.ful** *adj.*

dis.trib.ute (dis.TRIB.yoot, long "oo") *v.* **-utes, -ut.ed, -ut.ing 1** divide or pass out among many, esp. in shares: *Tips received are distributed equally among the staff.* **2** spread: *Distribute the manure evenly on the lawn; a magazine distributed nationwide to homeowners in selected areas;* **adj.**: *Spanish speakers are widely* **distributed** *in certain states.*
—**dis.trib.u.tion** (dis.truh.BYOO.shun) *n.*: *the distribution of food among the hungry; the distribution network of a marketing firm.*

dis.trib.u.tive (dis.TRIB.yuh.tiv) *adj.* having to do with distribution: *Multiplication is distributive over addition, i.e., x (y + z) = xy + xz; A* **distributive adjective** *such as "all" or "none" refers to all members of a set.* —**dis.trib.u.tive.ly** *adv.*

dis.trib.u.tor (dis.TRIB.yuh.tur) *n.* one that distributes, esp. a device that sends electricity to an engine's spark plugs in the correct order.

dis.trict (DIS.trict) *n.* an area or region, esp. one with a specific character or marked out for a judicial or administrative purpose: *business, electoral, farming, financial, residential, school, theater districts.*

district attorney *n.* the public prosecutor for a judicial district.

dis.trust (dis.TRUST) *n.* an absence of faith, confidence, trust, etc.: *the deep distrust between labor and management; the popular distrust of politicians.*
—*v.* not trust: *Everyone distrusts flatterers.* —**dis.trust.ful** *adj.*; **dis.trust.ful.ly** *adv.*

dis.turb (dis.TURB) *v.* **1** upset the peace, quiet, etc. of a place or person: *Don't disturb people who are asleep; The shots disturbed the quiet of the night; The picketer was charged with* **disturbing the peace** (= causing public disorder); **adj.**: *She was deeply* **disturbed** *to hear someone had broken into her home; She found the news quite* **disturbing**; *profoundly disturbing; a disturbing aspect, reminder, trend.* **2** upset mentally; **adj.**: *a ward for* **disturbed** *patients; a disturbed personality.* **3** trouble: *Don't disturb yourself for me.* —**dis.turb.er** *n.*: *arrested as a disturber of the peace.*

dis.turb.ance (dis.TUR.bunce) *n.* a disturbing; disorder or trouble: *to cause, create, make, put down, quell a disturbance; widespread political disturbances and riots.*

dis.u.nite (dis.yoo.NITE) *v.* **-nites, -nit.ed, -nit.ing** cause something or someone to become separate: *a family disunited by quarrels over an inheritance.* —**dis.u.ni.ty** (-YOO.ni.tee) *n.*

dis.use (dis.YOOSE) *n.* the state of not being used: *a railroad line that has fallen into disuse.* —**dis.used** *adj.*: *a disused mine shaft.*

ditch *n.* a trench dug in the earth, often containing water: *There are deep drainage ditches on the roadside; an irrigation ditch; to fight* **to the last ditch** (= to the end). —*v.* **1** dig a ditch around or in a place. **2** drive a car into a ditch; also, land a plane on water. **3** *Informal.* get rid of a person or thing; dump: *The project was ditched when funds ran out; He has a way of ditching his old buddies..*

dith.er (DITH.ur, "TH" as in "the") *n.* a state of nervous excitement or confusion: *He was all in a dither over his wedding.* —*v.* act indecisively: *He dithers instead of taking action.*

dit.to (DIT.oh) *n.* **dit.tos 1** the same as above: *The price of meat is up; ditto (for) potatoes.* **2** a mark ["] placed beneath something to be repeated; also **ditto mark.**

dit.ty (DIT.ee) *n.* **dit.ties** a simple little song: *a popular ditty.*

dit.zy *adj.* **dit.zi.er, -i.est** *Slang.* flighty: *ditzy blondes and brunettes.*

di.u.ret.ic (dye.yoo.RET.ic) *adj.* increasing the secretion of urine; *n.:* Digitalis, caffeine, and even water in large quantities are diuretics.

di.ur.nal (dye.UR.nul) *adj.* **1** daily: *the diurnal motion of the heavens due to the diurnal rotation of the earth.* **2** having to do with the daytime: *a diurnal, not nocturnal animal; Diurnal flowers close up at night.* —**di.ur.nal.ly** *adv.*

di.va (DEE.vuh) *n.* **-vas** or **-ve** (-vay) a leading female opera singer; prima donna.

di.va.gate (DYE.vuh.gate) *v.* **-gates, -gat.ed, -gat.ing** *Formal.* wander: *to divagate from the topic; divagating from his proper goal.* —**di.va.ga.tion** (-GAY.shun) *n.*

di.van (DYE.van, di.VAN) *n.* a couch, esp. one with neither back nor arms.

dive *v.* **dives,** *pt.* **dived** or **dove** (DOHV), *pp.* **dived, div.ing 1** plunge head-first: *Swimmers, submarines, aircraft, parachutists dive.* **2** enter vigorously into an activity: *He dives into homework as soon as he gets home.* **3** rush, dart, or plunge: *The rabbit dived into its hole as we approached; Stock prices dived* (= fell sharply) *during the Depression.* —*n.* a diving: *The submarine made a crash dive into the depths; a high dive from the diving board; a head-first dive; The pilot put his plane into a steep dive; The boxer took a dive* (= faked a knockout). —**div.er** *n.:* deep-sea, pearl, scuba, skin divers.

di.verge (duh.VURJ, dye-) *v.* **-verg.es, -verged, -verg.ing** move away from a direction or point: *rays that diverge from a central point; This is the point where our views diverge.* —**di.ver.gence** (-junce) *n.: a divergence of viewpoints.* —**di.ver.gent** (-junt) *adj.: widely divergent interests, paths, trends, views.*

di.vers (DYE.vurs) *adj. Formal.* several and various: *divers beliefs; the divers origins of words.*

di.verse (dye.VURSE) *adj.* different in kind; of various kinds: *people of diverse backgrounds.* —**di.verse.ly** *adv.*

di.ver.si.fy (dye.VUR.suh.fye) *v.* **-fies, -fied, -fy.ing** make various or diverse, esp. to extend business activities into different fields: *A company diversifies to protect itself from market changes; adj.: a well diversified investment portfolio.* —**di.ver.si.fi.ca.tion** (-fuh.CAY.shun) *n.*

di.ver.sion (di.VUR.zhun, dye-) *n.* **1** a pastime or entertainment: *golf, bridge, and such diversions.* **2** an action or maneuver that draws attention, activity, etc. aside: *a diversion of trade from one market to another; a diversion of funds from education to road maintenance.* **3** an alternative route for traffic bypassing a regular road that is closed for the time being; detour. —**di.ver.sion.ar.y** (-zhuh.nair.ee) *adj.: a diversionary attack, maneuver, raid, tactic.*

di.ver.si.ty (dye.VUR.si.tee) *n.* variety of things not related to one another: *a population with a diversity of backgrounds; a woman with a diversity of interests.*

di.vert (di.VURT, dye-) *v.* **1** turn aside: *to divert a stream from its natural course to a farm for irrigation.* **2** distract: *a false attack to divert the enemy fire.* **3** amuse: *video games to divert children.*

di.vest (dye.VEST, di-) *v.* deprive of clothes, property, rights, etc.; strip: *a boxer divested of his title; a company forced to divest itself of* (= get rid of) *some of its holdings.* —**di.vest.i.ture** (-VEST.i.chur) or **di.vest.ment** *n.*

di.vide (di.VIDE) *v.* **-vides, -vid.ed, -vid.ing 1** separate, esp. into parts or groups; distribute: *Divide the books into fiction and nonfiction; The kids divided up the pie among themselves; We divide the expenses and each pays a share; The path divides here into two branches; adj.: The country is getting* **divided** *along ethnic lines; A* **divided highway** *has a center strip separating traffic in opposite directions; a* **divided skirt** *(that looks like a skirt but is made like trousers); to draw a* **dividing line** (= line of separation) *between what is and what is not allowed.* **2** cause disagreement; disunite: *the policy of* **divide and rule** *(by setting parties against one another in order to have your own way); adj.: The caucus was sharply* **divided** *on or over the issue; a divided party.* **3** determine how many times one number is contained in another: *You get 3 when you divide 7 into 21; 36 divided by 9 is 4; 4 divides into 36 nine times.* —*n.* a dividing, esp. a watershed: *the Rockies are called the "Great Divide"; the great divide* (= death) *that everyone has to cross.*

div.i.dend (DIV.uh.dend) *n.* **1** a number to be divided: *10 is the dividend in "10 divided by 2."* **2** a stockholder's share of profits: *to declare a dividend; stock dividends.* **3** bonus: *Customer satisfaction carries or pays dividends in the form of better sales; generous, good, handsome, high, meager, rich dividends; the peace dividend from the end of the cold war.*

di.vid.er (di.VYE.dur) *n.* **1** one that divides, esp. a partition. **2** also **dividers**

divine / ¹do

pl. an instrument with two steel points used for measuring.

di.vine (di.VINE) *adj.* **-vin.er, -vin.est 1** of or like a god; having to do with God; theological: *Plato thought the planets were divine beings; King James I of England believed in the **divine right** of kings* (= God-given right to rule); *divine law, manifestation; the divine Savior; divine service, wisdom, worship.* **2** extremely good; superb; delightful: *a positively divine dress; His cooking is simply divine; divine weather.*
—*n.* a scholar or student of theology.
—*v.* **-vines, -vined, -vin.ing 1** foretell or predict by magic or special insight; *n.:* a ***divining rod*** *for finding water.* **2** conjecture or guess: *to divine her intentions; to divine what she means.*
—**di.vine.ly** *adv.* —**di.vin.er** *n.*
—**div.i.na.tion** (div.uh.NAY.shun) *n.*

di.vin.i.ty (di.VIN.i.tee) *n.* **-ties 1** the state of being divine. **2** a divine person; deity. **3** theology: *students of divinity; a Doctor of Divinity.* —**the Divinity** God.

di.vis.i.ble (di.VIZ.uh.bul) *adj p.* able to be divided, esp. evenly: *7 is not evenly divisible by 3.* —**di.vis.i.bil.i.ty** (-BIL.i.tee) *n.*

di.vi.sion (di.VIZH.un) *n.* **1** the act of dividing: *cell division; to do long division (e.g. Divide 37,428 by 59); the **division sign** [SoftKey]; Adam Smith advocated **division of labor*** (= each employee doing a part of the complete process). **2** the state of being divided: *There are sharp divisions in the party between Right and Left; The **division bells** of a legislature summon members to gather for voting.* **3** a line, boundary, etc. that divides: *an arbitrary division between young and old.* **4** the result of dividing; a part, portion, section, class, etc., esp. a large unit in the armed forces or a part of a league in sports: *airborne, armored, motorized divisions; the Yankees' place in the Eastern Division.*
—**di.vi.sion.al** *adj.*

di.vi.sive (di.VYE.siv) *adj.* tending to divide: *Abortion is a divisive issue.*
—**di.vi.sive.ly** *adv.;* **di.vi.sive.ness** *n.*

di.vorce (di.VORCE) *n.* **1** the complete legal termination of a marriage: *Dick and Jane got a divorce; She filed or sued for divorce; an uncontested divorce; The divorce was granted; divorce by mutual consent; divorce and reconciliation.* **2** a deep separation: *the divorce of church and state.* —*v.* **-vorc.es, -vorced, -vorc.ing** split up, as when a marriage is legally ended: *They got divorced; Dick divorced* (= split up with) *his wife;* *adj.:* *He's now divorced from his wife; a divorced couple; a dreamer divorced from the realities of daily life.*

di.vor.cé (di.vor.SAY) *n.* a divorced man. —**di.vor.cee** or **di.vor.cée** (di.vor.SEE, -SAY), *fem.*

div.ot (DIV.ut) *n.* a piece of ground torn out by the stroke of a golf club.

di.vulge (di.VULJ) *v.* **-vulg.es, -vulged, -vulg.ing** make known something secret: *He refused to divulge details of campaign expenses to the press.*

div.vy (DIV.ee) *v.* **div.vies, div.vied, div.vy.ing** *Informal.* divide: *robbers divvying up the loot.*

Dix.ie (DIX.ee) *n.* the Southern states of the U.S.

Dix.ie.land (DIX.ee.land) *n.* a jazz in duple time marked by improvisations.

diz.zy (DIZ.ee) *adj.* **diz.zi.er, diz.zi.est 1** having a whirling unsteady feeling in the head; giddy and prone to fall; also, causing this feeling: *a dizzy height, spell, speed; Looking down from the tower made him dizzy; He was dizzy from the height; Dizzy with success, he lost his head.* **2** *Informal.* silly or lightheaded: *a dizzy teenager.* —*v.* **diz.zies, diz.zied, diz.zy.ing** make dizzy: *She was dizzied by the height;* *adj a.:* *the **dizzying** heights of fame.* —**diz.zi.ly** *adv.;* **diz.zi.ness** *n.*

DNA *n.* a nucleic acid found in all living cells which transmits genetic information.

¹do (DOO) *v.* **does** (DUZ), *pt.* **did**, *pp.* **done** (DUN), **do.ing 1** perform: *to do a good job; We'll do our best to help; to do* (= fulfill) *one's duty; He did* (= completed) *five years in the military; What's done is done* (= it cannot be changed); *What do you do* (= work at) *for a living? Our class is doing* (= presenting) *"Hamlet."* **2** make: *to do a painting; Do* (= grant) *us a favor.* **3** cause or effect: *Kindness does wonders; Foul play does no good.* **4** deal with, work on, etc. to achieve an aim: *to do the dishes; Who does your hair? I can't do* (= deal successfully with) *this sum! He does* (*Informal* for uses or takes) *drugs; Let's do a lunch* (= have lunch together). **5** fasten; also **do up:** *Do your shirt* (*up*). **6** behave: *Do to others as you would like them to do to you; Do as I say, not as I do! Taking the knife to your mouth — it's just not **done*** (= not considered proper behavior). **7** suffice or serve: *This hat will do nicely, although I could have done with a better one; My knapsack will **do duty** for a pillow; We had to **make** the old carpet **do** for another year; When times are hard,* you **make do with** what you have or simply **do without;** We have to **do without** a lot of luxuries. **8** get on: *How are you doing in your new job?* [as a greeting to exchange on being introduced] *How do you do?* **9** move at a specified speed; travel: *Your car was doing 120 km/h; a 1990 book that tells you how to do* (= tour) *Europe on $50 a day.* **10** cook: *How do you like your steak done?* **11** cheat: *Many people were done out of their savings by the scam.* **12** [as an auxiliary verb in questions, negations, inversions; for emphasis; to refer to an earlier verb]: *Do you know what I know? I do not; Never did I see such a thing! I do declare! Run as fast as I do.* —**do a job** or **number on** *Slang.* treat someone roughly; confound, esp. by deception. —**do away with 1** get rid of something. 2 kill someone. —**do by** deal with or treat: *"Do as you would be done by," says the Golden Rule.* —**do for** attend to or care for someone: *They do for you in the rest home.* —**do in** *Slang.* 1 kill: *He was done in by gangsters.* 2 ruin: *She was done in by the scam.* —**do justice to** handle or treat as one deserves or requires. —**do the trick** produce the desired result. —**have to do with:** *She won't have anything to do* (= have any business) *with door-to-door sellers; This has to do with* (= is about) *selling her house.* —*n., pl.* **dos** or **do's** 1 something to be done: *Too many do's and don'ts* (= rules and customs) *cramp your style.* 2 *Informal.* a party or social event: *They had a big do at the country club.* —**do.a.ble** (DOO.uh.bul) *adj.*

²**do** (DOH) *n. Music.* the first or last tone of the diatonic scale.

dob.bin *n.* a patient, plodding farm horse.

Do.ber.man pin.scher (DOH.bur.mun. PIN.shur) *n.* a large, short-haired dog with a pointed snout.

doc *n. Informal.* 1 doctor. 2 guy or fellow: *What's up, doc?*

do.cent (DOH.sunt) *n.* a university teacher not on the regular faculty.

doc.ile (DOS.ul, -ile, DOH.sile) *adj.* easy to teach, control, etc.; submissive: *a docile child, horse, patient, pupil;* **doc.ile.ly** *adv.* —**do.cil.i.ty** (doh.SIL.i.tee) *n.*

dock *n.* 1 the place for the accused in a courtroom. 2 an area of water beside a pier or between piers: *Ships are brought into dock for repairs;* **Floating docks** are dry docks (in which a ship can lie out of the water); **graving docks** (for cleaning and tarring a ship's bottom); a **wet dock** (with water at a constant level, free from tides). 3 a pier or wharf; hence, a loading platform: *labor trouble at or in or on the docks.* —*v.* 1 cut off the end of something; hence, make a deduction from something due: *to dock a horse's tail; Wages are docked for being late.* 2 move or come into a dock; hence, link two spacecraft together in space; also, become so linked: *A ship docks at a port; A spacecraft docks with another;* **adj.:** *a docking maneuver.*

dock.age (DOCK.ij) *n.* 1 the use of a dock. 2 a charge for this.

dock.et (DOCK.it) *n.* a list, as of court cases tried or to be tried, things to be done, contents of a package, etc.: *What's on the docket today?* —*v.* put a summary of a case on a docket; list a case for action before a court.

dock.er, dock.hand or **dock.work.er** (DOK.wur.kur) *n.* a longshoreman: *a harbor closed by a dockers' strike.*

dock.yard *n.* a shipyard.

doc.tor (DOC.tur) *n.* 1 a physician; an M.D.: *Patients see doctors; Doctors see and treat their patients; This is not exactly what the doctor ordered* (= what is beneficial or desirable). 2 one who holds a doctorate degree, as a Ph.D.: *He got his doctor's (degree) last year; Who shall decide when doctors disagree* (= when the experts can't agree on it)? —*v.* 1 treat medically: *She was doctored back to health by our family physician.* 2 repair or mend: *My programmer has doctored the software so now it runs without a hitch.* 3 alter so as to deceive: *an accountant accused of doctoring the books or accounts; He didn't know the cat had been doctored* (= castrated) *when he paid for it;* **adj.: doctored** (= loaded) *dice; A doctored* (= drugged or strengthened) *wine has a different aroma.*

doc.tor.al (DOC.tuh.rul) *adja.* having to do with the academic doctorate: *a doctoral candidate, degree, hood; a postdoctoral research fellow.*

doc.tor.ate (DOC.tuh.rit) *n.* a university degree of the highest level: *She was awarded a doctorate in economics; D.Phil., Ed.D., Ph.D., etc. are usually earned doctorates* (based on attending a university); *D.D., D.Litt., LL.D., etc. may be honorary doctorates.*

doc.tri.naire (doc.truh.NAIR) *adj.* applying a preconceived doctrine without regard to reality or practical problems: *doctrinaire feminists, language, logic.* Also *n.*

doc.trine (DOC.trin) *n.* something

taught, as a set of theories, dogmas, basic beliefs, etc.: *the doctrines of the Church of England; to apply, disprove, establish, preach a doctrine; a sound doctrine.* —**doc.tri.nal** (DOC.truh.nul, doc.TRY.nul) *adj.*

doc.u.dra.ma (DOC.yuh.dram.uh) *n.* a dramatic piece based on historical facts produced for TV or as a movie: *They did a docudrama on the life and work of Einstein.*

doc.u.ment (DOC.yuh.munt) *n.* **1** an official paper, as a deed or birth certificate, forming the proof or basis of something; also, any book or similar item of a factual nature: *to submit a document as evidence in court; an authentic document;* **Document processing** involves data capture, storage, retrieval, duplication, etc., as done by word processors, printers, and copiers; document-processing software. **2** any computer data file. —*v.* (-ment) support with documents or references: *to document a claim, report, thesis; The historian documented her study by citing references.*

doc.u.men.ta.ry (doc.yuh.MEN.tuh.ree) **1** *adj.* a. concerning or being documents: *Citizenship certificates of two countries are documentary proof of dual citizenship; documentary evidence, material.* **2** *adj.* wholly factual and unbiased: *a documentary account, approach, style.* —*n., pl.* **-ries** a film or TV show of a factual nature: *a documentary on* or *about the harmful effects of pesticides;* **adj.**: *a documentary film, report, series.*

doc.u.men.ta.tion (doc.yuh.men.TAY.shun) *n.* (the providing of) documents or references: *The software comes with good documentation* (= operating instructions).

dod.der (DOD.ur) *n.* a parasitic vine of the morning-glory family that grows on other plants by means of suckers. —*v.* tremble or move shakily because of old age. —**dod.der.er** *n.*

dodge (DOJ) *v.* **dodg.es, dodged, dodg.ing** avoid by a trick or sudden movement; move trickily or quickly: *He went to Mexico to dodge the draft; to dodge a blow by ducking; He dodged behind a rock; He dodges in and out of traffic.* —*n.* **1** a dodging; means of evasion: *to use investments as a tax dodge.* **2** a clever scheme, expedient, or plan. —**dodg.er** *n.*: *draft, tax dodgers.*

do.do (DOH.doh) *n.* **1** a long-extinct, flightless bird: *The plan is dead as the* or *a dodo.* **2** a stupid or old-fashioned person.

doe (DOH) *n.* a full-grown female of the deer, antelope, rabbit, goat, etc. whose male is a buck.

do.er (DOO.ur) *n.* one who does, esp. a person of vigorous action.

does See DO.

doe.skin (DOH.skin) *n.* a soft leather of the skin of a doe or lamb.

does.n't (DUZ.unt) does not.

doff *v.* take off: *He doffed his coat and boots at the door; The President doffed* (= lifted) *his hat to the crowd.*

dog *n.* **1** a domesticated canine such as a poodle or beagle: *attack dogs like the pit-bull terrier, police dogs like German shepherds; guard, guide, mad, seeing-eye, sheep, sled, sporting, stray, working dogs; toy dogs* (= very small breeds); *Wild* (= not domesticated) *dogs include coyotes, foxes, jackals, and wolves; to curb one's dog; to work* **like a dog** (= very hard). **2** *Informal.* a fellow; also, a low worthless person: *a dirty dog; lucky dog; a running dog* (= lackey); *(an experience so bad) it shouldn't happen to a dog; He led* **a dog's life** (= wretched existence). **3** *Slang.* something considered a total failure: *The book was a dog; it never sold.* **4** an andiron; also, any of several devices for holding and gripping. —**a dog's age** *Informal.* a very long time. —**go to the dogs** *Informal.* be ruined, morally, physically, etc. —**let sleeping dogs lie** do not disturb a situation and cause unnecessary trouble. —**put on the dog** show off as though wealthy and refined.
—*v.* **dogs, dogged, dog.ging** track, pursue, etc. like a dog; hence, beset: *an expedition dogged by mishaps and problems.*

dog.bane *n.* any of several poisonous plants.

dog.cart *n.* a light two-wheeled carriage with a pair of seats back to back.

dog.catcher (DOG.cach.ur) *n.* one paid to capture and deal with stray dogs.

dog days *n.pl.* the hottest days of the summer.

doge (DOHJ) *n.* formerly, the chief magistrate of Genoa or Venice.

dog-ear *n.* a turned-down corner of a page; *adj.*: *a dog-eared book.*

dog-eat-dog *adj.* marked by ruthless competition: *this dog-eat-dog world; It's so dog-eat-dog in some courses that students turn to cheating.*

dog.fight *n.* **1** a rough fight, as between dogs. **2** an aerial combat between two or more fighter planes: *They engaged in a dogfight.*

dog.fish *n.* any of several small sharks.

dogged / dolly

dog.ged (DOG.id) *adj.* persistent or stubborn: *her dogged determination; his dogged efforts, loyalty, persistence.*
—**dog.ged.ly** *adv.;* **dog.ged.ness** *n.*

dog.ger.el (DOG.ur.ul) *n.* badly written, often humorous verse.

dog.gie, doggie bag same as DOGGY, DOGGY BAG.

dog.gone *adj. Informal.* damn: *Doggone it, how did it happen? That doggone pooch has eaten the cat food.*

dog.gy *n.* **dog.gies** [child's word] dog.

doggy bag *n.* a bag for taking leftovers from a restaurant, as if for one's dog.

dog.house *n.* a shelter for a dog. —**in the doghouse** *Informal.* in a state of disfavor.

do.gie or **do.gy** (DOH.gee) *n.* **-gies** a motherless calf.

dog in the manger *n.* one who selfishly guards something useless to prevent others from using it; *adj.:* a *dog-in-the-manger* policy.

dog.leg *n.* a sharp bend; hence, something so shaped, as a fairway.

dog.ma (DOG.muh) *n.* a belief or set of beliefs held strongly and often on the basis of authority, esp. that of a church.

dog.mat.ic (dog.MAT.ic) *adj.* **1** of dogma: *dogmatic theology* (concerned with the content of the Christian faith). **2** asserted by authority alone: *a dogmatic approach, assertion, statement, view; A scientist cannot be dogmatic* (= too assertive) *about questions that cannot be verified.* Also **dog.mat.i.cal**.
—**dog.mat.i.cal.ly** *adv.* —**dog.ma.tism** (DOG.muh.tiz.um) *n.*

do-good.er (DOO.good.ur) *n. Informal.* a well-meaning but impractical and naive social reformer.

dog-tired *adj.* quite exhausted.

dog.tooth *n.* a canine tooth.

dogtooth violet *n.* an early spring wildflower of the lily family.

dog.trot *n.* a gentle, slow trot; also *v.* **-trots, -trot.ted, -trot.ting**.

dog.wood *n.* a small tree or shrub with four-leaved greenish-white flowers and bright-red fruits.

dogy same as DOGIE.

doi.ly *n.* **-lies** a small, decorative lace or linen mat.

doings *n.pl.* things that are done or that occur.

do-it-yourself *adja.* having to do with use by the consumer rather than by a paid supplier: *a book on do-it-yourself plumbing repairs; a do-it-yourself backyard barbecue.* —**do-it-your.self.er** *n.*

dol.ce vi.ta (dole.chay.VEE.tah) *n.* a life of sweet self-indulgent luxury.

dol.drums (DOLE.drums, DOLL-) *n.pl.* **1** a region near the equator where there are light, changeable winds and many calms: *a sailing ship in the doldrums* (= becalmed). **2** a period or mood of depression, listlessness, inactivity, etc.: *He has been in the doldrums since losing his job.*

dole *n. Informal.* a grant of assistance, as food, clothes, or money, to the needy, esp. a payment by government to the unemployed: *He was on the dole for many months before he found a new job.* —*v.* **doles, doled, dol.ing** give out as charity, or sparingly, bit by bit: *a social worker who doles out sympathy to all and sundry.*

dole.ful *adj.* causing, having, or expressing sorrow: *doleful news.*
—**dole.ful.ly** *adv.*

doll *n.* **1** a small figure in the form of a human, esp. used as a child's toy: *baby, paper, rag dolls; a miniature **doll house**.* **2** *Informal.* an attractive or lovable person. —*v.* **doll up** *Informal.* dress finely, as for a special occasion: *She dolled herself up for the school prom.*

dol.lar (DOLL.ur) *n.* **1** the basic money unit in the U.S., Canada, Australia, and other countries: *the almighty dollar; a cheap, falling, strong, weak dollar; He repaid the loan in dearer dollars; to feel, look, smell **like a million dollars*** (*Informal for* splendid), *a **million-dollar** body, face, girl, view;* **Dollar for dollar** (= proportionately to the money involved), *this car is second to none; adja.: a **dollar-for-dollar** return for your money; on a dollar-for-dollar basis; a dollar bill, country, sign [$].* **2** *Informal.* money: *Everyone likes dollars; She was throwing dollars away by investing in that company; your entertainment, health, investment, dollar; adja.: a dollar amount, figure; dollar losses; in dollar terms.*

dollar day *n.* a day on which a store holds a special sale of low-priced goods.

dollar diplomacy *n.* **1** the use of a government's power to further its overseas economic or financial interests. **2** diplomacy helped by financial resources.

dollar store *n.* a store that sells goods priced no more than a dollar.

dollies See DOLLY.

dol.lop (DOLL.up) *n.* an amount or serving: *a dollop of whipped cream; We need large dollops of cash; You need an extra dollop of skill to do a good job.*

dol.ly (DOLL.ee) *n.* **dol.lies 1** [child's

word] a doll. **2** a low, wheeled platform, as used for moving heavy objects, for getting under an automobile, for moving a TV or movie camera around on, etc.

dol.men (DOLE.mun, DOLL-) *n.* a prehistoric monument formed by a large flat stone laid across upright stones.

do.lo.mite (DOH.luh.mite, DOL.uh-) *n.* a somewhat soft mineral or rock made up of calcium and magnesium carbonates.

do.lor (DOH.lur) *n. Poetic.* sorrow, mental distress. —**do.lor.ous** (DOH.luh.rus, DOL-) *adj.: dolorous lamentations; a dolorous misfortune;* **do.lor.ous.ly** *adv.* Also **do.lour** *Cdn.*

dol.phin (DOLL.fin) *n.* a small, whalelike sea mammal: *a school of dolphins; a bull* (= male) *dolphin; the calf* (= young) *and cow* (= female) *of a dolphin.*

dolt *n.* a stupid person; **dolt.ish** *adj.*

do.main (doh.MAIN) *n.* **1** an area under one's rule or control: *the King's domain; Our district has always been the domain of the Conservatives.* **2** a range or field of activity or concern: *Medicine is in the general domain of science; public domain.*

dome *n.* **1** a hemispherical roof, vault, etc.; *adj. & cpd: a* **domed** *building, ceiling, stadium, structure; a glass-domed skylight; our gold-domed capitol; an onion-domed Orthodox church.* **2** *Informal.* head: *Get that into thy thick dome!*

do.mes.tic (duh.MES.tic) *adj.* **1** of or concerning the household, home life, etc.: *a domestic quarrel between the maid and the homemaker; a domestic scene of love and peace; Butlers are in domestic service; She's not your domestic type of woman (who enjoys home life and working at home).* **2** having to do with one's own country; not foreign: *domestic crude oil, industries, markets, politics, prices, wines.* **3** tame, not wild: *cats, dogs, cows, ducks, pigs, and such domestic animals.* —*n.* a servant in someone's home, esp. a female. —**do.mes.ti.cal.ly** *adv.*

do.mes.ti.cate (duh.MES.tuh.cate) *v.* -cates, -cat.ed, -cat.ing make accustomed to living in human environments, out of the wild: *You can train an animal to work only after domesticating it; adj.: a* **domesticated** *variety of wheat; domesticated cattle;* **do.mes.ti.ca.tion** (-CAY.shun) *n.* —**do.mes.tic.i.ty** (-mes.TIS.i.tee) *n.*

domestic science same as HOME ECONOMICS.

dom.i.cile (DOM.uh.sile, -sul) *n.* the place of one's habitual residence: *Your will is settled according to the law of the place where you had your official domicile when you made the will even if you changed your domicile afterward.* —*v.* -ciles, -ciled, -cil.ing have or provide with a domicile; *an Iowan domiciled in California.* —**dom.i.cil.i.ar.y** (-SIL.ee.air.ee) *adj.*

dom.i.nant (DOM.uh.nunt) *adj.* **1** dominating or prevailing: *the dominant idea or theme in her books; English speakers are the dominant group in North America; a dominant influence in his life; a dominant passion; a dominant* (= overlooking) *cliff.* **2** in genetics, overpowering another gene or trait parallel to it; not recessive or latent: *Brown eyes are dominant over blue when genes for both are present.* —**dom.i.nance** (-nunce) *n.*

dom.i.nate (DOM.uh.nate) *v.* **-nates, -nat.ed, -nat.ing** **1** have control, authority, or influence: *Seniors try to dominate over the juniors; Our team dominated the league this year.* **2** overlook: *the cliffs dominating the city.* —**dom.i.na.tion** (-NAY.shun) *n.*

dom.i.neer (dom.uh.NEER) *v.* rule over, esp. tyrannically: *The stronger ones tend to domineer over the weaker; adj.: a big* **domineering** *bully.*

Do.min.i.can (doh.MIN.i.cun) *n.* **1** a person of or from the **Dominican Republic,** a country in the West Indies. **2** a member of a religious order of friars and nuns following the rule of St. Dominic. Also *adj.*

dom.i.nie (DOM.uh.nee) *n.* **1** *Scot.* a schoolteacher. **2** *Informal.* a clergyman.

do.min.ion (duh.MIN.yun) *n.* **1** sovereign power or its exercise: *in the days of the Empire, when Britain had dominion over land and sea; Many nations have been freed from the dominion of the colonial powers since World War II.* **2** the field or territory over which dominion is exercised; domain: *the king's dominions; British settler colonies were raised to the status of dominion (having self-rule but owing allegiance to the Crown); the Dominion of Canada.*

dom.i.no (DOM.uh.noh) *n.* **-nos** or **-noes** [takes *sing. v.*] **1** a game in which oblong pieces with one to six spots on either half are placed end to end so that the halves match each other. **2** such a piece.

domino effect *n.* the fall of one item of an arranged series causing the collapse of the next on or toward which it is leaning and so on down

the line; chain reaction.
domino theory *n.* the belief that a foreign takeover of one nation will lead to its neighbors also being taken over.
don *n.* **1 Don** a respectful term of address for men in Spanish: *Don Carlos.* **2** a Mafia leader. —*v.* **dons, donned, don.ning** put on clothing, hats, etc.
Do.ña (DOH.nyuh) *n.* a title used with a Spanish lady's first name.
do.nate (DOH.nate, doh.NATE) *v.* **-nates, -nat.ed, -nat.ing** give, esp. to a worthy cause: *We donate used clothes to the Salvation Army.* —**do.na.tion** (doh.NAY.shun) *n.*: *to make a donation; a donation to charity; political donations from corporations.*
done *pp.* of DO. —*adjp.* **1** cooked: *How do you like your steak done – rare, medium-rare, medium, or well? She likes it medium-rare and* **done to a turn** or **done to a T** (= just right). **2** *adja.* considered proper: *Eating peas with your knife – it's not* **the done thing**. **3** finished: *We're done with the dishes; a done deal; "You're done," he threatened; I'm* **done for** or **done in** or **done up** (= quite exhausted). —**done.ness** *n.: Degrees of doneness may be dialed on certain microwave ovens.*
Don Ju.an (don.WAHN) *n.* in Spanish legend, a notorious seducer of women; hence, a rake.
don.key (DONK.ee) *n.* **-keys 1** an ass: *A donkey brays; Donkeys go heehaw.* **2** a headstrong or stupid person.
—**a donkey's years** *Slang.* a long time.
donkey work *n. Informal.* the work of a drudge: *Computers take much of the donkey work out of our lives.*
Don.na (DON.uh) *n.* [Italian title] lady or madam.
don.ny.brook (DON.ee.brook) *n.* a wild brawl.
do.nor (DOH.nur) *n.* one who donates: *blood, bone-marrow, egg, organ, tissue donors; corporate campaign donors;* **adja.**: *donor nations; frozen donor embryos; donor sperm.*
Don Qui.xo.te (don.kee.HOH.tee) *n.* an idealistic, impractical fighter of evil, as the hero of a satiric novel of the same name by Cervantes, a 16th-century Spanish writer.
don't do not. —*n.* a prohibition or order not to do something: *do's and don'ts.*
do.nut (DOH.nut) *n.* a ring of leavened dough fried in fat: *People like to dunk donuts in coffee; He used to hang out in 24-hour donut shops.* Also **doughnut**.
doo.dad (DOO.dad) *n.* a small object or ornament, esp. one whose name has been temporarily forgotten: *the clutter of doodads on their coffee table.*
doo.dle (DOO.dul) *v.* **-dles, -dled, -dling** draw idly and aimlessly, esp. while preoccupied. —*n.* a drawing so made. —**doo.dler** *n.*
doodle bug *n.* the larva of the ant lion.
doom (long "oo") *n.* a judgment, esp. an adverse one; also, a grim fate: *The judge pronounced his doom and condemned him to death; He was sent to his doom in the electric chair; He awaited his doom on death row; The day of doom drew near; The soldier went to his doom bravely; messengers of* **doom and gloom**.
—*v.* consign to a bad fate; condemn: *They were doomed to die young; a plan doomed to failure from the beginning.*
dooms.day (DOOMZ.day) *n.* the end of the world; the day of God's final judgment on the world: *He's going to do nothing* **till doomsday**.
door (DORE) *n.* **1** a hinged, swinging, or sliding panel that covers an entrance, esp. to a house, room, etc.: *A door is hung on its hinges; to break down, close, force, lock, open, shut, slam a door; They knock, tap on the door; The door is ajar; back, double, front, revolving, side, sliding, storm doors; a meeting held* **behind closed doors** (= in secret); *adj. & cpd.:* automobile door handles; a door latch, lock, panel; a closed-door briefing; our next-door neighbors; an open-door policy; a four-door sedan. **2** a doorway; hence, a means or path of access: *the door to the next room; Visitors appear, arrive, are greeted* **at the door**; *The moment she walked* **in** or **through the door** *the lights came on; He just went* **out the door**; *Education* **opens the door to** *many careers; to* **show someone the door** (= ask politely to leave); *The boss* **laid the blame at the secretary's door**; *She told him never to* **darken her door** (= visit her) *again; The car accident* **closed** or **shut** or **slammed the door** on (= made impossible) *his hopes of a medical career; He earns his living by selling encyclopedias* **from door to door** (= house to house); *adja.*: *a door-to-door sales rep.*
door.jamb *n.* one of the upright pieces framing a doorway.
door.keep.er (DOR.kee.pur) *n.* a guardian at a door.
door.knob *n.* a knoblike handle for opening and shutting a door.
door.man *n.* **-men** an attendant who opens a building's door for people, calls taxis for them, etc.

door.mat *n.* **1** a mat for wiping the feet at a door. **2** *Informal.* one who passively suffers insults, etc. from others.

door.plate *n.* a plate mounted on a door bearing the occupant's name.

door.prize *n.* a prize awarded at a function to the winner of a ticket drawn from among those handed out at the door.

door.sill *n.* threshold.

door.step *n.* a step or steps in front of an outside door.

door.way *n.* an opening or entrance fitted with a door: *to stand in the doorway; the doorway to freedom, health, a new career.*

door.yard *n.* a yard near the door to a house.

do.pa (DOH.puh) *n.* an amino acid that produces a neural chemical, or **dopamine**, essential to normal nerve-functioning in the brain.

dop.ant (DOH.punt) *n.* an impurity added to an electrical semiconductor to affect its properties.

dope *n.* **1** a liquid, esp. a viscous one, used to give desired properties to a surface. **2** any adulterant or additive such as antiknock in gasoline, preservatives in foods, or stimulants for racehorses. **3** *Informal.* a narcotic or other intoxicating drug: *They don't take dope.* **4** *Slang.* a dull or half-witted person. **5** *Slang.* special information: *What's the latest dope about the project?* —*v.* **dopes, doped, dop.ing** apply or give dope to a person or thing: *to dope an athlete, a horse; the doping of blood to improve athletic performance; Silicon is doped with impurities in making transistors and chips.*

dope.ster (DOPE.stur) *n. Slang.* one who claims to know and be able to tell what will happen in the world of sports, politics, etc.

dop.ey (DOH.pee) *adj.* **dop.i.er, -i.est** *Slang.* dazed, as if drugged: *He was feeling dopey after the drink.* Also **dop.y.**

Dor.ic *adj.* of a style of architecture, having restrained simplicity, fluted columns, and plain capitals.

dorm *n. Informal* [short form] dormitory.

dor.mant (DOR.munt) *adj.* asleep or inactive: *Some plants and animals are dormant in winter; a dormant volcano; passions that lie dormant; ways of arousing our dormant interest in art.*
—**dor.man.cy** (-mun.see) *n.*

dor.mer or **dormer window** *n.* a window set upright in and projecting from a sloping roof.

dor.mi.to.ry (DOR.muh.tor.ee) *n.* **-ries** a room or building with sleeping accommodations for a large group: *college dormitories;* **adj.:** *a dormitory room; a dormitory* (= bedroom) *community or suburb.*

dor.mouse *n., pl.* **-mice** a nocturnal, squirrellike, Old World rodent that hibernates in winter.

dor.sal (DOR.sul) *adj.* of or on the back: *a dorsal fin.* —**dor.sal.ly** *adv.*

do.ry *n.* **-ries** a flat-bottomed, high-sided fishing boat.

dos.age (DOH.sij) *n.* the amount of a dose.

dose *n.* **1** an amount of medicine or treatment given at one time: *to administer, give, measure out, take a dose of medicine; to give someone or get a **dose of one's own medicine** (= give or get the same kind of treatment as one gives to others); a lethal or fatal dose.* **2** *Slang.* an infection of a venereal disease. —*v.* **dos.es, dosed, dos.ing** treat: *Mother used to dose us with vitamin pills in the winter.*

do.sim.e.ter (doh.SIM.i.tur) *n.* a machine for measuring the dosage of radiation received; **do.sim.e.try** (-tree) *n.*

dos.si.er (DOSS.yay) *n.* a file of papers about someone or something.

dost (DUST) [old word] the form of DO used with *thou.*

dot *n.* a small point, speck, etc., as over an *i* or *j*: *the dots and dashes of the Morse Code; She always arrives **on the dot*** (= exactly on time). —*v.* **dots, dot.ted, dot.ting** **1** mark or make with a dot: *Editors take care to **dot their i's and cross their t's*** (= to be precise, minutely correct, etc.); **adj.:** *a dotted line, necktie.* **2** form a dot or dots: *Fishing boats dot the lake; a park dotted with palms.* —**sign on the dotted line** agree fully to what is asked.

dot.age (DOH.tij) *n.* advanced old age with deteriorating mental faculties: *An old man in his dotage is said to be in his second childhood.*

dot.ard (DOT.urd) *n.* a person in his dotage.

dote *v.* **dotes, dot.ed, dot.ing** **1** be feeble-minded with old age. **2** be very fond of someone: *She just dotes on her son; a **doting** father and a loving husband.*

doth (DUTH) [old word] does.

dot matrix *n.* a pattern of dots, as an oblong with five dots across and seven down, from which letters, numbers, etc. are formed for computer output; **adj.:** *Most **dot-matrix** printers can also* produce letter-quality type.

dot.ty (DOT.ee) *adj.* **dot.ti.er, dot.ti.est** **1** full of dots. **2** *Informal.* feeble-minded; eccentric: *a dotty friend, idea, notion.*

Dou.ay Version (or **Bible**) (doo.AY-) *n.* an English translation of the Bible used by Roman Catholics.

dou.ble (DUB.ul) *adj.* **1** twice as much, many, strong, etc.; two instead of one: *a double thickness of paper; an egg with a double yolk; double exposure.* **2** twofold; in a pair: *double doors; a double boiler, date.* **3** for two: *a double bed, harness, room; double occupancy.* **4** having two senses, characters, etc.; hence, deceitful: *a word with a double meaning; The company kept double books, one with correct records and the other with false records to cheat on taxes; the double life of a double agent.* **5** having more petals than normal: *a double rose.* **6** an octave below normal: *a double bass.* —*adv.* twofold: *Fold it double; They ride double* (= two together) *on his bike; You may see double* (= two instead of one) *when hit on the head.* —*n.* **1** a double quantity, strength, etc.: *12 is the double of 6; Make it a double* (= twice the usual serving). **2** one that is just like another; hence, a substitute, as for an actor. **3** in baseball, a hit that allows the batter to get to second base. **4** a sharp turn or evasion while running. **5 doubles** *pl.* a game with two players on each side: *men's, mixed, women's doubles.* —**on the double** *Informal.* at an extra pace; very fast. —*v.* **-bles, -bled, -bling 1** make or become double: *how to double your money; House prices have doubled in ten years.* **2** fold in two; also, close up: *He doubled his fists in anger.* **3** go around a cape, headland, etc. **4** serve or stand in for another: *The stuntman doubled for the star in the fire scene.* **5** *Informal.* play a second role: *The cook doubles as our dishwasher.* **6** turn sharply or back on one's path: *The dogs doubled back to find the scent again.* —**double up 1** bend, esp. one's body, or fold double: *Hit in the stomach, he doubled up in pain.* **2** share, esp. accommodations, in pairs: *They doubled up to make room for everybody; Pat doubled up with Lou.*

double agent *n.* a spy working for both sides, as from within a government.

double bass *n.* the largest and the deepest-toned of the violin family of stringed instruments.

double bind *n.* a dilemma: *found herself or was caught in the double bind of racism and sexism.*

double blind *adj.* having to do with a test or clinical trial in which, in order to avoid bias, neither the subjects nor the researchers know which subjects are receiving what is being tested.

double boiler *n.* an upper saucepan for food set over a lower one holding boiling water.

double-breasted *adj.* overlapping in front with two rows of buttons: *a double-breasted blazer.*

double check *n.* a careful rechecking of something for accuracy or a similar purpose; **double-check** *v.*

double chin *n.* a chin with a fold of fatty flesh under it.

double-cross *v. Informal.* betray by doing the opposite of what was agreed to. —*n.* such an action; **double-crosser** *n.*

double date *n.* a date involving two couples. —**double-date** *v.* **-dates, -dat.ed, -dat.ing.**

double-deal *v.* **-deals, -dealt, -deal.ing** act with duplicity; deceive or cheat. —**double-dealing** *n. & adj.;* **double-dealer** *n.*

double-decker *n.* something that has two tiers or layers; *adja.: a double-decker bus, freeway, hamburger, garage.*

dou.ble en.ten.dre (doo.blahn.TAHN.druh) *n. French.* a word or phrase with two meanings, one of them usu. risqué.

double-header *n.* two baseball games between the same teams on the same day.

double indemnity *n.* an insurance policy provision by which the insurer pays double in case of the accidental death of the insured.

double jeopardy *n.* the position of an accused person being tried a second time for the same crime.

double-jointed *adj.* having a joint that permits a limb, digit, etc. to move with exceptional freedom.

double negative *n.* the substandard use of two negatives instead of one, as "I didn't do nothing" instead of "I didn't do anything."

double play *n.* in baseball, a play in which two runners are put out.

double standard *n.* a differential set of rules: *to apply, follow, use a double standard for hiring men and women.*

dou.blet (DUB.lit) *n.* **1** one of a pair, esp. of words such as *ward* and *guard,* with the same source but different lines of development. **2** a man's tightly fitted jacket once worn in Europe.

double take *n.* delayed reaction to

something unusual, as by a second glance, often used as a comic device: *to do a double take.*

double talk *n.* ambiguous or nonsensical talk that only appears to make sense.

double whammy *n. Informal.* a combination of two unwanted circumstances: *The car dealer was hit with a double whammy on sales by gasoline shortages and a recession.*

dou.bloon (dub.LOON) *n.* a former Spanish coin.

dou.bly (DUB.lee) *adv.* to twice the degree or amount; also, in a double manner: *He's doubly indebted to her as his wife and breadwinner; to be doubly sure.*

doubt (DOWT) *n.* **1** the state of being uncertain: *I'm in doubt* (= in uncertainty) *about the outcome of the race; He will beyond doubt* or *without doubt* (= certainly) *win the race; He'll no doubt* (= certainly) *win the race.* **2** a lack of certainty, conviction, or trust; disbelief: *Is there any doubt (as to) whether it will rain or snow? I have my doubts about his innocence; Many have expressed doubt that he is innocent; But I don't want to raise doubts in your mind; Let's give him the benefit of the doubt; To cast doubt on his intentions is not fair; to entertain, feel, harbor doubts about something; to dispel, express, resolve, voice a doubt about the matter; beyond the shadow of a doubt; deep, gnawing, lingering, reasonable, serious, slight, strong doubts.* —*v.* be uncertain or distrustful about something; also, think unlikely: *It's not that I doubt your words; I don't doubt that you are telling the truth; We doubt very much that he will come; We strongly doubt whether* or *if he is alive at all.*
—**doubt.er** *n.*

doubt.ful (DOWT.ful) *adj.* unsure or uncertain: *We are doubtful about tomorrow's weather; It's highly doubtful that it will be sunny; The outcome is still doubtful; a man of doubtful* (= questionable) *character.* —**doubt.ful.ly** *adv.*

doubting Thomas *n.* a persistent or habitual doubter.

doubt.less *adj. & adv.* without doubt; no doubt: *He will doubtless be here by supper time.* —**doubt.less.ly** *adv.*

douche (DOOSH, long "OO") *n.* a stream of water sent against a part or into a cavity of the body, esp. for washing: *a vaginal douche.*
—*v.* **douch.es, douched, douch.ing** apply or use a douche.

dough (DOH) *n.* **1** a soft, elastic mixture of flour, liquid, etc. prepared for baking: *to knead, mix, roll, work dough; firm, flaky, stiff dough; The dough has to rise before bread can be baked.* **2** *Slang.* money.

dough.nut (DOH.nut) *n.* [older spelling] DONUT.

dough.ty (DOW.tee) *adj.* **-ti.er, -ti.est** brave; valiant: *a doughty fighter.*

dough.y (DOH.ee) *adj.* like dough: *doughy bread* (= bread not baked long enough); *a doughy* (= soft and pale) *complexion.*

dour (DOO.ur, DOW.ur, *rhyme:* our) *adj.* **1** [in Scots use] stern or obstinate: *a dour Scot; dour and taciturn.* **2** gloomy; silent and ill-tempered: *a man who is dour in disposition; his dour determination, looks, silence.*

douse *v.* **dous.es, doused, dous.ing 1** plunge into a liquid; drench: *The arsonist doused the house with gasoline and set it on fire; We had pancakes doused in maple syrup.* **2** *Informal.* put out: *to douse the lights, enthusiasm, hopes, rumors.*

dove (DOHV) a *pt.* of DIVE.
—*n.* (DUV) **1** a pigeon, esp. a small, wild one: *Doves coo.* **2** a gentle or peaceful person, esp. one opposed to war or military threats; one who is not a hawk. —**dov.ish** (DUV.ish) *adj.*

dove-cote (DUV.coht, -cot) *n.* a nesting home for doves or pigeons; also **dove.cot.**

dove.tail (DUV.tail) *n.* a wedge-shaped projection fitted into a groove in another piece to make a joint firm and solid. —*v.* fit together thus: *One corner dovetails with the other; Your interests dovetail (with) ours; Our plans dovetailed neatly, nicely, perfectly;* **adj.**: *a cabinet with dovetailed corners.*

DOW same as DOW JONES INDUSTRIAL AVERAGE.

dow.a.ger (DOW.uh.jur, "OW" as in "HOW") *n.* **1** a widow having title or property from her dead husband: *an empress dowager; a dowager duchess.* **2** an older woman of social standing: *wealthy dowagers.*

dow.dy (DOW.dee, "OW" as in "HOW") *adj.* **-di.er, -di.est** shabby or plain in clothes or appearance. —**dow.di.ly** *adv.;* **dow.di.ness** *n.*

dow.el (DOW.ul) *n.* a peg fitting into a hole to join pieces or parts together.
—*v.* **-els, -eled, -el.ing** join with dowels. Also **dow.elled, dow.el.ling** *Cdn.*

dow.er (DOW.ur, "OW" as in "HOW") *n.* **1** a dowry. **2** a widow's share for life of her husband's property.

—*v.* provide with a dowry or dower.
Dow Jones industrial average (DOW, *rhyme:* cow) *n.* an average of selected stocks on the New York exchange, used as an economic indicator.

down *adv.* **1** at or toward a lower position, quieter or worse state, smaller volume, etc.: *The stars will come out when the sun goes down; Sit down! He came down with the flu; She's trying to quiet down the children; Cut down the essay to 2,000 words.* **2** southward; also, away from the speaker: *He's gone down to Florida; Let's walk down to the plaza.* **3** as partial payment, usu. in cash: *He paid $10,000 down on the house.* **4** in writing: *Put it down in your diary.* **5** in subjection: *They had been held down as slaves for centuries.* **6** toward a later time: *down through the ages.* —**down and dirty** *Informal.* cheap: *to get down and dirty in price*; *adj*.: *down-and-dirty merchandise, sex, stuff.* —**down and out** *Informal.* destitute, friendless, etc. —**down at the heels** *Informal.* in a shabby or run-down condition. —**down east** in or to eastern North America, as viewed from the West: *down east in Nova Scotia; down east music.* —**down home** in the southern U.S.: *down home in Louisiana.* —**down in the dumps** or **down in the mouth** *Informal.* depressed or sad. —**down on** *Informal.* hostile to someone: *People are down on him for always being late.* —**down on one's luck** *Informal.* unfortunate. —**down the drain** *Informal.* lost or gone. —**down to the ground** completely: *The promotion suits him down to the ground.* —*adj.* **1** in or at a low position: *The hydro lines were down after the storm; You don't hit or kick a man when he is down; the down elevator; The down pipe carries rain water from the roof; He's down on all fours under the table searching for the missing ring; The computer is down (= not working).* **2** out of play: *The ball is down on the 10-yard line.* **3** behind; trailing: *They're down 6-0 in the sixth inning.* **4** completed: *one down, two to go.* **5** less active, ill, or despondent: *She's down with a cold; He's feeling a bit down these days; Don't let these misunderstandings get you down (= bother you too much).*
—*prep.* **1** down along, through, etc.: *He ran down the hill; down the ages.* **2** to or at a lower or later point: *to sail down the river; That's two kilometers down the road; We have no idea what's going to happen ten years down the road.* **3** along: *I was walking down the road.*
—*n.* **1 downs** *pl.* grassy uplands. **2** a decline: *ups and downs; This is a real boost after the downs we've been having.* **3** in football, any of four attempts (three in Canadian football) to advance the ball 10 yards: *Second down and three yards to go.* **4** very fine fluffy feathers or hair: *the down on a teenager's chin.* **5** same as DOWNER, 1, 2.
—*v.* cause to go or be down: *The strikers downed tools; a heart condition made worse by downing too many cups of coffee; Phone lines were downed during the storm; He downed the ball on the 25-yard line; They downed (= defeated) the Dodgers 5-2;* *adj.*: *a downed spy plane.*

down-at-the-heels *adj.* shabby or run-down: *She's poor and down-at-the-heels; a down-at-the-heels hotel.*

down.beat *n.* a descending stroke of a conductor's baton showing the principal accent in a measure.
—*adj.* **1** gloomy; realistic and grim. **2** casual and relaxed.

down.burst *n.* a powerful downdraft or downward surge of air.

down.cast *adj.* pointed down; dejected: *with downcast eyes.*

down.draft *n.* a draft with a downward tendency: *a downdraft in the chimney caused by tall trees near it; A powerful downdraft was responsible for the airplane crash.*

down.er *n.* *Informal.* **1** a depressant drug, as a barbiturate or tranquilizer. **2** a depressing experience; bad trip.

down.fall *n.* **1** a heavy fall of snow or rain. **2** a sudden fall from power, wealth, etc. or the cause of this: *Addictions bring about people's downfall; We knew he was heading for a downfall; Drink was his downfall.* —**down.fall.en** (DOWN.fall.un) *adj.*

down.grade *n.* **1** a downward slope. **2** any path of decline: *an aging leader on the downgrade.* —*v.* **-grades, -grad.ed, -grad.ing** lower the status, pay, importance, etc. of a person or thing: *His condition has been downgraded from "serious" to "critical"; a hurricane downgraded to storm status.*

down.heart.ed (DOWN.har.tid) *adj.* depressed.

down.hill *adj.* downward along a hill or to a lower status, condition, etc.: *a downhill course, run, slide; It's all downhill from here on* (*Informal* for The hard part is over); *adv.*: *to go, roll, ski downhill.* —*n.* a downhill skiing race: *the World Cup downhill series.*
—**down.hill.er** (DOWN.hill.ur) *n.*

down-home *adj*. simple and informal

in a rural way: *a down-home atmosphere, feeling, look, image, personality; down-home advice, charm, cooking, humor, flavor, folks, hospitality, image, style, values.*

down.link *n.* communication from a satellite or spacecraft to the ground.

down.load *v.* transfer from one computer's storage to another's: *to download data, files, information, programs.* —*n.* the act of downloading or something downloaded: *Downloads are one method of information transfer.*

down.mark.et (DOWN.mar.kit) *adj. & adv.* downscale; not upscale.

down payment *n.* a first payment made at the time of purchase: *to make a down payment on a home.*

down.play *v.* play down; de-emphasize: *The company downplayed the seriousness of the oil spill.*

down.pour *n.* a very heavy rain: *a sudden torrential downpour.*

down.range *adv. & adj.* (further) along a missile's intended path.

down.right *adj.* **1** plainspoken or candid. **2** thoroughgoing or absolute: *a downright falsehood; adv.: He got downright hostile.*

down.scale *adj.* socially or economically inferior; not upscale.

down.shift *v.* shift to a lower gear.

down.side *n. Informal.* a downward trend or negative aspect: *There's a downside to it; The downside of that project is that it would cost a lot to implement; On the downside, it is also a waste of time; adj.: Better not say anything downside* (= negative) *on this issue; a downside analysis, risk, scenario.*

down.size (DOWN.size) *v.* **-siz.es, -sized, -siz.ing** to scale down in size and weight, as automobiles to make them more fuel-efficient: *to downsize a business, operation, store; adj.: a downsized model; n.: an era of corporate downsizing.*

Down's syndrome *n.* a chromosomal, congenital defect causing physical and mental retardation and slightly mongoloid appearance; mongolism. Also **Down syndrome.**

down.stage *adv. & adj.* of, at, or toward the front of the stage.
—*n.: to move to downstage.*

down.stairs *adv.* down a set of stairs; on or to a lower floor: *Who lives downstairs? Let's go downstairs.* —*adj.: She is downstairs; in the downstairs apartment; n.: painting the downstairs.*

down.stream 1 *adj. & adv.* in the direction of flow: *The boat floated downstream; The lamb was drinking downstream from the wolf; pollutants found downstream of or from the chemical company.* **2** *adj.* having to do with the latter stages of an industrial process: *Refining and marketing are the downstream end of the petroleum business; downstream assets, operations, products, profit; A downstream holding company owns the insurance company's miscellaneous interests.*

down.stroke *n.* a downward stroke, as of a bicycle pedal.

down.swing *n.* **1** a downward swing, as of a golf club. **2** same as DOWNTURN: *The TV program was canceled because of a downswing in the ratings; upswings and downswings in global temperatures.*

down.time *n.* time of inactivity, as of a machine or factory, or of leisure, as of a worker: *computer downtime; layover resulting in downtime for business travelers.*

down-to-earth *adj.* practical: *a down-to-earth approach, attitude, manner, nature, theory; down-to-earth advice, prices.*

down.town *n.* the lower, central, or business district of a city or town.
—*adj. & adv.* in or to downtown: *He has gone downtown; to downtown Montreal; a downtown business, office, store.*

down.trod.den (DOWN.trod.un) *adj.* trampled, as by tyranny; oppressed.

down.turn *n.* a decline, as in business: *an economic downturn; the downturn in worldwide stock markets; a global downturn; a downturn in the value of the dollar; cyclical downturns.*

down under or **Down Under** *n. & adv. Informal.* Australia or New Zealand: *The boomerang comes from down under; She's vacationing down under.*

down.ward *adj. & adv.* toward a lower, inferior, or later place, condition, etc.; also **down.wards** *adv.*

down.wind *adj. & adv.* in the direction the wind is blowing: *the downwind side of the mountains; people living downwind of the garbage dump.*

down.y *adj.* **down.i.er, -i.est** of, like, or covered with down: *the downy peach.*

dow.ry (DOW.ree) *n.* **-ries** the property that a woman brings to her husband at marriage; hence, a natural talent or gift: *Brains were the best dowry her family could provide for her.*

dowse (DOWZE) *v.* **dows.es, dowsed, dows.ing** use a divining rod.
—**dows.er** *n.*

dox.ol.o.gy (dox.OL.uh.jee) *n.* **-gies** a formula expressing praise of God.

doy.en (DOY.un) *n.* the senior member of a group; dean: *the doyen of French* historians; **doy.enne** (-en), *fem.*

doze *n.* a short nap; light sleep.
—*v.* **doz.es, dozed, doz.ing:** *He is dozing in the sun; Some tend to* **doze off** *while watching TV.*

doz.en (DUZ.un) *n.* a group of 12: *three dozen eggs; A baker's dozen is one more than a round dozen; Eggs are sold in dozens; We sell* **dozens of** (= lots of) *eggs every day.* —**doz.enth** *adj.*

doz.er (DOH.zur) *n. Informal.* bulldozer.

doz.y (DOH.zee) *adj.* **doz.i.er, -i.est** drowsy or sleepy.

drab *adj.* **drab.ber, drab.best** **1** grayish- or yellowish-brown. **2** dull; faded; monotonous: *It's a drab brown; the drab gray walls; the drab routine of an assembly-line job.* —*n.* drab color or a drab cloth. —**drab.ly** *adv.*; **drab.ness** *n.*

drach.ma (DRAK.muh) *n., pl.* **-mas** or **-mae** (-mee) the basic unit of money in Greece.

Dra.co.ni.an or **dra.co.ni.an** (dray.COH.nee.un) *adj.* very harsh or strict like **Draco,** a lawgiver of ancient Greece: *a Draconian law, measure, rule; the Draconian approach; its Draconian cruelty; a budget that is more Draconian than austere; a Draconian but pragmatic policy.*

draft *n.* **1** an act of drawing or pulling or what is drawn: *You're sitting in a draft* (= current of air) *by the window; a draft of fish* (= amount caught in a net at one time); *a draft* (= drink) *of water; We've beer* **on draft** (= to be drawn from a cask or keg). **2** a device for controlling air flow in a fireplace or wood stove. **3** the depth of water drawn by a ship: *a ship's draft* (= distance between water line and bottom of the keel); *vessels of shallow draft.* **4** a paper directing a bank to pay a specified amount to the person in whose favor it is drawn: *a bank draft for $1,000; a draft on a Boston branch of the bank.* **5** a sketch or plan of work to be done, made usu. by a draftsman. **6** a preliminary version of something written: *to make, prepare a draft of the speech; a preliminary, rough draft; the final, polished draft.* **7** a selection, as of new players by sports teams; also, of people for military service by a **draft board:** *During the Vietnam war, Americans used to dodge the draft by emigrating to Canada.* **8** the state of being forced, as by popular pressure: *He was unwilling to be a candidate but wouldn't refuse a draft.* —*adja.* **1** on draft: *draft beer.* **2** preliminary or rough: *a draft contract, manuscript; a draft version of the bill.* **3** used for pulling loads: *In the Third World,* **draft animals** *such as horses, oxen, mules, donkeys, and water buffalo still do much of the work of trucks and tractors.*
—*v.* **1** select by a draft: *to be drafted into an army.* **2** compose, sketch, or draw up, esp. in rough form: *to draft a letter, memo, proposal.*

draft.ee (draf.TEE) *n.* a person selected by a draft board for military service.

drafts.man (DRAFTS.mun) *n.* **-men** **1** one who prepares mechanical drawings, designs, plans, sketches, etc., as for making buildings and machines. **2** one who draws up official documents. **3** one who is skilled in drawing: *a gifted draftsman; An artist is more than a draftsman.* —**drafts.man.ship** *n.*

draft.y *adj.* **draft.i.er, -i.est** exposed to currents of air: *a drafty cottage, hallway, room.* —**draft.i.ness** *n.*

drag *v.* **drags, dragged, drag.ging** **1** pull or draw with difficulty, esp. along the ground; trail; hence, move or cause to move slowly, tediously, against one's will, etc.: *He had to drag the tree behind the cart; He dragged his son off to school; Don't drag me into your problems; Time drags near lunch hour; The meeting* **dragged on** *for hours; Don't* **drag out** *the meeting with useless questions.* **2** search or fish with a net, hook, etc.: *The police had the river dragged for the missing body.* **3** *Informal.* puff: *to drag on a cigar, cigarette, etc.*
—**drag one's feet** or **heels** move or act slowly and without making the required effort: *He was dragging his feet on the job.* —*n.* **1** something dragged, as a net, harrow, sledge, etc. **2** a dragging or something that slows or hinders, esp. the resistance of air or fluid to a moving body: *An airplane uses thrust to overcome (aerodynamic) drag; Drag increases with speed; a drag on the economy.* **3** *Informal.* a female attire worn by a man: *Tim appeared at the party in drag;* **adv.**: *Are you going to the party drag* (= with a female partner) *or stag?* **4** *Informal.* one that is boring: *Life can become a drag during summer; Dan is such a drag* (= bore) *when he starts talking about computers.* **5** *Informal.* a puff on a cigar, cigarette, etc.: *She took a drag on his cigar.* **6** *Slang.* a street: *the main drag.* **7** a drag race.
—**drag.ger** *n.*

drag.net *n.* **1** a fishing net pulled across the bottom of a body of water. **2** a set of coordinated procedures for

finding people wanted by police.
drag.on (DRAG.un) *n.* in myths, a large lizard or snake, winged and usu. fire-breathing: *Will science ever be able to slay the dragon of superstition?*
drag.on.fly (DRAG.un.fly) *n.* **-flies** a flying insect with four large, gauzy wings, which feeds on insects caught in flight.
Dragon Lady *n.* a powerful or intimidating woman.
dra.goon (druh.GOON) *n.* a heavily armed cavalryman. —*v.* harass or coerce: *He was dragooned into (joining) the organization.*
drag queen *n. Slang.* a male dressed as a female.
drag race *n.* an acceleration race over a short, straight course (**drag strip**), of ten between specially built cars (**dragsters**).
drain *v.* 1 draw or flow out of a place; hence, exhaust or make empty: *to drain gasoline from the tank;* **adjp.:** *Lou felt drained at the end of the exams.*
2 dry by drawing liquid from a place: *to drain land for farming; a creek that drains the region; The region drains* (= empties its water) *into the creek.*
3 become emptied or exhausted: *Her enthusiasm drained away.*
—*n.* 1 a means of draining, as a drainpipe: *to block, clean out, clear, clog, unclog a drain; Morality seems to be going down the drain and little is being done about it.* 2 a draining, depletion, etc.: *a drain on his financial resources; the brain drain to the U.S.*
drain.age (DRAY.nij) *n.* 1 a draining; also, a system of ditches, pipes, etc. for draining. 2 that which is drained off. 3 an area drained; also **drainage basin.**
drain.pipe *n.* a pipe for carrying off water or other unwanted liquid.
drake *n.* a male duck.
dram *n.* 1 a unit of weight equal to 3.888 grams. 2 a unit of capacity equal to 3.697 milliliters; fluid dram. 3 a small drink, esp. of alcohol: *Take a wee dram for your health.*
dra.ma (DRAH.muh, DRAM.uh) *n.* 1 a play for the stage, TV, or radio. 2 the art or institution of the theater or plays: *a student of Japanese drama.* 3 a unified series of exciting events: *a hostage drama at the embassy; The drama unfolded right in front of them.*
dra.mat.ic (druh.MAT.ic) *adj.* 1 having to do with drama (def. 3): *dramatic action, elements, unity; Events took a dramatic turn; the dramatic irony of the*

characters not being aware of what is happening but which the audience understands. 2 vivid, striking, exciting, etc.: *a rather dramatic entrance; a dramatic change, effect, impact, increase, influence, moment, move, performance; dramatic proof, results.* 3 **dramatics** *n.pl.* [usu. takes *pl. v.*] 1 dramatic behavior. 2 theatrical performance or production. —**dra.mat.i.cal.ly** *adv.*
dram.a.tist (DRAM.uh.tist) *n.* a playwright.
dram.a.tize (DRAM.uh.tize) *v.* **-tiz.es, -tized, -tiz.ing** 1 adapt for dramatic presentation. 2 present or regard dramatically: *He always dramatizes his problems.* —**dram.a.ti.za.tion** (-tuh.ZAY.shun, -tye-) *n.*
drank *pt.* of DRINK.
drape *v.* **drapes, draped, drap.ing** 1 cover or hang with cloth in loose folds; hang cloth thus: *a coffin draped with black cloth; He came out with a towel draped over his head.* 2 hang or rest casually or loosely: *His arm was draped over her shoulders.* —*n.* 1 draped cloth. 2 **drapes** *pl.* curtains: *window drapes; to draw, hang, open the drapes.*
drap.er (DRAY.pur) *n. Brit.* one who sells cloth, dry goods, etc.
dra.per.y (DRAY.puh.ree) *n.* **-per.ies** 1 draped cloth; also, the draping or arranging of material. 2 **draperies** *pl.* curtains.
dras.tic (DRAS.tic) *adj.* harsh or extreme: *The revolt was put down with drastic measures; The punishment was rather drastic; They took drastic steps.* —**dras.ti.cal.ly** *adv.*
draught (DRAFT), **draughtsman, draughty** same as DRAFT, DRAFTSMAN, DRAFTY.
draw *v.* **draws,** *pt.* **drew,** *pp.* **drawn, draw.ing** 1 pull with effort; hence, move gradually or slowly: *an engine drawing a long train; a carriage drawn by horses; The racer drew ahead; A small boat draws alongside (of) a ship; to draw* (= close) *the drapes; I had to* **draw him aside** *for a private chat.* 2 attract: *Sugar draws ants; a threat that draws no reply; a speech that drew cheers; May I draw your attention to the smoke rising from your roof?* 3 pull in; inhale: *He likes to draw at or on his pipe while thinking what to say; He says he will defend his country while he draws breath* (= as long as he lives); *He draws courage from her example; The cat drew in its claws; a chimney that draws* (= lets or causes air to flow) *well.* 4 pull out; extract: *She drew the sword from the scabbard; The*

gunfighter drew and fired; to draw lots; to draw water from a well; to draw money from the bank; a bank account drawing (= earning) good interest; to draw a chicken (= have its entrails taken out). **5** shape, make larger or longer, as by stretching or pulling: *Please draw the strings tight.* **6** move gradually and steadily: *The meeting is drawing to a close; Night draws on; Death draws nearer every moment.* **7** portray with lines or words; sketch; write out: *to draw a picture; She drew him in a thoughtful mood.* **8** infer or make: *to draw a conclusion; to draw an analogy between two things.* **9** of ships, etc., need a depth of water to float in: *Loaded boats draw more water than empty ones.* **10** bend a bow for shooting an arrow. **11** tie a contest: *Canada drew against the U.S.; We drew in the hockey game.* **12** steep: *The tea has to draw before being served.* —**draw a blank** have no result or answer. —**draw down** consume or deplete: *A war draws down military supplies.* —**draw on 1** approach or come near: *When winter drew on we were short of supplies; The brown horse is beginning to draw on the black one.* **2** take from somewhere: *He can draw on his great fund of knowledge; a check drawn on a bank; A check is drawn on or against an account.* —**draw out 1** prolong. **2** induce to talk: *He drew out the old-timer on the hardships of the Depression years.* —**draw the line** set a limit not to be gone past: *We have to draw the line at $10,000 for expenses.* —**draw up 1** set in order; also, straighten stiffly: *She drew herself up in her chair and listened intently.* **2** draft: *to draw up a plan, treaty, will.* **3** come to a stop: *The car drew up in front of us.* —*n.* **1** a drawing: *Lou is quick on the draw* (Informal for quick to react); *Pat is slow on the draw* (Informal for sluggish); *They held a lucky draw* (= raffle or lottery); *a fast-draw gunfighter.* **2** something drawn, esp. a tied contest: *The game ended in a draw.* **3** an attraction: *Niagara Falls is a powerful draw for tourists.* **4** a gully or valley.
draw.back *n.* a disadvantage or hindrance.
draw.bridge *n.* a bridge able to be raised or swung aside, as to let ships pass.
draw.down *n.* a reduction or depletion.
draw.er *n.* **1** one that draws. **2** a container in a desk, bureau, etc. that slides in and out: *to close, open, pull out, push in a drawer.* **3 drawers** *pl.* underpants.
drawing *n.* **1** the act or skill of portraying by drawn lines: *She's good at drawing.* **2** a representation so made: *Her pencil drawings are on display at the gallery; a draftsman's mechanical drawing; a freehand drawing; A line drawing has no shaded areas.*
drawing board *n.* a board used for drawing up plans: *She is at her drawing board all day; The project is on the drawing board;* **Back to the drawing board** (= Start again at the planning stage)!
drawing card *n.* attraction: *The hotel's drawing card is a good sandy beach.*
drawing room *n.* a room for receiving guests; parlor.
drawl *n.* a way of speaking that lengthens the vowel sounds: *a Texas drawl.* —*v.:* "*Naw,*" *he drawled,* "*no problem.*"
drawn 1 *pp.* of DRAW. **2** *adj.* strained and haggard: *a drawn look.*
draw.string *n.* a cord that is pulled to close a bag or to tighten clothing, curtains, etc.
dray *n.* a low cart or sled for heavy loads.
dread (DRED) *v.* fear greatly: *He dreads horror movies; She dreads being called up in the middle of the night.* —*n.* great fear: *The fugitive lived in dread of being caught.*
dread.ful *adj.* **1** causing dread: *dreadful consequences, news; a dreadful outcome, possibility, storm.* **2** very unpleasant or severe: *a dreadful mistake; It's dreadful to sit there and listen to speeches all day.* —**dread.ful.ly** *adv.*
dread.locks *n.pl.* an Afro-style hairdo of tightly curled and matted strands of hair.
dread.nought (DRED.nawt) *n.* a large battleship with heavy armor and big guns.
dream (DREEM) *n.* **1** a group of subjective images, thoughts, etc. in a sleeper's mind; also, a reverie or daydream: *Everyone has dreams; Some interpret dreams; a bad, recurring dream; a childhood dream about a pot of gold; Some dreams turn into nightmares.* **2** a vision or ideal, esp. if considered as unreal: *I have a dream of people living in harmony; What we achieved was beyond our wildest dreams; The wedding was like a dream come true; a field of dreams; wishes and dreams; visionary dreams; to achieve, fulfill, realize a dream; Her dream was to win an Olympic gold; an impossible dream; shattered dreams.* **3** something very desirable or excellent: *Our vacation was a dream; The new car runs*

dreamy / drew

like a dream (= without problems); *adj.*: *an expensive dream house; a* **dream factory** (= movie studio); *the* **dream machine** (= the TV industry); *A "dream team" won the basketball match at the Olympics.* —*v.* **dreams,** *pt. & pp.* **dreamed** *or* **dreamt** (DREMT), **dream.ing 1** have a dream: *Joe dreamed about waking up rich.* **2** be in a reverie; daydream. **3** suppose or imagine: *He never dreamed that one day he would win a Nobel Prize; I wouldn't* **dream of** *having you pay the bill; They tried hard to* **dream up** (= invent) *some excuse for being so late.* —**dream.er** *n.*

dream.y (DREE.mee) *adj.* **dream.i.er, -i.est 1** given to daydreaming: *a dreamy child, disposition; He's too dreamy to be a responsible babysitter.* **2** like a dream: *dreamy music; the dreamy quality of the scene; a dreamy recollection, smile, vision.* **3** *Informal.* perfect or lovely: *a dreamy car, companion, dress; It sounds dreamy; dreamy eyes.* —**dream.i.ly** *adv.*; **dream.i.ness** *n.*

drear.y (DREER.ee) *adj.* **drear.i.er, -i.est** causing boredom, low spirits, etc.; gloomy: *a dreary chore; It's very dreary working on the same book day after day.* Also **drear** *Poetic.* —**drear.i.ly** *adv.*; **drear.i.ness** *n.*

dreck *n. Slang.* something cheap and useless; rubbish or trash: *the dreck of downtown streets; We don't sell dreck to our customers.*

dredge *n.* **1** a scoop, bucket, net, etc. for dragging along the bottom of a body of water. **2** a ship fitted with this. —*v.* **dredg.es, dredged, dredg.ing 1** clean or deepen a channel or harbor with a dredge. **2** gather or search for something with or as if with a dredge: *to dredge oysters in the shallows; trying to* **dredge up** *news about the scandal.* **3** get sprinkled or coated with something: *to dredge fillets in crumbs; to dredge shrimp in flour.*

dregs *n.pl.* **1** the sediment from a liquid, esp. a drink. **2** the most worthless part: *the dregs of society.*

drench *v.* wet thoroughly or soak: *We were thoroughly drenched by a sudden downpour; drenched to the skin; a fugitive drenched in despair.*

dress *v.* **1** put clothes on a person: *A mother dresses her child; Don't come in, I'm dressing; to dress* (= put on formal clothes) *for dinner; Mourners dress in black; to dress casually, elegantly, lightly, smartly, tastefully, warmly; adj.: She went out to the costume party* **dressed** *as a fairy; dressed like a butterfly; neatly dressed children; well dressed guests; a fully dressed model; a nattily dressed gentleman; a richly dressed lady; scantily dressed bathers; on the fashion magazine's best-dressed list; half-dressed* (= half-naked) *people; "All dressed up and nowhere to go."* **2** decorate: *to dress a display window.* **3** comb and arrange hair; also, groom an animal. **4** put or get troops in straight lines. **5** prepare for cooking or use; finish; *adj.*: *a plain chicken* **dressed** *up with lemon and sage; dressed leather; dressed lumber.* **6** apply a dressing to a wound. —**dress down 1** scold vigorously. **2** dress less formally. —**dressed to the teeth** or **dressed to kill** dressed very finely or fancily. —**dress up** dress specially or formally: *She went out dressed up as a spacewoman; She dressed up her children as little goblins; Everyone came to the party nicely dressed up.*
—*n.* **1** clothing, esp. outer: *casual, formal, informal dress; He appeared in his native dress; neglect of one's dress.* **2** a woman's or girl's one-piece outer garment: *The ladies were in long cocktail dresses; low-cut, maternity, short, summer, tight dresses.* —*adj.* of clothes, formal: *a dress shirt; dress shoes; a dress affair* (requiring formal clothes).

dres.sage (druh.SAHZH) *n.* a kind of show riding in which a horse's maneuvers are controlled by barely visible motions of the rider.

dress circle *n.* the first tier of seats in a theater, where formal dress was once required.

dress.er *n.* **1** one who dresses: *a careful, fine, impeccable dresser.* **2** a bureau or chest of drawers, usu. with a mirror.

dressing *n.* **1** a bandage, medication, etc. applied to a wound: *to apply a dressing to a wound; put on, remove, replace a dressing.* **2** a sauce for salads, etc.: *a creamy French dressing.* **3** a bread-and-seasoning stuffing, as for poultry.

dressing gown *n.* an informal robe worn while lounging, preparing to dress, etc.

dressing room *n.* a room, as in a theater, to change costumes, makeup, etc. in.

dress rehearsal *n.* a rehearsal in full costume.

dress.y *adj.* **dress.i.er, -i.est 1** given to fancy dressing: *the dressy crowd; dressy women.* **2** stylish or formal: *dressy clothes for a dressy cocktail party; a dressy black suit good for dressy occasions.*

drew *pt.* of DRAW.

drib.ble (DRIB.ul) *v.* **drib.bles, drib.bled, drib.bling** 1 flow or fall in a small, unsteady stream; allow or cause to do so; also, slobber. 2 in sports, move the ball or puck by a series of bounces, taps, or kicks. —*n.* 1 what dribbles down: *A dribble of saliva fell from the baby's mouth; The donations came in dribbles.* 2 an act of dribbling: *a rapid dribble at center court.*
drib.let (DRIB.lit) *n.* a drop; also, a small amount.
dribs and drabs *n.pl. Informal.* tiny amounts: *They could save only in dribs and drabs.*
dried, drier, dries, driest See DRY, DRIER.
drift *n.* 1 aimless movement; also, one's course while drifting. 2 a movement; tendency; also, tenor, gist, etc.: *the drift of the political situation; the drift of their conversation; if you get the drift* (= meaning). 3 a bank of sand or snow piled up by wind. 4 a glacial deposit of rock debris. —*v.* 1 move aimlessly, esp. with a current, breeze, etc.: *a boat drifting south along the coast; It was drifting with the current; Some of the debris drifted back to the beach; Customers were still drifting in at closing time; We drifted off to sleep during the show; people drifting through life without even having learned to read; They started to* **drift apart** (= lose interest in each other) *over the years.* 2 cause to drift: *snow drifted by the wind.* 3 pile or be piled up in a drift; *adj.:* **drifting** *embers, sand, snow.*
drift.er *n.* one that drifts, esp. a homeless wanderer; bum.
drift.net or **drift net** *n.* a fishing net that moves like a wall catching everything in its path.
drift.wood *n.* wood drifting in or cast on shore by the water.
drill *n.* 1 a tool for making a hole in something hard: *a dentist's drill; to operate a power drill; a hand drill such as a brace; drill bits.* 2 a repeated series of physical or mental exercises used in teaching, esp. a military procedure for training in marching and use of weapons: *a military drill conducted by a drillmaster; fire, pronunciation, spelling drills.* 3 a furrow to plant seeds in; also, a machine that plants seeds in rows of holes and furrows: *a seed drill.* —*v.* 1 make a hole with a drill: *We are drilling for oil; adj.:* a **drilled** *well.* 2 *Informal.* throw a ball hard and fast or shoot a puck so as to penetrate the defense: *He drilled it through.* 3 train with or undergo a drill: *The teacher drilled his class in the multiplication tables; He had German* **drilled** (= instilled) *into him at school.* —**drill.er** *n.*
drill.mas.ter (DRIL.mas.tur) *n.* one who teaches military drill or trains others by means of drills.
drill press *n.* an upright power drill in which the drilling bit is lowered onto the work by a lever.
drill.ship *n.* a ship equipped for drilling on the sea bed, as for oil.
dri.ly (DRY.lee) same as DRYLY.
drink *v.* **drinks, drank, drunk, drink.ing** 1 swallow a liquid: *to drink water.* 2 take in mentally or with the senses: *tourists drinking in the sights of Paris.* 3 consume alcoholic beverages: *He drinks like a fish; He drinks to excess; n.: He sometimes goes missing after a bout of* **drinking.** 4 make or take part in a toast: *Let's* **drink to** *the bride and groom; Let's drink a toast to them; I'll* **drink to that** (= I agree). —**drink someone under the table** get one's drinking partner drunk while remaining sober oneself. —**drink up** finish one's drink. —*n.* 1 liquid for drinking or its amount: *a drink of water; food and drink; soft drinks; Coffees and colas are the top drinks.* 2 a beverage, esp. alcoholic: *Have a drink; a couple of drinks; Let me fix you a drink; to make, mix, nurse, pour, take, toss off a drink; mixed, stiff, strong drinks; The drinks are on the house.* 3 drinking of alcoholic beverages, esp. their excessive use: *He was driven to drink by loneliness; She took to drink.* —**drink.a.ble** *n. & adj.* —**drink.er** *n.: a hard* or *heavy drinker (of liquor).*
drip *v.* **drips, dripped, drip.ping** 1 fall or let fall in drops: *Water is dripping from the tap; water dripping off the roof; a dripping faucet.* 2 be overflowing or soaked: *a voice dripping with irony; adv.: He came in* **dripping** (= quite) *wet.* —*n.* a dripping or the noise of it: *the steady drip of a leaking faucet.*
drip coffee *n.* coffee made by pouring hot water over finely ground coffee (**drip grind**) in a pot, the coffee dripping into a lower section of the pot.
drip-dry *adj.* of clothes, made to dry while hung dripping wet.
drippings *n.pl.* juices that drip from cooking fat meat: *to make gravy from the drippings; Drippings help reinforce the flavor of the meat.*
drive *v.* **drives, drove** (DROHV), **driv.en, driv.ing** (DRY.ving) 1 make to move in some direction or to a tar-

get or goal: *to drive cattle to market; The golfer drove the ball from the tee; to drive a nail* (= hit it with a hammer) *into a wall; Scarcity drives up prices; Repression drives people underground; people driven out of their homes by invaders; What are you **driving at*** (= suggesting)? *The lecturer tried to make a point and **drive it home** with a story.* **2** force to move or work fast: *A south wind drove us on; The boss drives his workers very hard.* **3** bore; drill; dig: *to drive a tunnel under the canal; to drive a well.* **4** put into a state as specified: *He was driven to distraction and despair by the tragedy; The pain drove her mad; His behavior **drives me crazy** or **mad** (Informal for irritates me).* **5** give power or motion: *The engine is driven by steam; a mad man driven to murder;* **adj. & cpd.**: *a **driven** boss driven by the profit motive; driven snow; a chauffeur-driven limousine; a consumer-driven market; menu-driven computer searches; a motor-driven machine; wind-driven waves.* **6** operate, ride in, or convey in a vehicle: *to drive a car; She drives her children to school, then drives to work; Please drive me home; I saw him **drive down** the street; Let's **drive up** to the house over there and ask our way; He just **drove up** (= arrived) in a Cadillac; Labor strikes can **drive** consumers **up the wall** (Informal for annoy).* **7** carry on; conduct: *I got the car at a low price by **driving a hard bargain*** (= by negotiating skillfully). —*n.* **1** a driving, esp. a trip in a car: *Let's go for or go on or take a drive in the new car; a test drive; It's an easy 10-minute drive to work.* **2** a herding together or movement of animals: *a cattle drive.* **3** a driving of a ball: *a line drive to center field.* **4** a road; also, driveway: *Lakeshore Drive.* **5** a campaign: *a charity drive; to initiate, launch a drive for funds; a fund-raising drive.* **6** energy or dynamism: *a sales rep with plenty of drive; She has the drive to see the project through.* **7** a strong urge or impulse: *The sex drive is an elemental drive.* **8** a mechanism that transmits motion: *a belt drive; a motorcycle with a chain drive; the disk drive or tape drive in which a computer's magnetic storage media are rotated; fluid, four-wheel, front-wheel (automobile) drives.*

drive-in *adj.* providing service to patrons who remain in cars: *a drive-in bank, movie, takeout window.* Also *n.*

driv.el (DRIV.ul) *n.* meaningless or silly talk. —*v.* **-els, -eled, -el.ing** drool; let saliva dribble from the mouth; hence, speak foolish nonsense. —**driv.el.er** *n.* Also **driv.elled, driv.el.ling; driv.el.ler** *Cdn.*

drive.line same as DRIVETRAIN.

driv.er (DRY.vur) *n.* **1** one who drives: *a truck driver; Your **driver's license** is issued by the government; Who is in the **driver's seat*** (= controlling position)? **2** software by which a computer controls the operation of a peripheral: *a printer driver.*

drive shaft *n.* a shaft that transmits motion, as to the rear axle of an automobile.

drive-through *n.* **1** a drive through a place in one's automobile. **2** such a place. —*adj.* that one may drive through: *a drive-through carwash, game park, pickup window, zoo.*

drive.train *n.* the parts that carry power from an automobile's engine to the driving wheels, comprising the transmission, the drive shaft, universal joints, and the differential gears.

drive-up *adj.* same as DRIVE-IN: *the drive-up window of a bank.*

drive.way *n.* **1** a usu. short private road to one's garage, parking lot, house, etc.: *to pave or surface a driveway.* **2** a semi-private road, as through a housing complex or shopping center: *Vehicles may not be parked on driveways.*

driving *adj.* **1** having great force or producing a strong effect: *a driving ambition, concern, energy, force, influence, power, rain.* **2** having to do with the operation of a motor vehicle: *driving gloves; a driving lesson, school, test; safe driving practices; n.: careless, defensive, drunk, reckless driving.*

driz.zle (DRIZ.ul) *v.* **driz.zles, driz.zled, driz.zling** rain or sprinkle in fine droplets: *It's drizzling outside; Drizzle vinegar over the vegetables; Drizzle the cake with icing;* **adj.**: *a drizzling rain.* Also *n.*: *a misty drizzle; a drizzle of melted butter.* —**driz.zly** *adj.*: *a cold drizzly day.*

drogue (DROHG) *n.* **1** a cone-shaped device towed behind an aircraft as a target, for midair refueling of an aircraft, etc. **2** a parachute device used for braking an aircraft or space capsule.

droll (DROLE) *adj.* quaintly amusing: *a droll sense of humor.*

droll.er.y (DROH.luh.ree) *n.* **-er.ies** drollness; also, something droll.

drom.e.da.ry (DROM.uh.dair.ee) *n.* **-ries** a one-humped domesticated camel.

drone *n.* **1** a nonworking male honeybee serving only for reproductive purposes; hence, a parasitic idler. **2** a pilotless aircraft guided by remote control: *to send up drones for target practice.* **3** a low humming or monotonous sound or voice. **4** a pipe of a bagpipe that makes such a sound steadily. —*v.* **drones, droned, dron.ing** utter such a sound: *The speaker droned on with the financial report.*

drool *v.* **1** run or let saliva run from the mouth; *adj*.: *a drooling infant.* **2** *Informal.* show excessive pleasure at or in anticipation of something: *She's drooling over the chance to go to Europe.*

droop *v.* sag or hang down: *pants that droop down your rear end; She drooped her head in shame; My spirits drooped* (= I was dispirited) *at the bad news;* *adj.*: *a man with drooping shoulders.* —*n.*: *There's a slight droop to one eye; the vast droop of his belly.*

droop.y *adj.* sagging or floppy: *The flowers are droopy from the drought; droopy eyelids; modishly droopy* (= oversized) *knits such as cardigans and polo shirts; cpd: a droopy-eared rabbit; droopy-eyed workers.*

drop *n.* **1** a tiny, usu. globular mass of liquid: *a drop of water; Our coffee is "good to the last drop"; ear, eye, nose drops* (= medication); *knockout drops* (= drugs). **2** a tiny amount: *He's had a drop too much to drink* (= is drunk); *When we are trying to collect $40 million, $9.95 is a mere drop in the bucket, but every drop counts.* **3** a drop-shaped pendant, candy, etc.: *cough, gum, pearl drops.* **4** a falling, descent, or decrease: *the sheer drop of the mountain face; a sharp drop in the price of gas; a sudden drop in temperature; a drop in height from 20,000 to 10,000 ft; You're looking down a drop* (= cliff or slope) *of 5,000 ft.* **5** a dropping or deposit or a place for it: *The spy made the drop; He deposited the papers at the drop; a parachute drop of supplies; a mail drop for letters.* **6** something to be lowered, as a stage curtain (**drop curtain**) or a trapdoor. —**at the drop of a hat** promptly; without hesitation. —**get the drop on someone** *Informal.* have an advantage over someone. —*v.* **drops, dropped, drop.ping 1** fall or let fall, as in drops: *to drop a bomb; Drop a coin into the slot; Prices drop* (= decrease) *when demand is low; The troops were dropped* (= lowered) *by parachute.* **2** fall or cause to fall as from weakness, a blow, wounds, etc.: *to drop from exhaustion; The hunter dropped the moose with one shot; The wounded were dropping to the ground like flies.* **3** move to a position that is inferior, less active, or further back: *Our horse is beginning to drop back in the race; We never expected him to drop behind in class; to drop behind the others.* **4** say or write casually: *to drop a hint, a name; Do drop us a card when you get there.* **5** cease connection with a person or thing: *to drop a claim; Pat dropped his old friends and dropped out of sight* (= disappeared); *He drops* (= omits) *his g's and says readin', writin', etc.* **6** put down; deposit: *Please drop this letter in the mailbox; Can you drop me at Fifth Street?* **7** visit informally: *Please drop in on us sometime; I may drop around or drop by on Monday.* **8** *Informal.* take a narcotic in pill or capsule form: *He started smoking pot and dropping* (= swallowing) *acid.* —**drop dead** *interj. Informal.* get lost. —**drop off 1** decrease: *Attendance drops off toward the end of the month.* **2** leave: *She dropped off a package for you; to drop* (= fall) *off to sleep watching TV; Please drop* (= let) *me off at the next stop.* —**drop out** withdraw from a contest, school or program (before finishing it), from conventional society, etc.

drop-in *n.* **1** a casual visitor; *adj.*: *drop-in customers, parties, traffic.* **2** a place for informal visits; *adj.*: *a drop-in center for teens; drop-in shelters.* **3** something that is dropped into position; *adj.*: *an office-type drop-in ceiling; a drop-in replacement part; drop-in film cartridges.*

drop kick *n.* a kick made just as a dropped ball bounces from the ground; **drop-kick** *v.*

drop.let (DROP.lit) *n.* a small drop.

drop.off *n.* **1** a dropping off; decline. **2** *Informal.* delivery.

drop.out *n.* one who drops out: *a high-school dropout.*

drop.per (DROP.ur) *n.* a glass tube with a rubber bulb on one end and a small opening at the other, used to measure out drops.

droppings *n.pl.* animal excrement: *animal, bird droppings.*

drop.sy (DROP.see) *n.* a swelling caused by abnormal water retention in tissues; edema. —**drop.si.cal** *adj.*

dross *n.* **1** a scum of waste formed on molten metals. **2** worthless impurities; rubbish. —**dross.y** *adj.*

drought (DROWT) *n.* an extended period of unusually dry weather.

drove *pt.* of DRIVE. —*n.* a herd or large group, as of animals, moving or driven: *droves of cattle on the road to market;*

droves of flies; *People left the area* **in droves** *because of the chemical spill; others stayed home in droves.*

dro.ver (DROH.vur) *n.* one who herds animals, esp. to market.

drown (*rhyme:* down) *v.* **1** kill or die by submersion in liquid, esp. water: *He didn't drown himself, he was drowned; He had tried to drown* (= get rid of) *his sorrows at the local lounge.* **2** flood or overwhelm: *The preacher was drowned out by the noise of the traffic.*

drown.proof.ing (DROWN.proo.fing) *n.* a technique for avoiding drowning by relaxing and using one's natural buoyancy.

drowse (DROWZ) *v.* **drows.es, drowsed, drows.ing** sleep lightly; doze: *to drowse away the time.* —*n.:* *He was in a drowse when the book he was reading dropped to the floor.*

drow.sy (DROW.zee, "OW" as in "HOW") *adj.* **1** feeling or making one feel heavy and dull: *I feel drowsy after sitting in the sun; a drowsy day.* **2** quiet or inactive: *a drowsy village.* —**drow.si.ly** *adv.*; **drow.si.ness** *n.*

drub *v.* **drubs, drubbed, drub.bing** thrash or defeat soundly.

drudge *n.* one who does menial, boring, or plodding work: *Samuel Johnson described the dictionary maker as a harmless drudge.* Also *v.* **drudg.es, drudged, drudg.ing.**

drudg.er.y (DRUJ.uh.ree) *n.* **-er.ies** the work of a drudge: *He writes poetry to escape the drudgery of a dishwashing job; the sheer drudgery of housework.*

drug *n.* **1** a substance administered in medicines to affect the body; also, the medicine: *an over-the-counter drug like aspirin; prescription drugs; a proprietary, not generic drug; habit-forming, miracle, powerful, toxic, wonder drugs.* **2** a narcotic, hallucinogen, barbiturate, etc., esp. if addictive or abused: *hard and soft drugs; to peddle, push, sell, traffic in, take illicit* **drugs**; *He had been on* **drugs** *for some time when he was found dead;* **adja.**: *drug abuse, addicts, addiction, dealers, pushers.*

—*v.* **drugs, drugged, drug.ging 1** give a drug, esp. a narcotic, to someone: *The spy was drugged and carted away in a crate.* **2** mix a drug with something: *The drink was drugged.*

drug.gie same as DRUGGY, *n.*

drug.gist *n.* one who sells drugs, esp. a retail pharmacist.

drug.gy (DRUG.ee) **1** *n., pl.* **drug.gies** *Informal.* a drug addict. **2** *adj.* **drug.gi.er, drug.gi.est** having to do with drugs: *a druggy den, vision.*

drug.store *n.* a retail store that sells prescription drugs and a variety of other articles.

dru.id or **Dru.id** (DROO.id) *n.* a member of a pagan priestly order among the ancient Celts in Britain, Ireland, and Gaul. —**dru.id.ic** (droo.ID.ic) or **dru.i.di.cal** *adj.* —**dru.id.ism** (DROO-) *n.*

drum *n.* **1** a hollow cylinder or other shape with a membrane stretched over an open end, beaten as a percussion instrument: *to beat, play, roll a drum; a bass drum; the roll of the drums.* **2** eardrum. **3** a drumlike cylinder, as a barrel or a cartridge holder for a machine gun: *the brake drum of an automobile.* **4** the sound of a beaten drum; also **drum.beat.**

—*v.* **drums, drummed, drum.ming 1** play a drum; make a similar noise, as by tapping one's fingers or by beating the wings, as a bird does. **2** force by repetition: *It had been drummed into his head from early childhood that lying is bad.* —**drum out** expel from a group in disgrace. —**drum up** get by persistent canvassing or effort: *to drum up business, customers, interest, support.*

drum.beat *n.* the pounding of a drum, as in drumming up support for a cause: *a steady drumbeat of editorials.*

drum.brake *n.* an automobile brake operated by a pair of shoes pressed to the sides of a shallow metal drum attached to the moving wheel.

drum.lin *n.* an elongated hill of glacial earth and rock.

drum major *n.* a leader of a marching band.

drum ma.jor.ette (-may.juh.RET) *n.* a female baton twirler of a band.

drum.mer *n.* one who plays a drum: *individualists who march to (the beat of) a different drummer* (= are unconventional, doing their own thing).

drum.stick *n.* **1** a stick used to beat a drum. **2** the lower part of a leg of chicken, turkey, etc.

drunk *pp.* OF DRINK. —*adj.* intoxicated: *a drunk driver; drunk driving; He seemed drunk; drunk as a skunk; charged with drunk and disorderly conduct.*
—*n.* **1** a bout of drunkenness. **2** drunkard: *to roll* (= rob) *a drunk.*

drunk.ard (DRUNK.urd) *n.* one who is drunk, esp. habitually.

drunk.en (DRUNK.un) *adj.* **1** drunk: *They are not a drunken lot; drunken drivers.* **2** having to do with being drunk:

a drunken argument, incident, party, shouting match; a charge of drunken driving; He was staggering about in a drunken stupor. —**drunk.en.ly** adv.; **drunk.en.ness** n.

drunk tank n. a cell for people arrested for drunkenness.

drupe n. a fleshy, unsegmented fruit with a stone in the middle, as the peach, olive, and cherry.

druth.ers (DRUTH.urs, "TH" as in "the") n.pl. free choice: *If I had my druthers it wouldn't have happened that way.*

dry adj. **dri.er, dri.est** 1 not wet or moist: *the dry sand; dry as a bone;* **dry as dust** (= uninteresting); *There was not a dry* (= not crying) *eye at the funeral; a dry well* (that has no water); *The well has gone or run dry; dry land* (that is not under water); *a dry* (= not yielding milk) *cow.* 2 having or providing little rain: *a dry area, region, season; in dry weather.* 3 adj. having to do with solids, not liquids: *dry goods* such as cloth, clothing, groceries, etc.; ***Dry measure*** *uses pints, quarts, pecks, and bushels to measure grain, vegetables, etc.* 4 adj. served without butter or jam: *dry bread, toast.* 5 without moisture or lubrication: *a dry cough.* 6 prohibiting alcoholic drink: *a dry county, district; dry laws.* 7 not sweet: *a dry wine.* 8 plain or unadorned: *a dry* (= dull) *recitation of facts; his dry* (= subtly witty or ironic) *humor.* —**not dry behind the ears** *Informal.* immature or naive; wet behind the ears.
—v. **dries, dried, dry.ing** make or become dry: *clothes drying in the sun; We dry them in a dryer; adj.: Dried fish, food, fruit, meat, milk, etc. keep longer.* —**dry out** detoxify from the effects of alcohol. —**dry up** *Informal.* stop talking. —**dry.ly** adv.; **dry.ness** n.

dry.ad (DRY.ud, -ad) n. in myths, a nymph of the forest.

dry cell n. a battery cell having the electrolyte in paste form; also **dry battery**.

dry-clean v. clean clothes, etc. with a solvent other than water.
—**dry-cleaner** n.; **dry-cleaning** n.

dry dock n. a watertight dock that may be emptied of water to hold a ship under repair or one being built.
—**dry-dock** v. put a ship in a dry dock.

dry.er (DRY.ur) n. a machine, appliance, or person that dries: *an air dryer for the hands; a clothes washer and dryer; hair dryers.*

dry farming n. a method of cultivation adapted to dry areas, as in W. Texas; **dry-farm** v. —**dry-farmer** n.

dry goods See DRY, adj. 3.

dry ice n. solid carbon dioxide used as a cooling agent and for stage effects: *Dry ice passes from solid to vapor at $-78.5°C$;* **Dry Ice** *Trademark.*

dry measure See DRY, adj. 3.

dry rot n. 1 decay of seasoned wood from within by the action of fungi. 2 inner decay.

dry run n. a rehearsal or trial: *to do or make a dry run.*

dry.wall n. a panel of wallboard or plasterboard.

du.al (DEW.ul) adj. having to do with two; twofold; double: *a dual alliance, personality; dual citizenship, nationality; Training vehicles have dual controls; a truck trailer with dual tires; dual-purpose cattle* (raised for milk and beef).
—**du.al.i.ty** (dew.AL.i.tee) n.

du.al.ism (DEW.uh.liz.um) n. the belief that the world is composed of two basic principles or forces, as good and evil, matter and form, yin and yang, etc. —**du.al.ist** n. & adj.

dub v. **dubs, dubbed, dub.bing** 1 add new voices or sounds to a movie or sound track: *to dub in English dialogue for a French film; to dub a French film into English.* 2 dress leather by rubbing a greasy paste (**dubbin**) into it. 3 tap with a sword to make a knight: *The queen dubbed him a knight.* 4 give a new name, title, or nickname to someone: *They dubbed him "The King of Hearts."*
—n. 1 *Slang.* a bungler. 2 what is dubbed in a sound track.

du.bi.e.ty (dew.BYE.uh.tee) n. **-ties** a state of doubt.

du.bi.ous (DEW.bee.us) adj. 1 doubting or mistrustful: *She's dubious about or of your claims.* 2 causing doubt; questionable: *a dubious claim, behavior; dubious business practices; a man of dubious character.* —**du.bi.ous.ly** adv.

du.cal (DEW.cul) adj. of a duke or duchy: *families of ducal rank.*

duc.at (DUCK.ut) n. a former gold coin of Europe.

duch.ess (DUCH.is) n. 1 a duke's wife. 2 a woman who rules a duchy.

duch.y (DUCH.ee) n. **duch.ies** land ruled by a duke or duchess, as Luxembourg; dukedom.

duck n. 1 a web-footed water bird smaller than a goose: *Ducks and ducklings quack and waddle about; Jane has taken to computers* **like a duck to water** (= readily). 2 a strong, tightly woven, usu. cotton cloth for light-

duckbill / duffer

weight apparel. **3 ducks** *pl.* clothes, esp. pants, body of duck. **—like water off a duck's back** producing no effect. **—v. 1** lower oneself, one's head, body, etc. to avoid being seen or hurt: *He didn't duck fast enough to avoid the bullet; He should have ducked behind a car; boxers dodging and ducking in the ring; She came in late and ducked* (= moved quickly) *into her office.* **2** evade or dodge: *to duck issues, questions, reporters; She is ducking all phone calls this morning, but she won't **duck out of** her real obligations.* **3** submerge in water for a short time: *They ducked him in the pond.*
duck.bill *n.* a platypus.
duck.board *n.* a slatted board used as flooring or a walkway on wet or muddy areas.
duck.ling *n.* a young duck.
duck.pin *n.* **1** a short, thick bowling pin. **2 duckpins** *pl.* [with *sing. v.*] a game played with these.
duck soup *n. Informal.* a very easy thing to do.
duck.y *adjp.* **duck.i.er, -i.est** *Informal.* pleasing or excellent: *just ducky.* **—n.** a toy duck: *a rubber ducky.*
duct *n.* a tube, pipe, channel, etc. for the flow of air, liquids, etc. or for electrical wires and cables: *hot air ducts for heating the home; the tear ducts; The salivary and oil-producing glands also have ducts.* **—duct.less** *adj.*
duc.tile (DUCK.til, -tile) *adj.* **1** of solids, able to be stretched or drawn into shape without breaking: *Copper, aluminum, silver, etc. are ductile.* **2** docile or easily led.
ductless gland *n.* an endocrine gland, which releases its hormones into the blood or lymph system directly.
duct.work *n.* **1** pipes, fittings, etc., as used in a cooling, heating, or ventilation system. **2** a system of such ducts.
dud *n.* **1** *Informal.* a bomb or shell that fails to explode; hence, a failure, a worthless person, or something that is without effect; **adja.**: *a dud bomb, check, currency; dud assets.* **2 duds** *pl. Informal.* clothes; also, one's belongings: *a young guy dressed in Mountie duds; party duds.*
dude (DEWD) *n.* **1** *Informal.* a dandy or fop; hence, a city dweller or an easterner in the West. **2** *Slang.* a guy or fellow.
dude ranch *n.* a ranch run as a vacation spot for guests, sometimes called "guest ranch" or "resort ranch."
dudg.eon (DUJ.un) *n.* an angry fit of indignation: *He stalked out of the room in high dudgeon.*
due 1 *adjp.* to be paid or submitted, esp. payable immediately; owed: *Your rent is due on the first of each month; a loan that falls or comes due at the end of June.* **2** *adja.* proper or suitable: *after due consideration; You will hear from us in due course; with all due respect; It will be done in due time; with due diligence and dispatch; to conduct or do or perform **due diligence** (= a formal process of ensuring that others suffer no harm in a given situation).* **3** *adjp.* expected or scheduled: *The baby is due any day now; Our bus was due (to arrive) at 4:30; He is **due for** a pay raise* (= He can expect a pay raise); *A library book should be returned on the **due date** stamped on it.* **—due to 1** attributable to something: *game cancellations due to rain.* **2** *Informal.* because of something: *game canceled due to rain.* **—adv.** directly: *Miami is due south of Toronto on the same longitude; due east, north, west.* **—n. 1** something owed to or deserved by someone: *Let's **give the devil his due*** (= give deserved credit even to an enemy). **2 dues** *pl.* a fee, as for membership: *We pay annual membership dues of $50; He has **paid his dues** (Informal for earned what he is enjoying through hard work, suffering, etc.).*
du.el (DEW.ul) *n.* **1** a formal combat between two people, as to settle a point of honor: *Ho challenged Lou to a duel; But Lou doesn't fight duels.* **2** a contest between two: *a duel to the death; a duel of wits.* **—v. du.els, du.eled, du.el.ing. —du.el.ist** *n.* Also **du.elled, du.el.ling; du.el.list** *Cdn.*
du.en.de (doo.EN.day) *n. Spanish.* a magical and inspiring personal magnetism: *a flamenco dancer gifted with great duende.*
du.en.na (dew.EN.uh) *n.* a female chaperon, esp. for a young woman in a Spanish household.
due process *n.* the right to fair treatment according to the laws, as guaranteed by the constitution in democratic countries.
du.et (dew.ET) *n.* **1** a piece of music for two singers or players: *to play, sing a duet.* **2** the performing pair: *a male duet.*
duff *n.* **1** a flour pudding made in a cloth bag. **2** decaying matter covering the ground in forests. **3** *Slang.* buttocks: *to get off one's duff.*
duffel same as DUFFLE.
duf.fer (DUF.ur) *n. Informal.* one who is bumbling and incompetent, esp. such

a golfer.

duf.fle or **duf.fel** (DUF.ul) *n.* **1** coarse, thick-napped woolen cloth; *adja.: a duffel bag, coat, sock.* **2** [short form] duffle bag; duffel coat; duffel sock.

dug *pt. & pp.* of DIG.

dug.out *n.* **1** a canoe made of a hollowed-out tree trunk. **2** a rough shelter dug at least partly into the ground. **3** a roofed and sunken shelter for baseball players.

du jour (duh.ZHOOR) *adj.* [used after a noun] as prepared for serving on the particular day: *a restaurant's soup du jour; our price du jour; the thought du jour.*

duke *n.* **1** a nobleman of rank next below prince. **2** a ruler of a duchy or dukedom. **3 dukes** *pl. Informal.* fists: *to put up one's dukes; v.: to* **duke it out** (= fight it out).

duke.dom (DUKE.dum) See DUCHY.

dul.cet (DUL.sit) *adja.* sweet or soothing, esp. to the ear: *dulcet sounds, tones.*

dul.ci.mer (DUL.suh.mur) *n.* either of two musical instruments with steel strings; also **dul.ci.more.**

dull *adj.* **1** not perceiving sharply: *dull hearing; He's just a little dull, not stupid or dense; a* **dull-witted** (= slow in understanding) *fellow.* **2** sluggish; not active: *a week of dull trading on the stock exchange; a dull life, market, place; a dull* (= not intense) *ache.* **3** not sharp, bright, or clear: *a dull knife, light, sword; dull gray walls; dull sounds; a dull thud.* **4** boring or tedious: *a dull speech; The book is dull reading.* **5** overcast: *a dull day.* —*v.* make dull: *a mind dulled by drugs; Candy dulls the appetite; The knife has been dulled by rough use.*
—**dull.ness** *n.* —**dul.ly** *adv.*

dull.ard (DULL.urd) *n.* a stupid person.

du.ly (DEW.lee) *adv.* in a due and proper way, time, etc.: *a duly elected official.*

Du.ma (DOO.muh) *n.* in Russia, a legislative assembly.

dumb (DUM) *adj.* **1** unable to speak, either by birth or temporarily: *She was struck dumb with shock; a dumb animal, creature; n.pl. the deaf and the dumb* (= deaf-mutes). **2** silent: *He stayed dumb throughout the meeting; a dumb show.* **3** *Informal.* stupid: *He acted or played dumb; It was a dumb thing to do.*
—**dumb.ly** *adv.;* **dumb.ness** *n.*

dumb.bell *n.* **1** a short bar with often rounded weights on either end, lifted for exercise. **2** *Informal.* a stupid person.

dumb.found.ed (DUM.found.id) *adj.* made speechless for a moment, as with amazement: *He was dumbfounded to hear that he had been fired from his job; utterly dumbfounded at* or *by the news.*
Also **dumb.struck.**

dumb terminal *n.* a terminal without independent processing capability and operating only when connected to a computer; not a smart or intelligent terminal.

dumb.wait.er (DUM.way.tur) *n.* a small elevator for bringing food to a different floor.

dum.dum bullet *n.* a bullet that expands on impact, causing a jagged wound.

dum.found same as DUMBFOUND.

dum.my *n.* **dum.mies 1** a model human figure: *a dummy used by a ventriloquist; a tackling dummy (used for boxing practice); department-store dummies.* **2** an imitation or substitute for something, as one acting secretly for another person; *adja.: a dummy corporation; a dummy gun (that only looks like a real one).* **3** *Slang* [offensive] a mute person. **4** *Informal.* a stupid person. **5** the exposed hand of the declarer's partner in bridge. —*v.* **dum.mies, dum.mied, dum.my.ing** usu. **dummy up,** refuse to answer questions.

dump *v.* **1** unload, empty, or drop in a large mass: *They dump the garbage behind the building; Did she dump* (= drop) *him or was it the other way around? Data is dumped* (= transferred) *from computer memory to storage or to an output terminal.* **2** sell in large quantities abroad at a low price: *Surplus goods are sometimes dumped abroad to keep domestic prices up.*
—**dump on** *Informal.* unload bad feelings on someone, as by complaining or criticizing. —*n.* **1** a place for dumping something: *garbage, municipal, trash dumps; an* **ammunition dump** (= storage depot). **2** *Informal.* a rundown, dirty place: *This apartment is a real dump!* —**the dumps** *Informal.* a depressed state: *to feel down in the dumps over a defeat; an economy headed for the dumps.*

dump.ling *n.* a ball of dough boiled or steamed, stuffed with fruit as a dessert, or served unstuffed with meats.

dump.ster (DUMP.stur) *n.* a large bin for dumping trash; **Dumpster** *Trademark.*

dump truck *n.* a truck with a body that can be tilted up to unload through a tailgate.

dump.y *adj.* **dump.i.er, -i.est 1** short, squat, and plump: *a dumpy bird.* **2** shabby or grungy: *a dumpy dress,*

dun / dusky

restaurant, room.

dun *adj.* dull grayish-brown. —*n.* **1** this color; also, a dun horse. **2** a dunning. **3** one who duns. —*v.* **duns, dunned, dun.ning** ask a debtor repeatedly for payment.

dunce *n.* a slow-witted person: *He had to wear a* **dunce cap** *as punishment, which didn't help his self-esteem.*

dun.der.head (DUN.dur.hed) *n.* a stupid person: *Dan is no blundering dunderhead.*

dune *n.* a hill of sand made by the wind.

dune buggy *n.* a light automobile adapted, as by fitting with wide tires, for driving on soft sand.

dung *n.* excrement, esp. from animals, used as fertilizer. —**dung.y** *adj.*

dun.ga.ree (dung.guh.REE) *n.* **1** a coarse cotton cloth, esp. blue denim. **2 dungarees** *pl.* work clothes, esp. pants or overalls made of dungaree.

dun.geon (DUN.jun) *n.* a dark, usu. underground jail or cell.

dunk *v.* **1** submerge or dip into a liquid: *He likes to dunk his donut (in coffee).* **2** throw a basketball into the hoop with the hand reaching over the rim. —*n.* **1** a dunking; dip: *He had a good dunk in the lake.* **2** a basketball shot made by dunking; also **dunk shot.** —**dunk.er** *n.*

du.o (DEW.oh) *n.* **-os** a duet; hence, any pair.

du.o.dec.i.mal (dew.uh.DES.uh.mul) *adj.* having to do with 12 or 12ths: *a duodecimal system of measuring, as 12 inches to the foot, 60 minutes to the hour, or 24 hours to the day.*

du.o.de.num (dew.uh.DEE.num) *n.* **-nums** or **-na** the portion of the small intestine where it joins the stomach. —**du.o.de.nal** (-ul) *adj.*: *duodenal ulcers.*

dupe *v.* **dupes, duped, dup.ing** cheat by catching off guard or while suspecting nothing; make a fool of someone; trick: *He was duped into believing the car was new.* —*n.* one who is easily duped.

du.ple (DEW.pul) *adj.* double: *duple meter;* **duple time** *(with two beats to the bar).*

du.plex (DEW.plex) *adj.* double: *a duplex apartment, house; duplex (= two-ply) paperboard.* —*n.* **1** a house having two separate dwelling units; also **duplex house. 2** an apartment having rooms on two floors; also **duplex apartment. 3** transmission of computer data in both directions simultaneously between terminals: *to set a modem to*

full duplex.

du.pli.cate (DEW.pluh.cate) *v.* **-cates, -cat.ed, -cat.ing 1** make or become double; also, do or occur again: *It's a waste of time and money to duplicate our efforts; to duplicate achievements, experiences, feats, results, success.* **2** copy exactly, as with a **duplicating machine,** or duplicator. —*n.* (-kit) an exact copy; a double of something: *to make a duplicate of the application; an application prepared* **in duplicate** *(= with an exact copy of the original).* —*adj.* (-kit) double; being an exact copy: *a duplicate key; a duplicate set of keys;* In **duplicate bridge** *each hand is replayed by different players.* —**du.pli.ca.tion** (-CAY.shun) *n.* —**du.pli.ca.tor** (-cay.tur) *n.*

du.plic.i.ty (dew.PLIS.i.tee) *n.* **-ties** deception by acting so as to conceal one's real intent or feelings. —**du.plic.i.tous** (-tus) *adj.*

du.ra.ble (DURE.uh.bul) *adj.* long-lasting, esp. despite use and wear: *It's sturdy and durable; durable construction, equipment, fashions, friendships, leaders, products, relations; a durable peace; cars, appliances, furniture, and such* **durable goods.** —**du.ra.bil.i.ty** (-BIL.i.tee) *n.*

durable press *n.* a chemical process for fixing the shape, creases, etc. of a garment and making it wrinkle-resistant. —**durable-press** *adj.*

dur.ance (DYOOR.unce, DOOR-) *n.* imprisonment: *in durance vile.*

du.ra.tion (dew.RAY.shun) *n.* the time during which something lasts or continues to exist: *an illness of short duration; The facilities were closed* **for the duration** *(of the illness, strike, war, etc.).*

du.ress (dew.RES) *n.* illegal use of threats or force such as imprisonment to make someone do something: *One is not obliged to keep a promise made* **under duress.**

dur.ing (DURE.ing) *prep.* **1** throughout the course of time of something: *It's hot during the summer.* **2** at one point in the course of something: *He was wounded during the battle.*

durst [old form] *pt.* of DARE.

du.rum (DYOOR.um, DOOR-) *n.* a hardy wheat whose flour is used in macaroni, spaghetti, etc.

dusk *n.* the partial darkness of twilight: *Some flowers close at dusk; Dawn and dusk last very long at the poles during winter.*

dusk.y *adj.* **dusk.i.er, -i.est 1** dim; darkish; gloomy: *a dusky blue.* **2** dark-skinned; swarthy. —**dusk.i.ly** *adv.;* **dusk.i.ness** *n.*

dust *n.* **1** fine particles of solid matter; fine powdery earth: *A layer of dust covered the furniture lying in storage; Books were gathering dust in the library; Dust was collecting* or *settling everywhere; Children playing in the dirt kick up* or *raise quite a dust; Water is sprinkled on dirt roads to lay the dust; a cloud, layer, particle of dust; We return to dust when we die; The debate will resume* **when the dust settles** (= when the confusion is over). **2** something resembling dust: *The sun was formed from a swirling mass of gases and cosmic dust; gold dust; radioactive dust; volcanic dust.* —**bite the dust** die in battle; be defeated. —**dust and ashes 1** [indicating worthlessness]: *The king did penance for his misdeeds in dust and ashes* (put on the head as a sign of repentance). **2** [indicating disillusionment or disappointment]: *His hopes turned into dust and ashes.* —**shake the dust from one's feet** leave in anger or contempt. —**throw dust in someone's eyes** mislead or confuse. —*v.* **1** remove the dust from something: *Make sure you dust off the books as you take them down; n.: They need* **dusting**. **2** sprinkle with dust or any powder: *The detective dusted the fingerprints with white powder; She dusted sugar over the cakes; n.: There is a light* **dusting** *of snow on the ground.*
dust.bin *n.* garbage can.
dust bowl *n.* an area of dry blowing soil, no longer fertile.
dust devil *n.* a small whirlwind of dust, litter, etc.
dust.er *n.* **1** a person or implement that dusts: *a crop duster; a feather duster* (made with feathers). **2** a light housecoat.
dust jacket *n.* the printed protective wrapper of a hardcover book.
dust.pan *n.* a flat pan for collecting sweepings.
dust storm *n.* a windstorm or whirlwind bearing clouds of dust.
dust.up *n.* a quarrel or fight: *a dustup between two neighbors.*
dust.y *adj.,* **dust.i.er, -i.est** filled with or like dust: *a dusty old insurance policy; a dusty brown; a dusty village.*
Dutch *adj.* of the Netherlands, its people, or their language. —**the Dutch** *n.pl.* the people of the Netherlands. —**go Dutch** *Informal.* have each pay his or her own share, as on a date. —**in Dutch** *Informal* [derogatory] in trouble.
Dutch courage *n. Informal* [derogatory] bravery inspired by alcohol.
Dutch.man (DUCH.mun) *n.* -**men** a man of or from the Netherlands; Hollander. —**Dutch.wom.an** *n.* -**wom.en.**
Dutch treat *n. Informal.* a treat for which each person pays for his or her own share.
Dutch uncle *n. Informal* [derogatory] one given to making harsh and forthright criticisms: *He talked to her like a Dutch uncle.*
du.te.ous (DEW.tee.us) *adj.* [literary] dutiful: *a duteous wife.*
du.ti.a.ble (DEW.tee.uh.bul) *adj.* subject to duty: *goods dutiable at 25%.*
du.ti.ful (DEW.tuh.ful) *adj.* doing one's duty; obedient: *a dutiful child, servant, son.* —**du.ti.ful.ly** *adv.*
du.ty (DEW.tee) *n.* -**ties 1** a moral or legal obligation: *Do your duty; duty before pleasure; Her devotion to duty is well-known; He's always ready to answer* or *obey the call of duty; It's our democratic duty to vote; our patriotic duty to defend our country; our bounden duty to our country; He did it out of a sense of duty; an official charged with dereliction of duty; to take on a duty; to carry out, discharge, do, perform, shirk one's duty; a civic, moral, official, pleasant duty; When duty calls, she cannot wait; A doctor is* **duty bound** (= obliged by duty) *to save a life if possible.* **2** service: *He saw active duty during World War II; fatigue duty; guard duty; overseas duty; Marcie is* **on duty** *from 9 a.m.; She'll be* **off duty** *at 5 p.m.; My typewriter will* **do duty for** (= serve as) *my writing equipment while the word processor is being serviced;* **adja.:** *a duty nurse, officer* (who is on duty); *duty counsel.* **3** a tax, esp. one on imported or exported goods: *import and export duties; Customs duties are levied before sales taxes; Excise duties are paid on goods and services produced within a country; A duty was imposed on imported books and later lifted.*
duty-free *adj.* free of customs duties: *duty-free goods from a duty-free shop.*
du.vet (DEW.vay) *n.* a down-filled quilt used as bed covering; also called "continental quilt."
dwarf (DWORF) *n.* **dwarfs** or **dwarves** (DWORVZ) **1** an abnormally small adult person, plant, or animal. **2** in folk tales, a deformed or ugly dwarf with magical powers. —*v.* cause to be or remain too small: *the Japanese art of dwarfing trees; The aircraft carrier dwarfed the boats near it.* —**adja.:** *dwarf* (= undersized) *cattle that are born stunted; a dwarf tree* (such as a bonsai).
—**dwarf.ish** *adj.*

dwell / each

dwell *v.*, *pt. & pp.* **dwelled** or **dwelt** stay or remain for a long time; live in a place: *to dwell among the mountains, in a cottage, on an island.* —**dwell on** or **upon** think, speak, write, etc. about something at some length: *The speaker dwelt at length on choosing a career; Let's dwell a little* (= spend some time) *on this topic.* —**dwell.er** *n.*: *cave, city, forest, slum, urban dwellers.*

dwelling *n.* a building in which one lives; residence: *the humble dwelling of a poor peasant; a dwelling place.*

dwin.dle (DWIN.dul) *v.* **-dles, -dled, -dling** make or become less by steady degrees: *By 1830, the Beothuk population had dwindled to zero; adj.a.: our **dwindling** oil resources; a dwindling demand, market, number, supply.*

dy.ad (DYE.ad) *n.* a pair: *the buyer-seller dyad.*

dyb.buk (DIB.uk) *n.* **dyb.buks** or **dyb.buk.im** (dib.oo.KEEM) in Jewish folklore, a dead person's spirit that takes over a living person's body.

dye *n.* 1 a substance used to color or stain something, esp. fabrics, leather, hair, etc. 2 the resultant color: *a villain of the deepest dye* (= of the worst kind). —*v.* **dyes, dyed, dye.ing** to color or be colored in this way: *She dyed her hair brown; adj.: Does it look **dyed** or natural?* —**dy.er** *n.*

dyed-in-the-wool *adj.a.* firm or devoted: *a dyed-in-the-wool conservative, socialist; a dyed-in-the-wool establishment attitude.*

dying See DIE.

dyke *n.* Slang [offensive] a lesbian, esp. a masculine type; also **dike**. —**dyk.ey** *adj.*

dy.nam.ic (dye.NAM.ic) *adj.* having to do with motion; not static: *a dynamic period of history; a dynamic* (= energetic) *personality; a dynamic* (= active) *sales campaign; a dynamic* (= functional), *not organic disease; the **dynamic balancing** of a wheel while it is rotating; "Crescendo," "forte," "piano," etc. are **dynamic terms** used in **dynamic marking** of sheet music for loudness and softness.*
—*n.* 1 a force that produces change or action in society: *the inner dynamic that drives the young social reformer; the dynamics of social reform; population dynamics; The group dynamics of people working together is studied in sociology.* 2 **dynamics** *n.pl.* [with sing. v.] the physical study of motion and the forces producing it: *Dynamics is a branch of mechanics;* **cpd**: *aerodynamics, hydrodynamics, thermodynamics.* —**dy.nam.i.cal** *adj.*; **dy.nam.i.cal.ly** *adv.*

dy.na.mism (DYE.nuh.miz.um) *n.* 1 action or power arising from energy: *the dynamism of her personality.* 2 the theory that whatever happens is the result of forces acting on mind and matter.

dy.na.mite (DYE.nuh.mite) *n.* 1 an industrial blasting explosive: *a stick of dynamite.* 2 *Informal.* a person or thing having great energy and appeal: *The singer was hailed by her fans as dynamite; Our new sports car is 1,000 kg of pure dynamite; a vacuum-cleaner that is just dynamite for homes and offices.*
—*v.* **-mites, -mit.ed, -mit.ing** blow up with dynamite: *a bridge dynamited by terrorists.* —**dy.na.mit.er** *n.*

dy.na.mo (DYE.nuh.moh) *n.* **-mos** 1 an electrical generator. 2 a forceful and energetic person: *a dancing dynamo; stage dynamos; a heart-throbbing dynamo of a singer.*

dy.nas.ty (DYE.nuh.stee, DIN.uh-) *n.* **-ties** a series of rulers or powerful leaders of one family; also, their rule: *The Great Wall was built during the Ch'in dynasty which collapsed in 206 B.C.; Dynasties are established, founded, overthrown.* —**dy.nas.tic** (dye.NAS.tic) *adj.*

dys.en.ter.y (DIS.un.tair.ee) *n.* **-ter.ies** an infection of the large intestine marked by painful, often bloody diarrhea.

dys.func.tion (DIS.funk.shun) *n.* an impairment of normal functioning. —**dys.func.tion.al** *adj.*: *a dysfunctional family* (= broken home).

dys.lex.i.a (dis.LEX.ee.uh) *n.* abnormal difficulty in reading, often caused by brain damage. —**dys.lex.ic** *n. & adj.*

dys.pep.si.a (dis.PEP.see.uh) *n.* disturbed or difficult digestion; indigestion. —**dys.pep.tic** *n. & adj.*

dys.tro.phy (DIS.truh.fee) *n.* **-phies** 1 a disorder characterized by neural or muscular degeneration: *muscular dystrophy.* 2 faulty nutrition.

.... **E, e** ....

E or **e** (EE) *n.* **E's** or **e's** the fifth letter of the English alphabet; hence, the fifth in a series.

each (EECH) *pron.* every one of two or more taken separately: *He spoke to each of them; to each of the children; to **each and every one** of them;* [with *pl. v.*] *Lou and Pat each have a house; They each have their* (*Informal* for his or her) *house; Each of the houses is* or *are for sale; They looked at **each other** and their broker; They all looked at **each other** or **one another**.* —*adj.a.: a gift for each child.*

—*adv.* to or for each: *The tickets cost $50 each.*
ea.ger (EE.gur) *adj.* full of desire; keenly wanting: *a sales clerk eager to please customers; He is eager for appreciation; Lee is an* **eager beaver** (= overly diligent person) *who never rests.* —**ea.ger.ly** *adv.*; **ea.ger.ness** *n.*
ea.gle (EE.gul) *n.* **1** a large, powerful bird of prey having keen vision: *the bald eagle of the North; the golden eagle; An eagle soars; the scream of an eagle;* *adj.*: *The* **eagle-eyed** (= sharp-eyed) *forest ranger spotted smoke in the distance.* **2** in golf, a score of two under par on a hole.
ea.glet (EEG.lit) *n.* a young eagle
ear (EER) *n.* **1** the organ of hearing, esp. its visible, outer part; hence, the sense of hearing: *The hearing organ consists of the inner ear, middle ear, and outer ear (including the "ear canal"); He has a good ear for music; Dissonant voices grate on our ears; She had her ears pierced for earrings; He can wiggle his ears; Some animals* **perk up** or **prick up** *their ears when listening; Our ears perked up* or *pricked up* (= *We became attentive*) *as Joe went up to the mike to announce the winner; You have my ear* (= attention); *Tell me, I'm* **all ears** (= listening); *Friends and comrades,* **lend me your ears** (= pay attention)! *The boy genius set the computer world* **on its ear** (*Informal for* caused a revolution in the computer world); *I can play that song* **by ear** (= without written music); *I forgot my lines, so I* **played it by ear** (= improvised); *Dad* **turned a deaf ear** (= refused to listen) *to his pleas for more money; His pleas* **fell on deaf ears**; *He's* **up to his ears** (= deeply) *in debt.* **2** the grain-bearing spike of a cereal such as corn or wheat.
ear.drop *n.* a hanging ornament for the ear; also, an earring.
ear.drum *n.* a vibrating membrane between the outer ear and middle ear.
eared *adj. & comb.form.* having an ear or specified kind of ear: *The sea lion is an eared seal; a dog-eared book; golden-eared wheat; a sharp-eared listener.*
ear.ful (EER.ful) *n.* something startling or unpleasant: *She got an earful from her parents for being late.*
earl (URL) *n.* a British peer ranking below a marquis but above a viscount. —**earl.dom** *n.*
ear.lobe or **ear lobe** *n.* the lower part of the outer ear.
ear.ly (UR.lee) **-li.cr, -li.est 1** *adj. & adv.* before in time; not late: *I go to bed early and rise early; Spring is early this year; "The* **early bird** *catches the worm"* (= gets the prize); *Please reply* **at your earliest** (= soonest) **convenience.** **2** *adja. & adv.* in the beginning of a period: *Trees are in bud in early spring; I learned this early in life.* **3** *adja.* near the beginning of a historical period or epoch: **Early American** (= Colonial) *furniture;* **Early English** *(1200-1300);* **Early man** (= prehistoric humans) *chipped tools from stone;* **Early Victorian** (= of the earlier part of Queen Victoria's reign). —**early on** at or during an early stage *in* a period or activity.
ear.mark *n.* a mark to identify, designate, etc.: *a book that has all the earmarks* (= characteristics) *of sound scholarship.* —*v.* to mark specially; hence, assign or set aside: *to earmark funds for charity, emergencies, spending;* *adj.*: *earmarked funds, merchandise, purposes.*
ear.muffs *n.pl.* coverings for the ears against cold, noise, etc.
earn (URN) *v.* deserve or gain as reward, wages, profit, etc.: *to earn a living; Savings deposits earn interest; His community work earned him gratitude; It earned respect and admiration for him;* *adj.*: *You get two or more weeks of* **earned** *vacation in a year; Is your doctorate earned or honorary?* —**earn.er** *n.*
ear.nest (UR.nist) *adj.* serious and eager: *an earnest attempt to succeed; an earnest appeal, effort, worker.* —**in earnest** serious: *Surely, you can't be in earnest! I am in earnest about getting a degree; But he began studying in earnest* (= seriously) *only on the eve of the exam.*
—*n.* a pledge or surety: *His first poem was an earnest of greater works to come;* **earnest money** (paid as surety).
—**ear.nest.ly** *adv.*; **ear.nest.ness** *n.*
earnings *n.pl.* money that one earns: *his annual earnings; the average earnings of a postal worker; your net earnings after deducting expenses from gross earnings.*
ear.phone (EER.fone) *n.* a sound receiver worn in or on the ear.
ear.plug *n.* a plug for keeping sound or water out of the ear.
ear.ring (EER.ring, EER.ing) *n.* a ring, stud, etc. worn as an ear ornament.
ear.shot *n.* hearing range: *She was out of earshot when he called for help; Try to stay within earshot in case I need you.*
ear.split.ting (EER.split.ing) *adj.* painfully loud or high-pitched.
earth (URTH, "TH" as in "thin") *n.* **1** often **Earth**, the planet we live on: *The Earth rotates on its axis and revolves*

around the Sun; *The Moon circles or orbits the Earth once in about 30 days.* **2** the world and its inhabitants: *All earth rejoiced at the news.* **3** dry land; ground: *She is interested in everything that moves between the earth and the sky; the cultivation of the earth.* **4** soil or dirt: *a pot filled with earth.* —**down to earth** sensible and realistic. —**on earth 1** [as an intensive] of all things: *How (or Where, When, Why,* etc.) *on earth did this happen?* **2** on this planet: *our life on earth; as if he were the last man on earth.* —**run to earth** search and find someone or something.

earth.born *adj.* mortal.

earth.bound *adj.* **1** tied to earthly things. **2** worldly; unimaginative.

earth.en (URTH.un) *adj.* of earth or baked clay: *an earthen dam, floor, jar, jug, pot, tile.*

earth.en.ware (UR.thun.ware) *n.* pottery made of coarse porous clay.

earth.ly *adj.* **-li.er, -li.est 1** of the earth; also, worldly or temporal: *our earthly existence.* **2** *adj.a.* [used negatively] possible: *no earthly chance; Any earthly need for an umbrella today? What earthly use is that piece of junk?* —**earth.li.ness** *n.*

earth.mov.er (URTH.moo.vur) *n.* a bulldozer.

earth.quake *n.* a shaking of the earth: *a devastating earthquake; A major earthquake measuring 8.1 on the Richter scale struck Mexico in 1985.*

earth.shak.ing (URTH.shay.king) *adj.* of profound significance: *an earthshaking discovery, event; a matter of earthshaking importance.*

earth station *n.* a dish-shaped antenna for receiving TV signals directly from orbiting satellites; dish.

earth.work *n.* piled-up earth used for defense; embankment.

earth.worm *n.* a smooth, red-dish-brown, segmented worm that burrows in moist soil.

earth.y *adj.* **earth.i.er, -i.est 1** of or like earth: *earthy colors, shades, tones; warm earthy hues; an earthy, energetic, warm, sensuous woman.* **2** crude or vulgar: *earthy humor, wit; an earthy creature, style; No one can stand his earthy language.* —**earth.i.ness** *n.*

ear.wax *n.* the yellowish secretion from the ear; cerumen.

ear.wig *n.* a tiny insect having a pincerlike rear part.

ease (EEZ) *n.* **1** comfort; relaxation: *a millionaire's life of ease; Stand at ease* (= with feet apart)! **2** naturalness; poise: *the reassuring ease of her manner.* **3** facility: *She passed the exam with ease.* —**at ease** or **at one's ease** not feeling nervous or troubled. —**ill at ease** nervous or troubled. —**put someone at his** or **her ease** make someone feel at ease. —**take one's ease** relax.

—*v.* **eas.es, eased, eas.ing 1** make less painful or difficult: *The windfall check eased his money troubles; He was given an injection to ease the pain.* **2** move effortlessly or slowly: *She eased the car into the parking space; He eased himself into the corner of the sofa; Unwanted employees are eased out* (= relieved) *of their jobs.*

—**ease up** or **off** relax: *Ease off a little on a holiday;* **Ease up on** (= Don't be so hard on) *the poor fellow.* —**ease.ful** *adj.;* **ease.ful.ly** *adv.*

ea.sel (EE.zul) *n.* a frame or tripod to support an artist's canvas, a blackboard, etc.

ease.ment (EEZ.munt) *n.* in law, a limited right, as of passage, on land owned by another: *Your property deed may include an easement for a utility right-of-way.*

eas.i.ly (EE.zul.ee) *adv.* in an easy way; without doubt: *She won easily; She is easily the winner.* —**eas.i.ness** *n.*

east (EEST) *n.* where the sun rises; the direction opposite west: *The church is 20 miles to the east.* —**the East 1** the eastern part of the world, of a country, region, town, etc., esp. the countries in Asia: *the three wise men from the East; the Far East; the Middle East; the Near East; the East* (= people of the Orient) *trying to meet the West.* **2** the former Soviet Union and its East European allies: *The Berlin Wall was symbolic of the East-West divisions.* —**back east** or **down east** in or to the eastern part of the country, as viewed from the West. —*adj.a.: the east coast, wall; an east wind (from the east); Boston is east of New York;* **adv.**: *We are moving east next year; A ship sailing east* (= to the east).

East Asian *n. & adj.* (a person) of or from the region comprising E. China, Japan, North and South Korea, Taiwan, and nearby islands.

East.er (EES.tur) *n.* a Christian spring festival commemorating Christ's resurrection.

east.er.ly (EES.tur.lee) *adj. & adv.* **1** toward the east: *Cape Spear, Newfoundland, is Canada's most easterly point.* **2** from the east: *an easterly wind.* —*n., pl.* **-lies** an easterly wind.

east.ern or **East.ern** (EES.turn) *adj.* of, to, or from the east: *the eastern frontier, half, part, sector;* the **Eastern Hemisphere** (= the half of the earth composed of

Europe, Africa, Asia, and Australia); *the Eastern Orthodox churches;* **Eastern (Standard) Time** *used in Eastern U.S. and Canada.* —**east.ern.er** or **East.ern.er** *n.*

East Indian *n. & adj.* **1** (a person) of or from the Indian subcontinent. **2** formerly, (a person) of or from the **East Indies** (= Southeast Asia).

east.ward (EEST.wurd) *adj. & adv.* to the east: *an eastward journey, movement, tendency; to fly, sail, spread eastward; The ship sailed eastward across the Atlantic.* Also **east.wards** *adv.* —**east.ward.ly** *adj. & adv.*

eas.y (EE.zee) *adj.* **eas.i.er, -i.est** involving little effort; without constraints; not hard; smooth: *as easy as ABC; as easy as* (apple) *pie; an easy book; The type is easy to read; It's not easy getting a book published; It's easy for you to say that; an easy lesson, life, mind, pace, victory; to get a loan on easy terms; to repay a loan in easy installments; her affable, easy manners; to complete a journey* **by easy stages** (= a short distance at a time); *adv.*: *It's easier said than done.* —**easy come, easy go** easy to get and to spend: *With money, it was always easy come, easy go for him.* —**easy does it** do it in a relaxed manner. —**easy on the eyes** *Informal.* good to look at. —**go easy** use moderation: *Go easy on that cake, Billy.* —**on easy street** *Informal.* without financial worries. —**of easy virtue** of poor morals: *women of easy virtue.* —**take it easy** or **take things easy** relax.

eas.y.go.ing (EE.zee.GO.ing) *adj.* having a relaxed attitude.

easy mark *n.* one who is easy to impose upon.

easy money *n.* money obtained improperly.

easy touch *n.* one who is easy to get money out of.

eat (EET) *v.* **eats, ate, eat.en, eat.ing** take in with the mouth, as food: *something to eat; We eat to live; to eat a meal; to eat out* (at a restaurant); *to eat greedily, heartily, voraciously; Rust eats away* (= corrodes) *metal; The sea eats away at* (= takes away bit by bit; crodes) *our shores; Acids eat into* (= damage) *metal; Moths eat* (= make) *holes in cloth; What's eating* (*Informal.* bothering) *you? Inflation eats up* (= consumes) *whatever profit we make; He had to eat* (= take back) *his words when she proved him wrong.* —**eat one's heart out** be jealous; also, be bitterly sorry. —**eat out of one's hand** be submissive to another; obey eagerly.

—*n.* esp. **eats** *pl. Informal.* food.
—**eat.er** *n.*

eat.a.ble (EE.tuh.bul) *adj.* that is fit to eat: *These bananas are a bit too ripe to be eatable; n.: Any eatables in that basket?*

eat.er.y (EE.tur.ee) *n.* **-er.ies** *Informal.* restaurant.

eau de Co.logne (oh.duh.cuh.LONE) same as COLOGNE.

eaves (EEVZ) *n.pl.* the lower edges of a roof projecting beyond the walls of the house.

eaves.drop *v.* **-drops, -dropped, -drop.ping** listen secretly: *Lou was caught eavesdropping on their conversation; n.: electronic eavesdropping by the secret police.* —**eaves.drop.per** *n.*

eaves.trough (EEVS.trof) *n.* a channel along the eaves of a roof for carrying away rainwater.

ebb *n.* the flowing back of the tide; hence, a decline: *The fortunes of the party are at a low ebb these days; the* **ebb and flow** (= rise and fall) *of fortune.* —*v.*: *Life seemed to ebb away fast as he neared his end.*

e.bon.ics (i.BON.ics) *n.pl.* [with *sing. v.*] English as commonly spoken in the Southern U.S., esp. by Blacks; Black English.

eb.on.ite (EB.uh.nite) same as VULCANITE.

eb.on.y (EB.uh.nee) *n.* **-on.ies** the hard, dark wood of a tropical tree. —*adj.*: *an ebony statue; a child with ebony* (= black) *hair.*

e.bul.lience (i.BUL.yunce) *n.* a being ebullient; exuberance.

e.bul.lient (i.BUL.yunt) *adj.* bubbling, as with excitement or enthusiasm: *an ebullient optimism, personality, spirit, style; in an ebullient mood; She was her usual ebullient self.*

e.bul.li.tion (eb.uh.LISH.un) *n.* outburst: *an ebullition of joy.*

ec.cen.tric (ek.SEN.tric) *adj.* **1** odd or peculiar: *his eccentric behavior; He's eccentric in his habits; It's eccentric to wear a mismatched pair of socks.* **2** not concentric; off center: *Pluto moves in an eccentric orbit around the sun; an eccentric wheel for up-and-down movement.* —*n.* an eccentric person. —**ec.cen.tric.i.ty** (ek.sen.TRIS.i.tee) *n.* **-ties.**

ec.cle.si.as.tic (i.CLEE.zee.AS.tic) *n.* a clergyman. —**ec.cle.si.as.ti.cal** (-ti.cul) *adja.* having to do with the church as an institution: *ecclesiastical affairs, authority, calendar, controversy, history, power, provinces, superiors.*

ech.e.lon (ESH.uh.lon) *n.* a level of authority or responsibility: *Vice-presidents* are in the higher echelons of a company; the upper echelons of society.

ech.o (EK.oh) *n.* **-oes** a reflected or repeated sound, as heard around caves, in the mountains, etc.: *Some churches produce echoes; a radar echo.*
—*v.* **-oes, -oed, -o.ing 1** make an echo or reverberate: *His voice echoed across the valley.* **2** repeat: *a child echoing her mother's words.*

e.cho.ic (ek.OH.ic) *adj.* imitative in sound: *"Ding-dong" is echoic of a bell; an echoic word.*

ech.o.lo.ca.tion (EK.oh.loh.CAY.shun) *n.* location of objects by reflected sound, as bats do.

echo sounding *n.* determination of underwater distances by means of a sound-reflecting device called **echo sounder.**

é.clair (ay.CLAIR) *n.* an oblong piece of pastry with cream or custard filling.

é.clat (ay.CLAH) *n.* a splendid success that draws praise from everyone: *She performed the number with great éclat.*

ec.lec.tic (i.CLEC.tic) *adj.* drawing or drawn from various sources: *her eclectic taste in furniture.* —*n.* a philosopher, artist, etc. who uses eclectic methods. —**ec.lec.ti.cism** *n.*

e.clipse (i.CLIPS) *n.* the darkening of the sun (**solar eclipse**) by the moon's shadow or of the moon (**lunar eclipse**) by the earth's shadow: *a partial or total eclipse; He has been in eclipse* (= in darkness or hiding) *since his recent defeat at the polls.*
—*v.* **e.clips.es, e.clipsed, e.clips.ing** overshadow: *a movie star eclipsed by her more famous daughter.*

e.clip.tic (i.CLIP.tic) *n.* the sun's apparent annual path through the celestial sphere.

ec.logue (EC.log) *n.* a short pastoral poem.

eco- *adj. & comb.form.* ecological or environmental: *eco freaks, nerds, nuts, topics; eco-consciousness; eco-crisis; eco-friendly* (= ecologically friendly) *diapers.*

e.co.cide (EE.cuh.cide, EC.uh-) *n.* environmental destruction, esp. by pollutants.

e.col.o.gy (ee.COL.uh.jee) *n.* **1** (the study of) the relationship between organisms and their environment. **2** an environmental condition: *the ecology of a lake.* —**e.col.o.gist** (-jist) *n.*
—**e.co.log.i.cal** (ee.cuh.LOJ.i.cul) *adj.;* **e.co.log.i.cal.ly** *adv.*

e.co.nom.ic (ee.cuh.NOM.ic, ec.uh-) **1** *adja.* having to do with economics or economy: *the economic growth of a nation; Some nations claim an* **economic zone** *beyond their coastal waters for fishing and other purposes.* **2** *adj.* economical: *an economic measure to save money; A gas guzzler is not very economic.*

e.co.nom.i.cal (ee.cuh.NOM.i.cul, ec.uh-) *adj.* not wasteful of resources: *Spending money on a freezer is economical in the long run; It is economical to buy a freezer if you use food in large quantities; an economical solution;* **e.co.nom.i.cal.ly** *adv.*

economics (ee.cuh.NOM.ics, ec.uh-) *n.pl.* [takes *sing. v.*] the science of the production, distribution, and consumption of goods and services.

e.con.o.mist (i.CON.uh.mist) *n.* a specialist in economics.

e.con.o.mize (i.CON.uh.mize) *v.* **-iz.es, -ized, -iz.ing** be economical: *to economize on the use of energy and raw materials; to economize one's expenditures, scarce commodities, one's time; He economizes by bicycling to work.*
—**e.con.o.miz.er** *n.* —**e.con.o.miz.er** *n.*

e.con.o.my (i.CON.uh.mee) *n.* **-mies 1** management and use of resources, esp. how a country's money supply, industry, and trade work: *the state of our economy; how the economy is run; political economy* (= economics); *to achieve* **economies of scale** (= benefits of large-scale production that lowers unit cost). **2** thrift or an instance of it: *We try to practice economy; They did it with great economy of effort and expense; the little economies that help us save money.* **3** a system of managing resources: *We live in a free-enterprise economy; a planned economy; A major strike could cripple a capitalist economy; a rural economy.*
—*adj.* designed to save money: *an economy car such as a subcompact; We fly economy class; an economy drive* or *measure to cut costs; toothpaste in economy size.*

e.co.sys.tem (EE.coh.sis.tum, EC.uh-) *n.* the system of harmonious relationships between living and nonliving things of nature and their environment: *the ecosystem of a forest or lake.*

ec.ru (EC.roo) *n. & adj.* light tan or beige.

ec.sta.sy (EC.stuh.see) *n.* **-sies** rapture, esp. of delight: *pure, sheer ecstasy; He was in ecstasy over his wedding.*
—**ec.stat.ic** (ic.STAT.ic) *adj.*

-ectomy *comb.form.* surgical removal: *appendectomy, hysterectomy, vasectomy.*

ec.to.plasm (EC.tuh.plaz.um) *n.* the supposed vaporous emanation of a spiritualistic medium that may materialize as an apparition at a séance.

Ec.ua.do.ran (ek.wuh.DOR.un), **Ec.ua.do.re.an** or **Ec.ua.do.ri.an** (-DOR.ee.un) *n. & adj.* (a person) of or from **Ecuador**, a South American country.

ec.u.men.i.cal (ek.yoo.MEN.i.cul) *adj.* having to do with the Christian church as a whole; promoting church unity. —**ec.u.men.i.cal.ly** *adv.*

ec.u.men.ism (EK.yuh.muh.niz.um) *n.* the movement for church unity.

ec.ze.ma (eg.ZEE.muh, EC.suh.muh) *n.* a skin inflammation with redness, itching, and lesions. —**ec.zem.a.tous** (ig.ZEE.muh.tus, ig.ZEM.uh-) *adj.*

E.dam or **Edam cheese** (EE.dum-) *n.* a mild yellow cheese that comes in a round shape with a red rind.

ed.dy (ED.ee) *n.* **ed.dies** a circular current of water, wind, fog, dust, etc. —*v.* **ed.dies, ed.died, ed.dy.ing** to whirl: *Convention crowds eddied about in the hotel lobby.*

e.del.weiss (AY.dul.vice) *n.* an Alpine plant with white woolly flowers.

e.de.ma (i.DEE.muh) *n.* swelling, as of the ankles and feet, produced by accumulation of fluid in the tissues; dropsy.

E.den (EE.dun) *n.* in the Bible, the garden where Adam and Eve first lived; hence, a paradise.

edge (EJ) *n.* **1** the cutting side of a blade: *the cutting edge; the leading* (= front) *edge and trailing* (= back) *edge of an airplane's wing; Our company is* **on the cutting** or **leading edge** of (= is a leader in) *computer technology; Oil producing nations* **have an edge on** (= advantage over) *the world market; That cookie* **took the edge off** (= dulled) *my appetite.* **2** a border or brink; boundary: *to trim the edges of a lawn; at the water's edge; to look down from the edge of a precipice.* —**on edge** edgy or nervous. —*v.* **edg.es, edged, edg.ing 1** form a border or trimming: *The bag is edged with leather.* **2** move gradually, as to get in or put someone out of a place: *The child edged closer to its mother; We are all edging into old age; Houses edge up in price; They have edged past last year's highs; The Liberals* **edged out** *the Tories* (= put them out of place) *with just a handful of votes.* —**edg.er** *n.*

edge.ways or **edge.wise** *adv.* with the edge forward; sideways.

edg.y (EJ.ee) *adj.* **edg.i.er, -i.est** tense or anxious: *He's a bit edgy about what might happen; in an edgy mood.* —**edg.i.ness** *n.*

edh *n.* an Old Germanic letter [Ð, ð] used as a phonetic symbol for the *th* sound of *the.*

ed.i.ble (ED.uh.bul) *adj.* fit to eat; eatable: *an edible variety of mushroom.* —*n.* usu. **edibles** *pl.* food. —**ed.i.bil.i.ty** (-BIL.i.tee) *n.*

e.dict (EE.dict) *n.* an order of the highest authority; decree.

ed.i.fice (ED.uh.fis) *n.* an imposing building.

ed.i.fy (ED.uh.fye) *v.* **-fies, -fied, -fy.ing** improve morally; uplift: *A teacher's conduct is supposed to edify the students;* **adj.**: *an edifying example.* —**ed.i.fi.ca.tion** (-fuh.CAY.shun) *n.;* **ed.i.fi.er** (-fye.ur) *n.*

ed.it (ED.it) *v.* prepare a manuscript, newspaper, film, tape, etc. for publication or presentation.

e.di.tion (i.DISH.un) *n.* **1** the form in which a book, newspaper, or radio or TV program is presented to the public: *to bring out a new edition of Shakespeare; an abridged, annotated, critical, paperback, revised edition; the evening edition of the news; the city edition of a daily; a morning edition; all the 1997 editions* (= issues) *of a daily.* **2** the copies of a publication printed at one time; printing or impression: *The first edition of her book was sold out in a few weeks.* **3** a form in which something is presented or appears: *a specially equipped limited edition of 200 cars of a particular model; She is a younger edition of her mother; One edition of the Olympic coins in gold and 10 in silver were issued.*

ed.i.tor (ED.i.tur) *n.* **1** one who edits: *a newspaper's city editor; a copy editor; a technical editor.* **2** a viewing device for editing film or videotape. —**ed.i.tor.ship** *n.*

ed.i.to.ri.al (ed.i.TOR.ee.ul) *adja.* having to do with an editor, editors, or opinions: *an editorial article, opinion, page; our editorial director.* —*n.* an article containing an editor's opinion. —**ed.i.to.ri.al.ist** *n.* —**ed.i.to.ri.al.ly** *adv.*

ed.i.to.ri.al.ize (ed.i.TOR.ee.uh.lize) *v.* **-iz.es, ized, iz.ing** express opinions, esp. inappropriately: *It's not considered professional to editorialize in the news columns; Just give us the facts without editorializing.*

Ed.sel (ED.sul) *n.* a flop or failure, like an automobile of that name produced by Ford from 1958 to 1960.

ed.u.ca.ble (EJ.oo.cuh.bul) *adj.* capable of being educated or trained: *special classes for educable mentally handicapped* children. —**ed.u.ca.bil.i.ty** (-BIL.i.tee) n.

ed.u.cate (EJ.oo.cate) v. -cates, -cat.ed, -cat.ing **1** send to school or pay for someone's schooling: *Parents educate their children; She was educated* (= She went to school) *in Europe; educated at Cambridge;* adj.: *a highly educated* (= educationally accomplished) *writer.* **2** instruct in order to develop knowledge or skills: *to educate the public not to waste food;* adj.: *Children become educated about toys; educated consumers, shoppers; An educated guess* (based on some knowledge of the facts) *is likely to be right.*

ed.u.ca.tion (ej.uh.CAY.shun) n. **1** schooling: *The state provides free and compulsory education up to age 16; adult, college, continuing, high-school, in-service, liberal, physical, remedial, sex, university, vocational education; a good general education; higher educations and incomes.* **2** teaching; also, the study of teaching methods, principles, etc.: *boards of education; A faculty of education trains teachers.*

ed.u.ca.tion.al (ej.uh.CAY.shuh.nul) adj. **1** having to do with teaching: *an educational association, book, degree, film, foundation; educational materials, psychology, resources, standards, systems, television, theories.* **2** helping to improve the mind; instructive: *a very educational experience; educational influences; things of educational value.* —**ed.u.ca.tion.al.ly** adv.

ed.u.ca.tive (EJ.uh.cay.tiv) adj. educational or instructive: *an educative detail, experience, force; the educative value of field trips; educative work.*

ed.u.ca.tor (EJ.uh.cay.tur) n. a teacher, esp. a professional with long experience.

e.duce (i.DUCE) v. -duc.es, -duced, -duc.ing *Formal.* draw out; develop; also, deduce.

ed.u.tain.ment (ej.oo.TAIN.munt) n. something that is both educational and entertaining; adj.: *edutainment devices, programs, software.*

-ee n. suffix. **1** the recipient or subject of an action: *absentee, appointee, mortgagee, escapee, standee.* **2** one suggestive of another, esp. one of small size: *bootee, goatee.*

eel n. a snakelike fish: *slippery as an eel; Anglers bob for eels* (= fish for eels using a bundle of worms).

-eer n. suffix. a person or action having to do with (what is specified): *charioteer, mountaineer, profiteer.*

e'er (AIR) adv. *Poetical.* ever.

ee.rie or **ee.ry** (EER.ee) adj. -ri.er, -ri.est weird or mysterious in a frightening manner: *eerie shadows dancing on a wall; an eerie cry from the swamp; an eerie atmosphere, echo, silence.* —**ee.ri.ly** adv.

ef.face (i.FACE) v. **ef.fac.es, ef.faced, ef.fac.ing** remove or blot out something as if by rubbing away. —**ef.face.ment** n.

ef.fect (i.FECT) n. **1** what is produced by a cause; result: *The drug had some effect on him; to feel the effects of a drug; adverse, beneficial, dramatic, exhilarating, far-reaching, harmful, hypnotic, marginal, profound, salutary effects; a side effect; An effect wears off; Sometimes you sleep off the ill effects of a drug; All his counseling was to no effect; a former custom that is no more in effect* (= operation); *It has in effect* (= in practice) *fallen into disuse; a proclamation to give effect to a new law* (= make it produce the intended result); *The medicine took effect* (= produced the intended result) *immediately.* **2** a resulting impression: *Special sound effects are used in movies; a science-fiction movie with fancy special effects; You can start on Monday and I'll give you a letter to that effect* (= with that meaning); *He raises his voice merely for effect.* **3** effects pl. goods: *personal effects such as clothing and jewelry; household effects.*
—v. bring about; realize: *The treaty effected a settlement; The medication should effect a cure;* **ef.fect.er** n.

ef.fec.tive (i.FEC.tiv) adj. **1** producing the desired effect: *Antibiotics are effective against bacteria; The steps we are taking will be effective; effective communication, leaders, measures, methods, programs, ways; They will be effective in controlling crime; a forceful and effective speaker; The new timetable will be effective* (= in effect or operative) *as of Monday.* **2** actual: *the effective strength of an army after allowing for the sick and wounded; the effective membership of our organization after all the resignations.* —**ef.fec.tive.ly** adv.; **ef.fec.tive.ness** n.

ef.fec.tor (i.FEC.tur) n. a muscle, gland, etc. that can respond to a nerve impulse.

ef.fec.tu.al (i.FEC.choo.ul) adj. adequate to achieve a desired effect: *an effectual demand that brought a prompt response; The steps we took proved to be effectual; an effectual measure, punishment, remedy.*
—**ef.fec.tu.al.ly** adv.

ef.fec.tu.ate (i.FEC.choo.ate) v. -ates, -at.ed, -at.ing make effectual; put into

effeminate / egg

effect: *to effectuate a settlement.*
ef.fem.i.nate (i.FEM.uh.nit) *adj.* womanish; soft or delicate. —**ef.fem.i.na.cy** (-nuh.see) *n.*
ef.fen.di (i.FEN.dee) *n.* **-dis** a landowner or white-collar worker in an Arab country; formerly used as a Turkish title meaning "Master" or "Sir."
ef.fer.ent (EF.uh.runt) *adj.* carrying impulses from a central point, as the brain, outward to the muscles: *efferent nerves;* cf. AFFERENT.
ef.fer.vesce (ef.ur.VES) *v.* **-vesc.es, -vesced, -vesc.ing 1** of liquids, bubble and hiss as gas is let off. **2** be ebullient or excited. —**ef.fer.ves.cence** *n.;* **ef.fer.ves.cent** *adj.*
ef.fete (i.FEET) *adj.* worn-out or decadent: *the effete aristocracy, Athenians; an effete civilization.*
ef.fi.ca.cious (ef.uh.CAY.shus) *adj.* esp. of medicines, sure to have the desired effect: *an efficacious remedy.*
ef.fi.ca.cy (EF.uh.cuh.see) *n.* the quality of being efficacious: *a drug of proven efficacy; the efficacy of a cure, of advertising.*
ef.fi.cien.cy (i.FISH.un.see) *n.* the quality of being efficient: *A machine operates at peak* or *maximum efficiency when the energy put into it is the same as the work produced; degrees of efficiency; The less the friction, the higher the efficiency of a machine; conditions that impair, lower, reduce efficiency; An **efficiency apartment** usually consists of a room and kitchenette; An **efficiency expert** aims to make a business or system more efficient.*
ef.fi.cient (i.FISH.unt) *adj.* producing the desired result with the least waste of resources; capable: *an efficient executive, method, worker; a manager who is efficient in the use of resources; the efficient action of heat in raising temperature; Heat is the efficient cause of many chemical changes; Gas is more efficient than oil for home heating.* —**ef.fi.cient.ly** *adv.*
ef.fi.gy (EF.uh.jee) *n.* **-gies** a portrait or other representation of a notable person: *sculptured effigies on tombs, coins, etc.; the effigies* (= statues) *in Madam Tussaud's Wax Museum; The dictator was burned **in effigy*** (= in a crude representation).
ef.flo.resce (ef.luh.RES) *v.* **-resc.es, -resced, -resc.ing 1** blossom out. **2** become powdery or form a deposit. —**ef.flo.res.cent** *adj.;* **ef.flo.res.cence** *n.*
ef.flu.ence (EF.loo.unce) *n.* an outflow; emanation.
ef.flu.ent (EF.loo.unt) *adja.* flowing out, as a stream from a lake or reservoir: *effluent discharges, processing, treatment.* —*n.* chemically treated sewage or factory waste: *industrial effluents; chemical, liquid, sewage effluents.*
ef.flu.vi.um (i.FLOO.vee.um) *n.* **-vi.ums** or **-vi.a** (-vee.uh) an unpleasant vapor or odor.
ef.fort (EF.urt) *n.* energy required to do something; hence, a strong attempt or its result: *Power steering takes little effort; He spared no effort to make a success of the project; He made an all-out, conscious, desperate, frantic, gallant, heroic **effort** to succeed; He put forth a valiant **effort** to achieve his goal; His **efforts** were greatly appreciated; He redoubled his **efforts** toward the end.*
ef.fron.ter.y (i.FRUN.tuh.ree) *n.* **-ter.ies** boldness in defying norms of courtesy or propriety; impudence: *the effrontery to ask for a 25% raise when others are getting only 5%.*
ef.ful.gence (i.FUL.junce) *n.* splendor or brilliance. —**ef.ful.gent** (-junt) *adj.*
ef.fu.sion (i.FEW.zhun) *n.* an act of pouring out or something poured out, as feelings, body fluids such as lymph or blood escaping into surrounding tissues or cavities, etc.
ef.fu.sive (i.FEW.siv) *adj.* **1** marked by a pouring out: *an effusive volcanic eruption; effusive* (= poured out and solidified) *rocks formed from lava.* **2** marked by a pouring out of feelings; gushy: *an effusive speech, welcome; effusive praise.* —**ef.fu.sive.ly** *adv.;* **ef.fu.sive.ness** *n.*
eft *n.* a newt, esp. during the two to three years it lives on land before returning to water.
e.gad (i.GAD) *interj.* a mild oath: *Egad! He actually gave to charity?*
e.gal.i.tar.i.an (i.GAL.uh.TAIR.ee.un) *n. & adj.* (one) supporting equality for all: *an egalitarian attitude, society, spirit, view; egalitarian aims, ideals, principles; n.: a social egalitarian.* —**e.gal.i.tar.i.an.ism** *n.*
egg *n.* **1** the oval or round body laid by birds, reptiles, fishes, etc. that hatches into a living young: *Hens lay and hatch eggs; We beat, boil, fry, poach eggs; deviled, fried, hard-boiled, scrambled, soft-boiled eggs; how to separate the egg white from the yolk.* **2** an egg cell. **3** *Informal.* a person: *She's a good egg; bad, rotten eggs.* —**egg on one's face** *Informal.* embarrassment from having blundered. —*v.* **egg someone on** incite or

urge: *His companions egged him on to enter the race.*

egg.beat.er (EG.bee.tur) *n.* **1** a rotary device for beating eggs. **2** *Slang.* helicopter.

egg cell *n.* an ovum; female germ cell.

egg.head *n. Informal* [derogatory] an intellectual.

egg.nog *n.* a beverage made of eggs beaten up with milk and sugar, sometimes also containing liquor.

egg.plant *n.* a large, egg-shaped purplish fruit of a vegetable of the same name.

egg.roll *n.* a preparation of minced vegetables and meat rolled in an egg-dough casing and deep-fried.

egg.shell *n.* the covering of an egg: *You're **walking on eggshells*** (= trying to carry out a delicate operation).

e.gis (EE.jis) same as AEGIS.

eg.lan.tine (EG.lun.tine, -teen) *n.* a wild rose with sweetly scented leaves and flowers and bright red or orange fruits; sweetbrier.

e.go (EE.goh, EG.oh) *n.* **e.gos** **1** the thinking, feeling, and acting being as perceived by oneself: *one's alter ego* (= another self). **2** self-esteem: *Everyone tries to feed* or *flatter his ego; Being ignored hurt his ego; He had an inflated ego.*

e.go.cen.tric (ee.goh.SEN.tric, eg.oh-) *n. & adj.* (one) who is self-centered.

e.go.ism (EE.goh.iz.um, EG.oh-) *n.* self-centeredness or conceit; opposed to ALTRUISM. —**e.go.ist** *n.* —**e.go.is.tic** (-IS.tic) or **e.go.is.ti.cal** (-ti.cul) *adj.*

e.go.tism (EE.guh.tiz.um, EG.uh-) *n.* a more overt and annoying kind of egoism, expressed in speech and behavior; **e.go.tist** *n.* —**e.go.tis.tic** (-TIS.tic) or **e.go.tis.ti.cal** (-ti.cul) *adj.*

ego trip *n.* a self-centered or self-realizing activity. —**ego-trip** *v.* **-trips, -tripped, -trip.ping.** —**ego-tripper** (EE.goh.trip.ur, EG.oh-) *n.*

e.gre.gious (i.GREE.jus) *adj.* outstandingly bad: *an egregious blunder, error, waste; an egregious example of wasteful spending; the egregious Mr. Assman.* —**e.gre.gious.ly** *adv.*; **e.gre.gious.ness** *n.*

e.gress (EE.gres) *n.* an exit.

e.gret (EE.grit, EG.rit) *n.* a wading bird of the heron family that grows long plumes during its breeding season.

E.gyp.tian (i.JIP.shun) *n. & adj.* **1** (a person) of or from **Egypt**, a republic of N.E. Africa. **2** (having to do with) the extinct Hamitic language of ancient Egypt.

eh (AY) *interj.* [used at the end of an utterance in a doubtful or questioning way]: *from Canada, eh?*

ei.der (EYE.dur) *n.* a large sea duck of northern regions, whose soft down, or **eiderdown,** is used as stuffing in pillows, quilts, etc.

ei.det.ic (eye.DET.ic) *adj.* extremely vivid: *A person gifted with eidetic imagery has a photographic memory.*

eight (ATE) *n., adj. & pron.* one more than seven; the number 8 or VIII: *There are eight of them; eight girls; That's an eight (card).*

eight ball *n.* in pool, a black ball numbered 8. —**behind the eight ball** *Informal.* in a hazardous position.

eighth (AITTH) *n.* **1** the next after the seventh. **2** one of eight equal parts, as of an octave. —*adj. & adv.*: *the eighth part of the series; He came eighth.*

eight.y (AY.tee) *n., adj. & pron.* **-ties** **1** ten times eight; 80 or LXXX. **2** **the eighties** the numbers, years, etc. from 80 through 89. —**eight.i.eth** (-ith) *n. & adj.*

Ein.stein.i.an (ine.STY.nee.un) *adj.* having to do with Albert **Einstein**, a German-born American physicist (1879-1955) renowned for his theory of relativity: *Einsteinian physics.*

ein.stein.i.um (ine.STY.nee.um) *n.* an artificially produced radioactive element.

ei.ther (EE.thur, EYE-, "th" as in "the") *pron.* (the) one or the other: *Either of the twins can wear this;* **adj.**: *Sit on either stool; He can write with either hand* (= both hands); **conj.**: *Say either yes or no; Have either a candy bar, a yogurt, or an ice cream.* —*adv.* also: *If you don't go, I won't either.*

e.jac.u.late (i.JAK.yuh.late) *v.* **-lates, -lat.ed, -lat.ing** discharge, esp. semen. —**e.jac.u.la.to.ry** (-luh.tor.ee) *adj.*: *the ejaculatory duct.* —**e.jac.u.la.tion** (-LAY.shun) *n.*

e.ject (i.JECT) *v.* throw out: *The rowdies were ejected from the room; The pilot ejected* (= propelled himself out) *safely before the crash.* —**e.jec.tion** (i.JEC.shun) *n:* the ejection of a molded part from its mold; **adj.**: *an ejection system; The pilot bailed out of the disabled aircraft in her ejection seat.*

eke (EEK) *v.* **ekes, eked, ek.ing** add to something; supplement: *He had to take two jobs to **eke out** a living; to eke out an existence, increase, profit.*

e.lab.o.rate (i.LAB.uh.rit) *adj.* **1** worked out in great detail: *an elaborate plan, plot; elaborate excuses, precautions, prepa-*

rations. **2** ornate: *elaborate decorations; an elaborate costume, design, pattern.* —*v.* (-rate) **-ates, -at.ed, -at.ing** add more detail to something: *He hinted at the rumor but would not elaborate (on it).* —**e.lab.o.rate.ly** *adv.*; **e.lab.o.rate.ness** *n.* —**e.lab.o.ra.tion** (-RAY.shun) *n.*

e.lan (ay.LAHN) *n.* spirit or enthusiasm; dash or verve: *She joined the activities with great elan.*

e.land (EE.lund) *n.* an African antelope with spiraled horns.

e.lapse (i.LAPS) *v.* **e.laps.es, e.lapsed, e.laps.ing** of time, to pass; go by: *Many years elapsed before their first child was born; adj.: a display showing time elapsed.*

e.las.tic (i.LAS.tic) *adj.* **1** rubberlike or stretchable: *an elastic band, belt, tape; Knead the dough until it is smooth and elastic; the clown's elastic face.* **2** capable of returning to its original shape or form: *A steel spring is elastic; the elastic temperament of one who is never let down; her elastic optimism.* —*n.* **1** a fabric interwoven with rubber strands. **2** a garter or band made of this.

e.las.tic.i.ty (ee.las.TIS.i.tee) *n.* the quality of being elastic: *All substances have some elasticity; Rubber has great elasticity; Words in common use have much elasticity of meaning.*

e.las.ti.cize (i.LAS.tuh.size) *v.* **-ciz.es, -cized, -ciz.ing** make elastic; *adj.: an elasticized waistband.*

e.late (i.LATE) *v.* **e.lates, e.lat.ed, e.lat.ing** fill with high spirits, as by joy, pride, etc.: *Everyone was elated at or over the victory.* —**e.la.tion** (i.LAY.shun) *n.*

el.bow (EL.boh) *n.* **1** the outer part of the joint between the upper and lower arm, esp. bent, as when jostling, working, etc. **2** this bent shape or something in that shape; *adj.a.: an elbow pipe joint; elbow macaroni.* —**at one's elbow** close by. —**out at (the) elbows** in worn-out clothes; hence, poverty-stricken. —*v.* use the elbow to do something: *He elbowed everyone out of his way; He elbowed (his way) through the crowd; In hockey, elbowing an opponent (= hitting an opponent with the elbow) results in a penalty.*

elbow grease *n. Informal.* hard work.

elbow room *n.* space to move in comfortably: *There was no elbow room in the packed train; The new recruit was given plenty of elbow room (= freedom) for trying out new ideas.*

El Chea.po or **el chea.po** (el.CHEE.poh) *n. Informal.* a person or thing that is cheap or shoddy: *He's an El Cheapo; an el cheapo vacation.* Also **cheapie** or **cheapo.**

eld.er (EL.dur) *adj.* older or senior: *your elder brother; elder care* (= care of the elderly); *an elder statesman* (= senior retired politician). —*n.* **1** a respected older member of a tribe, community, church, family, etc.: *Listen to your elders; an elder of the Presbyterian church.* **2** a small tree or shrub bearing clusters of purple berries (**elderberry**), used in preserves, wines, etc.

el.der.ly (EL.dur.lee) *adj.* [respectful use] old or aged: *homes for the elderly.*

el.dest (EL.dist) *adj.* oldest, esp. of surviving family members.

El Do.ra.do or **El.do.ra.do** (el.duh.RAH.doh) *n.* **-dos** a legendary place that is rich in gold.

e.lect (i.LECT) *v.* choose, esp. in a formal way, as by voting: *Eloi was unanimously elected mayor as Eve's successor; They elected him to succeed Eve; Yves elected* (= chose) *law rather than politics for a career.* —*adj.* chosen: *the president elect* (who has not yet assumed charge); *the elect few.* —**the elect** *n.pl.* a specially chosen group: *the elect of God* (chosen for salvation).

e.lec.tion (i.LEC.shun) *n.* the act or process of electing: *to carry, concede, decide, fix, hold, lose, swing, win an election; close, free, rigged, runoff elections.*

e.lec.tion.eer (i.LEC.shuh.NEER) *v.* work for the success of a candidate or party in an election.

e.lec.tive (i.LEC.tiv) *adj.* having to do with an election or choice: *the elective office of president; an elective government, official; elective* (= nonessential) *surgery.* —*n.* an optional subject in a program of studies.

e.lec.tor (i.LEC.tur) *n.* one having the right to elect; voter. —**e.lec.tor.al** (-tuh.rul, ee.lec.TOR.ul) *adj.: electoral fraud, reform, politics; the electoral process, rolls, system; an electoral defeat, victory; the electoral votes cast by the **electoral college**, a body of electors chosen by the people to elect the U.S. President and Vice-President; an **electoral district*** (= constituency).

e.lec.tor.ate (i.LEC.tuh.rit) *n.* people qualified to vote, collectively.

e.lec.tric (i.LEC.tric) *adj.* **1** also **e.lec.tri.cal,** having to do with electricity: *an electric battery; an electric guitar, light, organ; electric heating; electrical activity, equipment, industries; an electrical circuit, discharge, engineer, worker; an **electric broom*** (= a small upright vacuum cleaner); *the electric eel* (= an eel capable of giving electric shocks); *an electrical storm* (= thunderstorm). **2** exciting or thrilling: *The reaction of the audience was electric; The air was electric with excitement; an electric performance, personality; electric* (= very bright) *blue.* —**e.lec.tri.cal.ly** *adv.*

electric chair *n.* **1** (sentence of) death by electrocution: *a killer sent to the electric chair.* **2** the chair used in this.

electric eye See PHOTOELECTRIC.

e.lec.tri.cian (i.lec.TRISH.un) *n.* one who installs, operates, or repairs electrical equipment.

e.lec.tric.i.ty (i.lec.TRIS.i.tee) *n.* **1** a form of energy generated by friction, induction, or chemical changes, and capable of producing heat, light, etc., as observed in natural phenomena such as lightning and in certain fishes and eels. **2** electric current, esp. as a public utility.

e.lec.tri.fy (i.LEC.truh.fye) *v.* **-fies, -fied, -fy.ing 1** charge with electricity; hence, excite or thrill: *The whole town was electrified by the news.* **2** provide or equip with electricity: *to electrify a rural area.* —**e.lec.tri.fi.er** (-fye.ur) *n.* —**e.lec.tri.fi.ca.tion** (-fuh.CAY.shun) *n.*

e.lec.tro.car.di.o.gram (i.lec.truh.CAR.dee.uh.gram) *n.* a tracing made by an electrocardiograph.

e.lec.tro.car.di.o.graph (i.lec.truh.CAR.dee.uh.graf) *n.* an instrument that detects and records the electrical impulses produced by heartbeats.

e.lec.tro.cute (i.LEC.truh.cute) *v.* **-cutes, -cut.ed, -cut.ing** kill by the action of electricity. —**e.lec.tro.cu.tion** (-CUE.shun) *n.*

e.lec.trode (i.LEC.trode) *n.* a conductor of outgoing or incoming current in an electrical circuit.

e.lec.tro.en.ceph.a.lo.gram (i.LEC.troh.en.SEF.uh.luh.gram) *n.* a tracing made by an **electroencephalograph,** an instrument that measures the electrical activity of the brain.

e.lec.trol.o.gist (i.lec.TROL.uh.jist) *n.* one trained to destroy hair roots, tumors, etc. with an electrified needle.

e.lec.trol.y.sis (i.lec.TROL.uh.sis) *n.* **1** the decomposition into its parts of an electrolyte. **2** the destruction of hair roots, tumors, etc. using an electrified needle.

e.lec.tro.lyte (i.LEC.truh.lite) *n.* a chemical solution that will conduct an electric current. —**e.lec.tro.lyt.ic** (-LIT.ic) *adj.;* **e.lec.tro.lyt.i.cal.ly** *adv.*

e.lec.tro.mag.net (i.lec.truh.MAG.nit) *n.* a magnet that has a coil of wire around it through which a current is passed to magnetize it. —**e.lec.tro.mag.net.ism** (-nuh.tiz.um) *n.* —**e.lec.tro.mag.net.ic** (-mag.NET.ic) *adj.: Radio waves, light, X rays, gamma rays, etc. are forms of electromagnetic radiation or electromagnetic waves produced when electric and magnetic fields act together.*

e.lec.tro.mo.tive force (i.lec.truh.MOH.tiv-) *n.* electric pressure that causes the flow of electricity through a circuit, usu. measured in volts.

e.lec.tron (i.LEC.tron) *n.* any of the negatively charged particles in an atom.

e.lec.tron.ic (i.lec.TRON.ic) *adj.* having to do with electronics: *an electronic flash camera; TV and such electronic journalism; the electronic cottage* (= home as computer-linked workplace); *electronic data processing using computers.* —**e.lec.tron.i.cal.ly** *adv.*

electronic funds transfer *n.* transfer of money from one account to another via computer communications, as by automatic teller machines and debit cards.

electronic mail same as E-MAIL.

electronic music *n.* music composed of sounds produced with electronic devices, assembled on magnetic tape, and played through loudspeakers.

electronics *n.pl.* the science of the behavior and control of electrons through vacuums, semiconductors, and gases for use in devices such as the electron tube, photoelectric cell, and transistor.

electronic surveillance *n.* the gathering of information by surreptitious means such as bugging, wiretaps, etc.

electron microscope *n.* a microscope that uses a beam of electrons instead of light to project enlarged images on a fluorescent surface or photographic plate.

electron tube *n.* a sealed glass or metal tube, either gas-filled or evacuated, for the controlled flow of electrons.

e.lec.tro.plate (i.LEC.truh.plate) *v.* **-plates, -plat.ed, -plat.ing** coat something with metal by electrolysis.

e.lec.tro.scope (i.LEC.truh.scope) *n.* a device for detecting minute electrical charges and identifying them as positive or negative.

e.lec.tro.shock therapy (i.LEC.truh.shok-) *n.* shock therapy using electric current.

e.lec.tro.stat.ic (i.lec.truh.STAT.ic) *adj.* having to do with static electricity: *Electrostatic printing, as xerography, reproduces originals without ink or pressure, using an electrically charged black powder.*

e.lec.tro.type (i.LEC.truh.type) *n.* a printing plate duplicated by electrolysis from a wax or plastic impression of the original type or engraving.

el.ee.mos.y.nar.y (el.i.MOS.uh.nair.ee) *adj.* of, for, or supported by charity: *eleemosynary activities, enterprises, institutions.*

el.e.gance (EL.uh.gunce) *n.* the quality of being elegant; refinement or polish: *the elegance of the furnishings; sartorial elegance; sheer elegance; a taste for elegance; She writes with grace and elegance; the elegance of a mathematical equation.*

el.e.gant (EL.uh.gunt) *adj.* rich and luxurious but restrained in style; graceful, tasteful, or polished: *an elegant diction, dresser, restaurant, writer; an elegant young man with elegant manners; a charming and elegant lady; She leads a life of elegant ease.*
—**el.e.gant.ly** *adv.*

el.e.gi.ac (el.e.gi.JYE.ac, i.LEE.jee.ac) *adj.* in the form of an elegy; hence, sad or mournful. —**el.e.gi.a.cal** (el.uh.JYE.uh.cul) *adj.*

el.e.gy (EL.uh.jee) *n.* **-gies** a melancholy poem, usu. one mourning the dead, as Thomas Gray's "Elegy."

el.e.ment (EL.uh.munt) *n.* **1** something basic, esp. a basic or constituent part: *Fire, air, earth, and water were once considered the four basic elements of nature; All matter is composed of 100-odd (chemical) elements; an essential, key, vital element of the story; the human element* (= factor); *There is an element* (= particle) *of truth in what he says; the* **elements** (= rudiments) *of algebra; the French element* (= component) *in the English vocabulary; criminal, extremist, subversive, undesirable elements* (= members) *of society; the heating element* (= unit) *of an electric kettle.* **2** the environment, esp. as made up of the forces of nature; hence, rough weather: *A storm-tossed vessel is at the mercy of the* **elements**; *Out of water, a fish is* **out of its element**; *She's* **in her element** (= doing what she likes best) *as a social worker.*

el.e.men.tal (el.uh.MEN.tul) *adja.* having to do with natural forces: *elemental gods representing the forces of nature; the elemental fury of a volcano in action; the elemental problem of survival; sex, hunger, and such elemental urges; an artist's elemental characters, music, themes.*

el.e.men.ta.ry (el.uh.MEN.tuh.ree) *adj.* basic or fundamental: *elementary arithmetic; "That's elementary, my dear Watson"; the electron, proton, and such supposedly indivisible* **elementary particles** *of matter; The first six (or sometimes eight) grades constitute* **elementary school**.

el.e.phant (EL.uh.funt) *n.* a huge mammal of Africa or Asia with a long snout, or trunk, and ivory tusks growing from either side of its upper jaw: *An elephant trumpets; a herd of elephants; a rogue elephant that has gone wild; the calf* (= young) *of an elephant; a cow* (= female) *elephant; a bull* (= male) *elephant.*

el.e.phan.ti.a.sis (EL.uh.fun.TYE.uh.sis) *n.* a tropical skin disease resulting in swelling and hardening of parts of the body.

el.e.phan.tine (el.uh.FAN.tine, -teen) *adj.* of or like elephants; huge, clumsy, etc.

el.e.vate (EL.uh.vate) *v.* **-vates, -vat.ed, -vat.ing** **1** lift or raise, esp. to a higher rank, plane, or quality: *a commoner elevated to the peerage; lawyers elevated to the bench;* **adj.**: *an* **elevated** *cholesterol level; An* **elevated railroad** *is elevated on tracks above street level allowing other traffic to pass underneath.* **2** make better in mind or soul; elate or exhilarate: *sagging spirits elevated by success;* **adj.**: *an* **elevating** *religious experience.*

el.e.va.tion (el.uh.VAY.shun) *n.* **1** a raising: *the elevation of a bishop to cardinal (status).* **2** height: *We were flying at an elevation of 30,000 ft; You get a good view of the countryside from this elevation* (= hill); *at an elevation* (= angular distance) *of 30 degrees above the horizon.* **3** the exterior design of a building: *front, rear, side elevations; a house model with a choice of three elevations.*

el.e.va.tor (EL.uh.vay.tur) *n.* **1** a cage or platform for traveling up and down in a building or mine: *There's a bank of elevators on the main floor; Take the up elevator to the top floor;* **adja.**: *an* **elevator** *lobby, operator, shaft.* **2** a tall structure in which grain is stored: *a prairie elevator.* **3** a movable horizontal flap on the tail section of an aircraft for making it go up and down.

el.ev.en (i.LEV.un) *n., adj. & pron.* one more than 10; the number 11 or XI: *There are eleven of them; eleven boys; a football eleven* (= team of 11 players).
—**e.lev.enth** *n. & adj.*

eleventh hour *n.* just before it is too late: *The program was canceled at the eleventh hour because of bad weather;* **adj**a.: *the eleventh-hour cramming for an exam; an eleventh-hour decision.*

elf *n.* **elves** (ELVZ) a mischievous little fairy. —**elf.in** or **elf.ish** *adj.*

e.lic.it (i.LIS.it) *v.* draw out: *a question that didn't elicit a response from anyone.* —**e.lic.i.ta.tion** (-i.TAY.shun) *n.*

e.lide (i.LIDE) *v.* **e.lides, e.lid.ed, e.lid.ing** drop or leave out a sound or syllable for euphony or rhythm, as "send'st" for "sendest."

el.i.gi.ble (EL.uh.juh.bul) *adj.* qualified or fit to be chosen: *Citizens are eligible to vote; Eve is eligible for admission to a university; an eligible bachelor or woman (who will make a suitable spouse); an eligible voter; eligible income for refundable tax credit.* —*n.* an eligible person: *a list of eligibles.* —**el.i.gi.bil.i.ty** (-BIL.i.tee) *n.*

e.lim.i.nate (i.LIM.uh.nate) *v.* **-nates, -nat.ed, -nat.ing** get rid of from within: *Body wastes are eliminated; In a tournament, losers in the first rounds are eliminated until a single champion remains; to tighten a budget by eliminating unnecessary expenses.* —**e.lim.i.na.tion** (-uh.NAY.shun) *n.*: *the elimination of poverty and hunger from the earth.*

e.li.sion (i.LIZH.un) *n.* an eliding.

e.lite (i.LEET, ay.LEET) *n.* **1** [takes *pl. v.*] a group considered to be superior: *a private school for the elite; the elite of society;* **adj**a.: *the creation of an elite force; a small elite group.* **2** a size of typewriter type that gives 12 characters to the linear inch.

e.lit.ism (i.LEE.tiz.um, ay.LEE-) *n.* rule by an elite. —**e.lit.ist** *adj.* having to do with the elite: *Is golf an elitist sport? an elitist approach, attitude, image;* **n.**: *college-educated elitists.*

e.lix.ir (i.LIK.sur) *n.* a fragrant alcoholic syrup containing medicine: *The alchemists sought the **elixir of life**, a mythical substance that would prolong life indefinitely.*

E.liz.a.be.than (i.liz.uh.BEETH.un) *n. & adj.* (a person) of the time of **Elizabeth I**, queen of England: *the Elizabethan age; Elizabethan drama, England.*

elk *n.* **1** a large mooselike deer of N. Europe. **2** the smaller North American wapiti.

ell *n.* **1** something L-shaped, as a joint of tubing or an annex to a building. **2** a former measure of cloth length, equal to 45 in. (112 cm): *"Give him an inch and he'll take an ell"* (= take too much).

el.lipse (i.LIPS) *n.* **el.lip.ses** (-siz) an oval-shaped symmetrical closed curve.

el.lip.sis (i.LIP.sis) *n., pl.* **-ses** (-seez) **1** an omission of a word or words from a grammatically complete sentence, as in "I can and I will." **2** a dash, periods, etc. indicating this, as "A stitch in time...."

el.lip.soid (i.LIP.soid) *n.* a slightly flattened sphere, as of the earth, whose plane sections are circles or ellipses; also *adj.* —**el.lip.soid.al** (i.lip.SOID.ul) *adj.*

el.lip.tic or **el.lip.ti.cal** (i.LIP.ti.cul) *adj.* **1** having to do with the ellipse: *an elliptic arch, curve; elliptic geometry, orbits, paths.* **2** marked by ellipsis: *elliptical language; Her writing is sometimes elliptical.* —**el.lip.ti.cal.ly** *adv.*: *The earth moves elliptically around the sun.*

elm *n.* a large, hardy tree valued for lumber and shade.

el.o.cu.tion (el.uh.CUE.shun) *n.* the art of public speaking. —**el.o.cu.tion.ist** *n.*

e.lon.gate (i.LONG.gate) *v.* **-gates, -gat.ed, -gat.ing** make or become longer, esp. out of proportion: *Stretching upward elongates your spine;* **adj**.: *an **elongated** (= disproportionately long) figure, form, shape; the giraffe's elongated neck.* —*adj.* elongated: *an elongate leaf.* —**e.lon.ga.tion** (ee.long.GAY.shun) *n.*

e.lope (i.LOPE) *v.* **e.lopes, e.loped, e.lop.ing** run away together to get married: *Jane eloped with Dick; They eloped.* —**e.lope.ment** *n.* —**e.lop.er** *n.*

el.o.quent (EL.uh.quent) *adj.* forceful or fluent in expression: *an eloquent speech; eloquent gestures;* **el.o.quent.ly** *adv.* —**el.o.quence** *n.*

else *adj*p. [follows modified pronoun or adverb] other: *Anyone else? someone else's book; everywhere else.* —*adv.* **1** in a different manner; at a different place or time: *How else? Where else shall we go?* **2** otherwise: *Finish the job, (or) else you won't be paid; Finish it in time **or else**, he was warned.*

else.where *adv.* somewhere else.

e.lu.ci.date (i.LOO.suh.date) *v.* **-dates, -dat.ed, -dat.ing** make something clear by illustrating or explaining: *to elucidate a meaning, problem, text.* —**e.lu.ci.da.tion** (-DAY.shun) *n.*

e.lude (i.LOOD, long "OO") *v.* **e.ludes, e.lud.ed, e.lud.ing** escape mental or physical grasp by some cunning quality: *The answer to this riddle eludes me; He was arrested after eluding the police for two years.* —**e.lu.der** *n.*

—**e.lu.sion** (-zhun) n.
e.lu.sive (i.LOO.siv) adj. hard to get, catch, or grasp: *an elusive concept; She's elusive like a will-o'-the-wisp.*
—**e.lu.sive.ly** adv.; **e.lu.sive.ness** n.
el.ver n. a young eel.
elves pl. of ELF.
E.ly.si.an (i.LIZH.un) adj. having to do with **Elysium**, or **Elysian Fields**, the paradise of Greek myth.
'em [short form] them: *Let 'em go.*
em n. a unit of type measure equal to about 1/16 in. (0.16 cm), originally the width of the letter M.
e.ma.ci.ate (i.MAY.shee.ate, -see.ate) v. **-ates, -at.ed, -at.ing** make very thin or waste away, as by hunger or illness.
—**e.ma.ci.a.tion** (-AY.shun) n.
e-mail n. transmission and distribution of messages by computer using telephone lines; electronic mail; *adja.: an e-mail address, message, system.* —v.: *You can always e-mail me at home; Please e-mail your notes to me.*
em.a.nate (EM.uh.nate) v. **-nates, -nat.ed, -nat.ing 1** originate, as from a source: *From where do these rumors emanate?* **2** emit: *the authority she emanates!* —**em.a.na.tion** (-NAY.shun) n.
e.man.ci.pate (i.MAN.suh.pate) v. **-pates, -pat.ed, -pat.ing** to free from slavery or restraint. —**e.man.ci.pa.tor** (-pay.tur) n.
e.man.ci.pa.tion (i.man.suh.PAY.shun) n. a freeing, as from slavery: *the emancipation of slaves from bondage; the emancipation of women; the emancipation of Irish Catholics in 1829.*
e.mas.cu.late (i.MASK.yuh.late) v. **-lates, -lat.ed, -lat.ing** castrate; hence, weaken: *freedom of speech emasculated by censorship.* —**e.mas.cu.la.tion** (-LAY.shun) n.
em.balm (im.BAHM) v. **1** preserve a dead body from decay using spices, chemicals, etc.; hence, preserve. **2** perfume.
em.bank (im.BANK) v. protect or support with an embankment.
em.bank.ment (im.BANK.munt) n. a bank of earth, stone, etc. raised to hold back water or support a roadway: *the embankment along the river Thames.*
em.bar.go (im.BAR.go) n. **-goes** a temporary government order prohibiting commerce with a foreign country, esp. the movement of ships or goods: *to impose, place, put an embargo on arms shipments to an enemy country; charged with shipping high tech items to Russia while under embargo; to lift or remove the economic embargo against trade with Cuba.*
—v. **-goes, -goed, -go.ing** prohibit or hold up: *Mail to Canada is embargoed in the U.S. during a postal strike; A press release embargoed till 6 p.m. may not be published before 6 p.m.*
em.bark (im.BARK) v. **1** put passengers or cargo on board a ship, airplane, etc. **2** get on board: *She embarked for Europe from Halifax; He is embarking (= setting out) on a new career as an engineer.*
—**em.bar.ka.tion** (em.bar.KAY.shun) n.
em.bar.rass (im.BAIR.us) v. **1** make or become uneasy or nervous: *parents embarrassed by a child's behavior; a sensitive child who embarrasses easily; adj.: She felt **embarrassed**; was embarrassed to find her name in the papers; embarrassed about or at or over the publicity she was subjected to; an embarrassed lady, response, silence; in an embarrassed way; It is **embarrassing** that so many people arrived after the guest of honor.* **2** hinder ease of movement; burden: *students embarrassed by heavy workloads; adj.: pensioners much **embarrassed** for life's necessities in inflationary times; financially embarrassed.*
—**em.bar.rass.ment** n.: *His shoplifting became an embarrassment to his family; social embarrassments of the underprivileged (who cannot afford good clothes, cars, etc.); a wealthy man's **embarrassment of riches** (= riches so excessive he doesn't know how to use them).*
em.bas.sy (EM.buh.see) n. **-bas.sies 1** a mission from one head of state to another. **2** an ambassador and his or her staff, the position of an ambassador, an ambassador's residence, or an ambassador's offices abroad: *You can find him at or in the embassy.*
em.bat.tled (em.BAT.uld) adj. engaged in battle: *an embattled city, presidency; to feel embattled.*
em.bed (im.BED) v. **-beds, -bed.ded, -bed.ding** fix firmly; also, plant: *Bricks are embedded in mortar; adj.: The human embryo begins to develop **embedded** in the uterus wall; to remove embedded dirt from carpets; a legend that has become embedded in the popular mind.*
em.bel.lish (im.BEL.ish) v. decorate with added ornamentation; enhance; *adj.: a somewhat **embellished** truth, though not a falsehood.* —**em.bel.lish.ment** n.
em.ber (EM.bur) n. a glowing piece of wood or coal in the remains of a fire: *the glow of burning embers; live embers; a dying, glowing ember; the last ember of hope; to fan the embers into a fire; an ember pit.*

em.bez.zle (im.BEZ.ul) *v.* **-bez.zles, -bez.zled, -bez.zling** steal money, securities, etc. entrusted to one's care: *An assistant manager was charged with embezzling $2 million from the bank; He had embezzled this money over several years.* —**em.bez.zle.ment** *n.* —**em.bez.zler** *n.*

em.bit.ter (em.BIT.ur) *v.* make bitter or resentful. —**em.bit.ter.ment** *n.*

em.bla.zon (im.BLAY.zun) *v.* **1** decorate with a coat of arms or other insignia. **2** extol. —**em.bla.zon.ment** *n.*

em.blem (EM.blum) *n.* an object or design used to represent something characteristic of it: *The beaver and the maple leaf are both emblems of Canada.* —**em.blem.at.ic** (em.bluh.MAT.ic) *adj.*: *The cross is emblematic of Christianity and symbolic of suffering.*

em.bod.y (im.BOD.ee) *v.* **-bod.ies, -bod.ied, -bod.y.ing 1** give form to an ideal, thought, feelings, etc.; personify: *Democratic ideals are embodied in our Constitution.* **2** incorporate: *The newer cars embody many gas-saving features.* —**em.bod.i.ment** *n.*: *Solomon was the embodiment of wisdom.*

em.bold.en (im.BOLE.dun) *v.* give someone the courage *to* do something.

em.bo.lism (EM.buh.liz.um) *n.* the blocking of an artery by an embolus.

em.bo.lus (EM.buh.lus) *n., pl.* **-li** (-lye) an object such as a blood clot, gas bubble, or globule of fat floating in the blood.

em.boss (im.BOSS) *v.* **1** make a design, lettering, etc. stand out on a surface. **2** decorate in relief; *adj.*: *an embossed business card; embossed stationery.* —**em.boss.ment** *n.*

em.bou.chure (ahm.boo.SHOOR) *n.* the method of applying the lips to the mouthpiece of a wind instrument; also called "lipping."

em.bow.er (em.BOW.ur) *v.* enclose in a bower.

em.brace (im.BRACE) *v.* **-brac.es, -braced, -brac.ing 1** clasp with the arms to show love or friendship; hug: *He embraced her; Father and son embraced.* **2** contain or include: *a program of education embracing the arts and sciences.* **3** accept or take up: *He left home to embrace the monastic life.* —*n.* hug: *a loving, tight, warm embrace; the passionate embraces of Romeo and Juliet.*

em.bra.sure (em.BRAY.zhur) *n.* a beveled opening in a wall with one side wider than the other, as for castle windows or in a parapet wall for firing guns through.

em.bro.cate (EM.bruh.cate) *v.* **-cates, -cat.ed, -cat.ing** rub a body part with a liniment. —**em.bro.ca.tion** (-CAY.shun) *n.* a liniment.

em.broi.der (im.BROY.dur) *v.* **1** embellish, esp. with embroidery. **2** exaggerate: *He embroidered the original story beyond recognition.*

em.broi.der.y (im.BROY.duh.ree) *n.* **-der.ies 1** the ornamenting of fabrics with needlework; also, embroidered work. **2** an embellishment or exaggeration.

em.broil (im.BROIL) *v.* involve a person or country in trouble, esp. in a quarrel: *He found himself embroiled in controversy.* —**em.broil.ment** *n.*

em.bry.o (EM.bree.oh) *n.* **-os** a developing plant in its seed or such an animal in its egg or mother's womb, esp. during the first two months of pregnancy in humans: *The researchers inserted rat genes into mouse embryos; the marketing of frozen Holstein embryos; adja.: an embryo implant, transfer, transplant; embryo research; the embryo stage.* —**in embryo** in an undeveloped state.

em.bry.ol.o.gy (em.bree.OL.uh.jee) *n.* the biology of the formation and development of embryos; **em.bry.ol.o.gist** *n.*

em.bry.on.ic (em.bree.ON.ic) *adja.* **1** developing: *a project in its embryonic stage; embryonic condition, development, growth, mice, stars; an embryonic human being.* **2** having to do with embryos: *embryonic cells, tissue; The embryonic membrane encloses an embryo in the womb.*

em.cee (EM.see) *n. Informal* [short form] master of ceremonies. —*v.* **-cees, -ceed, -cee.ing** act as emcee: *Who is emceeing? a Miss America pageant emceed by a TV star.*

e.mend (i.MEND) *v.* make scholarly corrections: *to emend a text.* —**e.men.da.tion** (ee.mun.DAY.shun) *n.*

em.er.ald (EM.ur.uld) *n.* a bright green precious stone or its color; *adj.*: *emerald green; "The Emerald Isle"* (= Ireland).

e.merge (i.MURJ) *v.* **e.merg.es, e.merged, e.merg.ing** come forth, as if from hiding; come out into view: *Venus emerged from the sea; to emerge from the shadows into light; After the first round, she emerged as the leading contender for the championship; New viruses have emerged* (= evolved as new forms) *recently.* —**e.mer.gence** (-junce) *n.*

e.mer.gen.cy (i.MUR.jun.see) *n.* **-cies** a situation arising suddenly that needs quick action, as a flood or heart attack: *In case of (an) emergency* or *In an emergency, don't panic; An emergency was declared in the area; a life-threatening, national, serious emergency; a state of emergency.* —*adja.*: *an emergency exit, landing, situation; a car's emergency lights; emergency relief; an emergency warning given on radio about a tornado; Cars are equipped with an* **emergency brake** or *parking brake for use if the foot brakes fail; She pulled the* **emergency cord** *and stopped the train;* **emergency equipment** *such as a first-aid kit, flares, and tow line; a hospital's* **emergency room** *(for treatment of medical emergencies); Ambulances, fire trucks, and such* **emergency vehicles.**

e.mer.gent (i.MUR.junt) *adja.* emerging or coming forth: *the newly emergent nations of Africa.*

e.mer.i.tus (i.MER.uh.tus) *adj.* [used after its noun] of a professional, retired from active service: *a professor emeritus;* *adja.*: *the emeritus organist of our cathedral.* —*n., pl.* **-ti** (-tye); *fem.* **-ta**, *pl.* **-tae** (-tee).

em.er.y (EM.uh.ree) *n.* **-er.ies** a hard, coarse corundum used for grinding and polishing, coated in powdered form on **emery board, emery cloth,** etc.

e.met.ic (i.MET.ic) *n. & adj.* (a substance) that induces vomiting.

em.i.grate (EM.uh.grate) *v.* **-grates, -grat.ed, -grat.ing** go *from* one country or region to settle in another: *They emigrated from Taiwan and immigrated to the U.S.; Canadians emigrate to the U.S. to live in the Sunbelt.* —**em.i.grant** (-grunt) *n. & adj.* —**em.i.gra.tion** (-GRAY.shun) *n.*

é.mi.gré (EM.uh.gray) *n.* a political fugitive, as the Cubans in the U.S.: *Russian émigrés;* *adja.*: *an émigré group, journal, poet, writer.*

em.i.nence (EM.uh.nunce) *n.* prominent or distinguished position: *a woman of great eminence as a physicist; We looked at the horizon from an eminence* (= elevated spot) *overlooking the sea; Your Eminence* [form of addressing a cardinal]; *His Eminence said so.* —**em.i.nent** *adj.*: *an eminent physician; He is eminent as a diplomat; She is eminent in her field.* —**em.i.nent.ly** *adv.*

eminent domain *n.* a government's right to appropriate private property for public use. —**em.i.nent.ly** *adv.*

e.mir (i.MEER) *n.* in Moslem countries, a ruler or chieftain.

e.mir.ate (EM.uh.rit, -rate) *n.* an emir's territory.

em.is.sar.y (EM.uh.sair.ee) *n.* **-is.sar.ies**
1 one sent on an official mission; messenger: *an emissary from the Vatican.*
2 a secret agent or spy.

e.mis.sion (i.MISH.un) *n.* an emitting or something discharged: *the emission of electrons from an electrode; Automobile emissions cause pollution.*

e.mit (i.MIT) *v.* **e.mits, e.mit.ted, e.mit.ting** send out or discharge heat, fumes, odors, sounds, etc.
—**e.mit.ter** *n.*

Em.my (EM.ee) *n.* **Em.mys** any of the annual awards for outstanding TV producers, performers, etc. made by the U.S. National Academy of Television Arts and Sciences.

e.mol.li.ent (i.MOL.yunt) *n. & adj.* softening or soothing (agent, medicine, etc.).

e.mol.u.ment (i.MOL.yuh.munt) *n.* usu. **emoluments** *pl. Formal.* reward for work, usu. other than wages: *health insurance, pension scheme, and such emoluments besides a salary; the emoluments* (= perks) *of an office; the emoluments* (= trappings) *of power.*

e.mote (i.MOTE) *v. Informal.* **e.motes, e.mot.ed, e.mot.ing** act or behave emotionally: *an actor who emotes too much.*

e.mo.ti.con (i.MOH.ti.con) *n.* a group of keyboard characters used, when viewed sideways, to express an emotion, esp. in e-mail messages, as :-(meaning "I'm sad."

e.mo.tion (i.MOH.shun) *n.* an intense feeling, as joy, anger, love, or fear: *The speech stirred up* or *whipped up the emotions of the mob; their pent-up emotions; the conflicting emotions of love of one's religion and loyalty to the nation; He left the scene with mixed emotions.*
—**e.mo.tion.al** *adj.*: *an emotional appeal, character, disorder, outburst, plea.*
—**e.mo.tion.al.ism** *n.* —**e.mo.tion.al.ly** *adv.*: *People sometimes act emotionally rather than rationally; an emotionally handicapped child with behavior problems.*

e.mo.tive (i.MOH.tiv) *adj.* causing strong feeling: *words with emotive associations; an emotive concept, expression; emotive language, words, utterances.*

em.pan.el (im.PAN.ul) *v.* **-els, -eled, -el.ing** same as IMPANEL. Also **em.pan.elled, em.pan.el.ling** *Cdn.*

em.path.ic (em.PATH.ic) *adj.* of or showing empathy: *an empathic response; She sounded empathic.*

em.pa.thize (EM.puh.thize, "th" as in "thin") *v.* **-iz.es, -ized, -iz.ing** have empathy: *to empathize with someone.*

empathy / empty

em.pa.thy (EM.puh.thee, "th" as in "thin") *n.* identification with another's feelings or ideas: *He has plenty of sympathy but little empathy with the poetry of suffering.*

em.pen.nage (ahm.puh.NAHZH, em.puh-) *n.* an aircraft's tail assembly.

em.per.or (EM.pur.ur) *n.* the male ruler of an empire.

em.pha.sis (EM.fuh.sis) *n., pl.* **-ses** (-seez) special stress put on syllables, words, thoughts, actions, etc. because of their relative importance.

em.pha.size (EM.fuh.size) *v.* **-siz.es, -sized, -siz.ing** stress: *The speaker emphasized each point by pounding the table with his fist.*

em.phat.ic (em.FAT.ic) **1** *adj.* expressed with force or spoken with emphasis: *an emphatic denial, gesture, opinion, statement; an emphatic "No"; "She does swim" is an emphatic form of utterance; "Herself," "himself," "itself," etc. are emphatic pronouns.* **2** *adjp.* sure or certain: *He's quite emphatic in his views; He's emphatic about having seen Bigfoot.* **3** *adja.* striking or telling: *an emphatic attempt, success, victory; an emphatic 95 percent.*
—**em.phat.i.cal.ly** *adv.*

em.phy.se.ma (em.fuh.SEE.muh) *n.* a lung disease in which the air sacs become enlarged, lose elasticity, and are unable to function efficiently.

em.pire (EM.pire) *n.* **1** a group of territories under a sovereign ruler, usu. an emperor: *to break up, build, consolidate, found, rule an empire; the collapse of the Soviet empire.* **2** sovereign rule: *an executive with no desire for empire.* **3** an extensive business or other organization with unified control: *to build up a financial empire; publishing empire; empire building.*

em.pir.ic (em.PEER.ic) *n.* one who relies on practical experience rather than on theory: *adj.:* empiric therapies.

em.pir.i.cal (em.PEER.i.cul) *adj.* **1** based on experiment and observation: *Your existence is an empirical fact, but that of ghosts is not; the empirical method of scientific procedure.* **2** based merely on practical experience: *an amateur doctor's empirical remedies.*

em.pir.i.cism (em.PEER.uh.siz.um) *n.* **1** the philosophy that all knowledge is derived from sense experience. **2** the method or practice of basing judgments on observation and experiment.
—**em.pir.i.cist** *n. & adj.*

em.place.ment (em.PLACE.munt) *n.* **1** positioning: *the emplacement of American missiles in Europe.* **2** a platform on which heavy guns are placed for firing.

em.plane (em.PLANE) *v.* board a plane: *We emplaned at 3 p.m. but were cleared for takeoff only at 4.*

em.ploy (em.PLOY) *v.* make use of or put to work on a regular basis: *I would like to hire you for occasional jobs but couldn't afford to employ you as a staffer; A housewife not gainfully employed doesn't pay income tax; methods employed to get votes; Skills not employed may go to waste; how to employ your spare time.*
—*n.* service: *They have 200 people in their employ.* —**em.ploy.er** (-PLOY.ur) *n.: an equal-opportunity employer.*

em.ploy.a.ble (em.PLOY.uh.bul) *adj.* that can be employed: *an employable immigrant with employable skills.*

em.ploy.ee (em.PLOY.ee, em.ploy.EE) *n.* one who is employed: *We're not taking on any more employees; to fire, hire, sack employees.* Also **em.ploy.e, em.ploy.es.**

em.ploy.ment (em.PLOY.munt) *n.* an employing or being employed, esp. a job: *a housewife who has no problem finding (outside) employment; to give, provide, seek employment; part-time, seasonal, steady employment; Employment peaks, rises, is up in the summer, down in the winter; An employment agency places workers and bills the employers for the service.*

em.po.ri.um (em.POR.ee.um) *n.* **-ri.ums** or **-ri.a** (-ee.uh) a large retail store with a variety of goods.

em.pow.er (em.POW.ur) *v.* **1** give someone power, authority, or ability *to do something.* **2** give self-actualizing power to a group: *ideas for empowering the homeless and unemployed; adj.:* newly **empowered** women and minorities.

em.press (EM.pris) *n.* an emperor's wife or the woman ruler of an empire.

emp.ty (EMP.tee) *adj.* **-ti.er, -ti.est** lacking the usual content: *an empty chair, lot, room; weasel words that are empty of meaning; "Empty vessels make the most sound"; The house is empty* (= the people who live in it are out) *but not vacant; an empty* (= valueless) *display; an empty* (= unreal) *dream; empty* (= idle) *hours; empty* (= hollow) *pleasures; an empty* (= meaningless) *promise; an empty* (= ineffective) *threat;* **empty calories** (from foods with no nutritive value); *to come up, leave, return, walk away* **empty-handed** (= without gaining anything); *an* **empty-headed** (= silly or stupid) *idea; I can't work* **on an empty stomach** (= without eating).
—*n., pl.* **-ties:** *Return the empties*

(= containers) *for refund or refill.* —*v.* **-ties, -tied, -ty.ing** make or become empty, as by pouring out the contents: *to empty a cup; rivers that empty* (= discharge) *into the Atlantic; The hall emptied* (= became empty) *at the sound of the siren; The streets seemed to have been emptied of traffic.* —**emp.ti.ly** (-tuh.lee) *adv.*; **emp.ti.ness** *n.*

empty nester *n.* one whose home is empty since the children have grown up and left.

empty set *n.* in mathematics, a set without members; null set.

empty word *n.* a word such as "from" or "but" that has a grammatical function more than meaning.

em.py.re.an (em.pye.REE.un, -PEER.ee.un) *n.* the highest heaven; also, the sky. —*adj.* heavenly or sublime. Also **em.py.re.al** (-PEER.ee.ul, -pye.REE.ul) *adj.*

e.mu (EE.mew) *n.* a large flightless bird of Australia, related to but smaller than an ostrich.

em.u.late (EM.yuh.late) *v.* **-lates, -lat.ed, -lat.ing** try to equal or excel an admired person or the person's qualities: *He tried to emulate his father's courage.* —**em.u.la.tion** (-LAY.shun) *n.* —**em.u.la.tor** (-lay.tur) *n.*

e.mul.si.fy (i.MUL.suh.fye) *v.* **-fies, -fied, -fy.ing** make an emulsion of two liquids. —**e.mul.si.fi.ca.tion** (-fuh.CAY.shun) *n.*

e.mul.sion (i.MUL.shun) *n.* **1** a dispersion in the form of fine droplets of one liquid in another in which it does not dissolve, as oil in water or pigments in latex to make "emulsion paints." **2** a light-sensitive coating used on camera film, plates, or paper.

en.a.ble (en.AY.bul) *v.* **-bles, -bled, -bling** give ability or capacity to someone, esp. legally: *Education enables one to qualify for better jobs;* **adja**.: *The U.S. Congress has to pass* **enabling** *legislation to enable a territory to become a state.*

en.act (in.ACT) *v.* **1** make into law: *to enact bills, legislation, statutes.* **2** act out on stage: *to enact a drama, play, role.* **3** put in practice: *to enact a ban, policy, treaty.* —**en.act.ment** *n.* —**en.ac.tor** *n.*

en.am.el (i.NAM.ul) *n.* **1** a hard, glasslike substance used to decorate and protect the surface of metal, glass, or pottery: *Kitchen appliances and bathroom fixtures are often finished in enamel;* **enamelware** *metal products.* **2** a kind of glossy paint, as used on walls, bicycles, and automobiles. **3** the hard outer covering of a tooth.

—*v.* **-els, -eled, -el.ing** decorate with or as with enamel; *adj.*: *an* **enameled** *brick, earring, plate.* —**en.am.el.er** *n.* Also **en.am.elled, en.am.el.ling; en.am.el.ler** *Cdn.*

en.am.ored (i.NAM.urd) *adj.* captivated or charmed: *He's quite enamored of her; Adults are not so enamored with computers as children are.* Also **en.am.oured** *Cdn.*

en bloc (ong.BLOC) *adv.* as a whole; all together: *They walked out en bloc; They voted en bloc to kill the legislation.*

en.camp (en.CAMP) *v.* camp or put soldiers, etc. in a camp; **en.camp.ment** *n.*

en.cap.su.late (en.CAP.suh.late) *v.* **-lates, -lat.ed, -lat.ing** encase (as if) in a capsule: *a theme encapsulated in his latest book.* Also **en.cap.sule** (-CAP.sul, -syool) **-sules, -suled, -sul.ing.** —**en.cap.su.la.tion** (-LAY.shun) *n.*

en.case (in.CASE) *v.* **-cas.es, -cased, -cas.ing** put (as if) in a case: *a bronze plaque encased in concrete.*

-ence See -ANCE.

en.ceph.a.li.tis (en.SEF.uh.LYE.tis) *n.* inflammation of the brain. —**en.ceph.a.lit.ic** (-LIT.ic) *adj.*

en.chain (in.CHAIN) *v.* **1** to chain. **2** captivate; hold fast.

en.chant (in.CHANT) *v.* charm, as if with magic; bewitch: *stories that enchant the reader;* **adj.**: *to be, become, feel* **enchanted**; *an* **enchanted** *castle, forest, garden;* **enchanting** *colors, fragrance, music; an enchanting performance, smile.* —**en.chant.er** *n.*; **en.chant.ress** (-tris) *fem.* —**en.chant.ment** *n.*

en.chi.la.da (en.chuh.LAH.duh) *n.* a rolled tortilla with a filling of meat or cheese, peppers, etc. —**the big enchilada** *Slang.* the boss. —**the whole enchilada** *Slang.* the whole thing.

en.ci.pher (en.SYE.fur) *v.* put a message into cipher; **en.ci.pher.ment** *n.*

en.cir.cle (en.SUR.cul) *v.* circle: *a bypass encircling the city;* **adj.**: *They felt* **encircled**; *an* **encircled** *fortress.* —**en.cir.cle.ment** *n.*

en.clave (EN.clave, AHN-) *n.* **1** a territory of one country lying inside the boundaries of another: *Goa was a Portuguese enclave in India.* **2** any exclusive or isolated territory: *Rosedale is an enclave of our city's well-to-do; The legal profession is no more a male enclave.*

en.close (in.CLOZE) *v.* **-clos.es, -closed, -clos.ing** **1** include, as in an envelope or parcel: *A $100 check is enclosed herewith; Please find enclosed a check for $100.* **2** shut up as with a fence: *a garden enclosed with a wall;* **adj.**: *an* **enclosed** *shopping mall;* **enclosed** *and open* spaces; an **enclosed convent** (*of cloistered nuns*).

en.clo.sure (in.CLOH.zhur) *n.* **1** something that shuts up, as surrounding walls. **2** an enclosed space, as a corral. **3** something enclosed, as a check with a covering letter.

en.code (in.CODE) *v.* **-codes, -cod.ed, -cod.ing** put a message into code or add codes to data or text: *A text is encoded by replacing its words with arbitrary symbols; to encode data for computer processing.*

en.cod.er (in.COH.dur) *n.* an encoding device: *In a color telecast, the three primary color signals are combined in an encoder for transmission.*

en.co.mi.um (en.COH.mee.um) *n.* **-mi.ums** or **-mi.a** (-mee.uh) *Formal.* an expression of high praise; eulogy.

en.com.pass (en.CUM.pus) *v.* **1** contain, as if encircled: *a mind that could encompass vast knowledge.* **2** accomplish: *a plot that encompassed his ruin.*

en.core (AHNG.core) *interj.* once more! repeat! *The audience shouted "Encore!"* —*n.* **1** a popular call to repeat a stage performance or act: *The audience insisted on an encore; v.: The audience encored the violinist three times.* **2** a repetition made in response to such a call: *to do, play, sing an encore.*

en.coun.ter (in.COWN.tur) *v.* come up against; confront: *to encounter difficulties.* —*n.* **1** an unexpected meeting: *brief, casual, chance, close, fleeting encounters.* **2** a confrontation: *an encounter with a burglar; a bloody, sudden, ugly encounter; Members of an* **encounter group** *meet in sensitivity-training sessions to talk about and act out hostile feelings and reactions to help them get along with others more effectively.*

en.cour.age (in.CUR.ij) *v.* **-ag.es, -aged, -ag.ing 1** give courage, hope, confidence, support, etc. to someone, esp. to do something: *A teacher encourages students to work harder; She doesn't encourage their disturbing others.* **2** stimulate or hearten: *We were encouraged to hear we had won; The news encouraged us; adj.: The news was quite encouraging.* —**en.cour.age.ment** *n.*

en.croach (in.CROHCH) *v.* trespass or intrude gradually *on* or *upon* someone's land, time, or other property: *The sea encroaches on land by erosion.* —**en.croach.ment** *n.*

en.crust (in.CRUST) *v.* cover with, form, or form into a crust: *The shoes were encrusted with mud; Ice encrusted the water in the tank.* —**en.crus.ta.tion** (en.crus.TAY.shun) *n.*

en.cum.ber (in.CUM.bur) *v.* burden, obstruct, or crowd so as to hinder freedom of movement or action: *He doesn't like to be transferred, as he is encumbered with a large family of dependents; an estate encumbered with debts; a backyard encumbered with junk; a page encumbered with footnotes.*
—**en.cum.brance** (-brunce) *n.*

en.cyc.li.cal (en.SIC.li.cul) *n.* a letter from the Pope to Catholic bishops worldwide.

en.cy.clo.pe.di.a (en.SYE.cluh.PEE.dee.uh) *n.* a book or set of books providing wide information on every field of knowledge or on a specific area if a specialized work: *an encyclopedia of science and technology.*
—**en.cy.clo.pe.dic** (-PEE.dic) *adj.* wide-ranging: *a scholar of encyclopedic knowledge.* Also **en.cy.clo.pae.di.a; en.cy.clo.pae.dic.**

en.cyst (en.SIST) *v.* enclose or become enclosed in a cyst. —**en.cyst.ment** *n.*

end *n.* **1** an extremity or limit, as of a line or of anything extended in space or time: *Tie a knot at each end of the rope; the front end and rear end of a car; The rope measures 10 m* **from end to end;** *I watched the game* **from beginning to end;** *We can't lend you any more money because you have reached* **the end of the line** – *you already owe too much; The news was broadcast to* **the ends of the earth** (= to the remotest places on earth); *The Minister was at* or *on the receiving end of the public outcry; Let's hear your end* (= side) *of the story; The unemployed find it hard to* **make (both) ends meet** (= make income equal expenditures); *It rained for days* **on end** (= continuously); *The gruesome sight made his hair* **stand on end** (= horrified him and made him feel as if the hair on his head was rising stiffly); *Ends* (= end players) *play at each end of the line of scrimmage in football.* **2** a finish: *at the end of the day; He fought for his rights to the bitter end; The meeting came to an end at midnight; to* **put an end to** *the nuisance; The old man was nearing his end* (= death); **In the end** (= At last), *everyone parted as friends; He gave us* **no end** (= a great deal) *of trouble.* **3** a piece of anything having extension: *Take all the candle ends off the cake; the odds and ends left over after a party.* **4** goal or purpose: *to accomplish, achieve one's ends; Have your end clearly in view; Does the* **end justify the means** (= Does the result justify the means used to achieve it)? —*v.* come or bring to a close: *High school ends with graduation; They end all meetings by singing the national anthem; We ended the dinner with a dessert; The game ended in a draw.* —**end up** finish: *The bellhop ended up owning the hotel; He ended up (as) company president; The gunman ended up in jail.*

en.dan.ger (en.DAIN.jur) *v.* put in danger, as of death: *Drunk drivers endanger lives; With so few left, whooping cranes are an* **endangered species** *(threatened with extinction).*

end-consumer same as END-USER.

en.dear (en.DEER) *v.* make dear or lovable: *Children have a way of endearing themselves to everyone;* **adj.:** *the endearing ways of children; an endearing nature, quality, trait.* —**en.dear.ing.ly** *adv.*

en.dear.ment (en.DEER.munt) *n.* expression of affection, as a word or touch: *a term of endearment such as "honey."*

en.deav.or (en.DEV.ur) *v. Formal.* make an attempt, esp. in an earnest and sustained manner: *Most parents endeavor to provide their children with a good education;* **n.:** *a lifetime of honest endeavor to reform the legal system.* Also **en.deav.our** *Cdn.*

en.dem.ic (en.DEM.ic) *adj.* belonging to a particular region because of favorable conditions, as certain plants and diseases: *Is complacency endemic to academic groups?* **n.:** *Epidemics come and go but an endemic tends to remain in a region or community.*

end.game or **end game** *n.* the final stage of a game, as in chess after the queens are exchanged and forces heavily reduced.

ending *n.* the last part: *a story with a happy ending; "Hamlet" has a tragic ending; the plural ending (= suffix) "-es."*

en.dive *n.* either of two varieties of a salad vegetable, one with curled leaves and the other (escarole) with broad, smooth leaves.

end.less (END.lis) **1** *adj.* without end, eternal or boundless, or seeming so: *the endless stretch of the heavens; The lecture seemed endless; an endless nuisance.* **2** *adj.* with the ends joined together, thereby making continuous: *the endless track of a snowmobile or bulldozer.* —**end.less.ly** *adv.*

end.most *adj.* farthest.

en.do.crine (EN.duh.crin, -crine) *adj.* having to do with a gland such as the thyroid, adrenal, or pituitary that secretes hormones directly into the bloodstream; hence, hormonal. —**en.do.cri.nol.o.gy** (-cruh.NOL.uh.jee) *n.;* **en.do.cri.nol.o.gist** *n.*

en.dog.a.my (en.DOG.uh.mee) *n.* the custom of marrying within one's own tribe; **en.dog.a.mous** (-mus) *adj.*

en.dog.e.nous (en.DOJ.uh.nus) *adj.* growing or developing from within, as spores within a cell or a disease from inside the body; **en.dog.e.nous.ly** *adv.*

end organ *n.* a terminal structure, as the nerve endings in the body: *The retina is the end organ of vision.*

en.dor.phin (en.DOR.fin) *n.* a hormone compound produced in the nerve cells of the body to relieve pain and tension: *Exercise stimulates the release of endorphins in the body.*

en.dorse (en.DORCE) *v.* **-dors.es, -dorsed, -dors.ing 1** sign a check, money order, or a document, usu. on the back, to indicate approval. **2** approve of or support: *to endorse a candidate, product, service.* —**en.dorse.ment** *n.*

en.do.scope (EN.duh.scope) *n.* an instrument for examining the inside of a hollow organ such as the bladder or rectum. —**en.do.scop.ic** (-SCOP.ic) *adj.*

en.do.the.li.um (en.duh.THEE.lee.um, "TH" as in "thin") *n.* a layer of cells forming the inner lining of blood vessels and body cavities. —**en.do.the.li.al** *adj.:* *endothelial cells.*

en.do.ther.mic (en.duh.THUR.mic) *adj.* having to do with absorption of heat: *Ice and salt form an endothermic mixture.* Also **en.do.ther.mal.**

en.dow (en.DOW, *rhyme:* HOW) *v.* provide someone with money, property, talents, or other assets: *Nature endowed her with beauty and wit.* —**en.dow.ment** *n.:* *The new school was provided with a million-dollar endowment (= fund); An* **endowment insurance policy** *matures at a specified date and is paid as a lump sum.*

end product *n.* the final result of a process or of a series of activities; finished product.

end run *n.* a football play in which the ball carrier tries to run around one end of the opponent's line; hence, a tactic for getting around opposition: *to make or try an end run around a person or situation.*

end table *n.* a small low table used beside a sofa or other piece of furniture.

en.due (en.DUE) *v.* **-dues, -dued, -du.ing** usu. **endued with,** provided with a quality.

en.dur.ance (en.DURE.unce) *n.* the state

endure / engage

or power of enduring or bearing: *You need great endurance to run a marathon; an athlete's powers of endurance; The agony was beyond her endurance* (= impossible to bear); *When the pain became past endurance she just fainted; a 19-day* **endurance race** *of automobiles; a grueling* **endurance test** *of one's patience.*
en.dure (en.DURE) *v.* **-dures, -dured, -dur.ing 1** bear something or someone, esp. for a long time; tolerate: *to endure noise, pain, suffering.* **2** continue in existence, esp. in spite of opposing influences; last: *Even great works of art do not endure forever;* **adj.**: *an enduring conflict, peace; the most enduring of all her works.* —**en.dur.a.ble** (-ruh.bul) *adj.*
end use *n.* the final use to which a product is put. —**end-user** or **end-consumer** *n.*
end.ways or **end.wise** *adj. & adv.* with the end forward; lengthwise.
end zone *n.* in a football field, the 10 yards behind either goal line.
en.e.ma (EN.uh.muh) *n.* [medical] the sending up of a liquid, as a purgative, into the rectum.
en.e.my (EN.uh.mee) *n.* **-mies 1** one who hates or wishes to harm another: *to conquer, overcome, rout an enemy; The escaped killer was considered public enemy number one; arch, bitter, common, mortal, political, powerful, sworn enemies.* **2** anything harmful or injurious: *A bad habit could be one's own worst enemy; Lethargy is the enemy of progress.*
en.er.get.ic (en.ur.JET.ic) *adj.* vigorous or forceful. —**en.er.get.i.cal.ly** *adv.*
en.er.gize (EN.ur.jize) *v.* **-giz.es, -gized, -giz.ing** rouse into action or give energy to a person or thing. —**en.er.giz.er** *n.*
en.er.gy (EN.ur.jee) *n.* **-gies 1** capacity for action; ability to do work: *a youngster full of energy; He starts each day in a burst of energy; Without proper guidance, he would dissipate his energy in useless pursuits; Hot weather saps his energy; He should concentrate his energy on doing one thing at a time; His energies have to be redirected in useful ways; Pat's energies are now being applied or devoted to winning a gold medal; Lou expended her energies in the cause of consumer rights; She's a person of boundless, limitless, unflagging energy; a sales rep with a high* **energy level**. **2** usable power: *Chemical, electrical, mechanical, and solar energy are different kinds of energy, while kinetic and potential energy are different forms of mechanical energy; Atomic energy was first harnessed in the 1940s; renewable sources of energy such as the sun, wind, and tides; We may be facing an* **energy crisis** (= acute energy shortage) *unless we conserve our nonrenewable oil and natural gas resources.*
en.er.vate (EN.ur.vate) *v.* **-vates, -vat.ed, -vat.ing** lessen the physical, mental, or moral vigor of someone, as by a hot, damp climate or overindulgence in luxury, alcohol, drugs, etc. —**en.er.va.tion** (-VAY.shun) *n.*
en.fi.lade (EN.fuh.lade, -lahd) *n.* gunfire along the length of a line of enemy troops.
en.fold (en.FOLD) *v.* wrap up; also, embrace.
en.force (en.FORCE) *v.* **-forc.es, -forced, -forc.ing** compel or force, esp. obedience, understanding, etc.: *Police enforce the law; Some laws are strictly enforced; to enforce an argument using facts and figures;* **adj.**: *a period of* **enforced** *idleness due to hospitalization.* —**en.force.a.ble** *adj.* —**en.force.ment** *n.*: *drug, law, speed enforcement;* **adj.**: *an enforcement agency, authority, mechanism, officer, program; enforcement efforts.*
en.forc.er (en.FOR.sur) *n.* **1** one who enforces: *law enforcers.* **2** one whose job is to enforce the will of a gang leader by threats and punishment: *gang enforcers; Professional hockey teams have enforcers who use intimidating tactics against opposing players.*
en.fran.chise (en.FRAN.chize) *v.* **-chis.es, -chised, -chis.ing 1** give voting rights to a group: *Women and minorities were enfranchised only in the 20th century;* **adj.**: *to become enfranchised as citizens; newly enfranchised voters.* **2** set slaves free. —**en.fran.chise.ment** (-chiz.munt, -chize.munt) *n.*
en.gage (en.GAGE) *v.* **-gag.es, -gaged, -gag.ing 1** be busy; occupy or involve: *Scientists are engaged in research; Japan is engaged in trade with many countries; matters that engage our attention all day; how to engage the interest of students; to engage someone in conversation; to engage in activities, arguments, negotiations, play; to engage in a sexual relationship, shouting match, struggle;* **adj.**: *politically* **engaged** *citizens; a book to keep you engaged.* **2** make involved, as machine parts meshing or people fighting: *As you release the clutch, it engages a flywheel connected to the engine; If the gears don't engage, you have a problem; He engaged the enemy in hand-to-hand combat.* **3** promise or bind oneself; **adj.**: *an* **engaged** *couple; Marc is engaged to (marry) Mia; Mia and Marc are engaged*

engagement / enigma

(to be married); They got engaged last week. **4** hire: *to engage a lawyer; We engaged a student as our tour guide; We engaged her to show us around her hometown.*

en.gage.ment (en.GAGE.munt) *n.* **1** an agreement or promise: *to announce an engagement* (= betrothal); *She broke off her engagement (to marry) and returned the* **engagement ring.** **2** an arrangement to meet someone: *The boss has canceled all outside engagements because of a cold; He has many luncheon, social, and speaking engagements; Previous* or *prior engagements prevent him from seeing surprise visitors.* **3** an action involving combat: *The territory was recaptured after a brief naval engagement with the enemy.*

engaging (en.GAY.jing) *adj.* pleasing or charming: *her engaging manner, smile; We found the movie quite engaging.*

en.gen.der (en.JEN.dur) *v.* give rise to or produce something: *Fear often engenders violence.*

en.gine (EN.jun) *n.* **1** a mechanism, esp. one that uses fuel energy to produce work: *air-cooled, diesel, gasoline, internal-combustion, jet, radial, reciprocating, rotary, steam, V-8 engines; to rev up, tune up, turn off, warm up an engine; Engines break down, idle, sputter, stall, work; Some engines burn too much gasoline; an engine that runs on alcohol.* **2** a machine used for military purposes: *medieval engines of warfare such as battering rams.*

en.gi.neer (en.juh.NEER) *n.* one who designs, manages, or operates machinery and systems to utilize power and materials: *a professional engineer such as a chemical, civil, electrical, electronic,* or *mechanical engineer; technicians such as* **operating engineers** *in charge of machines and plants, radio engineers, sound engineers, and* **stationary engineers** *in charge of generators, compressors, etc.*
—*v.* plan and make, as an engineer does: *a demonstration engineered* (= caused and managed) *by students; Some foods are scientifically engineered* (= fabricated) *for higher nutritional value and longer shelf life; adj.: a well* **engineered** *car.*

engineering *n.* **1** the study of the scientific use of energy and materials for practical purposes. **2** the profession of an engineer.

Eng.lish (ING.glish) *n.* **1** the Germanic language of England, used also in the British Commonwealth, the U.S., and other countries: *Old English* or *Anglo-Saxon (to about A.D. 1100),* Middle English (1100-1500), *and* Modern English; *British English is sometimes called "English English"; Correct English is called the King's* or *Queen's English; Current English is contemporary English; good English; in plain English* (= plainly speaking). **2 the English** *pl.* the people of England. —*adj.* having to do with England, its people, or their Germanic language: *the English Channel, foxhound, language, setter; English grammar, history, literature.*

Eng.lish.man (ING.glish.mun) *n.* -**men** a man of or from England;
Eng.lish.wom.an *n.* -**wom.en.**

en.gorge (en.GORJ) *v.* -**gorg.es, -gorged, -gorg.ing** **1** swallow greedily: *Leeches engorge on their victims' blood.* **2** distend with fluid or blood; *adj.: an* **engorged** *river ready to burst its banks; an engorged erectile organ.*

en.gram *n.* the supposed change in the nerve tissue of the brain for explaining memory, learning, etc.; also called "memory trace."

en.grave (en.GRAVE) *v.* -**graves, -graved, -grav.ing** **1** cut, carve, or etch letters or designs in wood, stone, metal, etc., esp. for printing from. **2** impress: *childhood experiences engraved in our memory.* —**en.grav.er** *n.;*
en.grav.ing *n.*

en.gross (en.GROSE, rhyme: DOSE) *v.* absorb the entire attention of someone: *Homework engrosses all her attention; adj.: a child deeply* **engrossed** *in her homework; an* **engrossing** *thriller; He can spend many engrossing hours doing crosswords.*

en.gulf (en.GULF) *v.* swallow up, as by waves: *The flames soon engulfed the building; He was engulfed by fear; Poverty and misery engulfed the family as a result of the disaster.*

en.hance (en.HANCE) *v.* -**hanc.es, -hanced, -hanc.ing** raise or increase value, beauty, or other desirable quality: *Home improvements enhance the value of property; Prestige is enhanced by victories; Beauty may be enhanced by makeup; A computer can enhance the quality of photographs transmitted from space by filling in missing bits of data; a computer's* **enhanced keyboard** *with 101 or 102 keys including function keys.* —**en.hance.ment** *n.*

e.nig.ma (uh.NIG.muh) *n.* **1** a person who is perplexing because of a mixture of conflicting qualities: *Nick is an enigma because he is kind to strangers and harsh to his neighbors.* **2** something that is ambiguous or cryptic in nature: *The* riddle of the Sphinx about the human being ("Who goes on four legs in the morning, on two at noon, and on three at night?") was an enigma to everyone except Oedipus who solved it. —**en.ig.mat.ic** (en.ig.MAT.ic) *adj.* difficult to interpret: *the Mona Lisa's enigmatic smile; an enigmatic figure, personality, style; The story remains enigmatic.* Also **en.ig.mat.i.cal.**

en.jamb.ment (in.JAM.munt) *n.* the running on of a sentence from one verse to the next, as in the lines "Nor tackle, sail, nor mast; the very rats / Instinctively had quit it." Also **en.jambe.ment.**

en.join (en.JOIN) *v. Formal.* command: *They were enjoined to keep the matter secret; enjoined not to speak to the press; Secrecy was enjoined* (= imposed) *on them.*

en.joy (en.JOY) *v.* take pleasure in something: *He likes school, enjoys games, enjoys doing homework; He is enjoying himself* (= having fun). —**en.joy.a.ble** (-JOY.uh.bul) *adj.*: *We had a highly enjoyable time at the party.* —**en.joy.ment** *n.*: *Hobbies provide enjoyment during leisure hours; She derives great enjoyment from watching hockey.*

en.large (en.LARGE) *v.* **-larg.es, -larged, -larg.ing** make or become larger: *a copier that enlarges and reduces originals.* —**enlarge on** or **upon** discuss at length. —**en.large.ment** *n.*

en.light.en (en.LITE.un) *v.* inform, esp. so as to remove misunderstanding, error, etc.: *Can you enlighten me on the nature of your research project? adj.: an enlightened* (= well-informed) *public; Enlightened self-interest guided Mexico and the U.S. in their trade negotiations; Her speech was instructive and enlightening.* —**en.light.en.ment** *n.*

en.list (en.LIST) *v.* join or get someone to join the military or a cause or undertaking: *to enlist in the armed forces for three years; She enlisted her young son in the navy; We enlisted the help of our neighbors in controlling street crime; an enlisted man* (not a commissioned officer) *in the armed forces.* —**en.list.ee** *n.* —**en.list.ment** *n.*

en.liv.en (en.LYE.vun) *v.* put life into a party, dull surroundings, etc.

en masse (en.MAS) *adv.* all together; in one body: *The staff resigned en masse.*

en.mesh (en.MESH) *v.* take in or as if in a net; entangle: *animal instincts that could enmesh and destroy us; adj.: He found himself enmeshed in his own web of lies; deeply enmeshed in a scandal.*

en.mi.ty (EN.mi.tee) *n.* **-ties** hostility or hatred, as between enemies: *to stir up enmity against, among, between, toward people; racial enmities.*

en.no.ble (en.NOH.bul) *v.* **-bles, -bled, -bling** raise to noble rank or add dignity; also, make noble: *Suffering purifies and ennobles character; adj.: Religion can be spiritually ennobling; ennobling influences, thoughts, words.* —**en.no.ble.ment** *n.*

en.nui (ahn.WEE) *n.* boredom; weariness.

e.nor.mi.ty (i.NOR.mi.tee) *n.* **-ties 1** outrageous or monstrous quality: *the enormity of a crime, of an offense, of his wickedness.* **2** *Informal.* vastness or immensity; enormousness: *the enormity of a problem, situation, task.*

e.nor.mous (i.NOR.mus) *adj.* very much exceeding the normal size, amount, or degree: *an enormous appetite; at enormous expense; a tragedy of enormous proportions; an enormous waste.* —**e.nor.mous.ly** *adv.*; **e.nor.mous.ness** *n.*

e.nough (i.NUF) *adj.* sufficient: *There are blankets enough* (= sufficient number) *for everyone; There is enough food* (= a sufficient quantity of it) *for everyone or food enough for everyone; enough people to help us or people enough to help us; money enough to buy more.* —*n. & pron.* a sufficient number or amount: *That will be enough; I have had enough of this* (= cannot tolerate this any more); *We have enough and to spare* (= more than sufficient); **Enough is enough** (= That's the limit); *He was enough of a fool* (= foolish enough) *to cheat on the exam.* —*adv.* sufficiently: *Sure enough, he was late (as usual); She's well enough to sit up in bed; glad enough* (= quite glad) *to get out of the hospital.*

en.plane (en.PLANE) *v.* **-planes, -planed, -plan.ing** board an aircraft.

enquire, enquiry same as INQUIRE, INQUIRY.

en.rage (en.RAGE) *v.* **-rag.es, -raged, -rag.ing** put in a rage or anger; infuriate: *A personal attack is likely to enrage your opponent; adj.: He was enraged to hear that he had been fired for no reason; quite enraged at or by or with the treatment he was receiving; an enraged bull, electorate, public; an enraged and outraged parent; an enraging remark; She found the Enquirer story more enraging than enthralling.*

en.rap.ture (en.RAP.chur) *v.* **-tures, -tured, -tur.ing** transport with joy: *TV enraptures and entrances children; adj.: an enraptured audience.*

en.rich (en.RICH) *v.* make rich; improve in quality: *Flour and rice are enriched by replacing the vitamins lost in milling the grain; a new laser process to enrich uranium (= increase its fissionable U-235 content) for use in nuclear reactors;* **adj. & cpd:** *white **enriched** bread (with added food value); fiber-enriched diets; oxygen-enriched air; vitamin-enriched cereals.* —**en.rich.ment** *n.*

en.roll (en.ROLE) *v.* **-rolls, -rolled, -roll.ing** enter on a roll or list, as a member of a body of students, electors, or of a club: *Students enroll in or for a course, program; to enroll at a school; A school enrolls students in courses;* **adj.:** *students **enrolled** in college, school, universities; people enrolled in insurance plans, medicare.* —**en.roll.ment** *n.: an enrollment of 3,000 students; college enrollment; heavy, large, small enrollments; an enrollment office.* Also **en.rol, en.rol.ment.**

en route (ahn.ROOT) *adv.* on the way to or *from* a place.

en.sconce (en.SCONCE) *v.* **-sconc.es, -sconced, -sconc.ing** establish oneself securely or snugly: *There she is, enjoying my book ensconced in her favorite chair.*

en.sem.ble (ahn.SAHM.bul) *n.* **1** an integrated set or whole whose parts together produce a single effect, as a matching costume and accessories. **2** music of several parts, a group of singers or actors performing cooperatively, etc.: *an ensemble called the New Chamber Orchestra.*

en.shrine (en.SHRINE) *v.* **-shrines, -shrined, -shrin.ing 1** enclose in or as in a shrine: *The pagoda enshrines two sacred hairs from the head of the Buddha.* **2** keep or cherish as sacred: *civil rights enshrined in the Constitution.*

en.shroud (en.SHROWD) *v.* to shroud or veil: *Clouds enshrouded the mountain top.*

en.sign (EN.sun) *n.* **1** the lowest rank of commissioned officer in the U.S. Navy. **2** (*also* EN.sine) a flag or emblem: *The Red Ensign was Canada's flag until 1965.*

en.si.lage (EN.suh.lij) *n.* ensiled green fodder.

en.sile (en.SILE) *v.* **-siles, -siled, -sil.ing** preserve fodder in a silo.

en.slave (en.SLAVE) *v.* **-slaves, -slaved, -slav.ing** make a slave of someone. —**en.slave.ment** *n.*

en.snare (en.SNARE) *v.* **-snares, -snared, -snar.ing** to snare or trap: *to ensnare a rabbit.*

en.sue (en.SUE) *v.* **-sues, -sued, -su.ing** follow, esp. as a consequence; result: *After the heavy rains a flood ensued;* **adj.:** *There was a drought and then a famine in the **ensuing** year; the ensuing controversy.*

en.sure (en.SURE) *v.* **-sures, -sured, -sur.ing** make certain or secure; guarantee: *Registration ensures delivery of mail; It ensures mail against loss, theft, etc. but does not ensure its being delivered on time; The weatherman cannot ensure that it will or will not rain tomorrow.*

en.tail (en.TAIL) *v.* make something a necessary requirement: *Success entails hard work.*

en.tan.gle (en.TANG.gul) *v.* **-gles, -gled, -gling 1** of hair, string, etc., make tangled or twisted together: *He got entangled in the net he was laying to catch birds.* **2** make or be tangled in a difficult or perplexing situation; **adj.:** *He became **entangled** in a dispute with neighbors; She doesn't like to get or become entangled with other people's problems.* —**en.tan.gle.ment** *n.: He doesn't like entanglements (= involvements) in or with his in-laws' affairs; Barbed-wire entanglements (= fences) were used as barriers in ground warfare.*

en.tente (ahn.TAHNT) *n.* **1** a friendly understanding, esp. between governments. **2** the parties to this, as a coalition.

en.ter (EN.tur) *v.* **1** go or come in: *Knock before entering; to enter by a side door; The burglar entered the house through the window;* [as a stage direction] *Enter Romeo* (= Romeo enters); *Enter the experts; Enter trouble.* **2** get into or join a group, list, record, etc.: *to enter the army, a profession, the practice of law; Words are entered in a dictionary; The accused entered a plea of guilty; It's time to enter* (= enroll) *your child in school; Don't **enter into** (= start) arguments with customers; to **enter on** or **upon** (= begin) a new career.*

en.ter.i.tis (en.tuh.RYE.tis) *n.* inflammation of the intestines

en.ter.prise (EN.tur.prize) *n.* **1** a project or undertaking that requires initiative and risk-taking: *a business enterprise; commercial enterprises; a joint enterprise; The company started as a private enterprise.* **2** initiative and risk-taking: *a woman of great enterprise; Ours is a **free-enterprise** society;* **adj.:** *She's quite **enterprising** (= marked by enterprise); an enterprising woman.*

en.ter.tain (en.tur.TAIN) *v.* **1** receive as a guest: *The Siegels were entertaining the*

enthrall / entrance

Khans last night; They entertain a lot on weekends. **2** please or amuse with something planned or prepared: *Clowns know how to entertain children with funny acts;* **adj.**: *The talk was instructive and* **entertaining. 3** be ready and willing to consider: *to entertain doubts, ideas, opinions, pleas, proposals, suggestions.* —**en.ter.tain.er** *n.*
—**en.ter.tain.ment** *n.*: *Stage shows provide live entertainment; TV affords entertainment for the bed-ridden; It is pure entertainment to watch babies playing.*
—**adj.**: *an entertainment tax (on stage and screen performances); an instructive book with some entertainment value; the* **entertainment industry** (= TV, radio, movies, music records, etc.).
en.thrall (en.THRAWL) *v.* **-thralls, -thralled, -thrall.ing** captivate by fascinating. Also **en.thral.**
en.throne (en.THRONE) *v.* **-thrones, -throned, -thron.ing** put on a throne; hence, exalt: *Elizabeth II was enthroned in 1953; Mercy is "enthroned in the hearts of kings."* —**en.throne.ment** *n.*
en.thuse (en.THOOZ, -THEWZ) *v.* **-thus.es, -thused, -thus.ing** *Informal.* show, feel, or express with enthusiasm: *"A marvelous movie," she enthused;* **adj.**: *We're all* **enthused***, but let us not get too enthused about it.*
en.thu.si.asm (en.THEW.zee.az.um) *n.* intense interest or admiration approaching zeal for a person, pursuit, cause, etc.: *to arouse, demonstrate, display, kindle, radiate, show, stir up enthusiasm for a cause; He expressed great enthusiasm about or over the new leader; her boundless, unbridled, wild enthusiasm; Let's not dampen her enthusiasm by telling her the party may be canceled.*
en.thu.si.ast (en.THEW.zee.ast) *n.* one who is keenly interested in an activity or cause: *a sports enthusiast; an enthusiast for women's rights.*
—**en.thu.si.as.tic** (-AS.tic) *adj.*: *He is an enthusiastic admirer of hers; She seems enthusiastic about or over her new responsibilities.* —**en.thu.si.as.ti.cal.ly** *adv.*
en.tice (en.TICE) *v.* **-tic.es, -ticed, -tic.ing** lure or tempt by skillful or crafty means: *The youth was enticed into running away from home; He was enticed with promises of becoming rich.*
—**en.tice.ment** *n.*
en.tire (en.TIRE) *adj.* unbroken as a unit; with no parts left out; complete in extent or degree: *Her entire savings amount to $19.98; The entire day was spent in conferences; an entire set of the encyclopedia; The skeleton was whole and entire; You have my entire support; I'm in entire agreement with you; He was in entire ignorance of what happened; an entire* (= not gelded or castrated) *horse.*
—**en.tire.ly** *adv.* completely: *I agree with you entirely; time spent entirely on useless pursuits; That's entirely different, unnecessary.* —**en.tire.ty** *n.*: *The proposal was rejected* **in its entirety.**
en.ti.tle (en.TYE.tul) *v.* **-tles, -tled, -tling 1** give a claim or right to something: *Your age entitles you to retirement benefits; You are entitled to your opinions.* **2** title: *a book entitled "Roots."*
—**en.ti.tle.ment** *n.*: *entitlements such as welfare and unemployment benefits.*
en.ti.ty (EN.ti.tee) *n.* **-ties** a person or thing that has independent existence: *Many believe that body and soul are separate entities; Ethnic groups are cultural entities; They try to preserve their entity* (= existence) *and individuality.*
en.tomb (en.TOOM, long "OO") *v.* to place in a tomb or mausoleum; bury.
—**en.tomb.ment** *n.*
en.to.mol.o.gy (en.tuh.MOL.uh.jee) *n.* a branch of zoology concerned with the study of insects; **en.to.mol.o.gist** *n.*
—**en.to.mo.log.i.cal** (-muh.LOJ.i.cul) *adj.*
en.tou.rage (ahn.too.RAHZH) *n.* a group of attendants; retinue: *the Queen's entourage.*
en.tr'acte (ahn.TRACT) *n.* **1** the interval between two acts of a stage performance. **2** a show put on during this period.
en.trails (EN.trailz) *n.pl.* the inner parts, esp. intestines, from a body; guts.
en.train (en.TRAIN) *v.* put or go on board a train.
[1]**en.trance** (EN.trunce) *n.* **1** the act of entering; entry: *His entrance was very dramatic, thanks to the marching band he had hired; He made a grand, triumphal entrance into the stadium; Actors have to know their exits and entrances; A woman's formal entrance into society used to be at a debut; Pearl Harbor marks America's entrance into World War II.* **2** a door or other passageway: *There is an entrance to the house from the garage; The service entrance is for deliveries; A guard is posted at the entrance; Do not block the entrance, or* **entranceway. 3** permission or right to enter; admission: *No one with a valid ticket is refused entrance; High school graduates are qualified for entrance to a university; There is no* **entrance fee** *for club members.*
[2]**en.trance** (en.TRANCE) *v.* **-tranc.es, -tranced, -tranc.ing** transport with joy,

as in a trance or dream; *adj.*: *They were* **entranced** *with the music, entranced at the pageantry, quite entranced over the whole show; The crowd stood entranced by the beauty of the pageant; It held them entranced for over an hour; an* **entrancing** *sight.* —**en.tranc.ing.ly** *adv.*

en.trant (EN.trunt) *n.* one who enters, esp. in a race or contest: *one of many entrants in the marathon.*

en.trap (en.TRAP) *v.* **-traps, -trapped, -trap.ping** catch in or as in a trap: *The police were accused of entrapping them into selling the drug.* —**en.trap.ment** *n.*

en.treat (en.TREET) *v.* ask earnestly and persuasively: *The child entreated her mother to let her watch a late movie.*

en.treat.y (en.TREE.tee) *n.* **-treat.ies** an earnest request: *Their entreaties for mercy fell on deaf ears.*

en.trée or **en.tree** (AHN.tray) *n.* **1** means of entering or the right to enter: *Eminent position or outstanding achievements are the usual entrées to the Who's Who; to gain entrée into an exclusive club.* **2** the main dish of a meal.

en.trench (en.TRENCH) *v.* put trenches around something; hence, fortify or make secure: *His success in the war further entrenched his position.* —**en.trench.ment** *n.*

en.tre.pre.neur (ahn.truh.pruh.NOOR) *n.* one who organizes and manages a business, assuming risks and seeking profits. —**en.tre.pre.neur.i.al** (-NOOR.ee.ul) *adj.*

en.tro.py (EN.truh.pee) *n.* **-pies** a property of matter by which the heat generated in doing work results in a lessening of available energy in a system and its gradual winding down; the tendency to inertness.

en.trust (en.TRUST) *v.* **1** trust someone with a responsibility: *I entrust you with my dog.* **2** trust a responsibility to someone: *I entrust Fido to your care.*

en.try (EN.tree) *n.* **-tries 1** the act, right, or a place of entering: *America's entry into World War II; The hero made a triumphal entry into the city; a burglar's forced entry into a house; He gained entry by breaking a window.* **2** the act of placing in a record or listing, as of words entered alphabetically in a dictionary; also, a thing or person so entered, as in a competition: *All entries have to be postmarked no later than December 31; Each entry starts with "Dear Diary"; A dictionary entry starts with the word's spelling; Bookkeepers make entries for each item of income and expense.*

—**adj.**: *An entry blank or form is filled out and submitted for entering a contest; entry criteria, fees, rules, visas; an* **entry-level** *(= lowest level) job such as dishwasher or stockroom clerk; an* **entry word** *(= headword) in a dictionary.*

en.twine (en.TWINE) *v.* **-twines, -twined, -twin.ing** twist or weave together or around.

e.nu.mer.ate (i.NEW.muh.rate) *v.* **-ates, -at.ed, -at.ing 1** list or name one by one: *My reasons are too many to enumerate; to enumerate the advantages, circumstances, facts, qualities, various items.* **2** count: *to enumerate the population of an area; to enumerate* (= make a census of) *an electoral district.*
—**e.nu.mer.a.tion** (-RAY.shun) *n.*
—**e.nu.mer.a.tor** (-ray.tur) *n.*

e.nun.ci.ate (i.NUN.see.ate) *v.* **-ates, -at.ed, -at.ing 1** pronounce distinctly: *Actors have to enunciate clearly for the audience to hear what they are saying.* **2** set forth systematically: *to enunciate a doctrine, principle, theory.*
—**e.nun.ci.a.tion** (-AY.shun) *n.*: *an announcer with good enunciation* (= manner of pronunciation).

en.u.re.sis (en.yoo.REE.sis) *n.* Med. habitual bed-wetting.

en.vel.op (en.VEL.up) *v.* **-ops, -oped, -op.ing** cover completely: *The mountain tops were enveloped in mist.*
—**en.vel.op.ment** *n.*

en.ve.lope (EN.vuh.lope, AHN-) *n.* a cover, esp. a flat paper container for mailing letters in: *We address, stamp, and seal envelopes before mailing; Please enclose a stamped, self-addressed envelope for a quick reply; A* **pay envelope** *contains a pay check or wages.* —**push the envelope** push the boundaries; expand: *to push the envelope of computer capacity.*

en.ven.om (en.VEN.um) *v.* **1** taint with venom or poison. **2** embitter.

en.vi.a.ble (EN.vee.uh.bul) *adj.* worthy of being envied: *My former helper is now in an enviable position as company president.* —**en.vi.a.bly** *adv.*

en.vi.ous (EN.vee.us) *adj.* feeling or showing envy: *Cinderella's sisters were envious of her beauty and jealous of her success with the prince.* —**en.vi.ous.ly** *adv.*

en.vi.ron.ment (en.VYE.run.munt, -urn.munt) *n.* **1** surroundings or habitat, esp. as affecting the development of an individual or community: *A child's own family should be the most healthy environment for its upbringing; to clean up, preserve, protect, pollute the environment* (= the air, water, soil, scenery, etc. around us); *the work environment.*

environs / epidemiology

2 a computer's hardware and its operating system: *the Windows environment; IBM and Mac environments; various operating environments.*
—**en.vi.ron.men.tal** (-MEN.tul) *adj.*: *Pesticides, exhaust fumes, and industrial wastes cause environmental pollution; Environmental art, sculpture, and theater involve or engage the viewer as well as artist; an environmental protection agency to deal with environmental problems;* **en.vi.ron.men.tal.ly** *adv.*
—**en.vi.ron.men.tal.ist** *n.*
en.vi.rons (en.VYE.runs, -urns) *n.pl.* **1** surroundings: *customer-friendly environs; factory environs.* **2** suburbs: *a city and its environs; commuters from outside the environs of the city.*
en.vis.age (en.VIZ.ij) *v.* **-ag.es, -aged, -ag.ing** form a mental picture of something, esp. under a particular aspect such as the future; visualize: *The lobbyist envisaged many problems in the proposed legislation; We envisage that the proposal will be accepted without delay.*
en.vi.sion (en.VIZH.un) *v.* form a mental picture of something, as if in a vision: *to envision a world full of peace and happiness.*
en.voy (EN.voy, AHN.voy) *n.* **1** a messenger, esp. a government official sent on a mission: *The president despatched his personal envoy to Rome to negotiate the treaty; An* **envoy extraordinary** *is a diplomatic official ranking next below an ambassador.* **2** a short farewell message in the form of a literary postscript or concluding stanza; also **en.voi.**
en.vy (EN.vee) *n.* **-vies 1** a feeling of wishing that one had what another enjoys: *Kay was consumed or green with envy; an object of envy; In a community racked by petty jealousies and envies many things are done out of mere envy; People feel, show envy; Others arouse or stir up envy by their behavior.* **2** the object of such feeling: *Lee's red convertible was the envy of the neighborhood.*
—*v.* **-vies, -vied, -vy.ing** feel envy toward someone: *Eve envies Flo; Many girls envy her curly hair; I envy your good fortune, but I don't envy you your job.*
en.zyme (EN.zime) *n.* a catalytic protein substance found in yeast and digestive juices: *Body irritants may be released by* **enzyme detergents** *used in dissolving stains.*
E.o.cene (EE.uh.seen) *n. & adj.* (of) the second epoch of the Cenozoic era of the earth beginning about 55 million years ago, marked by the rise of mammals: *Eocene rocks.*

eolian same as AEOLIAN.
e.o.lith (EE.uh.lith) *n.* a crude stone tool.
e.o.lith.ic (ee.uh.LITH.ic) *adj.* of the early Stone Age, characterized by eoliths.
e.on (EE.un, EE.on) *n.* a long and indefinite period of time; an age: *Eons have passed since the universe came into being.*
ep.au.let or **ep.au.lette** (EP.uh.let) *n.* an ornamental shoulder pad on a military uniform.
é.pee or **é.pée** (EP.ay, ay.PAY) *n.* a sharp-pointed, rigid sword with a circular guard used in fencing.
e.phed.rine (i.FED.rin) *n.* a drug that shrinks mucous membranes, used in treating asthma, hay fever, etc.
e.phem.er.al (i.FEM.uh.rul) *adj.* **1** short-lived or passing, as glory or pleasures: *art that has only ephemeral value; writings of ephemeral interest; He only had a temporary, if not ephemeral influence on poetry.* **2** originally, lasting no more than a few days, as certain plants, insects, etc.
ep.ic (EP.ic) *n.* **1** a long poem in a majestic style and with a heroic theme: *Greek and Roman epics by Homer and Virgil; The Ramayana is a Sanskrit epic.* **2** a long story that is full of adventure and heroism: *action-packed western movie epics.* —**adj***a.* heroic and adventurous: *the epic deeds of Ulysses; an epic battle, drama, struggle, voyage; a tragedy of epic (= vast) proportions.*
ep.i.cen.ter (EP.uh.sen.tur) *n.* the point on the earth's surface directly above the focus of an earthquake. Also **ep.i.cen.tre** *Cdn.* —**ep.i.cen.tral** (-SEN.trul) *adj.*
ep.i.cure (EP.uh.cure) *n.* a person with a highly refined taste for food and wine.
ep.i.cu.re.an (ep.uh.kew.REE.un) *adj.* given to sensuous pleasure, esp. of eating and drinking.
—*n.* same as EPICURE.
ep.i.dem.ic (ep.uh.DEM.ic) *adj.* spreading rapidly, as contagious diseases: *Measles could become epidemic if not controlled; an epidemic attack, fever; Dieting has reached epidemic proportions.*
—*n.* **1** an epidemic disease: *cholera, flu, typhoid epidemics; Epidemics break out, spread, if they are not contained or controlled; An epidemic touched off* or *triggered by a flu bug in 1918 became a pandemic.* **2** any rapid development, as of a fad: *The hula hoop started an epidemic in the 1950s.*
ep.i.de.mi.ol.o.gy (EP.uh.dee.mee.OL.

uh.jee) *n.* the branch of medicine concerned with epidemics; **ep.i.de.mi.ol.o.gist** *n.*

ep.i.der.mis (ep.uh.DUR.mis) *n.* the outer layer of the skin. —**ep.i.der.mal** *adj.*

ep.i.glot.tis (ep.uh.GLOT.is) *n.* a lidlike piece of elastic cartilage that closes the windpipe during swallowing.

ep.i.gram (EP.uh.gram) *n.* a terse witty saying, esp. one with a paradox in it, as "Revenge is a kind of wild justice." —**ep.i.gram.mat.ic** (-gruh.MAT.ic) *adj.*

ep.i.graph (EP.uh.graf) *n.* a motto or quotation written at the front of a building, statue, tomb, etc. or at the beginning of a book or chapter. **e.pig.ra.phy** (i.PIG.ruh.fee) *n.* the study of ancient inscriptions. —**ep.i.graph.ic** (ep.uh.GRAF.ic) *adj.*: *epigraphic evidence.*

ep.i.lep.sy (ep.uh.LEP.see) *n.* **-sies** a chronic nervous disorder marked by convulsions and unconsciousness. —**ep.i.lep.tic** (-tic) *n.* one who has epilepsy; *adja.: an epileptic fit, seizure, spike; epileptic symptoms.*

ep.i.logue (EP.uh.log) *n.* a concluding act or piece, as at the end of a play, poem, etc. Also **ep.i.log.**

ep.i.neph.rine (ep.uh.NEF.rin) *n.* an adrenal hormone used therapeutically to stimulate the heart, relax muscles, etc. Also **ep.i.neph.rin.**

e.piph.a.ny (i.PIF.uh.nee) *n.* a revelation or discovery, like the visit of the Magi to Jesus at Bethlehem, commemorated as **Epiphany,** a Christian festival held on January 6.

ep.i.phyte (EP.uh.fite) *same as* AIR PLANT.

e.pis.co.pa.cy (i.PIS.cuh.puh.see) *n.* **-cies 1** episcopal government. **2** episcopate.

e.pis.co.pal (i.PIS.cuh.pul) *adja.* having to do with bishops: *episcopal government, jurisdiction;* The (Protestant) **Episcopal Church** in the U.S. belongs to the Anglican communion. —**E.pis.co.pa.li.an** (-PAIL.yun) *n. & adj.* (a member) of this church.

e.pis.co.pate (i.PIS.cuh.pit) *n.* **1** a bishop's rank, term of office, or see. **2** bishops collectively.

ep.i.sode (EP.uh.sode) *n.* **1** an incident in a continuous course of events that is complete in itself, as in a literary or artistic work. **2** such a musical passage. **3** any occurrence or event: *a coronary episode; an episode of his childhood.* —**ep.i.sod.ic** (-SOD.ic) *adj.;* **ep.i.sod.i.cal.ly** *adv.*

e.pis.tle (i.PIS.ul) *n.* **1** *Formal.* a letter. **2 Epistle** one of the apostolic letters of the New Testament. —**e.pis.to.lar.y** (i.PIS.tuh.lair.ee) *adj.*

ep.i.taph (EP.uh.taf) *n.* a short inscription, as on a tombstone or tablet, in memory of a dead person.

ep.i.the.li.um (ep.uh.THEE.lee.um) *n., pl.* **-li.a** (-lee.uh) a kind of tissue that covers body surfaces, as the skin and mucous membrane. —**ep.i.the.li.al** (-lee.ul) *adj.*

ep.i.thet (EP.uh.thet) *n.* a word or phrase to characterize someone, usu. descriptive, as "doubting Thomas," often disparaging, as "silly goose": *a colorful epithet; a racist who often hurls or shouts or spews epithets at people; harsh, nasty, racial, vile epithets; His speeches are marked by epithet* (= name-calling) *and abuse.*

e.pit.o.me (i.PIT.uh.mee) *n.* **1** a summary or abstract giving essential features. **2** a person or thing that typifies a specified quality: *Satan is the epitome of evil.*

e.pit.o.mize (i.PIT.uh.mize) *v.* **-miz.es, -mized, -miz.ing 1** make a summary of something. **2** typify: *Satan epitomizes evil; a remark that epitomizes his attitude.*

ep.och (EP.uc, EE.poc) *n.* a period of time, esp. with reference to some memorable event; era: *The earth was covered by glaciers during the glacial epoch; Space exploration has ushered in a new epoch in human history; Our landing on the moon marks a new epoch; adj.: It was an epoch-making event.* —**ep.och.al** (EP.uh.cul) *adj.*

ep.o.nym (EP.uh.nim) *n.* a person from whom an institution, place, theory, movement, etc. is said to get its name: *A. G. Eiffel is the eponym of the Eiffel Tower.*

ep.on.y.mous (ep.ON.uh.mus) *adja.* giving one's name: *the eponymous edifice of A. G. Eiffel; the eponymous hero* (= Anne) *of "Anne of Green Gables."*

ep.ox.y (i.POX.ee) *n.* **-ox.ies** a durable synthetic resin used for adhesives, protective coatings, etc.; also called "epoxy resin"; *adja.: an epoxy coating, finish, glue, paint.* —*v.* **-ox.ies, -ox.ied, -ox.y.ing** to glue with epoxy resin.

ep.si.lon (EP.suh.lon) *n.* the fifth letter of the Greek alphabet (E, ε).

Ep.som salt (or **salts**) (EP.sum-) *n.* a white crystalline magnesium salt used as a laxative.

eq.ua.ble (EK.wuh.bul) *adj.* not liable to change suddenly; steady: *an equable temper;* **eq.ua.bly** (-blee) *adv.*

equal / equitation

—**eq.ua.bil.i.ty** (-BIL.i.tee) *n.*
e.qual (EEK.wul) *adj.* of the same amount, number, size, value, degree, spread, advantage, etc.: *We are all created equal; A dollar divides into four equal parts of 25 cents each; It's equal in value to four quarters; A quarter is equal to 25 cents; Minorities deserve equal employment opportunities (with the majority groups); Women fought for equal rights with men; We want equal pay for work of equal value; I don't feel* **equal to** (= fit enough for) *my usual walk today; to compete on (an)* **equal footing** *with others; An* **equal-opportunity** *employer gives an equal chance to everyone regardless of sex, race, religion, age, etc.; the* **equal sign** [=]; *the right to* **equal time** *on radio or TV to air an opposing view.* —*n.* one that is equal: *David and Goliath were not equals; Goliath had no equal in physical strength.* —*v.* **e.quals, e.qualed, e.qual.ing** be or make equal to a person or thing: *Two plus two equals four; Her record has not been equaled, let alone broken; There was no one to equal Goliath in strength.* Also **e.qualled, e.qual.ling** *Cdn.* —**e.qual.ly** *adv.*
e.qual.i.ty (ee.KWOL.i.tee) *n.* -**ties** the state or an instance of being equal: *to achieve* or *attain equality of opportunity; equality between the sexes; equality among the various sections of the population.*
e.qual.ize (EEK.wuh.lize) *v.* **-iz.es, -ized, -iz.ing** make equal, even, or uniform: **e.qual.i.zer** *n.* —**e.qual.i.za.tion** (-luh.ZAY.shun, -lye-) *n.*
e.qua.nim.i.ty (eek.wuh.NIM.i.tee) *n.* evenness of mind or temper: *She listened to the bad news with equanimity; It didn't upset her equanimity.*
e.quate (ee.QUATE) *v.* **e.quates, e.quat.ed, e.quat.ing** treat one thing as equal to another: *We don't equate happiness with wealth.* —**e.quat.a.ble** *adj.*
e.qua.tion (ee.QUAY.zhun) *n.* **1** an equating: *the equation of happiness with wealth.* **2** a sentence using symbols that says two expressions containing at least one variable element in them are equal: *a chemistry equation showing a reaction; a mathematical equation such as* "a + b = 0"; *to formulate, solve, state an equation.* **3** a variable element in a complex whole: *the human equation; the personal equation.* **4** a condition involving an equivalent relationship: *The movement of people between suburbs and cities is one of the prime equations of our social history; the supply-and-demand equation.*
e.qua.tor (ee.QUAY.tur) *n.* **1** an imaginary circle around a sphere, esp. the earth or a heavenly body, that divides it equally into two hemispheres: *North America is north of the equator.* **2** the corresponding circle in the celestial sphere: *the celestial equator.*
—**e.qua.tor.i.al** (eek.wuh.TOR.ee.ul) *adj.*: *an equatorial current.*
eq.uer.ry (EK.wuh.ree, i.KWER.ee) *n.* **eq.uer.ries 1** an officer attending on a member of the British royal family. **2** formerly, one in charge of horses.
e.ques.tri.an (i.QUES.tree.un) *adja.* on horseback: *equestrian events such as cross-country riding and show jumping; a circus performer's equestrian skills; an equestrian statue (showing the subject on horseback).* —*n.* a horseback rider; **e.ques.tri.enne** (i.ques.tree.EN), *fem.*
e.qui.dis.tant (eek.wuh.DIS.tunt) *adj.* equally distant: *Montreal and New York are equidistant from Vancouver.*
e.qui.lat.er.al (eek.wuh.LAT.uh.rul) *adj.* having all sides equal: *an equilateral triangle.*
e.qui.lib.ri.um (eek.wuh.LIB.ree.um) *n.* state of balance: *He lost his equilibrium and fell into the river; The canals of the inner ear are what help us maintain our equilibrium; Adding weights to one pan of a balance will upset the equilibrium.*
e.quine (EE.quine, EK.wine) *adj.* having to do with horses: *equine encephalitis, events, flu, research, vets.* —*n.* a horse.
e.qui.nox (EEK.wuh.nox) *n.* either of two times of the year when the sun crosses the equator and day and night are of equal length all over the globe: *the autumnal equinox; the spring* or *vernal equinox.* —**e.qui.noc.tial** (-NOK.shul) *adj.*
e.quip (i.QUIP) *v.* **e.quips, e.quipped, e.quip.ping** supply or provide with what is needed to make an occupation or function more efficient: *a car equipped with power steering; a party well equipped for camping out; First aid equips one to deal with life-and-death emergencies.*
—**e.quip.ment** *n.*: *military equipment; office equipment; sports equipment such as bats, gloves, masks, and helmets.*
e.quip.age (EK.wuh.pij) *n.* a carriage with horses, driver, and attendants.
e.qui.poise (EK.wuh.poiz) *n.* **1** even balance; equilibrium. **2** a force or weight that restores balance; counterbalance.
eq.ui.ta.ble (EK.wuh.tuh.bul) *adj.* characterized by equity: *Preferential hiring of minority candidates is considered equitable by some and unjust by others.*
—**eq.ui.ta.bly** *adv.*
eq.ui.ta.tion (ek.wuh.TAY.shun) *n.*

horsemanship.

eq.ui.ty (EK.wuh.tee) *n.* **-ties 1** fairness or justice; hence, a law that goes beyond common law and statutes, based on reason and the spirit of the law: *a court of equity.* **2** what a property is worth beyond what is owed on it: *The equity on your home increases as you pay off the mortgage.* **3 equities** *pl.* the ordinary shares of a corporation: *the equity market* (= stock market).

e.quiv.a.lent (i.QUIV.uh.lunt) *adj.* having equal force, value, effect, significance, etc.: *Send us $20 or an equivalent amount in pesos; A mile is equivalent to 1.609 km.* —*n.*: *Today's dollar is the equivalent of a quarter some years back; Few words have exact equivalents in different languages.* —**e.quiv.a.lence** *n.*

e.quiv.o.cal (i.QUIV.uh.cul) *adj.* **1** capable of more than one interpretation: *an equivocal answer, attitude, reply, statement; He sounded equivocal* (= ambivalent or deceptive) *about joining the party.* **2** of language or behavior, doubtful or questionable: *Does dual citizenship mean equivocal loyalties?*

e.quiv.o.cate (i.QUIV.uh.cate) *v.* **-cates, -cat.ed, -cat.ing** use words of double meaning in order to deceive. —**e.quiv.o.ca.tion** (-CAY.shun) *n.* —**e.quiv.o.ca.tor** (-cay.tur) *n.*

-er 1 *n. suffix.* agent or other person or thing related to something specified: *gardener, singer, six-footer.* **2** *adj. suffix* [forming comparatives]: *harder, taller, wiser.*

e.ra (EER.uh, AIR.uh) *n.* a period of time, esp. one starting from a particular event or one with distinctive characteristics: *Animals appeared in the Cenozoic era of the earth; The Christian era; in the Victorian era; The automobile ushered in a new era in transportation.*

e.rad.i.cate (i.RAD.uh.cate) *v.* **-cates, -cat.ed, -cat.ing** completely get rid of something that has established itself; uproot or eliminate: *reforms to eradicate social injustices; a program to eradicate poverty; to eradicate bad habits, crime, diseases, ignorance, illiteracy, vice.* —**e.rad.i.ca.tion** (-CAY.shun) *n.*

e.rase (i.RACE) *v.* **e.ras.es, e.rased, e.ras.ing** wipe out, esp. by rubbing or scraping, as a by a rubber **eraser**, or magnetically, as by a tape recorder's **erase head**. —**e.ras.a.ble** (-suh.bul) *adj.*

e.ras.ure (i.RAY.zhur) *n.* an erasing or where something has been erased.

er.bi.um (UR.bee.um) *n.* a rare-earth metallic element.

ere (AIR) *prep. & conj.* [old use] before.

e.rect (i.RECT) *adj.* upright, esp. straight, not bent or lying down: *Soldiers stand erect; an erect post; Apes don't have the erect posture of human beings.* —*v.* **1** make erect: *to erect* (= put up) *a building, flagpole, statue, tent.* **2** establish: *a monument erected in memory of war heroes.* —**e.rec.tion** *n.* —**e.rect.ly** *adv.*; **e.rect.ness** *n.* —**e.rec.tor** *n.*

e.rec.tile (i.REC.tul, -tile) *adj.* **1** capable of erecting: *an erectile organ; erectile tissue.* **2** having to do with erecting: *erectile dysfunction, failure, problems.*

ere.long (air.LONG) *adv.* before long.

erg (URG) *n.* the unit of energy in the metric system.

er.go (UR.goh) *adv.* therefore; hence.

er.go.nom.ics (ur.guh.NOM.ics) *n.pl.* the science of human work and efficient working conditions. —**er.go.nom.ic** *adj.*: *ergonomic design, furniture, products.*

er.gos.ter.ol (ur.GOS.tuh.role) *n.* a steroid alcohol, prepared from yeast or ergot, that produces vitamin D when exposed to ultraviolet light.

er.got (UR.gut) *n.* a parasitic fungus of cereal plants, esp. rye.

er.mine (UR.min) *n.* **1** the white winter fur of a weasel, that is valuable as trimming and is traditionally used on the robes of judges and European peers as a symbol of rank; **adj.**: *ermine caps, coats, jackets;* **adj. & cpd.**: *an ermined judge in her ermine-trimmed robe; ermine-lined boots.* **2** the animal itself.

e.rode (i.RODE) *v.* **e.rodes, e.rod.ed, e.rod.ing** wear away by gradual action, esp. of water, wind, acid, etc.: *Running water erodes soil and rocks; It erodes* (= forms by wearing away) *channels on the face of the earth;* **adj.**: *Canyons are spectacular examples of the* **eroding** *power of water; eroding prices, profits, standards; the eroding quality of life.*

e.rog.e.nous (i.ROJ.uh.nus) *adj.* sexually sensitive or arousing: *the erogenous parts of the body; erogenous zones.*

e.ro.sion (i.ROH.zhun) *n.* eroding or an act of eroding: *Canyons are the result of erosion; erosion by water and wind; the erosion of authority, popular support, trust.* —**e.ro.sive** (-ziv) *adj.*: *erosive arthritis.*

e.rot.ic (i.ROT.ic) *adj.* having to do with sexual desire: *erotic love, pleasure; erotic arousal, art, fantasies, feelings, literature, movies, novelties, toys.* —**e.rot.i.cal.ly** *adv.*

e.rot.i.ca (i.ROT.uh.cuh) *n.pl.* erotic literature, art, etc.

err (UR, AIR) *v.* do or be wrong: *"To err is human, to forgive divine"; You can* never **err on the side of** honesty (= You can never be too honest).

er.rand (ER.und) *n.* a trip to do something for someone else, as to deliver a message: *His job is to go on or run or do errands for everyone in the office; to send him on an errand; Florence Nightingale's errands of mercy as a nurse;* **adj.:** *an errand boy, service.*

er.rant (ER.unt) *adj.* **1** roving: *an errant knight.* **2** straying: *errant sheep.*

er.rat.a (uh.RAT.uh, uh.RAH-) *n.pl.* errors made in a book or other publication.

er.rat.ic (uh.RAT.ic) *adj.* irregular or eccentric: *erratic behavior, progress, weather; an erratic course, economy, heartbeat.* —**er.rat.i.cal.ly** *adv.*

er.ro.ne.ous (uh.ROH.nee.us) *adj.* mistaken or incorrect: *the erroneous assumption that the earth is flat; erroneous beliefs, ideas, notions.* —**er.ro.ne.ous.ly** *adv.*

er.ror (ER.ur) *n.* something mistaken, a wrong or incorrect action, a misplay or failure in a game, etc.: *an error in judgment; an error of taste; an error compounded by mismanagement; The accident was caused by human error; to commit, correct, make, rectify an error; a clerical, costly, egregious, flagrant, glaring, grievous, serious, tactical error; She's* **in error** (= mistaken) *about my birth date; Lou opened Lee's letter* **by** *or* **in error** (= by mistake); *He repented of his errors* (= moral wrongs) *in his old age;* **errors and omissions excepted** (= not liable for errors and omissions); **adj.:** *errors-and-omissions clauses, insurance, liabilities, suits.*

er.satz (UR.zahts, ER-) *adj.* substitute or imitated, hence inferior: *Margarine is ersatz butter; the ersatz culture of the newly rich.*

erst.while (URST.while) *adj.* of a little while ago; former: *Her erstwhile admirer is marrying someone else tomorrow.*

e.ruct (i.RUCT) *v.* belch. —**e.ruc.ta.tion** (i.ruc.TAY.sun) *n.*

er.u.dite (ER.yuh.dite, ER.uh-) *adj.* learned or scholarly: *an erudite man, scholar, woman; an erudite work in literary criticism.*

er.u.di.tion (er.yuh.DISH.un) *n.* learning and scholarship, esp. of the specialized kind: *a man of great erudition whose works are not for the masses; His books show amazing erudition without being pedantic.*

e.rupt (i.RUPT) *v.* break out or burst forth: *Volcanoes erupt (lava); Hot water and steam erupt from geysers; A riot erupted; Milk teeth erupt during a baby's first year.* —**e.rup.tion** *n.: rashes and other skin eruptions; a volcanic eruption.*

e.ryth.ro.cyte (i.RITH.ruh.cite) *n.* a red blood cell.

e.ryth.ro.my.cin (i.RITH.ruh.MY.sin) *n.* an antibiotic similar in action to penicillin.

-es *suffix.* **1** noun plural: *ashes, glasses, ladies, leaves.* **2** third pers. sing. pres. tense of verb: *defies, goes, washes.*

es.ca.late (ES.cuh.late) *v.* **-lates, -lat.ed, -lat.ing** rise as on an escalator; hence, increase, expand, intensify, develop, etc.: *A small incident escalates into a major confrontation;* **adj.:** *an* **escalating** *battle, crisis, debt, threat; escalating demands, prices, tension, violence, wages.*
—**es.ca.la.tion** (-LAY.shun) *n.*

es.ca.la.tor (ES.cuh.lay.tur) *n.* **1** a moving staircase on an endless belt: *the up escalator and the down escalator.* **2** same as **escalator clause**, a provision for adjusting wages, prices, etc. upward under specified conditions.
—**es.ca.la.tor.y** (-luh.tor.ee) *adj.: a settlement considered too escalatory.*

es.cal.lop (es.CAL.up, es.COLL.up) same as SCALLOP.

es.ca.pade (ES.cuh.pade) *n.* an adventurous act, esp. one involving freedom from restraint: *a childish Halloween escapade that turned into a tragedy; sexual escapades.*

es.cape (es.CAPE) *v.* **-capes, -caped, -cap.ing 1** get away or get away from somewhere: *Convicts try to escape from prison; Air has escaped from the tire; A cry of pain escaped her lips; Her name escapes* (= eludes) *me.* **2** stay free of something: *Many criminals escape being caught; He escaped death by sheer luck.*
—*n.* an escaping or a means of escaping: *a narrow, hairbreadth escape from death; to foil* or *thwart an escape; an escape from captivity; the escape of air from a tire; Romances are her favorite escape (from reality); He clambered down the fire escape* (= emergency staircase); *The burglar made good* (= effected) *his escape before the police arrived.*
—**adj.:** *an escape hatch, valve; an* **escaped** *convict, hostage, prisoner; an* **escape artist** (expert at escaping from any confining situation); *an* **escape clause** *to release a party from contractual obligations under specified conditions.*

es.cap.ee (es.CAY.pee, es.cay.PEE) *n.* one who has escaped, esp. from confinement. Also **es.cap.er** (es.CAY.pur).

escape literature *n.* literature that helps

to free the reader from the pressures of reality.

escape mechanism *n.* a mode of behavior such as daydreaming that helps people evade unpleasant realities and responsibilities.

es.cape.ment (es.CAPE.munt) *n.* a device, as in a timepiece or a typewriter, that regulates movement by means of a ratchet mechanism.

escape velocity *n.* the minimum velocity required to be free of a gravitational field and move into outer space.

es.cap.ism (es.CAY.piz.um) *n.* flight from unpleasant realities, responsibilities, etc. by means of diversions.
—**es.cap.ist** *n.*: *He's a dreamer and an escapist; adj.: an escapist attitude, fantasy, myth, show; escapist literature.*

es.car.got (es.car.GOH) *n.* **-gots** a garden snail that is eaten as a delicacy.

es.ca.role (ES.cuh.role) See ENDIVE.

es.carp.ment (es.CARP.munt) *n.* a steep slope or embankment of considerable length.

-escent *adj. suffix.* **1** beginning to be: *luminescent, obsolescent.* **2** displaying light: *incandescent, iridescent.* **-escence** *n.*

es.chew (es.CHOO) *v.* shun or avoid with special care: *to eschew vice and practice virtue; to eschew clichés, force, politics, rhetoric, violence.*
—**es.chew.al** *n.*

es.cort (ES.cort) *n.* a person or group accompanying another to give protection or as courtesy: *The police provided an escort for the procession; They proceeded under police escort; She came to the dance without an escort* (= male companion); *adj.: an escort (aircraft) carrier, fighter (plane), vessel; The madam running the escort service only provides dates.* —*v.* (es.CORT) go with someone as an escort: *The receptionist escorted the visitor to the door; Fifty aircraft escorted the royal yacht.*

es.crow (ES.croh) *n.* Law. esp. **in escrow,** of a grantor's money, deeds, bonds, etc., held by a third party or **escrow agent,** to be given to the grantee when terms stated in a contract are met.

es.cu.do (es.COO.doh) *n.* **-dos** the basic monetary unit of Chile and Portugal.

es.cutch.eon (is.CUTCH.un) *n.* a shield or similar plate on which a coat of arms is displayed: *a blot, blotch, smudge on one's escutcheon.*

-ese *suffix.* **1** *n. & adj.* (a person) of or from a specified country: *Assamese, Chinese, Portuguese.* **2** *n.* a jargon or occupational dialect: *bureaucratese, computerese, legalese.*

Es.ki.mo (ES.kuh.moh) *n.* **-mos 1** one of a native people of the Arctic, properly called "the Inuit." **2** their language.
—**Es.ki.mo** or **Es.ki.mo.an** (-MOH.un) *adj.*

Eskimo dog *n.* a powerful breed of dog used to pull sleds in the Arctic, including the Siberian husky and the Alaskan malamute.

e.soph.a.gus (i.SOF.uh.gus) *n., pl.* **-gi** (-jye) the tube that carries food down to the stomach; gullet.

es.o.ter.ic (es.uh.TER.ic) *adj.* unintelligible except to those initiated: *an esoteric doctrine, system; esoteric ideas, literature.*

es.pa.drille (ES.puh.dril) *n.* a light canvas shoe with plaited or rubber sole.

es.pal.ier (es.PAL.yur) *n.* **1** a shrub or tree trained to grow flat on a framework. **2** the lattice or other framework used.

es.pe.cial (es.PESH.ul) *adja.* special in a pre-eminent manner; exceptional: *Special consideration was given in her especial case because of the disability; a matter of especial interest to some operators.*
—**es.pe.cial.ly** *adv.*: *an especially hot day; movies, especially westerns; Use your headlights, especially after dark.*

Es.pe.ran.to (es.puh.RAHN.toh) *n.* an artificial international language based on common elements of European languages, e.g. "Esperanto meritas vian konsideron" (Esperanto deserves your consideration).

es.pi.o.nage (ES.pee.uh.nahzh, -uh.nij) *n.* spying for political, military, or industrial purposes: *to conduct* or *engage in espionage.*

es.pla.nade (es.pluh.NAHD, -NADE) *n.* a place designated as a public walk or drive, usu. along a shore.

es.pous.al (i.SPOW.zul) *n.* **1** an espousing of a cause or idea. **2 espousals** *pl.* formerly, betrothal or wedding ceremonies.

es.pouse (is.POWZE) *v.* **-pous.es, -poused, -pous.ing** advocate or take up: *to espouse a cause, doctrine, goal, idea, issue, measure, plan, policy, position, principle, theory, view; the values that we espouse in our society.*

es.pres.so (es.PRES.oh) *n.* **-pres.sos** coffee brewed under steam pressure.

es.prit (es.PREE) *n.* **1** lively wit. **2** esprit de corps.

es.prit de corps (es.PREE.duh.COR) *n.* group spirit; comradeship.

es.py (es.PYE) *v.* **-pies, -pied, -py.ing** catch sight of, esp. something small or partly hidden.

-esque *adj. suffix.* like what is specified: *Disneyesque, picturesque, statuesque.*

es.quire (ES.quire) *n.* an Anglo-Saxon title of courtesy used formally after a man's surname, esp. by lawyers, instead of "Mr." or other prefixed title: *Chris Capone, Esq., Barrister & Solicitor.*

-ess *n. suffix.* female: *empress, lioness, mistress;* [derogatory] *Jewess, negress, poetess.*

es.say (ES.ay) *n.* **1** a literary composition, usu. short and in prose, less formal than a treatise. **2** (*also* es.AY) a trial or attempt.
—*v.* (*usu.* es.AY) attempt: *Before leaping in, she essayed to find out how deep the water was;* **es.say.er** *n.*
—**es.say.ist** *n.* an essay-writer.

es.sence (ES.unce) *n.* **1** the basic or most important nature or quality, as the "greenness" of grass: *The essence of good manners is thoughtfulness; She is the very essence* (= embodiment) *of good manners; That is what it means* **in essence** (= essentially); *Time is of the essence* (= a most important consideration) *in an emergency.* **2** something abstracted, extracted, or distilled, as the gist of a speech, a meat extract, a perfume, etc.

es.sen.tial (i.SEN.shul) *adj.* having to do with what is basic or most important: *Food is necessary for survival, but life jackets are essential for safety in water; It's essential that everyone wear a life jacket; Breathing is essential to life; "Attar of roses" is an* **essential oil** *extracted from rose petals.* —*n.*: *The three R's are the essentials of a good education; the bare* or *basic* **essentials** *for survival in the jungle.*
—**es.sen.tial.ly** *adv.*

-est *suffix.* **1** *adj. & adv.* superlative degree: *greatest, soonest;* [Informal] *swingingest, winningest.* **2** *v.* Archaic. second pers. sing. pres. tense: *singest, walkest;* also **-st**: *canst, didst.*

est or **EST** *n.* a psychological training program for developing one's personality and potential.

es.tab.lish (is.TAB.lish) *v.* set up on a firm foundation: *a company established in 1827; A dentist establishes himself in a neighborhood; Much evidence is needed to establish a motive; It was finally established that he was innocent;* **adj.**: *It takes time for a practice to get* **established** (= accepted) *as a custom; Words get established by usage; Our dentist is now well established in our neighborhood; an established market, relationship; the established order; a long established system of government; the* **established church** (= state church) *of England.*

es.tab.lish.ment (is.TAB.lish.munt) *n.* **1** an establishing or thing established, as a household or business with all its members or employees. **2** a controlling group: *the literary establishment; the medical establishment.* **3 the Establishment**, the dominant social group; the elite: *the Washington Establishment; The Establishment prefers pinstripes to jeans.*

es.tate (is.TATE) *n.* **1** a large property, including a house: *He owns a large tea estate; a coffee estate; rubber estates.* **2** what one owns, esp. as left by a deceased person: *to come into an estate* (= inherit property); *real estate* (= immovable property); *an* **estate tax** (= succession duty); *an* **estate wagon** (*Brit. for* station wagon). **3** condition or stage in life: *A boy reaches man's estate* (= adulthood as a man); *The nobles, clergy, and common people were the three estates.*

es.teem (is.TEEM) *n.* great regard: *She is held in high* or *great esteem as a surgeon; She rose in the esteem of her staff as the years went by, while some fell in their esteem; public esteem; self-esteem.* —*v.* regard highly: *He esteems money above prestige; I esteem* (= consider) *it an honor to write for your paper;* **adj.**: *your* **esteemed** *journal; a highly esteemed lawyer.*

es.ter *n.* an organic compound resulting from the reaction of an acid with an alcohol, as fats and oils.

esthete, esthetic, etc. same as AESTHETE, AESTHETIC, etc.

es.ti.ma.ble (ES.tuh.muh.bul) *adj.* **1** worthy of esteem: *an estimable judge; her estimable skills.* **2** that can be estimated: *of estimable value; reliably estimable.*

es.ti.mate (ES.tuh.mate) *v.* **-mates, -mat.ed, -mat.ing** judge or give an approximate calculation of the worth, size, etc. of something: *We estimate that the project will cost $100,000; We estimate the cost to be $100,000; The cost is estimated at $100,000; to estimate the damage done to a car; to estimate a job in regard to cost or fee; to estimate a population.*
—*n.* (-mit, -mate) an opinion, esp. an approximate calculation: *to give, make, submit an estimate; What's your estimate for producing this book? ballpark, conservative, preliminary, rough estimates; By my estimate, it will cost around $750,000.*
—**es.ti.ma.tor** (-may.tur) *n.*

es.ti.ma.tion (es.tuh.MAY.shun) *n.* **1** an opinion or judgment: *In our estimation, the project is not workable.* **2** esteem: *She* was held in high estimation by all.

Es.to.ni.an (es.TOH.nee.un) *n. & adj.* **1** (a person) of or from **Estonia**, a country in N.E. Europe. **2** (having to do with) the Finno-Ugric language spoken there.

es.tranged (is.TRAINJD) *adj.* alienated from a friend or relative: *He lived alone, estranged from family and friends; an estranged couple, friendship, spouse; to be, become, feel estranged.* —**es.trange.ment** *n.*

es.tro.gen (ES.truh.jun) *n.* a group of sex hormones that are responsible for a woman's secondary female characteristics. —**es.tro.gen.ic** (-JEN.ic) *adj.*

es.trus *n.* the period of heat in female mammals excepting primates. —**es.trous** (-trus) *adj.*

es.tu.ar.y (ES.choo.air.ee) *n.* **-ar.ies** the mouth of a large river into which the tide flows from the sea.

e.ta (AY.tuh, EE-) *n.* the seventh letter of the Greek alphabet (H, η).

é.ta.gère or **e.ta.gere** (ay.tah.ZHAIR) *n.* a stand of shelves open on all sides for displaying small objects.

et al. (et.AL) *n.pl.* and the other people: *Luc, Guy, Mimi, et al.*

et cet.er.a (et.SET.uh.ruh, -SET.ruh) *n.pl.* [usu. shortened to "etc."] and the rest; and the like: *cats, dogs, hamsters, etc.; lawyers, doctors, engineers, etc.* (= and such people).

etch (ECH) *v.* **1** produce a drawing or other design on a metal or glass plate by the action of acid: *to etch a figure;* *adj.*: *an etched design.* **2** engrave deeply: *a tragic event etched forever in her memory; adj.*: *a sharply etched character, feature; deeply etched in our hearts and minds.* —**etch.er** *n.*

e.ter.nal (i.TUR.nul) *adj.* **1** having no beginning or end in time; timeless: *the eternal life of heavenly beings; Because of its long history, Rome has been called the "Eternal city"; The* **eternal triangle** *of a third party involved with a couple is a favorite theme in romances; the eternal* (= unchanging) *verities of truth and justice; God* **the Eternal**; *Hope* **springs eternal** *for the optimist in us; the eternal* (= perpetual) *flame burning at a memorial.* **2** *Informal.* seeming never to stop; ceaseless: *the eternal chatter of gossips; eternal complaining; an eternal nuisance.* —**e.ter.nal.ly** *adv.*

e.ter.ni.ty (i.TUR.ni.tee) *n.* **-ties 1** endlessness of time. **2** an infinite or seemingly endless period: *an eternity of anxious waiting; It seemed like an eternity; an* **eternity ring** *set with a continuous row of stones.*

-eth *v. suffix. Archaic.* third person sing. pres. tense: *cometh, doth, walketh.*

eth.ane (ETH.ane) *n.* a refrigerant or fuel gas obtained from natural gas and coal gas.

eth.a.nol (ETH.uh.nol) *n.* ethyl alcohol.

e.ther (EE.thur, "th" as in "thin") *n.* **1** a colorless, volatile, sweet-smelling liquid used as an anesthetic. **2** an invisible substance once thought to fill all space.

e.the.re.al (i.THEER.ee.ul, "TH" as in "thin") *adj.* heavenly; also, airy; light: *an ethereal beauty, effect, quality; ethereal harmonies, music.* —**e.the.re.al.ly** *adv.*

eth.ic (ETH.ic, "TH" as in "thin") *n.* **1** a rule of conduct; also, a system of such rules: *The Protestant work ethic says work is ennobling.* **2 ethics** *pl.* [takes *sing. v.*] moral philosophy; also, the moral quality of an action: *Ethics is taught in schools; Infants don't understand the ethics of taking things without asking.* **3 ethics** *pl.* [takes *pl. v.*] rules of conduct: *His professional ethics are faultless.*

eth.i.cal (ETH.i.cul) *adj.* agreeing with a professional standard: *The firing was quite legal though not ethical; Whatever be his morals, he's very ethical as a lawyer; the ethical, moral, and social questions raised by surrogate parenthood; ethical issues, standards, systems;* **ethical drugs** (= prescription drugs). —**eth.i.cal.ly** *adv.*

Eth.i.o.pi.an (ee.thee.OH.pee.un, "th" as in "thin") *n.* **1** *n. & adj.* (a person) of or from **Ethiopia**, an East African country. **2** [rarely] *adj.* black in complexion.

eth.nic (ETH.nic, "TH" as in "thin") *adj.* [sometimes hostile in the sense of "foreign"] having to do with people, esp. minorities, grouped according to language, nationality, race, or religion; ethno-cultural: *Spanish speakers form a major ethnic group in the U.S.; an ethnic background, community, custom, food, newspaper, restaurant, riding; ethnic culture, origins, sensibilities, theater; the ethnic vote; the ethnic Chinese of Singapore; an ethnic* (= racial) *joke, slur.* —**n.** [usu. derogatory] a member of an ethnic group: *Jews, blacks, and other ethnics.* —**eth.ni.cal.ly** *adv.*: *The Scots and the Irish are ethnically quite close.*

ethnic cleansing *n.* the elimination of a minority people for the benefit of the majority.

eth.nic.i.ty (eth.NIS.i.tee) *n.* the fact or quality of being ethnic: *immigration quotas based on ethnicity.*

ethno-centrism (eth.no.CEN.triz.um) *n.*

ethno-cultural / euro

ethnic chauvinism.
eth.no-cul.tur.al (eth.noh.CUL.chuh.rul) *adj.* ethnic.
eth.nog.ra.phy (eth.NOG.ruh.fee) *n.* the study of racial and cultural groups.
eth.nol.o.gy (eth.NOL.uh.jee) *n.* the anthropology of racial and cultural groups, their origins, distribution, and characteristics. —**eth.nol.o.gist** *n.* —**eth.no.log.ic** (eth.nuh.LOJ.ic) or **eth.no.log.i.cal** (-i.cul) *adj.*
e.thol.o.gy (ee.THOL.uh.jee) *n.* the biology of animal behavior. —**eth.o.log.i.cal** (-LOJ.i.cul) *adj.*
e.thos (EE.thos) *n.* the underlying moral and ethnic character of a person or group; code of values.
eth.yl (ETH.ul, "TH" as in "thin") *n.* the hydrocarbon base of common alcohol, ether, etc.
eth.yl.ene (eth.uh.LEEN) *n.* a gaseous hydrocarbon with an unpleasant odor, used as an anesthetic, to make polyethylene, and in **ethylene glycol**, automobile antifreeze.
e.ti.ol.o.gy (ee.tee.OL.uh.jee) *n.* -gies the study of origins or causes, esp. of diseases, as a branch of medicine. —**e.ti.o.log.ic** (EE.tee.uh.LOJ.ic) or **e.ti.o.log.i.cal** *adj.*
et.i.quette (ET.uh.kut, -ket) *n.* conventional rules of behavior, as in polite society, a particular profession, etc.: *the etiquette prescribed for weddings; courtroom etiquette; military etiquette; Social etiquette includes table manners.*
E.trus.can (i.TRUS.cun) *n. & adj.* (having to do with) the extinct language of or a tribe of people that lived in ancient Etruria in W.C. Italy.
et seq. *n.pl.* and the following ones, as pages of a book.
-ette *n.* suffix. 1 female: *majorette, suffragette, usherette.* 2 small: *cigarette, kitchenette, novelette.* 3 imitation or substitute: *leatherette, flannelette.*
é.tude (AY.tude) *n.* a piece of instrumental music written esp. for students to practice various techniques.
et.y.mol.o.gy (et.uh.MOL.uh.jee) *n.* -gies 1 the history of a particular word: *to determine* or *trace the etymology of "OK."* 2 the study of the origin and development of words. —**et.y.mol.o.gist** (-jist) *n.* —**et.y.mo.log.i.cal** (-muh.LOJ.i.cul) *adj.*
eu- *n. & adj.* prefix. good; well; true: *euphemism, euphonious, euphoria.*
eu.ca.lyp.tus (yoo.cuh.LIP.tus) *n.* a tall evergreen tree valued for its medicinal oil and timber.
Eu.cha.rist (YOO.cuh.rist) *n.* Commu-

nion or the consecrated bread and wine used in it: *Christians celebrate the Eucharist on Sundays; Catholics receive the Eucharist during Mass.* —**Eu.cha.ris.tic** (-RIS.tic) or **Eu.cha.ris.ti.cal** (-ti.cul) *adj.*
eu.chre (YOO.cur) *n.* a card game played with the 32 highest cards of the pack.
Eu.clid.e.an (yoo.CLID.ee.un) or **Eu.clid.i.an** *adj.* having to do with **Euclid**, a Greek mathematician of the 3rd cent. B.C.: *Euclidian geometry.*
eu.gen.ics (yoo.JEN.ics) *n.pl.* [takes *sing. v.*] the science of improving the human race by selective control of reproduction and thereby heredity. —**eu.gen.ic** *adj.;* **eu.gen.i.cal.ly** *adv.* —**eu.gen.i.cist** *n.*
eu.lo.gize (YOO.luh.jize) *v.* -giz.es, -gized, -giz.ing praise highly, as in a eulogy. —**eu.lo.giz.er** *n.*
eu.lo.gy (YOO.luh.jee) *n.* -gies a formal speech or a piece of writing in high praise of a person, as at a funeral: *The minister delivered a touching eulogy for the war dead; The letter was an eloquent eulogy to the leader of the expedition.* —**eu.lo.gist** *n.* —**eu.lo.gis.tic** (-JIS.tic) *adj.*
eu.nuch (YOO.nuk) *n.* a castrated boy or man.
eu.phe.mism (YOO.fuh.miz.um) *n.* an inoffensive term used in place of another considered overused or offensive, as "funeral director" for "undertaker." —**eu.phe.mis.tic** (yoo.fuh.MIS.tic) *adj.*
eu.pho.ni.ous (yoo.FOH.nee.us) *adj.* having euphony: *euphonious music; "Syllabication" is more euphonious than "syllabification."*
eu.pho.ny (YOO.fuh.nee) *n.* -nies pleasantness or smoothness of sounds, esp. spoken.
eu.pho.ri.a (yoo.FOR.ee.uh) *n.* a feeling of well-being or high spirits, esp. as produced by drugs such as amphetamines or cocaine: *in a state of euphoria; A feeling of euphoria came over her when she heard the great news.* —**eu.phor.ic** *adj.*
Eur.a.sian (yoo.RAY.zhun) 1 *adj.* having to do with Europe and Asia considered as one land mass. 2 *n.* a person of mixed European and Asian descent.
eu.re.ka (yoo.REE.kuh) *interj.* indicating triumph at a discovery, as Archimedes exclaimed ("I've found it" in Greek) on solving a problem.
eu.ro (YOOR.oh) 1 *n.* the basic money unit of a common currency for the

countries of the European Union. **2** *comb.form.* same as EUROPEAN.

Eu.ro.cur.ren.cy (YOOR.oh.cur.un.see) *n.* money held in European banks by non-European nations such as the U.S. and Japan for use in European money markets.

Eu.ro.dol.lars (YOOR.uh.doll.urs) *n.pl.* U.S. dollars deposited in foreign banks for use as currency in Europe.

Eu.ro.pe.an (yoor.uh.PEE.un) *n. & adj.* (a person) of or from Europe: *Asians and Europeans; European immigrants; The* **European Union** *of nations united as trading partners used to be the* **European Common Market** *and later the* **European (Economic) Community.**

European plan *n.* a hotel charging rate that covers room but not meals; cf. AMERICAN PLAN.

eu.ro.pi.um (yoo.ROH.pee.um) *n.* a rare-earth chemical element.

Eu.sta.chi.an tube (yoo.STAY.shun-) *n.* a tube that connects the middle ear with the throat and helps equalize pressure on both sides of the eardrum by taking in air, as when swallowing.

eu.tha.na.si.a (yoo.thuh.NAY.zhuh) *n.* the causing of death in order to end prolonged suffering in terminal cases; mercy killing.

eu.tha.nize (YOO.thuh.nize) *v.* **-niz.es, -nized, -niz.ing** kill mercifully: *to euthanize a dying animal.*

eu.then.ics (yoo.THEN.ics, "TH" as in "thin") *n.pl.* [takes *sing. v.*] improvement of the human race by control of environmental factors.

eu.troph.ic (yoo.TROF.ic) *adj.* polluted by excess of nutrients such as phosphates from human wastes. —**eu.troph.i.ca.tion** (-i.CAY.shun) *n.*

e.vac.u.ate (i.VAC.yoo.ate) *v.* **-ates, -at.ed, -at.ing 1** to empty: *to evacuate the bowels, stomach; to evacuate* (= discharge) *bodily wastes.* **2** withdraw from a place: *They were told to evacuate the area before the hurricane struck; to evacuate a city; to evacuate* (= remove) *people from a disaster area; The order to evacuate came in the middle of the night.* —**e.vac.u.a.tion** (-yoo.AY.shun) *n.*: *to carry out a mass evacuation from a disaster area.*

e.vac.u.ee (i.VAC.yoo.ee) *n.* an evacuated person.

e.vade (i.VADE) *v.* **e.vades, e.vad.ed, e.vad.ing** use trickery or skill to escape or dodge enemies, responsibilities, and other unwelcome things: *She successfully evaded the reporter's questions; Taxes may be legally avoided but not evaded; During the Vietnam war, many Americans moved to Canada to evade* (= dodge) *the draft.* —**e.vad.er** *n.*

e.val.u.ate (i.VAL.yoo.ate) *v.* **-ates, -at.ed, -at.ing** determine the amount, quality, or value of nonmaterial things: *to evaluate evidence, a performance, plan, play.* —**e.val.u.a.tion** (-AY.shun) *n.* appraisal: *to make a critical, fair, objective evaluation of a poem.*

ev.a.nes.cent (ev.uh.NES.unt) *adj.* fading away or vanishing: *Dreams are evanescent; an evanescent image, moment, perception; Wealth often proves evanescent.* —**ev.a.nes.cence** *n.*

e.van.gel.i.cal (i.van.JEL.i.cul) *adj.* **1** relating to the four Gospels. **2** of Protestant churches such as the Methodist and Baptist, stressing faith and the preaching of the Gospels rather than ritual and good works for salvation. —*n.* a member of such a church.

e.van.gel.ist (i.VAN.juh.list) *n.* **1 Evangelist** one of the four who wrote the Gospels: Matthew, Mark, Luke, or John. **2** a preacher, esp. a Gospel revivalist. —**e.van.gel.is.tic** (-LIS.tic) *adj.*

e.van.gel.ize (i.VAN.juh.lize) *v.* **-iz.es, -ized, -iz.ing** preach the Gospel to a people: *St. Thomas evangelized India.*

e.vap.o.rate (i.VAP.uh.rate) *v.* **-rates, -rat.ed, -rat.ing 1** change a liquid or solid into a gas: *Heat evaporates water;* **Evaporated milk** *is milk thickened for canning by evaporating it.* **2** become gaseous: *Water evaporates into vapor or steam; Hopes may evaporate* (= disappear). —**e.vap.o.ra.tion** (-RAY.shun) *n.*

e.vap.o.rite (i.VAP.uh.rite) *n.* a mineral deposit formed by the evaporation of sea water. —**e.vap.o.rit.ic** (-RIT.ic) *adj.*: *Gypsum, rock salt, and phosphate rocks are of evaporitic formation.*

e.va.sion (i.VAY.zhun) *n.* an act of evading: *a charge of tax evasion.*

e.va.sive (i.VAY.siv) *adj.* evading: *He's evasive about his past; The pilot took evasive action to avoid a midair collision; an evasive answer, maneuver, tactic.*

Eve (EEV) *n.* **1** in the Bible, the first woman and the wife of Adam. **2** also **eve**, the evening or day before: *Christmas Eve; It happened on the eve of the wedding; Oil was discovered in Saudi Arabia* **on the eve of** (= just before) *World War II.*

e.ven (EE.vun) *adj.* **1** of equal level: *The water level rose and was even with the pavement; an even* (= smooth) *surface.* **2** having equal intervals; uniform or regular: *the even hum of an engine.* **3** that divides equally, leaving no

remainder: *The property was divided in even shares among the three sons;* 2, 4, 6, 8, *etc. are even numbers; Give me an even* (= exact) *dozen.* **4** equal: *Give the girls an even break with the boys; an even* (= fifty-fifty) *chance; to* **bet even money** (= with odds of winning what one has risked); *The business is beginning to* **break even** (= have gains equaling losses) *after ten years; He vowed to* **get even** *with* (= get revenge on) *her for tricking him; Lee went* **even steven** *or* **stephen** (= with all debts settled) *with Lou and continued to be friends.*
—*adv.* [to emphasize a comparison]: *He can't even walk, let alone run; John is tall, but his sister is even taller; The patient died* **even as** (= just as) *the doctor arrived; She won't go* **even if** *she is invited; He is still sore,* **even so** (= still) *he should forgive her; Lou refuses to eat* **even though** (= although) *he is hungry.*
—*v.* make or become even or equal: *Use the trimmer to even the edges; Losses and gains* **even out** *over the years; Our team* **evened up** *the score in the second period.* —**e.ven.ly** *adv.*; **e.ven.ness** *n.*

even-handed *adj.* impartial: *A judge metes out even-handed justice; an even-handed approach, editorial, policy.*

eve.ning (EEV.ning) *n.* the final part of day and the early part of night: *Good evening* (to you)! *(Good) evening! I'll see you at seven (o'clock) in the evening* (= 7 p.m.); *a gala evening; We stay home* **evenings** (*Informal for* in the evenings).

evening primrose *n.* a tall herb with saucer-shaped white, yellow, or pink flowers that open in the evening.

evening star *n.* either of the two planets Venus or Mercury seen as bright stars in the evening sky.

e.ven.song (EEV.un.song) *n.* vespers.

e.vent (i.VENT) *n.* **1** a happening, esp. one of relative importance: *The first day of school is an event in a child's life; A birth is a blessed event; Read the papers for current events; A disastrous event took place* or *occurred last year on this day; the dramatic events of the hijacking and rescue of the passengers; a historical event such as the signing of a treaty; The publication of a book is a literary event; the main events of last year; a major event of her childhood; a media event; sporting events; tragic events;* **In that event** (= if that happens) *we shall have to sell our house and move into an apartment; Everyone can be* **wise after the event** (= can give advice about something after it has happened). **2** an item in a program of sports: *track and field events; swimming events.* —**at all events** *or* **in any event** whatever happens. —**in the event of** *or* **that** in case of.

even-tempered *adj.* calm: *an even-tempered woman.*

e.vent.ful (i.VENT.ful) *adj.* full of noteworthy events: *an eventful day at work.* —**e.vent.ful.ly** *adv.*

e.ven.tide (EE.vun.tide) *n.* [old use] evening.

e.ven.tu.al (i.VEN.choo.ul) *adj.* of an event, happening as a final effect: *the eventual defeat of the enemy; the eventual outcome of the war; our eventual victory.* —**e.ven.tu.al.ly** *adv.*

e.ven.tu.al.i.ty (i.VEN.choo.AL.i.tee) *n.* **-ties** a possible outcome: *In the eventuality of a hailstorm, an umbrella may not help much.*

e.ven.tu.ate (i.VEN.choo.ate) *v.* **-ates, -at.ed, -at.ing** turn out; result finally.

ev.er (EV.ur) *adv.* **1** at any time; by any chance: *Have you ever been to Los Alamos? Does Sue ever complain? Does she ever* (= She does)! *She is a complainer, if ever there was one* (= She is a perfect example of a complainer); [used after *how, what, when, where,* and *who* for added force] *How ever did this happen? Who ever told you that?* **2** at all times; forever: *Yours ever* or *Ever yours* or *Yours as ever* [used at the close of an informal letter]; *faithful as ever; lived happily ever after.* **3** [following a superlative]: *the greatest boxer ever* (= that ever lived)! —**ever and anon** *Poetic.* every now and then. —**ever so** *Informal.* very: *This has happened ever so often; in ever so many cases; Thank you ever so much.* —**for ever and a day** always.

ev.er.green (EV.ur.green) *n.* a plant or tree that has green leaves all year round, as the pine, spruce, etc.: *Most tropical plants are evergreens.* —*adj.* **1** nondeciduous: *evergreen shrubs, trees; the evergreen* (= always green) *Astroturf.* **2** of continuing interest: *an evergreen issue, song, title; merchandise with evergreen potential.* **3** that never expires: *an evergreen clause that prohibits termination of a contract; an evergreen license.*

ev.er.last.ing (ev.ur.LAST.ing) *adj.* lasting an eternity. —**ev.er.last.ing.ly** *adv.*

ev.er.more (ev.ur.MORE) *adv.* **1** [old use] forever. **2** more than ever: *our evermore crowded streets.*

eve.ry (EV.ree) *adj.* **1** each of a group [including all, or one after another if indefinite]: *Trains leave here every hour; It happens every day; Not every Tom, Dick, and Harry* (*Informal for* any ordinary person) *goes to college.* **2** [with abstract noun] all possible: *You have every reason to be proud of your children; perfect in every respect.* —**every last one** *Informal.* every one. —**every now and then** or **every now and again** occasionally; also **every once in a while** and **every so often.** —**every which way** *Informal.* in all directions.

eve.ry.bod.y (EV.ree.bod.ee, -bud.ee) *pron.* everyone: *Everybody loves somebody;* **Everybody and his brother** *walks over Jim's lawn.*

eve.ry.day (EV.ree.day) *adj*a. daily; hence, common or ordinary: *words that are in everyday use; An everyday occurrence is one that happens very commonly; everyday English, expenses, happenings, incidents, language, life, objects, shoes; clothes for everyday wear at home, work, or school.*

eve.ry.one (EV.ree.wun) *pron.* every person.

eve.ry.place (EV.ree.place) *n. & adv. Informal.* everywhere.

eve.ry.thing (EV.ree.thing) *pron.* every thing; all: *a gift for the woman who has everything; Children are everything* (= very important) *to her.*

eve.ry.where (EV.ree.where) *adv.* in or to every place: *Look everywhere; here, there, and everywhere else; Everywhere* (= *wherever*) *I went, the dog would follow me.* —*n.* all places: *for, from, to everywhere.*

e.vict (i.VICT) *v.* oust or discharge a tenant *from* a house or land by legal process. —**e.vic.tion** *n.;* **e.vic.tor** *n.*

ev.i.dence (EV.uh.dunce) *n.* something that supports an assertion: *Possession of stolen property is evidence of theft; The testimony of witnesses proved strong evidence that he had committed the crime; not mere hearsay evidence; a signed receipt produced in evidence against a defaulter; to dig up, find, furnish, gather, piece together, suppress, turn up, unearth, withhold evidence; The incriminating evidence had been planted on the accused; ample, circumstantial, compelling, conclusive, damaging, documentary, substantial, telltale evidence; a body of evidence; not a piece, scrap, shred of evidence against the accused; The bulk of the evidence is undeniable; The hit-and-run car was nowhere* **in evidence** (= to be seen); *One of the accused* **turned state's** or **King's** or **Queen's evidenc**e (= joined the prosecution) *and testified against the others.*
—*v.* -denc.es, -denced, -denc.ing be a sign of something: *Spontaneous tears evidenced his sorrow.*

ev.i.dent (EV.uh.dunt) *adj.* clear and plain to the understanding: *Her language showed her evident displeasure; It was evident that she was displeased.*
—**ev.i.dent.ly** *adv.*

ev.i.den.tiar.y (ev.i.DEN.shuh.ree) *adj.* having to do with evidence: *an item of evidentiary value; to conduct an* **evidentiary hearing** (at which evidence is presented).

e.vil (EE.vul) *n.* something very bad, harmful, or unlucky: *to root out the evils of drug abuse; Is idleness or money the root of all evil? When both candidates are unsuitable, one has to choose* **the lesser of two evils**; *Politics is a* **necessary evil** (that cannot be avoided). —*adj.*: *Alcohol is not necessarily evil; to ward off the* **evil eye** (= a look that is supposed to bring bad luck); *his* **evil genius** (that exerts an evil influence); *an* **evil-minded** (= malicious) *gossip; the* **Evil One** (= the Devil).
—**e.vil.do.er** (-doo.ur) *n.* —**e.vil.ly** *adv.*

e.vince (i.VINCE) *v.* **e.vinc.es, e.vinced, e.vinc.ing** *Formal.* reveal or manifest: *to evince a desire, feeling, quality, interest; as clearly evinced by her remarks.*

e.vis.cer.ate (i.VIS.uh.rate) *v.* -ates, -at.ed, -at.ing disembowel; hence, deprive of something vital.
—**e.vis.cer.a.tion** (-RAY.shun) *n.*

e.voc.a.tive (i.VOC.uh.tiv) *adj.* evoking: *an incident evocative of old times.*
—**ev.o.ca.tion** (ev.uh.CAY.shun) *n.*

e.voke (i.VOKE) *v.* **e.vokes, e.voked, e.vok.ing** call forth; elicit, esp. a response from the mind or emotions.

ev.o.lu.tion (ev.uh.LOO.shun) *n.* an evolving or development; also, a result of this: *The evolution of the horseless carriage into the automobile; the organic evolution of higher forms of life from the lower; Darwin's theory of evolution by natural selection; evolution as opposed to creation by God.* —**ev.o.lu.tion.ar.y** (-shuh.nair.ee) *adj.* —**ev.o.lu.tion.ism** *n.;* **ev.o.lu.tion.ist** *n. & adj.*

e.volve (i.VOLV) *v.* **e.volves, e.volved, e.volv.ing** develop gradually: *Did the modern horse evolve from the "Eohippus" of 65 million years ago?*

ewe (YOO) *n.* a female sheep.

ew.er (YOO.ur) *n.* a wide-mouthed water pitcher.

ex 1 *prep.* from; out of: *Goods are shipped ex warehouse; She is here ex officio.* **2** *prefix.* away from: *excommunicate, export, expurgate.* **3** *prefix.* former: *ex-convict, ex president, ex-wife.* **4** *n., pl.* **ex.es** *Informal.* one's divorced spouse.

ex.ac.er.bate (ig.ZAS.ur.bate) *v.* **-bates, -bat.ed, -bat.ing** aggravate or make worse: *to exacerbate anxieties, concerns,* *fears, problems, situations.* —**ex.ac.er.ba.tion** (-BAY.shun) *n.*

ex.act (ig.ZACT) *adj.* **1** agreeing in every detail; correct: *an exact copy; the exact size of a room; Passengers should pay exact fares in tickets, tokens, or cash since the driver carries no change; $2 to be exact; the **exact same** (Informal for very same) man I met yesterday.* **2** characterized by or capable of precision: *The calculations are exact in every detail; an exact aim, calculation; Psychology is not an **exact science** like physics or chemistry.* —*v.* obtain forcefully what is demanded: *a disciplinarian who exacts obedience from everyone; Tributes were exacted from conquered nations.* —**ex.ac.tion** *n.* —**exacting** *adj.*: *an exacting work schedule; a child who is very exacting in his demands;* **ex.act.ing.ly** *adv.* —**ex.act.ly** *adv.;* **ex.act.ness** *n.*

ex.ac.ti.tude (ig.ZAC.tuh.tude) *n.* the quality or an instance of exactness: *a woman of great exactitude.*

ex.ag.ger.ate (ig.ZAJ.uh.rate) *v.* -ates, -at.ed, -at.ing magnify or overstate something: *Cartoonists exaggerate facial features out of proportion; She always exaggerates;* *adj.*: *a greatly or grossly **exaggerated** account of what happened; exaggerated claims.* —**ex.ag.ger.a.tion** (-RAY.shun) *n.*

ex.alt (ig.ZAWLT) *v.* elevate or glorify: *the tendency to exalt commonplace things to the skies;* *adj.*: *He has an **exalted** opinion of himself; exalted religious fervor; an exalted sense of right and wrong; in an exalted state; exalted company, moments, tones.* —**ex.al.ta.tion** (eg.zawl.TAY.shun) *n.*: *the exaltation of capitalism; appreciation ranging from worship to exaltation.*

ex.am (ig.ZAM) *n. Informal.* an examination or a set of examination questions: *Students cheat on, fail, pass, sit for, take, undergo, write exams; annual, entrance, final, oral, written exams;* *adja.*: *exam fever, results, time.*

ex.am.i.na.tion (ig.ZAM.uh.NAY.shun) *n.* **1** a close inspection or study: *the examination of a new theory; A physician does a physical examination of or on a patient; careful, cursory, in-depth, superficial, thorough examinations; On close examination, the painting was found to be a fake.* **2** a test or set of questions: *competitive, comprehensive, difficult, easy, entrance, final, makeup, oral, placement, qualifying, written examinations; an examination in a subject, on a topic; Teachers administer, conduct, draw up, give, monitor, supervise examinations; Students fail, make up, pass, take examinations.*

ex.am.ine (ig.ZAM.in) *v.* -ines, -ined, -in.ing **1** closely inspect a patient, situation, etc.: *The insurance adjuster examined the car for damages; to examine carefully, closely, thoroughly.* **2** interview, question, or test an applicant, student, witness, etc.: *She was examined in all subjects.* —**ex.am.in.er** *n.*

ex.am.i.nee (ig.ZAM.uh.NEE) *n.* a person being tested at an examination.

ex.am.ple (ig.ZAM.pul) *n.* **1** a person or thing that is typical of the rest of a group: *Canines – dogs and wolves,* **for example**; *to cite, give, provide an example; a classic, concrete, glaring, illustrative, prime, typical example; the worst example of a polluted stream.* **2** one likely to be followed or copied: *He was punished as an example to or for the whole class; The teacher made an example of him; to follow an example; She's a shining, striking example of a model student; The rabbi taught* **by example** *rather than by preaching; Parents try to* **set a good example** *for their children.*

ex.as.per.ate (ig.ZAS.puh.rate) *v.* -ates, -at.ed, -at.ing irritate or annoy intensely: *Unnecessary delays exasperate everyone;* *adj.*: *The audience seemed bored and **exasperated**; We are exasperated at or by unnecessary delays in mail delivery; Delays can be very **exasperating**; his exasperating indifference.* —**ex.as.per.a.tion** (-RAY.shun) *n.*

ex.ca.vate (EX.cuh.vate) *v.* -vates, -vat.ed, -vat.ing **1** make by digging: *to excavate a mine, quarry, trench, tunnel;* *n.*: *an **excavating** machine to dig a building foundation.* **2** dig out or uncover: *Archaeologists excavate ancient ruins; Pompeii was excavated in 1748; They excavated a whole city;* *adj.*: *an **excavated** area.* **3** scoop out: *They excavated hundreds of tons of soil from the contaminated land.* **4** dig: *Check with the phone company before excavating in your backyard.* —**ex.ca.va.tion** (-VAY.shun) *n.*: *a city under excavation; an excavation site.* —**ex.ca.va.tor** (-vay.tur) *n.*

ex.ceed (ik.SEED) *v.* go beyond: *to exceed the speed limit; She exceeds (= surpasses) everyone in creativity.* —**ex.ceed.ing.ly** *adv.* extremely: *exceedingly difficult, simple, well.*

ex.cel (ik.SEL) *v.* -cels, -celled, -cel.ling surpass others: *He excels at tennis; She excels in math.*

ex.cel.lence (EK.sul.unce) *n.* excellent quality: *a student noted for excellence at or in piano playing; his excellence as a pi-*

anist; Music is just one of her many excellences (= things in which she excels).

Ex.cel.len.cy (EK.sul.un.see) *n.* -cies [a title of honor used in addressing a foreign head of state or ambassador, an archbishop, etc.]: *Her, His, Your Excellency; their Excellencies the American ambassador and his wife.*

ex.cel.lent (EK.sul.unt) *adj.* outstanding or very good: *an excellent job, player, record, student; I'm in excellent physical condition; Excellent* (= Superb)! —**ex.cel.lent.ly** *adv.*

ex.cel.si.or (ek.SEL.see.ur) *n.* soft fine wood shavings used for packing fragile things.

ex.cept (ik.SEPT) *v.* leave out; exclude: *No vehicles (buses excepted) may turn left here.* —**prep. & conj.** but: *Everyone except him was there; all veggies except spinach; I'm OK except (that) I have a slight headache; I'm OK except for a slight headache.*

ex.cep.tion (ik.SEP.shun) *n.* **1** an excepting or excluding; also, a person or thing excepted: *Everyone makes mistakes and I'm no exception; Our child eats all vegetables with the exception of broccoli and spinach; an honorable, important, notable exception; Latecomers are now the exception rather than the rule; "The exception proves the rule"* (= Without a rule, there could be no exception). **2** an objection: *She takes exception* (= objects) *to his language.* —**ex.cep.tion.a.ble** *adj.* objectionable.

ex.cep.tion.al (ik.SEP.shuh.nul) *adj.* unusual: *weather that is exceptional for this time of year; an exceptional case; exceptional* (= gifted or handicapped) *children.* —**ex.cep.tion.al.ly** *adv.*

ex.cerpt (ik.SURPT) *v.* take out passages *from* a source. —*n.* (EK.surpt) an extract; passage taken *from* a source.

ex.cess (ik.SES) *n.* what is greater than or exceeds a limit: *An excess of expenditure over income means you are in debt; He was given to gambling, drinking, and such excesses; The company has assets in excess of* (= more than) *$3 billion; He was left broken-hearted, having loved her to excess* (= too much).
—*adj.* (EK.ses): *A higher rate is charged for excess baggage; an excess profits tax.* —**ex.ces.sive** (ik.SES.iv) *adj.*; **ex.ces.sive.ly** *adv.*

ex.change (ix.CHANGE) *v.* -chang.es, -changed, -chang.ing give something in return for something else; give and receive: *a customer exchanging his gift for something better; We exchange greetings at New Year's; to exchange* (= change or swap) *seats with someone.*
—*n.* **1** a trade or swapping: *an exchange of prisoners after a war; a watch given in exchange for coupons; cultural exchanges between nations; an overseas **exchange student** under a scholarship program.* **2** a place for exchanging things or services: *a commodity exchange; stock exchange; telephone exchange (where lines are connected).* **3** money or a document for setting or adjusting payments, currency differences, etc.: *Exports earn foreign exchange; a bill of exchange* (= draft); *In those days, the **exchange rate** on the American dollar was $1.12 Canadian.* —**ex.change.a.ble** *adj.*

ex.cheq.uer (ix.CHEK.ur, EX.chek.ur) *n.* a national treasury: *the Japanese exchequer's reserve fund; His wife contributes more to their joint exchequer (Informal for finances) than he does.*

ex.cis.a.ble (ik.SYE.suh.bul) *adj.* on which excise may be charged: *an excisable commodity.*

¹**ex.cise** (EK.size, -sice) *n.* a tax or duty charged within a country on the manufacture and sale of goods such as liquor and tobacco, on purchases in the form of sales tax, and on services in the form of business licenses, entertainment tax, etc.

²**ex.cise** (ik.SIZE) *v.* -cis.es, -cised, -cis.ing remove by cutting out: *to excise an objectionable part from a book;* *adj.*: *the excised passages; an excised tumor.* —**ex.ci.sion** (-SIZH.un) *n.*: *the surgical excision of diseased tissue.*

ex.cite (ik.SITE) *v.* -cites, -cit.ed, -cit.ing **1** arouse the thoughts or feelings of someone; also, thrill: *The discovery excited the kids.* **2** stir up or make active: *Rumors excite curiosity; a speaker who excites passions.* —**ex.cit.a.ble** (-tuh.bul) *adj.* —**ex.cit.a.bil.i.ty** (-tuh.BIL.i.tee) *n.* —**ex.ci.ta.tion** (ex.si.TAY.shun) *n.* —**ex.cit.er** *n.*: *The exciter of an A-C generator supplies current to produce a magnetic field.*

excited *adj.* stirred up: *a hive of excited bees in hot pursuit; She was excited* (= thrilled) *to learn she had won; He got quite excited* (= angry) *about or at or over the treatment he received; electrons in an **excited state** of higher energy.* —**ex.cit.ed.ly** *adv.*

ex.cite.ment (ik.SITE.munt) *n.* the state of feeling excited about something pleasant; also, the thing itself: *She forgot her hat in her excitement; a trip full of excitements.*

exciting *adj.* thrilling: *an exciting adventure; an exciting bit of news; It's exciting* *to watch thrillers.*

ex.claim (ix.CLAIM) *v.* utter suddenly and vehemently: *"Ouch," she exclaimed in pain; He exclaimed: "I didn't do it!"* —**ex.cla.ma.tion** (ex.cluh.MAY.shun) *n.: an exclamation of joy; This [!] is an* **exclamation mark** *or* **point.** —**ex.clam.a.to.ry** (ix.CLAM.uh.tor.ee) *adj.: An exclamatory word or sentence is ended with an exclamation mark, as "Alas!"*

ex.clude (ix.CLOOD, long "OO") *v.* **-cludes, -clud.ed, -clud.ing 1** keep out or prohibit from somewhere: *No one can be excluded on the basis of age, sex, or color.* **2** leave out of consideration: *We cannot exclude the possibility of theft of the missing money; The bill comes to $400 excluding minor expenses.*

ex.clu.sion (ix.CLOO.zhun) *n.* what is excluded: *gifts, benefits, and other non-taxable exclusions (on a tax return); He studies algebra* **to the exclusion of** *(= so as to exclude) other branches of mathematics.*

ex.clu.sive (ix.CLOO.siv) *adj.* that excludes: *Ours used to be an exclusive neighborhood (with only people of one social group or income bracket); exclusive attention, jurisdiction, possession, privileges, use; an exclusive (not multiple) listing by a realtor; an exclusive news story (that no other media may carry); an exclusive feature (that no other product has); A patent gives exclusive rights to an inventor (= rights that no one else can have); Truth and untruth are mutually exclusive (= It's either the one or the other); an* **exclusive economic zone** *claimed by countries beyond their coastal waters to protect fishing and mineral rights; a car that costs $20,000* **exclusive of** *(= not including) optional items.* —*n.* an exclusive story or article. —**ex.clu.sive.ly** *adv.;* **ex.clu.sive.ness** *n.*

ex.cog.i.tate (ex.COJ.uh.tate) *v.* **-tates, -tat.ed, -tat.ing** think out: *to excogitate a device, plan.*

ex.com.mu.ni.cate (ex.cuh.MEW.nuh.cate) *v.* **-cates, -cat.ed, -cat.ing** formally cut someone off from membership, esp. of a church. —**ex.com.mu.ni.ca.tion** (-CAY.shun) *n.*

ex.co.ri.ate (ex.COR.ee.ate) *v.* **-ates, -at.ed, -at.ing 1** strip off the skin from a surface. **2** criticize a book, performance, person, etc. severely: *a play excoriated by the critics.* —**ex.co.ri.a.tion** (-ee.AY.shun) *n.*

ex.cre.ment (EX.cruh.munt) *n.* waste from the bowels: *human excrement.*

ex.cres.cence (ix.CRESH.unce) *n.* an abnormal growth on a plant or animal body, as a wart or bunion; **ex.cres.cent** *adj.*

ex.cre.ta (ix.CREE.tuh) *n.pl.* body wastes; excretions.

ex.crete (ix.CREET) *v.* **-cretes, -cret.ed, -cret.ing** eliminate from the body. —**ex.cre.tion** (ex.CREE.shun) *n.: Sweat, carbon dioxide, urine, etc. are bodily excretions.* —**ex.cre.to.ry** (EX.cruh.tor.ee) *adj.: the body's excretory functions.*

ex.cru.ci.at.ing (ix.CROO.shee.ay.ting) *adj.* **1** of mental or bodily pain, acute: *an excruciating agony, fear, pain.* **2** extreme or intense: *with excruciating care; excruciating delight; to describe something in excruciating detail; an excruciating regard for correctness.*

ex.cul.pate (EX.cul.pate) *v.* **-pates, -at.ed, -pat.ing** clear someone of alleged fault or blame. —**ex.cul.pa.tion** (-PAY.shun) *n.*

ex.cur.sion (ix.CUR.zhun) *n.* a journey made with the intention of returning to the starting-point; hence, a pleasure trip by air, train, ship, etc.: *We went on an excursion to collect specimens; a botany excursion from school; The excursion (party) was due back at 5 p.m.; a round-trip economy* **excursion ticket;** **ex.cur.sion.ist** *n.* **2** a digression; **ex.cur.sive** (-siv) *adj.* digressive.

ex.cur.sus (ix.CUR.sus) *n.* a scholarly or literary digression.

ex.cuse (ix.CUZE) *v.* **-cus.es, -cused, -cus.ing** overlook an offense or offending person: *Excuse me, ma'am; If you will excuse our interrupting; Please excuse us for interrupting; Excuse my (poor) French; We excuse you this time; We won't excuse your rudeness another time; I will* **excuse myself** *(= be absent) for the rest of this session; (Please)* **excuse me** *(= allow me to pass through, get out, etc.);* **Excuse me?** *(= What did you say? May I have your attention?); adj.: an excused absence; You're excused from classes till you are better; You are excused (= You may leave).* —*n.* (ix.CUSE) an act or instance of excusing: *to accept, find, make, reject an excuse; He tried to make up an excuse for being late; an excellent, good, plausible, valid excuse; the flimsy excuse that the watch is faulty; It sounds like a feeble excuse to get a new watch; A faulty watch is a lame excuse; There's no excuse (= justification) for always being late; That gadget is a poor excuse for (= example of) a watch.* —**ex.cus.a.ble** (-zuh.bul) *adj.: an excusable offense.*

ex.e.cra.ble (EX.uh.cruh.bul) *adj.* detestable: *an execrable crime; his execrable* manners; her execrable tastes. —**ex.e.cra.bly** adv.

ex.e.cute (EX.uh.cute) v. **-cutes, -cut.ed, -cut.ing 1** carry out to completion; put into effect: *to execute an agreement, plan, portrait, search warrant, transaction; The government executes what parliament legislates; Nurses execute doctors' orders; A deed is executed when it is signed, sealed, and delivered; Each step has to be executed gracefully in performing a dance; He died without naming anyone to execute his will; to execute* (= run) *a computer program.* **2** put a condemned person to death: *He was executed by hanging; was executed as a traitor.* —**ex.e.cut.a.ble** adj.

ex.e.cu.tion (ex.uh.CUE.shun) n. **1** an executing or the manner of it: *the execution of justice; the execution of a dance, plan, will.* **2** the putting to death of a condemned person: *The sentence was passed, but the execution was delayed by appeals; to carry out an execution; execution by electrocution, hanging; a public execution by firing squad.* —**ex.e.cu.tion.er** n.

ex.ec.u.tive (ig.ZEK.yuh.tiv) adja. having to do with the carrying out of a function; hence, managerial: *an executive committee, director, officer, secretary; The police are an executive arm of government; an executive* (= managerial) *chef; An* **executive chauffeur** *drives executives around; the* **Executive Mansion** (= White House); *The president is usually the* **chief executive officer** *of a corporation; official secrecy in the guise of* **executive privilege** *of confidentiality.* —n. **1** the executive branch of government: *the judiciary and the executive.* **2** a business manager: *the chief executive; the top executives of a corporation.*

ex.ec.u.tor (ig.ZEK.yuh.tur) n. one who is to carry out the provisions of a will. —**ex.ec.u.trix** fem.

ex.e.ge.sis (ex.i.JEE.sis) n., pl. **-ses** (-seez) the critical interpretation of a word or passage, esp. from the Bible.

ex.e.gete (EX.uh.jeet) n. an expert in exegesis.

ex.em.plar (ig.ZEM.plar, -plur) n. an ideal pattern or a model worthy of imitation.

ex.em.pla.ry (ig.ZEM.pluh.ree) adj. being an example to others: *She was praised for exemplary behavior; He was awarded* **exemplary damages** *(as a warning to others) besides compensation for the loss.*

ex.em.pli.fy (ig.ZEM.pluh.fye) v. **-fies, -fied, -fy.ing** serve as a typical example of something: *Mother Teresa exemplifies service.* —**ex.em.pli.fi.ca.tion** (-fuh.CAY.shun) n.

ex.empt (ig.ZEMPT) v. to free from a general obligation or requirement: *No one is exempted from paying taxes;* **adjp.**: *Certain goods are exempt from duty.* —**ex.emp.tion** (-ZEMP.shun) n.: *She was granted an exemption from jury duty; tax exemptions; Dependents may be claimed as exemptions (to reduce taxable income).*

ex.er.cise (EX.ur.cize) v. **-cis.es, -cised, -cis.ing 1** put to active use or work: *He walks the dog to exercise him; It's good to exercise (the body) for 30 minutes daily; to exercise hard, regularly, strenuously, vigorously.* **2** exert or apply: *to exercise restraint in the use of energy; In sending them to jail, the judge was only exercising his powers;* **adj.**: *They were quite* **exercised** (= troubled) *about or over his remarks.* —n. **1** the use or exertion of an organ, faculty, etc.: *Do or take a little exercise every day, says the doctor; regular exercise; Avoid strenuous exercise in the beginning; Swimming is an excellent form of vigorous exercise; physical exercises; warming-up exercises;* **adja.**: *a (stationary) exercise bike; an exercise break (from work); an exercise program.* **2** application or exertion: *Teaching requires the exercise of care and patience; The object of the exercise has to be kept in mind or it may become an* **exercise in futility** *(that yields no results); a mere academic exercise; a lesson followed by exercises* (= tasks); *an* **exercise book** *(for doing schoolwork).* **3 exercises** pl. a program or operation in many parts: *military exercises near the war zone; naval exercises in the Persian Gulf; to hold graduation or* **commencement exercises** (= ceremonies). —**ex.er.cis.er** n.

ex.ert (ig.ZURT) v. put or bring into action; exercise or wield: *to exert authority; You must* **exert yourself** (= try hard) *to achieve anything.* —**ex.er.tion** (ig.ZUR.shun) n.: *the exertion of undue influence; a diplomat's exertions* (= efforts) *in the cause of peace.*

ex.hale (ex.HALE) v. **-hales, -haled, -hal.ing** breathe out or give out vapor, smoke, odors, etc.: *We inhale oxygen and exhale carbon dioxide; Please exhale slowly; the odors exhaling* (= rising) *from the sewage plant.* —**ex.ha.la.tion** (ex.huh.LAY.shun) n.

ex.haust (ig.ZAWST) v. to empty out, drain off, or use up strength, supplies, or other contents: *Overspending exhausts our resources; He exhausted the subject* (= discussed it thoroughly) *within the hour;* **adj.**: *an* **exhausted** (= emptied) *oil* well; You must feel quite exhausted (= too tired to go on) after the climb; It was an **exhausting** (= very tiring) climb. —**n.** what exhausts or is exhausted: Use the fan as an air exhaust; Mufflers reduce the noise of car exhausts; Exhaust fumes are mostly carbon monoxide. —**ex.haus.ti.ble** adj.

ex.haus.tion (ig.ZAWS.chun) n. **1** great fatigue or tiredness: He collapsed on the floor out of sheer exhaustion; in a state of exhaustion. **2** a using up: the exhaustion of our resources, supplies.

ex.haus.tive (ig.ZAWS.tiv) adj. dealing completely with a subject; thorough: an exhaustive inquiry, search, study.

ex.hib.it (ig.ZIB.it) v. to display for public notice: Artists exhibit their work; evidence exhibited in court; He listened to the verdict without exhibiting (= showing) the least emotion. —**n.** something exhibited, as an art object or collection or a piece of legal evidence: to mount or organize an art exhibit; A work of art by Picasso was on exhibit; The murder weapon was entered as Exhibit A (= the first piece of evidence). —**ex.hib.i.tor** or **ex.hib.it.er** n.

ex.hib.i.tion (ex.uh.BISH.un) n. a public showing, esp. an organized display: an art exhibition; to put on or stage an exhibition; trade exhibitions (= fairs); He made an exhibition of himself (= made himself ridiculous) by crying like a baby.

ex.hi.bi.tion.ism (ex.uh.BISH.uh.niz.um) n. a tendency to attract attention to oneself excessively, as by indecent exposure; **ex.hi.bi.tion.ist** n. —**ex.hi.bi.tion.is.tic** (-NIS.tic) adj.

ex.hil.a.rate (ig.ZIL.uh.rate) v. **-rates, -rat.ed, -rat.ing** fill with high spirits: Some are scared rather than exhilarated by a roller-coaster ride; **adj.:** Young people find the ride an exhilarating experience; The climb was quite exhilarating. —**ex.hil.a.ra.tion** (-RAY.shun) n.

ex.hort (ig.ZORT) v. urge earnestly, as a preacher does: She exhorted them to study hard for the examinations. —**ex.hor.ta.tion** (eg.zor.TAY.shun) n.

ex.hume (iks.HUME, igz.HUME; rhyme: assume) v. **-humes, -humed, -hum.ing** dig a corpse out of its grave; hence, bring to light from a buried state. —**ex.hu.ma.tion** (ex.hyuh.MAY.shun) n.

ex.i.gen.cy (EX.uh.jun.see) n. **-cies** a situation of need requiring urgent action: An unexpected exigency arose; the **exigencies** (= demanding conditions) of life in a war zone.

ex.ig.u.ous (ig.ZIG.yoo.us) adj. sparing or scanty; meager: an exiguous diet; exiguous rations.

ex.ile (EG.zile, EK.sile) v. **-iles, -iled, -il.ing** force someone or oneself to leave home or country for a period: Napoleon was exiled from France; He was exiled to Elba. —**n.** an exiled person, the person's banishment, or its period: Napoleon was sent into exile twice; He died in exile on Saint Helena; Ugandan exiles in New York; exiles and émigrés; a writer forced into exile; living in enforced exile; a government-in-exile; the literature of exile; Ovid's poetry of exile; **adja.:** an exile community, government, network; exile literature.

ex.ist (ig.ZIST) v. to be; have being or life: Do ghosts exist? We can't exist without food; You can't exist long on bread and water.

ex.ist.ence (ig.ZIS.tunce) n. the state of existing: the existence of ghosts; Will the universe go out of existence? the miserable existence of the poor; the precarious existence (= life) of a wanted man; to eke out an existence (= a living) by taking in laundry. —**ex.ist.ent** (-tunt) adj.

ex.is.ten.tial (eg.zis.TEN.shul) adj. having to do with the philosophy of Jean-Paul Sartre and others that stresses living as the only reality and humans as responsible to themselves and for their own existence. —**ex.is.ten.tial.ism** n.; **ex.is.ten.tial.ist** n. & adj.

ex.it (EG.zit, EK.sit) n. **1** a way out, as from a stage, building, or highway: a plane's emergency exits; a window exit; There's no exit from the rear; The exit to the balcony was closed; **adja.:** an exit ramp, sign; an exit wound made by a bullet. **2** a going out, departure, or death: He felt sick and made a hasty exit from the meeting; **exits and entrances** (= when to come on stage and leave); **adja.:** exit papers, permits, visas; For honest feedback about work conditions, conduct an **exit interview** with an employee who is leaving employment; the **exit line** spoken by an actor before leaving a scene; an **exit poll** of voters as they come out after voting to find out how they voted. —**v. 1** go out: We exited from the highway to Main Street; Some exited by the fire escape, others through windows. **2** [as a stage direction] (He, she, or it) goes out: "(Antigonus) exit, pursued by a bear."

ex.o.bi.ol.o.gy (ex.oh.bye.OL.uh.jee) n. the biology of possible life in the universe outside the earth.

ex.o.crine gland (EX.uh.crin, -crine, -creen) n. a gland such as the salivary and tear glands that empties its secretion through a duct into the intestines or outside the body; cf. ENDOCRINE.

ex.o.dus (EX.uh.dus) *n.* a departure in large numbers, like that of the Israelites from ancient Egypt: *There's a mass exodus from the city to the country on summer weekends.*

ex of.fi.ci.o (ex.uh.FISH.ee.oh) *adj. & adv.* by virtue of one's official position: *She is a member of the board ex officio; an ex officio member of the board.*

ex.og.a.mous (ex.OG.uh.mus) *adj.* marrying only outside of one's tribe; **ex.og.a.my** (-mee) *n.*

ex.og.e.nous (ek.SOJ.uh.nus) *adj.* growing by additions on the outside, as tree stems; **ex.og.e.nous.ly** *adv.*

ex.on.er.ate (ig.ZON.uh.rate) *v.* **-ates, -at.ed, -at.ing** clear or free someone of guilt or responsibility for an action: *The verdict completely exonerated him of the charge; He was officially exonerated; to be exonerated from responsibility.* —**ex.on.er.a.tion** (-RAY.shun) *n.*

ex.or.bi.tant (ig.ZOR.buh.tunt) *adj.* excessive or unreasonable: *exorbitant demands, prices, profits.* —**ex.or.bi.tant.ly** *adv.*

ex.or.cise (EX.or.size) *v.* **-cis.es, -cised, -cis.ing** expel an evil spirit from a possessed person by solemn commands: *He exorcised the devil from Lu; He exorcised* (= freed) *Lu of the devil.* Also **ex.or.cize.** —**ex.or.cism** *n.;* **ex.or.cist** *n.*

ex.o.sphere (EX.us.feer) *n.* the outermost part of the atmosphere; **ex.o.spher.ic** (-FER.ic) *adj.*

ex.o.ther.mal (ex.oh.THUR.mul, "TH" as in "thin") *adj.* of a chemical change, attended by liberation of heat, as in combustion. Also **ex.o.ther.mic.**

ex.ot.ic (ig.ZOT.ic) *adj.* **1** of plants, fishes, foods, fashions, words, etc., introduced from abroad; not indigenous or native: *The African violet is an exotic plant that is native to Kenya and Tanzania.* **2** strangely fascinating or attractive: *an exotic appeal, atmosphere, feeling; exotic colors; an exotic nightclub dancer,*

ex.ot.i.ca (ig.ZOT.i.cuh) *n.pl.* exotic things collectively.

ex.pand (ik.SPAND) *v.* make or become larger, esp. in extent, by unfolding, opening, spreading, etc.: *Heat expands metals; A flooded river may expand into a lake; to expand a short story into a novel; A professor* **expands on** or **upon** (= explains at length) *a theme during a lecture.* —**ex.pand.a.ble** or **ex.pan.si.ble** *adj.*

ex.panse (ik.SPANCE) *n.* a large surface or stretch: *the broad expanse of his chest; the wide expanse of the grassy plain; the vast expanses of outer space.*

ex.pan.sion card (or **board**) *n.* a circuit board that allows a computer's memory or other capability to be increased: *An expansion card connects to a computer's* **expansion slot.**

ex.pan.sion.ism (ik.SPAN.shuh.niz.um) *n.* the policy or practice of expanding one's territory or power. —**ex.pan.sion.ist** *n. & adj.*

ex.pan.sive (ik.SPAN.siv) *adj.* **1** capable of or causing expansion: *the expansive force of heat on metals.* **2** of people, friendly and willing to talk: *She was in an expansive mood; A small compliment will make him expansive; an expansive personality.* —**ex.pan.sive.ly** *adv.;* **ex.pan.sive.ness** *n.*

ex par.te (ex.PAR.tee) *adj. & adv.* [legal use] without benefit to the other party: *an ex parte judgment, order; The case was heard ex parte* (= in the absence of the other party).

ex.pa.ti.ate (iks.PAY.shee.ate) *v.* **-ates, -at.ed, -at.ing** write or talk at length *on* or *upon* a subject. —**ex.pa.ti.a.tion** (-AY.shun) *n.*

ex.pa.tri.ate (iks.PAY.tree.ate) *v.* **-ates, -at.ed, -at.ing 1** withdraw oneself from one's native country and settle abroad: *He expatriated himself to England on retirement.* **2** exile; also, deprive of acquired citizenship: *a dissident expatriated from his homeland.* **3** to send to one's home country: *In some countries profits can be expatriated.*

—*n.* a person settled abroad in relation to his or her native country: *Ukrainian expatriates in North America;* **adja.:** *expatriate Americans in Japan; Bethune's expatriate heroism as a doctor in China.* —**ex.pa.tri.a.tion** (-AY.shun) *n.*

ex.pect (ik.SPECT) *v.* look forward to, usu. with certainty, often with hope or confidence: *Much is expected of or from a nation's leaders; People expect them to deliver on their election promises; I'm expecting company; I expect they'll be here by noon; They'll be here by noon,* **I expect** (= I suppose); *His wife is* **expecting** (= pregnant); *She's expecting twins.* —**ex.pect.a.ble** *adj.*

ex.pect.an.cy (ik.SPEC.tun.see) *n.* **-cies** the state of expecting or something expected: *There was an air of expectancy in the room when the hero was announced; life expectancy.* —**ex.pect.ant** (-tunt) *adj.: expectant fathers and mothers* (expecting a baby to be born). —**ex.pect.ant.ly** adv.

ex.pec.ta.tion (ex.pec.TAY.shun) n. **1** the act of expecting: *She had every expectation of winning the gold medal; He stayed home that day in expectation of* (= expecting) *a visit.* **2 expectations** pl. what is hoped for or the basis of hoping: *to have great* or *high expectations of winning; Contrary to expectations, everyone did well at school; He didn't fall short of expectations; He succeeded beyond all expectations; to come up to, exceed, meet, surpass expectations.*

ex.pec.to.rant (ik.SPEC.tuh.runt) n. a medicine that helps to expectorate.

ex.pec.to.rate (ik.SPEC.tuh.rate) v. -rates, -rat.ed, -rat.ing cough up phlegm; discharge sputum; also, spit. —**ex.pec.to.ra.tion** (-RAY.shun) n.

ex.pe.di.en.cy (ik.SPEE.dee.un.see) n. -cies suitability for a specific, usu. selfish purpose, without regard for principles: *political expediency.* Also **ex.pe.di.ence** (-unce).

ex.pe.di.ent (ik.SPEE.dee.unt) n. a device of convenience: *a phone call as an expedient for leaving a meeting.* —adj. politically wise: *The legislators thought it expedient to vote themselves a raise now rather than after re-election.*

ex.pe.dite (EX.puh.dite) v. -dites, -dit.ed, -dit.ing help speed up a plan, service, etc.: *Enclose a self-addressed stamped envelope to expedite a reply; Postal codes are used to expedite the processing of mail.* —**ex.pe.dit.er** or **ex.pe.di.tor** n.

ex.pe.di.tion (ex.puh.DISH.un) n. **1** a journey of people, ships, etc. organized for a specific purpose: *to go on, launch, lead, mount, organize an expedition; archaeological, military, scientific, whaling expeditions; an expedition to the Arctic; an expedition across the Sahara Desert; a cod-fishing expedition.* **2** the quality of being expeditious: *Food was dispatched with expedition to the famine-stricken area.*

ex.pe.di.tion.ar.y (ex.puh.DISH.uh.nair.ee) adj. having to do with a military expedition: *Cuban expeditionary forces in Angola.*

ex.pe.di.tious (ex.puh.DISH.us) adj. with easy and efficient speed; without delay: *fast and expeditious service; an expeditious answer, journey, method, move, plan.* —**ex.pe.di.tious.ly** adv.

ex.pel (ik.SPEL) v. -pels, -pelled, -pel.ling force out: *Air is expelled from the lungs in breathing; Students may be expelled* (= dismissed) *from school for se-*rious misbehavior. —**ex.pel.la.ble** adj. —**ex.pel.lee** (ex.puh.LEE) n.

ex.pend (ik.SPEND) v. use up large sums, resources, etc.: *the energies expended on* or *in tracking down Bigfoot.* —**ex.pend.a.ble 1** adj. that may be disposed of: *expendable income, jobs, supplies; an expendable regiment.* **2 expendables** n.pl. supplies such as paper, pencil, and ink.

ex.pend.i.ture (ik.SPEN.duh.chur) n. a spending or what is spent: *Every project requires the expenditure of time, money, energy, and other resources; We are trying to curb, curtail, cut down (on), reduce unnecessary expenditure; expenditures for luxuries.*

ex.pense (ik.SPENCE) n. **1** cost considered usu. as large: *She was put through college at her parents' expense; They were put to great expense; They went to great expense; They spared no expense to educate their children; Buying a car is a considerable expense for most families; to incur* or *run up an expense; to curb, curtail, cut down (on), defray, reduce, reimburse, share expenses; The school was built at government expense, not at our expense; They tried to increase volume* **at the expense of** quality; *A gas guzzler is a great expense* (= cause of expenditure). **2 expenses** pl. money for incidental expenditure: *a sales representative who gets a salary, car, and expenses.*

expense account n. a record of business expenses that are repaid to the employee.

ex.pen.sive (ik.SPEN.siv) adj. high-priced. —**ex.pen.sive.ly** adv.

ex.pe.rience (ik.SPEER.ee.unce) n. what one lives through, i.e., sees, feels, does, etc.; what happens to one; also, the knowledge gained: *Everyone learns by* or *from experience; We acquire, gain, get experience from doing things; broad, direct, first-hand, hands-on, practical, previous, wide experience; childhood experiences; to have an enlightening, harrowing, memorable, painful, pleasant, rewarding, unforgettable experience.* —v. -enc.es, -enced, -enc.ing have experience of something: *He had never experienced starvation;* adj.: *a qualified and* **experienced** *teacher; She's experienced at* or *in teaching the handicapped.* —**ex.pe.ri.en.tial** (-EN.shul) adj.

ex.per.i.ment (ik.SPER.uh.munt) n. a controlled action or process to discover something unknown or to test or demonstrate a known fact: *to carry out, conduct, perform an experiment; a chemistry experiment; an experiment in international*

cooperation. —*v.* (-ment) carry out experiments: *The Wright brothers experimented with different types of airplanes; Scientists experiment on mice and guinea pigs.* —**ex.per.i.men.tal** (-uh.MEN.tul) *adj.* having to do with experiments: *an experimental farm operated by the federal government to do agricultural research; an experimental variety of wheat; in the experimental stage of development; experimental* (= practical), *not theoretical knowledge; the experimental sciences;* **ex.per.i.men.tal.ly** *adv.*
—**ex.per.i.men.ta.tion** (-men.TAY.shun) *n.*

ex.pert (EX.purt) *n.* one who is highly skilled and knowledgeable: *a handwriting expert; an expert in arranging flowers; an expert on warranties; an expert at detecting flaws;* **adja.:** *an expert eye, job, typist, witness; expert advice, opinion, testimony, work.* —**adjp.** (also iks.PURT) having special skill and knowledge: *She's expert at calligraphy; very expert.*
—**ex.pert.ly** *adv.;* **ex.pert.ness** *n.*

ex.pert.ise (ex.pur.TEEZ) *n.* an expert's skill or knowledge: *technical expertise; Her expertise is or lies in labor relations; the expertise to mediate a dispute.*

ex.pi.ate (EX.pee.ate) *v.* -ates, -at.ed, -at.ing atone for a wrong: *to expiate a crime.* —**ex.pi.a.tor.y** *adj.:* expiatory prayers, sacrifices.—**ex.pi.a.tion** (-AY.shun) *n.*

ex.pi.ra.tion (ex.puh.RAY.shun) *n.* a breathing out or expiring: *expiration and inspiration; The mayor decided to run again at the expiration* (= end) *of his first term in office.* —**ex.pi.ra.to.ry** (ik.SPY.ruh.tor.ee) *adj.*

ex.pire (ik.SPIRE) *v.* -pires, -pired, -pir.ing breathe out; hence, breathe one's last: *He expired before next of kin could be called; Your license has expired* (= come to an end).

ex.pi.ry (ik.SPY.uh.ree, EX.puh.ree) *n.* -ries an expiring: *A driver's license may be renewed on expiry; the expiry date.*

ex.plain (ik.SPLAIN) *v.* make something clear and understandable: *You were absent yesterday – please explain; I can explain my absence; Al explained why he was absent; He explained that his wife was ill; He didn't try to* **explain it away** (= avoid an explanation by giving excuses). —**explain oneself 1** make one's meaning clear. **2** justify one's conduct. —**ex.plain.a.ble** *adj.*
—**ex.pla.na.tion** (ex.pluh.NAY.shun) *n.:* A full explanation is called for; the reasons given in explanation of his absence.* —**ex.plan.a.to.ry** (ik.SPLAN.uh.tor.ee) *adj.*

ex.ple.tive (EX.pluh.tiv) *n.* an obscenity: *a mild expletive; an edited story with expletives deleted.*

ex.pli.ca.ble (EX.pluh.cuh.bul, ik.SPLIC.uh-) *adj.* explainable: *puzzling but explicable behavior.*

ex.pli.cate (EX.pluh.cate) *v.* -ates, -at.ed, -at.ing analyze or interpret a passage, theory, etc. —**ex.pli.ca.tion** (-CAY.shun) *n.*

ex.plic.it (ik.SPLIS.it) *adj.* clearly stated, explained, or pictured; not implicit or vague: *The rules are explicit on that point; explicit language, sex, violence in movies.*
—**ex.plic.it.ly** *adv.*

ex.plode (ik.SPLODE) *v.* -plodes, -plod.ed, -plod.ing burst with a loud noise: *A boiler may explode under pressure; A bomb explodes or has to be exploded* (= blown up); *Pent-up discontent may explode* (= erupts) *into a riot; She exploded with fury* (= suddenly became furious) *when she realized she had been cheated; Science has exploded* (= disproved) *many myths and superstitions;* **adja.:** *an* **exploding** (= suddenly expanding) *demand, market, population.* —**exploded** *adj.* of a drawing, model, or view of a mechanism, showing components separated but in their relative positions: *an exploded view of a carburetor.*

ex.ploit (EX.ploit) *n.* a daring deed; feat: *the heroic exploits performed by Hercules.* —*v.* (ik.SPLOIT) make use of, often in an unfair or selfish manner: *They exploited her generosity.*
—**ex.ploit.a.tive** (-tuh.tiv) *adj.:* exploitative actions, treatment; an exploitative wage offer. Also **ex.ploit.ive.**
—**ex.ploi.ta.tion** (ex.ploy.TAY.shun) *n.*

ex.plo.ra.tion (ex.pluh.RAY.shun) *n.* an exploring: *space exploration.*

ex.plore (ik.SPLORE) *v.* -plores, -plored, -plor.ing search a new region so as to learn about it: *a lunar rover to explore the moon's surface; A surgeon explores a wound.* —**ex.plor.er** *n.*
—**ex.plor.a.to.ry** (-ruh.tor.ee) *adj.:* an exploratory voyage; exploratory surgery.

ex.plo.sion (ik.SPLOH.zhun) *n.* **1** an exploding or its noise: *What caused the explosion? A lighted match set off or touched off the explosion.* **2** sudden expansion or increase: *information, knowledge, population explosion; the explosion of interest in computers.*

ex.plo.sive (ik.SPLOH.siv) *n.* a substance that can cause an explosion: *TNT is a high explosive that detonates relatively fast; Gunpowder is a low explosive; plastic explosives* (= bombs); *to set off an explosive;*

The explosive had been planted in the baggage. —*adj.* capable of exploding: *an explosive charge; an explosive situation created by a public injustice; Lee has an explosive temper.* —**ex.plo.sive.ly** *adv.*; **ex.plo.sive.ness** *n.*

ex.po (EX.poh) *n.* **-pos** *Informal.* an international exhibition or world's fair: *the 1992 Seville expo.*

ex.po.nent (ik.SPOH.nunt) *n.* **1** one that expounds; hence, one that favors or promotes a policy, method, theory, etc.: *a leading exponent of free trade.* **2** in algebra, a symbol indicating an operation, as 3 in a³.

ex.po.nen.tial (ex.puh.NEN.shul) *adj.* very rapid: *A population that multiplies itself in a short period is increasing or growing at an exponential rate.* —**ex.po.nen.tial.ly** *adv.*

ex.port (ik.SPORT) *v.* **1** send or carry away to a foreign country, esp. goods for sale: *Cars are exported from Japan to North America; to export ideas, revolutions, skills, technology;* **adj.** domestic and **exported** goods; **adja.:** *petroleum exporting countries; an exporting venture.* **2** send data files or images from one application program to another. —*n.* (EX.port) an exporting or thing exported: *a country's exports and imports.* —**ex.port.er** *n*

ex.pose (ik.SPOZE) *v.* **-pos.es, -posed, -pos.ing 1** lay open; hence, display or reveal: *A bikini exposes some of the body; He was charged with exposing himself* (= displaying his body indecently) *on the beach.* **2** leave unprotected: *Children are exposed to much violence on TV; Ancient Spartans used to expose unwanted infants* (= kill by leaving them outside); *exposed to the elements.* **3** uncover sensitized film or plate for taking picture.

ex.po.sé (ex.poh.ZAY) *n.* an exposition, esp. an exposure of a crime or scandal.

ex.po.si.tion (ex.puh.ZISH.un) *n.* **1** an explanation in spoken or written form. **2** a large exhibition: *fairs and expositions.*

ex.pos.i.tor (ik.SPOZ.i.tur) *n.* one who explains or interprets. —**ex.pos.i.tor.y** (-tor.ee) *adj.:* expository writing.

ex post fac.to (-FAC.toh) after the fact: *An ex post facto law has retroactive force.*

ex.pos.tu.late (ik.SPOS.chuh.late) *v.* **-lates, -lat.ed, -lat.ing** plead or argue earnestly *with* someone about something requiring attention or to dissuade from an action: *She expostulated with us on the need for more editors.* —**ex.pos.tu.la.tion** (-LAY.shun) *n.*

ex.po.sure (ik.SPOH.zhur) *n.* **1** an exposing or being exposed: *a corrupt politician afraid of public exposure in the media; wide exposure* (= publicity); *The abandoned infant died of exposure (to the elements); charged with indecent exposure (of the body); a film with 24 exposures* (= pictures) *per roll; An exposure meter measures light intensity to determine the correct exposure time for a picture.* **2** aspect or facing: *Houses with a southern exposure get more sun in the winter.*

ex.pound (ik.SPOWND) *v.* set forth or explain a doctrine, theory, writings, etc. systematically, as by an authority on the subject: *to expound the theory of relativity; He expounded for hours on the need for pay equity.*

ex.press (ik.SPRESS) *v.* **1** put thoughts or feelings into words, music, signs, or symbols: *Parents express their concerns to teachers; to express belief, confidence, doubt, enthusiasm, hope, interest, optimism, resentment, satisfaction, views; A nod expresses assent; a sign* [+] *that expresses addition; He's learning to express himself in correct English;* **adja.:** *his expressed interest, desires, wishes.* **2** squeeze out juice, oil, milk, etc. from its source. **3** send by express: *We'll express the parcel to Vancouver.* —**adja. 1** clearly and directly stated: *express permission; He's here with the express purpose of talking to you; This was her express wish; She's the express* (= exact) *image of her mother.* **2** fast and direct: *an express elevator, highway, mail service, messenger, train.* —**adv.** by express: *Send it express to Houston.* —*n.* **1** a bus, train, or other service for transporting people or things quickly and directly. **2** the things thus transported.

ex.pres.sion (ik.SPRESH.un) *n.* **1** something that expresses thoughts and feelings; word or phrase: *colloquial, common, idiomatic, slang, technical expressions.* **2** a gesture, look, sigh, or tone of voice: *the expression of sadness on his face; angry, grave, happy, pained, puzzled, serious, vacuous expressions* (= looks). **3** the expressing of meaning, beauty, feelings, etc.: *She sings with expression; Her feelings sometimes **find expression** in poetic language; a statue that is beautiful **beyond expression*** (= beyond words).

ex.pres.sion.ism (ik.SPRESH.uh.niz.um) *n.* an artistic style developed as a reaction to impressionism that gives form to the artist's strong inner feelings and is exemplified by Van Gogh, Gauguin, O'Neill, and Kafka; **ex.pres.sion.ist** *n. & adj.* —**ex.pres.sion.is.tic** (-NIS.tic) *adj.*

ex.pres.sive (ik.SPRES.iv) *adj.* **1** serving to express: *words that are expressive of emotions.* **2** meaningful: *a very expressive gesture, look, word.* —**ex.pres.sive.ly** *adv.*

ex.press.ly (ik.SPRES.lee) *adv.* clearly or explicitly: *The rules expressly forbid it.*

ex.press.way (ik.SPRES.way) *n.* a limited-access divided highway for high-speed traffic.

ex.pro.pri.ate (ik.SPROH.pree.ate) *v.* **-ates, -at.ed, -at.ing** take land from the owner for public use, as for schools, parks, airports, etc. —**ex.pro.pri.a.tion** (-AY.shun) *n.*

ex.pul.sion (ik.SPUL.shun) *n.* an expelling or being expelled or forced out: *a student facing expulsion from school for cheating on exams.*

ex.punge (ik.SPUNJ) *v.* **-pung.es, -punged, -pung.ing** remove completely: *The judge ordered certain remarks expunged from the records.*

ex.pur.gate (EX.pur.gate) *v.* **-gates, -gat.ed, -gat.ing** purify a book or other writing of morally objectionable matter; *adj.*: *an expurgated edition of Shakespeare.* —**ex.pur.ga.tion** (-GAY.shun) *n.*

ex.qui.site (EX.kwuh.zit, ik.SQUIZ.it) *adj.* **1** of great excellence because of elaborate workmanship, delicate texture, keenness of taste, etc.: *exquisite beauty, grace, joy, taste; an exquisite* (= *finely made*) *design, lace.* **2** keenly felt: *exquisite agony, pain, torture.* —**ex.qui.site.ly** *adv.*

ex.tant (EX.tunt, ik.STANT) *adj.* of documents, paintings, life forms, etc., still existing: *Only one copy of the book is extant; one of the few extant varieties of the dying species.*

ex.tem.po.re (ik.STEM.puh.ree) *adj. & adv.* (spoken or done) without the use of notes or memory; *also* **ex.tem.po.rar.y** (-rair.ee) or **ex.tem.po.ra.ne.ous** (-RAY.nee.us) *adj.*

ex.tem.po.rize (ik.STEM.puh.rize) *v.* **-riz.es, -rized, -riz.ing** devise as something temporary; improvise: *An actor extemporizes when he forgets his lines; an extemporized shelter.*

ex.tend (ik.STEND) *v.* **1** stretch out in length, area, scope, time, etc.: *hands extended in welcome; Birds extend their wings when they fly; The drought-stricken area extends as far as the coast; The country extends* (= *reaches*) *from the Atlantic to the Pacific; Their sovereignty extends* (= *spreads*) *over the Arctic; to extend* (= *prolong*) *a vacation by another week; The deadline has been extended to Decem-*

ber 31; He **extended** *himself* (= *tried unusually hard*) *and suffered a nervous breakdown; adj.: an* **extended** *benefit program; with extended hands; an extended celebration, deadline, debate, period, stay, struggle, visit, warranty; extended leave, store hours; Nursing homes provide* **extended care** (*beyond what a hospital can*) *to the sick and disabled; an* **extended family** *of relatives under the same roof with the nuclear family.* **2** offer or convey: *to extend someone aid, credit, greetings, hospitality, an invitation, a loan, a welcome; She extended her sympathy to the bereaved family.*

ex.ten.sion (ik.STEN.shun) *n.* an extending or something extended as a continuation or addition: *He has been granted an extension of leave; Lou happened to listen in on the extension* (*telephone*) *when Pat called Lee; the extension of our knowledge; an extension to a house; an* **extension cord** *for an electrical appliance.*

ex.ten.sive (ik.STEN.siv) *adj.* having great extent of area, scope, influence, etc.: *She has extensive knowledge of her subject; Plentiful land is sometimes put to* **extensive farming** *though without intensive cultivation.* —**ex.ten.sive.ly** *adv.*

ex.tent (ik.STENT) *n.* the degree, scope, or area of extension: *the extent of one's hopes, influence, knowledge; We trust him to a certain extent and no further; to the extent of $500.*

ex.ten.u.at.ing (ik.STEN.yoo.ay.ting) *adj.* making an offense or guilt seem less serious: *His license was not suspended because of extenuating circumstances.* —**ex.ten.u.a.tion** (-AY.shun) *n.*: *the reasons given in extenuation of his conduct.*

ex.te.ri.or (ik.STEER.ee.ur) *n.* the immediate outside: *the brick exterior of a house; Her stern exterior hides a soft heart; shooting the exteriors* (= *outdoor scenes*) *for a movie.* —*adj.*: *a house with a handsome exterior design; exterior architectural features; an auto's exterior finish, styling, trim; Our car has two exterior mirrors; an oil-based exterior paint; an exterior staircase that serves as a fire escape; a building's exterior walls.* —**ex.te.ri.or.ly** *adv.*

ex.ter.mi.nate (ik.STUR.muh.nate) *v.* **-nates, -nat.ed, -nat.ing 1** destroy by killing: *a poison to exterminate rats.* **2** eliminate or wipe out: *Has smallpox been completely exterminated?* —**ex.ter.mi.na.tion** (-NAY.shun) *n.*: *the extermination of mice.* —**ex.ter.mi.na.tor** (-nay.tur) *n.*

ex.tern (EX.turn) *n.* one who is professionally connected with an institution, but does not live in it; cf. INTERN.

ex.ter.nal (ik.STUR.nul) **1** *adj.* on or from the outside, esp. as not related; not internal: *Rubbing alcohol is for external use; external evidence from outside the work under study; an external influence; the minister for* **external** (= foreign) *affairs.* **2 externals** *n.pl.* outward aspects or features such as one's clothing, manners, etc.: *the externals of religious practice.* —**ex.ter.nal.ly** *adv.*

ex.tinct (ik.STINCT) *adj.* no longer existing or active: *an extinct volcano; an extinct animal such as the dodo or dinosaur.* —**ex.tinc.tion** (-shun) *n.*: *the extinction of one's hopes; the extinction of the passenger pigeon.*

ex.tin.guish (ik.STING.wish) *v.* put out or put an end to something: *to extinguish a fire; to extinguish hopes, passions, rights.* —**ex.tin.guish.er** *n.*

ex.tir.pate (EX.tur.pate) *v.* **-pates, -pat.ed, -pat.ing** root out a race, family, species, evil, etc. —**ex.tir.pa.tion** (-PAY.shun) *n.*

ex.tol or **ex.toll** (ik.STOLE) *v.* **-tols** or **-tolls, -tolled, -tol.ling** praise highly; exalt: *The poem extols the virtue and courage of the heroine.*

ex.tort (ik.STORT) *v.* get something from someone by force or intimidation: *to extort confessions, money, promises.* —**ex.tor.tion** (-shun) *n.*: *extortion attempts, charges, demands, threats; to pay* **extortion money** *to gangsters.* —**ex.tor.tion.er** or **ex.tor.tion.ist** *n.*

ex.tor.tion.ate (ik.STOR.shuh.nit) *adj.* excessive: *extortionate demands, fees, interest rates, prices, taxes.*

ex.tra (EX.truh) *adj.* more or larger than normal: *available at no extra cost; more work for extra pay; adv.: an extra added attraction; an extra dry champagne; extra large eggs; an extra special quality.* —*n.* something or someone extra, as an additional favor, a special edition of a newspaper, or an actor for a minor role: *Extra! Extra! Read all about it! The epic film used 2,500 extras.*

ex.tract (ik.STRACT) *v.* draw out by physical or mental effort: *to extract* (= pull) *a tooth; to extract metal from ore* (by mechanical separation); *to extract* (= press) *juice from fruit; to extract* (= take out) *a passage from a book; to extract a confession (from an unwilling person).* —*n.* (EX.tract) something extracted: *an extract from Shakespeare; a cosmetic extract like musk; lemon, meat, vanilla extracts.* —**ex.trac.tor** *n.*

ex.trac.tion (ik.STRAC.shun) *n.* **1** an act of extracting: *the extraction of teeth.* **2** a person's ancestry: *a woman of noble extraction; people of British extraction.*

ex.trac.tive (ik.STRAC.tiv) *adj.* that extracts: *Lumbering, fishing, and mining are* **extractive industries**; *extractive agriculture, processes.*

ex.tra.cur.ric.u.lar (EX.truh.cuh.RIC.yuh.lur) *adj.* outside the regular curriculum: *sports, dramatics, hobbies, and such noncredit* **extracurricular activities** *of students.*

ex.tra.dite (EX.truh.dite) *v.* **-dites, -dit.ed, -dit.ing** deliver a prisoner *from* one country *to* another to be tried for a crime committed there. —**ex.tra.di.tion** (-DISH.un) *n.*

ex.tra.mar.i.tal (ex.truh.MAIR.uh.tul) *adj.* outside marriage; adulterous: *extramarital affairs, relationships, sex.*

ex.tra.mu.ral (ex.truh.MYOOR.ul) *adj.* outside the school or between schools: *extramural events, sports.*

ex.tra.ne.ous (ik.STRAY.nee.us) *adj.* **1** from outside: *pollution from extraneous substances.* **2** not relevant or germane: *an extraneous remark; an incident extraneous to the theme of the story.* —**ex.tra.ne.ous.ly** *adv.*

ex.traor.di.nar.y (ik.STROR.duh.nair.ee) *adj.* not ordinary; unusual. —**ex.traor.di.nar.i.ly** *adv.*

ex.trap.o.late (ik.STRAP.uh.late) *v.* **-lates, -lat.ed, -lat.ing** to follow a trend beyond the established range, as by extending a graph or curve: *We extrapolate costs, figures, findings, results, samples, surveys; a population estimate extrapolated* (= obtained by extrapolating) *from current census figures; In the late 1960s, demographers extrapolated* (= estimated) *that the world population would reach 10 billion by A.D. 2000; Scientists often extrapolate* (= extend their judgments) *from tests on animals to human risks in using a drug.* —**ex.trap.o.la.tion** (-LAY.shun) *n.*

ex.tra.sen.so.ry (ex.truh.SEN.suh.ree) *adj.* outside normal sense perception.

ex.tra.ter.res.tri.al (ex.truh.tuh.RES.tree.ul) *adj.* beyond the earth's atmosphere: *extraterrestrial beings, exploration, life, navigation.*

ex.tra.ter.ri.to.ri.al (EX.truh.ter.uh.TOR.ee.ul) *adj.* extending beyond one's territory: *extraterritorial ambitions, jurisdiction, privileges, rights.*

ex.trav.a.gance (ik.STRAV.uh.gunce) *n.* the quality or an instance of being extravagant: *the extravagance of her spending habits; He considers it an extravagance* to eat out frequently.

ex.trav.a.gant (ik.STRAV.uh.gunt) *adj.* **1** excessive: *extravagant claims, demands, praise, prices, spending.* **2** wasteful: *an extravagant lifestyle, spender; He's rather extravagant in his spending, in his tastes.* —**ex.trav.a.gant.ly** *adv.*

ex.trav.a.gan.za (ik.STRAV.uh.GAN.zuh) *n.* a spectacular stage or screen production; also, such an event: *a week-long extravaganza with stage shows, fiddler contests, livestock shows, beauty pageants, and fireworks.*

extravert See EXTROVERT.

ex.treme (ik.STREEM) **1** *adj.* farthest away, esp. from a middle: *the extreme edge of a cliff; the extreme rear; the extreme left wing of a political party; the extreme right; extreme examples.* **2** *adj.* of the highest degree: *the extreme heat of summer; in extreme cold, danger, old age, pain, poverty; with extreme joy, kindness, patience; an extreme case of insanity; extreme reactions to a drug; extreme caution.* **3** *adj.* of people and their behavior, not moderate: *extreme cruelty, opinions, views; to take extreme action; to use extreme (= excessive or drastic) measures.* —*n.* something that is extreme or situated at either end: *to go from one extreme to the other; the extremes of joy and despair; It was disappointing* **in the extreme** (= extremely); *She went to* **extremes** (= the utmost limits) *to save a few dollars.* —**ex.treme.ly** *adv.*

ex.tre.mism (ik.STREE.miz.um) *n.* a stance, philosophy, or activity that is not moderate, esp. the far left or far right in politics: **ex.tre.mist** *n. & adj.*

ex.trem.i.ty (ik.STREM.i.tee) *n.* **-ties** an extreme condition, degree, or part: *in the extremity of despair; Friends were a great help in her extremity; people driven* **to the last extremity** (= to death) *by famine; The* **extremities** (= hands and feet) *are the first to feel the cold.*

ex.tri.cate (EX.truh.cate) *v.* **-cates, -cat.ed, -cat.ing** free someone or oneself from a difficult situation: *to extricate oneself from a financial mess, a sticky situation, a web of lies.* —**ex.tri.ca.ble** (-cuh.bul) *adj.* —**ex.tri.ca.tion** (-CAY.shun) *n.*

ex.trin.sic (ik.STRIN.sic) *adj. Formal.* outside the essential nature of something; not intrinsic: *facts that are extrinsic to the subject under discussion.*

ex.tro.vert (EX.truh.vurt) *n.* one whose interests are in other people and in the world outside rather than in oneself: *There is more of the extrovert than introvert in the more outgoing among us;*

also **ex.tra.vert**. —**ex.tro.ver.sion** or **ex.tra.ver.sion** *n.* —*adj.*: *an extrovert personality;* also **ex.tro.vert.ed** or **ex.tra.vert.ed.**

ex.trude (ik.STROOD, long "OO") *v.* **-trudes, -trud.ed, -trud.ing 1** stick out or force out. **2** shape by forcing out a ductile material such as metals, plastics, and rubber through a die: *a pasta machine that extrudes everything from noodles to macaroni.* —**ex.tru.sion** (-TROO.zhun) *n.* —**ex.tru.sive** (-TROO.siv) *adj.*

ex.u.ber.ant (ig.ZOO.buh.runt) *adj.* **1** overflowing with cheer: *an exuberant youth; in an exuberant mood.* **2** profuse in growth: *the exuberant vegetation of a tropical jungle.* —**ex.u.ber.ance** (-runce) *n.*

ex.ude (ig.ZOOD, ik.SUDE) *v.* **-udes, -ud.ed, -ud.ing** come out or send out, as sweat through pores: *a hostess exuding charm.* —**ex.u.da.tion** (ex.yuh.DAY.shun) *n.*

ex.ult (ig.ZULT) *v.* rejoice in triumph; be jubilant: *to exult at her success; to exult in the victory; to exult over (winning) a gold medal; to exult (= crow) over someone's defeat.* —**ex.ult.ant** (-tunt) *adj.*; **ex.ult.ant.ly** *adv.* —**ex.ul.ta.tion** (EG.zul.TAY.shun, EX.ul-) *n.*: *the joy and exultation of an unexpected victory; a moment of exultation.*

ex.urb (ex.URB) *n.* a region beyond a city's suburbs, usu. inhabited by the well-to-do; **ex.ur.ban** *adj.*; **ex.ur.ban.ite** (-buh.nite) *n. & adj.*

ex.ur.bi.a (ex.UR.bee.uh) *n.* exurbs and the exurban way of life.

eye *n.* **1** the organ of sight: *He ran his eyes over the front page looking for his name; She was so attractive he couldn't take his eyes off her; He wears a patch over his blind eye; to blink, drop, lift, raise, rest, roll, squint, strain one's eyes; an eagle eye* (= keen sight); *blond hair and blue eyes* (= irises); *to give someone a black eye* (= bruised eye); *Feast your eyes on* (= Enjoy the sight of) *our manicured lawn; She is so calm she can be charged with theft and not* **bat an eye** (= show any emotion); *a confidential document* **for your eyes only** (= not to be copied or shared with anyone). **2** a look or glance: *to cast an eye on something; to fix one's eye on something; an anxious, critical eye; the green eye of jealousy; prying, piercing eyes; a sharp, suspicious eye; a watchful or weather eye; He's a flirt with a roving or wandering eye; to give someone the glad eye* (= a seductive glance); *to ward off the evil eye* (= a look that is sup-

posed to bring harm); *a jaundiced* (= jealous) *eye; There's more to it than* **meets the eye** (= more than is seen). **3** the power of seeing; hence, observation or judgment: *good, strong, weak eyes; He was guilty in the eyes* (= judgment) *of the law.* **4** one that detects: *an electric eye* (= photoelectric cell); *a private eye* (= detective). **5** something resembling an eye, as a needle's hole, buds on a potato, the calm center of a developing hurricane, a bull's-eye, etc. —**close** or **shut one's eyes to** ignore a situation that calls for action. —**eye for an eye** retaliation in kind. —**have an eye for** have the ability to see clearly: *She has an eye for detail; He has a good eye for bargains.* —**lay** or **set eyes on** look at or see the first time: *He loved her from the moment he set eyes on her.* —**make eyes at** look amorously at someone; ogle. —**see eye to eye with** agree with someone. —**throw dust in someone's eyes** deceive someone intentionally. —**with an eye to** having as one's purpose: *He asked to see the boss with an eye to asking for a loan.* —**with one's eyes open** fully aware of what may happen. —**with the naked eye** without the aid of an optical instrument such as a microscope or telescope.
—*v.* **eyes, eyed, ey·ing** or **eye·ing** look at, observe, or watch: *The policeman eyed him critically; The professor eyed her quizzically.*

eye appeal *n.* visual attractiveness: *Color is added to foods for eye appeal.*

eye.ball *n.* the ball-shaped part of an eye: *I'm up to my eyeballs in work.* —**eyeball to eyeball** *Informal.* face to face: *They went eyeball to eyeball with the Yankees;* **adj.**: *an eyeball-to-eyeball confrontation that makes one person blink.* —*v. Informal.* look closely at someone: *The guard was supposed to eyeball the prisoner at all times.*

eye.brow *n.* the arch of bone and growth of hair over each eye: *to pluck, tweeze one's eyebrows; a man with bushy, thick eyebrows; The court ruling* **raised eyebrows** (= caused a sensation) *around the country.*

eye-catching *adj. Informal.* striking; also, conspicuous: *an eye-catching design.* —**eye-catcher** *n.*

eye contact *n.* the meeting of two people's eyes: *She avoids eye contact with strangers in the big city.*

eyed (IDE) *adj. & comb.form.* having eyes or eyelike markings: *an eyed design; eyed like a peacock; almond-eyed,*
cockeyed, one-eyed, sharp-eyed.

eye.ful *n.* a sight, view, or person likely to please one: *Eve's quite an eyeful; He got an eyeful* (= more than he expected to see) *when he looked into the room.*

eye.glass *n.* a lens to aid vision, usu. **eyeglasses** *pl.*

eye.lash *n.* a hair or fringe of hairs on the edge of the upper or lower eyelid.

eye.let (EYE.lit) *n.* a small hole, usu. rimmed with metal, as for a shoelace to pass through, or edged with stitches, as in embroidered designs.

eye.lid *n.* the upper or lower fold of skin over an eye: *drooping, swollen eyelids.*

eye.lin.er (EYE.lye.nur) *n.* a cosmetic preparation applied to the base of the eyelashes.

eye-opener *n.* **1** something that surprises and enlightens: *The results of the literacy survey came as an eye-opener to educators.* **2** *Informal.* an early-morning drink.

eye.phone *n.* a headset containing a pair of wide-angle lenses used for viewing virtual-reality displays.

eye.piece *n.* the viewing lens of a microscope, telescope, etc.

eye-popping *adj.* impressive or astonishing: *eye-popping color; an eye-popping victory.*

eye.shade *n.* a green visor for shielding the eyes from strong light.

eye shadow *n.* a cosmetic preparation applied on the upper eyelids.

eye.sight *n.* vision: *bad, failing, poor eyesight.*

eyes-only *adj.* to be read only by the addressee: *an eyes-only document, message; information shared on an eyes-only basis.*

eye.sight *n.* vision.

eye.sore *n.* an unpleasant sight.

eye.tooth *n., pl.* **-teeth** an upper canine tooth: *It is a privilege anyone would* **give his eyeteeth** *for* (= It is a great privilege).

eye.wash *n.* **1** an eye lotion. **2** *Informal.* something said or done to impress or flatter.

eye.wit.ness (EYE.WIT.nis) *n.* one who can testify about a happening, having seen it in person: *an eyewitness to the accident; an eyewitness account.*

eying See EYE.

ey.rie (AIR.ee, EYE.ree) *n.* **-ries** a nest, as an eagle's, placed high: *The hawk swooped down from its eyrie; There's an eyrie of a restaurant atop the Tokyo Tower.* Also **aerie, aery, eyry.**

F, f

F or **f** (EF) *n.* **F's** or **f's** the sixth letter of the English alphabet; hence, the sixth in a series.

fa (FAH) *n.* in music, the fourth tone of the diatonic scale.

fab *adja. Informal* [short form] fabulous: *the Fab Four* (= the Beatles).

fa.ble (FAY.bul) *n.* **1** a story with a moral and animals as characters. **2** a myth or invention.

fa.bled (FAY.buld) *adj.* famous in legends or stories: *the fabled monster of Loch Ness; the fabled golden waves of prairie wheat; the most fabled of wines.*

fab.ric (FAB.ric) *n.* **1** a material, as flannel or other cloth, that is put together by weaving, knitting, or felting: *a fine fabric of linen fibers; synthetic, textile, and other fabrics.* **2** any structure of different elements: *None of the original fabric of the old cathedral remains today; the fabric of society weakened by civil wars.*

fab.ri.cate (FAB.ruh.cate) *v.* **-cates, -cat.ed, -cat.ing 1** create by putting parts together: *to fabricate a model; a new bronze alloy fabricated from copper and tin; adj.:* the separately **fabricated** *parts of a house; a pre-fabricated building; Margarine, bacon bits, coffee creamers, etc. are* **fabricated** *foods.* **2** make up in order to deceive: *to fabricate an excuse, explanation, falsehood, story.*
—**fab.ri.ca.tion** (-CAY.shun) *n.* falsehood: *That report was pure fabrication; an outright fabrication.* —**fab.ri.ca.tor** (-cay.tur) *n.*

fab.u.list (FAB.yuh.list) *n.* a teller or writer of fables, as Aesop.

fab.u.lous (FAB.yuh.lus) **1** *adja.* as in a fable: *fabulous dragons, heroes.* **2** *adj.* incredible or wonderful: *the fabulous treasures of sunken ships; I'm in fabulous health; You look fabulous.*
—**fab.u.lous.ly** *adv.: a fabulously wealthy man.*

fa.cade or **fa.çade** (fuh.SAHD, -SADE) *n.* **1** the front of a building: *the facade of a church; the south facade.* **2** a false or put-on appearance: *His modesty is a mere facade; the good-guy facade, to maintain a facade; behind the facade; The facade crumbled.*

face *n.* **1** the front of the human head; hence, an expression or look: *beautiful, familiar, moon, oval, round, ruddy, strange, ugly faces; Al made a face at Lu; Children make faces in the mirror; an angry, funny, poker, straight, serious face* (= expression); *She looked him* **in the face** (= directly); *They finally met face to face* (= in person); *He married her* **in the face of** (= facing) *opposition from her family; The new evidence* **flies in the face of** (= contradicts) *previous testimony; It seems a good plan* **on the face of it** (= judging by appearances); *He decided to* **put a good face on it** *and forget the embarrassing incident; She called him a liar* **to his face;** *A* **face guard** or **face mask** *is worn by players to protect the face from injury;* **adj.: in-your-face** (= aggressive) *audacity, competition, showmanship, style.* **2** the front, main, or outer surface: *the face of a clock; the faces of a crystal; Industry has changed the face* (= appearance) *of the land.* **3** dignity or prestige: *He* **lost face** *by refusing the challenge; She* **saved face** *by rewording her statement.* —*v.* **fac.es, faced, fac.ing 1** look or be turned toward something: *Our house faces south.* **2** meet a person in a brave or daring manner; confront: *He couldn't face his mother after telling a lie; He backed down when faced with the facts; Ming knew she was innocent and she calmly* **faced down** (= defeated) *the crowd without saying a word; They had to* **face up** *to the truth* (= accept it courageously). **3** provide a surface or trimming to something: *Our house is faced with brownstone;* **n.:** *a walnut veneer* **facing** (= front); *a military coat's* **facings** (= cuffs, collar, and trimmings).

face.down *n.* a confrontation or showdown. —*adv.* with the face down: *The body was lying facedown; Cards are dealt facedown on the table.*

face.less *adj.* having no distinctive character: *the faceless crowds of large cities.*

face.lift *n.* **1** cosmetic surgery for getting rid of facial wrinkles and such signs of age. **2** treatment to improve appearance: *The city hall got a facelift for the centennial.*

face-off *n.* **1** the opening play in hockey in which two opposing players face each other: *Our team won the face-off.* **2** a confrontation: *The Cuban missile crisis was a superpower face-off that brought the world to the brink of war.*

face-saving *adj.* that saves face or avoids embarrassment: *a face-saving compromise, formula, measure; The move was meant to be face-saving.*
—**face-saver** *n.*

fac.et (FAS.it) *n.* one of many sides, aspects, or phases, as a surface of a cut gem: *An insect's compound eye has six lensed facets; to study a problem in all its facets.*

fac.et.ed (FAS.it.id) *adj. & cpd.* having a facet or facets: *a faceted rock crystal; a*

facetious / fad

multi-faceted personality.

fa.ce.tious (fuh.SEE.shus) *adj.* aiming to be humorous, esp. by witty remarks in a serious or inappropriate situation: *facetious humor; a facetious remark, reply; He is being facetious.*

face-to-face *adj a.* direct: *a face-to-face confrontation, meeting, talk.*

face value *n.* 1 the stated value, as on a bond or bill. 2 apparent value or meaning: *I took his word at face value.*

fa.cial (FAY.shul) *adj.* of the face: *a facial expression, massage, treatment; facial features;* **facial tissue** *(paper) for use as a handkerchief.* —*n.* a treatment for the face, as given in a beauty parlor: *to get a facial.* —**fa.cial.ly** *adv.*

fac.ile (FAS.il, -ile) [sometimes derogatory, depending on context] 1 *adj.* shallow: *a facile answer, disposition, method, mind, nature, remark, solution, task, tongue, victory, wit; a sales rep's facile pitch.* 2 *adj.* saying or achieving easily: *a facile liar, narrator, pen, success, talker, writer.* —**fac.ile.ly** *adv.*

fa.cil.i.tate (fuh.SIL.uh.tate) *v.* **-tates, -tat.ed, -tat.ing** make a process, result, etc. easier: *to facilitate a reply, task; Labor-saving devices facilitate work.*
—**fa.cil.i.ta.tion** (-TAY.shun) *n.*
—**fa.cil.i.ta.tor** (-tay.tur) *n.*

fa.cil.i.ty (fuh.SIL.i.tee) *n.* **-ties** 1 the quality that makes a particular action easy or simple: *the dog's natural facility in swimming; Mia plays the piano with great facility; Yves has no facility with languages.* 2 something that helps an activity: *a correctional facility* (= prison); *recreational facilities; a university with excellent research facilities; Schools provide facilities for study such as books and libraries; swimming pools, tennis courts, and such sports facilities; an indoor swimming facility; airports, bus services, and other travel facilities; He operates a computer facility* (= installation); *Would you like to use the facilities* (= washroom)?

fac.sim.i.le (fac.SIM.uh.lee) *n.* 1 an exact copy, esp. of something graphic. 2 same as FAX.

fact *n.* something that is real, actual, or true: *Is the UFO story fact or fiction? Give me some* **facts and figures** (= precise information); *accepted, established, hard, historic, incontestable, irrefutable, proven, well-known facts; the bare facts; to ascertain, check, confirm, establish, ignore, verify a fact; to cite, distort, embellish, embroider, evaluate, face, interpret, marshal, present, twist (the) facts; The* **fact of the matter** *is that most people would rather drive to the corner store than walk; A helper in a crime could be an accessory* **before** *or* **after the fact** (= before or after the committing of the crime); **As a matter of fact** (= actually or really), *UFOs are fiction; No one,* **in fact,** *has touched a UFO;* **In point of fact** (= actually), *they don't exist.*

fact finder *n.* an investigator, esp. as a member of a committee, as in labor disputes; *adj.:* **a fact-finding** *committee, mission, tour.*

fac.tion (FAC.shun) *n.* 1 a minority group within an organization, working against its larger interests; clique: *a party torn by warring factions; an extremist faction.* 2 party strife. —**fac.tion.al** *adj.: factional conflicts, disputes, feuds, fighting, strife, warfare.* —**fac.tion.al.ism** *n.*

fac.ti.tious (fac.TISH.us) *adj.* contrived; sham: *a factitious demand caused by advertising.*

fact of life *n.* 1 something that is true and unavoidable: *Pollution is a fact of life.* 2 **facts of life** the basics of sex and reproduction.

fac.tor (FAC.tur) *n.* 1 a circumstance or element contributing to a result: *Strength of materials is a safety factor in construction; a cultural factor such as accent; common, deciding, major, risk factors.* 2 a number which when multiplied by another equals a given number: *3 and 6 are factors of 18.* 3 a trading agent: *a fur company factor.*
—**fac.to.ri.al** (fac.TOR.ee.ul) *n. & adj.: The factorial of 5 is 5 x 4 x 3 x 2 x 1; factorial mathematics.*

fac.to.ry (FAC.tuh.ree) *n.* **-ries** a building in which products are manufactured; industrial plant: *He works at or in an automobile factory; a factory hand* (= factory worker).

fac.to.tum (fac.TOH.tum) *n. Formal.* one who does all kinds of work around a house or office: *Sam is their secretary and general factotum.*

fac.tu.al (FAK.choo.ul) *adj.* agreeing with facts: *a factual account, claim, report; factual data, information, material.*
—**fac.tu.al.ly** *adv.*

fac.ul.ty (FAC.ul.tee) *n.* **-ties** 1 an ability or power: *the faculty of speech; a faculty for remembering names; a will made while in full possession of one's faculties.* 2 an academic division: *the faculty of arts.* 3 a teaching staff, esp. of a college or university: *She is on the medical faculty; The faculty is on strike; adj.: a faculty club, lounge, member.*

fad *n.* a temporary fashion or craze: *The hula hoop was a great fad of the 1950s; the denim fad; a food fad; the lat-*

est or *newest fad; passing fads.*
—**fad.dish** *adj.;* **fad.dist** *n.*
fade *v.* **fades, fad.ed, fad.ing** become faint: *The music faded in the distance; Childhood memories fade with age; worn brakes that fade* (= lose stopping power); *adj.: well-worn **faded** jeans.*
—**fade in** (or **out**) **1** of motion pictures, appear or make appear (or disappear) gradually. **2** of sounds, make or become more (or less) distinct.
faecal, faeces same as FECAL, FECES.
faer.ie or **faer.y** (FAIR.ee) *n.* **faer.ies** Archaic. fairyland; also, a fairy.
fag *v.* **fags, fagged, fag.ging** work hard until tired: *He's fagging away at his tasks; adj.: He's too **fagged** out to stay awake.* —*n.* Slang. **1** a cigarette. **2** [short form] faggot.
fag end *n. Informal.* the extreme end: *Everyone is tired at the fag end of the day.*
fag.got (FAG.ut) *n.* **1** *Slang* [derogatory] a male homosexual. **2** same as FAGOT.
fag.ot.ing (FAG.ut.ing) *n.* a zigzag stitch across two finished edges. Also **fag.got.ing**.
fag.ot (FAG.ut) *n.* a bundle of sticks or of iron rods. Also **fag.got**.
Fahr.en.heit (FAIR.un.hite) *adj.* having to do with a thermometer scale with 32° as the freezing point and 212° as the boiling point of water: *Ten degrees Fahrenheit; the Fahrenheit scale; a Fahrenheit thermometer.*
fa.ience or **fa.ïence** (fye.AHNCE, fay-) *n.* an opaquely glazed earthenware with colorful decorations.
fail *v.* **1** be wanting, lacking, or negligent: *He has brains but fails in diligence; Those failing to do their homework are given detentions; Words fail us when our hearts are full.* **2** be unsuccessful: *He failed the test; failed dismally, miserably; failed in math; Crops may fail during a drought; Trees fail to bear fruit; Businesses fail; Her confidence failed her when she got up to speak; Don't fail* (= disappoint) *me when I need you most; The teacher failed* (= did not pass) *those who scored below 50%.* —**without fail** surely: *I'll be there without fail.*
failing *n.* weakness or shortcoming: *Laziness is one of his failings; Her chief failing is tardiness; human, moral, social, technical failings; one's deepest, inner failings.* —*adj.: an old woman in failing* (= weakening) *health; my failing eyesight; a failing* (= not passing) *evaluation, grade.*
—*prep.* in the absence of something: *You have to produce your birth certificate, failing which you may not be registered.*
faille (FILE, FAIL) *n.* a ribbed silk or rayon fabric.
fail-safe *adja.* providing safety against failure: *a fail-safe device to open doors in an emergency.*
fail.ure (FAIL.yur) *n.* lack of success or an instance of it: *The party was a failure; business failures; businesses that end in failure; They prove to be failures; their failure to make a profit; crop, engine, heart, power failures; He was an abject, complete, dismal, hopeless, miserable, total failure in algebra, though not a failure in life.*
fain *adv. & adj.* [old use] glad(ly): *"I would fain die a dry death."*
faint *adj.* weak or feeble: *She felt faint and was about to collapse; He spoke in a faint voice, whisper; faint praise; I don't have the faintest idea where she is.*
—*v.* become unconscious: *He fainted on hearing the bad news.* —*n.* state of unconsciousness: *He fell into a faint; She came out of the faint in no time.*
—**faint.ly** *adv.;* **faint.ness** *n.*
faint-hearted *adj.* lacking courage; timid.
fair *adj.* **1** treating both sides alike without selfish considerations: *a fair and impartial judge; a fair businessman, decision, judgment; "Turn about is **fair play**"; to be fair to customers; He always gets what he wants by **fair means or foul*** (= with or without fraud); *It's not fair* (= according to the rules of boxing) *to hit below the belt; adv.: Let's play fair.* **2** good or pleasing: *a patient in fair condition; fair* (= light in color) *hair, skin; a fair* (= attractive) *maiden; fair* (= clear) *weather; a fair* (= favorable) *wind; the fair sex* (= women). **3** *adja.* moderately good: *a fair guess, number, price; Women and minorities are not **fair game*** (= legitimate objects) *for ridicule.*
—**fair and square** honest or honestly: *She is fair and square in her dealings; She deals fair and square with everyone; Lin hit Luc fair and square* (= straight) *on the nose.* —*n.* an exhibition of agricultural or industrial goods: *county, state, trade, world fairs.*
fair.ground or **fair.grounds** *n.* a place to hold fairs, carnivals, and other outdoor events.
fair-haired *adj.* having very light hair; hence, specially favored: *the **fair-haired** boy* (Informal for favorite) *of the firm.*
fair.ly *adv.* in a fair manner: *We treat our employees fairly* (= justly); *They look fairly* (= reasonably) *happy.* —**fair.ness** *n.*

fair shake n. *Informal.* an even chance: *to assure someone a fair shake; to get, give, have a fair shake.*

fair-trade agreement n. an agreement between nations to abide by minimum prices.

fair.way n. the mowed area of a golf course between tee and green.

fair-weather adj a. changeable; hence, untrustworthy: *a fair-weather friend.*

fair.y (FAIR.ee) n. **fair.ies** 1 a supernatural being resembling humans but usu. much smaller, sometimes winged, often mischievous and endowed with magical powers; **adj.**: *a fairy kind of thing; the fairy lights on a Christmas tree; fairy magic, voices, wings; Cinderella's **fairy godmother** was her sponsor and benefactor.* 2 *Slang* [derogatory] a male homosexual.

fair.y.land (FAIR.ee.land) n. the mythical land of fairies; hence, any beautiful or enchanting place.

fairy tale n. a story for children about fairies, fantasies, and magical happenings: *Grimm's Fairy Tales.*
—**fairy-tale** adj. having the qualities of fairy tales: *a fairy-tale house, princess, romance, valley; Your story is pure fairy-tale* (= all made up).

fait ac.com.pli (FATE.ah.cohm.PLEE), *pl.* **faits ac.com.plis** (FATE.ah.cohm.PLEE) an accomplished fact; hence, something that cannot be helped or changed.

faith n. 1 trust or belief: *She had faith in the justice system; Her faith was shaken by the jury's verdict; He didn't lose faith; a deep, enduring, strong faith; Labor and management bargained **in good faith*** (= with sincerity); *They showed **good faith*** (= good will) *by signing a contract;* **to keep** (not **break**) **faith** *with* (= be loyal, not disloyal to) *someone in good times and bad; a Hindu by faith and by conviction; We take many things **on faith** in the absence of proof.* 2 a particular belief or religion: *to keep the faith; renounce one's faith; He considers his religion the true faith; non-Christian faiths.*

faith.ful adj. loyal or dedicated: *a faithful dog, employee, husband, wife; spouses who are faithful to each other; faithful in everything.* —n. [takes *pl. v.*] practicing believers: *The faithful attend services regularly; the Jewish faithful; the Muslim faithful; the party faithful (of a political party); the fashion faithful.* —**faith.ful.ly** adv.; **faith.ful.ness** n.

faith.less adj. 1 that lacks faith: *a faithless suggestion.* 2 disloyal: *faithless spouses.*

fake v. **fakes, faked, fak.ing** pretend or counterfeit: *a painting style that is hard to fake; to fake an accident and collect insurance; to fake the goalie* (= draw the goalie out of position) *and shoot a goal.* —**adj.** false or sham: *Is your beard real or fake? It looks fake to me; a fake accent, check, identity, masterpiece, passport; fake bravado, fur; low-calorie fake foods; The fur seems **faked**; a faked scenario;* **n.**: *Her French accent is only a fake.*

fak.er n. a person who pretends or counterfeits; **fak.er.y** n.

fa.kir (fuh.KEER) n. a Moslem or Hindu holy beggar known for feats of magic and endurance.

fa.la.fel (fuh.LAH.ful) n. a Middle-Eastern sandwich, usu. containing fresh vegetables, beans, and spices.

fal.chion (FAL.chun, -shun) n. a broadbladed, curved medieval sword.

fal.con (FAL.cun) n. a hawk used in the sport of hunting birds.

fal.de.ral (FOL.duh.rol) n. a useless trifle; nonsense.

fall (FAWL) v. **falls, fell, fall.en, fall.ing** 1 drop or move down: *Leaves fall from trees in autumn; Soldiers fall in battle, dead or wounded; He slipped and fell on the floor; to fall headlong into a well; Children fall down on the ice; to fall down the stairs; to fall off a horse; to fall out of bed; During a storm, trees fall over, fall across power lines; Temperatures fall in the winter; The roof fell in* (= collapsed) *under the weight of the snow.* 2 occur, happen, or move into a new state or condition: *Night falls early in December; December 25 falls on a Sunday this year; People fall asleep, fall ill, fall in love with each other, fall into error, fall into evil ways, fall on hard times* (= become poor). 3 decline in power, position, value, etc.: *The ocean bed falls sharply a few kilometers from the shore; Stocks fell to their lowest value ever on Black Monday; A government falls* (= suffers defeat) *when it loses support; A country falls to* (= is conquered by) *the enemy; His face fell* (= suddenly took on a look of disappointment) *because the news was bad.* —**fall back** give way or retreat: *Troops were falling back all along the front.* —**fall back on** turn to for help: *a friend to fall back on in time of need.*
—**fall behind** fail to keep up with something: *Some runners soon fell behind; to fall behind in one's payments.*
—**fall down on the job** fail to do the job. —**fall flat** fail completely: *His plans and her jokes always fall flat.* —**fall for** *Informal.* 1 fall in love with some-

fallacy / fame

one: *He fell for her right away.* **2** be deceived by something: *We won't fall for that trick.* —**fall foul of** quarrel, clash, or lose favor with someone: *He fell foul of his boss; to fall foul of the law.* —**fall in** get in formation: *The troops were ordered to fall in.* —**fall into 1** begin: *to fall into conversation with someone.* **2** be classified: *People fall into different groups.* —**fall into line** comply or obey: *The dissidents won't fall into line.* —**fall in with** meet or join: *How did he fall in with criminal elements?* —**fall off** become less: *The membership of the party began to fall off after they lost the election.* —**fall on** or **upon 1** attack eagerly: *Hungry children fall on the food as soon as served; Troops fall upon an enemy.* **2** be the duty of someone: *It falls on her as the chair to preside over the meeting.* —**fall out (with)** quarrel (with): *Al and Lu fell out with each other over buying a new car; They had a **falling out.*** —**fall over backward(s)** or **fall (all) over oneself** try very hard; be very eager: *These waiters fall over backward to give good service; He fell (all) over himself trying to help me.* —**fall short** fail to reach a goal: *The results fell short of expectations.* —**fall through** fail: *Wild schemes often fall through.* —**fall to 1** belong, as right or as a duty: *It falls to her as the chair to preside over the meeting.* **2** begin doing something: *The children fell to doing their chores.* —*n.* **1** the act or result of falling; drop or collapse: *a fall on the ice; a fall from power; a sharp fall in demand, prices, temperature; the fall of a government; a free fall (under the pull of gravity alone); The tree branches helped break his fall; Niagara Falls is not a high fall or falls; his fall from grace; Since **the Fall** (= expulsion from paradise) of Adam and Eve, to err is human.* **2** autumn: *Schools open in the fall;* **adja.:** *fall colors, fashions; the fall session of a legislature.*

fal.la.cy (FAL.uh.see) *n.* **-cies** false or erroneous reasoning; an incorrect or deceptive idea: *Prejudices are based on old fallacies.* —**fal.la.cious** (fuh.LAY.shus) *adj.*

fall guy *n. Informal.* scapegoat: *to make someone the fall guy.*

fal.li.ble (FAL.uh.bul) *adj.* subject to error: *We are fallible creatures;* **fal.li.bly** *adv.* —**fal.li.bil.i.ty** (-uh.BIL.i.tee) *n.*

falling star *n.* a meteor.

fall line *n.* **1** where the mountains meet the plain. **2** in skiing, the fastest path down a slope.

Fal.lo.pi.an tube (fuh.LOH.pee.un-) *n.* either of a pair of tubes that carry the egg cells from the ovary to the uterus; also **fallopian tube.**

fall.out *n.* **1** radioactive particles from a nuclear explosion in the air: *radioactive fallout; a fallout shelter.* **2** an unforeseen result; side effect: *the fallout from a scandal; the social fallout from plant closures.*

fal.low (FAL.oh) *adj.* **1** unseeded or unused: *fields that **lie fallow**; a fallow field of alfalfa; a fallow imagination; a fallow period (of inactivity).* **2** light brownish yellow: *the fallow, spotted coat of the **fallow deer.***

false (FAWLSE) *adj.* **fals.er, fals.est** not true or correct: *What you heard was a false alarm set off by mistake; False arguments don't convince anyone; false (= illegal) arrest and imprisonment; Drugs were found in the **false bottom** (= secret compartment) of his suitcase; a false ceiling (hung below the ceiling joists); a ship flying false colors (to deceive the authorities); false (= fake) diamonds; a false (= unfaithful or disloyal) friend; to put up a false front (= deceptive appearance); He gained admission by false pretenses; false (= ill-founded) pride, sense of security; a false start before the starter's pistol is fired; A false step made her stumble and fall; a set of false (= artificial) teeth; a false (= incorrect) verdict; false weights (for cheating customers).* —**play false** cheat or trick someone. —**false.ly** *adv.;* **false.ness** *n.*

false.hood (FAWLSE.hood, short "oo") *n.* an untruth or lie: *an absolute, obvious, outright, utter falsehood.*

fal.set.to (fawl.SET.oh) *n.* **-set.tos** an artificially high singing voice, esp. of a tenor; *adv.*: *to sing falsetto.*

fal.sies (FAWL.seez) *n. Informal* [takes *pl. v.*] pads inside a brassiere.

fal.si.fy (FAWL.suh.fye) *v.* **-fies, -fied, -fy.ing** make or prove false: *a clerk fired for falsifying the records; The evidence falsifies your conclusion.* —**fal.si.fi.ca.tion** (-fuh.CAY.shun) *n.*

fal.si.ty (FAWL.si.tee) *n.* **-ties** falseness: *the truth or falsity of a claim.*

fal.ter (FAWL.tur) *v.* **-ters, -tered, -ter.ing** waver or hesitate in gait, resolve, speech, etc.: *He faltered and fell down the stairs; Our courage began to falter; She faltered out a few words before passing out; The engine faltered and stopped dead; He falters in his resolve to see the project through;* **adja.:** *a faltering attempt, enterprise; an infant's first faltering steps.* —**fal.ter.ing.ly** *adv.*

fame *n.* great reputation or renown: *an ambitious man eager for fame and fortune;*

famed / fanatic

to achieve, attain, seek, win fame; *At the height of his fame, he was still living in poverty.*

famed *adj.* famous: *a region famed for its lakes; Rio's famed carnival.*

fa.mil.ial (fuh.MIL.yul) *adj.* a. having to do with a family: *Most familial diseases are inherited; familial duty, history, relationships; a familial resemblance.*

fa.mil.i.ar (fuh.MIL.yur) *adj.* 1 well-known: *an all too familiar slogan; It sounds familiar; familiar to everyone; a familiar argument, example, face, scent, story, theme, voice; a long and familiar list of grievances; the strange and the familiar; both familiar and new; "Viewer discretion advised" has become familiar to TV viewers.* 2 intimate: *good friends on familiar terms; Children should not get familiar with strangers.* 3 acquainted: *to become familiar with an issue; We are thoroughly familiar with this problem, procedure, situation; sources familiar with the company.* —*n.* a close or everyday companion: *New shoes are not so comfortable as old familiars; A black cat was believed to be a witch's familiar* (= spirit in animal form). —**fa.mil.i.ar.ly** *adv.*: *"Jim," as the man is familiarly known.*

fa.mil.i.ar.i.ty (fuh.MIL.ee.AIR.i.tee) *n.* -ties closeness: *The lawyer showed lack of familiarity with* (= knowledge of) *the case; Pat resents such familiarities* (= liberties) *as necking and petting; She moves about with easy familiarity* (= informality) *among her guests.*

fa.mil.i.ar.ize (fuh.MIL.yuh.rize) *v.* -iz.es, -ized, -iz.ing make familiar: *He familiarized himself with the facts of the case.*

fam.i.ly (FAM.uh.lee) *n.* -lies 1 the social unit of parents and children: *a family of 12* (members); *a close, noble, royal family; broken families; Al comes from a good family; The nuclear family is your immediate family; an extended family; the ruling family* (to which the ruler belongs); *home and family; with family and friends; Love of music* **runs in the family** (= is hereditary to them); *They decided to keep the heirloom in the family; the Smith family; a fishing family; police families; the British family of nations;* **adja**: *a family budget, business, car, cemetery, dinner, farm, fortune, friend, history, movie, restaurant, reunion, sedan, skeleton; the family dog, income; family connections, finances, happiness, harmony, life, relationships, ties; a family-style restaurant; a* **family circle** (= close relatives as a group), *a* **family doctor** (= general practitioner) *in* **family practice**; *a lawyer who practices* **family law** *and appears in* **family courts** *that have jurisdiction in matters such as child abuse, custody, paternity, etc.; the* **family home** (where a family lives); **family name** (= last name); **family planning** (= birth control); *She's* **in the family way** (Informal for pregnant).
2 one's children as a group: *a couple without a family; to raise a family; to start a family; to clothe, feed, and support a family.* 3 any group or set with a common origin or with similar characteristics: *Cougars belong to the cat family; English and Hindi are in the Indo-Aryan family of languages; a plant family; a notorious Mafia family.*

family tree *n.* a chart showing the ancestors and descendants of a family; genealogical tree.

fam.ine (FAM.in) *n.* a widespread and serious shortage, esp. of food: *a country struck by famine.*

fam.ished (FAM.isht) *adj.* suffering from extreme hunger: *the famished look of war orphans; I missed breakfast, lunch, and supper – I'm famished* (Informal for very hungry).

fa.mous (FAY.mus) *adj.* very well-known and esteemed: *a famous professor; France is famous for its wines; famous as a wine-producing country.* —**fa.mous.ly** *adv.* Informal. very well: *They got along famously for 20 years.*

fan *n.* 1 a semicircular, often folding device for blowing air for ventilation or cooling: *a fan of feathers.* 2 something fan-shaped: *the* **fan hitch** *method of harnessing a team of sled dogs.* 3 a rotary device equipped with blades or vanes for blowing air: *a ceiling fan; electric, exhaust, table fans; to turn off, turn on a fan; the fan of a radiator.* 4 an enthusiastic follower or admirer; buff: *a football fan; an ardent fan of Anne Murray;* **adja**: *fan clubs, letters, magazines, mail.* —*v.* **fans, fanned, fan.ning**: *a room packed with people fanning themselves* (= using fans); *The speech helped fan* (= fire up) *the flames of rebellion; Their anger was fanned* (= raised) *into fury by the mob orator; Police and neighbors fanned out* (= spread out) *over the neighborhood in search of the missing child; a (baseball) batter who fans* (= fails after three attempts); *to fan* (= miss the hockey puck) *on a shot or pass.*

fa.nat.ic (fuh.NAT.ic) *n.* one who is uncritically enthusiastic about something religious, political, etc.: *a religious fanatic; Pin is a fanatic for vegetarianism.* —*adj*: *Mario is fanatic about fresh air; a fanatic cult.* —**fa.nat.i.cal** (-i.cul) *adj.*:

fanatical ideas; a fanatical sect.
—**fa.nat.i.cal.ly** adv.; **fa.nat.i.cism** n.
fan belt n. the belt that drives the fan of a radiator.
fan.ci.er (FAN.see.ur) 1 n. one with a special interest in particular types of birds, animals, plants, or articles.: *a dog fancier; an orchid fancier; a fancier of fine wines.* 2 comp. of FANCY.
fan.ci.ful (FAN.suh.ful) adj. overimaginative: *a fanciful poet; fanciful tales; Your idea sounds fanciful.*
fan.cy (FAN.see) n. an idea or imagination of a passing or trifling nature: *She can afford to do whatever strikes her fancy; Jo felt a sudden fancy for heart-shaped cookies; Advertisers use words and pictures to tickle your fancy; Aunt Ada took quite a fancy to her young niece; Science fiction is not mere fancy but the product of fertile imaginations; creatures of fancy such as fairies and dragons; a poet's flights of fancy; passing fancies.*
—*adj.* 1 **-ci.er, -ci.est** unusual or out-of-the-way: *a fancy costume; $50,000 seems a fancy price for a used car; Sensible children don't wear fancy shoes to school; Men now seem to want their dress shirts fancy.* 2 adja. having a pleasing quality: *fancy cakes, chocolates, dogs, foods, goods.*
—*v.* **-cies, -cied, -cy.ing** 1 imagine: *She fancies she'll be a doctor in five years; He fancies setting up a thriving business.* 2 like: *Pat doesn't fancy him as a doctor; Lu doesn't fancy working late.*
fancy dress n. imaginative costume, as for a masquerade.
fancy-free adj. free from serious romantic attachments.
fan.cy.work (FAN.see.wurk) n. crochet, embroidery, and other decorative needlework.
fan.dan.go (fan.DANG.goh) n. 1 a lively Spanish dance. 2 its music.
fan.dom (FAN.dum) n. a particular group of fans, as of a star.
fane n. a temple or church.
fan.fare n. 1 a sounding of trumpets; hence, a flourish. 2 publicity: *a narrow win announced with great fanfare.*
fan.fold adja. 1 that folds like a fan or accordion: *stackable fanfold, not cut-sheet paper.* 2 that is separable in layers: *multipart fanfold forms and labels.*
fang n. 1 one of the sharp and pointed teeth of carnivorous mammals; canine tooth: *The tiger bared its fangs menacingly.* 2 a venomous tooth of a reptile.
fan-jet n. a jet engine with a rotating fan for extra thrust.
fan.light n. a semicircular window, usu.
over a door.
fan.ny (FAN.ee) n. **fan.nies** *Informal.* the buttocks.
fan.tail n. a pigeon or goldfish with a fanlike tail or fin.
fan.ta.si.a (fan.TAY.zhuh, -tuh.ZEE.uh) n. a free-form, fanciful musical piece, as some of Bach's organ pieces or modern swing music.
fan.ta.size (FAN.tuh.size) v. **-siz.es, -sized, -siz.ing** daydream: *Everyone fantasizes now and then; The orphan child fantasizes that she is with her family; She is fantasizing about being reunited with her family; Pat fantasizes* (= daydreams about) *Ray and vice versa.*
fan.tas.tic (fan.TAS.tic) adj. 1 strange and unreal: *a fantastic story that no one will believe.* 2 *Informal.* incredible or wonderful: *a fantastic movie; a fantastic idea, price.* Also **fan.tas.ti.cal.**
—**fan.tas.ti.cal.ly** adv.
fan.ta.sy (FAN.tuh.see) n. **-sies** something imagined or invented in a literary or artistic way that has little correspondence with reality: *Tolkien's "Lord of the Rings" is high fantasy; Space travel is no longer a fantasy; He lives in a world of fantasy full of heroic deeds; He indulges in fantasies but doesn't act them out;* adja.: *a fantasy adventure, fair, film, island, land, life, world.* —**fan.ta.sist** n.
fan.zine (FAN.zeen) n. a magazine for fans, esp. of science fiction.
far adj. **far.ther** (FAR.thur, "th" as in "the") or **fur.ther** (FUR-), **far.thest** (-thist) or **fur.thest** distant or remote: *a far country; in the far future; the far ends of the earth; Detroit is farther from Texas than Chicago; the farthest of the three cities from Houston; Dictatorship is a **far cry*** (= a long way) *from democracy.*
—*adv.* at, to, or from a distance in time or position: *We like to travel far; He lives farther down the road; a job far* (= much) *easier than the old one;* **As** or **So far as** *I can tell, it won't rain today; This is the best deal* **by far** (= without doubt); *Lee is* **far and away** (= beyond doubt) *the best baker around here; She carried her message* **far and wide** (= everywhere); *The winter is* **far from** (= not quite) *over in March;* **Far be it from me to** (= I would never) *question his sincerity; Do I doubt his sincerity?* **Far from it!** *She will* **go far** (= succeed) *in her career;* **So far** (= till now), *she has done well.*
far.ad (FAIR.ud) n. the unit of electrical capacitance.
far.a.way (FAR.uh.way) adja. 1 distant: *faraway voices.* 2 dreamy: *a faraway look in his eyes.*

farce *n.* a humorous play full of funny situations and ridiculous happenings; hence, a mockery: *The new censorship laws make a farce of freedom of speech.* —**far.ci.cal** (FAR.si.cul) *adj.*

fare *v.* **fares, fared, far.ing** **1** get on; do: *How did he fare in his new job? She fared well at the exam; She couldn't have fared any better.* **2** [old use] go or travel. —*n.* **1** a fee paid for transportation: *The fare to the airport is $20; People pay the fare that is charged; cheap, economy, excursion, full, half, reduced fares; air, airplane, bus, plane, taxi, train fares.* **2** a paying passenger: *The cabby took his fare to the airport.* **3** food or diet: *plain, simple, wholesome fare.*

Far East *n.* eastern Asia, esp. China, Japan, Korea, and nearby islands; rarely, Southeast Asia.

fare.well (fare.WEL) *interj.* good-bye. —*n.* **1** an expression of good wishes at parting: *She made, said, took her farewell; He bade, wished her farewell; to say farewell to family and friends; one's final farewell.* **2** parting: *a fitting, fond, sad, tearful farewell; the moment of farewell;* **adja.:** *a farewell address, ceremony, dinner, gift, party, reception, speech, tour.*

far.fetched *adj.* contrived and unlikely: *a story too farfetched to be true; a farfetched claim, explanation, tale.*

far-flung *adj.* **1** widely scattered: *the far-flung oases of the Sahara.* **2** distant: *the far-flung corners of the earth.*

fa.ri.na (fuh.REE.nuh) *n.* finely ground meal or flour used as a breakfast cereal and in puddings.

far.i.na.ceous (fair.uh.NAY.shus) *adj.* starchy; mealy.

farm *n.* **1** a tract of land on which crops are grown and livestock raised: *to manage* or *run a farm; to work on a farm; chicken, dairy, fruit, poultry, sheep farms;* **adja.:** *farm credit, exports, income, labor, life, machinery, subsidies.* **2** a place where anything is raised for market: *fish, oyster farms; a fur farm (that raises animals for their fur).* **3** a minor-league baseball or hockey team associated with or owned by a major league club; also **farm club**.
—*v.* cultivate crops and raise livestock on a farm: *Over half the world's people farm for a living.* —**farm out** send work out to be done by others: *Many publishers farm out editorial work; The children were farmed out* (= sent) *to relatives when their mother was ill.*

farm.er *n.* one who farms: *grain farmers from the Prairies; a dirt farmer; Gentlemen farmers farm for pleasure; a sheep farmer from Australia; a farmer cooperative; a farmers' market.* —**farming** *n.:* *collective farming; subsistence farming; wheat farming.*

farm.hand *n.* one who works on a farm for wages.

farm.house *n.* the dwelling house on a farm.

farm.land *n.* land that is or can be used for agriculture.

farm.stead (FARM.sted) *n.* the land and buildings of a farm.

farm.yard *n.* the area next to or surrounded by buildings of a farm.

far-off *adja.* remote: *the far-off times and places of one's childhood.*

fa.rouche (fuh.ROOSH) *adj.* French. shy; also, uncouth; unsociable.

far-out *adja.* **1** very distant: *the far-out stars of our galaxy.* **2** *Informal.* far from the ordinary; unconventional: *a far-out design, sect; far-out music.*

far.ra.go (fuh.RAY.go, -RAH.go) *n.* **-goes** a jumble or mixture.

far-reaching *adj.* having wide-ranging effects or importance: *Far-reaching tax reforms have been proposed; Their effects will be far-reaching.*

far.ri.er *n. Brit.* someone who shoes horses, esp. a blacksmith.

far.row (FAIR.oh) *n. & v.* (give birth to) a litter of pigs.

far.see.ing (FAR.SEE.ing) *adj.* able to see far, esp. showing foresight; farsighted.

far.sight.ed (FAR.sye.tid) *adj.* **1** able to see ahead, esp. the future effects of one's actions; not shortsighted: *a farsighted leader.* **2** not able to see near objects as clearly as distant ones.
—**far.sight.ed.ness** *n.:* *Convex glasses are worn to correct farsightedness.*

fart [vulgar slang] *v.* expel gas through the anus. —*n.* **1** such an expelling. **2** an elderly person viewed with contempt: *an old fart.*

farther a *comp.* of FAR.

far.ther.most (FAR.thur.most, "th" as in "the") *adj.* remotest.

farthest a *superl.* of FAR.

far.thing (FAR.thing, "th" as in "the") *n.* **1** an old British coin worth one fourth of a penny. **2** something small or of little value; a small sum.

fas.ci.a (FASH.ee.uh) *n.* a narrow horizontal band around a house below the edge of a roof.

fas.ci.cle (FAS.i.cul) *n.* **1** a small cluster or bunch, as of fibers or flowers. **2** one of the parts of a volume published in installments. —**fas.ci.cled** *adj.*

fas.ci.nate (FAS.uh.nate) *v.* **-nates,**

-nat.ed, -nat.ing captivate, esp. in an irresistible or compelling way: *Poetry fascinates him;* **adj.:** *a fascinating personality, speech; I find her fascinating.* —**fas.ci.na.tion** (-NAY.shun) *n.*

fas.cism (FASH.iz.um) *n.* a political system or philosophy based on absolute loyalty to a one-party dictatorship, militarism, and usu. racism and nationalism. —**fas.cist** *n. & adj.*

fash.ion (FASH.un) *n.* **1** the manner or way of doing something: *He was questioned by customs in a friendly fashion; clothes arranged in an orderly fashion; people of all fashions* (= types); *He can speak Chinese* **after a fashion** (= moderately well). **2** what is current in styles of dress, speech, conduct, etc. at a particular time or place: *Designers set fashions; the latest fashions; Miniskirts come into fashion now and then; What is* **in fashion** *today may go* **out of fashion** *tomorrow; women* **of fashion** (= of social prominence); **adj.:** *a fashion design, magazine, show, trend.* **3** a fashionable item: *men's fashions; home fashions* (= bath, bedroom, table linen, and other accessories); *window fashions.* —*v.* make in a creative way: *a figure fashioned out of clay.*

fash.ion.a.ble (FASH.uh.nuh.bul) *adj.* stylish. —**fash.ion.a.bly** *adv.*

fast *adj.* **1** swift or rapid: *a fast runner; My watch is a couple of minutes fast* (= ahead of the actual time); **adj.:** *a fast return on investment; a fast highway* (on which you can drive fast); *at a* **fast and furious** *rate.* **2** firm or secure: *Make the rope fast.* **3** *adj.:* steadfast: *They've been fast friends since childhood.* **4** nonfading: *cloth dyed in fast colors.* **5** *adj.* dishonest or deceptive: *a fast* (= loose or forward) *woman; They pulled* **a fast one** (Informal for clever trick) *on me.* —*adv.:* *Pat is driving too fast; Another car is fast* (= quickly) *approaching us from behind; The child is fast* (= deeply) *asleep; to hold fast* (= securely) *to one's faith; He* **plays fast and loose** (= acts in an undependable way) *with his friends, with her affections.* —*v.* abstain from food for losing weight, as penance, in protest, etc.; *She fasts during Lent.* —*n.* **1** avoidance of food: *to observe a (religious) fast; He will break his fast only if his demands are met.* **2** one that fastens: *a door fast; A stern fast is a rope or cable.*

fast.back *n.* (an automobile with) a roof that is styled in an unbroken curve down the back.

fast-breeder reactor *n.* a breeder reactor using high-energy neutrons to produce nuclear fuel.

fast buck *n. Informal.* money made easily or dishonestly: *looking for a fast buck; pursuing the fast buck; He's out to make* or *turn a fast buck;* **adj.:** *a fast-buck artist, entrepreneur.*

fas.ten (FAS.un) *v.* make fast, as by tying or gluing: *a door fastened with a bolt and chain; He drives with his eyes fastened* (= fixed) *on the road in front.*

fas.ten.er or **fas.ten.ing** *n.* a device that fastens, as a zipper, hook, clip, etc.

fast food *n.* food such as hamburgers and hot dogs that may be prepared and served quickly. —**fast-food** *adj.:* *the fast-food industry; a fast-food chain, franchise, outlet, restaurant.*

fast-forward *n.* the fast winding of a tape forward: *VCRs equipped with fast-forward, rewind, playback, and other functions;* **adj.:** *a fast-forward button;* **v.:** *if you will fast-forward to December 31.*

fas.tid.i.ous (fas.TID.ee.us) *adj.* hard to please, being too critical of the quality of food, clothes, etc.; fussy: *She's a fastidious dresser; a man of fastidious tastes; She is fastidious about her china.* —**fas.tid.i.ous.ly** *adv.*; **fas.tid.i.ous.ness** *n.*

fast lane *n.* the passing lane of a highway.

fast.ness *n.* **1** a secure place or stronghold: *robbers hiding in the fastnesses of the jungle; the mountain fastnesses of the Rockies.* **2** the quality of being fast or firm.

fast-talk *v. Informal.* persuade by fast and often deceitful talking: *He fast-talked his way into a job selling used cars, then fast-talked me into buying a lemon.*

fast time same as DAYLIGHT SAVING TIME.

fast-track *v.* go or send faster through a program or operation than planned: *to fast-track a student through high school;* **adj.:** *a fast-track deal, method, procedure, student.*

fat *n.* **1** an oily substance of animal tissue; also, vegetable oil used as a cooking medium: *potatoes fried in deep fat; how to get rid of excess body fat; Some are more inclined to fat* (= to become fleshy) *than others.* **2** anything rich or superfluous: *to trim the fat off a heavy budget; He lives off* **the fat of the land** (= in luxury). —**chew the fat** or **rag** *Informal.* chat. —**the fat is in the fire** the damage is done; there will be trouble. —*adj.* **fat.ter, fat.test** filled out with fat: *He looks fat; fat cattle; a fat bank account* (with plenty of money in it); *He* charges fat (= heavy) fees; fat (= fertile) lands. —**fat (chance, lot of good,** etc.) *Informal.* very little (chance, good, etc.). —**fat.ly** *adv.*; **fat.ness** *n.*

fa.tal (FAY.tul) *adj.* causing death: *a fatal accident; fatal injuries; the **fatal flaw** that destroyed Hamlet; the **fatal hour** (that cannot be avoided).* —**fa.tal.ly** *adv.*

fa.tal.ism (FAY.tuh.liz.um) *n.* the belief or attitude that events, esp. unlucky ones, are predetermined and inevitable; **fa.tal.ist** *n.* —**fa.tal.is.tic** (-LIS.tic) *adj.*

fa.tal.i.ty (fuh.TAL.i.tee) *n.* **-ties** **1** deadliness: *the fatality of a disease like AIDS or cancer.* **2** a death as the result of a disaster: *highway fatalities; traffic fatalities during a snowstorm; The **fatality rate** is much worse on our highways than in the air.*

fat.back *n.* dried and salted fat from a hog's back.

fat cat *n. Informal.* a wealthy person: *the bankers and other fat cats of the financial world.*

fate *n.* **1** the inevitable outcome of events, often unfavorable: *blind, cruel fate; He met with a terrible fate being mauled to death by a bear; As sure as fate, the police were waiting around the corner; By a strange stroke of fate, the same thing happened the next day; It happened as fate decreed; The judgment sealed or decided his fate; the fate (= death) that awaits all of us; He was going out to meet his fate (= destiny) when he got on the highway.* **2 Fates** three goddesses of Greek and Roman myths who ruled people's lives.

fat.ed (FAY.tid) *adjp.* marked by fate: *Prisoners fated to die are said to be on "death row"; the ill-fated voyage of the Titanic.*

fate.ful (FATE.ful) *adja.* decisive for the future: *The fateful hour of the jury's fateful verdict.* —**fate.ful.ly** *adv.*

fat head *n. Slang.* stupidity: *He won't listen to anyone because of his fat head.* —**fat.head** *n.* a stupid person. —**fat.head.ed** *adj.*

fa.ther (FAH.thur, "th" as in "the") *n.* **1** a male parent; hence, originator: *the father of the child; the founding fathers of our nation; Edward Teller, the father of the hydrogen bomb; Satan, the father of lies; our fathers (= ancestors); Our Father (= God); He's a **father figure** (= one who has the stature and influence of a father) with a **father image**; Father Christmas (Brit. for Santa Claus); Father Frost (= winter personified).* **2 Father** [used also as a prefixed title] a Christian priest: *Dear Father Smith.* —*v.* be the father or begetter of someone: *Jim fathered the orphan child; The child was wrongly fathered (= imposed on as father) on Joe.* —**fa.ther.hood** *n.* —**fa.ther.less** *adj.* —**fa.ther.ly** (FAH.thur.lee); **fa.ther.li.ness** *n.*

father-in-law *n.* **fathers-in-law** the father of one's spouse.

fa.ther.land (FAH.thur.land) *n.* one's native or ancestral country.

Father's Day *n.* in North America, the third Sunday in June set apart for honoring fathers.

fath.om (FATH.um, "TH" as in "the") *n.* a measure of depth equal to 6 ft. (1.8 m). —*v.* to sound a depth; hence, get to the bottom of something; figure out: *He speaks so little, it's difficult to fathom his intentions; to fathom what he means.* —**fath.om.a.ble** *adj.*

fath.om.less (FATH.um.lis) *adj.* not fathomable or understandable: *a fathomless mystery; the fathomless depths of outer space.*

fa.tigue (fuh.TEEG) *n.* **1** weariness from exertion resulting in reduced capacity for work: *battle* or *combat fatigue; mental fatigue; physical fatigue;* **Metal fatigue** results from long use under stress. **2 fatigues** *pl.* work clothing: *army fatigues.* —*v.* **fa.tigues, fa.tigued, fa.tigu.ing** become weary or worn: *The raids confused and fatigued the army;* **adj.***: to be **fatigued** from a climb; a **fatigued axle** (with fatigued metal parts) may crack or break under continued strain.*

fatigue duty *n.* military duty of a menial nature, carried out in work clothes.

fats or **fat.so** *n. Informal* [nickname] a fat person.

fat.ted (FAT.id) *adj.* made fat: *to kill the fatted calf* (as in the Bible, to celebrate the return of the prodigal son).

fat.ten (FAT.un) *v.* make or become fat.

fat.ty (FAT.ee) *adj.* **fat.ti.er, fat.ti.est** **1** containing fat: *a fatty food; fatty meats, tissue; Fatty deposits could clog arteries by forming fatty plaque.* **2** *Informal.* overweight or too plump: *the fatty one over there.* —*n.*, *pl.* **fat.ties** *Informal.* a fat person.

fatty acid *n.* a substance consisting of long chains of carbon atoms with hydrogen atoms attached to them: *Foods derived from animals contain saturated fatty acids.*

fat.u.ous (FACH.oo.us) *adj.* stupid and self-satisfied.

fau.cet (FAW.sit) *n.* a fixture with a valve-device for drawing liquid from a pipe or cask; tap or spigot.

fault *n.* an imperfection, flaw, or error: *Everyone has faults; a service fault in tennis; to correct, overlook his faults; It happened through no fault of mine; The San Andreas Fault is a visible break in the rock stratum; The Islamic world is riven along the Sunni-Shiite* **fault line** (= rift); *Who was* **at fault** (= to blame) *in the accident? She's generous* **to a fault** (= excessively); *He is always trying to* **find fault with** (= blame) *someone.*
—*v.* blame: *You can't fault her driving for the flat tire; You can't fault it on her driving.* —**fault.find.er** (FAWLT.fine.dur) *n.*; **fault.find.ing** *n. & adj.*
—**fault.less** *adj.*; **fault.less.ly** *adv.*; **fault.less.ness** *n.*

fault.y (FAWL.tee) *adj.* **fault.i.er, -i.est** defective: *a faulty electrical connection; a fire resulting from faulty wiring; a faulty assumption, design, valve; faulty brakes, equipment, judgment, maintenance, reasoning, syntax.* —**fault.i.ly** *adv.*; **fault.i.ness** *n.*

faun (FAWN) *n.* a half-human, half-goat Roman deity of fields and herds.

fau.na (FAW.nuh) *n.* the animal life or animals of a particular period or region: *the flora and fauna of Iceland.*

Faust (FOWST) *n.* a dramatic character from German legends who sells his soul to the devil in return for magical powers.

fau.vism (FOH.viz.um) *n.* a French movement in art between 1903 and 1907 marked by bright colors and bold designs. —**fau.vist** *n.*

faux (FOH) *adj.* fake: *faux furs, jewelry, pearls.*

faux pas (FOH.PAH) *n., pl.* **faux pas** (FOH.PAH) a social blunder; also, an embarrassing mistake.

fave *n. Informal.* favorite: *a cult fave like "Star Trek";* **adj.**: *What's your fave sport?*

fa.vor (FAY.vur) *n.* **1** friendly regard or approval: *to look on someone with favor; to curry, find, gain favor with someone; Luck is in our favor; She fell* **out of favor** *with her boss; She's back* **in favor**; *We are all* **in favor of** *a holiday; a check made out* **in favor of** *John Doe (who is to get the money).* **2** a token of this, as a gift or an act of kindness: *Do me a small favor; noisemakers and such party favors; to bestow a favor on someone.*
—*v.* **1** have or show favor for a person or thing: *Which candidate do you favor for the post? He favors his nephew Al; She favored her cousin with* (= gave her cousin) *the job;* **adj.**: *He was heavily* **favored** *to get it; the most favored nation* (trading) *status; a favored candidate, location, target.* **2** resemble: *She favors her father.* —**fa.vor.a.ble** (FAY.vur.uh.bul) *adj.*: *weather that is favorable for a picnic;* **fa.vor.a.bly** *adv.* Also **fa.vour, fa.vour.a.ble; fa.vour.a.bly** *Cdn.*

fa.vor.ite (FAY.vur.it) *n.* a favored person or thing: *Al is her favorite; a heavy, strong favorite for the presidency;* **adj.**: *a child's favorite toy; a teacher's favorite pupil; one of America's* **favorite sons** (= popular and famous persons). Also **fa.vour.ite** *Cdn.*

fa.vor.it.ism (FAY.vur.it.iz.um) *n.* partiality toward particular people: *to show favoritism.* Also **fa.vour.it.ism** *Cdn.*

favour, etc. *Cdn.* FAVOR, etc.

fawn *n.* **1** a young deer less than a year old. **2** its pale yellowish brown color.
—*v.* show friendliness by cringing or flattery: *Some dogs fawn on people* (= show love by climbing on them, etc.); *He fawns on his bosses.*

fax *n.* **1** an electronic machine for transmitting documents and pictures via the telephone lines; also **fax** or **facsimile machine**. **2** a document or picture received by fax.
—*v.* communicate with or transmit by fax: *I faxed London; I'll fax the contract to you and put the check in the mail.*

fay *n.* an elf or fairy.

faze *v.* **faz.es, fazed, faz.ing** *Informal* [used negatively] upset: *Nothing could ever faze him.*

fe.al.ty (FEE.ul.tee) *n.* **-ties** allegiance, as of a vassal to his lord.

fear (FEER) *n.* an emotion felt in the presence of danger or some threat to one's well-being: *the fear of darkness; a fear of heights; to allay, arouse, express, feel, instill, kindle, overcome, show fear; The warning struck fear into our hearts; a grave, groundless, idle, lingering, mortal, sudden fear; the salutary fear* (= reverence) *of God; to administer justice* **without fear or favor;** *She tiptoed* **for fear of** *waking the baby.* —*v.* feel fear or be afraid: *She fears to fly; We fear for his life; He fears that her life may be in danger.* —**fear.ful** *adj.*; **fear.ful.ly** *adv.*; **fear.ful.ness** *n.*

fear.some *adj.* frightful: *the fearsome subject of AIDS, a fearsome disease; It has fearsome implications, prospects; It has already taken a fearsome toll; a tennis champion with a fearsome* (= intimidating) *forehand.*

fea.si.ble (FEE.zuh.bul) *adj.* **1** possible to carry out or do, esp. conveniently: *It's possible to drive 1,000 km nonstop, but hardly feasible; not a feasible plan.*

2 plausible: *a feasible story considering the circumstances.* —**fea.si.bil.i.ty** (-BIL.i.tee) *n.*

feast (FEEST) *n.* **1** an elaborate or sumptuous meal: *a wedding feast; The smorgasbord was a feast for the eyes and the palate.* **2** a religious festival: *"Hanukkah," the Feast of Lights.* —*v.* entertain with a feast: *He feasts his friends on his birthday; Feast your eyes on* (= Enjoy the sight of) *our manicured lawn.*

feat (FEET) *n.* a remarkable deed or exploit: *to perform herculean feats of strength; a brave, brilliant, outstanding, remarkable feat; It's no mean feat to climb Everest.*

feath.er (FETH.ur, "TH" as in "the") *n.* one of the light, soft, thin outgrowths covering a bird's body: *as light as a feather; to smooth her ruffled feathers* (= calm her down); *"Birds of a feather* (= of the same kind) *flock together."* —**feather in one's cap** an accomplishment.
—*v.* supply or furnish with feathers: *He was fired for trying to feather his nest* (= enrich himself by using his position); *adj.: a feathered arrow, dart; The birds are our feathered friends.* —**feath.er.y** (FETH.uh.ree) *adj.*

feath.er.edge (FETH.ur.ej) *n.* a thin and easily damaged edge.

feath.er.weight (FETH.ur.wait) *n.* a boxer weighing between 119 and 126 lb. (54 and 57 kg for Olympics).

fea.ture (FEE.chur) *n.* **1** an outstanding detail or quality: *the physical features of a region; characteristic, distinctive, distinguishing, noteworthy, redeeming features; a child with delicate, handsome, soft, striking features (of face).* **2** an outstanding item offered in a newspaper, store, etc.: *standard and optional features for a new car; a special feature; a double feature* (= two films shown one after another); *adja.: a feature article, presentation, story, writer; a feature-length* (= full-length) *movie.*
—*v.* **-tures, -tured, -tur.ing** be or make a feature of something: *a store that features discounts; Who was featured in that movie? featured as the hero.* —**fea.ture.less** *adj.: a featureless landscape; the featureless wastes of the Sahara.*

feb.ri.fuge (FEB.ruh.fyooj) *n. & adj.* (a substance) that reduces fever.

fe.brile (FEE.brul, FEB-) *adj.* having to do with fever: *febrile convulsions, illnesses, patients.*

Feb.ru.ar.y (FEB.roo.air.ee) *n.* **-ar.ies** the second month of the calendar year, with 28 days or, in leap years, 29 days.

fe.ces (FEE.seez) *n.pl.* waste from the intestines. —**fe.cal** (FEE.cul) *adj.*

feck.less (FEK.lis) *adj.* ineffective, futile, or irresponsible: *a young woman abandoned by her feckless lover; He thinks those who pay taxes are foolish and feckless and those who don't are smart; He plays the part of a virtuous, feckless, and wimpy youth.* —**feck.less.ly** *adv.;* **feck.less.ness** *n.*

fe.cund (FEC.und, FEE-) *adj.* fruitful or fertile: *the fecund earth; da Vinci's fecund genius.* —**fe.cun.di.ty** (fi.CUN.di.tee) *n.*

fe.cun.date (FEE.cun.date) *v.* **-dates, -dat.ed, -dat.ing** make fecund; fertilize. —**fe.cun.da.tion** (-DAY.shun) *n.*

fed *pt. & pp.* of FEED. —**fed up** *Informal.* tired and disgusted: *He's fed up with TV.* —**fed** or **Fed** *n. Informal.* **1** a federal government agent or official. **2 the feds** or **the Feds** *pl.* the federal government or its officials. **3 the Fed** a federal government agency.

fed.a.yeen (fed.ah.YEEN) *n.pl.* Arab guerrillas.

fed.er.al (FED.uh.rul) *adj.* **1** having to do with a federation: *a federal organization, party, union.* **2** having to do with a central government: *a federal affair, body, commission, district, policy, system; federal funding; a federal building* (housing federal government offices). —**fed.er.al.ly** *adv.*

fed.er.al.ism (FED.uh.ruh.liz.um) *n.* a system in which a central government has the authority in matters of national concern and states or provinces have the powers given them by the country's constitution, as in the U.S. and Switzerland. —**fed.er.al.ist** *n. & adj.*

fed.er.al.ize (FED.uh.ruh.lize) *v.* **-iz.es, -ized, -iz.ing** unite into a federal union or put under federal control.

fed.er.ate (FED.uh.rate) *v.* **-ates, -at.ed, -at.ing** unite into a federation.

fed.er.a.tion (fed.uh.RAY.shun) *n.* a union of many member nations, states, or organizations.

fe.do.ra (fi.DOR.uh) *n.* a man's soft felt hat with the crown creased lengthwise.

fee *n.* a charge or payment for a privilege or service: *We charge a fee for admission; fees for services rendered; contingency, entrance, lawyer's, membership, registration, tuition fees; For a (nominal) fee, the shop will hold an item for you; They waived his fee; She split her fees with him.*

fee.ble (FEE.bul) *adj.* **-bler, -blest**
1 weak from sickness or age: *a feeble old man; a feeble voice.* **2** ineffective: *a*

feeble attempt, cry; feeble efforts.
—**fee.bly** adv.

fee.ble.mind.ed (FEE.bul.mine.did) adj. mentally retarded. —**fee.ble.mind.ed.ly** adv.; **fee.ble.mind.ed.ness** n.

feed v. **feeds, fed, feed.ing 1** give (as) food: *Mother feeds the baby; Feed this to the cat; Caterpillars* **feed on** (= eat) *leaves; news to feed* (= satisfy) *your curiosity;* **n.:** *breast, forced, intravenous* **feeding. 2** supply or provide: *to feed data into a computer; A TV reporter feeds her stories to the network.*
—**n. 1** food for animals: *cattle feed.* **2** material to feed into a machine or furnace. **3** a feeding mechanism.

feed.back n. **1** in automatic systems, the return of part of the output as input, as in the on-and-off switching in a home heating system. **2** any similar process: *positive and negative feedbacks; This dictionary was compiled with the help of feedback from teachers and students.*

feed.bag n. a feed-filled bag fastened to a horse's head.

feed.er n. one that feeds: *local feeder airlines connecting with a major one.*

feed lot n. a farmlike place where cattle are fattened for market.

feed.stock n. raw material from which an industrial or synthetic product is made.

feel v. **feels, felt, feel.ing 1** be aware of or experience something or one's own state of being: *A nail or hair cannot feel; How do you feel? to feel bad, cold, fine, good, hot, proud, sorry, warm; He feels such an idiot to have done that; You will feel better after resting; She feels cheated; He feels for her in her misery; He feels pity for her; She feels like a fool; Do you* **feel like** *taking a walk? No, I don't* **feel up to** *it today.* **2** perceive by touching: *The doctor felt her pulse; She could feel it beat(ing); She felt about in her bag for the key; A blind man* **feels his way** *about in the dark; The room feels warm* (= One feels warm in it). **3** believe or think: *He feels strongly about cruelty to animals; feels that animals should not be killed for food; Let's* **feel out** (= find out the thinking of) *the membership on this question.* —**n. 1** the sense of touch: *She has a good feel* (= intuition) *for poetry that sells; She took a feel of* (= did an act of feeling) *his pulse.* **2** how something feels when touched: *the soft feel of silk.*

feel.er n. **1** one that feels, as an insect's antenna. **2** an observation or suggestion to find out what a person thinks: *to put out or throw out a feeler.*

feel-good adj. intended to make people feel good; promoting a sense of well-being: *feel-good ads, ethics, music, politics, products, projects, sales pitches.*

feeling n. **1** the sense of touch: *to lose feeling in one's foot.* **2** an experience of sensation or emotion, esp. as influencing one's thought: *a feeling of joy; a gut feeling; a numb feeling; to arouse or stir up popular feeling on an issue; a deep, eerie, friendly, gloomy, hostile, intense, queasy, sinking, uneasy feeling; What are your* **feelings** *on capital punishment? mixed feelings; to harbor feelings of hatred; no hard feelings; one's innermost, intimate, pent-up feelings; He sounds as if his* **feelings** (= sensitivities) *have been hurt; a man of delicate, sensitive feelings.*
—**adj.** sensitive or sympathetic: *a feeling remark.* —**feel.ing.ly** adv.

feet pl. of FOOT.

feign (FAIN) v. pretend: *to feign illness; He's only feigning he's ill; She wants to feign* (= make up) *an excuse for her absence;* **adj.:** *a* **feigned** (= pretended) *attack; feigned madness.*

feint (FAINT) n. pretense: *a surprise attack after (making) a feint of retreating.*
—v. pretend: *He dribbled the ball after feinting a pass.*

feist.y (FYE.stee) adj. **feist.i.er, -i.est** spirited or fighting: *a feisty lawyer, mood, politician; her feisty spirit.*

feld.spar n. a mineral found in crystalline rock and containing aluminum, silica, and other elements.

fe.lic.i.tate (fuh.LIS.uh.tate) v. **-tates, -tat.ed, -tat.ing** Formal. congratulate someone on an occasion of joy, as a wedding or graduation.
—**fe.lic.i.ta.tion** (-TAY.shun).

fe.lic.i.tous (fuh.LIS.uh.tus) adj. delightful or delightfully expressed: *a felicitous occasion, expression, outcome; a most felicitous way of expressing herself.*

fe.lic.i.ty (fuh.LIS.i.tee) n. **-ties 1** happiness or good fortune: *marital felicity.* **2** gracefulness of expression: *the felicity of her style, wit; felicity of phrasing; verbal felicities* (= graceful expressions).

fe.line (FEE.line) n. an animal of the cat family: *Lions and tigers are felines;* **adj.:** *He crept forward with feline* (= catlike) *stealth.*

fell 1 pt. of FALL. **2** v. strike down or cut down: *The giant felled the tree with one blow of the ax.* **3** adj. fierce or deadly: *He took care of everything* **at** *or* **in one fell swoop** (= suddenly and all at once). **4** n. an animal's hide; pelt.

fel.la (FEL.uh) n. Informal. fellow; also **fel.ler.**

fel.lah (FEL.uh) n. **fel.lahs, fel.la.hin**

(-HEEN) or **-heen** in Arab countries, a peasant or laborer.

fel.la.ti.o (fuh.LAY.shee.oh, -LAH.tee.oh) *n.* oral stimulation of the penis.

fel.ler *n.* **1** same as FELLA. **2** one who fells trees.

fel.loe (FEL.oh) same as FELLY.

fel.low (FEL.oh) *n.* **1** [familiar use] a male person: *a jolly good fellow; Ignore that fellow; the poor fellow.* **2** a companion: *They were fellows at school; Where's the fellow (= mate) to this glove? The world has not produced a fellow (= peer) to Shakespeare's genius;* **adj.**: *our fellow citizens; fellow humans; fellow feeling (= sympathy).* **3** a member of a learned society: *John B. Hancock Distinguished Fellow; resident, senior, visiting fellows.* **4** a student on a fellowship: *research, senior, teaching fellows.*

fel.low.man (FEL.oh.man) *n.* **-men** a fellow human being.

fel.low.ship (FEL.oh.ship) *n.* **1** companionship or community: *to foster or promote good fellowship in the neighborhood; the fellowship of humanity; united in fellowship with our brothers and sisters.* **2** at a university, a position or award given to a graduate student as a help.

fellow traveler *n.* a Communist sympathizer.

fel.ly (FEL.ee) *n.* **fel.lies** the rim of a wheel, or a section of it, that is supported by the spokes.

fel.on (FEL.un) *n.* one who has committed a felony.

fel.o.ny (FEL.uh.nee) *n.* **-nies** a crime such as arson, rape, or robbery that is more serious than a misdemeanor.

felt 1 *pt. & pp.* of FEEL: *a felt need.* **2** *n.* a fabric made of wool mixed with fur, hair, etc., matted together by steam and pressure instead of being woven or knitted: *a pool table covered with felt; a felt hat.* —*v.* make into felt; *adj.*: *a felted fabric; adja.: a felting needle.*
—**felting** *n.* felt cloth.

fe.male (FEE.male) *adj.* **1** of the sex that produces eggs or bears young: *a female animal; Is Chris male or female? a female companion, deity, fetus, figurine, function, patient, role, voice; female garb, health, hormones, membership; female prejudice; the female breast, domain, population, reproductive system, sex, symbol (♀).* **2** forming a receptacle for a corresponding male part: *the female organ of pollination; The vagina is a female structure; a female electric socket; A bolt turns in the female groove inside a nut.*
—*n.* a female person (including children) [derogatory in nonformal use]; also, a female animal, flower, etc.: *a condition that affects only females; older females; the female of the species; a normal athletic female; a study of black and white females with diabetes mellitus.*
—**fe.male.ness** *n.*

fem.i.nine (FEM.uh.nin) *adj.* having to do with women or their characteristics: *a feminine fashion, manner; lace that is soft and feminine; fresh and feminine; frilly and feminine; feminine appeal, beauty, feeling, graces, hygiene, looks, pink, qualities, shapes; the feminine gender, touch; the feminine suffix "-ess."* —*n.* a feminine word: *"She" and "actress" are feminines.*
—**fem.i.nin.i.ty** (-NIN.i.tee) *n.*

fem.i.nism (FEM.uh.niz.um) *n.* the women's rights movement or its principles. —**fem.i.nist** *n. & adj.*

fem.i.nize (FEM.uh.nize) *v.* **-iz.es, -ized, -iz.ing** make feminine; *adj.*: *the new feminized man; shopping as a feminized occupation; the feminizing influence of women.* —**fem.i.ni.za.tion** (-nuh.ZAY.shun, -nye-) *n.*: *divorce and the feminization of poverty, of power, of the work force.*

fem lib *n. Informal.* women's liberation.

femme fa.tale (fem.fuh.TAL) *n., pl.* **femmes fatales** (fem.fuh.TALS) a very seductive woman: *a beautiful but dangerous femme fatale..*

fe.mur (FEE.mur) *n.* **fe.murs** or **fem.o.ra** (FEM.uh.ruh) the thighbone.
—**fem.o.ral** (FEM.uh.rul) *adj.*: *a femoral artery.*

fen *n.* esp. in England, a marsh or swamp.

fence *n.* **1** a barrier of stakes, stones, or wire put around property for protection and privacy: *to build, erect, put up a fence; barbed-wire, chain-link, chicken-wire, picket fences.* **2** a receiver of stolen goods. **3** a place where such goods are bought and sold. —**on the fence** hesitating about which side of a dispute to join: *to sit on the fence.* —**to mend fences** *Informal.* to improve relations with people. —*v.* **fenc.es, fenced, fenc.ing 1** enclose or keep out with a fence: *"Don't fence me in."* **2** practice the sport of fencing. **3** parry questions. **4** buy and sell stolen goods.
—**fenc.er** *n.*

fence-sitter *n.* one who is undecided about which side to join. Also **fence-straddler.**

fence-mending *n.* the improving of a neglected relationship.

fencing *n.* **1** swordplay using a foil or saber. **2** material for putting up a fence.

fend *v.* defend: *She used judo to* **fend off**

her attacker; *He had to **fend** (= provide) for himself after his parents died.*

fend.er *n.* a protective or shielding device, as the metal covers over an automobile's tires, the screen in front of a fireplace, or a buffer for protecting a ship's side when docking: *the minor **fender benders** (= minor automobile collisions) that happen during a storm.*

fen.es.tra.tion (fen.uh.STRAY.shun) *n.* 1 the arrangement of windows in a building. 2 the cutting of a tiny window in the inner ear to treat deafness.

fen.nel (FEN.ul) *n.* an herb with fragrant leaves and aromatic seeds used in flavoring.

fe.ral (FEER.ul) *adj.* untamed or wild: *a feral cat; He fell into a feral rage.*

fer-de-lance (fair.duh.LAHNCE) *n. sing. & pl.* a large poisonous tropical American pit viper.

fer.ment (FUR.ment) *n.* 1 yeast, bacteria, or a similar substance that causes fermentation. 2 a state of agitation or unrest: *when the nation was in ferment; the ferment that swept Communist countries in 1989.* —*v.* (fur.MENT) cause fermentation: *Yeast ferments the starch in bread dough; adj.: Cheese is a fermented food (made by fermentation); newly fermented wine.*

fer.men.ta.tion (fur.mun.TAY.shun) *n.* a change such as the souring of milk or ripening of cheese brought about by the action of enzymes, bacteria, etc.

fer.mi.um (FUR.mee.um) *n.* an artificial radioactive metallic chemical element.

fern *n.* one of a large group of flowerless plants with stems and fronds which reproduce by means of spores: *the tree ferns found in wetlands.*

fern.er.y (FUR.nuh.ree) *n.* **-er.ies** a collection of ferns or the place where they are grown.

fe.ro.cious (fuh.ROH.shus) *adj.* 1 fierce or bloodthirsty: *a ferocious animal, beast, struggle.* 2 extreme: *pangs of ferocious hunger; ferocious ambition, energy, intensity.*

fe.roc.i.ty (fuh.ROS.i.tee) *n.* **-ties** fierce cruelty or a ferocious act.

-ferous *adj. suffix.* bearing. *coniferous, metalliferous, odoriferous, proliferous.*

fer.ret (FER.it) *n.* a weasellike animal trained for use by hunters and rat-catchers. —*v.* **ferret out** search out: *to ferret out facts, secrets, the truth.*

fer.ric (FER.ic) *adj.* of or derived from iron: *ferric oxide.*

Fer.ris wheel (FER.is-) *n.* an amusement device consisting of a large upright wheel with a fixed axis and seats swinging from its rim.

ferro- *comb.form.* iron: *ferroconcrete; ferro-magnetic; ferro-manganese.*

fer.ro.mag.net.ic (FER.oh.mag.NET.ic) *adj.* easily magnetized, as iron, steel, cobalt, or nickel.

fer.rous (FER.us) *adj.* of or derived from iron: *Steel is a ferrous alloy or ferrous metal; ferrous oxide.*

fer.rule (FER.ul, -ool) *n.* a metal ring or cap put at the end of a cane, tube, tool handle, etc. for added strength.

fer.ry (FER.ee) *n.* **fer.ries** a conveyance, as a boat, hydrofoil, or aircraft, esp. across water. —*v.* **fer.ries, fer.ried, fer.ry.ing** cross or convey, as by ferry: *People and cars are ferried to and from the island; Airplanes are ferried (= flown) from the factory to delivery points.*
—**fer.ry.boat** *n.* —**fer.ry.man** *n.* **-men**.

fer.tile (FUR.tul, -tile) *adj.* productive of young, crops, seeds, ideas, etc.: *fertile eggs, land, soil, women; a story-teller's fertile imagination.* —**fer.til.i.ty** (fur.TIL.i.tee) *n.*: *when the soil loses fertility; the decline of fertility in old age; adja.: fertility clinics, drugs, rites.*

fer.til.ize (FUR.tul.ize) *v.* **-iz.es, -ized, -iz.ing** make fertile, as by use of manure on land or by impregnating an egg cell; **fer.til.iz.er** (-lye.zur) *n.* —**fer.til.i.za.tion** (-luh.ZAY.shun, -lye-) *n.*

fer.ule (FER.ul, -ool) *n.* formerly, a ruler used for punishing schoolchildren.

fer.vent (FUR.vunt) *adj.* showing earnestness or devotion; impassioned: *a fervent plea for mercy; a fervent prayer;* **fer.vent.ly** *adv.*

fer.vid *adj.* fervent in a too eager manner: *a fervid preacher; fervid dogmatism, loyalty, vows;* **fer.vid.ly** *adv.*

fer.vor (FUR.vur) *n.* earnestness or enthusiasm; zeal: *patriotic, religious, revolutionary fervor.* Also **fer.vour** *Cdn.*

-fest *comb.form.* festival: *filmfest, funfest, Octoberfest, songfest, talkfest.*

fes.tal (FES.tul) *adj.* 1 having to do with a festal feast: *a festal assembly; festal ceremonies, solemnities.* 2 festive: *a festal celebration, day, occasion.*

fes.ter (FES.tur) *n.* a small ulcer or sore filled with pus. —*v.* 1 form pus: *Wounds fester.* 2 rankle or cause to rankle: *Hatred festered in his mind.*

fes.ti.val (FES.tuh.vul) *n.* a special period of celebration: *to hold a dance festival; drama, folk, music festivals; Hanukkah, the festival of lights; the Stratford Festival (of staged plays).*

fes.tive (FES.tiv) *adj.* having to do with a feast or festival; joyous or gay: *New Year's is a festive occasion; Everyone is in*

festivity / fiber

a festive mood; a festive air, atmosphere, celebration, crowd, event, feeling, season, spirit; festive garments.

fes.tiv.i.ty (fes.TIV.i.tee) *n.* **-ties** merrymaking; also, a festive activity: *an air of festivity; The festivities ended with fireworks.*

fes.toon (fes.TOON, long "OO") *n.* a garland of flowers or other decorative material for hanging in a loop.
—*v.: a room festooned with garlands and streamers for a party.*

fet.a cheese (FET.uh-) *n.* a firm white cheese made in Greece from goat's milk.

fe.tal (FEE.tul) *adj.* of a fetus: *fetal development; the curled-up* **fetal position** *characteristic of a fetus in the womb.*

fetch *v.* **1** bring or get: *I'll go and fetch some water from the well; Please fetch me a glass; The car will fetch $5,000 if you sell it now.* **2** draw forth: *to fetch a sigh, groan, tears.* **3** *Informal.* deal: *She fetched him one on the jaw.*
—**fetch up** stop: *The car skidded off the highway and fetched up against a tree.*

fetching *adj. Informal.* attractive or admirable: *a fetching appearance, hat, personality, smile; in a fetching pose.*
—**fetch.ing.ly** *adv.*

fete or **fête** (FAIT) *n.* a lavish entertainment or party, often one held outdoors. —*v.* **fetes** or **fêtes, fet.ed** or **fêt.ed, fet.ing** or **fêt.ing** honor with a fete: *The Olympic hero was feted everywhere he went.*

fet.id (FET.id, FEE.tid) *adj. Formal.* stinking: *The air was fetid with the smell of rotting garbage – Ugh!*

fet.ish (FET.ish, FEE.tish) *n.* **1** an idol, image, or other object carried around for its supposed magical powers. **2** a blind devotion: *He makes a fetish of washing his hands and feet before and after meals.* —**fe.tish.ism** *n.;* **fe.tish.ist** *n.*
—**fe.tish.is.tic** (-IS.tic) *adj.*

fet.lock *n.* the projection at the back just above a horse's or donkey's hoof with a tuft of hair on it.

fet.ter (FET.ur) *n.* **1** *usu.* **fetters** *pl.* leg irons: *a prisoner in fetters.* **2** a restraint: *The new rules are a fetter on freedom of the press; to be free from* or *to shed* or *shake off the fetters of superstition.*
—*v.* hamper or restrain.

fet.tle (FET.ul) *n.* **in fine fettle** in good physical condition.

fe.tus (FEE.tus) *n.* a developing animal embryo, esp. an unborn infant two months after conception.

feud (FEWD) *n.* a long-lasting quarrel, esp. between families or clans, often vengeful and bitter: *to stir up a feud; a family feud over an inheritance.* —*v.* carry on a feud: *The Smiths have been feuding with the Joneses since 1980.*

feu.dal (FEW.dul) *adj.* having to do with feudalism: *a feudal fief, lord, society, vassal; feudal laws, tenure; the feudal system.*

feu.dal.ism (FEW.dul.iz.um) *n.* the economic, social, and political system of medieval Europe binding vassals to the military service of their lords from whom they received fiefs of land and buildings and serfs or peasants to work the land.* —**feu.dal.is.tic** (-duh.LIS.tic) *adj.*

feu.da.to.ry (FEW.duh.tor.ee) *n.* **-ries** a feudal vassal or his fief.

fe.ver (FEE.vur) *n.* **1** abnormally high body temperature: *to come down with a fever; a high, intermittent, recurrent, slight fever.* **2** a disease: *glandular, hay, rheumatic, scarlet, typhoid, yellow fever.* **3** a state of excitement or restlessness: *exam, election, spring fever.*
—**fe.ver.ish** *adj.*

fever blister (or **sore**) *n.* a cold sore.

fever pitch *n.* a restless or excited state: *Emotions were at* or *had reached a fever pitch before the riot.*

few *n., adj. & pron.: Few* (= not many) *books are missing; 100 or fewer* (= a smaller number); *Only a few* (= some) *have been destroyed; Such cases are* **few and far between** (= rare); **Quite a few** (= a good many) *are lost;* **The few** (= the minority) *that are missing should be found.*

fey *adj.* fairylike, whimsical, or strange: *a fey character; a fey and chance event; She found the dress fey and amusing.*

fez *n.* **fez.zes** a red, brimless felt cap with a tassel hanging from the crown, worn by Arab men.

fi.an.cé (fee.ahn.SAY) *n.* a man engaged to be married; **fi.an.cée** (-SAY), *fem.*

fi.as.co (fee.AS.coh) *n.* **-cos** or **-coes** an utter failure: *The conference ended in a complete, total, utter fiasco.*

fi.at (FEE.at, -ut) *n.* an executive, usu. arbitrary, order; decree.

fib *n.* a trivial little lie. —*v.* **fibs, fibbed, fib.bing.** —**fib.ber** *n.*

fi.ber (FYE.bur) *n.* **1** a threadlike strand of an animal, vegetable, or mineral substance such as muscle tissue, wool, cotton, or asbestos: *Beans, bran, bread, and cereals are high in dietary fiber.* **2** this spun or woven into materials with strength and toughness: *Rayon, fiberglass, and nylon are synthetic fibers.*

fiberboard / field

3 strength or character: *a man of strong moral fiber.* Also **fi.bre** *Cdn.*

fi.ber.board (FYE.bur.bord) *n.* a building material pressed from wood and other fibers. Also **fi.bre.board** *Cdn.*

fi.ber.fill (FYE.bur.fil) *n.* a fluffy padding material made of synthetic fiber. Also **fi.bre.fill** *Cdn.*

fi.ber.glass (FYE.bur.glas) *n.* finespun glass woven into cloth, made into plastic material for boards, or in woolly form as insulation. Also **fi.bre.glass** *Cdn.*

fiber optics *n.pl.* [takes *sing. v.*] transmission of light around bends and in curves through a bundle of flexible filaments of glass or plastic. —**fiber-optic** *adj.* Also **fibre optics, fibre-optic** *Cdn.*

fibre *Cdn.* FIBER.

fi.bril (FYE.bril) *n.* a small fiber.

fi.bril.late (FIB.ruh.late) *v.* **-lates, -lat.ed, -lat.ing** split up into fibrils, esp. of the heart muscles.

fi.bril.la.tion (fib.ruh.LAY.shun) *n.* uncoordinated twitching or tremors of muscle fibers.

fi.brin (FYE.brin) *n.* a white, fibrous substance formed in blood clots from fibrinogen. —**fi.brin.ous** (-nus) *adj.*

fi.brin.o.gen (fye.BRIN.uh.jun) *n.* a protein present in blood serum.

fi.broid (FYE.broid) *n. & adj.* (having to do with) a benign tumor that grows in the muscle fibers of the walls of the uterus.

fi.bro.sis (fye.BROH.sis) *n.* excessive growth of fibrous tissue.

fi.brous (FYE.brus) *adj.* having fibers or like fiber: *fibrous board, grasses, protein, tissue, wood.*

fib.u.la (FIB.yuh.luh) *n., pl.* **-lae** (-lee) or **-las** the smaller of the two bones between the knee and the ankle; **fib.u.lar** *adj.*

-fic *suffix.* making: *acidific, deific, honorific, horrific, pacific.*

fiche (FEESH, FISH) *n.* [short form] microfiche.

fich.u (FISH.oo) *n.* a light triangular scarf worn by women draped over the shoulders and tied loosely at the breast.

fick.le (FICK.ul) *adj.* changeable like the weather; inconstant: *the fickle world of fashion; a fickle mind; fickle weather.*

fic.tion (FIC.shun) *n.* 1 something made up in the mind: *fact or fiction? pure fiction; a legal fiction* (= assumption of fact for a legal purpose). 2 literature of imagination including novels, short stories, and plays: *the world of fiction;* popular, romance, science fiction; **adj.:** *a fiction film, writer.* —**fic.tion.al** *adj.:* fictional characters, literature, roles.

fic.ti.tious (fic.TISH.us) *adj.* imaginary or invented: *a fictitious account; a fictitious character like Oliver Twist; fictitious heroes; He checked in under a fictitious* (= false) *name.*

fic.tive (FIC.tiv) *adj.* not genuine; also, fictional: *the fictive world of TV.*

fid.dle (FID.ul) *Informal. n.* 1 a violin: *to play the fiddle;* (as) **fit as a fiddle** (= quite healthy). 2 a falsification of accounts: *a tax fiddle.* —*v.* **fid.dles, fid.dled, fid.dling** 1 play on a violin. 2 tamper with, esp. accounts: *an accountant caught fiddling tax returns.* —**fid.dler** *n.*

fid.dle.sticks (FID.ul.sticks) *interj.* nonsense!

fi.del.i.ty (fuh.DEL.i.tee, fye-) *n.* **-ties** loyalty, esp. continuing faithfulness to a duty or trust: *to swear lifelong fidelity to one's marriage vows;* A **fidelity bond** insures against dishonesty or negligence.

fidg.et (FIJ.it) *v.* move or act nervously or restlessly: *to fidget with one's hands.* —*n.* this condition or a person who fidgets. —**the fidgets** *n.pl.* a fit of nervousness. —**fidg.et.y** *adj.*

fi.du.ci.ar.y (fi.DEW.shee.air.ee) *adj.* held or holding in trust; of a trustee: *Executors act in a fiduciary capacity; fiduciary duties, obligations, responsibilities, roles.* —*n., pl.* **-ar.ies** a trustee.

fie (FYE) *interj.* shame: *Fie on you!*

fief (FEEF) *n.* 1 an estate granted by a feudal lord to a vassal. 2 one's sphere of operation: *He runs the business as his private fief;* also **fief.dom.**

field (FEELD) *n.* 1 a piece of open land, esp. one put to a specific use, as for a crop, pasture, etc.: *a corn field; Farmers work in the fields; They plough, till, work the fields; a landing field (for aircraft); coal, gold, oil fields; baseball, football, playing fields; on the soccer field; a field of ice.* 2 an area of interest, influence, or activity: *Surgery is outside my field; in the field of medicine; one's field of vision; The Moon is within the Earth's gravitational field; the Earth's magnetic field; a* **field of fire** *(where shooting goes on), Lou doesn't go steady, but* **plays the field** (= dates various people); **adj.:** *a field guide, office, trial; field research.* —**adj.** having to do with a battlefield: *field artillery, batteries, hospitals, officers.* —*v.* 1 in baseball, cricket, etc., catch or stop a batted ball; hence, defend or tackle: *a skilled diplomat who fields reporters' questions with ease.* 2 put people on a field:

field day / figure

Our party fielded 200 candidates in the last election.
field day *n.* **1** a day for outdoor sports or activities. **2** an occasion of unrestricted freedom or enjoyment: *The Yankees had a field day against the Tigers.*
field glasses *n.pl.* binoculars for outdoor use; also **field glass.**
field goal *n.* **1** in football, a goal kicked from the field. **2** in basketball, a basket scored while the ball is in play.
field gun same as FIELD PIECE.
field hand *n.* a farm laborer.
field hockey *n.* hockey played on a field of grass.
field marshal *n.* in some countries, an army officer ranking next below a commander in chief.
field piece *n.* a cannon mounted on a carriage.
field test *n.* the test of a product or method under actual conditions of use; **field-test** *v.*
field trip *n.* a trip for students to gain knowledge outside of the classroom.
field.work *n.* work done in a field of activity, as by a sociologist or surveyor.
fiend (FEEND) *n.* **1** the devil; hence, an evil spirit or a wicked person. **2** *Informal.* one devoted or addicted to something: *bridge, fresh-air, hockey fiends.* —**fiend.ish** *adj.*
fierce (FEERCE) *adj.* **fierc.er, fierc.est 1** violent in temper or manner; ferocious: *a fierce attack, battle, civil war, dog; fierce fighting; It was fierce (Informal for very bad) of me to lose my temper.* **2** extreme or intense: *fierce competition, determination, hostility, intensity, loyalties, resistance, tenacity; the fierce heat of summer.* —**fierce.ly** *adv.;* **fierce.ness** *n.*
fi.er.y (FYE.uh.ree) *adj.* **fi.er.i.er, -i.est** like fire; burning: *a fiery sunset; a fiery* (= full of fire) *speech; a fiery* (= inflamed) *sore.*
fi.es.ta (fee.ES.tuh) *n.* esp. in Spanish-speaking countries, a religious or secular festival.
fife *n.* a flutelike musical instrument, used with drums.
FIFO (FYE.foh) *n.* the "first-in first-out" method of inventory valuation.
fif.teen (fif.TEEN) *n., adj. & pron.* five more than 10; 15 or XV. —**fif.teenth** *n. & adj.*
fifth *n., pron. & adj.* (the one) following the fourth; 1/5: *Who's the fifth? the fifth in line; the fifth boy; a fifth* (of a U.S. gallon of liquor); *to take* or *invoke the Fifth* or **Fifth Amendment** (of the U.S. Constitution against a person being forced to testify against himself or herself).
fifth column *n.* a subversive group working secretly for a foreign country.
fifth wheel *n.* a superfluous or burdensome person or thing.
fif.ty (FIF.tee) *n. & adj.* **-ties 1** one more than 49; 50 or L. **2 the fifties** *n.pl.* numbers, years, etc. ending in 50 through 59: *She's in her fifties; The fifties* (= 1950-59) *were a time of reconstruction in Europe.* —**fif.ti.eth** (-tee.ith) *n. & adj.*
fifty-fifty *adj. Informal.* equal: *a fifty-fifty joint venture; a fifty-fifty chance of winning; a fifty-fifty split.* —**adv.** equally: *Let's split it fifty-fifty.*
fig *n.* **1** a small tree bearing many-seeded pear-shaped fruit. **2** something contemptible: *She doesn't give* or *care a fig for* or *about his opinion; It's not worth a fig.*
fight (FITE) *v.* **fights, fought** (FAWT), **fight.ing 1** to struggle or contend against a person or thing: *to fight bravely, clean, desperately, dirty; to fight about* or *over a fence; to fight with* (= against) *one's neighbors; to fight with* (= using) *guns; to fight one's fear of the dark; to fight like dogs; Iraq fought against Iran; Children fight among themselves; We have to fight for survival; He couldn't **fight back** his tears; She **fought off** sleep by pinching herself; Pat is determined to **fight it out** or **fight to the finish;** Lee would never **fight shy of** (= avoid facing) the truth.* **2** achieve by fighting: *Fight your way through life; The battle was well fought.* —*n.* a struggle or conflict: *to get into, pick* or *provoke a fight with someone; to put up a last-ditch fight against the new bill; a bitter, desperate, fierce fight to the death; a fight to reduce taxes; a fight for justice; A fight breaks out* or *starts; a fist fight; Who won the fight? Though thrice beaten, he's still full of fight* (= fighting spirit). —**fight.er** *n.*
fighting chance *n.* a chance to win after a hard struggle: *to give everyone a fighting chance to earn a living; to get, have, stand a fighting chance.*
fig leaf *n.* a leaf used traditionally in sculpture to hide nudity.
fig.ment (FIG.munt) *n.* something made up: *a mere figment of the imagination.*
fig.u.ra.tion (fig.yuh.RAY.shun) *n.* a forming; also, a form or appearance.
fig.u.ra.tive (FIG.yuh.ruh.tiv) *adj.* using figures of speech; not literal. —**fig.u.ra.tive.ly** *adv.*
fig.ure (FIG.yur) *n.* **1** number or amount; also, a numeral: *Her salary runs to six figures; Did the sales rep men-*

figurehead / filler

tion a figure? ballpark, exact, round figures; Accountants should be good at **figures** (= math). **2** a shape or pattern: *A parabola is a geometric figure; the 69 "school figures" of figure skating; The airplane did a figure eight in the sky.* **3** the shape of one's body: *She diets to keep her figure; He's a handsome figure; an imposing, impressive, striking, trim figure; an artist good at figure drawing.* **4** personage: *familiar, national, political, prominent, public, underworld figures; Napoleon is a historical figure.* **5** an appearance or likeness; image: *Clowns cut funny figures; a ridiculous, sorry figure; She was the figure of misery; similes, metaphors, and such **figures of speech.***
—v. **-ures, -ured, -ur.ing 1** do sums: *That's too much to figure up without a calculator.* **2** imagine, picture, or estimate: *I figured we would be late; But I didn't figure on being* (= expect to be) *that late; I had figured* (= relied) *on or upon your helping us; It's difficult to figure out* (= understand) *what this poem means.* **3** appear prominently: *Galahad figures in Arthurian legends;* **adj.**: *plain, not figured* (= patterned) *wallpaper.*
fig.ure.head (FIG.yur.hed) *n.* **1** an ornamental carved figure on the bow of a ship. **2** a person in a high position but without real power.
figure skating *n.* ice skating using dance techniques and intricate patterns.
fig.u.rine (fig.yuh.REEN) *n.* a statuette.
fig.wort (FIG.wurt) *n.* a family of about 3,000 herbs, shrubs, and trees, some of which have medicinal value, as the foxglove.
fil.a.ment (FIL.uh.munt) *n.* a thread or a threadlike part, as the wire that glows in an electric bulb.
—**fil.a.men.tous** (-MEN.tus) *adj.*
fi.lar (FYE.lur) *adj.* threadlike.
fi.lar.i.a (fi.LAIR.ee.uh) *n.* a threadlike parasite that causes filariasis.
fil.a.ri.a.sis (fil.uh.RYE.sis) same as ELEPHANTIASIS.
fil.bert (FIL.burt) same as HAZELNUT.
filch *v.* steal something of small value casually: *to filch candy from a counter.*
—**filch.er** *n.*
file *n.* **1** a container such as a folder, drawer, or cabinet for keeping papers in order, usu. threaded with a wire, rod, or other device. **2** such a system or the set of papers: *to close, keep, make up, open a file on someone; Your application is on file,* says the *file clerk.* **3** a row of persons, animals, or things, one behind the other: *At the sound of the alarm, the pupils marched out in file; Indians walking their trail in single file.* **4** a smoothing or grinding metal tool with a ridged surface: *a nail file.*
—v. **files, filed, fil.ing 1** enter into an official record: *to file applications, lawsuits, tax returns; She filed* (= applied) *for divorce; Correspondents file* (= send) *stories for publication; Please file away these papers* (= enter them in the office records); *n.*: *a bankruptcy filing.* **2** move one behind the other: *Shoppers kept filing in all day; The Opposition filed out of the legislature in protest; Thousands filed past the coffin of the dead leader.* **3** smooth or grind away: *The rough edges should be filed away; n.*: *a carpentry floor sprinkled with iron filings* (= particles); *metal filings.*
fi.let (fi.LAY, FIL.ay) same as FILLET.
fil.i.al (FIL.ee.ul, FIL.yul) *adj.* of a son or daughter: *filial devotion, love, respect.*
fil.i.bus.ter (FIL.uh.bus.tur) *n.* the use of delaying tactics to obstruct passage of a bill in a legislature, esp. by prolonged speech-making: *In 1964, U.S. senators carried on or conducted or engaged in a filibuster against a civil rights bill for 75 days.* —v. use filibustering: *to filibuster a bill; U.S. Senator Huey Long filibustered 15 hours in 1935.*
fil.i.gree (FIL.uh.gree) *n.* ornamental, lacelike openwork of gold or silver wire. —v. **-grees, -greed, -gree.ing** adorn with or as if with filigree: *Our picture window was filigreed with frost.*
Fil.i.pi.no (fil.uh.PEE.noh) *n. & adj.* **-nos** (having to do with) a person of or from the Philippines.
fill *v.* **1** put something into a space so as to occupy it fully: *to fill a glass with water; Dentists fill cavities with porcelain; Please fill out this form; sails filled out by the wind; Please fill up my gas tank;* **adj.**: *a glass filled to overflowing; a room filled to capacity; filled with people.* **2** supply what is called for; fulfill: *to fill an order, doctor's prescription, requirement.* **3** put someone or oneself into a position or office: *An employment agency helps fill vacancies; Ms. Smith has filled the principalship; She was qualified enough to fill the bill* (= meet the job requirements); *The vice-principal fills in* (= substitutes) *for the principal when the latter is away; He later fills her in* (= brings her up to date) *on what happened during her absence.* —*n.* a filling or its amount: *Earth, gravel, and garbage are used as fills; They drank their fill; She had her fill* (of food); *He ate his fill from the buffet.*
fill.er *n.* a person or thing that fills,

such as ground wood added to synthetic resin for hardness and strength, a short item used to fill a newspaper column, the hose of a gas pump, etc.: *gas filler caps.*

fil.let (FIL.it, fi.LAY, FIL.ay) *n.* a slice of boneless, lean meat or fish; filet: *fillet of fish, sole; cod, salmon, trout fillets.* —*v.* to bone and slice fish or meat into fillets: *to clean and fillet a catch of fish.*

fill-in *n.* a substitute person or thing.

filling 1 *n.* something used to fill something else: *a cheese filling for a sandwich; The dentist put in a temporary filling; a plastic filling.* **2** *adj.* that fills: *a very filling meal; quite filling and satisfying;* **filling station** same as GAS STATION.

fil.lip (FIL.up) *n.* **1** an outward flip of a finger from the thumb, as in flicking a crumb off a sleeve. **2** something that goads or stimulates: *The tax was abolished as a fillip to industry.*

fil.ly (FIL.ee) *n.* **fil.lies** a young female horse.

film *n.* **1** a membrane or similar layer, as of oil in water. **2** a thin flexible material coated with a light-sensitive substance and made into sheets or rolls for taking photographs: *to develop, load, rewind, splice, wind film.* **3** a motion picture: *to ban, censor, direct, edit, make, produce, rate, release, review, shoot, show a film; action, adult, adventure, disaster, documentary, feature, gangster, propaganda, silent films.* —*v.* **1** photograph: *a movie filmed on location in Spain.* **2** coat: *a tabletop filmed with dust.*

film.dom (FILM.dum) *n.* the motion-picture industry or its personnel.

film.og.ra.phy (fil.MOG.ruh.fee) *n.* **-phies** a list of motion pictures according to actor, director, topic, etc.

film.set *n.* a motion-picture set. —*v.* set type photographically on film rather than in metal.

film.strip *n.* a length of film containing still pictures, diagrams, illustrations, etc. for use as a teaching aid.

film.y *adj.* **film.i.er, -i.est 1** thin: *a filmy curtain.* **2** hazy: *a filmy windowpane.*

fil.ter (FIL.tur) *n.* **1** a porous device for straining out dust, smoke, germs, or impurities from a liquid or gas medium in which they are suspended. **2** the porous material used, such as felt, paper, sand, or charcoal. **3** a device or substance for absorbing certain light rays and frequencies: *the color filter of a camera lens.* —*v.* **1** remove using a filter: *Air conditioners filter out dust and pollen from the air.* **2** subject to the action of a filter; *adj.:* Use **filtered** *water.* **3** pass or move slowly, as through a filter: *Refugees filter into the country; They filter through the border; Fashions filter down from the couture level to the mass market.*

fil.ter.a.ble (FIL.tur.uh.bul) *adj.* that can be filtered: *A filterable virus is small enough to pass through a bacteria-retaining filter.*

filth *n.* **1** foul dirt. **2** moral corruption or obscenity.

filth.y *adj.* **filth.i.er, -i.est** disgustingly dirty: *a filthy room, window; to work in filthy conditions;* **filthy lucre** (Informal for money); *adv.: a TV series featuring filthy* (= extremely) *rich characters.*

fil.tra.ble (FIL.truh.bul) same as FILTERABLE.

fil.tra.tion (fil.TRAY.shun) *n.* the process of filtering: *a city's water filtration plant.*

fin *n.* **1** a winglike or fanlike organ of a fish used for swimming, turning, and balancing its body in water. **2** any similar structure: *the tail fin of an aircraft; the cooling fins of a radiator.*

fi.na.gle (fuh.NAY.gul) *v.* **-gles, -gled, -gling** Informal. get something by devious or tricky means; wangle.
—**fi.na.gler** *n.*

fi.nal (FYE.nul) *adj.* last and decisive: *a final decision; the final hour; our final offer.* —*n.* something final, as a deciding game, the last examination in a course, etc.: *to take one's* **finals** *in Grade 12.*
—**fi.nal.ly** (-lee) *adv.*

fi.na.le (fuh.NAH.lee, -NAL.ee) *n.* the conclusion or last part, as of a play or piece of music: *the grand finale of her career.*

fi.nal.ist (FYE.nuh.list) *n.* one who takes part in the finals of a competition.

fi.nal.i.ty (fye.NAL.i.tee) *n.* **-ties** conclusiveness: *When Mom says something with finality, that's it, Dad!*

fi.nal.ize (FYE.nul.ize) *v.* **-iz.es, -ized, -iz.ing** make final: *Our plans have yet to be finalized.* —**fi.nal.i.za.tion** (-luh.ZAY.shun, -lye-) *n.*

final solution *n.* massacre, as of Jews by the Nazis.

fi.nance (fuh.NANCE, FYE.nance) *n.* **1** (the science of) the management of money, esp. public revenue: *an expert in finance; high finance; the Minister of Finance; A* **finance company** *makes short-term loans to individuals at higher rates of interest than banks.* **2 finances** *pl.* money resources; funds. —*v.* **-nanc.es,**

-nanced, -nanc.ing provide or get money for something: *The bank financed his new car.* —**fi.nan.cial** (-NAN.shul) *adj.*: *a family's financial affairs, difficulties, matters; insurance companies, banks, and such* **financial institutions**; *Bankers move in financial circles; the financial records; a financial* (= fiscal) *year.* —**fi.nan.cial.ly** *adv.*

fin.an.cier (fuh.nan.SEER) *n.* **1** an investor. **2** an expert in finance.

finch *n.* a small bird that has a sharp, cone-shaped bill for crushing seeds.

find (FINED) *v.* **finds, found, find.ing 1** come upon by accident or by searching: *The lost cat has been found; to find work; thoughts that found expression in verse; to find (the) time to do everything; to find* (= obtain) *funds for a project; A river finds its way* (= moves along) *to the sea; Please* **find out** (= learn or ascertain) *when the flight arrives.* **2** decide: *The jury found against the accused and for the defendant; He was* **found wanting** (= judged lacking what is required of him). **3** experience or perceive: *He finds moths interesting; She finds people forgetting her in her old age; He found himself in trouble.* —**find fault** complain about: *He finds fault with everything and everybody.* —**find oneself** discover one's own abilities: *After trying several jobs, he finally found himself as a social worker.* —*n.* a finding or something found: *The new recruit is a real find; Al held up a dime as the day's find; an archaeological find; a lucky find; rare find.* —**find.er** *n.*: *The child found a dime and shouted, "Finders keepers* (= One who finds something that has no owner has the right to keep it), *losers weepers"; A broker charges a* **finder's fee** *to arrange a mortgage on a house.*

fin-de-siè.cle (fan.duh.see.EK.luh) *adj.* having to do with the close of the 19th century: *the fin-de-siècle* (= decadent) *Versailles of Louis XIV.*

finding *n.* **1** discovery: *the findings of modern science.* **2** a decision, as of a jury. **3 findings** *pl.* things other than basic materials: *A notions department supplies a dressmaker's findings such as buttons, threads, and zippers.*

fine *adj.* **fin.er, fin.est:** *I feel fine* (= very good); *a fine* (= excellent) *young woman; fine* (= bright or clear) *weather; Gold alloy that is 18 carats fine is 75% pure gold; the fine* (= sharp) *edge of a knife; the fine point of a pen (that writes thin); fine* (= very small or thin) *wire; a fine* (= subtle or nice) *distinction; fine* (= delicate) *lace; Sand is finer* (= has smaller particles) *than gravel; one of the city's* **finest** (police officers); *their* **finest hour** (= moment of glory). —*adv. & cpd.: Friday will suit me fine* (= quite well); *walnuts chopped fine* (= in small pieces); **fine-drawn** (= thinly or delicately drawn) *wire, arguments, distinctions; Fiberglass is made of fine-spun glass.* —*n.* a sum of money paid as a penalty or punishment: *to impose, levy, slap a fine on someone; a heavy, mandatory, stiff fine.* —*v.* **fines, fined, fin.ing** impose a fine on someone: *The judge fined him $150 for speeding.*

fine art *n.* an art form that deals with the expression of beauty: *The fine arts are painting, sculpture, and architecture, sometimes also poetry, music, drama, and dancing; They have got their sales tactics down* **to a fine art** (= have perfected it).

fine print *n.* the less favorable parts of a contract or agreement, sometimes printed in small type.

fin.er.y (FYE.nuh.ree) *n.* **-er.ies** showy clothes, jewelry, etc.: *a bride in all her finery.*

fi.nesse (fuh.NES) *n.* **1** skillfulness: *a diplomat who can manage people with great finesse.* **2** cunning, as used in card games. —*v.* **-ness.es, -nessed, -ness.ing** use finesse; also, accomplish by finesse: *to finesse an appointment to the position; to finesse rather than resolve a dispute; He finessed my queen* (= took the card trick) *with his jack.*

fine-tune *v.* **-tunes, -tuned, -tun.ing** regulate by making small adjustments: *to fine-tune an engine; A government tries to fine-tune the economy* (= make it stable) *with tax cuts, spending increases, etc.*

fin.fish *n.* a true fish, not a shellfish such as an oyster or other mollusk.

fin.ger (FING.gur) *n.* **1** one of the five divisions of the hand, esp. any of the four exclusive of the thumb: *the index or trigger finger* (= forefinger); *middle finger; ring* (= third) *finger; little finger* (= pinkie); *Everyone jumps when she snaps her fingers; to* **point the finger** *or* **an accusing finger** *at someone; a warning finger; No one could* **lay** *or* **put their finger on** (= find out) *what had gone wrong; The finger of suspicion seemed to point to her* (= She was the suspect); *But no one dared* **lay a finger on** (= harm) *her or* **lift a finger against** (= oppose) *her.* **2** anything corresponding to or resembling a finger: *the finger of a glove; a finger of light coming through a hole in the roof.* —**give someone the finger** *or* **the one-finger salute** *Slang.* show

fingerboard / fire

someone contempt by making an upward-thrusting gesture with the middle finger. —**have a finger in the pie** have an interest; hence, meddle with: *Pat has a finger in every pie* (= in everything). —**keep** or **have one's fingers crossed** be hopeful. —*v.* **-gers, -gered, -ger.ing** 1 touch with or use the fingers on something, as a musical instrument in playing it. 2 *Informal.* point out a victim, potential loot, etc.

fin.ger.board (FING.gur.bord) *n.* the part of the neck of a violin or guitar against which the strings are pressed by the player's fingers to produce the desired tones.

finger bowl *n.* a small bowl for rinsing the fingers at a meal.

fin.gered (FING.gurd) *adj. & comb.form.* having or involving fingers: *giant trees with fingered roots; the keyboarder's fleet-fingered accuracy; a fumble-fingered fielder; a light-fingered pickpocket.*

finger food *n.* snacks that may be picked up and eaten with the fingers.

fingering (FING.guh.ring) *n.* the act, process, or method of using the fingers in playing a musical instrument.

finger painting *n.* painting by using the fingers, hand, or arm to spread paint on moistened paper; **finger-paint** *v.*

finger pier See PIER.

finger-pointing *n.* the act of making an accusation, esp. unfairly.

fin.ger.print (FING.gur.print) *n.* an impression of the lines that form arches, loops, and whorls on the fingertips, used as a positive means of identification: *a set of fingerprints*; *v.*: *The suspect was arrested, photographed, and fingerprinted.*

fin.ger.tip (FING.gur.tip) *n.* the tip of a finger: *He has several languages* **at his fingertips** (= at his command).

fin.i.al (FIN.ee.ul) *n.* an ornament forming the topmost part or apex of a peaked or arched structure, as the screw on top of a lampshade.

fin.i.cky (FIN.uh.kee) *adj.* fussy in taste or standards: *a finicky dresser, eater; finicky about the least things.* Also **fin.i.cal.**

fi.nis (FIN.is, FYE.nis) *n.* **-nis.es** a formal conclusion or end, as written at the end of a book, movie, etc.

fin.ish (FIN.ish) *v.* 1 bring to completion: *Of the 12 who started the race, only four finished; Jim finished in fourth place; Let me finish* (= reach the end of) *this chapter; We finished the meeting with or by singing the national anthem; She hopes to* **finish up** *at the top of her class.* 2 make complete: *a roughed-in fireplace that needs finishing; A* **finishing school** *prepares young women for social life; to* **put the finishing touches on** *an essay; to* **add** *or* **give a** *or* **the finishing touch** *to the decor.* —*n.* 1 the final part of something: *the close, hair-breadth, photo finish of a horse race; "The Charge of the Light Brigade" was a* **fight to the finish.** 2 something used in finishing: *paints, varnishes, waxes, and such finishes.* 3 a finished quality: *the glossy finish of art paper; His manner lacks finish* (= polish).

finished 1 *adjp.* in a state of having completed something: *a cabinet finished in black; We are finished for the day; But I'm not finished with you yet* (= Don't leave yet); *You're finished* (= ruined) *as a businessman; finished in business.* 2 *adja.* completed or perfected: *finished goods, products; a finished appearance, fabric, home, image; highly finished jeans; a finished* (= polished) *performance, work of art; a finished* (= accomplished) *pianist.*

fi.nite (FYE.nite) *adj.* having limits; neither infinite nor infinitesimal: *our finite existence; a finite amount, number, scope.* —**fi.nite.ness** *n.*

finite verb *n.* a verb with a definite person, number, and tense, as "goes" distinguished from the infinitive "to go."

fink *n. Slang.* an undesirable person such as a strikebreaker or informer. —**fink out** *Slang.* back out like a fink.

Finn *n.* a person of or from **Finland,** a N. European republic.

fin.nan had.die (FIN.un.HAD.ee) *n.* smoked haddock produced by a Scottish method.

finned (*rhyme:* wind) *adj.* having a fin or fins: *finned fishes; a finned pipe; finned coils.*

Fin.nish *n. & adj.* (having to do with Finland, Finns, or) the language of the Finns.

Fin.no-U.gric (fin.oh.OO.gric) *adj.* a subfamily of the Uralic group of languages to which Hungarian and Finnish belong.

fin.ny (FIN.ee) *adj.* **fin.ni.er, fin.ni.est** having to do with fins or fish: *the finny whale; the finny population (of fishes); the* **finny deep** (= ocean filled with fish).

fiord (FYORD) *n.* an inlet of the sea with steep cliffs on both sides, as in Norway.

fir *n.* a pyramid-shaped coniferous evergreen tree of the pine family.

fire *n.* 1 a burning or its flame: *to sit around a picnic fire; Your house may* **catch fire** (and burn) *if you smoke in bed; a house* **on fire** (= burning); *You're* **playing with fire** (= playing with something dangerous); *to bank, build, contain, douse, extinguish, kindle, light, make, put out, set, stamp out, start, stir, stoke a fire; to bring a fire under control; to strike fire using a flint; Fires break out, go out, rage, roar, smolder, spread;* **adj.**: *a fire alarm, brigade, hose.* **2** something resembling a fire, as strong feeling, zeal, or enthusiasm: *eyes full of fire; He didn't have to* **set the world on fire** (= do anything spectacular). **3** a discharge of firearms or an action resembling it: *Hold your fire! to cease, draw, exchange fire; cross fire; rapid fire; rifle fire; a baptism of fire; a decision still* **hanging fire** (= being considered); *We will* **open fire** (= start shooting) *when we sight the enemy; The politician was* **under fire** (= under attack) *from the media.* —*v.* **fires, fired, fir.ing 1** (cause to) burn, bake, get hot, etc.: *Pottery is fired* (= baked) *in a kiln; adventure stories that fire* (= excite) *the imagination; Sam left the meeting all* **fired up** (= excited) *at the imagined insult.* **2** shoot: *First he fired in the air, then into the crowd; fired point-blank at the bear; The press* **fired away** *with questions throughout the interview; He prefers to* **fire off** (= write and send) *memos rather than talk.* **3** dismiss from a job: *He was told to resign or be fired; got fired from his job.*

fire ant *n.* an ant with a burning sting that is a serious pest in the southern U.S.

fire.arm *n.* a hand weapon such as a rifle or pistol that fires a bullet or shell using gunpowder.

fire.ball *n.* **1** a ball of fire such as the great luminous cloud resulting from a nuclear explosion, or something resembling a ball of fire such as lightning or a brilliant meteor. **2** a very energetic person.

fire.base *n.* a military base delivering heavy gunfire.

fire.boat *n.* a boat with fire-fighting equipment.

fire.bomb *n.* a bomb designed to start a fire; *v.*: *Terrorists firebombed the embassy.*

fire.box *n.* **1** the fire-containing chamber of a furnace or boiler, as in a steam engine. **2** a box with a signaling device for alerting a fire station.

fire.brand *n.* **1** a piece of burning wood. **2** an agitator.

fire.break *n.* a strip of plowed or cleared land meant to stop a spreading fire.

fire.brick *n.* a brick made of fireclay to withstand high temperatures and used to line furnaces and kilns.

fire.bug *n. Informal.* a maniac who sets fire to things.

fire chief *n.* the head of a firefighting department.

fire.clay *n.* refractory clay used for making firebricks.

fire.crack.er (FIRE.crack.ur) *n.* a firework consisting of a paper roll of explosive and a fuse.

fire.damp *n.* the explosive methane-air mixture formed in coal mines.

fire.dog *n.* an andiron.

fire door *n.* a door for stopping a fire from spreading.

fire drill *n.* an exercise to teach the proper evacuation procedure in case of a fire.

fire engine *n.* a red automotive truck for transporting firefighters and their equipment; **adj.**: *a fire-engine red (color).*

fire escape *n.* **1** a fireproof stairway outside a building. **2** a ladder or other means of escaping a fire.

fire extinguisher *n.* a portable apparatus for spraying chemicals to put out fires.

fire.fight *n.* an exchange of gunfire.

fire.fight.er (FIRE.fye.tur) *n.* one trained to fight fires. —**fire.fight.ing** *n.*

fire.fly *n.* **-flies** a night beetle that gives off flashes of light; lightning bug.

fire.hall, fire.house same as FIRE STATION.

fire hat *n.* the helmet worn by a firefighter.

fire hydrant *n.* a street outlet to draw water from in case of a fire.

fire.log *n.* an artificial log made of sawdust and wax for use in the fireplace instead of wood.

fire.man (FIRE.mun) *n.* **-men 1** a firefighter: *the* **fireman's carry** (= two people taking a person's arm and leg on either side). **2** one who attends to a furnace.

fire.place *n.* a place for an open fire, esp. a framed one built in a room at the base of a chimney.

fire.plug same as FIRE HYDRANT.

fire.pow.er (FIRE.pow.ur) *n.* the firing capacity and effectiveness of a military unit or weapon.

fire.proof *adj.* that resists burning: *a fireproof building; fireproof clothing.* —*v.* **1** cover with fire resistants such as stone, brick, etc.: *to fireproof a building.* **2** treat with fire retardants such as ammonium phosphate, borax, and zinc chloride: *to fireproof clothing.*

fire sale *n. Informal.* a sale at a very low price, as of something damaged by fire.

fire.screen *n.* a screen placed in front of a fireplace as protection against flying sparks.

fire.side *n.* a hearth: *to sit by the fireside; The president went on TV with an informal* **fireside** *chat instead of giving a formal press conference.*

fire station *n.* a building in which fire engines and firefighters are housed.

fire.storm *n.* **1** a huge fire, as from a nuclear explosion or bombing raid, which generates inrushing winds fanning it. **2** a similar phenomenon: *A firestorm of telegrams and phone calls hit the White House.*

fire tower *n.* a tower used as a lookout by forest rangers.

fire.trap *n.* a place from which escape in case of fire would be practically impossible.

fire truck *n.* a fire engine.

fire.wall *n.* a wall for preventing a fire from spreading.

fire.wa.ter (FIRE.wot.ur) *n. Informal.* alcoholic liquor.

fire.wood *n.* wood for fuel.

fire.work *n.* **1** a device that produces noise and light, as a firecracker or rocket. **2 fireworks** *sing. & pl.* a spectacular display using firecrackers, rockets, etc.

firing line *n.* the front line of an activity, controversy, campaign, etc.

firing squad *n.* a group of soldiers that carries out a death sentence by firing or fires a volley of shots in salute.

firm *adj.* **1** not affected by pressure, movement, or change: *as firm as a rock; an infant that is firm on its feet; healthy, firm muscles.* **2** steady or strong: *a firm attachment, basis, belief, commitment, decision, foothold, foundation, grip, hand, handshake, hold, offer, opposition, price, voice; The dollar remained firm against the yen on the money market; Our side is* **on firm ground** (= sure of itself). **3** fixed or resolute: *She's firm in her religious beliefs; remains, stands firm; in firm control; firm discipline, leadership; The rebellion was put down with* **a firm hand**; *a teacher who is firm* (= strict) *with pranksters;* **adv.**: *Stand firm and do not yield; the basic beliefs that we all hold firm to.* —*v.* make or become firm: *Prices are firming up after going down; Let's firm up the contract and close the deal.* —*n.* a business enterprise or partnership: *He manages an advertising firm; law firms.* —**firm.ly** *adv.;* **firm.ness** *n.*

fir.ma.ment (FUR.muh.munt) *n.* the sky considered as a dome with stars fixed in it.

firm.ware *n.* software that comes with a computer, written into its read-only memory from which it cannot be accidentally erased.

first *adj.* coming before all others in time, position, rank, etc.: *the first prize; the first time; He takes a shower* **first thing** *in the morning; "First things first"* (= The most important duties should be done first). —*adv.* **1** before all others or everything else: *I have to finish my homework first; Who came in first?* **At first** (= In the beginning) *I didn't realize it; "First come, first served"* (= People are served in order of arrival); **First of all** or **First off** (= before anything else), *I would like to call the roll.* **2** for the first time: *when I first met you.* —*n. & pron.* a person, thing, place, etc. that is first: *She is a strong first; He is among the first; the first and the best of my pupils; She is first (in rank) in the class; I was* **the first** *to arrive; It has been like that* **from the (very) first** (= from the beginning); **from first to last** (= throughout).

first aid *n.* emergency care given to a sick or injured person: *to administer or give first aid;* **adj.**: *a first-aid kit; first-aid training, treatment, workers.*

first base *n.* in baseball, the base that a runner has to touch first. —**get to first base** *Informal.* take the first step toward a goal.

first.born *n.* the oldest child.

first class *n.* the first group in a classification system. —**first-class** *adj.*: *sealed letters and such first-class mail; a first-class passenger;* **adv.**: *She always flies first-class.*

first floor *n.* **1** the ground floor. **2** [in U.K. & Europe] the floor above the ground floor.

first-hand or **first.hand** *adj.* obtained from the original source; not secondhand: *It's first-hand information.* —*adv.* also **first hand:** *I learned it (at) first-hand; He experienced it at first hand.*

first lady *n.* **1** also **First Lady**, a woman chief of state or a chief of state's wife, as the wife of a male U.S. president. **2** the leading woman of an art or profession: *the first lady of ballet.*

first lieutenant *n.* a U.S. military officer ranking below captain and above second lieutenant.

first.ling *n.* the first of its kind, as produce or offspring.

first.ly *adv.* [used in listing items] in the first place; first: *Firstly, you are too young, secondly, you are still in school.*

first name *n.* given name, as opposed to

the family name or middle names.
—**first-name** *adja.* familiar or friendly: *The two are on a **first-name** basis.*

first person *n.* a pronoun or verb such as "I," "he," "you," or "we" and "am," "is," or "are" that refers to the speaker or writer: *An autobiography is written in the first person;* **adja.:** *a **first-person** account, narrative.*

first-rate *adj.* excellent: *a first-rate hotel with first-rate accommodation; The book is first-rate; a first-rate job, performance, player, scholar.*

first sergeant *n.* **1** a rank next below sergeant major. **2** in the U.S. Army and Marine Corps, a master sergeant serving as assistant to the commander of a company or battery.

first strike *n.* a nuclear attack in anticipation of one by the enemy.
—**first-strike** *adja.:* *the enemy's first-strike capability.*

first string *n.* the best group of players, not alternates or substitutes.
—**first-string** *adja.* first-rate.

firth *n.* esp. in Scotland, a narrow arm of the sea; estuary.

fis.cal (FIS.cul) *adja.* having to do with public revenue or corporate finance: *the nation's fiscal history; a fiscal analysis, crisis, deficit, policy; fiscal chaos, conservatives, control, responsibility; the **fiscal year** (= accounting period) ending March 31; the budget for fiscal 1998.*
—**fis.cal.ly** *adv.*

fish *n., pl.* **fish** or **fish.es** (fish species) **1** a water animal with fins, gills, and scales: *the birds of the air and the fishes of the sea; to catch fish; Fish bite at bait; a school or shoal of fish; Fish may be baked, broiled, filleted, fried, frozen, smoked; a queer fish (Informal for strange person); to feel like **a fish out of water** (= out of one's natural environment); something out of the way that is **neither fish nor fowl** (= not of a specific kind);* **adja. & cpd.:** *fish farming, filets, sandwiches, stock, tanks; a wide-angle **fish-eye** lens that gives a circular image.* **2** the flesh of fishes used as food: *tuna fish balls; fish and brewis.* —*v.* **1** try to catch fish: *He's fishing by the pond; She rarely goes fishing.* **2** search for, catch, or pull out: *Children fish for compliments; He fished out his will from a cabinet; to **fish in troubled waters** (= take advantage of a troubled situation);* **adja.:** *a **fishing** boat, community, fleet, hook, license, net, pole, rod, spot, trip, vacation, vessel; fishing rights, tackle.*

fish and chips *n.pl.* a dish of fried fish and French fries; also **fish-and-chips**.

fish.bowl *n.* a glass bowl for keeping live fish, open to view from all sides.

fish cake *n.* a fried food made of shredded fish and mashed potatoes.

fish fry *n.* a picnic or supper featuring fried fish.

fish.er *n.* **1** a marten. **2** one who catches fish; also **fish.er.man**, **-men**.

fish.er.y (FISH.uh.ree) *n.* **-er.ies 1** fishing as a business. **2** an establishment for processing fish.

fish.hook *n.* a hook used in angling for fish.

fishing expedition *n.* an inquiry undertaken in the hope of finding evidence of the required kind: *to go on a fishing expedition.*

fish-ladder *n.* a waterway built as an ascending series of connected pools that enables fish to pass over a dam or falls on their way to spawning grounds upstream.

fish stick *n.* an oblong piece of fried fish, often breaded.

fish story *n. Informal.* an exaggerated story, as of fishermen about their catches.

fish.tail *v.* swerve from side to side while moving.

fish.wife *n.* **-wives** a foul-mouthed woman.

fish.y *adj.* **fish.i.er**, **-i.est 1** dull-looking like a fish's eye. **2** slippery; hence, of doubtful value: *a fishy story; something fishy about the plan.*

fis.sile (FIS.ul) *adj.* that can be split; fissionable.

fis.sion (FISH.un) *n.* a splitting apart: *Nuclear fission releases energy, as in atomic bombs; Algae, amebas, and such simple organisms multiply by cellular fission.*
—**fis.sion.a.ble** (-un.uh.bul) *adj.*

fis.sure (FISH.ur) *n.* a crack or break, as in rocks, the skin, or a membrane.

fist *n.* a tightly closed or clenched hand, as in hitting: *to clench the fist; to shake one's fist at someone; the iron fist of the oppressor; a **fistfight** (using bare fists).*

fist.ful *n.* handful: *a fistful of awards, bills, dollars, flowers.*

fis.ti.cuffs (FIS.ti.cuffs) *n.pl.* a fight using fists: *to engage in fisticuffs.*

fis.tu.la (FIS.chuh.luh) *n.* **-las** or **-lae** (-lee) a wound or ulcer forming an abnormal body passage between two hollow organs, as the bladder and rectum, or connecting a hollow organ such as the stomach with the outside;
fis.tu.lous *adj.*

fit *adjp.* **fit.ter**, **fit.test** suited to a certain purpose, occasion, or use: *food that is fit for a king; news that is fit to be printed;*

The struggle for existence results in the survival of the fittest; She keeps fit as a fiddle by regular exercise; *adv.*: He **thought** or **saw fit** to invite some and leave out others. —*v.* **fits, fit.ted, fit.ting** to be right or the right size: "If the cap fits, wear it"; a punishment that fits the crime; His education and experience fit (= qualify) him for the job; But will he **fit into** (= be suitable for) our group? The new building **fits in** (= blends) with the surroundings; all **fitted out** (= equipped or dressed) for a costume party; a room **fitted up** as a studio. —*n.* **1** how something fits: The cut of his coat is good but the fit is poor; loose, snug, tight fits. **2** a sudden attack or convulsion; seizure: an epileptic fit; He fired her in a fit (= outburst) of fury; He throws a fit (= tantrum) now and then; She studies by **fits and starts** (= not regularly). —**fit.ness** *n.* —**fit.ter** *n.*

fit.ful *adj.* irregular or restless: She spent a fitful night with high fever; fitful sleep. —**fit.ful.ly** *adv.*

fitting *adj.* suitable or appropriate: a fitting answer to a rude question; a fitting occasion for a speech; It is fitting and proper that we honor her with a reception. —*n.* **1** a trying on of clothes being made to make sure they fit: a customer who insists on several fittings before her suit is finished; a fitting room. **2** a small, detachable machine part: elbows, clamps, and such pipe fittings. —**fit.ting.ly** *adv.*

five 1 *n., pron. & adj.* the number of the fingers of one hand; 5 or V: Give me five; five of them; five fiddlers. **2** *n.* a group of five or something numbered 5 or having five units, as a basketball team, playing card, domino, or five-dollar bill.

five-and-dime *n.* a store offering a variety of household and personal goods at a cheap price, formerly for five or 10 cents. Also **five-and-dime store, five-and-ten-cent store.**

five o'clock shadow *n.* facial hair that has grown since shaving in the morning.

fix *v.* **fix.es, fixed, fix.ing 1** make firm or steady: to fix the door with a doorstop. **2** fasten: to fix a shelf to a wall; On whom shall we fix the blame? Carl fixed his gaze on Chris. **3** repair or set right: to fix a leaking faucet; to fix a policy, problem; We need someone to **fix up** the house before we move in. **4** arrange or set up: to fix an appointment for 2 p.m.; The hairdresser will fix your hair; I could fix dinner for you; She fixed me up in a good hotel, then fixed me up with a new job. **5** *Informal.* influence dishonestly: The race was fixed; He tried to fix the jury; *n.*: a company charged with price **fixing. 6** *Informal.* punish: She threatened to fix him. —*n.* **1** position: Navigators used to get the fix of their ships from the stars; The executive with two luncheon appointments was **in a fix** (= awkward situation). **2** *Informal.* a dishonest influencing or a contest or situation so influenced. **3** *Slang.* a shot of a narcotic: a fix of heroin. **4** something to which one is addicted: He can't do without his weekly fix of golf. **5** a solution or repair: a quick fix; a technology fix.

fix.ate *v.* **-ates, -at.ed, -at.ing** have a fixation on a person or thing: The man was fixated on the idea that the young actress was in love with him.

fix.a.tion (fik.SAY.shun) *n.* a fixing of one's interest on a person or thing as an obsession: The man had a fixation on or for or over or with the young actress.

fixed (FIXT) *adj.* **1** arranged or set up: a fixed amount; Is the date fixed? on any fixed day; a race suspected of being fixed (= dishonestly arranged). **2** fastened or firm: a fixed boundary; fixed costs; the fixed (= unmoving) gaze of a dead person; a pensioner on a fixed (= unchanging) income; A **fixed star** is one so far away its position never seems to change. —**fix.ed.ly** (FIX.id.lee) *adv.*; **fix.ed.ness** *n.*

fixings *n.pl. Informal.* accessories: a turkey served with all the fixings.

fix.ture (FIX.chur) *n.* a person or thing that is part of a situation or place: A chandelier is a lighting fixture; plumbing fixtures; He's been so long with the company, he seems a fixture in the office.

fizz *n.* **1** a drink that gives out bubbles with a hissing sound. **2** liveliness: how to put more fizz into your business. —*v.* make a fizz: You can drink it while it fizzes.

fiz.zle (FIZ.ul) *v.* **fiz.zles, fiz.zled, fiz.zling** end feebly after a lively start; fail: The party fizzled out when most of the guests didn't arrive. —*n.* a fiasco.

fjord (FYORD) same as FIORD.

flab *n. Informal.* excess of flabby flesh: folds of flab; how to fight your flab.

flab.ber.gast.ed (FLAB.ur.gas.tid) *adj.* dumbfounded: They were flabbergasted to hear the best student had failed; completely, utterly flabbergasted.

flab.by (FLAB.ee) *adj.* **flab.bi.er, flab.bi.est** lacking firmness or strength: flabby flesh, muscles, will; the flabby generation of TV watchers.

flac.cid (FLAC.sid, FLAS.id) *adj.* **1** flabby: *flaccid muscles.* **2** limp or feeble: *droopy and flaccid from the heat; from erect to flaccid.*

flack *n.* **1** *Slang.* a press agent. **2** [nonstandard] flak or criticism. —*v. Slang.* act as a flack: *to flack for a movie star;* *adj.*: *a heavily flacked* (= publicized) *production.* —**flack.er.y** *n.* propaganda.

flac.on (FLAC.un) *n.* a small stoppered bottle for perfumes.

flag *n.* **1** a piece of fabric, usu. with a distinctive colored design, used as an emblem or banner, often hoisted on a **flagpole**, or **flagstaff**: *to dip, fly, lower, raise, run up, wave a flag; the white flag (of surrender); a ship sailing under the Liberian flag; a flag flying at half-mast.* **2** a slab of paving stone; flagstone.
—*v.* **flags, flagged, flag.ging 1** to signal: *We flagged down the first cab that came along.* **2** droop or slacken: *As time wore on, interest seemed to flag;* *adj.*: *a pep talk to revive their flagging spirits; a flagging campaign, economy, market; flagging confidence, demand, fortunes, interest, momentum, morale, profits, sales, support, vitality.*

flag.el.late (FLAJ.uh.late) *v.* **-lates, -lat.ed, -lat.ing** to whip; **flag.el.la.tion** (-LAY.shun) *n.*

fla.gel.lum (fluh.JEL.um) *n., pl.* **-gel.la** or **-gel.lums** a whip or whiplike organ that helps bacteria, sponges, etc. to move about.

flag.eo.let (flaj.uh.LET) *n.* a flutelike instrument, but blown like a recorder.

fla.gi.tious (fluh.JISH.us) *adj.* infamous; villainous.

flag.on (FLAG.un) *n.* a vessel with a spout, handle, and lid for holding wine or other liquor at the table.

fla.grant (FLAY.grunt) *adj.* of errors, offenses, etc., openly and notoriously bad: *flagrant cheating; a flagrant crime, error, injustice, mutiny, violation.*
—**fla.grant.ly** *adv.*

flag.ship *n.* **1** a ship carrying the officer (**flag officer**) in command of a fleet or squadron. **2** the most important of its group: *the flagship store of the company; a flagship brand, label, product.*

flag.stone *n.* a slab of paving stone.

flag-waving *n.* a patriotic but boastful appeal to the emotions.

flail *n.* a farm tool for threshing grain.
—*v.* strike with or wave arms about as with a flail.

flair *n.* a keen sense or taste: *She shows a distinctive flair for clothes.*

flak *n.* **1** antiaircraft gunfire. **2** *Informal.* criticism: *to take the flak when something goes wrong.*

flake *n.* **1** a small, thin piece or mass: *a flake of snow; flakes of rust; soap flakes; flakes of chocolate.* **2** *Slang.* an eccentric; nut. —*v.* **flakes, flaked, flak.ing** fall off in flakes: *Old paint tends to flake off.*
—**flake off** *Slang.* beat it. —**flake out** *Slang.* **1** collapse or lie down exhausted. **2** fail or flop.

flak jacket *n.* a bulletproof vest to protect the wearer from flying shell fragments.

flak.y (FLAY.kee) *adj.* **flak.i.er, -i.est 1** having to do with flakes: *a crisp and flaky pie crust.* **2** *Slang.* eccentric: *the oddball's flaky behavior.* —**flak.i.ly** *adv.*; **flak.i.ness** *n.*

flam.bé (flahm.BAY) *n.* a dessert or other dish served flaming.

flam.beau (flam.BOH) *n., pl.* **-beaux** (-BOZE) or **-beaus** a flaming torch.

flam.boy.ant (flam.BOY.unt) *adj.* flamelike in form or character; hence, ornate or showy: *a flamboyant artist, character, decor, design, fashion, figure, outfit, personality.* —**flam.boy.ance** (-unce) *n.*

flame *n.* **1** a brightly burning fire: *to kindle a flame; The car burst into flame on impact; It was in flames.* **2** *Informal.* a sweetheart: *my old flame; your first flame.*
—*v.* **flames, flamed, flam.ing 1** blaze, grow hot, glow, or burst out like a flame: *cheeks flaming with emotion; Her eyes flamed with fury;* *adj.*: *the flaming fall colors; flaming debris, houses, torches; flaming* (= passionate) *youth; flaming* (= utter) *radicals.* **2** *Slang.* leave an angry message on a computer network.

fla.men.co (fluh.MENG.coh) *n.* a kind of Spanish dance characterized by vigorous stamping, clapping, and singing to the rhythm of castanets and guitar music.

flame.out *n.* a jet-engine failure due to faulty fuel combustion.

flame thrower *n.* a military weapon for shooting burning fuel under pressure like water from a fire hose.

fla.min.go (fluh.MING.go) *n.* **-gos** or **-goes** a water bird with long legs and neck, curved bill, and pink feathers.

flam.ma.ble (FLAM.uh.bul) *adj.* that easily catches fire, as gasoline.
—**flam.ma.bil.i.ty** (-BIL.i.tee) *n.*

flange (FLANJ) *n.* a projecting rim of a wheel, rail, girder, etc. —*v.* **flang.es, flanged, flang.ing**: *pipe ends flanged and bolted together.*

flank *n.* **1** the fleshy side above the hips; also, a cut of beef corresponding to this part. **2** a side, as of a mountain,

a military or football formation, etc.
—v. **1** be placed beside: *She appeared in public flanked by bodyguards.* **2** attack from the side: *The troops were flanked and overpowered in a surprise attack.*

flan.nel (FLAN.ul) *n.* **1** a soft, warm woolen cloth with a napped surface. **2 flannels** *pl.* flannel trousers or woolen underwear.

flan.nel.et or **flan.nel.ette** (flan.uh.LET) *n.* a soft light napped cotton cloth.

flap *n.* **1** a broad, flat piece of material attached on one side, as the cover of a pocket, the gummed end of an envelope, or the hinged back sections of a plane's wings. **2** the sound of wings beating the air or of oars on water. **3** *Informal.* a stir or commotion: *The students were in a flap about or over the exam results.* —v. **flaps, flapped, flap.ping** make flaps or move by making flaps: *A young bird flaps its wings; Sails flapped in the wind.*

flap.jack *n.* a pancake.

flap.pa.ble (FLAP.uh.bul) *adj.* easily upset.

flap.per (FLAP.ur) *n.* **1** one that flaps, as a broad fin or a bird learning to fly. **2** a woman of the 1920s who was aggressively unconventional in dress and manners.

flare *n.* **1** an outburst of flame or a short-lived, unsteady blaze of light, as a rocket signal shot into the air or a solar eruption. **2** a candlelike light used as a marker on the ground: *They set up* or *set out flares at the crash site to warn approaching motorists.* **3 flares** *pl.* a pair of bell-bottomed trousers. —v. **flares, flared, flar.ing 1** burst into flame: *The candle sputtered, flared, and went out; when trouble flares* (= erupts); *He tends to flare up* (= get excited) *at the least provocation.* **2** widen toward the bottom: *He flared his nostrils in a grimace; adj.: A-line skirts are flared; flared cuffs.*

flare-up *n.* an outburst, sudden increase, or intensification: *a flare-up of hostilities.*

flash *n.* **1** a sudden, brief brilliance, as of lightning or of a camera flashbulb; hence, any similar feeling or display: *cameras with auto flash; the flashes of a strobe light; a flash of anger, inspiration, sunshine, wit; the hot flashes or flushes* (= feeling of warmth) *experienced during menopause.* **2** a brief period or something lasting only an instant: *I remembered the whole episode in a flash; First came a telex flash, then the full obituary; the flash of her smile.* —**a flash in the pan** a brilliant but short-lived effort or attempt. —v. **1** give out a sudden light: *a signal flashing every few seconds; a cursor that flashes* (= blinks) *off and on; His eyes were flashing* (= glowing) *with fury.* **2** happen or do something in a sudden or passing manner: *Headlights flashed* (= quickly passed) *by on the highway; A train flashed* (= suddenly came) *into view; The Associated Press flashed* (= sent out with speed) *the news across the nation; The policeman flashed* (= quickly showed) *his badge and walked in.* —**adj.** sudden or instantaneous: *flash calculations, lightning, storms.*

flash.back *n.* a narration or portrayal, esp. in a play or movie, of an episode from the past, as in suddenly recalling a past event.

flash.bulb or **flash.lamp** *n.* a lighting device that works with a camera shutter.

flash burn *n.* a burn caused by exposure to radiation.

flash.card *n.* any of a series of cards bearing words, pictures, etc. displayed before students to get quick responses in drilling them in math, reading, etc.

flash.er *n. Informal.* one who exposes himself indecently.

flash flood *n.* a sudden flood following a heavy rainfall.

flash-forward *n.* the showing of a future occurrence as a dramatic device in movies and TV.

flash gun *n.* a camera device for simultaneously triggering the shutter and the flash.

flash.ing *n.* sheet metal used to cover roof joints and angles.

flashlamp same as FLASHBULB.

flash.light *n.* a hand-held electric lamp.

flash point *n.* **1** the lowest temperature at which a flammable substance will catch fire in the presence of a flame. **2** a place where hostilities may flare up: *a flash point of racial unrest.*

flash.y *adj.* **flash.i.er, -i.est** gaudy or showy in a cheap way: *a flashy design, dress, lifestyle; flashy clothes;* **flash.i.ly** *adv.;* **flash.i.ness** *n.*

flask *n.* a container for carrying liquids.

flat *adj.* **flat.ter, flat.test 1** horizontal and plane, not round, high, or thick: *the flat top of a table; a flat* (= deflated) *tire.* **2** not changeable; absolute: *a flat denial, refusal; a flat rate of interest.* **3** not distinctive in regard to color, taste, sound, etc.: *a flat, not glossy paint; a flat musical note (that is below the normal pitch); soda pop that has gone flat*

(= stale). —**adv.** absolutely: *He placed flat last in the competition; The bridge will help islanders get to the mainland in nothing flat* (= in no time at all); *He fell flat on the floor; All his plans have fallen flat* (= failed). —**flat out 1** outright: *She flat out denied the charges; It was flat out incompetent of him to say such things;* **adja.:** *a **flat-out** assertion without any proof; flat-out lying, prohibitions.* **2** at full speed: *He drove flat out to the hospital.* —**n. 1** something flat, as a deflated tire, swampland, or the palm of the hand: *to change, fix, have a flat (tire); mud, salt flats; the flat of the hand.* **2** an apartment. **3** in music, a half pitch below the note, as indicated by the symbol [♭]. —**v. flats, flat.ted, flat.ting** make or become flat. —**flat.ly** *adv.*; **flat.ness** *n.*

flat.bed *n.* a truck or trailer whose body is a platform without sides.

flat.boat *n.* a flat-bottomed boat, usu. with square ends, for freight and passengers.

flat.car *n.* a railroad freight car without sides or roof.

flat.fish *n.* fish such as the flounder or sole that has a flat body with both eyes on the upper surface.

flat.foot *n., pl.* **-feet** a condition in which the arch of the instep has flattened.

flat.foot.ed (FLAT.foot.id) *adj. & adv.* Informal. in an unready condition: *to be caught flatfooted.*

flat.i.ron (FLAT.eye.urn) *n.* an iron for pressing clothes.

flat.ten (FLAT.un) *v.* make or become flat: *The toy was flattened when a truck ran over it;* **adj.:** *the **flattened** (= flat) body of the tapeworm.*

flat.ter (FLAT.ur) *v.* please a person by saying something that makes him or her feel good, as by praising: *He tried to flatter her about or on her good looks; The portrait flatters her* (= represents her favorably); *He **flatters himself** on* (= is pleased with) *his musical talent;* **adj.:** *I'm **flattered*** (= pleased) *to receive the award; flattered that I've been chosen; She feels flattered by or at all the attention she's getting; I find the award very **flattering*** (= pleasing) *for my self-esteem; quite flattering to my ego.* —**flat.ter.er** *n.*; **flat.ter.ing.ly** *adv.* —**flat.ter.y** *n.* **flat.ter.ies**; *base, servile flattery.*

flat.top *n. Informal.* an aircraft carrier.

flat.u.lence (FLACH.uh.lunce) *n.* accumulation of gas in the stomach or intestines.

flat.u.lent (FLACH.uh.lunt) *adj.* **1** having or causing flatulence. **2** windy or pompous.

flat.ware *n.* flat tableware such as plates, knives, and spoons.

flat.worm *n.* a worm with a flattened, segmented body, as tapeworms and flukes.

flaunt *v.* **1** display or parade what one possesses; show off: *to flaunt one's knowledge, power, wealth.* **2** flutter or wave proudly: *to flaunt a banner, flag.*

flau.tist ("au" as in "cause" or rhyming with "how") same as FLUTIST.

fla.vor (FLAY.vur) *n.* **1** the taste and smell that are characteristic of a substance: *Spices, fruit, etc. have natural flavors; the strong flavor of certain cheeses; They sell ice cream in 101 flavors; romances with an exotic flavor.* **2** a pleasing quality: *Spices impart flavor to bland foods.* —*v.* give a flavor to something: *Vanilla extract is used to flavor ice cream;* **adj.:** *plain and **flavored** yoghurt;* **n.:** *"Vanillin" is an artificial **flavoring**.* —**fla.vor.ful** or **fla.vor.some** *adj.* Also **fla.vour, fla.vour.ful, fla.vour.some** *Cdn.*

flaw *n.* an imperfection such as a crack or blemish that mars something structurally: *the flaw in a gem; the flaws and fallacies of your reasoning; a character flaw* (= weakness). —**flaw.less** *adj.*; **flaw.less.ly** *adv.*

flawed (FLAUD) *adj.* having a flaw: *a flawed diamond; a character flawed by a lack of will power.*

flax *n.* an herb or shrub that is raised for its fiber used to make linen and coarse yarns.

flax.en (FLAX.un) *adj.* **1** made of flax. **2** pale-yellow: *flaxen hair.*

flax.seed *n.* the seed of flax, used for making linseed oil.

flay *v.* **1** strip off the skin of a person or animal: *to flay a dead horse.* **2** criticize or scold harshly: *He was flayed alive for not doing his chores; legislators flaying each other.*

flea (FLEE) *n.* a tiny, wingless jumping insect that sucks the blood of animals.

flea collar *n.* an animal collar containing insecticide that repels fleas.

flea market *n.* an open-air bazaar that sells cheap, often used goods.

fleck *n.* a spot or patch: *floating flecks* (= flakes) *of snow.* —*v.* mark with flecks: *skin flecked with freckles.*

fled *pt. & pp.* OF FLEE.

fledge *v.* **fledg.es, fledged, fledg.ing** grow or equip with or as if with feathers: *to fledge an arrow;* **adj.:** *a full-fledged acrobat, enterprise, recession;* **n.:** *a*

flee / flight

mere **fledgling** or **fledgeling** (= beginner) of a poet.

flee v. **flees, fled, flee.ing** run away, as from danger or evil: *to flee from a fire; to flee a scene; to flee the country; to flee west* (= to the west).

fleece n. **1** a sheep's or similar animal's coat of wool. **2** a soft, warm, deep-piled fabric used for clothing: *natural fiber fleeces; the warmth of fleece without the weight of wool; fashion fleece; cotton, nylon, polyester fleece;* **adja.:** *fleece fabrics; a fleece blazer, garment, sweater, top.* —v. **fleec.es, fleeced, fleec.ing 1** shear sheep. **2** strip someone of belongings: *Con men fleeced him of his savings.*

fleec.y adj. **1** like, covered with, or made of fleece: *fleecy clouds.* **2** woolen: *warm fleecy underwear.*

fleet n. a unified group of vehicles: *a fleet of aircraft, automobiles, bicycles, ships.* —**adj.** swift: *Antelopes are fleet of foot; a fleet-footed animal.* —**fleet.ing** adj. passing swiftly: *Worldly joys are fleeting; a fleeting existence, fad, glimpse, sensation; in a fleeting instant; fleeting moments of fame; fleeting passions.*
—**fleet.ing.ly** adv.: *He thought she spoke to him fleetingly in a dream.*

fleet admiral n. the highest rank of U.S. naval officer with a five-star insignia.

Flem.ing n. a speaker of Flemish: *the Walloons and Flemings of Belgium.*

Flem.ish 1 n. a Germanic language allied to Dutch, spoken in **Flanders**, a medieval country in Europe, now a region divided among Belgium, France, and the Netherlands. **2** adj. having to do with Flanders, the Flemings, or their language.

flesh n. **1** the soft tissue beneath the skin, esp. the muscle and fat of animals: *Animal flesh is used as meat; stories that* **make your flesh creep** or **crawl** (= horrify you); **adj.:** *flesh-colored* (= yellowish pink) *tights.* **2** the body or bodily nature: *She dreamed she saw her dead child* **in the flesh** (= alive); *"The spirit is willing but the flesh is weak"; to* **mortify the flesh** *by penance; Your own* **flesh and blood** (= blood relatives) *are closer to you than in-laws.* —**press the flesh** shake hands with people, as when campaigning for election.
—v. feed, grow, or fill out with flesh: *An artist fleshes out a sketch with live figures;* **cpd.:** *firm-fleshed cod; a fully-fleshed vision; a well-fleshed steer.*

flesh.ly adj. **-li.er, -li.est** adj. having to do with the human body: *Venus's fleshly beauty; fleshly corruption, love, pleasures, scenes.* —**flesh.li.ness** n.

flesh.pot n. place of luxurious living: *to long for the fleshpots of one's native land; Saint-Tropez is one of the fleshpots of France.*

flesh.y adj. **flesh.i.er, -i.est 1** fat: *a soft and fleshy Cupid; Do I look a bit too fleshy?* **2** having to do with flesh: *the fleshy side of your fingertips; a fleshy intestinal growth; a fleshy fruit such as the apple.*

fleur-de-lis (flur.duh.LEE) n. **fleurs-de-lis** (flur.duh.LEEZ) a lilylike design used on early French flags.

flew pt. of FLY.

flex v. **1** bend: *to flex a limb.* **2** contract: *to flex a muscle.*

flex.i.ble (FLEX.uh.bul) adj. **1** that can be bent without breaking: *Wire, leather, etc. are flexible.* **2** adaptable: *a flexible mind, schedule; He's quite flexible in his decisions; flexible working hours, or* **flex-time.** —**flex.i.bly** (-blee) adv.
—**flex.i.bil.i.ty** (-BIL.i.tee) n.

flex.ure (FLECK.shur) n. a bending, curving, or folding. —**flex.ur.al** adj.

flib.ber.ti.gib.bet (FLIB.ur.tee.JIB.it) n. a flighty or gossipy person.

flick n. **1** a light, quick stroke or movement, as of a whip; also, the snapping sound made by it. **2** *Informal.* a movie.
—v. **1** make a flick or strike with a flick: *a pocket knife that can be flicked open or shut; He flicked a crumb off his sleeve; She flicked* (= switched) *on a light.* **2** flip: *to flick through a volume.*

flick.er v. waver or flutter: *The candle flickered and went out.* —n. a spark: *Is there a flicker of hope left? a pure liquid without a flicker of color or scent.*

flied a pt. of FLY (baseball sense).

fli.er (FLY.ur) same as FLYER.

flight (FLITE) n. **1** the act of flying: *a long flight over the Atlantic; the seasonal flights of birds to warmer climes; bumpy, chartered, connecting, domestic, scheduled, shakedown, solo, space, test flights; the flight of time; flights* (= soaring heights) *of ambition, fancy, imagination, rhetoric, wit; a* **flight attendant** *such as a steward or air hostess; a lightweight* **flight bag** (carried on one's shoulder) *containing sundries for use on board; Planes land on an aircraft carrier's* **flight deck**; *the large, stiff* **flight feathers** *on the wings and tails of birds; the* **flight path** *of an airplane, missile, or spacecraft; The* **flight recorder**, *or black box, of an aircraft records the voices in the cockpit and technical data; An astronaut has to be in top* **flightworthy** *condition.* **2** a scheduled airliner: *I put* her on a flight to Paris; The flight just left – it took off five minutes ago; the touchdown or landing of Flight 202 from London; *adja.*: flight arrivals, crews, delays, departures. **3** the act of fleeing: *the flight of slaves by the underground railroad to Canada; the flight* (= transfer) *of capital to foreign enterprises; The defeated armies were* **put to flight** (= made to flee); *They* **took flight** *or* **took to flight** (= fled). **4** a set or series: *We went up two flights of stairs; a flight of aircraft, geese; a new flight of ads, commercials, TV spots.* —**flight.less** *adj.* unable to fly: *the ostrich, emu, penguin, and such flightless birds.*

flight.y *adj.* **flight.i.er, -i.est** light-headed or frivolous. —**flight.i.ly** *adv.*

flim.flam *v.* **-flams, -flam.med, -flam.ming** *Informal.* cheat or trick. —*n.* deception; nonsense.

flim.sy (FLIM.zee) *adj.* **-si.er, -si.est** thin or frail: *a flimsy defense; flimsy evidence, excuses.* —*n.* a sheet of thin paper. —**flim.si.ly** *adv.*; **flim.si.ness** *n.*

flinch *v.* draw back from something painful or requiring courage: *She never flinches from doing what has to be done; He can take the worst news without flinching.*

fling *v.* **flings, flung, fling.ing 1** throw sharply and with force: *She flung her books on the table and strode out; He was flung into jail without being charged; Lou spoke out against the regime, flinging all caution to the winds.* **2** dash or rush: *He flung out of the room in a huff.* —*n.* **1** a casual attempt: *She had a fling at journalism before becoming a teacher; a last fling* (= spree of self-indulgence). **2** a Scottish dance: *the Highland fling.*

flint *n.* a hard quartz that gives off sparks when struck with steel.

flint glass *n.* a type of heavy glass used in optical instruments.

flint.lock *n.* a gun or its firing mechanism that uses a flint for igniting the charge.

flint.y *adj.* **flint.i.er, -i.est 1** having flint: *a flinty rock.* **2** hard and unyielding: *a flinty disposition, heart, look; a flinty general.*

flip *v.* **flips, flipped, flip.ping 1** toss or move something jerkily so that it turns on its side: *Let's flip a coin to settle the matter; She flipped through the book looking for pictures.* **2** flick or strike: *to flip at a fly; to flip marbles out of a ring; He flipped* (*Informal* for lost self-control) *when he was fired from his job.* —*n.* a flipping: *a flip of the coin; a* **flip chart** (of sheets hinged at the top for flipping

over); *the* **flip-down** *seats in a theater; a* **flip-top** *can of pop.* —*adj.* **flip.per, flip.pest** *Informal.* flippant: *She sounded flip but really meant it.*

flip-flop *n.* **1** a backward somersault. **2** a change, as of opinion, resembling a somersault: *Politicians do or make flip-flops on issues after hearing from the people.* **3** a flat, open-toed, backless shoe or slipper. —*v.* **flops, -flopped, -flop.ping** do a flip-flop.

flip.pant (FLIP.unt) *adj.* of attitudes and expressions, not respectful: *a flippant answer to a serious question.* —**flip.pan.cy** *n.*

flip.per (FLIP.ur) *n.* a broad, flat fin or blade: *Seals, sea lions, and whales have paddlelike flippers; a diver's rubber flippers.*

flip side *n. Informal.* the back of a phonograph record.

flirt *v.* **1** play at love: *to flirt with people; to flirt* (= trifle or toy) *with danger.* **2** flutter or flick: *the flirting of a bird's tail.* —*n.* one who flirts. —**flir.ta.tion** (-TAY.shun) *n.*; **flir.ta.tious** (-shus) *adj.*

flit *v.* **flits, flit.ted, flit.ting** flutter or fly about like a bee or butterfly: *thoughts flitting across a troubled mind; Time flits by.*

flitch *n.* a side of bacon.

float (FLOTE) *v.* **1** (make) stay on the surface of a fluid or move along lightly: *Cork floats on water; He doesn't swim, can't even float; to float* (= raise) *a sunken ship; A bond issue is floated* (= placed for sale) *on the market.* **2** launch: *to float a company, idea, loan, proposal, scheme.* —*n.* something that floats: *Cork is used as a float on a fishing line; the floats* (= exhibits on wheels) *in a parade; Planes that land on water have floats* (= airtight structures) *instead of wheels; an orange float* (= orange pop with a lump of ice cream floating on top); *a credit card company with a float* (= money in transit) *totaling billions of dollars because of uncashed traveler's checks; the yen's upward float* (= rise) *in value against the dollar.* —**float.er** *n.*

float.a.tion (floh.TAY.shun) See FLOTATION.

floating *adj.* that moves or changes: *the floating exchange value of a currency; a resort town with a floating population; The* **floating (decimal) point** *moves to the left of a display as a number like 1772.2532 is changed to 1.7722532 x 10^3; the two bottom* **floating ribs** (not attached in front).

flock *n.* **1** a group of animals of the same kind: *a flock of birds, geese, sheep.*

2 a group of worshipers: *A pastor tends his flock.* —*v.* group: *Children flocked around the ice-cream vendor;* "*Birds of a feather flock together.*"

floe *n.* a sheet or broken-off piece of floating ice.

flog *v.* **flogs, flogged, flog.ging 1** whip or beat with a stick: *to flog a mule; You're flogging a dead horse* (= fighting a dead issue). **2** *Informal.* sell or publicize: *a vendor flogging his wares.* —**flog.ger** *n.*

flood (FLUD) *n.* **1** a great flow or overflow of water, as of rivers after heavy rains, when the tide rises in a **floodtide**, or when a sluice, or **floodgate**, is opened in a dam: *a raging flood; The flood inundated the valley before beginning to subside.* **2** anything similar: *a flood of light, tears, words;* **the Flood** (= deluge) *of Noah's time.*
—*v.* flow or cause to flow like a flood: *The spring thaw flooded basements; The river flooded* (= overflowed).

flood.light *n.* a large light used for lighting the outdoors: *Niagara Falls is lit by floodlights.* —*v.* **-lights,** *pt. & pp.* **-light.ed** or **-lit, -light.ing** light by using floodlights.

flood plain *n.* a plain bordering a river and made fertile by the sediments left by its flood waters.

flood.tide See FLOOD, *n.* 1.

flood.way *n.* **1** the part of a floodplain that is closest to the river, hence at the greatest risk of being flooded. **2** a drainage system of ditches, levies, and streams for flood control, as in Wichita and Winnipeg.

floor (FLOR) *n.* **1** the inside bottom surface, as of a room: *a marble floor; a floor of hardwood; on the first floor of the house; ground, main, top, upper floors; the ocean floor; adja.: floor area, space; a floor plan; a floor-length ball gown.*
2 where a legislature or similar body meets: *on the floor of the Senate; to cross the floor (and join another party); a motion from the floor* (= where members sit, not from the platform). **3** the right to speak in a legislature: *Mr. Speaker, may I have the floor? to get, take the floor; to yield the floor to another member; to give someone the floor.* **4** a lower limit: *a floor (price) of $1,200 and a ceiling of $1,500.* —*v.* **1** provide with a floor, as of tiles or wood: *We floored the ground with tiles;* **n.**: *marble, parquet, and other types of* **flooring;** *flooring materials.*
2 knock down or defeat someone: *to floor a boxer;* **adj.**: *He seemed utterly* **floored** (= confounded) *by the question.*

floor.board *n.* a board or one of the strips forming a floor.

floor exercise *n.* a gymnastic exercise performed without an apparatus.

floor leader *n.* the leader of a party in a legislature.

floor manager *n.* a manager who supervises store clerks and looks after customers.

floor show *n.* an entertainment presented at a nightclub or restaurant.

floo.zy or **floo.zie** *n.* **-zies** *Slang.* a woman of low morals.

flop *v.* **flops, flopped, flop.ping** move about or drop down in a loose or clumsy way: *You could hear the fish flopping on the deck; She flopped into bed exhausted; The office is no place for flopping* (= lounging); *The play flopped* (= failed).
—*n.* *Informal.* failure: *The play was a total flop.*

flop.house *n.* a cheap hotel.

flop.py (FLOP.ee) **1** *adj.* **flop.pi.er, flop.pi.est** soft and flexible, like a hound's ear. **2** *n., pl.* **flop.pies** a flexible diskette for storing computer data; also **floppy disk**.

flops *n.* "floating (decimal) point operations per second," a measure of computer speed; **cpd:** *megaflops, gigaflops, teraflops.*

flo.ra (FLOR.uh) *n.* the plant life or plants of a specified region or period: *the flora and fauna of the Hebrides.*
—**flo.ral** (-ul) *adja.* having to do with flowers: *a floral arrangement, bouquet, emblem, wreath.*

flo.res.cence (flor.ES.unce) *n.* a blossoming state or period; **flo.res.cent** *adj.*

flor.id (FLOR.id) *adj.* **1** of a complexion, flushed, as with emotion. **2** ornate or showy: *a florid prose style.*

flor.in *n.* any of various silver or gold coins of European countries, as the Dutch guilder.

flor.ist (FLOR.ist) *n.* one who deals in or grows flowers.

floss *n.* **1** soft, silky fluff or fiber, as spun by silkworms, or candy spun from sugar. **2** silk yarn or thread, as used in embroidery or as "dental floss" to clean between teeth; *v.*: *Brush and floss your teeth daily, says the dentist.*

floss.y *adj.* **floss.i.er, -i.est** like floss, esp. showy or stylish.

flo.ta.tion (floh.TAY.shun) *n.* an act or process of floating; **adja.**: *a plane seat as a flotation cushion for use in case of a water landing; flotation devices.*

flo.til.la (floh.TIL.uh) *n.* a small fleet or a fleet of small ships.

flot.sam (FLOT.sum) *n.* floating debris, as from a shipwreck: *the flotsam and jetsam* (= discards and derelicts) *of a nation destroyed by war.*

flounce ("ou" as in "out") *v.* **flounc.es, flounced, flounc.ing** move *off* or *out* of a place with an abrupt or jerky motion, as if in impatience or disdain. —*n.* **1** such a movement. **2** a wide, rufflelike strip of cloth gathered and sewed on by its upper edge around a skirt. —**flounc.y** *adj.*

floun.der ("ou" as in "out") *v.* struggle or stumble about as in deep snow: *to flounder through a memorized speech; The government is floundering in red ink; The campaign floundered* (= failed); *adj.*: *a floundering attempt, business, economy; their floundering efforts to get out of the mess.* —*n.* **1** a floundering: *The team's flounder at the start of the season cost them the title.* **2** a saltwater fish with a flattened body and both eyes on the same side of the head.

flour (rhyme: our) *n.* the powdered and sifted meal of a cereal such as wheat for baking bread, biscuits, etc. —*v.* coat or cover with flour or a similar product; *adj.*: *a lightly floured rolling pin.* —**flour.y** *adj.*

flour.ish (FLUR.ish) *v.* **1** prosper or thrive: *The Aztec civilization flourished in Mexico before the Spanish conquest; She's flourishing as a lawyer.* **2** wave about or brandish: *to flourish a sword.*
—*n.* a waving or showy movement, writing, or musical passage: *She signs her name with a flourish; a flourish* (= fanfare) *of trumpets.*

flout *v.* treat advice, laws, orders, etc. with scorn. —*n.* a scornful act or speech. —**flout.er** *n.*

flow (FLOH) *v.* move or seem to move smoothly and steadily, as a stream of water: *Rivers flow into the ocean; eyes flowing with tears; hair that flows in the wind; wealth flowing out of an exploited nation; The flowing* (= rising) *tide swells a river.* —*n.* a smooth and steady pouring: *the flow of words from a fluent speaker; the ebb and flow of tides; the flow of electricity from the negative to the positive pole of a battery; to staunch the flow of blood; cash flow; the flow of traffic.*

flow chart *n.* a diagram showing the movement of materials and personnel in operating a plant or the steps in a complex process.

flow.er (rhyme: our) *n.* **1** the seed-producing part of a plant, usu. having colorful petals, scent, and honey: *a bouquet of fragrant flowers; to pick or pluck flowers; cut flowers for sale; Flowers bloom, fade, wilt, wither.* **2** a plant cultivated for its flowers: *to plant and grow flowers;* **adj.**: *flower beds, gardens.* **3** a blossoming or flourishing part or period: *Bamboos are rarely seen* **in flower**; *Lou was plucked from life* **in the flower** (= best part) *of youth.*
—*v.* bloom or develop: *Some plants flower once and wither away;* **n.**: *the early* **flowering** *of her poetical genius;* **adj.**: *the* **flowered** *design of a rose window; flowered patterns, wallpaper.*

flower child *n.* a hippie.

flower girl *n.* a young girl attending a bride with flowers.

flower head *n.* a composite flower such as the chrysanthemum or the sunflower that is made up of many little flowers.

flower people *n.pl.* hippies.

flow.er.pot (FLOW.ur.pot) *n.* a container for growing flowers.

flow.er.y (FLOW.uh.ree) *adj.* **-er.i.er, -er.i.est** **1** having to do with flowers: *a flowery dress, fragrance, pattern.* **2** ornate: *flowery language, speech, style, writing.*

flown (FLONE) *pp.* of FLY.

flu (FLOO) *n.* **flus** influenza: *Asian flu; swine flu; a new strain of flu (virus); a touch of (the) flu; to get, have, fight the flu; a bout, case of (the) flu;* **adj.**: *the flu season; to get an annual flu shot; flu symptoms, viruses.*

flub *v.* **flubs, flubbed, flub.bing** Informal. bungle: *He flubbed it; to flub a ball; to flub one's lines on the stage; The city flubbed its bid for the Olympics;* **n.**: *a bureaucratic flub.*

fluc.tu.ate (FLUK.choo.ate) *v.* **-ates, -at.ed, -at.ing** vary irregularly: *The value of the dollar fluctuates relative to other currencies; Temperatures fluctuate between highs and lows;* **adj.**: *a fluctuating demand; fluctuating interest rates, moods, standards, stock markets, temperatures, trends; wildly fluctuating fortunes.*
—**fluc.tu.a.tion** (-AY.shun) *n.*

flue (FLOO) *n.* a passage such as a pipe or tube for conveying smoke, air, etc., as in a chimney or pipe organ.

flu.ent (FLOO.unt) *adj.* esp. of writing or speech, flowing smoothly: *a fluent speaker; her fluent command of the language; She speaks fluent English;* **flu.ent.ly** *adv.* —**flu.en.cy** *n.*

fluff *n.* **1** soft fur or feathers, as inside a pillow. **2** nap, as on a woolen blanket. **3** something woolly or light: *Our cat is a fuzzy piece of fluff; a ball of fluff; The article reads like fashion fluff.* **4** a blun-

fluffy / flute

der, esp. in saying one's lines on the stage. —*v.* **1** make even or larger by shaking: *to fluff up a pillow.* **2** *Informal.* slip up on something: *I hope no one fluffs a line when we go on stage.*

fluff.y *adj.* **fluff.i.er, -i.est** appearing fluffed or made larger: *a fluffy angel cake; fluffy chicks.*

flu.id (FLOO.id) *n.* a liquid or gaseous substance such as water, mercury, or air: *Drink plenty of fluids; AIDS is transmitted through body fluids such as blood and semen.* —*adj.* flowing or flexible, not fixed or rigid: *Your muscles are at their most fluid when warmed up; light, fluid fabrics; an easy, fluid feeling; a dancer's fluid and graceful movements; a fluid diet (of nonsolid foods); cash, savings, and such fluid assets; The situation remains fluid* (= unstable). —**flu.id.i.ty** (floo.ID.i.tee) *n.*

fluid ounce *n.* a measure of capacity equal to 1.80 cu.in. or 29.57 ml.

fluid drive (or **clutch**) *n.* in an automobile, a power coupling that transmits motion by the spinning force of oil.

fluke *n.* **1** a flatfish; also, a flatworm or nematode. **2** the flat, triangular, pointed tip of each arm of an anchor or a similarly shaped head of an arrow, a lobe of a whale's tail, etc. **3** *Informal.* a stroke of luck: *She won by a fluke; It was a pure fluke.* —**fluk.y** (FLOO.kee) *adj.*

flume *n.* **1** a narrow, deep valley or channel. **2** a flowing channel or chute used in irrigation, logging, mining, etc.

flum.moxed (FLUM.uxt) *adj. Slang.* confused or confounded.

flung *pt.* of FLING.

flunk *v. Informal.* fail in school work: *Some students flunked the math test; They flunked in math, flunked calculus, several courses, but didn't **flunk out*** (= fail too badly to continue in school).

flun.ky (FLUNK.ee) *n.* **-kies** [contemptuous term] a menial servant or lackey; also **flun.key, -keys.**

flu.o.resce (floo.uh.RES) *v.* **-resc.es, -resced, -resc.ing** give off light by fluorescence.

flu.o.res.cence (floo.uh.RES.unce) *n.* **1** the property of transforming radiations such as ultraviolet rays and X rays into a different wavelength or color. **2** light thus emitted.

—**flu.o.res.cent** (-unt) *adj.* giving off light by fluorescence: *a fluorescent lamp or tube; fluorescent lights; a fluorescent screen (coated with fluorescent material).*

fluo.ri.date (FLOR.uh.date) *v.* **-dates,** **-dat.ed, -dat.ing** add fluorides to drinking water. —**fluor.i.da.tion** (-DAY.shun) *n.*

fluo.ride (FLOR.ide, FLOO.uh.ride) *n.* a fluorine compound, as used in water and toothpastes to prevent tooth decay.

fluo.rine (FLOR.een, FLOO.uh.reen) *n.* a gaseous chemical element.

fluor.o.car.bon (FLOO.ur.uh.CAR.bun) *n.* a fluorine-carbon compound used as a lubricant, refrigerant, or aerosol propellant.

fluor.o.scope (FLOO.ur.uh.scope) *n.* an instrument consisting of an X-ray machine and a fluorescent screen for viewing internal organs in operation.

flur.ry (FLUR.ee) *n.* **flur.ries** **1** a sudden gust of wind, fall of snow, or shower of rain: *the first flurry of rain; High winds, wet flurries (of wet snow), and snow squalls are forecast.* **2** a brief commotion: *a flurry of activity, announcements, calls, goals, letters, punches, trading on the stock exchange.* —*v.* **flur.ries, flur.ried, flur.ry.ing** **1** agitate or disturb; *adj.:* *He got all **flurried** when the boss asked to see him.* **2** fall in a flurry: *Her hair flurries in her face.*

flush *v.* **1** make or become red or glowing: *She felt her cheeks flush.* **2** make flow: *to flush a toilet; She flushed the picture down the toilet; They flushed the guerrillas out* (= made them come out) *with tear gas.* —*n.* **1** an excited condition; glow: *in the first flush of victory.* **2** a rapid flow or outgrowth: *the first flush of spring grass.* **3** a hand of the same suit of cards. —*adj.* **1** glowing with vigor: *the flush faces of healthy youth.* **2** abundant or prosperous: *oil-rich nations that are flush with money.* **3** even or level: *a flush door without panels; lines printed flush on the left; adv.: a flush left margin; The puck hit him flush* (= directly) *on the chin.*

flus.ter (FLUS.tur) *v.* upset or make nervous: *The speaker was visibly flustered by the heckling; adj.:* *to feel, get, grow, seem **flustered**.* —*n.* a state of nervousness or confusion: *The school was thrown into a fluster by the mayor's visit.*

flute (long "oo") *n.* **1** a high-pitched wind instrument consisting of a slender tube with finger holes along its stem and a hole at one end for blowing. **2** one of the ornamental grooves or furrows running parallel along a column. **3** a similar groove in a garment, furniture leg, or armor.

—**flut.ed** (FLOO.tid) *adj.: a fluted furniture leg, garment.* —**flut.ing**

(FLOO.ting) *n.*
flut.ist (FLOO.tist) *n.* one who plays a flute.
flut.ter (FLUT.ur) *v.* beat or flap rapidly and irregularly: *to flutter one's eyelids; The chick fluttered its wings as if to fly; Flags flutter in the wind; The patient's pulse fluttered awhile before regaining its rhythm; Waiters flutter about* (= move about quickly) *taking orders during the lunch hour.* —*n.* rapid flapping or agitation: *the flutter of wings; She put us in a flutter* (Informal for excited state) *by appearing unannounced; Bad acoustics could cause wow and flutter* (= rise and fall in pitch more rapid than wow) *in sound reproduction.*
flu.vi.al (FLOO.vee.ul) *adj.* having to do with a stream or river: *a fluvial channel, deposit, sediment.*
flux *n.* a flow or flowing: *the flux of the tides; the flux of electricity, particles, radiation, time; Spoken languages are in a continual state of flux* (= change).
fly *v.* **flies, flew** or **flied** (baseball sense), **flown** (FLONE), **fly.ing** move swiftly and lightly, as a bird through the air: *He would like to fly or at least learn to fly a plane; Lou has never flown in a plane; They fly (by) Air America; We fly* (= arrive by plane) *into New York; They flew (across) the Atlantic in a balloon; a pilot who flew refugees out of Ethiopia; He has flown many bombing missions; a ship flying before the wind; Windows flew open during the storm; The batter flied (the ball) to center field; a brilliant idea that would not fly* (Informal for succeed); *a testimony that* **flies in the face of** (= contradicts) *the facts as we know them; a man who* **flies into a rage** (= gets enraged) *when something goes wrong; He* **flies off the handle** (= gets angry) *at the least provocation; In her fury she* **let fly** (= burst out) *with four-letter words;* **adj.**: *flying debris, conditions, glass, machines; three hours of flying time; a flying* (= very short) *visit; She came out of the grilling* **with flying colors** (= victorious). —*n., pl.* **flies 1** a winged insect such as the housefly or dragonfly: *to swat a fly.* **2** a flying part, as the flapping edge of a flag. **3** a flap, as in a garment to hide buttons, zipper, etc. or one serving as the door of a tent. **4** a baseball batted high in the air; also **fly ball.** —**fly in the ointment** something that lessens the value or usefulness of what it affects, as an unwelcome guest at a party. —**on the fly** while flying: *Lou caught the ball on the fly; She's so busy she always eats on the fly* (= hurriedly). —**fly.a.ble** *adj.*
fly.blown *adj.* contaminated or spoiled, as covered with larvae of flies.
fly.by *n.* **-bys** a craft's flight close to or past an object under observation, esp. an object in space such as Mars or the moon.
fly-by-night *adj* a. that quits without paying debts or meeting contractual obligations: *a fly-by-night charity, operator, scheme.*
fly-cast *v.* to fish by use of flylike lures attached to the hook.
fly.catch.er (FLY.catch.ur) *n.* any of various birds that prey on insects in flight.
fly.er or **fli.er** *n.* **1** one that flies, as an aviator: *a frequent flyer.* **2** a notice distributed by hand. **3** Informal. a reckless enterprise.
flying boat *n.* a seaplane with a boatlike hull.
flying buttress *n.* in Gothic architecture, an arched prop or brace that supports a wall from the outside, its other end being set in a pier.
flying fish *n.* a fish of warm seas with fins that can be spread like wings for gliding over distances of up to 1,000 ft. (305 m) after a leap.
flying saucer *n.* a mysterious flying object, esp. one disk-shaped, reportedly seen in the skies.
flying squad *n.* a rapidly mobile unit, esp. of police, for special tasks.
flying squirrel *n.* a squirrel that can glide through the air using winglike folds of skin stretching between the forelegs and hind legs.
fly.leaf *n.* **-leaves** a blank leaf at the beginning or end of a book.
fly.pa.per (FLY.pay.pur) *n.* a strip of sticky paper for catching flies.
fly.speck *n.* a speck of dirt left by a fly; hence, a tiny spot or flaw.
fly.way *n.* the regular flight path of a migratory bird.
fly.weight *n.* a boxer weighing not more than 112 lb., or 51 kg for the Olympics.
fly.wheel *n.* a heavy wheel attached to the shaft of an engine to regulate its speed.
f-number (EF.num.bur) *n.* the ratio of the focal length of a camera lens to its diameter: *The lower the f-number the shorter the required exposure time.*
foal *n.* the young of an animal of the horse family; colt or filly. —*v.* give birth to a colt or filly.
foam *n.* **1** a mass of fine bubbles, as formed in or on a liquid by agitation,

fermentation, etc. **2** a rigid or spongy material made by the dispersal of bubbles in liquid rubber, plastic, etc.
—*v.* make foam: *boiling, foaming water; a rabid dog foaming at the mouth.*
—**foam.y** *adj.*

fob *n.* a short ribbon, chain, etc., often with an ornament, attached to a pocket watch or key ring: *"his and hers" key fobs.* —*v.* **fobs, fobbed, fob.bing** trick someone by imposing something: *They fobbed her off with a lemon of a car; They fobbed off a lemon on her.*

fo.cal (FOH.cul) *adja.* of or at a focus: *a focal distance, plane, range;* the **focal length** *of a lens or mirror* (= distance to its focus); *The Olympic Games become the* **focal point** *of world attention every four years.*

fo'c's.le (FOKE.sul) same as FORECASTLE.

fo.cus (FOH.cus) *n.* **-cus.es** or **-ci** (-sye) **1** the meeting point of rays of light, heat, or sound. **2** focal length or distance. **3** an adjustment of this to get a sharp image: *A photograph is* **in focus** (= clear) *or* **out of focus** (= blurred); *Bring the image* **into focus**. **4** center of attention: *a central, changing, clear, narrow, strong focus; Let's bring this issue into proper focus; The focus of her life was the poor and the downtrodden.*
—*v.* **-cus.es, -cused, -cus.ing 1** adjust a lens, the eyes, etc. so as to get a sharp image: *to focus the camera on a scene; adj.: a sharply* **focused** *light beam, image, picture.* **2** concentrate: *Let's focus our attention on the environment; He focuses his efforts on profitability; adj.: a highly* **focused** *effect, image, plan, product; More focused research is called for; Stay focused; You are too focused on the past.* Also **fo.cussed, fo.cus.sing** *Cdn.*

focus group *n.* a group of people used to test public reaction to a product or policy and find out changes required.

fod.der (FOD.ur) *n.* coarse or dried food for farm animals, as alfalfa, corn, hay, etc.

foe *n.* an enemy, esp. an actively hostile one: *a bitter, formidable, implacable foe; friend or foe?*

foehn (FANE, FURN) *n.* a warm, dry wind blowing down mountainsides in the Alps.

foe.tal, foe.tid, etc. same as FETAL, FETID, etc.

fog *n.* thick mist or cloud that is close to the ground and cuts visibility: *in dense, heavy, light fog; a patch of fog; Wait till the fog clears* or *lets up* or *lifts.*
—*v.* **fogs, fogged, fog.ging 1** cover with fog; *adj.: a* **fogged** *car window; fogged eyeglasses.* **2** obscure or confuse: *Liquor tends to fog the mind; questions that fog the real issues.*

fog.bank *n.* fog when seen as a dense mass.

fog.bound *adj.* hampered or prevented by fog: *a rash of accidents on a fogbound expressway; We were fogbound for many days; fogbound travelers.*

fogey See FOGY.

fog.gy (FOG.ee) *adj.* **fog.gi.er, fog.gi.est** full of fog; cloudy: *in foggy conditions, weather; I don't have the foggiest idea of what she means.* —**fog.gi.ly** *adv.;* **fog.gi.ness** *n.*

Foggy Bottom *n. Informal.* the U.S. State Department.

fog.horn *n.* a warning siren used on lighthouses and ships in foggy weather.

fo.gy (FOH.gee, "g" as in "go") *n.* **-gies** one who is old-fashioned in thinking and behavior: *an old fogy.* Also **fo.gey, -geys.**

foi.ble *n.* a minor personal weakness, esp. one easy to overlook: *human foibles; flaws and foibles.*

foil *n.* **1** a thin-rolled sheet of a metal such as tin, aluminum, lead, or gold, as used for wrapping. **2** a person or thing that acts as a sharp contrast setting another off, as a straight man for a comedian. **3** a blunted sword used in fencing. **4** a hydrofoil: *a boat with submerged foils; a foil-borne craft.*
—*v.* thwart or frustrate, as by throwing pursuers off a scent: *The guards foiled the prisoner's attempt to escape.*

foist *v.* palm off: *useless stuff foisted on unwary customers.*

fold *v.* **1** bend or double over, as to wrap or enclose: *A letter is folded to put in an envelope; candy folded* (= wrapped) *in foil; adj.: He stood there with* **folded** *arms* (crossed over his chest) *refusing to lend a hand; She knelt with hands folded* (= pressed together) *in prayer; the picture of a child folded in her mother's embrace* (= held to her breast); *adja. & cpd.: a* **folding** *chaise longue; a car's folding top; A* **folding screen** *made of hinged panels used as a room divider; an airplane's* **fold-down** *meal trays.* **2** *Informal.* fail: *A business folds* (up) *when broke.*
—*n.* **1** a folding or bend: *hidden in the folds of a drape.* **2** a sheep pen; also, a flock, esp. a church congregation: *the prodigal's return to the fold.*

-fold *comb.form.* number of parts or times as specified: *manifold, myriadfold, threefold, triplefold, twofold.*

fold.er *n.* something folded, as a file for papers or an advertising leaflet.

fol.de.rol or **fol.de.ral** (FOL.duh.rol) same as FALDERAL.

fold.out *n.* an oversize folded leaf, as in a magazine, that is folded out for viewing.

fo.li.age (FOH.lee.ij) *n.* leaves of a plant or tree.

fo.li.ate (FOH.lee.ate) *v.* -ates, -at.ed, -at.ing make into or like leaves; also, separate into layers; *adj. & cpd.*: graphite's foliate or **foliated** structure; a trifoliate cloverleaf. —**fo.li.a.tion** (-AY.shun) *n.*: the foliation of mica schist into layers.

fo.lic acid (FOH.lic-, FOL.ic-) *n.* a vitamin of the B complex found in leafy green vegetables.

fo.li.o (FOH.lee.oh) *n.* -os 1 a leaf of a book. 2 a page number. 3 formerly, the largest book size resulting from sheets of paper folded only once.

folk (FOKE) 1 *n. & comb.form.* the common people, esp. as a social or cultural group: *city folk, country folk, fisher folk, kinsfolk, gentlefolk, menfolk, womenfolk.* 2 **folks** *n.pl. Informal.* people: *old folks; How are your folks (= family, esp. parents)?* —*adj* a. that is traditional with the common people: *folk art, ethics, literature, medicine, psychology, speech, theater; a folk ballad, belief, custom, dance, singer, song, tale, tune; A* **folk epic** is one that has been handed down orally from prehistoric times.

folk.lore *n.* the traditional customs, beliefs, sayings, etc. of a people, handed down from generation to generation.

folk music *n.* music of the common people, including dance songs and folk songs, handed down from generation to generation.

folk rock *n.* folk songs sung to a rock rhythm.

folk song *n.* a traditional song of popular origin, as Negro spirituals, ballads, etc. —**folk.sing.er** *n.*; **folk.sing.ing** *n.*

folk.sy (FOKE.see) *adj.* -si.er, -si.est *Informal.* friendly or sociable in style: *folksy appeal, charm, humor, informality, style; in a folksy manner.*

folk.ways *n.pl.* habits or customs common within a social group: *local customs and folkways.*

folk.y same as FOLKSY.

fol.li.cle (FOL.i.cul) *n.* a body cavity or sac: *hair follicles in the skin; Graafian follicles contain egg cells in the ovary.*

fol.low (FOL.oh) *v.* 1 go or come after: *Christmas follows Thanksgiving; Your shadow follows you closely; The reasons are as follows; a sales representative who* **follows up** *letters with phone calls; The man emigrated and his family* **followed suit** (= did the same); *to* **follow through** (= go ahead) *with a plan;* **n.**: *service offered as a* **follow-through** *after sales; a* **follow-up** *visit.* 2 to result or ensue: *Wars follow from enmities.* 3 obey: *Buddhists follow Buddha's teachings; to follow blindly, faithfully; to follow (= go along) a coastline, course, path, river, road, route, track; Their behavior follows a pattern* (= They behave similarly); *Mom is* **a hard act to follow** (= difficult to emulate). 4 practice: *to follow a career, occupation, religion.* 5 understand: *a lecturer who is difficult to follow.* —**fol.low.er** *n.*

following (FOL.oh.ing) 1 *adj.* that follows: *for the following reasons; My reasons are* **the following.** 2 *n.* group of followers: *a political party with a large following.* 3 *prep.* after: *a dance following dinner.*

fol.ly (FOL.ee) *n.* **fol.lies** (-eez) 1 lack of good sense or an instance of it: *the folly of accepting rides from strangers; It was folly not to listen to advice; the follies and excesses of youth.* 2 **follies** *pl.* a revue: *ice follies.*

fo.ment (foh.MENT) *v.* 1 stir up something that is below the surface: *to foment discontent, hatred, rebellion, trouble.* 2 apply something hot and moist such as a compress or poultice to a painful body part. —**fo.men.ta.tion** (-men.TAY.shun) *n.*

fond *adj.* loving, often excessively: *a fond belief, husband, kiss, look, wife; a fond parent; fond and foolish hopes; with fondest love; He's* **fond of** *her.* —**fond.ly** *adv.;* **fond.ness** *n.*

fon.dle (FON.dul) *v.* -dles, -dled, -dling 1 pet or caress lovingly: *to fondle a child, kitten.* 2 caress sexually: *Some of the picketers complained of being fondled and kicked.*

fon.due (FON.dew) *n.* a preparation of wine-flavored melted cheese eaten by dipping bread in it; also **fon.du.**

font *n.* 1 a bowl or basin for holy water, esp. one used at baptism: *a baptismal font; a font (= fountain) of knowledge, wisdom.* 2 a style of printing type, as Helvetica and Baskerville: *Fonts come in various (point) sizes and styles* (= typefaces). 3 a complete set of type of the same size and style: *a desk-top printer with 14 resident* or *built-in fonts; scalable fonts that can be used in various sizes.*

food (long "oo") *n.* something to be consumed, esp. to sustain life or nourish growth: *People die for lack of food and* water; food and drink; Fertilizers are plant foods; the Scriptures as food for the soul; Food (= meat, vegetables, etc.) is grown on farms; **adja.**: food crops, fads, grains; A balanced meal should include food from the four food groups; food staples such as rice and wheat.

food bank n. an agency that collects food donations and distributes them to the needy.

food basket n. a list of basic food items used by statisticians to calculate living costs.

food chain n. a series of organisms that depend on one another for food, as mice on grass, owls on mice, bacteria on dead bodies which then become nutrients for the grass.

food cycle (or **web**) n. the cycle formed by the various food chains in an ecological system such as a forest or lake.

food group n. any of the groups of foods making up a balanced diet: *The four food groups are grain products, vegetables and fruit, milk products, and meat and alternates.*

food line n. a line of hungry people waiting to be served.

food processor n. an electrical kitchen appliance that chops, slices, mixes, shreds, etc.

food stamp n. a stamp issued by government to people on low incomes to exchange for food.

food.stuff n. anything such as grain, meat, vegetables, etc. that has food value.

food web same as FOOD CYCLE.

fool n. **1** a silly or idiotic person: *Don't make a fool of yourself.* **2** a jester, as in the Middle Ages. —v. **1** trick or deceive: *People get fooled on April 1; The eye is easily fooled because seeing is believing; Let's not fool ourselves into thinking that everything will turn out as desired.* **2** *Informal.* act like a fool: *I'm not fooling; Stop fooling around and start working; She fooled away her time till the eve of exams; It's dangerous to fool with explosives.*

fool.er.y (FOO.luh.ree) n. **-er.ies** a foolish action or foolish behavior.

fool.har.dy (FOOL.har.dee) adj. **-di.er, -di.est** foolishly daring.
—**fool.har.di.ness** n.

fool.ish (FOO.lish) adj. showing lack of good sense and judgment: *a foolish action, choice, hope, idea; mistake, young man; to feel foolish after doing something; to look foolish in front of others.*
—**fool.ish.ly** adv.; **fool.ish.ness** n.

fool.proof adj. too safe or simple to be mishandled, misunderstood, etc. even by a fool.

fools.cap n. a size of writing paper measuring about 13 in. (33 cm) by 17 in. (43 cm).

fool's paradise n. a state of happiness based on false hopes or illusions.

foot (short "oo") n., pl. **feet 1** the part of the leg that touches the ground when one is standing or walking: *to gain, shuffle, stamp one's feet; children in their stocking feet (without footwear); The whole city is at your feet from this hilltop; Children living nearby go to school on foot (= walking); to get on, rise, scramble, struggle to one's feet (= stand up for a special purpose); She put her foot down (= was firm) and refused to admit latecomers; Let's put our best foot forward (= appear at our best) for the interview; Small children tend to get under foot (= in the way).* **2** something corresponding to a foot: *the foot of a chair, stocking.* **3** a part opposed to the head or top part: *at the foot of the bed, hill, page, sail.* **4** a measure of length based on the human foot, equal to 12 in. (0.3048 m). **5** a unit of verse based on the syllable: *"Five and twenty sailors" has three feet.* —**foot in the door** entry: *To get, have, put a foot in the door of (= gain entry in) some professions is not easy.*
—**set foot** enter: *Troublemakers are not allowed to set foot in this country; Al was told never to set foot on American soil.*
—v. **1** find the sum of a column of figures. **2** pay costs, a bill, etc.: *to foot the bill.* —**foot it** walk: *They had to foot it home after missing the bus.*

foot.age (FOOT.ij) n. **1** length measured in feet: *cubic, linear, square footage.* **2** a length of motion-picture film: *action footage shot in Vietnam; newsreel, TV footage; library footage (from library stock).*

foot.ball n. **1** a game played using an inflated ball by two teams defending a goal at either end of a field; also, rugby or soccer. **2** the ball used in any of these games.

football pool n. a system for betting on football matches.

foot.board n. **1** an upright board forming the foot of a bed. **2** any board or plank used to rest the feet on.

foot.bridge n. a bridge for walking across.

foot-candle n. a unit of illumination equal to the light thrown by one candle at a distance of one foot.

foot-dragging n. failure to act with the required promptness.

foot.ed *adj. & comb.form.* having feet as specified: *a child's footed pajamas; barefooted; clubfooted; pussyfooted; splayfooted; We are two-footed animals; web-footed.*

foot.er *n.* a name, title, date, etc. repeated at the foot of each page of a document.

-footer *comb.form.* a person or thing in regard to height or length: *a strapping, big-boned six-footer; The superstore is a 100,000-square-footer; She putted a 25-footer on the twelfth hole; Greg fired a 10-footer (= hockey shot) into the open net.*

foot.fall *n.* the sound of a footstep.

foot.hill *n.* a hill at the foot of higher mountains: *a village nestled in the foothills of the Rockies.*

foot.hold *n.* **1** a place to hold on to with a foot. **2** a secure or advantageous position: *a firm foothold; to establish, gain, secure a foothold.*

foot.ing *n.* **1** a placing of the feet; hence, balance: *sure footing; to keep, lose, recover one's footing.* **2** basis or foundation: *a personal, sound, strong footing; on a war footing; businesses on solid footing; a firm financial footing.* **3** relationship: *on a competitive, equal, even, friendly footing with someone.*

foot.less *adj.* **1** having no feet or foundation. **2** clumsy or inept.

foot.lights *n.pl.* a row of stage lights at foot level.

foot.ling *adja. Informal.* trifling or silly: *a footling amount, award, film.*

foot.lock.er (FOOT.lock.ur) *n.* a chest kept at the foot of one's bed, esp. in barracks.

foot.loose *adj.* free to move about or do as one pleases: *footloose and fancy free.*

foot.man (FOOT.mun) *n.* **-men** a male servant doing odd jobs; doorman.

foot.note *n.* a note placed at the foot of a page or end of a chapter or book explaining or amplifying a text: *the footnotes to the volume.*

foot.pad *n.* a padded foot of a soft-landing spacecraft.

foot.print *n.* **1** an impression or mark made by a foot: *footprints in the sand; a set of footprints.* **2** the area occupied by a machine, as a computer on a desktop: *Copiers with smaller footprints are preferred; to cover, have, occupy a footprint.*

foot.race *n.* a running race.

foot.rest *n.* a support on which to rest the feet.

foot.sie (FOOT.see) *n.* [child's word] foot. **—to play footsie with** *Informal.* to flirt with an idea, group, plan, etc., like playing by touching feet under the table.

foot soldier *n.* a member of an infantry.

foot.sore *adj.* having feet that are sore, esp. from walking.

foot.step *n.* the sound or impression made by feet: *We saw footsteps leading to the spot where the body was found; to dog someone's footsteps; a disciple who follows **in the footsteps of** (= follows the example of) his master.*

foot.stool *n.* a low stool to rest the feet on.

foot.wear *n.* things to wear on the feet, as shoes, boots, and slippers.

foot.work *n.* the manner of using the feet, as in dancing or fencing.

fop *n.* a vain person; **fop.pish** *adj.* **—fop.per.y** *n.* **fop.per.ies.**

for (FOR, fur) *prep.* [indicating purpose, goal, object, fitness, exchange, duration, etc.]: *to go for a walk; to catch a plane for London; a gift for you; She has a good ear for music; We slept for 10 hours; The eggs are for hatching, not for eating; a restaurant famous for fine cooking; A lawyer acts for her clients; a child named for (= same as) her mother; I stayed home for (= because of) many reasons; a good guy for all I care (Informal for but I'm indifferent); a good guy for all I know (Informal for probably).* **—conj.** [not used to begin a sentence] because: *I'm not going, for I am ill.*

fora a *pl.* of FORUM.

for.age (FOR.ij) *n.* a search or what is searched out for food, esp. grass and winter fodder for farm animals. **—v. -ag.es, -aged, -ag.ing** wander in search, esp. of food: *Hunting and gathering tribes live by foraging; to forage for firewood.* **—for.ag.er** *n.*

for.ay (FOR.ay) *n.* **1** a raid or incursion: *to make a foray into enemy territory; He fended off several forays by corporate raiders; a scoring foray in football.* **2** an attempt or effort to get into something new or different: *to make forays into the U.S. market; the first, latest foray; an early, initial, opening, recent, tentative foray; occasional forays.* **—v.** make a raid.

forbad or **forbade** *pt.* of FORBID.

for.bear (for.BARE) *v.* **-bears, -bore, -borne** (-BORN), **-bear.ing 1** keep from doing or saying; also, be patient and control oneself. **2** same as FOREBEAR. **—for.bear.ance** (-unce) *n.*

for.bid (for BID) *v.* **-bids**, *pt.* **-had** or **-bade** (-BAD), *pp.* **-bid.den, -bid.ding**

forbidden fruit / forefront

order not to do something: *She had expressly forbidden her children to smoke; Strangers are forbidden use of the cottage; God forbid (such a calamity)! God forbid that I should ever say such a thing!*
forbidden fruit *n.* something wished for but not permitted.
forbidding *adj.* that causes fear or dislike: *The pool looks cold and forbidding; a man of forbidding appearance.*
—**for.bid.ding.ly** *adv.*
forbore, forborne See FORBEAR.
force *n.* **1** physical, mental, or moral power or strength, esp. its active use: *to apply* or *resort to* or *use force to open a door; We renounce the use of force; armed, brute, deadly, moral, physical force; a show of force; She can move objects by sheer force of will; "Absolutely" has greater force than "Yes"; the force of inertia as used in the wheels of toys; a centrifugal, centripetal, driving, irresistible, vital force; magnetic force* (= energy); *We go on making the same mistakes by* **force of habit**; *storms, earthquakes, floods and such* **forces of nature.** **2** a body of people: *air, armed, occupation, peace-keeping, police, sales forces; a task force to study speed limits; the work force* (= workers); *to* **join forces** (= unite) **with** *the opposition.* —**in force:** *Lower speed limits are now in force* (= in effect); *Volunteers came out in force* (= great numbers) *to help disaster victims.* —*v.* **forc.es, forced, forc.ing** get something done by overcoming resistance: *He forced the door (open); a confession forced from a prisoner; promises forced out of someone; a bribe forced on* or *upon an official; She had to force her way through the crowd; people forced out of* or *from their homes by a flood; He forces himself to be practical; She doesn't like to* **force herself on** *others* (= make others do what she wants).
forced (FORST) *adj.* done with the use of force: *a forced confession, entry; forced feeding; a plane's forced landing; smiles that look forced* (= artificial); *a forced-air heating system.*
force.ful *adj.* having force: *a forceful personality, presentation, speaker, style.*
—**force.ful.ly** *adv.;* **force.ful.ness** *n.*
for.ceps *n. sing. & pl.* a pair of pincers or tongs used by surgeons, dentists, and others for grasping, pulling, compressing, etc.
for.ci.ble (FOR.suh.bul) *adj.* **1** obtained or done by the use of force: *forcible confinement; a burglar's forcible entry; Rowdies are liable to forcible ejection from the nightclub.* **2** showing force: *a rather forcible argument; forcible language.*
—**for.ci.bly** *adv.*
ford *n.* a place in a stream that is shallow enough to cross by wading or driving through. —*v.* cross: *to ford a river.*
fore *adja.* in the front or forward, not back or aft: *the fore end of a firearm; a page's fore edge* (opposite the back or stitched edge); *the fore hatch of a ship.*
—*adv.* toward the bow of a ship.
—**fore and aft** at, to, or from bow and stern; *adj.:* *A schooner is a* **fore-and-aft** (= lengthwise) *rigged ship; a fore-and-aft cap in British army style.* —*n.* front: *a candidate who has* **come to the fore** *only recently.* —*interj.* used as a warning: *The golfer shouted "Fore" and swung her club.* —**comb.form.** before or front: *forefather, foreground, forerunner.*
fore.arm *n.* the part of the arm between elbow and wrist. —*v.* (for.ARM) arm beforehand: *to be forearmed with knowledge; "Forewarned is forearmed."*
fore.bear *n.* ancestor: *our immigrant forebears; The new car model is smaller than its forebears* (= predecessors). Also **for.bear.**
fore.bode (for.BODE) *v.* **-bodes, -bod.ed, -bod.ing** esp. of things, predict or warn about something unfavorable: *a dream foreboding a fatal crash.*
foreboding *n.* a feeling of something bad about to happen: *dark forebodings of disaster, of the end of the world, of apocalypse; a poem filled with foreboding; grim forebodings; a deep sense of foreboding;* *adj.:* *foreboding predictions, signs, words; Events are less foreboding than they appear.* —**fore.bod.ing.ly** *adv..*
fore.cast *v.* tell beforehand: *Snow is forecast for Christmas; economic indicators forecasting a recession.* —*n.* a foretelling or prediction.
fore.cas.tle (FOKE.sul) *n.* the raised deck near a ship's bow.
fore.close (for.CLOSE) *v.* **-clos.es, -closed, -clos.ing** close in advance: *A mortgage is foreclosed and the property sold if payments are not kept up; an embargo to foreclose trade with a nation.*
—**fore.clo.sure** (-CLOH.zhur) *n.*
fore.doom (for.DOOM) *v.* doom beforehand: *a plot foredoomed to failure because it was not kept secret.*
fore.fa.ther (FOR.fah.thur) *n.* an ancestor.
fore.fend (for.FEND) same as FORFEND.
fore.fin.ger (FOR.fing.gur) *n.* the finger next to the thumb.
fore.foot *n.* **-feet** one of the front feet of an animal or insect with four feet or more.
fore.front *n.* the extreme front; position

of the greatest importance: *at or in the forefront of a battle, movement, revolt, struggle; at the forefront of the agenda, of fashion, planning, technology; to bring* or *get a person or thing to the forefront; We are very much in the forefront of the market.*

fore.gath.er (for.GATH.ur, "TH" as in "the") same as FORGATHER.

fore.go (for.GO) *v.* **-goes, -went, -gone** (-GON), **-go.ing 1** go before or precede; *adj.:* From the **foregoing** *facts, we deduce that the earth is round; The case was so strong the verdict was a* **foregone conclusion** *(known in advance).* **2** same as FORGO.

fore.ground *n.* the part of a picture that appears closest to the viewer: *The children were in the foreground of the picture with a chalkboard in the background.*

fore.hand *n.* **1** in tennis and such racket games, a stroke with the palm of the hand turned forward. **2** a similar shot or pass in hockey.
—*adj.: a forehand drive, grip, stroke, volley.*

fore.head (FOR.id, FOR.hed) *n.* the part of the face above the eyebrows.

for.eign (FOR.in) *adj.* **1** of or from an outside country or place: *a foreign accent, currency, government, market, visitor; agencies serving foreign interests; English is a foreign language in Ethiopia; a language of foreign origin;* **cpd:** *native-born children of foreign-born parents; foreign-made goods; foreign-owned enterprises.* **2** having to do with foreign countries: *A* **foreign minister** *is in charge of a government's foreign affairs; foreign aid; our foreign policy, relations, trade.* **3** *Formal.* alien, not native or belonging to oneself: *Laziness is totally foreign to her nature; Dust, grit, and such foreign bodies get into our eyes; matters utterly foreign* (= irrelevant) *to our discussion.* —**for.eign.er** *n.*
—**for.eign.ness** *n.*

fore.know (for.NOH) *v.* **-knows, -knew, -known, -know.ing** have prior knowledge, esp. by use of divine or psychic power. —**fore.know.ledge** (NOL.ij) *n.*

fore.leg *n.* one of the front legs of an animal.

fore.limb *n.* a foreleg or a corresponding arm, fin, or wing.

fore.lock *n.* a lock of hair, as of a horse, growing just above the forehead.

fore.man (FOR.mun) *n.pl.* **-men 1** the leader of a jury. **2** one in charge of workers or a section of a plant;

fore.wom.an *n.* **-wom.en.**

fore.mast *n.* the mast near a ship's bow.

fore.most *adj.* first in position or importance: *the foremost champion of women's rights; the foremost among them; She is* **first and foremost** *a Basque, then a Spaniard;* **adv.:** *We have to hold that foremost in our minds.*

fore.named *adj.* before-mentioned; aforesaid.

fore.noon (for.NOON) *n.* the part of the day before noon; morning. —*adj.* (FOR.noon): *a forenoon session.*

fo.ren.sic (fuh.REN.sic) *adj.* having to do with courts of law or argumentation: *a lawyer's forensic abilities; A body is sent to a* **forensic laboratory** *for a postmortem;* **forensic medicine** (= medical science applied to legal questions).

fore.or.dain (for.or.DAIN) *v.* determine in advance; predestine.
—**fore.or.di.na.tion** (FOR.or.duh.NAY.shun) *n.*

fore.part *n.* the front or earlier part.

fore.play *n.* sexual stimulation before intercourse.

fore.quar.ter (FOR.quor.tur) *n.* the front half of a side of beef, lamb, pork, etc.

fore.run.ner (FOR.run.ur) *n.* **1** one who goes before another preparing the way; precursor. **2** a warning sign or symptom: *A sore throat is sometimes a forerunner of the flu.*

fore.sail *n.* the principal sail on the foremast of a ship.

fore.see (for.SEE) *v.* **-sees, -saw, -seen, -see.ing** see or realize in advance what is going to happen. —**fore.see.a.ble** (-SEE.uh.bul) *adj.: in the foreseeable future.*

fore.shad.ow (for.SHAD.oh) *v.* indicate something to follow; give advance warning of something: *events foreshadowing war.*

fore.sheet *n.* **1** one of the sheets of a foresail. **2 foresheets** *pl.* the forward part of an open boat.

fore.shore *n.* the part of a shore covered during high tide.

fore.short.en (for.SHOR.tun) *v.* portray an object shortened in front for proper perspective effect.

fore.sight *n.* the act or power of foreseeing: *The principal acted with foresight in sending the children home before the storm.*

fore.sight.ed (FOR.sye.tid) *adj.* having or using foresight: *Their foresighted planning averted a famine.*

fore.skin *n.* the fold of skin covering the end of the penis.

for.est (FOR.ist) *n.* a large wooded area; also, the trees and underbrush in it: *to clear a forest; dense, evergreen, hardwood, impenetrable, primeval, virgin forests; a (tropical) rain forest; a town hidden under a forest of TV antennas.* —**adj**.: *forest conservation; a forest fire, product, ranger, region, reserve;* **adj.**: a heavily **forested** (= wooded) *area; forested acres, hills.* —**for.est.a.tion** (-TAY.shun) *n.*

fore.stall *v.* take advance action to prevent or get ahead of something: *early negotiations to forestall a strike; how to forestall disaster, problems, violence.*

for.est.er (FOR.is.tur) *n.* 1 one trained in forestry. 2 one in charge of a park or forest; also **forest ranger.**

for.est.ry (FOR.is.tree) *n.* the science of forest cultivation and management of timber resources.

fore.taste *n.* a first experience of something to happen: *The balmy weather was a foretaste of spring; a foretaste of victory.* —*v.* (fore.TAIST) **-tastes, -tast.ed, -tast.ing.**

fore.tell (for.TELL) *v.* **-tells, -told, -tell.ing** indicate beforehand; predict: *to foretell the future.*

fore.thought *n.* 1 previous consideration: *Commitments require forethought.* 2 foresight: *With a little forethought the tragedy could have been averted.*

for.ev.er (fur.EV.ur) 1 *n.* an endlessly long time: *He was taking forever to finish his speech.* 2 *adv.* endlessly: *Nothing lasts forever; On a clear day you can see forever;* also **for.ev.er.more** (-MORE).

fore.warn *v.* warn in advance of something.

forewoman See FOREMAN.

fore.word (FOR.wurd) *n.* a short preface *to* a book.

for.feit (FOR.fit) *v.* lose or be deprived of something as punishment: *Drunk drivers forfeit their license.* —*n.* a forfeiting: *Murderers used to be punished by forfeit of their lives;* also **for.fei.ture** (-fi.chur) *n.*

for.fend (for.FEND) *v.* [old use] forbid: *Heaven forfend!*

for.gath.er (for.GATH.ur, "TH" as in "the") *v.* assemble or come together.

forgave *pt.* of FORGIVE.

forge (FORJ) *n.* 1 a furnace in which metal is heated or wrought. 2 a smithy. —*v.* **forg.es, forged, forg.ing** 1 to form or shape, as metal in a forge: *Blacksmiths forge metals by beating them into shape while red-hot on an anvil; to forge a horseshoe, tool, utensil; bonds of friendship forged at school.* 2 make or imitate falsely: *to forge a check, passport, signature;* **forg.er** *n.* 3 move suddenly with speed and power: *The horse that was last began forging into the lead toward the end; It* **forged ahead** *and won the race.*

for.ger.y (FOR.juh.ree) *n.* **-ger.ies** 1 a counterfeiting of checks and documents, paintings, signatures, etc. 2 something forged: *The Hitler diaries were found to be forgeries.*

for.get (fur.GET) *v.* **-gets, -got, -got.ten, -get.ting** 1 fail to remember: *I forgot to bring my homework to school; I forgot about bringing it* (= I didn't bring it); *I clean forgot; I completely forgot about it in the morning rush.* 2 neglect or disregard: *Let's forget about your unfinished work; Just forget it.* —**forget oneself** 1 say or do something improper. 2 be unselfish: *She forgets herself in the service of others.* —**for.get.ta.ble** (fur.GET.uh.bul) *adj.*

for.get.ful (fur.GET.ful) *adj.* apt to forget; also, negligent: *to be forgetful of the needs of others.* —**for.get.ful.ly** *adv.*; **for.get.ful.ness** *n.*

forget-me-not *n.* a tiny, yellow-centered, usu. sky-blue flower that grows in clusters, considered a symbol of true love.

for.give (fur.GIV) *v.* **-gives, -gave, -giv.en, -giv.ing** pardon, esp. give up the wish to punish: *I forgive and forget hurts, forgive enemies, but never forgive* (= cancel) *debts;* **adj.**: *our* **forgiven** *debts; a very* **forgiving** *kind of guy; The new car is harder to drive because it is less forgiving* (= tolerant) *of mistakes.* —**for.giv.a.ble** *adj.*

for.go (fur.GOH) *v.* **-goes, -went, -gone, -go.ing** do without something in a self-denying way, usu. because of practical considerations: *She worked nights, often forgoing sleep; to forgo conveniences, gains, opportunities, revenues, tax breaks.*

forgot, forgotten See FORGET.

fork *n.* 1 a tool with a handle and two or more prongs or tines for eating, pitching hay, etc. 2 something resembling it, as a tuning fork. 3 where branches of a tree, stream, or road meet; also, one of the branches: *a town situated at the fork of two rivers; the waters of the middle fork of the Salmon river.* 4 **forks** *pl.* area around a river fork. —*v.* 1 use a fork to lift, throw, dig, etc. 2 divide into forks or branches, as a river or road does. —**fork over** or **out** or **up** *Informal.* hand over money: *Fork it over; to fork over a million dollars.* —**forked** *adj.*: *a forked stick; forked*

(= zigzag) *lightning; the forked tongue of a serpent; to speak with a* **forked tongue** (= *to be untruthful*). —**fork.ful** *n.* **-fuls.**

fork.lift *n.* a vehicle with a pronged device in front that is slid under heavy objects for moving them, as in a warehouse; also **forklift truck.**

for.lorn (for.LORN) *adj.* wretched and forsaken: *the deserted and forlorn look of hungry children.* —**for.lorn.ly** *adv.*

forlorn hope *n.* a nearly hopeless enterprise.

form *n.* **1** shape or structure: *water in the form of ice and snow; The Greek god Proteus could assume or take or take on any form; the form and content of a poem; in an abridged, condensed, convenient, handy, revised form; light, heat, and other forms* (= *kinds*) *of energy; She is in excellent, good, superb form* (= *condition*) *today; He was not* **in form** (= *in good condition*) *yesterday.* **2** a way, method, or manner of doing something: *"Good morning" is the accepted form of greeting before noon; It's considered bad form* (= *behavior*) *to smoke at an interview; They don't like it in* **any manner, shape, or form;** *I'm not talking about mere* **forms and ceremonies. 3** a frame or mold: *Concrete is poured into forms for setting.* **4** a document to be filled out: *application, business, tax forms.* —*v.* to shape, take shape, put into shape, etc.: *Frost is forming on the window; Please form yourselves into circles; a party formed of friends and relatives; a figure formed out of clay; habits formed in childhood.*

-form *comb.form.* having form, as specified: *cruciform, uniform, vermiform.*

form.al (FOR.mul) *adj.* in accordance with a form, rule, custom, or convention: *A tuxedo is a formal costume; A contract is a formal agreement; a formal announcement, decision, invitation; They are getting more formal with their rules and regulations.* —**form.al.ly** *adv.* —**for.mal.ism** *n.*

for.mal.de.hyde (for.MAL.duh.hide) *n.* a colorless, pungent, water-soluble gas used as a disinfectant and preservative.

formal garden *n.* a garden laid out in geometrical designs.

for.mal.i.ty (for.MAL.i.tee) *n.* **-ties 1** attention to forms and ceremonies; hence, stiffness. **2** a rule, custom, or convention: *to complete, cut out, go through the formalities.*

for.mal.ize (FOR.muh.lize) *v.* **-iz.es, -ized, -iz.ing** make formal or give a form to: *language formalized as grammar rules; adj.: The fleur-de-lis is a formalized iris flower.* —**for.mal.i.za.tion** (-luh.ZAY.shun, -lye-) *n.*

for.mat (FOR.mat) *n.* shape, design, or arrangement: *Books are published in many formats, as hardcover, leatherbound, paperback, etc.; a meeting in the format of a panel discussion.* —*v.* **-mats, -mat.ted, -mat.ting** put in a format: *to format a diskette* (*in tracks and sectors*) *for recording data; to format text for printing out with appropriate margin widths, line spacing, etc.;* **n.:** *book* **formatting** *by computer.* —**for.mat.ter** *n.*

for.ma.tion (for.MAY.shun) *n.* a forming or something formed: *the formation of ice on a lake; battle, close, cloud, football, tight formations; planes flying in formation; Gibraltar is a huge rock formation.*

for.ma.tive (FOR.muh.tiv) *adj.* having to do with growth and formation: *the formative influences of home, school, and society; the formative years of childhood.*

for.mer (FOR.mur) *adj.* **1** previous: *stories of former times.* **2** the first-mentioned of two: *Of Lou and Lee, the former is a girl.* —**for.mer.ly** *adv.* in the past.

form.fit.ting (FORM.fit.ing) *adj.* close-fitting on the wearer's body.

for.mic *adj.* having to do with ants or an acidic fluid emitted by ants, spiders, and such insects.

for.mi.ca (for.MY.cuh) *n.* a heat-resistant plastic covering material for counters and tabletops. —**Formica** Trademark.

for.mi.da.ble (FOR.muh.duh.bul, for.MID.uh.bul) *adj.* **1** impressive: *a formidable list of qualifications; a formidable adversary, challenge, competition, display, record, rival, scholar; formidable gains, grace.* **2** frightening: *a formidable power, task, threat; to fight against formidable odds; more formidable than we thought.*

form.less *adj.* shapeless: *Fluids are formless; the voices of formless* (= *immaterial*) *beings.*

form letter *n.* a letter so written that copies of it may be dated and addressed to many people.

for.mu.la (FORM.yuh.luh) *n.* **-las** or **-lae** (-lee) **1** a set expression, esp. one for a specific use: *"You're welcome" is a polite formula for expressing thanks; "I baptize thee..." is a baptismal formula.* **2** a set of symbols expressing a scientific truth: *the chemical formula for water; a mathematical formula for the area of a circle.* **3** a set of specifications: *a soap-making formula; to devise a formula; a formula* *for success; a proven formula.* **4** something based on specifications: *to make up, prepare, warm up the baby's formula* (= milk mixture); ***formula investing*** (in selected securities according to a plan); *a **Formula One** racing car (built to specifications).*

for.mu.late (FORM.yuh.late) *v.* **-lates, -lat.ed, -lat.ing 1** express in a formula or systematically: *Einstein formulated relativity.* **2** prepare using a formula: *Pharmacists used to formulate prescriptions.* —**for.mu.la.tion** (-LAY.shun) *n.* —**for.mu.la.tor** (-lay.tur) *n.*

for.ni.cate (FOR.nuh.cate) *v.* **-cates, -cat.ed, -cat.ing** commit fornication; **for.ni.ca.tor** *n.*

for.ni.ca.tion (for.nuh.CAY.shun) *n.* sexual intercourse other than between husband and wife.

for.sake (fur.SAKE) *v.* **-sakes, -sook, -sak.ing** give up a person or thing to which one is attached: *Friends forsook him when he was in jail; bad habits that he forsook on marrying; adj.: a **forsaken** place.*

for.sooth (for.SOOTH) *adv. Archaic.* in truth; no doubt.

for.swear (for.SWARE) *v.* **-swears, -swore, -sworn, -swear.ing** swear solemnly to avoid something considered bad, as a habit. —**forswear oneself** perjure oneself.

for.syth.i.a (for.SITH.ee.uh, "TH" as in "thin") *n.* a shrub that bears clusters of yellow, bell-shaped blossoms in early spring; also called "golden bell."

fort *n.* a fortified place; also, a permanent army post: *Fort York in Toronto fell to the Americans in 1813; They went out shopping, leaving the children to **hold the fort*** (= look after the house).

¹**forte** (FORT) *n.* one's strong point: *I'm a plumber, carpentry is not my forte.*

²**for.te** (FOR.tay, -tee) *adj. & adv.* in music, loud(ly) and strong(ly).

forth *adv.* forward or onward: *He went forth to meet her; From that day forth* (= on), *they have been friends.* —**and so forth** et cetera. —**back and forth** to and fro.

forth.com.ing (FORTH.CUM.ing) *adj.* coming forward or approaching: *No help seemed forthcoming; our forthcoming movie attractions.*

forth.right *adj. & adv.* straightforward or frank: *He was very forthright in his answers; He told them forthright that the pay was too low.*

forth.with *adv.* at once: *He made his speech and forthwith left the meeting to catch his flight.*

for.ti.fy (FOR.tuh.fy) *v.* **-fies, -fied, -fy.ing** strengthen: *to fortify a town with a fortress; a soul fortified by suffering; Milk is fortified with vitamins and minerals.* —*adj. & cpd: a **fortified** castle, compound, town; calcium-fortified foods; fiber-fortified cereals; an iron-fortified infant formula; fortified breads, flour, grains; A **fortified wine** has up to 21% alcohol.* —**for.ti.fi.ca.tion** (-fuh.CAY.shun) *n.*

for.tis.si.mo (for.TIS.uh.moh) *adj. & adv. Music.* very loud(ly).

for.ti.tude (FOR.tuh.tude) *n.* strength of mind that enables one to endure pain, misfortune, etc. patiently: *intestinal fortitude* (= guts).

fort.night *n.* a period of two weeks.

fort.night.ly (FORT.nite.lee) *n.* a periodical appearing every two weeks; *adja.: a fortnightly issue, journal, publication; adv.: We publish fortnightly.*

for.tress (FOR.tris) *n.* a fortified place: *to besiege, storm, take a fortress; A fortress falls to the enemy.*

for.tu.i.tous (for.TUE.uh.tus) *adj.* of a fortunate event, happening by chance: *a fortuitous circumstance, encounter, event, meeting.* —**for.tu.i.tous.ly** *adv.*

for.tu.nate (FOR.chuh.nit) *adj.* of people and circumstances, lucky: *to be saved from fire by a fortunate change of wind; It's fortunate the wind changed; We were fortunate to be saved from the fire.* —**for.tu.nate.ly** *adv.*

for.tune (FOR.chun) *n.* **1** one's lot or luck: *It was her good fortune to be born in that family; the bad fortune to be hit by a truck; He left home to try his fortune as a sailor; our changing fortunes; A stroke of good fortune made her a millionaire; the **fortunes** of war* (= good and bad things brought about by war); *She tells fortunes* (= predicts good and bad things to come) *for a living; the goddess of fortune with her **Wheel of Fortune*** (= chance); *"Fortune* (= good fortune) *favors the brave"; when fortune smiles on us; a **fortune cookie** (containing a prediction or maxim on a piece of paper).* **2** wealth: *He's after fame and fortune; to accumulate, amass, come into, inherit, run through, squander a fortune; an enormous, vast, family fortune; That sofa will cost you **a fortune*** (= a large sum of money); *a **Fortune 500*** (= one of the top 500 in income) *company; a **fortune hunter*** (who seeks wealth, esp. by marriage).

for.ty (FOR.tee) *adj., pron. & n.* **1** four times 10; 40 or XL: *forty acres; some forty of them; She scored a forty; Give me an even forty.* **2 the forties** *n.pl.* numbers, years, etc. ending in 40 through

49: *The early forties were war years.*
—**for.ti.eth** (-tee.ith) *n. & adj.*
forty-five *n., adj. & pron.* **1** the number 45 or XLV or what it represents. **2** a forty-five caliber (.45) pistol, a phonograph record that plays 45 r.p.m., etc.
forty-niner *n.* one who went to California in the 1849 gold rush.
forty winks *n.pl. Informal.* a short nap.
fo.rum (FOR.um) *n.* **-rums** or **-ra** (-ruh) **1** a place for public discussion: *TV as a forum of public affairs; They held an open forum on* or *about traffic safety.* **2** a tribunal: *the forum of one's conscience; the internal forum.*
for.ward (FOR.wurd) *adj.* toward the front, not backward: *a forward leap, march, movement; a forward* (= pushy) *young man with very forward* (= bold) *views; forward planning (for the future); forward buying of grain (for later delivery).* —**adv.** to a front position: *to bring* or *put forward a proposal for reform; to come, rush, step forward; I look forward to our meeting (with pleasure); From that time forward* (= onward), *he was very careful; Put the clock forward* (= advance it) *by one hour in the spring.* Also **for.wards.** —*n.* a front-line player in team games such as hockey and basketball. —*v.* **1** send: *We will forward your mail to the new address; She had left a forwarding address.* **2** promote: *to forward a plan, scheme, someone's career, interests.* —**for.ward.er** *n.* —**for.ward.ly** *adv.;* **for.ward.ness** *n.*
forwent *pt.* of FORGO.
fos.sil (FOS.ul) *n.* **1** a hardened remnant of an animal or plant dating from a previous geological period, preserved in rock or in coal deposits: *animal, hominid, plant, rock fossils;* **adja.**: *fossil evidence; a fossil fern, relic, skull; the fossil record; the fast depletion of the earth's fossil fuels such as coal, oil, and natural gas.* **2** an antiquated person: *an old fossil of a philosopher.*
fos.sil.ize (FOS.uh.lize) *v.* **-iz.es, -ized, -iz.ing 1** change into a fossil; **adj.**: *the fossilized remains of prehistoric humans; fossilized peat; Amber is fossilized resin.* **2** become set or rigid in one's ways.
—**fos.sil.i.za.tion** (-luh.ZAY.shun, -lye-) *n.*
fos.ter *v.* **1** take care of a child who is not one's own or adopted. **2** help to grow or develop: *to foster good habits in children; hopes fostered by promises; to foster a culture.* —**adj.** having to do with fostering children: *to place* or *put a child in foster care* (= foster home); *a foster family, mother, parent, placement, son; Is she foster or adopted?*
foster child *n.* a child raised by foster parents: *A foster child is called a foster brother or foster sister in relation to other foster children.*
foster home *n.* a private home in which children needing special care are placed by agencies such as children's aid societies.
foster parent *n.* one acting in the place of a natural parent in taking care of children.
fought *pt. & pp.* of FIGHT.
foul (*rhyme:* howl) *adj.* **1** rotten or filthy; hence, disagreeable: *the foul air around a garbage dump; medicine with a foul taste; We were warned of foul* (= stormy) *weather; foul language* (= swearing); *a foul* (= violent) *crime; Chimney sweeps clean out the soot from foul* (= dirty) *chimneys.* **2** not fair; against rules: *A foul ball is one that lands outside the foul lines in foul territory; by fair means or foul* (= by honest or dishonest means). **3** tangled: *foul ropes.* —**adv.** in a foul manner: *to play foul; Those who go* or *fall* or *run foul of* (= get in trouble with) *the law may go to jail.* —*v.* make foul: *Auto exhausts foul the air; Their last-minute change of mind fouled up* (= spoiled or ruined) *our plans.*
—*n.* anything foul, as an infraction of a rule, a collision or entangling, or a foul ball. —**foul.ly** *adv.;* **foul.ness** *n.*
fou.lard (foo.LARD) *n.* a soft, lightweight silk or other fabric, usu. decorated with a printed pattern.
fouling *n.* a messy deposit, as in a sewage pipe or in the barrel of a gun after firing.
foul-mouthed *adj.* using foul language; abusive.
foul play *n.* **1** unfair play. **2** treacherous violence, esp. murder: *He met with foul play; The police suspected foul play when the missing person's clothes were found in the bush.*
foul-up *n. Informal.* a mixup or mess.
found *v.* **1** *pt. & pp.* of FIND. **2** establish: *The company was founded in 1847; an argument founded* (= based) *on facts, not hearsay evidence,* **adju.**: *a founding charter, conference, editor, member; our founding principles; in its founding years.* **3** cast metal, as in a foundry. —**adja. 1** discovered, not made as such: *Found fragments of writing from newsprint, laundry lists, etc. are used in composing found poems; Found art uses found objects such as driftwood, shells, and junk; You can't have a steady income from found money.* **2** furnished or equipped: *a fully found*

ship; *an all-found scholarship (that pays for fees, board, and lodging).*

foun.da.tion (fown.DAY.shun) *n.*
1 base: *Our house rests on a concrete foundation; a firm, solid, strong foundation; a cosmetic foundation for applying makeup; to undermine a foundation; a story without foundation* (= basis); *adj.: a foundation (garment) such as a corset or girdle with bra; to lay the* **foundation stone** *of a building.* **2** an endowed institution: *a charitable foundation; a science foundation; a foundation for humanitarian work.*

found.er (FOWN.dur) *n.* **1** one who founds an institution. **2** one who casts metals. —*v.* collapse or fail: *A horse founders from overwork and limps; a business that foundered during the recession; A ship foundered in the storm* (= filled with water and sank).

found-in *n.* a person arrested for being in an illegal establishment such as a gambling place or brothel.

founding father *n.* a person considered as a founder of an institution, nation, etc., as Benjamin Franklin and George Washington of the U.S.

found.ling *n.* an abandoned infant of unknown parents.

found.ry (FOUND.ree) *n.* **-ries** a shop where metal is molded into products such as engine blocks, dies, and printing type.

fount *n.* **1** a source or font. **2** a fountain.

foun.tain (FOWN.tun) *n.* **1** a spring of water, esp. an artificial jet or flow supplied by pipes and having a basin-like receptacle: *We first met at the office (water) fountain.* **2** source: *a fountain of ideas, knowledge, wisdom; He went in quest of the fountain of youth.*

foun.tain.head (FOWN.tun.hed) *n.* the original source, as of a stream: *God as the fountainhead of all wisdom.*

fountain pen *n.* a pen containing a reservoir of ink.

four (FOR) *n., pron. & adj.* one more than three; the number 4 or IV: *four limbs; four of them; Infants crawl around* **on all fours** (= hands and feet).

four-by-four *n.* **1** a cut piece of wood 4" x 4" thick: *a four-by-four post.* **2** an automobile with four-wheel drive; also **4 x 4, 4WD.**

four-flush *v. Informal.* to make a false claim or bluff; **four-flusher** *n.*

4-H club *n.* a usu. government-sponsored youth organization pledged to the improvement of skills ("head, heart, hands, and health") for social service, esp. in rural areas; **4-H.er** *n.*

four.fold *adj.* four times: *a fourfold gain, increase, rise; adv.: Our profits increased, grew, jumped fourfold.*

Four Hundred or **the 400** *n.* the exclusive social set of a community.

four-in-hand *n.* the simplest necktie with a slipknot and two hanging ends overlapping in front.

four-letter word *n.* **1** any of the most vulgar words of English that refer to sex, excretion, and related bodily parts. **2** any disgusting word or name.

four-o'clock *n.* a plant with fragrant white, pink, red, or yellow flowers that open in the afternoon.

four-poster *n.* a bed with four posts to support a canopy.

four.some *n.* a group of four persons, as for a game of golf.

four-speed or **four.speed** *adj.* having four gears or speeds: *a four-speed automatic transmission; a four-speed (camcorder) shutter.*

four-square or **four.square** *adj.* **1** square-shaped: *a four-square block, courtyard, piazza.* **2** solidly based, unyielding, or forthright: *We're foursquare against new taxes; adv.: They opted four-square for democracy.*

four.teen (for.TEEN) *n., adj. & pron.* four more than 10; the number 14 or XIV. —**four.teenth** *n. & adj.*

fourth (FORTH) **1** *adj. & adv.* next after third: *the fourth gear of a car; He placed fourth in the exam.* **2** *n.* one of four equal parts: *a fourth of those who passed.* —**fourth.ly** *adv.*

fourth estate *n.* the public press, journalists, or journalism.

Fourth World *n.* the poorest nations of the world.

four-wheel *adj.* having to do with four wheels: *four-wheel disc brakes, drives, steering.* —*n.* a vehicle in which all four wheels have engine power transmitted to them for better traction; also **four-wheel drive.**

fowl *n.* **1** a bird, esp. a large domestic bird such as a chicken, duck, goose, or turkey: *the fowls of the air and the fishes of the sea.* **2** the flesh of a bird used as food: *meat and fowl; fowl and game; neither fish nor fowl.* —*v.* hunt or catch wild fowl. —**fowl.er** *n.*

fowling piece (or **gun**) *n.* a lightweight shotgun.

fox *n.* **1** a small, wild, flesh-eating, bushy-tailed canine animal, usu. considered crafty and sly: *A fox yelps; a fox's cub* or *pup; a female fox* (= vixen).

2 a crafty or sly person: *a wise old fox.* —*v.* to trick by craftiness.
foxed *adj.* discoloured or stained.
fox.glove (FOX.gluv) *n.* a plant with bell-shaped flowers growing in long clusters that yield the drug digitalis.
fox.hole *n.* a hole dug as a shelter against gunfire for one or two soldiers.
fox.hound *n.* a breed of keen-scented hounds used in fox-hunting.
fox terrier *n.* a smooth-coated or wire-haired kind of small, lively, black-and-white pet dog formerly used to drive out foxes from hiding.
fox trot *n.* **1** a gait, as of a horse, that seems to combine a trot and a pace. **2** a ballroom dance in 4/4 time combining short rapid steps with slow ones. —*v.* **fox-trot, -trots, -trot.ted, -trot.ting.**
fox.y *adj.* **fox.i.er, -i.est** like a fox: *a foxy (= wily) old trader; the foxy (= soured or grapey) flavor of certain wines; foxy (= rotting) ice; a foxy (Slang for sexually attractive) woman.*
foy.er (FOY.ur, FOY.ay) *n.* an entrance hall or lobby, esp. one used as a lounge: *in the foyer of an apartment building, hotel, theater.*
fra.cas (FRAY.cus) *n.* a noisy fight or brawl.
frac.tal (FRAC.tul) *adj.* having to do with fractional dimensions, as of curves and surfaces: *fractal geometry; n.: Fractals are patterns that repeat themselves in smaller and smaller scales.*
frac.tion (FRAK.shun) *n.* **1** a broken part of a whole, esp. a fragment or insignificant portion: *Our candidate got only a fraction of the vote.* **2** in math, a quantity expressed with a numerator and denominator: *A common fraction such as 2/5 can be changed to the decimal fraction 0.4.* —**frac.tion.al** (-nul) *adj.*: *fractional currency such as dimes, nickels, and quarters.*
frac.tious (FRAK.shus) *adj.* rebellious; also, irritable or peevish: *a fractious coalition, community, group, spirit; fractious negotiations.*
frac.ture (FRAK.chur) *n.* a breaking, esp. a break or crack in a bone, rock, gem, etc.: *Fractures heal, knit; compound, greenstick, hairline, simple fractures; Physicians set fractures (= broken bones).* —*v.* **frac.tures, frac.tured, frac.tur.ing** break: *Bones fracture in various ways.*
frag.ile (FRAJ.ul, -ile) *adj.* easy to break or destroy: *a fragile toy, truce; in a fragile condition; a fragile environment;*

fragile happiness, health. —**fra.gil.i.ty** (fruh.JIL.i.tee) *n.*
frag.ment (FRAG.munt) *n.* a broken-off part; also, an incomplete part, as of a conversation, or an unfinished work, as Coleridge's poem "Kubla Khan." —*v.* (also -ment) break up or split up: *Is our society fragmenting as it gets more and more diversified?* **adj.**: *We face the prospect of fragmented families; a fragmented narrative (that lacks unity); a decentralized, fragmented organization, fragmented into small groups; a fragmented industry, market, society.* —**frag.men.tar.y** (-mun.tair.ee) *adj.* —**frag.men.ta.tion** (-mun.TAY.shun) *n.*
fra.grant (FRAY.grunt) *adj.* pleasant-smelling: *a fragrant air, flower, garden.* —**fra.grance** *n.*
frail *adj.* weak or delicate: *a man in frail health; a frail beauty, constitution, flower, smile, voice; frail excuses, hands, happiness, hopes, humanity.*
frail.ty *n.* **-ties** weakness or fault, esp. moral: *human frailty.*
frame *n.* **1** a structure, esp. a basic or skeletal system that gives something its shape or form: *a man of slender frame; the wooden frame of a frame house.* **2** the borders of a picture or of a pair of glasses: *Bright weather puts her in a cheerful frame of mind (= mood).* **3** something having a frame, as an individual picture on a strip of motion-picture film, one of the series of question-and-answer steps into which a topic is divided in programmed instruction, one of the 10 sequences in which scores are recorded at bowling, etc.: *a time frame of six months.*
—*v.* **frames, framed, fram.ing** **1** enclose in a border: *He stood there framed in the doorway; the constitution as originally framed (= put in shape) by our founding fathers.* **2** *Informal.* implicate fraudulently: *She was framed by agents who had planted the drugs in her room.* —**fram.er** *n.*
frame of reference *n.* a set of axes or coordinates: *a graph drawn with a time-temperature frame of reference; a judgment made without a clear frame of reference (= set of standards).*
frame-up *n. Informal.* fraudulent implication of an innocent person in a crime.
frame.work *n.* **1** structure: *an ancient ship with a wooden framework.* **2** set of standards: *free elections within the framework of a democratic society.*
franc *n.* the basic money unit of France,

Belgium, Switzerland, and about 20 other European and African countries.

fran.chise (FRAN.chize) *n.* **1** the right granted by a government to vote: *to exercise one's franchise; a universal franchise based on an equal vote for all.* **2** the right granted by a government or company to market a product or operate a service: *We have or hold a fried-chicken franchise;* **fran.chis.ee** (-chye.ZEE) *n.*

fran.chi.sor or **fran.chis.er** (FRAN.chye.sur) *n.* the grantor of a franchise.

Fran.cis.can (fran.SIS.cun) *adj.* having to do with a religious order founded by St. Francis of Assisi in the 13th century: *the Franciscan order; a Franciscan community, friar, nun.* Also *n.*

fran.ci.um (FRAN.see.um) *n.* a radioactive, metallic chemical element.

Franco- *comb.form.* French: *Franco-American, Franco-Canadian, Francophile.*

Fran.co.phone or **fran.co.phone** (FRANK.uh.fone) *n.* a French-speaking person in a multilingual society: *Canadian Francophones and Anglophones;* **adj.**: *the Francophone nations of Africa.*

fran.gi.ble (FRAN.juh.bul) *adj.* liable to break; **fran.gi.bil.i.ty** (-BIL.i.tee) *n.*

Frang.lais or **trang.lais** (frang.GLAY) *n. & adj.* French mixed with English, as "le cash, les girls."

frank *adj.* freely expressing what one feels or thinks: *a frank confession, exchange of views; I'll be frank with you; brutally frank; She's frank but fair.*
—v. send or mark mail for postage-free transmission, as by using an authorized sign instead of stamps; **adj.**: *a franked self-addressed envelope; franked or metered mail;* **n.**: *a franking machine.* **—n. 1** the franking privilege of members of Congress and certain U.S. officials. **2** a mark put on mail to indicate this. **3** *Informal.* a frankfurter. **4 Frank** a member of the group of Germanic tribes that established the **Frankish** empire which later broke up into France, Italy, and Germany.

Frank.en.stein (FRANK.un.stine) *n.* a monster that endangers its own creator.

frank.fur.ter (FRANK.fur.tur) *n.* a smoked sausage of beef or pork.

frank.in.cense (FRANK.in.sense) *n.* a gum resin of certain trees of Africa and Asia, burned as an incense.

fran.tic *adj.* wildly excited; frenzied: *a frantic rush to catch the bus; a frantic search for the wallet; It would drive anyone frantic* (= crazy). **—fran.ti.cal.ly** *adv.*

frap.pé (fra.PAY) *n.* a partly frozen drink or a dessert similar to sherbet.
—adj. partly frozen or chilled.

frappe (FRAP) *n.* a thick milkshake; rarely, a frappé.

frat *n. Informal.* a fraternity.

fra.ter.nal (fruh.TUR.nul) *adj.* **1** brotherly: *fraternal duty, love, relationships; fraternal societies* (of Elks, Foresters, Knights of Columbus, etc.). **2** developed from different egg cells, whether male or female: *fraternal quadruplets, twins;* cf. IDENTICAL. **—fra.ter.nal.ly** *adv.*

fra.ter.ni.ty (fruh.TUR.ni.tee) *n.* **-ties 1** brotherliness: *a feeling of fraternity; equality and fraternity; a fraternity* (= brotherly commonness) *of interests.* **2** a group of people of the same profession or interests: *the medical fraternity* (= physicians); *a Greek-letter fraternity* (of male students); *a fraternity pin or badge.*

frat.er.nize (FRAT.ur.nize) *v.* **-niz.es, -nized, -niz.ing** associate in a friendly manner: *Neighbors fraternize with one another.* **—fra.ter.ni.za.tion** (-nuh.ZAY.shun, -nye-) *n.*

frat.ri.cide (FRAT.ruh.cide) *n.* **1** one who kills a brother or sister. **2** such an act. **—frat.ri.ci.dal** (-SYE.dul) *adj.*

Frau (*rhyme:* how) *n., pl.* **Frau.en** (FROW.un) German for "Mrs."; also, a wife.

fraud *n.* a trick, trickster, or trickery: *The charity was a fraud* (= trick for exploiting people); *found guilty of fraud* (= trickery); *consumer fraud* (for tricking consumers); *vote fraud; welfare fraud* (for tricking the government of welfare money); *to commit, expose, perpetrate a fraud; a pious fraud* (= deception for religious purposes); *Is Flo a fraud* (= trickster) *or a genuine scholar?*

fraud.u.lent (FRAW.juh.lunt) *adj.* dishonest or deceptive: *a fraudulent claim, deal, scheme; fraudulent practices;* **fraud.u.lent.ly** *adv.* **—fraud.u.lence** (-lunce) *n.*

fraught (FRAUT) **1** *adjp.* loaded with something bad: *a scheme fraught with peril; an undertaking fraught with danger.* **2** *adj.* very tense; also, worrisome: *a controversy that is passionate and fraught; a fraught atmosphere, issue, situation.*

Fräu.lein (FROY.line) *n.* **1** German for "Miss." **2** an unmarried young woman.

fray *n.* a noisy quarrel or dispute: *to enter, get into, join the fray; to remain above the fray.* **—v.** wear through or become worn by rubbing: *Deer fray* their antlers against trees to rub off dry skin; *adj.*: *a frayed cable, cuff, leash; frayed* (= worn out or strained) *nerves, relations, tempers.*

fraz.zle (FRAZ.ul) *v.* **fraz.zles, fraz.zled, fraz.zling** make or become exhausted or frayed; *adj.*: *frazzled nerves after a frazzling birthday bash; frazzled businessmen, executives, motorists, parents, teachers.* —*n.* an exhausted condition: *worn to a frazzle.*

freak (FREEK) *n.* **1** a person or thing that is unusual, unexpected, odd, or queer: *a double-headed freak of nature; saved from ruin by a freak of fortune; adj.a.: a freak accident; the freak appeal of certain songs; A freak snowstorm hit us in July.* **2** *Slang.* a user of an illicit drug; hence, an addict or devotee, as of a cult: *an acid freak; baseball, eco, film, fitness, Jesus freaks.* —*v.* **freak** or **freak out** *Slang.* have or cause an extreme mental reaction: *When I told her to forget about it, It really freaked her out; to freak out on drugs; to freak out of* (= withdraw from) *society.*

freak-out *n. Slang.* the act of freaking out or one who has freaked out.

freck.le (FRECK.ul) *n.* a small, brownish spot on the skin.
—*v.* **-les, -led, -ling** mark or become marked with freckles: *The sun freckles the skin; The tendency to freckle diminishes as you grow older.* —**freck.led** *adj.*: *a freckled face, forehead, nose.*

free *adj.* **free.er, free.est** not bound or hampered: *All are born free and equal, but not free from care; free of debt; a prisoner free on parole; We enjoy free speech in a democracy; Feel free to browse around; He was fired for being too free with* (= for freely using) *company funds; to be free with advice* (= to give unasked-for advice); *I've two free* (= gratis) *tickets to the show; You can have it **for free*** (= without charge); *her engaging **free and easy*** (= relaxed and uninhibited) *manner; to give **free rein** to one's thoughts.* —**free on board** or **f.o.b.** placed without charge on board customer's vehicle: *goods free on board* (at) *our warehouse.* —*cpd.*: *lead-free gas; salt-free diet; sugar-free gum.*
—*adv.* without restraints: *Dogs should not run free in a people's park; Who sets or turns them free? Children are admitted free* (= without charge). See also FREELY. —*v.* **frees, freed, free.ing** make free: *to free people from slavery; to free a room of dust; to free up teachers for more teaching duties.*

free.base *v.* **-bas.es, -based, -bas.ing** *Slang.* purify cocaine chemically.

free.bie or **free.bee** *n. Informal.* something given free, as complimentary tickets.

free.boot.er (FREE.boo.tur) *n.* a plunderer.

free.born *adj.* not born in slavery.

freed.man *n.* **-men** one freed from slavery.

free.dom (FREE.dum) *n.* the state, right, or privilege of being free: *Do we enjoy the freedom to do what we like? to abridge, curtail, gain, secure, win freedom; academic, personal, political, religious freedom; a charter of rights and freedoms guaranteeing freedom of conscience and religion, freedom of thought and expression, freedom of assembly, and freedom of association; Children have **the freedom of*** (= privilege of moving about without restrictions in) *the house; Florence Nightingale was admitted to the Order of Merit and granted the Freedom of the City of London.*

free enterprise *n.* the capitalist economic system with a minimum of government control.

free fall *n.* a fall as if under the force of gravity alone: *The economy is in a free fall.*

free flight *n.* the flight of a rocket after its fuel is burned up.

free-for-all *n.* a contest in which anyone may take part, usu. with no rules; hence, a brawl.

free.hand *adj.* done without mechanical aids: *a freehand design, drawing, sketch; adv.*: *a picture drawn freehand.*

free.hold *n. & adj.* (an estate) held with some degree of ownership, not as a leasehold; **free.hold.er** *n.*

free lance *n.* one who is not committed to any one employer; also **free-lancer**.
—**free-lance** *adj.a.*: *a free-lance artist, editor, journalist.* —*v.* **-lanc.es, -lanced, -lanc.ing** work as a free lance: *Since resigning, she has been free-lancing as a consultant.*

free.load *v. Informal.* get things or make a living at another's expense; sponge.

free love *n.* sexual love without marriage or other social restrictions.

free lunch *n.* something with no hidden obligation or liability attached: *There's no such thing as a free lunch.*

free.ly *adv.* in a free manner: *People can roam freely through our malls; They can mingle freely with the crowds and spend freely in the shops; They speak freely and openly about restrictions; They pay freely agreed prices; He freely* (= without being forced) *admitted his guilt; leaflets freely*

available (= available free) *to anyone who asks.*
free.man (FREE.mun) *n.* **-men** one who is not a slave or serf; citizen.
free market *n.* an economy in which there is free competition; *adja.: a free-market approach, enterprise, society; free-market capitalism, forces, prices.*
Free.ma.son (FREE.may.sun) *n.* a member of the fraternal society, originally of the building trades, but now open to all professing belief in one God; **Free.ma.son.ry** *n.*
free port *n.* a port without import and export duties.
free-standing *adj.* **1** not having external supports: *The world's tallest free-standing structure is a tower; free-standing walls; a free-standing bookcase.* **2** independent; not attached: *a free-standing clinic (not attached to a hospital); a free-standing restaurant (that is not part of a hotel).*
free.stone *n.* a peach, cherry, or other such fruit whose pit does not cling to its flesh.
free.style *n.* swimming or figure skating with no specified style.
free.think.er (FREE.THINK.ur) *n.* a rationalist who shuns established religious beliefs based on the authority of a church or bible; **free.think.ing** *adj.*
free trade *n.* trade between nations without the restrictions of customs, duties, protective tariffs, etc.
free university *n.* a student-run university devoted to subjects of the students' own choice and without grades, credits, and such restrictions.
free verse *n.* verse without the structure imposed by a meter or rhyme.
free.ware *n.* computer software that is distributed without charge; *adja.: a freeware font, game, product, program.*
free.way *n.* **1** a main highway allowing free flow of traffic with fully controlled accesses and grade-separated interchanges. **2** a toll-free highway.
free.wheel.ing (free.WHEEL.ing) *adj.* moving along unrestrained or uninhibited: *a freewheeling discussion.*
free will *n.* the power of free choice, esp. in regard to one's salvation: *We are responsible for what we do* **of our own free will.** **—free-will** *adja.* voluntary: *a free-will offering.*
free world *n.* the countries outside totalitarian rule.
freeze *v.* **freez.es, froze, froz.en, freez.ing** harden or solidify with cold: *It's freezing (weather) all winter; It froze last night; The homeless may freeze to death; A bridge freezes (= ices) fast because of its exposure; The runner froze* (= stopped) *in his tracks when the police shouted "Freeze!" Dentists freeze the jaw (using an anesthetic) before pulling a tooth; to freeze* (= stop raises of) *prices, rents, wages; Lakes freeze over during a wintry night; You can argue until* **hell freezes over** (Informal for forever); *We'll believe you* **when hell freezes over** (Informal for We'll never believe you); *Water freezes at 0°C or 32°F, the* **freezing point** *of water.* **—***n.* a freezing or frozen condition: *The last ships to leave the canal were caught in the freeze; We were in a deep freeze all January; to impose a freeze* (= stopping of raises) *on prices and wages to halt inflation.*
freeze-dry *v.* **-dries, -dried, -dry.ing** dehydrate by freezing and evaporating; *adj.: freeze-dried coffee, foods, medicines.*
freeze-frame *n.* a still frame of a motion picture when stopped: *the freeze-frame button of a VCR.*
freez.er *n.* a chest or room in which perishable foods are preserved frozen: *A* **freezer wrap** *is used for keeping foods wrapped in the freezer.*
freeze-up *n.* the freezing up of water and soil in early winter or its duration.
freezing mixture *n.* a mixture of salt and crushed ice used for producing below-zero temperatures.
free zone *n.* an area around a free port.
freight (FRATE) *n.* **1** goods carried by water, land, or air transportation or the charge for it; *adja.: a freight car, forwarder, train.* **2** payment for such transportation; freightage. **3** charge or fees: *Most students pay the full freight without any financial aid.* **4** a freight train made up of freight cars: *He jumped a freight for San Francisco.* **—***v.* send by or load with freight: *merchandise freighted by air or air-freighted to Europe; a drama plot freighted with a subplot.* **—freight.age** (-ij) *n.*
freight.er *n.* a ship or plane carrying freight.
French *n.* **1** the language of France, Quebec, etc.: *Acadian, Canadian, Louisiana, Parisian French.* **2** **the French** the people who speak French, esp. the people of or from France.
—*adj.* having to do with France and other French-speaking countries and regions: *The French Academy; French colonial (architecture); French cuisine; The* **French and Indian War** *(1754-1763); the French Quarter (of New Orleans); the French Revolution.*
—French.man (-mun) *n.* **-men;**

French.wom.an *n.* -wom.en.
French door *n.* a door that opens in the middle and has glass panes from top to bottom.
French dressing *n.* a salad dressing of oil, vinegar, and seasonings.
French fries *n.pl.* deep-fried strips of potato. —**French-fry** *v.* **-fries, -fried, -fry.ing** fry potatoes, shrimps, onion rings, etc. in deep fat; also **french-fry.**
French horn *n.* a brass wind instrument with a coiled tube that flares out as a wide bell.
French kiss *n.* an open-mouth kiss involving the tongues of the partners.
French leave *n.* a departure made secretly or in a hurry.
French toast *n.* a slice of bread dipped in an egg-and-milk mixture and sautéed.
fre.net.ic (fri.NET.ic) *adj.* frenzied: *working at a frenetic pace; our frenetic city life; The search became desperate and frenetic.* —**fre.net.i.cal.ly** *adv.*
fren.zied (FREN.zeed) *adj.* full of frenzy: *He shook his fists in a frenzied rage; a frenzied battle, crowd, lifestyle, manner, pace; frenzied trading on the stock market.*
fren.zy (FREN.zee) *n.* **-zies** emotional agitation tending to violent activity: *in a wild frenzy; a frenzy of despair.*
fre.on (FREE.on) *n.* a commercially produced fluorocarbon fluid, used as a refrigerant, solvent, etc.; **Freon** *Trademark.*
fre.quen.cy (FREEK.wun.see) *n.* **-cies** the number of times that cycles, oscillations, or other repeated things or events are found in a given period or sample: *Our electric current has a frequency of 60 cycles per second; "The" has the highest frequency among English words; Accidents happen with alarming frequency during holiday weekends; Each radio station is on a different frequency (of radio waves); radio transmission by* **frequency modulation** *instead of amplitude modulation.*
fre.quent (FREEK.wunt) *adj.* occurring often: *a frequent visitor to the zoo.* —*v.* (free.KWENT) go to habitually: *a restaurant frequented by students* —**fre.quent.ly** *adv.*
fres.co (FRES.coh) *n.* **-cos** or **-coes** water-color painting on fresh plaster, as done on church ceilings. —*v.* **-cos** or **-coes, -coed, -co.ing:** *"The Creation of Adam" was frescoed by Michelangelo.*
fresh 1 *adj.* pure, not stale, used, preserved, etc.: *fresh as a daisy; a breath of fresh air; fresh clothes, flowers, fruit, milk, snow; I feel quite fresh after a shower;*

Fresh meat is not salted, canned, or frozen; fresh (= not salty) *water.* 2 *adja.* new and different: *to make a fresh start in life after failures; fresh evidence, fabrics, ideas, merchandise, vigor; a fresh approach, attack, danger, look, shock; fresh problems; a fresh* (= clear or healthy) *complexion; fresh* (= newly applied) *paint; fresh* (= relatively strong) *winds; a* **fresh breeze** *blowing at 29-39 km/h (18-24 mph).* 3 *adjp.* new and recent: *a tragedy still fresh in our minds; He's rather fresh on the job; fresh from a position as secretary;* **adv.***: She was fresh* (= recently) *out of school when she married; Don't* **get fresh** (*Informal for* bold *or* impudent) *with me!* **cpd:** *fresh-baked bread; a fresh-faced youth; a fresh-looking fashion; fresh-squeezed juice; oven-fresh cookies.*
—**fresh.ly** *adv.*: *freshly baked, cooked, ground, laundered, washed, waxed;*
fresh.ness *n.*
fresh.en (FRESH.un) *v.* make fresh: *a cream to freshen your complexion; Use the powder room to* **freshen up** *before dinner.* —**fresh.en.er** *n.*: *an air freshener; skin fresheners.*
fresh.et (FRESH.it) *n.* a rush of fresh water, as from a thaw or heavy rain.
fresh.man (FRESH.mun) *n.* **-men** a beginner, esp. a first-year student; **adja.***: freshman composition, English; a freshman congressman, M.P., senator.*
fresh.wa.ter (FRESH.waw.tur) *adja.* 1 having to do with lakes and streams, not salt water: *a freshwater fish, lake, spring, stream.* 2 inexperienced: *a freshwater sailor.* 3 out-of-the-way or obscure: *a freshwater college.*
fret *v.* **frets, fret.ted, fret.ting** 1 worry or be vexed: *He tends to fret and fume about or over trifles; a child fretting against parental control.* 2 eat away or corrode: *river banks fretted by the force of water.* —*n.* 1 *Informal.* state of agitation or irritation: *to get in a fret when something goes wrong.* 2 erosion. 3 one of the ridges as guides for fingering across the fingerboard of a guitar, banjo, etc. 4 a right-angled ornamental design or pattern, seen carved or in relief as **fretwork; adj.***: a fretted vault.* —**fret.ful** *adj.*; **fret.ful.ly** *adv.*
fret.saw *n.* a saw with a long and narrow blade for cutting curved outlines.
Freud.i.an (FROY.dee.un) *adj.* having to do with Sigmund **Freud**, the founder of psychoanalysis: *A* **Freudian slip** *is supposed to reveal something in the unconscious mind.*
fri.a.ble (FRY.uh.bul) *adj.* crumbly, as dry soil.

fri.ar (FRY.ur) *n.* a member of a mendicant Roman Catholic order of monks, as a Carmelite or Franciscan.

fri.ar.y (FRY.uh.ree) *n.* **-ar.ies** a monastery of friars.

fric.as.see (FRIC.uh.see, -uh.SEE) *n.* a dish of meat, esp. chicken, cut into pieces, stewed, and served with a thick gravy. —*v.* **-as.sees, -as.seed, -as.see.ing;** *adj.:* Will you have *fricasseed* chicken or veal?

fric.tion (FRIK.shun) *n.* **1** resistance from the rubbing of one thing against another: *Oil is used to reduce friction between moving metal parts.* **2** disagreement or unpleasantness: *to create friction between employees and management; office frictions due to personality differences; family frictions.*

Fri.day (FRY.dee, -day) *n.* **1** the sixth day of the week and the last of the customary workweek: *Thank God it's Friday!* **2** a faithful helper with a variety of duties: *my man Friday; girl Fridays; A clerk Friday wanted.*

fridge *n.* [short form] refrigerator.

fried *pt. & pp.* of FRY.

fried.cake *n.* a donut or cruller.

friend (FREND) *n.* **1** one who likes, has common interests with, and desires another's good without being related: *my good friend Flo; a close personal friend, but not a boyfriend or girlfriend; bosom, fair-weather, faithful, false, fast, intimate, life-long, loyal, mutual, special, staunch friends; a friend in need; the art of making and keeping friends; a friend of the poor;* a **friend of the court** (= advisor); *Who goes there, friend or foe? our friend* (= the person or stranger) *over there;* **man's best friend** (= dog). **2 friends:** *I'm friends* (= on friendly terms) *with Ray; He's trying to make friends with* (= be a friend of) *everyone; Al and Lu just made friends* (= made up) *after a good fight.* **3 Friend** a Quaker: *the Society of Friends.*

friend.ly (FREND.lee) *adj.* **-li.er, -li.est** of or like a friend: *friendly advice, arguments, disputes, dogs, games, greetings, smiles; a friendly manner, spirit, welcome; to be friendly to or toward or with someone; Soldiers on the battlefield are sometimes hit by friendly fire (from friends who mistake them for the enemy).* —**comb.form.** friendly or helpful as specified: *eco-friendly products; ozone-friendly aerosols; recession-friendly prices; user-friendly software.* —**friend.li.ness** *n.*

friend.ship *n.* the condition of being friends or an instance of it: *to break up, cement, cherish, cultivate, destroy, develop, promote, strike up a friendship; a firm, lifelong, strong, warm friendship between two people; the bonds of friendship among school chums; a long friendship; friendships that last.*

frier same as FRYER.

frieze (FREEZ) *n.* a decorative horizontal band, as the one containing carved figures on a classical building above the columns or one of wallpaper or similar design around the walls of a room below the ceiling.

frig.ate (FRIG.ut) *n.* a warship of 2,000 metric tons or more, formerly smaller, now sometimes larger than a destroyer.

frig.ging *adj. & adv.* [vulgar slang] damned.

fright (FRITE) *n.* fear, esp. when sudden and passing: *Your Halloween costume gave me quite a fright; Her hat was a real fright* (Informal for fearsome thing).

fright.en (FRY.tun) *v.* cause to feel sudden fear or become afraid: *a child frightened into submission; Her screams frightened off the attacker;* **adj.:** the *frightening* experience of being kidnapped; **adv.:** the *frighteningly* high numbers of highway deaths.

fright.ful *adj.* **1** terrible: *a frightful tragedy; frightful howls.* **2** *Informal* [intensifier]: *What a frightful snob! He left in a frightful hurry.*

fright.ful.ly (FRITE.fuh.lee) *adv.* **1** alarmingly: *driving frightfully fast.* **2** *Informal.* very: *I'm frightfully sorry.*

frig.id (FRIJ.id) *adj.* **1** extremely cold, as in the **Frigid Zone**, either of the two regions within the Arctic and Antarctic circles: *frigid air, temperatures, water, weather, winds.* **2** cold or aloof in manner: *He received a frigid reception; frigid relations between spouses.* —**frig.id.ly** *adv.* —**fri.gid.i.ty** (fri.JID.i.tee) *n.*

frill *n.* **1** a ruffle or similar edging or trimming: *frills and furbelows; frills, lace, and other finery.* **2** something serving as an ornament: *rebates, gifts, and other frills to attract shoppers: Some consider out-of-school trips educational frills; education without frills.* —**frill.y** *adj.*

fringe (FRINJ) *n.* **1** a border ornament or trimming of loose threads or cords, as on a shawl or rug, often tied in bunches: *a clipped fringe of hair over the forehead.* **2** the outer edge or limit: *criminals, drug pushers, thieves, and others on the fringes of society; the poor TV reception experienced in* **fringe areas** (= outer areas); *We provide pension, health insurance, and such* **fringe benefits**

frippery / front-end loader

to employees. —v. **fring.es, fringed, fring.ing** border: *trees fringing a lawn; The lawn was fringed by* or *with trees;* **adj.**: *a fringed rug; Some flowers have fringed petals* (= petals with borders); **adja.**: *a fringing coral reef growing outward from the shoreline.*

frip.per.y (FRIP.uh.ree) *n.* **frip.per.ies** 1 cheap finery. 2 affected elegance: *the fripperies of speech and behavior.*

fris.bee *n.* a saucer-shaped plastic disk for tossing back and forth in games; **Fris.bee** *Trademark.*

frisk *v.* 1 move in a lively, playful manner: *lambs frisking about in the sun.* 2 search a person for concealed weapons or goods, as police do after an arrest.

frisk.y *adj.* **frisk.i.er, -i.est** lively or playful: *a frisky little pup.* —**frisk.i.ly** *adv.;* **frisk.i.ness** *n.*

frit.ter (FRIT.ur) *n.* a small cake of fried batter containing corn, sliced fruit, fish, or other filling. —*v.* waste little by little: *to fritter away one's time and energies on* or *in useless pursuits.*

fritz *n.* usu. **on the fritz** *Slang.* out of order; on the blink: *a TV that goes on the fritz now and then.*

friv.o.lous (FRIV.uh.lus) *adj.* 1 trivial: *to waste money on frivolous baubles.* 2 lightminded or giddy: *frivolous behavior; a frivolous remark.* —**friv.o.lous.ly** *adv.* —**fri.vol.i.ty** (fri.VOL.i.tee) *n.*

friz or **frizz** *v.* form hair into tight little curls. —*n.* such hair.

friz.zle (FRIZ.ul) *v.* **friz.zles, friz.zled, friz.zling** 1 frizz or curl. 2 sizzle, fry, or broil.

friz.zly (FRIZ.lee) or **friz.zy** (FRIZ.ee) *adj.* curly: *frizzly hair.*

fro (FROH) *adv.* **to and fro** to somewhere and back; back and forth.

frock *n.* 1 formerly, an outer garment or robe worn by friars and monks; also, a man's double-breasted **frock-coat.** 2 a woman's or child's dress.

frog *n.* 1 a small, tailless, amphibious jumping animal with long hind legs and webbed feet: *the croaking of frogs.* 2 *Informal.* hoarseness; also **frog in the throat.**

frog.man *n.* **-men** a diver equipped with air supply, face mask, and flippers for long periods of exploration or demolition work under water.

frol.ic (FROL.ic) *n.* play or fun, esp. of a light-hearted, carefree nature: *fun and frolic on the beach.* —*v.* **-ics, -icked, -ick.ing** make merry; gambol about: *children frolicking in the snow.*

—**frol.ick.er** *n.* —**frol.ic.some** (-sum) *adj.*

from (FRUM, FROM) *prep.* 1 [indicating a starting point or source]: *It's 10 km from home to school; I know him from way back in the old country; It's a great idea from my point of view; cars priced from $20,000 to $30,000; Tell her from me she's wrong; A picture painted from life has to look lifelike.* 2 [indicating a cause or motive]: *shivering from the cold; It sounds fine from what I was told; speaking from envy.* 3 [indicating a difference or distinction]: *Humans are different from animals; Can you tell a frog from a toad?*

frond *n.* 1 a large leaf: *banana, fern, palm fronds.* 2 a tender coiled shoot: *the fronds of the "fiddlehead" fern.*

front (FRUNT) *n.* 1 the forward or most important part or side: *The driver is seated in front; a shirt front covered by a tie; Top marks place you in front; a cold front moving in from the Arctic; a stationary front; a warm front; to park in front of a house; They pay you up front* (= in advance); *Service is front and center* (= foremost) *in our work.* 2 a scene of activity: *No news from the western front* (of battle); *the fighting going on at the front; trouble brewing on the labor front; a war waged on many fronts.* 3 land or a road facing a body of water: *a villa on the lake front; river front; sea front.* 4 a face or cover: *His geniality is a mere front; He put on a bold, brazen front; a travel business used as a front* (= facade) *for a spy operation.* —**adja.** forward; fighting in or on the front lines; *a front seat; the front end and rear end of a car; The most important news makes the front page.* —*v.* 1 face: *The cottage fronts on a lake; windows fronting the street.* 2 pay as front money or capital; finance: *An investor fronts the money to start a venture; a fronting company.*

front.age (FRUNT.ij) *n.* 1 (extent of) land between a building and a street, river, or lake that it faces: *the frontage* (= width) *and depth of a building lot.* 2 a building's exposure: *a church with a southern frontage.*

front.al (FRUN.tul) *adj.* having to do with the front: *a direct, frontal assault, attack; the frontal lobe of the brain.*

front burner *n.* usu. **on the front burner,** in a position of priority; cf. BACK BURNER.

front-end *adja.* having to do with the front: *front-end activity, alignment, charges, fees; the front-end costs of buying a home.*

front-end loader *n.* a tracked construction vehicle with a scoop in front for picking up earth, fodder, etc.

fron.tier (frun.TEER) *n.* **1** the border between two countries: *a shooting incident on the Sino-Russian frontier.* **2** a region whose borders are being extended into newly explored territory: *the new frontiers opened up by space exploration; to advance, cross, extend a frontier; the frontiers of medicine; Outer space has been called the final frontier;* **adja.**: *in the frontier days when the pioneers were moving West; a frontier town, village; frontier (= rough) justice, life, values.*

fron.tiers.man (frun.TEERS.mun) *n.* **-men** a man living on the frontier.

front.line *n.* the front of a battleline: *to fight on the frontlines.*

front matter *n.* in a book, what precedes the text, as the title page, contents page, preface, etc.

front money *n.* *Informal.* advance payment for a product or service, as on signing a contract.

front office *n.* headquarters; hence, administrative authority.

front-runner *n.* the leading contender.

frost *n.* a freezing, the state of being frozen, or frozen dew, vapor, or hoarfrost: *There's a touch of frost in the air; a hint of frost; outdoor work to be finished before the first frost; the severe frost of January.* —*v.* cover with or like frost: *to frost a cake (with icing);* **adj.**: *a frosted car window* (covered with frost); *frosted* (= nontransparent) *glass for bathroom windows, electric bulbs, etc.; crunchy frosted flakes* (covered with sugar); *a frosted cake* (covered with icing).

frost.bite *n.* injury to skin and body tissue from exposure to cold.

frost.bit.ten (FROST.bit.un) *adj.* injured by frost: *to get frostbitten; a frostbitten foot; frostbitten skin.*

frost heave *n.* heaving of the ground caused by moisture freezing underneath.

frosting *n.* **1** icing: *chocolate frosting; to prepare a frosting mix.* **2** *Informal.* an extra bonus: *The bonus payment was the frosting on the cake.*

frost.y *adj.* **frost.i.er, -i.est 1** freezing or covered with frost. **2** cold or unfriendly: *a frosty reception, stare, welcome.*

froth *n.* foam, esp. as scum; hence, something worthless: *a discussion that was all froth and no substance.*
—*v.* produce froth: *an overworked horse frothing at the mouth; Dad will froth* (= will be angry) *when he hears this; how to froth* (= make froth in) *milk for making espresso;* **adj.**: *frothed coffee, cream,*

milk, soup; **adja.**: *a frothing attachment, device, pitcher;* **adv.**: *Mom is frothing mad.* —**froth.y** *adj.*: *Beat the egg whites until frothy* (= foamy); *a frothy dress, gown* (made of light material); *a frothy* (= silly) *adventure, discussion, narrative.*

frou.frou (FROO.froo) *n.* **1** rustling, as of a woman's skirts. **2** frilly trimming or ruffles that rustle or swish.

fro.ward (FROH.urd) *adj.* of people, difficult to manage; willful.
—**fro.ward.ness** *n.*

frown (rhyme: down) *v.* **1** wrinkle the forehead, as in disapproval; show displeasure: *It's no use frowning at your poor grades.* **2** disapprove of something: *Teachers frown on* or *upon latecomers.*
—*n.* a frowning expression or face.

frow.zy (FROW.zee, "OW" as in "how") *adj.* **-zi.er, -zi.est** untidy or unkempt; also **frow.sy.**

froze See FREEZE.

fro.zen (FROH.zun) *adj.* **1** hardened by cold: *Ice is water frozen solid; frozen hard in the cold; frozen food* (kept in a freezer); *a frozen lake, water main; the Frozen North* (= the Arctic). **2** made motionless, stiff, or fixed: *He stood there frozen with fear; Rents have been frozen* (= fixed) *for two years; All foreign assets were frozen* (= prohibited from being removed) *while the war was on.*

fruc.ti.fy (FRUC.tuh.fye) *v.* **-fies, -fied, -fy.ing** bear fruit; make productive: *plans that didn't fructify.*

fruc.tose *n.* fruit sugar, found combined with glucose (as sucrose) in sweet fruits and honey.

fru.gal (FROO.gul) *adj.* sparing, not wasteful; simple in regard to food, clothing, etc.: *a frugal diet, meal, people; frugal habits;* **fru.gal.ly** *adv.*
—**fru.gal.i.ty** (froo.GAL.i.tee) *n.*

fruit (FROOT) *n.* **1** the edible, often sweet, fleshy, and juicy part of a plant or tree, as apples, bananas, or grapes: *He grows fruits and vegetables in his front yard; Trees bear fruit; canned, dried, fresh, frozen, luscious fruit.* **2** any seed-bearing or useful plant product, as pea pods, cereal grains, green peppers, and such vegetables: *thanksgiving for the fruits of the earth.* **3** product or result: *the fruits of our labor; work that did not bear fruit.*
—**fruit.ful** *adj.;* **fruit.ful.ly** *adv.*
—**fruit.less** *adj.*: *fruitless efforts; a fruitless search; Our negotiations proved fruitless;* **fruit.less.ly** *adv.*

fruit.cake *n.* **1** a rich cake containing raisins, nuts, spices, etc. **2** *Informal.* an eccentric or insane person: *He's nutty as a fruitcake.*

fru.i.tion (froo.ISH.un) *n.* fulfillment or realization: *the fruition of our hopes; when our plans finally came to fruition; to bring them to fruition.*

fruit salad *n.* a mixture of fruit pieces served with cream and sugar.

fruit.y (FROO.tee) *adj.* **fruit.i.er, -i.est** rich or mellow in flavor, tone of voice, interest, etc.: *fruity aromas, flavors, fragrances, scents; a light fruity wine; a rich fruity taste; sweet and fruity.*

frump *n.* one who is shabby or dowdy, esp. a woman; also, this quality: *a dumpy frump; Frump is out, glamour is in.* —**frump.ish** or **frump.y** *adj.*: *a frumpy hat, image, maid; clothes that look frumpy.*

frus.trate (FRUS.trate) *v.* **-trates, -trat.ed, -trat.ing** make someone or something ineffective: *to frustrate aims, ambitions, aspirations, efforts, growth, strategies; adj.: She felt frustrated in her attempts to educate her child; It was frustrating for her to try to do it all by herself.* —**frus.tra.tion** (frus.TRAY.shun) *n.*: *a life of loneliness and frustration; It was no use venting his frustrations on his family; Some take to drinking to forget their frustrations.*

frus.tum *n.* **-tums** or **-ta** the base section of a pyramid or cone left after the top is cut off in a plane parallel to the base.

fry *v.* **fries, fried, fry.ing** cook in a pan or on a griddle, esp. using fat: *Please fry me two eggs; People are frying (= getting fried) in the summer heat; "We have other fish to fry"* (= other things to do); *"Out of the frying pan into the fire"* (= From something bad into something worse). —*n.* 1 usu. **fries,** *pl.* something fried: *a hamburger and (French) fries; home fries; stir-fries; a fry pan.* 2 an outdoor social gathering at which fried food is served: *a Saturday night fish fry.* 3 *sing. & pl.* little things, esp. young fish: *small fry.*

fry.er *n.* 1 a utensil for deep-frying. 2 a chicken suitable for frying, usu. larger than a broiler.

fuch.sia (FEW.shuh) *n.* 1 a plant bearing funnel-shaped red, white, or pink flowers that droop from long stalks. 2 the purplish red of its flowers.

fuck *v.* [vulgar slang] copulate with someone. —*n.* an act of copulation.

fud.dle *v.* **fud.dles, fud.dled, fud.dling** confuse or stupefy, as with drink.

fud.dy-dud.dy (FUD.ee.dud.ee) *n.* **-dud.dies** *Informal.* a fussy or old fashioned, usu. elderly person.

fudge (FUJ) *n.* 1 a rich, soft, often chocolate-flavored candy. 2 nonsense. —*v.* **fudg.es, fudged, fudg.ing** falsify or cheat: *to fudge on one's income tax return; to fudge* (= hedge) *on a promise; to fudge* (= dodge) *an issue.*

fu.el (FEW.ul) *n.* a substance such as coal, gasoline, ethane, or oil which, when burned, produces heat or power: *We ran out of fuel and were stranded on the highway; Uranium and hydrogen are atomic fuels liberating energy by fusion or fission; Fossil fuels will one day be exhausted; He only managed to add fuel to the fire* (= make the situation worse). —*v.* **fu.els, fu.eled, fu.el.ing** supply with or get fuel: *a plane fueling up before a flight.* Also **fu.elled, fu.el.ling** *Cdn.*

fuel cell *n.* a device, as used in spacecraft, for producing electricity from the chemical energy of the reaction of a fuel such as hydrogen with an oxidizer.

fu.gi.tive (FEW.juh.tiv) *n.* one who flees: *a fugitive from justice; Dogs were used to track down the fugitives.* —**adj.** fleeing: *fugitive convicts, drug-dealers, slaves.* —*adj.* fleeting: *He tried to finish the job during the fugitive hours of daylight; fugitive thoughts; Our dreams are fugitive.*

fugue (FYOOG) *n.* 1 a musical composition in the manner of a flight or chase interweaving several melodic strands or voices introduced in succession. 2 an amnesia patient's wandering away to a new place or life forgetting his real identity.

füh.rer or **fueh.rer** (FYOOR.ur) *n.* a fascist leader; the title of Adolf Hitler.

-ful *suffix.* 1 *n.* [*pl.* sometimes as "cups-ful"] amount for filling: *cupful, handful, spoonful.* 2 *adj.* full of, as specified: *sorrowful, soulful, tuneful.*

ful.crum ("ful-" as in "dull" or "full") *n.* **-crums** or **-cra** (-cruh) 1 the point of leverage or support, as of a crowbar. 2 the means of exerting pressure or influence.

ful.fill (full.FIL) *v.* **-fills, -filled, -fill.ing** perform, carry out, realize, etc. something that is expected or required: *to fulfill a duty, promise, prophecy; customers' orders to be fulfilled* (= filled); *She fulfilled herself as a physician after trying nursing and teaching; adj.: in search of a fulfilling* (= satisfying) *job.* Also **-fil, -fils, -fil.ing.** —**ful.fill.ment** or **ful.fil.ment** *n.*

full (short "oo") *adj.* complete in number, amount, extent, etc.; having everything needed to fill or satisfy: *The glass is full to the brim; It is full of water;*

"*Full speed ahead!*" *shouted the captain; I'll cooperate to the fullest extent; a full skirt that is generous with material; a garden in full bloom; a popular movie playing to full houses; an associate professor promoted to* **full professor***; a* **full-service** *gas station.* —*adv.: The ball hit her full* (= squarely) *in the face; Al knows full* (= quite) *well he is wrong.* —*n.: I was paid* **in full** (= all that had to be paid). —*v.* **fulls, fulled, full.ing 1** make full: *a dress fulled with wide folds.* **2** shrink and thicken wool and other cloths, as a **fuller** does. —**ful.ly** *adv.;* **full.ness** *n.*

full.back *n.* in football, an offensive back playing from a position directly behind the quarterback.

full-blooded *adj.* purebred; hence, vigorous or genuine: *full-blooded capitalism, patriotism, a full-blooded judicial inquiry.*

full-blown *adja.* fully grown or mature: *full-blown flowers; The roadside check could lead to a full-blown breath test at the police station; It was not a conference, but a full-blown convention; The nomination race was the start of a full-blown election campaign; The slowdown developed into a full-blown strike; a full-blown inquiry, personality, success.*

full-bodied *adj.* having much flavor or strength: *a rich, full-bodied, fruity wine; the brew's full-bodied taste; a glossy full-bodied production.*

full-course *adja.* **1** consisting of an appetizer or salad, main dish, dessert, and beverage: *a full-course dinner, lunch, meal.* **2** involving one complete lap of a racecourse: *a full-course caution flag, caution period.*

full-dress *adja.* observing all formalities: *a full-dress parliamentary debate; a full-dress rehearsal; a* **full-dress affair** *(requiring full formal costume).*

fuller's earth *n.* a bleaching clay used to shrink and thicken wool and other cloths.

full-fledged *adj.* fully developed: *a full-fledged acrobat, assault, campaign, democracy, enterprise, investigation, organization, project, recession, war.*

full-length *adj.* having regular length: *standing before a full-length mirror in a full-length dress; a full-length coat, movie, portrait.*

full moon *n.* the moon in its fully illuminated phase.

full-scale *adja.* not reduced in size; complete: *a full-scale model; a full-scale attack, investigation, operation, production, riot, war.*

full time *n.* the full working day, as from 9 to 5; *adv.: She works here full time;* *adja.: a* **full-time***, not part-time employee doing full-time work.*

ful.mar (FULL.mur) *n.* a sea bird of northern regions; petrel.

ful.mi.nate (FUL.muh.nate, "FUL-" as in "DULL") *v.* **-nates, -nat.ed, -nat.ing** thunder forth threats, denunciations, etc.: *the media fulminating against restrictions on freedom of the press.*
—**ful.mi.na.tion** (-NAY.shun) *n.*

ful.some (FULL.sum, short "oo") *adj.* excessive or insincere: *fulsome compliments, flattery, praise.*

fu.ma.role (FEW.muh.role) *n.* a volcanic vent or hole in the ground emitting steam, carbon dioxide, etc., as in Yellowstone National Park.

fum.ble *v.* **-bles, -bled, -bling 1** fail to catch a ball; hence, bungle: *to fumble with a ball; to fumble one's lines; to fumble a job, an issue, opportunity.* **2** grope clumsily: *He fumbled about in the dark for the key he dropped; Then fumbled with the lock* (= handled it clumsily in the dark); *a speaker fumbling for the right word.*

fume *n.* a choking or offensive gas, smoke, or vapor, as from an exhaust: *It's dangerous to inhale the fumes.*
—*v.* **fumes, fumed, fum.ing 1** treat: *Oak wood is fumed with ammonia gas for a darker color.* **2** be angry: *The boss is fuming about* or *at* or *over the slow mail delivery.*

fu.mi.gant (FEW.mi.gunt) *n.* a volatile chemical used in fumigating.

fu.mi.gate (FEW.mi.gate) *v.* **-gates, -gat.ed, -gat.ing** treat a room, tree, etc. with fumes to disinfect or kill pests.
—**fu.mi.ga.tor** (-gay.tur) *n.*
—**fu.mi.ga.tion** (-GAY.shun) *n.*

fum.y (FEW.mee) *adj.* **fum.i.er, -i.est** full of fumes; vaporous.

fun *n.* amusement or what provides amusement; sport: *Skating is fun; We had a lot of fun skating; It's not fun or funny to tease dumb animals; Children throw snowballs* **for fun** or **in fun;** *Guy likes to* **poke fun at** or **make fun of** *Cora's walk; The rain spoiled the fun; Life is not all* **fun and games.**
—*adj.* providing enjoyment: *We had a fun time at the party; It's more fun to watch this game than to play it.*

func.tion (FUNK.shun) *n.* **1** the kind of work that a person or thing is supposed to do: *The heart's function is to pump blood; a bodily function; the functions of a bank; the mathematical functions of a calculator; Each part has its* own *function to perform* or *fulfill.* **2** a formal occasion such as a wedding or an opening ceremony: *to attend a function; social functions.* **3** a variable quantity that is related to another: *A circle's radius is a function of its area.* —*v.* operate or perform: *The new computer is functioning well; We need someone to function as chairperson of the meeting.*

func.tion.al (FUNK.shuh.nul) *adj.* having to do with operation rather than structure or decoration: *functional architecture; We are fully functional* (= fully in operation); *A functional disorder has no organic causes for the organ's not working properly; A functional illiterate,* in spite of some schooling, is unable to perform minimally as a literate, such as filling out an application for a driver's license; *functional literacy* (= minimum standard of reading and writing).
—**func.tion.al.ly** *adv.*

func.tion.ar.y (FUNK.shuh.nair.ee) *n.* -**ar.ies** an official with routine duties.

function key *n.* a computer key with a specific function such as F3 for "help," as opposed to a key that types a letter or symbol.

function word *n.* a preposition, auxiliary verb, or conjunction that has little meaning of its own but has a grammatical function, as to connect subject and predicate in "She *is* good."

fund *n.* **1** a stock or supply, as of money: *Give to the Heart Fund; to establish* or *set up a fund; an entertaining speaker with a fund of anecdotes.* **2 funds** *pl.* money, esp. ready money: *We pay in U.S. funds; The check was returned because of insufficient funds (in the account); Welfare payments come out of public funds; to disburse, pay out, raise funds for a project; the funds required to get it going; Our funds dried up* or *ran out toward the end of the year; a hospital built out of private funds;* (*equal*) *matching funds offered by a government.*
—*v.* **1** provide funds for something: *Our library was funded by public donations; n.:* to obtain **funding** *for a project; adj.:* a federally **funded** *program.* **2** convert: *A short-term debt is funded into a long-term one at a fixed interest rate.*

fun.da.men.tal (fun.duh.MEN.tul) *adj.* essential or basic: *a citizen's fundamental rights and freedoms.* —*n.* a fundamental principle or fact: *the fundamentals of algebra.* —**fun.da.men.tal.ly** *adv.*

fun.da.men.tal.ism (fun.duh.MEN.tul.iz.um) *n.* belief in or the following of a literal interpretation of the rules of a religion. —**fun.da.men.tal.ist** *n. &*

functional / funnel

adj.

fu.ner.al (FEW.nur.ul) *n.* a ceremony honoring a dead person before cremation or burial: *to conduct* or *hold a funeral; family, military, state funerals;* **adj.:** *a funeral ceremony, cortege, oration, procession, pile* or *pyre; funeral rites; funeral director* (=undertaker or mortician). —**fu.ner.ar.y** *adj.: a funerary sculpture, tribute, urn.*

funeral home *n.* an establishment where the dead are embalmed and prepared for burial or cremation, often with a chapel for visiting mourners. Also **funeral parlor.**

fu.ner.ar.y (FEW.nuh.rair.ee) *adj.* having to do with a funeral: *a funerary sculpture, tribute, urn.*

fu.ne.re.al (few.NEER.ee.ul) *adj.* gloomy or dismal: *dressed in funereal black; wearing a funereal expression; a funereal stillness.*

fun.gal (FUNG.gul) *adj.* having to do with a fungus: *a fungal growth, infection, parasite;* also **fun.gous** (-gus).

fun.gi.ble (FUN.juh.bul) *adj.* generic in nature, hence exchangeable: *Money is fungible, but coins of sentimental value are not.*

fun.gi.cide (FUN.juh.cide) *n.* a fungus-destroying chemical.

fun.gus (FUNG.gus) *n., pl.* -**gi** (-jye) or -**gus.es** any of the lowest members of the plant kingdom having no stems, leaves, flowers, or chlorophyll, including mushrooms, molds, and mildews.

fu.nic.u.lar (few.NIC.yuh.lur) *n. & adj.* (a mountain railroad) worked by a rope or cable, as in the Alps.

funk *n. Informal.* **1** panic; lack of courage; also, a state of depression: *blue funk; in a deep funk.* **2** blueslike jazz music with an earthy quality: *shimmying to Sixties funk; street funk;* **adja.:** *a heavy funk beat; funk groups, records, rhythms.* —*v. Slang.* **1** jazz something up: *a funked-up version.* **2** dance to or play funk music: *Do you want to funk?* **3** back out of or avoid: *to funk out of a situation; to funk the hard choices.*

funk.y *adj.* **funk.i.er, -i.est** *Slang.* **1** smelly or earthy; hence, down-to-earth. **2** fashionable or trendy, not traditional: *funky fashions, jazz, jewelry, rock music; to get funky; the funky platform shoes of the 1970s.* —**funk.i.ness** *n.*

fun.nel (FUN.ul) *n.* **1** a wide-mouthed, tapering utensil for pouring liquids, grain, etc. into a narrow-mouthed container; hence, anything of similar shape: *the funnel of a tornado.* **2** a smokestack or flue. —*v.* **fun.nels,**

fun.neled, fun.nel.ing send through a funnel: *state secrets funneled out through the embassies;* **n.**: *the* **funneling** *of aid to poor countries.* Also **fun.nelled, fun.nel.ling** *Cdn.*

fun.nies *n.pl.* comic strips or a section of a newspaper containing these.

fun.ny (FUN.ee) *adj.* **fun.ni.er, fun.ni.est 1** amusing: *very funny; That's not funny!* **2** *Informal.* tricky or strange: *a funny feeling; There's something funny about his absence; Isn't it funny that there's no one home? funny* (= counterfeit) *money.* —**fun.ni.ly** *adv.*

funny bone *n.* **1** a sensitive spot at the back of the elbow that produces a painful tingling sensation when struck. **2** one's sense of humor.

fur *n.* **1** the soft, thick hair of mink, ermine, fox, etc. **2** this processed and made into a garment. **3** a furlike coating, as on a sick person's tongue or the lime deposit on a surface, as of a kettle. —*adj.* having to do with fur: *a fur coat, company, post, trail; the fur trade;* **fur farming** (on a ranch for raising fur-bearing animals). —**make the fur fly** *Informal.* create an uproar.

fur.be.low (FUR.buh.loh) *n.* a flounce, ruffle, or something showy or superfluous: *frills and furbelows.*

fur.bish *v.* burnish; also, renovate.

Fu.ries (FYOOR.eez) *n.pl.* three snake-haired female avengers of Greek and Roman myths.

fu.ri.ous (FYOOR.ee.us) *adj.* filled with fury; hence, wild or violent: *a furious attack, storm; working at a furious pace; Flo is furious about* or *at* or *over being bumped from the flight; furious that she missed her appointment;* **fu.ri.ous.ly** *adv.*

furl *v.* roll up; *adj.*: *a* **furled** *flag, sail, umbrella; a* **self-furling** *canopy.*

fur.long *n.* a unit of distance equal to 1/8 mile (0.2 km).

fur.lough (FUR.loh) *n.* leave of absence from duty, esp. in the military: *to be home on furlough.* —*v.* give furlough to someone.

fur.nace (FUR.nis) *n.* a chamber in which fuel is burned to heat buildings, melt metals, etc.: *a blast furnace; coal furnaces; to stoke a furnace; Home heating is done by gas and oil furnaces.*

fur.nish *v.* supply, provide, or equip with what is useful or needed: *a loan to furnish an apartment (with furniture, drapes, etc.); music furnished* (= provided) *by a band; Can you furnish* (= give) *one good reason why you're late? adj.*: *a library well* **furnished** *with books; a tastefully furnished living room.*

furnishings *n.pl.* **1** furniture, carpets, cushions, etc. **2** dress accessories, esp. men's.

fur.ni.ture (FUR.nuh.chur) *n.* the usu. movable equipment such as chairs, tables, and beds for living or working, as for a home, office, or ship: *garden, lawn, upholstered furniture; unfinished furniture (ready for painting, etc.).*

fu.ror (FYOOR.or) *n.* **1** a noisy outburst from a crowd; uproar: *The announcement caused* or *created* or *raised a furor in the audience; the furor over* or *about gas prices; A furor arises, dies down, subsides.* **2** an enthusiastic response. Also **fu.rore** *Brit.*

furred *adj.* covered with fur: *a furred kettle; furred, finned, and feathered (animal) species.*

fur.ri.er (FUR.ee.ur) *n.* one who processes or deals in furs.

fur.ring *n.* **1** the act of lining with fur or the fur used. **2** wooden strips attached to a wall to support the finished surface.

fur.row (FUR.oh) *n.* a track cut in the ground by a plough; also, anything similar, as a rut made by a wheel or a deep wrinkle on one's brow. —*v.* make a furrow: *His brow furrows when he tries to think hard;* **adj.**: *a face* **furrowed** *with age.*

fur.ry *adj.* made of, covered with, or soft like fur: *his furry chest; a furry beast, rodent, sweater, tongue.* —**fur.ri.ness** *n.*

fur.ther ("th" as in "the") **1** *adv.* [a comp. of FAR] farther; more distant: *Go no further; further complicated, divided, outside.* **2** *adj.* additional: *No further action is necessary; The show is over until further notice.* —*v.* advance or promote: *to further the aims of justice.* —**fur.ther.ance** (FUR.thur.unce) *n.*: *steps taken in furtherance of his aims.*

fur.ther.more (FUR.thur.more) *adv.* moreover.

fur.thest *adj. & adv.* a *superl.* of FAR.

fur.tive (FUR.tiv) *adj.* stealthy or sneaky: *The child took a few furtive steps and stole a glance into the room.* —**fur.tive.ly** *adv.*; **fur.tive.ness** *n.*

fu.ry (FYOOR.ee) *n.* **-ries 1** rage or frenzy tending to violence: *The pro- verbial fury of a scorned woman is a stereotype; He flew into a fury when told he had lost the bid; He vented his fury on* or *upon everyone around; pent-up, savage, unbridled fury; the fury of the elements* (= stormy weather). **2 Fury** any of the FURIES or one like them.

furze (FURZ) *n.* a spiny, evergreen shrub of the pea family with fragrant yellow flowers; gorse.

fuse (FEWZ) *n.* **1** a slow-burning wick ("safety fuse") as used in blasting: *Don't light the fuse yet.* **2** a mechanical or electrical device, usu. **fuze,** for setting off an explosive charge, as in guns and shells: *to arm or set a fuse; a percussion fuse; time fuses.* **3** a cartridge or plug containing a wire or metal strip that melts and breaks an electrical circuit as a safety device: *to blow (out) a fuse; What made the fuse blow (out)? to change a fuse.* —**blow a fuse** *Informal.* lose one's temper.
—*v.* **fus.es, fused, fus.ing 1** melt, esp. unite or blend by melting together: *furnaces to fuse zinc and copper into brass; One party fused with the other; a new party fused (= formed) out of many factions.* **2** equip a bomb, mine, etc. with a fuse; also **fuze.**

fu.see (few.ZEE) *n.* **1** a large-headed friction match. **2** a signal flare used on railroads and highways.

fu.se.lage (FEW.suh.lahzh) *n.* the body of an airplane housing the controls, crew, passengers, and cargo.

fu.si.ble (FEW.zuh.bul) *adj.* that can be fused: *Alloys are more fusible than pure metals.* —**fu.si.bil.i.ty** (-BIL.i.tee) *n.*

fu.sil.ier (few.zuh.LEER) *n.* a soldier armed with a **fusil,** a flintlock musket.

fu.sil.lade (FEW.suh.lade, -lahd) *n.* rapid gunfire: *a fusillade of questions from the press.*

fu.sion (FEW.zhun) *n.* **1** a fusing or melting: *the fusion of metals in making alloys.* **2** union: *the fusion of many cultures in a nation; the nuclear fusion of atoms in the hydrogen bomb,* also called **fusion bomb.** **3** popular music that is a blend of two styles, as jazz and rock.

fuss *n.* unnecessary bother, esp. about trivial things: *He kicked up a fuss (= row) because I spilled some soup; What a fuss she makes about* or *over her picture in the paper!* —*v.* make a fuss: *He fusses a lot about* or *over his wife and kids; Don't fuss with that dress, it looks all right; Flo* **fussed about** (= behaved anxiously) *all morning but achieved little.*

fuss.budg.et (FUSS.buj.it) or **fuss.pot** *n. Informal.* one who fusses over trifles.

fuss.y *adj.* **fuss.i.er, -i.est:** *He's very fussy (= particular) about his steaks; a dress too fussy (= full of details requiring much attention) to make in one day.*
—**fuss.i.ly** *adv.;* **fuss.i.ness** *n.*

fus.tian (FUS.chun) *n.* **1** a coarse twilled cloth with a velvety pile. **2** inflated talk or writing; bombast; claptrap.

fus.ty *adj.* **-ti.er, -ti.est 1** stale-smelling or musty. **2** old-fashioned; out-of-date.
—**fus.ti.ly** *adv.;* **fus.ti.ness** *n.*

fu.tile (FEW.tul, -tile) *adj.* of no use; ineffectual: *All his attempts proved futile; It's futile to argue with him; a futile question; a futile* (= frivolous) *young man.*
—**fu.tile.ly** *adv.* —**fu.til.i.ty** (few.TIL.i.tee) *n.*

fu.ton (FEW.ton, FOO-; *rhyme:* on) *n.* a thin mattress used for sleeping on the floor.

fu.ture (FEW.chur) *n.* **1** time to come after the present; also, events to come: *We face an uncertain future; bleak, bright, promising, unforeseeable future; to look into, plan, predict the future; in the distant, immediate, near future; Who knows what the future may bring; a career with a future* (= bright prospects); *He'll be more careful* **in future***; savings to provide* **for the future.** **2** an English verb form constructed with "shall" and "will," as "We will go." **3 futures** *pl.* commodities and stocks bought for future acceptance or delivery. —**adja.:** *the future tense of a verb; our future life (after death); the* **future shock** *or distress of coping with the rapid changes in modern society.*

fu.tur.ist (FEW.chuh.rist) *n.* **1** one who studies and forecasts future events and developments; futurologist. **2** a follower of an Italian art movement called futurism, lasting from about 1909 to 1916, that glorified the energy and speed of the machine age.
—**fu.tur.is.tic** (-RIS.tic) *adj.*
—**fu.tur.ism** *n.*

fu.tu.ri.ty (few.TURE.uh..tee, few.CHOOR-) *n.* **-ties 1** a future condition or event. **2** also **futurity race,** a horse race in which the contestants are nominated at birth.

fu.tur.ol.o.gy (few.chuh.ROL.uh.jee) *n.* a study of future trends based on the science and technology of the present; **fu.tur.ol.o.gist** *n.*

futz (FUTS) *v. Slang.* **futz around** loaf or fool around.

fuze See FUSE.

fuzee same as FUSEE.

fuzz (FUZ) *n. sing. & pl.* **1** loose, fluffy fibers, particles, or hairs, as of down or wool, or as on a peach or a caterpillar's back. **2 the fuzz** *Slang.* the police; a police officer. —*v.* make or become fuzzy: *to fuzz a distinction, an image, a party policy.*

fuz.zy (FUZ.ee) *adj.* **fuz.zi.er, fuz.zi.est** of or like fuzz; hence, blurred or indistinct: *a fuzzy photograph; fuzzy thinking; a politician whose speeches are fuzzy on the issues; the* **fuzzy set** *of "average*

Americans" (= a grouping with no sharply defined boundaries).
—**fuz.zi.ly** *adv.*; **fuz.zi.ness** *n.*
fuzzy logic *n.* a technology for assigning numerical values between zero and one to imprecise situations; *adj.*: *fuzzy-logic computing; a camcorder with fuzzy-logic autofocus.*
-fy *v. suffix.* make or become: *glorify, liquefy, magnify, simplify.*

.... **G, g** ....

G or **g** (JEE) *n.* **G's** or **g's** the seventh letter of the English alphabet; hence, the seventh in a series.
gab *v.* **gabs, gabbed, gab.bing** *Informal.* talk rapidly, excessively, or thoughtlessly; chatter. —*n.* esp. **the gift of (the) gab**, fluency of speech.
—**gab.ber** *n.*
gab.ar.dine (GAB.ur.deen) *n.* **1** a fabric of cotton, wool, or rayon with raised, diagonal ribs. **2** a garment made of this cloth. **3** a long, coarse cloak or smock worn in the Middle Ages, esp. by Jews. Also **gab.er.dine.**
gab.ble (GAB.ul) *v.* **gab.bles, gab.bled, gab.bling 1** talk quickly or incoherently; jabber or babble. **2** cackle.
—*n.* confused and voluble talk: *the gabble at a bazaar.*
gab.by (GAB.ee) *adj.* **gab.bi.er, gab.bi.est** *Informal.* talkative.
—**gab.bi.ness** *n.*
gaberdine See GABARDINE.
gab.fest *n. Informal.* **1** a gathering of people mainly for chatting. **2** a prolonged chat or gossiping.
ga.ble (GAY.bul) *n.* the triangular part of a wall at the end of a ridged roof: *a farmhouse called "Green Gables"; a* **gable window** (= a window in a gable or with a gable design). —**ga.bled** *adj.*
gad *v.* **gads, gad.ded, gad.ding** roam or wander about: *The government ministers were accused of gadding about at public expense.*
gad.a.bout (GAD.uh.bowt) *n. Informal.* a rambler looking for fun.
gad.fly *n.* **-flies 1** a horsefly. **2** a persistently annoying person.
gadg.et (GAJ.it) *n.* **1** a small mechanical device. **2** a trivial object.
—**gadg.et.ry** (-it.ree) *n.*
gaff *n.* **1** a pole with an iron hook used to land fish. **2** *Slang.* abuse. —**stand the gaff** endure harsh treatment.
—*v.* land a fish with a gaff.
gaffe (GAF) *n.* a clumsy social blunder: *to make a gaffe.*
gaf.fer (GAF.ur) *n.* an old man.

gag *v.* **gags, gagged, gag.ging 1** prevent speech by stopping up the mouth; hence, restrain free speech. **2** block off or obstruct; hence, choke or retch: *to gag a valve; He gagged on his first puff of tobacco.* **3** make or tell jokes.
—*n.* **1** anything that stops the mouth or prevents speech: *A gag kept the kidnapped man from crying for help; a dictator's gag on the press; Courts sometimes issue* **gag orders** *on the media.*
2 *Informal.* an amusing joke or trick: *The flying saucer turned out to be a gag; Someone did it for a gag.*
ga.ga (GAH.gah) *adj.p. Slang.* wildly enthusiastic: *The kids went gaga for or over Superman.*
gage (GAIJ) *n.* **1** a pledge or challenge to fight. **2** formerly, a glove, hat, or similar object thrown down as a gesture of defiance. **3** same as GAUGE.
—*v.* **gag.es, gaged, gag.ing.**
gag.gle (GAG.ul) *n.* a flock, group, or cluster: *a gaggle of geese, people, products; a gaggle of streamers flying from the car window.*
gag.man *n.* **-men** a writer of jokes or comic routines.
gai.e.ty (GAY.uh.tee) *n.* **-ties 1** the state of being gay or cheerful. **2** gay or festive entertainment: *to join in the gaieties of the season.* **3** bright, showy appearance: *gaiety of dress.*
gai.ly *adv.* in a gay manner: *a gaily caparisoned horse; gaily colored packages; gaily decorated lunchboxes; a house gaily painted in pink; a gaily wrapped gift.*
gain *v.* obtain or acquire, esp. as an achievement, addition, advantage, or profit: *He gained recognition by his memoirs; Our firm gained $10,000 in the deal; You gain weight by overeating; The climbers soon gained (= reached) the summit; This clock gains (= is faster by) a few seconds each day; She's slowly gaining strength after her recent illness; A faster runner was* **gaining on** *(= drawing nearer to) the champion; We tried to* **gain** *(= win)* **him over** *to our side.*
—*n.* something obtained or increased; profit: *the gains made last year in sales volume; a considerable, enormous, notable, tangible, tremendous gain; a gain in efficiency; losses and gains; a tax on capital gains; ill-gotten gains.*
gain.ful *adj.* profitable. —**gain.ful.ly** *adv.*: **gainfully employed** (= working for a living).
gain.say *v.* **-says, -said, -say.ing** deny or contradict: *It cannot be gainsaid that he is popular; There is no gainsaying his popularity.* —**gain.say.er** *n.*

gait *n.* **1** manner or style of moving on foot: *heavy, shambling, steady, unsteady gaits; the comic Charlie Chaplin gait; the loping gait of a one-legged walker.* **2** a horse's trot, pace, canter, or gallop: *After breaking stride at the half-mile mark, our horse got back on gait to finish second.*
—**gait.ed** *comb.form.* having a gait as specified: *heavy-gaited; slow-gaited; a smooth-gaited animal.*

gai.ter (GAY.tur) *n.* an outer covering for the leg reaching from the instep to ankle, mid-calf, or knee; legging or spat.

ga.la (GAY.luh, GAL.uh) *n.* a celebration or festival: *an opening-night gala.*
—*adj.* festive: *a gala affair, dinner, event, evening, occasion, party.*

ga.lac.tic (guh.LAC.tic) *adj.* **1** having to do with a galaxy: *the galactic center; galactic clusters, dust, fields, matter, nebulae; galactic noise from the Milky Way.* **2** huge or large: *a galactic amount, distance, sum; galactic forces, velocities; of galactic proportions.*

gal.ax.y (GAL.uk.see) *n.* **-ax.ies 1** one of the many systems of stars, gas, and cosmic dust that form the universe, esp. the **Galaxy**, or Milky Way. **2** a collection of illustrious people or things: *a galaxy of movie stars.*

gale *n.* **1** a strong wind: *a sudden gale;* **gale-force winds** *(32 to 63 mph or 51 to 102 km/h).* **2** an outburst: *gales of laughter.*

gall (GAWL) *n.* **1** a bitter secretion of the liver; bile. **2** anything bitter to endure; rancor or resentment. **3** *Informal.* impudence: *After cheating on the exam, the student had the unmitigated gall to accuse others of cheating.* **4** a sore caused by chafing. —*v.* rub a sore spot on the skin; hence, annoy: *It galls me to have to wait for latecomers.*

gal.lant (GAL.unt) *adj.* **1** brave or dashing: *a gallant knight, lady, soldier.* **2** [not used of people] stately or noble: *as gallant a ship as ever sailed; a gallant attempt, deed, display, effort, fight; a gallant* (= high-spirited) *horse.* **3** (guh.LANT) courteous, esp. polite to women: *the gallant attentiveness of a gallant escort; a gallant knight;* **n.**: a stylish young man, esp. a lady's man.

gal.lant.ry (GAL.un.tree) *n.* **-ries** brave, spirited, or courteous behavior or action: *a soldier's gallantry in battle; He displayed gallantry; courted her with little gallantries.*

gall.blad.der (GAWL.blad.ur) *n.* a sac situated under the liver in which excess bile is stored.

gal.ler.y (GAL.uh.ree) *n.* **gal.ler.ies 1** a long, narrow outdoor balcony; porch. **2** a balcony in a theater or public place, esp. the topmost balcony; also, the people seated in this area. **3** any group of spectators: *a performance applauded by the gallery; the parliamentary press gallery; the peanut gallery; They would much rather* **play to the gallery** (= cater to the tastes of the masses) *than try to impress the elite.* **4** a long, narrow room or passageway; underground tunnel or passage: *a shooting gallery* (= indoor range). **5** an institution for displaying or selling works of art: *a picture gallery; the National Art Gallery.*

gal.ley (GAL.ee) *n.* **1** a ship of former times propelled by oars and sails. **2** the kitchen of an airplane or ship. **3** in printing by hand, a tray holding type that has been set. **4** proof of typeset matter in single columns; also **galley proof.**

Gal.lic (GAL.ic) *adj.* having to do with Gaul or France: *Caesar's Gallic wars; a Gallic accent.*

Gal.li.cism (GAL.uh.siz.um) *n.* a French custom or characteristic.

gal.li.vant (GAL.uh.vant) *v.* roam about seeking fun.

gal.lon (GAL.un) *n.* a liquid measure equal to 4 quarts or 8 pints: *A U.S. gallon is 3.79 liters; The imperial gallon is 4.55 liters.*

gal.lop (GAL.up) *n.* the fastest pace of a horse or other four-legged animal: *She rode away at full gallop.* —*v.* to move at this pace: *a horse galloping across a field;* **adja.: galloping** *inflation.*

gal.lows (GAL.oze) *n.* **-lows** or **-lows.es** a structure of usu. two upright posts and a crossbeam used for hanging condemned criminals: *to be sent to the gallows.*

gallows humor *n.* humor based on a terrifying situation.

Gal.lup poll (GAL.up-) *n.* a survey of public opinion on a specific issue.

gal.lus.es (GAL.us.iz) *n.pl. Regional.* suspenders.

ga.lore (guh.LORE) *adjp.* [used after its noun] in great numbers: *a big sale with bargains galore.*

ga.losh (guh.LOSH) *n.* a high rainproof overshoe: *a pair of galoshes.*

gal.van.ic (gal.VAN.ic) *adj.* **1** having to do with electric current and its effects; electrolytic: *a galvanic battery, cell; Galvanic action does not affect plastics; water-induced galvanic corrosion where dissimilar metals are joined; a galvanic probe for* detecting oxygen in water. **2** electrical: *galvanic skin response; The announcement produced a galvanic reaction; a galvanic effect.*

gal.va.nize (GAL.vuh.nize) *v.* **-niz.es, -nized, -niz.ing 1** stimulate with electric current; hence, excite or startle: *The stock market was galvanized into activity by the encouraging news.* **2** to coat metal with rustproof zinc. —**gal.va.niz.er** *n.* —**gal.va.ni.za.tion** (-nuh.ZAY.shun, -nye-) *n.*

gam *n.* Slang. a leg, esp. of a woman.

gam.bit *n.* **1** a way of beginning a chess game by sacrificing a minor piece to gain an advantage. **2** an opening move, esp. a strategic one.

gam.ble (GAM.bul) *v.* **-bles, -bled, -bling 1** bet or play games of chance; risk or lose something by gambling: *He **gambled away** the money he had won.* **2** take a risk or speculate: *to gamble on the stock market; We gambled on having good weather for the picnic.* —*n.* a risky act: *to take a gamble on a new product.* —**gam.bler** *n.*

gam.bol (GAM.bul) *v.* **-bols, -boled, -bol.ing** run friskily: *The lambs gamboled on the hillside.*

gam.brel (GAM.brul) or **gambrel roof** *n.* a roof, as of barns, that has two slopes on each side.

game *n.* **1** a form of playing; diversion or pastime; also, a competitive activity: *a game of chance; games of skill; a board game such as chess or checkers; parlor games; video games; word games and puzzles; numbers game* (= lottery); *war games* (= maneuvers); *the Commonwealth, Olympic, summer, winter games* (= competitions). **2** a single contest in a competition: *to play a game; He won three out of four games; He threw the last game; The game was called because of rain; championship, close, fair games; a home game* (played at one's own place), *not an away game.* **3** the number of points needed to win: *21 points is a game in casino.* **4** any activity similar to sports in risk-taking, planning, competitiveness, etc.: *the game of diplomacy; the advertising game; a con or confidence game; the mating game; a waiting game* (= strategy); *We saw through his game* (= deception). **5** animals hunted for food or sport; also, their flesh: *to eat, hunt for, stalk game; deer and other game; big game such as lions and elephants; small game such as rabbits and squirrels; Anyone is fair game for the April Fool; a **game park** or **preserve** or **reserve** for the preservation of wild life.* —**the game is up** the plan has failed. —**to play the game** behave honorably according to rules. —*v.* **games, gamed, gam.ing** to gamble; *adj.a.:* Las Vegas, the **gaming** capital of North America; the gaming tables of our casino; the gaming business, industry, market; a gaming establishment, license. —*adj.* **1** plucky or brave: *a game youth.* **2** ready: *I'm game for a ride or to go on a ride; She's game too.* **3** lame: *a game leg; She's game in the leg.*

game fish *n.* a fish that is sought for sport with a hook and line.

game.keep.er (GAME.kee.pur) *n.* a person taking care of wildlife on a private reserve.

game plan *n.* planned strategy: *a politician's game plan.*

game point *n.* the point before the end of a game; also, the winning point.

game show *n.* a TV program featuring games of skill or chance.

games.man.ship (GAMES.mun.ship) *n.* skill in winning games, esp. by stratagems.

game.ster (GAIM.stur) *n.* a gambler.

gam.ete (GAM.eet, guh.MEET) *n.* a plant or animal reproductive cell capable of uniting with another to form a new individual. —**ga.met.ic** (guh.MET.ic) *adj.*

game theory *n.* a mathematical method of determining the best strategy in games, business, war, etc.

game warden *n.* an official who enforces hunting and fishing regulations.

gamey same as GAMY.

gam.in (GAM.un) *n.* a street urchin; waif.

ga.mine (guh.MEEN) *n.* a roguish but charming girl.

gam.mon (GAM.un) *n.* **1** a smoked ham or side of bacon. **2** nonsensical or deceptive talk.

gam.ut (GAM.ut) *n.* a complete musical scale; hence, the full range of anything variable: *the whole gamut of emotions from joy to despair; At this resort, accommodation runs the gamut from small guest houses to large luxury hotels.*

gam.y (GAY.mee) *adj.* **gam.i.er, -i.est 1** having the flavor of game, esp. when spoiled; hence, racy. **2** plucky. —**gam.i.ness** *n.*

gan.der (GAN.dur) *n.* **1** a male goose. **2** Slang. a look, esp. a close one, as if craning one's neck: *to take a gander at the goings-on.*

gang *n.* **1** a group of people working together: *a road gang repairing streets; a work gang; chain gangs.* **2** a band of criminals or delinquents: *a gang of*

gangland / garnet

thieves; *a juvenile gang; street gangs; to break up, form, join a gang.* **3** *adj.* being a set of similar items or units arranged to work together: *a gang drill, gang hook, gang plow, gang saw, gang switch.*
—*v.* form into groups: *Boys ganged (up) together at the corner; The children decided to* **gang up on** or **against** (Informal for join and attack) *the bully.*

gang.land *n.* the gangster world.

gan.gly (GANG.glee) *adj.* tall, thin, and awkward; loosely built: *a gangly youth; gangly arms and legs.* Also **gan.gling.**

gang.plank *n.* a removable ramp for boarding or leaving a ship.

gan.grene (GANG.green, gang.GREEN) *n.* the dying of body tissue due to interruption of the blood supply: *Gangrene may set in after a severe burn.*
—*v.* **-grenes, -grened, -gren.ing:** *A foot gangrened by frostbite may have to be amputated.* —**gan.gre.nous** (GANG.gruh.nus) *adj.*

gang.ster (GANG.stur) *n.* a criminal or racketeer.

gang.way *n.* **1** a passageway. **2** a gangplank. —*interj.* make way!

gaol (JAIL) *n. Brit.* jail. —**gaol.er** *n.*

gap *n.* **1** an opening or break: *A missing tooth leaves a gap; to bridge or close or fill a gap; a mountain gap in the Rockies; a wide gap.* **2** an obvious difference or disparity: *There's a gap of many years in your narrative; Lying builds up a credibility gap; the gender gap (between the sexes); the generation gap between parents and children; our trade gap (between imports and exports) with Japan.*

gape *v.* **gapes, gaped, gap.ing 1** open widely, as the mouth for yawning: *The abandoned quarry gaped before us; adj.: a gaping hole, void, wound.* **2** stare with the mouth open: *tourists gaping at the wonders of the Grand Canyon.* —*n.* a gaping: *to stifle a bored gape; with his mouth open in a gape of surprise.*

ga.rage (guh.RAHZH, -RAHJ) *n.* **1** a shelter for cars: *a house with an attached garage; a built-in garage; a (public) parking garage.* **2** a car repair shop.
—*v.* **-rag.es, -raged, -rag.ing** put or keep in a garage.

garage sale *n.* a sale of used household articles held at the seller's home.

garb *n.* **1** clothing or style of dress: *a nun's garb; Everyone came in formal garb.* **2** outward appearance: *to give confusion the garb of order.*
—*v.* wear as garb: *She was garbed in her graduation cap and gown.*

gar.bage (GAR.bij) *n.* **1** discarded food: *Garbage is disposed of separately from trash.* **2** anything discarded as worthless: *Garbage used to be picked up twice a week; No dumping of garbage on this lot; That's a lot of garbage* (= nonsense); *the green plastic* **garbage bag**; *a* **garbage can.**

gar.ble (GAR.bul) *v.* **-bles, -bled, -bling** distort, misrepresent, or intentionally scramble; *n.: a garble of gibberish; adj.: a* **garbled** *message; garbled speech, words.*

gar.den (GAR.dun) *n.* **1** a plot of land for growing flowers, fruit, or vegetables: *to maintain, plant, water, weed a garden; flower, kitchen, vegetable gardens; a* **garden hose** *for watering the lawn; tomatoes and other* **garden vegetables. 2** an area noted for good climate or fertile soil; *adj.: a lush resort in the garden spot of our state; a* **garden city** (= residential town with green areas). **3** an area for public recreation: *botanical, formal, rock, zoological gardens.* —*v.* work in a garden: *It is too cold here to garden in the winter; n.: landscape* **gardening** (= designing). —**gar.den.er** *n.*

garden variety *n.* a common or ordinary kind: *the garden variety of automobile; They come in a garden variety of shapes and colors; adj.: a* **garden-variety** *problem, restaurant, snake; the common garden-variety gangster film.*

gar.gan.tu.an or **Gar.gan.tu.an** (gar.GAN.choo.un) *adj.* enormous or huge: *a gargantuan appetite.*

gar.gle (GAR.gul) *v.* **-gles, -gled, -gling** rinse the throat with liquid kept in motion by exhaled breath.
—*n.* liquid for gargling: *a salt-water gargle for a sore throat.*

gar.goyle (GAR.goil) *n.* a grotesquely shaped waterspout projecting from the gutter of a building.

gar.ish (GAIR.ish) *adj.* gaudy or showy; glaring.

gar.land (GAR.lund) *n.* a wreath of leaves or flowers.
—*v.* decorate with a garland: *The bride was garlanded with roses.*

gar.lic *n.* **1** a plant related to the onion. **2** its strong-smelling bulb used in cooking: *a clove of garlic; There's a whiff of garlic in his office.* —**gar.lick.y** *adj.*

gar.ment (GAR.munt) *n.* an article of clothing: *a foundation garment; adj.: the garment district of the city; the garment industry; garment workers; a* **garment bag** (= travel bag that folds in two).

gar.ner (GAR.nur) *v.* gather for oneself: *to garner attention, pledges, sales, support, votes.*

gar.net (GAR.nit) *n.* a glossy mineral

gar.nish *v.* decorate or adorn, esp. food: *to garnish a platter with parsley;* *n.*: *a garnish of parsley.*
gar.nish.ee (gar.nuh.SHEE) *v.* **-ees, -eed, -ee.ing** legally withhold a debtor's money to pay the debts: *The loan company had his wages garnisheed.*
gar.nish.ment (GAR.nish.munt) *n.* a notice to garnishee.
ga.rotte same as GARROTE.
gar.ret (GAIR.it) *n.* an attic.
gar.ri.son (GAIR.uh.sun) *n.* **1** the troops stationed in a fortified place. **2** the fort itself. —*v.* to station troops, etc.: *Our troops were garrisoned in Europe during the war.*
garrison state *n.* a country dominated by military personnel.
gar.rote (guh.ROT, -ROTE) *n.* **1** strangulation by an iron collar, cord, wire, etc. **2** such a device. Also **ga.rotte**. —*v.* **gar.rotes, gar.rot.ed, gar.rot.ing** kill by garrote: *The robber garroted his victim with a wire.* Also **ga.rottes, ga.rot.ted, ga.rot.ting.**
gar.ru.lous (GAIR.uh.lus) *adj.* talkative or wordy. —**gar.ru.lous.ly** *adv.* —**gar.ru.lous.ness** or **gar.ru.li.ty** (guh.ROO.li.tee) *n.*
gar.ter *n.* a band or strap to hold up a stocking. —*v.* to support with a garter.
gas *n.* **gas.es** **1** a shapeless fluid like air which can expand indefinitely. **2** any gas or volatile liquid that is used as a fuel, anesthetic, poison, irritant, or illuminant, esp. gasoline: *The stalled car was out of gas; Step on the gas* (= accelerator pedal) *to go faster; coal gas; laughing gas; natural gas for home heating; Turn on the gas before lighting it; mustard gas; nerve gas; tear gas; toxic gas; stomach gas* (= flatulence); **adja.**: *a (poison) gas attack; gas heating (using natural gas); gas pipelines (carrying natural gas); a criminal executed in a **gas chamber** (with poison gas).* **3** *Slang.* a source of great pleasure or excitement: *The roller coaster is a real gas.*
—*v.* **gas.es, gassed, gas.sing 1** supply with gas: *to gas up a car before a trip.* **2** *Informal.* talk idly and boastfully: *He often gases about his fishing trips.*
gas-guzzler *n.* a large automobile with a low gas mileage.
gash *n.* a long, deep wound. —*v.* make a gash in something: *legs gashed by barbed wire.*
gas.o.line (GAS.uh.leen, gas.uh.LEEN) *n.* a flammable liquid distilled from petroleum and used as a motor fuel; gas: *high-octane, leaded, lead-free, premium, regular, unleaded gasolines.* Also **gas.o.lene.**
gasp *v.* **1** breathe in sharply, as from shock. **2** pant: *an asthmatic gasping for breath; The winded messenger gasped his story* (= told it while gasping for breath). —*n.* a gasping: *an audible gasp; to give, let out a gasp; a gasp for air.* —**at the last gasp** on the point of death.
gas range *n.* a range for cooking using household gas.
gas station *n.* where gasoline, oil, etc. for motor vehicles are sold.
gas.sy (GAS.ee) *adj.* **gas.si.er, gas.si.est** full of or producing stomach gas; flatulent: *gassy foods; a full and gassy feeling.*
gas.tric *adj.* having to do with the stomach: *gastric acid, cancer, ulcers, upsets;* **gastric juices** (= acidic digestive fluids produced by stomach glands).
gas.tri.tis (gas.TRY.tis) *n.* inflammation of the stomach lining.
gas.tro.en.ter.ol.o.gy (GAS.troh.en.tuh.ROL.uh.jee) *n.* a branch of medicine dealing with the digestive system. —**gas.tro.en.ter.ol.o.gist** *n.*
gas.tro.in.tes.ti.nal (GAS.troh.in.TES.tuh.nul) *adj.* of the stomach and intestines.
gas.tron.o.my (gas.TRON.uh.mee) *n.* the art of good eating. —**gas.tro.nom.ic** (-truh.NOM.ic) or **gas.tro.nom.i.cal** (-i.cul) *adj.*
gas.tro.pod (GAS.truh.pod) *n.* a single-shelled, soft-bodied mollusk such as snails and slugs.
gate *n.* **1** a movable barrier hung on a post which controls passage through an entrance in a fence, wall, castle, etc.: *to wait at the gate; the starting gate of a racetrack.* **2** a door or valve controlling water flow in a canal, dam, lock, etc.; also, a gateway. **3** the total amount of money taken or the number of spectators at an event. **4** a computer circuit having one output activated by a combination of signals to the inputs. —**give someone the gate** *Slang.* dismiss or reject someone.
gate-crash *v. Informal.* enter without an invitation or without paying: *to gate-crash a party.* —**gate-crash.er** *n.*
gat.ed (GAY.tid) *adj.* protected by a gate: *a private **gated community** with exclusive facilities for its residents and a gatekeeper controlling traffic.* —**gate.keep.er** *n.*
gate.way *n.* **1** an opening for a gate. **2** a means of entrance: *an arched gateway; St. Louis, the gateway to the West; the*

gateway of heaven; gateway cities. **3** software or hardware that connects dissimilar computer networks; also, software that facilitates access to a database; **adj**.: *a gateway connection, service; gateway protocols, software, systems.*

gath.er (GATH.ur, "TH" as in "the") *v.* **1** bring together: *He gathered his friends for a reunion; A farmer gathers his crop; Detectives gather evidence.* **2** come together; assemble: *Children gather around their teacher; They gathered at a workshop; The rockers gathered in a field;* **n.**: *a **gathering** of clouds before a storm; Thanksgiving and other family gatherings; a public gathering; social gatherings.* **3** accumulate or increase: *Old books gather dust in the library; A car gathers speed as it rolls downhill; a movement gathering momentum; as the drama gathers pace.* **4** draw: *She gathered a shawl around herself; to gather one's brows in a frown;* **adj**.: *a skirt **gathered** at the waist (into pleats or folds); a gathered waist.* **5** infer or conclude: *I gather you're not interested.* —**n.** a very small pleat: *She removed the gathers to remodel the dress.* —**gath.er.er** *n.*

gauche (GOHSH) *adj.* awkward, esp. socially.

gau.che.rie (goh.shuh.REE) *n.* a clumsy or tactless action; awkwardness.

gau.cho (GOW.choh, "OW" as in "HOW") *n.* **-chos** a cowboy of the South American plains.

gaud (GAWD) *n.* a cheap ornament or trinket.

gaud.y (GAW.dee) *adj.* **gaud.i.er, -i.est** tastelessly colorful; flashily ornamented. —**gaud.i.ly** *adv.;* **gaud.i.ness** *n.*

gauge (GAIJ) *n.* **1** a standard measurement, as for the widths of railway tracks, sizes of bores, wire thicknesses, etc.: *Trains run on broad, narrow, and standard gauges; a 12-gauge shotgun for duck-hunting; ordinary 12-gauge copper wire.* **2** a measuring instrument: *fuel, oil, pressure, rain, wind gauges; a water-level gauge.* **3** a means of estimating or judging: *Looks are no sure gauge of character.* —*v.* **gaug.es, gauged, gaug.ing** measure or judge: *a director gauging an actor's performance.*

gaunt *adj.* **1** thin-looking: *He was gaunt and weak; a gaunt (= elegant-looking) fashion model.* **2** desolate or grim-looking: *the gaunt brow of a cliff.* —**gaunt.ness** *n.*

gaunt.let (GAWNT.lit, GONT-) *n.* **1** a protective glove, esp. from a suit of armor. **2** two rows of armed people who strike a person forced to run between them; hence, any ordeal: *His work had to **run the gauntlet** of critics worldwide before being accepted.* —**pick up** or **take up the gauntlet** accept a challenge. —**throw down the gauntlet** challenge someone to fight.

gauze (GAUZ) *n.* a thin, transparent, loosely-woven fabric.

gave *pt.* of GIVE.

gav.el (GAV.ul) *n.* a small mallet used by a judge, auctioneer, or the chairperson of a meeting to call a meeting to order, close a session, etc.: *a rap of the gavel; The networks provided **gavel-to-gavel** (= beginning-to-end) coverage of the trial.*

gawk *v.* to stare stupidly: *to gawk at people.* —**n.** an awkward or clumsy person.

gawk.y (GAW.kee) *adj.* **gawk.i.er, -i.est** awkward or clumsy: *a growing boy's gawky limbs.* —**gawk.i.ness** *n.* —**gawk.ish** *adj.*

gay *adj.* **gay.er, gay.est 1** *Informal.* homosexual: *a gay bar; the gay community, lobby; gay liberation, men, rights; He's openly gay; gay, not straight;* **n.**: *gays and lesbians.* **2** joyous; lively; merry; given to (social) pleasure. **3** brightly colored: *a gay costume.* **4** licentious or immoral: *a gay dog.* —**gai.ly** or **gay.ly** *adv.* —**gay.e.ty** same as GAIETY.

gaze *v.* **gaz.es, gazed, gaz.ing** to look steadily and with fascination. —**n.** a gazing: *an admiring, intense, steady, wistful gaze; Their eyes met in a bewildered gaze.*

ga.ze.bo (guh.ZEE.boh, -ZAY.boh) *n.* **-bos** or **-boes** a belvedere.

ga.zelle (guh.ZEL) *n.* **-zelles** a small, swift, graceful antelope of Asia and Africa.

ga.zette (guh.ZET) *n.* **1** an official government journal. **2** [used in titles of newspapers]: *The Phoenix Gazette.* —*v.* **-zettes, -zet.ted, -zet.ting** publish or list in a gazette.

gaz.et.teer (gaz.uh.TEER) *n.* a dictionary of names of places, seas, rivers, mountains, etc.

gear (GEER, "G" as in "go") *n.* **1** a toothed wheel that meshes with another toothed element to transmit motion, often in a system of such gears: *Drivers change, reverse, shift gears; to put a car in low, high, reverse, top gear; Gears jam, lock, mesh, stick; a worm gear.* **2** equipment, esp. tools or clothing for a special purpose: *The soldier left his gear in the barracks; to pack camping gear for a trip; fishing, hunting, skiing gear.* **3** fashion: *dressed in the latest gear; trendy gear.*

gearbox / generality

—**in** (or **out of**) **gear** connected (or not connected) to the motor; hence, working (or not working) properly.
—**in high gear 1** in the highest speed range. **2** at high efficiency. —*v.* **1** connect, as by gears: *A car's rear wheels are geared to the motor; A factory's production is geared* (= adjusted) *to demand.* **2** equip or get ready: *a team gearing up for a game; hikers geared for an outing.*
gear.box *n.* an automobile transmission.
gear.shift *n.* a device for changing from one gear to another.
gear.wheel *n.* cogwheel.
gee (JEE) *interj.* expressing surprise: *Gee, aren't we lucky!*
geek ("g" as in "go") *n. Slang.* a weirdo or freak.
geese *pl.* of GOOSE.
gee whiz same as GEE.
—**gee-whiz** *adja. Informal.* surprisingly good: *a gee-whiz kid, look, movie.*
geez (JEEZ) same as GEE.
gee.zer (GEE.zur, "g" as in "go") *n. Slang.* an eccentric old man.
gel (JEL) *n.* a jellylike substance formed by the thickening of a colloidal solution. —*v.* **gels, gelled, gel.ling 1** form a gel: *Egg white gels when heated.* **2** take shape; jell: *Somehow our plans failed to gel.*
gel.a.tin or **gel.a.tine** (JEL.uh.tin) *n.* a gluelike substance used in drugs and cooking. —**ge.lat.i.nous** (juh.LAT.uh.nus) *adj.*
geld (JELD) *v.* to neuter a male animal; castrate: *a gelded horse.*
geld.ing *n.* a castrated animal, esp. a horse: *a mere gelding among stallions.*
gem (JEM) *n.* a precious or semiprecious stone cut and polished as a jewel; hence, anything highly valued: *A Picasso was the gem of his art collection.*
gem.i.nate (JEM.uh.nate) *v.* **-ates, -at.ed, -at.ing** make or become double or paired.
Gem.i.ni (JEM.i.nye, -nee) *n.* **1** a N. constellation and the third sign of the zodiac; also called "The Twins." **2** a person born under this sign.
gem.mol.o.gy or **gem.ol.o.gy** (jem.OL.uh.jee) *n.* the study of gems. —**gem.mol.o.gist** or **gem.ol.o.gist** *n.*
gem.stone *n.* a stone that may be cut and polished as a gem.
gen.darme (ZHAHN.darm) *n.* a soldier serving as a policeman, esp. in France.
gen.dar.mer.ie (zhahn.DAR.muh.ree) *n.* a body of gendarmes. Also **gen.dar.mer.y.**
gen.der (JEN.dur) *n.* **1** sex: *the female gender; male gender;* **adj.**: *gender differences, equality; the gender factor; gender orientation, politics, stereotyping; gender-neutral legislation.* **2** one of the grammatical categories into which words are grouped: *the feminine, masculine, neuter gender; the common gender of "baby."*
gender gap *n.* a difference in attitudes, values, etc. because of sex: *There was a gender gap that year in national politics, with five percent more women favoring one party over the other.*
gene (JEEN) *n.* a unit of chromosome that determines the inheritance of a certain characteristic.
ge.ne.al.o.gy (jee.nee.AL.uh.jee) *n.* **-gies** a record or study of family history; lineage or pedigree. —**ge.ne.al.o.gist** (-jist) *n.* —**ge.ne.a.log.i.cal** (jee.nee.uh.LOJ.i.cul) *adj.*
gene pool *n.* all the genes in a breeding population.
genera a *pl.* of GENUS.
gen.er.al (JEN.ur.ul) *adj.* **1** applicable to or true of the whole; common, prevalent, or widespread; not limited, specialized, precise, or detailed: *a general feeling of unrest in society; All bears have the same general features, but they differ in color and size; She quickly sketched the general outline of the scheme; reforms for the general welfare of the public; a general* (= national or provincial) *election.* **2** having the highest rank: *a store's general manager; the general secretary.* —*n.* **1** what is general: *His report concentrates on the general and ignores specifics; The weather,* **in general** (= usually), *is rainy throughout April.* **2** an officer of the highest rank, as in the military: *the general of the army; postmaster general; the superior general of a religious order.* **3** an officer ranking above a colonel: *brigadier, lieutenant, major generals; a four-star general.* —**gen.er.al.ship** *n.*
general assembly *n.* **1 General Assembly,** the supreme deliberative body of the United Nations. **2** the legislature of some U.S. states.
gen.er.al.is.si.mo (jen.uh.ruh.LIS.uh.moh) *n.* **-mos** the supreme commander of all armed forces in some countries.
gen.er.al.ist (GEN.uh.ruh.list) *n.* one who deals with a variety of subjects, goods, etc.: *a generalist, not a specialist;* **adja.**: *the generalist approach; generalist training.*
gen.er.al.i.ty (jen.uh.RAL.i.tee) *n.* **-ties 1** something general: *The lecturer spoke in generalities; sweeping generalities.* **2** the greater part: *The generality of people pay*

generalize / genitourinary

their taxes.

gen.er.al.ize (JEN.ur.uh.lize) *v.* **-iz.es, -ized, -iz.ing 1** speak in general terms: *He frequently generalizes without revealing specific plans; to generalize about a whole group based on experience with a few members.* **2** make general: *The scientist generalized a law from several experiments.* —**gen.er.al.i.za.tion** (-luh.ZAY.shun, -lye-) *n.*

gen.er.al.ly (JEN.ur.uh.lee) *adv.* in general: *Generally speaking, it's a friendly town; an obscure fact that is not generally known.*

general practitioner *n.* a physician who is not a specialist; family physician.

general-purpose *adj.* suitable for a variety of uses and users: *a general-purpose application, detergent, dictionary, tool, vehicle.*

general store *n.* a store selling a wide variety of merchandise but not in separate departments.

gen.er.ate (JEN.uh.rate) *v.* **-ates, -at.ed, -at.ing** bring into being, as by a process: *heat generated by burning coal; a diplomat generating good will; Insects generate countless offspring.* —**gen.er.a.tive** (-ruh.tiv, -ray.tiv) *adj.*: *generative organs, power, values.*

gen.er.a.tion (jen.uh.RAY.shun) *n.* **1** the act of generating: *the generation of electricity at Niagara Falls.* **2** all people of about the same age range considered as one step in the line of descent: *Children are the younger generation; Four generations* (= children, parents, grandparents, and great-grandparents) *of Smiths were at the family reunion; Parents talking to their teenagers help bridge the* **generation gap. 3** a span of 25 to 30 years: *a generation ago; The Smiths have been around for* **generations**; *traditions handed down from* **generation to generation. 4** people of a specific period: *the coming, next, older, post-war, present generation; earlier, future, later, lost, past generations.* **5** a stage of history: *a new generation of poets; a first-generation immigrant; third-generation computers.*

Generation X or **Gen X** *n.* people born in the 1960s and '70s; also **X Generation.** —**Generation Xer** or **Gen-Xer** *n.*

gen.er.a.tor (JEN.uh.ray.tur) *n.* one that generates, esp. a machine turning mechanical energy into electrical energy: *power generators; a revenue generator.*

ge.ner.ic (juh.NER.ic) *adj.* having to do with an entire group, class, or genus; hence, general, not specific: *Thorns are a generic feature in roses; generic software that is compatible with many computers; The generic* (= not trademarked) *name for Coke, Pepsi, etc. is cola; a generic* (= not brand-name) *drug.* —**ge.ner.i.cal.ly** *adv.*

gen.er.ous (JEN.ur.us) *adj.* **1** giving freely; noble or magnanimous: *He gave up his seat in a generous act; Gigi is generous in giving to the poor; Jean is quite generous with his time and money.* **2** ample or abundant: *She gave us a generous share of the profits;* **gen.er.ous.ly** *adv.* —**gen.er.os.i.ty** (-ROS.i.tee) *n.* **-ties.**

gen.e.sis (JEN.uh.sis) *n., pl.* **-ses** (-seez) the coming into being of something; origin: *The Book of Genesis starts with the creation of the universe.*

gene-splicing *n. Informal.* same as GENETIC ENGINEERING.

ge.net.ic (juh.NET.ic) **1** *adj.* having to do with origin and heredity. **2 genetics** *n.pl.* [takes *sing. v.*] the study of heredity and variations in related plants and animals. —**ge.net.i.cal.ly** *adv.* —**ge.net.i.cist** *n.*

genetic code *n.* the organization of chemical elements in the chromosome determining the characteristics passed on from generation to generation.

genetic engineering *n.* scientific manipulation of genes or gene processes to create or eliminate traits.

ge.nial (JEEN.yul) *adj.* **1** favorable to life or growth: *Oranges thrive in Spain's genial climate; a genial influence.* **2** cheerful and amiable: *a genial tolerance of different religions; a genial host; a genial, big-brotherly manner; a genial mood, nature, temperament, tone.* —**ge.nial.ly** *adv.* —**ge.ni.al.i.ty** (jee.nee.AL.i.tee) *n.*

-genic *adj. suffix.* producing: *carcinogenic, eugenic, photogenic.*

ge.nie (JEE.nee) *n.* **-nies** a supernatural being, often serving humans, like those in the Arabian Nights stories: *The threat of a holocaust is so great, people feel we should stuff the nuclear genie back in the bottle.* See also GENIUS.

genii *pl.* of GENIUS, 3.

gen.i.tal (JEN.uh.tul) *adj.* having to do with reproduction or reproductive organs: *the genital area* or *region of a body; genital contact, herpes, organs, sores.* —*n.pl.* genital organs: *female, male genitals.* —**gen.i.tal.i.a** (-TAIL.yuh) *n.pl., Formal.* genitals. —**gen.i.tal.ly** *adv.*

gen.i.tive (JEN.uh.tiv) *adj.* having to do with the grammatical case that expresses possession or source; *n.*: *"His" is in the genitive.*

gen.i.to.u.ri.nar.y (JEN.i.toh.YOOR.uh.nair.ee) *adj.* of the genital and

genius / geodesic dome

urinary organs.

gen.i.us (JEEN.yus) *n.* **-us.es 1** exceptional natural ability or inclination, esp. great intellectual capacity or creativity: *Gigi has a genius for learning languages; There's a spark of genius in everything she does.* **2** a person with such ability: *a budding genius; mathematical, mechanical, musical geniuses; Einstein was a rare genius; An I.Q. of 150 or more makes you a "genius" according to the Terman index.* **3** *pl.* **ge.ni.i** (JEE.nee.eye) the distinctive spirit of an age, nation, place, or group: *F. Scott Fitzgerald captured the genius of the "Lost Generation."* **4** one who strongly influences another: *his evil genius.*

gen.o.cide (JEN.uh.cide) *n.* the systematic destruction of a racial, political, or cultural group. —**gen.o.ci.dal** (-SYE.dul) *adj.*

ge.nome (JEE.nome) *n.* the complete DNA sequence of an organism: *mapping of the human genome.*

gen.o.type (JEN.uh.type) *n.* the genes making up an individual, as distinguished from its appearance, or phenotype.

-gen.ous *adj. suffix.* producing, generating, or produced by: *endogenous, erogenous, nitrogenous.*

gen.re (ZHON.ruh) *n.* a type or kind, esp. of literary or artistic composition: *Science fiction is a 20th-century genre.*

gent (JENT) *n. Informal.* a man.

gen.teel (jen.TEEL) *adj.* polite and stylish, esp. affectedly or prudishly elegant: *She learned the genteel arts in finishing school; an old lady living in genteel poverty; the genteel quarters of Georgetown.*

gen.tian (JEN.shun) *n.* one of many species of plants with brilliant, usually blue flowers that are fringed in the "fringed gentian."

gen.tile or **Gen.tile** (JEN.tile) *n.* **1** an outsider, as among Jews and Mormons: *a Jew married to a gentile.* **2** formerly, a heathen or pagan.

gen.til.i.ty (jen.TIL.i.tee) *n.* **-ties 1** the condition of being of gentle birth; refinement: *an air of old-fashioned gentility.* **2** people of gentle birth; aristocracy.

gen.tle (JEN.tul) *adj.* **-tler, -tlest 1** kind and considerate; of things, not harsh, rough, violent, etc.: *He was soothed by her gentle voice; a mother's gentle (= soft) touch; a gentle (= mild) detergent for dry skin; Apply gentle (= moderate) heat; I barely heard the gentle (= soft) knock; a wild horse now gentle (= tame) as a lamb;* *nearly flat terrain with only a gentle (= slow) incline.* **2** of the upper classes, refined or well-bred: *Do good manners go with gentle birth?* —*v.* **-tles, -tled, -tling** make gentle or tame: *Soft music gentles his nerves.* —**gen.tly** *adv.*; **gen.tle.ness** *n.*

gen.tle.folk or **gen.tle.folks** *n.pl.* people of good upbringing.

gen.tle.man (JEN.tul.mun) *n.* **-men 1** a polite or well-bred man: *Hello, ladies and gentlemen; an unwritten* **gentleman's agreement** *(based on trust); A valet used to be referred to as a "gentleman's gentleman."* **2** [polite use] man: *The police said the gentleman couldn't have raped so many old ladies within the same hour.*
—**gen.tle.man.ly** *adv.*

gen.tle.wom.an (JEN.tul.wom.an) *n.* **-wom.en** a lady; also, a female attendant of a woman of rank.

gen.tri.fy (JEN.truh.fye) *v.* **-fies, -fied, -fy.ing** improve or upgrade a deteriorating neighborhood, as when higher-income people move in: *whether to gentrify skid rows or to raze them;* *adj.*: *a* **gentrified** *area, district, neighborhood; gentrified looks.* —**gen.tri.fi.ca.tion** (-fuh.CAY.shun) *n.*

gen.try (JEN.tree) *n.* **-tries 1** people of gentle birth: *the fox-hunting gentry of England; the landed gentry (= traditional landlords, ranking just below nobles) of Britain.* **2** people of a specified class: *the boxing gentry; the colored gentry; the teaching gentry; The new governor entertained the local gentry.*

gen.u.flect (JEN.yuh.flect) *v.* bend the knee, esp. in worship.
—**gen.u.flec.tion** (-FLEC.shun) *n.*

gen.u.ine (JEN.yoo.in, -ine) *adj.* **1** real and not fake: *a genuine antique, coin, Picasso.* **2** true or sincere: *genuine sorrow.* —**gen.u.ine.ly** *adv.*; **gen.u.ine.ness** *n.*

ge.nus (JEE.nus) *n., pl.* **gen.er.a** (JEN.uh.ruh) or **ge.nus.es** a kind, sort, or class, esp. a plant or animal classification under "family," comprising many "species": *Genus Rosa includes hundreds of rose species.*

geo- *comb.form.* of the earth: *geocentric, geographical, geological.*

ge.o.cen.tric (jee.uh.SEN.tric) *adj.* with the earth as center: *the old geocentric theory of the universe.*

ge.ode (JEE.ode) *n.* a stonelike formation with a cavity lined with crystals.

ge.o.des.ic (jee.uh.DES.ic) *adj.* having to do with geodesy: *a geodesic path, sphere, structure.*

geodesic dome *n.* a strong though un-

geodesic line / germ cell

supported hemispherical framework of triangle-shaped blocks made up of short, straight bars in tension.

geodesic line *n.* the shortest line between two points, as an arc with the smallest curvature if the points are on a sphere.

ge.od.e.sy (jee.OD.uh.see) *n.* applied mathematics, used esp. in surveying, dealing with measurements on the curved surface of the earth. —**ge.od.e.sist** *n.*

ge.o.det.ic (jee.uh.DET.ic) *adj.* having do with land surveying using geodesy; geodesic: *Geodetic surveying takes into account the earth's curvature.*

ge.og.ra.phy (jee.OG.ruh.fee) *n.* **-phies** the science of the earth's natural features, climate, inhabitants, resources, etc. —**ge.og.ra.pher** *n.* —**ge.o.graph.ic** (jee.uh.GRAF.ic) or **ge.o.graph.i.cal** (-i.cul) *adj.*

ge.ol.o.gy (jee.OL.uh.jee) *n.* **-gies** the science of the structure and history of the earth's crust. —**ge.ol.o.gist** (-jist) *n.* —**ge.o.log.ic** (jee.uh.LOJ.ic) or **ge.o.log.i.cal** *adj.*; **ge.o.log.i.cal.ly** *adv.*

ge.om.e.try (jee.OM.uh.tree) *n.* the mathematics of points, lines, angles, surfaces, and solid figures. —**ge.o.met.ric** (jee.uh.MET.ric) or **ge.o.met.ri.cal** (-ri.cul) *adj.* —**ge.o.met.ri.cal.ly** (-cul.ee) *adv.*

ge.o.phys.ics (jee.uh.FIZ.ics) *n.pl.* the science of the earth's physical forces, including geology, meteorology, and seismology. —**ge.o.phys.i.cal** *adj.*; **ge.o.phys.i.cist** *n.*

ge.o.pol.i.tics (jee.uh.POL.uh.tics) *n.pl.* the study of politics in relation to geography, esp. as affecting foreign policies.

geor.gette (jor.JET) *n.* a sheer crepe of rayon or silk; **adja.:** *a georgette blouse, dress, jacket, skirt.*

Geor.gian (JOR.jun) *adj.* **1** having to do with the English kings George I-IV and the styles of architecture, furniture, etc. typical of their time: *a Georgian church, country house, four-poster, mansion, poet; the Georgian period, style.* **2** having to do with the State of **Geor.gia,** U.S.A.: *a Georgian drawl;* **n.:** *the Georgians of Atlanta.* **3** having to do with the country of **Georgia** in the Caucasus, its people, or their language: *the Georgian capital of Tbilisi; Georgian independence, nationalism.*

ge.o.sci.ence (jee.oh.SYE.unce) *n.* a science such as geography or geology that deals with the earth; **ge.o.sci.en.tist** *n.*

ge.o.sta.tion.ar.y (jee.oh.STAY.shuh.nair.ee) *adj.* of an artificial communications satellite, orbiting at the same speed and in the same direction as the earth so that it can act as a fixed relay station.

ge.o.ther.mal (jee.oh.THUR.mul) *adj.* of the earth's internal heat.

ge.ot.ro.pism (jee.OT.ruh.piz.um) *n.* the tendency, as of a plant's roots, to grow downward because of the earth's gravity.

ge.ra.ni.um (juh.RAY.nee.um) *n.* a garden plant or wildflower with showy scarlet, pink, white, or purple blossoms.

ger.bil (JUR.bil) *n.* a mouselike desert rodent with long hind legs.

ger.i.at.rics (jer.ee.AT.rics) *n.* [with *sing. v.*] a branch of medicine dealing with aging and the diseases of the aged. —**ger.i.at.ric** *adj.*

germ (JURM) *n.* **1** the seed, bud, or earliest form of a living thing: *the oil-rich wheat germ.* **2** source or origin: *Inspiration is the germ of poetry; the germ of an idea.* **3** a microscopic creature, as a bacterium; microbe; **adja.:** *germ fighters; the germ theory of the spread of infectious diseases; germ warfare using disease bacteria.*

Ger.man (JUR.mun) *adj.* having to do with **Germany,** a country in C. Europe, its language, or its people. —*n.* **1** a person of or from Germany. **2** the German language.

-german *comb.form.* **1** having the same parents: *a brother-german; sisters-german.* **2** closely related: *a cousin-german* (= first cousin).

ger.mane (jur.MAIN) *adj.* closely related: *Your sex is germane to the question of parenthood, but not even relevant to your becoming a lawyer.* —**ger.mane.ly** *adv.*; **ger.mane.ness** *n.*

Ger.man.ic (jur.MAN.ic) *adj.* German in origin: *The Germans, Dutch, English, etc. are Germanic peoples speaking Germanic languages.*

ger.ma.ni.um (jur.MAY.nee.um) *n.* a brittle, gray-white, metallic chemical element used in transistors.

German measles same as **RUBELLA.**

German shepherd *n.* an intelligent, wolflike dog trained for police work or for guiding the blind.

German silver *n.* an alloy of copper, nickel, and zinc; nickel silver.

germ cell *n.* a reproductive cell, as a sperm (male) or egg (female), whose hereditary substance is **germ plasm** consisting of chromosomes.

ger.mi.cide (JUR.muh.cide) *n.* a germ-destroyer, as an antiseptic. —**ger.mi.ci.dal** (-SYE.dul) *adj.*

ger.mi.nal (JUR.muh.muh.nul) *adj.* of germs; also, embryonic.

ger.mi.nate (JUR.muh.nate) *v.* **-nates, -nat.ed, -nat.ing** begin to grow; sprout; also, cause to sprout. —**ger.mi.na.tion** (-NAY.shun) *n.*

ger.on.tol.o.gy (jer.un.TOL.uh.jee) *n.* the scientific study of aging and the problems of the elderly; **ger.on.tol.o.gist** (-jist) *n.* —**ge.ron.to.log.ic** (juh.ron.tuh.LOJ.ic) or **ge.ron.to.log.i.cal** *adj.*

ger.ry.man.der (jer.ee.MAN.dur) *v.* **-ders, -dered, -der.ing** divide into voting areas that give one political party an advantage. —*n.* the practice of gerrymandering.

ger.und (JER.und) *n.* the "-ing" form of a verb used as a noun, as in "to enjoy *reading*" or "good *reading*."

gest or **geste** (JEST) *n.* [old use] a heroic exploit or a narrative of heroic deeds in verse.

ge.stalt or **Ge.stalt** (guh.SHTAHLT) *n.* a totality of form or structure that cannot be divided into parts or analyzed; **adj.***a.:* the Gestalt psychology of perception and behavior; gestalt therapy.

Ge.sta.po (guh.STAH.poh) *n.* **-pos** the Nazi German secret police.

ges.tate (JES.tate) *v.* **-tates, -tat.ed, -tat.ing** carry in the womb; hence, develop slowly.

ges.ta.tion (jes.TAY.shun) *n.* pregnancy or its period: *a ten-month period of gestation; a project that has been 10 years in gestation* (= development).

ges.tic.u.late (jes.TIK.yuh.late) *v.* **-lates, -lat.ed, -lat.ing** make vigorous gestures, esp. instead of words: *Too shocked to speak, he gesticulated helplessly.* —**ges.tic.u.la.tion** (-LAY.shun) *n.*

ges.ture (JES.chur) *n.* **1** a motion of the body expressing or emphasizing an idea or feeling: *Nodding is a common gesture for "Yes"; In East Indian classical dancing, every gesture and movement has a meaning; an angry gesture; a gesture of appreciation.* **2** any act or remark indicating attitude: *The offer was a conciliatory gesture; a bold, friendly, grand, noble gesture; She gave up her seat as a kind gesture to the man on crutches.* —*v.* **-tures, -tured, -tur.ing** communicate by gesture: *She gestured to the waiter to bring the tab.* —**ges.tur.al** (-rul) *adj.*

Ge.sund.heit (guh.ZOONT.hite) *interj.* [said when someone sneezes] Bless you!

get ("g" as in "go") *v.* **gets,** *pt.* **got,** *pp.* **got** or **got.ten 1** obtain or acquire, as by earning, buying, catching a disease, etc.: *I must get a better job; You must get some rest; How did he get such a good deal? She got herself new shoes; Go and get me a drink; You get 13 if you add 5 and 8; The children got colds.* **2** reach or cause to reach a place, condition, state, etc.: *We have to get home early; He's planning to get married; Let's not get* (= enter) *into an argument; Can you get* (= make) *him to listen? He didn't get the message; He got himself in trouble with the police; You have to get after* (= put pressure on) *him; Wayne doesn't want to get between* (= try to separate) *a man and his wife; to get* (= become) *angry, drunk, excited; to get even with someone; We're getting nowhere waiting for the bus; Let's get rid of the trash.* **3** *Informal.* overcome physically or emotionally, as by capturing, killing, irritating, puzzling, etc.: *The Mounties got* (= captured) *their man; Her pleas finally got* (= overcame) *him; Nothing gets* (= annoys) *me more than loud chewing.* **4** *Informal.* understand or hear: *I didn't get you.* **5** have, esp. as an obligation: *Our team has got to win!* **6** manage or contrive: *When will I get to see the dentist? We finally got the car going.* **7** communicate with someone: *Please get her on the phone.* **8** beget: *Abraham got Isaac.* —**get across** make or become clear: *to get a message across to the class.* —**get along** manage fairly well: *We used to get along on $100 a week; They find it hard to* **get along with** (= stay on good terms with) *each other.* —**get around 1** circulate: *Word got around that the boss had resigned.* **2** evade: *He tried to get around the rules.* **3** trick, esp. by flattery. **4** find the time for doing something: *I never got around to answering that letter.* —**get at 1** to reach: *Keep drugs where the kids can't get at them; to get at the truth by study and prayer.* **2** to reach indirectly: *He was accused of trying to get at* (= bribe) *the jury; What are you getting at* (= implying)? —**get away** leave or escape: *The burglars got away.* —**get away with** succeed in something: *People shouldn't be getting away with cheating; He practically got away with murder.* —**get back at** take revenge: *Jean is trying to get back at Marie for the snub.* —**get by** manage: *Can you get by without a loan?* —**get down** take up: *When you get down to it, it's no problem; Let's get down to business.* —**get it** *Informal.* be punished: *He got it for* being late. —**get it (all) together** or **get one's act together** *Informal.* to get organized or function in an organized way. —**get off** leave or escape: *Let's get off the bus; A smart lawyer got him off* (= helped him escape punishment). —**get off on** *Slang.* get pleasure or excitement from something: *to get off on drugs; She gets off on horror movies.* —**get on** go up on or into something: *to get on a train; Noisy children get on his nerves* (= make him nervous); *They are quite active though getting on* (= advancing) *in years; She gets on* (= is friendly) *with everyone.* —**get out** go out: *He quickly got out of town; if word of our plans gets out* (= escapes). —**get over** forget: *He'll soon get over the shock of her death.* —**get through 1** finish: *I get through my homework before bedtime.* **2** survive: *The homeless try to get through the winter.* **3** establish communication: *He couldn't get through to the operator.* —**get together** assemble: *Teachers get together with the principal now and then.* —**get to one** *Informal.* disturb: *His nagging is beginning to get to me.* —**get up** arise, as from bed or the table. —*n.* an animal offspring; also, the offspring of a male animal collectively.

get.a.way (GET.uh.way) *n. Informal.* escape: *The robbers made a quick getaway; adja.: a getaway car, resort, vacation.*

get-together *n.* an informal social gathering.

get-up *n.* costume: *He came to the party in a bizarre get-up; an elaborate get-up.*

get-up-and-go *n. Informal.* initiative or energy: *Vito has get-up-and-go; Leo lacks get-up-and-go.*

gew-gaw ("g's" as in "go") *n.* a bauble or trinket.

gey.ser (GUY.zur) *n.* a spring that periodically ejects columns of hot water and steam.

G-force *n.* the force of gravity: *Astronauts encounter high G-forces during blastoff and re-entry.* Also **g-force.**

ghast.ly (GAST.lee) *adj.* **-li.er, -li.est 1** terrifying or horrible; also, very unpleasant. **2** ghostlike or deathly; pale. —**ghast.li.ness** *n.*

ghat (GAWT, GAHT) *n.* in India, a flight of steps leading down to a river landing; also **ghaut.**

gher.kin (GUR.kin) *n.* a small cucumber used for pickling.

ghet.to (GET.oh) *n.* **-tos** or **-toes** a section of a city inhabited by a minority group obliged to live there for economic, legal, or social reasons: *the former Jewish ghettos of anti-Semitic countries; an inner-city ghetto; urban ghettos.*

ghost (rhyme: post) *n.* **1** the spirit of a dead person, supposed to appear to the living as a pale, shadowy form: *to see a ghost at night; a ghost story.* **2** a faint trace, suggestion, or shadow, as a secondary television or photographic image: *Ghosts result when the TV set receives direct as well as reflected images; a candidate without* **a ghost of a** (= the least) *chance.* **3** one who ghosts a book or speech. —**give up the ghost** *Informal.* die. —*v. Informal.* write another person's autobiography, speech, etc. for payment. —**ghost.ly** *adj.*

ghost town *n.* a deserted town which was once flourishing, as one abandoned after a gold rush.

ghost.write *v.* **-writes, -wrote, -writ.ten, -writ.ing** same as GHOST: *He ghostwrites for celebrities; adj.: a ghostwritten autobiography.* —**ghost.writ.er** *n.*

ghoul (GOOL) *n.* a legendary evil spirit that robs graves and feeds on the dead. —**ghoul.ish** *adj.*

GI (JEE.eye) *n., pl.* **GI's** or **GIs** a U.S. serviceman, esp. an enlisted soldier: *GI Joe.* —*adj.* conforming to military regulations: *a GI haircut.*

gi.ant (JYE.unt) *n.* a huge, imaginary humanlike being of enormous strength; hence, a person or thing of great size or powers: *Our phone company is a corporate giant; entertainment, industrial, media giants; the "San Francisco Giants"* (baseball team). —**adja.** huge or great in size: *a giant bank, corporation, leap, redwood tree, spider, step.*

gi.an.tess (JYE.un.tis) *n.* a female giant of folklore.

giantism same as GIGANTISM.

giant slalom *n.* a slalom on a longer and steeper course than the regular one.

gib.ber (JIB.ur, GIB-) *v.* speak rapidly and unintelligibly; chatter.

gib.ber.ish (JIB.ur.ish, GIB-) *n.* meaningless talk or chatter; nonsense.

gib.bet (JIB.it) *n.* a gallows. —*v.* **1** hang on a gibbet. **2** hold up to public ridicule.

gib.bon (GIB.un) *n.* a small, long-armed ape of Southeast Asia and the East Indies.

gib.bous (GIB.us) *adj.* **1** curved outward, protuberant; hence, humped or humpbacked. **2** of the moon or a planet, more than half full but less than a circle.

gibe (JIBE)) *v.* **gibes, gibed, gib.ing** make jeering remarks; taunt or sneer:

giblets / gin

Siblings gibe at each other. —*n.* a taunt or sneer: *siblings trading gibes.* Also **jibe.**

gib.lets (JIB.lits) *n.pl.* the edible viscera of a fowl, as the heart, liver, or gizzard.

gid.dy (GID.ee, "G" as in "go") *adj.* **gid.di.er, gid.di.est** 1 having or causing dizziness: *to climb to giddy heights.* 2 frivolous or fickle: *a giddy young flirt.* —**gid.di.ness** *n.*

gift ("g" as in "go") *n.* 1 something given; a present: *to give a birthday gift; wedding gifts; He lavished gifts on his spouse; a million-dollar gift to charity; an outright gift with no conditions attached.* 2 a natural ability or talent: *She has a gift for drawing; adj.: People are gifted in different ways; a gifted (= generally talented) child.* 3 the act or power of giving: *a job within the mayor's gift.*

gift certificate *n.* a certificate of a specified value issued by a store to customers to exchange for merchandise. Also **gift token, gift voucher.**

gift of tongues *n.* ecstatic speech that sounds like some unknown language.

gift.ware *n.* china, crystal, etc. that are suitable as gifts: *dinnerware and giftware; adja.: a giftware collection, showroom, shop; the giftware industry; a giftwares exhibition.*

gift.wrap or **gift-wrap** *v.* **-wraps, -wrapped, -wrapping** wrap for presentation as a gift; *adj.: a giftwrapped box; giftwrapped merchandise; adja.: giftwrapping paper.* Also *n.*

gig ("g's" as in "go") *n.* 1 an open, two-wheeled, horse-drawn carriage. 2 a long, light ship's boat. 3 a fishing spear. 4 *Slang.* a job, esp. a one-time engagement for a jazz or rock musician. Also *v.* **gigs, gigged, gig.ging.**

giga- (JIG.uh-) *comb.form.* one billion: *gigabit, gigabyte, gigacycle, gigaflops, gigaton, gigawatt.*

gi.gan.tic (jye.GAN.tic) *adj.* giantlike; huge or immense in size.

gi.gan.tism (jye.GAN.tiz.um) *n.* excessive growth of the body or of plants.

gig.gle ("g's" as in "go") *v.* **gig.gles, gig.gled, gig.gling** laugh in a silly or nervous way: *He kept giggling all through the speech.* —*n.* such a laugh: *She gave a shrill giggle at the remark.*

GI.GO (GUY.go, GEE-, "G" as in "go") *n.* "garbage in, garbage out" (= It's useless to process useless data).

gig.o.lo (JIG.uh.loh) *n.* **-los** a man paid as a woman's escort or lover.

Gi.la monster (HEE.luh-) *n.* a large, black-and-orange poisonous lizard of S.W. United States.

gild ("g" as in "go") *v.* **gilds,** *pt. & pp.* **gild.ed** or **gilt, gild.ing** 1 cover with gold leaf or gold-colored material: *It makes no sense to gild the lily* (= unnecessarily adorn something beautiful); *adj.: a gilded frame, mirror, rose; gilded silver; a gilded* (= showily wealthy) *life; to live in gilded luxury.* 2 make deceptively attractive in appearance; *adj.: a gilded image.* —*n.* same as GUILD.

gilding *n.* an outer layer of gold: *the gilding on a bracelet; a mere gilding* (= surface coating) *of politeness.*

gill ("g" as in "go") *n.* the breathing organ of fishes and other water animals. —**green around the gills** pale or nervous-looking. —**to the** (or **to one's**) **gills** *Informal.* up to the neck; totally.

gilt a *pt.* and *pp.* of GILD; *adja.:* gilt chairs; a gilt-framed mirror. —*n.* 1 same as GILDING: *gold, silver gilt.* 2 a gilt-edged security or investment: *Unlike market-ready hogs, females* (= breeding hogs) *are gilts; adja.: the gilts market; gilts prices; gilt holders, yields.*

gilt-edge or **gilt-edged** *adj.* edged with gold; hence, of the highest quality: *a gilt-edged mirror; Gilt-edge securities are safe investments; gilt-edged assets, bonds, stocks.*

gim.bals (GIM.buls, JIM-) *n.pl.* a device for keeping a ship's compass, etc. horizontal by counteracting motion.

gim.crack (JIM.crack) *n.* a showy, worthless object. —**gim.crack.er.y** *n.*

gim.let (GIM.lit, "G" as in "go") *n.* 1 a small hole-boring hand tool with a screw point. 2 a cocktail made with gin or vodka.

gim.me (GIM.ee, "G" as in "go") *Slang.* *v.* "give me": *Gimme a break.* —*n.* 1 something easily obtained: *A gimme goal has nothing to do with good hockey.* 2 the tendency of children to ask constantly for things they desire: *It's always gimme, gimme with kids who watch too much TV; Commercials promote the gimmes.*

gim.mick (GIM.ik, "G" as in "go") *n.* an ingenious device, scheme, deception, or concealed condition: *a sports car equipped with the latest gimmicks; pens given out as an advertising gimmick; promotional gimmicks.* —**gim.mick.ry** (-ree) *n.* **-ries.** —**gim.mick.y** *adj.*

gimp ("g" as in "go") *n.* a lame person or walk. —**gimp.y** *adj.*

gin (JIN) *n.* 1 an alcoholic liquor distilled from grain. 2 a trap or snare. 3 a machine for removing cotton seeds

from the fibers. —*v.* **gins, ginned, gin.ning** remove seeds from cotton.
gin.ger (JIN.jur) *n.* **1** a tropical plant with a pungent underground stem used as a spice. **2** the spice itself. **3** *Informal.* liveliness or spirit. —**gin.ger.y** *adj.*
ginger ale *n.* a ginger-flavored carbonated soft drink.
gin.ger.bread (JIN.jur.bred) *n.* **1** a ginger-flavored molasses cake. **2** gaudy or elaborate ornamentation, as on houses. —**adja.** elaborately ornamented: *gingerbread architecture; gingerbread clocks, design, men, trim.*
gin.ger.ly (JIN.jur.lee) *adv.* very carefully or cautiously: *He picked up the worm and held it gingerly between thumb and forefinger; to approach, step, tread gingerly.*
gin.ger.snap (JIN.jur.snap) *n.* a crisp ginger-flavored molasses cookie.
ging.ham (GING.um) *n.* a yarn-dyed cotton fabric often designed in checks, stripes, or plaids.
gin.gi.vi.tis (jin.juh.VYE.tis) *n.* inflammation of the gums.
gink.go (GING.koh, "G" as in "go") *n.* -**goes** an Asian ornamental tree with fan-shaped leaves; also **ging.ko.**
gin.seng (JIN.seng) *n.* an herb of Asia and North America with an aromatic root used in medicine.
gip, Gipsy same as GYP, GYPSY.
gi.raffe (juh.RAF) *n.* a cud-chewing African animal with a very long neck and legs and a tawny, spotted coat.
gird (GURD) *v.* **girds,** *pt. & pp.* **gird.ed** or **girt, gird.ing 1** encircle, as with a belt; surround: *a city girded by ramparts; "Thou hast girded* (= invested) *me with gladness."* **2** fasten or tie: *His sword was girded on; trousers girded up with rope; He girded himself* (= prepared) *for the blow.* —**gird (up) one's loins** prepare for action.
gird.er *n.* a main horizontal supporting beam of a building or bridge.
gir.dle (GUR.dul) *n.* an encircling or confining band, esp. a woman's elasticized undergarment worn about the hips and waist. —*v.* **-dles, -dled, -dling** encircle: *a park girdled by trees.*
girl (GURL) *n.* **1** a female child or a young unmarried woman: *chorus, dancing, flower, pinup girls; college girls and guys.* **2** [offensive when used instead of "woman"]: *a career girl; working girls.* **3** [offensive] a female servant. **4** a sweetheart or female companion; also, a girlfriend: *the girl of his dreams; the typical* **girl-next-door** (= conventional nice-girl) *image.* —**girl.hood** *n.;* **girl.ish** *adj.*
girl Friday See FRIDAY.
girl.friend *n. Informal.* **1** a female friend. **2** a sweetheart.
Girl Guide *n. Cdn.* a member of the **Girl Guides,** a youth organization corresponding to the Girl Scouts of America.
gir.lie (GUR.lee) *adj. Informal.* having to do with the physical aspect of women: *a design that is feminine without being girlie; a girlie calendar with girlie pictures; a girlie magazine.*
Girl Scout *n.* a member of the **Girl Scouts** of America, a character-building organization for girls aged 7 to 17 years.
girt 1 a *pt. & pp.* of GIRD. **2** *v.* put a girdle around; gird.
girth (GURTH) *n.* **1** the measurement around something; circumference: *waist and hip girth; girth measurements.* **2** a band around an animal's body to hold a saddle or pack on its back.
gis.mo (GIZ.moh) same as GIZMO.
gist (JIST) *n.* the essential or main point: *to get the gist of an article, conversation, message, report, statement, story; the gist of what he said; the gist of it.*
give (GIV) *v.* **gives, gave, giv.en, giv.ing 1** hand over: *Give her the book; Give it to him; to give to charity; How much will he give (as a price) for the car? He has given* (= devoted) *his life to the cause.* **2** provide or present: *to give a concert, party, reading, speech.* **3** yield or produce: *Cows give milk.* **4** yield; give way: *Any lock will give if forced; Something has got to give.* **5** afford a view; open: *The windows give onto the yard.* **6** reveal: *Don't give away the secret.* **7** stop doing, trying, or hoping: *to give up smoking; I give up (guessing the answer); They gave up* (= stopped trying to find) *the cat for lost.* —*n.* a yielding under pressure; elasticity or flexibility: *A concrete walk has no give; I see some give in their attitude.* —**give away 1** give as a gift. **2** present a bride to the groom. —**give in** yield: *He had to give in to her demands.* —**give it to someone** *Informal.* scold or beat. —**give or take** add or subtract a small number: *200 people, give or take a few.* —**give out 1** distribute or make known. **2** wear out; break down; become exhausted. —**give up 1** surrender or devote oneself, one's energies, life, time, etc. entirely to something: *She has given up her life to helping the poor.* —**give way** yield: *to give way to pressure; The bridge gave way*

(= collapsed). —**what gives?** *Informal.* what is the matter?: *What gives? What gives with him – is he mad or something?*

give-and-take *n.* a good-natured exchange, as of ideas or remarks: *the give-and-take of collaboration, family life, friendships, negotiations; the atmosphere, process, spirit of give-and-take; a give-and-take relationship.*

give.a.way (GIV.uh.way) *n.* **1** an unintentional revelation: *a dead giveaway.* **2** something given away without charge.

giv.en (GIV.un) **1** *pp.* of GIVE: *a boy given to* (= habitually disposed to) *bullying; Given that* (= considering that) *all are mortal, how can he hope to live forever? what I was given to understand* (= made to believe or understand). **2** *prep.* considering: *Given our mortality, it is meaningless to accumulate more than we can consume.* **3** *adj.* specified: *on a given date; within a given time.* **4** *n.* something known to be true: *Mortality is a given; One of the givens is nothing is guaranteed here.*

given name *n.* a name given to a person, as at baptism, not surname or family name; first name.

giz.mo (GIZ.moh, "G" as in "go") *n.* -**mos** *Slang.* a device or gadget.

giz.zard (GIZ.urd, "G" as in "go") *n.* the food-grinding second stomach of a bird.

gla.cé (gla.SAY) *adj.* candied or frozen; also, glossy; glazed: *peach glacé pie.*

gla.cial (GLAY.shul) *adj.* **1** relating to glaciers or to a **glacial epoch**, a period, as the Ice Age, when much of the earth was covered by glaciers: *glacial ice.* **2** very cold: *a glacial disposition.* **3** very slow: *The negotiations are moving at a glacial pace.* —**gla.cial.ly** *adv.*

gla.ci.ate (GLAY.shee.ate) *v.* -**ates, -at.ed, -at.ing** act on or cover with ice or glaciers. —**gla.ci.a.tion** (-AY.shun) *n.*

gla.cier (GLAY.shur) *n.* a huge body of ice slowly moving downhill or spreading across land.

glad *adj.* **glad.der, glad.dest 1** *adj.* causing or feeling joy or pleasure: *a glad occasion; glad tidings; to give someone the glad eye* (= a seductive glance). **2** *adjp.* pleased: *I'm glad to hear the good news; I'm glad it turned out that way; We are all glad about it.*

glad.den (GLAD.un) *v.* make or become glad.

glade *n.* an open space in a forest.

glad hand *n.* a jovial, often insincere greeting. —**glad-hand** *v.*: *a candidate glad-handing the voters.*

glad.i.a.tor (GLAD.ee.ay.tur) *n.* a man trained to fight for public entertainment in ancient Rome.

glad.i.o.lus (glad.ee.OH.lus) *n., pl.* -**li** (-lye) or -**lus.es** a plant with sword-shaped leaves and spikes of brightly colored flowers. Also **glad.i.o.la** (-OH.luh).

glad.some *adj.* joyful; cheerful; delightful: *the gladsome news.*

glad.stone (GLAD.stone) *n.* a small hinged suitcase that opens into two equal compartments; also **gladstone bag.**

glamor See GLAMOUR.

glam.or.ize (GLAM.uh.rize) *v.* -**iz.es, -ized, -iz.ing** make glamorous; idealize. —**glam.or.i.za.tion** (-ruh.ZAY.shun, -rye-) *n.*

glam.our (GLAM.ur) *n.* alluring charm, romance, or excitement: *the glamour of Hollywood; a woman with an aura of glamour; The glamour soon wore off; adj.: a glamour boy, drug, girl, queen.* Also **glam.or.** —**glam.or.ous** *adj.*: *a glamorous car, display, image, life; glamorous clothes, models, professions.*

glance *v.* **glanc.es, glanced, glanc.ing 1** strike and be deflected obliquely: *She threw the stone so that it glanced off the water; adj.: a glancing blow.* **2** look quickly: *She glanced at us as she passed by.* **3** to flash or gleam with light: *Swords glanced in the sun.*
—*n.* **1** a quick look: *to steal a glance at someone; to exchange glances; fleeting, furtive, knowing, shy, sidelong, wistful glances; She saw what was going on with a glance through the window.* **2** gleam: *the glance of swords in the sun.*

gland *n.* a fluid-producing organ such as the liver or kidneys: *The adrenal gland is a ductless gland; Sweat glands have ducts.*

glandes *pl.* of GLANS.

glan.du.lar (GLAN.juh.lur) *adj.* having to do with glands: *Mononucleosis is called "glandular fever."*

glans (GLANZ) *n., pl.* **glan.des** (-deez) the tip of the penis or of the clitoris.

glare *v.* **glares, glared, glar.ing 1** shine with a harsh, painfully bright light. **2** stare angrily or fiercely: *They glared at each other.* —*n.* **1** the effect of a harsh light: *to perform under the glare of television lights; in the full glare of publicity.* **2** an angry look: *Sam shot a glare of hatred at Lou.*

glaring 1 *adj.* that glares: *the glaring sun; harsh, glaring neon lights; glaring eyes.* **2** *adj.* conspicuous: *a glaring case of misconduct; a glaring abuse, deficiency,* discrepancy, disparity, error, example, inconsistency, injustice, lapse, omission, weakness; **glar.ing.ly** adv.

glas.nost (GLAS.nost) n. campaign of openness in dealing with the people, as started by the Soviet leader Mikhail Gorbachev.

glass n. 1 a hard, brittle, usually transparent substance made by melting sand with lime, potash, etc. 2 an object made of glass: *milk served in a glass; They clinked glasses and drank to each other's health; a wine glass; The glass (= mirror) reflected his face; He saw the moon through a glass (= telescope).*
3 **glasses** pl. eyeglasses or binoculars: *dark, field, opera, reading, sun glasses.*
4 the amount contained in a drinking glass: *a glass of milk;* also **glass.ful.**
—adj. made of glass: *a glass eye; "Those who live in glass houses should not throw stones"* (= Do not blame others when you are as bad as they).

glass blowing n. the art of forming molten glass into an object by blowing air into it through a tube; **glass blower** n.

glass ceiling n. prejudice, considered invisible, against the advancement of women and minorities to top positions in the workplace.

glassed adj. enclosed by glass: *a glassed patio;* a **glassed-in** *kitchen, office, viewing area.*

glass.ware n. glass objects, esp. drinking glasses.

glass wool n. glass spun into fibers like wool and used for filtering and insulation.

glass.y adj. **glass.i.er, -i.est** 1 smooth like glass: *a glassy sheet of ice.* 2 lifeless or expressionless: *a glassy stare.*
—**glass.i.ly** adv.

glau.co.ma (glaw.COH.muh) n. an eye disease in which pressure within the eyeball results in retinal damage and gradual loss of vision.

glaze v. **glaz.es, glazed, glaz.ing** 1 provide a window frame, etc. with glass. 2 cover pottery or food with a smooth, glossy surface; adj.: *glazed chicken breast* —n.: *Hot water dulled the china's glaze; There's a glaze of ice on the pond.*

gla.zier (GLAY.zhur) n. one who fits windows, etc. with glass.

gleam (GLEEM) n. 1 a brief flash or dim glow of light: *the gleam in her eyes; a gleam of sunshine.* 2 a brief or faint show: *a gleam of hope, interest.* —v.: *A fire gleamed in the dark; eyes momentarily gleaming with humor.* —**gleam.y** adj.

glean (GLEEN) v. 1 pick up the grain left by reapers. 2 gather facts, news, etc. bit by bit: *facts gleaned from old magazines.* —**glean.er** n.

glean.ings n.pl. things collected by gleaning.

glebe (GLEEB) n. a piece of land forming part of a clerical benefice.

glee n. 1 lively delight: *to dance with glee.* 2 an unaccompanied song for three or more different singing voices.
—**glee.ful** adj.; **glee.ful.ly** adv.

glee club n. a group organized for singing choral songs.

glen n. a narrow valley.

glen.gar.ry (glen.GAIR.ee) n. **-gar.ries** a woolen bonnet or cap, typical of Scottish Highlanders.

glib adj. **glib.ber, glib.best** smooth and fluent, often in an insincere way: *a glib excuse, judgment, sales pitch, solution, talker.* —**glib.ly** adv.; **glib.ness** n.

glide v. **glides, glid.ed, glid.ing** 1 move along smoothly and with ease. 2 descend in a plane without using the engine. —n.: *the prone glide and back glide in swimming; the plane's long glide to the ground.*

glid.er (GLY.dur) n. one that glides, esp. an engineless aircraft kept aloft by air currents: *A glider soars upward or across the sky.*

glim.mer (GLIM.ur) v. give a weak, flickering light; appear dimly: *stars glimmering in the distant sky.*
—n. a faint light: *the faint glimmer of distant candlelight; a glimmer of hope; a story without even a glimmer of truth.*

glimpse (GLIMPS) v. **glimps.es, glimpsed, glimps.ing** see or look at briefly and hastily. —n. a brief sight: *I caught a glimpse of the speeding car.*

glint n. 1 a flash or gleam of light. 2 a brief appearance.
—v. flash briefly: *Light glinted from the crystal glasses; With each turning, the story glints with a different light.*

glis.san.do (gli.SAHN.doh) adj. & adv. performed musically by gliding quickly up or down the scale.
—n., pl. **-di** (-dee) or **-dos** a part played in this way.

glis.ten (GLIS.un) v. shine brightly by reflecting light; sparkle: *Dew glistens on the grass; Her eyes glistened with tears;* adj.: *glistening eyes, hair, snows.*

glis.ter (GLIS.tur) v. [old use] glisten.

glitch n. 1 an unwanted surge of electricity or a false electronic signal. 2 *Informal.* a minor mishap or malfunction: *an unexpected glitch; the glitches and gremlins that bug computers.*

glit.ter (GLIT.ur) v. 1 shine brightly

with a flashing light; sparkle: *a glittering diamond.* **2** be showy or attractive: *the glittering costumes worn by rock singers.* —*n.* sparkle: *the glitter of diamonds; a circus parade's glitter; to decorate costumes with glitter* (= small, shiny objects). —**glit.ter.y** *adj.*: *beaded glittery costumes; the glittery lives of movie stars.*

glitz.y (GLIT.see) *adj.* **glitz.i.er, -i.est** showy or gaudy: *a glitzy image, party, restaurant.*

gloam.ing (GLOH.ming) *n.* [poetic] twilight or dusk.

gloat (GLOTE) *v.* take pleasure in a greedy, selfish, or sadistic manner: *to gloat over a rival's misfortune;* **n.**: *a gloat of triumph.*

glob *n.* a drop or globule; also, a rounded lump.

glob.al (GLOH.bul) *adj.* **1** of the whole earth; worldwide: *global changes, implications, issues; a global epidemic, strategy, war; AIDS on a global scale.* **2** all-inclusive: *a global command, view; a global search (of a database).*

glob.al.ism (GLOH.buh.liz.um) *n.* internationalism, esp. in plans or outlook. —**glob.al.ly** *adv.*

global village *n.* the concept of the world reduced to a small community by high-speed transportation and communications.

global warming same as GREENHOUSE EFFECT.

globe *n.* **1** anything spherical, esp. the earth or a model of it: *The equator girdles the globe.* **2** a nearly round glass object, as a fishbowl.

globe.trot.ting (GLOBE.trot.ing) *adja.* traveling all over the world: *a globetrotting businessman, career, executive, tour.* —**globe.trot.ter** *n.* Also **globe-trotting, globe-trotter.**

glob.u.lar (GLOB.yuh.lur) *adj.* **1** spherical: *globular droplets.* **2** composed of globules: *a globular cluster.*

glob.ule (GLOB.yool) *n.* a tiny ball or drop.

glob.u.lin (GLOB.yuh.lin) *n.* a protein in plant seeds, blood plasma, etc. that is soluble in dilute salt solutions but not in pure water.

glock.en.spiel (GLOK.un.speel) *n.* a percussion instrument of tuned metal bars played with light hammers and sounding like bells.

gloom (long "oo") *n.* darkness or dimness: *an all-pervading gloom; the gloom of winter; The bad news cast (a) gloom over the audience; a cloud, pall of gloom; tales of doom and gloom; There is gloom about* or *over the future of the environment.* —**gloom.y** *adj.*; **gloom.i.ly** *adv.*; **gloom.i.ness** *n.*

glo.ri.fy (GLOR.uh.fye) *v.* **-fies, -fied, -fy.ing 1** give praise, honor, worship, or glory to a person or thing; also, exalt to heaven: *a martyr glorified after death.* **2** make something seem more splendid than it actually is: *TV shows that glorify violence.* —**glo.ri.fi.er** (-fye.ur) *n.* —**glo.ri.fi.ca.tion** (-fuh.CAY.shun) *n.*

glo.ri.ous (GLOR.ee.us) *adj.* **1** having, giving, or deserving glory: *a glorious deed, past, reign, victory.* **2** magnificent or delightful: *the glorious fall weather; We had a glorious time at the party.* —**glo.ri.ous.ly** *adv.*

glo.ry (GLOR.ee) *n.* **-ries 1** great honor, fame, or praise, esp. of God: *Glory to God in the Highest; a painting of saints in heavenly glory; Olympic gold brings glory to a nation; to bask in the glory of victory; in the* **glory days** *of our youth.* **2** the source of renown; splendor or magnificence: *Long hair was her glory; the glory that was Rome.* —*v.* **-ries, -ried, -ry.ing** rejoice proudly: *to glory in one's exploits, over the vanquished.*

gloss *n.* **1** a shiny surface; luster: *a high gloss finish.* **2** a deceptive appearance. **3** a commentary on, a brief note within, or a translation of a text. —*v.* explain or annotate. —**gloss over** try to ignore or hide: *The report glosses over the details of the scandal.*

glos.sa.ry (GLOS.uh.ree) *n.* **-ries** a short dictionary of difficult or technical words: *a glossary at the end of a textbook.*

glos.so.la.li.a (glos.uh.LAY.lee.uh) *n.* unintelligible, meaningless speech occurring in religious ecstasy and schizophrenia.

glos.sy (GLOS.ee) *adj.* **gloss.i.er, -i.est 1** having a lustrous surface: *a glossy finish, glaze, look, paint, sheen; smooth and glossy.* **2** printed on glossy paper: *glossy magazines, pages, photos.* —*n.*, *pl.* **glos.sies** a magazine or photograph printed on smooth, shiny paper. —**gloss.i.ly** *adv.*; **gloss.i.ness** *n.*

glot.tis *n.* the narrow space in the larynx between the vocal cords. —**glot.tal** *adj.*

glove (GLUV) *n.* **1** a fitted hand covering with separated fingers: *kid, leather, rubber gloves; The nickname fits him* **like a glove;** *The gloves were coming off (in preparation for a fight) and charges were laid.* **2** a large padded leather covering used on the hand in baseball, boxing, etc.

glove box (or **compartment**) *n.* a

compartment in an automobile's dash for keeping small items.

gloved (GLUVD) *adj.* wearing gloves: *He was warmly gloved against the cold; a gloved hand.*

glow (GLOH) *v.* **1** shine brightly and steadily because or as though intensely heated; *adj.: glowing* embers; *a glowing* (= highly favorable) *account, description.* **2** have a bright, reddish color; flush or blush: *His cheeks glowed with embarrassment.* **3** show warm emotion: *glowing with pride in his son.*
—*n.* **1** brightness: *the glow of burning coal; the soft glow of a lamp.* **2** warmth or warm color: *the ruddy glow of health on her cheeks; to feel a glow of affection.*

glow.er (rhyme: flower) *v.* stare angrily or sullenly. —*n.* a scowl.

glow.worm (GLOH.wurm) *n.* an insect or insect larva that emits light, esp. a firefly.

glox.in.i.a (glok.SIN.ee.uh) *n.* a tropical American plant with velvety leaves and bell-shaped red, white, or purple flowers.

gloze *v.* **gloz.es, glozed, gloz.ing** gloss over.

glu.cose (GLOO.cose) *n.* **1** a sugar occurring naturally in animals and plants, esp. fruits, used by cells for energy. **2** a syrup made from starch and used to sweeten food.

glue (GLOO) *n.* a sticky substance used to join things, esp. one made from animal gelatin. —*v.* **glues, glued, glu.ing** stick: *a broken cup glued together.* —**glue.y** (GLOO.ee) *adj.*

glum *adj.* **glum.mer, glum.mest** gloomy, sullen, or morose. —**glum.ly** *adv.*; **glum.ness** *n.*

glut *v.* **gluts, glut.ted, glut.ting 1** fill or feed to excess: *to glut one's appetite.* **2** oversupply a market: *The price of gas went down when the world markets were glutted with oil.* —*n.* an oversupply: *There's a glut of cookbooks on the market.*

glu.ten (GLOO.tun) *n.* a sticky, elastic mixture of proteins found in grain; **glu.ten.ous** *adj.* gluten-containing: *Wheat is more glutenous than rye; glutenous bran.* —**glu.ti.nous** *adj.* sticky or gluey: *glutinous concrete, rice, sentimentality.*

glut.ton (GLUT.un) *n.* one who overeats or has a too large capacity for something: *He's a glutton for work.*
—**glut.ton.ous** *adj.* —**glut.ton.y** *n.* **glut.ton.ies.**

gly.cer.in or **gly.cer.ine** (GLIS.uh.rin) *n.* a thick, sweet, clear liquid made from fats and oils and used in lubricants, foods, and explosives; also **gly.cer.ol** (-rol).

gly.co.gen (GLYE.cuh.jun) *n.* a carbohydrate made and stored chiefly in the liver and converted into glucose when needed.

gly.col (GLYE.col) same as ETHYLENE GLYCOL.

G-man *n.* **G-men** an F.B.I. agent.

gnarl (NARL) *n.* a twisted, protruding knot on a tree.

gnarled or **gnarl.y** *adj.* knotty or misshapen.

gnash (NASH) *v.* grind together: *He gnashed his teeth in rage.*

gnat (NAT) *n.* any tiny, winged, usually biting insect.

gnaw (NAW) *v.* **1** consume, corrode, or produce by biting: *a dog gnawing (at) a bone; Mice gnaw holes.* **2** torment: *Remorse gnawed at his heart;* **adja.: gnawing** anxiety, hunger, pain.

gneiss (NICE) *n.* a coarse-grained rock made of layers of minerals, usually quartz, feldspar, and mica.

gnome (NOME) *n.* a dwarf of folklore who lives underground and guards treasures of precious ores: *the fabled gnomes* (= powerful bankers) *of Swiss banks.*

gno.mic (NOH.mic) *adj.* having to do with maxims and aphorisms: *gnomic poetry, quotations, verse.*

gnom.ish (NOH.mish) *adj.* dwarfish, like a gnome.

gnos.tic (NOS.tic) *adj.* claiming esoteric knowledge of spiritual matters: *gnostic insight;* **gnos.ti.cism** *n.*

gnu (NEW) *n.* a large, horned African antelope with high, massive shoulders.

go *v.* **goes** (GOZE), **went, gone** (GON, GAWN), **go.ing 1** move away to or from a place: *You can go now; I'll be gone by 5 p.m.* **2** move or pass on: *There's a rumor going through school; another year to go before I graduate; My eyesight is going* (= weakening); *Fifty dollars will not go far* (= purchase much) *at today's prices.* **3** be active: *The machine goes when you switch it on.* **4** move or tend to someone or something: *You shouldn't have gone to such trouble for me; This fact goes to prove he was wrong; She had to go to court to establish her claim.* **5** be, become, or be put in a certain way or condition: *Where will this sofa go? She will go mad when she hears this; Many go hungry all over the world; The battery had gone dead; Cats go missing; Some go broke; How did the interview go? The cork went pop.* —**go along** go forward in agreement: *They tried to go* along with his wishes; To get along with Joe you have to go along with him. —**go ape** Slang. go crazy: Fans are going ape over that star. —**go at** devote oneself to something: She goes at everything she takes up with energy. —**go back on** break: to go back on a promise. —**go by the board** be abandoned: The project went by the board when the director died. —**go down** be entered in the records: He'll go down in history as a great general. —**go for 1** apply to a person or thing: What I said about Al – the same goes for you too. **2** attack: The animal went for his face. **3** Informal. approve of: The government knew that the people wouldn't go for the increased taxes. —**go in for** take an interest in something: I don't go in for the latest fashions. —**go it alone** act alone: She decided to go it alone when her partner backed out. —**go off 1** take place: How did the meeting go off? **2** explode: The bomb didn't go off. —**go on 1** happen: What's going on in town? **2** judge by: We need some facts and figures to go on. **3** continue: Don't go on being late. —**go one better** do better: The competition tried to go one better by cutting prices. —**go out 1** go steady: Jack is going out with Jill. **2** **go out to** feel for someone: Our hearts go out to the children of broken homes. —**go over 1** examine: An accountant went over the company's books. **2** desert to another group: a spy who went over to the enemy. —**go through 1** pass: He went through a red light and got hit. **2** endure: the hard times she went through. —**go through with** carry out: to go through with a marriage, performance, plan. —**go under** fail: Many businesses go under during a recession. —**go up to** approach: She went up to the officer and asked the way. —**go with** go steady: Jack is going with Jill. —**go without** carry on wanting something: When food is scarce, some have to go without. —**let go 1** release: The child wouldn't let go of her mother's hand; A very reserved man at work, he lets himself go during office parties. —**to go** as takeout: ten hot dogs to go. —n. Informal. attempt: He will have another go at the top prize next year; to make a go (= success) of the new enterprise. —**from the word go** from the very start. —**no go** failure: It was no go each time he applied for membership. —**on the go** active: vitamins for people on the go from 9 to 5. —adjp. Informal. in perfect order: All systems are go for the blastoff. See also GOING, GONE.

goad (GODE) n. **1** a pointed rod used to urge animals forward. **2** a driving impulse. —v. drive: Examinations goad students into activity; Students are goaded to study hard.

go-ahead n. Informal. permission or signal to proceed: Wait for the leader to give the go-ahead; We got the go-ahead for the project.

goal (GOLE) n. **1** a desired aim, attained after some effort: to achieve or attain or reach or realize a goal; set a goal; an immediate goal; the ultimate goal of one's ambition. **2** in a race or in games such as hockey and football, the place to be reached for winning or scoring; also, such a score: to kick or make a goal; She scored two goals in one minute.

goal.ie (GOH.lee), **goal.keep.er** (GOLE.kee.pur) or **goal.tend.er** (-ten.dur) n. a player who defends a goal against the opposing team.

goal post n. one of a pair of posts marking the goal in hockey, soccer, lacrosse, etc.

goat (GOTE) n. **1** a cud-chewing, horned, and usually bearded animal related to the sheep: Goats baa or bleat; a young goat (= kid); a female goat (= doe or nanny); a male goat (= buck or billy goat). **2** Informal. a scapegoat: Education sometimes becomes the goat of government spending. —**get one's goat** Informal. make one feel annoyed or irritated.

goat.ee (goh.TEE) n. a small, pointed beard on the chin.

goat.herd n. one who tends goats.

goat.skin n. a container of leather made from a goat's skin.

gob n. **1** Slang. a sailor in the U.S. Navy. **2** Informal. a lump or mass; also **gob.bet** (GOB.it).

gob.ble (GOB.ul) v. **gob.bles, gob.bled, gob.bling 1** swallow greedily: He gobbled up the food in a hurry. **2** make the throaty sound of a male turkey, or **gob.bler**.

gob.ble.dy.gook or **gob.ble.de.gook** (GOB.ul.dee.gook, long or short "oo") n. Informal. speech or writing that is incomprehensible or meaningless because of its pompous or involved style.

go-between n. an intermediary or messenger between two parties.

gob.let (GOB.lit) n. a bowl-shaped drinking cup with a stem and foot but no handles.

gob.lin (GOB.lin) n. a mischievous elf or sprite of folklore.

go-cart n. **1** a small, low-slung toy wagon. **2** a kart.

god *n*. **1** a supreme being considered as supernatural and immortal; also, a male deity or idol: *heathen gods; the god of love.* **2 God** the creator and ruler of the universe for those who believe in one supreme being: *Thank God he's alive;* **God willing,** *I hope to pass my final exam;* *Compulsory arbitration means someone must* **play God** (= make a binding decision). **3** a deified person or thing. —**a sight** or **feast for the gods** something wonderful.

god.child *n*. **-chil.dren** one sponsored by a godparent, as at baptism; **god.daugh.ter** *n*.; **god.son** *n*.

god.dam or **god.damn** *n*., *adj*. & *adv*. [offensive] stronger forms of DAMN.

god.dess (GOD.is) *n*. a female god.

god.fa.ther (GOD.fah.thur) *n*. **1** a man who sponsors a person at baptism. **2** *Informal*. don or boss: *an underworld godfather;* **adj.a.:** *a godfather figure; the godfather image.*

god.for.sak.en (god.fur.SAY.kun) *adj*. desolate or dismal: *a godforsaken place.*

god.head *n*. **1** a divinity. **2 Godhead** God.

Go.di.va (guh.DYE.vuh) *n*. a legendary woman of Coventry, England, who rode naked through the streets on a horse to get a tax abolished: *Anyone to play Lady Godiva?*

god.less (GOD.lis) *adj*. not religious: *a godless world; the godless masses.* —**god.less.ness** *n*.

god.like *adj*. divine: *a godlike aura, grandeur, presence.*

god.ly (GOD.lee) *adj*. **-li.er, -li.est 1** devout: *a godly life, person.* **2** godlike. —**god.li.ness** *n*.

god.moth.er (GOD.muth.ur) *n*. a woman sponsoring a person at baptism.

god.par.ent (GOD.pair.unt) *n*. a godfather or godmother.

god.send *n*. something much-needed or desired that one gets as if sent by God: *A maid can be a real godsend to the busy homemaker.*

god.son See GODCHILD.

God.speed (god.SPEED) *n*. success: *to bid* or *wish someone Godspeed.*

go.fer (GOH.fur) *n Slang*. one who fetches things for another: *file clerks, receptionists, and assorted gofers.*

go-getter *n*. *Informal*. one who is aggressively ambitious.

gog.gle (GOG.ul) **1** *v*. **gog.gles, gog. gled, gog.gling** stare with bulging or surprised eyes *at* something. **2 goggles** *n.pl*. large protective eyeglasses as worn by welders, motorcyclists, and divers.

goggle-eyed *adj*. having staring eyes: *a goggle-eyed fish (with bulging eyes); The goggle-eyed audience never took their eyes off her.*

go-go *n*. **1** a discotheque. **2** discotheque dancing. —*adj*.: *a go-go dancer cavorting on the stage; the go-go* (= unrestrained) *pace of twentieth-century life; a go-go* (= speculative) *investment fund; a very go-go* (= stylish) *jacket and slacks.*

going 1 *n*.: *the coming and going* (= departure) *of winter; We find the going* (= progress) *tougher than expected; Let's leave the place* **while the going is good** (= while it is easy to leave). **2** *v*.: *a lucky young woman who has many things* **going for** (= in favor of) *her; She's 12*, **going on** (= approaching) *13; It's* **going to** (= about to) *rain.* **3** *adj*.: *the best candidate going* (= available); *The going* (= prevailing) *rate for this job is $150 an hour; a* **going concern** (= smoothly running business). **4** *comb.form*. going regularly as specified: *an easy-going guy; an ocean-going vessel; quiet-going kids; the theater-going public.*

going-over *n*. **1** a thorough examination. **2** a scolding or beating.

goings-on *n.pl*. *Informal*. happenings looked upon with disapproval: *The goings-on at that house were the talk of the town.*

goi.ter (GOY.tur) *n*. a thyroid disorder resulting in an abnormal swelling in the front of the neck. Also **goi.tre** *Cdn*.

gold *n*. **1** a bright-yellow precious metal used for jewelry and as international currency; hence, money: *to prospect for gold; We struck gold; Liz is as good as gold* (= very good). **2** a bright yellow: *dressed in gold and olive green;* **adj.a.:** *gold glitter, lettering, ribbon.* **3** a record that has sold one million copies or 500,000 copies as an album. **4** in Canada, a record or album that has sold between 50,000 and 100,000 copies. **5 gold medal:** *an Olympic gold.*

gold.brick *n*. *Slang*. one who shirks work; loafer.

gold digger *n*. *Slang*. a woman who uses her charms to get money from men.

gold.en (GOLD.un) *adj*. **1** made of gold: *the golden calf; a golden ring.* **2** bright yellow: *golden hair.* **3** flourishing or prosperous: *the golden age of poetry; the golden years of retirement; a golden* (= 50th year) *anniversary, jubilee; a golden* (= valuable) *opportunity.*

golden ager *n*. *Informal*. a person over 65 years old.

golden boy *n*. favorite: *the golden boy of*

our corporation.

golden calf *n.* **1** in the Bible, an idol worshiped by the Israelites. **2** wealth as an object of worship.

golden-haired boy same as GOLDEN BOY.

golden handshake *n.* a generous severance payment as an inducement for early retirement.

golden oldie *n. Informal.* something old but still popular, as a song.

golden parachute *n.* guarantee of a large severance payment to a top executive in the event of a company takeover.

gold.en.rod (GOLD.un.rod) *n.* a common wildflower with slender stems like wands, blooming in late summer with golden yellow flowers.

golden rule *n.* a basic rule of conduct, esp. "Treat others as you would like them to treat you."

gold.field *n.* a district in which gold is mined.

gold.filled *adj.* esp. of jewelry, with a gold layer over base metal.

gold.finch *n.* a common songbird whose male is bright yellow with a black patch on its head.

gold.fish *n.* a fancy variety of carp with bright colors ranging from gold to red, kept in glass bowls as ornamental fish.

gold.heart.ed (GOLD.har.tid) *adj.* having a generous nature.

gold leaf *n.* gold in the form of thin foil.

gold mine *n.* a mine yielding gold; hence, a source of something valuable: *We've hit a gold mine; You're sitting on a gold mine; a potential gold mine; a gold mine of information.* —**gold.min.ing** *n.*

gold.plate *n.* base metal coated with gold by electroplating: *a watch in 18-karat goldplate; goldplate bracelets;* also **goldplated** *adj.: goldplated buttons.*

gold.smith *n.* a worker skilled in making articles of gold; also, a dealer in them.

gold standard *n.* a system by which a country's basic monetary unit is made equal to and exchangeable for a specified amount of gold.

golf (GOLF, GAWLF) *n.* a game played with a small, hard ball and long-handled **golf clubs** on an outdoor **golf course,** or **golf links,** having a series of 9 or 18 holes: *to play a round of golf* (= complete circuit of all the holes). —*v.* play golf. —**golf.er** *n.*

Go.li.ath (guh.LYE.uth) *n.* in the Bible, a giant killed by David.

gol.ly (GOL.ee) *interj.* expressing surprise, pleasure, etc.: *By golly, he did it; Oh, golly gee!*

-gon *comb.form.* a figure with angles as specified: *octagon, pentagon, polygon.*

go.nad (GOH.nad) *n.* a male or female sex gland; an ovary or a testis.

go.na.do.trop.in (GOH.nad.uh.TROH.pin) *n.* a hormone that regulates the gonads; **go.na.do.trop.ic** (-TROP.ic) *adj.* Also **go.na.do.troph.in** (-TROH.fin), **go.na.do.troph.ic** (-fic).

gon.do.la (GON.duh.luh) *n.* **1** a long, narrow boat with peaked prow and stern, as used on the canals of Venice. **2** something resembling a gondola such as an enclosed suspended car used as a ski lift, a car suspended from under an airship, a low-sided open-topped railroad car, or **gondola car,** for bulk freight such as coal, etc.

gon.do.lier (gon.duh.LEER) *n.* one who rows or poles a gondola.

gone 1 *pp.* of GO: *He's gone to Africa; I've gone (= been) to Europe; Have you gone there?* **2** *adjp.* away: *I'll be gone for two days; Gone* (= departed) *are the days of cheap gas; The disease is too* **far gone** (= too advanced) *for us to do anything.* **3** *adj. Informal.* removed from reality: *He wore a gone expression; He's quite* **gone on** (= in love with) *her.*

gon.er (GON.ur) *n. Informal.* a person or thing beyond help: *One glance from her and you're a goner!*

gong *n.* a large metal disk that is struck for use as a bell or as a musical instrument.

gon.na (GON.uh) *Informal.* "going to": *It ain't gonna work.*

gon.o.coc.cus (gon.uh.COC.us) *n., pl.* **-coc.ci** (-COC.sye) the germ that causes gonorrhea; **gon.o.coc.cal** (-ul) *adj.*

gon.or.rhea (gon.uh.REE.uh) *n.* a venereal disease usually transmitted during sexual intercourse; **gon.or.rhe.al** (-ul) *adj.*

gon.zo (GON.zoh) *adj. Slang.* weird or bizarre.

goo *n. Slang.* **1** anything thick and sticky, as glue. **2** sentimentality: *nostalgia without the goo.* —**goo.ey** (GOO.ee) *adj.*

goo.ber *n. Informal* [Southern U.S.] a peanut.

good (short "oo") *adj., comp.* **bet.ter** (BET.ur), *superl.* **best** having a desirable quality: *Rain is good for crops, but bad for a picnic; She's good at or in manual work; good with her hands; good to her in-laws; Isn't it good to be home at last!*

Does 2 + 2 = 4 **hold good** (= be true) under all conditions? She's been away a good (= considerable) while; so tired I'm **as good as** (= almost) dead; a round-trip ticket that is **good for** (= valid for) a year; This pen is **no good** (= useless). —*n.* **1** what is good: *to do good and avoid evil; The laws work for the common good; Happiness is the highest good; What good is food you can't eat? I'm telling you for your own good; A teacher tries to bring out the good in every student; Some come to no good* (= yield no good result); *Sound advice, well taken, works* **to our good. 2 goods** *pl.* movable personal property; also, merchandise; things for sale: *capital, consumer, durable, manufactured goods; a* **goods-and-services** *tax.* —**for good (and all)** forever.
—**have the goods on someone** *Slang.* know something bad about a person that others don't. —*adv. Informal.* well: *I can't see good through the fog; It's raining good and* (= really) *heavy.*
—**make good 1** succeed: *Unsuccessful throughout life, he made good by marrying a wealthy widow.* **2** put into effect: *to make good one's escape; make good (on) a promise, a threat.* **3** pay for something: *to make good a loss.*
good-bye or **good.bye** *interj. & n., pl.* **-byes** farewell.
good-for-nothing *n.* one who is worthless or disreputable.
Good Friday *n.* the Friday before Easter, commemorating Christ's crucifixion.
good-hearted *adj.* kind and generous.
good.ish *adj.* fairly good, great, or large.
good-looking *adj.* handsome or pretty.
good.ly (GOOD.lee) *adj*a. **-li.er, -li.est** considerable: *a goodly sum of money.*
good-natured *adj.* likable or friendly; **good-naturedly** *adv.*
good.ness (GOOD.nis) *n.* the condition or quality of being good, esp. morally: *Goodness knows I tried; For goodness' sake, stop arguing.*
Good Sa.mar.i.tan (-suh.MAIR.uh.tun) *n.* one who takes pity on another in misery and offers help unselfishly; also **good samaritan.**
good-tempered *adj.* not easily annoyed; good-humored.
good turn *n.* a good deed or favor.
good.wife *n.* **-wives** *Archaic.* the mistress of a household; "Mrs."
good will *n.* **1** friendly feeling. **2** the reputation enjoyed by a business that is valued as one of its assets.
—**good.will** *adj*a. promoting good will: *a goodwill gesture, mission, tour.*
good.y (GOOD.ee) *n.* **good.ies** *Informal.* something good, esp. to eat. —*adj.* affectedly pious or moral. —*interj.* a child's exclamation indicating delight.
goody-goody *n.* one who is affectedly or abjectly good.
gooey See GOO.
goof (long "oo") *n. Slang.* **1** blunder. **2** a stupid person. —*v.* make a blunder: *Somebody goofed and the wedding cake never arrived; Those who* **goof around** (= waste time) *all day never get anything done; He was fired for* **goofing off** (= loafing) *on the job.*
goof.ball *n. Slang.* a barbiturate, stimulant, tranquilizer, etc. used nonmedically.
goof-off *n. Slang.* a shirker.
goof.y (GOO.fee) *adj.* **goof.i.er, -i.est** silly or crazy.
gook (long or short "oo") *n. Slang.* something sticky or slimy.
goon (long "oo") *n. Slang.* **1** a ruffian, as one hired to break up strikes or help prison guards: *a goon squad.* **2** a stupid person.
goop (long "oo") *n. Slang.* something semiliquid and sticky: *goops of ink from a ball-point pen.*
goose (rhyme: loose) *n., pl.* **geese** a web-footed bird that is smaller than a swan, to which it is related, and considered stupid: *A goose cackles* or *honks; a flock* or *gaggle of geese; a young goose* (= gosling); *a male goose* (= gander); *You silly goose!* **to kill the goose that lays golden eggs** (= to destroy a source of wealth out of greed). —**cook one's goose** See COOK. —*v.* **1** *Slang.* to startle a person by prodding him in the buttocks. **2** *Informal.* prod or urge forward: *to goose the economy by printing money;* to **goose up** (= raise) *sales, wages.*
goose.ber.ry (GOOSE.ber.ee) *n.* **-ber.ries** the small, oval, tart fruit of a thorny shrub related to the currant, commonly used in preserves and pies.
goose bumps *n.pl.* a skin condition resembling a plucked goose's skin caused by cold, fear, etc.; also **goose flesh, goose pimples.**
goose.neck *n.* a flexible neck, as used for the shafts of lamps: *a gooseneck kitchen faucet.*
goose.step *n.* an infantry marching step using high kicks.
go.pher (GOH.fur) *n.* **1** a burrowing rodent with large cheek pouches; also called "pocket gopher." **2** a ground squirrel of the prairies related to the chipmunk. **3** same as GOFER.

Gor.dian knot (GOR.dee.un-) *n.* something intricate like the knot that could not be untied and was cut by Alexander the Great with a quick, bold stroke.

gore *n.* 1 clotted blood. 2 a long, triangular or wedge-shaped piece of cloth inserted in a garment, sail, etc. to adjust width or shape. —*v.* **gores, gored, gor.ing** pierce or wound with a horn or tusk.

gorge (GORJ) *n.* 1 a narrow canyon with steep walls. 2 a mass, as of ice, choking a passage. 3 a seam on a coat where the collar meets the lapel. —**make one's gorge rise** of something gruesome, to disgust or make one want to vomit. —*v.* **gorg.es, gorged, gorg.ing** stuff with food: *children at a party gorging themselves with or on cake.*

gor.geous (GOR.jus) *adj.* splendid, esp. in a colorful way: *trees in gorgeous fall colors; gorgeous weather; a gorgeous day, display, sunset, view; Isn't she gorgeous! fifty gorgeous dancers kicking on the stage.*

go.ril.la (guh.RIL.uh) *n.* an African ape, the largest of the anthropoids.

gor.mand.ize (GOR.mun.dize) *v.* **-iz.es, -ized, -iz.ing** eat like a glutton; **gor.mand.iz.er** *n.*

gorm.less (GORM.lis) *adj. Informal.* senseless.

gorp *n. Informal.* a snack of high-energy food, as dried fruits, nuts, and seeds.

gorse same as FURZE.

gor.y (GOR.ee) *adj.* **gor.i.er, gor.i.est** bloody; hence, horrible: *a gory murder; Spare us the gory details.*

gosh *interj.* an exclamation of surprise: *By gosh!*

gos.hawk (GOS.hawk) *n.* the largest of a group of swift-flying hawks once used in falconry.

gos.ling (GOZ.ling) *n.* a young goose.

go-slow *adj.* going slow: *a go-slow approach, attitude, formula, plan, policy.*

gos.pel (GOS.pul) *n.* 1 something accepted without question, as from the Christian **Gospels**, the first four books of the New Testament: *the capitalist gospel; Some children take what is heard on TV as (the) gospel truth.* 2 Christianity: *to spread the gospel; St. Thomas preached the gospel in India.* 3 [short form] gospel music: *to sing gospel;* **adj.**: *a gospel choir, group, singer.*

gos.pel.er (GOS.pul.ur) *n.* a gospel preacher. Also **gos.pel.ler** *Cdn.*

gospel music *n.* church singing of devotional songs, as practiced by blacks of the American south.

gos.sa.mer (GOS.uh.mur) *n.* light and filmy substance, as of cobwebs seen floating in the air or sheer fabric resembling it; **adj.**: *gossamer veils, wings; gossamer (= light) construction.*

gos.sip (GOS.ip) *n.* 1 idle talk about other people and their private affairs: *Where did he pick up that piece of gossip? Who's spreading the gossip? the gossip about Dick and Jane.* 2 a person who indulges in gossip: *idle, malicious, vicious gossips.* —*v.*: *People gossip about unwed mothers and fathers.* —**gos.sip.y** *adj.*

got *pt. & pp.* of GET. —**have got** *Informal:* Have you got (= do you have) a match? I have got to (= must) go home now.

gotch.a (GOCH.uh) *Informal.* "I got you!"

Goth.ic (GOTH.ic) *n. & adj.* 1 (the language) of a Germanic people of the 3rd to 5th centuries A.D.: *a Gothic tribe.* 2 a style of architecture developed in Europe in the Middle Ages: *the pointed Gothic arch; Gothic cathedrals.* 3 fiction dealing with the supernatural and the grotesque: *Gothic books, fiction; 19th century Gothic novels.*

got.ta (GOT.uh) *Informal.* "have got to." See GOT: *Ya gotta love her.*

got.ten (GOT.un) a *pp.* of GET.

Gou.da (GOW.duh, GOO-) *n.* a flat, round cheese similar to Edam but with more fat.

gouge (GOWJ) *n.* 1 a chisel with a concave blade for cutting grooves and holes. 2 a channel or hole made with a gouge. —*v.* **goug.es, gouge, goug.ing** 1 dig or scoop out, as with a gouge: *to gouge out the meat of a coconut.* 2 *Informal.* extort money from someone: *The shopkeeper used to gouge his customers;* **n.**: *He was charged with (price)* **gouging.** —**goug.er** *n.*

gou.lash (GOO.lash) *n.* a highly seasoned stew of meat and vegetables.

gourd (GORD, GOORD) *n.* 1 the fruit of a vine such as the cucumber, pumpkin, or squash. 2 a hard-shelled fruit such as the calabash that is dried for use as a container.

gour.mand (GOOR.mund, -mahnd) *n.* a lover of good food and wine.

gour.met (GOOR.may) *n.* a discriminating expert of food and drink; also, such food and drink. —**adj.** having to do with good food and drink: *gourmet coffee, cooking, fare, merchandise; a gourmet cook, dish, food, item, meal, menu, restaurant, shop, show, store.*

gout (GOWT) *n.* a disease characterized by swelling of the joints, esp. that of the big toe. —**gout.y** *adj.* **gout.i.er, -i.est:** *gouty arthritis (caused by gout); a gouty joint; a gouty toe (suffering from gout).*

gov.ern (GUV.urn) *v.* control or regulate: *Children must learn to govern their temper; conduct governed by moral principles; The British Sovereign merely reigns and does not govern; Supply and demand govern prices; "to" governs "him," not "he" as in "Give it to him";* **adj.:** *a college's* **governing** *body.* —**gov.ern.a.ble** (-nuh.bul) *adj.* —**gov.ern.ance** (-nunce) *n.*

gov.ern.ess (GUV.ur.nis) *n.* a woman who teaches and supervises children in their home.

gov.ern.ment (GUV.urn.munt) *n.* **1** the act of governing; rule: *Democracy is government by the people; good, strong, weak government.* **2** a method or system of governing: *communist, democratic, parliamentary, totalitarian governments.* **3** a governing body of people such as the prime minister and cabinet: *the previous government; a Republican government; caretaker, central, coalition, federal, local, minority, municipal, national, provincial, provisional, state governments; to head, live under, overthrow, run, seize a government; government and opposition; Who will form the next government* (= *Who will be the next prime minister or premier*)? *The government was about to fall; the governments* (= *na- tions*) *represented at the U.N.;* **adja.:** *shouting from the government benches of parliament; the government leaders* (= *party spokesmen*) *of the house and senate.* —**gov.ern.men.tal** (-MEN.tul) *adj.*

gov.er.nor (GUV.ur.nur) *n.* **1** the appointed head of a state or colony. **2** a member of a governing body or "board of governors." **3** a mechanical device to control machine speed, as by operating a rheostat on an electric motor. —**gov.er.nor.ship** *n.*

governor general *n., pl.* **governors general** a chief governor: *The Governor General of Canada.*

gown (rhyme: down) *n.* **1** a long, loose outer garment or robe, as worn by judges and academics, or a woman's formal dress, as worn at a wedding. **2** a similar garment: *dressing gowns; a hospital gown.* —*v.* dress in a gown: *Candidates come capped and gowned for a graduation ceremony.*

grab *v.* **grabs, grabbed, grab.bing 1** grasp suddenly, esp. in an eager or greedy manner: *A dog grabs at a bone.* **2** *Informal.* take or get: *Grab a pencil and write this down; Something that grabs your attention; The Soviets grabbed the lead in the third period; He grabbed her by the arms; She* **grabbed hold** *of the* **grab bar** *when she slipped in the bath.* **3** *Informal.* make an impression on someone: *Five dollars for a cup of coffee – how does that grab you?* —*n.* a snatch or grasp: *an elected office* **up for grabs** *every four years.* —**grab.ber** *n.*

grab bag *n.* **1** a bag of assorted items sold at a fixed price. **2** miscellaneous assortment: *The politician offered a grab bag of promises.*

grab.by (GRAB.ee) *adj.* **grab.bi.er, grab.bi.est 1** that grabs: *grabby tires.* **2** avaricious: *grabby moneylenders.*

grace *n.* **1** a pleasing quality such as charm, beauty, or elegance: *Gazelles run fast with effortless grace; He's full of faults but for one saving grace* (= quality); *A defeated candidate concedes an election with* **good** *or* **bad grace;** *Jane puts on little* **airs and graces** *to impress people.* **2 Your** or **Her** or **His Grace** [title used in addressing or referring to an archbishop, duke, or duchess]. **3** favor or good will: *Adam's disobedience and fall from grace; divine grace; a state of grace; three days of grace, or a* **grace period,** *to return a book without penalty after it is due.* **4** a short prayer, as before or after a meal. —**in one's good** (or **bad**) **graces** favored (or disliked) by one. —*v.* **grac.es, graced, grac.ing 1** bring charm or elegance to something: *The mayor graced the occasion by* or *with her presence.* **2** honor someone, as with a title.

grace.ful *adj.* attractive in form, movement, or behavior: *a graceful animal, dance, gesture.* —**grace.ful.ly** *adv.;* **grace.ful.ness** *n.*

grace note *n. Music.* an extra note added for ornament.

gra.cious (GRAY.shus) *adj.* having or showing qualities befitting a high station in life, as courtesy, indulgence, and elegance: *her gracious smile; She's gracious toward everyone; a gracious gesture, speech; a suburban mansion fit for gracious living.* —**interj.** indicating surprise: *Good gracious!*

grack.le (GRAK.ul) *n.* a North American blackbird.

grad *n. Informal.* a graduate.

gra.da.tion (gruh.DAY.shun, gray-) *n.* a step or degree in something showing progressive change: *the gradations from violet to red in the rainbow.*

grade *n.* **1** one of a series of steps or

degrees: *school grades from 1 to 12; to skip a grade; He rose from the grade of warrant officer to the rank of captain.* **2** a classification according to quality: *prime, choice, and other grades of beef; There are several sizes of grade A eggs; different grades of coal, lumber, petroleum products; octane grades.* **3** an achievement rating, as A, B, C, D, E, F (fail), or S (satisfactory): *final, high, passing, school, top grades; to get, give, receive a grade; Everyone except those receiving F* **make the grade** (= pass). **4** a road level or ground level: *A basement is below grade; There is no grade separation between two tracks at a grade crossing.* **5** a grade crossing. **6** the slope of a road or railroad track: *Trains climb grades; gradual grades; steep grades.*
—*v.* **grades, grad.ed, grad.ing**
1 classify: *Only steer and heifer can be graded prime beef; a term paper graded "A".* **2** level or slope: *to clear a right of way and grade it for a highway.*

grade crossing *n.* a railroad track and another track or road crossing on the same level.

grade-point average *n.* the average obtained by dividing total points by the number of credits earned.

grad.er (GRAY.dur) *n.* **1** one that grades, esp. an earth-leveling machine: *a road grader.* **2** a school pupil in a specific grade: *a first grader.*

grade school *n.* in the U.S., an elementary school; also **the grades.**

grade separation *n.* a crossing that uses an overpass or underpass.

gra.di.ent (GRAY.dee.unt) *n.* a slope or its inclination.

grad.u.al (GRAJ.oo.ul) *adj.* by steps or degrees; little by little: *a gradual awakening, change, fall, improvement, process, rise, shift; The recession was more abrupt than gradual.* —**grad.u.al.ly** *adv.*

grad.u.al.ism (GRAJ.oo.uh.liz.um) *n.* the theory or policy of seeking social or political change gradually, not suddenly; **grad.u.al.ist** *n.*

grad.u.ate (GRAJ.oo.ate) *v.* **-ates, -at.ed, -at.ing 1** finish a course of study: *Al graduated from Georgetown; Our cook has graduated to baker after only six months on the job; the graduating class.* **2** give a diploma to someone: *Al was graduated with honors.* **3** mark or divide into gradations; *adj.: a thermometer graduated in degrees Celsius; a tax rate so graduated that higher incomes are taxed more than lower incomes.*
—*n.* (-oo.it) one who has graduated: *a Yale graduate; an honors graduate;* **adj.:** *a graduate degree, engineer, nurse, school; a graduate student working on her master's.* —**grad.u.a.tion** (-oo.AY.shun) *n.*

graf.fi.ti (gruh.FEE.tee) *n.pl.* crude drawings or writings done on a public wall, rock, etc. —**graf.fi.to** (-toh) *sing.*

graft *v.* **1** join a shoot or bud, called scion, from one plant or tree to another, called stock, and make it grow: *Several varieties of a plant may be grafted on to the same stock; adj.: a grafted bud.* **2** produce a new or improved fruit, flower, etc.; *adj.: a grafted variety, vine.* **3** transplant skin, bone, cells, etc. in this manner. **4** of politicians, public officials, etc., make money by illegal means. —*n.* **1** something grafted: *The tree is a graft between an orange and a quince; different types of graft such as cleft, splice, and saddle; A skin graft was done, but it didn't take; a bone graft from his pelvis.* **2** illegally made money: *graft in the form of protection money.*

gra.ham (GRAY.um) *adja.* made of fine, unsifted whole-wheat: *graham crackers, flour, wafers.*

Grail *n.* the cup used by Jesus at the Last Supper, sought by knights of medieval legend.

grain *n.* **1** a small, hard seed, esp. a cereal or its plant; also, cereal seeds collectively: *to grind, grow, mill, store grain; Our chief food grain is wheat; the world's grain consumption.* **2** a tiny, hard bit or particle: *grains of pollen, sugar; coarse, not fine grains of salt, sand, stone, etc.; Take tall tales* **with a grain of salt** (= with skepticism). **3** a unit of weight equal to 0.0648 gram or 50 milligrams (¼ carat) for gems. **4** the fiber pattern of wood, layer arrangement of coal, stone, etc.: *Punctuality goes* **against the grain** (= natural inclination) *of some people.*

grained *adj. & comb.form.* **1** marked like wood, marble, etc.: *a grained finish; long-grained wood; a yellow-grained variety.* **2** composed of grains; granulated: *coarse-grained sand; fine-grained rock.*

grain elevator *n.* a tall structure in which grain is loaded, cleaned, and stored for shipment.

grain.y *adj.* **grain.i.er, -i.est** having a grain or texture; consisting of particles: *the speckled, grainy appearance of a photographic enlargement.* —**grain.i.ness** *n.*

gram *n.* the basic unit of weight in the metric system, equal to 0.035 oz.; *Brit.* **gramme.**

-gram *comb.form.* **1** something recorded or drawn: *cablegram, diagram, mono-*

gram. 2 number of grams: *centigram, kilogram, milligram.*

gram.mar (GRAM.ur) *n.* 1 the rules governing the formation of words and the structure of sentences: *spelling and grammar.* 2 correctness of spoken or written expression: *your grammar; bad, sloppy, weak grammar; a program to check grammar.*

grammar school *n.* 1 in the U.S., an elementary school; grade school. 2 in the U.K., a nontechnical, academic secondary school.

gram.mar.i.an (gruh.MAIR.ee.un) *n.* an expert in grammar.

gram.mat.i.cal (gruh.MAT.i.cul) *adj.* having to do with grammar: *grammatical errors, lapses, mistakes, rules, skills, structures; (good) grammatical English.* —**gram.mat.i.cal.ly** *adv.*

Gram.my (GRAM.ee) *n.* **Gram.mys** or **Gram.mies** any of the annual awards made by the U.S. National Academy of Recording Arts and Sciences for achievements in the recording industry.

gram.o.phone (GRAM.uh.fone) *n. Brit.* phonograph.

gramps *n. Informal.* grandfather.

gran.a.ry (GRAN.uh.ree, GRAY.nuh-) *n.* **-ries** a storehouse for threshed grain: *The prairies are the granary (= grain-producing region) of our country.*

grand *adj.* 1 large in size or importance: *a grand finale, jury, piano, staircase, total.* 2 high in rank or dignity: *a grand old man, rabbi.* 3 *Informal.* very satisfying: *We had a grand time at the party; a grand day, view.* —*n. sing. & pl. Slang.* $1,000: *fifty grand (= $50,000).*

gran.dam or **gran.dame** *n.* [old use] an old woman, esp. a grandmother.

grand.child *n.* **-chil.dren** a child of one's son or daughter; a **grand.son** or **grand.daugh.ter.**

grande dame (grahn.DAHM) *n., pl.* **grandes dames** (grahn.DAHM) *French.* an elderly woman of prestige: *the grande dame of classical ballet.*

grand.daugh.ter (GRAN.daw.tur) See GRANDCHILD.

gran.dee (gran.DEE) *n.* 1 a Spanish or Portuguese nobleman of the highest rank. 2 an all-important personage.

gran.deur (GRAN.jur) *n.* greatness or magnificence of appearance, style, quality, nobility, etc.: *The dictator suffered from delusions of grandeur.*

grand.fa.ther (GRAN.fah.thur) See GRANDPARENT.

grandfather clause *n.* a legal provision for favoring a special group.

grandfather clock *n.* a large clock that stands on the floor in a tall, upright case.

gran.dil.o.quent (gran.DIL.uh.kwunt) *adj.* pompous in diction and tone.

gran.di.ose (GRAN.dee.ose) *adj.* 1 imposing or magnificent. 2 showy or pompous.

grand jury *n.* a jury of usually more than 12 persons that hears evidence and decides whether to indict an accused person for trial by a petit jury.

grand.ma (GRAN.mah, -muh) *n. Informal.* grandmother.

grand mal (grahn.MAL) *n.* the severest form of epileptic seizure.

grand.mas.ter (GRAN.mas.tur) *n.* an unusually skilled player, esp. an international winner in chess.

grand.moth.er (GRAN.muth.ur) See GRANDPARENT.

grand opera *n.* a musical drama with a serious theme and spectacular stage effects that is completely sung or recited.

grand.pa (GRAN.pah) *n. Informal.* grandfather.

grand.par.ent (GRAN.pair.unt) *n.* a parent of one's father or mother; grandfather or grandmother.

grand piano *n.* a large piano with horizontal frame and strings.

grand prix (grahn.PREE) *n., pl.* **grand prix** (-PREEZ) an international contest, esp. one of a series of races for Formula One cars.

grand slam *n.* 1 a winning of all the four major golf or tennis championships in one year. 2 in baseball, a home run hit with a runner on each base: *a grand slam homer.*

grandson See GRANDCHILD.

grand.stand *n.* the main seating place for the spectators at a sporting event. —*v. Informal.* make an attention-getting display, or **grandstand play,** as in baseball. —**grand.stand.ing** *n.*

grange (GRAINJ) *n.* a farm or farmhouse with its barn and other buildings.

gran.ite (GRAN.it) *n.* a hard rock with grains of minerals in it. —**gra.nit.ic** (gruh.NIT.ic) *adj.* like granite in firmness and endurance.

gran.ny or **gran.nie** (GRAN.ee) *n.* **gran.nies** *Informal.* 1 a grandmother or elderly woman. 2 a fussy person.

gra.no.la (gruh.NOH.luh) *n.* a prepared breakfast cereal of rolled oats and other ingredients that is used as a health food.

grant *v.* **1** allow a request, permission, claim, etc.: *to grant leave of absence to an employee; I grant that my statement was a bit misleading.* **2** confer property or other right or benefit: *Governments grant pensions to widows of veterans.*
—**take for granted** assume: *Don't take it for granted that you will get a raise every year; You can't take anyone for granted (as dependable) these days.*
—*n.* something granted, as money, lands, etc.: *to award* or *give a grant; to receive a grant for a project; a government grant; a grant to attend a convention;* **block grants** *of fixed amounts made by the federal government.* —**gran.tor** or **grant.er** *n.*

gran.tee (gran.TEE) *n.* one to whom a grant is made.

grant-in-aid *n.* **grants-in-aid** a money grant or subsidy given to a person or institution for an educational or public-service project.

grants.man.ship (GRANTS.mun.ship) *n.* the art of obtaining grants.

gran.u.lar (GRAN.yuh.lur) *adj.* grainy: *"Corn snow" is granular; granular tissue; the granular white cells in the bloodstream.* —**gran.u.lar.i.ty** (-LAIR.i.tee) *n.*

gran.u.late (GRAN.yuh.late) *v.* **-lates, -lat.ed, -lat.ing 1** form granules; *adj.:* *granulated garlic, honey, sugar.* **2** become granular or roughen: *A wound surface granulates in healing; adj.:* *granulated leather.* —**gran.u.la.tion** (-LAY.shun) *n.*

gran.ule (GRAN.yool) *n.* **1** a grain or small crystal, as of sugar or snow pellets. **2** one of the small, short-lived patches of gas in the sun's photosphere.

grape *n.* **1** the small, round, juicy berry that grows in clusters on various woody vines: *to pick grapes; press grapes for wine; a bunch of grapes.* **2** such a vine or the usually dark, purplish-red color of the fruit.

grape.fruit *n.* a large, round, yellowish citrus fruit.

grape hyacinth *n.* an herb of the lily family with spikes of bell-shaped blue or white flowers.

grape.shot *n.* small iron balls formerly used as cannon shot.

grape.vine *n.* **1** a grape-bearing vine. **2** *Informal.* word-of-mouth spreading of news, gossip, etc.: *We heard it by* or *on* or *through the office grapevine.*

graph (GRAF) *n.* a chart or drawing using lines, curves, bars, or circles ("pie chart") to present in picture form relationships between quantities: *a graph showing the changes of temperature during the day.* —*v.* show in graph form: *Student attendance may be graphed against school days along a pair of axes.*

-graph *comb.form.* a recording instrument or something recorded: *autograph, monograph, telegraph.*

graph.ic 1 *adj.* vivid or realistic: *a graphic description of the massacre; a graphic depiction, illustration, portrayal; in graphic detail; providing graphic evidence; too graphic for children to watch.* **2** *adj.* also **graphical,** having to do with graphs: *a graphic representation; graphical information, methods.* **3** *adj.* also **graphical,** having to do with the **graphic arts** of drawing, painting, printing, engraving, etc.: *a graphic design, display, image, pattern, print; graphic sweaters; graphic tops and bottoms; an information database with a graphic interface; graphic data;* **graphic artist** *n.* —*n.* **1** a work of graphic art: *a graphic of a globe; a graphic that no one can figure out; pie, bar, and line graphics; maps and graphics; graphics imported from clip art; a graphics library.* **2** a graphic display by computer on a video screen: *computer, VGA, video graphics; adj.:* *graphics adapters, boards, cards, chips, files, resolution, screens, software;* A **graphics tablet** *with pencil is used to input handwriting and such graphic data into a computer.* —**graphics** *n.pl.* [with *sing. v.*] design, including type, using graphic arts; also, graphic arts itself: *text and graphics; packaging with bold graphics.* —**graph.i.cal** *adj.* —**graph.i.cal.ly** *adv.*

graphical user interface *n.* a user interface that is icon-based rather than command-driven by input text characters.

graph.ite *n.* a soft, black carbon mineral used in lead pencils and for electrodes, crucibles, etc.

graph.ol.o.gy (graf.OL.uh.jee) *n.* the study of handwriting as indicative of character. —**graph.ol.o.gist** *n.*

-graphy *comb.form.* writing or something written, as a treatise or science: *biography, calligraphy, cryptography, geography.*

grap.nel (GRAP.nul) *n.* **1** a small anchor for boats and balloons, with several flukes or hooks. **2** an instrument with several claws at the end for seizing and holding, as an enemy ship.

grap.ple (GRAP.ul) *v.* **grap.ples, grap.pled, grap.pling 1** grip and hold. **2** struggle or wrestle: *There were more problems than she could* **grapple with** *in one day.* —*n.* **1** a struggle. **2** a grasping or holding device; also **grappling hook** or **iron**.

grasp *v.* seize and hold firmly, as with the hand: *The swimmer grasped at or for the rope thrown to her; She grasped it firmly; They grasped her by the arm and pulled her in; He's eager to grasp at any available opportunity; an idea that is not difficult to grasp* (= understand). —*n.* hold: *a firm grasp; He has a good grasp of Russian grammar; a thorough grasp of her subject; Success seems within her grasp* (= reach).

grasping *adj.* greedy or avaricious.

grass *n.* 1 any of various plants with jointed stems and long, narrow leaves eaten by grazing animals and cultivated on lawns: *blades of grass; a tuft of grass; to cut or mow the grass; Please don't walk on the grass* (= lawn). 2 any cereal grass such as wheat, barley, or corn. 3 *Slang.* marijuana. —**grass.y** *adj.* **grass.i.er, -i.est.**

grass hockey *n. Informal.* field hockey.

grass.hop.per (GRAS.hop.ur) *n.* a leaping insect that feeds on leaves and destroys crops.

grass.land *n.* pastureland: *Elephants live in the jungles and grasslands of Africa.*

grass roots *n.pl. Informal.* the common people who form the basic strength of any popular movement: *Power grows from the grass roots; Prosperity should trickle down to the grass roots; The defeated party had to be rebuilt from the grass roots up.* —**grass-roots** or **grass.roots** *adj.a.*: *at the grassroots level; a grass-roots movement for reform; a candidate with grassroots support.*

grass widow *n. Informal.* a woman temporarily separated from her husband.

grate *v.* **grates, grat.ed, grat.ing** 1 grind by scraping or rubbing: *to grate cabbage, cheese, chocolate.* 2 scrape or scratch or make a rasping sound, as an iron gate on its hinges: *Harsh voices grate on* (= irritate) *our ears.* —*n.* 1 a framework of bars forming a protective screen, as in a window; grill. 2 a horizontal framework of bars for holding burning fuel, as in a fireplace. —**grat.er** *n.*

grate.ful *adj.* 1 thankful: *We're grateful to you for helping us; grateful for your help; grateful that you could help.* 2 pleasing: *a grateful task.* —**grate.ful.ly** *adv.*

grat.i.fy (GRAT.uh.fye) *v.* **-fies, -fied, -fy.ing** give pleasure to; satisfy: *fancies that gratify one's desires;* **adj.**: *We are gratified at or by or over or with the results; gratified to learn of your success; The results are really gratifying.* —**grat.i.fi.ca.tion** (-fuh.CAY.shun) *n.*

grating 1 *n.* a protective framework: *subway gratings.* 2 *adj.* irritating: *a grating demeanor, personality, voice;* **grat.ing.ly** *adv.*

grat.is (GRAT.is, GRAY.tis) *adj. & adv.* free of charge: *tickets mailed gratis; gratis copies of a new book.*

grat.i.tude (GRAT.uh.tude) *n.* thankfulness: *our deep, profound, undying gratitude; to express, feel, show (one's) gratitude for favors received; We owe her a debt of gratitude.*

gra.tu.i.tous (gruh.TUE.uh.tus) *adj.* unjustified; uncalled-for: *gratuitous advice, violence; a gratuitous insult, remark.*

gra.tu.i.ty (gruh.TUE.i.tee) *n.* **-ties** a small money gift; tip.

gra.va.men (gruh.VAY.mun) *n.* **-va.mens** or **-vam.i.na** (-VAM.uh.nuh) the essential part of a complaint.

¹**gra.ve** (GRAH.vay) *adj. & adv. Music.* slow(ly).

²**grave** *adj.* **grav.er, grav.est** 1 serious and dangerous or threatening: *a grave condition, injustice, necessity, risk, situation, threat; grave concern, consequences, damage, doubts, harm, misgivings, peril; in grave danger of being killed.* 2 serious and solemn: *a mourner's grave expression; with a grave countenance; in a grave voice; a grave theme, warning.* —*n.* 1 a hole dug in the ground to bury a corpse: *to dig graves; freshly dug graves; A coffin is lowered into a grave; to lay flowers on a grave; People pray at his grave; a grave desecrated by body snatchers; bodies buried in mass graves; an unmarked grave; the watery grave of those who die at sea; from* **the cradle to the grave** (= all through life); *He has* **one foot in the grave** (= is near death); *It's enough to make him* **turn over in his grave** (= It's so shocking). 2 a mound of earth or tomb. 3 a mark originally indicating a vowel of low pitch, as in French words like *blasè*, used also to mark prominence of syllable, as in "an agèd genius"; also **grave accent**. —*v.* **graves,** *pt.* **graved,** *pp.* **grav.en** or **graved, grav.ing** 1 carve; hence, impress deeply; **adj.**: *idols and such* **graven images** *of stone and wood.* 2 clean and tar a ship's bottom; **adj.a.**: *the* **graving docks** *of shipyards.* —**grave.ly** *adv.*; **grave.ness** *n.*

grav.el (GRAV.ul) *n.* rock fragments, pebbles, etc. that are coarser than sand: *Streams and melting glaciers formed gravel pits; gravel in the urine* (= particles of kidney stones). —**grav.el.ly**

graven / greathearted

adj. harsh-sounding: *a gravelly voice.*
graven a *pp.* of GRAVE.
grave.stone *n.* an inscribed stone or monument marking a grave.
grave.yard *n.* a cemetery: *an auto graveyard; A **graveyard shift** (of workers) starts near midnight.*
gra.vim.e.ter (gruh.VIM.i.tur) *n.* a gravity-measuring device, used in determining the shape and depth of rock layers.
grav.i.tate (GRAV.uh.tate) *v.* **-tates, -tat.ed, -tat.ing** move or tend to or toward a place by or as if by gravity: *Heavier substances gravitate to the bottom of a liquid faster than lighter ones; two kindred spirits gravitating (= attracted) toward each other.* —**grav.i.ta.tion** (-TAY.shun) *n.* —**grav.i.ta.tion.al** *adj.*: *There's no gravitational force at the center of the earth.*
grav.i.ty (GRAV.i.tee) *n.* **-ties 1** the force of gravitation, esp. the earth's pull on objects: *the law of gravity; Gravity causes weight; The lower an object's center of gravity (= weight), the more stable it is.* **2** weightiness or seriousness: *to realize the gravity of a situation.*
gra.vure (gruh.VYOOR) *n.* **1** an intaglio process such as photogravure or rotogravure. **2** a plate or print made by it.
gra.vy (GRAY.vee) *n.* **-vies 1** sauce made by thickening with flour, seasoning, etc. the juice given off by meat in cooking. **2** *Slang.* a surplus beyond what is expected or needed: *pure gravy; in the gravy days of the postwar boom.*
gravy boat *n.* a gravy dish, originally boat-shaped.
gravy train *n.* source of easy money; sinecure.
gray *adj.* **1** of the dull color that is a blend of black and white or the color of aging hair: *gray hair; a gray suit.* **2** dismal or dreary: *in a gray and grouchy mood.* **3** vague or indeterminate: *a gray area of morality.* —*n.* a gray color, animal such as a gray horse, or gray cloth. —*v.* make or become gray: *hair grayed by age.* —**gray.ness** *n.*
gray.beard *n.* an old man.
gray eminence *n.* one who secretly exercises power.
gray.hound same as GREYHOUND.
gray.ish *adj.* somewhat gray.
gray.ling *n.* a troutlike freshwater game fish of cool or arctic regions.
gray.mail *n.* a kind of blackmail by threat of public exposure.
gray market *n.* a method of dealing based on the ability to pay without doing anything illegal as in black market.
gray matter *n.* the grayish tissue of the brain and spinal cord; hence, intelligence.
graze *v.* **graz.es, grazed, graz.ing 1** feed on grass: *Shepherds graze sheep; Sheep graze in our meadows.* **2** touch, scrape, or scratch in passing: *The bullet grazed his head.* —*n.* a grazing or abrasion.
grease (GREECE) *n.* a thick oily substance such as melted animal fat; lubricant: *a squeaky wheel that needs a spot of grease; a detergent that cuts (= dissolves) grease; nothing like elbow grease (= hard work) to get things done; Clowns, actors, etc. use makeup called **grease paint**.* —*v.* (GREECE, GREEZ) **greas.es, greased, greas.ing 1** smear with grease; lubricate: *Will higher pay **grease the wheels** of bureaucracy (= make it more efficient)?* **2** *Slang.* to bribe, esp. **grease the hand** or **palm** of someone.
greas.y (GREE.see) *adj.* **greas.i.er, -i.est 1** containing grease: *greasy food.* **2** soiled with grease: *greasy hands.*
greasy spoon *n. Slang.* a cheap, unsanitary restaurant.
great (GRATE) *adj.* **1** imposing in size or degree: *a great artist, friend, idea, judge, king, loss, man, occasion, ruler, writer; Alexander the Great; a great deal of fun; the great majority of people; A great many of us don't smoke; the great train robbery; once in a great while; the four or five great powers (= nations); He's **a great one for** (Informal for good at) throwing parties; the **Great War** of 1914-18.* **2** remarkable or surprising: *He shows great ignorance.* **3** *Informal.* very good: *You're great! It was great of you to come to our rescue; The party was great fun; Pat's the greatest! (= a remarkably good person).* —*adv. Informal.* very well: *She's doing great in school.*
—*comb.form.* two generations up or down: *great-granddaughter, great-grandfather, great-grandmother, great-grandson.* —**great.ly** *adv.*; **great.ness** *n.*
great circle *n.* a circle, esp. on the earth's surface, whose plane passes through the center of the sphere, as the equator: *A great-circle route is the shortest between two points.*
great.coat *n.* a heavy overcoat.
Great Dane *n.* a large, graceful, strong, short-coated dog.
great-grandchild *n.* **-chil.dren** a child of one's grandchild.
great.heart.ed (great.HAR.tid) *adj.* **1** noble or generous. **2** fearless.

Great Lakes *n.pl.* the lakes of Ontario, Erie, Huron, Michigan, and Superior.
great toe *n.* the big toe.
grebe (GREEB) *n.* a lobe-footed wading and diving bird related to the loon.
Gre.cian (GREE.shun) *n. & adj.* Greek: *Grecian art, columns, urns.*
Greco- (GREE.coh) *comb.form.* Greek (and): *Greco-Roman, Greco-Russian.*
greed *n.* excessive desire for money, food, power, etc.: *Midas showed insatiable greed for gold; He was consumed with greed.*
greed.y *adj.* **greed.i.er, -i.est** having great desire for food, money, etc.: *a child who is greedy for candy; to get greedy; a greedy moneylender.*
—**greed.i.ly** *adv.*; **greed.i.ness** *n.*
Greek *n.* a person of or from Greece; also, the language of Greece: *Your poetry is all Greek to* (= unintelligible to) *me; ancient warfare using Greek fire* (= chemical mixture that burns on contact with water); *Phi Beta Kappa, Phi Mu, and such Greek-letter fraternities and sororities.*
green *n.* **1** the color of greenery: *a room decorated in yellows and greens.* **2** a grassy plot, esp. a golf course: *the village green; a (golf) putting green; golf greens* (= golf courses); *adj.a.: green(s) fees.* **3** something green: *You can turn left only on a green* (= green light); *salad greens* (= vegetables). **4** *n.pl.* environmentalists: *The bill had to be withdrawn because of protests from the greens.*
—*adj.* **1** of the color of greenery: *The lawn has to look green and healthy; fresh and green; to be green with envy.* **2** immature or inexperienced: *a green team of reporters.* **3** having to do with the environment: *a green concern, movement, party; Go green!* —*v.* make or become green or younger; revitalize. *n.: the greening of deserts in Israel; Young immigrants help in the greening of the nation; the greening of recycling, thanks to sorters and stackers that make it more convenient.* —**green.ness** *n.*
green.back *n.* a piece of U.S. paper money.
green.bean *n.* a pod of the kidney bean
green belt *n.* a belt of trees and parks around a heavily built-up area.
Green Beret *n.* a member of the Special Forces of the U.S. Army.
green card *n.* official acceptance of an alien as a permanent resident in the U.S.
green.er.y (GREE.nuh.ree) *n.* **-er.ies** grass and other growing vegetation.

green-eyed monster *n.* jealousy.
green.groc.er (GREEN.groh.sur) *n. Brit.* a seller of fruits and vegetables.
green.horn *n. Informal.* a new arrival or recruit, esp. one who is easily duped.
green.house *n.* a glass- or plastic-covered building for climate-controlled cultivation of plants.
greenhouse effect *n.* the warming of the earth's lower atmosphere resulting from pollutants such as carbon dioxide (or **greenhouse gases**) blocking the escape of solar heat back into space.
green light *n.* permission to proceed, as indicated by a green traffic signal: *We got* or *received* or *have been given the green light to go ahead with the project.*
green.mail *n.* the forcing of a company to buy back its shares at a premium price from a speculator threatening a takeover.
green manure *n.* fertilizer made up of growing plants such as alfalfa, grasses, peas, beans, etc. plowed into the soil.
green onion *n.* a scallion.
green paper *n.* a government document containing proposals on a subject of reform for public discussion.
green pepper same as SWEET PEPPER.
green power *n.* power based on money.
green revolution *n.* increased production of food grains in developing countries, aided by fertilizers, pesticides, and new high-yield varieties.
green.room *n.* offstage waiting room for performers.
green.sward (rhyme: ford) *n.* grassy turf.
green thumb *n.* skill in gardening.
Greenwich time (GREN.ich, *Brit.* GRIN.ij) *n.* the local time at **Greenwich** in London, England, located on the prime meridian, which is the basis for time zones throughout the world.
green.wood *n.* a forest in full leaf; woodlands.
greet *v.* meet someone, esp. to welcome: *Guests are greeted at the door; The announcement was greeted with laughter.*
greeting *n.* **1** the act of one who greets or its expression: *a cordial, formal, friendly, warm greeting; The mayor extended an official greeting* (= welcome) *to the visitors; He began the letter with the greeting* (= salutation) *"Sir"; a greeting card bearing a message for a special occasion.* **2 greetings** *pl.* wishes: *to exchange greetings at Christmas; to extend* or *send greetings to friends; our cordial, friendly, warm, warmest greetings; birthday, holiday, season's greetings.*
gre.gar.i.ous (gruh.GAIR.ee.us) *adj.* **1** tending to herd or flock together:

the gregarious instinct in animals such as sheep; Some solitary bees and wasps are gregarious (= build their nests close together). 2 sociable, not solitary: *a witty and gregarious fellow.*

Gre.go.ri.an chant (gri.GOR.ee.un-) *n.* plainsong, as used in Roman Catholic ritual.

Gregorian calendar *n.* the present calendar introduced by Pope Gregory XIII in 1582 adjusting the Julian Calendar and decreeing a leap year every fourth year.

grem.lin *n.* a goblin usually blamed for mechanical mishaps: *The gremlins changed a letter and the forecast said "wild weather."*

gre.nade (gruh.NADE) *n.* a small bomb thrown by hand or fired from a rifle.

gren.a.dier (gren.uh.DEER) *n.* a soldier trained to throw hand grenades.

gren.a.dine (GREN.uh.deen) *n.* 1 a cordial syrup made from pomegranates. 2 a dress fabric of silk, wool, or cotton.

grew *pt.* of GROW.

grey same as GRAY.

grey.hound *n.* a swift-footed dog with long, powerful legs and keen sight, trained to hunt hares and in **greyhound racing** using a mechanical rabbit on an electric rail around a track.

grid *n.* 1 a framework resembling a grate or grill; gridiron. 2 something resembling a grid, as the lead plate in a storage battery, a football field, an interconnecting network of radio or television stations, a system of horizontal and vertical lines for locating points on a map, etc.: *the rectangular grid road system of certain cities.*

grid.dle (GRID.ul) *n.* a heavy, flat metal plate for cooking bacon, pancakes (**griddle cake**), etc.

grid.i.ron (GRID.eye.urn) *n.* 1 a grill for broiling. 2 anything resembling this, as a football field, the structure above a stage for manipulating scenery, or a clock pendulum with rods of different metals.

grid.lock *n.* a traffic jam so tight that no movement is possible.

grief (GREEF) *n.* acute sorrow, esp. one of short duration caused by some misfortune: *He almost went mad with grief when his wife died; Some have died of grief; Hopes of a lifetime came to grief* (= failed) *when the bank crashed; Good grief!* [exclamation of dismay]

griev.ance (GREE.vunce) *n.* a complaint or its real or imagined cause: *The fired worker nursed a grievance against his boss;* to air or vent a grievance publicly; He filed or launched or submitted a grievance to the higher authorities; They heard and redressed the grievance; the **grievance procedure** for settling a dispute.

grieve (GREEV) *v.* **grieves, grieved, griev.ing** 1 cause or feel grief: *It grieves us to hear Al is no more; Everyone grieves over his death; The whole village grieves for him.* 2 appeal as a grievance: *She grieved her dismissal to the labor union.*

griev.ous (GREE.vus) *adj.* causing suffering; hence, severe or grave: *a grievous crime, error, loss, wound, wrong; charges of brutality and causing grievous bodily harm; in grievous pain.*
—**griev.ous.ly** *adv.*; **griev.ous.ness** *n.*

grif.fin or **grif.fon** (GRIF.un) *n.* a mythical eagle with the hind legs and tail of a lion; also **gryph.on.**

grill *n.* 1 a gridiron. 2 a dish of broiled meat, fish, etc.: *a mixed grill of meats and vegetables.* 3 a small restaurant, or **grillroom.** 4 usually **grille**, a protective metal screen or grating, as in front of an automobile radiator. 5 a vent or window covered with a grating; *adj.: a grilled window.*
—*v.* 1 broil: *to grill a hamburger; adj.: grilled foods, meats, vegetables; a grilled cheese sandwich.* 2 torture with questions: *Lawyers grill witnesses.*

grill.work *n.* a pattern of grilles.

grim *adj.* **grim.mer, grim.mest** 1 unyielding or unrelenting: *a battle fought with grim resolve.* 2 gloomy or depressing: *the grim prospect of unemployment; a joke too grim to laugh at.* —**grim.ly** *adv.*; **grim.ness** *n.*

grim.ace (GRIM.is, gruh.MACE) *n.* a twisted or distorted face, as of one in pain or trying to amuse. —*v.* **-ac.es, -aced, -ac.ing** make a grimace: *She grimaced in disgust at the toad on the table.*

grime *n.* dirt, esp. soot, rubbed into a surface such as the skin.

grim reaper *n.* death personified.

grim.y (GRY.mee) *adj.* **grim.i.er, -i.est** covered with grime: *the grimy faces of miners.*

grin *n.* 1 a broad smile showing the teeth. 2 a baring of teeth in anger, pain, or scorn. —*v.* **grins, grinned, grin.ning** make a grin or express by a grin: *She nodded and grinned her approval; The pain was bad but he had to grin and bear it.*

grinch *n.* a person or thing that spoils a celebration, as in the story of the Grinch who stole Christmas gifts.

grind (GRINED) *v.* **grinds, ground,**

grind.ing 1 reduce to powder by friction, as grain in a mill: *to grind wheat into flour.* **2** rub or press together, as teeth by an angry person or when a crank turns: *to grind out music on a hand organ; The train* **ground to a halt** *just short of the landslide;* **n.**: *The strike brought the industry to a* **grinding halt.** **3** work hard or long: *a diligent worker grinding away at her tasks.*
—*n.* **1** hard work or study: *the dull grind of compiling a seed catalog.* **2** a grinding or its result: *coffee of a coarse grind* (= particle size). **3** *Informal.* a hard-working student: *He became a grind so as to get the best exam results.*

grind.stone *n.* **1** a millstone. **2** a sharpening and polishing instrument with a revolving stone.

grip *n.* **1** a firm hold or tight grasp: *to lose, relax, release, tighten one's grip; a firm, tight, viselike grip; a country in the grip of a famine; to get a good* **grip on oneself** (= have self-control); *a youngster who* **comes to grips with** (= tries to deal with) *reality.* **2** a way of holding a racket or golf club. **3** something to hold with, as a handle. **4** a handbag or small suitcase. **5** a stagehand in a film production crew. —*v.* **grips, gripped, grip.ping** have a firm hold: *The scared child gripped its mother's hand; a novel that grips your interest.* —**grip.ping.ly** *adv.*

gripe *v.* **gripes, griped, grip.ing** *Informal.* complain. —*n.* **1** *Informal.* complaint. **2 gripes** *pl.* pain in the intestines.

grippe (GRIP) *n.* influenza.

gris-gris (GREE.gree) *n. sing. & pl.* a charm, amulet, or fetish, as in voodoo cults.

gris.ly (GRIS.lee) *adj.* **gris.li.er, -li.est** horrible or ghastly: *a grisly murder.*

grist *n.* **1** ground grain such as meal or flour. **2** grain to be ground, as in a **grist.mill.** —**grist to** or **for one's mill** matter for profit or advantage to oneself.

gris.tle (GRIS.ul) *n.* cartilage, esp. in table meats. —**gris.tly** (GRIS.lee) *adj.*

grit *n.* **1** fine gravel, sand, or anything similar: *"All sand and no dirt, clear grit all the way through," said the leader about the kind of people he wanted.* **2 grits** *n.pl.* coarsely ground corn, oats, wheat, etc.; esp. in southern U.S., ground corn eaten boiled or fried. **3** obstinate courage or pluck: *true grit.* —*v.* **grits, grit.ted, grit.ting** clench or grind the teeth in determination: *She gritted her teeth and bore the pain.*

grit.ty (GRIT.ee) *adj.* **grit.ti.er, grit.ti.est 1** like grit; sandy: *medication with a gritty texture; the electric guitar's gritty wail; She complained of a gritty feeling in the eyes.* **2** plucky or brave: *a gritty effort; a gritty little girl.*

griz.zled (GRIZ.uld) *adj.* gray-haired; streaked with gray: *a grizzled beard.*

griz.zly (GRIZ.lee) **1** *n., pl.* **griz.zlies** a massive, grayish, ferocious bear of North America; also **grizzly bear.** **2** *adj.* grayish like a grizzly.

groan (GRONE) *n.* a deep sound made from the throat to express pain, disapproval, grief, etc.: *the groans of the wounded on a battlefield.* —*v.* make a groan: *She groaned with dismay on seeing her son's report card; a banquet table groaning under a load of food.*

groat (GROTE) *n.* a former British coin worth four pennies; hence, a trifling sum.

gro.cer (GROH.sur) *n.* a retailer of food and other household supplies.

gro.cer.y (GROH.suh.ree) *n.* **-cer.ies** a grocer's store or the food products sold in one: *Supermarkets sell* **groceries** *and nonfood items.*

gro.dy (GROH.dee) same as GROTTY.

grog.gy (GROG.ee) *adj.* **grog.gi.er, grog.gi.est** *Informal.* drunk or feeling like it, as from sleep; shaky or dazed. —**grog.gi.ly** *adv.*; **grog.gi.ness** *n.*

groin *n.* **1** the fold or depression between belly and thigh: *She kicked her attacker in the groin.* **2** in architecture, the curved edge formed by two intersecting vaults; *adj.*: *a groined vault.* **3** a jettylike structure to protect a coast from wave erosion.

grom.met (GROM.it) *n.* a ring or loop used as a fastening or reinforcement or to protect an opening or the thing passing through it.

groom (long "oo") *n.* **1** a bridegroom. **2** a man or boy who takes care of horses. —*v.* **1** take care of a horse, dog, etc. by cleaning and currying. **2** make neat and tidy in appearance; *adj.*: *He always appears well* **groomed**; *n.*: *Good* **grooming** *is a must for success.* **3** prepare someone for an office: *She is being groomed for the presidency.*

grooms.man (GROOMZ.mun) *n.* **-men** a bridegroom's attendant.

groove *n.* **1** a channel, furrow, or rut; hence, a routine. **2** *Slang.* something enjoyable. —**in the groove** *Slang.* in top form; working smoothly, like a needle playing in the groove of a phonograph record; groovy. —*v.* **grooves, grooved, groov.ing** *Slang.* react with

groovy / groundbreaking

empathy: *to groove to swing music; to groove with someone; everyone grooving* (= enjoying) *in his or her own way.*

groov.y (GROO.vee) *adj. Slang.*
  groov.i.er, -i.est swinging; excellent: *a groovy hairstyle.*

grope *v.* **gropes, grop.ed, grop.ing 1** feel one's way about as if blind or uncertain: *We groped around in the dark; a writer always groping for a better word.* **2** *Informal.* fondle sexually.
  —*n.* an act of groping.

gros.beak (GROSE.beek) *n.* a bird of the finch family with a strong beak for cracking seeds.

gros.grain (GROH.grain) *n.* a corded fabric of silk or rayon used for ribbons, etc.

gross (rhyme: dose) *adj.* **1** extremely bad or objectionable, as being coarse, vulgar, or indecent: *a gross error, injustice; gross misconduct, negligence; his gross table manners; That's gross!* **2** whole or entire, with nothing deducted: *a physician's gross income before overhead, salaries, etc. are paid out; a company's gross sales.* —*n.* **1** *pl.* **gross.es** the total amount. **2** *sing. & pl.* 12 dozen; 144: *six gross of eggs.* —*v.* earn before deductions: *How much did you gross last year?* —**gross out** *Slang.* disgust or shock, esp. by vulgarity.

gross national product *n.* the value of all goods and services produced in a country in a year.

gross ton *n.* 2,240 lb. (1,016 kg); long ton; See TON.

gro.tesque (groh.TESK) *adj.* unnatural or fantastic in appearance, shape, or manner; bizarre and ludicrous: *A gargoyle is a grotesque form of caricature.*
  —*n.* a painting or sculpture containing medallions, sphinxes, foliage, etc.

grot.to (GROT.oh) *n.* **-tos** or **-toes** a cave or a cavelike place, garden shelter, or shrine.

grot.ty (GROT.ee) *adj. Slang.* **1** grotesque; miserably bad: *a grotty ballroom.* **2** wretched: *feeling dead grotty!*

grouch *n. Informal.* **1** a grumbler. **2** a grumbling or sulky mood. **3** a complaint. —*v.* complain in a surly, ill-tempered manner. —**grouch.y** *adj.*
  —**grouch.i.ly** *adv.*

ground *pt.* of GRIND. —*n.* **1** the earth's surface, as distinguished from the air: *Leaves fall to the ground; to* **break ground** *for a new building; Keep your* **feet on the ground** (= Be practical in your thinking); *He built the company* **from the ground up**; *She knows about rockets* **from the ground up** (= thoroughly); *The new business has still to* **get off the ground** (= make a start); *adj. & cpd.:* The ground (connection) of an appliance conducts leaking electricity to earth; an airline's ground (= land) crew; Airline mechanics are ground-based; fighter planes directed by ground-controlled radar; a ground-to-air missile. **2** soil or land: *dry, firm, frozen, hallowed, wet ground; Plants grow in fertile ground.* **3** a part of the earth's surface: *We own a piece of ground in Florida; breeding, burial, camping, dumping, forbidden, hunting, parade, picnic, proving grounds; a flag with a gold crescent on a green ground* (= background). **4** the bottom: *the ground of the ocean where "groundfish" live.* **5** a position to defend or area of interest: *We are on common ground on this issue; on safe ground; on solid ground; You're on shaky ground if you say the earth is flat; on dangerous ground; Don't* **shift your ground** *in the middle of an argument; Continue fighting and don't* **give ground**; **Hold** *or* **stand your ground**; *Is mercy killing* **gaining** *or* **losing ground?** *Research theses are supposed to* **break new ground**, *not rehash old discoveries.*
  —**grounds 1** dregs: *coffee grounds left in a cup.* **2** a specific area: *the grounds of an estate, hospital, mansion, school; hunting and fishing grounds.* **3** basis or reasons: *On what grounds did she resign? Does she have any grounds to sue us? You've no grounds for complaint; ample, solid, sufficient grounds.* —**cut the ground from under someone's feet** destroy someone's plans or arguments, as by anticipating them. —**into the ground** till dead or exhausted: *to beat someone into the ground; to drive a car into the ground.* —*v.* put or base on the ground: *a pilot grounded by illness; aircraft grounded by fog; An appliance is grounded (electrically) by its own metal frame; adj.: arguments* **grounded** *on facts (as basis); You're grounded* (= punished by having privileges withdrawn) *for a week; a student well grounded* (= trained) *in the basics;* *n.: She has a good* **grounding** (= training) *in math.*

ground ball *n.* a baseball hit along the ground.

ground.break.er (GROUND.bray.kur) *n.* an innovator or pioneer in a field of activity.

ground.break.ing (GROUND.bray.king) *n.* starting of work on a new building, project, etc.: *Groundbreaking for the new facility is slated to begin in January; Groundbreaking is set or scheduled for May 1 and takes place at 9 a.m.; a* *groundbreaking ceremony.* —*adj.* innovative or pioneering: *a groundbreaking approach, book, decision, plan, solution, study, theory; groundbreaking research.*

ground cover *n.* low plants or shrubbery to decorate the ground and protect the topsoil against erosion.

ground crew *n.* the nonflying personnel of an airline, as mechanics.

ground-effect machine same as AIR CUSHION VEHICLE.

ground.er same as GROUND BALL.

ground.fish *n.* fish such as cod and halibut that live close to the bottom of a body of water; bottom fish.

ground floor *n.* 1 the floor nearest to the ground. 2 *Informal.* a position of advantage, as at the outset of a venture: *The man who owns the business got in on the ground floor.*

ground glass *n.* 1 nontransparent glass with a roughened surface. 2 glass in powder form.

ground.hog *n.* woodchuck: *the Groundhog Day tradition of determining the length of the winter by a shadow cast by the animal on February 2.*

ground.less *adj.* baseless.

ground.ling *n.* 1 a plant or animal whose habitat is close to the ground. 2 a person of inferior artistic taste.

ground rule *n.* a basic rule, as of a game.

ground speed *n.* the speed of an aircraft relative to the ground.

ground squirrel *n.* any burrowing animal of the squirrel family, as the groundhog, prairie dog, or woodchuck.

ground.swell *n.* 1 stormy water in the ocean, caused by a distant storm or earthquake. 2 a growing wave of popular concern, support, etc.: *There was a groundswell of public support for the nurses' demands.*

ground water *n.* the water that supplies wells and springs.

ground.work *n.* basis or foundation: *To lay the groundwork for a good education, start with the three R's; Have you done the groundwork* (= spadework) *for your project?*

ground zero *n.* 1 the point on the ground closest to an exploding atomic bomb. 2 the starting point: *The company has grown from ground zero to $100 million in sales; The competition is still at ground zero.*

group (GROOP, long "OO") *n.* a number of persons, animals, or things belonging, classed, or associated together: *a group of students; affinity, age, blood, encounter, ethnic, peer, pressure, special-interest, splinter groups; English and Dutch belong to the Germanic group of languages; Battalions and squadrons form military groups or units.* —*v.* form or arrange into a group: *They group around the leader; Foods are grouped* (= divided) *into four basic categories; All races are grouped* (= classed) *under the human species.*

group home *n.* a publicly funded home for deprived children or for the handicapped in need of care.

group.ie (GROO.pee) *n. Informal.* 1 a camp follower or fan. 2 a young, usually female fan of a pop group, esp. one who follows them for sexual relations.

group insurance *n.* insurance for a group of people, as the members of a club, under one contract and at low rates.

group practice *n.* medical practice (or **group medicine**) by many physicians working as a group.

group.ware *n.* software that enables a group to communicate and work together, as in an organization.

grouse *n. sing. & pl.* a game bird resembling domestic fowl: *the ruffed grouse; the Canada spruce grouse.* —*v.* **grous.es, groused, grous.ing** *Informal.* grumble. —*n. Informal.* a complaint. —**grous.er** *n.*

grout (GROWT) *n.* a thin mortar or plaster. —*v.* 1 fill up a space, as between tiles, finish a wall, ceiling, etc. with grout. 2 fix something with grout.

grove (GROHV) *n.* a small wood without underbrush; group of trees: *an orange grove; the groves of academe* (= the academic world).

grov.el (GRUV.ul, GROV.ul) *v.* **-els, -eled, -el.ing** crawl or cringe at the feet of or before someone feared: *to grovel in the dust; to grovel to the boss.* Also **grov.elled, grov.el.ling** *Cdn.*

grow (GROH) *v.* **grows, grew** (GROO), **grown** (GRONE), **grow.ing** develop, as animals and plants from seed, gradually getting bigger: *Trees and plants grow from seeds; Americans who grew up in Europe; Children grow up to become leaders of society; They grow out of their clothes* (which become too small for them); *A small business grows into a corporate giant; People grow their hair* (= let it get longer); *Days grow* (= gradually become) *shorter in the fall; Habits seem to grow on us like vines* (on walls); *the growing pains* (= stresses and strains) *of childhood and youth.* —**grow.er** *n.*

growl v. & n. **1** (make) a low, throaty sound, as a dog warning an approaching stranger, thunder in the distance, or the stomach of a hungry person; rumble: *Fido always growls at strangers.* **2** express with a growl: *Al growled his thanks and left.*

grown pp. of GROW. —*adj.* mature: *grown folks, men, women.*

grown-up n. & adj. adult: *kids and grown-ups; grown-up children; Act grown-up!* **grown-up goods** (= goods for grown-ups) *such as face creams and vacuums.*

growth (GROHTH) n. a growing, what has grown, or amount grown: *the rapid growth of grass in the spring; tumors and such cancerous growths; his growth in maturity; to foster, promote, retard, stunt growth; population growth; a* **growth company** *or* **growth industry** *with greater than average growth; A* **growth ring,** *or annual ring, shows a year's growth of wood.*

groyne (GROIN) n. a jettylike groin built to reduce sea erosion.

grub v. **grubs, grubbed, grub.bing** dig (up); also, rummage about: *A farmer grubs up tree roots and stumps to clear new land; to grub for potatoes; to grub around in the garbage for a missing ring; He grubs away at his menial tasks.*
—*n.* **1** an insect larva, as of a beetle. **2** a toiler; drudge. **3** *Slang.* food.

grub.by (GRUB.ee) adj. **grub.bi.er, grub.bi.est 1** grimy: *grubby hands.* **2** infested, as cattle or sheep, with fly maggots.

grub.stake n. food and equipment supplied in return for a share of the proceeds, as merchants used to supply gold prospectors in return for a share of their gold.

grudge (GRUJ) n. ill will against another: *to bear* or *owe someone a grudge; It's not healthy to harbor* or *nurse grudges; He acts as though he has* or *bears* or *carries* or *holds a grudge* (= reason for ill will) *against her; What's the use of carrying on a grudge? a* **grudge fight** *to avenge a defeat.* —*v.* **grudg.es, grudged, grudg.ing 1** resent: *I don't grudge doing him a favor although he charges for everything he does.* **2** envy: *I don't grudge him all the money he makes.* —**grudging** *adj.* reluctant or unwilling: *He's very grudging in his generosity; a grudging admiration, apology, approval, gesture, respect, support;* **grudg.ing.ly** *adv.*

gru.el (GROO.ul) n. liquid food, as for invalids, made by boiling meal in water or milk; a thin porridge.

gru.el.ing (GROO.uh.ling) adj. exhausting or tiring; demanding: *a grueling contest, experience, race, training session.* —*n.* something that is grueling. Also **gru.el.ling** *Cdn.*

grue.some (GROO.sum) adj. causing fear and loathing because of something frightful or hideous: *gruesome details; a gruesome scene of bloodshed.*
—**grue.some.ly** *adv.;* **grue.some.ness** *n.*

gruff adj. **1** rough, not polite: *gruff manners.* **2** having a deep and harsh voice: *a gruff reply, sergeant, voice.* —**gruff.ly** *adv.;* **gruff.ness** *n.*

grum.ble v. **grum.bles, grum.bled, grum.bling** growl, mutter, or rumble in a surly or peevish manner: *It's no use grumbling about* or *at* or *over the weather; He grumbled his thanks.*
—*n.* a grumbling or complaint.
—**grum.bler** *n.*

grump.y adj. **grump.i.er, -i.est** *Informal.* grouchy or ill-humored: *He's grumpy from work; in a grumpy mood.*
—**grump.i.ly** *adv.;* **grump.i.ness** *n.*

grunge n. *Slang.* the condition of being grungy; squalor or shabbiness.

grun.gy (GRUN.jee) adj. **-gi.er, -gi.est** *Slang.* shabby or squalid: *a grungy movie house.*

grun.ion (GRUN.yun) n. a small silvery fish of the California coast that comes up the beaches to spawn and may be caught by hand.

grunt n. **1** the short, deep guttural sound made by a hog. **2** an expression of boredom, disapproval, effort, etc. **3** an ocean fish of the Atlantic coast, such as the "pigfish" and "sailor's choice" that grunts when taken out of water.
—*v.* make or express with a grunt: *She was grunting and groaning with pain; He merely grunted his approval.*

Gru.yère (gri.YAIR) n. a variety of firm, light-yellow, whole-milk cheese.

gryphon (GRIF.un) same as GRIFFIN.

G-string n. **1** the string on a musical instrument that sounds the G note. **2** a loincloth to cover the genitals, as worn by strippers.

G-suit n. a garment worn by astronauts, pilots, etc. to withstand G-forces.

gua.nine (GWAH.neen) n. a crystalline substance, one of the four nitrogenous purine bases of DNA and RNA.

gua.no (GWAH.noh) n. **-nos** the waste matter of sea birds used as a fertilizer; also, any similar manure.

guar (GWAR) n. a legume grown as forage and for seeds that yield **guar gum.**

guar.an.tee (gair.un.TEE) n. a promise

or pledge to carry out a service or to replace, repair, or refund the price of a product if it proves unsatisfactory: *a TV set with a year's guarantee; a five-year guarantee against manufacturing defects; He has given a firm guarantee that the car won't break down; We insist on written guarantees; Health and wealth are no guarantees of happiness.* —*v.* **-tees, -teed, -tee.ing 1** stand behind: *We guarantee everything we sell.* **2** promise or pledge: *We guarantee satisfaction; We guarantee the car to be roadworthy; We guarantee that it will not break down; We guarantee it against all defects.* —**guar.an.tor** (GAIR.un.tor) *n.*

guar.an.ty (GAIR.un.tee) *n.* **-ties 1** a usually written agreement to pay another's debt if the latter fails to pay. **2** something given or taken as security for this promise. —*v.* **-ties, -tied, -ty.ing** same as GUARANTEE: *to put up collateral to guaranty a loan.*

guard (GARD) *v.* protect or defend, esp. by watching over someone or something against possible harm or danger or to prevent escape, as the Coast Guard or a sentry does: *to guard the borders from smugglers; a vaccination to guard against a disease; adj.: "We will see" was his* **guarded** (= cautious) *reply; guarded optimism.* —*n.* a person, group, or thing that guards: *an armed guard; crossing, honor, prison, security guards; The house is under guard; A watchdog keeps guard over a house; A sentry stands guard at a gate; He was hit when he* **let his guard** (= defensive stance as in boxing) **down**; *He was caught* **off guard** (= unprepared); *Citizens* **stand on guard** *over* (= ready to defend) *their country.* —**on** (or **off**) **one's guard** prepared (or unprepared).

guard.i.an (GAR.dee.un) *n.* a custodian, esp. one in charge of a minor, a mentally incompetent person, or of his or her property: *Parents are their children's "guardians by nature"; adj.: a guardian angel, spirit; guardian role.*

guard.rail *n.* a protective railing, as at the side of a staircase or highway.

guard.room *n.* **1** a room for the use of guards. **2** a room for keeping prisoners.

guards.man *n.* **-men** a member of the U.S. National Guard.

Gua.te.ma.lan (gwah.tuh.MAH.lun) *n. & adj.* (a person) of or from **Guatemala**, a country of N.W. Central America.

gua.va (GWAH.vuh) *n.* the yellow or red, round or pear-shaped fruit containing hard seeds surrounded by grainy flesh of a tropical tree of the myrtle family.

gu.ber.na.to.ri.al (GOO.bur.nuh.TOR.ee.ul) *adj.* of a governor or his or her office: *a gubernatorial campaign, candidate, election, nomination, race.*

guck *n. Slang.* a gooey or mucky substance. —**guck.y** *adj.*

Guern.sey (GURN.zee) *n.* **-seys** a breed of dairy cattle of fawn color with white markings.

guer.ril.la (guh.RIL.uh) *n.* a member of a volunteer force of irregulars fighting in small bands, usually behind enemy lines, using hit-and-run tactics, sabotage, kidnappings, and such terrorist actions; *adja.: a guerrilla attack, band, campaign, fighter, tactic, war; an urban guerrilla group; the guerrilla warfare of the Irish Republican Army.* Also **gue.ril.la.**

guess (GESS, "G" as in "go") *n.* a usually correct estimate or judgment made without sufficient evidence: *Your guess is as good as mine; It's anyone's* or *anybody's guess; I will hazard* or *make a guess.* —*v.* **1** make a guess: *Can you guess her height? Guess who's coming to dinner.* **2** *Informal.* suppose: *I guess I was wrong.*

guess.ti.mate (GES.tuh.mut) *n. Informal.* an estimate based on guessing.

guess.work *n.* guessing.

guest (GEST, "G" as in "go") *n.* **1** a person receiving hospitality or being entertained at a home, club, etc.: *We have guests tonight (for supper); honored, unexpected, unwelcome guests; wedding guests;* **Be my guest** (*Informal* for Help yourself)! **2** a patron of a hotel or restaurant: *a regular guest.* **3** one invited to take part in a show or program; *adja.: a guest appearance, column, editor, worker.*

guff *n. Informal.* empty talk: *No one will fall for that guff; I don't have to take any guff from you.*

guf.faw (guh.FAW) *n.* a coarse or loud laugh. —*v.* give a guffaw: *to guffaw at an off-color joke.*

guid.ance (GUY.dunce) *n.* **1** direction such as given to students on what courses to take ("educational guidance"), in choosing a career ("vocational guidance"), etc.: *parental guidance; under the guidance of a counselor.* **2** direction given to a missile in flight by means of radar, computers, etc.

guide (GIDE, "G" as in "go") *n.* **1** a person or thing that shows the way, as on a tour: *Let your conscience be your guide.* **2** a guidebook: *a guide to Paris.*

—v. **guides, guid.ed, guid.ing** act as a guide: *He guided us around Paris.*
guide.book n. a book of information for tourists and travelers.
guide.line n. 1 a line used as a guide or reference. 2 advice on policy by a controlling authority: *A guideline is not a rule; an operating, rough, simple guideline; a set of guidelines; to establish or give or issue or lay down or set up new guidelines for energy conservation; to adhere to or follow the guidelines set forth by the company.*
guide.post n. 1 a roadside sign for the guidance of travelers. 2 a guideline: *a navigational guidepost.*
guide.way n. a structure that supports and guides moving vehicles: *an electromagnetic guideway; a fixed-guideway technology; dedicated guideways.*
guide word n. a word placed at the top of a page showing the first or last entry on it, as "guidebook / gumption."
gui.don (GUY.dun, -don) n. an identifying flag, streamer, or pennant.
guild (GILD, "G" as in "go") n. 1 an association of people with a common interest, as of merchants or craftsmen of the same trade. 2 a labor union.
guil.der (GIL.dur) n. the basic money unit of the Netherlands and a silver coin worth 100 cents.
guild.hall n. a guild's meeting place.
guilds.man (GUILDS.mun) n. **-men** a member of a guild.
guile (GILE, "G" as in "go") n. slyness and cunning; deceit: *a man full of guile; She spoke without guile.*
—**guile.ful** adj.; **guile.less** adj.
guil.lo.tine (GIL.uh.teen, "G" as in "go") n. a heavy blade slid down grooves in an upright frame, used to execute people by beheading. —v. (gil.uh.TEEN) **-tines, -tined, -tin.ing** kill using a guillotine: *People were guillotined during the French Revolution.*
guilt (GILT, "G" as in "go") n. the fact or feeling of having done wrong: *a lawyer trying to establish guilt; to admit guilt in the accident; guilt by association; a guilt-ridden conscience.*
guilt.y adj. **guilt.i.er, -i.est** having done wrong: *The jury found Jim guilty of theft; They pronounced him guilty; guilty as charged; a verdict of guilty; a guilty verdict; He had pleaded not guilty; a not-guilty plea; a guilty conscience* (= feeling of guilt). —**guilt.i.ly** adv.
guinea fowl n. a W. African bird related to the pheasant and raised for its flesh and the eggs of the guinea hen.
guin.ea pig (GIN.ee, "G" as in "go") n. a furry rodent much used as a subject for scientific testing.
guise (GUYS) n. a garb or outward aspect, esp. a deceptive one: *treachery in* or *under the guise of friendship.*
gui.tar (guh.TAR) n. a musical instrument with six strings that are plucked or strummed. —**gui.tar.ist** n.
gu.lag (GOO.lahg) n. a forced-labor camp for prisoners, as in the Soviet Union.
gulch n. a deep, narrow ravine.
gulf n. 1 a large arm of an ocean extending into the land: *the **Gulf States** of Texas, Louisiana, Mississippi, Alabama, and Florida (near the Gulf of Mexico).* 2 a chasm or wide gap: *a yawning gulf; the widening gulf between rich and poor nations.*
gull n. 1 a long-winged, gray-and-white ocean bird useful as a scavenger around shore waters. 2 an easy victim of cheating; dupe.
—v. to dupe: *Con men gulled her out of her savings; She was gulled into thinking she would get rich quickly.*
gul.let (GULL.it) n. the throat, including the esophagus and pharynx.
gull.i.ble (GUL.uh.bul) adj. easily fooled, being too trusting: *a gullible youth.*
—**gul.li.bil.i.ty** (-BIL.i.tee) n.
gul.ly (GULL.ee) n. **gul.lies** a small ravine, esp. one worn by running water.
gulp v. swallow hastily or nervously: *He gulped it down and hurried to the door; She bravely gulped back* (= suppressed) *her tears.* —n.: *He drank the medicine in or at one gulp.* —**gulp.er** n.
gum n. 1 usually **gums** pl. the firm, pink supporting tissue around the base of the teeth. 2 a sticky, water-soluble sap of trees such as the plum and peach, used for drugs, candy, etc., esp. **gum arabic** obtained from an African tree: *to chew gum; a stick* or *wad of gum.*
—v. **gums, gummed, gum.ming** 1 smear or treat with something gummy. 2 *Informal.* clog or mess up: *Keep the plans secret and don't let anyone gum up* (= spoil) *the works.*
gum.bo n. **-bos** 1 the okra plant or its sticky pods. 2 a chicken-and-rice soup thickened with this. 3 fine, silty prairie soil that is sticky when wet. 4 a Black French dialect of Louisiana.
gum.drop n. a sweet and jellylike but stiff candy made with gum arabic.
gum.my (GUM.ee) adj. **gum.mi.er, gum.mi.est** covered with or giving off gum; sticky.
gump.tion n. *Informal.* readiness to act according to common sense; guts: *the*

gumption to say no without fear of offending.
gum.shoe *n.* 1 a rubber overshoe. 2 **gumshoes** *pl.* sneakers. 3 *Slang.* detective. —*v.* **-shoes, -shoed, -shoe.ing** go about quietly as if wearing sneakers.
gun *n.* 1 a weapon using an explosive, usually **gunpowder**, to shoot a bullet, shell, or other missile through a metal tube, esp. a cannon or machine gun; also, a rifle, pistol, or revolver: *to aim, carry, draw, fire, load, pack a gun; to hold a gun to someone's head; to turn a gun on someone; A gun fires, goes off, jams.* 2 something resembling a gun, as an "air gun" or an engine's throttle. 3 a gunman: *to hire a gun.* 4 *Slang* [jocular use] *"You son of a gun"* (= bastard)! —**great guns** *Informal.* fast and furiously toward success: *She's going or blowing great guns as a cabinet minister.* —**jump the gun** start too soon or get a head start: *The competition jumped the gun on our announcement.* —**spike one's guns** frustrate one's efforts. —**stick to one's guns** refuse to retreat. —**under the gun** under pressure *to* do something. —*v.* **guns, gunned, gun.ning** 1 shoot (at) with a gun: *a gangster gunned down by assassins.* 2 rev: *bikers gunning their motors.* —**gunning for** 1 trying to get something desired: *a prosecutor gunning for a conviction.* 2 trying to capture and punish someone: *The Oilers will be gunning for the Hawks in tomorrow's game.*
gun.boat *n.* a small, armed patrol boat.
gunboat diplomacy *n.* use of military threats to enforce treaties.
gun.cot.ton (GUN.cot.un) *n.* an explosive of cotton or other fiber soaked in a mixture of nitric and sulfuric acids, dried, and pressed into blocks.
gun.fight *n.* a fight using guns; **gun.fight.er** *n.*
gun.fire *n.* the firing of guns: *to come under heavy gunfire; a barrage, burst, hail of gunfire; an exchange of gunfire between police and snipers.*
gung-ho *adj. Informal.* eager and enthusiastic: *The union members were all gung-ho for about the strike; A gung-ho atmosphere reigned at the meeting; They were so gung-ho they had no doubt they would win.*
gunk *n. Informal.* something thick and messy: *where to dump the gunk dredged from the lake.*
gun.lock *n.* a mechanism that sets off the charge in a gun.
gun.man (GUN.mun) *n.* **-men** an armed gangster.

gun.met.al (GUN.met.ul) *n.* 1 a dark, bluish gray bronze used for gears, bearings, valves, and steam fittings. 2 a dark bluish gray.
gun.nel (GUN.ul) *n.* 1 a kind of eel-shaped fish of the N. Atlantic. 2 same as GUNWALE.
gun.ner *n.* a military man trained to use artillery or who has charge of a ship's guns.
gun.ner.y (GUN.uh.ree) *n.* heavy guns collectively or the science of making and using them.
gun.ny *n.* a burlap of jute or hemp; **gun.ny.bag** *n.*; **gun.ny.sack** *n.*
gun.play *n.* exchange of gunshots.
gun.point *n.* the point of a gun: *He was taken and held at gunpoint* (= under threat of being shot).
gunpowder See GUN, 1.
gun.run.ning (GUN.run.ing) *n.* smuggling of guns and ammunition.
guns and butter *n.* diplomacy using military and economic power.
gun.ship *n.* a heavily armed helicopter.
gun.shot *n.* a shot, shooting, or range of a gun: *They were fired on when they came within gunshot of the enemy.*
gun-shy *adj.* frightened by the sound of a gun, as some hunting dogs.
gun.sling.er (GUN.sling.ur) *n.* a gunman or gunfighter.
gun.smith *n.* one who makes or repairs small guns.
gun.wale (GUN.ul) *n.* the upper edge of a ship's or boat's side.
gup.py (GUP.ee) *n.* **gup.pies** a colorful tropical aquarium fish, also called "rainbow fish" or "peacock fish," whose grayish-green female bears living young.
gur.gle (GUR.gul) *n.* the bubbling sound of water poured from a narrow-neck bottle: *the happy gurgle of a baby.* —*v.* **-gles, -gled, -gling** make a gurgle: *dolls that gurgle and coo; Water gurgles out of* (= comes out gurgling from) *a pot; adja.: a gurgling baby, brook, sound.*
Gur.kha (GOOR.kuh, GUR-) *n.* a warlike people of Nepal.
gur.ney (GUR.nee) *n.* **-neys** a stretcher on four wheels.
gu.ru (GOOR.oo) *n.* 1 a Hindu religious teacher or guide. 2 a guide or leader in a specific field: *the communications guru Marshall McLuhan; Yogi Berra, the guru of baseball.*
gush *v.* 1 pour out copiously, as water from a spring: *Blood gushed forth from the wound.* 2 express oneself effusively. —*n.* a copious flow.

gush.er *n.* **1** one who gushes. **2** an oil well that flows without pumping.
gush.y *adj.* **gush.i.er, -i.est** *Informal.* effusive or sentimental.
gus.set (GUS.it) *n.* a triangular or diamond-shaped piece of cloth, metal, etc. used to strengthen or enlarge, as over a seam in a garment or at a truss joint.
gus.sy (GUS.ee) *v.* **gus.sies, gus.sied, gus.sy.ing** *Informal.* smarten or dress up: *to gussy up a store with displays; to get gussied up for a party.*
gust *n.* a sudden burst or rush of wind: *a gust of emotion, fire, rain, smoke; fitful gusts of wind.* —*v.* blow in gusts: *strong winds gusting to 60 km/h.*
gus.ta.to.ry (GUS.tuh.tor.ee) *adj.* of the sense of taste: *Your cooking is a gustatory delight!*
gus.to (GUS.toh) *n.* zest or relish: *She devours westerns with great gusto.*
gust.y *adj.* **gust.i.er, -i.est** marked by gusts: *a gusty day.*
gut *n.* the alimentary canal or a part of it, esp. intestines. —**guts** *n.pl.* **1** bowels or entrails. **2** *Informal.* the essential or working parts. **3** *Informal.* pluck or courage: *He doesn't have the guts to stand up to the bully, but has the guts (= impudence) to talk back to his mother.* —**hate someone's guts** dislike someone intensely. —*v.* **guts, gut.ted, gut.ting** disembowel; hence, destroy the inside of something: *a building gutted by fire.* —*adj.* *Informal.* **1** vital or basic: *the gut issues of the campaign; a gut (= easy-to-pass) course.* **2** from one's inner self: *to make a gut call on whether someone is lying; a gut feeling of what is right; his gut reaction.* —**gut.less** *adj.* *Informal.* cowardly.
guts.y *adj.* **guts.i.er, -i.est** *Informal.* bold or lusty.
gut.ter (GUT.ur) *n.* **1** a channel such as the ditch along the side of a street or the trough at the edge of a roof for carrying away rainwater or the groove on either side of a bowling alley. **2** a low or wretched place: *the language of the gutter; He was dragged down into the gutter by bad companions.* —*v.* to stream: *rainwater guttering downhill; wax running down the sides of a guttering candle.*
gut.ter.snipe (GUT.ur.snipe) *n.* a street urchin.
gut.tur.al (GUT.uh.rul) *adj.* of the throat; hence, rasping: *The hard "g" of "go" is a guttural sound; German may sound very guttural to the English.*
gut-wrenching *adj.* agonizing: *a gut-wrenching change, decision, moment,* *phone call, problem.*
gut.ty (GUT.ee) *adj.* **gut.ti.er, gut.ti.est** *Informal.* **1** gutsy. **2** basic or strongly evocative; having gut quality.
guy ("g" as in "go"; *rhyme:* my) *n.* *Informal.* **1** a fellow: *guys and girls; She was trying to be one of the guys; a great guy; a nice guy; a regular guy (= a good sport); a wise guy (= a conceited fellow); You guys (= boys and/or girls; fellows).* **2** a steadying or guiding rope, chain, or wire attached to a tent or tower. —*v.* **1** secure with a guy or guys; *adj.*: *a tower that is a free-standing, not guyed structure.* **2** *Informal.* tease or ridicule.
Guy.a.nese (guy.uh.NEEZ) *n.* & *adj., sing.* & *pl.* (having to do with) a person or from **Guyana**, a republic on South America's N.E. coast.
guz.zle (GUZ.ul) *v.* **guz.zles, guz.zled, guz.zling** eat or drink something greedily. —**guz.zler** *n.*
gym (JIM) *n.* [short form] **1** gymnasium. **2** physical education.
gym.kha.na (jim.KAH.nuh) *n.* **1** a place for athletic contests. **2** a contest or meet for horseriders or automobile drivers.
gym.na.si.um (jim.NAY.zee.um) *n.* **-si.ums** *or* **-si.a** a room or building equipped for physical training and indoor athletics.
gym.nast (JIM.nast) *n.* a gymnastic expert. —**gym.nas.tic** (jim.NAS.tic) *adj.*; **gym.nas.ti.cal.ly** *adv.*
gym.nas.tics *n.pl.* exercises for physical fitness, strength, and agility.
gym.nas.tic (jim.NAS.tic) **1** *adj.* having to do with gymnastics: *world gymnastic championships; gymnastic apparatuses, exercises, maneuvers, tumbles.* **2 gymnastics** *n.pl.* exercises for physical fitness, strength and agility: *She does gymnastics daily after school; There's more gymnastics (= the art) than choreography in jazz dancing; adj.: gymnastics championships, contests, teams.*
gym.no.sperm (JIM.nuh.spurm) *n.* a plant or tree whose fruit is not in an ovary as in angiosperms but exposed, as in conifers such as pines and firs.
gy.ne.col.o.gy (guy.nuh.COL.uh.jee, jye-) *n.* a branch of medicine that, together with obstetrics, deals with specifically female functions and diseases; **gy.ne.col.o.gist** *n.* —**gy.ne.co.log.ic** (-cuh.LOJ.ic) *or* **gy.ne.co.log.i.cal** *adj.*
gyp (JIP) *v.* **gyps, gypped, gyp.ping** *Slang.* cheat or swindle: *They gypped him out of his share of the booty.* —*n.* cheater or swindler; also, a cheating; *adj.*: *a gyp artist, joint.*

—**gyp.per** or **gyp.ster** n. swindler.
Gyp.sy (JIP.see) n. **-sies 1** a member of a wandering people, properly called "Romany," with a language of their own; also **gypsy**: *a passing gypsy; a band of gypsies;* **adj.**: *a gypsy caravan, fortuneteller.* **2** gypsy one who leads a wandering life: *a reporter who started as a newspaper gypsy;* **adj.**: *a gypsy life; a gypsy tour of Europe; an independent gypsy trucker;* a **gypsy cab** *(cruising for fares without a license).*
gy.rate (JYE.rate) v. **-rates, -rat.ed, -rat.ing** turn with a swinging motion in a circular or spiral course, as a tornado, a figure skater, or a spinning top: *to gyrate one's hips; dancers gyrating to music; His career has gyrated from prosperity to disaster;* **adj.**: *the gyrating hips of a rock singer; gyrating stock markets.* —**gy.ra.tion** (jye.RAY.shun) n.: *Elvis's pelvic gyrations; emotional gyrations; price gyrations on a wild stock exchange; the daily gyrations of the dollar.*
gyr.fal.con (JUR.fal.cun, -fawl.cun) n. an arctic falcon, the largest of the family.
gy.ro (JYE.roh) n. *Informal.* gyrocompass or gyroscope.
gy.ro.com.pass (JYE.roh.cum.pus) n. a compass with a motor-driven gyroscope.
gy.ro.scope (JYE.ruh.scope) n. a heavy wheel or disk mounted in a movable frame to spin on an axis that resists change by gravity or by any other force to counteract the rolling motion of a ship or aircraft.

.... **H, h** ....

H or **h** (AICH) n. **H's** or **h's 1** the eighth letter of the English alphabet; hence, the eighth in a series. **2** anything H-shaped.
ha.be.as cor.pus (HAY.bee.us.COR.pus) n. *Law.* a writ requiring a prisoner to be produced in court to determine if he is being held legally.
hab.er.dash.er.y (HAB.ur.dash.uh.ree) n. **-er.ies 1** hats, ties, shirts, socks, etc. for men. **2** a store that sells such items.
ha.bil.i.ment (huh.BIL.uh.munt) n. dress or attire. —**habiliments** pl. garments.
hab.it (HAB.it) n. **1** a settled tendency or disposition, acquired by practice, to perform an action almost automatically: *to acquire, develop, form good habits; an incurable, repulsive habit; It's dangerous to make a habit of smoking in bed; a disciplined woman with regular habits; She does it out of habit; He was in the habit of taking drugs; She gets up at the stroke of five by force of habit; It is hard to kick a habit (Informal for* to break a bad habit). **2** a costume, as of nuns and priests: *a Carmelite habit.* **3** mode of growth: *the prismatic or pyramidal habit of a crystal; the twining habit of a vine; habit and habitat.*
hab.it.a.ble (HAB.uh.tuh.bul) adj. able to be inhabited: *this habitable globe.*
—**hab.it.a.ble.ness** or **hab.it.a.bil.i.ty** (-BIL.i.tee) n.; **hab.it.a.bly** adv.
hab.it.ant (HAB.uh.tunt) n. a settler, esp. a farmer, of French Canada or Louisiana.
hab.i.tat (HAB.uh.tat) n. **1** natural habitation, esp. of a plant or animal. **2** an underwater laboratory.
hab.i.ta.tion (hab.uh.TAY.shun) n. **1** occupancy. **2** a home or settlement.
habit-forming adj. addictive: *Habit-forming drugs include narcotics, barbiturates, and tranquilizers.*
ha.bit.u.al (huh.BICH.oo.ul) adj. done by habit: *his habitual courtesy; Dad is a habitual snorer; his habitual* (= customary) *place at the head of the table.*
—**ha.bit.u.al.ly** adv.
ha.bit.u.ate (huh.BICH.oo.ate) v. **-ates, -at.ed, -at.ing** make used to something: *a dog habituated to being let out at night; She habituated herself to the harsh climate.*
—**ha.bit.u.a.tion** (-AY.shun) n.
ha.bit.u.é (huh.BICH.oo.ay) n. a frequenter or regular attender: *a habitué of the racetracks.*
ha.ci.en.da (hah.see.EN.duh) n. in Spanish America, a large country estate, farm, ranch, or plantation; also, the main dwelling on it.
hack v. **1** cut or chop crudely: *They hacked their way through the dense jungle; He hacked at the weeds with a hoe; to hack something to pieces; a wild beast found hacked to death.* **2** *Informal.* manage successfully: *He just couldn't hack it as a journalist.* **3** *Informal.* work as a hack driver: *a student who works part-time at hacking.* —n. **1** a common horse that may be hired for riding. **2** an old or worn-out horse: *a jaded old hack.* **3** a drudge or hireling: *a literary hack; a party hack; a hack job* (= drudgery). **4** *Informal.* a taxicab.
hack.a.more (HACK.uh.more) n. a halter for breaking horses.
hack.ber.ry (HACK.ber.ee) n. **-ber.ries** a tree related to the elms with cherrylike fruit; also called "nettle tree" and "netleaf hackberry."

hack.er *n.* **1** an amateur computer whiz, esp. one who uses his expertise to break into computer systems. **2** *Informal.* an amateur: *a miserable hacker of a golf player.*

hack hammer *n.* a tool for dressing stone.

hack.ie *n. Informal.* hackman.

hacking cough *n.* a dry cough without discharge of phlegm.

hacking jacket *n.* a jacket for use when riding, with **hacking** (= slanted and flapped) **pockets.**

hack.le (HACK.ul) *n.* **1** a neck feather of a fowl. **2 hackles** *pl.* hairs on a dog's neck that bristle when it is angry. —**raise the hackles of someone** or **get one's hackles up** *Informal.* make someone or become angry or ready to fight.

hack.man (HACK.mun) *n.* **-men** a cab-driver.

hack.ney (HACK.nee) *n.* **-neys** a common horse or a carriage or coach for hire. —**hack.neyed** (-need) *adj.* clichéd: *a hackneyed expression.*

hack.saw *n.* a saw for cutting metal.

hack.work *n.* the work of a hack, as done for hire.

had *pt. & pp.* of HAVE.

had.dock (HAD.uck) *n.* a N. Atlantic food fish related to but smaller than cod.

Ha.des (HAY.deez) *n.* **1** in Greek myth, the underworld. **2 hades** *pl. Informal.* hell.

had.n't (HAD.unt) had not.

hadst *Archaic.* the form of "had" used with THOU.

haf.ni.um (HAF.nee.um) *n.* a silvery metallic chemical element.

haft *n.* a hilt or handle.

hag *n.* an ugly old woman, esp. a witch.

hag.gard (HAG.urd) *adj.* careworn or emaciated: *a haggard face, look; a bit haggard after a long day.*
—**hag.gard.ly** *adv.*

hag.gis *n.* a Scottish dish of minced heart, liver, lungs, etc. of a sheep or calf boiled in the animal's stomach with suet, oatmeal, and seasonings.

hag.gle (HAG.ul) *v.* **hag.gles, hag.gled, hag.gling** argue about or over a price or bargain. —*n.* such a bargaining.

hag.i.og.ra.phy (hag.ee.OG.ruh.fee, hay.jee-) *n.* literature or a book dealing with lives of saints; **hag.i.og.ra.pher** *n.*

hah same as HA.

ha (HAH) *interj.* indicating surprise, joy, anger, etc.

ha-ha *interj.* an exclamation of delight.

hai.ku (HYE.koo) *n. sing. & pl.* a Japanese poem of three lines and a total of 17 syllables.

hail *n.* **1** a shout or cheer: *We were* **within hail** (= within hailing distance). **2** frozen raindrops falling during a thunderstorm. **3** a shower of bullets, blows, or anything similar.
—*v.* **1** greet or call to someone: *They hailed us as we drove by; Stand at the curb and hail a cab; He was hailed as the new leader; They hailed the decision a great victory.* **2** shower hail or like hail: *It was hailing on and off all afternoon; The mob hailed insults at him.* —**hail from** come from: *Our Chinese neighbors hail from Taiwan.* —*interj.* expressing greeting: *All hail! Hail to the chief!*

hail.er (HAY.lur) *n.* a bullhorn.

Hail Mary same as AVE MARIA.

hail.stone *n.* a pellet of hail.

hail.storm *n.* a storm with hail.

hair *n.* **1** any of the fine, threadlike outgrowths from the skin of mammals, esp. from the human head: *not a single hair.* **2** such hairs collectively: *a fine head of hair; a shock of hair; curly, kinky, straight, thick, thinning, unruly, wavy hair; a curl or lock of hair; auburn, black, blond, brown, dark, gray, light, red, white hair; to brush, comb, lose, part, stroke one's hair; Our dog sheds his hair everywhere; She braids, colors, cuts, does, dyes, shampoos, trims, washes her hair.* —**by a hair** by a small margin: *He lost the election by a hair.* —**by a hair's breadth** by a very short distance; narrowly: *We missed or escaped being hit by a hair's breadth.* —**get in one's hair** *Informal.* annoy one. —**let one's hair down** act in an uninhibited manner; be unrestrained. —**not turn a hair** show no reaction. —**split hairs** make too fine distinctions. —**to a hair** exactly. —**hair.less** *adj.*; **hair.like** *adj.*

hair.ball *n.* a small mass of hair found in the stomach of a cow, cat, and such animals that lick their coats.

hair-brained same as HARE-BRAINED.

hair-breadth *n.* a very small distance: *She came within a hair-breadth of winning the bronze medal; She was edged out by a hair-breath;* **adj.** *a.: We had a hair-breadth escape in the accident; hair-breadth timing.* Also **hairs-breadth, hair's-breadth.**

hair.brush *n.* a stiff brush for grooming the hair.

hair.cloth *n.* a fabric of cotton and horse's or camel's hair for use in upholstery and stiffening garments.

hair.cut *n.* the act or style of cutting the hair of the head.

hair.do (HAIR.doo) *n.* **-dos** (-dooz) way of arranging a woman's hair; coiffure.

hair.dress.er (HAIR.dress.ur) *n.* one who cuts and styles hair, esp. women's.

-haired *comb.form.* having hair as specified: *blond-haired; the curly-haired look; a dark-haired woman; a fair-haired youth; golden-haired boys; gray-haired grandpas.*

hair.line *n.* **1** the outline of the hair above the forehead: *the receding hairline of a balding man.* **2** a very thin line; *adj.a: a hairline crack or fracture; a questionable hairline decision; a hairline space.*

hair.piece *n.* a wig worn to cover baldness.

hair.pin *n.* a U-shaped metal or plastic pin used by women to keep their hair in place: *a hairpin bend in the road.*

hair-raiser *n.* something terrifying, esp. a story. —**hair-raising** *adj.*

hairs.breadth or **hair's-breadth** same as HAIR-BREADTH: *He escaped by a hairsbreadth.*

hair.split.ting (HAIR.split.ing) *n.* the making of too fine distinctions: *hairsplitting negotiations.*

hair.spray *n.* a spray to keep the hair in place.

hair.spring *n.* a fine spring used to regulate the balance wheel of a watch.

hair.style *n.* coiffure.

hair.styl.ing (HAIR.sty.ling) *n.* the work of cutting and arranging the hair. —**hair.styl.ist** *n.* hairdresser.

hair trigger *n.* a delicately adjusted trigger that operates by the slightest pressure. —**hair-trigger** *adj.*: *hair-trigger laughter, nerves; a hair-trigger temper.*

hair.y *adj.* **hair.i.er, -i.est 1** covered with hair: *a hairy chest; the hairy woodpecker.* **2** of or like hair: *a hairy growth.* **3** *Informal.* difficult or dangerous: *a hairy situation, time.*

hairy-chested *adj.* virile or robust.

Hai.tian (HAY.shun, -tee.un) **1** *n. & adj.* (a person) of or from **Haiti**, a West Indian republic. **2** the creole French spoken in Haiti.

hajj or **hadj** (HAJ) *n.* a pilgrimage to Mecca, the spiritual center of Islam.

haj.ji or **had.ji** (HAJ.ee) *n.* one who has made the hajj.

hake *n.* a marine food fish related to the cod.

hal.berd or **hal.bert** (HAL.burt, HAWL-) *n.* a medieval weapon that is a battle-ax and spear in one.

hal.cy.on (HAL.see.un) *adj.a.* peaceful and prosperous: *in the halcyon days of one's youth; a halcyon era, year.*

hale *adj.* **hal.er, hal.est** healthy: *a hale and hearty golden ager; hale, hearty, and wholesome.* —*v.* **hales, haled, hal.ing** haul: *He was haled into court to answer a charge.*

half (HAF) *n. & pron., pl.* **halves** (HAVZ) one of two equal parts making up something: *Seven is just half of 14; A year and a half has passed; One and a half years* or *One and one half years have passed; "Half a loaf is better than no bread"* (= Something is better than nothing); *I want my half of it; Divide the cake* **in half** or **into halves**; *one's* **better half** (*Informal* for spouse). —**by half** by far. —*adj. & pron.* being a half: *He'll be here in a half hour* or *in half an hour; sold at half price.* —*adv.* to half: *A half empty glass is half full; a potato that is only half cooked; We start work at half past eight* (= 8:30). —**not half bad** *Informal.* not at all bad; fairly good.

half-and-half *n., adj. & adv.* (a mixture, as of milk and cream) consisting of two equal parts.

half.back *n.* one of a pair of football players positioned with the fullback and quarterback behind the line of scrimmage.

half-baked *adj. Informal.* poor in planning or judgment: *a half-baked idea, scheme, visionary, youth.*

half-blood *n.* an offspring that is half-blooded.

half-blooded *adj.* **1** born of parents of different stocks or races. **2** related through only one common parent.

half-breed *n. & adj.* [usually offensive] (one) born of parents of differently colored races.

half boot *n.* a boot reaching halfway to the knee.

half brother (or **sister**) *n.* a brother (or sister) related through only one common parent.

half-caste *n. & adj.* [sometimes offensive] (one) of mixed European and Asian ancestry.

half-cocked *adj.* without full thought or consideration, like a firearm whose hammer is pulled back only halfway before firing.

half.heart.ed (HAF.har.tid) *adj.* unwilling or uninterested. —**half.heart.ed.ly** *adv.* Also **half-heart.ed, half.heart.ed.ly.**

half-life *n.* the time taken for half the atoms of a radioactive sample to break down in a steady proportion of decreasing amounts.

half-mast *n.* the position of flying a flag halfway from the top of its mast as a

sign of respect to a dead person or as a distress signal. Also **half-staff**.
half.pen.ny (HAY.puh.nee) *n. & adj.* (worth) half a British penny; *pl.* **half.pence** (sum of money) or **half.pen.nies** (coins).
half pint *n. Informal.* a small person; **half-pint** *adj.: a half-pint hero.*
half sister See HALF BROTHER.
half sole *n.* the front half of a sole. —**half-sole** *v.* -soles, -soled, -sol.ing: *to repair and half-sole a shoe, boot, etc.*
half-staff same as HALF-MAST.
half step *n.* 1 a short military marching step. 2 a musical half tone.
half.time *n.* an intermission between the halves of a game.
half.tone *n.* 1 a picture-printing method by which shades intermediate between black and white are engraved as dots of varying size by photographing the picture through a fine screen; *adja.: a halftone image, output, screen.* 2 a picture printed by this method: *halftones and text.*
half-track *n.* an army vehicle with tractor treads at the rear and wheels in front.
half-truth *n.* a deceptive statement giving only some of the facts.
half.way *adj. & adv.* 1 midway: *We live halfway between the two bus stops; She's halfway through the book; He had walked halfway across the street when he was hit.* 2 incomplete or incompletely: *a halfway measure, point; You can't leave halfway through a haircut.* —**go halfway** or **meet someone halfway** do one's share toward accomplishing something: *I'll take up the project only if you will go halfway with me; Joe agreed to meet Jim halfway.*
halfway house *n.* a center for housing former drug addicts, convicts, mental patients, etc. while they are being prepared to return to society.
half-wit *n.* fool; dolt.
half-witted *adj.* very stupid.
hal.i.but (HAL.uh.but, HOL-) *n.* a flatfish of the flounder group caught in northern seas and widely used as food.
hal.ite *n.* rock salt.
hal.i.to.sis (hal.i.TOH.sis) *n.* bad breath caused by a disorder of the stomach or mouth.
hall *n.* 1 a common passageway such as a corridor; hallway. 2 a foyer or lobby. 3 a large room for meetings, parties, etc.: *concert, convention, lecture, mess, study, town halls.* 4 an educational or residential building containing offices, housing a dormitory, etc.: *Athabasca Hall; the halls of ivy* (= academic life).
hal.le.lu.jah or **hal.le.lu.iah** (hal.uh. LOO.yuh) *interj.* "Praise the Lord." —*n.* a hymn with this theme.
hall.mark 1 *n. & v.* (put) an official mark guaranteeing quality, as Goldsmith's Hall in London used to stamp on gold and silver objects. 2 *n.* a distinguishing characteristic: *the hallmarks of a gentleman, of a good education.*
hal.lo (huh.LOH) *n., v. & interj.* **hal.los, hal.loed, hal.lo.ing** call or shout to greet or attract attention. Also **hal.loa** (huh.LOH).
hall of fame *n.* a memorial building in honor of celebrated people: *the Hockey Hall of Fame.*
hal.loo (huh.LOO) *n., v. & interj.* **-loos, -looed, -loo.ing** hallo, esp. as used to urge hounds on in hunting.
hal.lowed (HAL.ode) *adj.* blessed: *We are on hallowed ground.*
Hal.low.een or **Hal.low.e'en** (hal.oh. WEEN) *n.* Allhallows Eve; October 31, esp. the evening: *Children go seeking treats on Halloween; to scare away the goblins at Halloween; Happy Halloween! adja.: a Halloween costume, mask, night, parade, party, prank, robbery, tradition, treat.*
hal.lu.ci.nate (huh.LOO.suh.nate) *v.* **-nates, -nat.ed, -nat.ing** (cause) to see or experience things that are unreal or dreamlike, as when delirious or under the influence of a drug.
—**hal.lu.ci.na.tion** (-NAY.shun) *n.*
—**hal.lu.ci.na.to.ry** (-nuh.tor.ee) *adj.*
hal.lu.ci.no.gen (huh.LOO.suh.nuh.jun) *n.* a drug such as LSD that makes one hallucinate. —**hal.lu.ci.no.gen.ic** (-nuh.JEN.ic) *adj.*
hall.way *n.* a passageway or corridor.
ha.lo (HAL.oh, HAY.loh) *n.* **-los** or **-loes** a circle of light, as sometimes seen around the sun, moon, or other heavenly body and symbolically pictured around the heads of saints and similar personages as a mark of glory.
hal.o.gen (HAL.uh.jun) *n.* any of the five chemical elements astatine, fluorine, chlorine, bromine, and iodine that combine with metals to form salts: *a car equipped with high-intensity halogen lamps.*
halt (HAWLT) *n.* a stopping of movement: *The traffic came to a halt at the crash site; a grinding or screeching halt; The strike brought operations to a halt; effective steps to call a halt to wasteful spending.* —*v.* 1 (cause) to stop moving

or continuing: *Halt! Who goes there? measures to halt inflation; The marchers halted for refreshments.* **2** hesitate or waver. —*adj.* [old use] lame: *to cure the halt and the sick.*

hal.ter (HAWL.tur) *n.* **1** a rope or strap around the neck, as for leading a horse, a noose for hanging, etc. **2** death by hanging. **3** a woman's backless bodice, often **halter top**, held by a strap around the back of the neck; *adj***a.:** *a halter blouse, dress, gown, jacket, jumpsuit, neckline, style, suit.* —*v.* tie with or put a halter on a person or animal; hence, restrain.

halting *adj.* **1** faltering or wavering: *He testified in a halting voice.* **2** lame or limping: *his halting gait.* —**halt.ing.ly** *adv.*

halve (HAV) *v.* **halves, halved, halv.ing** **1** divide or share equally. **2** reduce to half: *The strength of the enemy was halved after the battle.*

halves (HAVZ) *n.pl.* of HALF. —**by halves** incompletely: *to do a job by halves.* —**go halves** share equally: *to go halves with someone.*

hal.yard (HAL.yurd) *n.* a rope or tackle for hauling a sail, flag, etc. up or down.

ham *n.* **1** the back of a thigh and buttock, as of a pig, esp. as salted and dried or smoked meat: *a breakfast of ham and eggs; He squatted on his* **hams.** **2** *Informal.* a showy performer: *a ham actor; a radio ham* (= amateur radio operator). **3** *Informal.* a theatrical demonstration: *a 90-minute TV special full of tears and ham; It was pure ham.* —*v.* **hams, hammed, ham.ming** overact: *He had to* **ham it up** *to make an impression.*

ham.burg.er (HAM.bur.gur) *n.* ground beef, a patty of such meat, or a patty grilled and sandwiched in a split bun.

Ham.ite *n.* a member of a Caucasoid people of N. and E. Africa including ancient Egyptians and Somalis. —**Ha.mit.ic** (ha.MIT.ic) *adj.*

ham.let (HAM.lit) *n.* a small village.

ham.mer (HAM.ur) *n.* **1** a pounding tool, usually with a metal head set crosswise at the end of a wooden handle. **2** anything similar, as one of the wooden mallets inside a piano, an auctioneer's gavel, the striking mechanism of a firing pin, or a bone of the middle ear: *Unclaimed articles go or come* **under the hammer** (= the auctioneer's gavel, for auction sale). —**hammer and tongs** with great vigor: *She went at it hammer and tongs.* —*v.* work with or as if with a hammer; strike with repeated blows; hence, work hard: *Lou hammers at her word processor six hours a day; She's* **hammering away** *at her Ph.D. thesis; to* **hammer out** *a solution to a vexing problem.*

hammer and sickle *n.* a Communist emblem symbolizing the laborer and the farmer, as on the flag of the former Soviet Union.

hammer-and-tongs *adja.* vigorous: *a hammer-and-tongs approach to a problem.*

ham.mer.head (HAM.ur.hed) *n.* a shark with a mallet-shaped head and eyes on each end.

ham.mer.lock (HAM.ur.lock) *n.* a wrestling hold in which the opponent's arm is held twisted behind his back.

hammer throw *n.* an athletic contest using a metal ball attached to a steel wire, thrown for distance.

ham.mer.toe (HAM.ur.toe) *n.* a bent and deformed toe.

ham.mock (HAM.uck) *n.* a cradlelike swinging couch, as one of netted cord slung by its ends between supports.

ham.per (HAM.pur) *v.* impede the movement or hinder the freedom of someone: *A heavy snowfall hampered our progress.* —*n.* a large covered basket or container, as for food, wine, laundry, or mail.

ham.ster *n.* a small rodent of the mouse family with large cheek pouches and a short tail.

ham.string *n.* **1** either of the two tendons at the back of the knee connecting the thigh muscles. **2** in four-footed animals such as the horse, a large tendon at the back of the hock. —*v.* **-strings,** *pt. & pp.* **-strung** or **-stringed, -string.ing** cripple or disable, (as if) by cutting the hamstring: *press freedom hamstrung by restrictions.*

hand *n.* **1** the end part of the forearm that is below the wrist, with fingers for grasping and holding: *We shook hands over the deal; to clasp, hold, take someone's hand; to clap, cup, lower, raise, wring one's hands; to* **lay one's hands on** (= seize; also, touch, as in blessings or religious ceremonies) *someone; to lead or take someone by the hand; He picked it up with his bare hands.* **2** a limb or other part similar to the human hand in appearance or use: *a monkey's hands* (= forelimbs) *and feet; a hand* (= bunch) *of bananas; The hands of a clock tell the time.* **3** a person or a person's action, skill, or power: *"All hands on deck"; hired hands; ranch hands; Please give or lend me a hand with this job; He would* have no hand in wrongdoing; He's an old hand at basket-weaving; She writes a legible hand; He rules with a firm hand; "an iron hand in a velvet glove"; He fell **into the hands** of the enemy. **4** what is given with the hand: The audience gave her a big hand (= round of applause); He decided to ask her hand (= promise) in marriage; the warm hand (= offer) of friendship. **5** the cards dealt to or held by a player in a game; also, a round of play: to have, hold, show, tip one's hand; a good, strong, weak hand. —**at hand** close by: A nurse is at hand if you need help; Peace was at hand after many years of war. —**from hand to mouth** on a day-to-day basis: With no money in the bank, we are practically living from hand to mouth. —**in hand** under control or in one's possession: The situation is well in hand; The money we have in hand is not sufficient. —**hand in glove** or **hand and glove** in close cooperation with someone. —**hand in hand** together: Lee and Lou walking hand in hand. —**hands down** easily: She won the game hands down. —**hands off** take your hands off: Hands off my bike! —**on hand** within reach: Please make sure coffee and donuts are on hand; I'll be on hand (= present) to help out. —**on one's hands** at one's disposal: When I have time on my hands no one needs me! —**on the one** (or **other**) **hand** from one (or another) point of view: On the one hand, we have a job opening; on the other hand, we can't afford to hire one more. —**out of hand** **1** out of control: Don't let the situation get out of hand. **2** forthwith: The petition was rejected out of hand. —**v.** give or do with the hand or as if with the hand: She handed him his drink; He courteously handed (= helped) her into the car; Did you **hand in** your work? She's so successful everyone **hands it** (= gives credit) to her. —**hand down** give: an opinion handed down by a court; a legend handed down (= passed along) from generation to generation. —**hand out** distribute: to hand out flyers, food. —**hand over** transfer to someone: The robber asked the teller to hand over the cash (to him); Mr. Lyon will hand over charge to the new teacher tomorrow.

hand.bag n. a small bag to hold in the hand, esp. a woman's purse.

hand.ball n. a game played by striking a rubber ball with the hand against a wall or board.

hand.bill n. a notice that is passed out or distributed by hand.

hand.book n. a manual or guidebook.

hand.car n. a small, open, four-wheeled railroad car used by workmen, formerly operated by pumping a handle.

hand.cart n. a cart that is pulled or pushed by hand.

hand.clasp n. a handshake.

hand.craft n. handicraft. —v.: make by manual skill: not machine-made but handcrafted parts.

hand.cuff n. one of a pair of metal rings joined by a short chain, used in restraining prisoners: She was led away in handcuffs. —v. **1** put handcuffs on someone; manacle. **2** check or hinder: The goalkeeper was handcuffed by the deflected shot.

-handed comb.form. having or using hands as specified: a left-handed writer; a two-handed stroke; empty-handed, even-handed, heavy-handed, high-handed, right-handed, single-handed.

hand.ed.ness (HAN.did.nis) n. one's natural preference for either the left or the right hand.

hand.ful n. **-fuls** **1** what a hand can hold; hence, a small number or amount. **2** Informal. a person or thing that is hard to manage.

hand.gun n. a firearm such as a pistol that is held and fired with one hand.

hand-held n. something that is held in the hand for operating, as a vacuum cleaner: corded hand-helds; adj a.: a hand-held blender, computer, mixer, phone, video game. Also **hand.held**.

hand.i.cap (HAN.dee.cap) n. **1** a disadvantage or hindrance: Poverty is a handicap to progress; The poor are under a handicap; We try to overcome our handicaps. **2** an adjustment of time, distance, or weight made for individual competitors in a contest or game to give the weaker ones an advantage or the stronger ones a disadvantage. **3** a game or race in which such handicaps are given, as in golf or horse racing. —v. **-caps, -capped, -cap.ping** **1** be at a disadvantage: He is handicapped by a speech defect; n.: the **handicapped** such as the deaf, blind, crippled, retarded, and mentally ill. **2** give a handicap to someone: In trapshooting, competitors may be handicapped up to nine meters.
—**han.di.cap.per** n.

hand.i.craft (HAN.dee.craft) n. **1** the skillful making of articles by hand. **2** a trade or art using such skill, as ceramics or basket-weaving. **3** a handicraft product or artifact. —**hand.i.craft.er** or **hand.i.crafts.man** n. **-men**.

hand.i.work (HAN.dee.wurk) n. handwork; also, work done personally; an individual achievement: *Some see the universe as the handiwork of God.*

hand.ker.chief (HANK.ur.chif) *n.* **-chiefs** or **-chieves** (-cheevz) **1** a usually square piece of cloth carried on one's person for blowing one's nose, wiping the face, etc. **2** a kerchief.

han.dle (HAN.dul) *n.* the part of a tool, door, cup, etc. for holding, grasping, or manipulating it. —**fly off the handle** *Informal.* lose one's temper. —**get a handle on** grasp mentally: *It took time for them to get a handle on the situation.* —*v.* **han.dles, han.dled, han.dling 1** take, operate, manage, or control (as if) with one's hand or hands: *A crowd has to be tactfully handled; The Oilers handled* (= defeated) *the Leafs with ease; n.: a case that requires delicate, gentle, tactful* **handling. 2** respond to control: *a car that handles well.*

han.dle.bar (HAN.dul.bar) *n.* **1** a bar with a handle at each end for steering a bicycle or motorcycle. **2** a moustache that resembles a handlebar, or **handlebar moustache.**

hand.made *adj.* made by hand, not by machine.

hand.maid or **hand.maid.en** (HAND.may.dun) *n.* **1** formerly, a female personal attendant. **2** helper: *Logic is the handmaid of philosophy.*

hand-me-down *n.* something, as a garment, handed down from an older person. —*adja.* secondhand or cheap: *an ill-fitting hand-me-down suit.*

hand.out *n. Informal.* something handed out as charity, as a free gift, as promotional literature, or as an official version of a news event.

hand.pick *v.* **1** pick fruits or vegetables. **2** choose: *to handpick one's supporters or aides.*

hand.picked *adj.* **1** personally selected, often unfairly: *a handpicked group of supporters.* **2** carefully selected: *The winning candidate had a group of handpicked advisors.*

hand.rail *n.* a rail fixed to the side of a stairway for use as a support.

hand.saw *n.* a saw that is used in the hand.

hand.set *n.* the hand-held receiver of a telephone with earpiece and mouthpiece at the ends.

hand.shake *n.* **1** a friendly clasping and shaking of each other's hands: *a warm handshake.* **2** a money gift made on parting: *a golden handshake.*

hands-off *adja.* noninterfering: *a hands-off approach, attitude, policy, stand.*

hand.some *adj.* **-som.er, -som.est**

handkerchief / hang

1 [esp. of males] good-looking: *a handsome design, face, fellow, horse, suitor, volume, woman, young man; a tall handsome stranger; handsome stationery; Our handsome hulk likes to flaunt himself in front of the mirror.* **2** generous: *a handsome amount, gift, payment, profit, settlement; handsome treatment.* —**hand.some.ly** *adv.*

hands-on *adja.* involving active participation: *a hands-on course, demonstration, experience.*

hand.spring *n.* a tumbling forward or backward on the hands, making a full circle in midair before landing on the feet.

hand.stand *n.* a standing on one's hands with the legs up.

hand-to-hand *adj. & adv.* close together; involving physical contact: *They fought hand-to-hand; a hand-to-hand combat.*

hand-to-mouth *adj.* spending or consuming with no provision for the future; precarious: *a hand-to-mouth existence.*

hand.work *n.* work done with one's hands; **hand.work.er** *n.*

hand.writ.ing (HAND.rye.ting) *n.* writing by hand or its style. —**hand.writ.ten** (-rit.un) *adj.*

hand.y *adj.* **hand.i.er, -i.est 1** readily available: *Keep your pencils handy.* **2** skilled, usually without training, in odd jobs: *Jean is handy at plumbing, Jan is handy with a lawnmower; Joe is handy around the house.* **3** convenient: *A food processor is very handy for kitchen chores; It's handy to have labor-saving gadgets; An eraser will* **come in handy** (= be convenient) *for corrections.* —**hand.i.ly** *adv.;* **hand.i.ness** *n.*

hand.y.man (HAN.dee.man) *n.* **-men** one who does odd jobs.

hang *v.* **hangs,** *pt. & pp.* **hanged** (in "kill" senses) or **hung, hang.ing**
1 attach, fasten, or suspend so as to swing or turn freely: *A coat is hung on a hook; Pictures hang on the wall; We hang out the laundry to dry; He hung his head in shame; was condemned to be hanged (by the neck); He was hanged for murder; He didn't have to hang himself;* **Hang it** (= Damn it)! **2** cover or furnish with something suspended, as a wall with tapestry or a window with drapes. **3** be or seem suspended, as when undecided, idle, etc.: *Time is hanging on his hands* (= He has free time) *since he quit his job; His career hangs* (= depends) *on your recommendation.* —**hang around** or **about** *Informal.* loiter or stand by idly.

—**hang back** be reluctant: *Billy is so shy*

he hangs back from group activities.
—**hang in there** *Informal.* don't give up; stay put. —**hang loose** *Informal.* be relaxed. —**hang on** keep one's hold or grip: *to hang on to a lifebuoy, to an heirloom, to old customs, to a piece of property.* —**hang out** *Informal.* live or stay: *Where do you hang out? The donut shop is where he hangs out* (= is often found); *Be careful who you hang out* (= keep company) *with.* —**hang up** put back on a hanger or hook, as the receiver at the end of a phone call: *She hung up on* (= cut off) *the harassing caller.* —**let it all hang out** *Informal.* let one's hair down; be uninhibited. —*n.* 1 the way something hangs: *I don't like the hang of that curtain.* 2 *Informal.* how something is done or what something means: *I'm trying to get the hang of this poem.* 3 *Informal.* a trifle: *I don't care a hang* or *give a hang about root beer.*
hang.ar (HANG.ur) *n.* a shed or shelter, as for aircraft.
hang.dog *adj.* sneaking or shamefaced: *a hangdog face, look.*
hanger-on *n.* **hangers-on** [contemptuous use] a follower or dependent.
hang gliding *n.* the sport of gliding or soaring using a kitelike device that carries the glider harnessed underneath it.
hanging *adj.* 1 that hangs: *a hanging basket, bookcase, plant; a hanging judge* (known for death sentences). 2 deserving death by hanging: *Murder used to be a hanging crime.* —**hangings** *n.pl.* things hung, as draperies or curtains: *silk hangings.*
hang-loose *adj.* relaxed; uninhibited: *a hang-loose investor, spirit, style.*
hang.out *n. Informal.* a place where one hangs out; a frequented resort.
hang.o.ver (HANG.oh.vur) *n. Informal.* aftereffects of a drinking bout, such as headache, dizziness, and depression.
hang.tag *n.* a hanging tag attached to a product, esp. a garment, with information about its material, how to take care of it, etc.; also **hang-tag, hang tag.**
hang-up *n. Informal.* 1 a mental or emotional problem: *employee hangups.* 2 a snag or impediment: *legal hangups.*
hank *n.* a coil or loop: *a hank of hair, thread.*
han.ker (HANK.ur) *v.* long or crave for something that makes one restless in its pursuit: *Some hanker after riches, others hanker for thrills; He has been hankering to go back to Europe ever since he landed here; In his old age he began to* long for peace and happiness after a lifetime of **hankering** for or after wealth.
han.kie or **han.ky** *n.* **-kies** *Informal.* handkerchief.
han.ky-pan.ky *n. Informal.* underhand dealings or affairs.
han.som (HAN.sum) *n.* a two-wheeled one-horse-drawn carriage with the driver's seat high up behind the cab; also **hansom cab.**
Ha.nuk.kah (HAH.nuh.kuh) *n.* a Jewish festival in December; also called "Feast of Lights."
hap *n.* [old use] happening; also, a chance or lot. —*v.* **haps, happed, hap.ping** occur by chance; happen.
hap.haz.ard (hap.HAZ.urd) *adj.* careless or chancy: *a haphazard filing of papers;* —*adv.: books left haphazard over the desks.* —*n.: gifts selected* **at haphazard.** —**hap.haz.ard.ly** *adv.*
hap.less (HAP.lis) *adj.* unlucky. —**hap.less.ly** *adv.*
hap.loid *n. & adj.* (a cell or gamete) with a single set of unpaired chromosomes in each nucleus.
hap.ly *adv.* by chance.
hap.pen (HAP.un) *v.* take place or be, esp. by chance: *The accident happened on the highway; I just happened to be at the scene; You're late, what happened?* **As it happens,** (= It turns out) *our new car had a flat tire; Accidents* **happen to** (= are experienced by) *lots of people.* —**happen on** or **upon** meet or find something by chance.
happening (HAP.un.ing) *n.* 1 what happens or takes place. 2 an event, activity, or performance of a spontaneous or vital nature with many participants, as "action painting" or "living theater."
hap.pen.stance (HAP.un.stance) *n.* a chance circumstance or happening: *as happenstance would have it; "Once may be happenstance, but twice is coincidence."*
hap.py (HAP.ee) *adj.* **hap.pi.er, hap.pi.est** 1 having peace and contentment: *a happy childhood, family, home, marriage.* 2 pleased: *We are happy to accept your invitation; happy that you are getting married; very happy about the marriage; Everyone is happy for (Informal for pleased with) you; a "happy face" sweater* (with such a design). 3 fortunate or lucky: *a happy chance, coincidence.* 4 apt or felicitous: *a happy choice of words; a happy idea, remark, thought.* —**hap.pi.ly** *adv.;* **hap.pi.ness** *n.*
-happy *comb.form.* happy with or dazed by something, as specified: *bomb-happy, slap-happy, trigger-happy.*
happy-go-lucky *adj.* easygoing or

light-hearted.
happy hour *n.* an early evening hour when a bar sells liquor at a discount.
ha.ra.ki.ri (HAH.ruh.KEER.ee) *n.* suicide by disembowelment, as once practiced by the samurai.
ha.rangue (huh.RANG) *n.* a long and loud, esp. scolding speech; tirade.
—*v.* -rangues, -rangued, -rangu.ing address in or deliver a harangue.
har.ass (huh.RAS, HAIR.us) *v.* bother or torment unceasingly, as by repeated calls, raids, demands, cares, worries, etc.; *adj.: a harassing caller, message; to trace harassing phone calls.*
—**har.ass.ment** *n.*
har.bin.ger (HAR.bin.jur) *n.* one that goes before another to announce what is to come: *The early-blooming primrose has been called the harbinger of spring.*
har.bor (HAR.bur) *n.* **1** a protected area of deep water on the coast of a sea or lake where ships may dock. **2** a place of safety or refuge; shelter.
—*v.* **1** come to anchor. **2** be or give a hiding place to an undesirable person, thing, or feeling: *hair that harbors fleas; to harbor feelings of revenge.*
—**har.bor.age** (-ij) *n.* Also **har.bour, har.bour.age** *Cdn.*
hard *adj.* **1** too firm to penetrate, cut, or crush: *a hard nut, rock, muscle.* **2** high in alcohol content: *Whiskey, gin, rum, etc. are hard liquors.* **3** backed by gold or readily convertible to other currencies: *hard currency such as dollars and pounds.* **4** not soft, weak, tentative, or visionary: *a hard and unyielding character; The police need hard evidence to get a murder conviction; It was a hard decision to let him go; the hard facts of reality; Let's take a good hard look before deciding.* **5** tough to endure: *No work is too hard for Lu; the school of* **hard knocks** (= hardships); *a* **hard luck story** (meant to get sympathy and help); *the hard* (= distressing) *times of unemployment; The fired employee left with no hard* (= harsh) *feelings; The baby gave us a hard* (= rough) *time when we ran out of milk; He said hard* (= unkind) *things to his best friend; hard* (= severe) *winter weather; Everyone hates* **hard and fast** (= very rigid) *rules; We were* **hard put to find** (= had great difficulty in finding) *a night's lodging in that strange city; a big spender who is* **hard up** *for (Informal for in great need of) money at the end of each month.* **6** demanding great physical or mental effort; not easy: *a hill that is hard to climb; the long, hard march to freedom; Some habits are hard to break; a list of hard words; an earphone for the* **hard of hearing** (= those who don't hear well); *a* **hard place** (= difficult to survive in); *adj.: Lee's just playing* **hard-to-get** (*Informal* for pretending to be not easily won over). —*adv.* in a hard manner: *The lake is frozen hard enough to skate on; Students work hard before a test; Try hard to succeed; Running makes you breathe hard; We are* **hard hit** (= We suffer) *by misfortunes; It will* **go hard with you** (= You will have a difficult time) *if you don't pay up; He took the defeat very hard* (= found it difficult to endure); *Superstitions* **die hard** (= remain in existence); *The church is* **hard by** (= close to) *the school.*
hard.back *n.* a book with hard covers.
hard.ball *n. Informal.* tough or aggressive action: *to play hardball* (= be callous or ruthless); *political hardball;* *adj.: hardball campaigns, politics, tactics.*
hard-bitten *adj.* tough or stubborn: *hard-bitten managers.*
hard.board *n.* board of pressed wood-chip fibers.
hard-boiled *adj.* **1** boiled with its shell until firm inside: *a hard-boiled egg.* **2** *Informal.* tough or callous: *a hard-boiled businesswoman.*
hard cider See CIDER.
hard copy *n.* a printout as distinguished from a video display.
hard-core *adj.* **1** chronic: *the hard-core unemployed and unemployables of a community; hard-core inflation.* **2** extremely bad: *(explicit) hard-core pornography.*
hard-cover or **hard.cov.er** (HARD. cuv.ur) *adj.* bound in cloth, board, or other stiff cover, not paperback: *a hard-cover book, edition, publication;* *n.: published in hardcover; hardcovers that outsell paperbacks.*
hard disk *n.* a computer's rigid disk for magnetic storage of data.
hard drug *n.* an addictive drug such as cocaine or heroine.
hard.en (HAR.dun) *v.* **1** make hard or become solidified. **2** make or become unfeeling or pitiless: *Do not harden your hearts; hardened by training;* *adj. & cpd: a* **hardened** *criminal; battle-hardened soldiers; campaign-hardened veterans; street-hardened toughs.*
hard goods same as DURABLE GOODS.
hard hat *n.* **1** a protective helmet worn by miners, construction workers, etc. **2** *Informal.* a construction worker. **3** an outspoken reactionary.
hard.head.ed (HARD.hed.id) *adj.* **1** stubborn. **2** practical or realistic: *a*

hardhearted / harmonium

hardheaded businesswoman.
hard.heart.ed (HARD.har.tid) *adj.* cruel or unfeeling.
har.di.hood (HAR.di.hood, short "oo") *n.* 1 daring or sturdiness. 2 audacity or boldness.
hard line *n.* an unyielding position: *The boss is taking a hard line against absenteeism.* —**hard-line** *adj.* unyielding in policy, esp. political: *a hard-line approach, government, nationalist, policy, position, record, regime, stand; hard-line opposition, views; He's too hard-line on the issue.* —**hard-liner** *n.*
hard lines or **hard.lines** *n.pl.* goods such as housewares and home-improvement and do-it-yourself products; not soft lines.
hard.ly *adv.* 1 barely; almost not: *I can hardly walk; Hardly anyone turned up at the meeting; You can hardly expect to be paid for such poor work.* 2 [old use] in a hard manner: *He was dealt with hardly and severely.*
hard-nosed *adj. Informal.* shrewd and tough: *a hard-nosed politician.*
hard.pan *n.* subsoil too cemented and compacted for roots to penetrate.
hard rock *n.* the original rock'n'roll with a loud and steady beat.
hard.scrab.ble (HARD.scrab.ul) *adja.* 1 earning a bare subsistence: *a hardscrabble existence.* 2 of land, barren: *hardscrabble coal country.*
hard sell *n. Informal.* high-pressure salesmanship: *the hard sell used to make kids eat wholesome foods.* —**adja.:** *a hard-sell campaign, commercial, hustler, promotion, tactic.*
hard.shell *adj. Informal.* uncompromising or rigid, esp. in religious matters.
hard.ship *n.* a hard-to-bear condition such as hunger, sickness, poverty, and pain.
hard.tack *n.* a hard, dry biscuit or unleavened bread, as once used by sailors and soldiers.
hard.top *n.* a convertible-style automobile with a rigid roof but no posts between front and rear windows.
hard.ware *n.* 1 metal articles, tools, utensils, etc.: *a hardware store.* 2 weaponry, equipment, etc.: *military hardware.* 3 apparatuses such as the physical units of a computer system, not programs or software.
hard water *n.* mineral-rich water that makes lathering difficult.
hard-wired or **hard.wired** *adj.* directly connected to a computer, not via the telephone or using software: *workstations hardwired to a network.*

hard.wood *n.* tough, compact wood, as of broad-leaved trees such as the oak, ebony, and mahogany; *adj.:* *a hardwood floor, tree; hardwood forests, lumber.*
har.dy (HAR.dee) *adj.* **hard.i.er, -i.est** strong and robust: *our hardy pioneers; hardy annuals that can endure the frost.* —**hard.i.ly** *adv.;* **hard.i.ness** *n.*
hare *n.* a rabbitlike furry animal but larger and with longer ears, a split upper lip, and powerful hind legs; jack rabbit: *Hares do not burrow but are very active in the spring; "to run with the hare and hunt with the hounds"* (= to play a double game, supporting both sides); *"mad as a March hare"* (when it is rutting).
hare.brained *adj.* giddy or flighty: *a harebrained scheme, undertaking; His ideas are somewhat harebrained.*
hare.lip *n.* cleft lip; **hare.lipped** *adj.*
har.em (HAIR.um) *n.* 1 a group of women kept by one man, as in a Moslem household. 2 an animal's mates collectively.
hark *v.* [literary use] listen! —**hark back** recall or refer back *to* an earlier subject or time.
harken same as HEARKEN.
har.le.quin (HAR.luh.quin) *n.* a comic character wearing a tight-fitting costume in diamond-shaped patches of color.
har.lot (HAR.lut) *n.* a prostitute; **har.lot.ry** (-luh.tree) *n.*
harm *n.* hurt with pain or distress: *drugs that do more harm than good; to undo the harm caused by pollutants; grave, grievous, irreparable, severe harm to the environment; There's no harm in watching a little TV.* —*v.* cause harm. —**harm.ful** *adj.;* **harm.ful.ly** *adv.*
har.mon.ic (har.MON.ic) *adj.* having to do with musical harmony: *a harmonic balance, concept, design, element.*
—*n.* 1 a musical overtone. 2 **harmonics** *pl.* [takes *sing.v.*] the science of musical sounds.
har.mon.i.ca (har.MON.i.cuh) *n.* a small wind instrument with metal reeds that is played with the mouth; mouth organ.
har.mo.ni.ous (har.MOH.nee.us) *adj.* 1 arranged so that the parts agree: *The structure is a harmonious mass of shapes and colors; nature and art forming a harmonious whole.* 2 agreeing in feelings, actions, etc.: *the harmonious relationships among our neighbors.* 3 concordant or well-sounding: *a harmonious melody.*
har.mo.ni.um (har.MOH.nee.um) *n.* a small type of reed organ.

har.mo.nize (HAR.muh.nize) *v.* **-niz.es, -nized, -niz.ing** be in or make harmony: *Complementary colors harmonize well; music harmonized in chords.* —**har.mo.ni.za.tion** (-nuh.ZAY.shun, -nye-) *n.*

har.mo.ny (HAR.muh.nee) *n.* **-nies** 1 musical agreement of sounds, esp. of various tones and chords. 2 agreement in thoughts, feelings, words, actions, etc.; accord: *to act in harmony with others; the peace and harmony in a happy family; racial harmony; to achieve social harmony.* 3 any orderly arrangement: *the harmony of color and form in a painting; the harmony of texture and shape.*

har.ness (HAR.nis) *n.* 1 a combination of straps, bands, etc. for hitching an animal to what it pulls, as a horse to a carriage or plough. 2 similar trappings to tie a person to a parachute, restrain an automobile driver for safety, or have a child or dog in one's control. —**in harness** at one's regular occupation: *He never took a vacation and died in harness.* —*v.* 1 put a harness on an animal: *to harness dogs to a sled.* 2 utilize the power of water, wind, atomic energy, etc.

harp *n.* an ancient stringed musical instrument, played by plucking its strings with the fingers. —*v.* play on a harp. —**harp on** or **upon** refer continually to a tiresome subject. —**harp.ist** *n.*

har.poon (har.POON) *n.* a spear with a long coiled line attached, thrown or shot to catch whales and such sea animals. —*v.* strike or catch with a harpoon; **har.poon.er** *n.*

harp.si.chord (HARP.si.cord) *n.* the medieval forerunner of the piano, whose strings are plucked by tabs connected to the keyboard.

har.py (HAR.pee) *n.* **-pies** a cruel and greedy person like the **Harpies** of Greek myth, winged monsters with a woman's head and bird's body.

har.ri.dan (HAIR.i.dun) *n.* a shrewish old woman.

har.ri.er (HAIR.ee.ur) *n.* 1 a breed of dog smaller than the English foxhound, used to hunt hares. 2 a cross-country runner. 3 one who harries. 4 a kind of hawk that preys on rodents, reptiles, and poultry.

har.row (HAIR.oh) *n.* an implement with a set of revolving disks (**disk harrow**) or one with spikes or teeth for breaking and smoothing the soil. —*v.* 1 break up and level plowed ground, as with a harrow. 2 lacerate, wound, or distress: *to be harrowed with guilt;* **adj.**: *The hijack- ing was a **harrowing** (= painful and distressing) experience; harrowing dramas, stories, tales; It's less harrowing to take pay cuts than lose jobs.*

har.ry (HAIR.ee) *v.* **har.ries, har.ried, har.ry.ing** 1 harass or torment; **adj.**: *a **harried** expression, lifestyle; harried consumers, executives, travelers.* 2 raid or pillage.

harsh *adj.* 1 disagreeably rough to the senses: *a harsh climate, color, flavor, portrait, sound.* 2 cruel or unfeeling: *a harsh parent; He is too harsh with his children.*

hart *n.* an antlered male of the European red deer.

har.te.beest (HAR.tuh.beest) *n.* a large, now scarce African antelope.

har.um-scar.um (HAIR.um.SCAIR.um) *adv.* in a reckless and irresponsible way.

har.vest (HAR.vist) *n.* 1 grain, fruit, vegetables, etc. gathered when mature: *We bring in* or *reap the harvest in the fall; abundant, bountiful, bumper, poor, rich harvests; a bountiful harvest of wheat; a record grain harvest; The seal harvest has suffered at the hands of animal rights activists;* **adj**.: *harvest tones; harvest wheat (color).* 2 the harvest season: *Farmers hire extra help during (the) harvest;* **adj**.: *a harvest festival; the harvest season, time.* 3 the fruit or reward of one's labors: *the harvest of our labors; a harvest of love, misfortune, resentment.* —*v.* gather for use, as grain when mature: *to harvest crops, grain; We harvest thousands of gallons of maple syrup each year; to harvest a new crop of cultures grown in the lab; A donated organ has to be used soon after it is harvested* (= removed from the body). —**har.vest.er** (HAR.vis.tur) *n.*

harvest moon *n.* the full moon nearest the September equinox.

has third person sing. of HAVE.

has-been (HAZ.bin) *n. Informal.* a person or thing whose heyday is past: *The singer was superrich and a has-been by age 20.*

hash *v.* 1 chop into small pieces for cooking. 2 make a mess of something. 3 *Informal.* discuss: *We hashed over it* or *hashed it over before making a decision.* —**hash out** settle a question by discussing. —*n.* 1 cooked food hashed and fried or baked. 2 a mixture or hodgepodge. 3 *Informal* [short form] hashish. —**make a hash of** make a mess of something. —**settle one's hash** *Infor-*

mal. subdue, silence, or put down someone.

hash browns *n.pl.* diced, boiled, and browned potatoes; also **hash brown potatoes.**

hash.ish (hash.EESH) *n.* an intoxicating drug prepared from an Asiatic plant; also **hash.eesh.**

has.n't (HAZ.unt) has not.

hasp *n.* a fastening device for a door or lid consisting of a hinged metal clasp fitting over a staple through which a peg or padlock is put to secure it.

has.sle (HAS.ul) *n. Informal.* a wrangle, argument, or tussle. —*v.* **has.sles, has.sled, has.sling 1** have a hassle: *to hassle with the referee* over or *about a foul call.* **2** harass or pester: *Will you stop hassling her?*

has.sock (HAS.uk) *n.* a cushioned seat or footstool.

hast [old use] the form of "have" used with THOU.

haste *n.* hurry, esp. in a careless manner: *"Haste makes waste"*; *"The more haste, the less speed"* (= The more you rush the less you achieve); *He* **made haste** (= hurried up) *and cooked up a tasteless meal; He did it* **in haste**; *In his haste, he even forgot to add salt.*

has.ten (HAY.sun) *v.* **1** hurry or speed up: *He was told to hasten and fix us something to eat.* **2** be quick: *Let me hasten to add that I didn't cook this dinner.*

has.ty (HAY.stee) *adj.* **hast.i.er, -i.est 1** quick: *He made a hasty exit after dinner.* **2** too quick or quick-tempered; rash: *a hasty decision.* —**has.ti.ly** *adv.*

hasty pudding *n.* **1** mush of cornmeal. **2** in Britain, mush of flour or oatmeal.

hat *n.* a head covering with a brim and crown for formal or outdoor wear: *to don and doff hats; a straw hat; top hat; Names were picked out of a hat* (= by lot); **Hats off** (= Congratulations) *to Jim for coming out first in his class; Three-D movies are* **old hat** (= nothing new); *You* **pass the hat** *around to take up a collection; She* **threw her hat into the ring** (= entered the contest) *as a candidate for election; You don't have to* **keep it under your hat** (*Informal* for keep it private or confidential). —**hat in hand** humbly.

hatch *n.* **1** an opening, as in a ship's deck for loading cargo: *Down the hatch it went.* **2** a trapdoor covering it: *to batten down the hatches before a storm.* **3** an opening or door in a spacecraft or aircraft: *an escape hatch.* **4** a set of hatched lines; also **hatching.**

—*v.* **1** draw or engrave fine parallel lines for a shading effect. **2** keep eggs warm so as to bring out the young. **3** bring forth young or come out from eggs. **4** plot or scheme: *prisoners hatching an escape plot.* —**hatch.er** *n.*

hatch.back *n.* an automobile with a trunk whose hinged door lifts all the way to the roof.

hat.check *adj.* having to do with the checking of coats and hats: *a hatcheck girl, stand.*

hatch.er.y (HACH.uh.ree) *n.* **-er.ies** a place where eggs are hatched.

hatch.et (HACH.it) *n.* a small, short-handled ax, as used to kill; tomahawk. —**bury the hatchet** make peace after a fight.

hatchet job *n. Informal.* an unfair attack in a publication: *The TV program did a hatchet job on the President.*

hatchet man *n. Informal.* one hired to deal viciously with opponents.

hatch.way *n.* a hatch or entrance.

hate *v.* **hates, hat.ed, hat.ing 1** dislike intensely, usually with malice and a tendency to hurt. **2** not like: *Cats hate water; He hates ice cream; She hates to disturb you.* —*n.* hostility or an object of it. —*adj.*: *a hate campaign; hate crimes, literature, propaganda; flooded by hate mail.* —**hate.ful** *adj.*; **hate.ful.ly** *adv.*

hath [old use] has.

ha.tred (HAY.trid) *n.* ill will or strong dislike: *Joe's hatred of* or *for skunks; to arouse, express, feel, show, stir up hatred toward people of other races and colors; Racists are consumed* or *filled with hatred.*

hat.ter *n.* one who makes or deals in hats.

hat trick *n.* three performances of a feat by the same player, as scoring three goals in a single game: *to do, pull off, score a hat trick.*

hau.berk (HAW.burk) *n.* a long tunic of chain mail.

haugh.ty (HAW.tee) *adj.* **-ti.er, -ti.est** proud in bearing or manner, esp. scornful of others. —**haugh.ti.ly** *adv.*; **haugh.ti.ness** *n.*

haul *v.* **1** pull or tug with sustained force; hence, transport: *the hauling of freight by truck and train.* **2** shift or change, as a wind or a sailing ship's course. —**haul off and** *Informal.* move suddenly to do something, as to hit: *So I hauled off and kissed him.* —**haul up** order to appear on trial: *He was hauled up before a judge.* —*n.* a load, amount, or distance hauled: *They fled with a million-dollar haul; a* **short-haul** (= short-distance) *flight.* —**in** or **over**

the long haul *Informal.* over a long period.
haul.age (HAW.lij) *n.* a hauling or charge for hauling.
haunch *n.* hindquarter, including hip, buttock, and top of thigh: *A dog sits on its haunches; a haunch* (= loin and leg) *of venison.*
haunt *v.* visit continually or seem to stay in a place, as a spirit inhabiting a house; hence, plague or obsess: *Memories from the past haunted her in her dreams; adj.: That house is haunted (by a ghost); a haunting melody (that stays in one's mind).* —*n.* a frequently visited place: *to revisit the haunts of one's youth; a favorite haunt of criminals.*
haut.boy (HOH.boy) *n.* an early version of the modern oboe; also **haut.bois** *sing. & pl.*
haute cou.ture (ote.coo.TOOR) *n.* leading fashion designers or their products.
haute cui.sine (ote.kwi.ZEEN) *n.* the art of master chefs or their specialties.
hau.teur (hoh.TUR) *n.* haughtiness.
Ha.van.a (huh.VAN.uh) *n.* a cigar made of Cuban tobacco.
have (HAV, huv, uv) *v.* **has** (HAZ, huz, uz), **had** (HAD, hud, ud), **hav.ing** 1 hold or possess: *We have a home; What are we having for dinner? Pizza. We're also having company; Please have a chair* (= Please sit down); *She's having* (= bearing or begetting) *a baby; She had two children by her first husband; Always have* (= keep) *my advice in mind; I won't have* (= tolerate) *any pranksters in my class; The police have nothing on* (= no evidence against) *us; We have nothing against* (= don't dislike) *the police.* 2 cause: *He's having his tonsils removed; We'll have someone (to) fix the faucets; Let's have a pizza delivered.* 3 [indicating necessity or obligation]: *It's midnight, I have (got) to go.* 4 [indicating completed action]: *Everyone has arrived; She'll have left by now.* —**have coming** deserve: *She had the raise coming to her after winning the contract.* —**have done with** cease or stop: *One last time and we shall have done with gambling for tonight.* —**have had it** *Informal.* reach an end with something: *I have had it – no more loans for you; I've had it up to here* (= up to the neck, as much as one can take). —**have it out** settle *with* someone by fighting or arguing. —**have on** be wearing: *I had nothing on when I came into the world.* —**have to do with** 1 be related to something: *Geology has to do with the earth.* 2 associate with something: *She won't have anything to do with him.* —**the haves and the have-nots** the rich and the not so rich.
ha.ven (HAY.vun) *n.* a harbor or refuge: *a safe haven for refugees; tax havens; a haven of peace, plenty, safety.*
have-not *n.* one that does not have something, esp. one with little material resources: *the haves and the have-nots of society; the nuclear powers and the have-nots.*
have.n't (HAV.unt) have not.
hav.er.sack (HAV.ur.sak) *n.* a bag for supplies or equipment, usually worn by soldiers, hikers, etc. with a strap over one shoulder.
hav.oc (HAV.uc) *n.* widespread harm or destruction, as caused by an earthquake or tornado: *The storm wreaked havoc on the town; a scandal that played havoc with* (= greatly damaged) *many reputations.*
haw *n.* 1 See HEM AND HAW. 2 the hawthorn or its berry.
Ha.wai.ian (huh.WYE.un) *adj.* having to do with **Hawaii,** a U.S. state composed of a group of islands in the N. Pacific. —*n.* 1 a person of or from Hawaii. 2 the Polynesian language of Hawaii.
hawk *n.* 1 a bird of prey with sharp eyesight, similar to eagles but smaller. 2 one who favors war, not a dove. —*v.* 1 hunt with or like hawks. 2 peddle wares by shouting, as a hawker does. 3 clear the throat noisily. —**hawk.ish** *adj.*
hawk.er *n.* a huckster: *the hawkers and vendors of downtown streets.*
hawk-eyed *adj.* sharp-eyed.
hawse (HAWZ) *n.* the part of a ship's bow containing the **hawseholes** through which a rope or cable, or **hawser,** for towing the ship is passed.
haw.thorn *n.* a thorny shrub or small tree with fragrant white, pink, or red flowers and fruits like little apples.
hay *n.* cut and dried grass, alfalfa, clover, etc. for use as fodder. —**hit the hay** *Informal.* go to bed. —**make hay while the sun shines** make the most of an opportunity. —*v.* mow grass, etc. and prepare hay.
hay.cock *n.* hay piled in a heap to dry in the field.
hay fever *n.* an allergic reaction with running nose, itchy eyes, sneezing, etc. caused by the pollen of trees and grasses.
hay.fork *n.* 1 a pitchfork. 2 a mechanical device for loading hay.
hay.loft *n.* a loft in a barn or stable for

storing hay.

hay.mak.er (HAY.may.kur) *n. Slang.* a knockout blow.

hay.mow *n.* **1** a pile of hay in a barn. **2** the mow or loft where it is stored.

hay.rick same as HAYSTACK.

hay.ride *n.* a pleasure ride taken by a group in an open vehicle, esp. at night.

hay.seed *n.* **1** grass, seed, chaff, etc. from hay. **2** *Slang.* a rustic or bumpkin.

hay.stack *n.* an outdoor stack of hay.

hay.wire *n.* wire for tying up bales of hay. **—go haywire** *Informal.* of a person or operation, go crazy or get upset.

haz.ard (HAZ.urd) *n.* **1** a risk or chance: *A stunt man's life is full of hazards; Careless smoking is* or *poses* or *presents a fire hazard, health hazard, safety hazard; a hazard to health; occupational hazards;* **adj.:** *hazard warning lights.* **2** an obstacle in golf. **—v.** expose to risk: *to hazard lives;* **hazard a guess** make a guess.

haz.ard.ous (HAZ.ur.dus) *adj.* risky or dangerous: *Smoking is hazardous to health; a hazardous journey, undertaking; hazardous materials, occupations; hazardous foods (that may get spoiled if not refrigerated); the disposal of hazardous industrial wastes that may contaminate the environment.*

haze *n.* **1** a mist, smoke, dust, etc. thinly spread in the air, reducing visibility: *A haze hung over the morning countryside.* **2** vagueness. **—v. haz.es, hazed, haz.ing** force newcomers to a group, as among students, to do humiliating things.

haz.el (HAY.zul) *adj.* light or yellowish brown. **—n.** a kind of shrub or tree bearing small, edible, light-brown nuts; **haz.el.nut** *n.*

ha.zy (HAY.zee) *adj.* **-zi.er, -zi.est** misty, smoky, or vague: *hot, humid, and hazy summer weather; hazy notions.* **—ha.zi.ly** *adv.;* **ha.zi.ness** *n.*

H-bomb *n.* a hydrogen bomb.

he (HEE) *n. & pron.,* objective HIM, possessive HIS; *pl.* THEY, objective THEM, possessive THEIR(S). **1** the male animal or human being referred to: *Is the calf a he or a she?* **2** he or she: *"He who hesitates is lost."*

head (HED) *n.* **1** the part of the body containing the brain, eyes, ears, nose, and mouth; the top part in humans and front part in quadrupeds: *to bare, bow, drop, hang, lift, nod, raise, scratch, shake, toss, turn one's head; hold one's head high (in self-respect); to hang one's head in shame.* **2** the chief, top, upper, or leading part of anything: *the head of a bed, column, corporation, department, family, household, pin, procession; Racism rears its ugly head in our cities; the head* (= source) *of a river; the head of a ship* (= the bow, etc.); *A movement* **gathers head** (= strength); *The head of our government, the President, is also the* **head of state;** *Is it* **heads or tails?** (= which side of the coin, the one with the head or the other side, is facing up when it is tossed to determine a choice?). **3** *sing. & pl.* individual(s): *500 head of cattle; The party costs $25 a head to cater.* **4** the cutting or hitting part of a hammer, golf club, ends of a drum, etc. **5** mind or brains: *He has a good head for figures; She keeps a clear head in difficult situations; She uses her head to solve problems; a level head; older and wiser heads than mine.* **6** [short form] headland; heading; headword. **—cannot make head or tail of something** cannot understand it. **—give someone his** or **her head** let one do as he or she likes. **—go to someone's head** affect one's mind, as to intoxicate or make conceited: *Success went to his head.* **—head over heels** completely or recklessly: *head over heals in love.* **—keep** (or **lose**) **one's head** keep (or lose) one's self-control. **—out of** or **off one's head** *Informal.* crazy. **—over one's head 1** beyond one's grasp. **2** without regard to one's claims or authority: *to complain to the boss over the supervisor's head.* **—to a head:** *A boil comes to a head before bursting; to bring matters to a head* (= crisis point). **—turn someone's head** make one giddy or conceited: *Success in the stock market turned his head.* **—adja. 1** having to do with the head: *a head cold.* **2** chief or leading: *a head clerk, gate, table.* **—v. 1** be the head of something: *A president heads a corporation; a letter headed with a place and date; She heads the committee.* **2** go in a certain direction: *We head home after school; They headed to the mall; to head east, home, out; to head* (= turn) *a boat toward shore; measures to* **head off** (= prevent) *trouble.*

-head *comb.form. Slang.* addict: *acidhead, pothead, teahead.*

head.ache (HED.ake) *n.* **1** pain in the head: *severe, sick, splitting headaches.* **2** *Informal.* a source of annoyance. **—head.ach.y** (-ay.kee) *adj.: a headachy feeling.*

head.board *n.* a board or frame at the head of something, as of a bed.

head cold *n.* a common cold affecting the nasal passages.

head.dress *n.* a usually elaborate covering for the head.

headed 1 *adjp.* going in the direction specified: *We are headed in that direction; headed west; The nation is headed into a recession; You are headed for trouble.* **2** *comb.form.* having a head as specified: *clear-headed, cool-headed, double-headed, hard-headed, light-headed, muddle-headed, soft-headed, wrong-headed.*

head.er *n.* a name, title, date, etc. repeated at the top of each page of a document.

head-first or **head.first** *adj. & adv.* (done or going) with the head first: *to dive head-first into a pool; a headfirst dive; to crash, jump, land headfirst.*

head.gear *n.* **1** headdress. **2** the harness for an animal's head.

head.hunt.er (HED.hun.tur) *n.* **1** formerly, a member of a tribe that killed their enemies and kept their heads as trophies. **2** an aggressive personnel recruiter.

heading *n.* **1** a topic or title placed at the beginning or top of a piece of writing. **2** the traveling direction of a ship or plane.

head.land *n.* a point of land projecting into water; cape.

head.light *n.* a bright light of a locomotive or automobile.

head.line *n.* a printed line at the top of a page or at the head of a news story: *a banner headline; a robbery that made* **headlines** (= important news) *all over the country.* —*v.* **-lines, -lined, -lin.ing** make or be the main attraction or news event.

head.lock *n.* a wrestling hold in which the opponent's head is held under one's arm.

head.long *adj. & adv.* **1** with the head first: *a headlong plunge.* **2** with uncontrolled speed or force; reckless(ly): *He ran headlong into oncoming traffic; a headlong drive, flight, retreat, rush.*

head.mas.ter (HED.mas.tur) *n.* in some schools, the principal.
—**head.mis.tress** *fem.*

head-on *adj.* frontal or direct: *head-on competition; a head-on collision, confrontation;* **adv.**: *The car ran head-on into a bus; The government decided to tackle the deficit head-on by cutting its wasteful spending; two companies competing head-on against each other.*

head.phone *n.* an earphone with a band to put over the user's head.

head.quar.ters (HED.kwor.turs) *n.pl.* [takes *sing.* or *pl.v.*] **1** administrative center. **2** a place from where orders are issued for a police force, army, etc.

head.rest *n.* **1** a support for the head, as in a barber's chair. **2** same as **head restraint**, a support at the top of an automobile seat's back to protect the occupant, esp. in a rear-end collision.

head.room *n.* overhead space or clearance.

head.set *n.* a pair of headphones or earphones, often with an attached transmitter.

head.ship *n.* the office or position of a head or chief.

head shop *n.* a shop selling accessories for the users of illicit drugs.

head start or **head.start** *n.* the advantage of a start ahead of one's peers or competitors: *to get a head start on the work lying ahead.*

head.stone *n.* a stone or tablet placed at the head of a grave.

head.strong *adj.* rash or foolish in having one's own way: *a headstrong child.*

head tax *n.* a tax levied on every person in a specific group, as those passing through an airport.

head.wait.er (HED.WAY.tur) *n.* a person in charge of waiters, as in a restaurant.

head.wa.ters (HED.wot.urs) *n.pl.* the streams that form the source of a river.

head.way *n.* **1** progress or advance: *to gain* or *make headway against something.* **2** headroom. **3** the interval between two successive buses, trains, etc. on the same route.

head wind *n.* a wind blowing directly opposite the direction something is traveling in.

head.word *n.* a word that forms the heading of a paragraph, dictionary entry, etc.

head.y *adj.* **head.i.er, -i.est** apt to affect the head, as an intoxicant: *Being mayor for a day was a heady experience; heady days, flavors, optimism, stuff, times; heady* (= rash or impetuous) *nationalists.*

heal (HEEL) *v.* **1** make or get well, as a wound, sore, burn, etc.; cure a disease or sick person. **2** end breached relations. **3** free from or get rid of something bad: *Time heals all sorrows.*
—**heal.er** *n.*

health (HELTH, "TH" as in "thin") *n.* **1** sound condition of body or mind: *to enjoy, promote good health; to recover* or *regain one's health; bad, broken, delicate, failing, fragile, robust health; mental, occu-*

pational, public health; **adj.**: health benefits, care, habits, insurance, issues, professionals, sciences. **2** a toast drunk to wish someone well: *We drank her health; To your health!*

health food *n.* food that is naturally health-giving, as grown without the use of chemicals and not subjected to processing.

health.ful *adj.* good for the health; health-giving: *a healthful climate; healthful eating; the healthful properties and value of spinach; healthful foods, music, snacks;* **health.ful.ly** *adv.;* **health.ful.ness** *n.*

health insurance *n.* an insurance program that covers hospital and medical expenses; also **health plan.**

health resort *n.* a place having a spa; also **health spa.**

health.y *adj.* **health.i.er, -i.est 1** having good health: *a sound mind in a healthy body.* **2** showing or giving health: *a healthy appearance, appetite, climate, habit.* —**health.i.ly** *adv.;* **health.i.ness** *n.*

heap (HEEP) *n.* **1** a mass or pile of things: *a heap of rubbish; a scrap heap; She has the ambition to be at the* or *on* **top of the heap** (= to be the leader). **2** *Informal.* a large amount: *a heap of sand; a heap of trouble.* —*v.* **1** form into a heap: *to heap* (= amass) *riches, wealth; to heap* (= load) *a plate with food;* **adj.**: *a* **heaping** (= heaped) *bowl, plate, spoonful.* **2** give a heap of something to someone: *to heap gifts, insults, praises on someone; to heap someone with gifts.*

hear (HEER) *v.* **hears, heard** (HURD), **hear.ing 1** perceive by the ear: *I hear the birds sing(ing); I hear you loud and clear; You heard what I said.* **2** listen to something: *to hear a lecture, recitation; You better hear what I have to say; Courts hear* (= listen to and try) *cases.* **3** receive information: *I never heard of such a thing; We heard from him yesterday; heard about the accident.*

hearing *n.* **1** the sense by which sounds are perceived: *acute, keen, impaired hearing; Some are* **hard of hearing**; *the hearing impaired* (people). **2** a range of this perception; earshot: *Parents are careful about what they say in the hearing of children.* **3** a listening or receiving of information: *He was given a patient hearing by the committee; to conduct* or *hold a hearing; to testify at a hearing; a fair, impartial, open hearing.*

hearing-aid *n.* a small sound-amplifying device worn in the ear.

heark.en (HAR.kun) *v.* [old use] listen *to prayer, etc.;* heed.

hear.say (HEER.say) *n.* something one has heard but not verified, as a rumor or gossip: *mere hearsay; hearsay evidence.*

hearse (HURSE) *n.* a vehicle for taking the dead to the grave.

heart (HART) *n.* **1** the hollow, muscular organ that pumps blood throughout the body, traditionally considered as the seat of one's feelings, esp. love, sympathy, courage, etc., and the center or most vital part of one's being: *a heavy, light heart* (in regard to feeling); *Hearts ache, beat, bleed, fail, palpitate, throb; a kind heart; a brave, faint, stout, strong, weak heart* (in regard to courage); *a hard* (= cruel) *heart; Let's not lose heart but take heart* (= courage); *a* **heart of gold** (= generous nature); *He broke her heart* (= made her very sad); *to gladden, harden, steal, win someone's heart; to speak from the heart* (= speak sincerely); *She is in the very heart* (= center) *of things; Pat has no heart for* (= does not like) *housework; He had a change of heart* (= of feeling). **2** a heart-shaped figure, as on a playing card. **3** a card so marked: *the queen of hearts.* —**after one's own heart** as one likes or desires it. —**at heart** in one's innermost nature. —**by heart** by or from memory: *to get, know, learn, recite a poem by heart.* —**from the bottom of one's heart** sincerely. —**have a heart** be kind; don't ask for so much. —**set one's heart:** *The announcement set our hearts at rest* (= made us feel at ease); *His heart is set against* (= He is opposed to) *marrying her; Her heart is set on winning* (= She is determined to win) *a gold medal.* —**take to heart:** *He took the warning to heart* (= was much moved by it). —**with all one's heart** with all sincerity and good will.

heart.ache (HART.ake) *n.* great sorrow or anguish.

heart attack same as CORONARY THROMBOSIS.

heart.beat *n.* one contraction and dilation of the heart.

heart.break (HART.brake) *n.* extreme sorrow or disappointment; **heart.break.ing** *adj.*: *heartbreaking news.* —**heart.bro.ken** (-broh.kun) *adj.*

heart.burn *n.* a burning feeling as if from near the heart, caused by the rising up of stomach acid.

heart.burn.ing (HART.burn.ing) *n.* intense jealousy or resentment.

-hearted *comb.form.* having a heart as specified: *broken-hearted, chicken-hearted, faint-hearted, gold-hearted, half-hearted, hard-hearted, large-hearted, light-hearted, stout-hearted, tender-hearted, warm-hearted,*

weak-hearted, whole-hearted.
heart.en (HAR.tun) *v.* cheer up.
heart.felt *adj.* sincere or genuine: *our heartfelt apology, sympathy, thanks.*
hearth (HARTH) *n.* **1** the floor near a fireplace; fireside. **2** home or family life.
hearth.side *n.* fireside.
hearth.stone *n.* **1** the stone forming a hearth. **2** home.
heart.land *n.* the central or vital region of a country, institution, movement, etc.
heart.less *adj.* without kindness, sympathy, or courage; **heart.less.ly** *adv.*; **heart.less.ness** *n.*
heart-rending *adj.* distressing.
heart.sick or **heart.sore** *adj.* sick at heart.
heart.strings *n.pl.* one's deepest feelings: *to tug at someone's heartstrings.*
heart.throb *n.* **1** a heartbeat. **2** *Informal.* a person one is infatuated with.
heart-to-heart *adj.* frank and sincere: *They made up after a heart-to-heart talk.*
heart.warm.ing (HART.war.ming) *adj.* kindling feelings of warmth and geniality.
heart.wood *n.* the wood forming the core of a tree trunk.
heart.y *adj.* **heart.i.er, -i.est 1** full of vigor and enthusiasm: *a hearty welcome.* **2** showing or promoting good health: *a hearty appetite, eater, meal.* —**heart.i.ly** *adv.*; **heart.i.ness** *n.*
heat (HEET) *n.* **1** the quality of being hot to the touch; high temperature; the form of energy that causes expansion, melting, etc.: *to generate, produce, radiate heat; to alleviate the heat of the summer; blistering, dry, extreme, intense, low, oppressive, radiant, red, stifling, white heat.* **2** great feeling or excitement: *He said it* **in the heat of** *the argument; a female mammal* **in heat** (= recurring period or condition of sexual excitement). **3** a single effort; hence, a preliminary round, as in a race, that qualifies candidates for the finals: *She won the first heat; a dead heat* (= a tie). **4** *Informal.* pressure: *to put the heat on someone; to apply the heat to force a confession; Someone has to* **take the heat** (= take the blame) *when things don't turn out as expected.* —*v.* **1** make or become hot or warm: *to heat water for coffee; adj.: a* **heated** *wire.* **2** excite or become excited; *adj.: a* **heated** *argument, discussion;* **heat.ed.ly** *adv.*
heat.er (HEE.tur) *n.* an appliance that provides heat: *a room heater.*
heat exchanger *n.* a device of the type of an automobile radiator for changing heat from one medium to another for elimination or for use.
heat exhaustion *n.* a mild form of heatstroke, brought on by excessive perspiration and resulting poor circulation.
heath (HEETH, "TH" as in "thin") *n.* **1** open wasteland covered by shrubs. **2** any of a family of shrubs and plants including the blueberry, cranberry, and arbutus.
heath.en (HEE.thun, "th" as in "thin") *n.* **-then** or **-thens 1** a person of no religion or culture. **2** formerly, one who is not a Christian, Jew, or Moslem: *heathen customs;* also **heath.en.ish**.
—**heath.en.dom** *n.* paganism; also **heath.en.ism.**
heath.er (HETH.ur, "TH" as in "the") *n.* a shrub of the heath family with scale-like leaves and purplish, bell-shaped flowers, common on moors in the British Isles; **heath.er.y** *adj.*
heating pad *n.* an electrically heated pad to apply warmth to the body.
heat lightning *n.* summer lightning that is not accompanied by the sound of thunder.
heat pump *n.* a refrigerating apparatus for extracting heat from the air, ground, water, etc. so as to cool the place that heat is taken from or to heat what it is delivered to.
heat.stroke or **heat stroke** *n.* illness from exposure to excessive heat.
heave (HEEV) *v.* **heaves,** *pt. & pp.* **heaved** or **hove** (HOHV), **heav.ing 1** lift and move something heavy: *A ship heaves anchor and sails away; They heaved the stone through the window.* **2** move in a rising and falling manner: *Her stomach heaves at the sight of blood; He heaved a sigh of relief; A ship* **heaves in** or **into sight** *on the horizon; The ground heaves* (= bulges) *from an earthquake; Sailors heave at* or **on** (= pull) *a rope; adj.: the heaving waves.* —**heave to** stop, as a sailing ship. —*n.* **1** rise and fall: *the heave of the sea; with a mighty heave* (= pull or throw). **2** a bulge or swelling, as because of water expanding as it freezes: *a frost heave.* **3 heaves** *pl.* a lung disease of horses, marked by difficult breathing and heaving sides.
—**heave ho!** the cry of sailors pulling in the anchor.
heave-ho *n. Informal.* dismissal: *to give someone, get the heave-ho.*
heav.en (HEV.un) *n.* **1** a place of great happiness. **2 Heaven** God's supposed dwelling place; where the blessed go after death. —**move heaven and earth**

heavy / hegemony

do one's utmost. —**the heavens** *pl.* the firmament. —**heavens!** or **for heaven's sake!** exclamation of surprise, protest, etc. —**heav.en.ly** *adj.* —**heav.en.ward** (HEV.un.wurd) *adj. & adv.*; also **heav.en.wards** *adv.*

heav.y (HEV.ee) *adj.* **heav.i.er, -i.est** having great weight; hence, hard: *a heavy load, rain; a heavy blow; heavy features, fighting, news, reading, traffic; They made it heavy going for him at work; a heavy* (= hard to digest) *meal; a heavy* (= sorrowful) *heart; a heavy* (= hard to endure) *odor; a heavy* (= sound) *sleeper; a heavy drinker and smoker (who drinks and smokes a lot); a heavy* (= abundant) *vote.* —*adv.: a deed that lies heavy on his conscience; Time **hangs heavy** on her hands* (= drags). —*n., pl.* **heav.ies** 1 something heavy, as a large wave. 2 a strong person hired for protection, as a bouncer, or one of consequence. 3 an actor in a nonheroic or villainous role. —**heav.i.ly** *adv.*; **heav.i.ness** *n.*

heavy-duty *adj.* designed for hard use; durable: *a heavy-duty shock absorber; heavy-duty machinery, shoes.*

heavy-handed *adj.* 1 awkward. 2 cruel or oppressive.

heavy-hearted *adj.* sad or gloomy.

heavy metal *n.* amplified electronic rock music with a heavy beat.

heav.y.set (HEV.ee.set) *adj.* having a stocky build.

heavy water *n.* water compounded with **heavy hydrogen,** or deuterium, used in nuclear reactors.

heav.y.weight (HEV.ee.wait) *n.* 1 a boxer weighing over 175 lb. (81 kg for Olympics). 2 *Informal.* a person of much intelligence or consequence.

He.bra.ic (hi.BRAY.ic) *adj.* of the Hebrews or their language, culture, etc.

He.brew (HEE.broo) *n.* 1 an Israelite or Jew. 2 the ancient or modern Semitic language of the Hebrews. —*adj.* Jewish; Hebraic.

heck *n. & interj. Informal.* hell: *What the heck! a heck of a job.*

heck.le (HEK.ul) *v.* **-les, -led, -ling** taunt or harass a speaker; **heck.ler** *n.*

hec.tare (HEC.tar, -tair) *n.* a metric unit of area equal to 10,000 square meters.

hec.tic (HEC.tic) *adj.* busy or exciting: *a hectic day, life, pace, period, time.*

hecto- *comb.form.* one-hundred: *hectogram, hectoliter, hectometer.*

hec.tor (HEC.tur) *n.* a bully or blusterer, like **Hector,** Trojan hero. —*v.: The Opposition tries to hector the Government whenever they get a chance.*

he'd (HEED) he had; he would.

hedge (HEJ) *n.* 1 a row of bushes planted as a fence. 2 a boundary, barrier, or means of protection, as against financial loss: *an investment as a hedge against inflation; a hedge fund.*
—*v.* **hedg.es, hedged, hedg.ing** enclose or protect: *hedged in* or *about by restrictions; to hedge against commodity price changes by selling futures; to **hedge a bet*** (= protect oneself) *by making one also on the opposite side; a politician accused of **hedging** on the issues* (= of being evasive). —**hedg.er** *n.*

hedge.hog *n.* an Old World animal similar to the American porcupine.

hedge.hop *v.* **-hops, -hopped, -hop.ping** fly a plane, as for crop-dusting, close to the ground.

hedge.row (HEJ.roh) *n.* a hedge of bushes.

he.don.ism (HEE.dun.iz.um) *n.* the philosophy of living only for pleasure; **he.don.ist** *n.* —**he.do.nis.tic** (-NIS.tic) *adj.*

heed *v.* pay attention to: *to heed a warning.* —*n.* attention or notice: *to pay* or *give heed to advice; He took no heed of warnings.* —**heed.ful** *adj.* —**heed.less** *adj.*; **heed.less.ly** *adv.*

hee.haw *n. & v.* bray; also, guffaw.

heel *n.* 1 the hindmost part of a foot, below the ankle. 2 anything resembling a human heel in shape, function, or position, as the hock of an animal or hind toe of a bird, the hind part of a shoe or sock, an end crust of bread, or any bottom part or portion. 3 *Informal.* a despicable person. —**be at someone's heel, on someone's heel, on the heels of someone** or **upon someone's heels** be close behind someone. —**cool one's heels** *Informal.* be kept waiting. —**down at the heel** (or **heels**) in a shabby condition. —**hard on the heels of** closely following a person or thing. —**take to one's heels** flee. —*v.* 1 furnish with a heel; also, follow closely behind, as a dog in pursuit. 2 lean to one side. 3 make a ship list.

heeled See WELL-HEELED.

heft *n. Informal.* weight or bulk. —*v.* lift or heave.

heft.y *adj.* **hef.ti.er, hef.ti.est** 1 heavy or bulky; well-built: *a hefty man, volume.* 2 considerable or large: *a hefty pay hike.* —**heft.i.ly** *adv.*; **heft.i.ness** *n.*

he.gem.o.ny (hi.JEM.uh.nee, HEJ.uh.moh.nee) *n.* **-nies** dominance, esp. of one nation over the others of a group.

he.gi.ra (hi.JYE.ruh) *n.* **1** a journey of safety or escape. **2 Hegira** Mohammed's flight from Mecca to Medina, A.D. 622, the beginning of the Moslem era.

heif.er (HEF.ur) *n.* a young cow that has not yet had a calf.

heigh-ho (HYE.hoh, HAY-) *interj.* expressing joy, surprise, boredom, etc.

height (HITE) *n.* **1** how high or tall a person or thing is: *The CN Tower is 553 meters in height.* **2** elevation or altitude: *flying at a height of 3,000 meters above sea level; the precipitous height of a cliff.* **3** the topmost point: *at the height of his career; It is the height of folly to say such a thing.* **4 heights** *pl.* an eminence or hill: *commanding heights; the dizzying heights of fame; the Golan Heights.*

height.en (HIGH.tun) *v.* **1** bring to a height or become high or higher. **2** make or become greater; increase.

Heim.lich maneuver (HIME.lik-) *n.* a method of forcing out what is lodged in a choking person's windpipe by hugging from behind and applying pressure to the abdomen.

hei.nous (HAY.nus) *adj.* hatefully bad: *a heinous act, crime, deed.*

heir (AIR) *n.* one who is in line to inherit another's property, as **heir apparent** if no stronger claimant is possible and **heir presumptive** till a nearer relative is born; *pl.* **heirs apparent, heirs presumptive.**

heir.ess (AIR.is) *n.* a female heir, esp. one inheriting great wealth.

heir.loom *n.* a personal possession handed down from generation to generation.

heist (HIGHST) *n. & v.* (commit) armed robbery: *to pull off a heist.*

held *pt. & pp.* of HOLD.

hel.i.cal (HEL.i.cul) *adj.* like a screw; spiral: *helical gears.*

helices a *pl.* of HELIX.

hel.i.cop.ter (HEL.uh.cop.tur) *n.* an aircraft that lifts off vertically, flies, and hovers with the aid of large rotor blades mounted horizontally on its top.

he.li.o.cen.tric (HEE.lee.uh.SEN.tric) *adj.* with the sun as center.

he.li.o.trope (HEE.lee.uh.trope) *n.* a plant with huge clusters of tiny, fragrant flowers colored lilac to dark-blue that always face the sun. —**he.li.o.trop.ic** (-TROP.ic) *adj.* of plants, turning toward the sun.

hel.i.pad (HEL.uh.pad) *n.* a helicopter-landing surface.

hel.i.port (HEL.uh.port) *n.* **1** a helicopter airport. **2** a helipad.

heli-ski (HEL.i.skee) *v.* **-skis, -skied, -ski.ing** to ski using a helicopter to reach the top of the slopes. —**heli-skiing** *n.*

he.li.um (HEE.lee.um) *n.* a lightweight gas used in industry, as a filler for balloons, and in medicine.

he.lix (HEE.lix) *n.* **-lix.es** or **-li.ces** (-luh.seez) a spiral.

he'll (HEEL) he will; he shall.

hell *n.* **1** in Christianity and other religions, a place of eternal torment as punishment for damned souls. **2** *Informal* [used to emphasize anything good or bad]: *Who the hell is he? It's cold like hell; like hell I would! to feel, fight, hope, run, work like hell; She's one* **hell of a** *lawyer, nice girl, nuisance.* —**all hell broke loose** conditions became very chaotic. —**just for the hell of it** *Informal.* for the thrill of it.

hell-bent *adj. & adv. Informal.* fully intent *on* achieving something; recklessly aiming *for* a goal or *to* achieve something.

hell.cat *n.* a witch or shrew.

hel.le.bore (HELL.uh.bor) *n.* **1** a plant of the crowfoot family with poisonous roots. **2** a white hellebore of the lily family.

Hel.len.ic (hel.LEN.ic) *adj.* Greek, esp. having to do with ancient Greek history, language, or culture; **Hel.len.ism** (HEL.uh.niz.um) *n.* —**Hel.len.ist** *n.*; **Hel.len.is.tic** (hel.uh.NIS.tic) *adj.*

hell-for-leather *adj. & adv. Informal.* hell-bent.

hell.gram.mite (HEL.gruh.mite) *n.* the larva of the dobson fly, used as fish bait.

hell.hole *n. Informal.* a detestable place.

hel.lion (HEL.yun) *n. Informal.* a rascal or troublemaker.

hel.lo (huh.LOH) *n. & interj.* an exclamation of greeting or response.

hel.lu.va (HEL.uh.vuh) [a respelling of the slang phrase "hell of a"] *Slang.* very good, bad, etc., as implied or expressed: *a helluva* (= very bad) *job; You're one helluva* (= very good) *guy.*

helm *n.* **1** a ship's steering wheel or gear. **2** a position of control: *to take over the helm of government; at the helm of the nation.*

hel.met (HEL.mut) *n.* a protective covering for the head: *crash, safety, steel helmets.* —**hel.met.ed** *adj.*

helms.man (HELMS.mun) *n.* **-men** one who steers a ship.

hel.ot (HEL.ut) *n.* a slave or serf, like the Helots of ancient Sparta.

help v. **1** provide someone with a useful thing or needed service: *Please help me set the table; to help with the dishes; to help us in our preparations; to help a patient (get) into a wheelchair; someone to* **help out** *in the kitchen; Do* **help yourself** *to the drinks;* n.: *Who'd like another* **helping** (= portion) *of cake?* **2** improve or make better: *a medicine to help your cough.* **3** avoid: *I couldn't help falling asleep during the show; He* **cannot help but** (= is obliged to) *admire her patience.* —n. **1** aid or assistance: *I went to her help.* **2** a person or other source of aid: *Help wanted; kitchen help at $25 an hour.* **3** in computer software, online documentation supplied as a help to the user. —**help.ful** *adj.;* **help.ful.ly** *adv.;* **help.ful.ness** *n.* —**help.less** *adj.;* **help.less.ly** *adv.;* **help.less.ness** *n.*
help.mate *n.* a helpful partner, as one's spouse; also **help.meet** [old use].
hel.ter-skel.ter (HEL.tur.skel.tur) *adv.* in confusion or disorderly haste.
—*adj.:* *a helter-skelter condition, militia, retreat.*
helve (HELV) *n.* a handle, as of a hatchet.
Hel.ve.tian (hel.VEE.shun) *n. & adj.* Swiss.
hem *n.* **1** the usually folded and sewn-down border or edge of a garment: *to let out, lower, raise, straighten, take up a hem.* **2** the sound of clearing the throat. —*v.* **hems, hemmed, hem.ming 1** put a hem on a garment. **2** enclose or confine: *a lake hemmed in or about or around by hills; He felt hemmed in on all sides by his enemies.* **3** make the sound of clearing the throat. —**hem and haw 1** hesitate in speech. **2** stall or put off doing something.
he-man *n.* **-men** *Informal.* an obviously virile man.
hem.a.tite (HEE.muh.tite) *n.* a reddish-brown mineral that is the chief ore of iron.
he.ma.tol.o.gy (hee.muh.TOL.uh.jee) *n.* the physiology of the blood; **he.ma.tol.o.gist** *n.*
heme (HEEM) *n.* the red-colored nonprotein part of hemoglobin.
hemi- *prefix.* half: *hemiplegia, hemisphere.*
hem.i.ple.gi.a (hem.i.PLEE.jee.uh) *n.* paralysis of one side of the body.
hem.i.sphere (HEM.is.feer) *n.* half of a sphere, esp. the northern, southern, western, or eastern half of the earth.
—**hem.i.spher.i.cal** (-FER.i.cul) *adj.*
hem.line *n.* a hem, esp. the bottom edge of a skirt as determining its length: *Hemlines tend to inch up and down; rising and falling hemlines.*
hem.lock *n.* **1** a parsleylike poisonous herb. **2** an evergreen tree of the pine family.
he.mo.glo.bin (HEE.muh.gloh.bin) *n.* the coloring matter of the red blood cells that transports oxygen from the lungs to the rest of the body.
he.mo.phil.i.a (hee.muh.FIL.ee.uh) *n.* a hereditary blood disorder affecting males that makes bleeding difficult to control because the blood does not clot normally; **he.mo.phil.ic** (-FIL.ic) *adj.*
—**he.mo.phil.i.ac** (-FIL.ee.ac) *n.* a hemophilic patient.
hem.or.rhage (HEM.uh.rij) *n. & v.* **-rhag.es, -rhaged, -rhag.ing** (have) a heavy bleeding. —**hem.or.rhag.ic** (-RAJ.ic) *adj.*
hem.or.rhoids (HEM.uh.roids) *n.pl.* swellings about the anus, often with bleeding; piles.
hemp *n.* a tall Asiatic plant of the mulberry family, kinds of which are the source of fiber for rope and cordage, marijuana, hashish, and oil.
—**hemp.en** *adj.*
hem.stitch *n. & v.* (stitch) an ornamental openwork pattern on fabric.
hen *n.* a female bird, esp. of the domestic fowl: *a cackling or clucking hen.*
hence *adv.* from this place, time, source, or origin: *Many years hence we shall all be gone; "Grapes are sour,"* hence (= therefore) *the sour-grapes philosophy.*
hence.forth (hens.FORTH) or **hence.for.ward** (-FOR.wurd) *adv.* from now on.
hench.man (HENCH.mun) *n.* **-men** a right-hand man, often a self-serving political follower.
hen.na (HEN.uh) *n.* an Egyptian privet whose orange-red dye is used widely, esp. to color nails and hair.
—*v.* **hen.nas, hen.naed, hen.na.ing:** *an Eastern beauty with hennaed nails.*
hen.peck *v.* domineer over one's husband.
hen.ry (HEN.ree) *n.* **-ries** or **-rys** the international unit of inductance.
hep *adj. Slang.* hip or aware.
hep.ar.in (HEP.uh.rin) *n.* an anticoagulant drug derived from the liver and used in thrombosis and embolism against blood clots.
he.pat.ic (hi.PAT.ic) *adj.* of the liver.
he.pat.i.ca (hi.PAT.i.cuh) *n.* liverwort.
hep.a.ti.tis (hep.uh.TYE.tis) *n.* inflammation of the liver, usually due to a virus.
hep.cat *n. Slang.* one who is hip or aware.

hepta- *comb.form.* seven: *heptagon* (= seven-sided figure); *heptameter* (= seven-footed verse); *heptarchy* (= rule by seven).

her (HUR, ur) *pron.* objective or possessive case of SHE: *I saw her; her face; I'm older than her (Informal for she); That's her (Informal for she).* —**hers** (HURS) *pron.*: *The purse is hers; his books and hers; Hers are newer.*

her.ald (HER.uld) *n.* 1 formerly, a public official in charge of announcements, ceremonies, coats-of-arms, etc. 2 an announcer or harbinger; *v.*: *birds heralding the dawn.* —**he.ral.dic** (huh.RAL.dic) *adj.*

her.ald.ry (HER.ul.dree) *n.* -**ries** 1 coats of arms or their science and art. 2 heraldic pomp: *with great pomp and heraldry.*

herb (URB, HURB) *n.* any seed plant with fleshy stems that is used for food and in medicines and perfumes.

her.ba.ceous (ur.BAY.shus, hur-) *adj.* green and fleshy, not woody like a tree or shrub: *a herbaceous border of perennials.*

herb.age (UR.bij, HUR-) *n.* green foliage; also, grass or pasturage.

her.bal (UR.bul, HUR-) *adj.* 1 having to do with herbs: *an herbal remedy.* 2 medicinal: *the herbal qualities of poison ivy.* —**her.bal.ist** *n.*

her.bar.i.um (ur.BAIR.ee.um, hur-) *n.* -**i.ums** or -**i.a** (-ee.uh) a botanical collection of dried plants.

her.bi.cide (UR.buh.cide, HUR-) *n.* a weed-killer. —**her.bi.ci.dal** (-SYE.dul) *adj.*

her.bi.vore (UR.buh.vore, HUR-) *n.* a plant-eating animal.

her.bi.vor.ous (ur.BIV.uh.rus, hur-) *adj.* plant-eating.

her.cu.le.an or **Her.cu.le.an** (hurk.yuh.LEE.un, hur.KEW.lee.un) *adj.* having or requiring great strength like that of **Hercules,** a hero of Greek and Roman myths, famous for feats of strength: *a herculean effort, feat, labor, task, workload; herculean dimensions, measures, proportions, strength.*

herd *n.* 1 a group of large animals such as cattle, horses, and elephants that are kept or that live together: *to round up, tend a herd.* 2 a crowd of common people or children: *the common herd; the **herd** instinct (to stay and act in a group).* —**ride herd on** supervise people closely like cowboys herding cattle. —*v.* form into or take care of as a herd or flock, as a herdsman does. —**herds.man** *n.* -**men**.

here (HEER) 1 *adv.* at, in, to, or into this place: *Come here, Joe; Here I come.* 2 *n.* at this point or time: *Let's pause here for a moment.* —**here below** on earth. —**here goes!** *Informal* [announcing something about to be done]. —**here you are!** *Informal* [said when handing over something asked for]. —**neither here nor there** not relevant. —**up to here** *Informal.* to the utmost: *People have had it up to here with all sorts of taxes.*

here.a.bout (HEER.uh.bowt) or **here.a.bouts** *adv.* about or near here.

here.af.ter (heer.AF.tur) 1 *adv.* in the future: *Hereafter we are going to be on time.* 2 *n.* the life after the present: *Who knows what may happen in the hereafter?*

here.by (heer.BY) *adv. Formal.* by this means, as by a document; in this way.

he.red.i.tar.y (huh.RED.uh.tair.ee) *adj.* 1 by inheritance: *a hereditary ruler, title.* 2 acquired by heredity: *a hereditary characteristic.* 3 traditional: *hereditary beliefs, customs, enemies, loyalties.*

he.red.i.ty (huh.RED.i.tee) *n.* -**ties** 1 the passing on of parental characteristics to offspring through genes. 2 such qualities, traits, etc. or the tendency to inherit them.

Her.e.ford (HUR.furd, HER.uh-) *n.* 1 a reddish-brown breed of beef cattle with white faces. 2 a similarly marked American breed of swine.

here.in (here.IN) *adv. Formal.* in this document, matter, etc.

here.of (heer.OV) *adv. Formal.* of or about this.

here.on (heer.ON) *adv. Formal.* on this.

here's (HEERS) here is.

her.e.sy (HER.uh.see) *n.* -**sies** an opinion or belief, esp. religious, that is opposed to the orthodox or established position: *He was accused of preaching heresy.* —**her.e.tic** (-uh.tic) *n. & adj.* —**he.ret.i.cal** (huh.RET.i.cul) *adj.*

here.to (heer.TOO) *adv. Formal.* to this document.

here.to.fore (HEER.tuh.for) *adv. Formal.* up to this time.

here.un.to (heer.UN.too) *adv. Formal.* to this.

here.up.on (heer.uh.PON) *adv. Formal.* upon this; also, immediately after.

here.with (heer.WITH, "TH" as in "the") *adv.* with this: *A check is enclosed herewith.*

her.it.a.ble (HER.i.tuh.bul) *adj.* that can be inherited.

her.it.age (HER.uh.tij) *n.* what is inherited, as a title, property, languages, traditions, etc.: *a cultural, family, priceless, proud, rich heritage; the teaching of* **heritage** (= ethnic) **languages** *in schools.*

her.maph.ro.dite (hur.MAF.ruh.dite) *n.* a person, animal, or organism with male and female organs. —**her.maph.ro.dit.ic** (-DIT.ic) *adj.* bisexual.

her.met.ic (hur.MET.ic) *adj.* airtight; also **her.met.i.cal.** —**her.met.i.cal.ly** *adv.*

her.mit (HUR.mit) *n.* a recluse, esp. a religious one.

her.mit.age (HUR.muh.tij) *n.* a hermit's secluded dwelling place.

her.ni.a (HUR.nee.uh) *n.* a bulging of an organ through weakened tissue surrounding it; rupture; **her.ni.al** *adj.*

her.ni.ate (HUR.nee.ate) *v.* **-ates, -at.ed, -at.ing** protrude so as to form a hernia; *adj.: a herniated* (= slipped or ruptured) *disk.* —**her.ni.a.tion** (-AY.shun) *n.*

he.ro (HEER.oh) *n.* **-roes 1** one admired for noble qualities or exploits, as the central characters in novels, plays, etc.: *folk, military, popular, war heros.* **2** a submarine sandwich.

he.ro.ic (hi.ROH.ic) *adj.* **1** of, about, or like heroes: *heroic qualities such as courage and nobility; The "Odyssey" is a heroic poem.* **2** daring and bold: *to take heroic measures.* **3 heroics** *n.pl.* extravagant or showy behavior. Also **he.ro.i.cal** *adj.;* **he.ro.i.cal.ly** *adv.*

her.o.in (HER.oh.in) *n.* a pain-relieving, habit-forming narcotic.

her.o.ine (HER.oh.in) *n.* a female hero.

her.o.ism (HER.oh.iz.um) *n.* **1** great courage or bravery. **2** the qualities and actions of a hero or heroine.

her.on (HER.un) *n.* a cranelike wading bird having a long neck, bill, and legs. —**her.on.ry** *n.* **-ries** a nesting place of herons.

hero sandwich *n.* a large sandwich with a roll sliced lengthwise and filled with cold cuts and vegetables.

her.pes (HER.peez) *n.* a blister-forming viral disease, **herpes simplex** forming "cold sores" or "fever sores" around the mouth and **herpes zoster**, or shingles, affecting nerves on one side of the chest and abdomen.

her.pe.tol.o.gy (hur.pi.TOL.uh.jee) *n.* the zoology of reptiles and amphibians; **her.pe.tol.o.gist** *n.*

Herr (HAIR) *n., pl.* **Her.ren** (HAIR.un) *German.* **1** a man. **2** [as title] Mr. or Sir.

her.ring (HER.ing) *n.* a small, widely used food fish of the North Atlantic.

her.ring.bone (HER.ing.bone) *n.* a pattern of rows of slanted lines arranged like the ribs on a herring's spine, as in twilled fabrics, bricklaying, or a climbing step in skiing.

hers See HER.

her.self (hur.SELF) *pron.* reflexive or emphatic of SHE: *Kay is proud of herself; sitting all by herself; She herself said it; She's not quite herself* (= as she normally is) *when unwell.*

hertz (HURTS) *n. sing. & pl.* a unit of frequency equal to one cycle per second.

he's (HEEZ) he is; he has.

hes.i.tant (HEZ.uh.tunt) *adj.* doubtful or undecided: *He was hesitant about accepting the job offer;* **hes.i.tant.ly** *adv.* —**hes.i.tan.cy** *n.* **-cies.**

hes.i.tate (HEZ.uh.tate) *v.* **-tates, -tat.ed, -tat.ing 1** be doubtful or undecided: *She hesitated before saying "yes"; He hesitated about jumping* or *hesitated to jump into the water.* **2** talk or act doubtfully or undecidedly: *"He who hesitates is lost."* —**hes.i.tat.ing.ly** *adv.* —**hes.i.ta.tion** (-TAY.shun) *n.*

hetero- *comb.form.* other or different: *heterodox, heterogeneous, heterosexual.*

het.er.o.dox (HET.ur.uh.dox) *adj.* not orthodox.

het.er.o.ge.ne.ous (het.ur.uh.JEE.nee.us) *adj.* composed of different kinds of things; not homogeneous: *a heterogeneous character, group, population.*

het.er.o.sex.u.al (het.ur.uh.SEK.shoo.ul) *adj.* **1** attracted to the opposite sex, not homosexual; also *n.* **2** of different sexes: *heterosexual twins.*

heu.ris.tic (hew.RIS.tic) *adj.* based on or involving trial and error: *a heuristic approach, computer program, teaching method.*

hew *v.* **hews,** *pt.* **hewed,** *pp.* **hewed** or **hewn, hew.ing 1** cut or form by cutting or chopping, as with an ax or chisel: *The enemy was hewn down in battle; to hew one's way through a jungle; a cave hewn out of a rock; adj. & cpd: hewn granite, timber; homemade, hand-hewn furniture; rock-hewn structures; a house built with stones* **rough-hewn** *on site.* **2** hold fast or adhere: *to hew to rules and regulations.* —**hew.er** *n.*

hex *n.* a magic spell. —*v.* put a hex on a person or thing; jinx. —*adj.* **1** hexagonal: *a bolt with a hex head; a hex wrench.* **2** hexadecimal: *a hex pad* or *keyboard with 16 keys.*

hexa- *comb.form.* six: *hexagon, hexameter, hexapod.*

hex.a.dec.i.mal (hex.uh.DES.uh.mul) *adj.* having to do with 16: *The hexadeci-*

mal code uses the base 16 instead of 10 used in the decimal code.

hex.a.gon (HEX.uh.gon) *n.* a polygon of six angles and sides. —**hex.ag.o.nal** (hek.SAG.uh.nul) *adj.*

hex.am.e.ter (hek.SAM.uh.tur) *n.* six-footed verse.

hex.a.pod (HEX.uh.pod) *n. & adj.* (an insect) having six legs.

hey (HAY) *interj.* used to ask a question, attract attention, or express surprise.

hey.day *n.* the time of greatest strength, prosperity, etc.: *in the heyday of colonialism.*

hi (HYE) *interj.* hello: *Hi there! Hi Joe! Hi neighbor!*

hi.a.tus (hye.AY.tus) *n.* **-tus.es** a break or gap in the continuity of something: *a two-month hiatus from work; to take a hiatus of several years.*

hi.ba.chi (hi.BAH.chee) *n.* **-chis** a charcoal-burning brazier and grill, as used for preparing food at the dining table: *a Japanese restaurant with hibachi cuisine.*

hi.ber.nate (HYE.bur.nate) *v.* **-nates, -nat.ed, -nat.ing** pass the winter in an inactive condition: *bats, bears, chipmunks, and such hibernating animals.* —**hi.ber.na.tion** (-NAY.shun) *n.* —**hi.ber.na.tor** (-nay.tur) *n.*

hi.bis.cus (hye.BIS.cus, huh-) *n.* a plant, shrub, or tree of the mallow family with large, colorful, usually bell-shaped flowers.

hic.cup or **hic.cough** (HIC.up) *n.* the sharp, clicking noise of a breathing spasm, or **hiccups** *pl.* —*v.* **hic.cups, hic.cupped** or **hic.cuped, hic.cup.ping** or **hic.cup.ing** make hiccups: *how to stop hiccupping.*

hick [derogatory] *n.* rustic: *Is he a hick or a city slicker? a mere hick town.*

hick.ey *n.* **-eys** *Informal.* a gadget or device.

hick.o.ry (HIK.uh.ree) *n.* **-ries** a hardwood tree of the walnut family, some bearing edible nuts, as the pignut and pecan; *adja.: a hickory switch, chair, walking stick.*

hi.dal.go (hi.DAL.go) *n.* **-gos** a Spanish noble ranking below a grandee.

hidden agenda *n.* secret plan.

hidden tax *n.* an indirect tax such as an excise or customs duty.

hide *v.* **hides, hid, hid.den** (HID.un), **hid.ing** (HYE.ding) **1** keep or remain secret or out of sight: *The sun is hidden by the clouds; a code word with a hidden meaning; n. & cpd: He has gone into hiding to escape the publicity; He'll come out of hiding soon; Children play*

hide-and-seek. 2 *pt.* **hid.ed** *Informal.* flog or thrash; *n.:* to give a good *hiding* to someone. —*n.* a raw or tanned skin of a large animal.

hide.a.way (HYE.duh.way) *n.* a place of seclusion, refuge, or retreat, as a quiet hotel; *adja.: The sofa opens out to show a hideaway bed; a hideaway cottage.*

hide.bound *adj.* **1** of cattle, with the skin sticking close to the body. **2** narrow-minded and obstinate.

hid.e.ous (HID.ee.us) *adj.* extremely ugly or revolting.

hide-out *n.* a place of hiding, as of guerrillas.

hie (HYE) *v.* **hies, hied, hy.ing** or **hie.ing** [old or poetic use] hasten: *Hie hither; He hied him(self) to the chase.*

hi.er.ar.chy (HYE.ur.ar.kee) *n.* **-chies 1** a graded or ranked organization, as of authority in the church, in a civil service, etc.: *the military hierarchy; He rose in the hierarchy from lieutenant to general.* **2** the body of people in higher authority: *They appealed to the hierarchy to bend a little.* **3** a graded series: *a hierarchy of values governing conduct.* —**hi.er.ar.chic** (-AR.kic) or **hi.er.ar.chi.cal** *adj.*

hi.er.o.glyph (HYE.ur.uh.glif) or **hi.er.o.glyph.ic** (hye.ur.uh.GLIF.ic) *n.* a picture or symbol expressing an idea, as in ancient Egyptian and Aztec writing. —**hieroglyphic** *adj.* **1** of or like hieroglyphics: *hieroglyphic prints.* **2** hard to read: *a pharmacist trying to figure out a hieroglyphic prescription.*

hi.fa.lu.tin (hye.fuh.LOO.tun) same as HIGHFALUTIN.

hi-fi (HYE.fye) *adj.* high-fidelity: *hi-fi equipment, quality, sets, systems.* —*n.* hi-fi equipment or a hi-fi component.

hig.gle.dy-pig.gle.dy (HIG.ul.dee.PIG.ul.dee) *adj. & adv.* in disorder; jumbled.

high *adj.* **1** being above the ground, esp. to a considerable distance: *a high mountain; How high is it? 1,000 m high; The cupboard is too high for me (to reach); the high (= top) shelf; a high dive (from a great height).* **2** great or advanced in quality or extent, importance, seriousness, etc.: *to drive at high speed; high crimes, principles, standards, treason; a high manner* (= conceit); *a high priest; high school; a high voice* (= high in pitch); *the higher apes* (= anthropoids). **3** *Informal.* intoxicated, esp. under the influence of a drug: *to get high on hashish.* —*adv.* at or to a height: *Birds fly high in the air; Stars shine high up in the sky; Tempers ran high during the debate.*

—n. something that is high: *a record that hits a new high; an all-time high; the highs and lows of atmospheric pressure; the highs induced by narcotics, yoga, jogging, etc.;* commands issued ***from on high*** (= as if from Heaven). **—high and dry** stranded; all alone: *The rising river left the cat high and dry on a treetop.* **—high and low** everywhere: *to search high and low.* **—high and mighty** important people: *the follies of the high and mighty.*

high.ball *n.* a mixed alcoholic drink served in a tall glass.

high beam *n.* a beam of headlight switched to illuminate the way far ahead.

high.born *adj.* of noble birth.

high.boy *n.* a high chest of drawers mounted on relatively tall legs.

high.brow *n. & adj. Informal.* (one) of supposedly great knowledge or culture.

high.chair *n.* a chair with long legs for infants to sit at the same table with adults.

high command *n.* the top leadership of an organization: *the Republican high command.*

High Commission *n.* the embassy of one Commonwealth country in another. **—High Commissioner** *n.*

high end *n.* the top range in merchandise: *During recessions there's a slowdown on the high end; Our goods were a bit too pricey for the high end; Sales at the high end are picking up.*

high-end *adj.* upscale: *High-end computers used to cost millions of dollars; a high-end clientele, customer, line, package, price, retailer; high-end sales, spending; the high-end marketplace.*

high-energy *adj.* **1** having to do with accelerated atomic particles: *a beam of high-energy protons; High-energy astronomy studies high-energy phenomena such as X rays and cosmic rays; high-energy lasers, physics.* **2** dynamic: *high-energy ads, children, efficiency, foods, jazz, music, organizations, snacks, workouts.*

higher education *n.* post-secondary education.

higher-up *n. Informal.* one in a higher rank or position.

high.fa.lu.tin or **high.fa.lu.ting** (hye.fuh.LOO.tun) *adj. Informal.* high-sounding or bombastic.

high fidelity *n.* sound reproduction with high accuracy and low distortion.

—high-fidelity *adj.: a high-fidelity amplifier; high-fidelity reception.*

high-five *n.* a slapping together of the raised palms of two people as a greet-ing or celebration.

high-flown *adj.* excessively high or bombastic: *high-flown praise.*

high-flyer *n.* **1** one that flies high, esp. a stock that rises in value more quickly than other stocks. **2** an extravagant or high-spending person. **—high-flying** *adj.: a high-flying financial company, real-estate dealer, specialty store.*

high frequency *n.* a radio frequency of 3 to 30 megahertz.

high-grade *adj.* of high quality or value: *high-grade bonds, ore, performances.*

high-handed *adj.* **1** overbearing in manner. **2** without consideration for others' feelings: *the new manager's high-handed way of running things.*

high-hat *adj. Informal.* snobbish: *to go high-hat.* **—v.** -hats, -hat.ted, -hat.ting treat snobbishly.

high jinks *n.pl.* boisterous fun; horseplay.

high.land (HYE.lund) *adj. & n.* (having to do with) a region that is higher than its surroundings: *the Highlands of northern and western Scotland; highland cattle, meadows; a Highland fling* (= dance of the Scottish Highlands). **—high.land.er** or **High.land.er** *n.*

high-level *adj.* **1** involving persons of high rank: *a high-level meeting of cabinet ministers.* **2** of a computer programming language, using almost the same language as the user, as Basic.

high.light *n.* a very prominent aspect or feature, as a light-reflecting spot on a shiny object: *the highlight of her career, of the evening, of a celebration.*

—v. -lights, -light.ed, -light.ing **1** be a highlight of something: *a year highlighted by achievements in science.* **2** give prominence to something: *Word-processing programs highlight misspelled words for correction; to highlight one's features using makeup; She prefers highlighting or streaking to coloring her hair.*

high.lin.er (HYE.lye.nur) *n.* **1** the member of a fishing fleet that brings in the largest catch. **2** its captain.

high.ly *adv.* **1** at a high level or standard: *a highly classified document; a highly placed official.* **2** very (much): *a highly entertaining act; He speaks highly* (= well) *of her.*

high-minded *adj.* marked by high principles or feelings.

high.ness (HYE.nis) *n.* high state. **—Her** or **His** or **Your Highness** [style of addressing or referring to royalty].

high noon *n.* **1** the middle of the day: *robbery at high noon.* **2** peak; high point: *in the high noon of her career.*

high-octane *adj.* of gasoline, having a high octane content; hence, high-powered or dynamic.

high-pressure *adj.* **1** using aggressive methods, esp. in selling. **2** involving much worry and tension: *a high-pressure job*.

high-rise *adj.* having many stories: *a high-rise apartment block*. **—n.** such a building: *There are high-rises, mid-rises, and walkups*.

high-riser *n.* **1** a high-rise. **2** a bicycle with high handlebars.

high.road *n.* **1** a main road. **2** a direct or easy route: *the highroad to fame*.

high roller *n.* one who spends freely or gambles recklessly.

high school *n.* secondary school consisting of grades 9 through 12, if four-year, or 10 through 12 if "senior high school."

high seas *n.pl.* the open ocean outside of national jurisdictions.

high-spirited *adj.* brave or proud: *a high-spirited youth; a high-spirited* (= frisky) *horse*.

high spirits *n.pl.* a feeling of liveliness and well-being: *Pat's in high spirits after exercising*.

high spot *n.* high point; highlight: *some of the high spots of our visit*.

high-sticking *n.* in hockey and lacrosse, a foul resulting from a player using the stick above shoulder level, esp. to hurt an opponent.

high-strung *adj.* easily excited.

high tech *n. Informal.* high technology. **—high-tech** *adj.*: *high-tech companies, equipment, research, solutions, ventures; to go high-tech*.

high technology *n.* technology used in highly sophisticated computers and other electronic devices.

high-tension *adj.* high-voltage: *a high-tension wire*.

high-test *adj.* **1** same as HIGH-OCTANE. **2** of high standard.

high-ticket *adj.* of goods and services, expensive: *Sewing machines, pianos, jewelry, etc. are high-ticket items; a high-ticket restaurant*.

high tide *n.* **1** (the time of) the highest level of the tide. **2** climax.

high time *n.* a time allowing no more delay: *It is high time we did something about this problem*.

high-water mark *n.* the highest point reached; acme: *Last year was the high-water mark for company profits*.

high.way *n.* **1** a public road: *divided, limited-access, inter-state highways*. **2** highroad: *the highway to success*.

high.way.man (HYE.way.mun) *n.* **-men** a highway robber.

highway robbery *n.* overcharging of prices.

high wire *n.* rope or cable stretched high for aerialists to perform on; tightrope.

hi.jack (HYE.jack) *v.* seize control of an airplane, bus, truck, etc. for extortion purposes. **—n.** a hijacking. **—hi.jack.er** *n.*

hike *v.* **hikes, hiked, hik.ing 1** go on a long walk; tramp or march. **2** *Informal.* pull up and hitch: *She hiked up her skirt and waded across the stream*. **3** raise or increase: *Prices are hiked to keep up with inflation*. **—n. 1** a long walk or march: *to go on a hike*. **2** a raising or increase: *the new hike in taxes*. **—take a hike** *Informal.* Go away! **—hik.er** *n.*

hi.lar.i.ous (huh.LAIR.ee.us) *adj.* causing great merriment: *a hilarious account, joke, party, spectacle, tale; her hilarious humor; This is downright hilarious!* **—hi.lar.i.ous.ly** *adv.* **—hi.lar.i.ty** *n.*

hill *n.* **1** an elevation on the earth's surface, smaller than a mountain: *the rolling hills of the prairies; a steep hill; to* **head for the hills** (*Informal for* run away and hide). **2** a pile, heap, or mound, as an anthill or molehill. **—over the hill** past one's prime, as a retired person.

hill.bil.ly (HIL.bil.ee) *n.* **-bil.lies** a person from a backwoods region, esp. of southeastern U.S.

hill.ock (HILL.uck) *n.* a small hill.

hill.side *n.* the slope of a hill.

hill.top *n.* the top of a hill.

hill.y *adj.* **hill.i.er, -i.est 1** full of hills: *a hilly region; hilly country*. **2** steep: *a hilly slope*.

hilt *n.* the handle of a sword, dagger, or similar weapon or tool. **—(up) to the hilt** to the maximum limit: *dressed to the hilt; in debt up to the hilt; She lived to the hilt and died poor*.

him *pron.* objective case of HE: *She knows him; She's older than him* (*Informal for* he); *It's him* (*Informal for* he) *all right*.

Hi.ma.la.yan (him.uh.LAY.un, huh.MAHL.yun) *adj.* having to do with the **Himalayas**, the world's highest mountain system.

him.self (him.SELF) *pron.* reflexive or emphatic form of HE: *He himself did it; He's not quite himself* (= as he normally is) *today; He likes to work* **by** *himself* (= alone).

hind (HINED) *n.* **1** the adult female of the red deer. **2** a British farm hand. **—adj. hind.er, hind.most** or

hind.er.most (HINE.dur.most) rear or back: *on its hind legs.*

hin.der (HIN.dur) *v.* prevent the progress of a person or thing: *We were hindered in our rescue efforts by a snowstorm; Thick underbrush hindered our movement; It hindered our moving forward; hindered us from moving forward.*

hinder, hind.er.most, hindmost See HIND, *adj.*

hind.quar.ter (HINED.kwor.tur) *n.* 1 the back half of a side of beef, lamb, etc. 2 **hindquarters** *pl.* a quadruped's hind pair of legs; haunches.

hin.drance (HIN.drunce) *n.* 1 an obstacle: *a hindrance rather than a help; a hindrance to progress; We need opportunities rather than hindrances.* 2 the act of hindering: *We have to be free to work without let or hindrance.*

hind.sight (HINED.site) *n.* a looking back after the event; understanding of what should have been done: *In hindsight* or *With (the benefit of) hindsight, he would have sent the letter by courier instead of mailing it.*

Hin.du (HIN.doo) *n.* a follower of Hinduism.

Hin.du.ism (HIN.doo.iz.um) *n.* the main religion of India, with worship of many gods, the caste system, and belief in reincarnation.

hinge (HINJ) *n.* 1 a natural or artificial joint on which a door, gate, lid, knees, clamshells, etc. move, turn, or depend. 2 a pivotal or determining factor. —*v.* **hing.es, hinged, hing.ing** 1 join: *a cover hinged to move up and down.* 2 depend: *Everything hinges on* or *upon her decision.*

hint *n.* an indirect or slight indication: *to drop a hint; Can you give me a hint? a hint about what you're up to; He left the place at the first hint of trouble; a broad* or *obvious hint; a gentle* or *subtle hint; the merest hint of suspicion; He can* **take a hint** (= understand what is meant); *There's a hint* (= trace) *of frost in the air; a hint of color, garlic, glamour, perfume, of a smile, of bitterness, guilt, irritation, success, trouble.* —*v.* give a hint: *She didn't suggest leaving, but hinted at the lateness of the hour; She hinted to us that it was getting late.*

hin.ter.land (HIN.tur.land) *n.* 1 the inland region behind a coast, as one served by a port. 2 a region far from any urban center.

hip *n.* 1 the joint of the thighbone with the ear-shaped **hipbone** of the pelvis; also **hipjoint.** 2 the fleshy side below the waist covering a hipjoint: *to wiggle one's hips; close-fitting* **hip-huggers** (= pants). —**shoot from the hip** *Informal.* act impulsively or recklessly. —*adj.* **hip.per, hip.pest** *Slang.* alert to or informed about what is new and modish; not square: *He is hip to what's going on; hip designer clothes; one of the city's hippest nightspots.* —*v. Slang.* 1 keep someone up to date; wise up. 2 make a person hip.

hipped *adj.* 1 *Slang.* obsessed: *hipped on golf.* 2 *adj. & comb.form.* having a hip or the specified type of hip: *A* **hipped roof,** *or* **hip roof,** *has all four sides sloping; pants for broad-hipped* or *wide-hipped people; narrow-hipped suits; the swivel-hipped Elvis.*

hip.pie or **hip.py** (HIP.ee) *n.* **hip.pies** a dropout from conventional society who lives a carefree life in communes, with long hair, practicing free love, mysticism, doing drugs, etc. —**hip.pie.dom** *n.*

hip.po (HIP.oh) *n.* **hip.pos** *Informal.* hippopotamus.

Hip.po.crat.ic oath (hip.uh.CRAT.ic-) *n.* an oath setting forth a physician's code of ethics.

hip.po.drome (HIP.uh.drome) *n.* an arena or indoor facility for horse racing, circuses, rodeos, etc.

hip.po.pot.a.mus (hip.uh.POT.uh.mus) *n.* **-mus.es** or **-mi** (-mye), a large-headed, short-legged, thick-skinned African animal that lives in rivers and marshy ponds.

hip roof See HIPPED.

hire *v.* **hires, hired, hir.ing** 1 engage for pay, esp. on a temporary basis: *to hire help, workers; Casual workers try to* **hire on** (= get hired) *during a strike; adj.:* a **hired** *gun; hired help; a newly hired nanny.* 2 get or give the use of a thing or the work or services of a person in return for payment: *to hire out a laborer or tool.* —*n.* a hiring, hired person, or payment for one: *to make a hire; a good worker worth every penny of his hire; cabs for hire; workmen on hire.*

hire.ling *n. & adj.* a. (one) who will do anything for pay; mercenary.

Hi.ro.shi.ma (heer.oh.SHEE.muh) *n.* a seaport of Japan where the first atomic bomb was dropped in 1945; hence, the death and destruction caused there: *No more Hiroshimas!*

hir.sute (HUR.soot, hur.SOOT, long "oo") *adj.* hairy.

his (HIZ) *adj. & pron.* of or to him: *Those are his; his neckties; a friend of his.*

His.pan.ic (his.PAN.ic) *adj.* of Spanish origin. —*n.* a Spanish-speaking Ameri-

can; also **His.pa.no** *n.* **-nos.**
hiss *v.* **1** make a sharp sound, as of air escaping from a tire or of geese and snakes when excited. **2** show disapproval by hissing: *The speaker was so unpopular the audience hissed at his jokes; He was hissed off the stage.* —*n.* a hissing: *He had to leave amid hisses and hoots from spectators.*
hist (PSST) *interj.* used to attract attention.
his.ta.mine (HIS.tuh.meen, -min) *n.* a substance of body tissues that is released in reaction to irritating substances from outside, causing symptoms of allergy.
his.tol.o.gy (his.TOL.uh.jee) *n.* the biology of tissue structure; **his.tol.o.gist** *n.*
his.to.ri.an (his.TOR.ee.un) *n.* a history scholar or writer of history.
his.tor.ic (his.TOR.ic) *adj.* **1** famous or important in history: *the historic event of the declaration of independence; the historic moment of the signing of a treaty; the historic interest of a "national historic park"; preserving a historic site; things of historic value.* **2** having to do with history: *certain historic practices in regard to hiring women and minorities; historic relationships between England and France; We have written records of events that have happened within* **historic times** (= from about 5,000 years ago).
his.tor.i.cal (his.TOR.i.cul) *adj.* **1** having to do with history or having reference to the past: *a historical event, novel, play, society, study; the historical method of working from the past to the present; certain historical relationships.* **2** factual, not fictitious: *historical characters and events.* —**his.tor.i.cal.ly** *adv.*
his.to.ric.i.ty (his.tor.IS.i.tee) *n.* genuineness as a historical fact: *the historicity of biblical stories.*
his.to.ri.og.ra.pher (HIS.tor.ee.OG.ruh.fur) *n.* **1** an official history writer. **2** a specialist in historiography.
his.to.ri.og.ra.phy (HIS.tor.ee.OG.ruh.fee) *n.* the study of history writing and research.
his.to.ry (HIS.tuh.ree) *n.* **-ries 1** a branch of knowledge dealing with the recording and study of past events: *ancient, cultural, medieval, military, modern history.* **2** historical records: *It will go down in history as a great success; ruins of an era before the dawn of history.* **3** a historical event: *The Summer Olympics was great news, but now it is history; The landing on the moon* **made history** (= It was so important). **4** a historical account: *a short history of Haiti; the case history of a patient; an oral history based on interviews.* **5** what has happened in the past, taken as a whole: *a patient with a history of heart trouble; to trace the history of a nation through the centuries; Does history repeat itself?*
his.tri.on.ics (his.tree.ON.ics) *n.pl.* [takes *sing.* or *pl. v.*] **1** dramatic representation; dramatics. **2** exaggerated or dramatic display of emotion.
—**his.tri.on.ic** *adj.*
hit *v.* **hits, hit, hit.ting 1** come against with force; strike, not miss: *The car hit (against) a tree; The driver hit his head on the roof; The dart hit the bull's-eye; a good fielder who couldn't hit* (= bat); *a nation* **hard hit** (= severely affected) *by famine; The media* **hit hard at** (= attacked) *the government; The minister hit back at the media; He hit out against his attackers.* **2** reach or find: *Drive on till you hit the highway; an event that hit the headlines; She hit on* or *upon* (= found by chance) *a clever plan; The two* **hit it off** (= got along well) *from the beginning.* —*n.* **1** a blow or stroke, esp. one getting to what is aimed at: *The player chalked up or scored more misses than hits; a direct hit; an unfair hit below the belt.* **2** success: *Our play was a box-office hit; a smash hit.* **3** *Slang.* dose or portion: *a hit of cocaine.* —*adja. Slang.* having to do with murder: *a (hired) hit man, squad, team.* —**hit-and-run** *adj.*: *a hit-and-run driver wanted by police; a hit-and-run military tactic; a hit-and-run baseball play;* *n.*: *the victim of a hit-and-run (accident or driver).* —**hit.ter** *n.*
hitch (HICH) *v.* **1** pull or move jerkily; yank: *to hitch up one's trousers before sitting down.* **2** fasten or attach: *a sleeve that hitches on to a doorknob; He hitched up a wagon and went on a tour of the country; authors who* **hitch up** (= join) *with an agent;* *adj.*: *a horse* **hitched** (= harnessed) *to a wagon; a trailer hitched behind* or *to the back of a car; His buddies were getting hitched* (Informal for getting married). **3** *Informal.* hitchhike: *He* **hitched a ride** *home instead of walking.* —*n.* **1** pull: *to give a hitch to a sock that won't stay up.* **2** knot: *He tied his donkey to a tree with a hitch of the rope.* **3** obstacle: *Everything went off without a hitch.* **4** stint or service: *He did a two-year hitch in the navy.*
hitch.hike *v.* **-hikes, -hiked, -hik.ing** travel by getting rides along the way.
—**hitch.hik.er** *n.*
hith.er (HITH.ur, "TH" as in "the") *adv.* to or on this side: *Come hither, darling!*

—**hither and thither** here and there; also **hither and yon.**

hith.er.to (hith.ur.TOO) *adv.* until now.

hit list *n.* a list or people, projects, etc. to be eliminated.

hit man *n.* a hired murderer.

hit-or-miss *adja.* aimless: *a hit-or-miss effort.*

hit parade *n.* a listing of popular hit songs.

HIV *n.* "human immunodeficiency virus," the cause of AIDS.

hive *n.* 1 a beehive; hence, a place of busy activity. 2 **hives** *pl.* [takes *sing.* or *pl.v.*] an itching and burning skin rash caused by allergies. —*v.* **hives, hived, hiv.ing** 1 put bees or settle in a hive: *Beekeepers hive bees; to hive off* (= separate) *one unit from a group.* 2 lay up for future use: *Bees hive honey.*

hmm *interj.* 1 expressing rumination, contemplation, etc.: *"Hmm. Not so fast!" "So you think I'm mistaken. Hmm."* 2 [with a rising tone, often magisterial] *What did you say?: "I think you're wrong"; "Hmm?"* Also **hmmm, hmmmm,** etc. depending on length of utterance.

hoa.gy or **hoa.gie** (HOH.gee, "g" as in "go") *n.* **-gies** a submarine sandwich.

hoard *v.* get and store away money, goods, etc. for future use or sale. —*n.* what is hoarded: *a squirrel's hoard of nuts for the winter; a miser's hoard of wealth; the profiteer's hoard of scarce commodities.* —**hoard.er** *n.*

hoarding *n.* 1 a temporary fence of boards put up around a work site. 2 *Brit.* a billboard.

hoar.frost *n.* white frost; frozen dew; ice crystals.

hoarse (HORSE) *adj.* **hoars.er, hoars.est** of sounds or voice, rough and husky. —**hoarse.ness** *n.*

hoar.y (HOR.ee) *adj.* **hoar.i.er, -i.est** 1 white or gray. 2 white-haired with age: *He shook his hoary head.* 3 ancient: *a hoary legend, past.* —**hoar.i.ness** *n.*

hoax (HOKES) *n.* a fraud or practical joke: *a literary hoax.* —*v.* trick: *The publisher was hoaxed into buying fake diaries of Hitler.* —**hoax.er** *n.*

hob *n.* 1 an elf or hobgoblin. 2 a shelf or ledge at the back or side of a fireplace. 3 the target peg in quoits. 4 a gear-cutting metal device. 5 *Informal.* mischief: *to play* or *raise hob.*

hob.ble (HOB.ul) *v.* **hob.bles, hob.bled, hob.bling** move in an awkward walk, as of a horse whose front legs are tied: *an injured skier hobbling around on crutches.* Also *n.*

hob.ble.de.hoy (HOB.ul.dee.hoy) *n.* a clumsy or gawky youth, esp. an adolescent.

hob.by (HOB.ee) *n.* **hob.bies** a leisure-time activity or pursuit outside of one's main occupation, indulged in for fun and profit: *to pursue a hobby.* —**hob.by.ist** *n.*

hob.by.horse (HOB.ee.horse) *n.* 1 a child's rocking horse or a stick with a horse's head. 2 one's favorite topic or pet theory.

hob.gob.lin (HOB.gob.lin) *n.* 1 a goblin. 2 a bogy.

hob.nail *n.* a large-headed nail for boot soles; *adj.:* a *hobnailed boot.*

hob.nob *v.* **-nobs, -nobbed, -nob.bing** associate familiarly *with* important or influential people.

ho.bo (HOH.boh) *n.* **-bos** or **-boes** a tramp.

Hob.son's choice (HOB.suns-) *n.* a choice with no alternative.

hock *n.* 1 the backward-bending hind-leg joint of a horse, cat, etc. or the corresponding joint of a fowl's leg. 2 *Slang.* pawn; also *v.* —**in hock** indebted: *He was in hock to loan sharks.*

hock.ey (HOK.ee) *n.* 1 ice hockey. 2 field hockey.

hock.shop *n.* pawnshop.

ho.cus-po.cus (HOH.cus.POH.cus) *n.* 1 a meaningless formula; deceptive talk. 2 trickery; sleight of hand.

hod *n.* 1 an open trough or box fixed to the top of a staff, used for carrying bricks or mortar up ladders, etc. 2 a coal scuttle.

hodge.podge *n.* a jumble or mixture.

Hodg.kin's disease (HOJ.kins-) *n.* a cancerous, sometimes fatal disease of the lymph nodes, spleen, etc.

hoe *n.* a farm tool consisting of a thin blade set across the end of a long handle. —*v.* **hoes, hoed, hoe.ing** cut, weed, or loosen soil with a hoe.

hoe.cake *n.* a thin cornmeal bread.

hoe.down *n.* a rollicking, rural kind of square dance of southern U.S. origin; also, the music for this.

hog *n.* 1 a pig, esp. one raised for meat. 2 a coarse, filthy, or selfish person. 3 one who is selfish: *a road hog.* —**eat** or **live off the hog, eat** or **live on the hog, eat** or **live high on the hog** *Informal.* live a luxurious life. —**go (the) whole hog** *Informal.* go all the way. —*v.* **hogs, hogged, hog.ging** grab or use selfishly: *Al likes to hog both lanes of the freeway.*

ho.gan (HOE.gahn) *n.* an earth-covered Navaho dwelling.

hog.gish *adj.* filthy, greedy, or selfish.
hogs.head *n.* 1 a large cask. 2 a liquid measure, varying from 63 to 140 gal. (238 to 530L).
hog-tie *v.* **-ties, -tied, -ty.ing** or **-tie.ing** make someone helpless, as by tying the feet.
hog.wash *n.* 1 swill. 2 baloney or nonsense.
hog-wild *adj. Informal.* wild with excitement: *to go hog-wild.*
ho-hum *interj.* expressing boredom. —*adj.* dull or boring: *a ho-hum routine.*
hoi pol.loi (HOY.puh.LOY) *n.pl.* the common people.
hoist *v.* raise or lift, as a flag or sail, usually with some mechanical means. —*n.* a hoisting or a hoisting machine, as derricks and cranes.
hoke *v.* **hokes, hoked, hok.ing** esp. **hoke up**, overplay a stage or screen part in a cheap or sensational manner.
hok.ey (HOH.kee) *adj.* cheaply sentimental; also, phony: *hokey humor; a hokey production number; Sounds a bit hokey to me.*
ho.kum (HOH.kum) *n. Slang.* bunk; humbug.
hold *v.* **holds, held, hold.ing** have or take in one's possession, as by the hand or in one's physical or mental power: *a mother holding a child; Hold yourself erect; a package being held for you at the post office; to hold* (= defend) *a fort against invaders; beliefs held* (= kept) *by people; Past mistakes will not be held* (= taken into account) *against you; She's held in great esteem by all; to hold someone* (= make him adhere) *to his word; to hold* (= consider) *life cheap; Borrowers are held* (= considered legally) *responsible for what they borrow; a staff meeting to be held* (= made to happen) *at 4 p.m.; The cease-fire seems to be holding* (= continuing); *But* **don't hold your breath** (= Don't be expecting it to happen); *to* **hold** (= adhere) **to** *a promise; a rule that* **holds good** *or* **true** (= applies) *in all cases; He's trying to* **hold down** (= stay in) *a job long enough to pay his debts; The preacher* **held forth** (= talked) *for over an hour.* —**hold it!** stop what you are doing! —**hold on** *Informal.* 1 keep on holding: *Hold on to your hat.* 2 wait: *Hold on, there!* —**hold one's own** keep one's position in the face of opposition. —**hold out** 1 continue resisting: *to hold out against the enemy; a labor union holding out for* (= refusing to settle and demanding) *more concessions.* 2 offer: *to hold out hopes of a settlement.* —**hold over** 1 postpone or retain. 2 keep or stay for a longer period: *The movie was held over for 10 weeks.* —**hold up** 1 maintain or continue: *to hold up under the strains of a job.* 2 stop, esp. by force: *to hold up a train.* —**left holding the bag** left responsible for someone else's unfinished work. —*n.* 1 a holding, manner of holding, thing to hold by or with, a holding influence, or an order to hold: *to relax, relinquish one's hold on something; a wrestler's hold; Put a hold* (= holding order or a stop) *on that.* 2 a cargo compartment in a ship or airplane. —**catch, get, grab, lay, seize** or **take hold of** seize or get possession of something. —**on hold** in waiting condition: *to put a telephone caller on hold; Our plans are on hold.* —**take hold** have an effect.
holding *n.* 1 land or other property. 2 **holdings** *pl.* stocks and bonds. —*adj*.: *a holding* (= delaying) *action; a holding* (= waiting) *area; a holding* (= temporary) *home for youths in trouble with the law; a holding tank* (for temporary storage); *a* **holding company** (controls other companies by ownership of stock).
holding pattern *n.* an oval flight course at a specified height for an aircraft awaiting clearance to land; hence, a stationary condition: *The candidates had to go into* or *were put in a holding pattern for half an hour.*
hold.out *n.* 1 refusal to agree or submit. 2 a person or group resisting thus: *the last holdout.*
hold.o.ver (HOLE.doh.vur) *n.* a person or thing remaining from a previous time: *Hippies are holdovers from the 1960s.*
hold.up *n.* a stoppage, esp. a forcible one for robbery.
hole *n.* 1 an opening in or through something; hence, a pit, cave, burrow, etc.: *to bore* or *dig a hole; fill in a hole; a gaping, yawning hole in the floor.* 2 a dingy or dirty place; an awkward position. 3 in golf, one of the usually 18 hollows on the green; also, a single play from tee to hole: *to shoot a* **hole in one**. —**in the hole** in difficulties, esp. in debt. —**pick holes in something** pick out errors or flaws, as in an argument. —*v.* **holes, holed, hol.ing** 1 make a hole in something. 2 drive into a hole. —**hole up** hide oneself: *Ann Frank was holed up in an attic for two years.*
-holic *comb.form.* addicted to what is specified: *alcoholic, chocoholic, workaholic.*

hol.i.day (HOL.uh.day) *n.* **1** a day of freedom from work, usually for a religious or other celebration: *We observe a holiday in honor of Columbus; legal, paid, public holidays; Sundays and other statutory holidays.* **2** a period of rest: *to take a holiday (from work).* **3** vacation: *He is on holiday; I go on holiday(s) next month; Schools are closed during the summer holidays.* —*adj*.: *a holiday mood; holiday pay;* **holiday weekend** (= "long weekend" of three days). —*v.* spend a holiday or vacation. —**hol.i.day.er** *n.*

holier-than-thou *adj.* implying superior goodness: *a holier-than-thou attitude, manner, politician, smugness.*

ho.li.ness (HOH.lee.nis) *n.* the quality or state of being holy. —**Your** or **His Holiness** [title used in addressing or referring to the Pope or a similar personage].

ho.lis.tic (hoh.LIS.tic) *adj.* having to do with the whole system rather than a part of it: *the holistic approach; holistic ecology, psychology;* **Holistic medicine** treats the whole body rather than affected parts.

hol.lan.daise sauce (HOLL.un.daze-) *n.* a creamy sauce of egg yolks, butter, etc.

Hol.land.er (HOLL.un.dur) *n.* a Dutch person or ship.

hol.ler (HOL.ur) *n. & v. Informal.* shout or yell.

hol.lo (huh.LOH) or **hol.loa** (huh.LOH) *n., interj. & v.* **hol.los, hol.loed, hol.lo.ing** [used esp. to attract attention] hello.

hol.low (HOL.oh) *adj.* **1** empty, not solid inside: *a hollow ball, tube.* **2** concave: *a hollow dish, lens.* **3** looking sunken: *hollow cheeks, eyes.* **4** sounding empty: *hollow laughter, voices.* **5** not real or genuine; false: *hollow hopes, promises, settlements; words that ring hollow.* —*n.* a cavity; depression; valley. —*v.* make hollow: *Erosion hollows river banks; The container was hollowed out of a gourd;* —*adj*.: *hollowed cheeks; a hollowed-out tree trunk.* —*adv. Informal.* thoroughly: *The boxer beat him hollow in no time.* —**hol.low.ness** *n.*

hol.low.ware (HOL.oh.ware) *n.* tableware such as bowls, cups, etc.; cf. FLATWARE. Also **hol.lo.ware**.

hol.ly *n.* **hol.lies** (-leez) an evergreen tree with glossy green leaves and bright red berries.

hol.ly.hock (HOLL.ee.hok) *n.* a tall, hardy plant of the mallow family with large stalks of colorful flowers.

Hol.ly.wood (HOL.ee.wood) *adj.* having to do with **Hollywood,** the home of the American motion-picture industry: *a play staged with Hollywood effects (suggestive of Hollywood); Hollywood dreams.*

hol.mi.um (HOLE.mee.um) *n.* a metallic chemical element.

hol.o.caust (HOL.uh.caust, HOH.luh-) *n.* a large-scale destruction, esp. of lives, as by fire: *a nuclear holocaust;* **the Holocaust** *of Jews under the Nazis.*

hol.o.gram (HOL.uh.gram, HOH.luh-) *n.* a three-dimensional image produced by laser: *Holograms are used on credit cards, etc. as a security device.*

hol.o.graph (HOL.uh.graf, HOH.luh-) *v.* make a hologram of something; produce by holography. —*n. & adj.* (a manuscript, letter, will, etc.) wholly written in the hand of the person whose name it bears. —**hol.o.graph.ic** (-GRAF.ic) *adj.* —**ho.log.ra.phy** (huh.LOG.ruh.fee) *n.*

Hol.stein (HOLE.steen, -stine) *n.* a breed of black-and-white dairy cattle.

hol.ster (HOLE.stur) *n.* a leather case for a pistol, usually attached to a belt.

ho.lus-bo.lus (HOH.lus.BOH.lus) *adj. & adv. Informal.* all at once: *They had to learn it holus-bolus; their heavy-handed holus-bolus approach.*

ho.ly (HOH.lee) *adj.* **-li.er, -li.est 1** worthy of worship or reverence, esp. because of spiritual perfection: *a holy man; the Holy Ghost* or *Holy Spirit.* **2** belonging to or devoted to God: *a holy day such as the Passover or Good Friday;* **Holy Communion** (= Eucharist); **the Holy Land** (= Palestine); *to take* **holy orders** (= ordination as a Christian priest or minister); **the Holy See** (= the Pope's authority or office); *the* **Holy Spirit** or **Ghost** (= the third person of the Trinity; also, the spirit of God); **holy water** (= water blessed for religious use); **Holy Writ** (= sacred scripture, esp. the Bible).

hom.age (HOM.ij) *n.* an act or show of reverence: *An eternal flame burns in homage to the war dead; People come to pay homage to them at the cenotaph.*

hom.burg *n.* a man's soft felt hat with a curved brim and the crown dented lengthwise.

home *n.* **1** one's dwelling place, where one belongs, often including family and surroundings: *"Home sweet home"; Some prefer to make their homes in the suburbs; University students often live away from home; to build, establish a home in Canada; provide a good home for the children; ancestral, country, foster, mobile, summer, winter homes; children of broken* homes (= families); *He feels quite at home* (= ease) *in this country; This country has been home to him for 50 years; She is not (at) home after 8* (= She is out or not receiving calls). **2** an establishment: *to manage* or *operate* or *run a home for the aged; convalescent, detention, funeral, nursing, rest, retirement homes.* **3** a native place or habitat: *Alaska is the home of the kodiak bear.* **4** in games, a goal or home plate. —**adj**a. having to do with home: *a home buyer, computer, office; on the home front.* —**adv**. **1** at or to one's home: *He's gone home; to bring the troops home from a U.N. mission abroad.* **2** to the point aimed at: *Drive the nail home; The point was brought home to* (= impressed on) *him.* —**v**. **homes, homed, hom.ing** go, return, or send home: *Guided missiles home in on their targets; An aircraft landing in fog will home onto a radar signal for guidance.*

home.base same as HOME PLATE.

home-based *adj.* based at home or conducted from home: *home-based businesses, entrepreneurs, services.*

home.bod.y (HOME.bod.ee) *n.* **-bod.ies** a person who prefers home and family to outside attractions: *a homebody who enjoys spending time with his wife and children.*

home.bound *adj.* forced to stay home all the time, as when disabled.

home.boy *n.* **1** a boy or man from one's own hometown or neighborhood. **2** a fellow gang member.

home.brew *n.* **1** home-made alcoholic beverage, esp. beer. **2** *Informal*. a professional player trained in one's own country, not an import.

home.com.ing (HOME.cum.ing) *n.* an arrival at or return to one's home or school, esp. an annual campus celebration.

home economics *n.pl.* [takes *sing. v.*] the management of a household as a course of study, including housekeeping, cooking, child care, etc.; domestic science.

home fries *n.pl.* potatoes served boiled, sliced, and fried.

home game *n.* a game played on home territory, not away.

home-grown *adj.* grown or produced at home: *home-grown fruit, politicians, talent, vegetables.*

home ice *n.* the hockey rink where a home game is played.

home.land *n.* **1** one's native land: *the question of a homeland for Palestinian Arabs.* **2** a semi-independent region established for a black tribe within South Africa during Apartheid.

home.ly *adj.* **-li.er, -li.est** having to do with home life: *homely pleasures; to give the story a homely touch; homely virtues; a homely* (= plain or plain-looking) *woman.* —**home.li.ness** *n.*

home.made *adj.* made at home, not commercially: *a homemade cake; furniture that looks homemade* (= lacking finish).

home.mak.er (HOME.may.kur) *n.* a manager of a household, esp. a housewife; **home.mak.ing** *n.*

ho.me.o.path (HOH.mee.uh.path) *n.* a practitioner of homeopathy; **ho.me.o.path.ic** (-PATH.ic) *adj.*

ho.me.op.a.thy (hoh.mee.OP.uh.thee) *n.* a medical system in which a disease is treated by giving minute doses of a drug which would produce symptoms of the disease in a healthy person

ho.me.o.sta.sis (HOH.mee.uh.STAY.sis) *n.* an organism's tendency or ability to maintain stability independently of its environment by regulation of its internal processes and systems such as respiration, circulation, hormones, etc.

home plate *n.* the slab beside which a baseball batter stands while batting.

hom.er (HOH.mur) *n. Informal.* a home run in baseball. —**v**. hit a homer.

Ho.mer.ic (hoh.MER.ic) *adj.* having to do with **Homer**, Greek epic poet.

home.room *n.* a room where all members of a class report.

home rule *n.* self-government, as of a colony.

home run *n.* a baseball hit that enables the batter to touch all bases and return to home plate.

home screen *n.* a TV screen: *seen on home screens.*

home.sick *adj.* sad because of being away from home. —**home.sick.ness** *n.*

home.spun *adj.* **1** plain: *homespun effects, looks, manners, values, wit; It looks very homespun.* **2** made using a spinning wheel: *a homespun bag, design, rug.* **3** homemade: *homespun fabrics, remedies, silk.* —*n.* cloth spun or made at home.

home.stead (HOME.sted) *n.* a place, including land and buildings, where a family settled and made its home: *the homestead rights of a farmer's wife.*

home.stead.er (HOME.sted.ur) *n.* one who has a homestead, esp. one who has acquired it by U.S. laws since 1862.

home.stretch *n.* the last stretch of a race track before the finish line: *In June, we are on the homestretch* (= in the conclud-

ing part) *of the school year.*
home.town *n.* a city or town where one lived while growing up.
home truth *n.* a basic fact of a somewhat embarrassing nature.
home.ward (HOME.wurd) *adj. & adv.* toward home: *homeward bound; a homeward trek; traveling homeward.* Also **home.wards** *adv.*
home.work *n.* work done at home, esp. schoolwork outside the classroom: *Both debaters had apparently done their homework* (= prepared themselves).
hom.ey (HOH.mee) *adj.* **hom.i.er, -i.est** having the atmosphere of a home; **hom.ey.ness** *n.*
hom.i.cide (HOM.uh.side) *n.* **1** one who kills another. **2** the crime itself: *justifiable homicide committed in self-defense; an allegation of negligent homicide against the driver;* **adj.**: *the homicide squad (of a police force); homicide rates, victims.*
—**hom.i.ci.dal** (-SYE.dul) *adj.*
hom.i.ly (HOM.uh.lee) *n.* **-lies** (-leez) **1** a sermon. **2** a moralizing speech.
—**hom.i.lec.tic** (-ee.LEC.tic) *adj.*
homing *adj.* capable of going home or to a destination as directed: *a homing device, system; the homing instinct of salmon; The homing pigeon is trained to carry written messages home over long distances.*
hom.i.nid (HOM.uh.nid) *n.* a primate mammal of the group that includes humans.
hom.i.ny (HOM.uh.nee) *n.* hulled corn, often coarsely ground, as "hominy grits."
homo- *comb.form.* same: *homogeneous, homograph, homosexual.*
ho.mo (HOH.moh) *n.* **1** [short form] homogenized milk. **2** *pl.* **-mos** [short form] homosexual.
ho.mo.ge.ne.ous (hoh.muh.JEE.nee.us) *adj.* of the same kind or of uniform composition, not heterogeneous: *a homogeneous and sometimes exclusive community, group, society, work force; a homogeneous blend, mass, mixture, whole; the homogeneous primal soup from which the universe was formed.* —**ho.mo.ge.ne.i.ty** (-juh.NEE.i.tee) *n.*
ho.mo.ge.nize (huh.MOJ.uh.nize) *v.* **-niz.es, -nized, -niz.ing** make homogeneous: *Homogenized milk has its fat particles evenly distributed so that cream does not separate and come to the top.*
ho.mog.e.nous (huh.MOJ.uh.nus) *adj.* **1** structurally similar because of common origin: *The forelimbs of birds and fishes are homogenous.* **2** [nonstandard] same as HOMOGENEOUS: *Was the early universe a homogenous soup?*

hom.o.graph (HOM.uh.graf) *n.* a word that is the same as another in spelling, but different in pronunciation and meaning, as "lead" (*n.*) and "lead" (*v.*).
ho.mol.o.gous (huh.MOL.uh.gus) *adj.* corresponding in origin, structure, etc.: *The flipper of a seal and the foreleg of a horse are homologous.*
hom.o.logue or **hom.o.log** (HOM.uh.log) *n.* a homologous thing or part: *The flipper of a seal is the homologue of a horse's foreleg.*
ho.mol.o.gy (hoh.MOL.uh.jee) *n.* structural likeness of body parts, esp. between different plants or animals.
hom.o.nym (HOM.uh.nim) *n.* **1** same as HOMOPHONE. **2** a word that is the same as another in pronunciation and spelling, but different in meaning, as "bear" (*v.*) and "bear" (*n.*).
hom.o.phile (HOM.uh.file) same as HOMOSEXUAL.
hom.o.pho.bi.a (hom.uh.FOH.bee.uh) *n.* fear of homosexuality.
hom.o.phone (HOM.uh.fone) *n.* a word that is pronounced like another, as "bear" and "bare," or "shoe" and "shoo."
Ho.mo sa.pi.ens (HOH.moh.SAY.pee.uns, -SAP.ee.uns) *n.* the "intelligent human being" as a species, from about 300,000 B.C.
ho.mo.sex.u.al (hoh.muh.SEK.shoo.ul) *n.* a person who is sexually attracted to those of the same sex. —*adj.* having to do with sexual attraction between members of the same sex: *a homosexual act, group, relationship; the homosexual community, condition, orientation.*
—**ho.mo.sex.u.al.i.ty** (-shoo.AL.i.tee) *n.*
hon.cho (HON.choh) *n.* **-chos** *Informal.* boss or chief: *the top news honcho of the local TV station.*
hone *n.* a fine-grained stone for whetting cutting tools. —*v.* **hones, honed, hon.ing** **1** sharpen a razor, knife, or other cutting tool using a hone: *She has honed her technique to a fine edge; to hone one's skills, tactics;* **adj.**: *a finely honed craft, delivery, perception, skill; an army honed to deadly efficiency.* **2 hone in on** focus on: *Businesses try to hone in on customer preferences.*
hon.est (ON.ist) *adj.* **1** of people, honorable and truthful; not lying, cheating, or stealing: *an honest politician; an honest broker* (= neutral mediator); *I do feel sorry, honest* (= I'm sincere). **2** having to do with an honest person: *an honest effort, face, living, mistake, opinion, piece of work; honest goods, profits.*
—**hon.est.ly** *adv.* —**hon.es.ty** *n.*

hon.ey (HUN.ee) *n.* **-eys 1** the sweet, thick, golden liquid made by bees (**honeybees**) from the nectar of flowers and stored in honeycombs. **2** anything sweet like honey. **3** *Informal.* darling: *Honey, I'm home; She thinks her new computer is a real honey.* —*v.* **hon.eys** or **hon.ies, hon.eyed** or **hon.ied, hon.ey.ing** sweeten: *He staved off eviction by honeying up* (= talking sweetly to) *the landlady; adj.:* **honeyed** *words (that are sweet like honey).*

hon.ey.comb (HUN.ee.come, rhyme: home) *n.* **1** a wax structure of six-sided cells, made by bees. **2** anything resembling this. —*v.:* **a landscape honeycombed with apartments.**

hon.ey.dew (HUN.ee.dew) *n.* **1** a sweet and sticky substance found on leaves and stems of plants. **2** a melon (**honeydew melon**) which has a whitish rind and sweet, green flesh.

honey locust *n.* a tree of the pea family with a slender trunk and featherlike foliage, whose pods contain a sweetish pulp.

hon.ey.moon (HUN.ee.moon) *n.* **1** the vacation taken by a newly married couple: *to go on a honeymoon.* **2** an initial period of harmonious relations, as between newly-weds: *The honeymoon has ended.* —*v.:* *They honeymooned in Las Vegas, Niagara Falls, and Paris.*
—**hon.ey.moon.er** *n.*

hon.ey.suck.le (HUN.ee.suck.ul) *n.* a shrub or vine with trumpet-shaped, nectar-filled flowers.

honk *n.* a wild goose's cry or a similar sound, as of an automobile horn.
—*v.* make a honk: *He parked outside and honked for his friend to come out; Cyclists don't like to be honked at.*

hon.ky or **hon.kie** (HONK.ee) *n. Slang* [offensive] a white person.

honky-tonk *n. Slang.* a cheap nightclub or dance hall; *adja.: honky-tonk music; a honky-tonk cafe, singer.*

hon.or (ON.ur) *n.* **1** keen personal sense of right and wrong: *a man of honor; I give you my word of honor; a duel fought as an affair of honor; a code of honor, to take a pledge on one's honor; an **honor box*** (= newspaper vending box) *based on the honor system.* **2** respect felt or shown to a person: *Dr. Bethune is held in high honor in China; He's an honor* (= source of respect) *to Canada; in honor of our war heroes; a guard of honor; Olympic winners bring* or *do honor to their countries; Your* or *Her* or *His Honor* [title of respect for judges and certain officials]; *to do the honors* (= observe the formalities of being a host or hostess); *buried with full military honors; the Queen's honors list.* **3** credit or distinction: *to confer an honor on someone; a dubious honor; the great, high honor of being chosen "woman of the year"; He passed with honors; an honor student on the honor roll.* —*v.* to respect: *He felt honored by the invitation; All credit cards are honored* (= accepted) *here.* Also **hon.our** *Cdn.*

hon.or.a.ble (ON.ur.uh.bul) *adj.* having, showing, causing, or worthy of honor: *an honorable deed, exception, motive, place in history, way out; an **honorable discharge** from the army after years of faithful service; the **honorable member*** (= M.P.) *for York; He didn't qualify for an award but received an **honorable mention*** (= citation). —**the Honorable** [title prefixed to the names of various justices, cabinet ministers, speakers of legislatures, etc.]: *the Honorable (John Doe,) Minister of Finance.* —**hon.or.a.bly** (-uh.blee) *adv.* Also **hon.our.a.ble**, **hon.our.a.bly** *Cdn.*

hon.o.rar.i.um (on.uh.RAIR.ee.um) *n.* **-i.ums** or **-i.a** (-ee.uh) a voluntary fee offered for a professional service.

hon.o.rar.y (ON.uh.rair.ee) *adj.* given or done as an honor: *an honorary consultant, degree, position;* **hon.o.rar.i.ly** *adv.*

hon.or.if.ic (on.uh.RIF.ic) *adj.* conferring or showing respect. —*n.* an honorific word or title, as "Excellency" or "Sir."

honor roll *n.* a list of outstanding students.

honor system *n.* a system based on trusting people to observe the rules.

honour, honourable, honourably See HONOR, HONORABLE.

hood (short "oo") *n.* **1** a covering for the head and neck or something looking like one, as the fold of cloth over the back of a parka, an automobile engine's metal cover, a canopy over a cooking range or window, the expanded neck of a cobra, the crests of certain birds, etc.: *to check under the hood (of a car for mechanical problems); adj.:* **hooded** (= having a hood) *crow, pitcher plant, seal.* **2** [short form] hoodlum.

-hood *n.* suffix. **1** state or quality: *childhood, falsehood.* **2** group: *brotherhood, neighborhood.*

hood.lum (long "oo") *n.* a young ruffian, esp. a member of a street gang.

hoo.doo *n.* **-doos 1** a strange rock formation in the shape of columns formed by wind and water erosion.

2 *Informal.* bad luck or a person or thing bringing it. **3** same as VOODOO.
hood.wink (short "oo") *v.* mislead or dupe, as if by blindfolding.
hoo.ey (HOO.ee) *n. & interj. Slang.* nonsense; bunk.
hoof (short or long "oo") *n.* **hoofs** or **hooves** the hard, horny covering on the feet of animals such as horses, pigs, and cattle: *the cloven hoof* (= sign of Satan); *Retail meat costs several times what it is worth* **on the hoof** (= as live animals). —*v. Informal.* walk: *Let's hoof it to the store.* —**hoofed** *adj.* having hoofs.
hook (short "oo") *n.* **1** a curved or bent piece of stiff material, as metal or wood, for catching, as a *fish hook,* to hang things on, as a *coat hook,* or as in a **hook and eye** (= fastening device with a hook and a loop). **2** a strike or blow, as in boxing, given with a curving motion. —**by hook or by crook** by any means, fair or foul. —**off the hook** *Informal.* out of trouble; free of responsibility. —*v.* catch fish, etc. with a hook or get by a trick: *She hooked herself a customer.* —**hook up** connect or set up a radio, telephone, etc.
hook.ah (HOOK.uh, short "OO") *n.* an Arabian smoking pipe connected by a long tube to a vase of water through which the smoke is drawn to cool it.
hooked *adj.* **1** bent like a hook, having hooks, or made by hooking: *a hooked nose, rug.* **2** *Informal.* addicted: *One visit to California and you are* or *get hooked; to get* or *become hooked on drugs, romances, soaps.*
hook.er *n. Slang.* a prostitute.
hook.up *n.* a radio or telephone setup, esp. a network of radio and television stations.
hook.worm *n.* a small round worm that enters the body through the skin and attaches itself to the intestinal wall, living as a parasite and causing "hookworm disease."
hook.y *n.* usually **play hooky** *Informal.* stay out of school without permission.
hoo.li.gan (HOO.luh.gun) *n.* a hoodlum.
hoop (long "oo") *n.* a large ring, as one of the flat bands holding the staves of a barrel together, any of the flexible rings forming a frame to hold out a skirt (**hoop skirt**), or a ring (**hula hoop**) used for twirling around the hips.
hoop.la (short "oo") *n. Informal.* ballyhoo; hullabaloo: *What's all the hoopla about?*

hoo.ray same as HURRAH.
hoose.gow (*rhyme:* how) *n. Slang.* jail.
Hoo.sier (HOO.zhur) *n.* [nickname] a person of or from Indiana.
hoot (long "oo") *n.* **1** the cry of an owl. **2** *Informal.* the least bit: *She doesn't* **care** or **give a hoot** or **two hoots** *that your car is new, whether you can drive, or about anything at all;* "*Give a hoot* (= care a little), *don't pollute.*" **2** *Slang.* something laughably funny: *It was a real hoot to see the teachers in their Halloween costumes.* —*v.* shout in disapproval or scorn: *The audience hooted at the speaker; He was hooted off the stage.* —**hoot.er** *n.*
hoot.en.an.ny (HOO.tun.an.ee) *n.* **-an.nies** an informal folk-singing party.
hooves a *pl.* of HOOF.
hop *n.* **1** a short leap on one foot, as in hopscotch, or on both feet, as birds do, or on all fours, as frogs. **2** *Informal.* a short trip or plane flight: *It's a short hop from New York to Washington.* **3** *Slang.* dope, esp. opium. **4** a vine whose dried flower clusters, or **hops,** are used to flavor beer, ale, etc.
—*v.* **hops, hopped, hop.ping** make a hop: *to hop out of bed when the alarm goes; rabbits hopping across a field; He had to hop about with one foot in a cast; to hop* (= board) *a train; a fence low enough to hop* (= leap over). —**hop up** *Informal.* supercharge: *to hop up an engine.* —**hopped up** *Slang.* under the influence of narcotics. —**hopping mad** *Informal.* very angry.
hope *n.* **1** a confident belief that something will be realized as desired: *Any hope of success? to dash, dispel, raise, thwart someone's hopes; high hopes; I'm writing you in hopes of* or *in the hope of finding my lost luggage; to abandon, give up, stir up hope; to cherish, entertain, express, nurse, voice a hope; faint, false, fervent, fond, idle, illusory, realistic, slight, vain hopes; in high hopes; Hopes come true, fade; Not a flicker, glimmer, ray, spark of hope was left; The thing seemed beyond* or *past hope.* **2** the thing hoped for, reason for hoping, or a person one has hopes in: *She's the hope of the family.* —*v.* **hopes, hoped, hop.ing** wish and expect: *Let's hope for the best; I hope so; I hope not; She didn't hope to recover, but kept hoping against hope.* —**hope.less** *adj.;* **hope.less.ly** *adv.;* **hope.less.ness** *n.*
hope chest *n.* formerly, a young woman's box of clothes and furnishings kept in anticipation of marriage.
hope.ful *adj.* feeling or giving hope: *We*

hophead / horse

are hopeful of victory; a hopeful sign; *n*.: young medical-school hopefuls (= aspirants). —**hope.ful.ly** *adv*.: She waited hopefully for the results; Hopefully (Informal for It is hoped), everyone will pass. —**hope.ful.ness** *n*.

hop.head *n. Slang.* a drug addict.

Ho.pi (HOH.pee) *n.* **1** (a member of) a Pueblo Indian tribe. **2** their Shoshonean language.

hop.per *n.* **1** one that hops, esp. an insect such as the locust. **2** a container that is emptied from the bottom, as a railroad car for bulk freight such as coal, a seeding machine or drill, etc.: *Your application is* **in the hopper** (= to be considered in its turn).

-hopping *comb.form.* sampling or checking one after another: *bar-hopping; career-hopping; (TV) channel-hopping, job-hopping, restaurant-hopping, table-hopping (at a restaurant).*

hop.scotch *n.* a children's game played by hopping through the squares of a figure drawn on the ground to pick up a stone tossed into it.

horde (HORD) *n.* a crowd or throng, esp. one considered as invading or rapacious: *the Tartar hordes; hordes of children, locusts, shoppers, tourists.*

ho.ri.zon (huh.RYE.zun) *n.* **1** where earth and sky seem to meet: *Ships appear on the horizon.* **2** the limit of one's experience or perception: *travel for broadening one's horizons.*

hor.i.zon.tal (hor.uh.ZON.tul) *n.* a line, surface, direction, etc. that is level, not vertical: *far below the horizontal;* **adj.:** *a horizontal direction, plane, position; horizontal and vertical axes; the horizontal scanning lines of a TV picture; horizontal and vertical blinds; a gymnast performing on the* **horizontal bars.** —**hor.i.zon.tal.ly** *adv.*

hor.mone *n.* a chemical substance produced in a particular part of an organism, as adrenalin or auxin, to regulate functions such as growth, sex, and metabolism. —**hor.mo.nal** (-MOH.nul) *adj.*

horn *n.* **1** either of a pair of hard, bony projections on the head of a hoofed animal. **2** a similar protrusion, as on the head of a snail or insect. **3** the substance that horns, birds' beaks, hoofs, fingernails, etc. are made of. **4** a container hollowed out of horn. **5** a brass-wind instrument or other sounding device: *a hunting horn, French horn, automobile horn; to blow* or *sound the horn; to* **blow** or **toot one's own horn** (= to boast). —**on the horns of a dilemma** perplexed. —**take the bull by the horns** be bold. —*v.* **horn in** *Informal.* intrude or butt in *on* a conversation, etc.

horn.book *n.* a flat board with a handle, containing the alphabet, numbers, or similar elementary teaching material, protected by a sheet of clear horn, used in the days when paper was scarce.

horned *adj.* having horns or hornlike things: *the horned owl, toad.*

hor.net (HOR.nit) *n.* any of several large social wasps that give painful stings: *to stir up a* **hornet's nest** (= provoke an angry reaction all around).

horn of plenty same as CORNUCOPIA.

horn.pipe *n.* a lively dance, once popular among sailors, or the music for it, played on a wind instrument made partly of horn.

horn.y *adj.* **horn.i.er, -i.est 1** *Slang.* lustful or excited. **2** made of horn; also, hard or calloused.

ho.rol.o.gy (hor.OL.uh.jee) *n.* **1** the science of measuring time. **2** the art of making timepieces. —**ho.rol.o.gist** *n.* —**hor.o.log.i.cal** (-uh.LOJ.i.cul) *adj.*

hor.o.scope (HOR.uh.scope) *n.* an astrological forecast based on the signs of the zodiac.

hor.ren.dous (hor.EN.dus) *adj.* liable to instill horror: *horrendous cruelties and atrocities; horrendous red tape.*

hor.ri.ble (HOR.uh.bul) *adj.* **1** dreadful: *a horrible torture chamber.* **2** *Informal.* extremely unpleasant: *a horrible odor.* —**hor.rib.ly** *adv.*

hor.rid (HOR.id) *adj.* frightful: *such horrid manners!* —**hor.rid.ly** *adv.*

hor.rif.ic (hor.IF.ic) *adj.* causing horror.

hor.ri.fy (HOR.uh.fye) *v.* **-fies, -fied, -fy.ing** cause to feel horror; shock: *He was horrified by the atrocities; horrified at the prospect of death;* **adj.:** *a horrifying scene.*

hor.ror (HOR.ur) *n.* **1** fear mixed with revulsion: *the horror of a child witnessing a crime; They looked on in horror.* **2** something that causes such feeling: *a story full of horror and suspense; the horrors of wasteful government spending;* **adja.:** *a horror film, movie, story.*

hors de com.bat (or.duh.cawm.BAH) *French.* put out of action; disabled.

hors d'oeu.vre (or.DURV) *n., pl.* **-vres** (-DURVZ) an appetizer such as anchovies, canapes, or olives.

horse *n.* **1** a strong, four-legged, solid-hoofed animal with a mane and a long tail of hair, used for riding and for pulling or carrying loads: *to break in,* *harness, mount, ride, saddle, shoe a horse; Horses buck, canter, gallop, neigh, trot, whinny; a young horse (= foal); a female horse (= mare); a young female horse (= filly); a male horse (= stallion); a young male horse (= colt); a castrated male horse (= gelding); to **back the wrong horse** (= be on the losing side); to **flog a dead horse** (= continue discussing a dead issue).* **2** a piece of gymnasium equipment used for vaulting. **3** a supporting frame, as a clotheshorse or sawhorse. —**from the horse's mouth** *Informal.* authoritatively: *I got my facts straight from the horse's mouth.* —**horse of another** or **of a different color** a different matter. —**look a gift horse in the mouth** criticize something received as a gift. —*v.* **horse around** *Informal.* fool around.

horse.back *adv.* on a horse's back: *to ride horseback; horseback riding.*

horse chestnut *n.* a shade tree or shrub bearing spikes of tiny white flowers and large brown poisonous seeds resembling chestnuts.

horse.feath.ers (HORS.feth.urs, "th" as in "the") *n. & interj. Slang.* nonsense.

horse.flesh *n.* **1** the flesh of a horse. **2** horses collectively.

horse.fly *n.* **-flies** a large insect that sucks the blood of cattle and horses.

horse.hair *n.* a stiff fabric made of hairs from a horse's tail or mane: *horsehair stuffing for a sofa.*

horse.hide *n.* leather from horse's hide.

horse latitudes *n.* regions of calm air around the earth at about 30°N. and S. latitudes.

horse.laugh *n.* a boisterous laugh.

horse.man (HORS.mun) *n.* **-men 1** a cavalryman. **2** one who rides or manages horses. —**horse.man.ship** *n.*

horse opera *n. Slang.* a cheap western.

horse.play *n.* boisterous play.

horse.pow.er (HORS.pow.ur) *n.* a unit of engine power: *a 2,000-horsepower engine; The runner suddenly lost horsepower and started trailing.*

horse race *n.* **1** a race between horses. **2** a closely fought race.

horse.rad.ish (HORS.rad.ish) *n.* **1** a pungent relish made of the grated root of an herb of the mustard family. **2** this herb.

horse sense *n. Informal.* common sense.

horse.shoe (HORS.shoo) *n.* **1** a U-shaped metal plate nailed to a horse's hoof for protection. **2 horseshoes** *pl.* a game of pitching horseshoes so as to get them around a stake 40 feet (12.20 m) away. —*adj.* horseshoe-shaped: *a horseshoe magnet, table.*

horseshoe crab *n.* a crablike sea animal with a horseshoe-shaped shell and long, spiny tail.

horse.tail *n.* a rushlike plant with a hollow, jointed stem, used as "scouring rush" because it contains the abrasive silica.

horse trading *n.* buying and selling with much bargaining, many concessions, etc.

horse.whip *n. & v.* **-whips, -whipped, -whip.ping** (beat with) a whip for driving horses.

horse.wom.an (HORS.wom.an) *n.* **-wom.en** *fem.* of HORSEMAN.

hors.y or **hors.ey** (HOR.see) *adj.* **hors.i.er, -i.est** having to do with horses or horse racing: *the horsey set frequenting the racetracks.* —**hors.i.ness** *n.*

hor.ta.to.ry (HOR.tuh.tor.ee) *adj.* exhorting; giving advice.

hor.ti.cul.ture (HOR.ti.cul.chur) *n.* the science and art of gardening, esp. of fruit trees, vegetables, and flowers. —**hor.ti.cul.tur.al** (-CUL.chuh.rul) *adj.;* **hor.ti.cul.tur.ist** *n.*

ho.san.na (hoh.ZAN.uh) *n. & interj.* praise to God.

hose (HOZE) *n.* **1** *pl.* **hos.es** a tube of flexible material for watering, putting out fires, etc.: *a garden hose; to train a hose on a mob.* **2** *sing. & pl.* same as HOSIERY. **3** *sing. & pl.* tight breeches formerly worn by men. —*v.* **hos.es, hosed, hos.ing** put water on with a hose: *to hose a lawn; to hose down a stone-throwing mob.*

ho.sier.y (HOH.zhuh.ree) *n.* socks and stockings.

hos.pice (HOS.pis) *n.* **1** a lodging for travelers. **2** a home for the sick or poor.

hos.pi.ta.ble (HOS.pit.uh.bul, hos.PIT.uh.bul) *adj.* **1** kind and courteous to guests and others seeking hospitality. **2** receptive: *Is your boss hospitable to new ideas?* —**hos.pi.ta.bly** *adv.*

hos.pi.tal (HOS.pit.ul) *n.* an institution where sick and injured are treated.

hos.pi.tal.i.ty (hos.puh.TAL.i.tee) *n.* **-ties** friendly and generous treatment of guests and strangers: *warm hospitality; to extend, offer, show hospitality; to abuse someone's hospitality; The hospitality suite of a hotel is for guests to socialize in at a convention.*

hos.pi.tal.ize (HOS.pit.ul.ize) *v.* **-iz.es, -ized, -iz.ing** put a patient into a hospital for medical, surgical, or related care. —**hos.pi.tal.i.za.tion** (-luh.ZAY.shun, -lye-) *n.*

host (*rhyme:* most) *n.* **1** one who receives and accommodates or entertains a guest: *a city to* **play host** *to* (= host) *the Olympics.* **2** an emcee of a radio or TV show. **3** an organism such as a plant or animal on which a parasite feeds, or an embryo into which a graft is transplanted. **4** in a computer system, a central database or the controlling computer of a network of terminals: *IBM hosts;* **adja.**: *the host computer; in the host mode; the host prompt; a host system.* **5** a large number, originally an army: *hosts of relatives; a host of applications, features, objections, plans.* **6** a wafer used in Holy Communion. **7 Host** such a consecrated wafer: *the sacred Host.* —*v.* act as a host or emcee for a TV show or other event: *to host the Olympics.*

hos.tage (HOS.tij) *n.* a person handed over or seized and held as a pledge or guarantee: *Twenty passengers were taken hostage during the hijacking.*

hos.tel (HOS.tul) *n.* an inexpensive lodging: *a hostel for the homeless; a supervised* **youth hostel** *for traveling youth.*

hos.tel.er (HOS.tul.ur) *n.* a hostel guest.

hos.tel.ry (HOS.tul.ree) *n.* **-ries** an inn or hotel.

host.ess (HOH.stis) *n.* **1** a woman who entertains invited guests. **2** a woman who works in an entertaining or service role, as in managing a hotel, in a restaurant or dance hall, as an airline stewardess, etc.

hos.tile (HOS.tul, -tile) *adj.* **1** of an enemy: *a hostile army, force, ruler.* **2** unfriendly: *a hostile book reviewer; His attitude was openly hostile; He was received with hostile looks; a hostile mood; A hot climate is hostile* (= unsuitable) *to polar bears.* —**hos.tile.ly** *adv.*

hos.til.i.ty (hos.TIL.i.tee) *n.* **-ties 1** a hostile act or condition: *to arouse, display, express, feel, show hostility; to stir up hostility between people; the strikers' hostility to* or *toward management.* **2 hostilities** *pl.* war. *the outbreak of hostilities between Arabs and Israel; the suspension of hostilities after the Six-Day War.*

hos.tler (HOS.lur) *n.* **1** one who takes care of horses at an inn. **2** one who services a locomotive or truck between runs.

hot *adj.* **hot.ter, hot.test 1** having a high temperature: *Fire is hot; a hot day; hot weather; boiling, piping, scalding hot water.* **2** sharp or pungent to the taste: *a hot curry, pepper.* **3** similar in effect to high heat or something that is hot: *Running makes you hot; a hot* (= fiery) *temper; a hot* (= fresh) *scent; police in hot* (= very close) *pursuit of a getaway car; a place getting too hot* (= dangerous) *for lawbreakers; a hot* (= live) *wire.* **4** *Informal.* causing heat; excited or passionate: *Some like it hot; a hot* (= wanted) *criminal; hot* (= stolen) *merchandise; hot* (= fashionable) *jazz; Radio is a hot medium unlike movies and TV because of more listener participation.* **5** *Informal.* extremely interesting: *a hot tip; hot news; what is hot and what is not* (hot); *He's a good student but* **not so hot** (= rather mediocre) *in athletics.* —**make it hot for someone** *Informal.* make things uncomfortable. —**hot.ly** *adv.;* **hot.ness** *n.*

hot air *n. Slang.* empty talk or writing.

hot.bed *n.* a place of rapid growth, as a glass-covered bed of earth heated by fermenting manure: *Slums are the hotbeds of vice and crime.*

hot-blooded *adj.* easily excited; reckless.

hot.box *n.* a bearing overheated by friction, as at the end of an axle of a railroad car.

hot button *n.* a question of vital importance that triggers an immediate emotional reaction in people: *Safety has become a hot button for car buyers; to hit, push, touch the hot button;* **adja.**: *a hot-button issue.*

hot.cake *n.* pancake. —**sell like hotcakes** *Informal.* sell rapidly.

hot dog *n.* **1** a sandwich made with a hot frankfurter in a split roll. **2** *Slang.* a skier or skateboarder who performs stunts, esp. one who shows off. —*interj. Slang.* an exclamation of approval or enthusiasm. —**hot.dog** *v.* **-dogs, -dogged, -dog.ging** *Slang.* to show off, as skiers and skateboarders. —**hot.dog.ger** *n.*

ho.tel (hoh.TEL) *n.* a commercial establishment providing food and lodging, esp. for travelers: *Hotel guests check in and out all day; A* **hotel clerk** *registers guests.*

ho.tel.ier (oh.tul.YAY) *n.* hotel-keeper.

hot flash *n.* sensation of heat passing over the body, often experienced by women during menopause.

hot.foot *n.* **-foots** the prank of lighting a match in the welt of a shoe of an unsuspecting person. —*adv. Informal.* in haste. —*v.* **hotfoot it** *Informal.* go hastily.

hot.head *n.* a rash or fiery-tempered

person. —**hot.head.ed** adj.
hot.house n. a heated greenhouse.
hot line n. **1** a direct telephone or other communication line set up for a special use, as in a crisis: *The first hot line was set up* or *installed between Moscow and Washington in 1963; Parents of missing children called into or on the hot line when the police reported finding a body in the woods; an AIDS hot line.* **2** a phone-in radio or TV show.
hot potato n. *Informal.* a troublesome question or subject that no one wants to handle.
hot rod n. *Slang.* an automobile modified for fast acceleration and speeds. —**hot rod.der** (HOT.ROD.ur) n.
hots n.pl. *Slang.* strong sexual desire: *to have **the hots** for someone.*
hot seat n. *Slang.* a situation or position in which one is subject to harassment or criticism.
hot.shot n. *Slang.* one who is flashily skillful: *a hotshot of an amateur; hotshots from Harvard;* **adja.**: *a hotshot amateur; her hotshot husband; hotshot bankers, prices.*
hot spot n. **1** a popular resort or meeting place. **2** a scene of social unrest, trouble, or hostilities. **3** a polluted or contaminated area. **4** a region of great heat, as inside the earth or near a spreading fire.
hot tub n. a large wooden tub of hot water to sit and socialize in.
hot water n. *Informal.* trouble: *He found himself in hot water.*
hot.wire v. **-wires, -wired, -wir.ing** start a car engine by short-circuiting the ignition.
hound n. **1** a short-haired, long-eared hunting dog that tracks its prey by scent: *a pack of hounds.* **2** *Informal.* an enthusiastic pursuer: *autograph, party, publicity hounds.* —v. keep chasing: *a debtor hounded by creditors; The creditors hounded him to pay up; He was hounded out of office by the media when they learned about his past.*
hour (OUR) n. **1** one of the 24 periods of 60 minutes each into which a day is divided: *a clock that shows* or *tells the hour, minute, and second; It strikes every hour on the hour; the wee* or *small **hours** of the morning (from 1 a.m. on); Casual workers are paid by the hour; The next train leaves within an hour.* **2** a moment in time: *She thinks 4 a.m. is an ungodly hour for waking up; Friends helped him in his hour of need; Everyone gathered at the appointed hour; The hour of decision had arrived; her **finest hour** (= moment or* period of greatest glory); *We work from 09:00* [pronounced "nine hundred"] ***hours** to 17:00* **hours** (= from 9 to 5). **3** any fixed period: *Our lunch hour is from 12:30 to 1:15 p.m.; Our office* **hours** *are from 9 to 5; the morning and afternoon rush hour; Buses are more frequent during peak hours; the zero hour (when an event is to begin).* —**after hours** after the regular school or business hours. —**keep late, odd, regular, strange,** etc. **hours,** go to bed late, work during odd, regular, strange, etc. hours.
hour.glass n. a time-measuring device consisting of two glass bulbs containing enough sand or liquid to run for an hour through the narrow neck connecting the top bulb to the bottom one: *her shapely **hourglass figure** (that is narrow at the waist).*
hou.ri (HOOR.ee, HOW-) n. **-ris** a beautiful nymph of the Moslem Paradise.
hour.ly adv. by the hour: *Some are paid hourly;* **adj.**: *an hourly rate of pay.*
house n. **hous.es** (HOW.ziz) **1** a living place, esp. as an establishment, often including a family and servants, headed by a parent and managed by a "lady of the house" or a "man of the house": *to build, demolish, put up, renovate, tear down a house; brick, country, detached, dilapidated, frame, haunted, prefabricated, ramshackle, rooming, row, summer, town houses; a swallow's hanging house; a snail with its house on its back; a fraternity house; Father **keeps house** (= does the housework) nowadays.* **2** family including ancestors and descendants: *Elizabeth II is from the royal House of Windsor; the house of David.* **3** an organization or institution: *boarding, disorderly, gambling, halfway, mail-order, publishing, safe houses; a house of correction, detention; In the long run, the odds favor the house (= casino), not the gamblers; The drinks are **on the house** (= free).* **4** an assembly or audience: *They played to a full or packed house, not to an empty house; Is there a doctor in the house? We are holding an open house (when everyone is welcome to drop in); Her singing never fails to **bring the house down** (Informal for be loudly applauded).* —v. (HOWZ) **hous.es, housed, hous. ing** put into a house: *The refugees were housed in tents; old furniture housed in the attic.*
house arrest n. the confinement of an arrested person in his or her own house.

houseboat / however

house.boat *n.* a barge fixed up as a dwelling.
house.boy *n.* a male servant of a household.
house.break.ing (HOUSE.bray.king) *n.* the act of breaking into a house to commit a crime.
house.bro.ken (HOUSE.broh.kun) *adj.* of a domestic pet, trained to live in a house, esp. knowing where to defecate and urinate.
house.call *n.* a visit by a professional to the home of a client: *Few doctors make housecalls any more.*
house.clean.ing (HOUSE.cleen.ing) *n.* getting rid of bad conditions, as in cleaning a house and its furnishings.
house.coat *n.* a woman's long-skirted garment for casual indoor wear.
house.fly *n.* **-flies** the common two-winged fly.
house.hold *n.* a group of people such as a family living in a house: *to run a household.* **—adja.** domestic: *household articles, effects, expenses.*
house.hold.er (HOUSE.hole.dur) *n.* the head of a house of family and servants.
household word *n.* a familiar name or saying.
house.hus.band (HOUSE.huz.bund) *n.* a man who manages a household while his wife has an outside job.
house.keep.er (HOUSE.kee.pur) *n.* one who manages a household.
house.keep.ing (HOUSE.kee.ping) *n.* 1 washing, cooking, and such work; housework: *light housekeeping.* 2 bookkeeping, paperwork, and such domestic details of business management. **—adja.** having kitchen facilities: *a large housekeeping suite at $300 a day; a housekeeping cabin.*
house.lights *n.pl.* lights in a theater auditorium, as opposed to stage lights.
house.maid *n.* a female servant doing housework.
house.moth.er (HOUSE.muth.ur) *n.* a woman in charge of young people living together, as in a dormitory.
House of Commons *n.* the lower house of parliament.
house of ill fame *n.* a brothel.
house.plant *n.* a plant that may be grown indoors.
house sitter *n.* a person who looks after a house during the absence of its regular occupant.
houses of heaven *n.pl.* the 12 portions of the zodiac, each with its own sign and name.
house style *n.* rules for spelling, punctuation, etc. used by a publisher's editor.
house.top *n.* roof: *This is private, don't shout it from the housetops.*
house.wares *n.pl.* dishes, small appliances, and such kitchen equipment and household articles.
house.warm.ing (HOUSE.warm.ing) *n.* a party to celebrate one's moving into a new home.
house.wife *n.* **-wives** the woman head of a household. **—house.wife.ly** *adj.*
house.wif.er.y (HOUSE.wye.fuh.ree) *n.* housekeeping.
house wine *n.* in restaurants, a common brand of inexpensive white wine that goes with a variety of foods.
house.work *n.* washing, cooking, and other housekeeping work.
housing *n.* 1 the providing of shelter: *low-income, public, student, subsidized, substandard housing.* 2 houses collectively; lodging: *open housing without racial discrimination; overpopulation and housing problems.* 3 a frame, box, plate, etc. for holding a mechanical part in place. 4 an ornamental saddle cover.
hove (*rhyme:* drove) a *pt. & pp.* of HEAVE.
hov.el (HOV.ul, HUV.ul) *n.* a miserable dwelling; hut.
hov.er (HOV.ur, HUV.ur) *v.* be in a fluttering, suspended, or lingering state: *a hummingbird hovering over its nest; The patient hovered between life and death; The temperature outside hovered around zero.*
how *adv.* 1 in what way, state, condition, etc.: *Hello, how are you? She will show you how to do it; No one knows how this happened.* 2 to what degree, extent, effect, etc.: *How old are you? How do you mean? Tell us how much you're asking; How* (= at what price) *do you sell these goods?* 3 *Informal.* why: *How is that?* 4 by what name: *How are you known around here?* **—and how!** *Informal.* very much so! **—how about** what do you say to (something): *How about buying me a drink?* **—how come?** *Informal.* Why: *How come* (= Why is it that) *you're late?* **how do you do?** [used formally on being introduced] hello! **—***n.*: *the hows and whys of a situation.*
how.dah *n.* a canopied seat for riding on an elephant or camel.
how.dy (HOW.dee) *interj. Informal.* hello.
how.e'er (how.AIR) [poetical form] however.
how.ev.er (how.EV.ur) *conj. & adv.* 1 in whatever way or to whatever extent: *I*

couldn't persuade her however hard I tried; However did you manage that? **2** nevertheless; but: *I'm busy; however, I will come.*

how.itz.er (HOW.it.sur) *n.* a short gun for firing shells and such projectiles at a high angle and low velocity.

howl *n.* a long, loud, and mournful cry, as dogs and wolves: *It let out a howl of pain.* —*v.* **1** give a howl: *The child howled with pain; The wind was howling all night.* **2** yell or shout from amusement or scorn: *The speaker was mercilessly howled down; They howled at him; He was howled off the stage.*

howl.er *n.* **1** one that howls. **2** *Informal.* a ridiculous blunder.

howling *adj.* a. that howls: *howling winds; a howling* (= desolate) *wilderness; a howling* (*Informal* for great) *success.*

how.so.ev.er (how.soh.EV.ur) *adv.* in whatever way or to whatever extent; however.

how-to *adj.* giving practical instructions on how to do something: *a how-to book on carpentry.*

hoy.den (HOY.dun) *n.* a saucy or boisterous girl; tomboy; **hoy.den.ish** *adj.*

Hoyle (HOIL), in **according to Hoyle**, according to the rules; exactly.

hua.ra.che (wuh.RAH.chee) *n.* a flat, leather-thonged sandal worn in Latin American countries.

hub *n.* **1** the central part around which a wheel turns. **2** a center of activity: *a city that proudly calls itself "the hub of the universe."*

hub.bub (HUB.ub) *n.* **1** confused noise, as of a milling crowd. **2** uproar.

hub.by (HUB.ee) *n.* **hub.bies** *Informal.* husband.

hub.cap *n.* a metal cap covering the end of an axle.

hu.bris (HEW.bris) *n.* extreme arrogance.

huck.le.ber.ry (HUK.ul.ber.ee) *n.* **-ber.ries** a shrub of the heath family with blueberrylike fruit.

huck.ster (HUCK.stur) *n.* **1** a peddler of small articles. **2** a loud or petty sales rep. **3** *Slang.* an adman, esp. a producer of commercials.
—*v.* peddle or promote: *a commercial that hucksters holiday homes in Florida.*

hud.dle (HUD.ul) *n.* a closely packed group, as of football players between plays. —*v.* **1** crowd together: *The dog huddled in a corner of the room; The children huddled together in front of the TV;* **adj.**: *the huddled masses of refugees; They stood huddled in a group; sitting huddled over a stool.* **2** confer in a huddle: *The leaders huddled at the party headquarters.*
—**hud.dler** *n.*

hue (HEW) *n.* color, esp. as the modification of a basic color; tint: *Vermilion is a darker hue of red.*

hue and cry *n.* a shouting of alarm; outcry: *They raised a hue and cry over the referee's decision.*

hued *adj.* colored: *a brightly hued outfit; They're finely shaped and hued;* **cpd**: *many-hued, multi-hued, reddish-hued.*

huff *n.* a fit of peevish anger: *He protested and walked out of the room in a huff.*
—**huff.y** *adj.*

hug *v.* **hugs, hugged, hug.ging 1** clasp closely in an embrace. **2** cling or stay close to something: *a low-slung car that hugs the road; The bus moved forward, hugging the right side of the highway.*
—*n.* a close embrace. —**hug.ger** *n.*

huge (HYOOJ) *adj.* **hug.er, hug.est 1** very large: *a huge amount, belly, chunk, deficit, portion, quantity.* **2** great: *a huge demand, potential, success, undertaking.* —**huge.ly** *adv.*; **huge.ness** *n.*

hug.ger-mug.ger (HUG.ur.mug.ur) *n.* a confused condition; disorder.

Hu.gue.not (HEW.guh.not) *n.* a French Protestant of the 16th and 17th centuries.

huh *interj.* expressing contempt, surprise, question, etc.

hu.la (HOO.luh) *n.* a Hawaiian dance marked by swaying of hips and graceful gestures.

hula hoop *n.* a light hoop for twirling around the hips for exercise or as a toy; **Hula-Hoop** *Trademark.*

hulk *n.* a heavy, unwieldy, or clumsy person or thing, as an old ship or automobile that is out of service: *a rusted old hulk of a vehicle; the hulk of the Titanic; the concrete-and-glass hulks dominating our city skyline; a hulk of a beast; a lumbering hulk;* **adj.**: *a big hulking heavyweight of a man.*

hull *n.* **1** the outer covering of a fruit or seed. **2** the calyx of some fruits such as the strawberry. **3** the outer frame on which a ship or similar vessel floats: *the double hull of a submarine.*

hul.la.ba.loo (HUL.uh.buh.loo) *n.* **-loos** clamor or disturbance.

hum *v.* **hums, hummed, hum.ming** make a low, continuous sound with lips closed, as in sounding out a melody without words: *to hum a tune; an office humming with activity.* —*n.* a humming: *the hum of bees, machines, a busy concourse.* —**hum.mer** *n.*

hu.man (HEW.mun, YOO.mun) *adj.*

having to do with the form and characteristics of people: *the human body; a human error; "To err is human"; a human-interest story; human consumption, existence, resources, rights, weaknesses.* —*n.* a person, or **human being.** —**hu.man.ly** *adv.*; **hu.man.ness** *n.*

hu.mane (hew.MANE) *adj.* **1** kind and sympathetic: *humane treatment of prisoners; a humane society for the protection of animals.* **2** humanistic: *humane studies; Doctor of Humane Letters.* —**hu.mane.ness** *n.*

hu.man.ism (HEW.muh.niz.um, YOO.muh-) *n.* a movement or philosophy emphasizing human worth and values, as opposed to a supernatural or ascetic view of life: *secular humanism;* **hu.man.ist** *n. & adj.* —**hu.man.is.tic** (-NIS.tic) *adj.*

hu.man.i.tar.i.an (hew.MAN.uh.TAIR.ee.un) *adj.* having to do with promoting human welfare and happiness: *humanitarian agencies, aid, assistance, concerns, efforts, grounds, missions, work.* —*n.* a humanitarian person such as a philanthropist. —**hu.man.i.tar.i.an.ism** (-uh.niz.um) *n.*

hu.man.i.ty (hew.MAN.i.tee) *n.* -**ties 1** human beings as a whole; mankind: *the good of humanity; Since World War II, deportation of civilians has been considered a crime against humanity.* **2** a human or humane quality. **3 the humanities** *pl.* branches of learning concerned with culture, not science, as religion, philosophy, languages, literature, history, and the fine arts.

hu.man.ize (HEW.muh.nize, YOO.muh-) *v.* -**iz.es,** -**ized,** -**iz.ing** make or become human or humane; **hu.man.iz.er** *n.* —**hu.man.i.za.tion** (-nuh.ZAY.shun, -nye-) *n.*

hu.man.kind (HEW.mun.kined) same as MANKIND.

hu.man.oid (HEW.muh.noid) *n.* a nearly human creature, as prehistoric types such as the Neanderthal man and the androids of science fiction.

human rights *n.pl.* fundamental civil, economic, political, and social rights, as of a free human being; **adja.:** *a human rights activist, campaign, commission, group, organization, record, violation; human rights abuses, crimes, laws.*

hum.ble (HUM.bul) *adj.* -**bler,** -**blest** modest and unpretentious: *She rose from humble beginnings or surroundings; a woman of humble background; She's of humble birth or origins; the mighty and the humble; humble apologies, folk, homes, jobs, pleas; Start your exercise equipment with the humble jump rope at $4.95; In my humble view or opinion, you are mistaken; I'm your humble servant; She was forced to eat* **humble pie** (= to make a humble apology). —*v.* -**bles,** -**bled,** -**bling** make humble: *a proud man humbled in defeat; The king humbled himself in penance.* —**hum.ble.ness** *n.* —**hum.bly** (-blee) *adv.*

hum.bug *n.* a person or thing that is a fraud. —*v.* -**bugs,** -**bugged,** -**bug.ging** deceive or trick. —*interj.* nonsense!

hum.ding.er (HUM.DING.ur) *n. Slang.* someone or something that is extraordinary or striking; beaut.

hum.drum *adj.* commonplace or boring: *a humdrum routine.*

hu.mer.us (HEW.muh.rus) *n., pl.* -**mer.i** (-muh.rye) the bone of the upper arm or forelimb. —**hu.mer.al** *adj.*

hu.mid (HEW.mid) *adj.* of the air, moist or damp. —**hu.mid.ly** *adv.*

Hu.mi.dex (HEW.mi.dex) *n.* a measure of discomfort based on the combined effect of heat and humidity.

hu.mid.i.fy (hew.MID.uh.fye) *n.* -**fies,** -**fied,** -**fy.ing** make the air humid. —**hu.mid.i.fi.er,** *n.*

hu.mid.i.ty (hew.MID.i.tee) *n.* dampness, esp. the amount of it in the air.

hu.mi.dor (HEW.muh.dor) *n.* a container or apparatus for keeping tobacco moist.

hu.mil.i.ate (hew.MIL.ee.ate) *v.* -**ates,** -**at.ed,** -**at.ing** to humble or disgrace someone; hurt someone's self-esteem; *adj.: a humiliating defeat.* —**hu.mil.i.a.tion** (-AY.shun) *n.*

hu.mil.i.ty (hew.MIL.i.tee) *n.* -**ties** the quality of being genuinely humble; lack of false pride.

hum.ming.bird (HUM.ing.bird) *n.* a tiny American bird that makes a humming sound by the extremely rapid vibration of their wings when hovering.

hum.mock (HUM.uk) *n.* a small, rounded hill; knoll.

hu.mon.gous or **hu.mun.gous** (hew.MUNG.gus) *adj. Slang.* large in size or extent: *a humongous birthday cake.*

hu.mor.ous (HEW.muh.rus) *adj.* amusing or funny. —**hu.mor.ous.ly** *adv.*

hu.mor (HEW.mur) *n.* **1** an amusing quality, as of a funny or ludicrous situation. **2** the capacity to appreciate this: *a good sense of humor.* **3** an expression of it in speech or writing: *black, deadpan, earthy, gallows, infectious, irrepressible, slapstick, subtle, wry humor; a humor magazine.* **4** a state of mind; also, a fancy or whim: *to be in bad humor; in good humor; She's in no humor* to be the butt of practical jokes. —**out of humor** in a bad mood. —v. indulge: *Children, the sick, and the cranky have to be humored now and then.* —**hu.mor.ist** *n.*

humour *Cdn.* HUMOR.

hump *n.* a lumpy formation, as on the back of a camel or as a deformity, as of a hunchback, or **humpback**; **hump.backed** *adj.* —**over the hump** *Informal.* past a difficult period or phase. —*v.* arch: *A cat humps its back when excited.*

humph *n. & interj.* a snorting sound expressing doubt, dissatisfaction, etc.

humungous same as HUMONGOUS.

hu.mus (HEW.mus) *n.* the dark part of soil that is rich in decaying matter.

Hun *n.* 1 one of a warlike Asiatic people who invaded Europe in the 4th and 5th centuries A.D. 2 **hun** a vandal.

hunch *n.* 1 *Informal.* a feeling of what is going to happen: *I took the umbrella on a hunch; I had a hunch it was going to rain.* 2 a hump; *v.*: *He has a way of hunching over the table when eating; adj.: pupils* **hunched** *in concentration over their books; He sat hunched up in a sulky mood.*

hunch.back *n.* a person with a curvature of the spine; humpback.

hun.dred (HUN.drid) *n., adj. & pron.* ten times ten; 100 or C: *three hundred boys; there are 300 of them; hundreds* (= a large number) *of boys.*

hun.dred.fold (HUN.drid.fold) *n., adj. & adv.* (being) a hundred times as much as or as many.

hun.dredth (HUN.dridth, "th" as in "thin") *n. & adj.* (being) a 100th part.

hun.dred.weight (HUN.drid.wait) *n.* a unit of weight equal to 100 lb. (45.36 kg) in the U.S. and Canada.

hung *pt. & pp.* of HANG.
—**hung up** *Slang.* having a hang-up or mental fixation: *Sam is so hung up about age; a kid who is really hung up on sports; Al is* **hung up on** (= infatuated by) *every girl he meets.*

Hun.gar.i.an (hung.GAIR.ee.un) *adj.* having to do with **Hungary**, a country of C. Europe. —*n.* a person of or from Hungary or their language.

hun.ger (HUNG.gur) *n.* 1 pain or discomfort of the stomach because of the body's need for food: *to alleviate, appease, gratify, satisfy one's hunger.* 2 starvation: *People die of hunger during a famine; People go on a* **hunger strike** (= go without food) *to enforce demands or in protest.* 3 any strong desire or craving: *the hunger for knowledge.* —*v.* have such a desire: *A child hungers for*

affection; *to hunger after justice.*

hung jury *n.* a jury that cannot agree on a verdict.

hun.gry (HUNG.gree) *adj.* **-gri.er, -gri.est** feeling hunger or a similar strong desire: *a hungry stomach; the hungry eyes of starving people; People go hungry in poor countries; the Hungry Thirties of the Depression years; souls hungry for salvation.* —**hun.gri.ly** *adv.*

hunk *n. Informal.* 1 a well-built man: *quite a hunk of a fellow.* 2 a large chunk or slice: *a hunk of bread, cheese, meat; She popped a hunk of jello into her gaping mouth.*

hun.ker (HUNK.ur) 1 *v.* squat *down* on one's haunches: *They hunkered down till the shooting stopped.* 2 **hunkers** *n.pl.* haunches.

hun.ky-do.ry (hunk.ee.DOR.ee) *adj. Slang.* quite satisfactory; fine.

hunt *v.* 1 chase, harry, kill, or catch game for food or sport. 2 search: *to hunt down an escaped convict; Researchers hunt for information in the library; Police hunt up evidence; adja.: the* **hunt-and-peck** *method of typing.* —*n.* a hunting, search, or a group hunting party: *to organize a hunt for big game.* —**hunt.er** or **hunts.man** (-mun) *n.* **-men**; **hunt.ress** (-tris) *fem.*

Hun.ting.ton's disease (HUN.ting.tuns-) *n.* an inherited chorea marked by emotional outbursts, forgetfulness, and jerky movements. Also **Huntington's chorea.**

hur.dle (HUR.dul) *n.* 1 an obstacle or barrier to jump over: *to clear* or *take a hurdle.* 2 **hurdles** *pl.* a race in which the competitors have to clear many hurdles. —*v.* **-dles, -dled, -dling** jump over or overcome an obstacle. —**hur.dler** *n.*

hur.dy-gur.dy (HUR.dee.GUR.dee) *n.* **-dies** a hand organ or barrel organ played by turning a handle.

hurl *v.* throw with force or violence, as a javelin or spear: *The two boxers hurled themselves at each other; The mob started hurling insults at the speaker.* —*n.* a forcible throw: *a hurl of the discus.*

hurl.y-burl.y (HUR.lee.bur.lee) *n.* **-burl.ies** turmoil or uproar.

hur.rah (huh.RAH) *n., v. & interj.* shout of joy or approval; cheer. Also **hur.ray** (-RAY).

hur.ri.cane (HUR.uh.cane) *n.* a whirling tropical storm with winds of 73 mi. (117 km) per hour or more: *the eye of a hurricane; A hurricane hits* or *strikes, then blows itself out; adja.: with hurricane force; a hurricane warning, watch; A* **hur-**

ricane lamp or lantern has a chimney that protects its flame from winds.

hur.ry (HUR.ee) v. **hur.ries, hur.ried, hur.ry.ing** make haste, often with some excitement and confusion: *Hurry up if you want to be on time.* —*n.*: *We were in a hurry to catch the train; In the hurry, she forgot her purse.* —*adj.*: *a hurried departure, lunch, meeting; too hurried to notice anything;* **hur.ried.ly** *adv.*

hurt v. **hurts, hurt, hurt.ing** feel or cause pain physically or mentally: *She hit a stone and hurt her foot; The injured foot hurts; She hurt herself; She was badly hurt; He hurt her feelings by saying "no"; She was deeply hurt; It hurts to see her suffer.* —*n.* a feeling of pain: *The hurts were forgotten but the scars remained.* —**hurt.ful** *adj.* harmful.

hur.tle (HUR.tul) v. **-tles, -tled, -tling** rush or move with a clattering or rattling sound: *A train hurtles past at a crossing; The truck skidded and hurtled across the street into a shop window; Rocks came hurtling down the mountainside.*

hus.band (HUZ.bund) *n.* a male spouse: *devoted, doting, jealous, unfaithful husbands; a common-law husband.* —*v.* manage economically: *to husband one's resources, strength.*

hus.band.man (HUZ.bund.mun) *n.* -men [old use] farmer.

hus.band.ry (HUZ.bund.ree) *n.* farming: *animal husbandry* (= care of farm animals).

hush *n., v. & interj.* quiet or silence: *A hush fell over the audience as a ghost appeared on the stage; to* **hush up** *a secret by paying* **hush money** *to the person likely to tell.*

hush-hush *adj.* secret or confidential: *a hush-hush air, manner, subject.*

hush puppy *n.* a cornmeal fritter.

husk *n.* the outer covering of cereals, esp. corn. —*v.* remove the husk of a cereal. —**husk.er** *n.*

husk.y *adj.* **husk.i.er, -i.est 1** hoarse: *a husky voice.* **2** big and strong: *a man of husky build.* —*n.* **husk.ies 1** a husky person. **2** a hardy sled dog of the Arctic; also called "Siberian husky." **husk.i.ly** *adv.;* **husk.i.ness** *n.*

hus.sar (huh.ZAR) *n.* a light cavalryman, originally of Hungary.

hus.sy (HUZ.ee, HUS.ee) *n.* **hus.sies 1** a mischievous girl. **2** a lewd woman.

hus.tings *n. sing. & pl.* in a political campaign, the speaking platform or stage: *Candidates for election hit* or *take to the hustings; their performance at* or *on the hustings.*

hus.tle (HUS.ul) v. **-tles, -tled, -tling 1** act aggressively to get something done: *You have to hustle in times of unemployment; to hustle to find work.* **2** rush or push someone to get something done: *a child hustled off to bed after watching TV late; The gate-crasher was hustled out the door; Cabbies were hustling people for rides.* **3** sell aggressively or deceitfully: *a boy caught hustling stolen goods; Tickets to the game were being hustled for $500 each.* —*n.* **1** a hustling quality: *a used-car sales rep who lacks hustle* (= drive); *the hustle and bustle of a big city; He makes a living by some hustle* (Informal for racket) *or other.* **2** a ballroom dance using disco music. —**hus.tler** *n.*

hut *n.* a small, plain or crudely built dwelling or cabin.

hutch *n.* **1** a cupboard with shelves for dishes, etc.: *a combined buffet and hutch for the dining room.* **2** a pen or coop, as a rabbit cage; also, a shack: *a hatchback model of an automobile equipped with a hutch* (= a foldable tent).

hutz.pa or **hutz.pah** (HOOT.spuh) same as CHUTZPAH.

huz.za or **huz.zah** (huh.ZAH) same as HURRAH.

hy.a.cinth (HYE.uh.sinth) *n.* a garden plant of the lily family with spikes of fragrant bell-shaped flowers.

hy.ae.na (hye.EE.nuh) same as HYENA.

hy.brid (HYE.brid) *adj.* of mixed origin or structure, as the mule (from a jackass and a mare) or "oramon" (from "orange" and "lemon"): *"Talkative" is a hybrid word that is half English and half Latin; a hybrid variety of corn;* **n.**: *The mule, "oramon," and the word "talkative" are hybrids.* —**hy.brid.ism** *n.*

hy.brid.ize (HYE.bruh.dize) v. **-iz.es, -ized, -iz.ing** crossbreed; **hy.brid.i.za.tion** (-duh.ZAY.shun, -dye-) *n.*

hy.dra (HYE.druh) *n.* a tiny freshwater polyp with stinging tentacles like the snakelike heads of **Hydra,** a monster of Greek myth.

hy.dran.ge.a (hy.DRAIN.jee.uh) *n.* a shrub bearing large, showy clusters of white, pink, or bluish flowers.

hy.drant (HYE.drunt) *n.* a discharge pipe with a nozzle, connected to a water main and serving as a street outlet for water to put out fires: *to turn on a fire hydrant.*

hy.drate *n.* a chemical compound of a substance with a definite amount of water, usually a salt containing "water of crystallization," as blue vitriol, which is hydrated copper sulfate. —*v.* **-drates, -drat.ed, -drat.ing**

combine with water; **hy.dra.tion** (-DRAY.shun) *n.*; **hy.dra.tor** (-dray.tur) *n.*

hy.draul.ic (hye.DRAW.lic) 1 *adj.* working with water or liquid pressure: *a hydraulic brake; Hydraulic cement hardens under water; hydraulic engineering.* 2 **hydraulics** *n.pl.* [takes *sing. v.*] physics dealing with the behavior of liquids at rest and in motion. —**hy.draul.i.cal.ly** *adv.*

hydro (HY.droh) 1 *comb.form.* water or hydrogen-containing: *hydrocarbon, hydroelectric, hydroplane.* 2 *n. Cdn.* hydroelectric power, electricity as a utility, or an agency that distributes it: *Toronto Hydro; Our hydro was cut off*; *adja.*: *hydro bills, dams, equipment, lines; a hydro project; hydro power.*

hy.dro.car.bon (hye.droh.CAR.bun) *n.* a compound of only hydrogen and carbon.

hy.dro.ceph.a.lus (hye.droh.SEF.uh.lus) *n.* abnormal enlargement of the head from excess of fluids in the brain.

hy.dro.chlo.ric acid (hye.droh.CLOR.ic-) *n.* a highly corrosive acid with a strong odor, widely used in industry.

hy.dro.dy.nam.ic (HYE.droh.dye.NAM.ic) *adj.* having to do with **hydrodynamics**, the hydraulics of liquids in motion.

hy.dro.e.lec.tric (HYE.droh.i.LEC.tric) *adj.* having to do with the generation of electricity by water power. —**hy.dro.e.lec.tric.i.ty** (-lec.TRIS.i.tee) *n.*

hy.dro.foil (HYE.droh.foil) *n.* 1 a vessel that skims over water at high speeds using winglike structures attached to its hull. 2 such a structure.

hy.dro.gen (HYE.druh.jun) *n.* a gaseous element that combines with oxygen to form water.

hy.dro.gen.ate (HYE.druh.juh.nate, hye.DROJ.uh-) *v.* **-ates, -at.ed, -at.ing** combine or treat with hydrogen: *Oils are hydrogenated to improve their quality*; **hy.dro.gen.a.tion** (-NAY.shun) *n.*

hydrogen bomb *n.* an extremely powerful nuclear weapon whose energy is derived from the fusion of hydrogen atoms.

hydrogen peroxide *n.* a colorless compound of hydrogen and oxygen, used as an antiseptic and bleach.

hy.drol.o.gy (hye.DROL.uh.jee) *n.* the study of water, water vapor, and ice formations around the globe and their linkages in the oceans, the atmosphere, and in the ground.

hy.drol.y.sis (hye.DROL.uh.sis) *n., pl.* **-ses** (-seez) decomposition by chemical reaction with water, as in the making of soap, sugar, alcohols, etc.

hy.drom.e.ter (hye.DROM.uh.tur) *n.* an instrument for testing the specific gravity of liquids.

hy.dro.pho.bi.a (hye.druh.FOH.bee.uh) *n.* 1 abnormal fear of water, as in rabies. 2 rabies.

hy.dro.phone (HYE.druh.fone) *n.* an instrument for detecting sounds transmitted through water, as from a submarine.

hy.dro.plane (HYE.druh.plane) *n.* a motorboat whose hull is so shaped as to enable it to skim over water at high speeds.

hy.dro.plan.ing (HYE.druh.plain.ing) *n.* the dangerous gliding of a rubber-tired vehicle on a wet pavement when the vehicle reaches a critical high speed.

hy.dro.pon.ics (hye.druh.PON.ics) *n.pl.* [takes *sing. v.*] the growing of plants in water, with nutrients added, instead of in soil. —**hy.dro.pon.ic** *adj.*; **hy.dro.pon.i.cal.ly** *adv.*

hy.dro.sphere (HYE.drus.feer) *n.* the water covering the earth's surface, as oceans, lakes, and rivers, distinguished from the land surface, or lithosphere.

hy.dro.ther.a.py (hye.druh.THER.uh.pee) *n.* medical treatment using water, as whirlpool baths, showers, sprays, etc.

hy.dro.ther.mal (hye.druh.THUR.mul) *adj.* having to do with igneous activity involving heated water.

hy.drous (HYE.drus) *adj.* containing water in chemical combination.

hy.drox.ide (hye.DROX.ide) *n.* a chemical ion containing one atom of hydrogen and one of oxygen.

hy.e.na (hye.EE.nuh) *n.* a wolflike animal of Africa and Asia, considered cowardly, with a weird cry like a hysterical laugh: *a pack of hyenas.*

hy.giene (HYE.jeen) *n.* the observance and practice of health standards: *dental, feminine, mental, personal, public hygiene.* —**hy.gi.en.ist** (HYE.jee.nist, hye.JEE-) *n.*

hy.gi.en.ic (hye.JEE.nic, hye.jee.EN.ic) *adj.* sanitary or healthful; **hy.gi.en.i.cal.ly** *adv.*

hy.grom.e.ter (hye.GROM.uh.tur) *n.* an instrument for measuring humidity; **hy.grom.e.try** (-tree) *n.*

hying *a pres.part.* of HIE.

hy.men (HYE.mun) *n.* a membrane partially closing the entrance to the vagina in virgins.

hymn (HIM) *n. & v.* (sing) a song of

praise, esp. in honor of God.

hym.nal (HIM.nul) *n.* a collection of hymns; also **hymn.book**.

hype *n. Slang.* **1** exaggerated promotion; hence, deception: *The book needs a little luck and a lot of hype to sell well; hard-sell hype; the poetic hype of copywriters; the hype about the redeeming social value of cheap movies.* **2** same as HYPODERMIC. **3** a drug addict. —*v.* **hypes, hyped, hyp.ing 1** promote in a sensational manner: *the business of hyping sex and violence on TV; a movie hyped as a hot romance.* **2** falsify or fake: *to hype production costs; adj.: a hyped package; hyped prices; a heavily hyped cure.* **3** stimulate or excite, as by a drug injection: *People get hyped for hockey games; They are hyped up by all the hoopla; adj.: a hyped-up* (= phony) *sales campaign.*

hy.per (HYE.pur) *adj. Slang.* **1** overactive: *a hyper child.* **2** overexcited: *Let's not get hyper about it.*

hyper- *prefix.* more than normal: *hyperactive, hyperinflation, hypersensitive.*

hy.per.a.cid.i.ty (HYE.pur.uh.SID.i.tee) *n.* acid indigestion, as if from excess of stomach acid.

hy.per.ac.tive (hye.pur.AC.tiv) *adj.* more active than normal; overactive: *a hyperactive child.* —**hy.per.ac.tiv.i.ty** (HYE.pur.ac.TIV.i.tee) *n.*

hy.per.bar.ic (hye.pur.BAIR.ic) *adj.* of greater-than-normal pressure: *a hyperbaric chamber; hyperbaric oxygen treatment.*

hy.per.bo.le (hye.PUR.buh.lee) *n.* a figure of speech using exaggeration for effect, as in "She looked daggers." —**hy.per.bol.ic** (hye.pur.BOL.ic) *adj.*

hy.per.crit.i.cal (hye.pur.CRIT.i.cul) *adj.* too critical.

hy.per.gly.ce.mi.a (HYE.pur.gly.SEE.mee.uh) *n.* an abnormal level of glucose in the blood; **hy.per.gly.cem.ic** *adj.*

hy.per.in.fla.tion (HYE.pur.in.FLAY.shun) *n.* economic inflation that is gone out of control.

hy.per.mar.ket (HYE.pur.mar.kit) *n.* a supermarket combined with a department store.

hy.per.me.di.a (hy.pur.MEE.dee.uh) *n.* a linked information system of data, graphics, text, video, and voice.

hy.per.sen.si.tive (hye.pur.SEN.suh.tiv) *adj.* too sensitive; **hy.per.sen.si.tiv.i.ty** (-TIV.i.tee) *n.*

hy.per.ten.sion (hye.pur.TEN.shun) *n.* high blood pressure; **hy.per.ten.sive** *adj.*

hy.per.text (HYE.pur.text) *n.* a method of organizing large interconnected bodies of textual and graphic information on specific topics in such a way that it can be accessed by a user as desired.

hy.per.thy.roid (hye.pur.THYE.roid, "TH" as in "thin") *n. & adj.* (having to do with) an overactive thyroid gland or a person suffering from it. —**hy.per.thy.roid.ism** *n.* this condition, as in goiter.

hy.per.ven.ti.late (hye.pur.VEN.tuh.late) *v.* **-lates, -lat.ed, -lat.ing** (cause someone) to breathe abnormally fast and deep: *Saying No to someone makes her hyperventilate; The patient was placed on a respirator and hyperventilated to relieve the pressure in the skull.*

hy.phen (HYE.fun) *n.* a punctuation mark used to show word division, as in compound words like "high-level," or in syllable division, as at the end of a line.

hy.phen.ate (HYE.fuh.nate) *v.* **-ates, -at.ed, -at.ing** use a hyphen in a word or at the end of a line to divide it: *A word like "bell-like" should be hyphenated; adj.: "High-level" is a hyphenated compound word; hyphenated names like Smith-Jones and Anglo-American; hyphenated Americans of supposedly divided loyalties.* —**hy.phen.a.tion** (-NAY.shun) *n.*

hyp.no.sis (hip.NOH.sis) *n., pl.* **-ses** (-seez) a trancelike condition in which a subject will act according to the suggestions of the person who induces the condition. —**hyp.no.tist** (HIP.nuh.tist) *n.* —**hyp.not.ic** (hip.NOT.ic) *adj.*

hyp.no.tize (HIP.nuh.tize) *v.* **-tiz.es, -tized, -tiz.ing** induce hypnosis in a subject.

hy.po (HYE.poh) *n.* **1** same as HYPE. **2** *Informal.* a hypodermic syringe or injection.

hypo- *prefix.* beneath or less than: *hypocenter, hypodermic, hypothyroid.*

hy.po.cen.ter (HYE.poh.cen.tur) same as GROUND ZERO. Also **hy.po.cen.tre** *Cdn.*

hy.po.chon.dri.a (hye.poh.CON.dree.uh) *n.* abnormal anxiety over one's health; **hy.po.chon.dri.ac** *n. & adj.*

hy.poc.ri.sy (hi.POC.ruh.see) *n.* **-sies** a pretending to be what one is not, esp. very good or religious.

hy.po.crite (HIP.uh.crit) *n.* one who pretends to be good or religious. —**hyp.o.crit.i.cal** (-CRIT.i.cul) *adj.* —**hyp.o.crit.i.cal.ly** *adv.*

hy.po.der.mic (hye.puh.DUR.mic) *adj.*

hypoglycemia / ice bag

beneath the skin: *a hypodermic syringe with a hypodermic needle for giving a hypodermic injection.*

hy.po.gly.ce.mi.a (HYE.poh.gly. SEE.mee.uh) *n.* deficiency of glucose in the blood; **hy.po.gly.cem.ic** *adj.*

hy.pot.e.nuse (hye.POT.un.yoose, -oose) *n.* the side of a right triangle opposite the right angle.

hy.po.thal.a.mus (hye.puh.THAL.uh. mus) *n.* a part of the brain that regulates body temperature and helps control the working of the internal organs.

hy.po.ther.mi.a (hye.puh.THUR.mee. uh) *n.* body temperature that is dangerously lower than normal.

hy.poth.e.sis (hye.POTH.uh.sis, "TH" as in "thin") *n.* **-ses** (-seez) an assumed or likely explanation of a set of facts for further study or verification: *a working hypothesis; to advance* or *propose a hypothesis; Later discoveries confirmed our hypothesis.*

hy.poth.e.size (hye.POTH.uh.size) *v.* **-siz.es, -sized, -siz.ing** make a hypothesis; assume on the basis of a set of facts: *to hypothesize about what might happen; Columbus hypothesized that he could reach India if he sailed west.*

hy.po.thet.i.cal (hye.puh.THET.i.cul, "TH" as in "thin") *adj.* conjectural: *Who will start a nuclear war is a hypothetical question.*

hy.po.thy.roid.ism (hye.puh.THYE. roid. iz.um, "TH" as in "thin") *n.* underac- tivity of the thyroid gland, as in cretinism; **hy.po.thy.roid** *n. & adj.*

hys.sop (HIS.up) *n.* an evergreen shrub used in salads and soups and formerly in medicine.

hys.ter.ec.to.my (his.tuh.REC.tuh.mee) *n.* **-mies** surgical removal of the uterus.

hys.te.ri.a (his.TEER.ee.uh, -TER.ee. uh) *n.* uncontrollable excitement, as in a neurotic condition brought on by an unbearable situation: *In a fit of hysteria, she smashed all her china; Mass hysteria resulted in a stampede; War hysteria led to the jailing of innocent civilians.*
—**hys.ter.ic** (-TER.ic) *n. & adj.*

hys.ter.i.cal (his.TER.i.cul) *adj.* **1** wildly excited: *Let's not get hysterical about it; hysterical behavior, laughter.* **2** *Informal.* wildly funny: *a hysterical joke.*

hysterics *n.pl.* a fit of uncontrollable laughter or crying.

.... **I, i** ....

I or **i** (EYE) *n.* **I's** or **i's** **1** the ninth letter of the English alphabet. **2** the Roman numeral for "1." —*pron., objective* ME, *possessive* MY, MINE; *pl.* WE, *objective* US, *possessive* OUR, OURS. the person who is speaking or writing.

i.amb (EYE.am) *n.* a metrical foot of one unstressed syllable followed by one stressed, as in "the knéll of párting dáy" (3 feet).

i.am.bic (eye.AM.bic) *n.* an iamb or a verse of iambs; *adj.: iambic verse.*
—**i.am.bus** (-bus) same as IAMB.

-iatric or **-iatrical** *comb.form.* medical; medicinal: *geriatric, pediatric, psychiatric.*

-iatrics *comb.form.* treatment of disease: *geriatrics, pediatrics.*

-iatry *comb.form.* medical treatment: *podiatry, psychiatry.*

I.be.ri.an (eye.BEER.ee.un) *n. & adj.* (having to do with) the European peninsula containing Spain and Portugal, also called "the Iberian Peninsula."

i.bex (EYE.bex) *n.* **i.bex.es** a type of wild goat found in the Alps and the Himalayas.

i.bis (EYE.bis) *n.* a wading bird related to the herons.

-ible same as -ABLE: *admissible, audible, expansible, forcible, intelligible.*

-ic *suffix.* **1** *adj.* having to do with: *hysteric, poetic, scenic;* also **-ical. 2** *n.* a person or thing: *arithmetic, emetic, lunatic.*

ice *n.* **1** water frozen solid or as a layer: *to form, make, melt, produce ice; crushed, dry, pack ice.* **2** a frozen dessert of sweetened fruit juice without milk or cream; water ice. **3** *Slang.* diamonds. **4** *Slang.* a crystalline form of methamphetamine. —*v.* **ic.es, iced, ic.ing** cover with, become covered with, turn to, or make cool with ice: *The bridge ices in cold weather and gets slippery.* —**break the ice** make a start, esp. by overcoming some initial difficulty. —**cut no ice with someone** *Informal.* have no effect on someone. —**on ice** *Informal.* **1** in reserve: *The remaining applications were put on ice.* **2** safely assured: *The bargain is on ice.*
—**on thin ice** in a dangerous position.

ice age *n.* the glacial epoch, esp. the Pleistocene Epoch or the **Ice Age.**

ice bag *n.* a bag of crushed ice applied

to the body to relieve pain or inflammation.

ice.berg *n.* a huge piece of ice broken off from a glacier floating in the sea with only its tip showing above water: *The Titanic hit or struck an iceberg and sank.*

ice.boat *n.* a craft resembling a sailboat but equipped with runners for running on ice.

ice.box *n.* a cabinet with ice in it for keeping foods cold; also, a refrigerator.

ice.break.er (ICE.bray.kur) *n.* a ship that can plow or smash a way through ice.

ice.cap *n.* a large ice-covered area in the polar regions.

ice cream *n.* a frozen dessert of sweetened and flavored cream.

iced *adj.* 1 containing ice: *iced coffee, tea.* 2 coated with icing: *an iced cake; a cake iced with chocolate.* 3 chilled with ice: *The champagne is iced and ready to serve; an iced cocktail glass.*

ice floe *n.* a sheet of floating sea ice.

ice hockey *n.* a game played on ice by opposing teams of six each, wearing skates and equipped with sticks having curved ends to drive a disk, or puck, into the opposite side's goal.

ice.house *n.* a building in which ice is made or stored.

Ice.land.er (ICE.lan.dur) *n.* a person of or from **Iceland,** an island republic between Greenland and Norway.

Ice.land.ic (ice.LAND.ic) *n. & adj.* (having to do with Iceland, its people, or) the N. Germanic language of Iceland.

ice milk *n.* a dessert similar to ice cream but made with skim milk.

ice pack *n.* 1 an ice bag or similar application. 2 an expanse of masses of broken, piled-up ice.

ice pick *n.* a sharp-pointed tool for chipping or breaking ice.

ice skate *n.* a boot or shoe fitted with a metal runner or blade for skating on ice. —**ice-skate** *v.* **-skates, -skat.ed, -skat.ing.** —**ice-skater** *n.*

ice storm *n.* a storm in which rain freezes as it falls, coating everything with a glaze of ice.

ice water *n.* 1 water from melting ice. 2 water chilled for drinking.

ice.wine *n.* a very sweet dessert wine made from grapes that are left on the vine until they freeze.

ich.thy.ol.o.gy (ic.thee.OL.uh.jee, "th" as in "thin") *n.* the scientific study of fishes. —**ich.thy.ol.o.gist** *n.*

i.ci.cle (EYE.si.cul) *n.* a hanging piece of ice formed by the freezing of dripping water.

ic.ing (EYE.sing) *n.* a sweet, creamy mixture for coating cakes and such baked goods; frosting. —**icing on the cake** pleasure or benefit beyond what is expected.

ick.y *adj.* **ick.i.er, -i.est** *Informal.* disgusting and distasteful.

i.con (EYE.con) *n.* 1 an image or figure, as a picture symbol shown on a video display representing a task to be performed by the computer at the click of a mouse. 2 in the Eastern Orthodox Church, a sacred painting or mosaic; ikon.

i.con.o.clast (eye.CON.uh.clast) *n.* one who attacks an established belief or institution. —**i.con.o.clas.tic** (-CLAS.tic) *adj.*

-ics *suffix.* a subject of study; also, the characteristics of something: *acoustics, aesthetics, mechanics.*

ic.tus *n.* stress or accent in verse.

i.cy (EYE.see) *adj.* **i.ci.er, i.ci.est** 1 of, covered with, or like ice: *an icy road; soft icy tones with blues and greens; an icy numbness.* 2 cold: *an icy reception, stare, wind: It's* **icy cold** *in here.* —**i.ci.ly** *adv.;* **i.ci.ness** *n.*

I'd (IDE) I had; I should; I would.

id *n.* the unconscious part of the psyche responsible for one's instinctual drives seeking pleasure and gratification.

i.de.a (eye.DEE.uh) *n.* 1 a mental image, thought, or meaning; concept: *Words express ideas; This was not my idea of a picnic; She has hit upon a new idea; to communicate, disseminate ideas; to dismiss, endorse, entertain, favor, implement, reject, toy with an idea; brilliant, clear, clever, crazy, daring, fixed, fantastic, farfetched, fresh, ingenious, novel, rough, silly, vague ideas; not the faintest or slightest idea what he means; Do you* **get the idea** (= understand)? 2 plan or scheme: *What's the big idea? a man of* **ideas** (= resourcefulness).

i.de.al (eye.DEE.ul, eye.DEEL) *n.* 1 a perfect type: *King Arthur as the ideal of chivalry.* 2 a goal to achieve: *a woman of high, lofty, noble ideals; to attain or realize an ideal.* —*adj.* 1 perfect: *This is ideal weather for a picnic.* 2 abstract or imaginary: *A geometrical point is a purely ideal concept.* —**i.de.al.ly** *adv.*

i.de.al.ism (eye.DEE.uh.liz.um, -DEEL.iz.um) *n.* 1 thought or behavior based on how things ought to be rather than how they are in reality; hence, the neglecting of practical matters. 2 in

idealize / idyll

art, literature, etc., representation of imagined types rather than of exact likenesses. —**i.de.al.ist** n.
—**i.de.al.is.tic** (-uh.LIS.tic) adj.; **i.de.al.is.ti.cal.ly** adv.

i.de.al.ize (eye.DEE.uh.lize, -DEEL.ize) v. **-iz.es, -ized, -iz.ing** 1 form an ideal: *We can't idealize from a few instances.* 2 think of as ideal: *Children sometimes idealize teachers;* **adj.**: *an idealized character, figure, image, model, past, self-image, view, vision of reality.* —**i.de.al.i.za.tion** (-luh.ZAY.shun, -lye-) n.

i.de.ate (EYE.dee.ate) v. **-ates, -at.ed, -at.ing** form ideas; form the idea of something; **i.de.a.tion** (-AY.shun) n.

i.dem (EYE.dem, EE-) pron. the same as mentioned already.

i.den.ti.cal (eye.DEN.ti.cul) adj. exactly alike: *the identical voice I heard yesterday; two men wearing identical ties; One tie is identical to or with the other; Unlike fraternal twins,* **identical twins** *develop from the same egg cell.*

i.den.ti.fy (eye.DEN.tuh.fye) v. **-fies, -fied, -fy.ing** 1 know or establish the identity of a person or thing; recognize: *Can you identify that voice? A voice can be identified by the speaker's accent; We can identify two main issues in this campaign.* 2 associate: *He's reluctant to identify (himself) with the radicals.* 3 empathize: *a dramatic character with whom the audience identifies.* —**i.den.ti.fi.a.ble** (-FYE.uh.bul) adj. —**i.den.ti.fi.ca.tion** (-fuh.CAY.shun) n.

i.den.ti.ty (eye.DEN.ti.tee) n. **-ties** 1 sameness: *We work together because of identity of interests.* 2 who somebody or what something is: *to establish the identity of an anonymous caller; a case of mistaken identity; A mask hides your identity; Come out and reveal your identity; Show your* **identity card** *as proof of your name and age; an adolescent suffering an* **identity crisis** *because of internal changes and social pressures.* 3 individuality: *Multiculturalism gives people of various origins a sense of identity; cultural identity.*

id.e.o.gram or **id.e.o.graph** (ID.ee.uh.gram, -graf, EYE-) n. a symbol such as a Chinese character or a picture that anyone can understand, as in pictographs, that stands for a whole idea instead of the words for it.

i.de.ol.o.gy (eye.dee.OL.uh.jee, id.ee-) n. **-gies** a set of doctrines characteristic of a person, group, or class: *Communist and capitalist ideologies.*
—**i.de.o.log.i.cal** (-uh.LOJ.i.cul) adj.

ides n. *sing. & pl.* in the ancient Roman calendar, the 15th of March, May, July, or October or the 13th of any other month.

id.i.o.cy (ID.ee.uh.see) n. **-cies** 1 great stupidity, as of an idiot. 2 a stupid expression or action.

id.i.om (ID.ee.um) n. 1 a particular language or dialect with its distinctive characteristics: *Shakespeare wrote in the idiom of the Elizabethans.* 2 an expression that is peculiar to a particular language: *"Get one's goat" is an idiom that is hard to translate into another language.* 3 an individualistic style: *the Shakespearean idiom.* —**id.i.o.mat.ic** (-uh.MAT.ic) adj.

id.i.o.syn.cra.sy (ID.ee.uh.SINC.ruh.see) n. **-sies** a peculiarity of style or behavior, as a mannerism, a writer's style, or one's reaction to a drug.
—**id.i.o.syn.crat.ic** (-sinc.RAT.ic) adj.

id.i.ot (ID.ee.ut) n. a very stupid person: *blithering, blooming, perfect idiots; the village idiot; "Stupid idiot" doesn't make sense to me.* —**id.i.ot.ic** (-ee.OT.ic) adj.; **id.i.ot.i.cal.ly** adv.

idiot box n. *Slang.* a television set; hence, TV.

idiot card n. *Slang.* a cue card for prompting a performer.

i.dle (EYE.dul) adj. **i.dler, i.dlest** 1 not active: *Money lies idle if not invested; Machinery stands idle during a strike; an idle but not lazy worker who happens to be on strike; an idle mind.* 2 lazy: *the idle rich; "Idle folks have the most labor."* 3 useless or worthless: *idle conversations, curiosity, gossip, pleasures, rumors, threats; It's idle to deny that the earth is round.* —v. **i.dles, i.dled, i.dling**: *workers idled by layoffs; to idle away* (= waste) *a summer; An automobile left idling* (= with the engine running but not engaged) *wastes gas.* —**i.dler** n.
—**i.dle.ness** n. —**i.dly** adv.

i.dol (EYE.dul) n. 1 an object of worship, esp. a statue; hence, a false god: *the worship of idols.* 2 an object of ardent admiration: *a fallen idol; matinee idols; movie idols.*

i.dol.a.try (eye.DOL.uh.tree) n. **-tries** idol worship. —**i.dol.a.ter** or **i.dol.a.tor** n. —**i.dol.a.trous** (-trus) adj.

i.dol.ize (EYE.duh.lize) v. **-iz.es, -ized, -iz.ing** regard or treat as an idol: *She was idolized as the incarnation of beauty;* **adj.**: *Mammon is wealth* **idolized**; *the idolized Elvis.*

i.dyll or **i.dyl** (EYE.dul) n. 1 a simple, charming, and picturesque, hence, usually rural scene or description: *the idylls of Theocritus.* 2 story: *Tennyson's "Idylls of the King" are stories about King*

Arthur; *idylls of family life.*

i.dyl.lic (eye.DIL.ic) *adj.* full of beauty and peace: *an idyllic existence without cares and worries; in the idyllic surroundings of a country home; an idyllic holiday, scene, setting, valley.*

if *conj.* **1** in case: *You'll get wet if it rains; I wouldn't do it if I were you; Please fly over, if at all possible.* **2** whether: *Ask if she will come.* **3** granting or allowing; even: *It will cost only $10, if that; Few, if any, lives were lost; I don't believe in UFOs because they are,* **if anything,** *illusions.* **4** though: *a welcome if unexpected change;* **as if** *I didn't know.* —*n.* condition: *It's a big if whether nuclear arms will be eliminated; Your money will be refunded with no* **ifs, ands,** or **buts.**

if.fy (IF.ee) *adj.* **if.fi.er, if.fi.est** *Informal.* uncertain or chancy: *The outcome is iffy.*

ig.loo (IG.loo) *n.* **-loos** a dome-shaped Inuit dwelling made of blocks of compact snow.

ig.ne.ous (IG.nee.us) *adj.* fiery; also, formed by the cooling of melted, usually volcanic material: *Pumice and granite are igneous rocks.*

ig.nite (ig.NITE) *v.* **-nites, -nit.ed, -nit.ing** catch or set on fire.
—**ig.nit.a.ble** (-tuh.bul) *adj.*

ig.ni.tion (ig.NISH.un) *n.* **1** an igniting: *accidental ignition of sleepwear; spontaneous ignition; the ignition of the fire;* **adja.:** *an ignition device; the ignition temperature.* **2** an apparatus or device for igniting the fuel in an engine: *The car keys are* **in the ignition;** *to turn or turn on, turn off or switch off the ignition;* **adja.:** *an ignition key; the ignition timing; a rocket's ignition system.*

ig.no.ble (ig.NO.bul) *adj.* not noble; shameful: *an ignoble end.* —**ig.no.bly** *adv.*

ig.no.min.y (IG.nuh.min.ee) *n.* **-min.ies** **1** disgrace or humiliation: *the ignominy of defeat.* **2** a disgraceful action, quality, or outcome: *He was subjected to many ignominies as a war prisoner.*
—**ig.no.min.i.ous** (-MIN.ee.us) *adj.;* **ig.no.min.i.ous.ly** *adv.*

ig.no.ra.mus (ig.nuh.RAY.mus) *n.* **-mus.es** an ignorant person.

ig.no.rance (IG.nuh.runce) *n.* the state of being ignorant: *abysmal, blissful, profound, total ignorance of* or *about the facts; to act in ignorance of the facts; to betray, display, show ignorance.*

ig.no.rant (IG.nuh.runt) *adj.* **1** lacking knowledge or education: *an ignorant answer, rustic.* **2** unaware: *He was ignorant of what went on behind his back.*

—**ig.no.rant.ly** *adv.*

ig.nore (ig.NOR) *v.* **-nores, -nored, -nor.ing** pay no attention to a person or thing: *to ignore an insult; Facts cannot be ignored; Dreams are best ignored;* **adj.:** *He felt* **ignored** *by the others; largely, virtually, wisely ignored; the long-ignored rights of women.*

i.gua.na (ig.WAH.nuh) *n.* a tropical New World lizard.

i.ke.ba.na (ee.kay.BAH.nah) *n.* the Japanese art of arranging flowers.

i.kon (EYE.con) *n.* a sacred painting or mosaic; icon.

il.e.i.tis (il.ee.EYE.tis) *n.* inflammation of the ileum.

il.e.um (IL.ee.um) *n., pl.* **il.e.a** (-uh) the lower portion of the small intestine.
—**il.e.ac** *adj.*

il.i.ac (IL.ee.ac) *adj.* having to do with the ilium.

il.i.um (IL.ee.um) *n.* the winglike portion of the hip bones.

ilk *n.* kind or class: *people* **of that** or **her** or **his** or **their ilk.**

I'll (ILE) I will; I shall.

ill *adj.* & *adv. comp.* **worse** (WURSE), *superl.* **worst** (WURST). —*adj.* **1** bad: *to stir up ill feeling among friends; He bore no one ill will; The place has fallen into ill repute.* **2** sick: *He's ill with the flu; She's fallen ill too; Everyone is taken ill and has gone home; to be desperately, gravely, seriously, terminally ill; All are physically ill; No one is emotionally or mentally ill; Lu is a little nervous and* **ill at ease** (= uncomfortable) *in company.*
—*adv.* badly: *He never speaks ill of his neighbors; She fared ill at the examination; He was generous when he could ill* (= scarcely) *afford to be.* —*n.* something bad, esp. sickness or evil: *the ills of our mortal existence, of our society.*
—*comb.form.* **1** badly: *ill-conceived, ill-considered, ill-defined, ill-equipped, ill-fitting, ill-founded, ill-informed, ill-prepared, ill-suited, ill-timed, ill-trained,* **2** bad: *ill-health, ill-treatment, ill-wisher.*

ill-advised *adj.* acting or done without good advice or proper consideration: *You would be ill-advised to call in sick when you want to go out shopping; an ill-advised move.* —**ill.ad.vis.ed.ly** (-VYE.zid.lee) *adv.*

ill-bred *adj.* badly brought up; rude: *an ill-bred cad.*

ill-disposed *adj.* unsympathetic: *We are ill-disposed to listen to complaints on a Monday morning; People are ill-disposed toward chronic complainers.*

il.le.gal (i.LEE.gul) *adj.* against the law,

esp. not permitted by the rules: *It is illegal to go through a red light; If you specify Drive 3 with only two on-line, that's illegal; an illegal move in chess; illegal possession of firearms; an illegal alien, immigrant.* —*n.* one who enters a country illegally. —**il.le.gal.ly** *adv.*
il.le.gal.i.ty (il.ee.GAL.i.tee) *n.* **-ties** 1 unlawfulness. 2 an illegal act.
il.leg.i.ble (i.LEJ.uh.bul) *adj.* impossible to read; **il.leg.i.bly** *adv.*
—**il.leg.i.bil.i.ty** (-BIL.i.tee) *n.*
il.le.git.i.mate (il.uh.JIT.uh.mit) *adj.* 1 born of parents not married to each other: *an illegitimate child, daughter, son.* 2 contrary to law, custom, or logic: *an illegitimate claim to property; an illegitimate conclusion, expression, use of funds.* —**il.le.git.i.mate.ly** *adv.*
—**il.le.git.i.ma.cy** (-uh.muh.see) *n.*
ill-fated *adj.* with an evil fate; unlucky: *the ill-fated voyage of the Titanic.*
ill-favored *adj.* ugly; also, unpleasant.
ill-gotten *adj.* obtained by evil means: *ill-gotten advantages, gains, goods, wealth.*
ill-humored *adj.* irritable; sullen.
il.lib.er.al (il.LIB.uh.rul) *adj.* narrow-minded; also, stingy.
il.lic.it (i.LIS.it) *adj.* not allowed by law or by the rules: *an illicit act, love affair, relationship; illicit sale of drugs; illicit trade.*
il.lim.it.a.ble (i.LIM.i.tuh.bul) *adj.* without limit; measureless; **il.lim.it.a.bly** *adv.*
il.lit.er.ate (i.LIT.ur.it) *adj.* 1 uneducated, esp. not knowing how to read or write. 2 lacking basic knowledge in one's field of study. —*n.* an illiterate person: *a functional illiterate who can't fill out an application for a job.*
—**il.lit.er.a.cy** (-ur.uh.see) *n.* **-cies.**
ill-mannered *adj.* having bad manners; rude.
ill-natured *adj.* of a mean disposition; disagreeable. —**ill-naturedly** *adv.*
ill.ness *n.* sickness: *to get over a slight illness; grave, mental, serious, sudden, terminal illnesses.*
il.log.i.cal (i.LOJ.i.cul) *adj.* not logical or sensible. —**il.log.i.cal.ly** *adv.*
—**il.log.i.cal.i.ty** (-CAL.i.tee) *n.* **-ties.**
ill-starred *adj.* ill-fated; unlucky.
ill-suited *adj.* badly suited; unsuitable.
ill-tempered *adj.* having a bad temper; irritable.
ill-timed *adj.* coming at the wrong time; inopportune.
ill-treat *v.* treat cruelly or unfairly; **ill-treatment** *n.*
il.lu.mi.nate (i.LOO.muh.nate) *v.* **-nates, -nated, -nating** 1 supply with light: *Gas lamps used to illuminate our streets; a neighborhood illuminated* (= decorated) *by Christmas lights.* 2 make clear or explain: *to illuminate an obscure passage;* *adj.*: *a very illuminating discussion.* 3 decorate initial letters, borders, etc. of a manuscript with colors and designs, as in the Middle Ages; *adj.*: *an illuminated manuscript.* Also **il.lu.mine** (i.LOO.min), **-mines, -mined, -min.ing.** —**il.lu.mi.na.tion** (-NAY.shun) *n.*
ill-usage *n.* ill-treatment; ill-use.
ill-use *n.* (IL.yoose) & *v.* (il.YOOZ) **-us.es, -used, -us.ing** (subject to) bad treatment.
il.lu.sion (i.LOO.zhun) *n.* a misleading effect produced on the eye or mind: *the illusion of movement produced by a series of still pictures; an optical illusion; He was under the illusion* (= false belief) *that wealth would make him happy; to cherish, create, dispel, harbor an illusion.*
il.lu.so.ry (i.LOO.suh.ree) *adj.* based on or due to an illusion; deceptive: *illusory hopes; an illusory peace; military prowess that is mostly illusory.* Also **il.lu.sive.**
il.lus.trate (IL.us.trate) *v.* **-trates, -trat.ed, -trat.ing** 1 provide with pictures, diagrams, etc.: *to illustrate a book, lecture; We illustrate word meanings with examples of usage.* 2 make clear or lucid: *Falling objects illustrate gravity.*
—**il.lus.tra.tor** (-tray.tur) *n.*
il.lus.tra.tion (il.us.TRAY.shun) *n.* an example or picture that illustrates: *Meanings are explained in this dictionary by illustration in context more than by definitions; verbal, not pictorial illustrations; to give, offer, provide an illustration; to draw an illustration* (= analogy).
il.lus.tra.tive (i.LUS.truh.tiv, IL.us.tray.tiv) *adj.* serving to illustrate: *an illustrative example; sentences that are illustrative of word meanings.*
il.lus.tri.ous (i.LUS.tree.us) *adj.* brilliantly eminent or distinguished: *our illustrious predecessors; an illustrious career, family, name;* **il.lus.tri.ous.ly** *adv.;* **il.lus.tri.ous.ness** *n.*
ill will *n.* dislike; hostility.
I'm (IME) I am.
im.age (IM.ij) *n.* 1 a graphic, optical, or electronic representation of a scene or object, as in a mirror, photograph, on TV, etc.: *a mirror image; a visual image; an image reflected in water.* 2 likeness: *the very image of her father; a spitting image of her mother; "God created man in his own image."* 3 a physical representation, as a statue or idol: *the worship*

imagery / imitation

of images. **4** a mental picture or concept: *the ivory-tower image of bankers; the corporate image of our company projected through the media; an image they didn't want to promote; They hired a public-relations firm to improve their public image.* **5** the expression of a mental concept, esp. a simile or metaphor: *drama as the image of life; the images of death in Shakespeare's plays.* —*v.* **-ag.es, -aged, -ag.ing 1** form an image of an object: *a bust of the king imaged in bronze; a slide that images sharply on the screen; The two are imaged as con men in the movie;* **n.**: *brain imaging; photographic imaging;* **adj.**: *an imaging device, process, system, technique; imaging software, technology.* **2** imagine: *a scene that is hard to image.*

im.age.ry (IM.ij.ree) *n.* mental images or their figurative expression, as in poetry: *poetry full of vivid imagery.*

i.mag.i.na.ble (i.MAJ.uh.nuh.bul) *adj.* capable of being visualized: *the worst imaginable scenario of a tragedy; the most beautiful sight imaginable;* **i.mag.i.na.bly** *adv.*

i.mag.i.nar.y (i.MAJ.uh.nair.ee) *adj.* not real but imagined: *UFOs may not be entirely imaginary; Many of our fears are imaginary; the imaginary square root of a negative quantity.*

i.mag.i.na.tion (i.maj.uh.NAY.shun) *n.* the power to imagine: *the fertile imagination of storytellers; to defy, excite, fire, stagger, stir someone's imagination; to use one's imagination; Try to see it in your imagination; an active, creative, feeble, lively, wild imagination; By no stretch of the imagination could such a thing happen; A resourceful executive has imagination and judgment; Your ghost story sounds like mere imagination* (= use of imagining power or an imagined object) *to me.*

i.mag.i.na.tive (i.MAJ.uh.nuh.tiv) *adj.* **1** able to picture things or form new ideas: *an imaginative child; Ida is imaginative but Ada is more practical.* **2** having to do with the imagination: *an imaginative answer; imaginative literature.* —**i.mag.i.na.tive.ly** *adv.*

i.mag.ine (i.MAJ.in) *v.* **-ines, -ined, -in.ing 1** form an image of something: *Imagine yourself flying like a bird.* **2** think or conceive of something: *Can you imagine someone living without TV for a whole year? I can imagine her becoming or as our next prime minister; I imagine* (= suppose) *that's what she wants to be.*

im.ag.ism (IM.uh.ji.zum) *n.* a school of poetry of the early 1900's stressing the use of clear images, free rhythms, and exact words from common speech: *Ezra Pound was the chief imagist.* —**im.ag.ist** *n.*

i.ma.go (i.MAY.goh) *n.* **i.ma.gos** or **i.mag.i.nes** (-MAY.guh.neez) an adult insect as it comes out of the pupa stage.

im.bal.ance (im.BAL.unce) *n.* lack of balance or proportion, as between two aspects of the same thing: *to correct the imbalance between our earning power and our spending habits; affirmative action to redress the imbalance in our hiring policies.*

im.be.cile (IM.buh.sul) *n.* one who is very foolish or stupid. —**im.be.cil.ic** (-SIL.ic) *adj.* —**im.be.cil.i.ty** (-SIL.i.tee) *n.*

im.bibe (im.BIBE) *v.* **-bibes, -bibed, -bib.ing 1** to drink, esp. alcoholic liquor. **2** absorb an atmosphere, ideas, principles, etc.: *You go to Paris to imbibe the true French spirit.*

im.bri.cate (IM.bruh.cate) *v.* **-cates, -cat.ed, -cat.ing** overlap, as fish scales, tiles, shingles, etc. —*adj.* (-kit) overlapping; also, ornamented with such a pattern. —**im.bri.ca.tion** (-CAY.shun) *n.* an overlapping (pattern).

im.bro.glio (im.BROLE.yoh) *n.* **-glios** a complicated and confusing situation, as in drama or politics.

im.brue (im.BROO) *v.* **-brues, -brued, -bru.ing** soak or stain with the blood of slaughter.

im.bue (im.BEW) *v.* **-bues, -bued, -bu.ing** soak or permeate; hence, inspire: *His teachers imbued him with the ambition to become a doctor; to be imbued with an idea, principle, spirit.*

im.i.ta.ble (IM.i.tuh.bul) *adj.* that can be imitated.

im.i.tate (IM.i.tate) *v.* **-tates, -tat.ed, -tat.ing** be, look, or act like another person or thing: *a successful novelist as a model for aspiring writers to imitate* (= emulate); *Do not imitate* (= mimic) *people as an ape or parrot does; She can imitate* (= reproduce) *any bird call; wallpaper imitating* (= resembling) *wood paneling.* —**im.i.ta.tor** (-tay.tur) *n.*

im.i.ta.tion (im.i.TAY.shun) *n.* an act of imitating or something that is a copy: *art as the imitation of life; "Imitation is the sincerest form of flattery"; Beware of cheap imitations; This is a pale imitation* (= poor copy) *of the original painting; He can do imitations* (= impressions) *of just about anyone; verses composed* **in imitation of** *a poet's style.* —*adj.* fake:

an imitation diamond; imitation leather.
im.i.ta.tive (IM.i.tay.tiv) *adj.* that follows a model: *Painting is an imitative art; imitative actions, behavior, products; He is cravenly imitative of his idol;*
im.i.ta.tive.ly *adv.*

im.mac.u.late (i.MAC.yuh.lit) *adj.* perfect or flawless: *a house in immaculate condition; an immaculate copy of the original painting; She left everything in immaculate order; the Immaculate Virgin Mary (conceived without original sin).*
—**im.mac.u.late.ly** *adv.*

im.ma.nent (IM.uh.nunt) *adj.* **1** indwelling or inherent; also, subjective. **2** of God, pervading the universe, not transcendent. —**im.ma.nence** *n.*
—**im.ma.nent.ly** *adv.*

im.ma.te.ri.al (im.uh.TEER.ee.ul) *adj.* **1** unimportant: *It's wholly immaterial how you get here provided you're on time.* **2** not material but spiritual.

im.ma.ture (im.uh.TURE, -CHOOR) *adj.* undeveloped; not mature.
—**im.ma.tu.ri.ty** *n.*

im.meas.ur.a.ble (im.MEZH.uh.ruh.bul) *adj.* vast; boundless; **im.meas.ur.a.bly** *adv.*

im.me.di.a.cy (i.MEE.dee.uh.see) *n.* -cies direct relevance to the present time, place, etc.: *a question that lacks immediacy and urgency; a sense of immediacy and excitement; the immediacies (= urgent needs) of life.*

im.me.di.ate (i.MEE.dee.ut) *adj.* with nothing coming between: *an immediate reply (without any delay); our immediate (= next-door) neighbor on the right; the immediate (= near), not remote cause of the death; one's immediate family (= spouse, children, parents, siblings and sometimes grandparents and grandchildren).* —**im.me.di.ate.ly** *adv.*

im.me.mo.ri.al (i.muh.MOR.ee.ul) *adj.* going back beyond memory: *the immemorial past; an immemorial (= ancient) custom; a custom that has come down to us from time immemorial.*

im.mense (i.MENCE) *adj.* **1** so large as to seem difficult to measure: *immense rocks of immense size; an immense amount of wealth; an immense difference; immense gains, importance, waste.* **2** *Informal.* splendid; very good: *an immense poem.*
—**im.mense.ly** *adv.* —**im.men.si.ty** (-si.tee) *n.*

im.merse (i.MURSE) *v.* **im.mers.es, im.mersed, im.mers.ing** **1** lower into a liquid so as to be covered by it: *To learn to swim, you've to be able to immerse yourself in water; Keep your head immersed.* **2** involve deeply: *He's deeply immersed in his homework; She sat immersed in thought.*

im.mer.sion (i.MUR.zhun) *n.* a dipping in: *baptism by immersion; total immersion in a language; an immersion program of language teaching (with the students using the language all the time and for all subjects); an immersion school; the electric coil of an immersion heater for liquids.*

im.mi.grant (IM.i.grunt) *n.* **1** a non-native admitted to a country to settle in it: *an immigrant from Ethiopia; an immigrant to this country; an illegal immigrant without a work permit; a landed immigrant (accepted as a permanent resident of Canada); hardworking immigrants; adja.: immigrant communities, groups, labor, workers; a native-born Canadian of immigrant parents; an immigrant visa.* **2** a new plant or animal observed in a region: *an immigrant bird.*

im.mi.grate (IM.i.grate) *v.* **-grates, -grat.ed, -grat.ing** come into a country to live in it: *People immigrate to North America from various parts of the world, but the native peoples migrated here from Asia in prehistoric times.*
—**im.mi.gra.tion** (-GRAY.shun) *n.*

im.mi.nent (IM.uh.nunt) *adj.* likely or about to happen soon without further warning: *A storm is imminent when black clouds gather; the imminent danger of an explosion.* —**im.mi.nence** *n.*

im.mo.bile (i.MOH.bul) *adj.* firmly fixed; also, motionless.
—**im.mo.bil.i.ty** (-moh.BIL.i.tee) *n.*

im.mo.bi.lize (i.MOB.uh.lize) *v.* **-liz.es, -lized, -liz.ing** make immobile or unable to move. —**im.mo.bi.li.za.tion** (-luh.ZAY.shun, -lye-) *n.*

im.mod.er.ate (i.MOD.uh.rit) *adj.* not moderate; excessive; **im.mod.er.ate.ly** *adv.;* **im.mod.er.ate.ness** *n.*

im.mod.est (i.MOD.ist) *adj.* **1** bold, not modest: *an immodest costume.* **2** indecent: *immodest behavior.* —**im.mod.es.ty** (-is.tee) *n.*

im.mo.late (IM.uh.late) *v.* **-lates, -lat.ed, -lat.ing** kill as a sacrifice: *The Buddhist monk immolated himself in a fire.*
—**im.mo.la.tion** (-LAY.shun) *n.*

im.mor.al (i.MOR.ul) *adj.* morally wrong, esp. in sexual matters.
—**im.mor.al.ly** *adv.*

im.mo.ral.i.ty (im.uh.RAL.i.tee) *n.* -ties **1** vice: *the social and sexual immorality of sleeping around.* **2** [old use] an immoral act or practice.

im.mor.tal (i.MOR.tul) *adj.* everlasting, not subject to death: *our immortal soul; Madame Curie's immortal fame as a physicist.* —**n.** **1** an immortal being: *the* immortals of the Roman pantheon. 2 a person of great fame: *the 40 immortals of the French Academy; our literary immortals.* —**im.mor.tal.i.ty** (im.or.TAL.i.tee) *n.*

im.mor.tal.ize (i.MOR.tul.ize) *v.* **-iz.es, -ized, -iz.ing** make immortal: *Shakespeare has been immortalized by his plays.*

im.mov.a.ble (i.MOO.vuh.bul) *adj.* that cannot be moved; hence, unyielding: *steadfast and immovable in purpose.* —*n.pl.*: *land, trees, buildings and such immovables.* —**im.mov.a.bly** *adv.* —**im.mov.a.bil.i.ty** (-BIL.i.tee) *n.*

im.mune (IM.yoon) *adj.* free or protected from something disagreeable to which one is normally liable: *To be immune from error is humanly impossible; a world made immune from smallpox; immune against attacks; immune to measles, polio, etc.; the body's immune defense system; TV viewers made immune (= insensitive) to violence; The immune response or reaction causes rejection of foreign tissue.*

im.mu.ni.ty (i.MEW.ni.tee) *n.* the state or condition of being immune: *An infant is born with passive immunity against* or *to certain diseases; acquired, active, developed, natural immunity; Diplomats are protected by diplomatic immunity from being charged for offenses.*

im.mu.nize (IM.yuh.nize) *v.* **-niz.es, -nized, -niz.ing** make immune, as by giving injections: *to immunize a traveler against typhoid.* —**im.mu.ni.za.tion** (-nuh.ZAY.shun, -nye-) *n.*

im.mu.nol.o.gy (im.yuh.NOL.uh.jee) *n.* a branch of medicine dealing with resistance to disease and reactions to foreign bodies, as in allergies; **im.mu.nol.o.gist** (-uh.jist) *n.* —**im.mu.no.log.ic** (-nuh.LOJ.ic) or **im.mu.no.log.i.cal** *adj.*

immuno- *comb.form.* immune; immunity; immunology: *immunoglobulin, immunosuppression, immunotherapy.*

im.mu.no.glob.u.lin (im.yuh.noh.GLOB.yuh.lin) *n.* the immunity-producing globulin (protein) component of serum; antibody.

im.mu.no.sup.pres.sion (IM.yuh.noh.suh.PRESH.un) *adj.* suppression of natural immune reactions, as to organ transplants.

im.mure (im.YOOR) *v.* **im.mures, im.mured, im.mur.ing** shut up within walls; also, entomb in a wall.

im.mu.ta.ble (im.YOO.tuh.bul) *adj.* unchangeable; —**im.mu.ta.bly** *adv.* —**im.mu.ta.bil.i.ty** (-BIL.i.tee) *n.*

imp *n.* **1** a young demon. **2** a mis-chievous child.

im.pact *n.* **1** a striking together; collision: *a steering column designed to collapse on impact (during a collision); an* **impact** *crater made by a meteorite hitting the earth; An* **impact printer** *that prints characters using a printhead and inked ribbon is not so quiet as laser printers.* **2** an influence for change; effect: *TV has considerable impact on* or *upon our culture; The family breakup had a strong emotional impact on the children; the social impact of AIDS; the visual impact of a movie; positive and negative impacts.* —*v.* **1** pack in: *refugees impacted into slums; adj.: An* **impacted** *wisdom tooth (pressing against another tooth) is taken out because it cannot break through the gum; a noise-impacted area.* **2** have an effect on something: *Laser printers have impacted (on) the publishing business considerably.*

im.pair (im.PAIR) *v.* harm or lessen the quality, value, strength, etc. of something: *Drugs could impair your health.* —**impaired** *adj.* **1** with one's faculties weakened by alcohol: *an impaired driver; a charge of impaired driving.* **2** handicapped: *hearing impaired (people); the visually impaired.* —**im.pair.ment** *n.*

im.pa.la (im.PAH.luh) *n.* an African antelope.

im.pale (im.PALE) *v.* **-pales, -paled, -pal.ing** pierce through with or fix upon something pointed, as a stake; **im.pale.ment** *n.*

im.pal.pa.ble (im.PAL.puh.bul) *adj.* that cannot be felt or perceived: *a too fine, impalpable distinction;* **im.pal.pa.bly** *adv.*

im.pan.el (im.PAN.ul) *v.* **-els, -eled, -el.ing 1** put a person on a list for jury duty. **2** select a jury. Also **im.panelled, im.panel.ling** *Cdn.*

im.part (im.PART) *v.* give, esp. by sharing: *the imparting of knowledge to pupils; stage lighting designed to impart an air of mystery to the scene; Spices impart flavors to foods.*

im.par.tial (im.PAR.shul) *adj.* not partial to any side; fair or unbiased: *an impartial judge;* **im.par.tial.ly** *adv.* —**im.par.ti.al.i.ty** (-shee.AL.i.tee) *n.* **-ties.**

im.pass.a.ble (im.PAS.uh.bul) *adj.* that cannot be traveled over or through: *an impassable road; a mountain pass made impassable by snow and ice.*

im.passe (IM.pas) *n.* **-pass.es** a deadlock, like a passage closed at one end: *The talks are at* or *have reached an impasse; To break the impasse, one party has to yield a little.*

im.pas.si.ble (im.PAS.uh.bul) *adj.* unable to suffer pain; hence, impassive. —**im.pas.si.bil.i.ty** (-BIL.i.tee) *n.*

im.pas.sioned (im.PASH.und) *adj.* full of feeling: *an impassioned appeal, defense, plea, speech; impassioned rhetoric; She becomes quite impassioned when the subject is mentioned.*

im.pass.ive (im.PAS.iv) *adj.* not showing emotion: *a face impassive in suffering; an impassive expression;* **im.pass.ive.ly** *adv.* —**im.pas.siv.i.ty** (im.pas.IV.i.tee) *n.*

im.pas.to (im.PAS.toh) *n.* **-tos** the technique or style of applying paint thickly to canvas, ceramics, etc.

im.pa.tience (im.PAY.shunce) *n.* **1** lack of patience: *His impatience with the screaming child didn't help much.* **2** eager restlessness: *In his impatience to drive away, he forgot to release the brake.*

im.pa.ti.ens (im.PAY.shuns) *n.* a plant of the balsam family that bursts its seed capsules with elastic force when ripe; touch-me-not.

im.pa.tient (im.PAY.shunt) *adj.* lacking patience: *a sales clerk who is impatient with customers; Pupils grow impatient for the class to be dismissed; a man in a hurry, always impatient of the least delay.* —**im.pa.tient.ly** *adv.*

im.peach (im.PEECH) *v.* **1** charge a public official such as a judge, senator, or president with misbehavior: *President Nixon was about to be impeached for the Watergate coverup.* **2** question or discredit: *to impeach a person's honor or motives.*
—**im.peach.a.ble** (-uh.bul) *adj.*; **im.peach.ment** *n.*

im.pec.ca.ble (im.PECK.uh.bul) *adj.* without error or flaw: *her impeccable taste.* —**im.pec.ca.bly** *adv.*

im.pe.cu.ni.ous (im.pic.YOO.nee.us) *adj.* having no money because of spending habits; penniless; **im.pe.cu.ni.ous.ness** *n.*

im.ped.ance (im.PEED.unce) *n.* the total effective resistance of an electric circuit to an alternating current, composed of reactance and ohmic resistance.

im.pede (im.PEED) *v.* **-pedes, -ped.ed, -ped.ing** slow up the movement or progress of someone or something by getting in the way.

im.ped.i.ment (im.PED.uh.munt) *n.* a hindrance or obstruction: *an impediment to growth, marriage, progress; a speech impediment* (= defect) *such as stuttering or stammering.*

im.ped.i.men.ta (im.PED.uh.MEN.tuh) *n.pl.* baggage, supplies, and such encumbrances, as of an army on the march: *Cameras, binoculars, maps, and other impedimenta of espionage.*

im.pel (im.PEL) *v.* **-pels, -pelled, -pel.ling** urge or drive forward, as by a strong desire: *Duty to society impelled Al to help the police; It impelled him into reporting the hit-and-run driver.*

im.pend (im.PEND) *v.* be about to happen, as if dropping from a suspended state; *adj.*: *an **impending** catastrophe, crisis, examination, trial; the impending doom.*

im.pen.e.tra.ble (im.PEN.uh.truh.bul) *adj.* **1** that cannot be penetrated or understood: *an impenetrable jungle, metal, mystery.* **2** not receptive to influences: *an impenetrable mind.*
—**im.pen.e.tra.bly** *adv.*
—**im.pen.e.tra.bil.i.ty** (-BIL.i.tee) *n.*

im.per.a.tive (im.PER.uh.tiv) *adj.* **1** having the nature of a command: *"Stop!" is in the **imperative mood**.* **2** that must be done: *It is imperative that we set out at once.* —*n.* something commanded: *Food and fresh air are physiological imperatives* (= necessities); *English imperatives* (= sentences in the imperative mood) *usually have no expressed subject, as in "Go home!"*

im.per.cep.ti.ble (im.pur.SEP.tuh.bul) *adj.* not easily perceived: *The difference in texture is imperceptible to the touch; Growth occurs by imperceptible* (= slow) *degrees.* —**im.per.cep.ti.bly** *adv.*

im.per.cep.tive (im.pur.SEP.tiv) *adj.* not perceiving; lacking perception or understanding. Also **im.per.cip.i.ent** (-SIP.ee.unt).

im.per.fect (im.PUR.fict) *adj.* not perfect; defective: *imperfect knowledge, understanding;* **im.per.fect.ly** *adv.*

im.per.fec.tion (im.pur.FEC.shun) *n.* lack of perfection; deficiency or fault: *Gems with slight imperfections are sold at reduced prices.*

im.pe.ri.al (im.PEER.ee.ul) *adj.* **1** of an empire, emperor, or empress: *Her Imperial Majesty; an imperial guard, power; the **imperial gallon*** (= about 1.2 times the U.S. gallon); *the imperial system of measurement.* **2** having or showing authority, majesty, or superior quality: *to live in imperial grandeur; the imperial presidency.*

im.pe.ri.al.ism (im.PEER.ee.uh.liz.um) *n.* the policy of ruling over smaller or weaker countries and exploiting them as colonies; **im.pe.ri.al.ist** *n. & adj.*
—**im.pe.ri.al.is.tic** (-LIS.tic) *adj.*

im.per.il (im.PER.ul) *v.* **-ils, -illed** or

-iled, -il·ling or **-il·ing** endanger or jeopardize.

im·pe·ri·ous (im.PEER.ee.us) *adj.* 1 overbearing or domineering: *an imperious aristocrat, face, gesture, look, manner, person, voice.* 2 imperative or urgent: *an imperious command, demand, need.* —**im·pe·ri·ous·ness** *n.*

im·per·ish·a·ble (im.PER.ish.uh.bul) *adj.* enduring or indestructible: *a statue cast in imperishable bronze.*
—**im·per·ish·a·bly** *adv.*

im·per·ma·nent (im.PUR.muh.nunt) *adj.* not permanent or lasting; **im·per·ma·nence** *n.*

im·per·me·a·ble (im.PUR.mee.uh.bul) *adj.* not permitting fluids to pass through, as clay, membranes, etc.

im·per·mis·si·ble (im.pur.MIS.uh.bul) *adj.* not permissible.

im·per·son·al (im.PUR.suh.nul) *adj.* 1 without reference to any person: *an impersonal directive, suggestion.* 2 having no personal feeling: *an impersonal force (as of the elements); Corporations tend to be quite impersonal.*

im·per·son·ate (im.PUR.suh.nate) *v.* **-ates, -at·ed, -at·ing** play the part of or pretend to be someone: *an actor impersonating a lunatic; charged with impersonating a police officer.*
—**im·per·son·a·tion** (-NAY.shun) *n.*
—**im·per·son·a·tor** (-nay.tur) *n.*

im·per·ti·nent (im.PUR.tun.unt) *adj.* 1 not showing due respect, esp. by interfering in another's business: *an impertinent child, intrusion.* 2 not relevant. —**im·per·ti·nent·ly** *adv.*
—**im·per·ti·nence** *n.*

im·per·turb·a·ble (im.pur.TUR.buh.bul) *adj.* that cannot be disturbed: *a calm and imperturbable temper.*

im·per·vi·ous (im.PUR.vee.us) *adj.* 1 not capable of being passed through: *cloth that is impervious to moisture.* 2 not affected by something: *one who is impervious to criticism, pity, reason.*

im·pe·ti·go (im.puh.TYE.go) *n.* **-gos** a contagious skin infection of the face, hands, and limbs, characterized by yellow, crusty sores.

im·pet·u·ous (im.PECH.oo.us) *adj.* 1 marked by impulsive force: *impetuous speed, torrents.* 2 rash, not thoughtful: *an impetuous nature, outburst.* —**im·pet·u·ous·ly** *adv.*
—**im·pet·u·os·i·ty** (-oo.OS.i.tee) *n.*

im·pe·tus (IM.puh.tus) *n.* a driving force or impulse: *A rock rolls downhill under the impetus acquired from gravity; a new agreement to give a fresh impetus to trade.*

im·pi·e·ty (im.PYE.uh.tee) *n.* **-ties** 1 lack of reverence. 2 an impious act.

im·pinge (im.PINJ) *v.* **-ping·es, -pinged, -ping·ing** 1 make an impact: *Billiard balls impinge on one another; where a ray of light impinges on a surface.* 2 encroach: *measures that impinge on or upon individual rights.* —**im·pinge·ment** *n.*

im·pi·ous (IM.pee.us, im.PYE.us) *adj.* irreverent or profane.

imp·ish *adj.* of an imp; mischievous: *an impish grin; the impish suggestion to echo Kennedy's famous Berlin speech and declare in Frankfurt, "I am a Frankfurter."*
—**imp·ish·ly** *adv.;* **imp·ish·ness** *n.*

im·plac·a·ble (im.PLAC.uh.bul, -PLAY.cuh.bul) *adj.* that cannot be appeased: *an implacable enemy, foe, hatred;* **im·plac·a·bly** *adv.* —**im·plac·a·bil·i·ty** (-BIL.i.tee) *n.*

im·plant (im.PLANT) *v.* plant or fix firmly, as in the mind: *high ideals implanted in children.* —*n.* (IM.plant) something implanted in living tissue: *When a transplant is not possible, an artificial heart implant may be the answer; a breast implant following surgical removal of the breast; dental implants (of false teeth).*

im·plau·si·ble (im.PLAW.zuh.bul) *adj.* not plausible; **im·plau·si·bly** *adv.*
—**im·plau·si·bil·i·ty** (-BIL.i.tee) *n.*

im·ple·ment (IM.pluh.munt) *n.* a tool or device used in some activity: *The plough and shovel are farm implements; A sword, gun, etc. are implements of war.*
—*v.* (-ment) to effect or carry out: *to implement a decision, order, plan, reform.*
—**im·ple·men·ta·tion** (-mun.TAY.shun) *n.*

im·pli·cate (IM.pluh.cate) *v.* **-cates, -cat·ed, -cat·ing** show someone to have a role, usually in something bad: *a confession implicating others in the robbery; He was implicated but not directly involved in the fraud.*

im·pli·ca·tion (im.pluh.CAY.shun) *n.* an implicating or something inferred: *the implications of being fired rather than resigning.*

im·plic·it (im.PLIS.it) *adj.* 1 implied or suggested, not expressed: *an implicit permission; obligations implicit in the contract.* 2 unhesitating; absolute: *implicit faith; Some parents expect implicit obedience from their children.*

im·plode (im.PLODE) *v.* **-plodes, -plod·ed, -plod·ing** burst inward, as when a vacuum tube breaks: *stars that implode;* *adj.:* *McLuhan wrote about the* **imploding** *(= contracting) energies of the* modern world. —**im.plo.sion** (im.PLOH.zhun) *n.*: *Buildings are demolished by implosion.* —**im.plo.sive** (-siv) *adj.*

im.plore (im.PLORE) *v.* **-plores, -plored, -plor.ing** beg someone earnestly, as if in distress: *We implore you to drop the case, not to sue us;* *adj.*: *an imploring look, tone, voice.* —**im.plor.ing.ly** *adv.*

im.ply (im.PLY) *v.* **-plies, -plied, -ply.ing** 1 hint at or suggest without saying: *His smile seemed to imply agreement; to imply that he had no objection.* 2 signify or suggest as a logical consequence without being expressed in words: *Rights imply duties; an implied warranty such as that a seller has the right to sell the goods, that what is sold is basically suitable for the intended purpose, etc.*

im.po.lite (IM.puh.lite) *adj.* not polite or courteous; **im.po.lite.ly** *adv.*; **im.po.lite.ness** *n.*

im.pol.i.tic (im.POL.uh.tic) *adj.* not politic or expedient; unwise.

im.pon.der.a.ble (im.PON.duh.ruh.bul) *n. & adj.* (something) that cannot be weighed or measured exactly: *the many imponderables* (= factors and circumstances) *of the human condition.*

im.port (im.PORT) *v.* 1 bring in, as merchandise, from a foreign country: *goods imported from abroad; goods imported into the U.S.* 2 mean or signify: *What does that remark import?* 3 bring a data file into one application program from another: *the importing and exporting of files.* —*n.* (IM.port) 1 something brought in from an external source: *Balance of trade depends on imports and exports.* 2 an imported professional hockey or football player. 3 signification; also, significance or importance: *the full import of his words; matters of great import; international, sociological import.* —**im.port.er** (im.POR.tur) *n.*

im.por.tance (im.POR.tunce) *n.* the quality of being important; significance: *Conservation is a subject of vital importance to* or *for the human race; great, historic, paramount, some, utmost importance; to acquire, assume importance; to attach* or *attribute importance to something.*

im.por.tant (im.POR.tunt) *adj.* 1 meaning much; of significant quality or value: *an important announcement; VIPs are very important people; Is a fancy car important to one's social status? not important for me; What's important is to do good and avoid evil; It's most important that everyone be happy.* 2 pretentious: *The mayor looks very important in her robe.* —**im.por.tant.ly** *adv.*: *"More importantly" is not as elegant a phrase as "What is more important."*

im.por.ta.tion (im.por.TAY.shun) *n.* an importing or something imported.

im.por.tu.nate (im.POR.chuh.nit) *adj.* persistent in asking: *an importunate beggar, petitioner; an importunate* (= pressing) *demand.*

im.por.tune (im.por.TUNE) *v.* **-tunes, -tuned, -tun.ing** ask someone repeatedly and annoyingly *to* do something. —**im.por.tu.ni.ty** (-TEW.ni.tee) *n.* -ties.

im.pose (im.POZE) *v.* **-pos.es, -posed, -pos.ing** 1 to place as a burden *on* or *upon* someone: *A fine is imposed on delinquents.* 2 take advantage of someone: *Uninvited guests impose themselves on their hosts; Sorry to impose on your generosity.* —**im.po.si.tion** (im.puh.ZISH.un) *n.*

imposing (im.POH.zing) *adj.* impressive because of size, excellence, or appearance: *an imposing building, display, personality.*

im.pos.si.ble (im.POS.uh.bul) *adj.* 1 that cannot be; not possible to be done, to be true, to tolerate, etc.: *It's impossible to please everyone; It's physically impossible for me to be in two places at once; That's impossible* (= cannot be true)*! The ancients thought it practically impossible to fly; almost, virtually, well-nigh impossible.* 2 difficult: *an impossible situation, student, task; He made life impossible for me.* —*n.*: *to attempt the impossible; The astronauts did the impossible by landing on the moon.* —**im.pos.si.bly** *adv.* —**im.pos.si.bil.i.ty** (-BIL.i.tee) *n.* -ties.

im.post (IM.pohst) *n.* 1 a duty or tax. 2 the top part of a column, pier, or wall on which the end of an arch rests.

im.pos.tor (im.POS.tur) *n.* one who deceives or cheats others by pretending to be someone else; also **im.pos.ter**.

im.pos.ture (im.POS.chur) *n.* a fraud or deception.

im.po.tent (IM.puh.tunt) *adj.* 1 lacking power or strength: *a new defense system that would make* or *render nuclear weapons impotent and obsolete; The UN has proved impotent in preventing hundreds of regional wars since it was established; Humans are impotent against the forces of nature; He ground his teeth in impotent fury.* 2 esp. of males, unable to complete the sexual act. —**im.po.tent.ly** *adv.* —**im.po.tence** or **im.po.ten.cy** *n.*

im.pound (im.POUND) *v.* **1** put in a pound, as a stray animal or towed vehicle. **2** seize and hold evidence in legal custody. **3** hold in a reservoir: *water impounded behind dams.* —**im.pound.ment** *n.*

im.pov.er.ish (im.POV.uh.rish) *v.* deprive of the essentials of a healthy existence: *Communist policies impoverished the economy; The forests were impoverished of timber, plants, animals, and people;* *adj.*: *the* **impoverished** *nations of the Fourth World; an impoverished land (without much plant or animal life or with its resources exhausted); impoverished inner city kids.* —**im.pov.er.ish.ment** *n.*

im.prac.ti.ca.ble (im.PRAC.ti.cuh.bul) *adj.* **1** not practicable or feasible; unrealistic: *an impracticable plan, policy, scheme, suggestion; It's impracticable to follow his advice.* **2** impossible to put to use: *an impracticable course, invention, path, road.*

im.prac.ti.cal (im.PRAC.ti.cul) *adj.* not sensible or realistic: *an impractical planner; It's impractical to keep a limousine to go to the corner store.* —**im.prac.ti.cal.i.ty** (-CAL.i.tee) *n.*

im.pre.cate (IM.pruh.cate) *v.* **-cates, -cat.ed, -cat.ing** call down evil on someone; hence, curse; **im.pre.ca.tor** *n.* —**im.pre.ca.tion** (-CAY.shun) *n.*

im.pre.cise (im.pri.SICE) *adj.* not precise; **im.pre.cise.ly** *adv.* —**im.pre.cis.ion** (-SIZH.un) *n.*

im.preg.na.ble (im.PREG.nuh.bul) *adj.* **1** that cannot be overcome by force: *an impregnable fortress, stronghold; an impregnable argument, belief.* **2** that can be impregnated. —**im.preg.na.bly** *adv.*

im.preg.nate (im.PREG.nate) *v.* **-nates, -nat.ed, -nat.ing** **1** make pregnant; fertilize ovum. **2** charge or fill: *The sea air is impregnated with salt; to impregnate wood with a preservative.* —**im.preg.na.tion** (im.preg.NAY.shun) *n.*

im.pre.sa.ri.o (im.pruh.SAH.ree.oh) *n.* **-os** an organizer or manager of an opera, concert company, or other musical entertainment.

im.press (im.PRES) *v.* **1** stamp or imprint: *a fossil impressed in rock.* **2** fix strongly on the mind or feelings: *He impressed us with his learning; He impresses us as a learned man; She impresses on everyone the urgency of her mission;* *adj.*: *Some children are not easily impressed; We are deeply, favorably, greatly, highly, strongly impressed.* **3** force someone to serve in the armed forces: *people impressed into the military;* **im.press.ment** *n.* —**im.pres.si.ble**

(-uh.bul) *adj.*

im.pres.sion (im.PRESH.un) *n.* an act of impressing or a result of it: *a thumb impression; to create an impression; to make a favorable impression on or upon the judges; deep, erroneous, false, lasting, pleasant, profound, strong, vivid impressions; I was under the impression that I had lost the bid; a 20,000-copy first impression* (= printing) *of a book; a comedian good at doing impressions* (= imitations) *of celebrities.*

im.pres.sion.a.ble (im.PRESH.un.uh.bul) *adj.* sensitive to influences; impressible: *the impressionable minds of children; Childhood is an impressionable period.*

im.pres.sion.ism (im.PRESH.un.iz.um) *n.* a style of painting, literature, etc. striving for suggestive impressions rather than execution of realistic detail; **im.pres.sion.ist** *n. & adj.* —**im.pres.sion.is.tic** (-NIS.tic) *adj.*

im.pres.sive (im.PRES.iv) *adj.* making a strong, esp. favorable impression on the mind or feelings: *an impressive ceremony, sight, speaker.* —**im.pres.sive.ly** *adv.*; **im.pres.sive.ness** *n.*

impressment See IMPRESS, 3.

im.pri.ma.tur (im.pruh.MAH.tur) *n.* official approval to publish, as in the Roman Catholic Church.

im.print (im.PRINT) *v.* mark by pressure; impress: *an unforgettable experience forever imprinted on our minds; A newborn animal may become permanently* **imprinted** (= attached) *to or on or by the parent, handler, etc. whom it first recognizes.* —*n.* (IM.print) **1** something imprinted: *the imprint left by feet on wet cement; a great teacher who left her imprint* (= distinctive mark) *on a whole generation of students; Her writings bear the imprint of genius; the imprint* (= lasting effect) *of years of suffering on his face.* **2** the publisher's name and the place and date of publication printed in a book, usually at the foot of the title page.

im.pris.on (im.PRIZ.un) *v.* put in prison; hence, confine; **im.pris.on.ment** *n.*

im.prob.a.ble (im.PROB.uh.bul) *adj.* not probable; unlikely: *a highly improbable story;* **im.prob.a.bly** *adv.* —**im.prob.a.bil.i.ty** (-BIL.i.tee) *n.*

im.promp.tu (im.PROMP.tyoo, -too) *adj.* done on the spur of the moment: *an impromptu concert, guided tour, press conference;* *adv.*: *remarks made impromptu.*

im.prop.er (im.PROP.ur) *adj.* not suitable, correct, in good taste, etc.: *Is it improper to cast your ballot in your own*

improper fraction / in

favor? —**im.prop.er.ly** adv.
improper fraction n. a fraction whose numerator is larger than or is equal to the denominator, as 4/4 or 4/3.
im.pro.pri.e.ty (im.prop.RYE.uh.tee) n. **-ties 1** lack of propriety: *the crass impropriety of chewing gum in church.* **2** an improper act, remark, language use, etc.
im.prove (im.PROOV) v. **-proves, -proved, -prov.ing** make or become better: *The patient is improving; how to improve your chances; land improved* (= made more valuable) *by cultivation; It's not easy to improve on or upon* (= do better than) *nature.* —**im.prov.a.ble** adj.
im.prove.ment (im.PROOV.munt) n. **1** the action of improving or getting better: *Your grades show signs of improvement; There is always, little, lots of, much, plenty of, some, still, substantial **room for improvement**.* **2** a result of improving; a positive change: *You have brought about a marked improvement in your work; added, decided, distinct, gradual, great, lasting, main, minor, significant, slight, some, steady, substantial improvements; a host of improvements; A "B" grade is **an improvement on** or **over*** (= is better than) *a "C".*
im.prov.i.dent (im.PROV.uh.dunt) adj. not providing for the future; thriftless: *his improvident habits, nature;* **im.prov.i.dent.ly** adv. —**im.prov.i.dence** n.
im.pro.vise (IM.pruh.vize) v. **-vis.es, -vised, -vis.ing** make or do something without preparation or prepared material: *a pop singer who improvises as he sings; The actor improvised her lines;* adj.: *We had to spend the night in an **improvised** shelter.* —**im.pro.vis.er** or **im.pro.vi.sor** n. —**im.pro.vi.sa.tion** (im.PROV.uh.ZAY.shun, IM.pruh.vuh.ZAY.shun, -vye-) n.
im.pru.dent (im.PROO.dunt) adj. not prudent; rash or indiscreet. —**im.pru.dence** n.
im.pu.dent (IMP.yuh.dunt) adj. shamelessly rude or impertinent; **im.pu.dent.ly** adv. —**im.pu.dence** n.
im.pugn (imp.YOON) v. attack a person's motives, character, action, or statement as false or worthless.
im.pulse (IM.pulse) n. **1** a sudden driving force or impetus; also, its effect: *He was acting on* or *under a mere impulse without any reflection; She felt an irresistible impulse to fly home; the impulse of curiosity, hunger; **impulse buying** by shoppers (who decide to buy on the spur of the moment).* **2** stimulus: *an electrical impulse; nerve impulses.*
im.pul.sion (im.PUL.shun) n. an impelling or impelling force; impetus.
im.pul.sive (im.PUL.siv) adj. **1** impelling: *an impulsive force.* **2** done or acting on impulse: *an impulsive child, demand, retort.* —**im.pul.sive.ly** adv.; **im.pul.sive.ness** n.
im.pu.ni.ty (imp.YOO.ni.tee) n. freedom from punishment, injury, or other consequence: *One seldom breaks the law with impunity.*
im.pure (imp.YOOR) adj. not pure, clean, or chaste.
im.pur.i.ty (imp.YOOR.i.tee) n. **-ties 1** contamination. **2** foreign matter, as in food, water, air, etc.
im.pute (imp.YOOT) v. **-putes, -put.ed, -put.ing** charge or attribute: *She is not guilty of the crimes imputed to her; to examine actions without imputing motives;* **im.put.a.ble** (-tuh.bul) adj. —**im.pu.ta.tion** (im.pyuh.TAY.shun) n.
in prep. **1** enclosed by limits of space, time, etc.: *She's in the house; It happened in a minute; He's rolling in the snow; Go in* (= into) *the house.* **2** [indicating various relationships]: *green in color; a girl in a million; degrees in science; a party in his honor; to go in search of help; It's not in him* (= characteristic of him) *to say "No" to a request for help; He's a generous man **in that*** (= because) *he gives to charities.* —adv.: *Come in, please; Don't let everyone **in on*** (= make them acquainted with) *the secret; Tell only those who are **in with*** (= friends with) *us.* —adj.: *She isn't in; The votes are in* (= have been received) *and counted; a train on the in* (= inside) *track; It is in* (Informal for fashionable) *to wear neckties; an in* (= private) *group, joke, word; All latecomers are **in for*** (= going to have) *trouble today.* —n.: *She has been here so long she knows all the **ins and outs*** (= detailed facts) *of the place; the **ins*** (= power group) *of a society; She could get you an **in with*** (Informal for introduction to) *her boss.* —comb.form: *in-depth study, in-service training; an in-crowd* (= clique); *drive-in, sit-in, stand-in, teach-in, wader-in.* —prefix.
1 to or on the inside: *inbound, incoming, indoors, insight.* **2** lack of something or being not able: *inability, inaccessible, inadmissible.* [Such compounds may be formed by prefixing "in" to many nouns, adjectives, and verbs. The spelling, meanings, pronunciation, and usages of such compounds remain the same as "in" plus

the base word in each case. The entries that follow are the most frequently used or the ones that are distinctive in one respect or another.]

in ab.sen.ti.a (in.ab.SEN.shuh) *Latin.* in his, her, or their absence: *He was tried in absentia; a degree conferred in absentia* (= without the candidate being present).

in.ac.cu.ra.cy (in.AC.yuh.ruh.see) *n.* -cies lack of accuracy or an instance of it: *a glaring inaccuracy; the many inaccuracies in the report.*

in.ac.tion (in.AC.shun) *n.* absence of action: *government inaction on the issue.*

in.ac.ti.vate (in.AC.tuh.vate) *v.* -vates, -vat.ed, -vat.ing make no longer active. —**in.ac.ti.va.tion** (-VAY.shun) *n.*

in.ad.e.quate (in.AD.uk.wit) *adj.* not adequate; unable to cope with a situation: *supplies that are inadequate to meet the demand; He feels very inadequate in his job.* —**in.ad.e.quate.ly** *adv.* —**in.ad.e.qua.cy** (-wuh.see) *n.* -cies.

in.ad.vert.ent (in.ud.VUR.tunt) *adj.* 1 inattentive. 2 unintentional. —**in.ad.vert.ent.ly** *adv.*: *She inadvertently left the door unlocked.* —**in.ad.vert.ence** *n.*

in.al.ien.a.ble (in.AIL.yuh.nuh.bul) *adj.* that cannot be taken away, as basic or fundamental rights; **in.al.ien.a.bly** (-blee) *adv.* —**in.al.ien.a.bil.i.ty** (-BIL.i.tee) *n.*

in.am.o.ra.ta (i.NAM.uh.RAH.tuh) *n.* one's sweetheart or female lover.

in.ane (in.ANE) *adj.* -an.er, -an.est empty of meaning; also, silly: *an inane expression, remark, smile.* —**in.an.i.ty** (in.AN.i.tee) *n.* -ties.

in.an.i.mate (i.NAN.uh.mit) *adj.* not animate: *the inanimate world; inanimate beings, objects.*

in.a.ni.tion (in.uh.NISH.un) *n.* starved condition; hence, lack of vigor or vitality.

in.ap.pro.pri.ate (in.uh.PROH.pree.ate) *adj.* not appropriate: *a costume that is inappropriate to the occasion; inappropriate behavior, remarks.*

in.ap.pre.ci.a.ble (in.uh.PREE.shuh.bul) *adj.* not appreciable; negligible; **in.ap.pre.ci.a.bly** *adv.*

in.apt (in.APT) *adj.* not apt or suitable: *an inapt companion, remark, term;* **in.apt.ly** *adv.;* **in.apt.ness** *n.*

in.ap.ti.tude (in.AP.tuh.tude) *n.* lack of aptitude or skill.

in.ar.tic.u.late (in.ar.TIK.yuh.lit) *adj.* 1 unable to speak fluently and readily: *an inarticulate child.* 2 incoherent or irrational: *He burst into an inarticulate rage.* —**in.ar.tic.u.late.ly** *adv.*

in.as.much as (in.uz.MUCH.as) *conj.* to the extent that; since.

in.au.gu.ral (in.AUG.yuh.rul) *n.* a ceremony or speech that inaugurates a function. —**adj.**: *the President's inaugural address, ball, parade; inaugural celebrations, festivities.*

in.au.gu.rate (in.AUG.yuh.rate) *v.* -rates, -rat.ed, -rat.ing 1 make a formal beginning of a new era, policy, institution, etc. 2 install a new president in office. —**in.au.gu.ra.tion** (-RAY.shun) *n.*

in.board *adj. & adv.* in the hull or toward the middle of a ship, boat, or other craft. —*n.* an inboard engine of a motorboat.

in.born *adj.* of qualities, existing at birth; innate: *an inborn talent.*

in.bound *adj.* inward bound: *an inbound flight; inbound traffic.*

in.bred *adj.* resulting from inbreeding; also, inborn.

in.breed (IN.BREED) *v.* -breeds, -bred, -breed.ing breed from closely related plants, animals, or persons, esp. in order to preserve purity of stock or strain: *Inbred corn has been fertilized with its own pollen;* **n.**: *hereditary illnesses due to* **inbreeding** *within a group, as by marriage between first cousins; Travel broadens the mind, inbreeding* (= narrow social or cultural life) *does not.*

In.ca (ING.cuh) *n.* a member of a highly civilized native people of South America who ruled in Peru and other countries before the Spanish conquest in the 1500's; **In.can** (-cun) *n. & adj.*

in.cal.cu.la.ble (in.CAL.kyuh.luh.bul) *adj.* 1 too great or too many to be counted: *incalculable benefits, effects, harm; The risks are incalculable; The pride they took in their accomplishments was incalculable.* 2 unpredictable: *an incalculable mood, temper; The costs of the operation would be incalculable.* —**in.cal.cu.la.bly** *adv.*

in.can.des.cent (in.can.DES.unt) *adj.* glowing red-hot or white-hot, as the filament of an electric lamp, or **incandescent lamp**. —**in.can.des.cence** (-unce) *n.*

in.can.ta.tion (in.can.TAY.shun) *n.* the use of words chanted as a magical formula or spell; also, such words.

in.ca.pa.ble (in.CAY.puh.bul) *adj.* not capable; **in.ca.pa.bil.i.ty** (-BIL.i.tee) *n.*

in.ca.pac.i.tate (in.cuh.PAS.i.tate) *v.* -tates, -tat.ed, -tat.ing disqualify; disable; make incapable.

in.ca.pac.i.ty (in.cuh.PAS.i.tee) *n.* **-ties** lack of capacity; also, a legal disqualification.

in.car.cer.ate (in.CAR.suh.rate) *v.* **-ates, -at.ed, -at.ing** imprison.
—**in.car.cer.a.tion** (-RAY.shun) *n.*

in.car.na.dine (in.CAR.nuh.dine) *v.* **-dines, -dined, -din.ing** make red like blood.

in.car.nate (in.CAR.nit) *adjp.* **1** existing in bodily form: *the devil incarnate; instincts incarnate in us.* **2** personified: *a moneylender who is greed incarnate; evil incarnate; a poet who is inspiration incarnate.* —*v.* (-nate) **-nates, -nat.ed, -nat.ing 1** make or be incarnate: *How do we come to incarnate on this planet?* **2** be the embodiment of something: *She incarnates all womanly virtues.*
—**in.car.na.tion** (-NAY.shun) *n.*: *He is the very incarnation of vice.*

in.case (in.CASE) same as ENCASE.

in.cen.di.ar.y (in.SEN.dee.air.ee) *n.* **-ar.ies** a person or thing that sets fire to something: *He was arrested as an incendiary; adj.: an incendiary bomb, crime; an incendiary speech (that stirs up violence).*

in.cense (IN.sense) *n.* the perfume or smoke from a gum or spice burned for fragrance, usually as part of a ritual. —*v.* (in.SENSE) **in.cens.es, in.censed, in.cens.ing** make someone very angry: *It incenses him that he's not getting paid for his work; Their behavior incenses him; adj.: He's incensed at or about or by or with their behavior; People are incensed against the premier; The premier is facing an incensed electorate.*

in.cen.tive (in.SEN.tiv) *n.* something such as an award, bonus, loan, pay, etc. tending or designed to stimulate or encourage someone to greater effort or output: *Pay raises are a powerful, strong incentive to work harder; a tax incentive for people to make charitable donations; adja.: an incentive award, bonus, pay.*

in.cep.tion (in.SEP.shun) *n.* beginning or commencement of a plan, undertaking, organization, business, program, etc.: *It has been a failure from its very inception.* —**in.cep.tive** *adj.*

in.cer.ti.tude (in.SUR.tuh.tude) *n.* uncertainty; also, insecurity.

in.ces.sant (in.SES.unt) *adj.* ceaseless or uninterrupted: *incessant chatter, complaining, demands, noises, phone calls, rain, squabbling;* **in.ces.sant.ly** *adv.*

in.cest (IN.sest) *n.* sexual relations between those closely related by blood, as father and daughter or uncle and niece. —**in.ces.tu.ous** (in.SES.choo.us) *adj.: an incestuous affair, marriage, rape, relationship; incestuous love.*

inch *n.* **1** a unit of length that is one-twelfth of a foot (2.54 cm). **2** a unit of rainfall, snow, or pressure, based on the height in inches of a liquid in a specified container, as of mercury in a barometer: *Three inches of rain fell during April.* **3** the smallest amount or least bit: *She wouldn't yield an inch.*
—**by inches 1** gradually; also **inch by inch. 2** only just: *He missed the target by inches.* —**every inch** completely: *She's every inch a lady.* —**within an inch of** very close to: *She came within an inch of losing the election.* —*v.* move little by little, or inch by inch, *along, back, forward,* etc.: *The shy child inched away and hid behind her mother.*

in.cho.ate (in.COH.it) *adj.* just begun; undeveloped: *"Begin to," "get going,"* etc. are inchoate or inceptive verb forms; also **in.cho.a.tive** (-uh.tiv).

inch.worm *n.* a looper; also called "measuring worm."

in.ci.dence (IN.suh.dunce) *n.* **1** the falling or striking of a projectile, ray, or beam on a surface: *the angle of incidence of light rays.* **2** the rate or frequency with which something occurs: *the incidence of an indirect tax on the manufacturer or consumer; the growing incidence of crime; There were only two incidences* (= occurrences) *of vandalism during the whole school year.*

in.ci.dent (IN.suh.dunt) *n.* an occurrence, esp. one of minor significance, usually related to something major: *a border incident leading to war; Incidents happen, occur, take place; to cover up, provoke, suppress an incident; amusing, curious, funny, humorous, strange, touching, ugly incidents; The gang leader was arrested without incident.* —*adj.* **1** falling or striking: *light incident on or upon a photographic subject.* **2** incidental: *duties incident to the office of principal.*

in.ci.den.tal (in.suh.DEN.tul) *adj.* that happens or is likely to happen along with something else that is more important: *problems incidental to setting up in business; incidental* (= casual) *expenses,* or **incidentals** *n.pl.*

in.ci.den.tal.ly (in.suh.DEN.tul.ee) *adv.* by the way.

in.cin.er.ate (in.SIN.uh.rate) *v.* **-ates, -at.ed, -at.ing** burn to ashes, as in an incinerator. —**in.cin.er.a.tion** (-RAY.shun) *n.* —**in.cin.er.a.tor** (-ray.tur) *n.*

in.cip.i.ent (in.SIP.ee.unt) *adj.* just beginning to be or become apparent: *a boy with an incipient growth of facial hair; the incipient life of a fetus; my incipient old age.* **—in.cip.i.ence** *n.*

in.cise (in.SIZE) *v.* **-cis.es, -cised, -cis.ing** cut into with a sharp tool, as to carve or engrave.

in.ci.sion (in.SIZH.un) *n.* a gash or cut, as in a surgical operation.

in.ci.sive (in.SYE.siv) *adj.* keen or cutting: *an incisive approach to problem-solving; an incisive mind.* **—in.ci.sive.ly** *adv.;* **in.ci.sive.ness** *n.*

in.ci.sor (in.SYE.zur) *n.* any of the sharp-edged cutting teeth in front of a mammal's upper and lower jaws.

in.cite (in.CITE) *v.* **-cites, -cit.ed, -cit.ing** **1** stir up: *to incite hatred; to incite a riot.* **2** urge: *to incite a person to action, violence; His speech incited the crew to mutiny.* **—in.cite.ment** *n.*

in.ci.vil.i.ty (in.suh.VIL.i.tee) *n.* **-ties** lack of civility; also, an uncivil act.

in.clem.en.cy (in.CLEM.un.see) *n.* **-cies** severity or harshness: *the inclemencies of the weather.*

in.clem.ent (in.CLEM.unt) *adj.* **1** severe or harsh: *an inclement judge, ruler.* **2** rough or stormy: *the inclement elements, weather.*

in.cli.na.tion (in.cluh.NAY.shun) *n.* an inclining: *the inclination (= angle) of an orbit from the equator; He led a life of ease following every inclination (= liking) of body and mind; an unwelcome visitor with no inclination (= disposition) to leave.*

in.cline (in.CLINE) *v.* **-clines, -clined, -clin.ing** **1** cause to slope, lean, or bend: *She inclined her head in prayer; adj.: an inclined roof; An inclined plane such as a plank or ramp at an angle is used for raising loads.* **2** be or make favorable, willing, or disposed: *Circumstances incline us to believe she's innocent; adjp.: She's inclined to think her son is innocent; We're inclined to agree.*
—*n.* (IN.cline) a slope.

inclose, inclosure same as ENCLOSE, ENCLOSURE.

in.clude (in.CLOOD, long "OO") *v.* **-cludes, -clud.ed, -clud.ing** take in as part of something: *Batteries are not included in the price; All are included in "human being"; Not all are included among the winners.*

in.clu.sion (in.CLOO.zhun) *n.* an including or something included: *the inclusion of a book in the approved list.*

in.clu.sive (in.CLOO.siv) *adj.* including: *February 1st to 10th inclusive (= including both days); an inclusive (= including much or all) charge, list, rate; It costs only $350 inclusive of (= including) taxes.* **—in.clu.sive.ly** *adv.;* **in.clu.sive.ness** *n.*

in.cog.ni.to (in.COG.nuh.toh, in.cog.NEE-) *adv.* with a concealed or disguised identity: *The king traveled incognito; n.: Some incognitos are hard to penetrate; adj.: He was incognito during the entire visit; an incognito visit.*

in.co.her.ent (in.coh.HEER.unt) *adj.* not coherent; **in.co.her.ent.ly** *adv.* **—in.co.her.ence** *n.*

in.com.bus.ti.ble (in.cum.BUS.tuh.bul) *n. & adj.* (something) that is not combustible.

in.come (IN.cum) *n.* money that comes in, or other benefit or gain received, on account of services or capital, esp. in a given period: *to earn an income; to live within, not beyond one's income; annual, fixed, net incomes; the per-capita income of a country; the* **income tax** *collected by governments based on the annual income of individuals and corporations.*

in.com.ing (IN.cum.ing) *n.* a coming in: *the incoming of the tide.* **—adja.:** *the incoming chairman, mail, traffic, year.*

in.com.men.su.rate (in.cuh.MEN.shuh.rit) *adj.* not commensurate; disproportionate; also **in.com.men.su.ra.ble.**

in.com.mode (in.cuh.MODE) *v.* **-com.modes, -com.mod.ed, -com.mod.ing** to inconvenience; annoy.

in.com.mu.ni.ca.do (IN.cuh.mew.nuh.CAH.doh) *adj. & adv.* (held) without means of communication, as prisoners.

in.com.pa.ra.ble (in.COM.puh.ruh.bul) *adj.* that cannot be compared, esp. being unequaled: *Jan's incomparable beauty, skill, wit.*

in.com.pat.i.ble (in.cum.PAT.uh.bul) *adj.* not compatible *with* one another, as different drugs, blood types, temperaments, etc. **—in.com.pat.i.bil.i.ty** (-BIL.i.tee) *n.*

in.com.pe.tent (in.COM.puh.tunt) *n. & adj.* (one) that is not competent; **in.com.pe.tent.ly** *adv.* **—in.com.pe.tence** or **in.com.pe.ten.cy** *n.*

in.com.plete (in.cum.PLEET) *adj.* not complete; **in.com.plete.ly** *adv.;* **in.com.plete.ness** *n.*

In.con.gru.ous (in.CONG.groo.us) *adj.* lacking agreement of parts or harmony with surroundings; not suitable or appropriate; **in.con.gru.ous.ly** *adv.* **—in.con.gru.ous.ness** or **in.con.gru.i.ty** (in.cong.GROO.i.tee) *n.* **-ties.**

in.con.se.quen.tial (IN.con.si.KWEN.shul) *adj.* of no consequence; unimportant; also, irrelevant; **in.con.se.quen.tial.ly** adv. —**in.con.se.quence** (in.CON.sik.wunce) n.

in.con.sid.er.a.ble (in.cun.SID.uh.ruh.bul) adj. not worth considering because trivial or small; negligible.

in.con.sid.er.ate (in.cun.SID.uh.rit) adj. without consideration for others; **in.con.sid.er.ate.ly** adv.; **in.con.sid.er.ate.ness** n.

in.con.sol.a.ble (in.cun.SOH.luh.bul) adj. that cannot be consoled: *an inconsolable child, grief, widow;* **in.con.sol.a.bly** adv.

in.con.spic.u.ous (in.cun.SPIC.yoo.us) adj. not conspicuous or attracting any attention; **in.con.spic.u.ous.ly** adv.

in.con.stant (in.CON.stunt) adj. not constant; changeable; **in.con.stant.ly** adv. —**in.con.stan.cy** n.

in.con.test.a.ble (in.cun.TES.tuh.bul) adj. not contestable; indisputable; **in.con.test.a.bly** adv. —**in.con.test.a.bil.i.ty** (-BIL.i.tee) n.

in.con.ti.nent (in.CON.tuh.nunt) adj. **1** not continent or having self-control, esp. in regard to sex. **2** unable to control one's bladder or bowels: *The paralysis made her incontinent.* —**in.con.ti.nent.ly** adv. —**in.con.ti.nence** n.

in.con.tro.vert.i.ble (IN.con.truh.VUR.tuh.bul) adj. that cannot be controverted; indisputable: *incontrovertible evidence, proof;* **in.con.tro.vert.i.bly** adv.

in.con.ven.ience (in.cun.VEEN.yunce) n. **1** lack of comfort or ease: *Dogs barking at night are a cause of much inconvenience to neighbors.* **2** something that is inconvenient: *considerable, great, slight inconveniences; to put up with the inconveniences of travel.* —v. **-ienc.es, -ienced, -ienc.ing** cause trouble or bother to someone: *I hope that my stay will not inconvenience you.* —**in.con.ven.ient** (-yunt) adj.

in.cor.po.rate (in.COR.puh.rate) v. **-rates, -rat.ed, -rat.ing 1** unite into or combine with so as to form one body: *a plan incorporating many suggestions.* **2** make into a legal body or corporation: *A business is incorporated for limiting the liability of investors;* adj.: *an **incorporated** business, company, municipality.* —**in.cor.po.ra.tion** (-RAY.shun) n.

in.cor.po.re.al (in.cor.POR.ee.ul) adj. not having material form, as angels and spirits; spiritual.

in.cor.rect (in.cuh.RECT) adj. not correct; also, inappropriate; **in.cor.rect.ly** adv.

in.cor.ri.gi.ble (in.COR.uh.juh.bul) adj. that cannot be changed or reformed: *an incorrigible habit, youth;* **in.cor.ri.gi.bly** adv. —**in.cor.ri.gi.bil.i.ty** (-BIL.i.tee) n.

in.cor.rupt.i.ble (in.cuh.RUP.tuh.bul) adj. not subject to corruption; esp., morally upright; **in.cor.rupt.i.bly** adv.

in.crease (in.CREECE) v. **-creas.es, -creased, -creas.ing** make or become greater in size, degree, number, etc.: *World population is increasing every minute; Prices increase with demand.* —n. (IN.creece) growth or its result: *an increase of 10° from the normal; a slight increase in productivity; Prices seem always **on the increase** in our economy.*

in.creas.ing.ly (in.CREE.sing.lee) adv. more and more.

in.cred.i.ble (in.CRED.uh.bul) adj. too unusual or improbable to believe: *an incredible feat of endurance; You're incredible! It's incredible to be able to do such a thing; incredible the way you go about your work; an incredible amount, deal, growth, opportunity, risk, success, value; This is just incredible!* —**in.cred.i.bly** adv.

in.cre.du.li.ty (in.cruh.DEW.li.tee) n. disbelief: *Incredulity was written all over his face.*

in.cred.u.lous (in.CREJ.uh.lus) adj. showing disbelief: *an incredulous expression, look, shaking of the head.* —**in.cred.u.lous.ly** adv.

in.cre.ment (IN.cruh.munt) n. amount or quantity of increase: *the annual increments in a wage scale.* —**in.cre.men.tal** (-MEN.tul) adj.

in.crim.i.nate (in.CRIM.uh.nate) v. **-nates, -nat.ed, -nat.ing** accuse someone of or involve someone in wrongdoing: *The gun in her possession seemed to incriminate her;* adj.: *He was suspected of the crime because of **incriminating** circumstances; incriminating documents, evidence, photographs, tapes.* —**in.crim.i.na.tion** (-NAY.shun) n. —**in.crim.i.na.to.ry** (-nuh.tor.ee) adj.

incrust, incrustation same as ENCRUST, ENCRUSTATION.

in.cu.bate (INK.yuh.bate) v. **-bates, -bat.ed, -bat.ing 1** sit on eggs or brood as a female bird does. **2** artificially develop eggs, cultures of microorganisms, premature infants, etc. **3** of germs, develop in a body before symptoms of the infection appear. —**in.cu.ba.tion** (-BAY.shun) n.: *Measles has an incubation period of 10 to 14 days.*

in.cu.ba.tor (INK.yuh.bay.tur) n. **1** an apparatus for keeping premature babies under controlled conditions till they are ready to live in a normal atmosphere. **2** an apparatus for keeping eggs warm while being hatched.

in.cu.bus (INK.yuh.bus) *n.* **1** an evil spirit supposed to lie on and oppress a sleeping person, as in a nightmare or "incubus attack." **2** anything oppressive or burdensome.

in.cul.cate (in.CUL.cate, IN.cul-) *v.* **-cates, -cat.ed, -cat.ing** impress ideas, habits, facts, etc. into the minds of others, esp. by frequent repetition: *Prejudice is often inculcated in children by parents.* —**in.cul.ca.tion** (in.cul.CAY.shun) *n.*

in.cul.pate (in.CUL.pate, IN.cul-) *v.* **-pates, -pat.ed, -pat.ing** same as INCRIMINATE.

in.cum.ben.cy (in.CUM.bun.see) *n.* **-cies 1** the term of office of an incumbent. **2** a duty or obligation.

in.cum.bent (in.CUM.bunt) *n.* a person holding an office or position: *Mr. Jones, the present incumbent.* —*adj.* **1** *adjp.* being an obligation or duty: *The judge felt it incumbent on or upon him to impose a jail term.* **2** *adja.* holding the specified office: *candidates challenging the incumbent mayor.*

incumber, incumbrance same as ENCUMBER, ENCUMBRANCE.

in.cu.nab.u.la (in.cue.NAB.yuh.luh) *n.pl.* **1** beginnings; first traces or earliest stages. **2** books printed before 1501. —**in.cu.nab.u.lum** *sing.*

in.cur (in.CUR) *v.* **-curs, -curred, -cur.ring** meet with or bring down on oneself something inconvenient or unpleasant: *to incur charges, costs, debts, expenses, liabilities, losses, obligations, penalties; to incur someone's dislike, displeasure, hatred, wrath.*

in.cur.a.ble (in.KYOOR.uh.bul) *adj.* that cannot be cured or remedied: *incurable diseases.*

in.cur.sion (in.CUR.zhun) *n.* an invasion or raid: *armed incursions by guerrillas into British territory.*

in.cus (INK.us) *n., pl.* **-cu.des** (in.CUE.deez) the small, anvil-shaped middle bone of the middle ear.

in.debt.ed (in.DET.id) *adj.* owing money, gratitude, etc.: *We are deeply indebted to you for taking care of our child.* —**in.debt.ed.ness** *n.*

in.de.cen.cy (in.DEE.sun.see) *n.* **-cies 1** lack of decency. **2** an obscene act: *a charge of committing a gross indecency in a public place.*

in.de.cent (in.DEE.sunt) *adj.* **1** not decent or becoming: *It's considered indecent to come out of the bathroom with nothing on; He married his brother's widow in indecent haste.* **2** morally bad or obscene: *Rape is a more serious crime than indecent assault; Sam was charged with indecent exposure (of genitals).* —**in.de.cent.ly** *adv.*

in.de.ci.pher.a.ble (in.di.SYE.fuh.ruh.bul) *adj.* that cannot be deciphered.

in.de.ci.sion (in.di.SIZH.un) *n.* tendency to hesitate; irresolution.

in.de.ci.sive (in.di.SYE.siv) *adj.* **1** not decisive or conclusive: *The battle was indecisive.* **2** vacillating: *Hamlet was indecisive about taking action against his father's murderer.*

in.dec.o.rous (in.DEC.uh.rus) *adj.* not decorous or seemly.

in.deed (in.DEED) *adv.* certainly; really. —*interj.* expressing surprise, doubt, irony, etc.

in.de.fat.i.ga.ble (in.di.FAT.uh.guh.bul) *adj.* untiring or tireless: *She was indefatigable in the service of the company.* —**in.de.fat.i.ga.bly** *adv.*

in.de.fea.si.ble (in.di.FEE.zuh.bul) *adj.* that cannot be done away with or annulled, as certain rights and claims; **in.de.fea.si.bly** *adv.*

in.de.fen.si.ble (in.di.FEN.suh.bul) *adj.* that cannot be defended; unjustifiable: *an indefensible position.*

in.de.fin.a.ble (in.di.FYE.nuh.bul) *adj.* that cannot be defined or described.

in.def.i.nite (in.DEF.uh.nit) *adj.* not definite; not defining, precise, or certain: *an indefinite answer such as "Maybe"; an indefinite period of time; an indefinite pronoun such as "some," "few," or "many"; an indefinite article (= "a" or "an").* —**in.def.i.nite.ly** *adv.*; **in.def.i.nite.ness** *n.*

in.del.i.ble (in.DEL.uh.bul) *adj.* that cannot be erased or blotted out: *an indelible ink, impression, memory;* **in.del.i.bly** *adv.*

in.del.i.cate (in.DEL.uh.kit) *adj.* lacking delicacy or propriety; coarse or tactless: *It was indelicate of him to point out her error in public.* —**in.del.i.ca.cy** (-cuh.see) *n.* **-cies.**

in.dem.ni.fy (in.DEM.nuh.fye) *v.* **-fies, -fied, -fy.ing** insure: *money set aside to indemnify workers against loss of job; to indemnify them against or for losses, damages, legal actions; to indemnify depositors in case of bank failure.* —**in.dem.ni.fi.ca.tion** (-fuh.CAY.shun) *n.*

in.dem.ni.ty (in.DEM.ni.tee) *n.* **-ties 1** security or insurance: *life insurance with double indemnity (= twice the* insured amount) *in case of accidental death.* **2** in Canada, the annual salary received by a member of Parliament or of a legislature, called **sessional indemnity. 3** compensation such as war reparations exacted from a defeated nation.

in.dent (in.DENT) *v.* **1** make a dent, notch, or recess on an edge or border: *The first line of a paragraph is indented a few spaces from the left margin; coves and capes that indent a coastline.* **2** make a dent or depression, as of a pattern on metal; hence, stamp: *an asphalt that indents easily.* —*n.* a notch or indention. —**in.den.ta.tion** (in.den.TAY.shun) *n.* —**in.dent.er** or **in.den.tor** *n.*

in.den.tion (in.DEN.shun) *n.* an indenting or the blank space left by indenting a line or paragraph: *Make a paragraph indention of five spaces.*

in.den.ture (in.DEN.chur) *n.* a written contract, usually **indentures**, esp. a contract binding one to someone else's service: *He was apprenticed to a carpenter by indentures.* —*v.* **-tures, -tured, -tur.ing** bind by indentures: *Plantation workers used to be slaves, indentured servants, or immigrants.*

in.de.pend.ence (in.duh.PEN.dunce) *n.* the quality of being independent; freedom: *The United States gained or won its independence from Britain; They declared independence on July 4, 1776; Many nations have achieved independence since World War II; Dependencies don't enjoy political independence; Some countries lose their independence to the superpowers.*

in.de.pend.ent (in.duh.PEN.dunt) *adj.* free from the rule, control, or influence of others: *Everyone would like to become independent (of others); an independent businessman, country, income, operator, opinion, thinker; a fiercely independent nationalist; She is a woman of independent means (having private resources); He has no income independent of* (= apart from) *his pension.* —*n.*: *He sits in the legislature as an independent (not belonging to any party).* —**in.de.pend.ent.ly** *adv.*

in-depth *adja.* profound or thorough: *an in-depth interview, report, study.*

in.de.scrib.a.ble (in.dis.CRY.buh.bul) *adj.* that cannot be described or is beyond description: *He was in indescribable pain;* **in.de.scrib.a.bly** *adv.*

in.de.struct.i.ble (in.dis.TRUC.tuh.bul) *adj.* that cannot be destroyed.

in.de.ter.mi.nate (in.di.TUR.muh.nit) *adj.* not determined; vague; inconclusive; **in.de.ter.mi.nate.ly** *adv.* —**in.de.ter.mi.na.cy** (-nuh.see) *n.*

in.dex (IN.dex) *n.* **-dex.es** or **-di.ces** (-duh.seez) **1** something that points or indicates: *Growth rings are an index of a tree's growth; "The face is the index of the mind."* **2** the forefinger, or **index finger. 3** a fist sign [☞] beside a note or paragraph. **4** same as THUMB INDEX. **5** a listing of authors or subjects, as at the end of a book or in a library catalog: *an author index; a card index* (= catalog); *subject index; to compile* or *do* or *make an index to a book; the former Roman Catholic Index of books prohibited as harmful to faith or morals; Standard & Poor's 500-stock index.* **6** the percentage variation from a normal, as in prices, wages, cost of living, etc.: *the consumer price index; cost-of-living index; index of leading economic indicators.* **7** a figure (as 3 in ab³) showing the power to which a mathematical quantity is raised. **8** the amount that a light ray bends, or **index of refraction**, in passing into a different medium: *The lower a gem's refractive index the less its luster.* —*v.* **1** provide with an index: *The book is well indexed.* **2** enter in an index: *All words are separately indexed in our database.* **3** adjust to the cost-of-living index: *to index wages, interest, etc.; adj.: an indexed pension.* —**in.dex.a.tion** (-AY.shun) *n.*

India ink *n.* an ink prepared from a pigment of lampblack with glue or gum, used for drawing and lettering.

In.di.an (IN.dee.un) *n.* **1** a member of one of the many groups of people considered natives of North America: *The Indians are also called Native Americans and Native Canadians; Navaho Indians; At work, Joe's just one of the Indians* (= not a chief). **2** a person of or from India; East Indian: *Indians and Pakistanis.* —*adja.* **1** having to do with North American Indians or their languages: *the Department of Indian Affairs; an Indian club* (= wooden club for exercise); *an Indian reservation* or, in Canada, *reserve.* **2** having to do with India or East Indians: *Indian police, politics; the Indian subcontinent (comprising India, Pakistan, and Bangladesh).*

Indian corn same as CORN, n. 1.

Indian file *n.* [old use] single file: *to walk in Indian file.*

Indian meal same as CORNMEAL.

Indian pipe *n.* an herb of the heath family that resembles a group of clay pipes because of its long stems having a white or pink bell-shaped flower at the end.

Indian summer *n.* a brief period of unusually mild weather sometimes occurring late in the fall.

India paper *n.* a very thin tough paper used for Bibles, air editions of newspapers, etc.

In.dic *adj.* having to do with the Indo-European languages of India such as Sanskrit, Hindi, and Bengali.

in.di.cate (IN.di.cate) *v.* **-cates, -cat.ed, -cat.ing** to point: *A clock's hands indicate* (= point out) *time; A nod indicates* (= means) *assent; She indicated* (= stated briefly) *that it was their last meeting; Lee's language is so poor that remedial English seems indicated* (= pointed to).
—**in.di.ca.tion** (-CAY.shun) *n.*
—**in.di.ca.tor** (-cay.tur) *n.*

in.dic.a.tive (in.DIC.uh.tiv) *adj.* indicating or pointing out something: *symptoms indicative of a disease; In "She is gone" and "Are you coming?" the verbs are in the* **indicative mood**, *not imperative.*

indices a *pl.* of INDEX.

in.di.ci.a (in.DISH.ee.uh) *n.pl.* **1** characteristic or distinctive marks. **2** postal markings put on mail.

in.dict (in.DITE) *v.* charge someone with a crime. —**in.dict.a.ble** (in.DYE.tuh.bul) *adj.*: *an indictable offense.*

in.dict.ment (in.DITE.munt) *n.* **1** an indicting: *Criminal cases are tried on indictment; A grand jury hands up an indictment to a judge; to issue, return, quash an indictment; to bring an indictment against someone for a crime.*
2 condemnation or accusation: *The accountant's report was a stinging indictment of wasteful spending; a sweeping indictment against the government.*

in.dif.fer.ence (in.DIF.uh.runce) *n.*
1 lack of interest: *to affect, display, feign indifference toward someone; a cool, studied indifference to flattery.* **2** lack of concern, esp. as to the importance of something: *Careless work shows his indifference; his indifference about good work habits; Her opinions are a matter of indifference to me; a marked indifference to the demands of justice.*

in.dif.fer.ent (in.DIF.uh.runt) *adj.*
1 showing no interest; apathetic: *She couldn't remain indifferent in a family dispute; He's not indifferent to the sufferings of the poor.* **2** mediocre: *a novel of indifferent quality.*

in.di.gence (IN.duh.junce) *n.* privation or need.

in.dig.e.nous (in.DIJ.uh.nus) *adj.* belonging or proper to a particular region, country, soil, or climate as native to it, not exotic or imported: *an indigenous people, species; The Australian aborigines are the indigenous inhabitants of the country; Koalas are indigenous to Australia.*

in.di.gent (IN.duh.junt) *adj.* needy: *an indigent widow;* **n.**: *a program for the indigent and unskilled.*

in.di.gest.i.ble (in.duh.JES.tuh.bul) *adj.* of foods, difficult to digest.

in.di.ges.tion (in.duh.JES.chun) *n.* poor digestion: *Some foods cause indigestion; an attack of indigestion; Arguing during meals gives me indigestion.*

in.dig.nant (in.DIG.nunt) *adj.* righteously angry or scornful: *She is indignant with her boss about or at or over not being given a raise.* —**in.dig.nant.ly** *adv.*

in.dig.na.tion (in.dig.NAY.shun) *n.* anger caused by an injustice: *public indignation; righteous indignation; to arouse, feel, show indignation; to express indignation about or at or over being kept waiting unnecessarily.*

in.dig.ni.ty (in.DIG.ni.tee) *n.* **-ties** something done or said that hurts one's dignity or self-respect: *indignities inflicted on the poor; to suffer indignities.*

in.di.go (IN.di.goh) *n.* **-gos** or **-goes** a deep blue dye once obtained from an Indian plant of the legume family but now made from aniline.

in.di.rect (in.duh.RECT) *adj.* **1** not straight or straightforward; devious: *an indirect answer, dealing, method, route; Unlike sales tax, an* **indirect tax** *is included in the price of a product.* **2** secondary: *an indirect cause;* **indirect discourse** (= reported speech); *In "Give me the pen," "me" is the* **indirect object.**
—**in.di.rect.ly** *adv.;* **in.di.rect.ness** *n.*

in.dis.creet (in.di.SCREET) *adj.* not discreet; **in.dis.creet.ly** *adv.*

in.dis.cre.tion (in.dis.CRESH.un) *n.*
1 lack of discretion; imprudence. **2** an indiscreet act or remark: *youthful indiscretions.*

in.dis.crim.i.nate (in.dis.CRIM.uh.nit) *adj.* **1** without care in making choices or decisions: *an indiscriminate reader; indiscriminate in her attacks, compliments, friendships, use of resources.* **2** adja. haphazard: *indiscriminate dumping; an indiscriminate mass, pile.*
—**in.dis.crim.i.nate.ly** *adv.*

in.dis.pen.sa.ble (in.dis.PEN.suh.bul) *adj.* absolutely essential: *Food is indispensable for or to living beings.*
—**in.dis.pen.sa.bly** *adv.*
—**in.dis.pen.sa.bil.i.ty** (-BIL.i.tee) *n.*

in.dis.posed (in.dis.POZED) *adj.* **1** not well disposed: *He's indisposed to help you.* **2** slightly ill: *The boss is indisposed.* —**in.dis.po.si.tion** (IN.dis.puh.ZISH.un) *n.*

in.dis.put.a.ble (in.dis.PEW.tuh.bul) *adj.* that cannot be disputed or denied.

in.dis.sol.u.ble (in.di.SOL.yuh.bul) *adj.* that cannot be undone; lasting.

in.dis.tinct (in.dis.TINCT) *adj.* not clearly defined or distinguishable; **in.dis.tinct.ly** *adv.*

in.dite (in.DITE) *v.* **-dites, -dit.ed, -dit.ing** compose a poem, speech, letter, etc.

in.di.um (IN.dee.um) *n.* a silver-white metallic chemical element.

in.di.vid.u.al (in.duh.VIJ.oo.ul) *n.* a separate person, animal, or thing: *the rights of the individual as opposed to those of society as a whole; treat children as individuals; each individual of a species; an obnoxious individual* (= person). —*adja.* having to do with an individual: *There is standing room besides individual seating for 200; lectures followed by individual coaching; Students get individual attention; an individual* (= distinctive) *style.* —**in.di.vid.u.al.ly** (-uh.lee) *adv.*

in.di.vid.u.al.ism (in.di.VIJ.oo.uh.liz.um) *n.* a doctrine stressing individual existence, freedom, importance, self-interest, etc.; **in.di.vid.u.al.ist** *n. & adj.* —**in.di.vid.u.al.is.tic** (-LIS.tic) *adj.*

in.di.vid.u.al.i.ty (IN.duh.vij.oo.AL.i.tee) *n.* **-ties 1** the sum of a person's distinctive characteristics. **2** one's individual condition or existence. **3** an individual characteristic or trait.

in.di.vid.u.al.ize (in.duh.VIJ.oo.uh.lize) *v.* **-iz.es, -ized, -iz.ing** make individual: *a style that individualizes* (= distinguishes) *her performance;* **adj.**: *individualized instruction of students.* —**in.di.vid.u.al.i.za.tion** (-luh.ZAY.shun, -lye-) *n.*

in.di.vid.u.ate (in.di.VIJ.oo.ate) *v.* **-ates, -at.ed -at.ing 1** make or become an individual. **2** distinguish or become distinctive. —**in.di.vid.u.a.tion** (-AY.shun) *n.*

in.doc.tri.nate (in.DOC.truh.nate) *v.* **-nates, -nat.ed, -nat.ing** fill someone's mind with the beliefs of a particular group or party: *People used to be indoctrinated in Communist theory; indoctrinated with falsehoods; a consultant hired to indoctrinate employees.* —**in.doc.tri.na.tion** (-NAY.shun) *n.*

Indo-European *n. & adj.* (having to do with) a family of languages originally spoken in India, Iran, and Europe, to which English belongs.

in.do.lent (IN.duh.lunt) *adj.* idle or lazy: *an indolent worker; an indolent* (= inactive) *ulcer; an indolent* (= painless) *cyst or tumor.* —**in.do.lence** (-lunce) *n.*

in.dom.i.ta.ble (in.DOM.uh.tuh.bul) *adj.* unconquerable or unyielding: *indomitable courage, spirit, will.* —**in.dom.i.ta.bly** *adv.*

in.door (IN.dore) *adja.* done, used, situated, etc. within a building: *an indoor facility, game, pool; indoor photography.* —**in.doors** (IN.DORS) *adv.*: *to go, keep, stay indoors.*

indorse same as ENDORSE.

in.du.bi.ta.ble (in.DEW.buh.tuh.bul) *adj. Formal.* that cannot be doubted; certain; **in.du.bi.ta.bly** *adv.*

in.duce (in.DUCE) *v.* **-duc.es, -duced, -duc.ing 1** bring about: *drugs to induce sleep;* **adj.**: *an* **induced** *abortion, labor;* **induced current** (induced by electrical conduction). **2** influence or persuade: *a carrot to induce a donkey to proceed.*

in.duce.ment (in.DUCE.munt) *n.* external influence or attempt to entice or tempt one to action: *to offer* or *provide inducements; a strong inducement; scholarships as inducements to study.*

in.duct (in.DUCT) *v.* install, enroll, or introduce someone *into* an office or position, the military, *to* a benefice, etc.; **in.duc.tor** (-tur) *n.* —**in.duct.ee** (in.duc.TEE) *n.*

in.duct.ance (in.DUC.tunce) *n.* the electrical property of inducing electromotive forces.

in.duc.tion (in.DUC.shun) *n.* **1** the process of inducing electrical or magnetic properties; **adj.**: *induction coils, heating.* **2** an inducting, as into military service or an office; **adj.**: *induction ceremonies, papers.* **3** process of reasoning from particular facts to general principles; also, a conclusion so reached; opposite of DEDUCTION. —**in.duc.tive** (in.DUC.tiv) *adj.*: *inductive logic, reasoning;* **in.duc.tive.ly** *adv.*

indue same as ENDUE.

in.dulge (in.DULJ) *v.* **-dulg.es, -dulged, -dulg.ing** yield or give in to one's pleasures, wants, wishes, or whims: *to indulge a fondness or craving for candy; a sick child who needs some indulging; She rarely* **indulges in** *abusive language.*

in.dul.gence (in.DUL.junce) *n.* **1** an indulging or something one indulges in. **2** in the Roman Catholic Church, remission of punishment due for sins. **3** tolerance or forbearance: *The lecturer craved the indulgence of a tired audience.*

—**in.dul.gent** *adj.*; **in.dul.gent.ly** *adv.*

in.du.rate (IN.dew.rate) *v.* **-rates, -rat.ed, -rat.ing** harden a substance, a tissue, a person in a habit, etc.; inure. —*adj.* (-rit) hardened or callous: *indurate to public opinion.* —**in.du.ra.tion** (-RAY.shun) *n.*: *induration of tissue around a wound.*

in.dus.tri.al (in.DUS.tree.ul) *adja.* having to do with industries: *modern industrial nations of the West; an industrial (= synthetic) diamond; Factory production was speeded up by machines during England's* **Industrial Revolution** *from about 1750.* —**in.dus.tri.al.ist** (-uh.list) *n.* —**in.dus.tri.al.ly** *adv.*

industrial estate same as INDUSTRIAL PARK.

in.dus.tri.al.ize (in.DUS.tree.uh.lize) *v.* **-iz.es, -ized, -iz.ing** make or become industrial: *Material progress lies in industrializing;* ***adj.*** *Japan is highly* ***industrialized;*** *the industrialized nations of the West.* —**in.dus.tri.al.i.za.tion** (-luh.ZAY.shun, -lye-) *n.*

industrial park *n.* a usu. suburban area set apart for businesses and industries.

industrial-strength *adja.* heavy-duty: *industrial-strength detergents, drills.*

in.dus.tri.ous (in.DUS.tree.us) *adj.* naturally hard-working: *an industrious clerk, housewife; industrious like ants and bees.* —**in.dus.tri.ous.ly** *adv.*; **in.dus.tri.ous.ness** *n.*

in.dus.try (IN.dus.tree) *n.* **-tries 1** a business activity or enterprise: *Primary or extractive industries such as fishing and mining; secondary or manufacturing industries; Distributive industries serve the consumer; basic, cottage, key industries; heavy, light, steel, textile, tourist, travel industries; Industries spring up;* to *build up* or *develop industries; American industry (= industries collectively).* **2** habitually hard-working quality; systematic effort: *Diligence and industry got her to the top.*

in.dwell.ing (IN.dwel.ing) *adj.* dwelling within: *an indwelling force, principle, spirit.*

In.dy (IN.dee) *n.* an automobile race similar to the "Indianapolis 500."

Indy car *n.* a racing car with a powerful rear-mounted engine; also "Indianapolis car": *Indy Car World Series;* ***adja.:*** ***Indy-car*** *champions, circuits, racing, rides, series.*

in.e.bri.ate (in.EE.bree.ate) *v.* **-ates, -at.ed, -at.ing** *Formal.* intoxicate. —*n.* (-it) a drunkard. —*adj.* drunk: *an inebriate driver.* —**in.e.bri.a.tion** (-AY.shun) *n.*

in.ef.fa.ble (in.EF.uh.bul) *adj.* not capable of being expressed in words: *that old ineffable charm; an ineffable mystery, sadness; the ineffable happiness of Heaven; ineffable beauty; the ineffable name of Jehovah (too sacred to be uttered).* —**in.ef.fa.bly** *adv.*

in.ef.fec.tive (in.i.FEC.tiv) *adj.* not effective; incapable: *ineffective controls, management, methods.*

in.ef.fec.tu.al (in.i.FEC.choo.ul) *adj.* not producing the expected effect: *ineffectual efforts.*

in.ef.fi.cient (in.uh.FISH.unt) *adj.* not working well enough to produce results quickly: *an inefficient administration, government, machine, manager, measure, method;* **in.ef.fi.cient.ly** *adv.* —**in.ef.fi.cien.cy** *n.*

in.el.e.gant (in.EL.i.gunt) *adj.* not elegant; coarse or crude; **in.el.e.gant.ly** *adv.* —**in.el.e.gance** *n.*

in.el.i.gi.ble (in.EL.i.juh.bul) *n. & adj.* (one who is) not eligible or suitable. —**in.el.i.gi.bil.i.ty** (-BIL.i.tee) *n.*

in.e.luc.ta.ble (in.i.LUC.tuh.bul) *adj. Formal.* not to be struggled with or avoided: *an ineluctable consequence, decline, effect, fate, link, necessity.* —**in.e.luc.ta.bly** *adv.*

in.ept (in.EPT) *adj.* utterly lacking in skill or dexterity; incompetent: *an inept comparison, question, remark; He's quite inept at* or *in handling people; a brave but inept (= bungling) military officer.* —**in.ept.ly** *adv.* —**in.ept.i.tude** or **in.ept.ness** *n.*

in.e.qual.i.ty (in.ee.KWOL.i.tee) *n.* **-ties** difference in status, opportunities, etc. between two or more social groups: *the inequalities between the rich and the poor.*

in.er.rant (in.ER.unt) *adj.* not erring. —**in.er.ran.cy** *n.*: *the inerrancy of the word of God.*

in.ert (in.URT) *adj.* lacking inherent power or quality, as to act or move: *The accident victim lay inert; An inert electorate; An* **inert gas** *such as neon does not combine with other elements.* —**in.ert.ly** *adv.*; **in.ert.ness** *n.*

in.er.tia (in.UR.shuh) *n.* **1** the tendency of matter to remain in its state of rest or motion unless acted on by an outside force: *the self-adjusting* **inertia reel** *of a safety belt; an aircraft engine with an* **inertia starter** *that has a wheel spun by hand.* **2** inertness or sluggishness: *Sheer inertia makes him stay in bed all morning.* —**in.er.tial** (-shul) *adj.*: *an inertial force; inertial resistance; a missile kept on course by means of an inertial guidance* or *navigation system.*

inescapable / inferior

in.es.ca.ble (in.uh.SCAY.puh.bul) *adj.* that cannot be escaped; inevitable, as a logical conclusion, moral necessity, etc. —**in.es.cap.a.bly** *adv.*

in.es.ti.ma.ble (i.NES.tuh.muh.bul) *adj.* too great or precious to be calculated; invaluable; **in.es.ti.ma.bly** *adv.*

in.ev.i.ta.ble (in.EV.i.tuh.bul) *adj.* unavoidable, as a natural occurrence or phenomenon: *Death is inevitable; an inevitable delay, result, war; a tourist with his inevitable camera.* —**in.ev.i.ta.bly** *adv.* —**in.ev.i.ta.bil.i.ty** (-BIL.i.tee) *n.*

in.ex.haust.i.ble (in.ig.ZAWS.tuh.bul) *adj.* 1 that cannot be exhausted: *the ocean's inexhaustible riches.* 2 tireless: *a man of inexhaustible energy.* —**in.ex.haust.i.bly** *adv.*

in.ex.o.ra.ble (in.EX.uh.ruh.bul) *adj.* that cannot be altered by begging or entreaty; relentless: *a dictator's inexorable demands; a condemned man awaiting his inexorable doom; the inexorable logic of her reasoning.* —**in.ex.o.ra.bly** *adv.*

in.ex.pe.ri.ence (in.ik.SPEER.ee.unce) *n.* lack of experience or consequent lack of skill, wisdom, etc. —**in.ex.pe.ri.enced** *adj.*

in.ex.pert (in.EX.purt, in.ik.SPURT) *adj.* inexperienced; also, unskilled.

in.ex.pi.a.ble (in.EX.pee.uh.bul) *adj.* that cannot be expiated or atoned for.

in.ex.pli.ca.ble (in.EX.plic.uh.bul, in.ex.PLIC-) *adj.* that cannot be explained or accounted for; mysterious; **in.ex.pli.ca.bly** *adv.*

in.ex.press.i.ble (in.iks.PRES.uh.bul) *adj.* that cannot be expressed or described; **in.ex.press.i.bly** *adv.*

in ex.tre.mis (in.ik.STREE.mis, -STRAY.mis) *Latin.* at the point of death.

in.ex.tri.ca.ble (in.EX.tric.uh.bul, in.ik.STRIC.uh.bul) *adj.* 1 impossible to extricate oneself from: *inextricable difficulties.* 2 impossible to disentangle: *an inextricable problem.* —**in.ex.tri.ca.bly** *adv.*

in.fal.li.ble (in.FAL.uh.bul) *adj.* not capable of failing or being wrong: *an infallible authority, method, remedy, test;* **in.fal.li.bly** *adv.* —**in.fal.li.bil.i.ty** (-BIL.i.tee) *n.*

in.fa.mous (IN.fuh.mus) *adj.* having or giving a scandalous reputation: *infamous and unprofessional conduct; an infamous crime, plot, traitor.*

in.fa.my (IN.fuh.mee) *n.* -mies 1 a disgraceful or wicked act. 2 disgrace or wickedness: *the infamy of Pearl Harbor.*

in.fan.cy (IN.fun.see) *n.* -cies 1 the state or period of being an infant.
2 any initial period: *in Caxton's days when printing was in its infancy.*

in.fant (IN.funt) *n.* a baby: *no extra charge for infants; to nurse, suckle, wean an infant; a newborn infant; premature infants;* **adj**a.: *Mozart was an infant prodigy; an infant (= young) nation.*

in.fan.ti.cide (in.FAN.tuh.side) *n.* 1 the killing of an infant. 2 the killer.

in.fan.tile (IN.fun.tile, -til) *adj.* having to do with infancy: *infantile behavior; infantile paralysis* (= polio).

infant mortality *n.* death before age one.

in.fan.try (IN.fun.tree) *n.* -tries 1 the branch of an army consisting of troops. 2 troops trained and equipped to fight on foot. —**in.fan.try.man** (-mun) *n.* -**men.**

in.farct (in.FARCT, IN.farct) *n.* an area of tissue killed by the blockage of an artery leading to it by a clot or embolus; **adj.**: *an infarcted area.* —**in.farc.tion** *n.*

in.fat.u.ate (in.FACH.oo.ate) *v.* -ates, -at.ed, -at.ing affect a person with a foolish, usually short-lived passion. —**in.fat.u.a.tion** (-AY.shun) *n.*

in.fect (in.FECT) *v.* 1 cause an unhealthy condition in a body part; become diseased, as with a germ or virus: *He was infected by the HIV virus;* **adj.**: *An open wound may become infected.* 2 to influence or affect: *The teacher infected the whole class with her enthusiasm.*

in.fec.tion (in.FEC.shun) *n.* 1 a disease caused by a spreading virus or bacterium: *airborne infections; a secondary infection such as sinusitis resulting from a virus cold.* 2 the act or process of infecting: *Infection sets in if a wound is not attended to; the rate, risk, route, source of infection; the infection (= affecting) of young minds with dangerous ideas.* —**in.fec.tious** (-shus) *adj.*: *infectious diseases; infectious (= spreading) enthusiasm, laughter.* —**in.fec.tive** (-tiv) *adj.*: *infective ability, agents, secretions, stages.* —**in.fec.tor** *n.*

in.fe.lic.i.tous (in.fuh.LIS.uh.tus) *adj.* not felicitous; inappropriate. —**in.fe.lic.i.ty** *n.* -ties.

in.fer (in.FUR) *v.* -fers, -ferred, -fer.ring 1 conclude from facts or evidence. 2 loosely, to imply. —**in.fer.ence** (IN.fuh.runce) *n.* —**in.fer.en.tial** (-REN.shul) *adj.* based on facts or evidence: *an inferential judgment.*

in.fe.ri.or (in.FEER.ee.ur) *n. & adj.* (one) that is lower in position, merit, or quality. —**in.fe.ri.or.i.ty** (-OR.i.tee) *n.*

in.fer.nal (in.FUR.nul) *adj.* hellish or damned: *an infernal region, scheme.* —**in.fer.nal.ly** *adv.*

in.fer.no (in.FUR.noh) *n.* **-nos** a hell-like place or condition: *a blazing, raging, roaring, towering inferno.*

in.fer.tile (in.FUR.tul) *adj.* barren or unproductive: *infertile couples, men, women.* —**in.fer.til.i.ty** (in.fur.TIL.i.tee) *n.*

in.fest (in.FEST) *v.* to overrun in large numbers, as with pests or parasites: *Slugs infest a green garden; adj. & cpd: hair infested with lice; a malaria-infested region; roach-infested homes; salmonella-infested chicken.* —**in.fes.ta.tion** (in.fes.TAY.shun) *n.*

in.fi.del (IN.fuh.dul) *n.* a religious unbeliever.

in.fi.del.i.ty (in.fuh.DEL.i.tee) *n.* **-ties** **1** (act of) disloyalty between spouses; unfaithfulness: *conjugal infidelity; marital infidelities.* **2** lack of religious faith.

in.field *n.* **1** an inner area such as is enclosed by a racetrack or bounded by the bases in a baseball field. **2** the defensive players, or **infielders**, who cover first, second, and third base and shortstop.

in.fight.ing (IN.fight.ing) *n.* **1** fighting within a group, as between associates. **2** fighting at close quarters, as in boxing or fencing. —**in.fight.er** *n.*

in.fill *n.* the filling in of empty spaces, as with new housing in a densely built-up area: *New housing has been created by infill, renovation, and conversion.* —**adja.:** *infill housing; an infill development, project, site; infill drilling of oil wells.*

in.fil.trate (IN.fil.trate, in.FIL.trate) *v.* **-trates, -trat.ed, -trat.ing** pass gradually through or into something; penetrate a region or organization secretly with hostile intent. —**in.fil.tra.tor** (-tray.tur) *n.* —**in.fil.tra.tion** (-TRAY.shun) *n.*

in.fi.nite (IN.fuh.nit) *adj.* endlessly great or vast: *God's infinite goodness; her infinite patience; God the Infinite (being).* —**in.fi.nite.ly** *adv.*

in.fin.i.tes.i.mal (IN.fin.i.TES.uh.mul) *adj.* that is extremely minute: *The chances of your contracting the disease are infinitesimal; The odds are infinitesimal.* —**in.fin.i.tes.i.mal.ly** *adv.*

in.fin.i.tive (in.FIN.uh.tiv) *n.* a verb form that is not limited to any person, number, or tense, as "to go" in "I (or We, They, etc.) want (or wanted) to go."

in.fin.i.tude (in.FIN.i.tude) *n.* **1** infinite condition. **2** something that is infinite in extent.

in.fin.i.ty (in.FIN.i.tee) *n.* **-ties** something infinite such as an indefinite number: *10/3 equals 3.333 to infinity.*

in.firm (in.FURM) *adj.* not firm or strong, esp. weak because of age.

in.fir.ma.ry (in.FUR.muh.ree) *n.* **-ries** **1** a small hospital. **2** a dispensary.

in.fir.mi.ty (in.FUR.mi.tee) *n.* **-ties** **1** weakness or illness. **2** a flaw of character.

in.flame (in.FLAME) *v.* **-flames, -flamed, -flam.ing** **1** make or become excited: *words apt to inflame a mob to fury; adj.: an inflamed mob, situation; inflamed passions, rhetoric, tensions.* **2** make or become sore or swollen: *an organ inflamed by an infection; adj.: an inflamed area, appendix, joint, wound.* —**in.flam.ma.tion** (in.fluh.MAY.shun) *n.*

in.flam.ma.ble (in.FLAM.uh.bul) *adj.* that catches fire easily: *Gasoline is highly inflammable; He has an inflammable* (= easily excitable) *temper.* —**in.flam.ma.bil.i.ty** (-BIL.i.tee) *n.*

in.flam.ma.to.ry (in.FLAM.uh.tor.ee) *adj.* apt to inflame: *an inflammatory lung condition; an inflammatory speech.*

in.flate (in.FLATE) *v.* **-flates, -flat.ed, -flat.ing** expand, as with air, or increase abnormally: *to inflate a balloon, tire; prices inflating at an annual rate of 30%; adj.: wildly inflated claims, prices; artificially inflated prices; an ego inflated with pride; an inflated ego, estimate, sense of self-importance.* —**in.flat.a.ble** (in.FLAY.tuh.bul) *adj.: an inflatable mattress, toy, vest.*

in.fla.tion (in.FLAY.shun) *n.* rise of prices and fall in the buying power of money: *creeping, double-digit, galloping, rampant, runaway inflation.*

in.fla.tion.ar.y (in.FLAY.shuh.nair.ee) *adj.* causing inflation: *Credit buying is inflationary; an inflationary wage settlement; unemployment during an inflationary recession; Wages and prices rise in an inflationary spiral.*

in.flect (in.FLECT) *v.* change or vary: *to inflect the tone or pitch of voice; to inflect the form of a word to show number, gender, tense, etc.* —**in.flec.tion** *n.* **1** tone: *"No!" has a falling inflection, but "No?" has a rising inflection.* **2** suffix showing a grammatical change: *"-ed," "-ing," "-est," and other inflections.* **3** a form so changed: *inflections of "go" such as "goes" and "gone."* —**in.flec.tion.al** *adj.*

in.flex.i.ble (in.FLEX.uh.bul) *adj.* rigid or unyielding in thought or will: *He's inflexible in his demands;* **in.flex.i.bly**

adv. —**in.flex.i.bil.i.ty** (-BIL.i.tee) *n.*
in.flex.ion (in.FLEC.shun) same as IN-FLECTION.
in.flict (in.FLICT) *v.* give or impose something painful: *to inflict casualties, damage, losses, misery, pain, punishments, suffering, terror, violence, wounds, etc. on or upon someone; The speech was so boring, the audience felt it was being inflicted on them; a self-inflicted wound.*
—**in.flic.tion** *n.* —**in.flic.tive** *adj.*
in.flight (IN.flite) *adj.* during flight: *an inflight movie; inflight refueling.*
in.flo.res.cence (in.fluh.RES.unce) *n.*
1 a growing flower cluster or its arrangement as a spike, panicle, etc. 2 a blossoming or flowering.
in.flow (IN.floh) *n.* a flowing in.
in.flu.ence (IN.floo.unce) *n.* indirect power or its effect: *the moon's influence on tides; a man of much influence but no real authority; to bring influence to bear on an issue; to exert influence on a person; to flaunt, strengthen, use one's influence; to wield influence; bad, civilizing, cultural, moderating, moral, outside, positive, powerful, restraining, salutary, waning influences; She's a good influence* (= person exerting influence) *on him; an influence for good; He was caught driving* **under the influence** *(of liquor); She was accused of* **influence peddling**.
—*v.* -enc.es, -enced, -enc.ing have or use influence: *Do stars influence our fate? a jury influenced by news stories.*
in.flu.en.tial (in.floo.EN.shul) *adj.* having or using much influence: *Many factors were influential in arriving at this decision; an influential lobbyist, senator.*
—**in.flu.en.tial.ly** *adv.*
in.flu.en.za (in.floo.EN.zuh) *n.* a contagious virus disease; flu; grippe.
in.flux *n.* a flowing in; inflow: *the influx of refugees into a country.*
in.fo (IN.foh) *n.* Informal. information.
in.fo.bit (IN.foh.bit) *n.* a bit of information as stored in a database.
infold same as ENFOLD.
in.fo.mer.cial (in.fuh.MUR.shul) *n.* a short TV feature advertising a product or service.
in.fo.tain.ment (in.fuh.TAIN.munt) same as EDUTAINMENT.
in.form (in.FORM) *v.* give facts or news to someone: *a letter to inform you of or about our decision; Neighbors sometimes inform on or against each other to the police.* —**in.form.er** *n.*
in.for.mal (in.FOR.mul) *adj.* not formal in style, esp. of speech or writing; colloquial; **in.for.mal.ly** *adv.* —**in.for.mal.i.ty** (in.for.MAL.i.tee) *n.* -ties.

in.for.mant (in.FOR.munt) *n.* one who supplies information, usually for professional use, as to the police.
in.for.ma.tion (in.fur.MAY.shun) *n.*
1 facts, data, news, etc.: *He is full of information but lacks judgment; to classify, collect, dig up, disclose, divulge, find, furnish, leak, provide information; to feed information into a computer; to retrieve information from a database; to withhold information from the public; classified, confidential, detailed, first-hand, inside, reliable, secondhand, secret information; information on or about enemy activities; adja.: the information industry; computerized information storage and retrieval; information systems.* 2 the communication of facts, news, etc.: *a director of information;* **For your information**, *we are closed on Sundays; adja.: an information agency, bureau, officer, service;* An **information utility** *provides dial-up services such as databases, electronic mail, stock quotes, travel information, and airline ticketing; the* **information superhighway** (= the Internet). —**in.for.ma.tion.al** (-shuh.nul) *adj.*
in.for.ma.tive (in.FOR.muh.tiv) *adj.* instructive: *an informative leaflet, lecture, talk.* —**in.for.ma.tive.ly** *adv.*
informed *adj.* knowing the facts: *Sterilization requires informed consent; Do keep us informed of your progress; a well-informed journalist.*
in.for.mer.cial (in.fur.MUR.shul) same as INFOMERCIAL.
infra- *prefix.* beneath; under: *infrared, infrasonic, infrastructure.*
in.frac.tion (in.FRAC.shun) *n.* infringement or violation: *a minor infraction of a rule.*
in.fra dig (IN.fruh.dig) *adjp.* beneath one's dignity.
in.fra.red (in.fruh.RED) *adj.* beyond the red end of the visible spectrum: *Infrared rays are used to detect heat from weather satellites and to photograph without light; infrared cameras, images, lights, night-vision, radiation, sensors, signals, telescopes, wavelengths; an infrared remote device for programming VCRs.*
in.fra.son.ic (in.fruh.SON.ic) *adj.* below audible range.
in.fra.sound (IN.fruh.sound) *n.* low-frequency sound.
in.fra.struc.ture (in.fruh.STRUK.chur) *n.* installations, facilities, roads, and such basic services and equipment to back up an undertaking.
in.fre.quent (in.FREEK.wunt) *adj.* not frequent; rare: *an infrequent visitor.*
—**in.fre.quent.ly** *adv.* —**in.fre.quence**

infringe / in-house

or **in.fre.quen.cy** *n.*
in.fringe (in.FRINJ) *v.* **-fring.es, -fringed, -fring.ing** break or violate: *a publication that infringes a copyright; something that infringes on or upon a private right or territory.* —**in.fringe.ment** *n.*
in.fu.ri.ate (in.FYOOR.ee.ate) *v.* **-ates, -at.ed, -at.ing** make furious; enrage; **in.fu.ri.a.ting** *adj.*; **in.fu.ri.a.ting.ly** *adv.*
in.fuse (in.FYOOZE) *v.* **-fus.es, -fused, -fus.ing** 1 pour liquid over something; hence, steep or let soak tea, herbs, etc. 2 instill: *Flagging spirits are infused with fresh courage; to infuse a fighting spirit into the underprivileged.* —**in.fu.sion** (in.FEW.zhun) *n.*: *the infusion of cash into the economy.*
-ing *suffix.* 1 *n.* as in *coming, happening, paintings.* 2 *pres.part.* as in *going, loving, moving, warring;* **adj.**: *a very loving child; warring factions.*
in.gath.er.ing (in.GATH.ur.ing, "TH" as in "the") *n.* a gathering in; harvest.
in.gen.ious (in.JEEN.yus) *adj.* inventive and skillful in thought or action: *an ingenious device, explanation, theory; He's ingenious at finding excuses.* —**in.gen.i.ous.ly** *adv.*; **in.gen.i.ous.ness** *n.*
in.ge.nu.i.ty (in.juh.NEW.i.tee) *n.* skill and cleverness in designing: *human ingenuity.*
in.ge.nue (AN.juh.noo) *n.* an artless and innocent young woman as a dramatic character.
in.gen.u.ous (in.JEN.yoo.us) *adj.* not trying to hide one's feelings or intentions; simple and artless: *a child's ingenuous answer, explanation, smile.* —**in.gen.u.ous.ly** *adv.*; **in.gen.u.ous.ness** *n.*
in.gest (in.JEST) *v.* take into the body like food; absorb. —**in.ges.tion** (-chun) *n.*; **in.ges.tive** (-tiv) *adj.*
in.gle *n.* a fire or fireplace.
in.gle.nook (ING.gul.nook) *n.* a fireplace.
in.glor.i.ous (in.GLOR.ee.us) *adj.* 1 disgraceful: *an inglorious end.* 2 obscure or little-known: *"Some mute inglorious Milton here may rest."*
in.got (ING.gut) *n.* metal cast into a bar or similar convenient shape.
ingraft same as ENGRAFT.
in.grain (in.GRAIN) *v.* work into the grain or fiber: *habits ingrained in us from childhood;* **adj.**: *deeply ingrained prejudices; an ingrained* (= out-and-out) *liar.* — *n.* (IN.grain) yarn, carpeting, etc. dyed before manufacture.

in.grate *n.* an ungrateful person.
in.gra.ti.ate (in.GRAY.shee.ate) *v.* **-ates, -at.ed, -at.ing** try to bring oneself into favor with someone: *The killer would first try to ingratiate himself into the confidence of his victims.* —**ingratiating** *adj.*: *his ingratiating behavior, cuteness, an ingratiating melody, voice, smile.*
in.grat.i.tude (in.GRAT.uh.tude) *n.* ungratefulness: *base, rank ingratitude.*
in.gre.di.ent (in.GREE.dee.unt) *n.* something that goes into the making of a mixture, esp. of a food or medicinal preparation: *the ingredients of a cocktail; basic ingredients; the essential ingredients of chivalry.*
in.gress *n.* entrance.
in.grow.ing (IN.groh.ing) or **in.grown** *adj.* growing or grown in, esp. embedded in the flesh: *an ingrown toenail.*
in.gui.nal (ING.gwuh.nul) *adj.* of or near the groin: *inguinal hernia.*
in.hab.it (in.HAB.it) *v.* live or dwell in a place. —**in.hab.i.ta.ble** (-tuh.bul) *adj.*
in.hab.it.ant (in.HAB.uh.tunt) *n.* one inhabiting a place: *America's original inhabitants; a city of two million inhabitants.*
in.hal.ant (in.HAY.lunt) *n. & adj.* (medicine or drug) that is inhaled.
in.ha.la.tor (IN.huh.lay.tur) *n.* an apparatus for administering medicinal vapors or oxygen in first aid.
in.hale (in.HALE) *v.* **-hales, -haled, -hal.ing** breathe in air, vapor, smoke, etc.; **in.hal.er** *n.* —**in.ha.la.tion** (in.huh.LAY.shun) *n.*
in.here (in.HEER) *v.* **-heres, -hered, -her.ing** *Formal.* belong or be inherent *in* something.
in.her.ent (in.HEER.unt, in.HAIR.unt) *adj.* existing as an inborn or inseparable quality: *the inherent goodness of human nature; basic rights inherent in citizenship.* —**in.her.ent.ly** *adv.*
in.her.it (in.HER.it) *v.* receive as a bequest in a will, as a hereditary trait, or as something passed along: *a chair he inherited from his grandfather; She inherited a financial mess from her predecessor.* —**in.her.it.a.ble** *adj.* —**in.her.it.ance** (-unce) *n.* —**in.her.i.tor** *n.*
in.hib.it (in.HIB.it) *v.* 1 forbid a person from doing something: *Clean-air signs inhibit most smokers from lighting up in public.* 2 hinder an action or process. —**in.hib.i.tor** *n.*
in.hi.bi.tion (in.huh.BISH.un) *n.* a check, esp. a mental blocking of one's own thinking or behavior.
in-house *adv.* inside a group or institution: *artwork for a book done in-house*

inhuman / inlaid

rather than by an agency; employees trained in-house; **adj.a.**: an in-house line of goods, program, publication, study, system; in-house education, staff, training.

in.hu.man (in.HEW.mun) *adj.* not human: *Cannibalism is cruel and inhuman; inhuman poverty and misery; His stamina seems inhuman.* —**in.hu.man.ly** *adv.*

in.hu.mane (in.hew.MAIN) *adj.* not showing humanity or kindness: *inhumane treatment of animals.*

in.hu.man.i.ty (in.hew.MAN.i.tee) *n.* -ties cruelty or barbarity: *man's inhumanity to man.*

in.hume (in.HUME) *v.* -humes, -humed, -hum.ing bury or inter.
—**in.hu.ma.tion** (in.hew.MAY.shun) *n.*

in.im.i.cal (i.NIM.i.cul) *adj.* **1** Formal. hostile: *an inimical attitude, force, glance.* **2** harmful: *drugs inimical to good health.* —**in.im.i.cal.ly** *adv.*

in.im.i.ta.ble (i.NIM.i.tuh.bul) *adj.* that cannot be imitated; matchless; **in.im.i.ta.bly** *adv.*

in.iq.ui.ty (i.NIK.wi.tee) *n.* -ties wickedness or a wicked act: *a den of iniquity.* —**in.iq.ui.tous** (-tus) *adj.*

in.i.tial (i.NISH.ul) *adj.* being the beginning of a series; first: *the initial letter of a word; in the initial stages of our negotiations; initial claims, impressions, plans, steps; My initial reaction was to refuse.*
—*n.* the first letter, esp. of a name: *John Q. Smith's initials* (= *J.Q.S.*).
—*v.* -tials, -tialed, -tial.ing mark with one's initials: *to initial a correction.*
—**in.i.tial.ly** *adv.* Also **in.i.tialled, in.i.tial.ling** *Cdn.*

in.i.tial.ize (i.NISH.ul.ize) *v.* -iz.es, -ized, -iz.ing of a computer process or device, to set to a starting position or value.

in.i.ti.ate (i.NISH.ee.ate) *v.* -ates, -at.ed, -at.ing **1** begin; get going: *to initiate a plan, project; to initiate talks.* **2** admit a person into a special group or to a field of knowledge or activity: *a day for initiating new members; He was initiated into the Knights of Columbus.*
—**in.i.ti.a.tion** (-AY.shun) *n.*
—**in.i.ti.a.tor** (-ay.tur) *n.;* **in.i.ti.a.to.ry** (-uh.tor.ee) *adj.*: *initiatory groups, rites.*

in.i.ti.a.tive (i.NISH.ee.uh.tiv) *n.* **1** the action of taking a first step: *She does things on her own initiative; a peace initiative; The stronger nation should take the initiative for peace talks.* **2** the ability required for this; hence, enterprise: *a woman who shows great initiative.*

in.ject (in.JECT) *v.* introduce or force into something, as serum into the bloodstream or fuel into the cylinders of an internal-combustion engine: *funds to inject new life into an ailing business.* —**in.jec.tion** *n.* —**in.jec.tor** *n.*

in.junc.tion (in.JUNK.shun) *n.* an order, esp. one issued by a court, to do or not do something, as during a labor strike: *A court delivers, grants, hands down, issues an injunction against picketing; an injunction to prevent picketing.*

in.jure (IN.jur) *v.* -jures, -jured, -jur.ing hurt or do harm or damage: *people injured in an accident;* **adj.**: *to be badly, fatally, seriously, severely, slightly injured; to put on a look of injured innocence* (= undeserved hurt).

in.ju.ri.ous (in.JOOR.ee.us) *adj.* harmful: *Bad publicity is injurious to a business; Smoking is injurious to health.*

in.jur.y (IN.juh.ree) *n.* -ries **1** bodily hurt: *injuries suffered in an accident; to inflict, receive, suffer, sustain an injury; bodily, fatal, great, internal, minor, physical, serious, severe, slight injuries; head injuries; injuries to the head.* **2** wrong or injustice: *an injury to one's pride, to one's reputation; the forgiveness of injuries; to add insult to injury* (= annoy besides hurting).

in.jus.tice (in.JUS.tis) *n.* **1** lack of justice: *a sense of injustice; social injustice.* **2** an unjust act: *to commit an injustice; to redress an injustice; a blatant, flagrant, gross injustice; rank injustice; the injustices of life; to do someone an injustice* (= judge him or her unfairly).

ink *n.* a colored liquid for writing, printing, or drawing: *a blob of ink; indelible, invisible, marking ink.*
—*v.* cover, mark, or stain with ink.

ink.blot *n.* **1** a blot of ink. **2** one of a set of irregular, inkblotlike figures used in a psychological test called "Rorschach test," or **inkblot test**.

ink.horn *n.* a container of horn formerly used to hold ink.

ink-jet printer *n.* a quiet, high-speed computer printer that works by spraying ink.

ink.ling *n.* a hint or vague notion: *to get, have an inkling of what it means; I didn't have the faintest or slightest inkling of it; to give someone an inkling of the problem.*

ink.stand *n.* a stand to hold pens, having also an inkwell.

ink.well *n.* a small pot of ink.

ink.y *adj.* **ink.i.er, -i.est 1** dark or black like ink. **2** stained with ink.
—**ink.i.ness** *n.*

in.laid (IN.laid, in.LAID) *adj.* decorated with a design, material, etc. set in the surface as an inlay: *an inlaid table top; rubber pieces inlaid in mid-sole.*

in.land (IN.lund) *adj.* **1** situated in or toward the interior of a country: *an inland town; inland waterways such as canals, rivers, and lakes; adv.: to go inland; travel inland by boat.* **2** domestic or internal: *sources of* **inland revenue** *such as income tax and excise, estate, and gift taxes.*

in-law *n. Informal.* a relative by marriage. —*comb.form:* brother-in-law, father-in-law, mother-in-law, sister-in-law, son-in-law.

in.lay *v.* **-lays, -laid, -lay.ing 1** set in or insert a piece of wood or metal, pattern, or illustration into a surface. **2** decorate thus. —*n.* something inlaid, as a mosaic, bone graft, or dental filling.

in.let *n.* a narrow strip of water extending or running from a sea, lake, or river, into the land, as a small bay or creek; hence, way of entry.

in.line skate *n.* a roller skate similar to an ice skate, with its rollers arranged in a straight line.

in.mate *n.* a person living with others, esp. one confined in a prison or institution.

in me.di.as res (in.MAY.dee.ahs.RACE) *adv. Latin.* in(to) the midst of it, as of a dramatic action.

in me.mo.ri.am (in.muh.MOR.ee.um) *Latin.* in memory of someone.

in.most *adj* a. most inward; secret: *one's inmost thoughts.*

inn *n.* **1** a hotel. **2** in names, a restaurant or tavern.

in.nards (IN.urds) *n.pl. Informal.* internal organs, parts, or workings.

in.nate (IN.ate, i.NATE) *adj.* existing in a person or thing from birth or by nature; inborn: *an innate defect, instinct, strength, vigor.* —**in.nate.ly** *adv.;* **in.nate.ness** *n.*

in.ner (IN.ur) *adj* a. situated farther in, esp. deep inside: *an inner organ of the body; the earth's inner core; inner* (= mental or spiritual) *peace; an influential* **inner circle** *of friends; the overcrowded, poverty-stricken, and crime-ridden* **inner city** *being abandoned in favor of the suburbs; a nonconformist* **inner-directed** *personality; one's* **innermost** (= most secret) *thoughts and desires.*

in.ner.sole (IN.ur.sole) *n.* insole.

in.ner.spring mattress (IN.ur.spring-) *n.* a mattress with a padded casing and coil springs inside.

inner tube *n.* the inflatable tube inside a tire, as of a bicycle.

in.ner.vate (i.NUR.vate, IN.ur-) *v.* -vates, -vat.ed, -vat.ing supply an organ or muscle with nerves. —**in.ner.va.tion** (in.ur.VAY.shun) *n.*

in.ning (IN.ing) *n.* **1** in baseball, a play period in which both teams have a turn at bat. **2** such a turn. **3 innings** *pl.* opportunity for action.

inn.keep.er (IN.kee.pur) *n.* the owner or manager of a hotel.

in.no.cence (IN.uh.sunce) *n.* the quality or state of being innocent: *to maintain, prove, show one's innocence; an air of injured innocence; people living in a state of* **primitive innocence** *(unspoiled by civilization).*

in.no.cent (IN.uh.sunt) *adj.* **1** doing or having done no harm or wrong; not deserving punishment for an offense: *He was declared innocent of the charge of theft; Many innocent people were killed in the bombing.* **2** harmless: *innocent enjoyment; We're having some innocent fun; innocent amusements, bystanders, pastimes, pleasures.* **3** without guile; hence, naive or simple: *an innocent infant, question; too innocent to be suspicious of anyone.* —*n.* a child or simple-minded adult. —**in.no.cent.ly** *adv.*

in.noc.u.ous (i.NOK.yoo.us) *adj.* **1** harmless or inoffensive: *an innocuous drug.* **2** unexciting: *an innocuous speech.* —**in.noc.u.ous.ly** *adv.;* **in.noc.u.ous.ness** *n.*

in.nom.i.nate bone (i.NOM.uh.nit-) *n.* the hipbone.

in.no.vate (IN.uh.vate) *v.* -vates, -vat.ed, -vat.ing **1** make changes: *You can't innovate without the boss's approval.* **2** bring in something new as a change: *Who innovated this procedure?* —**in.no.va.tive** (-vay.tiv) *adj.* —**in.no.va.tor** *n.*

in.no.va.tion (in.uh.VAY.shun) *n.* **1** introduction of a change: *The 1980s were a period of innovation in computer technology.* **2** the making of changes: *Progress comes about through innovation.* **3** a new method, device, or other change: *microwaves and such 20th-century innovations in kitchen equipment.*

in.nu.en.do (i.new.EN.doh) *n.* **-does** an indirect derogatory remark or hint: *His jokes are full of sexual innuendo; to make innuendoes about someone's private life.*

in.nu.mer.a.ble (i.NEW.muh.ruh.bul) *adj.* too numerous to be counted: *on innumerable occasions.*

in.oc.u.late (i.NOC.yuh.late) *v.* **-lates, -lat.ed, -lat.ing** introduce a serum or vaccine into the body, usually by injection, to give immunity *against* infectious diseases such as smallpox and measles. —**in.oc.u.la.tion** (-LAY.shun) *n.*

in.of.fen.sive (in.uh.FEN.siv) *adj.* unoffending: *an inoffensive remark.*

in.op.er.a.ble (i.NOP.uh.ruh.bul) *adj.* that cannot be surgically operated upon: *an inoperable tumor.*

in.op.er.a.tive (i.NOP.uh.ruh.tiv) *adj.* not working; without effect: *The previous boss's directives are inoperative today.*

in.or.di.nate (i.NOR.dun.it) *adj.* disorderly or immoderate: *an inordinate affection, delay, demand, passion.*
—**in.or.di.nate.ly** *adv.*

in.or.gan.ic (in.or.GAN.ic) *adj.* not organic or of vegetable or animal origin; mineral.

in.pa.tient (IN.pay.shunt) *n.* a patient who lives in the hospital while receiving treatment.

in.put *v.* **-puts,** *pt. & pp.* **-put.ted** or **-put, -put.ting** put into a machine or system as raw material for manufacturing, data for processing, etc.
—*n.* what is input, as a contribution or reaction: *A government tries to get input from the public on a proposed piece of legislation; capital, labor, and other inputs required for a new product.*

in.quest *n.* **1** a coroner's inquiry to find out the cause of a suspicious death. **2** the jury holding it or their finding.

in.qui.e.tude (in.KWYE.uh.tude) *n.* uneasiness of mind or body.

in.quire (in.QUIRE) *v.* **-quires, -quired, -quir.ing** *Formal.* ask: *to inquire about what happened last night; Mother inquires after you* (= asks about your health); *The police inquire into suspicious deaths;* *adja.:* *a child with an inquiring* (= curious and alert) *mind;* **in.quir.ing.ly** *adv.*
—**in.quir.er** *n.*

in.quir.y (in.QUIRE.ee, INK.wuh.ree) *n.* **-quir.ies 1** a request for information: *We made many discreet inquiries about her condition; Thanks for your kind inquiries.* **2** a formal investigation: *to conduct, hold, launch, make an official inquiry into a scandal.*

in.qui.si.tion (ink.wuh.ZISH.un) *n.* an intensive or ruthless questioning: *They conducted an inquisition into his teachings on religion and morals.* —**in.quis.i.tor** (in.QUIZ.i.tur) *n.* —**in.quis.i.to.ri.al** (-TOR.ee.ul) *adj.*

in.quis.i.tive (in.QUIZ.i.tiv) *adj.* questioning or curious in a prying manner; **in.quis.i.tive.ly** *adv.*; **in.quis.i.tive.ness** *n.*

in re (in.RAY, -REE) *prep. Latin.* in the matter of.

in-residence *comb.form.* of an artist or professional, having duties as a teacher, consultant, etc.: *a poet-in-residence at a university; a writer-in-residence.*

in.road *n.* usu. **inroads** *pl.* an invasion or encroachment: *Automation has made deep inroads into our work habits; to make inroads on* or *upon one's health, savings, time.*

in.sa.lu.bri.ous (in.suh.LOO.bree.us) *adj.* not healthful; noxious.

in.sane (in.SANE) *adj.* **1** formerly, mentally ill: *He drove her insane; She went insane; certifiably insane; an insane condition, man; an **insane asylum*** (for the mentally ill). **2** *Informal.* very foolish: *What an insane idea! insane prices.*
—**in.sane.ly** *adv.*

in.san.i.ty (in.SAN.i.tee) *n.* **1** severe mental illness: *He was judged not guilty of murder by reason of insanity; He pleaded temporary insanity due to a nervous condition.* **2** extreme foolishness: *outright, pure, sheer insanity.*

in.sa.ti.a.ble (in.SAY.shuh.bul) *adj.* that cannot be satisfied: *an insatiable appetite; his insatiable greed;* **in.sa.ti.a.bly** *adv.*

in.scribe (in.SCRIBE) *v.* **-scribes, -scribed, -scrib.ing** write in or engrave in a lasting manner: *a tombstone inscribed with one's name; words indelibly inscribed in her memory; to inscribe a book* (= autograph or dedicate it).
—**in.scrip.tion** (in.SCRIP.shun) *n.*

in.scru.ta.ble (in.SCROO.tuh.bul) *adj.* too mysterious to be understood by human scrutiny; **in.scru.ta.bly** *adv.*
—**in.scru.ta.bil.i.ty** (-BIL.i.tee) *n.*

in.seam (IN.seem) *n.* the inner seam of a trouser leg from the crotch to the bottom.

in.sect *n.* **1** a small, six-legged creature such as a fly, mosquito, or beetle. **2** a wingless or crawling creature such as a spider or tick.

in.sect.i.cide (in.SEC.tuh.cide) *n.* an insect-killing substance.
—**in.sect.i.cid.al** (-SYE.dul) *adj.*

in.sec.ti.vore (in.SEC.tuh.vore) *n.* an insect-eating plant or animal.
—**in.sec.tiv.o.rous** (in.sec.TIV.uh.rus) *adj.* insect-eating.

in.se.cure (in.si.CURE) *adj.* not secure or feeling safe: *an insecure child; He seems insecure in his job; an insecure job that may end any time; He feels insecure about going out at night; an insecure hold, lock.* —**in.se.cure.ly** *adv.*
—**in.se.cu.ri.ty** (-CURE.i.tee) *n.* **-ties.**

in.sem.i.nate (in.SEM.uh.nate) *v.* **-nates, -nat.ed, -nat.ing 1** put semen into a female animal or egg: *She was artificial-*

ly inseminated with the sperm of her husband; European queens inseminated by African drones. **2** inject a new element into something old: *to inseminate an old show with new characters.*
—**in.sem.i.na.tion** (-NAY.shun) *n.: artificial insemination by husband or donor.* —**in.sem.i.na.tor** (-nay.tur) *n.*

in.sen.sate (in.SEN.sate) *adj.* without sensation; also, stupid or unfeeling.

in.sen.si.ble (in.SEN.suh.bul) *adj.* **1** not sensitive: *to be insensible to the feelings of others.* **2** unconscious or numb: *He lay there insensible and bleeding; quite insensible of what was going on around him.* **3** not easy to sense or perceive: *It grew cold by insensible degrees.*

in.sen.si.tive (in.SEN.suh.tiv) *adj.* not emotionally or physically sensitive: *an insensitive critic, remark, response, spouse; insensitive to minorities, pain, women;* **in.sen.si.tive.ly** *adv.* —**in.sen.si.tiv.i.ty** (-TIV.i.tee) *n.*

in.sen.ti.ent (in.SEN.shee.unt) *adj.* not sentient; lacking life or feeling.
—**in.sen.tience** (-unce) *n.*

in.sep.a.ra.ble (in.SEP.uh.ruh.bul) *adj.* **1** that cannot be parted or separated: *inseparable companions; twins who are inseparable from each other.* **2** **inseparables** *n.pl.* inseparable persons or things. —**in.sep.a.ra.bil.i.ty** (-BIL.i.tee) *n.*

in.sert (in.SURT) *v.* put into the body of something: *to insert a key into a lock; to insert new names in a list.*
—*n.* (IN.surt) something inserted: *a **box insert** in a periodical article giving detailed information on a related subject; See the enclosed package insert for dosage information; an 8-page advertising insert* (= supplement) *of a newspaper.*
—**in.ser.tion** (in.SUR.shun) *n.: ornamental lace insertions in cloth.*

in-service *adj.* received in the course of one's employment: *in-service training.*

in.set 1 (in.SET) *v.* **-sets, -set, -set.ting** set in something: *a picture inset with the text.* **2** (IN.set) *n.* something inset or inserted.

in.shore *adj.* close to the shore, not offshore: *an inshore boat race; the gray whale of inshore waters; the annual inshore migration of codfish; inshore fishing, fishing grounds, fisheries, fleets, plants, winds; adv.: Fish that don't swim inshore get caught offshore.*

in.side (IN.side, in.SIDE) *n.* an inner side, position, part, etc.: *the inside of a room; one horse overtaking another on the inside* (= in the inside lane); *the insides* (Informal for internal organs) *of the body.* —**adj.:** *inside information; an inside page, pocket; the inside story.*
—**prep.:** *Fido is inside the house; We'll be back inside of or inside* (= within) *an hour.* —*adv.* (in.SIDE): *We stay inside when it rains; an umbrella turned inside out by the wind; She knows the place* **inside out** (= thoroughly).

inside job *n.* a crime committed with the help of someone inside the organization that is the victim.

in.sid.er (in.SYE.dur) *n.* one who belongs to a group or place, and is often specially privileged: *Stock market insiders have confidential information from company managers, directors, etc.; an* **insider trading** *scandal (resulting from exploiting confidential information on stocks).*

inside track *n.* position of advantage: *He has the inside track on getting the job.*

in.sid.i.ous (in.SID.ee.us) *adj.* treacherous; working secretly: *an insidious disease, influence, plot;* **in.sid.i.ous.ly** *adv.;* **in.sid.i.ous.ness** *n.*

in.sight *n.* power to see into and understand a situation: *to gain, have an insight into their mode of life; The book provides deep insights about their life.*
—**in.sight.ful** *adj.*

in.sig.ni.a (in.SIG.nee.uh) *n.* **-ni.a** or **-ni.as** a distinguishing mark of position or rank, as on a military uniform; emblem.

in.sin.cere (in.sin.SEER) *adj.* not sincere.
—**in.sin.cer.i.ty** (-SER.i.tee) *n.* **-ties.**

in.sin.u.ate (in.SIN.yoo.ate) *v.* **-ates, -at.ed, -at.ing 1** hint or imply something dishonorable about a person: *to insinuate that Joe is a thief.* **2** introduce oneself into a place artfully or slyly: *He insinuated himself into her affections.*
—**in.sin.u.a.tion** (-AY.shun) *n.*
—**in.sin.u.a.tor** (-ay.tur) *n.*

in.sip.id (in.SIP.id) *adj.* without flavor; dull or tasteless: *I find his poems insipid rather than inspired;* **in.sip.id.ly** *adv.*
—**in.si.pid.i.ty** (in.suh.PID.i.tee) *n.* **-ties.**

in.sist (in.SIST) *v.* be firm about a request, statement, or demand: *He insisted on accompanying her; He insisted that she shouldn't go out alone; He insisted and she agreed.* —**in.sist.ence** (-unce) *n.*
—**in.sist.ent** (-unt) *adj.;* **in.sis.tent.ly** *adv.*

in si.tu (in.SYE.too) *adj. & adv. Latin.* in its original place or position.

in.so.far (in.soh.FAR) *adv.* to such a degree or extent: *insofar as I'm concerned.*

in.so.la.tion (in.suh.LAY.shun) *n.* **1** solar radiation. **2** exposure to sun's rays.

in.sole *n.* an inside sole of a shoe.

in.so.lent (IN.suh.lunt) *adj.* openly defiant or insulting, esp. to a superior. —**in.so.lence** *n.*

in.sol.u.ble (in.SOL.yuh.bul) *adj.* **1** that cannot be dissolved. **2** not solvable. —**in.sol.u.bly** *adv.;* **in.sol.u.bil.i.ty** (-BIL.i.tee) *n.*

in.sol.va.ble (in.SOL.vuh.bul) *adj.* not solvable.

in.sol.vent (in.SOL.vunt) *adj.* unable to pay debts; bankrupt: *an insolvent bank, company, debtor, estate.* —**in.sol.ven.cy** *n.*

in.som.ni.a (in.SOM.nee.uh) *n.* sleeplessness; **in.som.ni.ac** *n. & adj.*

in.so.much (in.soh.MUCH) *adv.* **1** to such a degree: *insomuch that....* **2** inasmuch; insofar: *insomuch as....*

in.sou.ci.ant (in.SOO.see.unt) *adj.* Formal. pert and unconcerned: *an insouciant joy, manner, misanthrope; the insouciant telling of a story of starving children.* —**in.sou.ci.ance** *n.*

in.spect (in.SPECT) *v.* examine carefully and critically, as for errors or defects: *to inspect a factory for safety; to inspect a school; to inspect troops (officially); to inspect someone's work (for adequacy).* —**in.spec.tor** *n.*

in.spec.tion (in.SPEC.shun) *n.* an inspecting: *to carry out, conduct, make an inspection; a cursory, visual inspection; On closer inspection, the signature was found to be forged.*

in.spi.ra.tion (in.spuh.RAY.shun) *n.* **1** an influence of the mind or feelings that prompts one to be creative: *artistic inspiration; poetic inspiration; She started writing on a sudden inspiration; The classics often give* or *provide inspiration to a writer; Shakespeare has been the inspiration for many playwrights; lifelong companions who were a source of mutual inspiration; a lengthy essay without a flash* or *spark of inspiration; to derive* or *draw inspiration from Scripture; divine inspiration* (= inspiration from God). **2** a breathing in: *The chest expands during inspiration.* —**in.spi.ra.tion.al** (-shuh.nul) *adj.: inspirational literature, music, performance; an inspirational leader, manager, message, player, speaker.*

in.spire (in.SPIRE) *v.* **-spires, -spired, -spir.ing** breathe in; hence, be the cause of life, vigor, new thought or feeling, etc.: *The talk inspired his men with confidence; it inspired them to carry on with the struggle; Her warning inspired fear and respect in their hearts; rumors inspired by malice;* **adj.**: *a very inspiring talk.* —**in.spir.er** *n.*

inspired *adj.* **1** having creative power: *an inspired artist, poet; She speaks like someone inspired.* **2** resulting from creative power or inspiration: *inspired books, moments, scriptures, verses; a prophet's inspired words; a Sixties-inspired fashion.* **3** based on good intuition: *an inspired guess; inspired policies; His ideas are impulsive rather than inspired.*

in.spir.it (in.SPEER.it) *v.* put spirit into someone; hearten.

in.sta.bil.i.ty (in.stuh.BIL.i.tee) *n.* lack of stability, firmness, or determination.

in.stall (in.STAWL) *v.* **-stalls, -stalled, -stall.ing** put or establish a person, thing, or oneself in a place or position: *The faucet was installed by the plumber; a ceremony to install a new president; to install Jones as president; Software has to be installed in a computer; to install a keyboard, mouse, scanner, etc. on a computer; She installs herself in front of the TV after supper every day.* Also **in.stal.** —**in.stal.la.tion** (in.stuh.LAY.shun) *n.*

in.stall.ment (in.STAWL.munt) *n.* any of several parts, as of a large amount, long story or article, etc., that are due at regular intervals: *an encyclopedia published in installments; We paid for the freezer in installments; purchased it on the* **installment plan.** Also **in.stal.ment.**

in.stance (IN.stunce) *n.* **1** a person, thing, or event considered as a case or example: *We could cite* or *give many instances of her generosity; an isolated, rare instance;* **In the first instance,** *he wasn't invited, and then he stayed too long; Students need good reference books – dictionaries* **for instance.** **2** request or urging: *She was invited at my instance.*
—*v.* **-stanc.es, -stanced, -stanc.ing** illustrate or cite: *an attitude of disrespect instanced by his recent conduct.*

in.stant (IN.stunt) *n., adj. & comb.form.* a moment, esp. the present: *Come here this instant! your letter of the 14th instant* (= present month). —*adj. & cpd:* **In**stant coffee is quickly prepared; instant gratification, success; TVs with an **instant-on** button need no warm-up time; an **instant-start** fluorescent light.
—**in.stant.ly** *adv.*

in.stan.ta.ne.ous (in.stun.TAY.nee.us) *adj.* coming or happening in an instant: *instantaneous death by electrocution; an instantaneous reaction.*
—**in.stan.ta.ne.ous.ly** *adv.*

in.stan.ti.ate (in.STAN.shee.ate) *v.* **-ates, -at.ed, -at.ing** represent by an instance; **in.stan.ti.a.tion** (-AY.shun) *n.*

instant replay *n.* the immediate replay of a striking segment of a live telecast.

in.state (in.STATE) *v.* **-states, -stat.ed, -stat.ing** install a person in office.

in.stead (in.STED) *adv.* in place of a person or thing: *I'll have tea instead of coffee; He would like an ice cream instead; Instead of chairing the meeting herself, she sent us her husband.*

in.step *n.* the upper surface of the arch of the foot: *an instep kick in soccer.*

in.sti.gate (IN.stuh.gate) *v.* **-gates, -gat.ed, -gat.ing** incite or provoke a person, usu. to something considered bad: *to instigate an assassination, quarrel, rebellion; to instigate workers to strike.* —**in.sti.ga.tion** (-GAY.shun) *n.* —**in.sti.ga.tor** (-gay.tur) *n.*

in.still (in.STIL) *v.* **-stills, -stilled, -still.ing 1** put in drop by drop: *nose drops to be instilled in each nostril thrice daily.* **2** impart gradually: *Parents and teachers instill good habits in or into children; to instill knowledge, love of work, principles.* Also **in.stil.** —**in.still.ment** *n.*

in.stinct *n.* an unlearned, inborn tendency to behave in a certain way: *the basic instincts; the herd, hunting, mating, and survival instincts; the instinct for self-preservation; the maternal instinct to protect the young; a human, natural instinct; animal, predatory instincts; an unerring instinct* (= knack or gift) *for the right expression.* —**instinct with** filled or charged with: *a poem instinct with beauty.*

in.stinc.tive (in.STINK.tiv) *adj.* not thought out but spontaneous: *an instinctive awareness, dislike, fear, reaction, understanding.* —**in.stinc.tive.ly** *adv.*

in.stinc.tu.al (in.STINoo.ul) *adj.* having to do with instincts: *an instinctual experience, feel, knowledge, life.*

in.sti.tute (IN.stuh.tute) *v.* **-tutes, -tut.ed, -tut.ing** initiate or establish: *to institute a legal action, award, inquiry; to institute changes, charges, policies, criminal proceedings, programs, rules; to institute a halt to trading.* —*n.* **1** an organization for art, science, or education, esp. an advanced or specialized school, as one in technical subjects: *a technical institute; a collegiate institute; an institute for advanced study.* **2** a short teaching program: *a summer institute.* —**in.sti.tut.er** or **in.sti.tu.tor** *n.*

in.sti.tu.tion (in.stuh.TUE.shun) *n.* **1** an established organization: *charitable, educational, financial, social institutions; an institution endowed by the state.* **2** an establishing or thing established, as a law or custom: *the institution of marriage; slavery abolished as an institution;* *She is quite an institution around here* (= has been here for a long time).

in.sti.tu.tion.al (in.stuh.TUE.shuh.nul) *adj.* having to do with institutions: *Apartheid was condemned as institutional racism; institutional care for the infirm;* **institutional advertising** (as opposed to product advertising) *for generating good will.* —**in.sti.tu.tion.al.ly** *adv.*

in.sti.tu.tion.al.ize (in.stuh.TUE.shuh.nul.ize) *v.* **-iz.es, -ized, -iz.ing** make institutional or make into or put in an institution. —**in.sti.tu.tion.al.i.za.tion** (-luh.ZAY.shun, -lye-) *n.*

in.struct (in.STRUCT) *v.* give information to someone clearly and directly: *Teachers instruct pupils in a subject; A client instructs his lawyer; A judge instructs a jury; He was instructed* (= ordered) *to exercise daily.*

in.struc.tion (in.STRUC.shun) *n.* a direct command or set of directions: *to await, carry out, follow, give, issue, receive instructions; Pupils take instruction from teachers; English is our medium of instruction; She had left written instructions for us; Lawyers act on their client's instructions; a judge's instruction to the jury; A computer executes millions of instructions per second; Read the instructions before starting the engine; an instruction manual.* —**in.struc.tion.al** *adj.*

in.struc.tive (in.STRUC.tiv) *adj.* serving to teach: *an instructive and entertaining talk.*

in.struc.tor (in.STRUC.tur) *n.* one who instructs or teaches: *a language instructor; an instructor in music.* —**in.struc.tor.ship** *n.*

in.stru.ment (IN.struh.munt) *n.* a person or thing used as a means, esp. an implement for delicate scientific or artistic use: *a stringed musical instrument; a string instrument; to play an instrument; a blunt, sharp, surgical instrument; a navigational instrument such as a compass; A deed of conveyance is a legal instrument* (= document); *He refused to be used as an instrument of subversion; Only instruments are used in* **instrument flying** *and landing, as in fog.* —*v.* (-ment) equip with instruments; *adj.:* *a system fully* **instrumented** *for safety; an instrumented landing on Mars.*

in.stru.men.tal (in.struh.MEN.tul) *adj.* **1** serving as a means: *an editor instrumental in the publication of many books.* **2** having to do with instruments: *instrumental music.* —**in.stru.men.tal.ist** *n.* —**in.stru.men.tal.i.ty** (-TAL.i.tee) *n.* **-ties** a means or agency.

instrumentation / integral

in.stru.men.ta.tion (IN.struh.men.TAY.shun) *n.* **1** use of instruments. **2** arrangement or composition of music for instruments.

in.sub.or.di.nate (in.suh.BOR.dun.it) *adj.* not submitting to authority; disobedient; **in.sub.or.di.na.tion** (-NAY.shun) *n.*

in.sub.stan.tial (in.sub.STAN.shul) *adj.* **1** flimsy, as a cobweb. **2** imaginary, as dreams.

in.suf.fer.a.ble (in.SUF.uh.ruh.bul) *adj.* unbearable: *an insufferable bore; insufferable arrogance.* —**in.suf.fer.a.bly** *adv.*

in.su.lar (IN.suh.lur) *adj.* **1** of or like an island in being isolated from the surroundings: *an insular population, society.* **2** narrow-minded, as an islander is assumed to be: *his insular attitude; her insular group, scholarship, wisdom.* —**in.su.lar.i.ty** (-LAIR.i.tee) *n.*

in.su.late (IN.suh.late) *v.* **-lates, -lat.ed, -lat.ing** isolate or separate a conductor or source of energy such as heat, sound, or electricity with a nonconducting material so as to keep from losing or transferring energy: *Parents try to insulate their children from the cruelty of the real world; adj.: Our house is well insulated from the cold; the insulated lives of children growing up in a big city.* —**in.su.la.tion** (-LAY.shun) *n.* —**in.su.la.tor** (-lay.tur) *n.*

in.su.lin (IN.suh.lin) *n.* a sugar-reducing hormone.

in.sult (IN.sult) *n.* something insolent, rude, or contemptuous that humiliates another: *to avenge, take, swallow an insult; to fling* or *hurl insults at the speaker; The speech was an insult to their intelligence; to add insult to injury.*
—*v.* (in.SULT) do or say something that is an insult: *She just ignores people who insult her; adj.: He felt deeply insulted; a very insulting remark.*

in.su.per.a.ble (in.SOO.puh.ruh.bul) *adj.* that cannot be overcome or passed over: *an insuperable barrier, difficulty, obstacle, problem; insuperable odds.*

in.sup.port.a.ble (in.suh.POR.tuh.bul) *adj.* not supportable; that cannot be put up with or justified.

in.sur.a.ble (in.SHOOR.uh.bul) *adj.* capable of being or fit to be insured.

in.sur.ance (in.SHOOR.unce) *n.* **1** an undertaking to compensate or protect against specified losses in return for a fee: *to carry, take out, underwrite insurance; accident, automobile, collision, disability, fire, group, health, homeowner's, life, no-fault, term insurance; insurance on property; insurance against loss, fire, etc.; She's in insurance* (= the insurance business); *He collected $3,000 insurance (money) on his car; She pays $400 insurance (as premium) annually; Your insurance (policy) doesn't cover acts of God.* **2** protection: *Take your umbrella as insurance (against getting wet in case of rain).*

in.sure (in.SHOOR) *v.* **-sures, -sured, -sur.ing 1** give, take, or get insurance on a property, person, life, etc.: *You can insure your life for a huge sum of money; No one can be insured against dying.* **2** same as ENSURE. —**in.sur.er** *n.*

insured *n.* a person whose property or life is insured.

in.sur.gen.cy (in.SUR.jun.see) *n.* **-cies** a minor revolt.

in.sur.gent (in.SUR.junt) *n.* a person rising up or acting against an established government; rebel.
—**in.sur.gence** *n.*

in.sur.mount.a.ble (in.sur.MOWN.tuh.bul) *adj.* that cannot be overcome: *insurmountable difficulties, obstacles, problems;* **in.sur.mount.a.bly** *adv.*

in.sur.rec.tion (in.suh.REC.shun) *n.* an armed uprising or outbreak, usu. short-lived, against established authority: *to crush, foment, put down, quell, stir up an insurrection; The military was called out to suppress the insurrection; an armed insurrection.* —**in.sur.rec.tion.ist** *n.*

in.tact (in.TACT) *adjp.* untouched or whole in spite of something that might have impaired or damaged it: *The parcel was delivered intact; Nothing was left intact after the storm.*

in.tagl.io (in.TAL.yoh) *n.* **-ios** a design engraved into a hard surface, as seen on gems and used as a printing method.

in.take *n.* **1** an opening where a fluid enters a container: *The intake manifold of a carburetor connects it with the engine cylinders.* **2** a taking in, esp. of a fluid through a narrow opening. **3** the amount of liquid or gas taken in.

in.tan.gi.ble (in.TAN.juh.bul) **1** *adj.* that cannot be touched, felt, or grasped by the mind: *Goodwill is an intangible business asset; the intangible charisma of leadership.* **2** *n.pl.* nonmaterial things of value: *Assets include credit, patents, goodwill, and such intangibles.* —**in.tan.gi.bly** *adv.*

in.te.ger (IN.ti.jur) *n.* something that is whole, not a fraction, as a number or zero.

in.te.gral (IN.tuh.grul, in.TEG.rul) **1** *adj.* essential as part of a whole: *Limbs are integral parts of our bodies; they* are integral to our existence; *integral accessories, components, units; Minorities have an integral role to play in government.* **2** *adja.* formed of such parts: *an integral design, security system, wheel assembly.* **3** *adja.* whole or unbroken: *an integral number, personality, structure, technology.* —*n.* a whole number or a whole.

integral calculus *n.* the mathematics of finding the sum totals of extremely small numbers and using them to calculate their integrals, as the speed of a projectile from its rate of change.

in.te.grate (IN.tuh.grate) *v.* **-grates, -grat.ed, -grat.ing** make into or become a whole; bring parts together into one, as different racial groups in society: *Immigrants try to integrate into a new society; to integrate with the rest of the population;* **adj.:** *trying to get* **integrated***; transistors, resistors, and capacitors in one* **integrated circuit** *instead of being wired together; an* **integrated school** *(for members of various races, religions, etc.);* **integrated software** *combining a spreadsheet with word processing.* —**in.te.gra.tion** (-GRAY.shun) *n.* —**in.te.gra.tive** (-gray.tiv) *adj.*

in.teg.ri.ty (in.TEG.ri.tee) *n.* **1** trustworthy moral character: *a man of integrity.* **2** soundness or completeness of anything: *a treaty guaranteeing territorial integrity; a dramatization that lacks artistic integrity.*

in.teg.u.ment (in.TEG.yuh.munt) *n.* an organism's natural outer covering such as a skin, shell, or husk.

in.tel.lect (IN.tuh.lect) *n.* **1** mind or intelligence: *a woman of keen intellect.* **2** a person of great intelligence: *one of the greatest intellects of our time.*

in.tel.lec.tu.al (in.tuh.LEC.choo.ul) *adj.* having to do with or interested in things of the mind rather than of the body or emotions: *Chess is an intellectual game; reasoning, judgment, and such intellectual processes; a woman of intellectual tastes.* —*n.* an intellectual person: *Academics are intellectuals.* —**in.tel.lec.tu.al.ly** *adv.*

in.tel.lec.tu.al.ize (in.tuh.LEC.choo.uh.lize) *v.* **-iz.es, -ized, -iz.ing** make intellectual or treat intellectually, esp. without considering emotional aspects; philosophize.

intellectual property *n.* a creative work that is protected by a patent, trademark, or copyright.

in.tel.li.gence (in.TEL.uh.junce) *n.* **1** ability to learn, understand, remember, and respond to situations requiring use of the mind: *high, keen, limited, low, native, remarkable, sharp, superior intelligence; artificial intelligence;* **adja.:** *an intelligence test; The* **intelligence quotient** *(IQ) is a rating based on one's mental age relative to the chronological age.* **2** news or information of a vital nature: *Spies collect or gather intelligence; foreign, industrial, military intelligence;* **adja.:** *intelligence agencies, gathering, satellites, work.*

in.tel.li.gent (in.TEL.uh.junt) *adj.* having intelligence: *an intelligent child, dog, woman; an intelligent observation (showing intelligence); An* **intelligent** *or* **smart terminal** *can process data besides receiving and transmitting it like a dumb terminal.* —**in.tel.li.gent.ly** *adv.*

in.tel.li.gent.si.a (in.TEL.uh.JENT.see.uh) *n. sing.* or *pl.* the intellectual class of a society.

in.tel.li.gi.ble (in.TEL.uh.juh.bul) *adj.* that can be understood by the mind: *an unreasonable but intelligible explanation.* —**in.tel.li.gi.bly** *adv.* —**in.tel.li.gi.bil.i.ty** (-BIL.i.tee) *n.*

in.tem.per.ate (in.TEM.puh.rit) *adj.* not moderate or showing self-control: *an intemperate outburst; a man of intemperate habits (esp. in regard to drinking);* **in.tem.per.ate.ness** *n.* —**in.tem.per.ance** *n.*

in.tend (in.TEND) *v.* **1** have as an aim or purpose: *I intend to go home after school; What do you intend doing after getting married?* **2** mean: *an offense that was not intended.*

in.tend.ant (in.TEN.dunt) *n.* a government official supervising a district in South American countries.

in.tend.ed (in.TEN.did) *adj.* meant or planned: *the intended goal, purpose, use; well-intended advice; a book intended as a gift; a gift intended for the bride; the parents of the intended (= prospective) bride.* —*n.: a note from your intended (= prospective spouse).*

in.tense (in.TENCE) *adj.* **1** of a high degree; sharply focused; very keen: *intense happiness, heat, light, pain.* **2** strong in head and heart: *an intense personality, woman.* —**in.tense.ly** *adv.*

in.ten.si.fy (in.TEN.suh.fye) *v.* **-fies, -fied, -fy.ing** make or become more intense; strengthen: *to intensify activities, competition, concerns, cooperation, demands, efforts, a search; Attacks, charges, negotiations, pressure, problems, speculation, trends intensify.* —**in.ten.si.fi.ca.tion** (-fuh.CAY.shun) *n.* —**in.ten.si.fi.er** (-fye.ur) *n.*

in.ten.si.ty (in.TEN.si.tee) *n.* **-ties** the

state or quality of being intense; keenness: *intensity of emotion, heat, passion, vision; the intensity of a struggle; her passionate intensity.*

in.ten.sive (in.TEN.siv) *adj.* thorough or concentrated, not extensive: *intensive training; an intensive* (= in-depth) *study; a hospital's* **intensive care unit** *for critically ill patients;* **intensive farming** *to produce several crops each year with heavy use of labor, fertilizers, etc.* —*cpd.: capital-intensive farming; energy-intensive manufacturing; labor-intensive industries, skills; Selling hats is a service-intensive business.* —*n.* an intensive word such as *very, utter,* and *bloody;* intensifier. —**in.ten.sive.ly** *adv.;* **in.ten.sive.ness** *n.*

in.tent (in.TENT) *n.* what is intended or meant; intention: *malicious intent; assault with intent to kill; the intent* (= meaning) *of a message.* —**to all intents and purposes** in every way; practically. —*adj.* attentive or earnest: *an intent look; a student* **intent on** *passing her exams.* —**in.tent.ly** *adv.*

in.ten.tion (in.TEN.shun) *n.* **1** what is intended: *He had no intention of seeing her; She had every intention of seeing him; She stuck to her intention to see him.* **2 intentions** plans, as in regard to a person one is interested in: *What are his intentions in regard to her? honorable intentions; "The road to hell is paved with* **good intentions"** (= Good intentions are useless without good performance).

in.ten.tion.al (in.TEN.shuh.nul) *adj.* with an intended aim or purpose; deliberate: *an intentional snub.* —**in.ten.tion.al.ly** *adv.*

in.ter (in.TUR) *v.* -ters, -terred, -ter.ring *Formal.* bury a corpse.

inter- *comb.form.* between or among: *interact, interchange, interdependent, interface.*

in.ter.act (in.tur.ACT) *v.* act on or influence each other: *Students and teachers interact with each other.* —**in.ter.ac.tion** (-AC.shun) *n.*

in.ter.ac.tive (in.tur.AC.tiv) *adj.* acting on each other; two-way: *an interactive communication system; interactive cable TV; Spell checkers have to be interactive.*

in.ter a.li.a (in.tur.AY.lee.uh) *adv. Latin.* among other things.

in.ter.breed (in.tur.BREED) *v.* -breeds, -bred, -breed.ing same as HYBRIDIZE.

in.ter.cede (in.tur.SEED) *v.* -cedes, -ced.ed, -ced.ing plead with someone in authority for a favor: *The suspended student asked me to intercede with the principal for his reinstatement; I interceded on his behalf.*

in.ter.cept (in.tur.SEPT) *v.* cut off, stop, or seize a moving person or thing before reaching the destination: *to intercept a letter in the mail; to intercept a fleeing convict; to intercept a forward pass in football; to intercept the flow of oil.* —**in.ter.cep.tion** (-shun) *n.* —**in.ter.cep.tor** (-tur) *n.*

in.ter.ces.sion (in.tur.SESH.un) *n.* an interceding, as by prayer or mediation. —**in.ter.ces.sor** (-SES.ur) *n.* —**in.ter.ces.so.ry** (-SES.uh.ree) *adj.*

in.ter.change (in.tur.CHANGE) *v.* **1** to exchange. **2** cause two things to change places or to happen by turns. —*n.* (IN.tur.change) an interchanging, esp. a junction in the shape of a cloverleaf, diamond, etc. designed for unchecked flow of traffic between a highway or freeway crossing a secondary road or another freeway. —**in.ter.change.a.ble** (-CHAIN.juh.bul) *adj.*

in.ter.col.le.gi.ate (IN.tur.cuh.LEE.jit, -jee.it) *adj.* between or among colleges or universities.

in.ter.com (IN.tur.com) *n.* [short form] **intercommunication system,** a radio or telephone setup of amplifiers and loudspeakers for communicating between different parts of an office, factory, apartment building, etc.

in.ter.com.mu.ni.cate (IN.tur.cuh.MEW.nuh.cate) *v.* -cates, -cat.ed, -cat.ing communicate with each other. —**in.ter.com.mu.ni.ca.tion** (-CAY.shun) *n.*

in.ter.con.nect (in.tur.cuh.NECT) *v.* connect with one another; **in.ter.con.nec.tion** (-NEC.shun) *n.*

in.ter.con.ti.nen.tal (IN.tur.con.tuh.NEN.tul) *adj.* between or across continents: *an intercontinental ballistic missile; intercontinental migration.*

in.ter.cos.tal (in.tur.COS.tul) *adj.* situated between the ribs: *an intercostal muscle.*

in.ter.course (IN.tur.corse) *n.* dealings, as between people: *social intercourse; sexual intercourse* (= sexual act); *intercourse* (= communing) *with the Deity.*

in.ter.de.nom.i.na.tion.al (IN.tur.di.nom.uh.NAY.shun.ul) *adj.* involving different religious denominations.

in.ter.de.part.men.tal (IN.tur.di.part.MEN.tul) *adj.* involving different departments.

in.ter.de.pend.ent (IN.tur.di.PEN.dunt) *adj.* dependent upon one another. —**in.ter.de.pend.ence** *n.*

in.ter.dict (in.tur.DICT) *v.* prohibit or

forbid by decree: *measures to interdict the supply of illegal drugs.* —*n.* (IN.tur.dict) a prohibition. Also **in.ter.dic.tion** (-DIC.shun).

in.ter.dis.ci.pli.nar.y (IN.tur.DIS.uh.pluh.nair.ee) *adj.* involving different academic disciplines.

in.ter.est (IN.trist, -tuh.rist) *n.* **1** condition or feeling of wanting to know or learn about a person or thing: *to arouse, generate, lose, show, stir up, revive interest in the arts; a deep, intense, keen, lively interest; a story with much human interest; a conflict of interest between private and public interest; a story of some interest to the general public; The government has the national interest in view; She* **takes interest** *in education; That's not her only interest* (= subject of interest) *in life; a dull story without much interest* (= interesting quality); *Teachers work* **in the interest** or **in the interests** (= for the good) *of students.* **2** a group of people with a common concern: *an undertaking supported by the business interests of the town; banking interests; oil interests; shipping interests; steel interests; A ban on smoking is opposed by certain vested interests; a (special)* **interest group** *of tobacco growers.* **3** benefit or advantage: *People tend to look after their own interests; to guard, promote, protect their interests; Whose interests does this project serve? a clash of interests; He sold his interest* (= share) *in the farm.* **4** money charged or paid for the use of money: *The bank lends money at a certain interest; Savings deposits bear* or **pay** or **yield interest**; *Banks pay interest on deposits; Interest accrues to deposits; Interest is added to the principal; Interest is charged on loans.* —*v.* cause interest in someone: *Nothing interests him more than video games; Could I interest you in a new car? adj.: The car looks* **interesting**. —**in.ter.est.ing.ly** *adv.*

interested *adj.* **1** having or showing interest: *I'm interested in a new car at this time; interested in buying rather than leasing; You'll be interested to hear about our bargain prices; My wife is an interested party to a car deal; an interested look.* **2** having a personal interest: *a sales rep with an interested motive.*

in.ter.face (IN.tur.face) *n.* **1** hardware or software that connects two devices or the user with a computer. **2** a common surface or boundary through which two bodies, regions, or systems interact or communicate: *A union station is the transportation interface of a large city; Publishing is the interface between authors and the reading public.* —*v.:* *Authors interface with the public through publishers.*

in.ter.faith (IN.tur.faith) *adj.* involving different faiths or religions: *an interfaith conference.*

in.ter.fere (in.tur.FEER) *v.* **-feres, -fered, -fer.ing** get in the way of people or affairs: *to interfere in a family dispute; They hesitated to interfere between the spouses; Nothing unforeseen should interfere with our plans; The catcher interfered by hampering the batter's swing; adj.: a very* **interfering** (= meddlesome) *neighbor.* —**in.ter.fer.ence** (-unce) *n.:* *unwarranted foreign interference in a country's internal affairs; They will brook no interference from the superpowers; We won't tolerate any interference with our plans; His secretary was supposed to* **run interference** (Informal for handle the problems) *between him and his creditors.*

in.ter.fer.on (in.tur.FEER.on) *n.* a protein molecule produced by cells to fight a viral infection.

in.ter.ga.lac.tic (IN.tur.guh.LAC.tic) *adj.* between or among galaxies: *unending intergalactic space.*

in.ter.gla.cial (IN.tur.GLAY.shul) *adj.* between glacial epochs: *a warm interglacial period.*

in.ter.im (IN.tuh.rim) *n.* the time that comes between: *She was without a job in the interim while management changed hands; adj.: an interim arrangement, loan, payment, report.*

in.te.ri.or (in.TEER.ee.ur) *adj.* inside or inner, not exterior: *a house's interior walls; Style, color, pattern, etc. are elements of* **interior design** *used in* **interior decoration** *of houses, offices, automobiles, etc. to make them pleasant and comfortable.* —*n.* the inner or inside part: *the interior of a building; the interior of British Columbia* (away from the Pacific coast); *The U.S.* **Department of the Interior** *looks after the nation's natural resources.*

in.ter.ject (in.tur.JECT) *v.* throw in a remark, question, etc. abruptly between other things: *"Hold it!" he interjected as I was about to continue.*

in.ter.jec.tion (in.tur.JEC.shun) *n.* something interjected, esp. an exclamatory word considered as a part of speech, as "alas," "ouch," etc.; **in.ter.jec.tion.al** *adj.* —**in.ter.jec.tor** *n.*

in.ter.lace (in.tur.LACE) *v.* **-lac.es, -laced, -lac.ing** pass over and under each other, as reeds or fibers in basket-weaving: *Roads seem to interlace with rivers on a map; adj.: In the* **interlaced** *system of TV transmission odd-num-*

bered and even-numbered lines of a picture are scanned alternately, which results in flickering on the monitor; an interlaced variety of subjects; an **interlacing** pattern.

in.ter.lard (IN.tur.lard) *v.* mix or intersperse: *a speech interlarded with anecdotes.*

in.ter.leave (IN.tur.leev) *v.* **-leaves, -leaved, -leav.ing** insert alternately between pages: *illustrated pages interleaved with printed ones.*

in.ter.leu.kin (in.tur.LOO.kin) *n.* a protein produced in the body that helps the body's immune system by promoting the growth of white blood cells.

in.ter.line *v.* **-lines, -lined, -lin.ing** **1** (in.tur.LINE) insert between lines: *a text interlined with notes.* **2** (IN.tur.line) provide with an interlining. —*adj*. (in.tur.LINE) involving relationships between carriers: *interline agreements, cargo, services, shipments.*

in.ter.lin.e.ar (in.tur.LIN.ee.ur) *adj.* inserted between lines: *an interlinear translation.*

in.ter.lin.ing (IN.tur.lye.ning) *n.* an extra lining inserted in a garment; also, a middle layer, as of a quilt.

in.ter.link (in.tur.LINK) *v.* link together.

in.ter.lock (in.tur.LOCK) *v.* **1** lock or fit tightly together, as the pieces of a jigsaw puzzle. **2** operate together, as railroad signals. —*n.* an interlocking condition, device, or arrangement: *A microwave has two interlock systems to prevent it from operating if the door is even slightly open.*

in.ter.loc.u.tor (in.tur.LOC.yuh.tur) *n.* one who takes part in a dialogue, as the center man who questioned the end men in a minstrel show.

in.ter.loc.u.to.ry (in.tur.LOC.yuh.tor.ee) *adj.* happening or done during the course of something, as a decree with provisional force pronounced during a legal action.

in.ter.lope (in.tur.LOPE) *v.* **-lopes, -loped, -lop.ing** encroach, esp. into another's territory for trade or profit-making; **in.ter.lop.er** *n.*

in.ter.lude (IN.tur.lood, long "oo") *n.* an interval of musical or dramatic entertainment.

in.ter.mar.riage (in.tur.MAIR.ij) *n.* marriage across racial, religious, or familial boundaries: *intermarriage between Catholics and Protestants.*

in.ter.mar.ry (in.tur.MAIR.ee) *v.* **-mar.ries, -mar.ried, -mar.ry.ing** become connected by intermarriage: *Jews intermarrying with gentiles.*

in.ter.me.di.ar.y (in.tur.MEE.dee.air.ee) *n.* **-ar.ies** a person or thing with an in-between function: *Brokers act or serve as intermediaries between buyers and sellers; adj.: an intermediary role.*

in.ter.me.di.ate (in.tur.MEE.dee.it) *adj.* being in between two things: *an intermediate shade of green; The* **intermediate grades** (= usu. 7 through 10) *of school link junior and senior grades; an* **intermediate range ballistic missile** *(that travels up to 1,500 mi. or 2,414 km); an automobile of* **intermediate size** (= midsize, between standard and compact).

in.ter.ment (in.TUR.munt) *n.* an interring or burial.

in.ter.mez.zo (in.tur.MET.soh) *n.* **-mez.zos** or **-mez.zi** (-see) a short musical or other composition for playing between the acts of an opera or play.

in.ter.mi.na.ble (in.TUR.muh.nuh.bul) *adj.* endless-seeming; long and tiring; **in.ter.mi.na.bly** *adv.*

in.ter.min.gle (in.tur.MING.gul) *v.* **-gles, -gled, -gling** mingle or mix together: *The plainclothes police intermingled with the crowd.*

in.ter.mis.sion (in.tur.MISH.un) *n.* a temporary halt or break in an activity or performance, as between a play's acts.

in.ter.mit (in.tur.MIT) *v.* **-mits, -mit.ted, -mit.ting** stop for a time; also, stop and start again.

in.ter.mit.tent (in.tur.MIT.unt) *adj.* stopping and starting again: *an intermittent fever; an intermittent volcano erupting in cycles.* —**in.ter.mit.tent.ly** *adv.*

in.ter.mix (in.tur.MIX) *v.* intermingle.

in.ter.mo.dal (in.tur.MOH.dul) *adj.* of several modes: *an intermodal container that can be shipped by plane, rail, truck, or ship.*

in.tern (IN.turn) *n.* a medical or other professional receiving in-service training. —*v.* (in.TURN) **1** be an intern: *She interned in St. John's;* **in.tern.ship** *n.* **2** confine, esp. suspected aliens, in a certain place, as during wartime; **in.tern.ment** *n.*: *internment camps.*

in.ter.nal (in.TUR.nul) *adj.* inside or inner, not external: *Hormones are internal secretions; the internal combustion within an engine's cylinders; hence, the* **internal-combustion engine**; *A historical reference in a book is* **internal evidence** *of its date of publication;* **Internal medicine** *deals with the nonsurgical treatment of diseases of the heart, lungs, stomach, and such internal organs; a computer's* **internal memory** *(to hold data being processed) as opposed to its external storage; a* *government's* **internal revenue** *derived from taxing domestic goods and services, not from export and import duties.* —**in.ter.nal.ly** *adv.*

in.ter.na.tion.al (in.tur.NASH.uh.nul) *adj.* having to do with relationships between nations: *the U.S.-Canada international border; an* **international airport** *where planes land from foreign countries; the high seas, or* **international waters***, 200 miles (321.9 km) from a country's shore.* —**in.ter.na.tion.al.ly** *adv.* —**in.ter.na.tion.al.ism** *n.*

in.ter.na.tion.al.ize (in.tur.NASH.un.uh.lize) *v.* **-iz.es, -ized, -iz.ing** bring under international control.

international law *n.* the law dealing with war, peace, and neutrality.

interne same as INTERN.

in.ter.ne.cine (in.tur.NEE.sun, -sine) *adj.* of wars, struggles, feuds, etc., destructive to both sides.

in.ter.nee (in.tur.NEE) *n.* a person confined as an alien during wartime, as North Americans of Japanese ancestry during World War II.

In.ter.net (IN.tur.net) *n.* an international communication system made up of millions of computers and networks providing access to databases, e-mail, shopping, and other services.

in.tern.ist (in.TUR.nist) *n.* a specialist in internal medicine.

in.ter.nun.ci.o (in.tur.NUN.see.oh) *n.* **-os** (-oze) a papal envoy ranking below a nuncio.

in.ter.of.fice (in.tur.OF.is) *adj.* between or within the offices of an organization.

in.ter.per.son.al (in.tur.PUR.suh.nul) *adj.* (having to do with relations) between persons: *interpersonal communications, conflicts, relationships; a leader with good interpersonal skills (for managing people).*

in.ter.plan.e.tar.y (in.tur.PLAN.uh.tair.ee) *adj.* between planets or in their region: *interplanetary travel; an interplanetary probe into interplanetary space.*

in.ter.play (IN.tur.play) *n.* interaction: *the interplay of colored lights at Niagara Falls.*

In.ter.pol (IN.tur.pole) *n.* a Paris-based organization of the police forces of over 100 countries.

in.ter.po.late (in.TUR.puh.late) *v.* **-lates, -lat.ed, -lat.ing 1** insert new or spurious matter *into* a passage or text. **2** alter it thus: *interpolated passages in Shakespeare's plays.* —**in.ter.po.la.tion** (-LAY.shun) *n.*

in.ter.pose (in.tur.POZE) *v.* **-pos.es,** **-posed, -pos.ing** put forward or place *between* or *among* others: *a remark interposed at the wrong moment; Al got hurt when he interposed himself between the fighters.* —**in.ter.po.si.tion** (-ZISH.un) *n.*

in.ter.pret (in.TUR.prit) *v.* explain or bring out a meaning that is not apparent: *to interpret a dream; to interpret an author; to interpret a dramatic role (by one's acting); to interpret* (= translate) *for foreign tourists.* —**in.ter.pre.ta.tion** (-pri.TAY.shun) *n.* —**in.ter.pret.er** (-prit.ur) *n.* —**in.ter.pre.tive** (-pri.tiv) or **in.ter.pre.ta.tive** (-pri.tay.tiv) *adj.* explanatory; **in.ter.pre.ta.tive.ly** *adv.*

in.ter.ra.cial (in.tur.RAY.shul) *adj.* having to do with different races: *an interracial incident, marriage.*

in.ter.reg.num (in.tur.REG.num) *n.* an interval between two regimes; hence, a pause or break in a continuous activity.

in.ter.re.late (IN.tur.ruh.LATE) *v.* **-lates, -lat.ed, -lat.ing** have or bring into a mutual relationship. —**in.ter.re.la.tion.ship** *n.*

in.ter.ro.gate (in.TER.uh.gate) *v.* **-gates, -gat.ed, -gat.ing** question a prisoner, witness, etc. formally and systematically in a search for facts; **in.ter.ro.ga.tion** (-GAY.shun) *n.* —**in.ter.ro.ga.tor** (-gay.tur) *n.*

in.ter.rog.a.tive (in.tuh.ROG.uh.tiv) *adj.* used in asking a question: *an interrogative adverb such as "when," "where," or "why"; "Who" and "what" are interrogative pronouns.*

in.ter.rog.a.to.ry (in.tuh.ROG.uh.tor.ee) *n.* **-ries** a written question or set of questions for interrogating a witness.

in.ter.rupt (in.tuh.RUPT) *v.* **1** make a break in the continuity of something: *to interrupt a flow; An accident interrupts traffic; to interrupt study, work; High-rises interrupt* (= obstruct) *our view.* **2** break in upon a person, speech, etc.: *Sorry to interrupt you; Am I interrupting anything?* —*n.* a computer's ability to interrupt the execution of one routine and take up another without waiting for the first to finish —**in.ter.rupt.er** *n.* —**in.ter.rup.tion** *n.*

in.ter.scho.las.tic (IN.tur.scuh.LAS.tik) *adj.* between schools: *interscholastic sports;* also **in.ter.school** (-SCOOL).

in.ter.sect (in.tur.SECT) *v.* cut or cross each other, as two roads.

in.ter.sec.tion (in.tur.SEC.shun) *n.* a crossing or the place of crossing, as of lines, streets, etc.: *traffic accidents at a busy intersection; a railroad crossing that is* considered a dangerous intersection.

in.ter.sperse (in.tur.SPURCE) *v.* **-spers.es, -spersed, -spers.ing** put here and there between or among other things: *to intersperse statuary among the flowers in a garden; greenery interspersed with flowers.*

in.ter.state (in.tur.STATE) *adj.* between states, as of the U.S.: *an interstate highway.*

in.ter.stel.lar (in.tur.STEL.ur) *adj.* between stars or in their region: *interstellar cloud, space, travel.*

in.ter.stice (in.TUR.stis) *n.* **-stic.es** a narrow opening, crack, or similar intervening space, as in network. —**in.ter.sti.tial** (in.tur.STISH.ul) *adj.*

in.ter.tid.al (in.tur.TYE.dul) *adj.* between high-tide and low-tide levels: *fauna of the intertidal zone.*

in.ter.twine (in.tur.TWINE) *v.* **-twines, -twined, -twin.ing** twine together; interlace: *Four strands of wool are intertwined to make four-ply yarn.*

in.ter.ur.ban (in.tur.UR.bun) *adj.* between cities: *an interurban transportation system.*

in.ter.val (IN.tur.vul) *n.* a break or gap of space, time, pitch, or other factor: *a medication to be taken at regular intervals; Buses leave here at short intervals; labor pains at 10-minute intervals; a brief, lucid interval* (= limited period) *during an illness; A **major interval** (= pitch difference between two tones) chromatically reduced by a semitone becomes a **minor interval**.* —**at intervals** with breaks in time or space: *trees planted at intervals of 10 feet; At intervals* (= now and then) *the rain would get very heavy.*

in.ter.vene (in.tur.VEEN) *v.* **-venes, -vened, -ven.ing** 1 be, come, or go between events, persons, etc.: *to intervene in a family dispute; The government can intervene to end a strike; Before he could graduate, war intervened;* **adj.**: *the **intervening** period between their separation and reunion; the intervening years.* 2 [legal use] to act as an intervenor.

in.ter.ve.nor or **in.ter.ven.er** (in.tur.VEE.nur) *n.* an interested party given standing at a judicial hearing.

in.ter.ven.tion (in.tur.VEN.shun) *n.* an act of intervening: *armed, divine, military interventions.*
—**in.ter.ven.tion.ism** *n.*;
in.ter.ven.tion.ist *n. & adj.*

in.ter.view (IN.tur.vyoo) *n.* 1 a personal conversation, as between an employer and job applicant or a journalist and a subject: *to conduct, do, give, grant an interview; a live, telephone, taped, TV interview.* 2 a news story or article setting forth a conversation: *The interview appeared yesterday.* —*v.:* *The personnel manager interviews candidates for jobs; The politician refused to be interviewed on camera; She was interviewed via satellite.*
—**in.ter.view.er** *n.* —**in.ter.view.ee** (-EE) *n.* person interviewed.

in.ter.weave (in.tur.WEEV) *v.* **-weaves,** *pt.* **-wove** or **-weaved,** *pp.* **-wov.en** (-WOH.vun) or **-weaved, -weav.ing** weave together; interlace.

in.tes.tate (in.TES.tate, -tit) *n. & adjp.* (one who has died) without making a will: *to die intestate.*

in.tes.tin.al (in.TES.tuh.nul) *adj.* of the intestines: *an intestinal bypass operation;* **intestinal fortitude** (= pluck or guts).

in.tes.tine (in.TES.tin) *n.* the alimentary tube from the end of the stomach to the anus, divided into the narrow "small intestine" and the wider "large intestine"; bowel. —**adja.** within a country: *intestine strife.*

in.ti.ma.cy (IN.tuh.muh.see) *n.* **-cies** 1 personal closeness: *the intimacy between spouses.* 2 an intimate act, esp. sexual.

in.ti.mate (IN.tuh.mit) *adj.* personally close or familiar: *two friends on intimate terms; They are intimate with each other; the intimate atmosphere of a nightclub; an intimate nightclub; an intimate relationship; an intimate knowledge of the subject.*
—*n.* one who is intimate: *an intimate of Leslie's.* —*v.* (-mate) **-mates, -mat.ed, -mat.ing** Formal. suggest delicately or indirectly: *to intimate one's wishes; He has intimated to the family that he would like to sue them.* —**in.ti.mate.ly** *adv.*
—**in.ti.ma.tion** (-MAY.shun) *n.*

in.tim.i.date (in.TIM.uh.date) *v.* **-dates, -dat.ed, -dat.ing** frighten by display of superior strength, power, learning, etc.: *a witness intimidated into silence.*
—**in.tim.i.da.tion** (-DAY.shun) *n.*

in.to (IN.too) *prep.* [indicating movement toward or to the inside of]: *She went into the room; bumped into him by accident; to translate from French into English; She fell ill in October when she was a month into Grade 7; She is now into* (Informal for involved in) *cooking; She's so into cooking, she has no time to watch TV; 4 into 20* (= 20 divided by 4) *is 5.*

in.tol.er.a.ble (in.TOL.uh.ruh.bul) *adj.* too much to endure; unbearable: *He screamed in intolerable pain; The "Intolerable Acts" of the British Parliament drove the American colonies to war.*
—**in.tol.er.a.bly** *adv.*

in.tol.er.ance (in.TOL.uh.runce) *n.* 1 the quality of being intolerant: *racial* *intolerance; religious intolerance.* **2** allergy or sensitivity to something: *intolerance to specific drugs; A person with alcoholic intolerance should not touch liquor.*

in.tol.er.ant (in.TOL.uh.runt) *adj.* not tolerant, esp. of others' opinions or beliefs; bigoted: *He's too **intolerant** of opposition to be a democrat.*

in.to.na.tion (in.tuh.NAY.shun) *n.* **1** the act or style of intoning or chanting: *intonation of the Psalms.* **2** the rise and fall of the voice in speech: *Questions have a rising intonation.*

in.tone (in.TONE) *v.* **-tones, -toned, -ton.ing** recite a prayer, psalm, etc. in a singing voice or in a monotone.

in to.to (in.TOH.toh) *adv. Latin.* totally; as a whole.

in.tox.i.cant (in.TOX.i.kunt) *n. & adj.* (anything) that intoxicates, as an alcoholic liquor.

in.tox.i.cate (in.TOX.uh.cate) *v.* **-cates, -cat.ed, -cat.ing** make drunk or as if drunk: *Power intoxicates; He was intoxicated by the idea of getting rich by gambling.* —**in.tox.i.ca.tion** (-CAY.shun) *n.*

intra- *comb.form.* within; inside of: *intracity, intramolecular, intramural, intrastate.*

in.trac.ta.ble (in.TRAC.tuh.bul) *adj.* hard to manage; resisting control or direction.

in.tra.dos (IN.truh.dos, in.TRAY-) *n.* the inner curve of an arch or vault.

in.tra.mu.ral (in.truh.MYOOR.ul) *adj.* between members of the same school: *intramural sports.*

in.tran.si.gent (in.TRAN.suh.junt) *n. & adj.* (one who is) uncompromising, esp. in politics. —**in.tran.si.gence** *n.*

in.tran.si.tive (in.TRAN.suh.tiv) *adj.* of a verb, that does not need a direct object. —*n.* an intransitive verb such as "arrive," "seem," or "lie." —**in.tran.si.tive.ly** *adv.*

in.tra.u.ter.ine device (in.truh.YOO.tuh.rin, -rine) *n.* a birth control device such as a spiral or loop of plastic fitted in the uterus.

in.tra.ve.nous (in.truh.VEE.nus) *adj.* within or into a vein or veins: *intravenous feeding; an intravenous anesthetic, injection.* —**in.tra.ve.nous.ly** *adv.*

intrench same as ENTRENCH.

in.trep.id (in.TREP.id) *adj.* brave and fearless, esp. in regard to something new or unknown: *an intrepid explorer, firefighter, researcher.* —**in.tre.pid.i.ty** (in.truh.PID.i.tee) *n.*

in.tri.ca.cy (IN.truh.cuh.see) *n.* **-cies** the quality of being intricate or something that is intricate: *the intricacies of diplomacy, of a plot.*

in.tri.cate (IN.tri.kit) *adj.* hard to follow or understand, being complicated like a maze or elaborate like filigree work: *an intricate pattern, plot, problem.* —**in.tri.cate.ly** *adv.*

in.trigue (IN.treeg) *n.* a secret, often underhanded plot or scheme, as for the overthrow of someone or an illicit love affair: *to engage in domestic intrigue; The palace was a hotbed of intrigue; a web of intrigue.* —*v.* **-trigues, -trigued, -tri.guing 1** make or carry out a secret plan or plot: *He gets ahead by intriguing against his rivals.* **2** interest greatly: *a story opening that is likely to intrigue the reader; I'm intrigued by or with the happenings; **adj.**: Everyone is **intrigued**; intrigued in-laws; intrigued smiles; We find the revelations very **intriguing*** (= strangely fascinating or mysterious). —**in.tri.guing.ly** *adv.*

in.trin.sic (in.TRIN.sic) *adj.* existing within, as something essential or inherent, not extrinsic: *Beauty is intrinsic to beautiful objects; the intrinsic merit or worth of a painting besides its snob value; the intrinsic value of an object apart from its usefulness; The intrinsic value of a coin is what its metal is worth.*
—**in.trin.si.cal.ly** *adv.*

in.tro (IN.troh) *n.* **1** *Informal.* introduction. **2** in music, an introductory passage.

in.tro.duce (in.truh.DUCE) *v.* **-duc.es, -duced, -duc.ing 1** bring in or put in: *It's not advisable to introduce a knife into the mouth like a spoon; to introduce a new subject for discussion.* **2** bring forward for getting acquainted: *A chairman introduces a speaker (to the audience); I introduced myself to him; a party to introduce* (= begin or open) *the New Year.*

in.tro.duc.tion (in.truh.DUC.shun) *n.* an introducing: *the debut as a formal introduction to society; She replied to the introduction by saying "How do you do"; the introduction of printing in or into Europe in the 15th century; a letter of introduction; to write an introduction to a book.*
—**in.tro.duc.to.ry** (-tuh.ree) *adj.*

in.tro.it (in.TROH.it, IN.troh-) *n.* a psalm or hymn recited at the beginning of Mass or a similar Christian service.

in.tro.mit (in.troh.MIT) *v.* **-mits, -mit.ted, -mit.ting** insert; put in; **in.tro.mis.sion** *n.*

in.tro.spec.tion (in.truh.SPEC.shun) *n.* an examining of one's own thoughts and feelings. —**in.tro.spec.tive** (-tiv) *adj.;* **in.tro.spec.tive.ly** *adv.*

in.tro.vert (IN.truh.vurt) *n.* one who is

more concerned with his or her own thoughts and feelings than with the world outside, not an extrovert. —**in.tro.vert.ed** *adj.* —**in.tro.ver.sion** (-VUR.zhun, -VUR.shun) *n.*

in.trude (in.TROOD) *v.* **-trudes, -trud.ed, -trud.ing** thrust or push in where not invited or expected: *to intrude on a person's privacy; May I intrude? The enemy forces intruded into our territory; a bore who intrudes his views on everyone.* —**in.trud.er** *n.*: *He locks the gate to his backyard to keep out intruders.* —**in.tru.sion** (-TROO.zhun) *n.*

in.tru.sive (in.TROO.siv) *adj.* forcing in: *intrusive behavior, people; Molten magma forms intrusive rocks by pushing up from below the surface.* —**in.tru.sive.ly** *adv.*; **in.tru.sive.ness** *n.*

intrust same as ENTRUST.

in.tu.i.tion (in.tyoo.ISH.un, in.too-) *n.* **1** direct insight without conscious reasoning: *Experienced people sense things by intuition.* **2** something known or learned by such insight: *Our intuitions may fail in moments of panic.* —**in.tu.i.tive** *adj.*: *an intuitive feeling, judgment, sense, understanding; Software that is intuitive is supposed to be easy to use; an intuitive user interface;* **in.tu.i.tive.ly** *adv.*

In.u.it (IN.oo.it) *n. sing. & pl.* Eskimo (people or language): *the Inuit Tapirisat* (= *Eskimo Brotherhood*) *of Canada.*

in.un.date (IN.un.date) *v.* **-dates, -dat.ed, -dat.ing** overflow, as in a flood; deluge: *employers inundated with job applications.* —**in.un.da.tion** (-DAY.shun) *n.*

in.ure (in.YOOR) *v.* **-ures, -ured, -ur.ing** *Formal.* **1** accustom to something hard to bear: *Wartime experiences inure people to suffering;* adj.: *People become* **inured** *to cold, danger, hardship, hunger.* **2** be of advantage: *The benefits of a cleanup should inure to the whole community; The proceeds from the lottery will inure to the benefit of the public.* —**in.ure.ment** *n.*

in va.cu.o (in.VAC.yoo.oh) *adv. Latin.* (as if) in a vacuum.

in.vade (in.VADE) *v.* **-vades, -vad.ed, -vad.ing** enter another's territory to conquer or as if to take possession: *a household invaded by unexpected guests; Army worms invade fields.* —**in.vad.er** *n.*

in.va.lid (IN.vuh.lid) *n.* a person who is weak or sickly: *He remained an invalid all his life; a home for invalids.* —*v.* disable or render weak: *He was invalided by a bomb blast; He was then invalided* (= *released*) *out of the military.*

—*adj.* (in.VAL.id) not valid: *an invalid claim, check, marriage;* **in.val.id.ly** *adv.*

in.val.i.date (in.VAL.uh.date) *v.* **-dates, -dat.ed, -dat.ing** deprive of legal force or effect: *The most recent will invalidates any previous wills.* —**in.val.i.da.tion** (-DAY.shun) *n.*

in.va.lid.ism (IN.vuh.lid.iz.um) *n.* the state of being an invalid.

in.va.lid.i.ty (in.vuh.LID.i.tee) *n.* the state of being not valid.

in.val.u.a.ble (in.VAL.yoo.uh.bul) *adj.* of value that cannot be estimated; priceless. —**in.val.u.a.bly** (-blee) *adv.*

in.var.i.a.ble (in.VAIR.ee.uh.bul) *adj.* habitual and unchanging. —**in.var.i.a.bly** (-uh.blee) *adv.*: *He is invariably late on Monday mornings.*

in.va.sion (in.VAY.zhun) *n.* an invading, as by an attacking force, disease germs, etc.: *to carry out, launch, repel, repulse an invasion; the annual invasion of tourists in the summer; the invasion of privacy by electronic snooping.* —**in.va.sive** (-siv) *adj.* that invades the body: *an invasive cancer; A biopsy is an invasive diagnostic examination.*

in.vec.tive (in.VEC.tiv) *n.* a violent attack in words, spoken or written: *The media hurled a torrent of invective or invectives against the censorship laws.*

in.veigh (in.VAY) *v.* make a verbal attack against a person or thing.

in.vei.gle (in.VAY.gul, -VEE.gul) *v.* **-gles, -gled, -gling** mislead someone or obtain something by trickery: *He was inveigled into buying worthless stock.*

in.vent (in.VENT) *v.* make up or think up something new: *Who invented the ballpoint pen? a child good at inventing excuses.* —**in.ven.tor** *n.*

in.ven.tion (in.VEN.shun) *n.* an inventing or something invented: *Modern inventions make living comfortable; an ingenious invention; a report that is pure invention; "Necessity is the mother of invention"* (= *is what makes people invent things*).

in.ven.tive (in.VEN.tiv) *adj.* having the ability to invent: *an inventive mind; our inventive capacity, powers.* —**in.ven.tive.ly** *adv.*; **in.ven.tive.ness** *n.*

in.ven.to.ry (IN.vun.tor.ee) *n.* **-ries 1** an itemized list of goods in stock, property, etc., as for valuation: *to make or take an inventory of stock.* **2** the things so listed: *a sale to reduce inventory; the annual marking down of inventory; The shop will be closed next week for (checking) inventory; We like fast inventory turnover.* —*v.* **-ries, -ried, -ry.ing:** *We inventory stock monthly.*

in.verse (IN.vurse) *adj.* inverted or reversed, esp. mathematically: *an inverse function; Addition and subtraction are inverse operations.* —*n.*: *a/b is the inverse of b/a.* —**in.verse.ly** *adv.*: *Light intensity is inversely related to distance* (= The larger the distance the less intense the light).

in.ver.sion (in.VUR.zhun, -shun) *n.* a being inverted: *the inversion of subject and verb in "Did I?"*; **Temperature inversion** *with higher temperatures at higher altitudes traps smoke and noxious gases in the air.*

in.vert (in.VURT) *v.* turn in an opposite direction, esp. upside down: *A mirror reverses its image, a lens inverts it;* *adj.*: *an inverted image, pyramid; Quotation marks are inverted commas.*

in.ver.te.brate (in.VUR.tuh.brate, -brit) *n. & adj.* (an animal such as a worm or mollusk) that is backboneless.

in.vest (in.VEST) *v.* **1** spend or put out money, time, energy, and such resources with the expectation of later benefit: *People invest heavily in real estate;* **in.ves.tor** *n.* **2** *Formal.* endow a person *with* an office, dignity, authority, right, etc.; **in.ves.ti.ture** (in.VES.tuh.chur) *n.*

in.ves.ti.gate (in.VES.tuh.gate) *v.* **-gates, -gat.ed, -gat.ing** search into a situation or incident systematically so as to learn the facts. —**in.ves.ti.ga.tion** (-GAY.shun) *n.*: *to carry out, conduct, make an investigation; a criminal, cursory, impartial, perfunctory, thorough investigation; a case that is under police investigation.*
—**in.ves.ti.ga.tive** (-gay.tiv) *adj.*
—**in.ves.ti.ga.tor** (-gay.tur) *n.*

investiture See INVEST.

in.vest.ment (in.VEST.munt) *n.* an investing of money and such resources: *an investment of $5 million; a long-term investment; investments in blue chip stocks; Education is a good investment for life;* *adj.*: *an investment banker, company, counselor.*

in.vet.er.ate (in.VET.uh.rit) *adj.* **1** long-established: *an inveterate custom, habit, practice, prejudice.* **2** habitual: *an inveterate liar, smoker.* —**in.vet.er.a.cy** *n.*

in.vid.i.ous (in.VID.ee.us) *adj.* tending to cause envy or animosity: *an invidious comparison, discrimination, rule.*
—**in.vid.i.ous.ly** *adv.;* **in.vid.i.ous.ness** *n.*

in.vig.o.rate (in.VIG.uh.rate) *v.* **-rates, -rat.ed, -rat.ing** fill with vigor; *adj.*: *The swim was very invigorating; an invigorating climate, tonic.*

—**in.vig.o.ra.tion** (-RAY.shun) *n.*

in.vin.ci.ble (in.VIN.suh.bul) *adj.* that cannot be overcome or subdued: *invincible courage, ignorance;* **in.vin.ci.bly** *adv.* —**in.vin.ci.bil.i.ty** (-BIL.i.tee) *n.*

in.vi.o.la.ble (in.VYE.uh.luh.bul) *adj.* that must not or cannot be violated: *an inviolable sanctuary, promise; the inviolable gods;* **in.vi.o.la.bly** *adv.*
—**in.vi.o.la.bil.i.ty** (-BIL.i.tee) *n.*

in.vi.o.late (in.VYE.uh.lit) *adj.* not violated; sacred or pure: *to keep an oath inviolate; the shrine's inviolate sanctity.*

in.vis.i.ble (in.VIZ.uh.bul) *adj.* not visible; out of sight or hidden: *the invisible side of the moon; Germs are invisible to the naked eye;* **in.vis.i.bly** *adv.*
—**in.vis.i.bil.i.ty** (-BIL.i.tee) *n.*

in.vi.ta.tion (in.vuh.TAY.shun) *n.* an inviting: *to decline, extend, issue, send, spurn an invitation; to send out invitations to a wedding; printed invitations; an invitation to attend a wedding; a cordial, formal, informal invitation; Admission is by invitation only.* —**in.vi.ta.tion.al** *adj.*: *an invitational lecture not open to the public; an invitational tennis tournament.*

in.vite (in.VITE) *v.* **-vites, -vit.ed, -vit.ing** ask politely to be present somewhere or to do something: *to invite a guest; He was invited to the wedding; Your costume may invite* (= provoke) *comment;* *adj.*: *an inviting* (= attractive or alluring) *sight;* **in.vit.ing.ly** *adv.* —*n.* (IN.vite) an invitation.
—**in.vi.tee** (in.vye.TEE) *n.* **-tees.**

in vi.tro (in.VEE.troh) *adv.* artificially or mechanically, as an embryo maintained in a test tube, not in vivo; *adj.*: *an in-vitro fertilization; in-vitro diagnostic devices such as home kits and test strips for AIDS, diabetes, pregnancy, etc.*

in vi.vo (in.VEE.voh) *adv.* in the living body.

in.vo.ca.tion (in.vuh.CAY.shun) *n.* **1** an invoking or appeal to God or a similar higher power. **2** the words or formula used.

in.voice (IN.voice) *n.* a list of goods or services provided showing payment due for them: *an invoice for books shipped.* —*v.* **-voic.es, -voiced, -voic.ing** **1** enter on an invoice: *to invoice an order.* **2** bill: *to invoice a customer.*

in.voke (in.VOKE) *v.* **-vokes, -voked, -vok.ing** appeal to a higher power such as God or spirits or to an authority, as of a law, ruling, etc. for help or protection: *a prayer invoking God's blessing; penalties invoked only in times of national crises; to invoke aid, mercy, special privileges.*

in.vol.un.tar.y (in.VOL.un.tair.ee) *adj.* not willed or controlled by the will, as reflex actions: *an involuntary action, movement; the involuntary muscles of the intestines.* —**in.vol.un.tar.i.ly** (-TAIR.uh.lee) *adv.*

in.vo.lute (IN.vuh.loot) *adj.* **1** rolled inward, as the scrolls of an Ionic column. **2** curled in a spiral, as some shells. **3** intricate or involved: *an involute design.*

in.vo.lu.tion (in.vuh.LOO.shun) *n.* **1** an involving or entanglement. **2** an involute part.

in.volve (in.VOLV) *v.* **-volves, -volved, -volv.ing 1** enfold or include: *a job that involves manual work; Rights involve duties.* **2** concern or entangle: *I would like to help you without involving myself in or with your private life; And let's not involve the children in this.*
—**involved 1** *adj*e. closely connected or concerned: *She doesn't like to be or become or get involved in too many activities; Leo is emotionally involved with Lee; At first they didn't want to* **get involved** (= have a close relationship). **2** *adj.* complicated: *an involved explanation, question, sentence, style.*
—**in.volve.ment** *n.*

in.vul.ner.a.ble (in.VUL.nuh.ruh.bul) *adj.* that cannot be attacked or hurt: *an invulnerable argument, fortress, position; a fortress that is invulnerable to attack;* **in.vul.ner.a.bly** *adv.*
—**in.vul.ner.a.bil.i.ty** (-BIL.i.tee) *n.*

in.ward (IN.wurd) *adj*a. directed toward the inside; inner: *an inward curve, slant; one's inward nature.*
—*adv.*: *inward bound;* also **in.wards**.
—**in.ward.ly** (IN.wurd.lee) *adv.*: *He was inwardly happy at her discomfort.*

in.wrought (in.RAWT) *adj.* of a pattern or decoration, woven or worked in.

in-your-face *adj*a. *Informal.* provocative; confrontational: *in-your-face arrogance, audacity, showmanship.*

i.o.dide (EYE.uh.dide) *n.* a compound of iodine and another element.

i.o.dine (EYE.uh.dine, -din) *n.* a chemical element found in sea water and sea weed, used as an antiseptic.

i.o.dize (EYE.uh.dize) *v.* **-diz.es, -dized, -diz.ing** treat with iodine or an iodide: *iodized (table) salt.*

i.on (EYE.un, -on) *n.* an electrically charged atom or group of atoms; ANION or CATION.

I.on.ic (eye.ON.ic) *adj.* having to do with a style of architecture of Asiatic Greeks, characterized by scrolls in the capitals of the columns.

i.on.ize (EYE.uh.nize) *v.* **-iz.es, -ized, -iz.ing** (cause to) separate into ions, as acids, bases, and salts in solutions; **i.on.iz.er** *n.* —**i.on.i.za.tion** (-nuh.ZAY.shun, -nye-) *n.*

i.on.o.sphere (eye.ON.us.feer) *n.* the outer atmosphere of the earth that is ionized by solar radiation and cosmic rays. —**i.on.o.spher.ic** (-FER.ic) *adj.*

i.o.ta (eye.OH.tuh) *n.* **1** the ninth letter of the Greek alphabet, corresponding to "i." **2** the least bit or amount; jot: *I didn't get one iota of help from him.*

IOU (EYE.oh.YOO) *n.* **IOUs** a written promise ("I owe you") to repay money or debts owed.

I.o.wan (EYE.uh.wun) *n. & adj.* (a person) of or from **Iowa,** a Midwestern U.S. state.

ip.e.cac (IP.uh.cac) *n.* an expectorant made from the dried roots of a South American shrub of the same name.

ip.so fac.to (IP.soh.FAC.toh) *adv. Latin.* by the very fact.

IQ (EYE.cue) *n.* **IQs** "intelligence quotient," a measure of intelligence: *a high, low IQ; an IQ test.*

I.ra.ni.an (i.RAY.nee.un) *n.* **1** a person of or from **Iran,** a S.W. Asian country. **2** an Indo-European language such as Persian, Kurdish, or Pashto spoken in Iran. Also *adj.*

I.ra.qi (i.RAH.kee) *n.* **1** a person of or from **Iraq,** a republic W. of Iran. **2** the Arabic language spoken in Iraq. Also *adj.*

i.ras.ci.ble (i.RAS.uh.bul) *adj.* easily angered; hot-tempered. —**i.ras.ci.bil.i.ty** (-BIL.i.tee) *n.*

i.rate (eye.RATE) *adj. Formal.* angry: *an irate customer, driver.* —**i.rate.ly** *adv.*

ire *n.* wrath, as shown in looks, words, actions, etc.: *to arouse someone's ire.*
—**ire.ful** *adj.*

i.ren.ic (eye.REN.ic, -REE.nic) *adj.* promoting peace, esp. in religious disputes.

ir.i.des.cent (eer.uh.DES.unt) *adj.* displaying rainbowlike colors when seen from different angles, as mother-of-pearl. —**ir.i.des.cence** *n.*

i.rid.i.um (i.RID.ee.um) *n.* a white, heavy metallic chemical element.

i.ris (EYE.ris) *n.* **1** a plant with sword-shaped leaves bearing three-petaled flowers of varying color, stylized as the fleur-de-lis. **2** the colored part around the pupil of the eye.

I.rish (EYE.rish) *n.* **1** the **Irish** *pl.* the people of **Ireland,** an island W. of Britain. **2** the Celtic language of Ireland. —**get one's Irish up** *Informal.*

arouse one's temper. —*adj.* having to do with the people of Ireland or their language: *Pat sounds Irish; Irish fairy tales, literature, moss, potato famine, setter, stew, terrier, whiskey, wolfhound; Irish coffee contains whiskey and is topped with whipped cream.* —**I.rish.man** (EYE.rish.mun) *n.* **-men; I.rish.wom.an** (EYE.rish.woom.un) *n.* **-wom.en.**

irk *v.* cause a feeling of weariness or annoyance in someone: *It irks us to have to pay so much tax.* —**irk.some** *adj.*: *an irksome delay, task; irksome restrictions.*

i.ron (EYE.urn) *n.* **1** a hard, strongly magnetic, heavy metallic element used for tools and machinery, esp. as steel: *cast, crude, pig, scrap, wrought iron.* **2** any tool or weapon of iron, a golf club, etc.: *a branding iron* (= branding device); *climbing* or *grappling iron* (= a hook); *clothes iron* (for ironing clothes); to *pump iron* (= be a weightlifter). **3 irons** *pl.* handcuffs or shackles: *They put him in irons; leg irons.* —*v.* press and smooth cloth with a heated iron. —**iron out** smooth out confusion, differences, difficulties, etc. —*adj*.a. **1** containing iron: *iron ore.* **2** like iron in hardness: *an iron constitution, hand, lady; The dictator ruled with an iron fist for 25 years; an iron hand in a velvet glove* (= ruthlessness masked by softness). —**ironing** *n.* clothes ironed or for ironing: *Who'll do the ironing?*

Iron Age *n.* in human culture, the period when humans began to work and use iron.

i.ron.clad (EYE.urn.clad) *adj.* difficult to get out of, as if armored with iron plates: *an ironclad guarantee.*

Iron Curtain *n.* the barrier of censorship and secrecy that used to separate Communist E. Europe from non-communist countries.

ironic, ironical See IRONY.

iron lung *n.* an artificial respiratory chamber in which a paralyzed person can be kept alive for treatment.

i.ron.stone (EYE.urn.stone) *n.* **1** iron ore. **2** a type of hard white English pottery.

i.ron.ware (EYE.urn.ware) *n.* pots, tools, etc. of iron; hardware.

i.ron.work.er (EYE.urn.wur.kur) *n.* a person whose work is erecting and connecting the structural steel framework of buildings.

i.ron.works (EYE.urn.wurks) *n. sing. & pl.* a place where iron and steel products are made.

i.ro.ny (EYE.ruh.nee) *n.* **-nies** a saying, happening, or situation that is apparently contrary to what is intended or desirable, as when one says "Wonderful!" about something infuriating: *bitter irony; dramatic irony; a touch of irony; tragic irony; By an irony of fate, he received his inheritance the day he died.* —**i.ron.ic** or **i.ron.i.cal** (eye.RON.i.cul) *adj.* —**i.ron.i.cal.ly** *adv.*

Ir.o.quois (EER.uk.woy, -wah) *n., pl.* **-quois** (-woy, -woys, -wah, -wahz) **1** (a member of) any of six tribes of Indians of upper New York State. **2** any of their languages. —**Ir.o.quoi.an** (-WOY.un) *n. & adj.*

ir.ra.di.ate (i.RAY.dee.ate) *v.* **-ates, -at.ed, -at.ing** expose to rays of light or other radiation: *food preserved by being irradiated with gamma rays or electrons; a countenance irradiated by joy; adj.*: *irradiated cells, foods, soil, wheat.* —**ir.ra.di.a.tion** (-AY.shun) *n.*

ir.ra.tion.al (i.RASH.uh.nul) *adj.* **1** not endowed with reason: *Animals are irrational creatures; He became irrational with rage.* **2** contrary to reason: *Superstitions are irrational.* —**ir.ra.tion.al.ly** (-nuh.lee) *adv.* —**ir.ra.tion.al.i.ty** (-NAL.i.tee) *n.* **-ties.**

irrational number *n.* a real number that cannot be expressed in integers, as the square root of 2.

ir.re.claim.a.ble (eer.i.CLAIM.uh.bul) *adj.* that cannot be reclaimed; **ir.re.claim.a.bly** *adv.*

ir.rec.on.cil.a.ble (i.REC.un.SYE.luh.bul) *adj.* that cannot be reconciled or brought into harmony: *an irreconcilable enemy; irreconcilable differences, tastes, views.* —**ir.rec.on.cil.a.bly** (-luh.blee) *adv.*

ir.re.cov.er.a.ble (eer.i.CUV.uh.ruh.bul) *adj.* that cannot be recovered or remedied; **ir.re.cov.er.a.bly** *adv.*

ir.re.deem.a.ble (eer.i.DEE.muh.bul) *adj.* that cannot be brought back or exchanged; also, beyond remedy.

ir.re.duc.i.ble (eer.i.DEW.suh.bul) *adj.* that cannot be reduced or brought to a desired or simpler condition.

ir.ref.u.ta.ble (i.REF.yoo.tuh.bul, i.ref.YOO-) *adj.* that cannot be refuted or denied.

ir.re.gard.less (eer.uh.GARD.lis) *adj.* [nonstandard use] See REGARDLESS.

ir.reg.u.lar (i.REG.yuh.lur) *adj.* not obeying the usual rules, as in conduct, organization, or features: *an irregular coastline; irregular behavior, breathing; an irregular marriage (that is contrary to rules); irregular troops; "Go-went-gone"*

are parts of an *irregular verb*.
—**ir.reg.u.lar.ly** *adv*. —*n*. a soldier not of a regular army. —**ir.reg.u.lar.i.ty** (-LAIR.i.tee) *n*. **-ties**.
ir.rel.e.vant (i.REL.uh.vunt) *adj*. not pertinent or to the point; **ir.rel.e.vant.ly** *adv*. —**ir.rel.e.vance** *n*.
ir.re.li.gious (eer.i.LIJ.us) *adj*. not religious; also, impious.
ir.re.me.di.a.ble (eer.i.MEE.dee.uh.bul) *adj*. that cannot be remedied or corrected; **ir.re.me.di.a.bly** *adv*.
ir.rep.a.ra.ble (i.REP.uh.ruh.bul) *adj*. that cannot be repaired or put right: *to do irreparable harm*.
ir.re.place.a.ble (eer.i.PLAY.suh.bul) *adj*. that cannot be replaced.
ir.re.press.i.ble (eer.i.PRES.uh.bul) *adj*. that cannot be repressed or controlled.
ir.re.proach.a.ble (eer.i.PROH.chuh.bul) *adj*. blameless; **ir.re.proach.a.bly** *adv*.
ir.re.sist.i.ble (eer.i.ZIS.tuh.bul) *adj*. that cannot be resisted because too strong or fascinating; **ir.re.sist.i.bly** *adv*.
ir.res.o.lute (i.REZ.uh.loot) *adj*. not resolute; indecisive; **ir.res.o.lute.ly** *adv*. —**ir.res.o.lu.tion** (-LOO.shun) *n*.
ir.re.spec.tive (eer.uh.SPEC.tiv) *adjp*. regardless: *irrespective of color, creed, or sex*.
ir.re.spon.si.ble (eer.uh.SPON.suh.bul) *adj*. not responsible; **ir.re.spon.si.bly** *adv*. —**ir.re.spon.si.bil.i.ty** (-BIL.i.tee) *n*.
ir.re.triev.a.ble (eer.i.TREE.vuh.bul) *adj*. that cannot be retrieved or recovered.
ir.rev.er.ent (i.REV.uh.runt) *adj*. not reverent or respectful. —**ir.rev.er.ence** *n*.
ir.re.vers.i.ble (eer.i.VUR.suh.bul) *adj*. that cannot be reversed or changed.
ir.rev.o.ca.ble (i.REV.uh.cuh.bul) *adj*. that cannot be revoked or altered. —**ir.rev.o.ca.bly** (-blee) *adv*.
ir.ri.ga.ble (EER.i.guh.bul) *adj*. that can be irrigated.
ir.ri.gate (EER.uh.gate) *v*. **-gates, -gat.ed, -gat.ing** supply with flowing water or other liquid, as land for cultivation or a body part to cleanse it. —**ir.ri.ga.tion** (-GAY.shun) *n*. —**ir.ri.ga.tor** (-gay.tur) *n*.
ir.ri.ta.ble (EER.uh.tuh.bul) *adj*. **1** easily irritated. **2** highly sensitive to irritants, as skin or other plant or animal tissue. —**ir.ri.ta.bil.i.ty** (-BIL.i.tee) *n*.
ir.ri.tant (EER.uh.tunt) *n*. something causing irritation: *The barking at night proved an irritant to neighborly relations*; *adja*.: *an irritant poison*.
ir.ri.tate (EER.i.tate) *v*. **-tates, -tat.ed, -tat.ing 1** annoy in such a way that nothing can be done about it: *His comments irritated the speaker*. **2** stimulate biologically, as by light, heat, pressure, or touch. **3** make sore or sensitive, as mucous membranes by irritant poisons such as arsenic and lead: *Too much chlorine in the swimming pool irritates the eyes*. —**ir.ri.ta.tion** (-TAY.shun) *n*.
ir.rupt (i.RUPT) *v*. *Formal*. **1** rush in or burst in: *The drug squad irrupted into the apartment*. **2** of a species, to increase suddenly in numbers. —**ir.rup.tion** (-shun) *n*. —**ir.rup.tive** (-tiv) *adj*.
is (IZ) See BE.
-ish *adj. suffix*. of or like, esp. somewhat inclined to be: *girlish*; *reddish*; *sixish* (*Informal for about 6 o'clock*); *uppish*.
i.sin.glass (EYE.zin.glas) *n*. **1** a form of gelatin obtained from the air bladders of fishes such as the sturgeon. **2** thin sheets of mica used as an insulator against heat and electricity.
Is.lam.ic (is.LAH.mic) *adj*. having to do with the religion founded by Mohammed: *Islamic ceremonies, unity; the Islamic code, law, people, religion, republic, revolution, world*.
is.land (EYE.lund) *n*. **1** a usu. small land mass surrounded by water: *They live on Long Island; We live in Bowen Island; on an island in the Caribbean; Robinson Crusoe's deserted island; a tropical island*. **2** any isolated place such as a "traffic island" for the safety of pedestrians. —**is.land.er** *n*.
isle (ILE) *n*. a small island.
is.let (EYE.lit) *n*. a tiny island.
ism (IZ.um) **1** *n. Informal*. a doctrine or cause, as communism, fascism, jingoism, etc. **2** *suffix*. conduct, condition, or quality: *archaism, fascism, heroism, liberalism*.
is.n't (IZ.unt) is not.
iso- *comb.form*. equal or similar: *isobar, isometric, isotonic*.
i.so.bar (EYE.suh.bar) *n*. a line on a weather map connecting places of equal atmospheric pressure. —**i.so.bar.ic** (-BAIR.ic) *adj*.
i.so.late (EYE.suh.late) *v*. **-lates, -lat.ed, -lat.ing 1** separate from others: *to isolate one animal from the rest of the herd*; *adj*.: *a few isolated instances (that are not part of a general pattern)*. **2** obtain a substance in a free or uncombined state.
i.so.la.tion (eye.suh.LAY.shun) *n*. physical separation imposed by circumstances: *Robinson Crusoe's life of isolation; A*

hospital's **isolation ward** is for patients with contagious diseases. —**i.so.la.tor** (-lay.tur) n.

i.so.la.tion.ist (eye.suh.LAY.shuh.nist) n. & adj. (having to do with) an advocate of a policy of noninvolvement of one's country in international relations; **i.so.la.tion.ism** n.

i.so.mer (EYE.suh.mur) n. a chemical compound that is isomeric with another.

i.so.mer.ic (eye.suh.MER.ic) adj. composed of the same elements in the same proportion but in a different arrangement: *"Normal butane" and "isobutane" are isomeric forms of butane.* —**i.som.er.ism** (eye.SOM.uh.riz.um) n.

i.so.met.ric (eye.suh.MET.ric) adj. 1 having equality of measure: *An isometric crystal, as a cube-shaped one, has three equal axes; an isometric drawing, line, projection.* 2 involving contraction of muscles without shortening; not isotonic; **n.pl.**: *Isometric exercises, or isometrics, involve tensing (with little movement) of muscles against each other or against a fixed object.*

i.so.prene (EYE.suh.preen) n. a hydrocarbon used in making synthetic rubber.

i.sos.ce.les (eye.SOS.uh.leez) adj. of a triangle, having two equal sides.

i.so.therm (EYE.suh.thurm) n. a line on a map connecting places of the same average temperature; **i.so.ther.mal** (-THUR.mul) adj.

i.so.ton.ic (eye.suh.TON.ic) adj. 1 of solutions, having the same osmotic pressure. 2 involving shortening of a muscle, not isometric: *an isotonic contraction, exercise.*

i.so.tope (EYE.suh.tope) n. a form of a chemical element with the same chemical properties but different atomic weights: *Deuterium and tritium are isotopes of hydrogen.* —**i.so.top.ic** (-TOP.ic) adj.; **i.so.top.i.cal.ly** adv.

Is.ra.el (IZ.ree.ul, -ray.ul) n. the Jewish people or Hebrews.

Is.rae.li (iz.RAY.lee) n. & adj. (a person) of or from **Israel**, a country on the E. shore of the Mediterranean.

Is.ra.el.ite (IZ.ree.uh.lite, IZ.ray-) adj. having to do with the Jews of ancient Israel. —n. an Israelite Jew.

is.su.ance (ISH.oo.unce) n. an official issuing, as of a decree.

is.sue (ISH.oo) v. **is.sues, is.sued, is.su.ing** 1 put forth or put out: *to issue a proclamation, stamps and coins, a publication; clothing issued to G.I.s.* 2 come out: *smoke issuing from a chimney.* —n. 1 what is issued or comes out: *to bring out* or *publish a new issue of an old book; an issue consisting of 2,000 copies; back issues and current issues of a journal; a pair of* **government-issue** *boots; He died without issue* (= offspring). 2 result or outcome: *to await the issue of an election.* 3 subject of a dispute or controversy: *to address, bring up, face, raise, straddle an issue; Let's not make such an issue of it; to cloud, confuse, duck, evade, settle the issue; burning, dead, divisive, sensitive, side, substantive issues; That's not the issue* (= the point); *Let's not* **force the issue** (= force a decision); *The point* **at issue** (= in dispute) *is not how it happened but why; He hesitated to* **take issue** (= disagree) *with his boss.* —**is.su.er** n.

-ist n. suffix. person of specified occupation or persuasion: *atheist, botanist, communist, humorist, specialist.*

isth.mus (IS.mus) n. a narrow strip of land connecting two large areas across water, as of Panama or Corinth. —**isth.mi.an** (IS.mee.un) n. & adj.

it pron., possessive **ITS**, pl. **THEY**, objective **THEM**, possessive **THEIR** or **THEIRS**. 1 the understood subject to which an action refers: *We all heard it; Tell her about it; Don't make such a big deal of it.* 2 an indefinite or impersonal subject or object: *Who is it? "It never rains but it pours"; It's nice to see you.* 3 *Informal.* something disgusting: *He's full of it; That's a crock of it.*
—n. in children's games such as tag, the player who initiates the action, as catching, finding, etc.

I.tal.ian (i.TAL.yun) n. a person of or from Italy or the Romance language spoken there. —adj. having to do with Italy: *Italian immigrants; the Italian language.*

i.tal.ic (i.TAL.ic, eye-) n. a type or letter that slants to the right: *This is italic; It's printed in italics.* —adj. 1 **Italic** having to do with ancient Italy, its people, or their dialects. 2 having to do with italics: *italic type; an italic letter, passage, sentence (printed in italics).*

i.tal.i.cize (i.TAL.uh.size) v. **-ciz.es, cized, ciz.ing** print in italics or underline to indicate italics.

itch n. 1 skin irritation that makes one want to scratch: *an ointment to relieve your itch.* 2 a restless, uneasy longing or desire: *an itch for gold; Mites cause* **the itch**, *or scabies.* —v. have an itch: *I'm itching to get at him;* adj.: *I have* **itching** *ears (eager to hear what comes next); the itching palm of an avaricious man.* —**itch.y** adj. **itch.i.er, -i.est.**

—**itch.i.ness** *n.*

i.tem (EYE.tum) *n.* a separate unit or article in an enumeration, list, or group: *the first item on the agenda; collector's items; luxury items; news items.*

i.tem.ize (EYE.tuh.mize) *v.* **-iz.es, -ized, -iz.ing** list in detail; *adj.*: *I would like an itemized bill instead of a general statement.* —**i.tem.i.za.tion** (-muh.ZAY.shun, -mye-) *n.*

it.er.ate (IT.uh.rate) *v.* **-ates, -at.ed, -at.ing** repeat; do or say again; **it.er.a.tion** (-RAY.shun) *n.*

i.tin.er.ant (eye.TIN.ur.unt) *n.* one travelling from one place to another: *an itinerant judge, musician, preacher, seller.*

i.tin.er.ar.y (eye.TIN.uh.rair.ee) *n.* **-ar.ies 1** a plan, route, or record of a journey. **2** a traveller's guidebook.

-itis *n. suffix.* a disease or diseaselike condition: *appendicitis, bronchitis, electionitis* (= election fever).

it'll it will, it shall.

it's it is; it has.

its *adj. & pron.* possessive of IT: *Two of its legs are missing; They are its (legs).*

it.self (it.SELF) *pron.* emphatic or reflexive form of IT: *the very thing itself; A catalyst works without itself being affected; a machine able to run by itself; The book speaks for itself; TV watching is not bad in itself.*

it.ty-bit.ty (IT.ee.BIT.ee) or **it.sy-bit.sy** (IT.see.BIT.see) *adj. Informal.* tiny or small.

-ity *n. suffix.* quality or state: *ability, alkalinity; profanities* (= instances of profanity).

IV (eye.VEE) *n.* **IVs 1** an apparatus used to give an intravenous feeding or injection. **2** such a feeding or injection.

I've I have.

-ive *adj. suffix.* tending to or having the nature of something: *evasive, fugitive, talkative.*

i.vied (EYE.veed) *adj.* covered with ivy.

i.vo.ry (EYE.vuh.ree) *n.* **1** the hard, creamy-white substance of the tusks of elephants, walruses, etc. **2** *ivories pl. Informal.* things made of ivory, as piano keys, teeth, billiard balls, or dice. —*adj.* of or like ivory; creamy white.

ivory tower *n.* a place or state of existence away from the harsh realities of life: *Some universities as ivory towers.*

i.vy (EYE.vee) *n.* **i.vies** a creeping and climbing evergreen vine with smooth and shiny leaves, five-pointed in the common "English ivy."

-ize *v. suffix.* cause to be, become, or treat (like): *alphabetize, finalize, legalize.*

J, j

J or **j** (JAY) *n.* **J's** or **j's** the 10th letter of the English alphabet.

jab *n.* a quick poke with something pointed or a blow as in boxing: *to throw a jab; a left jab; right jab.* —*v.* **jabs, jabbed, jab.bing** give a jab: *Jan's umbrella jabbed me in the ribs.*

jab.ber (JAB.ur) *n. & v.* chatter *about something.*

jab.ber.wock.y (JAB.ur.wock.ee) *n.* gibberish; meaningless syllables.

ja.bot (zha.BOH, JAB.oh) *n.* a ruffle or frill on the front of a shirt or blouse.

jac.a.ran.da (jac.uh.RAN.duh) *n.* a beautiful tropical tree or shrub, esp. one species with clusters of tiny, fernlike leaves and bluish-white flowers.

jack *n.* **1** a male, esp. a young fellow or helper: *They fired every man Jack (of them); "A jack of all trades and master of none."* **2** a playing card with a picture of a knave: *A jack ranks below king and queen.* **3** a simple mechanism or device, as a machine to lift the wheel of an automobile, an outlet or receptacle for plugging in a telephone, etc. **4** something handy, as a small ball or flag. **5** a pebble or piece used in the children's game of **jacks.**
—*v.* **jack up** raise: *to jack up a car to change a tire; to jack up prices, wages, etc.*

jack.al (JACK.awl, -ul) *n.* a foxlike wild dog that hunts in packs by night and feeds on carrion: *a pack of jackals.*

jack.a.napes (JAK.uh.napes) *n.* a pert or forward fellow or child.

jack.ass *n.* **1** a male donkey. **2** a stupid person.

jack.boot *n.* a heavy military boot; hence, oppression or bullying behavior: *jackboot tactics.*

jack.boot.ed (JACK.boo.tid) *adj a.* ruthless: *jackbooted force, militarism.*

jack.daw *n.* the dusky-black common crow of Europe and N. Africa.

jack.et (JACK.it) *n.* **1** a short coat: *bomber, dinner, flak, life, sports, suit jackets.* **2** an outer covering: *a book's dust jacket; the jacket* (= skin) *of a potato; the jacket* (= sleeve) *of a record.*

Jack Frost *n.* frost personified; freezing weather.

jack.ham.mer (JAK.ham.ur) *n.* a pneumatic hammer for drilling rocks and concrete.

jack-in-the-box *n.* **-box.es** a toy consisting of a small box from which a figure springs when the lid is opened.

jack-in-the-pulpit *n.* **-pits** a North American wild plant having a club-

jackknife / jangle

shaped spike of flowers ("jack") arched over by a hoodlike flap ("the pulpit").

jack.knife *n.* **-knives 1** a large knife with a blade or blades that fold into the handle. **2** a dive in which the body is doubled up in midair before straightening up to hit the water.
—*v.* **-knifes, -knifed, -knif.ing** double up like a jackknife, as two railway cars in an accident: *A tractor-trailer jack-knifed on the main highway.*

jack-of-all-trades *n., pl.* **jacks-of-all-trades** one who can do different kinds of work though not as an expert in any of them.

jack-o'-lantern *n.* a lantern made of a hollowed-out pumpkin cut to look like a face.

jack.pot *n.* the accumulated stakes of a poker game or a similar big prize or windfall: *He* **hit the jackpot** (= won the biggest prize).

jack rabbit *n.* a long-eared North American hare with strong hind legs: *the jack-rabbit* (= sudden) *starts of a hot rodder.*

jack.straw *n.* a thin strip of wood or plastic used in the children's game of **jackstraws** in which such strips are thrown down in a pile to be picked up one at a time without disturbing the rest.

jack-tar *n.* a sailor.

jack-up *n.* an increase.

Jacob's ladder *n.* an herb with ladderlike leaves and large blue or white flowers.

jac.quard (juh.CARD) *n.* an elaborately figured weave done automatically on the **Jacquard loom** and used in table damask, brocades, tapestry, etc.; also, such fabric.

ja.cuz.zi (juh.KOO.zee) *n.* -**cuz.zis** a whirlpool bath. **Jacuzzi** *Trademark.*

jade *n.* **1** a hard, tough, green or white gemstone used for carvings and jewelry; *adj.* light-green. **2** a worn-out horse. **3** a disreputable woman.
—*v.* **jades, jad.ed, jad.ing** to dull or wear out, as with hard work or over-indulgence in something; *adj.: a jaded outlook, look.*

jag *v.* **jags, jagged, jag.ging** cut or tear unevenly. —*n.* **1** a pointed projection, as of rock. **2** a drinking bout or spree. **3** a fit: *a crying jag.*

jag.ged (JAG.id) *adj.* uneven or zigzag: *a jagged edge.*

jag.uar (JAG.wahr) *n.* a leopardlike but more heavily built ferocious cat of the W. hemisphere.

jai a.lai (HYE.lye, HYE.uh.lye) *n.* a fast Spanish game resembling handball but played with a basketlike container called "cesta" strapped to the player's forearm.

jail *n.* a prison, esp. one for temporary confinement or for minor offenses: *to go to jail; be sent to jail; to serve time in jail; He broke out of jail and is now missing.* —*v.* confine in or as if in jail.

jail.bird *n.* **1** *Informal.* a prisoner. **2** a habitual lawbreaker.

jail.break *n.* an escape from prison: *to attempt, make a jailbreak.*

jail.er or **jail.or** (JAY.lur) *n.* a person in charge of a jail or prisoners.

ja.la.pe.ño (hah.luh.PAIN.yo) *n.* a hot pepper used in Mexican cooking.

ja.lop.y (juh.LOP.ee) *n.* **-lop.ies** an old automobile or aircraft in poor condition.

jal.ou.sie (JAL.uh.see) *n.* a window or shutter made of horizontal slats or louvers that may be tilted, like Venetian blinds, to let in air and light but keep out rain.

jam *v.* **jams, jammed, jam.ming 1** press, squeeze, or wedge in between two surfaces: *a finger jammed in a car door.* **2** block or get blocked, get caught in, etc.: *logs jamming a river; clothes jammed into a suitcase; The car skidded when the driver jammed on the brakes; enemies jamming* (= interfering with) *each other's radio messages;* *adj.: A jammed lock or window is hard to open; a bus jammed (full) with passengers.*
—*n.* **1** a place with so many people or things that movement is impossible: *a log jam in a river; a traffic jam at a busy intersection; If you're* **in a jam** (*Informal* for tight spot) *give me a call.* **2** a fruit preserve: *to spread jam on toast; It's* **jam tomorrow, jam yesterday, but never jam today** (= Your present performance is never as good as your boasts about the past and the future).

Ja.mai.can (juh.MAY.cun) *n. & adj.* (a person) of or from **Jamaica**, a Caribbean island country.

jamb or **jambe** (JAM) *n.* a leglike upright piece forming part of a frame, as of a door.

jam.bo.ree (jam.buh.REE) *n.* **1** a large gathering for revelry or festivities. **2** a Boy Scout rally.

jam-packed *adj.* tightly packed, as a stadium with spectators.

jam session *n. Informal.* a lively gathering of musicians playing improvisations.

jan.gle (JANG.gul) *n.* a harsh, usu. metallic clashing noise, as of pots and pans: *Screaming children jangle on* (= upset) *his nerves.* —*v.* **-gles, -gled, -gling** make a jangle.

jan.i.tor (JAN.uh.tur) *n.* a person in charge of the cleaning, heating, and maintenance of a building; custodian. —**jan.i.tor.i.al** (-TOR.ee.ul) *adj.*

Jan.u.ar.y (JAN.yoo.air.ee) *n.* **-ar.ies** the first month of the calendar year, having 31 days.

ja.pan (juh.PAN) *n.* a hard varnish as used on Japanese lacquerware. —*v.* **-pans, -panned, -pan.ning** give a glossy finish with japan.

Jap.a.nese (jap.uh.NEEZ) *n. sing. & pl.* **1** a person of or from Japan. **2** *pl.* the people of Japan. —*adj.:* the Japanese cherry tree, language, maple, mink, porcelain, spaniel, yew.

Japanese beetle *n.* a voracious garden pest that entered the U.S. around 1916.

jape *n. & v.* **japes, japed, jap.ing** jest or gibe; **jap.er** n. —**jap.er.y** *n.*

ja.pon.i.ca (juh.PON.uh.cuh) *n.* **1** a species of camellia. **2** Japanese quince.

jar *n.* **1** a wide-mouthed container, usu. round, for holding liquids, cosmetics, canned fruit, etc.: *a cookie jar; a "Mason jar" for home canning.* **2** a harsh, esp. grating shock or sound. —*v.* **jars, jarred, jar.ring** cause a jar: *nerves jarred by the shaking and rattling of the long ride; It jars on one's nerves;* *adj.:* **jarring** (= discordant) *colors, opinions, sounds.*

jar.di.niere (jar.duh.NEER) *n.* an ornamental pot or stand for plants and flowers.

jar.gon (JAR.gun, -gon) *n.* **1** language that is unintelligible because it is meaningless or obscure. **2** the language of a particular occupational group or profession: *legal jargon; trade jargon.*

jas.mine (JAZ.min) *n.* a fragrant white or reddish flower of a vine or shrub of the olive family, originally from the Orient.

jas.per (JAS.pur) *n.* **1** an opaque, usu. red, yellow, or brown granular quartz. **2** *Slang.* guy.

ja.to (JAY.toh) *n.* the "jet-assisted take-off" system of an aircraft, using small rockets attached to its body; also **JA-TO.**

jaun.dice (JAWN.dis) *n.* a liver ailment resulting in a yellow discoloration of the skin and eyes. —*v.* **-dic.es, -diced, -dic.ing** be afflicted with jaundice; *adj.: a jaundiced* (= jealous or prejudiced) *eye, observer, view.*

jaunt *n.* a short pleasure trip or excursion: *to go on a jaunt through the hills.* —*v.* take a jaunt.

jaun.ty (JAWN.tee) *adj.* **-ti.er, -ti.est** stylish: *a hat set at a jaunty angle;* jaunty (= lively and carefree) *steps.* —**jaun.ti.ly** *adv.;* **jaun.ti.ness** *n.*

ja.va (JAH.vuh) *n. Slang.* coffee.

jav.e.lin (JAV.lin, JAV.uh.lin) *n.* a light wooden or metal spear, esp. one over 8.5 ft. (260 cm) long, thrown for distance as a field sport.

jaw *n.* **1** either of the two sets of bones containing teeth and forming the mouth: *the lower jaw; upper jaw; He dislocated his jaw; with her jaws set in determination; Jaws dropped in surprise.* **2 jaws** *pl.* an entrance to something undesirable: *the jaws of death, illiteracy; to snatch victory from the jaws of defeat.* **3** a gripping or holding part, as of a vise: *a wrecked car in the jaws of a crusher; ratchet jaws.* **4** *Slang.* a talk or chat: *a good jaw with an old friend.* **5** *Slang.* a lengthy, boring, or scolding talk. —*v. Slang.* to talk or talk to someone in a lengthy or boring manner: *He got jawed at; to jaw a situation out with someone.*

jaw.bone *n.* a bone of a jaw, esp. a lower jaw. —*v.* **-bones, -boned, -bon.ing** *Informal.* pressure or persuade using speech power, esp. to comply with government controls.

jaw.break.er (JAW.bray.kur) *n. Informal.* something that is hard on the jaws, as a kind of candy or a hard-to-pronounce word.

Jaws of Life *n. Trademark.* a cutting device used in rescuing people trapped in wreckage.

jay *n.* a crowlike but smaller and more colorful bird; also **jay.bird.**

Jay.cee *n.* a member of a junior chamber of commerce, a worldwide organization for leadership training and community work.

jay.walk *v.* of pedestrians, cross a street without regard to traffic regulations. —**jay.walk.er** *n.*

jazz *n.* **1** music developed by African Americans, characterized by emotional appeal, fast rhythms, and improvisation. **2** *Slang.* empty talk; nonsense: *... and all that jazz* (= and the rest of the stuff). **3** a style of gymnastic dancing based on rock music. —*adj.: a jazz band; jazz fans, music.* —*v.* play music as jazz. —**jazz up** *Informal.* add life, color, or appeal to something; *adj.: a news report that is too jazzed up to be true.*

jazz.y *adj.* **jazz.i.er, -i.est 1** like jazz. **2** *Informal.* lively or showy: *a jazzy new suit.* —**jazz.i.ly** *adv.*; **jazz.i.ness** *n.*

jeal.ous (JEL.us) *adj.* **1** fearful or suspicious about losing what is one's own to a rival, as a loved one or one's rights: *a jealous husband; a jealous guardian of religious freedom; Lee walked out in a jealous rage.* **2** envious: *rivals jealous of each other.* —**jeal.ous.ly** *adv.*

jeal.ous.y (JEL.uh.see) *n.* **-ous.ies** resentfulness against rivals; also, envy: *to arouse, feel jealousy; fierce, petty, professional jealousy.*

jeans (JEENS) *n.pl.* pants made of denim or similar cloth: *blue jeans.*

jeep *n.* a small, sturdy, usu. open automobile with four-wheel drive for use on rough terrain and in demanding jobs; **Jeep** *Trademark.*

jeer *n.* a scoffing cry or remark; ridicule. —*v.* scoff or ridicule a person or thing: *to jeer and taunt someone; an actor jeered off the stage.* —**jeer.ing.ly** *adv.*

jeez *interj.* expressing surprise; gee.

Je.ho.vah (ji.HOH.vuh) *n.* God, as in the Old Testament.

je.june (ji.JOON) *adj.* **1** empty or barren; without substance; not interesting or satisfying to the mind. **2** immature or childish.

je.ju.num (ji.JOO.num) *n.* portion of the small intestine between the duodenum and the ileum; **je.ju.nal** *adj.*

jell *v.* **1** become like jelly; set. **2** *Informal.* of ideas, plans, etc., take definite form: *He's been in a dozen careers that have not jelled.* —*n.* jelly.

jel.li.fy (JEL.uh.fye) *v.* **-fies, -fied, -fy.ing** change into jelly.

jel.ly (JEL.ee) *n.* **jel.lies 1** a semisolid, partly transparent food made from fruit juices, starch, etc. by the thickening action of gelatin. **2** any jellylike substance such as the tissue of jellyfish. —*v.* **jel.lies, jel.lied, jel.ly.ing** congeal as jelly; *adj.*: *a jellied salad.*

jel.ly.bean (JEL.ee.been) *n.* a candy made of jellied sugar.

jel.ly.fish (JEL.ee.fish) *n.* **1** an umbrella-shaped sea animal trailing stinging tentacles. **2** a spineless person.

jelly roll *n.* a rolled-up sheet of sponge cake spread with jelly.

jen.net (JEN.it) *n.* a female donkey.

jen.ny (JEN.ee) *n.* **jen.nies 1** the female of certain animals and birds. **2** same as SPINNING JENNY.

jeop.ard.ize (JEP.ur.dize) *v.* **-iz.es, -ized, -iz.ing** put in jeopardy; endanger or imperil.

jeop.ard.y (JEP.ur.dee) *n.* **-ard.ies** danger or peril: *The refugee claimed his life would be in jeopardy if he returned home.*

jer.e.mi.ad (jer.uh.MY.ad) *n.* a mournful complaint.

jerk *n.* **1** a quick, sharp pull, push, or twist. **2** a muscular contraction or twitch, as when the knee is tapped by a physician. **3** *Slang.* one considered as stupid, foolish, or irritating. —*v.* **1** pull quickly and sharply: *She jerked her arm away from her captor; a train jerking its way uphill.* **2** cut beef, etc. into strips for drying and preserving: *Reindeer meat may be jerked, smoked, or canned.* —**jerk.y** *adj.* **jerk.i.er, -i.est.** —**jerk.i.ly** *adv.*

jer.kin (JUR.kin) *n.* a short, sleeveless, close-fitting jacket, esp. one common in the 16th century.

jerk.wa.ter (JURK.wot.ur) *n.* a rural train. —*adja.* out-of-the way or unimportant: *a jerkwater town.*

jer.ry-built (JER.ee.bilt) *adj.* shoddily or cheaply constructed.

jer.sey (JUR.see) *n.* **-seys 1** a close-fitting pullover made of a plain-stitch knitted fabric. **2 Jersey** a breed of small dairy cattle, originally from Jersey, Channel Islands.

jess *n.* a short strap around a falcon's leg for attaching a leash.

jes.sa.mine (JES.uh.min) same as JASMINE.

jest *n.* something said for fun, often to tease or mock: *She said it only* **in jest** (= in fun). —*v.* laugh at or joke: *She doesn't jest about her work.*

jest.er *n.* a clown or fool, as in a medieval court.

Jes.u.it (JEZH.yoo.it, JEZ-) *n.* a member of the Society of Jesus, a Roman Catholic religious order.

jet *n.* **1** a stream of water, steam, flame, etc. sent out under pressure, as through a narrow nozzle or spout. **2** such an opening or vent. **3** a jet-propelled aircraft: *to fly, pilot a jet; adj.*: *a jet engine, fighter; jet fuel.* —*adj.* deep glossy black. —*v.* **jets, jet.ted, jet.ting 1** spout or gush: *water jetting from a fountain.* **2** travel by jet: *to jet over to London.*

jet-black *adj.* very black.

jet lag *n.* exhaustion felt after jetting through several time zones because of the disruption of the body's 24-hour biological rhythms. Also **jet fatigue, jet syndrome.**

jet.lin.er (JET.lye.nur) *n.* a commercial jet airliner.

jet.port *n.* an airport for jet airplanes.

jet-propelled *adj.* driven by jet propul-

jet propulsion / jinni

sion: *a jet-propelled aircraft, flying bomb, missile.*
jet propulsion *n.* the forward reaction of burned gases shooting backward from an engine through exhausts.
jet.sam (JET.sum) *n.* **1** jettisoned cargo washed ashore: *flotsam and jetsam.* **2** social derelicts and such rejected elements of society.
jet set *n.* fashionable people who make frequent air journeys, esp. in the pursuit of pleasure.
jet ski *n.* a small motorized boat equipped with skis, similar to a snowmobile, for skimming over water. —**jet-ski** *v.* **-skies, -skied, -ski.ing.**
jet stream *n.* **1** any of several wide bands of strong winds blowing at high altitudes from west to east. **2** a jet engine exhaust.
jet.ti.son (JET.uh.sun) *v.* throw goods overboard in an emergency so as to lighten a ship or aircraft. —*n.* such goods.
jet.ty (JET.ee) *v.* **jet.ties, jet.tied, jet.ty.ing** jut out into the water, as a landing pier. —*n.* a jettying wall or other structure.
jeu d'es.prit (zhuh.des.PREE) *n., pl.* **jeux d'es.prit** (zhuhz-) *French.* play of wit or a witticism.
Jew *n.* a follower of Judaism; Hebrew: *the Ashkenazic, Sephardic, and Oriental Jews; The child is a Jew if the mother is Jewish.* —**Jew.ish** *adj.*; **Jew.ish.ness** *n.*
jew.el (JOO.ul) *n.* **1** a precious stone or gem: *priceless jewels; to mount a jewel.* **2** a jeweled ornament; hence, something or someone very precious: *India was the jewel in the British Crown; Jo is a jewel of a wife.* —*v.* **-els, -eled, -el.ing** adorn or set with a jewel; *adj.*: *a jeweled crown; jeweled belts, clasps, straps.* —**jew.el.er** (JOO.ul.ur) *n.* Also **jew.elled, jew.el.ling; jew.el.ler** *Cdn.* —**jew.el.le.ry** *Brit.* JEWELRY.
jew.el.ry (JOO.ul.ree) *n.* jewels collectively: *costume jewelry.*
Jew.ish *adj.* having to do with Jews: *David is Jewish; He was born on 20 June 1945, or 9 Tammuz 5705 according to the Jewish* or **Hebrew calendar** *dating from Creation at 3760 B.C.; a Jewish community.* —**Jew.ish.ness** *n.*
Jew.ry (JOO.ree) *n.* **1** Jewish people. **2** formerly, a Jewish ghetto.
jez.e.bel (JEZ.uh.bel) *n.* a shameless or wicked woman like **Jezebel**, the wife of an Israelite king.
jib *n.* **1** a triangular sail set ahead of the foremast. **2** a shying horse. —*v.* **jibs, jibbed, jib.bing** refuse to move forward, as a shying horse.
jibe 1 *v.* **jibes, jibed, jib.ing** agree: *Your story doesn't jibe with his.* **2** same as GIBE.
jif.fy (JIF.ee) *n.* **jif.fies** *Informal.* moment: *I'll be back in a jiffy.*
Jiffy bag *Trademark.* a padded bag for mailing books, pictures, etc.
jig *n.* **1** a lively folk dance, often in triple time, or the music for it. **2** a device that works with an up-and-down motion, as a spoon-shaped fishing lure or a mechanical coal cleaner. **3** a device for holding machine work in position and guiding a tool that works on it, as in machine embroidery. —**the jig is up** it's hopeless; it's over. —*v.* **jigs, jigged, jig.ging 1** dance a jig. **2** jerk or move up and down.
jig.ger (JIG.ur) *n.* a measure for serving liquor, usu. 1.5 ounces.
jig.gle (JIG.ul) *n.* a slight shake or jerk. —*v.* **jig.gles, jig.gled, jig.gling** give a jiggle. —**jig.gly** *adj.*
jig.saw puzzle *n.* a picture sawed into small irregular pieces for fitting back together: *to assemble* or *put together a jigsaw puzzle.*
ji.had (ji.HAHD) *n.* a Moslem holy war or crusade for reform.
jilt *v.* cast off a lover faithlessly or unfeelingly. —*n.* one who jilts. —**jilt.er** *n.*
Jim Crow or **jim crow** *n.* discrimination against American blacks; **Jim Crow.ism** *n.*
jim-dandy *adj. & n.* **-dies** (a person or thing) that is excellent or first-rate.
jim.my (JIM.ee) *n.* **jim.mies 1** a short crowbar used especially by burglars. **2 jimmies** *pl.* bits of candy sprinkled on pastry and ice cream for decoration. —*v.* **jim.mies, jim.mied, jim.my.ing** pry open with a jimmy.
jim.son.weed (JIM.sun.weed) *n.* a large bushy plant with poisonous leaves and seeds; also called "Jamestown weed."
jin.gle (JING.gul) *n.* **1** a clinking sound like that of little bells, coins, or keys striking together. **2** a verse or music that is catchy because of the sound repetitions in it: *an advertising jingle.* —*v.* **-gles, -gled, -gling** make a clinking sound: *keys jingling in his pocket.* —**jin.gly** (-glee) *adj.*
jin.go (JING.go) *n.* **-goes** one who is jingoistic.
jin.go.ism (JING.go.iz.um) *n.* the attitude or policy of chauvinistic aggressiveness toward other countries. —**jin.go.ist** *n.* —**jin.go.is.tic** (-IS.tic) *adj.*
jin.ni (JIN.nee) *n., pl.* **jinn** in Moslem legend, a guardian spirit: *the good jinni that helped Aladdin.*

jin.rik.i.sha or **jin.rick.sha** (jin.RIK.shaw) *n.* a light, two-wheeled, hooded, man-drawn cart formerly used in Oriental countries as a taxicab.

jinx *v.* to bring bad luck to someone. —*n.* a person or thing that jinxes: *to put a jinx on someone.*

jit.ney (JIT.nee) *n.* **-neys** a cab or bus that travels a regular route serving a small community, as in some resort areas.

jit.ter.bug (JIT.ur.bug) *n.* a lively ballroom dance of the 1940's featuring acrobatic swings and lifts. —*v.* **-bugs, -bugged, -bug.ging:** *jitterbugging to swing music.*

jit.ters (JIT.urs) *n.pl. Informal.* the fidgets; a fit of nervousness: *a bad case of the jitters; something for easing jitters; She had last-minute jitters before going on stage; nervous jitters.*

jit.ter.y (JIT.uh.ree) *adj.* nervous.

jive *n.* **1** swing music or dancing of the 1940s; jazz; **adj.a.:** *a jive joint; jive dancing, records.* **2** *Slang.* talk that is phoney or tiring: *to be wise to the jive;* **adj.a.:** *jive talk; a jive word for the sex act.* —*v.* **jives, jived, jiv.ing 1** tease or kid: *Quit jiving.* **2** dance to or play jive music.

job *n.* **1** a piece of work, esp. one done for pay; task: *He does a good job in his present position; backbreaking, demanding, difficult, great, splendid jobs; a hatchet job; snow job; put-up job; a handyman hired to do odd jobs around the house; a job* (= unit of work) *to be run on the computer.* **2** a paid position of employment: *to find, get, give up, hold, hold down, hunt for, land, look for, lose, quit, take a job; a part-time or full-time job; cushy, desk, menial, soft, steady jobs; summer jobs for students; He was fired for drinking on the job* (= while on duty); **adj.a.:** *a job application, interview, offer, opportunity, site, title; job cuts, hunting, losses, markets, performance, security, training.* **3** *Informal.* a criminal act: *to do a job; an inside job; Pat pulled a job at* (= robbed) *the corner store.* —*v.* **jobs, jobbed, job.bing** sell goods purchased wholesale or in large quantities, piece by piece or in small quantities to retailers.

job action *n.* a tactic such as a slowdown, sick-out, or demonstration used by employees instead of striking.

job bank *n.* a computerized system that matches job vacancies with unemployed workers.

job.ber (JOB.ur) *n.* **1** one who does piecework or one who jobs as a middleman. **2** one who uses a position of trust for private ends.

job-hopping *n.* frequent changing of jobs for financial gain.

job.less (JOB.lis) **1** *adj.* unemployed: *the jobless poor; jobless workers; people left jobless;* **n.pl.:** *hope for the jobless; the number of jobless; the long-term jobless.* **2** *adj.* having to do with the unemployed: *jobless benefits; the jobless rate, total.*

job lot *n.* an assortment of goods, including inferior stuff, bought or sold in one lot.

job sharing *n.* the sharing of a full-time position by two people working in shifts.

jock *n. Informal* [short form] **1** disc jockey; jockey. **2** jockstrap. **3** a male athlete.

jock.ey (JOCK.ee) *n.* **1** one who rides horses in races. **2** one who guides the movement of something, as specified: *a disc jockey; bike, camel, car, gas, pump, tank jockeys.* —*v.* **-eys, -eyed, -ey.ing 1** ride a horse in a race. **2** try to gain an advantage by skillful maneuvering: *political parties jockeying to form a new government; to jockey for position; to jockey someone or something into position; to jockey a truck through city traffic.* **3** trick or cheat someone *into* doing something.

jock.strap *n.* **1** a pouched belt to protect the genitals of male athletes. **2** *Informal.* a male athlete.

jo.cose (joh.COSE) *adj.* given to joking or jesting; **jo.cose.ly** *adv.*; **jo.cose.ness** *n.* —**jo.cos.i.ty** (-COS.i.tee) *n.* **-ties.**

joc.u.lar (JOK.yuh.lur) *adj.* **1** fond of joking: *a jocular fellow.* **2** meant to be funny: *She said it in a jocular vein.* —**joc.u.lar.ly** *adv.* —**joc.u.lar.i.ty** (-LAIR.i.tee) *n.*

joc.und (JOH.cund) *adj.* merry or cheerful; **joc.und.ly** *adv.* —**jo.cun.di.ty** (joh.CUN.di.tee) *n.*

jodh.purs (JOD.purs) *n.pl.* breeches for riding that are loose and full above the knees and close-fitting below.

Joe or **joe** *n. Informal.* fellow or guy: *She's such a good Joe I don't feel threatened by her; not a dumb Joe but a mastermind.* —*adj.a.* ordinary: *She started at the bottom doing the Joe jobs.*

jog *n.* **1** a little shove or nudge. **2** a notch or a projecting part; also, unevenness. **3** a sharp and brief change of direction, as in a road. —*v.* **jogs, jogged, jog.ging 1** give a jog: *She has to jog her husband's memory sometimes.* **2** move along with a shaking motion: *a horse jogging along.* **3** run slowly: *People jog for exercise.* —**jog.ger** *n.*

John or **john** (JON) *n. Slang.* **1** a toilet. **2** a prostitute's client.
John Bull *n.* the English people or nation.
John Doe *n.* a name given to someone whose real name is unknown.
john.ny (JON.ee) *n.* **john.nies** a short gown worn by hospital patients.
Johnny Canuck See CANUCK.
Johnny-come-lately *n.* **-lies 1** a newcomer. **2** an upstart.
joie de vi.vre (zhwah.duh.VEEV.ruh) *n. French.* joy of living.
join *v.* **1** bring or come together with another person or thing: *broken pieces joined together; One piece is joined to another; a junction where one street joins another; to join two people in matrimony.* **2** associate with or come into the company of another or others: *to join the armed forces; She will join us in a minute; She'll join in with us; Let's join in the chorus; Let's join hands and say a prayer in silence; Later we will join forces with our allies and fight our common enemy; We'll join with them in the fight.* —**join battle** start fighting.
join.er *n.* **1** a person or thing that joins, esp. a carpenter or woodworker specializing in intricate joining work. **2** *Informal.* one who likes to join groups.
joint *n.* **1** a joining or place of joining: *a pipe joint; the ball-and-socket joint of the shoulder; dovetail, miter, mortise and tenon, riveted, universal, welded joints.* **2** a jointed part or division: *the middle joint of a finger; a butcher's joint* (= section) *of meat for roasting.* **3** *Slang.* a cheap establishment such as a hotel, restaurant, or other place where people meet: *two would-be burglars casing a joint; a booze joint; clip joints.* **4** *Slang.* a marijuana cigarette.
—*v.* **1** fit together for joining; *adj.*: *Insects have jointed legs; a perfectly jointed space suit.* **2** divide or cut up at the joints, as a butcher does.
—*adj.* shared or sharing: *a joint bank account; the Joint Chiefs of Staff (forming a military advisory board); divorced parents given joint custody of a child; a joint editor, secretary.* —**joint.ly** *adv.*
joist *n.* one of the parallel beams supporting a floor or ceiling from wall to wall.
joke *n.* **1** something that arouses laughter, as a funny story, remark, or prank: *to crack, take, tell a joke; a clean, coarse, crude, dirty, funny, off-color, practical, sick, stale joke; It's no joke to lose your job; Children play jokes on each other on April Fool's Day; Sometimes you can carry a joke too far; Better not make a joke of personal handicaps; the butt or object of a joke; The joke was on me.* **2** a person or thing to laugh at: *He's the joke of the village; The math test was a joke* (= was very easy). —*v.* **jokes, joked, jok.ing** jest or tease: *to joke with someone about something; n.: Joking aside, how serious is the loss?* —**jok.ing.ly** *adv.*
jok.er (JOH.kur) *n.* **1** one who jokes; also **joke.ster. 2** in some games, an extra card useful as a wild card or highest trump. **3** a tricky clause, phrase, or word inserted in a document to nullify its effect.
jol.lies (JOL.eez) *n.pl. Informal.* fun or pleasure: *They get their jollies by partying.*
jol.ly (JOL.ee) *adj.* **jol.li.er, jol.li.est** full of fun; merry. —*v.* **jol.lies, jol.lied, jol.ly.ing 1** to humor someone. **2** make fun of someone good-naturedly. —**jol.li.ly** *adv.* —**jol.li.ty** *n.*
jolt *n.* a sudden jerk, knock, or surprise: *The news of death came as a jolt to his loved ones; a severe jolt.* —*v.* give or experience a jolt: *It jolted everyone; It jolted us out of our smugness.* —**jolt.y** *adj.*
Jones.es (JONE.siz) *n.pl.* **keep up with the Joneses** slavishly follow what everyone else is doing, esp. in acquiring material things.
jon.gleur (JONG.glur) *n.* a wandering minstrel of the Middle Ages.
jon.quil (JONG.quil) *n.* a yellow narcissus of the amaryllis family.
Jor.da.ni.an (jor.DAY.nee.un) *n. & adj.* (a person) of or from **Jordan**, a S.W. Asian kingdom.
josh *v. Informal.* tease playfully. —**josh.er** *n.*
Joshua tree *n.* a small yucca tree of the deserts of S.W. United States.
jos.tle (JOS.ul) *v.* **-tles, -tled, -tling** push or shove, as in a crowd: *Children jostle with each other; They are jostling for position.* —*n.* a jostling.
jot *n.* a very small amount; iota: *I don't care one jot; There's not a jot of truth in the story.* —*v.* **jots, jot.ted, jot.ting** write down hastily and briefly; **jot.ter** *n.*
joule (JOWL, JOOL) *n.* a unit of energy equal to 10 million ergs.
jounce (JOWNCE) *n. & v.* **jounc.es, jounced, jounc.ing** jolt or bounce. —**jounc.y** *adj.*: *a jouncy ride in a jeep.*
jour.nal (JUR.nul) *n.* **1** a daily account or record such as a diary or log, a daily publication such as a newspaper, or a daily bookkeeping record: *He keeps a journal during the school term.* **2** a magazine or periodical: *a learned journal;*

professional journals; scholarly journals; to edit, publish, put out, subscribe to a journal. **3** the part of an axle or shaft turning in a bearing, or **journal box.**

jour.nal.ese (jur.nuh.LEEZ) *n.* language and style that is typical of newspapers and magazines.

jour.nal.ism (JUR.nuh.liz.um) *n.* **1** the gathering and publishing of news through the mass media: *I tried journalism for a career.* **2** journalistic writing: *Journalism is not always literature.* **3** newspapers and magazines collectively: *advocacy journalism; yellow journalism.* —**jour.nal.ist** *n.*
—**jour.nal.is.tic** (-LIS.tic) *adj.*

jour.ney (JUR.nee) *n.* a trip, usu. of some duration, to a definite place: *to go on, make, set out on, undertake a journey; a journey across the Sahara; a journey into or through the jungle; a long day's journey; a round-the-world journey; a pleasant, safe, sentimental, tiring journey; It's a journey* (= distance) *of 3,000 km.* —*v.* **-neys, -neyed, -ney.ing** go on a journey: *to journey from Montreal to Vancouver.*

jour.ney.man (JUR.nee.mun) *n.* **-men** a qualified and experienced though not a master workman; **adj.a.**: *a journeyman carpenter, mechanic, plumber, writer.*

joust (JOWST, JUST, JOOST) *n.* combat using lances between two knights on horseback, esp. as part of a medieval tournament, or **jousts** *pl.*
—*v.* engage in a joust.

jo.vi.al (JOH.vee.ul) *adj.* full of good humor and fun: *in a jovial mood;* **jo.vi.al.ly** *adv.* —**jo.vi.al.i.ty** (-AL.i.tee) *n.*

jowl (rhyme: howl) *n.* **1** the jaw: *a man with heavy jowls.* **2** the lower, hanging part of a face or head, as of cattle, fowl, the head and shoulders of salmon, etc.: *a messy desk with diskettes lying* **cheek by jowl** (= side by side) *with papers.* —**jow.ly** *adj.*

joy *n.* great delight or happiness: *Words cannot express our joy; We feel joy; Her face radiates joy; It's a joy to behold; He couldn't hide his joy that everyone was at the party; He finds* or *takes joy in teasing people; She leaped for* or *with joy on hearing the news; the joys and sorrows of life.*

joy.ful *adj.* full of or causing joy: *That was joyful news; Everyone is joyful about* or *over the victory.* —**joy.ful.ly** *adv.*

joy.ous (JOY.us) *adj.* full of or endowed with joy: *a joyous family, heart, mood, occasion.*

joy ride *n.* a ride taken for fun, often using unlawful means, as in a stolen automobile: *The boys were on a joy ride when they crashed.* —**joy rider** *n.;* **joy riding** *n.*

joy.stick *n.* **1** a lever that moves in many directions to control an airplane. **2** a similar tool used to control a computer display.

ju.bi.lant (JOO.buh.lunt) *adj.* showing great joy; exultant: *to be jubilant about* or *at* or *over something.* —**ju.bi.lant.ly** *adv.*

ju.bi.la.tion (joo.buh.LAY.shun) *n.* rejoicing; glee: *a poem expressing jubilation at the Olympic gold; Great jubilation was felt all over the country.*

ju.bi.lee (JOO.buh.lee) *n.* a time of rejoicing or celebration, esp. an anniversary: *a diamond jubilee* (= 60th year); *golden jubilee* (= 50th year); *silver jubilee* (= 25th year).

Ju.da.ic (joo.DAY.ic) *adj.* of the Jews or Judaism: *Judaic beliefs; the Judaic religion.*

Ju.da.ism (JOO.duh.iz.um) *n.* the Jewish religion or way of life: *Conservative Judaism; Orthodox Judaism; Reform Judaism; a policy of toleration of Judaism and opposition to Zionism.*

ju.das (JOO.dus) *n.* a traitor, like the disciple **Judas** who betrayed Jesus.

judge (JUJ) *n.* **1** one who decides, esp. a public official in a court of law who hears and decides cases; a justice: *a fair, impartial, harsh judge; a hanging* (= severe) *judge; a circuit, district, provincial, trial judge; a Supreme Court judge.* **2** one who decides questions of merit, taste, etc.; referee: *a fair judge; I'm a poor judge of wines.*
—*v.* **judg.es, judged, judg.ing** decide or settle: *the court's power to judge cases; It's not safe to judge by* or *from appearances; Better to judge from the facts; to judge a person guilty; to judge how old Jan is; motives that are hard to judge* (= criticize); *I judged it better to remain silent; Who's judging* (at) *the singing contest?* —**judge.ship** *n.*

judg.ment (JUJ.munt) *n.* **1** a judging: *to sit in judgment on a case; In my judgment, he's at fault; an error of judgment.* **2** a result of judging such as an opinion or a sentence: *to form* or *make a judgment; to hand down, pronounce, render a judgment; to reserve judgment on a case; a subjective value judgment; to pass judgment without hearing both sides; The judgment went against him; an accident that seemed* **a judgment on** (= punishment for) *his driving habits.* **3** the ability to judge: *to display, exercise judgment; She shows good judgment.* —**judg.men.tal** (-MEN.tul) *adj.* Also **judge.ment,**

judge.men.tal *Cdn.*
Judgment Day same as DOOMSDAY.
ju.di.ca.to.ry (JOO.di.cuh.tor.ee) *n. & adj.* (having to do with) a court of law or its administrative system.
ju.di.ca.ture (JOO.di.cuh.chur) *n.* 1 a court of law or its administration of justice. 2 a judge's position or jurisdiction.
ju.di.cial (joo.DISH.ul) *adj.* having to do with a judge: *a judicial decision, district, mind, process, review.* —**ju.di.cial.ly** *adv.*
ju.di.ci.ar.y (joo.DISH.ee.air.ee) *adj.* of the administration of justice: *judiciary proceedings.* —*n., pl.* **-ar.ies** the court system as a branch of government: *The legislature, executive, and the judiciary are the three branches of government; the independence of the judiciary; The judiciary* (= judges collectively) *helps mold our lives as social beings.*
ju.di.cious (joo.DISH.us) *adj.* wise in deciding; sound in judgment: *a judicious decision, parent, selection; the judicious use of one's powers.*
—**ju.di.cious.ly** *adv.*
ju.do (JOO.doh) *n.* a Japanese sport or weaponless method of self-defense in which balance, timing, leverage, etc. are used to throw an opponent.
ju.do.ka (joo.DOH.kuh) *n. sing. & pl.* a judo player.
jug 1 *n.* a large, narrow-mouthed container, usu. with a handle, for liquids: *juice, milk, water jugs; a jug of wine; a low-end generic* **jug wine** *sold in large bottles of 1.5 liters and up.* 2 *n. Slang.* jail. 3 *v.* **jugs, jugged, jug.ging** *Slang.* put in jail.
jug.ger.naut (JUG.ur.nawt) *n.* something massive and overpowering that crushes everything in its path.
jug.gle (JUG.ul) *v.* **jug.gles, jug.gled, jug.gling** manipulate or play tricks with figures, facts, or words, as one may do with balls, plates, etc. by tossing them up and catching them as a feat of dexterity. —**jug.gler** *n.*
jug.gler.y (JUG.luh.ree) *n.* **jug.gler.ies** sleight of hand; trickery; fraud.
jug.u.lar (JUG.yoo.lur) *adj.* of the neck or throat, esp. of the two chief **jugular veins** that take blood down from the head and neck to the heart. —*n.* a jugular vein: *They* **went for the jugular** (= attacked the weakest point).
juice (JOOSE) *n.* 1 the liquid part or essence of plant or animal tissue: *orange juice; the natural juices or gravy of meat; digestive juices; the* **gastric juice** *of the stomach; the* **creative juices** (= creative inspiration). 2 *Slang.* a fuel such as electricity or gasoline that supplies power; also, alcoholic liquor.
—*v.* **juic.es, juiced, juic.ing:** *music to* **juice up** (= enliven) *a party.*
juice.head *n. Slang.* an alcoholic.
juic.er (JOO.sur) *n.* a kitchen appliance for extracting juice from fruit.
juic.y (JOO.see) *adj.* **juic.i.er, -i.est** 1 full of juice: *a juicy tomato; juicy hamburgers.* 2 *Informal.* good or satisfying: *juicy bonuses, buys, incentives, jobs, secrets.* 3 *Informal.* exciting because of its being scandalous or racy: *a juicy biography, crime.* —**juic.i.ly** *adv.;* **juic.i.ness** *n.*
ju.jit.su or **ju.jut.su** (joo.JIT.soo) *n.* the Japanese system of wrestling from which judo developed.
ju.jube (JOO.jube, -joo.bee) *n.* a lozenge of gummy, fruit-flavored candy.
juke.box *n.* a coin-operated record player, formerly used in restaurants, bars, etc.
ju.lep (JOO.lup) *n.* an iced and sweetened drink of whiskey or brandy flavored with mint; also **mint julep**.
ju.li.enne (joo.lee.EN) *adj.* of vegetables, made into long thin strips: *julienne carrots, cuts, potatoes, strips;* **n.**: *a fried leek julienne; a julienne of lettuce and French bread; mixed vegetables cut in a julienne.* —*v.*: *a food processor that juliennes a variety of vegetables;* **adj.**: *served on a bed of* **julienned** *peas; julienned vegetables.*
Ju.ly (joo.LYE) *n.* **-lies** the seventh month of the calendar year, with 31 days.
jum.ble (JUM.bul) *n.* a disorderly mass or confusion. —*v.* **-bles, -bled, -bling** mix up in a jumble.
jum.bo (JUM.boh) *n.* **-bos** something very large of its kind; *adj.*: *a jumbo burger; a jumbo jet (airliner); a jumbo size bottle.*
jump *v.* move with sudden muscular effort using the feet and legs: *She jumps into bed at 10 p.m. and jumps out of bed at 5 a.m.; He jumped in and drove off; She escaped by jumping (into) a passing train; This is where the train* **jumped the tracks** (= got derailed); *He jumped clear of the building; Everyone jumped for or with joy; Grandpa dropped his book and jumped to his feet; He* **jumped to** (= came quickly to) *our defense; Cats jump from roof to roof; Horses jump over fences; Let us not* **jump to conclusions** *before all the facts are in; Prices jump as supplies dwindle; She* **jumped at** (= eagerly seized) *the long-awaited opportunity; He jumped* (= started ahead of) *the green light; He*

jumps on (= scolds) *his students at the slightest disturbance; The bondsman lost his money when the prisoner* **jumped bail** (= disappeared). —**jump the gun** See GUN. —*n.* a jumping: *He made a parachute jump; The high jump is a track-and-field event; a quantum* (= sudden and dramatic) *jump; Oil prices took a jump yesterday; to keep* **one jump ahead** (= one step ahead) *of the competition.* —**have** or **get the jump on someone** anticipate or get an advantage over someone.

jump.er *n.* **1** a person or thing that jumps: *Jump* or *Jumper cables close an electrical circuit by jumping or bypassing a break in it.* **2** a loose jacket or sleeveless dress worn to protect one's clothes. **3 jumpers** *pl.* same as ROMPERS.

jumping-off point (or **place**) *n.* point of departure.

jump-start *n.* the starting of a car using booster cables to recharge the battery; *v.: A "defibrillator" is used to jump-start failed hearts in emergency rooms.*

jump.suit *n.* a parachutist's one-piece suit or a similar woman's suit of top and trousers belted in the middle.

jump.y *adj.* **jump.i.er, -i.est** jittery or nervous: *What are you so jumpy about?* —**jump.i.ly** *adv.;* **jump.i.ness** *n.*

jun.co (JUNK.oh) *n.* **-cos** or **-coes** a small bird of the finch family, often seen in the winter; also called "snowbird."

junc.tion (JUNK.shun) *n.* **1** a joining. **2** a place of joining, as of roads.

junc.ture (JUNK.chur) *n.* a joining, esp. a critical moment in the coming together of events: *At that juncture he was lost for words.*

June (JOON) *n.* the sixth month of the calendar year, with 30 days.

june bug *n.* a large brown beetle that appears around June.

jun.gle (JUNG.gul) *n.* **1** a wildly overgrown tropical forest: *the dense jungles of central Africa, Brazil, etc.* **2** a place hard to survive in: *the jungle of city slums; the asphalt jungle; the blackboard jungle of teaching, the concrete jungle of our great cities; It's a jungle out there!*

jun.ior (JOON.yur) *n.* a person younger or lower in rank than another who is senior: *John Smith, Jr.* (= Junior, son of John Smith); *a college or high school junior (in his or her next-to-last year); She's my junior by two years.* —**adj:** *my junior brother; a junior member of the staff; a junior minister, partner; She's junior in rank; She's junior to me by two years.*

junior college *n.* a college offering two-year programs, either as the first two years for a bachelor's degree or as technical training for semiprofessional jobs.

junior high school *n.* usu., grades 7, 8, and 9 of school.

junior varsity *n.* a school or college team composed of those less qualified and experienced than the varsity.

ju.ni.per (JOO.nuh.pur) *n.* an evergreen shrub or tree of the cypress family having fragrant, berrylike cones.

junk *n.* **1** worthless stuff: *Children who eat junk, listen to junk, talk junk, and watch junk may grow up to be dopes.* **2** *Slang.* a narcotic, esp. heroin. **3** a Chinese flat-bottomed ship with four-cornered sails and a high poop. —*v.* discard as junk: *She junked her old car.*

junk bond *n.* a high-yield but speculative bond issued by a company for buying back its stocks or for financing a takeover.

junk.er *n. Informal.* something, esp. an automobile, that is bad enough to be junked.

junk.et (JUNK.it) *n.* an excursion or trip, esp. one taken by someone at public or company expense: *a Las Vegas gambling junket; She went on a free junket to hunt geese at James Bay.* —*v.* go on a junket.

junk food *n.* a food such as candy, potato chips, cake, or soda that has little nutritive value.

junk.ie or **junk.y** (JUNK.ee) *n.* **junk.ies** *Informal.* a drug addict.

junk mail *n.* unsolicited third-class mail such as advertising circulars; also called "direct mail."

junk.yard *n.* an area in which junk is kept: *an automobile junkyard; mean and tough as a* **junkyard dog.**

Juno Award *n.* any of the annual awards made by the Canadian Academy of Recording Arts and Sciences for achievements in the recording industry.

jun.ta (HOON.tuh, JUN-) *n.* a group of military men ruling a country after a coup d'état: *a revolutionary junta; government by junta.*

Ju.ras.sic (joo.RAS.ic) *n. & adj.* (having to do with) the second period of the Mesozoic era of the earth beginning about 180 million years ago when flying reptiles and birds appeared.

ju.rid.i.cal (joo.RID.i.cul) *adj.* having to do with the administration of justice. —**ju.rid.i.cal.ly** *adv.*

ju.ris.dic.tion (joor.is.DIC.shun) *n.* legal authority in regard to its extent or territory: *matters outside, under, within a court's jurisdiction; a court that has jurisdiction over a case; FTC had no jurisdiction in the matter, over the issue; people residing in our jurisdiction.*

ju.ris.pru.dence (joor.is.PROO.dunce) *n.* **1** the science or philosophy of law. **2** legal knowledge or skill.

ju.rist (JOOR.ist) *n.* a legal scholar such as a judge or lawyer. —**ju.ris.tic** (joor.IS.tic) *adj.*

ju.ror (JOOR.ur) *n.* one who takes an oath as a member of a jury: *A juror may be challenged before being selected.*

ju.ry (JOOR.ee) **1** *n., pl.* **-ries** a select group of people who hear evidence and give a verdict, as in a court trial, who determine the cause of a death in an inquest, or who decide the winner in a contest: *judge and jury; trial by jury; to charge, impanel, instruct, sequester, swear in a jury; to fix (= dishonestly influence) a jury; Citizens are called on to serve on a jury; a coroner's jury; grand jury; hung jury; petit jury; A jury reaches a verdict after deliberating; The jury is still out on the issue* (= The issue is still undecided); *adja.:* a jury box, trial; jury duty, selection, tampering; the jury system. **2** *adja.* for temporary use: *a jury mast, rig.*

ju.ry.man (JOOR.ee.mun) *n.* **-men** a juror. —**ju.ry.wom.an** *n.* **-wom.en.**

jury-rigged *adj.* makeshift: *a jury-rigged camera mount for shooting the action from various angles.*

just *adj.* due or appropriate according to a moral, social, esthetic, or other standard: *a just and upright man; He got his just reward; just deserts; a just and impartial decision; a just measure, praise, price.* —*adv.* **1** exactly or nearly as stated or at a certain time or place: *I saw her just now; I'm not sleepy just now; I'll do just as you say; That's just what I need; You just missed the bus; it just left.* **2** *Informal.* simply; truly; really: *I'm just fine; That looks just perfect.* —**just the same** even so; nevertheless. —**just.ly** *adv.;* **just.ness** *n.*

jus.tice (JUS.tis) *n.* **1** a being just; fairness: *peace on earth and justice to all.* **2** just treatment, esp. by process of law: *to dispense, mete out, obstruct, pervert, render justice; the frontier justice of pioneer days; the poetic justice of falling into one's own trap; a miscarriage of justice; travesty of justice; to bring someone to justice; justice tempered with mercy; Justice should prevail; "Justice delayed is justice denied"; The picture did not* **do justice** *to her* (= did not show her well); *Another portrait was ordered* **in justice to** (= in fairness to) *her demands; the U.S. Justice Department; The Department of Justice under the Minister of Justice looks after the administration of justice in Canada.* **3** a judge: *the Chief Justice of the United States; a Supreme Court justice; a* **justice of the peace** (= local magistrate).

jus.ti.fy (JUS.tuh.fye) *v.* **-fies, -fied, -fy.ing 1** make or show to be just or right: *conduct that is difficult to justify; Does a good end justify evil means?* **2** of printed lines, having even margins on either side: *A printed line is justified by spacing out the words;* **adj.:** *a justified margin.* —**jus.ti.fi.a.ble** (-FYE.uh.bul) *adj.;* **jus.ti.fi.a.bly** (-blee) *adv.* —**jus.ti.fi.ca.tion** (-fuh.CAY.shun) *n.*

jut *n.* a projection, part, etc. made or formed so as to stick out or stand out, as a balcony or jetty. —*v.* **juts, jut.ted, jut.ting** stick out: *Piers jut out into the water.*

jute *n.* a strong, shiny fiber made from a plant of the basswood family and used to make gunnysacks, cordage, rope, etc.

ju.ve.nile (JOO.vuh.nul, -nile) *n.* **1** a young and immature person. **2** a young plant or animal such as a two-year-old racehorse. —*adj.:* a juvenile acting role; a juvenile phase of development; A **juvenile court** *deals with* **juvenile delinquents** (= young offenders below the legal age, usu. 18); **juvenile diabetes** (that develops before age 20).

jux.ta.pose (JUX.tuh.poze) *v.* **-pos.es, -posed, -pos.ing** put close together or side by side *with* something, as for comparison or contrast. —**jux.ta.po.si.tion** (-puh.ZISH.un) *n.*

.... **K, k** ....

K or **k** (KAY) *n.* **K's** or **k's** the 11th letter of the English alphabet.

kabob same as KEBAB.

Ka.bu.ki (kuh.BOO.kee) *n.* a form of Japanese drama using pantomime, song, and dance.

kad.dish (KAH.dish) *n.* a Jewish hymn of praise used also as a mourner's prayer.

kaf.fee.klatsch (COF.ee.clach) *n.* an informal social gathering at which coffee is served.

kaf.fi.yeh (kah.FEE.yuh) *n.* an Arab headdress of cloth held in place by a cord wound round the head: *the Arab leader with his customary checkered kaffiyeh*

and dark glasses.
kai.ser (KYE.zur) *n.* an emperor, esp. one of the **Kaisers** of Germany and Austria up to 1918.
kale *n.* a cabbagelike vegetable with loose, curly leaves instead of a head.
ka.lei.do.scope (kuh.LYE.duh.scope) *n.* a tube fitted with mirrors that reflect colored beads and pieces of glass at one end in an endless variety of patterns as the tube is rotated and viewed. —**ka.lei.do.scop.ic** (-SCOP.ic) *adj.*
ka.mi.ka.ze (kah.muh.KAH.zee) *n.* a Japanese suicide attack or a plane or pilot making one. —*adj*a. suicidal, reckless, or self-destructive: *a kamikaze driver.*
kan.ga.roo (kang.guh.ROO) *n.* **-roos** an Australian mammal that carries its young in a pouch outside the mother's body and has powerful hind legs on which it hops about: *a mob of kangaroos.*
kangaroo court *n.* an unauthorized court, often a mock one, as set up by prison inmates.
ka.o.lin (KAY.uh.lin) *n.* a pure white clay of feldspar used in making high-grade pottery.
ka.pok (KAY.pok) *n.* a lightweight fiber obtained from the seed pods of an East Indian tree for use in mattresses, life jackets, etc.
kap.pa (CAP.uh) *n.* the 10th letter of the Greek alphabet (Κ, κ).
ka.put (kuh.POOT, long "OO") *adj*p. *Informal.* **be** or **go kaput** fail; be finished: *All our money is gone, vanished, kaput! Even the car is gone kaput.*
kar.a.kul (KAIR.uh.kul) *n.* **1** the curly, silky, usu. black fleece of young lambs of a broad-tailed sheep of C. Asia. **2** the sheep.
kar.at (CAIR.ut) *n.* a 1/24 part used as the unit for specifying the proportion of gold in an alloy: *In 10-karat gold, 10/24 of it is pure gold.*
ka.ra.te (kuh.RAH.tee) *n.* an Oriental form of unarmed combat using kicks, punches, and "chops" aimed at the most vulnerable parts of the opponent's body.
kar.ma (KAR.muh) *n.* **1** in Buddhism and Hinduism, life and actions as determining one's fate; hence, fate or destiny. **2** emanations from a person or thing: *bad, good karma.* —**kar.mic** *adj.*
karst *n.* a limestone region with a dry and barren surface, characterized by deep fissures and underground streams.
kart *n.* a small, low, four-wheeled, one-seater vehicle used for racing, or **kart.ing.**
ka.ty.did (KAY.tee.did) *n.* a large grasshopperlike long-horned green insect.
kay.ak (KYE.ak) *n.* a light Inuit canoe having a deck top covered with seal skin and a cockpit in the middle for the paddler.
kay.o (KAY.oh) *n.* a knockout in boxing. —*v.* **-os, -oed, -o.ing** knock out or beat out.
ka.zoo (kuh.ZOO) *n.* **-zoos** a toy musical instrument like an oboe consisting of a short tube stopped at one end with a membrane or paper that vibrates when the tube is hummed into.
ke.bab or **ke.bob** (kuh.BOB) *n.* a dish of pieces of marinated meat cooked with vegetables stuck on a skewer.
kedge *v.* **kedg.es, kedged, kedg.ing** move a boat by hauling on a rope attached to a small anchor thrown some distance in the water. —*n.* such an anchor.
keel *n.* **1** the main timber or steel piece laid lengthwise along the hull of a boat to support its framework. **2** a ridgelike part. —**on an even keel 1** in a level position. **2** stable or steady. —*v.* **keel over 1** turn over, as a boat. **2** *Informal.* collapse or faint.
keel.boat *n.* a freight boat with a keel and pointed prow.
keel.haul *v.* rebuke severely, like hauling one under a ship's keel.
keen *adj.* **1** having a fine edge: *a keen blade; a keen* (= alert) *mind.* **2** sharp or biting: *keen eyesight, pain, wind.* **3** very eager; full of enthusiasm: *keen competition; She's keen on winning; keen about learning to fly.* **4** *Informal.* wonderful. —*n.* a wailing or lamentation; *v.* make a sound suggesting it. —**keen.ly** *adv.*; **keen.ness** *n.*
keep *v.* **keeps, kept, keep.ing 1** continue to have and hold in one's possession, control, or care: *You may not keep library books beyond the due date; Parents don't keep their children from school without good reason; Pets should be kept off the streets; Please keep out of the way of the ambulance; Drivers must keep to the right of the road; Teachers keep students at their work; You keep saying* (= You continue to repeat) *that;* to **keep abreast of** (= stay informed of) *the latest advances in computers; Teachers have to* **keep after** (= urge) *students to make them do their best; Please* **keep off** (= stay away from)

the grass; Students should **keep on** (= continue) *attending school till graduation; He* **keeps very much to himself** (= avoids meeting people) *since his wife died.* 2 maintain or preserve without change of condition: *Salt keeps meat from spoiling; It helps to keep the roads clear of snow; A coat keeps you warm; We keep children amused; The family wanted to keep the wedding a secret; They wanted to keep it to themselves; a well-kept* (= well-preserved) *secret; What keeps* (= prevents) *you from going? They keep* (= raise) *hogs on the farm; We* **keep quiet** *in the library; Everyone, please* **keep to** (= remain in) *your rooms.* 3 be faithful to something: *to keep an appointment, the law, a promise, a treaty.* —**keep up** continue: *We have to keep up payments on a loan; to keep up the pace; Keep up the good work! Keep it up!*
—**keep up with** go as fast as a person or thing and not fall behind: *a fast runner who is difficult to keep up with; Supply has to keep up with demand; to keep up with the neighbors* (= do as well as one's neighbors); *to keep up* (= stay up to date) *with what's going on around us.* —*n.* 1 support or livelihood: *Maria earns her keep by taking care of the kids.* 2 the strongest part of a fort or castle. —**for keeps** *Informal.* 1 as one's own: *You can have it for keeps.* 2 on a continuing basis: *The winter has set in for keeps by January; The strikers are perfectly capable of* **playing for keeps** (= of carrying on in a ruthless manner till they achieve their ends). —**keep·er** *n.*

keep·ing *n.* 1 care: *something entrusted to your keeping.* 2 accordance: *a practice that is* **in keeping with** *custom.*

keep·sake *n.* something to keep in memory of someone; memento.

keg *n.* a small cask or barrel: *a powder keg.*

kelp *n.* an iodine-rich seaweed or its ashes.

Kelt, Keltic same as CELT, CELTIC.

Kel·vin *adj.* of a temperature-measuring scale with 273° as the freezing point of water and 373° as its boiling point.

ken *n.* range of knowledge: *matters within our ken; Some things are beyond our ken.* —*v.* **kens, kenned, ken·ning** *Scottish.* know or have knowledge of something.

ken·nel (KEN.ul) *n.* 1 a doghouse. 2 often **kennels** *pl.* a place that breeds or boards dogs. —*v.* **ken·nels, ken·neled, ken·nel·ing** keep in a doghouse. Also **ken·nelled, ken·nel·ling** *Cdn.*

ke·no (KEE.noh) *n.* a gambling game similar to bingo or lotto.

Ken·yan (KEN.yun, KEEN-) *n. & adj.* (a person) of or from **Kenya**, an E.C. African country.

ke·pi (KEP.ee) *n.* a French military cap with a flat top and a visor.

kept 1 *pt. & pp.* of KEEP. 2 *adja.* maintained for sexual relations: *a kept boy, woman.*

ker- *prefix.* forming interjections: *kerplunk, kerpow, kerthump!*

ker·a·tin (KER.uh.tin) *n.* the protein substance of horn, nails, hair, and feathers. —**ke.rat.i.nous** (kuh.RAT.un.us) *adj.* horny.

kerb *Brit.* CURB, *n.* 3.

ker·chief (KUR.chif) *n.* **-chiefs** or **-chieves** (-cheevz) 1 a usu. square piece of cloth used by women as a head covering or scarf. 2 a handkerchief.

kerf *n.* a cut or a channel carved by an ax or saw.

ker·fuf·fle (kur.FUF.ul) *n. Informal.* commotion or fuss.

ker·nel (KUR.nul) *n.* 1 a seed of the corn plant or a grain of wheat or other cereal. 2 the inner, edible part of a nut, fruit pit, etc. 3 the core or essence: *the kernel of an argument; a kernel of truth.*

ker·o·sene (KER.uh.seen) *n.* a thin fuel oil distilled from petroleum; also **ker·o·sine.**

kes·trel (KES.trul) *n.* a small European falcon; also called "windhover."

ketch *n.* a two-masted fore-and-aft-rigged ship.

ketch·up *n.* a seasoned sauce, esp. a thick one made of tomatoes.

ket·tle (KET.ul) *n.* a metal container for boiling liquids: *a boiling kettle.* —**kettle of fish** a matter or affair: *a different kettle of fish; a fine* or *pretty kettle of fish* (= a mess). —**the pot calling the kettle black** blaming someone when suffering from the same fault.

ket·tle·drum (KET.ul.drum) *n.* a drum made of parchment stretched over the flat top of a hollow copper or brass hemisphere.

key (KEE) *n.* **keys** 1 a small metal device with one end cut in a particular design for fitting into the keyhole of a door, padlock, etc. to lock or unlock it: *to cut, fit, insert, match, turn a key; the key to a room; a master key; skeleton key; a bunch of keys; car keys; ignition keys.* 2 something shaped or used like a key: *the key of a tin can; an old clock that is wound with a key.* 3 something that is wound with a key. **3** something that provides access or entry, as the solution to a problem or the explanation of a set of symbols: *a dictionary's pronunciation key; the key* (= answer) *to the exercises; the key to a mystery.* **4** one of a set of disks or buttons forming a keyboard operated with the fingers, as in playing certain musical instruments, operating a typewriter, or a keypunch machine: *Strike* or *Press the "shift" key to type a capital letter.* **5** a musical scale or system based on a basic tone or keynote, as "C major": *to sing on key; He spoke in a low key* (= tone or style of expression); *the key signature* (= sharps or flats placed after the clef) *of a staff of music.* **6** a low island or reef, esp. off the coast of Florida: *Florida Keys, Key West.* **7** the winged seed of the ash, elm, maple, etc. —*adj.* important or controlling: *a key advisor, area, factor, figure, issue, player, role; key personnel; Doing your homework is absolutely key to being promoted.* —*v.* **keys, keyed, key.ing 1** tune: *The speech was keyed to the mood of the audience; adj. & cpd.: a properly keyed violin; crazy fans keyed up* (= excited) *to a fever pitch; deluxe **color-keyed** seat belts (harmonized according to color).* **2** type: *to key in data for computer processing.*

key.board *n.* a set of disks or buttons on a computer, musical instrument, typewriter, etc. for its manual operation. —*v.* enter text, data, etc. into a processing system using a keyboard: *Matter had to be keyboarded for typesetting.*

key club *n.* a private club whose members usu. have keys to the premises.

key grip *n.* the head of a stage crew.

key.hole *n.* a hole in a door, padlock, etc. for inserting its key: *a child peeping through a keyhole.*

key.note *n.* **1** the basic note of a musical scale. **2** the basic idea or policy theme, as set forth in a **keynote speech** or **address** given at a convention. —*v.* **-notes, -not.ed, -not.ing** give the keynote or keynote address of a meeting. —**key.not.er** *n.*

key.pad *n.* a small keyboard, often handheld, having buttons for input of data: *a numeric keypad integrated with the computer keyboard.*

key.punch or **key punch** *n.* a machine for punching cards or tapes for data processing. —**key.punch** or **key.stroke** *v.* same as KEYBOARD.

key.stone *n.* **1** the central, topmost stone of an arch. **2** central principle: *Freedom is the keystone of democracy.*

key.stroke *n.* a tap of a key, as in keyboarding.

key.word *n.* a word that forms the key or guide to other words, as a guide word at the top of a dictionary page: *a computer program for showing the keywords of a document in their contexts; a **keyword-in-context** program.* Also **key word.**

kha.ki (KAK.ee, KAH.kee) *n.* **1** a strong, twilled, yellowish-brown cloth for uniforms, esp. military. **2** the color or a uniform made of khaki. **3 khakis** *pl.* such a uniform. —*adj.* **1** dull yellowish-brown. **2** made of khaki cloth.

khan (KAHN, KAN) *n.* a Turkish title, now used for "Mister" in some Central Asian countries.

khe.dive (kuh.DEEV) *n.* the title of the Turkish viceroys of Egypt between 1867 and 1914.

kib.ble (KIB.ul) *v.* **kib.bles, kib.bled, kib.bling** grind coarsely. —*n.* coarsely ground meal.

kib.butz (ki.BOOTS) *n., pl.* **kib.but.zim** (ki.boot.SEEM) an Israeli collective farm: *They live on the Kibbutz Eindor; were married at the same kibbutz.*

kib.itz (KIB.its) *v. Informal.* look on at a card game and offer unwanted advice: *to kibitz* (= chat) *with the crowd standing around.*

kib.itz.er (KIB.it.sur) *n.* one who kibitzes; hence, a meddler.

ki.bosh (KYE.bosh) *n. Slang.* **put the kibosh on** put an end to something; squelch.

kick *v.* **1** strike out with a foot, esp. forward: *Keep kicking to stay afloat; a horse that kicks; The cow kicked the pail.* **2** force or move by a kick: *A soccer ball is kicked; Slip-on shoes are easy to kick off.* **3** *Informal.* complain or grumble. **4** *Informal.* get rid of something: *to kick a habit.* —**kick around 1** discuss ideas, suggestions, etc. informally. **2** treat with no consideration: *When Dick retires, you won't have anyone to kick around any more.* —**kick in** *Informal.* **1** contribute one's share. **2** become active or operational. —**kick off** *Informal.* begin a campaign, proceedings, a project, etc. as by putting a ball in play with a kickoff. —**kick over** start operating, as an automobile engine beginning to fire. —**kick up** *Informal.* start or raise: *to kick up a dust* or *a fuss* or *a row, a storm; to kick up trouble.* —*n.* **1** a kicking: *a football kick; a free*

kickback / kin

kick in soccer; a penalty kick; a kick in the groin, behind; a **kick in the teeth** (= an embarrassing rejection); the kick (= recoil) of a gun when fired. **2** Informal. thrill: I get a kick out of studying words; Flat pop has no kick (= life or strength) to it; People start using drugs **for kicks**.

kick.back n. Informal. money illegally paid back to a patron in return for a benefit such as a job, business, contract, etc.: to take kickbacks for arranging mortgages.

kick.er n. **1** one that kicks. **2** Informal. something that gives a kick or jolt, as a punch line or a catch.

kick.off n. **1** in football and soccer, a place kick. **2** Informal. the start of an activity: the kickoff of a campaign.

kick.shaw n. a trifle such as a delicacy or bauble.

kick.stand n. on a bicycle or motorcycle, a short metal bar that is kicked into position to stand the vehicle up when not in use.

kick.y adj. **kick.i.er, -i.est** Informal. providing kicks; exciting.

kid n. **1** Informal. a child; also, a young man or woman; **adj**a.: my kid (= younger) brother; mere **kid stuff** (suitable for kids). **2** a young goat, its flesh for food, or its skin or leather, or **kidskin**, used for shoes and gloves. —v. **kids, kid.ded, kid.ding 1** tease: to kid a guy about his girlfriends. **2** fool: You're kidding! [exclamation of unbelief]. —**kid.der** n. —**kid.ding.ly** adv.

kid.dy or **kid.die** n. **kid.dies** a small child.

kid glove n. a glove made of the skin of a young goat: A temperamental person has to be handled **with kid gloves** (= carefully).

kid.nap v. **-naps, -nap.ped** or **-nap.ed, -nap.ping** or **-nap.ing** abduct someone, usu. for ransom or as a hostage. —**kid.nap.per** or **kid.nap.er** n.

kid.ney (KID.nee) n. **-neys 1** either of a pair of bean-shaped organs situated at the back above the waist that separates waste matter from the blood and passes it as urine into the bladder: A calculus or **kidney stone** is a hard mineral deposit in a kidney. **2** nature or sort: a man of a different kidney.

kidney bean n. a kidney-shaped bean such as the mottled "pinto bean" and the white "navy bean."

kidskin See KID.

kid.vid n. Informal. children's TV.

kiel.ba.sa (kil.BAH.suh, keel-) n., pl. **-sy** (-see) or **-sas** a smoked Polish sausage.

kill v. **1** cause death or cause the death of someone: "Thou shalt not kill"; Cain killed Abel; a soldier killed in action; **adj**a.: a **killing** (= exhausting) job. **2** do away with something: They played cards to kill time till dinner; Journalists kill stories they cannot use. **3** Informal. make one laugh to exhaustion: We killed ourselves laughing; **adj**p.: You're absolutely **killing** (= very funny). —**kill two birds with one stone** do two things by one effort. —n. a killing or something killed, as by a hunter or beast, an aircraft or missile shot down, etc.: Hounds move in for the kill when the exhausted prey is run to the ground.

kil.ler (KIL.ur) n. one that kills: a serial killer (who commits a series of murders); when the killer strikes again; **adj**a.: a killer satellite; An African breed of aggressive **killer bees** had been spreading northward from Brazil since 1957; a **killer whale** (= large voracious porpoise capable of killing a whale).

killing n. **1** slaughter: the killing of whales. **2** Informal. a profit or windfall, as from a sale: He made a killing in stocks by selling them when the market peaked.

kill-joy n. one who spoils others' fun.

kiln (KIL, KILN) n. a high-temperature furnace or oven for making lime, bricks, ceramics, pottery, etc. —v. burn, bake, or dry in a kiln.

ki.lo (KEE.loh, KIL.oh) n. **-los** [short form] kilogram or kilometer.

kilo- prefix. one thousand: kilobaud, kilobit, kilobyte, kilocycle, kilohertz, kilometer, kilopascal, kiloton, kilovolt, kilowatt.

kil.o.gram (KIL.uh.gram) n. a unit of weight equal to 1,000 grams. Also **kil.o.gramme** Cdn.

ki.lo.me.ter (kuh.LOM.uh.tur, KIL.uh.mee.tur) n. unit of length equal to 1,000 meters. Also **ki.lo.me.tre** Cdn.

kilowatt-hour (KIL.uh.wot.OUR) n. a unit of electrical energy equal to the work done by 1,000 watts acting for one hour.

kilt n. a knee-length pleated skirt, usu. of tartan, as worn by men in the Scottish Highlands; **adj**.: a **kilted** (= kilt-wearing) regiment.

kilt.er n. **out of kilter** Informal. not in proper working order.

ki.mo.no (kuh.MOH.noh) n. **-nos** the traditional Japanese outer garment of men and women, a long, loose robe with a wide sash around the waist.

kin n., sing. & pl. a relative or kinsman; also, relatives or kindred: He's no kin of mine; The boss likes to keep the jobs among kin (= for his relatives); An accident victim's identity is not disclosed before next of kin are informed; Her new book is close kin to an earlier work by John Smith; **adjp.**: The two books are clearly kin (= related).

-kin suffix. little: catkin, elfkin, lambkin, napkin.

kind (KINED) adj. sincerely sympathetic and considerate: Be kind to animals; He had a kind word for everyone; It was kind of her to baby-sit for us. —**n.** 1 a natural group of people, animals, plants, etc.: He's one of our own kind; our kind of people; birds of all kinds. 2 nature or characteristic: Being short or tall is a difference of degree, not of kind; He said nothing **of the kind** (= of that nature). —**in kind:** Payment used to be accepted in cash or in kind (= in goods or produce); The insult was paid back in kind (= in the same manner). —**kind of** Informal. same as SORT OF. —**of a kind** 1 of the same kind: two of a kind; something **one of a kind** (= unique). 2 of a poor quality.

kind.a (KINE.duh) Informal. kind of; sort of.

kin.der.gar.ten (KIN.dur.gar.tun) n. a class or school preparing four- and five-year-olds for first grade by games and other activities. —**kin.der.gart.ner** or **kin.der.gar.ten.er** (-gart.nur) n. a child or teacher in a kindergarten.

kind.heart.ed (KINED.HAR.tid) adj. kind by nature; kind and gentle.

kin.dle (KIN.dul) v. **-dles, -dled, -dling** 1 set on fire: to kindle firewood; Each substance has its own **kindling** temperature; to kindle (= light) a fire. 2 light up or arouse like fire: to kindle anger, interest, passion; a face kindled with joy.

kindling n. material such as dry wood that easily catches fire: We need tinder, kindling, and firewood to build a campfire.

kind.ly (KINED.lee) adj. **kind.li.er, -li.est** 1 disposed to be kind; friendly: a kindly old gentleman; kindly attentions. 2 agreeable: a kindly climate. —**adv.** in a kind manner: His words were kindly meant; Thank you kindly; Few dogs **take hindly to** (= accept or like) cats. —**kind.li.ness** n

kind.ness (KINED.nis) n. kind nature, treatment, or a kind act: to show kindness to or toward animals; the many kindnesses done to me; to repay or return kindnesses.

kin.dred (KIN.drid) adja. naturally related or similar: kindred facts, languages, natures, souls, spirits, tribes.

kine n.pl. Archaic. cows; also, cattle.

kin.e.scope (KIN.uh.scope) n. a television picture tube.

ki.ne.sics (kye.NEE.six) n.pl. the study of bodily movements and gestures as part of language.

kin.es.the.si.a (kin.is.THEE.zhuh, "TH" as in "thin") n. the sensation of muscle movements.

ki.net.ic (kye.NET.ic) adj. 1 of or by motion: A falling object has **kinetic energy**; a kinetic impact; kinetic weapons on satellites. 2 dynamic or energetic: I was feeling a bit kinetic; kinetic activity, art, effects, power, sexiness.

kin.folk or **kin.folks** n.pl. family or relatives. Also **kins.folk.**

king n. 1 a male sovereign: the King of Denmark; A king ascends or mounts the throne. 2 a male person or animal supreme in a certain sphere or class: The lion is the king of the beasts; a king among men; the king of the mountain; when comedy was king; an oil king (= tycoon). 3 a chess piece or playing card designated as king. —**king.ly** adj. —**king.ship** n.

king crab same as HORSESHOE CRAB.

king.dom (KING.dum) n. 1 a king's domain or territory: the kingdom of Alfred the Great; the kingdom of Jordan. 2 a division: the animal, vegetable or plant, and mineral kingdoms of the natural world. —**kingdom come** life after death. —**till kingdom come** forever.

king.fish.er (KING.fish.ur) n. a bright-colored crested bird with long, heavy bills with which they spear fish.

King James Bible or **King James Version** n. a version of the Bible published in 1611 under King James I; Authorized Version.

king.mak.er (KING.may.kur) n. a person with power and influence to make someone ruler or leader.

king.pin n. 1 in bowling games, the chief or front pin. 2 Informal. the most important person or thing: the kingpin of the underworld.

king's evidence See EVIDENCE.

king.size or **king.sized** adj. Informal. large: a kingsize cigarette, headache, meal; kingsize sheets for a **kingsize bed** (approximately 78 x 80 in. or 1.98 x 2.03 m).

kink n. 1 a twist or tight curl, as in hair, wire, or rope. 2 something that obstructs or prevents smooth operation: a few kinks to be ironed out in our plan; the only kink (= quirk) in his personality. 3 a muscle spasm. —**v.** bend or curve: Railroad tracks may expand and kink upward under intense heat.

kink.y (KINK.ee) *adj.* **kink.i.er, -i.est** 1 having kinks: *kinky hair; kinky goods* (*Informal* for goods obtained by crooked means). 2 *Informal.* unusual or bizarre: *kinky clothes;* **kinky sex** *involving spanking, chains, toys, etc.*
kins.folk (KINZ.folk) same as KINFOLK.
kin.ship *n.* family relationship: *Animal lovers feel a kinship with the animal world.*
kins.man (KINZ.mun) *n.* **-men** a relative, esp. a male. —**kins.wom.an, -wom.en.**
ki.osk (KEE.osk) *n.* a lightly built, open-sided structure, as a bandstand, newsstand, or booth: *a newspaper kiosk.*
kip *n.* the untanned hide of a young or small animal.
kip.per *v.* cure fish by salting and drying or smoking. —*n.* a kippered herring or salmon.
kirk *n.* in Scotland, a church.
Kir.li.an (KUR.lee.un) *adj.* having to do with a characteristic aura observed around an object when an electric charge is passed through it: *Kirlian photography.*
kir.tle (KUR.tul) *n.* 1 in the Middle Ages, a woman's gown or dress. 2 a man's tunic or coat.
kis.met (KIZ.mit) *n.* fate or destiny.
kiss *n.* 1 a caress with the lips: *to blow someone a kiss; to steal a kiss; loving, passionate, tender kisses.* 2 a gentle touch. 3 a small cake or candy: *chocolate kisses.* —*v.* caress or express with a kiss: *the moonlight kissing the treetops; She kissed him "good night"; He had to* **kiss good-bye to** (= give up) *his hopes of becoming a lawyer.* —**kiss off** *Slang.* dismiss a person or thing rudely. —**kiss.a.ble** *adj.*
kiss-and-tell *adj.* talking about one's confidential relationships: *the kiss-and-tell stories of a kiss-and-tell aide.*
kiss.er *n.* 1 one who kisses. 2 *Informal.* the face or mouth.
kissing cousin *n.* a close relative: *This sauce seems a kissing cousin to the commercial product.*
kissing disease same as MONONUCLEOSIS.
kiss of death *n.* a well-intentioned action that actually proves harmful or ruinous.
kiss-off *n. Slang.* a rude dismissal.
kit *n.* a set of tools, supplies, parts, etc. for a specific use: *a model airplane kit; first-aid, shaving, survival, traveling kits; a military* **kit bag.** —**the whole kit and caboodle** *Informal.* the whole lot.
kitch.en (KICH.un) *n.* a room or place for cooking food: *"Get out of the kitchen if you can't stand the heat."*
kitchen cabinet *n. Informal.* an unofficial advisory group that enjoys too much influence.
kitch.en.ette or **kitch.en.et** (kich.uh.NET) *n.* a small kitchen or cooking facility.
kitchen midden same as MIDDEN.
kitchen police *n.* 1 military personnel detailed to help in an army kitchen. 2 such a detail.
kitch.en.ware (KICH.un.ware) *n.* kitchen utensils or small appliances.
kite *n.* 1 a device for flying in the air at the end of a long string, made of a light, usu. geometrical framework covered with paper or plastic. 2 bird of prey of the hawk family noted for its long, narrow wings and graceful gliding. —**go fly a kite!** *Informal.* get lost! —*v.* to fly or soar: *Prices go on kiting as inflation soars; to kite checks* (= issue bad checks in an attempt to make or get money).
kith and kin *n.pl.* friends and relatives.
kitsch (KICH) *n.* trashy art or its pretentious quality. —**kitsch.y** *adj.*
kit.ten (KIT.un) *n.* a young cat.
kit.ten.ish (KIT.un.ish) *adj.* playful like a cat; coquettish.
kit.ty (KIT.ee) *n.* **kit.ties** 1 [pet name] cat or kitten. 2 a fund of money, esp. one pooled for a common purpose: *no money in the kitty.*
kitty-corner or **kitty-cornered** same as CATER-CORNER(ED).
ki.wi (KEE.wee) *n.* 1 a flightless, shaggy, long-billed bird of New Zealand. 2 *Informal.* a New Zealander. 3 an egg-sized fruit with fuzzy brown skin; also **kiwi fruit.**
Klan *n.* the Ku Klux Klan or one of its chapters. —**Klans.man** *n.* **-men.**
klatsch (CLACH) *n.* an informal social gathering.
klax.on (CLAX.un) *n.* a warning signal or horn, as used by ambulances and such emergency vehicles; **Klaxon** *Trademark.*
klee.nex *n.* a handkerchief made of tissue paper; **Kleenex** *Trademark.*
kleig light same as KLIEG LIGHT.
klep.to.ma.ni.a (klep.tuh.MAY.nee.uh) *n.* an obsessive impulse to steal, esp. things that the thief, or **kleptomaniac,** has no use for.
klieg light (KLEEG-) *n.* a high-intensity carbon-arc light used on motion picture sets.
klutz *n. Slang.* a clumsy person. —**klutz.y** *adj.*

knack (NAK) *n.* ability to do something with cleverness and skill: *It's easy once you get the knack of it; He has a knack for getting into trouble.*

knack.wurst (NAHK.wurst) same as KNOCKWURST.

knap.sack (NAP.sack) *n.* a soldier's or hiker's bag for supplies, carried strapped to the back.

knave (NAVE) *n.* 1 a rogue or dishonest person. 2 a jack (playing card). —**knav.ish** *adj.*

knav.er.y (NAY.vuh.ree) *n.* **-er.ies** rascality or roguery.

knead (NEED) *v.* work by pressing and squeezing dough, clay, muscles, etc. —**knead.er** *n.*

knee (NEE) *n.* the leg joint between thigh and lower leg, protected in front by the kneecap: *He dandled the child on his knee; Your first language is usually learned* **at your mother's knee** (= as a child); *to bring someone* **to his** or **her knees** (= force someone to obey or submit); *to ask for forgiveness* **on bended knee**(s). —*v.* **knees, kneed, knee.ing** touch or hit with the knee.

knee.cap *n.* the bone covering the knee.

knee-deep *adj.* sunk to the knees: *knee-deep in mud; found himself knee-deep in trouble.*

knee-high *adj.* reaching the knees: *She waded through knee-high water.*

knee.hole *n.* a space, as in a desk, for the user's knees.

knee-jerk *adj.* automatic like a reflex action: *a knee-jerk condemnation, reaction, response, view; in knee-jerk fashion; a knee-jerk conservative, follower.*

kneel (NEEL) *v.* **kneels,** *pt. & pp.* **knelt** or **kneeled, kneel.ing** go down on one's knee or knees, as in prayer: *to kneel before the altar.*

knell (NELL) *v.* ring a bell solemnly, as at someone's death. —*n.* such a ringing or its sound; hence, the indication of an end: *"The curfew tolls the knell of parting day"; Black Monday sounded the death knell of the enterprise.*

knelt a *pt. & pp.* of KNELL.

knew *pt.* of KNOW.

knick.ers (NIK.urs) *n.pl.* loose breeches gathered at the knee; also **knick.er.bock.ers** (NIK.ur.bok.urs).

knick.knack (NIK.nak) *n.* a small trivial or dainty article or trinket.

knife (NIFE) *n.* **knives** (NIVES) 1 a cutting tool with a blade and handle, as used with a fork for eating: *bread, butcher, carving, kitchen, paring, pocket, steak knives.* 2 a cutting blade, as of a lawnmower. —**under the knife** *Informal.* undergoing surgery. —*v.* **knifes, knifed, knif.ing** stab or cut through with or as if with a knife.

knight (NITE) *n.* 1 in the Middle Ages, a military man honored as a loyal servant of the king: *Francis was dubbed knight by the Queen.* 2 a British rank just below baronet with the title "Sir." 3 a man of chivalry: *a radiant bride on the arm of her* **knight in shining armor.** 4 a member of an order or society of "Knights" such as the **Knights of Columbus,** a Roman Catholic fraternal society. 5 a chess piece shaped like a horse's head. —*v.* make a knight: *He was knighted by the Queen.*

knight.hood *n.* 1 the rank of a knight; also, knights collectively. 2 chivalry.

knight.ly *adj.* chivalrous or brave.

knish (kuh.NISH) *n.* a baked or fried turnover with a filling usu. of mashed potato.

knit (NIT) *v.* **knits,** *pt. & pp.* **knit** or **knit.ted, knit.ting** 1 make a fabric or article of clothing by looping, instead of weaving, thread or yarn closely together with long needles: *to knit a sweater; A fractured bone knits* (= joins together) *in course of time; a close-knit group of researchers; adj.: a closely knit family; Her brow was knit* (= drawn together) *in a frown; n.: an individualist who sticks to his own* **knitting** (= minds his own business). —**knit.ter** *n.*

knit.wear *n.* knitted clothing.

knives *pl.* of KNIFE.

knob (NOB) *n.* 1 a rounded bulge made for ornament or as a handle fixed to a door, drawer, etc.: *Turn the knob to tune the radio; control knobs.* 2 a small rounded hill. —**knobbed** (NOBD) *adj.* —**knob.bly** (-lee) or **knob.by** *adj.*

knock (NOK) *n.* a sharp blow with something hard or solid, as a fist, knuckles, gavel, etc.: *a loud knock on the door; the hard knocks one has to take in the struggle to make a living; the lessons everyone learns* **in the school of hard knocks.** —*v.* strike, pound, or collide. *to knock at or on a neighbor's door; The boxer was knocked down in the first round; The ball knocked the vase off the table; No one likes to knock* (*Informal* for attack or criticize) *a colleague; An engine that knocks* (= makes a rattling noise) *needs antiknock in the fuel or no-knock gasoline.* —**knock about** or **around** 1 roam around. 2 treat someone roughly. —**knock back** consume, esp. a quantity of liquor. —**knock**

down 1 to fell. **2** indicate an auctioned item as sold, with a knock of the gavel. **3** disassemble: *furniture that comes knocked down in a carton.* —**knock off** *Informal.* **1** deduct: *We'll knock 10% off the price.* **2** stop work or other activity: *We knock off (work) at 5 p.m.; Will you please knock it off* (= stop behaving like that)? **3** finish routinely: *a prolific writer who knocks off one book after another.* **4** overcome or kill. —**knock out 1** defeat, as in boxing, or put a pitcher out of a game of baseball. **2** make inoperative: *power lines knocked out by a storm; Two drinks are enough to knock him out* (= make him unconscious). —**knock someone's socks off** *Informal.* amaze or overwhelm. —**knock together** put together or compose hastily. —**knock.er** *n.*

knock-kneed *adj.* with the legs bent inward at the knees so that they touch in walking. —**knock-knee** *n.*

knock.off *adj a.* routinely finished or cheaply copied: *"Ours is a brand-name computer, not some shoddy knockoff clone,"* the ad said. —*n.* a cheap copy: *a bogus knockoff of the original*

knock.out *n.* **1** a defeat: *He won it on a technical knockout;* **adj a.:** *It was a knockout blow; He was stupefied by knockout drops (that make one unconscious) in his drink.* **2** *Informal.* something outstanding: *You're a knockout! a knockout performance.*

knock.wurst (NOK.wurst) *n.* a thick, spicy frankfurter.

knoll (NOLE) *n.* a small rounded hill; mound.

knot (NOT) *n.* **1** a tie or fastening made with one or more cords, ropes, etc.: *to loosen, tie, undo, untie a knot.* **2** something that resembles a knot in closeness, intricacy, or lumpiness of form: *a figure-eight knot; knots of people standing around chatting; Why tie yourself in knots* (= get nervous) *over nothing?* **3** a hard, cross-grained mass formed in wood, as in knotty pine. **4** one nautical mile per hour. —**tie the knot** *Informal.* get married. —*v.* **knots, knot.ted, knot.ting 1** tie in a knot; tangle in knots. **2** unite closely or form into a hard lump.

knot.grass *n.* a weed of the buckwheat family with jointed stems.

knot.hole *n.* a hole left by a knot that has fallen out of a board or tree trunk.

knot.ty (NOT.ee) *adj.* **knot.ti.er, knot.ti.est** having knots: *knotty pine wood; a knotty* (= complex) *problem.*

knout (NOWT) *n.* a whip of a kind formerly used in Russia. —*v.* flog with a knout.

know (NO) *v.* **knows, knew** (NEW), **known** (NOHN), **know.ing** be well acquainted with a person or thing, having the subject firmly in the mind or memory: *Do I know you? You know me from school days; He knows her by name; She knows him to be a great spender; She knows it for a fact* (= knows it to be true); *He knows how to type; She knows the song by heart; Infants don't know* (= distinguish) *right from wrong; He should know better than to make promises he can't keep; I will let you know* (= inform you) *when the parcel arrives; Mother knows best* (= is the best guide). —*n.*: *people who are in the know* (*Informal* for having inside information); *Knowledge proceeds from the known to the unknown.* —**know.a.ble** (NOH.uh.bul) *adj.*

know-all same as KNOW-IT-ALL.

know-how *n. Informal.* expertise or practical knowledge: *the know-how to operate a business.*

knowing *adj a.* having knowledge in a special way: *a knowing glance, look, smile, wink.* —**know.ing.ly** *adv.*: *She wouldn't knowingly hurt a fly.*

know-it-all *n. Informal.* a person who pretends to know everything.

knowl.edge (NOL.ij) *n.* a knowing or understanding; also, what is known: *the knowledge of good and evil; knowledge of oneself; She denied all knowledge of the missing money; His resignation is a matter of common knowledge; It's common knowledge that he has resigned; a good working knowledge of Italian; extensive, intimate, intuitive, profound, rudimentary, superficial knowledge of a subject; Some things are beyond our knowledge; It has come to our knowledge that you are operating without a license; "Knowledge is power"; her great fund of knowledge; to absorb, accumulate, acquire, assimilate, communicate, gain, impart, soak up knowledge; to brush up, parade one's knowledge of a subject.* —**to (the best of) one's knowledge** as far as one knows.

knowl.edge.a.ble (NOL.ij.uh.bul) *adj.* well-informed; intelligent. —**knowl.edge.a.bly** *adv.*

knowledge engineer *n.* one who devises expert systems for computers to make decisions based on available knowledge or information.

knuck.le (NUCK.ul) *n.* **1** a finger joint, esp. one joining a finger to the rest of the hand: *She cracked her knuckles in* agony; *approached him with her fists clenched and knuckles white; to rap someone on* or *over the knuckles* (= punish or chastise). 2 the knee or hock joint of an animal such as a pig used as food. 3 a metal band worn over the fingers as a weapon in fist-fights; also **brass knuckles**. —*v*. **-les, -led, -ling; knuckle down** apply oneself earnestly: *to knuckle down to a job, task, to work.* —**knuckle under** submit or yield to a person or similar thing: *to knuckle under to threats; They never knuckle under.* —*cpd*: *bare-knuckle(d) fighting; white-knuckle adventures; scraped-knuckle car nuts; brass-knuckles strategy.*

knuck.le.head (NUCK.ul.hed) *n. Informal.* a stupid person.

knurl (NURL) *n*. 1 a small projection or knob. 2 a ridge formed of such, as the milling on the edge of a coin.

knurled (NURLD) *adj*. 1 milled, as the edge of a coin. 2 gnarled.

KO (KAY.oh) *v*. **KO's, KO'd, KO'ing** in boxing, to knock out; hence, defeat: *Leafs KO'd the Flyers.* —*n*. a knockout in boxing. Also **K.O., k.o.**

ko.a.la (koh.AH.luh) *n*. a small tree-dwelling Australian marsupial.

ko.di.ak bear (KOH.dee.ak-) *n*. a large brown bear native to Kodiak Island, Alaska.

kohl.ra.bi (cole.RAH.bee, COLE.rah-) *n*. **-bies** a vegetable related to the cabbage with leafstalks growing from its edible, bulb-shaped stem.

kola same as COLA.

ko.lin.sky (cuh.LIN.skee) *n*. **-skies** the golden-brown fur of an Asiatic mink, also called "China mink" or "Tartar sable."

kook (long "oo") *n. Informal.* one considered crazy or eccentric. —**kook.y** *adj*.; **kook.i.ness** *n*.

ko.peck or **ko.pek** (KOH.pek) *n*. a Russian money unit and coin equal to 1/100 of a ruble.

Ko.ran (koh.RAN) *n*. the sacred book of the Moslems.

Ko.re.an (koh.REE.un) *n*. 1 a person of or from **Korea,** an Asian peninsula opposite Japan. 2 the language of Korea. —*adj*. having to do with Korea, its people, or their language.

ko.sher (KOH.shur) *adj*. 1 of a food or establishment, meeting the requirements of Jewish dietary law: *kosher chicken.* 2 legitimate or proper: *a deal that's not quite kosher.*

kow.tow ("ow" as in "how") *v*. show slavish respect *to* someone. —*n*. an act of kowtowing.

kraal (KRAHL) 1 *n. & v*. (shut up in) an enclosed village for South African natives. 2 *n*. a pen or enclosure for animals in S. Africa.

kraft *n*. tough paper made from wood pulp for use in wrappers, etc.

kraut same as SAUERKRAUT.

Krem.lin *n*. 1 the government of the former Soviet Union. 2 the citadel of Moscow called "the Kremlin."

kro.na (CROH.nuh) *n*. 1 *pl*. **-nor** the basic money unit and a coin of Sweden. 2 *pl*. **-nur** the basic money unit and a coin of Iceland.

kro.ne (CROH.nuh) *n*., *pl*. **-ner** the basic money unit and a coin of Norway or Denmark.

Kru.ger.rand (CROO.guh.rand) *n*. a South African one-ounce gold coin.

kryp.ton (CRIP.ton, *rhyme:* on) *n*. a rare inert gaseous chemical element.

ku.dos (CUE.dos) *n*. [usu. takes *sing. v.*, rarely *pl.*; rarely "kudo" *sing.*] *Informal.* credit for an achievement; glory or fame: *to deserve, get, receive, win kudos; Kudos to the winners!*

kud.zu (COOD.zoo, short "OO") *n*. an Oriental vine of the pea family, grown to prevent soil erosion, for forage, and for its fiber.

Ku Klux Klan (KEW.KLUX.klan) *n*. a secret terrorist U.S. organization that is against non-whites, Jews, Catholics, etc.

ku.lak (coo.LAHK) *n*. a well-to-do Russian farmer of a class that opposed collectivization of the land in the 1930's.

kum.quat (CUM.kwot) *n*. a Chinese citrus fruit that looks like a miniature orange and has a sweet, edible skin.

kung fu (kung.FOO) *n*. the Chinese form of karate.

Kurd *n*. a member of a nomadic Moslem people of **Kurdistan,** a mountainous region of S.W. Asia lying in Turkey, Iran, and Iraq.

Kurd.ish 1 *n*. the Iranian language of the Kurds. 2 *adj*. having to do with the Kurds or Kurdish.

Ku.wait.i (koo.WAY.tee) *n, & adj* (a person) of or from **Kuwait,** an Arab emirate on the Persian Gulf.

kvetch *v. Slang.* complain in a nagging or whining manner; gripe. —*n*. one who complains thus.

kwa.shi.or.kor (kwah.shee.OR.kor) *n*. a protein-deficiency disease affecting esp. children and characterized by stunted growth and potbelly.

KWIC (KWIK) *n*. "keyword-in-context," a computer-generated index for retrieving keywords of a document together with portions of the surrounding text.

ky.mo.graph (KYE.muh.graf) *n.* an instrument for graphically recording on a drum wavelike motions such as muscular contractions or the pulse.

.... **L, l** ....

L or **l** *n.* **L's** or **l's** **1** the 12th letter of the English alphabet. **2** also **l**, the Roman numeral for 50. **3 L,** *pl.* **L's** something L-shaped, as an extension forming a right angle with the main building or a pipe-joint.

lab *n.* [short form] laboratory.

la.bel (LAY.bul) *n.* **1** a slip attached to something to identify or describe it, its ownership, or its destination: *clothes carrying a union label.* **2** designation: *the part-of-speech label of a dictionary entry.* —*v.* **-bels, -beled, -bel.ing** assign a person or thing to a particular class: *All luggage should be labeled with your name and address; He was labeled (as) a communist because of his leftist leanings.* —**la.bel.er** *n.* Also **la.belled, la.bel.ling; la.bel.ler** *Cdn.*

labia *pl.* of LABIUM.

la.bi.al (LAY.bee.ul) *n. & adj.* (a speech sound) made with the lips, as "b," "m," and "p": *labial consonants.*

la.bi.um (LAY.bee.um) *n., pl.* **-bi.a** (-bee.uh) a lip or liplike part such as the **labia majora** and **labia minora,** the outer and inner folds respectively of the vulva.

la.bile (LAY.bul, -bile) *adj.* unstable or fluctuating, as blood pressure.

la.bor (LAY.bur) *n.* **1** hard work or exertion, esp. physical: *He was sentenced to five years' hard labor; child, forced, manual, menial, slave labor; An electric dishwasher is a labor-saving device.* **2** the pains of childbirth: *A pregnant woman goes into labor; She was in labor for two hours; false labor; induced labor.* **3** a piece of work; task: *the labors of Hercules; Volunteers offer to help others as a* **labor of love** *(not for money).* **4** workers as distinguished from management; also, labor unions collectively: *migrant, organized, seasonal, skilled labor.* —*v.* work, esp. with much effort: *a truck laboring uphill with a heavy load; a practical-minded woman who labors under no delusions; She labors all day as a maid; Why labor a point that is so obvious?* *adj.*: *a* **labored** (= involving unnecessary work) *excuse, narrative, pun, style; the* **labored** (= heavy) *breathing of an asthmatic.* —**la.bor.er** *n.* Also **la.bour, la.bour.er** *Cdn.*

lab.or.a.to.ry (LAB.ruh.tor.ee, luh.BOR.uh-) *n.* **-ries** a place for scientific research or manufacture, esp. of drugs and chemicals.

Labor Day *n.* the first Monday of September observed as a holiday in honor of workers.

labor-intensive *adj.* investing much on labor: *Service industries are more labor-intensive than capital-intensive.*

la.bo.ri.ous (luh.BOR.ee.us) *adj.* **1** requiring much labor or hard work: *a laborious business, style of writing; laborious research, tasks; a slow and laborious climb; a laborious* (= labored) *excuse.* **2** industrious or hard-working: *a laborious craftsman, researcher, worker.*

labor union *n.* a workers' organization for the protection of their rights as wage-earners, esp. by collective bargaining.

labour *Cdn.* LABOR.

Lab.ra.dor (LAB.ruh.dor) *n.* a powerful breed of hunting dog, originally from Labrador, Canada; also **Labrador retriever.**

la.bur.num (luh.BUR.num) *n.* a small tree or shrub of the pea family having bright yellow blossoms hanging in clusters.

lab.y.rinth (LAB.uh.rinth) *n.* a confusing network of passageways; maze: *a hedge labyrinth; We got lost in a labyrinth of back alleys.*

lab.y.rin.thine (lab.uh.RIN.thin) *adj.* like a labyrinth; complicated.

lac *n.* a resinous substance deposited by insects on certain Asiatic trees.

lace *n.* **1** open fabric woven in patterns with threads of linen or similar soft material: *delicate, exquisite, fine lace;* *adj.*: *a lace border, edging;* **lace fern** *(with lacelike fronds).* **2** an ornamental braid used for trimming uniforms. **3** a string or cord pulled through eyelets to tie a shoe, tighten a corset, etc. —*v.* **lac.es, laced, lac.ing 1** tie with a lace: *to lace up a shoe.* **2** trim: *a uniform laced with gold (lace); a statement laced with accusations of wrongdoing; coffee laced with rum* (= with rum added).
—**lace into 1** attack physically. **2** criticize severely.

lac.er.ate (LAS.uh.rate) *v.* **-ates, -at.ed, -at.ing** tear flesh or tissues irregularly. —**lac.er.a.tion** (-RAY.shun) *n.*: *a laceration caused by a fishhook.*

lace.work *n.* lace; also, any lacelike decoration.

lach.ry.mal or **lac.ri.mal** (LAC.ruh.mul)

adj. tear-producing, as either of two glands, one above each eye.

lach.ry.mose (LAC.ruh.mose) *adj.* given to shedding tears; also, mournful.

lack *v.* be without or not have enough of something needed: *A novice lacks experience; She's not lacking in enthusiasm; So rich he seems to lack for nothing.*
—*n.* absence or shortage of something needed: *For lack of fresh air we had to move to another place; The plants died through lack of rain.*

lack.a.dai.si.cal (lack.uh.DAY.zi.cul) *adj.* lacking enthusiasm or interest.

lack.ey (LAK.ee) *n.* -eys 1 a footman. 2 a servile follower; toady.

lack.lus.ter (LACK.lus.tur) *adj.* dull or drab: *his lackluster performance on the job; The results so far have been lackluster; a lackluster demand for goods; a lackluster image; lackluster earnings, sales.* Also **lack.lus.tre** *Cdn.*

la.con.ic (luh.CON.ic) *adj.* brief to the point of seeming curt: *a laconic announcement, answer, reply; laconic in expression; a laconic person; his laconic wit, writing style.* —**la.con.i.cal.ly** *adv.*

lac.quer (LAK.ur) *n.* a resinous varnish made from the sap of certain Asiatic trees and from compounds of lac. —*v.* to coat metal, wood, etc. with lacquer; *adj.: a lacquered vase.* —**lac.quer.er** *n.*
—**lac.quer.work** or **lac.quer.ware** *n.*

lacrimal same as LACHRYMAL.

la.crosse (luh.CROS) *n.* a field game played between teams using sticks with a webbed pouch at one end to carry and throw a small rubber ball into the opposing team's goal.

lact- *comb.form.* derived from milk: *lactase, lactic, lactose.*

lac.tase (LAC.tace) *n.* an enzyme that helps in the digestion of milk sugar.

lac.tate *v.* -ates, -at.ed, -at.ing produce milk through a mammary gland: *A mother begins to lactate soon after the baby's birth.* —**lac.ta.tion** (lac.TAY.shun) *n.: Cows have a lactation period of about 10 months.*

lac.tic acid *n.* the acid of sour milk.

lac.tose *n.* the sugar of milk.

la.cu.na (luh.CUE.nuh) *n.* **-nas** or **-nae** (-nee) 1 a gap, esp. a missing part of a text or manuscript. 2 a cavity in a bone or cartilage.

lac.y (LAY.see) *adj.* **lac.i.er, -i.est** of or like lace. —**lac.i.ness** *n.*

lad *n.* a youth; also, a fellow: *a young lad and his lass.*

lad.der (LAD.ur) *n.* a climbing device, usu. a framework of two long sidepieces connected by rungs: *to climb, go up, mount a ladder; a rope ladder; up the social ladder (to membership in exclusive clubs).*

lad.die (LAD.ee) *n. Scottish.* lad.

lade *v.* **lades,** *pt. & pp.* **lad.ed** or **lad.en, lad.ing** load, as cargo on a ship; *n.: a bill of lading.*

lad.en (LAY.dun) *adjp.* burdened: *a tree laden with fruit; a ship fully laden with merchandise.*

la-di-da or **la-de-da** (lah.dee.DAH) *adj. Informal.* affectedly polished or refined; excessively genteel: *There's nothing fancy or la-di-da about their boutique.*

la.dle (LAY.dul) *n.* a long-handled spoon with a cup-shaped bowl.
—*v.* **la.dles, la.dled, la.dling** dip out with a ladle: *to ladle the gravy, soup.*
—**la.dler** *n.*

la.dy (LAY.dee) *n.* **-dies** 1 a woman of refinement or high social position: *lords and ladies; quite a lady; a lady by birth;* [hostile use] *Lady, you better watch your language!* 2 [as a title]: *Lady Chatterly; Lady Diana; Lady Luck* (= "luck" personified). 3 [as a polite term or euphemism] woman: *Ladies and gentlemen; the leading lady of the play; the young lady who baby-sits for us; the lady* (= mistress) *of the house; the* (homeless) *bag ladies of our streets;* **ladies of the evening** (= prostitutes).

lady beetle or **la.dy.bug** (LAY.dee.bug) *n.* a small round beetle with a bright red or yellow spotted back, useful against plant lice. Also **la.dy.bird.**

la.dy.fin.ger (LAY.dee.fing.gur) *n.* a finger-shaped spongecake.

lady-in-waiting *n.* **ladies-in-waiting** a queen's or princess's attendant.

la.dy.like (LAY.dee.like) *adj.* 1 like a lady: *Linda is quite ladylike; her ladylike manners; a ladylike touch.* 2 suitable for a lady: *ladylike clothes.*

la.dy.love (LAY.dee.luv) *n.* a sweetheart.

la.dy.ship (LAY.dee.ship) *n.* 1 a lady's rank or position. 2 **Ladyship** [preceded by "Her" or "Your," used in referring to or addressing a woman with the title "Lady"].

lady's man *n.* a man who is very attentive to women or fond of their company.

lady's-slipper *n.* a wild orchid with flowers shaped like a slipper; also **lady-slipper.**

lag *v.* **lags, lagged, lag.ging** fall behind instead of keeping up: *Those who lag behind in class need special help; As the speaker droned on, interest lagged; The order of play is decided by lagging* (= tossing balls toward a "lag line," as in marbles, or a boundary in billiards). —*n.* interval or amount by which a person or thing lags: *the time lag between the flash and the sound of the firing; the* **cultural** (or **culture**) **lag** *between social institutions and the advancement of science.*

la.ger or **lager beer** (LAH.gur-) *n.* a light, mellow beer that has been stored up to six months.

lag.gard (LAG.urd) *n.* one who falls behind: *He's no laggard when it comes to watching TV.* —**adj.***a.* slow: *a laggard operation; walking at a laggard pace; laggard merchandise (that sells slowly).*

la.gniappe or **la.gnappe** (lan.YAP) *n.* in the Southern U.S., a small gift given to a customer with his purchase.

la.goon (luh.GOON) *n.* a shallow body of water near or connected with a larger one: *the lagoons of Venice.*

laid *pt. & pp.* of LAY.

laid-back *adj. Informal.* relaxed in style; easy-going: *the look of a laid-back dude; the laid-back life of Californians.*

lain *pp.* of LIE.

lair *n.* the den of a wild animal.

laird *n.* in Scotland, a landowner.

lais.sez faire (les.ay.FAIR) *n.* the principle of noninterference by government in private enterprise. —**laissez-faire** *adj.*

la.i.ty (LAY.i.tee) *n.* **-ties** lay people, as distinguished from clergy.

lake *n.* **1** a body of water surrounded by land: *a cottage on* or *at the lake.* **2** a pool of oil, tar, lava, etc.

lake trout *n.* a char of the region of the Great Lakes.

lal.ly.gag (LAH.lee.lag) same as LOLLYGAG.

lam *v.* **lams, lammed, lam.ming** *Slang.* flee: *Let's lam out of here.* —*n.* **on the lam** in flight or in hiding: *He spent three years on the lam from the police.*

la.ma (LAH.muh) *n.* a Buddhist monk of Tibet or Mongolia.

La.ma.ism (LAH.muh.iz.um) *n.* Buddhism as practiced in Tibet and Mongolia; **La.ma.ist** *n. & adj.*

la.ma.ser.y (LAM.uh.sair.ee) *n.* **-ser.ies** a Lamaist monastery.

lamb (LAM) *n.* **1** the young of sheep: *the bleating of lambs; a sacrificial lamb; He was led like a lamb to the slaughter.* **2** a person thought of as young and innocent. **3** lamb's meat or skin: *New Zealand spring lamb.* —*v.* bring forth a lamb.

lam.bast or **lam.baste** (lam.BAIST, -BAST) *v.* **-bastes, -bast.ed, -bast.ing** *Informal.* thrash or scold severely.

lamb.da (LAM.duh) *n.* the 11th letter of the Greek alphabet (Λ, λ).

lam.bent (LAM.bunt) *adj.* playing lightly or gently over a surface: *lambent flames, light; her lambent* (= gently brilliant) *wit.* —**lam.bent.ly** *adv.* —**lam.ben.cy** *n.*

lamb.kin *n.* a little lamb.

lamb.skin *n.* (leather from) a lamb's skin.

lame *adj.* **lam.er, lam.est 1** crippled or limping: *a lame man; lame in one leg; a lame* (= painful) *back; a lame* (= weak) *excuse.* **2** *Slang.* square; not up to date. —*v.* **lames, lamed, lam.ing** make lame. —**lame.ly** *adv.;* **lame.ness** *n.*

la.mé (lah.MAY) *n.* a brocaded fabric of silk, wool, etc. interwoven with gold or silver.

lame.brain *n. Informal.* a slow-witted person.

lame duck *n.* **1** one who is disabled or helpless. **2** a public official serving the last part of his or her term after being defeated in a reelection. —**lame-duck** *adj.: a lame-duck president waiting out his lame-duck term.*

la.mel.la (luh.MEL.uh) *n., pl.* **-mel.lae** (-lee) or **-mel.las** a thin, platelike structure, as of a bivalve mollusk or one of the gills on the underside of a mushroom cap.

la.ment (luh.MENT) *n.* **1** an expression of grief, as by wailing or in a poem or song. **2** an elegy or dirge. —*v.* grieve or mourn: *a widow lamenting the death of her husband; Mothers lament for or over their missing children; adj.: our late* **lamented** (= mourned for) *friend; of lamented memory; a much lamented loss.* —**lam.en.ta.ble** (LAM.un.tuh.bul, luh.MEN-) *adj.: a lamentable tragedy; the lamentable* (= regrettable) *condition of our roads.* —**lam.en.ta.bly** *adv.* —**lam.en.ta.tion** (lam.un.TAY.shun) *n.*

lam.i.na (LAM.uh.nuh) *n., pl.* **-nae** (-nee) or **-nas** a thin plate or layer; hence, the blade of a leaf. —**lam.i.nar** (-nur) *adj.: the smooth laminar flow of air over an airplane wing;* also **lam.i.nal.**

lam.i.nate (LAM.uh.nate) *v.* **-nates, -nat.ed, -nat.ing 1** cover with a layer of clear plastic: *to laminate a diploma or picture.* **2** split, beat, or roll, as metal, into layers. **3** make in layers bonded together as plywood, safety glass, and plastics; *adj.: a laminated board.* —*adj.* (-nit) laminated: *a laminate beam, finish, tabletop.* —**lam.i.na.tion** (-NAY.shun) *n.*

lamp *n.* a device that gives light or heat

using electricity, gas, oil, kerosene, etc.: *floor, incandescent, reading, safety, table lamps; to light, turn down, turn off, turn on a lamp.*

lamp.black *n.* fine black soot used as a pigment; carbon black.

lam.poon (lam.POON) *n.* a satirical piece of writing ridiculing a person or organization. —*v.* attack someone using a lampoon. —**lam.poon.er.y** *n.*

lamp.post *n.* a post supporting a street lamp.

lam.prey (LAM.pree) *n.* -**preys** an eellike fish which, instead of jaws, has a mouth that it uses to suck blood from other fish.

lance *v.* **lanc.es, lanced, lanc.ing** pierce or cut open with a lance or lancet: *to lance a boil.* —*n.* 1 a sharp-pointed instrument such as the large, steel-tipped wooden spear used by medieval knights. 2 same as LANCET. 3 a cavalryman armed with a lance; also **lan.cer.**

lance corporal *n.* a U.S. marine ranking above a private first class and below a corporal.

lan.cet (LAN.sit) *n.* a small two-edged surgical knife.

land *n.* 1 the solid surface of the earth: *Columbus sighted land; He reached land; dry land; to travel by, on, over land; a small parcel of land; a plot of land; to clear land* (= the ground) *for cultivation; arable, barren, cultivable, fertile land* (= soil); *The house price is inclusive of land* (= plot). 2 country: *this land of ours; the Holy Land of Palestine; your native land; the Promised Land of Israel; in no man's land* (= neutral territory); *back in the land* (= realm) *of the living.* —*v.* 1 come or bring to land: *Passengers land at an airport; where to land a plane; how to land a fish.* 2 *Informal.* get: *She could easily land a job or contract; Theft could land you in jail; Pat landed him one* (*Informal for punched him*) *on the nose.*

lan.dau (LAN.dow, -daw) *n.* a four-wheeled carriage with two facing seats and two folding hoods meeting at the top from either end.

land bank *n.* parcels of land appropriated by government for a public project.

landed *adj.* having to do with land or landing: *the landed prices of imported goods; the landed gentry* (*who own land*); *a landed immigrant* (*who has legally taken up residence in Canada*); *landed property* (= real estate).

land.er *n.* a space vehicle designed to land, as on a planet.

land.fall *n.* 1 land sighted after a voyage by sea, balloon, etc.: *The Shetland Islands were important landfalls for the Vikings on their way to Britain.* 2 a landing: *The hurricane is on its way to landfall in Florida; It's expected to make landfall by dawn.*

land.fill *n.* disposal of garbage or rubbish by burying it layer by layer under earth: *a sanitary landfill site.*

land.form *n.* a physical feature of the earth's surface, as a hill or plateau.

land grant *n.* gift of land by a government for agricultural colleges, railroads, etc.

land.hold.er (LAND.hole.dur) *n.* an owner or occupant of land.

landing *n.* 1 a coming or bringing to land: *to make a safe, smooth, soft landing in heavy fog; bumpy, crash, easy, emergency, forced, hard landings; a landing by parachute; a **landing craft** for bringing people and equipment close to shore from a ship; The undercarriage or **landing gear** of an aircraft consists of wheels or floats; a **landing strip** (= air strip).* 2 the level part at either end of a flight of stairs: *I came to rest on the landing, with no broken bones at all.*

land.la.dy (LAND.lay.dee) *n.* -**dies** *fem.* of LANDLORD.

land.locked *adj.* 1 surrounded by land, as a bay, harbor, or inland country. 2 confined to fresh water, as fish: *landlocked salmon.*

land.lord *n.* 1 one who rents property to others: *an absentee landlord; slum landlords.* 2 the keeper of an inn or rooming house.

land.lub.ber (LAND.lub.ur) *n.* [sailor's term] one who is not used to the sea; **land.lub.ber.ly** *adj.*

land.mark *n.* 1 something that stands out on a landscape, serving to identify a locality. 2 a memorable event: *The moon-landing was a landmark in the history of space travel;* **adja.**: *a landmark decision of the Supreme Court; President Sadat's landmark visit to Israel.*

land.mass *n.* a continent or similar large unbroken area of land.

land mine *n.* an explosive placed just below the ground surface so as to go off when a person or thing passes over it.

land office *n.* a government office recording sales and transfers of public lands. —**land-office** *adja. Informal.* busy and rapid: *doing a land-office business; the land-office demand for a new product.*

land.scape *n.* 1 land scenery: *beautiful,*

landslide / lap

barren, bleak, desolate, gloomy, stark, wind-swept, wintry landscapes; the cultural, lunar, political, urban landscape; to scour the landscape for new talent; **adja.**: a landscape artist, painting, photograph. 2 a landscape painting.
—v. **-scapes, -scaped, -scap.ing** redesign land and what is on it so as to please the eye, as a **landscape architect** or **landscape gardener** does.

land.slide n. 1 the sliding of a mass of earth or rocks down a slope; also, such a displaced mass. 2 in an election, a large majority of votes: *She won by a landslide;* **adja.**: *a landslide defeat, re-election, victory.*

lands.man (LANDS.mun) n. **-men** one who lives on land, not a seaman.

lane n. a narrow way, path, or strip, esp. one marked out or designated for runners, aircraft, ships, automobiles, etc. going in the same direction: *to change, shift lanes; the fast lane (on the extreme left of a highway); an inside lane; the passing lane; The shoulder lane is the slow lane.*

lan.guage (LANG.gwij) n. 1 a system of communication, esp. human speech or the speech of one group of people: *your native language; her first language; national and official languages; English is a world language; ancient, classical, dead, foreign, modern, second, universal languages; colloquial, formal, idiomatic, informal, literary, nonstandard, spoken, standard, substandard, written language; African and Asian languages; Esperanto is an artificial, not a natural language; the sign language of the deaf; to acquire, butcher, enrich, learn, massacre, master a language; the language of the blind; high-level and low-level computer languages (used in programming); Machine language is a low-level programming language; a* **language laboratory** *with sound-recording and reproducing equipment for learning to speak languages.* 2 style of verbal expression: *abusive, bad, coarse, diplomatic, dirty, flowery, foul, obscene, offensive, plain, polite, rough, simple, strong language; Pardon my language!* the **language arts** *of reading, speaking, listening, and writing.*

lan.guid (LANG.gwid) adj. tired or bored, as on a hot and humid day; not disposed to exert oneself.
—**lan.guid.ly** adv.; **lan.guid.ness** n.

lan.guish (LANG.gwish) v. 1 suffer from languor; pine or droop: *a promising genius now languishing in prison.* 2 lose energy or vigor; **adj.**: *the* **languishing** *looks of a forlorn lover.*

lan.guor (LANG.gur) n. 1 weakness, sluggishness, or indifference caused by enervating conditions. 2 effeteness or softness: *the languor of a tropical existence.* —**lan.guor.ous** adj.: *a life of languorous ease;* **lan.guor.ous.ly** adv.

lank adj. 1 straight, with a tendency to bend, as tall grass or to lie limp, as hair; **lank.ly** adv.; **lank.ness** n. 2 awkwardly lean and tall; also **lank.y** adj. **lank.i.er, -i.est**: *a lanky body, model, youth; lanky-legged colts;* **lank.i.ly** adv.; **lank.i.ness** n.

lan.o.lin (LAN.ul.in) n. a waxlike substance made from a greasy coating on the wool of sheep, and used in ointments, cosmetics, as a dressing for fur, etc.; also called "wool wax."

lan.tan.a (lan.TAH.nuh) n. a tropical shrub with showy heads of brightly colored flowers and aromatic leaves.

lan.tern n. 1 a portable lamp with a light inside a frame: *Chinese, hurricane, kerosene lanterns.* 2 a chamber or case to hold or regulate a light, as the top part of a lighthouse or a small windowed turret crowning a dome. 3 an early projector called "magic lantern."

lantern-jawed adj. with the lower jaw projecting beyond the upper one.

lan.tha.num (LAN.thuh.num) n. a metallic element, the first of the **lanthanide** series of rare-earth elements.

lan.yard (LAN.yurd) n. a short rope or cord for holding or fastening something, as attached to a whistle, knife, or pistol and worn around the neck.

La.o.tian (lay.OH.shun) n. & adj. (a person) of or from **Laos**, a S.E. Asian republic.

lap n. 1 the knees and thighs of a sitting person forming a place where something may be held: *a child in her mother's lap; brought up in the lap of luxury; His fate is* **in the lap of the gods** (= beyond human help). 2 the loose front part of a garment when held up to hold or catch something. 3 an overlapping part. 4 one circuit, as of a racecourse: *He was running laps in the 200 miles-per-hour region; She swims 15 laps daily for exercise; Let's do two more laps; on the last lap* (= segment) *of our journey.* 5 a splashing sound. —v. **laps, lapped, lap.ping** 1 lay partly over another, as shingles on a roof; **adj.**: *a* **lapped** *seam.* 2 wrap or enfold, as with a canvas or in a blanket. 3 drink, as cats and dogs do: *Be wary of lapping up* (= eagerly consuming) *advice from strangers.* 3 beat gently with a splash-

ing sound: *waves lapping a shore.*
lap.a.ro.scope (LAP.uh.ruh.scope) *n.* an optical instrument inserted through the abdominal wall or the vagina for internal examinations.
lap belt *n.* a safety belt across the lap, as in an automobile.
lap.board *n.* a board placed over the lap for use as a table or desk.
lap.dog *n.* a small pet dog.
la.pel (luh.PEL) *n.* the folded-back part of a coat coming down from the collar.
lap.i.dar.y (LAP.uh.dair.ee) *n.* **-dar.ies** a craftsman of gems: *the lapidary art; a* **lapidary wheel** *(for cutting and polishing gems).*
lap.in *n.* rabbit fur.
lap.is laz.u.li (LAP.is.LAZ.yoo.lye, -lee) *n.* an azure-blue semiprecious stone or mineral.
Lapp *n.* a member of a Mongoloid people of the **Lapland** region of Norway, Sweden, Finland, and Russia, that lies above the Arctic Circle; **Lap.land.er** *n.*
lap.pet (LAP.it) *n.* a loose-hanging flap or fold, as the lobe of the ear or a bird's wattle.
lap robe *n.* a blanket or other covering for the lap.
lapse (LAPS) *n.* **1** a slip of the tongue, memory, or pen: *a lapse in judgment; literary lapses.* **2** a slipping back into depression, sin, savagery, etc. **3** a passing: *after a lapse of two years; a lapse into a coma, into silence.* **4** the ending of a privilege through neglect or of a custom through disuse.
—*v.* **laps.es, lapsed, laps.ing** **1** fall: *She lapsed into a coma; a once splendid palace now lapsed into ruin; adj.: a* **lapsed** (= nonpracticing) *Catholic; a lapsed hooker (who has returned to life as a hooker).* **2** end: *Your lease lapses unless renewed in three days; adj.: a* **lapsed** *insurance policy, treaty.*
lap.top *n.* a portable computer that is smaller than a briefcase.
lap.wing *n.* the crested European plover.
lar.board (LAR.burd) *n.* the port or left side of a ship.
lar.ce.ny (LAR.suh.nee) *n.* **-nies** [legal use] theft: *Grand larceny is theft of goods of greater value than in petty larceny.*
—**lar.ce.nist** *n.* —**lar.ce.nous** (-suh.nus) *adj.*
larch *n.* a tall, slender, coniferous tree valued for its durable wood.
lard *n.* the melted and clarified fat of hogs. —*v.* put bacon on or into slits in meat to improve its flavor: *a poor speech though larded with biblical quotations.*
lard.er *n.* **1** pantry: *a well stocked larder.* **2** food supply.
large (LARJ) *adj.* **larg.er, larg.est** big in dimensions or quantity: *the large calorie, intestine; a large fortune, household; large powers; on a large scale; pictures (as) large as (in) life; a* **larger-than-life** (= great) *personality.* —*adv.:* *a threat looming large on the horizon; Disappointment was writ large on his face.*
—**at large:** *The rapist is still at large* (= free); *The police are appealing to the public at large* (= as a whole); *cpd: A congress- man-at-large represents an entire state; An editor-at-large is not a staffer.*
—**by and large** in general.
large-hearted *adj.* generous.
large.ly *adv.* **1** for the most part: *Joe is largely to blame for what happened.* **2** generously: *They contributed largely of their wealth to the campaign.*
—**large.ness** *n.*
large-scale *adj.* large in scale or dimensions: *a large-scale map; large-scale abuses, cultivation, distribution, industries, operations, projects, waste.*
lar.gess or **lar.gesse** (lar.JES, LAR.jis) *n.* a generous or showily large bestowal or gift.
larg.ish (LAR.jish) *adj.* somewhat large.
lar.go *adj. & adv. Music.* (in a) stately or slow tempo. —*n.* such a musical piece.
lar.i.at (LAIR.ee.ut) *n.* **1** a lasso. **2** a rope for tethering a grazing animal.
lark *n.* **1** any of a family of small songbirds, esp. the skylark. **2** *Informal.* a frolic or prank: *For a lark, the wanted man dialed the police but got caught instead;* *v.:* *They were larking all night in the park.*
lark.spur same as DELPHINIUM.
lar.va (LAR.vuh) *n., pl.* **-vae** (-vee) or **-vas** the immature, usu. wormlike stage of an insect, as a caterpillar, grub, or maggot. —**lar.val** (-vul) *adj.*
lar.yn.gi.tis (lair.un.JYE.tis) *n.* hoarseness from inflammation of the throat.
lar.ynx (LAIR.inx) *n.* **lar.ynx.es** or **la.ryn.ges** (-IN.jeez) the sound-producing organ or "voice box" containing the vocal cords, situated above the windpipe. —**la.ryn.ge.al** (lair.IN.jee.ul) *adj.*
la.sa.gna (luh.ZAHN.yuh) *n.* a dish of noodles in ribbon form baked with layers of chopped meat, cheese, and tomato sauce; also **la.sa.gne.**
las.car (LAS.cur) *n.* an East Indian sailor.

las.civ.i.ous (luh.SIV.ee.us) *adj.* lewd or lustful; **las.civ.i.ous.ness** *n.*

lase (LAZE) *v.* **las.es, lased, las.ing** emit or subject to laser light.

la.ser (LAY.zur) *n.* a device producing an intense, penetrating beam of light which is used in scanning images, printing, playing records, surgery, cutting metal, etc. —*adj.*: *laser beams, light, scanners, technology.*

laser disc (or **disk**) same as COMPACT DISK.

laser printer *n.* a quiet non-impact computer printer that produces type of various fonts and sizes similar in sharpness to typesetting by traditional methods.

lash *n.* **1** the flexible striking part of a whip. **2** eyelash. **3** a stroke or blow, as with a whip. **4** something that hurts like a lash. —*v.* **1** beat or whip: *a tiger lashing its tail; sails lashed by a wind; We could hear the rain lashing against the window; The mob was lashed into a fury by one speaker after another; Editorials* **lash out at** or **against** (= attack) *injustices; The government lashed back at the media.* **2** tie or bind with a rope, cord, chain, etc.

lashing *n.* **1** material with which to tie or bind. **2** attack: *verbal lashing; tongue-lashings.* **3 lashings** *pl. Informal.* plenty: *lashings of whipped cream.*

lass *n.* a young girl; also, a sweetheart. Also **las.sie** (LAS.ee).

las.si.tude (LAS.uh.tude) *n.* weariness resulting from dejection, overexertion, etc.

las.so (LAS.oh, la.SOO) *n.* **-sos** or **-soes** a cowboy's rope with a noose at one end for catching or roping livestock. —*v.* **las.soes, las.soed, las.so.ing** rope or catch with a lasso. —**las.so.er** *n.*

last *adj.* a *superl.* of LATE. **1** coming at the end of a series: *the last boy in his class; the last man I want to see; a drug of last resort; "the last but not the least"; He is* **on his last legs** (= at the end of his resources). **2** coming after all others in time: *the last rites for the dying; her last will and testament; your last letter; on the* **last day but one** (= two days before the end) *of the school term.* —*adv.*: *Z comes last in the alphabet; She was fine when I last saw her.* —*v.* continue to exist and be useful: *Well-made goods last a long time; provisions to last a winter; The funds lasted us* (= were enough for) *a year.* —*n.* **1** a last person or thing: *Yesterday's game was the last of the series.* **2** a foot-shaped block on which to form or repair a shoe, used by cobblers. —**at (long) last** after a long time. —**breathe one's last** die. —**stick to one's last** mind one's own business. —**to the last** to the very end. —**last.ly** *adv.*

last-ditch *adj.* having to do with a final effort: *a last-ditch attempt, effort, measure; our last-ditch supporters.*

last hurrah *n.* the final moment of glory, as in politics.

lasting *adj.* continuing indefinitely: *a lasting effect, friendship, impression, solution; a just and lasting peace.*

Last Judgment *n.* God's judgment when the world ends.

last minute *n.* when it is almost too late: *She changed her mind at the last minute.*

last name *n.* a family name or surname.

last post *n.* a bugle call sounded at lights-out time, military funerals, and memorial services; taps.

last straw *n.* the last of many intolerable things, like the straw that broke the camel's back in the fable.

Last Supper *n.* the supper eaten by Jesus and his disciples before his crucifixion.

last word *n.* **1** the final say or authority: *Mom always has to have the last word in family disputes; Dad's book is the last word on how to conduct an argument.* **2** *Informal.* the latest or most fashionable thing: *The last word in beachwear has very little left.*

latch *n.* a fastening device inside a door, window, etc. consisting of a small lever falling into a notch, which may be opened from the outside by a latchkey or a **latchstring** passed outside through a hole in the door. —*v.* fasten: *a cabin door latched shut; a lonesome child looking for someone to* **latch on to** (*Informal* for attach oneself to).

latch.et (LACH.it) *n. Archaic.* strap or thong for fastening a shoe or sandal.

latch.key *n.* **1** a key to the front door of a house that is accessible from the outside. **2** a child left alone at home after school because the parents are at work; also **latchkey child.**

late *adj.* **lat.er** or **lat.ter, lat.est** or **last** **1** coming or happening after an expected time: *She's never late for work; was late in going to bed; a bit too late with his application; The supper was late.* **2** at an advanced time: *a late-night party; a late supper near midnight; the late city edition of a newspaper; the late 1990s* (= 1999, 1998, etc.). **3** recent in regard to death, retirement, or other

event: *her late husband; a late model car; our late mayor; the late floods.* —*adv.*
lat.er, lat.est or **last 1** after the usual or expected time: *We arrived late; We had lunch later on in the afternoon; We returned late at night.* **2** recently: *our late lamented friend; as late as last week.* —**of late** lately or recently. —**sooner or later** at some time in the future.
late.com.er (LATE.cum.ur) *n.* one who has come late or recently.
late.ly *adv.* recently.
la.tent (LAY.tunt) *adj.* lying hidden though in existence: *one's latent abilities, qualities; the latent undeveloped image captured on film;* **la.tent.ly** *adv.* —**la.ten.cy** *n.*
lat.er.al (LAT.ur.ul) *adj.* a. sideways: *a lateral movement; a lateral, not terminal bud; a* **lateral pass** *(thrown toward the sidelines or away from the opposing team's goal) in football.* —**lat.er.al.ly** *adv.*
la.tex (LAY.tex) *n.* **1** the milky juice of the bark of plants and trees such as rubber. **2** a rubber or plastic emulsion, as used in paints and adhesives.
lath ("th" as in "the" or as in "thin") *n.* one of the thin, narrow strips of wood or metal forming a lattice or a framework for plastering, as for the walls of a frame house. —*v.* cover or line with laths.
lathe (LAITH, "TH" as in "the") *n.* a machine for shaping pieces of wood, metal, etc. by turning them against a cutting tool. —*v.* **lathes, lathed, lath.ing** shape on a lathe.
lath.er (LATH.ur, "TH" as in "the") *n.* **1** froth or foam, as produced by soap and water or by a sweating horse. **2** *Informal.* state of excitement: *The guests were late and she was in a lather; Why get or whip or work yourself into a lather over nothing?* —*v.* cover with or form lather: *Lather your face before shaving; Soap does not lather in hard water.* —**lath.er.y** *adj.*
lath.ing ("th" as in "the" or as in "thin") or **lath.work** *n.* laths or their installation.
Lat.in *n.* **1** the language of ancient Rome. **2** one who speaks a language such as French, Italian, Portuguese, or Spanish that is descended from ancient Latin; one who is from the Mediterranean region; *adja.*: *a Latin nation; the Latin temperament; a* **Latin American** *country (of the Western Hemisphere south of the U.S.); the* **Latin Church** (= Roman Catholic Church).
La.ti.no (luh.TEE.no) *n.* -**nos** a Latin American.

lat.ish (LAY.tish) *adj. & adv.* somewhat late.
lat.i.tude (LAT.uh.tude) *n.* **1** the distance north or south of a point on the globe from the equator, measured in degrees: *Columbus, Ohio, is at a latitude of 40 degrees North.* **2** a place or region with reference to its latitude: *cold, high, low latitudes.* **3** degree of freedom of thought or action: *Older children are allowed greater latitude than younger ones in regard to watching TV.*
—**lat.i.tu.di.nal** (-TEW.dun.ul) *adj.*
lat.i.tu.di.nar.i.an (LAT.uh.tew.dun.AIR.ee.un) *n. & adj.* (one who is) liberal in his views, esp. in religious matters.
la.trine (luh.TREEN) *n.* a toilet for the use of many, as in a barracks, camp, or factory.
lat.te (LAT.ay) *n.* a stronger kind of espresso made from finer beans.
lat.ter (LAT.ur) *adj.* a *comp.* of LATE. **1** later or more recent: *the latter half of May* (= May 16 to May 31). **2** the last-mentioned, usu. the second of two: *Of Jack and Jill, the latter is the younger; Of Tom, Dick, and Harry, the latter* (= Harry) *is the baby.*
latter-day *adj.* of recent times: *a latter-day problem; a latter-day Shakespeare; a* **Latter-day Saint** (= Mormon).
lat.ter.ly (LAT.ur.lee) *adv.* recently.
lat.tice (LAT.is) *n.* **1** a framework of crossed wooden or metal strips. **2** a window, door, or gate with such a framework. —**lat.ticed** (LAT.ist) *adj.*
lat.tice.work (LAT.is.wurk) *n.* a lattice or lattices collectively.
Lat.vi.an (LAT.vee.un) *n. & adj.* **1** (a person) of or from **Latvia,** a country on the Baltic Sea. **2** (having to do with) the Baltic language of Latvia.
laud *n. & v.* praise or acclaim.
—**laud.a.ble** (LAW.duh.bul) *adj.*; **laud.a.bly** (-blee) *adv.*
laud.a.num (LAW.dun.um) *n.* a solution of opium in alcohol.
laud.a.to.ry (LAW.duh.tor.ee) *adj.* expressing praise: *a laudatory speech; laudatory verses.*
laugh (LAF) *v.* make the sounds, facial expressions, and bodily movements of one who is amused, joyous, scornful, etc.: *People laugh at his jokes; They laugh with him; Some burst out laughing; "He who laughs last laughs longest"* (= The one who succeeds in the end is the best). —**laugh at** ridicule: *People used to be laughed at for wanting to go to the moon.* —**laugh off** dismiss with a laugh, as something of no conse-

quence. —**laugh someone out of court** ridicule and get rid of someone. —**laugh up one's sleeve** laugh or ridicule secretly. —*n.* **1** an act of laughing: *anything to get a laugh; He did it for laughs.* **2** *Informal.* something that causes laughter. —**have the last laugh** be successful over the others in the end. —**laugh.a.ble** (LAF.uh.bul) *adj.*; **laugh.a.bly** (-blee) *adv.* —**laugh.ing.ly** *adv.* in a laughing manner.

laugh.er *n. Informal.* a game that is an easy win.

laughing gas *n.* nitrous oxide which sometimes causes laughter when inhaled.

laugh.ing.stock (LAF.ing.stok) *n.* an object of ridicule: *He made a laughingstock of himself with his claims of UFO sightings.*

laugh.ter (LAF.tur) *n.* the sound or action of laughing: *His wild claims provoked laughter; contagious, convulsive, derisive, hearty, hysterical, infectious, raucous, uproarious, subdued laughter; The audience broke up in gales of laughter.*

launch *v.* set in motion, as a ship slid into water or a missile shot into the air: *money to launch her in business; to launch an attack against the enemy; to launch threats; to launch into a tirade against gambling.* —*n.* **1** a launching. **2** an open motorboat used for short trips. **3** a large boat carried by a warship.

launch (or **launching**) **pad** *n.* a platform from which a missile or spacecraft is launched, usu. at a **launch** (or **launching**) **site** such as Cape Canaveral, Florida, by means of a **launch vehicle** (= a rocket system to boost a spacecraft into orbit).

launch window *n.* a limited period suitable for launching a spacecraft depending on the position of the planets.

laun.der (LAWN.dur) *v.* **1** wash and iron clothes, linens, etc. **2** improve or make acceptable: *a public-relations firm hired to launder the image of the corporation; adj.: a laundered version of the real story.* **3** make illegal funds clean by channeling through a third party such as a foreign bank to hide their source; *adj.: laundered money.* —**laun.der.er** *n.*; **laun.dress** (-dris) *fem.*

laun.dro.mat (LAWN.druh.mat) *n.* a self-service laundry; **Laundromat** Trademark.

laun.dry (LAWN.dree) *n.* **-dries 1** a place for laundering clothes, etc. **2** a batch of such items before or after laundering: *clean, dirty laundry; to do, dry, fold, iron the laundry.*

laundry list *n.* a long and routine list of items.

lau.re.ate (LOR.ee.it) *n.* one honored with a special prize or title: *a poet laureate; Nobel laureates.* —**lau.re.ate.ship** *n.*

lau.rel (LOR.ul) *n.* **1** a tropical tree or shrub with aromatic leaves used by the ancient Greeks to crown victorious athletes. **2 laurels** *pl.* fame or victory: *He was never content to rest on his laurels* (= be satisfied with his accomplishments).

la.va (LAH.vuh, LAV.uh) *n.* **1** melted rock from a volcano. **2** this solidified.

la.vage (luh.VAHZH) *n.* the medicinal washing out of an organ such as the stomach.

lav.a.lier or **lav.a.liere** (lav.uh.LEER) *n.* **1** an ornament worn on a necklace. **2** a microphone used that way.

lav.a.to.ry (LAV.uh.tor.ee) *n.* **-ries** a toilet, a washbowl with running water, or a washroom equipped with either or both.

lave *v.* **laves, laved, lav.ing** [poetical use] wash or bathe.

lav.en.der (LAV.un.dur) *n.* **1** the pale-purple flowers and leaves of a fragrant European mint: *He's all lavender and old lace* (= very gentle-mannered). **2** a pale-purple: *lavender roses.*

lav.ish (LAV.ish) *adj.* spending or spent very generously and freely: *lavish expenditure, gifts, praise; He's lavish in his praise and lavish with her money.* —*v.* bestow or spend liberally: *the love and care lavished on children.* —**lav.ish.ly** *adv.*; **lav.ish.ness** *n.*

law *n.* **1** a written or unwritten rule or regulation governing conduct, recognized by a society: *the laws of hospitality, morality; the law of the land; A bill becomes law when passed by parliament; According to the law, you have to drive on the right; It is against the law to drink and drive; Governments maintain law* (= control imposed by laws) *and order in society; He went to law* (= a court of law) *to establish his claim; You read or study law for several years before entering the law* (= legal profession) *to practice law; Try not to get into trouble with the law* (= police); *No one is above the law* (= free from it); *Better leave it to the police and not take the law into one's own hands* (= not try to enforce the law oneself); *Observe the Law* (= God's commands in the Old Testament) *and the prophets; to administer, adopt, annul,* break, challenge, cite, enact, flout, interpret, promulgate, repeal, strike down, violate a law; blue, dietary, just, lemon, licensing, stringent, unwritten, zoning laws. **2** a type of law: canon, civil, common, constitutional, criminal, family, international, Islamic, labor, maritime, martial, military, municipal, statutory law; the Mosaic law (of Moses); She's a Doctor of Laws. **3** any rule or principle: Newton's laws of motion; a law of nature such as gravitation; the law of supply and demand; the **law of the jungle** (based on who is stronger or more powerful).

law-abiding adj. obedient to the law: a law-abiding citizen.

law.break.er (LAW.bray.kur) n. one who goes against the law; **law.break.ing** n. & adj.

law.ful adj. according to the law: a lawful arrest, claim, heir; by all lawful means. —**law.ful.ly** adv.; **law.ful.ness** n.

law.giv.er (LAW.giv.ur) n. one who makes laws. —**law.giv.ing** n. & adj.

law.less (LAW.lis) adj. **1** without laws: a lawless life, tribe. **2** breaking the law; disorderly: lawless behavior, violence; a lawless gang. —**law.less.ness** n.

law.mak.er (LAW.may.kur) n. one who helps make laws, as a legislator.

law.man (LAW.mun) n. **-men** a law officer such as a sheriff or marshal.

lawn n. a plot of close-cropped, grass-covered land for recreation or as part of landscaping: to mow a lawn. —**lawn.y** adj.

lawn bowling n. a game played on a bowling green using wooden balls that are rolled toward a ball.

lawn mower n. a machine for mowing lawns.

law.ren.ci.um (law.REN.see.um) n. a short-lived radioactive element.

law.suit n. a case in a law court: to bring, file, lose, settle, win a lawsuit against a party.

law.yer (LAW.yur, LOY.ur) n. one qualified to practice law: to hire or retain a lawyer. —**law.yer.ly** adj.: lawyerly caution, fees, skills.

lax adj. loose or relaxed, not tight or strict: lax habits, morals; a school that is somewhat lax in discipline; lax fiber, tissue; lax soil (in texture); **lax.ly** adv. —**lax.i.ty** or **lax.ness** n.

lax.a.tive (LAX.uh.tiv) n. a medicine that helps to make the bowels loose.

lay v. **1** pt. of LIE: He lay down to sleep. **2 lays, laid, lay.ing** cause to lie; hence, set or put down, esp. in a particular way: A bricklayer lays bricks; to lay chairs around a room; See the cat laying (Nonstandard for lying) there; Our teacher lays (= puts) much emphasis on neatness; a well-laid (= well-made) plan; I'll lay (= make) a bet the baby will be a boy; I'll lay (= bet) you $50 it will be a girl; Birds lay (= produce) eggs; A good rain will lay (= settle) the dust; The exorcist tried to lay (= get rid of) the ghost; He lost his cool and started to **lay about him** (= hit out) with his hockey stick; She **lays claim to** (= claims) her uncle's estate; a committee to **lay down** (= declare authoritatively) rules and regulations; They managed to **lay hold of** (= grab) the burglar; It's wise to **lay in** (= store up) provisions for winter; The paint has been **laid on** (= applied) rather thick; Please **lay out** (= arrange) these pages in proper order; You **lay over** (= stop and wait) in Rome and catch a flight the next day for Bombay; the cemetery where grandpa was **laid to rest** (= buried); It's time to lay the book aside and **lay** (= arrange) **the table** for dinner; She is **laid up** (= sick in bed) with the flu. —**lay off 1** make workers idle: Thousands were laid off when the factory closed. **2** stop doing something bad: The superpowers should lay off (= stop interfering with) Third World countries; Better lay off (= stop using) drugs; Lay off (= Stop your annoyance), will you? —**n. 1** the way something is laid or lies: the lay of the land as seen from the air. **2** Slang. partner for sexual intercourse: an easy lay. **3** a narrative poem for singing; also, a song or tune: "The Lay of the Last Minstrel." —**adj.** nonprofessional, esp. not of the clergy: lay people; a book that is too technical for lay readers.

lay.a.bout (LAY.uh.bowt) n. an idle and lazy person.

lay.a.way (LAY.uh.way) n. an article reserved for a customer on payment of a deposit to be claimed later after the full price is paid: We buy Christmas gifts in October on the **layaway plan**.

lay.er (LAY.ur) n. **1** one that lays: All our hens are good layers. **2** one thickness or stratum, esp. one of several: an even, outer, protective, uneven layer; the bottom, top layer; a **layer cake** with a filling between the layers; the **layered look** of clothes worn one over the other.

lay.er.ing (LAY.ur.ing) n. **1** the wearing of clothes in layers. **2** a method of growing roots for a new plant from a twig or shoot still attached to its parent.

lay.ette (lay.ET) n. an outfit of clothes, blankets, etc. for a newborn infant.

lay.man (LAY.mun) or **lay.wom.an** (LAY.woom.un) *n.* **-men** or **-wom.en** one who is an outsider in relation to a particular profession, as one who is not a clergyman.

lay.off *n.* **1** a temporary dismissal of an employee. **2** the duration of such unemployment.

lay.out *n.* the arrangement of parts of something organized: *the layout of an advertisement, camp, newspaper page.*

lay.o.ver (LAY.oh.vur) *n.* a break or stop in the course of a journey.

lay.per.son (LAY.pur.sun) same as LAYMAN or LAYWOMAN.

la.zar (LAZ.ur) *n.* a leper.

laze *v.* **laz.es, lazed, laz.ing** be lazy or idle.

la.zy (LAY.zee) *adj.* **-zi.er, -zi.est 1** not willing to work or exert oneself: *a lazy fellow, youth.* **2** having to do with a lazy person: *a lazy excuse, habit.* **3** slow-moving or sluggish: *a lazy current, stream; a lazy eye* (= poor vision resulting from weak eye nerves). —**la.zi.ly** *adv.*; **la.zi.ness** *n.*

la.zy.bones (LAY.zee.bones) *n. Informal.* a lazy person.

Lazy Su.san (-SOO.zun) *n.* a revolving tray used on the table to place small items of food within easy reach of everyone.

L-dopa (el.DOH.puh) *n.* an isomer of dopa used to treat Parkinson's disease.

lea (LEE) *n.* a meadow or pasture.

leach (LEECH) *v.* **1** be subject to washing action: *Silver-plated cups that leech too much lead are a health hazard; the **leaching** field of a sewage system.* **2** remove by washing action: *Heavy rainfall can leach out minerals from fertile soil; the **leaching** method of separating metal from ore.*

¹**lead** (LEED) *v.* **leads, led, lead.ing 1** show the way by going in front, directing, or guiding: *You lead, we follow; Please lead the way; a mob led by a troublemaker; He leads them by promises; What led* (= induced or made) *them to follow him? He will **lead them down the garden path*** (= deceive them); *He'll **lead them (on) a merry chase*** (= send them on a useless pursuit); *the events **leading up to*** (= preparing the way for) *the war.* **2** be first in something: *She leads (the class) in all subjects; the float that leads the parade; the batter who leads off in an inning.* **3** pass life, time, etc. in a particular way: *She leads a happy life.*
—*n.* **1** one that leads, as the principal part in a play: *to play the lead; to be cast in the lead; The story has a good lead* (= opening paragraph); *police tracking down leads* (= clues) *on a murder; Dogs should be on a lead* (= leash); **adj.**: *the lead car, dog, hand, singer; the lead* (= leading) *role of Macbeth.* **2** a leading: *someone to take the lead in organizing the show; We'll follow his lead.* **3** a being first, as in a race: *We are in the lead; We've to hold* or *maintain the lead; We have a commanding lead over* (= wide margin by which we lead) *the competition.* —**lead.er** *n.*; **lead.er.ship** *n.*

²**lead** (LED) *n.* **1** a soft, heavy, bluish-gray metallic element that is poisonous in compounds such as "lead acetate" and "lead arsenate." **2** something made of lead, as bullets, a plumb bob, or a strip of metal to space out lines of type. **3** the graphite used in pencils. —**get the lead out** *Slang.* hurry up; hustle. —*v.* to cover, mix, treat, weight, or fix glass in position with lead. —**adja.** having to do with lead: *a lead pipe; a lead* (= graphite) *pencil.*

lead.ed (LED.id) *adj.* containing lead: *leaded gasoline.*

lead.en (LED.un) *adj.* made of or like lead in weight, color, dullness, etc.: *leaden limbs, skies, spirits, thoughts.*

leading *adj.* (LEE.ding) **1** that leads: *the leading character in a play; one of our leading* (= influential) *citizens; a **leading question*** (so worded as to suggest the desired answer). **2** front: *the leading edge of an airfoil, of a warm front; at the leading edge of technology.*
—*n.* (LED.ing) **1** metal strips for spacing out lines of type. **2** such spacing.

lead-pipe *adja. Informal.* absolutely certain: *a lead-pipe certainty, cinch.*

lead poisoning *n.* poisoning caused by lead being absorbed into the body.

lead time (LEED-) *n.* the time required before a plan or project is carried out, as in manufacturing a new product.

leaf (LEEF) *n.* **leaves** (LEEVZ) **1** one of the thin, flat, green parts of a tree or plant: *a fig leaf; tea leaves; Leaves rustle in the wind.* **2** something similar to a leaf such as a flower petal, a sheet of paper or metal, a movable part of a table's top, a door, or a gate: *The dome was covered with gold leaf.* —*v.* **1** to bear leaves: *Many trees and plants leaf in the spring.* **2** look through casually: *to leaf through a book, magazine.*

leaf.age (LEE.fij) *n.* leaves or foliage.

leaf.hop.per (LEEF.hop.ur) *n.* an insect that feeds on plant juices.

leaf insect *n.* an insect that resembles a leaf.

leaflet / leasehold

leaf.let (LEEF.lit) *n.* **1** a printed, often folded sheet, as for direct-mail advertising: *a propaganda leaflet.* **2** a small leaf or a part of a compound leaf.

leaf mold *n.* **1** decayed leaves forming a top layer of soil. **2** a mold affecting foliage.

leaf.stalk (LEEF.stawk) *n.* the narrow part of the leaf connecting the blade to the stem of the plant or tree.

leaf.y (LEE.fee) *adj.* **leaf.i.er, -i.est** having many leaves: *leafy vegetables such as lettuce.*

league (LEEG) *n.* **1** an alliance of organizations with common interests, as in politics or sports: *the League of Nations (1920-1946); major-league* (= major class or category) *baseball; big, bush, minor leagues.* **2** formerly, a measure of distance, usu. equal to three nautical miles (5.556 km). —**in league** allied with someone. —**out of one's league** *Informal.* out of one's own class.

leak (LEEK) *v.* allow something to go in or out, as through a hole or crack: *a leaking boat; Water leaks into a boat; They are accused of leaking state secrets to the press; Air is leaking out* (= escaping) *from the tire; Truth will leak out.* —*n.* a leaking or something that leaks: *The pipe sprang a leak; to stop the leak; to plug a security leak; a politically inspired news leak.*

leak.age (LEE.kij) *n.* a leak, what has leaked out, or its amount.

leak.y (LEE.kee) *adj.* **leak.i.er, -i.est** that leaks: *a leaky boat, faucet, roof.*

lean (LEEN) *v.* **leans,** *pt. & pp.* **leaned** or **leant** (LENT), **lean.ing** bend or incline from a normal position *toward, against, on,* or *upon* something, as for support: *to lean a ladder against a wall; the Leaning Tower of Pisa; a doctrine leaning toward heresy; Friends lean* (= rely) *on each other in times of crisis.* —**lean on** *Informal.* force or urge someone to do something. —**lean over backward(s)** try very hard to please someone; bend over backward. —*n.* inclination; also **leaning.** —*adj.* **1** without much fat: *lean meat, He's of a lean and wiry build.* **2** meager or scanty: *a fuel mixture that is too lean* (= not rich enough) *for proper burning.* —**lean.ness** *n.*

lean-to (LEEN.too) *adj.* of a roof, having a single slope, usu. set against a larger structure. —*n., pl.* **-tos** a shelter, shed, or extension with a lean-to roof.

leap (LEEP) *n.* a jump or spring, esp. one suggesting lightness: *a great leap forward.* —**by leaps and bounds** rapidly or swiftly. —*v.* **leaps,** *pt. & pp.* **leaped** or **leapt** (LEEPT, LEPT), **leap.ing** jump or cause to jump over something: *horses leaping a fence; "Look before you leap"; An idea leaped to her mind; to leap at* (= grasp eagerly) *an opportunity.*

leap.frog *v. & n.* **-frogs, -frogged, -frog.ging** (leap over as in) a game in which players jump, with legs spread wide, over the bent back of each of the other players: *to play leapfrog; One labor union tries to leapfrog* (= get more than) *the wages gained by another; to leapfrog ahead of* or *past the competition;* **adja.:** *leapfrog advances, technologies;* **n.:** *to do* **leapfrogging; adja.:** *leapfrogging oil prices.*

leap year *n.* a year of 366 days, with February 29 as the extra day, occurring every fourth year.

learn (LURN) *v.* **learns,** *pt. & pp.* **learned** (LURND) or **learnt, learn.ing 1** acquire a skill or knowledge, as by study or experience: *to learn a poem by heart; Children learn to walk; They learn by* or *from experience; to learn dancing* or *to dance* or *how to dance;* **adj.:** *a* **learned** *habit, lesson, response, skill.* **2** come to know: *I learned about the lottery; learned that he is now a millionaire; I learned the news from TV.* —**learn.er** *n.*

learn.ed (LUR.nid) *adj.* having to do with learning; scholarly: *a learned book, profession, scholar, society.*

learning *n.* **1** knowledge, esp. of the formal or advanced kind: *a man of great learning; higher learning; not mere book learning.* **2** the act of learning: *programmed learning; A child with a* **learning disability** *may need special help with reading and math; A* **learning curve** or **graph** *shows progress in learning relative to the time required; a* **learning module** (= unit).

lease (LEECE) *n.* **1** a contract by which one person (**lessor**) lets another (**lessee**) have the use of property such as land, buildings, automobiles, etc. for a certain period on payment of a rent: *A lease may expire* or *run out if not renewed.* **2** the right thus acquired, its period, or the property itself: *Surgery could give you a* **new lease on life** (= chance to continue living). —*v.* **leas.es, leased, leas.ing** give or take a lease on something: *to lease a car from a dealer.* —**leas.er** *n.*

lease.hold *n.* property held by a lease. —**lease.hold.er** *n.*

leash (LEESH) *v.* check or hold an animal on a leash. —*n.* a line, chain, or strap: *a child* **straining at the leash** (= trying hard) *to be free of parental control.*

least (LEEST) *adj.* a superl. of LITTLE; smallest, slightest, or lowest: *I'm not the least bit worried; The* **least** (or **lowest**) **common denominator** *of ½, ¼, and ¾ is 12, the same as the* **least** (or **lowest**) **common multiple** *of 2, 3, and 4.*
—*n.* what is smallest, slightest, or lowest: *The least I ask is 25 cents;* **At least** *say "Thank you."* —**not in the least** not at all. —*adv.* a superl. of LITTLE: *He likes Mondays least.*

least.wise *adv. Informal.* at any rate.

leath.er (LETH.ur, "TH" as in "the") *n.* **1** animal skin prepared for making shoes, coats, gloves, etc. **2** such an article. —*adj.* made of leather; also **leath.ern.**

leath.er.neck (LETH.ur.nek) *n. Slang.* a U.S. marine.

leath.er.y (LETH.uh.ree) *adj.* tough and pliable like leather.

leave (LEEV) *v.* **leaves, left, leav.ing 1** go or depart from a place: *a flight leaving (New York) for London; She just left (here).* **2** let a person or thing be; let remain: *Don't leave the baby alone; She left the door open; There was no one left in the house; The injured dog was left for* (= abandoned as) *dead; I left* (= forgot) *my wallet at school; I leave it to your good judgment; The decision is left up to you; His arguments* **leave me cold** (= unimpressed). **3** let a person have: *His rich uncle left him a fortune.* **4 leaves, leaved, leav.ing** put forth leaves.
—**leave off** stop or cease. —**leave out** omit or ignore. —**leave something** or **somewhat** or **a great deal** or **a lot** or **much to be desired** be not as good as it should be: *Your homework leaves somewhat to be desired.*
—*n.* **1** permission: *He asked leave to speak; She has a year's leave* (= free time away from duty); *maternity, sick leave; terminal leave (before retirement); a sailor on shore leave; He was granted* **leave of absence** (= permission to be absent) *from duty; She's back home* **on leave**; *It was time to* **take leave of** (= to leave) *his family; He seems to have* **taken leave of his senses** (= He's acting strangely). **2 leaves** See LEAF.
—**leaved** *adj. & cpd:* having leaves as specified: *a lovely tree when fully leaved; broad-leaved trees; a four-leaved clover.*

leav.en (LEV.un) *n.* **1** a substance such as yeast or baking powder, also called **leavening**, that causes fermentation in batter or dough by releasing carbon dioxide which lightens and raises it. **2** a spreading influence bringing about change. —*v.* **1** make batter or dough rise. **2** lighten, temper, or enliven: *poetry leavened with wit.*

leaves *pl.* of LEAF.

leave-taking *n.* parting or farewell.

leavings *n.pl.* what is left; leftovers or remnants.

Leb.a.nese (leb.uh.NEEZ) *n. & adj., sing. & pl.* (a person) of or from **Lebanon**, an Asian country at the E. end of the Mediterranean.

lech.er *n.* a man who indulges in lechery or lust. —**lech.er.ous** (-uh.rus) *adj.;* **lech.er.ous.ly** *adv.* —**lech.er.y** (LECH.uh.ree) *n.*

lec.i.thin (LES.uh.thin) *n.* a fatty substance of plant and animal tissues, found esp. in egg yolk, soybeans, corn, etc.

lec.tern (LEC.turn) *n.* a tall reading stand, usu. with a slanted top, as used by a lector.

lec.tor (LEC.tur) *n.* a person who reads to the congregation at a church service.

lec.ture (LEC.chur) *n.* **1** an instructive talk, as given to a class of students: *Professors deliver, students attend lectures.* **2** a scolding. —*v.* **-tures, -tured, -tur.ing** give a lecture to someone; also, scold: *The teacher lectured him on his poor marks.* —**lec.tur.er** *n.: a lecturer in* or *on English.* —**lec.ture.ship** *n.*

led *pt. & pp.* of LEAD.

le.der.ho.sen (LAY.dur.hoh.zun) *n.pl.* short leather pants worn by men and boys in Bavaria.

ledge (LEJ) *n.* a narrow shelf or ridge standing out from an upright surface: *a window ledge; a ledge of rock near a shore.*

ledg.er (LEJ.ur) *n.* a book in which money transactions are recorded.

lee *n.* **1** a side, as of a ship or island, that is sheltered from the wind. **2** shelter: *in the lee of a wall.*
—*adj.* a. sheltered or away from the wind; leeward, not windward: *a lee shore, tide; the lee side of a ship.*

leech *n.* **1** a small worm, also called "bloodsucker," once used in medicine to remove blood from patients. **2** a hanger-on. —*v.* drain or exhaust: *work that leeches one's energy.*

leek *n.* an onionlike but mild-flavored vegetable.

leer *n.* a sly, suggestive, or evil glance. —*v.* look with a leer at someone.

leer.y *adj.* **leer.i.er, -i.est** *Informal.* suspicious or wary *of* someone or something.

lees (LEEZ) *n.pl.* dregs or sediment, as of wine during fermentation.

lee.ward (LEE.wurd, LOO.wurd) *adj. & adv.* away from the wind; toward the lee. —*n.* the lee side.

lee.way *n.* **1** leeward drift of a ship or aircraft from its true course; also, the degree of such deviation. **2** a margin of safety or tolerance; freedom or elbow room: *Allow some leeway for human error; Don't give too much leeway to laziness.*

left *n.* **1** the side of the body or the hand to the north when one is facing east: *Your heart is on your left.* **2** a left turn: *Take a left at the lights.* **3 the left** or **the Left,** in politics, a liberal or radical position, party, or person, esp. one advocating social and economic reform: *the extreme, far Left.* **4** a punch with the left hand: *to deliver* or *throw a left.* —*adv. & adj.* on or toward the left: *Turn left at the lights; No left turn on a red light.* —*pt. & pp.* of LEAVE.

left-handed *adj. & adv.* using or done with the left hand: *He is left-handed; a left-handed pitch; He pitches left-handed; a left-handed* (= insincere) *compliment.*

left.ist *n.* a member of the political Left: *liberals and leftists; adj.: leftist candidates, leanings, positions, views.*

left.o.ver (LEFT.oh.vur) *n.* something that is left or unused, as scraps of food: *We don't serve leftovers to our guests; The project is a leftover from the previous government.*

left wing *n.* **1** a front-line player or position to the left of center, as in hockey. **2** the more radical section of a political party. —**left-wing** *adj.* —**left-wing.er** *n.*

left.y *n.* **left.ies** *Informal.* a left-handed person.

leg *n.* **1** one of the limbs in humans and animals used for support and for moving about: *to cross one's legs in sitting; Walk around the room to stretch your legs a little; a cat's hind legs; He does not have a leg to stand on* (= has no valid defense). **2** any part suggesting a leg, as of trousers, of a table, chair, etc. **3** one of the stages of a course, as in a relay race or journey: *She is on the last leg of her journey.* —**break a leg** *Informal.* good luck! —**on one's last legs** near collapse. —**pull someone's leg** *Informal.* tease; also, trick in fun, not maliciously. —*v.* **legs, legged, leg.ging** *Informal.* go on foot: *The car broke down and we had to leg it the rest of the way.*

leg.a.cy (LEG.uh.see) *n.* **-cies 1** an inheritance or bequest. **2** anything handed down from the past or by predecessors: *a lasting legacy of the war.*

le.gal (LEE.gul) *adj.* involving the law or its knowledge or use: *to take legal action; legal advice; in her legal capacity as the child's guardian; in legal control, ownership; the legal profession; your legal rights and responsibilities; a legal system; the **legal age*** (= age of majority); *a **legal holiday*** (set by law) *such as Thanksgiving.* —**le.gal.ly** *adv.* —**le.gal.i.ty** (lee.GAL.i.tee) *n.*

le.gal.ism (LEE.guh.liz.um) *n.* **1** strict adherence to the letter of the law. **2** a legal expression or rule. —**le.gal.is.tic** (-LIS.tic) *adj.*

le.gal.ize (LEE.guh.lize) *v.* **-iz.es, -ized, -iz.ing** make legal: *Gambling has been legalized in the form of government-run lotteries.* —**le.gal.i.za.tion** (-luh.ZAY.shun, -lye-) *n.*

legal pad *n.* a pad of ruled legal-size paper; also **legal tablet.**

legal-size paper *n.* paper measuring 8.5 x 14 in. or about 22 x 36 cm.

legal tender *n.* money acceptable in payment of a debt: *One thousand pennies may not be legal tender for $10.*

leg.ate (LEG.ut) *n.* a special envoy of the pope.

leg.a.tee (leg.uh.TEE) *n.* one to whom a legacy is bequeathed.

le.ga.tion (li.GAY.shun) *n.* **1** a legate's mission. **2** a diplomatic mission headed by a minister and ranking below an embassy.

le.ga.to (li.GAH.toh) *adj. & adv. Music.* (performed) in a smooth and connected manner.

leg.end (LEJ.und) *n.* **1** a story or tradition connected with the history of a people, as the story of St. George and the Dragon: *Mother Teresa's work with the poor made her a living legend; She became a legend in her own lifetime.* **2** an inscription, as on a medal. **3** an explanation, as of an illustration or of symbols used on a chart or map.

leg.end.ar.y (LEJ.un.dair.ee) *adj.* having to do with legend: *the legendary tales about Charlemagne; He became a legendary figure even during his life.*

leg.er.de.main (lej.ur.duh.MAIN) *n.* sleight of hand, as when a magician takes rabbits out of a hat; hence, trickery or deception.

leg.ged (LEG.id, LEGD) **1** *adj.* having a leg or legs: *a legged desk, seat, sofa.*

2 *comb.form.* with legs as specified: *to sit cross-legged; four-legged animals; full-legged trousers; a long-legged colt; spindly legged jeans; a three-legged stool; wide-legged pajamas.*

leg.ging *n.* a leg-covering: *woolen leggings for children.*

leg.gy (LEG.ee) *adj.* **leg.gi.er, leg.gi.est** having long legs: *a leggy brunette, sprinter; Leggy colts look awkward.*

leg.horn or **Leg.horn** (LEG.horn, -urn) *n.* a breed of small chicken, developed in Italy, the best in egg-laying.

leg.i.ble (LEJ.uh.bul) *adj.* clear enough to read: *She writes a legible hand;* **leg.i.bly** *adv.* —**leg.i.bil.i.ty** (-BIL.i.tee) *n.*

le.gion (LEE.jun) *n.* **1** an army, esp. a unit of 3,000 to 6,000 soldiers in ancient Rome: *the French Foreign Legion; an armed legion of terrorists.* **2** a large number: *Tax evaders – their name is legion; Horror stories are legion; the growing legion of informers.* **3** usu. **Legion**, a society, as of ex-servicemen: *the American Legion; a university's Legion of Honor; a legion hall (of the American Legion).* —**le.gion.ar.y** (-nair.ee) *n. & adj.* **-ar.ies.**

le.gion.naire (lee.juh.NAIR) *n.* a member of a Legion.

leg.is.late (LEJ.is.late) *v.* **-lates, -lat.ed, -lat.ing 1** make laws: *The government can only legislate on what it can control.* **2** bring about something by legislating: *to legislate equal pay for work of equal value; to legislate strikers back to work; No one can legislate quality of life.* —**leg.is.la.tor** *n.*

leg.is.la.tion (lej.is.LAY.shun) *n.* the making of laws or statutes: *to adopt, enact, introduce, pass legislation to ban smoking.*

leg.is.la.tive (LEJ.is.luh.tiv) *adj.* having to do with legislation: *a legislative body, decree, measure; legislative authority, reforms.*

leg.is.la.ture (LEJ.is.luh.chur) *n.* a lawmaking body of elected representatives of a state or province.

le.git (luh.JIT) *adj. Informal.* legitimate: *He has switched from nightclub circuits to legit theater; He's gone legit.* —*n.:* strictly **on the legit** (= within the law).

le.git.i.mate (luh.JIT.uh.mit) *adj.* rightful according to law or other standard: *a legitimate candidate, claim, conclusion, heir, purpose; a legitimate movie star, play;* **Legitimate theater** is drama of literary merit, not musical comedies, motion pictures, etc. —**le.git.i.ma.cy** (-muh.see) *n.*

le.git.i.mize (luh.JIT.uh.mize) *v.* **-miz.es, -mized, -miz.ing** make or declare to be legitimate. Also **le.git.i.ma.tize** (-muh.tize).

leg.man *n.* **-men** one engaged in work that involves much moving about, esp. an on-the-scene reporter or an assistant on routine duties outside the office.

leg.room *n.* room for the legs while seated, as in a car.

leg.ume (LEG.yoom, lig.YOOM, long "oo") *n.* (the pod or seed of) a plant of the pea family, as the bean, peanut, alfalfa, or clover. —**le.gu.mi.nous** (-YOO.mi.nus) *adj.*

leg.work *n.* the work of a legman.

lei (LAY, LAY.ee) *n., pl.* **leis** a Hawaiian garland or wreath of flowers.

lei.sure (LEE.zhur, LEZH.ur) *n.* time that one may spend for rest and recreation: *Do it at your leisure* (= convenience). —*adj.:* leisure homes, hours, time, wear; **the leisure class** (of people not working for a living).

lei.sure.ly (LEZH.ur.lee) *adj.* unhurried: *He works at a leisurely pace; a leisurely meal; adv.: We drove leisurely* (= unhurriedly) *around town.*

leisure suit *n.* a suit for casual wear consisting of a shirtlike jacket and trousers.

leit.mo.tif or **leit.mo.tiv** (LITE.moh.teef) *n.* leading or dominant theme.

lem.ming *n.* a mouselike arctic animal noted for periodic migrations during which large numbers starve to death or get killed.

lem.on.ade (lem.uh.NADE) *n.* a drink made of water, sugar, and lemon juice.

le.mur (LEE.mur) *n.* a fluffy-furred, long-tailed primate of Madagascar.

lend *v.* **lends, lent, lend.ing 1** give money, goods, or services temporarily: *to lend someone $5,000 at 10% interest for one year; Please lend him your car for an hour;* **Lend me an ear** (= Listen to me); *to* **lend a hand** (= to help); *a subject that* **lends itself to** (= is suitable for) *dramatic treatment.* **2** give or impart: *Her presence lends distinction to the proceedings.* —**lend.er** *n.*

length *n.* how long or extended something is: *the length and width of a room; throughout the length and breadth of the land; The room is 10 m in length; People you don't want to get involved with should be kept* **at arm's length** (= at some distance); *She described what happened* **at great length** (= in detail or fully); *He* will **go to great lengths** (= make a great effort) *to help a friend; Our horse won the race by a length* (= horse's length); *a length of rope (of a specific length); a full-length movie (not a short one);* **At length** (= Finally), *somebody spoke up;* **adj**.: *the difference between an* **arm's-length** *relationship between strangers and a family relationship; an arm's-length policy, transaction.*

length.en (LENG.thun) *v.* make or become longer.

length.wise *adj. & adv.* in the direction of the length. Also **length.ways**.

length.y *adj.* **length.i.er, -i.est** very long, often too long: *a lengthy essay, lecture, speech.* —**length.i.ly** *adv.*

le.ni.ent (LEE.nee.unt, LEEN.yunt) *adj.* **1** mild: *a lenient climate.* **2** merciful: *a lenient judge; lenient rules.* —**le.ni.ence** or **le.ni.en.cy** *n.*

len.i.tive (LEN.uh.tiv) *n. & adj.* (something) that soothes or lessens; palliative. —**len.i.ty** *n.* leniency.

lens *n.* **1** a piece of glass or other transparent body that focuses or spreads light rays, as in the eye on in a camera, microscope, or telescope: *concave and convex lenses; Contact lenses are corrective lenses for the eyes.* **2** any focusing device for sound waves, electrons, etc.

lent *pt. & pp.* of LEND.

Lent.en (LEN.tun) *adj.* having to do with **Lent**, a 40-day (excluding Sundays) period of penitence in Christian churches, lasting from Ash Wednesday to Easter Sunday.

len.til *n.* **1** an ancient food plant of the pea family, valued for its nutritious, lens-shaped seeds. **2** the seed.

Le.o (LEE.oh) *n.* **1** a N. constellation and the fifth sign of the zodiac. **2** a person born under this sign.

le.o.nine (LEE.uh.nine) *adj.* of or like a lion.

leop.ard (LEP.urd) *n.* a large fierce cat of Asia and Africa valued for its black-spotted skin: *a young leopard* (= cub); *"A leopard cannot change its spots."*

le.o.tard (LEE.uh.tard) *n. usu.* **leotards**, *pl.* **1** a tight-fitting, one-piece garment for the torso, as worn by acrobats. **2** tights.

lep.er (LEP.ur) *n.* **1** one who has leprosy. **2** an outcast. —**lep.rous** (-rus) *adj.*

lep.re.chaun (LEP.ruh.cawn) *n.* a fairy of Irish folklore.

lep.ro.sy (LEP.ruh.see) *n.* a chronic infectious and ulcerous disease of the skin and nerves that causes disfigurement.

les.bi.an (LEZ.bee.un) *n. & adj.* (a female) homosexual. —**les.bi.an.ism** *n.*

lese majesty (LEEZ.MAJ.us.tee) *n.* an offense against the sovereign, esp. treason.

le.sion (LEE.zhun) *n.* an injury to tissue, as an ulcer, tumor, or abscess: *an open lesion.*

less *adj.* a *comp.* of LITTLE; not as much or as many; smaller, fewer, or lower in rank, importance, quality, etc.: *She's no less a person than the president; He uses little salt and less sugar; Grandma is less than pleased with the rising cost of food; Coffee used to cost 10 cents or less; 10 items or less (Informal for fewer).* —**adv**. not as much or as often: *to sleep less and work longer.* —**prep**. minus: *$10,000 less deductions; two years less a day.* —**n**. a smaller amount: *a little less of it.* —**adj**. *suffix* [freely added to nouns] not having or involving what is specified: *endless, painless, useless.*

les.see (les.EE) See LEASE.

less.en (LES.un) *v.* make or become less: *to lessen chances, expenses, hostility, the amount, impact, interests, the need for something, the pain of something; to lessen someone's dependence, liability, loss.*

less.er *adj.* a *comp.* of LITTLE; smaller or less important: *He was found guilty on a lesser charge of manslaughter;* the **lesser panda** (= not the black-and-white "giant panda," but the red one).

les.son (LES.un) *n.* **1** a learning exercise or something learned: *to take driving lessons* (= instruction); *In our school,* **lessons** *begin at 9 a.m.; a lesson in French; The accident will be a lesson* (= warning) *to him; That should teach him a lesson* (= make sure he doesn't do it again). **2** a passage from the Bible for reading at a church service.

les.sor (LES.or) See LEASE.

lest *conj.* for fear that: *He was cautious lest he be misunderstood; Lest we forget; He was afraid lest he should miss the bus.*

-let *n. suffix.* **1** small person or thing: *booklet, leaflet, piglet, starlet.* **2** small article of attire: *anklet, bracelet, wristlet.*

let *v.* **lets**, *pt. & pp.* **let, let.ting** allow to go, have, pass, etc.: *to let the cat out; We can't let him (come) in; Let us* (= I propose that we) *pray; Surgeons used to* **let blood** (run out) *as a cure; a house* **to let** (= for rent); *Please let* (= leave) *it alone; He doesn't have the training,* **let alone** (= not to mention) *experience for the job; He feels badly* **let down** (= disappointed) *by friends; Only friends were*

let in on (= told) *the secret; As a first offender, she was **let off** (= allowed to leave) with a warning; He likes to **let on** (Informal for pretend) that he has a rich uncle.* —**let out** 1 release or make known. 2 rent: *to let out the basement to boarders.* 3 make larger: *to let out a couple of inches at the waist of the pants.* —**let up** *Informal.* stop or pause: *The housing shortage will not let up for another year.* —*n.* in a racket game, an interference with play. —**without let or hindrance** without obstacles.

let.down *n.* a slowing up; also, a disappointment: *the letdown after the buildup for the Olympics.*

le.thal (LEE.thul, "th" as in "thin") *adj.* capable of causing death: *rifles, pistols, and such lethal weapons; a lethal injection (given to one condemned to death); a lethal* (= deadly) *dose.* —**le.thal.ly** *adv.*

leth.ar.gy (LETH.ur.jee) *n.* a dull, sluggish, or tired state. —**le.thar.gic** (luh.THAR.gic) *adj.*

let's let us.

let.ter (LET.ur) *n.* 1 a character of the alphabet, as A, B, C, etc.: *in block letters; a capital* or *upper-case letter; lower-case* or *small letters; follow orders **to the letter*** (= precisely); *He observes **the letter of the law*** (= its literal meaning) *but not its spirit.* 2 a written communication: *the art of writing letters; business, chain, dead, express, fan, form, love, open, poison-pen letters; Our letters must have crossed in the mail; **letter quality** printing that resembles typewriting.* 3 **letters** [takes *sing.* or *pl. v.*] literature; also, learning: *a man, woman of letters* (= an author or a literary scholar); *a Doctor of Letters.* —*v.* mark with or inscribe in letters: *to letter a poster.* —**let.ter.er** *n.*

letter bomb *n.* a bomb in the form of a postal envelope that explodes when opened.

letter box *n.* mailbox.

letter carrier *n.* one who delivers mail.

lettered *adj.* 1 marked with letters: *a lettered design; Streets are either numbered or lettered, like 6th and K streets; a boldly lettered T-shirt; a hand-lettered sign.* 2 literate; also, learned.

let.ter.head (LET.ur.hed) *n.* 1 writing paper printed with one's name and address. 2 such name and address.

lettering (LET.ur.ing) *n.* 1 the art of making drawn, printed, or stamped letters. 2 such letters.

letter-perfect *adj.* correct in every detail.

let.ter.press (LET.ur.pres) *n.* printing from raised type.

letter quality *n. & adj.* (appearance in regard to sharpness) that is similar to typewriting: *letter quality printers; in letter quality mode; near letter quality.*

letters patent *n.pl.* an official document granting a person some right or authority, as a title to land.

let.tuce (LET.is) *n.* the large, crisp, green leaves of a plant much used in salads: *a head of lettuce; leaf lettuce.*

let.up *n. Informal.* pause or slackening: *a letup in the rain.*

leu.ke.mi.a (loo.KEE.mee.uh) *n.* a cancerous, often fatal, uncontrolled growth of leukocytes; **leu.ke.mic** *adj.* Also **leu.ce.mia, leu.ce.mic.**

leu.ko.cyte (LOO.kuh.cite) *n.* a white blood cell; also **leu.co.cyte.**

lev.ee (LEV.ee) *n.* 1 a wall of banked-up earth and sandbags put up along a river's bank to contain floods. 2 a formal reception, as by a sovereign, governor, mayor, etc.: *a New Year's levee.*

lev.el (LEV.ul) *adj.* equal in height everywhere; horizontal: *Adjust the legs to make the table level; The flood waters were level with the second floor; a level* (= not heaping) *teaspoonful; He always keeps a level* (= sensible) *head; a **level-headed** woman; a level* (Informal for steady) *voice; a **level crossing** (Brit.* for grade crossing); *to compete on a **level playing field*** (with both sides having equal opportunities); *adv.*: *We'll do our **level best*** (= very best). —*n.* 1 something that is level: *a parking level; Did we park on this level?* 2 a height or depth: *We can see best at eye level; Basements are below the ground level; the oil level in a car engine; a lake above sea level; The water rose to a level of three meters; a high level of achievement; a clerk at a low level; In 1988, an income of $20,000 a year was below the **poverty level** (or **line**) for a family of four; Water finds or seeks **its own level*** (= reaches the same height at all points if allowed); *at the federal, local, municipal, national levels; the highest levels of government.* 3 an instrument used to determine if a plane is horizontal. —**on the level** of a person or conduct, blameless or genuine. —*v.* **-els, -eled, -el.ing** make horizontal or on the same level: *a town leveled by an earthquake; words leveled* (= directed) *at his critics; Prices are expected to rise and then **level off*** (= stay the same); *Come on now, **level with*** (= be honest) *me.* —**lev.el.er** *n.* Also **lev.elled, lev.el.ling; lev.el.ler** *Cdn.*

lev.er (LEV.ur, LEE.vur) *n.* 1 a device such as a crowbar for exerting force.

2 a means of exerting power or moral force: *He used his position as a lever to get votes.*

lev.er.age (LEV.ur.ij) *n.* 1 means of applying force: *The longer the crowbar the greater the leverage.* 2 advantage, effectiveness, or influence: *Teachers have much leverage with the principal.*

leveraged buyout *n.* the buying out of a company using borrowed money.

le.vi.a.than (luh.VYE.uh.thun) *n.* a huge and monstrous thing or animal.

Le.vis (LEE.vize) *n.pl.* close-fitting heavy blue-denim trousers; **Levi's** *Trademark*.

lev.i.tate (LEV.uh.tate) *v.* **-tates, -tat.ed, -tat.ing** rise and float in the air: *Magnets are used to propel and levitate vehicles;* *adj.*: *a magnetically levitated transportation system.* —**lev.i.ta.tion** (-TAY.shun) *n.*

lev.i.ty (LEV.i.tee) *n.* **-ties** lack of proper seriousness; frivolity.

lev.y (LEV.ee) *v.* **lev.ies, lev.ied, lev.y.ing** 1 raise taxes, armies, etc. by legal authority. 2 seize property in satisfaction of a claim. 3 wage: *to levy war on* or *against a nation.* —*n., pl.* **lev.ies** 1 a fine or tax that is imposed on a person or thing. 2 enlistment for military service or the men enlisted. —**lev.i.er** *n.*

lewd (LOOD) *adj.* indecent or obscene. —**lewd.ly** *adv.;* **lewd.ness** *n.*

lex.i.cal (LEX.i.cul) *adj.* having to do with word meaning rather than grammar. —**lex.i.cal.ly** *adv.*

lex.i.cog.ra.phy (lex.i.COG.ruh.fee) *n.* the work or art of researching words and compiling dictionaries; also, the profession. —**lex.i.cog.ra.pher** *n.* —**lex.i.co.graph.ic** (-cuh.GRAF.ic) or **lex.i.co.graph.i.cal** *adj.*

lex.i.con (LEX.i.cun) *n.* 1 vocabulary: *Violence is not in her lexicon.* 2 a dictionary, esp. of a classical language.

li.a.bil.i.ty (lye.uh.BIL.i.tee) *n.* **-ties** the condition of being liable: *No one would accept* or *admit liability* (= responsibility) *for the accident; to acknowledge, assume, take on a liability; a limited, not full liability* (= obligation); *One's sex or color should be neither a liability* (= disadvantage) *nor an asset in job hunting; Heavy liabilities* (= debts) *forced him into bankruptcy.*

li.a.ble (LYE.uh.bul) *adj.p.* subject to a responsibility or risk: *a carrier that is not liable to anyone for damage to luggage; If you play with fire, you are liable to get burned; Everyone is liable to make mistakes now and then.*

li.aise (lee.AIZ) *v.* **-ais.es, -aised,** **-ais.ing** to have liaison *with* someone for cooperative action.

li.ai.son (lee.AY.zon, LEE.uh.zon) *n.* 1 communication between different parts of an army, of civilian bodies, etc. for cooperation. 2 illicit sexual relationship.

li.ar (LYE.ur) *n.* [offensive in direct speech] one who tells lies.

lib *n.* [short form] liberation: *women's lib.*

li.ba.tion (lye.BAY.shun) *n.* 1 a ceremonial pouring out of wine, oil, etc. as an offering to a god. 2 the liquid poured out thus. 3 *Informal.* a drink or drinking that intoxicates.

lib.ber *n. Informal* [often derogatory] a liberationist, esp. a feminist: *a women's libber.*

li.bel (LYE.bul) *n.* 1 the hurting of someone's good name by publishing something written, printed, drawn, etc. unjustly. 2 material that libels. —*v.* **-bels, -beled, -bel.ing** defame someone by a libel. —**li.bel.er** *n.* —**li.bel.ous** *adj.* Also **li.belled, li.bel.ling; li.bel.ler; li.bel.lous** *Cdn.*

lib.er.al (LIB.uh.rul) *adj.* 1 free or broad-minded; not narrow, strict, or prejudiced: *He's quite liberal in his interpretation of the Bible.* 2 generous: *a liberal donation, tipper; He's very liberal with other people's money; a liberal* (= plentiful) *supply of provisions.* —*n.* 1 one who is in favor of progress and reform. 2 **Liberal** a member of a Liberal Party, as in Canada and Britain. —**lib.er.al.ism** *n.* —**lib.er.al.i.ty** (-RAL.i.tee) *n.*

liberal arts *n.pl.* subjects of cultural interest and value, as languages, literature, philosophy, history, etc. —**liberal education** *n.*

lib.er.al.ize (LIB.uh.ruh.lize) *v.* **-iz.es, -ized, -iz.ing** make or become liberal or more liberal: *to liberalize economic reforms, election laws, trade;* *adj.*: *the agitation for liberalized abortion laws.* —**lib.er.al.i.za.tion** (-luh.ZAY.shun, -lye-) *n.*

lib.er.al.ly (LIB.uh.ruh.lee) *adv.* generously.

lib.er.ate (LIB.uh.rate) *v.* **-ates, -at.ed, -at.ing** set free, as from slavery, confinement, dictatorship, enemy occupation, etc. —**lib.er.a.tion** (-RAY.shun) *n.;* **lib.er.a.tion.ist** *n.* —**lib.er.a.tor** (-ray.tur) *n.*

lib.er.tar.i.an (lib.ur.TAIR.ee.un) *n.* one who believes in freedom, sometimes absolute freedom, in thought and action: *a civil libertarian.*

—**lib.er.tar.i.an.ism** *n.*

lib.er.tine (LIB.ur.teen) *n. & adj.* (one) without moral restraints; (one who is) licentious.

lib.er.ty (LIB.ur.tee) *n.* **-ties** freedom from restraints such as slavery: *liberty of action, thought, etc.; May I take the liberty of telling you that it's getting late? She doesn't let boys* **take liberties** (= be too familiar) *with her on dates.* —**at liberty** free: *to set prisoners at liberty; A telephone operator is not at liberty to give out unlisted numbers.*

li.bi.do (li.BEE.doh, li.BYE-) *n.* energy derived from the instincts, esp. the sexual urge. —**li.bid.i.nal** (li.BID.un.ul) *adj.*

li.bid.i.nous (li.BID.uh.nus) *adj.* lustful; lewd; lascivious.

Li.bra (LYE.bruh, LEE-) *n.* **1** a S. constellation and the seventh sign of the zodiac. **2** a person born under this sign.

li.brar.i.an (lye.BRAIR.ee.un) *n.* **1** one in charge of a library. **2** one trained in library science.

li.brar.y (LYE.brair.ee) *n.* **-brar.ies** a collection of books, manuscripts, tapes, etc. or where it is housed: *circulating, lending, mobile, public, reference, research libraries.*

li.bret.to (li.BRET.oh) *n.* **-bret.tos** or **-bret.ti** (-tee) (a book containing) the words of an opera or similar long musical composition. —**li.bret.tist** *n.*

Lib.y.an (LIB.ee.un) *n. & adj.* (a person) of or from **Libya**, a N. African republic on the Mediterranean.

lice *pl.* of LOUSE.

li.cense (LYE.sunce) *n.* **1** a formal or legal permission to do something as a member of society, as driving, marrying, or practicing a profession: *to grant, issue, revoke, suspend a license; a driver's license* (= document granting license to drive); *poetic license* (= ignoring language rules for the sake of poetic effects). **2** irresponsible use of freedom. Also **li.cence**.
—*v.* **-cens.es, -censed, -cens.ing** to grant a license to someone: *A pharmacist is licensed to dispense drugs;* **adj.**: *a licensed medical practitioner; a licensed establishment that sells liquor.*

li.cen.see (lye.sen.SEE) *n.* one granted a license.

li.cen.ti.ate (lye.SEN.shee.it) *n.* **1** one licensed to practice an art or profession. **2** a university degree between a bachelor's and a doctor's.

li.cen.tious (lye.SEN.shus) *adj.* immoral or lewd. —**li.cen.tious.ly** *adv.*;

li.cen.tious.ness *n.*

li.chen (LYE.cun) *n.* a flowerless plant resembling moss that grows on bare rocks, tree stumps, etc.

lic.it (LIS.it) *adj.* permitted by law; not forbidden. —**lic.it.ly** *adv.*

lick *v.* **1** pass the tongue over an object: *She licked her fingers; licked them clean; flames licking the walls.* **2** *Informal.* beat or thrash; also, conquer: *If you can't lick them, join them; She has the problems licked* (= solved); *a thesis* **licked into shape** (*Informal* for put in proper form) *for submission;* **n.**: *He got a good* **licking.** —**n.** a licking: *One lick of that ice-cream cone satisfied her.* —**lick and a promise** *Informal.* a hasty performance, as of washing and cleaning.

lick.e.ty-split (lick.uh.tee.SPLIT) *adv. Informal.* at full speed.

lic.o.rice (LIC.uh.ris, -rish) *n.* **1** an extract of the sweet roots of an herb of the pea family. **2** a black-colored candy flavored with this extract.

lid *n.* **1** a movable cover, as of a pot or box. **2** an eyelid. **3** a curb or check: *tighter measures to* **keep the lid on** *excess spending; The company has decided to put the lid on further expansion.* —**lid.ded** *adj.*

li.do (LEE.doh) *n.* **-dos** a beach resort or bathing facility.

lie (LYE) *n.* **1** a deliberate falsehood, esp. a cowardly one: *His entire life seemed a lie; Facts* **give** or **put the lie to** (= show to be untrue) *his claims; a barefaced, brazen, downright, monstrous, outright, whopping lie; a white lie; a web of lies.* **2** the way in which something lies; lay: *the lie of the land.* —*v.* **1 lies, lied, ly.ing** utter a lie: *He's lying! Don't lie to me.* **2 lies, lay, lain, ly.ing** of a person or heavy body, place oneself or be in a horizontal position, as when tired: *Bathers lie on the beach; Let me lie down for a while; He lay on the floor; to* **take** *something* **lying down** (= to be meek or submissive); *He was fired for* **lying down on the job** (= for being too lazy). **3** stay or exist, as specified: *Who lies buried here? Mexico lies (to the) south of the U.S.; Fields lie fallow; Her future lies in medicine, not law; There's someone* **lying in wait for you** (= waiting to surprise you) *around the corner.*

lied (LEED) *n., pl.* **lied.er** a German song of the Romantic era.

lie detector *n.* a device for measuring changes in blood pressure, pulse, breathing, etc. as reflecting the mind of a subject under questioning.

lief (LEEF) *adv. Archaic.* **would** (or **had**)

as lief would (or had) as willingly (do something).
liege (LEEJ) *adj.* **1** of a feudal lord, having a right to homage and loyal service: *his liege lord, sovereign.* **2** of a vassal, obliged to give homage and loyal service. —*n.* lord: *My liege!* —**liege.man** (-mun) *n.* **-men** vassal.
lien (LEEN, LEE.un) *n.* [legal use] a claim on property because of a debt incurred on it, as when a contractor is not paid for work done on a house: *a mechanic's lien; to place a lien on or against a property; to have a lien discharged.*
lieu (LOO) *n.* **in lieu of** instead of: *bonus payments in lieu of salary increases.*
lieu.ten.ant (loo.TEN.unt, *Cdn.* lef-) *n.* an officer who acts in place of a higher one; also, a corresponding rank just below captain: *first, flight, second lieutenants; a lieutenant colonel, commander, general.* —**lieu.ten.an.cy** *n.* **-cies.**
lieutenant governor *n.* **1** (loo.TEN.unt-) a public official next in rank to the governor, as in the U.S. **2** (lef.TEN.unt-) the representative of the Crown in a Canadian province.
life *n.* **lives 1** the state of being alive or active: *Is there life after death? He ran for dear life; She gave, laid down, risked, sacrificed her life to save her child; to claim, ruin, restore, snuff out, take a life; to breathe new life into a dying project; The missing child stood there **as big** or **large as life** (= in person); a story that is **true to life** (= as in reality); a picture painted **from** (*real*) *life* (= based on a living subject); the facts of life (about sex and reproduction).* **2** one that lives, esp. a person: *Two lives were lost in the fire; No animal or plant life is found on the moon; marine life; Does a computer virus qualify as a **life form**? a life form that is an intermediate step between viruses and bacteria.* **3** a period of existence: *the three-year life of a car lease; the shelf life of fresh bread; The murderer got life (= a sentence of life in prison).* **4** a way or kind of living: *He led a dog's life; a busy, dull, hectic, happy, hard, miserable, nomadic, peaceful, solitary, stormy life; adult, city, civilian, love, married, sex, social life; the quality of your working life.* **5** biography: *Levy's life of Napoleon.* **6** liveliness or spirit; also, its source: *Let's put some life into the singing; Carlos was the life of the party.* —**for life** as long as one lives: *president for life.* —**for the life of me** or **her** or **him** [used in negative statements] however hard I try: *I can't figure it out for the life of me.* —**of one's life** the most important: *He's facing the fight of his life.*
life.belt *n.* a beltlike life preserver.
life.blood *n.* something life-giving, as blood to the body.
life.boat *n.* a boat built for rescue work or one carried on a ship for use if the ship is to be abandoned.
life.buoy *n.* a ring-shaped float thrown to drowning people.
life-care *adj.* elder-care: *a life-care center, community, facility.*
life cycle *n.* life history: *the life cycle of a butterfly (from egg to death).*
life expectancy *n.* the expected duration of a person's life under specific conditions: *In the mid-1980s, the life expectancy of North American women was 80 years and of men 72 years.*
life.guard *n.* a person trained in life-saving, esp. in water.
life insurance *n.* insurance to pay a sum of money to one's heirs in case of death: *to take out life insurance on your spouse.*
life jacket *n.* a life preserver made like a sleeveless jacket.
life.less (LIFE.lis) *adj.* having no life: *Unlike plants and animals, minerals are lifeless; a lifeless body; a quite lifeless performance (without energy or vigor).*
life.like *adj.* exactly like the subject in real life: *a lifelike statue.*
life.line *n.* **1** a rope or line thrown to save a person in water. **2** the only means or route for sending help to one in distress.
life.long *adj.* involving a lifetime: *lifelong enmity, friends, habits, health, immunity, love; a lifelong ambition, bachelor, commitment, dream, friendship, interest, struggle, student, sufferer.*
life net *n.* a large sheet or net of canvas held on the ground for people from a burning building to jump into.
life preserver *n.* a device in the shape of a belt, jacket, or ring, usu. filled with air or cork, to keep a person afloat.
lif.er (LYE.fur) *n. Informal.* **1** one sentenced to life imprisonment. **2** a career member of the military.
life raft *n.* an inflatable boat or raft for use in case of a shipwreck or an airplane crash at sea.
life.sav.er (LIFE.say.vur) *n.* **1** one trained in lifesaving. **2** *Informal.* a person or thing helpful to someone in distress.
life.sav.ing (LIFE.say.ving) *adj.* designed or used for the saving of

lives: *a lifesaving apparatus, drug.*

life science *n.* a science dealing with life and living things, as biology, biochemistry, medicine, or sociology.

life-size or **life-sized** *adj.* of a painting, statue, etc., of the same size as the subject represented.

life span *n.* an organism's average length of life: *The maximum life span of a turtle is 123 years.*

life.style *n.* a way of life characteristic of a person or group: *Is the Canadian lifestyle less hectic than the American? the lifestyles of the eighties; affluent, criminal, grandiose, laid-back, luxurious, ritzy, traditional lifestyles;* **Lifestyle advertising** *shows people having a good time, as in beer commercials.*

life-support system *n.* a system designed to provide oxygen, food, water, and such essentials of life to people who are critically ill, those in space, under water, etc.

life.time *n.* the entire life of a person or thing: *It will last a lifetime; the chance of a lifetime* (= a rare chance); *a lifetime occupation (that lasts a lifetime).*

life vest same as LIFE JACKET.

life.work *n.* the main work of one's life.

lift *v.* **1** raise or rise to a higher level or position: *He can lift his own weight; a small car with a trunk door that lifts back; a pleasure trip to* **lift your spirits** (= to cheer you up); *He refused to* **lift a finger** (= do anything) *to help us.* **2** remove or withdraw: *to lift a ban, blockade, embargo; The fog will lift at dawn; when the rain lifts* (= stops for a time). **3** *Informal.* steal: *He was caught lifting things from shops; a passage lifted from a copyrighted work.* —*n.* **1** an act of lifting or its result or extent: *An airfoil creates a lift in reaction to gravity; The victory gave his spirits quite a lift; A lift of 100 kg is beyond me; the haughty lift of her chin; Let's give him a lift* (= ride) *home.* **2** anything that lifts or elevates, as a "chair lift" or "ski lift," an elevator, or a promotion.

lift.off *n.* the vertical blastoff of a space vehicle or missile.

lift truck same as FORKLIFT TRUCK.

lig.a.ment (LIG.uh.munt) *n.* a strong fibrous band of tissue fastening bones together or holding organs in place.

li.ga.tion (lye.GAY.shun) *n.* a tying: *tubal ligation to prevent pregnancy.*

lig.a.ture (LIG.uh.chur) *n.* a binding, something to tie with, as a thread used by a surgeon to tie off a blood vessel, or something tied together, as the letters *ffl* and *ae* combined into single characters.

light (LITE) *n.* **1** that by which we see, including ultraviolet and infrared radiation: *the light of the sun; a bright, dull, faint, harsh, soft, strong light; to read by the light of a lamp; Facts* **come to light** (= become known); *to* **see the light** (= understand the truth). **2** a source or supply of light, as the sun, a lamp, a match or cigarette lighter, a lighthouse or traffic signal, a window, or a famous person or "luminary": *to dim, extinguish, shine, switch on, turn down, turn off, turn on, turn up a light* (= lamp); *backup, dome, parking lights* (on an automobile); *a pilot light* (of a clothes dryer or furnace); *a traffic light* (= signal); *to cross against, go through, stop at a red (traffic) light; Lights* (= lamps) *flicker, are off, on, out; Florence Nightingale was a guiding light* (= source of inspiration) *for nurses; the northern and southern* **lights** (= auroras). **3** the quality or condition of being lit or illumined: *the contrasts of light and shade in a picture; the harsh light of reality; the light* (= gleam) *in her eyes.* **4 lights** *n.pl.* the lungs of sheep, pigs, etc. used as food. —**in (the) light of** considering. —**see the light of day** come to be or be made public. —**shed** or **throw light on a subject** make clear or clarify a subject.

—*adj.* **1** bright or pale in color: *a light complexion; as light as dawn; a light hallway.* **2** not heavy: *light as a feather; a light jacket, punishment, snowfall;* **Light industries** *produce consumer goods;* **adv.**: *Let's travel light (without too much baggage).* **3** having qualities suggesting little weight; delicate, nimble, cheerful, etc.: *a light body frame; light music; light (not heavy) sleep; light spirits; a light step; a light beer or wine (with less alcohol); light opera* (= operetta). **4** lacking due weight or seriousness: *light of purpose; a bit* **light in the head** (= foolish or crazy; also, dizzy); *Don't* **make light of** (= consider as not serious) *his misbehavior.*

—*v.* **lights,** *pt. & pp.* **light.ed** or **lit, light.ing 1** cause to give light: *Let's light a candle; streets lit by electricity; Six o'clock is lighting-up time; She lighted up* (= lit a cigarette); *a face lit by joy; Her face lit up with pleasure;* **adj.**: *a lighted candle, match, sign.* **2** come down from an animal's back, from flight, etc.: *A bird lights on a tree; Her eyes lighted on* (= found) *a face in the crowd.* —**light into** *Informal.* attack or scold. —**light out** [*pt. & pp.* **lit out**]

Informal. leave in a hurry *for* a place.

light bulb *n.* an incandescent lamp.

light.en (LYE.tun) *v.* make or become lighter or more cheerful: *The confession lightened her heart.*

light.er *n.* 1 a person or thing that lights: *a cigarette lighter.* 2 a boat or barge for carrying cargo between ships and shore.

light.er.age (LYE.tuh.rij) *n.* a fee for using a cargo lighter.

light.face *n.* light printing type, not boldface; **light.faced** *adj.*

light-fingered *adj.* having light fingers; also, thievish.

light-footed *adj.* stepping gracefully.

light-headed *adj.* silly or frivolous; also, dizzy.

light-hearted *adj.* without cares and worries; happy and gay; **light-heartedly** *adv.*

light.house *n.* **-hous.es** a tower with a flashing light at the top to warn or guide ships.

light.ing *n.* 1 the arrangement of lights, as in a room. 2 the act of supplying or kindling a light.

light.ly *adv.* 1 with little or less-than-usual weight, amount, force, etc.: *Snow fell lightly outside; We dress lightly in hot weather.* 2 delicately, nimbly, cheerfully, etc.: *He took the bad news lightly; She stepped aside lightly.* 3 without due weight or seriousness: *a matter too serious to be treated lightly; He speaks lightly of his elders.*

light meter *n.* a light-measuring instrument; exposure meter.

light.ning *n.* a flash of light in the sky caused by electrical discharges from clouds: *Thunder and lightning struck the town; forked, heat, sheet lightning; a bolt, flash, stroke of lightning; The enemy attacked with lightning speed;* **lightning bug** (= firefly); *a* **lightning raid** *(that is quick as lightning); a* **lightning rod** *(fixed to a roof for grounding electricity).*

light pen (or **pencil**) *n.* a pen-shaped photoelectric device for using on a cathode-ray-tube screen to activate a computer to change or modify images, as in editing a text.

lights *n.pl.* the lungs of sheep, pigs, etc. used as food.

light.ship *n.* a ship designed and built for use as a floating lighthouse.

light show *n.* a kaleidoscopic display of lights and colors accompanied by rock music.

light.some *adj.* light and elegant; light-hearted; nimble: *a lightsome heart; lightsome steps.*

light.weight *n.* a boxer weighing between 126 and 135 lbs. (57 and 61 kg for Olympics). —*adj.* 1 light in weight: *lightweight cloth, construction, metals.* 2 not serious or important: *a lightweight approach.*

light-year *n.* a unit of astronomical distance equal to the distance that light travels in one year, approximately 9.5 trillion km (6 trillion miles).

lig.ne.ous (LIG.nee.us) *adj.* woody or hard: *a ligneous tumor.*

lig.ni.fy (LIG.nuh.fye) *v.* **-fies, -fied, -fy.ing** make into or become like wood by deposits of a celluloselike substance called **lignin.**

lig.nite *n.* a low-quality, brownish-black coal with a woody texture; also called "brown coal."

lik.a.ble (LYE.kuh.bul) *adj.* easy to like: *a likable character, fellow, guy, personality.* —**lik.a.ble.ness** *n.*

like *prep.* [indicating similarity]: *She swims like a fish; She is like her brother; I don't feel like (taking) a walk; It looks like (it is going to) rain; citrus fruits like (Informal for such as) oranges and lemons; It's just like (= characteristic) her to be generous.* —*adj.* similar: *as like as two peas; Like (magnetic) poles repel; a like amount.* —**like crazy, like the devil, like hell** or **like mad** furiously: *It works like crazy when you turn it on.* —**comb.form.** similar to or characteristic of a person or thing: *bell-like, catlike, childlike, milklike.* —*adv. Informal.* probably: *Like enough it will rain.* —*conj.* 1 *Informal.* as: *The candy tastes good like it should; It looks like (= as if) it's going to rain.* 2 *Slang* [used expletively]: *He's really, like, hyper, you know.* —*n.* 1 a similar person or thing: *When shall we see her like again? He prefers boas, chimps,* **and the like** *to humans; The community had no place for* **the likes** *of him.* 2 what one likes: *I have my own* **likes and dislikes** *(= preferences and aversions).* —*v.* **likes, liked, lik.ing** 1 feel well toward a person or thing: *He likes company; I like candy, but not now.* 2 wish to have something: *She'd like a drink; As you like; I wouldn't like you to get wet; I like it as it is.*

like.a.ble (LYE.kuh.bul) same as LIKABLE.

like.li.hood (LIKE.lee.hood, short "oo") *n.* probability: *the likelihood of raining; In all likelihood it'll rain tonight; There's every likelihood that it'll rain.*

like.ly (LIKE.lee) *adj.* **-li.er, -li.est** probable: *There's a likely chance of rain tonight; It's likely to* or *likely that it will*

like-minded / limpid

rain; *a likely night for rain;* ***adv.***: *It'll most* or *very likely rain tonight.*

like-minded *adj.* of the same way of thinking: *like-minded people.*

lik.en (LYE.kun) *v.* consider one as similar *to* another; compare.

like.ness *n.* similarity or resemblance: *She bears no likeness to her mother; This statue is a good likeness* (= representation) *of her.*

like.wise *adv.* **1** in the same way as another. **2** moreover; besides.

liking (LYE.king) *n.* what one likes or prefers: *Everything was not to her liking; She has developed a liking for fish; She has* or *shows a special liking for seafood; Everyone has taken a liking for her.*

li.lac (LYE.luc, -lac) *n.* **1** a shrub bearing clustered blossoms that are usu. light purple; ***adj.***: *lilac blossoms; a lilac bush.* **2** light purple or mauve color; ***adj.***: *a lilac color, dress, gown, robe.*

Lil.li.pu.tian (lil.i.PEW.shun) *adj.* **1** small or tiny like an inhabitant of **Lilliput** in Swift's *Gulliver's Travels.* **2** small or narrow-minded.

lilt *n.* a lively rhythm: *an Irish lilt; She answered with a delighted lilt.* —*v.* play, sing, or move in a lilt; ***adj.***: *a lilting quality; in a lilting voice.*

lil.y (LIL.ee) *n.* **lil.ies** a plant with stemless leaves growing from a bulb and flowers with six parts, typically white, as in the **lily of the valley.**

lily-livered *adj.* cowardly.

lily pad *n.* a floating leaf of the water lily.

lily-white *adj.* **1** pure white. **2** innocent: *not so lily-white as she claims.* **3** of or for white people only: *a lily-white community, neighborhood, organization.*

li.ma bean (LYE.muh-) *n.* a common tropical bean that bears broad pods.

limb (LIM) *n.* **1** a leg, arm, or wing. **2** something similar, as the branch of a tree. —**out on a limb** *Informal.* in a dangerous or precarious position.

lim.ber *adj.* supple or nimble: *a lean and limber acrobat.* —*v.* make limber: *some exercises to help you **limber up.***

lim.bo *n.* **-bos 1** the state of being forgotten or unwanted: *The book is in limbo and may never get published.* **2 Limbo** in Christian theologies, a region of confinement for those barred from Heaven because of not being baptized.

Lim.bur.ger (LIM.bur.gur) *n.* a semisoft ripened cheese with a strong odor.

lime *n.* **1** a citrus fruit resembling a lemon but greener, smaller, and more acid. **2** a white calcium compound used in making mortar and cement.

—*v.* **limes, limed, lim.ing** treat or cover with lime: *agricultural liming materials.*

lime.ade (lye.MADE) *n.* a sweet beverage made with lime juice.

lime.light *n.* a spotlight, formerly produced by incandescent lime: *in the limelight of publicity.*

lim.er.ick (LIM.uh.rick) *n.* a rhymed five-line humorous verse, as Edward Lear's: *There was an Old Man with a beard, / Who said, 'Tis just as I feared! / Two owls and a hen, / Four larks and a wren, / Have all built their nests in my beard!*

lime.stone *n.* rock containing calcium that is the chief source of lime.

lim.it *n.* **1** a point in time or space that forms a boundary: *to lower the age limit for voting; to break* or *exceed the speed limit on a highway; the legal limit; to impose, place, put, raise, reach, set a limit; to stretch resources to the limit; As far as our growth is concerned,* **the sky is the limit** (= there is no limit); *Pat is* **the limit** (*Informal* for as much as one can put up with)! **2 limits** *pl.* boundaries: *outside the city limits; within the limits of decency; Trust him, but* **within limits** (= moderately); *The boys' change room is* **off limits** *to* (= not to be entered by) *girls.* —*v.* set a limit to something: *Please limit your call, limit yourself to five minutes; The time is limited by.*
—**lim.i.ta.tion** (-uh.TAY.shun) *n.*

limited *adj. & comb.form.* having a limit or limits; restricted: *a limited (not all-out) war; We are severely limited in spending; strictly limited to $500; a limited-access highway; a time-limited test; a limited-stop bus or train service; a* **limited company** (with liability limited to its assets); *a* **limited edition** *of a book with a small print run.*

limn (LIM) *v.* **limns, limned, limn.ing** (LIM.ing, -ning) paint or draw; hence, portray; describe; **lim.ner** (LIM.ur, LIM.nur) *n.*

lim.o (LIM.oh) *n.* **-os** [short form] limousine.

lim.ou.sine (LIM.uh.zeen) *n.* a chauffeured luxury automobile.

limp *n.* a lameness or a halting way of walking. —*v.* walk or proceed with or as if with a limp. —*adj.* droopy or weak: *a limp argument, body, handshake, leaf; a body limp with exhaustion.*

limp.et (LIMP.it) *n.* a mollusk that clings to rocks, moving about at high tide.

lim.pid *adj.* softly clear or transparent: *a limpid stream; limpid eyes; a limpid* *prose style.* —**lim.pid.ly** *adv.*

lim.y (LYE.mee) *adj.* **lim.i.er, -i.est** 1 of or containing lime: *a limy deposit.* 2 covered with birdlime. 3 sticky.

lin.age (LYE.nij) *n.* 1 the number of lines of print or writing. 2 a rate or charge per line.

linch.pin *n.* 1 a pin that keeps a wheel in place on its axle. 2 a key person or element: *the linchpin of an argument, business, strategy, system.*

lin.den (LIN.dun) *n.* a soft-wooded shade tree with heart-shaped leaves, bearing white or yellow clusters of flowers full of nectar.

line *n.* 1 a piece of thread or wire considered in its length but not width or thickness; hence, anything resembling it: *a clothes line for drying laundry; an angler's hook and line; a plumb line; the lines on an aging face; a stanza of four lines (of verse); Please form a line* (= queue); *Drop me a line* (= brief letter) *when you get there; The starlet fluffed* or *forgot her* **lines** (= words to speak) *in the middle of the play; What's your bottom line, prestige or profit?* 2 a long fine mark: *lines drawn on paper; Sign on the dotted line; broken, curved, heavy, straight, thin, vertical, wavy lines.* 3 something thought of as forming a line: *The (phone) line is busy; It's a party line; communication lines between two cities; the hot line between the superpowers; the gas line leading from tank to engine; power lines (carrying electricity); a supply line; a county, foul, goal, service, snow, state, tree line; a faulty line of reasoning; a line (= row) of trees along an avenue; the line (= circle) of the equator; a noble line (= family) of kings; to follow the* **line of least resistance** (= go the easy way); *an artillery's* **line of fire**; *the front* **line of battle**; *Battle* **lines** *are drawn and the fight is about to start.* 4 something organized or laid down, as a plan, policy, business, occupation, etc.: *All party members have to fall in line with the rest; We take a firm, hard line on women's issues; a statement in line with our policies; a policeman killed* **in the line of duty** (= while doing his duty); *What line* (= business) *are you in? We work on an assembly line; I'm in line* (= It's my turn) *for a raise; to* **hold the line on** *wage increases* (= keep wages from rising); *Stamp collecting is not (in)* **my line** (= one of my interests); *A store cannot carry every* **line of goods** (= type of merchandise); *There was no truth in the* **official line** (= statement) *handed out to the press.* —**along the lines** in the way specified: *He said something along the lines of changing our approach; along the lines of Freud* (= as Freud would have thought); *along Freudian lines; Family members tend to think along the same lines.* —**bring into line** cause to agree or conform. —**down the line** from the top to the bottom in an ordered series: *They try to set a good example all* **down the line** *from the principal to the janitor.* —**draw the** or **a line** set a limit: *We have to draw a line somewhere.* —**on line** connected for operation: *to be, come, get, go, put on line.* —**on the line** *Informal.* in a position of high risk: *Your job is on the line.* —**out of line** against the normal way of being or doing: *Your price is out of line; It's way out of line* (= not compatible) *with what I can afford; He got out of line* (= became rude) *and started swearing.* —**toe the line** conform. —*v.* **lines, lined, lin.ing** 1 mark with lines; *adj.*: **lined** *writing paper; a forehead lined with age.* 2 arrange or form a line: *People lined the route of the parade; to line up speakers for a function; Athletes* **line up** *for a race; We have to* **line up behind** (= support) *our leader.* 3 put or serve as a lining in something: *a coat lined with fur; Bookshelves line the library walls; People in power sometimes try to* **line their pockets** (= make money illicitly).

lin.e.age (LIN.ee.ij) *n.* 1 the line of descent from an ancestor. 2 such descendants.

lin.e.al (LIN.ee.ul) *adj.* 1 in a direct line of descent, as from father to son: *a lineal descendant, heir.* 2 hereditary: *a lineal feud, right.*

lin.e.a.ment (LIN.ee.uh.munt) *n.* usu. **lineaments**, *pl.* distinctive features of a face.

lin.e.ar (LIN.ee.ur) *adj.* 1 having to do with lines: *a linear, not pictorial form of writing; a linear design, dimension, series; a linear equation (whose graph is a straight line).* 2 having to do with length: *A meter is a unit of linear measure; an air cushion vehicle propelled by the magnetic waves of a* **linear motor** *(that does not rotate).* 3 sequential in structure: *a linear learning pattern, procedure, technique.*

line.back.er (LINE.back.ur) *n.* a football player positioned behind the defensive line.

line drive *n.* a baseball hit in almost a straight line close to the ground.

line.man (LINE.mun) *n.* **-men** 1 one

linen / lion

who works on a telegraph, telephone, electric, or railroad line. 2 a football player positioned on the line of scrimmage.

lin.en (LIN.un) *n.* 1 a tough yarn or cloth woven of fibers of flax. 2 sheets, tablecloths, napkins, etc. made of linen: *fine linen; fresh linen; to change the linen* (= bed sheets).

line of credit *n.* the maximum amount that a customer is allowed to borrow from a bank.

line of scrimmage *n.* in football, an imaginary line parallel to the goal lines at the most forward point of the ball when it is on the ground.

line printer *n.* a computer printer that handles data line by line, not character by character, as in a serial printer.

lin.er (LYE.nur) *n.* 1 an airplane or ship belonging to a transportation line. 2 material used as lining.

line score *n.* in baseball, a summary of the hits, runs, and errors made by each team.

lines.man (LINES.mun) *n.* **-men** 1 a sports official who watches the lines during play to assist the referee or umpire, as in football and tennis. 2 a lineman.

line.up *n.* an arrangement or listing of persons or things, as of suspects for identification or players taking part in a game: *a police lineup (of suspects); the fall lineup of TV shows; the long gasoline lineups during the oil embargo.*

ling *n.* a North American marine food fish of the cod family.

-ling *n. suffix.* small or dependent: *cageling, hireling, princeling, sapling, underling.*

lin.ger (LING.gur) *v.* take time, as if reluctant to leave: *Some people linger at the door with a long good-bye; He lingers over his coffee; Doubts lingered in my mind;* **adja.:** *a lonely* **lingering** *death; lingering anxieties, doubts, effects, fears, feelings, odors, suspicions; a longing lingering look.*

lin.ge.rie (lan.zhuh.REE, lahn.zhuh.RAY) *n.* women's underclothing and night clothes.

lin.go (LING.go) *n.* **-goes** *Informal* [sometimes derogatory] 1 speech that sounds foreign or is unintelligible to one. 2 jargon: *to speak the lingo of one's profession.*

lin.gua fran.ca (LING.gwuh.FRANK.uh) *n.* a common language for easy communication between speakers of different languages, as a hybrid mixture or pidgin.

lin.gual (LING.gwul) *adj.* having to do with the tongue. —*n.* a lingual sound, as "l" or "d."

lin.guist (LING.gwist) *n.* 1 a specialist in linguistics. 2 one who speaks many languages; polyglot.

lin.guis.tics (ling.GWIS.tics) *n.pl.* [takes sing. v.] the science of language, including the study of pronunciation, syntax, meaning, derivation, etc. —**lin.guis.tic** *adj.;* **lin.guis.ti.cal.ly** *adv.*

lin.i.ment (LIN.uh.munt) *n.* a soothing medication for rubbing on the skin.

lin.ing (LYE.ning) *n.* a covering material of a surface: *the inner lining of a coat; worn brake linings; "Every cloud has a silver lining"* (= Every misfortune has a bright side).

link *n.* 1 a connection: *We maintain close links with people back home; no links to the underworld; The present forms a link with the past and the future; cuff links for a shirt sleeve.* 2 a connected part: *the links of a chain; sausage links.* 3 **links** *pl.* a golf course. —*v.* join or connect: *persons linked with a crime; Spacecrafts link up with each other.*

link.age (LINK.ij) *n.* a linking or a system of links.

linking verb *n.* a verb such as "be" or "seem" (as in "Books are good" and "She seems OK") that links subject and predicate.

link-up *n.* a linking together or rendezvous: *a link-up of space vehicles, military forces.*

lin.net (LIN.it) *n.* a small Old World finch, usu. brown, with dark streaks on its back.

li.no.le.um (li.NOH.lee.um) *n.* a hard, canvas-backed floor covering made from linseed oil.

lin.seed *n.* flaxseed, which yields an oil (**linseed oil**) used in paints, varnishes, and in making linoleum.

lin.sey-wool.sey (LIN.zee.WOOL.zee) *n.* a coarse cloth of linen and wool.

lint *n.* 1 a soft fleecy material scraped from linen, formerly used as a dressing for wounds. 2 bits of fluff or fuzz of any material. —**lint.y** *adj.*

lin.tel (LIN.tul) *n.* the horizontal beam or bar over a window or door.

lin.y (LYE.nee) *adj.* 1 resembling a line. 2 marked with or full of lines.

li.on (LYE.un) *n.* 1 a large, strong animal of the cat family whose male has a distinctive flowing mane: *The lion is the king of the beasts; the cub of a lion; a pride* (= group) *of lions.* 2 a person distinguished by bravery, strength, or

fame: *a social lion.* —**li.on.ess** (-uh.nis) *fem.*
lion-hearted *adj.* very brave or courageous.
li.on.ize (LYE.uh.nize) *v.* **-iz.es, -ized, -iz.ing** treat a person as a hero or celebrity. —**li.on.i.za.tion** (-nuh.ZAY.shun, -nye-) *n.*
lion's share *n.* the biggest portion.
lip *n.* 1 either of two fleshy folds forming the mouth: *the upper and lower lips; to part, pucker, purse one's lips; chapped lips; to lick* or *smack one's lips with delight; His name is* **on everyone's lips** (= He is famous); *My* **lips are sealed** (= I can't reveal it); *A* **lip consonant** *such as "b," "m," or "p" is formed with the lips.* 2 a liplike part or a lip-shaped edge of an opening: *the lip of a bell, crater, pitcher.* 3 *Informal.* insolent talk: *Don't give me any of your lip.*
lipped *adj. & comb.form.* having a lip or as specified: *a lipped pitcher; full-lipped and sexy; loose-lipped killers; mean-lipped; a thin-lipped mouth; tight-lipped silence; two-lipped* (= two-petaled) *blossoms.*
lip.py *adj.* **lip.pi.er, lip.pi.est** *Informal.* insolent. —**lip.pi.ness** *n.*
lip.read.ing (LIP.reed.ing) *n.* understanding what someone is saying by noting lip movements, as done by the deaf.
lip service *n.* service only by words: *to give* or *pay lip service to a cause.*
lip.stick *n.* a small stick of cosmetic paste for coloring the lips.
lip-sync or **lip-synch** (LIP.sink) *v.* **-synchs, -synched, -synch.ing** synchronize lip movements with previously recorded sound, or speech sounds with lip movements, as in dubbing a motion picture in a different language. —*n.* a lip-synching.
liq.ue.fy (LIK.wuh.fye) *v.* **-fies, -fied, -fy.ing** change to a liquid state. —**liq.ue.fac.tion** (-FAC.shun) *n.*
li.queur (li.CUR) *n.* a sweetened and flavored syrupy alcoholic liquor.
liq.uid (LIK.wid) *n.* a substance that flows readily, as water: *a clear liquid.* —*adja.* 1 being a liquid: *liquid bleach, oxygen, soap; a liquid lunch of beverages;* **liquid air** (at about –190°C). 2 flowing like a liquid: *liquid fire from a flame thrower; liquid food; a bird's liquid notes; liquid verse.* 3 clear or bright: *liquid blue; her liquid eyes; the liquid sky.* —**liq.uid.i.ty** (luh.QUID.i.tee) *n.*
liquid assets *n.pl.* cash on hand and bank deposits, bills receivable, etc. that can be quickly converted to cash.
liquid crystal *n.* an organic substance in semisolid state with crystalline optical properties: *a digital watch with a* **liquid crystal display** (LCD).
liquid measure *n.* a system of measurement of liquid volume using units such as the quart and the liter.
liq.ui.date (LIK.wuh.date) *v.* **-dates, -dat.ed, -dat.ing** 1 clear off a debt, accounts, mortgages, etc. by paying what is owed. 2 settle the affairs of a bankrupt business by dividing up its assets among the creditors. 3 get rid of someone, often by violent means: *rivals liquidated by a dictator.* —**liq.ui.da.tion** (-DAY.shun) *n.* —**liq.ui.da.tor** (-day.tur) *n.*
liq.uor (LIK.ur) *n.* a distilled alcoholic drink such as whiskey or gin: *hard liquor; strong liquor;* **adja.**: *liquor laws, licenses, stores.*
li.ra (LEER.uh) *n., pl.* **li.re** (-ray) or **li.ras** the basic money unit of Italy equal to 100 centesimos.
lisle (LILE) *n.* a fine, tightly twisted thread, originally from Lille, France, used to make knitted garments and hosiery.
lisp *v.* speak like a child or imperfectly, esp. to substitute "th" for "s" and "z," as in "kithing cuthinth" (kissing cousins). —*n.* a lisping or lisping sound.
lis.some or **lis.som** (LIS.um) *adj.* lithe or nimble in a delicate, esp. feminine way.
list *n.* 1 a series of names, words, figures, etc.: *to compile, draw up, make up a list; a patient on the critical list; laundry, mailing, shopping lists; I am at the top of the waiting list; A new computer is high on her list of priorities.* 2 a tilt to one side, as of a leaking ship. —**enter the lists** enter a struggle or contest. —*v.* 1 set forth in a list or series: *Not all numbers are listed in the phone book;* **n.**: *the alphabetical* **listing** (= entry) *of words in the dictionary.* 2 to tip or tilt. 3 [old use] to please: *"The wind bloweth where it listeth."*
lis.ten (LIS.un) *v.* try to hear, understand, or follow: *to listen to advice, to a speech, to the radio, to one's teachers; You may* **listen in to** *what is being broadcast, but you had better not* **listen in on** *a private conversation.* —**lis.ten.er** *n.*
list.less (LIST.lis) *adj.* having no energy or enthusiasm; **list.less.ly** *adv.;* **list.less.ness** *n.*
list price *n.* the price of a product as posted or given in a catalog, the usual price at which it is sold.
lit *a pt. & pp.* of LIGHT.
lit.a.ny (LIT.un.ee) *n.* **-nies** a form of

prayer consisting of a series of supplications.

li.tchi (LEE.chee) *n.* an evergreen Chinese tree bearing clusters of bright-red raisinlike fruits, called **litchi nuts** when dried.

lite *adj.* [popular spelling] light: *lite beer, ice cream, mayonnaise, whiskey.*

li.ter (LEE.tur) *n.* a metric unit of capacity equal to 1,000 cc. Also **li.tre** *Cdn.*

lit.er.a.cy (LIT.uh.ruh.see) *n.* **1** ability to read and write: *adult literacy; functional literacy; to enhance, promote literacy*; **adja.**: *a literacy campaign, level, program, test; literacy skills.* **2** basic competence in a specified subject: *business, computer, consumer, scientific literacy.*

lit.er.al (LIT.ur.ul) *adj.* **1** following the exact words: *a literal interpretation, translation; the literal* (= not figurative) *meaning.* **2** matter of-fact, not exaggerated: *a literal account, version; the literal truth.* —**lit.er.al.ly** *adv.*

lit.er.al.ism (LIT.uh.rul.iz.um) *n.* **1** adherence to the literal meaning of a text. **2** realism in artistic representation. —**lit.er.al.ist** *n.*

lit.er.ar.y (LIT.uh.rair.ee) *adj.* having to do with literature: *a literary journal, style, treatise; the literary profession; a **literary agent*** (= authors' representative).

lit.er.ate (LIT.ur.it) *n.* **1** one who can read and write: *one of the few literates among them*; *adj.*: *a barely literate society.* **2** one that is well-read or learned; *adj.*: *a passionately literate artist; a literate public; her witty and literate style; a very literate periodical.*

lit.e.ra.ti (lit.uh.RAH.tee) *n.pl.* the educated class.

lit.er.a.ture (LIT.ur.uh.chur) *n.* **1** writings of a period, country, or language having lasting appeal because of subject, style, etc.: *American literature; French literature; medieval literature.* **2** writings on a particular subject: *the literature on classical music; There is a considerable body of literature on UFOs; travel literature.* **3** any printed material such as pamphlets and notices: *the literature you call junk mail; pulp* (= cheap) *literature.*

lithe (LITHE, "TH" as in "thin") *adj.*
lith.er, lith.est having a supple, slender, or nimble grace; **lithe.ly** *adv.*; **lithe.ness** *n.*

lithe.some (LITHE.sum, "TH" as in "the") *adj.* having graceful vigor; lissome: *a lithesome gymnast.*

lith.i.um (LITH.ee.um, "TH" as in "thin") *n.* a soft, silver-white chemical element, the lightest of metals.

lith.o.graph (LITH.uh.graf, "TH" as in "thin") *n. & v.* (make) a print or copy by lithography.

li.thog.ra.phy (li.THOG.ruh.fee) *n.* a printing process using a flat plate so treated that only the portions to be printed are ink-receptive;
li.thog.ra.pher *n.* —**lith.o.graph.ic** (lith.uh.GRAF.ic) *adj.*;
lith.o.graph.i.cal.ly *adv.*

li.thol.o.gy (li.THOL.uh.jee) *n.* the study of rocks.

lith.o.sphere (LITH.us.feer) *n.* the earth's solid part, excluding the hydrosphere.

lith.o.trip.sy (LITH.uh.trip.see) *n.* the breaking up of kidney stones or gallstones with ultrasound waves using a device called lithotripter.
—**lith.o.trip.ter** *n.*

Lith.u.a.ni.an (lith.oo.AY.nee.un, "th" as in "thin") *n. & adj.* **1** (a person) of or from **Lithuania**, a N.E. European country. **2** (having to do with) the Baltic language of Lithuania.

lit.i.gant (LIT.uh.gunt) *n.* a party to a lawsuit.

lit.i.gate (LIT.uh.gate) *v.* **-gates, -gat.ed, -gat.ing 1** engage in a lawsuit. **2** contest: *to negotiate rather than litigate; to litigate a case, issue, suit.*
—**lit.i.ga.tion** (-GAY.shun) *n.*

li.ti.gious (li.TIJ.us) *adj.* **1** disputable at law. **2** given to engaging in lawsuits; quarrelsome: *a litigious society; litigious consumers.*

lit.mus *n.* a dye that turns red when put into acid and blue in alkalis, used as a chemical indicator: *blue litmus and red litmus paper; a decisive **litmus test** of their intent to achieve peace.*

li.tre (LEE.tur) *Cdn.* LITER.

lit.ter *n.* **1** scattered rubbish; hence, untidiness or disorder: *Keep litter in a litter bag.* **2** the young borne at one birth by an animal: *a litter of kittens, puppies.* **3** a single-passenger vehicle consisting of a couch, often curtained, borne on the shoulders of four men. **4** a stretcherlike device for transporting a sick or injured person. **5** straw, hay, leaves, etc. forming a bedding for animals or used to absorb animal excrement. **6** a layer formed on a forest floor by decaying leaves.
—*v.* cover or scatter with litter: *Wood shavings littered the shop floor; hallways littered with paper.* —**lit.ter.er** *n.*

lit.ter.bug (LIT.ur.bug) *n.* a person who litters parks, highways, etc. —*v.* **-bugs, -bugged, -bug.ging:** *fined $500 for*

litterbugging.
lit.tle (LIT.ul) *adj. comp.* **lit.tler, less** or **less.er,** *superl.* **lit.tlest** or **least 1** small, esp. in an endearing way: *a little child; the little finger; a dear little man.* **2** not much or long; short: *Please stay a little while.* **3** small-minded or petty: *the little thoughts of little minds.* —*adv. comp.* **less,** *superl.* **least 1** slightly; somewhat: *a little tired; He is little known around here.* **2** not at all: *He thinks little of the prices of things he buys; It matters little to him; mighty little; precious little; She* **made little of** (= ignored) *the incident.* —*n.* a small amount, short time or distance, etc.: *Wait a little; Walk a little; Have a little of this pie; It evaporated* **little by little** (= gradually). —**lit.tlish** *adj.* —**lit.tle.ness** *n.*
little slam *n.* in bridge, the winning of 12 tricks.
little theater *n.* amateur or experimental drama.
lit.to.ral (LIT.uh.rul) *adj.* of or near a seashore: *littoral currents, land rights.*
lit.ur.gy (LIT.ur.jee) *n.* -**gies** ritual for public worship, as in a Christian church; **lit.ur.gist** *n.* —**li.tur.gi.cal** (li.TUR.ji.cul) *adj.*
liv.a.ble (LIV.uh.bul) *adj.* **1** endurable: *a livable climate, environment, existence.* **2** that can be lived in; habitable: *a livable apartment, city, room.* **3** that can be lived with: *a livable community, person, wage.* —**liv.a.ble.ness** or **liv.a.bil.i.ty** (-BIL.i.tee) *n.*
live (LIV) *v.* **lives, lived, liv.ing** have life or continue in life: *You may live long; You may live to (the age of) 100; Many have lived to be 90; Good neighbors live in harmony; They live and let (others) live; Spouses live together (in the same house); The birds live from day to day (with no worries about the future); He's living, not dead; They say we shouldn't live to eat (with eating as the main purpose), but eat to live* (= to survive); *He lives* (= subsists) *on mere bread and water; Most parents live* (= exist) *only for their children; Where do you live* (= reside)? **to live by** (= adhere to) *the rules; Some people* **live beyond their means** (= spend more than they earn); *A hero's memory* **lives on** (= continues to exist); *Some rules are hard to* **live with** (= tolerate). —**live down** cause to be forgotten: *to live down a scandalous past.* —**live from hand to mouth** to make a bare living. —**live it up** *Informal.* spend freely: *He lived it up and went broke.* —**live up to** act in accordance with something: *to live up to an ideal,*
expectations, a promise, one's reputation, a responsibility. —*adj.* (rhyme: five) having life or its qualities such as movement, growth, heat, energy, etc.: *a live cigar, coal, issue, lobster, topic; a live audience* (of actual people); *Don't touch a live wire; a live telecast* (not a recorded one); *This is Tom Jones live* (= reporting live, not from a recording) *at the murder scene.* —*adv.* (rhyme: five) directly, not from tape or film: *It is being broadcast live.*
live.a.ble (LIV.uh.bul) same as LIVABLE.
-lived (LIVED, LIVD) *comb.form.* having life as specified: *long-lived, short-lived; the nine-lived* (-LIVED) *cat.*
live-in (LIV.in) *adj.* **1** having to do with living where one works: *a live-in job, maid.* **2** cohabiting: *a live-in partner, relationship.*
live.li.hood (LIVE.lee.hood) *n.* means of living, esp. money for food, clothing, and shelter.
live.long (LIV.long) *adj.* the whole wearisome length of time: *all the livelong day, night, summer.*
live.ly (LIVE.lee) *adj.* -**li.er,** -**li.est** full of life: *a lively conversation, imagination, time; lively colors.* —*adv.* in a lively manner: *Step lively* (= hurry up). —**live.li.ness** *n.*
liv.en (LYE.vun) *v.* make or become lively: *Let's liven things up a bit.*
liv.er (LIV.ur) *n.* **1** a gland that secretes bile, once considered the seat of emotion. **2** an animal's liver used as food: *braised liver with vegetables.* **3** one who lives as specified: *a clean liver; loose livers.*
liv.er.ied (LIV.uh.reed) *adj.* wearing livery; uniformed, as a chauffeur or other servant.
liver spot *n.* a patchy discoloration of the skin often seen during pregnancy.
liv.er.wort (LIV.ur.wurt) *n.* a liver-shaped, mosslike little plant that grows on rocks, tree trunks, etc. in damp and shady places.
liv.er.wurst (LIV.ur.wurst) *n.* a sausage made of ground liver.
liv.er.y (LIV.uh.ree) *n.* -**er.ies** a characteristic uniform or garb, as formerly issued to servants, esp. retainers in charge of horses. —**liv.er.y.man** (-mun) *n.* -**men** a liveried servant.
lives *pl.* of LIFE.
live.stock (LIVE.stok) *n.* farm animals such as cattle, pigs, sheep, poultry, geese, and rabbits.
live.ware (LIVE.ware) *n. Informal.* computer personnel.
live wire *n.* **1** a wire carrying electric

current. **2** *Informal.* an energetic and enterprising person.

liv.id *adj.* **1** blue-gray; back-and-blue. **2** very pale: *livid with cold, illness, rage.* **3** very angry: *She was livid about or at or over the story; livid with him.*

living *adj.* **1** having life: *a living being; An earthquake hasn't struck here* **in living memory** (= as long as anyone can remember); *a living language, monument; n.:* **the living** (= living people) *and the dead.* **2** having to do with life: *our living conditions, quarters, standards.* —*n.* **1** the way one lives: *a woman of plain living and high thinking; a country with a high standard of living.* **2** livelihood: *He begs for a living; to earn, eke out a living; to make a comfortable, honest living.*

living room *n.* a room for relaxing, entertaining, etc. in a home.

living standard See STANDARD OF LIVING.

living wage *n.* a wage that is sufficient for maintaining a reasonable standard of living.

living will *n.* a written request to be allowed to die rather than be kept alive artificially.

liz.ard (LIZ.urd) *n.* a reptile such as the chameleon and the iguana having four legs and tail and a long body with dry, scaly skin.

lla.ma (LAH.muh) *n.* a smaller and humpless camel of South America, related to the alpaca.

lla.no (LAH.noh) *n.* **-nos** a vast, treeless plain of Spanish America that is rich with grass in the wet season.

lo (LOH) *interj.* look: *Lo and behold!*

load (LODE) *n.* **1** something carried, as in a cart or on an animal's back (as a pack): *to carry, transport a load; to lessen, lighten a load; That's a load* (= burden) *off my mind; The electric utility runs at peak load* (= power) *in extreme hot and cold weather; a social worker's case load; a student carrying a full load (of courses); a teacher's heavy work load; Lu has* **loads** (*Informal* for plenty) *of experience.* **2** a definite quantity, also a load considered as a unit of weight: *three loads of laundry; a busload of students; two truckloads of gravel.* —*v.* **1** put a load on a carrier or into a receptacle: *to load a ship with grain; Grain is loaded into or onto ships; The ships are loaded to (maximum) capacity; A gun or camera is loaded before shooting; Flight 213 is now* **loading** (= taking on passengers) *at Gate 45; Data from storage is loaded* (= transferred) *into the main memory of a computer for processing.* **2** to burden or weight: *a mind* **loaded down** *with* (= suffering from) *anxiety.*

loaded *adj.* **1** carrying a load or charge: *a loaded truck; loaded with gold; Is the gun loaded? Cheaters use* **loaded dice** *that fall as desired; A loaded question, remark, or word has a hidden or allusive meaning.* **2** *Slang.* drunk. **3** equipped with extra features or accessories. —**loaded for bear** *Informal.* ready for a fight.

load.star, load.stone same as LODESTAR, LODESTONE.

loaf (LOHF) *n.* **loaves** a mass of baked bread in a handy shape or other food such as meat or fish molded like bread. —**loaves and fishes** personal gain or profit. —*v.* **1** spend time idly. **2** idle *away time on a job.*

loaf.er (LOH.fur) *n.* **1** idler or vagabond. **2** a step-in leather shoe.

loam (LOME) *n.* a fertile, easy-to-work soil that is a mixture of sand, clay, and silt; **loam.y** *adj.*

loan (LONE) *n.* a lending or something lent, esp. money: *a bank loan; to negotiate, raise, repay or pay off, secure, underwrite a loan; the loan of your car for a few days; an inter-library loan; a loan of $100; a temporary loan (which must be returned); The books are* **on loan** *from Joe;* **adja.:** *a loan default, guarantee; a bank's loan officer.* —*v.* lend: *Will you loan me your car for a few days? I can loan you $10 any time.*

loan.er *n.* something on loan, as a replacement car given for temporary use.

loan shark *n. Informal.* one who lends money at illegal interest rates. —**loan-sharking** *n.*

loan.word *n.* a word recently borrowed from a foreign language: *"Beef," "mutton," "veal," and "pork" were originally loanwords from French, like "pizza" and "spaghetti" in modern times from Italian.*

loath (LOHTH, "TH" as in "thin") *adj.* strongly unwilling *to do something: loath to admit it; loath to risk their lives.*

loathe (LOHTH, "TH" as in "the") *v.* **loathes, loathed, loath.ing** hate with disgust; abhor. —**loathing** *n.: fear and loathing; self-loathing.*

loath.some *adj.* disgusting: *a loathsome aspect, sight, smell.*

loaves (LOHVZ) *pl.* of LOAF.

lob *v.* **lobs, lobbed, lob.bing** in games such as tennis, baseball, and soccer, to hit, throw, or kick a ball in a high arc but without much force. —*n.* such a stroke, throw, or kick. —**lob.ber** *n.*

lob.by (LOB.ee) *n.* **lob.bies 1** a vestibule or entrance hall of a theater, apartment building, etc.: *We met in the hotel lobby.* **2** a group that lobbies: *an education lobby; the anti-gun lobby; the tobacco lobby.* —*v.* **lob.bies, lob.bied, lob.by.ing** attempt to influence the decisions of lawmakers, officials, etc., as by talking to legislators outside the room where they deliberate: *to lobby against free trade; to lobby for cleaning up the Great Lakes.* —**lob.by.ist** *n.*

lobe *n.* a rounded, projecting, usu. fleshy part, as a division of the lung, brain, or liver, the lower ear, etc.: *Maple leaves have three to seven fingerlike lobes.* —**lobed** *adj.* divided into lobes: *a stork's lobed feet; the lobed maple leaf.*

lo.bot.o.my (luh.BOT.uh.mee) *n.* **-mies** a surgical operation on the front lobe of the brain.

lob.ster *n.* a crustacean with two large pincerlike claws and a fanlike tail, relished as a sea food.

lo.cal (LOH.cul) *adj.* having to do with a particular place or body part: *national and local news; a local anesthetic for pulling a tooth; the* **local area network** formed by office computers wired together to share resources and equipment; *a feeder or local-service airline; Regional dialects, customs, etc. lend* **local color** *to writing.* —*n.* a local person or thing, as a bus service, a branch of a library, union, etc.: *I'm one of the locals here; a local (chapter) of a teachers' union; a teachers' local; a union local.* —**lo.cal.ly** *adv.*

lo.cale (loh.CAL) *n.* the setting of a story or scene of an event.

lo.cal.i.ty (loh.CAL.i.tee) *n.* **-ties 1** a neighborhood or region. **2** awareness or recognition of where one is: *a good sense of locality.*

lo.cal.ize (LOH.cul.ize) *v.* **-iz.es, -ized, -iz.ing** limit to a particular area or location: *a legend that is difficult to localize* (= determine its origin); *adj.: a localized disease, outbreak, pain.* —**lo.cal.i.za.tion** (-luh.ZAY.shun, -lye-) *n.*

local option *n.* a local government's legal right: *a municipality's local option to prohibit liquor.*

lo.cate (LOH.cate, loh.CATE) *v.* **-cates, -cat.ed, -cat.ing 1** find out the position or location of a person or thing: *to locate former friends, a hidden treasure, a place on a map.* **2** establish in a place: *a news correspondent located in London; a suitable place to locate one's business.* —**lo.ca.tor** (-tur) *n.*

lo.ca.tion (loh.CAY.shun) *n.* **1** where something is: *a good location for a facto-*
ry; The star was hiding at an undisclosed location. **2** a locating: *a Hollywood movie shot* **on location** *in Spain* (where the action is supposed to take place, not at a studio).

loch (LOK, LOKH) *n.* [Scottish] **1** a lake. **2** a partially landlocked narrow bay, or "sea loch."

loci *pl.* of LOCUS.

lock *n.* **1** something that closes, fastens, or fixes so as to stop movement or action: *combination, deadbolt, safety, time locks; to pick a lock; Keep your valuables* **under lock and key**; *A series of locks* (= watertight chambers) *helps ships move from one water level to another through a canal; He moved out of the house* **lock, stock and barrel** (= leaving nothing). **2** a bunch or tuft: *a lock of cotton, hair, wool.* —*v.* close with or as if with a lock: *Please lock and bolt the door; Cattle lock* (= jam) *horns in a fight; a pension plan with funds* **locked in** (so that money cannot be taken from it for a certain length of time); *A missile* **locks on to** *its target by radar; Employers* **lock out** *strikers* (= close the plant) *to make them agree to their demands; to* **lock up** *a convict in jail; adj.: wrestlers* **locked** *in combat; a couple walking with arms locked* (= joined); *She got locked in a closet; a locked door; It was locked shut.*

lock.er *n.* a storage chest, closet, or compartment that can be locked.

locker room *n.* a room with lockers for athletes to change clothes. —**locker-room** *adja.* coarsely funny: *locker-room humor, jokes.*

lock.et (LOK.it) *n.* a small ornamental case containing a keepsake, usu. attached to a necklace.

lock.jaw *n.* a severe tetanus attack preventing opening of the jaws.

lock.nut *n.* a nut that locks in place or keeps another nut in place.

lock.out *n.* the closing of a plant by an employer to force settlement of a strike.

lock.smith *n.* a maker or repairer of locks.

lock.step *n.* marching one behind another in tight formation: *Canada and Mexico breaks lockstep with the U.S. in many matters.*

lock-up *n. Informal.* a jail, esp. one for temporary custody.

lo.co (LOH.coh) *adj. Slang.* crazy, as cattle after eating the narcotic **locoweed** of western North America: *He's gone loco.* —*n.* [short form] locomotive.

lo.co.mo.tion (loh.cuh.MOH.shun) *n.* motion from place to place.

lo.co.mo.tive (LOH.cuh.moh.tiv) *adj.* having or causing locomotion: *a locomotive engine; Plants have no locomotive faculty.* —*n.* an engine that moves a train: *an electric locomotive; a **locomotive engineer*** (= engine driver).

lo.co.mo.tor (loh.cuh.MOH.tur) *adja.* having to do with organs used in locomotion: *locomotor activation, coordination.*

locoweed See LOCO.

lo.cus (LOH.cus) *n., pl.* **-ci** (-sye) the variable central point of a system: *The family is the locus of affection (where love and trust are systematically practiced); The locus of economic wealth seems to be shifting to Asia.*

lo.cust (LOH.cust) *n.* 1 a short-horned grasshopper that usu. moves about in swarms destroying crops; also, a cicada. 2 a shrub or shade tree of the pea family, esp. the spiny "black locust" tree with fragrant white flowers.

lo.cu.tion (loh.CUE.shun) *n.* 1 a set phrase or other form of expression: *the unique locutions of dialect speakers.* 2 manner of expression: *His locution is sloppy and riddled with obscenities.*

lode *n.* 1 a vein or stratum of metal ore, esp. one with magnetic properties; hence, a source: *a mother lode of secret documents.* 2 a piece of such rock, or **lodestone.**

lo.den (LOH.dun) *n.* 1 a sturdy woolen cloth. 2 its grayish green color.

lode.star *n.* a guiding star, esp. the North Star which shows the way like a lodestone used as a compass.

lodestone See LODE.

lodge (LOJ) *n.* 1 a place for temporary stay, as an inn, a hunter's cottage, rented room, etc.: *hunting, motor, mountain, ski lodges.* 2 an Indian dwelling such as a wigwam or tepee. 3 a den or lair of a beaver or otter. 4 a branch of a fraternal society: *a Masonic lodge.* —*v.* **lodg.es, lodged, lodg.ing** 1 to house or be housed: *a house that lodges students; He's lodging* (= staying) *at a motel; a bullet lodged* (= stuck) *in a bone;* —*n.:* *to find a **lodging*** (= accommodation) *for the night; students' **lodgings*** (= rooms); *a **lodging*** (= rooming) ***house.*** 2 put or lay formally: *to lodge an appeal, a protest, a complaint with the police against someone.* —**lodg.er** *n.: She takes in lodgers to supplement her income.*
—**lodg.ment** *n.*

lo.ess (LOH.is, LES) *n.* a wind-borne, silt-size dust forming a fertile topsoil, as in C. and S.W. United States.
—**lo.ess.i.al** (loh.ES.ee.ul) *adj.*

loft *n.* 1 an upper room or place, as an attic, the place in a barn where hay is stored, the gallery of a church where the organ is kept, a pigeon's house, etc. 2 in golf, the slope of the hitting face of a club. 3 a high stroke or the height given to a lofted ball. —*v.* in golf, bowling, and marbles, to shoot or throw relatively high into the air.

loft.y (LOF.tee) *adj.* **loft.i.er, -i.est** high in an imposing or conspicuous way: *a lofty mountain, spire; a woman of lofty ideals; a lofty* (= grand) *style of writing; a lofty* (= haughty) *manner, sneer.*
—**loft.i.ly** *adv.;* **loft.i.ness** *n.*

log *n.* 1 a felled trunk or large branch of a tree: *logs of firewood; a raft of logs; to sleep like a log* (= soundly); *a **log cabin*** (made of logs). 2 a block of wood, or "log chip," at the end of a line thrown into water from a ship to determine its speed. 3 a ship's daily record of progress: *to keep a log.* 4 a similar record of an operation or performance, as of an airplane or computer.
—*v.* **logs, logged, log.ging** 1 cut down trees; also, cut trees into logs; *n.: a forest destroyed by **logging**.* 2 to measure speed: *The police logged the speeder at 120 miles.* 3 travel: *a pilot who has logged a million miles.* 4 check in or out of a computer system: *To use a database, you **log in** or **on** by typing in your ID and password; Type in "OFF" to **log off** or **out*** (when you have finished).

-log See -LOGUE.

lo.gan.ber.ry (LOH.gun.ber.ee) *n.* **-ber.ries** a blackberrylike, purplish-red fruit that grows in clusters on a trailing vine.

log.a.rithm (LOG.uh.rith.um, "th" as in "the") *n.* in algebra, an exponent: *In 3^5 (i.e. $3 \times 3 \times 3 \times 3 \times 3 = 243$), the logarithm of 243 to the base 3 is 5.*
—**log.a.rith.mic** (-RITH.mic) *adj.*

log.book *n.* a book kept as a log or record of progress.

loge (LOHZH) *n.* 1 a booth, stall, or a box in a theater or opera house. 2 the forward part of a theater mezzanine.

log.ger (LOG.ur) *n.* one who cuts down trees and makes them into logs; lumberjack.

log.ger.head (LOG.ur.hed) *n.* [regional] a blockhead. —**at loggerheads** disputing or arguing *with* someone.

log.gi.a (LOJ.ee.uh) *n.* a gallery or arcade protected from the sun but open to the air.

log.ging *n.* the harvesting and transportation of trees from the forest to the sawmill.

log.ic (LOJ.ic) *n.* the science of reasoning and inference; also, its principles, a particular system of logic, reasoning itself, or a logical result or outcome: *deductive, inductive, symbolic logic; the clear, cold logic of her reasoning; There's little logic in his argument; The logic unit of a computer carries out operations involving AND, OR, and NAND.* —**log.i.cal** *adj.*; **log.i.cal.ly** *adv.*

lo.gi.cian (loh.JISH.un) *n.* a person skilled in logic.

lo.gis.ti.cal (loh.JIS.ti.cul) *adj.* having to do with logistics: *to provide logistical aid such as helicopters to the rebel army; logistical capability, equipment, problems, support.* Also **lo.gis.tic.** —**lo.gis.ti.cal.ly** *adv.*

lo.gis.tics (loh.JIS.tics) *n.pl.* 1 [takes *sing. v.*] the science of planning and carrying out operations, esp. military, involving transport of people, equipment, and supplies; *adja.: a logistics* (= logistical) *expert, manager, system; a company providing transportation and logistics support.* 2 logistical operations: *The logistics of the rock group included two moving vans full of crew and equipment; the logistics of an election campaign.*

log.jam *n.* 1 obstruction caused by logs jamming a watercourse: *to break* or *break up* or *clear a logjam.* 2 piled-up work, a deadlock, or a similar obstacle to progress.

log.o (LOH.goh, LOG.oh) *n.* **-os** an identifying symbol of an organization, for use in advertising and promotion of its image: *the five-ring Olympic logo.*

log.o.type (LOG.uh.type) *n.* [original form] logo.

log.roll.ing (LOG.roh.ling) *n.* in politics, cooperation between parties, as in a legislature by voting for each other's bills, like pioneers helping to roll logs off each other's clearings.

-logue *comb.form.* 1 something spoken or written: *catalogue, dialogue, epilogue, monologue;* also **-log.** 2 specialist: *ideologue; sinologue* (= China specialist).

-logy *comb.form.* 1 a way of speaking or writing: *analogy, eulogy, tautology.* 2 a subject: *biology, geology, zoology.*

lo.gy (LOH.gee, "g" as in "go") *adj.* **-gi.er, -gi.est** *Informal.* sluggish, as from overeating; also, groggy.

loin *n.* 1 the back of the body between the hips and the ribs considered as the seat of strength and generative power: *a child of his loins* (= his natural child). 2 the corresponding part of an animal's body: *a loin (cut) of pork.* —**gird (up) one's loins** prepare for action.

loin.cloth *n.* a piece of cloth worn by men in warm countries, wrapped around the hips and between the thighs.

loi.ter *v.* 1 move around aimlessly: *No loitering on these premises; to loiter around the mall.* 2 spend time idly: *He likes to loiter away his leisure hours.* —**loi.ter.er** *n.*

loll (*rhyme*: doll) *v.* 1 move about in a relaxed or lazy manner. 2 droop or hang loosely, as a dog's tongue in hot weather.

lol.li.pop or **lol.ly.pop** (LOLL.ee.pop) *n.* a piece of hard candy stuck on a short stick or handle: *to lick, suck a lollipop.*

lol.ly.gag (LOLL.ee.gag) *v.* **-gags, -gagged, -gag.ging** *Informal.* loaf or dawdle.

lone *adja.* [literary use] solitary or lonesome: *the lone nights; the lone traveler in the desert.*

lone.ly *adj.* **-li.er, -li.est** 1 being alone and gloomy: *a lonely widow; matrimonial ads appearing in the* **lonely hearts** *columns of newspapers.* 2 *adja.* alone and isolated: *a lonely house, place, tree, village.* —**lone.li.ness** *n.*

lon.er (LOH.nur) *n. Informal.* one who prefers to live or work alone.

lone.some *adj.* 1 feeling lonely: *a lonesome bachelor, orphan.* 2 causing one to feel lonely; solitary: *a lonesome existence, road.* —**lone.some.ly** *adv.;* **lone.some.ness** *n.*

lone wolf *n.* one who prefers to live and work alone.

long *adj.* **long.er** (LONG.gur), **long.est** (LONG.gist) 1 extending from end to end: *ten meters long and two wide; a book 250 pages long; a long* (= not short) *rope.* 2 longer than it is broad: *a long board, skull.* 3 lasting relatively much in time: *It's been a long stretch without a holiday; a long memory; the long vowels of "food," "feed," and "foe."* 4 little likely to succeed; risky: *a long chance, shot; the long odds of 10 to 1.* —**in the long run** or **over the long haul** as time passes; eventually. —**long on** having plenty of something: *He's long on anecdotes, brains, excuses, kindnesses.* —**adv.** for a long time past or to come: *It happened long ago; long before Columbus; She sat up all night long* (= throughout the night). —**as long as** or **so long as** provided that. —*n.* a long time or something lasting long: *The next bus will be here before long; You won't have long to wait; Is the "o" sound of "dog" a long or a short?* —**the long and short**

of it the substance or gist of something that may be condensed. —v. have a strong desire; yearn: *The prisoner longs to be free; longs for freedom.*
long.boat n. the largest boat carried by a sailing ship.
long.bow (LONG.boh) n. a bow drawn by hand to shoot a feathered arrow; cf. CROSSBOW.
long distance n. a telephone service connecting a relatively great distance, esp. when not "local." —**long-distance** (long.DIS.tunce) adja. having to do with a great distance: *a long-distance call, mover, runner;* adv.: *to call home long-distance.*
lon.gev.i.ty (lon.JEV.i.tee) n. the condition of living for a long time: *Increased longevity results from better health care.*
long-faced adj. looking glum or sad.
long-hair n. *Informal.* 1 an intellectual with preference for classical rather than popular music: *long-hair music.* 2 a hippie.
long.hand n. regular handwriting, not shorthand.
long.horn n. a breed of cattle with long horns.
longing n. a desire for something hard to attain: *the longing to go back home; a longing for the good old days;* adja.: *He cast a longing eye on Lolita; longing looks.* —**long.ing.ly** adv.
lon.gi.tude (LON.juh.tude) n. distance east or west of the prime meridian, measured in degrees from 0 to 180 in either direction: *lines of longitude; Memphis is on the 90-degree west longitude.*
lon.gi.tu.di.nal (lon.juh.TUE.dun.ul) adj. 1 of longitude: *The longitudinal lines run north to south from pole to pole.* 2 lengthwise: *a longitudinal measurement; longitudinal* (= not transverse) *stripes, waves.* —**lon.gi.tu.di.nal.ly** adv.
long.johns n.pl. *Informal.* long underwear.
long jump n. an athletic jump with distance as the aim.
long-lived (LONG.livd, -lived) adj. having a long life or existence.
long-playing adj. of a 12-inch phonograph record, playing up to half an hour at 33⅓ r.p.m.
long-range adj. having a long range of time or distance: *a long-range benefit, effect, forecast, goal, missile, objective, plan, prospect, trend, view; long-range planning.*
long.shore.man (LONG.SHOR.mun) n. -men one who loads and unloads ships on a waterfront.

long shot n. *Informal.* a promising person or thing whose success is possible but not likely, as a bet at long odds: *Lili is considered a long shot for the principalship; Our horse is a long shot to win the race.* —**not by a long shot** not at all.
long.stand.ing (LONG.stand.ing) adj. that has existed for a long time: *a longstanding complaint, feud, invitation.*
long.suf.fer.ing (LONG.SUF.ur.ing) adj. enduring insults, pain, injury, etc. for a long time: *Don't put on that longsuffering look; a longsuffering spouse.*
long-term adja. based on a rather long period: *a long-term asset, commitment, loan, loss, solution; long-term planning.*
long.time adja. longstanding: *a longtime adviser, ally, commitment, friend, popularity.*
long ton See TON.
lon.gueur (long.GUR) n. a long and dull passage in a book or a similar period in a performance.
long-winded adj. 1 tiresomely long: *a long-winded narrative, report, speech, statement.* 2 not getting out of breath easily: *a long-winded horse, runner.*
loo n. *Informal.* washroom or toilet.
look (short "oo") v. 1 direct the eyes in order to see: *If you want to see, look! Look at her; Look at him jumping; "Look before you leap"* (= Be cautious); *She looked him in the face and said No; to look in or into a mirror; to look out (of) the window; to look through a telescope; I look through* (= examine) *the morning paper during breakfast.* 2 face or be turned: *The window looks south; It looks out onto a park; a church looking on a highway;* Ladies, **look out for** (= watch) *your purses.* 3 appear to be: *She doesn't look her age; He's 70 and looks it; He looks old and wrinkled; You* **look like a winner**; *It* **looks like** *(it's going to) rain.* 4 turn one's mind, memory, hopes, etc.: *They are looking for jobs; Parents* **look after** (= take care of) *their children; Travelers* **look ahead** *to a safe journey; He* **looks down on** (= regards with some contempt) *the unemployed; I* **look forward to** (= anticipate with pleasure) *your birthday party; The police* **look into** (= investigate) *complaints; We need someone to* **look to** (= turn to) *for help in trouble; Business is* **looking up** (= improving). —**look up** 1 check: *to look up words in a dictionary.* 2 visit: *Do look us up when you are in town.* 3 respect: *Children* **look up to** *their teachers.* —n. 1 a directing of the eyes: *to have, steal, take a look; baleful, cold, curious,*

dirty, distant, faraway, furtive, grim, hard, hungry, inviting, knowing, loving, nasty, puzzled, sinister, sullen, vacant, withering looks. **2** appearance: *We can't judge people by or from their looks; From the look of things, we're in for a storm; I don't like the look of that lawn; His good looks got him the job; mere good looks.* —**look.er** *n.*

look-alike *n.* one that looks like another: *the prince's look-alike* (= double); *an Elvis Presley look-alike* (= imitation); **adja.:** *a look-alike* (= fake) *pill that could cause heart failure; look-alike* (= similar-looking) *boy and girl mannequins.*

looker-on *n.* **lookers-on** an observer or onlooker.

looking glass *n.* a mirror.

look.it *interj. Informal.* look here!

look.out *n.* **1** a person keeping watch: *Lookouts are posted at strategic points.* **2** a watching: *Keep a sharp lookout for intruders; That's your lookout* (= worry); *The police are **on the lookout** for the escaped convicts; a lookout system to prevent criminals from entering the country.* **3** an esp. high place from which to watch: *to watch birds from a lookout; a lookout tower.*

look-see *n. Informal.* a quick visual inspection.

loom (long "oo") *n.* a machine for weaving thread or yarn into cloth. —*v.* **1** weave using a loom. **2** come into view dimly, often threateningly, as in mirages over the horizon: *Unemployment looms large in our view of the future.*

loon (long "oo") *n.* **1** a water bird that looks like a large duck, is a good swimmer and diver, and has a weird cry: *as crazy as a loon.* **2** a stupid or crazy person.

loon.y (LOO.nee) *n.* **loon.ies** *Informal.* **1** a lunatic or crazy person. **2** the Canadian dollar coin with a loon bird on one side; also **loon.ey, loon.y, loon.ie.** —*adj. Informal.* crazy: *He's just a bit eccentric, not quite loony; Loonies used to be sent to the **loony bin*** (= insane asylum).

loop (long "oo") *n.* **1** the shape of a curve that crosses itself, as in a written "l." **2** anything in this shape: *Fingerprints have arches, loops, and whorls; A belt is passed through loops; a **loop antenna** attached to a TV set; the **loop knot** of a lasso.* **3** a series of computer instructions that repeat themselves till the desired end is reached. —**knock** or **throw someone for a loop** *Informal.* startle or shock someone. —*v.* form a loop: *ridges that loop on the tip of a finger; An aerialist **loops the loop*** (= turns in vertical loops).

loop.er *n.* a caterpillar such as the cankerworm or the inchworm that crawls by looping its body.

loop.hole *n.* **1** an opening in a fortress wall for shooting through or for observation. **2** a means of escape: *a legal loophole in the wording of a contract; to close a loophole; to find tax loopholes.*

loop.y *adj.* **loop.i.er, -i.est** *Slang.* crazy.

loose *adj.* **loos.er, loos.est 1** not tight, compact, or firm: *a loose jacket, soil, tooth, weave.* **2** untied, relaxed, or slack: *a dog that is loose at night; It's running loose; Who let or set or turned him loose? loose change (of coins); a man of loose morals; a reputation ruined by the loose tongue of a loose talker; Lu **let loose*** (= released) *a volley of abuse; A mad dog **broke loose*** (= got away); *The dog is now **on the loose*** (= roaming free); *Don't get uptight, just **hang loose*** (*Informal.* for relax). —*v.* **loos.es, loosed, loos.ing** make loose: *to loose a grip, knot; to loose* (= shoot) *a volley or blast.* —**loose.ly** *adv.;* **loose.ness** *n.*

loose cannon *n. Informal.* one whose behavior is unpredictable, like a cannon not secured on deck.

loose-leaf *adja.* allowing the leaves or pages to be rearranged or replaced: *a loose-leaf binder, file, notebook.*

loos.en (LOO.sun) *v.* make or become loose or looser: *Laxatives loosen bowels; Liquor may loosen the tongue; Why not **loosen up*** (= relax) *a bit?*

loose end *n.* an unfinished thing or condition, as the strands at a rope's end: *He found himself **at loose ends*** (= uncertain what to do) *when suddenly laid off from work.*

loot (long "oo") *n.* **1** goods of value taken away, as during a riot or following a natural disaster; plunder. **2** *Informal.* money or gifts received. —*v.* sack: *stores looted and burned by vandals.*

lop *v.* **lops, lopped, lop.ping 1** cut off a limb or branch: *how to lop off $50 from your heating bill.* **2** hang limply; droop; **adja. & cpd.:** *the lop ears of a lop-eared rabbit.* —*n.* cut-away or discarded parts, as of trees.

lop.sid.ed (lop.SYE.did) *adj.* leaning to one side; unsymmetrical or unbalanced: *a lopsided pumpkin, smile; a lopsided attitude; a lopsided vote of 120 against 7.* —**lop.sid.ed.ly** *adv.;* **lop.sid.ed.ness** *n.*

lope *v.* **lopes, loped, lop.ing** move at an easy, bounding gait or stride; also *n.*

lo.qua.cious (loh.QUAY.shus) *adj.* inclined to talk at length with fluency or ease; talkative. —**lo.quac.i.ty** (-QUAS.i.tee) *n.*

lord *n.* **1** one who has power over others: *the feudal lord of the manor; the lord of the jungle.* **2 Lord** [as a title]: *the Lord Mayor of London; the House of Lords* (= British nobles) or **the Lords.** **3 Lord** [as a title of reverence]: *Lord Buddha; the Lord God; The Lord* (= God) *knows I didn't do it.* —**lord it (over)** act in an authoritarian way toward someone: *Our new supervisor lords it over us.*

Lord Chancellor *n., pl.* **Lords Chancellor** Britain's highest judicial official who presides over the House of Lords. Also **Lord High Chancellor.**

lord.ly *adj.* **-li.er, -li.est 1** noble: *a lordly farewell; lordly homes; the lordly Longhurst.* **2** haughty: *his lordly contempt, disdain.* —*adv.* in a lordly manner.

Lord's Day *n.* Sunday.

lord.ship *n.* the rank of a lord; [as a title]: *Your* or *His Lordship.*

Lord's Prayer *n.* the Christian prayer beginning with "Our Father."

Lord's Supper *n.* Holy Communion; Eucharist.

Lord.y (LOR.dee) *interj.* expressing surprise.

lore *n.* the traditional knowledge of a people, esp. on a particular subject: *bird lore; Irish lore; sacred lore; the traditional lore of the gypsies.*

lor.gnette (lorn.YET) *n.* eyeglasses fixed to the end of a handle.

lorn *adj. Archaic.* forsaken; desolate.

lor.ry (LOR.ee) *n.* **lor.ries** *Brit.* a truck.

lose (LOOZ) *v.* **los.es, lost, los.ing** **1** cease to have; fail to keep, get, exist, etc.: *to lose one's life in an accident; to lose one's balance, patience, wallet; Mia lost the election to Lu; She lost (to him) by a small margin; Don't lose time by making too frequent stops;* "*He who hesitates is lost*"; *adj.: She got lost in the crowd; a lost chance, generation, opportunity, soul; lost health, property, time; adja.: to play a losing game (that cannot be won); You're fighting a losing battle; Look for your watch in the lost-and-found department.* **2** cause the loss of a person or thing: *A bad error lost him his job.* —**be lost on** or **upon** be wasted upon someone: *The advice, humor, kindness was lost on him.* —**get lost!** *Informal.* go away! —**lose oneself** become engrossed or occupied: *I can lose myself in a good book.* —**lose out** fail or be defeated: *Jim lost out; He lost out to his rival; He lost out on the contract.* —**lost in** ab-sorbed: *lost in thought, contemplation.* —**los.er** *n.*: *bad, born, good, poor, sore losers.*

loss *n.* a losing, being lost, or a lost person, thing, etc.: *an airplane crash with a great loss of life; losses and gains in business; the heavy losses inflicted on the enemy; an irreparable, irretrievable, total loss; to incur, make up, offset, recoup, suffer, sustain losses; He was at a loss for words* (= did not know what to say).

loss leader *n.* an article put on sale at a loss to attract customers by its low price.

lost *pp.* of LOSE.

lost cause *n.* a failed or hopeless cause.

lot *n.* **1** the deciding of something by chance, as in a lottery by picking one out of many bits of paper, wood, etc.: *turns decided by lot; They cast* or *drew lots to decide who would keep the loot.* **2** fate or fortune: *It fell to his lot to raise his brother when they were orphaned; She decided to throw or cast her lot with* (= join) *the rebels.* **3** a plot of land: *an empty* or *vacant lot; parking lots; a used-car lot.* **4** a set of persons or things: *goods for auction divided into lots; They're not a bad lot (of people); a happy lot; a miserable, sorry lot.* **5** *Informal.* a great deal or amount: *Thanks a lot; She had to pay a lot (of money) for the car; quite a lot of money; We had lots to eat and drink at the party; lots of food.*

loth (LOHTH, "TH" as in "thin") same as LOATH.

Lo.thar.i.o (loh.THAIR.ee.oh) *n.* -**os** a philanderer.

lo.tion (LOH.shun) *n.* a liquid medicinal or cosmetic preparation to apply to the skin: *after-shave, body, hand, skin, suntan lotions.*

lot.ter.y (LOT.uh.ree) *n.* **lot.ter.ies** a gambling game in which prizes are awarded to ticket holders by the drawing of lots.

lot.to (LOT.oh) *n.* a game of chance similar to bingo.

lo.tus (LOH.tus) *n.* **1** a water plant and flower sacred to Egyptians, Hindus, and Chinese. **2** in Greek myth, a fruit inducing a state of dreamy languor if eaten, as in the "lotus-eaters" of the *Odyssey.*

lotus position *n.* a sitting posture in yoga with legs folded and the arms resting on the knees.

loud ("ou" as in "out") *adj.* **1** having great intensity of sound; not quiet: *a loud blast, noise, outcry; loud applause, laughter, music, snoring.* **2** not tasteful in style: *a loud dress; loud colors, people; a rather loud necktie.* **—adv.** in a loud manner: *to speak out loud; to think loud; to turn up the radio loud; You're talking too loud.* **—loud and clear 1** quite audible: *to speak in a loud and clear voice;* **adv.**: *I hear you* or *You're coming through loud and clear.* **2** quite unmistakable: *The customer feedback was loud and clear;* **adv.**: *That says it loud and clear.* **—loud.ly** *adv.;* **loud.ness** *n.*

loud.mouth *n.* one who is outspoken and indiscreet; **adj.**: *a loudmouthed politician.*

loud.speak.er (LOUD.SPEE.kur) *n.* an electrical sound-amplifying device: *The police warned them over a loudspeaker to stay away from the contaminated area.*

lounge (LOWNJ) *v.* **loung.es, lounged, loung.ing 1** stand, sit, or move about in a relaxed or lazy manner: *She lounges around the pool on sunny days.* **2** pass time thus: *He lounges away his leisure hours on the beach.* **—n. 1** a room for relaxing: *the cocktail lounge of a club, hotel, restaurant; a faculty lounge (of a university); the transit lounge and the VIP lounge at an airport.* **2** a couch or sofa.

lounge lizard *n. Slang.* one who lounges around, as a fop, womanizer, or sponger.

lour same as ²LOWER.

louse *n.* **1** *pl.* **lice** a small wingless parasitic insect or pest that lives on the sap of plants, as aphids, or on the blood of animals, as crab lice and body lice. **2** *pl.* **lous.es** *Slang.* someone considered as mean and contemptible. **—v. louse up** *Slang.* spoil or mess something up.

lous.y (LOU.zee, "OU" as in "out") *adj.* **lous.i.er, -i.est 1** infested with lice. **2** *Informal.* bad or miserable: *It's lousy to have to watch the same shows everyday; a lousy business, day; lousy food; I feel lousy.* **3** *Informal.* oversupplied: *Midas was lousy with riches.*

lout (rhyme: out) *n.* a clumsy or ill-mannered man. **—lout.ish** *adj.;* **lout.ish.ness** *n.*

lou.ver (LOO.vur) *n.* **1** an arrangement of sloping slats or boards over an opening to regulate light and air. **2** one of these slats or boards. **—lou.vered** (LOO.vurd) *adj.: a louvered door, window.* Also **lou.vre, lou.vred** *Cdn.*

lov.a.ble (LUV.uh.bul) *adj.* loving or endearing: *a lovable fellow; There's something lovable about him; a lovable and capable woman.*

love (LUV) *n.* **1** a strong liking or affection for a thing or person: *Teaching is a labor of love to good teachers; Some won't do it for love or for money; blind, platonic, true, undying, unrequited love; your love of ice cream; the love for* or *of one's family; Please give them our love* (= kind regards); *Ma sends her love;* Hippies were called **love children** *in the days of lovebeads, love-ins, and flower power; Saint Valentine's Day is the time to be bitten by the* **lovebug** *and for* **love letters. 2** the object of such affection: *Come, my love!* **3** a zero score in tennis: *Fifteen love* (= 15 for the serving side, nothing for the receiver). **—in love** affected by love: *Jack is in love; hopelessly in love with Jill; He has fallen in love with her; He's head over heels in love with her.* **—make love 1** show one's love, as by embracing or kissing; pet. **2** have sexual intercourse: *to make love to someone;* **love.mak.ing** *n.* **—v. loves, loved, lov.ing 1** feel love toward someone: *He loves his wife and children; loves them dearly, deeply, very much; Lovers often love blindly, passionately; He loves her the way she is.* **2** *Informal.* to like very much: *Jan just loves ice cream; Lou loves to go on dates; Tim loves watching TV.* **—love.a.ble** (LUV.uh.bul) same as LOVABLE.

love affair *n.* a romantic attachment between two people not married to each other; hence, any similar attachment: *her love affair with expensive cars.*

love.beads *n.pl.* a necklace of beads worn as a love-and-peace symbol.

love.bird *n.* **1** a small parrot, often kept as a cage bird, remarkable for its affectionate manner toward its mates. **2** one of an openly affectionate pair.

love-crossed *adj.* disappointed in love.

love handles *n.pl. Informal.* a ring of loose fat seen around the middle in some persons; also called "spare tire."

love-in *n.* a gathering for expressing mutual love.

love.knot *n.* a knot tied as a token of love.

love.lorn *adj.* suffering because of unreturned love.

love.ly (LUV.lee) *adj.* **-li.er, -li.est 1** beautiful: *a lovely child, home, sight, story.* **2** *Informal.* delightful: *Isn't he lovely! We had a lovely time at the party.* **—love.li.ness** *n.*

lov.er (LUV.ur) *n.* **1** sweetheart: *a jilted lover.* **2** devotee: *a lover of music.*

love seat *n.* a sofa for two persons.

love.sick *adj.* **1** suffering with love. **2** expressing such suffering: *a lovesick*

poem. —**love.sick.ness** n.
love triangle n. the situation of two parties romantically involved with a third one.
loving adj. full of love; affectionate: *your loving sister;* **lov.ing.ly** adv.
loving cup n. a large, two-handled ornamental vessel, often with cover, used formerly for ceremonial drinking at weddings and banquets, now as athletic trophies.
low (LOH) adj. **1** near the ground or bottom: *a low light, level, wall.* **2** not high: *a low grade, neckline, position, price, temperature; low-level radiation;* the **Low Countries** (= Belgium, Netherlands, and Luxembourg). **3** not great or noble: *in low company; a low blow, deed, opinion, thought, trick.* —*adv.* in a low manner: *We're running low on gas; to aim, fly low; to speak low* (= quietly).
—**lay low 1** knock down. **2** conquer or kill. **3** *Informal.* remain hidden.
—**lie low** remain hidden.
—n. **1** something low, as a gear, pressure, region, etc. **2** the characteristic call of a cow. —*v.* make such a call: *the lowing herd.* —**low.ness** n.
low.ball v. **-balls, -balled, -ball.ing** quote a deceptively low price or amount: *to lowball bids, estimates, expenses, quotations; I suspect they're lowballing;* n.: *That figure sounds like a lowball; to engage in* **lowballing**; *the lowballing of incomes to evade taxes.* —*adja.*: *a lowball contractor, figure, item, price, quote; lowball leasing, pricing.* —**low.ball.er** n.
low beam n. beam of headlight switched to show the way immediately in front of the vehicle.
low.born adj. of low or humble birth.
low.brow n. & adj. *Informal.* (one) having little interest in intellectual or cultural matters.
low-cal adj. low-calorie.
low.down n. *Informal.* true and factual information: *Give me* **the lowdown** *on Saturday's party; Here's the lowdown.*
—*adja.* *Informal.* mean or contemptible: *a filthy lowdown beast; a lowdown dirty trick.*
low-end adja. *Informal.* cheap or inexpensive: *a low-end computer; Unauthorized photocopying of books is a type of low-end piracy.*
¹**low.er** (LOH.ur) **1** adj. comp. of LOW: *the lower, middle, and upper voice ranges; the lower* (= down the river) *St. Lawrence;* **adv.**: *to aim, fly, speak lower.* **2** *v.* make or become lower: *to lower a flag; to lower expenses, one's voice; Do not* **lower yourself** *(in dignity or self-respect).*

²**low.er** (rhyme: our) *v.* look dark and threatening, as skies, clouds, faces, etc.: *the lowering skies.*
lower case n. in printing, small, not capital letters; *adj.*: *upper-case and lower-case letters.* Also **low.er.case, lower-case**.
lower class n. farm laborers, the unskilled, unemployed, etc. as a social class.
lower house n. the more representative house of a bicameral legislature.
low.er.most (LOH.ur.most) adj. lowest.
lowest common denominator, lowest common multiple See LEAST.
low frequency n. a radio frequency between 30 and 300 kilohertz.
low-grade adj. **1** of inferior grade or quality: *low-grade oil.* **2** low in range: *a low-grade fever.*
low-key adj. subdued or restrained in style or intensity: *a low-key approach, campaign, ceremony, response, speech; He is a quiet, charming, low-key personality.* Also **low-keyed**.
low.land (LOW.lund) n. a low or flat region, as in the **Lowlands** of Scotland.
low-level adj. of a computer programming language, using almost the same language as the machine, as machine language.
low.life n., pl. **-lifes** one who leads a disreputable life: *the lowlifes of skid row; lowlife characters.*
low.ly (LOH.lee) adj. **-li.er, -li.est 1** humble and meek: *a lowly opinion of oneself; lowly individuals.* **2** low in rank or position: *a lowly job, occupation, status; a man of lowly origin; the lowly pencil.* —*adv.* in a low manner or voice; also, humbly. —**low.li.ness** n.
low.mind.ed (low.MINE.did) adj. low or mean.
low profile n. a style or behavior that is inconspicuous or unobtrusive: *to keep a low profile.*
low-rise adja. only a few stories high: *a low-rise apartment building.*
low-spirited adj. dejected.
low-tension adja. low-voltage.
low tide or **low water** n. **1** the level or time when the tide is lowest. **2** the lowest point reached by anything; also **low-water mark**.
lox n. **1** also **LOX**, liquid oxygen, as used in rockets. **2** a kind of smoked salmon.
loy.al (LOY.ul) adj. staunchly faithful: *to be loyal to one's country, employer, friends, king, spouse; a loyal friend, husband, servant, subject, wife.*

—**loy.al.ly** *adv.*

loy.al.ist *n.* one who does not join a popular revolt but supports the government, as the **Loyalists** during the American Revolution and the Spanish Civil War.

loy.al.ty (LOY.ul.tee) *n.* **-ties 1** faithfulness: *an employee's loyalty to the company; to swear loyalty to the Sovereign; unswerving loyalty to one's party.* **2** attachment: *conflicting loyalties; the divided loyalties of a double agent.*

loz.enge (LOZ.inj) *n.* a candy, cough drop, etc., originally diamond-shaped.

LP *n., pl.* **LPs** or **LP's** long-playing record.

LSD *n.* "lysergic acid diethylamide," a powerful hallucinogenic drug.

lu.au (LOO.ow, *rhyme:* how) *n.* a Hawaiian feast.

lub.ber (LUB.ur) *n.* **1** a big or clumsy sailor. **2** a landlubber. —**lub.ber.ly** *adj. & adv.*

lube *n.* a lubricating oil: *a lube job* (= automobile lubrication).

lu.bri.cant (LOO.bruh.kunt) *n. & adj.* (an oil, grease, etc.) that reduces friction between moving parts, as of a machine.

lu.bri.cate (LOO.bruh.cate) *v.* **-cates, -cat.ed, -cat.ing 1** apply a lubricant to machinery. **2** make smooth or slippery. —**lu.bri.ca.tion** (-CAY.shun) *n.* —**lu.bri.ca.tor** (-cay.tur) *n.*

lu.bri.cious (loo.BRISH.us) or **lu.bri.cous** (LOO.bri.cus) *adj.* slippery; also, lewd. —**lu.bric.i.ty** (-BRIS.i.tee) *n.* **-ties.**

lu.cent (LOO.sunt) *adj.* giving off light; also, clear; **lu.cent.ly** *adv.*

lu.cerne (loo.SURN) *n. Brit.* alfalfa.

luces *a pl.* of LUX.

lu.cid (LOO.sid) *adj.* **1** shining or clear; easy to understand: *a lucid analysis, passage, style, text, view.* **2** clear-headed: *a will made during a lucid interval; in a lucid state; his last lucid words.* —**lu.cid.ly** *adv.* —**lu.cid.i.ty** (loo.SID.i.tee) *n.*

Lu.ci.fer (LOO.suh.fur) *n.* "light-bearer," Satan's name before his fall from heaven; hence, the Devil.

lu.cite (LOO.site) *n.* a tough acrylic resin or plastic, often used instead of glass; **Lucite** *Trademark.*

luck *n.* chance or fortune, esp. good fortune or prosperity: *As luck would have it, we lost the race; We had bad, tough luck; It was pure* or *sheer luck that they won; I wish we had a bit* or *stroke of luck; Good luck (to you)! Try your luck at setting up in business; Your luck may improve, run out, turn; a hard luck story; Don't press* or **push your luck** (= Don't depend too much on luck). —**down on one's luck** unlucky, esp. having no money to spend. —**out of luck** unlucky, esp. being unable to do or get what is desired. —*v.* esp. **luck out** *Informal.* to be lucky.

luck.y *adj.* **luck.i.er, -i.est** fortunate, esp. by mere chance: *a lucky escape; It's lucky that you passed; You're lucky to be alive; a lucky star, winner.* —**luck.i.ly** *adv.;* **luck.i.ness** *n.*

lu.cra.tive (LOO.cruh.tiv) *adj.* producing wealth; profitable: *a lucrative business, career, contract, market;* **lu.cra.tive.ly** *adv.;* **lu.cra.tive.ness** *n.*

lu.cre (LOO.cur) *n.* riches: *the worship of filthy lucre.*

lu.cu.bra.tion (loo.cue.BRAY.shun) *n.* a laborious or elaborate work or composition.

lu.di.crous (LOO.di.crus) *adj.* laughably incongruous or ridiculous; **lu.di.crous.ly** *adv.;* **lu.di.crous.ness** *n.*

luff *v.* sail into the wind. —*n.* the act of turning a ship's bow toward the wind.

lug *v.* **lugs, lugged, lug.ging** pull or tug; carry something heavy: *A central vacuum saves you the trouble of lugging a vacuum cleaner around.* —*n.* a projecting piece or part by which to hold or support something: *The large* **lug nuts** *holding the wheels of an automobile are unscrewed by using a* **lug wrench**.

luge (LOOZH) *n.* a sled used in the sport of coasting down an icy chute. —**lug.er** *n.*

lug.gage (LUG.ij) *n.* suitcases and such traveler's baggage: *many pieces of luggage; carry-on* or **hand luggage**; *luggage to be checked into a plane;* **check-in luggage**.

lu.gu.bri.ous (loo.GOO.bree.us, short "loo," long "GOO") *adj.* looking or being sad or mournful in an exaggerated way.

luke.warm *adj.* **1** tepid or barely warm: *water that is lukewarm to the touch.* **2** lacking warmth or enthusiasm: *He seems lukewarm about* or *to our proposal.*

lull *v.* to calm or become calm: *to lull a person's fears, suspicions; to lull a child to sleep.* —*n.* a period of calm or lessened activity: *a lull in the fighting; a lull in a conversation, storm; a lull in trade.*

lull.a.by (LUL.uh.bye) *n.* **-bies** a song to lull an infant to sleep: *to hum a lullaby; to sing a lullaby to the baby.*

lu.lu (LOO.loo) *n. Informal.* a person or thing that is remarkable in some way:

Our new logo is a lulu!
lum.ba.go (lum.BAY.go) *n.* muscular rheumatism in the lower back.
lum.bar (LUM.bur, -bar) *adj.* lowerback: *the lumbar region; seats with lumbar support; lumbar vertebrae.*
lum.ber (LUM.bur) *n.* 1 logs sawn and dressed into boards, planks, etc.: *seasoned lumber.* 2 useless furniture and household articles taking up room. —*v.* 1 cut down trees and saw logs into lumber. 2 move along heavily and noisily, as a bear or elephant.
lum.ber.jack (LUM.bur.jack) *n.* a logger: *a lumberjack's appetite, skills;* **adj.:** *a red-and-white checkered lumberjack coat, jacket, shirt.*
lum.ber.man (LUM.bur.man) *n.* **-men** a logger or one who deals in lumber.
lum.ber.yard (LUM.bur.yard) *n.* a place where lumber is kept for sale.
lu.men (LOO.mun) *n.*, *pl.* **-mi.na** muh.nuh) or **-mens** a unit of light measurement.
lu.mi.nar.y (LOO.muh.nair.ee) *n.* **-nar.ies** 1 a light-giving body such as the sun or moon. 2 a famous person: *a literary luminary.*
lu.mi.nes.cence (loo.muh.NES.unce) *n.* light without burning or heat, as given off by fireflies and by fluorescence; cold light. —**lu.mi.nes.cent** (-unt) *adj.*
lu.mi.nous (LOO.muh.nus) *adj.* giving off light: *a luminous celestial body; a watch's luminous dial; luminous paints; a luminous* (= *enlightening*) *performance;* **lu.mi.nous.ly** *adv.* —**lu.mi.nos.i.ty** (-NOS.i.tee) *n.*
lum.mox (LUM.ux) *n. Informal.* a stupid or clumsy person.
lump *v.* heap together or make into a heap or heaps. —**lump it** *Informal.* endure it: *"Like it or lump it."*
—*n.* 1 a shapeless solid mass: *a lump of coal, sugar; cube-shaped* **lump sugar**, *not grain sugar.* 2 a swelling or bump: *a painful lump on the head; One overcome by emotion feels a* **lump in the throat.** 3 **lumps** *pl.* punishment: *He takes his lumps gracefully when attacked in the press.* —**in the lump** in one mass. —**lump.ish** *adj.*
lump.ec.to.my (lum.PEC.tuh.mee) *n.* **-mies** surgical removal of a breast cancer.
lump.y *adj.* **lump.i.er, -i.est** 1 full of lumps: *lumpy porridge.* 2 heavy and clumsy, as the "lumpfish" or "lumpsucker" of Northern waters.
—**lump.i.ness** *n.*
lu.na.cy (LOO.nuh.see) *n.* **-cies** 1 great folly: *It's sheer lunacy to go skating during the spring breakup; I have had enough of his lunacies.* 2 madness or insanity.
lu.nar (LOO.nur) *adj.* of the moon: *a lunar day, eclipse, month, probe;* A **lunar (excursion) module** takes astronauts to the moon's surface and back from a command module that stays in orbit.
lu.na.tic (LOO.nuh.tic) *n.* one who is insane or utterly foolish; *adj.: a lunatic idea; a* **lunatic asylum** (for the insane).
lunatic fringe *n.* an extremist or fanatical section of a movement, society, etc.
lunch *n.* a light meal at midday: *The boss is out for lunch; not a box lunch, picnic lunch, or working lunch but a three-martini business lunch; We'll discuss it at lunch; I took her out to lunch; We went out to eat, but her mind was totally* **out to lunch** (*Informal for* crazy); *"There's no such thing as a free lunch"* (= Nothing comes free). —*v.* have a lunch: *We lunch at the cafeteria.*
lunch.eon (LUNCH.un) *n. Formal.* lunch: *a business luncheon at Claridges; I met him at an Empire Club luncheon; an awards luncheon; state luncheons.*
lunch.eon.ette (lunch.uh.NET) *n.* a small restaurant serving light meals.
luncheon meat *n.* ready-to-eat, packaged meat in the shape of a loaf.
lunch.room *n.* 1 a room, as in a school or place of work, in which to eat lunch. 2 a luncheonette.
lu.nette (loo.NET) *n.* a crescent-shaped figure or opening.
lung *n.* 1 either of a pair of baglike breathing organs in humans and other vertebrates: *congested lungs; smoking and lung cancer.* 2 a device such as an iron lung.
lunge (LUNJ) *n.* a sudden thrust, as with a sword, or a forward leap: *He made a lunge at the burglar.*
—*v.* **lung.es, lunged, lung.ing** make a lunge: *The thief lunged toward him with a knife.*
lung.fish *n.* a fish that has an air bladder besides gills to enable it to breathe in the air and in water.
lunk or **lunk.head** *n. Informal.* a dolt.
lu.pine (LOO.pin) 1 *n.* a plant of the pea family with star-shaped compound leaves and long clusters of usu. yellow or bright-blue flowers as in the bluebonnet; also **lu.pin.** 2 *adj.* of a wolf or wolves; also, wolflike.
lu.pus (LOO.pus) *n.* a disease marked by skin eruptions on the face and hands.
lurch *v.* stagger or lean suddenly to one

side: *The boat lurched to the right and sank.* —*n.* a lurching movement to a side or forward: *The leaking boat gave a lurch and hit a ship close by.* —**leave someone in the lurch** desert a friend or colleague who expects help.

lure *n.* 1 a device such as a bait or decoy used to tempt or entice. 2 an attraction or the power of such attraction: *the lures of Las Vegas.* —*v.* **lures, lured, lur.ing** tempt or entice with or as with a lure: *She was lured away by false hopes; They lured her into signing the contract.*

lu.rid (LOOR.id) *adj.* 1 shining with a red or fiery light: *a lurid sunset.* 2 gruesome or sensational: *a lurid tale of murder; lurid crimes, details, imagery.* —**lu.rid.ly** *adv.*; **lu.rid.ness** *n.*

lurk *v.* lie in wait or move about stealthily: *an intruder lurking in the shadows; Doubts still lurked in his mind.*

lus.cious (LUSH.us) *adj.* sweet and delicious; appealing to the senses: *a luscious apple, peach, pear, pie; luscious lips, poetry, scenery;* **lus.cious.ly** *adv.*; **lus.cious.ness** *n.*

lush *adj.* 1 luxuriant in growth: *lush jungles, vegetation.* 2 luxurious: *a lush brocade, green color, lifestyle; lush fabrics; the lush liberal patronage.* —*n.* Slang. an excessive drinker; alcoholic.

lust *n.* an intense longing or desire, esp. sexual: *to arouse, feel, gratify, satisfy one's lust; the lusts of the flesh; the lust for gold, power.* —*v.* to have intense desire: *to lust after* or *for someone.* —**lust.ful** *adj.*; **lust.ful.ly** *adv.*

lus.ter (LUS.tur) *n.* brightness or brilliance of polish, beauty, reputation, etc.: *Lili will add luster to her new position as president; The new position takes on a new luster because of her.* Also **lus.tre** *Cdn.*

lus.ter.ware (LUS.tur.ware) *n.* pottery glazed with metallic oxides. Also **lus.tre.ware** *Cdn.*

lus.trous (LUS.trus) *adj.* glossy or brilliant.

lus.trum *n.* a ceremonial purification held in ancient Rome every five years; **lus.tral** *adj.*

lust.y *adj.* **lust.i.er, -i.est** full of vigor; robust: *a lusty eater, young man; lusty cheers.* —**lust.i.ly** *adv.*; **lust.i.ness** *n.*

lu.ta.nist or **lu.te.nist** (LOO.tun.ist) *n.* a lute player.

lute *n.* an ancient stringed musical instrument with a flat-topped, pear-shaped body and a distinctive bent-back head.

lu.te.ti.um (loo.TEE.shee.um) *n.* a rare-earth metallic element.

Lu.ther.an (LOO.thuh.run, "th" as in "thin") *n. & adj.* (a member) of the church originated by Martin **Luther**, German theologian and leader of the Reformation; **Lu.ther.an.ism** *n.*

lut.ist (LOO.tist) *n.* 1 a lute player. 2 one who makes lutes.

lux *n.* **lux.es** or **lu.ces** (LOO.seez) a unit of light intensity equivalent to 0.0929 foot-candle.

luxe (LOOKS, LUX) *adj.* luxurious: *the luxe look in women's fashions; luxe fibers, lace; a very luxe collection.*

lux.u.ri.ant (lug.ZHOOR.ee.unt) *adj.* 1 rich or abundant in growth: *luxuriant jungle vegetation; luxuriant hair.* 2 rich in ornament; florid. —**lux.u.ri.ance** *n.*

lux.u.ri.ate (lug.ZHOOR.ee.ate) *v.* **-ates, -at.ed, -at.ing** indulge oneself; revel: *bathers luxuriating in the summer sun.* —**lux.u.ri.a.tion** (-AY.shun) *n.*

lux.u.ri.ous (lug.ZHOOR.ee.us) *adj.* contributing to luxury: *a luxurious existence, hotel; luxurious food, surroundings;* **lux.u.ri.ous.ly** *adv.*

lux.u.ry (LUK.shuh.ree, LUG.zhuh.ree) *n.* **-ries** 1 ease and comfort provided by expensive food, clothes, amusements, etc. beyond the basic necessities: *He lived in luxury all his life; in the lap of luxury; to afford, enjoy the luxury of a heated swimming pool; to wallow in luxury; It would be pure, sheer luxury;* **adja.:** *a luxury apartment, hotel; luxury cars, goods.* 2 the use of luxuries or the things themselves: *Cake would be a luxury for people who can't afford bread.*

-ly *suffix.* 1 like the one specified: *knightly, manly, queenly, scholarly.* 2 occurring every specified period: *daily, hourly, yearly.* 3 in the manner specified: *childishly, happily, icily, musically.*

ly.ce.um (lye.SEE.um, LYE.see-) *n.* an adult-education organization providing lectures, concerts, etc.; also, a lecture hall.

ly.cra (LYE.cruh) *n.* an elastic synthetic textile used for swimsuits; **Lycra** *Trademark.*

lye *n.* a strong alkaline solution or solid, usu. of sodium hydroxide or potassium hydroxide, used in making soap and for household cleaning.

lying (LYE.ing) 1 *pres. part.* of LIE. 2 *n.* the telling of lies or the habit: *Your lying has to stop;* **adja.:** *lying lips, words; a lying scoundrel, tongue.*

lying-in *n.* confinement in childbirth. —**adja.:** *a lying-in hospital, period.*

Lyme disease *n.* a tick-transmitted inflammatory disease characterized by joint pains and neurological disorders.

lymph (LIMF) *n.* a plasmalike transparent yellowish fluid of body tissue. —**lym.phat.ic** (lim.FAT.ic) *adj.*

lymph node (or **gland**) *n.* a knotlike formation along a lymphatic vessel that occurs in clusters in the groin, neck, armpits, etc.

lymph.oid (LIM.foid) *adj.* having to do with lymph or the tissue of lymph nodes.

lym.pho.ma (lim.FOH.muh) *n.* a tumor of lymphoid tissue.

lynch (LINCH) *v.* of a mob, to kill an accused person without trial, often by hanging.

lynx *n.* a short-tailed wild cat related to the bobcat, with pointed and tufted ears, valued for its coat. —**lynx-eyed** *adj.* sharp-eyed.

ly.on.naise (lye.uh.NAZE) *adja.* prepared with finely sliced fried onions: *lyonnaise potatoes, sauce.*

lyre *n.* an ancient stringed musical instrument like a small harp, used by the Greeks for accompanying songs and recitations.

lyr.ic (LEER.ic) *n.* **1** a short poem with a songlike quality, expressing the poet's deeply felt personal reactions to things, as an elegy, ode, or sonnet. **2 lyrics** *pl.* the words of a song as distinguished from the music. —*adja.: a lyric poet; a lyric* (= melodic) *quality; a lyric tenor* (with a higher and lighter voice). —**lyr.i.cism** (-uh.siz.um) *n.*

lyr.i.cal (LEER.i.cul) *adj.* expressive of emotion: *Her poetry is all lyrical; There's a lyrical ring to it; a lyrical ballad, passage, theme, tune; the lyrical impulse; lyrical intensity, power, works; The reunion was a humdrum affair, nothing to **wax** or **be lyrical*** (= excited) *about.* —**lyr.i.cal.ly** *adv.* —**lyr.i.cism** *n.*

lyr.i.cist (LEER.uh.sist) *n.* **1** a writer of verses for songs. **2** a lyric poet.

lyr.ist *n.* **1** (LIRE.ist) a lyre player. **2** (LEER.ist) a lyricist.

ly.ser.gic acid (lye.SUR.jic-) See LSD.

-lysis *comb.form.* disintegration or decomposition: *catalysis, electrolysis, paralysis.*

.... **M, m** ....

M or **m** (EM) *n.* **M's** or **m's 1** the 13th letter of the English alphabet. **2** the Roman numeral for 1,000.

Ma or **ma** (MAH) *n. Informal.* mother: *Look, Ma!* —*adja.: Our motel is a **ma-and-pa*** (= private and independent) *operation, not part of a chain.*

ma'am (MAM) *n. Informal* [in direct address] madam.

Ma Bell *n.* a Bell Telephone company.

Mac or **Mack** *n. Informal.* fellow or guy: *Who do you think you are, Mac?*

ma.ca.bre (muh.CAH.bruh, -bur) *adj.* dealing with death, esp. its gruesome aspects: *a macabre sense of humor; a macabre description, story, twist.*

mac.ad.am (muh.CAD.um) *n.* (a road surface or pavement made of) crushed stone or gravel packed firmly in layers, often with tar or asphalt as binding material. —**mac.ad.am.ize** *v.* **-iz.es, -ized, -iz.ing:** *a macadamized road.*

ma.caque (muh.CAHK, -CAK) *n.* a large, short-tailed monkey of S. Asia, as the rhesus.

mac.a.ro.ni (mac.uh.ROH.nee) *n.* dried flour paste, usu. in the form of short tubes, that is boiled or baked for food.

mac.a.roon (mac.uh.ROON) *n.* a small, sweet cookie made of egg white and crushed almonds or coconut.

ma.caw (muh.CAW) *n.* a gaudily plumed, long-tailed parrot of tropical America with a screeching cry.

mace *n.* **1** a medieval hand weapon or club with a spiked metal head. **2** a ceremonial, club-shaped staff used, esp. in legislatures, as a symbol of authority. **3** a spice made from the dried outer covering of the aromatic seeds of an East Indian tree.

Mac.e.do.ni.an (mas.uh.DOH.nee.un) *n. & adj.* (a person) of or from **Macedonia,** an ancient kingdom of S.E. Europe, now a region of Greece, Yugoslavia, and Bulgaria.

mac.er.ate (MAS.uh.rate) *v.* **-ates, -at.ed, -at.ing** soften by soaking, as flowers to extract perfume: *Ants make nests with macerated plant tissue.* —**mac.er.a.tion** (-RAY.shun) *n.*

Mach (MAHK) *n.* the ratio of the speed of an object to the speed of sound: *Mach 2 is twice the speed of sound.* Also **mach.**

ma.che.te (muh.SHET.ee) *n.* a large, heavy knife of Latin America, used for cutting and as a weapon.

Mach.i.a.vel.li.an (mak.ee.uh.VEL.ee.un) *adj.* crafty or deceitful, as counseled by Niccolo **Machiavelli,** 1469-1527, Italian writer on statecraft.

mach.i.na.tion (mak.uh.NAY.shun, mash-) *n.* a cunning plot or scheme; intrigue.

ma.chine (muh.SHEEN) *n.* **1** a mechanical device or appliance, esp.

one with coordinated moving parts to transmit power for a desired end: *A lever is a simple machine; adding, answering, calculating, composing, computing, copying, duplicating, earthmoving, printing, sewing, slot, vending, voting, washing, X-ray machines; Machines break down, function, run;* **adj.**: *a* **machine-made**, *not handmade product.* **2** a person or group that works like a machine, without thought or will: *the Big Blue Machine; a party machine; propaganda machine; the Nazi war machine.* —**v.** **-chines, -chined, -chin.ing** process or finish with a machine. —**ma.chin.a.ble** (-nuh.bul) *adj.*

machine gun *n.* an automatic weapon that fires ammunition fed into it from a belt or magazine continuously and rapidly. —**machine-gun** *v.* **-guns, -gunned, -gun.ning.** —**machine gunner** *n.*

machine language *n.* a system of signs, characters, or symbols readable by a computer, as one consisting of binary digits.

machine-readable *adj.* that is directly usable by a computer: *machine-readable data, texts.*

ma.chin.er.y (muh.SHEE.nuh.ree) *n.* **-ries 1** machines or machine parts collectively: *well-oiled machinery* (= mechanism). **2** the means by which something functions: *We have different machineries for the sales and service functions.*

machine translation *n.* a translation made by a computer.

ma.chin.ist (muh.SHEE.nist) *n.* one skilled in the making and operation of machines or machine tools.

ma.chis.mo (mah.CHEEZ.moh) *n.* strong or aggressive masculinity, as displayed in swearing, fighting, drinking, and such aspects of a macho.

Mach number same as MACH.

ma.cho (MAH.choh) *adj.* openly and aggressively virile: *a macho actor; macho humor.* —*n.* a macho man: *Hockey is not just for machos.*

macintosh same as MACKINTOSH.

mack.er.el (MAK.ur.ul) *n.* a food fish of the North Atlantic, colored silvery white below and blue or green with wavy black stripes on its back; *adja.:* a *mackerel sky* (*marked like a mackerel's back*); *mackerel clouds.*

mack.i.naw (MAK.uh.naw) *n.* a short heavy winter coat, usu. in a plaid pattern.

mack.in.tosh (MAK.in.tosh) *n.* a waterproof raincoat.

mac.ra.me (MAC.ruh.may) *n.* the art of knotting cord, rope, or string into articles such as purses, belts, and other accessories.

mac.ro (MAC.roh) *n.* a computer instruction containing several operations to be carried out in sequence. —*adja. & comb.form.* large or large-scale: *a macro lens, unit; macrocosm, macroorganism, macroscopic.*

mac.ro.bi.ot.ics (MAK.roh.bye.OT.ics) *n.pl.* [takes *sing. v.*] the science of prolonging life, esp. by a diet of unprocessed natural foods. —**mac.ro.bi.ot.ic** *adj.*: *a Zen macrobiotic diet of vegetables and cereals; a macrobiotic food cult.*

mac.ro.cosm (MAC.ruh.coz.um) *n.* a large and complex whole, as the universe. —**mac.ro.cos.mic** (-COZ.mic) *adj.*

ma.cron (MAY.crun) *n.* a mark placed over a vowel, as in ā, ē, or ō, to indicate length or stress.

mac.ro.scop.ic (mac.ruh.SCOP.ic) *adj.* large enough to be seen by the naked eye; also, large-scale: *a macroscopic issue;* **mac.ro.scop.i.cal** *adj.*

mac.u.la (MAK.yuh.luh) *n.* a spot or blotch, esp. on the skin or cornea. —**mac.u.lar** (-lur) *adj.*: *macular lesions and rashes* (*on the skin*); *age-related* **macular degeneration** *leading to loss of vision.*

mad *adj.* **mad.der, mad.dest 1** angry: *He was mad at her because she was late; hopping mad.* **2** crazy: *It's mad to quit school when you're doing so well; stark raving mad; His drinking drives me mad; I'll go mad at this rate; mad with frustration.* **3** insane: *a mad bomber; That dog may be mad* (= have rabies). **4** overly enthusiastic: *She's mad about flying, but not about her flying instructor; He works* **like mad** (*Informal for* furiously) *on the eve of a test.* —**mad.ly** *adv.*; **mad.ness** *n.*

mad.am (MAD.um) *n.* **1** *pl.* **-ams** a woman who keeps a brothel. **2** *pl.* **mes.dames** (may.DAHM) [used in addressing] a lady.

mad.ame (MAD.um, muh.DAM) *n.* [French title used in addressing a French-speaking married woman, as "Dear Madame," or prefixed like "Mrs."] *pl.* **mesdames** (may.DAHM): *Madame Sauvé.*

mad.cap *n.* a reckless or impulsive person: *a madcap scheme to raise money.*

mad.den (MAD.un) *v.* make or become mad, esp. irritate.

mad.der (MAD.ur), **mad.dest**

(MAD.ist) See MAD.

mad.ding (MAD.ing) *adj.* frenzied; also, maddening: *the madding crowd.*

made *pt.* of MAKE.

Ma.deir.a or **madeira** (muh.DEER.uh) *n.* a dessert wine made in Madeira Islands off the N.W. coast of Africa.

ma.de.moi.selle (mad.uh.muh.ZEL) *n.,* French, *pl.* **mes.de.moi.selles** (made.mwah.ZEL) an unmarried, usu. young French-speaking woman. [also used like "Miss" as a title]

made-to-measure *adj.* made to the customer's measurements; custom-tailored.

made-to-order *adj.* made according to the customer's requirements.

made-up *adj.* 1 invented: *a made-up excuse, story, word.* 2 finished with make-up: *a made-up clown; made-up with a clown face.*

mad.house *n.* 1 a scene of uproar and confusion. 2 *Informal.* an asylum for the mentally ill.

mad.man *n.* **-men** a lunatic. —**mad.wom.an** *n.* **-wom.en.**

mad money *n. Informal.* a small amount of money for spending on impulse, for emergencies, etc.

Ma.don.na (muh.DON.uh) *n.* 1 Mary as the mother of Jesus. 2 a picture or statue of her.

mad.ras (MAD.rus) *n.* a plain-weave fabric, originally from Madras, India, noted for its bleeding colors.

mad.ri.gal (MAD.ruh.gul) *n.* a type of short love poem popular in the 16th century.

mael.strom (MAIL.strum) *n.* a violently confused or turbulent condition or situation, like **Maelstrom,** a dangerous whirlpool off the Norwegian coast: *caught up in the maelstrom of war.*

maes.tro (MICE.troh, mah.ES.troh) *n.* **-tros** or **-tri** (-tree) 1 a great musical composer, teacher, or performer. 2 a masterly performer in any art.

Ma.fi.a or **ma.fi.a** (MAH.fee.uh) *n.* 1 an underworld organization of criminals, Sicilian in origin: *the New York Mafia;* **adj.:** *a Mafia assassin, boss, chief* or *"capo," don, family, film, wife; the Mafia lifestyle.* 2 **mafia** any dominant group with similar interests or backgrounds: *the Harvard mafia of Kennedy's White House; the Communist mafia; a drug mafia.*

ma.fi.o.so (mah.fee.OH.soh) *n., pl.* **-si** (-see) a member of the Mafia.

mag 1 *n. Informal.* magazine. 2 *adj.* made of magnesium alloy: *mag wheels.*

mag.a.zine (mag.uh.ZEEN) *n.* 1 an often illustrated periodical of popular interest carrying a variety of articles: *newspapers and magazines; a fashion magazine; news magazines; A TV* **magazine show** *dealing with a variety of topics.* 2 a place where a supply is stored, as of film in a camera or cartridges inside a machine gun, or a place for storing military supplies and ammunition: *a gunpowder magazine* (= supply depot).

mag.da.len (MAG.duh.lun) or **mag.da.lene** (-leen) *n.* a reformed prostitute, as Mary Magdalene in the Bible.

ma.gen.ta (muh.JEN.tuh) *n.* a purplish red dye.

mag.got (MAG.ut) *n.* the wormlike larva of a two-winged fly. —**mag.got.y** *adj.*

Ma.gi (MAY.jye) *n.pl.* in the Bible, the "Three Wise Men" from the East who visited Jesus in his crib. —**magus** *sing.*

ma.gic (MAJ.ic) *n.* 1 the art of creating illusions by sleight of hand and other tricks: *Magicians perform magic; Caterpillars become butterflies* **as if by magic.** 2 the supposed supernatural power of influencing natural events or of controlling human actions by ritual use of incantations, spells, rites, fetishes, talismans, etc.: *black magic; Witchcraft and sorcery are kinds of magic.* 3 any mysterious power: *the magic of love.* —**adj.:** *a magic potion; King Midas's magic touch; a magic trick, wand; a magic* (= wonderful) *moment.* —**mag.i.cal** *adj.: the magical adventures of Alice in Wonderland; magical events, happenings, powers, stories; the magical touch; the magical million-dollar figure; a magical mystery tour, transformation.* —**mag.i.cal.ly** *adv.*

magic bullet *n.* a swift remedy or solution: *There's no magic bullet against baldness; no magic bullet to make you lose weight.*

ma.gi.cian (muh.JISH.un) *n.* one who practices magic; sorcerer.

mag.is.te.ri.al (maj.us.TEER.ee.ul) 1 *adj.* authoritative: *a magisterial interpretation, performance, quality.* 2 *adj.* having to do with a magistrate: *magisterial proceedings.* 3 *adj.* overbearing: *a magisterial air, pronouncement, tone.*

mag.is.trate (MAJ.us.trate) *n.* a government official administering the law, esp. a minor judicial officer, as a justice of the peace. —**mag.is.tra.cy** (-truh.see) *n.* **-cies.**

mag.ma (MAG.muh) *n.* molten rock, the source of igneous rock: *Magma is extruded as lava.* —**mag.mat.ic**

(mag.MAT.ic) *adj.*
mag.nan.i.mous (mag.NAN.uh.mus) *adj.* noble or generous-spirited, as in forgiving wrongs, not being petty, etc. —**mag.nan.i.mous.ly** *adv.* —**mag.na.nim.i.ty** (mag.nuh.NIM.i.tee) *n.*
mag.nate *n.* a person of wealth, position, and influence in business or industry: *an oil magnate; a shipping magnate.*
mag.ne.sia (mag.NEE.zhuh) *n.* magnesium oxide, a white, alkaline powder used as a laxative and in industry.
mag.ne.si.um (mag.NEE.zhee.um) *n.* a light, silver-white, metallic element.
mag.net (MAG.nit) *n.* an object that attracts, because of the force of a **magnetic field** around it.
mag.net.ic (mag.NET.ic) *adj.* **1** having to do with magnetism: *Iron and nickel are magnetic elements; A magnetic recording tape is used to record sound; the magnetic bubbles of a computer's bubble memory; A* **magnetic disk** *is used to record computer data; A* **magnetic needle** *points to the earth's* **magnetic poles** *lying near the geographic poles; the* **magnetic north** *as shown by a compass needle.* **2** having strong personal attractive power: *a leader with a magnetic personality.* —**mag.net.i.cal.ly** *adv.*
magnetic resonance imaging *n.* computerized imaging of the body's internal tissues using a magnetic field and low-energy radio waves.
mag.net.ism (MAG.nuh.tiz.um) *n.* magnetic force or the power of attraction: *the earth's magnetism; your personal magnetism; a singer who has lost her magnetism.*
mag.net.ite (MAG.nuh.tite) *n.* a black mineral that is an important source of iron.
mag.net.ize (MAG.nuh.tize) *v.* **-iz.es, -ized, -iz.ing 1** make or become magnetic so as to attract. **2** to charm or hypnotize: *an audience magnetized by a singer's voice.* —**mag.net.i.za.tion** (-tuh.ZAY.shun, -tye-) *n.*
mag.ne.to (mag.NEE.toh) *n.* **-tos** a small generator in which electricity is produced in a coil of wire moving through a magnetic field.
mag.ne.tom.e.ter (mag.nuh.TOM.i.tur) *n.* an instrument for measuring the strength of a magnetic field.
mag.ne.to.sphere (mag.NEE.tus.feer) *n.* the upper atmospheric region dominated by the earth's magnetism; **mag.ne.to.spher.ic** (-FEER.ic) *adj.*
mag.nif.i.cent (mag.NIF.uh.sunt) *adj.* impressive because of beauty, richness, or splendor: *a magnificent mansion, palace, tribute, voice;* **mag.nif.i.cent.ly** *adv.* —**mag.nif.i.cence** *n.*
mag.nif.i.co (mag.NIF.i.co) *n.* **-cos** or **-coes** a person of high rank; grandee.
mag.ni.fy (MAG.nuh.fye) *v.* **-fies, -fied, -fy.ing 1** make or make seem larger, as with a lens, or **magnifying glass**. **2** exaggerate: *Don't magnify your problem.* —**mag.ni.fi.er** (-fye.ur) *n.* —**mag.ni.fi.ca.tion** (-fuh.CAY.shun) *n.*
mag.nil.o.quent (mag.NIL.uk.wunt) *adj.* grandiloquent; **mag.nil.o.quence** *n.*
mag.ni.tude (MAG.nuh.tude) *n.* greatness of size or strength; degree of importance: *the direction and magnitude of a force; an earthquake of magnitude 7.6 on the Richter scale; The faintest stars are of the sixth magnitude; a problem* **of the first magnitude**.
mag.no.li.a (mag.NOH.lee.uh) *n.* a tree or shrub with large, dark-green leaves, sweet-smelling, usu. snowy-white flowers, and conelike fruits.
mag.num *n.* a double-size bottle of wine or liquor containing 1.5 liters; also, this size. —*adj.* unusually large: *a magnum cartridge, a .458 magnum rifle.*
magnum o.pus (-OH.pus) *n.* one's greatest work; masterpiece.
mag.pie *n.* a noisy bird related to the jays, usu. black-and-white with a long tail.
Magus See MAGI.
Mag.yar (MAG.yar, MOJ.ar) *n. & adj.* (a member or the Finno-Ugric language) of the chief people of Hungary; Hungarian.
ma.ha.ra.ja or **ma.ha.ra.jah** (mah.huh.RAH.juh) *n.* a former ruler of an Indian state; **ma.ha.ra.ni** or **-nee** (-nee) *fem.*
ma.ha.ri.shi (mah.huh.RISH.ee) *n.* a Hindu sage or spiritual leader.
ma.hat.ma (mah.HAHT.muh, -HAT.muh) *n.* in India, a great and holy man, as "Mahatma Gandhi."
Mahican See MOHICAN.
mah jong or **mah jongg** (mah.JONG, -ZHONG) *n.* a game of Chinese origin, played by four people using 144 engraved tiles.
ma.hog.a.ny (muh.HOG.uh.nee) *n.* **-nies 1** the dark reddish-brown wood of a large tropical American tree of the same name. **2** its color. —*adj.: mahogany furniture; a beach boy with a mahogany tan.*
Ma.hom.et (muh.HOM.it) same as MO-

HAMMED.

ma.hout (muh.HOWT) *n.* an elephant-driver or keeper.

maid *n.* 1 a female servant. 2 a maiden.

maid.en (MAY.dun) *n.* a young unmarried woman. —*adj.* 1 having to do with being a maiden: *a maiden aunt.* 2 first-time: *a rocket's maiden flight; an M.P.'s maiden speech in a legislature; the Titanic's maiden voyage.* —**maid.en.hood** (short "oo") *n.* —**maid.en.ly** *adj.*

maid.en.hair (MAY.dun.hair) *n.* a species of fern with finely divided fronds. —**maidenhair tree** same as GINKGO.

maid.en.head (MAY.dun.hed) *n.* the hymen; also, virginity.

maiden name *n.* one's surname before marriage: *Ms. Ann Smith continues to use her maiden name* (= i.e. Smith) *though married to Mr. Jones*

maid-in-waiting *n.* **maids-in-waiting** a queen's or princess's female attendant.

maid of honor *n.* 1 a woman as a chief bridesmaid. 2 a maid-in-waiting.

maid.serv.ant (MADE.sur.vunt) *n.* [old use] a woman servant; housemaid.

mail *n.* 1 a postal or similar messaging system: *Your check is in the mail; electronic mail; a reply by return mail* (= "within 24 hours"); *the origin of the mails in Europe.* 2 what is sent through the mail, as letters and parcels: *to address, stamp, and send out mail; to deliver, forward, sort the mail; a bag of mail (containing many pieces of mail); certified, domestic, express, fan, first-class, hate, junk, registered, second-class, special-delivery, surface, third-class mail.* 3 a body armor of metal plates, rings, etc.: *chain mail; a coat of mail; adj.: a **mailed** (= protected with metal or armor) fist, knight.* —*adj.:* a *mail carrier, chute, clerk; mail delivery.* —*v.* send by mail: *to mail a letter; adj.: a **mailed** application, catalog, gift, questionnaire; n.: posters, mailings, and brochures; mass mailings.*

mail.box *n.* 1 a box into which outgoing mail is dropped by the public. 2 a private box for receiving mail. 3 a computer storage file for receiving e-mail.

mail drop *n.* a receptacle, pigeonhole, etc. used for dropping off mail.

mail.er *n.* 1 a person or machine that addresses, stamps, or mails. 2 a small container for mailing things, or an advertising leaflet.

mail fraud *n.* use of the mails for cheating purposes.

mail.man *n.* -men a male letter carrier.

mail order *n.* an order for goods by mail. —**mail-order** *adj.: a mail-order business, catalog; a **mail-order house*** (= a firm that sells by mail).

maim *v.* cripple or mutilate.

main *adj.* of a system or connected whole, chief or principal: *the main subject of a program of study; a sentence's main and subordinate clauses; a hustler with an eye to or on or for the **main chance*** (= the most advantageous opportunity); *the **main course*** (= main dish or entrée) *of a meal; a computer's **main memory*** (= random access memory in which data is processed). —*n.* 1 a principal channel, as of water, gas, sewage, or electricity: *The water main burst.* 2 [old use] the ocean: *the western main.* 3 [old use] mainland: *the Spanish main.* —**in the main** for the most part. —**with might and main** with all one's strength. —**main.ly** *adv.*

main.frame *n.* 1 a computer's central processing unit, not a peripheral such as a printer. 2 a large computer, not a micro or minicomputer.

main.land (MAIN.land, -lund) *n.* the main landmass, as distinguished from outlying islands: *the Chinese mainland.* —**main.land.er** *n.*

main.line *n.* 1 the principal road, route, etc. 2 *Slang.* a large vein; *v.* **-lines, -lined, -lin.ing** inject heroin or other narcotic into a large vein.

main.mast *n.* the principal mast of a vessel.

main.sail *n.* the largest sail on the mainmast.

main.spring *n.* 1 the principal spring of a watch, clock, gun, etc. 2 chief incentive: *Is money the mainspring of your life?*

main.stay *n.* 1 a mainmast's supporting wire or rope. 2 chief support: *The quarterback was the mainstay of the football team.*

main.stream *n.* the principal current; the main direction of flow; the prevailing trend: *in the mainstream of politics; adj.: a mainstream brand, breakfast cereal, candidate, consumer, political party, product; Microcomputers are now mainstream; mainstream appeal, Christianity, Islam; adv.: Health food is going mainstream.* —*v.:* to mainstream *specialty items; Women and minorities are beginning to be mainstreamed; n.: the **mainstreaming** of special students in regular programs.*

Main Street or **main street** *n.* 1 a small town's principal street. 2 the masses, esp. as typifying materialism, mediocrity, provincialism, etc.

—main.street *v.* campaign for election along main streets. **—main.street.er** *n.*
main.tain (main.TAIN) *v.* **1** keep in existence; keep active or unimpaired: *Police maintain law and order; An automobile has to be maintained in running condition; income sufficient to maintain a family.* **2** argue for something: *He couldn't maintain his innocence in the face of all that evidence; Mimi still maintains that the moon landing never took place.* **—main.tain.a.ble** *adj.*
main.te.nance (MAIN.tun.unce) *n.* **1** a maintaining or support: *health maintenance; preventive maintenance of a car; road maintenance;* **adj.:** *a maintenance engineer, man; maintenance staff.* **2** means of livelihood: *a hobby that provides maintenance; to pay maintenance to one's former spouse and children.*
mai.son.ette (may.zuh.NET) *n.* a duplex apartment or small house.
mai.tre d' (may.tur.DEE) *n., pl.* **mai.tre d's** (-DEEZ) [short form] maître d'hôtel.
maî.tre d'hô.tel (may.truh.doh.TEL) *n., pl.* **maî.tres-** (may.truh-) a head waiter or chief steward.
maize (MAIZ) same as CORN, *n.* 1.
ma.jes.tic (muh.JES.tic) *adj.* having majesty or grandeur; stately and lofty in appearance; also **ma.jes.ti.cal.** **—ma.jes.ti.cal.ly** *adv.*
maj.es.ty (MAJ.is.tee) *n.* **1** lofty grandeur: *the Rocky Mountains in all their majesty.* **2 Her, His, Your Majesty,** *pl.* **Their, Your Majesties** [title used in speaking of or to a king, queen, emperor, etc.].
ma.jol.i.ca (muh.JOL.i.kuh) *n.* Italian white-glazed pottery; faience; delft.
ma.jor (MAY.jur) *adj.* relatively greater in size, importance, etc., not minor: *a major disagreement, improvement, poet, portion, subject of study;* [in music] *a **major chord** based on a major scale; major surgery* or *a major operation (requiring general anesthesia).* *—v.* of a student, specialize: *She's majoring in history.* *—n.* **1** a student majoring in a specified subject or the subject itself: *She's a history major, His major is music.* **2** in the armed forces, a commissioned officer ranking above a captain and below a lieutenant colonel: *A **major general** ranks above a brigadier general and below a lieutenant general.*
major-do.mo (MAY.jur.DOH.moh) *n.* **-mos** a chief steward or butler.
majorette [short form] same as DRUM MAJORETTE.
ma.jor.i.ty (muh.JOR.i.tee) *n.* **-ties 1** more than half the total number of votes, people, etc.; also, votes or people in excess of a required number: *an absolute, bare, large, narrow, overwhelming, simple, small, working majority; to get, receive, win by a slim majority; in the majority of cases; A **majority government** (with the governing party having a majority in parliament) is more secure than a minority government.* **2** the legal age of responsibility or adulthood: *the age of majority; You attain or reach majority in most countries at 18 or 21.* **3** the military rank of a major.
major league *n.* in baseball, either the American League or the National League. **—major-league** *adj.* **1** having to do with a major league: *major-league baseball; major-league clubs, players; to play at the major-league level.* **2** toprated: *a major-league image, organization, player, sports stadium; major-league prospects.*
major scale *n.* a diatonic musical scale having half tones after the third and seventh notes.
make *v.* **makes, made, mak.ing 1** bring something into being; create, form, shape, or put together: *Who made the universe? Sam makes dresses; Lou makes a living as a plumber; He died without making a will; Everyone makes mistakes; Poets, they say, are born, not made; "Haste makes waste"; Make peace, not war; a soup made of* or *out of* or *with vegetables; She makes* (= arranges) *her bed in the morning; What do you **make of** (=* How do you interpret*) this telegram?* **2** cause to be or cause oneself to be or become: *Please make sure the door is locked; He's trying to make himself understood; to make someone president; She can make children do their homework; Their work makes her happy; She'll make* (= become) *a good teacher; He was made to wait.* **3** attain or reach; achieve: *A story has to be sensational to make the front page; What grade did you make on the test? a challenge that could either make you* (= *get you success*) *or break you; He had to run to make* (= catch) *the 5 o'clock bus.* **—make away with 1** get rid of or kill. **2** steal. **—make believe** pretend or imagine. **—make do** manage with something that is not so good: *to make do with fewer clothes; How do you make do on your tiny salary?* **—make for** move toward: *When the alarm sounds, make for the exits; Being prepared makes for* (= leads to) *safety.* **—make it** succeed: *You have to work hard to really make it.* **—make off** run away. **—make**

off with steal. —**make out 1** see or understand: *It's too faint for me to make out.* **2** (try) to prove: *It is not the cure-all the ads make it out to be.* **3** write or fill out: *Please make this out in duplicate.* **4** *Informal.* succeed: *How are you making out in your new job?* —**make over 1** change or alter. **2** transfer the ownership of something: *The title to the house was made over to his son.* —**make up 1** put together; compose: *an audience made up of students; She's good at making up excuses; It's time to make up your mind* (= decide); *Friends make up* (= become reconciled) *after a fight.* **2** restore or compensate for something lost: *He works longer hours to make up for lost time; to make up a loss; I'll make it up to you for losing your books.* **3** put on cosmetics, stage masks, etc. —*n.* the origin of a product: *a bicycle of Canadian make; the year and make* (= brand, as Ford, GM, etc.) *of a car.* —**on the make** *Informal.* seeking profit, adventure, etc.

make-believe *n.* a pretending or imagining: *His exploits are mere make-believe; the make-believe of drama; a make-believe picnic on the moon.*

make-over *n.* a remodeling or beauty treatment: *You see a genuine change in the man, not just an image make-over.*

mak.er (MAY.kur) *n.* one that makes: *a film maker; the maker* (= manufacturer) *of a car; to meet one's maker* (= to die).

make.shift *adj.* temporary or substitute: *a makeshift arrangement, bed of hay, operating room, shelter.* Also *n.*

make.up or **make-up 1** *n.* cosmetics, masks, etc. that are applied on the face: *to apply, put on, remove, wear makeup; to take off one's makeup;* **adj.**: *a makeup artist, counter, expert.* **2** *n.* how something is put together; composition: *the ethnic makeup of a community; the economic makeup of a population; the genetic makeup of a species; the page makeup and design of a newspaper; a makeup editor.* **3** *adj. Informal.* compensatory: *a makeup examination for students who were ill.*

make-work *n.* work devised mainly to keep people employed: *a make-work government project.*

making *n.* a being made or becoming: *The trouble was not of his own making; the making* (= compilation) *of dictionaries; Publicity spoiled our plans while they were still* **in the making** (= being made); *a youngster with the* **makings of** (= potential for becoming) *a rocket scientist; His marriage was the making of him* (= cause of his success).

mal- *prefix.* bad(ly); poor(ly): *maladapted, maladroit, malcontent.*

mal.a.chite (MAL.uh.kite) *n.* **1** a green copper ore used for making ornamental articles. **2** its green color.

mal.ad.just.ed (mal.uh.JUS.tid) *adj.* not well adjusted to one's environment. —**mal.ad.just.ment** *n.*

mal.a.droit (mal.uh.DROIT) *adj.* not adroit; clumsy or awkward. —**mal.a.droit.ly** *adv.;* **mal.a.droit.ness** *n.*

mal.a.dy (MAL.uh.dee) *n.* **-dies** a bodily disorder, often one that is deep-seated or that may prove fatal.

ma.laise (mal.AIZ) *n.* **1** a disordered condition. **2** a vague feeling of discomfort.

mal.a.mute (MAL.uh.mute) *n.* a strong, heavy-coated sled dog of Alaskan origin.

mal.a.prop.ism (MAL.uh.prop.iz.um) *n.* a ludicrous mixing up of similar words, as "We got the R.I.P. treatment" instead of saying "V.I.P. treatment."

ma.lar.i.a (muh.LAIR.ee.uh) *n.* a mosquito-borne parasitic disease characterized by periodic chills and fever. —**ma.lar.i.al** *adj.*

ma.lar.key or **ma.lar.ky** (muh.LAR.kee) *n. Slang.* bunk; nonsense.

mal.a.thi.on (mal.uh.THY.on, "TH" as in "thin") *n.* a general-purpose phosphate insecticide of low toxicity.

Ma.lay (MAY.lay, muh.LAY) *n. & adj.* (having to do with) a brown-skinned Mongoloid people of Malaysia, the Philippines, and Indonesia or any of their languages: *the* **Malay Archipelago** (of islands between S.E. Asia and Australia, chiefly Indonesia and the Philippines); *the* **Malay Peninsula** (extending from Singapore to the Isthmus of Kra, Thailand).

Mal.a.ya.lam (mal.uh.YAH.lum) *n.* a Dravidian language of S.W. India.

Ma.lay.an (muh.LAY.un) same as MALAY.

Ma.lay.sian (muh.LAY.zhun) *n. & adj.* (having to do with) a S.E. Asian federation of states including most of the Malay Peninsula ("West Malaysia") and "East Malaysia" (Sabah and Sarawak).

mal.con.tent (MAL.cun.tent) *n. & adj.* (one) who is dissatisfied or rebellious.

male *adj.* **1** of the kind in plants, animals, and humans that fertilizes the female for begetting offspring: *A male plant has only flowers with stamens; The stamen and the penis are male reproductive organs.* **2** having to do with males and their qualities: *a male chauvinist; a male* (= projecting) *electrical plug; the male bonding* (= close personal relationships) *among men.* —n. a male person, animal, plant, or flower. —**male.ness** *n.*

mal.e.dic.tion (mal.uh.DIC.shun) *n.* 1 a curse. 2 slander. —**mal.e.dic.tor.y** *adj.*

mal.e.fac.tor (MAL.uh.fac.tur) *n.* an evildoer or criminal; **mal.e.fac.tress** (-tris) *fem.* —**mal.e.fac.tion** (-FAC.shun) *n.*

ma.lef.ic (muh.LEF.ic) *adj.* baleful or malicious.

ma.lef.i.cent (muh.LEF.uh.sunt) *adj.* doing evil; harmful. —**ma.lef.i.cence** *n.*

ma.lev.o.lent (muh.LEV.uh.lunt) *adj.* wishing others evil; malicious. —**ma.lev.o.lence** (-lunce) *n.*

mal.fea.sance (mal.FEE.zunce) *n. Law.* misconduct by a public official.

mal.for.ma.tion (mal.for.MAY.shun) *n.* an abnormal or faulty formation of a body or body part, as a hunched back: *a congenital malformation.* —**mal.formed** *adj.*

mal.func.tion (mal.FUNK.shun) *v.* fail to function properly. —*n.* a malfunctioning.

mal.ice (MAL.is) *n.* desire to harm another: *He bore no malice toward anyone.*

ma.li.cious (muh.LISH.us) *adj.* meant to harm someone; spiteful: *malicious attacks, behavior, cruelty, gossips, remarks.* —**ma.li.cious.ly** *adv.*

ma.lign (muh.LINE) *v.* speak evil of someone; slander. —*adj.* 1 injurious; also, malicious: *a malign doctrine, influence, purpose, view.* 2 cancerous: *a malign tumor.*

ma.lig.nant (muh.LIG.nunt) *adj.* 1 malign: *a malign look, spell.* 2 likely to spread and prove fatal if not checked; not benign: *a malign growth, lump in the breast; malign cholera, hypertension.* —**ma.lig.nan.cy** (-nun.see) *n.* —**ma.lig.ni.ty** (-ni.tee) *n.*

ma.lin.ger (muh.LING.gur) *v.* pretend illness in order to escape duty. —**ma.lin.ger.er** *n.*

mall (MAWL) *n.* 1 a shopping center, usu. enclosed: *shopping malls.* 2 a pedestrians-only street lined with shops: *a pedestrian mall.* 3 a broad, parklike walk or promenade.

mal.lard (MAL.urd) *n.* a common wild duck.

mal.le.a.ble (MAL.ee.uh.bul) *adj.* 1 of metals, that can be hammered or pressed into thin sheets, as gold, silver, copper, etc., not stiff like cast iron. 2 easily changed, shaped, or trained: *a malleable character; one* malleable student in a class of stubborn rebels. —**mal.le.a.bil.i.ty** (-BIL.i.tee) *n.*

mal.let (MAL.it) *n.* a hammer with a wooden head, short-handled for driving a chisel or long-handled for use in polo and other games.

mal.low (MAL.oh) *n.* a herb, shrub, or tree such as the marshmallow with hairy stems and leaves.

mal.nour.ished (mal.NUR.isht) *adj.* poorly nourished.

mal.nu.tri.tion (mal.new.TRISH.un) *n.* a malnourished condition resulting from improper diet.

mal.oc.clu.sion (mal.uh.CLOO.zhun) *n.* improper meeting of teeth because of a receding or protruding lower jaw.

mal.o.dor.ous (mal.OH.dur.us) *adj.* having a bad odor; stinking.

mal.prac.tice (mal.PRAC.tis) *n.* improper conduct or treatment by a professional, esp. neglect of a patient by a physician.

malt (MAWLT) *n.* barley or other grain that is first soaked and allowed to sprout, then kiln-dried and aged for use in beer-making and distilling: *Dried milk and malt extract powder are mixed in milk to make **malted milk.***

Mal.tese (mawl.TEEZ) *n. & adj.* (a person) of or from **Malta**, an island republic S. of Sicily.

Mal.thu.sian (mal.THOO.zhun, "TH" as in "thin") *n. & adj.* (a believer in the theory) of Thomas **Malthus**, 1766-1834, that population increases would result in world food shortages. —**Mal.thu.sian.ism** *n.*

malt liquor *n.* beer, ale, etc. made from malt by fermentation.

malt.ose (MAWL.tose) *n.* malt sugar formed from starch by the action of an enzyme.

mal.treat (mal.TREET) *v.* treat brutally; abuse or hurt. —**mal.treat.ment** *n*

ma.ma or **mam.ma** (MAH.muh) *n. Informal.* mother: *Tony is no **mamma's boy*** (= sissy).

mam.bo (MAHM.boh) *n.* **-bos** a musical form or dance of Cuban Negro origin.

mam.mal (MAM.ul) *n.* a vertebrate such as a human being, dog, bat, or whale whose females nourish their young with milk from the breast. —**mam.ma.li.an** (ma.MAY.lee.un) *n. & adj.*

mam.mar.y (MAM.uh.ree) *adj.* having to do with the breasts: *a mammary gland.*

mam.mo.gram (MAM.uh.gram) *n.* an X ray of the breast for detecting abnor-

mammon / mandible

malities. —**mam.mog.ra.phy** (ma.MOG.ruh.fee) *n.*

mam.mon (MAM.un) *n.* the greedy pursuit of wealth, personified as **Mammon.**

mam.moth (MAM.uth) **1** *n.* a huge prehistoric hairy kind of elephant with large curved tusks. **2** *adja.* gigantic or colossal: *a mammoth enterprise, job, plan, structure, undertaking.*

man *n., pl.* **men 1** an adult human male, in roles such as suitor, husband, servant, follower, or a person with virile qualities: *He was man enough to apologize; Be a man! Take it like a man! a man of action; a man of letters; a man of his word (who will keep promises); a best man; a con or confidence man; advance, enlisted, hatchet, hit, leading, maintenance, marked, organization, right-hand, straight, straw, stunt men; to live together as man* (= husband) *and wife; all the king's men* (= followers). **2** a member of the human race; a person or individual: *Is man descended from the apes? the Neanderthal man; Man is mortal; He's running a one-man show; a chess man* (= piece); *They fought the invaders* **as one man** or **as a man** (= Everybody fought); *They were wiped out* **to a man** (= All were lost); **man's best friend** (= dog). —*v.* **mans, manned, man.ning 1** supply with people, usu. men, for defense or hard work: *Sailors man a ship.* **2** put courage into oneself: *He manned himself for the ordeal.*

—*comb.form.* **1** person, esp. a male: *batsman, chairman, freshman, spokesman.* **2** person: *man-eater, manhandle, man-hour, manpower.*

man-about-town *n.* **men-about-town** a man of society who spends much time in clubs, theaters, etc.

man.a.cle (MAN.uh.cul) *n.* usu. **manacles** *pl.* handcuffs or fetters: *a prisoner in manacles.* —*v.* **-cles, -cled, -cling** restrain with or as if with manacles: *Totalitarian regimes manacle the press.*

man.age (MAN.ij) *v.* **-ag.es, -aged, -ag.ing 1** handle or make use of people, resources, etc. efficiently: *someone to manage the sales department; a horse that is difficult to manage* (= control); *adj.:* *a well* **managed** *business; a* **managed health-care** *plan (that delivers only appropriate, cost-effective medical care); adja.:* *a* **managing** *director, editor, partner.* **2** cope: *Can you manage with just one helper? It's impossible to manage without a pay check; He seems to manage well on such a low income; She managed to return* (= succeeded in returning) *the book on time.* —**man.age.a.ble** (-ij.uh.bul) *adj.;* **man.age.a.bly** *adv.*

man.age.ment (MAN.ij.munt) *n.* a managing, being managed, or a group of managers: *the management of a business; labor and management; senior management* (= managers); *a shop under new management* (= owners). —**man.age.men.tal** (-MEN.tul) *adj.*

man.ag.er (MAN.ij.ur) *n.* one who manages: *our bank manager; general, office, sales, service managers; an assistant manager; the branch manager of our bank.* —**man.a.ge.ri.al** (man.uh.JEER.ee.ul) *adj.:* *a managerial position, responsibility, role; the managerial class, ranks.*

ma.ña.na (mun.YAH.nuh) *n.* [implying the habit of putting things off] tomorrow: *Saying mañana won't get your homework done; adja.:* *the mañana attitude, habit, philosophy.*

man-at-arms *n., pl.* **men-** a soldier, esp. one heavily armed and mounted.

man.a.tee (MAN.uh.tee) *n.* a large plant-eating mammal of warm coastal waters and rivers with flippers in front and a flat, rounded tail; also called "sea cow."

Man.chur.i.an (man.CHOOR.ee.un) *adj.* having to do with **Manchuria,** a historic region of N.E. China.

man.da.rin (MAN.duh.rin) *n.* **1 Mandarin** the dialect of northern China, the most widely spoken form of Chinese. **2** a high military or civil official, as of the former Chinese empire: *Chinese mandarins; Ottawa mandarins such as deputy ministers.* **3** a tangerine orange.

man.date *n.* **1** an order or command. **2** authority or commission: *Elected representatives get their mandate from the people; He claims to be carrying out a mandate from Heaven; He doesn't have a clear mandate, though; Britain had a mandate from the League of Nations to administer Iraq; adj.:* *Iraq was a* **mandated** *territory.*

man.da.to.ry (MAN.duh.tor.ee) *adj.* **1** obligatory: *Seat belts were made mandatory long ago; a prisoner free on mandatory supervision; a mandatory drug-testing program, jail sentence, retirement age.* **2** [legal use] having the nature of a mandate: *a mandatory injunction, order.* —**man.da.to.ri.ly** *adv.*

man.di.ble (MAN.duh.bul) *n.* a movable mouth part used for chewing or biting, as the lower jaw in humans, the upper or lower part of a bird's beak, an insect's jawlike appendages, etc. —**man.dib.u.lar** (man.DIB.yuh.lur) *adj.*

man.do.lin (MAN.duh.lin, -LIN) *n.* a musical instrument with a pear-shaped body like a lute's and four to six pairs of strings. —**man.do.lin.ist** (-LIN.ist) *n.*

man.drake *n.* 1 a plant of the nightshade family with a forked root; also **man.drag.o.ra** (-DRAG.uh.ruh). 2 a May apple.

man.drel or **man.dril** (MAN.drul) *n.* 1 a tool-carrying shaft or spindle of a lathe. 2 a bar or rod around which metal or glass tubing is shaped.

man.drill *n.* a large W. African baboon whose male has a blue and scarlet face and rump.

mane *n.* the long and heavy hair around the neck of animals such as lions and horses. —**maned** *adj.*

man-eater *n.* 1 a cannibal. 2 an animal that eats human flesh, as a tiger or shark. —**man-eating** *adj.*

ma.nege (muh.NEZH) *n.* 1 horsemanship or a trained horse's movements. 2 a riding school.

ma.nes (MAY.neez) *n.* the revered spirit of a dead person, like the **Manes**, or dead ancestors, of ancient Romans.

ma.neu.ver (muh.NOO.vur) *n.* 1 a tactical movement, as of the military or of warships: *NATO conducts* **maneuvers** (= *military exercises*) *in the Atlantic.* 2 a skillful use of people, situations, etc. for private ends, as to achieve or escape something; manipulation or stratagem: *clever, political, tactical maneuvers.* —*v.* move skillfully or tactically: *to maneuver for position in a power struggle; Small cars are easy to maneuver into and out of a parking space; He managed to maneuver* (= *force by maneuvers*) *the vice-president out of his job.* —**ma.neu.ver.a.ble** *adj.* Also **ma.noeu.vre, ma.noeu.vra.ble** *Cdn.*

man Friday See FRIDAY.

man.ful *adj.* courageous or resolute as befits a man. —**man.ful.ly** *adv.*

man.ga.nese (MANG.guh.neez) *n.* a grayish-white metallic chemical element used in alloys such as bronze and steel.

mange (MAINJ) *n.* an itchy skin disease of domestic animals caused by mites.

man.ger (MAIN.jur) *n.* a long box or trough for livestock to eat from, as in a stable.

man.gle (MANG.gul) *v.* -**gles**, -**gled**, -**gling** 1 tear, hack, or crush so as to mutilate; hence, botch or ruin something; *adj.:* *The wrecked car was just* **mangled** *metal; a mangled reputation.* 2 press or smooth linens using a mangle. —*n.* an ironing machine equipped with rollers.

man.go (MANG.go) *n.* -**goes** or -**gos** the delicious and sometimes acid, pulpy, kidney-shaped fruit of a tropical tree of the same name.

man.grove (MANG.grohv) *n.* a tropical tree of salty coastal waters that grows in thickets formed by roots sent down from its own branches.

man.gy (MAIN.jee) *adj.* -**gi.er**, -**gi.est** 1 having the mange: *a mangy dog.* 2 shabby or contemptible. —**man.gi.ness** *n.*

man.han.dle (MAN.han.dul) *v.* -**dles**, -**dled**, -**dling** handle or treat roughly.

man.hat.tan (man.HAT.un) *n.* a cocktail of whiskey and sweet vermouth.

man.hole *n.* a covered hole for access to a sewer, ship's tank, etc.: *Open manholes are a threat to pedestrians.*

man.hood (short "oo") *n.* 1 the state of being a man: *to grow to or reach manhood.* 2 manly character. 3 men collectively: *the manhood of the nation.*

man-hour *n.* a unit of one hour's work by one person.

man.hunt *n.* an organized hunt for a criminal or fugitive: *to carry out, conduct, organize a manhunt for the escapees.*

ma.ni.a (MAY.nee.uh) *n.* 1 a mental disorder characterized by an uncontrollable urge or excitement: *an arsonist with a mania for setting fire to buildings.* 2 excessive enthusiasm or a craze: *She has a mania for fresh air.* —*comb.form.* mania or craze for specified subject: *kleptomania, megalomania, seafood mania.*

ma.ni.ac (MAY.nee.ac) *n.* 1 one who is wildly insane: *a raving maniac; sex maniacs; suicidal maniacs.* 2 one who is excessively enthusiastic about something: *an exercise maniac; hockey maniacs; a maniac for organization; a maniac about quality.* —**ma.ni.a.cal** (muh.NYE.uh.cul) *adj.:* *with maniacal force; a maniacal hatred, laugh, rage, shriek, urge.*

man.ic *adj.* 1 suffering from mania: *Recurrent bouts of manic depression drove him to suicide.* 2 resembling mania: *a woman of manic energy; manic delight, enthusiasm, intensity, rhythms.*

manic-depressive *adj.* having to do with a psychosis involving alternating periods of mania and depression. —*n.* a manic-depressive patient.

man.i.cure (MAN.i.cure) *v.* -**cures**, -**cured**, -**cur.ing** trim, clean, and polish fingernails; *adj.:* *the* **manicured** *grounds of Memorial Park; a well-manicured hand; a manicured lawn*

manifest / mannish

(kept like one's hand). —*n.* the care of or treatment for the hands, esp. the fingernails. —**man.i.cur.ist** *n.*

man.i.fest (MAN.uh.fest) *adj.* plain and clear to the mind: *facts that are manifest to the view; a manifest error, truth;* In the 19th century, some thought territorial expansion was America's **manifest destiny**. —*n.* an itemized cargo or passenger list: *a shipping manifest; Your name is on the manifest.* —*v.* display or reveal: *She manifested little interest in the proceedings; Her true feelings began to manifest themselves later; the facts as manifested (= proved) by documents.* —**man.i.fes.ta.tion** (-TAY.shun) *n.*: *A dog wags its tail in manifestation of joy; a strike as a manifestation of political support.* —**man.i.fest.ly** *adv.* clearly: *manifestly absurd, false, unfair.*

man.i.fes.to (man.uh.FES.toh) *n.* **-tos** or **-toes** a public declaration of plans or policies, issued by a government or political party.

man.i.fold (MAN.uh.fold) *adj.* 1 many and various: *the manifold duties and responsibilities of a mayor; The reasons for the decision are manifold.* 2 having many parts or facets: *his manifold wisdom; a manifold personality, plan, program of action.* —*n.* a pipe fitting with many lateral connections: *an automobile engine's intake manifold; an exhaust manifold.* —*v.* 1 make manifold. 2 to duplicate, as in making carbon copies.

man.i.kin (MAN.i.kin) same as MANNEQUIN.

Manila hemp *n.* a strong fiber from the leaves of the "Abaca" banana plant, esp. useful for making ropes, formerly also used in **Manila paper**, a tough, buff-colored wrapping paper. Also **manila hemp, manila paper.**

man in the street *n.* the average person.

man.i.oc (MAN.ee.oc) same as CASSAVA.

ma.nip.u.late (muh.NIP.yuh.late) *v.* **-lates, -lat.ed, -lat.ing** handle with skill, dexterity, or craftiness: *He's good at manipulating marionettes; He manipulated the electorate to win the election; The accounts were manipulated in anticipation of the audit.*
 —**ma.nip.u.la.tive** (-luh.tiv) *adj.*
 —**ma.nip.u.la.tion** (-LAY.shun) *n.*
 —**ma.nip.u.la.tor** (-lay.tur) *n.*

man.kind *n.* 1 (man.KINED) the human race; human beings. 2 (MAN.kined) men, as distinguished from women or womankind.

man.ly *adj.* **-li.er, -li.est** 1 befitting a man: *manly sports.* 2 as a man should be; courageous, honorable, etc.: *a very manly youngster.* —*adv.* in a manly way. —**man.li.ness** *n.*

man-made or **man.made** *adj.* 1 made by human beings, not natural: *man-made climatic changes, pollution; man-made calamities, disasters, famines; Traffic, taxation, and such man-made laws.* 2 synthetic: *a man-made fiber, material, virus.*

man.na (MAN.uh) *n.* 1 in the Old Testament, food dropped from heaven to aid the Israelites in the wilderness. 2 a miraculous supply. 3 spiritual nourishment.

manned (MAND) *adj.* controlled by or carrying human beings: *a manned bomber, satellite, spacecraft, torpedo.*

man.ne.quin (MAN.i.kin) *n.* 1 a model of the human body, as used to display clothes in shop windows or by artists, tailors, etc. 2 a woman who models clothes for buyers.

man.ner (MAN.ur) *n.* 1 a way of behaving, esp. one characteristic of a person or that is conventional within a group: *an aristocratic, awkward, businesslike, cavalier, charming, courteous, flippant, friendly gentle, gracious, grand, ingratiating, matter-of-fact, obnoxious, overbearing, pretentious, servile, sheepish, sloppy, statesmanlike, stern, sullen manner; our doctor's fine bedside manner; Hold your fork in this manner (= way); They don't like it in* **any manner, shape, or form;** *He's a bit of a barbarian,* **in a manner of speaking** *(= if I may say so); He speaks French as if* **to the manner born** *(= as if French were his mother tongue); All* **manner of** *(= kinds of) people were there.* 2 **manners** *pl.* social behavior: *Mind your manners; Children have to learn (good) manners; Bad manners won't be tolerated; the manners and customs of the Saxons.*

man.nered (MAN.urd) 1 *comb.form.* having a certain way of behaving: *an ill-mannered clerk; mild-mannered people; a well-mannered child.* 2 *adj.* artificial or affected; showing a mannerism: *a mannered style, walk, writer.*

man.ner.ism (MAN.uh.riz.um) *n.* a manner or style that is considered excessive or peculiar: *Men and women differ in their mannerisms.*

man.ner.ly (MAN.ur.lee) *adj. & adv.* polite or politely. —**man.ner.li.ness** *n.*

man.ni.kin (MAN.uh.kin) same as MANNEQUIN.

man.nish (MAN.ish) *adj.* suggestive of a man's traits or manners; masculine: *her rather mannish bearing; a mannish style, way.*

manoeuvre / manuscript

ma.noeu.vre (muh.NOO.vur) *n. & v. Cdn.* MANEUVER.

man of the cloth or **man of God** *n.* a clergyman.

man of the world *n.* a worldly man.

man-of-war *n., pl.* **men-** formerly, a warship.

ma.nom.e.ter (muh.NOM.i.tur) *n.* an instrument for measuring the pressure exerted by a gas or liquid, as the sphygmomanometer used to take blood pressure.

man.or (MAN.ur) *n.* **1** a mansion on a large estate. **2** formerly, the house of a feudal lord, or "lord of the manor"; also **manor-house.** —**ma.no.ri.al** (muh.NOR.ee.ul) *adj.*

man.pow.er (MAN.pow.ur, *rhyme:* our) *n.* **1** the power of human strength. **2** the supply of people for work, including the unemployed and the retired seeking work: *manpower policies.*

man.qué (mahng.KAY) *adj.* [used after its noun] unfulfilled or frustrated: *a connoisseur manqué; poets manqué.*

man.sard (MAN.sard) *n.* **1** a gambrel roof with ridges on four sides instead of two. **2** the story immediately below it.

manse *n.* a parsonage, esp. a Scottish Presbyterian one.

man.ser.vant (man.SUR.vunt) *n.* **men.ser.vants** a male servant.

man.sion (MAN.shun) *n.* a stately or imposing residence: *a 15-room mansion; the governor's mansion; their Paris mansion; a Victorian mansion.*

man-size or **man-sized** *adj.* full-size or large: *a man-size dinner, job, portion (of food).*

man.slaugh.ter (MAN.slaw.tur) *n.* [legal use] the unlawful killing of one human being by another though not with malice as in murder: *a charge of manslaughter in the death of a bicyclist run over by a car.*

man.sue.tude (MAN.swi.tude) *n.* Archaic. gentleness or meekness.

man.ta (MAN.tuh) *n.* **1** a square-shaped scarf worn as a cape by Latin American women. **2** the wide-finned **manta ray** or "devil fish."

man.teau (man.TOH) *n.* a woman's mantle or cloak.

man.tel (MAN.tul) *n.* **1** the framework, often with stone or marble facing, around a fireplace. **2** the shelf above a fireplace, or **mantelpiece.**

man.til.la (man.TIL.uh) *n.* a light scarf worn over the head and shoulders by Spanish and Latin American women.

man.tis *n.* **-tis.es** or **-tes** (-teez) an insect with long forelegs for catching their prey, often seen lifted as if in prayer, hence "praying mantis"; also **man.tid.**

man.tis.sa (man.TIS.uh) *n.* in a common logarithm, the part to the right of the decimal point.

man.tle (MAN.tul) *n.* anything that covers or envelops, as a loose outer garment, the burning hood of meshwork covering the flame in a gas lamp, the outer body wall of mollusks that secretes the shell material and forms oyster pearls, the part of the earth between crust and core, etc.: *A mantle of snow covered the mountain; A mantle of darkness descended on the city when the power failed.* —*v.* **-tles, -tled, -tling 1** cover or be covered, as a pond with scum. **2** flush or blush.

man.tra (MAN.truh) *n.* a Hindu or Buddhist sacred utterance or chant: *Profitability is the mantra for capitalists.*

man.u.al (MAN.yoo.ul) *adj.* involving use of the hands or requiring physical skill; not automatic: *manual labor, workers; a five-speed manual transmission; the* **manual alphabet** *used by deaf-mutes; manual training in arts and crafts.* —*n.* **1** a handbook: *a car owner's manual; instruction, teacher's, training, user's manuals.* **2** the formal handling routine of a rifle or other weapon, called "manual of arms." **3** the manual keyboard of an organ. —**man.u.al.ly** *adv.*

man.u.fac.to.ry (man.yuh.FAC.tuh.ree) *n.* **-ries** a factory.

man.u.fac.ture (man.yuh.FAC.chur) *v.* **-tures, -tured, -tur.ing 1** make from raw materials, esp. by use of machines and on a large scale: *to manufacture and market goods; to manufacture products, product lines; Extractive industries like mining supply raw materials to related* **manufacturing** *industries; adj.:* hand-made *and* **manufactured** *goods; natural and manufactured gases.* **2** invent or make up; *adj.: a* **manufactured** *excuse.* —*n.* a product or the act or process of making it: *goods of foreign manufacture.* —**man.u.fac.tur.er** *n.*

man.u.mit (man.yuh.MIT) *v.* **-mits, -mit.ted, -mit.ting** free from slavery; **man.u.mis.sion** (-MISH.un) *n.*

ma.nure (mun.YOOR) *n.* animal excrement or dung used as fertilizer: *Spread the manure on your lawn; They sell fertilizers and manures.* —*v.* **-nures, -nured, -nur.ing** fertilize with manure.

man.u.script (MAN.yuh.script) *n.* something written, not printed: *the typed* manuscript of a book; a manuscript submitted for publication; an illuminated medieval manuscript; learned theses lying **in manuscript** (= unpublished).

Manx *adj.* having to do with the **Isle of Man** (of the British Isles), its inhabitants, or their extinct Celtic language. —*n.* **1** the Manx language. **2** *pl.* the Manx people.

man.y (MEN.ee) *adj., comp.* **more**, *superl.* **most** (MOHST) consisting of a large number; numerous: *many cats, men, things; Marc told him to get lost* **in so many** (= in those exact) *words*. —*n. & pron.* a large number of persons or things: *Many of them were absent; A* **good many** (= larger number) *passed;* **Many a** *student* (= Many students) *failed*.

man.y.fold (MEN.ee.fold) *adv.* many times.

many-sided *adj.* having many sides, aspects, or possibilities.

Mao.ism (MOW.iz.um) *n.* the philosophy and practices of Mao Zedong, 1893-1976, Chinese communist leader; **Mao.ist** *n. & adj.*

Ma.o.ri (MOW.ree) *n.* **1** a Polynesian native of New Zealand; *adj.*: *a Maori chief*. **2** the language of the Maoris.

map *n.* **1** a representation of a part of the earth on a plane surface showing the more important places, rivers, mountains, seas, etc.: *to read a map; relief, road, weather maps; Our village is not on the map; It was wiped off the map* (= completely destroyed) *by a tornado*. **2** a similar chart of the heavens to show positions of the stars. —**on the map** well known: *A writeup in a national newspaper put her on the map* (= made her well-known); *The Who's Who entry keeps him on the map.* —*v.* **maps, mapped, map.ping 1** make a map of a place: *James Vancouver mapped Canada's Pacific coast in the 1790s.* **2** plan: *to* **map out** *a project, one's time.* —**map.per** *n.*

ma.ple (MAY.pul) *n.* **1** any of over 100 species of shady trees of temperate regions, bearing double-winged seeds, or "keys," and having leaves that grow opposite each other: *The "sugar maple" yields a sap which is boiled to make* **maple syrup** *and* **maple sugar.** **2** the hard, light-colored wood of the maple. **3** the flavor of maple syrup or sugar.

mar *v.* **mars,** *pt. & pp.* **marred, mar.ring** spoil the beauty of something; damage slightly: *furniture marred by scratches; Nothing could mar her happiness.*

mar.a.bou (MAIR.uh.boo) *n.* the adjutant stork.

ma.ra.ca (muh.RAH.cuh) *n.* a rattle made of a gourd with seeds or lead inside, used in pairs as a percussion instrument in Latin American countries.

mar.a.schi.no cherry (mair.uh.SKEE.noh, -SHEE.noh) *n.* an artificially colored cherry used in desserts and beverages for flavor, originally preserved in **maraschino,** a liqueur made from a black Dalmatian cherry.

mar.a.thon (MAIR.uh.thon, "th" as in "thin") *n.* **1** a long-distance (52.2 km) foot race, as at the Olympics: *Fitness buffs run marathons.* **2** an activity requiring great endurance: *a dance marathon to raise money; a grueling marathon; Friday afternoons are marathons in our office;* **adja.**: *a marathon campaign, run, runner, session, week.* —**mar.a.thon.er** *n.*

ma.raud (muh.RAWD) *v.* raid and plunder; pillage. —**ma.raud.er** *n.*

mar.ble (MAR.bul) *n.* **1** a hard limestone rock, cut for use in architecture and carved into sculptures: *The Taj Mahal is built of white marble; a slab of marble for a tabletop.* **2** a small ball of marble, glass, or stone used in the children's game of "marbles": *a bad loser who picks up his marbles and leaves as soon as he's beaten.* —*adja.* of or like marble, esp. hard, white, and cold: *a marble floor; marble walls;* **adj.**: *a* **marbled** *hallway.* —*v.* **-bles, -bled, -bling** to color or make like the variegated pattern of marble; *adj.*: *a book with* **marbled** *edges; marbled effects, jade; well-marbled prime beef;* **n.**: *meat with a* **marbling** *of fat.* Also **mar.ble.ize, -iz.es, -ized, -iz.ing:** *a marbleized candle.*

March *n.* the third month of the calendar year, with 31 days.

march *v.* **1** to walk in military style: *We could hear the troops marching outside; She marched out of the room as if displeased; At the fire alarm, march* (= lead) *the children out in single file.* **2** progress steadily: *History marches on.* —*n.* **1** a marching or its manner or extent: *It's a day's march to the camp; A slow march suits a funeral procession; death, forced, peace marches; The protesters organized a march on Parliament Hill; We'll be* **on the march** (= moving along) *after breakfast; She* **stole a march on** (= outwitted) *us by camping out near the box office to buy the first ticket.* **2** a piece of music to accompany a march, as "When Johnny comes marching home": *funeral, military, wedding marches; to play* or *strike up a march.* **3** a border or frontier (district), as the **Marches** of Wales or Scotland separating them from England. —**march.er** *n.*

marching orders *n.pl. Informal.* **1** orders of dismissal from a job. **2** job instructions.

marchioness See MARQUESS.

march-past *n.* a procession, as of troops in review.

Mar.di Gras (MAR.dee.GRAH) *n.* carnival celebration of Shrove Tuesday in the French tradition, as in New Orleans.

ma.re (MAIR.ee) *n., pl.* **-ri.a** (-ee.uh) one of the dark, flat areas of the moon or Mars, once thought to be seas.

mare *n.* a mature female horse, donkey, etc.: *a brood mare (used for breeding).*

mare's nest *n.* **1** a "discovery" that turns out to be deceptive. **2** a mess.

mar.ga.rine (MAR.juh.rin) *n.* a butter substitute made from fats and vegetable oils.

mar.gin (MAR.jin) *n.* an edge or border, as the blank space around the written or printed matter on a page: *a text annotated with notes in the margins; to set a typewriter margin of five spaces; a letter printed out with justified margins; a comfortable, handsome, safe, slender, small, wide margin; within the allowed margin of error; a price markup with a large profit margin; a margin of safety; He won the election by a narrow margin* (= small majority or plurality).
—**mar.gin.al** (-ul) *adj.: a marginal case, difference, factor; to cut staff by eliminating marginal* (= borderline; barely acceptable) *staff positions;* **marginal land** *(whose yield will barely cover costs).*
—**mar.gin.al.ly** *adv.*

mar.gi.na.li.a (mar.juh.NAY.lee.uh) *n.pl.* notes in the margins.

mar.gue.rite (mar.guh.REET) *n.* **1** a species of daisy. **2** a single-flowered chrysanthemum.

ma.ri.a.chi (mar.ee.AH.chee) *n.* **-chis 1** an itinerant Mexican band of musicians and singers. **2** their music. **3** a member of the group.

Mar.i.an (MAIR.ee) *adj.* having to do with the Virgin Mary.

mar.i.gold (MAIR.uh.gold) *n.* a garden plant related to chrysanthemums with orange or yellow flower heads.

mar.i.jua.na or **mar.i.hua.na** (mair.uh.WAH.nuh) *n.* a drug prepared from the hemp plant, smoked as a narcotic.

ma.rim.ba (muh.RIM.buh) *n.* an African type of xylophone, having resonating tubes or gourds underneath the wooden bars for a richer tone.

ma.ri.na (muh.REE.nuh) *n.* a small harbor for pleasure craft with service and restaurant facilities.

mar.i.nade (mair.uh.NADE) *n.* a spicy solution or sauce to tenderize meat or add flavor to foods. —*v.* same as MARINATE.

mar.i.nate (MAIR.uh.nate) *v.* **-nates, -nat.ed, -nat.ing** soak in marinade or oil and vinegar; *adj.: a marinated leg of lamb; marinated vegetables served as salads.* —**mar.i.na.tion** (-NAY.shun) *n.*

ma.rine (muh.REEN) *adj.* **1** of the sea: *marine biology, life, stories.* **2** nautical or naval: *marine engineering; marine insurance; a marine propeller.* —*n.* **1** a soldier specially trained for assault operations by sea and land. **2 Marine** a member of the U.S. Navy's **Marine Corps. 3** the ships of a country collectively: *the merchant marine.*

mar.i.ner (MAIR.uh.nur) *n.* a sailor.

mar.i.o.nette (MAIR.ee.uh.NET) *n.* a puppet controlled by strings or wires held by the puppeteer hidden above the stage.

mar.i.tal (MAIR.i.tul) *adj.* having to do with marriage; conjugal: *marital bliss, counseling, tax deductions, ties, vows.*
—**mar.i.tal.ly** *adv.*

mar.i.time (MAIR.i.time) *adj.* relating to the sea: *a maritime nation* or *power with a good navy; maritime laws (of shipping and navigation); Canada's* **Maritime Provinces,** *or* **the Maritimes,** *are New Brunswick, Nova Scotia, and Prince Edward Island.* —**Mar.i.tim.er** *n.*

mar.jo.ram (MAR.juh.rum) *n.* an aromatic herb of the mint family used for flavoring foods.

mark *n.* **1** a scratch, spot, trace, etc. made on an object: *Sign at the "X" mark; a punctuation mark such as the comma and period; a question mark; quotation marks; Spots are the distinguishing marks of a leopard; "On your marks, get set, go!" said the starter before firing her pistol; He* **made his mark** (= gained recognition) *as an inventor.* **2** a target or goal; person or thing aimed at: *to find, hit, miss, overshoot the mark; I don't feel* **up to the mark** (= well enough) *on Monday mornings; Her replies to questions were all* **off the mark**

markdown / marriage

or **wide of the mark**; *Drunks are easy marks* (= victims) *for pickpockets*. **3** indication of some quality: *the marks of a gentleman; She gets high marks* (= grades) *in history; An M16 rifle is much more sophisticated than a Mark 1, or M1 rifle*. **4** the basic money unit of Germany worth 100 pfennigs.
—*v.* carry a mark or other indication: *a face marked by scars; The room was marked "Private"; Fireworks marked the end of the celebrations; Mark* (= Note) *my words well; items* **marked down** *for quick sale; She's* **marking time** (= waiting) *before springing the surprise on him*.
—**mark.er** *n.*

mark.down *n.* a price reduction or its amount.

marked *adj.* **1** easily distinguished: *a marked change, decline, improvement; in marked contrast; marked differences of color; a marked shift toward the left; a marked success; a* **marked man** *(with no chance of escape from attack, suspicion, etc.)*. **2** destined: *a promising youth marked for success*. **3** *comb.form:* a *pock-marked face; marked-down merchandise*.

mark.ed.ly (MAR.kid.lee) *adv.* plainly or noticeably.

mar.ket (MAR.kit) *n.* **1** a place for buying and selling goods: *a farmer driving to market; an expensive product priced right* **out of the market** *(so nobody can buy it); Excess supply creates a buyer's market with low prices; Publishers put books on the market; There's no market* (= demand) *for air conditioners in the winter; the labor market* (= supply); *the youth market* (= consumer group); *I'm* **in the market** *for* (= interested in buying) *a new car every five years*. **2** a shop or store: *farmer's, fish, food, fruit, meat, vegetable markets*. **3** the activity of buying and selling: *active, depressed, falling, firm, lively, rising, sluggish, steady markets; black, bond, commodities, futures securities, wheat markets*. **4** the stock market: *Speculators play the market; The market opened weak, but closed strong; bear* (= falling) *markets and bull* (= rising) *markets*. —*v.* sell: *the art of marketing used cars; a talent difficult to market because no one needs it*. —**mar.ket.a.ble** *adj.* —**mar.ket.er** *n.* Also **mar.ket.eer** (mar.ki.TEER) *n.*

mar.ket.place (MAR.kit.place) *n.*
1 where a market is held. **2** the world of business and trade: *the language of the marketplace; competition in the marketplace*.

marking *n.* **1** evaluation: *the marking of essays, projects, tests*. **2** a mark, marks, or their arrangement, as on a bird or animal.

mark.ka (MAR.kah) *n., pl.* **mark.ka** (-kah) the basic money unit of Finland.

marks.man (MARKS.mun) *n.* **-men** one who is skilled at shooting; **marks.wom.an** *n.* **-wom.en.**
—**marks.man.ship** *n.*

mark.up *n.* the increase in the price of an article from its production cost to its selling price.

marl *n.* a soil mixture of clay, sand, and calcium carbonate, as "shell marl" or "greensand marl," used for fertilizer.

mar.lin *n.* a large marine game fish with a spear like a swordfish's; also called "spearfish."

mar.line.spike (MAR.lin.spike) *n.* a pointed iron tool used by sailors to separate strands of rope; also **mar.lin.spike**.

mar.ma.lade (MAR.muh.lade) *n.* a clear jelly made of a fruit such as orange and pieces of its rind.

mar.mo.re.al (mar.MOR.ee.ul) *adj.* of or like marble; smooth, white, cold, etc.; also **mar.mo.re.an.**

mar.mo.set (MAR.muh.zet) *n.* a small, thick-furred, long-tailed monkey of S. and C. America.

mar.mot (MAR.mut) *n.* a ground-dwelling rodent of the squirrel family: *The woodchuck and groundhog are species of marmot; the hoary marmot of Siberia*.

ma.roon (muh.ROON) *v.* be left stranded and helpless: *The rising waters left people marooned on rooftops*.
—*n.* **1** a very dark brownish red: *Latvia's maroon-and-white flag*. **2** one left marooned like the fleeing black slaves on West Indian islands in the 18th century.

marque (MARK) *n.* a brand or make, as of a luxury or racing car: *the Mercedes marque*.

mar.quee (mar.KEE) *n.* **1** a canopy over an entrance, as of a theater or hotel. **2** a large tent.

mar.quess or **mar.quis** (both MAR.kwis) *n.* a nobleman ranking below a duke and above an earl or count; **mar.quise** (-KEEZ) or **mar.chio.ness** (MAR.shuh.nis) *fem.*

mar.que.try (MAR.kit.ree) *n.* inlaid work of shell, ivory, etc. in furniture.

mar.qui.sette (mar.ki.ZET) *n.* a sheer, meshed fabric used for mosquito nets, curtains, etc.

mar.riage (MAIR.ij) *n.* **1** the act of taking as husband or wife: *to annul, ar-*

range, break up, consummate, dissolve, enter into, propose, walk away from a marriage; common-law, communal, mixed, secret, trial marriages; Anne was given away (in marriage) by her father; a **marriage of convenience** (entered into for gaining some advantage, not out of love). **2** wedding: *the day of the marriage;* **adja.**: *the marriage bed, ceremony, night, reception.* **3** married life: *a long and happy marriage.*
—**mar.riage.a.ble** (-juh.buhl) *adj.*

mar.ried (MAIR.eed) **1** *adj.* living together as husband and wife: *She's single, not married; She may get married some day; a married couple; a much-married movie star.* **2** *adja.* having to do with the married state: *married bliss, life; married quarters (for married people).* —**n.** a married person: *young marrieds; newly marrieds (= married couples).*

mar.row (MAIR.oh) *n.* **1** the soft fatty substance filling the cavities of bones: *a bone-marrow transplant.* **2** the best or inmost part: *She felt chilled to the marrow.*

mar.ry (MAIR.ee) *v.* **mar.ries, mar.ried, mar.ry.ing** **1** take as husband or wife: *Lou married Lee; Each has married into a good family.* **2** unite, as in marriage: *Our pastor married Lou to Lee; Parents used to* **marry off** *their daughters; to marry urban development with environmental concerns.*

Mar.seil.laise (mar.suh.LAIZ) *n.* France's national anthem.

marsh *n.* a tract of low, hence often wet, soft land; swamp or bog.
—**marsh.y** *adj.*

mar.shal (MAR.shul) *n.* **1** an official with duties in a public place or at a public event: *a fire marshal (= head of a fire department); a parade marshal (in charge of parades, processions, etc.); A U.S. marshal is an officer of the federal court.* **2** an officer in the military or in the police force of a town or village: *an air marshal; a field marshal in the British army; a provost marshal (= head of a military police force).* —*v.* **-shals, -shaled, shal.ing** usher or present in an orderly fashion: *to marshal people into the auditorium; to marshal arguments, facts, forces.* Also **mar.shalled, mar.shal.ling** *Cdn.*

marsh gas same as METHANE.

marsh.mal.low (MARSH.mel.oh, -mal.oh) *n.* **1** a soft spongy candy made from corn syrup, sugar, albumen, and gelatin, originally from the root of the "marsh mallow" plant: *to roast or toast marshmallows.* **2** a person or thing that is soft and sweet: *She started work as a marshmallow and ended up a tough union leader; Some consider Walt Disney movies mere marshmallows because they don't show sex or violence.*

marsh marigold *n.* a marsh plant of the buttercup family with bright yellow flowers.

mar.su.pi.al (mar.SOO.pee.ul) *n.* a mammal such as the kangaroo, koala, or opossum that carries its young in a pouch outside the mother's body.

mart *n.* marketplace or center of trade.

mar.ten (MAR.tun) *n.* **1** a weasellike animal: *the pine marten of the northern coniferous forests.* **2** its soft, thick fur.

mar.tial (MAR.shul) *adj.* of war; warlike: *a martial air; his martial bearing; her martial spirit;* **martial arts** such as karate and judo. —**mar.tial.ly** *adv.*

martial law *n.* military rule imposed on civilians in a crisis.

Mar.tian (MAR.shun) *n.* a supposed inhabitant of Mars. —*adj.* having to do with Mars: *the Martian landscape, surface; Martian rocks and soils, visitors.*

mar.tin (MAR.tun) *n.* a bird of the swallow family, esp. the "purple martin" with long, pointed wings and forked tail.

mar.ti.net (mar.tuh.NET) *n.* a very rigid disciplinarian: *a martinet of an editor.*

mar.tin.gale (MAR.tun.gale) *n.* a strap of a horse's harness fastening the nose-band to the girth for preventing rearing.

mar.ti.ni (mar.TEE.nee) *n.* **-nis** a cocktail made of gin or vodka and dry vermouth: *a dry martini; a two-martini lunch.*

mar.tyr (MAR.tur) *n.* one who suffers much and even submits to death because of his or her beliefs or principles, as the early Christians did for their faith: *a martyr in the cause of freedom; a martyr for the feminist cause; to* **make martyrs** *of people (= make them suffer and become heroes).* —*v.* cause to suffer or be killed as a martyr.
—**mar.tyr.dom** (-dum) *n.*

mar.vel (MAR.vul) *v.* **-vels, -veled, -vel.ing** **1** to be filled with astonishment. **2** express wonder at something: *Everyone marvels at her patience.*
—*n.* something that causes one to marvel: *a marvel of architectural achievement; Our cook can do marvels with the right ingredients.* Also **mar.velled, mar.vel.ling** *Cdn.*

mar.vel.ous (MAR.vuh.lus) *adj.* wonderful or splendid; **mar.vel.ous.ly** adv.; **mar.vel.ous.ness** n. Also **mar.vel.lous, mar.vel.lous.ly, mar.vel.lous.ness** Cdn.

Marx.ism (MARX.iz.um) n. a theory of class struggle supposed to lead to a classless society and a "proletarian heaven," as developed by Karl Marx, 1818-1883. —**Marx.ist** or **Marx.i.an** n. & adj.

mar.zi.pan (MAR.zuh.pan) n. an almond-flavored candy shaped into fruits, meats, and toys.

mas.ca.ra (mas.CAIR.uh) n. cosmetic coloring for the eyelashes. —v. **-ras, -raed, -ra.ing**: *Chris arrived heavily mascaraed for the party.*

mas.cot n. a person, animal, or thing symbolizing good luck.

mas.cu.line (MASK.yuh.lin) adj. referring to or distinctive of the male: *masculine aggressiveness, courage; a masculine voice; French "soleil" for "sun" is of the masculine gender.*
—**mas.cu.lin.i.ty** (-LIN.i.tee) n.

ma.ser (MAY.zur) n. an electronic device that emits and amplifies microwaves.

mash n. a soft, pulpy mass, as of crushed malt or grain in hot water for making beer, whiskey, etc. or of bran or meal in water for feeding horses; adj**a**.: *mash beans, onions.* —v. **1** reduce to a mash: *to mash vegetables;* adj.: *a dish of* **mashed** *potatoes; garlic mashed to a paste.* **2** crush: *a finger mashed by a door;* adj.: *a* **mashed** *toe.*

mash.er n. a man who frequently makes passes at women.

mash note n. a flattering letter meant to soften up a member of the opposite sex.

mask n. **1** an artificial likeness of a person's face: *a death mask; Halloween masks; a hypocrite wearing the mask of friendship.* **2** a piece of material worn over part of the face: *Fencers and baseball catchers wear masks; gas, oxygen, ski, surgical masks; a stocking mask worn by a robber.* —v. cover or conceal, as with a mask: *She tried to mask her true feelings by smiling;* adj.: *a* **masked** *gunman; masked dancers at a* **masked ball**; n.: *A painter protects areas not to be painted by using* **masking tape**. —**mask.er** n.: *a masker taking part in a masquerade.*

mas.och.ism (MAS.uh.kiz.um) n. the pleasure or sexual satisfaction derived from one's own pain and suffering; **mas.och.ist** n. —**mas.och.is.tic** (-KIS.tic) adj.

ma.son (MAY.sun) n. **1** one who builds with stone, clay, brick, or concrete. **2 Mason** same as FREEMASON; **Ma.son.ic** or **ma.son.ic** (-SON.ic) adj.

mason jar n. a tight-closing glass jar used in home canning; also **Mason jar**.

ma.son.ry (MAY.sun.ree) n. **-ries 1** a structure built by a mason, as stonework or brickwork. **2** a mason's trade or skill. **3 Masonry** same as FREEMASONRY.

masque (MASK) n. **1** a theater entertainment of the 1600s having an allegorical theme, with actors wearing masks, and characterized by singing, dancing, and pageantry. **2** a masked ball or masquerade: *a Twelfth Night court masque.*

mas.quer.ade (mas.kuh.RADE) n. **1** a party at which masks and fancy costumes are worn. **2** a disguise or false pretense. —v. **-ades, -ad.ed, -ad.ing** pose: *A charlatan was caught masquerading as a physician.*

mass n. **1** bulk or quantity of matter, esp. large: *An elephant's body has mass.* **2** large size or number; also, the greater part or majority: *The mass of an iceberg is under water; Individuals showed interest, but* **in the mass** (= as a whole) *people didn't care.* **3** an amount or lump: *a chimney spewing masses of smoke; The flower beds were masses of color; a plastic, shapeless, sticky mass of dough; Asia and Europe form one land mass* (= expanse); *a politician's appeal to* **the masses** (= common people). **4 Mass** or **mass** a celebration of the Eucharist in the Roman Catholic and other churches: *The faithful assist at or attend or hear Mass; Priests celebrate or say Masses; to offer a Mass for the dead (souls in purgatory); a solemn high Mass on Easter Sunday, not a low* (= ordinary) *Mass; one of Palestrina's Masses* (= musical settings of the Mass).
—adj**a**. having to do with mass or bulk: *a crowd seized with mass hysteria; a mass meeting of citizens; mass* (= large-scale) *buying.* —v. form or gather into a mass: *Enemy troops were massing along the border.*

mas.sa.cre (MAS.uh.cur) n. a large-scale, esp. merciless slaughter of people or animals. —v. **-cres, -cred, -cring** slaughter: *Innocent infants were massacred in the war.*

mas.sage (muh.SAHZH, -SAHJ) n. a rubdown of the body or a part of it by kneading, stroking, etc. to relax muscles or stimulate activity in an organ: *a cardiac massage; a facial* massage given in a beauty parlor; **adja.**: *a massage center, parlor, technique, treatment.* —*v.* **mas.sag.es, mas.saged, mas.sag.ing 1** give a massage: *to massage someone's body; to massage* (= flatter) *one's ego.* **2** manipulate data, as by a computer. —**mas.sag.er** or **mas.sag.ist** *n.* Also **mas.seur** (ma.SUR) *n.,* **mas.seuse** (ma.SOOZ) *fem.*

mass-cult *n. Informal.* popular culture as spread through TV and other mass media.

mas.sif (MAS.if, ma.SEEF) *n.* a compact group of mountains and peaks.

mas.sive (MAS.iv) *adj.* having a large mass; large in quantity, scope, or degree: *a man of massive build; massive rocks; a massive assault, hemorrhage; threat of massive retaliation using atomic weapons; The patient suffered a massive stroke and is in critical condition; a massive structure.*

mass media *n.pl.* [usu. takes *pl. v.*] means of communication with the masses, as motion pictures, newspapers, magazines, radio, and TV; also called the **media.** —**mass medium** *sing.*

mass-produce *v.* **-duc.es, -duced, -duc.ing** produce on a large scale, esp. by use of machinery. —**mass production** *n.*

mass transit *n.* subways and such transportation for the masses.

mast *n.* **1** a long vertical pole or spar supporting a ship's sails, yards, rigging, etc. **2** any supporting post, as of a flagpole, crane, derrick, aerial, or antenna. **3** fallen nuts of forest trees serving as food for swine.

mas.tec.to.my (mas.TEC.tuh.mee) *n.* **-mies** surgical removal of a breast.

mas.ter (MAS.tur) *n.* **1** a person with power or authority, as the male head of a household, the captain of a merchant ship, a male teacher or tutor, the employer of a servant, etc.: *You are your own master when self-employed; The* **taxing master** *of a court can have your legal bills reduced if found to be excessive.* **2 Master** [courtesy title for a boy not old enough to be called "Mister"]: *Master John, son of Mr. Smith.* **3** one who heads an institution or activity: *the Master of Massey College.* **4** the holder of a university degree between bachelor and doctor: *Master of Arts, Education, Science; She's working on her master's (degree).* **5** a great artist, musician, or author; also, one who has reached a high level of learning or skill: *a past master of the art; a master of deceit; apprentices, journeymen, and masters; a chess master; the old masters;* **adja.**: *a masters competition in swimming, track and field, etc. for people over a certain age; the* **Masters tournament** *for golf masters.* **6** a controlling source or original, as the matrix of a phonograph record or a duplicating stencil or plate. —**adja.** principal or chief: *a master builder, craftsman, hand; The master bedroom is the largest in the house; a master plumber, not just an apprentice or journeyman; a master* (= main) *switch; the master* (= original) *tape of a motion picture.* —*v.* become master of or expert in an area: *Can humans master the elements? Kay has mastered calculus.*

mas.ter.ful (MAS.tur.ful) *adj.* **1** domineering, esp. by force of personality: *Lin had become too masterful for Lee to live with.* **2** showing great ability; masterly: *a masterful answer, performance, timing; the masterful Sherlock Holmes.* —**mas.ter.ful.ly** *adv.*

master key *n.* a key that opens many locks.

mas.ter.ly *adj.* expert or skillful: *a masterly command of the language;* **adv.**: *a masterly* (= skillfully) *executed plan.*

mas.ter.mind (MAS.tur.mined) *n.* one who plans and directs an operation or enterprise; *v.*: *a plot masterminded by the deposed king.*

master of ceremonies *n.* **1** one in charge of the formalities of a ceremonial function, as at a church service. **2** one who hosts an entertainment program or banquet, introducing guests, performers, etc.

mas.ter.piece (MAS.tur.peece) *n.* an extraordinary piece of workmanship; one's greatest work: *an enduring masterpiece.*

master plan *n.* an overall or general plan, as of a city.

master sergeant *n.* a high-ranking noncommissioned officer of the U.S. Army, Air Force, or Marine Corps.

mas.ter.stroke (MAS.tur.stoke) *n.* a masterly action or its effect: *a masterstroke of genius.*

mas.ter.work (MAS.tur.wurk) *n.* a masterpiece.

mas.ter.y (MAS.tuh.ree) *n.* **-ter.ies** command or control: *her mastery of English; an election giving one party mastery* (= the upper hand) *over another.*

mast.head *n.* **1** the top of a ship's mast. **2** in a newspaper or magazine, the title, address, etc. usu. carried at the top of the editorial page. **3** the "flag" or name plate at the top of the front page of a periodical.

mas.tic *n.* the pale yellowish resin of a Mediterranean tree used for caulking and in varnishes, plasters, etc.

mas.ti.cate (MAS.tuh.cate) *v.* **-cates, -cat.ed, -cat.ing** chew food or crush rubber to a pulp. —**mas.ti.ca.tion** (-CAY.shun) *n.*

mas.tiff *n.* a breed of dog with a broad head, drooping ears, and short muzzle.

mas.to.don (MAS.tuh.don) *n.* a huge extinct type of elephant with distinctive nipplelike projections on its molars.

mas.toid *n. & adj.* (having to do with) a bony projection behind the ear: *a mastoid infection.*

mas.tur.bate (MAS.tur.bate) *v.* **-bates, -bat.ed, -bat.ing** stimulate the genitals for sexual pleasure. —**mas.tur.ba.tion** (-BAY.shun) *n.* —**mas.tur.ba.tor** (-bay.tur) *n.*

mat *n.* **1** a plaited, woven, or felted piece of coarse material or small rug for use on the floor as covering, protective padding, for wiping shoes on, etc.: *bath, door, exercise, welcome mats; a* **place mat** *(for an individual's dishes, silverware, etc. at an eating table).* **2** a thick tangle or knotted condition: *a mat of messy hair.* **3** a border or background, as for a picture in framing it. **4** a dull surface or finish given to colors, glass, metals, etc.; also **mat, matte. 5** *Informal.* a matrix or printer's mold.
—*v.* **mats, mat.ted, mat.ting 1** make into or cover with a mat: *The hair is all matted; a wall matted with ivy.* **2** put a border or background around a picture, etc. **3** give a dull surface to metals, glass, etc.

mat.a.dor (MAT.uh.dor) *n.* a star bullfighter.

match *n.* **1** a person or thing that is like another, hence considered in an equal or opposite role: *A flyweight is no match for a heavyweight; Cy met his match in Sue; Sue is more than his match in* (= is better at) *problem-solving.* **2** a matching, as a contest: *a chess match; football match; to promote, stage a match; championship, play-off, return matches.* **3** a mating, as a marriage: *They're a good match as husband and wife; Jo and Ed will make a perfect match.* **4** a splinter of wood or a cardboard strip tipped with a substance that will catch fire under friction, as when struck on the specially prepared surface of a "safety match": *to light* or *strike a match; The arsonist put* or *set a match to the house; a box of matches.* —*v.* be or get a match for a person or thing: *Red and green don't match; Her beauty is matched by her wit; A blue sock cannot be matched with a red one; She finds herself matched against a world champion; She doesn't* **match up** (= is not equal) *to her rival;* **adj.:** *matching accessories; a* **matching grant** or **matching funds** *to induce the recipient to come up with half the costs, as of a project; a matching set of clothes.*

match.book *n.* a cardboard folder of safety matches on a strip of paper.

match.less *adj.* without equal; peerless.

match.mak.er (MATCH.may.kur) *n.* **1** one who makes matches for burning. **2** one who arranges marriages or boxing matches. —**match.mak.ing** *n.*

match.wood *n.* pine, aspen, and such wood splintered for making matches.

mate *v.* **mates, mat.ed, mat.ing** join as a pair or couple, esp. in sexual union: *Some animals don't mate in captivity; You get a mule if you mate a horse with a donkey; A queen bee mates with a drone; Birds mate in the spring;* **adja.:** *Spring is the* **mating** *season; an animal's mating call; mating behavior, dances, patterns, rituals.*
—*n.* **1** either individual of a matched pair or couple: *a bird crying for its mate; Where is the mate to this sock?* **2** a companion: *He's my apartment mate, not really a roommate; The running mate of the presidential candidate in U.S. elections runs for vice-president.* **3** an assistant or helper. **4** a deck officer of a merchant ship or a naval petty officer.
—**comb.form.** companion: *bedmate, classmate, helpmate, housemate, playmate, roommate, schoolmate.*

ma.té or **ma.te** (MAH.tay, MAT.ay) *n.* an aromatic tea made from the leaves of a South American holly and drunk from a gourd container.

ma.te.ri.al (muh.TEER.ee.ul) *n.* basic matter or resource from which other things may be made: *He has enough material to write a book; material for a book; building materials; packing material; padding material; promotional material such as buttons and banners; radioactive material; raw material(s); reading material such as books and papers; paper, pencil, and other writing materials; She's promotable because she's executive material; material* (= cloth) *for dresses.*
—*adja.* **1** physical and tangible, not spiritual or ideal: *the material world; our material comforts, possessions, well-being.* **2** tending to corrupt: *material greed.* —**material to something** having

materialism / matter

substance or importance: *evidence, facts, testimony, etc. that are material to a case or argument; A bystander was held as a material witness to the crime.* —**ma.te.ri.al.ly** *adv.*

ma.te.ri.al.ism (muh.TEER.ee.uh.liz.um) *n.* a theory, doctrine, or tendency that stresses matter and material aspects to the prejudice of the intellectual and the spiritual; **ma.te.ri.al.ist** *n. & adj.* —**ma.te.ri.al.is.tic** (-uh.LIS.tic) *adj.*

ma.te.ri.al.ize (muh.TEER.ee.uh.lize) *v.* **-liz.es, -lized, -liz.ing** 1 take physical form or give physical form to something: *A spirit may materialize at a séance.* 2 become real: *Impractical plans don't materialize.* —**ma.te.ri.al.i.za.tion** (-luh.ZAY.shun, -lye-) *n.*

ma.te.ri.el or **ma.té.ri.el** (muh.teer.ee.EL) *n.* military or industrial equipment, supplies, etc. as distinguished from manpower.

ma.ter.nal (muh.TUR.nul) *adj.* 1 having to do with being a mother: *the maternal instinct to protect children; maternal affection, feelings, leave, trust.* 2 on or from the mother's side of the family: *a maternal aunt, grandfather, inheritance, uncle.* —**ma.ter.nal.ly** *adv.*

ma.ter.ni.ty (muh.TUR.ni.tee) *n.* pregnancy and motherhood; *adj.:* *maternity benefits, dresses, leave; a hospital's maternity ward;* **maternity wear** (for the pregnant).

math *n.* [short form] mathematics.

math.e.mat.ics (math.uh.MAT.ics) *n.pl.* [takes *sing. v.*] the science of quantities and their relationships, using numbers, as in arithmetic, symbols, as in algebra, and figures, as in geometry. —**math.e.mat.i.cal** *adj.;* **math.e.mat.i.cal.ly** *adv.* —**math.e.ma.ti.cian** (-muh.TISH.un) *n.*

maths *Brit.* MATH.

mat.i.nee or **mat.i.née** (mat.un.AY) *n.* an afternoon performance of a play, opera, motion picture, etc.: *a* **matinee idol** (= male actor admired by women).

mat.ins (MAT.ins) *n.pl.* a morning prayer service.

matri- *comb.form.* mother: *matriarch, matricide, matrimony.*

ma.tri.arch (MAY.tree.ark) *n.* a mother who is the head of a family group or tribe. —**ma.tri.ar.chy** (-kee) *n.* **-chies.**

ma.tri.cide (MAT.ruh.cide, MAY.truh-) *n.* 1 one who kills his or her mother. 2 the crime itself. —**ma.tri.ci.dal** (-SYE.dul) *adj.*

ma.tric.u.late (muh.TRIK.yuh.late) *v.* **-lates, -lat.ed, -lat.ing** enroll in or be admitted to a college as a student. —**ma.tric.u.la.tion** (-LAY.shun) *n.*

mat.ri.mo.ny (MAT.ruh.moh.nee) *n.* **-nies** 1 marriage, esp. as a sacrament. 2 the married state. —**mat.ri.mo.ni.al** (-MOH.nee.ul) *adj.*

ma.trix (MAY.trix) *n., pl.* **-tri.ces** (-seez) or **-trix.es** a mold by which something is formed or shaped, as the skin at the base of a fingernail, the rock or groundmass in which crystals are found embedded, a female die for casting types, or a papier-mâché impression for making printing plates.

ma.tron (MAY.trun) *n.* 1 a motherly type of sophisticated or well-to-do woman. 2 a mature woman in a supervisory role, as in a hospital, dormitory, jail, or school. —**ma.tron.ly** *adj.*

matron of honor *n.* a married woman as chief bridesmaid.

matte (MAT) *n.* 1 unrefined metal, as copper, that sinks to the bottom of a smelter. 2 dull surface or finish; mat. —*adj.* finished with a dull, not shiny surface: *a matte finish, glaze, photographic print, projection screen, surface; a semi-matt print;* also **matt**.

mat.ter (MAT.ur) *n.* 1 material or substance that makes up something, esp. physical: *Matter exists in solid, liquid, and gaseous states; the mind's sway over matter* (= material part of the universe). 2 a subject of thought, speech, activity, etc.: *business matters; a matter of common knowledge; a matter of life and death; Aging is a matter of time; Owning a home is a matter of time and money; to arrange, clear up, complicate, settle, simplify, straighten out matters; to pursue or take up a matter; We'll give the matter serious consideration; Going to university is no easy matter; Committing a crime is no laughing matter; a matter of grave importance; to bring matters to a head; Matters came to a head; He's not an expert in matters of constitutional law; a matter of some urgency; Compatibility is at the heart of the matter;* **What's the matter?** (= What's wrong?); *We will give you our opinion* **without mincing matters** (= candidly); **For that matter** (= concerning that), *he is not even a lawyer.* 3 material or things: *printed matter; reading matter; organic, solid, vegetable matter; foreign matter in one's eye; postal matter such as letters and parcels; the subject matter of a poem.* —**as a matter of fact** actually. —**no matter** of no importance: *I forget who said it, but it's no matter; No matter who asks you,* refuse; Assert yourself, **no matter what** (= whatever happens). —v. have importance; count: *Does it matter who said it? It matters little (to me).*

matter of course n. something routine or happening regularly.

matter-of-fact adj. factual and prosaic: *a matter-of-fact account, report, tone of voice; quite matter-of-fact.* —**matter-of-fact.ly** adv.; **matter-of-fact.ness** n.

mat.tock (MAT.uk) n. a digging and cutting implement resembling a pickax but with a flat blade.

mat.tress (MAT.ris) n. a padding of straw, foam rubber, cotton, etc. to sleep on, usu. on a bed: *a firm mattress; soft mattresses; a spring mattress (supported by coil springs).*

mat.u.ra.tion (mach.oo.RAY.shun) n. a maturing process.

ma.ture (muh.TYOOR, -CHOOR) adj. fully developed or grown: *mature fruits; a mature wine; her mature wisdom.* —v. **-tures, -tured, -tur.ing** become mature: *Some mature faster than others; A wine has to mature to have body; a bond that matures* (= becomes due for payment) *in 10 years.* —**ma.ture.ly** adv.

ma.tu.ri.ty (muh.TYOOR.i.tee, -CHOOR.i.tee) n. a matured condition: *to reach maturity.*

ma.tu.ti.nal (mach.uh.TYE.nul, muh.TEW.tun.ul) adj. of the morning; early in the day.

mat.zo (MAHT.suh, -soh) n., pl. **-zoth** (-sote) or **-zos** (a piece of) unleavened bread eaten at the Passover.

maud.lin (MAWD.lin) adj. sentimental in a tearful or silly way: *a maudlin soap opera; He gets maudlin at family reunions.*

maul n. a heavy mallet or hammer for driving stakes, wedges, etc. —v. handle roughly; bruise or mangle: *mauled by a tiger; a new play mauled* (= badly criticized) *by critics.* —**maul.er** n.

maun.der (MAWN.dur) v. talk or act in a rambling or confused manner. —**maun.der.er** n.

mau.so.le.um (maw.suh.LEE.um, maw.zuh-) n. **-le.ums** or **-le.a** (-LEE.uh) a magnificent tomb built above ground, as the Taj Mahal or the original Mausoleum of Halicarnassus, Turkey, one of the "seven wonders" of the ancient world.

mauve (MOHV, MAUV) n. **1** a delicate shade of purple or violet. **2** such a dye. Also *adj.*

mav.er.ick (MAV.uh.rick) n. *Informal.* nonconformist: *a political maverick; an engineering maverick;* **adja.**: *a maverick financier, leader; her maverick talent.*

ma.ven or **ma.vin** (MAY.vun) n. *Informal.* expert or connoisseur: *fashion mavens; our microwave maven.*

ma.vis (MAY.vis) n. the European "song thrush."

maw n. the oral or similar cavity through which a bird, animal, machine, etc. devours something.

mawk.ish adj. sentimental in an excessive or insincere style: *a mawkish scene from Dickens.* —**mawk.ish.ly** adv.; **mawk.ish.ness** n.

max.i (MAK.see) n., adj. & *comb.form, pl.* **max.is** maximum; very long: *She wore a maxicoat over a miniskirt; A dress of maxi length is a maxi; a maxi-taxi* (= very large taxi).

max.il.la (mak.SIL.uh) n., pl. **-il.lae** (-lee) **1** the upper jaw bone. **2** either of a pair of insect mouth-parts used for handling food. —**max.il.lar.y** (MAX.uh.lair.ee) n. **-il.lar.ies**: *The mandible is the inferior maxillary;* **adja.**: *the maxillary bone.*

max.im (MAX.im) n. a proverb or precept, esp. a practical rule of conduct, as "A stitch in time saves nine."

maxima a *pl.* of MAXIMUM.

max.i.mal (MAX.uh.mul) adj. having to do with a maximum: *at maximal intensity;* **max.i.mal.ly** adv.

max.i.mize (MAX.uh.mize) v. **-miz.es, -mized, -miz.ing** magnify or increase to the utmost; intensify highly: *to maximize our efforts to achieve an end; to maximize profits with minimum capital; He stayed just long enough on the job to maximize his pension before retiring.*

max.i.mum (MAX.uh.mum) n. **-mums** or **-ma** the greatest possible or attained quantity, number, value, etc.: *The noise is at its maximum on weekends; the maximum allowed;* **adja.**: *the maximum speed limit on a highway; a maximum-security prison; yesterday's maximum temperature.*

may auxiliary v., pt. **might** (MITE) **1** [expressing possibility]: *I may be late; You might have asked yesterday; It may rain tonight; then again, it might not.* **2** [expressing permission]: *You may come in; May I have an apple?* **3** [expressing hope, contingency, etc.]: *He goes to work so that his family may be happy; May you be happy!*

May n. the fifth month of the calendar year, having 31 days: *the merry month of May.*

Ma.ya (MAH.yuh) n. one of a highly civilized tribe of Central American Indians or their language; **Ma.yan** n. & *adj.*

May apple *n.* a North American perennial herb of the barberry family that has dark-green, umbrellalike leaves with five to seven lobes, and whose roots are often used as a purgative.

may.be (MAY.bee) *adv.* perhaps: *Maybe I shouldn't have said that; He is maybe about 70 years old.*

May Day *n.* **1** May 1, a spring festival in some countries. **2** in socialist countries, a day in honor or workers.

May.day *n.* a distress signal used by ships and aircraft to radio for help.

may.flow.er (MAY.flow.er) *n.* a plant that flowers in early spring, esp. the trailing arbutus or an anemone.

may.fly *n.* **-flies** a short-lived, four-winged fly of ponds and streams, common in early spring, serving as food for fish; also called "day fly." Also **May fly.**

may.hem (MAY.hem, -hum) *n.* **1** [legal use] a crime of violence that maims a person. **2** violent or willful havoc: *murder and mayhem; the mayhem in our hockey rinks; the mayhem on Children's TV.*

may.n't (MAINT) may not.

may.o (MAY.oh) *n.* [short form] mayonnaise.

may.on.naise (MAY.uh.naze) *n.* a thick salad dressing made of egg yolks, oil, and vinegar.

may.or (MAY.ur) *n.* the elected head of a city or borough. —**may.or.al** *adj.*; **may.or.ship** *n.*

may.or.al.ty (MAY.uh.rul.tee) *n.* **-ties** a mayor's term of office or position.

May.pole *n.* a decorated pole around which merrymakers dance on May Day.

May queen *n.* a girl chosen as queen of May Day festivities.

maze *n.* **1** a labyrinth. **2** anything intricate or confusing. —**maz.y** *adj.*

ma.zur.ka (muh.ZUR.kuh) *n.* a lively Polish folk dance or the music for it.

M.C. (EM.see) same as MASTER OF CEREMONIES.

Mc.Coy (muh.COY) *n.* **the real McCoy** *Informal.* the real or genuine person or thing.

me (MEE) *pron.* **1** objective case of "I": *Give it to me; people like you and me; the* **me generation** *of people concerned about their own well-being.* **2** *Informal.* "I": *me and my friend; Not me! Me too!*

mead (MEED) *n.* **1** an alcoholic drink made from honey. **2** [old use] meadow.

mead.ow (MED.oh) *n.* a tract of moist, low-lying, level grassland; also **mead.ow.land.** —**mead.ow.y** *adj.*

mead.ow.lark (MED.oh.lark) *n.* a North American songbird with a yellow breast marked with a black "V."

mead.ow.sweet (MED.oh.sweet) *n.* a species of spiraea.

mea.ger (MEE.gur) *adj.* **1** poor or scanty: *a meager attendance, diet; a meager fare of bread and soup; a meager income.* **2** thin, not fleshy or rich: *a meager face, soil.* —**mea.ger.ly** *adv.*; **mea.ger.ness** *n.* Also **mea.gre, mea.gre.ly, mea.gre.ness** *Cdn.*

meal (MEEL) *n.* **1** food for eating at any time, usu. at a **mealtime** such as morning, noon, and evening; breakfast, lunch, dinner, etc.: *to cook, eat, enjoy, fix, have, order, prepare, serve a meal; heavy, light, skimpy, square, sumptuous meals; Dinner is our main meal of the day.* **2** coarsely ground unbolted grain, esp. corn. **3** any substance ground to powder: *bone meal.*

meal.y (MEE.lee) *adj.* **meal.i.er, -i.est** **1** covered with a meallike powder: *a mealy bug, insect; Butterflies and moths have mealy wings.* **2** same as MEALY-MOUTHED.

meal.y.bug (MEE.lee.bug) *n.* a sap-sucking scale insect covered with a white sticky powder.

mealy-mouthed *adj.* not speaking plainly or sincerely; given to mincing matters.

mean (MEEN) *v.* **means, meant** (MENT), **mean.ing 1** signify or refer: *What does "lark" mean? "Smoke" means a cigar to him, but to her it means fire; Do you know what it means to be an orphan? Your patronage means much* (= is of great importance) *to us.* **2** have in mind, as thought, intention, or purpose: *I didn't mean to hurt you; I mean you no harm; I meant it as a joke; It was meant for everyone; He* **means well** (= has good intentions). —*adj.* **1** bad by nature or disposition; petty, selfish, hard to manage, etc.: *Backbiting is mean; I feel mean after saying that; She's always generous to the poor, never mean* (= stingy). **2** *Informal.* skillful: *an excellent pitcher who throws a mean curve; He plays a mean banjo* (= plays the banjo skillfully); *She can run a mean mile* (= run a mile easily). **3** low; humble; poor: *the meanest flower of the field; a mean cottage; An Oscar is* **no mean** (= is a fine) *tribute to a young actress.* **4** in the middle or halfway between greater and lesser things, opposites, or extremes; average: *the mean annual temperature of a region.* —*n.* **1** something that is mean or average: *7 is the mean of 3, 5, 9, and*

11; the **golden mean** between too much and too little of anything. **2 means** *n.pl.* [takes *sing.* or *pl. v.*] agency or resource by which a purpose is achieved: *by fair means or foul; a means to an end; The end does not justify the means; You run into debt if you live beyond your means* (= income); *people of moderate means* (= wealth); *He got through* **by means of** *cheating;* **By all means** (= certainly) *let's help her if we can; It's* **by no means** (= not at all) *the last word on the subject; the* **ways and means** *of avoiding a tax; a* **means test** *to determine how poor you are.* —**mean.ly** *adv.;* **mean.ness** *n.*

me.an.der (mee.AN.dur) *n.* a winding course, as of a stream with a series of U-bends. —*v.* follow a winding course: *Children meander* (= wander aimlessly) *through the park;* **adja.**: *a* **meandering** *course, narrative, river.*

mean.ie or **mean.y** (MEE.nee) *n.* **mean.ies** *Informal.* one who is mean or petty.

meaning (MEE.ning) *n.* what is meant, as by a word, action, gesture, or other expression: *the meaning of "lexicographer"; clear, double, figurative, literal meanings; The meaning is obscure; the accepted meaning* (= sense) *of a word; Lexicographers never* **lose their meaning** (= importance); *Childhood experiences often* **define the meanings** (= things of significance) *in your life; if you* **get my meaning** (*Informal* for if you understand me). —**mean.ing.ful** *adj.;* **mean.ing.ful.ly** *adv.* —**mean.ing.less** *adj.*

meant *pt. & pp.* of MEAN.

mean.time *n.* **in the meantime** during the time between two happenings; also **mean.while.**

meany same as MEANIE.

mea.sles (MEE.zuls) *n.pl.* [takes *sing.* or *pl. v.*] **1** a contagious virus disease characterized by inflammation of the mucous membranes, high fever, and a rash; also called "seven-day measles." **2** a milder disease characterized by a pink rash; also called "German measles" and "three-day measles."

mea.sly (MEEZ.lee) *adj.* **-sli.er, -sli.est** **1** having measles. **2** *Informal.* worthless or contemptible: *a measly job; a measly $2,000; a measly 3% raise.*

meas.ur.a.ble (MEZH.uh.ruh.bul) *adj.* that can be measured: *a measurable difference, effect, improvement; measurable success; in measurable terms;* **meas.ur.a.bly** *adv.* —**meas.ur.a.bil.i.ty** (-BIL.i.tee) *n.*

meas.ure (MEZH.ur) *n.* **1** the length, weight, area, capacity, etc. of something according to a standard or system: *A hectare is a measure of area; cubic, dry, liquid, metric, square measure; a measure of time such as the minute or hour; The tailor will take your measure for a suit; a suit that has been* **made to measure** (= made to fit the customer); *The boss may* **take your measure** (= judge you) *by how you dress; My success is* **in a measure** or **in some measure** or **in a large measure** (= to some or to a large degree) *due to her; My gratitude to her is* **beyond measure** (= without limit). **2** a measuring instrument: *Use a tape measure.* **3** something measured: *six measures of grain; She had some measure of success as a lawyer; the full measure of my gratitude; I'll add $10 to what I owe you* **for good measure** (= as extra). **4** something measured rhythmically, as a foot of verse, a bar of music, or a dance. **5** a course of action: *to carry out* or **take measures against** *crime; coercive, drastic, extreme, harsh, preventive, safety, security, stern, stop-gap, stringent measures.* **6** an act of a legislature; statute: *a measure awaiting a vote in the House of Commons.*
—*v.* **-ures, -ured, -ur.ing** take the measure of a person or thing: *Tailors measure customers; This room measures 10 by 12* (= is 10 feet wide and 12 feet long); *You can't measure her performance against* (= compare her performance with) *his; He lost his job because he didn't* **measure up (to expectations).**
—**measured** *adj.* **1** having been measured: *a measured mile* (for checking speed); *a measured portion.* **2** regular or rhythmical: *the measured beat of a drum; walking at a measured pace; the measured tread of a walk.* **3** careful and precise: *a measured response.*

meas.ure.ment (MEZH.ur.munt) *n.* a way, act, result, or system of measuring: *the measurements of a room; exact measurements; the* **measurements** *of a human figure* (around the bust or chest, waist, and hips).

meat (MEET) *n.* **1** animal flesh used as food, esp. the "red meat" of cattle, hogs, and sheep: *cooked meats; to carve, cure, cut, fry, roast, slice meat; chopped, kosher, lean, minced, tender, tough meat.* **2** food; also, edible part: *to scoop out the meat of a coconut; "One man's meat is another man's poison"* (= What is good for one may be harmful to another); *the meat* (= substance or essence) *of his argument;*

Thrillers are **meat and drink** to her (= She gets a lot of satisfaction from reading thrillers).
meat.ball *n.* a ball of ground or chopped meat: *spaghetti and meatballs.*
meat.head *n. Slang.* a dunce or blockhead.
meat.pack.ing (MEET.pack.ing) *n.* the industry of slaughtering animals and preparing their meat for sale.
meat.y (MEE.tee) *adj.* **meat.i.er, -i.est** 1 having meat or fat: *a meaty morsel, texture, wrestler.* 2 having substance and content for thought: *a meaty essay, letter, speech.* —**meat.i.ness** *n.*
mec.ca (MEC.uh) *n.* a place one longs to visit, as Mecca in Saudi Arabia, the chief holy city of Moslems: *Our new mall is a shopper's mecca; Las Vegas, the mecca for high rollers.*
me.chan.ic (muh.CAN.ic) *n.* a person skilled in the use of tools and machinery; machinist or repairman: *an auto mechanic.*
me.chan.i.cal (muh.CAN.i.cul) *adj.* having to do with machines or mechanics: *Mary has great mechanical aptitude; a mechanical dummy who can't change a light bulb; a puppet's mechanical* (= machine-like) *movements; The longer a crowbar, the greater its* **mechanical advantage** (= the amount of work done relative to the force applied); *A draftsman's* **mechanical drawing** *made with instruments shows the exact shape and size of an object to be made;* **Mechanical engineering** *deals with mechanical power and machinery; A* **mechanical pencil** *has a supply of lead that may be pushed forward as you write.* —**me.chan.i.cal.ly** *adv.*
mechanics *n.pl.* 1 [takes *sing. v.*] the physics of forces acting on bodies when at rest and in motion: *fluid mechanics; quantum mechanics.* 2 [takes *pl. v.*] practical or functional details: *the mechanics of a contract; the mechanics of playing on an instrument; the mechanics of punctuation.*
mech.a.nism (MEC.uh.niz.um) *n.* a mechanical part, system, or machinery: *the mechanism of a watch; the mechanism of the universe; a defense mechanism for protection against having to face disagreeable situations; an escape mechanism such as daydreaming.* —**mech.a.nis.tic** (-NIS.tic) *adj.*
mech.a.nize (MEC.uh.nize) *v.* **-niz.es, -nized, -niz.ing** 1 do work by machine rather than by hand: *The post office has mechanized the sorting of mail.* 2 equip with machinery, as an army with armored vehicles, tanks, etc.

—**mech.a.ni.za.tion** (-nuh.ZAY.shun, -nye-) *n.*
med.al (MED.ul) *n.* a metal disk resembling a coin, to commemorate a person or event, given as an award for achievement, or bearing a religious emblem or picture: *a medal struck in honor of a hero; to award, earn, give a medal; the gold, silver, and bronze medals of the Olympics.* —**med.al.ist** (MED.ul.ist) *n.;* also **med.al.list** *Cdn.*
me.dal.lion (muh.DAL.yun) *n.* 1 a large medal. 2 a medal design, as on a tablet, an architectural panel, or a carpet.
med.dle (MED.ul) *v.* **med.dles, med.dled, med.dling** interfere improperly: *to meddle in* or *with other people's affairs.* —**med.dler** *n.*
med.dle.some (MED.ul.sum) *adj.* having a tendency to meddle: *a meddlesome busybody, relative; his meddlesome nature.*
me.di.a (MEE.dee.uh) *n.pl.* 1 [often used as *sing.*] same as MASS MEDIA: *electronic media such as radio and TV; the news media; print media such as newspapers and magazines; The media find* [rarely *finds*] *that bad news makes good headlines; the newer media* [rarely *medias*] *such as radio and TV; a media relations officer; a* **media circus** *with new albums, press releases, fan hysteria, etc.* 2 *pl.* of MEDIUM.
media event *n.* an event that has been stage-managed for its publicity value.
me.di.ae.val (mee.dee.EE.vul, med.ee-) same as MEDIEVAL.
me.di.al (MEE.dee.ul) *adj.* being in the middle: *a medial position; the medial, not initial "p" of "principal."*
me.di.an (MEE.dee.un) *n.* 1 a middle or intermediate number, line, etc.: *The median* (= average of the middle figures) *of 1, 3, 5, 7, and 11 is 5; The median of 1, 3, 5, and 7 is 4.* 2 same as MEDIAN STRIP. —*adj.*: *the median income of high school teachers; the* **median strip** *separating the opposite lanes of a highway.*
me.di.ate (MEE.dee.ate) *v.* **-ates, -at.ed, -at.ing** 1 act as a go-between in a dispute: *to mediate between the two factions in a dispute.* 2 to help settle something by mediating: *to mediate a conflict, dispute, issue.* 3 to achieve something by mediating: *to mediate an agreement; to mediate the release of prisoners.* —*adj.* (-dee.it) with something intervening or in the middle; not direct or immediate: *a mediate contact* (through a third party); **me.di.ate.ly** *adv.* —**me.di.a.tion** (-AY.shun) *n.* —**me.di.a.tor** (-ay.tur) *n.;* **me.di.a.trix** (-AY.trix) *fem.*

med.ic *n. Informal.* a medical student, practitioner, or a member of a medical corps.

med.i.ca.ble (MED.i.cuh.bul) *adj.* that may be medically treated; hence, curable.

Med.i.caid or **med.i.caid** (MED.uh.caid) *n.* a medical program to help the needy, as in the U.S.

med.i.cal (MED.i.cul) *adj.* having to do with medicine: *a medical condition, emergency, practitioner, school; medical care, ethics, literature.* —**med.i.cal.ly** *adv.*

medical examiner *n.* a coroner or similar public officer.

med.i.ca.ment (MED.i.cuh.munt, muh.DIC-) *n.* a medicine.

Med.i.care or **med.i.care** (MED.uh.care) *n.* 1 a program of medical and hospital services run by a government. 2 a similar program for people aged 65 and over, as in the U.S.

med.i.cate (MED.uh.cate) *v.* **-cates, -cat.ed, -cat.ing** treat with medicine: *Physicians are not supposed to medicate themselves;* **adj.:** **medicated** *cough drops, lotions, shampoos.*

med.i.ca.tion (med.uh.CAY.shun) *n.* medicine as administered: *a patient on* or *under medication for a heart condition; He'll be off medication in a month; to dispense, give, receive, take medication; oral medication.*

me.dic.i.nal (muh.DIS.un.ul) *adj.* having to do with the curing of diseases: *the medicinal properties of herbs.*
—**me.dic.i.nal.ly** *adv.*

med.i.cine (MED.uh.sin) *n.* 1 a substance or preparation used in preventing or treating disease: *Take some medicine for your cough; Doctors prescribe medicines* (= drugs); *nonprescription, over-the-counter, patent, proprietary medicines; The punishment proved strong medicine* (= cure); *They* **took their medicine** *(Informal for* accepted their punishment*) cheerfully.* 2 the science or art of treating and preventing diseases: *Doctors practice, study medicine; clinical, folk, holistic, internal, preventive, socialized, veterinary medicine.*

medicine ball *n.* a ball thrown from player to player for exercise.

medicine man *n.* a healer who relies on supernatural power, as a witch doctor.

med.i.co (MED.uh.coh) *n.* **-cos** *Informal.* a medical student or practitioner.

me.di.e.val (mee.dee.EE.vul, med.ee-) *adj.* of the Middle Ages: *medieval castles, churches, cities, costume, Europe, heritage, monasteries, studies, times,* warfare. —**me.di.e.val.ism** *n.;* **me.di.e.val.ist** *n.*

me.di.o.cre (mee.dee.OH.cur) *adj.* of average or ordinary quality; relatively inferior. —**me.di.oc.ri.ty** (-OC.ri.tee) *n.* **-ties.**

med.i.tate (MED.uh.tate) *v.* **-tates, -tat.ed, -tat.ing** 1 think with concentration of mind: *to meditate on* or *upon the quality of our lives.* 2 consider or contemplate an action: *Hamlet meditated revenge.* —**med.i.ta.tion** (-TAY.shun) *n.* —**med.i.ta.tive** (-tay.tiv) *adj.;* **med.i.ta.tive.ly** *adv.*

Med.i.ter.ra.ne.an (med.uh.tuh.RAY.nee.un) *n.* the sea enclosed by Europe, Africa, and Asia: *a cruise in the Mediterranean (Sea);* **adj.:** *the Mediterranean origin of Western civilization; a Mediterranean route.*

me.di.um (MEE.dee.um) *n., pl.* **me.di.a** 1 a means of conveying or communicating: *Speech is a medium of communication; Money is a medium of exchange for goods; French is the medium of instruction in French schools; the press as an advertising medium; advertising media such as billboards, direct mail, TV, radio, and periodicals; print and electronic media; local and national media.* 2 *pl.* **mediums** a person through whom spirits communicate with the living: *a spiritualistic medium.* 3 a substance or environment in which something exists or operates: *a culture medium for bacteria; ether as the medium through which light is transmitted; an artist who paints in the oil medium* (= pigment with oil as vehicle). 4 a middle condition or quality: *a happy medium between two extremes;* **adj.:** *a man of medium height; a medium income group; a medium radio frequency range* (between high and low); *a medium-security* (not minimum- or maximum-security) *prison.*
—**me.di.um.is.tic** (-uh.MIS.tic) *adj.* of or like a spiritualistic medium.

med.lar (MED.lur) *n.* a tree of the rose family bearing fruit resembling crab apples.

med.ley (MED.lee) *n.* **-leys** 1 mixture of various elements or parts: *a musical medley of marches; a* **medley relay** *in swimming* (in which team members swim the butterfly, backstroke, breaststroke, and freestyle in that order). 2 a hodgepodge or jumble.

me.dul.la (muh.DUL.uh) *n.* a core or cavity, as of a bone, hair, or kidney.

medulla ob.long.a.ta (-ob.long.GAH.tuh) *n.* an extension of the spinal cord into the back of the brain containing nerve centers of the body's vital functions.

meed *n.* [literary use] deserved portion: *meed of praise, victory.*

meek *adj.* patient and submissive, not self-assertive: *the meek and gentle nature of a religious person; She was meek and mild; I find him too meek and spineless.* —**meek.ly** *adv.*; **meek.ness** *n.*

meer.schaum (MEER.shum, -shawm) *n.* **1** a soft, white, clayey mineral. **2** a tobacco pipe with a bowl made of it.

meet *v.* **meets, met, meet.ing 1** come into contact or communication: *We were both at the party but didn't meet; Please meet me at home; Parallel lines never meet; (the corner) where King Street meets Second Avenue; We met all night over the matter; The Government and the Opposition meet head-on during question period; I have to meet the 8 o'clock flight from New York; There's* **more to this than meets the eye** (= This is not so simple as it seems); *We'll meet* (= play against each other) *in the finals; I'd like you to meet* (= be introduced to) *my family.* **2** deal with as required: *to meet a challenge, deadline, debt, enemy, threat.*
—**meet with 1** meet by chance; come across; come upon: *Cab drivers meet with all sorts of people; I met with an accident on my way home; met up with an old buddy at the fair; Her plans met with success* (= were successful); *His idea met with* (= received) *approval.* **2** meet and talk with someone: *We met with the demonstrators; We met face-to-face with their leaders to resolve our differences.*
—*n.* a coming together for a competition, the place where it is held, or the people at it: *a swimming meet; track-and-field meets.*
—*adj.* [old use] proper or becoming: *It is meet and just that we should do this.*

meeting *n.* a gathering or assembly, esp. to discuss or decide on something: *to adjourn, arrange, break up, call, call off, cancel, conduct, convene, hold, organize, preside over a meeting; chance, clandestine, closed, open, public, secret meetings; board, business, cabinet, committee, prayer, staff meetings; a mass meeting of students; a meeting between the two; She was at the meeting; The chair calls a meeting to order; a* **meeting of minds** (= understanding).

mega- *comb.form.* **1** large: *megalomania, megaproject, megavitamins.* **2** one million: *megadeath, megahertz, megaton.*

meg.a.bit (MEG.uh.bit) *n.* one million bits of computer data.

meg.a.bucks (MEG.uh.bucks) *n.pl. Informal.* money in millions of dollars.

meg.a.byte (MEG.uh.byte) *n.* one million bytes.

meg.a.death (MEG.uh.deth) *n.* in atomic warfare, a unit of one million deaths.

meg.a.flops (MEG.uh.flops) *n.* a computer speed of 10 million flops per second.

meg.a.hertz (MEG.uh.hurts) *n. sing. & pl.* a unit of frequency equal to one million cycles per second.

meg.a.lo.ma.nia (MEG.uh.loh.MAY.nee.uh) *n.* a mental disorder marked by delusions of personal grandeur, power, wealth, etc. —**meg.a.lo.ma.ni.ac** *n. & adj.*

meg.a.lop.o.lis (meg.uh.LOP.uh.lis) *n.* a continuous region of several metropolitan areas.

meg.a.phone (MEG.uh.fone) *n.* a funnel-shaped, hand-held device for making a voice louder, as used by cheerleaders.

meg.a.ton (MEG.uh.tun) *n.* the explosive power of one million tons of TNT.

meg.a.vi.ta.mins (MEG.uh.vye.tuh.mins) *n.pl.* vitamins in large quantities; *adj*a.: *a megavitamin supplement, tablet, therapy.*

me.gil.lah (muh.GIL.uh, "G" as in "go") *n. Slang.* a boringly detailed account: *the whole megillah.*

meg.ohm *n.* one million ohms.

mei.o.sis (mye.OH.sis) *n., pl.* **-ses** (-seez) in sexually reproducing organisms, a two-stage division to halve the number of chromosomes in a sex cell; **mei.ot.ic** (-OT.ic) *adj.*

mel.a.mine (MEL.uh.meen) *n.* a thermosetting plastic used for dinnerware, tabletops, electrical parts, etc.

mel.an.cho.li.a (mel.un.COH.lee.uh) *n.* a mental illness marked by extreme depression. —**mel.an.cho.li.ac** *n. & adj.*

mel.an.chol.ic (mel.un.COL.ic) *adj.*
1 suffering from melancholia.
2 melancholy.

mel.an.chol.y (MEL.un.col.ee) *adj.* gloomy, depressing, or pensive: *a melancholy person, scene, smile, song, thought.*
—*n.* a melancholy condition or mood; *afflicted with melancholy.*

Mcl.a.ne.sian (mel.uh.NEE.zhun) *n. & adj.* (a person) of or from **Melanesia,** an island group N.E. of Australia: *Melanesian languages, peoples.*

mé.lange (may.LAHNZH, -LAHNJ) *n. French.* an incongruous mixture; hodgepodge.

me.lan.ic (muh.LAN.ic) *n. & adj.* (one) having melanism or melanosis.

mel.a.nin (MEL.uh.nin) *n.* the dark pigment of the skin, hair, iris, feathers, etc.

mel.a.nism (MEL.uh.niz.um) *n.* abnormal development of melanin; opposite of ALBINISM.

mel.a.no.ma (mel.uh.NOH.muh) *n.* a blackish tumor such as a malignant mole.

mel.a.no.sis (mel.uh.NOH.sis) *n.* a melanin abnormality, as seen after a sunburn.

Mel.ba (MEL.buh) *n.* a very thin, crisp toast; also **melba toast.**

meld *n.* 1 in card games, a scoring card or combination. 2 a mixture or blend. —*v.* announce or show a meld of cards.

me.lee (MAY.lay, may.LAY) *n.* a confused hand-to-hand fight among a number of people.

mel.io.rate (MEEL.yuh.rate) *v.* **-rates, -rat.ed, -rat.ing** make or become better; **mel.io.ra.tive** (-ray.tiv) *adj.* —**mel.io.ra.tion** (-RAY.shun) *n.*

mel.lif.lu.ous (muh.LIF.loo.us) *adj.* flowing like honey: *mellifluous speech, voices, words.* —**mel.lif.lu.ous.ly** *adv.*

mel.low (MEL.oh) *adj.* soft, sweet, etc., as fruit when it ripens; not sharp, harsh, or strident: *mellow apples, colors; mellow soil that is rich and loamy; the mellow tones of a violin; mellow* (= mature) *wines, wisdom.* —*v.* make or become mellow: *People tend to mellow with age.* —**mel.low.ness** *n.*

me.lod.ic (muh.LOD.ic) *adj.* 1 of or like a melody: *the melodic pattern of a poem; a melodic, not harmonic sequence.* 2 melodious. —**me.lod.i.cal.ly** *adv.*

me.lo.di.ous (muh.LOH.dee.us) *adj.* pleasant-sounding; tuneful. —**me.lo.di.ous.ly** *adv.;* **me.lo.di.ous.ness** *n.*

mel.o.dra.ma (MEL.uh.drah.muh) *n.* drama of a sensational kind with much action and play of emotion. —**mel.o.dra.mat.ic** (-druh.MAT.ic) *adj.*

mel.o.dy (MEL.uh.dee) *n.* **-dies** 1 sweet music. 2 a song or tune: *to hum, play, sing a melody; a haunting melody.* —**mel.o.dist** *n.*

mel.on (MEL.un) *n.* the usu. large, juicy fruit of a trailing plant of the gourd family, as the watermelon and cantaloupe.

melt *v.* 1 change or pass from solid to liquid state: *Ice melts to form water;* **adj*a*.:** *melting ice, snows, temperature; the melting season.* 2 dissolve: *Sugar melts in coffee.* 3 disappear gradually, as clouds or mist in the sun; blend or merge: *The spy melted into the crowd.* —*n.* melted metal, esp. a quantity melted at one time.

melt.down *n.* 1 the melting of the uranium core of a reactor resulting in release of radioactivity. 2 a devastating change: *the stock-market meltdown* (= crash) *of October 1987.*

melting point *n.* the temperature at which a solid begins to melt: *Wax has a low melting point.*

melting pot *n.* a place where people of different races become assimilated: *Immigration has made America the melting pot or crucible of many cultures.*

mel.ton (MEL.tun) *n.* a short-napped, heavy, smooth, woolen cloth used for overcoats.

melt.wat.er (MELT.waw.tur) *n.* water from melted snow and ice.

mem.ber (MEM.bur) *n.* 1 a limb or similar organ of a plant or animal. 2 a distinct part or unit of a whole: *a member of a family; a Member of the Legislative Assembly; active, card-carrying, charter, corresponding, life, ranking members; the five members of the set of odd numbers less than 10.* —**mem.ber.ship** *n.* the state of being a member, members as a whole, or their number.

mem.brane *n.* a soft, thin, pliable sheet or layer of tissue covering a body surface or separating spaces, as the eardrum. —**mem.bra.nous** (MEM.bruh.nus) *adj.*

me.men.to (muh.MEN.toh) *n.* **-tos** or **-toes** a souvenir or keepsake.

mem.o (MEM.oh) *n.* **-os** [short form] memorandum.

mem.oir (MEM.wahr, -wor) *n.* 1 a biographical notice or a report based on personal knowledge of a person or subject. 2 **memoirs** *pl.* a wide-ranging first-hand record of events, as of a war, or of recollections, as of one's life. 3 **memoirs** *pl.* the proceedings of a learned society.

mem.o.ra.bil.i.a (mem.uh.ruh.BIL.ee.uh) *n.pl.* 1 things and events worth remembering about a subject. 2 an account of them.

mem.o.ra.ble (MEM.uh.ruh.bul) *adj.* worth remembering; notable. —**mem.o.ra.bly** *adv.*

mem.o.ran.dum (mem.uh.RAN.dum) *n.* **-dums** or **-da** (-duh) 1 a short or informal note, as to help one to remember something. 2 an internal business communication: *an inter-office memorandum about* or *on leaking secrets to the media.*

me.mo.ri.al (muh.MOR.ee.ul) *adj*a*.* that

commemorates an event or person: *a memorial dinner, holiday, service, statue.* —*n.* a memorial statue, publication, holiday, etc.: *a war memorial; to build, erect* or *put up, unveil a memorial to the war dead.*

Memorial Day *n.* a U.S. holiday in honor of members of the armed forces dead in wars, usu. the last Monday in May.

mem.o.rize (MEM.uh.rize) *v.* **-riz.es, -rized, -riz.ing** learn by heart. —**mem.o.ri.za.tion** (-ruh.ZAY.shun, -rye-) *n.*

mem.o.ry (MEM.uh.ree) *n.* **-ries 1** the capacity to keep something in mind and recall it afterward: *to commit a formula to memory; to recite a poem from memory; to jog someone's memory during a lapse of memory; She lost her memory as the result of an accident; I have a good memory for faces, a bad memory for names; It slipped my memory* (= I forgot). **2** what is stored or recalled: *a scene that evokes* or *stirs up memories of the past; bitter, blessed, dim, fond, photographic, pleasant, poignant, sacred memories; a monument erected in memory of war heroes; walking down memory lane* (= recalling the past with nostalgia). **3** a storage and recall system: *a computer memory; random access memory; a memory bank* (= data bank); *to add more memory* (= memory chips) *to a computer.*

men *pl.* of **MAN**.

men.ace (MEN.is) *n.* a threat or danger: *Hoodlums are a menace to society.* —*v.* be a menace to someone: *hoodlums menacing people in elevators;* adj.: *a menacing* (= threatening) *look.* —**men.ac.ing.ly** *adv.*

mé.nage or **me.nage** (may.NAHZH, muh-) *n. French.* a household.

me.nag.er.ie (muh.NAJ.uh.ree) *n.* a collection of wild animals, as for a zoo or circus.

mend *v.* of things damaged or needing improvement, to make or become as good as before or as they should be: *Use glue to mend a broken toy; a loafer told to mend his ways or be fired.* —*n.* a mending or what is mended: *The mend in his coat was showing.* —**on the mend** improving in health or recovering from an injury. —**men.der** *n.*

men.da.cious (men.DAY.shus) *adj.* lying; not truthful; **men.da.cious.ly** *adv.*

men.dac.i.ty (men.DAS.i.tee) *n.* **-ties 1** untruthfulness; also **men.da.cious.ness. 2** a lie.

men.de.le.vi.um (men.duh.LEE.vee.um) *n.* a synthetic radioactive chemical element.

men.di.cant (MEN.duh.kunt) *adj.* begging alms: *The Franciscans are a mendicant order of friars.* —*n.* a begging friar.

men.folk or **men.folks** *n.pl. Informal.* men, esp. of a family or other social group.

men.ha.den (men.HAY.dun) *n.* a herring of Atlantic coastal waters, used for feed, oil, and fertilizer.

me.ni.al (MEE.nee.ul) *adj.* domestic and lowly: *a menial task; menial work.* —*n.* [derogatory] a domestic servant: *the menials of their household.* —**me.ni.al.ly** *adv.*

men.in.gi.tis (men.in.JYE.tis) *n.* a dangerous brain disease caused by viruses or bacteria.

me.nis.cus (mi.NIS.cus) *n.* **-cus.es** or **-ci** (-sye, -skye) **1** the concave or convex top surface of a liquid in a tube. **2** anything crescent-shaped, as a lens that is concave on one side and convex on the other. —**me.nis.coid** *adj.*

Men.non.ite (MEN.uh.nite) *n.* a member of a Christian sect noted for their simple living and worship and opposition to military service, taking oaths, etc.

men.o.pause (MEN.uh.paws) *n.* the normal cessation of menstruation, occurring in most women between 45 and 50.

men.o.rah (muh.NOR.uh) *n.* the seven- or nine-branched candelabrum used in Jewish rites.

men.ses (MEN.seez) *n.pl.* the usu. monthly flow of blood from the uterus; period.

men.stru.al (MEN.stroo.ul) *adj.* having to do with menstruation: *the menstrual discharge, flow; menstrual pain.*

men.stru.a.tion (men.stroo.AY.shun) *n.* discharge of the menses. —**men.stru.ate** (MEN.stroo.ate) *v.* **-ates, -at.ed, -at.ing.**

men.sur.a.ble (MEN.shuh.ruh.bul) *adj.* measurable; **men.sur.a.bil.i.ty** (-BIL.i.tee) *n.*

men.sur.a.tion (men.suh.RAY.shun) *n.* the geometrical measurement of lengths, areas, and volumes.

mens.wear *n.* clothing for men.

-ment *n. suffix.* indicating act, state, result, etc., usu. of a verbal action: *abutment, government, statement; merriment.*

men.tal (MEN.tul) *adj.* **1** of the mind: *mental development, health, illness, retardation; a man with a mental age* (= intelligence level) *of 12 years;* **Mental cruelty** (= inflicting mental suffering) *is sometimes charged in divorce cases.* **2** having

to do with mental disorders: *a mental case, hospital, patient.* —**men.tal.ly** *adv.*
men.tal.i.ty (men.TAL.i.tee) *n.* **-ties** mental capacity or attitude.
mental reservation *n.* a qualification of a statement that is not expressed by the speaker.
mental retardation *n.* condition of below-normal mental development; formerly **mental deficiency.**
men.thol (MEN.thawl, -thole) *n.* a soft white substance with the pleasant odor and cooling properties of peppermint. —**men.tho.lat.ed** (-thuh.lay.tid) *adj.* containing or treated with menthol.
men.tion (MEN.shun) *v.* refer to or cite: *No one even mentioned it to me; The president mentioned her by name and praised her work;* **Don't mention it** (= "You're welcome," in acknowledgment of thanks); *The room costs $200 a night,* **not to mention** (= not counting) *extras.* —*n.* a reference or citation: *He made no mention of what happened; She winces at the very mention of the incident; He received only an honorable mention, not a prize.* —**men.tion.a.ble** *adj.*
men.tor (MEN.tor, -tur) *n.* a trusted adviser or teacher.
men.u (MEN.yoo) *n., pl.* **-us** **1** list of food dishes or the food served, as at a restaurant: *What's on the menu today?* **2** list of choices in using a computer program as shown on the video display; **adja. & cpd:** *menu options shown on a menu bar; a* **menu-driven** *computer that uses icons; menu-driven, not command-driven software.*
me.ow (mee.OW) *n.* the cry of a cat; also **me.ou.**
me.phit.ic (muh.FIT.ic) *adj.* bad-smelling; hence, noxious.
mer.can.tile (MUR.cun.til, -tile, -teel) *adj.* having to do with merchants or trade: *a mercantile economy, firm; mercantile law.*
mer.ce.nar.y (MUR.suh.nair.ee) *n.* **-nar.ies** a soldier or other hired person working mainly for money; hireling: *greedy foreign mercenaries;* **adja.:** *a mercenary force, motive, soldier, war; the mercenary aspect; mercenary troops.*
mer.cer (MUR.sur) *n. esp. Brit.* a dealer in textiles.
mer.cer.ize (MUR.suh.rize) *v.* **-iz.es, -ized, -iz.ing** treat fine cotton chemically for added luster, strength, and deeper dye: *mercerized cotton, denims.*
mer.chan.dise (MUR.chun.dise, -dize) *n.* goods or commodities: *the lines of merchandise carried by a store; general merchandise as well as specialty items.* —*v.* (-dize) **-dis.es, -dised, -dis.ing** trade in goods or commodities, esp. by use of market research, packaging, and promotion methods. —**mer.chan.dis.er** *n.* Also **mer.chan.dize** *v.;* **mer.chan.diz.er** *n.*
mer.chant (MUR.chunt) *n.* a trader such as a wholesaler, retailer, or shopkeeper.
mer.chant.a.ble (MUR.chun.tuh.bul) *adj.* fit for marketing; marketable.
mer.chant.man (MUR.chunt.mun) *n.* **-men** a cargo ship; also **merchant ship.**
merchant marine *n.* **1** a nation's cargo and passenger ships collectively. **2** their personnel.
merciful, merciless See MERCY.
mer.cu.ri.al (murk.YOOR.ee.ul) *adj.* **1** changeable in mood: *a mercurial temperament.* **2** of or containing mercury; also **mer.cur.ic, mer.cur.ous.** —**mer.cu.ri.al.ly** *adv.*
mer.cu.ry (MURK.yuh.ree) *n.* **1** a heavy, silver-white, normally liquid metallic element used in thermometers, barometers, etc. **2** a column of mercury; hence, temperature: *The mercury dipped* or *fell* or *plunged* or *plummeted to minus 20 degrees Celsius last night.* **3 Mercury** in Roman myths, the swift-footed messenger of the gods.
mer.cy (MUR.see) *n.* **-cies** kindness or compassion shown to someone out of generosity: *justice tempered with mercy; Have mercy on us; It's a mercy* (= blessing) *he wasn't killed in the fire; When the tax evader gets caught, he is* **at the mercy of** (= in the power of) *the government; left* **to the tender mercies** (= at the kind disposal) *of the tax department; The convict threw himself* **at** or **upon the mercy of** *the court.* —**mer.ci.ful** *adj.;* **mer.ci.ful.ly** *adv.* —**mer.ci.less** *adj.;* **mer.ci.less.ly** *adv.*
mercy killing same as EUTHANASIA.
mere (MEER) *adja.* nothing more or better than: *a mere child; He gets mad at the mere mention of the affair; mere words.*
mere.ly (MEER.lee) *adv.* simply or only: *You don't get money merely by asking for it; An air-conditioned room is not merely cool, but also dust-free.*
mer.est (MEER.ist) *superl.* of MERE; least: *at the merest suspicion of wrongdoing; attention to the merest detail.*
mer.e.tri.cious (mer.uh.TRISH.us) *adj.* alluring or attractive in a deceptive way: *a hooker's meretricious charms.* —**mer.e.tri.cious.ly** *adv.;* **mer.e.tri.cious.ness** *n.*

mer.gan.ser (mur.GAN.sur) *n.* a fish-eating duck equipped with a bill notched at the edges and having a crested head, esp. the **hooded merganser.**

merge (MURJ) *v.* **merg.es, merged, merg.ing** combine so as to lose identity or become part of something else: *The colors of the rainbow merge gradually, imperceptibly into one another; A small company may merge with a larger one; Many companies are merged* (= consolidated) *into large corporations.*

merg.er (MUR.jur) *n.* a merging or absorption: *to carry out or effect a merger of one company with another.*

me.rid.i.an (muh.RID.ee.un) *n.* **1** an imaginary line drawn from pole to pole passing through a particular point on the globe for measuring its longitude. **2** the highest point; culmination; prime: *in the meridian of his glory; at the meridian of her greatness.*

me.ringue (muh.RANG) *n.* a dessert topping for pies, puddings, etc., made with egg whites and sugar beaten stiff and baked: *a crisp meringue;* **adja.**: *meringue powder, tarts; Here's a lemon meringue pie for you!*

me.ri.no (muh.REE.noh) *n.* **-nos 1** a fine-wooled Spanish breed of sheep. **2** its soft heavy fleece. **3** the wool, cloth, etc. made from it.

mer.it *n.* real worth; what one has earned: *The picture is a mere copy with no artistic merit; intrinsic merit; Hiring for jobs should be based on merit alone; the relative merits of law and medicine as careers; a question decided on its* **merits***;* **adja.**: *a Boy Scout wearing a merit badge; merit pay; the merit system.*
—*v.* earn or deserve: *an important issue that merits your consideration;* **adj.**: *a well* **merited** *award.*

mer.i.tor.i.ous (mer.uh.TOR.ee.us) *adj.* full of worth or merit: *a meritorious action, deed; meritorious conduct, service.*
—**mer.i.tor.i.ous.ly** *adv.;*
mer.i.to.ri.ous.ness *n.*

merit system *n.* a system of appointing and promoting people in jobs based on competence.

Mer.lin (MUR.lin) *n.* a magician and seer who helped King Arthur.

Mer.lot (MUR.loh) *n.* a dry red wine made from dark-blue grapes; also **mer.lot.**

mer.maid (MUR.maid) *n.* an imaginary sea creature in the shape of a woman's body above the waist and a fish's body from the waist down.
—**mer.man** *n.* **-men.**

mer.ri.ment (MER.ee.munt) *n.* hilarious fun; gaiety.

mer.ry (MER.ee) *adj.* **mer.ri.er, mer.ri.est** full of fun and laughter: *a merry Christmas party, laugh, tune; We* **make merry** (= have fun) *at a celebration.*
—**mer.ri.ly** *adv.;* **mer.ri.ness** *n.*

merry-go-round *n.* **1** an amusement ride with wooden animals such as horses going up and down on a revolving platform. **2** a busy whirl of activities.

mer.ry.mak.ing (MER.ee.may.king) *n.* fun or merry entertainment.
—**mer.ry.mak.er** *n.*

me.sa (MAY.suh) *n.* a steep-sided hill with a flat top.

mé.sal.li.ance (may.zuh.LYE.unce, -zal.YAHNCE) *n. French.* a marriage with a person of lower social position.

mes.cal (mes.CAL) *n.* **1** an alcoholic drink made by Mexicans from the sap of certain agaves. **2** such a cactus plant. **3** same as PEYOTE; also **mes.ca.line** (MES.cuh.leen, -lin).

mesdames *pl.* of MADAM or MADAME.

mesdemoiselles *pl.* of MADEMOISELLE.

mesh *n.* **1** one of the openings between the cords or wires of a net, sieve, screen, etc.: *A 60-mesh screen has 60 meshes to the inch.* **2** a woven netlike material: *fine or coarse mesh; a wire mesh; caught in the* **meshes** (= threads or network) *of a spider's web, of the legal system;* **adja.**: *a mesh bag for shopping; a mesh knit; a wire-mesh kitchen basket.*
—**in mesh** interlocked.
—*v.* engage or interlock, as gears or zippers: *The two systems don't mesh; One doesn't mesh with the other.*

mesh.work *n.* network; meshes.

mes.mer.ism (MEZ.muh.riz.um, MES-) *n.* [former term] hypnotism.

mes.mer.ize (MEZ.muh.rize, MES-) *v.* **-iz.es, -ized, -iz.ing** same as HYPNOTIZE.

meso- *comb.form.* middle; midway: *mesosphere, Mesozoic.*

mes.o.sphere (MEZ.us.feer) *n.* the layer of the atmosphere between stratosphere and thermosphere.
—**mes.o.spher.ic** (-FER.ic) *adj.*

Mes.o.zo.ic (mez.uh.ZOH.ic) *n. & adj.* (having to do with) the era of geologic time intermediate between Paleozoic and Cenozoic eras, beginning about 220 million years ago.

mes.quite (mes.KEET) *n.* a thorny tree or shrub of the pea family that grows in hot, dry climates, common in S.W. United States and Mexico.

mess *n.* **1** an untidy, unpleasant, or confused condition: *What a mess! He made a mess of the job he was given; His office was in a real mess; to clean up* or *sweep up a mess; Use paper towels to mop up the mess.* **2** a group of people, as in the army, who regularly eat together. **3** such eating together or their eating place: *the officers' mess; They are at mess now; A mess sergeant is in charge of the kitchen.* **4** a portion of food, esp. a dish of something, as of meal or cereal: *a savory mess; a mess of pottage.* —*v.* **1** make untidy, unpleasant, confused, etc.: *an office messed up by a birthday party; The sales rep liked to* **mess about** or **around** (= putter around) *in the office instead of getting out to sell, but he did not* **mess with** (Informal for treat improperly) *the other employees.* **2** eat together, as in the army: *Chris was invited to mess with the officers.*

mes.sage (MES.ij) *n.* a communication: *the Queen's Christmas message to the Commonwealth; to convey, deliver, garble, scramble, send, transmit a message; clear, direct, hidden, strong, subliminal, subtle messages; a message* (= commercial) *from our sponsor; a poem with a message* (= theme or idea). —**get the message** Informal. take the hint or understand what is implied. —*v.* send as a message or send a message to a place or person: *The captain had messaged "fire on board" before crash-landing; to message someone's voice-mail box; a telecommunications carrier providing voice, data, and messaging services.*

Messeigneurs *pl.* of MONSEIGNEUR.

mes.sen.ger (MES.un.jur) *n.* one who carries a message or goes on a mission or errand.

messenger RNA *n.* a ribonucleic acid that carries the message or code for the formation of a particular protein.

Mes.si.ah (muh.SYE.uh) *n.* **1** the "deliverer" promised to Israel by the prophets, identified with Jesus by Christians: *They await the Messiah's arrival; the coming of the Messiah.* **2 messiah** a leader who promises a bright future: *She is being hailed as our next musical messiah; false messiahs; political messiahs.*

Mes.si.an.ic (mes.ee.AN.ic) *adj.* having to do with a Messiah: *the Messianic age of peace and freedom; the Messianic prophecy; Messianic times.*

messieurs *pl.* of MONSIEUR.

Messrs. (MES.urs) *pl.* of MR: *Messrs. T. Jones & Co.; Messrs. Jones, Smith, and McGrath.*

mess.y *adj.* unpleasant or untidy. —**mess.i.ly** *adv.;* **mess.i.ness** *n.*

mes.ti.zo (mes.TEE.zoh) *n.* **-zos** or **-zoes** a Latin American of mixed parentage, esp. of white and American Indian descent; **mes.ti.za** *fem.*

met *pt. & pp.* of MEET.

meta- *prefix.* beyond; over; after: *metabolism, metamorphosis, metaphysics.*

me.tab.o.lism (muh.TAB.uh.liz.um) *n.* the process by which a living being transforms food into energy (destructive metabolism, or catabolism) and into living tissue (constructive metabolism, or "anabolism"): *the basal metabolism of a body at rest; Vigorous exercise after a meal may disturb* or *upset your metabolism.* —**met.a.bol.ic** (met.uh.BOL.ic) *adj.*

me.tab.o.lite (muh.TAB.uh.lite) *n.* a substance that is essential to or that is produced by metabolism.

me.tab.o.lize (muh.TAB.uh.lize) *v.* **-liz.es, -lized, -liz.ing** subject to or undergo metabolism.

met.a.car.pus (met.uh.CAR.pus) *n., pl.* **-pi** (-pye) the part of the hand between wrist and fingers. —**met.a.car.pal** (-pul) *adj.*

met.al (MET.ul) *n.* **1** a mineral substance such as iron, lead, or copper that has a shiny surface, conducts heat and electricity, can be melted, etc.: *base metals; precious metals; Metals corrode, rust.* **2** an alloy or anything made out of metal: *The car was good only for scrap metal after the crash; sheet metal.* **3** basic material; also, mettle.

me.tal.lic (muh.TAL.ic) *adj.* like metal: *a metallic gray, luster, sound, voice; a car finished with metallic paint* (that glistens from bits of metal in it).

met.al.lif.er.ous (met.uh.LIF.uh.rus) *adj.* yielding metal: *metalliferous rocks, deposits, compounds.*

met.al.loid (MET.ul.oid) *n. & adj.* (an element such as silicon or arsenic) having metallic properties.

met.al.lur.gy (MET.ul.ur.jee) *n.* the extraction of metals from their ores and their modification for use. —**met.al.lur.gic** (-UR.jic) or **met.al.lur.gi.cal** *adj.* —**met.al.lur.gist** *n.* —**met.al.ware** *n.*

met.al.work (MET.ul.wurk) *n.* **1** artistic work using metal. **2** artistic things made of metal. —**met.al.work.er** *n.;* **met.al.work.ing** *n.*

met.a.mor.phic (met.uh.MOR.fic) *adj.* that has been changed in appearance and composition by heat, pressure, etc.: *Marble and slate are metamorphic rocks.* —**met.a.mor.phism** (-fiz.um) *n.*

met.a.mor.phose (met.uh.MOR.foze) *v.*

-phos.es, -phosed, -phos.ing change in form: *Tadpoles and caterpillars are metamorphosed into frogs and butterflies; rocks metamorphosed by heat.* —**met.a.mor.phous** (-fus) *adj.*

met.a.mor.pho.sis (met.uh.MOR.fuh.sis) *n., pl.* **-ses** (-seez) a complete change of form, character, etc. as if by magic: *the metamorphosis of a butterfly, frog.*

met.a.phor (MET.uh.fur, -for) *n.* a figure of speech using words in a meaning different from their literal sense, implying a comparison: *"The dawn of civilization" is a good metaphor; "The dawn and fall of civilizations" is a* **mixed metaphor**; *The Vietnam War has become a* **metaphor for** (= symbolic of) *disaster.* —**met.a.phor.ic** (met.uh.FOR.ic) or **met.a.phor.i.cal** *adj.*; **met.a.phor.i.cal.ly** *adv.*

met.a.phys.ics (met.uh.FIZ.ics) *n.pl.* [with *sing. v.*] a division of philosophy that studies fundamental problems of knowledge and reality beyond those of the physical world, as existence, essence, and causality; also called "speculative philosophy." —**met.a.phys.i.cal** *adj.*; **met.a.phys.i.cal.ly** *adv.* —**met.a.phy.si.cian** (-ZISH.un) *n.*

me.tas.ta.sis (muh.TAS.tuh.sis) *n., pl.* **-ses** (-seez) 1 the transfer of a disease, esp. cancer, from one part of the body to another. 2 a secondary tumor caused in the process. —**me.tas.ta.size** *v.* **-siz.es, -sized, -siz.ing.**

met.a.tar.sus (met.uh.TAR.sus) *n., pl.* **-si** (-sye) the part of the foot between ankle and toes. —**met.a.tar.sal** *adj.*: *the metatarsal arch.*

me.tath.e.sis (muh.TATH.uh.sis) *n., pl.* **-ses** (-seez) transposition of letters or sounds in a word, as "perty" for "pretty."

mete (MEET) *v.* **metes, met.ed, met.ing** usu. **mete out,** measure out; apportion or allot: *to mete out justice, punishment, rewards.*

met.em.psy.cho.sis (muh.tem.sye.COH.sis) *n., pl.* **-ses** (-seez) reincarnation of a soul in a different body, as in Buddhist belief.

me.te.or (MEE.tee.ur) *n.* the streak of light seen as a "shooting star" or "falling star" in the sky when a meteoroid glows on entering the earth's atmosphere.

me.te.or.ic (mee.tee.OR.ic) *adj.* of or like a meteor in swiftness, brilliancy, etc.: *a movie star's meteoric rise to fame; her meteoric career; a meteoric climb, growth, inflation rate.*

me.te.or.ite (MEE.tee.uh.rite) *n.* the part of a meteoroid that does not burn up before reaching the earth. —**me.te.or.it.ic** (-RIT.ic) *adj.*

me.te.or.oid (MEE.tee.uh.roid) *n.* a chunk of metal or rock falling to Earth from space.

me.te.or.ol.o.gy (MEE.tee.uh.ROL.uh.jee) *n.* the study of the atmosphere, esp. weather; **me.te.or.ol.o.gist** *n.* —**me.te.or.o.log.i.cal** (-ruh.LOJ.i.cul) *adj.*

me.ter (MEE.tur) *n.* 1 a measuring and often recording instrument, as for gas, electricity, distances, parking time, etc. 2 rhythm in music or verse, based on units such as beats, length or stress of syllables, etc.: *The time signature shows 4/4 meter or common time; the four-line ballad meter.* 3 the basic unit of length in the metric system, equal to 39.37 in.; also **me.tre** *Cdn.* —*v.* measure: *to meter office mail (with a postage meter); a seeder with a* **metering** *device to meter the spacing.* —**comb.form.** 1 a metric unit of length: *centimeter, kilometer, millimeter.* 2 a measuring device: *odometer, speedometer, thermometer.*

meter maid *n.* a female police employee who issues tickets for parking violations.

meth.a.done (METH.uh.dohn) or **meth.a.don** *n.* a substitute narcotic drug used in the treatment of addiction to heroin, morphine, and opium.

meth.am.phet.a.mine (meth.am.FET.uh.meen) *n.* a stimulant amphetamine, also used in weight control; speed (*Slang*).

meth.ane (METH.ane) *n.* a flammable gaseous hydrocarbon formed in marshes and mines by the decomposition of vegetable matter.

meth.a.nol (METH.uh.nol) *n.* a poisonous industrial chemical used as a solvent and in fuels and antifreezes; wood alcohol.

me.thinks (mi.THINKS) *v., pt.* **-thought** [old use] It seems to me.

meth.od (METH.ud) *n.* an orderly way or procedure for doing something: *the proper method of brushing the tooth; new teaching methods; to adopt, employ, use a method; antiquated, modern, up-to-date methods; deductive, inductive, scientific methods; There's (a)* **method in his madness** (= What he's doing is not as crazy as it seems). —**me.thod.i.cal** (muh.THOD.i.cul) *adj.*; **me.thod.i.cal.ly** *adv.*

Meth.od.ist (METH.uh.dist) *n. & adj.* (a member) of a protestant denomination based on the teachings of John Wesley; Wesleyan; **Meth.od.ism** n.

meth.od.ol.o.gy (meth.uh.DOL.uh.jee) n. **-gies** 1 the science of method. 2 a particular system: *the methodology of teaching.*

meth.yl (METH.ul) n. a hydrocarbon radical found in methyl alcohol and other organic compounds. —**methyl alcohol** same as METHANOL.

me.tic.u.lous (muh.TIK.yuh.lus) adj. careful, often finicky about minute details: *a meticulous dresser; meticulous in her work.* —**me.tic.u.lous.ly** adv.; **me.tic.u.lous.ness** n.

mé.tier (mait.YAY) n. a field of work in which one is specially skilled; forte: *Though trained as a teacher, her true métier was journalism.*

Mé.tis (may.TEES, may.TEE, MAY.tee) n. sing. & pl. a person of mixed white and native Indian descent.

me.tre (MEE.tur) Cdn. METER, n. 3.

met.ric adj. having to do with the meter as the basic unit of length: *The decimal metric system of measurement has meter, gram, and liter as basic units; a metric ton of 1,000 kg or one tonne; metric conversion (to the metric system).*

met.ri.cal (MET.ri.cul) adj. having to do with rhythm: *metrical form, rhythm, regularity; a metrical pattern, stanza, translation.*

met.ri.cate (MET.ruh.cate) v. **-cates, -cat.ed, -cat.ing** change into the metric system. Also **met.ri.cize** (MET.ruh.cize) v. **-ciz.es, -cized, -ciz.ing.** —**met.ri.ca.tion** (-CAY.shun) n.

met.ro or **Met.ro** (MET.roh) n. **-ros** 1 an underground railroad: *Montreal, Paris, Moscow, Washington, etc. have metros; We go to work on the metro; Most take the metro instead of driving;* **adj**a.: *a Metro station* or *stop, subway, transit system.* 2 a large city or its administration: *Our town is part of Metro; Mr. Lee is a member of Metro;* **adj.**: *the Charleston metro area; She's on the Metro board; a seat on Metro Council; a metro suburb.*

met.ro.nome (MET.ruh.nome) n. a device that ticks to mark time at an adjustable speed, used by musicians; **met.ro.nom.ic** (-NOM.ic) adj.

me.trop.o.lis (muh.TROP.uh.lis) n. 1 a large, important, or capital city. 2 the center of a specified activity: *a city once called the crime metropolis (= capital) of North America.*

me.tro.pol.i.tan (met.ruh.POL.uh.tun) adj. 1 having to do with a large city: *A metropolitan area includes a city and its suburbs; a metropolitan center, newspaper; metropolitan Washington; the metropolitan and rural markets.* 2 having to do with a federation of several municipalities: *a metropolitan police force, region.* —n. the head of an ecclesiastical province, usu. an archbishop: *In the Eastern Orthodox Church, a metropolitan ranks above an archbishop and below a patriarch.*

met.tle (MET.ul) n. 1 quality of character or temperament. 2 spirit or courage: *to prove* or *show one's mettle.* —**on one's mettle** ready to do one's best.

met.tle.some (MET.ul.sum) adj. high-spirited: *a mettlesome horse.*

mew 1 n. & v. same as MEOW. 2 v. to cage a hawk, etc. or shut someone up. 3 **mews** n.pl. [with sing. v.] an alley or street.

mewl (MYOOL) v. make a feeble or whining cry; **n.**: *None of your* **mewling** *here;* **adj**a: *a* **mewling** *baby.*

Mex.i.can (MEX.i.cun) n. & adj. (a person) of or from **Mexico**, a republic just S. of the U.S.

Mexican standoff n. a confrontation that results in an impasse.

mez.za.nine (MEZ.uh.neen) n. 1 a middle story between a building's first floor and second floor. 2 a balcony over the main floor, as of a theater, esp. its forward part.

mezzo-soprano (MET.soh.suh.PRAN.oh, MEZ.oh-) n. **-nos** (a singer with) a voice between contralto and soprano.

mi.aow or **mi.oaw** (mee.OW) same as MEOW.

mi.as.ma (my.AZ.muh) n. an evil-smelling vapor, considered infectious, as of swamps. —**mi.as.mic** or **mi.as.mal** adj.

mi.ca (MY.cuh) n. a mineral that is formed of very thin transparent layers.

mice pl. of MOUSE.

mick.ey (MICK.ee) n. *Slang.* 1 a doctored alcoholic drink; also **Mickey Finn.** 2 *Cdn.* a half-bottle of wine or liquor.

Mick.ey Mouse (MICK.ee-) adj.a. *Informal.* trivial, petty, or second-rate: *a Mickey Mouse computer system, contract, effort, job.*

Mic.mac n. & adj. (a member) of an Algonquian Indian tribe of E. Canada.

mi.cro (MY.croh) n. **-cros** [short form] microcomputer. —**comb.form.** very small: *microcosm, microfilm, microorganism.*

mi.crobe (MY.crobe) n. a disease-causing microorganism. —**mi.cro.bi.al** (my.CROH.bee.ul) or **mi.cro.bic** adj.

mi.cro.bi.ol.ogy (MY.croh.bye.OL.uh.jee) *n.* a branch of biology dealing with microorganisms; **mi.cro.bi.ol.o.gist** *n.*

mi.cro.burst (MY.croh.burst) same as WIND SHEAR.

mi.cro.chip (MY.croh.chip) *n.* an integrated circuit on a tiny wafer of silicon. Also **mi.cro.cir.cuit** (MY.croh.sur.kit).

mi.cro.com.put.er (MY.croh.cum.PEW.tur) *n.* a computer system built around one or more microprocessors.

mi.cro.cosm (MY.croh.coz.um) *n.* a little world: *the universe in microcosm* (= miniature). —**mi.cro.cos.mic** (-COZ.mic) *adj.*

mi.cro.e.lec.tron.ics (MY.croh.i.lec.TRON.ics) *n.pl.* [with *sing. v.*] the electronics of microminiaturized circuits.

mi.cro.fiche (MY.cruh.feesh) *n. sing. & pl.*, rarely **-fich.es** *pl.* a card-size sheet of microfilm containing many pages.

mi.cro.film (MY.croh.film) *n.* a film copy of a document, book, etc. in highly reduced size.

mi.cro.form (MY.croh.form) *n.* microfiche, microfilm, or other such method of information storage.

mi.cro.lite (MY.cruh.lite) *n.* a very light aircraft for one person.

mi.crom.e.ter (my.CROM.uh.tur) *n.* an instrument for measuring very small dimensions, used in microscopes, surveyor's instruments, and the **micrometer calliper** which can measure accurately to 0.00254 mm (0.0001 in.).

mi.cro.min.i.a.ture (my.croh.MIN.ee.uh.chur) *adja.* of extremely small electronic circuits: *a microminiature component*. Also **mi.cro.min.i.a.tur.ized** *adj.*.

mi.cron (MY.cron) *n.* one millionth of a meter.

Mi.cro.ne.sian (my.cruh.NEE.zhun) *n. & adj.* (a person or language) of **Micronesia**, the part of Oceania E. of the Philippines, including Guam and the Caroline, Gilbert, and Marshall Islands.

mi.cro.or.gan.ism (my.croh.OR.gun.iz.um) *n.* a microscopic animal or vegetable organism such as a bacterium, fungus, or virus.

mi.cro.phone (MY.cruh.fone) *n.* an instrument for changing sound into electrical signals, for transmission as in a telephone or for magnification as in a public-address system.

mi.cro.proc.es.sor (my.croh.PROS.uh.sur) *n.* a data-processing unit built on a tiny silicon chip.

mi.cro.scope (MY.cruh.scope) *n.* an optical instrument for viewing very minute objects. —**mi.cro.scop.ic** (-SCOP.ic) *adj.*; **mi.cro.scop.i.cal.ly** *adv.* —**mi.cros.co.py** (my.CROS.cuh.pee) *n.*

mi.cro.sur.ger.y (my.cruh.SUR.juh.ree) *n.* operation on microscopic structures such as blood cells.

mi.cro.wave (MY.cruh.wave) *n.* **1** a radio wave varying between 1 mm and 30 cm in length, as used in radar, TV, and the **microwave oven** for cooking food electronically. **2** a microwave oven: *microwave cooking; Is that bowl microwave-safe?* —*v.* cook in a microwave: *Microwave it uncovered on "high" for six minutes; adj.: He likes his bacon microwaved; microwaved popcorn.*

mid 1 *prep.* [old use] amid; also **'mid**: *Fox sat down and Burke rose to speak, mid visible emotion.* **2** *adja. & comb.form.* middle: *in mid career, ocean, winter; since the mid 1990s; mid-January; mid-morning; in her mid-fifties; mid-term.*

mid.air *n.* in the air well above the ground: *left suspended in midair; adja.: a midair collision of aircraft; midair refueling.*

Mi.das (MY.dus) *n.* in Greek myth, a king who had the power to change whatever he touched into gold: *a billionaire with the Midas touch.*

mid.cult *n.* middle-class culture, only moderately intellectual; middlebrow culture.

mid.day *n.* the middle of the day; noon: *Is it hottest at midday? adja.: a midday meal; the midday heat, sun.*

mid.den (MID.un) *n.* a refuse heap, esp. an archeological find containing tools, pottery, etc. left by prehistoric people.

mid.dle (MID.ul) *adj.* intermediate or in between two extremes of length, duration, size, attitude, etc.: *the middle distance (between foreground and background, as in a picture); Most of the tax is collected from the middle-income group; a middle position politically between Right and Left.* —*n.* a middle point, part, etc.: *the middle of the night, room, street; Pat measures 25 in.* (= 63.5 cm) *round the middle* (= waist).

middle age *n.* **1** the time of life between youth and old age, usu. 40 to 65 years; **middle-aged** *adj.* **2 Middle Ages** *pl.* the period of European history between about A.D. 500 and 1500.

Middle America *n.* **1** the American middle class with moderate political views. **2** the Midwest. —**Middle American** *n. & adj.*

mid.dle.brow (MID.ul.brow, *rhyme:* how)

middle class / Midwest

adj. moderately intellectual, neither highbrow nor lowbrow. —*n.* such a person.

middle class *n.* the social class between the upper class and the lower working class, with an above-average education and standard of living. —**middle-class** *adj.*

middle ear *n.* the part of the ear between the external ear and the inner ear, including the eardrum and three small bones in humans.

Middle East *n.* a large region of northeastern Africa and southwestern Asia, including Iran, Iraq, the Arabian Peninsula, Turkey, Egypt, and the Sudan; **Middle Eastern** *adj.*

middle ground *n.* a position of moderation: *to find a middle ground between socialism and democracy; to take the middle ground.*

middle initial *n.* the initial letter of a person's middle name.

mid.dle.man (MID.ul.man) *n.* **-men 1** a go-between or intermediary. **2** a trader such as a broker, packer, wholesaler, or retailer who buys from a producer for sale to consumers.

middle management *n.* managerial personnel intermediate between supervisors and senior administrators.

middle name *n.* a name used between a person's first name and surname: *The middle name of John H. Doe is "Henry."*

middle-of-the-road *adj.* of moderate views, esp. in politics, avoiding extremes of Right and Left.
—**middle-of-the-roader** *n.*

middle school *n.* a school linking elementary and high school, usu. grades 5 to 8.

mid.dle.weight (MID.ul.wait) *n.* a person of average weight, esp. a boxer weighing between 147 and 160 lb. (67 and 75 kg for Olympics).

mid.dling (MID.ling) *adj.* of average size, degree, or quality, often mediocre.

mid.dy *n.* **mid.dies** *Informal.* **1** midshipman. **2** a loose blouse with a sailor collar; also **middy blouse.**

Mid.east same as MIDDLE EAST.

midge (MIJ) *n.* a small fly or insect such as a gnat.

mid.get (MIJ.it) *n.* a person or thing proportionately small of its kind: *a circus featuring midgets; France and Britain are nuclear midgets, not giants; You're not playing midgets in this game; She races midgets.* —**adj.**: *midget car racing; midget championships, drivers, submarines;* **midget golf** (= miniature golf).

mid.i (MID.ee) *n.* a coat, dress, or skirt reaching to the middle of the calf.

mid.land (MID.lund) *n.* the middle or interior of a country.

mid.life crisis *n.* the anxious situation that sometimes results when people realize that they are not young anymore.

mid.most *n., adj. & adv.* (the part or area) nearest the middle.

mid.night *n. & adj.* of or at the middle of the night; 12 o'clock at night.
—**burn the midnight oil** study or work late at night.

midnight sun *n.* the sun seen above the horizon continuously for six months of the year in the polar regions, as in parts of Norway, the "land of the midnight sun."

mid.point *n.* the middle part or stage of anything having duration or extension.

mid.riff *n.* **1** the middle portion of the human body between chest and waist. **2** a section of a woman's garment that covers or exposes this: *a lace midriff.*

mid-rise *n.* an apartment building that is not a high-rise or walkup.

mid.ship.man (MID.ship.mun) *n.* **-men** a student naval officer.

mid.ships same as AMIDSHIPS.

mid.size *adj.* intermediate in size: *A midsize car is larger than a compact.*

midst *n.* a middle or surrounded position: *a traitor in our midst; I found time to help him* **in the midst of** *my other preoccupations.* —*prep.* [old or poetic use] amidst; also **'midst.**

mid.stream *n.* the middle of a stream: *It's wasteful to abandon a project in midstream.*

mid.sum.mer (MID.sum.ur) *n.* the middle of summer, esp. the summer solstice.

mid.term *n. & adj.* (in) the middle of a term of office, school, etc.

mid.town *n.* the middle section of a town between downtown and uptown: *a taxi ride to midtown;* **adj.**: *a midtown apartment; midtown Manhattan.*

mid.way *n.* an avenue containing amusements, side shows, and concessions at a fair or carnival. —*adj. & adv.* in the middle: *a midway point; The bus broke down midway between home and school.*

mid.week *n. & adj.* (in) the middle of the week; **mid.week.ly** *adj. & adv.*

Mid.west *n.* the north central region of the U.S. forming the American heartland, bounded by the Rockies, the southern boundaries of Kansas and Missouri, the Ohio River, and the Appalachians. —**Mid.west.ern** *adj.*;

Mid.west.ern.er n.
mid.wife n. -**wives** a woman who helps mothers in childbirth.
mid.wife.ry (mid.WIF.ree, -WYE.fuh.ree) n. the work of a midwife.
mid.win.ter (MID.WIN.tur) n. the middle of winter, esp. the winter solstice.
mien (MEEN) n. one's appearance, bearing, or demeanor as expressive of character or mood: *a man of sorrowful mien.*
miff v. *Informal.* put someone into a peevish fit: *He was miffed by her remarks;* **adj.**: *He was miffed at her; miffed about being snubbed.* —**miff.y** *adj.* touchy.
MIG or **Mig** (MIG) n. a Russian jet fighter.
might pt. of MAY. —n. overwhelming strength, power, or authority: *a dictator who thinks might is right; She attacked the problem with all her might; He fought with might and main* (= with all his strength).
might.y *adj.* **might.i.er, -i.est** extremely strong or great: *the mighty warrior; a mighty blow; How the mighty (people) have fallen!* —*adv. Informal.* extremely; very: *That's mighty nice of you; It matters mighty little.* —**might.i.ly** *adv.*; **might.i.ness** n.
mi.gnon.ette (min.yuh.NET) n. 1 a hardy garden plant with soft-green leaves and tall spikes of fragrant, tiny, yellowish-green flowers. 2 the yellowish-green color.
mi.graine (MY.grain) n. a severe kind of repeatedly occurring headache, usu. on one side, sometimes accompanied by nausea and vomiting.
mi.grant (MY.grunt) *adj.* migrating: *a migrant camp, farm laborer, worker; migrant birds;* n.: *hordes of migrants; economic, homeless, rural migrants.*
mi.grate (MY.grate) v. -**grates, -grat.ed, -grat.ing** 1 move to another region or country periodically, as birds and animals to warmer climates in the winter. 2 move away, as emigrants.
—**mi.gra.tion** (my.GRAY.shun) n.; **mi.gra.tion.al** *adj.*
mi.gra.to.ry (MY.gruh.tor.ee) *adj.* migrating: *a migratory bird, habit, pattern.*
mi.ka.do (mi.KAH.doh) n. -**does** the ancient title of Japanese emperors, given up in 1945.
mike n. *Informal.* a microphone.
mil n. a 1/1000 unit, as of an inch, of a liter, etc.
mi.la.dy or **mi.la.di** (mi.LAY.dee) n. 1 an English-speaking noblewoman. 2 a woman of fashion.
milch (MILK, MILCH) *adja.* of cows and such domestic animals, kept for milking, not for meat or draft.
mild (MILED) *adj.* moderate or agreeable, not severe or harsh: *a mild cheese, cigarette, concussion, fever, rebuke, recession, shampoo, winter.* —**mild.ly** *adv.*; **mild.ness** n.
mil.dew n. a minute whitish fungus that forms on plants and materials such as paper, leather, and cloth in damp weather. —v. affect or be covered with mildew. —**mil.dew.y** *adj.*
mile n. a unit of length equal to 5,280 ft. (1.609 km): *a teacher's commitment to go the extra mile* (= go out of one's way) *for students.*
mile.age (MY.lij) n. 1 a per-mile or per-meter traveling allowance, car-rental rate, etc. 2 the number of miles or kilometers traveled, covered, etc.: *the mileage on a car; Smaller cars give better mileage; There's not much mileage* (= wear) *left on those tires (which are nearly bald); political mileage* (= advantage or benefit) *from dirty tricks;* **adj.**: *the mileage figure shown on an odometer; a mileage test of fuel consumption; an air mileage* (= air distance) *chart.*
mile.post n. a signpost indicating distance from a given point in miles or kilometers.
mil.er (MY.lur) n. one who competes in a mile race.
mile.stone n. 1 a stone put up as a milepost. 2 a significant stage or event, as during a journey or career.
mi.lieu (meel.YUR, -YOO) n. the immediate environment, esp. social.
mil.i.tant (MIL.i.tunt) *adj.* aggressive or warlike, esp. in fighting for a cause or movement: *a militant attitude, churchman, conservationist; militant trade unionism.* —n. one who is militant.
—**mil.i.tant.ly** *adv.* —**mil.i.tan.cy** n.
mil.i.ta.rism (MIL.i.tuh.riz.um) n. the spirit, policy, or condition of being aggressively prepared for war; **mil.i.ta.rist** n. —**mil.i.ta.ris.tic** (RIS.tic) *adj.*
mil.i.ta.rize (MIL.i.tuh.rizc) v. -**riz.es, -rized, -riz.ing** 1 prepare and equip an army, nation, etc. for war. 2 give a military character to a government.
—**mil.i.ta.ri.za.tion** (-ZAY.shun) n.
mil.i.tar.y (MIL.i.tair.ee) 1 *adja.* having to do with soldiers or an army: *a military government, uniform; the military spirit; military law, personnel, service, valor;* **Military police** *have police duties*

within the army. **2** *n. sing. & pl.*, also **-tar.ies** *pl.* armed forces: *to call in the military; the militaries of various countries.* —**mil.i.tar.i.ly** (-TAIR.uh.lee) *adv.*

mil.i.tate (MIL.i.tate) *v.* **-tates, -tat.ed, -tat.ing** have force or weight *against* [rarely *for* or *in favor of*] something or someone: *Facts, evidence, concepts, etc. that militate against national unity.*

mi.li.tia (muh.LISH.uh) *n.* **1** an organization of civilians drafted to help their country in an emergency: *to call out the militia.* **2** an organization of part-time members of the army, as the National Guard in the U.S. —**mi.li.tia.man** (-mun) *n.* **-men.**

milk *n.* **1** the white liquid from the mammary glands of a female mammal; also, this in processed form: *(human) breast milk; condensed, evaporated, fresh, homogenized, pasteurized, skim, whole milk; manufacturers of infant milks* (= formulas); *the milk of human kindness* (= natural sympathy and kindness). **2** a similar liquid, as found in a coconut, the latex of trees and plants, etc. —*v.* **1** draw milk from a domestic animal: *to milk cows.* **2** draw from a resource capable of yielding something useful: *Some rattlers are milked for venom for use as an antidote; an estate milked dry by litigation; Merchants milk* (= exploit) *the commercial aspect of Christmas.*

milk.er *n.* **1** one that milks. **2** an animal that yields milk.

milk glass *n.* a whitish glass resembling porcelain.

milk.maid *n.* a dairymaid or a woman who milks cows.

milk.man *n.* **-men** a man who sells or delivers milk.

milk of magnesia *n.* a milklike suspension of magnesium hydroxide in water used as an antacid and laxative.

milk.shake *n.* a frothy drink of milk shaken with flavoring and ice cream.

milk.sop *n.* a sissy.

milk tooth *n.* any of the first set of 20 teeth a baby gets that later fall out.

milk.weed *n.* a plant with stem containing a milky juice and pods of seeds with tufts of silky hair on them.

milk.y *adj.* **milk.i.er, -i.est** white like milk or containing or yielding milk: *the milky juice of the lettuce; milky white teeth; rich, milky tea.* —**milk.i.ness** *n.*

mill *n.* **1** a machine that grinds grain, traditionally between two huge, flat stones, one turning against the other, powered by a **millwheel** driven by a current of water or a canal called a **millrace**, or **millstream**, often flowing from a **millpond**, or **milldam**. **2** a machine that grinds coffee, pepper, or stones, that presses the juice of sugar cane, apples, etc., or that stamps coins. **3** a factory: *cotton, flour, lumber, paper, rolling, steel, textile mills.* **4** an establishment with a routine or repetitive operation: *diploma, divorce, photocopying, propaganda mills.* **5** a thousandth part of a dollar, one tenth of a cent, as used in accounting: *A two-mill levy was added to the property tax last year.* —**through the mill** *Informal.* through hard practical training or experience. —*v.* **1** to process using a mill: *Grain is milled into flour or meal; adj.: the milled* (= ridged) *edge of a coin; n.: the milling* (= notches or ridges) *given to a coin.* **2** move about in circles or confusion: *Convention crowds milled about in the hotel lobby.*

mil.age (MIL.ij) *n.* a taxation rate expressed in mills per dollar.

mil.len.ni.um (mil.EN.ee.um) *n.* **mil.len.ni.ums** or **mil.len.ni.a 1** a thousand-year period, esp. the one starting with the year 2000. **2** *the millennium* an era of peace and happiness prophesied in the Bible. —**mil.len.ni.al** *adj.*

millepede same as MILLIPEDE.

mil.ler *n.* the owner or operator of a grain mill.

mil.let (MIL.it) *n.* **1** a widely used food cereal bearing creamy white seeds on long stalks. **2** similar grasses used as forage.

milli- *comb.form.* thousandth part: *milliampere, millibar, milligram, milliliter, millimeter, etc.*

mil.li.ner (MIL.uh.nur) *n.* one who makes or deals in millinery.

mil.li.ner.y (MIL.uh.nair.ee) *n.* **-ner.ies 1** women's hats. **2** the hat business.

milling machine *n.* a machine with toothed cutters for shaping metal into slots, gears, etc.

mil.lion (MIL.yun) *n.* a thousand thousands; 1,000,000: *The painting was sold for five million dollars; an aircraft costing millions of dollars.* —**mil.lionth** (MIL.yunth) *adj.*

mil.lion.aire (mil.yuh.NAIR) *n.* a very wealthy person, esp. one who has a million or more dollars, pounds, francs, etc. Also **mil.lion.naire.**

mil.li.pede (MIL.uh.peed) *n.* a many-legged, wormlike arthropod that feeds on decaying plant matter.

millpond, millrace See MILL.

mill.stone *n.* **1** either of two huge, flat, round stones that turn against each other to grind grain into flour. **2** a crushing burden: *The scandal proved a political millstone around the minister's neck.*

millstream, mill wheel See MILL.

mill.wright (MILL.rite) *n.* one who sets up or repairs machinery in a mill or factory.

milque.toast or **Milque.toast** (MILK.tohst) *n.* a very timid person.

milt *n.* the sperm or sperm-filled reproductive glands of a male fish, or milter. —**milt.er** *n.*

mime *n.* **1** acting without speech, using only bodily movements and gestures: *The action of the play is all in mime; a mime theater.* **2** a mimic or the performance of one.
—*v.* **mimes, mimed, mim.ing** act without speech, as in a pantomime.

mim.e.o (MIM.ee.oh) *n.* [short form] mimeograph.

mim.e.o.graph (MIM.ee.uh.graf) *n.* a stencil duplicating machine. —*v.* to copy graphic matter using a mimeograph.

mi.me.sis (mi.MEE.sis) *n.* **1** artistic imitation. **2** mimicry.

mi.met.ic (mi.MET.ic) *adj.* imitative: *the mimetic art; mimetic gestures, movements; A leaf insect's mimetic coloring imitates its surroundings.*

mim.ic *v.* **-icks, -icked, -ick.ing 1** resemble or imitate: *A leaf insect mimics its surroundings; A parrot mimics speech.* **2** imitate or ape, esp. for fun.
—*n.* one skilled in mimicking; also **mim.ick.er**.

mim.ic.ry (MIM.ic.ree) *n.* **-ries 1** artistic imitation of someone's speech, style, or mannerisms for comic effect: *humor by mimicry.* **2** the imitation of its surroundings by a bird or animal for hiding from its enemies, as by the chameleon or the "stick insect."

mi.mo.sa (mi.MOH.suh) *n.* a tree, shrub, or herb of warm climates whose featherlike leaves respond to stimuli by closing and drooping.

min.a.ret (min.uh.RET) *n.* a slender tower, usu. attached to a mosque, with a surrounding balcony at the top, from which people are called to prayer.

min.a.to.ry (MIN.uh.tor.ee) *adj.* menacing or threatening.

mince *v.* **minc.es, minced, minc.ing 1** chop up into very small pieces: *to mince meat; adj.: minced beef, garlic, onion, parsley.* **2** affect a daintiness of speech or delicacy of manner, as by restraining one's words or walking with shortened, or **mincing**, steps.
—**not to mince matters** or **words** to be plain or outspoken.

mince.meat *n.* a mixture of minced meat, beef fat, apples, raisins, currants, spices, etc.: *The Government made mincemeat of the Opposition* (= beat them soundly); *adja.: a mincemeat cake, filling; a mince pie* (filled with mincemeat).

mind (MINED) *n.* **1** the faculty by which a person remembers, thinks, understands, reasons, wills, etc.: *What's on your mind? What do you have in mind? Let's keep that in mind* (= remember it); *Did it ever cross your mind* (= occur to you) *that you could be wrong? She has an analytical mind; He has a mind of his own* (= is independent in his thinking); *I've half a mind to* (= I am tempted to) *say no to her and give her a bit* or *piece of my mind* (= tell her bluntly what I think). **2** a person with mind as specified: *clear, closed, inquiring, keen, narrow, one-track, twisted minds.* —**blow one's mind** *Informal.* **1** experience hallucinations, as by use of LSD. **2** be overwhelming, as to surprise or baffle.
—**change one's mind** change one's intention or opinion. —**make up one's mind** decide; also, decide *to* do something. —**out of one's mind** mentally ill; crazy. —**put in mind** remind someone. —*v.* pay attention to something: *Mind the step (ahead of you); Do you mind* (= object to) *closing the door? Do you mind? Who's minding* (= looking after) *the store? Mind your own business* (= Don't meddle in other people's affairs); *Never mind* (= It does not matter).

mind-bending *adj.* **1** hallucinogenic. **2** *Informal.* mind-blowing or mind-boggling.

mind-boggling *adj.* emotionally or mentally overwhelming: *a mind-boggling idea; a mind-boggling ten million dollars; with mind-boggling speed and efficiency;* also **mind-blowing**.

mind-expanding *adj.* hallucinogenic.

minded *adj. & comb.form.* having a mind as specified: *if you're so minded* (= inclined); *People are becoming ecologically minded; absent-minded; feeble-minded; high-minded; like-minded; narrow-minded; open-minded; right-minded; simple-minded; single-minded; tough-minded.*

mind.ful *adjp.* aware or careful: *to be mindful of our duties; mindful that duty comes first.*

mind.less *adj.* stupid or careless: *mindless assembly-line jobs; our mindless pursuit of*

mind reader / minimal

wealth; **mind.less.ly** *adv.;* **mind.less.ness** *n.*
mind reader *n.* **1** one who seems to guess another's thoughts. **2** one gifted with extrasensory perception.
mind-set *n.* the way one habitually thinks: *your liberal mind-set; her status-quo mind-set.*
mind's eye *n.* imagination: *I saw it in my mind's eye; Two images of that event linger in the mind's eye.*
mine *pron.* possessive case of "I": *your children and mine; a friend of mine* (= belonging to me). —*adj.* [formerly used before a vowel or "h" or after a noun]: *Mine eyes have seen thy salvation; O sister mine!* —*n.* **1** an excavation for extracting a mineral from the earth: *to close down, open, work a mine; an abandoned mine; strip mines and open-pit mines.* **2** a deposit of such a mineral: *salt mines.* **3** an abundant source or supply: *This book is a gold mine of information.* **4** an explosive charge laid under water or ground to blow up an enemy's fortifications, vehicles, or ships: *a land mine; to detect, detonate, disarm a mine; to sweep mines.*
—*v.* **mines, mined, min.ing 1** dig out something valuable: *Gold used to be mined here; They're mining* (= digging) *for coal.* **2** blow up using a mine: *The ship sank after being mined; a highway mined by terrorists.* —**min.er** *n.*
mine.field *n.* **1** an area in which explosive mines have been laid by the enemy. **2** a potentially dangerous subject or situation: *Reducing the old age benefits proved a political minefield for the government.*
mine.lay.er (MINE.lay.ur) *n.* a ship or submarine used to lay mines under water.
min.er.al (MIN.ur.ul) *n.* a substance such as a metal, a precious stone, salt, coal, petroleum, natural gas, calcium, and sulfur that is mined or quarried from the earth: *Is it (an) animal, (a) vegetable, or (a) mineral? adj.a.: diseases due to mineral deficiencies in the diet; a mineral deposit.*
min.er.al.ize (MIN.ur.uh.lize) *v.* **-iz.es, -ized, -iz.ing 1** treat with minerals; *adj.: mineralized water (containing minerals).* **2** convert to mineral; *adj.: Metal deposits occur mineralized as ore.*
—**min.er.al.i.za.tion** (-luh.ZAY.shun, -lye-) *n.*
min.er.al.o.gy (min.uh.ROL.uh.jee, -RAL.uh.jee) *n.* the science of minerals; **min.er.al.o.gist** *n.*
—**min.er.a.log.i.cal** (-ruh.LOJ.i.cul) *adj.;* **min.er.a.log.i.cal.ly** *adv.*
mineral oil *n.* an oil of mineral origin, esp. an oily liquid with no color, taste, or odor that is obtained from petroleum and used as a laxative and in cosmetics.
mineral spring *n.* a spring whose water contains dissolved minerals.
mineral water *n.* water containing mineral salts or gases, sold bottled.
Mi.ner.va (mi.NUR.vuh) *n.* the Roman goddess of wisdom and warfare.
mi.ne.stro.ne (min.uh.STROH.nee) *n.* a thick vegetable soup, originally Italian.
mine.sweep.er (MINE.swee.pur) *n.* a ship equipped to remove enemy mines laid under water.
min.gle (MING.gul) *v.* **-gles, -gled, -gling** mix or blend, esp. without losing identity: *Boys mingle with girls at parties; adj.: mingled feelings of joy and sorrow.*
ming tree *n.* a bonsai.
min.gy (MIN.jee) *adj.* **-gi.er, -gi.est** *Informal.* mean and stingy: *a mingy amount; He's rather mingy about spending money; mingy supplies.*
min.i (MIN.ee) *adj. & comb.form.* very small: *a mini coat, dress, tour, van; a supplementary minibudget; minibus, minicamera, minicomputer, minifloppy (diskette), miniskirt.* —*n., pl.* **min.is** a dress, coat, etc. that is considered small of its kind.
min.i.a.ture (MIN.ee.uh.chur) *n.* a copy or representation on a much smaller scale than its original, as a painting on ivory or vellum: *a miniature* (= tiny bottle) *of whiskey; the Taj Mahal carved in miniature; adj.a.: a miniature doll house; miniature golf (played with a putter and golf ball on a miniature course).*
—**min.i.a.tur.ist** *n.* —**min.i.a.tur.ize** (-chuh.rize) *v.* **-iz.es, -ized, -iz.ing;** *adj.: a miniaturized circuit, electronic component; the miniaturized computer.*
—**min.i.a.tur.i.za.tion** (-ruh.ZAY.shun, -rye-) *n.*
min.i.bike (MIN.ee.bike) *n.* a small motorcycle for use on country roads and trails.
min.i.bus (MIN.ee.bus) *n.* a very small bus for 10 to 15 people.
min.i.com.put.er (MIN.ee.cum.PEW.tur) *n.* a small computer designed to do many jobs.
min.im *n. & adj.* (smallest) amount or portion, as a half note in music, 1/60 of a fluid dram, or a downward stroke in writing.
min.i.mal (MIN.uh.mul) *adj.* the smallest or least possible: *a minimal charge; minimal standards, terms.* —**min.i.mal.ly** *adv.*

minimal art *n.* abstract painting or sculpture in simple shapes and minimum colors.

min.i.mal.ism (MIN.uh.muh.liz.um) *n.* **1** same as MINIMAL ART. **2** artistic style marked by extreme simplicity.

min.i.mize (MIN.uh.mize) *v.* **-miz.es, -mized, -miz.ing 1** reduce to a minimum: *to minimize a risk.* **2** belittle: *Let's not minimize the importance of education.*

min.i.mum *n.* **-mums** or **-ma** the least or lowest amount: *We are cutting expenses to a minimum; to the (absolute) minimum required for survival; There is a minimum (speed) to be maintained on a highway.* —*adja.* least or lowest: *yesterday's minimum temperature; the* **minimum wage** *fixed by government.*

min.ion (MIN.yun) *n.* a servile follower; favorite servant.

min.is.cule [rare spelling] same as MINUSCULE.

min.i.se.ries (MIN.ee.seer.eez) *n.* a TV drama presented in a series of parts spread over many days: *a 12-hour, 8-part miniseries.*

min.i.skirt (MIN.ee.skirt) *n.* a short skirt with the hemline well above the knee; *adj.: a miniskirted drum majorette.*

min.is.ter (MIN.is.tur) *n.* **1** a high public servant, as a member of a government cabinet, a diplomat ranking below ambassador, etc.: *a* **minister without portfolio** *(not in charge of any particular government department).* **2** a protestant clergyman. —*v.* serve: *Nurses minister to (the needs of) the sick and dying; adja.: the nurse as a ministering angel.* —**min.is.te.ri.al** (-TEER.ee.ul) *adj.* —**min.is.trant** (-trunt) *n. & adj.* (one) who ministers. —**min.is.tra.tion** (-TRAY.shun) *n.*

min.is.try (MIN.is.tree) *n.* **-tries** a minister's office, term, or duties: *a Tory ministry* (= government or cabinet); *the foreign ministry* (= government department); *She was called to the ministry* (= to join the clergy); *the lay ministry* (= religious work carried out by the laity).

mink *n.* a small weasel or its lustrous, deep-brown fur made into a coat, cape, or stole.

min.ne.sing.er (MIN.uh.sing.ur) *n.* a German love poet and singer of the Middle Ages.

min.now (MIN.oh) *n.* a fish of the carp family, often used as bait, as the "common shiner."

Mi.no.an (mi.NOH.un) *n. & adj.* (an inhabitant) of Crete at the time of its Bronze Age civilization, till 1100 B.C.

mi.nor (MY.nur) *adj.* lesser in importance, rank, size, extent, etc.; not major: *a minor baseball league; a minor operation, repair; minor surgery; a minor subject (of a program of studies).* —*n.* **1** a person under the age of 18: *A minor may not vote or buy liquor.* **2** a minor or secondary subject of study: *German is her minor; v.: a history major minoring in German.*

mi.nor.i.ty (my.NOR.i.tee) *n.* **-ties 1** a part, group, or number that is less than half, not a majority: *the Catholic minority of Northern Ireland; Catholics are in a minority there; In a minority of cases, a drug may do more harm than good; Orientals, South Asians, and blacks form visible minorities in a white society;* adja.*: Jews, blacks, and such minority groups; a* **minority government** *(by a party with less than half the seats in a legislature).* **2** the state of being a minor: *You can't vote during your minority.*

minor scale *n.* **1** a diatonic musical scale having half tones after the second, fifth, and seventh notes in the "harmonic" form. **2** a diatonic musical scale having half tones after the second and seventh notes while ascending and the sixth and third notes while descending in the "melodic" form.

min.ster *n.* **1** a church attached to a monastery. **2** a great cathedral such as Westminster or York in England.

min.strel (MIN.strul) *n.* **1** a traveling poet-musician of the Middle Ages: *a wandering minstrel.* **2** a member of a **minstrel show,** an American variety show of the 19th century featuring comics with blackened faces.

—**min.strel.sy** *n.* **-sies.**

mint *n.* **1** a strongly scented plant such as peppermint or lavender, whose fragrant leaves or oil is used in perfumes, flavoring, medicine, etc.: *a sprig of mint; n.: after-dinner mints* (= minted sweets); *breath mints;* **adja.***: mint leaves, sauce, tea;* **adj.***: fresh minted iced tea; waxed and minted dental floss.* **2** mint-flavored candy: *breath mints; after-dinner mints.* **3** a place where money is coined. —**a mint of money** a vast sum of money. —**in mint condition** of collectibles such as books, stamps, and coins, as good as new. —*v.* **1** to coin money, medals, etc.: *He's so wealthy he literally or practically mints money;* **adj.***: freshly minted graduates; a newly minted democracy; n.: coins marked with their name, place of* **minting***, and year of issue.* **2** invent or fabricate; *adj.: Many trademarks are newly minted words; a new-*

mint julep / misalliance

minted approach to the problem.
mint julep See JULEP.
mint.y adj. having the flavor of mint.
min.u.end (MIN.yoo.end) n. a number from which another is to be subtracted.
min.u.et (min.yoo.ET) n. **1** a slow, stately 17th century dance for couples. **2** the music for it.
mi.nus (MY.nus) prep. [indicating subtraction or negation]: *3 minus 2 is 1; a temperature of minus five degrees* (= five below zero); *Al returned home minus* (Informal for without) *his hat.* —n. the sign [–] indicating subtraction or negation: *Every career has its pluses and minuses* (= drawbacks); adj.: *a minus quantity such as "–2ab"; the **minus sign**; a minus temperature; a B minus* (= B–) *grade.*
mi.nus.cule (mi.NUS.cule, MIN.us-) n. a small or lowercase letter. —adj. very small: *a minuscule script; a minuscule difference, fraction, increment, percentage.*
¹**mi.nute** (my.NEWT) adj. **-nut.er, -nut.est** very small or insignificant; requiring close scrutiny: *minute details, insects; minute* (= detailed) *instructions.* —**mi.nute.ly** adv.; **mi.nute.ness** n.
²**min.ute** (MIN.it) n. **1** a 60th part of an hour; hence, a moment: *Wait a minute* (= a short while); *There were too many applications **at the last minute*** (= close to the deadline); *I want my money back **this minute*** (= right now); *an up-to-the-minute news update;* **The minute that** or **The minute** (= as soon as) *the teacher turns her back, the children start talking;* adj.: *a clock's minute hand; quick-cooking minute rice.* **2** a 60th part of an angular degree. **3 minutes** pl. the official record of the proceedings at a meeting: *The secretary is supposed to keep* or *take minutes of meetings, then read the minutes to the members who may vote to accept or reject the minutes.*
min.ute.man (MIN.it.man) n. **-men** a volunteer of the American Revolutionary War trained to fight "at a minute's notice": *the "Minuteman" ballistic missile.*
minute steak (MIN.it-) n. a thin beefsteak for fast frying.
mi.nu.ti.ae (muh.NEW.shee.ee) n.pl. minute details; **mi.nu.ti.a** (-shee.uh), sing.
minx n. a pert or saucy girl; **minx.ish** adj.
Mi.o.cene (MY.uh.seen) n. & adj. (of) the fourth epoch of the Cenozoic era of the earth, beginning about 26 million years ago.
mir.a.cle (MEER.uh.cul) n. **1** an action or event that is beyond human power or understanding, as raising the dead to life: *It's a miracle that she survived the crash; She survived by a miracle; to accomplish, perform, work a miracle; Antibiotics were hailed as **miracle drugs*** or *wonder drugs; a miracle worker.* **2** a marvelous person or thing: *She's a miracle of patience.*
mi.rac.u.lous (muh.RAK.yuh.lus) adj. surprising and fortunate like a miracle: *his miraculous good fortune; her miraculous recovery from cancer.* —**mi.rac.u.lous.ly** adv.
mi.rage (muh.RAHZH) n. **1** an optical illusion of water or phantom images caused by refraction of light in hot air: *The travelers in the desert rushed toward the water hole only to find it was a mirage.* **2** something unattainable or illusory.
mire n. **1** a marsh. **2** slush or deep mud: *The wheels got stuck in the mire; He dragged her name through the mire* (= brought her shame) *by publishing his exploits.* —v. **mires, mired, mir.ing 1** soil with mud: *hands all mired from gardening.* **2** get or cause to get stuck or to sink in mud or as if in mud: *The factory closing will mire hundreds of families in poverty;* adj.: *Our car got **mired** (down) in the mud hole; a mired economy; people mired in debt, intrigue, materialism, politics; a government mired in a fiscal crisis.*
mir.ror (MEER.ur) n. a glass with its back coated with silver so as to reflect images; also, a similar shiny surface: *a full-length mirror; a car's rear-view mirror; side-view mirror; the face as a mirror of character.* —v. reflect, as in a glass: *a building mirrored in a reflecting pool; The election results mirrored the mood of the nation.*
mirth n. gaiety and fun, esp. with laughter: *His costume provoked mirth;* **mirth.ful** adj.
MIRV (MURV) n. **MIRV's** "Multiple Independently-targeted Re-entry Vehicle," a long-range missile with multiple warheads for different targets.
mir.y (MIRE.ee) adj. **mir.i.er, -i.est** muddy; swampy; dirty.
mis- prefix [with negative sense]: *mislead, mismanage, misshapen.*
mis.ad.ven.ture (mis.ud.VEN.chur) n. mishap or misfortune: *The case was ruled death by misadventure* (= accident), *not homicide.*
mis.al.li.ance (mis.uh.LYE.unce) n. unsuitable alliance, esp. in marriage.

mis.al.lo.ca.tion (MIS.al.uh.CAY.shun) *n.* improper allocation of funds, resources, etc.

mis.an.thrope (MIS.un.thrope) *n.* one who mistrusts or hates everyone. —**mis.an.throp.ic** (-THROP.ic) *adj.* —**mis.an.thro.pist** (mis.AN.thruh.pist) *n.*; **mis.an.thro.py** (-pee) *n.*

mis.ap.ply (mis.uh.PLY) *v.* **-ap.plies, -ap.plied, -ap.ply.ing** apply funds or resources illegally or wastefully. —**mis.ap.pli.ca.tion** (MIS.ap.luh.CAY.shun) *n.*

mis.ap.pre.hend (MIS.ap.ri.HEND) *v.* misunderstand; **mis.ap.pre.hen.sion** (-HEN.shun) *n.*

mis.ap.pro.pri.ate (mis.uh.PROH.pree.ate) *v.* **-ates, -at.ed, -at.ing** take funds, etc. wrongly or dishonestly. —**mis.ap.pro.pri.a.tion** (MIS.uh.proh.pree.AY.shun) *n.*

mis.be.got.ten (mis.bi.GOT.un) *adj.* illegitimate or bastard.

mis.be.have (mis.bi.HAIV) *v.* **-haves, -haved, -hav.ing** behave badly: *He got drunk at the party and misbehaved.* —**mis.be.hav.ior** *n.* Also **mis.be.hav.iour** *Cdn.*

mis.brand *v.* brand or label misleadingly.

mis.cal.cu.late (mis.CAL.kyuh.late) *v.* **-lates, -lat.ed, -lat.ing** wrongly calculate or estimate a result or outcome. —**mis.cal.cu.la.tion** (-LAY.shun) *n.*

mis.call (mis.CAWL) *v.* misname.

mis.car.riage (mis.CAIR.ij) *n.* failure of an intended or proper result: *Mary had a miscarriage* (= "spontaneous abortion" or expulsion of an embryo or fetus from the uterus); *The jury was fixed and the trial was a gross miscarriage of justice; The freight was not delivered because of miscarriage* (= failure to arrive). —**mis.car.ry** (mis.CAIR.ee) *v.* **-car.ries, -car.ried, -car.ry.ing.**

mis.cast (mis.CAST) *v.* **-casts, -cast, -cast.ing** cast in an unsuitable role: *Mimi was miscast as the cowardly lion.*

mis.ceg.e.na.tion (mis.EJ.uh.NAY.shun) *n.* marriage between a white and a member of another race.

mis.cel.la.neous (mis.uh.LAY.nee.us) *adj.* **1** of varied or mixed items though similar: *a miscellaneous collection; miscellaneous comments, expenses, matters.* **2** many-sided: *a miscellaneous feeling, talent, writer.* —**mis.cel.la.neous.ly** *adv.*

mis.cel.la.ny (MIS.uh.lay.nee) *n.* **-nies** a miscellaneous collection, esp. a literary one.

mis.chance *n.* a piece of bad luck.

mis.chief (MIS.chif) *n.* harm or injury caused by irresponsible behavior: *to cause, do, make mischief; Lou is always up to some mischief or other; Lee can't stay out of mischief; It's hard to keep him out of mischief; He's always getting into mischief; a prankster charged with public mischief for pulling the fire alarm; Her eyes are full of mischief* (= playful teasing). —**mis.chie.vous** (MIS.chuh.vus) *adj.*: *a mischievous child, gossip, look, rumor;* **mis.chie.vous.ly** *adv.*

mis.ci.ble (MIS.uh.bul) *adj.* of a liquid, capable of being mixed with another.

mis.com.mu.ni.ca.tion (MIS.cuh.mew.nuh.CAY.shun) *n.* defective or erroneous communication.

mis.con.ceive (mis.cun.SEEV) *v.* **-ceives, -ceived, -ceiv.ing 1** plan or think out badly; *adj.*: *a wholly misconceived approach, attempt, method, plan, policy.* **2** misinterpret. —**mis.con.cep.tion** (-SEP.shun) *n.*

mis.con.duct (mis.CON.duct) *n.* **1** improper behavior, esp. adultery. **2** mismanagement, esp. in public office: *gross, professional misconduct.* **3** a penalty in hockey: *The referee handed out or gave out 20 minor penalties, 16 majors, two misconducts* (= 10-minute suspensions), *and five game misconducts* (= suspensions for the remainder of the game).

mis.con.strue (mis.cun.STROO) *v.* **-strues, -stru.ing, -stru.ing** misinterpret or misconceive. —**mis.con.struc.tion** (-STRUC.shun) *n.*

mis.cre.ant (MIS.cree.unt) *n.* one who is villainous or depraved.

mis.cue (mis.CUE) *v.* **-cues, -cued, -cu.ing** give a performer a wrong cue. —*n.* an error, esp. by a player in baseball, football, etc.

mis.deal (mis.DEEL) *v.* **-deals, -dealt** (-DELT), **-deal.ing** deal playing cards wrongly. —*n.* such a deal.

mis.deed (mis.DEED) *n.* a wrong or wicked deed; crime.

mis.de.mean.or (mis.di.MEE.nur) *n.* **1** a violation such as a traffic offense or assault that is less serious than a felony. **2** a misdeed. Also **mis.de.mean.or** *Cdn.*

mis.di.rect (mis.duh.RECT) *v.* direct wrongly. —**mis.di.rec.tion** (-REC.shun) *n.*

mis.do.ing (mis.DOO.ing) *n.* wrongdoing; **mis.do.er** *n.*

mise-en-scène (mee.zahn.SEN) *n. French.* a stage setting; hence, surroundings or milieu.

mi.ser (MY.zur) *n.* a stingy person who

hoards money, loving it for its own sake. —**mi.ser.ly** *adj.*; **mi.ser.li.ness** *n.*

mis.er.a.ble (MIZ.uh.ruh.bul) *adj.* wretched, poor, or unhappy: *the miserable life of the poor; miserable slums, weather; a miserable failure; You can't get a coffee with a miserable 50 cents; a miserable* (= unfriendly) *fellow.* —**mis.er.a.bly** *adv.*

mis.er.y (MIZ.uh.ree) *n.* **-er.ies** a cause or condition of being miserable: *a life of misery; the miseries of war; to alleviate, cause, relieve misery; He lived in misery all his life; abject, sheer, untold misery.*

mis.fea.sance (mis.FEE.zunce) *n. Law.* illegal performance of a lawful action.

mis.file *v.* **-files, -filed, -fil.ing** file a paper, etc. in the wrong place.

mis.fire *v.* **-fires, -fired, -fir.ing** fail to fire or to achieve the intended effect: *Engines, cylinders, guns, spark plugs, efforts, people, plans may misfire; adj.: a misfired shot.* —*n.* a misfiring: *the misfire in a badly tuned automobile engine; an ignition misfire; a lean misfire.*

mis.fit *n.* **1** one not well adjusted socially or in a job. **2** a badly fitted garment. —*v.* **-fits, -fit.ted, -fit.ting** fit badly: *a boy misfitted in his older brother's clothes.*

mis.for.tune (mis.FOR.chun) *n.* a piece of bad luck: *to have* or *suffer a misfortune; She had the misfortune to get hurt in an accident.*

mis.giv.ing (mis.GIV.ing) *n.* usu. **misgivings** *pl.* feelings of doubt or lack of confidence: *We had misgivings about hiring him; misgivings that he might prove undependable.*

mis.gov.ern (mis.GUV.urn) *v.* govern badly; **mis.gov.ern.ment** *n.*

mis.guide (mis.GIDE, "G" as in "go") *v.* mislead, esp. into wrongdoing.

mis.guid.ed (mis.GUY.did) *adj.* mistaken; in error: *He's very misguided in his aims, though well-meaning; a misguided genius.* —**mis.guid.ed.ly** *adv.*

mis.han.dle (mis.HAN.dul) *v.* **-dles, -dled, -dling** treat or manage badly.

mis.hap *n.* an unlucky, usu. minor accident.

mis.hear (mis.HEER) *v.* **-hears, -heard** (-HURD), **-hear.ing** hear incorrectly.

mish.mash *n.* a hodgepodge.

mis.in.form (mis.in.FORM) *v.* give someone false or misleading information; *adj.: I'm afraid you're grossly misinformed about what's going on at the office; He's either lying or misinformed; misinformed criticism; a misinformed public.* —**mis.in.for.ma.tion** (MIS.in.fur.MAY.shun) *n.*

mis.in.ter.pret (mis.in.TUR.prit) *v.* understand or interpret incorrectly. —**mis.in.ter.pre.ta.tion** (-pruh.TAY.shun) *n.*

mis.judge (mis.JUJ) *v.* **-judg.es, -judged, -judg.ing** judge wrongly or unjustly. —**mis.judg.ment** *n.* Also **mis.judge.ment** *Cdn.*

mis.la.bel (mis.LAY.bul) *v.* **-bels, -beled, -bel.ing** label incorrectly or falsely. Also **mis.la.belled, mis.la.bel.ling** *Cdn.*

mis.lay (mis.LAY) *v.* **-lays, -laid, -lay.ing** misplace or lose something.

mis.lead (mis.LEED) *v.* **-leads, -led, -lead.ing** to lead someone to go, think, or act in error or badly: *We are misled by bad advice, by illegible writing, by a candid manner; I was misled about the whole business; the serious charge of misleading the House* (= lying to a legislature); *adj.: It's misleading to give only the good news; misleading advertising.*

mis.man.age (mis.MAN.ij) *v.* **-ag.es, -aged, -ag.ing** manage badly or dishonestly. —**mis.man.age.ment** *n.*

mis.match (mis.MATCH) *v.* match badly; *adj.: a mismatched pair of socks; They are a mismatched couple; Siamese twins are clearly mismatched.* —*n.:* *The boxers were an obvious mismatch; the mismatch between educations and job requirements; the **mismatching** of supply and demand.*

mis.name (mis.NAME) *v.* **-names, -named, -nam.ing** name incorrectly or inappropriately.

mis.no.mer (mis.NOH.mur) *n.* a wrongly given name: *It's a misnomer to call a whale a fish because it is a mammal; a misnomer to call this stuff food.*

mi.sog.a.mist (mi.SOG.uh.mist) *n.* one who hates marriage. —**mi.sog.a.my** *n.*

mi.sog.y.nist (mi.SOJ.uh.nist) *n.* one who hates women. —**mi.sog.y.ny** *n.*; **mi.sog.y.nous** (-nus) *adj.*

mis.place (mis.PLACE) *v.* **-plac.es, -placed, -plac.ing** put in a wrong place: *Grandma often misplaces her glasses; Only after being jilted did he realize that his affections had been misplaced* (= bestowed on the wrong person); *adj.: A misplaced key is often lost; misplaced commas, faith, hopes, priorities, trust, zeal.*

mis.play (mis.PLAY) *v.* play a game wrongly. —*n.* a wrong play.

mis.print (MIS.print) *n.* a printing error. —*v.* (mis.PRINT) print incorrectly.

mis.pri.sion (mis.PRIZH.un) *n. Law.* criminal neglect of duty, actively or passively: **misprision of felony** (= concealment of another's felony).

mis.pro.nounce (mis.pruh.NOUNCE) *v.* **-nounc.es, -nounced, -nounc.ing** pronounce incorrectly.
—**mis.pro.nun.ci.a.tion** (MIS.pruh.nun.see.AY.shun) *n.*

mis.quote (mis.QUOTE) *v.* **-quotes, -quot.ed, -quot.ing** quote incorrectly. —**mis.quo.ta.tion** (-kwuh.TAY.shun) *n.*

mis.read (mis.REED) *n.* **-reads, -read** (-RED), **-read.ing** read wrongly; hence, misunderstand.

mis.rep.re.sent (MIS.rep.ri.ZENT) *v.* represent incorrectly or falsely.
—**mis.rep.re.sen.ta.tion** (-zen.TAY.shun) *n.*

mis.rule (mis.ROOL) *n.* **1** bad government. **2** disorder or anarchy. —*v.* **-rules, -ruled, -rul.ing** govern badly.

miss *v.* **1** fail to attain, get, hit a person or thing: *She missed the target; to miss an aim, appointment, bus, joke, meeting, opportunity, point; to miss* (= fail to notice) *someone in a crowd; I just missed* (= escaped) *being hit by the ball; You can't miss it* (= It's so obvious); *People living in the country often miss out on what is going on in town.* **2** notice the absence of a person or thing: *When did you first miss the child?* **3** feel the absence of a person or thing: *I'll miss you when you're gone; You'll be sorely missed; I'll miss working with you; I seem to be missing my wallet.* —*n., pl.* **miss.es 1** a missing: *Is that a hit or a miss? a clean miss; near miss; strikes, spares, and misses in bowling.* **2** a usu. young unmarried woman or girl: *May we have the check, Miss?* **3 Miss** [title used before an unmarried girl's or woman's name]: *Miss (Mary) Jones* [or rarely] *Miss Mary; Miss America* (= winner of a personality contest for young American women).

mis.sal (MIS.ul) *n.* a book used by the celebrant at a Mass, containing prayers, readings, etc.

mis.shap.en (mis.SHAY.pun) *adj.* deformed: *a misshapen limb.*

mis.sile (MIS.ul) *n.* something directed at a target, esp. a weapon such as a stone, spear, bullet, rocket, etc.: *to fire, intercept, launch a missile; ballistic, cruise, guided, nuclear, strategic, tactical missiles.*

mis.sile.ry or **mis.sil.ry** (MIS.ul.ree) *n.* **1** military missiles collectively. **2** their design and operation. —**mis.sile.man** (-mun) *n.* **-men**.

missing *adj.* not where someone or something should be: *Our cat has gone missing; When everyone had taken their seats, one child was missing; soldiers **missing in action*** (= unaccounted for after a war); *the theory of the evolutionary missing link between apes and humans.*

mis.sion (MISH.un) *n.* the sending of people on an assignment; also, the people thus sent or their assigned task: *a combat mission; dangerous missions; a diplomatic mission to China; He was on a goodwill mission; a rescue mission; a search-and-destroy mission; an Apollo space mission (of exploration); Japanese pilots flew suicide missions (with little chance of survival) during the war; a trade mission to Italy; a pilot who has flown numerous (bombing) missions over Vietnam; to accomplish, carry out, perform, undertake a mission; a mission (to preach the Gospel) to the Indies; her lifelong mission* (= calling or vocation) *of caring for the sick; to collect money for the **missions*** (= organizations for spreading Christianity).

mis.sion.ar.y (MISH.uh.nair.ee) *n.* **-ar.ies** a person on a religious mission.
—*adj.*: *a missionary priest, society; Mother Teresa's missionary zeal.*

mission control *n.* the command center on the ground for space flights.

mis.sion.er (MISH.un.ur) *n.* a missionary.

mission statement *n.* a declaration of the aims and objectives of an organization.

mis.sis (MIS.uz) *n. Informal* [written "Mrs." when used as title] **1** one's wife: *Mrs. Smith.* **2** the mistress of a household: *Is the missis home?*

Mis.sis.sip.pi.an (mis.uh.SIP.ee.un) *n. & adj.* **1** (a person) of or from **Mississippi**, a U.S. state. **2** (the geological period) of the earlier half of the Carboniferous.

mis.sive (MIS.iv) *n.* an epistle or long letter sent to someone.

Mis.sour.i (mi.ZOOR.ee) *n.* a state of the U.S., nicknamed the "Show Me State": *I am from Missouri (Informal for unwilling to accept anything without proof).* —**Mis.sour.i.an** (-ee.un) *n. & adj.*

mis.spell (mis.SPEL) *v.* **-spells**, *pt. & pp.* **-spelled** or **-spelt, -spell.ing** spell incorrectly. —**mis.spell.ing** *n.*

mis.spend (mis.SPEND) *v.* **-spends, -spent, -spend.ing** spend improperly; also, waste or squander; *adj.*: *a misspent youth.*

mis.state (mis.STATE) *v.* **-states, -stat.ed, -stat.ing** state incorrectly or falsely; **mis.state.ment** *n.*

mis.step *n.* a wrong step; also, a mistake.

mis.sus same as MISSIS.

mist *n.* **1** a fog that is not too thick to see through nor so thin as a haze: *a mist* (= fine spray) *of perfume.* **2** something that dims or blurs vision: *a historian who got lost in the mists of antiquity.* —*v.* make or become misty, as eyes with tears.

mis.take (mis.TAKE) *n.* an error of observation, judgment, expression, action, etc.; misunderstanding: *Our mistake, Sir! She opened his letter by mistake; to correct, excuse, forgive, make, rectify a mistake; bad, glaring, foolish, slight mistakes; It was a mistake to take on that assignment.* —**make no mistake** (about it), You may be sure. —*v.* **-takes, -took, -tak.en, -tak.ing** make a mistake or take wrongly: *I mistook her words; Twins are often mistaken for each other.* —**mis.tak.a.ble** (-kuh.bul) *adj.*

mis.tak.en (mis.TAY.cun) *adj.* wrong: *He could be mistaken; a mistaken notion; He was mistaken about what she said; quite mistaken in finding fault with her.* —**mis.ta.ken.ly** *adv.*

mis.ter *n.* **1** the full form of MR. **2** *Informal.* sir: *Hey, mister!*

mis.time (mis.TIME) *v.* **-times, -timed, -tim.ing** say or do at the wrong time.

mis.tle.toe (MIS.ul.toh) *n.* a parasitic evergreen plant associated with Christmastime: *the Christmas tradition of kissing under the mistletoe.*

mistook *pt.* of MISTAKE.

mis.tral (MIS.trul, mi.STRAHL) *n.* a cold northerly wind from the W. Alps blowing over S. France and causing frost damage to crops.

mis.treat (mis.TREET) *v.* ill-treat. —**mis.treat.ment** *n.*

mis.tress (MIS.tris) *n.* **1** a woman in a ruling or controlling position, as the female head of a household or a teacher or expert, esp. in a special subject: *our dancing mistress; Britain used to be the mistress of the seas; "a mistress in her own house, though a daughter in her mother's."* **2** a woman who regularly has sex with a man she is not married to. **3 Mistress** [old use] Mrs.; Miss.

mis.tri.al (MIS.try.ul) *n.* a judgment that a trial is of no legal effect: *The judge declared a mistrial as the jurors could not agree on a verdict.*

mis.trust (mis.TRUST) *n.* a lack of trust or confidence: *The smooth-talking politician arouses mistrust; to have a deep, profound mistrust of strangers.* —*v.* feel mistrust toward: *He mistrusts his ability to edit his own writing; He mistrusts himself as his own editor.* —**mis.trust.ful** *adj.*; **mis.trust.ful.ly** *adv.*

mist.y *adj.* **mist.i.er, -i.est 1** covered with mist: *the misty air, hills; a misty morning; eyes misty with tears.* **2** blurred: *a misty memory, view.* —**mist.i.ly** *adv.*; **mist.i.ness** *n.*

mis.un.der.stand (MIS.un.dur.STAND) *v.* **-stands, -stood, -stand.ing** fail to understand a message, person, etc. correctly.

mis.un.der.stand.ing (MIS.un.dur.STAN.ding) *n.* **1** a failure to understand properly. **2** a quarrel or falling out.

mis.use (mis.YOOZ) *v.* **-us.es, -used, -us.ing** use a thing or treat a person improperly. —*n.* (-YOOSE): *a misuse of authority, words.*

mite *n.* **1** a tiny, insectlike, usu. parasitic creature that sucks the blood of animals, juice of plants, or torments human beings: *a bird mite; grain mite; itch mite.* **2** a tiny amount, small coin, or very small creature. —*adv. Informal.* a little: *His joke is wearing a mite thin.*

mi.ter (MY.tur) *n.* **1** the tall, pointed ceremonial headdress of ecclesiastics of the rank of bishop and higher, which is joined in two folding halves facing front and back. **2** a corner joint of two beveled or rabbeted pieces fitting together in a right angle. —*v.* **-ters, -tered, -ter.ing** join in a miter: *two boards mitered together.* Also **mi.tre, mi.tres, mi.tred, mit.ring** *Cdn.*

miter box *n.* a device used as a guide for sawing wood at the proper angle for making a miter joint.

miter joint same as MITER, 2.

mit.i.gate (MIT.uh.gate) *v.* **-gates, -gat.ed, -gat.ing** make or become mild or less harsh: *to mitigate one's anger; to mitigate the cold; to mitigate a disaster; to mitigate pain.* —**mit.i.ga.tion** (-GAY.shun) *n.* —**mit.i.ga.tive** (-gay.tiv) *adj.*; **mit.i.ga.tor** *n.*

mi.to.sis (my.TOH.sis) *n.* cell division that leaves the new cells with their own nuclei and the same number of chromosomes as the original cell; **mi.tot.ic** (my.TOT.ic) *adj.*

mi.tral (MY.trul) *adj.* resembling a miter: *the mitral valve of the heart.*

mi.tre *Cdn.* MITER.

mitt *n.* **1** a protective covering for the hand but without fingers: *a (baseball) catcher's mitt; an oven mitt.* **2** mitten.

mit.ten (MIT.un) *n.* a glove that covers the four fingers together and the thumb separately.

mix *v.* **mix.es,** *pt. & pp.* **mixed** (MIXT) or **mixt, mix.ing** combine so as to associate together: *Oil and water don't mix; Please mix me a drink; to mix ingredients for a cake; a visit mixing business with pleasure; a sociable woman who mixes well with people of all ages.* —**mix up 1** confuse: *She got Tim mixed up with his twin brother Tom.* **2** involve: *He was mixed up in a scandal; Better not get mixed up with that crowd.* —*n.* something mixed or for mixing: *cake, cement, pancake, soup mixes; gin with his favorite mix (such as tonic).*
—**mix.a.ble** *adj.*

mixed (MIXT) *adj.* of different kinds: *a mixed group (of men and women); The movie received mixed (= good and bad) reviews; a **mixed bag** (of assorted items); Nuclear power may be considered as a **mixed blessing** (that has good and bad aspects); No locker-room jokes in **mixed company** (of men and women); a **mixed drink** (= alcoholic drink with several ingredients); something of doubtful value received with **mixed feelings** (such as joy and regret); a **mixed marriage** (between persons of different religions or races); a **mixed media** presentation (using film, photographs, slides, tapes, etc.); a **mixed metaphor** (with clashing comparisons); A **mixed number** has an integer and a fraction, as 2¾.*

mixed-up *adj.* confused: *a mixed-up youth.*

mix.er *n.* one that mixes: *an electric food mixer; She's too shy to be a good mixer (in society).*

mix.ture (MIX.chur) *n.* a mixing, being mixed, or something mixed: *Sand and sugar form a mixture, not a compound.*

mix-up *n.* a confusion or a confused state: *There's been a mix-up; a mix-up over who sits where; a mix-up about the seats; a mix-up in the seating arrangements.*

miz.zen (MIZ.un) *n.* **1** a fore-and-aft sail. **2** mizzenmast.

miz.zon.mast (MIZ.un.mast) *n.* in a ship with two or three masts, the one nearest the stern.

mne.mon.ic (ni.MON.ic) *adj.* of or meant to help the memory: *jingles, rhymes, and such mnemonic devices.*

moan (MONE) *n.* a low and mournful sound: *the moans of the injured and dying.* —*v.* say with or utter in a moan: *a patient moaning with pain; "Oh no," she moaned, when she heard the news.*

moat (MOTE) *n.* a deep and wide ditch, usu. water-filled, as around a fortress wall or zoo display area.

mob *n.* **1** a disorderly or riotous crowd: *to control, disperse, inflame, stir up, subdue a mob; an angry mob of demonstrators;* **adj.a.:** *mob rule, violence.* **2** the common people or masses: *the tastes of the mob;* **adj.:** *mob orators, reactions.* **3** *Informal.* a criminal group or gang: *a mob of gangsters;* **the Mob** (= the Mafia). —*v.* **mobs, mobbed, mob.bing** crowd around a person or into a place, as a mob: *a movie star mobbed by autograph hunters; shoppers mobbing sales counters.*

mo.bile (MOH.bul, -beel) **1** *adj.* moving or movable: *a mobile library; the upwardly mobile middle class; a mobile (= changeable in expression) face; Are you mobile? (= Do you have a car?).* **2** (-beel) *n.* a delicately balanced, usu. suspended decoration or art object made of pieces of metal or plastic attached to wires and rods so as to move in currents of air. —*comb.form.* something moving: *artmobile, bloodmobile, bookmobile, snowmobile, popemobile.*
—**mo.bil.i.ty** (moh.BIL.i.tee) *n.*

mobile home *n.* a large trailer used as a home.

mobile lounge *n.* a vehicle used for carrying passengers between aircraft and air terminal.

mobile phone same as CELLPHONE.

mo.bi.lize (MOH.buh.lize) *v.* **-liz.es, -lized, -liz.ing 1** put into motion or active use. **2** organize or get ready, as troops for war. —**mo.bi.li.za.tion** (-luh.ZAY.shun. -lye-) *n.*

Mö.bi.us band (or **strip**) (MOH.bee.us-) *n.* a band made by twisting a rectangular strip of material lengthwise through 180° before sticking its ends together.

mob.ster (MOB.stur) *n.* a member of a criminal group or mob; gangster.

moc.ca.sin (MOC.uh.sin) *n.* a heelless sandal or slipper of soft leather, originally used by North American Indians.

mo.cha (MOH.cuh) *n.* a fine variety of coffee, originally shipped from Mocha, Yemen. —*adj.* flavored with coffee or coffee and chocolate: *mocha cakes, ice cream, puddings.*

mock *v.* make fun of a person or thing, esp. by imitating or caricaturing; ridicule: *The bully mocked him, mocked his accent, and jeered at him;* **adj.:** *a **mocking** gesture; mocking laughter; Her style is critical and gently mocking; self-*

mockheroic / modish

mocking humor; **mock.er** n. —*adj*. pseudo or imitation: *a mock battle, parliament, turtle soup*. —**mock.er.y** n. -**ries**: *The new rules make a mockery of human rights* (= make it look worthless).

mock.he.ro.ic (mock.hi.ROH.ic) *adj*. imitative of heroic style or character, as "Don Quixote" or Alexander Pope's poem "The Rape of the Lock."

mocking bird n. a grayish bird that can imitate the calls of other birds.

mock-up n. an accurately built model, usu. full-size, for studying, testing, or display, as of an airplane.

mod n. & *adj*. (one who is) bold and unconventional in dress and behavior: *Mods wear mod clothes; mod styles*.

mode n. a method, manner, or style, esp. one that is usual, customary, or current: *the mode of life of the Inuit; a mode of operation, transport; the pause mode of a VCR; a company in expansion mode; Dad is dressed in the latest mode* (= style); *the major and minor modes* (= scales or keys) *in music*. —**mod.al** (MOH.dul) *adj*. —**mo.dal.i.ty** (moh.DAL.i.tee) n.

mod.el (MOD.ul) n. **1** one that is to be imitated or copied: *a wax model for a marble statue; an artist's model; She's a model* (= perfect example) *of decorum; a role model for her children*; *adj*.: *a model farm, hospital; his model* (= exemplary) *behavior; a model* (= excellent) *husband, pupil, teacher, wife;* a **model home** (for viewing by potential buyers). **2** one made in the same pattern as others: *the make and model* (= particular design, as Chevrolet, Mustang, or Corolla) *of your car; a Model T Ford; a new model of computer; an airplane model* (= a small representation). **3** a person who displays clothes by wearing them: *a fashion model*. —*v*. **-els, -eled, -el.ing** **1** follow as a model: *a university modeled after Oxford; She models herself on* (= admires and imitates) *her mother*. **2** work as a fashion model: *She models hats at fashion shows, also models for customers; She models* (= does modeling) *at $200 an hour*. **3** make models: *He models in clay*. —**mod.el.er** n. Also **mod.elled, mod.el.ling; mod.el.ler** Cdn.

mo.dem (MOH.dem) n. a "modulator-demodulator" device for converting computer data for transmission or reception via telephone lines.

mod.er.ate (MOD.uh.rit) *adj*. within proper bounds, esp. not excessive: *She is moderate in her ambitions, demands, expenditures; a man of moderate habits, means; a moderate amount, drinker, position, risk, tone of voice, view; moderate exercise, gains, growth, prices*. —*n*.: *a political moderate, more liberal than conservative*. —*v*. (-rate) **-ates, -at.ed, -at.ing** **1** make or become less excessive: *Inflationary prices have now begun to moderate;* *adj*.: *She exercises a moderating influence on her husband*. **2** act as moderator: *Who's moderating the panel discussion?* —**mod.er.ate.ly** *adv*; **mod.er.ate.ness** n. —**mod.er.a.tion** (-RAY.shun) n.

mod.er.a.tor (MOD.uh.ray.tur) n. one who presides: *the moderator of an examination, meeting, panel discussion*.

mod.ern (MOD.urn) *adj*. **1** recent or current: *The computer is a modern invention; The New World was settled by Europeans in modern times;* **Modern English** (since about 1500). **2** up-to-date: *modern architecture, fashions, views*. —*n*. one who is modern: *ancients and moderns; moderns and ultramoderns*. —**mod.ern.ly** *adv*. —**mod.ern.ness** or **mod.er.ni.ty** (-DUR.ni.tee) n.

mod.ern.ism (MOD.urn.iz.um) n. **1** modern views or methods, esp. as departing from tradition. **2** a modern idiom or usage. —**mod.ern.ist** n.; **mod.ern.is.tic** (-NIS.tic) *adj*.

mod.ern.ize (MOD.ur.nize) *v*. **-iz.es, -ized, -iz.ing** make or become modern; **mod.ern.iz.er** n. —**mod.ern.i.za.tion** (-nuh.ZAY.shun, -nye-) n.

mod.est (MOD.ist) *adj*. proper in one's behavior or appearance, being unassuming, shy, decent, etc.: *a modest sales pitch, not loud or vulgar; He's modest about his qualifications; quite modest in his claims; a modest little cottage; a modest demand; A bikini is not modest enough to wear to church;* **mod.est.ly** *adv*.

mod.es.ty (MOD.is.tee) n. the quality of being properly humble, shy, decent, etc.: *the false modesty of keeping piano legs covered;* the **modesty panel** *of a desk for hiding the legs of a woman seated behind it*.

mod.i.cum (MOD.uh.cum) n. a small amount: *a modicum of manners, taste, truth, wine*.

mod.i.fy (MOD.uh.fye) *v*. **-fies, -fied, -fy.ing** change or alter, esp. to limit or moderate: *to modify a behavior, demand, method, one's tone of voice; In "too little," "too" modifies "little."* —**mod.i.fi.er** n. —**mod.i.fi.ca.tion** (-fuh.CAY.shun) n.

mod.ish (MOH.dish) *adj*. overly fashionable or stylish: *too modish for my tastes*. —**mod.ish.ly** *adv*.; **mod.ish.ness** n.

mod.u.lar (MOJ.uh.lur) *adj.* having to do with modules; standardized: *a modular telephone cable, cord, coupler, jack; modular equipment; modular house construction; a modular system.*
—**mod.u.lar.i.ty** (-LAIR.i.tee) *n.*

mod.u.late (MOJ.uh.late) *v.* **-lates, -lat.ed, -lat.ing** regulate or adjust, as the tone or pitch of one's voice in speaking, from one key to another in a musical composition, the frequency or amplitude of video and audio signals in broadcasting, etc.
—**mod.u.la.tion** (-LAY.shun) *n.*;
mod.u.la.tor (-lay.tur) *n.*

mod.ule (MOJ.ool) *n.* **1** a structural unit or component with a specific function in a larger unit or system: *building modules; the astronauts in a command module; a lunar excursion module; a spacecraft's service module; work modules making up an office; problem-solving in action modules responding to specific needs.* **2** a standard size or measure: *toothpaste in six metric modules from 25 to 150 ml.*

mo.dus o.pe.ran.di (MOH.dus.op.uh.RAN.dye, -dee) *n. Latin.* mode of operation or procedure.

modus vi.ven.di (MOH.dus.vi.VEN.dye, -dee) *n. Latin.* mode of living or coexisting.

mo.gul (MOH.gul) *n.* **1** magnate: *a movie mogul.* **2** a bump on a ski run.

mo.hair (MOH.hair) *n.* a fabric made of the hair of the Angora goat, usu. blended with wool.

Mo.ham.med.an (mo.HAM.id.un) *n. & adj.* Moslem. —**Mo.ham.med.an.ism** *n.*

Mo.hawk (MOH.hawk) *n. & adj.* (a member of) an Iroquois Indian people who originally lived in the region of the Mohawk River.

Mo.he.gan (moh.HEE.gun) *n. & adj.* (a member) of an Algonquian Indian people formerly living in W. Connecticut.

Mo.hi.can (moh.HEE.cun) *n. & adj.* (a member) of an Algonquian Indian people, including the Mohegans, formerly living along the Hudson River.

mol.e.ty (MOY.i.tee) *n.* **-ties 1** a portion, esp. half of something. **2** a basic part of a chemical compound: *a sweetener made by hydrogenation of the glucose moiety.*

moil *v.* **1** work hard as a drudge. **2** churn.

moi.ré (mwah.RAY, maw-) *n. & adj.* (a silk or rayon) having a wavelike pattern or clouded appearance.

moist *adj.* moderately wet: *skin that is moist with perspiration.* —**moist.ly** *adv.*; **moist.ness** *n.*

mois.ten (MOY.sun) *v.* make or become moist: *Don't wet the stamp, just moisten it before sticking.*

mois.ture (MOIS.chur) *n.* a liquid that causes moistness, esp. water vapor, as in the air.

mois.tur.ize (MOIS.chuh.rize) *v.* **-iz.es, -ized, -iz.ing** make skin, air, etc. moist, as a cosmetic cream does; **mois.tur.iz.er** *n.*

mo.lar (MOH.lur) *n.* a tooth adapted for grinding: *The four wisdom teeth are the rearmost of the three molars on each side of the jaws; an impacted molar (tooth); We have 12 molars in all.*

mo.las.ses (muh.LAS.iz) *n.* a thick, sticky, brown syrup obtained as a by-product during the refining of cane sugar.

mold (MOLD) *n.* **1** a frame, matrix, hollow, etc. that gives form or shape to what is put in it: *monotonous characters cast in the same mold.* **2** the shape or form or what is formed in a mold, as a jelly or pudding: *a jello mold; plaster molds.* **3** a greenish or whitish fungous growth, as seen on bread, cheese, etc.: *Books gather mold in a wet basement.* **4** crumbly rich soil: *a planter filled with leaf mold.* —*v.* **1** form or shape: *a figure molded out of clay; a character molded by experience.* **2** become covered with mold: *cheese starting to mold.* Also **mould** *Cdn.*

mold.board *n.* a type of plow that lifts and turns the soil away from the furrow as it tills. Also **mould.board** *Cdn.*

mold.er 1 *n.* one that molds or shapes something. **2** *v.* crumble or decay, esp. by turning into dust; *adj.*: *the moldering ruins of an ancient temple.* Also **moul.der** *Cdn.*

molding *n.* **1** the act or process of molding. **2** a continuous molded surface or strip for decoration or finish, as on buildings or on the side of an automobile's body. Also **moulding** *Cdn.*

mold.y *adj.* **mold.i.er, -i.est 1** mold covered. **2** stale or musty.
—**mold.i.ness** *n.* Also **mould.y** *Cdn.*

mole *n.* **1** a congenital, usu. dark protuberance on the skin. **2** a small furry burrowing animal that lives underground. **3** a tunneling machine. **4** a spy lying in wait to act as a double-agent: *a mole planted by the Soviets in the CIA.* **5** a breakwater, esp. one formed of large stones, earth, or masonry.

mol.e.cule (MOL.uh.cule) *n.* a small particle, esp. the smallest particle of a chemical element or compound, composed of atoms. —**mo.lec.u.lar** (muh.LEK.yuh.lur) *adj.*

mole.hill *n.* a small mound of earth thrown up by a mole.

mole.skin *n.* **1** the skin of the mole used as fur. **2** a cotton fabric used for work clothes.

mo.lest (muh.LEST) *v.* annoy a weaker person such as a child, esp. sexually; **mo.lest.er** *n.*: *a child molester.* —**mo.les.ta.tion** (moh.les.TAY.shun) *n.*

moll (MOL) *n. Slang.* a gangster's mistress or girl friend.

mol.li.fy (MOL.uh.fye) *v.* **-fies, -fied, -fy.ing** calm or soothe a person or his or her feelings.

mol.lusk (MOL.usk) *n.* a soft-bodied, shell-enclosed creature such as a snail, oyster, or octopus. Also **mol.lusc** *Cdn.*

mol.ly.cod.dle (MOL.ee.cod.ul) *v.* **-cod.dles, -cod.dled, -cod.dling** to pamper or fuss over someone. —*n.* a boy used to being pampered.

Mo.lo.tov cocktail (MOL.uh.tof-) *n.* a crude hand grenade made of a bottle of gasoline and a wick.

molt *v.* of a bird, insect, snake, etc., shed its feathers, skin, shell, or similar worn-out body covering. —*n.* this act or process. Also **moult** *Cdn.*

mol.ten (MOLE.tun) *adj.* melted: *molten lava, metal.*

mo.ly (MOH.lee) *n.* **1** in Greek myth, a magical herb. **2** the European wild garlic.

mo.lyb.de.num (muh.LIB.duh.num) *n.* a hard, heat-resistant element used in alloys such as steel.

mom *n. Informal.* mother.

mom-and-pop *adj. Informal.* of businesses, small and independent; **ma-and-pa**: *a mom-and-pop store.*

mo.ment (MOH.munt) *n.* **1** a short space of time; instant: *I'll be with you in a moment; crucial, opportune, rash moments; She got up and protested on the spur of the moment* (= without deliberation); *Let's forget it* **for the moment** (= now); *She had to* **seize the moment** (= take advantage of the opportunity). **2** weight or importance: *matters of great pith and moment.*

mo.men.tar.i.ly (moh.mun.TAIR.ee.lee) *adv.* **1** for a moment: *He was lost for words momentarily.* **2** from moment to moment: *We are expecting the flight to take off momentarily.* **3** in a moment; soon; presently: *He'll see you momentarily.* —**mo.men.tar.i.ness** *n.*

mo.men.tar.y (MOH.mun.tair.ee) *adj.* lasting only a moment: *a momentary dilemma, glance, kiss, pause; momentary appeal, pleasure, relief.*

mo.men.to (moh.MEN.toh) *n.* **-toes** [substandard form] See MEMENTO.

moment of truth *n.* a moment of crisis that helps one to arrive at the truth.

mo.men.tous (moh.MEN.tus) *adj.* of great moment or weight: *a momentous announcement, decision, occasion; something of momentous significance.*

mo.men.tum (moh.MEN.tum) *n.* **-tums** or **-ta** the force of a moving body; impetus: *A stone gains* or *gathers momentum as it rolls downhill.*

mom.my (MOM.ee) *n.* **mom.mies** [child's word] mother.

mommy track *n. Informal.* the career path of a woman who has children while holding down a job.

mon.arch (MON.urk) *n.* **1** a supreme ruler such as a king, queen, emperor, or sultan: *A constitutional monarch cannot be an absolute monarch.* **2** an orange-and-black migratory butterfly. —**mo.nar.chic** (muh.NAR.kic) or **mo.nar.chi.cal** (-ki.cul) *adj.*

mon.arch.y (MON.ur.kee) *n.* **-arch.ies** a country ruled by a monarch, usu. with limited power, as in the U.K.: *to establish, overthrow, set up a monarchy.* —**mon.arch.ist** *n.*

mon.as.ter.y (MON.uh.stair.ee) *n.* **-ter.ies** a place where a community of monks or nuns lives an ascetic life.

mo.nas.tic (muh.NAS.tic) *adj.* characteristic of monks and nuns; ascetic: *a monastic life, retreat, sect; monastic solitude;* **mo.nas.ti.cal.ly** *adv.*

mo.nas.ti.cism (muh.NAS.tuh.siz.um) *n.* the condition or system of living a monastic life.

mon.au.ral (mon.OR.ul) same as MONOPHONIC; **mon.au.ral.ly** *adv.*

Mon.day (MUN.dee, -day) *n.* the day following Sunday, usu. the first working day of the week: *We love weekends and hate Mondays.*

M-1 (EM.wun) *n.* the basic money supply of an economy, consisting of cash and bank deposits.

mon.e.tar.y (MON.uh.tair.ee) *adj.* having to do with money, esp. coinage or currency: *a monetary policy, system, unit, value; monetary issues* or *questions;* **mon.e.tar.ism** *n.*

mon.ey (MUN.ee) *n.* **mon.eys** or **mon.ies 1** an authorized medium of exchange, esp. coins or paper notes: *to change, circulate, coin, counterfeit money.*

2 wealth or property: *to bank, borrow, deposit, earn, invest, launder, lend, make, put up, raise, refund, save, squander, tie up, withdraw money; They sink money into speculative ventures; a man of money; conscience, earnest, easy, hush, mad, marked, pin, pocket, prize, seed money; She wouldn't do it for love or for money; He's out of money at the end of a month; We put money into* (= invest in) *savings bonds; the moneys* (= sums of money) *owed by you.* —**in the money** *Informal.* **1** rich or prosperous. **2** among the top prize-winners of a race or contest. —**money talks** *Informal.* You can accomplish things with money. —**on the money** *Informal.* exactly as expected or desired: *He made a firm pass right on the money.*

mon.ey.bags (MUN.ee.bags) *n.pl.* [with sing. v.] *Informal.* a rich and avaricious person.

mon.eyed (MUN.eed) *adj.* rich and wealthy.

mon.ey.lend.er (MUN.ee.len.dur) *n.* one who lends money at interest.

mon.ey.mak.er *n.* (MUN.ee.may.kur) *n.* **1** one skilled in acquiring wealth. **2** a profit-making scheme or product. —**mon.ey.mak.ing** *n. & adj.*

money market *n.* the buying and selling of short-term bonds and certificates.

money of account *n.* a monetary denomination such as the mill used only in reckoning, not issued as a coin or note.

money order *n.* a document issued at a post office or bank ordering payment of a specified amount on the purchaser's behalf to another person.

money supply *n.* the amount of money circulating in an economy.

-monger *comb.form* [derogatory] dealer in what is specified: *gossipmonger, peacemonger, rumormonger, scandalmonger, warmonger.*

Mon.gol (MON.gul, -gole) or **Mon.go.li.an** (mong.GO.lee.un) *n. & adj.* (a native) of **Mongolia**, an E.C. region of Asia.

Mon.gol.ic (mong.GOLL.ic) *n. & adj.* (having to do with) a subfamily of languages in Mongolia.

Mon.gol.ism (MONG.gul.iz.um) [usu. offensive] same as DOWN'S SYNDROME.

Mon.gol.oid (MONG.guh.loid) *n. & adj.* (a member) of a race of peoples characterized by stocky build, yellowish skin, and slanted eyes, including the Inuit and the peoples of China, Japan, Indonesia, etc.

mon.goose (MONG.goose) *n.* -**goos.es** a small carnivorous mammal of S. Asia and Africa, related to the civet cat and noted as a destroyer of rats and poisonous snakes such as the cobra.

mon.grel (MUNG.grul, MONG-) *n.* a dog of no recognizable breed. —*adj.* mixed in origin or character: *a mongrel dialect.*

monied same as MONEYED.

monies a *pl.* of MONEY.

mon.i.ker or **mon.ick.er** (MON.uh.kur) *n. Informal.* a nickname: *Eire, the Emerald Isle, Erin, and Irish Free State are monikers for the Republic of Ireland.*

mo.nism (MOH.niz.um, MON-) *n.* the metaphysical doctrine of the oneness of reality, etc., as opposed to dualism, pluralism, etc.; **mo.nist** *n.* —**mo.nis.tic** (muh.NIS.tic) *adj.*

mo.ni.tion (moh.NISH.un) *n.* **1** admonition. **2** an intimation or warning of danger.

mon.i.tor (MON.uh.tur) *v.* to watch or check on the performance of a person or operation: *His movements were monitored closely by the police; adja.: a monitoring service for house alarm systems; a monitoring station listening to broadcasts.* —*n.* **1** a student helping a teacher in class. **2** an output device for receiving audio or video signals: *a tape recorder with a telephone monitor; video monitor; TV monitor; a heart monitor in an operating room.* **3** software for monitoring a system. —**mon.i.to.ry** *adj.*

monk (MUNK) *n.* a male religious living in a monastery: *Benedictines, Carthusians, and such Christian monks; a Buddhist monk.* —**monk.ish** *adj.*

mon.key (MUNK.ee) *n.* -**keys** a small long-tailed ape or primate: *a horde of monkeys; to* **make a monkey out of** (*Informal for* to fool) *someone.* —*v. Informal.* fool or tamper: *He doesn't like cooks monkeying with his favorite dish.*

monkey business *n. Informal.* tricky or mischievous behavior.

mon.key.shines (MUNK.ee.shines) *n.pl. Slang.* clownish jokes or pranks.

monkey wrench *n.* a wrench with a jaw that is adjustable to various sizes of nuts. —**throw a monkey wrench into something** disrupt or obstruct the functioning of something going smoothly.

monks.hood same as ACONITE.

mon.o (MON.oh) *n.* [short form] **1** mononucleosis. **2** a monophonic phonograph record.

mono- *comb.form.* one or single: *monochrome, monogamy, monograph.*

mon.o.chro.mat.ic (MON.uh.croh.MAT.

ic) *adj.* of one color; consisting of a single wavelength.

mon.o.chrome (MON.uh.crome) *n.* a painting, print, etc. in a single color or shades of one color: *a monochrome* (= black and white) *TV signal.*

mon.o.cle (MON.uh.cul) *n.* an eyeglass for one eye; **mon.o.cled** *adj.*

mon.o.clo.nal (mon.uh.CLOH.nul) *adj.* having to do with cells derived from a single biological clone: *monoclonal antibodies, diagnostics, tumors.*

mon.o.cot.y.le.don (MON.uh.cot.uh.LEE.dun) *n.* a flowering plant such as grasses, palms, and lilies that has a single cotyledon in its seed embryo; **mon.o.cot.y.le.don.ous** (-LEE.dun.us) *adj.*

mon.o.dy (MON.uh.dee) *n.* **-dies** 1 a mourning or dirge, esp. as sung by a single person. 2 a musical composition for a single voice; **mon.o.dist** *n.*; —**mo.nod.ic** (muh.NOD.ic) *adj.*

mo.nog.a.my (muh.NOG.uh.mee) *n.* marriage with one person at a time. —**mo.nog.a.mist** *n.*; **mo.nog.a.mous** (-uh.mus) *adj.*

mon.o.gram (MON.uh.gram) *n.* a design combining the initials of a name. —*v.* **-grams, -grammed, -gram.ming** print a monogram on something; *adj.:* **monogrammed** *jewelry, linen, stationery.*

mon.o.graph (MON.uh.graf) *n.* 1 a scholarly work treating a single subject exhaustively. 2 a single volume, not a series. 3 a booklet explaining a single commercial product such as a drug.

mon.o.lin.gual (mon.uh.LING.gwul) *adj.* limited to one language: *a monolingual population.*

mon.o.lith (MON.uh.lith) *n.* 1 a single massive block of stone, as a monument or column. 2 a person or thing that is massive and unyielding. —**mon.o.lith.ic** (-LITH.ic) *adj.: a monolithic monument or column (of one stone); a monolithic society (that is massive and rigid); a monolithic integrated circuit (on a single silicon chip).*

mon.o.logue (MON.uh.log) *n.* 1 a long speech by one person of a group: *to recite a monologue.* 2 a soliloquy or other dramatic piece involving one actor. Also **mon.o.log.**

mon.o.ma.ni.a (mon.uh.MAY.nee.uh) *n.* a mental disorder involving one fixed idea; **mon.o.ma.ni.ac** *n. & adj.*

mon.o.mer (MON.uh.mur) *n.* a combining molecule of a polymer.

mon.o.nu.cle.o.sis (MON.uh.new.clee.OH.sis) *n.* a blood disease of young people caused by an abnormality of single-nucleus blood cells; also called "glandular fever" and "kissing disease."

mon.o.phon.ic (mon.uh.FON.ic) *adj.* having to do with sound reproduction using a single channel: *a monophonic, not a stereophonic system.*

mo.nop.o.list (muh.NOP.uh.list) *n.* one who has a monopoly or favors monopoly. —**mo.nop.o.lis.tic** (-LIS.tic) *adj.*

mo.nop.o.lize (muh.NOP.uh.lize) *v.* **-liz.es, -lized, -liz.ing** have, get, or keep something exclusively: *to monopolize a conversation.*

mo.nop.o.ly (muh.NOP.uh.lee) *n.* **-lies** 1 exclusive marketing control of a commodity or service, as most public utilities: *The Post Office has* or *holds a monopoly on* or *over mail.* 2 a company enjoying such absence of competition: *Governments try to break up monopolies.*

mon.o.rail (MON.uh.rail) *n.* a single rail or a vehicle traveling on one, with the cars either suspended from the rail or balanced on top of it.

mon.o.so.di.um glu.ta.mate (mon.uh.SOH.dee.um.GLOO.tuh.mate) *n.* a salt used to enhance the flavor of foods; also called "MSG."

mon.o.syl.la.ble (MON.uh.sil.uh.bul) *n.* a word of one syllable. —**mon.o.syl.lab.ic** (-suh.LAB.ic) *adj.*

mon.o.the.ism (MON.uh.thee.iz.um, "th" as in "thin") *n.* the belief or doctrine that there is only one God; **mon.o.the.ist** *n.* —**mon.o.the.is.tic** (-IS.tic) *adj.*

mon.o.tone (MON.uh.tone) *n.* sameness of tone of utterance, style of writing, etc.: *He reads in a dull monotone.*

mo.not.o.nous (muh.NOT.uh.nus) *adj.* tiresome because of unvarying tone or style: *a monotonous routine; It's monotonous to eat the same lunch every day.* —**mo.not.o.ny** *n.: VCRs break* or *relieve the monotony of TV watching.*

Mon.sei.gneur (mon.sen.YUR) *n., pl.* **Mes.sei.gneurs** (may.sen.YUR) a French title of honor given to persons of high rank.

mon.sieur (mus.YUR) *n.* **mes.sieurs** (MES.urz) 1 a gentleman. 2 **Monsieur** French title equivalent to "Mr." or "Sir."

Mon.si.gnor (mon.SEEN.yur) *n.* **-gnors** or **-gno.ri** (mone.seen.YOR.ee) a title given to certain dignitaries of the Roman Catholic Church.

mon.soon (mon.SOON) *n.* a seasonal wind blowing over the Indian Ocean, esp. in the summer, accompanied by heavy rains.

mon.ster (MON.stur) *n.* **1** a huge, ugly, or wicked creature such as a dragon. **2** a grossly malformed birth. —*adj*a. huge: *a monster rally; the demolition of small bungalows for building* **monster homes** *in old neighborhoods.*

mon.strance (MON.strunce) *n.* in the Roman Catholic Church, a vessel for displaying the consecrated host for adoration.

mon.strous (MON.strus) *adj.* **1** like a monster: *monstrous in appearance.* **2** wicked: *a monstrous crime; It's monstrous to abuse children; It's monstrous that criminals go unpunished.* —**mon.strous.ly** *adv.* —**mon.stros.i.ty** (mon.STROS.i.tee) *n.* **-ties.**

mon.tage (mon.TAHZH) *n.* in photography, motion pictures, etc., a combining or blending of many distinct pictures for a special effect.

month (MUNTH) *n.* one of the 12 divisions of the year, from 28 to 31 days long, January through December: *The lunar month of about 29½ days is the period of one revolution of the moon around the earth.*

month.ly (MUNTH.lee) *adj. & adv.* every month; once a month. —*n., pl.* **-lies** a monthly publication.

mon.u.ment (MON.yuh.munt) *n.* a tablet, statue, pillar, building, etc. put up in commemoration of a person or event: *The pyramids of Egypt are ancient monuments; The book is a monument to its author's creative genius; A place of historic or scenic interest in the U.S. may be set apart as a* **national monument** *for public use.*

mon.u.men.tal (mon.yuh.MEN.tul) *adj.* **1** being, like, or having to do with a monument: *a monumental event, figure, sculpture, work; monumental marble and stone.* **2** exceptionally large or great: *an event of monumental importance, significance; a monumental advantage, challenge, change, crisis, step, task, work.* **3** exceptionally bad: *a monumental blunder, error, failure, waste; his monumental ignorance.* —**mon.u.men.tal.ly** *adv.*

moo *v. & n.* **moos, mooed, moo.ing** (make) the sound of the call of a cow.

mooch (long "oo") *v. Slang.* get money, food, etc. by begging; sponge or cadge; **mooch.er** *n.*

mood (long "oo") *n.* **1** a state of mind; feeling or attitude: *angry, festive, holiday, genial, jovial, joyful, melancholy, pensive, sullen moods; Talk to him when he is in a good mood; in the mood to listen to you; She's in no mood for playing games; Could drugs modify one's moods? There is a mood of optimism in the country; Don't approach him when he is* **in a mood** *or* **in one of his moods** (= when he is in a bad mood); *He is a man of* **moods** (= uncertain temper). **2** a grammatical aspect of the action of a verb: *"He is going" is in the indicative mood* (i.e., aspect of action as a fact); *"Please go" is in the imperative mood* (i.e., aspect of action as a command).

mood.y *adj.* **mood.i.er, -i.est** gloomy or sullen. —**mood.i.ly** *adv.*; **mood.i.ness** *n.*

moon (long "oo") *n.* **1** often **Moon**, a heavenly body that is the earth's natural satellite, taking about 29½ days for a full circle, from one "new moon" to the next, during which period it waxes from "crescent" to "full moon" and then wanes: *The moon comes out when the sun goes down.* **2** any satellite of a planet: *the moons of Jupiter.* —*v.* **1** spend time or wander *about* or *around* idly. **2** *Slang.* show one's bare buttocks as a prank or gesture of contempt: *Mo never moons moms.*

moon.beam *n.* a ray of moonlight.

Moon.ie (MOO.nee) *n.* **Moon.ies** a member of a religious cult founded by Sun Myung Moon.

moon.light *n.* the light of the moon: *to walk by moonlight; to go swimming in the moonlight.* —*v. Informal.* work at a job, as at night, in addition to a regular one; **moon.light.er** *n.*

moon.lit *adj.* lighted by the moon: *a moonlit night.*

moon.scape *n.* a view of the moon's surface.

moon.shine *n.* **1** moonlight. **2** foolish notions; empty talk. **3** *Informal.* illegally made alcoholic liquor.

moon.shot *n.* the launching of a spacecraft toward the moon.

moon.space *n.* a view of the moon's surface.

moon.stone *n.* a whitish variety of gem.

moon.struck *adj.* dazed, dreamy, or mentally unbalanced.

moon.walk *n.* an astronaut's walk on the moon.

Moor *n.* a northwest African, esp. a member of the people that conquered Spain in the 8th century A.D. —**Moor.ish** *adj.*

moor *n.* a tract of marshy wasteland, usu. heather-covered; heath; also **moor.land.** —*v.* secure a ship, boat, etc. in place by fastening it by rope or chain to a pier or to the shore or by anchors.

mooring *n.* also **moorings** *pl.* **1** the

place to which a craft is moored. **2** the anchors or chains by which something is secured in place. **3** a person's ties or attachments, as of religion or society, that are a source of security.

moose *n.* a North American elk with flattened antlers: *a bull* (= male) *moose; calf* (= young) *moose; cow* (= female) *moose.*

moot *adj.* debatable: *a moot point, question; a dismissal* **made moot** (= of no consequence) *by resignation; a* **moot court** (= mock court for law students to practice in). —*v.* raise for discussion: *The Bigfoot, as is mooted, may not be a myth after all.*

mop *n.* **1** an implement for wiping floors, usu. a handle with a bundle of rags or a sponge at the end: *dry, dust, wet mops.* **2** a thick head of unruly hair. —*v.* **mops, mopped, mop.ping** wipe: *a handkerchief to mop your brow; to mop the floor clean.* —**mop up 1** wipe up: *to mop up a spill.* **2** dispose of remaining members of a group: *to mop up the remnants of a defeated army; n.: mopping up operations.*

mope *v.* **mopes, moped, mop.ing** be gloomy or in low spirits. —*n.* **1** a gloomy person. **2 mopes** *pl.* low spirits.

mo.ped (MOH.ped) *n.* a light motorcycle that can be pedaled.

mop.ey (MOH.pee) *adj.* given to moping; dejected; also **mop.ish** (MOH.pish) or **mop.y.** —**mop.i.ness** *n.*

mop.pet (MOP.it) *n. Informal.* a little child.

mo.raine (muh.RAIN) *n.* rock, dirt, sand, etc. deposited by a moving glacier.

mor.al (MOR.ul) *adj.* **1** having to do with accepted standards of good conduct: *our moral behavior; moral law, lessons; to lead a moral life; a moral man, person, woman; a moral novel, tale (that teaches a moral lesson); You sound very moral* (= virtuous); *Infants are not moral beings* (= They don't know right from wrong). **2** based on what one thinks is right and wrong: *a moral duty, question, responsibility, sense, victory; the moral courage or fiber to stand up to a bully; a bully's moral cowardice; the moral indignation of the public toward injustices; to exert moral pressure on someone to get something done; Though I can't contribute to your cause, you have my moral support.* **3** based on high probability: *That a mother loves her child is a moral though not an absolute certainty.*
—*n.* **1** a moral lesson: *The story has a moral to it.* **2 morals** *pl.* moral principles, esp. in regard to sex: *a man of good morals; to corrupt the morals of youth; to protect or safeguard the morals of society; adja.: a morals charge, conviction, offense.* —**mor.al.ly** *adv.*

mo.rale (muh.RAL) *n.* mental or moral condition in regard to discipline and confidence: *The good news helped to boost* or *lift* or *raise his morale; The morale of an army, team, etc. may be high, low; A leader's bad example may destroy* or *undermine morale.*

mor.al.ist (MOR.uh.list) *n.* **1** an expert in morals. **2** one who favors or is concerned with regulating morals, as through censorship. —**mor.al.is.tic** (-LIS.tic) *adj.*

mo.ral.i.ty (muh.RAL.i.tee) *n.* -**ties 1** moral quality, system, instruction, etc.: *standards of morality; Christian, Hindu, Moslem, private, public morality; a medieval* **morality play** *with virtues and vices as characters.* **2** goodness or rightness: *the morality of killing animals for meat.*

morality squad *n.* a police division concerned with gaming and prostitution.

mor.al.ize (MOR.uh.lize) *v.* **-liz.es, -lized, -liz.ing** [derogatory] think, talk, or write about morals in a superior way: *to moralize about* or *on* or *over* or *upon sin and punishment; an editorial moralizing against abortion; n.: This is a critical analysis, not moralizing; pompous, prim, self-righteous, sentimental moralizing; adja.: moralizing attitudes, preachers, rhetoric, writers.* —**mor.al.i.za.tion** (-luh.ZAY.shun. -lye-) *n.*

moral philosophy *n.* ethics as a branch of philosophy.

moral victory *n.* victory based on what is right: *We lost the election but won a moral victory because we deserved to win.*

mo.rass (muh.RAS) *n.* a swamp or marsh; hence, a messy situation: *A dictionary user should not get bogged down in a morass of meanings.*

mor.a.to.ri.um (mor.uh.TOR.ee.um) *n.* **-ri.ums** or **-ri.a** an official delay or suspension, as on legal action to collect a debt, testing of nuclear weapons, etc.: *to declare a moratorium; to lift a moratorium on the sale of foreign car.*

mo.ray (MOR.ay, muh.RAY) *n.* a large, thick-bodied, fierce eel of tropical seas.

mor.bid *adj.* diseased or sickly; gruesome: *a morbid curiosity, growth, interest in death; the morbid details of a crime;* **mor.bid.ly** *adv.*; **mor.bid.ness** *n.*

—**mor.bid.i.ty** (-BID.i.tee) *n.*
mor.dant (MOR.dunt) *adj.* incisive; caustic; pungent: *mordant criticism, wit.* —*n.* **1** a chemical that fixes colors. **2** an etching agent. —**mor.dant.ly** *adv.* —**mor.dan.cy** *n.*
more *comp.* of MANY or MUCH.
—*adj.* a greater or additional amount, number, or part: *We need more food; a few more donuts; a little more coffee; More guests have arrived.*
—*adv.: I couldn't agree with you more; He doesn't write to me any more; I shall be* **more than** (= quite) *happy to help you; People are eating out* **more and more** (= in larger numbers); *The baby is* **more or less** (= almost) *asleep;* **What's more** (= in addition), *it is past midnight.*
—*n. & pron.: the more the merrier; Some more, please; a few more of the donuts you sold us yesterday; Many were killed, more* (= an additional number; also, a greater number) *were wounded.*
mo.rel (muh.REL) *n.* an edible mushroom.
more.o.ver (mor.OH.vur) *adv.* besides; in addition.
mo.res (MOR.aiz, -eez) *n.pl.* the traditional morally binding rules and customs of a society: *our social manners and mores; "One spouse at a time" is part of our sexual mores.*
morgue (MORG) *n.* **1** a place where unidentified bodies are kept temporarily, as of victims of accidents or violent deaths. **2** formerly, a newspaper reference library stocking obituaries, news clippings, etc.
mor.i.bund (MOR.uh.bund) *adj.* in the process of dying out: *a moribund civilization, custom; Are monarchies moribund?*
Mor.mon (MOR.mun) *n.* a member of the Church of Jesus Christ of Latter-day Saints; **Mor.mon.ism** *n.*
morn *n.* [poetic use] morning.
morn.ing *n.* the period from dawn to noon, esp. the beginning of a day: *Good morning (to you)! from morning till noon; on a wintry morning; the morning of January 31; a drinking bout and a hangover the morning after;* **adj.:** *a* **morning-after** *headache following a binge.*
morning glory *n.* a climbing plant with trumpet-shaped flowers that stay open only in the morning.
morning sickness *n.* the sickness felt in the morning during the first few months of pregnancy.
morning star *n.* a planet, esp. Venus, seen in the morning sky.
Mo.roc.can (muh.ROC.un) **1** *n. & adj.* (a person) of or from **Morocco**, a country in N.W. Africa. **2** *n.* a kind of fine leather made from goat skins.
mo.ron (MOR.on) *n.* **1** a foolish or stupid person. **2** formerly, a classification of a mentally retarded person with an I.Q. between 50 and 75. —**mo.ron.ic** (muh.RON.ic) *adj.*
mo.rose (muh.ROSE) *adj.* glum and unsociable; gloomy. —**mo.rose.ly** *adv.;* **mo.rose.ness** *n.*
morph *n.* **1** a variant form of a morpheme: *In "illegal," "impotent," "inactive," and "irrational," "il-," "im-,"in-," and "ir-" are morphs of the prefix meaning "not."* **2** a variant form of a plant or animal, as the queen bee and the worker bee. **3** the digital transforming of one image into another, as of a bear into a bull; also *v.*
mor.pheme (MOR.feem) *n.* any of the smallest word units of a language, as affixes, inflections, roots, etc.
—**mor.phem.ic** (mor.FEE.mic) *adj.*
mor.phine (MOR.feen) *n.* a narcotic drug made from opium and used medically to relieve pain.
mor.phol.o.gy (mor.FOL.uh.jee) *n.* (the study of) form and structure, as of animals and plants, of words and inflections, etc.; **mor.phol.o.gist** *n.*
—**mor.pho.log.i.cal** (-fuh.LOJ.i.cul) *adj.*
mor.ris *n.* a vigorous folk dance of rural England performed by trained men.
mor.row (MOR.oh) *n.* [poetic or literary use] **1** morning. **2** the next day.
Morse code *n.* an alphabet of dots and dashes for use in telegraphy: *a message in Morse code.*
mor.sel (MOR.sul) *n.* **1** a mouthful or small portion of food: *a dainty* or *tasty morsel; a bite-size morsel.* **2** a piece or amount: *There's hardly a morsel of energy left in me; with only a few morsels of evidence.*
mor.tal (MOR.tul) *adj.* having to do with death: *in mortal fear of being killed; a mortal threat, torment; mere mortal man; two people locked in a mortal combat; a mortal* (= fatal) *blow, injury, wound; one's mortal* (= deadly or hated) *enemy; They live in mortal* (= intense) *danger; They did mortal* (= great) *damage; our mortal* (= human) *limitations; a* **mortal sin** (*that causes spiritual death*); *to* **shuffle off this mortal coil** (= to die). —*n.* a human being: *They are mere mortals; She is no ordinary mortal.* —**mor.tal.ly** *adv.*
mor.tal.i.ty (mor.TAL.i.tee) *n.* death,

esp. its rate in proportion to population: *infant mortality;* A **mortality table** *shows life expectancy.*

mor.tar (MOR.tur) *n.* **1** a bowl of porcelain or other hard material for pounding substances to a powder using a pestle. **2** a short-range cannon that fires shells (dropped down its muzzle) in a high arc, as over a hill or fortification. **3** a hardening mixture of lime, cement, etc. for use between bricks or stones in building.

mor.tar.board (MOR.tur.bord) *n.* **1** a square board used by masons to hold and work mortar. **2** an academic cap with a square board on top from which a tassel hangs.

mort.gage (MOR.gij) *n.* **1** a pledging of property as security for the payment of a loan or debt to the lender, or **mort.ga.gee** (mor.guh.JEE): *to take out a mortgage on one's home; to give, hold, pay off a mortgage.* **2** the deed by which this is conveyed by the owner of the property, or **mort.ga.ger** or **mort.ga.gor** (-guh.jur).
—*v.* **-gag.es, -gaged, -gag.ing** transfer one's rights by or as if by a mortgage: *to mortgage one's house, happiness, future.*

mor.ti.cian (mor.TISH.un) *n.* an undertaker.

mor.ti.fy (MOR.tuh.fye) *v.* **-fies, -fied, -fy.ing** punish oneself: *Saints mortify their bodies, desires, etc. by fasting and penance; to mortify the flesh; adj.: She felt deeply mortified* (= embarrassed) *by her child's behavior in public;* a **mortifying** *defeat, experience, failure, mistake.*
—**mor.ti.fi.ca.tion** (-fuh.CAY.shun) *n.*

mor.tise (MOR.tis) *n.* a hole or notch in one part of a joint of a piece of wood into which the tenon of the other part fits; *adj*a.: *mortise joints, locks; mortise-and-tenon construction.* —*v.* **-tis.es, -tised, -tis.ing** join with a mortise: *beams mortised, not nailed together.* Also **mor.tice.**

mor.tu.ar.y (MOR.choo.air.ee) *n.* **-ar.ies** a place where dead bodies are kept before burial or cremation; funeral home; *adj*a.: *a mortuary chapel, service.*

mo.sa.ic (moh.ZAY.ic) **1** *n.* a picture or design made with small colored pieces of stone, glass, etc. inlaid on a surface such as a floor, ceiling, or wall: *Our nation is a mosaic of many cultures; adj*a.: *a mosaic design, floor, pavement.* **2 Mosaic** *adj.* having to do with Moses: *The Mosaic law includes the Ten Commandments.*

Mo.ses (MOH.ziz) *n.* the lawgiver of the Israelites who led them out of slavery in Egypt: *Holy Moses!*

mo.sey (MOH.see) *v.* **-seys, -seyed, -sey.ing** *Informal.* move *along* at a leisurely pace.

Mos.lem (MOZ.lum) *n.* a follower of the religion founded by Mohammed.

mosque (MOSK) *n.* an Islamic place of public worship.

mos.qui.to (mus.KEE.toh) *n.* **-tos** or **-toes** a two-winged, blood-sucking insect that is often a carrier of disease germs, as of malaria and yellow fever: *A mosquito net is used to keep mosquitoes out.*

moss *n.* a tiny green plant that grows in cushionlike clusters on damp banks, rocks, and trees. —**moss.y** *adj.*

moss.back *n.* **1** an old turtle with algae growing on its back. **2** *Informal.* an old fogey; very conservative person.

most (MOHST) *superl.* of MANY & MUCH. —*n. & pron.* the greatest amount, degree, or number: *Boys form most of the group; a group that is noisier than most; a car that gives only 10 km to the liter* **at (the) most** (= as a maximum). —*adj. & adv.:* *a most interesting subject; Most people like dogs; She loves children most;* as **most** (*Informal* for almost) *anyone will tell you; The show was good* **for the most part** (= almost completely); *the hostess with the* **mostest** (*Informal* for the most charming hostess). —**comb.form** [forming superlative]: foremost, topmost, uppermost.

most.ly *adv.* for the most part; mainly: *It snows mostly in January.*

mot (MOH) *n.* **mots** (MOZE) a witty saying.

mote *n.* a speck of dust.

mo.tel (moh.TEL) *n.* a roadside establishment providing furnished rooms and parking spaces for travelers.

mo.tet (moh.TET) *n.* a polyphonic vocal composition, usu. of a religious nature.

moth *n.* an insect that resembles a butterfly but is less brightly colored, that flies mostly at night, and whose larvae eat wool, fur, etc.

moth.ball *n.* a small ball of camphor or similar material used to keep moths away from clothing: *The new project has been* **put in** or **into mothballs** (= shelved or stored away).

moth-eaten *adj.* out-of-date: *a moth-eaten idea.*

moth.er (MUTH.ur, "TH" as in "the") *n.* **1** a female parent: *an expectant, foster, step, surrogate, welfare, working mother; the* **mother superior** (= head) *of a convent.* **2** a source or origin of

motherboard / motor home

anything: *the **mother church** (of all the Christian churches); your **mother country** (= country of birth); the **mother house** (= headquarters or original convent) of the nuns.* —*v.* produce, nourish, or protect, as a mother does: *She has mothered many orphans; Do men like to be mothered?* *n.*: **Mothering** *comes naturally to most women;* *adja.*: *the mothering instinct; her mothering days, period, role.*
—**moth.er.ly** *adj.*: *motherly care, fondness, image; a motherly woman.*
—**moth.er.li.ness** *n.*

moth.er.board (MUTH.ur.bord) *n.* a slotted board on which other boards containing a computer's circuitry are mounted.

moth.er.hood *n.* the state of being a mother: *Education is like motherhood; No one attacks **motherhood and apple pie** (as they stand for basic North American values).* —*adja.* of basic importance: *a motherhood issue, proposal, statement.*

mother-in-law *n.* **mothers-in-law** the mother of one's spouse.

moth.er.land (MUTH.ur.land) *n.* one's native or ancestral country.

mother lode *n.* a rich source, as in mining: *a database that is a mother lode of information.*

Mother Nature *n.* nature personified as a creative and nurturing force.

mother-of-pearl *n.* the glossy inner lining of the shells of the pearl oyster and other mollusks, used in making buttons, beads, etc.

mother tongue *n.* one's first-learned and still-understood language.

mo.tif (moh.TEEF) *n.* in art, literature, and music, a dominant theme, main feature, or recurring pattern: *Love is the leading motif of romances.*

mo.tile (MOH.tul, -tile) *adj.* of organisms, capable of motion. —**mo.til.i.ty** (moh.TIL.i.tee) *n.*

mo.tion (MOH.shun) *n.* **1** a moving: *Newton's laws of motion; the line of motion of a skier; Who set the universe in motion? Do not get off a train when it is in motion.* **2** a formal proposal made in a meeting, legislature, or court of law: *a motion for adjournment; to accept, defeat, make, second, vote down, vote on, withdraw a motion; A motion carries or is passed.* **3** gesture: *I saw Tim **go through the motions of** (= routinely or halfheartedly) brushing his teeth.*
—*v.* gesture: *The chairman motioned us to be seated.*

mo.tion.less *adj.* without moving: *He sat there motionless.*

motion picture *n.* **1** a series of contiguous pictures giving the impression of movement when projected; moving picture. **2** a story in this form. Also **moving picture** or **movie**.

motion sickness *n.* nausea felt by passengers on a ship, plane, etc.

mo.ti.vate (MOH.tuh.vate) *v.* **-vates, -vat.ed, -vat.ing** provide with or influence as a motive; impel: *What motivates students to complete high school?*
—**mo.ti.va.tion** (-VAY.shun) *n.*
—**mo.ti.va.tion.al** (-VAY.shuh.nul) *adj.*: *motivational analysis, drives, experts, research.*

mo.tive (MOH.tiv) **1** *n.* the cause of an action: *Revenge was the motive for the murder; to establish, find a motive; to question someone's motives; altruistic, base, honorable, noble, selfish, ulterior motives; people acting from the highest motives; the profit motive of corporations; an underlying motive for the kidnaping; Did he have some motive to commit the crime?* **2** *n.* a basic melody or motif, as the first four notes of Beethoven's "Fifth Symphony." **3** *adj.* moving: *the motive power* of steam; *cpd.*: *automotive, electromotive, locomotive.*

mot.ley (MOT.lee) *adj.* **1** many-colored, as a clown's garment: *a motley dress.* **2** varied in character: *a motley band, collection, crew, crowd, team;*
—**mot.ley.ness** *n.*

mo.to.cross (MOH.tuh.cros) *n.* a cross-country motorcycle race.

mo.tor (MOH.tur) *n.* one that gives motion, esp. an engine: *a lawnmower powered by an electric motor; a gas motor; the outboard motor of a boat; A motor runs, stalls, works; to start, turn off a motor; The brain's **motor area** controls neurons that impart motor impulses to muscles; a **motor vehicle** running on an internal combustion engine.* —*v.* go or convey by automobile; **mo.tor.a.ble** *adj.*: *a motorable road.*

mo.tor.bike (MOH.tur.bike) *n. Informal.* motorcycle.

mo.tor.boat (MOH.tur.boht) *n.* a boat propelled by a motor.

mo.tor.cade (MOH.tur.cade) *n.* a procession of motor vehicles.

mo.tor.car (MOH.tur.car) *n.* automobile.

motor court *n.* a motel.

mo.tor.cy.cle (MOH.tur.sye.cul) *n.* a heavier and larger type of bicycle powered by an internal combustion engine. —*v.* **-cles, -cled, -cling** travel by motorcycle. —**mo.tor.cy.clist** *n.*

motor home *n.* an automotive recreational vehicle built on a truck chassis and having living facilities.

motor hotel (or **inn**) *n.* a hotel with parking facilities for guests.

mo.tor.ist (MOH.tur.ist) *n.* a traveler by automobile.

mo.tor.ize (MOH.tuh.rize) *v.* **-iz.es, -ized, -iz.ing 1** equip with a motor; *adj.*: *motorized bicycles, film advance and rewind; motorized shoulder belts; motorized traffic (of motor vehicles); No motorized vehicles are allowed in the park.* **2** equip with motor vehicles; *adj.*: *motorized forces; a motorized regiment.* —**mo.tor.i.za.tion** (-ruh.ZAY.shun, -rye-) *n.*

motor lodge same as MOTOR HOTEL.

mo.tor.man (MOH.tur.mun) *n.* **-men** a driver of an electric train or streetcar.

motor scooter *n.* a scooterlike vehicle with an engine mounted over the rear wheel and the driver seated with feet on a floorboard.

motor truck *n.* an automotive truck for carrying freight.

motor vehicle *n.* an automotive vehicle such as an automobile, bus, truck, etc. for use on roadways.

mot.tle (MOT.ul) *v.* **mot.tles, mot.tled, mot.tling** mark with blotches or streaks of different colors; *adj.*: *a mottled finish, leaf, skin.*

mot.to (MOT.oh) *n.* **-tos** or **-toes** a rule of conduct, usu. a brief expression such as "Be prepared," put on a coat of arms or badge.

moue (MOO) *n.* a pout or grimace.

mould, mould.er, molding, mouldy, moult See MOLD, etc.

mound (*rhyme:* round) *n.* **1** a bank of earth or stones: *a burial mound.* **2** a knoll. —*v.* heap up as a mound.

mount (*rhyme:* count) *v.* **1** climb on or toward the top of a thing or animal: *to mount a horse, ladder, platform; adj.*: *the state **mounted** police (on horseback); the **mounting** (= rising) cost of living.* **2** place or fix in proper position: *to mount a specimen on a slide, stamps in an album, gems in gold, guns on a gun carriage.* **3** set up or organize: *to mount an attack, campaign, challenge, defense, demonstration, exhibition, offensive, protest.* —*n.* **1** [used in names] mountain: *Mount Everest; Mt. Logan.* **2** an animal or machine on which one is mounted. **3** a place to mount something on, as a backing or support: *a cardboard mount for a picture; an engine mount; the vacuum mount of a pencil sharpener; the mount* (= bastion) *of a castle.*

moun.tain (MOWN.tun) *n.* a very high hill or mass of land, often rising to a peak; also, the peak: *to climb, scale a mountain; the Matterhorn mountain; the height* or *elevation of a mountain; a chain* or *range of mountains; rugged, snow-covered, volcanic mountains; Everest, the world's highest mountain, is in the Himalayan **Mountains*** (= a mountain formation); *a mountain* (= huge pile) *of garbage; a mountain of work awaiting a vacationer; Let us not **make a mountain out of a molehill*** (= magnify small difficulties).

mountain ash *n.* a tree that grows in high places and has pinnate compound leaves, clusters of white flowers, and red, berrylike fruits.

moun.tain.eer (mown.tuh.NEER) *n.* **1** one who lives in the mountains. **2** a skilled climber of mountains. —*v.* climb mountains as a sport.

mountain goat same as ROCKY MOUNTAIN GOAT.

mountain laurel *n.* an evergreen shrub or tree with dark, glossy leaves and pink, white, or purple flowers.

mountain lion *n.* a wildcat of W. North America, smaller than a jaguar.

moun.tain.ous (MOWN.tun.us) *adj.* **1** full of mountains. **2** huge like a mountain.

moun.te.bank (MOWN.tuh.bank) *n.* a charlatan or quack.

Mount.ie or **Mount.y** (MOWN.tee) *n.* **Mount.ies** *Informal.* a member of the Royal Canadian Mounted Police.

mounting *n.* a backing or support, as for a picture; mount.

mourn (MORN) *v.* feel or express sorrow or grief for a dead person: *to mourn a death, loss; mourning for* or *over a dear one.*

mourn.ful *adj.* sorrowful. —**mourn.ful.ly** *adv.*; **mourn.ful.ness** *n.*

mourning *n.* the expression of grief at someone's death, the usu. black clothes worn as a sign of it, or the period of such expression: *A nation goes into mourning when its head of state dies; The government declares* or *proclaims a period of mourning; national mourning; The country was in mourning for a month.*

mouse *n., pl.* **mice 1** a small gnawing animal with soft fur and pointed snout, esp. the "house mouse" found worldwide and used in laboratories: *Cats catch mice; as quiet as a mouse; a field mouse; white mice.* **2** a timid person. **3** *pl.* **mouses**, a hand-held, button-operated device attached to a microcomputer for manipulating the cursor on its monitor and selecting

routine operations without using the keyboard. **4** *Slang.* a black eye.
—*v.* (MOWZE) **mous.es, moused, mous.ing** hunt for mice, as a cat does; **mous.er** *n.*

mouse.trap *n.* a trap for catching mice: *"Make a better mousetrap and the world will beat a path to your door"* (= Inventors are in great demand).

mousey same as MOUSY.

mousse (MOOSE) *n.* **1** a light, molded, chilled dessert made with gelatin and whipped cream: *banana, coffee, maple mousse.* **2** a hairstyling foam.

mous.tache (mus.TASH, MUS.tash) same as MUSTACHE.

mous.y or **mous.ey** (MOW.see, -zee) *adj.* **mous.i.er, -i.est** like a mouse; timid or stealthy. —**mous.i.ness** *n.*

mouth *n.* **1** an opening through which food is taken into the body, and in which speech sounds are made: *to cram* or *stuff one's mouth with cake; It makes your mouth water* (= tempts you); *a big mouth* (= gossip); *Study the subject before you **shoot your mouth off*** (*Informal for* before you talk as if you know all about it). **2** any opening or entrance resembling a mouth, as of a cave, jar, or of a river where it empties into a larger body of water.
—**down in** or **at the mouth** *Informal.* in low spirits. —*v.* ("TH" as in "the") **1** utter words in an affected manner; declaim. **2** form words with the mouth silently.

mouthed *adj. & comb.form.* having a mouth or one as specified: *a mouthed shell; close-mouthed, foul-mouthed, loud-mouthed, mealy-mouthed, open-mouthed; wide-mouthed.*

mouth.ful *n.* **-fuls 1** a small quantity, as will fill a mouth. **2** *Informal.* a hard-to-pronounce word or a string of words. **3** *Informal.* an appropriate or significant remark: *You said a mouthful.*

mouth.piece *n.* **1** a part or structure that serves as a mouth, as of a water pipe, or that is placed at or near a person's mouth, as of a musical instrument that is blown into, of a tobacco pipe, or of a telephone. **2** a person or periodical that speaks for another: *a press attaché who serves or acts as a mouthpiece for his country.*

mouth.wash *n.* a liquid preparation for rinsing the mouth.

mouth.wa.ter.ing (MOUTH.waw.tur.ing) *adj.* very appetizing or tasty.

mou.ton (MOO.ton, *rhyme:* on) *n.* fur made from a sheepskin, dyed to look like beaver or seal.

mov.a.ble (MOO.vuh.bul) **1** *adj.* that can be moved from place to place, as furniture. **2 movables** *n.pl.* personal property. Also **move.a.ble.**

move (MOOV, long "OO") *v.* **moves, moved, mov.ing 1** change place or position: *Stand still without moving; Who moved this desk? People move from inner cities to suburbs; Our office is moving to Vancouver; We're moving our warehouse to a small town; He moved out of the old neighborhood when he got a new job; Our new neighbors move in on Monday; She moved up through the ranks to become vice-president; Luxury goods are difficult to move* (= sell) *in hard times.* **2** act or operate: *A door moves on hinges; Everyone was profoundly* or *deeply moved by the story; a story that moves* (= stirs) *people to tears; to move* (= be active) *in academic circles; Purgatives move* (= evacuate) *bowels.* **3** go or come; proceed: *A train going at 120 km/h is moving fast; Police try to keep the crowds moving; Let's move on; People started moving toward the exits.* **4** apply formally or propose: *The lawyer moved for a new trial; She moved that a new trial be held.* —**move in 1** close in: *The police surrounded the place and then moved in on the kidnappers; Hunters move in for the kill.* **2** start living with someone: *His mother-in-law wanted to move in with them.* —**move over** to make room for someone more important. —*n.* a changing of place or position: *He dared not make a move for fear of being shot; One false move and you are a dead duck; the moves of a chess game; a brilliant move that ended the game; We made a move from California to New York; a move to the east; clever, decisive, smart, wrong moves; A warning is given as a first move* (= step or action) *before firing someone; Orders keep three waiters constantly **on the move*** (= moving).

move.ment (MOOV.munt) *n.* **1** the motion of a person or thing in a particular manner or direction: *the movement of the earth around the sun; troop movements along a border; a sonata in three movements* (= parts); *a 17-jewel watch movement* (= mechanism); *to have a bowel movement* (= emptying of stool). **2** organized effort to reach a goal: *civil-rights, labor, peace, political movements; the movement for reform; a movement against smoking in the workplace; to launch, oppose, support, suppress a movement.*

mov.er (MOO.vur) *n.* one that moves, esp. in the business of moving furniture and equipment belonging to residences, offices, homes, etc. from one place to another: *the movers and shakers* (= people of power and influence) *of the country's foreign policy.*

mov.ie (MOO.vee) *n.* **1** also **moving picture,** a motion picture: *to make a home movie;* **adj** *a.: a movie camera, projector.* **2** a motion-picture theater: *a drive-in movie.* —**the movies** *n.pl.* **1** a movie showing: *We go to the movies on weekends.* **2** the moving-picture industry: *She hopes to get into the movies and become a star.*

moving violation *n.* a traffic violation while the vehicle is in motion, as not stopping at a stop sign.

mow 1 (*rhyme:* how) *n.* a haymow; hayloft. **2** (MOH) *v.* **mows,** *pt.* **mowed,** *pp.* **mowed** or **mown** (MONE), **mow.ing** cut down grass, grain, etc.: *to mow a lawn; The troops were mercilessly mowed down* (= killed) *by the enemy.* —**mow.er** (MOH.ur) *n.: to work a hand mower; to operate a lawn mower; a power mower; a rider mower.*

mox.ie (MOX.ee) *n. Informal.* pluck or guts and know-how.

moz.za.rel.la (mot.suh.REL.uh) *n.* a soft, white, mild-flavored Italian cheese.

Mr. (MIS.tur) *n.* **1** *pl.* **Messrs.** (MES.urs) [prefixed title used with a man's surname or title]: *Mr. T. Jones; Mr. Jones; Mr. Chairman.* **2** a product or service personified: *Mr. Coffee, Donut, Escort.*

Mrs. (MIS.iz), *pl.* **Mmes.** (may.DAHM) [prefixed title for a married woman who has taken her husband's surname]: *Mrs. (Mary) Jones, née Chan.*

Ms. (MIZ), *pl.* **Ms.es** (MIZ.uz) [prefixed title used with a woman's surname]: *Ms. (Mary) Jones.*

much *adj. & n. comp.* **more,** *superl.* **most** (in) a great amount, degree, quantity, etc.: *He spent much time on the project; How much profit did she make? The results didn't amount to much; She doesn't have much of a chance; We have much to learn from older and wiser people; He tends to* **make much** *of the little he does; A dollar a week is* **not much of** *a contribution.* —*adv.: Prices are much higher than two years ago; How much will you pay? Wages are much* (= nearly) *the same as last year.*

mu.ci.lage (MEW.sil.ij) *n.* a sticky vegetable substance used as an adhesive, usu. made by dissolving gum arabic in water: *The glue on a postage stamp is a mucilage made with dextrin.*

—**mu.ci.lag.i.nous** (-LAJ.uh.nus) *adj.: Seaweeds, flaxes, etc. are mucilaginous* (= mucilage-producing).

muck *n.* **1** farmyard manure. **2** dirt or filth. **3** dark soil rich in decaying matter. —**muck about** or **around** *with Informal.* be involved with a person or thing in a careless manner. —**muck up** *Informal.* make a mess of something. —**muck.y** *adj.*

muck.rak.er (MUCK.ray.kur) *n.* a journalist who searches for and writes sensationally about corruption in government, big business, etc. —**muck.rake** *v.* **-rakes, -raked, -rak.ing.**

mu.cous (MEW.cus) *adj.* **1** secreting mucus, as the **mucous membrane** lining body cavities. **2** slimy.

mu.cus (MEW.cus) *n.* a thick, slimy fluid produced by the inner lining of the nose, vagina, windpipe, etc. for lubrication and protection.

mud *n.* **1** soft, sticky, wet earth: *a layer of mud; Mud cakes as it dries; Mud oozes, squishes: to spatter someone with mud.* **2** an abusive, malicious attack: *to sling or throw mud at someone.*

mud.dle (MUD.ul) *n.* a mess or disorder: *He found it difficult to get out of the muddle he was in; He made a muddle of the project.* —*v.* **mud.dles, mud.dled, mud.dling** confuse or make confused: *to muddle an issue, plan, task; Liquor tends to muddle one's thinking; Some children put off doing their homework but at the last moment* **muddle through** *somehow* (instead of doing it in an organized manner). —**mud.dler** *n.*

mud.dle.head.ed (mud.ul.HED.id) *adj.* confused; bungling; inept: *a muddleheaded manager, policy; muddleheaded thinking.*

mud.dy (MUD.ee) *adj.* **mud.di.er, mud.di.est 1** containing or covered with mud: *muddy shoes, terrain, tires, water.* **2** resembling mud: *muddy slush; Taupe, olive, brown, and such muddy colors.* **3** murky or confused: *a muddy area of ethics; muddy thinking.* —*v.* **mud.dies, mud.died, mud.dy.ing 1** make or become covered with mud: *to muddy one's clothes;* *adj.: a* **muddied** *floor.* **2** make cloudy or confused: *to muddy an issue; to* **muddy the waters** *by irrelevant arguments; adj.:* **muddied** *reasoning.* —**mud.di.ness** *n.*

mud.guard *n.* **1** a covering over a vehicle's wheel for protection from mud thrown up by it; fender. **2** same as SPLASHGUARD.

mud room *n.* a room near an entrance where street shoes may be left so as not to track mud into the house.

mud.sling.ing (MUD.sling.ing) *n.* slanderous attack against an opponent. —**mud.sling.er** *n.*

muen.ster (MUN.stur) *n.* a semisoft cheese made from whole milk.

mu.ez.zin (mew.EZ.in) *n.* at a mosque, an official who calls the people to prayer.

muff *n.* 1 a short, tubelike covering of fur or other warm material into which the hands are inserted to keep them warm. 2 a bungling or awkward handling. —*v.* bungle or miss a catch, esp. in baseball.

muf.fin *n.* a small round cake of wheat flour or corn meal.

muf.fle (MUF.ul) *v.* **muf.fles, muf.fled, muf.fling** cover closely so as to keep warm or to deaden a sound: *She was muffled in a scarf; adj.: a muffled voice.*

muf.fler (MUF.lur) *n.* something that muffles, as a scarf or the silencing device attached to an automobile engine.

muf.ti (MUF.tee) *n.* civilian costume, not a uniform.

mug *n.* 1 a cylindrical metal or earthenware cup with a handle, formerly often decorated with a grotesque face: *a drinking mug; shaving mug.* 2 *Slang.* face or mouth. —*v.* **mugs, mugged, mug.ging** 1 *Slang.* make faces, as a ham actor. 2 *Slang.* make a mug shot of a person's face. 3 attack a person to rob. —**mug.ger** *n.*

mug.gy (MUG.ee) *adj.* **mug.gi.er, mug.gi.est** hot and humid: *a muggy day; muggy weather.* —**mug.gi.ness** *n.*

mug shot *n.* a police photograph of a prisoner's face.

mug.wump *n.* one who withdraws support from his political party, esp. in an aloof or self-important manner.

Mu.ham.mad.an (muh.HAM.uh.dun) same as MOSLEM.

muk.luk (MUCK.luck) *n.* a boot in the style of a usu. knee-high Inuit boot made of the skin of seal or reindeer.

mu.lat.to (muh.LAT.oh) *n.* **-lat.toes** a person of mixed white and black descent, esp. one born of a white and a black parent.

mul.ber.ry (MUL.ber.ee) *n.* **-ber.ries** a tree that bears small edible purplish or reddish fruits resembling blackberries and whose leaves, esp. of the "white mulberry," have been used as food for the silkworm since ancient times.

mulch *n.* loose vegetable material such as straw, leaves, and wood chips spread around plants to reduce evaporation, enrich the soil, etc. —*v.* spread mulch on or around: *to mulch the ground, an orchard, a tree.*

mulct *n.* a fine or penalty. —*v.* get by fraud or extortion: *clients mulcted of their savings.*

mule *n.* 1 the usu. sterile hybrid offspring of a jackass and a horse: *stubborn as a mule.* 2 *Informal.* one who is stubborn. 3 a backless slipper for women. —**mul.ish** *adj.*; **mul.ish.ly** *adv.*; **mul.ish.ness** *n.*

mule deer *n.* a North American deer with a black-tipped tail and ears like a mule's.

mu.le.teer (mew.luh.TEER) *n.* a mule driver; also **mule skinner** *Informal.*

mull *v.* 1 ponder: *to mull over a possibility, problem, proposal.* 2 make a warm, sweetened spiced drink of wine, cider, or other beverage; *adj.: mulled ale, cider, wine.*

mul.lein or **mul.len** (MULL.in) *n.* a plant of the figwort family, esp. the "common mullein" with thick, velvety leaves and clusters of yellow flowers on tall spikes.

mul.let (MUL.it) *n.* an edible fish of warm waters, esp. the "gray" and "red" mullets.

mul.li.gan stew (MUL.uh.gun-) *n.* a stew of odds and ends of meat, fish, etc.

mul.li.ga.taw.ny (mul.i.guh.TAW.nee) *n.* a highly seasoned soup, usu. of chicken stock, originally from India.

mul.lion (MUL.yun) *n.* a slim, vertical bar dividing window panes.

multi- *comb.form.* many: *multicolored, multi-event, multilingual, multimillionaire, multi-user.*

mul.ti.cul.tur.al (mul.tee.CUL.chur.ul) *adj.* having to do with many cultures: *a multicultural program; Ours is a multicultural society.* Also **mul.ti.eth.nic** (-tee.ETH.nic).

mul.ti.far.i.ous (mul.tuh.FAIR.ee.us) *adj.* diverse or varied: *multifarious activities, duties, problems.*

mul.ti.lin.gual (mul.tee.LING.gwul) *adj.* using many languages.

mul.ti.me.di.a (mul.tee.MEE.dee.uh) *adj.* using several communications media, as text, sound, and pictures: *a multimedia computer application; a multimedia kit, presentation, program; multimedia publishing; multimedia CD-ROMs.*

mul.ti.na.tion.al (mul.tee.NASH.uh.nul) *adj.* having to do with several countries: *a multinational company, issue, labor union; n.: U.S. multinationals* (= multinational companies).

mul.ti.ple (MUL.tuh.pul) *n.* a number

obtained by multiplying a whole number by itself two or more times.
—*adja. & cpd:* many at the same time: *multiple applications, births, copies, entries, partners, submissions; multiple contradictory versions of an incident; multiple ownership; a multiple-line sales rep; a multiple-mirror telescope; the multiple-personality disorder; multiple-use zoning of land; a* **multiple-choice** question with several answers to choose from.

multiple sclerosis *n.* a disease of the nervous system characterized by hardening of tissues and eventual paralysis of the legs, hands, eyesight, speech, etc.

mul.ti.plex (MUL.tuh.plex) *adj.* having to do with the transmission of many signals at once on the same carrier wave: *multiplex radio transmission, channel.*

mul.ti.pli.cand (mul.tuh.pli.CAND) *n.* a number that is to be multiplied by another, or multiplier.

mul.ti.pli.ca.tion (mul.tuh.pli.CAY.shun) *n.* **1** a multiplying or increase. **2** a short method of adding equal numbers many times, in an operation indicated by a **multiplication sign** [x].

mul.ti.plic.i.ty (mul.tuh.PLIS.i.tee) *n.* a great number or variety: *a multiplicity of interests.*

mul.ti.ply (MUL.tuh.ply) *v.* **-plies, -plied, -ply.ing 1** increase in number: *Rabbits multiply fast.* **2** find the mathematical product of two numbers: *2 multiplied by 3 is 6.* —**mul.ti.pli.er** *n.*

mul.ti.pur.pose (mul.tee.PUR.pus) *adja.* serving several purposes: *a multipurpose fabric, kit.*

mul.ti.ra.cial (mul.tee.RAY.shul) *adj.* of several races: *a multiracial society.*

mul.ti.stage (mul.tuh.STAGE) *adja.* having several stages: *a multistage pump, rocket.*

mul.ti.task.ing (mul.ti.TAS.king) *n.* a computer's execution of more than one program at the same time.

mul.ti.tude (MUL.tuh.tude) *n.* a large number, esp. of people.

mul.ti.tu.di.nous (mul.tuh.TUE.dun.us) *adj.* very numerous.

mul.ti.vi.ta.min (mul.tuh.VYE.tuh.min) *adja.* containing all the vitamins essential to health: *a multivitamin tablet.*

mum 1 *adjp. & interj.* silent: *Let's keep mum on or about this;* **Mum's the word** (= Don't talk)! **2** same as MOM. **3** [short form] chrysanthemum.
—*v.* same as MUMMER.

mum.ble (MUM.bul) *v.* **-bles, -bled, -bling** speak in a low, indistinct mutter, as because of embarrassment; **mum.bler** *n.*

mum.ble.ty-peg (MUM.bul.tee.PEG) *n.* a game of throwing a knife so as to make it stick in the ground. Also **mumble-the-peg.**

mum.bo jum.bo (mum.boh.JUM.boh) *n.* **1** meaningless or ritualistic talk: *the mumbo jumbo of witchcraft.* **2** a fetish or idol.

mum.mer (MUM.ur) *n.* a person who wears a fancy costume or a mask, as at a festival or in a pantomime.
—*v.* perform or go visiting as a group of mummers: *Newfoundlanders go mummering during Christmas.*

mum.mer.ies (MUM.uh.reez) *n.pl.* a dumb show or other performance by mummers.

mum.mi.fy (MUM.uh.fye) *v.* **-fies, -fied, -fy.ing** make into or like a mummy; *adj.: a mummified corpse, custom.*
—**mum.mi.fi.ca.tion** (-fuh.CAY.shun) *n.*

mum.my (MUM.ee) *n.* **mum.mies 1** a dead body embalmed for burial and preservation, as in ancient Egypt. **2** [child's word] mother.

mumps *n. sing. & pl.* a contagious virus disease of the salivary glands characterized by painful swelling of the sides of the face and neck: *to come down with the mumps.*

munch *v.* chew vigorously or with a crunching sound.

mun.dane (MUN.dane) *adj.* commonplace or everyday: *mundane activities, affairs; our mundane existence.*

mu.nic.i.pal (mew.NIS.uh.pul) *adja.* having to do with a municipality: *a municipal council, district, government, library, police.*

mu.nic.i.pal.i.ty (mew.NIS.uh.PAL.i.tee) *n.* **-ties** a locally self-governing, usu. incorporated city, town, or borough.

mu.nif.i.cent (mew.NIF.uh.sunt) *adj.* generous or lavish in a princely way: *munificent benefits, gifts, people.*
—**mu.nif.i.cence** *n.*

mu.ni.tion (mew.NISH.un) usu. **munitions** *n.pl.* military supplies such as guns, bombs, and equipment; *adja.: a munitions factory, plant, ship; a munition stockpile.*

mu.ral (MYOOR.ul) *n.* a large-size painting or decoration done on a wall: *the murals of Tintoretto; adja.: a mural design, painting.* —**mu.ral.ist** *n.*

mur.der (MUR.dur) *n.* **1** the crime of killing a person, esp. on purpose: *a cold-blooded, grisly, mass, ritual, vicious, wanton, premeditated murder; serial mur-*

murderous / music

ders by a serial killer; *Capital murder* used to carry the death penalty. **2** *Informal.* something hard or unpleasant, as a job, the weather, etc.: *Paperwork can be murder; It is murder on one's creativity.* —*v.* **1** commit murder on a person or thing: *He was brutally murdered.* **2** botch or mangle: *to murder a song, the English language.* —**mur.der.er** *n.;* **mur.der.ess** *fem.*

mur.der.ous (MUR.dur.us) *adj.* having to do with murder: *a murderous blow; murderous hate, heat, intent.* —**mur.der.ous.ly** *adv.*

mur.i.at.ic acid (mew.ree.AT.ic-) same as HYDROCHLORIC ACID.

murk *n.* darkness and gloom, as because of a vapor or mist.

murk.y (MUR.kee) *adj.* **mur.ki.er, -ki.est** dark and gloomy, as because of a vapor or mist: *the murky, smoke-filled air;* murky (= muddled) *logic.* —**murk.i.ly** *adv.;* **murk.i.ness** *n.*

mur.mur *n.* a soft, low, continuous but indistinct sound or voice, as of a grumbling person, the flow of a stream, distant voices, or a diseased heart valve. —*v.* utter in a murmur: *to murmur a prayer; to murmur one's thanks; to murmur* (= complain) *about poor wages.* —**mur.mur.er** *n.*

Mur.phy's Law (MUR.fees-) *n.* the satirical observation that if anything can go wrong, it will.

mur.rain (MUR.in) *n.* **1** an infectious disease of cattle, as anthrax. **2** *Archaic.* plague.

mus.ca.tel (mus.cuh.TEL) *n.* a sweet dessert wine made from **muscat** grapes that have the odor of musk.

mus.cle (MUS.ul) *n.* **1** a fibrous body tissue distributed in bands and bundles, esp. as organs, helping in work and movement: *the biceps, heart, stomach muscles; to contract, flex, tense, move, pull, strain, wrench a muscle; to develop one's muscles; muscle spasms.* **2** physical strength or power: *a he-man with more muscle than brains; a labor union with political muscle;* **adj***.:* those *high-powered muscle cars with animal names;* **n.***:* a bit of *muscle-flexing* (= show of force). —*v.* **mus.cles, mus.cled, mus.cling** force by or as if by using muscles: *He jumped the queue and muscled his way in; Criminals tried to muscle in on his business* (= get a share of it by force). —**muscled** *adj. & cpd.:* *muscled bodies, legs; heavily muscled mercenaries; hard-muscled, well-muscled.*

muscle-bound *adj.* **1** too muscular, as from too much exercise: *the muscle-bound figure of Serena Schwarz.* **2** rigid or inflexible: *a muscle-bound administration; muscle-bound competition.*

mus.cle.man (MUS.ul.man) or **muscle man** *n.* a man with strong muscles, as a bouncer or bodyguard.

mus.cu.lar (MUSK.yuh.lur) *adj.* having to do with muscles: *a muscular activity, arm; a man of a muscular build (having good muscles); muscular power, strain, strength.* —**mus.cu.lar.i.ty** (-LAIR.i.tee) *n.*

muscular dystrophy *n.* an inherited disease that causes muscles to weaken and waste away.

mus.cu.la.ture (MUSK.yuh.luh.chur) *n.* system or arrangement of muscles.

muse (MYOOZ) *n.* **1** the source of inspiration, esp. of a poet. **2 the Muses** *pl.* in Greek and Roman myths, nine goddesses of the arts and sciences. —*v.* **mus.es, mused, mus.ing** ponder or reflect meditatively: *a poet musing on* or *about* or *over* or *upon her past.*

mu.sette (mew.ZET) *n.* a small canvas or leather knapsack; also **musette bag.**

mu.se.um (mew.ZEE.um) *n.* a place where objects of cultural and scientific value are stored and exhibited: *art, science, wax museums.*

mush *n.* **1** a soft, thick, pulpy mass like corn meal boiled in water. **2** *Informal.* weak sentimentality. **3** *n. & v.* travel over snow with a dog sled. —*interj.* a shout to urge sled dogs forward.

mush.room *n.* a usu. umbrellalike, rapidly-sprouting, fleshy fungus; **adj***.a.:* a *mushroom cap, sauce, soup;* the (fast) *mushroom growth of a boom town; the umbrella-shaped* **mushroom cloud** *following a nuclear blast.* —*v.* grow like mushrooms: *Fast-food outlets keep mushrooming.*

mush.y *adj.* **mush.i.er, -i.est** **1** soft and pulpy like mush: *vegetables cooked tender but not mushy; mushy meat; when the brakes feel mushy.* **2** weakly sentimental: *mushy emotion.*

mu.sic (MEW.zic) *n.* **1** a rhythmic sound or sequence of sounds that is pleasing to the ear: *a poem set to music, background, chamber, country, folk, modern, organ, rock, soul music; The news was music* (= pleasing) *to my ears.* **2** the art of making such sounds systematically, using the voice or instruments: *lessons in music.* **3** written music: *to compose* or *write, perform, play, read music; a piece of music.* —**face the music** *Informal.* face the consequences, as of one's actions.

mu.si.cal (MEW.zi.cul) *adja.* having to do with music: *a musical instrument; a musical ear (that is sensitive to music); a musical family (of members who are skilled in music); a musical* (= melodious) *voice.* —*n.* a play or motion picture having a sentimental or humorous theme worked out with much singing and dancing, as "My Fair Lady." Also **musical comedy.** —**mu.si.cal.ly** *adv.*

musical chairs *n.pl.* [with *sing. v.*] **1** a game in which the players move around a row of chairs numbering one less than the number of players and sit down on them when the music stops, leaving one player out of the game, and so on till there are only two players and one chair left: *to play musical chairs.* **2** a situation in which there is much changing of seats.

mu.si.cale (mew.zuh.CAL) *n.* a party featuring a musical program.

mu.si.cian (mew.ZISH.un) *n.* one skilled in music, esp. as a composer or performer. —**mu.si.cian.ly** *adj.*

mu.si.col.o.gy (mew.zi.COL.uh.jee) *n.* the study of the principles, history, etc. of music; **mu.si.col.o.gist** *n.*

music video *n.* a video dramatizing a popular song.

musk *n.* a strong-smelling substance from a gland of the **musk deer** and other animals that is used in making perfume. —**musk.y** *adj.*: *a musky cologne, fragrance, perfume.*

mus.keg *n.* a mossy bog or swamp of the far N. regions of North America.

mus.kel.lunge (MUS.kuh.lunj) *n. sing. & pl.* a prized North American game and food fish, the largest of the pike family; also **mus.kie** (-kee).

mus.ket (MUS.kit) *n.* a heavy muzzle-loading shoulder firearm of former times. —**mus.ket.eer** (mus.kuh.TEER) *n.*

musk.mel.on (MUSK.mel.un) *n.* a vine of the gourd family such as the honey dew and the cantaloupe that bear sweet fruit with a distinctive musklike flavor.

musk ox *n.* a shaggy-haired wild ox of the Arctic that gives off a musky smell.

musk.rat *n.* a ratlike rodent with a musky odor that lives in burrows near streams and rivers and is valued for its coat of long, shiny hair.

Mus.lim (MUZ.lim) same as MOSLEM.

mus.lin (MUZ.lin) *n.* **1** a closely woven cloth used for sheets. **2** in Britain, a sheer cotton fabric, originally made in Iraq and India.

muss *n.* a rumpled or disordered condition. —*v.* put into a muss: *wrinkle-free, hard-to-muss clothes.* —**muss.y** *adj.*

mus.sel (MUS.ul) *n.* a clamlike bivalve mollusk, valued as food and for mother-of-pearl.

must *auxiliary v., pres. & past* **1** [expressing obligation]: *I must go now; You must not be late.* **2** [expressing possibility, certainty, etc.]: *You must be tired; This book must be Lin's.* —*n.* **1** *Informal.* something obligatory: *A black tie is a must; adja.: a must book, item of clothing.* **2** the fermenting juice of grapes; new wine.

mus.tache (mus.TASH, MUS.tash) *n.* hair growing on a man's upper lip: *to grow, trim a mustache; a handlebar mustache.*

mus.tang *n.* a small, hardy horse of southwestern U.S.

mus.tard (MUS.turd) *n.* a pungent condiment in paste or powder form prepared from the seed of a plant used also in plasters and poultices.

mustard gas *n.* a poison gas with a mustardlike odor, used in chemical warfare.

mustard plaster *n.* a poultice made with mustard.

mus.ter *v.* **1** of troops, assemble: *They mustered behind the barricades.* **2** collect soldiers, resources, etc.: *He tried to muster all the support he could from the voters; to muster up courage.* —**muster in** (or **out**) enlist in (or discharge from) the military. —*n.* an assembly. —**pass muster** be up to the required standard.

must.n't (MUS.unt) must not.

mus.ty (MUS.tee) *adj.* **-ti.er, -ti.est 1** stale or mouldy, as from dampness or lack of fresh air: *musty air; a musty odor; water with a musty and metallic taste.* **2** antiquated: *musty customs, ideas.* —**mus.ti.ly** *adv.*; **mus.ti.ness** *n.*

mu.ta.ble (MEW.tuh.bul) *adj.* changeable by nature; also, fickle; **mu.ta.bly** (-blee) *adv.* —**mu.ta.bil.i.ty** (-BIL.i.tee) *n.*

mu.tant (MEW.tunt) *n. & adj.* (an animal such as the white turkey or a plant such as the pink grapefruit) produced by mutation.

mu.tate (MEW.tate) *v.* **-tates, -tat.ed, -tat.ing** (cause) to undergo mutation. —**mu.ta.tive** (-tuh.tiv) *adj.* marked by change.

mu.ta.tion (mew.TAY.shun) *n.* gene change caused by radiations, chemicals, etc. resulting in the appearance of new characteristics that are trans-

mitted to offspring; **mu.ta.tion.al** *adj.*
mute *adj.* dumb or silent: *deaf and mute; He was mute with astonishment; the mute "b" of "tomb."* —*n.* **1** a dumb person. **2** a silencing device, as on a musical instrument: *the mute button of a TV remote.* —*v.* **mutes, mut.ed, mut.ing** muffle or soften the sound of a voice, violin string, etc.: *The Opposition muted its criticism of the new legislation while giving it a second look.* —**mute.ly** *adv.*; **mute.ness** *n.*
mu.ti.late (MEW.tuh.late) *v.* **-lates, -lat.ed, -lat.ing** deprive a person, literary work, song, etc. of an essential part, as by maiming or crippling. —**mu.ti.la.tion** (-LAY.shun) *n.* —**mu.ti.la.tor** (-lay.tur) *n.*
mu.ti.ny (MEW.tuh.nee) *n.* **-nies** a rebellion, esp. by soldiers or sailors against their officers: *to crush, put down, quell, stir up a mutiny; when a mutiny breaks out.* —*v.* **-nies, -nied, -ny.ing** rebel: *The army mutinied against the junta.* —**mu.ti.neer** (mew.tuh.NEER) *n.* —**mu.ti.nous** (-nus) *adj.*
mutt *n. Slang.* **1** a mongrel dog. **2** a stupid or despised person.
mut.ter *v.* speak words, curses, etc. in a low and indistinct voice, as if angry or dissatisfied. —*n.* what is muttered; grumble.
mut.ton (MUT.un) *n.* the flesh of mature sheep used as food. —**mut.ton.y** *adj.*
mut.ton.chops (MUT.un.chops) *n.pl.* sideburns that are narrow at the top and broad and rounded at the bottom.
mu.tu.al (MEW.choo.ul) *adj.* relating to or shared by each other: *the mutual affection between spouses; Marc and Luc are mutual enemies; Mia is their* **mutual friend** (= friend of both); **mu.tu.al.ly** *adv.* —**mu.tu.al.i.ty** (-AL.i.tee) *n.*
mutual fund *n.* an investment company whose members pool their capital to invest in stocks and other securities.
muu.muu (MOO.moo) *n.* a long, loose-fitting dress for informal wear, originally from Hawaii.
Mu.zak (MEW.zak) *n. Trademark.* recorded background music transmitted by telephone line or FM radio.
muz.zle (MUZ.ul) *n.* **1** the mouth of an animal such as a dog, horse, or cow that is at the end of the projecting part of the head. **2** the mouth of the barrel of a gun or pistol: *a muzzle-loading firearm.* **3** a cover made of straps or wires put around an animal's muzzle. —*v.* **muz.zles, muz.zled, muz.zling 1** put a muzzle on an animal. **2** restrain a person, newspaper, etc. from speaking out; gag.
my *adj.* possessive case of "I": *My dear fellows, this is my date!* —*interj.:* Oh, my!
my.col.o.gy (my.COL.uh.jee) *n.* the branch of botany dealing with fungi; **my.col.o.gist** *n.* —**my.co.log.i.cal** (-cuh.LOJ.i.cul) *adj.*
my.e.li.tis (my.uh.LYE.tis) *n.* inflammation of the spinal cord or of the bone marrow.
my.lar (MY.lar) *n.* polyester film used for electrical insulation, magnetic tape, etc.; **Mylar** *Trademark.*
my.na or **my.nah** (MY.nuh) *n.* a bird of the starling family, native to India, esp. a "talking" species often kept as a pet.
my.o.pi.a (my.OH.pee.uh) *n.* nearsightedness or shortsightedness. —**my.op.ic** (my.OP.ic) *adj.*
myr.i.ad (MEER.ee.ud) *n.* an indefinitely large number: *Myriads of voices joined in the chant;* **adj.:** *the myriad voices chanting slogans; myriad details, facets, tasks.*
myr.mi.don (MUR.muh.don, *rhyme:* on) *n.* an unquestioning, esp. unscrupulous follower, like the **Myrmidons** of Greek myth, a warlike people who followed Achilles to the Trojan War.
myrrh (MUR) *n.* a fragrant gum resin used in making incense and perfume since ancient times; **myrrh.ic** *adj.*
myr.tle (MUR.tul) *n.* **1** an evergreen Mediterranean shrub with fragrant flowers, leaves, and berries. **2** the common periwinkle.
my.self (my.SELF) *pron.* reflexive or emphatic of "I" or "me": *I speak only for myself; I fell on the ice and hurt myself; I'm not myself* (= as well as usual) *today.*
mys.ter.y (MIS.tuh.ree) *n.* **-ter.ies** something hidden from human knowledge or hard to understand or explain: *the mystery of three persons in one God; the mysteries of the universe; Her disappearance has remained a mystery; an unsolved mystery; Her whereabouts are a mystery to us; to clear up, fathom, unravel a mystery; The mystery deepens as people start talking; a project shrouded in mystery; the air of mystery* (= secrecy) *surrounding the baby's birth; the mysteries* (= rites) *of the Christian religion; a mystery or* **mystery novel** (= detective story); *to go on a* **mystery tour** (*without knowing in advance where you are going*). —**mys.te.ri.ous** (mis.TEER.ee.us) *adj.*; **mys.te.ri.ous.ly** *adv.*; **mys.te.ri.ous.ness** *n.*

mys.tic (MIS.tic) *n.* one who seeks to learn about God and supernatural things through intuition rather than by use of reason. —*adj.* **1** of mystics or mysticism: *a mystic experience, influence.* **2** mysterious or occult: *the mystic arts; mystic rites and ceremonies.* Also **mys.ti.cal.** —**mys.ti.cal.ly** *adv.*

mys.ti.cism (MIS.tuh.siz.um) *n.* the philosophy or doctrines of mystics, esp. in regard to the knowledge of God through meditation and spiritual insight.

mys.ti.fy (MIS.tuh.fye) *v.* **-fies, -fied, -fy.ing** puzzle or perplex: *Children's questions sometimes mystify adults;* **adj.**: *the mystified look on her face.*
—**mys.ti.fi.ca.tion** (-fuh.CAY.shun) *n.*

mys.tique (mis.TEEK) *n.* the air of mystery about a person or thing: *the feminine mystique of the Mona Lisa; the mystique (= impressive professionalism) of bullfighting.*

myth (MITH) *n.* **1** a primitive, often supernatural story current among a people that seeks to explain something in nature, as stories of creation of the universe. **2** such stories collectively; mythology: *Greek myth and legend.* **3** a false belief; also, a person or thing considered as imagined or invented: *the myth of male superiority; My uncle's fabulous wealth proved to be a mere myth; to debunk, dispel, explode a myth.*
—**myth.i.cal** *adj.*: *mythical animals such as the unicorn.*

my.thol.o.gy (mi.THOL.uh.jee) *n.* **-gies 1** the study of myths. **2** a group of myths: *Greek mythology.*
—**my.thol.o.gist** *n.* —**myth.o.log.i.cal** (mith.uh.LOJ.i.cul) *adj.*

.... **N, n** ....

N or **n** (EN) *n.* **N's** or **n's** the 14th letter of the English alphabet. —**'n'** and: *kiss 'n' ride; park 'n' fly; rock 'n' roll; show 'n' tell.*

nab *v.* **nabs, nabbed, nab.bing** *Informal.* seize quickly, esp. arrest a person: *The police nabbed the thief before he could escape.*

na.bob (NAY.bob) *n.* a wealthy or important man.

na.celle (nuh.SEL) *n.* the metal casing enclosing an engine on or in the wing of an airplane.

na.cre (NAY.cur) *n.* mother-of-pearl.

na.dir (NAY.dur) *n.* the lowest point; opposite of ZENITH: *His hopes were at a nadir; Their decadence reached a nadir just before the fall.*

nag *v.* **nags, nagged, nag.ging 1** find fault with or worry someone continually: *Stop nagging her; It's no use nagging at me all day.* **2** annoy or vex: *to be nagged by doubts, questions, suspicions;* **adj.**: *a nagging backache.* —*n.* **1** one who nags; scold. **2** an old or worn-out horse.

nai.ad (NAY.ad, NYE-) *n.* **1** in Greek and Roman myths, the guardian nymph of a river or stream. **2** the incomplete adult stage of insects such as dragonflies and damselflies when they are wingless and live in water.

na.if (nah.EEF) *n.* one who is naive.

nail *n.* **1** the thorny growth at the ends of fingers and toes: *to cut or pare one's nails; to bite, file, manicure, polish one's nails.* **2** a pointed metal spike with a broadened head that is hit with a hammer to drive it into pieces of wood or other material for fastening them: **hard as nails** (= having no feeling); *to* **hit the nail on the head** (= say it exactly right). —*v.* fasten or secure, as with a nail: *a sign nailed to a wall; Let's* **nail down** *the offer with a small deposit.*

nain.sook (NAIN.sook, short "oo") *n.* a soft, light muslin.

na.ive or **na.ïve** (nah.EEV) *adj.* **1** simple or unsophisticated; hence, foolishly simple: *a naive attitude, creature, outlook, person, philosophy, remark; his naive ignorance, judgment.* **2** [technical use] untutored: *a naive informant, rat, subject.* —**na.ive.ly** or **na.ïve.ly** *adv.*

na.ive.té or **na.ïve.té** (nah.eev.TAY, -EEV.tay) *n.* **1** artlessness. **2** a naive action or remark. Also **na.ive.ty** (nah.EEV.tee) *n.* **-ties.**

na.ked (NAY.kid) *adj.* unclothed; hence, uncovered or plain; bare: *a body lying naked; completely naked; bare* or *buck* or *stark naked; a naked sword (out of its sheath); naked aggression, ambition, fear; the naked truth.* —**na.ked.ly** *adv.*; **na.ked.ness** *n.*

naked eye *n.* the eye unaided by a magnifying glass, microscope, or telescope: *invisible to the naked eye.*

nam.a.ble (NAY.muh.bul) same as NAMEABLE.

nam.by-pam.by (NAM.bee.PAM.bee) *n. & adj.* **-bies** (a person or talk that is) silly or sentimental.

name *n.* **1** word or words by which a person, animal, place, or thing is called or known: *your name and address; assumed, brand, code, common, family, fancy, first, given, legal, maiden, married, middle, pet, proper, stage, trade*

name-calling / narcotic

names; I know him only by name (not personally); The booking was made in my name; Joe registered under an assumed name; She called him **names** (= bad names). **2** reputation or fame: *He earned a good name as a journalist; made a name for himself in the community; A scandal gives one a bad name; It besmirches or smears one's name; She had to go to court to clear her name; the greatest name* (= person) *in boxing; to drop names* (= boast of one's connections); *a name-brand* (= well-known) *soap.* —**in name only** not in reality; without power or influence: *the boss in name only.* —**in the name of 1** by the authority of God, the king, the law, etc. **2** on behalf of someone: *He claims to speak in the name of the moral majority.* —*v.* **names, named, nam.ing** give a name to someone or call by name: *a baby named for or after his father; a general accusation without naming any offenders; Can you name the signs of the zodiac? Lin was named to the chair; Lin was named (as the) chairperson; You name* (= mention) *it, we've got it.*
—**name.a.ble** *adj.*
name-calling *n.* the calling of bad names: *to engage in or resort to name-calling when arguments fail.*
name-dropping *n.* the mentioning of important persons or places in a familiar way in order to impress others. —**name-dropper** *n.*
name.less *adj.* without a name for various reasons: *a nameless ancestor, crime, feeling, infant; My detractors shall remain nameless for the present.* —**name.less.ly** *adv.*
name.ly *adv.* that is to say; viz.
name of the game *n. Informal.* the essential thing; a goal or the means of attaining it: *The name of the game is profitability..*
name.plate *n.* a plate, plaque, etc. bearing a person's name.
name.sake *n.* one with the same name as another, esp. if named after that other person.
NAND (NAND) *n.* in computer logic, the operator that is the opposite of "and"; adja. The NAND gate (= device or circuit) *performs NAND operations; The NAND output of statements A and B is true if either A or B is false, and false if both A and B are true.*
nan.keen (nan.KEEN) *n.* a firm-textured cloth finished without size or bleach, originally made in China from a yellowish kind of cotton; also **nan.kin**.

nan.ny (NAN.ee) *n.* **nan.nies 1** a child's domestic nurse. **2** a babysitter: *English nannies for hire; live-in nannies.*
nanny goat *n.* a female goat.
nano- (NAN.oh) *comb.form.* billionth: *nanogram, nanometer, nanosecond.*
nap 1 *n.* a brief, light sleep: *Have or take a nap when you feel tired.* **2** *n.* a soft or downy surface, as of fur, velvet, etc.; *adj.: a napped fabric, flannel, silk.* —*v.* **naps, napped, nap.ping** take a nap: *to catch one napping* (= catch one off guard).
na.palm (NAY.pahm) *n.* highly flammable jellied gasoline, used in bombs and flame throwers; *v.: the napalming of enemy territory.*
nape *n.* the back of the neck.
naph.tha (NAF.thuh, NAP-, "th" as in "thin") *n.* a flammable petroleum product used as a cleaning agent and solvent.
naph.tha.lene (NAF.thuh.leen, NAP-) *n.* a white crystalline hydrocarbon obtained from coal tar for use in mothballs, dyes, etc.
nap.kin *n.* **1** a small towel or piece of cloth or paper used for wiping the lips, etc. while eating: *He always eats with the napkin tucked under his chin.* **2** a sanitary pad or napkin.
na.po.le.on (nuh.POH.lee.un) *n.* a pastry with a custardlike filling.
Na.po.le.on.ic (nuh.poh.lee.ON.ic) *adj.* having to do with **Napoleon** Bonaparte, 1769-1821, French general and conqueror of Europe: *the Napoleonic civil code, wars.*
nap.py *n.* **nap.pies** *Informal.* a diaper. —*adj.* downy: *nappy hair.*
narc or **nark** *n. Informal.* a police agent enforcing narcotic laws.
nar.cis.sism (NAR.suh.siz.um) *n.* preoccupation with one's own beauty. —**nar.cis.sist** *n. & adj.* —**nar.cis.sis.tic** (-SIS.tic) *adj.*
nar.cis.sus (nar.SIS.us) *n.* **-cis.sus.es** or **-cis.si** (-sye) a plant of the amaryllis family with sword-shaped leaves and tall shoots of fragrant, six-petaled white or yellow flowers.
nar.co.lep.sy (NAR.cuh.lep.see) *n.* an illness characterized by irresistible attacks of sleep.
nar.co.sis (nar.COH.sis) *n.* a state of stupor induced by a narcotic.
nar.cot.ic (nar.COT.ic) *n.* a drug such as opium, codeine, or heroin that deadens pain and causes stupor: *a charge of trafficking in narcotics;* **adj.**: *a narcotic addict, effect, substance.*
—**nar.co.tism** *n.*

nar.co.tize (NAR.cuh.tize) *v.* **-tiz.es, -tized, -tiz.ing** subject to a narcotic; dull or deaden. —**nar.co.ti.za.tion** (-tuh.ZAY.shun. -tye-) *n.*
nard same as SPIKENARD.
nar.es (NAIR.eez) *n.pl.* nostrils; **nar.is** *sing.*
nark 1 *n.* Brit. Informal. a spy or informer for police. **2** same as NARC.
Nar.ra.gan.sett (nair.uh.GAN.sit) *n.* (a member of) an American Indian tribe that lived in the region of Narragansett Bay, Rhode Island.
nark 1 *v. & n.* Brit. Informal. (turn) spy or informer for police. **2** same as NARC.
nar.rate (NAIR.ate) *v.* **nar.rates, nar.rat.ed, nar.rat.ing** relate or tell a story, adventures, experiences, etc. —**nar.ra.tion** (nair.AY.shun) *n.* —**nar.ra.tor** (NAIR.ay.tur, nuh.RAY.tur) *n.*
nar.ra.tive (NAIR.uh.tiv) *n. & adj.* a story or tale that recounts events: *a fast-paced narrative; long narrative;* **adja.:** *a narrative poem; his narrative prose style.*
nar.row (NAIR.oh) *adj.* limited or small in width: *a narrow margin, street;* (= *not liberal*) *viewpoint; a narrow* (= *limited*) *circle of friends; a narrow* (= *close*) *escape, majority; narrow* (= *close*) *scrutiny; "Meat" means animal flesh in its narrowest sense.*
—*v.* make or become narrower: *You see people narrowing their eyes in bright light; The road narrows round the curve;* to **narrow down** *the choice of candidates to a few.* —*n.* something narrow, esp. **narrows** *pl.* a narrow passage, as a strait or mountain pass. —**nar.row.ly** *adv.;* **nar.row.ness** *n.*
nar.row.cast (NAIR.oh.cast) *v.* televise by cable, not broadcast.
narrow-minded *adj.* limited in outlook, not broad-minded. —**narrow-mindedness** *n.*
nar.whal (NAR.wul) *n.* an arctic whale whose male has a long spiral tusk like the fabled unicorn's.
nar.y (NAIR.ee) *adj.* **nary a** or **an** not one: *with nary a cent in his pocket.*
na.sal (NAY.zul) *adj.* having to do with the nose: *a nasal bone, sound, voice; A cold could block your nasal passages.* —*n.:* "M," "n," and "ng" are nasals (= sounds produced through the nose); *the nasals* (= nasal bones) *forming the bridge of the nose.* —**na.sal.ly** *adv.*
na.sal.ize (NAY.zuh.lize) *v.* **-iz.es, -ized, -iz.ing** utter or speak nasally: *Our news reader tends to nasalize her vowels;* **adj.:** *the nasalized vowels of the French "un bon vin."* —**na.sal.i.za.tion** (-luh.ZAY.shun. -lye-) *n.*
nas.cent (NAY.sunt, NAS.unt) *adj.* being born or formed; beginning to develop: *a nascent gas; a nascent intellectual; hydrogen in a nascent state during a chemical reaction; nascent tumors.* —**nas.cence** *n.*
na.stur.tium (nuh.STUR.shum) *n.* a trailing or climbing garden plant having brightly-colored, spurred flowers with five sepals and petals and long-stalked umbrella-shaped leaves.
nas.ty (NAS.tee) *adj.* **-ti.er, -ti.est** disgusting or offensive to good taste: *a nasty feeling, job, remark, smell, temper, wound; nasty behavior; nasty* (= very unpleasant) *weather.* —**nas.ti.ly** *adv.;* **nas.ti.ness** *n.*
na.tal (NAY.tul) *adj.* of or from birth: *a natal day* (= birthday); *the natal hour; the natal death rate* (= rate of deaths at birth). —**na.tal.i.ty** (nuh.TAL.i.tee) *n.* -ties.
na.ta.to.ri.um (nay.tuh.TOR.ee.um) *n.* **-ri.ums** or **-ri.a** (-ree.uh) an indoor swimming facility.
na.tion (NAY.shun) *n.* a people with a common history and culture, usu. living under one government in a country of their own and using the same language: *a newly independent African nation; the Jewish nation; a member nation of the United Nations; favored, friendly, peace-loving, sovereign nations; two warring nations; It snowed across the nation* (= all over the country) *yesterday; the Six Nations* (= tribes) *federation of Iroquois.* —**na.tion.hood** *n.*
na.tion.al (NASH.un.ul) *adj.* having to do with a nation: *a national academy, anthem, disaster, disgrace, emergency, flag, food, forest, government, holiday, monument, park; the national character, income; national defense, health and welfare, revenue, unity; the national debt* (= what a nation owes other countries); *the Jimmy Carter national historic site in Plains, GA.* —*n.* a citizen or subject: *an Israeli who was a U.S. national; Foreign nationals are granted citizenship after a few years' residence.* —**na.tion.al.ly** *adv.*
National Guard *n.* a volunteer reserve group organized in each state as part of the U.S. Army and Air Force.
na.tion.al.ism (NASH.un.uh.liz.um) *n.* devotion to one's country, esp. in protecting its independence: *rampant nationalism; the cash-register nationalism that encourages foreign imports at the expense of home industry.* —**na.tion.al.ist** *n. & adj.* —**na.tion.al.is.tic** (-LIS.tic)

adj.: nationalistic feeling, fervor, spirit.

na.tion.al.i.ty (nash.uh.NAL.i.tee) *n.* **-ties** national or ethnic origin: *Immigrants belong to many nationalities; The refugee claimed Russian nationality.*

na.tion.al.ize (NASH.un.uh.lize) *v.* **-iz.es, -ized, -iz.ing** make national, esp. take an industry, institution, land, etc. under national control. —**na.tion.al.i.za.tion** (-luh.ZAY.shun.-lye-) *n.*

national park *n.* a park, monument, historic site, or recreational area set aside by a national government for public use.

na.tion.wide (NAY.shun.wide) *adj.* existing throughout the nation; national: *a nationwide alert, broadcast, computer network, trend; She went on nationwide television; agencies, consumers, teachers, universities nationwide;* **adv.:** *The disease has spread nationwide; The program is offered nationwide.*

na.tive (NAY.tiv) *adj.* 1 inborn, not acquired: *one's native abilities, instincts, qualities, talents.* 2 having to do with birth or place of origin: *native African customs; the native rights of the Inuit; native silver (in its natural state); native peoples, tribes; The panda is native to China; her **native land** (= land of birth); her **native language** or **native tongue** (= mother tongue); a **Native American** (= American Indian); a **native-born** Italian with British parents; **Native Canadians** (= Canadian Indians or Inuit); a **native Indian** (= North American Indian, not one from India); the **native peoples** (= Indians and Inuit) of Canada; New England is proud to count poet Robert Frost as a **native son** because he was raised there though born elsewhere; Some tourists like to **go native** (= take on the ways and customs of the natives).* —*n.* a person, animal, or plant that belongs to a specified region by origin or birth: *The koala is an Australian native; Joe is a native of Japan; natives and foreigners.*

native speaker *n.* 1 one who has been speaking a language since adolescence: *an educated native speaker; Even native speakers make language errors.* 2 one who is a proficient user of a language: *The book should have been translated into French by a native speaker of the language; Jacques uses English with native-speaker ability (= with proficiency).*

na.tiv.ism (NAY.tuh.viz.um) *n.* a self-protective attitude or policy typical of natives toward immigrants and foreigners.

na.tiv.i.ty (nuh.TIV.i.tee) *n.* **-ties** 1 birth: *population shown by nativity; your country of nativity.* 2 **the Nativity** the birth of Christ; also, Christmas: *Feast of the Nativity.*

NATO (NAY.toh) *n.* the North Atlantic Treaty Organization composed of U.S.A., Canada, and European countries.

nat.ter (NAT.ur) *v. Informal.* 1 chatter *on* or *away.* 2 grumble *about* something.

nat.ty (NAT.ee) *adj.* **nat.ti.er, nat.ti.est** of dress or appearance, neat and trim: *a natty dresser; a natty leisure suit.* —**nat.ti.ly** *adv.*

nat.u.ral (NACH.uh.rul) *adj.* 1 having to do with nature: *the natural beauty of the countryside; the natural mother of Liz (who gave birth to Liz); a natural language like English (not artificial like Esperanto or a computer language such as Fortran); a natural (= illegitimate) son of the king;* **natural phenomena** *such as storms, earthquakes, and floods.* 2 having to do with the innate character or nature of a person or thing; not artificial or formal: *You look more natural without makeup; her natural gifts, voice; a* **natural-born** *entertainer, genius, problem-solver.* 3 containing no additives or preservatives; processed very little: *natural fiber, flavor, foods.* —*n.* one naturally suited for a job, role, etc.; also, the thing itself: *He's a natural to play the part of the wizard; Acting is a natural for her.* —**nat.u.ral.ness** *n.*

natural childbirth *n.* delivery by a mother emotionally and physically trained to bear the pain without the help of an anesthetic.

natural gas *n.* a hydrocarbon gas formed in the earth from organic matter, much used as fuel.

natural history *n.* the nontechnical, popular study of the animals, plants, minerals, and other things in nature.

nat.u.ral.ism (NACH.uh.rul.iz.um) *n.* in art, fiction, drama, etc., the use of what is natural and realistic, instead of the unscientific and the supernatural.

nat.u.ral.ist (NACH.uh.rul.ist) *n.* 1 one who studies natural history. 2 an advocate of naturalism. —**nat.u.ral.is.tic** (-ruh.LIS.tic) *adj.*

nat.u.ral.ize (NACH.uh.ruh.lize) *v.* **-iz.es, -ized, -iz.ing** make or become native or like a native: *a government program for naturalizing immigrants; The African violet was naturalized long ago;*

adj.: "Spaghetti" is a **naturalized** Italian word; not native-born but a **naturalized** American (= an immigrant who has become a citizen). —**nat.u.ral.i.za.tion** (-luh.ZAY.shun. -lye-) *n.*

nat.u.ral.ly (NACH.uh.ruh.lee) *adv.* **1** by nature: *naturally curly hair; the naturally unsuspecting child.* **2** in a natural, not artificial manner: *He can't talk naturally when on stage.* **3** as might be expected: *Naturally, he'll be upset by the bad news.*

natural note *n.* in music, a note without a sharp or flat.

natural resources *n.pl.* useful things in nature, as water, minerals, land, and forests.

natural science *n.* a science dealing with nature, as biology, chemistry, geology, or physics, as distinguished from the humanities and social sciences. —**natural scientist** *n.*

natural selection *n.* the process by which only the fittest or best-adapted of a species survive in the struggle for food, shelter, and other necessities of life.

na.ture (NAY.chur) *n.* **1** the world of animals, plants, minerals, forces such as instincts, and phenomena such as wind and rain that are not made by humans: *Everyone loves nature; We try to harness the forces of nature; the back-to-nature philosophy of people tired of city life; freaks of nature; Nudists socialize **in a state of nature** (= nude).* **2** real quality or character: *It is the dog's nature to bark; It's not in his nature to attack letter carriers; It's human nature to make mistakes; Helping others is second nature to Sam; Tim's true nature comes out when he has to deal with people; Let's appeal to their better natures; Lee is not lazy **by nature**; Digging for artifacts is a pursuit of a scholarly nature (= kind); It's all in the **nature of things** (= things as they are).*

nature study *n.* the study of the life and phenomena in nature at the elementary level.

nature trail *n.* a path laid out in a natural environment for the study of animals, plants, etc.

na.tur.ist (NAY.chur.ist) *n.* a nudist.

naught (NAWT) *n.* nothing; zero: *All our efforts came to or went for naught; It was all for naught.*

naugh.ty (NAW.tee) *adj.* **-ti.er, -ti.est 1** disobedient or mischievous: *a naughty child; It's not nice to be naughty.* **2** mildly indecent in behavior: *a naughty joke, lady, remark; naughty words referring to body parts; Jack and Jill having naughty fun; naughty black lingerie.* —**naugh.ti.ly**

adv.; **naugh.ti.ness** *n.*

nau.sea (NAW.zhuh, -zee.uh) *n.* **1** sickness of the stomach that makes one want to vomit. **2** loathing or disgust.

nau.se.ate (NAW.see.ate, -zee.ate, -shee.ate, -zhee.ate) *v.* **-ates, -at.ed, -at.ing** make one want to vomit: *The very mention of snails nauseates her;* **adj.**: *She feels nauseated; a very nauseating experience, sensation.* —**nau.se.a.tion** (-AY.shun) *n.*

nau.seous (NAW.shus, -zee.us) *adj.* **1** feeling or causing nausea; nauseated or queasy: *These days, she feels nauseous in the mornings.* **2** disgusting or loathsome; nauseating: *foods that are nauseous to some.*

nau.ti.cal (NAW.ti.cul) *adj.* having to do with sailors, ships, or navigation: *a nautical college, uniform; "amidships," "fo'c'sle," and such nautical terms; The international **nautical mile** (= distance unit of 6,076 ft. or 1,852 m), or "sea mile," is used in air and sea navigation.*

nau.ti.lus (NAW.tul.us) *n.* **-lus.es** or **-li** (-lye) a mollusk with a spiral shell divided into many chambers lined with mother-of-pearl.

Nav.a.jo or **Nav.a.ho** (NAV.uh.hoh) *n., pl.* **-jos** or **-hos** a member or the language of a Native American people of New Mexico, Arizona, and Utah.

na.val (NAY.vul) *adj.* having to do with a navy: *a naval academy, base, battle, cadet, installation, officer, power, vessel.*

naval stores *n.pl.* products such as pitch, tar, rosin, turpentine, etc. used for repairing sailing ships.

nave *n.* the central or main part of a church where the congregation is seated.

na.vel (NAY.vul) *n.* a depression in the center of the belly where the umbilical cord was attached at birth: *the navel-fixed gaze of a self-satisfied person in contemplation.*

navel orange *n.* a seedless orange with a navellike formation at its apex.

nav.i.ga.ble (NAV.uh.guh.bul) *adj.* that can be navigated: *a navigable river (that is wide and deep enough for craft); navigable waters; a navigable* (= steerable) *balloon.* —**nav.i.ga.bly** *adv.* —**nav.i.ga.bil.i.ty** (-BIL.i.tee) *n.*

nav.i.gate (NAV.uh.gate) *v.* **-gates, -gat.ed, -gat.ing 1** steer, guide, or manage a ship, plane, etc. through the sea, air, etc. **2** make one's way past or through something: *We had a difficult time navigating the snowbound schoolyard.* **3** get through a river, sea, etc. in a craft: *to navigate the Niagara River.*

navigation / necessitate

4 *Informal.* move or walk steadily: *He finds it difficult to navigate after a couple of drinks.*

nav.i.ga.tion (nav.uh.GAY.shun) *n.* **1** the science of guiding a craft on its course through water, air, or space. **2** a navigating.

nav.i.ga.tor (NAV.uh.gay.tur) *n.* **1** one who navigates. **2** an explorer of the seas.

na.vy (NAY.vee) *n.* **-vies 1** a nation's warships collectively or the whole naval establishment including yards, offices, and personnel. **2** [short form] navy blue.

navy bean *n.* a white variety of bean, as used for "Boston baked beans."

navy blue *n.* a dark purplish blue.

navy yard *n.* a shipyard for naval vessels.

nay *adv.* **1** not only that but also: *She's poor, nay, destitute!* **2** [old use] no; opposite of AYE. —*n.* a negative vote or voter: *"The nays have it"* (= The negative side has won).

nay.say.er (NAY.say.ur) *n.* a person with a negative or pessimistic attitude.

Na.zi (NAHT.see) *n. & adj.* (a member) of the German fascist party that ruled from 1933 to 1945 under Adolph Hitler; **Na.zi.sm** *n.*

N-bomb (EN.bom) same as NEUTRON BOMB.

Ne.an.der.thal (nee.AN.dur.thawl) *n.* **1** a primitive human of the Stone Age, the **Neanderthal man. 2 neanderthal** one who is backward or primitive: *the neanderthals who set fire to our forests;* **adja.:** *a neanderthal male chauvinist; her neanderthal mentality; their neanderthal views on computers.*

Ne.a.pol.i.tan (nee.uh.POL.uh.tun) *n. & adj.* (a person) of or from Naples, Italy.

neap tide *n.* either of the two lowest high tides of a month; cf. SPRINGTIDE.

near (NEER) *adj.* close in distance, relationship, feelings, time, etc.: *Her house is near, not far from here; in the near distance, near future; a near friend, relative; Holidays are near* (= coming soon); *the nearest* (= most direct) *route;* **Near beer** *has less than 0.5 percent alcohol; a move to abolish the sales tax on* **near foods** *such as candies and soft drinks; A* **near miss** *is almost a hit.* —*adv.:* *Holidays are drawing near; We came near to scoring a goal; The water is near* (*Informal* for nearly) *frozen.* —**near at hand** close by in time or place: *Peace seemed near at hand; Keep your calculator near at hand.* —*v.* approach: *We are nearing the end of our journey.* —**near.ness** *n.*

near.by (NEER.bye, neer.BYE) *adv.* close by: *She lives nearby;* **adja.:** *in a nearby town; in nearby Delhi; seated at a nearby table.*

Near East *n.* **1** the countries of southwestern Asia and northeastern Africa. **2** the Middle East. —**Near Eastern** *adj.*

near.ly (NEER.lee) *adv.* closely: *We are nearly related; It's nearly* (= almost) *noon.*

near.sight.ed (NEER.sye.tid) *adj.* not able to see far because of defective eyesight; **near.sight.ed.ness** *n.*

neat (NEET) *adj.* **1** clean and orderly: *a neat drawing; He writes a neat hand; She's quite neat in all her homework; a neat and tidy kitchen; a neat mind looking for nice distinctions.* **2** *Informal.* pleasing: *That's really neat! a neat dress, haircut; a neat* (= net) *profit of $100,000.* **3** undiluted: *neat brandy; He likes his brandy neat; Two glasses of port and one neat whiskey, please.* —**neat.ly** *adv.;* **neat.ness** *n.*

'neath or **neath** (NEETH, "TH" as in "thin") [poetical] beneath.

neb *n. Scottish.* **1** a tip, esp. a beak; nib. **2** a snout or a person's mouth.

neb.bish (NEB.ish) *n. Slang.* a pitifully inept or dull person.

neb.u.la (NEB.yuh.luh) *n.* **-las** or **-lae** (-lee) a cloudlike hazy patch seen in the sky at night. —**neb.u.lar** (-lur) *adj.*: *the nebular hypothesis of the origin of the solar system.*

neb.u.lous (NEB.yuh.lus) *adj.* **1** cloudy or hazy: *a nebulous liquid, state.* **2** confused or vague: *a nebulous concept, idea, notion.* —**neb.u.los.i.ty** (-LOS.i.tee) *n.* **-ties.**

nec.es.sar.y (NES.uh.sair.ee) *adj.* needed or required in a pressing manner though not essential: *Food, shelter, and clothing are necessary to or for our existence; It's necessary to eat or that we eat in order to live; the necessary repairs for a car after a collision; It's necessary that we visit the dentist regularly; Visits to the dentist are a necessary* (= unavoidable) *evil; the necessary* (= logical) *consequence of un action.* —*n.* **-es.sar.ies** something that is necessary: *Children have a right to the* **necessaries of life** *such as food, shelter, clothing, medical care, and some education.* —**nec.es.sar.i.ly** (-SAIR.uh.lee) *adv.*

ne.ces.si.tate (nuh.SES.uh.tate) *v.* **-tates, -tat.ed, -tat.ing** make necessary: *Crime necessitates punishment; A jail term necessitates living away from home.*

ne.ces.si.ty (nuh.SES.i.tee) *n.* **-ties** an urgent or pressing need or thing needed: *Food is a necessity; a dire necessity; He managed to survive with the bare, daily necessities of life; Most people go to work out of necessity; "Necessity is the mother of invention"; She was forced to go on welfare by family necessity* (= poverty); *I must, **of necessity**,* (= forced by circumstances) *limit my speech to five minutes because I've a plane to catch.*
—**ne.ces.si.tous** (-tus) *adj.* in great need or poverty: *necessitous circumstances;* **ne.ces.si.tous.ly** *adv.*

neck *n.* **1** the narrow, slender part connecting the head to the rest of the body: *to crane one's neck for a better view; to **break one's neck** (= try too hard) on a job; He **risked his neck** (= risked his life) by going down Niagara Falls in a barrel; He was saved **by a neck** (= narrowly); She was only trying to **save her (own) neck** (= life) by telling a lie; He'll **get it in the neck** (Informal for be severely dealt with) for ignoring warnings.* **2** anything resembling a neck, as a narrow strip of land, the narrowest part of a bottle, violin, tooth, etc.
—**breathe down someone's neck** *Informal.* get too close to someone, as if to use power or influence. —**in one's neck of the woods** *Informal.* in one's part of the country. —**neck and neck** running equal, as two horses in a race. —**stick one's neck out** act too boldly or foolishly. —**up to one's neck** deeply involved: *I'm up to my neck in work; He's up to his neck in debt.*
—*v. Informal.* kiss passionately: *Milton frowns on necking in the library.*

neck.er.chief (NEK.ur.chuf, -cheef) *n.* **-chiefs** or **-chieves** (-cheevz) a handkerchieflike piece of cloth worn about the neck.

neck.lace (NECK.lis) *n.* an ornamental chain or string of jewels, beads, etc. worn around the neck.

neck.line *n.* the line formed by the edge of a garment around, esp. at the front of the neck: *high, low, low-cut, plunging necklines.*

neck.tie *n.* a strip of cloth worn around the neck under a collar, tied at the front of the neck with its loose ends hanging down.

neck.wear *n.* neckties, scarves, etc. collectively.

ne.crol.o.gy (nuh.CROL.uh.jee) *n.* **-gies** an obituary list or record, as kept by a church.

nec.ro.man.cy (NEC.ruh.man.see) *n.* sorcery or fortune-telling by communicating with the dead; **nec.ro.man.cer** *n.*

ne.crop.o.lis (nuh.CROP.uh.lis) *n.* a cemetery, as found on the site of an ancient city.

ne.cro.sis (nuh.CROH.sis) *n.* death of body tissues, as after a severe burn or in gangrene; **ne.crot.ic** (-CROT.ic) *adj.*

nec.tar (NEC.tur) *n.* **1** the drink of the gods of Greek myth. **2** a sweet or delicious drink, as the liquid that bees gather from flowers.

nec.tar.ine (nec.tuh.REEN) *n.* a variety of peach with a smooth skin.

née or **nee** (NAY, NEE) *adj.* [used before a married woman's maiden name] born as: *Mary Jones, née Smith* (= born as Miss Mary Smith).

need *n.* a lack of something useful, desired, or required; also, the thing lacked: *She's badly in need of vitamins; There's no need for junk food; no need for you to lose weight; the urgent need to put out a fire; men's daily needs such as toiletries; a nun's simple needs; Our needs come before our wants; to create, feel, fill, meet, minister to, obviate, satisfy a need; Sewers are a crying need in this town; a desperate, dire, material, pressing need; The poor live in constant need; "A friend in need (who helps when one is in trouble) is a friend indeed"; There's no need* (= You are not required) *to apologize; She is prepared to sacrifice her life for her child, **if need be*** (= if the need arises).
—*v.* have need of a person or thing: *People desperately need jobs; A crossing guard is badly, sorely needed at the school; Everyone needs to work; She need not have hurried since she missed the flight anyhow; He didn't need to hurry to catch the flight since he was much too early; Yvette need not hurry since her flight has been canceled; Need I say more? The unemployed need* (= are required) *to look for jobs;*
adj.: much needed rain. —**needs must** necessarily: *She needs must go back to get her hat when everyone else is ready to leave!*

need.ful *adj.* required or necessary: *a patient needful of love and care.*

nee.dle (NEE.dul) *n.* **1** a slender, pointed piece of steel with a hole at the thicker end through which a thread is passed for sewing: *to look for **a needle in a haystack*** (= something impossible to find). **2** a similar instrument for carrying a thread for knitting, hooking, etc. **3** anything resembling a needle, as the pointer of a gauge or meter, the vibrating pin in the pickup

mechanism of a phonograph, the pointed leaf of a pine, or the injecting end of a surgical syringe: *a hypodermic needle.* **4** *Informal.* an injection of a drug: *my weekly needle for allergies.*
—*v.* **-dles, -dled, -dling** tease or annoy someone with gibes, provocative comments, etc.

nee.dle.leaf (NEE.dul.leef) *adj.* of a tree, having needlelike or scalelike leaves: *Pines, firs, spruces, and such conifers are needleleaf trees.*

nee.dle.point (NEE.dul.point) *n.* embroidery made on an open-mesh canvas background; *adj.*: *a needlepoint design; Needlepoint lace is made with a needle instead of a bobbin.*

need.less *adj.* unnecessary: *Needless to say, we're tired and hungry; the needless suffering of the poor; needless apologies, controversies, fears, injustices, worries; This is needless and unwarranted.*
—**need.less.ly** *adv.*; **need.less.ness** *n.*

nee.dle.wom.an (NEE.dul.woom.un) *n.* **-wom.en** a woman who does needlework.

nee.dle.work (NEE.dul.wurk) *n.* embroidery, needlepoint, knitting, and such work done with a needle.

need.n't (NEED.unt) need not.

need.y *adj.* **need.i.er, -i.est 1** in need; poor or destitute: *needy children; feeling needy and insecure; financial aid for the neediest students.* **2** lustful: *Lee looked at passers-by with needy eyes; needy looks.*
—*n.*: *Let's not forget the needy at Thanksgiving; the needy of our city; the truly needy.* —**need.i.ness** *n.*

ne'er (NAIR) [poetic] never.

ne'er-do-well *n. & adj.* (one who is) worthless or irresponsible.

ne.far.i.ous (ni.FAIR.ee.us) *adj.* extremely wicked or villainous: *a nefarious activity, deed, scheme.* —**ne.far.i.ous.ly** *adv.*; **ne.far.i.ous.ness** *n.*

ne.gate (ni.GATE) *v.* **-gates, -gat.ed, -gat.ing 1** nullify. **2** deny the existence of something. —**ne.ga.tion** (-GAY.shun) *n.*

neg.a.tive (NEG.uh.tiv) *adj.* **1** saying "no"; opposite: *the negative side of a debate.* **2** against or on the other side of something considered positive: *the negative electrode of a battery; negative film (with reversed image); a negative TB test; negative three degrees Celsius; −3 has a negative sign* (= minus sign) *before it.*
—*n.* something negative, as a word, vote, or reply, a minus sign or quantity, a film or photographic image, a battery terminal to which current flows, etc.: *He replied* **in the negative** (= said "no"). —*v.* **-tives, -tived, -tiv.ing 1** vote against or deny. **2** disprove. —**neg.a.tive.ly** *adv.*
—**neg.a.tiv.ism** (-iz.um) *n.*
—**neg.a.tiv.i.ty** (-TIV.i.tee) *n.*

negative income tax *n.* a subsidy paid by government to the poor to guarantee a minimum income.

negative option *n.* the choice of either returning unsolicited merchandise or keeping it and paying for it.

neg.lect (nig.LECT) *v.* give too little attention or care to a person or thing: *Do not neglect your health or your duties; She neglected* (= omitted) *to write home; adj.*: *a neglected* (= uncared-for) *child.*
—*n.* a neglecting or failure to look after a person or thing: *a vacant house in a state of neglect; parental neglect of children; fired for neglect of duty; the policy of benign neglect as a tactic for avoiding an issue or not doing justice to a cause; child neglect* (= neglect of a child).
—**neg.lect.ful** *adj.*; **neg.lect.ful.ly** *adv.*

neg.li.gee (neg.li.ZHAY) *n.* **1** a woman's light and loose-fitting dressing gown. **2** careless or informal attire.

neg.li.gent (NEG.li.junt) *adj.* habitually or extremely careless: *fired for being grossly negligent in his duty.*
—**neg.li.gence** *n.*: *contributory, criminal, willful negligence.* —**neg.li.gent.ly** *adv.*

neg.li.gi.ble (NEG.li.juh.bul) *adj.* that can be neglected; trifling or unimportant: *The money may seem negligible to you, but it's substantial for me; a negligible amount, effect, error, impact, increase, level, loss; a negligible 1%; It's almost negligible; n.: That's a negligible.*

ne.go.ti.a.ble (ni.GOH.shee.uh.bul, -shuh.bul) *adj.* that may be negotiated: *a negotiable claim, contract* (that may be discussed and modified); *Our offer is not negotiable* (= cannot be modified or made better); *The road is not negotiable* (= passable) *during the flood; A check, money order, or draft that is negotiable* (= can be exchanged for money) *is a* **negotiable instrument.**

ne.go.ti.ate (ni.GOH.shee.ate) *v.* **-ates, -at.ed, -at.ing 1** discuss and arrange: *Labor negotiates with management about or over wages, for raises and better working conditions; to negotiate an agreement, loan, sale, settlement, treaty; While both sides negotiated, the strike dragged on.* **2** sell, transfer, or assign something negotiable, as a check, funds, etc. **3** successfully go past, over, etc.: *to negotiate a curve, fence, hill.*

ne.go.ti.a.tion (ni.goh.shee.AY.shun) *n.* **1** discussion for reaching an agree-

ment: *Everything is a matter of* or *for negotiation; We are in negotiation with the management; The pay is* **under negotiation**. 2 usu. **negotiations** *pl.*: *diplomatic, high-level, peace, round-the-clock negotiations; to break off, conduct, enter into, open, resume negotiations with someone.*
—**ne.go.ti.a.tor** (-shee.ay.tur) *n.*
ne.gri.tude (NEG.ruh.tude, NEE.gruh-) *n.* the fact of being a Negro, esp. the value of black or African culture; also **Ne.gro.ness** (NEE.groh.nus) *n.*
Ne.gro (NEE.groh) *n.* **-groes** [historical use; offensive in reference to contemporary people] a member of the Negroid group or black human race; *adja.*: *a negro (baseball) league, college, face, slave, veteran, woman.*
Ne.groid (NEE.groid) *n.& adj.* (having to do with) an African race distinguished by dark skin, kinky hair, and broad lips and nose.
neigh (NAY) *v. & n.* the characteristic cry of a horse.
neigh.bor (NAY.bur) *n.* one living near another: *our next-door neighbor; good neighbors; "Love thy neighbor"* (= fellow humans). —*v.* live or be situated nearby: *a state neighboring the Canadian border; Mexico neighbors on* or *upon the U.S.;* **adja.**: *two* **neighboring** *countries like Norway and Sweden.* Also **neigh.bour** *Cdn.*
neigh.bor.hood (NAY.bur.hood, short "oo"] *n.* a particular region, place, or district with the people living there: *a high-income neighborhood; poor neighborhoods; Ask your friendly neighborhood banker for a loan.* —**in the neighborhood of** *Informal.* near: *We used to live in the neighborhood of the church; The job pays in the neighborhood of* (= approximately) *$150,000 a year.* Also **neigh.bour.hood** *Cdn.*
neigh.bor.ly (NAY.bur.lee) *adj.* like good neighbors; friendly: *neighborly friendliness, relations; The neighborly thing to do is to report prowlers to the police.*
—**neigh.bor.li.ness** *n.* Also **neigh.bour.ly, neigh.bour.li.ness** *Cdn.*
neighbour, etc. *Cdn.* NEIGHBOR, etc.
nei.ther (NEE.thur, NYE-, "th" as in "the") *adja., pron. & conj.* not the one or the other: *The shoe would fit neither foot; would fit neither of the feet; It would fit neither the left foot nor the right.*
—*adv.* [used with "no," "not," or other negative in previous clause] also not: *He doesn't smoke; neither do I* or *me neither* (*Informal.* for and I don't either).
Nel.ly or **nel.lie** (NEL.ee) *n., pl.* **Nel.lies** or **nel.lies** *Slang.* a weak or effeminate person: *He's a bit on the nellie side; a* **nervous Nellie** (= a worrier); *a* **nice Nelly** (= prude).
nel.son (NEL.sun) *n.* a wrestling hold in which leverage is applied with one arm ("half nelson") or both ("full nelson") passed from behind and under the opponent's arm (or arms) against his neck and head.
nem.a.tode (NEM.uh.tode) *n.* a roundworm, as the hookworm or pinworm, with an unsegmented body pointed at both ends, that lives in soil, water, or as parasites in animals and plants.
nem.e.sis (NEM.uh.sis) *n., pl.* **-ses** 1 a fate which the victim deserves; retribution: *to meet one's nemesis.* 2 the punishing agent, like **Nemesis**, the Greek goddess of vengeance: *The parking meter is often the shopper's nemesis.*
neo- (NEE.oh) *comb.form.* new or recent: *neocolonial, neonatal, neo-Nazi.*
ne.o.clas.si.cism (nee.oh.CLAS.uh.siz.um) *n.* the revival of classical principles or practices in literature and the arts. —**ne.o.clas.sic** or **ne.o.clas.si.cal** *adj.*
ne.o.co.lo.ni.al.ism (NEE.oh.cuh.LOH.nee.uh.liz.um) *n.* domination by the great powers of smaller countries through economic, political, and military influence. —**ne.o.co.lo.nial** *adj.;* **ne.o.co.lo.nial.ist** *n. & adj.*
ne.o.dym.i.um (nee.oh.DIM.ee.um) *n.* a rare-earth metallic element.
ne.o.im.pres.sion.ism (NEE.oh.im.PRESH.un.iz.um) *n.* a French movement of the late 1800's based on pointillism as a reaction against impressionism.
ne.ol.o.gism (nee.OL.uh.jiz.um) *n.* a newly coined word or phrase, or a new meaning for an established word. Also **ne.ol.o.gy** (-uh.jee) *n.* **-gies.**
ne.on (NEE.on) *n.* 1 an inert gaseous element used in lamps and advertising signs for the bright glow it gives when an electric current is passed through it; *adja.*: *neon lamps* or *lights; neon colors, signs; bathed in a neon glow.* 2 a fluorescent color.
ne.o.na.tal (nee.oh.NAY.tul) *adj.* of the newborn, esp. less than a month old: *the neonatal period; neonatal care, deaths, diseases, medicine, mortality; a neonatal intensive care unit.*
ne.o.nate (NEE.uh.nate) *n.* a newborn infant.
ne.o.phyte (NEE.uh.fite) *n.* 1 a new convert. 2 a novice or beginner: *a political neophyte;* **adja.**: *a neophyte actor, computerist, politician.*

ne.o.plasm (NEE.uh.plaz.um) *n.* a new or abnormal growth such as a tumor; **ne.o.plas.tic** (-PLAS.tic) *adj.*

ne.o.prene (NEE.uh.preen) *n.* a synthetic rubber resistant to heat, oil, weather, gasoline, etc., used for making hose, insulation, shoe soles, etc.

Nep.a.lese (nep.uh.LEEZ) *adj.* having to do with **Nepal**, a Himalayan kingdom on India's N. border. —*n. sing. & pl.* a person of or from Nepal.

Ne.pa.li (nuh.PAW.lee) *n.* the Indic official language of Nepal.

neph.ew (NEF.yoo, NEV-) *n.* a son of one's brother, sister, brother-in-law, or sister-in-law.

neph.rite (NEF.rite) *n.* a variety of jade.

ne.phri.tis (nuh.FRY.tis) *n.* inflammation of the kidneys. —**ne.phrit.ic** (-FRIT.ic) *adj.*

ne plus ul.tra (nee.plus.UL.truh) *n.* the acme or culmination, as of something attained.

nep.o.tism (NEP.uh.tiz.um) *n.* favoritism shown to relatives, as in giving jobs.

nep.tu.ni.um (nep.TUE.nee.um) *n.* a radioactive metallic element.

nerd (NURD) *n. Slang.* one considered as unpleasant or insignificant: *computer nerds.*

nerve (NURV) *n.* **1** a strand or fiber that carries impulses of sensation and motion between the sense organs and the brain: *sensory nerves; a spinal nerve; The question about her past hit a (raw) nerve* (= touched a sensitive point). **2** a vein of a leaf or rib of an insect's wing. **3 nerves** *pl.* nervousness: *She had an attack of nerves; She is a* **bundle of nerves** (= very nervous person); *Some of his puns* **get on her nerves** (= annoy her); *to calm, fray, frazzle, settle one's nerves.* **4** a mental or bodily strength; courage or vigor: *strong, taut, weak* **nerves**; *She has* **nerves** *of steel; She likes to* **strain every nerve** (= try her very best) *on the eve of a test; Don't* **lose your nerve** *and give up at the last moment.* **5** boldness or impudence: *the teenage son's nerve to ask for a Ferrari after totaling a Ford.* —*v.* **nerves, nerved, nerv.ing** give strength or courage to do something: *She nerved herself to receive the tragic news.*

nerve cell *n.* a neuron.

nerve center *n.* **1** a group of nerve cells controlling a specific function such as respiration or vision. **2** a headquarters or center of activity.

nerve gas *n.* a poisonous gas used in warfare whose principal effect is on the nervous system.

nerve.less *adj.* **1** without strength or vigor. **2** without nervousness. —**nerve.less.ly** *adv.*; **nerve.less.ness** *n.*

nerve-racking or **nerve-wracking** *adj.* very trying on one's nerves: *a nerve-racking job, ordeal, time.*

ner.vous (NUR.vus) *adj.* **1** jumpy or restless: *Gigi feels nervous at the end of the month; She's nervous about the bills waiting to be paid; He's a* **nervous wreck** *before an examination.* **2** animated or vigorous: *the nervous energy that drives her forward.* **3** of the nerves: *nervous excitement.* —**ner.vous.ly** *adv.*; **ner.vous.ness** *n.*

nervous breakdown *n.* a sudden emotional illness accompanied by depression, fatigue, lack of appetite, feelings of inadequacy, etc.

nervous system *n.* the bodily system consisting of the brain, spinal cord, nerves, and nerve endings.

nerv.y (NUR.vee) *adj.* **nerv.i.er, -i.est** **1** brash or impudent: *nervy scrambling for power.* **2** showing or requiring courage; bold or courageous: *a nervy risk.* **3** nervous or excitable: *in a nervy and troubled mood.* —**nerv.i.ly** *adv.*; **nerv.i.ness** *n.*

-ness *n. suffix.* quality or state: *fastness, forgiveness, goodness.*

nest *n.* **1** a cozy place for retiring into, esp. a structure built of twigs or straw in which birds lay and hatch eggs. **2** a place similarly used by insects, fishes, and other animals. **3** a place swarming with something bad; hangout: *a nest of criminals, spies, thieves, vice.* **4** a group of articles, often of gradually varying size, fitting into one another: *a nest of drinking cups, tables.* —*v.* **1** make or form a nest: *Storks nest on roofs and chimneys.* **2** of the members of a series of objects, fit one into the next or another; *adj.*: *a* **nested** *subroutine* (to be carried out within a computer program); *stacking chairs and* **nesting** *tables.*

nest egg *n.* money set aside as a reserve or to start a fund.

nes.tle (NES.ul) *v.* **-tles, -tled, -tling** shelter or settle cozily: *a village nestled in a valley; She nestled down into the chair by the fire; Guy* **nestled up** *to his mom; Mother nestled* (= pressed) *the frightened child in her arms.*

nest.ling (NEST.ling) *n.* a bird too young to leave its nest.

net *n.* **1** a fabric knotted or woven of string, thread, hair, etc. with regularly spaced meshes, esp. something made of such fabric for catching fish, butterflies, etc., for dividing a court in games such as tennis and volleyball, for protection against mosquitoes, to keep hair in place, etc.: *to cast or spread a net for fish; butterfly, mosquito, safety nets.* **2** a trap or snare. **3** what is left over after deductions from gross; **adj.**: *a net amount, benefit, price; net earnings, income, profit.* **4 the Net** [short form] the Internet. —*v.* **nets, net.ted, net.ting 1** catch in a net or as if in a net: *to net fish.* **2** clear or yield as profit: *We netted $20,000 from the sale.*

neth.er (NETH.ur, "TH" as in "the") *adja.* lower or under: *The team's success rate places it in the nether regions of NHL statistics;* the **nether world** (= Hades or hell). —**neth.er.most** *adj.* lowest.

net.i.quette (ET.i.kut, -ket) *n.* rules of behavior when communicating on computer networks such as the Internet.

netting *n.* **1** the making of a net. **2** fishing with a net. **3** net material.

net.tle (NET.ul) *n.* a weed with stinging bristles. —*v.* **net.tles, net.tled, net.tling** irritate or annoy someone.

net.tle.some (NET.ul.sum) *adj.* irritating or annoying.

net.work *n.* **1** a mesh or something resembling it, as a system of roads, veins, etc. that cross each other. **2** a group of radio or television stations that may broadcast the same programs simultaneously: *News is broadcast over the national networks;* **adja.**: *network operations, television.* **3** an association or club: *a feminist network; old-boy networks.* **4** a computer system of databases, terminals, printers, and such devices for exchange of information.

net.work.ing (NET.wurk.ing) *n.* **1** the making or using of a computer network. **2** a supportive system of people with the same interests and objectives for sharing services and information.

net worth *n.* one's assets minus liabilities; also **net assets.**

neu.ral (NEW.rul) *adj.* of a nerve or of the nervous system. —**neu.ral.ly** *adv.*

neu.ral.gia (new.RAL.jee.uh) *n.* sharp pain along the route of a nerve; **neu.ral.gic** *adj.*

neu.ras.the.ni.a (new.rus.THEE.nee.uh, "TH" as in "thin") *n.* a neurotic condition; **neu.ras.then.ic** (-THEN.ic) *adj.*

neu.ri.tis (new.RYE.tis) *n.* inflammation of a nerve or nerves, as in shingles or sciatica; **neu.rit.ic** (-RIT.ic) *adj.*

neuro- *comb.form.* nerve: *neurology, neurosis, neuroscience.*

neu.rol.o.gy (new.ROL.uh.jee) *n.* a branch of medicine dealing with the nervous system and its diseases; **neu.rol.o.gist** *n.* —**neu.ro.log.i.cal** (-ruh.LOJ.i.cul) *adj.*

neu.ron (NEW.ron) *n.* a nerve-cell body and its processes such as dendrites. —**neu.ron.al** (-ruh.nul) *adj.*: *neuronal activity, degeneration, function.*

neu.ro.science (new.roh.SYE.unce) *n.* a science dealing with the nervous system or mental phenomena, as psychology; **neu.ro.sci.en.tist** *n.*

neu.ro.sis (new.ROH.sis) *n., pl.* **-ses** (-seez) a mental disorder characterized by anxiety, phobias, insecurity, and depression. —**neu.rot.ic** (new.ROT.ic) *n. & adj.* —**neu.rot.i.cal.ly** *adv.*

neu.ter (NEW.tur) *n.* **1** a grammatical form or word: *Is the word in the masculine, feminine, or neuter?* **adj.**: *The pronoun "it" is neuter; the neuter gender.* **2** an animal, plant, or insect that is neither masculine nor feminine, or sexless, as a worker bee or a spayed animal. —*v.* to make neuter, as by castrating an animal: *The victors proceeded to neuter the vanquished militarily;* **adj.**: *a neutered dog, tomcat;* **n.**: *the neutering* of Japan after World War II.

neu.tral (NEW.trul) *adj.* belonging to neither side, as a nation not joining a war: *Switzerland remained neutral in the two world wars; the neutral corners of a boxing ring; Beige is a neutral* (= bland or weak) *color; Water is chemically neutral* (= neither acid nor alkaline). —*n.*: *Change gears from reverse to neutral; the colors of gray, beige, and such neutrals; Austria, Spain, Switzerland, and such neutrals of World War II.* —**neu.tral.ly** *adv.*

neu.tral.ism (NEW.truh.liz.um) *n.* the policy or practice of keeping neutral, esp. in international relations; non-alignment; **neu.tral.ist** *n. & adj.* —**neu.tral.i.ty** (new.TRAL.i.tee) *n.*

neu.tral.ize (NEW.truh.lize) *v.* **-iz.es, -ized, -iz.ing** make neutral chemically, politically, in artistic effect, etc.; **neu.tral.iz.er** *n.* —**neu.tral.i.za.tion** (-luh.ZAY.shun, -lye-) *n.*

neutral spirits *n.pl.* ethyl alcohol of 190 proof or over.

neu.tri.no (new.TREE.noh) *n.* **-nos** an elementary particle with no electric charge and a mass near zero.

neu.tron (NEW.tron) *n.* a chargeless subatomic particle that combines with protons to form the nucleus of all atoms except those of hydrogen.

neutron bomb *n.* an atomic bomb that would release radioactive neutrons taking lives but without the blast that is destructive to property.

nev.er (NEV.ur) *adv.* not ever; at no time; also, not at all: *I've never been to China; **Never mind**, I'm going there next year; Never mind the expense; Never mind that I've still to learn Chinese; A bikini will **never do** for something to wear to church; a gas bar that is **never ever** closed* (Informal for open 24 hours and 7 days).

nev.er.more (NEV.ur.more) *adv.* never again.

never-never land *n.* a never-attainable, imaginary condition or unreal place.

nev.er.the.less (NEV.ur.the.LES) *adv.* however. **—new.ness** *n.*

ne.vus (NEE.vus) *n., pl.* **-vi** (-vye) a birthmark or mole.

new *adj.* **1** now or recently come into being, use, possession, etc.: *a new car; a new hand at car repair; Our new home is only about 25 years old; a new arrival, fashion, idea, look.* **2** seen or known for the first time: *the discovery of the New World; new evidence on an old murder; Greece is new to us; **So what else is new?*** (Informal for "As if what you are saying is something new"). **3** not yet accustomed: *We are new to Greece; I'm new at driving.* **—new.ness** *n.*

New Age *adj.* **1** having to do with a cultural movement based on new approaches to religion, medicine, the environment, etc.: *New Age customers, design, movements, mysticism, pursuits.* **2** having to do with a soothing style of popular instrumental music.

new blood *n.* new people who bring fresh ideas or vigor into an organization.

new.born *adj.* **1** just born: *a newborn child, nation, star; a newborn nursery (for newborns).* **2** born anew: *newborn depths of emotion; a newborn interest.*
—*n.* a newborn child: *an abandoned newborn; care of the newborn and the elderly; problems of drug-exposed newborns.*

new.com.er (NEW.cum.ur) *n.* a new or recent arrival, often a beginner: *a newcomer to Newfoundland; a relative newcomer to the business; a political newcomer.*

new.el (NEW.ul) *n.* **1** a post or pillar supporting the handrails of a staircase, esp. at either end of it; also **newel post. 2** the central pillar of a winding staircase.

new.fan.gled (NEW.FANG.guld) *adj.* [derogatory] newly put together: *newfangled devices, gadgets, ideas, notions.*

new-fashioned *adj.* of a new fashion in form or style: *a new-fashioned way of using money to make money; new-fashioned songs.*

new.found or **new-found** *adj.* newly found or discovered: *a newfound ally, friend, hero; their newfound confidence, fame, freedom, wealth.*

New.found.land or **Newfoundland dog** (new.FOUND.lund, new.fun.LAND-) *n.* **1** a big, strong working dog with a black or black-and-white coat. **2** a breed of short-haired dog from which the Labrador retriever was bred.

New Left *n.* the radical social and political movement of the 1960's among American youth.

new.ly *adv.* recently or freshly: *a newly arrived immigrant; newly formed companies; newly industrialized nations; a newly married couple; a newly paved driveway.*

new.ly.wed or **newly-wed** (NEW.lee.wed) *n.* one recently married; bride or bridegroom.

new moon *n.* the beginning of the first phase of the moon when it appears totally dark before waxing from a thin crescent to a half moon.

news *n.pl.* [takes *sing. v.*] new or recent events, esp. as reported in a newspaper or broadcast on radio or TV: *to announce, break, cover, distort, flash, hear, spread, suppress the news; Quintuplets always make news; If you do something remarkable, you will be in the news; We heard it on the Late News; to turn on the news (on radio or TV); Our victory made front-page news; the latest news; the nightly news; a **bit** or **piece of news**; several items of news; bad, good, sensational, startling, welcome news; Yesterday's news is today's history;* **adj.**: *a news beat, clip, column, item, program, report, story; news media.*

news.box *n.* a newspaper-vending box.

news.boy *n.* a boy who distributes newspapers; newspaper carrier.

news.cast *n.* a radio or TV broadcast of news. **—news.cast.er** *n.*

news conference *n.* a conference for announcing something to the media.

news.deal.er (NEWS.dee.lur) *n.* a retailer of newspapers and magazines.

news.group *n.* a group interested in a specific subject that holds discussions on a computer network.

news.hound *n.* a dedicated news reporter.

news.let.ter (NEWS.let.ur) *n.* a bulletin or report periodically issued to a group to keep them informed of happenings in their field of interest.

news.mag.a.zine (NEWS.mag.uh.zeen) *n.* a magazine that summarizes and comments on current events.

newsmaker / nick

n. a magazine that summarizes and comments on current events.
news.mak.er (NEWS.may.kur) n. a newsworthy person.
news.man n. -men 1 a news reporter. 2 a newsdealer.
news.pa.per (NEWS.pay.pur) n. a periodical, esp. a daily publication, containing news and comments, features, and advertising; **adja.:** *a newspaper ad, bureau, carrier, clipping, column, columnist, critic, editorial, headline, report, reporter, stand; newspaper jargon.*
news.pa.per.man (NEWS.pay.pur.man) n. -men a newspaper publisher, editor, reporter, etc. —**news.pa.per.wom.an** n. -wom.en.
new.speak (NEW.speek) n. a style of official language meant to deceive the public.
news people n.pl. news reporters.
news.per.son (NEWS.pur.sun) n. a news reporter.
news.print n. 1 paper used for printing newspapers, esp. cheap paper made from wood pulp: *Magazines are printed on glossy paper rather than on newsprint.* 2 old newspapers: *the de-inking and recycling of newsprint.*
news.reel n. a short motion picture of news events, as shown in a movie theater.
news.stand n. a stand at which newspapers, etc. are sold.
news.wire n. a news service via teletypewriter: *Associated Press newswire.*
news.wor.thy (NEWS.wur.thee, "th" as in "the") adj. having interest or importance as news.
news.y (NEW.zee) adj. **news.i.er, -i.est** *Informal.* 1 containing much news: *newsy letters, reports.* 2 being the subject of news: *a newsy design; newsy photos; The media chose her as the newsiest woman of the year.*
new.ton (NEW.tun) n. a unit of force equal to the force required to produce an acceleration of one meter per second per second on a mass of one kilogram.
new town n. a city planned and built as a small self-contained community away from a large urban area to reduce overcrowding.
new wave n. 1 a new movement or trend in art, cinema, cooking, music, etc. 2 a type of rock music of the 1970s; **adj.:** *the new-wave culture of punk rockers.*
New Year or **New Year's** n. the first day or days of a new year.
New Year's Day n. January 1.
New Year's Eve n. the evening of December 31.
New York.er n. a person of or from New York City or New York State.
next adj. nearest, esp. after a person or thing: *the next house; the house next to ours; We'll see you next week; Who's next (in line)?* *to catch the next train* (= the train after this train or closest to a specified one). —**adv.:** *The number 4 comes next after 3; What did she do next? the next best* (= second best) *solution to a problem; He did next to* (= almost) *nothing to help us.*
next door adv. very close, esp. in the next house: *They live next door; right next door; next door to us; the girl next door; the girl-next-door image; Cuba is next door to Haiti;* **adja.:** *our next-door neighbors.*
next of kin n. nearest relative(s).
nex.us n. 1 a link or connection within a system or situation: *There should be no nexus between the government and the judiciary.* 2 core or center: *a family that is the nexus of a vast fortune.*
Nez Percé (NEZ.PURCE) n. (one of) an American Indian people now confined to a small reservation in Idaho.
ni.a.cin (NYE.uh.sin) n. nicotinic acid.
Ni.ag.a.ra (nye.AG.ruh) n. a cataract or torrent, like **Niagara Falls:** *a Niagara of facts and figures.*
nib n. a point or tip, esp. of a fountain pen.
nib.ble (NIB.ul) v. **nib.bles, nib.bled, nib.bling** take a small, gentle, or cautious bite: *Fish nibble at bait; Rising prices* **nibble** *away at the value of the dollar;* **n.:** *The book proposal got only nibbles from publishers, no real bites.* —**nib.bler** n.
Nic.a.ra.guan (nik.uh.RAH.gwun) n. & adj. (a person) of or from **Nicaragua,** a Central American country.
nice adj. **nic.er, nic.est** 1 agreeable; good; proper: *a nice boy, girl, man, party, person, time; nice weather; Is Toronto a nicer place to live than New York?* 2 requiring care or exactness; subtle or refined: *a nice legal distinction, shade of meaning, ear for music.* —**nice.ly** adv.; **nice.ness** n.
ni.ce.ty (NYE.suh.tee) n. -ties daintiness; exactness; also, something dainty or refined: *the niceties of courteous behavior; She does everything she touches* **to a nicety** (= with exactness).
niche (NICH) n. 1 a recess in a wall, as for a statue or vase. 2 a secure position: *He occupies a special niche in the organization; She has carved out a niche*

niche for herself in her profession.
nick n. a small or superficial cut or chip: *a table top with nicks and scratches; A collision was avoided by braking **in the nick of time*** (= just in time). —v.: *He nicked himself while shaving.*
nick.el (NICK.ul) n. **1** a hard silver-white metallic element used in alloys. **2** a five-cent piece.
nickel-and-dime adj. small or small-time: *a nickel-and-dime dealer, job.* —v. weaken or reduce little by little: *a government whose taxation policies nickel-and-dime people to death.*
nick.el.o.de.on (nick.uh.LOH.dee.un) n. **1** an early type of jukebox operated with a nickel. **2** an early movie theater that charged a nickel for admission.
nickel silver same as GERMAN SILVER.
nick.er n. & v. neigh.
nick.name n. a familiar name given to a person or place, either a descriptive term, as "Tricky Dick," "Winter playground," etc. or a pet name, as "Lizzie." —v. **-names, -named, -nam.ing:** *a president nicknamed "Old Hickory."*
nic.o.tine (NICK.uh.teen) n. a poisonous alkaloid found in tobacco.
nic.o.tin.ic acid (nick.uh.TIN.ic-) n. a vitamin of the B group, used against pellagra.
niece (NEECE) n. the daughter of one's brother, sister, brother-in-law, or sister-in-law.
nif.ty (NIF.tee) adj. **-ti.er, -ti.est** *Informal.* smart or stylish: *a nifty feature, hairstyle, pair of gloves; nifty leisure-time activities; nifty new gadgets, products.*
Ni.ge.ri.an (nye.JEER.ee.un) n. & adj. (a person) of or from **Nigeria,** a republic of W. Africa.
nig.gard (NIG.urd) n. a stingy person. —**nig.gard.ly** adj. stingy: *a niggardly giver; niggardly praise; Our teacher is never niggardly in her praise of good students.* —**nig.gard.li.ness** n.
nig.ger (NIG.ur) n. **1** [offensive except in bona fide black use] a Negro. **2** a member of an underprivileged group of society.
nig.gle (NIG.ul) v. **nig.gles, nig.gled, nig.gling** work fussily; be finicky: *Lou tends to niggle about or over trivial things;* **adj.:** *niggling* (= trifling or petty) *annoyances, faults, problems.*
nigh adj. & adv. near: *a nigh fantastical tale; The time drew nigh; The end was nigh; She was **nigh unto** death; The job is **well nigh*** (=nearly or almost) *finished; It seemed well nigh impossible.* —**prep.** [old use] near: *the nigh horse.*

night (NITE) n. **1** the period from dusk to dawn when it is dark: *dark, restless, sleepless, starlit, stormy nights; a weird sound in the dead of (the) night; the opening night of a play; a wedding night; The lights went out on the night of October 31; He wished me good night and went to a late night movie; We don't watch movies late **at night**; Some people have to work **nights*** (= at night); *San Francisco **by night*** (= during the night) *is more colorful than by day.* **2** darkness of night; also, a period of gloom or unhappiness: *the dark night of the soul.*
night blindness n. inability of the eye to adjust to faint light.
night.cap n. **1** a cap worn with night clothes. **2** *Informal.* an alcoholic drink taken at bedtime: *to have a nightcap.* **3** *Informal.* the second game of a doubleheader.
night clothes n.pl. clothes such as pajamas for wearing while in bed.
night.club n. a place of night-time entertainment that serves food and liquor with music and dancing.
night crawler n. a large earthworm.
night.dress same as NIGHTGOWN.
night.fall (NITE.fall) n. the coming of night; dusk: *The stars appear at nightfall.*
night.gown (rhyme: down) n. a loose, light garment that a woman or girl wears in bed.
night.hawk n. a bird related to the whippoorwill that feeds on flying insects at dusk and dawn.
night.ie (NYE.tee) n. *Informal.* a nightgown.
night life n. pleasure-seeking activity at night, esp. in nightclubs.
night.ly (NITE.lee) adj. **1** at or by night: *his nightly journey;* **adv:** *a bird that is seen nightly; a comic who appears nightly.* **2** every night: *our nightly walk; the nightly news;* **adv.:** *We pray nightly.*
night.mare n. **1** a distressing dream. **2** a frightening experience. —**night.mar.ish** adj.: *a nightmarish experience; nightmarish images, qualities.*
night owl n. *Informal.* one who stays up at night.
night.rid.er (NITE.rye.dur) n. a member of a mounted gang committing acts of violence by night.
night.shade n. a family of poisonous tropical plants such as jimsonweed, belladonna, and bittersweet as well as useful ones such as potato, tomato, tobacco, and eggplant.
night.shift n. **1** the people assigned to work during the night, as in a factory.

nightshirt / nitrify

2 the period: *to work (on) the nightshift.*
night.shirt *n.* a long, loose shirt that gave way to pajamas early in the 20th century.
night.soil *n.* human waste used as fertilizer.
night.spot *n. Informal.* nightclub.
night.stand *n.* a small bedside table; also **night table.**
night.stick *n.* a policeman's club.
night.time *n.* the period of darkness from dusk to dawn.
night.walk.er (NITE.walk.er) *n.* one who goes out at night as a thief, prostitute, etc.
night.wear same as NIGHT CLOTHES.
ni.hil.ism (NYE.uh.liz.um) *n.* in politics, philosophy, etc., the rejection of all traditional and existing beliefs, practices, institutions, etc.; **ni.hil.ist** *n. & adj.* —**ni.hil.is.tic** (-LIS.tic) *adj.*
-nik *n. suffix.* one devoted to what is specified: *beatnik, computernik, nogoodnik, peacenik; sputnik* (= "travel companion").
nil *n.* nothing: *Your chances of visiting the moon are practically nil; almost, virtually nil.*
nim.ble (NIM.bul) *adj.* light and quick: *a young dancer's nimble feet; the nimble fingers of a piano player; a nimble mind, wit.* —**nim.ble.ness** *n.* —**nim.bly** *adv.*
NIM.BY or **Nim.by** (NIM.bee) *n.* **NIM.BYS** or **Nim.bys** [short form] **1** the "not in my backyard" objection to something one doesn't like (such as a landfill site) being established close to where one lives. **2** such a person. —**nim.by.ism** *n.*
nim.bus *n., pl.* **-bi** (-bye) or **-bus.es 1** a dark-gray rain cloud. **2** a disk-shaped halo; a circle of radiant light.
nim.rod *n.* a hunter.
nin.com.poop (NINK.um.poop) *n.* a foolish or silly person.
nine *n., adj. & pron.* one more than eight; the number 9 or IX. —**to the nines** elaborately; to perfection: *dressed to the nines.* —**ninth** (NINETH) *n., adj. & adv.*
nine.pins *n.pl.* a bowling game using nine instead of 10 pins.
nine.teen (NINE.TEEN) *n., adj. & pron.* one more than 18; the number 19 or XIX; **nine.teenth** *n. & adj.*
nine-to-five or **9 to 5** *adj.* from 9 a.m. to 5 p.m.: *a nine-to-five job, operation, routine; the nine-to-five grind, rat race.* —**nine-to-fiv.er** *n.*
nine.ty (NINE.tee) *n., adj. & pron.* **-ties 1** nine times 10; 90 or XC. **2 the nineties** numbers, years, etc. from 90 through 99. —**nine.ti.eth** (-tee.ith) *n. & adj.*
nin.ny (NIN.ee) *n.* **nin.nies** fool.
ninth See NINE.
ni.o.bi.um (nye.OH.bee.um) *n.* a soft, gray, metallic element.
nip *v.* **nips, nipped, nip.ping 1** to pinch or bite, as a crab with its claws: *A gardener nips off shoots to check growth; a dog nipping at a stranger's pants.* **2** blight or destroy, as by frost: *Trouble was brewing, but the principal **nipped it in the bud** by effective action.* **3** drink liquor in nips or sips. **4** *Informal.* enter quickly: *The child was hurt while nipping in and out of traffic handing out flyers.* —*n.* **1** a pinch or bite; also, a bit. **2** a biting cold: *the nip of a wintry night.* **3** pungent flavor or tang, as of cheese. **4** a sip of liquor: *a nip of sherry.*
nip and tuck *Informal.* **1** *adv.* neck and neck; closely matched. **2** *n.* cosmetic surgery.
nip.per (NIP.ur) *n.* **1** one that nips, as the claw of a crab. **2** *Informal.* a little boy: *a cute little nipper with rosy cheeks.* **3 nippers** *pl.* pliers, pincers, etc.
nip.ple (NIP.ul) *n.* **1** a small projection on a breast or udder through which milk is drawn; teat. **2** a teatlike part, as on a nursing bottle.
nip.py (NIP.ee) *adj.* **nip.pi.er, nip.pi.est** sharp or biting: *nippy cheese, fall weather.*
nir.va.na (nur.VAH.nuh, -VAN.uh) *n.* in Buddhism, the state of supreme bliss.
Ni.sei (NEE.say) *n. sing. & pl.* one born in North America of Japanese immigrant parents.
ni.si (NYE.sye) *adj. Law.* of a decree or order, not absolute or final.
nit *n.* the egg or young of a louse or similar insect.
nite [popular spelling] same as NIGHT.
ni.ter (NYE.tur) *n.* a nitrate used in making gunpowder or as fertilizer.
nit.pick.ing or **nit-pick.ing** *n.* (NIT.pick.ing) *n.* fault-finding in a petty manner: *mere nitpicking; adj.: nitpicking criticisms, issues, rules.* Also *v.* **nit.pick, nit.picks, nit.picked, nit.pick.ing.** —**nit.pick.er** *n.*
ni.trate (NYE.trate) *n.* a salt or ester of nitric acid.
ni.tre (NYE.tur) *Cdn.* NITER.
ni.tric acid (NYE.tric-) *n.* a strong, nitrogen-containing acid used in making explosives, fertilizers, and drugs.
ni.tri.fy (NYE.truh.fye) *v.* **-fies, -fied, -fy.ing 1** treat with nitrogen or a ni-

trogen compound. **2** produce nitrates, nitrites, etc. by bacterial action. —**ni.tri.fi.ca.tion** (-fuh.CAY.shun) *n.*
ni.trite(NYE.trite) *n.* a salt or ester of nitrous acid.
ni.tro (NYE.troh) *n. Informal.* nitroglycerine.
ni.tro.cel.lu.lose (nye.troh.SEL.yuh.lohs) *n.* a highly flammable ester of cellulose; guncotton.
ni.tro.gen (NYE.truh.jun) *n.* a colorless, odorless gas that makes up four fifths of the atmosphere. —**ni.trog.e.nous** (nye.TROJ.uh.nus) *adj.*
ni.tro.glyc.er.ine or **ni.tro.glyc.er.in** (nye.troh.GLIS.uh.rin) *n.* a heavy, oily, explosive liquid used in dynamite, rocket propellants, and to dilate blood vessels for easing cardiac pain.
nitrous oxide (NYE.trus-) *n.* a gas that is sweetish in odor, used as an anesthetic; laughing gas.
nit.ty-grit.ty (NIT.ee.GRIT.ee) *n. Informal.* the basic facts of a situation, problem, etc.: *when you get down to the nitty-gritty; the nitty-gritty of details.*
nit.wit *n.* an idiot.
nix *v. Informal.* say "No" to something. —*adv. & interj.* no; stop!
no (NOH) *adv.* [used to deny, refuse, etc.]: *Do you want it, yes or no? No, I don't! That is no small job.* —*adj.*: *He works for no pay; That's no* (= not any) *job for me.* —*n., pl.* **nos** or **noes 1** a refusal or denial: *a flat no.* **2** a negative vote or voter: *The nos (not ayes) have it.* **3** *sing. & pl.* the oldest type of Japanese classical drama, performed by masked actors using music and dancing, accompanied by a chorus; also **Noh.**
No.bel.ist (noh.BEL.ist) *n.* a Nobel-prize winner.
no.be.li.um (noh.BEE.lee.um) *n.* a synthetic radioactive chemical element.
No.bel prize (noh.BEL-) *n.* any of the six annual international awards for achievements in physics, chemistry, physiology or medicine, literature, peace, and economics, the first five founded by Alfred **Nobel** (1833-96), a Swedish chemist: *Economist James Buchanan won the Nobel in 1986;* **adja.**: *a Nobel award; the Nobel committee; Nobel laureates; the Nobel Peace Prize.*
no.bil.i.ty (noh.BIL.i.tee) *n.* **-ties 1** the state of being noble or high in social rank. **2** nobles as a class.
no.ble (NOH.bul) *adj.* **no.bler, no.blest 1** famous or excellent: *a woman of noble birth; a noble deed, family, gesture, sentiment; a noble* (= lofty) *edifice.* **2** chemi-

cally stable; unaffected by oxygen: *helium, neon, and such noble* (= inert) *gases; Gold and silver are noble* (= precious) *metals.* —*n.* a person of noble birth or rank. —**no.ble.ness** *n.* —**no.bly** (-blee) *adv.*
no.ble.man (NOH.bul.mun) *n.* **-men** a peer.
no.blesse o.blige (noh.BLES.oh. BLEEZH) *n.* the moral obligation implied by the maxim, "Noble birth obliges one to be noble in conduct and behavior."
no.ble.wom.an (NOH.bul.woom.un) *n.* **-wom.en** a peeress.
no.bod.y (NOH.bud.ee, -bod.ee) *pron.* no one. —*n., pl.* **-bod.ies** a person of no importance.
no-brainer *n.* something that requires little intelligence to understand or operate.
nock *n.* a notch, as at either end of a bow where the bowstring is tied or that of the arrow where it fits over the bowstring. —*v.* fit an arrow over the bowstring for shooting.
noc.tur.nal (noc.TUR.nul) *adj.* of or during the night: *nocturnal creatures, imaginings, visits; A* **nocturnal animal** *such as a bat or owl is active at night; childhood memories of nocturnal bed-wetting;* **nocturnal emission** (= wet dream). —**noc.tur.nal.ly** *adv.*
noc.turne (NOC.turn) *n.* a form of dreamy or romantic musical composition, esp. for the piano.
noc.u.ous (NOK.yoo.us) *adj.* harmful; damaging; **noc.u.ous.ly** *adv.*
nod *v.* **nods, nod.ded, nod.ding** bend the head downward briefly, as in greeting an acquaintance, to indicate agreement, or when sleepy: *She nodded to the class when she entered the room; He nodded assent; flowers nodding in the wind; I nodded off* (= fell sleep) *in front of the TV; "Even Homer sometimes nods"* (= makes mistakes). —*n.* a nodding of the head: *A project gets or is given* **the nod** (= permission to go ahead with it).
nod.dy *n.* **nod.dies** a tropical tern with a rounded tail.
node *n.* **1** a knot or joint, as the points along a stem from which leaves grow. **2** a receiving or transmitting terminal where several branches of a computer network come together. —**nod.al** (NOH.dul) *adj.*
nod.ule (NOJ.ool) *n.* a small knob, lump, or swelling. —**nod.u.lar** (NOJ.uh.lur) *adj.*
No.el or **No.ël** (noh.EL) *n.* **1** Christmas. **2** noel or noël a Christmas song or

carol.

no-fault *adj.* involving no fixing of blame: *no-fault auto insurance, benefits, coverage, divorce, laws.* —*n.* a no-fault system: *Lawyers may be the main losers under no-fault.*

no-frills *adj.* of a service or product, without nonessential features that add to cost: *a no-frills air fare, government, grocery store, operation, service; the no-frills approach.*

nog *n.* an alcoholic eggnog.

nog.gin (NOG.in) *n.* **1** a small cup or mug of liquor, originally ¼ pint. **2** *Informal.* one's head: *The retort was like a knock on the noggin.*

no-good *n. & adj. Informal.* worthless person or thing.

Noh same as NO, *n.* 3.

no-hitter *n.* a baseball game in which a pitcher allows the opposing team no base hits.

no.how (NOH.how) *adv. Informal.* in no way.

noise *n.* a harsh, disagreeable, or unwanted sound: *the noise of a city street; Traffic makes* or *produces noise; Walls reduce* or *cut down on the noise; deafening, loud, shrill noises; I'd like to go to bed when the noise abates* or *dies down; animal noises and barbaric behavior at hockey games; static noise in radio reception; "snow" caused by noise* (= unwanted signals) *in TV equipment.* —*v.* **nois.es, noised, nois.ing** spread *about* or *abroad,* as a story or report by rumor. —**noise.less** *adj.*; **noise.less.ly** *adv.*

noise.mak.er (NOIS.may.kur) *n.* a horn or similar device used to make noise at a party.

noise pollution *n.* pollution of the environment by noise from airports, automobiles, industry, etc.

noi.some (NOY.sum) *adj.* foul-smelling or harmful: *a noisome odor.*

nois.y (NOY.zee) *adj.* **nois.i.er, -i.est** causing noise: *Rock music is loud to some, noisy to others; noisy neighbors; a noisy quarrel.* —**nois.i.ly** *adv.*; **nois.i.ness** *n.*

nol.le pros.e.qui (NOL.ee.PROS.uh.kwye) *n. Law.* a prosecutor's notice of "not proceeding further with the suit."

no-load *n.* a mutual fund that charges no commission on sales.

no.lo con.ten.de.re (NOH.loh.cun.TEN.duh.ree) *n. Law.* declaration of no defense but without admitting guilt; "no contest."

no.mad (NOH.mad) *n.* a member of a people such as Bedouins and Gypsies with no settled home but wandering about from place to place; *adj.:* *a nomad tribe; nomad ants, camps, sailors.* —**no.mad.ic** (noh.MAD.ic) *adj.:* *nomadic clans, herdsmen, people, tribes; their nomadic life, pastoralism; a nomadic lot.*

no man's land *n.* **1** an area or scope of activity that is indefinite or ambiguous. **2** land separating opposing armies.

nom de guerre (nom.duh.GAIR) *n.* French, *pl.* **noms de guerre** pseudonym.

nom de plume (nom.duh.PLOOM) *n., pl.* **noms de plume** (nom.duh-) a pen name used by a writer.

no.men.cla.ture (NOH.mun.clay.chur) *n.* a naming system: *the binomial nomenclature used in biology, as "Felis domestica" for "cat."*

nom.i.nal (NOM.uh.nul) *adj.* in name only; hence, slight or negligible: *a nominal amount, leader, salary;* **nom.i.nal.ly** *adv.*

nom.i.nate (NOM.uh.nate) *v.* **-nates, -nat.ed, -nat.ing** name, often appoint, to an office or position: *He was nominated but not elected; to be nominated for the mayoralty; She was nominated as* or *to be the executor of the estate.*
—**nom.i.na.tion** (-NAY.shun) *n.:* *Mimi's name was put in nomination for mayor; to accept, reject a nomination.*
—**nom.i.na.tor** (-nay.tur) *n.*

nom.i.na.tive (NOM.uh.nuh.tiv) *adj.* naming the subject of a verb: *"He" is the nominative case of "him."* —*n.* a nominative word or its grammatical case: *"He" is in the nominative.*

nom.i.nee (nom.uh.NEE) *n.* a nominated person.

non- [a prefix freely added, usu. without a hyphen except before capitalized words, to adjectives and adverbs to mean "not" and to nouns to mean "not a," "opposite of," or "lack of." The basic meaning and pronunciation of such compounds are usu. the same as in the base word. The more unusual compounds are entered and explained below].

non.a.chiev.er (non.uh.CHEE.vur) *n.* one who does not succeed as expected, esp. a student who does not get passing grades.

non.age (NON.ij, NOH.nij) *n.* **1** the period of being legally a minor. **2** the period before maturity; immaturity.

non.a.ge.nar.i.an (non.uh.juh.NAIR.ee.un) *n. & adj.* (a person) aged 90 to 99.

non.a.ligned (non.uh.LINED) *adj.* in international politics, neutral: *a non-*

aligned nation. —**non.a.lign.ment** (-LINE.munt) *n.*

no-name *n.* a person or thing that has no name or is undistinguished; generic: *He was a no-name before joining the Blue Jays;* *adj.*: *a no-name brand of gasoline; cheap no-name products.*

nonce usu. **for the nonce**, for the time being.

nonce word *n.* a word made up for the occasion, as "Anglo-saxophone," "Coca-colonize," or "nowhereness": *Many nonce words gain currency, as "O.K." did.*

non.cha.lant (NON.shuh.lunt, -shuh.LAHNT) *adj.* coolly indifferent; unconcerned; **non.cha.lant.ly** *adv.* —**non.cha.lance** (-lunce, -LAHNCE) *n.*

non.com *n.* [short form] noncommissioned officer.

non.com.bat.ant (non.com.BAT.unt, -COM.buh.tunt) *n. & adj.* (a nurse, chaplain, or civilian) not taking part in actual combat.

non.com.mis.sioned officer (non.cuh.MISH.und-) *n.* in the armed forces, an enlisted man of the ranks of corporal through sergeant major.

non.com.mit.tal (non.cuh.MIT.ul) *adj.* not committing oneself: *"We will see" is his usual noncommittal reply.*

non com.pos men.tis (non.COM.pus.MEN.tis) *adj. Latin.* not of sound mind.

non.con.duc.tor (non.cun.DUC.tur) *n.* a substance that does not conduct heat, electricity, or sound; insulator.

non.con.form.ist (non.cun.FOR.mist) *n.* **1** one who does not conform to prevailing attitudes or behavior. **2 Nonconformist** in the 1600s, one who refused to conform to the Church of England. —**non.con.form.i.ty** (-mi.tee) *n.*

non.co.op.er.a.tion (NON.coh.op.uh.RAY.shun) *n.* refusal to cooperate, esp. as civil disobedience.

non.cred.it (non.CRED.it) *adja.* not having academic credit, as toward a degree: *a noncredit course.*

non.dair.y (non.DAIR.ee) *adja.* not made with milk or milk products: *a nondairy coffee creamer.*

non.de.script (NON.duh.script) *adj.* not easily described, being not distinctive. —*n.* such a person or thing.

non.drink.er (NON.drink.ur) *n.* one who does not use alcoholic beverages.

none (NUN) *pron.* no one: *None of them is* or *are here; She wants none but the best; That was none other than Joe; "None so deaf as those who will not hear."*

—*adv.* not at all: *Because of new taxes, I'm none the richer for the pay raise.*

non.en.ti.ty (non.EN.ti.tee) *n.* **-ties** **1** one, esp. a person, of little importance. **2** something that has no real existence.

none.such (NUN.such) *n. & adj.* (a person or thing) that is unequaled or unique.

none.the.less (nun.the.LESS) *adj.* nevertheless; however.

non.e.vent (non.i.VENT) *n.* an event that is made too much of, esp. when it does not take place as predicted.

non.fat *adj.* of foods, not fatty: *nonfat buttermilk, dressings, milk, yogurt; nonfat dairy products, protein supplements.*

non.fic.tion (non.FIC.shun) *n.* writings such as history, biography, and essays.

non.he.ro (non.HEER.oh) same as ANTIHERO.

non.in.ter.laced (non.IN.tur.laced) *adj.* having the odd- and even-numbered lines of a transmitted picture refreshed at once, which results in little flicker on the screen: *a noninterlaced display, monitor, signal, video.*

non.in.ter.ven.tion (NON.in.tur.VEN.shun) *n.* avoidance of intervention, esp. in the affairs of another nation or in another jurisdiction.

non.met.al (non.MET.ul) *n.* an element such as a gas, bromine, sulfur, etc. that does not have metallic qualities. —**non.me.tal.lic** (-muh.TAL.ic) *adj.*: *the nonmetallic luster of quartz.*

no-no *n. Informal.* something forbidden, esp. as not good for one: *Chewing gum is a no-no in most churches.*

no-nonsense *adj.* practical and businesslike: *a no-nonsense approach, manager, voice; Her appearance and manner are strictly no-nonsense.*

non.pa.reil (non.puh.REL) *n. & adj.* (person or thing) that is unequalled or peerless.

non.par.ti.san (non.PAR.tuh.zun, -zan) *adj.* not partisan, esp. in regard to political parties.

non.per.son (NON.pur.sun) *n.* one who is considered as not existing or as rejected, unperson: *Stalin became a nonperson after his death.*

non.plus (NON.plus, non.PLUS) *v.* **-plus.ses** or **-plus.es, -plussed** or **-plused, -plus.sing** or **-plus.ing** perplex or puzzle utterly or hopelessly.

non.pre.scrip.tion (non.pri.SCRIP.shun) *adj.* available without a doctor's prescription: *nonprescription drugs, products, sunglasses.*

non.prof.it (non.PROF.it) *adj.* not run

nonproliferation / normal

for profit, as cultural foundations, the Red Cross, etc.: *a nonprofit group, organization, society.*

non.pro.lif.er.a.tion (NON.pruh.lif.uh.RAY.shun) *n.* the stoppage of the spread of nuclear weapons: *a nonproliferation treaty.*

non.res.i.dent (non.REZ.uh.dunt) *n.* a person living elsewhere, not where doing business, working, going to school, etc.; *adj.: a nonresident alien, citizen, corporation, investor, employer, member, student; nonresident earnings, purchases, tax returns, tuition, etc. (that have to do with nonresidents).*

non.re.sist.ant (non.ri.ZIS.tunt) *n. & adj.* (a person) who submits passively to unjust authority or force; **non.re.sist.ance** *n.*

non.re.stric.tive (non.ri.STRIC.tiv) *adj.* not grammatically restrictive: *a nonrestrictive clause.*

non.rig.id (non.RIJ.id) *adj.* not rigid, esp. of airships that remain in shape by gas pressure; **non.ri.gid.i.ty** (-ri.JID.i.tee) *n.*

non.sched.uled (non.SKEJ.oold) *adj.* not serving a particular route or following a regular timetable: *a nonscheduled airline, charter, flight.*

non.sec.tar.i.an (non.sec.TAIR.ee.un) *adj.* not restricted to a particular religion.

non.sense *n.* something that makes no sense or is worthless or stupid: *What nonsense to say I stole your purse; He always speaks* or *talks nonsense after a couple of drinks; complete, outright, perfect, pure, sheer, utter nonsense; No one has to put up with* or *tolerate that kind of nonsense;* *adja.: a nonsense syllable (without sense associations); the nonsense verses of "Jabberwocky."* —**non.sen.si.cal** (non.SEN.si.cul) *adj.*

non se.qui.tur (non.SEK.wuh.tur) *n.* an inference or observation that does not logically follow from what was said before it.

non.skid (NON.SKID) *adj.* that resists skidding: *a nonskid floor, sole, surface.*

non.start.er (NON.STAR.tur) *n.* an idea, move, proposal, etc. that is not likely to be effective or successful.

non.stick *adja.* not allowing food to stick: *a nonstick coating of Teflon; a nonstick frying pan, surface.*

non.stop *adj.* that goes without stopping: *a nonstop flight to Paris;* **adv.:** *In 1986, the "Voyageur" aircraft flew nonstop around the world without refueling.*

non.sup.port (non.suh.PORT) *n.* failure to provide for one's legal dependent.

non-U (NON.YOO) *adj. Informal.* not upper-class.

non.un.ion (non.YOON.yun) *adj.* not made by, belonging to, or recognizing a labor union: *a nonunion company, job, worker.*

non.vi.o.lence (non.VYE.uh.lunce) *n.* avoidance of the use of force, as in civil rights movements. —**non.vi.o.lent** *adj.*

noo.dle (NOO.dul) *n.* **1** a flour paste, usu. made with egg, in ribbon form. **2** a simpleton. **3** *Informal.* the head.

nook (short "oo") *n.* a secluded corner or spot: *a breakfast nook in the kitchen; a cozy nook in a library; She looked in* ***every nook and cranny*** (= everywhere).

noon *n. & adj.* 12 o'clock in the daytime; midday: *at high noon on a hot July day.* Also **noon.day, noon.time;** **noon.tide** [old use].

no one *pron.* nobody; no person: *No one knows what will happen tomorrow; No one believed men would land on the moon in 1969; She reports to no one but the president.*

noose *n.* a loop made in a rope with a slipknot that tightens as the free end is pulled: *They voted against* **the noose** (= death by hanging). —*v.* **noos.es, noosed, noos.ing** catch or snare in a noose.

no-par *adj.* having no nominal or par value, only a market value: *no-par stocks.*

nope *adv. Informal.* no.

nor *conj.* [used after a negative, esp. "neither" or "not"] and not; and not either: *Neither Joe nor Jan was there; They will not eat, nor will they drink anything.*

Nor.dic (NOR.dic) **1** *adj.* of the Northern European countries, esp. Scandinavian: *Nordic features are blue eyes, blond hair, tall stature, and elongated head; She looks Nordic.* **2** *adja.* having to do with ski jumping and cross-country skiing: *Nordic equipment, events, skiing.*

nor'east.er (nor.EES.tur) *n.* same as NORTHEASTER.

no-return *adja.* not to be returned for refund of deposit: *a no-return bottle.*

norm *n.* **1** a standard or model for a group to follow: *to establish* or *set a norm for children to follow; the norms of society.* **2** a group's average performance as a measuring standard.

nor.mal (NOR.mul) *adj.* standard or usual: *Frost is normal in wintertime; a man of normal intelligence; It's perfectly normal for adults to cry at times; "Loves her he" is not the normal word order in*

normalcy / nose

English. —*n.* a condition, level, amount, etc. that is normal: *Ten degrees Celsius is above (the) normal for this time of year; Business is returning to normal after the recession.* —**nor.mal.ly** *adv.* —**nor.mal.i.ty** (nor.MAL.i.tee) *n.*

nor.mal.cy (NOR.mul.see) *n.* the condition of being normal: *the return to normalcy after a war.*

nor.mal.ize (NOR.muh.lize) *v.* **-iz.es, -ized, -iz.ing** make normal: *to normalize relations.* —**nor.mal.i.za.tion** (-luh.ZAY.shun, -lye-) *n.*

Nor.man (NOR.mun) *n.* **1** a member of an originally Viking group from **Normandy,** a region of N.W. France, which conquered England in 1066: *the Norman Conquest.* **2** a person of or from Normandy.

norm.a.tive (NOR.muh.tiv) *adj.* setting a norm or standard: *a normative influence, grammar, principle.*

Norse *n. & adj.* (the people or the language) of Norway or of ancient Scandinavia; Norwegian.

Norse.man (NORS.mun) *n.* **-men** a Scandinavian of ancient times.

north ("th" as in "thin") *n.* the direction to the left of one facing the east or rising sun, to which a compass needle points: *The magnetic North Pole lies close to the geographic north or true north; Canada is north of the U.S.* —**the North 1** the northern U.S. comprising the states north of Maryland, the Ohio River, and Missouri. **2** the northern part of Canada, esp. the Territories. —*adj.* **1** toward the north: *The north magnetic pole is near Bathurst Island, N.W.T.* **2** from the north: *a north wind.* —*adv.*: *People from the south go up north in the summer; to drive, fly, sail, turn, walk north.*

North American *n. & adj.* (a person) of or from the northern continent of the Western Hemisphere, from Greenland to Panama, including also the West Indies.

north.east (north.EEST) *n.* (a region in or toward) the direction midway between N. and E. —*adj. & adv.* from, in, or toward the northeast.

north.east.er (north.EES.tur) *n.* a wind or storm from the northeast; also **nor'easter.** —**north.east.er.ly** *adj. & adv.* —**north.east.ern** *adj.* —**north.east.ward** (-wurd) *adj. & adv.;* also **north.east.wards** (-wurds) *adv.*

north.er ("th" as in "the") *n.* a strong north wind or storm, esp. a winter wind over Texas and the Gulf of Mexico.

north.er.ly (NOR.thur.lee, "th" as in "the") *adj.* **1** from the north: *a cold northerly wind.* **2** toward the north: *Inuvik, NWT, is Canada's most northerly town; adv.: The truck was proceeding northerly on Main Street when hit by the bike.* —*n.* **1** a northerly wind. **2** same as NORTHER.

north.ern (NORTH.urn, "TH" as in "the") *adj.* **1** of, from, in, or toward the north. **2 Northern** of the North. —**north.ern.er** *n.* —**north.ern.most** *adj.*

northern lights same as AURORA BOREALIS.

North.man (NORTH.mun) *n.* **-men** Norseman.

North Star *n.* a bright star that appears fixed in the sky with other stars rotating around it.

north.ward (NORTH.wurd) *adj. & adv.* toward the north. Also **north.wards** *adv.*

north.west (north.WEST) *n.* **1** a region in or toward the direction midway between north and west. **2 the Northwest** in the U.S., the region consisting of the states of Washington, Oregon, and Idaho. —*adj. & adv.* from, in, or toward the northwest. —**north.west.er.ly** *adj. & adv.* —**north.west.ern** *adj.* —**north.west.ward** *adj. & adv.;* **north.west.wards** *adv.*

north.west.er (north.WES.tur) *n.* **1** a northwest wind or storm; also **nor'wester.** **2 Northwester** a native of the Northwest. —**north.west.er.ly** *adj.*

Northwest Passage *n.* an Arctic route linking the Atlantic and the Pacific through the waters north of the Canadian mainland.

Nor.we.gian (nor.WEE.jun) *adj.* having to do with **Norway,** a country of N. Europe. —*n.* a person of or from Norway or the Scandinavian language spoken there.

nor'west.er (nor.WES.tur) same as NORTHWESTER.

nose (NOZE) *n.* **1** the breathing and smelling organ with two openings forming part of the face just above the mouth: *to blow, pick, wipe one's nose; to tweak someone's nose; aquiline, bloody, bulbous, running or runny noses; to* ***follow one's nose*** (= go straight forward). **2** the sense of smell: *Dogs have good noses; a reporter's nose for news.* **3** the projecting front part of a ship, plane, etc. —**count noses** count those present. —**cut off one's nose to spite one's face** take action that harms one's own interests. —**hold one's nose** get ready to do something unpleasant: *Just hold your nose and vote for them.* —**lead by the nose** control someone completely. —**on the nose** *Informal.* precisely. —**pay through the nose** pay too much for a product or service. —**thumb one's nose at** to defy someone. —**turn up one's nose at** treat something with scorn; also, sneer at someone. —**under one's nose** in plain view. —*v.* **nos.es, nosed, nos.ing 1** smell out, as a dog: *Dogs nose out mice.* **2** discover as if by smelling: *a scandal nosed out by a reporter.* **3** nuzzle: *She nosed the blanket closer.* **4** push something off, one's way into, etc. with a forward part, as a bulldozer: *homeowners nosed out by developers.* **5** search or pry into someone's affairs: *a committee nosing around on what took place.* —**nose out** defeat one's opponent by a narrow margin.

nose.bleed *n.* a bleeding from the nose.
nose cone *n.* the cone-shaped front section of a rocket or missile.
nose dive *n.* **1** a swift downward plunge of an airplane, kite, etc. **2** a sudden drop in price: *Prices went into* or *took a nose dive; the economy's nose dive into recession.* —*v.* **nose-dive, -dives, -dived, -div.ing**: *The Dow Jones index nose-dived 200 points yesterday; The party's popularity had nose-dived just before the election was called; adj.a.: nose-diving grades, profits, stocks.*
nose.drops *n.pl.* medication for dropping into the nose.
nose.gay *n.* a bouquet.
nose job *n.* a purely cosmetic job like changing the shape of a nose by surgery.
nose.piece *n.* something that goes over the nose or that is like a nose in position, as the rotating piece holding the objective lenses of a microscope.
nosey same as NOSY.
nosh *n. Informal.* a snack: *We asked them in for a nosh and a chat.*
no-show *n.* a not showing up as expected without a previous cancellation; also, such a person: *Jack's absence wasn't really a no-show because his letter was in the mail; adj.a.: no-show employees, jobs, managers, passengers.*
nos.ing (NOH.zing) *n.* a projecting part or edge.
nos.tal.gia (nos.TAL.juh) *n.* a sentimental interest in a former period or condition; **nos.tal.gic** *adj.*
nos.tril *n.* either of the openings of the nose.

nos.trum *n.* a cure-all offered by a quack.
nos.y or **nos.ey** (NOH.zee) *adj.* **nos.i.er, -i.est** *Informal.* prying or inquisitive: *to be nosy about what's going on in someone's backyard; nosey neighbors.* —**nos.i.ly** *adv.;* **nos.i.ness** *n.*
not *adv.* [negative in function]: *Black is not white; Tell him not to worry; It may not rain – I hope not; She's **not at all** (= certainly not) my kind of woman.*
no.ta be.ne (NOH.tuh.BEE.nee) *Latin.* note well.
no.ta.ble (NOH.tuh.bul) *adj.* noteworthy or distinguished: *a notable contribution to science; a notable event; a notable figure.* —*n.* a notable person: *celebrities and other notables; industry, political, wine notables.* —**no.ta.bly** *adv.* —**no.ta.bil.i.ty** (-BIL.i.tee) *n.*
no.ta.rize (NOH.tuh.rize) *v.* **-riz.es, -rized, -riz.ing** certify a document, as a lawyer or notary does: *Affidavits have to be notarized; adj.: a notarized document.*
no.ta.ry (NOH.tuh.ree) *n.* **-ries** a person legally authorized to certify documents, take oaths, etc.; also **notary public.**
no.ta.tion (noh.TAY.shun) *n.* **1** a noting down or what is noted down; annotation. **2** a method or system of representing words, quantities, and such technical data using signs and symbols, as in mathematics and music. —**no.ta.tion.al** *adj.*
notch *n.* **1** a V-shaped cut on an edge or surface, as on a stick to keep a tally. **2** anything resembling it, as a narrow mountain defile or the angle formed by a coat's collar with the lapel. —*v.* make a notch: *to notch up (= score) a gain, victory, win; adj: a notched collar, edge, lapel.*
note *n.* **1** what is jotted down, esp. a short letter or memorandum: *to address, deliver, drop, send someone a note; a diplomatic note; protest notes; to take notes during a lecture; to compare notes with colleagues on a project.* **2** observation or notice: *to make a note of the license plate of a car; a mental note; No one seemed to take note of (= pay attention to) her.* **3** a piece of paper money: *a pound note.* **4** a bank note or promissory note: *a demand note; treasury notes; when a note matures.* **5** a musical tone or sound: *to hit* or *strike the high notes of a song; the notes of a trumpet.* **6** an expression with a certain signification: *the note of triumph in her voice; festive, fresh, jarring, optimistic, pessimistic, sour,*

triumphant notes. **7** distinction: *men of note; a woman of note in public life.*
—*v.* **notes, not.ed, not.ing** make a note of something: *Please note down what I say; I noted how she spells her name; She noted that I am good at spelling; Did you note the color of her hair?*

note.book *n.* a book to make notes in: *loose-leaf, school, spiral notebooks;* **adj.a.**: *notes made on notebook paper; A* **notebook computer** *is the size of a notebook, about 10 x 12 x 2 in., weighing around 5 lb.*

noted (NOH.tid) *adj.* widely known: *a noted surgeon; noted for heart transplants.*

note.wor.thy (NOTE.wur.thee, "th" as in "the") *adj.* remarkable or impressive: *a noteworthy accomplishment.*

noth.ing (NUTH.ing, "TH" as in "thin") *pron.* no thing; not any thing: *There's nothing in his pocket; We've nothing to lose and everything to gain by trying; The watch is good for nothing* (= worthless); *You can have it* **for nothing** (= for free); *Pat means nothing* (= is not important) *to me; a student who is* **nothing if not** *ambitious* (= who is quite ambitious).
—*n.* **1** something that does not exist; zero: *Something cannot come out of nothing.* **2** a person or thing of no consequence: *little nothings; They exchanged a few polite nothings; whispering sweet nothings in her ear.* —*adv.* not at all: *That is nothing remarkable; He went ahead nothing daunted by reverses.* —**nothing doing** *Informal.* definitely not! —**in nothing flat** *Informal.* in no time at all; very fast. —**think nothing of** consider something as easy to achieve or as unimportant.

noth.ing.ness (NUTH.ing.nis) *n.* nonexistence: *into the depths of nothingness; to pass or sink into nothingness.*

no.tice (NOH.tis) *n.* **1** warning or notification: *He was fired with a month's notice in writing; She was put on notice that her work was not satisfactory; He gave us notice to move; We had to leave the place at or on short notice; No more classes until further notice; She* **served notice** *on her boss that she was quitting.* **2** attention: *facts that escaped his notice; Your scanty costume may attract notice.* **3** a posted sign or published account for drawing attention to something: *to put up a notice on the bulletin board; The new book received scant notice in the papers; newspaper notices of births and deaths.*
—*v.* **-tic.es, -ticed, -tic.ing** see with the mind: *Did you notice her hairdo? Did you notice him getting off the bus? The play was favorably noticed* (= reviewed) *in the press.*

no.tice.a.ble (NOH.tuh.suh.bul) *adj.* easily noticed or worth noticing: *a noticeable improvement.* —**no.tice.a.bly** *adv.*

no.ti.fy (NOH.tuh.fye) *v.* **-fies, -fied, -fy.ing** inform someone officially or formally: *to notify a customer of the arrival of the goods ordered; Please notify us in writing.* —**no.ti.fi.ca.tion** (-fuh.CAY.shun) *n.*

no.tion (NOH.shun) *n.* **1** a vague idea, intention, or belief; also, a whim or fancy: *We don't have the slightest notion about* or *of what's on his mind; foggy, hazy, preconceived, vague, widespread notions; It took ages to dispel the notion that the earth is flat.* **2 notions** *pl.* miscellaneous small articles such as sewing things. —**no.tion.al** *adj.*

no.to.ri.e.ty (noh.tuh.RYE.uh.tee) *n.* a being notorious; ill fame: *people who gain notoriety as drug dealers; the notoriety surrounding his disappearance.*

no.to.ri.ous (nuh.TOR.ee.us) *adj.* famous in a bad way: *a notorious drug dealer; He's notorious for cheating customers; quite notorious as a cheater;* **no.to.ri.ous.ly** *adv.*

not.with.stand.ing (not.with.STAN.ding) *prep.* in spite of: *The party went on, notwithstanding the lateness of the hour.* —*conj.*: *The party went on, notwithstanding the hour was late.* —*adv.*: *The lateness of the hour notwithstanding, the party went on.*

nou.gat (NOO.gut) *n.* a candy made of sugar paste with nuts and sometimes fruit in it.

nought (NAWT) same as NAUGHT.

noun *n.* a word that is the name of a person, thing, place, action, etc.: *an* **abstract noun** *such as "beauty"; a* **collective noun** *such as "class" or "team"; Jones and Smithtown are* **proper nouns**, *not* **common nouns**; *"Woman" is a feminine noun; masculine nouns; neuter nouns; A* **mass noun** *like "sugar" or "paper" is generally not a* **countable noun**, *unlike "sugars" (as in "Two sugars and no cream") and "papers" (as in "the daily papers"); "Flying" as in "Flying is fun" is a* **verbal noun** *derived from the verb "to fly."*

nour.ish (NUR.ish) *v.* feed and thus help to grow; foster. —*adj.*: *Milk is* **nourishing** (= has food value); *nourishing* (= suckling) *mothers; a nourishing* (= healthful) *climate, diet, environment, food, meal, relationship; Children need nourishing* (= fostering) *support.*

nour.ish.ment (NUR.ish.munt) *n.* something that nourishes, as food: *Plants draw nourishment from the soil.*

nou.veau riche (noo.voh.REESH) *n.*, *pl.* **nou.veaux riches** (-voh.REESH) French. a newly rich person; parvenu.

nou.velle cui.sine (noo.VEL.kwi.ZEEN) *n.* French. a style of cooking using light ingredients, wholesome foods such as vegetables, and smaller and more flavorful portions presented artistically.

no.va (NOH.vuh) *n.* **-vas** or **-vae** (-vee) a star that "explodes" into sudden brilliance and then fades away.

nov.el (NOV.ul) *adj.* new in an unusual or strange way: *Your first snowfall is a novel experience; a novel idea, sensation, suggestion.* **—n.** a book-length work of prose fiction dealing with human life and experience: *detective, historical, mystery novels.*

nov.el.ette (nov.uh.LET) *n.* a short novel.

nov.el.ist (NOV.uh.list) *n.* the author of a novel.

nov.el.ize (NOV.uh.lize) *v.* **-iz.es, -ized, -iz.ing** make a novel of a play, biography, etc. **—nov.el.i.za.tion** (-luh.ZAY.shun, -lye-) *n.*

no.vel.la (noh.VEL.uh) *n.* a short novel.

nov.el.ty (NOV.ul.tee) *n.* **-ties 1** novel quality: *The novelty of your first snowfall wears off after some shoveling.* **2** something novel, esp. a small decorative or useful article: *a shop selling novelties and souvenirs.*

No.vem.ber (noh.VEM.bur) *n.* the 11th month of the calendar year, with 30 days.

no.ve.na (noh.VEE.nuh) *n.* in the Roman Catholic Church, a series of prayers or services spread over nine days or occasions.

nov.ice (NOV.is) *n.* a beginner, or new recruit, as in a religious order: *a rank novice at* or *in window dressing; a computer novice; political novices and veterans;* **adj.a.:** *a novice nun; novice bicyclists, investors, users; novice and experienced drivers.*

no.vi.ti.ate (noh.VISH.ee.it, -ate) *n.* **1** a novice's training period. **2** novices' quarters.

now *adv.* **1** at this instant, time, juncture, etc.: *I want my dinner now; right now; It's too bad I've had to wait until now; I haven't complained up to now; A pizza will be here just now* (= very soon). **2** [used more as an interjection than as an adverb of time]: *Now hear this; Well, now, what do you think? Now, now, don't do that!* **—conj.** since: *Now that you're 18, you can vote.* **—n.** the present time, hour, age, etc.: *From now on, we'll try harder; By now she must be home;* **adj.a.:**
up-to-date fashions for the now generation. **—now and again** or **now and then** occasionally; from time to time.

now.a.days (NOW.uh.days) *adv.* in these days; at the present time.

no.way or **no.ways** *adv.* in no way.

no.where *adv.* not anywhere: *She is nowhere to be seen; Our search is getting or going nowhere; We're nowhere near* (= not nearly at) *the end of our journey;* **n.:** *It came from* or *out of nowhere.*

no-win *adj.* not helping to win: *a no-win game, situation, struggle.*

no.wise *adv.* not at all: *nowise different; in nowise concerned.*

nox.ious (NOK.shus) *adj.* harmful or injurious to health: *noxious fumes, weeds; noxious influences (that corrupt).*

noz.zle (NOZ.ul) *n.* a vent or spout shaped for controlling the flow of a gas or liquid, as of a bellows or garden hose.

nth (ENTH) *adj.* multiplied an indefinite or "n" number of times. **—to the nth degree** to the utmost.

nu.ance (NOO.ahnce) *n.* a subtle variation of meaning, tone, or color.

nub *n.* **1** knob or lump. **2** *Informal.* point or gist; also **nub.bin.**

nub.ble (NUB.ul) *n.* a knob or lump.

nub.bly (NUB.lee) *adj.* **nub.bli.er, nub.bli.est** of a surface, knotted or lumpy; also **nub.by** (NUB.ee).

nu.bile (NEW.bul, -bile) *adj.* of a girl, ready for marriage; marriageable.

nu.cle.ar (NEW.clee.ur, NUKE.yuh.lur) *adj.* **1** forming a nucleus or core: *Parents and children form the nuclear family.* **2** having to do with the atomic nucleus or nuclear energy: *the nuclear age; nuclear fission, fusion, physics, power, radiation, waste; a nuclear warhead, weapon; the nuclear club* (of nations that have exploded an atomic device); a **nuclear-free** zone (that is free of nuclear weapons and nuclear energy); **Nuclear medicine** uses radioisotopes to diagnose and treat diseases; *a nuclear power* (= nation with nuclear weapons). **—n.** *Informal.* nuclear energy: *Is nuclear better than solar?*

nuclear reactor *n.* an apparatus for controlled production of atomic energy.

nuclear winter *n.* a worldwide condition of extreme cold, devastation, and darkness that would result from a nuclear war.

nu.cle.ate (NEW.clee.ate) *v.* **-ates, -at.ed, -at.ing** form as or into a nucleus; **nu.cle.a.tion** (-AY.shun) *n.*

nu.cle.ic acid (new.CLEE.ic-) *n.* a com-

plex organic acid such as DNA or RNA found in the nuclei of cells.
nu.cle.on (NEW.clee.on) *n.* a neutron or proton. —**nu.cle.on.ic** (-ON.ic) *adj.*
u.cle.us (NEW.clee.us) *n., pl.* **-cle.i** (-clee.eye) or **-cle.us.es** 1 core or center of activity, esp. the central part of a plant or animal cell containing genetic material. 2 the positively charged particle at the center of an atom in which matter and energy are concentrated.
nude *adj.* **nud.er, nu.dest** unclothed or naked, esp. as in art: *a nude model, picture; nude* (= flesh-colored) *stockings.* —*n.* the unclothed human figure, as in art: *Picasso's nudes; Some models pose in the nude* (= naked). —**nu.di.ty** (NEW.di.tee) *n.: movies without nudity and violence; frontal nudity.*
nudge (NUJ) *n.* a gentle push or jog, as with the elbow. —*v.* **nudg.es, nudged, nudg.ing** give a nudge.
nu.die (NEW.dee) *n. Informal.* a show, magazine, etc. featuring nudes.
nud.ism (NEW.diz.um) *n.* principle or practice of social nudity. —**nud.ist** *n.: nudist colonies.*
nu.ga.to.ry (NEW.guh.tor.ee) *adj. Formal.* trifling; hence, invalid or futile in effect: *The rewards of running in a marathon may be nugatory.*
nug.get (NUG.it) *n.* a lump of something precious from the earth: *gold nuggets.*
nui.sance (NEW.sunce) *n.* a troublesome or annoying person, thing, or situation: *Mosquitoes make a nuisance of themselves in the summer; They are a perpetual nuisance in hot climates; A mischief-maker is a public nuisance; He created or caused a nuisance by pulling the fire alarm; One who commits a nuisance can be sued for damages; a confounded nuisance; Sales tax and other government levies collected in small amounts directly from consumers are called* **nuisance taxes***; To the government they have more than* **nuisance value.**
nuke (rhyme: duke) *n. Informal.* a nuclear weapon or power-generating station.
null *adj.* 1 of no effect, esp. legal; invalid: *a law declared* **null and void** *by a court.* 2 amounting to nothing; zero or empty: *a null effect, result.*
nul.li.fy (NUL.uh.fye) *v.* **-fies, -fied, -fy.ing** make valueless; declare null and void; annul. —**nul.li.fi.ca.tion** (-fuh.CAY.shun) *n.*
nul.li.ty (NUL.i.tee) *n.* something that is null: *The court ruled that the discharge of the employee was a nullity; a decree of nullity in a divorce case.*
null set *n.* in math, a set with no members; empty set: *Two-sided polygons belong to a null set.*
numb (NUM) *adj.* **numb.er, numb.est** insensible or benumbed, as with cold, shock, etc.: *Her left side is numb; He was numb with fear.* —*v.* make numb: *The painkiller numbed the pain; adj.: a* **numbing** *effect, experience, sensation; the* **mind-numbing** *tedium of the assembly line.* —**numb.ly** *adv.;* **numb.ness** *n.*
num.ber (NUM.bur) *n.* 1 a numeral figure that tells how many, as 70 or LXX: *cardinal numbers such as 1, 2, 3, etc. and ordinal numbers such as 1st, 2nd, 3rd, etc.; 1, 3, 5, 7, etc. are odd numbers and 2, 4, 6, 8, etc. are even numbers.* 2 a countable group or collection: *the growing number of traffic deaths on holiday weekends; Their number is large; A good number will go hungry this winter; the total number of 1,007; a round number such as 1,000;* **A number of** *others are homeless.* 3 one of a series: *The back number of a magazine is not its current issue; the call number of a library book; The serial number of an automobile is much longer than its license number; What number did you dial? She has an unlisted* (phone) *number; a very popular number* (= item, as of a program). 4 in grammar: *"Fish" could be* (in the) *singular or plural number; "Goes" is the singular number of "go."* —**beyond** or **without number** too many to be counted. —**do a number on** *Slang.* criticize or humiliate someone. —**numbers** 1 arithmetic: *Accountants are good at numbers.* 2 a large group: *People like to travel together because there's safety in numbers.* —*v.* 1 give a number instead of a name to something; *adja.: a* **numbered** *account, corporation.* 2 count: *to be numbered among the chosen few; a* **numbering** *machine.* 3 limit the number of something; *adj.: A terminally ill patient's days are* **numbered.** 4 amount to; add up to; total: *The dead numbered 100.*
num.ber.less (NUM.bur.lis) *adj.* countless.
numbers game *n.* game of betting on the appearance of specific numbers in daily published statistics such as bank financial balances; also **numbers pool, numbers racket.**
numbskull same as NUMSKULL.
nu.mer.a.cy (NEW.muh.ruh.see) *n.* **-cies** skill in the use of numbers: *the basic skills of literacy and numeracy.*
nu.mer.al (NEW.muh.rul) *n.* a symbol or expression denoting a number or

numbers: *The Roman numeral LIV is 54 in Arabic numerals; a numeral system.*
nu.mer.ate (NEW.muh.rate) *v.* **-ates, -at.ed, -at.ing** count or list; enumerate. —**nu.mer.a.tion** (-RAY.shun) *n.*
nu.mer.a.tor (NEW.muh.ray.tur) *n.* in a fraction, the number above the line.
nu.mer.ic (new.MER.ic) *adj.* using figures, not letters: *a numeric code, computer, keypad, readout.*
nu.mer.i.cal (new.MER.i.cul) *adj.* having to do with numbers: *numerical control; in numerical order; a numerical analysis, quantity, value.* —**nu.mer.i.cal.ly** *adv.*
nu.mer.ol.o.gy (new.muh.ROL.uh.jee) *n.* fortune telling using numbers such as birthdates; **nu.mer.ol.o.gist** *n.*
nu.me.ro u.no (NOO.muh.roh.OO.noh) *n. Informal.* oneself as the "number one" or most important member of a group.
nu.mer.ous (NEW.muh.rus) *adj.* **1** very many: *numerous books, complaints, gifts, occasions.* **2** consisting of a large number: *a numerous clientele, progeny; the numerous middle class.* —**nu.mer.ous.ly** *adv.;* **nu.mer.ous.ness** *n.*
nu.mis.mat.ics (new.miz.MAT.ics) *n.pl.* [with *sing. v.*] the study or collecting of coins, paper money, medals, tokens, credit cards, and such items of monetary interest; **nu.mis.mat.ic** *adj.* —**nu.mis.ma.tist** (-MIZ.muh.tist) *n.*
num.skull or **numb.skull** *n.* a blockhead or dunce.
nun *n.* a woman living in a convent under religious vows.
nun.ci.o (NUN.shee.oh, -see.oh) *n.* **-os** a papal ambassador.
nun.ner.y (NUN.uh.ree) *n.* **nun.ner.ies** [former term] a convent.
nup.tial (NUP.shul) **1** *adj.* of a wedding: *a nuptial ceremony, day, Mass, song.* **2 nuptials** *n.pl.* a wedding ceremony.
nurse *n.* **1** a person trained to take care of the sick: *general-duty, hospital, male, private-duty nurses; A professional nurse is usually a Registered Nurse (R.N.); R.N.s include* **visiting nurses** *who give home care and implement public-health programs.* **2** a woman hired to care for another's children; also **nurse.maid.** —*v.* **nurs.es, nursed, nurs.ing** **1** suckle: *to nurse a baby; a* **nursing mother.** **2** take care of patients: *to nurse the sick; to nurse people back to health; n.: the profession of* **nursing.** **3** take care of something in a protective manner: *He's staying home nursing a cold; It seems healthier to forgive than to nurse a grudge; He has been at the bar nursing the same drink all evening.*

nurse practitioner *n.* a nurse trained to carry out the more routine functions of a physician.
nurs.er.y (NUR.suh.ree) *n.* **-er.ies 1** a children's room. **2** a nursery school or day-care center: *a child in a day nursery.* **3** a place where plants are grown for transplanting, experimentation, etc. —**nurs.er.y.man** (-mun) *n.* **-men.**
nursery rhyme *n.* a simple poem such as "Little Jack Horner" or "Sing a song of sixpence."
nursery school *n.* a pre-kindergarten school.
nursing home *n.* a private institution that takes care of the aged, sick, and disabled.
nurs.ling *n.* a suckling child.
nur.ture (NUR.chur) *n.* caring help in development: *Nurture builds on nature.* —*v.* **-tures, -tured, -tur.ing** give nurture to a person or thing: *to love and nurture our children; to nurture good habits, qualities, relationships, talents; A greenhouse nurtures plants; a friendship nurtured from childhood;* **adj.***: a well* **nurtured** *child; long nurtured hopes; a carefully nurtured image.*
nut *n.* **1** a dry, hard fruit with a seed or kernel enclosed in a shell of woody fiber, as the walnut, peanut, or coconut. **2** a small metal block with a threaded hole to screw on to and lock a bolt in place: *nuts and bolts.* **3** *Slang.* an eccentric or crazy person: *It's no use talking to that nut; He's* **off his nut** (= crazy). **4** *Slang.* a devotee or enthusiast: *an ecological nut; an aircraft nut who builds model airplanes in his spare time.* —**nuts** *adjp. Slang.* crazy: *He's not only misinformed, he's nuts! She* **went nuts** *at the news; He's* **nuts about** *skateboarding; Carl is* **nuts about** *(= very fond of) Claire.* —*interj.* expressing scorn: *Nuts to you!*
nut.crack.er (NUT.crak.ur) *n.* **1** an implement for cracking nuts open. **2** a bird of the crow family with sharp claws for holding nuts, esp. pine cones, while opening them.
nut.hatch *n.* a climbing bird that has a habit of wedging nuts in the bark of a tree to hack them open with its bill.
nut.meat *n.* the edible kernel of a nut.
nut.meg *n.* **1** a spice obtained from the aromatic seed of an East Indian tree. **2** the seed.
nut.pick *n.* a table implement for digging out the kernels of cracked nuts.
nu.tri.a (NEW.tree.uh) *n.* **1** the short blue-brown fur of the coypu. **2** a coypu.

nutrient / obdurate

nu.tri.ent (NEW.tree.unt) *n.* a substance or ingredient that is nourishing: *diets rich in nutrients; critical, healthful, staple, vital nutrients;* **adja.**: *the nutrient content of a salad; the nutrient value of beef; In hydroponics, a water-based nutrient solution is used instead of soil;* **cpd**: *a nutrient-conscious generation; nutrient-packed cells; nutrient-poor water; nutrient-rich foods.*

nu.tri.ment (NEW.truh.munt) *n.* something that is nourishing; food.

nu.tri.tion (new.TRISH.un) *n.* **1** the study of the process by which food is assimilated by an organism. **2** nourishment. —**nu.tri.tion.al** *adj.* having to do with nutrition: *nutritional aspects, claims, data, deficiency, needs, value;* **nu.tri.tion.al.ly** *adv.* —**nu.tri.tion.ist** *n.*

nu.tri.tious (new.TRISH.us) *adj.* having food value: *delicious and nutritious dishes; Spinach is very nutritious; a nutritious breakfast, diet, food, meal.*

nu.tri.tive (NEW.truh.tiv) *adj.* having to do with nourishment: *nutritive functions, plasma; the nutritive process.*

nuts and bolts *n.pl. Informal.* practical aspects: *Profit-making is the nuts and bolts of most businesses; the nuts and bolts of retailing.* —**nuts-and-bolts** *adja.* dealing with practical aspects: *Nan works in the nuts-and-bolts business area; She is a good nuts-and-bolts organizer; the nuts-and-bolts approach; the nuts-and-bolts end of a business; a nuts-and-bolts affair, difference, job, program, workshop; nuts-and-bolts knowledge, help.*

nut.shell *n.* the shell enclosing a nut. —**in a nutshell** in a few words; concisely.

nut.ty (NUT.ee) *adj.* **nut.ti.er, nut.ti.est 1** nutlike or containing nuts: *a nutty cookie, flavor, taste; nutty as a fruitcake.* **2** *Informal.* nuts or crazy: *a nutty idea.* **3** enthusiastic: *She's nutty about new fashions.* —**nut.ti.ness** *n.*

nuz.zle (NUZ.ul) *v.* **nuz.zles, nuz.zled, nuz.zling 1** rub or push against with or as if with the nose or snout. **2** snuggle or nestle: *A baby nuzzles up against its mother.* —**nuz.zler** *n.*

ny.lon (NYF.lon) *n.* **1** a strong, elastic synthetic product widely used as fibers, sheets, tubes, etc.: *stockings of sheer nylon.* **2 nylons** *pl.* nylon stockings: *a pair of nylons.*

nymph (NIMF) *n.* **1** in Greek and Roman myths, a goddess of nature inhabiting the water, woods, and hills. **2** the wingless but adultlike larva stage in the metamorphosis of insects such as grasshoppers and chinch bugs.

nym.pho.ma.ni.a (nim.fuh.MAY.nee.uh) *n.* excessive sexual desire in a woman; **nym.pho.ma.ni.ac** *n. & adj.*

.... **O, o** ....

O or **o** (OH) *n.* **O's** or **o's 1** the 15th letter of the English alphabet. **2 O** [old use] same as OH: *O Canada! O Lord!*

oaf (OHF) *n.* a stupid or awkward fellow. —**oaf.ish** *adj.*

oak (OKE) *n.* a strong and sturdy tree of the beech family that bears nuts called acorns: *woods of oak; furniture in oak (wood);* **adja.**: *the oak tree; oak forests, leaves, wood.* —*adj.* also **oak.en**, of the wood of an oak: *oak barrels, casks, finishes, floors, handles, scents, tables, veneers; an oaken door, shaft, vessel.*

oa.kum (OH.kum) *n.* a caulking material used in the seams of wooden ships, for packing joints in pipes, etc.

oar (OR) *n.* a broad-bladed implement used in rowing a boat. —**rest on one's oars** rest after doing some work. —**oars.man** (ORS.mun) *n.* **-men.**

oar.lock *n.* a U-shaped support or notch in one side of a boat for holding the oar in place.

o.a.sis (oh.AY.sis) *n., pl.* **-ses** (-seez) in a desert, a fertile spot with water and some vegetation.

oat (OHT) *n.* **1** a cereal grass bearing grain used as livestock feed and in making oatmeal, etc. **2 oats** *sing. & pl.* the seed of this grass: *a breakfast of rolled oats; to* **sow one's wild oats** (= be promiscuous, esp. in youth). —**oat.en** *adj.*

oat.cake *n.* a thin flat oatmeal cake or bread.

oath (*rhyme:* both) *n.* **1** a solemn promise, often calling on God as witness: *to take* or *swear the oath of allegiance to the king; A justice administers the oath of office to a minister; Witnesses testify under oath (to tell the truth).* **2** a swearing or a swearword; curse: *to mutter* or *utter an oath.*

oat.meal (OHT.meel) *n.* **1** meal or flakes made from oats. **2** this cooked as porridge; also called "hot cereal."

ob- *prefix.* toward or against: *obverse, obnoxious, obdurate.*

ob.bli.ga.to (ob.luh.GAH.toh) *n.* **-tos** or **-ti** (-tee) an instrumental part accompanying a solo: *an aria with trumpet obbligato.*

ob.du.rate (OB.dyuh.rut, -duh.rut) *adj.* obstinate or hardhearted: *an obdurate attitude, refusal, sinner.* —**ob.du.rate.ly**

adv. —**ob.du.ra.cy** (-ruh.see) *n.*

o.be.di.ence (oh.BEE.dee.unce) *n.* the act of obeying or willingness to obey: *The army demands* or *exacts obedience from soldiers; Schools try to instill obedience to rules and regulations; respect and obedience; obedience to a command, to authority; the religious vows of poverty, chastity, and obedience; absolute, blind, enthusiastic, perfect, unquestioning obedience; a puppy trained in obedience;* **adja.**: *an obedience course, lesson, trial.*

o.be.di.ent (oh.BEE.dee.unt) *adj.* obeying or submissive: *an obedient child; obedient to its parents;* **o.be.di.ent.ly** *adv.*

o.bei.sance (oh.BAY.sunce, oh.BEE-) *n.* (a gesture of) homage or deference; **o.bei.sant** *adj.*

ob.e.lisk (OB.uh.lisk, OH.buh-) *n.* a four-sided tapering pillar of stone with a pyramidal top, originally erected near ancient Egyptian temples.

o.bese (oh.BEECE) *adj.* excessively fat; **o.be.si.ty** (-BEE.si.tee) *n.*

o.bey (uh.BAY) *v.* **1** carry out: *to obey an order.* **2** be guided by someone: *to obey the authorities, one's conscience.*

ob.fus.cate (OB.fus.cate, ob.FUS.cate) *v.* **-cates, -cat.ed, -cat.ing** confuse or obscure: *drugs that obfuscate the mind; arguments obfuscating the issues.* —**ob.fus.ca.tion** (-CAY.shun) *n.*

o.bit (OH.bit, OB-) *n. Informal.* obituary.

ob.i.ter dic.tum (OH.bi.tur.DIC.tum, OB-) *n., pl.* **ob.i.ter dic.ta** an incidental observation.

o.bit.u.ar.y (uh.BICH.oo.air.ee) *n.* **-ar.ies** a notice of a person's death or a short biography accompanying it.

ob.ject (OB.jikt) *n.* **1** a person or thing that a feeling, thought, or action is directed toward: *the object of his attentions; an object of derision; an unidentified flying object; In "Joe loves Jan," "Jan" is the grammatical object of the verb; I try to look sexy but I resent being considered as a mere sex object.* **2** goal or purpose: *What's the object of your research? Money is* **no object** (= no problem) *when we are looking for the best.* —*v.* (ub.JECT) oppose or disapprove strongly; be opposed: *"I object," shouted the lawyer; People object to smoking in the workplace.*

ob.jec.ti.fy (ub.JEC.tuh.fye) *v.* **-fies, -fied, -fy.ing** make objective: *Women are sometimes objectified and commoditized.* —**ob.jec.ti.fi.ca.tion** (-fuh.CAY.shun) *n.: sexual objectification.*

ob.jec.tion (ub.JEC.shun) *n.* an expression of or the reason for objecting: *to deal with, make, meet, raise, withdraw an objection; A judge may overrule or sustain an objection raised by a lawyer; We have no objection to your opening the window; I know you wouldn't open the window over our objections.*

ob.jec.tion.a.ble (ub.JEC.shuh.nuh.bul) *adj.* open to objection; unpleasant or disagreeable: *an objectionable report; objectionable language.*

ob.jec.tive (ub.JEC.tiv) *n.* something in the position of object, esp. an intended object or a definite goal: *a great achiever who always aims at clear objectives; The objective of a microscope or telescope is the part closest to the object being viewed.* —*adj.* **1** having to do with an object: *"Me," "them," "whom," etc. are in the* **objective case** (= they function as objects of verbs). **2** dealing only with facts, not influenced by emotions; not subjective: *an objective analysis, look, report; An* **objective test** *has a choice of alternative answers to be checked and no questions requiring essay-type answers.* —**ob.jec.tive.ly** *adv.* —**ob.jec.tive.ness** or **ob.jec.tiv.i.ty** (-TIV.i.tee) *n.*

object lesson *n.* a practical illustration of a principle, esp. one that teaches a lesson.

ob.jec.tor (ub.JEC.tur) *n.* one who objects: *a conscientious objector.*

ob.jet d'art (ob.zhay.DAR) *n., pl.* **ob.jets d'art** (ob.zhay.DAR) *French.* a small object of artistic value.

objet trou.vé (OB.zhay.troo.VAY) *n. French.* a found-art object. See FOUND ART.

ob.jur.gate (OB.jur.gate) *v.* **-gates, -gat.ed, -gat.ing** *Formal.* scold or rebuke harshly. —**ob.jur.ga.tion** (-GAY.shun) *n.*

ob.late (OB.late) *adj.* flattened at the poles, as a spheroid: *The earth is not quite round but a somewhat oblate sphere.*

ob.la.tion (ub.LAY.shun) *n.* a sacrifice or offering to God.

ob.li.gate (OB.li.gate) *v.* **-gates, -gat.ed, -gat.ing** bind morally or legally: *freebies that obligate you to order from a catalog;* **adjp.**: *He did not feel* **obligated** *to shop there in spite of gifts received.*

ob.li.ga.tion (ob.li.GAY.shun) *n.* what one is obliged to do because of an agreement or by one's position, occupation, relationships, etc.: *You are under no obligation to tip our staff; He felt some obligation to pay for the damage; the duties and obligations of a job; to assume, discharge, fulfill, meet an obligation.* —**ob.lig.a.to.ry** (ob.LIG.uh.tor.ee) *adj.*

o.blige (uh.BLIGE) *v.* **o.blig.es, o.bliged, o.blig.ing** bind people by

oblique / obstacle

force of law, custom, conscience, etc.: *The law obliges us to drive on the right; She's ready to oblige* (= do a favor) *whenever she can;* **adj.**: *I'm much* **obliged** *by* (= grateful for) *your kindness; a very* **obliging** (= accommodating) *neighbor.* —**o.blig.ing.ly** *adv.*

ob.lique (oh.BLEEK) *adj.* **1** slanting, not perpendicular or parallel: *Acute and obtuse angles are oblique angles.* **2** indirect, often underhand: *an oblique accusation, glance, reference.* —**ob.lique.ly** *adv.* —**ob.lique.ness** or **ob.liq.ui.ty** (ub.LIK.wi.tee) *n.*

ob.lit.er.ate (ub.LIT.uh.rate) *v.* **-ates, -at.ed, -at.ing** destroy all traces of something; wipe out signs, marks, etc. completely. —**ob.lit.e.ra.tion** (-RAY.shun) *n.* —**ob.lit.e.ra.tor** (-ray.tur) *n.*

ob.liv.ion (ub.LIV.ee.un) *n.* **1** the condition of being forgotten: *People pass or sink into oblivion by death, neglect, etc.* **2** forgetfulness or unconsciousness: *The patient sank back into oblivion.*

ob.liv.i.ous (ub.LIV.ee.us) *adj.* forgetful or unaware: *We are oblivious of the passage of time while asleep; to be oblivious of danger.* —**ob.liv.i.ous.ly** *adv.*; **ob.liv.i.ous.ness** *n.*

ob.long (OB.long) *adj.* longer than it is broad; rectangular, not square: *an oblong table.* —*n.* an oblong object or rectangular figure.

ob.lo.quy (OB.luk.wee) *n.* **-quies** shame or disgrace: *The deposed president lived in obloquy till death.*

ob.nox.ious (ob.NOK.shus) *adj.* unbearably offensive or objectionable: *the obnoxious manners of an obnoxious person; He became obnoxious to everyone.* —**ob.nox.ious.ly** *adv.*; **ob.nox.ious.ness** *n.*

o.boe (OH.boh) *n.* a double-reed woodwind instrument with a high-pitched tone; **o.bo.ist** *n.*

ob.scene (ob.SEEN) *adj.* **1** immoral or indecent: *obscene dancing, gestures, language, literature, phone calls.* **2** excessive: *an obscene amount of money; obscene prices, profits.* —**ob.scene.ly** *adv.* —**ob.scen.i.ty** (ob.SEN.i.tee) *n.*

ob.scu.rant.ism (obs.CURF.un.tiz.um) *n.* opposition to progress and enlightenment. —**ob.scu.rant.ist** *n. & adj.*

ob.scure (obs.CURE) *adj.* **1** not clear or distinct; hard to understand: *an obscure corner, meaning; an obscure passage in a book.* **2** little known: *an obscure genius, village.* —*v.* **-scures, -scured, -scur.ing** make dark or hide from view: *Clouds obscure the sun.* —**ob.scure.ly** *adv.* —**ob.scur.i.ty** (-i.tee) *n.*

ob.se.quies (OB.suh.kweez) *n.pl.* funeral rites.

ob.se.qui.ous (ub.SEEK.wee.us) *adj.* obedient in a servile or fawning manner. —**ob.se.qui.ous.ly** *adv.*; **ob.se.qui.ous.ness** *n.*

ob.ser.vant (ob.ZUR.vunt) *adj.* **1** mindful of rules, customs, etc.: *an observant Jewish community.* **2** watchful: *He's usually alert and observant while driving; to be observant of what is happening around one.* —**ob.ser.vance** *n.*: *observance of human rights; religious observances such as Easter and Passover.*

ob.ser.va.tion (ob.zur.VAY.shun) *n.* **1** the act or process of examining or studying: *an error of observation; a patient placed* or *kept under close observation.* **2** a remark or comment: *to make a shrewd observation; astute, keen, penetrating, wise observations.*

ob.serv.a.to.ry (ub.ZUR.vuh.tor.ee) *n.* **-ries** a building equipped with a telescope, etc. for astronomical research.

ob.serve (ub.ZURV) *v.* **-serves, -served, -serv.ing 1** abide by or keep: *to observe a custom, holiday, law.* **2** to notice: *changes observed at puberty.* **3** examine or study: *Astronomers observe the stars; to observe everything attentively, carefully, closely.* **4** to comment or remark: *He observed wisely that pride goes before a fall.* —**ob.ser.va.ble** (-vuh.bul) *adj.* —**ob.ser.ver** *n.*

ob.sess (ub.SES) *v.* occupy one's mind in an unreasonable or unhealthy manner: *Ideas, feelings, and impulses could obsess the mind; Some are obsessed by fear, others with making money;* **adj.**: *Jean is so* **obsessed** *about cleanliness he washes every hour.* —**ob.ses.sion** (-SESH.uh) *n.*; **ob.ses.sion.al** (-uh.nul) *adj.* —**ob.ses.sive** (-SES.iv) *adj.*; **ob.ses.sive.ly** *adv.*

ob.sid.i.an (ub.SID.ee.un) *n.* a natural black-colored glass formed by the cooling of lava.

ob.so.les.cence (ob.suh.LES.unce) *n.* the state of being obsolescent or out of date: *Planned obsolescence (for making a product become out of date) is often built into goods.* **ob.so.les.cent** (-unt) *adj.* becoming obsolete or out of date: *an obsolescent custom; sailing as an obsolescent mode of travel.*

ob.so.lete (OB.suh.leet, ob.suh.LEET) *adj.* fallen into disuse; outmoded: *an obsolete expression, implement, word; Is the horse and buggy obsolete?* —**ob.so.lete.ly** *adv.*; **ob.so.lete.ness** *n.*

ob.sta.cle (OB.stuh.cul) *n.* something that stands in the way of one's progress: *an obstacle to progress; to clear, encounter, overcome, remove, surmount, take an obstacle; a formidable, insurmountable obstacle; the fences, ditches, hurdles, etc. of an* **obstacle course** *used in military training.*

ob.stet.ric (ub.STET.ric) **1** *adj.* having to do with childbirth: *obstetric forceps; an obstetric nurse, ward;* also **ob.stet.ri.cal. 2 obstetrics** *n.pl.* [takes *sing. v.*] the branch of medicine concerned with childbirth. —**ob.ste.tri.cian** (ob.stuh.TRISH.un) *n.*

ob.sti.nate (OB.stuh.nit) *adj.* not yielding to reason or remedies: *He remained obstinate in his beliefs till death; He's obstinate about everything he advocates; an obstinate fever, habit.* —**ob.sti.nate.ly** *adv.* —**ob.sti.na.cy** (-nuh.see) *n.*

ob.strep.er.ous (ub.STREP.uh.rus) *adj.* noisy or disorderly in an unruly way: *obstreperous behavior, youth.*

ob.struct (ub.STRUCT) *v.* block movement or activity by placing obstacles in the way: *a pile-up obstructing traffic; Tall buildings obstruct our view.* —**ob.struc.tion** *n.: an obstruction in the windpipe; charged with* **obstruction of justice** *for trying to bribe the jury.* —**ob.struc.tive** *adj.*

ob.struc.tion.ist (ub.STRUC.shuh.nist) *n.* one that obstructs: *A filibusterer is an obstructionist; adj.: an obstructionist organization, policy, tactic.* —**ob.struc.tion.ism** *n.*

ob.tain (ub.TAIN) *v.* **1** secure or get through effort, planning, etc.: *how to obtain a license; evidence obtained by the police; to obtain approval, credit, knowledge, results.* **2** be prevalent or in use: *superstitious practices still obtaining in some societies.* —**ob.tain.a.ble** (-nuh.bul) *adj.*

ob.trude (ub.TROOD, long "OO") *v.* -trudes, -trud.ed, -trud.ing **1** push out: *The bird obtruded its head and looked out of the nest.* **2** thrust oneself or one's concerns forward where not wanted: *He never obtruded his ideas on others.* —**ob.tru.sion** (-TROO.zhun) *n.*

ob.tru.sive (ub.TROO.siv) *adj.* pushing or showy: *an obtrusive color, influence, manner.* —**ob.tru.sive.ly** *adv.;* **ob.tru.sive.ness** *n.*

ob.tuse (ub.TYOOSE, -TOOSE) *adj.* **1** not acute or sharp: *An obtuse angle is more than 90 degrees.* **2** blunt and insensitive: *He is too obtuse to get the point.* —**ob.tuse.ly** *adv.;* **ob.tuse.ness** *n.*

ob.verse (OB.vurse) *n.* the front, as the side of a coin or medal with the head or other main design.

ob.vi.ate (OB.vee.ate) *v.* -ates, -at.ed, -at.ing remove a difficulty, need, etc. by anticipating it: *Spending wisely obviates the need for borrowing.*

ob.vi.ous (OB.vee.us) *adj.* plain to the view: *an obvious truth; It's obvious that they like each other; It's obvious to everyone; n.: to state the obvious.* —**ob.vi.ous.ly** *adv.*

oc.a.ri.na (oc.uh.REE.nuh) *n.* an egg-shaped molded wind instrument that produces a soft whistling sound when blown into.

oc.ca.sion (uh.CAY.zhun) *n.* **1** a particular time, esp. one favorable to an event's taking place: *a propitious occasion; I'd like to take this occasion to thank the principal; I've not yet had an occasion to talk to your parents; I'll do it as the occasion arises; A reunion is a good occasion for making a speech; I've warned you about this on numerous occasions; on the rare occasion of an earthquake; The football game was the occasion (though not cause) of the fight.* **2** an event or happening: *on great occasions such as weddings; festive, gala, fitting, happy, joyous, memorable, special occasions.* —**rise to the occasion** meet the challenge. —**on occasion** now and then. —*v.* bring about: *Their enmity is well-known, but what occasioned the fight?*

oc.ca.sion.al (uh.CAY.zhuh.nul) *adj.* **1** happening now and then, not regularly: *a forecast of occasional showers; occasional appearances, efforts, errors, misuse, problems, references.* **2** having to do with particular occasions: *your son as an occasional driver; occasional furniture (for auxiliary use); occasional music (for special occasions);.* —**oc.ca.sion.al.ly** *adv.*

oc.ci.dent (OK.suh.dunt) *n.* the West, esp. **the Occident**, Europe and the Americas, as distinguished from the Orient.

oc.ci.den.tal or **Oc.ci.den.tal** (ok.suh.DEN.tul) *adj.* of the West. —*n.* a native of the West.

oc.clude (uh.CLOOD, long "OO") *v.* **oc.cludes, oc.clud.ed, oc.clud.ing** close or block so as to prevent passage: *Clots occlude the blood supply in a coronary artery; Upper and lower teeth should occlude* (= meet properly)*; n.: An* **occluded front** *is formed by cold air overtaking and forcing up a warm air mass.* —**oc.clu.sion** (-CLOO.zhun) *n.* —**oc.clu.sive** (-ziv) *adj.*

oc.cult (uh.CULT, OC.ult) *adj.* hidden or concealed from ordinary human knowledge: *Astrology, alchemy, and* magic are occult sciences; *an occult practice*; *n*.: *Fortunetellers claim to know **the occult*** (= occult matters). **—oc.cult.ism** *n*.; **oc.cult.ist** *n*.

oc.cu.pan.cy (OK.yuh.pun.see) *n*. **-cies** the act or period of occupying a place: *a room rate based on **double occupancy*** (= two in a room); *adj.a.*: *a hotel's occupancy level or rate; occupancy taxes*. **—oc.cu.pant** (-punt) *n*.: *junk mail addressed to the occupant of a dwelling; rear-seat occupants*.

oc.cu.pa.tion (ok.yuh.PAY.shun) *n*. **1** an occupying by an enemy: *a territory that is under occupation by a foreign army*. **2** work that one is trained to do or does habitually; profession: *The unemployed man is a cab driver by occupation; A rewarding occupation such as running a free health clinic need not be a profitable occupation*. **—oc.cu.pa.tion.al** (-shuh.nul) *adj.*: *The bends is an occupational disease of divers; **Occupational therapy** helps overcome handicaps by participation in selected activities*. **—oc.cu.pa.tion.al.ly** *adv*.

oc.cu.py (OK.yuh.pye) *v*. **-pies, -pied, -py.ing 1** take up or engage: *Matter occupies space; A good book occupies our attention; Hobbies occupy my spare time*; *adj.p.*: *The baby-sitter kept the children **occupied** and out of trouble*. **2** have possession of a place: *She moved in and occupied the house*; *adj.*: *an **occupied** seat; an occupied position that will soon fall vacant*. **3** take possession by force: *when Afghanistan was occupied by the Soviets*; *adj.a.*: *an **occupied** territory*. **—oc.cu.pi.er** *n*.

oc.cur (uh.CUR) *v*. **oc.curs, oc.curred, oc.cur.ring** of an event, thing, etc., happen to be found: *When did his death occur? "The" occurs more frequently than any other word; Did that ever **occur to you*** (= come to your mind)? **—oc.cur.rence** (-unce) *n*.: *common, daily, regular occurrences*.

o.cean (OH.shun) *n*. **1** one of the great expanses of water around the globe: *the Atlantic, Pacific, Indian, Arctic, and Antarctic oceans*. **2** a great number or quantity: *oceans of funds, time, trouble, words*.

o.cean.ar.i.um (oh.shun.NAIR.ee.um) *n*. **-i.ums** or **-i.a** an aquarium with large tanks in which fishes are placed together without separation.

o.cean.go.ing (OH.shun.go.ing) *adj*. **1** naval: *an oceangoing vessel*. **2** maritime: *oceangoing commerce; the oceangoing world*.

o.ce.an.ic (oh.shee.AN.ic) *adj*. having to do with the ocean: *an oceanic climate, current; the oceanic depths; oceanic life; the oceanic* (= oceanlike) *vastness of a desert*.

o.cean.og.ra.phy (oh.shuh.NOG.ruh.fee) *n*. the study of oceans and marine life; **o.cean.og.ra.pher** *n*. **—o.cean.o.graph.ic** (-nuh.GRAF.ic) *adj*.

o.ce.lot (OS.uh.lot, OH.suh-) *n*. a medium-sized spotted wild cat found from Texas to Paraguay.

o.cher or **o.chre** (OH.cur) *n*. **1** earth containing iron oxide, used as a pigment. **2** its yellow to brownish-red color.

o'.clock (uh.CLOC) *adv*. according to the clock: *8 o'clock in the morning* (= 8 a.m.).

oct-, octa- or **octo-** *comb.form*. eight: *octagon, octane, octette, octopus*.

oc.ta.gon (OC.tuh.gun, -gon) *n*. an eight-sided plane figure. **—oc.tag.o.nal** (oc.TAG.uh.nul) *adj*.

oc.tane (OC.tane) *n*. a petroleum hydrocarbon that gives quality to gasoline: *The higher the **octane number** or rating of a gasoline, the less the engine knocks*.

oc.tave (OC.tiv, -tave) *n*. **1** an interval of eight full musical tones. **2** the series of tones making up such an interval or the eighth full tone from any given tone. **3** a group of eight verses, festival days, etc.

oc.ta.vo (oc.TAH.voh) *n*. **-vos 1** the page size of 6 in. by 9 in. (15.24 cm by 22.86 cm). **2** a book with octavo pages.

oc.tet (oc.TET) *n*. **1** a musical composition or group of singers or players with eight voices or instruments. **2** a set of eight. Also **oc.tette**.

Oc.to.ber (oc.TOH.bur) *n*. the 10th month of the calendar year, with 31 days.

oc.to.ge.nar.i.an (oct.tuh.juh.NAIR.ee.un) *n. & adj*. (a person) aged 80 to 89.

oc.to.pus (OC.tuh.pus) *n*. **-pus.es** or **-pi** (-pye) a soft-bodied sea mollusk with eight arms or tentacles.

oc.to.syl.lab.ic (oc.tuh.si.LAB.ic) *n. & adj*. (a verse) of eight syllables.

oc.u.lar (OC.yuh.lur) *adj*. of the eye or by eyesight; visual. **—***n*. the eyepiece lens of a microscope or telescope.

oc.u.list (OC.yuh.list) *n*. [former term] ophthalmologist.

OD (OH.dee) *n*. **OD's** *Informal*. **1** an overdose of a drug, esp. a narcotic. **2** one who has taken an OD. **—***v*. **OD's, OD'd, OD'ing** take sick or die from an OD: *to OD on drugs.*

o.da.lisque or **o.da.lisk** (OH.dul.isk) *n.* a concubine in a harem.

odd *adj.* **1** remaining as extra: *an odd stocking without its mate; Keep the odd change after payments;* **the odd man out** *after the others have paired off; hundred-odd* (= 100 plus a few); *He worked at odd* (= casual or occasional) *jobs while seeking employment.* **2** not even: *the odd numbers 1, 3, 5, 7, etc.* **3** strange or peculiar: *an odd hairstyle; an odd-looking creature.* —*n.pl.* chances: *The odds favor Sam 3 to 1; The* **odds are** *Sam will win; The odds for Jim's winning are not good* or *The odds are long against his winning; The question for him is how to improve* or **better the odds;** *Sam is* **by all odds** *the luckiest; The soldiers died fighting against* **heavy odds** (= disadvantages). —**at odds** in disagreement: *two brothers at odds with each other.* —**beat the odds** overcome disadvantages; also **fight** or **defy the odds.** —**odds and ends** miscellaneous things. —**odd.ly** *adv.*; **odd.ness** *n.*

odd.ball *n. & adj. Informal.* eccentric.

odd.i.ty (OD.i.tee) *n.* **-ties** a peculiar person or thing

odd.ment (OD.munt) *n.* an odd bit or remnant.

odds-on *adja.* sure to win: *She's the odds-on favorite to succeed the mayor.*

ode *n.* a ceremoniously lyric poem in an exalted style: *an ode to Napoleon.*

o.di.ous (OH.dee.us) *adj.* hateful in an offensive or disagreeable way: *odious cruelty; an odious epithet.* —**o.di.ous.ly** *adv.*; **o.di.ous.ness** *n.*

o.di.um (OH.dee.um) *n.* widespread hatred of the kind that results in disgrace.

o.dom.e.ter (oh.DOM.uh.tur) *n.* an instrument that records the distance traveled by a vehicle.

o.dor (OH.dur) *n.* what makes anything smell good or bad: *the detection of odors; body odor; to emit, give off, perceive, recognize an odor; fetid, foul, musty, pleasant, pungent, rank, strong odors; natural and synthetic odors; the odor of scandal; a company* **in bad odor** (= having a bad name) *with the law.* —**o.dor.less** *adj.* Also **o.dour, o.dour.less** *Cdn.*

o.dor.ous (OH.duh.rus) *adj.* giving forth an odor. Also **o.dor.if.er.ous** (-RIF.uh.rus) *adj.*: *Onions are not so odoriferous as garlic.*

odour *Cdn.* ODOR.

od.ys.sey (OD.uh.see) *n.* **od.ys.seys** a long wandering or journey, as of the Greek hero Odysseus in the ancient epic poem "Odyssey": *Our cruise was a 10-day odyssey one can never forget.*

oed.i.pal or **Oed.i.pal** (ED.uh.pul, EED-) *adj.* relating to the Oedipus complex.

Oedipus complex *n.* in psychoanalysis, an unconscious childhood attachment to one's parent of the opposite sex, as explaining personality disorders in adult life.

oe.no.phile (EE.nuh.file) *n.* a lover or connoisseur of wine.

o'er (OR, OHR) [poetic use] over.

oe.soph.a.gus (ee.SOF.uh.gus) same as ESOPHAGUS.

oes.tro.gen (EES.truh.jun) same as ESTROGEN.

oeu.vre (URV.ruh) *n. French.* the body of works of an author or artist.

of (ov, uv) *prep.* **1** [indicating origin or cause]: *born of noble blood; He died of hunger; a house of cards; north of* (= from) *Yellowknife.* **2** [indicating a relationship]: *children of God; the works of Shakespeare; love of* (= for) *truth.* **3** having to do with: *words of advice; the state of Idaho; a house of prayer.* **4** before: *The time is 10 minutes of 8* (= 7:50). **5** during: *of a summer evening.*

off (OF) *adv.* away: *He took his hat off; He went off without a word; Turn off the tap; to pay off a loan; He's way off in his estimate; Taiwan is far off in the east; He saw me off at the airport.* —**off and on** now and then. —*prep.* away from: *His hat is off his head; a ship anchored off the coast; We get off work at 5 p.m.; to get the tops off of bottles (nonstandard for off bottles); cpd:* an *off-camera interview; a hockey player's off-ice behavior; an off-the-rack* (= ready-to-wear, not custom-made) *suit.* —*adj.* away: *I'll be off soon; The lights are off* (= not on); *adja.:* an *off* (= unlikely) *chance.* —*interj.* away: *Off with mosquitoes!*

of.fal (AWF.ul, OF-) *n.* **1** garbage. **2** waste animal parts such as viscera, industrial by-products, etc.

off-base See BASE, *n.*

off-beat *n. Music.* a weakly accented beat. —*adj.* **1** off the regular rhythm. **2** of an unusual kind: *off-beat theater.*

off-color *adj.* **1** not the right color. **2** improper or risqué: *an off-color joke; off-color language.* **3** not feeling well.

offence *Cdn.* OFFENSE.

of.fend (uh.FEND) *v.* hurt one's sense of right and wrong; do wrong or displease: *Mom will be offended if you do that; It offends against good manners; It offends good taste.* —**of.fen.der** *n.*

of.fense (uh.FENCE) *n.* **1** what offends against the law, one's conscience, feelings, etc.: *Speeding is a traffic offense; capital, criminal, indictable, minor, petty offenses; Luc apologized and explained the offense was not intended; Strong language is likely to* **give offense** (= to offend); *He's too meek to* **take offense** (= be offended) *at anything.* **2** (OH.fence) attack: *weapons of offense and defense.* Also **of.fence** *Cdn.*

of.fen.sive (uh.FEN.siv) *adj.* **1** unpleasant or insulting: *offensive language; an offensive fellow, smell.* **2** attacking or aggressive: *an offensive army, weapon.* —*n.* attack: *an army on the offensive; a new offensive; to take the offensive; to carry out, launch, mount, undertake an offensive; a* **peace offensive** (= aggressive move for peace). —**of.fen.sive.ly** *adv.*; **of.fen.sive.ness** *n.*

of.fer (OF.ur) *v.* **1** hold out for acceptance: *Many offered to help her; They offered advice, help, suggestions.* **2** present: *prayers and sacrifices offered to God; The enemy offered little resistance; They didn't even offer* (= attempt) *to defend themselves; Do it if the opportunity offers* (= presents) *itself.* —*n.* an offering or what is offered: *He refused all offers of help; an offer to purchase (something); We've received an offer of $200,000 on the house; an offer so good you can't refuse; job offers; an offer of marriage; to accept, decline, make, reject, spurn, withdraw an offer.*

offering (OF.ur.ing) *n.* an act of presenting or what is presented: *the offering of prayers and sacrifices; an offering to the Almighty; a plate to collect church offerings; a school's course offerings.*

of.fer.to.ry (OF.ur.tor.ee) *n.* **-ries** **1** the offering of bread and wine at a church service, esp. the Mass, and the prayers accompanying this. **2** the taking up of the offerings of the congregation at public worship.

off.hand *adj.* said or done without preparation: *an offhand manner, remark, suggestion, tone;* **adv.**: *a speech delivered offhand.* —**off.hand.ed** *adj.*; **off.hand.ed.ly** *adv.*; **off.hand.ed.ness** *n.*

off-hour *adj.* outside of business hours or rush hours: *off-hour callers, deliveries, processing.*

of.fice (OF.is) *n.* **1** a place from which a service is carried out: *booking, branch, home, main offices; a box office; a lawyer's office; the patent office; post offices; Sam works at or in a dentist's office; Our office is open Monday through Friday.* **2** a position of responsibility, esp. public: *The highest office of the nation is that of President; to assume an office; to resign from an office; to hold, run for, seek, take office; A government is* **in office** *while in power; A party goes* **out of office** *when it loses an election.* **3** prayers: *to recite the divine office; the last* **offices** (= rites for the dead). —**good offices** *pl.* service: *He got the job through the good offices of a friend.*

of.fice.hold.er (OF.is.hold.ur) *n.* a public or government official.

office hours *n.pl.* hours of business.

of.fi.cer (OF.uh.sur) *n.* anyone holding a position of authority: *the chief executive officer of a company; commissioned and warrant officers of the armed forces; personnel officers; police officers.*

of.fi.cial (uh.FISH.ul) *adj.* **1** having to do with an office: *an official manner, occasion, position, uniform.* **2** authorized or recognized: *an official announcement; Romansch is a national but not an official language in Switzerland; Is the appointment official? an official record.*
—*n.* a person holding office; officer: *public officials; school officials.*
—**of.fi.cial.dom** (-dum) *n.*
—**of.fi.cial.ism** *n.* —**of.fi.ci.al.ly** *adv.*

of.fi.ci.ant (uh.FISH.ee.unt) *n.* an officiating clergyman.

of.fi.ci.ate (uh.FISH.ee.ate) *v.* **-ates, -at.ed, -at.ing** perform official duties: *to officiate at a ceremony; to officiate as chairperson of the meeting.*

of.fi.cious (uh.FISH.us) *adj.* meddlesome, esp. from a position of authority. —**of.fi.cious.ly** *adv.*; **of.fi.cious.ness** *n.*

off.ing *n.* **1** the distant sea as seen from the shore. **2** the immediate future: *Reforms are* **in the offing** (= impending).

off.ish *adj. Informal.* aloof or reserved in manner.

off-key *adj.* not on the right musical note; not harmonious.

off-limits *adj.* out of bounds: *Bars are off-limits to children.*

off-line *adj. & adv.* not directly connected to a computer; not on-line: *an off-line printer.*

off.load *v.* unload.

off.print *n.* a separate print or small edition made from a larger publication, as of a magazine article.
—*v.* make an offprint.

off-putting *adj.* that puts one off; that turns one away: *The formality of the design could be off-putting to some; a financial package with the off-putting title "collateralized mortgage obligation."*

off-season *n.* the period outside the

regular season: *Ski resorts are closed during the off-season;* **adj.**: *a low off-season fare to Florida; off-season rates.*

off.set *n.* **1** a transferring, as printing from an impression made by type on a rubber cylinder instead of directly on paper. **2** make-up or replacement; **adj.**: *an offset arrangement, job.* **3** a bend in a screwdriver to enable it to reach a hidden screwhead.
—*v.* (of.SET) **-sets, -set, -set.ting** balance or compensate for something: *higher wages to offset rising prices.*

off.shoot *n.* something proceeding from a main part, as a branch growing from a main stem.

off.shore *adj.* **1** away from the shore: *an offshore oil well;* **adv.**: *winds blowing offshore.* **2** overseas or foreign: *two domestic and three offshore companies; offshore students.*

off.side *adj. & adv.* in hockey, soccer, etc., illegally ahead of the puck, ball, etc.

off.spring *n., pl.* **-spring** or **-springs** **1** descendants or progeny: *to produce offspring; numerous offspring; Those kids are the offsprings* (= *children*) *of movie stars.* **2** outcome: *Famine is often the offspring of war.*

off.stage *n.* the part of a stage not visible to the audience. —**adj. & adv.** private or privately; behind the scenes.

off-the-cuff *adj. Informal.* offhand: *off-the-cuff advice; an off-the-cuff remark, style of humor;* **adv.**: *comments made off-the-cuff.*

off-the-record *adj.* not to be quoted.

off-the-wall *adj. Informal.* unusual or unorthodox.

off.track *adja.* away from the race track: *offtrack betting.*

off-white *adj.* grayish or yellowish white.

off-year *n.* **1** a year of reduced activity or production. **2** a year outside of a regular presidential election year in the U.S.

oft *adv.* [poetic] often.

of.ten (OF.un, -tun) *adv.* frequently; also **of.ten.times.**

o.gle (OH.gul) *v.* **o.gles, o.gled, o.gling** glance with love and desire at someone: *boys and girls ogling each other; Sam ogles at every passing girl.*
—*n.* an amorous glance. —**o.gler** *n.*

o.gre (OH.gur) *n.* a man-eating monster of folklore; **o.gress** (OH.gris) *fem.*
—**o.gre.ish** *adj.*

oh *interj.* calling someone's attention, expressing surprise, etc.: *Oh John! Oh boy! Oh yes? Oh no!* [with rising and falling tone] *Uh-oh* (= something wrong)!

ohm *n.* a unit of electrical resistance; **ohm.ic** *adj.*

o.ho (oh.HOH) *interj.* expressing surprise, taunting, etc.

oil *n.* **1** a greasy or fatty liquid that is lighter than water, obtained from mineral, animal, or vegetable matter: *Oil and water do not mix; A film of oil covered the driveway.* **2** petroleum: *to hit or strike oil; to pump, produce, refine oil; an oil slick on the water; an oil spill from a tanker.* **3** oil color or oil painting: *to paint in oils; Picasso painted his first oil at age 9.* —**adja.** having to do with oil: *an oil medium, painting, tanker.*
—*v.* treat, supply, or lubricate with oil: *to oil the levers of power;* **adj.**: *an oiled bowl, finish, pan; nicely tanned and oiled; Keep the engine oiled;* **well-oiled** *machinery.*

oil.cloth *n.* heavy waterproof cloth treated with oil or paint and used as covering for tables, walls, etc.

oil color *n.* paint in which oil is the vehicle.

oil-shale *n.* shale containing oil.

oil.skin *n.* **1** same as OILCLOTH. **2** usu. **oilskins** *n.pl.* clothes made of oilskin.

oil well *n.* a well drilled for obtaining petroleum.

oil.y (OY.lee) *adj.* **oil.i.er, -i.est 1** of or like oil; greasy: *oily cloth, hair, hands, skin.* **2** fawning, esp. in an oily way: *his oily tongue; her oily smile.*

oink *v.* make the noise of a hog.

oint.ment (OINT.munt) *n.* a fatty medicinal or cosmetic preparation to put on the skin.

O.jib.wa (oh.JIB.way, -wah) *n.* (a member of) an Algonkian-speaking Indian people who formerly lived around Lake Superior; also **O.jib.way.**

OK or **o.kay** (oh.KAY, OH.kay) *adj., adv. & interj. Informal.* all right: *Is she OK? Is it OK to smoke here? an OK guy; Are you doing OK? OK!*
—*n., pl.* **OK's** or **o.kays** approval: *to get the boss's OK; The boss has given his OK to the plan.* —*v.* **OK's** or **o.kays, OK'd** or **o.kayed, OK'ing** or **o.kay.ing** approve: *The boss had to OK it first.*

o.key-doke (OH.kee.DOKE) *adj. & interj. Informal.* same as OK; also **o.key-do.key** (-kee).

o.kra (OH.cruh) *n.* a shrub of the mallow family bearing sticky green pods used in stews, to thicken soup, etc.

ol' or **ole** (OLE) *adj. Informal.* old: *good ol' boys back home; ol' man winter; Ol' Man River (Mississippi).*

old *adj.* **1** grown in years; not young:

an old lady; a grand old age; at the ripe old age of 90; died of old age; in an **old-age home.** 2 having existed, been in use, etc. for some time: *old clothes; an old friend.* 3 in regard to age: *How old is the baby? She's a year old.* 4 former: *a teacher's old students; old school ties.* —*n.* the past time: *in days of old.* —**the old** old persons or things. —**old.ness** *n.*
old boy *n.* 1 an alumnus of a boys' school: *an old boys' association.* 2 a member of a long-established and privileged social or professional clique; *adj*a.: *an old-boy club; the old-boy establishment; old-boy connections; the* **old-boy network** *that hinders women and minorities from getting jobs.*
old country *n.* an immigrant's original country.
old.en (OLE.dun) *adj.* [poetic] old: *in olden days.*
old-fashioned *adj.* 1 old in fashion, ways, tastes, etc.: *an old-fashioned gentleman; a woman of old-fashioned goodness; old-fashioned oats; Do it the old-fashioned way.* 2 out of fashion: *an old-fashioned dress; old-fashioned music, standards, thinking, values, washboards.*
old fogy (or **fogey**) See FOGY.
Old Glory *n.* the U.S. national flag.
old guard *n.* the older and more conservative members of a group.
old hand *n.* an experienced person.
old hat *n. Informal.* something that one is accustomed to: *Your new idea is old hat to me.*
old.ie (OLE.dee) *n. Informal.* an old person or thing, esp. a musical piece: *a golden oldie;* **adj**a.: *an* **oldies** *concert, show, station.*
old.ish *adj.* somewhat old.
old lady *n. Informal.* one's mother or wife.
old-line *adj.* established or conservative: *an old-line neighborhood store, preacher, statesman; the old-line moderate wing of the party.*
old maid *n.* 1 a woman who has never married. 2 a prim or fussy person. —**old-maid.ish** *adj.*
old man *n. Informal.* one's father or husband.
old master *n.* 1 a distinguished European painter before 1700. 2 a work by an old master.
old money *n.* inherited wealth.
old school *n.* the conservative or old-fashioned group of society; *adj*a.: *an old-school liberal, manager, traditionalist; old-school paternalism.*
old.ster (OLD.stur) *n. Informal.* an old person.

old-time *adj.* of the past; of long standing: *old-time favorites, radio, traditions, virtues, wine-makers; an old-time crafts fair, snake oil peddler.*
old-timer *n. Informal.* a veteran or other old person.
old wives' tale *n.* an old and foolish belief.
Old World *n.* Europe, Asia, and Africa; the Eastern Hemisphere: *Old World charm;* [in reference to W. Europe] *Old World hospitality.*
o.lé (oh.LAY) *interj. & n. Spanish.* a shout of approval.
ole same as OL'.
o.le.ag.i.nous (oh.lee.AJ.uh.nus) *adj.* 1 producing oil. 2 oily or fawning.
o.le.an.der (OH.lee.an.dur) *n.* a poisonous shrub with lance-shaped leaves and roselike flowers.
o.le.o (OH.lee.oh) *n.* [short form] oleomargarine.
o.le.o.mar.ga.rine (OH.lee.oh.MAR.juh.rin) same as MARGARINE.
ol.fac.to.ry (ole.FAC.tuh.ree) *adj.* of the sense of smell: *olfactory nerves; the olfactory organ* (= nose).
ol.i.gar.chy (OL.uh.gar.kee) *n.* -**chies** 1 a state or corporation ruled by a small group. 2 such a group or their government. —**ol.i.gar.chic** (-kic) or **ol.i.gar.chi.cal** (-ki.cul) *adj.*
Ol.i.go.cene (OL.uh.go.seen) *n. & adj.* (of) the third epoch of the Cenozoic era of the earth, beginning about 40 million years ago.
ol.ive (OL.iv) *n.* a Mediterranean evergreen tree with soft gray-green leaves, bearing small, oval fruit that is purple to black when ripe and contains much oil. —*adj.* yellow to yellow-green.
olive branch *n.* the branch of an olive as a peace emblem: *to extend* or *hold out* or *offer the olive branch.*
olive drab *n.* a dark olive cloth, formerly used for army uniforms.
olive green *n.* the color of unripe olive; yellowish green.
ol.i.vine (OL.uh.veen) *n.* a greenish silicate of magnesium and iron.
O.lym.pi.ad or **o.lym.pi.ad** (oh.LIM.pee.ad) *n.* 1 the Olympic games. 2 in ancient Greece, a period of four years as between two Olympic games.
O.lym.pi.an (oh.LIM.pee.un) *adj.* 1 of or from **Olympia**, a plain in ancient Greece where the ancient Olympic games were held every four years. 2 having to do with Mount Olympus in northern Greece, the supposed home of the gods; hence, lofty: *Olympian heights; decisions handed down*

Olympic / once

from the Olympian detachment of the highest court of the land; two women facing Olympian (= superior) *odds in a group dominated by 132 men.* —*n.* **1** an Olympic athlete. **2** a god.

O.lym.pic (oh.LIM.pic) *adj.* **1** having to do with the Olympics: *The Olympic games are held every four years; Olympic gold; an Olympic athlete, hero, medal.* **2** having to do with Mount Olympus; Olympian. —**Olympics** *n.pl.* a series of athletic contests held every four years, as in ancient Greece: *The modern international Olympics started in 1876; the summer and winter Olympics;* also **Olympic games.**

Om (OHM) *n.* a Hindu mantra or sacred syllable suggestive of the ultimate reality.

om.buds.man (OM.buds.mun, om.BUDS-) *n.* **-men 1** an independent government official investigating citizens' complaints against the government. **2** any resident mediator: *media, prison, university ombudsmen.*

o.me.ga (oh.MEE.guh, -MAY.guh) *n.* the last letter of the Greek alphabet [Ω, ω].

om.e.let or **om.e.lette** (OM.lit, -uh.lit) *n.* eggs beaten and cooked in a pan without stirring: *cheese, Spanish, Western omelets.*

o.men (OH.mun) *n.* something considered as foretelling a future event: *Some people consider a howling dog an omen of death; not a good omen for a journey.*

om.i.nous (OM.uh.nus) *adj.* as if threatening evil: *an ominous sign, sound, trend.* —**om.i.nous.ly** *adv.*

o.mis.sion (oh.MISH.un) *n.* an omitting or thing omitted: *a glaring omission.*

o.mit (oh.MIT) *v.* **o.mits, o.mit.ted, o.mit.ting 1** fail to include: *to omit a name from a list.* **2** fail to do: *Do not omit to call me when you arrive.*

omni- *comb.form.* all: *omnibus, omnipotent, omniscience.*

om.ni.bus (OM.ni.bus) *n.* **-bus.es** formerly, a bus. —*adj.* dealing with many items at once: *omnibus bills, packages, talks.*

om.nip.o.tent (om.NIP.uh.tunt) *adj.* all-powerful, as God. —**om.nip.o.tence** *n.*

om.ni.pres.ent (om.ni.PREZ.unt) *adj.* present everywhere at all times, as God. —**om.ni.pres.ence** *n.*

om.nis.cient (om.NIS.ee.unt, om.NISH.unt) *adj.* knowing all things, as God. —**om.nis.cience** *n.*

om.ni.um-gath.er.um (OM.nee.um. GATH.uh.rum, "TH" as in "the") *n.* a miscellaneous collection or assemblage.

om.ni.vore (OM.nuh.vor) *n.* one that is omnivorous.

om.niv.o.rous (om.NIV.uh.rus) *adj.* eating any sort of food indiscriminately, as a bear: *an omnivorous animal, insect, reader.* —**om.niv.o.rous.ly** *adv.;* **om.niv.o.rous.ness** *n.*

on *prep.* **1** [indicating position implying contact from above or imposition]: *the food on the table; shoes on your feet; pictures on the wall; a tax on profits; He heaped insult on insult; She is on the phone all the time; to sit on a committee* (as a member); *The police have nothing on* (= no evidence against) *you; The drinks are on me* (= I'm paying for them). **2** toward: *a march on Parliament Hill.* **3** by means of: *as seen on TV.* **4** [indicating engaged condition or process]: *a house on fire; cars on sale; men on business; operators on duty.* **5** [indicating time]: *on a clear day; on our departure; on your birthday.* **6** concerning: *a lecture on poetry; books on Milton; bent on mischief.* —*adv.* **1** [indicating position implying contact from above or imposition]: *Put your coat on.* **2** [indicating the beginning of an activity]: *Turn on the lights.* **3** [indicating continuation of an activity]: *Let's move on; Hold on to the ropes; Go on with your speech! She's well on* (= advanced) *in years; The speech went on and on* (= without stopping). —**on and off** now and then. —**on to** *Informal.* aware of: *He seems to be on to something.* —**and so on** and so forth; et cetera. —*adj.* in progress or operation: *The switch was on, not off; Press the on button; The movie is on now; You're on* (*Informal* for in the business or competition); *an on-again off-again friendship.*

on-air *adja.* by means of air waves, not by cable: *on-air radio and TV programs.*

on-camera *adja. & adv.* before a TV or movie camera: *an on-camera interview.*

once (WUNCE) *adv.* at one time; on one occasion: *He visits us once a year; a once* (= formerly) *wealthy man; She is never once* (= ever) *late for work.* —**once for all** or **once and for all** finally and conclusively. —**once in a while** now and then. —**once upon a time** long ago. —*conj.* as soon as: *You can ask him once he is here.* —*n.* one time: *Lend me the car just this once.* —*adja.* former: *T. H. White's "The Once and Future King [Arthur]."* —**at once 1** immediately: *Come here at once!* **2** simultaneously: *I can't be in two places at once.*

once-over *n. Informal.* a quick, evaluating look or action: *to give someone the once-over; a quick once-over.*

on.com.ing (ON.cum.ing) *adja.* approaching: *He ran into oncoming traffic; an oncoming attack, crisis, truck; in oncoming years;* **n.:** *the oncoming of winter.*

one (WUN) *n.* **1** the cardinal number 1: *It's one o'clock now; one p.m.* **2** something marked one, as a card or bill: *Two fives and three ones make $13.* —**pron.** a person or thing: *Are you the one who phoned? He is one of them; the ones who are homeless; There's room for only one; One* (= any person) *should watch one's language; One* (= I, you, we, or people) *would like to think jogging is good for your health; We are* **at one** (= in agreement) *on this issue; I,* **for one** (= certainly), *am against smoking; family members who love* **one another** (= each other); **One by one** (= one after another) *they came back; We are* **one up on** (= We have an advantage over) *the competition with our offer of free tickets instead of discount coupons; We deal with each other* **one on one** (= directly); **adja.:** *a* **one-on-one** (= direct or individual) *relationship.* —**adja.** being a single thing or individual: *one book; two people of one* (= same) *mind; One* (= a certain) *John Smith called.* —**one.ness** *n.*

O.nei.da (oh.NYE.duh) *n.* (a member of) an Iroquois Indian people formerly living in C. New York state.

one-liner *n.* a joke or wisecrack in one sentence, as "After she kissed him, he was still a frog."

one-night stand *n.* a one-time performance (as of a play) or experience (as of making love to someone).

one-off *adja.* occurring only once: *a one-off situation.*

101 (wun.oh.WUN) *comb.form.* elementary level in a subject: *You start the program with Rocket Science 101; The brash new recruit had skipped Modesty 101.*

on.er.ous (ON.ur.us) *adj.* burdensome or laborious: *an onerous duty, task.*

one.self (wun.SELF) *pron.* one's own self: *a job difficult to do all* **by oneself** (= without help). —**be oneself 1** act naturally: *Be yourself!* **2** feel well or normal: *I'm not myself today.*

one-shot *adja.* achieved or effective by only one action: *a one-shot affair, approach, answer, deal, lead, remedy, solution, victory.*

one-sided *adj.* **1** having one side more prominent or more developed: *a one-sided leaf.* **2** unequal or uneven: *a one-sided game.* **3** prejudiced: *a one-sided decision, umpire.*

one-time *adja.* **1** former: *a one-time professor of Yale.* **2** being or made only once: *a one-time offer.*

one-to-one *adj.* **1** of two sets, matching every element in one set with one and only one in the other: *There is no one-to-one correspondence between English letters and their sounds, as the sound of "c" in "cat," "ice," "chat," etc.* **2** direct; one on one: *The volunteers worked on a one-to-one basis with the children needing help; a one-to-one dialogue, ratio, relationship.* —**adv.:** *They fought* **one to one** *against the enemy.*

one-track *adja. Informal.* thinking about just one thing: *a one-track mind.*

one-two punch *n.* in boxing, a left-hand jab and right punch in quick succession.

one-up *adj. Informal.* one step ahead of one's competitor; hence, in a position of advantage: *We are one-up on the competition;* **v.:** *two kids trying to one-up each other.* —**one-up.man.ship** (-mun.ship) *n.*

one-way *adj.* in one direction only: *a one-way street; one-way traffic; a one-way* (= not return) *ticket home; a* **one-way mirror** *(that you can hide behind and look through).*

on.go.ing (ON.go.ing) *adj.* moving forward or continuing: *an ongoing business, problem, relationship, research project.*

on.ion (UN.yun) *n.* **1** the pungent edible bulb of a plant of the lily family. **2** the plant.

on.ion.skin (UN.yun.skin) *n.* a tough, thin, translucent paper.

online or **on-line** *adj.* directly connected to a computer: *For online Help, press F1; an on-line printer, service;* **adv.:** *a printer operating on-line.*

on.look.er (ON.look.ur) *n.* one who is looking on.

on.ly (OHN.lee) *adj.* alone of its kind; sole: *the only child of her parents; the only one for me; a club for men only.* —**adv.** solely: *I've only one pair of hands; I did it only for you; He only got* (= got nothing more than) *a C+ in the test; I can only walk or run, not fly; He's only* (= just) *a child; I would fly* **if only** *I could; I would be* **only too** (= very) *glad to fly.* —**conj.** but: *I would fly, only I can't afford it.*

on.o.mat.o.poe.ia (ON.uh.mat.uh.PEE.uh) *n.* imitation of sounds, as in word-formation (e.g. "meow," "crash"), or the use of words suggestive of sense, as in Dryden's "The double

Onondaga / open

double double beat of the thundering drum"; **on.o.mat.o.poe.ic** or **on.o.mat.o.po.et.ic** (-poh.ET.ic) *adj.*

On.on.da.ga (on.un.DAW.guh, -DAH.guh) *n.* a member of an Iroquois Indian people formerly living in C. New York state.

on.rush *n.* a rushing forward: *the onrush of change.* —**on.rush.ing** *adj.*: *the onrushing stream, tide, wind.*

on.set *n.* a vigorous start or attack: *the onset of a disease, of an enemy, of winter.*

on.shore *adj.* on or toward the shore; not offshore: *onshore oil;* **adv.**: *winds blowing onshore.*

on.side *adv.* to the side as support, not offside: *to get more people to come onside and work for them.*

on-site *adj.a.* at the site of a particular activity: *on-site day care, investigation, parking, se testing.*

on.slaught (ON.slawt) *n.* a violent attack.

on.to (ON.too) *prep.* 1 to and upon: *thrown onto the ground.* 2 *Informal.* on to; aware of: *Don't let the other guy get onto our plans.*

on.tog.e.ny (on.TOJ.uh.nee) *n.* (the history of) the development of an individual organism from egg to birth and growth.

on.tol.o.gy (on.TOL.uh.jee) *n.* metaphysics, esp. the branch dealing with existence and reality.

o.nus (OH.nus) *n.* burden or responsibility: *the onus of proving a charge.*

on.ward (ON.wurd) *adj.* forward: *the onward march of events; an onward journey, shipment; from January 1 onward; from this point onward; from that time onward.* —*adv.*: *They moved onward; progressing ever onward and upward;* also **on.wards.**

on.yx (ON.ix) *n.* a banded variety of marble or agate used as a gem, esp. for carving cameos.

oo.dles (OO.duls) *n.pl. Informal.* a great amount; lots: *toast with oodles of marmalade; There are oodles of things to do.*

ooh and aah *v.* express joy or surprise by sighing: *The children started oohing and aahing when Santa appeared with the gifts;* *n.*: *Santa was greeted with* **oohs and aahs** *by the children.*

o.o.lite (OH.uh.lite) *n.* a limestone rock or deposit with a concentric or radial crystalline structure. —**o.o.lit.ic** (-LIT.ic) *adj.*: *oolitic chert, limestone.*

oomph (OOMF) *n. Informal.* 1 sex appeal. 2 vigor or vitality.

oops same as WHOOPS.

ooze (OOZ) *v.* **ooz.es, oozed, ooz.ing** leak out or seep gradually, as through small holes: *blood oozing from a wound; a broken pot oozing water; Our hostess oozes hospitality; Her hubby oozes with* (= is full of) *charm.* —*n.* 1 something that oozes. 2 mud or slime, esp. the deposit at the bottom of a body of water. 3 a bog or marsh.

oo.zy (OO.zee) *adj.* **-zi.er, -zi.est** 1 oozing. 2 slimy. —**oo.zi.ness** *n.*

op or **op art** *n.* abstract painting in geometric patterns creating optical illusions of flickering movement; also called "optical art."

o.pac.i.ty (oh.PAS.i.tee) *n.* **-ties** a being opaque or something opaque.

o.pal (OH.pul) *n.* a gemstone remarkable for reflecting light in a rainbow-like play of colors. —**o.pal.es.cent** (-LES.unt) *adj.*; **o.pal.es.cence** *n.*

o.paque (oh.PAKE) *adj.* 1 impenetrable by light, sound, heat, etc., esp. not transparent or translucent. 2 mentally obtuse; stupid. —**o.paque.ness** *n.*

op art See OP.

ope *v.* **opes, oped, op.ing** [old use] open.

Op-Ed or **Op-Ed page** *n.* a newspaper page, usu. facing the editorial page, containing special features.

o.pen (OH.pun) *adj.* 1 not closed, covered, confined, clogged, etc.: *an open box, view, wound; Walk in through the open door; We're open for business from 9 to 5; Public parks are open to everyone; the wide open spaces of the countryside; By publishing it, you're laying yourself open to public criticism; She's quite open* (= straightforward) *with us; in open* (= not frozen) *waters.* 2 having holes: *Netting is an open fabric.* 3 public, not secret: *an open challenge, letter, violation.* 4 undecided: *an open question.* 5 receptive, not prejudiced: *an open mind; I'm* **open to** *suggestions.* 6 generous: *He gives to charity with an open hand; We received, waited for, welcomed her* **with open arms** (= warmly).

—*v.* make or become open: *to open a carton; Open your mouth wide for the dentist; The door of the fridge opens on the left; Schools open in September; We open* (= start) *our meetings with a hymn; Children* **open up** (= feel free) *and start talking when you gain their confidence.*

—*n.* **the open** 1 open land or water; the outdoors. 2 public knowledge: *Let's bring the dispute out into the open and try to settle it by discussion.* 3 a tournament open to amateurs and professionals: *the U.S. Open (tennis tournament); the U.S. Golf Open.*

open air / operative

—**o.pen.er** n. —**o.pen.ly** adv.; **o.pen.ness** n.

open air n. air that is not confined; outdoors: *out of the house and into the open air.* —*adj.*: *an* **open-air** (= outdoor) *café, market, theater.*

open-and-shut case n. *Informal.* an issue that is easily settled, being straightforward or obvious.

open book n. a person or thing that has nothing hidden about it: *Our plans are an open book to the competition;* **adj***a*.: *the* **open-book** *approach, manager; open-book accounting, relationships, testing.*

open-door policy n. a nation's policy of admitting immigrants of all nationalities without bias.

open-ended adj. not closed at one end; adaptable in regard to time and such limits: *an open-ended container, contract, mortgage, program, schedule; an open-ended return ticket; open-ended talks; An essay is an open-ended, not multiple-choice question.*

open-faced adj. **1** candid-looking. **2** without a top slice of bread: *an open-faced sandwich.*

open-handed adj. liberal in giving: *an open-handed policy.*

open-hearted adj. frank or benevolent: *an open-hearted attitude; her open-hearted collaboration, intimacy.*

open house n. hospitality that is open to everyone, esp. a social event at an institution for a promotional purpose: *Realtors have* or *hold* or *keep open houses to attract buyers for their homes; On Sundays, I hold (an) open house for lexicographers.*

open housing n. housing without discrimination based on age, race, religion, etc.

opening n. **1** a gap or hole; also, a clearing: *an opening in the jungle.* **2** a beginning of operations: *a grand opening of the new building with free coffee and donuts for everyone.* **3** a vacant position or job: *We have an opening for a receptionist.*

open-line adj. hot-line or phone-in: *an open-line radio program.*

open-minded adj. free from prejudices, receptive to new ideas.

open-mouthed adj. with the mouth open: *an open-mouthed pitcher; He gazed in open-mouthed* (= gaping) *astonishment.*

open-pit adj*a*. having to do with mining by excavating the surface of the earth, as for copper, diamonds, and phosphates: *open-pit mines, mining, operations; open-pit deposits and reserves.*

open season n. the legal period of the year for hunting protected game or fish: *the open season on ducks; After the budget is presented, it's open season for the Opposition to attack the Government.*

open sesame n. magical door: *A university degree used to be the open sesame to a good job.*

open shop n. a business employing union and nonunion workers, not a closed shop.

o.pen.work (OH.pun.wurk) n. ornamental work with openings in it.

op.er.a (OP.ur.uh) n. **1** a *pl.* of OPUS. **2** a dramatic composition in which the text is set to music, usu. with orchestral accompaniment: *a comic opera; grand opera; light opera.* **3** something similar to an opera: *a soap opera; horse opera.* —**op.er.at.ic** (op.uh.RAT.ic) adj.

op.er.a.ble (OP.ur.uh.bul) adj. **1** practicable or feasible. **2** that can be surgically operated on: *an operable cancer.*

opera glasses n.pl. small binoculars.

op.er.ate (OP.uh.rate) v. **-rates, -rat.ed, -rat.ing 1** work or run: *He operates a ferry service; It operates day and night; the unfavorable factors operating against us.* **2** perform surgery: *He was operated on for a hernia.*

operating system n. a piece of software for a computer's routine operations such as startup, input and output, filing of data, running programs, etc.

op.er.a.tion (op.uh.RAY.shun) n. **1** an action or procedure: *the smooth operation of a machine; the operation of a factory, law, plan; a surgical operation to remove a tumor; to have* or *undergo, perform an operation; major and minor operations; addition, subtraction, and other arithmetical operations; Computers carry out arithmetical, logical, and transfer operations as specified by instructions; The plant is now* **in operation** (= functioning). **2** a planned and executed mission or project: *military operations; Operation Breadbasket; to conduct, launch an operation; covert, drilling, mopping-up, rescue operations.*

op.er.a.tion.al (op.uh.RAY.shun.ul) adj. **1** functioning: *Our computer network is now operational.* **2** having to do with operation: *operational costs, problems, research.*

op.er.a.tive (OP.uh.ruh.tiv) adj. **1** effective: *the operative clause, phrase, principle, word; The new rules are* or *become operative as of Monday: They will remain operative.* **2** having to do with a surgical operation: *operative treatment.*
—n. an operator, esp. a spy or detective.

op.er.a.tor (OP.uh.ray.tur) *n.* **1** a skilled worker: *computer, crane, radio, telephone operators.* **2** *Informal.* a skillful user of people and materials for one's own purposes: *a slick* or *smooth operator; big-time operators.* **3** a mathematical symbol or instruction: *the AND, NAND, OR, and OR ELSE operators of computer logic.*

op.er.et.ta (op.uh.RET.uh) *n.* a light, short opera such as Gilbert and Sullivan's "The Mikado."

oph.thal.mic (of.THAL.mic, "TH" as in "thin") *adj.* having to do with the eyes: *an ophthalmic dispenser, hospital, vein; ophthalmic drops.*

oph.thal.mol.o.gy (of.thal.MOL.uh.jee) *n.* a branch of medicine dealing with the eyes and eye diseases.
—**oph.thal.mol.o.gist** *n.*

oph.thal.mo.scope (of.THAL.muh.scope) *n.* an optical instrument for viewing the interior of the eye.

o.pi.ate (OH.pee.it, -ate) *n.* **1** a narcotic drug containing opium. **2** anything that soothes or dulls pain.

o.pine (oh.PINE) *v.* **o.pines, o.pined, o.pin.ing** express an opinion in a formal manner: *The researcher opined that children watch too much TV.*

o.pin.ion (uh.PIN.yun) *n.* a conclusion or judgment that seems true or probable though open to dispute: *a matter of opinion, not a certainty; to air, entertain, express, form, hold, offer, venture, voice an opinion; an opinion about* or *on a subject; considered, dissenting, expert, informed, lay opinions; He has a good opinion of the applicant; a high opinion of her; a lawyer's professional opinion; Get a second opinion from another lawyer; In my humble opinion, I deserve a promotion; He is of the opinion that the death penalty should be restored; an opinion* (= decision) *handed down by a court.*

o.pin.ion.at.ed (uh.pin.yuh.NAY.tid) *adj.* dogmatic in one's opinions.

o.pos.sum (uh.POS.um) *n.* a furry, tree-dwelling North American marsupial that will pretend to be dead if surprised on the ground.

op.po.nent (uh.POH.nunt) *n.* one who opposes, esp. in a formal contest such as a game or election: *a formidable opponent.*

op.por.tune (OP.ur.tune) *adj.* done or happening at a favorable time; timely: *an opportune arrival, moment; It was quite opportune;* **op.por.tune.ly** *adv.*

op.por.tun.ism (op.ur.TUE.niz.um) *n.* the taking selfish advantage of opportunities regardless of principles;

op.por.tu.nist *n.* —**op.por.tu.nis.tic** (OP.ur.tue.NIS.tic) *adj.*

op.por.tu.ni.ty (op.ur.TUE.ni.tee) *n.* **-ties** a favorable occasion: *to afford, find, give, have, lose, miss, seize an opportunity; to take the opportunity to do something; attractive, lost, missed, rare opportunities; a job opportunity; an opportunity for mischief; when an opportunity arises; When opportunity knocks* (= offers itself), *seize it; an equal-opportunity employer.*

op.po.sa.ble (uh.POH.zuh.bul) *adj.* that may be opposed or placed against: *the opposable thumb of humans and the great apes.*

op.pose (uh.POZE) *v.* **op.pos.es, op.posed, op.pos.ing** be or place in the way of, against, or in contrast: *We oppose war; We resolutely, vehemently oppose your fighting; We oppose the resolution* (that is being debated); *You pick up objects by opposing thumb to fingers;* **adj.**: *Truth is **opposed to** falsehood; Humans, **as opposed to** beasts, can talk.*

op.po.site (OP.uh.zit) *adj.* set against or contrary to something: *"Truth" and "falsehood" have opposite meanings; They are as diametrically opposite as north and south; the house opposite to ours* (across the street); *the opposite camp* or *side;* **adv.**: *the tree standing opposite.*
—**n.**: *Truth is the opposite of lying; "Truth" and "falsehood" are direct opposites.* —**prep.**: *the house opposite ours; An actor plays opposite* (= in a complementary role; e.g., as husband and wife) *an actress or another actor.*

opposite number *n.* a person or thing corresponding to another in a different system or organization; counterpart.

op.po.si.tion (op.uh.ZISH.un) *n.* **1** an act of opposing or the state of being opposed or in contrast: *the opposition to the death penalty; A full moon is **in opposition to*** (= directly facing) *the sun; to arouse, crush, offer, overcome, put up, run up against, stir up opposition; fierce, stiff, vehement opposition; The bill was passed over the opposition of the other parties.* **2** one that opposes: *the Democratic opposition; The Government faces the Opposition during Question Period;* **adja.**: *an opposition party in parliament; opposition groups, leaders.*

op.press (uh.PRES) *v.* **1** keep down in a cruel way: *people oppressed by heavy taxes;* **adj.**: *an **oppressed** minority; They felt oppressed.* **2** weigh down; burden: *minds oppressed with anxiety.*
—**op.pres.sion** (-PRESH.un) *n.*
—**op.pres.sive** (-PRES.iv) *adj.*: *the*

opprobrious / orangery

oppressive heat of summer; an oppressive policy, regime, system, weight; oppressive forces, humidity, laws, taxation; **op.pres.sive.ly** adv.; **op.pres.sive.ness** n. —**op.pres.sor** (-PRES.ur) n.

op.pro.bri.ous (uh.PROH.bree.us) adj. scornful or abusive: an opprobrious epithet. —**op.pro.bri.ous.ly** adv.

op.pro.bri.um (uh.PROH.bree.um) n. scornful condemnation; infamy: a term of opprobrium.

opt v. decide in favor of something: to opt for a course of action; to opt to do something; to opt out of a group; Half the membership **opted** (= dropped) **out**.

op.tic (OP.tic) adj. of the eye or eyesight: the optic nerve.

op.ti.cal (OP.ti.cul) adj. 1 having to do with light: an optical illusion, instrument; **optical character recognition** software for converting text into digital form with an **optical character reader**; an **optical fiber** (= a fiber-optic strand); **optical scanning** of graphic matter, as coded prices on goods, for computer processing; **optical storage** of music, text, and video on compact discs, or **optical discs**, read by laser beams. 2 visual: an optical defect such as myopia. —**op.ti.cal.ly** adv.

op.ti.cian (op.TISH.un) n. one who makes or sells eyeglasses.

op.tics n.pl. [takes sing. v.] a branch of physics dealing with light and its properties and phenomena.

op.ti.mal (OP.tuh.mul) adj. optimum: optimal amounts, dosages, efficiency, use; an optimal compromise, number, solution; **op.ti.mal.ly** adv.

op.ti.mism (OP.tuh.miz.um) n. the philosophy of looking at the bright side of things or taking the most hopeful view: The President expressed optimism about the future of the country; **op.ti.mist** n. —**op.ti.mis.tic** (-MIS.tic) adj. hopeful: The politician was cautiously optimistic about or over the future.

op.ti.mum (OP.tuh.mum) 1 adj. best or most favorable for some end: the optimum temperature for eggs to hatch. 2 n. an amount, degree, condition, etc. that is optimum: 99.86°F is the optimum for hatching eggs.

op.tion (OP.shun) n. 1 the right or privilege of choosing: A publisher contracts for an option on an author's future work; They may exercise the option to bid on her next novel; a stock option to buy or sell stocks at a given price within a specified period. 2 a choice: There are several options before you; the option of paying a fine or going to jail; a range of options; career, menu, treatment options.

op.tion.al (OP.shun.ul) adj. not required: Ties are optional but shirts are a must; an optional course of study; **op.tion.al.ly** adv.

op.tom.e.try (op.TOM.uh.tree) n. the testing of eyes for vision and prescribing of glasses to correct defects. —**op.tom.e.trist** n.

op.u.lent (OP.yuh.lunt) adj. Formal. suggestive of great wealth and luxury: the opulent court of a prince; opulent surroundings; an opulent (= abundant) growth of hair. —**op.u.lence** n.

o.pus (OH.pus) n., pl. **op.er.a** or **o.pus.es** a work, esp. a musical composition, its number indicating the order of publication: Beethoven's Symphony No. 8 in F major, Opus 93.

or conj. introducing an alternative, as "black or white," or equivalent, as "opus, or work".

-or n. suffix. 1 one that does as specified: actor, creator, objector. 2 an abstract quality or condition: horror, pallor, terror.

or.a.cle (OR.uh.cul) n. 1 a very wise person or his or her prophetic utterance. 2 in ancient Greece and Rome, an answer, often cryptically worded, given by a god to a crucial question put through a priest concerning the future. 3 such a priest or priestess. 4 a place such as Delphi where oracles were delivered. —**o.rac.u.lar** (aw.RAC.yuh.lur) adj.; **o.rac.u.lar.ly** adv.

o.ral (OR.ul) adj. 1 having to do with the mouth: Does a mouthwash help oral hygiene? oral cancer; an oral dose, medication; an **oral contraceptive** (such as the Pill). 2 spoken: an oral (not written) agreement, argument, communication, decision, examination, exchange, source, testimony, tradition, transmission; an **oral history** in the form of tape-recorded interviews with people of the time, oral accounts of aboriginal peoples, etc. —n.: He passed his orals (= oral tests). —**o.ral.ly** adv.

or.ange (OR.inj) n. 1 a round, reddish-yellow, citrus fruit or the tree: a mandarin orange; navel orange. 2 a reddish yellow. —adj. 1 of the color of orange: a bright orange necktie. 2 **Orange** Irish-Protestant: an Orange lodge; the Orange order; We are becoming less and less Orange as immigration increases.

or.ange.ade (or.in.JADE) n. a drink made with orange juice, sugar, and water.

orange pekoe n. a larger size or grade of pekoe.

or.ange.ry (OR.in.juh.ree) n. -ries a

orangutan / order

hothouse for growing oranges in a cold climate.

o.rang.u.tan (o.RANG.oo.tan) *n.* a large arboreal ape of Borneo and Sumatra; also **o.rang.ou.tang.**

o.rate (o.RATE) *v.* **o.rates, o.rat.ed, o.rat.ing** speak in a pompous manner.

o.ra.tion (o.RAY.shun) *n.* a rhetorical or ceremonial speech: *to deliver a funeral oration.*

or.a.tor (OR.uh.tur) *n.* an eloquent public speaker. —**or.a.tor.i.cal** (-TOR.i.cul) *adj.*

or.a.tor.i.o (or.uh.TOR.ee.oh) *n.* **-os** a musical composition, originally on a biblical theme, as in Handel's Messiah, sung to orchestral accompaniment by soloists and a chorus.

or.a.to.ry (OR.uh.tor.ee) *n.* **-ries** 1 skill in or the art of public speaking: *campaign oratory; mob oratory.* 2 a small chapel. —**or.a.tor.i.cal** (-TOR.i.cul) *adj.*

orb *n.* a globe, esp. the sun, moon, or other heavenly sphere.

or.bit *n.* a circular path, as of a planet or satellite: *"Sputnik" was the first artificial earth-satellite put into* or *in orbit; to launch a space capsule and place it in orbit; a service module in a parking orbit around* or *of* or *round the moon; the orbit* (= range) *of one's ambitions.*
—*v.* move in or put into an orbit: *Planets orbit the sun; NASA orbits scientists aboard space shuttles; adj.: an orbiting observatory, satellite.* —**or.bit.al** (-tul) *adj.: an orbital flight, launcher, path, (space) station.* —**or.bit.er** *n.*

or.chard (OR.churd) *n.* 1 a plot containing fruit trees or nut trees. 2 the trees collectively. —**or.chard.ist** *n.*

or.ches.tra (OR.cuh.struh) *n.* 1 a group of musicians playing together on various stringed, wind, and percussion instruments: *to conduct* or *direct* or *lead an orchestra; An orchestra performs; a chamber, philharmonic, string, symphony, pops orchestra;* **adja.:** *an orchestra concert, piece.* 2 the space, or **orchestra pit,** between the audience and the stage in a theater. 3 the whole main floor of a theater. —**or.ches.tral** (-KES.trul) *adj.*

or.ches.trate (OR.cuh.strate) *v.* **-trates, -trat.ed, -trat.ing** 1 compose or arrange music, as for an orchestra: *to orchestrate a ballet.* 2 organize: *a general strike orchestrated by the unions; to orchestrate an election, offensive, publicity campaign; adj.: a well-orchestrated effort, presentation, production, show of solidarity.*
—**or.ches.tra.tion** (-TRAY.shun) *n.*

or.chid (OR.kid) *n.* 1 any of a large family of beautiful flowers with three petals, including a specially shaped "lip," as in the lady-slipper. 2 the plant. 3 a pale purple.

or.dain (or.DAIN) *v.* 1 invest with one's office: *to ordain a minister, priest, rabbi; Joe was ordained priest by his bishop;* see ORDINATION. 2 decree or establish, as by a supreme power: *It happened as God had ordained from eternity;* **or.dain.ment** *n.*

or.deal (or.DEEL, OR.deel) *n.* a severe test or experience: *In ancient justice systems, the accused would undergo ordeals by combat, fire, water, etc.; The cross-examination was a trying ordeal.*

or.der (OR.dur) *n.* 1 an authoritative telling of what one wants; command or requisition: *"Go home" is an order, not a request; to carry out, execute, issue, obey, rescind, revoke, take, violate an order; an order to report for duty; a court, gag, restraining order; confined to bed on doctor's orders; marching orders; The sentry is under orders to shoot on sight.* 2 a request for goods or services in return for payment; also, such goods: *to cancel, fill, place, take a customer's order; delivery of an order; two orders of coffee; a money order* (= ordering document) *purchased at a bank.* 3 arrangement according to a system: *words in alphabetical order; events in chronological order; numerical order; arranged according to order of importance; She left the room in good order.* 4 systematic procedure: *a **point of order** raised by a member in parliament; You're **out of order**, please withdraw your remark, declared the president.* 5 harmony with what is considered good: *Governments establish order in society; Police try to maintain law and order; to restore order after a fight.* 6 a rank, grade, or class: *The squirrel, beaver, and rat families belong to the rodent order of the mammal class; Barons are the lowest order of nobles; an intellect of a high order; Brahmins were at the top of the pecking order in Hindu society; "The **old order** changeth giving place to the new"* (= An old social order gives way to a new one); *efforts to restore the old order.* 7 an organized religious or social group: *the Carmelite Order; a cloistered order; the Loyal Order of Moose.* 8 a form or style: *the Doric, Ionic, and Corinthian orders of Greek architecture.*
—**call to order** order a group or a member to be quiet: *The chair calls a meeting to order.* —**in order** proper: *Celebrations are in order after a victory.*
—**in order that** so that. —**in order to** as a means to; so as to. —**in (or out**

order-in-council / organization

of order working (or not) working properly, as a machine. **—on order** ordered but not yet received. **—on the order of** in the range of: *They got raises on the order of 10%.* **—to order** as required by buyer: *a suit made to order.* **—v. 1** tell authoritatively; command: *Doctors order patients to bed; just what the doctor ordered; She ordered (food) for the whole family.* **2** arrange according to a system: *to order one's affairs, life.* **—order about** or **around** tell someone to do this and that in a domineering way.

order-in-council *n., pl.* **orders-in-council** an order passed by a provincial or federal cabinet.

or.der.ly (OR.dur.lee) *adj.* **1** well-behaved. **2** well-organized. **—adv.** in a well-organized manner. **—n.,** *pl.* **-lies** a male attendant, as in a hospital or in the service of an army officer. **—or.der.li.ness** *n.*

order of business *n.* a task to be dealt with as scheduled: *The first order of business was a roll call.*

order of the day *n.* what is generally happening or is approved of: *Is vegetarianism becoming the order of the day?*

order paper *n.* the agenda of a legislature: *Many bills die on the order paper (without being considered).*

or.di.nal (OR.duh.nul) *adj.* expressing order in a series: *the ordinal numbers.* **—n.** a number such as 1st, 2nd, 3rd, etc.

or.di.nance (OR.dun.unce) *n.* a law or regulation, esp. one issued by a local authority such as a municipality: *a fire-prevention ordinance prohibiting the construction of wooden sheds; zoning ordinances; to adopt, apply, enforce an ordinance.*

or.di.nar.y (OR.duh.nair.ee) *adj.* **1** usual or normal: *an ordinary experience; Snow in summer is something* **out of the ordinary.** **2** common; hence, average or somewhat inferior: *an ordinary dress, poet, wine.* **—or.di.nar.i.ly** (-NAIR.uh.lee) *adv.*

or.di.nate (OR.dun.it, -ate) *n.* the distance of a point on a graph along its vertical axis.

or.di.na.tion (or.duh.NAY.shun) *n.* an ordaining or being ordained as a priest, minister, or rabbi: *the ordination of women to the priesthood.*

ord.nance (ORD.nunce) *n.* **1** military weapons and ammunition: *naval ordnance.* **2** the tools used in their manufacture and maintenance.

Or.do.vi.cian (or.duh.VISH.un) *n. &* *adj.* (of) the second period of the Paleozoic era of the earth, beginning about 400 million years ago.

or.dure (OR.jur) *n.* dung or filth; excrement.

ore *n.* rock or mineral from which gold, silver, iron, sulfur, fluorides, and such deposits may be extracted.

o.reg.a.no (uh.REG.uh.noh) *n.* the Mediterranean marjoram.

or.gan (OR.gun) *n.* **1** a keyboard musical instrument used esp. in churches for the solemnity and grandeur of its sound effects which are produced by air forced through pipes, as in a "pipe organ," or electrically, as in an "electronic organ." **2** any similar instrument such as a "hand organ" or "mouth organ." **3** a body part with a specific function: *the organs of digestion, locomotion, speech; the reproductive organs of plants and animals; sense, sensory, vital organs.* **4** means of action or communication: *The army is an organ of government; the official organ (= periodical publication) of a group or party.*

or.gan.dy or **or.gan.die** (OR.gun.dee) *n.* **-dies** a thin, stiff, transparent cotton fabric used for evening dresses, trimmings, etc.

or.gan.ic (or.GAN.ic) *adj.* **1** having to do with a bodily organ: *an organic (= not functional) disorder.* **2** relating to organization into a unit or whole, like that of a living organism: *the organic unity of a literary work;* **organic architecture** *that seems to grow out of its surroundings.* **3** having to do with living things; animal or vegetable: *organic evolution, fertilizers; organic matter such as peat;* **organic chemistry** *(of carbon compounds that make up living tissues).* **—or.gan.i.cal.ly** *adv.*

or.gan.ism (OR.guh.niz.um) *n.* a living thing: *harmful, healthy, living organisms; A virus is a microscopic organism.*

or.gan.ist (OR.guh.nist) *n.* an organ player.

or.gan.i.za.tion (or.guh.nuh.ZAY.shun, -nye-)) *n.* **1** an arranging of parts into a whole: *An essay has to have some organization; Your work shows poor organization; Our party needs more organization and muscle.* **2** something organized, esp. a group: *to disband, dissolve, form an organization; business, charitable, non-profit, philanthropic, professional, religious, student, youth organizations; The United Nations is an international organization; An* **organization chart** *shows company officers and departments; an* **organization man** *(dedicated to his*

company). —**or.gan.i.za.tion.al** *adj.*
or.gan.ize (OR.guh.nize) *v.* **-iz.es, -ized, -iz.ing 1** make or form into a working unit or whole: *to organize a campaign, an essay, one's thoughts, themselves; celebrations organized around a theme; production organized along capitalist lines; organized into two groups; adj.: a small but well **organized** army; Let's get organized; become better organized; our organized efforts; She's an organized student leading an organized life; earthworms and such less organized forms of life that can be cut in two and will continue to live separately.* **2** form into a union or organization: *to organize the workers into a labor union; adj.: **organized** crime, labor, religion.* —**or.gan.iz.er** *n.*
or.gan.za (or.GAN.zuh) *n.* a dress fabric similar to organdy made of silk or a synthetic.
or.gasm (OR.gaz.um) *n.* the climax of sexual excitement. —**or.gas.mic** (or.GAZ.mic) *adj.*
or.gi.as.tic (or.jee.AS.tic) *adj.* being like an orgy: *orgiastic celebration, spending.*
or.gy (OR.jee) *n.* **-gies 1** unrestrained indulgence in eating, drinking, sex, etc. **2** a party for it: *a drunken orgy.*
o.ri.el (OR.ee.ul) *n.* an upper-story bay window projecting outward from the wall face.
o.ri.ent (OR.ee.unt) *n.* **1 the orient** [poetic use] the east. **2 the Orient** East Asia, as distinguished from Europe and America. —*adj.* rising: *the orient sun.* —*v.* (-ent) place something or oneself in a specific direction: *Businesses are oriented toward profit-making; Employees have to orient themselves accordingly; to orient oneself* (= adjust) *to a new place.*
O.ri.en.tal (or.ee.EN.tul) *n.* a native of the Orient: *Chinese, Japanese, Koreans, and other Orientals.* —*adj:* *Oriental arts, cooking, eyes, food, glory, languages, music, pagodas, religions, rugs, silk, splendor, tastes; an oriental-looking bungalow; the difference between the Oriental and Occidental minds.* Also **oriental.**
o.ri.en.tate (OR.ee.en.tate) *v.* **-tates, -tat.ed, -tat.ing 1** same as ORIENT. **2** to place facing east. —**o.ri.en.ta.tion** (-TAY.shun) *n.: to give recruits an orientation* (= introduction) *to the new life; the orientation of new members; orientation rites.*
-oriented *comb.form.* directed toward: *action-oriented, profit-oriented, sports-oriented.*
o.ri.en.teer.ing (OR.ee.un.TEER.ing) *n.* the sport of navigating through the woods with a map and compass.
or.i.fice (OR.uh.fis) *n.* a mouthlike opening or aperture, as of a tube.
o.ri.flamme (OR.uh.flam) *n.* a brightly colored banner, as once carried to battle as an emblem; hence, a rallying point.
o.ri.ga.mi (or.uh.GAH.mee) *n.* the Japanese art of folding paper to make decorative objects.
or.i.gin (OR.uh.jin) *n.* **1** how or where something comes into being; beginning: *the origin of the universe; the origin of a river.* **2** ancestry or parentage: *one's land of origin; a man of humble origin; The word "orgy" is of Greek origin* (= etymology); *"Dab" is of uncertain origin.* **3 origins** *pl.* where something originates; roots: *her aristocratic origins; the origins of civilization.*
o.rig.i.nal (uh.RIJ.uh.nul) **1** *adj.* initial or earliest: *the original inhabitants of the New World; a book translated from the original Latin (text).* **2** *adj.* new; not copied: *a very original idea; an original work, not a translation; her original* (= inventive) *mind.* —*n.* the very first source or specimen: *a translation that is close to the original; Who was the original of the Mona Lisa?* —**o.rig.i.nal.ly** *adv.*
o.rig.i.nal.i.ty (uh.rij.uh.NAL.i.tee) *n.* the quality of being original, fresh, or creative.
o.rig.i.nate (uh.RIJ.uh.nate) *v.* **-nates, -nat.ed, -nat.ing** come or bring into being, esp. as new: *Where did the rumor originate? Who originated it? Gossip originates from curiosity; It originates with people talking too much.* —**o.rig.i.na.tion** (-NAY.shun) *n.* —**o.rig.i.na.tor** (-nay.tur) *n.*
o.ri.ole (OR.ee.ole) *n.* an insect-eating songbird with beautiful feathers that weaves a hanging nest.
or.i.son (OR.uh.sun) *n.* Archaic. prayer.
Or.lon *adj.* Trademark. an acrylic fiber used esp. for fabrics.
or.mo.lu (OR.muh.loo) *n.* brass or bronze resembling gold, used to decorate furniture.
or.na.ment (OR.nuh.munt) *n.* something added for greater beauty, as rings, bracelets, Christmas-tree decorations, etc.: *Beauty needs no ornament; a woman who is not just an ornament to her home; garden ornaments such as statuary, fountains, and lamps.* —*v.* (-ment) beautify or embellish: *lace to ornament a dress.* —**or.na.men.ta.tion** (-men.TAY.shun) *n.* —**or.na.men.tal** (-MEN.tul) *adj.*
or.nate (or.NATE) *adj.* much orna-

ornery / osteopathy

mented: *an ornate vase; ornate* (= flowery) *prose.* —**or.nate.ly** *adv.*; **or.nate.ness** *n.*
or.ner.y (OR.nuh.ree) *adj. Informal.* mean or irritable: *an ornery beast, remark; a downright mean and ornery character;* **or.ner.i.ness** *n.*
or.ni.thol.o.gy (or.nuh.THOL.uh.jee) *n.* the scientific study of birds; **or.ni.thol.o.gist** *n.* —**or.ni.tho.log.i.cal** (-thuh.LOJ.i.cul) *adj.*
o.ro.tund (OR.uh.tund) *adj.* 1 of utterance, full-voiced or resonant. 2 bombastic or pompous.
or.phan (OR.fun) *n.* a child who has lost its parents or guardians: *a war orphan.* —*adj.*: *an orphan child; an orphan home* (for orphans). —*v.* make orphan: *Children are orphaned by war, death, fire, etc.; satellite countries orphaned by the collapse of the Soviet Union; adj.: an orphaned child; Tax law changes result in orphaned computer software.* —**or.phan.hood** *n.*
or.phan.age (OR.fuh.nij) *n.* an institution that takes care of orphans.
or.ris *n.* a species of iris whose underground stem, or **orrisroot,** yields a fragrant oil used in perfumes.
ortho- *comb.form.* straight or correct: *orthodontics, orthodox, orthopedist.*
or.tho.don.tics (or.thuh.DON.tics) *n.pl.* [takes *sing. v.*] a branch of dentistry dealing with the correction of tooth irregularities, as by use of braces. —**or.tho.don.tic** *adj.* —**or.tho.don.tist** *n.*
or.tho.dox (OR.thuh.dox) *adj.* generally accepted or traditional, esp. in religious doctrine, practices, etc.: *an orthodox community, establishment, politician; orthodox communism, doctrine, economics, theology, views.* —**or.tho.dox.y** *n.*
or.thog.ra.phy (or.THOG.ruh.fee) *n.* -**phies** the study or a system of spelling. —**or.tho.graph.ic** (or.thuh.GRAF.ic) *adj.*
or.tho.pe.dics (or.thuh.PEE.dics) *n.pl.* [takes *sing. v.*] surgical correction and treatment of deformities, diseases, fractures, etc. of bones and joints. —**or.tho.pe.dic** *adj.* —**or.tho.pe.dist** *n.*
Or.well.i.an (or.WELL.ee.un) *adj.* of society, dehumanized and regimented, as in the novel "1984" by George Orwell.
O.sage (oh.SAGE) *n.* a member of a Siouan Indian people now living in Oklahoma.
Os.car (OS.cur) *n.* a statuette awarded annually by the Academy of Motion Picture Arts and Sciences of America to the best stars, directors, producers, etc.
os.cil.late (OS.uh.late) *v.* -**lates, -lat.ed, -lat.ing** 1 swing like a pendulum; also, vacillate or waver: *to oscillate between hope and despair.* 2 vary, as an electric current. —**os.cil.la.tion** (-LAY.shun) *n.* —**os.cil.la.tor** (-lay.tur) *n.*
os.cil.lo.scope (os.SIL.uh.scope) *n.* an instrument that shows variations of electrical current on a fluorescent screen.
os.cu.late (OSK.yuh.late) *v.* -**lates, -lat.ed, -lat.ing** kiss; **os.cu.la.tion** (-LAY.shun) *n.*
-**ose** *suffix* 1 *n.* carbohydrate: *cellulose, fructose, glucose.* 2 *adj.* full of or fond of something, as specified: *bellicose, jocose, verbose.*
o.sier (OH.zhur) *n.* a willow whose pliable twigs are used in making baskets and furniture.
-**osis** *suffix.* process or condition: *acidosis, metamorphosis, neurosis.*
os.mi.um (OZ.mee.um) *n.* a hard, brittle, metallic chemical element used in alloys.
os.mo.sis (oz.MOH.sis) *n.* the tendency of liquids and gases to pass through a semipermeable membrane or other porous material in order to equalize concentration on both sides: *Plant roots absorb minerals and oxygen enters the blood by osmosis.* —**os.mot.ic** (oz.MOT.ic) *adj.*: *osmotic pressure.*
os.prey (OS.pree) *n.* a bird of the hawk family that catches fish with its sharp talons by diving into water feet first.
os.si.fy (OS.uh.fye) *v.* -**fies, -fied, -fy.ing** 1 change into bone, as cartilage in old people. 2 make or become hardened, as in practices, attitudes, etc. —**os.si.fi.ca.tion** (-fuh.CAY.shun) *n.*
os.su.ar.y (OS.yoo.air.ee) *n.* -**ar.ies** a cave, vault, or urn containing bones of the dead.
os.ten.si.ble (os.TEN.suh.bul) *adj.* professed or seeming: *the ostensible goal, purpose, reason;* **os.ten.si.bly** *adv.*
os.ten.ta.tion (os.tun.TAY.shun) *n.* a showy or pretentious display of wealth. —**os.ten.ta.tious** (-shus) *adj.*; **os.ten.ta.tious.ly** *adv.*
os.te.o.ar.thri.tis (OS.tee.oh.ar.THRY.tis) *n.* arthritis of aging people, marked by degeneration of the bones and joints.
os.te.op.a.thy (os.tee.OP.uh.thee) *n.* a system of medicine that emphasizes the relationship of bones and muscles to the functioning of body organs.

osteoporosis / out

—**os.te.o.path** (OS.tee.uh.path) *n.*; **os.te.o.path.ic** (-PATH.ic) *adj.*
os.te.o.po.ro.sis (OS.tee.oh.puh.ROH.sis) *n.* a disorder in which bones become porous, brittle, and easily fractured.
os.tler (OS.lur) *n. Rare.* hostler.
os.tra.cize (OS.truh.size) *v.* **-ciz.es, -cized, -ciz.ing** banish someone from society, as in ancient Greece. —**os.tra.cism** (-siz.um) *n.*
os.trich *n.* a large, heavy, long-legged, flightless but swift-footed African bird, fabled to hide its head in the sand when frightened.
Os.we.go tea (os.WEE.go-) *n.* a North American mint or the tea brewed from its leaves.
oth.er (UTH.ur, "TH" as in "the") *adja.* different person or thing from one already mentioned or implied: *my other car; Any other question? Some other time, not now;* ***pron.****: One is Tom, who is the other? Tom, Dick, and others.* —**every other** every second person or thing: *We eat meat every other week.* —**other than** except (for): *Other than denying everything, he wouldn't talk; Other than that, I've nothing to say; other than to say I'm sorry; I haven't spoken to him other than by phone.* —**the other day** or **evening** or **morning** or **night** or **week**, recently.
oth.er.wise (UTH.ur.wize) *adv.* **1** in other respects: *an otherwise good record (except in math); an otherwise honest fellow.* **2** differently: *He should be alive today, but Fate willed otherwise;* ***adjp.****: How could it be otherwise? whether living or otherwise* (= not). —***conj.****: Let's hurry, otherwise we may be late.*
oth.er.world.ly (uth.ur.WURLD.lee) *adj.* having to do with a world to come, as after death, or with things of the mind or imagination: *a man of otherworldly* (= spiritual) *concerns.*
—**oth.er.world.li.ness** *n.*
o.ti.ose (OH.shee.oze, OH.tee-) *adj.* purposeless or useless: *otiose criticism, remarks.*
o.to.lar.yn.gol.o.gy (OH.toh.lair.ing.GOL.uh.jee) *n.* a medical specialty dealing with ailments of the ear, nose, and throat.
ot.ter (OT.ur) *n.* an animal of the weasel family that lives close to water and feeds on fish.
ot.to.man (OT.uh.man) **1** *n.* a low, cushioned seat or footstool. **2 Ottoman** *n. & adj.* Turk(ish).
ou.bli.ette (oo.blee.ET) *n.* a dungeon that can be opened only from the top.

ouch *interj.* expressing sudden pain.
ought (AWT) *auxiliary v.* [expressing what is right, desirable, due, etc.]: *You ought to* (= should) *know better; She ought not be kept waiting.*
ought.n't (AWT.unt) ought not.
Oui.ja board (WEE.juh-) *n. Trademark.* an oblong board with letters and numbers printed on it and a pointer that is supposed to be guided by spirits when it indicates answers to questions, as at a séance.
ounce *n.* **1** a unit of weight equal to 1/16 pound avoirdupois (28.35 g) or 1/12 pound troy (31.10 g). **2** a fluid ounce.
our (OWR, AR) *adj.* possessive case of WE: *our books, dog, family.* —**ours** *pron.*: *None of these is ours; Ours is a poodle.*
our.self (owr.SELF) *pron.* [used by courts, editors, and others using "we" instead of "I"] myself.
our.selves (owr.SELVZ) *pron.* reflexive or emphatic form of WE or US: *We ourselves did it; We speak only for ourselves.*
-ous *adj. suffix.* having: *ambitious, glorious, porous.*
oust (OWST) *v.* drive or force out; expel: *an unruly player ousted from a game.*
oust.er (OWS.tur) *n.* expulsion or eviction.
out *adv.* [used after its verb] **1** away from the usual place, condition, etc., esp. away from the center or inside of something; hence, into the open: *when the moon comes out; He stuck out his tongue; to farm out work; He dropped out of school; to let the dog out; She has gone out; an umbrella turned* **inside out**; **adja.**: *a* **coming-out** (= coming into society) *party.* **2** to completion or exhaustion: *She cried her heart out; fought it out with him; The lights are going out* (= off); *The batter flied out* (= was retired). **3** lacking or short: *I was out $10 after paying the bills; She was a few meters out* (= in error) *in her estimate.* —**comb.form. 1** do something better than another: *outbid, outdistance, outfox; to out-Ripley Ripley.* **2** outside: *outdoors, outhouse, outlying, outpatient.*
—**out of 1** away from: *Get out of the way; She was bilked out of her savings; We are out of luck; Such a high raise is* **out of the question** (= cannot be considered); *He is* **out of work** (= unemployed). **2** because of: *He cried out of pain.* **3** from: *a statue carved out of wood.* —**adjp. 1** away: *Fashions are in* (style) *now and out* (of style) *later; The jury is still out* (= undecided) *on the*

case; before the year is out (= finished); *Lights are out* (= not on); **adja.:** an out tray for papers going out; *the Out Islands of the Bahamas.* **2** gone forth or beyond; not inside: *to paint a house inside and out; He is out for a walk; She's out to a meeting; They are out on strike; His calculations are out* (= incorrect) *by $100; The book will be out* (= published) *in the fall.* —**out for** in search of something: *At a party, we're out for fun.* —**out of it** *Informal.* unaware or uninitiated: *He is so out of it, he doesn't know who the latest hockey stars are.* —**out to** intent on: *He's out to make money.* —*v.* be discovered: *Murder will out.* —*prep.* through or along: *He went out the door; We were driving out Lakeshore Road when the news was heard on the radio.* —*n.* **1** one that is out: *people considered outs in an exclusive society.* **2** exit or excuse: *He was without an out or alibi; She knows all the ins and outs* (= details) *of the business.* **3** the act or instance of a player having his or her turn as a batter, base runner, etc. ended. —**on the outs** *Informal.* at odds: *He's on the outs with his colleagues.*

out.age (OW.tij) *n.* an interruption or suspension, as a power failure.

out-and-out *adja.* utter or complete: *an out-and-out denial, falsehood, radical.*

out.back *n.* back country; hinterland: *the Australian outback; Elliot Lake is in the outback of Ontario; an outback town.*

out.bal.ance (out.BAL.unce) *v.* **-anc.es, -anced, -anc.ing** outweigh.

out.bid (out.BID) *v.* **-bids,** *pt. & pp.* **-bid** or **-bid.den, -bid.ding** make a higher bid than another: *She outbid him for the contract.*

out.board *adja.* outside the hull or body of a boat or other craft: *An outboard motor is fitted to a boat's stern.* —*n.* an outboard motor or a boat equipped with one.

out.bound *adj.* traveling outward.

out.break *n.* a sudden occurrence or development, as of a war, disease, etc.

out.build.ing (OUT.bild.ing) *n.* a building separate from the main building.

out.burst *n.* a bursting out, as of applause, fury, laughter, joy, etc.: *angry, sudden, violent outbursts.*

out.cast *adj.* cast out from home or society. —*n.* an outcast person or animal.

out.caste (OUT.cast) *n.* a member of the lowest caste of Hindus; an untouchable.

out.class (out.CLAS) *v.* surpass.

out.come *n.* result or consequence: *the final outcome of the negotiations.*

out.crop *n.* an exposed surface of a rock or stratum. —*v.* to project or appear on the surface.

out.cry *n.* **-cries** a crying out or scream; hence, an uproar: *a public outcry against the proposed new taxes.*

out.dat.ed (out.DAY.tid) *adj.* out-of-date or obsolete: *Clothes fast become outdated; They begin to look outdated as fashions change; outdated customs, equipment, practices, technology.*

out.dis.tance (out.DIS.tunce) *v.* **-tanc.es, -tanced, -tanc.ing** outstrip.

out.do (out.DOO) *v.* **-does, -did, -done, -do.ing** do better than others, previously, etc.

out.door *adja.* of the outdoors; open-air: *outdoor activities, cafes, sports, theaters.*

out.doors (OUT.DORS) *n.* open air: *a lover of the great outdoors; as big as all outdoors.* —*adv.* in or into the open air: *He's gone outdoors; Lee likes to sleep outdoors.*

out.draw (out.DRAW) *v.* **-draws, -drew, -draw.ing** **1** attract a larger crowd than another person or thing: *The football game outdrew the movie.* **2** draw a gun faster than someone else.

out.er *adj.* **1** farther out: *an outer circle; the outer city* (= suburbs). **2** external: *the outer ear; an outer garment.*

out.er.most (OU.tur.most) *adj.* farthest from the center.

outer space *n.* **1** space immediately beyond the atmosphere. **2** interstellar space.

out.er.wear (OU.tur.ware) *n.* clothes worn on the outside or over other clothes, as gloves, sweaters, jackets, coats, etc.

out.face *v.* **-fac.es, -faced, -fac.ing** face someone boldly.

out.field *n.* in baseball, the playing area or players beyond the infield. —**out.field.er** *n.*

out.fit *n.* **1** a group such as a business organization or military unit. **2** equipment for an activity. **3** a set of clothes: *a cowgirl outfit; a holiday outfit.* —*v.* **-fits, -fit.ted, -fit.ting** equip: *to outfit an expedition; He came outfitted for a camping trip; an academic work outfitted with footnotes, appendices, index, etc.; She came to the party outfitted in a spacesuit.* —**out.fit.ter** *n.*

out.flank (out.FLANK) *v.* outmaneuver or outwit, as by getting around the flank of enemy troops.

out.flow *n.* a flowing out or what flows out.

out.fox v. outwit or outsmart.

out.gen.er.al (out.JEN.ur.ul) v. surpass in leadership.

out.go n. **-goes** expenditure: *to keep income and outgo in balance.*

out.go.ing (OUT.go.ing) adj. 1 having initiative: *She is very outgoing as a sales rep; her outgoing personality.* 2 going out: *outgoing calls, mail, shipments; the outgoing tide; the outgoing* (= retiring or defeated) *president.*

out.grow (out.GROH) v. **-grows, -grew, -grown, -grow.ing** grow faster than someone, grow too large for clothes, or grow out of early habits, friendships, etc.

out.growth n. a growing out; offshoot; hence, a result or development: *a natural outgrowth.*

out.guess (out.GUESS) v. defeat by anticipating; outwit: *She outguessed the others and was first to get in when the doors opened.*

out.house n. a small outbuilding, as one used as a toilet.

out.ing n. a short pleasure trip, ride, walk, etc.: *They went on an outing in the park.*

out.land.ish (out.LAN.dish) adj. very strange or bizarre.

out.last (out.LAST) v. last longer than something else; outlive.

out.law n. a person deprived of legal rights, as a notorious criminal. —v. declare a person to be an outlaw or make something illegal: *Chemical warfare has been outlawed.*

out.law.ry (OUT.law.ree) n. the condition of being an outlaw.

out.lay n. 1 a spending of money or other resources as an investment: *to make outlays for installing new machinery.* 2 what is spent: *a huge outlay of $10 million.* —v. (out.LAY) **-lays, -laid, -lay.ing** expend.

out.let n. 1 a means of letting something out, as from a container: *an outlet from a lake; an outlet to the sea; to plug a lamp into an electrical outlet; an outlet for one's energies, emotions.* 2 a market or store: *a factory outlet; retail outlets.*

out.line n. 1 the shape or main features of a subject: *to draw up* or *make an outline; to draw a map* **in outline**; *the outlines of a project.* 2 a drawing, plan, or summary giving an outline: *the rough outline of a plan; an outline of English literature.* —v. **-lines, -lined, -lin.ing** give or define in outline: *He outlined his proposals for a settlement; a skyscraper outlined against the sky.*

out.live (out.LIV) v. **-lives, -lived, -liv.ing** live longer than something else; survive: *Cannons have outlived their usefulness.*

out.look n. 1 what one sees with the mind, esp. about the future; point of view or prospects: *Gita has a cheerful outlook on life; bright, dismal, gloomy, healthy, long-range, positive outlooks; the outlook for the future.* 2 what one sees on looking out; view: *the outlook from the top of the tower.* 3 a place to look out from; lookout.

out.ly.ing (OUT.ly.ing) adja. lying outside the limits or away from the center: *outlying areas, districts, suburbs, villages.*

out.ma.neu.ver (out.muh.NEW.vur) v. **-vers, -vered, -ver.ing** defeat by maneuvering; outwit. Also **out.ma.noeu.vre** Cdn.

out.mod.ed (out.MOH.did) adj. out of fashion or out-of-date.

out.num.ber (out.NUM.bur) v. exceed in number: *Girls outnumber boys in our school.*

out-of-bounds adj. & adv. outside one's limits, as in a game or when straying.

out-of-date adja. old-fashioned or obsolete: *out-of-date fashions, merchandise, records, technology.*

out-of-doors same as OUTDOORS.

out-of-pocket adja. paid out in cash: *petty cash for out-of-pocket expenses.*

out-of-the-way adj. 1 not commonly known; unusual: *out-of-the-way information; There's nothing out-of-the-way about his manner.* 2 remote or unfrequented: *an out-of-the-way eating place, farm.*

out-of-town.er n. *Informal.* someone from out of town.

out.pa.tient (out.PAY.shunt) n. a patient not staying in the hospital while being treated.

out.per.form (out.pur.FORM) v. achieve better results than another: *The new car outperforms the old one.*

out.place.ment (OUT.place.munt) n. help provided by a company in finding a new job for an employee being terminated.

out.play (out.PLAY) v. play better than another.

out.point (out.POINT) v. win more points than someone else.

out.post n. 1 a base or camp, esp. military, away from the main camp: *the last outposts of a vanishing empire.* 2 the personnel assigned to an outpost. 3 a frontier settlement.

out.pour.ing (out.POR.ing) n. a pouring out, esp. an uncontrolled expression:

the outpourings of a tortured soul; an outpouring of grief, rage, sympathy.

out.pull (out.PULL) *v.* attract a larger crowd than something else.

out.put *n.* **1** what is produced, as by a machine: *an engine's heat output; horsepower output; power output; Hollywood's output (of movies); the monthly output of the oil well; to increase* or *step up the output; our annual output of goods and services; adja.: output data, quotas, voltage.* **2** a form in which processed information is put out by a computer: *printout, visual display, and other outputs; adja.: an output device, display, format; output quality, resolution.* —*v.* **-puts, -put.ted, -put.ting** produce as output: *to open a file and output it on the monitor.*

out.rage *n.* a gross violation of the rights or feelings of others or the anger aroused by it: *an outrage against humanity; It's an outrage that such a crime could go unpunished.* —*v.* **-rag.es, -raged, -rag.ing** anger or offend extremely: *a massacre that outraged humanity; adj.: He felt outraged by the false report; an outraged public; outraged at or over or about the shootings; outraged by the new taxes; morally outraged; an outraged response from taxpayers.*

out.ra.geous (out.RAY.jus) *adj.* extremely offensive or shocking: *an outrageous crime, demand, insult; outrageous prices.* —**out.ra.geous.ly** *adv.*

out.rank (out.RANK) *v.* rank higher than another: *An army major outranks a captain.*

out.ré (oo.TRAY) *adj.* outlandish or unconventional.

out.reach (out.REECH) *v.* **1** reach out. **2** exceed: *aspirations that outreach one's achievements.* —*n.* the act of reaching out or its extent: *the social outreach of our ministry; adja.: an outreach program for the disadvantaged; our outreach campaigns, efforts, groups, services.*

out.rid.er (OUT.rye.dur) *n.* **1** an attendant on horseback accompanying a carriage or wagon: *the outriders of a chuckwagon (in chuckwagon racing).* **2** any mounted attendant.

out.rig.ger (OUT.rig.ur) *n.* a boat or canoe equipped with a projecting bracket or framework on either side for supporting the oars or for steadying the craft.

out.right *adj.* complete or utter: *an outright denial, falsehood; an outright and unconditional offer.* —*adv.: She denied the story outright; The fox was run over and killed outright (= then and there).*

out.run (out.RUN) *v.* **-runs, -ran,** **-run.ning 1** run faster than someone else. **2** exceed: *He went broke when he allowed his spending to outrun his income.*

out.sell (out.SEL) *v.* **-sells, -sold, -sell.ing** sell more than another.

out.set *n.* a setting out; start: *at the outset of her career; From the outset, he has been doing well in his job.*

out.shine (out.SHINE) *v.* **-shines,** *pt. & pp.* **-shone** or **-shined, -shin.ing** shine more brightly than another; hence, surpass.

out.side (OUT.side, out.SIDE) *n.* an outer side or location: *to wash the outside of a car; a favorable impression from the outside; To people on this island, the rest of the world is the outside.* —*adja.* **1** exterior: *a house in need of inside and outside repairs.* **2** remote: *an outside chance, possibility.* —*adv. & prep.* on or to the outside of something: *She's waiting outside (the door).* —**at the outside** at the most. —**outside of** *Informal.* with the exception of: *She wouldn't accept any money outside of expenses.*

out.sid.er (out.SYE.dur) *n.* one from outside a group or region: *Nonresidents are outsiders to the islanders.*

out.size *n.* **1** an unusually large size. **2** an outsize garment. —**out.size** or **out.sized** *adj.: outsize cargo, earrings, personalities; an outsized claim, version.*

out.skirts *n.pl.* districts away from the center, as of a city; outer borders: *suburbs on the outskirts of a metropolis.*

out.smart (out.SMART) *v.* outdo in smartness or by cunning.

out.spend (out.SPEND) *v.* **-spends, -spent, -spend.ing** spend more than a limit, another person, etc.

out.spo.ken (out.SPOH.kun) *adj.* open and blunt in speech: *an outspoken critic; He's quite outspoken in his comments.* —**out.spo.ken.ly** *adv.;* **out.spo.ken.ness** *n.*

out.spread (out.SPRED) *adj.* extended: *a bird with its wings outspread; with outspread arms.*

out.stand.ing (out.STAN.ding) *adj.* **1** standing out from the rest; prominent: *an outstanding citizen; She's quite outstanding as a lawyer; outstanding in her accomplishments as a lawyer.* **2** unsettled: *debts still outstanding.* —**out.stand.ing.ly** *adv.*

out.sta.tion (OUT.stay.shun) *n.* an outpost in an unsettled area.

out.stay (out.STAY) *v.* stay longer than someone; overstay: *to outstay one's welcome.*

out.stretched (out.STRECHT) *adj.* stretched out; outspread: *He came for-*

ward with an outstretched hand; with outstretched arms.

out.strip (out.STRIP) v. **-strips, -stripped, -strip.ping** go faster; hence, surpass: *Demand sometimes outstrips supply.*

out.vote (out.VOTE) v. **-votes, -vot.ed, -vot.ing** defeat someone in voting.

out.ward (OUT.wurd) adj. **1** external: *the outward man; outward appearance, beauty, behavior.* **2** moving or turned toward the outside: *an outward journey.* —adv. toward the outside: *lines diverging outward from the center; an outward-bound journey;* also **outwards.** —**out.ward.ly** adv.: *the outwardly respectable hypocrite; the outwardly cautious and inwardly conniving schemer.*

out.wear (out.WARE) v. **-wears, -wore, -worn, -wear.ing 1** of fabrics, etc., last longer than another fabric in wearing: *Handmade goods often outwear machine-made ones.* **2** wear out: *to outwear one's welcome.* **3** become out of date; adj.: **outworn** *furniture, ideas, machinery, metaphors, values.* —n. outerwear: *sportswear and outwear.*

out.weigh (out.WAY) v. exceed in weight, importance, etc.: *These reasons far outweigh the others.*

out.wit (out.WIT) v. **-wits, -wit.ted, -wit.ting** overcome by superior intelligence or cleverness.

out.work n. a small defensive fortification outside the main one.
—v. (out.WURK) outdo by working harder, better, etc.

out.worn See OUTWEAR.

ou.zel (OO.zul) same as WATER OUZEL.

ou.zo (OO.zoh) n. **-zos** an unsweetened but flavored Greek cordial.

ova pl. of OVUM.

o.val (OH.vul) n. & adj. (anything) egg-shaped or like an ellipse.

Oval Office n. the U.S. President's office; hence, the Presidency.

o.va.ry (OH.vuh.ree) n. **-ries** the egg-containing reproductive organ of a female: *A flowering plant's ovary is the seed-producing part.* —**o.var.i.an** (oh.VAIR.ee.un) adj.: *ovarian cancer, cyst, follicles.*

o.vate (OH.vate) adj. egg-shaped, as certain leaves.

o.va.tion (oh.VAY.shun) n. enthusiastic applause, with clapping or cheering: *The ballerina got or received a standing ovation; a thunderous ovation.*

ov.en (UV.un) n. a chamber in a stove or near a fireplace for baking, heating, etc.: *to light, turn off, turn on an oven; convection, microwave, self-cleaning ovens.*

o.ver (OH.vur) prep. **1** above: *a roof over our heads; Who's over you at work?* **2** all through: *We flew over the city; That happened over (= during) a long period.* **3** beyond: *Europe lies over the ocean; She is doing over 100 km/h; He leaped over the wall.* **4** about: *to brood over failures.* **5** by means of: *news sent over the air waves.* —adv. [indicating an action as carried across or beyond a place or time]: *Hand it over to us; He fell over on his face; Let's talk things over; She's sleeping over at her friend's; Turn over the page; I'm not over (= very) tired; Read it over and over (= again and again) till you know it by heart.*
—adj. finished: *The game is over; We are over with it; It's all over between Guy and Gigi; He isn't over borrowing her car, though.* —**over and out** message finished. —*prefix* [added without a hyphen to adjectives to mean "too" and to nouns and verbs to mean "too much." Such compounds whose basic meaning and pronunciation are not the same as in the base word are entered and explained below].

o.ver.a.chieve (oh.vur.uh.CHEEV) v. **-chieves, -chieved, -chiev.ing** perform at a better than normal level; adj.: *an overachieving student; the overachieving type.* —**o.ver.a.chiev.er** n.

o.ver.act (oh.vur.ACT) v. exaggerate in acting a part.

o.ver.age 1 (oh.vur.AGE) adj. past the age of usefulness, eligibility, etc. **2** (OH.vur.ij) n. surplus or excess.

o.ver.all (OH.vur.all) **1** adj*a*. including everything: *overall expenses; an overall operating budget;* adv.: *It measures two meters overall.* **2** **overalls** n.pl. loose-fitting trousers with an attached piece to cover the chest, worn by workers to protect their clothes.

o.ver.arm (OH.vur.arm) adj. with the arm raised over the shoulder, as in swimming; also, overhand.

o.ver.awe (oh.vur.AW) v. **-awes, -awed, -aw.ing** awe someone into submission; inspire awe in someone.

o.ver.bal.ance (oh.vur.BAL.unce) v. **-anc.es, -anced, -anc.ing 1** outweigh in amount or value. **2** cause to lose balance and tip over.

o.ver.bear.ing (oh.vur.BAIR.ing) adj. domineering or dictatorial.

o.ver.bite (OH.vur.bite) n. an overlapping of the upper front teeth over the lower.

o.ver.blown (oh.vur.BLONE) adj. exaggerated or inflated: *overblown demands,* *legends, nationalism, praise, tales.*

o.ver.board *adv.* over the side of a ship into the water: *to fall overboard.* —**go overboard** *Informal.* act in an overenthusiastic manner: *He is going overboard over* or *about* or *for the new car.*

o.ver.cast (oh.vur.CAST) *adj.* cloudy or dark: *an overcast sky, weather.*

o.ver.charge (oh.vur.CHARJ) *v.* **-charg.es, -charged, -charg.ing** 1 charge extra or too much. 2 overload with burden or force. —*n.: an overcharge of $25.*

o.ver.clothes (OH.vur.clothes) same as OUTERWEAR.

o.ver.cloud (oh.vur.CLOUD) *v.* cloud over or darken.

o.ver.coat (OH.vur.coat) *n.* a usu. heavy outer coat worn in cold weather.

o.ver.come (oh.vur.CUM) *v.* **-comes, -came, -come, -com.ing** conquer or overpower: *to be overcome by desire, embarrassment, smoke; overcome with admiration, emotion, excitement, gratitude, grief.*

o.ver.do (oh.vur.DOO) *v.* **-does, -did, -done, -do.ing** do too much or carry to excess: *She overdid* (= overacted) *her part in the play;* **adj.***: the overdone glitz; The panic seems overdone; an overdone* (= overcooked) *steak.*

o.ver.dose (OH.vur.dose) *n.* a larger dose than is safe: *The actress took a fatal* or *lethal overdose of sleeping pills.* —*v.* **-dos.es, -dosed, -dos.ing***: She overdosed on sleeping pills.*

o.ver.draft (OH.vur.draft) *n.* an overdrawing or the sum overdrawn.

o.ver.draw (oh.vur.DRAW) *v.* **-draws, -drew, -drawn, -draw.ing** 1 draw from an account more money than there is in it. 2 exaggerate in drawing or portraying.

o.ver.dress (oh.vur.DRES) *v.* dress too elaborately or showily.

o.ver.drive (OH.vur.drive) *n.* in an automobile transmission, a gear available at higher speeds.

o.ver.due (oh.vur.DUE) *adj.* due some time back; late: *an overdue payment, train; Your payment is past overdue; an overdue baby (who should have been born by now)*

o.ver.es.ti.mate (oh.vur.ES.tuh.mate) *v.* **-mates, -mat.ed, -mat.ing** set or provide too high an estimate for something.

o.ver.ex.pose (OH.vur.ix.POZE) *v.* **-pos.es, -posed, -pos.ing** expose a photographic film too long.
—**o.ver.ex.po.sure** (OH.vur.ex.POH.zhur) *n.*

o.ver.flight (OH.vur.flite) *n.* a flight in an aircraft over a territory.

o.ver.flow (oh.vur.FLOH) *v.* flow over: *A river overflows (its banks) during a flood; The crowd overflowed into the hallways; hearts overflowing with happiness;* **adj.***: an overflowing basket, creek, cup; overflowing abundance; overflowing crowds; our overflowing landfill sites;* **n.***: The rooms were full to overflowing.* —*n.* something that overflows; hence, a surplus or excess: *a storm overflow; sewer overflow; measures to stem the overflow; the overflow of people from a convention;* **adj.***: an overflow audience, crowd, pipe, tank; overflow seating.*

o.ver.fly (oh.vur.FLY) *v.* **-flies, -flew, -fly.ing** fly over a place in an airplane.

o.ver.grow (oh.vur.GROH) *v.* **-grows, -grew, -grown, -grow.ing** 1 grow over: *a garden overgrown with weeds.* 2 outgrow or grow too fast. —**o.ver.growth** *n.*

o.ver.hand (OH.vur.hand) *adj.* made with the hand raised above the elbow, as in playing tennis; overarm: *an overhand stroke in tennis or handball; an overhand throw.*

o.ver.hang (oh.vur.HANG) *v.* **-hangs, -hung, -hang.ing** 1 hang or project over something: *A lace cloth overhangs the tablecloth.* 2 hang over in a gloomy or threatening manner: *The threat of war overhangs our plans;* **adj.***: an overhanging roof; the overhanging threat of war.* —*n.* (OH.vur.hang) a jutting out or something that overhangs: *the overhang of an upper story over the lower; the massive overhang of foreign debt; the inventory overhang of unsold merchandise.*

o.ver.haul (oh.vur.HAWL) *v.* examine machines thoroughly and repair as necessary. —*n.* (OH.vur.hawl) an overhauling: *an engine overhaul; a complete, major, thorough overhaul.*

o.ver.head (oh.vur.HED) *adj.* being or from above: *the sun overhead; a garage's overhead door; an overhead projector* to throw images above the lecturer; *an overhead* (= overhand) *smash;* **adv.***: cables running overhead.* —*n.* (OH.vur.hed) business expenses such as rent, maintenance, utilities, etc. covering all operations: *The company's overhead is only about 8% of its earnings.*

o.ver.hear (oh.vur.HEER) *v.* **-hears, -heard, -hear.ing** hear a speaker or what is spoken without the speaker's being aware of it.

o.ver.joy (oh.vur.JOY) *v.* fill with great joy; **adj.***: We're overjoyed to hear about your victory.*

o.ver.kill (OH.vur.kil) *n.* capacity in excess of what is required to achieve an objective, esp. to kill with nuclear power; excessive killing power: *The media blitz was a promotional overkill.* Also *v.*

o.ver.land (OH.vur.land) *adj.* across, by, or on land: *an overland invasion, route;* *adv.*: *They traveled overland to the East.*

o.ver.lap (oh.vur.LAP) *v.* **-laps, -lapped, -lap.ping** lap or lay over: *roof shingles that overlap (each other).* —*n.* (OH.vur.lap) an overlapping: *There's an hour's overlap between the day and night shifts.*

o.ver.lay (oh.vur.LAY) *v.* **-lays, -laid, -lay.ing** place over another; also, cover or finish with something: *a dome overlaid with gold.* —*n.* (OH.vur.lay) something laid over: *a map with color overlays showing special features.*

o.ver.lie (oh.vur.LYE) *v.* **-lies, -lay, -lain, -ly.ing** lie on or over: *The puppy was overlain (and smothered) in sleep by its own mother.*

o.ver.load (OH.vur.lode) *n.* too heavy a load: *an overload of inventory; We having an information overload; A starving person may experience* **sensory overload** *when faced with an abundance of food.*
—*v.* (oh.vur.LODE): *Air-conditioners overloaded the circuit; a jeep overloaded with machines and tools; a young recruit overloaded with responsibilities;* *adj.*: *an* **overloaded** *truck; overloaded supplies; an overloaded transportation system.*

o.ver.look (oh.vur.LOOK) *v.* **1** look over from above; hence, watch or oversee: *Our room overlooks (= gives us a view of) the harbor.* **2** fail to see: *She was not ignored but overlooked in the hurry.* **3** ignore or excuse: *a taskmaster who never overlooks our shortcomings.*

o.ver.lord (OH.vur.lord) *n.* one with power over other lords.

o.ver.ly (OH.vur.lee) *adv.* too much; excessively: *I'm not overly excited about the plan.*

o.ver.much (oh.vur.MUCH) *adj., adv. & n.* too much.

o.ver.night (oh.vur.NITE) *adja.* during the night: *an overnight journey, stay, stop, telegram.* —*adv.*: *They got ready overnight to start at dawn; a problem difficult to solve overnight (= quickly).*

o.ver.pass (OH.vur.pass) *n.* a crossing at a higher level, as a bridge over a road or railroad: *a pedestrian overpass.*

o.ver.play (oh.vur.PLAY) *v.* exaggerate the importance of something or be overoptimistic about an advantage one has: *He lost his bid by overplaying his hand.*

o.ver.pow.er (oh.vur.POW.ur) *v.* conquer by superior power; overwhelm.

o.ver.qual.i.fied (oh.vur.KWOL.uh.fide) *adj.* too highly qualified, esp. for a job.

o.ver.rate (oh.vur.RATE) *v.* **-rates, -rat.ed, -rat.ing** rate or value too highly.

o.ver.reach (oh.vur.REECH) *v.* reach beyond one's capability: *He overreached by borrowing more than he could afford; He overreached himself;* *adj.*: *her* **overreaching** *ambition, ardor; overreaching investors, politicians;* *n.*: *He was careful to avoid* **overreaching** *when buying the house.*

o.ver.re.act (oh.vur.ree.ACT) *v.* react in an excessive or uncalled-for manner, as by an outburst.

o.ver.ride (oh.vur.RIDE) *v.* **-rides, -rode, -rid.den, -rid.ing** overrule or prevail over something: *The U.S. Congress could override a presidential veto; A constitutional change is required for overriding the Charter of Rights;* *adj.*: *an* **overriding** *concern, factor, interest, reason.*

o.ver.rule (oh.vur.ROOL) *v.* **-rules, -ruled, -rul.ing** set aside or decide against something: *His objection was overruled.*

o.ver.run (oh.vur.RUN) *v.* **-runs, -ran, -run.ning** **1** of enemies, weeds, vermin, etc., run over or occupy a place causing harm: *a lawn overrun with weeds.* **2** go beyond: *to overrun a time limit.* —*n.* (OH.vur.run) an overrunning: *a cost overrun of 50%.*

o.ver.sea (oh.vur.SEE) *adja.* beyond the sea; abroad: *oversea communications; an oversea trip.* —**o.ver.seas** (-SEEZ) *adj. & adv.*: *He went overseas for higher studies; an overseas assignment, investment, territory.*

o.ver.see (oh.vur.SEE) *v.* **-sees, -saw, -seen, -see.ing** supervise or manage. —**o.ver.se.er** (OH.vur.see.ur) *n.*

o.ver.sexed (oh.vur.SEXT) *adj.* having excessive sexual desire.

o.ver.shad.ow (oh.vur.SHAD.oh) *v.* be more brilliant than someone else; surpass.

o.ver.shoe (OH.vur.shoo) *n.* a galosh or similar outer shoe.

o.ver.shoot (oh.vur.SHOOT) *v.* **-shoots, -shot, -shoot.ing** **1** shoot over or beyond a target. **2** go or pass beyond a limit: *The aircraft overshot the runway and ended up in a ditch.*

o.ver.sight (OH.vur.site) *n.* **1** an overseeing. **2** an overlooking: *an error due to (an) oversight; We left her name*

o.ver.size or **o.ver.sized** *adj.* larger in size than ordinary.

o.ver.sleep (oh.vur.SLEEP) *v.* **-sleeps, -slept, -sleep.ing** sleep longer than intended; sleep in.

o.ver.spread (oh.vur.SPRED) *v.* **-spreads, -spread, -spread.ing** spread over or cover something: *At the mention of the name, a blush overspread his countenance.*

o.ver.state (oh.vur.STATE) *v.* **-states, -stat.ed, -stat.ing** exaggerate: *to overstate a case.* —**o.ver.state.ment** *n.*

o.ver.stay (oh.vur.STAY) *v.* stay beyond: *He tends to overstay his leave, time, visa, welcome; She never overstays.*

o.ver.step (oh.vur.STEP) *v.* **-steps, -stepped, -step.ping** go beyond the limits of something; exceed.

o.ver.stuff (oh.vur.STUF) *v.* stuff with too much of something; *adj.: He uses overstuffed upholstery for extra comfort.*

o.vert (OH.vurt, oh.VURT) *adj.* done or manifested openly: *an overt act; overt behavior, hostility.* —**o.vert.ly** *adv.*

o.ver.take (oh.vur.TAKE) *v.* **-takes, -took, -tak.en, -tak.ing** catch up with or pass a moving person or thing: *He was ticketed for overtaking a school bus while its signals were flashing; Fate overtook the Titanic on its maiden voyage.*

over-the-counter *adja.* sold directly: *over-the-counter drugs (sold without a prescription); over-the-counter trading (of securities not listed on a stock exchange).*

o.ver.throw (oh.vur.THROH) *v.* **-throws, -threw, -thrown, -throw.ing** defeat or destroy: *charged with plotting to overthrow the government.* —*n.* (OH.vur.throh) defeat or destruction.

o.ver.time (OH.vur.time) *n.* **1** time in excess of what is standard. **2** the pay for working overtime: *Casual workers get no overtime.* —*adja.: fined for overtime parking; a game still tied at the end of two overtime periods; adv.: He works overtime to double his income.*

o.ver.tone (OH.vur.tone) *n.* **1** in music, a higher tone heard in harmony with a fundamental note that is sounded. **2** a suggestion or implication: *The air was tense with overtones of rebellion; a question with racial overtones.*

o.ver.ture (OH.vur.chur) *n.* **1** a proposal or offer to negotiate: *We made several overtures to the other party for a settlement of the dispute.* **2** a musical composition designed as a prelude or introduction, esp. to an opera: *to compose, perform, play an overture.*

o.ver.turn (oh.vur.TURN) *v.* turn something over; upset: *The truck overturned while cornering; to overturn a ban, conviction, decision, judgment, law, ruling, statute, verdict, veto; The decision was overturned on appeal; adj.: an overturned truck; dresser drawers found overturned.* —*n.* (OH.vur.turn) an overturning.

o.ver.view (OH.vur.view) *n.* a brief survey or summary.

o.ver.ween.ing (oh.vur.WEE.ning) *adj.* conceited or arrogant: *overweening pride, vanity.*

o.ver.weigh (oh.vur.WAY) *v.* **1** outweigh. **2** weigh down or oppress.

o.ver.weight (OH.vur.wait) *n.* a weight over the standard or normal weight: *He is suffering from overweight; adj.: Is she overweight? our overweight boss.*

o.ver.whelm (oh.vur.WHELM) *v.* **1** engulf: *a swimmer overwhelmed by the waves.* **2** overcome: *She was overwhelmed by superior forces; overwhelmed with grief at her child's death; adj.: overwhelming (= great) gratitude, indifference, majority, odds, sorrow, victory.*
—**o.ver.whelm.ing.ly** *adv.*

o.ver.win.ter (oh.vur.WIN.tur) *v.* pass the winter.

o.ver.wrought (oh.vur.RAWT) *adj.* **1** exhausted by too much work or excitement. **2** too elaborate or ornate.

ov.i.duct (OH.vi.duct) *n.* a tube carrying an egg from the ovary to the uterus; a Fallopian tube.

o.vip.a.rous (oh.VIP.uh.rus) *adj.* reproducing by laying eggs, not viviparous.

o.void (OH.void) *n. & adj.* (something) egg-shaped.

o.vu.late (OHV.yuh.late, OV-) *v.* **-lates, -lat.ed, -lat.ing** produce and discharge eggs from the ovary; **o.vu.la.tion** (-LAY-) *n.*

o.vule (OHV.yool, OV-) *n.* an unfertilized or immature egg or seed; **o.vu.lar** (OV.yuh.lur) *adj.*

o.vum (OH.vum) *n., pl.* **-va** (-vuh) an unfertilized egg.

owe (OH) *v.* **owes, owed, ow.ing** be in debt for something to someone: *I owe you nothing; We owe much to our country; a chronic borrower always* **owing** *for something; Joe owes* (= bears) *her a grudge.* —**owing to** because of; on account of.

owl *n.* a nocturnal bird of prey with large round eyes, characterized by its hooting call. —**owl.ish** *adj.;* **owl.ish.ly** *adv.*

owl.et (OW.lit) *n.* a young or small owl.

own (OIN) *v.* have as one's property or as belonging to one: *I only work*

here, I don't own the place; a waif whom his parents would not own; He owned (= admitted) he had been misled; owned to having lied; She had to **own up** (= confess) to the deed or to doing it.
—*adj*. [used with possessive pronoun] : my own children; your own business; her own neck; *pron.*: to each his own.
—**come into one's own** get what is rightfully one's: Women have been coming into their own since the 1970s.
—**hold one's own** defend oneself.
—**of one's own** belonging to oneself: problems of his own that are not our fault.
—**on one's own** doing what one wants without help. —**own.er** n.
—**own.er.ship** n.
ox n., pl. **ox.en** (OX.un) **1** a heavy-bodied, long-tailed, cloven-hoofed, cud-chewing animal such as a cow, buffalo, bison, or yak: the bellowing of oxen; strong as an ox. **2** a castrated bull used for beef or as a draft animal.
ox.al.ic acid (ok.SAL.ic-) n. a toxic organic acid found in plants such as the "wood sorrel," used in bleaching and removing stains, rust, etc.
ox.a.lis (OX.uh.lis) n. a group of plants with an acidic taste, including the "wood sorrel," mostly used as ornamentals.
ox.blood (OX.blud) n. a deep red color.
ox.bow (OX.boh) n. the U-shaped part of a yoke that passes under and around the neck of the draft animal.
oxen pl. of OX.
ox.ford (OX.furd) n. **1** a low shoe that is laced over the instep. **2** a cloth of cotton or rayon with a plain or basket weave used for shirts and blouses.
Oxford gray n. a dark gray color.
ox.i.dant (OX.i.dunt) n. oxidizer; *adj*. oxidizing.
ox.i.da.tion (ox.i.DAY.shun) n. an oxidizing or being oxidized.
ox.ide n. an oxygen compound.
ox.i.dize (OX.i.dize) v. **-diz.es, -dized, -diz.ing** combine with oxygen, as metal in rusting or when a substance burns in air. —**ox.i.diz.a.ble** (-dye.zuh.bul) *adj*. —**ox.i.diz.er** n.
ox.y.a.cet.y.lene (OX.ee.uh.SET.ul.een) *adj*. using an oxygen-acetylene mixture: the oxyacetylene flame of a welding torch.
ox.y.gen (OX.i.jun) n. a colorless, odorless gaseous element occurring in the atmosphere, essential to life and for combustion. —**ox.y.gen.ic** (-JEN.ic) *adj*.
ox.y.gen.ate (OX.i.juh.nate) v. **-ates, -at.ed, -at.ing** treat or combine with oxygen, as in making hydrogen peroxide or in a heart-lung machine.
—**ox.y.gen.a.tion** (-NAY.shun) n.
—**ox.y.gen.a.tor** (-nay.tur) n.
oxygen tent n. a hood or canopy put over the bed of a patient to provide an extra supply of oxygen.
ox.y.mo.ron (ok.si.MOR.on) n. a figure of speech involving an apparent contradiction: "Progressive conservative" may seem an oxymoron to the Liberals.
—**ox.y.mo.ron.ic** (-muh.RON.ic) *adj*.
oys.ter (OY.stur) n. a bivalve marine mollusk valued as food and for the pearls found in certain kinds: "The world's mine oyster" (= place for making a profit, like extracting a pearl from an oyster). —*adj*.: oyster farmers, harvests, shells; an **oyster bar** (where oysters are served); an **oyster bed** (where oysters breed); **oyster sauce** (= a variety of soy sauce).
oys.ter.ing (OY.stur.ing) n. the work of taking oysters from the sea.
O.zark (OH.zark) *adj*. having to do with a region of hills extending over Illinois, Missouri, Arkansas, and Oklahoma: the Ozark culture of S. Missouri.
o.zone (OH.zone) n. a form of oxygen with a sharp odor, formed in air by electric discharges and remaining as a layer in the ozonosphere: Skin cancer could result from exposure to the sun's ultraviolet rays if the protective ozone layer or shield is depleted by pollution.
—**o.zon.ic** (oh.ZON.ic) *adj*.
ozone layer n. a layer of ozone about 25 miles (40 km) above the earth protecting it from the sun's ultraviolet rays: The ozone layer may develop ozone holes because of atmospheric pollution. Also **o.zon.o.sphere** (oh.ZON.us.feer.)

.... **P, p** ....

P or **p** (PEE) n. **P's** or **p's 1** the 16th letter of the English alphabet. **2** something symbolized by P, as the 16th in a series, or something shaped like the letter. —**mind one's P's and Q's** be very careful about every detail: Typists have to mind their P's and Q's.
pa (PAH, PAW) n. Informal. father.
pab.lum n. a food, esp. something watered down or simplified: The book is poor pablum for a 12-year-old; **Pablum** Trademark. Also **pab.u.lum** (PAB.yuh.lum).
pace n. **1** a step in walking: It's three paces from my desk to the door. **2** relative speed of movement: the fast pace of city

life; *He works at a leisurely pace; a brisk, frantic, slow, sluggish, snail's pace; A change of pace will make you less tense; an energetic person who **sets the pace** (for others to keep up with) at work; He's too fast to **keep pace with.*** **3** a manner of walking, esp. a horse's ambling gait.
—**put someone through his** or **her paces** test or demonstrate someone's abilities. —*v.* **pac.es, paced, pac.ing 1** walk with regular steps: *The anxious parents paced up and down outside the operation theater; We **paced off** the room to measure it (as so many steps long or wide).* **2** lead as a pacer does: *a TV show that always paces the others in popularity ratings.*
pa.ce (PAY.see) *prep. Latin.* without annoyance to someone: *Let me say this pace the competition.*
pace.mak.er (PACE.may.kur) *n.* a tiny electronic device implanted near the heart to regulate its beat.
pac.er (PAY.sur) *n.* **1** one who sets the pace in a race: *a pacer car.* **2** same as PACEMAKER.
pace.set.ter (PACE.set.ur) *n.* **1** a leader. **2** one who sets the pace or speed.
pach.y.derm (PAK.i.durm) *n.* a large, thick-skinned mammal, as the elephant, rhinoceros, or hippopotamus.
pach.y.san.dra (pak.i.SAN.druh) *n.* a woody, evergreen, low-growing plant often used as ground cover.
Pa.cif.ic (puh.SIF.ic) **1** *n.* the ocean between Asia and the Americas; also **Pacific Ocean:** *a trip across the Pacific.* **2** *adja.* of the Pacific: *the Pacific coast (of North America); the Pacific region.* **3 pacific** *adj.* tending to pacify; calm or peaceful: *a pacific world order.*
—**pa.cif.i.cal.ly** *adv.* —**pacification** See PACIFY.
Pacific Rim *n.* the region bordering the Pacific, including Australia, Japan, New Zealand, Philippines, South Korea, and the W. coast of North America.
pac.i.fi.er (PAS.uh.fye.ur) *n.* one that pacifies, esp. something for an infant to suck or chew on.
pac.i.fism (PAS.uh.fiz.um) *n.* opposition to war or military action. —**pac.i.fist** *n.*: *a pacifist who refuses to fight;* **adja.**: *a pacifist approach to a settlement; pacifist idealism, leanings;* also **pac.i.fis.tic** (-FIS.tic) *adj.*
pac.i.fy (PAS.uh.fye) *v.* **-fies, -fied, -fy.ing** make peaceful or quiet: *to pacify a country, nation, situation;* **adj.**: *to keep the people **pacified**; a **pacifying** influence.* —**pac.i.fi.ca.tion**

(-fuh.CAY.shun) *n.*
pack *n.* **1** things wrapped up and tied together as a bundle for carrying, as on one's back: *a back pack; parachute pack.* **2** things considered in sets or groups: *Cigarettes come in packs of 20; beer in 6-packs; a year's pack of salmon (caught in one season).* **3** something compactly put together, as a compress for applying heat, cold, or pressure to a body part: *a cosmetic beauty pack, face pack, or mud pack (= paste); an undercover police officer wearing a body pack (= recording device); an ice pack (= ice bag or pack ice).* **4** persons, animals, or things grouped together for a common purpose: *a pack of hunting dogs, thieves, wolves; to run with the pack; a Brownie pack; submarine pack; a pack of lies; a pack (= deck) of cards.*
—*v.* **1** make, put, or crowd into a pack: *Pack everything in two bags; Pack the bags tight; The refugees were **packed into** the boats like sardines; We **pack off** the kids to school after breakfast; It's time to **pack up** and go home; The inept were **sent packing** (= were dismissed).* **2** treat so as to make compact or leak-proof: *A plumber packs a pipe joint; A road roller packs the earth; A dentist packs a bleeding gum.* **3** *Informal.* carry in a pack; be loaded with something: *He packed a change of clothes in his briefcase; dark clouds packing a storm; I want a word that packs (= has) more punch.* **4** arrange with corrupt motives: *to pack a jury (with sympathizers).* —**pack it in** put an end to what one is doing.
pack.age (PAK.ij) *n.* **1** a parcel or bundle: *to deliver, mail, send, wrap packages; food, gift packages; a **package insert** with information on the product; an American **package store** (= liquor store).* **2** a proposal, plan, offer, etc. containing many items to be accepted as a whole: *a software package (of programs for general use by the public); a **compensation package** (= salary, bonus, etc.); a **buyout package** (offered to employees) instead of laying them off;* **adja.**: *a package holiday, tour; a **package deal** (in which many related items are included in the price).* —*v.* **-ag.es, -aged, -ag.ing** put in a package, esp. put together as a unit for presentation or sale: *to package gifts; a candidate packaged by the media;* **adj.**: **packaged** *goods, software, vacations;* **n.**: *The **packaging** (= container) is sometimes more expensive than the product; a truth-in-packaging law.*
pack animal *n.* a load-carrying animal, as a camel, mule, or **packmule,** or

packhorse, often equipped with a **pack saddle.**

pack.et (PAK.it) *n.* **1** a small parcel, as of mail. **2** a boat plying a regular route carrying passengers, freight, and mail; also **packet boat.**

packet switching *n.* the breaking up of electronic messages into fixed-length units, or packets, and despatching them to their destinations by the most efficient routes.

pack ice *n.* an expanse of masses of broken, piled-up ice; ice pack.

packing *n.* **1** material used to prevent or stop a leakage of water, steam, or air. **2** the processing and packing of food, esp. meat, for wholesale, as is done in a **packing house** or **packing plant.**

pack mule *n.* a load-carrying mule.

pack rat *n.* **1** a North American rodent that carries away small articles and hides them in its nest. **2** one who hoards odd, unnecessary articles.

pack.sack *n.* a traveling bag of sturdy material, strapped to one's back.

pack saddle See PACK ANIMAL.

pack.thread *n.* a strong thread for sewing up bags.

pack.train *n.* a line of pack animals.

pact *n.* a treaty or agreement: *the auto pact between the U.S. and Canada; the free-trade pact; a peace pact; a secret pact between nations; The arms race between the superpowers was like a suicide pact; a pact of friendship.*

pad *n.* **1** a mass of soft material or a cushionlike container: *a heating pad; a scouring pad of steel wool or plastic mesh for pots and pans; knee pads, leg pads, and shoulder pads worn for protection while playing; an inked stamp pad (for pressing rubber stamps on).* **2** a frameless flexible saddle. **3** a water plant's floating leaf. **4** the soft under part of fingers and toes, esp. of the feet of animals. **5** a launch pad. **6** *Slang.* a place to sleep: *a hippie at his pad; a crash pad.* —**on the pad** *Slang.* receiving bribes: *a cop suspected of being on the pad.*

—*v.* **pads, pad.ded, pad.ding** stuff or fill out: *an essay padded with quotations; adj.: She shuns padded bras; padded shoulders; a heavily padded (= inflated) expense account; a well-padded chair; a padded cell for violent inmates.* —**pad about** walk noiselessly: *a child padding about on bare feet.*

padding *n.* material used to pad or fill out.

pad.dle (PAD.ul) *n.* **1** an oar with a broad, flat blade. **2** a similar implement, as a board of a water wheel or the **paddle wheel** of a steamboat, a table tennis racket, or one used in **paddle ball,** a game similar to squash, and in **paddle tennis,** an outdoor game resembling tennis: *a Mississippi River paddle boat* or *"paddle-wheeler" of the 19th century; a paddle raft (that is rowed).* **3** an instrument used in stirring, mixing, or beating, shaped like a paddle, as a potter's pallet: *a glass finisher's paddle for shaping objects; drinking, pasta, stirring paddles; a paddle beater for non-stick cookware.* **4** a handled board formerly used for spanking.

—*v.* **pad.dles, pad.dled, pad.dling:** *Children paddled (= splashed) about in the wading pool; In college, Jane paddles her own canoe (= manages all by herself).* —**pad.dler** *n.*

pad.dock (PAD.uck) *n.* an enclosure adjoining a stable, for feeding, exercising, or displaying animals, esp. racehorses.

pad.dy (PAD.ee) *n.* **pad.dies 1** rice in the husk, esp. when standing in the field. **2** a field of rice, often called **paddy-field. 3 Paddy** *Slang.* an Irishman.

paddy wagon *n. Informal.* a patrol wagon.

pad.lock *n.* a lock that can be put on a staple or chain by means of a U-shaped link that snaps shut and stays shut until unlocked; *v.: The door was shut and padlocked.*

pa.dre (PAH.dray, -dree) *n.* in Latin countries, a title for a priest; Father.

pae.an (PEE.un) *n.* a song of exultation or triumph: *The media sang paeans to her triumph at the Olympics.*

pa.gan (PAY.gun) *n.* one who has no recognized religion; formerly, not a Christian, Jew, or Muslim; *adj.: pagan beliefs, customs, idols.* —**pa.gan.ism** *n.*

page *n.* **1** one side of a leaf of a book: *the sports page of a newspaper; a book's title page; to tear out a page (= leaf) of a book.* **2** an event or series of events: *a glorious page in our life; a page from real life; in the pages of history.* **3** an attendant or messenger, as at a hotel, theater, or in a legislature.

—*v.* **pag.es, paged, pag.ing 1** arrange into pages; paginate a volume. **2** turn the pages: *to page through a volume.* **3** summon someone using a loudspeaker or similar device; *adj.a: a paging service, system; adj.: when the paged party answers.* —**pag.er** *n.*

pag.eant (PAJ.unt) *n.* a spectacular show, parade, or procession: *a pageant* at which Mister and Miss Monte Carlo are crowned. —**pag.eant.ry** (PAJ.un.tree) *n.: the pomp and pageantry of a royal wedding.*

page boy or **page.boy** *n.* **1** a boy who works as a page. **2** a shoulder-length hair style.

pag.i.nate (PAJ.uh.nate) *v.* **-nates, -nat.ed, -nat.ing 1** arrange a document or volume into pages. **2** number the pages of a document or volume. —**pag.i.na.tion** (-NAY.shun) *n.*

pa.go.da (puh.GOH.duh) *n.* a many-storied pyramidal tower of India and the Far East: *an eight-sided Chinese pagoda.*

paid *pt. & pp.* of PAY.

pail *n.* **1** a cylindrical vessel, usu. with a handle, for liquids; bucket: *a milk pail.* **2** the amount a pail will hold: *two pails of water;* also **pail.ful, -fuls.**

pain *n.* **1** suffering of body or mind: *aches and pains; acute, dull, excruciating, gnawing, nagging, severe, sharp, shooting, stabbing, throbbing pain; The child cried out in pain; to allay, bear, ease, endure, kill, relieve, soothe, stand, suffer pain; to inflict pain on someone.* —**pains** *pl.* **1** effort or care: *He went to some pains to satisfy her demands; She took great pains to research her book thoroughly; She spared no pains; He was* **at pains** *to quiet rumors about his resignation.* **2** physical suffering: *labor pains (of childbirth); the "growing pains" of children.* —**pain in the neck** *Informal.* nuisance. —**under** (or **on** or **upon**) **pain of** under penalty of something: *He was told to surrender on pain of death.*
—*v.* feel or cause pain: *It pains me to hear you are hurt;* **adj.**: *I am* **pained** (= distressed) *to hear about the tragedy; a pained expression, face, look, voice.*
—**pain.ful** *adj.;* **pain.ful.ly** *adv.*
—**pains.tak.ing** *n. & adj.;* **pains.tak.ing.ly** *adv.*

pain.kill.er (PAIN.kil.ur) *n.* something that relieves pain, as a drug.
—**pain.kill.ing** *adj.*

paint *v.* **1** apply color, as with a brush: *to paint a portrait in oil.* **2** make something in color, as a picture, or **paint-ing. 3** put cosmetics on the face.
—**paint the town red** *Informal.* go on a merrymaking spree. —*n.* a usu. liquid mixture or pigment for coating a surface for decoration or protection: *to apply paint to a surface; to daub paint on something; to scrape paint off a surface; a blob, coat, speck, splash of paint; flat, glossy, grease, latex, war paint; to apply two coats of paint; "Caution – wet paint!"*
—**paint.er** *n.*

painting *n.* **1** the art of using paints to create pictures: *the painting of a portrait;* **finger painting** *in kindergarten.* **2** such a picture: *a landscape painting by Matisse; oil and water-color paintings.*

pair *n.* **1** two persons, animals, or things connected in some way: *four pair* or *pairs of socks; a newly married pair; The skating pairs are next on the program; a pair of brackets, compasses, gloves, headlamps, oxen, shoes, skis, spectacles; The animals entered Noah's Ark* **in pairs** (= two by two). **2** something with two equal parts: *a pair of pants, scissors, shorts.* —**pair off** or **pair up with** form into pairs: *The guests paired off for the dance; The men paired up with the women.* —**paired** *adj.* formed into a pair or pairs.

pai.sa (PYE.sah) *n., pl.* **-se** (-SAY) or **-sas** a money unit of India, Pakistan, Oman, and Bangladesh.

pais.ley (PAIZ.lee) *n.* a colorful cloth design of curved and swirled figures; **adj.**: *a paisley design, shawl.* Also **Paisley.**

pa.ja.mas (puh.JAM.uz, -JAH.muz) *n.pl.* a loose-fitting sleeping suit of pants and shirt. —**adj.**: *pajama bottoms, tops; a teen* **pajama party** (= slumber party).

Pak.i.stan.i (pak.i.STAN.ee) *n. & adj.* (a person) of or from **Pakistan,** a S. Asian republic.

pal.ace (PAL.is) *n.* **1** a large, splendid residence, esp. of a sovereign, archbishop, or other dignitary: *an imperial palace.* **2** a similar building for exhibitions, entertainments, etc. —**adj.** involving intimacy and influence with persons in power: *palace politics, guards, revolutions.*

pal.a.din (PAL.uh.din) *n.* a knight or champion.

pal.an.quin (pal.un.KEEN) *n.* a covered litter formerly used in Eastern countries, borne on the shoulders of servants by means of poles; also **pal.an.keen.**

pal.at.a.ble (PAL.uh.tuh.bul) *adj.* **1** tasty: *Food has to be palatable to the eater.* **2** agreeable: *palatable advice.*

pal.ate (PAL.it) *n.* **1** the sense of taste: *a wine pleasing to the palate; We've delicacies to tickle your palate* (= very tasty delicacies). **2** the roof of the mouth, with the **hard palate** at the front and **soft palate** at the back.

pa.la.tial (puh.LAY.shul) *adj.* of or like a palace: *the palatial surroundings of the governor's mansion.*

pa.lat.i.nate (puh.LAT.un.ate, -it) *n.* the territory of a palatine, as the Upper and Lower Palatinates of S.W. Germany until 1620.

pal.a.tine (PAL.uh.tine) *n.* a lord or count having royal prerogatives: *Carolina was a palatine colony.*

pa.lav.er (puh.LAV.ur) *n.* extended talk, esp. between traders. —*v.* **1** talk profusely. **2** talk flatteringly; cajole.

pale *adj.* **pal.er, pal.est** of the face, bloodless; light or weak: *to go* or *turn pale with fear; a deathly pale color; a pale blue; a pale* (= poor) *imitation.*
—*v.* **pales, paled, pal.ing** become pale; hence, fade: *Paola pales at the sight of blood; His accomplishments pale into insignificance when you compare them with hers; They pale before hers.*
—*n.* **1** a picket or stake. **2** an enclosed area. —**beyond** or **outside** (or **within**) **the pale** beyond or outside (or within) the limits of the law, of the church, of respectability, etc. —**pale.ly** *adv.;* **pale.ness** *n.*

pale.face *n.* [Indian term] a white person.

paleo- *comb.form.* prehistoric: *Paleocene, paleographic, Paleolithic.*

Pa.le.o.cene (PAY.lee.uh.seen) *n.* the first epoch of the Cenozoic era of the earth, beginning about 65 million years ago: *Paleocene rock formations.*

pa.le.og.ra.phy (pay.lee.OG.ruh.fee) *n.* the study of ancient documents; **pa.le.og.ra.pher** *n.* —**pa.le.o.graph.ic** (-GRAF.ic) or **pa.le.o.graph.i.cal** *adj.*

Pa.le.o.lith.ic (PAY.lee.uh.LITH.ic) *n.* the earliest part of the Stone Age; *adj.: a Paleolithic tool chipped out of stone; the Paleolithic Neanderthal man;* also **paleolithic** *adj.*

pa.le.on.tol.o.gy (PAY.lee.un.TOL.uh.jee) *n.* the study of fossils as a clue to earlier forms of life; **pa.le.on.tol.o.gist** *n.*

Pa.le.o.zo.ic (PAY.lee.uh.ZOE.ic) *n.* the geologic era from 600 million to 225 million years ago: *Amphibians and reptiles appear in the Paleozoic era.*

Pal.es.tine (PAL.uh.stine) *n.* the land between the Mediterranean and the Jordan River, the birthplace of Judaism and Christianity, and sacred also to Muslims; also called "the Holy Land." —**Pal.es.tin.i.an** (-STIN.ee.un) *n. & adj.: Many Palestinians are Palestinian Arabs.*

pal.ette (PAL.it) *n.* **1** an artist's handheld board for mixing colors: *A palette knife is used to mix and apply colors.* **2** a range of colors: *He paints in a wide palette; the color palette of a computer's graphics.*

pal.frey (PAWL.free) *n.* [old use] a saddle horse, esp. one for a woman to ride.

pal.i.mo.ny (PAL.uh.moh.nee) *n.* a form of alimony awarded by a court to a partner when a couple who have lived together separates.

pal.imp.sest (PAL.imp.sest) *n.* a document or writing material such as vellum or parchment bearing evidence of more than one writing, the earlier one(s) having been imperfectly erased.

pal.in.drome (PAL.in.drome) *n.* a sentence (as "Madam, I'm Adam"), phrase, or word (as "Malayalam") that reads the same backward or forward.

pal.ing (PAY.ling) *n.* **1** a pale, picket, or stake. **2** a collection of them or a fence made with them.

pal.i.sade (PAL.uh.sade) *n.* **1** a fortification of stakes or pales. **2** one of the stakes used in such a fence. **3** **palisades** *pl.* a line of cliffs. —*v.* **-sades, -sad.ed, -sad.ing** surround with or as with a palisade: *Tall cliffs palisade the shore.*

pall (PAWL) *v.* **palls, palled, pall.ing** get boring; cloy: *This show is beginning to pall on me.* —*n.* a covering, as on a coffin: *A pall of smoke hangs over the city; Her death cast a pall over* or *on the school reunion* (= made the occasion gloomy).

pal.la.di.um (puh.LAY.dee.um) *n.* a silvery-white, metallic chemical element.

pall.bear.er (PAWL.bair.ur) *n.* one who escorts or helps to carry a coffin at a funeral.

pal.let (PAL.it) *n.* **1** a paddlelike wooden tool used by potters for mixing and shaping clay. **2** same as PALETTE: *a broad pallet of colors.* **3** a low, portable platform for storing or moving objects; *adja.: pallet delivery, handling, loads, racks, storage.* **4** a makeshift bed or mattress used on the floor.

pal.li.ate (PAL.ee.ate) *v.* **-ates, -at.ed, -at.ing** lessen the severity of a crime, illness, pain, evil, etc. —**pal.li.a.tion** (-AY.shun) *n.* —**pal.li.a.tive** (-ay.tiv) *n.: a mere palliative and no cure; adj.: the palliative care of people with AIDS.*

pal.lid (PAL.id) *adj.* pale, as by illness: *a pallid complexion, face.*

pal.lor (PAL.ur) *n.* paleness of the skin due to fear, illness, weakness, etc.

palm (PAHM) *n.* **1** the inner surface of the hand from the wrist to the base of the fingers: *a palm-sized camcorder,*

palmate / pancreas

camera, TV. **2** a part corresponding to this, as of a glove or the blade of a paddle. **3** a family of trees without branches but only a trunk and crowns of hand-shaped leaves: *the coconut palm;* ***adja.:*** *palm fronds, leaves, oil, trees.* **4** a palm leaf as a symbol of victory. —**bear** or **carry off the palm** win a personal victory. —**grease the palm of someone** to bribe. —**have an itching palm** *Informal.* be greedy for money. —*v.* conceal in the palm, as a card; hence, pass off: *The con man palmed off a fake diamond on the young lady; He palmed it off as a genuine diamond.*

pal.mate or **pal.mat.ed** (PAL.may.tid) *adj.* shaped like an open hand with extended fingers, as palm leaves or antlers.

pal.met.to (pal.MET.oh) *n.* **-tos** or **-toes** a palm with fan-shaped leaves, common in South Carolina ("Palmetto State").

palm.ist (PAH.mist) *n.* one who tells fortunes by reading the lines on a person's palms.

palm.is.try (PAH.mis.tree) *n.* the palmist's art.

palm.top *n.* a small computer that fits in one's palm.

palm.y (PAH.mee) *adj.* **palm.i.er, -i.est** flourishing or prosperous: *the palmy days of one's youth.*

pal.my.ra (pal.MY.ruh) *n.* a fan-leaved palm of India and Africa with durable wood, edible fruits, and leaves used for thatching.

pal.o.mi.no (pal.uh.MEE.noh) *n.* **-nos** a light-colored horse with white mane and tail.

pal.pa.ble (PAL.puh.bul) *adj.* **1** that can be felt; hence, obvious: *a palpable advantage; in palpable form; palpable fear, frustration, pleasure, strength; The tension in the crowd became palpable.* **2** [medical use] that can be examined by palpating: *a palpable lump.*

pal.pa.bly (PAL.puh.blee) *adv.* obviously: *The story is palpably absurd.*

pal.pate (PAL.pate) *v.* **-pates, -pat.ed, -pat.ing** feel with the hand, as in a medical checkup: *Physicians palpate the breasts to check for lumps.* —**pal.pa.tion** (pal.PAY.shun) *n.*

pal.pi.tate (PAL.puh.tate) *v.* **-tates, -tat.ed, -tat.ing** throb rapidly: *The heart palpitates under exertion or excitement.* —**pal.pi.ta.tion** (-TAY.shun) *n.*

pal.sy (PAWL.zee) *n.* **-sies 1** paralysis or a disorder characterized by trembling, as Parkinson's disease: *cerebral palsy; facial palsies.* **2** a paralyzing influence. —*v.* **-sies, -sied, -sy.ing** paralyze: *He stood still, palsied by fear;* *adj.: a palsied child, limb.*

pal.ter (PAWL.tur) *v.* use trickery; trifle: *a matter too serious to palter with.*

pal.try (PAWL.tree) *adj.* **-tri.er, -tri.est** trifling or contemptibly small: *a paltry amount; paltry concessions, contributions; a paltry 2% raise; a paltry ration of soup and tea; a paltry sum of money.* —**pal.tri.ness** *n.*

pam.pas (PAM.pus) *n.pl.* the vast treeless plains of South America, esp. in Argentina; **pam.pa** *sing.*

pam.per (PAM.pur) *v.* treat with indulgence: *to pamper one's vanity;* ***adj.:*** *a pampered child.* —**pam.per.er** *n.*

pam.phlet (PAM.flit) *n.* an unbound booklet on a current topic.

pam.phlet.eer (pam.fluh.TEER) *n.* one who issues pamphlets, esp. as propaganda; **pam.phlet.eer.ing** *n.*

pan *n.* **1** a flat, open dish for cooking: *frying pans; pots and pans.* **2** a shallow receptacle, depression, cover, etc.: *the pans* (= dishes) *of a balance; a* ***gold pan*** (= dish for washing ore). —*v.* **pans, panned, pan.ning 1** sift, esp. gravel for gold. **2** *Informal.* criticize harshly: *a movie panned by reviewers.* **3** turn a movie camera in a sweeping motion for a panoramic view. —**pan out** *Informal.* of an enterprise, turn out well: *Our plans did not pan out.*

pan- *comb.form.* all: *Pan-American, Panarctic, panhuman, pantheism.*

pan.a.ce.a (pan.uh.SEE.uh) *n.* a cure-all remedy: *no panacea for world hunger.*

pa.nache (puh.NASH) *n.* an air of confidence and ease; flamboyance: *He plays Romeo with great panache; She wears new fashions with style and panache.*

Pan.a.ma.ni.an (pan.uh.MAY.nee.un) *n. & adj.* (a person) of or from **Panama**, a Central American republic.

panama or **panama hat** *n.* a straw hat woven from leaves of a palmlike plant common in South and Central America.

Pan-American *adj.* pertaining to the Americas: *Pan-American Games; the Pan-American Highway.*

pan.a.tel.a (pan.uh.TEL.uh) *n.* a long, slender cigar.

pan.cake *n.* a thin batter cake cooked on both sides and served hot.

pan.cre.as (PAN.cree.us) *n.* a long, fleshy gland near the stomach that secretes a hormone called insulin and the **pancreatic juice** which helps in digestion. —**pan.cre.at.ic** (-AT.ic) *adj.*

pan.da (PAN.duh) *n.* a black-and-white bearlike animal of China and Tibet, also called the **giant panda**: *The lesser panda is a smaller, raccoonlike, reddish Asiatic animal.*

pan.dem.ic (pan.DEM.ic) *n.* an epidemic spread over a wide area; *adj.*: *Influenza was pandemic in 1918-19 and killed about 20 million.*

pan.de.mo.ni.um (pan.duh.MOH.nee.um) *n.* wild disorder: *to cause* or *create, stir up a pandemonium; Pandemonium broke loose* or *broke out, prevailed* or *reigned when the teacher was late for class.*

pan.der (PAN.dur) *n.* a procurer or pimp. —*v.* act as a pander: *movies that pander to the public's taste for violence; They pander to the vulgar crowd; people who pander sex for profit.* —**pan.der.er** *n.*

Pandora's box (pan.DOR.us-) *n.* a source of endless trouble, as in the Greek myth of **Pandora,** the first mortal woman, who caused all earthly ills by opening a box against the advice of the gods.

pan.dow.dy (pan.DOW.dee) *n.* -**dies** a deep-dish pie of sliced apples.

pane *n.* **1** a division of a window or door framing a sheet of glass. **2** the glass itself.

pan.e.gyr.ic (pan.uh.JEER.ic) *n.* a formal eulogy or tribute to a person or event.

pan.el (PAN.ul) *n.* **1** a usu. rectangular piece, section, or division of a surface such as a ceiling, wall, or door, often at a different level from its surroundings: *a control panel; instrument panel; the panels of a skirt; the panels of an airplane wing.* **2** a number of persons forming a group to discuss or investigate something: *a jury panel; A panel of experts held a panel discussion on AIDS.* —*v.* **pan.els, pan.eled, pan.el.ing** cover with panels: *to panel the walls of a basement;* **n.**: *glass, wall, wood* **paneling;** *adj.*: *a* **paneled** *dining room, hallway, wall; an pine-paneled office; a paneled shirt with its front in a different color or pattern.* Also **pan.elled, pan.el.ling** *Cdn.*

pan.el.ist (PAN.ul.ist) *n.* a member of a panel of experts or judges. Also **pan.el.list** *Cdn.*

panel truck *n.* a small delivery truck with a fully enclosed body.

pang *n.* a sharp, sudden attack of pain: *pangs of hunger, fury, jealousy, remorse; birth pangs; to feel pangs of conscience.*

pan.han.dle (PAN.han.dul) *n.* a strip of territory projecting like the handle of a pan: *the Texas panhandle between Oklahoma and New Mexico.* —*v.* -**dles, -dled, -dling** beg on the street. —**pan.han.dler** *n.*

pan.ic *n.* a sudden fear, esp. one that spreads, as when a bank fails or a fire breaks out: *to avert, cause, create, prevent panic; He was in a panic over* or *about the missed flight; We felt panic at the sight of a car coming head-on; We escaped being hit and the panic subsided.* —**hit** or **press** or **push the panic button** react in a panicky manner. —*v.* -**ics, -icked, -ick.ing** feel or cause panic: *Don't panic, it's only a rumor; The passengers panicked at the mention of a bomb; Their screams panicked the children; adj.*: **panicked** *children, selling, traders.* —**panic-stricken** *adj.*: *a panic-stricken animal, crowd, herd.* —**pan.ick.y** *adj.*

pan.i.cle (PAN.i.cul) *n.* a flower cluster branched like a tree, as in oats and other grasses. —**pan.i.cled** *adj.*

pan.jan.drum (pan.JAN.drum) *n.* a pretentious or pompous official.

pan.nier (PAN.yur) *n.* **1** a basket for carrying loads. **2** one of a pair of baskets slung across a pack animal's back or across the front or rear of a bicycle.

pan.o.ply (PAN.uh.plee) *n.* -**plies 1** a complete suit of armor. **2** a splendid array: *He was waited on by a full panoply of servants.*

pan.o.ra.ma (pan.uh.RAM.uh) *n.* **1** a view in all directions: *a panorama of the countryside from a hilltop.* **2** an unlimited, comprehensive, or continuous view: *The book depicts the changing panorama of history.* —**pan.o.ram.ic** *adj.*: *a panoramic view; the Panoramic Camera with a 360-degree view.*

pant *v.* **1** breathe in gasps, as from exertion; also, gasp: *He rushed in panting for breath; "Water!" he panted* (= said gaspingly). **2** yearn desperately: *a mother panting for the return of her missing child.* —*n.* a gasp or puff of breath. —**pants** *n.pl.* **1** *Informal.* trousers: *ski pants; adj.a.*: *pant belts, cuffs, legs, pressers.* **2** panties. —**beat** or **knock the pants off someone** *Informal.* clobber or trounce. —**with one's pants down** *Informal.* in an embarrassing position.

pan.ta.loons (PAN.tuh.loons) *n.pl.* men's loose, baggy trousers, as worn in the 19th century.

pant.dress *n.* a dress with a divided skirt.

pan.the.ism (PAN.thee.iz.um) *n.* the belief that God is the same as the forces and manifestations of nature; **pan.the.ist** *n.* —**pan.the.is.tic** (-IS.tic) *adj.*

pan.the.on (pan.THEE.un) *n.* **1** a temple dedicated to all the gods. **2** the gods themselves: *a pantheon of national heroes.*

pan.ther *n.* **1** a large black cat, esp. a leopard. **2** a cougar or puma.

pan.tie or **pan.ty** (PAN.tee) *n.* usu. **panties** *pl.* a woman's or child's short underpants.

pan.ti.hose (PAN.tee.hoze) same as PANTYHOSE.

pan.to.mime (PAN.tuh.mime) *n.* expression using gestures without words, as in the dramatic art form of the same name. —*v.* **-mimes, -mimed, -mim.ing** use pantomime: *Knowing only English, he had to pantomime his way through China.* —**pan.to.mim.ist** (-mye.mist) *n.*

pan.try (PAN.tree) *n.* **-tries** a room or closet for storing food and table accessories such as china and linens.

pant.suit or **pants suit** *n.* a woman's jacket-and-trouser outfit.

panty See PANTIE.

pan.ty.hose *n. sing. & pl.* a woman's undergarment combining panties and stockings.

pan.ty.waist (PAN.tee.waist) *n.* **1** a child's outfit of shirt and pants buttoned together. **2** *Slang.* a sissy.

pap *n.* **1** soft food, as for infants. **2** anything handed out for consumption that lacks substance or vigor: *The book is mere political pap.*

pa.pa (PAH.puh) *n. Informal.* father.

pa.pa.cy (PAY.puh.see) *n.* **-cies 1** a pope's position, authority, or term of office: *the papacy of John Paul II.* **2** popes collectively: *the Italian papacy.* **3** the system of government of the Roman Catholic Church: *The pope is the head of the papacy.*

pa.pa.in (puh.PAY.in) *n.* an enzyme extracted from the fruit of the papaya, used esp. as a meat tenderizer.

pa.pal (PAY.pul) *adj.* of the pope: *papal authority; the Papal States; the papal succession.*

pa.pa.raz.zo (pah.puh.RAHT.so) *n., pl.* **-raz.zi** (-RAHT.see) a journalist who doggedly pursues news stories and pictorial subjects.

pa.paw (PAW.paw, puh.PAW) same as PAWPAW.

pa.pa.ya (puh.PYE.uh) *n.* a tropical tree resembling a palm, bearing a yellowish-orange melonlike fruit; often erroneously called "papaw"

or "pawpaw."

pa.per (PAY.pur) *n.* **1** a thin, pliable sheet material made of pulp prepared from wood or rags and used for writing, printing, wrapping, covering, etc.: *bond, carbon, filter, litmus, manila, scrap, scratch, tissue, toilet, wax paper.* **2** a piece or sheet of this: *Keep paper and pencil handy; A contract is not a mere scrap of paper; Useless paper is recycled; a plan that looks good* **on paper** (= in theory). **3** something written or printed, as an essay or newspaper: *to deliver, give, present, read a paper to a learned society; Students do, hand in, write papers; term papers; a school paper; to get a paper out* (= publish a periodical); *You are in today's paper* (= newspaper). **4** document: *background, discussion, green, white papers; a* **negotiable paper** (= negotiable instrument).

—**papers** *pl.* **1** documents: *Show your papers to Immigration; citizenship papers; a ship's papers.* **2** students' work: *Teachers correct, grade, mark, read papers.* —*v.* cover with wallpaper: *a statement designed to* **paper over** (= hide) *the cracks in their administration.*

—**pa.per.er** *n.*

paper-and-pencil *adj.* having to do with writing, esp. written tests: *paper-and-pencil assessment, employment, exams, honesty, integrity, methods, tests.*

pa.per.back (PAY.pur.back) *n.* a book with paper covers.

pa.per.board (PAY.pur.board) same as CARDBOARD.

paper boy *n.* a male newspaper carrier.

paper clip *n.* a wire or plastic clasp for holding papers together.

pa.per.hang.er (PAY.pur.hang.ur) *n.* one who decorates with wallpaper.

paper tiger *n.* a threatening but ineffectual person or thing.

paper trail *n.* a record of transactions as showing something or leading somewhere.

paper-train *v.* train a pet to defecate or urinate only on paper when indoors.

paper tray *n.* a tray for holding paper: *a printer with dual paper trays for different sizes of paper.*

pa.per.weight (PAY.pur.wait) *n.* a weight used to keep papers from being blown away.

pa.per.work (PAY.pur.wurk) *n.* clerical duties incidental to one's main occupation: *trying to catch up on last week's paperwork.*

pa.per.work.er (PAY.pur.wur.kur) *n.* a worker in a paper factory.

pa.per.y (PAY.puh.ree) *adj.* thin like

papier-mâché / parakeet

paper: *the papery skin of garlic.*
pa.pier-mâ.ché (PAY.pur.muh.SHAY) *n.* a plastic material made of paper pulp.
pa.pil.la (puh.PIL.uh) *n., pl.* **-pil.lae** (-PIL.ee) a nipplelike projection on a body surface, as on the tongue: *A wart is an overgrowth of a skin papilla.*
—**pap.il.lar.y** (PAP.uh.lair.ee) *adj.*
pap.il.lon (PAP.i.lon) *n.* a European toy spaniel with butterflylike ears.
pa.pist (PAY.pist) *n. & adj.* [hostile use] Roman Catholic.
pa.pist.ry (PAY.pis.tree) *n.* a papist's beliefs and practices.
pa.poose (puh.POOSE) *n.* a young North American Indian child.
pa.pri.ka (puh.PREE.kuh) *n.* a mild seasoning made from some red peppers.
Pap test (or **smear**) *n.* a test for cancer of the vagina using a mucus specimen.
pap.ule (PAP.yool) *n.* a non-pus-forming pimple. —**pap.u.lar** (-yuh.lur) *adj.*
pa.py.rus (puh.PYE.rus) *n.* **-rus.es** or **-ri** (-rye) a writing material, document, or scroll of paper made from the pith of an Egyptian reed.
par *n.* **1** standard or common value: *to sell stocks or shares at, above, below par; The Canadian dollar is sometimes accepted* **on a par with** or **at par with** (= equal to) *the U.S. dollar; His performance has to be* **up to par** (= average) *for him to be confirmed in the job.* **2** in golf, the standard score for a hole or a course: *A little exaggeration is* **par for the course** (= normal) *in commercial pitches.*
para- *prefix.* related or accessory: *paralegal, paramedical, paramilitary, paraprofessional, parapsychology, paratyphoid.*
par.a.ble (PAIR.uh.bul) *n.* a simple story with a moral: *the parable of the prodigal son.* —**par.a.bol.i.cal** (-BOL.i.cul) *adj.*
pa.rab.o.la (puh.RAB.uh.luh) *n.* a curve, as of a ball thrown at an angle.
—**par.a.bol.ic** (pair.uh.BOL.ic) *adj.*
par.a.chute (PAIR.uh.shoot) *n.* **1** an umbrella-shaped contrivance used for a slow, safe descent from the air to the ground: *A* **drag parachute** *is used as a brake behind a landing plane;* **adj.:** *a parachute drop of food and medicine; Paratroops make parachute jumps; parachute jackets, pants.* **2** a payment made to make an exit easy; compensation package: *She was eased out of her job with a* **golden parachute** *of $30 million;* **adja.:** *parachute packages, payments.*
—*v.* **-chutes, -chut.ed, -chut.ing** drop by parachute: *Troops and supplies were parachuted into the jungle.*
—**par.a.chut.ist** *n.*
pa.rade (puh.RADE) *n.* a showy display, esp. an organized public procession: *to hold* or *stage a parade; May Day, military, New Year's Day, ticker-tape parades.* —*v.* **-rades, -rad.ed, -rad.ing** go or put on parade: *models parading on a stage; They parade in front of spectators; The prisoners were paraded before a jeering mob; The superrich like to parade* (= display) *their wealth.*
par.a.digm (PAIR.uh.dim, -dime) *n.* **1** a model or pattern: *The "Queen's English" is considered the paradigm of correct usage by most Brits.* **2** in grammar, a set of the complete inflectional forms of a noun, pronoun, or verb, as "ride, rides, riding, rode, ridden."
—**par.a.dig.mat.ic** (-dig.MAT.ic) *adj.*
paradigm shift *n.* a fundamental change in approach: *Einstein's theory of relativity is a major paradigm shift in explaining the universe.*
par.a.dise (PAIR.uh.dice) *n.* a place of supreme happiness, as heaven or Eden (Paradise): *Niagara Falls used to be a honeymooners' paradise; an earthly paradise.* —**par.a.dis.al** (-DYE.sul), **par.a.di.si.a.cal** (-duh.SYE.uh.cul) or **par.a.di.sa.i.cal** (-duh.SAY.i.cul) *adj.*
par.a.dox (PAIR.uh.dox) *n.* a seemingly contradictory statement, situation, or person, as a bather in a three-piece suit. —**par.a.dox.i.cal** (-DOX.i.cul) *adj.:* *"Hasten slowly" sounds paradoxical;* **Paradoxical sleep** *is characterized by rapid eye movements.* —**par.a.dox.i.cal.ly** *adv.*
par.af.fin (PAIR.uh.fin) *n.* **1** a waxy substance made from petroleum and used for candles, waterproofing the inside of milk cartons, etc. **2** *Brit.* kerosene.
—*v.* **par.af.fins, par.af.fined, par.af.fin.ing** treat with paraffin: *Wax paper, airtight lids, etc. are paraffined.*
par.a.gon (PAIR.uh.gun) *n.* a model: *a paragon of a wife; a paragon of excellence, purity, virtue, old world charm and hospitality.*
par.a.graph (PAIR.uh.graf) *n.* **1** a subdivision of a written piece, starting on a new line. **2** a short piece complete in itself, as a news item in a paper.
—*v.* divide into paragraphs; *adj.: a neatly* **paragraphed** *essay.*
—**par.a.graph.ic** (-GRAF.ic) *adj.*
Par.a.guay.an (pair.uh.GWYE.un, -GWAY.un) *n. & adj.* (a person) of or from **Paraguay,** a South American republic.
par.a.keet (PAIR.uh.keet) *n.* a small

long-tailed parrot, as a budgie or lovebird.
par.a.le.gal (pair.uh.LEE.gul) *n.* a legal assistant trained to carry out certain tasks for which a lawyer is not required.
par.al.lax (PAIR.uh.lax) *n.* the apparent difference in position of an object viewed from different directions, as when an extended finger is seen with one eye closed and then with the other.
par.al.lel (PAIR.uh.lel) *adj.* **1** side by side lengthwise but an equal distance apart: *two lines parallel to each other; Parallel lines never meet.* **2** simultaneous, not one after another or serial: *a **parallel printer** to which the bits of a byte can be transmitted on separate channels at once; **parallel processing** of data in which more than one arithmetic operation can be carried out at the same time; **parallel transmission** of data in several bits at a time.* —*n.* **1** something parallel: *The **parallels of latitude** around a globe show angular distances from the equator; Winnipeg is on the 50th parallel; Batteries may be connected in series or **in parallel** (= negatives together and positives together); The vice-principal works **in parallel with** the principal.* **2** comparison: *a striking parallel; The moon-landing is **without parallel** (= equal) in history; The preacher **drew a parallel** (= made a comparison) between Easter and spring festivals.* —*v.* **-al.lels, -al.leled, -al.lel.ing** form a parallel with a person or thing: *a creative genius paralleling Shakespeare.* Also **par.al.lelled, par.al.lel.ling** *Cdn.* —**par.al.lel.ism** *n.*
parallel bars *n.pl.* a set of two bars set horizontally on posts for gymnastic exercises.
par.al.lel.o.gram (pair.uh.LEL.uh.gram) *n.* a four-sided figure with opposite sides parallel and equal, but usu. not a rectangle.
parallel parking *n.* the parking of a car parallel to the curb.
parallels of latitude, parallel printer, parallel processing, parallel transmission See PARALLEL.
pa.ral.y.sis (puh.RAL.uh.sis) *n., pl.* **-ses** (-seez) **1** the partial or complete loss of sensation and movement in the body or in an organ: *partial paralysis following a stroke; infantile paralysis* (= polio). **2** a state of powerlessness: *the paralysis of governments overburdened with debt; fiscal, moral, political paralysis.*
—**par.a.lyt.ic** (pair.uh.LIT.ic) *n.*: *a paralytic in a wheelchair; adj.*: *a paralytic illness, stroke; paralytic polio.*
par.a.lyze (PAIR.uh.lize) *v.* **-lyz.es, -lyzed, -lyz.ing** cause paralysis in a body: *Paraplegia paralyzes the lower body; a city paralyzed by a transit strike.*
—**par.a.lyz.ing.ly** *adv.* Also **paralyse; par.a.lys.ing.ly** *Brit.*
par.a.me.ci.um (pair.uh.MEE.shee.um) *n., pl.* **-ci.a** or **-ci.ums** a one-celled oval-shaped amoebalike animal of fresh waters that swims about by means of hairlike cilia.
par.a.med.ic (PAIR.uh.med.ic) *n.* an auxiliary medical worker, as a nurse's aide, lab technician, or midwife.
—**par.a.med.i.cal** (-MED.i.cul) *adj.*: *paramedical work such as giving injections, taking X rays, etc.*
pa.ram.e.ter (puh.RAM.uh.tur) *n.* a factor, characteristic, or feature of a system: *Temperature, pressure, and density are the parameters of the atmosphere; to study a problem in all its parameters.*
—**par.a.met.ric** (pair.uh.MET.ric) or **par.a.met.ri.cal** *adj.*
par.a.mil.i.tar.y (pair.uh.MIL.uh.tair.ee) *adj.* auxiliary to a military force: *a paramilitary force; paramilitary training.*
par.a.mount (PAIR.uh.mount) *adj.* supreme or primary: *The privileges of kings used to be paramount over people's rights; a question of paramount importance.*
par.a.mour (PAIR.uh.moor) *n.* an illicit lover, esp. a mistress.
par.a.noi.a (pair.uh.NOY.uh) *n.* a mental disorder characterized by delusions of grandeur, persecution, etc.
—**par.a.noi.ac** (-ac) *n. & adj.*
par.a.noid (PAIR.uh.noid) **1** *n.* a paranoia patient. **2** *adja.* having to do with paranoia: *a paranoid delusion, personality, schizophrenic.* **3** *adj.* scared and anxious: *You don't have to get paranoid about one anonymous phone call; paranoid fears, people, reactions.*
par.a.pet (PAIR.uh.pet) *n.* a low wall or railing at the edge of a balcony, roof, bridge, or atop a rampart.
par.a.pher.na.li.a (pair.uh.fur.NAY.lee.uh) *n. sing. & pl.* equipment or gear proper to an activity or office.
par.a.phrase (PAIR.uh.fraze) *n.* a restatement of a text to give the meaning, often in simpler form.
—*v.* **-phras.es, -phrased, -phras.ing** **1** make a paraphrase of: *a poem that is difficult to paraphrase.* **2** adapt or quote creatively: *To paraphrase Kennedy, Ask not what I can do for you, but rather what you can do for me!*
par.a.ple.gi.a (pair.uh.PLEE.jee.uh) *n.*

parapsychology / parenthesis

paralysis of the lower half of the body. —**par.a.pleg.ic** (-jic) *n. & adj.*
par.a.psy.chol.o.gy (pair.uh.sye.COL.uh.jee) *n.* the psychology of psychic phenomena. —**par.a.psy.chol.o.gist** *n.*
par.a.sail.ing (PAIR.uh.say.ling) *n.* the sport of soaring using a parachute.
par.a.site (PAIR.uh.site) *n.* one that exists at another's expense; sponger: *The mistletoe and bacteria are biological parasites; Spongers are parasites of society.* —**par.a.sit.ic** (-SIT.ic) or **par.a.sit.i.cal** (-i.cul) *adj.* —**par.a.sit.ism** (-suh.tiz.um) *n.*
par.a.sit.ize (PAIR.uh.suh.size) *v.* **-iz.es, -ized, -iz.ing** live with as a parasite: *Aphids parasitize plants.*
par.a.sol (PAIR.uh.sol) *n.* an umbrella used as a sunshade.
par.a.sym.pa.thet.ic nervous system (PAIR.uh.sim.puh.THET.ic-) *n.* a subsystem of the nervous system controlling involuntary activities and working in opposition to the sympathetic nervous system, as in slowing down the heartbeat that sympathetic impulses speed up.
par.a.thi.on (pair.uh.THYE.on, "TH" as in "thin") *n.* a poisonous insecticide used against plant lice.
par.a.thy.roid (pair.uh.THYE.roid, "TH" as in "thin") *adja.* having to do with glands located near the thyroids, which produce hormones regulating the body's use of calcium and phosphorus: *parathyroid disease, glands, hormones.*
par.a.troops (PAIR.uh.troops) *n.pl.* soldiers trained to parachute from airplanes. —**par.a.troop.er** *n.*
par.a.ty.phoid (pair.uh.TYE.foid) *n.* an intestinal infection caused by food poisoning.
par.boil *v.* boil partially; precook; *adj.: parboiled rice.*
par.cel (PAR.sul) *n.* 1 a wrapped package or bundle; *adj.: parcel delivery, service.* 2 a collection or group of persons, animals, or things: *a parcel of liars.* 3 a piece or portion: *a parcel of land; parcels of a forest; Growing one's hair is* **part and parcel** (= an essential part) *of growing up.*
—*v.* **-cels, -celed, -cel.ing** make into a package: *goods parceled up for shipping; work parceled out to free-lancers.* Also **par.celled, par.cel.ling** *Cdn.*
parcel post *n.* a postal service for parcels.
parch *v.* to dry, as by the sun's heat: *land parched by drought; parched throats thirsting for a drink; adja.: parched earth, farmland, skin; parched* (= roasted) *corn.*
parch.ment (PARCH.munt) *n.* 1 fine writing material made from skins, as vellum, or paper specially processed. 2 a document on such material, as a diploma.
pard *n. Archaic.* leopard.
par.don (PAR.dun) *n.* 1 forgiveness: *He begged pardon of her for keeping her waiting.* 2 release from a penalty of law: *a full pardon granted by the Queen.*
—**I beg your pardon** [a polite formula of apology, as for not hearing something said, or, in a rising tone, a challenge to repeat what was said].
—*v.* forgive: *We try to pardon each other's faults; Pardon me for interrupting; Pardon my rudeness;* **Pardon me** (= Sorry about not hearing you, offending you, etc.). —**par.don.a.ble** *adj.*; **par.don.a.bly** *adv.*
par.don.er (PAR.dun.ur) *n.* formerly, one licensed to raise money by dispensing papal pardons.
pare *v.* **pares, pared, par.ing** 1 clip or cut the edge or shave the surface of something: *to pare one's nails; n.: a paring knife to pare an apple with.* 2 reduce: *to pare down a budget; to pare down expenses to a minimum.*
par.e.gor.ic (pair.uh.GOR.ic) *n.* an opium preparation used to relieve intestinal pain and diarrhea.
par.ent (PAIR.unt) *n.* 1 a father or mother: *adoptive, foster, loving, natural, permissive parents; Children obey their parents; a* **single parent** (without a spouse). 2 originator or source: *the U.S. parent of a Mexican subsidiary; adja.: a parent company, firm, organization.*
—**par.ent.hood** *n.*; **par.ent.ing** *n.*
par.ent.age (PAIR.un.tij) *n.* ancestry: *a man of noble parentage.*
par.en.tal (puh.REN.tul) *adja.* having to do with a parent: *parental authority, consent, control, custody, duties, guidance, influence, love, neglect, responsibility, rights.*
parental leave *n.* paid or unpaid leave from work granted to either or both parents of a newborn or newly adopted child.
pa.ren.the.sis (puh.REN.thuh.sis) *n., pl.* **-the.ses** (-seez) 1 one of a pair of round brackets ( ) used to enclose words, numbers, or other symbols. 2 a word or clause inserted within a sentence and set off from it by a pair of such brackets, commas, or dashes, i.e., **in** or **within parentheses.**
—**par.en.thet.ic** (-ren.THET.ic) or

par.en.thet.i.cal *adj.*
—**par.en.thet.i.cal.ly** *adv.*
par.en.the.size (puh.REN.thuh.size) *v.* **-siz.es, -sized, -siz.ing** put something as a parenthesis or in parentheses.
pa.re.sis (puh.REE.sis) *n., pl.* **-ses** (-seez) partial paralysis: *General paresis is a brain disease resulting from syphilis.*
—**pa.ret.ic** (-RET.ic) *n. & adj.*
par ex.cel.lence (par.EK.suh.LAHNCE) *adjp.* preeminent: *a writer par excellence though a poor speaker.*
par.fait (par.FAY) *n.* **1** a frozen dessert of cream and eggs. **2** ice cream in several layers.
parfait glass *n.* a tall, slender glass with a short stem.
pa.ri.ah (puh.RYE.uh) *n.* an outcast.
pa.ri.e.tal (puh.RYE.uh.tul) *adj.* having to do with walls: *Parietal bones form the sides and roof of the skull; Parietal regulations affect life within college walls, such as dormitory visiting hours.*
par.i-mu.tu.el (pair.ee.MEW.choo.ul) *n.* **1** a betting system in which the winners share the total amount wagered minus a percentage for the management. **2** a machine used to register bets and calculate payoffs.
parings *n.pl.* what is pared off; leavings or shavings.
pa.ri pas.su (PAIR.ee.PASS.oo) *adj. & adv. Latin.* at an equal rate.
par.ish (PAIR.ish) *n.* **1** an administrative division of a diocese, with a priest or minister in charge; also, its members collectively; *adja.*: *a parish church, hall, priest, school.* **2** a county in Louisiana. —**pa.rish.ion.er** (puh.RISH.uh.nur) *n.*
Pa.ri.sian (puh.RIZH.un) *n.* a person of or from Paris, France; *adj.*: *a Parisian accent; Parisian fashions, French.*
par.i.ty (PAIR.i.tee) *n.* **-ties** (-teez) **1** equality, esp. in purchasing power: *parity between prices and incomes; to achieve, attain, establish parity; Firefighters want parity of pay with the police.* **2** the property of being odd or even, as in binary-coded data: *4 and 6 have the same parity; A parity check determines whether there is an odd or even number of zeros or ones in a set of binary digits.*
park *n.* **1** an area of land set aside for public recreation: *an amusement park; a national historic park; a state or provincial park; public, trailer, theme parks;* **Park rangers** and **park wardens** take care of national and provincial parks. **2** a commercial area: *a car park* (= parking lot); *a suburban industrial park with offices and facilities for parking, recreation, etc.* —*v.* **1** put a vehicle in a place and leave temporarily. **2** *Informal.* put or leave a person or thing somewhere for a time: *No parking of gum under the table, please; The kids were parked with Grandma.*
par.ka (PAR.kuh) *n.* **1** a hooded fur jacket for winter wear. **2** a similar warm garment of cloth.
park.ade (par.KADE) *n.* an automobile parking facility that is one or more stories high.
park.ette (par.KET) *n.* a small public park.
parking lot *n.* an area for parking motor vehicles.
parking meter *n.* a coin-operated clock device for regulating the use of a parking space.
parking orbit *n.* an orbit from which a space vehicle may be launched.
Par.kin.son's disease (PAR.kin.suns-) *n.* a nervous disorder of advancing age characterized by muscular tremors of the hand, face, and other parts of the body; also called **parkinsonism** and "shaking palsy."
Parkinson's Law *n.* the satirical observation that work expands to fill the time available.
park.land *n.* wooded land suitable for use as a public park.
park.way *n.* a broad boulevard or landscaped highway.
par.lance (PAR.lunce) *n.* style of speech: *In common parlance "inebriated" would be "drunk."*
par.lay *n.* a bet or series of bets with a previous wager plus winnings as the next bet. —*v.* bet or risk something in increasing amounts: *She parlayed a small inheritance into a fortune.*
par.ley (PAR.lee) *n.* **-leys** a negotiation for coming to terms with an adversary. —*v.* negotiate: *At first Israel refused to parley with the P.L.O.*
par.lia.ment (PAR.luh.munt) *n.* the highest lawmaking body, esp. of Britain and other Commonwealth countries: *A parliament adjourns, convenes, meets; to adjourn, convene, convoke, dissolve a parliament; M.P.s sit in parliament; Parliament is now in session; Parliament rises at the end of a session; Candidates stand for parliament* (= election).
par.lia.men.tar.i.an (PAR.luh.men. TAIR.ee.un) *n.* an expert in parliamentary procedure.
par.lia.men.ta.ry (par.luh.MEN.tuh.ree) *adj.* having to do with parliaments: *parliamentary language, practice, procedure; the parliamentary system.*

par.lor (PAR.lur) *n.* **1** a semiprivate room for social conversation: *A sun parlor* or *sun porch lets in plenty of sunshine;* *adja.*: *a parlor chair, game, piano; a Victorian parlor setting.* **2** a specially designed business establishment: *beauty, beer, funeral, ice cream, massage, milking, pizza, video parlors.* Also **par.lour** *Cdn.*

parlor car *n.* a railroad car with superior individual accommodation; chair car.

parlour *Cdn.* PARLOR.

par.lous (PAR.lus) *adja.* perilous or risky: *the parlous state of his campaign; We live in parlous times.* —*adv.* [old use] extremely: *The night was parlous cold.*

Par.me.san (PAR.muh.zahn) *n.* a hard, dry cheese with a sharp flavor.

par.mi.gia.na (par.muh.JAH.nuh) or **par.mi.gia.no** (-noh) *adjp.* prepared with Parmesan cheese: *eggplant parmigiana; veal parmigiana.*

pa.ro.chi.al (puh.ROH.kee.ul) *adj.* **1** of a parish: *a parochial school.* **2** narrow-minded: *very parochial in her interests;* **pa.ro.chi.al.ly** *adv.*. —**pa.ro.chi.al.ism** *n.*

par.o.dist (PAIR.uh.dist) *n.* a writer of parodies.

par.o.dy (PAIR.uh.dee) *n.* **-dies 1** imitation and exaggeration of a person's style for ridiculing: *a parody of Milton.* **2** a poor imitation; travesty: *a mere parody of a court of justice.* —*v.* **-dies, -died, -dy.ing** make a parody of a person or thing: *Smith likes to parody Shakespeare.*

pa.role (puh.ROLE) *n.* a conditional release from prison before a term is fully served: *a convict on day parole; early parole for good behavior; to release or free someone on parole; back in prison for violating his parole.* —*v.* **-roles, -roled, -rol.ing** to free on parole: *Paolo was paroled (from prison) for good conduct.*

pa.rol.ee (puh.roh.LEE) *n.* one who has been paroled.

pa.rot.id gland (puh.ROT.id-) *n.* either of the two salivary glands at the base of each ear.

par.ox.ysm (PAIR.uk.siz.um) *n.* a sudden outburst: *a paroxysm of despair, joy, laughter, pain, rage.* —**par.ox.ys.mal** (-SIS.mul) *adj.*

par.quet (par.KAY) *n.* **1** the part of a theater's main floor from the orchestra pit to the **parquet circle**, the part beneath the rear balcony. **2** a floor of parquetry. —*v.* **-quets** (-KAZE), **-quet.ed** (-KADE), **-quet.ing** (-KAY.ing) finish with parquetry: *wainscoting parqueted with cedar.*

par.quet.ry (PAR.kit.ree) *n.* **-ries** a mosaic of inlaid wood.

par.ra.keet (PAIR.uh.keet) same as PARAKEET.

par.ri.cide (PAIR.i.cide) *n.* **1** a murderer of a parent or other close relative. **2** such a murder. —**par.ri.ci.dal** (-SYE.dul) *adj.*

par.rot (PAIR.ut) *n.* **1** one of a family of colorful tropical birds with hooked bills and the ability to mimic speech. **2** one who repeats something without understanding it; *v.*: *The brighter students try to emulate their teachers instead of parroting them.*

parrot fever *n.* a viral lung infection caught from sick birds.

par.ry (PAIR.ee) *v.* **par.ries, par.ried, par.ry.ing 1** turn aside a blow, as in fencing. **2** evade adroitly: *He parried reporters' questions with a "No comment."* —*n.*, *pl.* **par.ries** a parrying or evading: *the parry and thrust of political debates.*

parse *v.* **pars.es, parsed, pars.ing** give a grammatical description of a sentence, phrase, word, etc.: *"Parries" may be parsed as noun, plural of "parry" or as verb, singular of "to parry."*

par.si.mo.ny (PAR.suh.moh.nee) *n.* **1** thrift. **2** stinginess or niggardliness. —**par.si.mo.ni.ous** (-MOH.nee.us) *adj.*

pars.ley (PAR.slee) *n.* a plant whose crinkled leaves are used as a garnish: *Sprinkle with chopped fresh parsley (leaves) before serving.*

pars.nip *n.* a vegetable of the carrot family with a long whitish edible root.

par.son (PAR.sun) *n.* a clergyman, usu. a Protestant one.

par.son.age (PAR.sun.ij) *n.* a parson's residence.

Parson's table *n.* a rectangular table with straight legs at the corners.

part *n.* **1** a portion or division of something: *Petals are parts of a flower; spare parts for an automobile; The three R's are an essential part of education; an integral part of the system; the major part of the day; Oxygen is a constituent part* (= component) *of water; for* **the better part** (= more than half) *of an hour; a remote part* (= area) *of Africa; the part* (= dividing line) *in your hair; I like the music only* **in part** (= not completely); *People here* **for the most part** (= mostly) *like to get out and vote.* **2** a person's share or role in an activity: *You did your part well; Al played the part of Othello; He acts and looks the part; Jane took her*

partake / partitive

mother's part (= side) *in the family dispute*; *One of the actors flubbed his part* (= lines) *because he didn't learn or memorize or study his part*; *A bit part* (= role) *in a movie has little or no speaking*; *I didn't take part* (= partici- pate) *in the fight, at least not an active part*; **For my part** (= personally), *I like peace and quiet*; *There was some hesitation* **on the part of** (= by) *John*. **3 parts** *pl.*: *a man of parts* (= abilities); *She's traveling in foreign parts* (= regions); *the private parts* (= genitals). —**in good part** graciously: *He took the criticism in good part.*
—*v.* divide or separate: *The referees parted the fighting teams*; *They parted as friends*; *She parts her hair in the middle*; *We must* **part company** (= leave each other) *in London*; *He will* **part from** (= leave) *us in a few hours*; *We* **part with** *everything we have when we die.*

par.take (par.TAKE) *v.* **-takes, -took, -tak.en, -tak.ing** take a share or part in something: *The whole town partook in the festival*; *to partake of a meal.*
—**par.tak.er** *n.*

par.terre (par.TAIR) *n.* **1** a garden area of flower beds. **2** same as PARQUET CIRCLE.

par.the.no.gen.e.sis (par.thuh.noh.JEN.uh.sis) *n.* reproduction by unfertilized egg, as in honeybees and wasps.

par.tial (PAR.shul) *adj.* **1** not total: *a partial eclipse of the moon.* **2** unfairly favoring one side; biased: *a referee who is* **partial to** *one side*; *He is partial toward his relatives.* —**par.ti.al.i.ty** (-shee.AL.i.tee) *n.*

par.tial.ly (PAR.shuh.lee) *adv.* to a certain degree: *a student partially dependent on his parents.*

par.ti.ci.pant (par.TIS.uh.punt) *n.* one who takes part in something: *an active participant in sports*; *a willing participant in the crime.*

par.ti.ci.pate (par.TIS.uh.pate) *v.* **-pates, -pat.ed, -pat.ing** take part: *to participate in social activities.*
—**par.ti.ci.pa.tion** (-PAY.shun) *n.*
—**par.tic.i.pa.tor** (-pay.tur) *n.*

par.ti.ci.pa.to.ry (par.TIS.uh.puh.tor.ee) *adj.* involving direct or active participation, as of the audience in **participatory theater**: *participatory management, politics, processes*; **Participatory democracy** *involves the people directly in political decision-making instead of through their elected representatives.*

par.ti.ci.ple (par.TIS.uh.pul) *n.* a word with characteristics of verb and adjective, as "acting" in "He is acting" (present participle) and "an acting president" (adjectival participle).
—**par.ti.cip.i.al** (-tuh.SIP.ee.ul) *adj.*

par.ti.cle (PAR.ti.cul) *n.* **1** a tiny bit; smallest unit of matter: *dust particles in the air*; *minute particles*; *not a particle of evidence against him*; *protons, electrons, and other atomic particles*; *Sawdust or wood particles are used to make* **particle board**. **2** an uninflected part of speech or an affix, as "in," "and," "the," "bi-," and "oh."

parti-colored *adj.* having more than one color: *a parti-colored marble*; *parti-colored* (= various and diverse) *thoughts about the future.*

par.tic.u.lar (pur.TIK.yuh.lur) *adj.* **1** relating to an individual person or thing; specific: *This particular case is an exception to the rule.* **2** special: *a matter of particular concern to me.* **3** exact or careful: *She is very particular about punctuation.* —*n.* a detail or specific: *Rica's OK in every particular*; *Flo was fired, but I won't go into particulars*; *He likes seafood, lobsters* **in particular** (= especially). —**par.tic.u.lar.i.ty** (-LAIR.i.tee) *n.*

par.tic.u.lar.ize (pur.TIK.yuh.luh.rize) *v.* **-iz.es, -ized, -iz.ing** specify or give details: *He condemned the whole gang without particularizing about individuals.*

par.tic.u.lar.ly (pur.TIK.yuh.lur.lee) *adv.* especially: *Gino is generally good as a student but particularly good at math*; *particularly* (= specifically) *in algebra.*

par.tic.u.late (pur.TIK.yuh.lit, -late) *adj.* formed of particles: *airborne particulate fallout*; *n.*: *cytoplasmic particulates.*

parting *n.* separation: *a tearful parting of friends*; *They agreed on a* **parting of the ways** *after 50 years together.* —*adj.* final: *a dying man's parting words*; *a parting shot from the getaway car.*

par.ti.san (PAR.tuh.zun, -sun) *n.* **1** a strong supporter of a party, esp. a militant. **2** a guerrilla. —*adj.* favoring one party: *He's too partisan to serve on this committee*; *partisan politics, propaganda, spirit.* —**par.ti.san.ship** *n.*

par.tite *adj. & comb.form.* divided; cleft: *a partite leaf*; *a tripartite treaty.*

par.ti.tion (par.TISH.un) *n.* division or separation: *a partition between rooms*; *the partition of Germany and Korea after World War II.* —*v.*: *The dining area was partitioned off*; *India was partitioned into two nations in 1947*; *adj.*: *a* **partitioned** *area, enclosure, locker.*

par.ti.tive (PAR.tuh.tiv) *adv. Grammar.* serving to divide: *"Some of us" is a partitive construction*; *n.*: *"Some," "few,"* "any," etc. are partitives; **par.ti.tive.ly** adv.

part.ly adv. in part: *You're partly right and partly wrong; He's the culprit, but you're partly to blame too.*

part.ner (PART.nur) n. one who shares in some activity or business with another or others: *an active partner in my business, not a silent or sleeping partner; dancing partners; partners in crime.*
—**part.ner.ship** n.: *to dissolve, form a partnership.*

part of speech n. one of the grammatical classes of words, as noun, pronoun, verb, adjective, adverb, preposition, conjunction, or interjection.

partook pt. of PARTAKE.

par.tridge (PAR.trij) n. a plump-bodied game bird such as the quail or grouse.

part-song n. a usu. unaccompanied song for several voices.

part-time adj. & adv. for less than the usual time: *to work part-time on a part-time job.* —**part-timer** n.

par.tu.ri.tion (par.too.RISH.un) n. childbirth.

part.way adv. part of the way; partly: *Partway through the book, Flo fell asleep.*

par.ty (PAR.tee) n. -**ties 1** a group taking part in an organized cause or activity: *a hunting party; the ruling party; to establish, dissolve, form a political party; Party politics is not for the common good.* **2** a group on a specific mission: *boarding, landing, rescue, search parties.* **3** a gathering for amusement or celebration: *birthday, cocktail, dinner, farewell, going-away, office, pajama, surprise, tea parties; to arrange, attend, crash, give, throw a party; The party broke up late at night; Al is such a **party animal** he is usually the last to leave.* **4** a person: *An innocent party got hit; aggrieved, controlling, interested, willing parties; a disinterested third party; the opposite party (in a legal action); the party (Informal for person) who called yesterday; Yves would not **be a party to** (= participant in) the deal.*
—v. -**ties, -tied, -ty.ing** hold or attend parties: *She parties too much for a final-year student; partying with the rich and famous;* **adj.**: *a **partying** crowd;* **n.**: *wild partying; too much partying.*

party line n. **1** a telephone circuit with more than one subscriber. **2** a party's policies and principles: *to deviate from, follow, hew to the party line.*

party poop (or **pooper**) n. Slang. one who spoils the fun of a party.

party spirit n. **1** social spirit. **2** narrow loyalty.

party wall n. a common wall between two properties.

par.ve.nu (PAR.vuh.new) n. one who is new to his wealth and social position; upstart.

pas (PAH) n., pl. **pas** (PAHZ) a dance step or a series of steps.

pas.cal (pas.CAL) n. a unit of pressure of one newton per square meter.

Pasch (PASK) n. Passover or Easter.
—**pas.chal** (PAS.cul) adj.: *a paschal candle; the **paschal lamb** (eaten at Passover); the **Paschal Lamb** (= Jesus or a symbolic representation).*

pa.sha (PAH.shuh) n. a title of rank once used after the name of Turkish officers.

pass v. **1** get to or cause to get to and past a person or thing: *We passed each other on the street; She passed by my window; Many years have passed (by) since my graduation; Please pass (= hand) me the salt; This story passes belief (= is incredible).* **2** proceed or depart: *That was a bit insulting, but let it pass; She passed (= died) quietly in her sleep.* **3** be or cause to be accepted or approved: *Peg passed the test; The teacher passed her with a C grade; A law is passed; A bill passes (a legislature); The judge passed sentence; The forger tried to pass a bad check; Nylon will not pass for silk.* —**bring to pass** cause to happen or exist: *Space travel has brought to pass many fancies of former ages.* —**come to pass** happen: *How did this ever come to pass?* —**pass away** or **on** die: *Grandma passed away last year.* —**pass off** get accepted: *The shopkeeper passed off a cheap imitation as the real thing.* —**pass out 1** hand out: *The teacher passed out free tickets for the show.* **2** Informal. faint: *He passed out when he heard about the tragedy.* —**pass over** ignore: *No one was passed over at promotion time.* —**pass up** refuse or give up: *Who would pass up such an opportunity?* —n. **1** a movement: *A magician makes passes with a wand; a bomber's pass over its target; Cora is annoyed by strangers **making passes at** (= unwelcome advances to) her on the street; a forward pass (= ball thrown forward) during play.* **2** a resulting state or condition: *What a pretty pass (= state of affairs) we have reached!* **3** something indicating acceptance or allowing progress: *to cancel, issue, revoke a pass; a free pass (= ticket) to the games; a convoy advancing through a mountain pass (= narrow passage); a pass with honors; a **pass-fail** system instead of grades.*

pass.a.ble (PAS.uh.bul) adj. that can be

passage / past

passed: *a bridge that is passable* (= useable) *only in the dry season; a passable* (= adequate) *knowledge of the subject.* —**pass.a.bly** *adv.: Her French is passably good.*

pass.age (PAS.ij) *n.* **1** a passing: *I forgot the hurt with the passage of time; The bill had a stormy passage in parliament; We were refused passage* (= transit) *without a visa; a passage* (= journey) *to Europe by boat.* **2** a way: *an underground passage; nasal passages* (= channels). **3** a selection or quotation: *a passage from Shakespeare.*

pass.age.way (PAS.ij.way) *n.* a way for passing through, as a hallway or alley.

pass book same as BANKBOOK.

pas.sé (pas.AY) *adj.* outmoded or oldish: *a fashion that is passé; a passé idea from the eighties.*

pas.sel (PAS.ul) *n. Informal.* a group or assortment; parcel.

pas.sen.ger (PAS.un.jur) *n.* one being conveyed in a public or private vehicle: *Buses carry, drop off, leave off, pick up, take on passengers; a transit passenger; The passenger* (= right) *side of a vehicle is the driver side in many countries.*

pas.ser (PAS.ur) *n.* one who passes: *buck, check, examination passers.*

passer-by *n.* **passers-by** a person passing by: *seated atop her car in full view of every passer-by.*

pass.er.ine (PAS.uh.rine) *n. & adj.* (having to do with) the largest order of birds, including blackbirds, finches, jays, sparrows, and warblers.

pas.sim *adv. Latin.* here and there in the book specified.

passing *adj.a.* getting past: *C is the passing* (= satisfactory) *grade; the passing* (= changing) *scene; The hero got only a passing* (= casual) *mention in the press; Use the **passing lane** for passing slow vehicles.* —*n.*: *The passing* (= death) *of our leader left a void in our hearts; I spoke to her in passing* (= briefly) *before boarding my plane; a **passing bell*** (= death bell). —**pass.ing.ly** *adv.*

pas.sion (PASH.un) *n.* **1** a strong feeling, esp. of love, lust, hate, anger, or enthusiasm: *poetry without passion; Pride is his ruling passion; She has a passion* (= enthusiasm) *for journalism; The child flew into a passion* (= angry outburst); *to arouse, excite, inflame, stir up passion; to curb, gratify, restrain, satisfy one's passion; Passions ran high during the debate.* **2** an object of such feeling: *Journalism was one of her early passions.* **3 Passion** Christ's sufferings, from after the Last Supper to the Crucifixion: *The Passion is dramatized in **Passion plays**; **Passion Sunday** ushers in **Passion Week**, the week before Easter.* —**pas.sion.less** *adj.*: *a passionless performance of "Hamlet."*

pas.sion.ate (PASH.un.it) *adj.* full of passion: *a passionate appeal for help, mercy; a passionate attempt, belief, believer, character, conviction, embrace, interest, kiss, youth; passionate devotion, feelings, love, support.* —**pas.sion.ate.ly** *adv.: She's passionately fond of the outdoors.*

pas.sive (PAS.iv) *adj.* not active but receiving or acted upon: *a passive audience; passive* (= meek) *submission to authority; In **passive euthanasia**, treatment is withheld to allow the patient to die; **passive immunity** (by injecting a serum containing disease-fighting antibodies); **passive resistance** (= civil disobedience); a **passive restraint** such as an automatic safety belt or airbag for the driver's protection; **passive smoking** (by nonsmokers inhaling smoke from smokers).* —**pas.sive.ness** *n.*; **pas.siv.ism** *n.*; **pas.siv.ist** *n.*

passive voice *n.* the verb form used to show that the receiver of the action is the grammatical subject, as in "Ray was seen by Pat."

pas.siv.i.ty (pa.SIV.i.tee) *n.* the state or quality of being passive: *female passivity; the weary passivity of couch potatoes; to slip into passivity; passivity and apathy.*

pass.key *n.* a master key.

Pass.o.ver (PAS.oh.vur) *n.* the commemoration of the deliverance of Israel from slavery in Egypt.

pass.port *n.* **1** a government document identifying the bearer's citizenship for purposes of travel abroad: *to issue, lose, revoke a passport; Renew your passport when it expires.* **2** something guaranteeing acceptance or admission: *A university degree used to be a passport to many careers.*

pass.word *n.* a secret identifying word or phrase, as used to pass through a guarded gate or gain access to a database: *Give the password to the sentry.*

past *adj.* **1** passed by; gone by in time: *Night comes after the day is past; the past year; in years past; the past few days; the past several months; the past three days; this past night; "Ran" is the **past tense** of "run."* **2** former or previous: *past achievements, generations, glory; from past experience; a past president of a society.* —*n.* former time or time of life: *memories from the past; the country's glorious past; a checkered, dark, murky*

past; the distant past; In the past this would not have happened; The politician's past (= something embarrassing that happened earlier in life) *was revealed during the election campaign.*
—**prep. & adv.** beyond: *It is 10 minutes past (the hour); A car sped past (us); Miracles are past human understanding; past all hope; Your payment is long past due;* **adj.:** *a past-due account, bill; the past-due balance, interest.*

pas.ta (PAS.tuh, PAH.stuh) *n.* **1** unleavened dough for making spaghetti and such Italian foods. **2** a dish made with pasta.

paste *n.* **1** a sticky or plastic mixture, as of flour and water or like toothpaste. **2** pasta. **3** a soft food prepared by pounding and mixing: *almond, anchovy, tomato pastes.* **4** any soft mixture or substance, as paper adhesives, clay used in pottery, etc. **5** a plastic kind of glass or a gem made with it.
—*v.* **pastes, past.ed, past.ing 1** stick: *a wall pasted with posters.* **2** *Slang.* thrash: *The thugs pasted him;* **n.:** *They gave him a good* **pasting***; The Detroit Tigers took a 7-3 pasting from the Minnesota Twins.*

paste.board *n.* a board made of layers of paper pasted together.

paste job *n. Informal.* pastiche.

pas.tel (pas.TEL) *n.* **1** a chalklike pigment mixed with gum and made into crayons for painting in soft colors. **2** a painting made with such crayons: *oils and pastels.*
—**adj.** soft and delicate in color effects: *a pastel floral print; pastel colors, tones; the pure pastel shades of a painting by Degas; soft pastel pink walls.*

pas.tern *n.* the part of a horse's foot between the hoof and the fetlock.

pas.teur.ize (PAS.chuh.rize) *v.* **-iz.es, -ized, -iz.ing** sterilize, esp. milk, by heating to kill bacteria; **adj.:** *pasteurized cheese, egg, milk.*
pas.teur.iz.er *n.* —**pas.teur.i.za.tion** (-ZAY.shun) *n.*

pas.tiche (pas.TEESH) *n.* **1** a musical or other artistic composition that is a patchwork of borrowings from various sources; potpourri. **2** hodgepodge: *The poem is a pastiche of clichés.*

pas.ties n.pl. **1** (PAY.stees) a pair of adhesive coverings for the nipples, worn by exotic dancers. **2** *pl.* of PASTY.

pas.tille (pas.TEEL) *n.* **1** a medicated lozenge or tablet: *throat pastilles.* **2** a pellet for fumigation. **3** a crayon of pastel.

pas.time *n.* an activity pursued as a diversion: *America's national pastime is baseball; Flo's favorite pastime is reading; the international pastime of keeping up with the Joneses.*

past master *n.* an expert or adept *in* or *of* an art, occupation, etc.: *a past master of the piano.*

pas.tor (PAS.tur) *n.* a minister heading a parish or congregation.

pas.to.ral (PAS.tuh.rul) *adj.* **1** having to do with leadership of a religious group: *a priest's pastoral duties, responsibilities; a bishop's pastoral letter.* **2** of rural life: *Virgil's pastoral poetry; "As You Like It" is pastoral drama; a pastoral scene, setting, theme.*

pas.to.rale (pas.tuh.RAL) *n.* a musical composition with a pastoral theme.

past participle *n.* a verb form or adjective showing completed action, as in "She is *lost*" or "a *lost* cat."

pas.tra.mi (puh.STRAH.mee) *n.* a highly seasoned smoked beef.

pas.try (PAY.stree) *n.* **-tries** sweet goods baked from flour paste, as pies, tarts, turnovers, etc.: *light pastry; rich pastry; a Danish pastry.*

pas.ture (PAS.chur) *n.* **1** food for grazing animals. **2** land on which grass and such vegetation grows or is grown; also, a piece of such land; also **pas.ture.land, pas.tur.age** (-ij)
—*v.* **-tures, -tured, -tur.ing** feed on growing grass: *sheep pasturing on a hillside; Farmers pasture livestock.*

pas.ty (PAY.stee) *adj.* **-ti.er, -ti.est** **1** like paste; sticky and doughy: *a pasty mixture, sludge;* in a pasty state. **2** dull and pale: *a pasty complexion, face.*
—*n.* (PAS.tee), *pl.* **-ties** a pie with a meat filling.

pat *n.* **1** a light tap or stroke with a flat surface, as with the palm of the hand: *a pat on the back* (in encouragement or to congratulate). **2** a small flat portion made by or as if by a pat: *a pat of butter for a toast.*
—*v.* **pats, pat.ted, pat.ting** give a light stroke to a person or animal: *The child patted her cat; Tim* **patted** *himself on the* **back** (= was pleased with himself) *and kept up the good work.* —**adj. & adv.** prompt or promptly: *a resourceful girl with a pat answer for everything; The book was published* **pat** *on schedule.* —**have** or **have down** or **know something pat** *Informal.* know perfectly, esp. from memory. —**stand pat** *Informal.* **1** stand firm, without budging. **2** resist change.

patch *n.* **1** a small piece of material that serves to mend, cover, or decorate where it is applied: *a jacket with* *patches at the elbows; the general with an eye patch over his blind eye; a shoulder patch* (= insignia); *a patch* (= change) *in a computer program to correct or modify it.* **2** something similar to a patch in appearance: *a black dog with a patch of white on its back; a potato or cabbage patch* (= area or plot). —*v.* **1** put on a patch to mend something: *Sam patched Lou's torn pants; The friends soon **patched up** (= settled) their differences.* **2** connect with: *Radio hams try to **patch into** secret communications.*

patch pocket *n.* a pocket sewn on to the outside of a garment.

patch test *n.* an allergy test for a substance made by using a pad saturated with it on one's skin.

patch.work *n.* a piece of work or a design made up of many patches: *Our street is a patchwork of badly laid asphalt;* **adja**: *a patchwork apron, coalition, design, dress, pillow, quilt; a patchwork* (= irregular or patchy) *appearance, effect, job, outline, policy.*

patch.y (PACH.ee) *adj.* **patch.i.er, -i.est 1** having or being in patches; uneven: *patchy color, fog, sunlight; a patchy lawn, pattern.* **2** not uniform; sketchy or incomplete: *patchy evidence, information.* —**patch.i.ly** *adv.;* **patch.i.ness** *n.*

pate *n. Informal.* head or brain: *a bald pate.*

pâ.té (pah.TAY) *n. French.* a paste or spread: *pâté of mushrooms.*

pâté de foie gras (pah.TAY.duh.fwah. GRAH) *n. French.* pâté made of the liver of geese or ducks.

-pated *comb.form.* having a head as specified: *addlepated, bald-pated.*

pa.tel.la (puh.TEL.uh) *n.* **-tel.las** or **-tel.lae** (-TEL.ee) kneecap.

pat.en (PAT.un) *n.* a flat piece of metal, esp. a small plate used for the Eucharistic bread.

pat.ent 1 (PAY.tunt) *adj.* plain or evident on inspection: *a patent falsehood; It is patent to everyone; granted by letters patent* (= a public document open for general inspection). **2** (PAT.unt) *n.* an exclusive right to an invention or process granted to a person by the government: *to award, grant, hold, infringe, issue a patent; to take out a patent on a new gadget;* **adja.**: *patent infringements, law, protection, rights, searches, (infringement) suits; A **patent attorney** handles cases relating to patents and trademarks; patent disputes, drugs; A **"patent pending"** notice, showing that a patent has been applied for, discourages imitators.* —*v.* take out a patent for something

new: *A better mousetrap should be patented.* —**pat.ent.a.ble** *adj.*

pat.en.tee (pat.un.TEE) *n.* one to whom a patent is granted.

patent leather *n.* a glossy smooth black leather.

pat.ent.ly (PAT.unt.lee) *adv.* clearly: *a theory that is patently absurd.*

patent medicine *n.* a medicine protected by a trademark and usu. sold without a prescription; proprietary medicine.

patent office *n.* the government agency that regulates patents and trademarks.

pat.en.tor (PAT.un.tur) *n.* a government authority that grants patents, as the Patent Office.

pa.ter (PAY.tur) *n.* **1** *Brit. Informal.* one's father. **2** a paternoster.

pa.ter.fa.mil.i.as (PAT.ur.fuh.MIL.ee.us) *n.* the father of a household.

pa.ter.nal (puh.TUR.nul) *adj.* of, like, or from a father: *paternal affection; a paternal employer, government; one's paternal grandmother;* **pa.ter.nal.ism** (-nuh.liz.um) *n.* —**pa.ter.nal.is.tic** (-LIS.tic) *adj.*

pa.ter.nos.ter (pah.tur.NAW.stur) *n.* the Lord's Prayer; also **Pater Noster.**

pa.ter.ni.ty (puh.TUR.ni.tee) *n.* the state of being a father: *Many employers grant **paternity leave** to new fathers; An unwed mother may bring a **paternity suit** to establish paternity and the father's responsibility; A **paternity test** compares the blood groups of child, mother, and alleged father.*

path *n.* a track or trail: *to beat* or *blaze* or *clear* or *make a path through a forest; A fallen tree blocked our path; an obstacle in our path; a beaten path; mountain paths; progress along predictable paths; This path goes* or *leads nowhere; Are we on the right path? to stray* or *wander from the path of virtue; on the path to fame, ruin; paths of glory; the path of democracy, war; the cyclical path* (= orbit) *of a comet; the flight path* (= course or route) *of a satellite; the path of directories and subdirectories leading to a computer file; to lead someone **up the garden path** (by false promises) and **down the primrose path** (in a vain search for pleasure).*

pa.thet.ic (puh.THET.ic) *adj.* causing feelings of pity; pitiful or pitiable: *a futile and pathetic attempt; pathetic efforts; What a pathetic sight! a pathetic story of starving children; It's pathetic that people should be starving.* —**pa.thet.i.cal.ly** *adv.*

pathetic fallacy *n.* a figure of speech

attributing feelings to nature, as in "the cruel sea" and "the happy autumn fields."

path.find.er (PATH.fine.dur) *n.* one who finds a way or route, as through unexplored territory.

path.less *adj.* having no paths: *the pathless desert; a pathless wilderness.*

path.o.gen (PATH.uh.jun, "TH" as in "thin") *n.* a disease-causing microorganism or substance. —**path.o.gen.ic** (-JEN.ic) *adj.*

path.o.log.i.cal (path.uh.LOJ.i.cul) 1 *adj.* having to do with pathology or diseases: *a pathological analysis, aversion, examination, test; a pathological condition (caused by a disease); pathological evidence; the dumping of pathological waste from hospitals.* 2 *adja.* compulsive: *a pathological drinker, gambler, liar.*

path.ol.o.gy (path.OL.uh.jee) *n.* **-gies** the study of the origin, nature, and symptoms of diseases, esp. as affecting body tissues. —**path.ol.o.gist** (-jist) *n.*

pa.thos (PAY.thos) *n.* the quality of arousing pity and tenderness: *There was an element* or *touch of pathos in his resignation speech.*

path.way *n.* a path or way leading to a place: *pathways and roadways; sensory pathways; the pathways of the brain; pathways to success; pathways toward peace; to build pathways between people of different races; a pathway to reconciliation; the pathway of a food chain.*

-pathy *comb.form.* 1 feeling or emotion: *antipathy, sympathy, telepathy.* 2 disease or treatment: *hydropathy, naturopathy, psychopathy.*

pa.tience (PAY.shunce) *n.* capacity to endure suffering and put up with inconveniences without complaining: *the patience of Job; patience in adversity; the patience to read every word of a boring essay; It taxes* or *tries your patience; You may lose your patience* or *run out of patience; I'm out of patience with pranksters; My patience is wearing thin; to display, have, show patience; endless, great, infinite patience with everyone.*

pa.tient (PAY.shunt) *adj.* having patience: *a patient listener; the patient Griselda; She was patient in suffering; patient with everyone.* —*n.* a person receiving medical care: *to cure, treat a patient; a patient discharged from a hospital.* —**pa.tient.hood** *n.* —**pa.tient.ly** *adv.*

pat.i.na (PAT.un.uh, puh.TEE.nuh) *n.* **-nas** or **-nae** (-nee) 1 a glossy green film or coating formed on copper, bronze, etc. by oxidation that is considered elegant: *a head of Zeus aged to a weathered patina; a mellow patina finish.* 2 any surface finish, natural or artificial: *gleaming with the patina of age; a patina of good manners.*

pa.ti.o (PAT.ee.oh) *n.* **-os** 1 an open courtyard. 2 an area adjoining a dwelling, used for outdoor lounging, dining, etc.: *breakfast on the patio.*

pat.ois (PAT.wah) *n., pl.* **-ois** (-wahz) a nonstandard variety of a language, as a provincial dialect or the jargon of an occupational class.

patri- *comb.form.* father: *patriarch, patricide, patrimony.*

pa.tri.arch (PAY.tree.arc) *n.* 1 the head of a tribe or founder of a family, as Abraham, Isaac, and Jacob in the Bible. 2 any venerable male leader or founder, as Joseph Smith in the Mormon Church. 3 a high-ranking bishop of the Eastern Orthodox Church. —**pa.tri.ar.chal** (-AR.cul) *adj.*: *It is a patriarchal custom for a married woman to take her husband's name.*

pa.tri.ar.chate (PAY.tree.ar.kit, -kate) *n.* a church patriarch's office or jurisdiction.

pa.tri.ar.chy (PAY.tree.ar.kee) *n.* **-chies** a social organization or institution in which power is held by male leaders.

pa.tri.cian (puh.TRISH.un) *n. Formal.* one belonging to a family of high social rank; aristocrat; *adj.*: *his patrician air; a patrician family.*

pat.ri.cide (PAT.ruh.cide) *n.* 1 the murder of one's father. 2 the murderer. —**pat.ri.ci.dal** (-SYE.dul) *adj.*

pat.ri.mo.ny (PAT.ruh.moh.nee) *n.* **-nies** a legacy from one's father or ancestors. —**pat.ri.mo.ni.al** (-MOH.nee.ul) *adj.*

pa.tri.ot (PAY.tree.ut) *n.* one who loves his or her country: *an ardent, zealous patriot.* —**pa.tri.ot.ic** (-OT.ic) *adj.*: *the patriotic spirit.* —**pa.tri.ot.ism** (-uh.tiz.um) *n.*

pa.tris.tic (puh.TRIS.tic) *adj.* of the early church fathers: *patristic writings;* also **pa.tris.ti.cal.**

pa.trol (puh.TROLE) *v.* **-trols, -trolled, -troll.ing** make a regular circuit of a territory for service, security, etc.: *to patrol the skies; patrolling in the Mediterranean.*

—*n.* a patrolling or a patrolling person or group of people, ships, planes, etc.: *The police are out on patrol; beach, border, highway, military, police, school patrol; (police) foot patrol; a (naval) shore patrol; a Boy Scout patrol with eight members and a patrol leader;* **adja.**: *patrol* agents, duty, units, vehicles; *a patrol car* (= squad car). —**pa.trol.ler** *n.*

pa.trol.man (puh.TROLE.mun) or **pa.trol.wom.an** (-woom.un) *n.* **-men** or **-wom.en** a police officer on patrol duty.

patrol wagon *n.* a small, enclosed police truck for transporting prisoners.

pa.tron (PAY.trun) *n.* **1** a special benefactor, guardian, or protector: *a wealthy patron of the arts; St. George, the patron saint of England.* **2** a regular customer of a shop, library, or other establishment. —**pa.tron.ess** *fem.*

pa.tron.age (PAY.trun.ij, PAT.run-) *n.* **1** protection, support, etc. given by a patron: *royal patronage; under the patronage of the premier.* **2** the business brought by a customer: *Thank you for your patronage.* **3** the power to grant favors, esp. political; also, such favors, as appointments, contracts, financial support, etc.: *the politics of privilege and patronage; pork barrel and patronage; adj*.: *a patronage appointment, job, network, position, post, role, system.*

pa.tron.ize (PAY.truh.nize, PAT.ruh-) *v.* **-iz.es, -ized, -iz.ing** **1** be a patron of an establishment: *We don't patronize that store any more.* **2** be condescending toward someone: *Don't patronize me!* *adj.*: *He sounds patronizing; a patronizing air, attitude, comment, manner, tone, view.* —**pa.tron.iz.ing.ly** *adv.*

pat.ro.nym.ic (pat.ruh.NIM.ic) *adj.* derived from or indicating a father's name: *"Mc," meaning "son," is a patronymic prefix.* —*n.*: *patronymics such as "Simpson," and "O'Brian"* (= descendant of Brian).

pa.troon (puh.TROON) *n.* a feudal landholder under the Dutch colonial regimes of New York and New Jersey.

pat.sy (PAT.see) *n.* **-sies** *Slang.* one who is easily victimized, imposed upon, etc.

pat.ter (PAT.ur) *n.* **1** quick, light tapping: *the patter of rain on a roof.* **2** the gabble or chatter of a rapidly talking hawker, comedian, or other performer. —*v.* **1** hit or move with light tapping sounds: *rain pattering on the window; The children pattered down the hallway as the bell rang.* **2** to chatter or gabble: *The magician pattered away while we watched.* —**pat.ter.er** *n.*

pat.tern (PAT.urn) *n.* **1** an ideal, model, or guide: *She was a pattern* (= model) *of domestic virtues; a paper pattern* (= guide) *for making a dress.* **2** a design with a repeating, hence predictable arrangement of elements: *a paisley pattern; wallpaper patterns; a series of murders with a pattern to them; a behavior pattern; group behavior following a cultural pattern; a winter weather pattern; the holding pattern* (= flight course) *over a busy airport.* —*v.* to model: *Children tend to pattern themselves after or on or upon their parents.*

pat.ty (PAT.ee) *n.* **pat.ties** a small, flat, disk-shaped form of chopped or minced meat, fish, or other food: *a hamburger patty; a patty shell of baked dough to hold a creamed-meat, vegetable, or fruit filling.*

pau.ci.ty (PAW.si.tee) *n.* smallness or fewness; lack: *a paucity of good speakers; the paucity of evidence in a case.*

Paul.ine (PAWL.ine) *adj.* having to do with **St. Paul**, an apostle of the 1st century: *Pauline principles; the Pauline school.*

paunch *n.* a potbelly. —**paunch.y** *adj.*

pau.per (PAW.pur) *n.* a poor person living on public charity.

pau.per.ize (PAW.puh.rize) *v.* **-iz.es, -ized, -iz.ing** make poor: *a nation pauperized by drought, corruption, and inflation.*

pause (PAWZ) *n.* **1** a partial stop, esp. in reading or speaking: *Commas indicate pauses in a sentence; a pregnant pause during an announcement; a long, awkward pause during the wedding ceremony; a serious matter that should **give one pause*** (= make one stop and think). **2** a lengthening of a musical note indicated by [⌣] or [⌢] placed over it. —*v.* **paus.es, paused, paus.ing** make a pause: *Let's pause and catch our breath.*

pave *v.* **paves, paved, pav.ing** cover or overlay a path, street, or an area with asphalt, concrete, tiles, etc.: *to pave a driveway; The road to ruin is paved* (= full of) *with good intentions; negotiations to **pave the way for*** (= prepare for) *a peace treaty.* —**pav.er** *n.*

pave.ment (PAVE.munt) *n.* **1** a paved surface, esp. of a street: *to tear up the pavement for laying cables; Pavements buckle during a heat wave; to **pound the pavement*** (= go about wearily) *looking for a job.* **2** *Brit.* a sidewalk. **3** material used to pave; also **paving**.

pa.vil.ion (puh.VIL.yun) *n.* **1** a tent. **2** a light, tentlike open or temporary structure, as for an exhibit: *a band pavilion; the national pavilions at an expo.* **3** a special part of a building complex: *a hospital's maternity pavilion.*

Pav.lov.i.an (pav.LOH.vee.un) *adj.* having to do with Ivan **Pavlov** (1849-1936), Russian physiologist, noted for his theory of "conditioned reflexes."

paw *n.* **1** a foot of an animal with claws, distinguished from a hoof. **2** *Informal.* a human hand. —*v.* **1** use the paws to kick, touch, etc. **2** to touch or grasp in a rude manner: *She resented being pawed by the crowd.*

pawl *n.* a pivoted or hinged catch working with a ratchet wheel to drive it forward or to prevent backward rotation, as on a windlass.

pawn *n.* **1** a chessman of the lowest value. **2** someone under someone else's control: *a helpless pawn.* **3** something given as surety: *The jewels were held in pawn against the payment of the loan.* —*v.* give as surety: *He pawned his guitar for ten dollars.*

pawn.bro.ker (PAWN.broh.kur) *n.* a person who lends money in exchange for personal goods left as security.

pawn.shop *n.* a pawnbroker's place of business.

paw.paw *n.* a North American tree that bears small greenish fruit containing pulp with a bananalike flavor.

Pax *n. Latin.* peace, esp. as enforced by a military power: *Pax Romana* (= Roman peace); *Pax Americana* (= American peace).

pay *n.* money given for work or service; wages or salary: *equal pay for work of equal value; back, overtime, severance, take-home pay; a writer in the pay of a corporation;* **adj.a.:** *pay envelope, telephone, TV.* —*v.* **pays, paid, pay.ing 1** give money or a similar amount in return for a product or service: *We paid $55,000 for the car; He pays rent on his house; She pays handsomely; Employees pay into a pension fund; I pay for purchases by check, in cash, out of my own pocket;* **adj.a.:** *a pay-as-you-go* (= as and when an obligation is incurred) *system of paying bills or taxes.* **2** be profitable or worthwhile: *It pays to advertise; The business closed because it didn't pay; The job pays $2,000 a week; She is highly or well paid for her work.* **3** give something that is due, fair, or proper: *to pay attention to a lecture; to pay compliments; to pay a penalty; to pay a visit to someone; to pay back* (= punish in return) *in the same coin; Jane pays her way* (= pays her expenses) *through college.* —**pay off 1** pay someone in full: *to pay off a mortgage.* **2** be profitable; bring returns: *Hard work pays off in the long run.* **3** *Informal.* to bribe someone. —**pay one's dues** suffer patiently, esp. life's hardships. —**pay out** [*pt.* **payed**] let out a rope or cable gradually.

—**pay the piper** or **fiddler 1** pay for one's pleasure. **2** suffer the consequences of one's action. —**pay through the nose** pay excessively. —**pay up** pay fully what is due.

pay.a.ble (PAY.uh.bul) *adj.* to be paid or due: *accounts payable and receivable; a check payable to John Doe; Admission is payable at the door; a draft payable on demand; prices payable in cash and in full; dividends payable (on) January 1 or within 14 days; It's payable annually.*

pay.back *n.* the recouping of an original investment by the net income received on it.

pay-cable *n.* pay-TV via cable.

pay.check *n.* a check in payment of salary or wages: *a weekly paycheck.*

pay.day *n.* the day on which wages are paid.

pay dirt *n.* **1** earth or ore containing enough mineral to make the mining profitable: *to hit pay dirt.* **2** a profitable find or discovery.

pay.ee (pay.EE) *n.* one who receives a payment.

pay.er or **pay.or** *n.* one who pays.

pay.load *n.* **1** the revenue-producing load in a plane, train, truck, etc. **2** the passengers, instruments, etc. in a spacecraft as distinguished from fuel and other operational loads. **3** a missile's warhead or bomb load.

pay.mas.ter (PAY.mas.tur) *n.* an official in charge of paying wages and salaries.

pay.ment (PAY.munt) *n.* a paying or its amount: *cash payments; a down payment (made initially); a payment for goods; payments on a loan; to stop payment on a check; to suspend payments; $100 in full and final payment* (= settlement) *of a claim.*

pay.off *n.* **1** a paying off of a mortgage, profits, bribe money, etc.; also, what is paid: *Someone made a payoff to the kidnappers; The payoff was $3 million.* **2** what one gets from an investment: *The payoff of laser printers is near-typeset quality.*

pay.o.la (pay.OH.luh) *n. Informal.* bribe.

payor (PAY.ur) same as PAYER.

pay.out *n.* what is paid out as a winning or dividend.

pay phone (or **station**) *n.* a coin-operated public telephone.

pay.roll *n.* **1** a list of employees and the pay they receive: *to be put on the payroll.* **2** the amount of money needed to pay employees in a given period: *Unable to meet the payroll, the company*

declared bankruptcy.
pay-TV *n.* the system of broadcasters selling program packages to viewers on a subscription basis.
pa.zaaz (puh.ZAZ) same as PIZAZZ.
pea (PEE) *n.* **1** the small, round edible seed borne in the pods of certain vines. **2** any of these vines or a related plant. —**as like as two peas** exactly alike.
peace (PEECE) *n.* **1** a state of calm and quiet; freedom from war: *The war is over and peace is at hand; to achieve peace; bring about peace in society; to break, disturb, shatter the peace; a durable, fragile, just, lasting peace; a breach of the peace; Peace reigned in Jerusalem; to be or to feel at peace; You have* **peace of mind** (= a mind without worries) *when* **at peace** *with yourself; Everyone wants to live in* **peace and quiet;** **Hold your peace** (= stay quiet) *when your mother is talking; Christmas is a good time to* **make (one's) peace** *with enemies; The court ordered him to* **keep the peace** (= obey the laws); *adja.: a peace conference; the Indian peace pipe; the Nobel Peace Prize; a peace treaty; the U.S.* **Peace Corps** (of volunteers) *working in Third World countries.* **2** an agreement, esp. between nations, to end a war or not to fight; treaty: *to negotiate a peace with the enemy; the 1763 Peace of Paris.*
peace.a.ble (PEE.suh.bul) *adj.* peace-loving: *the right of peaceable assembly; a peaceable country like Canada; "the peaceable kingdom"; a peaceable citizen, man, society, woman.* —**peace.a.bly** *adv.*
peace.ful (PEECE.ful) *adj.* having peace; free from worry, trouble, violence, etc.: *to lead a peaceful life; peaceful coexistence between the superpowers.* —**peace.ful.ly** *adv.;* **peace.ful.ness** *n.*
peace.keep.ing (PEECE.keep.ing) *adja.* helping to keep the peace: *a U.N. peacekeeping force; peacekeeping duties, operations, troops; the U.N.'s peacekeeping function or role; n.: Our aim is peacekeeping, not warmaking.*
peace.mak.er (PEECE.may.kur) *n.* one who helps settle quarrels: *"Blessed are the peacemakers."*
peace.nik *n.* [disparaging term] a demonstrator for peace.
peace officer *n.* a civil officer such as a police officer, sheriff, or justice of the peace.
peace pipe *n.* a pipe smoked ceremonially by native North Americans at a peace conference.
peace sign *n.* a sign made with the forefinger and middle-finger turned outward in the form of a V.
peace.time *n.* a period of peace: *in peacetime and wartime; adja.: peacetime economy; peacetime emergencies such as earthquakes and other natural disasters; peacetime uses of nuclear energy.*
peach (PEECH) *n.* **1** a small, roundish, orange-yellow, fleshy fruit of a low-growing, widely cultivated tree: *a* **peaches-and-cream** (= healthy and smooth) *complexion.* **2** *Informal.* a highly admired person.
peach.y *adj.* **1** peach-colored. **2** *Informal.* fine: *The future looks peachy; just peachy.*
pea.cock (PEE.cock) *n.* a large Asiatic bird, the male of the **peafowl**, having long greenish blue (**peacock blue**) feathers with tips marked like eyes which it spreads out at the back like a fan in the presence of the female: *proud as a peacock.* —**pea.hen** *fem.*
pea jacket *n.* a heavy, woolen, double-breasted outer coat.
peak (PEEK) *n.* **1** a pointed top, as of a mountain, pyramid, or conical cap; summit: *to scale the peak of Mount Everest.* **2** any tapered end or high point: *the peak of a beard; at the peak of her career; traffic at the peak of the rush hour; Prices reach a peak and then level off; adja.: an engine running at peak efficiency; Summer is the peak season for travel.* **3** the visor of a cap. —*v.* **1** reach a high: *House prices peak in the spring.* **2** look sickly; waste away: *to peak and pine.*
peaked (PEEKT) *adj.* having a peak: *a peaked cap, helmet, lapel, roof.*
peak.ed (PEE.kid) *adj.* pale and wan.
peal (PEEL) *n.* **1** a long, loud sound, esp. of bells; also, any similar sound: *peals of laughter, thunder, trumpets.* **2** a set of tuned bells; carillon; also, changes rung on it.
—*v.* ring or sound loudly: *Church bells pealed (out) to usher in the New Year; A carillon pealed forth the victory anthem; the* **pealing** *organ.*
pea.nut (PEE.nut) *n.* **1** a tropical vine whose pods ripen underground, yielding seeds, also called "groundnuts" or "goobers," used in preparations such as **peanut brittle,** a candy, **peanut butter** (= a butterlike spread), and **peanut oil.** **2** *Informal.* a small or insignificant person. **3 peanuts** *pl. Informal.* a trivial sum of money: *No one likes to work for peanuts.* —*adja.* petty or cheap: *peanut politics; a peanut sum of $8; The* **peanut gallery** *of a*

theater has cheap seating.

pear (PAIR) *n.* a fleshy, sweet, cone-shaped fruit borne by varieties of trees widely cultivated in temperate regions: *a **pear-shaped figure** (that is wide toward the bottom); the **pear-shaped** (= full and resonant) tones of a singer.*

pearl (PURL) *n.* a white or bluish-gray, satiny gem obtained from inside some oyster shells: *a string of pearls; cultured pearls; imitation pearls; "a pearl of great price."* —**cast pearls before swine** give something valuable to people who cannot appreciate it. —**pearl.y** *adj.* white and lustrous: *her pearly white teeth; the **Pearly Gates** (of Heaven).*

pearl.es.cent (pur.LES.unt) *adj.* iridescent like pearl: *a pearlescent finish, glow, sheen, skin.* —**pearl.es.cence** *n.*

pearl gray *n.* bluish gray.

peas.ant (PEZ.unt) *n.* **1** a tiller of the soil; rustic. **2** an uncultured person. —**adj.**: *a peasant girl; peasant labor; We are of peasant stock.*

peas.ant.ry (PEZ.un.tree) *n.* peasants as a class: *The peasantry of England led by Wat Tyler revolted in 1381.*

pea soup *n.* **1** a thick soup made with peas as the chief ingredient. **2** *Informal.* a very thick fog; also **pea.soup.er.**

peat (PEET) *n.* partially decayed vegetable matter dug from marshy places and used as fertilizer and, in dried form, as fuel: *Sphagnum, or **peat moss**, forms soft, spongy peat.* —**peat.y** *adj.*

peb.ble (PEB.ul) *n.* a small, smoothly worn stone, as found on a beach. —*v.* **peb.bles, peb.bled, peb.bling 1** cover or finish with pebbles; *adj.*: *a **pebbled** road.* **2** make to look pebbly: *to pebble leather* (= to give it a grainy surface).

peb.bly (PEB.lee) *adv.* full of or covered with pebbles or little bumps: *a pebbly design, texture; a pebbly shore.*

pe.can (pi.CAN, -CAHN) *n.* the oval, edible nut of a hickory tree common in southern U.S.

pec.ca.dil.lo (pec.uh.DIL.oh) *n.* **-dil.los** or **-dil.loes** a petty sin or fault.

pec.ca.ry (PEC.uh.ree) *n.* **-ries** a tropical animal related to the wild hog.

pec.ca.vi (pe.CAH.wee) *n.* an acknowledgment of guilt.

peck *n.* **1** a unit of dry measure equal to eight quarts: *"a peck of pickled peppers"; a pretty peck of troubles.* **2** a quick jab or stroke with a beak or as if made with a beak, as a light, quick kiss: *a peck on the cheek.* —*v.* pick, pick at, or pick up, as with a beak: *Using just two fingers, she pecked out the note on her old typewriter; He's just pecking at his food because he's not really hungry.*

pecking order *n.* an order of social dominance or precedence, as in a flock of poultry in which a weaker bird will submit to a stronger one while dominating others weaker than itself: *The No. 2 position in the Cabinet pecking order used to be held by the Finance Minister.*

pec.tin *n.* a white, colloidal substance found in ripe fruits, used in making jellies because of its solidifying properties.

pec.to.ral (PEC.tuh.rul) *adj.* on the chest or breast: *the pectoral fin of a fish; a bishop wearing a pectoral cross.*

pec.u.late (PEK.yuh.late) *v.* **-lates, -lat.ed, -lat.ing** embezzle. —**pec.u.la.tion** (-LAY.shun) *n.* —**pec.u.la.tor** (-lay.tur) *n.*

pe.cul.i.ar (pi.CULE.yur) *adj.* **1** particular or special: *an item of peculiar interest to collectors; a custom **peculiar to** certain peoples.* **2** strange or odd: *Peg's peculiar behavior.* —**pe.cul.iar.ly** *adv.* —**pe.cu.li.ar.i.ty** (-lee.AIR.i.tee) *n.* **-ties.**

pe.cu.ni.ar.y (pi.CUE.nee.air.ee) *adj.* having to do with money: *a pecuniary interest, motive, value.*

ped- *comb.form.* **1** foot: *pedicab, pedicure, pedometer;* See also **PEDE- 2** child: *pedagogue, pediatrician, pedodontist.*

ped.a.gogue (PED.uh.gog) *n.* a teacher of a pedantic or dogmatic kind; also **ped.a.gog.**

ped.a.go.gy (PED.uh.goh.jee) *n.* the art and science of teaching. —**ped.a.gog.ic** (-GOJ.ic) or **ped.a.gog.i.cal** (-GOJ.i.cul) *adj.*; **ped.a.gog.i.cal.ly** *adv.*

ped.al (PED.ul) *n.* **1** a lever worked by the foot, as used in an automobile, on musical instruments such as the piano, and on machines such as the bicycle and old sewing machines: *the brake pedal; to depress or step on the gas pedal; adj.*: *pedal action, power, strokes.* **2** (also PEE.dul) *adj.* relating to the foot or to a pedal. —*v.* **ped.als, ped.aled, ped.al.ing** move by pedals: *The bicyclists pedaled uphill; Keep pedaling* (= working the pedals). Also **ped.alled, ped.al.ling** *Cdn.*

ped.a.lo (PED.uh.loh) *n.* a small boat with a paddle wheel turned by pedals.

pedal pushers *n.pl.* women's calf-length slacks.

ped.ant (PED.unt) *n.* one who makes a show of his or her learning, esp. by too much attention to trivial things. —**pe.dan.tic** (pi.DAN.tic) *adj.*: *It's* pedantic to refer to a flea unnecessarily as "Pulex irritans" or to say "It is I" instead of "It is me" in ordinary speech.

ped.ant.ry (PED.un.tree) *n.* **-ries** a pedantic manner or an instance of it: *pedantry parading as scholarship; the pedantries of grammar and pronunciation.*

ped.dle (PED.ul) *v.* **ped.dles, ped.dled, ped.dling** 1 sell articles by going from place to place: *to peddle encyclopedias, insurance, newspapers; a street vendor peddling his wares;* **n.:** *drug* ***peddling****; influence peddling.* 2 circulate: *to peddle gossip, lies.*

ped.dler (PED.lur) *n.* a hawker or seller: *Pimps are peddlers of vice; dope, drug, influence, smut, street peddlers.*

-pede or **-ped** *comb.form.* foot or feet: *biped, centipede, millipede, quadruped.*

ped.e.rast (PED.uh.rast) *n.* one who practices pederasty.

ped.er.as.ty (PED.uh.ras.tee) *n.* anal intercourse with a boy.

ped.es.tal (PED.us.tul) *n.* the supporting base of a column or statue.
—**put on a pedestal** glorify: *People are beginning to put quality of life on a higher pedestal than material wealth; A* ***pedestal desk*** *has a set of drawers supporting its top on one or both sides; a powder room with a* ***pedestal basin*** *or sink that is supported on a column.*

pe.des.tri.an (puh.DES.tree.un) 1 *n.* a walker, esp. one out on a street. 2 *adj.* having to do with pedestrians: *pedestrian malls, traffic; a* ***pedestrian overpass*** *across a highway.* 3 *adj.* commonplace: *a pedestrian style of writing.*
—**pe.des.tri.an.ism** *n.*

pe.des.tri.an.ize (puh.DES.tree.uh.nize) *v.* **-iz.es, -ized, -iz.ing** convert for pedestrian use: *a street pedestrianized into a shopping mall with no vehicular traffic allowed.*

pedi- same as PED-.

pe.di.at.ric (pee.dee.AT.ric) 1 *adj.* relating to pediatrics: *pediatric hospital wards, nasal drops, nurses.* 2 **pediatrics** *n.pl.* a branch of medicine dealing with the care of children.
—**pe.di.at.ri.cian** (PEE.dee.at.RISH.un) *n.*

ped.i.cab (PED.i.cab) *n.* a three-wheeled vehicle pedaled like a bicycle, with passengers seated at the back, used as a taxicab in Asian countries.

ped.i.cure (PED.i.cure) *n.* treatment of the feet and toenails.

ped.i.gree (PED.i.gree) *n.* 1 ancestry: *a man of noble pedigree; dogs of unknown pedigree;* **adj.** of known ancestry: *a pedigree Alsatian; pedigree pets.* 2 a list or record, as a family tree, showing ancestry: *Good cats come with pedigrees.* 3 affiliation or connection: *academic, intellectual, political pedigrees.*

pedigreed *adj.* of pure stock: *pedigreed cattle, corn, dogs, horses, poultry, wheat.*

ped.i.ment (PED.i.munt) *n.* a triangular, gablelike structure over a row of columns, a doorway, etc.

pedlar same as PEDDLER.

pedo- See PED-.

pe.do.don.tist (pee.duh.DON.tist) *n.* a dentist specialized in the care of children's teeth.

pe.dom.e.ter (pi.DOM.uh.tur) *n.* an instrument worn for measuring distances walked.

pe.do.phile (PEE.duh.file) *n.* an adult with a sexual desire for young children.

pe.dun.cle (PEE.dunk.ul, pi.DUNK.ul) *n.* the stalk of a flower or fruit, esp. of a cluster, as of the lily of the valley.

pee *v.* **pees, peed, pee.ing** [child's word] urinate.

peek *n.* a quick stealthy look; a peeping. —*v.* **take a peek:** *to peek at, in, into, through, under something; to peek out from behind the curtains.*

peek.a.boo (PEE.kuh.boo) *n.* a game played with infants by covering one's face, then uncovering it, and saying "Peekaboo!" —*adja.* see-through: *a peekaboo curtain.*

peel *n.* a skin, rind, or bark that is relatively thin: *banana, lemon, orange peels.* —*v.* to skin: *Boiled potatoes peel easily; Peel the banana to eat it; An aircraft* ***peels off*** *(= separates and turns off) from a flight formation;* **adj.:** *a* ***peeled*** *carrot; I'll keep my eyes peeled (Informal for be on the alert) for a job vacancy;* **adja.:** ***peeling*** *paint, plaster, skin, walls.*
—**peeling** *n.* esp. **peelings** *pl.* parts peeled off: *potato peelings.*

peen *n.* the rounded or wedgelike end of a hammer head opposite the face.

peep *n.* 1 a brief look taken from a hidden position: *the peep of dawn in the eastern sky.* 2 the high-pitched cry of young birds, mice, etc.; cheep. 3 a complaining sound: *No one ever hears a peep out of her.* —*v.* 1 **take a peep:** *She peeped at her kid brother through the keyhole.* 2 utter a peep: *The child wouldn't stop peeping; You can hear "peeper" frogs peeping in early spring.*

peep.er (PEE.pur) *n.* 1 one who peeps, as a frog. 2 **peepers** *pl. Informal.* one's eyes.

peep.hole *n.* a hole, as in a door or wall, for peeping through.

Peeping Tom *n.* a voyeur.
peep show *n.* a usu. erotic show viewed through a coin-operated machine.
peep sight *n.* a plate with a small hole used by a marksman to line up the target and front sight.
peer *v.* 1 look closely, often with narrowed eyes; squint: *She peered at him over her glasses; He peered into her eyes.* 2 appear partly or slowly: *the sun peering through the clouds; The mechanic peered out from under the car.*
—*n.* 1 an equal in rank, value, ability, etc.: *Children learn language from their peers; the right to be tried and judged by one's peers; Has there been a peer to Einstein? adja.: peer groups, reviews; peer(-review) panels; peer pressure.* 2 a British noble, as a baron, viscount, earl, marquis, or duke (in ascending order). —**peer.ess** *fem.*
peer.age (PEER.ij) *n.* the nobility consisting of peers: *Jack has just been raised to the peerage.*
peer.less (PEER.lis) *adj.* without equal: *Toscanini was peerless as a conductor.*
peeve (PEEV) *n.* 1 an irritation or grudge: *"Not warm enough" is a pet peeve of Ray's; He shouldn't take out petty peeves from work on his family.* 2 a bad mood: *You'll rarely find Paola in a peeve.* —*v.* **peeves, peeved, peev.ing** irritate or annoy: *Peg is easily peeved by loud talkers.*
pee.vish *adj.* cross or complaining; also, showing ill temper: *a peevish child, expression, remark; What's Peg so peevish about?* —**pee.vish.ly** *adv.*; **pee.vish.ness** *n.*
pee.wee *n.* 1 *Informal.* a tiny person or thing; *adja.: a peewee baseball league, golf course, Saturday-morning match.* 2 same as PEEWEE.
peg *n.* 1 a small, often tapered bolt of wood or metal used to fasten, as a tent to the ground, to plug, as a barrel, to hang things, as on a peg-board, or to tighten, as violin strings: *He's a **square peg in a round hole*** (= He's badly matched with his position). 2 a degree or step: *In the reshuffle, some were **taken down a peg** or two* (= humbled); *Pat was moved **up a peg** to office manager.* 3 in baseball, a hard throw of the ball aimed at putting out a runner. —*v.* **pegs, pegged, peg.ging** 1 fasten, mark, plug, etc. using pegs: *Roosevelt had pegged* (*Informal* for identified) *Hitler as a mad man; adj.: a **pegged** wooden rack; If you think you've got her pegged* (*Informal* for categorized), *you're in for a surprise; pegged* (= peg-top) *pants, skirts, trousers.* 2 work hard: *She pegs away at math all year.* 3 hold at a certain mark or level: *Pay raises are pegged to inflation; Oil was once pegged at $40 a barrel; adj.: a **pegged** (= fixed) rate of exchange.*
peg.board *n.* a board with evenly spaced holes into which hooks are inserted for hanging or displaying articles.
peg leg *n. Informal.* a wooden leg or a person having one.
peg top *n.* 1 a child's spinning top with a metal peg at its base. 2 **peg tops** *pl.* trousers that are narrow at the ankles; also **peg-top trousers.**
peign.oir (pain.WAHR) *n.* a woman's dressing gown.
pe.jo.ra.tive (pi.JOR.uh.tiv) *adj.* tending to make worse or lower: *"Silly" got its present meaning by a pejorative change from "happy" as in the old expression "silly sheep."* —*n.* a pejorative word, as "egregious" or "knave."
—**pe.jo.ra.tive.ly** *adv.*
Pe.kin.ese or **Pe.king.ese** (pee.ki.NEEZ) *adj.* having to do with **Peking** (now Beijing), capital of China, or its people. —*n., pl.* **-ese** 1 a person of or from Peking. 2 the Chinese dialect of Peking. 3 a Chinese breed of dog with long hair, flat face, and curled tail.
pe.koe (PEE.koh) *n.* a high grade of black tea from India and Sri Lanka.
pel.age (PEL.ij) *n.* the hair, fur, or wool covering of a mammal.
pe.lag.ic (puh.LAJ.ic) *adj.* of the oceans, as distinguished from the coast: *pelagic fauna, as crustaceans and whales; pelagic driftnets, whaling.*
pelf *n.* [contemptuous use] wealth: *the tyranny of pelf and power.*
pel.i.can (PEL.uh.cun) *n.* a large web-footed bird with an elastic pouch under its long bill for scooping up and storing fish, fabled to feed starving young with its own blood.
pel.la.gra (puh.LAG.ruh, -LAY.gruh) *n.* a chronic disease caused by lack of niacin and protein in the diet, first affecting the skin and mucous membranes. —**pel.la.grous** (-grus) *adj.*
pel.let (PEL.it) *n.* 1 a tiny, well-packed mass or ball: *a pellet of fertilizer, medication, snow.* 2 a piece of lead shot; small bullet: *shotgun pellets.* —*v.* hit with or make into pellets: *pelleted seed.*
pel.let.ize (PEL.uh.tize) *v.* **-iz.es, -ized, -iz.ing** make into pellets; *adj.: pelletized rat poison.*
pell-mell *adv.* in confusion; recklessly: *to rush pell-mell in panic.* —**adja.** dis-

orderly: *pell-mell investment; The early 1980s was a time of pell-mell expansion in the computer industry.*

pel.lu.cid (puh.LOO.sid) *adj.* clear and transparent: *Addison's pellucid prose style.*

pelt *v.* hit continuously; strike repeatedly: *hail pelting a roof; The children pelted each other with snowballs; The angry mob pelted stones at the embassy; Rain pelted down on the crowd.* —*n.* **1** a pelting: *the pelt of hailstones; The horses ran away at full pelt* (= at full speed). **2** an untanned or undressed skin of a fox, mink, beaver, etc.

pel.vic *adj.* having to do with the pelvis: *the pelvic fins of fish; The bony* **pelvic girdle** *or* **arch** *supports a vertebrate's hind limbs.*

pel.vis *n.* -**vis.es** *or* -**ves** (-veez) the basinlike framework of bones of the hip.

pem.mi.can (PEM.i.cun) *n.* a concentrated food of dried and powdered meat mixed with fat and fruit; also **pem.i.can.**

pen *n.* **1** an instrument for writing with ink or other fluid: *ball-point, felt-tip, fountain, quill pens; With a stroke of the pen, the country was declared independent; Can the computer do away with pen and paper? "The pen* (= written expression) *is mightier than the sword."* **2** an enclosure, as for domestic animals: *pig pens; a submarine pen* (= dock). **3** *Informal.* a penitentiary. —*v.* **1** pens, penned, pen.ning write carefully: *to pen a note, poem, tribute; adj.: a hurriedly penned invitation; a well-penned essay.* **2** pens, *pt. & pp.* penned *or* pent, pen.ning confine in or as in a pen: *"Don't pen me in"; The Minotaur was penned in the Labyrinth; illegal immigrants penned up with convicts.* See also PENT-UP.

pe.nal (PEE.nul) *adj.* having to do with punishment: *a penal colony, institution; penal labor, servitude; a penal offense* (that is subject to punishment); *the* **penal code** (of laws dealing with crime).

pe.nal.ize (PEE.nul.ize) *v.* -**iz.es**, -**ized**, -**iz.ing** punish: *You may not be penalized if you confess; The poor man was penalized for someone else's crime; In North American football, a team charged with a foul may be penalized 5, 10, or 15 yards* (i.e., loss of so much distance). —**pe.nal.i.za.tion** (-luh.ZAY.shun, -lye-) *n.*

penal servitude *n.* imprisonment with hard labor.

pen.al.ty (PEN.ul.tee) *n.* -**ties** punishment: *a penalty for speeding; the death penalty; to impose, pay, rescind a penalty;*

pellucid / penetrate

light, severe, stiff penalties; ordered to pay the fine **on** *or* **under penalty of** *going to jail; A hockey player is sent to the* **penalty box** (to sit on a bench for two to 12 minutes as penalty); *a free* **penalty kick** (awarded to a player in soccer); *a* **penalty shot** (in hockey).

pen.ance (PEN.unce) *n.* punishment based on repentance: *For the crimes of his youth, St. Paul* **did penance** *for the rest of his life; A sinner receives the* **sacrament of penance** *or* **of reconciliation** *from a priest by going to confession, as in the Roman Catholic Church.*

pence a *pl.* of the British PENNY.

pen.chant (PEN.chunt) *n.* a strong inclination: *a writer with a penchant for detail.*

pen.cil (PEN.sul) *n.* **1** a drawing, writing, or marking implement, esp. one with "lead" enclosed in a cylinder of wood: *a lead pencil; mechanical pencils.* **2** a stick of crayon, cosmetic material, etc.: *cosmetic, eyebrow pencils.* —*v.* -**cils**, -**ciled**, -**cil.ing** mark with a pencil: *He penciled some changes on the manuscript; He penciled them in.* Also **pen.cilled, pen.cil.ling** *Cdn.*

pen.dant (PEN.dunt) *n.* a suspended ornament or fixture, as a locket, chandelier, etc.; also **pen.dent.** —**pendent** *or* **pendant** *adj.* suspended or hanging: *a balcony pendent over a porch.*

pending *adj.* not settled; being processed: *The case is still pending* (in the courts); *bills pending in Congress; pending legislation, matters, suits; Charges are pending; patent pending* (= applied for). —*prep.* while awaiting: *The museum is closed pending repairs; She is free pending an appeal; matters pending approval; pending a review.*

pen.du.lar (PEND.yuh.lur, -juh.lur) *adj.* relating to a pendulum: *pendular oscillations.*

pen.du.lous (PEND.yuh.lus) *adj.* hanging: *Some birds build pendulous nests; his pendulous breasts; her pendulous* (= drooping) *belly.*

pen.du.lum (PEND.yuh.lum, PEN.juh-) *n.* a freely swinging suspended body, as the regulating mechanism of a clock: *a swing of the political pendulum to the Left.*

penes a *pl.* of PENIS.

pen.e.trate (PEN.uh.trate) *v.* -**trates**, -**trat.ing**, -**trat.ing 1** force a way into and through something: *The wound has penetrated to the bone; a jungle that is too dense to penetrate; to penetrate deep into a forest; a preacher who can penetrate hardened hearts.* **2** see into something: *to*

pen.e.tra.tion (pen.uh.TRAY.shun) *n.* penetrate a mystery; to penetrate someone's disguise. —**pen.e.tra.ble** (-truh.bul) *adj.*
penetrating *adj.* **1** that penetrates the senses: *a penetrating look, odor, shriek.* **2** that penetrates the mind: *a penetrating intellect, mind, question, study.*
pen.e.tra.tion (pen.uh.TRAY.shun) *n.* a penetrating: *the penetration of a knife through an animal's heart; An ad campaign tries to achieve penetration of a market; one's powers of (mental) penetration; the penetration (= insertion) of a penis into a vagina.*
pen friend See PEN PAL.
pen.guin (PENG.gwin) *n.* a flightless, web-footed, short-legged sea bird with paddlelike flippers instead of wings.
pen.i.cil.lin (pen.uh.SIL.in) *n.* a powerful antibiotic.
pe.nile (PEE.nile) *adj.* having to do with the penis: *the penile opening, shaft; penile cancer, erections, hygiene, implants; penile-vaginal intercourse.*
pen.in.su.la (puh.NIN.suh.luh) *n.* a land area almost surrounded by water: *the Arabian Peninsula.*
pen.in.su.lar (puh.NIN.suh.lur) *adj.* having to do with a peninsula: *a peninsular region; Napoleon's **Peninsular War** in Spain and Portugal.*
pe.nis (PEE.nis) *n.* **-nis.es** or **-nes** (-neez) the erectile male sex organ.
pen.i.tence (PEN.i.tunce) *n.* the state of being penitent; repentance: *David showed true penitence for his sins.*
pen.i.tent (PEN.i.tunt) *n.* one who is sorry for having sinned: *a penitent sinner.* —**pen.i.ten.tial** (-TEN.shul) *adj.*: *King David's penitential psalms; a Lenten penitential service.*
pen.i.ten.tia.ry (pen.i.TEN.shuh.ree) *n.* **-ries** a prison for serious crimes: *a federal penitentiary; a **penitentiary offense** (punishable by a jail term).*
pen.knife *n.* **-knives** a small pocket knife.
pen.light *n.* a small flashlight resembling a fountain pen.
pen.man (PEN.mun) *n.* **-men** a person skilled in handwriting or calligraphy. —**pen.man.ship** *n.*
pen name *n.* a writer's assumed name; pseudonym: *Charles Dodgson wrote under the pen name of Lewis Carroll.*
pen.nant (PEN.unt) *n.* a long, tapering flag used for signaling, identification, or as a championship emblem: *Who won the Eastern Division (baseball) pennant in 1981?*
pen.ni.less (PEN.i.lis) *adj.* very poor; destitute.
pen.non (PEN.un) *n.* a banner or pennant.
Penn.syl.va.ni.an (pen.sul.VAY.nee.un) *n. & adj.* **1** (a person) of or from **Pennsylvania,** a Northeastern U.S. state. **2** (the period) of the second half of the Carboniferous.
pen.ny (PEN.ee) *n.* **pen.nies 1** in the U.S. and Canada, a cent. **2** a British money unit equal to 1/100 of a pound; *pl.* [collectively] **pence**: *a few pence, tenpence.* —**cost a pretty penny** cost a good deal of money. —**pinch pennies** be thrifty or frugal. —**turn an honest penny** earn a little money honestly.
penny ante *n.* a poker game with a penny as the highest bet. —**penny-ante** *adja.* cheap: *a penny-ante gambler; penny-ante stuff.*
penny arcade *n.* a coin-operated amusement center.
penny pincher *n. Informal.* a miser. —**penny-pinching** *n. & adj.*: *Pat's penny-pinching attitude, spouse, ways.*
pen.ny.roy.al (pen.ee.ROY.ul) *n.* a mint with a strongly pungent odor.
pen.ny.weight (PEN.ee.wait) *n.* a unit of weight equal to 24 grains or 1/20 of a troy ounce.
penny-wise *adj.* thrifty in minor things: *"penny-wise and pound-foolish."*
pen.ny.worth (PEN.ee.wurth) *n.* a small amount, value, or bargain.
pe.nol.o.gy (pee.NOL.uh.jee) *n.* prison management and treatment of offenders; **pe.nol.o.gist** *n.*
pen pal *n.* a friend with whom one communicates without having met: *electronic pen pals.* Also **pen friend.**
pen.sion (PEN.shun) *n.* **1** a regular payment that an employee receives on retirement: *a disability pension; It is hard to live on a fixed pension because of inflation; old-age pensions; to award, draw, grant, revoke a pension; adja.: a pension fund, plan; pension benefits, payments.* **2** (pahn.SYONG) *French.* a boarding house; also, board and lodging. —*v.* to retire someone: *Some are pensioned off before 65.*
—**pen.sion.a.ble** (-nuh.bul) *adj.*: *the pensionable age of 65 (at which one may retire from a job with a pension); a pensionable disability (that qualifies for a pension).*
pen.sion.er (PEN.shun.ur) *n.* one receiving a pension.
pen.sive (PEN.siv) *adj.* thoughtful or melancholic: *a pensive mood; She looked pensive, almost sad.* —**pen.sive.ly** *adv.*; **pen.sive.ness** *n.*
pent a *pt. & pp.* of PEN.

penta- *comb.form.* five: *pentagon, pentameter, pentathlon.*

pen.ta.cle (PEN.tuh.cul) *n.* a five-pointed star.

pen.ta.gon (PEN.tuh.gun) *n.* **1** a five-sided figure with five angles. **2 the Pentagon** a pentagon-shaped building housing the U.S. Department of Defense; hence, the U.S. military establishment. —**pen.tag.o.nal** (pen.TAG.uh.nul) *adj.*

pen.ta.gram (PEN.tuh.gram) same as PENTACLE.

pen.tam.e.ter (pen.TAM.i.tur) *n.* a verse or verse form with five feet: *"The curfew tolls the knell of parting day" is an iambic pentameter.*

pen.tath.lon (pen.TATH.lon) *n.* an Olympic contest of five events, namely, horseback riding, fencing, pistol shooting, running, and swimming.

Pen.ta.teuch (PEN.tuh.tuke) *n.* the first five books of the Bible; Torah.

Pen.te.cost (PEN.tuh.cost) *n.* a church festival on the seventh Sunday after Easter, celebrating the descent of the Holy Spirit on Christ's apostles. —**Pen.te.cos.tal** (-COS.tul) *adj.*: *"Assemblies of God" is a Pentecostal church; the Pentecostal gift of speaking in various tongues.* —**Pen.te.cos.tal.ism** *n.*

pent.house *n.* an apartment or structure built on the roof of a tall building: *a penthouse suite.*

pent-up *adj.* repressed or bottled up: *His pent-up fury was unleashed in violence; pent-up animosity, emotion, energy, frustration.*

pe.nu.che (puh.NOO.chee) *n.* a fudge made of brown sugar: *walnut penuche.*

pe.nul.ti.mate (pi.NUL.tuh.mit) *n. & adj.* (the one) next to the last.

pe.num.bra (pi.NUM.bruh) *n., pl.* **-brae** (-bree) or **-bras** a partial shadow formed around a totally dark area, or umbra, as in an eclipse.

pen.u.ry (PEN.yuh.ree) *n.* extreme poverty: *He lived in penury all his life.* —**pe.nu.ri.ous** (pi.NEW.ree.us) *adj.*: *the penurious years of famine and drought.*

pe.on (PEE.on) *n.* formerly, a laborer forced to work to pay off a debt.

pe.on.age (PEE.uh.nij) *n.* the Mexican system of employing peons, illegal since 1917: *a charge of holding 13 workers in peonage.*

pe.o.ny (PEE.uh.nee) *n.* **-nies** a plant of the buttercup family bearing large red, pink, or white flowers.

peo.ple (PEE.pul) *n.* **1** *pl.* human beings, esp. of a particular place, group, or nation: *"Let my people go," pleaded Moses; a government of the people; the people of Peru; boat people; common, little, old, ordinary, primitive, working, young people; my people (Informal for relatives) from Peoria.* **2** *sing., pl.* **peoples** a race or social group: *a chosen people; the English-speaking peoples; the peoples of Asia; the ant people* (= species; group of creatures). —*v.* **-ples, -pled, -pling** populate: *to people the staff with women and minorities; Slums are peopled by the poor.*

people meter *n.* a hand-held push-button electronic device hooked up to a computer that measures TV-viewing habits on an individual basis.

people mover *n.* **1** a mass-transport system or vehicle. **2** a horizontal escalator.

people's *adj.* **1** formerly, socialist or communist: *a people's democracy, republic.* **2** populist or popular: *the People's Bible; a people's party.*

people's park *n.* a park without restrictions.

pep *n.* energy or vigor: *Please put some pep into your talk; plenty of pep and punch; pep and vigor.* —*adj.* morale-raising: *a pep rally, talk.* —*v.* **peps, pepped, pep.ping** put vigor or life into something: *The coach pepped up their spirits.*

pep.per (PEP.ur) *n.* **1** a pungent condiment obtained by grinding the dried berries, or **peppercorns,** of an East Indian vine: *Ordinary pepper is black pepper; White pepper is made from fully ripe berries; There's a dash of pepper in this dish.* **2** capsicum: *green, red, sweet peppers; hot cayenne pepper; chili peppers used in sauces; peppers stuffed with rice.* —*v.* **1** season with pepper; *adj.*: *a hot peppered sauce.* **2** shower or pelt: *The media peppered the president with questions; They peppered away at him for an hour.*

pepper mill *n.* a hand mill for grinding peppercorns.

pep.per.mint (PEP.ur.mint) *n.* **1** a confection flavored with an aromatic mint. **2** the mint.

pep.per.o.ni (pep.uh.ROH.nee) *n.* **-nis** a highly seasoned Italian sausage: *sliced pepperoni; pepperoni pizza.*

pepper shaker *n.* a container for sprinkling powdered pepper.

pep.per.y (PEP.uh.ree) *adj.* **pep.per.i.er, -i.est 1** pungent: *a peppery sauce.* **2** hot-tempered or fiery: *a peppery general, orator.*

pep pill *n. Informal.* a stimulating drug, as an amphetamine.

pep.py (PEP.ee) *adj.* **pep.pi.er, pep.pi.est** having pep: *a peppy veteran who can never sit idle.*

pep.sin *n.* an enzyme of the stomach aiding the digestion of proteins.

pep.tic *adj.* relating to pepsin or to digestion: *peptic ulcers (of the stomach and duodenum).*

pep.tide *n.* any of the amino acids that are linked together in chains to make up proteins: *peptide bonds.*

per *prep.* **1** for each: *two scoops per child; The price is $2 per (item); a speed of 80 km per (= an) hour.* **2** through: *money sent per bearer of this letter; The order has been filled* **as per** (Formal for according to) *your instructions.*

per.ad.ven.ture (per.ud.VEN.chur) *adv.* [old use] perhaps. —**beyond a peradventure** beyond doubt.

per.am.bu.late (puh.RAMB.yuh.late) *v.* **-lates, -lat.ed, -lat.ing** walk through, over, up and down, etc. a place. —**per.am.bu.la.tion** (-LAY.shun) *n.*

per.am.bu.la.tor (puh.RAMB.yuh.lay.tur) *n. Brit.* a baby carriage; pram.

per annum (per.AN.um) *adv.* each year; annually: *an income of $50,000 per annum;* **adj.:** *the* **per-annum** (= annual) *growth, income, increase, yield.*

per.cale (pur.CALE) *n.* a closely woven cotton fabric used for shirts, dresses, pajamas, etc.

per cap.i.ta (pur.CAP.uh.tuh) *adv.* per person: *an allowance of $100 per capita;* **adj.:** *on a* **per-capita** *basis; the per-capita allowance, consumption, income, output.*

per.cei.va.ble (pur.SEE.vuh.bul) *adj.* that can be perceived: *Ultrasound is not perceivable by the human ear;* **per.cei.va.bly** (-blee) *adv.*

per.ceive (pur.SEEV) *v.* **-ceives, -ceived, -ceiv.ing** become aware of through the senses, esp. sight, or through the mind: *By the smoke from the chimney, we perceived that the house was occupied; We perceived that lives were in danger unless we acted fast;* **adj.:** *a* **perceived** *change, threat, value.*

per.cent (pur.SENT) *adja. & adv.* per hundred: *a five percent sales tax; I agree with you a hundred percent.* —*n.* **1** a hundredth part: *Ten percent of 1,000 is 100.* **2** percentage: *a percent of your earnings.* Also **per cent**

per.cent.age (pur.SEN.tij) *n.* **1** a part or portion, esp. of a hundred: *Only a small percentage of pupils were absent.* **2** *Informal.* profit: *There's no percentage in drilling here for oil.*

per.cen.tile (pur.SEN.tile) *n.* a value or range of distribution of a variable within a series of 100 parts: *A score in the 75th percentile is higher than 75% of all the scores.*

per.cept (PUR.sept) *n.* an impression received by the senses, not one conceived in the mind.

per.cep.ti.ble (pur.SEP.tuh.bul) *adj.* capable of being perceived: *Outside the home, the animosity between the two is hardly perceptible; the barely perceptible outline of a flying object; a perceptible change, effect, impact;* **per.cep.ti.bly** (-blee) *adv.* —**per.cep.ti.bil.i.ty** (-BIL.i.tee) *n.*

per.cep.tion (pur.SEP.shun) *n.* **1** the act or power of perceiving or understanding: *Good perception of depth is important for a pilot; The survivors had no clear perception of what happened in the crash; extrasensory perception; She has a keen perception of scents.* **2** what is perceived: *perceptions and feelings; perceptions of reality; public perceptions of commercial products.*

per.cep.tive (pur.SEP.tiv) *adj.* understanding: *Hearing is a perceptive faculty; a quiet youth with a keen and perceptive mind.* —**per.cep.tive.ly** *adv.*

per.cep.tu.al (pur.SEP.choo.ul) *adj.* having to do with perception: *the perceptual skills of a child; An optical illusion is a perceptual problem.* —**per.cep.tual.ly** *adv.*

perch (PURCH) *n.* **1** a spiny freshwater food fish. **2** a bird's roost. **3** a place to sit, esp. a high position; hence, vantage point: *From her perch up in the tree, Eve could see everything around.* —*v.* come to rest at a height; also, be placed thus: *Children perched on trees to watch the parade;* **adjp.:** *a village* **perched** *on a mountain height.*

per.chance (pur.CHANCE) *adv.* [old use] perhaps.

per.cip.i.ence (pur.SIP.ee.unce) *n.* perception or discernment. —**per.cip.i.ent** (-unt) *adj.* discerning.

per.co.late (PUR.cuh.late) *v.* **-lates, -lat.ed, -lat.ing** pass or make a liquid pass through a porous medium; filter or filter through: *to percolate coffee; ideas that percolate through the student community.* —**per.co.la.tion** (-LAY.shun) *n.*

per.co.la.tor (PUR.cuh.lay.tur) *n.* a coffee pot in which boiling water is made to percolate through ground coffee.

per con.tra (-CON.truh) *adv. Latin.* on the contrary.

per.cus.sion (pur.CUSH.un, "USH" as in "rush") *n.* **1** a striking or hitting.

per diem / perfunctory

2 a section of a band or orchestra containing instruments such as drums, xylophone, etc.: *percussion instruments;* **per.cus.sion.ist** (pur.CUSH.un.ist) *n.*

per di.em (pur.DEE.um) *adv.* by the day: *Supply teachers are paid so much per diem;* **adj.**: *a per diem* (or *per-diem*) *amount, basis, charge, cost, rate.*
—*n., pl.* **per diems** a daily allowance.

per.di.tion (pur.DISH.un) *n.* damnation or hell.

per.dur.a.ble (pur.DEW.ruh.bul) *adj.* extremely durable; lasting: *hard and perdurable like granite; the perdurable author of over 100 books.*
—**per.dur.a.bil.i.ty** (-BIL.i.tee) *n.*

per.e.grine (PER.uh.grin) *adj.* traveling about; migratory; cosmopolitan, as the *peregrine falcon* used in falconry.

per.e.gri.nate (PER.uh.gri.nate) *v.* -nates, -nat.ed, -nat.ing travel around or abroad, esp. on foot; **per.e.gri.na.tion** (-NAY.shun) *n.*

per.emp.to.ry (puh.REMP.tor.ee) *adj.* 1 allowing no appeal or refusal: *A proposed juror may be rejected by a* **peremptory challenge** *(with no reasons given).* 2 abrupt and dictatorial: *a peremptory manner, order.*
—**per.emp.to.ri.ly** *adv.*

per.en.ni.al (puh.REN.ee.ul) *adj.* 1 constantly occurring: *a perennial complaint, conflict, problem.* 2 lasting throughout the year: *a perennial stream (that never dries up); The iris is a perennial plant; A great book is a perennial source of inspiration.* —*n.* a perennial plant: *hardy perennials such as roses.* —**per.en.ni.al.ly** *adv.*

per.e.stroi.ka (per.es.TROY.kuh) *n.* overhauling and restructuring of the Soviet economic and political system started in the 1980s.

per.fect (PUR.fict) *adj.* flawless; without faults: *No one is perfect; "Practice makes perfect"; a perfect circle, stranger; perfect nonsense; perfect weather for a picnic;* **per.fect.ly** *adv.* —*v.* (pur.FECT) make perfect: *Practice helps to perfect a skill;* **per.fec.ti.ble** *adj.*; **per.fect.i.bil.i.ty** (-tuh.BIL.i.tee) *n.*: *the perfectibility of human nature.*

per.fec.tion (pur.FEC.shun) *n.* the act of making or state of being perfect: *It takes years to bring an invention to perfection; to achieve* or *attain perfection; Jean does everything* **to perfection** (= perfectly). —**per.fec.tion.ism** *n.*

per.fec.tion.ist (pur.FEC.shuh.nist) *n.* one who demands perfection: *Being a perfectionist, Jan is not very popular with co-workers;* **adj.**: *the perfectionist approach; perfectionist tendencies.*
—**per.fec.tion.is.tic** (-NIS.tic) *adj.*

per.fec.to (pur.FEC.toh) *n.* -tos a cigar tapered at both ends.

per.fi.dy (PUR.fuh.dee) *n.* -dies (-deez) *Formal.* the quality or an act of being deceitful or treacherous.
—**per.fid.i.ous** (per.FID.ee.us) *adj.*

per.fo.rate (PUR.fuh.rate) *v.* -rates, -rat.ed, -rat.ing bore or punch through, esp. make a line of holes, as on sheets of postage stamps: *An ulcer may perforate through the stomach wall.*
—**per.fo.ra.tion** (-RAY.shun) *n.*
—**per.fo.ra.tor** (-ray.tur) *n.*

per.force (pur.FORCE) *adv.* necessarily: *Much of science fiction, perforce, is speculative.*

per.form (pur.FORM) *v.* 1 carry out a task, promise, function, duty, etc. that requires effort or skill: *A surgeon performs an operation; Magicians perform tricks; They perform live on stage; to perform an abortion, ceremony, computation, contract, piece of music, service, task; to perform as promised; to perform in the role of "Hamlet"; to perform penance for one's sins.* 2 put on a show: *a bear that performs; Acrobats perform on the high wire;* **adja.**: *performing artists, bears, groups; in her performing years; the* **performing arts** *such as drama, dancing, and music.* 3 behave as expected: *Joe is highly qualified, but can he perform (on the job)? Our new car is performing well;* **adj.**: *the best performing products;* **top-performing** *mutual funds.* —**per.form.er** *n.*

per.form.ance (pur.FORM.unce) *n.* 1 the carrying out of an action: *Promises are meaningless without performance; She's very conscientious in the performance of her duties.* 2 a show: *a beautiful ballet performance; an evening performance; benefit, command, daring, gala, live, repeat performances.* 3 functioning or behavior: *an engine's poor performance on the highway.*

per.fume (PUR.fume) *n.* 1 a pleasant odor: *fragrant, but not heavy perfumes.* 2 a sweet-smelling fluid preparation: *to dab on* or *put on perfume; Ray came in reeking of some cheap perfume.* —*v.* (pur.FUME) -fumes, -fumed, -fum.ing put on or fill with perfume: *a temple perfumed with incense.* —**per.fum.er** *n.*

per.fum.er.y (pur.FEW.muh.ree) *n.* -er.ies a perfumer's art, products, or place of business.

per.func.to.ry (pur.FUNK.tuh.ree) *adj.* casual or indifferent: *He goes about his work in a perfunctory fashion; a perfunctory inspection, job, manner, worker.*

pergola / perishing

—**per.func.to.ri.ly** adv.
per.go.la (PUR.guh.luh) n. an arbor or walk having a roof of trellis work with climbing vines.
per.haps (pur.HAPS) adv. possibly or maybe: *Perhaps I'm mistaken, perhaps not; For perhaps one split second I was asleep at the wheel; Perhaps I'm being too careful; Well, perhaps.*
peri- prefix. around; about; near: *perimeter, perinatal, peripheral.*
per.i.gee (PER.i.jee) n. the point in a satellite's orbit that is nearest to the earth's center.
per.i.he.li.on (per.uh.HEE.lee.un) n. **-li.ons** or **-li.a** the point in a solar orbit that is nearest to the sun.
per.il (PER.ul) n. danger or a source of danger: *to avert, face a peril; the perils of skydiving; Enter at the peril of being arrested; Enter* **at your peril** (= your own risk); *Tax evaders live* **in peril of** *the law* (= risk being caught).
per.i.lous (PER.uh.lus) adj. dangerous or hazardous: *a perilous course, journey, situation, undertaking; in perilous straits, times.* —**per.i.lous.ly** adv.
pe.rim.e.ter (puh.RIM.uh.tur) n. **1** the outer boundary or border of a figure, area, etc.: *exhibits placed around the perimeter of the room; perimeter walls.* **2** the length of a perimeter.
per.i.na.tal (per.uh.NAY.tul) adj. around the time of birth: *Perinatal care of infants lasts from conception to several months after birth; perinatal medicine, mortality, (hospital) unit.*
per.i.ne.um (per.uh.NEE.um) n., pl. **-ne.a** (-uh) the area between the genitals and the anus. —**per.i.ne.al** adj.
pe.ri.od (PEER.ee.ud) n. **1** a portion of time, esp. one well marked: *a school day divided into eight periods; The Cambrian period began 600 million years ago; the Civil War period; cooling-off, incubation, question-and-answer, rest, waiting periods.* **2** a punctuation mark [.] put at the end of a sentence or abbreviation; *interj.* [used for emphasis]: *Freedom of speech is a question of freedom, period.* **3** a well-proportioned sentence, esp. one in which the principal clause is placed at the end. **4** the menses: *to have, miss a period.* —*adj.* belonging to a specific historical period: *period costumes, flavor, furniture, a period comedy, play.*
pe.ri.od.ic (peer.ee.OD.ic) adj. **1** occurring at regular intervals: *the periodic migration of birds to warmer regions; on a periodic basis; periodic changes, cycles, inspections, tides, tune-ups.* **2** occurring repeatedly; intermittent: *periodic binges, eruptions, interruptions, outbreaks, slowdowns.* —**pe.ri.o.dic.i.ty** (-ee.uh.DIS.i.tee) n.
pe.ri.od.i.cal (peer.ee.OD.i.cul) adj. periodic, esp. published at regular intervals: *periodical announcements, newsletters, reports.* —**n.** a weekly, monthly, yearly, etc. publication; **adj.**: *periodical articles, indexes, listings, reviews, titles.* —**pe.ri.od.i.cal.ly** adv.
periodic sentence same as PERIOD, 3.
periodic table n. a chart showing the chemical elements arranged according to their atomic numbers.
per.i.o.don.tics (peer.ee.uh.DON.tics) n.pl. [takes *sing. v.*] a branch of dentistry that deals with diseases of the bones and tissue around the teeth; **per.i.o.don.tal** adj.
period piece n. a work of art or architecture peculiar to a historical period.
per.i.pa.tet.ic (per.uh.puh.TET.ic) adj. **1** involving walking; itinerant. **2 Peripatetic** having to do with Aristotle or his philosophy: *the Peripatetic school.* —**n.** a Peripatetic or itinerant philosopher.
pe.riph.er.al (puh.RIF.uh.rul) adj. **1** of a periphery; outer or external: *The peripheral nervous system branches out from the central nervous system;* **peripheral vision** (outside the area of direct sight). **2** incidental: *Having fun working is peripheral to getting the work done.* —**n.** an external device or unit connected to a computer, as a keyboard, display terminal, or printer. —**pe.riph.er.al.ly** (-ruh.lee) adv.
pe.riph.er.y (puh.RIF.uh.ree) n. **-er.ies** an outer boundary or surface; outskirts: *Suburbs are on the periphery of a metropolitan city.*
pe.riph.ra.sis (puh.RIF.ruh.sis) n., pl. **-ses** (-seez) a roundabout way of speaking; circumlocution. —**per.i.phras.tic** (per.uh.FRAS.tic) adj.
per.i.scope (PER.uh.scope) n. an optical instrument that enables one to see above or around an obstacle, used esp. in submarines. —**per.i.scop.ic** (-SCOP.ic) adj.
per.ish v. be destroyed: *Hundreds perished in the fire; Many perished from famine; "Those who take the sword shall perish by the sword."* —**perish the thought!** [said of something one does not want to happen].
per.ish.a.ble (PER.ish.uh.bul) adj. liable to spoil or decay quickly: *perishable foods; n.: perishables such as fruit, vegetables, and eggs.* —**per.ish.a.bly** adv.
perishing adv. very or quite: *It's perish-*

peristalsis / peroxide

ing cold out there; How utterly perishing true!

per.i.stal.sis (per.uh.STAWL.sis) *n.*, *pl.* **-ses** the wavelike contractions of a tubular structure such as the intestines or the bile duct which tends to force its contents forward. —**per.i.stal.tic** *adj.*

per.i.to.ne.um (per.uh.tuh.NEE.um) *n.* the membrane lining the cavity of the abdomen; **per.i.to.ne.al** *adj.*

per.i.to.ni.tis (per.uh.tuh.NYE.tis) *n.* inflammation of the peritoneum.

per.i.wig (PER.i.wig) *n.* a men's wig, esp. a peruke.

per.i.win.kle *n.* **1** an evergreen plant of the dogbane family whose creeping variety is also called "running myrtle." **2** a small snail with a conical shell.

per.jure (PUR.jur) *v.* **-jures, -jured, -jur.ing** usu. **perjure oneself**, give false evidence or withhold a truth after taking an oath; *adj.:* **perjured** (= false) *evidence, testimony.* —**per.jur.er** *n.*

per.jur.y (PUR.juh.ree) *n.* the act of perjuring oneself or an instance of it: *To lie on the witness stand is to commit perjury.*

perk *n.* [short form] perquisite: *A chauffeur-driven car is one of the perks of the presidency.* —*v.* **1** [short form] percolate; *adj.:* freshly **perked** *coffee.* **2** move or behave in a smart, brisk, lively, or pert manner: *The horse perked up an ear at the sound; She's beginning to* **perk up** *(= become active) after her long illness; He came for the interview* **perked out** *in his Sunday best.*

perk.y (PUR.kee) *adj.* **perk.i.er, -i.est 1** lively: *a perky little girl; a perky hairdo.* **2** saucy: *They are a brash and perky lot.* —**perk.i.ly** *adv.;* **perk.i.ness** *n.*

per.lite (PUR.lite) *n.* a pearly volcanic glass similar to obsidian.

perm *n.* Informal. permanent wave.

per.ma.frost (PUR.muh.frost) *n.* subsoil that is permanently frozen, as in the Arctic.

per.ma.nent (PUR.muh.nunt) *adj.* lasting long or indefinitely, not temporary: *Baby teeth are replaced by 32 permanent teeth; a permanent home, job, resident;* **per.ma.nent.ly** *adv.* —**per.ma.nence** (-nunce) *n.*

permanent or **permanent wave** *n.* a hair wave that lasts through several washings.

permanent press *n.* a fabric treated for wrinkle resistance; durable press.

per.me.a.ble (PUR.mee.uh.bul) *adj.* capable of being permeated; having pores or openings to allow fluids to pass through, as limestone; **per.me.a.bly** *adv.* —**per.me.a.bil.i.ty** (-BIL.i.tee) *n.*

per.me.ate (PUR.mee.ate) *v.* **-ates, -at.ed, -at.ing 1** pass through or *into* every part of something: *Gases can permeate (through) charcoal.* **2** spread through or into a place or thing: *The smell of cooking permeated the house; adj.: a philosophy* **permeated** *with (= full of) pragmatism.* —**per.me.a.tion** (-AY.shun) *n.*

Per.mi.an (PUR.mee.un) *n.* the last period of the Paleozoic era of the earth, beginning about 275 million years ago; *adj.: Permian fossils; Cone-bearing trees appeared in the Permian period.*

per.mis.si.ble (pur.MIS.uh.bul) *adj.* that may be permitted: *permissible evidence; It's not permissible to eat in our library.* —**per.mis.si.ble.ness** or **per.mis.si.bil.i.ty** (-BIL.i.tee) *n.*

per.mis.sion (pur.MISH.un) *n.* a permitting or allowing: *The teacher may give or grant you permission to leave the classroom.*

per.mis.sive (pur.MIS.iv) *adj.* excessively lenient; indulgent: *permissive child discipline; our modern permissive society.* —**per.mis.sive.ly** *adv.;* **per.mis.sive.ness** *n.*

per.mit (pur.MIT) *v.* **-mits, -mit.ted, -mit.ting** allow to do or exist: *If the weather permits, we'll eat in the patio; Weather permitting, we'll have a picnic; Smoking is not permitted here; an urgent matter that* **permits** *of no delay.* —*n.* (PUR.mit) **1** permission or license: *building, fishing, work permits; to cancel, give, grant, rescind, revoke a permit.* **2** the pompano fish.

per.mu.ta.tion (pur.mew.TAY.shun) *n.* an arrangement of a set of things in a particular order: *CBA is one of the six permutations possible with A, B, and C; all sorts of* **permuations and combinations.**

per.ni.cious (pur.NISH.us) *adj.* severely harmful; deadly: *a pernicious doctrine, effect, habit, influence; Failure of the body to absorb vitamin B_{12} results in* **pernicious anemia.** —**per.ni.cious.ly** *adv.*

per.nick.e.ty (pur.NIK.uh.tee) same as PERSNICKETY.

per.o.ra.tion (per.uh.RAY.shun) *n.* the concluding part of a formal discourse.

per.ox.ide (pur.OX.ide) *n.* an oxide containing an unusual proportion of oxygen, esp. "hydrogen peroxide"; *adja. & cpd:* peroxide bleaching, prod-

perpendicular / persona

ucts, solutions; *peroxide-based sanitizers; a peroxide-bleached filter; peroxide blond hair* (= bleached with peroxide); *adj.*: *a peroxided redhead.*

per.pen.dic.u.lar (pur.pen.DIK.yuh.lur) *adj. & adv.* at a 90-degree angle, esp. upright or vertical: *in a perpendicular plane; cliffs rising perpendicular to the shore.* —*n.*: *a tower leaning 10 degrees from the perpendicular.*
—**per.pen.dic.u.lar.ly** *adv.*
—**per.pen.dic.u.lar.i.ty** (-LAIR.i.tee) *n.*

per.pe.trate (PUR.puh.trate) *v.* **-trates, -trat.ed, -trat.ing** commit, esp. a crime, blunder, or other outrageous act.
—**per.pe.tra.tion** (-TRAY.shun) *n.*
—**per.pe.tra.tor** (-tray.tur) *n.*

per.pet.u.al (pur.PECH.oo.ul) *adj.* continuing indefinitely; ceaseless: *a perpetual nuisance; a land of perpetual sunshine; A **perpetual calendar** can be used for many years; A **perpetual motion** machine is supposed to run forever.*
—**per.pet.u.al.ly** *adv.*

per.pet.u.ate (pur.PECH.oo.ate) *v.* **-ates, -at.ed, -at.ing** make perpetual: *Superstitions help perpetuate myths; an elixir that claims to perpetuate life.*
—**per.pet.u.a.tion** (-AY.shun) *n.*
—**per.pet.u.a.tor** (-ay.tur) *n.*

per.pet.u.i.ty (pur.puh.TUE.i.tee) *n.* **-ties** indefinite duration: *The house was bequeathed to her and her heirs **in perpetuity*** (= forever).

per.plex (pur.PLEX) *v.* puzzle and worry: *I'm perplexed by or about or at or over her sudden change of mind; adj.*: *He gave her a **perplexed** look; a perplexed* (= complicated) *issue; torn by **perplexing** doubts.* —**per.plex.ed.ly** *adv.*
—**per.plex.ing.ly** *adv.*

per.plex.i.ty (pur.PLEX.i.tee) *n.* **-ties** something that perplexes: *the perplexities of a student's first day in a new school.*

per.qui.site (PURK.wuh.zit) *n.* a bonus, fringe benefit, or a peculiar privilege, esp. one attached to a position or office, as a sales rep's expense account or company car.

per se *adv. Latin.* by or in itself: *Drinking per se, as opposed to drunk driving, is not criminal.*

per.se.cute (PUR.suh.cute) *v.* **-cutes, -cut.ed, -cut.ing 1** harass, esp. because of one's beliefs: *She was persecuted for her religious beliefs.* **2** annoy constantly; pester; *adj.*: *The minister felt **persecuted** by a hostile press; a persecuted minority.*
—**per.se.cu.tion** (-CUE.shun) *n.*: *bloody, political, racial, relentless, religious persecution; to suffer persecution for justice's sake.* —**per.se.cu.tor** (-cue.tur) *n.*

per.se.vere (pur.suh.VEER) *v.* **-veres, -vered, -ver.ing** continue doing, esp. something hard; be steadfast: *to persevere in one's efforts to get a gold medal; to persevere at or with your studies.*
—**per.se.ver.ance** (-unce) *n.*

Per.sian (PUR.zhun) *n.* **1** a person of or from **Persia**, the former name of Iran. **2** the chief language of Iran, esp. its ancient and literary forms.
—*adj.*: *Persian carpets, literature; the **Persian cat** with long silky hair.*

Persian lamb *n.* **1** the fur of karakul sheep. **2** the lamb.

per.si.flage (PUR.suh.flahzh) *n.* light banter or writing.

per.sim.mon (pur.SIM.un) *n.* **1** the pulpy, edible, plumlike fruit of a tree of the ebony family. **2** the tree.

per.sist (pur.SIST) *v.* **1** continue being or doing, esp. with a purpose: *She persisted in taking her daily walk despite her illness.* **2** continue to last: *Mountain snows persist till early summer.*
—**per.sis.tence** (-tunce) *n.*: *his quiet persistence in doing things the right way; She shows dogged persistence in her efforts; Only Pat has the persistence to fight to the finish; The continuity of moving pictures is based on persistence of vision.*
—**per.sis.tent** (-tunt) *adj.*: *a persistent cough, questioner; A persistent pesticide or virus takes a long time to get out of a system;* **per.sis.tent.ly** *adv.*

per.snick.e.ty (pur.SNIK.uh.tee) *adj. Informal.* extremely fastidious; fussy.

per.son (PUR.sun) *n.* **1** a human being: *a displaced person; missing persons; stolen by persons unknown; She's a natural person (with nothing artificial about her); The child found a friend **in the person of** the police officer; adj.*: *A **person-to-person** phone call used to be operator-handled.* **2** a legal entity having rights and duties: *A company is a legal person.* **3** an individual physically considered: *They threatened him but didn't touch his person; He couldn't find a penny on her person; The president was here **in person*** (= personally). **4** any of the three pronoun categories, as the **first person** (= I, we), **second person** (= you), **third person** (= he, she, it, they).
—*comb.form* [as a neutral substitute for "man" and "woman"]: *chairperson, person-hour, personhood, spokesperson.*

per.so.na (pur.SOH.nuh) *n., pl.* **-nae** (-nee) **1** a character in a play or novel. **2** an author's personality seen through his or her works. **3** *pl.* **-nas** in psychology, a personality assumed by an individual as a mask.

per.son.a.ble (PUR.suh.nuh.bul) *adj.* pleasing in appearance or personality. —**per.son.a.bly** (-nuh.blee) *adv.*

per.son.age (PUR.suh.nij) *n.* a person of rank or importance.

per.son.al (PUR.suh.nul) *adj.* having to do with a particular person; private: *a personal and confidential letter; your personal history; a personal assistant, newspaper column; a highly personal remark bordering on slander; a personal* (= live) *appearance by a movie star;* **personal hygiene** *(of the body); Lack of* **personal space***, as in a crowd, makes one tense.* —**per.son.al.ly** *adv.*

personal computer *n.* a microcomputer, esp. a desk-top.

personal effects *n.pl.* belongings such as clothing and toiletry.

personal equation *n.* variation in observation or judgment because of one's personality.

per.son.al.i.ty (pur.suh.NAL.i.tee) *n.* -ties a person's distinctive character: *a woman with some personality; charming, dynamic, forceful, magnetic, multiple, split, strong, weak personalities; a well-known TV personality* (= person); *to indulge in* **personalities** (= offensive personal remarks); *adja.: personality development, differences, traits, types; the Soviet* **personality cult** *of Stalin; Pat and Ray have a* **personality problem** (= They can't get along well).

per.son.al.ize (PUR.sun.ul.ize) *v.* -**liz.es**, -**lized**, -**liz.ing** make identifiable as one person's; *adj.: a* **personalized** *greeting card.*

personal property *n.* [legal use] chattels, not real estate. Also **per.son.al.ty** (PUR.sun.ul.tee).

persona non gra.ta (-GRAH.tuh) *n., pl.* **per.so.nae non gra.tae** (pur.SOH.nee. non.GRAH.tee) one who is not acceptable: *A diplomat suspected of being a spy is declared persona non grata.*

per.son.ate (PUR.suh.nate) *v.* -**ates**, -**at.ed**, -**at.ing** [legal use] same as IMPERSONATE. —**per.son.a.tion** (-NAY.shun) *n.*

person-day *n.* the duration of a person's average work day.

per.son.i.fy (pur.SON.uh.fye) *v.* -**fies**, -**fied**, -**fy.ing** make into a person; *adj.: the Mississippi* **personified** *as "Ol' Man River"; He thinks Bo is beauty personified.* —**per.son.i.fi.ca.tion** (-fuh.CAY.shun) *n.*

per.son.nel (pur.suh.NEL) *n.* employees as a body: *army, enlisted, government, military, sales personnel; 500 personnel; The office personnel are on their coffee break;* **adja.:** *personnel management; a personnel department.*

per.spec.tive (pur.SPEC.tiv) *n.* the look of objects as affected by their dimensions and distance from the viewer: *a picture drawn out of perspective; the proper, true, wrong perspective; to see events in the right perspective; a new perspective of history.* —**per.spec.tive.ly** *adv.*

per.spi.ca.cious (pur.spuh.CAY.shus) *adj.* discerning: *a perspicacious analysis of an obscure issue;* **per.spi.ca.cious.ly** *adv.* —**per.spi.cac.i.ty** (-CAS.i.tee) *n.*

per.spi.cu.i.ty (pur.spuh.CUE.i.tee) *n.* the quality of being perspicuous or lucid: *the perspicuity of his argument, writing.*

per.spic.u.ous (pur.SPIC.yoo.us) *adj.* 1 clearly expressed; lucid: *a perspicuous style.* 2 expressing oneself clearly: *a perspicuous writer.* —**per.spic.u.ous.ly** *adv.;* **per.spic.u.ous.ness** *n.: the perspicuousness of her prose.*

per.spire (pur.SPIRE) *v.* -**spires**, -**spired**, -**spir.ing** to sweat: *We perspire profusely in a sauna.* —**per.spi.ra.tion** (-spuh.RAY.shun) *n.*

per.suade (pur.SWADE) *v.* -**suades**, -**suad.ed**, -**suad.ing** move or win over to think or act as desired: *She persuaded him to stop smoking; persuaded him of the need to stop smoking;* **adj.:** *Are you* **persuaded** (= convinced) *that smoking is bad for your lungs?*

per.sua.sion (pur.SWAY.zhun) *n.* 1 power of persuading: *a convincing speaker with great powers of persuasion; We used friendly persuasion to get him to change his mind.* 2 a group or party with a particular set of beliefs; denomination: *Protestants of all persuasions; a Calvinist of the strictest persuasion; various persuasions; a gentleman of the feminist persuasion.* —**per.sua.sive** (-ziv) *adj.;* **per.sua.sive.ly** *adv.;* **per.sua.sive.ness** *n.*

pert *adj.* 1 saucy or flippant: *a pert answer; a pert little girl.* 2 jaunty or lively: *He's feeling pert and refreshed.* —**pert.ly** *adv.;* **pert.ness** *n.*

per.tain (pur.TAIN) *v.* refer or relate: *evidence that pertains to the mystery; new facts pertaining to the case.*

per.ti.na.cious (pur.tuh.NAY.shus) *adj.* stubbornly clinging to an opinion or course of action: *a pertinacious newshound; a lawyer's pertinacious cross-examination;* **per.ti.na.cious.ly** *adv.* —**per.ti.nac.i.ty** (-NAS.i.tee) *n.: a bill collector's pertinacity in dunning creditors.*

per.ti.nence (PUR.tun.unce) *n.* relevance.

pertinent / petard

per.ti.nent (PUR.tun.unt) *adj.* clearly and directly relevant: *a pertinent question; matters that are not pertinent to the case.* —**per.ti.nent.ly** *adv.*: *a question pertinently put at the right moment.*

per.turb (pur.TURB) *v.* agitate mentally; upset: *He's easily perturbed by or about or over unforeseen events; adj.: a perturbing revelation.* —**per.tur.ba.tion** (-tur.BAY.shun) *n.*

per.tus.sis (pur.TUSS.is) *n.* whooping cough.

pe.ruke (puh.ROOK, long "OO") *n.* a men's wig with a tie at the back, fashionable in the 17th and 18th centuries; periwig.

pe.ruse (puh.ROOZ) *v.* **-rus.es, -rused, -rus.ing** 1 read or study casually: *to peruse a display, face, menu, picture.* 2 [former use] read or study carefully: *"Let me peruse this face."* —**pe.ru.sal** (-zul) *n.*

Pe.ru.vi.an (puh.ROO.vee.un) *n. & adj.* (a person) of or from **Peru,** a South American republic.

per.vade (pur.VADE) *v.* **-vades, -vad.ed, -vad.ing** spread through all parts of something: *The spirit of camaraderie soon pervaded the camp; an atmosphere pervaded with animosity.* —**per.va.sive** (-VAY.ziv) *adj.*: *a pervasive influence;* **per.va.sive.ly** *adv.*; **per.va.sive.ness** *n.*

per.verse (pur.VURSE) *adj.* contrary to what is desirable, reasonable, or established as normal: *an obstinate and perverse nature; to take a perverse pleasure in doing something wrong-headed; a perverse desire, fascination, thrill.* —**per.verse.ly** *adv.*; **per.verse.ness** *n.*

per.ver.sion (pur.VUR.zhun) *n.* a distortion: *The translation seems a perversion of the author's original sense.*

per.ver.si.ty (pur.VUR.si.tee) *n.* **-ties** 1 the quality of being perverse: *political perversity.* 2 something perverse: *the perversities of human nature.*

per.vert (pur.VURT) *v.* turn or cause something normal or desirable to turn to something bad; corrupt or lead astray: *a charge of perverting the course of justice by influencing a trial; a verdict that perverts the ends of justice; adj.: their perverted art, concepts, standards; sick or perverted; the perverting influence of TV violence.* —*n.* (PUR.vurt) a perverted person: *a sexual pervert.*

pe.se.ta (puh.SAY.tuh) *n.* a silver coin and the basic monetary unit of Spain and Spanish dependencies.

pes.ky (PES.kee) *adj.* **-ki.er, -ki.est** *Informal.* annoying, as gnats or mosquitoes.

pe.so (PAY.soh) *n.* **-sos** the basic money unit of many Latin American countries and the Philippines.

pes.si.mism (PES.uh.miz.um) *n.* the tendency to expect the worst possible outcome: *the pessimism about or over the future of the environment;* **pes.si.mist** *n.* —**pes.si.mis.tic** (-MIS.tic) *adj.*; **pes.si.mis.ti.cal.ly** *adv.*

pest *n.* 1 a harmful plant or animal, as insects, mice, and weeds: *Snails and larvae are garden pests.* 2 an annoying person; nuisance: *Gossips are pests of society.*

pes.ter (PES.tur) *v.* annoy or vex: *Rob kept pestering his friend for money; Stop pestering me about the loan; I won't be pestered into lending you any more money.*

pest.hole *n.* a place so unsanitary it helps the spread of disease.

pes.ti.cide (PES.tuh.cide) *n.* a chemical or other agent used against harmful plants and animals.

pes.tif.er.ous (pes.TIF.ur.us) *adj.* 1 disease-causing: *pestiferous germs, vermin.* 2 *Informal.* annoying: *pestiferous telephone solicitations.*

pes.ti.lence (PES.tul.unce) *n.* a fatal epidemic disease, as the plague: *We have survived pestilence, war, and famine.* —**pes.ti.len.tial** (-LEN.shul) *adj.*: *a pestilential threat;* **pes.ti.len.tial.ly** *adv.*

pes.tle (PES.ul) *n.* a club-shaped tool used with a mortar for pounding or grinding ingredients, as in a laboratory.

pet *v.* **pets, pet.ted, pet.ting** 1 fondle or caress: *Children like to pet and feed animals; adj.a.: a zoo with a petting pen; petting zoos.* 2 *Informal.* to caress and kiss someone; *n.*: *No petting in the library; to engage in heavy petting (leading to the sex act).* —*n.* 1 a domesticated animal kept for companionship, as a cat, dog, or goldfish: *a household pet.* 2 a young person treated by someone with special care; favorite: *a teacher's pet; adj.a.: one's pet peeves; a pet project, rock, theory.* 3 a peevish mood: *She spent all day in a pet.* —**pet.tish** *adj.*

PET (PET) *n.* a computerized scanning device that shows the functioning of internal organs using cross-sectional images; *adj.a.: a PET evaluation, scan, study.* —**PET scanner** *n.*

pet.al (PET.ul) *n.* one of the separate leaflike parts of a flower's corolla: *a basket of rose petals.* —**pet.aled** *adj. & cpd.*: *Most flowers are petaled; the many-petaled daisy;* also **pet.alled** *Cdn.*

pe.tard (pi.TARD) *n.* an explosive device: *The schemer was* **hoist with** *or* **by his own petard** (= became his own victim, like one blown up by his own bomb).

pet.cock *n.* a small valve or faucet for draining radiators, boilers, etc.

Pete (PEET) *n.* in **for Pete's sake** [an oath of entreaty]: *For Pete's sake, stop fighting!*

pe.ter (PEE.tur) *v.* in **peter out**, come to an end gradually; be exhausted: *The case dragged on, but finally petered out; Oil wells gradually peter out; **n**.: the **petering** out of one's energies, hopes, provisions.* —**St. Peter** *n.* the chief of Christ's disciples, supposed to be guarding the gates of Heaven: *the chair of St. Peter* (= papacy). —**rob Peter to pay Paul** satisfy one need by creating another, as by using the rent money to make a car payment.

Peter Principle *n.* the satirical observation that employees tend to get promoted till they reach their level of incompetence.

pet.i.ole (PET.ee.ole) *n.* **1** a leafstalk. **2** a stalklike connecting part between thorax and abdomen, as in the wasp.

pe.tit (PET.ee) *adj.* [legal use] small or minor; opposed to GRAND: *petit jury, petit larceny.*

pe.tite (puh.TEET) *adj.* of a woman, small and slender in figure.

pe.tit four (pet.ee.FOR) *n., pl.* **petits fours** (pet.ee.FORS) or **petit fours** a small frosted cake.

pe.ti.tion (puh.TISH.un) *n.* **1** a formal request to someone in authority: *to circulate, deny, file, grant, present, reject, withdraw a petition.* **2** a document making such a request: *a petition for retrial.* —*v.* ask formally: *It's the people's constitutional right to petition the government; They petitioned the mayor for a new hospital.* —**pe.ti.tion.er** *n.*

petit jury *n.* a jury of 12 members; also **petty jury.**

petit larceny *n.* theft of property below a certain specified value; also **petty larceny.**

pet name *n.* a nickname, as "Bettina" for "Beth."

pet.nap.ping (PET.nap.ing) *n.* the stealing of pets, as for sale to laboratories for use in experiments. Also **pet.nap.ing.**

pet.rel (PET.rul) *n.* a black-and-white sea bird with long wings, esp. the "storm petrel."

Pe.tri dish (PEE.tree-) *n.* a small glass dish with a cover used in a biological laboratory: *A test-tube baby is conceived in a Petri dish.*

pet.ri.fy (PET.ruh.fye) *v.* **-fies, -fied,** **-fy.ing 1** make or become like rock; *adj.*: *a **petrified** tree; The petrified forests of Arizona are made up of tree trunks buried in rock millions of years ago.* **2** stun or daze; *adj.*: *He stood motionless, **petrified** by or with fear; He's petrified* (= scared) *of flying.* —**pet.ri.fi.ca.tion** (-fuh.CAY.shun) *n.*

petro- *comb.form.* **1** having to do with petroleum: *petrochemical, petrodollars.* **2** having to do with rock: *petroglyph, petrography.*

pet.ro.chem.i.cal (pet.roh.KEM.i.cul) *n.* a chemical made from crude oil and natural gas and used in plastics, synthetics, fertilizers, etc.
—**pet.ro.chem.is.try** (-is.tree) *n.*

pet.ro.dol.lars (PET.roh.doll.urs) *n.pl.* revenue made from the sale of petroleum.

pet.ro.glyph (PET.roh.glif) *n.* something carved on rock; rock art.

pe.trog.ra.phy (pi.TROG.ruh.fee) *n.* the science of the description and classification of rocks.

pet.rol (PET.rul) *n. Brit.* gasoline.

pet.ro.la.tum (pet.ruh.LAY.tum) *n.* a yellowish jellylike substance made from petroleum for use in ointments, dressings, etc.; also **petroleum jelly.**

pe.tro.le.um (puh.TROH.lee.um) *n.* a dark, oily, bituminous liquid found in rock strata, which yields paraffin, gasoline, etc.; crude oil; also called "black gold."

pe.trol.o.gy (puh.TROL.uh.jee) *n.* a branch of geology dealing with rocks; **pe.trol.o.gist** *n.*

PET scan See PET.

pet.ti.coat (PET.ee.coat) *n.* a woman's underskirt; *adja.* [derogatory]: *petticoat government* (= rule by women).

pet.ti.fog (PET.ee.fog) *v.* **-fogs, -fogged, -fog.ging** quibble over trifles, esp. in legal matters; *adja.*: *pettifogging details, objections, rules.*
—**pet.ti.fog.ger** *n.*

pet.tish *adj.* peevish or petulant.

pet.ty (PET.ee) *adj.* **pet.ti.er, pet.ti.est** **1** small or unimportant; low in rank: *a petty detail, grievance.* **2** mean or small-minded: *petty partisanship, spite.*
—**pet.ti.ly** *adv.*; **pet.ti.ness** *n.*

petty cash *n.* money for small expenses.

petty jury, petty larceny See PETIT.

petty officer *n.* a naval rank of enlisted personnel varying from **master chief petty officer** down to **petty officer third class** which is just above seaman.

pet.u.lance (PECH.uh.lunce) *n.* petty irritability; peevishness. —**pet.u.lant**

petunia / pheasant

(-lunt) *adj.*; **pet.u.lant.ly** *adv.*

pe.tu.ni.a (puh.TUNE.yuh) *n.* a garden plant with large, velvety, funnel-shaped flowers.

pew *n.* a bench with a back, fixed in rows for seating in churches.

pe.wee (PEE.wee) *n.* a small bird related to the flycatcher; also **pee.wee.**

pew.ter (PEW.tur) *n.* **1** a silver-gray alloy of tin used for cooking utensils and tableware; **adja.**: *pewter chandeliers, craftsmen, hardware.* **2** such articles.

pe.yo.te (pay.OH.tee) *n.* **1** a psychedelic drug made from a cactus called mescal; mescaline. **2** the cactus mescal.

pfen.nig (FEN.ig) *n.* a German unit of currency equal to 1/100 of a mark.

pha.e.ton (FAY.uh.tun) *n.* **1** a light, four-wheeled carriage. **2** an early type of automobile or touring car.

phage (FAIJ) *n.* [short form] bacteriophage.

pha.lanx (FAY.lanx) *n.* **-lanx.es** a body of troops in compact formation.

phal.a.rope (FAL.uh.rope) *n.* a small wading bird similar to a sandpiper but with lobed toes.

phal.lic (FAL.ic) *adj.* **1** genital, esp. as related to a child's psychosexual development: *phallic display.* **2** pertaining to the generative power whose symbol is the penis: *a phallic sculpture, symbol.*

phal.lus (FAL.us) *n.* **phal.lus.es** or **phal.li** (-lye) the penis as a symbol.

phan.tasm (FAN.taz.um) *n.* a figment of the imagination; specter or phantom. —**phan.tas.mal** (fan.TAZ.mul) or **phan.tas.mic** *adj.*

phan.tas.ma.go.ri.a (FAN.taz.muh.GOR.ee.uh) *n.* a constantly changing scene or succession of images as in a dream.

phan.ta.sy (FAN.tuh.zee) *n.* **-sies** same as FANTASY.

phan.tom (FAN.tum) *n.* a specter or ghost: *a phantom of one's fantasies; the elusive phantom of hope.* —**adja.** **1** illusory or ghostlike: *A phantom ship upside down in the sky is a common illusion of sailors.* **2** imaginary or fictive: *a phantom figure, image, opponent; phantom revenues, transactions, voters.*

phar.i.sa.ic (fair.ih.SAY.ic) or **phar.i.sa.i.cal** (-i.cul) *adj.* self-righteous or hypocritical, as the Pharisees.

Phar.i.see (FAIR.uh.see) *n.* a member of an ancient Jewish sect noted for their strict practices.

phar.ma.ceu.ti.cal (far.muh.SOO.ti.cul) *adj.* having to do with pharmacy: *a pharmaceutical chemist; pharmaceutical advertising.* —**n.** a medical drug.

phar.ma.ceu.tics (far.muh.SOO.tics) *n.pl.* [takes *sing. v.*] the science of preparing and dispensing drugs; pharmacy.

phar.ma.cist (FAR.muh.sist) *n.* one who sells drugs; druggist.

phar.ma.col.o.gy (far.muh.COL.uh.jee) *n.* the science of drugs and their effects, including therapeutics, toxicology, etc. —**phar.ma.col.o.gist** *n.* —**phar.ma.co.log.ic** (-cuh.LOJ.ic) or **phar.ma.co.log.i.cal** *adj.*

phar.ma.co.poe.ia (FAR.muh.cuh.PEE.uh) *n.* a book with authoritative information on drugs, their properties, dosages, etc.: *the U.S. Pharmacopoeia; in the herbal pharmacopoeia.* Also **phar.ma.co.pe.ia.**

phar.ma.cy (FAR.muh.see) *n.* **1** the profession dealing with the preparation and dispensing of drugs; also, this science. **2** a drugstore.

pha.ryn.ge.al (fuh.RIN.jee.ul) *adj.* having to do with the pharynx: *a pharyngeal muscle.*

phar.yn.gi.tis (fair.in.JYE.tis) *n.* sore throat.

phar.ynx (FAIR.inx) *n.* **-ynx.es** or **-yn.ges** (fuh.RIN.jeez) the tract connecting the mouth with the esophagus and serving as both a food and air passage.

phase (FAZE) *n.* a particular, esp. changing aspect of something; stage of development: *the phases of the moon (as "full moon," "new moon," "first quarter," and "third quarter"); the color phases of the red fox; the final phase of a war; Windshield wipers have to work* **in phase** (= in a reciprocal relationship, so as not to clash). —**out of phase** not synchronized; out of step: *Drug addicts drift out of phase with the rest of the world.* —*v.* **phas.es, phased, phas.ing** plan or carry out in stages: *An addict is* **phased off** *a drug; Operations were* **phased down** *in Vietnam long before the U.S. pullout; Innovative changes are* **phased in** *at a plant; An obsolete product line is* **phased out** (= gradually taken off the market); *adj. & cpd.: a carefully* **phased** *army withdrawal; phased payments; a phased plan, revolution, troop reduction; phased deregulation, disarmament; a five-phased plan; a phased-in program.* —**phase-down** *n.* —**phase-out** *n.*

phase-locked *adj.* in precise synchronization *with* something.

pheas.ant (FEZ.unt) *n.* a bird of the same family as the peacock and the domestic fowl with beautiful feathers that are often used to trim hats.

phe.no.bar.bi.tal (fee.nuh.BAR.bi.tawl) *n.* a barbiturate used as a sedative.

phe.nol (FEE.nole, -nawl) same as CARBOLIC ACID. —**phe.nol.ic** (-NOH.lic, -NOL.ic) *adj.: A phenolic resin is used in molded plastic products, varnishes, adhesives, etc.*

phe.nom.e.nal (fuh.NOM.uh.nul) *adj.* extraordinary: *a phenomenal growth, speed, success.* —**phe.nom.e.nal.ly** *adv.*

phe.nom.e.non (fuh.NOM.uh.non) *n.* 1 *pl.* **-e.na** (-uh.nuh) anything observable or apparent: *natural phenomena such as storms, eclipses, and sunsets.* 2 *pl.* **-nons** a remarkable person, thing, or event, as a child prodigy: *The Guinness Book of Records is a publishing phenomenon.*

phe.no.type (FEE.nuh.type) *n.* 1 an organism's observable properties collectively. 2 a group of organisms with common characteristics.

pher.o.mone (FER.uh.mohn) *n.* a scented chemical secretion, usu. in the females of species such as insects, for eliciting specific responses in others of the species, as to find food or mates. —**pher.o.mo.nal** (-MOH.nul) *adj.*

phew (FEW) *interj.* expressing impatience, astonishment, etc.

phi.al (FYE.ul) same as VIAL.

Phi Be.ta Kap.pa (FYE.bay.tuh.CAP.uh) *n.* (a member of) an American honor society of outstanding students, founded in 1776.

phi.lan.der (fuh.LAN.dur) *v.* of a man, have love affairs in a casual or frivolous manner. —**phi.lan.der.er** *n.*

phi.lan.thro.pist (fuh.LAN.thruh.pist) *n.* one who is generous with gifts of money to help fellow humans, esp. the poor.

phi.lan.thro.py (fuh.LAN.thruh.pee) *n.* **-pies** 1 the desire to help humanity. 2 a humanitarian effort, gift, or institution, as a charitable foundation. —**phi.lan.throp.ic** (fil.un.THROP.ic) *adj.*

phi.lat.e.ly (fuh.LAT.uh.lee) *n.* stamp collecting as a hobby; **phi.lat.e.list** (-uh.list) *n.* —**phil.a.tel.ic** (fil.uh.TEL.ic) *adj.*

-phile *comb.form.* one fond of what is specified: *Anglophile, audiophile, bibliophile, Francophile; oeonophile.*

phil.har.mon.ic (fil.har.MON.ic) *n.* a symphony orchestra or a society sponsoring one: *the Berlin Philharmonic;* **adja.**: *a philharmonic concert, player (who is a member of an orchestra); a philharmonic society (devoted to music).*

phi.lip.pic (fuh.LIP.ic) *n.* a bitter attack or denunciation; tirade.

Phil.ip.pine (FIL.i.peen) *adj.* having to do with the **Philippines,** or **Philippine Islands,** a republic off the coast of S.E. Asia.

phil.is.tine (FIL.is.teen) *n.* an uncultured person who is hostile to the arts, like the biblical **Philistines,** a non-Semitic people at war with the Israelites. —**phil.is.tin.ism** *n.*

Phil.lips (FIL.ips) *adja.* having to do with screws whose head has a cross slot: *Phillips screws, screwdrivers.*

phil.o.den.dron (fil.uh.DEN.drun) *n.* a vine of the arum family, esp. a species with heart-shaped leaves.

phi.lol.o.gy (fuh.LOL.uh.jee) *n.* 1 the study of language. 2 [old use] linguistics, esp. historical. —**phi.lol.o.gist** (-jist) *n.* —**phi.lo.log.i.cal** (fil.uh.LOJ.i.cul) *adj.*

phi.los.o.pher (fuh.LOS.uh.fur) *n.* 1 a student or teacher of philosophy. 2 one who seeks truth and wisdom and faces trying situations with calmness. —**phil.o.soph.ic** (fil.uh.SOF.ic) or **phil.o.soph.i.cal** (-SOF.i.cul) *adj.: a philosophical doubt; the philosophic mind; Jan was philosophical about her defeat* (= accepted it with calmness and courage).

phi.los.o.phize (fuh.LOS.uh.fize) *v.* **-phiz.es, -phized, -phiz.ing** to see things with calmness and in a rational way: *Jon tried to philosophize about his defeat.*

phi.los.o.phy (fuh.LOS.uh.fee) *n.* 1 the study of the most fundamental nature and principles of things, as causality, space and time, God, etc. 2 learning, esp. in the arts and sciences: *a Doctor of Philosophy in engineering.* 3 *pl.* **-phies** a system, theory, or the sum total of one's beliefs, esp. as helpful to peace of mind: *to bear sufferings with philosophy; the Epicurean philosophy that right living leads to inner peace; her* **philosophy about** (= attitude to) *getting married; Everyone has their own* **philosophy of life** (= attitude to life and its purpose).

phil.ter or **phil.tre** (FIL.tur) *n.* a magic drink or drug, esp. a love potion.

phle.bi.tis (fli.BYE.tis) *n.* inflammation of a vein, usu. in the leg.

phle.bot.o.my (fli.BOT.uh.mee) *n.* **-mies** an opening of a vein to let out blood in the treatment of disease.

phlegm (FLEM) *n.* 1 thick mucus brought up by coughing. 2 apathy; also, the quality of not getting too easily excited. **phleg.mat.ic** (fleg.MAT.ic) *adj.: a phlegmatic temperament;*

She's too phlegmatic to get excited about anything.

phlo.em (FLOH.em) *n.* food-conducting tissue of the stems, roots, and leaves of higher plants and trees.

phlox *n.* any of a group of garden plants with brilliantly colored flowers, as the sweet William.

-phobe *comb.form.* one who fears or hates a person or thing, as specified: *Anglophobe, homophobe, xenophobe.*

pho.bi.a (FOH.bee.uh) *n. & comb.form.* an irrational and morbid fear or hatred: *our fears and phobias; agoraphobia; claustrophobia; hydrophobia.* —**pho.bic** *adj.*

Phoe.ni.cian (fi.NISH.un, -NEESH.un) *n. & adj.* (a person) of or from **Phoenicia**, an ancient country in the region of the coasts of Syria, Lebanon, and Israel.

phoe.nix (FEE.nix) *n.* a mythical bird, fabled to burn itself after 5,000 years of life, and rise again from its ashes; hence, a symbol of immortality.

-phone *comb.form.* sound: *megaphone, telephone, xylophone.*

phone (FONE) *n. & v.* **phones, phoned, phon.ing** *Informal.* same as TELEPHONE.

phone book same as TELEPHONE DIRECTORY.

phone-in *n.* a TV or radio program in which listeners phone the host with their views on the topic being discussed; call-in.

pho.neme (FOH.neem) *n.* a distinctive speech sound of a language: *"Cat," "kit," and "chord" begin with the same phoneme.*

pho.ne.mic (fuh.NEE.mic) **1** *adj.* having to do with phonemes: *For many speakers there is no phonemic difference between "Mary," "merry," and "marry."* **2 phonemics** *n.pl.* the study of the sound systems of languages. —**pho.ne.mi.cal.ly** *adv.*

pho.net.ic (fuh.NET.ic) **1** *adj.* corresponding to speech sounds: *English spelling is not phonetic; a phonetic alphabet, pronunciation, script, transcription.* **2 phonetics** *n.pl.* the study of the production and transcription of speech sounds; *adja.: a phonetic association; a phonetics laboratory.* —**pho.net.i.cal.ly** *adv.*

pho.ne.ti.cian (foh.nuh.TISH.un) *n.* an expert in phonetics.

phoney same as PHONY.

phon.ic (FON.ic) **1** *adj.* having to do with speech sounds, esp. phonics. **2 phonics** *n.pl.* a method of teaching reading using the sound values of letters. —**phon.i.cal.ly** *adv.*

pho.no (FOH.noh) *n.* **-nos** [short form] phonograph.

pho.no.graph (FOH.nuh.graf) *n.* a machine that reproduces sound as transcribed in a spiral groove on a cylinder or disk, or **phonograph record.** —**pho.no.graph.ic** (-GRAF.ic) *adj.;* **pho.no.graph.i.cal.ly** *adv.*

pho.nol.ogy (foh.NOL.uh.jee) *n.* the study of the sounds and sound changes of a language; **pho.nol.o.gist** (-jist) *n.* —**pho.no.log.i.cal** (-nuh.LOJ.i.cul) *adj.*

pho.ny (FOH.nee) **1** *adj. Informal.* **-ni.er, -ni.est** not genuine; sham or fake. **2** *n., pl.* **-nies** or **-neys** a fake or charlatan: *The new therapist proved to be a phony.* —**pho.ni.ly** *adv.;* **pho.ni.ness** *n.*

phoo.ey (FOO.ee) *interj. Informal.* expressing scorn or disgust: *Phooey to fried chicken!*

phos.phate (FOS.fate) *n.* a chemical compound occurring naturally as **phosphate rock**, and used in fertilizers, detergents, and soft drinks.

phos.phor (FOS.fur, -for) *n.* a phosphorescent substance, as used in fluorescent lamps and television tubes.

phos.pho.res.cence (fos.fuh.RES.unce) *n.* **1** the giving of light with little or no burning or heat, as in fireflies. **2** the light thus produced. —**phos.pho.res.cent** (-unt) *adj.*

phos.pho.rus (FOS.fuh.rus) *n.* a nonmetallic easily-burning chemical element occurring in minerals such as apatite and in animal tissue.

pho.tic (FOH.tic) *adj.* having to do with light activity: *The photic driving effect of the lights and sounds of a discotheque makes people feel dizzy; the uppermost **photic zone** of the ocean that light penetrates.*

pho.to (FOH.toh) **1** *n.* **-tos** [short form] photograph. **2** *comb.form.* light or photographic: *photocopy, photoelectric, telephoto, wirephoto.*

pho.to.com.po.si.tion (FOH.toh.com.puh.ZISH.un) *n.* typesetting using photographic images of characters projected on film.

pho.to.cop.i.er (FOH.toh.cop.ee.ur) *n.* a copier for making photocopies.

pho.to.cop.y (FOH.toh.cop.ee) *n.* **-cop.ies** a photographic copy of something written, drawn, or printed. —*v.* **-cop.ies, -cop.ied, -cop.y.ing** make a photocopy of something: *Copyrighted materials may be photocopied only*

pho.to.e.lec.tric (FOH.toh.i.LEC.tric) *adj.* electrically affected by light: *Automatic doors and burglar alarms are operated by **photoelectric cells**, or electric eyes, that convert light into electrical energy.*

pho.to.en.grav.ing (FOH.toh.en.GRAY.ving) *n.* **1** a photographic process for making printing plates, esp. of pictures. **2** such a picture or its printing plate.

photo finish *n.* a race finish so close that only a photograph can determine the winner: *It ended in a photo finish.*

pho.to.gen.ic (foh.toh.JEN.ic) *adj.* good for being photographed: *a picturesque and photogenic spot; cute and photogenic twins; a photogenic location, setting, show, star.*

pho.to.graph (FOH.tuh.graf) *n.* a picture taken by a camera on light-sensitive film, developed, and printed on paper: *a family photograph; group photographs; to blow up or enlarge, mount, pose for, touch up a photograph.* —*v.* **1** take a picture of an object: *a bullet photographed in flight.* **2** look good in pictures: *Marc always photographs well.* —**pho.to.graph.ic** (-GRAF.ic) *adj.*; **pho.to.graph.i.cal.ly** *adv.* —**pho.tog.ra.pher** (fuh.TOG.ruh.fur) *n.*

pho.tog.ra.phy (fuh.TOG.ruh.fee) *n.* the art or process of taking pictures using cameras: *still photography; trick photography (to create illusions, as of a train about to hit someone).*

pho.to.gra.vure (FOH.toh.gruh.VYOOR) *n.* **1** photoengraving using an intaglio plate. **2** a plate or print made by this process.

pho.to.li.thog.ra.phy (FOH.toh.li.THOG.ruh.fee) *n.* a lithographic process using photography for preparing the printing surface.

pho.tom.e.ter (foh.TOM.i.tur) *n.* an instrument for measuring the intensity of light; light meter; **pho.tom.e.try** (-tree) *n.* —**pho.to.met.ric** (-toh.MET.ric) *adj.*

pho.to.mi.cro.graph (foh.toh.MYE.cruh.graf) *n.* a photograph taken using a microscope.

pho.ton (FOH.ton, *rhyme:* on) *n.* a quantum of electromagnetic energy, as given out in X rays, gamma rays, etc.

photo-offset *n.* offset printing using plates prepared by photolithography.

photo opportunity *n.* an occasion for the media to take pictures, as of celebrities. Also **photo op** [short form].

pho.to.play (FOH.toh.play) *n.* a play filmed as a motion picture.

photoelectric / physiatry

pho.to.sen.si.tive (foh.toh.SEN.suh.tiv) *adj.* sensitive to light.

pho.to.sphere (FOH.tus.feer) *n.* the innermost part of the atmosphere of the sun or of a star.

pho.to.stat (FOH.tus.tat) *n.* a copy made with a photocopier; **Photostat** Trademark.

pho.to.syn.the.sis (foh.tuh.SINTH.uh.sis) *n.* a chemical process by which green plants make food by the action of sunlight and give off oxygen. —**pho.to.syn.thet.ic** (-sin.THET.ic) *adj.*

pho.tot.ro.pism (foh.TOT.ruh.piz.um) *n.* the bending of a plant, usu. stalks and leaves, as of the sunflower, toward light or, as some roots do, away from light. —**pho.to.trop.ic** (foh.toh.TROP.ic) *adj.*

phrase (FRAZE) *n.* **1** a group of words, esp. as a unit within a sentence: *apt, catchy, pithy, tuneful phrases; a Czech-English phrase book for the use of tourists.* **2** a short, pithy expression, as "Peace with honor" or "go the whole hog": *to coin a new phrase; a well-turned phrase.* **3** in music, a section of a composition, usu. a passage of four measures. —*v.* **phras.es, phrased, phras.ing** express in choice words; *adj.*: *a beautifully phrased lyric; a carefully phrased apology; an elegantly phrased remark; a neatly phrased observation; a tactfully phrased question; a well-phrased toast; delicately, judiciously phrased; n.*: *inelegant phrasing.* —**phras.al** *adj.*

phra.se.ol.o.gy (fray.zee.OL.uh.jee) *n.* **-gies** style of expression, esp. choice of words.

phre.nol.o.gy (fri.NOL.uh.jee) *n.* the science that claims to tell a person's character from the shape of the skull; **phre.nol.o.gist** *n.*

phy.lac.ter.y (fi.LAC.tuh.ree) *n.* **-ter.ies** either of two small, cubical leather cases holding scriptural texts, worn on the forehead and left arm by orthodox Jewish men during prayers.

phy.log.e.ny (fye.LOJ.uh.nee) *n.* the evolutionary development of a type of animal or plant or of a language stock.

phy.lum (FY.lum) *n., pl.* **-la** (-luh) a subkingdom in the classification of animals and plants.

phys ed (fiz.ED) *n.* [short form] physical education.

phy.si.a.try (fi.ZYE.uh.tree) *n.* treatment of illnesses and injuries using massages, exercise, heat therapy, etc.; physical medicine.

phys.ic (FIZ.ic) *n.* a medicine, esp. a laxative. —*v.* **-ics, -icked, -ick.ing** treat with medicine.
phys.i.cal (FIZ.i.cul) *adj.* **1** material: *the physical universe; Ghosts are not physical beings; a university's* **physical plant** (= buildings, equipment, etc.); *a* **physical science** *such as physics, chemistry, or astronomy.* **2** having to do with the body: *a physical examination; The hockey player got very physical* (= rough); **Physical education** *promotes physical fitness by means of games, gymnastics, etc.;* **physical geography** (= physiography); **physical medicine** (= physiatry); **physical therapy** (= physiotherapy). **3** having to do with the laws of nature, esp. of matter and energy: *Thawing is a physical change; To go back in time is a physical impossibility;* **Physical chemistry** *studies the chemical properties of matter.*
—*n.* a physical examination by a doctor: *Doctors do physicals; to get or have a physical.* —**phys.i.cal.ly** *adv.*
phy.si.cian (fuh.ZISH.un) *n.* a medical doctor; **phy.si.cian.ly** *adj.*
phys.ics (FIZ.ics) *n.pl.* [with *sing. v.*] the science of matter and energy and their interactions. —**phys.i.cist** *n.*
phys.i.og.no.my (fiz.ee.OG.nuh.mee) *n.* **-mies** external features, esp. of the face, as indicative of character: *the physiognomy of the moon.*
phys.i.og.ra.phy (fiz.ee.OG.ruh.fee) *n.* geography dealing with the earth's physical features such as land forms and climates. —**phys.i.o.graph.ic** (-ee.uh.GRAF.ic) *adj.*
phys.i.ol.o.gy (fiz.ee.OL.uh.jee) *n.* the branch of biology that deals with the vital functions and processes of living organisms; **phys.i.ol.o.gist** *n.*
—**phys.i.o.log.ic** (-ee.uh.LOJ.ic) or **phys.i.o.log.i.cal** *adj.*
phys.i.o.ther.a.py (FIZ.ee.oh.THER.uh.pee) *n.* the treatment of disease by physical means such as massages, exercise, light, heat, etc.; physical therapy. —**phys.i.o.ther.a.pist** *n.*
phy.sique (fuh.ZEEK) *n.* bodily build: *a man of fine physique; powerful physique.*
pi (PYE) *n.* **1** *pl.* **pis** (PIZE) the 16th letter of the Greek alphabet [Π, π]. **2** *pl.* **pies** (PIZE) mixed-up printing type; also **pie.** —*v.* **pies, pied, pi.ing** or **pie.ing** mix up: *How did the type get all pied?*
pi.a.nis.si.mo (pee.uh.NIS.i.moh) *Music. adj. & adv.* very soft; more softly than piano.
pi.an.ist (pee.AN.ist, PEE.uh.nist) *n.* one who plays the piano.

pi.an.o (pee.AH.noh) **1** *n.* a large percussion instrument with wire strings that are struck by playing on a keyboard: *to play the piano; This should be played on the piano; to tune a piano; A piano is either in* **in tune** *or* **out of tune**; *grand piano; upright piano;* **adj.a.:** *a piano concerto, piece, quartet, recital, sonata, virtuoso.* **2** *adj. & adv. Music.* soft or softly: *a piano passage, tone.* **3** *n., pl.* **-nos** a passage to be performed softly.
pi.an.o.for.te (pee.AN.oh.fort, -FOR.tee) same as PIANO.
pi.as.tre or **pi.as.ter** (pee.AS.tur) *n.* 1/100 of a pound in Egypt, Lebanon, Sudan, and Syria.
pi.az.za (pee.AZ.uh) *n.* **1** (*usu.* pee.AT.suh) an open public square in Italy. **2** a veranda.
pic *n.* **pics** or **pix** *Informal.* **1** a picture. **2** a movie.
pi.ca (PYE.cuh) *n.* a size of printing type giving six lines to the inch vertically; 12-point type.
pic.a.resque (pic.uh.RESK) *adj.* of fiction, dealing with roguish heroes and their adventures.
pic.a.yune (pik.ee.YOON) *adj.* trivial or petty.
pic.co.lo (PIC.uh.loh) *n.* **-los** a small, high-pitched flute.
pick *v.* **1** take up, separate, or pull off with the fingers, beak, or a pointed instrument: *Please pick me some flowers; to pick one's teeth or nose* (in order to clean it); *to pick a bone clean; to pick* (= start) *a fight with someone; to pick* (= shred) *rags; We have to obey all the laws without* **picking and choosing.**
2 choose or select: *She picked her words carefully as she spoke; to pick* (= steal from) *somebody's pocket; A child* **picking at** *her food* (= eating it little by little) *may be either ill or not hungry.* **3** dig or pierce: *Rocky soil is hard to pick; a lock that no thief can pick; a watertight alibi you can't pick holes in.* **4** pluck the strings of a banjo or guitar; hence, play: *to pick a guitar.* —**pick off** dispose of someone: *From his ambush, the gunman picked off his victims one by one.*
—**pick on** tease or nag: *Why do you always pick on your kid brother?* —**pick one's way** walk carefully: *She slowly picked her way through the crowd.* —**pick out 1** select: *Please pick out a red tie for me from the rack.* **2** distinguish or make out: *It's hard to pick her out in the picture.* **3** play on a keyboard: *to pick out a melody on the piano.* —**pick over** handle: *He picked over the ties for a long time before buying one.* —**pick up** take

or get: *Please pick up the phone and order a pizza; a suspect picked up by police for questioning; I'll pick you up at the bus stop; I'll pick up the tab* (= I'll pay) *for our dinner; a tie he picked up* (= purchased) *at the store; Where did you pick up* (= learn) *your French? We'll pick up* (= regain) *our trail in the morning; She's slowly picking up* (= recovering) *after the operation; It's someone he picked up* (= persuaded to accompany him) *in town; Parents shouldn't have to **pick up after*** (= clean up for) *you as you grow up.* —**pick up on** *Informal.* become aware of or refer to something: *to pick up on a previous statement.*
—*n.* **1** a picking or choosing; hence, chosen person or thing: *Please take your pick* (= choice); *These apples are the pick* (= the best) *of the crop.* **2** a pickax; also, a tool for breaking: *an ice pick.* **3** a small device for plucking the strings of a musical instrument.

pick.a.back (PICK.uh.back) *adj. & adv.* same as PIGGYBACK.

pick.a.nin.ny (PIK.uh.nin.ee) *n.* **-nin.nies** [unfavorable term] a black child.

pick.ax *n.* a heavy, T-shaped tool for digging. Also **pick.axe.**

pick.er.el (PIK.uh.rul) *n.* a small North American freshwater fish of the pike family.

pick.er.el.weed (PIK.uh.rul.weed) *n.* a blue-flowered plant of shallow waters with arrow-shaped leaves.

pick.et (PICK.it) *n.* **1** a pointed stake or pale; one of the posts forming a **picket fence. 2** a person posted as a guard; also, a body of such persons; hence, a striking member of a union stationed outside a place of work, often in a group called a **picket line.**
—*v.* **1** post pickets at a place; also, act as a picket: *to picket a factory.* **2** enclose or secure with a picket: *He picketed* (= tethered) *his horse before going indoors.* —**pick.et.er** *n.*

pickings *n.pl.* what is picked or gathered; hence, returns or profits: *lean pickings; slim pickings for so much trouble.*

pick.le (PICK.ul) *n.* **1** salt water or vinegar for preserving foods in; hence, an article of food thus preserved: *dill pickles; a sweet pickle relish.* **2** *Informal.* a predicament: *in a sad, fine, pretty, sorry pickle.* —*v.* **-les, -led, -ling 1** preserve in salt water and vinegar: *to pickle onions; adj.:* **pickled** *foods, meats, vegetables.* **2** give a streaked or yellowed finish to wood; *adja.: a pickled effect; pickled pine, woodwork;* **n.:** *a lacquered finish in pale pickle.*

pick.lock *n.* a burglar.

pick-me-up *n.* a tonic.

pick.pock.et (PICK.pock.it) *n.* one who steals from somebody's pocket.

pick.up *n.* **1** *Informal.* a casual lover. **2** a light truck with an open body. **3** an electronic device for changing vibrations (as from a record player) or sounds and images (as in radio and TV reception) into electrical energy. **4** acceleration: *an engine with good pickup.*

Pick.wick.i.an (pik.WIK.ee.un) *adj.* like Samuel Pickwick, a Dickens character: *words used in a Pickwickian sense* (to avoid giving offense).

pick.y *adj.* **pick.i.er, -i.est** choosy or fussy: *Pat's very picky about her clothes.*

pic.nic *n.* **1** an informal meal eaten outdoors; also, an outing for it: *to go on a picnic; a picnic shelter for motorists.* **2** *Informal.* a pleasant job or experience: *It's no picnic working in the warehouse.*
—*v.* **-nics, -nicked, -nick.ing** have a picnic. —**pic.nick.er** —**pic.nick.y** *adj.: to eat on the lawn in picnicky style.*

pico- *comb.form.* one trillionth: *picocurie, picogram, picosecond.*

pi.cot (PEE.coh) *n.* one of a series of ornamental loops forming an edging on lace, ribbon, etc.

pic.to.graph (PIC.tuh.graf) *n.* **1** picture writing, as seen in ancient caves. **2** a picture or symbol: *a car and dangling keys is a pictograph for "car rental."*
—**pic.to.graph.ic** (-GRAF.ic) *adj.*
—**pic.tog.ra.phy** (pic.TOG.ruh.fee) *n.*

pic.tor.i.al (pic.TOR.ee.ul) *adj.* having to do with pictures: *a pictorial history of the war;* **pic.tor.i.al.ly** *adv.*

pic.ture (PICK.chur) *n.* **1** something drawn, painted, or photographed: *to draw, frame, hang, paint a picture;* (= motion picture); *Let's take a picture* (= photograph). **2** a visual image or an idea: *clear, gloomy, realistic pictures; She looks the picture of health;* **Get the picture** (*Informal for* Get the idea)? —*v.* **-tures, -tured, -tur.ing** make into or form a picture: *Judas is pictured as a villain; I pictured* (= imagined) *myself at my wedding; adj.: a pictured urn (decorated with pictures).*

Pic.ture.phone (PICK.chur.fone) *Trademark.* a telephone that shows a TV picture of the person one is talking to.

pic.tur.esque (pik.chuh.RESK) *adj.* having a picturelike quality: *a cottage with a picturesque setting in the mountains; a picturesque style of writing.*
—**pic.tur.esque.ly** *adv.;*
pic.tur.esque.ness *n.*

picture tube *n.* a cathode-ray tube displaying a picture, as in TV.

picture window *n.* a large window giving a wide view of the outside.

pid.dle (PID.ul) *v.* **pid.dles, pid.dled, pid.dling** trifle or dawdle: *Let's not piddle over petty expenses;* **adj.**: *It's only a piddling* (= trifling) *sum.*

pid.gin (PIJ.in) *n.* a trade jargon used as a bridge between languages, with minimal vocabulary and grammar, as **pidgin English** which has Chinese or South Pacific elements: *The slogan in pidgin English said: "Yumi Bilong Olgeta New Guinea"* (= You and me all together belong to Papua New Guinea).

pie *n.* **1** a baked dish of meat, vegetables, or fruit, usu. having a top crust of pastry: *cherry, lemon meringue, meat pies; pizza pies; Give me a piece or slice or wedge of the pie; It's easy as pie; as American as apple pie; how to increase your share of the national pie* (= wealth). **2** mixed-up printing type; pl. **3** a parti-colored bird or animal, esp. the magpie. —**pie in the sky** *n. Informal.* a vainly hoped-for benefit or reward.

pie.bald (PYE.bauld) *adj.* of two colors, esp. black-and-white. —*n.* a piebald horse.

piece (PEECE) *n.* **1** a part, portion, or bit of something: *a piece of chalk, cheese, fruit, paper; a cup broken to pieces; a piece of advice, news.* **2** a single article or amount, often from a larger class or whole: *one piece of luggage; a piece of music; a chess piece; a 50-cent piece; a three-piece suit; cloth sold only by the piece* (= standard length); *a conversation piece* (= subject); *a fowling piece* (= light gun for hunting fowl); *I spoke my piece* (= what I had to say) *and sat down.* —**go to pieces 1** break into pieces. **2** collapse or break down. —**of a piece with** in keeping with something: *His performance is of a piece with his character.* —**piece of cake** *Informal.* something very easy. —**piece of one's mind** *Informal.* a scolding. —**piece of the action** a share of the benefits or profits. —*v.* **piec.es, pieced, piec.ing** make into one piece or whole; patch: *to piece a quilt; to piece out a personal account by hearsay; odds and ends pieced together in one volume.*

pièce de ré.sis.tance (pee.ES.duh.ray. zees.TAHNCE) *n.* the main item or event, esp. a main dish: *The pièce de résistance of the magic show was a woman walking away after being sawn in half.*

piece goods *n.pl.* cloth sold by the meter or yard from bolts.

piece.meal *adv.* piece by piece: *to buy piecemeal; to do a job piecemeal;* **adja.**: *piecemeal changes, operations, reforms; a piecemeal approach, expansion, process; in a piecemeal fashion.*

piece of eight *n.* an old Spanish peso worth eight reals.

piece.work *n.* work based on the amount produced, not the time taken.

pied (PIDE) *adj.* parti-colored in color or outfit: *a pied-billed diving bird; the Pied Piper of Hamelin.*

pied-à-terre (pee.AY.duh.TAIR) *n., pl.* **pieds-** (pee.AY.duh-) an occasional dwelling.

pie-eyed *adj. Slang.* drunk.

pie.plant *n.* the rhubarb, used in pies.

pier (PEER) *n.* **1** a bridgelike structure that juts out, as into the sea for use as a landing place, promenade, or breakwater: *Mobile lounges are used instead of finger piers to go from boarding gates to aircraft.* **2** a pillar or post supporting an arch or bridge, esp. where two spans meet. **3** a section of a wall between windows.

pierce (PEERCE) *v.* **pierc.es, pierced, pierc.ing** go into or through something, esp. at a particular point or with a sharp object: *A nail pierces a tire; a heart pierced with grief;* **adj.**: *a piercing tenor; piercing high notes; piercing anguish, clarity, eyes, intensity, pain, screams, smells, voices; in piercing detail; an armor-piercing grenade; an ear-piercing shriek;* **adj.**: *She has a pierced earlobe for wearing a pierced earring.* —**pierc.ing.ly** *adv.*

pier glass *n.* a tall mirror set in a wall pier.

pies *pl.* of PI or PIE.

pi.e.ty (PYE.uh.tee) *n.* **-ties** devotion and respect, as for God and religious things: *Almsgiving is an act of piety; filial piety* (= love and respect shown to one's parents).

pif.fle (PIF.ul) *n. Informal.* trivial talk; *adj.*: *a piffling* (= worthless) *figure, matter, sum.*

pig *n.* **1** a domesticated animal, raised for pork meat, ham, bacon, etc. and thought of as stupid, filthy, and greedy; swine or hog: *Pigs grunt, oink, and squeal; a female pig* (= sow); *male pig* (= boar). **2** [offensive] a hated person: *a male chauvinist pig.* **3** a bar into which molten iron is cast; also **pig iron.** —**pig out** *Slang.* eat too much; gorge oneself: *Peg pigged out on lemon pie.*

pi.geon (PIJ.un) *n.* **1** a bird of the dove family, usu. tame, and often trained as homing and carrier pigeons: *the cooing pigeon.* **2** one considered easy to dupe, gentle, and timid; hence **pigeon-hearted** or **pigeon-livered** *adj.*

pi.geon.hole (PIJ.un.hole) *n.* a small compartment in a desk or cabinet resembling a pigeon's nesting hole.
—*v.* **-holes, -holed, -hol.ing** classify or shelve: *The collection was pigeonholed and forgotten.*

pigeon-toed *adj.* having toes or feet pointed inward.

pig.gish (PIG.ish) *adj.* resembling a pig: *a piggish manner of eating.* —**pig.gish.ly** *adv.*

pig.gy (PIG.ee) *n.* a little pig.

pig.gy.back (PIG.ee.back) *adja.* on the back or shoulders: *three piggyback commercials during the same break; a spacecraft carrying piggyback capsules; a piggyback ride on her dad's back; adv.: a truck trailer carried piggyback on a railroad flatcar.* —*v.* travel as on someone's back: *He missed the flight but piggybacked home on a charter.*

pig.gy.bank (PIG.ee.bank) *n.* a coin bank in the shape of a piggy.

pig.head.ed (PIG.hed.id) *adj.* stubborn: *too pigheaded to listen to advice.*

pig in a poke *n. Informal.* something unseen that turns out to be valueless: *to buy a pig in a poke.*

pig iron See PIG, *n.* 3.

pig Latin *n.* a coded jargon, as "agic-may ords-way" for "magic words."

pig.let (PIG.lit) *n.* a little pig.

pig.ment (PIG.munt) *n.* a coloring substance, as added to paints, inks, plastics, etc. or as found in plant and animal tissues, esp. in skin and hair; *adja. & cpd:* pigment colors, printing; pigment spots on the skin from exposure to the sun; pigment-dyed clothes; pigment-rich cells.
—*v.* color; *adj.: a deeply pigmented tissue; pigmented inks.* —**pig.men.ta.tion** (-TAY.shun) *n.: Albinos lack pigmentation.*

Pig.my (PIG.mee) *n. & adj.* **-mies** same as PYGMY.

pig.nut *n.* the brown hickory or its nut.

pig.pen or **pig.sty** *n.* an enclosure for pigs: *The place is filthy as a pigpen.*

pig.skin *n.* **1** leather from the skin of a pig. **2** *Informal.* a football.

pig.tail *n.* a tight braid of hair worn at the back or side of the head.

pike *n.* **1** [short form] turnpike: *the first good dictionary to come down the pike (Informal for appear) in a long time.* **2** a wooden shaft with a pointed metal head, once carried by foot soldiers, or **pikemen** (*sing.* **-man**). **3** a freshwater food fish with a long snout such as the muskellunge and walleye; also **pike.perch.**

pik.er (PYE.kur) *n. Informal.* a stingy person; cheapskate.

pike.staff *n.* **-staves 1** the shaft of a pike. **2** a traveler's spiked staff.

pi.laf or **pi.laff** (pi.LAHF) *n.* a flavored rice dish with meat, fish, etc. boiled together.

pi.las.ter (pi.LAS.tur) *n.* a rectangular column that supports a wall, into which it is set, though partially projecting from it.

pi.lau or **pi.law** (pi.LAW) same as PILAF.

pil.chard (PIL.churd) *n.* **1** a small saltwater fish of the herring family; the European sardine. **2** any related fish, as the "California pilchard."

pile *n.* **1** a heap, as of books, garbage, logs, dishes, etc.: *He made his pile (of money) by the time he was 30.* **2** the raised surface of rugs, fabrics such as velvet, etc.; nap: *shaggy, smooth, soft, thick piles; adj: deep-piled carpeting.* **3** a heavy post or beam forming a support or foundation for a dock, bridge, etc. or one driven into the earth with a **pile driver** or **pile engine** (= hammering machine): *to sink a pile.* **4** same as ATOMIC PILE. **5** *pl.* hemorrhoids.
—*v.* **piles, piled, pil.ing** heap or cause to heap: *Snow was piled high on the driveway; Five people piled into the back seat; They soon piled out of the car; Telegrams piled up on the M.P.'s desk; See the dishes piled in the sink; a backyard piled with garbage.*

pile-up *n.* a piling up or heap: *a bad pile-up (of vehicles in collision) on a fogbound expressway.*

pil.fer (PIL.fur) *v.* steal or take away in small amounts; filch; **pil.fer.er** *n.*

pil.fer.age (PIL.fur.ij) *n.* pilfering or the amount of goods pilfered: *Store losses by pilferage (= shoplifting) alone amount to millions of dollars.*

pil.grim *n.* **1** a traveler or wanderer, esp. one going on a pilgrimage to a holy place. **2 Pilgrim** or **Pilgrim Father** any of the English Puritans who first came to America in 1620.

pil.grim.age (PIL.gruh.mij) *n.* a journey to a shrine or sacred place such as Jerusalem or Mecca: *to go on* or *make a pilgrimage to Mecca.*

pill *n.* **1** a tiny ball, pellet, or capsule of medicine for swallowing whole: *to take a pill; to pop pills (Informal for take narcotics); sleeping pills.* **2 the Pill** *Informal.* an oral contraceptive: *Peg is on*

the Pill. —**a bitter pill to swallow** something unpleasant to accept or endure.
pil.lage (PIL.ij) v. -ag.es, -aged, -ag.ing to loot or plunder. —n. a pillaging or things pillaged; booty or spoils. —**pil.lag.er** n.
pil.lar (PIL.ur) n. 1 a vertical, usu. cylindrical supporting structure; column: *He was a pillar of strength in times of trouble.* 2 such a pillar set up as a memorial, as the Washington Monument. —**driven from pillar to post** driven desperately from one resource to another.
pil.lared (PIL.urd) adj. having pillars: *the pillared majesty of the Parthenon; a pillared front porch.*
pill.box n. 1 a shallow cylindrical container for pills. 2 a small, low, concrete-and-steel gun emplacement: *to storm a pillbox.*
pill.head n. Slang. one addicted to drugs in pill or capsule form.
pil.lion (PIL.yun) n. an extra seat behind a horse's saddle or motorcycle seat.
pil.lo.ry (PIL.uh.ree) n. -ries formerly, a wooden post and framework in which an offender had head and hands locked while exposed to public scorn as punishment. —v. -ries, -ried, -ry.ing ridicule publicly: *a play pilloried by the critics.*
pil.low (PIL.oh) n. a cushion to rest the head on while one sleeps: *to fluff up the pillows when making a bed.* —v. rest as if on a pillow: *The child slept, pillowed on her mother's breast.*
pil.low.case (PIL.oh.case) or **pil.low.slip** (PIL.oh.slip) n. a removable cover for a pillow.
pillow talk n. intimate chatting, as by people in bed.
pil.low.y (PIL.oh.ee) adj. soft like a pillow.
pi.lot (PYE.lut) n. 1 a person or thing that leads or guides, as the operator of an aircraft, the helmsman of a ship, or an engine sent ahead of a train to see that the line is clear. 2 a sample or the first episode of a proposed TV series. 3 a pilot lamp or pilot light. —adj. serving to activate, guide, test, etc.: *a pilot program, project, study.* —v. guide or steer: *to pilot a ship through rough seas.* —**pi.lot.less** adj.: *a pilotless aircraft; a gas range with electronic pilotless ignition.*
pilot balloon n. a balloon sent up to test the wind's direction and velocity; trial balloon.
pilot film or **pilot tape** n. a film or tape of a TV series for advance viewing by sponsors.
pi.lot.house (PYE.lut.house) n. an enclosed structure atop the deck of a ship from which it is navigated.
pilot lamp (or **light**) n. 1 a flame kept lit for igniting a main burner when needed, as in a home heating furnace. 2 an indicator light.
Pil.sener or **Pil.sner** (PILS.nur, PILZ-) n. a light lager beer, usu. served in a tall, conical, footed glass. Also **pilsener** or **pilsner**.
pi.men.to (pi.MEN.toh) n. -tos 1 allspice or the evergreen shrub that yields the spice. 2 a sweet pepper used esp. for stuffing olives; also **pi.mien.to** (pim.YEN.toh) n.
pimp n. a prostitute's agent; pander. —v. act as a pimp or procurer.
pim.per.nel (PIM.pur.nul) n. a small, wild-growing plant of the primrose family with scarlet, white, or blue flowers that close in cloudy weather.
pim.ple (PIM.pul) n. a small, inflamed swelling on the skin. —**pim.pled** or **pimply** adj.: *a pimpled face; a pimply shape, teenager.*
pin n. 1 a short, stiff piece of wire having a sharp point and tiny head, used in various designs for fastening papers, cloth, etc. together: *pin pricks.* 2 a similar peg of wood or metal: *bobby, bowling, cotter, hair, hat, rolling pins.* 3 an ornament or badge with a pin or clasp: *a tie pin.* 4 **pins** pl. Informal. legs. —v. **pins, pinned, pin.ning** fasten or hold firmly: *Rico is so busy it's hard to pin him down to a definite time or place for a meeting; Jane tried to pin the blame on someone else; a leader on whom people had pinned their hopes.*
pin.a.fore (PIN.uh.for) n. a sleeveless garment worn like an apron over a dress or blouse.
pin.ball machine n. a game machine on which points are scored as a spring-driven ball slides down a board hitting various targets such as pins and bumpers.
pince-nez (PANCE.nay, pl. also -nayz) n. sing. & pl. a pair of eyeglasses that are clipped to the bridge of the nose.
pin.cers (PIN.surz) n.pl. a tool like the claws of a crab that is used for gripping or nipping things and worked like a pair of pliers.
pinch v. 1 squeeze between finger and thumb: *She pinched herself to make sure she was awake.* 2 to act or suffer in a tightening or pressing manner: *Tight*

shoes pinch; I'm pinched for time; the look of faces pinched by famine. **3** *Informal.* steal: *Who's pinching my pencils?* **4** *Informal.* arrest: *The fellow was pinched on a vagrancy charge.* —**pinch pennies** be stingy: *Pat never pinches pennies when entertaining friends.* —*n.* a pinching: *a friendly pinch on the cheek; the pinch of poverty; Take tall tales with* **a pinch of salt** (= with doubts); *a friend who never failed me* **in a pinch** (= hardship or emergency). —*adj.* a in a baseball game, having to do with playing as a substitute: *a pinch hit, homer, runner, single.* —**pinch.er** *n.*: *a penny pincher's dream.*

pinch hit *n.* in baseball, a base hit made while pinch-hitting. —**pinch-hit** *v.* **-hits, -hit, -hit.ting** act as a substitute for someone: *a volunteer ready to pinch-hit for colleagues in emergencies.* —**pinch-hitter** *n.*

pin curl *n.* a curl of hair held in place by a bobby pin while setting.

pin.cush.ion (PIN.cush.un, "ush" as in "push") *n.* a small cushion that pins and needles are stuck into for storage.

pine *v.* **pines, pined, pin.ing 1** to long or yearn: *He was pining for or after his absent wife and family; He pined to be reunited with his family.* **2** waste away through grief. —*n.* **1** an evergreen tree with needlelike leaves and cones. **2** its wood.

pin.e.al (PIN.ee.ul) *adj.* resembling a pine cone: *The* **pineal body** *or* **gland**, *which regulates body cycles, is an organ at the center of the brain.*

pine.ap.ple (PINE.ap.ul) *n.* the juicy fruit, shaped like a pine cone, of a spiny tropical plant.

pine nut *n.* a nut of the piñon.

pine tar *n.* a dark, viscous liquid obtained from pine wood and used in paints, varnishes, disinfectants, etc.

pin.feath.er (PIN.feth.ur, "th" as in "the") *n.* a young feather that is just emerging from the skin.

ping *n.* **1** a sharp ringing sound as of a bullet striking metal. **2** the knock in a badly burning engine. —*v.* make a ping: *an auto engine that pings under loud.*

ping-pong *n.* **1** same as TABLE-TENNIS: *the ping-pong diplomacy of a foreign team going to play ping-pong in China.* **2** a table-tennis set; **Ping-Pong** *Trademark.* —*v.* move or send back and forth: *the ping-ponging of patients from one physician to another.*

pin.head *n.* **1** something tiny or trifling. **2** a stupid person; **pin.head.ed** *adj.*

pin.hold.er (PIN.hole.dur) *n.* a holder for cut flowers that has a pin-studded base.

pin.hole *n.* a minute hole, as if made by a pin.

pin.ion (PIN.yun) *n.* **1** a bird's wing, esp. the outer rear edge having flight feathers. **2** a small gear whose teeth mesh with a larger wheel or rack: *a rack-and-pinion movement.* —*v.* **1** hamper or restrain, as by cutting off a bird's pinions. **2** disable a person by holding or binding the arms to the sides of the body.

pink *n.* **1** a pale red color. **2** any of a group of plants bearing beautiful and fragrant flowers that have reddish petals with crinkled edges, as the carnation and sweet William. —**in the pink** *Informal.* in the best condition or state: *in the pink of condition, fashion, health, repair.* —*adj.* **1** of the color pink: *a pink dress, elephant;* **pink-collar** (= traditionally female) *occupations such as nursing and homemaking.* **2** with left-wing or Communist leanings. **3** emotionally excited: *Pat was tickled pink at the suggestion.* —*v.* **1** stab gently; prick. **2** cut with shears (**pinking shears**) to make a zigzag pattern. **3** decorate with a scalloped edge.

pink.eye *n.* reddening of eyes in acute conjunctivitis.

pink.ie or **pink.y** (PINK.ee) *n.* **pin.kies** the little finger.

pink.o *n.* [hostile use] a Communist sympathizer.

pink slip *n. Informal.* a notice terminating one's employment: *to get the pink slip.*

pin money *n.* money given or set aside for minor expenses.

pin.na.cle (PIN.uh.cul) *n.* **1** a spire, mountain peak, or other tall, tapering form. **2** its highest point: *to reach a pinnacle; the pinnacle of the profession, season; at the pinnacle of civilization, evolution, fashion, power; at the pinnacle of one's career, glory, success.*

pin.nate (PIN.ate) *adj.* of compound leaves, featherlike in formation, as of the sumac, ash, etc.

pi.noc.le or **pi.noch.le** (PEE.nuc.ul, -noc.ul) *n.* a card game played with a deck of 48 cards.

pi.ñon (PIN.yun, -yone) *n.* a pine tree of southwestern U.S. bearing edible nuts called **pine nuts**.

pin.point *n.* the point of a pin or something tiny, esp. a spot precisely marked, as with a pin on a map:

pin.prick *n.* 1 a prick, as with a pin. 2 a petty annoyance.

pins and needles *n.pl.* a tingling sensation, as in a limb after numbness: *She's been on pins and needles* (= anxious) *awaiting her exam results.*

pin.stripe *n.* 1 a very narrow stripe on a fabric; also, such a fabric: *fabrics in solids and pinstripes; banker's pinstripes;* **adja.:** *pinstripe blazers, gray flannel, shirts, shorts, suits;* **adj.:** *pinstriped shirts, navy blue suits.* 2 **pinstripes** a suit with such stripes, typical of business executives: *He wears pinstripes to board meetings; the conservative pinstripes image.*

pin.strip.er (PIN.stry.pur) *n. Informal.* a business executive.

pint ("i" as in "pine") *n.* a unit of capacity equal to 16 oz.; ½ quart; 0.55L.

pin.to (PIN.toh) *adj.* spotted or mottled. —*n.*, *pl.* **-tos** such a horse.

pinto bean *n.* a spotted or mottled variety of kidney bean.

pint-size *adj.* 1 that can hold one pint: *a pint-size carton, mug, package.* 2 *Informal.* very small: *a pint-size computer, hurricane, pundit, singer, version.* Also **pint-sized.**

pin.up *adja.* designed or suitable for putting up, esp. as a picture for viewing. —*n.* such a picture: *pinups of movie stars.*

pin.wheel *n.* a paper toy having vanes pinned down in the middle and revolving like a wheel.

pin.worm *n.* a small roundworm.

pin.yin (PIN.YIN) *n.* a system of writing Chinese characters in Roman letters.

pi.o.neer (pye.uh.NEER) *n.* an explorer of a new area: *A wagon train of pioneers headed west; a pioneer in heart transplants; a civil-rights pioneer;* **adja.:** *pioneer days; life in a pioneer settlement; the pioneer spirit.* —*v.* be a pioneer: *The Wright brothers pioneered in aviation; Armstrong and Aldrin pioneered the way to the moon.*

pi.ous (PYE.us) *adj.* 1 showing religious devotion: *a pious act, hope, pilgrim, profession of faith.* 2 showing false piety: *He's a pious fraud; mere pious and empty rhetoric; pious hypocrisy.* —**pi.ous.ly** *adv.*

pip *n.* 1 a dot with a number value, as on dice or dominoes. 2 a small seed, as of the orange or apple. 3 a short, high-pitched signal; also, a blip. 4 a disease of chickens, marked by a crust formed on the tongue. 5 *Slang.* any annoying or depressing disease. 6 *Informal.* a person or thing that is wonderful: *a bright pip of a lad.*

pipe *n.* 1 a tube for conveying water, gas, oil, etc.: *drain, exhaust, overflow pipes.* 2 a tube with a small bowl at one end for smoking tobacco, etc.: *to puff on a pipe.* 3 a musical tube blown by air, as in a bagpipe or in a **pipe organ.** —**pipes** *pl.* 1 bagpipe. 2 *Informal.* organs of respiration or singing. —*v.* **pipes, piped, pip.ing** 1 play on a pipe. 2 convey by pipes: *to pipe oil from a well into a refinery.* —**pipe down** *Informal.* stop talking. —**pipe up** 1 begin to play or sing. 2 *Informal.* speak up.

pipe dream *n. Informal.* a fantasy or vain hope.

pipe.line *n.* 1 a line of connected pipes: *a pipeline for natural gas.* 2 any channel or process: *a pipeline of information, supplies, etc.; Raises for everyone are* **in the pipeline** (= coming or expected).

pipe of peace same as PEACE PIPE.

pip.er (PYE.pur) *n.* in **pay the piper** See PAY.

pi.pet or **pi.pette** (pye.PET) *n.* a suction tube for measuring or transferring liquids.

pip.ing (PYE.ping) *n.* 1 a system of pipes. 2 pipe music. 3 a pipelike trimming material for edges or seams. —**piping hot** very hot.

pip.it *n.* a small, larklike songbird.

pip.kin *n.* a small pot of metal or earthenware.

pip.pin *n.* a yellowish-green variety of apple with excellent flavor.

pip.squeak *n.* a small or insignificant person.

pi.quant (PEEK.unt) *adj.* agreeably pungent, lively, vivid, etc.: *a piquant sauce, wit; Carla's piquant charm;* **pi.quant.ly** *adv.* —**pi.quan.cy** (-un.see) *n.*

pique (PEEK) *n.* feeling of hurt vanity or pride: *He stomped out of the party in a pique; She said it in a fit of pique.* —*v.* **piques, piqued, piqu.ing** 1 hurt the pride of someone: *It piqued her not to be invited.* 2 arouse or excite interest, curiosity, etc.: *Her exotic style piques my curiosity.*

pi.qué or **pi.que** (pi.KAY) *n.* a plain or printed fabric of cotton, rayon, or silk, with raised cords usu. running the length of the material.

pi.quet (pi.KET, -KAY) *n.* a card game for two, played with 32 cards.

pi.ra.cy (PYE.ruh.see) *n.* **-cies** the action of a pirate: *laws against air piracy; piracy on the high seas; literary piracy by* infringing copyright; TV piracy via satellite dishes.

pi.ra.nha (puh.RAH.nuh) *n.* a fierce little fish of South American rivers that attacks humans and animals in large groups.

pi.rate (PYE.rit) *n.* **1** a robber of the high seas or a hijacker. **2** one who violates a copyright or patent. —*v.* **pi.rates, pi.rat.ed, pi.rat.ing** rob or steal: *In some countries, underground publishers pirate textbooks and drive established publishers out of business; adj.: a pirated edition, tape, textbook.* —**pi.rat.i.cal** (pye.RAT.i.cul) *adj.*

pir.ou.ette (peer.oo.ET) *n.* a whirling around on the toe or on the ball of the foot, as in ballet. Also *v.* **-ettes, -et.ted, -et.ting.**

pis.ca.to.ri.al (pis.cuh.TOR.ee.ul) *adj.* having to do with fishing or fishermen; also **pis.ca.to.ry** (PIS.cuh.tor.ee).

Pis.ces (PYE.seez, PIS.eez) *n.* **1** a N. constellation and the 12th sign of the zodiac; also called "the Fishes." **2** a person born under this sign.

pis.mire *n.* **1** an ant. **2** a contemptible person.

piss [vulgar slang] *n.* urine. —*v.* urinate. —**piss off** make someone angry; *adj.: He's still **pissed off** at me; She's pissed off about everything at work; She easily gets pissed off.*

pis.ta.chi.o (pi.STASH.ee.oh) *n.* **-os** a tree of warm and dry regions yielding clusters of seeds called "pistachio nuts" or "green almonds" that have an edible kernel.

pis.til *n.* the seed-bearing, female organ of a flower, made up of one or more carpels. —**pis.til.late** (-it, -ate) *adj.* of a flower, having a pistil, esp. without stamens.

pis.tol (PIS.tul) *n.* a small firearm that can be fired with one hand: *an automatic pistol with a magazine of shells.*

pistol-whip *v.* **-whips, -whipped, -whip.ping** beat with the barrel of a pistol.

pis.ton (PIS.tun) *n.* a flat, round device used in pumps and engines, that moves back and forth by the pressure of a fluid inside a cylinder in which it is fitted tightly by **piston rings**, the resulting motion being transmitted by a **piston rod** attached to the flat, round device.

pit *n.* **1** the stone of a fruit: *He collects the pits of almonds, avocadoes, cherries, dates, olives, peaches, plums, and prunes.* **2** a hole or cavity in the ground, naturally formed or one dug for burial, mining, trapping, etc.: *"He who digs a pit shall fall into it."* **3** a place or area resembling a pit, as for servicing automobiles, the orchestra's place in front of a stage, a body depression or hollow such as a pock mark, the armpit, or an enclosure for bear-baiting or cockfights: *the **pit of the stomach** (= depression below the breastbone); It's **the pits** (Informal for a disgusting situation or place).* —*v.* **pits, pit.ted, pit.ting 1** remove the pit from a fruit: *to pit cherries; adj.: **pitted** dates.* **2** to place or set: *an unequal contest with one man pitted against three.* **3** to mark with pits or pock marks: *The moon's surface is pitted with craters; adj.: pocked and **pitted** skin; pitted highways; a road surface pitted with potholes.*

pi.ta (PEE.tah) *n.* a flat, round bread of the Middle East.

pit-a-pat (PIT.uh.pat) *n.* a throbbing motion or sound; *adv.: Her heart went pit-a-pat when her name was called.*

pitch *v.* **1** put up; also, set or fix in a particular manner: *to pitch a tent; a voice pitched too low to be heard; hopes pitched too high; adj. & cpd: the **pitched** monotone of his preaching style; a high-pitched voice that almost sounds shrill; low-pitched roofs (with a low slope).* **2** throw, toss, or hurl: *to pitch hay into a hay rack with a pitchfork; A baseball pitcher pitches the ball to the batter; a boat pitching and rolling in the waves; The heckler was pitched out of the hall; the kind of merchandise being pitched at children.* **3** *Informal.* promote or hype: *The mayor went to Switzerland to pitch his city's bid for the Olympics; She went to Hollywood to pitch an idea for a movie.* —**pitch in** contribute: *If everyone pitches in, we will finish the work soon.* —**pitch into** join enthusiastically in an activity: *We pitched into the food as soon as we were served.* —**pitch on** choose someone, esp. for something unwelcome: *Jones pitched on me to propose the toast.* —*n.* **1** a pitching or throw: *a bowler's fast pitch; the pitch of a voice (= its sound quality based on vibrations of the sound waves); emotion stirred to a fever pitch (= intensity).* **2** *Informal.* sales talk: *A free trip to Florida was included in the sales pitch.* **3** a black, sticky substance made from coal tar or petroleum and used for waterproof- ing, filling cracks, etc. **4** a court or playing ground for sports such as cricket and horseshoe pitching.

pitch-black or **pitch-dark** *adj.* extremely

pitchblende / place

black or dark: *the pitch-black darkness, night; a pitch-dark sky.*
pitch.blende (PICH.blend) *n.* a pitchlike mineral ore containing radium, uranium, and actinium.
pitched battle *n.* a planned and organized fight: *The demonstrators fought a pitched battle with the police but were hosed down.*
pitch.er *n.* 1 one who pitches in a baseball game. 2 a large jug for liquids, with a handle on one side and a lip for pouring on the other.
pitcher plant *n.* a plant that feeds on insects which it traps in its pitcher-shaped leaves.
pitch.fork *n.* a large long-handled fork for pitching hay.
pitch.man *n.* **-men** *Informal.* one who makes a sales pitch.
pitch pipe *n.* a pipe producing a standard tone, used in tuning.
pitch.y *adj.* **pitch.i.er, -i.est** full of or like pitch.
pit.e.ous (PIT.ee.us) *adj.* deserving or causing pity: *a piteous sight.* —**pit.e.ous.ly** *adv.*
pit.fall *n.* 1 a concealed pit for catching animals or people. 2 any hidden danger: *to avoid a pitfall; the pitfalls of hitchhiking.*
pith *n.* 1 the spongy core tissue of plant stems; also, a similar substance lining orange skins, inside a feather's shaft, etc.: *white pith;* **adj.:** *pith hats, helmets.* 2 the core or gist: *"matters of great pith (= importance) and moment."*
pith.y *adj.* **pith.i.er, -i.est** brief and full of meaning: *a pithy maxim, style, utterance.* —**pith.i.ly** *adv.;* **pith.i.ness** *n.*
pit.i.a.ble (PIT.ee.uh.bul) *adj.* arousing regrettable pity: *the pitiable condition of starving children.* —**pit.i.a.ble.ness** *n.;* **pit.i.a.bly** *adv.*
pit.i.ful (PIT.i.ful) *adj.* so miserable as to evoke pity: *a pitiful amount, comedy, minority, offer, performance, situation.* —**pit.i.ful.ly** *adv.;* **pit.i.ful.ness** *n.* —**pit.i.less** *adj.*
pi.ton (PEE.ton, *rhyme:* on) *n.* a spike or wedge that is driven into ice surfaces or fissures in rock for passing ropes through in mountain-climbing.
pit stop *n.* a stop for fueling, refreshments, etc., as during an automobile race.
pit.tance (PIT.unce) *n.* a meager allowance or remuneration: *a mere pittance.*
pit.ter-pat.ter same as PATTER.
pi.tu.i.tar.y (puh.TUE.uh.tair.ee) *n.* **-tar.ies** an endocrine gland attached to the brain, that secretes hormones controlling growth and other bodily functions; *adj.:* *the pituitary gland, growth hormone; pituitary dwarfism, tumors.*
pit viper *n.* a viper with a deep hollow in the side of the head, as a rattlesnake, copperhead, or water moccasin.
pit.y (PIT.ee) *n.* 1 sorrow for another's suffering: *to arouse, feel, show pity; Have or Take pity on a poor beggar; pity for the poor; I gave her my money out of pity; a sense of pity;* **For pity's sake**, *be kind to animals.* 2 a cause for regret: *What a pity we lost!* —*v.* **pit.ies, pit.ied, pit.y.ing** feel pity for someone: *We pity the homeless.* —**pit.y.ing.ly** *adv.*
piv.ot (PIV.ut) *n.* 1 a shaft or point on which something turns. 2 a person or thing in a key position, as the **pivotman** or center in basketball, ice hockey, etc. —*v.* turn: *A ballerina pivots on the tip of her toes; His entire future pivots (= depends) on his examination results.* —**piv.ot.al** (-tul) *adj.* central: *a decision of pivotal significance to her career.*
pix a *pl.* of PIC.
pix.el (PIX.ul) *n.* the smallest element of a picture formed on a video display.
pix.ie or **pix.y** (PIX.ee) *n.* **pix.ies** a mischievous fairy; sprite. —**pix.y.ish** *adj.* resembling a pixy: *her pixyish charm.*
pi.zazz or **piz.zazz** (puh.ZAZ) *n. Informal.* vigor or style: *accessories to give your car a little pizazz.*
piz.za (PEET.suh) *n.* a pie consisting of thinly rolled dough baked with tomato sauce, cheese, meat, vegetables, spices, etc. on it. Also **pizza pie.**
piz.ze.ri.a (peet.suh.REE.uh) *n.* an establishment where pizza is made and sold.
piz.zi.ca.to (pit.si.CAH.toh) *adj. & adv. Music.* played by plucking the strings. —*n., pl.* **-ti** (-tee) a passage or note so played.
pj's (PEE.jaze) *n.pl. Informal.* pajamas.
plac.ard (PLAY.card, PLACK.urd) *n.* a notice posted in a public place; poster. —*v.* 1 announce with placards: *The visit of the circus was placarded in advance.* 2 cover, as with placards: *The walls were placarded with ads.*
pla.cate (pluh.CATE, PLAC.ate) *v.* **-cates, -cat.ed, -cat.ing** soothe or satisfy; appease: *a spoiled child who is hard to placate with gifts.* —**pla.ca.tion** (pluh.CAY.shun) *n.*
place *n.* 1 a definite portion of occupied space, as a city, street, courtyard, building, home, particular spot, etc.:

placebo / plain-vanilla

"No place like home"; "a place for everything and everything in its place"; A mosque is a place of worship; a meeting place; Dad's place is at the head of the table; Who took my place (at the table)? to lay or set a place for a guest; *Let's meet at our place* (= dwelling); 2 a position, esp. one of rank, office, function, etc.: *a teacher's place in society; A prince and a pauper traded places; to give up a place in line* or *in a queue; It's not my place to criticize you, Sir; A servant had to know his place or he would be **put in his place*** (= rebuked); *The computer network is now **in place*** (= established); *We now use word processors **in place of*** (= instead of) *typewriters.* —**go places** *Informal.* start to succeed: *You're going places, boy!* —**take place** happen. —*v.* **plac.es, placed, plac.ing** put: *He was placed third in the race; to place an order for books; The orphan child has been placed with foster parents; We place service above sales; to place your con- fidence in your secretary; The name is familiar, but I can't place* (= identify) *his face; to place* (= present) *the facts before a jury.*

pla.ce.bo (pluh.SEE.boh) *n.* **-bos** or **-boes** a preparation, as sugar pills or colored water that has no medicinal effect, often given to patients used as a control group in a medical test: *Some arthritic cures have only a **placebo effect**.*

place card See PLACE SETTING.

place kick *n.* the kicking of a ball held on the ground, as in football.

place mat See PLACE SETTING.

place.ment (PLACE.munt) *n.* a placing: *the placement of children in foster homes; A **placement agency** finds jobs for people.*

pla.cen.ta (pluh.SEN.tuh) *n.* **-tas** or **-tae** (-tee) a disc-shaped organ attached to the uterus, through which a fetus is nourished by its mother. —**pla.cen.tal** *adj.*

plac.er (PLASS.ur) *n.* an alluvial or glacial deposit containing minerals: *placer mining.*

place setting *n.* china and silver for one person at a table, usu. on a **place mat**, sometimes with a **place card** bearing the guest's name.

place value *n.* the value of a digit because of its position in a numeral: *In 22.2, each 2 has a different place value – namely, two tens, two units, and two tenths.*

plac.id (PLAS.id) *adj.* calm and without agitation: *a placid lake; the lake's placid surface; her placid temperament;* **plac.id.ly** *adv.;* **plac.id.ness** *n.*

—**pla.cid.i.ty** (plas.ID.i.tee) *n.*

plack.et *n.* a finished slit at the top of a skirt, shirt, etc. to make it easier to put on and take off.

pla.gia.rize (PLAY.juh.rize) *v.* **-riz.es, -rized, -riz.ing** use or pass off another's ideas or writings as one's own. —**pla.gia.rism** *n.;* **pla.gia.rist** *n.*

plague (PLAIG) *n.* an affliction, esp. a deadly epidemic: *the drug plague; a plague of locusts; She avoids TV **like the plague**.* —*v.* **plagues, plagued, plagu.ing** inflict suffering on someone: *a society plagued by high taxes and rising prices; Stop plaguing* (= annoying) *your mom for this and that.*

plaid (PLAD) *n.* 1 a pattern of checks or colored stripes crossing at right angles, as on the woolen scarf worn over the shoulder by Scottish Highlanders; *adj.a.: a plaid pattern, shirt, skirt, tie.* 2 such a garment: *glen plaids; tartan plaids.*

plain *adj.* 1 easy to see, hear, understand, etc.: *It's plain to the view; plain and clear; in plain English; in plain language.* 2 without ornament, color, seasoning, beauty, etc.: *a plain face; a police officer in **plain clothes*** (= not in uniform). 3 flat: *plain ground.*
—*n.* level land: *a coastal plain; The battle was fought on a plain; lava plains.*
—*adv.* simply: *just plain bored.*
—**plain.ly** *adv.;* **plain.ness** *n.*

plain.clothes.man (PLAIN.cloze.mun, -clothes.mun) *n.* a police officer, esp. a detective, who wears plain clothes while on duty.

plain fare *n.* simple food.

plain-Jane or **plain Jane** *adj.* ordinary; unsophisticated: *the plain-Jane shopper looking for basic values; very plain-Jane.*

plain sailing *n.* progress that is smooth and easy.

plains.man *n.* an inhabitant of the plains.

plain.song or **plain.chant** *n.* ancient church music sung in unison; Gregorian chant.

plain-spoken *adj.* plain and frank: *a plain-spoken farm boy; a plain-spoken account.*

plaint *n.* 1 [poetic use] lamentation. 2 [legal use] complaint.

plain.tiff *n.* one who brings a lawsuit.

plain.tive (PLAIN.tiv) *adj.* mournful: *a plaintive appeal, lament, note, plea, voice; the plaintive lowing of cattle; the plaintive sound of the violin.* —**plain.tive.ly** *adv.*

plain-vanilla *adj.* of the ordinary kind: *plain-vanilla ice cream; a plain-vanilla computer without any bells and whistles;*

the plain-vanilla version; My work is not so plain-vanilla as you think.

plait n. & v. braid; adj.: a **plaited** fabric; plaited grass, hair.

plan n. a drawing or outline of some action; scheme: a building plan drawn to scale; a five-year plan; your plans for the summer; brilliant, elaborate, grandiose, ingenious, well-laid, well-thought-out plans; contingency, flight, floor, master plans; to pay for appliances on the installment plan; a plan to cut down on waste; to carry out, concoct, devise, draw up, execute, foil, formulate, frustrate, implement, propose, reject, shelve, thwart, unveil a plan; pension plans; retirement plans. —v. **plans, planned, plan.ning** make plans; intend or contemplate: Are you planning to attend our meeting? I'm planning for my retirement; I'm planning on leaving for Florida next week. —**plan.ner** n.

pla.nar (PLAY.nur) adj. lying in one plane: a planar surface.

plane n. 1 a flat or level surface; also, a level: an inclined plane; a high plane of achievement; He kept the discussion on a lofty plane; the supernatural plane; adja.: plane (= level or flat) surfaces, figures. 2 a carpenter's tool for shaping and smoothing. 3 airplane: Before boarding his plane, the premier had a **planeside** chat with the press; a **planeload** of refugees. —v. **planes, planed, plan.ing** make flat and smooth using a plane: to plane a surface smooth. —**plan.er** n. —**plane.ness** n.

plan.et (PLAN.it) n. a heavenly body revolving around the sun whose light it reflects, esp. Mercury, Venus, Earth, Mars, Jupiter, Saturn, Uranus, Neptune, and Pluto. —**plan.e.tar.y** (-uh.tair.ee) adj.

plan.e.tar.i.um (plan.uh.TAIR.ee.um) n. -i.ums or -i.a (-ee.uh) 1 an optical device for showing the pattern and movement of the planets, sun, moon, and stars projected inside a dome. 2 a building housing this.

plan.e.tol.o.gy (plan.uh.TOL.uh.jee) n. -gies the study of planets; **plan.e.tol.o.gist** n.

plane tree n. a tree such as the sycamore, with leaves that are broader than they are long.

plan.gent (PLAN.junt) adj. resounding, esp. mournfully: the plangent sounds of a flute; plangent notes, voices; She sang in a plangent and complaining tone; "pulse of water plangent like a knell."

plank n. 1 a board that is at least 2 in. (5.08 cm) thick and 8 in. (20.32 cm) wide, as used in flooring a stage or platform. 2 an item of a political platform: A higher minimum wage was one of his campaign planks. —**walk the plank** be forced to kill oneself, as the crew of a ship captured by pirates made to jump overboard from a plank. —v. 1 cover with planks. 2 Informal. put down with some force: She planked down the change and strode out of the room. 3 cook and serve fish, steak, etc. on a board.

planking n. a covering of planks or the planks themselves: new planking for the kitchen floor.

plank.ton (PLANK.tun) n. the mass of tiny, drifting animal and plant life in bodies of water, as protozoans, jellyfish, and algae. —**plank.ton.ic** (-TON.ic) adj.

planned adj. organized or regulated: a planned affair, community; a carefully planned production; a government-controlled **planned economy**, not a free one; **planned obsolescence** (= designing that makes a product useless or out of date after a short time); **planned parenthood** (= birth control, esp. as an organized movement).

planning n. the act or process of making a plan: estate, family, financial, town planning.

plant n. 1 a living thing that is typically rooted in the ground and nourishes itself with food from air, sunlight, and water; an herb, vine, soft-stemmed shrub, or young tree: annual, climbing, exotic, perennial, tropical plants. 2 a machine or machinery used to make a product or provide a service: a gas plant; power plants. 3 a factory or building and its equipment: an automobile plant; heating plant; a college's physical plant; the school plant. —v. 1 put in the ground, as a sapling or seed: to plant flowers; to plant a field with wheat. 2 place in a certain way, esp. firmly: Parents plant good habits in the young early in life; He stood in a threatening attitude with arms akimbo and feet planted wide apart; The boxer planted one on his opponent's left jaw. 3 place secretly so as to deceive or hurt: He was suspected as an undercover agent planted by the enemy; to plant a bomb.

plan.tain (PLAN.tin) n. 1 a kind of banana plant or its large greenish fruit that is eaten cooked. 2 a low-growing herb or weed such as the "broadleaf" and "ribgrass."

plan.tar (PLAN.tur) adj. having to do with the sole of the foot: plantar warts.

plantation / platform

plan.ta.tion (plan.TAY.shun) *n.* **1** a large estate growing a crop such as cotton, rubber, tobacco, sugar cane, or tea with the help of laborers who live on the estate. **2** a colony or settlement.

plant.er *n.* **1** one that plants, as a machine, farmer, or plantation owner. **2** a container for houseplants.

plan.ti.grade (PLAN.tuh.grade) *adj.* walking on the sole of the foot: *plantigrade animals such as bears, apes, and humans.*

plant louse *n.* an aphid.

plaque (PLAK) *n.* **1** a thin, flat piece, as a tablet of wood or metal commemorating some event, an ornamental brooch or badge, etc.: *a memorial plaque; to put up a plaque in honor of the dead warrior.* **2** surface coating or deposit: *Dentists remove plaque from teeth.*

plash *n. & v.* (make) a gentle splash.

plasm (PLAZ.um) *n.* **1** genetic or cell-forming material; ***comb.form:*** *cytoplasm, ectoplasm, protoplasm.* **2** plasma.

plas.ma (PLAZ.muh) *n.* **1** the liquid part of blood, milk, etc. **2** a gas containing equal numbers of positive and negative particles: *A **plasma jet** is used in satellites to steer through space; A **plasma torch** is used in melting and vaporizing solids.* —**plas.mat.ic** (plaz.MAT.ic) or **plas.mic** *adj.*

plas.ter (PLAS.tur) *n.* a pasty mixture that hardens on drying, used to coat walls, ceilings, etc.: *to apply plaster to a wall; the crumbling plaster of an old building.* —*v.* stick with or as if with plaster: *He plasters down his wet hair; a wall plastered with posters.* —**plas.ter.er** *n.*

plaster of Paris *n.* calcined gypsum in white, powdery form, used for statuary, in **plaster casts** to hold fractured bones, and for making sheets of board, or **plasterboard**, used for walls, ceilings, etc.

plas.tic *adj.* **1** having molding, shaping, or pliable qualities: *Clay, wax, plaster, etc. are plastic substances; the plastic (= easily shaped) mind of a child; sculpture, painting, ceramics, and such **plastic arts**; A **plastic bomb** is a puttylike explosive; **Plastic bullets** (made of plastic) are used in riot control; **Plastic surgery** restores deformed or maimed body parts to their original shape.* **2** changeable in form; hence, artificial or insincere: *our plastic culture; his plastic smile.* —*n.* **1** a synthetic, moldable substance such as nylon or vinyl. **2** same as **plastic money**, credit cards used instead of cash: *They don't take plastic at the village post office.* —**plas.tic.i.ty** (-TIS.i.tee) *n.*

plat *n.* **1** a plot of land, esp. a building lot. **2** a map or plan indicating such plots.

plate *n.* **1** a flat, shallow circular dish, esp. for serving food; also, dishes and plated utensils collectively: *dinner plates; paper plates; to pass the collection plate (for donations) in church; gold and silver plate.* **2** food served on a plate: *salad and vegetable plates; tickets at $300 a plate (including service).* **3** a sheet of metal, glass, plastic, etc., as for taking photographs, for printing engraved impressions, etc.: *an automobile license plate; a printing plate; plate-glass windows.* **4** a print made with an engraving, esp. a full-page picture in color: *the plates and illustrations in a book.* **5** a piece of metal or plastic fitted with false teeth; denture: *lower and upper plates.* **6** a protective piece of material such as makes up a ship's steel hull or the horny or bony covering of reptiles and fishes: *a shield of armor plate.* **7** same as HOME PLATE. **8** any of the large movable pieces making up the earth's crust: *tectonic plates.*
—*v.* **plates, plat.ed, plat.ing 1** cover with plate or with a precious metal: *He ordered the faucets plated with gold;* *adj. & cpd:* ***plated*** *flatware, steel; armor-plated cars; chrome-plated accessories; gold-plated fixtures; a silver-plated spoon.* **2** make into plates; *adj.:* *a book all **plated** and ready for printing.* **3** put into plates: *Let's plate (out) the food for serving; adj.:* ***plated*** *entrées.*

pla.teau (plat.OH) *n.* **-teaus** or **-teaux** (-TOZE) **1** an elevated flat or level region; tableland: *a high plateau.* **2** a leveling off in a trend; stable period: *House prices reached a plateau (= leveled off) in the winter.*

plat.en (PLAT.un) *n.* **1** in a printing press, a plate that presses the paper against the printing surface. **2** the roller of a typewriter.

plate tectonics *n.pl.* the theory that the earth's crust is made up of huge plates, the friction between which causes earthquakes and forms mountains, volcanoes, etc.

plat.form *n.* **1** an elevated floor, esp. a stage for speakers: *to mount (= ascend) a platform; the launching platform or pad of a spacecraft.* **2** a statement of principles and policies of a political party or candidate: *to adopt, draft, draw up a platform; a party platform; the planks of a political platform.* **3** a major computer operating system under which applications software are designed to run;

also called "software platform": *Macintosh, MS-DOS, Unix, and Windows platforms.* **4** a group of computers that can run the same software; also called "hardware platform": *a program that runs on any hardware platform.*

plat.i.num (PLAT.num, -in.um) *n.* a silver-white, noncorrosive, metallic element; *adja.: a platinum album (with sales of 1 million units), record (2 million); a music video that has achieved platinum status (50,000 units); a **platinum blonde** (with silver-white hair).*

plat.i.tude (PLAT.i.tude) *n.* a solemnly made but well-worn or flat statement, as "Whatever will be, will be": *to mouth platitudes.* —**plat.i.tu.di.nous** (-TUE.dun.us) *adj.*

pla.ton.ic (pluh.TON.ic) *adj.* purely intellectual or spiritual, with no sexual interest: *platonic friendships, love; Our relationship is strictly platonic.*
—**pla.ton.i.cal.ly** *adv.*

pla.toon (pluh.TOON) *n.* a military unit usu. forming part of a company.

plat.ter (PLAT.ur) *n.* **1** a usu. oval dish for serving food: *a serving platter.* **2** a course of a meal: *a salad platter with cauliflower, broccoli, eggs, and olives.* **3** *Informal.* phonograph record. —**on a platter** as if served; received without effort: *Some children expect everything to be handed (to) them on a silver platter.*

plat.y.pus (PLAT.uh.pus) *n.* **-pus.es** or **-pi** (-pye) an aquatic, egg-laying mammal of Australia, with a bill like a duck's, webbed feet, and a paddle-shaped tail.

plau.dit (PLAW.dit) *n.* usu. **plaudits** *pl.* an expression of approval; applause: *to earn, receive, win plaudits.*

plau.si.ble (PLAW.zuh.bul) *adj.* believable, esp. as it appears: *It's plausible that life exists on other planets; Her story seems plausible; a plausible argument, candidate, theory;* **plau.si.bly** (-blee) *adv.*
—**plau.si.bil.i.ty** (-BIL.i.tee) *n.*

play *n.* **1** amusing or recreational activity; sport or fun: *All work and no play makes for a dull life.* **2** the way such activity is carried on or a stage or act in it: *fair, foul, rough play; A volley ball is **in play** till it hits the ground; a subject that brings her writing powers **into play**; "The good life depends on the liver" is a **play on words** (= pun).* **3** an organized fun activity, esp. a drama or similar performance: *Shakespeare's plays; to perform, produce, put on, rehearse a play; A play closes, opens, runs (in a place, at a theater).* **4** movement, activity, etc., esp. as being free, light, or quick: *the play of a poet's fancy; There should not be too much play in a steering wheel; the play of moonlight on the lake.*
—*v.* **1** do something for fun: *Children like to play all day; to play at (= have a game of) teacher and pupil; Canadians playing (= having a game against) Russia; It's dangerous to play (= do foolish things) with matches.* **2** work or perform: *to play a trick on someone; The circus plays (= gives performances in) southern cities in the winter; to play (= perform on) the piano; The officer played (= directed) her flashlight under the car; A possum plays (= pretends to be) dead; Will you **play back** (= replay) the recording for me? The media may **play down** (= make little of) or **play up** (= make much of) a story; to **play into the hands of** (= become a victim of) someone; Let's **play it cool** (Informal for stay calm); to **play off** (= set) one side against the other; The car dealer **played on** or **upon** (= took advantage of) his inexperience to sell him a lemon; a student trying to **play up to** (= gain the favor of) the teacher.* —**play.er** *n.* —**play.ful** *adj.;* **play.ful.ly** *adv.;* **play.ful.ness** *n.*

play.act.ing (PLAY.ac.ting) *n.* **1** acting on the stage. **2** pretense.

play.back *n.* the replaying of a recording.

play bill *n.* **1** a theatrical announcement. **2** a program of a play.

play book *n.* a notebook with diagrams of plays for a football team.

play.boy or **play.girl** *n.* one given to pleasure-seeking, esp. sexual.

play-by-play *adja.* detailed: *a play-by-play account of an event.*

player piano *n.* a piano played by a mechanical device.

play.fel.low (PLAY.fel.oh) same as PLAYMATE.

play.go.er (PLAY.go.ur) *n.* one who frequents the theater.

play.ground *n.* an area for outdoor play.

play.house *n.* **1** a theater. **2** a building for children to play in.

playing card *n.* one of a set of small rectangular cards used in card games.

playing field *n.* a stretch of ground for playing a game: *success on the playing field; A **level playing field** would give both sides an equal chance to win.*

play.let (PLAY.lit) *n.* a short play.

play.list *n.* a list of recordings to be broadcast by radio.

play.mate *n.* a companion for playing with.

play.off *n.* a contest for breaking a tie

or deciding a championship at the end of a tournament.
play.pen *n.* a portable enclosure for an infant to play in.
play.suit *n.* a play outfit consisting of a blouse and shorts.
play.thing *n.* a toy.
play.wright *n.* the author of a play.
pla.za (PLAH.zuh, PLAZ.uh) *n.* **1** a public square: *the plazas of Madrid; Rockefeller Plaza.* **2** a commercial area: *a service plaza (for motorists); shopping plaza (= shopping center); toll plaza (containing toll booths).*
plea (PLEE) *n.* **1** an appeal: *a fervent, impassioned, urgent plea; a plea for mercy.* **2** defense, esp. in answer to a charge: *Ignorance of the law is no plea; A defendant enters* or *makes* or *puts forward a plea through a lawyer; to* **cop a plea** (Informal for plead guilty for avoiding trial on a more serious charge); *a reduced charge as a result of* **plea bargaining** *between prosecuting and defending attorneys.*
plead (PLEED) *v.* **pleads,** *pt. & pp.* **plead.ed** or [regional use] **pled, plead.ing 1** argue a case: *Lawyers plead in court.* **2** answer a charge: *How do you plead – guilty or not guilty? He pleaded innocent* (= not guilty). **3** offer as an excuse for something: *to plead insanity when charged with murder.* **4** beg: *He pleaded for more time; She pleaded with her mother to let her watch the late movie.*
plead.er (PLEE.dur) *n.* a person qualified to plead in court.
plead.ings *n.pl.* statements made by the lawyers for the plaintiff and the defendant in a suit.
pleas.ant (PLEZ.unt) *adj.* having a pleasing effect: *We had a pleasant time at the party; a medicine that is pleasant to the taste;* **pleas.ant.ly** *adv.;* **pleas.ant.ness** *n.*
pleas.ant.ry (PLEZ.un.tree) *n.* **-ries 1** joking or fun. **2** a joke or a pleasant remark: *to exchange pleasantries.*
please (PLEEZ) *v.* **pleas.es, pleased, pleas.ing 1** be agreeable to someone: *a salesclerk eager to please* (= satisfy) *customers;* **adj.**: *We're greatly, highly, very* **pleased** *to meet you; His manner was most* **pleasing***; pleasing qualities; pleasing to the eye; It's pleasing to know you like my book.* **2** [as a polite formula]: *Please come in; Please stop;* **If you please,** *I'd like the window closed;* **Yes, please** (= I accept your offer with thanks); [as an order] *Stop please!* —**pleas.ing.ly** *adv.*
pleas.ur.a.ble (PLEZH.ur.uh.bul) *adj.* enjoyable: *a pleasurable experience.* —**pleas.ur.a.bly** *adv.*
pleas.ure (PLEZH.ur) *n.* **1** the feeling of being pleased; enjoyment: *the pleasure of your company; He took secret pleasure in his rival's defeat; It gives me great pleasure to accept this award; Pastimes afford pleasure; a life of pleasure; to feel, find, take pleasure in sports; to experience pleasure; She derives no pleasure from watching boxing; to mix business with pleasure on a trip; I do it for pleasure rather than for money; The dying patient couldn't find any pleasure in living.* **2** something that pleases: *to forgo a pleasure; It's a pleasure to introduce the next speaker; a genuine, rare, real pleasure; the pleasures of country living.*
pleat (PLEET) *n.* a fold, as on a skirt or drapes, stitched flat at the top: *Dry cleaners charge for skirts by the pleat; forward and reverse pleats; wide two-inch pleats;* **adja.**: *pleat pants; triple-pleat trousers.* —*v.*: *to pleat a skirt;* **adj.**: *a skirt with* **pleated** *ruffles; a pleated front;* **n.**: *top-selling* **pleateds** (= pleated drapes); *vertical drapes and pleateds; lace* **pleating** *and embroidery.*
plebe (PLEEB) *n.* a freshman at the U.S. Military Academy or Naval Academy.
ple.be.ian (pli.BEE.un) *n.* one of the common people, not a patrician. —*adj.* vulgar or coarse: *plebeian habits, humor, tastes.*
pleb.i.scite (PLEB.uh.site, -sit) *n.* a vote by all the people of a nation or section of it to elicit their opinion on a political issue: *to hold a plebiscite on school financing; A plebiscite is less binding on a government than a referendum.*
plebs *n., pl.* **ple.bes** (PLEE.beez) the lowest class of people in ancient Rome; also, the masses.
plec.trum *n.* **-trums** or **-tra** (-truh) a pick for playing a stringed musical instrument such as a banjo or mandolin.
pled a *pt. & pp.* of PLEAD.
pledge *n.* **1** a promise or vow: *to take a pledge of allegiance to the flag; to honor a pledge; Politicians make campaign pledges; to* **take the pledge** (not to drink). **2** a person or thing placed as security or guarantee: *a diamond ring as a pledge of his fidelity.* **3** a member accepted but not yet initiated into a club, fraternity, etc. **4** the state of being held as a pawn or hostage: *Innocent passengers were held* **in pledge** *by the hijackers.* —*v.* **pledg.es, pledged, pledg.ing 1** give as a pledge: *She pledged her jewelry as security for the loan; He pledged $100 to the Heart Fund.* **2** bind sol-

emnly: *The oath pledged him to secrecy.* **3** promise: *He pledged his support for the cause; to pledge allegiance to the Queen; The students pledged not to smoke, drink, or use drugs.*

Pleis.to.cene (PLY.stuh.seen) *n. & adj.* (of) the first epoch of the Quarternary period in the Cenozoic era of the earth, beginning about two million years ago.

ple.na.ry (PLEE.nuh.ree, PLEN.uh-) *adj.* full or complete, esp. in membership: *a plenary meeting* or *session of the council; plenary* (= full) *powers;* **n.**: *Send it to plenary* (= a plenary meeting) *for ratification.*

plen.i.po.ten.ti.ar.y (plen.i.puh.TEN.shee.air.ee) *adj.* having full powers or authority. —*n.* **-ar.ies** such a diplomat: *"ambassador extraordinary and plenipotentiary," the highest rank of diplomat.*

plen.i.tude (PLEN.i.tude) *n.* fullness or completeness: *a queen appearing in the plenitude of her majesty.*

plen.te.ous (PLEN.tee.us) *adj.* [poetical] plentiful: *a plenteous harvest.*

plen.ti.ful (PLEN.ti.ful) *adj.* existing in large numbers or amounts: *plentiful goods, harvests, supplies.* —**plen.ti.ful.ly** *adv.*

plen.ty (PLEN.tee) *n.* a large number or amount: *We get plenty of homework; We've plenty to do on weekends; We live in times of plenty* (= well supplied with life's necessities). —**in plenty 1** in large supply: *We have apples in plenty.* **2** having an abundance of goods: *They live in plenty.* —*adj. Informal.* sufficient: *There's plenty food.* —*adv. Informal.* very: *I got plenty hungry.*

ple.num (PLEE.num) *n.* **-nums** or **-na 1** a full space or enclosure, not a vacuum: *The fan of a heating furnace regulates the warm-air plenum and the cold-air return duct.* **2** a full assembly, esp. of a legislative body: *a central committee plenum.*

pleth.o.ra (PLETH.uh.ruh) *n.* an overabundance; fullness to excess: *a plethora of job applications, praise, problems.*

pleu.ri.sy (PLOOR.uh.see) *n.* inflammation of the membrane that covers each lung and lines the chest cavity.

plex.i.glas (PLEX.i.glass) *n.* a light but tough acrylic plastic used in aircraft windows, lenses, helmet shields, etc. —**Plexiglas** *Trademark.*

plex.us *n.* a network of arteries, lymphatic vessels, or nerves.

pli.a.ble (PLY.uh.bul) *adj.* **1** easy to bend or twist: *Leather is pliable; a pliable twig.* **2** easy to persuade or influence: *The power brokers thought a novice minister would be pliable to their influence.* —**pli.a.bil.i.ty** (-BIL.i.tee) *n.*

pli.ant (PLY.unt) *adj.* willing to comply. —**pli.an.cy** (-un.see) *n.*

pli.ers (PLY.urs) *n. sing. & pl.* a tool with a pair of jaws for gripping, bending, cutting wires, etc.

plight (PLITE) *n.* **1** an unfortunate condition: *the sad plight of refugees.* **2** [old use] a solemn promise. —*v.* [old use, as in the marriage formula]: *"Till death do us part ... I plight* (= promise) *thee my troth."*

plinth *n.* the square base of a column, pedestal, statue, vase, a piece of furniture, etc.

Pli.o.cene (PLY.uh.seen) *n. & adj.* (of) the last epoch of the Cenozoic era of the earth, beginning about 14 million years ago.

plod *v.* **plods, plod.ded, plod.ding 1** walk heavily or with effort: *The weary travelers plodded along.* **2** apply oneself steadily to a difficult task: *children plodding away at their chores.* —**plod.der** *n.* —**plod.ding.ly** *adv.*

plop *v.* **plops, plopped, plop.ping** set, drop, or throw down, as a stone into water. —*n.* a plopping or its sound.

plot *n.* **1** a small piece of ground, esp. a measured area, as on a ground plan: *a garden plot; a plot of land.* **2** a map, chart, or graph: *the plot of a ship's course.* **3** the plan of events in a literary work such as a novel or play: *a plot built around a wedding; The plot thickens as the wedding day draws near.* **4** a secret plan of action to hurt a person, group, or nation: *to devise, expose, foil, hatch, thwart a plot; a diabolic plot to kidnap a child; a sinister plot against the government.* —*v.* **plots, plot.ted, plot.ting 1** to mark, as on a map, graph, or chart: *to plot a temperature curve; Time is plotted against temperature; X and Y coordinates are used to plot the position of a ship; a subdivision* **plotted out** (= marked into plots) *for new housing.* **2** plan: *to plot the overthrow of a dictator; to plot a course of action, coup, revolt, strategy; politicians plotting while the country burns; He was plotting with his fellows to play tricks on the others; adj.: a poorly* **plotted** *thriller; a thickly plotted story; well-plotted novels.* —**plot.ter** *n.*

plough *Cdn.* **PLOW.**

plov.er (PLUV.ur, PLOH.vur) *n.* a small, stout shore bird of the lapwing family with a short body and pointed wings.

plow (rhyme: how) *n.* **1** a farm implement for turning up the soil in furrows and drawn by animals or a tractor. **2** a snowplow. —*v.* work, as with a plough: *to plow a field; He plows a **lonely furrow*** (= works all by himself); *Profits are **plowed back*** (= reinvested) *into our business; She **plows into*** (= gets busy with) *her work soon after breakfast; a book that is difficult to **plow through*** (= laborious to go through) *in a week.* —**plow.a.ble** (-uh.bul) *adj.* —**plow.er** *n.* Also **plough, plough.a.ble, plough.er** *Cdn.*

plow.man *n.* **-men** a farm worker. Also **plough.man** *Cdn.*

plow.share *n.* the blade of a plow. Also **plough.share** *Cdn.*

ploy *n.* a tactic or device: *a clever ploy to make a fast buck; a marketing ploy.*

pluck *v.* **1** pull off: *to pluck a bird's feathers; to pluck flowers or fruit from a tree; to **pluck a chicken*** (= pull the feathers off the dead bird). **2** pull or tug at something: *a singer plucking away at his guitar; Someone in the crowd plucked at her sleeve; I couldn't **pluck up*** (= summon) *enough courage to protest.* —*n.* boldness or courage: *the pluck to try and try again.*

—**pluck.y** *adj.* **pluck.i.er, -i.est** characterized by pluck: *a plucky little girl who plays hockey on a boys' team; a plucky escape, game, spirit.* —**pluck.i.ly** *adv.*

plug *n.* **1** a small piece of material used to stop up a hole: *an ear plug; a plug* (= lump) *of tobacco for chewing.* **2** something similar: *an automobile spark plug; an **electrical plug*** (with prongs to connect with an electrical outlet); *They didn't have the heart to **pull the plug on*** (Informal for disconnect the life-support system of) *the dying patient; adja.: a **plug-in** adaptor, clock, shaver; a **plug-and-play** home theater with audio and video components.* **3** *Informal.* a favorable bit of publicity, esp. on TV or radio: *a commercial plug.* —*v.* **plugs, plugged, plug.ging 1** put something into a hole to stop a flow, make a connection, etc.: *measures to plug the leak of top secret information; to plug a loophole in the arrangements; An electric kettle is plugged* (= connected by inserting its plug) *into a wall outlet; Please plug in the toaster; adj.: a **plugged** filter, nozzle, oil well; language students **plugged into** (= connected and listening to) *a tape player.* **2** *Informal.* promote: *a bestseller plugged by the networks.* —**plug away** work laboriously: *She plugs away at her homework till bedtime.*

plug-compatible *adj.* of computers and peripherals, substitutable with another maker's models.

plug.o.la (plug.OH.luh) *n. Informal.* a payola or bribe given for a plug or favorable publicity.

plum *n.* **1** a smooth-skinned, juicy dark-red or yellow fruit with a large stone. **2** the tree it grows on. **3** a raisin, as used in a "plum cake" or "plum pudding." **4** something attractive or desirable: *That job is a real plum; politicians craving for the plums of office; adja.: a plum assignment, job, position, role.*

plum.age (PLOO.mij) *n.* a bird's feathers.

plumb (PLUM) *n.* a device consisting of a small weight (**plumb bob**) attached to a line (**plumb line**) to measure the depth of water or to test whether a wall is vertical. —**out of plumb** or **off plumb** not vertical or straight. —*adj.* **1** *Informal.* downright: *a plumb fool; adv.: Your figures are plumb wrong; We're plumb out of stock.* **2** vertical: *The post has to be (erected) plumb; a plumb doorway.* —*v.* to understand fully: *to plumb (the depths of) a mystery.*

plumb.er (PLUM.ur) *n.* one skilled in plumbing: *A plunger is often called a "plumber's friend or helper."*

plumbing (PLUM.ing) *n.* **1** the occupation of putting in and repairing of pipes and fixtures for water, gas, sewage, etc. **2** the pipes and fixtures themselves.

plume (PLOOM) *n.* **1** a large feather used as an ornament; also, a tuft of feathers. **2** a feathery part, as of a seed, leaf, or insect: *"Plume hyacinth," "plume moth," and "plume poppy" have plumes.* **3** a formation resembling a feather; trail: *a plume of smoke rising from a chimney or volcano.* —*v.* **plumes, plumed, plum.ing 1** provide with plume; *adj.: a **plumed** helmet; a white-plumed bird.* **2** preen: *A swan plumes its feathers; The boss **plumes himself on*** (= boasts of) *his secretary's achievements.*

plum.met (PLUM.it) *n.* a plumb bob or line. —*v.* plunge: *Stock prices plummeted on Black Monday.*

plum.my (PLUM.ee) *adj.* **plum.mi.er, plum.mi.est 1** good and desirable; plum. **2** characterized by an affected upper-class style of speaking: *a plummy accent, enunciation, voice.*

plump *adj.* **1** rounded or chubby: *Paula is pleasantly plump.* **2** direct or blunt: *A plump "no" was her answer.*

—*adv.* heavily or suddenly: *He dropped himself plump into the chair.* —*v.* **1** make or become plump: *The child is eating*

plumy / poach

well and gradually plumping up; He plumped up the pillows before getting into bed. **2** let fall or drop: She plumped her books down on the bed. —**plump for** support or champion: Each teacher seemed to plump for her own pupils.

plum.y (PLOO.mee) adj. **plum.i.er, -i.est 1** adorned with plumes. **2** feathery.

plun.der (PLUN.dur) v. rob, esp. on a large scale, as invaders do; loot or pillage. —**n.** what is taken in robbery, as a bribe, etc.: a pirate ship loaded with plunder; a price so high it borders on plunder. —**plun.der.er** n.

plunge (PLUNJ) v. **plung.es, plunged, plung.ing 1** go or send down suddenly into water or as if into water or other deep place: She plunged her burned hand into the water; He plunged into the pool to save the drowning child; He was plunged in grief by the death of his wife; **adj.**: a woman with a **plunging** neckline (of a top that is revealing); plunging crude oil prices; the plunging dollar. **2** Informal. to gamble or speculate rashly: She plunged into the stock market and lost a fortune.
—**n.** an act of plunging: a plunge in the pool; a plunge in the stock market; He wants to give up his job to start a business, but hesitates to **take the plunge.**

plung.er (PLUN.jur) n. **1** a long-handled suction cup for freeing clogged drains. **2** one who plunges, esp. a rash speculator.

plunk n. a metallic or twanging sound, as made by plucking on a stringed musical instrument. —v. fall or drop heavily; plump: He plunked the change down on the counter and walked out.

plu.ral (PLOOR.ul) adj. indicating more than one: a plural noun; a plural component adhesive; a plural political system; a plural (= multicultural) society.
—**n.** a word form indicating more than one: "Boys," "boxes," "oxen," "fish," and "women" are plurals; The nouns are in the plural.

plu.ral.ism (PLOOR.uh.liz.um) n. the having or existence of more than one, as various ethnic groups with equal rights living in the same society.
—**plu.ral.is.tic** (-LIS.tic) adj.: We live in a pluralistic society.

plu.ral.i.ty (ploo.RAL.i.tee) n. **-ties 1** in an election, the number of a winner's votes if less than a majority. **2** the excess of such a winner's votes over the nearest rival's.

plu.ral.ize (PLOOR.uh.lize) v. **-iz.es, -ized, -iz.ing** make into plural: "Fish" is pluralized in "Fish swim."

—**plu.ral.i.za.tion** (-luh.ZAY.shun, -lye-) n.

plus n. **1** the addition sign [+]: the plus sign. **2** something added; hence, an advantage: One of the pluses of our new car is air-conditioning; Each car has its pluses and minuses. —**prep.** added to something: Two plus two is four; qualifications plus experience. —**adj.** extra: She got a B plus in math; a plus factor, quantity; on the plus (= positive) side.
—**conj.** Informal: He's jobless, plus (= and besides) he's in debt.

plush n. a fabric similar to velvet but with a thicker pile. —**adj.** soft or luxurious: plush carpeting, fabrics, offices; a plush toy; He dines in plush (= luxurious) surroundings. —**plush.ly** adv.; **plush.ness** n.

plu.toc.ra.cy (ploo.TOC.ruh.see) n. **-cies 1** government by the wealthy. **2** the wealthy class. —**plu.to.crat** (PLOO.tuh.crat) n.; **plu.to.crat.ic** (-CRAT.ic) adj.

plu.to.ni.um (ploo.TOH.nee.um) n. a radioactive metallic element used in nuclear reactions.

plu.vi.al (PLOO.vee.ul) adj. having do with rain.

ply n. **plies** a layer, fold, or strand of a material such as woven cloth, twisted rope, or plywood: a tire built with four plies of polyester cord; **cpd.**: a two-ply paper towel; four-ply silk; a bias-ply tire.
—v. **plies, plied, ply.ing 1** travel regularly: a ferry plying between the mainland and the islands; It has been plying the same route for years. **2** work at steadily: She plied the child with questions to get her to tell the truth; a cutter plying (= using) his shears; to **ply one's trade** (= work at one's occupation).

ply.wood n. a building material made of sheets of wood glued and pressed together.

pneu.mat.ic (new.MAT.ic) **1** adj. having to do with air under pressure: a pneumatic drill, hammer, tire; pneumatic tubes to shoot messages between two points, as in an office or a plant. **2 pneumatics** n.pl. [takes sing. v.] the study of the properties of gases.
—**pneu.mat.ic.al.ly** adv.

pneu.mo.nia (new.MOH.nee.uh) n. a disease of the lungs ("double pneumonia" when both lungs are affected) usu. caused by viruses or bacteria.

poach v. **1** cook egg, fish, or fruit without its shell or skin in a boiling liquid or over steam: bass poached in cider; pears poached in wine and honey. **2** take game or fish illegally.

poach.er *n.* **1** one who poaches game or fish. **2** a covered pan or baking dish for poaching food.

pock *n.* **1** an eruption on the skin caused by a disease such as smallpox. **2** a pitlike mark or scar left by it.

pock.et (POCK.it) *n.* **1** a small bag forming part of one's clothing, for carrying a handkerchief, money, etc.: *People stood around with hands in their pockets* (= idle); *Don't let someone pick* (= steal from) *your pocket.* **2** a similar hollow or isolated space: *a billiard pocket; a pocket* (= small area) *of unemployment; air pockets.* —**in someone's pocket** under someone's control. —**out of pocket** short of cash: *He was out of pocket after paying off the mortgage.* —**pock.et.ful** *n.* **-fuls.**

pock.et.book (POCK.it.book) *n.* **1** a book in a small format. **2** a purse or wallet; hence, financial resources: *things that hurt* or *hit consumers in the pocketbook; adja.: a pocketbook issue, vote; pocketbook patriotism.*

pock.et.knife (POCK.it.nife) *n.* **-knives** a knife with a blade or blades folding into the handle.

pocket money *n.* money given for small personal expenses.

pocket veto *n.* an indirect veto of a bill by the President's not signing it before Congress adjourns.

pock.mark *n.* the scar left by a pock. —**pock.marked**: *a pockmarked complexion, road; the pockmarked surface of the moon;* also **pock.y** *adj.* **pock.i.er, -i.est.**

po.co (POH.coh) *adv. Music.* somewhat: *poco allegro.* —**poco a poco** little by little.

pod *n.* **1** a seed case or shell, as of beans or peas, that splits open when ripe. **2** a cocoon or egg capsule. **3** a container, enclosure, or housing outside a craft for carrying fuel, instruments, etc.: *the engine pod of an aircraft; a rest pod* (= recessed area) *for factory workers to relax in.* **4** a group of animals: *a pod of seals, whales.* —*v.* **pods, pod.ded, pod.ding** to form pods.

-pod *comb.form.* footed: *arthropod, cephalopod.*

po.di.a.try (puh.DYE.uh.tree) *n.* a branch of medicine dealing with foot ailments; **po.di.a.trist** *n.*

po.di.um (POH.dee.um) *n., pl.* **-di.a 1** a small platform for standing on, as for an orchestra conductor: *The skyscraper stands on a three-story podium at the corner of King and Bay streets.* **2** a lectern.

po.em (POH.um) *n.* a piece of creative writing in verse form with emotional and imaginative content: *to compose, recite, write a poem.*

po.e.sy (POH.uh.see) *n.* [old use] poetry.

po.et (POH.it) *n.* one who composes poetry. —**po.et.ic** (poh.ET.ic) or **po.et.i.cal** *adj.* —**po.et.i.cal.ly** *adv.*

po.et.as.ter (POE.it.as.tur) *n.* a second-rate poet.

po.et.ess (POE.it.is) *n.* [uncomplimentary use] female poet: *a prairie poetess; the poetess of doom and gloom.*

poetic justice *n.* the rewarding of good and punishing of evil as seen in uncaused events: *the poetic justice of a pickpocket being robbed.*

poetic license *n.* freedom to ignore a rule or convention for the sake of an artistic effect, as in writing verse.

poet laureate *n.* a nation's official poet.

po.et.ry (POE.i.tree) *n.* **1** the art of writing poems. **2** poems collectively: *the poetry of Milton; Elizabethan poetry.*

po.gey (POH.gee, "g" as in "go") *n. Slang.* welfare, unemployment benefits, or charity: *to go on the pogey while looking for a job.*

po.go stick (POH.goh-) *n.* a stilt with handles at the top and springy footrests at the bottom with which a child makes short leaps for moving around.

po.grom (poh.GROM, POH.grum) *n.* an organized massacre, as of Jews in Czarist Russia.

po.gy same as POGEY.

poi *n.* a pasty Hawaiian food made from taro root.

poign.ant (POIN.yunt) *adj.* painful to the mind and feelings: *poignant memories, sights, sorrow, tales;* **poign.ant.ly** *adv.* —**poign.an.cy** *n.*

poin.ci.a.na (poin.see.AN.uh) *n.* a flowering tree of the pea family with fernlike leaves and fiery red blossoms.

poin.set.ti.a (poin.SET.ee.uh, -SET.uh) *n.* a tropical plant with yellow flowers and red, petallike leaves.

point *n.* **1** a tapering end, as of a pencil; tip: *a sharp point; a hostage taken* **at the point of** (= using) *a gun;* [in place names] *Point Pelee; Hanlan's Point.* **2** a dot or mark made with a tip: *the decimal point in 1.5* (= one point five); *an exclamation point* [!]. **3** a position in time or space: *the point at which the lines meet; focal, rallying, starting, turning, vantage points; the high and low points of one's career; The patient was* **at the point of** *death last night; adja.: Information from* **point-of-sale** *transaction terminals helps to keep store records up to* *date.* **4** a mark as a unit or measure: *You score 10 points if you win; the* **set point** *of a game (that may decide the set in favor of the player who is leading); the boiling and freezing points* (= degrees of temperature) *of water; N.N.E. is a* **point of the compass** (= one of 32 directions). **5** a single detail, item, or particular: *Let me answer you point by point; You've raised an interesting point* (= matter); *to argue, concede, emphasize, illustrate, labor, stress, win a point; He has good and bad points* (= sides) *as a writer; Sometimes he misses* **the point** (= the main idea) *altogether; Her good looks are* **beside the point** (= irrelevant); *This essay is* **a case in point** (= a relevant example); *You've* **made your point** (= proved your case); *In* **point of fact** (= in regard to fact), *only a few attended the meeting*. **6** purpose or urgency: *There's no point in arguing further.* —*v.* **1** make into a point: *Use a sharpener to point a pencil*. **2** show or indicate: *to* **point out** *a place on a map; All the symptoms* **point** *to stomach ulcers; Errors of grammar and spelling* **point up** *the need for remedial English*. **3** to aim: *The gun was pointed at his head; It's rude to point at people (with the finger when they are looking).*

point-blank *adj.* from a close position: *He was gunned down at point-blank range; a point-blank* (= direct) *denial of the charge;* —*adv.: She refused him point-blank* (= bluntly).

pointed *adj.* **1** having a point: *a pointed end, hat, instrument.* **2** aimed at someone: *a pointed finger; a pointed attack, message, question, reminder; a pointed remark that made the listeners uneasy.*
—**point.ed.ly** *adv.*

point.er *n.* **1** one that points, as a rod or needle: *She gave us a few* **pointers** (= hints or advice) *on what to look for in a used car.* **2** a breed of hunting dog that sniffs out game and stays pointing to it.

poin.til.lism (PWAHN.tul.iz.um) *n.* painting in small dots of primary color that blend into the desired tones when seen at a distance; **poin.til.list** *n. & adj.*

point.less *adj.* without a point or purpose; meaningless. —**point.less.ly** *adv.;* **point.less.ness** *n.*

point man *n.* a leading player; one in the forefront.

point of departure *n.* a starting point: *a book that is a new point of departure for writers on the subject.*

point of no return *n.* a point at which turning back is impossible, like an airplane without enough fuel to return to its starting point; hence, a critical point: *a terminal case of cancer past the point of no return.*

point of view *n.* standpoint: *from a selfish point of view.*

point.y *adj.* **point.i.er, -i.est 1** having many points: *a pointy clown's cap.* **2** pointed: *boots with pointy toes; a* **pointy-headed** (= egghead) *bureaucrat.*

point zero *n.* the place of explosion of an atomic bomb.

poise (POIZ) *n.* **1** self-possession: *a woman of great poise; with poise and confidence; to keep, lose, maintain one's poise.* **2** the way one carries oneself; carriage: *her graceful poise.*
—*v.* **pois.es, poised, pois.ing** balance or be balanced: *to poise oneself for a dive;* —*adj.:* to appear, seem poised; *a company poised for strong growth in the next quarter; her poised performance; The diver stands poised at the edge of the diving board.*

poi.son (POY.zun) *n.* **1** a substance that causes illness or death in a living organism. **2** anything destructive or harmful, such as certain chemicals, plants, snake bites, and stings of insects. —*v.* put poison in something: *The drink was poisoned; books that poison young minds; She was poisoned* (= killed by poisoning); *adj.: a* **poisoned** *arrow, atmosphere; poisoned air, fish, food, water.*
—*adj*a. containing poison: *poison gas, ivy, oak.* —**poi.son.ous** (-us) *adj.*

poison ivy *n.* a vine or shrub with trifoliate leaves and whitish berries, whose tissues contain a poisonous oil that causes a rash when touched.

poison-pen letter *n.* a malicious, harassing letter, usu. by an anonymous writer.

poison pill *n.* a legal provision that would make the takeover of a company too costly for the buyer.

poke *v.* **pokes, poked, pok.ing 1** prod or jab; push: *Someone in the crowd poked her; He poked his head in my door to announce the visitor; to poke around in the bushes for a lost ball; a dawdler* **poking along** (= proceeding slowly) *with his work; He likes to* **poke fun at** (= tease) *his sister.* **2** *Informal.* punch.
—*n.* a prod or push: *a friendly poke in the ribs; She* **took a poke at him** (*Informal for* gave him a punch).

pok.er (POH.kur) *n.* **1** a metal rod for stirring a fire. **2** a card game in which bets are placed on the value of the cards held.

poker face *n. Informal.* a face without any expression.

pok.ey or **pok.y** (POH.kee) *adj.* **pok.i.er, -i.est** 1 annoyingly slow. 2 dull, dowdy, or stuffy and cramped.
— *n. pl.* **pok.eys** or **pok.ies** *Slang.* a jail: *doing time in the pokey.* — **pok.i.ly** *adv.*; **pok.i.ness** *n.*

pol *n.* [short form] politician.

po.lar (POH.lur) *adja.* 1 having to do with the North or South Pole: *a polar ice cap, region, route; the polar orbit of a spacecraft (passing over the poles); the large, white-furred* **polar bear** *of the Arctic; the* **polar circles** (= Arctic and Antarctic circles); *the* **polar lights** (= the auroras). 2 directly opposed: *Falsehood is the polar opposite of truth; polar alternatives, differences, inequalities.*

po.lar.i.ty (puh.LAIR.i.tee) *n.* **-ties** 1 the condition of having opposed poles: *A magnet or battery has negative and positive polarities;* **adja.**: *polarity changes, checks, reversal.* 2 opposition: *the political polarity between capital and labor.*

po.lar.ize (POH.luh.rize) *v.* **-iz.es, -ized, -iz.ing** 1 give or get polarity; *adj.*: *Polarized sunglasses cut out much reflected light; a camera with a polarizing filter.* 2 divide into opposing groups: *a community polarized by rivalries.*
— **po.lar.i.za.tion** (-ruh.ZAY.shun, -rye-) *n.*

pole *n.* 1 a long, slender, and usu. rounded piece of wood or metal, as used to push a boat with: *ski, telephone, tent poles.* 2 either end of an imaginary rotating axis, as of the earth: *North Pole; South Pole.* 3 either of two opposing forces or principles: *the opposite poles of a magnet; The negative pole* (= terminal) *of one battery is to be connected to the positive pole of the other when using a booster cable; The two sides were* **poles apart** (= widely separated) *when they started talks.*

Pole *n.* a person of or from **Poland**, a central European country.

pole.ax or **pole.axe** *n.* a battle-ax with a short handle and usu. with a spike or hook opposite its blade.

pole.cat *n.* 1 a weasellike animal of Europe, related to the ferret. 2 a skunk.

po.lem.ic (puh.LEM.ic) 1 *adj.* having to do with controversy; also **po.lem.i.cal.** 2 *n.* a controversy. 3 **polemics** *n.pl.* [takes *sing. v.*] the art of controversy.
— **po.lem.i.cist** (-uh.sist) *n.*

pole.star *n.* the North Star; hence, a guiding principle: *Duty was the polestar of his life.*

pole vault *n.* an athletic jump over a high crossbar using a flexible pole.

po.lice (puh.LEECE) *n.* 1 a department of government that prevents crime, maintains public peace and safety, enforces laws, etc.; also, its members: *to call the police; mounted, plainclothes, state police;* **adja.**: *a police car, officer, outpost, patrol, post.* 2 any similar private organization providing security services: *campus, military, secret, security police.*
— *v.* **-lic.es, -liced, -lic.ing** 1 guard: *to police a neighborhood.* 2 keep a military area clean and orderly. — **po.lice.man** (-mun), **-men** *n.*; **po.lice.wom.an** *n.* **-wom.en.**

police dog *n.* a dog trained to help police, esp. a German shepherd.

police officer *n.* a policeman or policewoman.

police state *n.* a state in which social, political, and economic life is repressed, usu. by use of secret police.

pol.i.cy (POL.uh.see, "OL" as in "doll") *n.* **-cies** 1 a principle, conduct, or plan of action: *"Satisfaction or money back" is our store policy; the foreign policy of peaceful coexistence; to adopt, carry out or implement, formulate, pursue, set, shape a policy; a company policy; America's foreign policy.* 2 an insurance contract: *to issue, take out, write up a policy.*

pol.i.cy.hold.er (POL.uh.see.HOLE.dur) *n.* one to whom an insurance policy has been issued.

po.li.o (POH.lee.oh) *n.* [short form] poliomyelitis.

po.li.o.my.e.li.tis (POH.lee.oh.my.uh.LYE.tis) *n.* an acute viral infection of the central nervous system, which sometimes leads to paralysis.

pol.ish ("ol" as in "doll") *n.* 1 a glossy surface finish, as of glass. 2 a substance used to give this finish: *nail polish; shoe polish.* 3 refinement or culture. — *v.* give polish to something: *to polish floors, furniture, shoes;* **adj.**: *highly polished* (= refined) *manners, prose, style.* — **polish off** finish: *He polished off his dinner in no time.* — **polish up** practice and improve: *Better polish up your French before going to Paris.*

Pol.ish (POH.lish) *n. & adj.* (the Slavic language) of the Poles.

Po.lit.bu.ro (POLL.it.byoor.oh, "OLL" as in "doll") *n.* a communist party's top policy-making group. Also **politburo.**

po.lite (puh.LITE) *adj.* **-lit.er, -lit.est** 1 proper in one's behavior toward others: *a polite young woman; At least be polite if you can't be friendly; polite applause; polite* (= subtle) *prejudice.* 2 cultured, polished, or elegant: *a man of*

polite learning; She moves in polite society. —**po.lite.ly** *adv.;* **po.lite.ness** *n.*
pol.i.tesse (pol.i.TES) *n.* formal politeness; decorousness.
pol.i.tic (POL.i.tic, "OL" as in "doll") *adj.* shrewd and tactful: *She thought it politic not to disagree with the boss.*
po.lit.i.cal (puh.LIT.i.cul) *adj.* having to do with government or politics: *The Arab diplomat sought political asylum in the U.S.; a political office, party; political economy, patronage; amnesty for political prisoners;* **political science** (= science of government). —**po.lit.i.cal.ly** *adv.:* **Politically correct** language and practices help avoid offending sensibilities in regard to race, sex, religion, etc.
pol.i.ti.cian (pol.i.TISH.un, "ol" as in "doll") *n.* 1 one who is busy with political affairs, esp. one in political office: *astute, great, honest, shrewd politicians.* 2 an opportunist: *a crooked politician; just a scheming politician, not a statesman.*
po.lit.i.cize (puh.LIT.uh.size) *v.* **-ciz.es, -cized, -ciz.ing** make political in character: *to politicize the Olympics.* —**po.lit.i.ci.za.tion** (-suh.ZAY.shun, -sye-) *n.*
pol.i.tick (POL.i.tic, "OL" as in "doll") *v.* be busy with political activities.
po.lit.i.co (puh.LIT.uh.coh) *n.* **-cos** or **-coes** a party politician.
pol.i.tics (POL.i.tics, "OL" as in "doll") *n.pl.* 1 [takes *sing. v.*] the science of government: *Politics is her major.* 2 [takes *sing.* or *pl.v.*] political principles or activities, including intrigue or rivalry: *Politics are to blame for the fiasco; Is politics a dirty game? to play, talk politics; office, partisan, party, power politics.*
pol.i.ty (POL.i.tee) *n.* **-ties** 1 government or a form of government. 2 a state or other political unit.
pol.ka (POLE.kuh, POH.kuh) *n.* 1 a fast Bohemian dance for couples. 2 the music for this.
pol.ka dot (POH.kuh-) *n.* 1 a round dot repeated as a pattern on fabric. 2 such a pattern, a fabric with this pattern, or an item of girls' or women's wear made of such a fabric: *a display of polka dots, florals, and full skirts;* **adja.:** *a* **polka-dot** *design; a white polka-dot dress.* Also **pol.ka.dot** *n. & adja.*
poll (POLE) *n.* 1 a voting, its results, or the counting of votes: *A heavy poll is expected; The poll was light because of bad weather; a straw poll.* 2 **polls** *pl.* voting places: *The polls close at 8 p.m.;* **We go to the polls** (= vote) *on election day.* 3 an opinion survey on a specific issue: *to carry out* or *conduct* or *take a poll of the student population on the voting age; Gal-*
lup, exit, Harris, public-opinion polls. —*v.* 1 survey by means of a poll: *A random sample of the population was polled on the issue;* **n.:** *Yesterday's* **polling** *was heavy;* **adja.:** *a* **polling** *booth, day, district, firm, place, site, station.* 2 receive as votes: *The winner polled 60% of the votes.* 3 shear or crop wool, horns, head hair, etc. —**poll.er** *n.*
pol.lack (POL.uk, "OL" as in "doll") *n.* a food fish of the cod family.
pol.len (POL.un, "OL" as in "doll") *n.* a fine powder produced by flowers for the fertilization of other flowers by the agency of wind, insects, etc.
pollen count (or **index**) *n.* an estimate of the number of pollen grains in the air for warning hay-fever victims.
pol.li.nate (POL.uh.nate, "OL" as in "doll") *v.* **-nates, -nat.ed, -nat.ing** fertilize a flower by pollen. —**pol.li.na.tion** (-NAY.shun) *n.* —**pol.li.na.tor** (-nay.tur) *n.*
pol.li.wog (POL.ee.wog, "OL" as in "doll") *n.* a tadpole.
poll.ster (POLE.stur) *n.* one who conducts a poll of public opinion.
poll tax (POLE-) *n.* a uniform per-head tax, not based on income or property; also called "capitation tax."
pol.lu.tant (puh.LOO.tunt) *n.* something that pollutes the environment, as smoke, noise, wastes, or exhausts.
pol.lute (puh.LOOT, long "OO") *v.* **pol.lutes, pol.lut.ed, pol.lut.ing** make unclean; defile, esp. the environment. —**pol.lu.ter** *n.* —**pol.lu.tion** (-LOO.shun) *n.: air, noise, soil, sound, water pollution; the* **pollution index** (= measure of impurities in the air).
Pol.ly.an.na (poll.ee.AN.uh, "oll" as in "doll") *n.* one who sees an optimistic side in even the most tragic events.
pollywog same as POLLIWOG.
po.lo (POH.loh) *n.* a ball game played on horseback using mallets.
po.lo.naise (pol.uh.NAIZ) *n.* 1 a dignified processional dance of Polish origin. 2 the music for it.
po.lo.ni.um (puh.LOH.nee.um) *n.* a radioactive metallic element.
polo shirt *n.* a short-sleeved, knitted pullover of cotton or jersey.
pol.ter.geist (POLE.tur.guyst; *rhyme:* iced) *n.* the supposed spirit behind the phenomena of haunted houses such as fire-raising, stone-throwing, china-smashing, and door-slamming.
pol.troon (poll.TROON, "oll" as in "doll") *n.* a contemptible coward.
poly- (POL.ee-, "OL" as in "doll") *comb.form.* much or many: *polyandry,*

polyglot, polygon.

pol.y.an.dry (POL.ee.an.dree) *n.* the practice or custom of having more than one male spouse at a time.

pol.y.chlo.ri.nat.ed bi.phen.yl (pol.ee.CLOR.uh.nay.tid.bye.FEN.ul, -FEE.nul) *n.* an industrial chemical compound, similar to pesticides, that contaminates the environment and enters the food chain.

pol.y.clin.ic (pol.ee.CLIN.ic) *n.* a clinic with various specialist departments.

pol.y.es.ter (pol.ee.ES.tur) *n.* a synthetic material used in making paints, fibers, films, plastics, etc.

pol.y.eth.yl.ene (pol.ee.ETH.uh.leen) *n.* a plastic used for containers, kitchenware, tubing, etc.

po.lyg.a.mous (puh.LIG.uh.mus) *adj.* 1 that practices polygamy: *a polygamous society, tribe.* 2 having both bisexual and unisexual flowers: *Certain ashes and maples are polygamous.*

po.lyg.a.my (puh.LIG.uh.mee) *n.* marriage with more than one spouse at the same time, esp. having more than one wife. —**po.ly.gam.ist** (-guh.mist) *n.*

pol.y.glot (POL.ee.glot) *adj.* speaking, writing, or containing several languages: *a polyglot edition, population.*
—*n.* a multilingual person or text.

pol.y.gon (POL.ee.gon, *rhyme:* on) *n.* a closed plane figure, usu. one with five or more straight sides. —**po.lyg.o.nal** (puh.LIG.un.ul) *adj.*

pol.y.graph (POL.i.graf) *n.* a lie detector. —*v.:* *arrested, fingerprinted, polygraphed, and released.*

pol.y.he.dron (pol.ee.HEE.drun) *n.* a solid figure with five or more plane surfaces. —**pol.y.he.dral** (-drul) *adj.*

pol.y.math (POL.ee.math) *n.* a person of wide-ranging knowledge.

pol.y.mer (POL.uh.mur) *n.* a substance composed of molecules that have combined with each other, as polyethylene which is made by the polymerization of ethylene gas. —**po.lym.er.ize** (-rize) *v.* -**iz.es, -ized, -iz.ing; po.lym.er.i.za.tion** (-ruh.ZAY.shun, -rye-) *n.*
—**pol.y.mer.ic** (-MER.ic) *adj.*

Pol.y.ne.sian (pol.uh.NEE.zhun) *n. & adj.* 1 (a person) of or from **Polynesia**, a region of the C. Pacific including Hawaii, Samoa, Tonga, and nearby islands. 2 (having to do with) any of the languages spoken by Polynesians or their culture.

pol.y.no.mi.al (pol.ee.NOH.mee.ul) *n.* in algebra or biology, an expression with more than two terms, as "x + y - z" or "Populus nigra italica" (Lombardy poplar); *adj.:* *a polynomial equation; polynomial nomenclature.*

pol.yp (POL.ip) *n.* 1 a simple sea animal such as a coral that has a hollow cylindrical body with one end attached to the sea bottom while the other, equipped with tentacles, acts as its mouth. 2 a tumor projecting from the mucous membrane of the bladder, intestine, nose, or uterus.

po.lyph.o.ny (puh.LIF.uh.nee) *n.* a musical composition of two or more harmonizing melodies; counterpoint.
—**pol.y.phon.ic** (pol.ee.FON.ic) *adj.*

pol.y.sty.rene (pol.ee.STY.reen) *n.* a tough, clear plastic used for housewares, toys, electrical insulation, radio cabinets, etc.

pol.y.syl.lab.ic (POL.ee.suh.LAB.ic) *adj.* of many syllables: *a polysyllabic word.*

pol.y.tech.nic (pol.ee.TEK.nic) *n.* a school providing instruction in many technical subjects.

pol.y.the.ism (pol.ee.THEE.iz.um, "TH" as in "thin") *n.* a religion with more than one god; **pol.y.the.ist** *n.* —**pol.y.the.is.tic** (POL.ee.thee.IS.tic) *adj.*

pol.y.un.sat.u.rat.ed (POL.ee.un.SACH.uh.ray.tid) *adj.* of a fatty acid or vegetable oil, lacking four or more hydrogen atoms: *Margarine and most vegetable oils are sources of polyunsaturated fats.*

pol.y.u.re.thane (pol.ee.YOOR.uh.thane) *n.* a synthetic rubber used in flexible and rigid forms as foams, molded products, etc.

pol.y.vi.nyl chloride (pol.ee.VYE.nil-) *n.* a thermoplastic material used for imitation leather, phonograph records, etc.

po.made (poh.MADE, -MAHD) *n.* a scented ointment for the hair: *a waxy pomade of beeswax.* —*v.* **-mades, -mad.ed, -mad.ing** apply pomade to something; *adj.:* *pomaded hair.*

pome.gran.ate (POM.gran.it) *n.* a round tropical fruit full of seeds with a hard rind and tart, crimson pulp.

Pom.er.a.ni.an (pom.uh.RAY.nee.un) *n.* a breed of small dog with long, silky hair.

pom.mel (PUM.ul) *n.* a knoblike projection, as on a sword's hilt or the front end of a saddle.

pomp *n.* a showy display: *a ceremony full of pomp and pageantry; an emperor's life of pomp and circumstance.*

pom.pa.dour (POM.puh.dore) *n.* a hairdo that rises straight up from the forehead, over a pad or roller in the case of women.

pom.pa.no (POM.puh.noh) *n.* a food fish of the Atlantic, the largest type of which is the permit or "great pompano."

pom-pom *n.* an ornamental tuft or ball of soft material; also **pompon**.

pom.pous (POM.pus) *adj.* showy or pretentious: *a pompous manner, speech, style;* **pom.pous.ly** *adv.* —**pom.pous.ness** or **pom.pos.i.ty** (pom.POS.i.tee) *n.*

ponce *n. Slang.* same as PIMP.

pon.cho (PON.choh) *n.* **-chos** 1 a cloak resembling a blanket with a hole through it for the wearer's head. 2 a similar garment, esp. a raincoat.

pond *n.* a body of water smaller than a lake.

pon.der (PON.dur) *v.* weigh mentally; consider deeply: *a philosopher pondering a truth; to ponder on* or *over* or *upon one's future.*

pon.der.a.ble (PON.duh.ruh.bul) *adj.* appreciable in regard to weight or importance.

pon.der.o.sa pine (pon.duh.ROH.suh-) *n.* a tall pine of W. North America valued as timber.

pon.der.ous (PON.duh.rus) *adj.* heavy, clumsy, or dull: *an elephant's ponderous gait; a ponderous essay, lecture.*

pone *n.* cornmeal bread in oval loaves, common in southern U.S.

pon.gee (PON.jee) *n.* a soft, light-brown cloth of Chinese silk.

pon.iard (PON.yurd) *n.* a dagger.

pon.tiff *n.* a bishop, esp. the **Pontiff** or **Supreme Pontiff** (= pope).

pon.tif.i.cal (pon.TIF.i.cul) *adj.* 1 papal: *a pontifical institute; pontifical robes.* 2 pompous or dogmatic. 3 **pontificals** *n.pl.* a pontiff's ceremonial vestments and insignia.

pon.tif.i.cate (pon.TIF.uh.kit) *n.* a pontiff's office or term of office. —*v.* (-cate) **-cates, -cat.ed, -cat.ing** 1 officiate as a pontiff. 2 speak pompously: *to pontificate on a subject one knows little about.*

pon.toon (pon.TOON) *n.* 1 a flat-bottomed boat: *a temporary* **pontoon bridge** *(that is supported by pontoons).* 2 one of the floats on the landing gear of a seaplane; also, any similar float.

pon.y (POH.nee) *n.* **-nies** 1 a small horse. 2 a small glass of liqueur. 3 *Informal.* a crib, as notes used by a student to cheat on a test.

pony express *n.* a system of transporting mail by a relay of horses, once used in western U.S.

po.ny.tail (POH.nee.tail) *n.* hair tied behind the head and hanging down like a pony's tail.

pooch *n. Informal.* a dog.

poo.dle *n.* a breed of dog with thick curly hair that is clipped or shaved in various styles.

pooh *interj.* indicating impatience or contempt.

pooh-bah *n.* a self-important official with much authority.

pooh-pooh *v.* treat with contempt; dismiss as of no worth.

pool *n.* 1 a small basin or body of water: *indoor, shallow, stagnant, swimming, wading pools.* 2 a puddle or small collection of liquid: *The accident victim lay in a pool of blood.* 3 a form of billiards, played on a six-pocket **pool table**, often in a **pool hall** or **pool room**: *He was shooting pool all evening.* 4 a group or combination of people or resources for a common purpose: *We formed a car pool (to share the driving to work); a gene pool; a typing pool (of available typists); football pools.* 5 a business combine or cartel for controlling a market. —*v.* put in a common fund: *We pooled our talents to make the show a success.*

poop *n.* 1 a raised deck at the stern of a ship; also **poop deck**. 2 *Informal.* excrement: *dog poop; A* **poop scoop** *bylaw requires dog owners to clean up after their pets in public places.* 3 *Informal.* inside information: *Here's the straight poop on video games; a* **poop sheet** *handed out to journalists.* —*v. Informal.* be exhausted: *Pat's all* **pooped out** *at the end of the day.*

poor *adj.* 1 lacking in quality or amount: *a poor essay, job, performance; a poor showing at the polls; poor English; He's poor in spelling.* 2 needy: *one of the poorer Third World countries; the poor people; a poor widow; the rich and* **the poor** *(people).* 3 needing pity: *a poor orphan; Poor me!* —**poor.ly** *adv.*

poor.house *n.* formerly, a publicly supported institution for the poor.

poor-mouth *v. Informal.* portray oneself as poor for complaining, excusing oneself, etc.

pop *n.* 1 *Informal.* father. 2 a carbonated drink: *orange pop; soda pop.* 3 **pops** *pl.* pop music: *Boston pops orchestra.* 4 **pop** or **Pop**, art that uses everyday subjects and techniques based on commercial art; also **pop art** or **Pop art**; **pop artist** or **pop.ster** *n.* 5 a light explosive sound, as a gun shot: *The cork went pop.* 6 in baseball, a short, high fly ball; also **pop fly, pop-up**. —*adj.* popular in artistic or cultural appeal: *pop art, culture, evangelism, fiction,*

music, psychology, singers.
—v. **pops, popped, pop.ping** do or make happen lightly, quickly, or with a sound: *You will pop* (= burst) *the balloon if you prick it; He popped* (= dropped) *into her office for a short visit; to **pop the question*** (= propose marriage); *hippies popping* (= putting into their mouths quickly) *pills and blowing marijuana; There's no end to the problems that **pop up*** (= rise suddenly) *at work.* —**pop off** *Informal.* **1** die suddenly. **2** talk or write carelessly.

pop.corn *n.* the white kernels of Indian corn puffed out by heating, usu. in a popper.

pope *n.* the head of the Roman Catholic Church.

pop.eyed *adj.* having bulging eyes.

pope.mo.bile (POPE.muh.beel) *n.* a security vehicle used by the pope.

pop fly See POP.

pop.gun *n.* a toy gun that fires a cork or pellets with a popping sound.

pop.in.jay (POP.un.jay) *n.* a vain person; fop.

pop.lar (POP.lur) *n.* a fast-growing tall tree such as the aspen.

pop.lin *n.* a tightly woven ribbed fabric with a plain weave.

pop-off *n. Informal.* a person who pops off in speech or writing.

pop.o.ver (POP.oh.vur) *n.* a light, puffy muffin that pops over the edge of the pan in which it is baked.

pop.per *n.* a utensil for popping corn.

pop.py (POP.ee) *n.* **pop.pies** an herb with large, usu. red flowers and a milky juice: *Bakery products are sometimes flavored with **poppy seed**.*

poppy-cock *n. Informal.* nonsense.

pop.si.cle (POP.si.cul) *n.* a flavored ice on a stick: *He saves his **popsicle sticks** for household uses.* **Popsicle** *Trademark.*

popster same as POP ARTIST.

pop-top *n. & adj.* (a soda or beer container) having a ring for pulling the top open.

pop.u.lace (POP.yuh.lis) *n.* the common people; the masses.

pop.u.lar (POP.yuh.lur) *adj.* of or for the common people, esp. appealing to or liked by them: *a popular belief, figure, government, politician, price; popular opinion; the popular will; teachers who are popular with students; left-wing parties united in a popular front against fascism; a president elected by direct popular vote;* **pop.u.lar.ly** *adv.* —**pop.u.lar.i.ty** (LAIR.i.tee) *n.*

pop.u.lar.ize (POP.yuh.luh.rize) *v.* **-iz.es, -ized, -iz.ing** make popular.

pop.u.late (POP.yuh.late) *v.* **-lates, -lat.ed, -lat.ing** inhabit or supply with people to inhabit: *Animal life existed before humans populated the earth;* *adj.:* *densely, heavily, sparsely **populated** areas.*

pop.u.la.tion (pop.yuh.LAY.shun) *n.* the people or the number of people of a place or group: *the adult male population of a country; aging, expanding, growing, rising, shrinking, transient populations; the falling population of urban areas; The recent **population explosion*** (= rapid rise in population) *all over the world is due to improved living conditions and lower rates of infant mortality.*

pop.u.list (POP.yuh.list) *n.* a member of a political party devoted to helping the common people as against moneyed interests; *adj.:* *a populist agenda, image, movement, party, politician; a populist crusade against conservatives; Is she populist or liberal?* —**pop.u.lism.**

pop.u.lous (POP.yuh.lus) *adj.* thickly populated: *Cities are the most populous areas of a country.* —**pop.u.lous.ness** *n.*

pop-up *n.* a pop-fly.

pop-up menu *n.* a menu that appears on a computer screen when the mouse is clicked and held on a particular selection.

por.ce.lain (POR.sul.in) *n.* a fine-grained, white, translucent, glazed ceramic ware; china.

porch *n.* **1** a roofed entrance to a building. **2** a veranda: *a glass-covered sun porch.*

por.cine (POR.sine, -sin) *adj.* of or like pigs or hogs.

por.cu.pine (PORK.yuh.pine) *n.* a large rodent with a covering of long, sharp spines for protection.

pore *n.* a tiny opening on leaves, skin, etc. for the absorption or passage of fluids, as when sweating. —*v.* **pores, pored, por.ing** study long and intently: *She has been poring over that book all day.*

pork *n.* the meat of a pig or hog, esp. when cured.

pork barrel *n.* financial resources used for the political benefit of elected representatives: *a privileged group that draws its nourishment from the pork barrel;* *adja.:* *the **pork-barrel** trough; pork-barrel politicians, politics, projects.*

pork.er *n.* a young hog raised for food.

pork.y *adj.* **pork.i.er, -i.est** like pork: *a porky* (= fat) *fellow.*

porn *n.* [short form] pornography: *hard-core porn; child porn and prostitu-*

tion; **adj.:** *a porno bookstore, film, movie, producer, queen, shop, star.*

por.no [short form] *adj.* pornographic: *nude without being porno; porno films, movies, videotapes.*

por.nog.ra.phy (por.NOG.ruh.fee) *n.* writings and pictures meant to arouse sexual desire: *hard-core, soft-core pornography.* —**por.no.graph.ic** (-nuh.GRAF.ic) *adj.*

po.rous (POR.us) *adj.* full of pores; allowing light, air, etc. to pass through; **po.rous.ly** *adv.* —**po.rous.ness** or **po.ros.i.ty** (puh.ROS.i.tee) *n.*

por.phy.ry (POR.fuh.ree) *n.* **-ries** an igneous rock containing large crystals of one kind, as feldspar, in a mass of smaller crystals, as in some granites. —**por.phy.rit.ic** (-RIT.ic) *adj.*

por.poise (POR.pus) *n.* **-pois.es** 1 a smaller kind of sea mammal than a whale. 2 a dolphin.

por.ridge (POR.ij) *n. Brit.* a soft food of cereal or oatmeal boiled in milk until thick.

por.rin.ger (POR.in.jur) *n.* a small basin or bowl for serving porridge, soup, etc., esp. to a child.

port *n.* 1 a harbor: *to arrive at, call at a port; to make* or *reach port; return to port; to put into port (and stay there for a time); clear* (= leave) *a port.* 2 a harbor city, esp. a port of entry for cargo and people into a country: *a port city; a port authority.* 3 a strong, dark-red wine of Portugal: *port wine.* 4 a ship's or aircraft's left side for one facing front. 5 an opening, as in a fortress wall. 6 a porthole. 7 a socket or interface for connecting a computer to its peripherals: *joystick, keyboard, mouse, printer ports; parallel and serial ports.* 8 one's bearing or carriage.

port.a.ble (POR.tuh.bul) *adj.* easy to carry or move, as a small TV or computer: *a portable pension plan for employees changing jobs or moving to another region.* —*n.* one that is portable: *classes housed in portables.* —**port.a.bil.i.ty** (-BIL.i.tee) *n.*

port.age (POR.tij) *n.* a place or route for carrying boats and provisions overland, as from one river to another; **adj.:** *a portage path, road, route, track.* —*v.* **-ag.es, -aged, -ag.ing** carry boats and cargoes at a portage: *They rode the rapids and portaged around the waterfalls.*

por.tal (POR.tul) *n.* an entrance, esp. an imposing one.

portal-to-portal *adj.* relating to a workman's time between entering the employer's premises and leaving it, irrespective of the actual place of work: *portal-to-portal pay.*

port.cul.lis (port.CULL.is) *n.* an iron grating that is slid down grooves to close the gateway of an ancient fortress.

porte-co.chere (port.coh.SHARE) *n.* a roofed porch at the entrance to a building for vehicles to stop to let off or take in people.

por.tend (por.TEND) *v.* be a warning of some future event; bode.

por.tent (POR.tent) *n.* a foreboding or omen.

por.ten.tous (por.TEN.tus) *adj.* 1 ominous or foreboding: *a portentous forecast, statement, warning.* 2 arousing awe; amazing; hence, pompous: *portentous ruminations, utterances; portentous obscurity; a portentous pretender.*

por.ter *n.* 1 a servant such as baggage carrier, doorman, or janitor in a hotel, train, etc. 2 a heavy, dark-brown beer.

por.ter.house (POR.tur.house) *n.* a choice cut of beef between sirloin and tenderloin; also **porterhouse steak.**

port.fo.li.o (port.FOH.lee.oh) *n.* **-os** 1 a thin, flat case, usu. of leather, for papers and documents. 2 the office or department of a cabinet minister: *A minister without portfolio has general functions.* 3 a list of one's investments such as stocks and bonds.

port.hole *n.* an opening in a ship's or aircraft's side as a window.

por.ti.co (POR.ti.coh) *n.* **-cos** or **-coes** a porch with a row of columns supporting its roof. —**por.ti.coed** (-code) *adj.: a porticoed entrance, hotel.*

por.tiere (port.YAIR) *n.* a curtain hung over a doorway.

por.tion (POR.shun) *n.* 1 a shared part of something, as a serving of food, an inheritance, or a dowry. 2 one's lot in life: *Sorrow was her portion all life long.* —*v.* distribute: *The aged farmer portioned out the land among his children.*

portland cement *n.* a fine cement made by burning limestone and clay, used in making concrete that originally had the color of stone from Portland, England.

port.ly *adj.* **-li.er, -li.est** fat but stately in bearing: *a portly gentleman.* —**port.li.ness** *n.*

port.man.teau (port.MAN.toh) *n.* **-teaus** or **-teaux** a suitcase that opens into two compartments hinged together.

portmanteau word *n.* a word formed by joining two words together, as

"motel" (*mo*tor + h*otel*) or "smog" (*s*moke + f*og*).
port of call *n.* a port where ships stop for repairs, supplies, cargo, etc.
port of entry *n.* an official port for cargo and people to enter a country.
por.trait (POR.trit, -trait) *n.* **1** a picture or representation, esp. of a person or persons: *to commission, paint, pose for or sit for a portrait; family portraits.* **2** a graphic or dramatic portrayal: *The book is a portrait of a very controversial figure.*
por.trait.ist (POR.tray.tist) *n.* one who paints portraits.
por.trai.ture (POR.truh.chur) *n.* **1** the art of portraying; portrayal. **2** a portrait.
por.tray (por.TRAY) *v.* **1** draw or paint a picture of a person or thing: *An artist portrays a scene; a book that portrays (in words) pioneer life; people portrayed as heroes.* **2** act out or enact: *a character hard to portray on the modern stage.*
—**por.tray.al** (-ul) *n.*: *the portrayal of women in the media; the actor's portrayal of Portia.*
Por.tu.guese (por.chuh.GEEZ, "G" as in "go") *n. sing. & pl.* **1** a person of or from **Portugal**, a country of S.W. Europe. **2** the language of Portugal and Brazil. Also *adj.*
Portuguese man-of-war *n.* a jellyfish that is a colony of animals attached to a gas-filled float from which hang long tentacles for grasping at fish, stinging, etc.
por.tu.lac.a (por.chuh.LAC.uh) *n.* a low-growing fleshy tropical plant of the purslane family bearing brilliant flowers.
port-wine *adja.* having to do with a large birthmark of purplish color, usu. on the face or neck: *port-wine birthmarks, stains; port-wine stain birthmarks.*
pose (POZE) *v.* **pos.es, posed, pos.ing 1** assume or make assume a certain position: *Pat can pose for hours; to pose for a photograph; A photographer poses a group for a picture; Pat only poses (= works as a model) for artists.* **2** affect a posture or attitude; pretend to be someone else: *He gained entry by posing as a detective.* **3** raise a question, esp. a baffling one: *Overpopulation poses many problems; to pose a challenge, danger, question, threat.* —*n.* a posing: *He assumes the pose of a martyr; to strike a pose; his pose as a pundit; His piety is a mere pose.*
pos.er (POH.zur) *n.* **1** one who poses. **2** something baffling.

po.seur (poh.ZUR) *n.* one who poses for effect.
posh *adj. Informal.* elegant or luxurious: *a posh hotel, job, neighborhood.*
pos.it (POZ.it) *v.* put forward as a fact; postulate.
po.si.tion (puh.ZISH.un) *n.* **1** a place or location, esp. in relation to other factors: *Troops move into position before a parade; to take a safe position behind a wall; to negotiate from a position of strength; I'm not in a position to tell you what is going on; defensive, dominant, embarrassing, impregnable, leading, ludicrous, prominent, vulnerable positions; opposing parties maneuvering for position* (= a position of advantage); *to attack, hold, occupy, regain, storm, surrender, take up a position* (= military site). **2** a posture: *to assume a kneeling position; awkward, prone, sitting, squatting, supine positions; the fetal and lotus positions.* **3** a stand, as on an issue: *to take a firm, radical, strong position on the death penalty; I don't agree with your position; a position paper for discussing policy.* **4** a post of employment: *clerical, government, permanent, teaching, temporary, vacant positions; to apply for, find, seek a position.* **5** a high rank: *men and women of position in our company.* —*v.* to place or post: *Troops are positioned in readiness for action.* —**po.si.tion.al** *adj.*
pos.i.tive (POZ.uh.tiv) *adj.* **1** not negative: *"Yes" is a positive answer; Current flows from a battery's positive terminal; a positive pregnancy test; a positive (photographic) print; a positive integer* (= whole number greater than zero) *such as 3.* **2** definite: *He's not just sure but quite positive about it; a positive refusal; We need helpful, positive* (= creative) *criticisms.* —*n.* something positive: *Two negatives make a positive.*
—**pos.i.tive.ly** *adv.*; **pos.i.tive.ness** *n.*
pos.i.tron (POZ.i.tron) *n.* the positive antiparticle of an electron.
pos.se (POS.ee) *n.* a body of persons having legal authority: *a posse of constables.*
pos.sess (puh.ZES) *v.* **1** have as a natural or acquired quality or skill; own: *a beggar who possesses nothing; an orator possessing great powers of persuasion*; *adjp.*: *a woman possessed of initiative and enterprise.* **2** gain control over someone; dominate: *What possessed you to behave like that?* *adjp.*: *a woman possessed with fury; an apostle possessed by missionary zeal; adj.*: *to exorcise a possessed person* (= one controlled by an evil spirit). —**pos.ses.sor** *n.*

pos.ses.sion (puh.ZESH.un) *n.* **1** ownership: *to get or take possession of a newly bought house; a will made while in possession of one's senses.* **2** something owned: *Guam was made a possession of Spain in 1561; He gave away all his (material) possessions and became a monk.*

pos.ses.sive (puh.ZES.iv) *adj.* having to do with possession: *the possessive instinct; a possessive nature, parent;* **adja.:** *a possessive adjective such as "my", "his," or "your"; "Mine" and "theirs" are* **possessive pronouns;** *The words are in the possessive case.* —*n.* the possessive case or a word in the possessive.
—**pos.ses.sive.ly** *adv.;*
pos.ses.sive.ness *n.*

pos.si.ble (POS.uh.bul) *adj.* that can exist, happen, or be done: *Please apply as soon as possible; at the earliest possible date; It's possible to beat cancer; anything that is humanly possible.* —**pos.si.bil.i.ty** (-BIL.i.tee) *n.* **-ties.**

pos.si.bly (POS.uh.blee) *adv.* **1** by any chance: *How could you possibly do such a thing?* **2** perhaps: *She's away, possibly out of town.*

pos.sum (POS.um) *n. Informal.* same as OPOSSUM. —**play possum** pretend to be asleep or dead.

post- *prefix.* after in time or place: *postgraduate, postlude, post-mortem.*

post (*rhyme:* most) *n.* **1** an upright piece of wood or metal supporting or displaying something, as a bedpost, lamppost, or signpost: *Two goal posts define the goal.* **2** a place of duty; job: *Stay at your posts; the post of Secretary of State.* **3** station: *command, listening, observation, trading posts.* **4** postal service: *book post; parcel post.* **5** *Brit.* mail: *My post is full of praise for the new book; Please reply* **by return of post** (= by return mail).
—*v.* **1** put up or display: *We'll post it on the bulletin board; The new business is posting sales of $1 million a year;* **adja.:** *Obey* **posted** *speed limits; posted prices, signs.* **2** to place on duty; station: *A sentry is posted at a gate; He has been posted to London.* **3** mail: *a letter posted in London;* **adjp.:** *We'll* **keep you posted** (=keep you informed) *on what happens.*

post.age (POSE.tij) *n.* the charge for mailing something, usu. paid by means of **postage stamps** or a **postage meter** that imprints mail and records the charges.

post.al (POSE.tul) *adj.* having to do with the post office: *the postal system; the U.S. Postal Service* (= department); *Unlike a picture postcard, a* **postal card** *has a postage stamp printed on it; The Ca-*
nadian **postal code** *consists of six alternating letters and numbers that identify a mail delivery area, as L4W 2C3.*

post.card *n.* **1** a card with a picture on one side and space on the other for a short message; also called a "picture postcard." **2** a postal card.

post chaise *n.* a four-wheeled closed carriage.

post.code *n.* the British postal code, as OX2 6DP.

post.date (post.DATE) *v.* **-dates, -dat.ed, -dat.ing** to date a check, letter, etc. later than the actual time of writing it; *adj.:* a *postdated* check, document.

post.er *n.* a placard for posting, as in a public place: *a campaign poster; to put up wall posters.*

poster boy *n.* a person seen as a publicity symbol for a cause or movement.

pos.te.ri.or (pos.TEER.ee.ur) *n.* the buttocks. —*adj.* coming after in position or time.

pos.ter.i.ty (pos.TER.i.tee) *n.* descendants; future generations.

pos.tern (POH.sturn) *n.* a back door or gate: *a postern door.*

post exchange *n.* a store at a military post.

post.grad.u.ate (post.GRAJ.oo.it) *adja.* following a bachelor's degree; graduate: *postgraduate degrees such as M.A. and Ph.D.* —*n.* a postgraduate student.

post.haste *adv.* with all speed.

post.hu.mous (POS.choo.mus) *adja.* after one's death: *a posthumous award received by his widow; her posthumous daughter* (born after the father's death).
—**post.hu.mous.ly** *adv.: a book published posthumously* (= after the author's death).

post.hyp.not.ic (post.hip.NOT.ic) *adj.* made during hypnosis for carrying out afterward: *a posthypnotic suggestion.*

post.ie (POSE.tee) *n. Informal.* a postal worker, esp. a letter carrier.

pos.til.ion (pose.TIL.yun) *n.* in horse-drawn vehicles, one who guides the team of horses by riding the leading horse. Also **pos.til.lion** *Cdn.*

post.im.pres.sion.ism (post.im.PRESH.un.iz.um) *n.* a school of late 19th-century painting in revolt against impressionism.

post-industrial *adj.* having to do with the era following industrialization: *from an industrial to a post-industrial or information age; a post-industrial future, society, world.*

post.lude *n.* **1** a concluding piece of

music. 2 a final phase.
post.man (POST.mun) *n.* **-men** a mailman; letter carrier.
post.mark *n.* a mark stamped on mail by the post office to show the place and date of mailing: *a February 29 postmark.* —*v.*: *an envelope postmarked London.*
post.mas.ter (POST.mas.tur) *n.* a person in charge of a post office: *The Postmaster General heads the U.S. Postal Service.* —**post.mis.tress** (POST.mis.tris) *fem.*
post.mod.ern (POST.mod.urn) *adj.* in art, architecture, and literature, having to do with a departure from modern tendencies: *the first truly postmodern automobile; Is the postmodern "whole language" method of teaching reading responsible for illiterate high-school graduates?* Also **post-modern.** —**post.mod.ern.ism** *n.*; **post.mod.ern.ist** *n. & adj.*
post.mor.tem (POST.mor.tum) *n.* 1 the examination of a body after death, as by a coroner, to determine the cause of death: *to carry out* or *conduct a post-mortem on a body;* **adja.:** *a post-mortem examination, finding, report.* 2 an inquiry following an event: *a post-mortem on the failure of a bank.* —**post mortem** *adv.* after the event: *The study was conducted post mortem by the experts.*
post.na.sal drip (post.NAY.zul-) *n.* the dripping of mucus from the sinuses down the back of the throat.
post.na.tal (post.NAY.tul) *adj.* following childbirth: *postnatal care.*
post office *n.* 1 a place where mail is received for distribution, stamps are sold, etc.: *A private post office box or "lock box" may be rented for receiving mail.* 2 esp. **Post Office,** a government agency in charge of mail.
post.op.er.a.tive (post.OP.uh.ruh.tiv) *adj.* following a surgical operation: *postoperative care, fever, infection, pain; the postoperative period.*
post.paid *adv.* with the postage already paid: *We'll send it postpaid for a few dollars;* **adj.:** *a postpaid* (= stamped) *envelope for reply.*
post.par.tum (post.PAR.tum) *adj.* of the period after childbirth: *postpartum blues, care, depression, women.*
post.pone (post.PONE) *v.* **-pones, -poned, -pon.ing** put off or delay: *"Do not postpone till tomorrow what you can do today."* —**post.pone.ment** *n.*
post road *n.* a road over which mail is or was carried.
post.script *n.* something written as an afterthought: *She added a postscript to the letter saying "P.S. I love you."*
post time *n.* the time scheduled for the start of a horse race.
pos.tu.lant (POS.chuh.lunt) *n.* a candidate seeking admission to a religious order.
pos.tu.late (POS.chuh.late) *v.* **-lates, -lat.ed, -lat.ing** assume as a basic truth or axiom; hence, require logically: *Do natural phenomena postulate the existence of the supernatural?* —*n.* a fundamental principle.
pos.ture (POS.chur) *n.* 1 a way of holding the body: *an erect posture; in a reclining posture; exercises to improve the posture.* 2 a state, condition, or attitude: *a holier-than-thou posture; a defensive posture against the enemy.* —*v.* **-tures, -tured, -tur.ing** assume a posture, esp. for effect. —**pos.tu.ral** (POS.chur.ul) *adj.*
post.war *adja.* after-the-war: *the postwar population increase.*
po.sy (POH.zee) *n.* **-sies** [old use] 1 same as POESY. 2 a motto in verse. 3 a bouquet.
pot *n.* 1 a round vessel for domestic use: *to scour pots and pans; a chamber pot; a melting pot of many cultures.* 2 *Informal.* in betting, the entire stake; kitty. 3 *Informal.* marijuana. —**go to pot** go to ruin. —*v.* **pots, pot.ted, pot.ting** put into a pot for keeping or cooking; **adj.:** *a room full of **potted** plants; a potted* (= condensed; also, canned) *history of China.*
po.ta.ble (POH.tuh.bul) *n. & adj.* (something) drinkable. —**po.ta.bil.i.ty** (-BIL.i.tee) *n.*: *water of doubtful potability.*
pot.ash *n.* a potassium compound obtained from wood ashes for use mainly as a fertilizer.
po.tas.si.um (puh.TAS.ee.um) *n.* a soft, silver-white metallic chemical element.
potassium carbonate *n.* a potassium compound used in glass-making, soaps, etc.
potassium cyanide *n.* a poisonous compound used as an insecticide.
potassium nitrate *n.* a salt used in explosives, to preserve meat, and in medicine.
po.ta.tion (poh.TAY.shun) *n.* a drink, esp. of alcoholic liquor.
po.ta.to (puh.TAY.toh) *n.* **-toes** the round, hard, starchy underground stem of a widely cultivated plant, eaten baked, boiled, mashed, or fried crisp in slices called **potato chips** or in strips called **French fries.**

potato salad *n.* boiled and sliced potatoes mixed with dressing, served cold, as at delis.

pot.bel.ly (POT.bel.ee) *n.* **-bel.lies** a protruding belly; *adj.*: *a potbellied stove (with a rounded body).*

pot.boil.er (POT.boy.lur) *n.* a usu. second-rate work, esp. a book written for one's livelihood.

po.tent (POH.tunt) *adj.* powerful or effective: *a potent argument, brew, dose, drug, force, issue, medicine, ruler, weapon; He's no longer potent* (= capable of sexual intercourse) *after his illness;* **po.tent.ly** *adv.* —**po.ten.cy** (-tun.see) *n.*

po.ten.tate (POH.tun.tate) *n.* a ruler or sovereign.

po.ten.tial (puh.TEN.shul) *adj.* capable of coming into being: *I see in her a potential leader; Our profits are potential rather than actual; A coiled spring has* **potential energy.** —*n.* what one can become: *a new recruit with great potential for high positions; full potential; growth potential; market potential.*
—**po.ten.tial.ly** *adv.* —**po.ten.ti.al.i.ty** (-shee.AL.i.tee) *n.*

po.ten.ti.ate (puh.TEN.shee.ate) *v.* **-ates, -at.ed, -at.ing** make more powerful: *alcohol potentiated by drugs.*
—**po.ten.ti.a.tion** (-AY.shun) *n.*

pot.head *n. Slang.* a habitual marijuana user.

poth.er ("th" as in "thin") *n. & v.* fuss or bother.

pot.herb *n.* an herb used as a vegetable or in flavoring, as the mustard plant or mint.

pot.hole *n.* a rounded hole or depression, as in a rocky river bed or worn-out road surface.

pot.hook *n.* a hook for hanging a pot over a fire or for lifting hot pots and lids.

po.tion (POH.shun) *n.* a drink, esp. one that is medicinal, poisonous, or supposedly magical: *a love potion.*

pot.luck *n.* food that is available as regular fare: *Surprise visitors are invited to take potluck with the family; We had a* **potluck supper** (*party with the guests bringing their own favorite dishes*).

pot.pie *n.* a meat pie baked in a pot, with only a top crust.

pot.pour.ri (poh.poo.REE) *n.* a medley of musical or literary pieces.

pot.roast *n.* beef browned and cooked slowly in a closed pot with only a little water.

pot.sherd *n.* a broken bit of pottery.

pot.shot *n.* a random or casual shot with no regard for rules: *The new play seemed an easy target for critics to* **take potshots at.**

pot.tage (POT.ij) *n.* [old use] a kind of thick soup or stew: *a mess of pottage.*

pot.ter (POT.ur) same as PUTTER.
—*n.* one who makes pottery.

pot.ter.y (POT.uh.ree) *n.* **-ter.ies 1** pots, pans, vases, etc. made of clay. **2** the potter's art. **3** a potter's workshop.

pot.ty (POT.ee) *n.* a child's toilet: *a baby potty with a music box attached.*
—*adj. Informal.* crazy or eccentric: *a potty aristocrat, comedy; Pat's gone completely potty.*

pouch (POWCH) *n.* **1** a small bag or sack, as for keeping or carrying something: *a diplomatic pouch (for documents or messages); a mail pouch; a tobacco pouch.* **2** an animal's baglike body part, as a kangaroo's pocket or the one under a pelican's bill.
—*v.* put in a pouch: *a pocket gopher pouching nuts under a tree;* **adj.**: *Marsupials are* **pouched** *animals (that have an external pouch for carrying their young).*
—**pouch.y** *adj.*: *cheeks pouchy with age.*

poult (POHLT) *n.* a young fowl, esp. a turkey.

poul.ter.er (POHL.tur.ur) *n. Brit.* one who deals in poultry.

poul.tice (POLE.tis) *n.* a warm, pulpy mass, as of mustard, herbs, flour, etc., applied to a body part as a dressing.

poul.try (POLE.tree) *n.* domestic fowls such as chickens, turkeys, ducks, and geese: *a poultry farmer.*

pounce *v.* **pounc.es, pounced, pounc.ing** swoop down, as if to seize a person or thing: *He greedily pounces on every opportunity to make some money.*

pound *n.* **1** an enclosure for confining stray dogs, cattle, or for cars impounded by police. **2** a trap for fish, forming part of a "pound net." **3** a pounding or its sound. **4** the basic money unit of the U.K. and certain African and Middle Eastern countries. **5** a unit of weight equal to 16 oz. (0.4536 kg). —*v.* strike or hit heavily and repeatedly: *Knock once, don't pound on my door; Use a mortar and pestle to pound the medication; His heart was pounding with terror; She* **pounded out** *the story on her old typewriter; The unemployed* **pound the pavement** (= walk the streets) *looking for work;* **adj**.: *a* **pounding** *headache, heart, rhythm.*

pound.age (POUND.ij) *n.* **1** the weight in pounds. **2** the per-pound rate of tax, etc. **3** a confining or the fee charged at an animal pound.

pound cake *n.* a cake rich in eggs,

which used to be made with a pound each of flour, butter, sugar, etc.

pound-foolish *adj.* careless about large sums of money: *"penny-wise and pound-foolish."*

pour (POR) *v.* flow or cause to flow, as a stream, flood, or heavy rain, freely, copiously, or steadily: *Please pour me a glass of water; a child pouring forth his tale of sorrow with tears pouring down his cheeks; Rush-hour crowds pour out of the subway.*

pour.boire (poor.BWAR) *n.* a tip or gratuity.

pout (POWT) *v.* show displeasure by pushing out the lips; sulk. —*n.* a sulk: *She continued in a pout till she had her way.* —**pout.er** *n.*

pov.er.ty (POV.ur.tee) *n.* the condition of being poor; want or deficiency: *Many people live in poverty all their lives; to eliminate, eradicate, wipe out poverty; abject, dire, grinding poverty; a poverty of talent; People live above, at, or below the* **poverty line** or **poverty level** (= the minimum income needed for buying food, shelter, and clothing) *which, in 1990, was $12,675 for an American family of four;* *adj.*: *the poverty-stricken countries of the Third World.*

pow.der (POW.dur) *n.* **1** a dry material of fine particles such as some cosmetics, medicines, etc.: *bleaching, dusting, scouring, talcum powder.* **2** gunpowder: *That fight is not worth* **powder and shot**; *Watch out and* **keep your powder dry** (= stay calm). —*v.*: *She powders* (= puts powder on) *her nose;* *adj.*: *powdered faces, hair; a drug in powdered form;* **powdered milk** (= milk in powder form). —**pow.der.y** *adj.*

powder keg *n.* **1** a cask containing gunpowder. **2** a potentially explosive situation.

powder puff *n.* a pad or ball for applying face powder. —**powder-puff** *adja.* *Informal.* of appeal mainly to women: *powder-puff journalism.*

powder room *n.* a lavatory equipped with a toilet and sink, as near the entrance to a home.

pow.er *n.* **1** authority or strength: *the discretionary powers of a judge; to assume, exercise, seize, wield power; the government* **in power**; *A new government* **comes (in)to power** *after a general election.* **2** capability: *your powers of observation; bargaining, earning, purchasing power; supernatural powers; a nation's air, fire, military, naval, sea power.* **3** a person or state having authority and strength: *an economic summit of the seven major powers; a world power; nuclear powers;* **The powers that be** (= the authorities) *willed otherwise.* **4** source of energy: *to cut off, turn off, turn on the power; electric, nuclear, solar, water, wind power.* —*v.* provide with power: *a small car powered by a big engine.* —*adj.*: *an automobile equipped with* **power brakes** *and* **power steering**; *a power mower, saw; a party's* **power base** (= center of support) *eroded by scandals; The Mayor was a* **power broker** (= influence peddler) *for politicians; a* **power line** (= wire conducting electricity) *downed by a storm; The vice-president was jobless after a* **power struggle** *in the company.* —**pow.er.ful** *adj.*; **pow.er.ful.ly** *adv.*

power of attorney *n.* a document authorizing another to act for one in a legal matter.

power pack *n.* a device for converting electricity to the voltage required for an electronic circuit.

power plant *n.* **1** the engine and related parts of an automobile, aircraft, or ship. **2** a plant in which electricity is generated; also **powerhouse, power station**.

power structure *n.* a controlling group or system: *the power structure of a male-dominated society.*

power train *n.* the mechanism by which power is transmitted from an automobile engine to its axle, including the clutch, transmission, and drive shaft.

pow.wow *n.* **1** a get-together of or with North American Indians. **2** *Informal.* any conference.

pox *n.* **1** a disease such as "chicken pox" or "smallpox" that leaves pock marks on the skin: *A* **pox** (= curse) *on drug-pushers!* **2 the pox** syphilis.

prac.ti.ca.ble (PRAC.ti.cuh.bul) *adj.* that can be put into practice; feasible: *A trip to the moon may be practicable but is hardly a practical idea for a holiday;* **prac.ti.ca.bly** *adv.* —**prac.ti.ca.bil.i.ty** (-BIL.i.tee) *n.*

prac.ti.cal (PRAC.ti.cul) *adj.* **1** having to do with practice rather than theory or ideas: *a scheme full of practical difficulties; It's too unwieldy for practical purposes, a practical mind.* **2** engaged in practice or work: *a practical farmer, physicist.* **3** virtual: *Jack is the boss, but Jill is in practical control.*

—**prac.ti.cal.ly** (-tic.lee) *adv.*
—**prac.ti.cal.i.ty** (-CAL.i.tee) *n.*

practical joke *n.* a trick played on someone for causing embarrassment, as the hotfoot.

practical nurse *n.* a nurse who helps

professional nurses with day-to-day tasks of caring for the sick.

prac.tice (PRAC.tis) *n.* **1** a custom: *superstitious practices such as fortune-telling and voodoo.* **2** a habit: *Sam makes a practice of arriving late; It's a common practice around here.* **3** exercise: *He's out of practice on the violin; target practice; "Practice makes perfect"; a plan that is difficult to* **put into practice** (= carry out). **4** business of a professional nature: *a flourishing law practice; the practice of accountancy, medicine, nursing; group practice (by many professionals on the same premises); a lucrative private practice.* **5** business method: *fair-trade, sharp, unethical practices.*
—*v.* (PRAC.tis) *v.* **-tic.es, -ticed, -tic.ing** **1** do something habitually: *He practices what he preaches.* **2** do something customarily: *to practice one's religion;* **adj.a.:** *a* **practicing** *Catholic, Jew.* **3** do something repeatedly; exercise: *She practices the piano daily; to practice charity, economy, patience, singing;* **adj.a.:** *He bore it with* **practiced** (= skilled) *coolness; a practiced pickpocket.* **4** do something professionally: *to practice accountancy, law, medicine; to practice as a dentist;* **adj.a.:** *a* **practicing** *lawyer.*

practise *Cdn.* PRACTICE.

prac.ti.tion.er (prac.TISH.uh.nur) *n.* one who practices a profession such as medicine: *family, general, nurse practitioners.*

prae.tor (PREE.tor) *n.* a law official of ancient Rome, with rank next below consul.

prae.to.ri.an guard (pree.TOR.ee.un-) *n.* a Roman emperor's bodyguard.

prag.mat.ic or **prag.mat.i.cal** (prag.MAT.i.cul) *adj.* **1** concerned with practical values; matter-of-fact. **2** having to do with pragmatism: *pragmatic philosophy.* —**prag.mat.i.cal.ly** *adv.*

prag.ma.tism (PRAG.muh.tiz.um) *n.* the philosophy of judging things by how they work rather than by abstract values of truth and goodness.
—**prag.ma.tist** *n. & adj.*

prai.rie (PRAIR.ee) *n.* a region of level or rolling land with tall grass but few trees: *a house on the windswept prairie; the Canadian* **Prairie Provinces** *of Alberta, Saskatchewan, and Manitoba.*

prairie dog *n.* a squirrellike rodent of the North American prairies with a shrill doglike bark.

prairie schooner *n.* a large covered wagon used by pioneers to travel across the prairies.

praise (PRAIZ) *v.* **prais.es, praised, prais.ing** **1** worship: *the Lord be praised!* **2** speak of a person or thing with admiration: *He was praised by some and hated by others; She was highly praised for her courage.*
—*n.* a praising: *The principal's speech was in praise of his teachers; a cook who receives only praises; to bestow, heap, lavish praise on someone; faint, glowing, unstinting praise; She bores me by* **singing the praises** *of her children all day long; Praise be to God* (= May God be worshiped)!

praise.wor.thy (PRAIZ.wur.thee, "th" as in "the") *adj.* worthy of praise: *a praiseworthy act; praiseworthy behavior.*
—**praise.wor.thi.ly** *adv.;*
praise.wor.thi.ness *n.*

pra.line (PRAY.leen, PRAH-) *n.* a candy made of brown sugar and nuts.

pram *Brit.* [short form] perambulator.

prance *v.* **pranc.es, pranced, pranc.ing** **1** raise the forelegs and spring, as a horse does. **2** strut about; swagger: *to prance around the stage.* Also *n.*

prank *n.* a mischievous trick played on someone. —**prank.ish** *adj.*
—**prank.ster** *n.*

pra.se.o.dym.i.um (PRAY.zee.oh.DIM.ee.um) *n.* a yellowish-white metallic chemical element.

prate *v.* **prates, prat.ed, prat.ing** talk foolishly and at length. —**prat.er** *n.*

prat.fall *n. Informal.* a fall on one's buttocks.

prat.tle (PRAT.ul) *v.* **prat.tles, prat.tled, prat.tling** **1** prate: *when politicians prattle about family values; Let them prattle on.* **2** babble. —**prat.tler** *n.*

prawn *n.* a shellfish that is larger than a shrimp.

pray *v.* **1** worship God; also, ask for divine favor: *She prays before going to bed; They pray (to) God for help; a hopeless case that is* **past praying for.** **2** ask humbly; entreat: *He prayed his dad not to ground him.* **3** *Formal.* please: *Pray be careful.*

pray.er (PRAY.ur) *n.* one who prays.

prayer (PRAIR) *n.* an act of praying: *to offer a fervent prayer in a moment of danger; a prayer for the dead; Columbus knelt down in prayer on landing in the New World; He says his* **prayers** *every night; The* **Book of Common Prayer** (= Church of England's official liturgy); *Mail-order businesses would* **not have a prayer** (= not have a chance) *without an 800 number; Everything is riding* **on a wing and a prayer** (= on chance); **adj.a.:** *a prayer book, room,* service. **—prayer.ful** *adj.*; **prayer.ful.ly** *adv.*

praying mantis same as MANTIS.

pre- *prefix.* before in time, position, etc.: *prearranged, precursor, prefix.*

preach (PREECH) *v.* **1** deliver a sermon: *to preach to our congregation.* **2** set forth or urge in a moralistic tone, usu. in a tiresome way: *always preaching (about) social justice; He likes to preach in his classes; Stop preaching at me and start practicing.* **—preach.er** *n.* **—preach.y** *adj.*

pre.am.ble (PREE.am.bul) *n.* an introduction to a constitution, statute, etc.

pre.ar.range (pree.uh.RAINJ) *v.* **-ar.rang.es, -ar.ranged, -ar.rang.ing** arrange beforehand; **pre.ar.range.ment** *n.*

Pre.cam.bri.an (pree.CAM.bree.un) *n. & adj.* (of) the earliest era of geological time, ending about 570 million years ago.

pre.can.cer.ous (pree.CAN.suh.rus) *adj.* of tissue, that may develop into cancer: *precancerous lesions, polyps, sores.*

pre.car.i.ous (pri.CAIR.ee.us) *adj.* dependent on chance; uncertain: *a precarious existence in a war-torn country; a precarious hold, position.* **—pre.car.i.ous.ly** *adv.*; **pre.car.i.ous.ness** *n.*

pre.cau.tion (pri.CAW.shun) *n.* care taken against danger, failure, etc. or to ensure good results: *a fire-safety precaution; elaborate precautions against being robbed.* **—pre.cau.tion.ar.y** (-shuh.nair.ee) *adj.*: *a precautionary measure.*

pre.cede (pri.SEED) *v.* **-cedes, -ced.ed, -ced.ing** be or happen before in time, position, order, etc.: *A precedes B in alphabetical order;* **adja.:** *the preceding example; in the preceding year.*

prec.e.dence (PRESS.uh.dunce, pri.SEE.dunce) *n.* higher position, rank, importance, etc.: *Emergency cases take precedence over routine ones.*

prec.ed.ent (PRESS.uh.dunt) *n.* a previous case that serves as an example: *Judgments cite, create, establish, set precedents, The destruction of Hiroshima and Nagasaki is without precedent in human history.* **—adj.** (pri.SEE.dunt) preceding: *precedent circumstances.*

pre.cen.tor (pri.SEN.tur) *n.* one who heads a church choir or congregational singing.

pre.cept (PREE.sept) *n.* a rule of behavior; maxim: *to persuade by example rather than by precept; A familiar precept is "Look before you leap."*

pre.cep.tor (pree.SEP.tur) *n.* a teacher or instructor: *a preceptor to the prince.*

pre.ces.sion (pri.SESH.un) *n.* a forward movement, as the **precession of the equinoxes**, the earlier occurrence of the equinoxes in each successive year caused by the gyration of the earth's rotating axis; **pre.ces.sion.al** *adj.*

pre.cinct (PREE.sinct) *n.* **1** a subdivision or district: *election, police, voting precincts.* **2 precincts** *pl.* grounds or enclosure: *No smoking within the school precincts.*

pre.ci.os.i.ty (presh.ee.OS.i.tee) *n.* **-ties** a being affected or fastidious.

pre.cious (PRESH.us) *adj.* **1** of great value: *gold, silver, and such precious metals; a precious gem, stone; precious qualities; a precious* (= beloved) *child.* **2** affected or overstylized: *a model's precious manner.* **—adv.** very: *precious few, little.* **—pre.cious.ly** *adv.*; **pre.cious.ness** *n.*

prec.i.pice (PRES.uh.pis) *n.* a steep cliff or vertical rock face.

pre.cip.i.tan.cy (pri.SIP.uh.tun.see) *n.* undue haste or suddenness.

pre.cip.i.tant (pri.SIP.i.tunt) *adj.* hasty or sudden. **—n.** what is precipitated, as from a solution.

pre.cip.i.tate (pri.SIP.uh.tate) *v.* **-tates, -tat.ed, -tat.ing 1** cause to happen abruptly: *a border incident that precipitated a crisis; to precipitate a conflict, decision, downfall, revolution, strike; It precipitated* (= pushed) *the country into war.* **2** cause to fall, as from a surrounding medium: *Salt precipitates as its solution cools.* **—n.** a substance, usu. in crystal form, obtained by precipitation. **—adj. 1** hasty or rash: *to be precipitate in one's actions.* **2** very steep or sudden: *a precipitate drop, slope; the precipitate fall of communism; a precipitate decline in sales.* **—pre.cip.i.tate.ly** *adv.*

pre.cip.i.ta.tion (pri.SIP.uh.TAY.shun) *n.* **1** what falls from the atmosphere: *forms of precipitation such as rain, snow, and hail; a region of heavy precipitation; acid precipitation.* **2** precipitancy.

pre.cip.i.tous (pri.SIP.uh.tus) *adj.* very steep, almost vertical: *a precipitous decline, descent, drop, hillside;* **pre.cip.i.tous.ly** *adv.*; **pre.cip.i.tous.ness** *n.*

pré.cis (pray.SEE, PRAY.see) *n., pl.* **-cis** (-SEEZ, -seez) a summary or concise statement.

pre.cise (pri.SICE) *adj.* correct or exact: *a precise account of the incident; very precise in her utterances; Be precise about facts and figures; He's too prim and pre-*

cise for my tastes. —**pre.cise.ly** *adv.*; **pre.cise.ness** *n.*

pre.ci.sion (pri.SIZH.un) *n.* accuracy or exactness: *the precision of a watch; the unerring precision of his aim; A chronometer tells time with the utmost precision; It is a precision instrument.* —**pre.ci.sion.ist** *n.*

pre.clude (pri.CLOOD, long "OO") *v.* to bar or prevent: *The barbed-wire fence precluded all possibility of escape.* —**pre.clu.sion** (-CLOO.zhun) *n.*

pre.co.cious (pri.COH.shus) *adj.* showing early maturity: *a very precocious child;* **pre.co.cious.ly** *adv.*; **pre.co.cious.ness** *n.* —**pre.coc.i.ty** (-COS.i.tee) *n.*

pre.cog.ni.tion (pree.cog.NISH.un) *n.* advance knowledge of an event before it happens. —**pre.cog.ni.tive** (-COG.ni.tiv) *adj.*: *precognitive clairvoyance.*

pre-Columbian (pree.cuh.LUM.bee.un) *adj.* of the period before Christopher Columbus in America: *pre-Columbian America, artifacts, civilizations, history, roots; the pre-Columbian world.*

pre.con.ceive (pree.cun.SEEV) *v.* -ceives, -ceived, -ceiv.ing form an idea or opinion beforehand; *adj.*: *our preconceived notions.* —**pre.con.cep.tion** (-SEP.shun) *n.*

pre.con.cert.ed (pree.cun.SUR.tid) *adj.* arranged beforehand.

pre.con.di.tion (pree.cun.DISH.un) *v.* condition or train beforehand. —*n.* prerequisite.

pre.cook *v.* cook beforehand partially or completely.

pre.cur.sor (pri.CUR.sur) *n.* forerunner: *The drought was a precursor of or to the famine.*

pre.date (PREE.date) *v.* -dates, -dat.ed, -dat.ing same as ANTEDATE.

pre.da.tion (pri.DAY.shun) *n.* the act of preying on another, as a predator does: *sheep losses from predation; male predation (of females).*

pred.a.tor (PRED.uh.tur) *n.* one who plunders or preys on others, as a bird of prey or child molester: *Caterpillars are agricultural predators; garden, livestock predators; sexual predators; predators of children; keeping predators at bay.*

pred.a.to.ry (PRED.uh.tor.ee) *adj.* **1** preying or plundering: *predatory birds such as eagles and hawks; predatory animals, crime, habits, instincts.* **2** exploitative: *predatory businesses, practices, pricing.*

pre.de.cease (pree.di.SEECE) *v.* -ceas.es, -ceased, -ceas.ing die before someone.

pred.e.ces.sor (PRED.uh.ses.ur, PREE.duh-) *n.* one who has gone before a person or thing in a specific capacity: *the prime minister's predecessor; the vinyl predecessor of the compact disc.*

pre.des.ti.na.tion (PREE.des.tuh.NAY.shun) *n.* the theological doctrine that God has predestined certain souls to salvation and others to damnation.

pre.des.tine (pree.DES.tin) *v.* -tines, -tined, -tin.ing determine the future of someone, as by fate; foreordain: *She was predestined to become great.*

pre.de.ter.mine (pree.di.TUR.min) *v.* -mines, -mined, -min.ing determine beforehand. —**pre.de.ter.mi.na.tion** (-muh.NAY.shun) *n.*

pre.dic.a.ment (pri.DIC.uh.munt) *n.* a perplexing or difficult situation.

pred.i.cate (PRED.i.cate) *v.* -cates, -cat.ed, -cat.ing **1** assert something as characteristic of someone: *to predicate goodness of God.* **2** base an assertion or statement on something: *The company's plans are predicated on improving quality, not on growth.* —*n.* (-kit) what is said of a grammatical or logical subject: *In "She is great," "is great" is the predicate.* —**pred.i.ca.tion** (-CAY.shun) *n.*

pre.dict (pri.DICT) *v.* tell what one believes is going to happen; foretell: *to predict the future; to predict when it will rain.* —**pre.dic.ta.ble** (-tuh.bul) *adj.*; **pre.dic.ta.bly** *adv.* —**pre.dic.tion** (-shun) *n.*

pre.dic.tive (pri.DIC.tiv) *adj.* having to do with anticipating what may happen: *predictive ability, analysis, failure, information, power, value.*

pre.di.gest (pree.di.JEST, -dye.JEST) *v.* treat food, as with enzymes, to make it easier to digest; **pre.di.ges.tion** (-JES.chun) *n.*

pre.di.lec.tion (pree.duh.LEC.shun, pred.uh-) *n.* a special liking: *a predilection for spiced foods.*

pre.dis.pose (pree.dis.POZE) *v.* -pos.es, -posed, -pos.ing incline in advance; be susceptible: *Military life predisposed him to a strict regimen.* —**pre.dis.po.si.tion** (PREE.dis.puh.ZISH.un) *n.*

pre.dom.i.nant (pri.DOM.uh.nunt) *adj.* that predominates: *a predominant factor, fear, feature, position, reason, role, share, source, standard, theme, trend, use; Our company was predominant in sales;* **pre.dom.i.nant.ly** *adv.* —**pre.dom.i.nance** (-nunce) *n.*

pre.dom.i.nate (pri.DOM.uh.nate) *v.* -nates, -nat.ed, -nat.ing be greater in number, power, influence, etc.: *Reason*

pree.mie (PREE.mee) *n. Informal.* a prematurely born infant.

pre.em.i.nent (pree.EM.uh.nunt) *adj.* outstanding or surpassing: *a surgeon who is preeminent in her specialty;* **pre.em.i.nent.ly** *adv.*
—**pre.em.i.nence** (-nunce) *n.*

pre.empt (pree.EMPT) *v.* **1** acquire or appropriate something before others. **2** in radio and TV, take the place of something: *a news special preempting regular programs.* —**pre.emp.tion** (-shun) *n.*

pre.emp.tive (pree.EMP.tiv) *adj.* preventive or forestalling: *a preemptive strike on a nuclear facility (to prevent it from making bombs); a preemptive attack, seizure.*

preen *v.* **1** of a bird, clean and smooth its feathers with the beak. **2** dress oneself carefully: *He primps and preens in front of the mirror before going to school.* **3** pride oneself on something: *He preens himself too much on his sharp business deals.*

pre.ex.ist (pree.ig.ZIST) *v.* exist before something or someone; antedate; **pre.ex.is.tence** (-ZIS.tunce) *n.*; **pre.ex.is.tent** *adj.*

pre.fab (PREE.fab) *n.* [short form] a prefabricated building.

pre.fab.ri.cate (pree.FAB.ruh.cate) *v.* **-cates, -cat.ed, -cat.ing** make in sections that can be easily assembled; *adj.:* A **prefabricated** *house can be assembled in a few days.*
—**pre.fab.ri.ca.tion** (-CAY.shun) *n.*

pref.ace (PREF.is) *n.* a statement at the beginning of a book, speech, etc.
—*v.* **pref.ac.es, pref.aced, pref.ac.ing** begin: *The speaker prefaced his remarks with a quotation from Shakespeare.*

pref.a.to.ry (PREF.uh.tor.ee) *adj.* being a preface: *a prefatory note; prefatory remarks.*

pre.fect (PREE.fect) *n.* **1** an administrative official, as of ancient Rome, the head of a department in France, etc. **2** a student monitor.

pre.fec.ture (PREE.fek.chur) *n.* a prefect's office, territory, or residence.

pre.fer (pri.FUR) *v.* **-fers, -ferred, -fer.ring 1** like better than another: *She prefers tea to coffee; He prefers to read rather than watch TV; We prefer taking the bus rather than riding to work;* **adj.a.:** *the* **preferred** *candidate, fuel, method, option, seat; the least preferred of the alternatives; a preferred customer, item.* **2** [legal use] bring forward: *to prefer a charge against someone; to prefer a claim to something.* —**pref.er.a.ble** (PREF.ur.uh.bul) *adj.;* **pref.er.a.bly** (-blee) *adv.* —**pref.er.ence** (-unce) *n.*

pref.er.en.tial (pref.uh.REN.shul) *adj.* showing favor: *a preferential shop favoring union members in hiring; a preferential tariff rate for friendly nations; preferential treatment of favorites.*

preferred stock *n.* stock that has priority over common stock in the sharing of dividends and assets.

pre.fig.ure (pree.FIG.yur) *v.* **-ures, -ured, -ur.ing** be a prototype of a person or thing; foreshadow.

pre.fix (PREE.fix) *n.* a word element used at the beginning of a word, as "ante-," "dis-," "ex-," or "pre-."
—*v.* (PREE.fix, pree.FIX) add before: *"Ms." may be prefixed to a woman's name.*

preg.nant (PREG.nunt) *adj.* **1** carrying a developing offspring in the uterus: *a pregnant woman.* **2** filled with or rich in something: *"Cocacolonize" is pregnant with meaning; an idea pregnant with possibilities; a pregnant (= significant) pause.* —**preg.nan.cy** (-nun.see) *n.* **-cies.**

pre.heat (PREE.heet) *v.* heat beforehand; *adj.:* **preheated** *intake air; Place the TV dinner in an oven preheated to 400°F.*

pre.hen.sile (pree.HEN.sil. -sile) *adj.* that can seize or grasp: *a monkey's prehensile tail.*

pre.his.tor.ic (pree.his.TOR.ic) *adj.* of the time before recorded history, i.e. up to 5,000 years ago: *Dinosaurs are prehistoric animals; prehistoric art found in caves.*

prej.u.dice (PREJ.uh.dis) *v.* **-dic.es, -diced, -dic.ing 1** harm a right, claim, etc.: *behavior that prejudiced his chances of promotion.* **2** cause bias in someone: *A jury could be prejudiced by news reports of the crime.*
—*n.* bias: *popular prejudices; to arouse, eliminate, stir up prejudice against minorities; racial prejudice; sexual prejudice; a statement made* **without prejudice** *(= without harm to one's existing rights).* —**prej.u.di.cial** (-DISH.ul) *adj.*

prel.ate (PREL.it) *n.* a high-ranking clergyman, as a bishop.

pre.lim (PREE.lim, pri.LIM) *n. & adj.* [short form] preliminary.

pre.lim.i.nar.y (pri.LIM.uh.nair.ee) *adj.* coming before; introductory: *a judge's preliminary hearing on a case; a preliminary discussion.* —*n., pl.* **-nar.ies:** *competitors eliminated in* **the preliminaries** *(= rounds of matches before the main event).*

prel.ude (PREL.yood, PRAY.lood, long "oo") *n.* **1** an action or event leading to something major: *a ceasefire as a prelude to a peace treaty.* **2** in music, an opening movement of an opera or similar work. **3** a separate concert work. —*v.* **-udes, -ud.ed, -ud.ing** introduce: *the calm that preluded the storm.*

pre.mar.i.tal (pree.MAIR.i.tul) *adj.* before marriage: *premarital counseling, relations, sex.*

pre.ma.ture (pree.muh.TYOOR, -CHOOR) *adj.* before the proper or usual time, as a baby born more than two weeks early: *a premature birth, delivery; It's premature to arrange for celebrations when we are not sure of victory.* —**pre.ma.ture.ly** *adv.*

pre.med (PREE.med) *n. & adja.* [short form] premedical.

pre.med.i.cal (pree.MED.i.cul) *adja.* preparatory to the study of medicine: *a premedical course, exam, student.*

pre.med.i.tate (pree.MED.i.tate) *v.* **-tates, -tat.ed, -tat.ing** think out or consider beforehand; *adj.*: *a premeditated murder;* **pre.med.i.ta.tion** (-TAY.shun) *n.*

pre.mier (prim.YAIR, PREE.mee.ur) *adja.* first in rank or importance: *the premier dancer of a ballet; a matter of premier importance.* —*n.* a chief minister, as of a province. —**pre.mier.ship** *n.*

pre.miere (prim.YAIR, prim.EER) *n.* **1** the first public performance of a star. **2** the first showing of a movie or play: *a world premiere; to stage a premiere.* —*v.* **-mieres, -miered, -mier.ing** **1** give a premiere: *The new TV sitcom premieres tonight.* **2** appear as a star for the first time: *The star of the show is premiering in the new sitcom.*

prem.ise (PREM.is) *n.* **1** the logical basis for drawing a conclusion: *major and minor premises.* **2 premises** *pl.* a piece of land with the buildings on it: *No picnicking on these premises; an off-premises cafeteria; office premises* (= building or a portion of it). —*v.* **-is.es, -ised, -is.ing** state or imply as a premise: *policies premised on gender differences.*

pre.mi.um (PREE.mee.um) *n.* **1** an incentive bonus or reward; a gift offered as an inducement to buy a product or service: *the premiums offered with breakfast cereals.* **2** an extra payment: *to pay a premium for a special product; theater tickets bought* **at a premium** (= high price) *at the last moment; tax loopholes that* **put a premium** (= unusual value) *on dishonesty.* **3** the fee paid on an insurance policy; *adja.*: *a premium discount for nonsmokers.* —**adja.** higher-priced: *premium brands, business, products, quality, wines; goods priced at the premium end of the market; premium* (= high grade) *gasoline.*

pre.mo.ni.tion (pree.muh.NISH.un) *n.* a foreboding or presentiment: *premonitions of trouble to come; a premonition that something was about to go wrong.*

pre.na.tal (pree.NAY.tul) *adj.* before birth: *Mothers need prenatal care; prenatal injury to infants.*

pre.oc.cu.py (pree.OK.yuh.pye) *v.* **-pies, -pied, -py.ing** take up the undue attention of someone: *Some issues seem to preoccupy the news media; adj.*: *a student* **preoccupied** *with outside activities.* —**pre.oc.cu.pa.tion** (-PAY.shun) *n.*

pre.or.dain (pree.or.DAIN) *v.* decree beforehand: *Events seem to happen as if preordained by Providence.*

prep *adj.* [short form] preparatory: *a prep school.* —*v.* **preps, prepped, prep.ping** prepare a patient for surgery, etc.

pre.pack.age (pree.PAK.ij) *v.* **-ag.es, -aged, -ag.ing** package in standard units or grades for sale; *adj.*: *prepackaged foods, plans, software, teaching materials.*

prep.a.ra.tion (prep.uh.RAY.shun) *n.* an act of preparing or something prepared: *to pack up in preparation for a trip; to make last-minute preparations for a wedding; a preparation* (= medicine) *for colds.*

pre.par.a.to.ry (pri.PAIR.uh.tor.ee) *adj.* that prepares: *a countdown preparatory to a takeoff; A* **preparatory school** *prepares students for college.*

pre.pare (pri.PARE) *v.* **-pares, -pared, -par.ing** make or get ready: *Who will prepare dinner? Layoffs prepare the way for automation; adj.*: *to be* **prepared** *for emergencies; I'm not* **prepared** (= willing) *to tell you.* —**pre.pared.ness** (-PAIR.id.nis) *n.*: *to test our preparedness for war.*

pre.pay (pree.PAY) *v.* **-pays, -paid, -pay.ing** pay beforehand: *the right to prepay mortgages without penalty; adj.*: *a* **prepaid** *ticket.* —**pre.pay.ment** *n.*

pre.pon.der.ance (pri.PON.dur.unce) *n.* the state of being greater than something else in numbers, weight, power, etc.: *the preponderance of women over men in recent censuses.*

—**pre.pon.der.ant** (-runt) *adj.* dominating: *Was wealth or ambition the preponderant influence of his life?*

prep.o.si.tion (prep.uh.ZISH.un) *n.* a word such as "on," "above," or "by" used with a noun or pronoun as its object.

pre.pos.sess (pree.puh.ZES) *v.* influence in a favorable way; *adj.:* He seemed *prepossessed* by the leader's zeal; a woman of *prepossessing* charm.
—**pre.pos.ses.sion** (-ZESH.un) *n.*

pre.pos.ter.ous (pri.POS.tuh.rus) *adj.* contrary to reason and common sense; ridiculous: *He was making preposterous demands on my time and patience.* —**pre.pos.ter.ous.ly** *adv.*

prep.py or **prep.pie** (PREP.ee) *n.* **prep.pies** *Informal.* a product of a private school that prepares students for university, considered typical in regard to fashion, behavior, etc.; *adja.:* the preppy image, look, set; preppie styles.

pre.pro.gram (pree.PROH.gram) *v.* **-grams, -grammed** or **-gramed, -gram.ming** or **-gram.ing** program in advance: *to preprogram a computer.*

pre.quel (PREEK.wul) *n.* a movie, play, novel, or other work that portrays the earlier life of the characters of the main work.

pre.req.ui.site (pree.REK.wuh.zit) *n.* something required beforehand: *Basic courses are prerequisites for or to the more advanced ones.*

pre.rog.a.tive (pri.ROG.uh.tiv) *n.* a special privilege or right: *a royal prerogative; It's a woman's prerogative to have babies; the Prime Minister's prerogative to appoint senators.*

pres.age (PRES.ij) *n.* **1** a sign or omen. **2** a presentiment. —*v.* (*usu.* pri.SAGE) **-ag.es, -aged, -ag.ing** predict or forebode.

pres.by.ter.y (PRES.buh.tair.ee) *n.* **-ter.ies 1** a governing body of the Presbyterian church or of the United Church of Canada. **2** a parish priest's residence.

pre.school (PREE.school) *n.* kindergarten or nursery school: *education from preschool to college.* —*adja.* before school-going age: *a daycare center for preschool children; preschool day care, education, programs.* —**pre.school.er** *n.*

pre.sci.ence (PREE.shee.unce, PRESH.ee-) *n.* foreknowledge. —**pre.sci.ent** *adj.*

pre.scribe (pri.SCRIBE) *v.* **-scribes, -scribed, -scrib.ing** order or direct with authority the use of books, medicines, etc. or to follow a course of action: *to prescribe eyeglasses, remedies, strategies; The doctor prescribes that you abstain from smoking; adj.: a prescribed course of study, treatment; for a prescribed period.*

pre.scrip.tion (pri.SCRIP.shun) *n.* **1** something prescribed, esp. a doctor's order for a medicine: *Doctors write, pharmacists fill prescriptions; Some drugs are sold by prescription only; prescription drugs; You can get it only on a doctor's prescription; a prescription for peace in the Middle East.* **2** the medicine itself.

pres.ence (PREZ.unce) *n.* **1** the state of being present: *a contract signed in the presence of witnesses; troops to maintain the U.S. presence in Europe; He makes his presence felt or known by acting foolishly; to act with presence of mind (= calmness) in a panicky situation.* **2** one's bearing or personality; an impressive appearance: *a woman of commanding presence.*

pres.ent (PREZ.unt) *adj.* existing here and now as specified or understood: *All students were present yesterday; In the present case, no action is called for; from ancient times to the present day.*
—*n.* **1** the present time: *"Do" is in the present (tense); She's too busy at present; a light meal to satisfy you for the present.* **2** a gift: *birthday, Christmas, wedding presents.* **3** [old use] a document: *Know ye, by these presents, that....*
—*v.* (pri.ZENT) *Formal.* **1** offer or give: *A lawyer presents arguments in a case; A new diplomat presents his or her credentials; Graduates are presented with diplomas.* **2** introduce: *A visiting dignitary is presented at court; to present a guest to a gathering.* —**present arms** [military use] salute by holding a weapon vertically with the point down. —**pre.sen.ta.tion** (prez.un.TAY.shun, pree.zun-) *n.*

pre.sent.a.ble (pri.ZEN.tuh.bul) *adj.* respectable in appearance: *Get a haircut and make yourself presentable for the interview.* —**pre.sen.ta.bly** *adv.*

present-day *adja.* contemporary: *present-day fashions, historians, society; present-day Russia.*

pre.sen.ti.ment (pri.ZEN.tuh.munt) *n.* a feeling that something, esp. bad, is about to happen; premonition or foreboding.

pres.ent.ly (PREZ.unt.lee) *adv.* **1** at present: *They are presently in Europe.* **2** soon: *The bus will be here presently.*

present participle *n.* the "-ing" form of a verb used to express duration and progression of an activity.

pres.er.va.tion (prez.ur.VAY.shun) *n.* a preserving or being preserved.

pre.ser.va.tive (pri.ZUR.vuh.tiv) *n.* one that preserves: *Salt is a food preservative; no preservatives (= chemicals)* added; **adj.**: *a preservative medium for a photographic solution.*

pre.serve (pri.ZURV) *v.* **-serves, -served, -serv.ing** keep or maintain without harm: *May God preserve you (from danger)! Fruits may be preserved (from decay) by cooking with sugar; laws to preserve* (= keep safe) *our natural resources.* —**n.** **1** a fruit preparation: *a strawberry preserve.* **2** grounds: *No poaching on private game preserves; wild-life preserves.* —**pre.serv.er** *n.*: *A life preserver is worn against drowning.*

pre.set (pree.SET) *v.* **-sets, -set, -set.ting** set beforehand; **adj.**: *a long-range missile with a preset guidance system; a preset speed; a credit card with a preset spending limit.*

pre.shrunk (PREE.shrunk) *adj.* of a fabric, shrunk during manufacture to reduce shrinkage in use.

pre.side (pri.ZIDE) *v.* **-sides, -sid.ed, -sid.ing** have authority or control, esp. as chairperson: *Judges preside at trials; to preside over a meeting.*

pres.i.dent (PREZ.uh.dunt) *n.* **1** the chief executive of a republic, company, college, club, etc. **2** the chairperson of a meeting. —**pres.i.den.cy** (-dun.see) *n.* **-cies.**

pres.i.den.tial (prez.uh.DEN.shul) *adj.* having to do with a president: *the presidential address, chair, oath of office; presidential powers.*

pre.sid.i.um (pre.SID.ee.um) *n.* **-i.ums** or **-i.a** (-ee.uh) in communist countries, a permanent executive committee.

pre.spot.ter (pree.SPOT.ur) *n.* a dry-cleaning worker who removes certain stains before cleaning.

press *v.* **1** act upon with steady force: *She pressed the picture to her heart; Press the button for help; to press grapes for wine; Clothes pressed while you wait; Phonograph records, cotton bales, etc. are pressed* (= made by pressing); *Metal is pressed* (= shaped) *into coins; Her responsibilities are beginning to **press on*** (= weigh heavily on) *her mind; Candidates for election **press the flesh*** (*Informal* for shake hands with people) *all day;* **adj.**: *fresh juice just pressed; She had ner nose pressed flat against the windowpane; She is pressed for time;* **hard pressed** *to pay her debts; hard pressed for capital, cash, finances; a* **hard-pressed** *debtor; people hard-pressed by poverty.* **2** urge: *She pressed him to stay for dinner; Politicians press the need for reform; an angry public pressing the government for an inquiry; The police decided not to*

press charges *and dropped the case; Women and children were* **pressed into** *service* (= forced to serve) *at the height of the war; an army* **pressing on** *to victory;* **adj.**: *He's away on* **pressing** (= urgent) *business; a pressing need.*

—**n.** **1** a pressing or its result: *driven forward by the press of ambition; a fabric that keeps its press; permanent press; He elbowed his way through the press* (= crowd) *of people.* **2** a machine that presses: *printing, wine presses; Morning papers* **go to press** (= are printed) *after midnight; The book is* **in** *or* **on press** (= being printed). **3** newspapers or journalists: *a free press; the yellow press.* **4** publicity: *Her performance received a good press; A* **press agent** (= publicity agent) *worked hard to ensure it.*

press box *n.* a space reserved for reporters, esp. at a sports event.

press conference same as NEWS CONFERENCE.

press kit *n.* promotional materials handed out to the press.

press.man (PRES.mun) *n.* **-men** the operator of a printing press.

press.room *n.* **1** where the presses are installed in a printing plant. **2** a room for journalists.

press secretary *n.* the public relations officer of a prominent person or organization..

pres.sure (PRESH.ur) *n.* the action of pressing or the condition of being pressed: *Atmospheric pressure decreases with altitude; barometric, high, low pressure; Hypertension is high blood pressure; He studies under pressure of exams; to exert* or *put pressure on someone; to* **bring pressure to bear** *on someone; to build up, ease, face, relieve, resist pressure; intense, parental, peer, public, relentless pressure; As time goes on, pressure builds up, eases, falls, rises; A* **pressure cooker** *cooks fast with steam under pressure.*

—*v.* **pres.sures, pres.sured, pres.sur.ing** force by applying pressure: *people pressured into signing sales contracts.*

pressure group *n.* a group that exerts pressure on governments and legislatures to further its own interests.

pres.sur.ize (PRESH.ur.ize) *v.* **-iz.es, -ized, -iz.ing** **1** keep under normal pressure in spite of altitude; **adj.**: *the* **pressurized** *cabin of an airplane; pressurized space suits.* **2** raise to a higher-than-normal pressure; **adj.**: *pressurized air, gas cylinders, steam.* **3** pressure someone: *She was pressurized to sign the sales contract;* **adj.**: *pressurized executives, work environments.*

pressure suit / prevent

—**pres.sur.iz.er** n.
pressure suit n. a suit designed to keep the wearer under normal pressure at high altitudes.
pres.tige (pres.TEEZH) n. reputation based on outstanding achievement: *to gain prestige by achievements; great, high, low prestige.* —**pres.ti.gious** (-TIJ.us) adj.: *a prestigious award, institution, position, prize, title, university.*
pres.to (PRES.toh) interj. behold: *Hey presto! And the rabbit vanished.*
pre.stressed concrete (PREE.strest-) n. concrete cast around steel cables held under tension.
pre.sume (pri.ZOOM) v. **-sumes, -sumed, -sum.ing 1** assume: *Everyone is presumed innocent until proven guilty; "Dr. Livingstone, I presume* (= suppose)*?"* **2** venture: *He presumes to advise his parents; It would be **presuming on** *(= making free use of) *his generosity to ask for another loan;* adj.: *a very **presuming*** (= presumptuous) *young man.* —**pre.su.ma.ble** (-muh.bul) adj. —**pre.su.ma.bly** (-blee) adv.
pre.sump.tion (pri.ZUMP.shun) n. the act of presuming or something presumed or taken for granted: *the presumption of innocence; It's only a presumption, not a proven fact; It was considered presumption* (= nerve) *for women to want to vote.*
pre.sump.tive (pri.ZUMP.tiv) adj. presumed: *the heir presumptive; The stolen goods in his car seem presumptive evidence against him.*
pre.sump.tu.ous (pri.SUMP.choo.us) adj. arrogant or excessively forward; presuming; **pre.sump.tu.ous.ly** adv.
pre.sup.pose (pree.suh.POZE) v. **-sup.pos.es, -sup.posed, -sup.pos.ing 1** assume: *Let's not presuppose anything before looking at the facts.* **2** require as a logical precondition: *A product presupposes a producer.* —**pre.sup.po.si.tion** (PREE.sup.uh.ZISH.un) n.
pre.tax (PREE.tax) adj. before tax: *pretax earnings.*
pre.teen (PREE.teen) n. a child who is in the 9-12 age group; adj.: *preteen fashions, styles, years, the preteen set.*
pretence Cdn. PRETENSE.
pre.tend (pri.TEND) v. **1** make believe: *Let's pretend we are in space; She pretended not to hear.* **2** claim, esp. falsely: *to pretend illness as an excuse; The young Stuarts **pretended to** the throne of England.* —**pre.tend.er** n.
pre.tense (pri.TENSE, PREE.tense) n. **1** a pretending: *begging under the pretense of poverty; He gained entry by or on* or *under false pretenses; without any pretense* (= attempt) *at truthfulness; a plain-spoken manner free from all pretense* (= phoniness). **2** appearance: *to maintain some pretense of decorum.*
pre.ten.sion (pri.TEN.shun) n. claim: *a journalist with no pretensions to scholarship.*
pre.ten.tious (pri.TEN.shus) adj. **1** making undue claims to excellence or worth: *a pompous and pretentious style of writing.* **2** showy or ostentatious: *Sam is stylish without being pretentious; a pretentious lifestyle, pundit, title.*
pre.ter.nat.u.ral (pree.tur.NACH.uh.rul) adj. **1** out of the ordinary: *a man of preternatural strength.* **2** supernatural or psychic: *miracles and such preternatural phenomena.* —**pre.ter.nat.u.ral.ly** adv.
pre.test (pree.TEST) n. & v. test in advance.
pre.text (PREE.text) n. a false purpose or reason; pretence: *espionage under the pretext of missionary work.*
pret.ty (PRIT.ee) adj. **pret.ti.er, pret.ti.est 1** moderately pleasing and attractive to look at: *not just another pretty face; a pretty little girl.* **2** Informal. considerable in amount: *a pretty mess you're into; The car cost me a pretty sum.* —adv. fairly: *looks pretty good; He'll be here pretty soon; Everything went pretty much as we expected.* —**sitting pretty** in a fairly advantageous position. —v. **pret.ties, pret.tied, pret.ty.ing** Informal. make pretty: *We'll pretty up our basement for the party.* —**pret.ti.ly** adv.: *a prettily wrapped gift;* **pret.ti.ness** n.
pre.vail (pri.VAIL) v. be stronger, more usual, or more common: *Reason prevailed against or over prejudices; The children prevailed on or upon* (= succeeded in persuading) *their mother to take them to the movie;* adj.: *Youth tend to follow the **prevailing** fashions; The **prevailing*** (= generally current) *westerly winds make flying from west to east faster in the Northern Hemisphere.*
prev.a.lent (PREV.uh.lunt) adj. widespread: *a trend prevalent among teenagers.* —**prev.a.lence** (-lunce) n.
pre.var.i.cate (pri.VAIR.uh.cate) v. **-cates, -cat.ed, -cat.ing** evade the truth by quibbling or a similar tactic. —**pre.var.i.ca.tion** (-CAY.shun) n. —**pre.var.i.ca.tor** (-cay.tur) n.
pre.vent (pri.VENT) v. stop from doing or happening; hinder: *measures to prevent disease; No one can prevent our catching cold; Only prompt action can prevent a fire from spreading.*

preventive / prima facie

—**pre.ven.ta.ble** or **pre.ven.ti.ble** adj.
—**pre.ven.tion** (-VEN.shun) n. the act of preventing: *fire prevention; the prevention of cruelty to animals; "Prevention is better than cure."*
pre.ven.tive (pri.VEN.tiv) adj. helping to prevent something: *a habitual criminal held without bail in preventive detention; Vaccination is a preventive measure; the field of preventive medicine.*
—n. a preventive measure or agent, as a drug.
pre.view (PREE.view) n. **1** an advance showing or viewing of a play, movie, or TV program: *a sneak preview;* v.: *to preview new merchandise.* **2** foretaste.
pre.vi.ous (PREE.vee.us) adj. earlier: *I cannot be at tomorrow's meeting because of a previous engagement; a commitment made* **previous to** (= before) *your request.* —**pre.vi.ous.ly** adv.
pre.war (PREE.wor) adj. before the war, esp. World War II: *in prewar days, years; the prewar era; the great prewar Depression (1929-39).*
prey (PRAY) n. *sing.* **1** an animal hunted for food. **2** a victim: *an easy prey; He* **fell prey to** (= became a victim of) *loansharks.* —v. make a prey of someone: *Larger beasts prey on smaller ones; Guilt preyed on or upon her mind.*
price n. the amount of money to be paid to the seller of something; cost or worth: *to bring, fetch, fix, pay, put, quote, set a price; to bring down, cut, freeze, hold down, mark down, mark up, raise, slash prices; asking, bargain, exorbitant, going, inflated, reasonable, retail, sale, stiff, wholesale prices; prices drop, fall, go down, go up, skyrocket, slump; Governments impose price controls to fight inflation; They would not agree to peace* **at any price** (= at too heavy a price); *There are anti-trust laws against* **price-fixing** *by members of a trade or profession.*
—v. **pric.es, priced, pric.ing** put a price on something: *It's priced too high for my pocket; Houses have* **priced themselves out of the market** (= Houses have become too expensive).
price.less adj. having great value: *a priceless antique, asset, gem, heirloom, treasure.*
price tag (or **ticket**) n. a tag or ticket showing the price of the item to which it is attached.
price war n. a competition in which retailers repeatedly cut prices below those of their rivals.
pric.ey (PRY.see) adj. **pric.i.er, -i.est** *Informal.* expensive: *pricey artwork, customers, professionals, technology.*

prick n. **1** a little mark or puncture made by a sharp point, as of a pin or thorn. **2** a pricking or the sharp pain thus caused: *the pricks of conscience.*
—v. give pain or make a small hole, as with a pin or thorn: *A balloon bursts if pricked; Thickly growing seedlings are* **pricked out** (= transplanted) *uniformly in larger pans.* —**prick up one's ears** listen closely.
prick.le (PRIK.ul) n. **1** a thorn or spine. **2** a sharp sensation. —v. **-les, -led, -ling** tingle.
prick.ly (PRIK.lee) adj. **-li.er, -li.est** having sharp points: *the prickly porcupine; the itchy reddish rash of* **prickly heat** *or "heat rash"; the* **prickly pear** *cactus.*
pride n. **1** a sense of one's own worth: *to appeal to one's pride; The low marks hurt his pride; great, injured, wounded pride; to pocket* or *swallow one's pride and accept defeat.* **2** pleasure over one's qualities, possessions, or achievements: *We take pride in a job well done.* **3** a source of such esteem: *David was the pride and joy of her old age.* **4** false esteem of oneself or contempt of others: *"Pride goes before a fall."* **5** the best part; prime: *in the days of her pride; Shakespeare's* **pride of place** (= highest position) *among dramatists.* **6** a group of animals: *a pride of lions, peacocks.*
—v. **prides, prid.ed, prid.ing** be proud of something: *He prides himself on his high marks.* —**pride.ful** adj.; **pride.ful.ly** adv.
priest (PREEST) n. a religious official who performs religious rites and other functions, esp. a member of the clergy ranking next below a bishop: *Pat was ordained priest yesterday.*
—**priest.ess** n.: *a priestess of Venus; Phyllis Diller, the High Priestess of Charm.* —**priest.hood** (short "oo") n. —**priest.ly** adj. —**priest.li.ness** n.
prig n. a rigid and smug observer of morals and manners.
prig.gish (PRIG.ish) adj. like a prig: *He's too priggish to dress casually.*
prim adj. **prim.mer, prim.mest** overprecise or formal: *a prim and proper fashion.* —**prim.ly** adv.; **prim.ness** n.
pri.ma.cy (PRY.muh.see) n. **-cies 1** superiority or preeminence. **2** the rank or office of a church primate.
pri.ma don.na (PREE.muh.DON.uh) n., *pl.* **prima donnas 1** the leading woman singer in an opera. **2** a vain or temperamental person.
pri.ma fa.ci.e (PRY.muh.FAY.shee.ee) adj. & adv. [legal use] adequate

without further examination: *a prima facie case; prima facie evidence.*

pri.mal (PRY.mul) *adj.* more basic than primitive in time: *The Earth evolved out of primal material; the primal forces of matter and energy; primal elements, fears, struggles; the **primal scream** therapy for relieving tensions.*

pri.ma.ry (PRY.mair.ee) *adja.* first in time, rank, or importance: *Your 20 primary* (= baby or milk) *teeth are replaced by 32 permanent ones;* ***Primary care*** *physicians such as family doctors; A **primary cell**, as used in a flashlight, cannot be recharged; Blue, red, and yellow are the **primary colors**; The **primary school** comprises kindergarten through Grade 3.* —**pri.ma.ri.ly** (pry.MAIR.uh.lee) *adv.*

pri.mate (PRY.mate) *n.* 1 an animal of the highest order such as the human being, ape, or monkey. 2 (*also* PRY.mit) an archbishop.

prime *n.* 1 the earliest or best stage or period: *The year is at its prime in the spring; She died in the prime of youth.* 2 a number that is not composed of other numbers, as 1, 2, 3, 5, 7, 11, or 13; *also* **prime number.**
—*adj.* first or chief: *The **prime meridian** of 0 degree longitude passes through Greenwich, England; the **prime minister** of a country.* —*v.* **primes, primed, prim.ing** make ready or prepare, as a gun with powder for firing, a water pump by pouring in some water, a painting surface with a first coat, a witness with facts, etc.

prim.er *n.* 1 (PRY.mur) one that prepares, as a first coat of paint, a device to set off an explosive charge, etc. 2 (PRIM.ur) a beginner's textbook: *a primer on Chinese cooking.*

prime rate *n.* the rate of interest charged to a bank's best customers.

prime time *n.* on radio and TV, the evening hours, usually 6 to 11, when most people tune in.

pri.me.val (pry.MEE.vul) *adj.* of the earliest times: *the earth's primeval uninhabited condition; primeval forests, jungles.* —**pri.me.val.ly** *adv.*

prim.i.tive (PRIM.uh.tiv) *adj.* 1 of early times; undeveloped: *primitive instincts, living conditions, tribes, weapons.* 2 crude; lacking modern conveniences: *The accommodation at the camp was rather primitive.*
—*n.* 1 a member of an undeveloped civilization: *Some groups of people used to be called primitives.* 2 one not trained or sophisticated: *She's a primitive in her artistic leanings.* —**prim.i.tive.ly** *adv.;* **prim.i.tiv.ism** *n.*

pri.mor.di.al (pry.MOR.dee.ul) *adj.* primeval: *a primordial joy, urge, voice; Did matter originate as a primordial fireball of radiation? the primordial "soup" from which life arose according to some theories; a primordial swamp.* —**pri.mor.di.al.ly** *adv.*

primp *v.* dress or groom oneself in a fussy manner: *She's busy primping her hair; to primp for a photograph.*

prim.rose *n.* an early-flowering ornamental plant with yellowish flowers.
—**primrose path** or **way** path of pleasure or temptation.

prince *n.* 1 a male member of a royal family: *a crown prince; the prince and the pauper; the Prince of Wales.* 2 the ruler of a small country: *a European prince; the Prince of Monaco.* 3 the chief or excellent one: *a prince among men; a prince of peace; a **prince of the church*** (= cardinal).

prince consort *n.* a reigning queen's husband.

prince.ling *n.* a petty prince.

prince.ly *adj.* **-li.er, -li.est** 1 noble or generous: *in princely style; We paid a princely sum for that house.* 2 having to do with a prince: *a princely family, state; princely power.*

prin.cess (PRIN.sis, -ses) *n.* a female member of a royal family.

prin.ci.pal (PRIN.suh.pul) *adj.* chief: *the principal ally, character, city, clause, ingredient, interest, source.* —*n.* the most important one, as the head of a school, a capital sum bearing interest, the chief actor in a play, a main accomplice in a crime, or the main body of an estate. —**prin.ci.pal.ly** *adv.* —**prin.ci.pal.ship** *n.*

prin.ci.pal.i.ty (prin.suh.PAL.i.tee) *n.* **-ties** a prince's territory, as Monaco or Andorra.

principal parts *n.pl.* a set of the main inflected forms of a verb, usu. the present tense, past tense, and past participle, as "take-took-taken."

prin.ci.ple (PRIN.suh.pul) *n.* 1 a fundamental truth, law, or rule: *the principles of mathematics; We agree **in principle*** (= in fundamentals) *but we have to work out the details.* 2 the basis of an action or operation, esp. behavior: *the principles of good government; two machines built on the same principle; basic, guiding, high, sound, strict principles; to adhere to, apply, enunciate, formulate, lay down a principle; a matter of principle; Men and women **of principle*** (= having principles) *do everything on principle* (= according to principles); *adj.: a high-principled woman* (= woman with high standards of moral conduct).

print *n.* **1** a mark made by pressure, as a fingerprint, type impression, design on cloth, etc.: *print patterns.* **2** a cloth or paper with such marks: *a Japanese color print; a floral print; adja.: print cloths, dresses, jackets, ties.* **3** something printed: *clear, dark, large print; when you first break into print* (= get something published); *Read the fine* or *small print* (= something important printed in small type) *before signing a contract; There are millions of copies of the Bible in print* (= published and available); *It has never gone out of print* (= stopped being published); *adja.: print ads, campaigns, versions; the print media such as the press.* **4** a photograph made from a negative.
—*v.* **1** reproduce letters, words, pictures, etc. mechanically: *Gutenberg started printing from movable type in 1440; words printed in boldface, italics, roman; Please print your name (using printed letters) instead of writing it; a book printed* (= manufactured) *in Singapore; Press "P" (on the keyboard) to print out the essay.* **2** stamp: *Patterns are printed on cloth.* —**print.a.ble** (-uh.bul) *adj.*

printed circuit *n.* an electronic circuit in which the connections are printed on an insulated base instead of being wired together.

printed matter *n.* a category of mail that includes books, magazines, newspapers, greeting cards with messages of five words or fewer, etc.; also **printed papers.**

print.er *n.* **1** a machine that prints type: *a computer printer; line printers; dot-matrix, ink-jet, laser printers.* **2** a person whose work or business is printing: *printers and publishers; an error of the printer's devil* (= printer's young helper); *printer's proof* (= trial print).

printing *n.* **1** the art or business of producing books, periodicals, etc. with type or plates: *letterpress, litho, offset printing; adja.: a printing plant, plate, press.* **2** a printing or the copies printed at one time; impression: *The first printing was sold out in a week.*

print.out *n.* a computer's printed output.

pri.or (PRY.ur) *adja.* **1** earlier in time: *I am unable to accept your invitation because of a prior engagement (made before you asked); He was in farming prior to* (= before) *entering politics.* **2** preceding in importance or rank: *I must give prior consideration to business engagements.* —*n.* the superior of a priory; **pri.or.ess** (-ris) *fem.*

pri.or.i.tize (pry.OR.uh.tize) *v.* **-tiz.es, -tized, -tiz.ing** put in order of priority: *We need to prioritize; to prioritize customers, lists, merchandise, methods, one's time.*

pri.or.i.ty (pry.OR.i.tee) *n.* **-ties** a relative degree of importance or urgency: *to establish, reexamine, set priorities; the right priorities; Top priority is given for emergency relief; It gets priority; high priority; Our first* or *number one priority* (= something important or urgent) *is feeding the hungry; It takes priority over* (= becomes more important or urgent than) *everything else.* —*adja.: priority lists, mail, seating; a priority project, scale, setting.*

pri.o.ry (PRY.uh.ree) *n.* **-ries** a monastery.

prism (PRIZ.um) *n.* a solid with similar, equal, and parallel ends, and sides that are parallelograms.

pris.mat.ic (priz.MAT.ic) *adj.* having to do with a prism or prisms: *prismatic binoculars, glass, lenses; prismatic light* (displayed as a spectrum); *prismatic colors* (= colors of the rainbow).

pris.on (PRIZ.un) *n.* a place of confinement, esp. for convicted criminals: *to break out of, escape from, be sent to, be sentenced to, spend time in prison; adja.: behind prison bars* or *walls; a prison cell, sentence, term, warden, yard.*

pris.on.er (PRIZ.un.ur) *n.* a captive: *Over 100 soldiers were taken prisoner; political prisoners; a prisoner of conscience* (= political prisoner); *a prisoner of war* (= person taken prisoner in war).

pris.sy (PRIS.ee) *adj.* **pris.si.er, pris.si.est** *Informal.* prim or prudish. —**pris.si.ly** *adv.;* **pris.si.ness** *n.*

pris.tine (PRIS.teen, pris.TEEN) *adj.* in its original unspoiled condition : *a painting restored to its pristine beauty; in pristine environments like the Arctic; nature in its pristine state; a white pristine dress.*

prith.ee (PRITH.ee, "TH" as in "the") *interj.* [old use] I pray thee; please.

pri.va.cy (PRY.vuh.see) *n.* the quality or state of being private; secrecy: *in the privacy of my home; data banks as a threat to privacy; the invasion of one's privacy by electronic snooping.*

pri.vate (PRY.vit) *adj.* having to do with one person or group; not public: *private dealings that serve private ends; a* *private office*; *a private school that charges fees.* —*n.* **1** a soldier or marine of the lowest rank. **2 privates** *pl.* genitals. —**in private** privately, not openly.

pri.va.teer (pry.vuh.TEER) *n.* **1** formerly, an armed, privately owned ship in the service of a country. **2** a crew member or commander of such a vessel.

private enterprise same as FREE ENTERPRISE.

private eye *n.* an investigator or detective.

private first class *n.* an enlisted person ranking above a private and below a corporal or lance corporal.

private parts *n.pl.* genitals.

pri.va.tion (pry.VAY.shun) *n.* the condition of being deprived of life's ordinary necessities: *the many privations imposed by war.*

pri.va.tize (PRY.vuh.tize) *v.* **-iz.es, -ized, -iz.ing** make private: *to privatize the post office.* —**pri.va.ti.za.tion** (-tuh.ZAY.shun, -tye-) *n.*

priv.et (PRIV.it) *n.* an evergreen shrub widely grown for hedges.

priv.i.lege (PRIV.uh.lij, PRIV.lij) *n.* a benefit or advantage granted to an individual or attached to a position: *to abuse, enjoy, grant, suspend a privilege; kitchen privileges for boarders; It's a pleasure and a privilege to work with Pat; no special privileges for anyone; the rights and privileges of membership; a question of parliamentary privilege* (= right).

privileged (PRIV.uh.lijd, PRIV.lijd) *adj.* **1** enjoying a privilege: *We are privileged to live in an affluent society; a privileged class of people.* **2** legally protected: *a privileged communication between lawyer and client; A damaging statement about someone that is privileged in a legislature could be slanderous if repeated outside.*

priv.y (PRIV.ee) *adj.* [old use] private or secret: *privy parts..* —**privy to** Formal. privately informed about something. —*n., pl.* **priv.ies** an outhouse, esp. a toilet.

privy council *n.* a formal body of advisors appointed by a sovereign: *The Federal cabinet acts as the Canadian Privy Council.*

privy purse *n.* a sovereign's allowance for private expenses, as in the U.K.

prize *n.* something worth competing for or that is offered to a winner in a competition, lottery, etc.: *to award or give, receive, win a prize; booby, cash, consolation, door, first, grand, runner-up prizes; the Nobel prize;* **adj.:** *prize money,*

privateer / probe

packages, winners, winnings; prize cattle, herds, horses, salmon (that have won prizes). —*v.* **priz.es, prized, priz.ing** **1** value highly: *She prizes her independence more than money;* **adj.:** *a highly* **prized** *triple-A rating; our most prized possessions.* **2** estimate the value of something: *to prize a painting.* **3** force open with a lever; pry.

prize.fight *n.* a professional boxing match. —**prize.fight.er** *n.*

prize money *n.* money offered as prize.

prize ring *n.* a square enclosure of ropes for prize fights.

prize.win.ner (PRIZE.win.ur) *n.* the winner of a prize; **prize.win.ning** *adj.:* *a prizewinning essay, poem, poet.*

pro- *prefix.* **1** forward in place or time: *prologue, provision.* **2** in place of: *proconsul, pronoun.* **3** favorable to: *pro-choice, pro-life, pro-Republican.*

pro (PROH) *n.* **pros** **1** *Informal.* professional: *a football pro; She drives like a pro.* **2** something in favor: *to weigh the pros and cons of capital punishment.* —**pro and con** *adv.* for and against: *He spoke at length pro and con;* **prep.:** *gave arguments pro and con capital punishment;* **adja.:** *the various* **pro-and-con** *arguments.*

pro.ac.tive (proh.AC.tiv) *adj.* anticipatory, not reactive: *a proactive approach to problem-solving; a proactive role.*

prob.a.bil.i.ty (prob.uh.BIL.i.tee) *n.* **-ties** a being probable or something that is probable: *There is a 25% probability of rain today; An accident is one of the probabilities of how he died;* **In all probability,** *she will win a gold medal.*

prob.a.ble (PROB.uh.bul) *adj.* likely because reasonable or logical: *It's possible to win $5 million dollars in the draw, but only a few are probable winners; the probable cause of the accident.* —**prob.a.bly** *adv.*

pro.bate (PROH.bate) *n.* in law, the official proving of a will's genuineness: *a probate court.* —*v.* **-bates, -bat.ed, -bat.ing** legally establish a will as genuine and valid.

pro.ba.tion (pruh.BAY.shun) *n.* a trial of a person's conduct or worth: *a six months' probation for new employees; A first offender is given a suspended sentence and placed on probation for one year under a* **probation officer.** —**pro.ba.tion.al** *adj.* —**pro.ba.tion.er** *n.* —**pro.ba.tion.ar.y** (-nair.ee) *adj.: a probationary appointment, employee, period, status; on a probationary basis.*

probe *n.* **1** an investigation: *to conduct, launch a probe; a probe into corruption; a*

police probe; DNA probes. **2** an instrument for probing, as a surgeon's slender metal device for exploring a wound or body cavity: *a meat probe.* **3** same as SPACE PROBE: *a Venus probe.*
—*v.* **probes, probed, prob.ing** investigate: *a committee probing charges of corruption; Scuba divers probe the hull of a sunken ship.*

pro.bi.ty (PROH.bi.tee) *n.* uprightness of morals; honesty: *a model of probity.*

prob.lem (PROB.lum) *n.* **1** a question put forward for solution: *to do or solve a mathematical problem; a simple problem; problem solving.* **2** a difficult or perplexing situation or person: *to address, cause, confront, conquer, create, pose, tackle, settle, solve a problem; acute, complicated, difficult, emotional, involved, knotty, perennial, serious, social, thorny problems; when problems arise;* **No problem** (*Informal for* You're welcome); **adj.**: *a problem area, child, drinker.*

prob.lem.at.ic (prob.luh.MAT.ic) *adj.* posing a problem: *Testing students for promotion or failure is problematic; problematic passages in a book; a problematic aspect, economy, issue, personality, situation.* Also **prob.lem.at.i.cal** (-ti.cul).

pro.bos.cis (pruh.BOS.is, -kis) *n.* **-cis.es** a long, flexible snout, such as an elephant's trunk or a butterfly's tubelike organ for sucking nectar.

pro.caine (PROH.cain) *n.* a synthetic compound used as a local anesthetic, esp. by dentists.

pro.ce.dur.al (pruh.SEE.juh.rul) *adj.* having to do with procedure: *The meeting was delayed by procedural problems.*

pro.ce.dure (pruh.SEE.jur) *n.* **1** method of doing something: *legal procedure; parliamentary procedure; the procedure to be followed in applying for a passport; established, normal, standard procedure.* **2** a particular form of action: *operations and such medical procedures.*

pro.ceed (pruh.SEED) *v.* go forward: *Stop and proceed slowly at 10 km/h; She thanked him and proceeded to untie the parcel; He was unable to proceed with his studies; to proceed* (= take legal action) *against violators; quarrels proceeding* (= arising) *from old enmities.*
—**proceeding** *n.* **1** [legal use] action: *to initiate or institute legal proceedings against someone; divorce proceedings; an adversarial proceeding.* **2** **proceedings** *pl.* the activities of a society or their record.
—**proceeds** (PROH.seeds) *n.pl.* [takes *pl.v.*] returns or profit: *The proceeds of this concert will go to charity; net proceeds.*

proc.ess (PROH.ses, PROS.es) *n.* **-ess.es** (-es.iz) **1** a course or series of actions or their method: *a manufacturing process; He was deported by due process of law; the judicial process; mental or thought processes; in the process of setting up a business; He lost some money* **in the process** (= while doing so). **2** an outgrowth or projecting part, as the appendix of the intestine. —**adj.** made by or involving a special process: **Process art** *reflects the artist's conceptual process; The mass-produced* **process cheese** *is blended from several cheeses; the* **process engineer** *in charge of an assembly-line operation.*
—*v.* put through methodically: *to process applications, data, food, orders, recruits;* **n.**: *the* **processing** *of immigrants; word processing.*

pro.ces.sion (pruh.SESH.un) *n.* an orderly, formal movement, esp. of people: *funeral, graduation, wedding processions.*

pro.ces.sion.al (pruh.SESH.uh.nul) *n.* a hymn book or music for processions.

proc.es.sor (PROH.suh.sur, PROS.uh.sur) *n.* **1** one that processes: *a food processor; word processors.* **2** a computer or its part that operates on data.

pro-choice *adj.* favoring a woman's right to abortion: *a pro-choice advocate, group, supporter; the pro-choice movement; Are they pro-choice or pro-life?*

pro.claim (proh.CLAIM) *v.* **1** announce publicly and officially: *a public holiday proclaimed in honor of a returning hero; to proclaim a country independent; to proclaim a region a disaster area; to proclaim war; to proclaim a law* (= to put it into effect). **2** glorify: *an ad proclaiming the virtues of a new computer.*
—**proc.la.ma.tion** (proc.luh.MAY.shun) *n.*: *to issue a royal proclamation; a proclamation of amnesty.*

pro.cliv.i.ty (proh.CLIV.i.tee) *n.* **-ties** a natural weakness for something: *a proclivity for making rash judgments; a patient with a proclivity to epileptic seizures.*

pro.cras.ti.nate (proh.CRAS.tuh.nate) *v.* **-nates, -nat.ed, -nat.ing** put off doing things from day to day.
—**pro.cras.ti.na.tion** (-NAY.shun) *n.*
—**pro.cras.ti.na.tor** (-nay.tur) *n.*

pro.cre.ate (PROH.cree.ate) *v.* **-ates, -at.ed, -at.ing** beget offspring.
—**pro.cre.a.tion** (-AY.shun) *n.*
—**pro.cre.a.tive** (-ay.tiv) *adj.*;
pro.cre.a.tor (-ay.tur) *n.*

Pro.crus.te.an (proh.CRUS.tee.un) *adj.*

ruthless in enforcing conformity, like **Procrustes** (-teez) of Greek myth, who stretched his victims to fit his beds.
proc.tor (PROC.tur) *n.* an administrative official of a college; *v.: graduate students hired to proctor* (= supervise) *an exam.* —**proc.to.ri.al** (-TOR.ee.ul) *adj.: proctorial duties.*
proc.u.ra.tor (PROC.yuh.ray.tur) *n.* an agent or manager, esp. a financial or legal official.
pro.cure (pruh.CURE) *v.* **-cures, -cured, -cur.ing 1** obtain, esp. by some effort: *to procure votes; to procure* (= bring about) *an abortion.* **2** get someone for prostitution.
—**pro.cure.ment** (-munt) *n.: the procurement of military supplies.*
—**pro.cur.er** *n.* a pimp.
prod *v.* **prods, prod.ded, prod.ding** poke; hence, urge: *to prod cattle; prodded into activity by the approaching exams.*
—*n.* **1** a thrust or jab. **2** a pointed instrument: *a cattle prod.* —**prod.der** *n.*
prod.i.gal (PROD.uh.gul) *n.* a wastefully extravagant person; *adj.: an inheritance depleted by prodigal spending, as in the parable of the **prodigal son**; Nature's prodigal* (= abundant and seemingly wasteful) *resources.*
—**prod.i.gal.ly** *adv.* —**prod.i.gal.i.ty** (-GAL.i.tee) *n.* **-ties.**
pro.di.gious (pruh.DIJ.ee.us) *adj.* very great or marvelous: *a prodigious amount, energy, memory, output, performance; a man of prodigious strength.*
—**pro.di.gious.ly** *adv.*;
pro.di.gious.ness *n.*
prod.i.gy (PROD.uh.jee) *n.* **-gies** something amazing or extraordinary, esp. a marvelously talented child: *Mozart was a musical prodigy; child prodigies.*
pro.duce (pruh.DUCE) *v.* **-duc.es, -duced, -duc.ing 1** bring or put forward: *evidence produced in court; Cows produce* (= give) *milk.* **2** bring into existence in any of various ways: *a method that produces results; Causes produce effects; She produces* (= prepares for public presentation) *the plays she directs; a book printed and produced* (= manufactured) *abroad.* —*n.* (PROD.uce) what is produced by a farm, esp. fruits and vegetables.
pro.duc.er (pruh.DEW.sur) *n.* **1** one who produces commercial goods or services. **2** one who produces movies, plays, or shows.
producer goods *n.pl.* raw materials, tools, machinery, etc. for the production of consumer goods.
prod.uct (PROD.uct) *n.* **1** what is produced: *commercial products such as factory goods; milk, cheese, and such dairy products; farm products such as crops and livestock; a finished product; waste products; the **product line*** (= various goods) *of a manufacturer.* **2** result: *an end product; This poem is a product of genius; These children are products of the 1990s; Six is the product of* (= result of multiplying) *2 and 3.*
pro.duc.tion (pruh.DUK.shun) *n.* the act of producing or something produced: *the production of goods and services; The movie was hailed as a great production* (= show); *a factory's **production line*** (= assembly line).
pro.duc.tive (pruh.DUC.tiv) *adj.* **1** producing much: *a productive worker.* **2** producing good results: *productive labor, time.* **3** capable of producing: *Suspicion is **productive** of enmities.*
—**pro.duc.tive.ly** *adv.*
—**pro.duc.tive.ness** or **pro.duc.tiv.i.ty** (prod.uc.TIV.i.tee) *n.*
prof *n. Informal.* professor.
pro.fane (pruh.FANE) *adj.* not showing the reverence due to sacred things: *a profane man's profane language.*
—*v.* **-fanes, -faned, -fan.ing** make profane: *temples profaned by marauders.*
—**pro.fane.ly** *adv.* —**prof.a.na.tion** (prof.uh.NAY.shun) *n.*
pro.fan.i.ty (pruh.FAN.i.tee) *n.* **-ties 1** lack of reverence; profaneness. **2** vulgar or irreverent speech or its utterance: *a mouthful of profanities.*
pro.fess (pruh.FES) *v.* **1** declare one's faith in something; affirm: *He renounced Buddhism and professed (faith in) Islam.* **2** to practice law, medicine, or another profession. **3** claim: *He professes to know nothing of what happened; professes total ignorance; adj.: a **professed*** (= acknowledged or self-declared) *abortionist; a professed desire to get involved; their professed admiration, commitment, dislike, goal, ideals, ignorance, interest, love, patriotism, views.*
pro.fess.ed.ly (pruh.FES.id.lee) *adv.* admittedly: *She's a professedly poor piano player; He's professedly a radical.*
pro.fes.sion (pruh.FESH.un) *n.* **1** the act of professing: *a profession of faith, loyalty.* **2** a vocation that involves training or skill: *Law, medicine, and divinity used to be called the learned professions; to practice a profession; a nun by calling but a teacher by profession; Cook by name but doctor by profession; a national body's call to the **profession*** (= to people practicing the profession).
pro.fes.sion.al (pruh.FESH.uh.nul) *adj.*

professor / program

1 having to do with a profession: *a professional nurse; a lawyer's professional ethics.* 2 expert: *professional advice; a professional pickpocket; The break-in seems a professional job.* 3 playing for pay: *a professional boxer, not an amateur; a professional hockey player.* —*n.* 1 one who practices a profession: *Librarians are professionals; real, true professionals; a football professional.* 2 one who plays for pay: *An Olympic champion may* **turn professional** *(to play for pay).*
—**pro.fes.sion.al.ism** *n.*
—**pro.fes.sion.al.ly** *adv.*

pro.fes.sor (pruh.FES.ur) *n.* a teacher in a college or university: *a professor of physics; an emeritus professor* or *professor emeritus; adjunct, assistant, associate, full, visiting professors.* —**pro.fes.sor.ship** *n.*
—**pro.fes.sor.i.al** (prof.uh.SOR.ee.ul, proh.fuh-) *adj.*

prof.fer (PROF.ur) *n. & v.* **prof.fers, prof.fered, prof.fer.ing** *Formal.* offer: *to proffer advice; a night's lodging proffered in friendship; to accept a proffered hand.*

pro.fi.cient (pruh.FISH.unt) *adj.* skilled: *He's proficient in* or *at cooking, though not an expert;* **pro.fi.cient.ly** *adv.*
—**pro.fi.cien.cy** *n.*

pro.file (PROH.file) *n.* 1 the side view of a face: *Lily looks better in profile.* 2 an outline of features or characteristics: *a company profile; patient's medication profile; Keep a* **low profile** (= do not draw attention to yourself) *and avoid talking to the media; cpd: a low-profile executive; a high-profile job (with high exposure to the public).* 3 an outline biography: *Kennedy's "Profiles in Courage" contains biographies of U.S. senators.*
—*v.* **-files, -filed, -fil.ing** 1 show in profile: *The Queen is profiled on Canadian coins.* 2 describe: *The "Most Wanted" show profiles the worst criminals.*

prof.it (PROF.it) *n.* 1 financial gain: *to make a clear, gross, handsome, net, quick profit; to earn, reap, turn a profit on a sale; business profits; excess profits; The sale brought in* or *yielded a profit; The car was repaired and sold* **at a profit**; *the* **profit and loss** *statement at the close of a financial year.* 2 benefit or advantage: *What profit is there in arguing?*
—*v.* benefit: *to profit by* or *from one's mistakes.*

prof.it.a.ble (PROF.i.tuh.bul) *adj.* yielding a profit: *a profitable undertaking; It's not profitable* (= beneficial) *to go on pumping money into a failing business;* **prof.it.a.bly** *adv.* —**prof.it.a.bil.i.ty** (-BIL.i.tee) *n.*

prof.i.teer (prof.i.TEER) *n.* one who makes excessive profits in a time of scarcity. —*v.* do thus; *n.:* hoarding and **profiteering**.

prof.li.gate (PROF.luh.git, "g" as in "go") *adj.* dissipated or extravagant; *n.* such a person; **prof.li.gate.ly** *adv.*
—**prof.li.ga.cy** (-guh.see) *n.*

pro for.ma (proh.FOR.muh) *adj. Latin.* as advance information: *A* **pro forma invoice** *is sent as notice, not to ask for any payment due.*

pro.found (pruh.FOUND) *adj.* deep: *in profound sleep; my profound apologies, sympathy; a profound thinker; a profound bow; profound* (= thoroughgoing) *changes in society.*

pro.found.ly *adv.* completely or totally: *profoundly deaf, disturbing, divided, mistaken, moved; Tomorrow's vote may profoundly change the course of history.*

pro.fun.di.ty (pruh.FUN.di.tee) *n.* **-ties** depth: *the profundity of a philosopher's thought; Confucian profundities* (= deep thoughts).

pro.fuse (pruh.FUSE, *rhyme:* produce) *adj.* excessively plentiful: *He shed profuse tears; her profuse thanks; He was profuse in his praise;* **pro.fuse.ly** *adv.*
—**pro.fu.sion** (-FEW.zhun) *n.* excessive amount: *Rain fell in profusion after the long drought.*

pro.gen.i.tor (proh.JEN.uh.tur) *n.* ancestor or begetter.

prog.e.ny (PROJ.uh.nee) *n.* **-nies** offspring.

pro.ges.ter.one (proh.JES.tuh.rohn) *n.* a steroid sex hormone that prepares the uterus to receive a fertilized ovum.

prog.na.thous (PROG.nuh.thus) *adj.* (having the jaws) projecting.

prog.no.sis (prog.NOH.sis) *n., pl.* **-ses** (-seez) an estimate of the course, duration, and effect of a patient's illness.

prog.nos.tic (prog.NOS.tic) *adj.* predictive: *a prognostic sign, symptom, weather chart.*

prog.nos.ti.cate (prog.NOS.ti.cate) *v.* **-cates, -cat.ed, -cat.ing** foretell from a sign or symptom: *It is difficult to prognosticate the survival of the present government; Few rely on what the weatherman prognosticates.*
—**prog.nos.ti.ca.tion** (-CAY.shun) *n.*
—**prog.nos.ti.ca.tor** (-cay.tur) *n.*

pro.gram (PROH.gram) *n.* 1 a list of items or events, as for a performance: *the program of the evening.* 2 a broadcast item or performance: *phone-in,*

radio, TV *programs*. **3** a plan of doing something step by step: *to draw up a program of studies; to carry out, launch, terminate a program; building, development, honors, school programs; a program in literature; a program to cut spending; What's on our program (= schedule) today?* **4** a series of instructions for a computer: *to boot up, debug, execute, run, write a program*. —*v.* **-grams, -grammed** *or* **-gramed, -gram.ming** *or* **-gram.ing 1** plan a program of something: *to program a ceremony, function*. **2** instruct: *to program a computer to do tax returns using a* **programming language** *such as Cobol, Fortran, and Pascal.* —**pro.gram.ma.ble** *or* **pro.gram.a.ble** (proh.GRAM.uh.bul) *adj.: a programmable calculator.* —**pro.gram.mer** (PROH.gram.ur) *or* **pro.gram.er** *n.* Also **pro.gramme** *Cdn.*
pro.gress (PROH.gres, PROG.res) *n.* forward movement; advance: *the progress of civilization through the centuries; to hinder, impede, make progress in doing something; our progress toward reaching an agreement; A meeting is* **in progress** (= going on). —*v.* (pruh.GRES) **-gress.es, -gressed, -gress.ing** make progress: *How's the patient progressing? to progress toward perfection.*
—**pro.gres.sion** (pruh.GRESH.un) *n.: a drinker's progression toward alcoholism.*
pro.gres.sive (pruh.GRES.iv) *adj.* **1** going forward: *a progressive disease, idea, nation*. **2** favoring continual reform, esp. in government: *a progressive party; She is progressive in her thinking*. —*n.* one who favors political reform.
—**pro.gres.sive.ly** *adv.*
pro.hib.it (pruh.HIB.it) *v.* forbid authoritatively: *Smoking is strictly prohibited here; You are prohibited from smoking here*; *adj.: a* **prohibited** *activity, area, author, category, chemical; prohibited goods, literature*.
pro.hi.bi.tion (proh.uh.BISH.un) *n.* a prohibiting, esp. of alcoholic liquors: *Prohibition has failed in most countries; a prohibition against smoking.*
—**pro.hi.bi.tion.ist** *n.*
pro.hib.i.tive (pruh.HIB.uh.tiv) *adj.* **1** preventing from buying, doing, etc.: *prohibitive legal fees, house prices, tax rates*. **2** too expensive: *Buying a house these days is becoming prohibitive.*
—**prohibitive favorite** *Informal.* one who is sure to win; sure bet.
—**pro.hib.i.tive.ly** *adv.*
pro.hib.i.to.ry (pruh.HIB.uh.tor.ee) *adj.* prohibiting: *a prohibitory order against a publication; prohibitory measures.*

proj.ect (PROH.ject, PROJ.ect) *n.* **1** a proposed or actual undertaking, often on a large scale: *a highway construction project; a Grade 9 science project*. **2** a group of apartments or houses forming a unit, usu. built and run with public funds: *a housing project*. —*v.* (pruh.JECT) **1** propose: *A tax hike is projected for next year*. **2** extend in space or time: *a cape projecting into the sea; to project* (= estimate by extending known information) *population increases of the next decade*. **3** cause to appear on a surface: *pictures projected on a screen; a world map made by mathematically projecting the globe on a flat surface.*
pro.jec.tile (pruh.JEC.tile, -til) *n.* anything thrown or hurled forward, as a missile or rocket: *to launch a projectile.*
pro.jec.tion (pruh.JEC.shun) *n.* **1** a jutting out: *the projections on a surface*. **2** an estimate of something in the future: *to make a projection of population increases*. **3** something thrown on a surface: *the projection of a picture on a screen; the Mercator projection* (= map) *of the globe; a* **projection booth** *from which movies are projected*. **4** in psychology, the ascribing or attribution of one's own feelings or motives to other persons or things, often as a defense mechanism. —**pro.jec.tion.ist** *n.* a projector operator.
pro.jec.tor (pruh.JEC.tur) *n.* a machine for projecting pictures: *a movie projector; overhead projector; slide projectors.*
pro.lapse (proh.LAPS) *n.* the downward slipping of an organ from its normal position because of weakness of supporting tissue, as of the rectum or uterus. —*v.* **-laps.es, -lapsed, -laps.ing**; *adj.: a* **prolapsed** *cord, heart valve, uterus.*
pro.le.tar.i.an (proh.luh.TAIR.ee.un) *n.* a member of the proletariat.
—*adj.* having to do with the proletariat: *proletarian art, literature, rule, virtues; a proletarian district, government, revolution; the proletarian class, state.*
pro.le.tar.i.at (proh.luh.TAIR.ee.ut) *n.* the industrial working class.
pro-life *adj.* opposed to abortions, euthanasia, and such ways of ending life: *a pro-life candidate, group, position; the pro-life movement*. —**pro-lifer** *n.*
pro.lif.er.ate (pruh.LIF.uh.rate) *v.* **-ates, -at.ed, -at.ing** multiply or grow rapidly, esp. in an uncontrolled manner: *Corals proliferate by budding.*
—**pro.lif.er.a.tion** (-RAY.shun) *n.: the U.N. treaty to prohibit the proliferation of nuclear weapons.*

—**pro.lif.er.ous** (-ur.us) *adj.*: *a proliferous growth of new tissue.*
pro.lif.ic (pruh.LIF.ic) *adj.* producing much: *a prolific writer; Rabbits and hamsters are prolific* (= fertile) *animals.*
pro.lix (proh.LIX, PROH.lix) *adj.* verbose or long-winded; **pro.lix.ly** *adv.*
—**pro.lix.i.ty** (proh.LIX.i.tee) *n.*
pro.logue (PROH.log) *n.* **1** an introductory part: *the prologue to a play, poem, novel.* **2** any introductory act or event: *the prologue to a new era; if the past is prologue* (= if the past indicates what is to come). Also **pro.log.**
pro.long (pruh.LONG) *v.* make longer, esp. in time: *Why prolong the agony? a visit prolonged into the night;* **adj**.: *a prolonged illness, period; prolonged applause, relief, use.* —**pro.lon.ga.tion** (proh.long.GAY.shun) *n.*
prom *n. Informal.* a formal dance held by a school or college class: *the senior prom.*
prom.e.nade (prom.uh.NAHD, -NADE) *n.* **1** a public walk or ride taken for pleasure. **2** a public place for walking, as a ship's "promenade deck."
—*v.* **-nades, -nad.ed, -nad.ing** **1** walk about, esp. in display: *Prendergast and his dog like to promenade on the beach.* **2** parade someone, as if for display: *The best of the bunch were promenaded on the stage for the benefit of the judges.*
Pro.me.the.an (pruh.MEE.thee.un, "th" as in "thin") *adj.* life-bringing; daringly creative, like **Prometheus,** a Titan of Greek myth who stole fire from heaven for human benefit.
pro.me.thi.um (pruh.MEE.thee.um) *n.* a rare-earth metallic chemical element.
prom.i.nence (PROM.uh.nunce) *n.* a being prominent or something that is prominent: *a paper that gives prominence to sports stories; Churchill came into prominence during World War II; an iceberg first noticed as a prominence on the horizon; Solar prominences erupt as huge arches of gas.*
prom.i.nent (PROM.uh.nunt) *adj.* **1** projecting: *an insect's prominent eyes; a prominent chin, nose.* **2** conspicuous, distinguished, or eminent: *a prominent leader; prominent people; a prominent position in public life.* —**prom.i.nent.ly** *adv.*
pro.mis.cu.ous (pruh.MIS.cue.us) *adj.* disorderly or indiscriminate, esp. in regard to sex: *a promiscuous life; promiscuous behavior, youth;*
pro.mis.cu.ous.ly *adv.* —**pro.mis.cu.ous.ness** or **prom.is.cu.i.ty** (prom.is.CUE.uh.tee) *n.*

prom.ise (PROM.is) *n.* **1** one's word that binds one to do or not do something: *to break, fulfill, keep, make a promise; He went back on his promise; He was sued for breach of promise; broken, empty, solemn promises; a promise to deliver on time.* **2** an expectation of hope or success: *a juvenile poem that shows much promise; the land of promise flowing with milk and honey; great promise but poor performance.*
—*v.* **-is.es, -ised, -is.ing** make a promise: *I promise you help; I promise to marry you; An honest politician never **promises the moon*** (= something that cannot be delivered); **adj**.: *a promised raise; the* **Promised Land** *of Canaan (as promised by God to the Israelites).*
promising *adj.* likely to give success or good results: *The weather looks promising; a promising start in life;*
prom.is.ing.ly *adv.*
prom.is.so.ry (PROM.uh.sor.ee) *adj.* containing a promise to pay back: *a **promissory note** for $5,000 due for payment in 60 days.*
pro.mo (PROH.moh) *n.* **-mos** *Informal.* promotional announcement; commercial: *all those promos for junk food.*
prom.on.to.ry (PROM.un.tor.ee) *n.* **-ries** a headland; cape.
pro.mo.ta.ble (pruh.MOH.tuh.bul) *adj.* that can be promoted: *a promotable candidate; The name "Ryan" is more promotable in the French media than "Regan."*
pro.mote (pruh.MOTE) *v.* **-motes, -mot.ed, -mot.ing** **1** raise in rank: *They promoted her from major to colonel.* **2** further the popularity of a person or thing: *to promote an author, book; a new movie well promoted by ads.* **3** help to establish: *to promote peace and understanding.* —**pro.mot.er** (-MOH.tur) *n.*
—**pro.mo.tion** (-shun) *n.*
—**pro.mo.tion.al** (-shun.ul) *adj.*: *promotional activity, hype; a promotional ad campaign, event, tour.*
prompt *v.* **1** make someone do something: *Good examples prompt others to do the same.* **2** cause something to be: *a gift prompted by charity.* **3** remind by supplying cues or lines: *to prompt an actor.* —*adj.* acting or done quickly: *prompt action to put out a fire; prompt deliveries, replies, service; He's prompt at or in answering questions; We expect prompt obedience from students.* —*n.* **1** a prompting, as a suggestion or reminder. **2** a symbol appearing on a computer screen to indicate readiness to accept an instruction from the user.

—**prompt.er** n. —**prompt.ly** adv.
—**prompt.ness** n.: *promptness of payment, service; her promptness and energy;* also **promp.ti.tude** (-tuh.tude).

prom.ul.gate (PROM.ul.gate, proh.MUL.gate) v. **-gates, -gat.ed, -gat.ing** 1 put into force officially: *a regulation promulgated by executive order.* 2 make widespread: *to promulgate ideas, knowledge, policies.*
—**prom.ul.ga.tion** (-GAY.shun) n.

prone adj. 1 liable or inclined: *Human beings are prone to error; a nervous and accident-prone driver.* 2 *Formal.* (lying) on one's face: *The body was stretched prone on the pavement; the prone glide in swimming.* —**prone.ly** adv.; **prone.ness** n.

prong n. the pointed end of a part that is a branch of something, as a tine of a fork, fang of a tooth, or tip of an antler.

pronged adj. branched: *the pronged antlers of the "pronghorn" antelope;* cpd: *a two-pronged tuning fork; a three-pronged attack by the invading army.*

pro.noun (PROH.noun) n. a word such as "I," "you," "he," "herself," or "anybody" that functions like a noun.
—**pro.nom.i.nal** (proh.NOM.uh.nul) adj.

pro.nounce (pruh.NOUNCE) v. **-nounc.es, -nounced, -nounc.ing** 1 declare formally or officially: *The judge pronounced a sentence; Lu was pronounced guilty; Jo was pronounced dead on arrival at the hospital.* 2 give the pronunciation of a word: *"Waskatenau" is pronounced* (wuh.SET.nah).
—**pro.nounce.a.ble** (-suh.bul) adj.: *"Chomley" is more pronounceable than "Cholmondeley."* —**pro.nounce.ment** (-munt) n. a formal declaration.

pronounced adj. strongly marked or perceived: *a change that is becoming more pronounced; a pronounced accent, difference, effect, feature, tendency.*

pron.to (PRON.toh) adv. *Informal.* quickly or promptly.

pro.nun.ci.a.men.to (proh.NUN.see.uh. MEN.toh) n. **-tos** a public announcement or proclamation.

pro.nun.ci.a.tion (pruh.nun.see.AY.shun) n. the way of saying a word, syllable, or sound of a language.

proof (long "oo") n. 1 the act or process of proving; test or trial: *"The proof of the pudding is in the eating"; to put a new bike* **to the proof** (= try it out). 2 something that establishes truth or correctness; sure evidence: *A postal receipt is proof of delivery; to furnish, produce, provide proof; ample, clear, convincing, positive proof; The burden of proof is on the accuser.* 3 the strength of liquor: *Alcohol that is 100% proof has 57.1% alcohol by volume; A* **proof spirit** *is 100 proof.* 4 a trial print: *a photographer's or printer's proof; the galley proofs and page proofs of a book.*
—adj. 1 adjp. of proven value or strength: *a good coat of paint that is* **proof against** *the ravages of the weather;* cpd: *a foolproof plan (that is supposed to succeed); a rustproof paint (that prevents rust); a waterproof watch (that water cannot enter).* 2 adja. of coins, having a shiny surface and struck for collectors: *a proof coin, set; of proof quality.*

proof.read (PROOF.reed) v. **-reads, -read** (-red), **-read.ing** read something for correcting errors before presentation or publication. —**proof.read.er** n.

prop n. 1 a support or stay: *The prop of his old age was an only son; a corn plant's prop roots.* 2 [short form] propeller. 3 [short form] stage property.
—v. **props, propped, prop.ping** support something in a certain way: *to prop a door open; a poor defense propped up by shady witnesses.*

prop.a.gan.da (prop.uh.GAN.duh) n. ideas or doctrines spread by an interested party to influence others: *political propaganda; war propaganda; to spread propaganda against the opposition;* adja.: *a propaganda effort; radio and TV as propaganda instruments.*
—**prop.a.gan.dist** n. —**prop.a.gan.dize** v. **-diz.es, -dized, -diz.ing.**

prop.a.gate (PROP.uh.gate) v. **-gates, -gat.ed, -gat.ing** spread, as with seeds or cuttings: *to propagate a breed of animals, a plant; Trees propagate themselves; Insects propagate diseases; to propagate news; a story propagated on the air waves.*
—**prop.a.ga.tion** (-GAY.shun) n.: *sexual propagation of the species; propagation of radio waves; the propagation of ideas, of the faith, of a philosophy, of a vision.*
—**prop.a.ga.tor** (-gay.tur) n.: *a malicious propagator of lies.*

pro.pane (PROH.pane) n. a flammable gas obtained from petroleum and natural gas for use as a fuel, in refrigeration, etc.

pro.pel (pruh.PEL) v. **-pels, -pelled, -pel.ling** drive something forward: *a man propelled by ambition; Her recent book has propelled her to the top of her profession;* cpd: *a jet-propelled aircraft; rocket-propelled grenades; a self-propelled vehicle.* —**pro.pel.lant** or **pro.pel.lent**

n.: a rocket propellant composed of a fuel and an oxidizer; **adja.:** *Liquid hydrogen is the propellent fuel.*
pro.pel.ler (pruh.PEL.ur) *n.* a revolving device for propelling an aircraft, ship, etc.; also **screw propeller.**
pro.pen.si.ty (pruh.PEN.si.tee) *n.* **-ties** *Formal.* a natural inclination: *a propensity for punning; a propensity to tell fibs; the human propensity to selfishness.*
prop.er 1 *adj.* right, correct, or suitable, as if belonging or related: *Please put everything back in its proper place; proper conduct for a pupil; Suburbs are outside the city proper* (= the main city); *Hank received a proper* (*Informal for* thorough and well-deserved) *tongue-lashing from his uncle; We are experiencing weather* **proper to** (= typical of) *this time of year.* **2** *adja.* designating one, not many; not common: *Trademarks are considered proper adjectives; a* **proper noun** *or* **name** *such as "Ohio" or "the Joneses."* —**prop.er.ly** *adv.*
propertied (PROP.ur.teed) *adj.* owning property: *the propertied classes.*
prop.er.ty (PROP.ur.tee) *n.* **-ties 1** what is owned by one, esp. real estate and movable goods: *a piece of property; Get off my property! This is not stolen property; common, joint, personal, public property; stage properties; a man* **of property** (= of wealth). **2** a quality or characteristic: *Density is one of the properties of matter.*
proph.e.cy (PROF.uh.see) *n.* **-cies** a foretelling or something foretold, esp. if divinely inspired: *to make a prophecy about the end of the world; The prophecy did not come true or turned out to be false or was not fulfilled.*
proph.e.sy (PROF.uh.sye) *v.* **-sies, -sied, -sy.ing** predict that something will happen: *Peg prophesied that Gigi would become president.*
proph.et (PROF.it) *n.* one who tells the future, esp. if divinely inspired or claimed to be: *a false prophet; The weatherman is often a poor prophet; to obey the law and the prophets (of the Old Testament).* —**proph.et.ess** (-is) *fem.*
pro.phet.ic (pruh.FET.ic) *adj.* foretelling: *Jeremiah's prophetic utterances; a gloom that is prophetic of doom;* also **pro.phet.i.cal.** —**pro.phet.i.cal.ly** *adv.*
pro.phy.lac.tic (proh.fuh.LAC.tic) *n.* a preventive agent or device: *prophylactics such as the Salk vaccine and the condom; effective prophylactics.* —**adja.** preventive: *prophylactic agents, drugs, treatment, use.*
pro.phy.lax.is (proh.fuh.LAX.is) *n.* prevention or protection: *scaling and cleaning as prophylaxis against tooth decay.*
pro.pin.qui.ty (proh.PINK.wi.tee) *n. Formal.* **1** nearness in place or time: *geographic propinquity.* **2** nearness of relationship; kinship: *degrees of propinquity.*
pro.pi.ti.ate (pruh.PISH.ee.ate) *v.* **-ates, -at.ed, -at.ing** win the favor of someone of influence, esp. of someone who should be appeased: *to propitiate the gods.* —**pro.pi.ti.a.tion** (-AY.shun) *n.* —**pro.pi.ti.a.to.ry** (-uh.tor.ee) *adj.: a propitiatory invocation, offering, sacrifice.*
pro.pi.tious (pruh.PISH.us) *adj.* auspicious or favorable: *The weather seems propitious for the trip; Fortune is propitious to us.*
prop.jet same as TURBOPROP.
prop.man *n.* a person in charge of stage properties; property man.
pro.po.nent (pruh.POH.nunt) *n.* one who proposes or espouses something: *a proponent of free trade.*
pro.por.tion (pruh.POR.shun) *n.* **1** the proper relation of things one to another as of parts to a whole: *Everyone is paid* **in proportion to** *work done; The arms are somewhat* **out of proportion to** *the statue's body; The cost of living has risen out of all proportion to wages.* **2** ratio: *"1/2 : 3/6" is a proportion.* **3** part or share: *the proportion of silver in the coin; your proportion* (= share) *of the work; a disease of epidemic* **proportions** (= dimensions or size).
—*v.* be or make in due proportion: *We have to proportion our expenses to our earnings;* **adj.:** *Chris has a nicely* **proportioned** *figure; Exercise can keep you well proportioned; a perfectly proportioned swimming pool.*
pro.por.tion.al (pruh.POR.shun.nul) *adj.* in due proportion: *Achievement in life is often directly proportional to one's intelligence and inversely proportional to the lack of it; In most political systems, parties get* **proportional representation** *in a legislature based on the votes cast; Monospaced printing does not look as good as* **proportional spacing** *with "i," "m," etc. occupying spaces in proportion to their width;* **pro.por.tion.al.ly** *adv.*
—**pro.por.tion.ate** (-nit) *adj.* proportional: *a proportionate balance; proportionate cuts, shares; of proportionate size; on a proportionate basis;* **pro.por.tion.ate.ly** *adv.*
pro.pos.al (pruh.POH.zul) *n.* a proposing or something proposed, as an offer or request: *to make a marriage pro-*

posal to someone; to accept or adopt, entertain, put forward a proposal; a proposal to reform the tax system; a proposal for reform.

pro.pose (pruh.POZE) v. **-pos.es, -posed, -pos.ing** **1** put forward for consideration or acceptance: *We propose Jones for mayor; I propose that we accept the report; I proposed (marriage) and she accepted.* **2** plan or intend: *I propose to go abroad in the summer.*

prop.o.si.tion (prop.uh.ZISH.un) n. **1** a statement, esp. a resolution at a meeting: *the proposition that sales taxes be abolished.* **2** *Informal.* a proposed deal or something to be dealt with, as a problem or a person: *That's a tough proposition.* **3** *Informal.* a proposal, esp. for sexual intimacy; v.: *Chris has never been propositioned by anyone.* —**prop.o.si.tion.al** *adj.*

pro.pound (pruh.POUND) v. put forward for consideration: *to propound a doctrine, question, riddle, scheme, theory.*

pro.pri.e.tar.y (pruh.PRY.uh.tair.ee) *adj.* pertaining to ownership: *a proprietary interest, right;* **proprietary medicine** (= patent medicine).

pro.pri.e.tor (pruh.PRY.uh.tur) *n.* an owner, as of a business; **pro.pri.e.tress** (-tris) *fem.*

pro.pri.e.ty (pruh.PRY.uh.tee) *n.* **1** the quality or condition of being proper or fitting, esp. in regard to behavior: *the questionable propriety of chewing gum in church.* **2 -ties** *pl.* standards or requirements of proper behavior: *Children are taught to follow certain domestic proprieties; social proprieties.*

pro.pul.sion (pruh.PUL.shun) *n.* a propelling or its force: *jet propulsion; rocket propulsion.* —**pro.pul.sive** (-siv) *adj.*: *a propulsive beat, dance, rhythm; a dynamic and propulsive role.*

pro ra.ta (proh.RAY.tuh, -RAT.uh) *adj.* proportionate or proportionately; prorated: *The money was distributed to the claimants, large and small, on a pro rata basis; pro rata shares; payment pro rata;* *adv.*: *Creditors were paid pro rata based on the amounts owed.*

pro.rate (proh.RATE) v. **-rates, -rat.ed, -rat.ing** divide, distribute, or assess proportionately to other factors such as share or interest of each individual: *Each extra hour is prorated at $30 per half hour;* *adj.*: *Part-timers are paid prorated amounts of the full salary.* —**pro.ra.tion** (-RAY.shun) *n.*

pro.rogue (proh.ROHG) v. **-rogues, -rogued, -rogu.ing** formally dismiss a legislature; adjourn. —**pro.ro.ga.tion** (-ruh.GAY.shun) *n.*

pro.sa.ic (proh.ZAY.ic) *adj.* matter-of-fact or dull: *a prosaic existence, job, occupation.* —**pro.sa.i.cal.ly** *adv.*

pro.sce.ni.um (proh.SEE.nee.um) *n.* **-ni.ums** or **-ni.a** (-nee.uh) the front part, esp. the apron of a stage framed by the arch (**proscenium arch**) containing the curtain.

pro.scribe (proh.SCRIBE) v. **-scribes, -scribed, -scrib.ing** *Formal.* prohibit a person or practice as dangerous. —**pro.scrip.tion** (-SCRIP.shun) *n.*

prose (PROZE) *n.* ordinary language that is not in verse form.

pros.e.cute (PROS.uh.cute) v. **-cutes, -cut.ed, -cut.ing** **1** pursue: *to prosecute a claim, an investigation, a war on drugs; to prosecute a study.* **2** bring a criminal action: *Shoplifters will be prosecuted for theft; Lawyers defend and prosecute cases; to prosecute a charge, crime, robbery; Shopkeepers don't prosecute in every case of theft; a* **prosecuting attorney** (= government lawyer or prosecutor). —**pros.e.cu.tor** (-cue.tur) *n.*

pros.e.cu.tion (pros.uh.CUE.shun) *n.* **1** a bringing of a criminal action: *Shoplifters face prosecution for theft; the prevention and prosecution of drunk driving.* **2** the prosecuting party, usu. the government: *witnesses for the prosecution.*

pros.e.lyte (PROS.uh.lite) *n.* a convert from one religion to another.

pros.e.lyt.ize (PROS.uh.luh.tize) v. **-iz.es, -ized, -iz.ing** to convert, esp. by inducements.

pro.sit (PROH.sit) *interj.* [used as a toast] to your health! Also **prost** (*rhyme:* most).

pro.sod.ic (pruh.SOD.ic) *adj.* having to do with prosody: *prosodic features such as meter and rhyme.*

pros.o.dy (PROS.uh.dee) *n.* verse structure or its study; **pros.o.dist** *n.*

pros.pect (PROS.pect) *n.* **1** an extensive view or outlook: *a prospect of the countryside from a hilltop.* **2** an expectation of something; also, someone expected: *She seems a good prospect as a client; a job with good* **prospects** (= chances) *for promotion.* —*v.* search: *to prospect for gold, oil, minerals.* —**pros.pec.tor** *n.*

pros.pec.tive (pros.PEC.tiv) *adja.* hoped for or expected: *the prospective bride; a prospective candidate for election;* **pros.pec.tive.ly** *adv.*

pros.pec.tus (pros.PEC.tus) *n.* an outline, esp. of something proposed, giving its main features: *the prospectus of a book in preparation, of a business, of an* educational institution.

pros.per (PROS.pur) *v.* thrive, esp. financially; succeed.

pros.per.i.ty (pros.PER.i.tee) *n.* a prospering or thriving: *to enjoy prosperity in business; "Prosperity makes friends, adversity tries them."*

pros.per.ous (PROS.pur.us) *adj.* **1** thriving: *a prosperous business, economy, era, farmer, future, land, landlady, nation, society.* **2** favorable: *prosperous weather for tomatoes.* —**pros.per.ous.ly** *adv.*

pros.tate *n.* a male gland surrounding the urethra. —**pros.tat.ic** (pros.TAT.ic) *adj.*

pros.ta.ti.tis (pros.tuh.TYE.tis) *n.* inflammation of the prostate.

pros.the.sis (pros.THEE.sis, PROS.thuh-, "th" as in "thin") *n., pl.* **-ses** (-seez) **1** the replacement of a missing tooth, eye, or limb. **2** a replacement part, as a denture or artificial eye.

pros.thet.ic (pros.THET.ic) **1** *adj.* being a replacement part: *A denture is a prosthetic device.* **2** **prosthetics** *n.pl.* a branch of surgery dealing with artificial body parts.

pros.ti.tute (PROS.ti.tute) *n.* a person who provides sex for pay. —*v.* **-tutes, -tut.ed, -tut.ing** sell one's talents for base purposes: *A journalist would be prostituting himself if he wrote a paid review of a worthless book.* —**pros.ti.tu.tion** (-TUE.shun) *n.*: *the prostitution (= selling out) of literary talent for political propaganda.*

pros.trate (PROS.trate) *v.* **-trates, -trat.ed, -trat.ing 1** lie stretched out, usu. with the face downward: *Worshipers prostrate themselves before the altar.* **2** lay low: *David prostrated Goliath with one slingshot.* **3** weaken or exhaust: *We were prostrated by heat.* —*adj.* lying flat; also, laid low or overcome: *his prostrate body; our prostate economy, thanks to overspending; The Nazis lay or were prostrate at the end of the war.* —**pros.tra.tion** (pros.TRAY.shun) *n.*: *heat prostration* (= heat exhaustion); *nervous prostration* (= nervous breakdown).

pros.y (PROH.see) *adj.* **pros.i.er, -i.est 1** resembling prose: *the prosiness of free verse.* **2** prosaic or dull: *a prosy tale.*

pro.tac.tin.i.um (proh.tac.TIN.ee.um) *n.* a radioactive metallic chemical element.

pro.tag.o.nist (proh.TAG.uh.nist) *n.* **1** the main character in a play or story. **2** champion or leader.

pro.te.an (PROH.tee.un, proh.TEE-) *adj.* **1** like the Greek god **Proteus** who could assume any form; hence, changeable: *a protean art form.* **2** versatile: *a protean artist.*

pro.tect (pruh.TECT) *v.* guard against harm, esp. with or as if with a cover or barrier: *Roofs protect us from or against the elements; tariffs to protect industries from foreign competition;* *adj.*: *The whooping crane is an endangered and therefore* **protected** *species (protected from collectors, hunters, etc.).* —**pro.tec.tion** (-TEK.shun) *n.*: *to afford or give or provide protection; police protection; the protection of domestic industries, wild life.* —**pro.tec.tion.ism** (-iz.um) *n.;* **pro.tec.tion.ist** *n.*

protection money *n.* money extorted by racketeers or paid as bribe for protection.

pro.tec.tive (pruh.TEC.tiv) *adj.* protecting or guarding: *Camouflage is protective coloration against the enemy; Parents are protective of their children; a drunk kept in* **protective custody** *by the police; A* **protective tariff** *is placed on imports to give domestic producers a price advantage;* **pro.tec.tive.ly** *adv.* —**pro.tec.tor** (-tur) *n.*

pro.tec.tor.ate (pruh.TEC.tur.it) *n.* a state or territory dependent on another for defense, foreign relations, etc.: *Solomon Islands was a British protectorate till 1978.*

pro.té.gé (PROH.tuh.zhay) *n.* a person to whom one is patron; **pro.té.gée** (-zhay) *fem.*

pro.tein (PROH.teen) *n.* a complex chemical compound occurring as an essential part of all living things: *Milk, eggs, fish, and lean meat are rich in protein.*

pro tem (proh.TEM) *adj.* [short form] pro tempore: *a pro tem administration; appointed as bishop pro tem.*

pro tem.po.re (proh.TEM.puh.ree) *adj. & adv. Latin.* temporary or temporarily: *Al was appointed chairman pro tempore.*

pro.test (pruh.TEST, PROH.test) *v.* **1** object to something: *Women and minorities protest (against) discrimination in hiring; We protested (to the government) that the new tax was unjust.* **2** declare solemnly: *Joan of Arc died protesting her innocence.* —*n.* (PROH.test) a protesting: *loud protests from the public; to enter, file, lodge a protest; to register a strong protest with the authorities against interference in internal matters; Everyone resigned* **in protest;** *an unjust levy paid* **under protest** (= unwillingly). —**pro.test.er** or

pro.tes.tor (-TES.tur) *n.*
Prot.es.tant (PROT.is.tunt) *n.* a Christian not of the Catholic Church or the Eastern Orthodox Church: *Are you turning Protestant?* **adja.:** *a Protestant church, denomination, minister; The **Protestant (work) ethic** considers work as the road to salvation.* —**Prot.es.tant.ism** (-tun.tiz.um) *n.*
pro.tes.ta.tion (prot.is.TAY.shun) *n.* a strong declaration: *her protestations of innocence.*
proto- *comb.form.* 1 first in time, importance, etc.: *protohistory, protomartyr, prototype.* 2 earliest form: *the Indo-European proto-language; proto-Tamil.*
pro.to.col (PROH.tuh.col) *n.* 1 a code of etiquette to be observed on state occasions: *She broke or violated protocol by offering her gloved hand to the Queen; a breach of protocol; to observe diplomatic protocol; military protocol.* 2 an initial draft of a document, esp. a treaty: *to draw up a protocol; the 1925 Geneva Protocol outlawing chemical warfare; a protocol agreement.* 3 a set of rules for the formatting of messages in computer communications.
pro.ton (PROH.ton, *rhyme:* on) *n.* the positively charged elementary particle in the nucleus of all atoms.
pro.to.plasm (PROH.tuh.plaz.um) *n.* the essential living matter of all animal and plant cells; **pro.to.plas.mic** (-PLAZ.mic) *adj.*
pro.to.type (PROH.tuh.type) *n.* a working model of a new idea or product: *to build a prototype for the city of the future; a prototype of an electric car; a working prototype;* **adja.:** *a prototype city, model, superstore; a new gadget in prototype form.*
pro.to.zo.an (proh.tuh.ZOE.un) *n.* a one-celled, microscopic animal, as an amoeba or paramecium.
pro.tract (proh.TRACT) *v.* lengthen or prolong; **adj.:** *a protracted affair, campaign, conflict, delay, effort, process, struggle, war; protracted court battles, negotiations, talks.*
pro.trac.tor (proh.TRAC.tur) *n.* an instrument in the form of a semicircular graduated disc used for plotting and measuring angles.
pro.trude (pruh.TROOD, long "oo") *v.* **-trudes, -trud.ed, -trud.ing** jut or stick out: *vertebrae that protrude and press on nerves;* **adj.:** *protruding eyes, tissue; his protruding tongue.* —**pro.tru.sion** (-TROO.zhun) *n.*
pro.tu.ber.ance (pruh.TUE.buh.runce) *n.* a bulge: *the protuberance of baby boomers in our population (curves).*
—**pro.tu.ber.ant** (-TUE.buh.runt) *adj.* bulging: *protuberant eyes.*
proud *adj.* 1 feeling or showing self-esteem: *He is justly proud of his achievements; feeling proud; Jean is too proud to beg; a mother **proud** of her many children; a proud parent; the proud* (= glorious) *moment of breaking a world record; a proud* (= spirited) *steed.* 2 having or showing too high an opinion of oneself: *proud as a peacock; proud and arrogant.* —**do one proud** *Informal.* make one feel gratified.
—**proud.ly** *adv.*
proud flesh *n.* in a wound, overgrown granular tissue that has yet to heal.
prove (PROOV) *v.* **proves, pt. proved, pp. proved** or **prov.en, prov.ing** 1 demonstrate or show: *Prove that you can lift this weight; Later events proved my suspicions; They proved him guilty; a charge that you cannot prove beyond a reasonable doubt; to prove conclusively; The new recruit proved herself in three days; "The exception proves the rule"* (because every rule has an exception); **adj.:** *a **proven** car that has sold well for many years; a woman with a proven track record.* 2 turn out: *The new recruit proved to be a good choice; The book proved fascinating.* —**prov.a.ble** (-vuh.bul) *adj.* —**prov.a.bil.i.ty** (-vuh.BIL.i.tee) *n.*
prov.e.nance (PROV.uh.nunce) *n.* place of origin; source: *the content and provenance of the crates; goods of Korean provenance.*
Pro.ven.çal (proh.vun.SAHL, prov-) *adj.* having to do with the Romance language of **Provence,** a region of S.E. France: *the Provençal troubadours of the Middle Ages.* —*n.* the language of Provence or a person of or from the region.
prov.en.der (PROV.un.dur) *n.* 1 hay, corn, oats, and such dry food for livestock. 2 *Informal.* provisions or food.
pro.ve.ni.ence (proh.VEE.nee.unce) same as PROVENANCE.
prov.erb (PROV.urb) *n.* a short, wise saying that has been long in use among a people: *As the proverb goes or runs, "Haste makes waste."*
pro.ver.bi.al (pruh.VUR.bee.ul) *adj.* well-known: *Solomon's proverbial wisdom; the proverbial "sleeping dog"; the proverbial 800-pound gorilla.*
—**pro.ver.bi.al.ly** (-uh.lee) *adv.*: *Dogs are proverbially faithful animals.*
pro.vide (pruh.VIDE) *v.* **-vides, -vid.ed, -vid.ing** see to or supply a need or

contingency: *Sheep provide us with wool; Rules provide penalties for offenses; They provide that offenders be punished; insurance to provide for old age and to provide against accidents; It provides him with an opportunity to make money; I provide for my family* (= pay for my family's needs). **—provided** or **providing** *conj.* on the condition that; if: *provided (that) the shoes fit.* **—pro.vid.er** *n.*

prov.i.dence (PROV.i.dunce) *n.* a being provident; prudent management: *Some see the hand of (divine) Providence in everything that happens to them.*

prov.i.dent (PROV.i.dunt) *adj.* careful about future needs, as by saving money: *the provident housewife;* **prov.i.dent.ly** *adv.*

prov.i.den.tial (prov.i.DEN.shul) *adj.* fortunate in happening at exactly the right moment: *It was providential that a doctor happened to be on the plane.* **—prov.i.den.tial.ly** *adv.*

prov.ince (PROV.ince) *n.* **1** an administrative division of a country: *the provinces of Canada.* **2** a sphere of activity or interest: *Marriage counseling is outside the province of a divorce lawyer.*

pro.vin.cial (pruh.VIN.shul) *adj.* **1** having to do with a province: *a provincial highway, legislature, park, parliament.* **2** of outlying areas rather than cities; rustic or unsophisticated: *a provincial accent.* **3** narrow: *His concerns remained rather provincial even after traveling abroad.* **—pro.vin.cial.ism** *n.* **—pro.vin.cial.ly** *adv.*

proving ground *n.* a place for the systematic testing of new equipment, theories, etc.

pro.vi.sion (pruh.VIZH.un) *n.* **1** the act of providing or something provided; arrangement: *There is a provision in the will for gifts to charity; The will makes provision for it.* **2 provisions** *pl.* food supplies or stocks.

pro.vi.sion.al (pruh.VIZH.uh.nul) *adj.* for the time being: *provisional data, figures, plans; a provisional estimate of unemployment in the next decade; a provisional government in exile.* **—pro.vi.sion.al.ly** *adv.*

pro.vi.so (pruh.VYE.soh) *n.* **-sos** or **-soes** a legal stipulation or condition: *with one proviso; She accepted the job with the proviso that no one interfere with her work; a racing bug's insurance policy with a no-speeding proviso.*

prov.o.ca.tion (prov.uh.CAY.shun) *n.* a provoking or something that provokes: *The police fired under extreme provocation; There was much provocation for their behavior; He tends to shout at the slightest provocation; Various provocations were provided or offered to make her fight.*

pro.voc.a.tive (pruh.VOC.uh.tiv) *adj.* **1** tending to arouse a negative feeling or reaction: *provocative behavior; highly provocative language; a very provocative* (= sexually attractive) *costume.* **2** thought-provoking or stimulating: *a provocative essay; a provocative Chopin recital; a controversial and provocative figure; her provocative artistic vision.* **—pro.voc.a.tive.ly** *adv.*

pro.voke (pruh.VOKE) *v.* **-voked, -vok.ing** **1** make angry or annoyed: *A cool-headed man is not easily provoked; She was provoked into saying things she now regrets; adj.: his very provoking behavior.* **2** cause: *artless comments that provoked laughter; comments that provoke arguments; to provoke controversy, jealousy, rage, resentment, responses, riots; adj.: a thought-provoking speech.* **—pro.vok.ing.ly** *adv.*

pro.vost (PROH.vohst, PROV.ust) *n.* **1** a high-ranking official, esp. of a college. **2 provost guard** (PROH.voh-) soldiers on police duty in an army under a **provost marshal.**

prow (rhyme: how) *n.* the front part of a ship, boat, aircraft, etc.

prow.ess (PROW.is, "OW" as in "how") *n.* [literary use] personal bravery or extraordinary ability: *his prowess in battle; She demonstrated* or *displayed her great prowess as a skier; her prowess on the slopes; sexual prowess.*

prowl (rhyme: howl) *v.* go about cautiously like a beast of prey: *enemy subs prowling along our coast; troublemakers prowling the streets; Birders prowl for owls.* **—n.** a prowling: *an all-night prowl by birders; There's a bear* **on the prowl** (= prowling) *in this park; The police arrived in a* **prowl car** (= squad car) *when a prowler was reported in the neighborhood.* **—prow.ler** *n.* a suspected burglar

prox.i.mate (PROX.uh.mit) *adj.* nearest in order, location, or time: *a proximate cause, objective; the proximate future; Our proximate goal is to graduate and get a job, the ultimate goal is happiness.*

prox.im.i.ty (prok.SIM.i.tee) *n. Formal.* nearness: *a house located in close proximity to a garbage dump; geographical proximity; a marriage between first cousins forbidden because of proximity of blood; adja.: proximity locations;* **proximity searching** *of a database (for related words occurring within a few words of each other).*

prox.i.mo (PROX.uh.moh) *adj. Formal.* in the next month; cf. INSTANT, ULTIMO.

prox.y (PROX.ee) *n.* **prox.ies** a substitute with authority to act for another person or a document giving such authority: *Marriage by proxy is not so common as voting by proxy, as at business meetings; The* **proxy statement** *(sent to stockholders with information on company affairs for soliciting their proxies) showed the chairman of the board holding 18,000 shares.*

prude *n.* one who affects excessive modesty in speech and manners: *a Victorian prude.* —**prud.ish** *adj.;* **prud.ish.ly** *adv.;* **prud.ish.ness** *n.*

pru.dence (PROO.dunce) *n.* the quality of being prudent: *Exercise prudence; as simple prudence suggests; fiscal, lending, retail prudence.*

pru.dent (PROO.dunt) *adj.* cautious and circumspect: *a prudent and thrifty housekeeper; Cats don't like prudent mice; a prudent course of action; a prudent investor; to act in a prudent manner; It's prudent to make a will as you get older.* —**pru.dent.ly** *adv.*

pru.den.tial (proo.DEN.shul) *adj.* having to do with being prudent: *Be prudential (= use prudence) in buying insurance; a prudential (Formal for advisory) committee with discretionary powers.* —**pru.den.tial.ly** *adv.*

prud.er.y (PROO.duh.ree) *n.* **-er.ies** a being prudish or an instance of it: *Victorian prudery dictated such pruderies as saying "limb" for "leg."*

prune (PROON) *n.* a dried sweet plum; also, a plum suitable for drying: *prune juice; pitted prunes; At 100 years, I see a dried-up prune in my mirror.*
—*v.* **prunes, pruned, prun.ing** 1 cut out superfluous or dying parts from a plant or tree. 2 trim: *a thesis pruned of unnecessary jargon; n.: a wordy essay that needs* **pruning.**

pru.ri.ent (PROO.ree.unt) *adj.* having to do with lustful desires: *literature appealing* or *catering to the prurient interest.* —**pru.ri.ence** (-unce) *n.*

Prus.sian (PRUSH.un) *n. & adj.* (a person) of or from **Prussia,** a N. European kingdom and empire (1701-1919), in a region now covered by Germany, Poland, and Russia.

pry *v.* **pries, pried, pry.ing** 1 snoop: *No one likes people to pry into their private affairs; adj.: Pat is very* **prying** *(= inquisitive); prying eyes.* 2 force out with or as if with a lever: *to pry open a lid; to pry secrets out of someone.*
—*n.* a tool for prying, as a crowbar.

psalm (SAHM) *n.* a sacred song or poem, especially one from the **Psalms**, a book of the Old Testament, believed to be by King David, the **Psalmist**.

psalm.o.dy (SAH.muh.dee) *n.* 1 the singing of psalms. 2 *pl.* **-dies** an arrangement of psalms. 3 a psalm book.

Psal.ter (SAWL.tur) *n.* Psalms or a collection of psalms for use in worship; also **psalter, psalm book.**

pseu.do (SUE.doh) *adja. & comb.form.* counterfeit or false: *pseudo currency, learning, statistics; pseudo-economists; pseudo-scientific.*

pseu.do.nym (SUE.duh.nim) *n.* an assumed name: *Sam Clemens wrote under the pseudonym Mark Twain.*
—**pseu.don.y.mous** (sue.DON.uh.mus) *adj.: The pseudonymous author of "Tom Sawyer" is really Sam Clemens.*

pshaw (SHAW) *interj.* expressing contempt, disbelief, etc.

psit.ta.co.sis (sit.uh.COH.sis) same as PARROT FEVER.

pso.ri.a.sis (suh.RYE.uh.sis) *n.* a skin disease forming itchy, red patches covered with loose silver-white scales.

psst *interj.* made to attract someone's attention quietly: *Psst! Your slip is showing.*

psych (SIKE) *v. Informal.* 1 get oneself mentally ready: *to psych oneself up; She can psych herself to wake up on time; She took a few moments to get psyched up for the dive.* 2 probe someone's mind; hence, figure out: *to* **psych out** *her insomnia; We'll psych him out with this story.* 3 intimidate or be intimidated: *He was really psyched.* 4 [short form] psychology: *pop psych.* —**adja.** *Informal.* having to do with psychotherapy: *a psych case, emergency, nurse, patient.*

psy.che (SYE.kee) *n.* one's soul or mind: *to explore the human psyche; the psyche of an addict.*

psy.che.del.ic (sye.cuh.DEL.ic) 1 *adj.* relating to hallucinogenic drugs such as LSD or their abnormal effects on the mind: *a psychedelic experience; psychedelic lights, music.* 2 *n.* a psychedelic drug or its user.

psy.chi.a.try (suh.KYE.uh.tree, sye-) *n.* a branch of medicine dealing with mental and emotional disorders; **psy.chi.a.trist** *n.* —**psy.chi.at.ric** (sye.kee.AT.ric) *adj.*

psy.chic (SYE.kik) *n.* one who is sensitive to forces outside the physical world, as a spiritualistic medium.
—*adj.* spiritualistic: *I don't know what she thinks, I'm not psychic; psychic energy,*

psycho / public

power; a psychic force, healer. —**psy.chi.cal** (SYE.ki.cul) adj.: psychical research into spiritualism, ESP, and such psychical phenomena. —**psy.chi.cal.ly** adv.

psy.cho (SYE.coh) **1** n. -cos Informal. psychopath: drunk psychos behind wheels; adj.: psycho killers, wards. **2** comb.form. mental: psychoactive, psychobabble, psychology.

psy.cho.ac.tive (sye.coh.AC.tiv) adj. acting on the mind: a psychoactive drug that can change behavior.

psy.cho.a.nal.y.sis (SYE.coh.uh.NAL.uh.sis) n. the probing of a person's repressed desires, fears, and anxieties for treating mental and emotional disorders.
—**psy.cho.an.a.lyst** (-AN.uh.list) n.
—**psy.cho.an.a.lyt.ic** (-an.uh.LIT.ic) or **psy.cho.an.a.lyt.i.cal** adj.
—**psy.cho.an.a.lyt.i.cal.ly** adv.

psy.cho.an.a.lyze (sye.coh.AN.uh.lize) v. -lyz.es, -lyzed, -lyz.ing treat by psychoanalysis. Also **psy.cho.an.a.lyse** Brit.

psy.cho.bab.ble (SYE.coh.bab.ul) n. the jargon used by psychologists.

psy.cho.chem.i.cal (sye.coh.KEM.i.cul) n. a psychoactive chemical such as LSD or nerve gas; also **adj.**

psy.cho.dra.ma (sye.coh.DRAH.muh) n. a form of group mental therapy in which patients act out problem situations in order to understand and face them.

psy.cho.gen.ic (sye.coh.JEN.ic) adj. caused by mental or emotional conflicts; originating in the mind: psychogenic amnesia, phantom pain, symptoms.

psychological moment n. the most favorable moment: the psychological moment for popping the question.

psy.chol.o.gy (sye.COL.uh.jee) n. -gies **1** the science of mental processes and behavior of people and animals: abnormal, child, clinical, educational psychology; Teachers use psychology (Informal for understanding of people) when dealing with students. **2** the way a person or group behaves: group psychology; mob psychology. —**psy.chol.o.gist** n. —**psy.cho.log.i.cal** (-cuh.LOJ.i.cul) adj.

psy.cho.path (SYE.coh.path) n. a mentally ill person. —**psy.cho.path.ic** (-PATH.ic) adj.

psy.cho.sis (sye.COH.sis) n., pl. -ses (-sees) a major mental disorder, either functional, as schizophrenia, or with an organic cause such as brain damage.

psy.cho.so.mat.ic (sye.cuh.soh.MAT.ic) adj. of a physical disorder, involving both the mind and the body, as certain stomach ulcers, high blood pressure, etc.

psy.cho.ther.a.py (sye.coh.THER.uh.pee) n. treatment of mental and emotional disorders by psychological rather than physical means.
—**psy.cho.ther.a.pist** n.

psy.chot.ic (sye.COT.ic) n. a person affected by a psychosis: psychotics on the loose; adj.: psychotic behavior; in a psychotic frenzy; psychotic killers.

psy.cho.trop.ic (sye.coh.TROP.ic) n. & adj. (a drug) tending to alter the mind, as a tranquilizer or hallucinogen.

ptar.mi.gan (TAR.mi.gun) n. a grouse of mountainous and cold regions that has brown feathers in the summer and white in the winter and completely feathered feet.

pter.o.dac.tyl (ter.uh.DAC.tul) n. an extinct winged reptile with wingspans up to 50 ft. (15.24 m) that lived more than 60 million years ago.

Ptol.e.ma.ic (tol.uh.MAY.ic) adj. having to do with Claudius **Ptolemy**, an ancient Greek astronomer: In the Ptolemaic system, Earth was the center of the universe.

pto.maine (TOH.main) n. a poisonous chemical compound produced by decaying foods.

pub n. Brit. Informal. a licensed tavern or bar.

pu.ber.tal (PEW.bur.tul) adj. having to do with puberty: pubertal boys, changes, development, girls, growth, processes.

pu.ber.ty (PEW.bur.tee) n. the age at which one is capable of sexual reproduction: Girls usually reach puberty before boys.

pu.bes (PEW.beez) **1** n. sing. & pl. pubic hair or region. **2** pl. of PUBIS.

pu.bes.cent (pew.BES.unt) adj. arriving at or having reached puberty.
—**pu.bes.cence** (-unce) n.

pu.bic adj. having to do with the genital region: the pubic area, bone; pubic hair.

pu.bis (PEW.bis) n., pl. **pu.bes** (-beez) a bone of the pelvis on either side, arching together at the front.

pub.lic adj.n. **1** having to do with the people as a whole: the public interest; public knowledge, morals; a survey of public opinion; a public cause, park, place; a public (= nonprofit) broadcasting system; What is not copyrighted, patented, or trademarked is in the **public domain**; public domain software. **2** civic or governmental: public health, officials,

service; *a paid* **public holiday** *such as Christmas or Thanksgiving.* **3** *adj.* not private; well-known: *a public figure; his public life; a secret made public; A private company goes public (and sells shares on the stock exchange); a crime committed* **in public** (= *publicly*). —*n.* the people or a section of it: *the reading public, traveling public, and other publics.*
—**pub.lic.ly** *adv.*
public address system *n.* an amplification system of microphones and loudspeakers for addressing a large audience.
pub.li.can (PUB.li.cun) *n.* **1** a tax collector of ancient Rome. **2** the keeper of a pub in Britain.
public assistance *n.* government aid to the needy.
pub.li.ca.tion (pub.li.CAY.shun) *n.* **1** something published: *an official publication of the government.* **2** the process of publishing, including printing and distribution: *to begin, start, suspend publication.*
public defender *n.* a lawyer assigned to defend poor people at public expense.
public domain 1 *adja.* not enjoying an intellectual property right such as a copyright or patent: *public domain poetry, programs, software, titles.* **2** *n.* the realm of such works considered public property: *After a time, original works enter* or *go into the public domain; The Bible is in the public domain.*
public eye *n.* public notice: *As a senator, she is always in the public eye; to disappear from the public eye; to stay out of the public eye.*
public house *n. Brit.* a licensed tavern or bar.
pub.li.cist (PUB.luh.sist) *n.* one who publicizes; press agent.
pub.li.ci.ty (pub.LIS.i.tee) *n.* **1** public notice and the getting of it: *to avoid, gain, give, provide, receive, seek, shun publicity; She launched her campaign in a blaze of publicity; wide publicity.* **2** articles, announcements, etc. used in the process: *Bad publicity doesn't help the box office.*
pub.li.cize (PUB.luh.size) *v.* **-ciz.es, -cized, -ciz.ing** give publicity to a person or thing.
public mischief *n.* intentionally misleading a police officer.
public relations *n.pl.* [takes *sing. v.*] the promotion of a favorable public image by means of publicity: *As a job title, "public information officer" is preferred to "public relations officer" because of negative connotations.*

public school *n.* in North America, a free school supported by taxes.
public-spirited *adj.* having the good of the public as one's concern: *a public-spirited citizen, housewife.*
public television *n.* noncommercial TV for public information and instruction.
public utility See UTILITY.
public works *n.pl.* the building of highways, dams, bridges, etc. for the use of the public, as by a **public works department.**
pub.lish *v.* make known publicly, esp. print and distribute something written or drawn, as books, art, and music.
—**pub.lish.er** *n.*
puck *n.* **1** the disk used in ice hockey. **2** a mischievous spirit, like Puck in Shakespeare's "Midsummer Night's Dream." —**puck.ish** *adj.*
puck.er *v.* draw into folds or wrinkles: *She puckered up* (= contracted the lips) *and blew us a kiss; adj.: the puckered stripes of seersucker cloth; a puckered knit; n.: Shrinkage could cause puckering.*
—*n.* such folds or wrinkles or a puckered fabric: *pucker cotton Lycra.*
pud.ding (POOD.ing, short "OO") *n.* a soft, thick, sweet, cooked dessert, as "rice pudding" or a baked one, as "plum pudding."
pud.dle (PUD.ul) *n.* **1** a small pool of liquid, usu. of muddy water. **2** a pasty mixture of clay and sand for waterproofing; *v.: to puddle* (= stop) *up a hole.*
pu.den.da (pew.DEN.duh) *n.pl.* the genital organs, esp. of a woman.
—**pu.den.dum** *n.* the vulva.
pudg.y (PUJ.ee) *adj.* **pudg.i.er, -i.est** fat or thickset: *pudgy fingers; People on the pudgy side need to go on a diet.*
pueb.lo (PWEB.loh) *n.* **-los 1** an Indian village of S.W. United States, having compactly built, terraced adobe houses. **2** one of such houses.
pu.er.ile (PEW.uh.ril) *adj.* childish or silly; **pu.er.ile.ly** *adv.* —**pu.er.il.i.ty** (-RIL.i.tee) *n.* **-ties:** *name-calling and such puerilities.*
Puer.to Ri.can (pwer.toh.REE.cun) *n. & adj.* (a person) of or from **Puerto Rico,** a Caribbean island commonwealth, associated with the U.S.
puff *n.* **1** a short, quick blast or draw of air, smoke, or other gas: *puffs of steam from an iron; a puff of breath; a statement punctuated by puffs on his pipe.* **2** a swelling, as if full of air, or something air-filled or fluffy: *hair done in puffs; cream puffs and such* **puff pastry.**

3 overblown praise: *The review was a puff for the book.*
—*v.* **1** move or come in puffs: *smoke puffing out from chimneys; She puffed out the candles one by one; He puffs away at his cigar when thinking hard; She came in huffing and puffing for air.* **2** swell with air: *a trumpeter with his cheeks puffed out; a young hero all puffed up with pride.* **3** praise: *an ad puffing a product to the skies.* —**puf.fer.y** (PUF.uh.ree) *n.*

puff.ball *n.* a white, round, mushroom-like fungus that bursts at the touch releasing a cloud of tiny spores.

puf.fin *n.* a black-and-white sea bird with an enormous beak and a puffy body.

puf.fy *adj.* **puf.fi.er, puf.fi.est** swollen: *a boxer's face puffy with bruises.*
—**puff.i.ness** *n.*

pug *n.* **1** a small dog with a short turned-up nose and a tail curled up over its back. **2** a nose like a pug's. **3** [short form] pugilist.

pu.gil.ist (PEW.juh.list) *n. Formal.* a boxer. —**pu.gil.ism** (-liz.um) *n.* boxing; **pu.gil.is.tic** (-LIS.tic) *adj.*

pug.na.cious (pug.NAY.shus) *adj.* fond of fighting: *the pugnacious offspring of a quarrelsome family;* **pug.na.cious.ly** *adv.*
—**pug.nac.i.ty** (-NAS.i.tee) *n.*

pug-nosed *adj.* having an upturned nose like a pug's.

pu.is.sant (PEW.i.sunt, PWIS.unt) *adj. Archaic or poetic.* powerful; mighty; **pu.is.sant.ly** *adv.* —**pu.is.sance** *n.*

puke *n. & v.* **pukes, puked, puk.ing** *Slang.* vomit.

puk.ka or **puck.a** *adj.* first-rate; genuine.

pul.chri.tude (PUL.cri.tude) *n.* [literary] beauty; comeliness. —**pul.chri.tu.di.nous** (-TUE.di.nus) *adj.*

pule *v.* **pules, puled, pul.ing** cry feebly; whine.

pull (short "oo") *v.* **1** use force to get action in the direction of the force; opposite of PUSH: *Don't push that door, pull it (toward you); She pulled my hair; a child pulling at her mother's sleeve; Pull your horse back; Let's pull this sled up the hill; Please lock the door and pull the drapes (closed).* **2** use or suffer force in various ways: *The cat pulled the paper to shreds; a toy pulled apart by kids; A dentist pulls (= extracts) teeth; She's pulling (= plucking) weeds in the garden; I pulled (= sprained) a muscle in my leg; He pulls (= sucks) on his pipe while thinking.* **3** move: *She stepped on the gas and pulled ahead of the other cars; Trains pull into the station and pull out of it;* *The officer asked the speeder to pull over to the curb; A car pulls up at a stoplight; The ball pulled to the left and missed the pins.* —**pull for 1** support: *Let's pull for the winning team.* **2** row toward: *The boat is leaking, let's pull for or toward the shore.* —**pull off** accomplish: *That was a neat trick he pulled off.* —**pull oneself together** compose oneself: *He pulls himself together in no time after each defeat.* —**pull through** *Informal.* **1** recover: *All those taken to hospital pulled through within a week.* **2** get through: *Somehow, we managed to pull through the horrendous week.* —**pull up** reprimand: *He was pulled up for being late.* —*n.* a pulling, its force, or what is pulled: *the pull of gravity; You need some pull (= influence) to get that job; It was a hard or long pull (= big effort) getting to the top of the hill; Everyone had a long pull (= drink) at the bottle.* —**the long pull** the long term: *You are in it for the long pull; Short-term plans won't help you in or over the long pull.*

pull date *n.* the date stamped on perishable goods after which they are not to be sold.

pull-down menu *n.* on a computer screen, a list of choices that appear beneath the option selected.

pul.let (PULL.it, short "oo") *n.* a young hen.

pul.ley (PULL.ee, short "oo") *n.* **pul.leys** a wheel with a grooved rim for driving a belt that transmits power or for running a rope for raising weights.

Pull.man (PULL.mun, short "oo") *n. Trademark.* **-mans** a railroad parlor car; also **Pullman car.**

pull-out *n.* **1** a withdrawal, as of troops. **2** something to be pulled out, as a magazine insert.

pull.o.ver (pull.OH.vur, short "oo") *n.* a sweater or shirt that is put on by being pulled over the head.

pul.mo.nar.y (PUL.muh.nair.ee) *adj.* of the lungs: *pulmonary disease, edema, embolism, infection.*

pulp *n.* **1** a soft moist mass, as the juicy part of a fruit, the soft tissue inside a tooth, the ground mixture of pulpwood, rag, etc. from which paper is made, etc. **2** a cheap or sensationalistic book or magazine, printed on inferior paper made from wood pulp. —*v.* make into pulp: *Newsprint is pulped and recycled;* **adj.:** *a pulping machine; the pulping industry, process.*
—**pulp.y** *adj.:* *pulpy orange juice; the pulpy material inside vertebral discs.*

pul.pit (PULL.pit, short "OO"; also as in "dull") *n.* **1** an enclosed raised structure set up in church for preaching from. **2** the clergy or ministry: *to be called to the pulpit; the role of women in the pulpit.*

pul.sar (PUL.sar) *n.* a type of celestial objects known by the pulsations of radio, light, and X-ray waves received from them.

pul.sate (PUL.sate) *v.* **-sates, -sat.ed, -sat.ing** beat or throb with a regular rhythm, as the heart or pulse does. —**pul.sa.tion** (pul.SAY.shun) *n.*

pulse *n.* **1** a regular beat, as of the heart pumping blood which is felt in the arteries, esp. at the wrist: *erratic, irregular, weak pulse.* **2** an indication of life or feeling: *a Gallup poll reflecting the pulse of the nation.* —*v.* **puls.es, pulsed, puls.ing 1** beat or throb: *Life pulses in our veins.* **2** move as if with a pulse: *Traffic pulses through a city during rush hour.*

pul.ver.ize (PUL.vuh.rize) *v.* **-iz.es, -ized, -iz.ing** reduce to or become powder. —**pul.ver.i.za.tion** (-ruh.ZAY.shun, -rye-) *n.*

pu.ma (PEW.muh) *n.* a cougar.

pum.ice (PUM.is) *n.* a lightweight, porous, volcanic rock used as a scouring and polishing powder.

pum.mel (PUM.ul) *v.* **pum.mels, pum.meled, pum.mel.ing** pound on someone or something repeatedly, esp. with the fists. Also **pum.melled, pum.mel.ling** *Cdn.*

pump *n.* **1** a machine for forcing fluids in or out of places, esp. by up-and-down action, as of a lever: *a gasoline pump; heat, stomach, sump pumps; a pump-action rifle or shotgun (that is readied for firing by sliding a lever backward and forward).* **2** a low-cut slip-on shoe for formal evening wear. —*v.* use a pump or work up and down like a pump: *The flooded basement had to be pumped out; We pumped it dry; to pump up a bicycle tire; a teacher pumping knowledge into pupils; The reporters pumped (Informal for tried to get information out of) Yves, but he would only say "No comment"; a politician kissing babies and pumping (= shaking) hands; The terrorists pumped (= shot) three bullets into him; Lasers are pumped (= excited to for energy radiation) by light, radio waves, electricity, etc.* —**pump iron** lift weights for exercise.

pump.er.nick.el (PUM.pur.nik.ul) *n.* a kind of heavy, dark bread, usu. made from whole-meal rye.

pump.kin (PUM.kin) *n.* a large, round, orange-yellow, edible gourdlike fruit.

pumpkin head *n. Slang.* a dolt.

pump-priming *n.* government expenditure on public works, relief, etc. in order to stimulate business and employment during a recession.

pun *n. & v.* **puns, punned, pun.ning** play on words, as "Mr. Dole is doleful news." —**pun.ner** or **pun.ster** *n.*

punch *v.* **1** strike with the fist: *The bully punched him on the nose; punched him out; punched his lights out; They got up shouting and punching their fists in the air;* **n.**: *A boxer practices on a suspended punching bag.* **2** cut, stamp, etc. with a quick thrust: *A ticket is inspected and punched; to punch holes in a card; to punch in computer data; She sat down at the terminal and punched out her report; to punch down dough; Workers punch in and punch out of a factory by thrusting a timecard into a time clock;* **n.**: *Coded data were punched on a punch card in a key-punch machine.* **3 punch up** *Informal.* enliven. —*n.* **1** a blow or a thrust of the fist: *a boxer's one-two punch (with the left and right hands in quick succession); to throw* or *land a punch; a hard, knockout, powerful punch.* **2** a punching device: *a three-hole paper punch.* **3** *Informal.* vigor or force: *a pep talk full of punch; ads that lack punch; how to add extra punch to your speech; strong editorials that pack a punch.* **4** a sweetened drink of juices, wines, liquors, etc. usu. mixed in a large **punch bowl** and ladled out, as at a party. —**beat someone to the punch** *Informal.* do something before someone else does it, like hitting a boxing opponent before he hits you. —**pull one's punches** *Informal.* be ineffective on purpose.

punch-drunk *adj.* dazed by blows.

pun.cheon (PUNCH.un) *n.* a large cask to hold up to 120 gallons of liquor.

punch line *n.* the last part of a joke designed to get a laugh at the end of telling it.

punch-out or **punch-up** *n.* a brawl or fistfight.

punch.y *adj.* **punch.i.er, -i.est** having vigor or force: *a punchy comment.*

punc.til.i.o (punc.TIL.ee.oh) *n.* **-os** a fine point of conduct or ceremony. —**punc.til.i.ous** (-ee.us) *adj.*: *a diplomat's punctilious attention to protocol.*

punc.tu.al (PUNK.choo.ul) *adj.* on time, esp. habitually: *He's always punctual in arriving at work;* **punc.tu.al.ly** *adv.* —**punc.tu.al.i.ty** (-AL.i.tee) *n.*

punc.tu.ate (PUNK.choo.ate) *v.* **-ates,**

puncture / pure

-at.ed, -at.ing show pauses, emphases, etc., esp. in written language, using **punctuation marks** such as the comma, question mark, and exclamation point: *a speech punctuated* (= interrupted) *by frequent cheers; a busy day punctuated with phone calls.* —**punc.tu.a.tion** (-AY.shun) *n.*

punc.ture (PUNK.chur) *n.* a tiny hole, esp. one made with or as if with a point: *a thorn puncture; punctures in the skin.* —*v.* **-tures, -tured, -tur.ing** make to puncture: *to puncture a balloon, blister; adj.: to repair a puncured tire; a punctured myth; punctured pride.*

pun.dit *n.* 1 a learned person. 2 a supposed authority: *TV weather pundits.*

pun.gent (PUN.junt) *adj.* 1 sharp to the taste and smell: *Horse radish is pungent.* 2 keen or biting: *pungent satire.* —**pun.gent.ly** *adv.* —**pun.gen.cy** (-see) *n.*

Pu.nic (PEW.nic) *adj.* of ancient Carthage: *"Punic faith" meant treachery to Romans.*

pun.ish *v.* cause suffering or discomfort, usu. for some offense; penalize: *Offenders are punished; Thievery used to be punished by hanging; The boxer continued to punish* (= hurt) *his fallen opponent; adja.: It was a punishing* (= exhausting) *climb to the top; the punishing* (= hurting) *summer heat; punishing inflation, schedules, setbacks, tax rates.* —**pun.ish.a.ble** (-uh.bul) *adj.*

pun.ish.ment (PUN.ish.munt) *n.* 1 a punishing: *The punishment should fit the crime; to escape, impose or mete out, suffer punishment; cruel and unusual punishment; capital, corporal, summary punishment; There's a limit to the punishment one can take.* 2 *Informal.* rough use: *A taxicab gets more punishment than the cabby.*

pu.ni.tive (PEW.ni.tiv) *adj.* 1 having to do with punishment; punishing: *punitive action, measures, raids, reparations, tariffs; the punitive approach to drug use; punitive damages awarded against willful wrongdoers.* 2 harsh: *punitive laws, taxation.* —**pu.ni.tive.ly** *adv.*

punk *n.* 1 a slow-burning, spongy preparation of dried fungi or decayed wood used as tinder. 2 *Slang.* a petty hoodlum or ruffian. 3 an inexperienced youngster, as a child hobo. 4 a punk rock musician; also **punk.er.** —*adj. Slang.* of poor quality: *the punkest grub he ever ate.*

punk rock *n.* rock 'n' roll of the late 1970s characterized by rowdy costumes, language, and performing style.

punk.y *adj. Informal.* having to do with punks or hoodlums: *a punky hairdo with flashes of color in it.*

pun.ster (PUN.stur) *n.* one fond of making puns.

punt *n.* 1 a flat-bottomed boat propelled with a long pole. 2 a kick given to a football dropped from one's hands and before it touches the ground. —*v.* 1 travel by, convey by, or propel a punt boat. 2 give a punt kick to a football.

pu.ny (PEW.nee) *adj.* **-ni.er, -ni.est** inferior in size, strength, or importance; petty. —**pu.ni.ness** *n.*

pup *n.* 1 a young dog, fox, wolf, etc. 2 a young seal, shark, or whale.

pu.pa (PEW.puh) *n., pl.* **-pae** (-pee) or **-pas** an insect in its middle stage of development, between larva and adult, when it is encased in a cocoon; **pu.pal** (-pul) *adj.*

pu.pil (PEW.pul) *n.* 1 a young student, esp. one under a teacher's personal supervision; hence, follower. 2 the black, circular portion inside the iris of the eye. —**pu.pil.lar.y** (-puh.lair.ee) *adj.*

pup.pet (PUP.it) *n.* a doll-like, hand-controlled figure of a person or animal used in a **puppet show.** —**pup.pet.ry** (-it.ree) *n.* —**pup.pet.eer** (-uh.TEER) *n.*

pup.py (PUP.ee) *n.* **pup.pies** same as PUP.

puppy love *n.* juvenile love for one of the opposite sex.

pup tent *n.* a small, wedge-shaped shelter tent for one or two persons.

pur.blind (PUR.blined) *adj.* 1 nearly blind; dimsighted. 2 obtuse.

pur.chase (PUR.chus) *v.* **-chas.es, -chased, -chas.ing** *Formal.* buy: *to purchase aircraft, computers, real estate, stocks; adja.: a purchasing decision, department; The purchasing power of the dollar goes down with rising prices.* —*n.* a purchasing or thing purchased: *to make a purchase; Where are my purchases? a major purchase such as a house, car, or appliance.* —**pur.chas.a.ble** *adj.*

pur.dah (PUR.duh) *n.* 1 the seclusion of women from public view. 2 a veil or curtain used for this, as in India.

pure (PYOOR) 1 *adj.* **pur.er, pur.est** free from taint, defects, errors, etc.; unmixed: *pure as snow; "the pure in heart"; pure English; a pure breed.* 2 *adja.* sheer or absolute: *It happened by pure accident; That's pure nonsense; nonsense pure and simple.* 3 *adja.* abstract or theoretical: *pure* mathematics. —**pure.ly** adv.

pure.blood n. an individual of unmixed ancestry: *a pureblood Indian.* Also **pure-blooded** adj.

pure.bred n. an animal of unmixed breed: *Arabian purebreds* (= purebred horses); adj.: *purebred cattle, livestock, pups.*

pu.rée (pew.RAY) n. **1** a cooked vegetable that has been rubbed through a sieve and made into a paste or suspension. **2** a puréed vegetable soup. —v. **pu.rées, pu.réed, pu.rée.ing:** *to purée fruit in a blender;* adj.: *coarsely puréed carrots; puréed strawberries.*

pur.ga.tion (pur.GAY.shun) n. the act of purging: *the purgation of the soul.*

pur.ga.tive (PUR.guh.tiv) n. a purging agent, as a cathartic; adj.: *the purgative action of castor oil; purgative confession.*

pur.ga.to.ry (PUR.guh.tor.ee) n. -ries in Roman Catholic theology, a state of temporary punishment that purifies souls for entry into heaven.
—**pur.ga.to.ri.al** (-TOR.ee.ul) adj.

purge (PURJ) v. **purg.es, purged, purg.ing** clear or cleanse by getting rid of something undesired: *a drug that purges the bowels; to purge away dross from metal; a political party purged of undesirable elements; souls purged of sin.* —n. a purging or something that purges: *They conducted* or *carried out a sweeping purge of the party; Stalin's purges of the 1930s.*

pu.ri.fy (PYOOR.uh.fye) v. -fies, -fied, -fy.ing make or become pure: *to purify water for drinking; He purified himself by bathing in the Ganges;* adj.: *purified air; a highly purified form of Vitamin E.*
—**pu.ri.fi.er** n. —**pu.ri.fi.ca.tion** (-fuh.CAY.shun) n. —**pu.ri.fi.ca.to.ry** (pew.RIF.i.cuh.tor.ee) adj.

Pu.rim (POOR.im) n. a Jewish holiday commemorating Esther's deliverance of the Jews from a massacre.

pu.rine (PYOOR.een) n. **1** a colorless crystalline substance that is the parent of compounds of the uric-acid group. **2** a derivative of it, as caffeine or guanine.

pur.ism (PYOOR.iz.um) n. **1** the too strict adherence to what is traditionally correct in language matters without regard for the changing nature of vocabulary, usage, etc. **2** an instance of this, as saying "It is I" instead of "It is me." —**pur.ist** n. —**pu.ris.tic** (pyoor.IS.tic) adj.

pu.ri.tan (PYOOR.i.tun) n. one who is very strict in matters of religion or morals, as the Puritan group of the Church of England in the 16th and 17th centuries. —**pu.ri.tan.ism** or **Pu.ri.tan.ism** n. —**pu.ri.tan.i.cal** (-TAN.i.cul) adj.

pu.ri.ty (PYOOR.i.tee) n. the quality or state of being pure; pureness; freedom from dirt, evil, or foreign elements: *the purity of our water; the purity of a gold coin; Apartheid laws were aimed at racial purity; ideological purity; the tonal purity of her voice.*

purl v. **1** knit with inverted stitches so as to produce a ribbed appearance. **2** of a stream, flow with a murmuring sound. Also n.

pur.lieu (PUR.lew) n. **1** a bordering or outlying region. **2 purlieus** pl. environs.

pur.loin (pur.LOIN) v. *Formal.* steal; adj.: *a publisher of purloined manuscripts.*

pur.ple (PUR.pul) n. crimson color, indicative of high rank: *"clothed in purple and fine linen"; a bishop raised to the purple* (= created cardinal).
—adj. **1** bluish red: *a purple dye; purple grapes; Her ears turned purple in the cold; He was purple with rage.* **2** adja. ornate or gaudy in style: *He writes a dull prose except for the occasional purple patch* or *passage.* **3** *Informal.* off-color: *a purple joke.* —**pur.plish** adj.

pur.port (PUR.port) n. general meaning or intent; gist: *the purport of the message.* —v. (also pur.PORT) intend or mean supposedly: *The offer was purported to be a generous one; The skin cream purports* (= claims) *to erase wrinkles;* **pur.port.ed.ly** (-POR.tid.lee) adv.

pur.pose (PUR.pus) n. intention, esp. with determination: *the purpose of our visit; to accomplish, achieve, fulfill, serve a purpose; A small car will do for all practical purposes* (= in reality); *He ignored the letter on purpose* (= deliberately) *to snub him; remarks quite to the purpose* (= pertinent). —v. **-pos.es, -posed, -pos.ing** intend: *She purposed to stay awake but fell asleep.* —**pur.pose.ful** adj.; **pur.pose.ful.ly** adv. —**pur.pose.ly** adv. on purpose.

purr n. the low murmuring sound of a contented cat. —v. **purrs, purred, pur.ring** make a purr.

purse n. **1** a small bag, originally one with drawstrings. **2** a woman's handbag: *Beware of pickpockets and purse snatchers on the street.* **3** amount of money; means: *The fraud artist retired with a poor pension but a well-lined purse; a prize fight with a $1 million purse* (= stake); *He was presented with a gold*

watch and a purse (= gift of money).
—v. **purs.es, pursed, purs.ing** pucker: *She pursed her lips in disapproval.*

purs.er *n.* an official in charge of money matters on a ship or of cabin service on an airliner.

purse-proud *adj.* vainly proud of one's wealth.

purse strings *n.pl.* power to manage someone's finances: *to control, hold, loosen, tighten the purse strings.*

purs.lane (PURS.lin, -lane) *n.* an annual trailing weed, sometimes used in salads.

pur.su.ance (pur.SUE.unce) *n. Formal.* a carrying out: *a letter written in pursuance of a client's wishes.* —**pur.su.ant** (-unt) *adj.: goods shipped pursuant to* (= according to) *a customer's instructions.*

pur.sue (pur.SUE) *v.* **-sues, -sued, -su.ing** 1 follow someone in order to catch up: *police pursuing a getaway car; She was pursued by reporters everywhere she went.* 2 have as an aim, esp. to accomplish something: *She's pursuing her studies at the university; She'll pursue a career in politics.* —**pur.su.er** *n.*

pur.suit (pur.SUIT) *n.* 1 a pursuing or chase: *our pursuit of happiness; The police crossed the border in hot pursuit of the fleeing car.* 2 occupation or hobby: *Her many pursuits include fishing.*

pu.ru.lent (PURE.uh.lunt, -yuh.lunt) *adj.* containing or forming pus.
—**pu.ru.lence** *n.*

pur.vey (pur.VAY) *v.* supply, esp. as food or a commodity.

pur.vey.or (pur.VAY.ur) *n.* supplier: *purveyors of fast foods; The TV networks are purveyors of culture to or for the masses; purveyors of hate such as racists.*

pur.view *n.* range or scope of authority or perception: *This is outside or beyond the purview of our department; It's currently in or under the purview of Customs and Immigration; We can only deal with matters within our purview.*

pus *n.* a thick, yellow discharge from an infected body part.

push (short "OO") *v.* 1 press against a person or thing so as to move forward: *You pull that door open and push it shut; to push for* (= urge) *a strike, the right to strike; Grandpa is pushing* (= close to) *90; Everyone hates being pushed around* (= harassed). 2 force one's way: *to push into an overcrowded bus; to push through a crowd; Let's not push it* (= overdo it); *Don't push your luck* (= take unnecessary risks).
3 move: *At the sound of the alarm, people pushed toward the exits; Let's push on till we reach home.* 4 *Informal.* sell or promote the sale of something: *Get the mayor to push the lottery; Pushing drugs is illegal.* —*n.* a pushing: *a self-starter who never needs a push; A good sales rep has push* (= drive) *but is not pushy;* "*when push comes to shove*" (= when things get worse). —**push.er** *n.*

push button *n.* a button that is pushed to operate something: *an elevator operated by push buttons;* **adj.**: *a push-button telephone; Robots would control push-button warfare.*

push.cart *n.* a cart that is pushed, as for supermarket shopping.

push.o.ver (PUSH.oh.vur) *n. Informal.* 1 one easy to impose upon: *He's a pushover for a loan any time.* 2 an easy job; cinch: *It's a pushover to get our lawn mowed by the neighbors when we go on holidays.*

push-up *n.* an exercise done by raising and lowering the body held stiffly extended in a prone position.

push.y (short "OO") *adj.* **push.i.er, -i.est** *Informal.* unpleasantly aggressive.

pu.sil.lan.i.mous (pew.si.LAN.uh.mus) *adj.* faint-hearted; timid.
—**pu.sil.la.nim.i.ty** (-la.NIM.i.tee) *n.*

puss (short "OO") *n.* **puss.es** *Informal.* 1 a cat; pussy. 2 face: *She socked him in the puss.*

¹**pus.sy** (PUSS.ee) *adj.* like or containing pus.

²**puss.y** (POOS.ee, short "OO") *n.*
1 *Slang.* a vulva. 2 same as PUSSYCAT, 1.

puss.y.cat (POOS.ee.cat, short "OO") *n.*
1 a cat; pussy. 2 an agreeable or quiet-going person: *He has an aggressive style, but is really a pussycat at heart.*

puss.y.foot (POOS.ee.foot) *v. Informal.* be overly cautious and noncommittal: *to pussyfoot around an issue like bilingualism.*

puss.y.wil.low (POOS.ee.wil.oh) *n.* a small tree with fur-covered grayish-white catkins.

pus.tule (PUS.chool) *n.* a pus-filled pimple.

put (short "OO") *v.* **puts, put, put.ting**
1 to place, esp. move something onto a position: *to put food on the table; to put sugar in your coffee.* 2 make someone or something be in a certain way; set: *Children are put to bed; an idea difficult to put into words; to put one's affairs in order; to put words to music; to put someone to shame.* 3 (rhyme: but) throw: *putting the shot (in shot put).*
—**put across** convey an idea

putative / pyramid

successfully. —**put down 1** crush: *to put down a revolt.* **2** write down: *You can put me down for a $10 contribution; Put down the main points in writing.* **3** *Informal.* snub or belittle. **4** kill mercifully, as a pet. —**put in** *Informal.* **1** contribute: *She puts in a lot of work on holidays.* **2** apply: *He put in for a loan.* —**put off 1** postpone: *She wanted to put off buying a new car; I advised her not to put it off.* **2** turn one away: *The high prices of cars put me off.* —**put on 1** apply: *The work is putting too much strain on my nerves.* **2** *Informal.* tease: *You're putting me on!* —**put something over on** pass something off on someone by trickery: *The class put one over on the teacher so she thought it was a Friday.* —**put out 1** in baseball, retire a batter or runner. **2** begin a voyage: *We put out to sea in a boat.* **3** offend: *Dina was put out by his bad manners.* —**put paid to something** wipe out, like an account stamped "paid." —**put up:** *a house put up* (= offered) *for sale; Why don't you put up* (= justify yourself or get ready to fight) *or shut up? He put up a good fight* (= fought well); *She'll put you up* (= lodge you) *for the night; Who put him up to* (= made him do) *this? an unsociable character difficult to **put up with*** (= bear or tolerate). —**put upon** impose upon. —*adjp. Informal.* in place: *Stay put till I return.* —*n.* (rhyme: but) a throw: *a shot put.*

pu.ta.tive (PEW.tuh.tiv) *adja.* supposed: *an orphan child's putative father.*

put.down *n. Informal.* an act or statement that belittles, criticizes, etc.

put-on *n. Informal.* a pretense or hoax.

put-out *n.* of a batter or runner in baseball, a being retired.

pu.tre.fy (PEW.truh.fye) *v.* **-fies, -fied, -fy.ing** be or make putrid or rotten: *putrefying flesh.* —**pu.tre.fac.tion** (-FAC.shun) *n.*

pu.tres.cent (pew.TRES.unt) *adj.* becoming putrid; **pu.tres.cence** *n.*

pu.trid (PEW.trid) *adj.* **1** rotting or decayed: *the putrid smell of putrid meat.* **2** corrupt or foul: *the putrid air of a porn shop.* —**pu.trid.ness** *n.*

putsch (POOCH, short "OO") *n.* a secretly plotted attempt to overthrow a government.

putt (rhyme: but) *v.* strike a golf ball across the green (**putting green**) to try to drop it into the hole. —**putt.er** *n.*

put.tee (puh.TEE, PUTT.ee) *n.* a strip of cloth wound round the calf like a gaiter.

put.ter ("put" as in "but") **1** *n.* a golf club used for putting. **2** *v.* busy oneself aimlessly *in* or *around* something: *to putter around the garden;* also **pot.ter.**

put.ty ("put" as in "but") *n.* **put.ties** a doughlike cement used in fixing window panes, to fill holes in wood, etc.: *wood putty; He's like putty in her hands.* Also *v.* **put.ties, put.tied, put.ty.ing.**

put-up *adj. Informal.* prearranged in a sly or crafty manner: *a put-up job.*

puz.zle (PUZ.ul) *v.* **puz.zles, puz.zled, puz.zling** bewilder: *a stranger puzzled by local customs; He's good at **puzzling out*** (= solving) *conundrums; She **puzzled over*** (= tried to think of) *a solution all night.* —*n.* a problem or task that puzzles or is designed to puzzle: *a crossword puzzle; jigsaw puzzle; The disappearance of the child remained a puzzle to the police; The driver was in a puzzle when he reached the crossroads.* —**puz.zle.ment** (-munt) *n.* —**puz.zler** *n.*

pyg.my (PIG.mee) *n.* **-mies** a person or thing of small stature like a **Pygmy**, a Negroid African people of short stature. —*adj.* dwarfish: *pygmy chimps, goats, hippos; Most of the species in Biosphere II were pygmy; The **pygmy antelope** is only 25.4 cm (10 in) tall; The **pygmy owl** is about 17.8 cm (7 in) long.*

py.ja.mas (puh.JAM.uz) *Brit.* same as PAJAMAS.

py.lon (PYE.lon, -lun) *n.* **1** a gateway of an ancient Egyptian temple, esp. one consisting of two pyramidal towers. **2** a framework of steel used to support overhead cables. **3** a post, tower, or conical marker for guiding air or road traffic. **4** a supporting structure, as of an airplane engine.

py.or.rhe.a (pye.uh.REE.uh) *n.* a pus-forming disease affecting the roots of the teeth.

pyr.a.mid (PEER.uh.mid) *n.* **1** a solid figure with a polygon base and sloping sides that meet at the top. **2** any of the huge structures with a square base and triangular sides meeting at the top built in ancient Egypt for royal tombs. **3** any structure or scheme resembling a pyramid, often an inverted pyramid; *adja. & cpd.: a pyramid telephone system for passing on messages* (by one person telling many, each of whom in turn tell others, and so on); *a **pyramid-fire** cooking arrangement at a camp; a **pyramid scheme** for raising money, as by chain letters.* —*v.* put in the form of a pyramid; hence, increase or raise: *a financial empire built by pyramiding*

pyre / quadruplicate

subsidiaries within a holding company; Profits may be pyramided by speculative buying or selling of stock. —**py.ram.i.dal** (puh.RAM.i.dul) *adj.*: *a pyramidal army tent, chain of command, class structure.*

pyre *n.* a woodpile for burning a dead body: *a funeral pyre.*

pyr.i.dine (PEER.i.deen) *n.* a pungent-smelling liquid base distilled from coal tar.

py.rim.i.dine (pye.RIM.i.deen) *n.* an organic base or a derivative of it that is a constituent of DNA or RNA.

py.rite (PYE.rite) *n.* a gold-colored compound of iron and sulfur; iron pyrites; also called "fool's gold." —**py.rit.ic** (pye.RIT.ic) *adj.*

py.ri.tes (puh.RYE.teez) *n.pl.* a sulfur-bearing mineral.

pyro- *comb.form.* fire; heat: *pyromania, pyrometer, pyrotechnics.*

py.rol.y.sis (pye.ROL.uh.sis) *n.* chemical decomposition by the action of heat.

py.ro.ma.ni.a (pye.ruh.MAY.nee.uh) *n.* a compulsive urge to set fire to things; **py.ro.ma.ni.ac** *n. & adj.*

py.rom.e.ter (pye.ROM.i.tur) *n.* an instrument for measuring the unusually high temperatures of glass, pottery, and metal work.

py.ro.tech.nics (pye.roh.TEK.niks) *n.pl.* 1 fireworks. 2 any brilliant display, as of rhetoric or emotion: *verbal pyrotechnics.* —**py.ro.tech.nic** or **py.ro.tech.ni.cal** *adj.*

Pyr.rhic victory (PEER.ic-) *n.* a victory won at heavy cost, esp. of lives.

Py.thag.o.re.an (pi.thag.uh.REE.un) *adj.* having to do with **Pythagoras,** a Greek philosopher-mathematician of the 6th c. B.C.: *The Pythagorean theorem states that the square of the hypotenuse of a right triangle is equal to the sum of the squares of the other two sides.*

py.thon (PYE.thon, -thun) *n.* a large, nonvenomous snake such as the anaconda or the boa constrictor that crushes its prey within its coils.

pyx (PIX) *n.* a small container for holding a Eucharistic wafer.

.... **Q, q** ....

Q or **q** (CUE) *n.* **Q's** or **q's** the 17th letter of the English alphabet.

q.t. or **Q.T.** *Informal.* quiet. —**on the q.t.** quietly or confidentially.

qua (QUAH, QUAY) *adv.* in the capacity of; as: *Humans are called rational animals qua rational, not qua animals.*

quack (QUAK) *n.* 1 a duck's cry; also *v.* 2 one who pretends to have medical skills; *adj.a.: a quack cure, product, therapy, treatment.* 3 any charlatan: *quack politicians.* —**quack.er.y** *n.* -**er.ies:** *arthritic victims of quackeries.*

quad (QUOD) *n.* [short form] quadrangle; quadruplet.

quad.ran.gle (QUOD.rang.gul) *n.* 1 a flat figure with four sides and four angles. 2 such a four-sided area surrounded by buildings. —**quad.ran.gu.lar** (quod.RANG.gyuh.lur) *adj.*

quad.rant (QUOD.runt) *n.* 1 one quarter of a circle or its circumference; 90-degree arc. 2 an instrument for measuring angles to determine altitudes.

quad.ra.phon.ic (quod.ruh.FON.ic) *adj.* relating to sound reproduction that uses four separate channels; cf. STEREOPHONIC.

quad.rat.ic (quod.RAT.ic) *adj.* in algebra, relating to the square of a number: "$ax^2 + bx + c = 0$" *is a* **quadratic equation.**

quad.ren.ni.um (quod.REN.ee.um) *n.* -**ren.ni.ums** or -**ren.ni.a** (-ee.uh) a period of four years. —**quad.ren.ni.al** (-ee.ul) *adj.*

quad.ri.lat.er.al (quod.ruh.LAT.uh.rul) *adj.* having four sides. —*n.* a four-sided figure; quadrangle.

qua.drille (kwuh.DRIL) *n.* a French square dance of the 1800's.

quad.ril.lion (quod.RIL.yun) *n.* 1 in the U.S. and Canada, a billion millions or 1 followed by 15 zeros. 2 in the U.K., 1 followed by 24 zeros.

quad.ri.ple.gi.a (quod.ruh.PLEE.jee.uh) *n.* paralysis from the neck down, affecting all four limbs. —**quad.ri.ple.gic** (-PLEE.jic, -PLEJ.ic) *n. & adj.*

quad.ru.ped (QUOD.ruh.ped) *n.* a four-footed animal.

quad.ru.ple (QUOD.ruh.pul, quod.ROO.pul) *v.* -**ples,** -**pled,** -**pling** multiply by four: *Government spending had quadrupled by the end of the decade; You quadruple (= increase fourfold) the risk of breast cancer by certain therapies.* —**adj.** 1 four times: *a quadruple amount;* in quadruple time (with four beats per measure). 2 containing four parts: *a quadruple alliance, birth, (coronary) bypass, (DPTP) vaccine.*

quad.ru.plet (QUOD.ruh.plit) *n.* 1 one of four born at a single birth. 2 a group of four: *a quadruplet of musical notes.*

quad.ru.pli.cate (quod.ROO.pli.kit) *adj.* multiplied by four; *n.:* Prepare the in-

voice *in* **quadruplicate** (= in four copies). —*v.* (-cate) **-cates, -cat.ed, -cat.ing** provide four of something; **quad.ru.pli.ca.tion** (-CAY.shun) *n.*
quaff (QUOF, QUAF) *v.* drink with zest. —*n.* drink: *a hearty quaff of ale.*
quag.mire (QUAG.mire) *n.* damp ground that yields underfoot; bog.
qua.hog (QUOH.hog, QUAW-) *n.* a hard-shelled, edible clam of the E. coast of North America; also **qua.haug.**
quail *n.* a game bird of the grouse and partridge families, esp. the bobwhite. —*v.* lose courage and shrink back in fear: *I quail at the thought of going through that ordeal again; The lion quailed under its trainer's whip.*
quaint *adj.* old-fashioned or odd in an interesting or unusual way: *a quaint refrain; his quaint style of writing.*
quake *v.* **quakes, quaked, quak.ing** shake violently, as from fear or shock: *He quaked with fright; the quaking aspen.* —*n.* a shaking or shivering, esp. an earthquake. —**quak.y** (QUAY.kee) *adj.*
Quak.er (QUAY.kur) *n.* [used by outsiders] a member of the religious group called the Society of Friends; Friend.
qual.i.fi.ca.tion (quol.uh.fi.CAY.shun) *n.* **1** a condition: *an answer accepted without qualification.* **2** an accomplishment or skill: *a necessary qualification for the job; a principal with impressive qualifications and experience for her job.*
qual.i.fy (QUOL.uh.fye) *v.* **-fies, -fied, -fy.ing 1** make suitable or competent for an occupation, calling, task, etc.: *Our team has qualified for the finals; Not everyone qualifies; Her answer qualifies as a yes;* **adj. & cpd.**: *a **qualified** applicant; She is qualified to practice medicine; ill-qualified; well-qualified;* **adja.**: *a **qualifying** applicant, degree, examination.* **2** modify: *Adjectives qualify nouns.* **3** limit or moderate: *to qualify a scolding with a smile;* **adja.**: *Her answer was a **qualified** yes.* —**qual.i.fi.er** *n.*
qual.i.ta.tive (QUOL.i.tay.tiv) *adj.* having to do with quality: *a qualitative change, edge, difference; qualitative criteria, improvements, tests;* **qual.i.ta.tive.ly** *adv.*
qual.i.ty (QUOL.i.tee) *n.* **-ties 1** essential nature or characteristic feature: *the qualities of a good student.* **2** worth or excellence: *the fine quality of his singing; fabric of poor quality; a bad movie with few redeeming qualities; a woman of quality; The **quality of life** in a place is measured in terms of crime, pollution,* *health care, living expenses, climate, etc.;* **adja.**: *quality ice cream (of high quality); a quality newspaper;* **quality control** *of a manufactured product by sampling and testing; After work, she spends **quality time** with the family every day.*
qualm (QUAHM) *n.* **1** a temporary feeling of sickness or faintness. **2** a feeling of doubt or uneasiness about the rightness of an action: *She had no qualms about letting her child walk home alone.* —**qualm.ish** *adj.*: *He felt qualmish as he was about to parachute.*
quan.da.ry (QUON.duh.ree, -dree) *n.* **-ries** a state of uncertainty and hesitation: *She was placed in a quandary as a result of two appointments for the same hour.*
quanta *pl.* of QUANTUM.
quan.ti.fy (QUON.tuh.fye) *v.* **-fies, -fied, -fy.ing** determine or indicate the quantity of something: *It's impossible to quantify the value of a good education.*
quan.ti.ta.tive (QUON.ti.tay.tiv) *adj.* having to do with quantity: *a quantitative analysis, approach, measure, test, value; in quantitative terms.*
quan.ti.ty (QUON.ti.tee) *n.* **-ties** amount or number: *a small quantity of sugar; Stores buy goods **in quantity** (= in bulk or in large amounts); It's on sale at $4.95 while quantities (= stocks or supplies) last.*
quan.tize (QUON.tize) *v.* **-tiz.es, -tized, -tiz.ing** express or measure energy in quanta.
quan.tum (QUON.tum) *n., pl.* **-ta** (-tuh) a specific quantity; esp. in the **quantum theory**, one of the basic indivisible amounts (**quanta**) in which energy is given out or absorbed by a substance.
quantum jump (or **leap**) *n.* **1** an abrupt transition from one state to another: *Within an atom, electrons make quantum jumps or leaps as they change orbits absorbing or giving off energy.* **2** any sudden change: *The discovery of the wheel was a quantum leap (= great step forward) in human civilization.*
quantum mechanics *n.pl.* [with *sing. v.*] a theory of the mechanics of atomic structures and phenomena in terms of measurable quanta.
quantum theory See QUANTUM.
quar.an.tine (QUOR.un.teen) *n.* **1** the detaining of ships, people, animals, etc. in isolation to prevent disease from spreading. **2** the place or time in which they are so held.
—*v.* **-tines, -tined, -tin.ing** put in

quarantine: *a ship quarantined for 40 days at a port of entry.*
quark *n.* a hypothetical subatomic particle carrying a fractional electric charge and being the supposed basic constituent of known particles such as protons and neutrons.
quar.rel (QUOR.ul) *n.* **1** an angry dispute: *bitter, domestic, family quarrels; to pick a quarrel with someone.* **2** cause for complaint: *I have no quarrel with or about the money you are offering me, but I don't like the job.* —*v.* **quar.rels, quar.reled, quar.rel.ing 1** disagree: *I must quarrel with your decision.* **2** dispute angrily: *to quarrel with a neighbor about or over the location of a fence.* Also **quar.relled, quar.rel.ling** *Cdn.*
quar.rel.some (QUOR.ul.sum) *adj.* given to quarreling: *the quarrelsome Donald Duck; a quarrelsome labor union; He is touchy and quarrelsome; Kay is in a quarrelsome mood.*
quar.ry (QUOR.ee) *n.* **quar.ries 1** an object of pursuit, esp. a hunted animal: *to stalk one's quarry.* **2** a place where rock or limestone is dug from the earth: *an abandoned quarry.* —*v.* **quar.ries, quar.ried, quar.ry.ing** dig: *machines for drilling, mining, and quarrying; road workers quarrying for materials; adj.: locally quarried stone.*
quart (QUORT) *n.* **1** one fourth of a gallon; two pints or 1.14 liters. **2** a dry measure equaling 1/8 peck.
quar.ter (QUOR.tur) *n.* **1** a fourth part, as of an hour (15 minutes), a year (3 months), a dollar (25 cents or the coin), an animal's carcass (one leg and adjacent parts), etc.: *The time is a quarter to or of six (= 5:45); at a quarter past or after six (= 6:15).* **2** a region or place; hence, a special district: *the Latin Quarter of Paris; the French quarter of New Orleans.* **3** mercy or compassion: *They give or show no quarter to the enemy.*
—**quarters** *pl.* **1** accommodation: *bachelor, married, military, officers' quarters.* **2** sources: *news from reliable quarters.* —**at close quarters** close together: *Boxers fight at close quarters.* —*v.* **1** divide into four: *to quarter an apple.* **2** provide with shelter: *Horses are quartered in the stables; soldiers quartered in barracks.* **3** assign troops to a lodging place: *The troops were quartered on the local population.*
quar.ter.back (QUOR.tur.back) *n.* a football player who calls the signals and directs the team's play: *An armchair quarterback is better at talking than doing things;* One who plays **Monday morning quarterback** *talks wisely after the event.* —*v.* play the quarterback position; hence, to lead or direct: *He quarterbacks the sales side of the business.*
quar.ter.deck (QUOR.tur.deck) *n.* part of a ship's upper deck near the stern.
quarter horse *n.* a strong muscular horse originally bred in the U.S. for short races and later used as a range and rodeo horse.
quar.ter.ly (QUOR.tur.lee) *n.* **-lies** a publication issued every three months. —*adj.: quarterly dividends, earnings, journals; adv.: a report issued quarterly.*
quar.ter.mas.ter (QUOR.tur.mas.tur) *n.* **1** an army officer who supplies food, clothing, etc. to soldiers. **2** a naval petty officer who looks after a ship's steering, signals, etc.
quarter note *n.* a musical note held one fourth the time of a whole note.
quar.ter.staff (QUOR.tur.staf) *n., pl.* **-staves** a large wooden staff formerly used as a weapon.
quar.tet (quor.TET) *n.* **1** a piece of music for four instruments or people: *to play a string quartet.* **2** the group performing this. **3** any group of four. Also **quar.tette** *Cdn.*
quar.to (QUOR.toh) *n.* **-tos 1** the page size, usu. 9½ x 12 in. (24 x 30 cm) resulting from folding one sheet into four leaves. **2** a book printed on such pages.
quartz (QUORTS) *n.* a hard mineral found in rocks and in crystalline form in amethyst: *The* **quartz crystal** *of a radio transmitter or electric clock vibrates with a natural frequency.*
qua.sar (QUAY.sar, -zar) *n.* a very distant, starlike object that emits brilliant light and often powerful radio waves.
quash *v.* **1** crush or suppress: *to quash a rebellion.* **2** void legally: *a decision quashed by a higher court.*
qua.si (QUAY.sye, -zye; QUAH.see, -zee) *adj. & comb.form.* resembling but not quite: *a quasi contract, joke; quasi utilities such as banking and insurance; a quasi-humorous situation; to act in a quasi-judicial capacity.*
quasi-stellar object same as QUASAR.
Qua.ter.nar.y (kwuh.TUR.nuh.ree) *n.* the second of the two periods of the Cenozoic era; *adj.: Human beings developed in the Quaternary period.*
quat.rain (QUAW.train) *n.* a stanza of four lines.
quat.re.foil (CAT.ur.foil) *n.* **1** a leaf or flower with four parts or petals. **2** a four-lobed architectural ornament.

qua.ver (QUAY.vur) *v.* tremble or quiver: *His voice quavered with fright.* —*n.* **1** a trembling or quivering. **2** such a sound. **3** in music, an eighth note.

quay (KEE) *n.* wharf.

quea.sy (QUEE.zee) *adj.* **-si.er, -si.est 1** nauseated: *a queasy stomach; a queasy feeling in my stomach; She's beginning to feel a bit queasy in the mornings.* **2** uneasy: *I feel queasy about it; We get queasy at the thought of people being murdered in cold blood; When the truth was told, people grew queasy.* **3** troublesome: *a queasy moment, problem.* —**quea.si.ly** *adv.*; **quea.si.ness** *n.*

Que.bec.er or **Que.beck.er** (qui.BEK.ur) *n.* a person of or from Quebec, a Canadian province.

Que.be.cois (cay.buh.QUAH) *n. sing. & pl.* a person of or from Quebec, esp. a speaker of French. —*adj.* having to do with Quebec or the Quebecois: *Quebecois cuisine, culture, French; a Quebecois poet, singer, writer.*

queen *n.* **1** a female sovereign: *Queen Elizabeth II; the Queen's accession or succession to the throne in 1952; She was crowned queen in June 1953.* **2** the wife or widow of a king. **3** a woman noted for beauty, power, etc.: *beauty queens; movie queens; Queen City* (= a capital city). **4** a mature egg-laying ant, bee, etc. of a colony. —*v.*: *an actress who likes to* **queen it over** (= act like a queen toward) *her admirers.* —**queen.ly** *adj.*; **queen.li.ness** *n.*

queen consort *n.* the wife of a reigning king.

queen mother *n.* the mother of a reigning monarch.

Queen's English *n.* English usage that is considered as standard or correct.

queen-size *adj.* approximately 60 x 80 in. (1.5 x 2 m): *a queen-size bed, sheet;* also **queen-sized**.

queer *adj.* unusual or strange, esp. abnormal: *a queer sensation in the stomach; a queer idea.* —*v.* spoil: *Doping queered his chances for an Olympic medal.* —*n. & adj. Slang* [offensive] homosexual. —**queer.ly** *adv.*; **queer.ness** *n.*

quell *v.* put an end to; crush: *to quell a rebellion, uprising; to quell one's doubts, fears.*

quench *v.* cool suddenly, esp. something burning: *Steel is tempered by quenching it while red-hot; Water quenches thirst; The outburst quenched his fury.*

quer.u.lous (QUER.uh.lus, -yuh.lus) *adj.* complaining or fretful: *a querulous invalid.* —**quer.u.lous.ly** *adv.*

que.ry (QUEER.ee) *n.* **que.ries 1** question or inquiry. **2** a question mark, esp. one used to express doubt about something; *v.*: *The proofreader queried the author's spelling of the word.*

quest *n.* a search or expedition: *a prospector's quest for gold; our quest for happiness; immigrants* **in quest of** *a better life.*

ques.tion (QUES.chun) *n.* **1** a sentence or phrase asking for an answer from someone, as "Who is it?": *Send your questions in writing; to address, answer, bring up or pose, field a question; put a question to someone; burning, crucial, hypothetical, leading, loaded, moot, rhetorical, relevant, thorny questions; a question about or concerning capital punishment; He popped the question (of marriage) after dinner; The question is academic* (= of no value); **to beg the question** (= take as true something that has to be proved); *a question-and-answer session.* **2** doubt: *There's* **no question** *of his age or Age is not* **in question;** *No question he's of age; But there is some question about his qualifications; The decision was called* **into question;** *His honesty is* **beyond** *or* **without question.** **3** a subject of doubt, discussion, or dispute: *The chairman put the question to the vote; to clear up or resolve a question; the book* **in question** (= being considered or discussed); *It is* **out of the question** (= impossible). —*v.* **1** ask someone a question or questions: *The reporter questioned the mayor about or on the allegation; Most of those questioned said "No"; The driver was stopped and questioned by the police; n.: She didn't break down under their* **questioning.** **2** challenge: *I must question your claim.* —**ques.tion.er** *n.*

ques.tion.a.ble (QUES.chun.uh.bul) *adj.* that raises questions of truth, goodness, honesty, value, etc.: *a questionable activity, assertion, assumption; questionable ethics; It's questionable whether he can be trusted; a man of questionable reputation.* —**ques.tion.a.bly** (-blee) *adv.*

question mark *n.* the punctuation mark [?] put at the end of a written question; interrogation mark.

ques.tion.naire (ques.chuh.NAIR) *n.* a list of questions on a particular subject, as for an opinion survey: *to draw up, fill out, formulate, send out a questionnaire.*

queue (CUE) *n.* **1** a braid of hair which hangs down the back. **2** a line of people waiting in order of arrival: *to form, stand in a queue at a cashier's counter; to join, jump the queue.* **3** in a computer system, a sequence of items waiting

for action, as files to be printed.
—*v.* **queues, queued, queu.ing** form a line: *Eager fans queued up for tickets.*

quib.ble (QUIB.ul) *v.* **quib.bles, quib.bled, quib.bling** make petty distinctions, esp. in order to evade an issue: *It's no use quibbling with the tax department about or over a small payment.*
—**quib.bler** *n.*

quiche (KEESH) *n.* a custard pie filled with cheese and often bacon, mushrooms, etc.

quick *adj.* fast or prompt, esp. in reacting to a stimulus; live and active: *a dog with a quick ear; a quick response to a call; The ambulance was quick to respond to our call; He is quick with figures; She's quick in math* (= in understanding math); **quick breads** such as muffins and scones (baked quickly using baking powder, not yeast); a **quick-change** act, artist, fixture, magician, system (that quickly changes from one to another).
—*n.* **the quick 1** a sensitive point: *The child clipped her nails to the quick; Her criticism* **cut him to the quick** (= hurt his feelings). **2** [old use] living persons: *the quick and the dead.* —**quick.ly** *adv.;* **quick.ness** *n.*

quick buck *n. Informal.* money made without much effort: *how to make a quick buck; He's out for or after a quick buck;* **adj**.: *a quick-buck artist, hustler.*

quick.en (QUIK.un) *v.* make or become more quick, alive, or fast: *Quicken your pace to catch up with him; The pulse quickens under fear; stories that quicken one's imagination; **n**.: the* **quickening** (= movements) *felt in the womb as pregnancy advances.*

quick fix *n. Informal.* a fast though superficial fixing of a problem: *There is no quick fix to unemployment;* **adj**.: *a quick-fix casserole, policy, solution.*

quick-freeze *v.* **-freez.es, -froze, -fro.zen, -freez.ing** freeze food rapidly in preparation for long-term storage at low temperatures.

quick.ie (QUIK.ee) *n. Informal.* something done or prepared in a hurry, as a cheap movie or publication; **adj**.: *quickie crash diets, marriages, solutions; a quickie* (= wildcat) *strike.*

quick.lime *n.* lime that has not been slaked.

quick-lunch *n.* a place specializing in quickly prepared food; luncheonette.

quick.sand *n.* soft, wet sand that yields to pressure and sucks down heavy objects on its surface: *She found herself in the quicksand of a rash decision.*

quick.sil.ver (QUIK.sil.vur) *n.* mercury.

quick.step *n.* **1** lively music for a military march in quick time, a pace of 120 steps a minute. **2** a lively dance step.

quick study *n.* one who is quick at learning or studying something new.

quick-tempered *adj.* easily angered: *He's too quick-tempered to control himself.*

quick-witted *adj.* showing a sharp and alert mind.

quid *n.* **1** a piece of chewing tobacco. **2** *Brit. Informal.* a pound sterling; sovereign.

quid pro quo (QUID.pro.QUO) *n.* something expected or given as a return for something else; a consideration.

qui.es.cent (kwy.ES.unt) *adj.* inactive for a time; quiet: *a tourist town that is quiescent though not dormant during the winter;* **qui.es.cent.ly** *adv.*
—**qui.es.cence** *n.*

qui.et (KWY.ut) *adj.* calm or peaceful: *the quiet countryside; a quiet stream; a man of quiet disposition; decorated in quiet colors; the quiet diplomacy that characterizes U.S.-Canada relations.* —*n.* the state of being quiet: *The teacher asked for absolute quiet; neighbors living in peace and quiet; The riot shattered the quiet of the neighborhood.* —*v.* make quiet: *He quieted the frightened animals; The class quieted down when the teacher arrived.*
—**quiet.ly** *adv.;* **quiet.ness** *n.*

qui.e.tude (KWY.uh.tude) *n.* tranquility or repose.

qui.e.tus (kwy.EE.tus) *n.* something, esp. death, that ends all activity: *The newspaper story gave the rumors their quietus.*

quill *n.* **1** a stiff, hollow, pointed shaft, as a porcupine's spine or the stem of a goose's feather. **2** the feather itself. **3** an object made from it, as a pen or toothpick.

quilt *n.* a padded blanket or coverlet with its filling kept in place by lines of stitching, often in a pattern: *a patchwork quilt; a quilt pattern.*
—*v.* make a quilt or something similar: *to quilt a bag; We're quilting tomorrow;* **adj**.: *a* **quilted** *bag, design, effect, jacket, robe;* **n**.: *a* **quilting bee** (= social gathering for making quilts).

quince *n.* the hard, yellow, acid fruit of a small tree related to apples and pears.

qui.nine (KWY.nine) *n.* a bitter crystalline substance prepared from cinchona bark and used to treat malaria and other fevers.

quin.sy (QUIN.zee) *n.* a throat inflammation with an abscess near the tonsils.

quint *n.* [short form] quintuplet.

quin.tal (QUIN.tul) *n.* **1** in the metric system, 100 kilograms. **2** a hundredweight.

quin.tes.sence (quin.TES.unce) *n.* the purest form or best example: *the Good Samaritan as the quintessence of charity.*
—**quin.tes.sen.tial** (-SEN.shul) *adj.*

quin.tet or **quin.tette** (quin.TET) *n.* **1** a piece of music for five voices or instruments. **2** a group of five singers, team of five basketball players, etc.

quin.tu.ple (QUIN.tup.ul, quin.TUE.pul) *v.* **-ples, -pled, -pling** multiply or increase by five: *a plan to quintuple sales in one year.* —*n.*: *20 is the quintuple of 4.* —*adj.* having five parts: *a quintuple heart bypass operation.*

quin.tu.plet (QUIN.tuh.plit, quin.TUP.lit) *n.* one of five offspring of a single birth.

quip *n.* a pointed, neatly turned remark or retort. —*v.* **quips, quipped, quip.ping.** —**quip.ster** *n.*

quire *n.* a set of 24 or 25 sheets of the same kind of paper.

quirk *n.* a peculiar characteristic; a turn or twist from what is usual: *the quirks of an eccentric character; by some strange quirk of fate.* —**quirk.y** *adj.*
—**quirk.i.ness** *n.*

quirt *n.* a short-handled riding whip with a braided leather lash.

quis.ling (QUIZ.ling) *n.* a traitor, esp. the puppet of a foreign power occupying one's country.

quit *v.* **quits,** *pt. & pp.* **quit** or **quit.ted, quit.ting 1** leave a place or situation; cease doing something; give up: *He quit school; She quit smoking; He quit all claims for damages; The engine suddenly quit on us.* **2** free oneself of a person or thing: *He paid up and quit his debts; She left the party to be quit of his company.* See also QUITS.

quit.claim *n.* **1** the formal giving up of a claim or title to a property, right, etc. **2** a document to this effect, or **quitclaim deed.**

quite (KWITE) *adv.* completely: *He's quite wrong; She's quite (= very) anxious; Micawber is quite a (= really a) character.* —**quite a few** *Informal.* a good number.

quits *adj. Informal.* finished: *After one more game, I'll be quits with you* (= on even terms with you); *We'll call it quits* (= stop or give up) *for today if it rains.*

quit.tance (QUIT.unce) *n.* **1** release from debt, responsibility, etc. **2** repayment.

quit.ter (QUIT.ur) *n. Informal.* one who gives up without trying hard enough.

quiv.er (QUIV.ur) *n.* **1** a carrying case for arrows. **2** a trembling; quaver: *a quiver of desire, excitement, rage.*
—*v.* tremble: *to quiver with indignation;* **adja.:** *a quivering mass of jelly; a quivering voice, wimp.*

qui vive? (kee.VEEV) *n.* a French sentry's challenge, "Who goes there?": *Be on the qui vive* (= watchful) *against pickpockets.*

quix.ot.ic (quik.SOT.ic) *adj.* like the romantic hero Don Quixote, running into danger trying to do the impossible: *a quixotic adventure, attempt, character, demand, dream, effort, policy, quest.*

quiz *n.* **quiz.zes** a series of questions, esp. a short test. —*v.* **quiz.zes, quizzed, quiz.zing** question: *Father quizzed him about his activities.*

quiz.zi.cal (QUIZ.i.cul) *adj.* questioning or puzzled: *a quizzical (facial) expression, eyebrow, glance, look.*
—**quiz.zi.cal.ly** *adv.*

quoin (COIN, QUOIN) *n.* **1** an external angle or corner of a wall. **2** a stone helping to form this; cornerstone.

quoit *n.* a flat metal ring thrown to encircle a peg in the game of **quoits** *pl.* [takes *sing. v.*].

quon.dam (QUON.dum) *adj.* that once was; former: *a quondam friend, now archenemy.*

Quon.set hut (QUON.sit-) *n. Trademark.* a prefabricated building made of corrugated metal and shaped like a half cylinder.

quo.rum (QUOR.um) *n.* the minimum number of a group's members that must be present to transact business legally: *One third of the membership shall constitute or make up a quorum.*

quo.ta (QUOH.tuh) *n.* that proportion of a total due from or to a person, group, etc.: *a sales rep's quota of business; to meet a quota; He had exceeded his quota before the end of the year; immigration quotas for ethnic groups; a quota system.*

quo.ta.ble (QUOH.tuh.bul) *adj.* worth quoting: *a quotable author, line, poet.*

quo.ta.tion (quoh.TAY.shun) *n.*
1 words repeated exactly: *biblical quotations; a quotation from Shakespeare; a pair of "quotation marks"* [as used here]. **2** current price: *today's stock market quotations.* **3** a stated price: *The contract went to the company that submitted the lowest quotation.*

quote *v.* **quotes, quot.ed, quot.ing**
1 repeat exactly; give words from a source: *to quote a line, maxim, poem, saying; to quote (from) an author; She was quoted as saying that he did it;* **adj.:** *the most* **quoted** *author, authority; a frequently, widely quoted source; quoted words.*
2 present as examples; cite: *I could quote many instances of his bravery.*
3 state the price of goods or services: *It was quoted at $1,995; They quoted $3,000 for the antique;* **adj.:** *a* **quoted** *price.* —*n.* **1** quotation: *a quote from Milton.* **2** [used at the beginning of a quotation]: *She's some,* **quote unquote** *poet* or *She's some, quote, poet, unquote* (= She is some "poet").

quoth (*rhyme:* both) *v.* [old use] said.

quo.tid.i.an (quoh.TID.ee.un) *adj.* daily: *the quotidian chills and fever of malaria; quotidian life, truths.*

quo.tient (QUOH.shunt) *n.* the number that results from dividing one quantity by another, as 3 from 21/7: *the intelligence quotient* (= IQ).

.... **R, r** ....

R or **r** (AR) *n.* **R's** or **r's** the 18th letter of the English alphabet. —**the three R's** reading, writing, and arithmetic, as the basics of education.

rab.bet (RAB.it) *n.* a groove cut in or near a board's edge so that another piece can fit into it; *v.:* *two boards rabbeted together.*

rab.bi (RAB.eye) *n.* **rab.bis** the spiritual leader of a Jewish congregation. —**rab.bin.ic** (ra.BIN.ic) or **rab.bin.i.cal** (-i.cul) *adj.*

rab.bin.ate (RAB.i.nit) *n.* the office or tenure of a rabbi.

rab.bit (RAB.it) *n.* a small, long-eared, short-tailed burrowing animal with soft fur: *Rabbits breed fast.*

rabbit ears *n.pl.* *Informal.* an indoor TV antenna consisting of two adjustable rods.

rabbit punch *n.* a sharp blow on the back of the neck.

rab.ble (RAB.ul) *n.* a disorderly crowd; mob.

rabble-rouser *n.* one who tries to arouse a crowd to violent emotions or actions. —**rabble-rousing** *n. & adj.*

Rab.e.lai.si.an (rab.uh.LAY.zee.un) *adj.* having to do with broad or coarse humor in the style of François **Rabelais** (1494–1553), French satirist.

rab.id (RAB.id) *adj.* **1** afflicted with rabies: *a rabid cat, dog, wolf.* **2** violent or fanatical: *a rabid thirst; his rabid zeal; He's rabid about spreading his ideas.* —**rab.id.ly** *adv.*

ra.bies (RAY.beez) *n.* a serious disease which attacks the central nervous system of warm-blooded animals and is transmitted by a bite of an infected animal: *Our dog got rabies and was destroyed.*

rac.coon (ra.COON) *n.* a furry, gray-brown animal with a bushy, ringed tail and black, masklike hair around its eyes.

race *n.* **1** a major division of humanity: *the Caucasoid, Mongoloid, and Negroid races of old.* **2** an animal species: *the canine race; the human race.* **3** any group with similar ancestry or characteristics: *a noble race of warriors.* **4** a contest, esp. of speed, to reach a point or achieve an aim: *to run (in) a race; boat, cross-country, drag, horse, relay races; the 9-to-5 rat race; the arms race between the superpowers; a race against time; a race between Republicans and Democrats; the race for mayor; Americans won the race to the moon.* **5** a steady, onward movement on a regular course, as of a river, life, etc.
—*v.* **rac.es, raced, rac.ing 1** compete or engage in a race: *I'll race you to that tree.* **2** run at top speed: *The ambulance raced to the hospital; Don't race the engine when it is cold; With the deadline fast approaching, you are racing against time.* —**rac.er** *n.*

race.course *n.* a course for racing, esp. a usu. oval one for racing horses or dogs.

race.horse *n.* a horse used for racing.

ra.ceme (ra.SEEM) *n.* a flower cluster with short-stemmed individual flowers at regular intervals on a main stalk, as in oats.

race.track, race.way same as RACECOURSE.

ra.chi.tis (ruh.KYE.tis) same as RICKETS.

ra.cial (RAY.shul) *adj.* having to do with the human races: *racial backgrounds, bias, conflicts, differences, discrimination, groups, hatred, jokes, minorities, segregation.* —**ra.cial.ly** *adv.*

racialism, racialistic See RACISM.

racily, raciness See RACY.

racing (RAY.sing) *n.* the sport of holding or engaging in trials of speed: *auto, bicycle, car, dog, horse, sailboat racing.*

ra.cism (RAY.siz.um) *n.* **1** belief in the relative superiority of individual races. **2** discrimination based on this belief: *to stamp out racism; institutionalized racism.* Also **ra.cial.ism** (RAY.shuh.

liz.um) *n.* —**ra.cial.is.tic** (-LIS.tic) *adj.*
ra.cist (RAY.sist) *n.* one who believes in or practices racism: *Hitler was a racist;* *adj.*: *White supremacists are racist in their philosophy; racist attitudes, bigotry, governments, jokes, overtones, policies.* Also **ra.cial.ist.**
rack *n.* **1** a framework for storing or displaying various items: *clothes, hat, magazine, storage, towel racks; a luggage rack over the seats in a bus; a three-tiered* **rack car** *for transporting automobiles by rail.* **2** a toothed bar that meshes with another toothed structure such as a pinion: *a* **rack-and-pinion** *movement, railroad, steering.* **3** an instrument of torture on which limbs are stretched; hence, any torment: *Martyrs used to die on the rack.* **4** a front quarter or rib cut of meat: *rack of lamb.* —**rack and ruin** See WRACK. —**rack one's brains** think hard. —*v.* torture or torment: *racked by arthritis, doubts, coughing, remorse; He's racked with pain; adja.: a* **racking** *cough, headache.* —**rack up** *Informal.* score: *Our team quickly racked up 10 points.*
rack.et (RACK.it) *n.* **1** a long-handled oval frame strung with netting, used in tennis, squash, etc.; racquet. **2** loud noise, as of revelry: *The party made a terrible racket.* **3** a dishonest scheme or activity, esp. for obtaining money: *to run a blackmail racket.*
rack.et.eer (rack.i.TEER) *n.* one who runs a racket: *a big-time racketeer; petty racketeers;* *n.*: *charges of fraud and* **racketeering;** *adj.*: *a racketeering case, enterprise, law.*
rac.on.teur (rack.on.TUR) *n.* a skillful storyteller.
rac.quet (RACK.it) same as RACKET, 1.
rac.y (RAY.see) *adj.* **rac.i.er, -i.est 1** having the characteristic flavor, vigor, etc. of something; hence, piquant or spicy: *racy fruit.* **2** suggestive or stimulating to the senses: *Some consider "The Catcher in the Rye" too racy a book for the young; his racy sense of humor; a racy tabloid; clothes that are light, racy, and carefree.* —**rac.i.ly** *adv.*; **rac.i.ness** *n.*
ra.dar (RAY.dar) *n.* a "radio detecting and ranging" device for locating faraway objects such as missiles or mountains by reflecting radio waves.
ra.dar.scope (RAY.dar.scope) *n.* a radar receiver with a fluorescent screen display.
ra.di.al (RAY.dee.ul) *adj.* branching out like rays from a center: *An amphitheater has radial seating; A* **radial engine** *has its cylinders arranged like the spokes of a wheel instead of at an angle as in the V-type; A* **radial tire** *has its ply cords laid at right angles to the center line of the tread instead of diagonally as in bias-ply tires.* —**ra.di.al.ly** *adv.*
ra.di.ant (RAY.dee.unt) *adj.* **1** giving off rays, as of light or heat: *Radiant energy is transmitted in waves; radiant heating using hot-water pipes, baseboards, or loops of electric cable.* **2** glowing or happy: *a radiant bride; a face radiant with joy; a necklace radiant with diamonds.* —**ra.di.ance** *n.*
ra.di.ate (RAY.dee.ate) *v.* **-ates, -at.ed, -at.ing 1** give out rays of something: *The sun radiates energy; a sales rep radiating confidence.* **2** spread out from a center: *Spokes radiate from a wheel's center.*
ra.di.a.tion (ray.dee.AY.shun) *n.* emission of rays, esp. X rays: *Radium emits radiation; The Geiger counter is a radiation detector; nuclear radiation; the sun's thermal radiation; The Van Allen* **radiation belt** *around the earth contains high-energy-charged particles;* **radiation sickness** *caused by overexposure to radioactive matter.*
ra.di.a.tor (RAY.dee.ay.tur) *n.* one that radiates, esp. a cooling, heating, or transmission device: *an automobile radiator; heating radiators.*
rad.i.cal (RAD.i.cul) *adj.* **1** basic or fundamental: *a radical error, idea, principle.* **2** affecting the foundation: *a radical change, position, view.* **3** favoring fundamental change of the social structure: *a radical politician, student group; academe's* **radical chic** *(= voguish association with radicals).*
—*n.* **1** one who is radical. **2** *Math.* a root, indicated by a **radical sign** as in $^3\sqrt{9}$ (= cube root of 9). —**rad.i.cal.ism** *n.* —**rad.i.cal.ly** *adv.*
rad.i.cal.ize (RAD.i.cuh.lize) *v.* **-iz.es, -ized, -iz.ing** make politically radical. —**rad.i.cal.i.za.tion** (-luh.ZAY.shun, -lye-) *n.*
radii a *pl.* of RADIUS.
ra.di.o (RAY.dee.oh) *n.* **-os 1** the sending and receiving of sound and picture signals using electromagnetic waves without connecting wires, as in broadcasting. **2** a broadcast receiving set or broadcasting as a business, medium, etc.: *Let's turn on the radio for the latest weather; to turn down, turn up, turn off the radio; I listened to the weather on or over my car radio; AM, clock, FM, transistor radios.* —**adja.**: *a radio announcer, engineer, program, wave.*
—*v.* **-oes, -oed, -o.ing** communicate

with someone or transmit a message by radio: *He radioed for help, radioed to all the ships in the vicinity, radioed instructions; She radioed back.*

radio- *comb.form.* **1** radio: *radiogram, radiosonde, radiotelephone.* **2** radiation: *radiology, radiometer, radiotherapy.*

ra.di.o.ac.tive (RAY.dee.oh.AC.tiv) *adj.* having to do with radioactivity: *radioactive contamination, decay, dust, elements, emissions, fallout, isotopes, materials, substances, waste.*

ra.di.o.ac.tiv.i.ty (RAY.dee.oh.ac.TIV.i.tee) *n.* the process by which substances such as radium and uranium give off atomic particles or rays: *a dangerous level of radioactivity.*

radio astronomy *n.* the study of radio waves from heavenly bodies such as the sun, Jupiter, pulsars, quasars, etc.

ra.di.o.car.bon (RAY.dee.oh.CAR.bun) same as CARBON 14.

radio frequency *n.* an electromagnetic wave frequency ranging from 3 kilohertz to 300 gigahertz that is suitable for TV and radio broadcasting.

radio galaxy *n.* a galaxy that is a source of radio waves.

ra.di.o.gram (RAY.dee.oh.gram) *n.* a telegram sent by radio.

ra.di.o.graph (RAY.dee.oh.graf) *n.* an X-ray photograph. —*v.* make a radiograph of an object. —**ra.di.o.graph.ic** (-GRAF.ic) *adj.*; **ra.di.o.graph.i.cal.ly** *adv.* —**ra.di.og.ra.phy** (-OG.ruh.fee) *n.*

ra.di.o.i.so.tope (RAY.dee.oh.EYE.suh.tope) *n.* a radioactive form of a substance such as iodine or iron used in diagnosis and treatment, esp. of cancer.

ra.di.ol.o.gy (RAY.dee.oh.OL.uh.jee) *n.* a branch of medicine dealing with the use of radiant energy such as X rays in diagnosis and treatment; **ra.di.ol.o.gist** *n.* —**ra.di.o.log.i.cal** (-dee.uh.LOJ.i.cul) *adj.*

ra.di.om.e.ter (RAY.dee.oh.OM.i.tur) *n.* an instrument for measuring radiant energy; **ra.di.om.e.try** (-uh.tree) *n.* —**ra.di.o.met.ric** (-oh.MET.ric) *adj.*; **ra.di.o.met.ri.cal.ly** *adv.*

ra.di.o.phone (RAY.dee.oh.fone) same as RADIOTELEPHONE.

ra.di.o.sonde (RAY.dee.oh.sond) *n.* a meteorological device consisting of a balloon carrying instruments for recording weather data which are transmitted by radio to ground stations.

ra.di.o.tel.e.graph (RAY.dee.oh.TEL.uh.graf) *n.* wireless telegraphy; **ra.di.o.tel.e.graph.ic** (-GRAF.ic) *adj.*; **ra.di.o.te.leg.ra.phy** (-tuh.LEG.ruh.fee) *n.*

ra.di.o.tel.e.phone (RAY.dee.oh.TEL.uh.fone) *n.* a telephone using radio waves as the transmission medium, as in moving vehicles; **ra.di.o.te.leph.o.ny** (-tuh.LEF.uh.nee) *n.*

radio telescope *n.* the telescope used in radio astronomy, equipped with an antenna to pick up radio waves from beyond the reach of optical telescopes by means of a giant dishlike reflector.

ra.di.o.ther.a.py (RAY.dee.oh.THER.uh.pee) *n.* therapy using X rays, radium, and other radioactive substances; **ra.di.o.ther.a.pist** *n.*

rad.ish *n.* the usu. white or red and spherical crisp, sharp-tasting, edible root of a plant of the mustard family.

ra.di.um (RAY.dee.um) *n.* a very unstable radioactive metallic element, used in luminous paints and in cancer therapy (**radium therapy**).

ra.di.us (RAY.dee.us) *n.*, *pl.* **-di.i** (-dee.eye) or **-di.us.es 1** a straight line from the center to the outside of a circle or sphere: *the radius of the earth.* **2** the area or distance covered by a radius: *people living within a radius of 20 miles from downtown.*

ra.don (RAY.don) *n.* a radioactive gas formed by the natural breakdown of uranium in the earth's crust, as found in the polluted air of tightly sealed homes.

raf.fi.a (RAF.ee.uh) *n.* (fiber from) a large-leaved palm tree of Madagascar.

raff.ish (RAF.ish) *adj.* showy; rakish; disreputable: *a playboy's raffish memoirs; the city's raffish district; the raffish hint of gambling.*

raf.fle (RAF.ul) *n.* the casting of lots for prizes: *They held a raffle for the Heart Fund; raffle tickets.* —*v.* **raf.fles, raf.fled, raf.fling** hold a raffle or sell off an article by a raffle. —**raf.fler** *n.*

raft *n.* **1** a floating structure of logs or timbers fastened together: *to launch a raft.* **2** a similar craft made of canvas, plastic, etc.: *an inflatable life raft.* **3** *Informal.* collection: *charged with a whole raft of offenses.* —*v.* make logs, boards, etc. into a raft, send by raft, or carry on a raft: *We went rafting* (= riding by raft) *on the Niagara.*

raft.er *n.* one of the sloping beams supporting a roof.

rag *n.* **1** a small, valueless, or torn piece of cloth: *clad in rags* (= worn-out clothes); *to chew the rag* (*Informal* for chat); *adj.*: *a rag doll; rag paper; the rags-to-riches story of a self-made millionaire.* **2** a tune in ragtime.
—*v.* **rags, ragged, rag.ging** *Informal.*

tease or taunt: *They ragged him about his poor marks*; **n.:** *bully* **ragging.**
rag.a.muf.fin (RAG.uh.muf.in) *n.* a ragged and dirty person, esp. a child.
rag.bag *n.* 1 a bag for rags. 2 a miscellaneous collection.
rage *n.* 1 fury or a fit of fury: *a blind, drunken, jealous, sudden, towering, uncontrollable, violent rage; He flew into a rage; She drove off in a rage but had to stop and fix a flat.* 2 a fad or vogue: *The rage then was bed-racing; Ray grew up when skateboarding was* **all the rage.**
—*v.* **rag.es, raged, rag.ing** 1 be in a rage: *He would rage at or against anyone who opposed him.* 2 go on uncontrollably: *A fire raged out of control; while a storm raged outside.*
rag.ged (RAG.id) *adj.* 1 tattered or torn: *in ragged clothes; a ragged dress, shirt.* 2 shabby or shaggy: *a ragged beard, boy; ragged hair.* 3 uneven or jagged: *to trim a ragged edge; lines printed with a ragged right margin.*
—**rag.ged.ly** *adv.;* **rag.ged.ness** *n.*
rag.ged.y (RAG.id.ee) *adj. Informal.* ragged: *a shoeless raggedy kid; a Raggedy Ann doll.*
rag.lan (RAG.lun) *adja.* of a sleeve, extending to the collar with slanted underarm seams: *raglan sleeves.*
—*n.* an overcoat with raglan sleeves.
ra.gout (ra.GOO) *n.* a highly seasoned stew of meat and vegetables.
rag.tag *n.* worthless or disreputable people; riffraff.
rag.time *n.* a strongly rhythmic style of piano playing, a forerunner of jazz.
rag.weed *n.* a weed with hairy, toothed leaves and long spikes of flowers full of pollen.
rah *interj.* hurrah.
rah-rah *adj. Informal.* spirited or enthusiastic like cheerleaders: *the rah-rah spirit of the centennial celebration;* **n.:** *the public relations rah-rah* (= hoopla).
raid *n.* a sudden, hostile attack or invasion: *The U.S. carried out or conducted an air and naval raid against Libya; Libya's raid into Chad; bombing, border, guerrilla, police, retaliatory, suicide raids; a raid on or upon drug traffickers.*
—*v.* make a raid on a place: *Police raided the gambling joint; to raid the fridge for snacks.* —**raid.er** *n.*
rail *n.* 1 either of a pair of parallel connected steel bars forming a track for a train or similar vehicle; hence, a railroad: *to travel by rail.* 2 a horizontal bar connecting posts and forming a guard or barrier, as on a fence. 3 a marsh bird such as the coot that has a thin body for slipping through reeds and grasses. —*v.* 1 complain bitterly *against* or *about* or *at* a person or thing; **rail.er.y** *n.* **rail.er.ies.** 2 fence with rails; **n.:** *Be careful about leaning on the* **railing;** *wooden railings;* **adj.:** *a brass-railed spiral staircase.*
rail.road *n.* 1 a track of rails for locomotives, streetcars, etc.; **adja.:** *a railroad car, crossing, station, track.* 2 such a transportation system: *a commuter railroad; the Union Pacific Railroad.* —*v.* 1 send by railroad. 2 *Informal.* rush a person, business, etc. through a system without careful consideration: *The bill was railroaded through the legislature; They tried to railroad* (= force) *him off the job.*
rail.way 1 *Cdn.* railroad. 2 [older and special uses] a track of rails: *cog railways; scenic railways;* **adj.:** *a railway carriage, engineer, museum, post office.*
rai.ment (RAY.munt) *n.* [old use] clothing.
rain *n.* 1 water falling in drops from the sky: *The rain came down in buckets or torrents; acid, driving, freezing, heavy, intermittent, light, pouring, soaking, steady, torrential rain; The rain beats, falls, lets up, patters, pours, starts, stops; Pat's always punctual,* **come rain or shine** (= whatever the weather); *spring* **rains** (= seasonal rainfalls). 2 anything resembling rain: *a rain of bullets, kisses, tears.* —*v.* fall as or like rain: *It's raining outside; They rained flowers on the returning hero; Tears rained down her cheeks; It's* **raining cats and dogs** *or raining hard; "It never rains but it pours"* (= Things happen in quick succession); *Polish voters* **rained on** *the Communist* **parade** (= beat the Communists); *The game was* **rained out** (= postponed because of rain).
rain.bow (RAIN.boh) *n.* an arch of colorful light seen in mist or spray: *the seven colors of the rainbow; A rainbow appears after a rain; a* **rainbow coalition** (*of people of all colors*).
rainbow trout *n.* a brightly colored North American trout with a rosy band along its body on either side.
rain.check *n.* an offer that is extended for a future occasion, as a ticket from a game stopped by rain or a coupon for a sales item that is sold out: *I'll take a raincheck on that offer.*
rain.coat *n.* a waterproof outer coat.
rain.drop *n.* a drop of rain.
rain.fall *n.* 1 a fall of rain: *a region of heavy rainfall.* 2 its amount: *annual, average, light rainfall.*

rain forest *n.* an evergreen tropical forest of equatorial regions characterized by dense growth, with treetops forming a canopy shading the forest floor.

rain.mak.ing (RAIN.may.king) *n.* the making of rain by artificial means. —**rain.mak.er** *n.*

rain.storm *n.* a storm with heavy rain.

rain.y (RAY.nee) *adj.* **rain.i.er, -i.est** having to do with rain: *rainy weather; to save for a rainy day* (= future time of need).

raise (RAZE) *v.* **rais.es, raised, rais.ing 1** move a person or thing to a higher level or position: *to raise the flag; to raise the standard of living; to raise the dead (to life); to raise the Titanic from the bottom of the sea; He never raises his voice (as in excitement); People are raised* (= elevated) *to positions of authority; to raise the people's consciousness.* **2** to bring up: *to raise children, crops, horses, turkeys; a telethon to raise* (= collect) *funds; to raise* (= cause) *a laugh; to raise* (= erect) *a monument; to raise a point* (= bring it up for discussion). **3** end: *to raise a siege.* —*n.* an increase: *a 10% raise in wages; The company gave an across-the-board raise to its employees; Some deserved a higher raise (in salary); She got a hefty raise.*

rai.sin (RAY.zin) *n.* a sweet sun-dried grape.

rai.son d'être (ray.zon.DET.ruh) *n. French.* the reason for being what something is: *the raison d'être for the male-female difference.*

ra.ja or **ra.jah** (RAH.juh) *n.* a prince of India.

rake *n.* **1** a long-handled tool or machine equipped with prongs for gathering leaves or hay, smoothing the ground, etc. **2** the slant or slope, as of a mast or funnel toward the stern, or of a floor from the horizontal, etc. **3** a dissolute man. —*v.* **rakes, raked, rak.ing 1** to remove, gather, etc. with or as if with a rake: *to rake leaves off a lawn; Hay is raked into piles; to rake in* (= gather quickly and abundantly) *profits; Why rake up* (= stir up) *long-forgotten enmities?* **2** to slant or slope: *a ship with a short mast raked well forward.*

rake.off *n. Informal.* a cut or share of profits.

rak.ish (RAY.kish) *adj.* **1** smart or trim, suggesting speed: *a rakish ship.* **2** jaunty or dashing: *a hat set at a rakish angle.* **3** dissolute: *a rakish life, look.*

ral.ly (RAL.ee) *v.* **ral.lies, ral.lied, ral.ly.ing 1** come or bring together for a renewed or united effort: *He rallied his forces for a renewed attack; They rallied to their country's defense; to rally round (to the side of) a leader; They rallied round; rallied round the flag, the menorah, their slogan;* **adja.:** *their rallying cry, point.* **2** recover or revive: *Our spirits rallied on hearing the good news; We rally from an illness; The price of gold rallied to the $350 level; The Canadians rallied with two last-minute goals; Tremblay rallied the Canadians to a 2-2 tie; The Penguins rallied on goals by Don and Chris; They rallied for a 5-2 victory over the Canucks.* —*n., pl.* **ral.lies 1** a rallying, as of the stock market. **2** a coming together of people such as scouts, sports-car enthusiasts, or worshipers for a group activity: *to hold, organize a rally; peace, pep, political rallies.*

RAM *n.* the random access memory of a computer: *In a computer memory,* **dynamic RAM**, *unlike* **static RAM**, *keeps data one bit at a time at an address and for only a fraction of a second.*

ram *n.* a male sheep, usu. with outward-curving horns. —*v.* **rams, rammed, ram.ming** butt or strike violently against, down, or into something: *Piles are rammed into a river bed; Cars ram into each other in a demolition derby; I can't ram it down his throat if he won't believe me.*

ram.ble (RAM.bul) *v.* **-bles, -bled, -bling 1** go about in an aimless or leisurely manner: *He likes to ramble in the woods; She rambles the woods; adj.: a* **rambling** (= spread out irregularly) *house; a rambling narrative (that tends to stray from topic to topic); a rambling* (= wandering) *vine.* **2** wander away, as from a subject while talking: *The lecturer rambled on; He rambled on for an hour about how he got lost.* —*n.* a roaming or excursion: *a ramble in the woods.*

ram.bler (RAM.blur) *n.* **1** a walker or one who rambles about. **2** one that rambles: *Some roses are ramblers, others are climbers.* **3** a large one-story home; ranch house.

ram.bunc.tious (ram.BUNK.shus) *adj.* boisterous and unruly: *a crowd of rambunctious students.*

ram.e.kin (RAM.i.kin) *n.* a small baking dish or an individual portion cooked in it.

ram.ie (RAM.ee) *n.* **1** an Asiatic nettle. **2** the fiber obtained from it.

ram.i.fi.ca.tion (ram.uh.fi.CAY.shun) *n.* **1** a ramifying or branching out: *the ramifications of a system.* **2** [usu. in *pl.*] consequence or outgrowth: *the* far-reaching or *widespread ramifications of a decision; the ramifications of a problem; an intricate plot with many ramifications.*

ram.i.fy (RAM.uh.fye) *v.* **-fies, -fied, -fy.ing** branch out; spread out.

ramp *n.* a sloped means of access to a different level, as at a highway interchange or the staircase used to board a plane: *wheelchair ramps for sidewalks; a steep ramp; to go down, up a ramp; a ramp speed of 35 mph.*

ram.page (RAM.page) *n.* a spell of reckless or violent behavior: *The merrymakers went **on the** or **on a rampage.*** —*v.* (ram.PAGE) **-pag.es, -paged, -pag.ing** rush about wildly or in excitement: *elephants rampaging through a forest; Merrymakers rampaged through the mall and broke windows.*

ram.pant (RAM.punt) *adj.* unchecked in growth or movement: *Inflation was running rampant at about 25% a year; rampant (= rank) vegetation.*
—**ram.pan.cy** *n.*

ram.part (RAM.part) *n.* a defensive barrier, esp. one built around a fort with a parapet on top: *The enemy stormed the ramparts.*

ram.rod *n.* a rod used to ram a charge into a muzzle-loading firearm.

ram.shack.le (RAM.shack.ul) *adja.* rickety: *ramshackle dwellings, tenements, vehicles.*

ran *pt.* of RUN.

ranch *n.* **1** a large farm for raising cattle, sheep, or horses: *a cattle ranch; a dude ranch for tourists; He works at a ranch but doesn't live on it.* **2** a specialty farm: *a chicken, fruit, mink ranch.* **3** a low-roofed one-story dwelling; also **ranch house.** —*v.* manage or work on a ranch. —**ranch.er** *n.*

ran.cher.o (ran.CHAIR.oh) *n.* in southwestern U.S., a ranch owner or ranch worker; rancher.

ranch.hand *n.* one employed on a cattle ranch.

ran.cid (RAN.cid) *adj.* tasting or smelling like spoiled fat, butter, etc.: *rancid fish.* —**ran.cid.i.ty** (ran.CID.i.tee) *n.*

ran.cor (RANK.ur) *n.* bitter or spiteful hatred: *to express, feel, show, stir up rancor; He was full of rancor against or toward the enemy.* —**ran.cor.ous** *adj.*; **ran.cor.ous.ly** *adv.* Also **ran.cour** *Cdn.*

rand *n. sing. & pl.* the basic money unit of South Africa, equal to 100 cents.

ran.dom (RAN.dum) *adj.* made or done without a purpose, plan, or aim: *random shots; to take* or *select a **random sample** or a sample chosen **at random** as representative of a large group.*
—**ran.dom.ly** *adv.*

random access *n.* access to data in a computer memory in the order desired by user; **random access memory.**

ran.dom.ize (RAN.duh.mize) *v.* **-iz.es, -ized, -iz.ing** make at random; *adj.*: *a randomized selection of items.*
—**ran. dom.i.za.tion** (-muh.ZAY.shun, -mye-) *n.*

ran.dy *adj.* **-di.er, -di.est 1** lecherous: *randy as a rabbit; randy songs.* **2** sexually aroused: *You don't seem randy at all!*

ra.nee (RAH.nee) *n.* a raja's wife; rani.

rang *pt.* of RING.

range (RAINJ) *v.* **rang.es, ranged, rang.ing 1** vary within an area or distance: *The price ranges from $30 to $50 or between $30 and $50; a fine ranging up to $100 a day; Buffalo once ranged (= roamed) our plains; **adja. & cpd:** Radar is a **ranging** (= distance-finding) device; a far-ranging discussion; a free-ranging herd; wide-ranging essays, surveys, vision.* **2** arrange or classify in groups: *eggs ranged small, medium, and large; The collaborators **ranged themselves with** (= joined) the invaders; They were ranged (= aligned) against us.*
—*n.* **1** distance or extent: *a wide range of vision; within range of gunfire; The target seemed out of range; price, salary, size ranges; at close, point-blank range; goods in the $50 to $75 price range; **cpd:** Let's take a long-range view of the matter; long-range missiles, planning; short-range radio.* **2** variety: *We cater to a broad range of clients; We carry a full range of hats; a wide* or *diverse range of goods; a whole range of perils.* **3** a place for a continuing activity: *artillery, firing, rifle, rocket ranges; a driving range (for golf).* **4** row or series: *a mountain range.* **5** a cooking stove, usu. with oven and storage compartment: *electric and gas ranges.*

rang.er (RAIN.jur) *n.* **1** one who patrols or guards a region: *a forest ranger.* **2** a commando or special police officer: *Texas Rangers.* **3 Ranger** a senior Girl Guide, 16 years or older.

rang.y (RAIN.jee) *adj.* **rang.i.er, -i.est 1** able to range about. **2** long-limbed: *rangy cattle or horses; his tall rangy good looks.*

rani same as RANEE.

rank *n.* **1** a row, as of a lineup of soldiers: *to form a rank; to **break ranks** and run; Closing down of businesses swell the **ranks** of the unemployed; to enroll in, enter, join, move up in, rise in, serve in*

rank and file / rapture

the ranks (= army); *a general who came up or rose from the ranks (of the enlisted); to close ranks* (= unite) *to meet a challenge.* 2 a position according to grade and seniority, esp. of a military officer: *He holds the rank of colonel; to pull rank on someone* (= to use one's position) *to get an advantage; an official of high rank; cabinet rank.*
—*v.* to rate or be rated: *Canadian actors rank among the best in the world; He ranks as an outstanding poet; He does not rank with Shakespeare; Shakespeare ranks above all dramatists; A major ranks below a colonel; A colonel ranks* (= outranks) *a major.* —*adj.* 1 coarse and vigorous in growth, as weeds. 2 bad-smelling: *rank tobacco.* 3 *adja.* complete or utter: *a rank amateur, beginner; rank ingratitude, injustice, nonsense.* —**rank.ly** *adv.*; **rank.ness** *n.*
rank and file *n.* 1 ordinary soldiers. 2 the ordinary membership or people: *the Republican rank and file; The rank and file of the union rejected the offer.*
ranking *adja.* of high rank: *a ranking educator, officer; the ranking* (= highest-ranked) *senator.*
ran.kle (RANK.ul) *v.* **-kles, -kled, -kling** be a source of irritation or soreness: *It rankled her that she was not invited; an insult that still rankles (in her mind).*
ran.sack *v.* 1 search a place thoroughly, as if to plunder. 2 to plunder or pillage.
ran.som (RAN.sum) *n.* a price demanded for freeing a person from captivity: *a child kidnaped and held for ransom; to demand, exact, pay a ransom.*
—*v.* free someone by paying a ransom: *The child was rescued by police before being ransomed.*
rant *v.* talk wildly and loudly: *He rants and raves whenever things go wrong; dare not rant at his wife, though.*
—*n.* a noisy or bombastic speech.
rap *n.* 1 a sharp knock: *a rap on the door; He received a rap on the knuckles* (= mild punishment or reproof) *from the teacher for being lazy.* 2 *Slang.* blame or punishment: *looking for someone to take the rap; He got a bad or bum rap* (= was unfairly punished); *jailed on a burglary rap* (= charge); *looked for ways to beat* (= escape) *the rap.* 3 *Slang.* chat or talk: *a rap session.* 4 *Informal.* the least bit: *I don't give or care a rap.* 5 a kind of popular monotone music with a strong beat and rhymes like "The bat hit the cat, and the cat went scat."
—*v.* **raps, rapped, rap.ping** 1 tap or knock sharply, as on a door. 2 *Slang.* chat or talk: *He wastes a lot of time rapping on the phone.* —**rap.per** *n.*
ra.pa.cious (ruh.PAY.shus) *adj.* plundering; greedy; grasping: *the rapacious wolf; a rapacious tyrant.*
—**ra.pa.cious.ness** or **ra.pac.i.ty** (-PAS.i.tee) *n.*
rape *n.* 1 a forcing, esp. of a woman, to have sexual intercourse: *to commit rape; attempted, gang, marital rapes; rape victims.* 2 a plant of the mustard family, the source of **rapeseed** and **rapeseed oil**, now called canola.
—*v.* **rapes, raped, rap.ing** commit rape; ravish or violate.
rap.id (RAP.id) *adj.* moving at a swift pace; quick: *a rapid pulse, stream; the rapid growth of weeds;* **rapid-fire** (= like firing in rapid succession) *questioning; the rapid eye movement and rapid breathing and heart rates associated with the dreaming phase of sleep; a rapid transit public transportation system using fast trains.* —*n.* usu. **rapids** *pl.* a part of a river with swift currents and rocks beneath the surface: *a shallow boat or raft for riding or shooting the rapids of the Niagara.* —**rap.id.ly** *adv.*
—**ra.pid.i.ty** (ruh.PID.i.tee) *n.*
ra.pi.er (RAY.pee.ur) *n.* a narrow-bladed, pointed dueling sword used for thrusting: *the rapier thrust of his wit.*
rap.ine (RAP.in) *n.* plundering; pillage.
rap.ist (RAY.pist) *n.* one who commits a rape.
rap.pel (ruh.PEL) *v.* **rap.pels, rap.pelled, rap.pel.ling** slide *down* a cliff face using a rope.
rap.port (ra.POR) *n.* a close relationship implying mutual sympathy and harmony: *to establish a rapport with her colleagues; She works in close rapport with them.*
rap.proche.ment (ra.PROHSH.mahng) *n.* the establishment of cordial relations: *to bring about a rapprochement between the warring factions.*
rap.scal.lion (rap.SCAL.yun) *n.* a rogue or rascal.
rap session *n. Slang.* an informal group discussion.
rap sheet *n. Slang.* a police record.
rapt *adj.* absorbed or engrossed in a thinking state or emotion: *He was rapt in thought; They listened with rapt attention;* **rapt.ly** *adv.*; **rapt.ness** *n.*
rap.ture (RAP.chur) *n.* the state of being rapt in a feeling of bliss: *She spent the night in rapture over her wedding; a rapture of joy.* —**rap.tur.ous** *adj.*

ra.ra a.vis (RAIR.uh.AY.vis) *n.* a rare bird; rarity.

rare *adj.* **rar.er, rar.est 1** not frequent; without many instances or specimens: *It's rare to see this bird in January; a rare phenomenon; He's a rare bird at these meetings.* **2** *adja.* unusually good: *a rare book, beauty, event, talent.* **3** not dense: *the rare mountain air; the rarer regions of the atmosphere.* **4** of meat, not cooked much: *a rare steak; He wants it (done) medium rare.* —**rare.ly** *adv.*

rare.bit same as WELSH RABBIT.

rare-earth element (or **metal**) *n.* any of a series of metallic elements from lanthanum to lutetium with similar chemical properties.

rar.e.fied *adj.* **1** less dense: *the rarefied air of the mountains; a rarefied gas.* **2** exalted: *the rarefied atmosphere of the corporate elite; rarefied lives, realms.* **3** esoteric: *the rarefied world of art; rarefied aspects, exhibits, societies, tastes, views.* Also **rar.i.fied.**

rar.e.fy (RAIR.uh.fye) *v.* **-fies, -fied, -fy.ing** make or become less dense. —**rar.e.fac.tion** (-FAC.shun) *n.*

rar.ing (RAIR.ing) *adj. Informal.* very eager: *He is raring to go.*

rar.i.ty (RAIR.i.tee) *n.* **-ties 1** rareness. **2** an unusual person or thing.

ras.cal (RAS.cul) *n.* **1** a scoundrel; rogue. **2** [used jokingly] a naughty or mischievous person. —**ras.cal.ly** *adv.* —**ras.cal.i.ty** (ras.CAL.i.tee) *n.*

rash *n.* **1** a skin eruption, often itchy, usu. covering an area of the body in spots or patches, as in measles and prickly heat: *diaper, heat, nettle rashes; A rash breaks out; She* **broke out in** (= became covered with) *a rash.* **2** sudden appearance in large numbers: *a rash of accidents on an icy highway.* —*adj.* hasty or thoughtless; precipitate: *a rash action, decision, driver, promise.* —**rash.ly** *adv.;* **rash.ness** *n.*

rash.er *n.* **1** a slice of bacon. **2** a serving of several slices of bacon.

rasp *n.* **1** a coarse file with a surface of points or teeth. **2** the grating sound made as if or when a rasp is used: *a cricket's rasp, the rasp of a saw.* —*v.* utter with a grating sound: *He rasps out his orders; voices that rasp* (= irritate) *one's nerves.* —**rasp.y** *adj.*

rasp.ber.ry (RAZ.ber.ee, -buh.ree) *n.* **-ber.ries 1** a small, round, usu. red or purple fruit of a bush of the rose family. **2** *Informal.* a rude noise of disapproval made by sticking out the tongue and blowing strongly: *Ray gave him the raspberry; to blow raspberries.*

ras.ter *n.* **1** a set of horizontal lines composed of pixels which form the image on a computer screen. **2** a set of parallel scanning lines on which a TV image is projected.

rat *n.* **1** a destructive rodent larger than a mouse. **2** *Slang.* a person considered low or mean, as an informer; also **rat fink.** —*v.* **rats, rat.ted, rat.ting** act in a low way. —**rat on 1** inform on someone. **2** go back on a promise: *He ratted on his word.* —**smell a rat** suspect something tricky.

ratch.et (RACH.it) *n.* **1** a wheel that is so toothed that it can move in only one direction, working with a pawl; also called **ratchet wheel. 2** the pawl itself. —*v.* move by degrees: *Interest rates seem to be ratcheting lower; to ratchet up prices, rates, rhetoric, a risk, spending, taxes; Unemployment is ratcheting up slowly; It has ratcheted up or upward two percentage points; The phone rates are being ratcheted down.*

rate *n.* a measurement of something variable in relation to something else: *The annual birth rate is about 17 per 1,000 of the population; to fix or set the minimum wage rate; annual, flat, high, hourly, low, moderate, reduced, regular, seasonal, slow, steady rates; accident, crime, death, discount, divorce, fertility, inflation, metabolic, mortality, pulse, tax rates; Money is loaned at a certain rate of interest; the postal rate for first-class mail; Al is a first-rate* (= top-class), *not second- or third-rate mind.* —**at any rate** in any case: *At any rate, we are not backing out; I hope to make a small profit at any rate* (= at least). —*v.* **rates, rat.ed, rat.ing 1** rank or be ranked: *Al is rated in the top 10% of his class; On a scale of 1 to 10, we would rate him about 2; He's rated among the best students; He rates with the best; He is rated as excellent; is rated very highly.* **2** *Informal.* deserve: *Her work is so good she rates a promotion.* **3** scold or berate.

rate.pay.er (RATE.pay.ur) *n.* one who pays taxes to a municipality.

rat.fink same as RAT, *n.* 2.

rath.er (RATH.ur, "TH" as in "the") *adv.* **1** more readily, properly, etc.: *He would rather play than work; prefers to play rather than work; prefers playing rather than working; He would rather not work at this hour; I would rather you did your homework than watch TV; He was let go, rather* (= more correctly), *he resigned.* **2** somewhat: *a rather chilly reception.*

raths.kel.ler (RAHT.skel.ur) *n.* a German-style basement restaurant.

rat.i.fy (RAT.uh.fye) *v.* **-fies, -fied, -fy.ing** give formal approval of an agreement, law, treaty, etc., usu. by vote. —**rat.i.fi.ca.tion** (-fuh.CAY.shun) *n.*

rating (RAY.ting) *n.* **1** a comparative estimate: *a fuse wire with a 15 amp. rating; a four-star credit rating; a high rating; a politician's approval rating; efficiency, octane, power ratings; a TV show canceled because of low ratings* (as determined by popularity surveys); *adja.: a rating firm, system; a credit-rating agency.* **2** a rank or grade; also, a placement in one.

ra.tio (RAY.shee.oh, -shoh) *n.* **-tios** the relation in quantity, amount, or degree between two things or this expressed as the quotient of two numbers; proportion: *The ratio of length to width for our flag is 2 to 1; The ratio between length and width is 2; Length and width are in the ratio of 2 to 1.*

ra.ti.o.ci.nate (rash.ee.OH.suh.nate) *v.* **-nates, -nat.ed, -nat.ing** go through the formal process of reasoning; **ra.ti.o.ci.na.tion** (-NAY.shun) *n.*

ra.tion (RASH.un, RAY.shun) *n.* a share or allotment, esp. of food: *daily, monthly rations; emergency, food, gasoline rations; to be on short rations* (= scanty food supply or provisions). —*v.* distribute as rations: *Food is strictly rationed during a war; Scarce supplies are rationed out to or among the most needy; Each person is rationed* (= limited) *to so much per week;* **n.:** *wartime rationing; to end, introduce, terminate rationing.*

ra.tion.al (RASH.uh.nul) *adj.* **1** based on reasoning: *rational behavior, suggestions; a rational explanation of a mystery.* **2** able to reason: *Humans are rational animals.* **3** sensible: *Let's be rational; the rational thing to do in a situation.* —**ra.tion.al.ly** *adv.* —**ra.tion.al.i.ty** (-NAL.i.tee) *n.*

ra.tion.ale (rash.uh.NAL) *n.* the underlying reasons or rational basis of a belief, custom, phenomenon, etc.: *the rationale of superstitious behavior; Your rationale* (= explanation) *is not quite convincing.*

ra.tion.al.ism (RASH.uh.nuh.liz.um) *n.* the principle or practice of using reason as the ultimate authority for knowledge, as opposed to faith or sense experience; **ra.tion.al.ist** *n.* —**ra.tion.al.is.tic** (-LIS.tic) *adj.*

ra.tion.al.ize (RASH.uh.nuh.lize) *v.* **-iz.es, -ized, -iz.ing 1** treat in a rational manner: *to rationalize a miracle, myth, superstition; attempts to rationalize* (= make rational) *English spelling.* **2** try to justify as a defense mechanism: *He's merely rationalizing; to rationalize an unreasonable behavior, fear, feeling, prejudice.* —**ra.tion.al.i.za.tion** (-luh.ZAY.shun, -lye-) *n.*

rat race *n. Informal.* the frantic struggle for survival in a highly competitive environment: *fed up with the 9-to-5 rat race.*

rat.tan (ruh.TAN) *n.* a tough material from the reedy stems of various East Indian climbing palms used for wickerwork, furniture, etc.

rat.tle (RAT.ul) *n.* **1** a baby's toy that makes noise when shaken. **2** a series of short, sharp sounds: *the squeaks and rattles in a car's body.* **3** the horny pieces joined together at the end of a rattlesnake's tail or the warning sound it makes. **4** the gurgling sound made by a dying person; also called "death rattle." —*v.* **rat.tles, rat.tled, rat.tling 1** make the sound of a rattle: *to rattle sabers; a rattling noise.* **2** talk in an incessant chatter: *He can rattle off or away a whole list of names.* **3** *Informal.* disturb one's composure; upset: *It rattled him to hear that his secretary had quit.*

rat.tle.brain (RAT.ul.brain) *n.* a frivolous or giddy person. —**rat.tle.brained** *adj.*

rat.tler (RAT.lur) or **rat.tle.snake** (RAT.ul.snake) *n.* a venomous American snake with a rattle on the end of its tail: *when the rattler strikes.*

rattling *n.* the act of making a sound like a rattle's: *saber rattling.* —*adja.* **1** that rattles: *rattling bones, chains, windows.* **2** *Informal.* lively; splendid: *a rattling business;* **adv.:** *a rattling good time.*

rat.trap *n.* **1** a trap for rats. **2** *Informal.* a run-down building.

rat.ty *adj.* **rat.ti.er, rat.ti.est** suggestive of or infested with rats; hence, shabby or wretched.

rau.cous (RAW.cus) *adj.* roughsounding or rowdy: *The crowd was getting raucous; raucous activism, discussions, entertainment, mayhem, music, parties, rebels, voices; a raucous campaign, debate, fray, laugh, performance, session.* —**rau.cous.ly** *adv.;* **rau.cous.ness** *n.*

raun.chy (RAWN.chee) *adj.* **-chi.er, -chi.est** earthy; lustful; vulgar: *a raunchy magazine; a raunchy TV show; too raunchy for family viewing.* —**raun.chi.ness** *n.*

rav.age (RAV.ij) *v.* **-ag.es, -aged,**

-ag.ing cause destruction or devastation: *Floods ravaged the area.* —*n*.: *to repair the ravages of war.*

rave *v.* **raves, raved, rav.ing** 1 talk wildly or furiously, as when delirious: *to rant and rave about* or *at* or *against a person or thing; adj.: a raving activist, lunatic, maniac, tantrum; adv.: He's raving mad; n.: his ravings against capital punishment.* 2 talk with great, often excessive enthusiasm: *He often raves to his boys about* or *over his exploits in the war; adj.: a raving* (= unusually impressive) *beauty, success.* —*n. Informal.* 1 enthusiastic praise: *There were raves in the media; adja.: The book drew* or *earned* or *garnered* or *got* or *received* or *won rave reviews; The show played to rave notices.* 2 a subject of such praise: *Garlic was the rave last year; It has never been a fave rave of mine.*

rav.el (RAV.ul) *v.* **-els, -eled, el.ing** 1 tangle or confuse. 2 untwist or unravel. —*n.* 1 a raveled part; also **raveling.** 2 a tangle or confusion: *a ravel of roads; caught in the ravels of the rush-hour traffic.* Also **rav.elled, rav.el.ling** *Cdn.*

rav.en (RAY.vun) *n.* 1 a larger-size type of crow with black and lustrous feathers. 2 black and lustrous: *her raven hair.* —*v.* feed or prey like a raven; *n.: the ravenings of sex.*
—**ravening** or **rav.en.ous** (-uh.nus) *adj.* 1 very hungry. 2 rapacious: *ravening wolves.* —**rav.en.ous.ly** *adv.*

ra.vine (ruh.VEEN) *n.* a long, narrow, deep depression in the earth's surface, smaller than a valley or canyon.

ra.vi.o.li (rav.ee.OH.lee) *n.pl.* [takes *sing. v.*] small casings of pasta filled with meat or cheese.

rav.ish (RAV.ish) 1 transport with joy: *She was ravished with delight.* 2 to rape.
—**ravishing** *adj.* enchanting: *His act is simply ravishing; a ravishing beauty, book, show, view of the mountains.*

raw *adj.* 1 in the natural state: *raw* (= uncooked) *meat; a raw* (= untrained) *recruit; a raw* (= unfinished) *draft; raw* (= unprocessed) *data, fiber, hide, materials, sewage, wool* 2 rough or harsh: *a raw deal, weather, wind; a raw cut; a raw spot* (on the body with the skin removed, as by a wound). —**in the raw** 1 in a natural state: *to experience life in the raw.* 2 naked: *Sam may sleep in the raw, but never goes swimming in the raw.*

raw.boned *adj.* gaunt, not fleshed: *his rawboned build.*

raw.hide *n.* (a whip made with) untanned cattle hide.

ray *n.* 1 a thin line of light radiating from a central source such as the sun: *to emit, send forth, send out rays; cathode, cosmic, death, gamma, heat, infrared, light, ultraviolet, X rays; a ray* (= gleam) *of hope.* 2 any similar line or a raylike part, as a petal of the daisy or an arm of the "starfish." 3 any of a group of fishes including manta rays and skates that have a flat, disklike body, pectoral fins like large wings, and a whiplike tail.

ray.on (RAY.on, *rhyme:* on) *n.* a silklike shiny fabric made from cellulose fiber.

raze *v.* **raz.es, razed, raz.ing** to level or demolish: *The earthquake razed the city, with buildings razed to the ground.*

ra.zor (RAY.zur) *n.* a shaving implement: *a straight razor; to hone* or *sharpen a razor; a double-edged safety razor; adj.: an election won with a razor-thin majority.*

razz *v.* tease or ridicule.

raz.zle-daz.zle (RAZ.ul.daz.ul) *v.* **-daz.zles, -daz.zled, -daz.zling** *Informal.* bewilder or deceive with something dazzling or exciting.

razz.ma.tazz (RAZ.muh.taz) *n. Informal.* liveliness or flashiness.

¹**re** (RAY, REE) *prep.* regarding: *re your inquiry of March 13th.*

²**re** (RAY) *n. Music.* the second tone of the diatonic scale.

re- prefix [freely added to verbs and nouns, using a hyphen to emphasize or distinguish, as in "re-cover"] again or anew: *reactivate, reassurance, re-cover* (= cover again); *re-election.*

reach (REECH) *v.* get to a person, place, or thing: *You can reach me by phone; His fame reaches far and wide; He quickly reached for his coat; Please reach me the hat; She cannot be reached* (= got at or influenced) *by bribes; Reach out* (= extend) *your hand; He tried to reach* (toward) *the extended hand; Parents try hard to* **reach out** *to* (= communicate with) *their children because of the generation gap.*
—*n.* a reaching or its extent: *Tall hockey players have a long reach with their sticks; Drugs are kept* **out of reach** (= beyond reaching length) *of children; He lives within easy reach* (= travel) *by subway; Infinity is beyond the reach* (= grasp) *of the human imagination; in the outer* **reaches** (= limits or extent) *of the atmosphere; the upper reaches of the Nile; the vast reaches of the Sahara.*
—**reach.a.ble** (-uh.bul) *adj.*

re.act (ree.ACT) *v.* 1 act back or in response to someone or something: *If I ask for a raise, how will he react? She reacted with kindness; People react against cruelty; They react strongly; to react to a stimulus; He didn't react to the insult.* **2** act chemically: *Carbon reacts with oxygen to form carbon dioxide.*

re.act.ance (ree.ACT.unce) *n.* electrical opposition: *Ohms express electrical reactance to the flow of alternating current.*

re.act.ant (ree.ACT.unt) *n.* a chemical that reacts with another, as carbon with oxygen.

re.ac.tion (ree.AC.shun) *n.* **1** a response or acting back: *allergic reaction to smoke; Allergens cause* or *trigger reactions; the action and reaction of colliding bodies; your reaction to the new tax; The new tax met with* or *encountered a strong reaction from the public; an adverse* or *negative reaction; public reaction against the tax; a chain, delayed, favorable, knee-jerk, natural, normal, nuclear, positive, strong, weak reaction; A catalyst speeds up a chemical reaction; reaction time.* **2** a political or social tendency to return to a former state of affairs.

re.ac.tion.ar.y (ree.AC.shuh.nair.ee) *adj.* opposed to progress or reform: *a reactionary force, party, spirit; reactionary behavior, politics, prejudices.* —*n., pl.* **-ar.ies** such a person: *progressives and reactionaries.*

re.ac.ti.vate (ree.AC.tuh.vate) *v.* **-vates, -vat.ed, -vat.ing** make or become active again: *to reactivate a case, disease, fear, program, tendency.*
—**re.ac.ti.va.tion** (-VAY.shun) *n.*

re.ac.tive (ree.AC.tiv) *adj.* that tends to react: *a reactive impulse, tendency; He's reactive to change; reactive and responsive; She's proactive rather than reactive; a reactive dye* (that reacts with a material to make it nonfading).

re.ac.tor (ree.AC.tur) *n.* **1** one that reacts, esp. positively in a medical test. **2** a device or vessel in which a chemical process is carried out: *atomic, fission, nuclear reactors.*

read (REED) *v.* **reads, read** (RED), **read.ing 1** get the meaning, esp. from something written: *Can he read? He reads books, Braille, English; He also reads gestures, minds, thoughts; You can read all* (= get all the information) *about it in the papers; I read* (= hear or understand) *you loud and clear; adj.: a widely read writer.* **2** say what is written: *Please read aloud; Read to me while I sew; Volunteers read for the sick.* **3** study or learn: *He's reading law; reading for a degree; Better read up on your history before the exam; adj.: He's well read* (= informed) *in the classics; widely read in literary criticism.* **4** show, mean, or be: *The clock reads 10; "Thimk" should read "think"; The memo reads as follows; It reads like a shopping list.* **5** transfer data from an outside storage medium into computer memory. —**read between the lines** look for or see a hidden meaning. —**read something into** see something that is not expressed.
—**read someone out of** expel someone from membership in a political party, etc. —**read.a.ble** (-duh.bul) *adj.;* **read.a.bly** (-blee) *adv.*
—**read.a.ble.ness** or **read.a.bil.i.ty** (-BIL.i.tee) *n.*

read.er (REE.dur) *n.* **1** one who reads: *an avid, voracious reader.* **2** a book containing selections for one learning to read: *a basic, elementary reader.* **3** a selection of articles on a given subject: *a history reader.*

read.er.ship (REE.dur.ship) *n.* **1** an audience of readers: *a magazine with a wide readership.* **2** a reader's position or office.

read.i.ly (RED.i.lee) *adv.* **1** willingly: *They answer readily to requests.* **2** easily: *This is readily available in stores.*

read.i.ness (RED.ee.nis) *n.* the state or quality of being ready: *her readiness to help; A nurse holds herself in readiness for emergencies.*

reading (REE.ding) *n.* **1** the act of one who reads: *Children learn reading and writing; remedial reading; the final reading* (= consideration) *of a bill in parliament; adja.: your reading level, skills; a poetry reading session.* **2** reading material: *the assigned reading for a course; light, serious, solid, suggested reading.* **3** what is read, studied, or learned: *a man of wide reading* (= learning); *Take a reading* (= what the meter shows) *every hour; a new reading* (= interpretation) *of Milton.*

read-only *adj.* of computer data, that can be read but not manipulated: *read-only files, storage; a compact disc read-only memory (CD-ROM).*

read.out (REED.out) *n.* **1** recorded or displayed data from a computer: *digital readouts.* **2** the process or device used. **3** transmission of data, as from a space vehicle.

read.y (RED.ee) *adj.* **read.i.er, -i.est 1** prepared or willing to do as specified or implied without delay: *Are you ready? We are ready to leave; always ready with an answer; She'll be ready* (= apt) *to find fault.* **2** immediately available: *Dinner is ready; I need ready cash, money; You have a ready reply for everything; Ambulances are ready for emergencies; The troops moved up with guns* **at the ready** (= state of being ready); *adj.:* **ready-to-wear** (= ready-made) *clothes.* —*v.* **read.ies, read.ied, read.y.ing** make oneself ready: *They readied themselves for battle.*

ready-made *adj.* **1** made ready for use or sale, not made-to-order: *a ready-made TV dinner, dress.* **2** lacking individuality; commonplace: *a ready-made answer, opinion, solution.*

re.a.gent (ree.AY.junt) *n.* a chemical used for its reaction to substances in laboratory testing, industrial manufacture, etc., as bicarbonate of soda and oxalic acid.

¹**re.al** (REE.ul, REEL) *adj.* existing in fact, not as appears or imaginary: *a real experience, not a dream; A concave lens does not have a real focus or form a real image that may be projected on a screen; Is that diamond real* (= genuine) *or fake? real* (= immovable) *property or real estate.* —*adv. Informal.* very: *Her aunt was real nice to us.* —**for real** *Informal.* serious or seriously: *Practicing is over, let's do it now for real.* —**real.ness** *n.*

²**re.al** (REE.ul, ray.AHL) *n.* a former Spanish coin worth an eighth of a piece of eight.

real estate *n.* land including any houses built on it.

re.al.ism (REE.uh.liz.um) *n.* philosophy or action based on things as they are, not as they should be, esp. in the artistic portrayal of life: *The colors lend realism to the scene.* —**re.al.ist** *n.:* She's a down-to-earth realist.* —**re.al.is.tic** (-LIS.tic) *adj.*, **re.al.is.ti.cal.ly** *adv.*

re.al.i.ty (ree.AL.i.tee) *n.* -**ties 1** the quality of being real: *We have to accept reality, it's no use denying it; It has no basis* **in reality** (= in fact); *to do or take or run a* **reality check** (*to find out about what is really happening*). **2** a real person or fact: *the grim, harsh, sober realities of life.*

re.al.ize (REE.uh.lize) *v.* -**iz.es, -ized, -iz.ing 1** be aware of something: *I didn't realize I was in Mexico; When he fully realized what had happened, it was too late.* **2** make real: *to realize an ambition.* **3** convert into money: *to realize an investment; to realize bonds and stocks; We realized* (= obtained as money) *very little from the sale.* —**re.al.iz.a.ble** (-lye.zuh.bul) *adj.* —**re.al.i.za.tion** (-luh.ZAY.shun, -lye-) *n.*

re.al.ly (REE.uh.lee) *adv.* **1** actually: *Are we really late? Not really.* **2** [as intensifier]: *It was really* (= very) *cold last night; I really* (= very much) *love him; You really ought to see this movie; Really?* —**interj.** indeed: *Well, really!*

realm (RELM) *n.* domain or region: *the realm of fancy, philosophy, science.*

re.al.po.li.tik (ray.AHL.poh.li.teek) *n.* practical politics based on reality.

real time *n.* computer system of simultaneous input and processing of data: *Most process-control systems operate in real time;* **adj.:** *Airline bookings must be processed by a* **real-time** *system; on a real-time basis; real-time messaging, software, speech translation.*

re.al.tor (REE.ul.tur) *n.* an accredited real-estate agent; **Realtor** *Trademark.*

re.al.ty (REE.ul.tee) *n.* -**ties** real estate.

ream (REEM) *n.* **1** a package of 500 sheets of paper. **2 reams** *pl. Informal.* a large quantity: *reams of unpublished poetry.* —*v.* widen an existing hole or to bore using a rotating tool with a ridge or spiral surface. —**ream.er** *n.*

reap (REEP) *v.* to cut, as with a scythe: *to reap grain; to reap* (= gather) *crops; "You reap* (= harvest) *what you sow."* —**reap.er** *n.*

rear (REER) *v.* **1** to raise: *The animal reared its head; Unemployment rears its ugly head during a recession;* **adj.:** *a* **rearing** *horse (rising on its hind legs).* **2** bring up: *We reared our children to be good citizens; to rear* (= breed) *livestock.* —*n.* the back part or position: *in the rear of the house; a car with its engine in the rear; seated in the rear (seat) of the car; The army was attacked from the rear; He got kicked in the rear; In a procession, the most important people* **bring up the rear** (= come last). —**adj.:** *the rear bumper, wheels; a* **rear admiral** (= officer of rank just below vice admiral); *the* **rear end** *of a car; an infant's* **rear-facing** *carseat; a* **rear-ender** (= rear-end collision); *the* **rear-view mirror** *of an automobile.*

rear guard *n.* soldiers guarding the rear of an army; **adj.:** *to fight a* **rear-guard** *action.*

rear.most (REER.most) *adj.* farthest at the back; last: *the rearmost car of the train.*

rear.ward (REER.wurd) *adj. & adv.* at or toward the rear: *a rearward movement, thrust, tilt; to move rearward.* Also **rear.wards** *adv.*

rea.son (REE.zun) *n.* **1** a cause or occasion that explains something: *to cite or give reasons; cogent, compelling, convinc-*

ing, logical, personal, plausible, sound, strong, underlying, urgent, valid reasons; We had every reason to suspect fraud; You can't fire someone without sufficient reason; There's no reason to be concerned; the reasons for and against a course of action; The real reason behind their move was something else; The reason why he did it is not clear; He resigned for personal reasons; for reasons of health; not guilty **by reason of** (= because of) insanity; She was fired **with reason** (= with justification). **2** thinking and judging capacity: Animals and infants lack reason; He lost his reason in his final days. **3** logic or good sense: Please listen to reason; When will you see reason? It **stands to reason** (= is logical) that workers be paid; We're prepared to accommodate you **within reason** (= within reasonable limits). —v. **1** use one's thinking capacity: our capacity to reason; Let's reason out a solution based on the evidence available. **2** argue: He's too headstrong to reason with; He reasons that it is too late now.

rea.son.a.ble (REE.zun.uh.bul) adj. **1** according to reason: We are all rational, but not everyone is reasonable; He is always reasonable about paying his dues; It seems only reasonable that we give him more time; The accused was acquitted because the jury didn't think him guilty **beyond a reasonable doubt**. **2** moderate or fair: a reasonable price, demand, excuse; a reasonable house (that is moderately priced). —**rea.son.a.bly** adv.

reasoning n. the use of reason or an instance of it: cogent, deductive, faulty, inductive, shrewd, solid, sound reasoning; His reasoning (= argument) sounds a bit specious.

re.as.sure (ree.uh.SURE) v. **re.as.sures, re.as.sured, re.as.sur.ing** assure so as to remove the fears of or restore confidence to someone: She reassured us about or of the health of our child; reassured us he would survive; **adj.:** Her words were **reassuring**; It's reassuring that help is available. —**re.as.sur.ance** (-unce) n.

re.bate (REE.bate) n. a partial refund of payment: We got or received a tax rebate.

reb.el v. (ri.BEL) **-els, -elled, -el.ling 1** actively resist or fight against authority: The slaves rebelled; They rebelled against the colonial government. **2** oppose or feel repelled by something: Everyone rebels at injustices. —n. (REB.ul) one who rebels: famous rebels of history; **adja.:** a rebel army, soldier, movement.

re.bel.lion (ri.BEL.yun) n. a defiance of authority, esp. armed resistance to one's government: to foment or stir up a rebellion; to crush or put down or quash or quell a rebellion; They were in open rebellion against the government; The rebellion broke out suddenly, but it failed. —**re.bel.lious** (ri.BEL.yus) adj.: rebellious troops; children who are rebellious by temperament.

re.birth (REE.birth) n. **1** a second birth, as in reincarnation. **2** a revival or renaissance: the rebirth of learning in Europe.

re.born (ree.BORN) adj. born again: I felt reborn and rejuvenated; a reunited and reborn Germany.

re.bound (REE.bownd) n. a springing back: The other players were waiting to grab the rebound if he missed; She hit the ball **on the rebound**; He married the first woman he met **on the rebound** (= after being rejected). —v. (ree.BOWND) bounce back; also, recover from a setback or frustration.

re.buff (ri.BUF) v. repulse or reject: She offered Omar a ride but was rebuffed; to rebuff an accusation, initiative, proposal, request; **n.:** She met with a rebuff; a polite, not sharp rebuff.

re.buke (ri.BYOOK) v. **-bukes, -buked, -buk.ing** blame or reprove sharply: to be mildly, sternly rebuked. —**n.:** to administer or deliver or give a rebuke to someone; He drew or received a rebuke from his superiors for his tardiness.

re.bus (REE.bus) n. a riddle composed of pictures, letters, and numbers.

re.but (ri.BUT) v. **-buts, -but.ted, -but.ting** refute by use of arguments, evidence, etc., as in court or in a debate.

re.but.tal (ri.BUT.ul) n. a rebutting: to make a rebuttal of the arguments.

rec (REC) n. [short form] recreation: a rec room.

re.cal.ci.trant (ri.CAL.si.trunt) adj. defiantly resisting control or authority: a rare case of a recalcitrant teenager! —**re.cal.ci.trance** (-trunce) n.

re.call (ri.CALL) v. **1** call back: an ambassador recalled to London; defective cars recalled by a manufacturer; We've been recalled (to work) from vacation; recalled after a long layoff; recalled to active duty. **2** remember: I don't recall her name but do recognize the face; I can recall her distinctly or vividly; I recall seeing her as a young child; cannot recall where I met her; I suddenly recalled I had a dental appointment. —**n.** (also REE-) a recalling: a retentive memory with almost complete or total recall; Nothing is lost beyond recall; the safety recall of defective cars; Return to camp when the recall (signal) sounds.

re.cant (ri.CANT) v. formally withdraw or renounce a belief, opinion, etc.: *He recanted only on his deathbed.*
—**re.can.ta.tion** (ree.can.TAY.shun) n.

re.cap (REE.cap, ri.CAP) v. **-caps, -capped, -cap.ping** 1 retread a worn tire. 2 *Informal.* recapitulate. —n. (REE.cap) 1 a recapped tire. 2 a recapitulation.

re.ca.pit.u.late (ree.cuh.PICH.uh.late) v. **-lates, -lat.ed, -lat.ing** sum up; repeat main points briefly.
—**re.ca.pit.u.la.tion** (-LAY.shun) n.

re.cede (ri.SEED) v. **-cedes, -ced.ed, -ced.ing** go backward: *when the tide recedes from the harbor; The threat has receded;* adj.: *a receding* (= backward-sloping) *chin; the receding* (= moving away from the forehead) *hairline of a balding man.*

re.ceipt (ri.SEET) n. 1 an act of receiving something: *We reply immediately on receipt; We acknowledge receipt of letters.* 2 a written confirmation of something received: *to give, make out or write out a receipt for payments received; Always get receipts; Keep your receipts for tax purposes.* 3 receipts pl. money received: *Each day's receipts are deposited at the bank daily.* —v. issue a receipt for something: *to receipt goods; to receipt* (= mark as paid) *a bill or invoice;* n.: *automated processing and* **receipting** *of deliveries;* adj.: *a dated and* **receipted** *invoice.*

re.ceiv.a.ble (ri.SEE.vuh.bul) adj. that may be received or on which payment is to be received: *accounts receivable.*
—**receivables** n.pl.: *a list of receivables; payables and receivables.*

re.ceive (ri.SEEV) v. **-ceives, -ceived, -ceiv.ing** 1 take what is offered or delivered: *to receive a hit, letter, gift; The mind receives ideas; boats receiving loads; He received a crushing blow.* 2 accept; adj.: *a widely received opinion; received ideas, views, wisdom; The British standard is the **Received Pronunciation** (as used by the educated people of Southern England).* 3 welcome: *Guests are received at the door; to be received coldly, coolly, favorably, warmly, with open arms; He was received as a returning hero; to receive a convert into the church.*

re.ceiv.er (ri.SEE.vur) n. 1 one that receives: *a wireless receiver; a receiver of stolen goods.* 2 the listening end of a telephone line: *to pick up the receiver; hang up or put down or replace the receiver.* 3 a football player who receives a kickoff or punt. 4 the judicial manager of property in a bankruptcy: *The firm's assets are in the hands of the receiver.* —**re.ceiv.er.ship** n.: *A bankrupt firm is put or goes into receivership; It has been in receivership since last year.*

receiving line n. the host, hostess, and guests of honor standing in a row to greet guests; also **reception line.**

re.cent (REE.sunt) adj. of a time just passed: *a recent event; a recent acquaintance (made not long ago);* **re.cent.ly** adv. —**re.cen.cy** n.

re.cep.ta.cle (ri.SEP.tuh.cul) n. 1 a container. 2 the containerlike base of a flower. 3 an electrical outlet to insert a plug into.

re.cep.tion (ri.SEP.shun) n. 1 the receiving of a person or thing: *chilly, cold, cordial, diplomatic, formal, friendly, hospitable, mixed, official, rousing, warm receptions; His proposal got or met with a cool reception; The returning hero was accorded or given an enthusiastic reception;* adj.: *an office's reception area, desk, room.* 2 a social function for receiving guests: *to give or hold a reception; to host a reception; We met at the Mayor's reception; civic, public, wedding receptions; a formal reception* (= receiving) *line.* 3 the quality of the sound in receiving radio or TV broadcasts: *cable reception; We usually have good or strong reception; We are experiencing poor or weak reception because of the weather.*

re.cep.tion.ist (ri.SEP.shuh.nist) n. one employed to receive callers, esp. in an office.

re.cep.tive (ri.SEP.tiv) adj. able or ready to receive stimuli, suggestions, etc.: *The boss is receptive to new ideas.*
—**re.cep.tiv.i.ty** (ree.sep.TIV.i.tee) n.

re.cep.tor (ri.SEP.tur) n. the receiver of a stimulus, as the light-sensitive retina and the nerve endings inside a muscle; sense organ.

re.cess (REE.ses, ree.SES) n. 1 an inner place, as a niche or alcove. 2 a secluded place: *the innermost recesses of one's heart.* 3 a break in an activity for rest or recreation: *to take a ten-minute recess, the summer recess; Parliament is in recess.* —v. 1 put into a recess: *The light fixtures are recessed in the ceiling;* adj.: **recessed** *lighting, lights, shelving.* 2 take a break: *We recess for lunch at noon.*

re.ces.sion (ri.SESH.un) n. 1 a going backward. 2 a temporary decline in business activity, less severe than a depression: *a business or economic recession; Countries go into and come out of*

recessional / recognition

recessions.

re.ces.sion.al (ri.SESH.uh.nul) *n.* a piece of music for the end of a church service.

re.ces.sion.ar.y (ri.SESH.uh.nair.ee) *adj.* having to do with an economic recession: *recessionary fears, pressures, times; a recessionary bite, economy, environment, period, year.*

re.ces.sive (ri.SES.iv) *adj.* receding, esp. of a genetic character or trait that is latent, not dominant.

re.cher.ché (ruh.sher.SHAY, -SHER.shay) *adj.* of manner, diction, etc., studied; excessively refined.

re.cid.i.vism (ri.SID.uh.viz.um) *n.* tendency to relapse into crime or other behavior or illness pattern: *how to reduce recidivism; high and low recidivism rates.* —**re.cid.i.vist** *n. & adj.*: *a recidivist alcoholic.*

rec.i.pe (RES.uh.pee) *n.* 1 a list of ingredients and set of directions for preparing something to eat or drink. 2 a formula or procedure: *a recipe for happiness, peace, success.*

re.cip.i.ent (ruh.SIP.ee.unt) *n.* one who receives: *a worthy recipient of the award.*

re.cip.ro.cal (ruh.SIP.ruh.cul) *adj.* involving exchange between two parties or a back-and-forth relationship, as when Tom helps Mary and vice versa: *reciprocal trade agreements between countries; "Each other" is a **reciprocal pronoun**.* —**re.cip.ro.cal.ly** *adv.*

re.cip.ro.cate (ruh.SIP.ruh.cate) *v.* -cates, -cat.ed, -cat.ing give back in mutual exchange: *to reciprocate a compliment; to reciprocate hospitality, kindness, love; One favor is reciprocated by or with another; We would like to reciprocate for your generosity; adj.: the **reciprocating** (= back-and-forth) motion of a piston.* —**re.cip.ro.ca.tion** (-CAY.shun) *n.*

rec.i.proc.i.ty (res.uh.PROS.i.tee) *n.* -ties mutual exchange between two parties: *a relationship that began on the basis of reciprocity; It died because of lack of reciprocity between them.*

re.cit.al (ri.SYE.tul) *n.* 1 a reciting of facts; account. 2 a performance, as by a musician or group of dancers: *to give a modern dance recital; organ, piano, violin recitals.* —**re.cit.al.ist** *n.*

rec.i.ta.tion (res.uh.TAY.shun) *n.* 1 a reciting, esp. from memory. 2 something that is recited.

rec.i.ta.tive (RES.i.tuh.TEEV) *n.* a portion of an opera's text that is sung in a speechlike style, often with little accompaniment.

re.cite (ri.CITE) *v.* -cites, -cit.ed, -cit.ing 1 repeat aloud from memory: *to recite a poem, speech, the alphabet.* 2 repeat or enumerate by reading from a text: *The citizens' group recited a litany of complaints.*

reck.less (RECK.lis) *adj.* very careless and unconcerned about consequences; extremely rash: *It was reckless of him to drive while drunk; reckless driving;* **reck.less.ly** *adv.;* **reck.less.ness** *n.*

reck.on (RECK.un) *v.* 1 count or compute: *to reckon the per-unit cost; We reckoned* (= counted) *on your helping us; We have to reckon with* (= settle accounts) *with everyone we have done business with.* 2 consider: *He was reckoned peerless in his time; We have to **reckon with*** (= seriously consider) *their suggestions; They are a force to be **reckoned with*** (= faced or dealt with). 3 *Informal.* suppose; guess: *I reckon you're right.*

reckoning (RECK.un.ing) *n.* 1 calculation: *the reckoning of a ship's location; By my reckoning we are close to shore; dead reckoning.* 2 an account or its settlement: *a reckoning with the enemy; The **day of reckoning*** (= day for settling an account or fulfilling an obligation) *is drawing near.*

re.claim (ri.CLAIM) *v.* get back what was considered given up or lost: *Wasteland is reclaimed by irrigation and drainage; processes to reclaim rubber, metal, etc. from waste; checked baggage to be reclaimed* (= claimed back) *on landing; adj.: a **reclaimed*** (= reformed) *sinner.* —**re.claim.a.ble** (-muh.bul) *adj.: recycling of reclaimable wastes.* —**rec.la.ma.tion** (rec.luh.MAY.shun) *n.: land reclamation.*

re.cline (ri.CLINE) *v.* -clines, -clined, -clin.ing 1 lean back: *I was reclining against the tree when it broke; Recline your head on the pillow; adja.: a **reclining** chair, figure, seat.* 2 lie down: *to recline on a couch; Snoopy reclining atop his doghouse.*

re.clin.er (ri.CLY.nur) *n.* a chair with adjustable back and footrest: *a three-position recliner; a rocker recliner.*

rec.luse (REC.loose, ri.CLOOSE) *n.* one living a secluded or cloistered life, as a hermit or monk: *The old lady was a virtual recluse in her home.* —**re.clu.sive** (ri.CLOO.siv) *adj.*

rec.og.ni.tion (rec.ug.NISH.un) *n.* 1 a recognizing: *a book burned beyond recognition; The dazed child showed or gave no signs of recognition.* 2 favorable notice: *to gain, give, grant recognition; a scientist who has won worldwide recognition; He received recognition for his achievements* from the government; general, official, public, universal, wide recognition; an award in recognition of his services to the community. **3** conversion of words or images to computer-readable form: *optical character recognition by scanning.*

re.cog.ni.zance (ri.COG.nuh.zunce) *n.* a legal undertaking entered into before a court: *The accused was released on his own recognizance* (= without payment of surety).

rec.og.nize (REC.ug.nize) *v.* **-niz.es, -nized, -niz.ing 1** know from memory; identify: *a face difficult to recognize.* **2** take notice of formally: *Speakers have to be recognized by the chair; He recognized* (= realized) *that his chances were nil; The U.N. recognized* (= accepted) *Communist China in 1971.* **3** take notice of favorably: *His work was recognized only after his death; She is recognized as an authority on the subject; recognized generally, universally, officially, widely;* **adj.:** *a recognized authority on Egypt.* —**rec.og.niz.a.ble** (-nye.zuh.bul) *adj.;* **rec.og.niz.a.bly** *adv.*

re.coil (ri.COIL) *v.* spring back in reaction, as at an ugly sight or as a gun does when fired: *She recoils in horror at the sight of blood; recoils from it instinctively; Evil deeds often recoil on or upon* (= react against) *the doer.* —*n.* a recoiling or its distance.

rec.ol.lect (rec.uh.LECT) *v.* remember something forgotten; recall something from the past: *I cannot recollect what happened next; She cannot recollect being taken to the hospital; She only recollects that she fell off her horse.*

rec.ol.lec.tion (rec.uh.LEC.shun) *n.* memory: *I have no recollection of making any promises; hazy, painful, vague, vivid recollections of childhood.*

re.com.bi.nant (ree.COM.buh.nunt) *adja.* combining genes from different sources: *recombinant progeny; recombinant DNA technology* (= genetic engineering).

re.com.bine (ree.cum.BINE) *v.* **-bines, -bined, -bin.ing** combine again or anew. —**re.com.bi.na.tion** (REE.com.buh.NAY.shun) *n.*

rec.om.mend (rec.uh.MEND) *v.* **1** favor or speak favorably of a person or thing: *I recommend him for admission; I recommend that he be admitted; I recommend your admitting him; to recommend enthusiastically, strongly; We recommend this book to you;* **adj.:** *a recommended dose, method, practice, reading; He came to the job highly recommended.* **2** suggest as a cure: *We've nothing to recommend for a cold.* **3** commend: *He died recommending his soul to God.*

rec.om.men.da.tion (rec.uh.men.DAY.shun) *n.* an act of recommending or something recom- mended: *We gave him a letter of recommendation; We provided or wrote a re- commendation for him; made a recommen- dation to appoint him to the vacancy; lukewarm, negative, positive, strong, weak recommendations; They didn't act on or carry out or implement our recommendation; Good grooming is itself a recommendation in a job applicant; recommendations for safe driving.*

rec.om.pense (REC.um.pence) *n.* a compensation or return: *a cash recompense; in recompense for his services.* —*v.* **-pens.es, -pensed, -pens.ing** compensate with money: *He was amply, highly, well recompensed for his services.*

rec.on.cile (REC.un.cile) *v.* **-ciles, -ciled, -cil.ing 1** restore to harmony: *Soon after each fight they are reconciled; They are reconciled with each other; to reconcile accounts, claims, demands, discrepancies, figures, plans, versions; a story difficult to reconcile* (= make agree) *with the facts;* **adj.:** *reconciled couples, discrepancies, enemies.* **2** settle: *to reconcile differences.* **3** resign oneself to something: *She found it hard to reconcile herself to life in a wheelchair; was finally reconciled to her lot.* —**rec.on.cil.a.ble** (-SYE.luh.bul) *adj.* —**rec.on.cil.i.a.tion** (-sil.ee.AY.shun) *n.:* to bring about or effect a reconciliation with his family.

rec.on.dite (REC.un.dite) *adj.* Formal. abstruse or obscure: *a recondite author, style, subject.*

re.con.di.tion (ree.cun.DISH.un) *v.* repair and put in good condition: *to recondition a used car.*

re.con.nais.sance (ri.CON.uh.sunce) *n.* a military survey to explore or spy for information, esp. about the enemy: *to carry out or conduct an aerial reconnaissance;* **adja.:** *a reconnaissance mission, patrol, plane, satellite.*

rec.on.noi.ter (rec.uh.NOY.tur, ree.cuh-) *v.* **-ters, -tered, -ter.ing** make a reconnaissance of a place. Also **rec.on.noi.tre** *Cdn.*

re.con.sid.er (ree.cun.SID.ur) *v.* consider again with a view to changing a decision, view, etc. —**re.con.sid.er.a.tion** (REE.cun.sid.uh.RAY.shun) *n.*

re.con.sti.tute (ree.CON.sti.tute) *v.* **-tutes, -tut.ed, -tut.ing 1** restore powdered milk, frozen juice, etc. to its original consistency by adding water; **adj.:** *not fresh but made from* **reconstitut-**

ed *orange juice.* **2** put together again in a different way: *to reconstitute a committee, legislature, meeting.*

re.con.struct (ree.cun.STRUCT) *v.* rebuild in original form using remaining parts, evidence, etc.: *Plastic surgery reconstructs deformed or maimed body parts; to reconstruct a city, extinct languages.* —**re.con.struc.tion** (-shun) *n.*

re.cord (ri.CORD) *v.* **1** put or register something heard, felt, seen, etc. on paper, magnetic tape, film, phonograph discs, etc. in a lasting form: *the date as recorded on the birth certificate; The VCR is now recording; Annual rings record a tree's age; adj.: a recorded, not live broadcast.* **2** show: *A thermometer records temperature.*

—*n.* (REC.urd) **1** the act of recording or being recorded; also, what is recorded, as a document, disc, tape, etc. containing anything written, spoken, sung, etc.: *to keep accurate records of everything; to cut or make a long-playing phonograph record; to play a record; to keep a record of the day's events; You're on record as saying so; It's a matter of public record; the wettest day* **on record** (= officially noted); *Let's* **set the record straight** (= correct an error or misunderstanding); *In 1982, AIDS became a disease* **of record** (= having to do with official records); *a statement made* **off the record** (= not for putting down or publication). **2** past performance: *a good, clean driving record; a poor safety record; a distinguished record as a public servant; your employment record; a record of convictions; academic, criminal, police, service records; excellent, impeccable, mediocre, spotty records.* **3** the highest, lowest, biggest, etc. in regard to something: *The 1978 record for a man's weight was 1,069 lb.; A record set or established today is broken later; Records fall; to equal or tie a record held by someone; an unbroken record; national, Olympic, speed, world records;* **adja.:** *a record attendance, height, temperature.*

re.cord.er (ri.CORD.ur) *n.* **1** one that records, esp. an instrument or machine such as a tape recorder. **2** a flutelike wooden musical instrument.

recording *n.* **1** what is recorded, as on magnetic tape. **2** the device, as a disc, containing it.

re.cord.ist (ri.COR.dist) *n.* one who records.

record player *n.* a phonograph.

re.count (ri.COWNT) *v.* **1** narrate; also, enumerate. **2** also **re-count**, count again. —*n.* (REE.count) the act of counting again.

re.coup (ri.COOP) *v.* regain something one has lost: *to recoup one's fortune, health, losses, strength; He needed time to recoup.*

re.course (REE.corse, ree.CORSE) *n.* **1** a seeking of help or protection: *to have recourse to legal measures.* **2** a source of aid: *I was left with no recourse.*

re.cov.er (ri.CUV.ur) *v.* get back or regain: *Police recover stolen property; Work harder to recover lost time; to recover damages (by process of law); to recover oneself in a fall; to recover consciousness; to recover from an illness; to recover (= gain control of) a fumbled ball.* —**re.cov.er.a.ble** (-ruh.bul) *adj.: a country with large recoverable coal reserves.*

re.cov.er.y (ri.CUV.uh.ree) *n.* **-er.ies** a recovering: *the recovery of stolen vehicles; A quick recovery saved the skidding car; to make a rapid, remarkable, slow, speedy recovery; an economic recovery following a recession; the recovery in the bond market; the recovery of the Canadian dollar (in value) against the American dollar; the* **recovery room** *where patients are wheeled in from surgery to recover from the effects of anesthesia.*

rec.re.ant (REC.ree.unt) *n. & adj.* (one who is) cowardly or disloyal.

rec.re.ate (REC.ree.ate) *v.* **-ates, -at.ed, -at.ing** **1** take recreation: *Children prefer to recreate outdoors.* **2** See RE-CRE-ATE. —**rec.re.a.tive** (-ay.tiv) *adj.*

re-cre.ate (ree.cree.ATE) *v.* **-ates, -at.ed, -at.ing** create again: *to re-create the scenes of one's childhood; to re-create an atmosphere, historical moment, image.* Also **re.cre.ate.**

rec.re.ate (REC.ree.ate) *v.* **-ates, -at.ed, -at.ing** to refresh oneself physically or mentally. —**rec.re.a.tive** *adj.*

rec.re.a.tion (rec.ree.AY.shun) *n.* means of refreshment after work, as games, picnics, and other leisure-time activities: *He watches birds for recreation; a government department of culture, fitness, and recreation; reading and recreation; rest and recreation;* **adja.:** *recreation ministry, services, therapy; a recreation area, center, room.* —**rec.re.a.tion.al** (-shun.ul) *adj.: recreational activities, facilities, use; a* **recreational vehicle** *such as a trailer, camper, or motor home.*

re.crim.i.na.tion (ri.CRIM.uh.NAY.shun) *n.* an act of blaming each other: *Why waste time on recriminations when we are both responsible for what happened? mutual recriminations leading to divorce proceedings.* —**re.crim.i.na.tive** or

re.crim.i.na.to.ry (-nuh.tor.ee) *adj.*
rec room *n.* recreation room.
re.cru.des.cence (ree.croo.DES.unce) *n.* a new outbreak of a disorder or a worsening, as of a disease; **re.cru.des.cent** *adj.*
re.cruit (ri.CROOT, long "OO") *v.* enlist new personnel for an army, navy, or other organization: *to recruit volunteers from the public.* —*n.* a newly enlisted soldier, sailor, or member of a group: *fresh, green, raw recruits.* —**re.cruit.er** *n.* —**re.cruit.ment** *n.*
rec.tal (REC.tul) *adj.* having to do with the rectum: *rectal cancer; a rectal examination, thermometer;* **rec.tal.ly** *adv.*
rec.tan.gle (REC.tang.gul) *n.* a four-sided figure with four right angles, but usu. not a square. —**rec.tan.gu.lar** (rec.TANG.gyuh.lur) *adj.*
rec.ti.fy (REC.tuh.fye) *v.* **-fies, -fied, -fy.ing** to correct by conformity to a standard: *to rectify an injustice, mistake, situation;* **adj.**: *rectified* (= purified) *spirits;* **adja.**: *A rectifying device or rectifier changes alternating current to direct current.* —**rec.ti.fi.ca.tion** (-fuh.CAY.shun) *n.* —**rec.ti.fi.er** *n.*
rec.ti.lin.e.ar (REC.tuh.LIN.ee.ur) *adj.* having to do with straight lines: *the rectilinear propagation of light.*
rec.ti.tude (REC.tuh.tude) *n.* uprightness of character or conduct.
rec.to (REC.toh) *n.* **-tos** a right-hand page; cf. VERSO.
rec.tor (REC.tur) *n.* **1** a minister or clergyman in charge of a parish. **2** the head of a seminary, college, or school.
rec.to.ry (REC.tuh.ree) *n.* **-ries** a rector's residence.
rec.tum (REC.tum) *n.* the straight final portion of the intestine leading to the anus.
re.cum.bent (ri.CUM.bunt) *adj.* lying down or reclining: *a figure shown in a recumbent position.*
re.cu.per.ate (ri.COO.puh.rate) *v.* **-ates, -at.ed, -at.ing** regain health or strength: *to recuperate from an illness; It takes time to recuperate after a flu attack.* —**re.cu.per.a.tion** (-RAY.shun) *n.* —**re.cu.per.a.tive** (-ray.tiv) *adj.*
re.cur (ri.CUR) *v.* **-curs, -curred, -cur.ring** occur again: *a disease that tends to recur after treatment; The nightmare keeps recurring* (= returning) *to him in his dreams;* **adja.**: *on a recurring basis; a recurring concern, expression, nightmare, question, theme; recurring charges, costs, problems; When you divide 10 by 3, you get the recurring decimal 3.33333....*

—**re.cur.rent** (-unt) *adj.*: *recurrent characteristics, costs, episodes, headaches, rumors, signs.* —**re.cur.rence** (-unce) *n.*
re.cy.cle (ree.SYE.cul) *v.* **-cles, -cled, -cling** put waste materials through a process or treatment for using again: *to recycle glass, paper, scrap, wastes; incentives to recycle; the push to recycle;* **n.**: *the full recycle of bleach effluents; garbage recycling;* **adja.**: *recycle strategies; the recycle symbol;* **adj.**: *recycled paper.* —**re.cy.cla.ble** (-cluh.bul) *adj.*: *Returnable containers are preferred to recyclable ones.*
red *n.* **1** the color of fresh blood: *bright, dark, deep, light red; No turn on red allowed at these lights; We are operating $3 million in the red* (= in debt) *this year; The boss will see red* (= get angry) *if he finds out.* —**adj. red.der, red.dest** of the color red: *There are red and white blood cells or corpuscles; He appeared with red* (= bloodshot) *eyes; There were many red faces* (= embarrassed people) *following the fiasco.* —**red.dish** *adj.*; **red.dish.ness** *n.*
Red *n.* a communist or an extreme radical. —**adj.** communist: *Some African nations went Red after independence; Red China.*
re.dact (ri.DACT) *v.* **1** prepare a redaction of a work. **2** draw up a statement, proclamation, etc. —**re.dac.tor** *n.*
re.dac.tion (ri.DAC.shun) *n.* a revised or rearranged edition, as of parts of the Bible.
red alert *n.* the final stage of warning of an enemy attack: *The army was on red alert for a couple of hours.*
red alga *n.* a class of marine algae such as agar, useful as gelatin substitutes.
red-blooded *adj.* vigorous or lusty: *Every red-blooded Canadian resents being typed as American and vice versa.*
red.breast (RED.brest) *n.* a robin.
red.bud *n.* an ornamental tree of the pea family that bears delicate pink blossoms early in the spring before its leaves appear.
red.cap *n.* a porter at a bus or railroad station.
red carpet *n.* an impressive or ceremonial welcome: *They rolled out or pulled out the red carpet for the visiting dignitary;* **adja.**: *a red-carpet ceremony; He received or was given red-carpet treatment.*
red cedar *n.* a North American tree of the cypress family, esp. the juniper, or "eastern red cedar," and arborvitae, or "western red cedar."
red cent *n. Informal.* even a trifling

amount: *Don't expect one red cent from the government; Handouts are not worth a red cent;* **I don't give a red cent** (= I don't care) *for green grapes and avocados.*

red.coat *n.* **1** a red-coated British soldier of the American Revolutionary War. **2** *Informal.* a Mountie.

red deer *n.* a large Old World deer related to the elk, with a reddish brown coat and a yellow-to-orange patch on the rump.

red.den (RED.un) *v.* make or become red; flush or blush.

re.deem (ri.DEEM) *v.* get back something or someone in another's possession by paying a price: *jewelry redeemed by repaying a loan; The government redeems savings bonds; to redeem* (= pay off) *a mortgage; Christians believe humanity has been redeemed from sin by a redeemer, or the Redeemer Jesus;* **n.:** *the* **redeeming** *of slaves;* **adj.:** *a poor show with few* **redeeming** (= saving) *features.*
—**re.deem.a.ble** (-muh.bul) *adj.*
—**re.deem.er** *n.*

re.demp.tion (ri.DEMP.shun) *n.* a redeeming, being redeemed, or something that redeems: *She prayed for his redemption from debt; She left him when she thought he was past or beyond redemption.* —**re.demp.tive** (-tiv) *adj.: redemptive force, power; a redemptive mission.*

Red Ensign *n.* a red flag with the Union Jack at the upper corner.

red.eye *n. Informal.* a flight leaving late at night for arrival early in the morning: *to catch, take the redeye; fly a redeye; a redeye flight.*

red-faced *adj.* embarrassed: *He was red-faced when told of his mistake; red-faced bureaucrats.*

red fox *n.* a fox with reddish fur.

red-handed *adv.* in the act of committing a crime: *The shoplifter was caught red-handed.*

red.head *n.* a red-haired person, esp. a woman; **red.head.ed** *adj.*

red herring *n.* something irrelevant used to divert attention from the main issue.

red-hot *adj.* **1** glowing red with heat: *red-hot iron.* **2** exciting or sensational: *a red-hot campaign, fanatic; red-hot news, rumors.*

red-letter day *n.* a memorable or happy occasion.

re.dis.trict (ree.DIS.trict) *v.* organize into new districts.

red light *n.* a warning light or signal, as one requiring traffic to stop: *He went through* or *ran the red light and got ticketed.*

red-light district *n.* a part of a town with many brothels.

red.lin.ing (RED.lye.ning) *n.* economic discrimination against a poor neighborhood, as when a bank refuses mortgages or loans.

red man *n.* a redskin.

red meat *n.* the meat of cattle, hogs, and sheep, distinguished from white meat.

red.neck *n. Informal.* a white farmer of Southern U.S. considered as bigoted or narrow-minded.

re.do (ree.DOO) *v.* **re.does** (-DUZ), **re.did, re.do.ing, re.done** (-DUN) **1** do something again: *to redo a display, one's makeup, a test, one's will.* **2** redecorate: *to redo a house, kitchen, room.*

red.o.lent (RED.ul.unt) *adj.* smelling or evocative of something: *a kitchen redolent of garlic; a custom redolent of pioneer days; New Orleans is redolent with Old World charm.* —**red.o.lence** *n.*

re.dou.ble (ree.DUB.ul) *v.* **-bles, -bled, -bling** increase greatly; intensify: *Her enthusiasm redoubled; She redoubled her efforts to win the scholarship.*

re.doubt (ri.DOWT) *n.* a small temporary fortification.

re.doubt.a.ble (ri.DOW.tuh.bul) *adj.* formidable or eminent: *a redoubtable adversary, inventor, warrior.*

re.dound (ri.DOWND) *v.* have a result or reaction: *actions that redound to one's credit.*

red pepper *n.* **1** a seasoning ground from the fruit or seeds of a red capsicum. **2** the plant.

re.dress (ri.DRESS) *v.* set right or repair a wrong, grievance, etc.
—*n.* (also REE.dress) reparation or the means of finding a remedy: *We sought legal redress when persuasion failed.*

red shift *n.* a shift in the spectral lines of distant objects such as quasars toward the red end because of movement away from the earth.

red.skin *n.* [derogatory] a North American Indian.

red snapper *n.* a Caribbean species of snapper fish.

red squirrel *n.* the noisiest of the squirrel family with reddish fur on its back.

red.start *n.* an American wood warbler whose male has red markings on its wings and tail.

red tape *n.* excessive adherence to rules and regulations, as in government service; bureaucratic routine: *They got caught up* or *involved in red tape; We cut* through the red tape and talked to the minister in charge.

red tide n. a red discoloration of sea water due to the sudden increase of certain organisms that kill marine life.

re.duce (ri.DUCE, rhyme: produce) v. -duc.es, -duced, -duc.ing make less, lower, smaller, simpler, etc.: *how to reduce expenses, weight; a family reduced to poverty by unemployment; The heckler was reduced to silence by the retort; The corporal was reduced in rank; was reduced to the rank of private; 3/9 can be reduced to 1/3;* adja.: *a reducing diet; Hydrogen acts as a reducing agent in recovering a metal from an ore by removing the oxygen and uniting with it to form water.* —**re.duc.er** n. —**re.duc.i.ble** adj.

re.duc.tion (ri.DUC.shun) n. a reducing, being reduced, the amount reduced, or a result of reducing: *the reduction of an argument to absurdity; the reduction of iron ore to metal; Employees can buy the same goods at a substantial reduction* (= discount); *The president took a reduction* (= cut) *in salary.* —**re.duc.tive** (-tiv) adj.

re.dun.dan.cy (ri.DUN.dun.see) n. 1 pl. -cies an instance of wordiness, as "consensus of opinion." 2 a being redundant: *redundancy of effort; redundancy and inefficiency.* Also **redundance**.

re.dun.dant (ri.DUN.dunt) adj. 1 superfluous or unnecessary: *jobs made redundant by automation.* 2 wordy: *redundant expressions such as "exact same"; a redundant style.* —**re.dun.dant.ly** adv.

re.dux (ri.DUX) adjp. returned or brought back: *the Dark Ages redux*.

red.wood n. a giant evergreen tree of western U.S. of the sequoia group; also called "California redwood."

reed n. 1 a tall, slender grass plant with a hollow, jointed stem that is often used for musical pipes, arrows, etc. 2 the stem itself. 3 a thin piece of material used in the mouthpiece of a reed instrument. 4 same as **reed instrument**, a wind instrument such as a clarinet that makes its sound by the vibration of a reed in the mouthpiece.

reed.y adj. **reed.i.er, -i.est** of or like a reed or sounding like a reed instrument: *a high reedy voice; its reedy quality.* —**reed.i.ness** n.

reef n. a ridge of rocks, sand, or coral lying covered near the surface of the water: *The ship struck a reef and sank.* —**reef.y** adj.

reef.er (REE.fur) n. 1 *Slang.* a marijuana cigarette. 2 *Informal.* a refrigerated van, freight car, etc.

reek v. send out a strong, unpleasant smell: *He walked in reeking of alcohol; a department reeking with corruption.*

reel n. 1 film, thread, cable, etc. wound on a revolving device such as a roller or spool; also, the device: *a film in two reels; a reel-to-reel tape deck; a fishing rod and reel.* 2 a whirling motion. 3 a lively folk dance of the Scottish Highlands. —v. 1 wind on a reel. 2 be or cause to be in a whirl: *The blow sent him reeling; His head was reeling under the blow; banks reeling from bad loans; Chris came out of the bar and reeled* (= staggered) *down the street.* —**reel in** pull in a fish using a reeled line: *Atlanta reeled in the 1996 Summer Olympics.* —**reel off** repeat a list, text, etc. with ease and speed; rattle off.

re.en.force (ree.un.FORCE) same as REINFORCE.

re-en.ter or **re.en.ter** (ree.EN.tur) v. 1 enter again: *to re-enter a bus, business, competition, market, race, scene, the work force.* 2 make enter again: *to re-enter a computer command, order, term, word.*

re-en.try or **re.en.try** (ree.EN.tree) n. -tries 1 a second entry: *a re-entry permit.* 2 a re-entering, as of the earth's atmosphere by a space vehicle: *a fiery re-entry; a re-entry vehicle.*

reeve (REEV) v. **reeves**, pt. & pp. **reeved** or **rove, reev.ing** pass a rope through a ring or cleat. —n. 1 in Canada, the elected head of a rural municipality or of a village council. 2 a chief official of a municipality. 3 formerly, a bailiff.

ref n. & v. **refs, ref fed, ref.fing** [short form] referee.

re.face (ree.FACE) v. -fac.es, -faced, -fac.ing put a new face or covering on something.

re.fec.tion (ri.FEC.shun) n. food and drink; also, a meal or repast.

re.fec.to.ry (ri.FEC.tuh.ree) n. -ries a dining hall in a monastery or convent.

re.fer (ri.FUR) v. -fers, -ferred, -fer.ring 1 direct or send someone or something for information, action, help, etc.: *He referred me to a lawyer; Let's refer the dispute to a judge.* 2 direct one's attention: *He referred to many authorities on the subject; Does this remark refer* (= apply) *to me?* —**ref.er.a.ble** (REF.uh.ruh.bul, ri.FUR.uh-) adj. —**re.fer.rer** (ri.FUR.ur) n.

ref.er.ee (ref.uh.REE) n. one who supervises a game, enforcing the rules; umpire: *In many games, as in football and tennis, umpires and referees have different functions.* —v. **-ees, -eed, -ee.ing**

act as a referee: *Who's refereeing the basketball game today?*

ref.er.ence (REF.ur.unce) *n.* **1** a referring, being referred, or thing referred to: *There are many references to the Bible in Shakespeare's plays; job applications filed for future reference; a scholarly book with many footnote references; books kept on the desk for easy or ready reference; articles alphabetically arranged for ease of reference; Everyone has a personal frame of reference in terms of which to discuss a subject; a direct reference; an indirect or oblique reference;* **with** or **in reference to** *your letter of January 31st; hiring* **without reference to** *sex, race, or religion.* **2** a source of information on a subject: *May I cite you as a (personal) reference? He showed me excellent references* (= letters of recommendation) *from former employers; to give* or *provide good, positive, satisfactory references.*
—*adj.*: *a reference librarian, library; a* **reference book** *such as a dictionary, atlas, or encyclopedia; a* **reference mark** *such as the asterisk.*

ref.er.en.dum (ref.uh.REN.dum) *n.* -**dums** or -**da** (-duh) a reference, as of legislative measures, to the direct vote of the people; also, such a vote: *to conduct* or *hold a referendum on a subject of national interest.*

ref.er.ent (REF.uh.runt) *n.* a thing referred to, as the animal by the word "horse"; object of a reference.

re.fer.ral (ri.FUR.ul) *n.* the act or an instance of referring a person or thing to someone: *Our clients come mostly by referral; Specialists receive referrals; a referral made from the President's office to the Dean of Studies; income derived from fees, commissions, and referrals.*

re.fill (ree.FIL) *v.* fill again. —*n.* (REE.fil) a refilling, as of a drug prescription, or something used to refill, as in a ball-point pen. —**re.fill.a.ble** (-uh.bul) *adj.*: *a refillable container.*

re.fine (ri.FINE) *v.* -**fines, -fined, -fin.ing** **1** make finer or less coarse. **2** purify: *to refine oil; the refining process.* —**refine on** or **upon** improve or improve on something: *to refine upon an invention, method.*

re.fined (ri.FINED) *adj.* **1** made free from impurities: *refined petroleum, sugar.* **2** polished: *refined language; a woman of refined manners, tastes; a refined* (= cultured) *young woman.* **3** subtle: *a refined distinction.*

re.fine.ment (ri.FINE.munt) *n.* **1** fineness of feeling or behavior: *a man of refinement.* **2** an act or result of refining: *Wrought iron is a refinement of pig iron; sarcasm as a refinement of cruelty.*

re.fin.er.y (ri.FYE.nuh.ree) *n.* -**er.ies** a plant for refining raw materials such as oil or sugar.

re.fla.tion (ree.FLAY.shun) *n.* stimulation of inflation to cure an economic recession.

re.flect (ri.FLECT) *v.* **1** throw back light, heat, sound, etc.: *Mirrors reflect light, images, one's face; Editorials reflect* (= express) *the views of the paper; Great deeds reflect* (= bring) *credit on their doers; Bad manners often reflect on* (= bring discredit to) *one's parents.* **2** turn one's thoughts back on a subject; seriously consider: *He blurted out nonsense without reflecting; Please reflect (up)on what you said.*

re.flec.tion (ri.FLEC.shun) *n.* **1** a reflecting, being reflected, or something reflected; image: *We see a laterally inverted reflection in a mirror.* **2** thinking or consideration; also, its expression: *quiet, serious, sober reflection; Sorel's reflections on violence; On* or *after further reflection, he decided not to quit school.* **3** a remark or observation, esp. one casting blame; hence, blame or discredit: *My comments are no reflection on your motives.* —**re.flec.tor** (-tur) *n.*

re.flec.tive (ri.FLEC.tiv) *adj.* **1** reflecting: *We wear reflective clothing for safety in the dark; Copper foil is used as reflective insulation against heat.* **2** thoughtful: *I found him in a reflective mood.*

re.flex (REE.flex) *n.* a usu. inborn, automatic reaction to a stimulus: *The doctor hit his knee with a hammer to test his reflexes; The mouth watering at the mention of food is a conditioned reflex.*
—*adj.* **1** coming as a reaction: *the reflex speed of a boxer in the ring; You jerk back your hand from a flame by* **reflex action**; *A reflex action works in a* **reflex arc** (= nerve path). **2** reflected back: *A reflex image is used for focusing a "reflex camera."* —**re.flex.ly** *adv.*

re.flex.ive (ri.FLEX.iv) *adj.* **1** referring back to the subject of a sentence: *a reflexive noun, pronoun.* **2** being a reflex; reactive: *the reflexive awareness of the will; behavior that is reflexive and automatic; a reflexive response.*
—*n.* a reflexive verb or pronoun, as *bethink, hurt oneself, myself, yourselves,* etc. — **re.flex.ive.ly** *adv.*;
re.flex.ive.ness *n.*

re.flux (REE.flux) *n.* **1** a flowing back: *a reflux condenser.* **2** heartburn: *acid reflux.*

re.for.est (ree.FOR.ist) *v.* replant land with trees, as after a fire.
—**re.for.est.a.tion** (-is.TAY.shun) *n.*

re-form (REE.form) *v.* form again.
—**re-for.ma.tion** (-MAY.shun) *n.*

re.form (ri.FORM) *v.* make or become better, as by removing faults; *adja.: a reformed criminal, young offender; the Dutch Reformed Church.*
—*n.* an improvement in conditions: *to carry out* or *effect social reforms; an agrarian* or *land reform; spelling reform in English; adja.: a reform bill; a reform group versus the establishment.*
—**re.form.a.ble** (-uh.bul) *adj.*
—**re.form.a.tive** (-muh.tiv) *adj.*

ref.or.ma.tion (ref.ur.MAY.shun) *n.* a reforming or being reformed, esp. **the Reformation**, the European religious movement of the 1500s leading to the founding of Protestant churches.

re.form.a.to.ry (ri.FOR.muh.tor.ee) *n.* **-ries** an institution for young offenders; a correctional training school: *He spent time at* or *in a reformatory; The maximum reformatory sentence is two years less a day, so he was sent to the penitentiary.* Also **reform school.**

re.form.er (ri.FOR.mur) *n.* **1** one who works for reform. **2 Reformer** a leader of the Reformation.

re.fract (ri.FRACT) *v.* subject to refraction; bend: *Water refracts light.*

re.frac.tion (ri.FRAC.shun) *n.* **1** the bending of waves of light, sound, etc. when passing from one medium to another obliquely. **2** measuring of the eye's bending of light waves: *The optometrist does a refraction before prescribing corrective lenses.* —**re.frac.tive** (-tiv) *adj.: Water has a lower refractive index,* or *index of refraction, than glass* (= Water bends light less than glass).

re.frac.to.ry (ri.FRAC.tuh.ree) *adj.* **1** stubbornly resisting control or irection: *a refractory group of people.* **2** able to withstand great heat: *a refractory material such as fireclay.*

re.frain (ri.FRAIN) *n.* a phrase or verse that is repeated at intervals in a poem or song, esp. at the end of a stanza; chorus or burden: *to sing a refrain.*
—*v.* hold oneself from doing something one is inclined to do: *People refrain from smoking in church.*

re.fresh (ri.FRESH) *v.* **1** make or become fresh again: *a few hints to refresh his memory; We refresh ourselves with a drink, warm bath, etc.; adj.: a refreshing breeze, experience, sleep.* **2** refill: *to refresh glasses after each drink; to refresh supplies.* —**re.fresh.er** *n.: a refresher course for reviewing what one learned some time back.*

re.fresh.ment (ri.FRESH.munt) *n.* a refreshing or that which refreshes: *A lemonade is a good refreshment on a warm day; They offer* or *serve light refreshments* (= food and drink) *such as coffee and donuts.*

re.frig.er.ant (ri.FRIJ.uh.runt) *adj.* that refrigerates: *a refrigerant device such as a heat pump.* —*n.* a refrigerant fluid, as freon.

re.frig.er.ate (ri.FRIJ.uh.rate) *v.* **-ates, -at.ed, -at.ing** make or keep food, etc. cold to keep from perishing: *Most food has to be refrigerated for later use.*
—**re.frig.er.a.tion** (-RAY.shun) *n.: Perishables are kept under refrigeration.*

re.frig.er.a.tor (ri.FRIJ.uh.ray.tur) *n.* a cabinet or room for keeping food, etc. from perishing: *a frost-free refrigerator; Raiding the refrigerator (for snacks) during commercials is a common practice.*

ref.uge (REF.yooj, long "oo") *n.* a place of shelter or of protection from danger or trouble: *The Salvation Army gives* or *provides refuge to the homeless; a place of refuge for the night; They found* or *took refuge from the storm in a bus shelter; Jasper National Park is a large wildlife refuge; Having nowhere to hide, they sought refuge in flight.*

ref.u.gee (REF.yoo.jee, -JEE) *n.* one who flees from one's country to another for protection: *political refugees; a refugee from persecution.*

re.ful.gent (ri.FUL.junt) *adj.* shining or radiant; **re.ful.gent.ly** *adv.*
—**re.ful.gence** *n.*

re.fund (ri.FUND) *v.* pay back a deposit, an excess payment, the price of an unsatisfactory purchase, etc.
—*n.* (REE.fund) a refunding or a refunded amount: *to give* or *pay a refund; They got* or *received a tax refund.*
—**re.fund.a.ble** (-duh.bul) *adj.*

re.fur.bish (ri.FUR.bish) *v.* **1** brighten or polish up: *to refurbish one's image.* **2** renovate: *to refurbish a hotel, store.*
—**re.fur.bish.ment** *n.*

re.fus.al (ri.FEW.zul) *n.* **1** a refusing: *We met with a curt, flat, outright, point-blank refusal; an adamant refusal to help.* **2** right or option to acquire something before it is offered to others: *The publisher got first refusal on the author's next book; the right of first refusal.*

re.fuse (ri.FYOOZ) *v.* **-fus.es, -fused, -fus.ing** not do, give, grant, or accept something directly or bluntly: *She refused to change her mind; She refused*

them permission; *refused them outright; refused categorically, completely, point-blank; The horse refused to jump; It refused the carrot; an offer (so good) you can't refuse; She also refused* (= rejected) *the presidency, advice, gifts.*
—*n.* (REF.yoose, -yooze) what is rejected; garbage or trash: *kitchen refuse; paper refuse for recycling; a poor man ready to accept even the refuse of the job market; adj.: refuse disposal, dumps, recycling, sorters.*

re.fute (ri.FUTE, *rhyme:* cute) *v.* **-futes, -fut.ed, -fut.ing** prove a person or argument to be wrong by use of evidence, reasoning, etc. —**re.fut.a.ble** (-tuh.bul) *adj.* —**ref.u.ta.tion** (ref.yuh.TAY.shun) *n.*

re.gain (ri.GAIN) *v.* get back: *to regain one's confidence, consciousness, footing, health, popularity; territory regained from the enemy; to regain* (= get back to) *the shore.*

re.gal (REE.gul) *adj.* royal, esp. majestic or splendid as a king or queen: *her regal bearing, dignity, splendor.*
—**re.gal.ly** *adv.*

re.gale (ri.GALE) *v.* **-gales, -galed, -gal.ing** entertain *with* something delightful or delicious. —**re.gale.ment** *n.*

re.ga.li.a (ri.GAY.lee.uh) *n.pl.* **1** the crown, scepter, and such emblems of royalty; hence, the insignia or emblems of any office or order. **2** finery.

re.gard (ri.GARD) *v.* consider mentally or with the eyes in a specified manner, as with favor or respect: *He regarded her lovingly; The painting is regarded with suspicion; It is regarded as a fake, as of no value; adj.: a highly regarded* (= esteemed) *surgeon.*
—*n.* **1** consideration: *Have or show some regard for safety; He acted without regard to the rights of others; to be held in high, low, some regard* (= esteem).
2 regards *pl.* good wishes: *Please give him my regards; Convey or send my regards to him; with my best regards; with cordial, friendly, kind, kindest, sincere, warmest, personal regards from yours truly.* —**as regards** or **in regard to** or **regarding** or **with regard to** concerning: *As regards or in regard to or regarding or with regard to your application, I have yet to decide; You are all right as regards* (= according to) *height and weight.* —**re.gard.ful** *adj.* —**re.gard.less** *adj.*: *to be regardless* (= careless) *of the rights of others;* **adv.**: *Do it regardless of* (= in spite of) *costs; Do it regardless* (= in spite of costs).

re.gat.ta (ri.GAT.uh) *n.* a boat race or a series of boat races.

re.gen.cy (REE.jun.see) *n.* **-cies 1** the government of a regent or its period of rule, as **the Regency** (1811-1820) in English history. **2** a body of regents.

re.gen.er.ate (ri.JEN.uh.rate) *v.* **-ates, -at.ed, -at.ing 1** be reborn spiritually. **2** regrow a part, as plants and lower animals do: *The human body regenerates hair, nails, etc.* —**re.gen.er.a.tion** (-RAY.shun) *n.*

re.gent (REE.junt) *n.* **1** one who rules a country when the monarch is absent, too young, or ill. **2** a member of a governing body of a school, library, museum, etc.

reg.gae (REG.ay) *n.* a popular form of West Indian music blending calypso, blues, and rock 'n' roll.

reg.i.cide (REJ.uh.cide) *n.* **1** the killing of a king. **2** the killer.

re.gime (ruh.ZHEEM, ray-) *n.* **1** a system of government, its rule, or its period: *to establish a democratic regime; The totalitarian puppet regime was overthrown; during the previous regime.*
2 regimen. Also **ré.gime.**

reg.i.men (REJ.uh.mun) *n.* a way of living in regard to diet, exercise, sleep, etc.; hence, a course of treatment: *He went on a strict regimen to control his weight; a grueling, low-calorie regimen; She was put on a megavitamin regimen; exercise, fitness, moisturizing, single-drug regimens.*

reg.i.ment (REJ.uh.munt) *n.* a military unit composed of battalions or squadrons: *an infantry regiment.* —*v.* (-ment) organize, as a school system, in a strict or uniform manner. —**reg.i.men.tal** (-MEN.tul) *adj.* —**reg.i.men.ta.tion** (-men.TAY.shun) *n.*

re.gion (REE.jun) *n.* a usu. indefinite area or division with certain common characteristics: *the Atlantic region; border, metropolitan, mountainous, outlying, remote, polar, tropical, uninhabited regions.* —**re.gion.al** (-nul) *adj.*: *a matter of regional rather than national interest; a regional dialect, expression, flavor; regional geography, government.*
—**re.gion.al.ism** *n.* —**re.gion.al.ly** *adv.*

reg.is.ter (REJ.is.tur) *n.* **1** a record: *to keep a case register; a hotel register.* **2** in computers, a temporary storage device for arithmetic, logic, and other operations: *a buffer register.* **3** a particular compass or range: *A bass sings in a different register from a soprano; "Informal" and "Slang" are different registers* (= levels of usage). **4** a grille over a hole in a wall or floor to

regulate the air from a heating or cooling system.
—*v.* **1** record officially: *Births, deaths, etc. are registered at the registry; Guns have to be registered with the police; to register a complaint, protest, trademark;* **adj.**: *a registered automobile, gun, home ownership plan, retirement savings plan, trademark, voter;* **Registered mail** (which is entered in the records) can be traced. **2** show or indicate: *Her face registered no surprise; The thermometer registered a high of 95°F yesterday; The earthquake registered 6.5 on the Richter scale; The polls registered an approval rating of only 51 percent; Christmas sales registered an all-time high last year; Stores registered $10 billion in sales; The candidate didn't register* (= make an impression). **3** enrol: *She registered as a Republican; At the college, he registered for four courses; was registered by the registrar herself; Many are registered in the course;* **adj.**: *a registered student; a registered* (= licensed) *architect, dietician, nurse.*

reg.is.trar (REJ.is.trar) *n.* an official in charge of records.

reg.is.tra.tion (rej.is.TRAY.shun) *n.* a registering, an entry in a register, the number of those registered, or a certificate of registering, as of an automobile: *gun registration; voter registration;* **adj.**: *a registration board, certificate, fee, form, plate.*

reg.is.try (REJ.is.tree) *n.* **-tries 1** an office of registration. **2** a register book. **3** registration, esp. of a ship: *a ship of Liberian registry.*

reg.nal (REG.nul) *adj.* having to do with a reign: *in Queen Elizabeth's 25th regnal year.*

reg.nant (REG.nunt) *adj.* reigning; predominant; prevalent.

re.gres.sion (ri.GRESH.un) *n.* the act of going backward: *the behavior regression of an older child acting like an infant; a regression in one's health, skills; a regression made to reread something you have missed; the biological regression* (= reversion) *to type.* —**re.gress.ive** (-GRES.iv) *adj.*: *an unfair and regressive payroll tax; in a regressive fashion or way; a regressive feature, idea, measure, step, style, trend.* —**re.gres.sor** (-ur) *n.*

re.gret (ri.GRET) *v.* **-grets, -gret.ted, -gret.ting** feel sorrow or dissatisfaction about an action or any unfortunate occurrence: *I regret to have to or regret having to say this; He regrets his absence; regrets deeply* or *very much that he cannot be present.* —*n.* a feeling or expression of regret: *to feel, show regret at or over what happened; She expressed regret(s) for her behavior, regret at not being able to attend the function; our deep, keen regret; We sent our* **regrets** (= a polite note) *declining the invitation.* —**re.gret.ful** *adj.*: *I felt regretful* (= bad) *about what happened;* **re.gret.ful.ly** *adv.*
—**re.gret.ta.ble** (-tuh.bul) *adj.*: *I felt bad about the whole regrettable incident;* **re.gret.ta.bly** *adv.*

re.group (ree.GROOP) *v.* group again, esp. reorganize one's forces for a renewed fight.

reg.u.lar (REG.yuh.lur) *adj.* **1** according to rule or custom; normal; usual: *Nine to five are regular business hours; "Fix" is a regular* or *weak verb with endings "-es," "-ed," and "-ing"; A regular size is not so large as king size; regular and premium* (grade) *gasoline.* **2** habitual or predictable: *a regular customer, reader, subscriber; a regular* (= likeable) *guy; a regular* (*Informal for* thorough) *nuisance.* **3** even; symmetrical; orderly: *a face with regular features; a regular heartbeat; the regular life of a camp.* **4** professional or recognized: *the regular soldiers of a regular army, not draftees, reserves,* or *mercenaries; the regular* (= religious, not secular) *clergy; a regular* (= official) *nominee of the party.* —*n.* **1** a regular soldier, clergyman, or player, not a substitute. **2** *Informal.* a regular contributor, customer, or attender (as at church services). —**reg.u.lar.ly** *adv.*
—**reg.u.lar.i.ty** (-LAIR.i.tee) *n.*

reg.u.lar.ize (REG.yuh.luh.rize) *v.* **-iz.es, -ized, -iz.ing** make regular or normal: *They regularized their status by becoming permanent residents; to regularize the spelling and style of a publication.*

reg.u.late (REG.yuh.late) *v.* control or maintain in a controlled state: *Signals regulate the flow of traffic;* **adj.**: *expansion at a regulated pace; a regulated economy, market; regulated businesses, substances, utilities; a well-regulated* (= well-adjusted) *clock, life, household.*
—**reg.u.la.tive** (-lay.tiv) *adj.*: *a regulative instrument, principle, system.*
—**reg.u.la.tor** (-lay.tur) *n.*

reg.u.la.tion (reg.yuh.LAY.shun) *n.* **1** control: *unnecessary government regulation; the regulation of traffic during rush hour.* **2** a rule for the enforcement of a law: *to adopt* or *enact a regulation; to apply* or *enforce the traffic regulation that cars would be towed during a snow emergency; to violate a regulation; army, government, military, parking, police, security regulations.*
—**adj.**: *as required by regulations: the*

regulatory / rejoice

regulation size; a regulation uniform.
reg.u.la.to.ry (REG.yuh.luh.tor.ee) *adj.* **1** that regulates: *a regulatory agency, authority, body, gene, measure, move, sign, step, system.* **2** subject to control: *a regulatory product that is dangerous to handle.*
re.gur.gi.tate (ri.GUR.juh.tate) *v.* **-tates, -tat.ed, -tat.ing** throw back what is contained inside; vomit. —**re.gur.gi.ta.tion** (-TAY.shun) *n.*
re.hab (REE.hab) *n.* [short form] **1** rehabilitation: *to go into rehab; drug rehab;* **adja.:** *a rehab center, clinic, house, patient, program, project.* **2** renovation or restoration: *to do a kitchen, office, store rehab; rehab and refurbishment;* **adja.:** *rehab activity; rehab* (= renovated) *buildings, space, properties.* **3** a renovated property. —*v.* **re.habs, re.habbed, re.hab.bing** renovate: *whether to rebuild or rehab a house.*
re.ha.bil.i.tate (ree.huh.BIL.uh. tate) *v.* **-tates, -tat.ed, -tat.ing** restore to the original good or healthy condition: *to rehabilitate a cardiac patient, prison inmate, run-down neighborhood; a building rehabilitated to its previous condi- tion; She has been politically rehabilitated* (= reinstated). —**re.ha.bil.i.ta.tion** (-TAY.shun) *n.* —**re.ha.bil.i.ta.tive** (-tay.tiv) *adj.*: *rehabilitative programs, services, treatment.*
re.hash (ree.HASH) *v.* work up old material in a new form without much improvement. —*n.* (REE.hash): *Is this lunch a rehash of yesterday's leftovers?*
re.hears.al (ri.HUR.sul) *n.* a rehearsing: *a wedding rehearsal; a camera rehearsal (before a TV show); a dress rehearsal (in full costume).*
re.hearse (ri.HURSE) *v.* **-hears.es, -hearsed, -hears.ing** practice a play, role, concert, ceremony, etc. for public performance.
reign (RAIN) *n.* a sovereign's being in power or its period: *during the long reign of Queen Victoria.*
—*v.* **1** be the sovereign: *A sovereign is said to reign, not rule; She reigned over England for 63 years.* **2** prevail: *Peace reigned in Jerusalem; a modern office where computers reign supreme.*
re.im.burse (ree.im.BURSE) *v.* **-burs.es, -bursed, -burs.ing** pay a person for money spent: *He was reimbursed amply, fully, generously for all his travel expenses; His expenses were reimbursed* (= paid). —**re.im.burse.ment** *n.*
rein (RAIN) *n.* **1** one of a pair of long, narrow straps or lines connected to the bridle of an animal for its driver or rider to control it: *to draw in or tighten a rein.* **2** a check or control: *to assume, seize the reins of government; She kept a tight rein on all company expenditure; Unlike reporters, storytellers can* **give free** *or* **full rein** *to their imagination.*
—*v.* guide or curb: *A rider* **reins** *in a horse before dismounting; to rein (in) one's passions* (= have them under control).
re.in.car.na.tion (REE.in.car.NAY.shun) *n.* the supposed rebirth of a soul in another body. —**re.in.car.nate** (-CAR. nate) *v.* **-nates, -nat.ed, -nat.ing.**
rein.deer (RAIN.deer) *n. sing. & pl.* a large antlered deer of N. Europe and Asia.
re.in.force (ree.in.FORCE) *v.* **-forc.es, -forced, -forc.ing** strengthen: *A military force is reinforced with more troops, ships, planes, etc.; In a learning process, a response to a stimulus may be reinforced, as by pairing the taste of a food with a sound or tone as an added stimulus;* **Reinforced concrete** *is strengthened with metal inside it.* —**re.in.force.ment** *n.*: *to bring up, commit, send* **reinforcements** (= military units).
re.in.state (ree.in.STATE) *v.* **-states, -stat.ed, -stat.ing** restore to a former position or condition: *He was fired without cause but was reinstated with full pay and seniority in his former position; was reinstated as office manager.* —**re.in.state.ment** *n.*
re.it.er.ate (ree.IT.uh.rate) *v.* **-ates, -at.ed, -at.ing** repeat a request, warning, belief, etc. insistently: *She reiterated her warning; reiterated that we were heading for bankruptcy.* —**re.it.er.a.tion** (-RAY.shun) *n.* —**re.it.er.a.tive** (-ray.tiv) *adj.*
re.ject (ri.JECT) *v.* **1** refuse to accept, agree to, or submit to something: *to reject an application, claim, offer, plea, protest note, suggestion; She rejected his advances; to reject the Church's authority; to reject help; He was rejected for the army; She rejected the plan completely, flatly, outright, totally.* **2** discard or throw out something or someone: *adj.*: *The underprivileged feel* **rejected** *by society; a rejected apple, child, lover.*
—*n.* (REE.ject) a rejected person or thing: *Bad apples are discarded as rejects; the rejects and derelicts of society.*
—**re.jec.tion** (ri.JEC.shun) *n.*: *an organism's immunological rejection of a transplanted organ or foreign tissue; a publisher's* **rejection slip** *sent back with an unsuitable manuscript.*
re.joice (ri.JOICE) *v.* **-joic.es, -joiced, -joic.ing** be full of great joy: *Let's rejoice; We rejoice to hear you have won;*

We rejoice in or at or over her win; It rejoices (= gladdens) our hearts. —**re.joic.ing** n.

re.join (ree.JOIN) v. **1** join again: to rejoin (= go back to) a company, discussion, the work force; The two Germanys were rejoined (= reunited) as one nation. **2** reply formally, as to a plaintiff in court.

re.join.der (ri.JOIN.dur) n. Formal. an answer to a reply: "So what?" was her rejoinder to the report; He argued in rejoinder that the new rule was impossible to enforce; a formal rejoinder.

re.ju.ve.nate (ri.JOO.vuh.nate) v. **-nates, -nat.ed, -nat.ing** make young again or give new vigor to a person or thing: to rejuvenate a dying organization; to rejuvenate our sagging economy; a company that rejuvenated itself and avoided bankruptcy. —**re.ju.ve.na.tion** (-NAY.shun) n.

relaid See RELAY, v. 2.

re.lapse (ri.LAPS) v. **-laps.es, -lapsed, -laps.ing** fall back into a previous condition: to relapse into a bad habit, coma, former routine; to relapse into error, heresy, obscurity, silence; The patient relapsed when he was sent home from hospital. —n. a relapsing, as a return of symptoms that had disappeared: to have a relapse; The patient suffered a complete or total relapse; His relapse proved fatal.

re.late (ri.LATE) v. **-lates, -lat.ed, -lat.ing 1** tell or narrate: to relate an adventure, story; She related how she escaped from the fire. **2** connect: Children **relate to** (= form personal ties with) their peers more easily than to elders; adj. & cpd: The Smiths are **related** to the Joneses by marriage; "Frail" and "fragile" are related through Latin; a related article, lawsuit; related aspects; drug-related deaths; tax-related information. **3** refer: We're all interested in what relates to ourselves; I don't see how it relates; one of the biggest problems **relating to** our economy. —**re.lat.er** or **re.la.tor** (-tur) n. —**re.lat.ed.ness** n.

re.la.tion (ri.LAY.shun) n. **1** an account or narration. **2** a connection, esp. as a relative: Bara Yogi is no relation of Mahesh Yogi; They are not close relations; Results should bear some relation to costs. **3 relations** pl. dealings or affairs: The two had no (sexual) relations though living together; to establish, have or maintain, renew relations with Moscow; to break off or sever relations; to strain relations among or between countries; business, diplomatic, foreign, friendly, labor, public, trade relations; an expert in international **relations** (= dealings or affairs). —**in relation to 1** concerning: The memo is in relation to our talks. **2** compared with: Delaware is a small state in relation to California. —**re.la.tion.al** adj.

—**re.la.tion.ship** n.: The point you raise does not bear or have any relationship to what we are discussing; to have a casual, close, intimate, direct, meaningful, warm relationship with someone.

rel.a.tive (REL.uh.tiv) n. one related by blood or marriage: a blood relative; close, distant, near relatives.

—adj. related to each other or to something else; comparative: the relative merits of coffee and pop as beverages; to live in relative comfort (compared with others less fortunate); "Hot" and "cold" are relative (= variable from person to person); Ten times in 2 days is a higher **relative frequency** than 10 times in 3 days. —**relative to 1** concerning: a memo relative to our talks. **2** compared with: The cost is nothing relative to its importance. —**rel.a.tive.ly** adv.; **rel.a.tive.ness** n.

relative humidity n. percentage of moisture in the air compared to the maximum it can hold at the same temperature.

relative pronoun n. a pronoun such as that, which, what, who, whom, or whose that introduces a relative clause, as in "the house that Jack built."

rel.a.tiv.ism (REL.uh.tuh.viz.um) n. the philosophical theory of notions of right and wrong being relative, not absolute; **rel.a.tiv.ist** n. —**rel.a.tiv.is.tic** (-VIS.tic) adj.

rel.a.tiv.i.ty (rel.uh.TIV.i.tee) n. **-ties** the quality or condition of being relative: Einstein's theory of relativity; the relativity of time and space because of motion.

re.lax (ri.LAX) v. make or become less stiff, tense, or severe: to relax one's muscles; Discipline is relaxed at certain times; Sit back and relax (= rest); adj.: It's **relaxing** to take a hot shower; soothing and relaxing; a relaxing activity, experience, time.

re.lax.ant (ri.LAX.unt) n. a drug that relaxes muscles: a muscle relaxant; adj.: the relaxant effect of tranquilizers.

re.lax.a.tion (ree.lak.SAY.shun) n. **1** the act of relaxing. **2** rest or recreation: We play for fun and relaxation.

re.lay (REE.lay) n. a linking of one stage with the next in a continuous operation, as in a relay race: to run a relay; Volunteers worked in relay(s), one

relieving the next, to put out the fire; the relay (= *conveying*) *of a puck from one player to another;* **adja.:** *a relay antenna, station, switch, team; the green postal* **relay boxes** *for letters awaiting delivery; A* **relay race** *is a contest among several teams of contestants, each teammate running a part of the distance in sequence with the others; a* **relay satellite** *for TV and other signals.*
—*v.* **1** convey or pass on: *the relaying of messages to remote regions; to relay information, orders, signals.* **2** supply in groups: *People were relayed to fight the fire.* **3 re-lay** or **re.lay** (ree.LAY) **-lays, -laid, -lay.ing** lay again.

re.lease (ri.LEECE) *v.* **-leas.es, -leased, -leas.ing** free or let go from a confined or restricted condition: *Prisoners are released; a priest released from his vows; property released (legally) to a claimant; a statement released for publication on Monday morning.* —*n.* a releasing: *release from jail; a release of pressure, tension; a feeling of release; a statement for immediate release (to the media); a movie awaiting release (to the theaters); He obtained a settlement after signing a release (from further claims).*

rel.e.gate (REL.i.gate) *v.* **-gates, -gat.ed, -gat.ing** put away or assign *to* a lower position; hence, cast out or demote: *Women used to be relegated to second-class positions; relegated to the archives, margins, sidelines.* —**rel.e.ga.tion** (-GAY.shun) *n.*

re.lent (ri.LENT) *v.* become less stern or more merciful: *The teacher relented and canceled the penalty.*

re.lent.less (ri.LENT.lis) *adj.* that does not relent; unyielding: *the lawyer's relentless cross-examination; a relentless door-to-door campaign; her relentless logic; the relentless passage of time.*
—**re.lent.less.ly** *adv.*

rel.e.vant (REL.uh.vunt) *adj.* having some bearing on a matter; pertinent: *testimony relevant to a case.*
—**rel.e.vance** (-vunce) *n.*: *a question of little relevance to the present crisis; a matter of great relevance for youth; social relevance;* also **rel.e.van.cy:** *a sense of relevancy; consistency and relevancy.*

re.li.a.ble (ri.LYE.uh.bul) *adj.* that may be relied on: *a reliable piece of information; reliable information, news; a reliable product, source, witness;* **re.li.a.bly** *adv.*
—**re.li.a.bil.i.ty** (-BIL.i.tee) *n.*

re.li.ance (ri.LYE.unce) *n.* trust or confidence: *He didn't place much reliance on miracle cures.* —**re.li.ant** (-unt) *adj.*

rel.ic *n.* something from the past, as an object kept as a souvenir or keepsake, a part of a saint's body venerated as a memorial, or an ancient custom or practice: *a relic from the past; a relic of the Buddha; relics of antiquity; the* **relics** (= ruins or remains) *of ancient Rome.*

rel.ict *n.* something residual or remaining unchanged from a previous era, esp. geologic: *a Carboniferous relict; glacial relicts; a relict mountain.*

re.lief (ri.LEEF) *n.* **1** a removal or lessening of suffering or strain: *to express, feel, find, give* or *provide, receive, seek relief; a big relief; great, instant, permanent, sweet relief; debt relief; The medication brought only temporary relief from pain; Comic scenes provide comic relief in Shakespeare's tragedies; a feeling, measure, murmur, sense, sigh of relief; It's a relief to be home from work; It's a relief that the day is finished; To my immense relief, the parcel had arrived.* **2** replacement: *working long hours without relief;* **adja.:** *a relief agency, effort, fund, pitcher, worker.* **3** money, food, clothes, etc. given to the poor: *The family is* **on relief** (= receiving public aid). **4** a figure or design made to stand out from its surface, as "high relief" or "low relief" (= bas relief): *A* **relief map** *shows the hills, valleys, etc. of a region; The distant hills stood out* **in bold** or **sharp relief** *against the night sky.*

re.lieve (ri.LEEV) *v.* **-lieves, -lieved, -liev.ing** **1** remove or lessen suffering, pressure, etc.: *Aspirin relieves pain; measures to relieve misery; I'm relieved* or *It relieves me to hear you're safe; Anecdotes relieve the monotony of a speech.* **2** replace: *You'll be relieved in a few minutes when the next shift arrives; The ambassador was relieved of his charge and called back home.*

re.liev.er (ri.LEEV.vur) or **relief pitcher** *n.* in baseball, a pitcher who relieves another during a game.

re.li.gion (ri.LIJ.un) *n.* **1** the worship of God, gods, or the supernatural; also, a belief in or devotion to such worship: *natural religion and revealed religions; freedom of religion; a man of religion; He suddenly got religion when struck by tragedy; Animals are not capable of religion.* **2** a system of worship: *the great religions of the world; the Christian, Jewish, Moslem, pagan religions; the state religion of a theocratic state; We are tolerant of all religions; He practices the Hindu religion; Sun worship is not an established* or *organized religion in California; At 21 she entered religion* (= the life of a religious). **3** something

that is practiced with devotion: *She makes a religion of watching hockey on TV.*
re.li.gi.os.i.ty (ri.LIJ.ee.OS.i.tee) *n.* religiousness.
re.li.gious (ri.LIJ.us) **1** *adj.* a. having to do with religion: *a religious figure, group, house, life, order, sect, service; religious beliefs, duties, fundamentalists, values, worship; secular and religious views.* **2** *adj.* pious or devout: *a deeply or profoundly religious person.* **3** *adj.* scrupulous or conscientious: *with religious attention to detail; his religious observance of decorum; her religious devotion to duty; with religious care, neatness.*
—*n. sing. & pl.* a monk, nun, or other member of a religious order.
—**re.li.gious.ly** *adv.*; **re.li.gious.ness** *n.*
re.lin.quish (ri.LINK.wish) *v.* give up something one has a claim to or is interested in keeping: *He finally relinquished all hope of getting custody of the child; She relinquished her business interests to her son.*
rel.i.quar.y (REL.i.quair.ee) *n.* **-quar.ies** a small receptacle for a relic.
rel.ique (REL.ic, ruh.LEEK) *n. Archaic.* relic.
rel.ish (REL.ish) *n.* **1** olives, pickles, sardines, etc. or a slightly sweet preparation of chopped pickles that gives one a zest for food: *green tomato relish; tart corn relish.* **2** zest or appetite: *Some children have great relish for foods advertised on TV; Ray shows little relish for racy humor.* —*v.* to like the taste of something; enjoy: *He doesn't relish (the prospect of) going on a diet.*
re.live (ree.LIV) *v.* **-lives, -lived, -liv.ing** live or undergo an experience again mentally: *to relieve an episode, experience, the past, one's youth.*
re.lo.cate (ree.LOH.cate, ree.loh.CATE) *v.* **-cates, -cat.ed, -cat.ing** move to a new location; settle in another place; **re.lo.ca.tion** (ree.loh.CAY.shun) *n.*
re.luc.tant (ri.LUC.tunt) *adj.* **1** not inclined to do something: *reluctant to answer questions; a reluctant helper.* **2** unwilling: *a reluctant answer; reluctant obedience.* —**re.luc.tant.ly** *adv.*
—**re.luc.tance** (-tunce) *n.*
re.ly (ri.LYE) *v.* **-lies, -lied, -ly.ing** have confidence that a person or thing will do or be as expected: *He relies on weather forecasts; Rely on my assistants for help* or *to help, but don't depend on them for everything.*
REM (REM) *n.* the "rapid eye movement" or dreaming phase of sleep.

re.main (ri.MAIN) *v.* continue, keep on, or be left, as when others have departed: *Nothing remained of the house after the fire; She remained a poor woman all her life; We remain standing while the anthem is played; The outlook remains bright in spite of the recent losses; It remains to be seen if he'll do as told; Three remains if you take away 8 from 11;* **adj.**: *the remaining members of the once popular club; the remaining 5%.*
re.main.der (ri.MAIN.dur) *n.* **1** what is left: *The remainder of 11 minus 8 is 3, of 21 divided by 3 is zero.* **2** a copy or the copies of a published book for disposal at a very low price after its sales have dropped off. —*v.* sell as remainder: *The present edition will be remaindered when the revised one is out.*
re.mains (ri.MAINS) *n.pl.* **1** what is left of something broken up or ruined, as of a destroyed civilization, a dead writer's unpublished works, etc. **2** a dead body: *animal remains; Her mortal remains were laid to rest yesterday.*
re.mand (ri.MAND) *v.* **1** order back, esp. judicially: *an accused remanded in custody* (= kept in prison until the trial). **2** order or commit: *a case remanded to a lower court, to a later date.*
—*n.* a remanding.
re.mark (ri.MARK) *n.* a brief comment or casual observation: *She made a remark that it was getting late; biting, casual, caustic, closing, complimentary, concluding, cryptic, cutting, derogatory, facetious, flattering, nasty, off-the-cuff, opening passing, pointed, sarcastic, slanderous, snide, suggestive, trite, trivial, witty remarks.* —*v.* **1** comment on something: *No one else remarked on* or *upon the lateness of the hour.* **2** observe or point out: *"It's near midnight," she remarked; She remarked to us that it was getting late.*
re.mark.a.ble (ri.MARK.uh.bul) *adj.* worthy of notice; extraordinary: *At 80, he's a remarkable man with a remarkable memory; He's remarkable for his memory; It's remarkable that he remembers so well; It's remarkable how he remembers so well;* **re.mark.a.ble.ness** *n.*
—**re.mark.a.bly** *adv.*
re.me.di.a.ble (ri.MEE.dee.uh.bul) *adj.* that can be remedied: *a remediable defect, flaw, weakness.*
re.me.di.al (ri.MEE.dee.ul) *adj.* serving to remedy: *remedial action, classes, courses, education, English, exercises, measures;* **re.me.di.al.ly** *adv.*
rem.e.dy (REM.uh.dee) *n.* a cure or treatment for an illness or some other unhealthy condition such as an evil,

loss, etc.: *to prescribe, resort to a remedy; to pursue a (legal) remedy; a certain, effective, efficacious, reliable, sure remedy for coughs and colds; a folk remedy for hiccups.* —*v.* **-dies, -died, -dy.ing** provide a remedy for something; cure: *to remedy a defect, evil, grievance, problem, shortage, situation.*

re.mem.ber (ri.MEM.bur) *v.* **1** keep in mind: *Please remember to phone me; She's doing well, thanks to the rich uncle who remembered her (in his will); I didn't remember (= I forgot) to go there.* **2** recall: *I don't remember going there; She remembers me as a child.* **3** mention someone as sending greetings to another: *Remember me to your friends.*

re.mem.brance (ri.MEM.brunce) *n.* **1** the act of remembering; memory: *our remembrance of the past; To the best of my remembrance, no such thing happened; I have many happy remembrances of our life together; prayers offered in remembrance of the dead; Veterans Day is* **Remembrance Day** *in Canada, celebrated on November 11.* **2** something given or kept as a remembrance: *I keep this book as a remembrance (= memento or keepsake) of the dear one; She sends her kind* **remembrances** (= greetings).

re.mind (ri.MINED) *v.* put in mind; cause to remember: *She reminded him of or about the date; reminded him that it was their anniversary; reminded him to take his pills; She reminds him of his mother, which reminds me next week is my mother's birthday.* —**re.mind.er** *n.*

rem.i.nisce (rem.uh.NIS) *v.* **-nisc.es, -nisced, -nisc.ing** recall or tell about one's past experiences.

rem.i.nis.cence (rem.uh.NIS.unce) *n.* the act of reminiscing; also, an account of usu. pleasurable recollections, or **reminiscences** *pl.*
—**rem.i.nis.cent** (-unt) *adjp.: a song that is* **reminiscent** *of the 1950s; Grandpa is becoming more and more reminiscent (= reminiscing) as he gets older;* **adja.:** *His speech was punctuated by reminiscent asides; a reminiscent comment, mood, style.*

re.miss (ri.MIS) *adj.* careless or negligent *in* or *about* performing a task or duty. —**re.miss.ly** *adv.;* **re.miss.ness** *n.*

re.mis.sion (ri.MISH.un) *n.* a remitting: *The medication brought about a complete remission of the disease; The disease is now in remission; the remission of old debts, sins.* Also **re.mit.tal** (ri.MIT.ul) *n.*

re.mit (ri.MIT) *v.* **-mits, -mit.ted, -mit.ting 1** send money as expected or due payment: *Please remit the balance due.* **2** let off or free from punishment, debts, etc.: *the power to remit (= forgive) sins.* **3** lessen efforts, pain, symptoms, etc. —**re.mit.tance** (-unce) *n.: to make, send a remittance; A remittance of $500 is enclosed with the letter.*

rem.nant (REM.nunt) *n.* a small remaining part or piece: *broadloom remnants; the remnants of a defeated army; a* **remnant sale** *(of ends of bolts of cloth, carpet pieces, etc.).*

re.mod.el (ree.MOD.ul) *v.* **-els, -eled, -el.ing** alter the structure or design of a building, clothes, etc. Also **re.mod.elled, re.mod.el.ling** *Cdn.*

re.mon.strance (ri.MON.strunce) *n.* an act or instance of remonstrating.

re.mon.strant (ri.MON.strunt) *n. & adj.* (a person) who remonstrates; **re.mon.strant.ly** *adv.*

re.mon.strate (ri.MON.strate) *v.* **-strates, -strated, -strat.ing** reason or plead with someone about something objected to; expostulate; **re.mon.stra.tor** (-stray.tur) *n.* —**re.mon.stra.tion** (ree.mon.STRAY.shun) *n.*

re.mor.a (REM.uh.ruh) *n.* a tropical ocean fish that attaches itself to marine animals and ships with a disklike sucking organ on its head.

re.morse (ri.MORSE) *n.* a torturing sense of guilt: *to show, express, feel remorse for or over a crime; a bitter, deep, profound remorse; The killer didn't display a twinge of remorse.* —**re.morse.ful** *adj.;* **re.morse.ful.ly** *adv.* —**re.morse.less** *adj.;* **re.morse.less.ly** *adv.*

re.mote (ri.MOTE) *adj.* **-mot.er, -mot.est** far removed in space or time, esp. from a central point: *a remote village in the mountains; in the remote past, future; a remote (= slight) possibility; radio-operated* **remote control** *for garage doors, missiles, planes, toys, etc.*
—*n.* a remote-control device: *TV-VCR remotes; universal remotes; pre-programmed and learning remotes.*
—**re.mote.ly** *adv.;* **re.mote.ness** *n.*

re.mov.al (ri.MOO.vul) *n.* a removing: *snow removal; furniture removal; his removal from office.*

re.move (ri.MOOV) *v.* **-moves, -moved, -mov.ing** move or take away: *He removed his hat and coat as he entered the house; to remove stains from clothes; Spots are easily removed by regular cleaning; He was removed from office; He removed himself (= moved away) to Europe to start a new life;* **adjp.:** *a life* **far removed** *from the real world; I'm his first cousin* **once removed** (= child of his first cousin).
—*n.* an interval or degree of distance:

Al lives at a few removes from his old neighborhood. —**re.mov.a.ble** (-vuh.bul) *adj.* —**re.mov.er** *n.*

re.mu.ner.ate (ri.MEW.nuh.rate) *v.* **-ates, -at.ed, -at.ing** pay someone *for* a service or trouble; recompense. —**re.mu.ner.a.tion** (-RAY.shun) *n.*

re.mu.ner.a.tive (ri.MEW.nuh.ray.tiv) *adj.* profitable or gainful: *a remunerative business, price, rate of pay; remunerative employment.*

ren.ais.sance (REN.uh.sahnce) *n.* rebirth or revival: *the Renaissance of art and literature in Europe from the 14th to the 17th century.*

re.nal (REE.nul) *adj.* having to do with the kidneys: *renal arteries, calculus, diseases.*

re.nas.cence (ri.NAS.unce, ri.NAY-) same as RENAISSANCE; **re.nas.cent** *adj.*

rend *v.* **rends, rent, rend.ing** split or tear apart with violence: *Their shrieks rent the air;* *adj.: a heart-rending scene of families being torn apart; a rent garment.*

ren.der (REN.dur) *v.* **1** give: *to render aid, judgment, services, thanks to God; bills payable when rendered* (= presented); *a city rendered up* (= surrendered) *to the enemy.* **2** cause to be in a specified condition: *people rendered helpless, homeless, speechless (as by fright).* **3** melt: *to render fat for lard;* *adj.: the stench of carcasses from a rendering plant.* **4** interpret artistically by painting, acting, singing, translating, etc.: *It takes a great actor to render Macbeth well;* **n.***: a rendering of the Psalms into Modern English.*

ren.dez.vous (RON.day.voo) *n., pl.* **-vous** (-vooz) **1** a previously agreed-on meeting or the agreement to meet. **2** the meeting place. —*v.* **-vouses** (-vooz), **-voused** (-vood, long "oo"), **-vous.ing** (-voo.ing) meet or bring together people, ships, spacecraft, etc.

ren.di.tion (ren.DISH.un) *n.* an artistic rendering: *He gave a new rendition* (= performance) *of the national anthem; a letter-perfect rendition* (= translation) *of the Greek original.*

ren.e.gade (REN.uh.gade) *n.* a traitor to one's faith or party; deserter; turncoat.

re.nege (ri.NEG, ri.NIG) *v.* **-neg.es, -neged, -neg.ing** **1** go back *on* a promise or commitment. **2** fail to follow suit in a card game in violation of rules.

re.new (ri.NEW) *v.* make new or like new something that has lost its force or effect: *to renew an attack, contract, subscription; to renew supplies; to renew one's efforts, enthusiasm.* —**re.new.a.ble** (ri.NEW.uh.bul) *adj.: renewable energy; a renewable resource; renewable sources of energy such as wind, sun, tides, and garbage.* —**re.new.al** (-ul) *n.: urban renewal.*

ren.net (REN.it) *n.* a substance containing rennin found in the stomach of an unweaned calf; also, a similar substance made from fungi: *calf, recombinant, vegetable rennets.* —*v.* curdle: *the renneting of heated milk.*

ren.nin (REN.in) *n.* a milk-curdling enzyme found in the stomachs of cud-chewing animals.

re.nounce (ri.NOWNCE) *v.* **-nounc.es, -nounced, -nounc.ing** give up a person or thing that one is attached to: *to renounce worldly pleasures, one's religion; She renounced the world and became a religious; renounced all claims to his fortune; She would never renounce her kith and kin.*

ren.o.vate (REN.uh.vate) *v.* **-vates, -vat.ed, -vat.ing** restore a building, painting, etc. to good condition by cleaning, repairing, etc. —**ren.o.va.tion** (-VAY.shun) *n.:* to make renovations in a building; a costly renovation of the old house. —**ren.o.va.tor** (-vay.tur) *n.*

re.nown (ri.NOWN) *n.* great distinction or fame: *men of great renown; She achieved or attained wide renown as an educator;* *adj.: a renowned* (= famous) *warrior; He is renowned as a scientist; renowned for his discoveries.*

rent **1** *pt. & pp.* of REND. **2** *n.* a torn place in a fabric; split: *a rent in her gown.* **3** *n.* regular payment for the use of a piece of property: *The landlord just raised the rent on our room; evicted for nonpayment of rent; Now he has more rooms for rent.* —*v.* give or get the use of something in return for payment: *She rents out rooms to students; We rented a car at the airport; We rented it from Rentals Inc.; They rent cars to the public; What does a car rent for nowadays?* —**rent.er** *n.*

rent.al (REN.tul) *n.* a renting, renting agency, a piece of property rented out, or the payment for it: *boat, car, film, office rentals.* —*adj.: a rental agreement, car, charge; A rental library charges for books lent.*

rent.als.man (REN.tuls.mun) *n.* **-men** an ombudsman of landlord-tenant relations.

re.nun.ci.a.tion (ri.NUN.see.AY.shun) *n.* a renouncing or giving up: *the* renunciation of an agreement, claim, course of action, hope, policy, right, title.

re.or.gan.i.za.tion (ree.OR.guh.nuh.ZAY.shun, -nye-) *n.* an organizing again or anew: *Our company underwent a reorganization.* —**re.or.gan.ize** (-guh.nize) *v.* **-iz.es, -ized, -iz.ing.**

rep *n.* [short form] representative: *field, sales, state reps.*

re.pair (ri.PAIR) *v.* **1** restore, esp. something damaged, to good condition. **2** remedy a loss, harm, wrong, etc. **3** betake oneself *to* a place. —*n.* **1** a repairing or an instance of it: *to do* or *make the necessary repairs to an old home; extensive, major, minor repairs; a body shop for car repairs; damaged beyond repair; The road is closed while under repair.* **2** condition with respect to repairs: *a house kept in (good) repair; It was in bad repair after years of neglect.* —**re.pair.a.ble** (-ruh.bul) or **rep.a.ra.ble** (REP.uh.ruh.bul) *adj.* —**re.pair.man** (ri.PAIR.mun) *n.* **-men.**

rep.a.ra.tion (rep.uh.RAY.shun) *n.* a making of amends for a wrong: *War reparations are levied on defeated nations.*

re.par.a.tive (ri.PAIR.uh.tiv) *adj.* having to do with reparation or repairs.

rep.ar.tee (rep.ur.TEE) *n.* cleverness or skill in replying wittily: *She's good at repartee.*

re.past (ri.PAST) *n.* meal; food and drink: *light, meager, rich repasts.*

re.pa.tri.ate (ree.PAY.tree.ate, ree.PAT-) *v.* **-ates, -at.ed, -at.ing** return a person or thing to the home country: *to repatriate illegal aliens, migrant workers, prisoners of war; Foreign businesses may not repatriate their profits.* —*n.* (-tree.it) a repatriated person. —**re.pa.tri.a.tion** (-tree.AY.shun) *n.:* *the repatriation of Hong Kong from Britain to China in 1997.*

re.pay (ree.PAY) *v.* **-pays, -paid, -pay.ing** pay back; make a return for something to someone: *to repay a loan, kindness; She became a social worker to repay her debt to society; to repay a creditor, lender; He repaid Jane for her kindness; Love is sometimes repaid with ingratitude.* —**re.pay.a.ble** (-uh.bul) *adj.*; **re.pay.ment** *n.*

re.peal (ri.PEEL) *v.* cancel or annul, esp. a law. —*n.* a repealing.

re.peat (ri.PEET) *v.* do or say something again: *He never repeats a mistake; to repeat a formula after someone, as when being sworn in; to repeat a lesson to a class from memory; a tiresome lecturer who tends to repeat himself* (= say again what he said already). —*n.* **1** a repeating or anything repeated, as a rerun TV program. **2** in music, a passage to be repeated or a symbol indicating this. —**re.peat.er** *n.*

repeated *adj.* **1** said or done again: *repeated attempts, mistakes, occurrences, warnings.* **2** renewed: *a repeated failure, pattern, request.* —**re.peat.ed.ly** *adv.*

re.pel (ri.PEL) *v.* **-pels, -pelled, -pel.ling** force or drive back: *to repel an attack, enemy, invasion; Like (magnetic) poles repel (each other); adj.: It's repelling* (= disgusting) *in appearance, odor; a repelling sight.*

re.pel.lent (ri.PEL.unt) *n.* something that repels: *insect repellents; adj.: a mosquito repellent spray; a water repellent substance, surface; Tobacco smoke is repellent to her.* Also **re.pel.lant** (-unt).

re.pent (ri.PENT) *v.* feel sorry for something and seek forgiveness, as a sinner: *He repented (of) his past; a foolish decision that he lived to repent* (= regret). —**re.pent.ance** (-tunce) *n.*; **re.pent.ant** (-tunt) *adj.*

re.per.cus.sion (ree.pur.CUSH.un, rhyme: discussion) *n.* a reaction or effect, often far-reaching, of some action or event: *without fear of repercussion(s); to have damaging, disastrous, serious repercussions.*

rep.er.toire (REP.urt.war) *n.* the stock of plays, parts, pieces, etc., that musicians, performers, or companies have at their command. Also **rep.er.to.ry** (-tor.ee) *n.* **-ries.**

repertory theater *n.* a company that has a repertory of prepared plays or operas to put on in rotation during a season.

rep.e.ti.tion (rep.uh.TISH.un) *n.* a repeating or something repeated.

rep.e.ti.tious (rep.uh.TISH.us) *adj.* tending to repeat; hence, tiresome: *a speaker's repetitious habit; a repetitious job, speaker, task, theme.* —**rep.e.ti.tious.ly** *adv.*; **rep.e.ti.tious.ness** *n.*

re.pet.i.tive (ri.PET.uh.tiv) *adj.* characterized by repetition: *the repetitive nature of rhymes; mundane and repetitive tasks; repetitive strain* (or *stress* or *motion*) *injuries,* or *disorders,* such as "carpal tunnel syndrome" (resulting from repetitive tasks involving short and fast movements that strain muscles, tendons, and nerves). —**rep.e.ti.tive.ly** *adv.*

re.place (ri.PLACE) *v.* **-plac.es, -placed, -plac.ing 1** take the place of someone or something that is gone or no longer usable: *We replace a burned-out light bulb with a new one; The retired principal was replaced by Ms. Lee; She is* now difficult to replace (= find a good substitute for). **2** put back: *to replace books on a shelf; He was ordered to replace* (= pay for) *the broken china.* —**re.place.a.ble** (-suh.bul) *adj.* —**re.place.ment** *n.*

re.play (ree.PLAY) *v.* play over or again. —*n.* (REE.play) a playing again; repetition: *the instant replay (from videotape) of an action just broadcast.*

re.plen.ish (ri.PLEN.ish) *v.* to refill: *to replenish glasses, inventories, reserves, supplies; to replenish a wardrobe with new fashions;* —**re.plen.ish.ment** *n.*

re.plete (ri.PLEET) *adj.* filled to the maximum: *a book replete with absurdities, errors; a day replete with thrills; Lou fell asleep replete* (= very full) *with food and drink.* —**re.ple.tion** (ri.PLEE.shun) *n.*

rep.li.ca (REP.li.cuh) *n.* a duplicate or copy, esp. one made by the original artist.

rep.li.cate (REP.li.cate) *v.* **-cates, -cat.ed, -cat.ing** duplicate or produce an exact copy of something. —**rep.li.ca.tion** (-CAY.shun) *n.*

re.ply (ri.PLY) *v.* **-plies, -plied, -ply.ing** answer orally or in writing, esp. in kind or appropriately: *He replied immediately or promptly to her phone call; replied that he would see her the next morning.* —*n.*: *to give or make a reply; At first his letter didn't draw or elicit a reply; Then he got or received a curt, gruff, stinging, sullen reply; He sent an immediate, prompt, succinct, terse, witty reply; She waved in reply to his hello.*

re.po (REE.poh) *n. Informal.* **1** something repossessed. **2** repurchase agreement for securities. —*adj.* repossession: *the repo business; Two repo men came to get his car.*

re.port (ri.PORT) *v.* give information about or an account of what one has seen or done: *a journalist reporting on a disaster from the scene; to report a prowler to the police; She reported him to the police for breaking in; He's reported to be still around or It's reported that he's still around; UFOs were reported seen by the villagers or They reported having seen the UFOs or They reported (their) seeing UFOs; A child has been reported missing; Sorry to report (to you that) I'm ill; My friend has already reported sick; We will not report* (= present ourselves) *for duty tomorrow; Our manager reports* (= answers) *directly to the president; The journalist reports back to his editor;* **adj.**: *your reported earnings; a widely reported story; A reported 300 fell ill.* —*n.* **1** a reporting or account: *He will file or give, make, present, submit a report on or about the incident to his boss; He has to draw up or make out, write out, write up the report; She has heard but cannot confirm the report that he has resigned; accurate, annual, biased, classified, confidential, daily, detailed, exhaustive, favorable, first-hand, interim, minority, top-secret, unconfirmed, written reports; a man of good report* (= reputation). **2** rumor: *an idle report; as report has it.* **3** a sound, as of a gun or explosion. —**re.port.a.ble** (-tuh.bul) *adj.*

re.port.age (ri.POR.tij) *n.* a reporting, esp. in the style of newspapers: *accurate, up-to-date news reportage.*

report card *n.* a report sent periodically by a school to parents about a pupil's progress.

re.port.ed.ly (ri.POR.tid.lee) *adv.* according to report: *UFO's were reportedly seen by the villagers.*

re.port.er (ri.POR.tur) *n.* one who reports, esp. news for the media. —**re.por.to.ri.al** (rep.ur.TOR.ee.ul) *adj.*: *reportorial coups, credentials, skills.*

re.pose (ri.POZE) *v.* **-pos.es, -posed, -pos.ing 1** put or place trust, confidence, etc. in someone or something. **2** to rest following activity: *He reposed her head on his shoulder; bodies reposing* (= lying at rest) *in their graves undisturbed.* —*n.* **1** rest following activity: *The body looked serene in repose; the eternal repose of departed souls.* **2** poise: *her self-assured repose of manner.* —**re.pose.ful** *adj.*

re.pos.i.to.ry (ri.POZ.i.tor.ee) *n.* **-ries 1** a storage place or container. **2** a person or institution to which something is entrusted: *He is the repository of her confidences; Books are repositories of knowledge.*

re.pos.sess (ree.puh.ZES) *v.* take possession of property, as a seller does because of the buyer's default in payments. —**re.pos.ses.sion** (-ZESH.un) *n.*

rep.re.hend (rep.ri.HEND) *v.* rebuke or blame.

rep.re.hen.si.ble (rep.ri.HEN.suh.bul) *adj* blameworthy: *reprehensible behavior, conduct, deeds.*

rep.re.sent (rep.ri.ZENT) *v.* **1** stand for as a symbol: *Words represent ideas; Let T represent time.* **2** act or speak in place of another: *Lawyers represent their clients.* **3** present: *Satan is always represented as evil; The physician was not licensed as represented to the public; This chart graphically represents the data we* have gathered.

rep.re.sen.ta.tion (REP.ri.zen.TAY.shun) *n.* **1** a representing or being represented: *"No taxation without representation"; proportional representation; a good representation* (= picture or statue) *of Venus.* **2** representatives as a group: *the representation from Iceland.* **3** a formal statement of facts or arguments in support of a demand or viewpoint: *in spite of representations made to the government.*
—**rep.re.sen.ta.tion.al** *adj.*

rep.re.sen.ta.tive (rep.ri.ZEN.tuh.tiv) *adj.* **1** representing: *a representative collection, sample, selection; a painting that is representative of a style.* **2** based on elections: *a representative form of government; a representative assembly, government, institution.* —*n.* **1** one who represents a person or group, as a delegate, sales rep, or agent. **2 Representative** a member of the lower house of a U.S. state legislature or of Congress.

re.press (ri.PRES) *v.* **1** keep down, as an undesirable impulse or an unpleasant memory from the conscious mind. **2** put down something developing or seeking an outlet: *She tried to repress her laughter; to repress a rebellion.*
—**re.pres.sion** (-PRESH.un) *n.: to live under repression.* —**re.pres.sive** (-PRES.iv) *adj.: a repressive measure; under a repressive regime that is repressive of civil rights.*

re.prieve (ri.PREEV) *v.* **-prieves, -prieved, -priev.ing** give temporary relief from trouble or danger, esp. from death by execution.
—*n.* a reprieving or being reprieved, esp. a temporary suspension of a sentence of death: *He got or received or was given or was granted a last-minute reprieve from execution.*

rep.ri.mand (REP.ruh.mand) *n.* a formal or sharp rebuke, often public, as from one in authority: *The judge administered or issued a reprimand to the offending attorney; a mild reprimand; He received a severe, stern, written reprimand.*
—*v.* give a reprimand to someone.

re.print (ree.PRINT) *v.* to print an edition of a book again. —*n.* (REE.print): *They have issued a reprint of the 1950 classic.*

re.pris.al (ri.PRY.zul) *n.* an act of retaliation, esp. military or political: *They were threatened with reprisals; The terrorist camps were bombed in reprisal for their attacks on civilians; a reprisal carried out against terrorist attacks.*

re.prise (ruh.PREEZ) *n.* **1** a renewal or repetition of an action: *a reprise of his previous efforts.* **2** esp. in music, the return to an original theme: *a reprise of an old tune.* —*v.* **re.pris.es, re.prised, re.pris.ing** repeat or reenact: *to reprise a role.*

re.proach (ri.PROHCH) *v.* find fault with, esp. in a resentful manner: *He was reproached for something he didn't do.*
—*n.* a reproaching, the cause of it, or the resulting discredit or disgrace: *a look of reproach; a term of reproach; the reproaches heaped on her; He earned the reproach of the community; He was thought to be* **above** *or* **beyond reproach** (= faultless). —**re.proach.ful** *adj.: a reproachful critic, tone, word;* **re.proach.ful.ly** *adv.*

rep.ro.bate (REP.ruh.bate) *n.* one who is depraved or very wicked.

rep.ro.ba.tion (rep.ruh.BAY.shun) *n.* censure or condemnation.

re.pro.duce (ree.pruh.DUCE) *v.* **-duc.es, -duced, -duc.ing** produce copies from an original, sound from a recording, offspring from eggs or by means of spores, etc.
—**re.pro.duc.tion** (-DUC.shun) *n.*
—**re.pro.duc.tive** (-tiv) *adj.*

re.prog.ra.phy (ri.PROG.ruh.fee) *n.* duplication of graphic material, as by photocopiers. —**re.pro.graph.ic** (ree.pruh.GRAF.ic) *adj.*

re.proof (ri.PROOF) *n.* a reproving: *a mild reproof.*

re.prove (ri.PROOV) *v.* **-proves, -proved, -prov.ing** find fault with someone. —**re.prov.ing.ly** *adv.*

rep.tile (REP.tile) *n.* a crawling, scaly, cold-blooded vertebrate such as a snake, lizard, crocodile, or turtle: *a creeping* or *slithering reptile.*
—**rep.til.i.an** (rep.TIL.ee.un) *n. & adj.*

re.pub.lic (ri.PUB.lic) *n.* a state or a form of government headed by an elected president and run by elected representatives, as in France, U.S.A., India, etc.: *Communist states used to call themselves democratic, people's,* or *socialist republics.*

re.pub.li.can (ri.PUB.li.cun) *adj.* **1** having to do with a republic: *a republican government, party, system.* **2** favoring republics: *republican ideas, movements, sympathies.* **3 Republican** having to do with the U.S. Republican Party: *a Republican candidate.* —*n.* **1** one who favors a republic. **2 Republican** a member of the U.S. Republican Party.

re.pu.di.ate (ri.PEW.dee.ate) *v.* **-ates, -at.ed, -at.ing** disown or reject: *to repudiate a charge, doctrine, friend, treaty.*

—**re.pu.di.a.tion** (-AY.shun) *n.*

re.pug.nance (ri.PUG.nunce) *n.* a strong dislike or aversion: *Ray feels no repugnance to eating snails; Sam turns away from it in deep repugnance.*

re.pug.nant (ri.PUG.nunt) *adj.* disagreeable or objectionable to one's tastes, ideas, liking, etc.: *Food is repugnant to a sick stomach; We think slavery repugnant.* —**re.pug.nant.ly** *adv.*

re.pulse (ri.PULSE) *v.* **-puls.es, -pulsed, -puls.ing** repel by force, coldness, discourtesy, etc.; rebuff: *to repulse an attack, attacker, enemy; to repulse an offer of friendship; She is repulsed (= disgusted) by creeping things.* —*n.* a repulsing or being repulsed; rejection.

re.pul.sion (ri.PUL.shun) *n.* **1** a being repelled or a repulse: *magnetic attraction and repulsion.* **2** strong aversion or disgust.

re.pul.sive (ri.PUL.siv) *adj.* repelling or disgusting: *a repulsive creature, force, sight; His manners are utterly repulsive to her;* **re.pul.sive.ly** *adv.;* **re.pul.sive.ness** *n.*

rep.u.ta.ble (REP.yuh.tuh.bul) *adj.* having a good reputation: *a reputable business, dealer, lawyer;* **rep.u.ta.bly** *adv.*

rep.u.ta.tion (rep.yuh.TAY.shun) *n.* a normally good public estimation of character or quality: *a witch-hunt that destroyed many reputations; She enjoys a good reputation as a lawyer; international, local, worldwide reputation; to acquire, build, establish a reputation; to compromise, guard, live up to, protect, ruin, tarnish one's reputation; a reputation for being sharp; Sam has the reputation of (being) a swindler; He staked his reputation on the outcome of the trial.*

re.pute (rip.YOOT) *n.* reputation: *He's held in high repute, not in low repute; a lawyer of* **repute***; a* **house of ill repute** (= brothel).

re.put.ed (ri.PEW.tid) *adj.* **1** reputable: *a widely reputed authority.* **2** generally believed: *the reputed father of the orphan; the book's reputed author; He is reputed (to be) the world's richest man.* —**re.put.ed.ly** *adv.*: *He's reputedly (= as generally believed) the oldest living person.*

re.quest (ri.QUEST) *v.* ask politely or formally: *We request the pleasure of your company; We request a favor of or from the public; We request you not to smoke or We request that you do not smoke.*

—*n.* a requesting, being requested, or something requested: *She filed a request with the authorities; He made a request to her parents; told them he had a request to make of them; They submitted a joint request to the school; considered whether to deny or reject the request; to grant a request; The school agreed to act on the request; a request for more time or a request that they be given more time; desperate, formal, modest, reasonable, simple, special, urgent, written requests; She's here at your request; a performance repeated* **by request***; Refunds are made on or upon request.* —**adj.** that involves asking: *a request card, item, (bus) stop, system.*

Re.qui.em (REK.wee.um, RAY-) *n.* (the musical setting of) a Mass for the repose of departed souls.

re.quire (ri.QUIRE) *v.* **-quires, -quired, -quir.ing** demand, as by rule or necessity: *Drivers are required to stop at red lights; It is required by law from or of all drivers; Piano playing requires (= calls for) practice; It requires that you (should) practice regularly;* **adj.**: *This book is* **required** *reading for all students; the required amount, notice, repairs.*

re.quire.ment (ri.QUIRE.munt) *n.* something required or needed: *He has fulfilled or met or satisfied the requirements set or established for the Ph.D. program; admission, entrance, minimum requirements; the requirement that a test of English proficiency be passed.*

req.ui.site (REK.wuh.zit) *adj.* needed or required: *the quorum requisite for a business meeting; the requisite amount, number; the requisite qualifications and experience for a job.* —**n.**: *Air and water as the prime requisites for survival.*

req.ui.si.tion (rek.wuh.ZISH.un) *n.* a formal demand for something required, as of military supplies or personnel: *Our only jeep was in constant requisition.*

—*v.* request formally: *Help had to be requisitioned from outside the town.*

re.quite (ri.QUITE) *v.* **-quites, -quit.ed, -quit.ing 1** make return for an act or to a person: *to requite the community for help received.* **2** retaliate against or avenge. —**re.quit.al** (ri.KWY.tul) *n.*: *harm done in requital.*

rere.dos (REER.dos, RAIR-) *n.* a decorated wall or screen rising behind an altar.

re.run (REE.run) *n.* another showing of a motion picture or TV program after the first run: *a theater that shows only reruns of old movies.*

re.sale (REE.sale) *n.* a selling again of an item to a third party or subsequent buyer.

re.scind (ri.SIND) *v.* annul or cancel: *to*

rescind laws; to rescind an agreement, decision, license, measure, order, permit, policy, resolution, treaty; to rescind one's actions, approval, endorsement.
—**re.scis.sion** (ri.SIZH.un) *n.*

re.script (REE.script) *n.* an order or decree, as from the pope, in answer to a question or petition.

res.cue (RES.cue) *v.* **-cues, -cued, -cu.ing** free or save someone in trouble by quick action: *The child was rescued from the fire.* —*n.* a rescuing: *to attempt, effect, make, mount a rescue; a daring, heroic rescue of the hostages from the hands of the terrorists.* —**res.cu.er** *n.*

re.search (REE.surch, ri.SURCH) *n.* a careful search or investigation, esp. an organized scholarly or scientific inquiry: *to conduct or pursue research in a specific area; an exhaustive, extensive, laborious, original, painstaking, thorough research into the causes of cancer; a book based on solid market research on buying habits.* —*v.* do research on a subject: *Scientists are researching the causes of cancer;* *adj.: a carefully, meticulously, well researched essay, report, study.*
—**re.search.er** *n.*

re.sec.tion (ri.SEC.shun) *n.* the surgical removal of a portion of an organ or bone.

re.sem.blance (ri.ZEM.blunce) *n.* similarity, esp. in outward appearance: *The sisters bear a close resemblance to each other; the striking, strong family resemblance between them; a remote resemblance to their cousins.*

re.sem.ble (ri.ZEM.bul) *v.* **-bles, -bled, -bling** be similar to a person or thing in appearance or qualities: *a son closely resembling his mother.*

re.sent (ri.ZENT) *v.* feel or show anger at something offensive or toward an offender: *We strongly resent his jumping the queue; We bitterly resent being left behind.* —**re.sent.ful** *adj.: We are resentful of queue-jumpers; resentful at or about being left behind;* **re.sent.ful.ly** *adv.*

re.sent.ment (ri.ZENT.munt) *n.* indignation and ill will resulting from an offense: *The injustice aroused or stirred up resentment in the community; People felt and expressed or voiced their bitter, deep, sullen resentment about it; resentment against authority; resentment toward the police; They harbored a resentment; felt resentment that they were unjustly dealt with.*

re.ser.pine (ri.SUR.pin, -peen) *n.* a tranquilizing drug used to treat high blood pressure.

res.er.va.tion (rez.ur.VAY.shun) *n.* **1** a reserving or something reserved, as an advance booking of a room at a hotel: *We have reservations for four people; to make, confirm, cancel a reservation.* **2** a tacit or expressed condition: *a mental reservation; our wholehearted support without reservations.* **3** a tract of land set apart for the exclusive use of a Native American group: *on the Omaha Reservation.*

re.serve (ri.ZURV) *v.* **-serves, -served, -serv.ing** hold back or keep for a particular person, another occasion, later use, etc.: *to reserve a right, room, seat, space, table; to reserve judgment till all the facts are in; all rights (in the book) reserved by the author; He wisely reserved (= saved) his energies till the final act.* —*n.* **1** something reserved, as money or resources kept **in reserve** for later use, a body of trained people (or reservists), ships, or aircraft standing by for military service when needed, etc.: *the nation's energy and gold reserves; our oil reserves, reserves of capital; bird, forest, game, wildlife reserves* (= tracts of public land); *adja.: a reserve army, first-baseman (in baseball), fund, soldier, unit; the reserve forces.* **2** a Canadian Indian reservation: *the Kahnawake Reserve; reserve lands.* **3** the keeping of one's thoughts or feelings to oneself; aloofness: *to display or show reserve in one's dealings; a cool reserve that was hard to break down; He unburdened his mind* **without reserve** (= freely).

re.served (ri.ZURVD) *adj.* **1** set aside: *a reserved seat.* **2** restrained in speech or manner: *He's reserved about his background, reserved toward or with strangers.*
—**re.ser.ved.ly** (-vid.lee) *adv.*

re.ser.vist (ri.ZUR.vist) *n.* a member of a military reserve.

res.er.voir (RES.urv.wahr) *n.* a large supply or store, esp. of water: *natural and artificial reservoirs.*

re.side (ri.ZIDE) *v.* **-sides, -sid.ed, -sid.ing** **1** live, esp. in a settled way: *to reside in a country; to reside at a hotel.* **2** exist; be vested: *In a democracy, power resides in the people.*

res.i.dence (REZ.i.dunce) *n.* a residing or where one resides; home: *to establish, take up residence in Mexico; a poet who is* **in residence** (= living or working on a regular basis) *at a university.* —**res.i.den.cy** (-dun.see) *n.* **-cies.**

res.i.dent (REZ.i.dunt) *n.* **1** one that resides in a place: *a U.S. resident; a permanent resident* (= immigrant) *in Canada; adj.: a resident Alaskan; She is*

resident abroad; a resident poet, representative, scholar; a printer with 14 resident fonts of type (built into its ROM) and a slot for removable cartridges with extra fonts. **2** a physician in training or on full-time duty at a hospital. —**res.i.den.tial** (rez.i.DEN.shul) adj.: a residential district, hotel, neighborhood, school.

residua pl. of RESIDUUM.

re.sid.u.al (ri.ZIJ.oo.ul) adj. having to do with a residue or remainder: residual air, damage, guilt, heat, use, value, waste; a residual effect, estate, feeling, product, right. —**n. 1** a remainder. **2** in television, a fee paid to a performer for each rerun of a show or commercial.

re.sid.u.ar.y (ri.ZIJ.oo.air.ee) adj. having to do with what remains of an estate after bequests are made: a residuary clause, legacy.

res.i.due (REZ.uh.due) n. what remains at the end of a process: the residue of salt left after evaporation of a (salt) solution; the residue of an estate after settlement of claims. Also **re.sid.u.um** (ri.ZIJ.oo.um), pl. **-sid.u.a** (-oo.uh).

re.sign (ri.ZINE) v. **1** give up a job or position: He resigned from the board; resigned as chairman; resigned his membership. **2** be ready to endure: He had to resign himself to a life on or to living on welfare.

res.ig.na.tion (rez.ig.NAY.shun) n. **1** a resigning or a formal notice of it: to hand in, offer, submit, tender, withdraw one's resignation. **2** passive acceptance of suffering or misfortune.

re.signed (ri.ZINED) adj. submissive: He is resigned to his lot in life; She's quite resigned to the life of a widow. —**re.sign.ed.ly** (-nid.lee) adv.

re.sil.ient (ri.ZIL.yunt) adj. springing back to the original form or position, as rubber or a spring: "Silicone rubber" makes a resilient caulk; a resilient floor tile; a resilient disposition, economy; a sitcom with a resilient cheerfulness about it; a **resilient currency** (that recovers its exchange value after a fall). —**re.sil.i.ence** (-yunce) or **re.sil.i.en.cy** (-yun.see) n.: emotional resilience; the resiliency of rubber.

res.in (REZ.in) n. an organic substance such as shellac secreted by certain plants, trees, and insects, and much used in paints and varnishes. —**res.in.ous** (-nus) adj.

re.sist (ri.ZIST) v. act against an attack, enemy, temptation, etc. that is trying to overcome one: I couldn't resist laughing at his jokes. —**re.sist.er** n.

—**re.sist.i.ble** adj.

re.sist.ance (ri.ZIST.tunce) n. **1** a resisting or the power to resist: to break down, crush, offer, overcome, put down, put up resistance to something; They met with armed, determined, fierce, passive, stiff, strong, stubborn resistance; to take the line or course or path **of least resistance** (= take the easiest way). **2** the opposition offered by a substance to the passage of electricity. **3** secretly conducted opposition to foreign military occupation, often **the Resistance.** —**re.sist.ant** (-tunt) adj.

re.sis.tor (ri.ZIS.tur) n. a device with electrical resistance used in controlling voltage, to heat furnaces, etc.

res.o.lute (REZ.uh.loot, long "oo") adj. determined or firm in one's purpose. —**res.o.lute.ly** adv.; **res.o.lute.ness** n.

res.o.lu.tion (rez.uh.LOO.shun) n. **1** determination to achieve an aim; resolve: She acted with firm resolution; Hamlet lacked resolution. **2** what is resolved upon: a New Year's resolution to quit smoking; a resolution (= statement) proposed, adopted or passed by the city council. **3** a solving: the resolution of a dramatic plot; the resolution of our doubts. **4** a breaking up or separation: the resolution of a chemical compound into its elements; The sharp, high resolution of an electron microscope enables the viewer to distinguish objects; a video display with a resolution of 1,024 x 768 pixels; high and low resolutions; a printer with resolution enhancement technology.

re.solve (ri.ZOLV) v. **-solves, -solved, -solv.ing 1** decide or determine: He resolved to give up smoking; It was resolved that smoking be banned; **adjp.:** He is firmly **resolved** never to smoke again. **2** solve: to resolve a conflict, crisis, dispute, issue, mystery, problem. **3** break up: White light is resolved into the colors of the spectrum; the **resolving power** of a telescope or microscope to provide separate images of closely spaced parts of an object. —**n.** resolution: to make a firm resolve never to smoke. —**re.solv.a.ble** (-vuh.bul) adj.

res.o.nance (REZ.uh.nunce) n. a resounding quality; an echoing, strengthening, or prolonging of sound, as by a hollow or cavity: a quartz crystal vibrating in resonance with (= at the same frequency as) a generator; the **resonance box**, or resonator, of a guitar or violin.

res.o.nant (REZ.uh.nunt) adj. having resonance: Vowels are more resonant than consonants; A resonant voice depends on one's mouth, throat, and nasal cavities. —**res.o.nant.ly** adv.

res.o.nate (REZ.uh.nate) v. **-nates, -nat.ed, -nat.ing** produce resonance; resound. —**res.o.na.tion** (-NAY.shun) n. —**res.o.na.tor** (-nay.tur) n.

re.sort (ri.ZORT) v. **1** go often to a place, esp. habitually: *Tourists resort to a beach, shrine, spa*. **2** turn to, as for help: *to resort to force, tears, trickery, violence, war*. —*n*. a resorting or a place or thing resorted to: *health, holiday, seaside, summer, winter resorts; without resort to force; He took to prayer as the or as a* **last resort** (= last means of help); *a drug of last resort*.

re.sound (ri.ZOUND) v. sound loudly; echo or ring. —**resounding** adj. emphatic or unmistakable: *resounding cheers; a resounding cry, effect, failure, success, victory; a resounding "Yes"; a resounding 90% vote*; **re.sound.ing.ly** adv.

re.source (REE.sorce, ri.SORCE) n. a means or source of help, relief, supply, etc. that may be drawn upon when needed: *a man of resource; the earth's natural resources such as land, water, and minerals; to develop, exploit, tap a country's resources; to pool one's resources; borrowing as a last resource; the financial resources to undertake a project; A* **resource center** *such as a library contains learning resources; a* **resource person** (= general consultant).

re.source.ful (ri.SORCE.ful) adj. good at finding ways and means of solving a problem: *The boy who stuck his finger in a hole in the dike and saved his town from a flood had to be resourceful; The resourceful Amish use windmills to pump water*. —**re.source.ful.ly** adv.; **re.source.ful.ness** n.

re.spect (ri.SPECT) v. have or show esteem for a person or thing: *to respect one's elders; I respect his rights; I respect him as a teacher;* **adj.**: *He's a highly* **respected** *member of our club*; **prep.**: *a suggestion* **respecting** (= concerning) *yesterday's announcement*.
—*n*. **1** esteem or proper regard: *He talks of his teacher with respect; pays respect to what she says; She inspires respect; She commands respect from her students; She is held in high respect by them; She has earned, won their respect; Jim lost his respect by behaving badly; He shows little respect for rules; He ought to behave better at least out of respect for his teacher*. **2 respects** pl. respectful regards: *I'd like to send her my respects; Please give her my respects; He's come to pay his respects to her; our* **last respects** (= tribute after death). **3** a point considered: *a great man in many respects; In some respects he's not so great; a memo* **in** or **with respect to** (= regarding) *the raise you asked for*.

re.spect.a.ble (ri.SPEC.tuh.bul) adj. **1** worthy of respect: *a respectable family, gentleman; to look respectable; in respectable society*. **2** impressive: *a respectable income, number; an audience of respectable size*. —**re.spect.a.bly** adv. —**re.spect.a.bil.i.ty** (-BIL.i.tee) n.

re.spect.ful (ri.SPECT.ful) adj. having or showing respect: *a respectful manner; He's respectful to or of his elders*. —**re.spect.ful.ly** adv.

re.spect.ive (ri.SPEC.tiv) adj. as relates to each individually: *Everyone please get back to your respective seats*.

re.spect.ive.ly (ri.SPEC.tiv.lee) adv. in order: *I, II, and III are 1, 2, and 3, respectively*.

res.pi.ra.tion (res.puh.RAY.shun) n. breathing by means of lungs or gills in animals and through leaves and buds in plants: *We gave him artificial respiration till help arrived*.

res.pi.ra.tor (RES.puh.ray.tur) n. **1** an artificial breathing device. **2** a mask worn over the nose and mouth to prevent the breathing in of harmful substances.

res.pi.ra.to.ry (RES.puh.ruh.tor.ee, ris.PYE.ruh-) adj. having to do with respiration: *respiratory diseases, distress, organs*.

re.spire (ri.SPIRE) v. **-spires, -spired, -spir.ing** breathe: *Produce will continue to ripen and respire in storage; All respiring animals give off carbon dioxide*.

res.pite (RES.pit) n. a temporary relief from an exertion or suffering: *He works without respite from 8 to 12; A coffee break allows* or *gives some respite from work; a brief, temporary respite; The rain brought a respite from the heat*.

re.splend.ent (ri.SPLEN.dunt) adj. full of splendor; shining brightly: *He was resplendent with joy; She looked resplendent in glory as carnival queen*; **re.splend.ent.ly** adv. —**re.splend.ence** (-dunce) n.

re.spond (ri.SPOND) v. **1** react, as in answer: *to respond to an appeal, call, letter, plea, question, stimulus; We phoned the police and they responded promptly*. **2** show a favorable reaction: *to respond to a medication, to kindness, treatment; The patient did not respond for a couple of hours*.

re.spond.ent (ri.SPON.dunt) n. **1** one

who responds to a poll, questionnaire, survey, etc. **2** a defendant. —*adj.* responding.

re.spond.er *n.* one that responds, esp. a signal-returning electronic device, as in radar.

re.sponse (ri.SPONSE) *n.* a responding, as a reply or any reaction to a stimulus: *At first, our pleas elicited* or *evoked no response; Nothing was heard in response to our calls; The initial response was glib, lukewarm, sullen; She gave a witty response to the heckler's question; a computer's* **response time** *between receiving a command and executing it.*

re.spon.si.bil.i.ty (ri.SPON.suh.BIL.i.tee) *n.* **-ties** a being responsible or accountable; obligation: *A greater sense of responsibility is required; the responsibility to do a good job; the responsibilities of the office; He is old enough to accept* or *assume* or *bear, exercise, shoulder, take (on) full responsibility for his actions; to dodge* or *evade* or *shirk responsibility; We have to share, if not bear, the responsibility* (= *blame*) *for what happens around here instead of laying the responsibility at someone else's door; The collective responsibility lies with all of us; The ultimate responsibility for a product is the manufacturer's; an awesome, clear, grave, great, heavy responsibility; the responsibility to inform the next of kin after a body is identified; a terrible responsibility; The terrorists admitted, in fact claimed, responsibility for the explosion; They had done it* **on their own responsibility** (= *initiative*).

re.spon.si.ble (ri.SPON.suh.bul) *adj.* **1** accountable or answerable for an action or happening, often to someone: *We are responsible for our actions, for carrying out our duties; Someone has to be responsible when a fire alarm goes off; Teachers are directly responsible to the principal; The brakes failed and the mechanic was held responsible; a responsible approach, attitude;* **Responsible government** *is answerable to the people; A storm was responsible for* (= *was the cause of*) *the airplane crash.* **2** *trustworthy: a very responsible child; responsible adults, citizens, officials; Dogs are more responsible than cats.* **3** involving important duties: *a highly responsible job, position, role.* —**re.spon.si.bly** *adv.*

re.spon.sive (ri.SPON.siv) *adj.* reacting favorably: *to be responsive to an appeal, to changes, to needs, to a treatment, to one's wishes; a responsive chord, performance, service.* —**re.spon.sive.ly** *adv.;*

re.spon.sive.ness *n.*

rest *n.* **1** a break from activity, as for relaxation; pause: *to have* or *take a day of rest from work; to take rest now and then; a well-earned rest; The doctor ordered bed rest; complete rest for body and mind; objects at rest and in motion; an explanation to set your mind* **at rest** (= free from anxiety); *The car went out of control and* **came to rest** (= stopped) *against a wall; a stool as a rest* (= support) *for the feet; a symbol indicating a half rest* (= interval of silence) *between notes in music; souls gone* **to their rest** (= repose in another world); *Bodies are* **laid to rest** (= buried). **2 the rest** what remains or is left: *the rest of us; We'll do the rest; For the rest, I have nothing to say.*

—*v.* **1** stop doing or saying anything; be inactive: *He rests only at night; never rests his horses* (= lets them be inactive); *The prosecution rests (from arguing a case); I rest my case.* **2** be at ease; relax: *He wouldn't let me rest till I said "yes"; The patient is resting.* **3** support or be supported; lean: *a pillow to rest your head on; a house resting on a weak foundation.* **4** remain: *Please* **rest assured** *we'll do our best; The decision* **rests with** (= is the responsibility of) *the court.* —**rest.ful** *adj.;* **rest.ful.ly** *adv.*

res.tau.rant (RES.tuh.runt, -rahnt) *n.* a commercial eating place: *He manages, operates, runs a fast-food restaurant; an elegant, first-class restaurant; a licensed restaurant (where liquor is served).*

res.tau.ra.teur (res.tuh.ruh.TUR) *n.* a restaurant operator; also [nonstandard] **res.tau.ran.teur.**

rest home *n.* a nursing home.

res.ti.tu.tion (res.tuh.TUE.shun) *n.* restoration to the owner of the property that he or she was deprived of; the making good of loss or damage: *the restitution of stolen property; to claim, demand, owe, pay, seek restitution; He offered restitution; to make full restitution to her for the broken china.*

res.tive (RES.tiv) *adj.* balky, as a horse; restless or impatient, as if under restraint; **res.tive.ly** *adv.;* **res.tive.ness** *n.*

rest.less *adj.* without rest; always busy or moving: *a restless crowd; the restless waves; a restless desire, eye, mind, nature, night, sleep.* —**rest.less.ly** *adv.;* **rest.less.ness** *n.*

res.to.ra.tion (res.tuh.RAY.shun) *n.* a restoring or being restored: *restoration of civilian rule; the restoration of a historic site; the restoration of an old* *painting.*

re.stor.a.tive (ri.STOR.uh.tiv) *adj.* that restores: *restorative dentistry, powers, therapy.*

re.store (ri.STOR) *v.* **-stores, -stored, -stor.ing 1** bring back to its original condition: *to restore a ruined building, damaged paintings, one's health.* **2** return: *to restore books to a shelf, order in class, property to its owner, a job to a fired employee, an employee to his former position.* —**re.stor.a.ble** (-ruh.bul) *adj.*

re.strain (ri.STRAIN) *v.* keep in check, esp. by use of force or authority: *a leash to restrain a dog from attacking people; Restrain your curiosity, temper; adj.: a cool and restrained* (= controlled) *manner; a restrained image, reaction, style, treatment; restrained passions.*

re.straint (ri.STRAINT) *n.* **1** a restraining, being restrained, or means of restraining: *an animal kept or put under restraint; to apply restraint; A restraint* (= leash) *is sometimes put on the more difficult cases.* **2** control: *She cast off or flung off or shook off all restraint; He sobbed without restraint; the social restraints against smoking; She spoke with restraint, choosing her words carefully; The police exercised, displayed or showed great restraint in dealing with the demonstrators.*

re.strict (ri.STRICT) *v.* confine within limits: *Student activities are restricted to school hours; Restrict your speed to 90 km/h; She restricts herself to a vegetarian diet; adj.: a restricted area, circle of friends, field, range, vocabulary; restricted to 500 words; restricted access, hours; a salt-restricted diet* (without salt).
—**re.stric.tion** *n.*: *to impose, lift, place or put restrictions on wages and prices.*

re.stric.tive (ri.STRIC.tiv) *adj.* confining or limiting: *restrictive clothing, policies, quotas, regulations; price fixing, monopolies, and such restrictive trade practices.* —**re.strict.ive.ly** *adv.*

rest room *n.* a public lavatory.

re.sult (ri.ZULT) *n.* a final effect or consequence of an action, esp. a desired effect: *We work to achieve, get, produce results; No sure-fire results; The net, overall results are good; Results are evaluated, measured, tabulated; a direct, logical result of the action; It had no lasting results; examination results; All got the same result* (= answer to a problem).
—*v.* have or follow as a result: *Death could result if people drink this; Carelessness results in* (= has as its result) *accidents; Accidents result* (= follow as a result) *from carelessness.*

re.sult.ant (ri.ZUL.tunt) *adj a.* resulting: *the resultant effect of more people taking public transport to work; the resultant higher prices, increase in costs;* **adj.**: *the legal fees resultant thereof.*

re.sume (ri.ZOOM, long "OO") *v.* **-sumes, -sumed, -sum.ing** return to an activity or position: *The talks will resume on January 1; We will resume work(ing) after lunch; We resume at 2 p.m.; to resume breathing, control, habits, negotiations, production; to resume one's position.* —**re.sump.tion** (ri.ZUMP.shun) *n.*

ré.su.mé or **re.su.me** (REZ.oo.may, rez.oo.MAY) *n.* **1** a summary of one's qualifications and employment experience; vita: *the résumé of a job applicant.* **2** any summary: *a résumé of the evidence, of a book, speech.*

re.sur.gent (ri.SUR.junt) *adj.* tending to rise again: *resurgent inflation, racism; the resurgent Right; a resurgent economy, industry, interest, movement, nation, threat; Japan was resurgent soon after the war.*
—**re.sur.gence** *n.*: *the resurgence of hopes, interest, nationalism, spirits.*

res.ur.rect (rez.uh.RECT) *v.* raise or revive: *Lazarus was resurrected from the dead; to resurrect dead issues, old practices.*

res.ur.rec.tion (rez.uh.REC.shun) *n.* a rising from the dead, as Christ's **Resurrection.**

re.sus.ci.tate (ri.SUS.uh.tate) *v.* **-tates, -tat.ed, -tat.ing** revive from apparent or near death; bring back to consciousness. —**re.sus.ci.ta.tion** (-TAY.shun) *n.*: *to give mouth-to-mouth resuscitation.* —**re.sus.ci.ta.tor** (-tay.tur) *n.*

re.tail (REE.tail) *n.* the sale of goods in small quantities to consumers: *Shops buy wholesale and sell at retail.*
—*v.* **1** sell at retail: *the retailing of meat; These radios retail* (= are sold) *at or for $500 each.* **2** retell or relate stories, gossip, slander, etc.
—*adj.*: *a retail merchant, price, store; the retail trade;* **adv.**: *Stores buy wholesale and sell retail.* —**re.tail.er** *n.*

re.tain (ri.TAIN) *v.* continue to hold or keep, esp. against opposing forces: *insulated so as to retain heat; a good memory that retains everything; to retain a lawyer* (so that services will be available as needed); *adj.: a retaining fence, screw, tank, wall; retaining power; an earth-retaining structure.*

re.tain.er (ri.TAIN.ur) *n.* **1** one that retains: *a retainer for use after braces have been removed from teeth.* **2** a fee to secure the services of a lawyer or other professional: *Put down a retainer and we're in business.* **3** an employee in a wealthy household.

retaining wall *n.* a wall put up to hold back a mass of earth, flood waters, or racing cars.

re.tal.i.ate (ri.TAL.ee.ate) *v.* **-ates, -at.ed, -at.ing** return injury or evil, usu. in kind: *They retaliated against the guerrillas for their attack on the village; retaliated with a bombing of their hide-outs.* —**re.tal.i.a.tion** (-AY.shun) *n.*: *in retaliation for their attacks; an act of retaliation; massive retaliation against the enemy; swift retaliation.*
—**re.tal.i.a.to.ry** (-ee.uh.tor.ee) *adj.*: *a retaliatory attack, measure, policy, strike, threat; retaliatory action, sanctions.*

re.tard (ri.TARD) *v.* slow down; check the progress or movement of something: *to retard development, growth, progress.* —*n.* (REE.tard) [derogatory] a retarded person. —**re.tar.da.tion** (-DAY.shun) *n.*: *mental retardation.*

re.tard.ant (ri.TAR.dunt) *n.* a chemical or other substance that slows down a process or resists an action: *a fire retardant; rust retardants.*

retarded *adj.* mentally handicapped: *a child born retarded; retarded children; the care of the retarded* (= retarded people).

retch *v.* want to vomit: *She retched at the sight.*

re.ten.tion (ri.TEN.shun) *n.* a retaining or retaining capacity. —**re.ten.tive** (-tiv) *adj.*: *Al has a very retentive memory; retentive powers; moisture-retentive mulch;* **re.ten.tive.ly** *adv.*; **re.ten.tive.ness** *n.*

ret.i.cent (RET.uh.sunt) *adj.* not speaking freely, esp. from reserve or embarrassment: *She was reticent about what happened;* **ret.i.cent.ly** *adv.*
—**ret.i.cence** *n.*

ret.i.na (RET.un.uh) *n.* **-nas** or **-nae** (-nee) the light-sensitive back part of the eye on which images are formed.
—**ret.i.nal** (-nul) *adj.*

ret.i.nue (RET.un.yoo) *n.* a body of retainers, attendants, or assistants following an important person.

re.tire (ri.TIRE) *v.* **-tires, -tired, -tir.ing** **1** of a person, withdraw from work or activity at the end of the day, of a career, etc.: *Employees may retire from service with full pension after 30 years; He retires to his den for study; to retire from a game such as basketball or cricket by being put out; She retires daily (to bed) at 11 p.m.; She likes a hot bath before retiring.* **2** withdraw: *We'll just retire him to make room for a better worker; to retire bonds, loans, etc. (from circulation);* ***adj.***: *a shy* **retiring** (= reserved) *man.*

retired 1 *adj.* no longer in service: *a retired teacher; retired people.* **2** *adja.* having to do with retirement: *to lead a retired life; the retired list (of retired people); a retired allowance or pay (for retired people).* **3** *adj.* withdrawn: *a reserved and retired character;* ***adja.*** *a retired* (= secluded) *spot.*

re.tir.ee (ri.tye.REE) *n.* one who has retired.

re.tire.ment (ri.TIRE.munt) *n.* the state of being no longer in service: *He went into early retirement at 50; compulsory, forced retirement; Al lives in retirement in Florida; She came out of retirement and started a new business.*

re.tool (ri.TOOL) *v.* change over to new tools, dies, and such machinery, as at the beginning of a new production season.

re.tort (ri.TORT) *n.* **1** a container, usu. of glass, for distilling substances. **2** a quick, sharp, or witty reply: *He made an angry retort.* —*v.*: *He retorted angrily that he was quitting.*

re.touch (ri.TUCH) *v.* improve a photograph, composition, etc. by slight changes.

re.trace (ri.TRACE) *v.* **-trac.es, -traced, -trac.ing** go back over the way one came, over past actions, etc.: *to retrace a route, one's steps, the story of one's life.*

re.tract (ri.TRACT) *v.* **1** draw back, as claws or fangs. **2** withdraw a statement, promise, etc. —**re.trac.tion** *n.*: *to issue, make a retraction.*

re.tract.a.ble (ri.TRAC.tuh.bul) *adj.* that can be drawn back: *the retractable roof of our domed stadium; an aircraft's retractable landing gear.*

re.trac.tile (ri.TRAC.tile, -til) *adj.* having the quality of being retractable: *a cat's retractile claws.*

re.tread *v.* (ree.TRED) **-treads, -tread.ed, -tread.ing** same as RECAP, *v.* 1.
—*n.* (REE.tred) **1** a retreaded tire. **2** a new tread.

re.treat (ri.TREET) *n.* **1** a going back or withdrawal, as from battle: *The retreat was hasty, precipitate, but carried out in good order; a tactical retreat.* **2** a signal for a military retreat: *A retreat is sounded on a bugle or drum; The retreat played at dusk ends the working day; They* **beat a retreat** (= ran away). **3** a temporary withdrawal from regular occupations for self-improvement: *We went on a weekend retreat; We go into retreat every year.* **4** a place of seclusion; refuge: *a country retreat; mountain retreats.* —*v.* make a retreat: *The enemy*

retreated before the advancing armies; They retreated to the mountains; The government retreated from its previous position on wage-and-price controls.
re.trench (ri.TRENCH) *v.* reduce expenses, staff, etc. for economy; **re.trench.ment** *n.*
ret.ri.bu.tion (ret.ruh.BYOO.shun) *n.* deserved punishment for one's actions: *Divine retribution was visited on the unjust; They were determined to exact retribution from the ruling party.* —**re.trib.u.tive** (-TRIB.yuh.tiv) *adj.a.* punishing: *the retributive God of the Old Testament; retributive justice.*
re.trieve (ri.TREEV) *v.* **-trieves, -trieved, -triev.ing** regain by making an effort, as a dog, or **retriever**, trained to fetch killed or wounded game: *to retrieve misplaced articles, one's reputation, data from computer storage.* —**re.triev.a.ble** (-vuh.bul) *adj.* —**re.triev.al** (-vul) *n.*
re.triev.er (ri.TREE.vur) *n.* a dog trained to fetch killed or wounded game.
retro- *comb.form.* back or backward: *retroactive, retrofire, retrofit.*
ret.ro.ac.tive (ret.roh.AC.tiv) *adj.* covering a period that is past: *a retroactive law; a decision with retroactive effect; a pay raise retroactive to January 1;* **ret.ro.ac.tive.ly** *adv.* —**ret.ro.ac.tiv.i.ty** (RET.roh.ac.TIV.i.tee) *n.*
ret.ro.fire (RET.roh.fire) *v.* **-fires, -fired, -fir.ing** fire a retrorocket. —*n.* such firing.
ret.ro.fit (RET.roh.fit) *v.* **-fits, -fit.ted, -fit.ting** modify a machine, vehicle, etc. by fitting it with newly designed parts or equipment: *an oil furnace retrofitted with new devices to increase efficiency.*
ret.ro.grade (RET.roh.grade) *adj.* tending to take one backward; hence, not progressive: *retrograde ideas, policies, steps.*
ret.ro.gress (ret.ruh.GRES) *v.* move backward; **ret.ro.gres.sion** (-GRESH.un) *n.* —**ret.ro.gress.ive** (-GRES.iv) *adj.*
ret.ro.rock.et (RET.roh.rock.it) *n.* on a spacecraft, a small rocket that fires in the direction of flight in order to slow the craft down.
ret.ro.spect (RET.ruh.spect) *n.* esp. **in retrospect,** when looking back at what is past: *In retrospect, we shouldn't have done that; What happened last night looks funny in retrospect.* —**ret.ro.spec.tion** (-SPEC.shun) *n.* —**ret.ro.spec.tive** (-SPEC.tiv) *adj.;* **ret.ro.spec.tive.ly** *adv.*

ret.ro.vi.rus (RET.roh.vye.rus) *n.* an RNA virus such as HIV that makes DNA using RNA instead of the other way round.
re.turn (ri.TURN) *v.* come, go, give, take, or send back: *We return home from school at 4; He'll return to work on Monday; Return all borrowed books; to return a blow, compliment, visit; to return* (= give) *thanks to God; A jury returns* (= reports) *a verdict; A candidate is returned* (= elected) *to a legislature or political office; an enterprise that returns* (= yields as profit or earnings) *$10 million annually.* —**n.** a returning or thing returned: *Service will resume on our return to work from holidays; to file an income-tax return* (= report); *a joint* (tax) *return by husband and wife; to do a favor* **in return** (= in compensation) *for another; a business that folded because of poor returns* (= yield); *The return on investment* (= profit) *was just 5%; We wish you* **many happy returns** (= many more days like this); *The election* **returns** (= results) *are not in yet.* —**adj.**: *a return address, date, journey, match, trip; the return air fare, postage;* **by return mail** (= as soon as possible). —**re.turn.a.ble** (ri.TUR.nuh.bul) *adj.*: *a returnable container;* **n.**: *returnables and recyclables.*
re.turn.ee (ri.tur.NEE, ri.TUR.nee) *n.* one who has returned, as from service overseas.
re.un.ion (ree.YOON.yun) *n.* a uniting again: *a touching reunion of family members separated by war; to hold annual, class, family reunions; to hope for a reunion after a divorce.*
rev *n. Informal.* a revolution of a motor. —*v.* **revs, revved, rev.ving** increase the speed of a motor, as by pressing the gas pedal of an automobile: *The company is revving up* (= increasing) *its public relations.*
re.vamp (ree.VAMP) *v.* patch up; hence, reconstruct or revise: *a dissertation revamped into a book; a company trying to revamp its corporate image;* **adj.**: *a revamped idea, exhibit, look, menu, product line, project.*
re.vanche (ruh.VAHNSH) *n. French.* revenge.
re.vanch.ism (ruh.VANCH.iz.um) *n.* the aggressiveness of a defeated nation seeking to recover lost territory; **re.vanch.ist** *n.*
re.veal (ri.VEEL) *v.* make known or visible something that is hidden: *to reveal a secret; He revealed to us that he was the child's true father;* **adj.**: *a very*

revealing gown (that exposes more of the body than is customary).

rev.eil.le (REV.uh.lee) n. a bugle call for awakening soldiers in the morning.

rev.el (REV.ul) v. -els, -eled, -el.ing 1 take part in a revel. 2 take much pleasure in an activity: *a playboy who revels away his nights; Writers revel in words; Some children revel in mischief-making.* —n. same as REVELRY. —**rev.el.er** n. Also **rev.elled, rev.el.ling; rev.el.ler** *Cdn.*

rev.e.la.tion (rev.uh.LAY.shun) n. a revealing or something revealed, esp. something startling and usu. pleasing: *He made an astounding, startling, stunning revelation; Her royal roots were a revelation to us; the revelation that her father was of royal blood; the divine revelation made to Moses.* —**re.vel.a.to.ry** (REV.uh.luh.tor.ee) *adj.*

rev.el.ry (REV.ul.ree) n. -ries a boisterous merrymaking.

re.venge (ri.VENJ) v. -veng.es, -venged, -veng.ing avenge a wrong or wronged person in a retaliatory or malicious spirit. —n. a revenging; also, a desire or opportunity for taking vengeance: *something done in the spirit of revenge; Hamlet was told to exact or get or have or take (his) revenge on Claudius for his father's murder; to kill him in revenge for his father's murder; "Revenge is sweet" to the unforgiving.* —**revenge oneself** or **be revenged** take vengeance *on* someone. —**re.venge.ful** *adj.*

rev.e.nue (REV.uh.new) n. 1 income, esp. from an investment: *Sales generate, produce, yield revenue; annual, monthly, yearly revenues.* 2 a government's income from taxes, customs, duties, etc.: *The tax department collects revenue; adja.: revenue collection, figures, growth, loss, shortfall, structure; Federal **revenue sharing** with state and local governments; A **revenue stamp** is proof of payment of a government tax.* —**rev.e.nu.er** n. a tax official.

re.verb (ri.VURB) n. [short form] 1 reverberation: *reverb acoustics, effects, levels; digital reverb technology.* 2 a device for producing reverbs: *digital reverbs; reverb units.*

re.ver.ber.ate (ri.VUR.buh.rate) v. -rates, -rat.ed, -rat.ing reecho; hence, resound: *The applause reverberated through the hallways; The whole town reverberated with the good news; It reverberated across the nation; Oil prices doubled and caused a reverberating inflation in the economy.* —**re.ver.ber.a.tion** (-RAY.shun) n.

re.vere (ri.VEER) v. -veres, -vered, -ver.ing regard, usu. a person, with great respect and love: *Indians revere Gandhi as the father of their nation; an emperor revered as a god; adj.: someone so universally revered as Mother Teresa; a woman revered for her humanitarian work; the revered dollar; a revered leader, name, patriarch.*

rev.er.ence (REV.uh.runce) n. love and respect mixed with awe: *a name held in reverence by everyone; He felt, showed a deep reverence for life; reverence for ancestors, religious values, tradition; She treated them with reverence.* —v. -enc.es, -enced, -enc.ing regard with reverence.

rev.er.end (REV.uh.rund) *adja.* 1 worthy of being revered: *the reverend gentlemen over there.* 2 **Reverend** [used as title for a member of the clergy]: *the Reverend Anne Jones; the Reverend A. Jones; the Reverend Miss Jones; the Reverend Sister Smith; the Reverend Father Smith.* —n. *Informal.* a member of the clergy, esp. a minister: *He is a reverend; Ask the reverend; Hi, Reverend!*

rev.er.ent (REV.uh.runt) *adj.* feeling or showing reverence: *a reverent attitude, awe, hush, posture, spirit; reverent singing of the psalms.* —**rev.er.en.tial** (-REN.shul) *adj.* cause by reverence: *a reverential account, bow, pose, tone, zeal.* —**rev.er.en.tial.ly** *adv.*: *Her ashes are reverentially preserved in a glass case; He spoke reverentially of his parents.* —**rev.er.ent.ly** (-runt.lee) *adv.*: *He was reverently referred to as "Father."*

rev.er.ie (REV.uh.ree) n. a pleasant daydream: *Sam reads romances and indulges in reveries.* Also **rev.er.y, -er.ies.**

re.vers (ruh.VEER, -VAIR) n., pl. -vers (-VEERS, -VAIRS) a part of a garment such as a lapel that has been turned back and stitched to show the underside of the material.

re.ver.sal (ri.VUR.sul) n. a reversing.

re.verse (ri.VURSE) n. 1 the opposite or contrary. *Selling is the reverse of buying.* 2 something that is opposite, esp. in direction: *to put a car in reverse (gear); Watch the rear before you go into or shift into reverse; the obverse and the reverse (= back) of a coin; He suffered or sustained many financial reverses (= setbacks or misfortunes) before reaching his present position.* —*adja.*: *Z, Y, X, W ... is in reverse alphabetical order; the reverse image in a mirror;* **reverse**

revert / revolt

discrimination (against members of the majority group); the **reverse video** mode of screen display with the colors of the characters and background reversed.
—v. -vers.es, -versed, -vers.ing turn to the other side or in an opposite direction: *Children learning to write sometimes reverse their letters; to reverse a car* (= drive backward); *to reverse* (= cancel) *a judicial decision; to reverse a policy, trend; to reverse the charges (of a telephone call so that the recipient, not caller, pays).* —**re.verse.ly** *adv* —**re.vers.i.ble** (-suh.bul) *adj.*

re.vert (ri.VURT) *v.* **1** go back or return, as offspring to an ancestral type or thoughts to a previous subject or something recalled. **2** of property, go back to a prior owner: *Copyright reverts to the author (from the publisher) when a book goes out of print.* —**re.ver.sion** (ri.VUR.zhun) *n.*

re.vet.ment (ri.VET.munt) *n.* **1** a facing of stone, concrete, or brick protecting an embankment. **2** a retaining wall.

re.view (riv.YOO) *n.* **1** a looking at or examination, as of work or events at the end of a period, a higher court's examination of a lower court's decision, or the inspection of troops at a parade: *a comprehensive review of the war; to hold a review of the troops; Your pay is under review; As she lay dying, her whole life passed in review before her.* **2** a critical evaluation of a new book, movie, play, concert, etc.: *to do or write a (book) review; The book got or received favorable, positive, rave reviews in the media;* **adja.:** *a review article; review copies (of books for review).* **3** a magazine dealing with current affairs, including also book reviews: *cultural, financial, literary reviews.* **4** same as REVUE.
—v. to study or examine: *to review a decision, movie, situation; to review evidence, options, policies; to review a book (in a journal); He's reviewing (lessons) for the exam; to review* (= inspect) *a parade;* **adj.:** *a reviewing room, system; The soldiers marched past the reviewing stand.* —**re.view.er** *n.: book reviewers.*

re.vile (ri.VILE) *v.* -viles, -viled, -vil.ing abuse with words; slander.
—**re.vile.ment** *n.;* **re.vil.er** *n.*

re.vise (ri.VIZE) *v.* -vis.es, -vised, -vis.ing to change, correct, or improve something already done: *to revise an agreement, book, estimate, list, plan, system;* **adj.:** *a revised edition, estimate, plan, treaty; the 1881-85 Revised Version of the King James Bible; the 1952 Revised Standard Version of the*

American Standard Version of the Bible.
—*n.* a revised form of something.
—**re.vis.er** or **re.vi.sor** *n.* —**re.vis.ion** (-VIZH.un) *n.*

re.vi.tal.ize (ree.VYE.tul.ize) *v.* -iz.es, -ized, -iz.ing give new vigor or vitality to something: *to revitalize a business, career, community, company, the economy, a movement, neighborhood, one's spirit;* **adj.:** *a revitalized city, industry, leadership, society.* —**re.vi.tal.i.za.tion** (-luh.ZAY.shun, -lye-) *n.*

re.viv.al (ri.VYE.vul) *n.* **1** a reviving or being revived; also, a revitalization: *a revival of our ailing economy; We are experiencing a revival of family values; the* **Revival of Learning** (= the Renaissance) *in Europe.* **2** a new presentation of a play, fresh publication of a book, etc.: *a Broadway revival.* **3** an evangelistic meeting for renewal of religious fervor: *a revival meeting, preacher.*
—**re.viv.al.ism** *n.;* **re.viv.al.ist** *n.*

re.vive (ri.VIVE) *v.* -vives, -vived, -viv.ing **1** bring back a person, idea, hope, practice, activity, etc. from a lifeless, unconscious, or inactive condition: *Fresh air seemed to revive her spirits; The news story revived old memories; to revive confidence, hopes, interest, one's fortunes; to revive an attempt, economy, feeling, image, influence, threat, tradition;* **adj.:** *a revived dispute, effort, fashion, interest, nation, project, rumor.* **2** come back to an active condition: *The dying plant soon revived; Fears of fresh violence revived.*

re.viv.i.fy (ree.VIV.uh.fye) *v.* -fies, -fied, -fy.ing give new life or vigor to something: *Germany was reunited and revivified.* —**re.viv.i.fi.ca.tion** (-fuh.CAY.shun) *n.*

re.voke (ri.VOKE) *v.* -vokes, -voked, -vok.ing cancel a privilege, trust, grant, or license by withdrawing it.
—**rev.o.ca.tion** (rev.uh.CAY.shun) *n.*

re.volt (ri.VOLT) *n.* an uprising: *The Peasants' Revolt of 1381 against oppressive conditions was quickly put down; to incite, stir up a revolt; They tried to crush, quell the revolt; the revolt of the American colonies; labor, peasant, popular, rent, slave, student, tax revolts.*
—*v.* **1** turn away in protest; rebel: *The colonies revolted (against Britain).* **2** disgust: *Cannibalism is a practice that revolts human nature; something that every normal person revolts against* (= finds disgusting); **adj.:** *a revolting* (= disgusting) *act, creature, crime, habit, practice; The movie is revolting and grotesque.*

rev.o.lu.tion (rev.uh.LOO.shun) *n.* **1** the overthrow of something established, esp. a regime: *to foment, organize, stir up a revolution; to crush, defeat, put down a revolution; the French Revolution of 1789-99.* **2** a radical or complete change: *the Industrial Revolution; cultural, sexual, social revolutions; the electronic revolution of the 1980s.* **3** a going around in an orbit: *The annual revolution of the earth round the sun causes the revolution* (= cycle) *of the seasons; a motor that makes 5,200 revolutions* (= rotations) *per minute.*
—**rev.o.lu.tion.ar.y** (-nair.ee) *n. & adj.* -**ar.ies.** —**rev.o.lu.tion.ist** *n.*
rev.o.lu.tion.ize (rev.uh.LOO.shuh.nize) *v.* -**iz.es,** -**ized,** -**iz.ing** change completely or radically: *Automation has revolutionized industry.*
re.volve (ri.VOLV) *v.* -**volves,** -**volved,** -**volv.ing 1** (cause) to move in a circle around a center or axis: *Satellites revolve around their planets; a life of leisure revolving around TV; adja.: a revolving chair, restaurant, showcase; At work, we take holidays on a revolving basis.* **2** (cause) to turn over in the mind; reflect upon: *She's revolving the pros and cons before deciding.*
re.volv.er (ri.VOL.vur) *n.* a handgun with five to seven cartridges contained in a revolving cylinder: *to aim, level, point a revolver at someone; to cock, draw, fire, load, whip out a revolver; A revolver is fired, goes off, jams, misfires.*
revolving credit *n.* a system in which credit is automatically renewed as bills are paid off, as in using charge cards.
revolving door *n.* a four-leaved entrance door that turns around a vertical axis to keep out drafts: *In* ***revolving-door medicine,*** *patients are whisked in and out of doctors' offices with minimal checking and treatment.*
re.vue (ri.VUE, *rhyme:* view) *n.* a variety show consisting of songs, skits, chorus dances, etc.: *to put on* or *stage a revue.*
re.vul.sion (ri.VUL.shun) *n.* a strong feeling of reaction in disgust or horror: *to express, feel revulsion against* or *at* or *toward mass murderers; a feeling of deep, utmost revulsion.*
re.ward (ri.WORED) *n.* something in return for a service, esp. in recognition of merit: *The police offered, paid, posted a reward for information about the wanted man; to claim, reap, receive a reward; a due, just, tangible, well-deserved reward; Is virtue its own reward? the intellectual rewards of scholarship.*
—*v.* give a reward to someone: *They rewarded him with a life-time pension; adjp.: He felt amply rewarded* (= recompensed) *for his time and effort; adj.: a rewarding* (= satisfying or gratifying) *experience.*
re.wind (ree.WINED) *v.* **re.winds, re.wound** (-WOWND), **re.wind.ing 1** wind back, as exposed film in a camera. **2** wind again.
—*n.* (REE.wined) a rewinding: *a vacuum with automatic cord rewind; the rewind button of a VCR.*
re.word (ree.WURD) *v.* word differently: *to reword a statement.*
re.write (ree.RITE) *v.* -**writes,** -**wrote,** -**writ.ten,** -**writ.ing** write something differently or in an improved form; revise: *They rewrite rules to suit their own agenda; A party coming to power tries to* ***rewrite history*** (= improve on the past; also, ignore it).
—*n.* (REE.rite) a rewritten story or script; *adja.: the rewrite desk (of a newspaper); our rewrite man.*
rhap.so.dize (RAP.suh.dize) *v.* -**diz.es,** -**dized,** -**diz.ing** go into raptures *about* or *over* something.
rhap.so.dy (RAP.suh.dee) *n.* -**dies 1** a highly enthusiastic expression of feeling, esp. of delight: *rhapsodies of flowery speeches.* **2** a musical composition such as Liszt's "Hungarian Rhapsodies." —**rhap.so.dist** *n.* —**rhap.sod.ic** (rap.SOD.ic) or **rhap.sod.i.cal** *adj.;* **rhap.sod.i.cal.ly** *adv.*
rhe.a (REE.uh) *n.* a South American bird resembling but smaller than the ostrich.
Rhen.ish (REN.ish) *n. & adj.* (a wine) of the region of the Rhine river in Europe.
rhe.ni.um (REE.nee.um) *n.* a rare, silvery-white, metallic element used in alloys.
rhe.o.stat (REE.uh.stat) *n.* a resistor for regulating the flow of electric current, as used in dimmer switches.
—**rhe.o.stat.ic** (-STAT.ic) *adj.*
rhe.sus monkey (REE.sus-) *n.* a macaque of S.E. Asia in which the Rh factor was discovered in 1940.
rhet.o.ric (RET.uh.ric) *n.* **1** the art of effective writing and speaking; hence, skill in this: *rhetoric and oratory.* **2** showy eloquence: *to indulge in, resort to rhetoric; eloquent, heated, impassioned, soothing rhetoric; mere empty political rhetoric; more rhetoric than reality.*
—**rhet.o.ri.cian** (-RISH.un) *n.*
rhe.tor.i.cal (ri.TOR.i.cul) *adj.* having to do with rhetoric; empty: *A* ***rhetorical***

question such as "Is everything satisfactory?" is asked mostly for effect.

rheum (ROOM) *n.* a watery discharge or flow, as mucus or tears.

rheu.mat.ic (roo.MAT.ic) *adj.* having to do with rheumatism: *a rheumatic patient.* —*n.* one who has rheumatism.

rheu.ma.tism (ROO.muh.tiz.um) *n.* any of several diseases affecting the muscles and joints, as rheumatic fever, arthritis, etc.

rheu.ma.toid arthritis (ROO.muh.toid-) *n.* an often crippling disease characterized by inflammation and stiffness of the joints.

Rh factor (AR.AICH-) *n.* an antigen present in the red blood cells of most people, or **Rh positive** people: *Rh factor incompatibility* (= **Rh negative** people not being able to safely receive Rh positive transfusions).

rhine.stone (RINE.stone) *n.* **1** an imitation diamond of cut glass or paste. **2** faceted rock crystal, originally from Germany.

rhi.ni.tis (rye.NYE.tis) *n.* inflammation of the nasal mucous membranes, caused by hay fever, a cold, etc.

rhi.no (RYE.noh) *n.* [short form] rhinoceros.

rhi.noc.er.os (rye.NOS.uh.rus) *n.* a huge beast with one or two upward-curving horns on its nose.

rhi.zome (RYE.zome) *n.* the rootlike but usu. horizontal underground stem of wild ginger, mint, and such perennials.

Rh negative, Rh positive See RH FACTOR.

rho.di.um (ROH.dee.um) *n.* a hard, silvery-white metallic element.

rho.do.den.dron (roh.duh.DEN.drun) *n.* an evergreen woody plant of the heath family bearing spectacular clusters of flowers.

rhom.boid (ROM.boid) *n.* an oblique-angled parallelogram having opposite sides equal. —*adj.* shaped like a rhombus or rhomboid; also **rhom.boi.dal** (rom.BOY.dul).

rhom.bus (ROM.bus) *n.* **-bus.es** or **-bi** (-bye) an oblique-angled parallelogram having all sides equal.

rhu.barb (ROO.barb) *n.* **1** a perennial vegetable with reddish, juicy stalks that are used in desserts. **2** *Slang.* a heated argument: *to get into a rhubarb about something.*

rhyme (RIME) *n.* **1** similarity of end sounds between words, as in "beside/decried" and "wall/fall," esp. as used at the ends of lines of verse: *He gets mad at people without **rhyme or reason*** (= without sense or logic). **2** verse or poetry, esp. a simple verse composition that rhymes: *a nursery rhyme.* —*v.* **rhymes, rhymed, rhym.ing** make rhymes or put into rhymes: *"Head" doesn't rhyme with "bead"; They don't rhyme; the art of rhyming; Rickman is an operator with a **"rhymes with slick"** image;* **adj.**: *Blank verse is so called because it is not **rhymed**;* **adja.**: *rhyming lines, slang, words; fast-rhyming rap music.*

rhym.er or **rhyme.ster** (RIME.stur) *n.* [derogatory] one who makes rhymes; versifier.

rhythm (RITH.um, "TH" as in "the") *n.* a regularly repeated sound forming a pattern suggesting movement, as the tread of marching soldiers, the beating of the heart, the beat of strong and weak syllables in verse, the duration of musical bars, etc.: *We danced to the frenzied rhythm of the music; heavy, pulsating, steady, strong rhythms; a children's **rhythm band** of percussion instruments.* —**rhyth.mic** or **rhyth.mi.cal** *adj.* —**rhyth.mi.cal.ly** *adv.*

rhythm and blues *n.* popular American music influenced by rock-and-roll and blues.

rhythm method *n.* birth control involving avoidance of intercourse during ovulation.

ri.al (ree.AWL, -AHL) *n.* the basic money unit of Iran and Oman. See also RIYAL.

rib *n.* **1** one of the 12 pairs of curved bones attached to the backbone and forming the chest cavity enclosing the heart, stomach, and other organs: *to break* or *fracture a rib; She made the child laugh by poking him **in the ribs**.* **2** anything resembling a rib, as the metal strips supporting an umbrella's cloth, the keel-to-deck timbers of a ship's frame, etc. —*v.* **ribs, ribbed, rib.bing** **1** form or furnish with ribs; *adj.: a **ribbed** cardigan; ribbed like corduroy.* **2** *Informal.* tease, like poking in the ribs: *Al sometimes gets ribbed about being a househusband;* **n.**: *He took a **ribbing** about it from his buddies.*

rib.ald (RIB.uld) *adj.* vulgarly or indecently humorous: *ribald humor, jokes, remarks, tales.* —**rib.ald.ry** *n.*

rib.and (RIB.und) *n. Archaic.* ribbon.

rib.bon (RIB.un) *n.* a narrow strip or band of material, as used to tie hair or packages, to decorate costumes, or as a badge of honor or membership: *to change a printer ribbon; His shirt was*

cut or torn to **ribbons** (= tatters); *it hung in ribbons.*
rib cage *n.* the chest cavity.
ri.bo.fla.vin (RYE.buh.flay.vin) *n.* a growth-promoting vitamin of the B complex found in liver, milk, eggs, etc.
ri.bo.nu.cle.ic acid (RYE.buh.new. CLEE.ic-) *n.* a nucleic acid that functions in protein synthesis and as a carrier of genetic codes; RNA.
ri.bose (RYE.bose) *n.* a sugar present in all animal and plant cells.
ri.bo.some (RYE.buh.sohm) *n.* one of the cell structures that are the site of protein synthesis. —**ri.bo.so.mal** (-SOH.mul) *adj.*
rice *n.* **1** a cereal grass of warm countries, grown esp. in Asia for food. **2** its grains boiled for food: *converted rice; polished rice; wild rice.* —*v.* **ric.es, riced, ric.ing** make cooked potatoes, etc. into ricelike grains.
rich *adj.* having more resources, esp. money, property, etc. than is required for normal needs: *a rich banker; Arab nations rich in oil; They* **struck it rich** *during the 1970s; a rich cake, fuel mixture, soil; rich colors, food, furnishings, tones; That's rich (Informal for very amusing)!* —**the rich** *n.pl.* wealthy people: *the life of the idle rich.* —**rich.es** *n.pl.* wealth: *to amass riches; the story of his rise from rags to riches.* —**rich.ly** *adv.;* **rich.ness** *n.*
Rich.ter scale (RIK.tur-) *n.* a scale of numbers for measuring the strength of an earthquake, 8 or more being the most destructive and 4 and below being hardly noticeable.
rick *n.* an outdoor stack of hay, straw, etc.
rick.ets (RIK.its) *n.* a vitamin-deficiency disease affecting esp. children, resulting in bowlegs, knock-knees, etc. from softened bones.
rick.ett.si.a (ri.KET.see.uh) *n., pl.* **-ae** (-ee) a rod-shaped microorganism responsible for parrot fever, typhus, and other diseases; **rick.ett.si.al** *adj.*
rick.et.y (RIK.uh.tee) *adj.* feeble or shaky: *a rickety old structure.*
rick.rack *n.* a zigzag braid used as trimming on clothes.
rick.sha or **rick.shaw** (RIK.shaw) same as JINRIKISHA.
ric.o.chet (RIK.uh.shay) *n.* a glancing rebound or skip from a surface, as a bullet off a wall or a flat stone off a water surface. —*v.* **-chets,** *pt. & pp.* **-cheted** (-shayed), **-chet.ing** (-shay.ing) make a ricochet: *The bullet ricocheted*

rib cage / rider

off the windshield. Also **ric.o.chet.ed** (-shet.id), **ric.o.chet.ing** (-shet.ing) Brit.
rid *v.* **rids,** *pt. & pp.* **rid** or **rid.ded, rid.ding** make free of something undesirable: *to rid a dog of fleas; to be rid of the nuisance; I tried to* **get rid of** *it.*
rid.dance (RID.unce) *n.* a ridding: *Good riddance to bad rubbish! It was* **good riddance** (= welcome relief) *when the noisy party left.*
rid.den *pp.* of RIDE. —*comb.form.* dominated by what is specified: *crime-ridden, debt-ridden, disease-ridden, drug-ridden, guilt-ridden.*
rid.dle (RID.ul) *n.* **1** a puzzling question, often sounding contradictory, and requiring a witty answer, as "What grows bigger the more you take from it?" (A hole): *to pose, solve a riddle; to speak in riddles like a sphinx, like an oracle.* **2** a coarse sieve, as for grading potatoes or sifting coal.
—*v.* **rid.dles, rid.dled, rid.dling** **1** talk in riddles; also, solve: *Riddle me this.* **2** make holes in something: *The car was riddled with bullets; a road riddled with potholes; a department* **riddled with** (= full of) *corruption; cpd.: a bullet-riddled wall; loophole-riddled contracts.* **3** sift with a riddle.
ride *v.* **rides, rode, rid.den** (RID.un), **rid.ing** **1** sit on and manage an animal or vehicle: *to ride a bicycle, horse; a child riding her father piggyback; a mind* **ridden** (= dominated) *by fears.* **2** travel or be carried by an animal or vehicle: *He rides to work by bus; He has never ridden on or in a train; She just rode by; A ship rides the waves; rides at anchor in the harbor; a kite riding the winds; a car that rides* (= runs) *smoothly; The future of the company rides* (= depends) *on this publication; The government decided to* **ride out** *the storm* (= wait patiently for it to pass); *He's never been known to* **ride roughshod over** (= mistreat) *his employees.* —*n.* **1** a riding: *to go for* or *go on* or *take a ride; to get a ride from someone; to give someone a ride; a joy ride in a stolen car; to bum* or *hitch* or *thumb a ride (Informal for* hitchhike). **2** something to ride, as a Ferris wheel: *to go on the rides at a fair.* —**let ride** *Informal.* let pass or leave undisturbed. —**take someone for a ride** *Informal.* cheat or victimize someone.
rid.er (RYE.dur) *n.* **1** one who rides. **2** something appended to a contract, bill, etc. as an amendment or addition. —**rid.er.ship** *n.: Transit ridership* (= number of riders) *is up this year.*

ridge (RIJ) *n.* a long and narrow, usu. horizontal line formed by the meeting of two rising surfaces: *the ridge of a mountain range, of an animal's back, of the nose; the ridges on a corded fabric, on plowed land between furrows, of high pressure on a weather map; the ridge of a roof topped by a* **ridgepole** *to which rafters are fastened.* —*v.* **ridg.es, ridged, ridg.ing** form into or extend in ridges: *The floor of the Atlantic ridges in the middle from north to south; adj.: a* **ridged** *edge for a better grip.*

rid.i.cule (RID.i.cule) *n.* mockery, esp. using words: *The new scheme has drawn or incurred the ridicule of the media; Today's cartoon holds it up to ridicule; The editorial heaps or pours ridicule on the scheme.* —*v.* **-cules, -culed, -cul.ing** subject a person or thing to ridicule.

ri.dic.u.lous (ri.DIK.yuh.lus) *adj.* arousing laughter; absurd: *It's ridiculous to spend so much money on the scheme; It's ridiculous that they want $500 million for the project.* —**ri.dic.u.lous.ly** *adv.*

riding (RYE.ding) *n.* a Canadian electoral district; constituency.

ri.el (ree.EL) *n.* the basic money unit of Cambodia.

rife *adjp.* widespread: *Rumors about his death are rife, esp. in his hometown; His hometown is* **rife with** (= full of) *rumors of his death.*

riff *n.* a recurring melodic phrase in jazz.

rif.fle (RIF.ul) *n.* 1 a choppy stretch of water formed by a shoal or reef. 2 the patch of ripples caused thus. 3 a way of shuffling cards by combining the separate decks into one while their edges are bent and rapidly released against each other.
—*v.* **rif.fles, rif.fled, rif.fling** 1 shuffle cards in this manner. 2 leaf rapidly: *to riffle through a book, through files, pages, papers.* 3 make ripples in water, sand, etc.: *See the breeze riffling the water on the lake.*

riff.raff *n.* worthless or disreputable people.

ri.fle (RYE.ful) *v.* **-fles, -fled, -fling** 1 cut spiral grooves in a gun barrel, as of a rifle. 2 search as a robber: *to rifle through office files.*
—*n.* 1 a long-barreled gun that fires its bullets with a spinning motion: *to aim, fire, handle, level, load, point a rifle; air, assault, automatic, hunting rifles; Rifles fire, go off, misfire;* **adja.:** *rifle barrels, butts, fire, ranges; to take the* **rifle approach** *to selling (aimed at specific groups of customers) instead of the scatter-gun approach.* 2 a body of riflemen: *the Queen's Rifles.* —**ri.fler** *n.*

ri.fle.man (RYE.ful.mun) *n.* **-men** a soldier armed with a rifle.

rift *n.* 1 a cleft or fissure. 2 a breach of friendship: *to cause a rift among the partners; to heal the rift between the two.* —*v.* split or cleave.

rig *v.* **rigs, rigged, rig.ging** 1 fit out, as a ship, with rigging: *She came to the party rigged out in her best attire.* 2 manipulate dishonestly, as the outcome of a prizefight or election, market prices, etc. —*n.* 1 the kind and arrangement of a ship's rigging: *the fore-and-aft rig of a schooner.* 2 a large vehicle: *to drive a tractor-trailer rig.* 3 equipment: *an oil-drilling rig.*

rig.a.ma.role (RIG.uh.muh.role) same as RIGMAROLE.

rigging (RIG.ing) *n.* 1 ropes, chains, etc. supporting a ship's masts, sails, etc. 2 the similar network of ropes and chains controlling theater scenery.

right *adj.* 1 good, true, correct, just, or proper; not wrong: *You're right; She's right to say "No"; He's right in saying "No"; It's right of you to say "No"; It's not right that they should force you to say "Yes"; the right thing to say; That's just right for me; That's all right; the right clothes to wear.* 2 not left: *He writes with his right hand; the right side; He's politically* **Right** (= conservative). 3 straight, not slanting: *a* **right angle** *(of 90°); a right (circular) cone.*
—*adv.* 1 well, truly, correctly, justly, or properly: *You guessed right; Everything turned out right in the end.* 2 to the right side: *You face east if you turn right from north.* 3 straight: *I'll be right back; Let's do it right now; Come home* **right away** *or* **off** (= immediately); *(You're)* **right on!** (Informal for quite right); *the* **Right Honorable** *Chris Smith, the* **Right Reverend** *Pat Smith* [British titles used with the names of certain high officials and bishops, respectively].
—*n.* 1 that which is good, true, correct, etc.: *Infants can't tell right from wrong; She was in the right in saying "No."* 2 that to which one has a just claim: *You are within your rights to say "No"; a bill of rights; our social rights and responsibilities; to assert, claim, enjoy, exercise, gain, protect, relinquish, renounce, safeguard, sign away, waive a right; the divine right of kings; basic, civil, conjugal, exclusive, fundamental, human, inalienable, inherent, legal, natural, sole rights; women's rights; the right to exist, to remain silent; the right to life, liberty, etc.*

as in the Constitution. **3** the right side or wing: *We drive on the right (of the road); The boxer delivered or threw a stiff right (= blow) to the jaw.* **4 right** or **Right** a conservative or reactionary position, person, view, etc.: *a party of the right; the extreme, far right in politics.* —**by right** or **rights** justly: *By rights, she should have got the job.* —*v.* **1** put in order what is wrong: *to right an error, imbalance, injustice, wrong.* **2** make straight what is slanting or overturned: *to right the picture on the wall.* **3** become straight: *The boat righted itself.* —**right.ly** *adv.;* **right.ness** *n.*
right.eous (RYE.chus) *adj.* **1** upright; morally blameless: *a righteous person.* **2** justifiable: *righteous indignation, zeal.* —**right.eous.ly** *adv.;* **right.eous.ness** *n.*
right.ful (RITE.ful) *adj.* according to just claims; by right: *the rightful owner; his rightful rank; a woman's rightful place in society.* —**right.ful.ly** *adv.*
right-hand *adj a.* **1** having to do with the right side: *on the driver's right-hand side; the minister's right-hand (= trusted) man.* **2** having to do with the right hand: *a right-hand blow, glove.*
right-handed *adj.* **1** having a tendency to use the right hand rather than the left: *a right-handed pitcher;* **adv.:** *He throws right-handed.* **2** turning clockwise: *a right-handed propeller, screw.* —**right-handedly** *adv.;* **right-handedness** *n.*
right.ist *n. & adj.* conservative or reactionary.
right-minded *adj.* morally or intellectually right: *a right-minded citizen, employer.*
right of way *n.* **rights of way 1** the right to go first, as of pedestrians at a crossing; precedence: *At a pedestrian crossing, people have the right of way over vehicles; Vehicles yield right of way to pedestrians.* **2** right to use land owned by another, as to walk through. **3** such land or land used by a public utility, railroad, or highway: *a power-line right-of-way.* Also **right-of-way, rights-of-way.**
right-to-life same as PRO-LIFE.
right wing *n.* **1** a front-line player or position to the right of center, as in hockey. **2** the rightist or most conservative group in a party; **adj a.: *right-wing** extremism, politics, views; a right-wing administration, group, Republican.* —**right-winger** *n.*
rig.id (RIJ.id) *adj.* stiff or strict, not bending or yielding: *the rigid frame of a rigid airship; a rigid disciplinarian;* *He's rigid about rules; rigid economic controls; rigid rules.* —**rig.id.ly** *adv.;* **rig.id.ness** *n.* —**ri.gid.i.ty** (ri.JID.i.tee) *n.:* *strength and rigidity; structural rigidity; ideological, intellectual rigidity.*
rig.ma.role (RIG.muh.role) *n.* words or action without sense; something too involved or incoherent.
rig.or (RIG.ur) *n.* **1** strictness or exactness: *a life of rigor and discipline; the rigor of his logic.* **2** severity or harshness: *the rigor of military training; the rigors of the Arctic climate.* —**rig.or.ous** *adj.;* **rig.or.ous.ly** *adv.;* **rig.or.ous.ness** *n.* Also **rig.our** *Cdn.*
rigor mor.tis *n.* stiffening of the muscles following death.
rile *v.* **riles, riled, ril.ing** *Informal.* irritate or anger: *It riled him that* or *He was riled that few turned up for the meeting.*
rill *n.* a small brook; rivulet.
rim *n.* a circular or curving edge, as the lip of a cup, the spectacle frame around the lenses, or the outer part of a wheel over which a tire is fitted: *He was standing on the rim of the canyon when he fell in.* —*v.* **rims, rimmed, rim.ming 1** form a rim around: *Skyscrapers rim the park;* **adj. & cpd.:** *a rimmed cookie sheet, pattern; gold-rimmed dishes; horn-rimmed, wire-rimmed glasses; eyes red-rimmed from nights without sleep.* **2** roll around the rim, as a basketball before dropping into the basket.
rime *n.* **1** [old use] same as RHYME: *"The Rime of the Ancient Mariner."* **2** hoarfrost; *v.* **rimes, rimed, rim.ing** cover with rime. —**rim.y** *adj.*
rind (RINED) *n.* the thick outer covering or skin of certain fruits such as the lemon and melon, of bacon, or of cheese.
¹**ring** *n.* **1** something curved round like a circle, as the ornamental band worn on a finger: *diamond, engagement, key, napkin, nose, wedding rings; the rings of Saturn; rings under the eyes (from old age); onion rings; piston rings; to blow smoke rings; the growth of tree rings; She can **run rings around** (= far outperform) him.* **2** an enclosed area for a circus or prizefight: *a wrestling ring; a three-ring circus; She threw her hat into **the ring** (= entered the contest as a candidate).* **3** a close group of people working with a selfish or secret aim: *crime, drug, prostitution, sex, smuggling, spy rings.* —*v.* **rings, ringed, ring.ing 1** encircle: *A highway rings the city; The house is ringed (about) with trees.* **2** place or put a ring, as in the nose of an ani-

mal or around a tree by cutting away bark.

²ring *v.* **rings, rang, ring.ing 1** give forth a clear sound, as a bell: *A phone rings; The story rings true (like a genuine coin) but it doesn't* **ring a bell** (= remind me of anything); *Our phone has been* **ringing off the hook** (= ringing constantly) *since the want ad appeared;* **adja.:** *a* **ringing** (= strong) *endorsement.* **2** use a bell as signal: *Please ring me at the office; Ring (the bell) for service; to* **ring down** *the curtain on* (= conclude) *a performance or action; Sales clerks* **ring up** (= record and total) *customers' purchases (on the cash register).* **3** be filled with a sound; resound: *a room* **ringing with** *laughter; a neighborhood ringing with a scandal; Her ears were still ringing with the scolding she got.* —*n.* **1** a sound of or like ringing: *Give me a ring* (= phone call) *when you're ready.* **2** its characteristic quality: *His story has the ring of truth; There's a false or hollow ring to her tale.*

ring binder *n.* a loose-leaf binder with pages held by metal rings that snap open and shut.

ring.er *n.* **1** one that rings: *a bell ringer.* **2** one that encircles: *She made a ringer with every toss of her horseshoe; She got or threw a ringer.* **3** a look-alike or substitute, often false: *a dead ringer for Jackie.* **4** See also **WRINGER**.

ring.ette (ring.ET) *n.* a less aggressive form of hockey played with a straight stick and a rubbery donutlike puck.

ring finger *n.* the finger next to the little finger.

ring.lead.er (RING.lee.dur) *n.* **1** the leader of a plot. **2** the leader of a ring of criminals.

ring.let (RING.lit) *n.* a small ring, as a curl of hair.

ring.mas.ter (RING.mas.tur) *n.* the director of performances in a circus ring.

ring.side *n.* a place close to a boxing or circus ring: *a ringside seat for a close view of the action.*

ring.worm *n.* a contagious fungus infection of the skin that spreads out in a ring.

rink *n.* **1** a smooth floor or surface prepared for hockey, skating, curling, etc.: *ice rinks.* **2** a building housing it: *We met at a rink.*

rink.y-dink (RINK.ee.dink) *adja.* *Slang.* shoddy or cheap: *rinky-dink crime, politics; a rinky-dink job, operation.*

rinse (RINCE) *v.* **rins.es, rinsed, rins.ing 1** wash lightly or cleanse thus,

as the mouth with water: *Rinse the soap out of your hair.* **2** to dye or tint hair, fabrics, etc. —*n.* a rinsing or something used for washing or tinting the hair: *a dental rinse for oral hygiene; the rinse cycle of a clothes washer.*

ri.ot (RYE.ut) *n.* **1** a violent outbreak or disturbance by a group of people: *Riots break out, erupt; to cause, crush, incite or instigate, put down, quell, spark a riot; communal, food, prison, race riots.* **2** something wild or unrestrained: *Our garden is a riot of color in the spring; You're a riot (Informal for extremely funny).* —**read the riot act** give official warning of consequences: *The coach read the riot act to his hockey team and they responded with a 3-2 victory.* —**run riot 1** be wild or unrestrained: *when conspicuous consumption runs riot.* **2** grow luxuriantly: *Weeds run riot in a neglected garden.* —*v.* engage in a riot: *The inmates rioted at the penitentiary; They rioted against the warden.* —**ri.ot.ous** (-tus) *adj.*; **ri.ot.ous.ly** *adv.*; **ri.ot.ous.ness** *n.*

rip *v.* **rips, ripped, rip.ping 1** tear or split apart quickly, esp. along a joining such as a seam or along the grain of wood, as with a ripsaw. **2** *Informal.* rush violently: *He came ripping up the street;* **ripped out with** (= uttered) *profanities; merciless* **ripped into** *her* (= attacked her verbally). —**rip off** *Informal.* **1** steal or rob: *taxes that rip off people; Tax evaders rip off the government.* **2** exploit or cheat: *the public ripped off by big business.* —*n.* a tear or rent: *a rip in his pants.* —**rip.per** *n.*

rip cord *n.* a cord by which a parachute is pulled open during descent.

ripe *adj.* **rip.er, rip.est 1** fully developed or mature: *The harvest is ripe; tomatoes ripe for the picking; ripe cheese, wine, wisdom; garbage that is pretty ripe* (= smelly); [often ironical] *The smoker died at the* **ripe old age** *of 35.* **2** ready for use, action, etc.: *The time is ripe for action, change, expansion.* —**ripe.ly** *adv.*; **ripe.ness** *n.*

rip.en (RYE.pun) *v.* make or become ripe: *Their relationship ripened into love;* *n.*: *the* **ripening** *of corn, cheese, fruit.*

rip-off *n. Informal.* an act of theft or exploitation: *income-tax rip-offs by corporations; the massive rip-off of medical insurance by overbilling; Third World rip-offs by capitalist countries; The show was a clever rip-off designed to plug a new movie; a rip-off artist.* Also **rip.off.**

ri.poste (ri.POHST) *n.* **1** a sharp, quick retort like a fencer's counterattack or thrust following a parry. **2** such a thrust.

rip.ple (RIP.ul) *n.* a series of little waves, as when still water is disturbed: *The wind makes ripples on our swimming pool; She has ripples in her hair; a ripple of laughter; Raising the minimum wage has a **ripple effect** (= spreading effect) on other wages.* —*v.* make a ripple: *sand rippled by the tide; breeze rippling a field of corn; Laughter rippled through the audience.*

rip-roaring *adj. Informal.* **1** boisterous; hilarious: *rip-roaring laughter, races.* **2** impressive: *a rip-roaring growth of sales; a rip-roaring 500%.*

rip.saw *n.* a saw that cuts wood in the direction of the grain.

rip.tide *n.* a surface current formed by waves returning after breaking on the shore.

rise (RIZE) *v.* **ris.es, rose, ris.en** (RIZ.un), **ris.ing** go up or get up, esp. gradually: *The sun rises in the east; smoke rising from a chimney; He rises (from bed) at 6 a.m.; Wages and prices keep rising; The rebels rose against the government; The general rose (in his career) from the ranks; the order to **rise and shine** (= get out of bed); a river that rises (= has its origin) in the Rockies; A resourceful person will **rise to the challenge, to the occasion** (= meet it successfully).* —*adj.*: *the risen sun (that has come up); the risen Christ (who has come back from the dead); the risen wind; the rising sun; rising rivers, storms, temperatures, tides; her rising indignation, tone of anger; the rising (= growing) generation.* —*n.* **1** an upward movement, slope, increase, etc.: *You can't see far because of a rise in the road; His meteoric rise to stardom; the rise and fall of the Roman Empire; the sharp rise in prices; Prices are **on the rise** (= increasing).* **2** origin or beginning: *the rise of the Fraser River in the Rockies; the rise of a storm; the theory of the rise of animals from lower forms of life; the rise of separatism.* —**get a rise out of** *Informal.* get an emotional response or reaction from someone. —**give rise to** originate something unwanted: *Unemployment gives rise to poverty and crime.*

ris.er (RYE.zur) *n.* **1** one that rises: *early, late risers.* **2** the vertical part between two steps. **3** a display platform, as in a store, that is raised above its surroundings.

ris.i.ble (RIZ.uh.bul) *adj.* having to do with laughter; funny. —**ris.i.bil.i.ty** (-BIL.i.tee) *n.* **-ties:** *It tickled his risibilities* (= sense of humor).

risk *n.* **1** the possibility of danger or loss of something: *a risk to life and limb, to safety; to assume, face, incur risks; calculated, grave, great, high, low risks; You* **run** *or* **take a risk** *by stepping into heavy traffic; You do so* **at the risk of** *being killed; You're putting your life* **at risk;** *Use the unfinished road* **at your own risk** *(= without claims for accidents, etc.).* **2** a person considered in regard to a risk: *She is a security risk; He was rejected for life insurance as a poor risk* (= hazard); *A healthy person is a good risk (for life insurers).* —*v.* incur or expose to a risk, esp. voluntarily: *You risk your life by driving while drunk; risk being killed and killing others.*

risk arbitrage *n.* the buying up of the stocks of firms threatened by takeover in the hope of selling them at the higher price resulting from the takeover.

risk capital same as VENTURE CAPITAL.

risk.y *adj.* **risk.i.er, -i.est** involving risk: *a risky life, undertaking, venture; It's risky to smoke in bed.* —**risk.i.ness** *n.*

ris.qué (ris.KAY) *adj.* close to being indecent; off-color: *risqué humor, lyrics, stories.*

rite *n.* **1** a ceremonial form or act: *to perform a rite; pagan, religious, solemn rites; initiation, funeral, marriage rites; to administer the **last rites** to a sick person; a Lenten rite* (= liturgy); *a **rite of passage** (= a ritual marking passage from one status to another, as at marriage or from childhood to adulthood).* **2** a church denomination: *the Greek Catholic Rite.*

rit.u.al (RICH.oo.ul) *n.* a system of rites or procedure as established for a usu. religious ceremony: *the Easter ritual; the ritual of voodoo; to go through a ritual for form's sake; She makes a ritual of her Sunday dinners;* **adj.**: *a ritual dance; ritual laws; the ritual slaughter of kosher chicken.* —**rit.u.al.ly** *adv.* —**rit.u.al.ism** *n.;* **rit.u.al.ist** *n.* —**rit.u.al.is.tic** (-LIS.tic) *adj.;* **rit.u.al.is.ti.cal.ly** *adv.*

ritz.y (RIT.see) *adj.* **ritz.i.er, -i.est** *Informal.* high-class; luxurious; plush: *a ritzy hotel, neighborhood, restaurant.* —**ritz.i.ness** *n.*

ri.val (RYE.vul) *n.* one trying to equal or surpass another; competitor: *They are rivals in rental cars; rivals for the same business; closest, main, primary rivals;* **adj.**: *a rival camp, company, gang, group, theory.* —*v.* **-vals, -valed, -val.ing** equal or excel: *We try harder every day to rival the leader of the market.*

Also **ri.valled, ri.val.ling** *Cdn.*
ri.val.ry (RYE.vul.ree) *n.* **-ries** competition between evenly matched opponents: *sibling rivalry; long-standing political rivalries; to stir up rivalry between partners; There is intense, keen, strong rivalry among them; rivalry for the top job.*
rive *v.* **rives,** *pt. & pp.* **rived** or **riv.en** (RIV.un), **riv.ing** split or tear apart violently.
riv.er (RIV.ur) *n.* a natural stream larger than a brook or creek, normally confined within banks, and flowing into a sea, lake, or another river: *to go up, down (the) river; His partner sold him down the river* (= betrayed him).
river basin *n.* the region drained by a river and its tributaries.
riv.er.bed (RIV.ur.bed) *n.* the channel in which a river flows.
riv.er.boat (RIV.ur.boat) *n.* a boat with shallow draft used on a river.
riv.er.front (RIV.ur.frunt) *n.* the area fronting a river: *along the city's riverfront;* *adja.:* *riverfront land; a riverfront development, park, property, site.*
riv.er.side (RIV.ur.side) *n.* the side of a river: *a building on the riverside;* *adja.:* *a riverside park, frontage, jetty, warehouse.*
riv.et (RIV.ut) *n.* a metal bolt whose plain end is flattened into another head after being passed through the parts to be joined together. —*v.* **-ets, -et.ed, -et.ing** fasten with a rivet: *steel beams riveted together; a preacher who can rivet your attention for an hour;* *adj.:* *They stood riveted to the spot; with all eyes riveted on her; the most riveting* (= attention-holding) *performer in rock 'n' roll.* Also **riv.et.ted, ri.vet.ting** *Cdn.*
riv.u.let (RIV.yuh.lit) *n.* a small river or stream.
ri.yal (ree.YAHL, -YAWL) *n.* the basic money unit of Saudi Arabia, Qatar, and Yemen; also **ri.al.**
RNA same as RIBONUCLEIC ACID.
roach (ROHCH) *n.* **1** [short form] cockroach. **2** *Slang.* a butt of a marijuana cigarette, held with a **roach clip.**
road (RODE) *n.* a usu. public path, way, or course for traveling to a destination: *This is the road to take; back, country, dirt, impassable, main, mountain, service, toll, wrong roads; paved, rough, smooth, straight, winding roads; "All roads lead to Rome"; Obey the rules of the road; Demonstrators took to the road in large numbers; the royal road to success; A traveling sales rep is **on the road** much of the time; to get a show on the road* (= touring); *Pat's **on the road***

to (= moving toward) *recovery; Forget about **one for the road*** (= an extra drink); *inventions waiting for us **down the road*** (= in the future).
road.bed *n.* the foundation laid for a highway, railroad, etc.
road.block *n.* **1** a barrier placed across a road, as by police at checkpoints: *to establish, run, set up a roadblock.* **2** any hindrance: *The Government has placed roadblocks in the way of the inquiry commission.*
road hog *n. Informal.* an unmannerly driver, esp. a motorist who drives in the middle of the road.
road.house *n.* an out-of-town restaurant and bar on a main route.
road rage *n.* anger directed by a driver toward other drivers who do not observe the rules of the road.
road runner *n.* a cuckoo of the deserts of S.W. North America that is better able to run than fly; also called "chaparral cock."
road.show *n.* a touring theatrical show.
road.side *n.* the side of a road: *to stop on the roadside;* *adja.:* *a roadside park, picnic table, restaurant.*
road.stead (ROAD.sted) *n.* a sheltered anchorage for ships near a shore.
road.ster *n.* **1** an early open-bodied automobile with a single wide seat. **2** a horse for riding or driving on a road.
road test *n.* **1** the testing of a vehicle for roadworthiness. **2** a test of driving ability.
road.way *n.* **1** a road: *a major roadway.* **2** the part of a road used by vehicles: *the roadway of a bridge.*
road.work *n.* running exercise for boxers in training.
road.wor.thy (RODE.wur.thee) *adj.* of vehicles, in good condition.
—**road.wor.thi.ness** *n.*
roam (ROME) *v.* go about in a large area without a plan or aim; wander over: *pirates roaming the seas; He roamed about* or *around* or *over* or *through the country after dropping out of school.*
roan (RONE) *adj.* of a brownish or blackish color sprinkled with white or gray. —*n.* **1** a horse or other animal of this color. **2** the color.
roar (RORE) *n.* a loud, full, and rumbling sound: *the roar of a lion: the roar of a cheering crowd, engine, waterfall; the roar of the wind; the roar of thunder, of traffic on a highway; greeted with roars of laughter.*
—*v.* make a roar: *The lion roared; The crowd roared with laughter; The officer roared out his commands.* —**roaring** *adja.*

very great: *The play was a roaring success; We did a roaring trade;* **adv.**: *Ray came in roaring* (= very much) *drunk.*

roast (ROHST) *v.* **1** cook by dry or radiant heat in an oven or over an open fire: *to roast coffee beans, meat, metal ore; The turkey is roasting; I'm roasting in this heat.* —**adj.**: *a roasting chicken, duck, pan, rack;* **adj**: *It's roasting* (= hot and dry) *out there; a roasting hot afternoon.* **2** *Informal.* subject a person to ridicule or criticism; *n.: They gave him a good* **roasting.**
—*n.* **1** roasted meat or meat suitable for roasting: *to make a roast; chuck, eye, lamb, pork, pot, rib roasts;* **adj.**: *roast beef, chicken, pig, potatoes.* **2** a picnic at which food is roasted: *corn, steer roasts.* **3** an event at which a person is ridiculed, usu. good-naturedly: *There was a roast for the premier last night.*

rob *v.* **robs, robbed, rob.bing** deprive a person or establishment of property, good name, etc. by violence, fraud, or any unjust means: *A swindler robbed the old man of his savings; He robs banks; children caught robbing an orchard; They rob* (= steal) *apples.* —**rob.ber** *n.: a band* or *gang of robbers.*

rob.ber.y *n.* **rob.ber.ies** theft by violence or any unjust means: *to commit (a) robbery; armed, bank, daylight, highway robbery.*

robe *n.* **1** a long, loose outer garment, as worn wrapped around when lounging or as a bathrobe. **2** a ceremonial garment, as worn by a priest or judge: *a judge dressed in black robes.*
—*v.* clothe with a robe: *a priest robed in gold-trimmed vestments.*

rob.in *n.* either or two thrushes, a common American bird with a reddish breast or a smaller European species, also called "redbreast."

Robin Hood *n.* in English legend, a hero of the common people who robbed the rich to give to the poor.

ro.bot (ROH.bot) *n.* **1** a mechanical person or human automaton. **2** an insensitive, machinelike human being.

ro.bot.ics (roh.BOT.ics) *n.pl.* the technology involved in making and operating robots; **adj.**: *a robotics expert, lab, researcher; a robotic arm, assembly line, machine tool, system.*

ro.bust (roh.BUST, ROH.bust) *adj.* healthy and vigorous in body or mind, not sickly: *a robust young man; his robust* (= vigorous, not delicate) *humor; robust* (= full-bodied) *coffee; robust* (= sturdy) *faith.* —**ro.bust.ly** *adv.;* **ro.bust.ness** *n.*

rock *n.* **1** the hard, firm, solid part of the earth's crust made up of minerals: *a house built on rock; granite rock; firm, solid, steady as a rock;* **adj.**: *rock climbing, formations, quarries; rock solid; a* **rock-solid** *relationship, trust.* **2** a large mass of this or a piece: *"Danger: Falling Rocks"; He threw a rock* (= stone) *at the rook; I found myself* or *was caught* **between a rock and a hard place** (*Informal for* was in a difficult situation). **3** a style of popular music and dance based on blues and country-and-western music, and characterized by heavy rhythms, common melodies, and popular lyrics; rock'n'roll: *hard rock; punk rock;* **adj.**: *rock concerts, lyrics, music; a rock band, group, hit, quartet, song, video.* **4** a rocking movement. —**on the rocks 1** *Informal.* ruined or bankrupt. **2** of a drink, served on ice cubes: *rum on the rocks.*
—*v.* move back and forth upon a base: *to rock a baby to sleep; a building rocked* (= shaken) *by an explosion; waves rocking a boat; Team players should not* **rock the boat** (*Informal for* try to upset a situation).

rock-and-roll same as ROCK, *n.* 3.

rock bottom *n.* the very lowest level: *The stock has just hit rock bottom; She has lost everything and is at rock bottom;* **adj.**: *a* **rock-bottom** *bid, offer; rock-bottom levels, justice, prices, rates.*

rock.bound *adj.* of a coast, covered with rocks.

rock candy *n.* large, hard sugar crystals.

rock.er *n.* a chair mounted so as to be rocked by its occupant; also **rocking chair**. —**off one's rocker** *Informal.* crazy.

rock.et (ROCK.it) *n.* a spacecraft or projectile powered by a cylinder containing fuel which, when rapidly burned, creates thrust by the force of the escaping gases, as used in shooting fireworks, war missiles, space probes, etc.: *to fire, launch a rocket; a booster rocket.*

rock.et.ry (ROK.it.ree) *n.* the science of making and using rockets.

rocket ship *n.* a rocket-propelled spacecraft.

rock-fall *n.* **1** the fall of rock down a slope, as in a cave or mine. **2** fallen rock.

rock garden *n.* a flower garden on rocky ground or among rocks.

Rock.ies *n.pl. Informal.* the **Rocky Mountains** of W. North America.

rocking chair See ROCKER.

rocking horse *n.* a toy horse on rockers for a child to ride.

rock'n'roll or **rock 'n' roll** (ROCK.un.role) same as ROCK, *n.* 3.

rock salt *n.* salt that is mined from the earth, not sea salt.

rock wool *n.* an insulating material made from molten rock by blowing a jet of steam through it.

rock.y *adj.* **rock.i.er, -i.est 1** shaky: *a rocky ride; a rocky history, marriage, period, relationship, start, weather, year; rocky times.* **2** *Informal.* dizzy or weak: *feeling a bit rocky after the tumble.* **3** full of rocks; consisting of rocks; also, firm or hard as a rock: *a rocky layer, road, shore, soil, surface, terrain, trail.*
—**rock.i.ness** *n.*

Rocky Mountain goat *n.* a goatlike antelope with a dense, shaggy coat, found in the Rockies.

Rocky Mountain sheep same as BIGHORN.

ro.co.co (ruh.COH.coh) *n.* a highly ornate and elaborate artistic style of the 1700s, more delicate in design than baroque. —*adj.* overelaborate or quaint.

rod *n.* a thin, straight stick or bar, as used to fish with, as a measuring unit (16.5 ft. or 5.029 m), or one carried as a symbol of authority: *curtain, divining, fishing, lightning, piston, traverse rods; The king ruled the land with a **rod of iron** (= harshly); "Spare the rod (= punishment) and spoil the child."*

rode *pt.* of RIDE.

ro.dent (ROH.dunt) *n.* any of an order of mammals such as squirrels, beavers, and rats having incisors suited to gnawing.

ro.de.o (ROH.dee.oh, roh.DAY.oh) *n.* -os an exhibition of or contest in cowboy skills: *to hold* or *stage a rodeo.*

roe (ROH) *n.* **1** fish eggs or sperm: *to spawn roe.* **2** a small, tailless Old World deer whose male, or **roebuck**, has short, three-tined antlers.

roent.gen (RENT.gun) *n.* the international unit for measuring radiation such as gamma rays and X rays.

rog.er (ROJ.ur) *interj.* esp. in radio communications, "OK!"

rogue (ROHG) *n.* a scoundrel; rascal. —*adj.* not controllable; hence, renegade: *a rogue cop, elephant, institution, state.* —**ro.guer.y** (ROH.guh.ree) *n.* —**ro.guish** (ROH.gish, "g" as in "go") *adj.* **1** dishonest: *a roguish accountant, lawyer, politician.* **2** mischievous: *a roguish farce, look; roguish wit.* —**ro.guish.ly** *adv.*; **ro.guish.ness** *n.*

roil *v.* to muddy water, etc. by stirring up sediment; hence, vex or irritate; rile: *He is easily roiled by criticisms;* **adj.**: *the **roiled** waters of popular discontent; to get roiled;* **adja.**: *a **roiling** sea; the roiling boil of America's melting pot; a roiling controversy.* —**roil.y** *adj.* **roil.i.er, -i.est** turbid; also, irritated.

roist.er *v.* make merry boisterously; **roist.er.er** *n.*

role *n.* **1** an actor's part: *to act out, assume, perform, play, take on a role; cast in the role of Macbeth; to assign roles to players; leading, supporting, title roles.* **2** a part played in real life: *He plays an active role in running the school; She had a key role in organizing the show; The prime minister had to fulfill his role as a father and his political role as the nation's leader; the social role of a teacher; the conflict between her roles as breadwinner and as wife; Children often imitate their parents as **role models**.* Also **rôle**.

roll (ROLE) *v.* **1** move or cause to move or go forward with a turning motion, as a ball, wheel, or something on wheels: *She rolled me the ball; Tears rolled down his cheeks; He rolled over and played dead; She rolled up her sleeves and started working; Let's get it rolling; Roll the cameras; The years rolled by; to **start** or **get** or **set the ball rolling** (Informal for make a beginning);* **Heads will roll** (= People will be punished); *She has learned to **roll with the punches** (= accept adversity without resisting too much); Orders for new cars are **rolling in**; The boss is **rolling it in** (= making money fast); She's **rolling in it** (= very rich);* **adja.**: *a **rolling** stone; First bring the gravy to a rolling boil; lift trucks and such rolling equipment; a rolling fleet of 300 cars; A **rolling stop** (with the wheels moving slowly) won't do for a full stop at a stop sign.* **2** move or cause to sway from side to side, as a ship tossed by waves; hence, walk with a swagger: *a rolling gait.* **3** have a rising and falling surface;* **adj.**: *the **rolling** countryside, fields, hills, landscape, plain, prairie.* **4** of sounds, have a full or reverberating quality: *to roll one's r's* (= utter them with a trill); **adja.**: *the **rolling** drum, thunder.* **5** flatten by using a roller: *to roll a road surface; rolled oats; This year we're celebrating Christmas and your birthday **rolled into one** (= combined).* **6** *Slang.* rob a drunk, lush, stiff, or other helpless person. —**roll back** move back, as prices to a former level. —*n.* **1** something rolled up: *a roll of film, money, paper.* **2** a food that is round, rolled, or folded: *cabbage, dinner, jelly, kaiser, sausage rolls.* **3** a list of names: *to call* or *take the roll; an honor roll of the top students; the roll of honor; Six were* **struck off the rolls** (= removed from the list) *for misbehavior.* **4** a rolling movement: *He walks with the roll of a sailor (swaying from side to side).* **5** a rising and falling surface: *the roll of the land.* **6** a rolling sound: *the roll of distant thunder, of drums; the roll* (= long, deep sound) *of his verse.* —**on a roll** *Informal.* enjoying a series of wins.

roll.back *n.* a rolling back: *government-ordered price rollbacks; a rollback of plans, programs, reforms, sanctions, taxes.*

roll bar *n.* a metal bar across the roof inside an automobile to protect the driver if the vehicle should roll over.

roll call *n.* the reading aloud of a list of names, as of soldiers, to find out who is absent.

roll.er *n.* **1** one that rolls, as a long swelling wave. **2** a cylinder used to roll a surface or one on which something is rolled. **3** a jaylike bird whose male has the habit of tumbling in the air to attract the attention of the female.

roller coaster *n.* an elevated track with ascents, descents, and abrupt turns, carrying passengers in open cars on amusement rides.

roller derby *n.* a contest between roller-skating teams.

roller skate *n.* a skate with small wheels instead of a runner for use on floors. —**rol.ler-skate** *v.* -**skates**, -**skat.ed**, -**skat.ing.**

rol.lick (ROL.ik) *v.* behave in a carefree, frolicsome manner: *children rollicking in the snow;* **adj.:** *a **rollicking** cheerful woman; rollicking dance, fun, joy, music, songs, wit.*

rolling pin *n.* a long cylindrical piece of wood or other material for rolling out dough.

rolling stock *n.* all the wheeled vehicles of a railroad or trucking company.

roll.o.ver (ROLE.oh.vur) *n.* **1** a rolling over; **adj.:** *cars with rollover bars; for rollover protection.* **2** reinvestment of funds: *pension-plan rollovers.*

roll-top *adj.* of a desk, having a sliding top that closes and locks over the desk's working surface.

ro.ly-po.ly (roh.lee.POH.lee) *adj.* of a person or animal, short and plump.

ROM (ROM) *n.* the "read-only memory" of a computer comprising system software that cannot be manipulated like the random-access memory; **adj.:** *a ROM card, chip.*

ro.maine (roh.MAIN) *n.* a variety of lettuce with a long roll of leaves curled inside each other.

ro.man (ROH.mun) *n.* a type or print that is upright, as "this," not *"this."*

Roman candle *n.* a firework that shoots out balls of fire: *The stocks I bought took off like a Roman candle.*

Roman Catholic *n. & adj.* (a member) of the Christian church that has the Pope as its head.

ro.mance (roh.MANCE, ROH.mance) *n.* **1** a novel of love and adventure involving characters and events somewhat remote from real life, as of medieval knights: *Scott's historical romances.* **2** this quality or atmosphere: *love and romance; to put romance back into a marriage.* **3** a love affair: *a whirlwind romance; the new nation's romance with democracy.* **3 Romance** *adj.* having to do with the languages derived from Latin, as Italian, French, Spanish, and Portuguese.
—*v.* (roh.MANCE) -**manc.es**, -**manced**, -**manc.ing** exaggerate, indulge in fancies, or woo someone romantically. —**ro.manc.er** *n.*

Ro.ma.ni.an (roh.MAY.nee.un) *n. & adj.* (a person of or from or the language) of **Romania,** a country of S.E. Europe.

Roman numeral *n.* a numeral written in Roman letters using I, V, X, L, C, D, and M.

ro.man.tic (roh.MAN.tic) *adj.* **1** having to do with romance, esp. love and adventure: *a romantic affair, scene, situation, story.* **2** impractical or visionary: *romantic notions.* —*n.* a romantic person; romanticist. —**ro.man.ti.cal.ly** *adv.*

ro.man.ti.cism (roh.MAN.tuh.siz.um) *n.* in literature and the fine arts, a movement or style marking a departure from classicism, based on emotion and inspiration rather than reason and logic and freedom and spontaneity of expression as opposed to restraint and order; **ro.man.ti.cist** *n.*

ro.man.ti.cize (roh.MAN.tuh.size) *v.* -**ciz.es**, -**cized**, -**ciz.ing** make or be romantic; **adj.:** *a highly **romanticized** story; a romanticized view.*

Rom.a.ny (ROM.uh.nee, ROH.muh-) *n.* **1** a Gypsy. **2** the Indic language of the Gypsies.

Ro.me.o (ROH.mee.oh) *n.* an ardent lover, like the hero of Shakespeare's "Romeo and Juliet."

romp *v.* run or jump about in

boisterous play: *Our team romped to easy victories at the Olympics.* —*n.*: *children out for a romp in the park.*
romp.er *n.* 1 one who romps. 2 usu. **rompers** *pl.* a child's playsuit consisting of pants and top.
rood (RUDE) *n.* 1 a crucifix or cross. 2 a unit of area equal to ¼ acre (0.10117 hectare).
roof (long "oo") *n.* roofs the top covering of a building or a similar part: *the roof of a car; the roof of the mouth* (= palate); *homeless people without a roof over their heads* (= with nowhere to live); *Prices go through or hit the roof in times of scarcity; She hit the roof* (Informal for got very angry) *when she heard the bad news; a roof deck* (= flat part of roof for gardening, sunbathing, etc.); *roof garden* (= garden on a roof). —*v.* cover with a roof; *adj. & cpd.: a roofed enclosure; a patio roofed with a skylight; a gable-roofed house; glass-roofed, tile-roofed, tin-roofed.* —**roof.less** *adj.*
roofing *n.* material for roofs; *adja.: roofing material, shingles, tiles.*
roof.top *n.* the top of a building: *a hotel rooftop; You don't shout something secret from the rooftops; adja.: a rooftop antenna, garden, restaurant, terrace; rooftop parking.*
rook (short "oo") *n.* 1 a chess piece shaped like a castle tower. 2 a bird of the crow family noted for its cunning. —*v. Slang.* cheat or swindle: *Car owners complain of being rooked right and left.*
rook.er.y (ROOK.uh.ree) *n.* **-er.ies** a colony of rooks or their nesting place.
rook.ie (ROOK.ee) *n. Informal.* an inexperienced recruit or a novice; *adja.: a rookie constable, politician, teacher; in my rookie year.*
room (long or short "oo") *n.* 1 a part of a building set apart by walls or partitions, as for an office or as living quarters: *We waited in an adjoining room; banquet, dining, furnished, family, guest, locker, men's, reading, rented, rest, spare, storage, utility rooms; a room to work in; He addressed the whole room* (= the people in it); *adja.: room air-conditioners, temperature, visits.* 2 space: *plenty of room for four passengers; standing room only; Make room for Daddy; a table that takes up too much room; bargaining, breathing, maneuvering room; There's much room for* (= scope for) *improvement in your work.* —*v.* to lodge: *He's rooming at our house; used to room with her;* **room.er** *n.*
room and board *n.* lodging and meals.

room clerk *n.* a hotel's front-desk clerk.
room.ette (roo.MET) *n.* a private compartment in a railroad sleeping car.
rooming house *n.* a house with furnished rooms for rent.
room.mate *n.* one sharing a room or rooms with others.
room service *n.* food service in a hotel room.
room.y (ROO.mee) *adj.* **room.i.er, -i.est** spacious. —**room.i.ness** *n.*
roost (long "oo") *n.* a perching place for birds, esp. domestic fowls: *She* **rules the roost** (Informal for is in charge) *here; Al began to regret what he did when the chickens he hatched* **came home to roost** (= when what he did began to backfire). —*v.* 1 perch on a roost. 2 settle for the night.
roost.er *n.* a male domestic fowl; cock: *Roosters crow; they go "cock-a-doodle-doo."*
root (long "oo") *n.* 1 the usu. underground part of a plant that serves as support and draws nourishment from the soil; also, a similar part of a hair, tooth, etc.: *Weeds should be pulled up by the roots; Plants* **strike** or **take root** (in the soil); *We have* **struck root** or **roots** (= settled down) *in Canada.* 2 a source or origin: *to get at the root of the matter; The words "material," "metro," and "mother" have the same root; social problems that are cultural* **at root**; *Blacks have African roots; the* **root cause** *of all this trouble.* —*v.* 1 fix or settle, as in the ground: *customs and practices deeply rooted in our culture.* 2 become fixed or begin growing by sending out roots: *Plants root best in the spring.* 3 poke, search, or dig up, as with the snout: *Pigs root for potatoes; They root about or around in the fields; Someone has been rooting around among my papers; We should try to* **root out** (= destroy) *this habit.* 4 *Informal.* cheer: *Let's root for Jane, for the home team.*
root beer *n.* a sweetened carbonated drink flavored with extracts of the roots of plants such as sarsaparilla and trees such as sassafras.
root canal *n.* a procedure for replacing the diseased tissue of a tooth's pulp cavity: *to undergo a root canal; adja.: root canal surgery, therapy, work.*
root crop *n.* a crop such as carrots, potatoes, and turnips grown for their edible roots.
root.let (ROOT.lit) *n.* a small root.
root.stock same as RHIZOME.
root vegetable same as ROOT CROP.
rope *n.* a thick, strong cord made of twisted or braided strands of fiber or

similar material and traditionally used for ships' rigging, to tether animals, etc.; also, a piece of this for a particular purpose: *a length* or *piece of rope; a skipping rope; to jump* or *skip rope; tighten a rope; The rope* (= hanging as punishment) *has been abolished.* —**give one enough rope** or **plenty of rope** let one act freely and take the consequences. —**know** or **learn the ropes** *Informal.* know or learn a job or activity: *to learn the ropes of diplomacy.* —**on the ropes** in a helpless position, like a boxer about to be knocked out.
—*v.* **ropes, roped, rop.ing** 1 mark off an area, catch, etc. with a rope. 2 tie with a rope: *mountaineers roped together.* —**rope in** *Informal.* induce someone to do something for another person or cause: *How did he get roped in?*

Roque.fort cheese (ROKE.furt-) *n.* a strong-tasting, mold-ripened cheese made from sheep's milk, originally in Roquefort, France.

Ror.schach test (ROR.shahk-) *n.* a psychological test based on the subject's interpretation of a series of ink-blot designs.

ro.sa.ry (ROH.zuh.ree) *n.* **-ries** (a string of beads used by Roman Catholics to keep count of) a series of prayers to the Virgin Mary.

rose (ROZE) *n.* **1** the beautiful, usu. fragrant flower of a shrub with a prickly stem: *Roses are red, violets are blue; a long-stemmed rose; a bouquet of roses; Life is not a **bed of roses** (= something easy or pleasant); Everything was **coming up roses** (= happening as desired) when tragedy struck.* **2** the shrub itself. **3** the flower's commonly reddish color. —*adj.*: *a rose color, flower; a rose leaf; I never promised you a **rose garden** (= that things would be easy or pleasant).* —*v. pt.* of RISE.

ro.sé (roh.ZAY) *n.* a light pink wine.

ro.se.ate (ROH.zee.it, -ate) *adj.* rose-colored.

rose.bud *n.* the bud of a rose.

rose.bush *n.* a shrubby rose.

rose-colored *adj.* rosy: *She sees the world through rose-colored glasses* (= is very optimistic).

rose.mar.y (ROZE.mair.ee) *n.* **-mar.ies** an evergreen mint with fragrant leaves and pale blue flowers.

ro.sette (roh.ZET) *n.* a rose-shaped ornament, as of ribbon or as used in architecture.

rose water *n.* a watery perfume containing a rose extract.

rose window *n.* a circular window with roselike tracery.

rose.wood *n.* (the dark, reddish-brown wood of) a tropical tree of the pea family.

Rosh Ha.sha.na (ROHSH.huh.SHAH. nuh, ROSH-) *n.* the Jewish New Year.

ros.in (ROZ.in) *n.* the resin of pine trees, used in paints and varnishes and to rub on smooth surfaces to keep them from being slippery.

ros.ter (ROS.tur) *n.* a list, esp. of personnel on duty.

ros.trum (ROS.trum) *n.* **-trums** or **-tra** (-truh) **1** a platform or stage for public speaking: *He mounted the rostrum to address the meeting.* **2** a beaklike part or structure.

ros.y (ROH.zee) *adj.* **ros.i.er, -i.est** **1** rose-colored; pinkish red: *rosy. cheeks.* **2** optimistic or promising: *a rosy future.* —**ros.i.ly** *adv.*; **ros.i.ness** *n.*

rot *v.* **rots, rot.ted, rot.ting** decompose; decay: *a promising artist rotting in a dead-end job.* —*n.* **1** decay. **2** a disease of plants and trees, as "potato rot" and "dry rot." **3** a worsening situation: *Stop the rot; Act now before the **rot sets in.*** **4** *Informal.* nonsense: *Don't talk rot.*

ro.ta.ry (ROH.tuh.ree) *adj.* wheellike, circular, or rotating: *a rotary dial phone, not a push-button; a rotary engine, press; the cogwheel emblem of the Rotary Club.* —*n.* **-ries** a rotary machine or setup.

ro.tate (ROH.tate) *v.* **-tates, -tat.ed, -tat.ing 1** turn around a center or axis, as a wheel or top: *The earth rotates on its axis every 24 hours.* **2** (cause to) take turns: *The Olympics are rotated among the continents; a position that rotates among the vice-presidents; to rotate employees through different jobs; to rotate work shifts; to rotate the wheels of a car* (= switch them around for even wear); *to **rotate crops** (= alternate them in a field from year to year) for preserving the soil.* —**ro.ta.tion** (roh.TAY.shun) *n.*; **ro.ta.tion.al** (-shun.ul) *adj.* —**ro.ta.tor** (ROH.tay.tur) *n.*; **ro.ta.to.ry** (-tuh.tor.ee) *adj.*

rote *n.* a repetitive or routine way of doing something: *Math tables are best learned **by rote*** (= memorized by repetition); *adj.*: *rote behavior, learning, memory, skills, tasks; Her response was rote; a job that is considered rote.*

rot.gut *n. Slang.* cheap liquor.

ro.tis.ser.ie (roh.TIS.uh.ree) *n.* **1** a restaurant or shop featuring roasted meat. **2** a grill with an electrically rotated spit.

ro.to.gra.vure (roh.tuh.gruh.VYOOR)

n. a printing process using cylinders on which print and pictures have been engraved.

ro.tor (ROH.tur) *n.* a rotating part, as of a motor or a generator or the system of blades of a helicopter.

rot.ten (ROT.un) *adj.* **1** corrupt or foul-smelling: *a rotten egg, smell, tooth; a scheme that is* **rotten to the core;** *There's a* **rotten apple** (= undesirable character) *in every group;* **rotten ice** *or* **snow** *(that is melting).* **2** *Informal.* unpleasant or bad: *a rotten day at work; a rotten feeling, shame; rotten weather.* —**rot.ten.ness** *n.*

ro.tund (ROH.tund) *adj.* plump or rounded out: *a rotund gentleman, matron, singer.* —**ro.tun.di.ty** (roh.TUN.di.tee) *n.*

ro.tun.da (roh.TUN.duh) *n.* **1** a round, usu. dome-covered building. **2** a room under a dome, usu. a lobby or concourse: *We'll meet in the rotunda.*

rou.ble (ROO.bul) same as RUBLE.

rou.é (roo.AY) *n.* a dissolute or dissipated man; rake.

rouge (ROOZH) *n.* **1** a reddish powder used as a cosmetic. **2** a reddish powder used for polishing metal, glass, etc. —*v.* **roug.es, rouged, roug.ing** color with rouge.

rough (RUF) *adj.* not smooth, even, or level: *a rough ride on a rough road; We had a rough time in Soviet Russia; rough* (= not gentle) *language, manners; rough* (= stormy) *weather; rough* (= unskilled) *work; rough* (= harsh) *voices; a rough* (= general) *estimate, idea sketch; a rough translation (that is not exact).* —*adv.* in a rough manner. —*n.* **1** a rough or violent person. **2** rough ground, esp. uncleared land along a golf fairway. **3** a rough condition: *to take the rough with the smooth.* —*v.* **1** subject a person to roughness: *Al was roughed up by the bigger boys.* **2** do incompletely, without finishing: *He roughed in the whole job first; The cavity was roughed out to within a ¼ inch of the finished dimension;* **adja.:** *a* **roughed**-*in washroom; a roughed-in* (= roughly sketched) *outline; a* **roughing**-*out operation; a roughing cut; n.: lathe* **roughing.** —**rough it** live a rough life: *She's used to roughing it.*

rough.age (RUF.ij) *n.* coarse material, esp. fibrous foodstuff such as bran eaten for bulk.

rough-and-ready *adj.* effective in a crude way: *a rough-and-ready calculation, device, method, toughness; in a rough-and-ready way.*

rough-and-tumble *adj.* rough and disorderly: *our rough-and-tumble existence.*

rough diamond *n.* a worthy but crude person.

rough.en (RUF.un) *v.* make or become rough: *to roughen up a floor before refinishing it;* **adj.:** *a* **roughened** *area, surface, texture.*

rough-hew *v.* **-hews,** *pt. & pp.* **-hewed** or **-hewn, -hew.ing 1** hew stone, timber, etc. without smoothing. **2** give something a rough form; **adj.: rough-hewn** *furniture; the rough-hewn lifestyle of loggers; a rough-hewn but generous person.*

rough.house *v.* **-hous.es, -housed, -hous.ing** *Informal.* take part in or subject to rough play or fun.

rough.ly (RUF.lee) *adv.* approximately: *It costs roughly $10,000; We received roughly 500 inquiries; Roughly 25% of the calls were from Mexico.* —**rough.ness** *n.*

rough.neck *n.* **1** a coarse or rowdy person. **2** a worker on a drilling rig.

rough.shod *adj.* of horses, with shoes having projecting nail heads. —**ride roughshod over** treat a person, feelings, etc. roughly.

rou.lette (roo.LET) *n.* a gambling game using a ball rolled over a small revolving wheel (**roulette wheel**) with numbers on it: *People play "parking roulette" by parking illegally, not knowing when they might get a ticket.*

round *adj.* **1** shaped like a circle, ball, or cylinder: *Balls are round; round eyes; a round face, column, table; a round vowel such as "O"* (pronounced with rounded lips). **2** filled out in form or figure: *her round figure; A round figure or number or sum* (= an approximate number) *such as 1,000 (instead of 998 or 1,003); round* (= curved) *shoulders; a round* (= full) *dozen.* **3** vigorous: *She scolded him in round terms; a round scolding; to move at a round pace.* —*n.* **1** something round, as a ball, a rung of a ladder, a cut of beef below the rump, etc.: *figures sculptured* **in the round** (= not in relief). **2** a course or activity that ends where it begins: *a guard making his rounds; a rumor now going the rounds; the endless round of parties; the earth's yearly round.* **3** something forming a part of the action in a group or sequence, as a section of a boxing match, one shot from a weapon such as a firearm or the ammunition for it, etc.: *Three rounds were fired; a round of applause; He ordered a round of drinks for everyone present; "Three Blind Mice" is a round, or musical canon.*

roundabout / rove

—*v.* **1** make or become round: $2,995.75 **rounds off** to $3,000; *A year abroad* **rounded out** *her studies;* **adj.:** *"O" is said with* **rounded** *lips; rounded teaspoonfuls; a rounded corner, design, edge, stone; a well-rounded education.* **2** go or turn round: *Slow down to round the corner.* —**round up** drive or gather together: *A cowboy rounds up cattle; A party whip tries to round up a majority to vote for a bill.* —**adv. & prep. 1** in a circular path by a place or person, back to one's position, etc.: *I just saw her going round (the corner); We talked him round to vote for us.* **2** on all sides of a person or place: *We gathered round (the leader); to show visitors round (the displays).* **3** throughout a place or period; around: *It rains all round the year in the rain forests; all year round; We spread the news round (the town); He kept watch* **round the clock** (= 24 hours).

round.a.bout (ROWN.duh.bowt) *adj.* going round or indirect: *a roundabout course, route, way.*

roun.de.lay (ROWN.dul.ay) *n.* a song or poem with a refrain.

round file *n. Informal.* wastebasket.

round.house *n.* **1** a round building for repairing locomotives, with a turntable in the center. **2** *Informal.* a punch thrown with a wide swing: *John landed a roundhouse right.*

round.ly *adv.* **1** vigorously or fully: *She scolded Lee roundly; to be roundly booed, condemned, criticized, defeated, denounced.* **2** widely: *to be roundly entertained; roundly described as a great success.*

round robin *n.* **1** a petition with signatures in a circle so as not to show who signed first. **2** a letter sent round to a group for comments. **3** a tournament in which each player meets every other in turn; **adja.:** *a round-robin competition.* **4** a series or round: *a round robin of tax deductions.*

round table *n.* a conference of a group of people meeting as equals or without consideration of precedence, as among King Arthur's "Knights of the Round Table": *the groups gathered* or *sitting at the Round Table; The National Round Table on the Environment;* **adja.:** *a* **round-table** *agreement, conference, discussion, session; round-table negotiations, participants, talks.*

round-the-clock *adja.* continuing day and night: *a round-the-clock bodyguard, vigil, watch;* **adv.:** *He watched at her bedside round the clock.*

round trip *n.* a trip to and back from a place; **adv.:** *We drove 884 miles round trip from Atlanta to Orlando;* **adja.:** *a* **round-trip** *fare, flight, ticket.*

round.up *n.* **1** a rounding up or gathering of cattle, scattered members of a group, news items for a summary, etc. **2** the people and horses rounding up cattle on a ranch. **3** the herd alone.

round.worm *n.* a nematode, esp. one found in the intestines of children.

rouse (ROWZE) *v.* **rous.es, roused, rous.ing 1** stir, as from sleep; arouse: *He was roused from sleep in the middle of the night.* **2** stir up game from cover or a person to a state of excitement or anger: *She roused the crowd to a fever of excitement; rousing the rabble toward war;* **adj.:** *The singer was given a* **rousing** (= enthusiastic) *welcome; a rousing cheer, ovation, reception, rendition, send-off, speech, start, success.* —**rous.er** *n.: a rouser of the rank and file.*

roust.a.bout (ROW.stuh.bout, "OW" as in "how") *n.* a usu. unskilled workman doing odd jobs as a deck hand, longshoreman, or one taking down tents, etc. in a circus.

rout (ROWT) *n.* **1** an utter defeat and resulting flight: *The enemy was put to rout; the rout of the enemy forces; Many got trampled in the rout that ensued.* **2** a disorderly crowd. —*v.* **1** defeat utterly; hence, put to flight: *The enemy forces were completely routed.* **2** dig or scoop out, as pigs root out things from the ground.

route (ROOT; *also* ROWT) *n.* a regular course or road, as of one making deliveries: *to follow, map out, plan, take a route; circuitous, devious, direct, roundabout, scenic routes; bus, mail, newspaper, overland, streetcar, trade, truck routes.*
—*v.* **routes, rout.ed, rout.ing** send goods, traffic, etc. by a route or arrange the route for it: *We routed the memo to all key personnel.*

rou.tine (roo.TEEN) *n.* a regular series of actions or operations: *our office routine; a daily, dull, ordinary, usual routine; to write installation* or *setup routines for computer software; a comedy or dance routine* (= act or bit). —*adj.* habitual, not special: *a routine assignment, checkup, inquiry, task; routine maintenance; as routine as brushing your teeth; This job is getting a bit routine* (= dull); *The program was somewhat routine.* —**rou.tine.ly** *adv.*

rou.tin.ize (roo.TEE.nize, ROO.tun.ize) *v.* make routine or regular: *to routinize a process.*

rove (ROHV) a *pt.* of REEVE.
—*v.* **roves, roved, rov.ing** go about or

wander over a place, usu. with a purpose; **adj**.: *a roving ambassador, reporter; his roving eye* (= tendency to admire other women). —**rov.er** *n*.

¹**row** (ROH) **1** *n*. a line of persons or things: *a row of seats; seats placed in rows; on death row (awaiting execution); on skid row (as a derelict); She lives on millionaires' row* (= street); *three years* **in a row** (= in succession). **2** a trip in a boat that is rowed. —*v*. **1** move a boat using oars: *He went rowing for fun; It's hard to row a boat upstream;* **adj**.: *a rowing expedition, machine, regatta, shell.* **2** carry people or goods in a rowboat: *She rowed her family out to Ward's Island.*

²**row** (rhyme: how) *n*. a noisy quarrel; squabble: *to kick up, make, raise a row; He had a row with the neighbors; a row about* or *over their noisy parties.*

row.boat (ROH.boat) *n*. a boat that is rowed, not a sailboat.

row.dy ("ow" as in "how") *n*. & *adj*. **-di.er, -di.est** (one who is) quarrelsome or disorderly; **row.di.ness** *n*. —**row.dy.ish** *adj*. —**row.dy.ism** *n*.

row.el (ROW.ul, "OW" as in "how") *n*. & *v*. **-els, -eled, -el.ing** (urge a horse with) a small wheel with projections which is attached to the end of a spur. Also **row.elled, row.el.ling** *Cdn.*

row house (ROH-) *n*. one of a series of connected houses of identical design.

roy.al (ROY.ul) *adj*. **1** having to do with a sovereign, a kingdom, or its government: *the royal couple, family;* **Royal assent** *is given to a piece of legislation for it to become law in Canada;* *n*.: *the royals of Buckingham Palace.* **2** regal; majestic or splendid. **3** *Informal* [used as intensifier]: *a royal pain in the neck.* —**roy.al.ist** *n*. & *adj*. —**roy.al.ly** *adv*.

roy.al.ty (ROY.ul.tee) *n*. **-ties 1** royal persons or their rank, quality, etc. **2** a share of receipts from a property or creative work paid to its owner, author, or composer: *Publishers pay authors royalties on books; They earn handsome royalties for their authors; Some books continue to bring in royalties long after publication.*

R.S.V.P. or **RSVP** [used with invitations] Please reply. —*v*. *Informal*. reply: *Only a few RSVP'd "yes" to the invitation.*

rub *v*. **rubs, rubbed, rub.bing** (cause) to move while pressing against something: *Rub hands (together) to keep warm; An eraser rubs off writing; to rub a surface dry; a tire rubbing against the fender; His shoulder rubbed hers in the crowded elevator; They* **rub elbows** or **shoulders** (= associate) *with royalty;* *n*.: *the hobby of making* **rubbings** *of old coins (by rubbing with a colored substance on paper placed over them).* —**rub down 1** rub something to polish, clean, etc.; *n*.: *a good rubbing down with soap and water.* **2** massage. —**rub it in** irritate someone by repeatedly mentioning something unpleasant: *She's already miserable about losing - don't rub it in anymore.* —**rub off on** or **onto** of a quality or activity, spread by close contact: *I hope some of her virtues rub off on you.* —**rub out 1** erase. **2** *Slang*. kill. —**rub someone the wrong way** irritate. —*n*. a rubbing: *Give it a good rub; Body rubs* (= massages) *are relaxing; But there's* **the rub** (= difficulty).

rub.ber (RUB.ur) *n*. **1** one that rubs, esp. an eraser. **2** an elastic substance obtained from the latex of certain trees: *crude rubber; natural rubbers.* **3** a similar synthetic product: *acrylic, foam, sponge rubber.* **4** the rubber tree. **5 rubbers** *pl*. rubber overshoes. —*adj*. made of rubber: *rubber balls, bullets, gloves, shoes, tires; circular elastic* **rubber bands** *to put round things as a fastener.* —**rub.ber.y** *adj*.

rubber cement *n*. an adhesive consisting of rubber in an evaporating solvent.

rubber check *n*. *Informal*. a check that is returned because of insufficient funds; an "N.S.F." check.

rubber-chicken *adj*. having to do with speaking engagements: *He took to the rubber-chicken circuit after retirement; a rubber-chicken campaign dinner.*

rub.ber.ize (RUB.uh.rize) *v*. **-iz.es, -ized, -iz.ing** coat or impregnate with rubber; *adj*.: *rubberized asphalt, cotton, handles, heels.*

rub.ber.neck (RUB.ur.nek) *n*. *Informal*. a gawking sightseer. —*v*. gawk: *a traffic jam due to drivers rubbernecking at a crash site.*

rubber stamp *n*. **1** a device for stamping dates, signatures, endorsements, etc. **2** *Informal*. one who routinely approves decisions made by others. **3** such approval. —**rub.ber.stamp** (rub.ur.STAMP) *v*. put a rubber stamp on something: *Does the upper house merely rubberstamp what has been passed in the lower house?*

rubbing alcohol *n*. an alcohol-containing liquid for external uses.

rub.bish (RUB.ish) *n*. something worthless or discarded; trash: *garbage and rubbish disposal; a heap* or *pile of rubbish; He talks rubbish* (= nonsense).

rub.ble (RUB.ul) *n*. a mass of broken stones, bricks, etc.; debris of destroyed

buildings: *The earthquake reduced the town to rubble.*
rub.down *n.* a massage: *a rubdown parlor.*
rube (long "OO") *n. Informal* [derogatory] a person from the country who does not understand city ways.
ru.bel.la (roo.BEL.uh) same as MEASLES, *n.* 2.
ru.be.o.la (roo.BEE.uh.luh) same as MEASLES, *n.* 1.
ru.bi.cund (ROO.bi.cund) *adj.* ruddy; reddish.
Ru.bi.con (ROO.bi.con) *n.* something irrevocable: *Once you cross or pass the Rubicon* (= commit yourself to a course of action), *there's no turning back.*
ru.bid.i.um (roo.BID.ee.um) *n.* a soft, potassiumlike metallic element.
ru.ble (ROO.bul) *n.* the basic money unit of the former Soviet Union and its successor states, equal to 100 kopecks.
ru.bric (ROO.bric) *n.* **1** a procedural guide or rule; formula: *A priest has to observe certain rubrics when saying Mass;* "And they lived happily ever after" has become a rubric of storytellers. **2** the heading of a classification: *services provided under the rubric "added value."*
ru.by (ROO.bee) *n.* **-bies 1** a red variety of corundum, one of the costliest of gems. **2** its usu. deep-red color. —*adj.* deep-red.
ruck.sack *n.* a knapsack.
ruck.us *n. Informal.* a row or uproar: *The parents raised a ruckus over their child's low marks.*
rud.der *n.* a hinged piece of wood or metal at the rear end of a boat or aircraft for steering it.
rud.dy (RUD.ee) *adj.* **rud.di.er, rud.di.est** reddish in complexion; healthy-looking. —**rud.di.ly** *adv.;* **rud.di.ness** *n.*
rude *adj.* **rud.er, rud.est 1** rough in manner; discourteous: *It's rude to contradict your elders; fired for being rude to customers.* **2** of primitive times; barbarous: *a rude implement; our rude forefathers.* **3** rough in effect: *a rude sketch; a rude awakening, shock.* —**rude.ly** *adv.;* **rude.ness** *n.*
ru.di.ment (ROO.duh.munt) *n.* usu. **ru.di.ments** *pl.* basics; elements: *the rudiments of algebra.*
ru.di.men.ta.ry (roo.duh.MEN.tuh.ree) *adj.* undeveloped or beginning: *the rudimentary wings of flightless birds; He has only a rudimentary knowledge of Latin.*
rue (ROO) *n.* an evergreen herb formerly used in medicines. —*v.* **rues, rued, ru.ing** regret: *You will rue the day you quit school.* —**rue.ful** *adj.;* **rue.ful.ly** *adv.;* **rue.ful.ness** *n.*
ruff *v.* to trump in a card game. —*n.* **1** a trumping. **2** a stiff, crimped or pleated, frill-like collar once worn by men and women. **3** a similar band of fur or feathers, as around the neck of birds such as the grouse (**ruffed grouse**).
ruf.fi.an (RUF.ee.un) *n.* one who is rough or rowdy: *a gang of ruffians.* —**ruf.fi.an.ly** *adj.*
ruf.fle (RUF.ul) *v.* **ruf.fles, ruf.fled, ruf.fling 1** make uneven, rough, or disturbed what is smooth: *to ruffle hair, calm waters; to ruffle one's composure, disposition, temper;* *adj.*: *a chiffon ruffled gown; a ruffled shirt, skirt; ruffled hair; to smooth or soothe some ruffled feathers* (= annoyed people). **2** shuffle or flip through pages, playing cards, etc. —*n.* **1** a disturbance; ripple. **2** a strip of material with a frilly edge used as trimming on dresses. **3** the ruff on a bird's neck. **4** a low vibrating drumbeat: *The dignitary was announced with ruffles and flourishes.*
rug *n.* **1** a piece of fabric used as a floor covering: *a scatter rug; throw rugs.* **2** a lap robe. —**pull the rug (out) from under** suddenly withdraw support from a person, project, etc. —**sweep something under the rug** conceal something one wishes to disregard or forget about.
rug.by (RUG.bee) *n.* a British football game distinguished by continuous play by players wearing little protective gear; also **rug.ger.** —**adja.**: *rugby football; a rugby field, league, union.*
rug.ged (RUG.id) *adj.* irregular or rough in feature: *a rugged coast, shoreline; rugged ground, terrain; a rugged face with rugged features; the rugged conditions of pioneer life; her rugged individualism.* —**rug.ged.ly** *adv.;* **rug.ged.ness** *n.*
ru.in (ROO.in) *n.* a state or cause of complete destruction or damage beyond repair: *the ruin of one's plans; Drinking was his ruin; They sifted through the ancient ruins; a pile of ruins; a city lying in ruins.* —*v.* come or bring to ruin: *crops ruined by frost; The scandal ruined his career.* —**ru.in.a.tion** (-uh.NAY.shun) *n.* —**ru.in.ous** (-uh.nus) *adj.;* **ru.in.ous.ly** *adv.*
rule *n.* **1** the way something normally happens or is usu. done: *the rules of grammar; Snow is the exception rather*

than the rule at this time of year; The golden rule says you should do to others as you would wish them to do to you; **As a rule** we don't work on Sundays. **2** a regulation or a set of regulations governing life or conduct: *Everyone has to obey the ground rules of a game; to adopt, apply, break, enforce, rescind, revoke, violate a rule; firm, general, hard-and-fast, inflexible, strict rules; the prime rule; We have made it an invariable rule to pay (in) cash; Everything is done according to rule; No one should be found in violation of the rules; the rule against smoking in elevators; the rules of parliamentary procedure; It's against the rules to drive with the parking lights on; Drivers have to observe many **rules and regulations**; "Drive right" is one of the **rules of the road**; We **bend** or **stretch the rules** a bit in special circumstances.* **3** government: *the rule of law; to establish, extend one's rule; British rule over India ended in 1947; benevolent, despotic, for- eign, majority, mob, popular rule; The monastic rule does not allow talking after hours; during the long rule (= period of government) of the Liberals.* **4** a ruler: *a slide rule.*
—*v.* **rules, ruled, rul.ing 1** lay down as a rule; make an official decision: *The judge was asked to rule on the matter; She ruled (that) the evidence (was) inadmissible; She ruled against him, not in his favor; ruled him (to be) out of order; We can now **rule out** (= exclude) other possibilities.* **2** govern by exerting authority: *Our heads should rule our hearts; He ruled (over) the country with an iron hand;* **n.:** *the rulers and the ruled;* **cpd:** *a British-ruled island; the Liberal-ruled legislature.* **3** mark lines on something; **adj.:** *ruled writing paper with lines across them; ruled pads (of ruled paper).*
rule of thumb *n.* a practical though not precise method of deciding or estimating.
rul.er (ROO.lur) *n.* **1** one who governs; sovereign. **2** a strip of wood, metal, etc. for marking straight lines and measuring short distances.
ruling (ROO.ling) *n.* an official decision, as by a court or umpire: *to give, hand down, make a ruling; a ruling about or on the evidence.* —**adj.** governing or controlling: *the ruling classes, party; one of the ruling families; one's ruling ambition, passion.*
rum *n.* an alcoholic liquor made from molasses.
Ru.ma.ni.an (roo.MAY.nee.un) same as ROMANIAN.

rum.ba (RUM.buh) *n.* **1** a ballroom dance of Cuban origin in quadruple time. **2** the music for it.
rum.ble (RUM.bul) *v.* **-bles, -bled, -bling** make a low, heavy rolling sound: *Thunder rumbled in the distance; The truck rumbled (= moved with a rumbling sound) down the cobbled street; The dispute rumbled on;* **adj.:** *a rumbling sound;* **n.:** *rumblings* (= expressions of dissatisfaction) *about the heavy tax burden; rumblings of discontent.*
—*n.* **1** a rumbling sound: *the rumble of distant thunder; a deep, low rumble; a rumble of assent.* **2** a complaining sound: *rumbles of discontent.* **3** a street fight, as between teen gangs.
rumble strip *n.* a part of a pavement with slightly raised strips of asphalt for making a rumbling sound when tires go over it.
ru.mi.nant (ROO.muh.nunt) *n.* a cud-chewing animal such as the cow, sheep, camel, or giraffe. —*adj.* **1** cud-chewing: *ruminant mammals.* **2** meditative: *in a ruminant mood.*
ru.mi.nate (ROO.muh.nate) *v.* **-nates, -nat.ed, -nat.ing 1** chew the cud. **2** meditate or muse *about* or *on* something. —**ru.mi.na.tion** (-NAY.shun) *n.*
rum.mage (RUM.ij) *v.* **rum.mag.es, rum.maged, rum.mag.ing 1** search thoroughly *through* a drawer, attic, files, old clothes, etc. by moving things about. **2** find out or turn up something by rummaging.
—*n.* **1** a rummaging. **2** miscellaneous articles, as offered at a **rummage sale**, usu. to raise money for charity.
rum.my (RUM.ee) *n.* a card game in which players try to form matching sets and sequences.
ru.mor (ROO.mur) *n.* general talk or a story that is not authentic or verifiable: *to circulate, confirm, deny, dispel, spread rumors; Rumors fly; as rumor has it; There's a rumor that he is broke.*
—*v.* tell or spread by rumor: *It is rumored that he is broke; He is rumored to have gone broke.* Also **ru.mour** *Cdn.*
rump *n.* **1** buttocks. **2** a corresponding cut of beef; **adj.:** *rump roasts, steaks.* **3** a remnant, as of a body of people: *A rebel rump of 16 M.P.s broke ranks and voted against the bill.*
rum.ple *v.* **-ples, -pled, -pling** crush a sheet of paper, garment, etc. or tousle hair; **adj.** a **rumpled** bed, blouse, hat; *rumpled clothes, hair, paper.*
—*n.* a wrinkle or crease.
rum.pus *n. Informal.* a row or uproar: *to raise a rumpus.*

rumpus room *n.* a room set apart for recreational activities, parties, etc.

run *v.* **runs, ran, run.ning** **1** (cause) to move at a pace faster than walking: *He runs for exercise; She is out running her horse.* **2** (cause) to go or move quickly or violently: *He left what he was doing and ran for his life; a ship run aground; She ran her eyes over the page; The car was hit by another running a red light; He was shot trying to run the blockade; He's running* (= contesting the election) *for mayor.* **3** (cause) to go on or keep going: *a train running between Boston and New York; We need a manager to run the business; An engine left running wastes gas.* **4** exist in a specified way: *"Streets" and "avenues" run at right angles to each other; Prices run high as demand increases; Inflation is running rampant; a talent that runs in his family; Our mail is running 10 to 1 in favor of our plan; Their writs don't run* (= are not valid) *here;* [Informal] *People run scared as factories close.* **5** drop stitches or ravel: *a fabric that will not run.* **6** publish: *a story they ran in yesterday's editions.* **7** chase: *to run a rabbit down.* **8** smuggle: *He was charged with running guns across the border.* **9** process or get processed by computer: *to run a Windows application; It doesn't run on our computer.* —**run across** or **into someone** meet someone by chance. —**run down** **1** decline in strength; deteriorate. **2** hunt down; knock down. **3** speak badly of someone. —**run in** **1** *Informal.* arrest and put in jail. **2** break in a new car, shoes, a young horse, etc. —**run out** come to the end of some resource: *Our money ran out; We ran out of* (= had no more) *money.* —**run short** be lacking in a resource: *He runs short of money toward the end of each month.* —**run to** extend or amount to the specified limit: *The book runs to 900 pages.* —**run up** *Informal.* accumulate: *He ran up a huge telephone bill.* —*n.* **1** a running, its duration, or result: *a 12-hour run; a print run of 10,000 copies; The children have the run* (= free use) *of the house when we are out of town; a bombing run* (= a short straight flight for aiming bombs); *a dry run* (= trial or test). **2** a trip or route: *a bus on the Boston-New York run.* **3** a series or succession of things: *a run of bad luck; a run (of withdrawals) on a bank.* **4** a track or area: *dog, sheep, ski runs.* **5** a ravel, as in stockings. —**a run for one's money** **1** satisfaction. **2** challenge. —**in the long run** ultimately. —**on the run** (while) running or fleeing: *a wanted man on the run, with the police looking for him.*

run.a.bout (RUN.uh.bowt) *n.* a light, usu. one-seater vehicle.

run.a.round (RUN.uh.round) *n. Informal.* a being referred from place to place in a frustrating manner: *They gave us the runaround at City Hall.*

run.a.way (RUN.uh.way) *n.* one that has run away: *The young runaway was back home for supper.* —**adj.**: *a runaway* (= fugitive) *slave; a runaway team of horses; runaway inflation (that has gotten out of hand); a runaway* (= very successful) *bestseller, victory.*

run-down *adj.* not running; declining or deteriorating: *a building in a run-down condition; a run-down factory, neighborhood, operation; to feel, get run-down* (= exhausted).

run.down *n.* a summary: *a rundown on or of today's main events.*

rune (ROON) *n.* **1** any letter of an ancient Germanic alphabet used in inscriptions. **2** a mystical or obscure poem. —**ru.nic** *adj.*

rung **1** *n.* a crosspiece forming a step of a ladder or one holding together two legs of a chair: *bottom, lowest, highest, top rung of a ladder.* **2** *v.* a *pp.* of RING.

run-in *n. Informal.* encounter or quarrel: *He has frequent run-ins with the police.*

run.let (RUN.lit) or **run.nel** (RUN.ul) *n.* a small stream.

run.ner (RUN.ur) *n.* **1** one who runs, as a racer, messenger, a football player carrying the ball, or a "base runner" in baseball. **2** a piece or strip placed along the length of something, as the blade of a skate. **3** a narrow carpet. **4** a horizontally growing stem that takes root at nodes, forming on it new plants, as the strawberry. **5** such a plant.

runner-up *n.* **runners-up** a competitor who finishes in second place: *Sam was runner-up in the election, in the race; the runner-up to the champion.*

running *n.* **1** the act or operation of one that runs or manages: *the running of an engine, business, race.* **2** contest: *Some of the candidates who are* **in the running** *for mayor at the start will soon be* **out of the running.** —**adj.** **1** having to do with movement: *She made a running leap over the stream; a running target; a train's running time between Chicago and New York; She kept a running account, tally of her exploits; He gave a running commentary* (= oral play-by-play comments) *on the game.* **2** flowing: *a* *running sore* (discharging *pus*); *running water; a running waterfall.* **3** continuous or continuing: *The wire costs $2.50 per running foot; a running pattern, script; a thump-thump-thump running sound.* —*adv.: The neighbors came running to put out the fire; He hasn't slept for three nights running* (= continuously).

running gear *n.* a vehicle's wheels and axles.

running knot *n.* a knot that slips along the rope around which it is tied.

running lights *n.pl.* a pair of lights on an automobile, aircraft, or other vehicle that are on all the time it is moving.

running mate *n.* a candidate for election on the same ticket as another for a higher office.

running shoes same as SNEAKERS.

running water *n.* water supplied through pipes.

run.ny (RUN.ee) *adj.* **run.ni.er, run.ni.est 1** thin in consistency: *a runny jam.* **2** flowing, as with mucus: *a runny nose.*

run.off *n.* **1** a final contest between the leading candidates in an election; *adj.: a runoff election, vote.* **2** what drains or runs off from a source: *the winter runoff; runoff from factories polluting rivers.* **3** cashing in: *the runoff of Canada Savings Bond holdings.*

run-of-the-mill *adj.* of a product or specimen, commonplace; ordinary: *a run-of-the-mill actor, evening, movie, theme.*

runt *n.* a stunted or undersized plant, animal, or [derogatory] person: *the runt of the litter; That grandstanding little runt!* —**runt.y** *adj.*

run-through *n. Informal.* **1** a rehearsal. **2** a rundown or summary.

run time *n.* the time or duration of executing a task or program on computer. —**run-time** *adj.* generic or inexpensive: *a royalty-free run-time copy or version of Windows software.*

run.way *n.* a special track or way for the movement of people, animals, machines, etc., as the paved strip used by aircraft for takeoffs and landings, or a narrow extension of a stage from its center into the audience.

ru.pee (roo.PEE) *n.* the basic money unit of India, Pakistan, Sri Lanka, Mauritius, etc., equal to 100 paise or cents.

ru.pi.ah (roo.PEE.uh) *n.* the basic money unit of Indonesia.

rup.ture (RUP.chur) *n.* **1** a break or tear, as of the spleen, or a weakening of the muscular wall, as in a hernia. **2** a break in relations: *a rupture of diplomatic relations.* —*v.* cause or suffer a rupture: *An infected appendix may rupture;* *adj.:* **ruptured** *pipelines, relations, seals, tanks, unity.*

ru.ral (ROOR.ul) *adj.* having to do with the country, as opposed to the city: *rural (mail) delivery; a rural municipality, scene; a rural route* (= rural mail service). —**ru.ral.ism** *n.;* **ru.ral.ly** *adv.*

ruse (ROOZE, ROOSE) *n.* a trick used to mask something, as illness feigned to skip class: *a clever ruse.*

rush *v.* **1** move with great speed or haste: *The doctor rushed to see the patient; rushed to her aid; had her rushed to hospital; She rushed through the sale; rushed headlong into marriage; You're rushing me!* *adj.: the* **rushing** *process of selecting freshmen for fraternities and sororities.* **2** attack with speed and force: *The assailant rushed at his victim with a knife; Commandos had to rush the hijacked plane.* —*n.* **1** a rushing or rushed activity: *She forgot her hat in the rush; the rush of modern life; the rush to buy lottery tickets; the California gold rush; Drugs give a sudden rush* (= kick) *that makes the heart race and the body quiver.* **2 rushes** *pl.* the first prints of a movie scene for review by the director: *rushes of the previous day's filming.* **3** a grasslike plant with round stems that grows in marshy places.

rush hour *n.* the time of the heaviest traffic during the day, esp. morning and evening.

rusk *n.* a dry and crisp piece of twice-baked bread or cake.

rus.set (RUSS.it) *adj.* reddish brown, as the cloth that English peasantry used to wear or a kind of winter apple. —*n.* russet cloth or apple.

Rus.sian (RUSH.un) *n.* a person of or from Russia; also its official language. Also *adj.*

Russian roulette *n.* the firing of a revolver at one's own head as an act of bravado without knowing if its only cartridge is in the firing chamber: *Hitchhiking is like* **playing Russian roulette with** (= taking chances on) *your life.*

rust *n.* **1** a reddish brown coating formed on exposed metal, esp. iron; also, the color. **2** a fungus disease of plants, esp. cereals such as wheat, that leaves spores resembling metal rust. —*v.* become covered with rust; hence, deteriorate.

rus.tic (RUS.tic) *adj.* **1** of the country:

rustic charm, simplicity. **2** rough, crude, or unpolished: *rustic furniture, humor, manners.* —*n.* one from the country, esp. an uncouth person. —**rus.tic.i.ty** (rus.TIS.i.tee) *n.*

rus.ti.cate (RUS.ti.cate) *v.* **-cates, -cat.ed, -cat.ing 1** send to the country; also, in Britain, punish by suspension from school. **2** lead a rural life. —**rus.ti.ca.tion** (-CAY.shun) *n.* —**rus.ti.ca.tor** (-cay.tur) *n.*

rus.tle (RUS.ul) *n.* the sound of dry leaves, papers, silk, etc. rubbing lightly together.
—*v.* **-tles, -tled, -tling 1** make or move with a rustle. **2** act or move with energy or speed: *to* **rustle up** (= gather or get ready) *a list of items, players for a team, things for a meal.* **3** steal cattle, horses, etc.; **rust.ler** *n.*

rust.proof *adj.* that resists rust: *a rustproof coating, material; a rustproof warranty (that warranties against rust).*
—*v.* make an automobile safe from rusting; **rust.proof.ing** *n.*

rust.y (RUS.tee) *adj.* **rust.i.er, -i.est 1** coated with rust or rust-colored. **2** in need of polishing, as a skill lying unused: *My Greek is a bit rusty.*

rut *n.* **1** a track or furrow, as made by wheels on a road: *deep ruts in the road.* **2** a settled, routine, or monotonous way of life or course of action: *He felt he was* **(stuck) in a rut***; longed to get out of the rut and do some traveling.* **3** a period or state of sexual excitement or heat, as of the male deer: *during a rut.* —*v.* **ruts, rut.ted, rut.ting 1** make a rut. **2** be in heat. —**rut.ty** *adj.* **rut.ti.er, rut.ti.est; rut.ti.ness** *n.*

ru.ta.ba.ga (root.uh.BAY.guh) *n.* a yellow turnip of the mustard family.

ru.the.ni.um (roo.THEE.nee.um) *n.* a silver-white metallic chemical element used in alloys.

ruth.less (ROOTH.lis) *adj.* merciless or cruel: *He is quite ruthless in his criticism.* —**ruth.less.ly** *adv.*; **ruth.less.ness** *n.*

R value *n.* the thermal resistance value of insulation: *To diminish heat loss through the roof of a house, attic insulation to an R value of R30 is recommended.*

Rx (AR.EX) *n.* **1** a medical prescription: *an Rx for survival.* **2** remedy: *the first-line Rx for angina.*

rye *n.* **1** a cereal similar to wheat, used to make bread and liquors: *corned beef on rye (bread).* **2** a whiskey distilled from rye.

rusticate / saccharin

.... **S, s** ....

S or **s** *n.* **S's** or **s's 1** the 19th letter of the English alphabet. **2** anything S-shaped.

s 1 [added to make plural form]: *boys, girls, the ABC's.* **2** [added to make the third person singular ending of verbs in the present indicative]: *loves, kills, kisses.* **3** [added with apostrophe to make the possessive case of nouns]: *boy's, children's.* **4** [added with apostrophe to make the contracted form of "is," "has," "us," and "does"]: *It's; He's gone; Let's go;* [Informal] *What's it mean?*

Sab.bath (SAB.uth) *n.* a day of rest and worship, as Sunday in Christian practice: *to break, keep the Sabbath.*

Sab.bat.i.cal (suh.BAT.i.cul) **1** *adj.* having to do with the Sabbath: *Sabbatical observances.* **2 sabbatical** *n.* a year or a shorter period of leave for rest, study, etc. such as may be granted to teachers or professors; also **sabbatical leave:** *She's on a sabbatical; He will be taking a sabbatical next year; a sabbatical from work; an executive on a skiing sabbatical;* **adja.:** *to be on sabbatical leave; a sabbatical grant, year.*

sa.ber (SAY.bur) *n.* **1** a heavy cavalry sword for cutting and thrusting, usu. having a curved blade. **2** a fencing foil. Also **sa.bre** *Cdn.*

saber rattling *n.* a menacing show of strength, esp. military.

saber saw *n.* a small electric jigsaw.

Sa.bin vaccine (SAY.bin-) *n.* an oral polio vaccine.

sa.ble (SAY.bul) *n.* **1** a marten of N. Europe and Asia or its fur which is dark-brown to black; hence, black color. **2 sables** *pl.* mourning garments.

sab.o.tage (SAB.uh.tahzh) *n.* damage done to something, esp. property, as a vengeful or subversive act, as by enemy agents or striking workers: *an act of sabotage;* **adja.:** *a sabotage mission, plot, squad.* —*v.* **-tag.es, -taged, -tag.ing** commit sabotage on something: *attempts to sabotage a bill; to sabotage the talks.*

sab.o.teur (sab.uh.TUR) *n.* one who sabotages.

sa.bra (SAH.bruh) *n.* a native-born Israeli.

sabre *Cdn.* SABER.

sac *n.* a baglike part of an animal or plant usu. containing liquid, as the bladder in humans.

sac.cha.rin (SAC.uh.rin) *n.* a very sweet coal-tar product used as a sugar

sac.cha.rine (SAC.uh.rin) *adj.* sugary; also, affectedly sweet: *his saccharine poetry, sentimentality, style; her saccharine smile, voice.*

sac.er.do.tal (sas.ur.DOH.tul) *adj.* priestly: *sacerdotal ordination, vestments.*

sa.chem (SAY.chum) *n.* the chief of some native Indian tribes: *party sachems of local politics.*

sa.chet (sa.SHAY) *n.* a small sealed bag containing perfume, shampoo, powder, etc. for one-time use: *a sachet of dried yeast, hand lotion, soup mix; cedar sachets; herbal sachets; sachet bags.*

sack *n.* **1** a large bag of coarse cloth: *Sam* **got the sack** (*Informal* for dismissal) *for drinking on the job; a late worker who* **hits the sack** (*Informal* for goes to bed) *about midnight.* **2** a dry, white wine popular in the 16th and 17th centuries. —*v. Informal.* **1** fire or dismiss someone. **2** plunder or pillage: *Rome was sacked by the barbarians.*

sack.cloth *n.* a coarse cloth for making sacks; also **sack.ing**. —**sackcloth and ashes** the traditional garb of a humble penitent or mourner.

sack.ful *n.* what a sack will hold.

sa.cral (SAY.crul) *adj.* of the sacrum.

sac.ra.ment (SAC.ruh.munt) *n.* a Christian rite or ceremony considered especially sacred. —**sac.ra.men.tal** (-MEN.tul) *adj.*

sa.cred (SAY.crid) *adj.* **1** set apart or dedicated to someone holy, esp. to the worship of a divine being; holy; inviolable: *a mountain sacred to the Muses; the sacred altar.* **2** worthy of reverence or solemn attention: *the sacred writings of the Bible, Koran, and other holy books; a sacred duty.* —**sa.cred.ness** *n.*

sacred cow *n.* something treated with unquestioning devotion.

sac.ri.fice (SAC.ruh.fice) *n.* an offering or giving up of something valuable for a higher purpose; also, the thing so offered: *a lamb killed as a sacrifice to God; The Aztecs used to offer prisoners as human sacrifices; the sacrifice of one's time and energies in the cause of education; a house sold* **at a sacrifice** (= at a loss); *A baseball batter's* **sacrifice fly** *or* **sacrifice hit** *advances a base runner while the batter is put out.* —*v.* **-fic.es, -ficed, -fic.ing** make a sacrifice: *He sacrificed his health in the pursuit of wealth; John (the batter) sacrificed Jack (the base runner) to second base* (= got Jack to second while himself being put out). —**sac.ri.fi.cial** (sac.ruh.FISH.ul) *adj.*: *a sacrificial lamb, role;* **sac.ri.fi.cial.ly** *adv.*

sac.ri.lege (SAC.ruh.lij) *n.* a violation of something sacred; gross irreverence. —**sac.ri.le.gious** (-LIJ.us) *adj.*

sac.ris.tan (SAC.ris.tun) *n.* an official in charge of a sacristy.

sac.ris.ty (SAC.ris.tee) *n.* **-ties** a place, usu. near the sanctuary, where sacred vessels, vestments, etc. are kept; vestry.

sa.cro.il.i.ac (say.croh.IL.ee.ac) *n. & adj.* (the joint) between the ilium and the sacrum.

sac.ro.sanct (SAC.roh.sanct) *adj.* most sacred; consecrated: *Social benefits are considered politically sacrosanct.*

sa.crum (SAY.crum) *n., pl.* **-cra** (-cruh) or **-crums** the lower end of the spinal column.

sad *adj.* **sad.der, sad.dest** full of or causing sorrow; not happy. —**sad.ly** *adv.;* **sad.ness** *n.*

sad.den (SAD.un) *v.* make or become sad: *We were deeply saddened to learn of Al's passing; It saddened everyone who knew him; adj.: a saddening experience; his saddened colleagues.*

sad.dle (SAD.ul) *n.* **1** the usu. padded and curved seat for a rider of a horse, bicycle, etc. **2** something shaped like a saddle, as a cut of lamb, mutton, or venison consisting of the loins and the connecting back portion. —**in the saddle** in a controlling position. —*v.* **sad.dles, sad.dled, sad.dling** put a saddle upon an animal or person; hence, burden: *Sam is saddled with a heavy mortgage.* —**sad.dler** *n.*

sad.dle.bag (SAD.ul.bag) *n.* one of a pair of bags hung on each side behind a saddle.

sad.dle.bow (SAD.ul.boh) *n.* the arched front part of a saddle.

saddle horse *n.* a horse for riding.

saddle shoe *n.* a casual-wear white oxford with a band of contrasting color across the instep.

Sad.du.cee (SAJ.uh.see) *n.* a member of a Jewish sect opposed to the Pharisees and accepting only the written law of the Bible; **Sad.du.ce.an** (-SEE.un) *adj.*

sad.i.ron (SAD.eye.urn) *n.* a heavy flatiron.

sad.ism (SAD.iz.um, SAY.diz.um) *n.* the getting of pleasure, esp. sexual, from inflicting pain on another; **sad.ist** *n.* —**sad.is.tic** (suh.DIS.tic) *adj.*

sad.o.mas.o.chism (sad.oh.MAS.uh.kiz.um, say.doh-) *n.* sadism and masochism in the same person; **sad.o.mas.o.chist** *n.*

sad sack *n. Informal.* a typically inept

or stupid person.

sa.fa.ri (suh.FAR.ee) *n.* **-ris 1** a hunting expedition, esp. in Africa. **2** the people and animals in it. **3** a vacation trip to observe animal life: *to go on an East African safari.*

safe *adj.* **saf.er, saf.est** free from danger, harm, risk, etc.: *A locked door is safe; a dark but safe street; Stay at a safe distance from drugs and guns; The police officer made her feel safe; safe from enemies; Children should be safe in school; safe and secure; to make the world safe for our children; a drug that is touted as safe and effective; Time was when it was not safe to say the earth goes round the sun; She's quite **safe and sound** (= without harm or injury); a safe (= not risky) guess; a safe (= reliable) driver, guide; a safe (= sure-to-win) seat for the Republicans; Let's **play it safe** (Informal for* Let's take no risks); *a **safe bet** (that you can't lose);* **cpd.***: a microwave-safe casserole; dishwasher-safe.*
—n. a place for keeping something safe, as a steel container: *to crack a safe; an office safe.* **—safe.ly** *adv.*

safe-conduct *n.* permission to pass safely through hostile territory: *He was given safe-conduct through the camp; to issue a safe-conduct (pass).*

safe-deposit *adj.* of a box or vault, for storing valuables, as in a bank: *safe-deposit boxes;* also **safety-deposit.**

safe.guard *n.* protection: *a safeguard against fires; built-in safeguards in the security system.*

safe.house *n.* **1** a refuge. **2** a house that gives protection for plotters, criminals, etc. Also **safe house.**

safe.keep.ing (SAFE.keep.ing) *n.* a keeping or being kept safe; custody.

safe period *n.* the period of the menstrual cycle when pregnancy is unlikely.

safe risk *n.* a person whom it is safe to insure, as a healthy man for life insurance.

safe sex *n.* sexual activity without the risk of sexually transmitted diseases, as by using condoms.

safe.ty (SAFE.tee) *n.* **-ties 1** the state of being safe; security: *to assure, not jeopardize her safety; She found safety in flight, in numbers; to live in safety without fear of being attacked; a margin of safety.* **2** a safety device: *to release the safety.* **3** in football, a play worth two points for the defensive team when the ball carrier is downed in his own end zone or steps out of his end zone; also, a defensive back close to his team's goal line. **—adj.***: a safety factor, fuse, helmet, measure, patrol, precaution, rule; safety equipment; for safety reasons; a **safety-deposit box** (= safe-deposit box); shatterproof **safety glass**; A **safety match** will strike fire only on a prepared surface; A **safety net** protects circus performers in case of a fall; A clasplike **safety pin** has its point held inside a guard; A **safety razor** has its blade between guards for protection; the **safety valve** of a steam boiler for release of excessive pressure.*

saf.flow.er (SAF-; *rhyme:* flower) *n.* a thistlelike plant with orange flowers whose seeds yield an oil used in medicine and cooking.

saf.fron (SAF.run) *n.* a bright orange dyestuff and cooking spice obtained from a crocus.

sag *v.* **sags, sagged, sag.ging** sink or hang down in the middle under weight or pressure, as a stretched rope, horizontal beam, or plank; hence, fall to a lower level: *The roof is sagging; a sagging dollar, economy, morale; sagging prices, spirits, trade; shoulders sagging under the weight of responsibility; Business, confidence, fortunes, prices sag.* **—n.** a sagging place or condition: *the recent sag in consumer demand.*

sa.ga (SAH.guh) *n.* a long story of heroic deeds, like a medieval Norse historical narrative.

sa.ga.cious (suh.GAY.shus) *adj.* of keen mind and sound practical judgment: *a sagacious decision; Guide dogs are sagacious animals.* **—sa.gac.i.ty** (-GAS.i.tee) *n.*

sag.a.more (SAG.uh.more) *n.* a subordinate chief among some North American Indians.

sage *n.* **1** a small shrubby mint whose leaves and stems are used in seasonings: *Garnish with fresh sage;* **adj.***: a sage green color; dried sage leaves.* **2** an elderly man who is wise and discerning: *One of the seven sages of ancient Greece said "Know thyself"; an investment sage.* **3** sagebrush. **—adj.** wise and discerning: *sage advice, counsel.* **—sage.ly** *adv.*

sage.brush *n.* a low-growing aromatic American shrub of the composite family.

sag.gy (SAG.ee) *adj.* **sag.gi.er, sag.gi.est** having a tendency to sag; sagging: *saggy pants.* **—sag.gi.ness** *n.*

Sag.it.ta.ri.us (saj.i.TAIR.ee.us) *n.* **1** a S. constellation and the ninth sign of the zodiac. **2** a person born under this sign.

sa.go (SAY.go) *n.* **-gos** the starch or flour from the pith of an East Indian

saguaro / salesman

palm.

sa.gua.ro (suh.GWAH.roh) *n.* **-ros** the giant, candelabra-shaped cactus of Arizona, S.E. California, and N.W. Mexico.

Sa.ha.ran (suh.HAR.un, -HAIR.un) *adj.* having to do with **Sahara,** the world's largest desert, stretching across N. Africa: *Saharan heat, oases, sand; sub-Saharan* (= black) *Africa.*

said *pt. & pp.* of SAY. —*adj.* [legal use] above-mentioned: *(the) said witness; (the) said amount.*

sail *n.* **1** a sheet of cloth spread to catch the wind for power to move a boat. **2** sails collectively; also, a ship. **3** voyage. **4** the arm of a windmill. —**set sail** begin a voyage. —*v.* **1** move upon a body of water or be moved forward using sails; also, begin a voyage; set sail: *She sails from Boston for Europe tomorrow; Naomi James sailed solo around the world; It was smooth or plain sailing* (= trouble-free) *all the way.* **2** manage a sailing vessel. **3** glide smoothly like a ship with outspread sails or under sail: *He sailed through the exams.* —**sail into** *Informal.* attack or criticize someone.

sail.board *n.* a surfboard equipped with a sail and rudder.
—**sail.board.ing** *n.*

sail.boat *n.* a boat moved by a sail.

sail.cloth *n.* canvas or other cloth for sails, tents, etc.

sail.fish *n.* a large marlin with a saillike dorsal fin.

sail.or (SAY.lur) *n.* one who sails, esp. an enlisted person in a navy.

sail.plane *n.* a glider plane designed for soaring.

saint *n.* a holy person, esp. one officially recognized by a Christian church.
—**saint.hood** *n.* —**saint.ly** *adj.* **-li.er, -li.est.** —**saint.li.ness** *n.*

Saint Ber.nard (-bur.NARD) *n.* a large powerful dog originally bred by monks for rescuing lost travelers in the Swiss Alps.

Saint Valentine's Day *n.* February 14, on which valentines are exchanged.

Saint Vi.tus dance (-VYE.tus) or **Saint Vi.tus's dance** (-tus.iz) See CHOREA.

saith (SETH) [old form] says.

¹**sake** *n.* interest or consideration: *For our children's sake, please stop arguing; For the sake of our children, please stop arguing; Please stop arguing, for goodness sake;* [for added force] *For Heaven's sake, please stop arguing; I'm saying this for both our sakes, for your sake and*

Page 956, *User's*™ *Webster,* © 2000, T. M. Paikeday

mine; Let's not argue for arguing's sake (= because we like to argue); *Let's suppose, for argument's sake* (= as a starting point), *that life does exist on Mars.*

²**sake** or **sa.ki** (SAH.kee) *n.* a Japanese rice wine, usu. served warm.

sa.laam (suh.LAHM) *n.* an Eastern or Muslim greeting that means "peace" in Arabic.

sal.a.ble (SAY.luh.bul) *adj.* that can be sold: *salable merchandise.*

sa.la.cious (suh.LAY.shus) *adj.* obscene; pornographic; **sa.la.cious.ly** *adv.;* **sa.la.cious.ness** *n.*

sal.ad (SAL.ud) *n.* a cold dish of green vegetables and fruit: *Caesar salad; tossed salads; Waldorf salad;* **adj.***: a salad bowl; a restaurant's self-service* **salad bar***; the* **salad days** (= naive period) *of one's youth; a* **salad dressing** (= sauce used with a salad).

sal.a.man.der (SAL.uh.man.dur) *n.* **1** a lizardlike amphibian that lives in streams and ponds. **2** a mythical reptile said to live in fire.

sa.la.mi (suh.LAH.mee) *n.* a thick, highly seasoned Italian sausage.

sal.a.ried (SAL.uh.reed) *adj.* having a salary: *a salaried officer; the salaried staff; a salaried job (that pays a salary, not wages).*

sal.a.ry (SAL.uh.ree) *n.* **-ries** remuneration calculated on a monthly or annual basis and paid regularly, usu. for nonmanual services, in contrast to wages: *to earn, negotiate, pay a salary; to raise someone's salary.*

sale *n.* **1** a selling: *a cash sale (to be paid for at time of sale); clearance, closeout, discount, fire, garage, going-out-of-business, liquidation, rummage, storewide, warehouse sales; a company with annual* **sales** (= gross receipts) *of $20 million; She works in* **sales,** *not promotion (department); The boots are* **for sale.** **2** a selling at reduced prices: *spring sale of winter boots; We have a sale on boots; The boots are* **on sale.** —**sales 1** *adj.:**a sales agent, check, director, executive, force, manager, organization, promotion, quota, register, representative, slip, tax; sales resistance; the number-one sales spot in the market.* **2** *cpd.:* salesclerk, salesgirl, saleslady, salespeople, salesroom.
—**saleable** same as SALABLE.

sales.clerk *n.* one who helps sell goods in a store; also **sales.per.son.**

sales.man (SAILS.mun) *n.* **-men** a man who sells goods or services: *a door-to-door salesman; traveling salesmen.*
—**sales.girl** *n.* —**sales.la.dy** *n.* **-dies.**

—sales.wom.an *n.* **-wom.en.**
—sales.man.ship *n.*
sales.per.son (SAILS.pur.sun) *n.* a salesman or saleswoman; also **sales representative** or **sales rep** [short form]. **—sales.peo.ple** (-pee.pul) *n.pl.*
sales slip *n.* a receipt acknowledging payment for something sold; also **sales receipt.**
sales talk *n.* talk aimed at selling or persuading people to buy something.
sal.i.cyl.ic acid (sal.uh.SIL.ic-) *n.* a chemical used in making aspirin.
sa.lient (SAIL.yunt) *adj.* prominent: *the salient features of this dictionary; its salient characteristics, points.*
—n. an angle, part of a fortification, etc. that points outward; projection: *The Battle of the Bulge is named after a salient; the Rafah salient south of the Gaza Strip.* **—sa.lience** *n.*
sa.line (SAY.leen, -line) *adj.* of salt; salty: *a saline solution.* **—sa.lin.i.ty** (suh.LIN.i.tee) *n.*
sa.li.va (suh.LYE.vuh) *n.* a digestive juice produced in the mouth by the salivary glands. **—sa.li.var.y** (SAL.uh.vair.ee) *adj.*
sal.i.vate (SAL.uh.vate) *v.* **-vates, -vat.ed, -vat.ing** produce saliva, esp. excessively; **sal.i.va.tion** (-VAY.shun) *n.*
Salk vaccine (SAWLK-) *n.* a polio vaccine given as injections.
sal.low (SAL.oh) *adj.* yellowish or sickly in complexion.
sal.ly (SAL.ee) *v.* **sal.lies, sal.lied, sal.ly.ing** go *forth* or set *out* suddenly (as if) to attack. **—n.** 1 a sallying forth or sortie: *to make a sally into enemy lines; bombing sallies.* 2 a witty remark: *sallies of wit; an opening sally.* 3 an excursion or jaunt.
Sally Ann *n. Informal.* the Salvation Army, a Christian evangelistic and social service organization.
salm.on (SAM.un) *n.* a large food fish that swims back from the ocean to spawn in freshwater streams.
sal.mo.nel.la (sal.muh.NEL.uh) *n.* any of a genus of bacteria that cause food poisoning, paratyphoid, etc.
sa.lon (suh.LON) *n.* 1 a reception hall or fashionable gathering place: *a hotel salon.* 2 a business place dealing in goods and services related to women and fashion: *beauty, couture, dress, hairstyling, shoe salons; a networking salon.*
sa.loon (suh.LOON) *n.* 1 a tavern; *adj.: a saloon bar, girl; swinging saloon doors.* 2 a large room for a specified social purpose: *a dining saloon.*
sa.loon.keep.er (suh.LOON.kee.pur) *n.*

a tavern operator.
sal.si.fy (SAL.suh.fee, -fye) *n.* **-fies** a garden vegetable whose fleshy roots have an oysterlike flavor.
sal soda same as WASHING SODA.
salt (SAWLT) *n.* 1 a white, crystalline substance obtained from sea water and mines and widely used as a seasoning and preservative: *Add salt to taste; Use common salt or table salt; salt-and-pepper holders, sets;* **adj.:** *salt* (= salted) *beef, pork; Salt flats, mines, pits, and wells have salt deposits.* 2 that which adds piquancy or liveliness to anything. 3 *Informal.* a sailor: *an old salt.* 4 **salts** *pl.* a laxative such as "Epsom salts" or a preparation such as "smelling salts" that is inhaled to relieve faintness, headache, etc.
—rub salt into or **pour salt on the wound** make one's pain even worse.
—salt of the earth the finest of people. **—take with a grain** or **pinch of salt** accept with some skepticism.
—worth one's salt worth one's pay.
—v. 1 season or preserve with salt: *to salt fish, meat, nuts;* **adj.:** *lightly salted butter, fish, meat, water; Her speech is heavily salted with expletives.* 2 tamper with something so as to change its character or quality: *to salt a mine; The ore samples were salted with gold dust.*
—salt away lay away safely; put aside or save.
salt.box *n.* a two-story dwelling, as of colonial days, having its roof extended at the back to cover a kitchen annex.
salt.cel.lar (SAWLT.sel.ur) *n.* a salt container used on the table.
salt.ine (sawl.TEEN) *n.* a thin salted cracker: *a new saltine flavor.*
salt lick *n.* rock salt occurring above the ground which animals lick.
salt pan *n.* a natural depression in the earth containing a deposit of salt.
salt.pe.ter or **salt.pe.tre** (SAWLT.pee.tur) *n.* 1 naturally occurring potassium nitrate; niter. 2 a nitrate of sodium or calcium.
salt.shak.er (SAWLT.shay.kur) *n.* a salt container for sprinkling salt on food.
salt.wa.ter (SAWLT.wot.ur) *adj.* having to do with salty water: *a saltwater lake, fish.*
salt.y *adj.* **salt.i.er, -i.est** 1 that tastes of salt: *salty foods, soups, taste.* 2 racy: *salty anecdotes, humor, language.* **—salt.i.ness** *n.*
sa.lu.bri.ous (suh.LOO.bree.us) *adj.* healthful or invigorating: *a salubrious climate; the salubrious mountain air.*
sal.u.tar.y (SAL.yuh.tair.ee) *adj.* health-

ful or beneficial even if unpleasant: *a salutary exercise, experience, influence, medicine, warning; salutary advice, penance, suffering.*

sal.u.ta.tion (sal.yuh.TAY.shun) *n.* an act or expression of greeting, such as a bow, raising the hat, or "Dear Sir or Madam" at the beginning of a letter.

sa.lute (suh.LOOT) *v.* **-lutes, -lut.ed, -lut.ing** greet, esp. to show honor or respect using a standard gesture such as a bow or a formal act such as raising the right hand or firing a cannon. —*n.* a saluting act or gesture; greeting: *a 21-gun salute.*

sal.vage (SAL.vij) *n.* **1** the saving of useful property from loss or waste, as ship or cargo from a shipwreck, scrap metal, etc. **2** property salvaged; also, compensation for salvage work. —*v.* **-vag.es, -vaged, -vag.ing** save property from being lost or destroyed: *He escaped with his dignity barely salvaged; to salvage an agreement, career, reputation, vacation;* **adja.:** *salvage efforts, plans, value;* **adj.:** *salvaged brick, food, wastepaper.* —**sal.vage.a.ble** (-juh.bul) *adj.*

sal.va.tion (sal.VAY.shun) *n.* **1** the saving of a person from damnation; redemption: *Missionaries preach salvation; sinners seeking salvation from hell; He found salvation in faith and good works.* **2** any saving from a great loss or calamity; also, that which effects it: *The timely arrival of the police proved his salvation (from assault); They found salvation in religion; Her only salvation was in fleeing the fire; Your salvation lies in laying off drugs.*

salve (SAV) *v.* **salves, salved, salv.ing** soothe: *a balm to salve the wound; words to salve her conscience; to salve his ego.* —*n.* a balm, ointment, or anything that soothes.

sal.ver (SAL.vur) *n.* a serving tray.

sal.vo (SAL.voh) *n.* **-vos** or **-voes** simultaneous discharge of guns as a salute or in attack; volley: *to fire a salvo; a salvo of bombs, cheers, insults.*

samaritan See GOOD SAMARITAN.

sa.mar.i.um (suh.MAIR.ee.um) *n.* a rare-earth metallic element.

sam.ba (SAM.buh) *n.* **1** a Brazilian ballroom dance of African origin in duple time. **2** the music for it.

same *adja. & pron.* (being) the one referred to or implied: *He sleeps in the same bed every day; This is the same lunch as* or *that you ate yesterday* (= same in kind, appearance, amount, etc.); *the same as yesterday's; They are both the same* (= alike); *They are one and the same* (= exactly similar); *It's all the same to me;* **All the same** (= In spite of it), *I'm not eating today; Fill in the form and forward same* (Nonstandard for it) *to us.* —*adv.* in the same manner: *I feel the same (as you); same with me; same here.* —**same.ness** *n.*

Sa.mo.an (suh.MOH.un) *adj.* having to do with a group of 16 islands in the S. Pacific.

sam.o.var (SAM.uh.var) *n.* a metal urn with an internal tube containing burning charcoal, used in Russia to heat water for tea.

sam.pan (SAM.pan) *n.* an Oriental boat having a small cabin often used as a dwelling and equipped with a sail and propelled by an oar at the stern.

sam.ple (SAM.pul) *n.* a part or specimen that shows the quality of the whole: *free samples of a new toothpaste; a random sample of the population; a fair sample* (= instance or specimen) *of his wit.* —*v.* **-ples, -pled, -pling** take as a sample; test a part of something.

sam.pler (SAM.plur) *n.* **1** one who samples; also, a collection of samples. **2** a piece of cloth embroidered in various designs for practice or display.

Sam.son (SAM.sun) *n.* in the Bible, an Israelite famed for his strength.

sam.u.rai (SAM.uh.rye) *n. sing. & pl.* (a member of) a warrior class in feudal Japan.

san.a.to.ri.um (san.uh.TOR.ee.um) *n.* **-ri.ums** or **-ri.a** (-ree.uh) **1** an establishment for treating a particular group of patients: *a TB sanatorium; a sanatorium for the mentally ill.* **2** a convalescent home.

sanc.ti.fy (SANC.tuh.fye) *v.* **-fies, -fied, -fy.ing** make holy; consecrate: *a day sanctified by God as the Sabbath; a practice sanctified by custom.*
—**sanc.ti.fi.ca.tion** (-fuh.CAY.shun) *n.*

sanc.ti.mo.ni.ous (sanc.tuh.MOH.nee.us) *adj.* pious in a showy way; **sanc.ti.mo.ni.ous.ly** *adv.*
—**sanc.ti.mo.ny** (SANC.tuh.moh.nee) *n.* pretended piety or virtue.

sanc.tion (SANC.shun) *n.* **1** official or authoritative approval: *a bill that has received the sanction of Parliament; to give sanction to a bill.* **2** penalty provided by a law for its enforcement: *to apply economic sanctions such as trade boycotts and embargoes, instead of military sanctions, to force a nation to obey international law; trade sanctions imposed against a hostile nation; to lift sanctions.*
—*v.* approve of something officially: *Many churches don't sanction divorce;*

customs sanctioned by tradition.

sanc.ti.ty (SANC.ti.tee) *n.* sacredness: *the sanctity of marriage; the* **sanctities** (= duties, obligations, etc. considered as sacred) *of family life.*

sanc.tu.ar.y (SANC.choo.air.ee) *n.* **1** a consecrated place such as a place of worship, esp. the part of a church containing the altar. **2** a place of refuge or protection: *a bird, wild life sanctuary; to find, offer, provide, seek sanctuary; Hijackers are given sanctuary in certain countries; a sanctuary for political refugees.*

sanc.tum (SANC.tum) *n.* **1** a sacred place: *the inner sanctum of one's conscience.* **2** *Informal.* one's private place of seclusion; den.

sand *n.* loose grains of worn-down rock, finer than gravel but coarser than silt, found in river beds, on seashores, etc.: *the* **sands** (= sandy tract) *of the desert; to bury* or *hide one's head in the sand* (= to ignore realities). —*v.* **1** put sand over or into something: *to sand an icy road.* **2** smooth a surface, as of wood, with "sandpaper" or with a "sanding machine."
—**sand.er** *n.*

san.dal (SAN.dul) *n.* a slipper or low shoe with straps joining the sole to the foot: *a pair of sandals; beach sandals.*

san.dal.wood (SAN.dul.wood) *n.* the heavy, straight-grained, fragrant, yellowish wood of several trees of the East Indies that is used for carving and whose oil is used for cosmetics.

sand.bag *n.* a sand-filled bag used for ballast, protection, etc. —*v.* **-bags, -bagged, -bag.ging 1** put sandbags in or around a place for protection. **2** hit someone, as with a sandbag: *The Opposition tried to sandbag the Government into adopting its policies.*

sand.bank *n.* a shoal, ridge, etc. formed by a deposit of sand, as at the mouth of a river; also **sand.bar.**

sand.blast *n. & v.* (clean, engrave, etc. with) a blast of air or steam containing sand; **sand.blast.er** *n.*

sand.box *n.* a small enclosure filled with sand for children to play in.

sand.hog *n.* a laborer working underground or under water, as in a caisson.

sand.lot *adja.* of sports and games, informal or unorganized: *sandlot baseball, games; a sandlot free-for-all.*

sand.man *n.* the folklore genie who makes children sleepy.

sand.pa.per (SAND.pay.pur) *n. & v.* (rub with) paper coated with sand for polishing surfaces.

sand.pip.er (SAND.pye.pur) *n.* a small bird with a long, soft-tipped bill seen on seashores.

sand.stone *n.* a rock composed of sand particles cemented together by silica, clay, calcium, etc.

sand.storm *n.* a desert storm driving clouds of sand through the air.

sand.wich *n.* two slices of bread with a layer of meat, cheese, jam, or other filling between them: *cheese, club, corned-beef, grilled-cheese, ham, tomato-and-lettuce, tuna sandwiches; the* **sandwich generation** *of people who have both their children and elders to look after.*
—*v.* to place or crowd in between two other persons or things: *to sandwich a doctor's appointment between meetings.*

sand.y (SAN.dee) *adj.* **sand.i.er, -i.est 1** containing or covered with sand: *sandy beaches.* **2** yellowish-red: *sandy hair.*

sane *adj.* **san.er, san.est** mentally sound; also, sensible. —**sane.ly** *adv.*

sang *pt.* of SING.

sang-froid or **sang.froid** (sang. FRWAH) *n.* coolness or composure: *the sang-froid of our banker.*

san.gui.nar.y (SANG.gwuh.nair.ee) *adj.* bloody: *a sanguinary war; a cruel and sanguinary* (= bloodthirsty) *tyrant.*

san.guine (SANG.gwin) *adj.* **1** disposed to be cheerful and confident: *a sanguine temperament; his sanguine hopes.* **2** ruddy: *a sanguine complexion.*

san.i.tar.i.an (san.i.TAIR.ee.un) *adj.* a sanitation specialist.

san.i.tar.i.um (san.i.TAIR.ee.um) *n.* **-i.ums** or **-i.a** (-ee.uh) **1** a health resort. **2** a sanatorium.

san.i.tar.y (SAN.i.tair.ee) *adj.* **1** having to do with cleanliness: *the sanitary environment of a hospital; sanitary measures to combat disease; sanitary gloves; the sanitary* (= hospital-clean) *appearance of Dr. Smith's residence; a disposable* **sanitary pad** or **napkin** *worn to absorb the menstrual flow.* **2** having to do with waste disposal: *sanitary fittings; a sanitary landfill site; A* **sanitary engineer** *deals with aspects of public health such as water supply, sewage disposal, etc.*

san.i.ta.tion (san.i.TAY.shun) *n.* aspects of public health that include sewage disposal, water treatment, pollution control, and food processing.

san.i.tize (SAN.i.tize) *v.* **-tiz.es, -tized, -tiz.ing 1** make sanitary: *a new product for sanitizing kitchen counters;* **adja.**: *a hot water* **sanitizing** *cycle; sanitizing agents.* **2** remove objectionable features

from something to be published; *adj.*: a *sanitized* film version. —**san.i.tiz.er** *n.*: *a toothbrush sanitizer.*
san.i.ty (SAN.i.tee) *n.* **1** sound mental health: *to keep, lose, maintain, preserve* or *retain one's sanity.* **2** soundness of judgment.
sank *pt.* of SINK.
sans *prep.* without: *hockey sans violence.*
San.skrit *n.* the Indo-European classical language of India, with records from around 1000 B.C.
San.ta Claus (SAN.tuh.claws) *n.* the red-suited, white-bearded, jolly old man that children believe brings them Christmas gifts.
sap *n.* **1** the vital juice that circulates through a plant carrying food and water: *The sap of the sugar maple begins to run in spring when the days are warm and nights cold.* **2** health and vigor. **3** *Slang.* a dupe or fool. **4** a trench dug for approaching or undermining an enemy's position. —*v.* **saps, sapped, sap.ping** dig under or undermine; hence, weaken or wear away: *strength sapped by heat.* —**sap.less** *adj.* lacking in health and vigor.
sa.pi.ent (SAY.pee.unt) *adj.* wise or discerning; **sa.pi.ent.ly** *adv.* —**sa.pi.ence** *n.*
sap.ling *n.* **1** a young tree. **2** a young person.
sap.o.dil.la (sap.uh.DIL.uh) *n.* a tropical tree that bears delicious, apple-shaped, rusty-brown fruit and whose latex is used for gum chicle.
sap.per *n.* a trench-digging soldier.
sap.phire (SAF.ire) *n.* a bright-blue gem or its color. —*adj.*: *Our swimming pool is a sapphire blue; a sapphire necklace, ring.*
sap.py (SAP.ee) *adj.* **sap.pi.er, sap.pi.est** **1** full of sap; also, full of vitality. **2** *Slang.* foolish. —**sap.pi.ness** *n.*
sap.ro.phyte (SAP.ruh.fite) *n.* an organism that draws nourishment from dead or decaying matter.
—**sap.ro.phyt.ic** (-FIT.ic) *adj.*
sap.suck.er (SAP.suck.ur) *n.* a woodpecker that gets sap out of trees.
sap.wood *n.* the light-colored, sap-carrying part of a tree trunk between bark and heartwood.
Sar.a.cen (SAIR.uh.sun) *n.* an Arab or Moslem, esp. at the time of the Crusades. —**Sar.a.cen.ic** (-SEN.ic) *adj.*
sa.ran (suh.RAN) *n.* a synthetic plastic material used as a film or sheet, esp. for wrapping, and as a textile fiber for draperies, upholstery, etc.
sar.casm (SAR.caz.um) *n.* an ironical and cutting type of humor or remark, often used to ridicule: *His tongue was dripping with sarcasm; biting, keen, piercing, mild sarcasm.* —**sar.cas.tic** (sar.CAS.tic) *adj.* —**sar.cas.ti.cal.ly** *adv.*
sar.co.ma (sar.COH.muh) *n.* **-mas** or **-ma.ta** (-muh.tuh) a cancer of connective tissues, esp. of bones or muscles.
sar.coph.a.gus (sar.COF.uh.gus) *n., pl.* **-gi** (-jye) or **-gus.es** a stone coffin, esp. an inscribed or ornamented one.
sar.dine (sar.DEEN) *n.* a small herring, usu. canned for food or dried and powdered for fish meal: *a bus packed like a can of sardines* (= a very crowded bus).
sar.don.ic (sar.DON.ic) *adj.* scornful or sarcastic: *a sardonic expression; sardonic humor, laughter.* —**sar.don.i.cal.ly** *adv.*
sarge *n. Informal.* sergeant.
sa.ri or **sa.ree** (SAH.ree) *n.* a S. Asian, esp. Indian garment of women, consisting of a decorated length of lightweight cloth draped around the body.
sa.rin (SAH.rin) *n.* a lethal nerve gas.
sa.rong (suh.RONG) *n.* a colorful piece of cloth worn like a skirt by men and women of the East Indies.
sar.sa.pa.ril.la (sas.uh.puh.RIL.uh, sar.suh-) *n.* (the fragrant root of) a tropical vine of the smilax group, used to flavor carbonated drinks.
sar.to.ri.al (sar.TOR.ee.ul) *adj.* of tailoring, esp. of men's clothes: *sartorial elegance; a sartorial masterpiece; in sartorial splendor.*
sash *n.* **1** a broad strip of cloth worn either as a belt or over one shoulder as a dress accessory or sign of rank. **2** the frame holding the glass in a door or window; also, the sliding frame of a double-hung window (**sash window**).
sa.shay (sa.SHAY) *n. Informal.* walk or move in a gliding manner, esp. sideways: *to sashay across a stage.*
Sas.quatch (SASK.watch) *n.* a hairy monster of western Canadian folklore; Bigfoot.
sass *n. Informal.* saucy talk; also, style: *a woman with sass and sweetness; sass and verve; sass and wit.* —*v.* answer impudently.
sas.sa.fras (SAS.uh.fras) *n.* (the aromatic root bark of) a North American laurel with pale yellow flowers and irregularly-shaped leaves.
sass.y (SAS.ee) *adj.* **sass.i.er, -i.est** *Informal.* **1** saucy: *a sassy little girl.* **2** fresh; lively; stylish: *sassy albums, essays.* —*v.* **sass.ies, sass.ied, sass.y.ing** make sassy or stylish: *a little*

car sassied up with a lot of accessories.
sat *pt. & pp.* of SIT.
Sa.tan (SAY.tun) *n.* the Devil.
sa.tan.ic (suh.TAN.ic, say-) *adj.* **1** fiendish or evil like Satan: *satanic pride.* **2** having to do with the worship of Satan: *a satanic cult.*
satch.el (SACH.ul) *n.* a bag for carrying books to school, clothes, etc.
sate *v.* **sates, sat.ed, sat.ing** satisfy a desire or appetite so fully that it dies: *sated with food and drink.*
sa.teen (suh.TEEN) *n.* an imitation satin cloth, usu. all-cotton.
sat.el.lite (SAT.ul.ite) *n.* **1** a person or thing following another that is larger or more important, as a small planet that revolves around a larger one: *The moon is the earth's only satellite; to put an artificial satellite in orbit; to launch a communications satellite; spy, weather satellites;* **adja.:** *the satellite campuses of a university; a satellite city near a metropolis.* **2** one of many nations controlled by a great power: *the former Soviet satellites of Eastern Europe.*
sa.ti.ate (SAY.shee.ate) *v.* **-ates, -at.ed, -at.ing** satisfy a desire or appetite to excess; sate: *satiated with food and drink.* —**sa.ti.a.tion** (-AY.shun) *n.* —**sa.ti.e.ty** (suh.TYE.uh.tee) *n.*: *filled to satiety with food and drink.*
sat.in (SAT.un) *n.* a smooth and glossy silk or other fabric woven with a lustrous face. —**sat.in.y** *adj.*
sat.in.wood (SAT.un.wood) *n.* (an East Indian tree that has) a yellowish-brown wood with a satiny luster.
sat.ire (SAT.ire) *n.* **1** the use of irony and sarcasm to expose folly and vice, as in cartoons, comedies of manners, and the literature of such writers as Swift and Pope. **2** such a work or works collectively. —**sat.i.rist** (-uh.rist) *n.* —**sa.tir.i.cal** (sa.TEER.i.cul) *adj.;* **sa.tir.i.cal.ly** *adv.*
sat.i.rize (SAT.uh.rize) *v.* **-riz.es, -rized, -riz.ing** attack using satire.
sat.is.fac.tion (sat.is.FAC.shun) *n.* a satisfying or something that satisfies, esp. the discharge of a debt or claim or making up for harm done: *to afford, express, feel, find, give satisfaction; to take satisfaction in doing a good job; deep, quiet satisfaction about a job well done; The work was done to our complete satisfaction; "Satisfaction guaranteed or your money back"; Teaching has many satisfactions, job satisfaction being one; The customer demanded, sought satisfaction* (= compensation); *He got, had, received satisfaction for the loss suffered.*

sat.is.fac.to.ry (sat.is.FAC.tuh.ree) *adj.* adequate: *a satisfactory though not outstanding performance; A settlement has to be satisfactory to both parties; mutually satisfactory; a satisfactory arrangement, alternative, deal, level, outcome, relationship, result, reply, service, solution, substitute.* —**sat.is.fac.to.ri.ly** *adv.*
sat.is.fy (SAT.is.fye) *v.* **-fies, -fied, -fy.ing 1** fulfill: *to satisfy one's appetite; to satisfy a condition, demand, desire, hope, need; to satisfy her curiosity; to satisfy the requirements for a Ph.D.; to satisfy* (= pay) *a claim for damages.* **2** make happy or contented: *a spoiled child who is hard to satisfy; We're completely, perfectly, thoroughly satisfied with what we bought;* **adj.:** *a* **satisfied** *customer; a self-satisfied smile; a* **satisfying** *career, experience, life, performance; completely, deeply, extremely, highly, immensely, richly, supremely satisfying; The pay raise was a satisfying 15%.* **3** convince: *She satisfied herself that the insult was not intended; We are satisfied that's the truth.*
sa.to.ri (suh.TOR.ee) *n.* spiritual awakening that is the goal of Zen Buddhism.
sa.trap (SAY.trap, SAT-) *n.* a subordinate or petty ruler, as in the ancient Persian Empire.
sat.u.rate (SACH.uh.rate) *v.* **-rates, -rat.ed, -rat.ing** (cause) to be filled, charged, or soaked to the maximum: *soil saturated by water from heavy rains;* **adj.:** *a* **saturated** *solution of a substance in water; Air saturated with moisture will condense if cooled;* **Saturated fats** *contain the maximum number of hydrogen atoms in their molecules; A* **saturated market** (*with plentiful supplies*) *is a buyer's market.* —**sat.u.ra.tion** (-RAY.shun) *n.* maximum in regard to capacity or limit: *employment saturation in a population or occupation; market saturation of a product;* **adja.:** *The computer market has reached the saturation point; an evangelist with saturation coverage on TV; saturation advertising, bombing, level, limit, marketing, strategy.*
Sat.ur.day (SAT.ur.dee, -day) *n.* the last day of the week, following Friday.
Saturday night special *n.* a cheap, dangerous, easily concealed handgun.
Sat.urn *n.* the planet sixth in distance from the sun and the second largest, with three rings around it.
sat.ur.nine (SAT.ur.nine) *adj.* gloomy or forbidding in aspect.
sat.yr (SAY.tur, SAT-) *n.* in Greek myth, a lecherous woodland deity with the lower half of his body like a

goat's. —**sa.tyr.ic** (suh.TEER.ic) *adj.*

sat.y.ri.a.sis (sat.uh.RYE.uh.sis) *n.* excessive sexual desire in the male.

sauce *n.* **1** a liquid or soft preparation served with food or as a topping with dessert to add flavor: *barbecue, soy, spaghetti, steak, tomato sauce.* **2** *Informal.* impudence. —*v.* **sauc.es, sauced, sauc.ing 1** season; add flavor to a food. **2** *Informal.* be saucy to someone.

sauce.pan *n.* a metal cooking pot with a handle.

sau.cer *n.* a small, shallow dish for holding a cup.

sauc.y (SAW.see) *adj.* **sauc.i.er, -i.est** flippant and disrespectful in behavior. —**sauc.i.ly** *adv.*; **sauc.i.ness** *n.*

Sa.u.di (SOW.dee, sah.OO.dee) *n. & adj.* **-dis** (a person) of or from **Saudi Arabia**, a kingdom occupying most of the Arabian peninsula.

sau.er.kraut (SOUR.crowt) *n.* finely cut cabbage fermented in brine.

sau.na (SAW.nuh) *n.* **1** a steam bath in which water is thrown on hot stones to produce steam. **2** the room housing the bath.

saun.ter (SAUN.tur) *n. & v.* walk in a leisurely manner; stroll.

sau.ro.pod (SOR.uh.pod) *n.* a gigantic plant-eating dinosaur such as the brontosaurus.

sau.sage (SOS.ij) *n.* **1** a tubular casing stuffed with chopped and seasoned meat. **2** one such casing or link: *pancakes and sausages.*

sau.té (soh.TAY) *v.* **-tés, -téed** (-TAID), **-té.ing** (-TAY.ing) fry quickly in a little fat: *to sauté mushrooms in butter and garlic*; *adj.*: *tomatoes with sautéed zucchini.* —*n.* sautéed food.

sau.terne (soh.TURN) *n.* a sweet white table wine; also **sau.ternes** (-TURN).

Sau.vi.gnon (SOH.VIN.yohn) *n.* a dry, red wine made from a blue-black variety of grape.

sav.age (SAV.ij) *n.* one who is fierce, brutal, or rough-mannered: *drunken savages; Rousseau's "noble savage" considered as superior to the civilized man.* —*adj.* utterly uncivilized or brutal: *a savage act, attack, dog, spending cut, struggle; savage criticism; a savage* (= fierce) *temper.* —*v.* **-ag.es, -aged, -ag.ing** attack violently or brutally: *a child savaged by an attack dog; a country savaged by fighting; The Republicans ridiculed and savaged the Democrats for their turnabout.* —**sav.age.ly** *adv.*; **sav.age.ness** *n.* —**sav.age.ry** (-ij.ree) *n.* **-ries.**

sa.van.na or **sa.van.nah** (suh.VAN.uh) *n.* tropical grassland lying between forests and deserts, as of sub-Saharan Africa, the velds of South Africa, and the pampas of South America.

sa.vant (suh.VAHNT, SAV.unt) *n.* one who is learned in a particular area: *a literary savant.*

save *v.* **saves, saved, sav.ing 1** make or keep free from danger, risk, loss, etc.: *The seat belt saved the driver's life; Take a plane to save time; Flying will save us time; Read in good light to save your eyes; how to save marriages that are breaking up.* **2** preserve or keep for future use: *He's saving money* (= putting money aside) *for a vacation; tips to help you save (money); She's trying to save* (= economize) *on travel expenses; to save* (= copy) *computer data onto a disk; It's no use trying to persuade him – save your breath.* —*n.* an act, as of a goalkeeper, that prevents an opponent from scoring: *He made a spectacular save.*
—*prep. Formal.* except(ing): *All were rescued, save for a missing cat; all save one*; *conj.*: *I agree with you on everything save that life exists on Mars.* —**sav.er** *n.*

saving *n.* **1** reduced expenditure: *saving and investment; saving and thrift.* **2 savings** *pl.* money saved: *to deposit, dip into, withdraw one's savings; a savings account in a savings bank; a high-interest, fixed-term savings certificate; a savings and loan association* (= cooperative savings bank) *owned and operated by shareholders.*

sav.ior (SAVE.yur) *n.* **1** one who saves: *the savior of the economy.* **2** in Christian religions, Jesus Christ, **the Savior.** Also **sav.iour, Saviour** *Cdn.*

sa.voir-faire (sav.wahr.FAIR) *n.* tact or ability to get along well in social situations.

sa.vor (SAY.vur) *n.* the distinctive taste, smell, or other quality of something: *the savor of soy sauce.* —*v.* enjoy the savor of something: *She savored the wine slowly; His style savors* (= smacks) *of arrogance.* Also **sa.vour** *Cdn.*

sa.vor.y (SAY.vuh.ree) *adj.* **-vor.i.er, -vor.i.est 1** pleasing to the smell and taste: *a savory dish, treat; the savory aromas from her kitchen; so savory it makes your mouth water.* **2** [used negatively] pleasant or acceptable, esp. morally: *the less savory side of his character.* Also **sa.vour.y** *Cdn.*

sav.vy (SAV.ee) *n.* practical know-how: *an aide with political savvy; a taxi driver with plenty of savvy; a woman with a lot of fashion savvy; marketing savvy.* —*adj.* **sav.vi.er, sav.vi.est** having practical know-how: *He is more savvy than smart;*

a savvy businessman, consumer, merchant; the savvier seniors; America's savviest cola drink; computer-savvy children. —v. **sav.vies, sav.vied, sav.vy.ing** know or grasp: *Do you savvy this, young man?*

saw *pt.* of SEE. —**saw** *n.* **1** a wise saying; maxim. **2** a tool that has a metal blade with teeth on a straight or circular edge for cutting hard substances. —*v.* **saws,** *pt.* **sawed,** *pp.* **sawed** or **sawn, saw.ing** cut (as if) with a saw with a back-and-forth motion: *He sawed the air trying to make gestures;* **adja.:** *a sawed-off shotgun.*

saw.bones *n. Slang.* a surgeon.

saw.buck *n. Slang.* a ten-dollar bill.

saw.dust *n.* fine fragments of wood produced in sawing.

saw.horse *n.* a frame with four legs for supporting wood being sawn by hand.

saw.mill *n.* a factory in which logs are sawn into lumber.

saw.toothed *adj.* serrated like a saw's teeth: *a sawtoothed pattern; sawtoothed responses.*

saw.yer (SAW.yur) *n.* one who saws wood.

sax [short form] saxophone: *alto, baritone, soprano, tenor saxes; a sax player.*

Sax.on (SAK.sun) *n. & adj.* (a dialect or member) of a Germanic people who settled in Britain in the fifth century; also, Anglo-Saxon.

sax.o.phone (SAX.uh.fone) *n.* a wind instrument with a curved body, usu. made of brass; **sax.o.phon.ist** (-FOH.nist) *n.*

say *v.* **says** (SEZ), **said** (SED), **say.ing** **1** utter; speak; tell: *Please say what is on your mind; She said a few words in reply; What do you say about that? What do you say (in reply) to that? He's saying his prayers; She left without saying goodbye; What can you say for* (= in justification of) *yourself? The clock says* (= shows) *12.* **2** state; declare: *hard to say whether he's telling the truth; It says here, "Take as directed"; He said he would be late; He did not say it in jest; He's said to be a learned man.* **3** [used parenthetically] let us suppose as an example, estimate, etc.: *You would make, say, $200 a day.* —*n.* expression of one's opinion: *a chance to have her say (on the subject); The boss has the final say* (= power of deciding) *in the matter.*

saying *n.* **1** something said, esp. a commonly heard statement: *common, popular, wise sayings; the sayings of Confucius; as the saying goes.* **2 there is no saying** it is impossible to say: *There's no saying what will happen next.*

say-so *n. Informal.* **say-sos** a supposedly authoritative assertion or assurance; hence, authority: *It was done on the say-so of the secretary.*

scab *n.* **1** a blood clot on the surface of a wound or the crust formed on a healing wound. **2** a plant disease producing scablike spots. **3** a worker who takes the place of a striker. **4** *Slang.* a scoundrel. —*v.* **scabs, scabbed, scab.bing 1** of a wound, become covered with a scab. **2** act as a scab (worker).

scab.bard (SCAB.urd) *n.* a sheath for a sword or dagger.

scab.by *adj.* **scab.bi.er, scab.bi.est** covered with scabs; hence, low or mean.

sca.bies (SCAY.beez) *n.pl.* a skin condition with much itching caused by a burrowing mite.

scab.rous (SCAB.rus, SCAY.brus) *adj.* **1** rough or scaly: *a scabrous leaf.* **2** scabby; hence, vile; indelicate; obscene.

scads *n.pl. Informal.* a large amount or number: *scads of appointments, bank loans, fun, money, people, time.*

scaf.fold (SCAF.uld, -old) *n.* **1** a raised framework, usu. of poles and planks, to stand on while working on a building. **2** formerly, a platform from which criminals were hanged. —*v.* furnish with a scaffolding.

scaffolding (SCAF.ul.ding) *n.* a scaffold for workers; also, the poles, planks, etc. forming it: *to erect, put up, take down scaffolding.*

scal.a.ble (SCAY.luh.bul) *adj.* that can be scaled up or down: *a scalable font of type.*

scal.a.wag (SCAL.uh.wag) *n. Informal.* a rascal, scamp, or reprobate: *the scalawags and carpetbaggers of the Reconstruction period in the U.S.*

scald (SCAWLD) *v.* burn (as if) with a hot liquid or steam. —*n.* a burn caused thus.

scale *n.* **1** a series or sequence forming a classifying and measuring system: *the Celsius and Fahrenheit temperature scales; The Richter scale measures the strength of earthquakes; a salary scale of $50,000 to $60,000; the eight-tone musical scale; How does Chris rate* **on a scale of** *one to ten?* **2** relative size or proportion: *a map drawn to scale; a scale of one centimeter to ten kilometers; bribery on a large scale; He threw a party on a grand scale; on a scale unseen in modern times; a* **scale drawing** *or* **model** *of an airplane (made according to a scale).* **3** any of the thin, flat, horny pieces covering a fish or reptile; also, any layer or piece resembling this. **4** a weighing machine: *Stand on the (bathroom) scale; Let's weigh it on the kitchen scale; a balance with a pair of* **scales** (= pans, or **scalepans**); *She* **tips the scales at** (= weighs) *61 kg*. —**tip** or **turn the scales** decide or settle an issue: *The speaker's vote tipped the scales in favor of the motion.* —*v.* **scales, scaled, scal.ing 1** climb up, as on a ladder. **2** scrape scales from fish or remove in layers or pieces, as bark from trees, tartar from teeth, etc. **3** weigh on a scale. —**scale up** (or **down**) increase (or reduce) in proportion.

scale insect *n.* an insect such as mealybugs that resemble scales as they cluster on the plants on which they feed.

sca.lene (scay.LEEN, SCAY.leen) *adj.* having the sides all of unequal length: *a scalene triangle.*

scal.lion (SCAL.yun) *n.* an onion that has not developed a bulb; also, a leek or green onion.

scal.lop (SCOL.up, SCAL-) *n.* **1** a bivalve mollusk with fanlike rounded and ribbed shells; also, a scallop shell. **2** a scallop-shaped decoration, as on the edge of a dress. —*v.* **1** bake in a casserole with a milk sauce and bread crumbs. **2** decorate or trim with scallops.

scalp *n.* the hair-covered skin and flesh of the head. —*v.* **1** tear the scalp from the head. **2** *Informal.* buy and sell theater tickets, stocks, etc. at a high, often illegal profit. —**scalp.er** *n.*

scal.pel (SCAL.pul) *n.* a surgeon's dissecting knife.

scal.y (SCAY.lee) *adj.* **scal.i.er, -i.est** (as if) having scales: *scaly fish; dry, scaly skin; scaly patches.*

scam *n. Informal.* a scheme to swindle or defraud.

scamp *n.* a rascal.

scamp.er *v.* run quickly, as small animals or children when scared. —*n.* a playful running or scurrying.

scam.pi (SCAM.pee) *n.pl.* the Norwegian lobster or shrimp cooked in Italian style.

scan *v.* **scans, scanned, scan.ning 1** look at closely; go over an object part by part, as a television camera in transmitting a picture or a radar beam in searching an area: *to scan text and graphics into a computer;* **adj***a.*: *scanning cameras, equipment, software, systems, wands;* **adj.***:* *a scanned document, image.* **2** go over quickly: *I had time only to scan* (= go quickly over) *the morning's headlines during breakfast.* **3** mark off lines of verse into feet. —*n.* a scanning or its result: *brain, CAT, PET, radar, ultrasonic scans.* —**scan.ner** *n.*

scan.dal (SCAN.dul) *n.* **1** action or conduct that is shocking and shameful; also, the feeling of general outrage that results from it: *to cause, cover up, create, uncover a scandal; a sensational scandal; when a scandal bursts, erupts; a breath* or *hint* or *suggestion of scandal.* **2** slander or evil gossip: *to enjoy, listen to, repeat, spread, talk scandal.*

scan.dal.ize (SCAN.duh.lize) *v.* **-liz.es, -lized, -liz.ing** outrage the feelings of someone: *The story of corruption scandalized public opinion; He was convicted of contempt for scandalizing the court.*

scan.dal.mon.ger (SCAN.dul.mung.gur, -mong.gur) *n.* one who spreads slander.

scan.dal.ous (SCAN.duh.lus) *adj.* causing scandal: *scandalous behavior; a scandalous state of affairs.* —**scan.dal.ous.ly** *adv.*

scandal sheet *n.* a sensational newspaper or magazine carrying much gossip.

Scan.di.na.vi.an (scan.duh.NAY.vee.un) *n.* **1** a person of or from **Scandinavia**, a region comprising Norway, Sweden, Denmark, Iceland, and Finland. **2** any of the Germanic languages spoken there. —*adj.:* *Scandinavian countries, design, furniture.*

scan.di.um (SCAN.dee.um) *n.* a soft, gray metallic element.

scan.sion *n.* metrical scanning of verse.

scant *adj*a. falling short of the required size or quantity; barely enough: *He spoke with scant regard for truth; She paid scant attention to what was said; a scant three minutes of her time;* **adj***p.:* *We were scant of breath after the run.* —*v.* skimp: *a period scanted by historians.*

scant.ling *n.* a small beam or piece of timber, esp. one used as an upright in building.

scant.y *adj.* **scant.i.er, -i.est** falling short; barely enough: *a scanty attendance, bathing suit, breakfast; a region of scanty rainfall; The news from home was scanty.* —**scant.i.ly** *adv.:* *a scantily clad bather;* **scant.i.ness** *n.*

scape.goat *n.* one made to take the blame for others.

scap.u.la (SCAP.yuh.luh) *n.* **-las** or **-lae** (-lee) the shoulder blade; **scap.u.lar** *adj.*

scar *n.* a mark, as of a healed wound or burn: *The experience left many scars; hideous, permanent, psychological scars;*

She bore or carried the scars all her life.
—v. **scars, scarred, scar.ring** form or leave a scar.

scar.ab (SCAIR.ub) n. a dung beetle, sacred to the ancient Egyptians, or its carved image.

scarce (SCAIRCE) adj. **scarc.er, scarc.est** not easily available: *Water is scarce this summer; a scarce* (= rare) *book; He* **makes himself scarce** *(Informal for goes or stays away) when help is needed.*

scarce.ly adv. hardly; almost not: *He's so tired he can scarcely walk; Scarcely had he stood up when he collapsed; He has scarcely any strength left in his legs; He scarcely ever walks any more; He could scarcely* (= certainly not) *have come here walking.* —**scarce.ness** n.

scar.ci.ty (SCAIR.si.tee) n. **-ties** inadequate supply: *a period of scarcity; acute scarcity of information, labor, resources, transportation, water; economic scarcity; food scarcity.*

scare v. **scares, scared, scar.ing** fill a person or animal with fear, often resulting in flight: *She tried to scare away the intruder; She was scared out of her wits; scared to death by the intruder; The experience scared her into fleeing the city; Potential customers were scared away;* adj.: *Some are too* **scared** *to fly; scared stiff; very scared of heights; scared for their jobs; Let's not get scared.* —**run scared** to panic. —**scare up** *Informal.* get together supplies, etc. to meet a need. —n. fright: *to get, give someone a scare; to put, throw a scare into somebody.*

scare.crow n. a ragged figure set up in a field to scare birds away from crops.

scarf n. **scarfs** or **scarves** 1 a long strip of cloth or a neckerchief worn for ornament or protection around the neck, head, waist, etc. 2 a long and narrow table covering.

scar.i.fy (SCAIR.uh.fye) v. **-fies, -fied, -fy.ing** 1 scratch, cut, or break up a surface, as the skin for vaccination, topsoil in agriculture, etc. 2 hurt a person by severe criticism.
—**scar.i.fi.ca.tion** (-fuh.CAY.shun) n.

scar.let (SCAR.lit) n. a bright red color, as of the robes of persons of rank: *bright oranges and flaming scarlets;* adj.: *A scarlet dress tunic is part of a Mountie's formal outfit;* **scarlet fever** (= disease marked by fever and red spots on the skin); *the* **scarlet pimpernel** (= plant with small, red starlike flowers); *a* **scarlet woman** (= prostitute).

scarp n. & v. (make into) a steep slope or escarpment, as of a cuesta.

scar.y (SCAIR.ee) adj. **scar.i.er, -i.est** *Informal.* 1 frightening: *It was scary going in there; scary movies, stories; the scary facts, truth.* 2 easily frightened: *scary little mice.* —**scar.i.ly** adv.

scat v. **scats, scat.ted, scat.ting** 1 to go away. 2 in jazz, sing or speak scat.
—n. nonsense sounds or syllables: *a tune with a dash of scat;* adj.a.: *improvised, no-rule scat singing; scat syllables; Yodeling is a type of scat vocalizing.*
—**interj.** used to drive away an animal.

scath.ing (SCAY.thing, "th" as in "the") adj. severe or harsh: *a scathing attack, commentary, report; scathing criticism, remarks.* —**scath.ing.ly** adv.

sca.tol.o.gy (scuh.TOL.uh.jee) n. obscene literature, esp. dealing with excrement. —**scat.o.log.i.cal** (scat.uh.LOJ.i.cul) adj.

scat.ter (SCAT.ur) v. go or send in different directions, as papers by a wind or a flock when driven.

scat.ter.brain (SCAT.ur.brain) n. one who cannot concentrate on a subject.
—**scat.ter.brained** adj.

scatter rug n. a small rug.

scav.enge (SCAV.inj) v. **-eng.es, -enged, -eng.ing** 1 search among or gather discarded objects: *a bear scavenging for food.* 2 feed on rubbish or dead matter, as vultures and hyenas.
—**scav.eng.er** n.

sce.nar.i.o (suh.NAIR.ee.oh) n. **-os** 1 a sequence of events as planned or imagined, esp. a film director's script containing instructions on camera shots, etc.: *Who wrote the scenario?* 2 what might happen: *a possible scenario; In or under a worst-case scenario, we could be facing famine.* —**sce.nar.ist** n.

scene (SEEN) n. 1 the place or stage of an action or incident: *No one was at the scene of the crime when it happened; a reporter on the scene of the accident.* 2 a sphere of activity or way of life: *disco, drug, national, sports scenes.* 3 an act or episode of a play. 4 a view, esp. one that has artistic appeal, as a landscape: *a scene depicted on canvas; beautiful, familiar, gruesome, revolting, tragic scenes.* —**behind the scenes** backstage: *The visitor was taken behind the scenes; No one knew what was going on* **behind the scenes** (= secretly); adj.a.: *a* **behind-the-scenes** (= secret) *activity, effort, player, role, struggle.* —**make a scene** make an embarrassing display of one's emotions.

scen.er.y (SEE.nuh.ree) n. **-er.ies** 1 the features of a landscape: *We paused to* admire the scenery; beautiful, majestic, picturesque scenery. **2** the painted screens and such accessories used on a stage to represent the place of an action: *to dismantle, move, set up, shift scenery; A change of scenery is called for.*

sce.nic (SEE.nic) *adj.* **1** having fine scenery: *a scenic drive, highway, trail; an amusement park with a miniature* **scenic railway;** *We lost our way and took the* **scenic route** (*Informal for* a roundabout way). **2** having to do with natural scenery: *scenic artists, beauty, effects; the scenic Rockies.* —**sce.ni.cal.ly** *adv.*

scent (SENT) *n.* **1** a perfume. **2** a smell or the trail left by a smell: *The hounds picked up and followed the scent of the fox; They were thrown off the scent by water; a faint, not pungent scent* (= odor); *a keen scent* (= sense of smell) *for game.* —*v.* to smell or suspect: *to scent danger, game, trouble.*

scented *adj.* perfumed: *The air is heavily scented with allspice; a scented garden with scented foliage and fragrant flowers; scented candles, cosmetics, lotions; mint-scented whipped cream.*

scep.ter (SEP.tur) *n.* **1** a staff carried by a sovereign as a symbol of power. **2** sovereignty: *"Sceptre and crown / Must tumble down."* —*adj.*: *the* **sceptered** *isle* (= Britain). Also **scep.tre** *Cdn.*

scep.tic, etc. See SKEPTIC, etc.

scep.tre *Cdn.* SCEPTER.

sched.ule (SKEJ.ool, SHEJ.ool) *n.* **1** a plan of procedure such as a timetable: *airline, bus, production, publishing, train schedules; to draw up, make up, plan a schedule; Our flight arrived according to or* on *schedule, not ahead of schedule; The train was* **behind schedule** (= late). **2** an agenda; also, a list: *a schedule of events; a full schedule for the day; a* **price schedule** (= list). —*v.* **-ules, -uled, -ul.ing** enter in a schedule: *The meeting is scheduled to begin at 9 a.m.; It is scheduled* (= planned) *for 9 a.m.;* ***adj.***: *a movie star's* **scheduled** *appearances, arrival; the scheduled completion date; Charter flights are not scheduled flights; the scheduled opening of a show; We paid only the scheduled price; the scheduled stops of a tour.*

sche.mat.ic (skee.MAT.ic) *n.* a diagram or scheme: *the schematic of a heating system; the schematics showing the trajectory of the bullets; This doesn't fit into our market schematic* (= plan). ***adj.***: *a schematic design, diagram, drawing, flowchart, model; The plot is schematic* (= planned) *and predictable.*
—**sche.mat.i.cal.ly** *adv.*

scheme (SKEEM) *n.* **1** a plan or systematic arrangement: *a coordinated color scheme; AABBA is the rhyme scheme of a limerick; In our* **scheme of things** (= in the way we want things organized), *this is not very important; our place in the general scheme of things.* **2** a project: *a drainage scheme; a grandiose scheme to make the desert bloom; the wildest schemes.* **3** an underhand plan or plot: *to devise or think up, foil or thwart a scheme; diabolical, fantastic, preposterous schemes; a scheme to rig the vote; a forgery scheme.*
—*v.* **schemes, schemed, schem.ing** plot or intrigue: *He was scheming to get rich quickly;* **n.**: *color* **scheming;** *We could see through his sinister, subtle scheming;* ***adj.***: *a scheming competitor, politician, rival.* —**schem.er** *n.*

scher.zo (SCAIR.tsoh) *n.* **-zos** or **-zi** (-tsee) a lively movement of a symphony or sonata.

schil.ling (SHIL.ing) *n.* the basic money unit of Austria.

schism (SIZ.um, SKIZ.um) *n.* **1** a division or split within a church, as the Great Schism of the 1300s with rival popes: *to cause, create a schism within the church.* **2** the offense of causing religious schism or a resulting sect of such a split. —**schis.mat.ic** (skis.MAT.ic) *n. & adj.*

schist (SHIST) *n.* mineral rock that splits easily into layers, as mica and talc. —**schist.ose** *adj.*

schiz.oid (SKIT.soid) *n. & adj.* (a person) showing schizophrenic symptoms.

schiz.o.phre.ni.a (skit.suh.FREE.nee.uh) *n.* a mental disorder characterized by hallucinations and delusions, the emotional side of the patient being disturbed. —**schiz.o.phren.ic** (-FREN.ic) *n. & adj.*

schle.miel (shluh.MEEL) *n. Slang.* a bungler or chump.

schlep (SHLEP) *n. Slang.* an awkward or dull person.

schlock (SHLOK) *n. Informal.* trashy stuff: *all the schlock that gets published as literature;* ***adja.***: *a schlock movie, novel, show.* —**schlock.y** *adj.*

schmaltz (SHMAHLTS) *n. Slang.* excessive sentimentalism in art, music, etc.

schmo (SHMOH) *n.* **schmos** or **schmoes** *Slang.* a dolt or jerk.

schnapps (SHNAHPS) *n.* a ginlike alcoholic liquor.

schnau.zer (SHNOW.zur) *n.* a terrier-like German breed of dog.

schnook (SHNOOK, short "OO") *n. Slang.* a sucker or dupe.

schnoz.zle (SHNOZ.ul) *n. Slang.* the

nose.
schol.ar (SCOL.ur) *n.* **1** a learned person: *a distinguished classical scholar; an eminent scholar.* **2** a student: *a history scholar; serious scholars; a Rhodes scholar* (= scholarship holder). —**schol.ar.ly** *adj.*: *scholarly habits, methods, research; a scholarly pursuit, thesis, treatise, work.*

schol.ar.ship (SCOL.ur.ship) *n.* **1** a grant of money or other aid to help a student: *to apply for, award, establish, found, get, grant, receive, win a scholarship; a scholarship for graduate study; a scholarship to study abroad.* **2** the knowledge or erudition of a learned person: *to foster, promote scholarship; solid, sound, thorough scholarship.*

scho.las.tic (scuh.LAS.tic) **1** *adj.* having to do with schools or scholars: *scholastic aptitude, distinction, performance.* **2** *adj.* having to do with **scholasticism,** a medieval Christian system of philosophy.

scholastic aptitude test *n.* a test for determining a candidate's areas of special fitness, used for college admission.

school (SCOOL) *n.* **1** a place for teaching and learning: *Children must attend school till they are 16; She goes to school in Trenton; goes to a good school; He works at* or *in a school; a school district.* **2** an educational course or session: *Try not to be late for the beginning of school; He is sometimes kept after school (hours) as punishment; school work.* **3** the course of formal education: *She started school at age five; At 18, she left school and went to work; He finished school and graduated from Harvard; David dropped out of* or *left* or *quit school at 16; Her other children are still at* or *in school; during my school days.* **4** a particular type of school or a department of instruction: *accredited, boarding, correspondence, dental, elementary, graduate, high, junior high, medical, primary, nursing, secondary, undergraduate, vocational schools; a school for the handicapped.* **5** a group of people who agree in their views, methods, etc.: *an educator of the old school; an avant-garde school of art; a radical school of thought; various schools of opinion on a subject; schools of philosophy.* **6** an activity or experience having training value: *the school of adversity, hard knocks, life; "Example is the school of mankind."* **7** a group of teachers and students: *The whole school assembled in the gym.* **8** a group of the same kind and size of fish or other water animal swimming together.

—*v.* **1** teach or train: *Soldiers are schooled to obey; Children should be thoroughly schooled in the basics; adja.: a superbly schooled voice; schooled in psychology; well schooled discipline;* **n.:** *Your education partly depends on where you receive your schooling; Many geniuses have had no formal schooling.* **2** swim together, as tuna and sardines.

school board *n.* a local group managing a school system.

school.boy *n.* a boy attending school; **school.girl** *fem.*

school.fel.low (SCOOL.fel.oh) *n.* schoolmate.

school figure *n.* any of a series of movements used to test competitors in skating, horseback riding, etc.

school.house *n.* a school building.

school.marm or **school.ma'am** (SCOOL.mahm, -mam) *n. Informal.* **1** a woman schoolteacher. **2** one who is pedantic or priggish.

school.mas.ter (SCOOL.mas.tur) *n.* [old-fashioned] a male schoolteacher; **school.mis.tress** *fem.*

school.mate *n.* one going to the same school as another.

school.room *n.* a room in which teaching is done.

school.teach.er (SCOOL.tee.chur) *n.* one who teaches in a school.

school.yard *n.* a piece of ground near or around a school; school playground.

school year *n.* the period of the year when school is in session, usu. September to June in North America.

schoon.er (SKOO.nur) *n.* a fore-and-aft-rigged ship with two or more masts.

schtick (SHTIC) same as SHTICK.

schuss (SHOOS, short "OO") *n.* a fast run on skis down a steep course.
—*v.* make a schuss.

schuss.boom.er (SHOOS.boo.mur) *n.* one who schusses downhill.

schwa (SHWAH) *n.* **1** a neutral vowel sound, as of the "a" and "e" of "*another.*" **2** the phonetic symbol "ə" representing this.

sci.at.ic (sye.AT.ic) *adj.* having to do with the hip or hip nerves: *sciatic nerve, pain.*

sci.at.i.ca (sye.AT.i.cuh) *n.* inflammation of the large sciatic nerve running down the back of each thigh.

sci.ence (SYE.unce) *n.* **1** systematized knowledge based on observed and tested facts, as distinguished from art: *to advance, foster, promote science.* **2** a branch of it, as mathematics, logic, and the physical and biological sciences: *applied, domestic, information, library, linguistic, military, natural, physical, political, social, space science; Linguistics is not an exact science; the* **sciences** *(= natural sciences and mathematics) as distinguished from the arts.* **3** a skill or technique: *the science of boxing.*

science fiction *n.* fiction based on imaginative and fantastic applications of science and technology to life on other planets, the future, etc.

sci.en.tif.ic (sye.un.TIF.ic) *adj.* dealing with or based on science: *scientific evidence, inquiry, knowledge, methods, research, thinking.* —**sci.en.tif.i.cal.ly** *adv.*

sci.en.tist (SYE.un.tist) *n.* one trained in science, esp. the physical and biological sciences: *computer, physical, political, rocket, social scientists.*

sci-fi (SYE.fye) *n.* [short form] science fiction.

scim.i.tar (SIM.i.tur) *n.* a curved sword of Eastern origin.

scin.til.la (sin.TIL.uh) *n.* spark; a shred or trace: *not one scintilla of evidence; without a scintilla of truth.*

scin.til.late (SIN.tul.ate) *v.* **-til.lates, -til.lat.ed, -til.lat.ing** sparkle brilliantly, as a diamond. —**scin.til.la.tion** (-LAY.shun) *n.*

sci.on (SYE.un) *n.* **1** a branch or shoot for grafting. **2** a descendant; offspring.

scis.sion (SIZH.un) *n.* a cutting or splitting.

scis.sor (SIZ.ur) *v.* cut with scissors.

scis.sors *n. sing. & pl.* a cutting instrument for cloth, paper, hair, etc. consisting of two pivoted blades that are squeezed against each other by the action of the hand inserted through two rings at one end of the blades.

scissors kick *n.* a swimming kick used with a sidestroke in which the legs are moved like scissors.

scle.ro.sis (scluh.ROH.sis) *n., pl.* **-ses** (-seez) hardening of tissues, as of the arteries or nerves. —**scle.rot.ic** (-ROT.ic) *adj.*

scoff *v.* mock or jeer *at* a person or thing that deserves respect. —*n.* a scoffing.

scoff.law *n.* one who habitually flouts the law.

scold *v.* find fault with or rebuke, esp. in an ill-tempered way: *He was scolded for wasting food; scolded about his eating habits; n.: He was given a good* **scolding***; He got or received a scolding from his mother.* —*n.* one who scolds, esp. a woman: *a humorless scold.*

sco.li.o.sis (skoh.lee.OH.sis, skol.ee-) *n.* abnormal lateral curvature of the spine.

sconce *n.* a light fixture bracketed to a wall, usu. for a candle.

scone (SCONE, SCON) *n.* a quick bread or biscuit baked on a griddle or in an oven.

scoop *n.* **1** a shovellike tool or utensil used to dig or ladle out coal, dirt, flour, grain, ice cream, mashed potatoes, sugar, etc. **2** a scooping or the amount taken up in one scooping: *two scoops of ice cream.* **3** *Informal.* a piece of news published by a paper ahead of its rivals. —*v.* **1** take up or hollow out with a scoop: *the "stoop and scoop" regulation against pets fouling public places.* **2** *Informal.* beat rival newspapers by publishing a story first.

scoot *v.* be off in a hurry; dart; decamp: *students ready to scoot out of the room when the class is dismissed.*

scoot.er *n.* **1** a child's two-wheeled vehicle consisting of two tandem wheels connected by a footboard, with a steering post connected to the front wheel. **2** a motor scooter.

scope *n.* **1** extent or range of perception or activity: *matters beyond, outside, within the scope of an inquiry; The scope of the human mind is limited; a plan with much scope* (= room or opportunity) *for expansion.* **2** [short form of words ending in **-scope,** *comb.form* meaning "observing instrument"] microscope, stethoscope, telescope: *optic scopes; a scope exam.*

scor.bu.tic (scor.BYOO.tic) *adj.* having to do with scurvy; also **scor.bu.ti.cal** *adj.*

scorch *v.* burn the outside surface of cloth, vegetation, etc. so as to discolor or damage: *fields scorched by the sun; adj.: a* **scorched** *landscape; scorched hillsides; the sun-scorched desert; the* **scorched earth** *policy of devastating an area before yielding it to invaders.* —*n.* a superficial burn.

score *n.* **1** a mark, scratch, or notch, as in keeping tally. **2** a record or account, as of points in a game: *to keep the score; We quickly ran up a score of 10 points; a score of 20 to 4 in the deciding game; The score stood (at) 20 to 4 or 20-4; We won by a lopsided score; an even score of 4-4* (= a tie score); *We* **paid off** or **settled** *some old scores* (= grievances); *I have no regrets* **on that score** (= account); *It's good to* **know the score** (*Informal* for know the favorable and unfavorable facts of a situation) *before*

sitting down to negotiate. **3** a set of 20: *She lived three score years and ten (= 70 years); three score and ten years; We've seen them scores of (= many) times; They came in scores (= in large numbers).* **4** the notation of a musical work containing one or more parts, as for an orchestra: *Who wrote the score?*
—*v.* **scores, scored, scor.ing** **1** make or assign as points: *The home team scored 10 points against the visitors; She tried to score (points) off her rival (= beat him in an argument); n.: She did most of the scoring for their team.* **2** keep a record of the number of points. **3** make a mark or line: *The editor scored out the lines to be deleted.* **4** arrange a piece of music in a score: *the art of scoring for an orchestra.* **5** succeed: *It is hard to score with a poorly organized program; She scored high in math but low on the other subjects.*
—**scor.er** *n.*
score.board *n.* a large board that shows the score in a game.
score.card *n.* a card for keeping the score in a game.
sco.ri.a (SCOR.ee.uh) *n., pl.* **-ri.ae** (-ree.ee) **1** slag or dross, as from the reduction of metal ores. **2** a coarse pumice.
scorn *v.* regard with contempt: *a know-it-all who scorns advice.*
—*n.* contempt: *an expert who treats lay people with scorn; to express, feel scorn; He heaped scorn on the speaker at the rally.* —**scorn.ful** *adj.;* **scorn.ful.ly** *adv.*
Scor.pi.o (SCOR.pee.oh) *n.* **1** a S. constellation and the eighth sign of the zodiac; also **Scor.pi.us.** **2** a person born under this sign.
scor.pi.on (SCOR.pee.un) *n.* an arachnid with a venomous sting at the end of a curved tail.
Scot *n.* a person of or from Scotland.
—**Scots** *n. & adj.* same as SCOTTISH.
Scotch **1** *n. & adj.* [less preferred form] Scots or Scottish. **2** same as SCOTCH WHISKY.
scotch *v.* **1** wound without killing: *to scotch a snake.* **2** stamp out or crush: *to scotch an idea, move, plan, report, rumor, theory.*
Scotch.man (SCOCH.mun) *n.* **-men** [less preferred form] Scotsman; **Scotch.wom.an, -wom.en** *fem.*
scotch tape *n.* an adhesive tape; **Scotch tape** *Trademark.* —**scotch-tape** *v.* **-tapes, -taped, -tap.ing:** *to scotch-tape pictures to a wall.*
Scotch terrier same as SCOTCH TERRIER.

Scotch whisky *n.* a whiskey distilled from barley in Scotland.
scot-free *adj.* unpunished; without loss or injury: *She got off, was let off scot-free.*
Scots *n. & adj.* Scottish.
Scots.man (SCOTS.mun) *n.* **-men** a person of or from Scotland.
—**Scots.wom.an, -wom.en.**
Scot.tie or **Scot.ty** *n.* **Scot.ties** *Informal.* **1** Scottish terrier; also **scottie, scotty.** **2** Scotsman.
Scot.tish (SCOT.ish) *adj.* having to do with Scotland or its people: *Scottish brogue, dancing, dialects, English, generosity, humor, tweed.* Also *n.*
Scottish terrier *n.* a strong and plucky, short-legged terrier of Scottish breed with a hard, wiry coat and small upright ears.
scoun.drel (SCOWN.drul) *n.* a villain or rascal.
scour *v.* **1** clean or polish pots, pans, etc. by rubbing with something abrasive, as a **scouring pad.** **2** dig or wear away by the force of something in motion, as a channel by a stream. **3** search an area, one's memory, etc. by going over it quickly and thoroughly. —*n.* **1** a scouring. **2 scours** *pl.* diarrhea in newborn cattle.
scourge (SCURGE) *n.* **1** a whip. **2** any large-scale punishment or widespread affliction such as a plague or war.
—*v.* **scourg.es, scourged, scourg.ing** punish as with a whip.
scout *v.* **1** to reconnoiter or survey, as a military or police **scout car,** a space vehicle, etc. **2** search: *to scout for firewood; to scout around for fresh talent; to scout out a site for our business; We were scouting three locations; They scouted the hills and valleys for the missing child;* **adj.:** *a scouting expedition, group, report.*
—*n.* **1** one sent out to scout: *a talent scout interviewing persons with talent.* **2** a member of the Scouts move-ment: *Boy Scouts; an American Girl Scout.*
scouting *n.* activities of scouts, esp. of the Boy Scouts or Girl Scouts.
scout.mas.ter (SCOUT.mas.tur) *n.* the adult leader of a band of scouts.
scow (*rhyme:* how) *n.* **1** a barge used for bulk cargo. **2** a sailboat with a square stern and rounded bow.
scowl *n.* an ill-humored or sullen look or frown with contracted eyebrows.
—*v.* look with a scowl: *He scowled in annoyance; to scowl at someone.*
—**scowl.er** *n.*
scrab.ble (SCRAB.ul) *n. & v.*

scrab.bles, scrab.bled, scrab.bling scrape, scramble, or scribble. —**scrab.bler** n.

scrag.gly (SCRAG.lee) *adj.* **scrag.gli.er, scrag.gli.est** irregular or ragged: *a scraggly beard, ear of corn, tree.*

scrag.gy (SCRAG.ee) *adj.* **scrag.gi.er, scrag.gi.est** rugged or scrawny: *scraggy cliffs; a scraggy neck.*

scram *v.* **scrams, scrammed, scram.ming** *Informal.* go away; also *interj.*

scram.ble (SCRAM.bul) *v.* **-bles, -bled, -bling 1** move forward by climbing, crawling, etc.; struggle: *to scramble up a rock; Football players scramble to get the ball; People scramble for government grants, for a living, for power, seats, wealth.* **2** mix or jumble; *adj.:* a **scrambled** (= deliberately garbled) radio or TV signal; **scrambled eggs** *(that are stirred while frying).* —*n.* something scrambled or disorganized: *Life is a mad, wild scramble; a shanty town that is a scramble of mud and stucco houses.*

scram.bler *n.* an electronic device that mixes transmission signals, esp. so that they may not be picked up by unauthorized persons: *They use a scrambler phone to avoid wiretaps; Pay-TV operates on a scrambler-descrambler system.*

scrap *n.* **1** a piece or fragment, as of torn paper, leftover meat, or a brief extract from something written or printed: *scraps of information, paper, vegetables, writing; a* **scrap book** *for collecting pictures, clippings, etc.* **2** discarded metal or trash: *The car was sold for scrap;* *adj.:* *scrap iron, metal, paper, wood.* **3** *Informal.* a fight or struggle: *She put up a good scrap; minor scraps.*
—*v.* **scraps, scrapped, scrap.ping 1** make into scraps; discard as junk: *We scrapped the car when it rusted.* **2** *Informal.* fight or quarrel: *The children scrapped over where to sit.* —**scrap.per** *n.*

scrape *v.* **scrapes, scraped, scrap.ing 1** rub or scratch against or with something rough or sharp: *to scrape paint off with a knife; She fell and scraped her knee; The tire is scraping against the fender.* **2** get by trying very hard: *They scraped together enough money to pay the rent; He scraped through the exam with a bare pass; manages to scrape along on a small income; He scrapes by as a furniture mover.* —*n.* **1** a scraping (sound) or a scraped place. **2** a predicament.
—**scrap.er** *n.*

scrap.heap or **scrap heap** *n.* a pile of discarded things: *the scrapheap of discarded fashions; headed for the scrapheap of history.*

scrap.per (SCRAP.ur) *n.* fighter: *What a scrapper he is!*

scrap.py (SCRAP.ee) *adj.* **scrap.pi.er, scrap.pi.est 1** made up of fragments; disconnected: *scrappy quotes.* **2** *Informal.* quarrelsome; also, tough or gritty: *scrappy fighters, fun, kids.* —**scrap.pi.ly** *adv.;* **scrap.pi.ness** *n.*

scratch *v.* **1** mark, cut, or scrape lightly with something sharp or pointed: *furniture scratched by movers; The dog scratches at the door when it wants out; Al is* **scratching his head** *(= thinking hard)* **over** *what to do next; The lecturer hasn't even* **scratched the surface of** *(= made a start on) the subject;* "*You scratch my back and I'll scratch yours*" *(Informal for* Help me and I'll help you*).* **2** write or draw hurriedly: *to scratch one's name on a park bench.* **3** draw a line through as in striking out a name: *Two candidates were scratched (= withdrawn) from the race.* **4** scrape money together: *We managed to scratch together a small down payment.*
—*n.* **1** a scratching or a mark or cut made by it: *He came out of the ordeal without a scratch; a* **scratch test** *made on the skin using various substances and noting reactions for determining a person's allergies.* **2** a line marking the starting point of a race: *Let's scrap everything and start* **from scratch** *(= from zero or with nothing to build on).* —**up to scratch** up to the point of readiness; in acceptable condition: *None of the candidates was up to scratch.* —*adj.* **1** for making quick notes: *scratch paper; a* **scratch pad** *(of scrap paper for making informal notes).* **2** hastily put together: *a scratch meal, performance, team.*

scratch.y *adj.* **scratch.i.er, -i.est** that scratches: *scratchy clothes; the scratchy sounds of a scratchy recording; scratchy writing made with a scratchy quill pen; a scratchy shirt, voice; scratchy hair.*
—**scratch.i.ness** *n.*

scrawl *v.* write carelessly or hastily.
—*n.* such writing: *an illegible scrawl that is hard to make out.* —**scrawl.er** *n.*
—**scrawl.y** *adj.*

scraw.ny (SCRAW.nee) *adj.* **scraw.ni.er, -ni.est** *Informal.* thin and bony: *a turkey's scrawny neck; Annie is lithe without being scrawny; a scrawny teenager.*

scream (SCREEM) *n.* **1** a sharp, shrill cry of pain, fright, etc.: *She heard a bloodcurdling scream outside her window; a loud scream of pain followed by screams of laughter.* **2** *Informal.* a very funny person or thing: *The play is a scream and so is its director!*

—*v.* utter a scream: *The child was carried out kicking and screaming; She was screaming her head off; She screamed that she had been lied to; She was not screaming with pain; She screamed and shouted at them; The child screamed blue murder when it couldn't get what it wanted; They screamed for help.*

screech *n.* a harsh, shrill, piercing sound or cry; shriek: *the screeches of a frightened child; The "screech owl" is noted for its harsh cry.* —*v.* make a screech: *The subways screeched to a halt as the strikers walked out;* **n.:** *the screeching of brakes; The subway system ground to a screeching halt.* —**screech.y** *adj.*

screen *n.* **1** a covered frame or something similar put up to hide, protect, or separate: *Let's put up a screen here; a painted Japanese screen; a wire mesh screen to keep out flies.* **2** a projection surface for movies, slides, or other images: *a radar screen; the TV screen; home screen or small screen (= TV); A movie made its debut last week on only 32 screens (= theaters) and made money at a whopping $20,000 a screen.* **3** a sieve or other straining device.
—*v.* **1** shield to protect or separate: *A row of trees screened (= blocked) our view; a dining area screened (= partitioned) off from the living room; a sheltered life screened (= protected) from unhealthy influences; adj.: a screened pavilion, porch, terrace, window.* **2** show a motion picture on a theater screen; **n.:** *to do a screening for a select audience; screening booths.* **3** sift or separate: *Candidates are carefully screened for sensitive jobs; to screen donated blood for the AIDS virus (to prevent its spread);* **adj.:** *carefully screened visitors; screened-in refugees;* **adja.:** *breast screening exams; screening tests;* **n.:** *employment screening; genetic screening of fetuses, employees, etc. for detecting inherited disorders.*

screen.play *n.* the script of a motion picture.

screen saver *n.* a moving graphic display switched on to a computer screen to prevent its being damaged when there is no user input for a specific length of time.

screen test *n.* filmed audition, as given to aspirants to movie or TV stardom.

screen.writ.er (SCREEN.rye.tur) *n.* one who writes screenplays.

screw *n.* **1** a naillike but spirally threaded metal piece for fastening things by turning a tool called **screwdriver** in its slotted head. **2** any mechanical device working like a screw on an advancing spiral, as a jack for lifting loads, the propeller (**screw propeller**) of a ship or airplane, a corkscrew, thumbscrew, etc. —**have a screw loose** *Informal.* be crazy. —**put the screws on** *Informal.* use pressure on someone. —*v.* **1** twist or turn, as a screw; hence, fasten or tighten: *He screwed the lid on tight; She has her head screwed on right (= She is sensible); He had to screw up his courage (= get brave) to do it.* **2** twist out of shape; contort one's face. **3** to hurt vindictively: *a hate list of political enemies to be screwed.* —**screw around** *Slang.* **1** to fool around. **2** [vulgar use] be sexually promiscuous. —**screw up** *Slang.* **1** mess up or mismanage: *to screw up a deal, job; to screw up figures, plans: She screwed up the arrangements at the last minute; a movie about guys who are screwed up (= crazy or confused).* **2** make someone nervous: *She got all screwed up waiting for her turn in the dentist's chair.*

screw.ball *n. Slang.* one who is eccentric.

screw.up *n. Slang.* a botched job; blunder.

screw.worm *n.* **1** a blowfly whose maggots burrow into the flesh of living animals. **2** its larva.

screw.y *adj.* **screw.i.er, -i.est** *Slang.* crazy or eccentric.

scrib.ble (SCRIB.ul) *n.* marks or writing made in a careless or hasty manner: *an illegible scribble.* —*v.* **scrib.bles, scrib.bled, scrib.bling** make a scribble: *to scribble graffiti on walls.*
—**scrib.bler** *n.*

scribe *n.* a writer, esp. a copyist of manuscripts before the invention of printing.

scrim *n.* **1** a loosely woven cotton fabric used for lining, curtains, etc. **2** a gauze curtain used on a stage for special effects.

scrim.mage (SCRIM.ij) *n.* **1** a play in football beginning at the "line of scrimmage" when the ball is snapped back. **2** a football team's practice game. —*v.* **scrim.mag.es, scrim.maged, scrim.mag.ing** take part in a scrimmage or struggle.

scrimp *v.* be sparing or niggardly with food, money, and other resources: *She scrimped to pay for piano lessons; People buy houses by scrimping on luxuries; Some seniors have to manage by scrimping and saving.* —**scrim.py** *adj.*

scrim.shaw *n.* **1** a carved or engraved object of ivory, bone, shells, etc., as made by whalers during long voyages. 2 such objects collectively or their craft.

scrip *n.* a receipt or certificate of entitlement to a share of stock, land, money, etc.

script *n.* 1 a handwriting or a type style resembling it. 2 the written text of a motion picture, play, etc.

scrip.tur.al (SCRIP.chuh.rul) *adj.* having to do with sacred writings, esp. the Bible. —**scrip.tur.al.ly** *adv.*

Scrip.ture (SCRIP.chur) *n.* 1 the Bible; also **the Scriptures** *pl.* 2 **scripture** any sacred book.

scriv.ner (SCRIV.nur) *n. Archaic.* a scribe or copyist.

scrod *n.* young cod or other fish boned and cut into strips for cooking. —*v.* **scrods, scrod.ded, scrod.ding** to fillet a fish for cooking.

scrof.u.la (SCROF.yuh.luh) *n.* a tuberculosis of the lymph nodes, esp. of the neck; **scrof.u.lous** (-lus) *adj.*

scroll (SCROLE) *n.* 1 a roll of paper or parchment usu. used for writing on: *the Dead Sea Scrolls written by a Jewish sect.* 2 a scroll-shaped ornamentation as on the head of a violin or, in architecture, the top part of an Ionic column. —*v.* move text up, down, or across a computer screen so as to view a new portion.

Scrooge or **scrooge** (SCROOJ) *n.* a mean and miserly person: *Sam is miserly like Scrooge, but Jan is generous like Santa.*

scro.tum (SCROH.tum) *n., pl.* **-ta** or **-tums** the pouch containing the testicles. —**scro.tal** *adj.: scrotal hernia, swelling; the scrotal sac.*

scrounge (SCROWNJ) *v.* **scroung.es, scrounged, scroung.ing** *Informal.* go about or collect by searching, begging, pilfering, etc.: *They had to scrounge around for the firewood; Finally they scrounged it from High Park.* —**scroung.er** *n.*

scrub *v.* **scrubs, scrubbed, scrub.bing** 1 wash or clean utensils, hands, floors, etc. by rubbing hard, usu. with a "scrub brush": *to scrub a floor; to scrub the floor clean; to scrub a stain* (= remove it by scrubbing) *off a floor; Keep scrubbing* (= rubbing hard) *till the stain comes off.* 2 *Informal.* cancel: *Many space missions were scrubbed after the 1986 "Challenger" disaster.* —*n.* 1 small or stunted trees or shrubs: *scrub growth.* 2 land with such growth: *scrub land.* 3 one considered insignificant or inferior. 4 a player not on the regular team. 5 a scrubbing: *facial scrubs;* **adj.**: *scrub brushes, nurses, pads; hospital scrub suits worn by surgeons.* 5 a cosmetic preparation used for scrubbing. —**scrub.ber** *n.*

scrub.by (SCRUB.ee) *adj.* **scrub.bi.er, scrub.bi.est** 1 stunted: *scrubby growth, vegetation.* 2 covered with scrub: *scrubby land.*

scrub nurse *n.* a nurse who assists surgeons in the operating room.

scrub.wom.an (SCRUB.woom.un) *n.* **-wom.en** a cleaning woman.

scruff *n.* the back of an animal's neck, esp. the loose skin covering it.

scruf.fy (SCRUF.ee) *adj.* **scruf.fi.er, scruf.fi.est** shabby or grubby: *a scruffy dresser; He works in a scruffy office in the old part of town; The teenagers formed a scruffy grassroots movement for fighting drugs.* —**scruf.fi.ly** *adv.;* **scruf.fi.ness** *n.*

scrump.tious (SCRUMP.shus) *adj. Informal.* splendid or delicious: *a scrumptious candy bar.* —**scrump.tious.ly** *adv.*

scrunch *v.* crush or squeeze. —*n.* a scrunching noise.

scru.ple (SCROO.pul) *n.* a feeling of uneasiness about doing what may not be right or proper: *The fellow has no scruples about drinking and driving; It shows a lack of scruples.* —*v.* **-ples, -pled, -pling** hesitate to do something; have scruples: *The Film Review Board will not scruple to cut certain passages from a film.*

scru.pu.lous (SCROOP.yuh.lus) *adj.* conscientious; careful about fine points of morality, accuracy, etc.: *We are very scrupulous about giving the devil his due; a scholar's scrupulous attention to detail; a job done with scrupulous care.* —**scru.pu.lous.ly** *adv.* —**scru.pu.los.i.ty** (-LOS.i.tee) *n.*

scru.ti.nize (SCROO.tun.ize) *v.* **-niz.es, -nized, -niz.ing** examine carefully with attention to particulars: *to scrutinize the ballots cast.*

scru.ti.ny *n.* **-nies** a careful inspection: *Employees complain of being under constant scrutiny; What is done in public is open to scrutiny by the public; a politician whose record will not bear close scrutiny; the strict scrutiny of the tax auditor.*

scu.ba (SCOO.buh) *n.* underwater breathing equipment, as used by a diver, or **scuba diver.**

scud *v.* **scuds, scud.ded, scud.ding** move fast, as clouds or a boat driven by wind: *clouds scudding across the sky.* —*n.* a scudding of clouds, etc. driven by wind.

scuff *v.* **1** walk dragging the feet: *a streetwalker scuffing the sleazy side of town.* **2** scratch, scrape, or wear out; *adj.*: *scuffed bottles, (wooden) floors, shoes.* —*n.* **1** a rough or worn spot on a surface: *scuffs and scratches; scuff marks; scuff-resistant finishes.* **2** a light, flat, backless house slipper.

scuf.fle (SCUF.ul) *n.* a rough, confused fight at close quarters: *A scuffle broke out between the two groups.* —*v.* **scuf.fles, scuf.fled, scuf.fling** to struggle *with* someone at close quarters.

scull *n.* **1** a light oar, either one mounted at the stern or one used in pairs by oarsmen in a race. **2** a light racing boat. —*v.* propel a boat using a scull.

scul.ler.y (SCUL.uh.ree) *n.* **scul.ler.ies** a dish-washing and cleaning room attached to a kitchen.

scul.lion (SCUL.yun) *n. Archaic.* a kitchen servant.

sculpt *v.* [short form] to sculpture: *desert sands sculpted by the wind into undulating dunes; adj.: The mannequin is a **sculpted** version of his beloved; sculpted arches, cheekbones, columns, figures, foreheads, forms; n.: He enjoys painting, **sculpting**, and baking; ice sculpting.*

sculp.tor (SCULP.tur) *n.* one who produces sculpture; **sculp.tress** (-tris) *fem.*

sculp.ture (SCULP.chur) *n.* **1** the art of carving out or otherwise making three-dimensional works of art. **2** the products of such art collectively or a statue, carving, or other figure carved out, cast, or modeled in clay, wax, etc. —*v.* **-tures, -tured, -tur.ing** carve as in sculpture; *adj.*: *a **sculptured** carpet with a raised design; a sculptured three-dimensional look; sculptured contours, figures; a sculptured design, face, fit, trim.*
—**sculp.tur.al** *adj.*: *sculptural elegance, form, object, pieces, quality, style, work.*

scum *n.* dross or such refuse that rises to the top of a liquid or body of water, as the "green scum" formed by organisms on the surface of a pond: *the scum* (= despised people) *of society.* —*v.* **scums, scummed, scum.ming** become covered with or form scum.
—**scum.my** *adj.* **scum.mi.er, scum.mi.est.**

scum.bag *n.* [vulgar slang] a despicable person.

scup *n.* a food fish of the N. Atlantic coast of the U.S.

scup.per (SCUP.ur) *n.* an opening in the side of a ship at deck level for water to run off. —*v. Informal.* ruin or destroy: *The support of the media actually scuppered her chances of becoming party leader.*

scurf *n.* scaly or flaky dead matter such as dandruff; **scurf.y** *adj.*

scur.ril.ous (SCUR.uh.lus) *adj.* foully abusive or jesting: *scurrilous attacks, language, remarks, writers;* **scur.ril.ous.ly** *adv.* —**scur.ril.i.ty** (scuh.RIL.i.tee) *n.* **-ties.**

scur.ry (SCUR.ee) *v.* **scur.ries, scur.ried, scur.ry.ing** scamper: *Some scurried for cover; scurried for safety; Others scurried around like mice.*
—*n.* a scamper or hurrying.

scur.vy (SCUR.vee) *n.* a disease caused by lack of vitamin C in the diet.
—*adj.* **-vi.er, -vi.est** mean or contemptible: *a scurvy fellow.*
—**scur.vi.ly** *adv.*

scutch.eon (SCUCH.un) same as ESCUTCHEON.

scut.tle (SCUT.ul) *n.* **1** a metal pail for carrying and pouring coal. **2** a lidded opening in the hull or deck of a ship. **3** a scamper or scurry.
—*v.* **scut.tles, scut.tled, scut.tling 1** sink a ship by cutting a hole in it. **2** scrap or abandon: *Plans for the picnic were scuttled by the rain; to scuttle an agreement, deal, proposal; to scuttle negotiations.* **3** to scurry or scamper: *Crabs scuttle across the sand.*

scut.tle.butt (SCUT.ul.but) *n.* **1** a ship's drinking fountain. **2** *Informal.* rumor or gossip.

scuzz.y *adj.* **scuzz.i.er, -i.est** *Slang.* repulsive or abhorrent.

scythe (SITHE, "TH" as in "the") *n.* an L-shaped mowing and reaping implement with a long curved blade and a handle swung by both hands.
—*v.* **scythes, scythed, scyth.ing** cut or work with a scythe.

sea (SEE) *n.* a large body of salt water connected to an ocean; also, the ocean: *the Mediterranean Sea; the landlocked Caspian Sea; The Sea of Galilee is really a freshwater lake; Jim went to sea* (= became a sailor) *at 12; He put (out) to sea in a junk; The boat drifted out to sea; an invasion by sea and land; choppy, heavy, high, open, raging, rough, stormy, turbulent sea(s); blessed with calm seas; a pirate on the high seas; An old salt who has sailed the seven seas* (= traveled the world); *a **sea of*** (= large number of) *documents, faces, troubles; a sea of* (= vast amount or extent of) *change, color(s), data, debt, publicity, red ink, sand, slime.*
—**at sea** in the ocean: *ships at sea; a sailor buried at sea; He was completely **at sea*** (= bewildered) *when he sat down to take the test.* —**adj.** having to do with

the sea; marine: *the sea air; sea animals, captains, duty, fish, routes, water.*
sea anemone *n.* an anemonelike polyp with brightly colored tentacles.
sea.bed *n.* the floor of a sea.
sea.bird *n.* a bird that lives on or by the sea, as the albatross or petrel.
sea.board *n.* land bordering the sea: *on the Atlantic seaboard; the eastern seaboard.* Also **sea.coast.**
sea change *n.* a transformation: *to undergo a sea change.*
sea chest *n.* a sailor's storage chest.
sea cow *n.* a manatee or other sea animal.
sea dog *n.* a veteran sailor.
sea.far.er (SEE.fair.ur) *n.* a traveler of the seas; sailor; **sea.far.ing** *n. & adj.*
sea.food *n.* saltwater fish and shellfish eaten as food.
sea.go.ing (SEE.go.ing) *adj.* **1** oceangoing: *a seagoing container, tanker, vessel.* **2** seafaring: *a seagoing life.*
sea gull same as GULL, *n.* 1.
sea horse *n.* a fish of warm waters with a head resembling a horse's and a prehensile tail.
seal (SEEL) *n.* **1** a sea animal with four flippers that usu. lives in coastal waters, esp. in polar regions: *a colony of seals; the bark of a seal; a bull* (= male) *seal; a cow* (= female) *seal; the killing of* **pup seals** (= baby seals) *for pelt.* **2** a seal's pelt. **3** a stamped design, usu. on **sealing wax** made of shellac, etc., that is put on a document to make it official or on a letter, bottle, door, etc. to make it secure; also, the stamp or wax used: *the Great Seal of England; to affix a corporate seal; Contract bids are received* **under seal***; a seal of approval; negotiations carried out under a seal of secrecy; a wax seal; Who broke the seal? an* **Easter seal** (= decorative paper stamp). —*v.* **1** to hunt seals. **2** close tightly or as if with a seal: *to seal an envelope; The doors were sealed shut; to seal a surface with shellac (against moisture, etc.); Police may* **seal off** *an area under investigation (to prevent anyone entering or escaping); We have a promising new player* **signed, sealed, and delivered;** *adj.: a* **sealed** *jar of preserves; a tightly sealed container, home; Sealed bids or tenders are invited for a contract.* **3** secure something or make it final or decisive: *a promise sealed with a kiss.* **4** make something certain: *The evidence of the last witness sealed his fate; to seal one's doom, future, victory, win.*
sea lane *n.* a sea traffic lane or route.
seal.ant (SEEL.unt) *n.* a sealing agent or substance such as shellac.
sea legs *n.pl.* ability to adjust to the rolling of a ship by keeping one's balance, not being seasick, etc.: *to find, get one's sea legs.*
seal.er *n.* **1** one engaged in hunting seals. **2** one that seals, as a basecoat of paint.
sea level *n.* the average level of the surface of the sea, used as a measuring standard for heights and depths on land: *New York is at sea level; Mt. Everest is 29,000 ft. (8.84 km) above sea level; the Dead Sea is 1,300 ft. (396 m) below sea level.*
sea lion *n.* a seal with a coat of short, coarse hair and small ears, often trained as a circus performer.
seal.skin (SEEL.skin) *n.* the pelt of a seal or a garment made from it: *sealskin coats.*
seam (SEEM) *n.* **1** the line formed by the joining of two edges, esp. of cloth sewn together; also, of boards, as of a boat: *to let out a seam; a crowded apartment* **bursting at the seams;** *The plan* **came apart** *or* **fell apart at the seams** (= entirely). **2** a layer or bed of coal or other mineral: *coal seams.*
—*v.* **1** join together forming a seam; *adj.: a* **seamed** *pattern, skirt, stocking.* **2** mark with seamlike features such as wrinkles, scars, fissures, etc.
sea.man (SEE.mun) *n.* **-men** a sailor, esp. one in a naval rank below petty officer: *able, leading, master, ordinary seamen; the* **seaman's rest** (= lodging).
—**sea.man.ship** *n.*
seam.less *n.* **1** without seams: *seamless pipes, stockings, tubes.* **2** having no breaks or faults of texture or design: *a seamless blend, pattern, web; Sam returned from Saint-Tropez with a seamless tan.*
sea.mount *n.* a large volcanic mountain under the sea.
seam.stress (SEEM.stris) *n.* a woman who sews, esp. for a living.
seam.y (SEE.mee) *adj.* **seam.i.er, -i.est** sordid or squalid: *the seamy side of life.*
—**seam.i.ness** *n.*
sé.ance (SAY.ahnce) *n.* a spiritualist session to communicate with the dead: *Mediums conduct or hold séances; others attend séances; They sit and wait at a séance for spirits to materialize (in bodily form).*
sea.plane (SEE.plane) *n.* **1** an airplane with floats for landing or taxiing on water. **2** a flying boat.
sea.port *n.* a port for seagoing vessels.
sear (SEER) *v.* **1** burn the outside tis-

sue so as to harden it, as in branding, cauterizing, or in browning toast. 2 wither or dry up grain, etc.

search (SURCH) *v.* look through or examine a place, person, etc. to find something: *Police searched all the baggages for firearms.* —*n.* a searching: *the search for a missing child; careful, exhaustive, fruitless, painstaking, thorough searches; a body search; The* **search and replace** *function of a word processor can find specified words in a document and substitute them with others; the right "to be secure against unreasonable* **search or seizure"***; We are all* **in search of** *happiness.* —**search.er** *n.*

searching *adj.* thorough or penetrating: *a searching examination, investigation, look; The committee asked some searching questions.*

search.light *n.* 1 an apparatus on a swivel for projecting a powerful beam of light in any direction. 2 the beam.

search warrant *n.* a document issued by a court authorizing a police search.

sea.scape *n.* a view of the sea or a picture representing one.

sea.shell *n.* the shell of a sea mollusk.

sea.shore *n.* 1 a place where land and sea meet; seacoast. 2 [legal] the ground between high and low tides.

sea.sick *adj.* sick from or as if from the rolling motion of a ship: *She felt or got seasick.* —**sea.sick.ness** *n.*

sea.side *n.* a seashore or seacoast: *a walk by the seaside;* **adj**.: *a seaside cottage, resort, town, village.*

sea.son (SEE.zun) *n.* 1 one of the four divisions of the year, i.e., spring, summer, autumn, and winter. 2 any special period: *baseball, dry, fishing, harvest, holiday, hurricane, low, mating, off, planting, rainy, slack, tourist seasons; The Santa Claus parade ushers in the Christmas season; The Christmas shopping season opens with Thanksgiving; to close, usher out a season; She wears her hat* **in season and out of season** (= at all times). —*v.* 1 make food tasty with the use of salt, pepper, spices, etc.: *He likes to season everything with ground cumin; She seasons* (= livens up) *her lectures with wit and humor;* **adj**.: *a highly* **seasoned** *sauce; seasoned flour, salt; seasoned dry bread;* **n**.: *no-salt* **seasoning** (= condiment). 2 to condition or become conditioned; mature; age; **adj**.: *Seasoned lumber does not warp or shrink; seasoned air travelers, ideas, observers, performers, Republicans.* —**sea.son.er** *n.*

sea.son.a.ble (SEE.zun.uh.bul) *adj.* happening or suited to the season, occasion, etc.: *seasonable advice, clothes, gifts; We're having normal, seasonable temperatures.* —**sea.son.a.bly** *adv.*

sea.son.al (SEE.zun.ul) *adj.* having to do with or dependent on a season: *seasonal blooms, employment, migrations, hotel rates.* —**sea.son.al.ly** *adv.*

season ticket *n.* a ticket for a series of games or shows, transportation, etc. that is good for a specified period.

seat (SEET) *n.* 1 a place to sit on: *Please have a seat; Take a seat; Take your seat; We assign seats on a first-come basis; a room with seats for 200; to give up, keep, relinquish one's seat; box, bucket, driver's, front-row, ringside seats; the seat of one's pants* (= the part on which one sits). 2 where one gets a right to sit: *a reserved seat on a flight; She won a seat in parliament; held her seat for eight years; lost her seat in the last election.* 3 where something is based; center: *the seat of government; a county seat; Universities are seats of learning.* 4 a dominant or advantageous position: *A small deposit will put you in the driver's seat.* —*v.* cause to sit or provide with a seat: *Guests are seated first; This room seats* (= has seats for) *200 people;* **adj**.: *Please be* **seated***; Remain seated till the aircraft comes to a stop; a seated figure, position; deep-seated animosities, fears.*

seat belt or **seat.belt** *n.* a safety belt across the lap and often the chest and shoulder to secure a person, as in an automobile: *to wear a seatbelt;* **Fasten your seatbelts** (= Brace yourself).

seating *n.* sitting accommodation or seats: *rows of seating; indoor and outdoor seating; seating for 200; limited seating; No one is denied seating;* **adja**.: *seating areas, arrangements, capacities, comfort, positions.*

seat-of-the-pants *adj.* based on experience and intuition rather than technology: *a seat-of-the-pants feeling; seat-of-the-pants ability, approach, decision, flying, judgment, know-how, logic, operation, strategy; It's all very seat-of-the-pants.*

sea urchin *n.* a sea animal related to the starfish that has a body enclosed in a hard round shell covered with long, movable spines.

sea wall *n.* a wall or embankment built to protect a shore from the waves.

sea.ward (SEE.wurd) *adja.* 1 coming from the sea: *seaward winds.* 2 toward the sea: *the seaward edge of town; the seaward side; the seaward tide (going out to sea).* —**sea.ward** or **sea.wards** *adv.* toward the sea: *The boat was carried seaward; We're heading seaward.*

sea.way *n.* **1** an inland waterway with access from the sea for oceangoing ships: *the St. Lawrence Seaway.* **2** a sea traffic route.
sea.weed *n.* a sea plant or plants, esp. a marine alga.
sea.wor.thy (SEE.wur.thee) *adj.* of a ship, fit for sailing; **sea.wor.thi.ness** *n.*
se.ba.ceous (si.BAY.shus) *adj.* oil-secreting: *Sebaceous glands open into the hair follicles of the skin.*
seb.or.rhe.a (seb.uh.REE.uh) *n.* abnormal secretion of the sebaceous glands; **seb.or.rhe.ic** *adj.*: *seborrheic dermatitis.*
se.cede (si.SEED) *v.* **-cedes, -ced.ed, -ced.ing** of a group, cut itself off as a part *from* a state, religious body, etc. —**se.ces.sion** (-SESH.un) *n.;* **se.ces.sion.ist** *n.*
se.clude (si.CLOOD) *v.* **-cludes, -clud.ed, -clud.ing** shut oneself off from others; *adj.*: *a secluded area, beach, lake, resort, spot; secluded from public view; the secluded life of a convent.*
se.clu.sion (si.CLOO.zhun) *n.* isolation: *to go into seclusion; Monks used to live in seclusion all their lives; a period of seclusion; in the seclusion of a prison cell.* —**se.clu.sive** (-siv) *adj.*
sec.ond (SEC.und) *adj.* next after the first: *her second child; He is second in command; Jack placed first in the race, John came in second; He came off* **second best***; But he is second* (= inferior) *to none in studies; He'll get a second* (= another) *chance; We meet every second* (= alternate) *year.* —*adv.*: *the horse that finished second; November is the second last month.* —*v.* **1** support, esp. for parliamentary consideration: *He was proposed and seconded for election to the office; to second a motion, nomination, resolution.* **2** transfer an officer temporarily to another position: *seconded to overseas duty.* —*n.* **1** a person, thing, or place that is second: *Jill came in, finished, ran, was a close second; Put the car in second (gear); It happened on the second (day of the month); on the second (day) of last April.* **2 seconds** *pl.*: *The cake was so good she asked for* **seconds** (= a second helping); *a cheap store that sells rejects and* **seconds** (= defective articles). **3** a 60th part of a minute: *a car that goes from zero to 60 miles per hour in 7.9 seconds.* **4** a moment or instant: *I'll be with you in a second; It happened in a split second; Please wait a second; One second!* —**sec.ond.er** *n.*: *proposer and seconder.* —**sec.ond.ly** *adv.*
sec.ond.ar.y (SEC.un.dair.ee) *adj.* that is second, subordinate, or inferior; not primary: *secondary feathers, sources; A* **secondary color** *such as orange or green is produced by mixing two primary colors; The teacher feels that punctuation is* **secondary to** *correct spelling; There is a* **secondary accent** or **stress** *on the third syllable of "secondary"; Elementary school is followed by* **secondary school** (= high school). —**sec.ond.ar.i.ly** *adv.*
second childhood *n.* period of senility; dotage.
second-class *adj.* **1** of the second class: *a second-class ticket; Newspapers and periodicals qualify as* **second-class mail** *for reduced postal rates.* **2** inferior: *Immigrants are not second-class citizens; relegated to second-class status; She complained of second-class treatment as a female applicant.* —*adv.*: *Magazines are sent second-class; Except when on business, he goes or travels second-class* (= economy or tourist accommodation by train, ship, air, etc.).
second fiddle *n.* subordinate role: *She's tired of playing second fiddle to her boss.*
second-guess *v. Informal.* use hindsight to criticize someone for something already done.
sec.ond.hand (SEC.und.hand) *adj.* not from the original source: *secondhand information; secondhand* (= used or not new) *goods from a secondhand dealer; the dangers of nonsmokers inhaling secondhand smoke (from smokers).* —*adv.*: *He got the car secondhand* (= in used condition); *She gets most of her news* **at secondhand** (= through someone else).
second nature *n.* an acquired characteristic or tendency that has become firmly fixed in a person: *Punctuality is second nature to* or *for* or *with her.*
second opinion *n.* the opinion of another professional: *Let's get a second opinion before deciding on surgery.*
second person *n.* a pronoun or verb form referring to the person spoken to, as "you," "yours," "are," etc.
second-rate *adj.* of inferior quality; second-class: *a second-rate author, candidate, genius, mind, performance, poet.*
second-string *adj. Informal.* in sports, not of the regular team; reserve or substitute.
second thought (or **thoughts**) *n.* reconsideration of a first opinion or judgment: *His wife provides sober second thought to decisions he makes in a hurry; I jumped in without giving the matter a second thought; Then I had second thoughts about it;* **On second thought***, I decided not to swim in the cold water.*
second wind *n.* renewal of regular

strength, as by regaining one's breath: *She gets* or *catches her second wind after an afternoon nap.*

se.cre.cy (SEE.cruh.see) *n.* -**cies** a being secret or kept secret: *Mark it "Confidential" to ensure secrecy; The meeting has to be held in the strictest secrecy; We'll swear everyone to secrecy and meet in secrecy at a remote location.*

se.cret (SEE.crit) *adj.* having to do with concealing or keeping from general knowledge or view: *Let's keep the matter secret from the rest of the family; a secret admirer, door, passage, plot, society.*
—*n.* something secret or mysterious: *to betray, blurt out, divulge* or *reveal, ferret out, guard, keep, uncover a secret; She doesn't make a secret of her beliefs; a closely guarded, military, open, state, trade secret; It's a secret between us; Discoveries unlock the secrets of nature; I know the secret* (= secret cause) *of her many successes; They met **in secret*** (= secretly or unknown to others) *to plan the surprise party.* —**se.cret.ly** *adv.*

sec.re.tar.i.al (sec.ruh.TAIR.ee.ul) *adj.* of a secretary: *a secretarial chair, job; secretarial duties, help.*

sec.re.tar.i.at (sec.ruh.TAIR.ee.ut) *n.* the administrative staff of a government department: *the U.N. Secretariat in New York.*

sec.re.tar.y (SEC.ruh.tair.ee) *n.* -**tar.ies** 1 an employee who handles the correspondence, keeps records, etc. of a person or organization: *executive, personal, press secretaries; He works as private secretary to the mayor.* 2 a company officer with similar duties. 3 the head of a government department: *defense, foreign, labor secretaries; the U.S. **Secretary of State*** (= president's advisor on foreign affairs). 4 a writing desk. —**sec.re.tar.y.ship** *n.*

se.crete (si.CREET) *v.* -**cretes, -cret.ed, -cret.ing** 1 hide in a secret place; cache. 2 discharge, as from a gland; **se.cre.tion** (si.CREE.shun) *n.*; **se.cre.to.ry** (-tuh.ree) *adj.: a secretory duct.*

se.cre.tive (SEE.cruh.tiv, si.CREE.tiv) *adj.* tending to conceal rather than communicate; not frank or open: *She's naturally very secretive about her sex life.*
—**se.cre.tive.ly** *adv.*; **se.cre.tive.ness** *n.*

secret police *n.* a secretly operating police organization that enforces a government's political policies.

secret service *n.* a department of government in charge of security.

sect *n.* a group following a particular doctrine or leader, often a dissenting group: *a heretical sect; warring sects; religious sects* (= denominations).

sec.tar.i.an (sec.TAIR.ee.un) *n.* a person devoted to a sect, esp. in a narrow-minded way; *adj.: sectarian violence in the Middle East; sectarian armies, fanatics, rivalries.* —**sec.tar.i.an.ism** *n.*

sec.ta.ry (SEC.tuh.ree) *n.* -**ries** a sectarian.

sec.tion (SEC.shun) *n.* 1 a cutting or a cut-off part: *a cesarian section; conical, cross, vertical sections.* 2 a division or part of something larger: *the business, classified, news, sports, travel sections of a newspaper; a city's business, residential sections; the sections of a bookcase (to be assembled); the sections of a chapter, fruit, pie; to play in the brass, percussion, string,* or *woodwind section of an orchestra; a section of a railroad maintained by a group of workers (**section gang**).*
—*v.* divide into sections or divide so as to display a section.

sec.tion.al (SEC.shuh.nul) *adj.* 1 having to do with a section: *a sectional drawing, view.* 2 local or regional: *sectional interests, prejudices, quarrels, rivalries.* 3 made up of sections; modular: *a sectional bookcase, sofa; sectional furniture.*
—**sec.tion.al.ly** *adv.* —**sec.tion.al.ism** *n.*

sec.tor (SEC.tur) *n.* 1 part of a circle between two radii. 2 area of operation or activity: *in the public and private sectors of industry.*

sec.u.lar (SEC.yuh.lur) *adj.* of the world, not of the church, of a religion, or of religious life: *secular education, society;* **secular clergy** (= diocesan clergy, not belonging to a religious order). —**sec.u.lar.ism** *n.*

sec.u.lar.ize (SEC.yuh.luh.rize) *v.* -**iz.es, -ized, -iz.ing** make secular; transfer to civil or lay use or control, as church schools. —**sec.u.lar.i.za.tion** (-ruh.ZAY.shun, -rye-) *n.*

se.cure (si.CURE) *adj.* protected against danger, harm, risk, fear, worry, etc.; safe: *She feels secure with the doors locked; secure against intruders; a nation secure from attack, feels happy and secure in her beliefs; a secure investment; a secure* (= firm) *knot.*
—*v.* -**cures, -cured, -cur.ing** make secure: *A door is secured by locking it; Banks secure their loans by collaterals; to secure our borders against traffickers; Let's secure our seats* (= purchase tickets) *before the show is sold out.*
—**se.cure.ly** *adv.*

se.cur.i.ty (si.CURE.i.tee) *n.* -**ties** 1 protection or the feeling of being protected or secure: *a child brought up in the security of the home; a feeling, sense of security against attack; to compromise, ensure, provide, strengthen, tighten, undermine security; collective, internal, national, personal security; Social Security or Social Insurance is instituted by governments to provide people with social benefits;* **adja.:** *maximum and minimum security prisons; He was refused the job as a security risk; A child clings to its* **security blanket** *as if for protection; the U.N.* **Security Council** *for safeguarding world peace.* **2** something that protects or secures: *His signature is good security for a loan.* **3 securities** *pl.* stocks and bonds: *to issue, register securities; gilt-edged securities; government securities.*

se.dan (si.DAN) *n.* **1** an automobile having an enclosed body with center posts between front and back windows to support the roof, not a hardtop. **2** a covered portable chair carried on poles like a litter, usu. by two men; also **sedan chair.**

se.date (si.DATE) *adj.* calm and composed in manner or style: *sedate apparel, styling; a sedate approach, character, fashion, interior, life, pace.*
—*v.* **-dates, -dat.ed, -dat.ing** put someone under sedation using a sedative; *adj.:* **She was so** ***sedated*** *she would have walked into a lion's den; mildly sedated; the* ***sedating*** *effect of certain drugs.*
—**se.date.ly** *adv.;* **se.date.ness** *n.*
—**se.da.tion** (-DAY.shun) *n.:* an operation carried out while under heavy sedation.

sed.a.tive (SED.uh.tiv) *n.* a substance such as a barbiturate or bromide that tends to soothe and calm the nerves.

sed.en.tar.y (SED.un.tair.ee) *adj.* involving much sitting: *sedentary habits; a sedentary life, occupation.*

Se.der (SAY.dur) *n.* the domestic observance of the beginning of the Jewish Passover, esp. on its first night.

sedge *n.* a grasslike plant but with triangular, solid stems that grows in marshy places. —**sedg.y** *adj.:* sedgy banks, grass, swamps.

sed.i.ment (SED.uh.munt) *n.* **1** matter settling at the bottom of a liquid; dregs. **2** matter deposited by ice, water (as by a receding flood), wind, etc. —**sed.i.men.ta.ry** (-MEN.tuh.ree) *adj.* containing or formed by sediment: *Shale, limestone, and sandstone are sedimentary rocks.* —**sed.i.men.ta.tion** (-mun.TAY.shun) *n.*

se.di.tion (suh.DISH.un) *n.* **1** the stirring up of discontent or rebellion against a government: *to foment, incite sedition; To advocate the violent overthrow of one's government would be an act of sedition.* **2** such action or speech.
—**se.di.tious** *adj.*

se.duce (si.DUCE, *rhyme:* produce) *v.* **-duc.es, -duced, -duc.ing** persuade to do something wrong or unlawful, esp. to have sexual intercourse. —**se.duc.er** *n.;* **se.duc.tress** (si.DUC.tris) *fem.*
—**se.duc.tion** (-shun) *n.* —**se.duc.tive** (-tiv) *adj.: a seductive image, performer, song, voice; the seductive lure of riches;* **se.duc.tive.ly** *adv.;* **se.duc.tive.ness** *n.*

sed.u.lous (SEJ.uh.lus) *adj.* diligent in pursuing an objective till it is reached: *the sedulous imitation of a model writer;* **sed.u.lous.ly** *adv.*

see *v.* **sees, saw, seen, see.ing 1** be aware of through the eyes: *We can't see anything in the dark; I saw him crossing the street* (= in the middle of the street), *but I can't say I saw him cross the street* (= get to the other side). **2** look at a person or thing: *See this picture; Will you see* (= look and find) *who is at the door?* **3** perceive with the mind: *Do you see what I mean? I see that you're right; I see from the papers that there are no survivors; What do you see in her* (that is so attractive to you)? *He prepared to leave,* **seeing** (= considering) *that it was getting late.* **4** experience or have knowledge of something: *an old house that has seen better times; She would like to see her children settled.* **5** visit: *time to see a lawyer; She doesn't like her boyfriend seeing* (= dating) *other girls.* **6** receive: *The boss will see you now.* **7** make sure; take care: *Please see that the lights are turned off when you leave; Please see* (= escort) *the last visitor out.* **8** consider: *Can you see her as a future President? Please hire him if you see* (= judge) *fit to do so.* —**see about** or **after** take care of something: *The boss wants you to see about the invitations.* —**see eye to eye** agree: *Mom and Dad don't always see eye to eye with each other on* or *about everything.* —**see into** have knowledge of something: *She claims to be a prophet who can see into the future.* —**see off** say goodbye to someone: *He's gone to the airport to see her off.* —**see through** **1** understand the real nature of a person, scheme, etc.: *It's easy to see right through him.* **2** take care of a person or undertaking till the end of something: *I'll see you through this crisis; I have to see the project through to its completion.*
—**see to** attend to something: *He'll see*

seed / segregation

to the arrangements; *His boss will see to it that the arrangements work.*
—*n.* a bishop's office, authority, or diocese: *the see of Rome; the Apostolic or Holy See.*

seed *n.* **1** the usu. grainlike part of a plant from which a new plant will sprout: *to broadcast, plant, sow, spread seeds; Seeds germinate, grow; a bag of lettuce seed* (= seeds), *grass seed;* **cpd.:** green-**seeded** *and white-seeded varieties of bean.* **2** source or origin: *tales that sowed seeds of suspicion in her mind.* **3** descendants: *the seed of Abraham.* **4** a tournament player in regard to ranking: *John is top seed in the men's event.* —**go** or **run to seed** be finished with flowering and production: *People like to keep working even after retirement lest they go to seed* (= become useless or unproductive).
—*v.* **1** sow seeds over a field: *to seed a field; a field seeded with wheat; Clouds are seeded with crystals of dry ice and other chemicals to make rain or snow;* **n.:** *spring seedings;* **adj.:** *the seeded acreage; a seeded plant bed.* **2** develop by providing seed money: *to seed a corporation, idea, industry, market, project.* **3** remove seeds from fruit; **adj.:** *seeded grapes, pears.* **4** to rank according to ability or worth; **cpd:** *Top-seeded players meet last in a tournament; the top-seeded car of the year; the third-seeded TV network.*
—**seed.er** *n.* —**seed.less** *adj.*

seed.ling *n.* **1** a plant grown from a seed. **2** a young tree smaller than a sapling.

seed money *n.* money for starting an enterprise.

seed.time *n.* the sowing season.

seed.y *adj.* **seed.i.er, -i.est 1** full of seeds. **2** gone to seed; unproductive: *a seedy business, commercial area.* **3** shabby-looking: *the seedy side of town; seedy bars, hotels, neighborhoods.*
—**seed.i.ly** *adv.;* **seed.i.ness** *n.*

Seeing Eye or **Seeing Eye dog** *n.* Trademark. a blind person's guide dog.

seek *v.* **seeks, sought, seek.ing** try to find or get: *to seek advice, fortune, shelter; We seek to please our customers; to seek (after) the truth; We've got the funds we sought (for);* **cpd:** *a much sought-after speaker; a long-sought goal.* —**seek.er** *n.: a status seeker.*

seem *v.* appear: *She seems happy; seems like a happy person; What seems to be the problem? We seem to have lost our way; It seems (to me) we have lost our way; It seems a waste of time;* **adj.:** *a seeming* (= apparent) *coincidence, contradiction;*

his seeming indifference, sincerity, willingness. —**seem.ing.ly** *adv.*

seem.ly *adj.* **-li.er, -li.est** that looks appropriate or proper: *Clothes should be seemly if not attractive; in a seemly fashion; seemly* (= pleasing) *behavior.*
—**seem.li.ness** *n.*

seen *pp.* of SEE.

seep *v.* flow out slowly through cracks of a ceiling, etc. or fine pores, as of sand: *water seeping into a basement.*
—**seep.age** (-ij) *n.*

seer *n.* one who claims to see into or foretell the future; prophet; **seer.ess** *fem.*

seer.suck.er (SEER.suck.ur) *n.* a crinkly, lightweight fabric for dresses, jackets, etc.

see.saw *n.* **1** a plank supported in the middle for children to sit on at opposite ends and ride up and down; teeter-totter. **2** an up-and-down or back-and-forth movement, as in warfare or in a game. —*v.* move up and down or back and forth: *The match was so close, the lead seesawed between the two sides for a long time.*

seethe ("th" as in "the") *v.* **seethes, seethed, seeth.ing** be agitated or disturbed, as boiling water: *a nation seething with rebellion; He seethed with fury, resentment.*

see-through 1 *adja.* that can be seen through: *a see-through building, crisper, dress, window;* also *n.* **2** *adj.* transparent: *Chiffon is see-through; see-through fabrics.*

seg.ment (SEG.munt) *n.* **1** a natural section or part: *the segments of an orange, earthworm's body, the various segments of the population; a 15-minute segment of a TV program.* **2** a portion of a circle cut off by a plane or that between two parallel planes. —*v.* (-ment) divide into segments: *Consumers are segmented into many groups;* **adj.:** *The market is becoming more and more segmented; a segmented approach to marketing; displaying goods in a segmented fashion; a segmented market, society.*
—**seg.men.ta.tion** (-mun.TAY.shun) *n.*

seg.re.gate (SEG.ruh.gate) *v.* **-gates, -gat.ed, -gat.ing** to separate, esp. as a group and for reasons of race, sex, contagion, etc.: *to segregate the boys from the girls; students segregated into academic and nonacademic streams;* **adj.:** *a segregated area, beach, school; Some parts of the world are still racially segregated.*

seg.re.ga.tion (seg.ruh.GAY.shun) *n.* (policy of) separation of racial groups in housing, education, transportation facilities, etc.: *to maintain, practice segregation; racial, religious, sex segregation.* —**seg.re.ga.tion.ist** *n.*

se.gue (SEG.way) *v.* **-gues, -gued, -gue.ing** *Music.* proceed without pause to or into the following movement. —*n.* such a direction.

sei.gneur (seen.YUR) *n.* a feudal lord. —**sei.gno.ri.al** or **sei.gnio.ri.al** (-YOR.ee.ul) *adj.*

seine (SAIN) *n.* a weighted net for encircling and hauling in schools of fish. —*v.* **seines, seined, sein.ing** fish with a seine.

seis.mic (SIZE.mic) *adj.* having to do with earthquakes: *seismic activity, changes, design, forces, safety, shock, waves;* **seis.mi.cal.ly** *adv.*

seis.mo.gram (SIZE.muh.gram) *n.* a recording made by a seismograph.

seis.mo.graph (SIZE.muh.graf) *n.* an instrument that records the duration, intensity, and direction of an earthquake. —**seis.mo.graph.ic** (-GRAF.ic) *adj.* —**seis.mog.ra.phy** (size.MOG.ruh.fee) *n.;* **seis.mog.ra.pher** (-ruh.fur) *n.*

seis.mol.o.gy (size.MOL.uh.jee) *n.* the science of earthquakes; **seis.mol.o.gist** *n.* —**seis.mo.log.i.cal** (-muh.LOJ.i.cul) *adj.*

seize (SEEZ) *v.* **seiz.es, seized, seiz.ing** take hold or possession of a thing or person suddenly and with force: *He seized the food without waiting to be served; contraband seized by customs; the right of police to search and seize; He likes to seize on* or *upon* (= understand and use) *every opportunity to plug his candidate; Jan was seized* (= stricken) *with remorse soon after the deed; Some brakes have a tendency to seize* (= stick fast).

sei.zure (SEE.zhur) *n.* a seizing or being seized: *unwarranted search and seizure of goods; cardiac, heart, epileptic seizures.*

sel.dom (SEL.dum) *adv.* rarely; not often: *a bird seldom seen in these parts; Things are seldom as they seem; his seldom neat appearance.*

se.lect (si.LECT) *v.* choose or pick out of many, using care and discrimination: *to select a jury; She was selected from among many who applied; We selected her to fill the vacancy.* —*adj.* carefully chosen: *Only a select few were admitted; a select* (= exclusive) *group of friends.* —**se.lec.tion** (si.LEC.shun) *n.: Make a selection; Take your selection to the cashier; She was happy to play their* (musical) *selection.* —**se.lec.tor** (-tur) *n.*

se.lec.tive (si.LEC.tiv) *adj.* careful in selecting: *She's very selective in her choices; the* **selective service** *system of compulsory military service based on the classification in which each one falls.* —**se.lec.tiv.i.ty** (-TIV.i.tee) *n.*

se.lect.man (si.LECT.man, -mun) *n.* **-men** a member of a board of officers chosen annually to manage the affairs of a New England town.

sel.e.nite (SEL.uh.nite) *n.* a transparent, crystalline variety of gypsum.

se.le.ni.um (si.LEE.nee.um) *n.* a metalloid element used in photoelectric cells, rectifiers, etc.

sel.e.nog.ra.phy (sel.uh.NOG.ruh.fee) *n.* the science of the moon's physical features. —**sel.e.nog.ra.pher** *n.*

self *n.* **selves** (SELVZ) one's own person: *He appeared quite like his old self; her former self* (= as she was before); *by his very self* (= by himself); *their true selves* (= their true natures); *He puts self* (= his own interests) *above all else; a check payable to self* (= oneself). —*comb.form.* of, by, to, or for oneself or itself: *self-criticism, self-employed, self-respect, self-worth.*

self-addressed *adj.* addressed to oneself: *a stamped self-addressed envelope for a quick reply.*

self-assurance *n.* confidence in oneself.

self-assured *adj.* self-confident: *a relaxed and self-assured manner; She was quite poised and self-assured as a witness; He sounded supremely self-assured and competent.*

self-binder *n.* a farm machine that cuts grain and ties it into bundles.

self-centered *adj.* selfish. —**self-centeredness** *n.*

self-composed *adj.* in control of one's emotions; calm and cool.

self-conceit *n.* too much pride in oneself; vanity.

self-concept *n.* self-image.

self-confidence *n.* confidence in oneself: *to acquire, display, gain, have, instill, show self-confidence; to restore, not undermine her self-confidence; the self-confidence to stand up for her rights.* —**self-confident** *adj.*

self-conscious *adj.* **1** aware of oneself: *An animal is conscious but never self-conscious.* **2** unduly aware of oneself; ill at ease: *A good actor shouldn't be self-conscious.*

self-contained *adj.* **1** complete within itself; independent: *a self-contained classroom, living unit.* **2** showing self-control. **3** reserved: *silent and self-contained.*

self-contradiction *n.* **1** a statement con-

taining a contradiction. **2** a contradiction of oneself or itself.
—**self-contradictory** *adj*.

self-control *n*. control of one's actions, feelings, desires, etc.: *to exercise, lose self-control; She displays admirable, complete, total self-control in public.*
—**self-controlled** *adj*.

self-defense *n*. defense of oneself, one's rights, actions, etc.: *the art of self-defense; She acted in self-defense; It is unfortunate to have to kill in self-defense.*

self-denial *n*. a sacrifice of one's own desires: *Ascetics exercise, practice self-denial.*

self-deprecating *adj*. putting oneself down: *his self-deprecating charm and wit; She's a little self-deprecating; her self-deprecating sense of humor; She mentioned her achievements in a self-deprecating way.*

self-destruct *v*. destroy oneself or itself: *Perishable foods self-destruct if kept long outside the fridge; a price sticker designed to self-destruct (= come off in pieces) if tampered with.*

self-determination *n*. freedom to make one's own decisions, esp., of a people, to determine for themselves what form of government they shall have: *the right to self-determination; to achieve, give or grant, want self-determination.*

self-effacing *adj*. minimizing one's own achievements.

self-esteem *n*. a sense of one's own worth: *your sense of self-esteem; lack of self-esteem; Lu suffers from low self-esteem; how to develop high self-esteem; to build up, diminish, gain, raise, restore self-esteem; to boost, build, destroy, enhance, improve, lose, raise one's self-esteem; when your self-esteem crumbles.*

self-evident *adj*. obvious, and needing no explanation.

self-explanatory *adj*. explaining itself; obvious without explanation.

self-expression *n*. expression of oneself, esp. in the arts.

self-fertilization *n*. fertilization of a plant or animal by its own pollen or sperm.

self-fulfilling *adj*. becoming fulfilled because predicted or expected: *a self-fulfilling prophecy, as when a manager gets a rush job done by telling her employees that she is confident they can finish it by day's end.* —**self-fulfillment** *n*.: *to achieve, attain, seek self-fulfillment.*

self-government *n*. government by one's own people, esp. elected representatives. —**self-governing** *adj*.

self-image *n*. conception of one's own worth, identity, etc.

self-important *adj*. showing too high an opinion of oneself; **self-importance** *n*.

self-interest *n*. the seeking of one's own advantage over the interests of others; selfishness: *Most of us act in our own self-interest; the policy of enlightened self-interest.*

self.ish (SEL.fish) *adj*. caring too much for oneself without regard for the rights of others. —**self.ish.ly** *adv*.; **self.ish.ness** *n*.

self.less (SELF.lis) *adj*. unselfish.
—**self.less.ly** *adv*.; **self.less.ness** *n*.

self-made *adj*. who has reached a position largely through personal efforts: *a self-made businesswoman, man, millionaire.*

self-pity *n*. pity for oneself: *to indulge in self-pity.*

self-pollination *n*. pollination of the same flower or another flower of the same plant.

self-possession *n*. self-control; **self-possessed** *adj*.

self-propelled *adj*. propelled by its own power: *self-propelled artillery, missiles.*

self-regard same as SELF-RESPECT.

self-regulating *adj*. **1** of machines, regulating itself; automatic: *a self-regulating heating system.* **2** governing itself: *law, medicine, and such self-regulating professions.*

self-reliance *n*. reliance on one's own powers, esp. mental; **self-reliant** *adj*.

self-respect *n*. respect for one's own worth as a person: *He kept his self-respect and ignored the insult; If I quit now I'd lose my self-respect.*
—**self-respecting** *adj*.

self-righteous *adj*. convinced that one is more righteous and moral than others: *a moralistic and self-righteous person; self-righteous and hypocritical; self-righteous convictions, purposes.*
—**self-righteously** *adv*.;
self-righteousness *n*.

self.same *adj a*. the very same; identical: *the selfsame day; the selfsame Mr. Smith I met yesterday.*

self-sealing *adj*. sealing by itself: *a self-sealing tire (that seals itself when punctured); a self-sealing envelope (that is sealed by applying pressure).*

self-seeker *n*. a seeker of one's own advantage; selfish person. —**self-seeking** *n. & adj*.

self-serve *adj a*. self-service: *a self-serve gas station.*

self-service *n*. the practice of customers serving themselves, as at a gas station, cafeteria, etc.; *adj*.: *a self-service gas station, laundry, vending machine.*

self-serving *adj.* self-seeking; selfish.
self-starter *n.* 1 an electrical device for starting an internal combustion engine without cranking. 2 *Informal.* a person with initiative. —**self-starting** *adj.*
self-styled *adj.* so named by oneself without justification: *a self-styled "president for life."*
self-sufficiency *n.* the condition of needing no outside help: *Many countries have achieved or attained self-sufficiency in food.* —**self-sufficient** *adj.*
self-willed *adj.* obstinate or stubborn.
self-worth same as SELF-ESTEEM.
sell *v.* **sells, sold, sell.ing** 1 exchange goods, services, etc. for money or other return: *He sells cars; buys wholesale and sells retail; sells them by the dozen; a used car sold as is* (= with no guarantees) *for $200; It was sold at a loss; He doesn't like to sell to family; a store that sells groceries in bulk; He's in jail for selling state secrets to the enemy; Lottery tickets* **sell like hot cakes** (= sell quickly and in large quantities); *n.: panic* **selling** *of stocks because of falling prices;* **adja. & cpd:** *a selling point, price, season, technique; best-selling; fast-selling; top-selling.* 2 (cause to) be sold or accepted: *Snow tires sell best in winter; He sold his voters on* (= convinced them about) *capital punishment; He is* **sold on** (= completely persuaded about) *capital punishment; Her excuse just wouldn't sell* (= be accepted). —**sell someone down the river** *Informal.* betray. —**sell off** get rid of something by selling it: *They are selling off their winter stock to make room for spring clothes.* —**sell out** 1 dispose of completely by selling: *We just sold out today's paper; We are completely sold out (of today's paper); We are planning to sell out (the business) to the competition.* 2 *Informal.* betray. —**sell short** act on the basis of undervaluing something: *My broker advised me to sell Columbus short (because the stock is going to drop in price); You are selling your kids short* (= cheating them) *by neglecting to read aloud to them.*
—*n.* 1 a selling or its method: *hard, soft, tough sells.* 2 *Informal.* hoax. —**sell.er** *n.: It's a* **seller's market** *when goods are scarce and prices high.*
sell.out *n.* 1 a selling out or a show for which all seats are sold: *The fund-raising show was a sellout;* **adja.:** *A sell-out audience attended the preview; sellout crowds.* 2 *Informal.* a betrayal: *a sellout of national interests.*
Selt.zer water (SELT.sur-) *n.* 1 mineral water. 2 usu. **seltzer water,** carbonated water.
sel.vage or **sel.vedge** (SEL.vij) *n.* the edge of a cloth woven so as to prevent raveling.
selves *pl.* of SELF.
se.man.tics (suh.MAN.tics) *n.pl.* [takes *sing. v.*] the study of meanings in language. —**se.man.tic** *adj.*
—**se.man.ti.cist** *n.*
sem.a.phore (SEM.uh.for) *n.* a visual signaling system based on different positions of arms or hand-held flags.
sem.blance (SEM.blunce) *n.* outward appearance or likeness that differs from the reality: *a story without even the semblance of truth; a semblance of legitimacy, order, reality, wealth; a feeble semblance of authority.*
se.men (SEE.mun) *n.* the male reproductive fluid.
se.mes.ter (suh.MES.tur) *n.* one of the two terms into which an academic year is divided.
semi- *comb.form.* half; partly; incompletely: *semicentennial, semicolon, semi-independent, semipermanent.*
sem.i.an.nu.al (sem.ee.AN.yoo.ul) *adj.* 1 occurring every half year. 2 lasting a half year.
sem.i.au.to.mat.ic (SEM.ee.aw.tuh.MAT.ic) *n. & adj.* (a gun) that is self-loading though not like a machine gun in firing automatically.
sem.i.col.on (SEM.ee.coh.lun) *n.* the punctuation mark [;].
sem.i.con.duc.tor (SEM.ee.cun.DUC.tur) *n.* a material such as silicon that conducts electricity better than an insulator but not as well as a conductor, hence used in electronic devices such as transistors, lasers, and solar batteries.
sem.i.con.scious (sem.ee.CON.shus) *adj.* only partly conscious or awake.
sem.i.de.tached (SEM.ee.di.TACHT) *n. & adj.* (one) of two dwellings joined side by side, sharing a common wall or garage.
sem.i.fi.nal (sem.ee.FYE.nul) *adja.* next to the last, as in a tournament.
—*n.* a semifinal match or round.
sem.i.flu.id (sem.ee.FLOO.id) *n. & adj.* (a substance such as molasses or pitch) that is thick but flowing.
sem.i.for.mal (sem.ee.FOR.mul) *adj.* partly formal: *a semiformal dance at a semiformal wedding; in semiformal attire (without formal gowns, tuxedos, etc.);* also **semi-formal.**
sem.i.month.ly (sem.ee.MUNTH.lee) *adj. & adv.* issued twice a month.
—*n.* a semimonthly periodical.

sem.i.nal (SEM.uh.nul) *adj.* **1** having to do with seed or semen: *the seminal fluid.* **2** containing the seeds for later development: *a seminal idea, influence, moment, study, work; Woodstock was one of the seminal rock events of the 1960s.* —**sem.i.nal.ly** *adv.*

sem.i.nar (SEM.uh.nar) *n.* a meeting of a group of people doing research or studying under someone's guidance: *Executives attend, conduct, hold seminars on management methods.*

sem.i.nary (SEM.uh.nair.ee) *n.* **-nar.ies** an educational institution for preparing priests, ministers, rabbis, etc.; **sem.i.nar.i.an** (-NAIR.ee.un) *n.*

Sem.i.nole (SEM.uh.nole) *n.* (a member of) an American Indian people of Florida and Oklahoma.

sem.i.per.me.a.ble (sem.ee.PUR.mee.uh.bul) *adj.* of a membrane, allowing the passage of only certain substances: *He has a semipermeable mind.*

sem.i.pre.cious (sem.ee.PRESH.us) *adj.* of a gemstone, of less value than precious stones, as amethyst or turquoise: *semiprecious jewelry, stones.*

sem.i.pri.vate (sem.ee.PRY.vit) *n. & adj.* (a hospital room) that is shared with one other patient.

sem.i.pro.fes.sion.al (SEM.ee.pruh.FESH.un.ul) *n.* a player who gets paid on a part-time basis; also **sem.i.pro**; *adj.*: *a semiprofessional sport, player, team; a semipro ball club.*

sem.i.skilled (SEM.ee.skild) *adj.* partly skilled or requiring limited training.

sem.i.soft (SEM.ee.soft) *adj.* of a cheese, medium soft, as Limburger.

Sem.ite (SEM.ite) *n.* a person speaking a Semitic language.

Se.mit.ic (suh.MIT.ic) *n. & adj.* (of) the group of languages comprising Arabic, Aramaic, Assyrian, Hebrew, Phoenician, Syrian, etc.

sem.i.trail.er (SEM.ee.tray.lur) *n.* a cargo-carrying trailer with wheels at the rear and in the middle and supported at the front by a truck tractor.

sem.i.trop.i.cal (sem.ee.TROP.i.cul) *adj.* partly tropical.

sem.i.vow.el (SEM.ee.vow.ul) *n.* a consonantlike vowel, esp. "w" or "y."

sem.i.week.ly (sem.ee.WEEK.lee) *adj.* published twice a week: *a semiweekly magazine;* **n.**: *a weekly that used to be a semiweekly;* *adv.*: *We publish semiweekly.*

sen.ate (SEN.it) *n.* **1** the upper branch of a legislature. **2** a legislative or governing council, as of a university: *to convene, convoke, disband, dissolve a senate; A senate adjourns, meets.* —**sen.a.tor** (-uh.tur) *n.* —**sen.a.to.ri.al** (-uh.TOR.ee.ul) *adj.*

send *v.* **sends, sent, send.ing 1** cause a person or thing to go without oneself going: *We send children to school; Please send the message to him; Send him the message; Send it by courier; We'll send her on a mission; Send her as our delegate; to send the children to camp; The wind sent the papers flying; Send him to get coffee; Send him for (= to get) coffee.* **2** *Informal.* excite or thrill: *the kind of music that really sends her.* —**send for** send a request or messenger for a person or thing: *Please send for the plumber; He likes to send away for (= order) everything offered free.* —**send out:** *to send out invitations; a reporter sent out to cover an event; We send out for Chinese food (= order it delivered) on busy evenings.* —**send packing** dismiss without ceremony. —**send.er** *n.*

send-off *n. Informal.* a farewell in honor of someone leaving a group on a new venture, going on a trip, etc.: *Her students gave her a big send-off.*

send-up *n.* a takeoff: *a TV feature that is a send-up of the news media.*

Sen.e.ca (SEN.uh.cuh) *n.* (a member of) an Iroquoian-speaking people of W. New York State.

Sen.e.ga.lese (sen.i.guh.LEEZ) *n. & adj., sing. & pl.* (a person) of or from **Senegal**, a country of W. Africa.

se.nile (SEE.nile) *adj.* relating to weakness of old age, esp. loss of mental powers: *senile condition, deterioration, psychosis; He is 90 but not at all senile.* —**se.nil.i.ty** (suh.NIL.i.tee) *n.*

sen.ior (SEEN.yur) *n.* **1** a student in a graduating class. **2** one who is older or of higher rank: *reduced rates for seniors* (= senior citizens); *John Smith, Sr.* (= Senior, father of John Smith, Jr.). —*adj.* older in age, rank, etc.: *He is senior to me by two years; middle and senior management; the senior partner of the firm.*

senior citizen *n.* an elderly, usu. retired person, normally 65 and up.

senior high school *n.* grades 10, 11, and 12 of high school.

sen.ior.i.ty (seen.YOR.i.tee) *n.* **-ties** superiority in age; priority because of length of service in a job: *promotion by or according to seniority rather than by merit alone.*

sen.na (SEN.uh) *n.* a laxative made from the dried leaves of a cassia plant.

se.ñor (sain.YOR) *n.* **-ño.res** (-YOR.es) *Spanish.* a gentleman; [as a title] Mr.

or Sir; **se.ño.ra** (-YOR.ah) *fem.*
se.ño.ri.ta (sain.yuh.REE.tah) *n. Spanish.* a young lady; [as a title] Miss.
sen.sa.tion (sen.SAY.shun) *n.* **1** sense impression, esp. of touch or feeling: *sensations of heat and cold; a sensation of giddiness; burning, choking, numbing, pleasant sensations.* **2** (cause of) a widespread feeling of excitement: *The announcement caused, created a sensation; She is a great sensation as a singer.*
sen.sa.tion.al (sen.SAY.shuh.nul) *adj.* arousing or meant to arouse general excitement: *a sensational show, story, trial; sensational headlines, journalism; She looked sensational in her bridal gown;* **sen.sa.tion.al.ly** *adv.*
—**sen.sa.tion.al.ism** *n.*
sense *n.* **1** a power of feeling or awareness: *a sense of security;* the *five senses* of sight, hearing, smell, taste, and touch. **2** understanding or appreciation: *your sense of beauty, responsibility; I wish he had a grain of sense in his head; He showed a poor sense of timing; She displays a wry sense of humor; had the good sense to say "Yes"; common sense; horse sense.* **3** a particular meaning: *true in every sense of the word; the figurative, literal, narrow, strict senses of a term;* **In a sense** (= to a certain extent), *you're right.* **4 senses** *pl.* normal state of mind: *How can we bring him to his senses? It may be too late when she comes to her senses.* —**make sense** have meaning: *Your reasons don't make sense; It makes sense to drive within the speed limit; Can you make any sense out of this letter?* —*v.* **sens.es, sensed, sens.ing** be aware of something; perceive: *She sensed the danger; sensed right away that something was wrong; A smoke detector can sense (the presence of) smoke; He doesn't seem to have sensed your meaning.* —**sense.less** *adj.;* **sense.less.ly** *adv.*
sen.si.bil.i.ty (sen.suh.BIL.i.tee) *n.* **-ties 1** ability to sense or perceive. **2** fineness of feelings: *a woman of sense and sensibility; Let's not hurt her* **sensibilities** (= sensitive feelings).
sen.si.ble (SEN.suh.bul) *adj.* **1** having good sense; reasonable and practical: *a sensible young woman; Take a sensible stand; Be sensible; It is sensible of her to withdraw; These are sensible* (= appropriate) *shoes for gym wear.* **2** perceiving or aware: *She is sensible of the feelings of others.* **3** that can be perceived: *sensible differences, phenomena; a sensible* (= appreciable) *reduction in price.*
—**sen.si.ble.ness** *n.* —**sen.si.bly** *adv.*
sen.si.tive (SEN.si.tiv) *adj.* **1** able to feel and be affected easily or readily: *a sensitive skin, woman; Lou is sensitive to criticism but not to flattery; a sensitive thermometer; a* **sensitive plant** *such as the mimosa whose leaves fold up if touched.* **2** keen or perceptive: *a sensitive and intelligent child; a sensitive soul.* **3** having to do with delicate or secret information: *a sensitive position in government; politically sensitive material; a sensitive issue such as language rights.*
—**sen.si.tive.ly** *adv.;* **sen.si.tive.ness** *n.*
—**sen.si.tiv.i.ty** (-TIV.i.tee) *n.*
sensitivity training See ENCOUNTER.
sen.si.tize (SEN.si.tize) *v.* **-tiz.es, -tized, -tiz.ing** make or become sensitive: *Children have to be sensitized to the dangers of the street;* **adj.**: *to become* **sensitized**; *sensitized film, materials, paper.* —**sen.si.ti.za.tion** (-tuh.ZAY.shun, -tye-) *n.*
sen.sor (SEN.sur) *n.* a sensing device for a physical stimulus such as heat or light: *motion sensors; The burglar tripped a sensor and set off the alarm; sensors planted on the sea floor by spy submarines.*
sense organ *n.* any of the bodily organs, as the eye, ear, nose, tongue, and skin, that receive the stimuli of the senses; receptor.
sen.so.ry (SEN.suh.ree) *adj.* of the senses or sensation: *sensory nerves, organs, perception, stimulation.*
sen.su.al (SEN.shoo.ul) *adj.* having to do with the gratification of the senses: *sensual appetites, enjoyment, life, music, pleasures;* **sen.su.al.ist** *n.* —**sen.su.al.ly** *adv.* —**sen.su.al.i.ty** (-shoo.AL.i.tee) *n.*
sen.su.ous (SEN.shoo.us) *adj.* **1** having to do with the enjoyment of sense impressions: *sensuous appeal, colors, delight, music, verse.* **2** voluptuous: *sensuous body lines, contours, eyes, lips, looks; a sensuous mouth, woman.* —**sen.su.ous.ly** *adv.;* **sen.su.ous.ness** *n.*
sent *pt. & pp.* of SEND.
sen.tence (SEN.tunce) *n.* **1** a group of words forming a complete statement, question, or command. **2** a decision, as of a judge, esp. on the punishment for an offense; also, the punishment: *to carry out, commute, execute, impose, pass, pronounce, reduce, serve out, suspend a sentence; He was waiting on death row under sentence of death; a death sentence; a prison sentence; harsh, light, stiff sentences.* —*v.* **-tenc.es, -tenced, -tenc.ing** punish judicially: *He was convicted and sentenced to three years in prison.*
sen.ten.tious (sen.TEN.shus) *adj.* wise and moralistic in tone: *a sententious speech, lecturer; the sententious voice of*

Polonius.

sen.tient (SEN.shunt) *adj.* that can feel; conscious: *sentient beings.*

sen.ti.ment (SEN.tuh.munt) *n.* an attitude or disposition of mind influenced or refined by feelings, as patriotism (duty influenced by love of country): *Politicians voice patriotic sentiments; the growing sentiment in favor of banning liquor ads; the strong public sentiment against pornography; a speech full of lofty, noble sentiments.*

sen.ti.men.tal (sen.tuh.MEN.tul) *adj.* having to do with sentiment rather than reason: *the sentimental behavior of a sentimental parent; He is very sentimental about or over his old school; a picture with more sentimental than commercial value.* —**sen.ti.men.tal.ly** *adv.* —**sen.ti.men.tal.ism** *n.;* **sen.ti.men.tal.ist** *n.*

sen.ti.men.tal.i.ty (sen.tuh.mun.TAL.i.tee) *n.* **-ties** too much sentiment or its expression: *maudlin, mawkish sentimentality.*

sen.ti.men.tal.ize (sen.tuh.MEN.tul.ize) *v.* **-iz.es, -ized, -iz.ing** **1** make sentimental. **2** indulge in sentiment *about* or *over* a person or thing.

sen.ti.nel (SEN.tun.ul) *n.* a sentry.

sen.try (SEN.tree) *n.* **-tries** a member of a military guard: *The sentry posted at the gate is relieved at night.*

sentry box *n.* a shelter for a sentry to stand in.

se.pal (SEE.pul) *n.* one of the usu. green, leaflike parts at the base of a flower or enclosing a bud.

sep.a.ra.ble (SEP.uh.ruh.bul) *adj.* capable of being separated: *distinct and separable components; Trim all separable fat before cooking; Easily separable waste materials help in recycling.* —**sep.a.ra.bly** *adv.*

sep.a.rate (SEP.uh.rit) *adj.* distinct from another; not together: *Keep them separate (from each other); seated at separate tables; They went their separate ways; the outdated doctrine of separate but equal treatment of minorities.* —*n.* a blouse, skirt, pants, etc. for wearing in different combinations: *coordinated separates.* —*v.* (-rate) **-rates, -rat.ed, -rat.ing** (cause to) be apart; divide: *War separates families; She was separated from the group and got lost; a wall separating two apartments; The couple separated* (= decided to live apart). —**sep.a.rate.ly** (-rit.lee) *adv.* —**sep.a.ra.tion** (-RAY.shun) *n.: the painful separation of a married couple; the separation of church and state.*

sep.a.ra.tist (SEP.uh.ruh.tist) *n.* a member of a group that wants to withdraw from a large, esp. political body: *The Basque separatists want their own country;* *adj.*: *There are separatist groups in most large nations; separatist factions, forces, movements, sentiments, trends.* —**sep.a.ra.tism** *n.*

sep.a.ra.tor (SEP.uh.ray.tur) *n.* one that separates: *A centrifugal separator is used to separate cream from milk; A metal separator is used in garbage recycling.*

se.pi.a (SEE.pee.uh) *n. & adj.* dark-brown (pigment or a drawing done in it).

sep.sis *n., pl.* **-ses** (-seez) poisoning caused by disease germs.

Sep.tem.ber (sep.TEM.bur) *n.* the ninth month of the calendar year, with 30 days.

sep.tet (sep.TET) *n.* **1** a group of seven, esp. musicians. **2** a musical piece for a septet.

sep.tic *adj.* **1** resulting from or causing poisoning by disease germs: *He died of a septic wound.* **2** having to do with decay: *Sewage decomposes in a* **septic tank** *by bacterial action.*

sep.ti.ce.mi.a (sep.tuh.SEE.mee.uh) *n.* blood poisoning.

sep.tu.a.ge.nar.i.an (SEP.choo.uh.juh.NAIR.ee.un) *n. & adj.* (a person) aged 70 to 79.

Sep.tu.a.gint (SEP.too.uh.jint) *n.* the oldest Greek translation of the Old Testament.

sep.tum *n.* partition, as in the heart or nose.

sep.ul.cher (SEP.ul.cur) *n.* a tomb. Also **sep.ul.chre** *Cdn.*

se.pul.chral (suh.PUL.crul) *adj.* suggestive of the grave or burial: *sepulchral gloom, voices; a sepulchral* (= hollow and deep) *groan.*

sep.ul.ture (SEP.ul.chur) *n.* burial.

se.quel (SEEK.wul) *n.* something following or resulting from an earlier happening, as a continuation of a story with the same characters: *the sequels to "Anne of Green Gables"; Walt Whitman's "Sequel to Drum Taps."*

se.quence (SEEK.wunce) *n.* **1** an order of succession: *words in alphabetical sequence; Tell us what happened in chronological sequence; the natural sequence of events; The scenes lack sequence* (= continuity of progression). **2** a connected series: *Ace, King, and Queen form a sequence in cards; Any set of terms in a specific order is a mathematical sequence.* **3** an episode: *a movie sequence.* —*v.* **se.quenc.es, se.quenced,**

se.quenc.ing arrange in a sequence: *to sequence customers, genes, offspring; to sequence an album, genome, program;* **adj.**: *a **sequenced** approach; a fully sequenced genome;* **n.**: *mapping and **sequencing** of information;* **adja.**: *sequencing machines, technology.*
—**se.quen.tial** (see.QUEN.shul) *adj.*; **se.quen.tial.ly** *adv.*

se.ques.ter (si.QUES.tur) *v.* **1** seclude; **adj.**: *the **sequestered** life of a convent.* **2** separate or remove: *to sequester oneself from worldly distractions; Jury members are sequestered* (= cut off from family, news, etc.) *during a trial.*

se.ques.tra.tion (see.ques.TRAY.shun) *n.* **1** separation or isolation: *a life of sequestration.* **2** the temporary placing of a disputed property in the hands of a third party pending a court award; hence **se.ques.trate** *v.* **-trates, -trat.ed, -trat.ing.**

se.quin (SEE.quin) *n.* any of the shiny discs of metal sewn on to dresses, etc. for decoration; spangle. —**se.quined** (-quind) *adj.* **1** adorned with sequins: *a sequined dress, gown, skirt; sequined looks, women.* **2** sequin-shaped: *sequined hearts, motifs.*

se.quoi.a (si.QUOY.uh) *n.* a group of the largest and oldest trees, including the redwood and the "giant sequoia" of W. California.

sera a *pl.* of SERUM.

se.rag.lio (si.RAL.yoh) *n.* **-lios** a sultan's palace or its harem.

se.ra.pe (suh.RAH.pee) *n.* a bright-colored woolen shawl used by Latin American men.

ser.aph (SER.uf) *n.* **-aphs** or **-a.phim** an angel of the highest order.
—**se.raph.ic** (si.RAF.ic) *adj.*; **se.raph.i.cal.ly** *adv.*

Serb (SURB) or **Ser.bi.an** (-bee.un) *n.* **1** a person of or from **Serbia**, a Balkan country. **2** Serbo-Croatian as used in Serbia. —**adj.** of Serbia, its people, or their language: *a Serb nationalist group; under Serbian rule.*

Serbo-Croatian (SUR.boh.croh.AY.shun) *n.* the major Slavic language of Yugoslavia. —**adj.** having to do with this language or the people who speak it.

sere (SEER) *adj.* [poetic] dry or withered.

ser.e.nade (ser.uh.NADE) *n.* music played or sung by a lover under his sweetheart's window. —*v.* **-nades, -nad.ed, -nad.ing** play or sing a serenade to someone.

ser.en.dip.i.ty (ser.un.DIP.i.tee) *n.* **-ties** **1** the gift for making fortunate discoveries when least expecting them. **2** such discovery: *Dictionary browsing offers the word lover opportunities for serendipity.* —**ser.en.dip.i.tous** (-tus) *adj.*: *the serendipitous discovery of a star.*

se.rene (suh.REEN) *adj.* **1** calm and clear: *serene skies.* **2** calm and dignified: *a serene life, look, smile.* **3 Serene** [used of or to royalty of certain countries]: *His, Her, Your Serene Highness.*
—**se.rene.ly** *adv.* —**se.rene.ness** or **se.ren.i.ty** (suh.REN.i.tee) *n.*

serf (SURF) *n.* a feudal peasant bound to the soil and to the service of his lord. —**serf.dom** *n.*

serge (SURJ) *n.* a fabric with a twill weave showing diagonal ridges, used for dresses, suits, etc.

ser.geant (SAR.junt) *n.* **1** a noncommissioned military officer ranking above corporal and below warrant officer. **2** a police officer ranking above a constable.

sergeant-at-arms *n.* **sergeants-at-arms** an officer who keeps order in a legislature or court.

se.ri.al (SEER.ee.ul) *adj.* forming a series or succession with others: *the serial number on a check; serial murders by a **serial killer** (who kills one after another); a **serial novel** (appearing chapter by chapter in a periodical); first **serial rights** (to publish a piece of writing first in a periodical); **serial transmission** of data bit by bit, not parallel transmission (of several bits simultaneously); a serial cable, connector, interface, port, printer.*
—*n.* a serial story or publication: *a TV serial (broadcast part by part).*
—**se.ri.al.ly** *adv.*

se.ri.al.ize (SEER.ee.uh.lize) *v.* **-iz.es, -ized, -iz.ing** make serial: *to serialize a novel on TV.* —**se.ri.al.i.za.tion** (-luh.ZAY.shun, -lye-) *n.*

se.ries (SEER.eez) *n. sing. & pl.* a number of things or events connected with each other: *a series of accidents, lectures, publications; a TV series; an unbroken series.*

ser.i.graph (SER.i.graf) *n.* an artist's own handmade print using the silk-screen process. —**se.rig.ra.pher** (suh.RIG.ruh.fur) *n.*; **se.rig.ra.phy** *n.*

se.ri.ous (SEER.ee.us) *adj.* **1** showing or requiring earnestness: *He shows serious interest in his studies; She's serious about her duties; serious attention, consideration.* **2** important or grave: *He told the joke in a serious manner; Murder is a serious crime; a serious matter; serious damage to the car; It's deadly serious; a patient in se-*

rious but not critical condition.
—**se.ri.ous.ly** *adv.*; **se.ri.ous.ness** *n.*
ser.mon (SUR.mun) *n.* **1** a religious or moral talk usu. based on Scripture: *Christ's* **Sermon on the Mount** *contains the Lord's Prayer.* **2** any moralistic talk: *The minister says he doesn't preach sermons but delivers homilies.* —**ser.mon.ize** *v.* **-iz.es, -ized, -iz.ing**: *to stop sermonizing and start working.*
se.rol.o.gy (si.ROL.uh.jee) *n.* the study of serums and their properties; **se.rol.o.gist** *n.* —**se.ro.log.ic** (seer.uh.LOJ.ic) or **se.ro.log.i.cal** *adj.*
se.rous (SEER.us) *adj.* having to do with blood serum: *serous drainage, excretion, fluid.*
ser.pent (SUR.punt) *n.* a big snake, thought of as sly and treacherous.
ser.pen.tine (SUR.pun.teen, -tine) *adj.* like a serpent; twisted, cunning, etc.
ser.rate (SER.ate) *adj.* having a saw-toothed edge, as certain leaves; also **serrated**: *a serrated blade, edge, knife, wheel.* —**ser.ra.tion** (suh.RAY.shun) *n.*
ser.ried (SER.eed) *adj.* in close order: *soldiers in serried ranks.*
se.rum (SEER.um) *n.* **-rums** or **-ra 1** the clear fluid part of blood left after clotting: *how to lower your serum cholesterol level.* **2** a blood serum preparation containing antibodies for injection into patients with hepatitis, measles, etc.
ser.vant (SUR.vunt) *n.* **1** a person employed in household work: *domestic, faithful, loyal, trusted servants.* **2** a person in the service of a government: *a civil servant; public servants.*
serve (SURV) *v.* **serves, served, serv.ing 1** carry out duties; function: *People serve as teachers, on juries, at (the) table, under supervisors, with their colleagues; Store clerks serve* (= help) *customers; Soldiers serve* (= work) *in the army; to serve with the marines.* **2** satisfy a purpose; suit: *A carrot will serve our purpose; It induces the donkey to move on; His illness served as an excuse.* **3** put a ball or similar thing in play: *It's my turn to serve; He always serves to the weaker opponent.* **1** supply food, needs, etc.: *It's time to serve lunch; enough food to serve four people; Being ticketed for speeding seemed to* **serve him right**; *adj.*: *a community well* **served** *with health care; ill served; n: a* **serving** (= portion or helping) *of fish; generous, liberal, second, small serving*s. **5** undergo: *She has to serve three years as an apprentice; He has served his term in jail;* **adj.**: *the time* **served.** **6** present an order, warrant,
etc.: *The typist served notice (on her boss) that she was quitting; He was served with a summons to appear in court.* —*n.* a serving of a ball or similar thing: *an underhand serve; a serve to the backhand.*
serv.er *n.* **1** one that serves: *cake, salad, wine servers.* **2** a program or service on a computer network that provides clients with access to databases, programs, peripheral devices, etc.: *an Internet server.*
serv.ice (SUR.vis) *n.* **1** the function or occupation of serving: *He was on active service in World War II; She's in the Federal Service; meritorious, military, public, regular, slow, yeoman service; to introduce, restore service; This car will give good service for five years; civil, customer, door-to-door, express, professional service; diplomatic, intelligence, secret service; a medal for distinguished service; She has* **seen service** (= been in the armed forces) *in many parts of the world; Our china has seen plenty of service* (= been put to much use) *over the years; I am* **at your service** (= ready to serve or be of use); *He applied to* **be of service** *as a cook.* **2** what is produced by serving, as work, benefit, etc.: *We offer, provide service with a smile; to do, hold, perform, render, suspend a service; ambulance, answering, burial, bus, dating, delivery, employment, ferry, janitorial, laundry, limousine, news, placement, postal, repair, room, telephone, towing, wire services; a bill for services rendered by a professional; to break, lose one's service* (= opening play in a game); *funeral, marriage, prayer services* (= ceremonies).
—*adja.*: *the service area (at a gas station); the service bays of an auto repair shop; service centers (for highway travelers); a service charge for processing a check; a service contract; her service record.* **3** a set of dishes, spoons, etc. used for serving food: *coffee, dinner, silver, tea service.* —*v.* **-ic.es, -iced, -ic.ing** do work on something or for someone as something due: *to service accounts, automobiles, customers, machines, markets, needs; to* **service a debt** (*by paying interest due*); *A heifer is serviced* (= made to copulate with) *by a bull.*
serv.ice.a.ble (SUR.vis.uh.bul) *adj.* useful or operative: *We want a serviceable, not a luxury car; A bicycle is sometimes more serviceable than a limousine.*
service company *n.* a company that sells a service, not a material product, as banks, hotels, and movers.
service line *n.* the boundary line from which a ball is served, as in tennis.

serv·ice·man (SUR.vis.man, -mun) *n.*, *pl.* **-men** 1 a person in military service. 2 one who maintains and repairs machines, appliances, etc.
—**serv·ice·wom·an, -wom·en.**

service mark *n.* the trademark of a service such as those offered by a financial or utility company.

service module *n.* the part of a manned aircraft between the landing module and command module, containing the propulsion, retrofire, and thrust systems.

service road *n.* an access road or a road parallel to an expressway.

service sector *n.* the group of companies that supply services, not goods; *adja.*: *service-sector companies, industries, jobs.*

service station *n.* a facility for supplying gas and repair services to motorists.

servicewoman See SERVICEMAN.

ser·vi·ette (sur.vee.ET) *n.* Cdn. a table napkin.

ser·vile (SUR.vile) *adj.* 1 having to do with slaves: *the servile masses.* 2 cringing or submissive: *his servile attitude, manner, spirit; done out of servile fear; She's servile to none.* —**ser.vile.ly** *adv.* —**ser.vil.i.ty** (sur.VIL.i.tee) *n.*

serving *n.* a portion or helping of food.

ser·vi·tor (SUR.vi.tur) *n.* a servant or attendant.

ser·vi·tude (SUR.vi.tude) *n.* bondage or slavery: *a life of servitude.*

ser·vo (SUR.voh) *n.* **-vos** [short form] servomechanism; servomotor.

ser·vo·mech·a·nism (SUR.voh.mec.uh.niz.um) *n.* a control system for detecting and correcting errors in an automatic system, as one helping to keep an automatic pilot on course.

ser·vo·mo·tor (SUR.voh.moh.tur) *n.* a motor supplying power for moving a servomechanism.

ses·a·me (SES.uh.mee) *n.* an East Indian herb whose seeds yield an oil used in cooking and flavoring: *A university degree used to be the **open sesame** (= magical door) to a good job.*

ses·qui·cen·ten·ni·al (SES.kwi.sen.TEN.ee.ul) *n. & adj.* (of) a 150th anniversary.

ses·qui·pe·da·li·an (SES.kwi.puh.DAY.lee.un) *adj.* 1 of words, many-syllabled. 2 of a style, using long words; pedantic.

ses·sile (SES.il, -ile) *adj.* fixed to a spot, as barnacles, leaves attached to stem without stalk, etc.

ses·sion (SESH.un) *n.* the sitting or assembly of a group of people to discuss, deliberate, learn, etc., as of a court, legislature, school, etc., esp. its duration: *a long morning session on safety; during the afternoon session; briefing, bull, jam, joint, plenary, practice, rap, special, summer, winter, working sessions; They met in secret sessions; a new session of a legislature; The court is **in session** from 10 a.m.* —**ses.sion.al** *adj.*

set *v.* **sets, set, set.ting** 1 put or place with a purpose, direction, or in a certain manner or condition: *She set the flowers on the table; He set a match to the dry grass, paper, and kindling; The house was set on fire; styles set in Paris; a ladder set against a wall; Compositors used to set type for printing; Manuscripts were set in type; a manner that sets everyone at ease; What value do you set on the missing diamond? He loved her from the moment he set his eyes on her; She has her **sights set on** (= She aspires to) a Ph.D.* 2 assign: *to set a task; She set them to write an essay.* 3 arrange: *to set the table for dinner; Let's set a date for the meeting; to set the stage for a performance; to set a trap for mice; a sonnet set (= adapted) to music.* 4 (cause) to be firm or settled in position: *Concrete sets in a mold; to set hair in a perm; The doctor set the broken bone.* 5 go down: *The sun sets in the west.* 6 make (a hen) sit on eggs for hatching; also, sit. —**set about** or **to** begin: *She set about writing her thesis; As soon as they had been served, the kids set to (= began eating).* —**set apart** distinguish: *Speech sets humans apart from animals.* —**set aside** 1 put away money, etc. *for a purpose.* 2 reject, as a decision by a higher court. —**set forth** make known views, plans, etc. —**set in** of an undesirable condition, begin and continue: *Bad weather, a disease, infection, rot may set in.* —**set off** 1 cause something to be suddenly active: *to set off an alarm, bomb, chain reaction, crisis, fireworks, riot; The shooting set off violence in the streets.* 2 begin, as on a journey: *He sets off for work at 8 a.m. every day; They set off on a spending spree.* —**set on** or **upon** attack: *Sam was set upon by hoodlums.* —**set out** 1 begin: *to set out for work in the morning; Let's finish what we set out to do.* 2 arrange or spread: *goods set out for viewing; to set out breakfast on the patio.* —**set sail** leave by ship: *to set sail for Europe.* —**set up** 1 establish; put up: *a roadblock set up by police; to set up in business; to set up practice as a lawyer; to set up shop.* 2 raise: *to set up a cry or shout.*

—*n.* **1** a group or collection of persons or things belonging together: *They belong to the jet set; the fast, international, smart set; a set of numbers, twins; to lose, play, win a set (of games); a dining-room set (of furniture); a dinner set (of dishes); to break (up), make (up) a set; carving, chemistry, chess, geometry, tea sets; radio, transistor, TV sets* (= assembled equipment). **2** the scenery of a play or motion picture: *to dismantle a set.* **3** the way in which something is formed or forming: *the set of his shoulders; the set of public opinion on the subject.* —*adj.* fixed or established: *a set piece (of literature) for recitation; a man of set views; a set time for everything; He is set* (= intent) *on winning; She is dead set against drinking; We are* **all set** (= ready or prepared) *for takeoff, to begin; Get ready, get set, go!*

set.back *n.* a reversal of or check to progress: *to have, receive, suffer a setback; business, financial, political setbacks.*

set.screw *n.* a screw that is threaded through one metal part and tightened against the surface of another to prevent relative motion between them.

set.tee (se.TEE) *n.* a benchlike sofa with back and arms.

set.ter *n.* a long-haired hunting dog trained like a pointer.

setting *n.* **1** what is set, as eggs that a hen sits on for hatching, the music for a poem or other text, or dishes or silverware for one person at a table: *place settings for 12 guests; to adjust the setting of a thermostat.* **2** what something is set in, as the mounting of a jewel, or the time, place, and surroundings of a play or story: *natural, romantic, stage settings.*

set.tle (SET.ul) *v.* **set.tles, set.tled, set.tling** **1** reach a final decision or agreement *with* a party, *for* something, or *on* a time, place, or plan: *The strikers settled for a 10% raise; an argument that is hard to settle peacefully; We'll try to settle the case out of court; There are accounts to be settled* (= paid) *before leaving; The property was divided and* **settled on** or **upon** *his children* (= formally given to them). **2** (cause) to take up residence: *Immigrants settle in a country; The government tries to settle doctors in rural areas; The Dutch settled* (= colonized) *Indonesia.* **3** establish oneself or itself: *It takes time to settle into a new job; Marriage helps youth* **settle down** (*in life*); *School helped them settle down to study, into a new routine; It was 1 a.m. when they settled down* (= came to rest) *for the night;* **adj.**: *Some old people are too* **settled** (= established) *in their ways.* **4** (cause) to be in a more stable, composed, or compact state: *A tranquilizer will settle your nerves; Rains help settle* (loose) *dust; A new house settles* (in its foundation); *Dust settles* (= comes to rest) *on everything.*

set.tle.ment (SET.ul.munt) *n.* **1** a settling, as an agreement or its terms, bestowal of property on someone, etc.: *to come to, make, negotiate, reach a settlement; fair, lump-sum, marriage, out-of-court, tentative settlements.* **2** a being settled, as a colony or colonization. **3** a social institution or welfare center for improvement of living conditions.

set.to (SET.too) *n.* **-tos** *Informal.* a fight or argument.

set.up *n.* what is set up, as an arrangement, plan, etc.

sev.en (SEV.un) *n., adj.* & *pron.* one more than six; the number 7 or VII: *seven boys and girls; There are seven of them; They are seven in all.*
—**sev.enth** *n., adj.* & *adv.*: *the seventh hour; You're seventh in line; He is seventh; He came seventh.*

seven seas *n.pl.* all the oceans of the world: *to sail the seven seas.*

sev.en.teen (sev.un.TEEN) *n., adj.* & *pron.* seven more than 10; 17; XVII; **sev.en.teenth** *n.* & *adj.*

seventh heaven *n.* a state of bliss or extreme happiness.

sev.en.ty (SEV.un.tee) *n., adj.* & *pron., n.pl.* **-ties 1** seven times ten; 70 or LXX. **2 the seventies** the numbers, years, etc. from 70 through 79.
—**sev.en.ti.eth** (-tee.ith) *n.* & *adj.*

seven-year itch *n.* an urge to have an affair after seven years of marriage.

sev.er (SEV.ur) *v.* cut so as to separate: *a limb that has been severed from the body; to sever a branch, communication line, connection, rope.*

sev.er.al (SEV.ur.ul) *adja.* **1** more than two; a few: *several occasions, people, times.* **2** different; separate: *They went their several ways; a joint and several liability.* —**pron.** some: *Several of us were present; I saw several (of the kind mentioned).*

sev.er.al.ly (SEV.ur.uh.lee) *adv.* individually or separately: *The makers are held jointly and severally responsible for a product.*

sev.er.ance (SEV.ur.unce) *n.* a severing or separation: *severance of relations; the* **severance pay** *given on termination of employment.*

se.vere (suh.VEER) *adj.* **-ver.er, -ver.est**

1 strict or rigorous: *a severe test of endurance; severe looks, reasoning.* **2** hard to endure: *a severe attack, headache, illness, scolding; severe weather conditions; a severe* (= violent) *storm.* —**se.vere.ly** *adv.* —**se.ver.i.ty** (suh.VER.i.tee) *n.* **-ties.**

sew (SOH) *v.* **sews**, *pt.* **sewed**, *pp.* **sewn** or **sewed, sew.ing 1** fasten with stitches: *to sew pages together to make a book; to sew buttons on a shirt.* **2** make by sewing: *to sew a book, buttonhole, shirt.* —**sew up** close with stitches: *to sew up a seam, torn shirt, wound; We had the game all **sewn up*** (= made certain) *by the third quarter.* —**sew.er** *n.*

sew.age (SOO.ij) *n.* waste matter carried in sewers and drains: *raw, treated, untreated sewage.*

sew.er (SOO.ur) *n.* a pipe or drain, usu. underground, for water and wastes: *a sanitary sewer; storm sewers.*

sew.er.age (SOO.uh.rij) *n.* a sewer system; *adja.: a sewerage project, scheme, service.*

sewing (SOH.ing) *n.* **1** something sewn or to be sewn by hand or with a machine, or **sewing machine. 2** the occupation: *He's adept at cooking, sewing, and typing.*

sex *n.* **1** the male-female distinction: *discrimination based on age and sex; members of the opposite sex* (= male or female group). **2** sexual activity, esp. intercourse: *explicit sex in films; illicit sex; premarital sex; all the sex and violence on TV; the joys of sex; Spouses **have sex with** each other; adja.: sex abuse, drive, education, functions, lives, objects, organs; a sex test for athletes; a **sex act*** (= copulation); *people with **sex appeal*** (= sexual attractiveness). —*v.* **1** to identify in regard to sex: *to sex chicks, fish, herring; adj.: the ambiguously **sexed** Ariel; sexed connectors.* **2 sexed** *adj. & cpd.* having sexual appetite as specified: *highly sexed people; an over-sexed kid; under-sexed nerds.* **3 sex up** *Informal.* make sexually more exciting: *to sex up a play, scene; adj.: a **sexed-up** costume, movie, show.* —**sex.er** *n.*

sex.a.ge.nar.i.an (sex.uh.juh.NAIR.ee.un) *n. & adj.* (a person) aged 60 to 69.

sex chromosome *n.* either of two chromosomes that are alike (XX) in the female and different (XY) in the male, by the pairing of which the sex and sex-linked characteristics of offspring are determined.

sex hormone *n.* any of the various hormones secreted by the gonads which control the development of sexual organs and characteristics.

sex.ism *n.* prejudice or discrimination based on sex, esp. against women. —**sex.ist** *adj.: a sexist attitude, bias, comment, remark; sexist language; a male-dominated sexist society.* —*n.* a sexist person.

sex.ploi.ta.tion (sex.ploy.TAY.shun) *n.* exploitation of sex, as in movies and commercials.

sex.pot *n. Informal.* a very sexy woman.

sex symbol *n.* an entertainer noted for sex appeal.

sex.tant (SEX.tunt) *n.* an instrument for measuring angular distance between points, used esp. in navigation.

sex.tet (sex.TET) *n.* **1** a group of six, esp. musicians. **2** a musical composition for six voices.

sex.ton (SEX.tun) *n.* a custodian of church property and equipment.

sex.u.al (SEK.shoo.ul) *adj.* having to do with sex: *sexual behavior, harassment, intercourse, morality, reproduction, revolution;* **sexual assault** (= rape, attempted rape, or molestation); **sexual relations** (= sexual activity between people). —**sex.u.al.ly** *adv.* —**sex.u.al.i.ty** (-AL.i.tee) *n.*

sex.y (SEK.see) *adj.* **sex.i.er, -i.est 1** sexually stimulating or provocative: *a sexy design, dress, movie; Jan's sexy image.* **2** attractive or appealing: *Is British English sexier than American English? a sexy business, issue, outlook.* —**sex.i.ly** *adv.;* **sex.i.ness** *n.*

sh *interj.* hush!

shab.by (SHAB.ee) *adj.* **shab.bi.er, shab.bi.est 1** in a much-worn, poor, or run-down condition: *shabby clothes, interiors; a shabby-looking fellow.* **2** unworthy or mean: *rather shabby treatment.* —**shab.bi.ly** *adv.;* **shab.bi.ness** *n.*

shack *n.* **1** a small, crude dwelling: *dilapidated, run-down, tar-papered shacks.* **2** room: *a ham operator's basement radio shack.* —*v.* **shack up** *Informal.* cohabit: *Jack used to shack up with Jill.*

shack.le (SHACK.ul) *n.* **1** a manacle or fetter; hence, any restraint: *Slaves throw off their **shackles** and regain freedom.* **2** a fastening or coupling device. —*v.* **shack.les, shack.led, shack.ling** restrain with shackles: *a prisoner with his legs shackled; the shackling of press freedom.*

shad *n.* a fish of N. Atlantic waters valued for its flesh and roe.

shade *n.* **1** a place that is not in direct light and heat, esp. of the sun: *to rest in the shade of a tree.* **2** a partly dark condition or relative obscurity: *the lights and shades of a picture;* **the shades** (= darkness) *of evening; He was* **put in** or **into the shade** (= surpassed) *by his more brilliant brother.* **3** a device to control light, as of a lamp, or to shut out light, as used over a window: *a window shade; to draw, drop, lift, lower, pull down, raise the shades.* **4** gradation of color: *Maroon is a shade of red; delicate, dark, light, pale, pastel, soft shades; a shade of doubt, fear; many shades* (= slight differences) *of meaning; 33°F is* **a shade** (= slightly) *above freezing point.* **5 shades** *pl. Informal.* sunglasses: *a movie star hiding behind his shades.* **6** [literary] ghost: *"shades of night";* **Shades of** *Chernobyl* (= This reminds one of what happened at Chernobyl). —*v.* **shades, shad.ed, shad.ing 1** screen from light: *a hat with a wide brim to shade your eyes from the sun.* **2** make dark or darker in lighting or coloring: *Shade it a little;* **n.:** *The picture needs a little* **shading** (= filling in) *to show darkness.* **3** change little by little, as into a different shade: *The red patches* **shade off** (= merge) *into pink.*

shad.ow (SHAD.oh) *n.* **1** the shade cast by an object blocking the light: *the shadow of a dog; Shadows fall on the ground; to cast, produce, throw a shadow; dark, long, sharp, soft shadows; The dog saw its own shadow* (= image) *in the water; He's his master's shadow* (= follower); *He walks* **in her shadow** (= is close to her or under her influence); *to emerge from* **the shadows** (= obscurity) *and get into politics; Indonesian shadow play using puppets.* **2** something unsubstantial or ghostlike: *Ill health has made him a mere shadow of his former self; a pale shadow; the shadow of power;* **adja.:** *shadow negotiations; the* **shadow economy** *of black markets, bartering, bribes, and tax evasion.* **3** a shaded area, as in a picture; hence, darkness or gloom: *The death cast a shadow on his life; The nuclear accident* **cast a long shadow** *on or over the use of nuclear energy.* **4** slight trace: *beyond the or a* **shadow of a doubt;** *to cast a* **shadow of doubt on** *the proposal.* —*v.* **1** cast a shadow on a person or thing. **2** follow or watch unobserved: *He was being shadowed by the secret police.*

shadow-box *v.* to box with an imaginary opponent for training or exercise.

shadow cabinet *n.* in a parliament, a cabinet of opposition members, each studying the work of a real cabinet member.

shad.ow.y (SHAD.oh.ee) *adj.* **1** indistinct: *a shadowy figure, form.* **2** full of shadows: *shadowy corners, corridors, forests.* **3** mysterious: *his shadowy past; the shadowy world of spies.*

shad.y (SHAY.dee) *adj.* **shad.i.er, -i.est 1** in the shade or giving shade: *a shady bough, tree.* **2** *Informal.* dishonest: *a shady character, deal.* —**shad.i.ness** *n.*

shaft *n.* **1** a long handle or stem: *the shaft of an arrow, spear.* **2** formerly, a dart or similar thrown missile: *shafts of ridicule, wit.* **3** a beam of light: *a shaft of lightning.* **4** a polelike, round, often hollow bar: *the drive shaft of a car connected to the axles.* **5** a structure or passage resembling the shaft: *the shaft of a mine; to bore, sink a shaft; An elevator moves in a shaft.* —**get the shaft** *Informal.* get unfairly treated. —*v. Informal.* **1** cheat or trick: *He got shafted in the deal.* **2** deal unfairly with someone: *a politician shafted by the media.*

shag *n.* **1** cloth, carpet, etc. with long, rough nap. **2** a mass of coarse hair, fiber, or finely shredded tobacco. —*v.* **shags, shagged, shag.ging** chase after and return a ball when it goes out of play.

shag.gy (SHAG.ee) *adj.* **shag.gi.er, shag.gi.est 1** looking unkempt or needing a shave or haircut: *a youth with long shaggy hair.* **2** covered with rough coarse fiber or hair: *shaggy eyebrows; a shaggy dog.*

shaggy dog story *n. Informal.* a long story ending in a sudden anticlimax; dumb joke.

shah *n.* formerly, a king of Iran.

shake *v.* **shakes, shook** (short "oo"), **shak.en, shak.ing 1** (cause to) move jerkily up and down or back and forth: *Shake the bottle before use; to shake (dust from) a rug; He swore and shook his fists at Joe; She shook her head* (= said "No"); *They* **shook hands** (= clasped each other's hands in greeting, in congratulation, in agreement); *They* **shook hands on** *the deal* (= made a gentleman's agreement). **2** (cause to) tremble or totter: *Earthquakes shake buildings; The news shook* (= upset) *the nation;* **adj.:** *She seems* **shaken;** *A visibly shaken premier announced the bad news.* **3** waver or weaken: *Nothing could shake his faith in his leader; to shake one's confidence;* **adj.:** *a* **shaken** *economy; his shaken morale; the company's shaken reputation; the shaken stock market.* —**shake down 1** get by shaking, as fruit from a tree. **2** *Informal.* extort money from a victim.

3 cause to settle down; hence, get adjusted or accustomed. —**shake off** get rid of something: *to shake off a sense of dread, a feeling of exhaustion.* —**shake up** give someone a bad shock: *The news of the defeat was enough to shake him up; He was all shook up.*
—*n.* a shaking or something shaken: *Give the rug a good shake; She ordered a shake* (= milkshake); *He has got* **the shakes** (= a trembling disease); *I want a* **fair shake** (*Informal* for fair deal); *He's* **no (great) shakes** (*Informal* for not especially good) *as a journalist.*
—**shake.a.ble** *adj.*
shake.down *n.* **1** *Informal.* extortion of money, as by graft. **2** a getting adjusted or accustomed, as of new equipment, of people to a new environment, etc.; *adja.: a shakedown* (= test) *cruise, flight, run.*
shake.out *n.* a reorganization, as in a business or industry, which results in the survival of only the best.
shak.er (SHAY.kur) *n.* **1** one that shakes: *a cocktail shaker* (for mixing drinks). **2** a container used for shaking out something: *cheese, pepper, salt, sugar shakers; a shaker set.* **3 Shaker** a member of a Quaker sect well known for their austere and functional furniture; *adja.: a shaker print, sweater, table; the purity of Shaker design.*
Shake.spear.e.an (shake.SPEER.ee.un) *adj.* having to do with William **Shakespeare** (1564-1616), the greatest English poet and playwright: *Shakespearean blank verse; the Shakespearean comedy, stage, tragedy; The* **Shakespearean sonnet** *has the rhyme scheme "abab cdcd efef gg."* —*n.* a Shakespeare scholar.
shake-up *n.* a drastic reorganization, esp. of personnel.
shak.y (SHAY.kee) *adj.* **shak.i.er, -i.est** weak, not firm: *a shaky foundation, partnership, table, voice.* —**shak.i.ly** *adv.*; **shak.i.ness** *n.*
shale *n.* a soft sedimentary rock that easily splits into layers.
shale oil *n.* petroleum from bituminous shale.
shall (SHAL) *auxiliary v., pt.* **should** (SHOOD, short "OO" or shud) *Formal.* **1** [expressing future time in the first person]: *I shall be away on business; We shall see.* **2** [expressing necessity or obligation]: *You shall not smoke; She shall be your boss; They shall not pass; Should I give up smoking? You should not have done that.*
shal.lot (SHAL.ut, shuh.LOT) *n.* an onionlike herb with bulbs clustered like garlic, used to flavor cooked foods.
shal.low (SHAL.oh) *adj.* **1** not deep: *a shallow dish, bowl, grave, pan, pool; shallow breathing; at a* **shallow angle** (close to the horizontal). **2** superficial: *shallow explanations, profundities, understanding, victories; They sound shallow.*
—**shallows** *n.pl.* [takes *sing.* or *pl. v.*] the shallow part of a body of water.
sha.lom (shah.LOME) *n. & interj.* [used as a Hebrew greeting] peace!
shalt [old form, used with "thou"] shall: *Thou shalt not steal.*
sham *n.* a false or fake person or thing.
—*v.* **shams, shammed, sham.ming** feign or pretend. —**sham.mer** *n.*
sha.man (SHAH.mun, SHAY-) *n.* a medicine man.
sham.ble *v.* **-bles, -bled, -bling** walk awkwardly; shuffle.
—*n.* **1** a shambling gait. **2 shambles** *n.pl.* [takes *sing. v.*] (a scene or state of) disorder or destruction: *The room was turned into a shambles; They made a shambles of it; The economy is in (a) shambles; a hopeless, total shambles.*
shame *n.* **1** (a feeling of) great dishonor or disgrace: *It's a shame to behave or that you behave like that; You've brought shame on or to or upon your family; We felt shame at his behavior; an awful, bloody, crying, dirty shame; He hung his head in shame; He'll remember this day to his eternal shame; Her cheeks burned with shame; What a shame we lost! Shame on us!* **2** a cause of such feeling: *He's a shame to his profession.* —**put to shame 1** make ashamed. **2** surpass. —*v.* **shames, shamed, sham.ing 1** make ashamed: *He was shamed into admitting defeat.* **2** send away in disgrace: *He was shamed out of his position.* —**shame.ful** *adj.*; **shame.ful.ly** *adv.*; **shame.ful.ness** *n.*
shame.faced *adj.* **1** bashful. **2** showing shame. —**shame.fac.ed.ly** (shame.FAY.sid.lee) *adv.*
shame.less *adj.* having or showing no shame; impudent: *a shameless act of robbery; a shameless attempt to cheat; a shameless display, braggart;* **shame.less.ly** *adv.*; **shame.less.ness** *n.*
sham.poo (sham.POO) *n.* **1** a soaplike preparation for washing the hair and scalp. **2** a shampooing. —*v.* **-poos, -pooed, -poo.ing 1** use shampoo on the hair or wash the hair of a person with shampoo. **2** clean a rug with liquid soap. —**sham.poo.er** *n.*
sham.rock *n.* a three-leaved clover or similar plant.
shang.hai (SHANG.hye) *v.* **-hais,**

-haied, -hai.ing 1 drug someone and put on board ship. **2** kidnap or trap in this manner.

shank *n.* **1** the part of the human leg between knee and ankle or a corresponding part in animals. **2** in a tool, device, etc., a connecting or essential part, usu. straight, as a shaft, stem, or handle: *the shank of a fish hook; the shank* (= side) *of a shoe; the* **shank end** (= early part) *of the afternoon.*

shan't shall not.

shan.tung (shan.TUNG) *n.* a silky fabric, heavier than pongee, used for curtains, robes, etc.

shan.ty *n.* **-ties 1** same as chantey; also **shan.tey, -teys. 2** a shack or hut.

shan.ty.town (SHAN.tee.town) *n.* an area of mostly shacks.

shape *n.* **1** outline or form, esp. of something having mass and bulk; configuration: *the shape of an S, boat, pear; The god Proteus could appear in or assume different shapes; Customers come in all shapes and sizes; In* **no way, shape, or form** (= by no means) *would he join the family business; Ideas* **take shape** *as realities.* **2** good condition: *She's in excellent shape for a 60-year-old; I'm in no shape to go back to work; He keeps* **in shape** *by lifting weights; exercises to help you* **get into shape.**
—*v.* **shapes, shaped, shap.ing** make in a particular shape: *a statue shaped out of marble; experiences that shape one's character; The employee was told to* **shape up** (= perform satisfactorily) *or ship out.* —**shape.less** *adj.*: *a shapeless blob, disorder, mass.*

shape.ly *adj.* **-li.er, -li.est** having a pleasing shape: *a shapely dress, figure, jacket, leg, model.* —**shape.li.ness** *n.*

shard *n.* **1** potsherd. **2** a fragment: *shards of glass; The bomb scattered steel shards over a wide area.*

share *n.* **1** a part or portion belonging to or done by one: *his share of the loot; a share of the blame, burden, credit, market, responsibility; Each girl did her share; received a share of the profits; equal, fair, full, large, lion's, major shares; the shares* (of ownership) *held by each stockholder, or shareholder, of a corporation.* **2** a plowshare. —*v.* **shares, shared, shar.ing** use or have something among a group or with others: *Three girls shared the prize; Jan shared the prize with the others; The prize was shared among them; Everyone shared* (= took part) *in the celebrations;* ***n.***: *profit* **sharing** *by employees; revenue sharing by the provinces.*

share.crop *v.* **-crops, -cropped, -crop.ping** work another's land for a share of the crop; **share.crop.per** *n.*

share.hold.er (SHARE.hold.ur) *n.* one who owns shares in a corporation; stockholder.

share.ware *n.* software that is initially distributed free of charge to users who are expected to pay a fee to the author if they continue to use it.

shark *n.* **1** a usu. large, meat-eating ocean fish with a torpedolike body, reputed to attack humans. **2** one who ruthlessly exploits others: *a card shark; loan sharks.*

shark.skin *n.* **1** a shark's hide or leather. **2** a smooth fabric with steplike twill weave.

sharp *adj.* **1** having a thin cutting edge or fine point: *a sharp knife, pencil; a sharp* (= pointed) *nose; a sharp* (= abrupt) *turn.* **2** pricking or biting: *a sharp taste; sharp words; sharp* (= cold) *weather.* **3** shrill or high-pitched: *a sharp cry of pain; a sharp musical note* (half a tone above natural pitch). **4** having qualities of keenness, quickness, smartness, etc.: *sharp desire, ears; a sharp lawyer; sharp* (= smart) *clothes.* **5** clear-cut: *a sharp contrast; in sharp relief.* —*n.* **1** a musical note or tone raised above its normal pitch by a half tone. **2** the symbol [#] used to indicate such a note or tone: *a symphony in the key of C sharp.* —*v.* **1** raise by one half tone. **2** sound such a note. —*adv.* in a sharp manner: *at 8 p.m. sharp; to sing sharp* (= above the correct pitch); *Look sharp* (= watch out)! —**sharp.ly** *adv.*: *Production has been sharply reduced; Prices have risen sharply; She spoke sharply to the child; a sharply defined issue; a sharply critical review.* —**sharp.ness** *n.*

sharp.en (SHARP.un) *v.* make or become sharp; **sharp.en.er** *n.*

sharp.er *n.* a professional gambler or swindler.

sharp-eyed *adj.* keen in sight or watchfulness; also **sharp-sighted.**

sharp.ie (SHAR.pee) *n.* **1** *Informal.* a clever or cunning person. **2** a sharper.

sharp.shoot.er (SHARP.shoo.tur) *n.* marksman; **sharp.shoot.ing** *n.*

sharp-tongued *adj.* harsh or severely critical in speech.

sharp-witted *adj.* having a keen mind and quick tongue.

shat.ter (SHAT.ur) *v.* break into scattering pieces: *Safety glass will not shatter if broken; Her hopes and dreams were shattered;* ***adj.***: *It was a* **shattering** *blow to his pride; absolutely shattering; an earth-shattering defeat, experience.* —**shat.ter.proof**

(SHAT.ur.proof) *adj.*

shave *v.* **shaves,** *pt. & pp.* **shaved** or **shav.en, shav.ing 1** remove hair from the body with a razor: *He shaves daily; shaves himself; shaved off his beard; Barbers shave customers; Women shave their legs;* *adj.*: *skinheads with* **shaven** *heads; a freshly shaven look; a clean-shaven youth.* **2** slice ham, etc. thin: *a plane for shaving wood;* *n.*: *chocolate, pencil, wood* **shavings** (= thin pieces or slices that have been shaved off). **3** graze a surface or pass very close to it: *The bullet only shaved her leg.*
—*n.* an act or result of shaving: *He has a shave and a shower in the morning; shaves of beef; That was a close shave* (= narrow escape).

shav.er (SHAY.vur) *n.* **1** a shaving instrument, esp. an electric razor. **2** *Informal.* a youngster.

shawl *n.* a square or oblong piece of cloth used esp. by women as a covering for the head or shoulders.

Shaw.nee (shaw.NEE) *n.* **1** (a member of) an Algonquian Indian people now living in Oklahoma. **2** their language.

shay *n. Informal.* chaise.

she (SHEE) *n. & pron., objective* HER, *possessive* HERS, *pl.* THEY, *objective* THEM, *possessive* THEIR(S). the female human or animal referred to; also, a person or thing thought of as female: *She is their queen; Is the puppy a he or a she? There she* (= the whale) *blows!*

sheaf (SHEEF) *n.* **sheaves** a bundle: *a sheaf of arrows, papers; a sheaf of wheat* (= stalks cut and bound).

shear (SHEER) *v.* **shears,** *pt. & pp.* **sheared** or **shorn, shear.ing 1** strip an animal of its covering, esp. sheep of its wool: *to shear lamb, sheep; sheep shearing time;* *adj.*: *shorn sheep; perfectly shorn lawns.* **2** strip off wool, fur, etc.: *adj.*: *sheared beaver, fox, furs, mink;* **shorn** *wool.* **3** deprive of something: *Samson was shorn of his strength; a dictator shorn of his powers.* **4** cut or break by the action of two forces sliding in opposite directions, as causes materials to split into layers: *A truck sideswiped the car shearing off the left-side doors;* *adja.*: *a shearing action, force, stress; shearing machines.*
—*n.* **1** a shearing or a blade of a pair of **shears** (= large scissors): *pinking, pruning, sheep shears; tin shears* (for cutting tin); *garden, kitchen shears.* **2** a shearing force or stress: *a plane crash caused by wind shear.* —**shear.er** *n.*

shear.ling (SHEER.ling) *n.* **1** a yearling sheep. **2** leather from the hide of such a sheep; *adja.*: *a shearling coat; shearling and leather jackets.*

sheath (SHEETH, "TH" as in "thin") *n.* **1** a case for the blade of a knife. **2** a similar covering over a cat's claw or the base of a grass's leaf that wraps around its stem. **3** a woman's straight, close-fitting dress.

sheathe (SHEETH, "TH" as in "the") *v.* **sheathes, sheathed, sheath.ing** put into or enclose in a sheath.

sheathing (SHEETH.ing, "TH" as in "the") *n.* the inner layer of boards used under the siding or roofing of a frame house.

sheave (SHIV, SHEEV) *n.* a wheel or pulley with a grooved rim.

she.bang (shuh.BANG) *n. Informal.* business; affair; outfit: *Pat was made head of* **the whole shebang.**

she'd (SHEED) she had; she would.

shed *n.* a one-story structure sometimes open on one side, used for shelter or storage: *garden, tool, wood sheds.*
—*v.* **sheds, shed, shed.ding 1** let drop or fall: *to shed tears; Snakes shed* (= cast off) *their skin; We shed* (= remove and leave) *our coats at the door; a revolution achieved without* **shedding blood** (= killing). **2** give forth; send out: *She sheds joy around her; The sun sheds light; to* **shed light on** (= clear up) *a mystery.*

sheen *n.* the shiny quality of satin, silk, etc.; soft luster: *polished to a high sheen; the silky sheen of her hair.* —**sheen.y** *adj.*

sheep *n. sing. & pl.* **1** an animal related to the goat, raised for its wool, milk, and meat, i.e., mutton and lamb. **2** one considered meek and submissive, like sheep being shorn; hence, a mindless follower, esp. as one of a group.

sheep dog *n.* a dog trained to herd and watch sheep.

sheep.fold *n.* a pen or shelter for sheep; also **sheep.cote.**

sheep.ish *adj.* bashful or embarrassed: *a sheepish grin, look, smile.* —**sheep.ish.ly** *adv.*

sheep range *n.* land used for grazing sheep.

sheep.skin *n.* **1** the skin of a sheep. **2** leather or parchment made from it. **3** *Informal.* a diploma.

sheer *v.* swerve or deviate, as a ship from its course: *to sheer away from or sheer off something.* —*adj.* **1** very thin or transparent: *a sheer fabric such as chiffon; sheer drapes, hosiery, nylons.* **2** *adja.* pure or unmixed: *sheer absurdity, beauty, delight, determination, folly, ignorance, luck, nonsense, pleasure, poppycock.* **3** *adja.*

mere: *by sheer coincidence; in sheer size alone; their sheer numbers.* **4** very steep; precipitous: *sheer cliffs; a sheer rock face.* —*n.* a sheer fabric, garment, etc.: *voile sheers* (= sheer curtains) *for the window.* —*adv.* directly; also, steeply: *a rock face rising sheer from the beach.*

sheet *n.* a broad, thin piece of material or something resembling it: *bed sheets; white as a sheet; to change sheets for a new guest* (when making a bed); *a sheet of glass, ice, paper, water; a company's balance sheet; The police officer made out a charge sheet; The rain came down* **in sheets** (= as masses of water).

sheeting *n.* material for covering or lining purposes.

sheet lightning *n.* lightning seen in broad flashes from beyond the horizon.

sheet metal *n.* thin-rolled sheets of metal.

sheet music *n.* music printed on unbound sheets of paper.

sheik or **sheikh** (SHEEK, SHAKE) *n.* an Arab chief; also, a Muslim title; **sheik.dom** or **sheikh.dom** (-dum) *n.*

shek.el (SHEK.ul) *n.* the basic money unit of Israel.

shelf *n.* **shelves** (SHELVS) **1** a board attached at a height horizontally to a wall or inside a cabinet for holding things, as books in a bookcase: *to put up shelves; a room with built-in shelves; shelves stocked with books.* **2** a ledge of rocks, esp. one under water: *the continental shelf off the Atlantic coast.* —**on the shelf** put aside as useless.

shelf life *n.* how long a packaged product will keep if stored.

she'll (SHEEL) she will; she shall.

shell *n.* **1** the hard outer covering of oysters, snails, and other mollusks, insects such as beetles, and of turtles, eggs, seeds, and nuts: *adj.:* **shelled** *almonds, crabmeat, peas, shrimp, walnuts.* **2** a shell-like outer covering, as the framework of a house or ship, a sleeveless pullover blouse, or the case of a pie. **3** a racing rowboat. **4** an artillery projectile filled with explosive: *to lob shells into enemy territory; to fire shells at enemy ships.* **5** a cartridge case for a shotgun or other small arms. **6** a menu-driven or graphical interface for easy use of an operating system. —*v.* **1** remove the shell or husk: *to shell nuts.* **2** bombard with artillery shells. —**shell out** *Informal.* pay or hand out an amount of money, candy, etc.: *Be ready to shell out soon after dusk on Halloween.*

shel.lac (shuh.LAC) *n.* **1** varnish made of refined lac dried into flakes and dissolved in alcohol. **2** lac used in sealing wax and molded articles. —*v.* **shel.lacs, shel.lacked, shel.lack.ing** **1** varnish with shellac. **2** *Informal.* thrash; also, beat decisively; *n.:* *to get, give, take a* **shellacking** (= thrashing or defeat).

shell bean *n.* the edible seed of a bean that is shelled for use, as lima bean.

shell company *n.* a company that exists only in name.

shell.fire *n.* the firing of artillery shells.

shell.fish *n.* an oyster, clam, lobster, etc. that is not a true fish.

shell game *n.* a dishonestly played game involving substitution; hence, a cheating or swindle.

shell shock *n.* nervous breakdown resulting from battlefield experiences.

shel.ter (SHEL.tur) *n.* a roof or other cover for protection from the elements or a specific threat: *food, clothing, and shelter; bomb, bus, fall-out shelters; Get under shelter when bombs start falling; to afford, give, offer, provide shelter; shelter for the homeless; to find, take shelter from the rain; the shelter of a roof, of an umbrella.* —*v.* protect or provide a shelter for a person or thing: *to shelter a child from evil influences; We sheltered* (= found shelter) *under the trees; adj.: a* **sheltered** (= protected) *spot; the sheltered life of a convent; a life of sheltered ease; a tax-sheltered investment.*

shelve *v.* **shelves, shelved, shelv.ing** **1** put something on a shelf: *Leave the books for the librarian to shelve.* **2** put off or put aside: *The plans were shelved because of lack of funds.* **3** furnish with shelves.

shelves *pl.* of SHELF.

shelving *n.* boards, posts, etc. for putting up shelves.

she.nan.i.gans (shuh.NAN.uh.guns) *n.pl. Informal.* mischievous, devious, or tricky behavior.

shep.herd (SHEP.urd) *n.* one who tends sheep; **shep.herd.ess** *fem.* —*v.* herd or look after as a shepherd: *a teacher shepherding children across a street.*

sher.bet (SHUR.but) *n.* an ice made with fruit juice, sugar, and low-fat milk or egg white.

sher.iff *n.* **1** in the U.S., the chief law-enforcement officer of a county. **2** in Canada, an official who serves summonses, maintains order in the courts, and executes judgments.

Sher.pa (SHUR.puh) *n.* a member of a Nepalese people famed as porters and guides in the Himalayas.

sher.ry (SHER.ee) *n.* **sher.ries** a usu. yellowish-to-brown fortified wine.
she's (SHEEZ) she is; she has.
Shet.land pony (SHET.lund-) *n.* the smallest breed of horse, with long, thick hair, originally from the Shetland Islands, N.E. of Scotland.
shew (SHOW) *n. & v.* **shews,** *pt.* **shewed,** *pp.* **shewed** or **shewn, shew.ing** [old use] same as SHOW.
shib.bo.leth (SHIB.uh.luth) *n.* **1** a custom or usage, esp. in language, narrowly applied as a criterion of membership in a particular class or faction. **2** a false or outdated notion.
shied *pt. & pp.* of SHY.
shield (SHEELD) *n.* a piece of armor held in one hand for protection in battle. —*v.* protect or defend with or as if with a shield: *She shielded her child from the falling debris; to shield someone against attack; He tried to shield his accomplice by giving false evidence.*
shier, shies, shiest See SHY.
shift *v.* **1** change location, position, or direction in an unstable or restless manner: *The wind has shifted to northeast; He kept shifting in his chair nervously; shifted his weight from one leg to the other; He had to* **shift for himself** (= take care of himself) *without a home or friends.* **2** move: *We shift into top gear for cruising; He tried to* **shift (the) blame** *onto his employees; Now you're* **shifting your ground** (= changing the basis of your reasoning). —*n.* **1** change: *a shift in the wind; to bring about a shift in attitudes, policy; a shift of interest, responsibility; Press the* **shift key** *to type capitals.* **2** a group or period in which people work in a relay system: *He works the day shift; Everyone works an eight-hour shift; graveyard, night, split, swing shifts.* **3** a gearshift: *an automatic shift; a manual, standard, stick shift.* **4** a sheathlike but beltless dress. **5** a slip: *She stood there in the cold in nothing but her shift.* —**make shift** manage as best one can with available resources.
shift.less *adj.* lazy: *a stupid, dirty, and shiftless fellow.*
shift.y *adj.* **shift.i.er, -i.est** evasive or tricky: *shifty behavior, looks; shifty-eyed merchants.* —**shift.i.ly** *adv.;* **shift.i.ness** *n.*
shill *n. Informal.* a person hired to lure customers into buying, betting, gambling, etc. by posing as a customer himself.
shil.le.lagh (shi.LAY.lee) *n. Irish.* a cudgel.
shil.ling (SHIL.ing) *n.* **1** the basic money unit of Kenya, Tanzania, and Uganda. **2** formerly, a British money of account equal to 1/20 of a pound.
shil.ly-shal.ly (SHIL.ee.shal.ee) *v.* **-shal.lies, -shal.lied, -shal.ly.ing** dawdle over a decision.
shim *n.* a thin wedge or strip of material. —*v.* **shims, shimmed, shim.ming** level up or support something by using shims.
shim.mer (SHIM.ur) **1** *n.* a wavering or unsteady light; glimmer. **2** *v.* shine with a shimmer: *The lake shimmered in the moonlight.* —**shim.mer.y** *adj.*
shim.my (SHIM.ee) *v.* **shim.mies, shim.mied, shim.my.ing 1** shake or wobble, as the front wheels of an automobile that need balancing. **2** dance with shaking movements.
—*n.* **1** a shaking or vibration. **2** a jazz dance of the 1920s.
shin *n.* the front of the leg between the knee and the ankle: *Al barked* or *scraped his shins climbing trees.*
—*v.* **shins, shinned, shin.ning** climb *up* a tree trunk, pole, etc. using hands and legs.
shin.bone *n.* the larger of the two bones of the lower leg.
shin.dig *n. Informal.* a large and lively social gathering.
shine *v.* **shines, shone** (SHON), **shin.ing 1** send out or reflect light, as the sun, moon, lights, etc.: *The sun is shining; It shines on the rich and the poor; Shine the lights* (= make the lights shine) *on the dark side of the house;* **adj.:** *a* **shining** *light, star; "from sea to shining sea."* **2** be brilliant or conspicuous in some respect, at some skill, etc.: *He shines at math; true talent shining through;* **adj.:** *a* **shining** *example of self-sacrifice; a shining future, moment of glory, performance.* **3** [*pt.* usu. **shined**] make shiny; polish: *Jon shines shoes.* —*n.* brightness; also, gloss: *a flat finish with no shine; Jon will give you a shine* (= will shine your shoes). —**take a shine to** *Informal.* become fond of someone.
shin.er (SHY.nur) *n. Informal.* a black eye.
shin.gle (SHING.gul) *n.* **1** a flat, thin piece of wood or other material laid in overlapping rows to cover roofs or walls: *asphalt shingles; roofing shingles;* **adj.:** *a* **shingled** *cottage, house, roof.* **2** *Informal.* a small sign as used by a physician or other professional: *The young lawyer hung out* or *up her shingle and started her practice.* **3** a woman's short haircut tapered at the nape. **4** small well-rounded pebbles or a

beach covered with them: *children playing in the shingle.* **5 shingles** *sing. & pl.* a painful skin disease characterized by blisters: *to develop shingles.* —**shin.gly** *adj*

shin.guard *n.* protective padding worn on the shin while playing soccer, baseball, etc.

shin.ny *v.* **shin.nies, shin.nied, shin.ny.ing** same as SHIN.

shin.splints *n.pl.* [takes *sing. v.*] strain or injury to lower leg muscles from running on hard surfaces.

Shin.to (SHIN.toh) *n.* the traditional religion of Japan that centers around the worship of ancestors and the basic forces and processes of nature; **Shin.to.ism** *n.*

shin.y (SHY.nee) *adj.* **shin.i.er, -i.est** bright or shining; also, polished: *a shiny day; bright and shiny; smooth and shiny; to powder a shiny nose; a shiny finish, new penny, skin, surface; shiny hair, shoes.*

-ship *n. suffix.* **1** state or condition: *authorship, fellowship; workmanship* (= skill of a worker). **2** group: *membership, readership.*

ship *n.* **1** a large seagoing vessel: *to board, build, christen, launch, load, navigate, refit, sail, scuttle, sink, torpedo, unload a ship; capital, cruise, hospital, merchant, passenger, sailing, supply ships; to disembark from a ship; to raise a sunken ship; to* **abandon ship** *(when it is sinking); to* **jump ship** *(= desert from a ship's crew); The boss* **runs a tight ship** *(= operates efficiently).* **2** the officers and crew of a ship. **3** an aircraft or spacecraft: *a lunar ship; the rocket ships of science fiction.* —**when your ship comes in** or **comes home** when you become rich. —*v.* **ships, shipped, ship.ping 1** put on board a ship; hence, transport by sea, rail, road, or air: *We ship goods; Goods are shipped out to distant parts; He was shipped off* (= sent away) *to boarding schools and summer camps as a child.* **2** take in or install in a ship: *to ship oars, rudders; The boat began to* **ship water** (= be flooded) *in the storm.* **3** go on board a ship to travel, for service, etc.: *At just 16, Conrad shipped out on a trading ship; Sam has to shape up or* **ship out** *(= leave).* —**ship.per** *n.*

ship.board *adj.* on board a ship: *a shipboard riot, romance, summit meeting; n.: It happened on shipboard.*

ship.build.er (SHIP.bild.ur) *n.* one whose business is shipbuilding.

ship.build.ing (SHIP.bild.ing) *n.* the designing and construction of ships.

ship.fit.ter (SHIP.fit.ur) *n.* one who fits a ship's parts together.

ship.mate *n.* a fellow sailor.

ship.ment (SHIP.munt) *n.* goods shipped or their shipping.

shipping *n.* **1** the ships of a nation, business, etc. collectively: *merchant shipping.* **2** the transportation of goods: *a shipping company; the* **shipping clerk** *in a warehouse; The price doesn't include* **shipping and handling** *(charges for packaging, freight, etc.).*

ship.shape *adj. & adv.* trim and tidy; in good order: *She keeps her room shipshape; to appear shipshape; in shipshape condition.*

ship.worm *n.* a clamlike mollusk that bores holes in wood.

ship.wreck *n.* **1** the loss or destruction of a ship at sea: *the shipwreck of the Titanic; Many sailors have experienced or suffered shipwrecks; the shipwreck* (= ruin or failure) *of his hopes and ambitions.* **2** wreckage or a wrecked ship: *the richest shipwreck ever uncovered in our waters.* —*v.* cause or suffer shipwreck: *The Titanic was shipwrecked off Newfoundland; We were shipwrecked and marooned on an island.*

ship.wright *n.* a shipbuilder or repairer, esp. a carpenter.

ship.yard *n.* an establishment for the building and repair of ships: *a naval shipyard.*

shire *n.* in Britain, a county.

shirk *v.* avoid doing one's work or duty: *to shirk one's duty, responsibilities; shirk a role; how to reduce shirking (at work);* **shirk.er** *n.*

shirr *v.* **1** bake shelled eggs in a shallow dish with butter. **2** gather cloth together by means of short parallel stitches. —*n.* such a gathering; also **shirr.ing.**

shirt *n.* **1** a garment for the upper part of the body with a front opening, collar, and short or long sleeves, as usu. worn by men: *dress and sport shirts; (a knitted pullover) polo shirt; (a close-fitting) body shirt; a hair shirt worn as penance.* **2** an undershirt. —**keep one's shirt on** *Informal.* remain calm during an argument. —**lose one's shirt** *Informal.* lose all one's money or property.

shirt.dress *n.* a dress with a shirtwaist.

shirt.ing *n.* cloth for shirts.

shirt.sleeve *n.* the sleeve of a shirt: *He's so busy at work he's always found* **in (his) shirtsleeves** *(= not wearing a jacket); adja.: shirtsleeve temperature, weather (so warm one doesn't need a coat when going out).*

shirt.tail *n.* the part of a shirt that is usu. tucked inside one's trousers.
shirt.waist *n.* a blouse fashioned like a shirt.
shish kebab *n.* a skewered kebab.
shit *n. & interj.* [vulgar slang] human excrement. —*v.* **shits, shit.ted, shit.ting** excrete. —**shit.ty** *adj.*
shiv *n. Slang.* a knife.
shiv.er (SHIV.ur) **1** *v.* tremble, as from fear or cold: *He was so scared he was shivering in his shoes; Kay was shivering with cold; Some shiver at the very thought of winter.* **2** *n. & v.* splinter.
—*n.* a shivering or shaking: *a chilling story that will send shivers down (or up and down) your spine; It gives you* **the shivers.** —**shiv.er.y** *adj.*
shlemiel, shlep, shlock, shmaltz, shmo, shnook, etc. same as SCHLEMIEL, etc.
shoal (SHOLE) *n.* **1** a large group: *a shoal (= school) of fish.* **2** a shallow place with sand or rocks underneath: *They hit a shoal; a ship stranded on the shoals.* **3 shoals** *pl.* a dangerous situation: *a company grounded on the shoals of bad investments.*
shoat (SHOTE) *n.* a weaned young hog.
shock *n.* **1** a sudden violent shake or jolt, as felt when electric current passes through the body or an earthquake strikes: *The news of his tragic death came as a shock; a shock to everyone in the family; It was a shock to learn of his death; It gave her a shock; She felt, got or had a shock; People expressed shock at the tragedy; culture, electric, future, mild, profound, rude, severe, terrible shocks;* **adj.:** *He uses four-letter words for their shock effect; The name of the movie has shock value; (electric) shock treatment.* **2** a failure or collapse of the circulatory system resulting from a serious injury or burn; also, a dazed condition brought on by some disaster or personal loss: *cardiac, insulin, psychic, shell shock; She was in shock for several days after the incident; to go into shock; send, plunge someone into shock.* **3** a thick bushy mass: *a shock of hair.* **4** [short form] shock absorber (as of automobile wheels). —*v.* cause shock to someone: *It shocked him to hear that she had died; He was shocked to hear the news; She was shocked into silence by the obscenities hurled at her.*
shock absorber *n.* anything that lessens a shock, esp. a piston device used on automobiles, to reduce the shock of rough rides or impacts.
shock.er *n.* a person or thing that shocks, esp. a sensational story.
shocking *adj.* causing great surprise, disgust, etc.: *shocking language, news; It was shocking to find out what was going on.*
shocking pink *n.* a very bight pink.
shock.proof *adj.* protected against shocks: *a shockproof watch.*
shock therapy *n.* treatment of severe mental illness using electric current administered to the brain producing momentary unconsciousness and convulsions; in full "electroconvulsive therapy" or ECT.
shock troops *n.pl.* troops specially trained to lead attacks.
shock wave *n.* the blast from an explosion: *The news of the murder sent shock waves through the community.*
shod a *pt. & pp.* of SHOE.
shod.dy *n.* **shod.dies 1** cloth made of woolen waste. **2** anything of inferior quality though looking good.
—*adj.* **shod.di.er, shod.di.est 1** inferior: *shoddy goods, merchandise, workmanship.* **2** shabby: *shoddy business practices, service, treatment.* —**shod.di.ly** *adv.;* **shod.di.ness** *n.*
shoe (SHOO) *n.* **1** an outer covering for a foot, usu. made of leather: *to break in new shoes; shoes that pinch; basketball, dress, gym, high-heeled, running, sports, tennis, track shoes.* **2** something resembling a shoe in function, position, etc., as a horseshoe, the outer casing of a pneumatic tire, etc. —**fill someone's shoes** take the place vacated by someone. —**the shoe is on the other foot** the situation is reversed. —**where the shoe pinches** where the problem is.
—*v.* **shoes,** *pt. & pp.* **shod** or **shoed, shoe.ing** furnish or cover with a shoe: *Blacksmiths shoe horses; shod with steel; well-shod feet.*
shoe.horn *n.* an implement with a curved blade used to ease one's heel into a shoe.
shoe.lace *n.* a length of string or strap for lacing or tying a shoe.
shoe.mak.er (SHOO.may.kur) *n.* one who makes or repairs shoes.
shoe.shine *n.* a cleaning and polishing of a pair of shoes.
shoe.string *n.* **1** shoelace. **2** *Informal.* a small or barely adequate amount of capital: *to operate on a shoestring;* **adja.:** *We're on a shoestring budget; a shoestring operation; a* **shoestring catch** *(made just before a ball hits the ground).*
shoe tree *n.* a foot-shaped form of wood inserted in a shoe to preserve its shape.

sho.gun (SHOH.gun) *n.* the title of the hereditary commander-in-chief and virtual ruler of Japan till 1867.
shone *pt.* of SHINE.
shoo *interj.* [used to drive away birds, flies, etc.] go away! —*v.* **shoos, shooed, shoo.ing** drive away by calling "shoo."
shoo-in *n. Informal.* an easy winner: *a shoo-in to win* or *for the nomination.*
shook *pt.* of SHAKE. —**shook up** *Informal.* upset or agitated.
shoot (long "oo") *v.* **shoots, shot, shoot.ing 1** send forth suddenly and swiftly like a bullet, arrow, or other missile; also, fire at a person or thing: *to shoot arrows, guns; He shot two rounds; The fleeing man was shot at; The robber was shot by the police; was shot dead; to shoot to kill; an order to shoot on sight; The planes were shot down; Reporters shoot questions during interviews; The flames shot up; cars shooting past spectators; a canoe for shooting* (= passing quickly along) *the rapids of the river;* **adj.:** *a shooting incident* (involving firing a weapon); *a shooting gallery* (= a covered place for target practice); *a shooting range* (= an outdoor place for target practice); *a shooting war* (= not a cold war). **2** get by shooting: *He shot three goals; Cameras shoot pictures; Let's shoot* (= aim) *for the top.* —**shoot from the hip** act hastily. —**shoot up** *Informal.* inject: *Addicts shoot up amphetamines; He's given up shooting (up) heroin.*
—*n.* **1** a shooting: *to go on a tiger shoot; He lost the shoot* (= shooting match). **2** a new young growth from a plant: *the tender shoots of a fern; bamboo shoots.*
shooting script *n.* a script with scenes arranged in the order required for filming.
shooting star *n.* a small meteor falling to earth seen as a streak of light.
shoot.out *n. Informal.* a gunfight.
shop *n.* **1** a small retail store: *a book shop; paint shops.* **2** a place where goods are produced or a service is provided; workshop or factory: *barber, beauty, (auto) body, butcher, carpenter's, machine, printing shops.* —**talk shop** indulge in or use shoptalk.
—*v.* **shops, shopped, shop.ping** visit stores, as at a mall, or buy from a store: *He's out shopping; shopping for a hat; He shops (at) the World Mall; But first he shops* (= studies) *the ads.* —**shop around** search around, as at stores: *to shop around for a bargain, a better job.*
—**shop.per** *n.* —**shop.keep.er** *n.*

shop.lift.er (SHOP.lif.tur) *n.* one who steals goods displayed for sale in a store. —**shop.lift** *v.* —**shop.lift.ing** *n.*
shoppe (SHOP) *n.* [old spelling used for quaint effect in names] shop: *Ye Computer Shoppe.*
shopping *n.* the act of buying from stores: *We do all our shopping on Saturdays; arcade, Christmas, convenience, impulse shopping; comparison shopping* (for the best prices). —**adj.:** *a shopping bag, cart, list, pattern, season, spree, trip; shopping habits; a **shopping center** with many shops and a parking area; an enclosed **shopping mall** with central heating and air-conditioning.*
shopping-bag lady same as BAG LADY.
shopping plaza *n.* a shopping center.
shop.talk *n.* **1** discussion of one's business, as with a colleague, esp. using jargon. **2** such jargon.
shop.worn *adj.* **1** of articles displayed for sale, soiled or frayed by having been handled or on display. **2** not fresh or attractive: *a shopworn appearance, cliché, look, theme.*
shore *n.* **1** land along the edge of a sea, lake, etc.; coast: *a cottage on the shore of a lake; cities along the shores of Lake Michigan; a ship anchored many miles **off shore** carrying goods not allowed **on shore**; Immigrants arrive on our **shores*** (= in our country). **2** a prop or brace to support a structure, esp. on its side.
—*v.* **shores, shored, shor.ing** support or prop: *to shore up a shaky wall; to shore up falling interest rates, the falling dollar.*
shore bird *n.* a wading bird such as a plover or sandpiper.
shore.line *n.* the line formed by a coast; coastline.
shore patrol *n.* members of the U.S. Navy or Coast Guard carrying out police duties on shore.
shorn *pp.* of SHEAR.
short *adj.* **1** relatively small in extent or duration; not long or tall: *a short distance, time; a man relatively short in stature; the short vowels of "pat," "pet," "pit," "pot," and "put"; He has a short* (= bad) *memory; You may make some money **in the short run*** (= at first or for a short time). **2** less than sufficient: *Food is in short supply; He cheats his customers with short weight and short change; She is **short of** breath after the run; We are (running) short of supplies; Being short* (= curt) *didn't help him keep customers; We don't want to be **caught short*** (= in acute need); *She wants nothing **short of*** (= less than) *what was*

promised. **3** *adja.* of pastry and such baked foods, crumbly or flaky: *a short crust.* **4** *adjp.* not yet owning securities, goods, etc. sold in advance: *We are short of cotton.* —**get the short end of the stick** *Informal.* receive unfair treatment. —**make short work of** deal with or dispose of something quickly. —*adv.*: to sell cotton short (for future delivery); She stopped short (= abruptly) in the middle of her speech; He would stop at nothing **short of** (= except) murder; He **cut short** his vacation and returned to work; Her performance **fell short** of expectations. —*n.* **1** something short or shortened, as a short form, item, movie, etc.: "Deli" is **short for** (= the short form of) "delicatessen." **2** a short circuit. **3 shorts** *pl.* short trousers or drawers: *a pair of Bermuda shorts; boxer shorts.* —**in short** briefly. —*v.* **1** to shortchange: *The store clerk shorted us.* **2** to short-circuit: *The kettle shorted out with an explosion.*

short.age (SHOR.tij) *n.* a deficiency or its amount: *an acute shortage of water; food, housing, labor shortages.*

short.bread *n.* a rich crumbly cake or cookie.

short.cake *n.* a pastry cake served with sugared or cooked fruit: *strawberry shortcake; down-home turkey shortcake.*

short.change *v.* **-chang.es, -changed, -chang.ing** *Informal.* **1** give less than the correct change. **2** deprive someone of what is due; cheat.

short circuit *n.* a usu. dangerous high flow of electric current between two points bypassing the main circuit. —**short-circuit** *v.*

short.com.ing (SHORT.cum.ing) *n.* a failing or fault.

short.cut *n.* **1** a way that is shorter than the regular route: *to take a shortcut through the fields.* **2** any way of saving time or effort: *There are no shortcuts to fame and fortune.*

short.en *v.* **1** make or become shorter: *Please shorten your speech to three minutes; Shorten it by two minutes.* **2** make pastry crisp and flaky by use of shortening.

shortening *n.* butter, lard, etc. added to doughs and batters to make short pastry: *vegetable shortening made from soybean oil.*

short.fall *n.* a falling short of something expected or its amount; deficiency: *production, revenue, sales shortfalls; to make up a shortfall.*

short fuse *n. Informal.* a quick temper.

short.hand *n.* a system of rapid writing using abbreviations and symbols: *The reporter took it down in shorthand; Can you take shorthand?*

short.hand.ed (SHORT.hand.id) *adj.* short of helpers.

short.horn *n.* a roan-colored breed of beef cattle having short horns, originally from England.

short list *n.* a list of candidates selected for consideration: *Jon made the short list but Jane got the job.*

short-lived (SHORT.lived, -livd) *adj.* lasting only a short time: *short-lived fads, fashions, pleasures; a short-lived affair, career, craze, enterprise, relationship, triumph, victory; The crisis was short-lived.* Also **short.lived.**

short.ly *adv.* **1** in a short time; soon. **2** briefly; in summary. **3** abruptly or curtly. —**short.ness** *n.*

short order *n.* **1** an order for food that can be quickly cooked; *adja.*: *We need a short-order cook for the lunch counter.* **2** the food so ordered. —**in short order** at short notice; quickly: *Sometimes it is difficult to get a substitute teacher in short order.*

short-range *adja.* having a short range in distance or time; not long-range.

short shrift *n.* little consideration; curt treatment: *to get short shrift; give somebody short shrift; He* **made short shrift of** *the proposal* (= got rid of it quickly).

short.sight.ed *adj.* **1** nearsighted. **2** lacking in foresight. —**short.sight.ed.ly** *adv.*; **short.sight.ed.ness** *n.*

short-spoken *adj.* using few words; hence, curt.

short.stop *n.* in baseball, the infielder or the position between second and third base.

short story *n.* a compact work of prose fiction, as published in magazines, with a single plot and a limited number of characters.

short subject *n.* a cartoon, newsreel, or other short item shown before or between feature films.

short-tempered *adj.* quickly angered.

short-term *adj.* having to do with a relatively short period of time; not long-term: *short-term benefits, employment, gains.*

short ton See TON.

short.wave *n.* electromagnetic radiation of wavelength less than 100 meters, as used in FM broadcasting.

short-winded *adj.* easily getting out of breath; having difficulty in breathing.

Sho.sho.ni or **Sho.sho.ne** (shoh.SHOH.nee) *n.* (a member of) a Native American people living in Idaho, Nevada, Utah, and Wyoming. —Sho.sho.ne.an *adj.*

shot *pt. & pp.* of SHOOT. —*adjp.* **1 shot with** flecked or streaked with something: *a sky shot with patches of cloud; red silk shot with gold thread; an essay* **shot through with** (= full of) *humor.* **2** worn out or broken, as an automobile part needing replacement: *His health is shot.* —*n.* **1** a shooting or anything similar, as a scoring attempt in a game, an injection or dose of a drug, a pointed remark, or a random guess: *to fire* or *take a shot at a target; to fire the first* or *opening shot; cheap, parting, passing, penalty, pistol, random, rifle, warning shots; a flu shot* (= injection); *They were warned not to approach* **within shot** (= range) *of the rifles; We will have* **a shot at it** (= make an attempt to get or accomplish it); *a shot* (= drink) *of whiskey.* **2** *Informal.* a person: *a big shot.* **3** a marksman or markswoman: *bad, crack, good shots.* **4** a solid metal ball, esp. a large one for a cannon. **5** small lead pellets collectively: *bird shot; lead shot.* **6** a camera picture or film sequence: *a good shot of his face.* —**call the shots** *Informal.* give orders. —**shot in the arm** something to stimulate or invigorate. —**shot in the dark** a wild guess.

shot.gun *n.* a smooth-bore hunting gun that fires lead pellets: *a sawed-off shotgun.* —**ride shotgun** watch protectively: *Governments tend to ride shotgun on* or *over municipal affairs.* —*adja.* **1** forced: *shotgun mergers; a* **shotgun wedding** or **marriage** (*forced on a couple by pregnancy*). **2** aggressive: *He had to use a shotgun approach to marketing to sell his new gadget.*

shot put *n.* the contest of throwing a heavy metal ball for distance. —**shot-putter** *n.* —**shot-putting** *n.*

should *pt.* of SHALL.

shoul.der (SHOLE.dur) *n.* **1** where the arm is joined to the trunk: *to put one's* **shoulder to the wheel** (= work hard); *to stand or work* **shoulder to shoulder** (= side by side or in a united way); *adja.: a shoulder bag; a carrying case with should strap; protective* **shoulder pads** *for football players.* **2** a shoulder-like part, esp. the usu. unpaved edge of a road: *Caution – soft shoulders.*
3 shoulders *pl.* the upper part of the back, esp. as bearing burdens: *a man with broad shoulders; square shoulders; He shrugged his shoulders in dismay; The responsibility rests on your shoulders; Ray* **rubs shoulders** (= associates) *with important people.* —**straight from the shoulder** frankly or directly. —*v.* push, support, or bear a burden, blame, etc. (as if) with a shoulder or shoulders: *to shoulder a burden, responsibility.*
—**shouldered** *adj. & cpd.* having shoulders or as specified: *a shouldered coat; the shouldered look; broad-shouldered men; a full-shouldered silhouette; wide-shouldered jackets.*

shoulder belt *n.* an anchored belt worn over one shoulder attached to a lap belt for safety in an automobile: *rear-seat shoulder belts;* also **shoulder harness.**

shoulder blade *n.* either of the two flat, triangular bones at the back of the shoulder; scapula.

shoulder season *n.* the period between high or peak season and low season: *Spring and fall are shoulder seasons for international travel.*

should.n't should not.

shout *n.* a sudden loud cry or call: *Give me a shout if you need help; a shout of recognition; shouts of despair, hatred, joy, triumph.* —*v.* utter a shout: *The drowning man shouted for help; No one likes to be shouted at; to* **shout down** *an opponent* (= make him or her stop talking by continued shouting). —**shout.er** *n.*

shove (SHUV) *v.* **shoves, shoved, shov.ing** push roughly, often to get a person or thing out of one's way: *He shoved his job and left home; to engage in a* **shoving match** (= power struggle). —**shove around** order about. —**shove off** *Informal.* leave, as by pushing one's boat away. —*n.* a shoving: *to give someone a shove.*

shov.el (SHUV.ul) *n.* an implement with a broad, hollowed-out blade and handle for scooping out loose material such as earth, coal, and snow: *Diesel power shovels have replaced steam shovels for digging.* —*v.* **-els, -eled, -el.ing** dig or throw out with a shovel: *to shovel earth, sand, snow.* Also **shov.elled, shov.el.ling** *Cdn.*

shov.el.ful (SHUV.ul.ful, *rhyme:* full) *n.* how much a shovel will hold.

show (SHOH) *v.* **shows,** *pt. & pp.* **shown** (SHOHN) or **showed, show.ing 1** (cause to) be seen: *He showed me a picture; showed me through the building; Your slip is showing; Children like to* **show off** (= be watched while doing something they are proud of); *He likes to show off* (= display) *his new car; Half of those who reserved seats failed to* **show up** (= arrive). **2** explain or demon-

strate: *She'll show you how it works; an experiment to show that light travels faster than sound.* **3** direct or guide: *The hostess showed us around; showed us to our seats;* **n.**: *The Labor party made a good* **showing** (= a good impression or performance) *at the polls.*
—**n. 1** a showing: *They voted 112-25 in a show of hands.* **2** a display, exhibition, or performance: *a show of strength, temper; to produce, promote, put on, sponsor, stage a show; to catch or see or take in a show while in the city; a floor show at a night club; a talent show by children; air, auto, dog, flower, horse, TV, variety shows; The show starts at 8;* **Good show!** (= Very good!); *Let's* **get the show on the road** (*Informal* for get things going); *He's just* **putting on a show** (= just pretending); *The kindergarten kids* **stole the show** (= attracted the most attention); *Sam was in charge of* **the whole show** (= the complete operation).

show biz or **show.biz** (SHOH.biz) *n. Informal.* show business; *adj*a.: *a show-biz musical, success, theme; their showbiz instincts.*

show.boat *n.* formerly, a large boat equipped as a traveling theater.

show business *n.* the entertainment industry.

show.case *n.* a glass case for displaying articles in a store or museum: *Expo 86 was the showcase of the nation.*
—*v.* -cas.es, -cased, -cas.ing: *Much young talent was showcased at the school fair.*

show.down *n. Informal.* the bringing out of a dispute into the open in order to force a settlement: *to come to or have, force a showdown with the opposition.*

show.er (*rhyme:* our) *n.* **1** a brief fall of rain or anything similar: *heavy, light, passing, scattered showers; April showers; thunder showers; a shower of arrows, hail, meteorites, stones.* **2** a party for giving gifts to a woman on a special occasion: *baby, bridal, engagement, wedding showers.* **3** (a bathroom fixture for) an overhead spray of water; *adj*a.: *a shower curtain, stall; a* **shower head** (= nozzle). **4** a wash taken under a shower, or a **shower bath**: *to take a shower.* —*v.* **1** rain briefly. **2** come or send in a shower: *to shower compliments, gifts on* or *upon someone; He was showered with insults.* **3** take a shower bath: *He likes to shower and shave before breakfast.* —**show.er.y** *adj.*

show.girl *n.* **1** a woman performer who is more of a decoration than a star: *slick showgirls.* **2** a woman dancer or singer in a stage show: *cabaret showgirls.*

show.man (SHOW.mun) *n.* **-men 1** a man skilled in presenting things in an impressive or dramatic manner. **2** a producer of shows. —**show.man.ship** *n.*

shown a *pp.* of SHOW.

show.off *n.* one who vainly displays his or her good points.

show.piece *n.* something considered the best of its kind, as fit for display.

show.place *n.* a place that is proudly shown to tourists.

show.room *n.* a room in which goods are displayed for viewing.

show-stopper *n.* something arresting or riveting; also **show stopper.**

show window *n.* a shop's outside display window.

show.y *adj.* **show.i.er, -i.est** striking or gaudy in appearance. —**show.i.ly** *adv.;* **show.i.ness** *n.*

shrank a *pt.* of SHRINK.

shrap.nel (SHRAP.nul) *n.* the flying fragments from an exploding bomb, shell, or mine: *a piece of shrapnel.*

shred *v.* **shreds, shred.ded, shred.ding** cut or tear into narrow strips or fragments: *They shred tires before dumping them; a paper shredding machine; adj.: shredded cheese, coconut, lettuce.*
—*n.* a torn or cut off strip: *His shirt was torn to shreds; There was not a shred* (= bit) *of evidence against her; some shred of hope.* —**shred.der** *n.*

shredded wheat *n.* a breakfast cereal made from dried wheat that is shredded and molded into biscuits.

shrew (SHROO) *n.* **1** a small aggressive mouselike mammal. **2** a bad-tempered scolding woman. —**shrew.ish** *adj.*

shrewd (SHROOD, long "oo") *adj.* sharp and clever in practical matters: *a shrewd businessman, guess, observer; shrewd at guessing.* —**shrewd.ly** *adv.;* **shrewd.ness** *n.*

shriek (SHREEK) *n.* a sharp, shrill cry of extreme fear, delight, pain, or other emotion; screech: *shrieks of laughter; an unearthly shriek.* —*v.* make a shriek: *She shrieked at the sight of blood; to shriek with delight, pain, terror.*

shrift *n.* [old use] confession or shriving. See SHORT SHRIFT.

shrike *n.* a usu. gray or brownish bird with a shrieking call, noted for its habit of impaling its prey on a thorn with its hooked beak before tearing it apart; also called "butcherbird."

shrill *adj.* **1** of cries and such sounds, high-pitched and sharp, as of a cricket, whistle, etc.: *A voice gets shrill after some shouting; a shrill outburst, scream, voice.* **2** insistent but ineffectual: *their shrill activism, efforts, extremism, opposition.* —*v.* utter with or make such a sound. —**shril.ly** *adv.*; **shrill.ness** *n.*

shrimp *n.* **1** a small shellfish related to crabs and lobsters, valued as sea food. **2** *Informal.* a small insignificant person.

shrine *n.* **1** a place sacred to the memory of a venerated person: *a Shinto shrine; to pray at a shrine; the shrines of rock and roll.* **2** a tomb or a place in which relics are preserved.

shrink *v.* **shrinks**, *pt.* **shrank** or **shrunk**, *pp.* **shrunk** or **shrunk.en, shrink.ing 1** contract in extent, scope, volume, etc., as fabrics when laundered: *shrinking fortunes, influence, inventory; how to shrink wool* (= make it shrink). **2** draw back instinctively *from* something unpleasant or frightening, as a dog from the whip.
—*n. Slang.* a psy- chiatrist, psychotherapist, or psychoanalyst.

shrink.age (SHRINK.ij) *n.* the process of shrinking or its result: *puckering caused by shrinkage of thread; shrinkage in employment, of world markets; Retail shrinkage from employee thefts, shoplifting, accounting errors, etc. amount to nearly 2% of total sales; inventory shrinkage.*

shrinking violet *n.* a shy or timid person.

shrink-wrap *v.* **-wraps, -wrapped, -wrap.ping** wrap and seal goods in plastic film: *shrink-wrap packaging; adj.: a book sold shrink-wrapped together with its tape.*

shrive *v.* **shrives**, *pt.* **shrove** (SHROHV) or **shrived**, *pp.* **shriv.en** or **shrived, shriv.ing** [old use] hear someone's confession, as a priest does.

shriv.el (SHRIV.ul) *v.* **-els, -eled, -el.ing** dry up or wither into a wrinkled state, as a leaf or fruit from the heat of the sun: *The crops shriveled up in the heat wave; adja.: shriveling criticism, remarks.* Also **shriv.elled, shriv.el.ling** *Cdn.*

shroud *n.* **1** a burial cloth for a dead body. **2 shrouds** *pl.* the set of ropes supporting a ship's mast.
—*v.* cover or hide: *The kidnaping is shrouded in mystery.*

shrove a *pt.* of SHRIVE. —**Shrove Tuesday** *n.* the last day before Lent begins.

shrub *n.* a woody-stemmed plant smaller than a tree; bush. —**shrub.by** *adj.*

shrub.ber.y (SHRUB.uh.ree) *n.* **shrub.ber.ies 1** shrubs collectively: *hiding in the shrubbery.* **2** a place planted with shrubs.

shrug *v.* **shrugs, shrugged, shrug.ging** raise the shoulders momentarily to show indifference, doubt, etc.: *She didn't say anything, but shrugged her shoulders; He shrugged at the idea; "I wonder," he shrugged* (= said with a shrug); *He* **shrugged it off** (= dismissed it as unimportant). —*n.* a shrugging gesture: *He dismissed it with a shrug and a smile; a* **gallic shrug** (using one shoulder).

shrunk, shrunken See SHRINK.

shtick *n. Slang.* **1** a comic routine. **2** a gimmicky thing or quality: *his whole artistic shtick.*

shuck *n.* **1** a husk, pod, shell, or similar outer covering. **2** something of little or no value: *not worth shucks.*
—*v.* re- move the shucks or shell: *to shuck corn, oysters, peanuts.* —**shucks** *interj.* ex- pressing impatience or disappoint- ment: *Aw, shucks!*

shud.der (SHUD.ur) *n.* a sudden shaking or trembling of the body from horror, disgust, etc. —*v.* experience a shudder: *I shudder to think what might have happened; I shudder at the thought; It makes me shudder; The world shudders with fear of another war.*

shuf.fle (SHUF.ul) *v.* **shuf.fles, shuf.fled, shuf.fling 1** walk or move in a dragging manner: *He shuffled along; to shuffle* (= drag) *one's feet.* **2** mix and rearrange a deck of cards. **3** disarrange papers, etc. usu. in search of something.
—*n.* a shuffling of cards or a shuffling movement, dance, action, etc.

shuf.fle.board (SHUF.ul.bord) *n.* a game played by pushing disks using a long cue over the scoring areas marked on a narrow, smooth-surfaced court.

shun *v.* **shuns, shunned, shun.ning** avoid a person or thing because of aversion or dislike: *a modest man who shuns publicity; Kay shuns society.*

shunt *v.* move or turn off to one side, as in switching a train from one track to another: *to shunt someone aside or away or off to the sidelines.*
—*n.* a shunting.

shush *interj. & v.* hush!

shut *v.* **shuts, shut, shut.ting** close so as to keep one in or out: *Please shut the door; Blinds shut out light; A factory* **shuts down***; It is shut down by a strike; We were* **shut in** *for several days by the snowstorm; Turn the tap to* **shut off** *the water; Tall buildings shut off our view.*

—**shut up** *Informal* [not polite as "Shut up!"] stop talking: *No one could make the child shut up.*
shut.down *n.* a shutting down of a factory, usu. temporarily.
shut.eye *n. Informal.* sleep: *to catch some shuteye during a break.*
shut-in *n.* one confined indoors by illness.
shut.out *n.* a preventing of the opposite side from scoring: *to score a shutout.*
shut.ter *n.* one that shuts, as a hinged cover for a window or the opening-and-closing device of a camera aperture. —*v.* furnish with a shutter or shutters; *adj.: a shuttered window; shuttered* (= closed) *businesses.*
shut.ter.bug (SHUT.ur.bug) *n.* a photography enthusiast.
shut.tle *v.* **shut.tles, shut.tled, shut.tling** move back and forth over a course, as the needlelike device carrying threads from side to side in a loom or a vehicle carrying passengers back and forth over a route: *The bus shuttles between the city and the suburbs.* —*n.* something designed to shuttle back and forth: *a shuttle plying between the city and the airport; a reusable space shuttle; a* **water shuttle** *transporting people and goods between two islands; adja.: a shuttle bus, crew, flight, launch,* (weaving) *loom, route, service, train.*
shut.tle.cock (SHUT.ul.cock) *n.* a light, feathered object, called "bird" or "birdie," that is hit back and forth in badminton.
shuttle diplomacy *n.* negotiation by diplomats traveling back and forth between countries.
shy *adj.* **shy.er** or **shi.er, shy.est** or **shi.est** reserved or timid in manner; bashful: *He feels a bit shy about posing for a picture; We* **fight shy of** (= try to avoid) *publicity; We are $100* **shy of** (= short of) *the target figure.* —*v.* **shies, shied, shy.ing 1** shrink or draw back, esp. suddenly, as a horse startled by something in its way: *The horse shied at the barking dog; Gina shies away from* (= avoids) *publicity.* **2** fling a stone, stick, etc. sideways at a target. —**shy.ly** *adv.;* **shy.ness** *n.*
shy.lock *n.* a hardhearted moneylender.
shy.ster (SHY.stur) *n. Informal.* a professional, esp. a lawyer, who uses tricky methods.
Si.a.mese twins (sye.uh.MEEZ-) *n.pl.* twins born joined together.
Si.ber.i.an (sye.BEER.ee.un) *n. & adj.* (a person) of or from **Siberia,** the cold and isolated N. Asian part of Russia.

sib.i.lant (SIB.uh.lunt) *n.* a sound such as *s, sh, z,* or *zh* that has a hissing quality; *adj.: a sibilant murmur, protest, whoosh.*
sib.ling *n.* a fellow offspring; brother or sister; *adja.: sibling jokes, love, rivalry, rivals.*
sib.yl (SIB.ul) *n.* a prophetess of the ancient Greeks and Romans; **sib.yl.line** (-line, -leen) *adj.*
sic 1 *adv. Latin.* thus [used within square brackets to confirm that something that seems questionable, as a spelling error, is faithfully reproduced]. **2** *v.* **sics, sicked, sick.ing** incite a dog to attack: *She sicked Tiger on(to) the burglar; Sic* (= attack) *him, Tiger!*
Si.cil.ian (si.SIL.yun) *n. & adj.* (a person) of or from **Sicily,** an island off the S. tip of Italy.
sick *adj.* suffering from something bodily or mental: *You look sick; She's worried sick about her child; sick at heart; sick at* or *to one's stomach* (= nauseated); *a sick* (= morbid or macabre) *joke; He's sick* (= longing) *for home; a sick* (= migraine) *headache; She is* **sick and tired of** (= quite fed up with) *eating in restau- rants; Nurses care for* **the sick** (people). —**sick.ish** *adj.*
sick bay *n.* part of a ship or clinic used as a hospital.
sicked, sicking See SIC.
sick.en (SICK.un) *v.* make or become sick: *It sickens one to watch the fighting going on in families; The child sickened and died; adj.: a sickening experience; It was quite sickening to watch; a sickening stench;* **sick.en.ing.ly** *adv.*
sick.ie (SICK.ee) *n.* **-ies** *Informal.* one who behaves in a queer or perverted manner.
sick.le (SICK.ul) *n.* a short-handled tool with a curved blade for mowing grass and grain.
sickle-cell anemia *n.* a hereditary blood disorder found in people of African origin in which red blood cells change to a sickle shape.
sick.ly *adj.* **-li.er, -li.est 1** having to do with sickness: *a sickly complexion.* **2** frequently sick: *a sickly child.*
sick.ness (SICK.nis) *n.* **1** illness: *"in sickness and in health, till death do us part."* **2** a particular disease: *radiation sickness; sleeping sickness; Both morning sickness and motion sickness cause nausea.*
sick-out *n.* the labor tactic of claiming illness as a group, esp. when unable to strike.
sick.room *n.* a sick person's room.

side *n.* **1** a boundary surface or line, away from the center, esp. of something considered as not having a front or back: *the four sides of a square; the north, east, south, and west sides of a building; the two sides of a street; the debit and credit sides of a ledger; on a mountain side; the sunny side of a house; Opposition came from all sides.* **2** the left or right of something considered as having a front, back, etc.: *the passenger side of a car; a driver-side airbag; two people seated* **side by side** (= next to each other); *the* **side door** or **side entrance** *of a house; a* **side of beef** (= lengthwise half of a carcass); *She* **split her sides** *laughing* (= laughed uproariously). **3** a group or party in relation to another: *the opposing sides of a dispute; the losing and winning sides; the sales side* (= department) *of the business; Referees shouldn't take sides* (= favor either side). **4** either surface of something flat or considered as having only two sides: *the reverse and obverse sides of a coin; the dark side of the moon; the windward side of the island; There are two sides to every question; to see the humorous side* (= aspect) *of an issue; Let's look* **on the bright side.** —**on the side** in addition to the regular or main thing. —*adj.:* *a side* (= not main) *deal, dish, issue, street; a side* (= not front) *view.* —*v.* **sides, sid.ed, sid.ing** take a side: *Dad naturally sides with* (= favors) *Mom in family arguments; Tim usually sides against* (= opposes) *his sister.*

side arm *n.* a sword, pistol, or other weapon worn at the waist. —**side.arm** *adj. & adv.* of a throw or stroke, not overhand or underhand but made with the arm relatively parallel to the ground.

side.bar *n.* **1** a magazine story or article that throws a sidelight on a main feature. **2** a brief conference between judge and lawyers out of the jury's hearing.

side.board *n.* a low cabinet that holds dining accessories, its top being used as a side table.

side.burns *n.pl.* hair grown down the sides of a man's face.

side.car *n.* a small car attached to the side of a motorcycle.

side dish *n.* a dish of food served along with the main course.

side effect *n.* a usu. adverse secondary effect or reaction, esp. of a drug.

side.kick *n.* a pal or partner.

side.light *n.* an incidental bit of information that helps to understand a subject or character.

side.line *n.* **1** a business carried on in addition to one's main business or job. **2** the side boundary of a playing field or court: *to watch from the sidelines; to sit on the sidelines and cheer.* **3** an inactive state: *a player on the sidelines; an issue relegated to the sidelines.* —*v.* **-lines, -lined, -lin.ing** put out of action, as a player.

side.long *adj.* directed to one side: *a sidelong glance.*

side.man (SIDE.man, -mun) *n.* **-men** a supporting player, esp. in a jazz band.

side.piece *n.* a piece that forms the side of something.

si.de.re.al (sye.DEER.ee.ul) *adj.* having to do with the stars: *Astronomers use* **sidereal time** *based on the earth's rotation in reference to the stars.*

side.sad.dle (SIDE.sad.ul) *n. & adv.* (a saddle designed to be used) with both legs of the rider on the same side of the animal.

side.show *n.* a small show, as of a circus, that is not part of the main show.

side.split.ting (SIDE.split.ing) *adj.* extremely funny: *a sidesplitting comedy, joke, story.*

side.step *v.* **-steps, -stepped, -step.ping** **1** step aside. **2** dodge or avoid a blow, responsibility, etc. by stepping aside: *to sidestep an issue.*

side.stroke *n.* a swimming stroke executed on the side in combination with a scissors kick.

side.swipe *v.* **-swipes, -swiped, -swip.ing** give a glancing blow or hit: *A car sideswiped her at a crossing; n.: She gave him a few sideswipes during the melee.*

side.track *v.* **1** switch a train to a railroad siding; *n.* such a siding. **2** distract someone or turn aside from the main issue.

side.walk *n.* a usu. paved walkway at the side of a street: *A* **sidewalk artist** *paints on sidewalks.*

side.wall *n.* the side of a tire.

side.ways *adj. & adv.* **1** to or from a side: *She avoids snoring by sleeping sideways; a sideways access, escape, glance, look, movement.* **2** with a side forward: *Before dieting, Sam could only make it through the door sideways; a sideways move.* Also **side.wise.**

side.wind.er (SIDE.wine.dur) *n.* a rattlesnake of S.W. United States and Mexico that moves with sideways loops.

sid.ing (SYE.ding) *n.* **1** boards or shingles covering the outside of a frame house: *aluminum, cedar, steel, vinyl* sidings; *a siding that looks like wood.* **2** a short railroad track branching from a main one.

si.dle (SYE.dul) *v.* **-dles, -dled, -dling** move sideways in a shy or furtive manner: *The child sidled up to her mom and whispered in her ear.*

siege (SEEJ) *n.* **1** a surrounding of a place, as a fortress, to force a surrender: *a city under siege* or *in a state of siege; The mob* **laid siege to** *City Hall; The siege was lifted* or *raised after a few days.* **2** the condition of being threatened (as if) from all sides, as by an enemy: *The company is going through a siege of financial problems; Luc has come out of a long siege of* or *with cancer; the* **siege mentality** *of people who consider themselves besieged.*

si.er.ra (see.ER.uh) *n.* a range of mountains with a jagged outline of peaks.

si.es.ta (see.ES.tuh) *n.* a midday nap.

sieve (SIV) *n.* a utensil with holes for straining out the large particles of a mixture or the solid parts of a liquid.

sift *v.* **1** pass through a sieve: *to sift flour.* **2** examine carefully: *to sift evidence; He sifted through the debris looking for the ring.* **3** separate: *to sift fact from fiction.* —**sift.er** *n.*

sigh (SYE) *n.* a long, deep breathing sound, as in relief, sadness, etc.: *to breathe* or *heave a sigh of relief.*
—*v.* make a sigh: *She sighed in pain; a mother sighing* (= yearning) *for her missing child.*

sight (SITE) *n.* **1** the act, power, or range of seeing: *an eagle with keen sight; She lost her sight in an accident; Kay cannot stand the sight of blood; We had* **caught sight of** *him* (= seen him for a moment); *but* **lost sight of** (= were no longer able to see) *him in the crowd; He was* **out of sight** *in no time; "Out of sight, out of mind"* (= We tend to forget people and things we don't see for some time); *Soon we were* **within sight of** (= able to see) *the city; Our goal seemed* **within sight** (= near). **2** something seen: *familiar, horrible, lovely, sorry, ugly sights; to take in* or *see the (interesting) sights of a city; He's quite* **a sight** (= looks odd) *in that hat.* **3** a seeing device: *a telescopic sight; A marksman adjusts his sights;* **takes a sight** (= takes aim) *before firing; She has her* **sights** (= aspirations) *set on a Ph.D.* **4** *Informal.* a good deal: *Now things are a damn sight better; not by a darn sight.*
—**at** or **on sight** as soon as seen: *orders to shoot on sight; love* **at first sight.**
—**know by sight** be able to recognize upon seeing. —**sight unseen** without seeing in advance: *We bought the house sight unseen.* —*v.* see or take aim, esp. by use of a seeing device. —**sight.ing** *n.: reported UFO sightings.*

sight.ed *adj. & comb.form.* having sight or as specified: *Is she sighted or blind? a sighted firearm (that has a sight attached); clear-sighted, farsighted, shortsighted.*
—**sight.less** *adj.* blind.

sight.ly *adj.* **-li.er, -li.est** pleasant-looking; not ugly; **sight.li.ness** *n.*

sight reading *n.* the skill of performing written music, of reading something in a foreign language, etc. without previous preparation. —**sight-read** *v.* **-reads, -read** (-red), **-read.ing.**

sight.see.ing (SITE.see.ing) *n.* the visiting of places of interest, as a tourist or visitor: *Let's go sightseeing;* **adj***.: a sightseeing day, spot, stop, tour.*
—**sight.see** *v.: off to town to sightsee and shop; to sightsee the city;* **sight.see.er** *n.*

sig.ma (SIG.muh) *n.* the 18th letter of the Greek alphabet (Σ, σ, ς).

sign (SINE) *n.* **1** a mark, symbol, gesture, etc. that stands for or means something: *a dollar sign; the multiplication sign; the signs of the zodiac; the* **sign language** *of deaf-mutes.* **2** a marker bearing a sign: *a "No trespassing" sign; traffic signs; to post* or **put up** or **set up** *a sign; The sign says the house is sold.* **3** evidence or indication: *Breathing is a sign of life; the body's vital signs; signs of forced entry into a home; encouraging, sure, telltale, unmistakable signs.*
—*v.* **1** write one's name or signature on a document: *to sign a contract; Sign on the dotted line.* **2** agree legally to something: *Some authors* **sign away** *their rights in return for small payments.*
—**sign on** or **up 1** enlist: *We signed on 25 volunteers today; Lots of people want to sign up.* **2** start broadcasting: *TV and radio stations* **sign on** *in the morning and* **sign off** (= stop broadcasting) *at the end of the day.* —**sign.er** *n.*

sig.nal (SIG.nul) *n.* **1** a sign with an agreed-on meaning, used to warn, inform, etc.: *red, green, and amber traffic signals; the turn signals of an automobile; smoke signals; "SOS" and "Mayday" are distress signals; to flash, give, pick up, send signals; The attack began on* or *at a signal from the captain.* **2** an electrical or electromagnetic transmission that conveys a message, as in telegraphy, radio, and TV. —*v.* **-nals, -naled, -nal.ing 1** give warning, notice, etc. to someone by a signal or signals: *The Titanic signaled for help to other ships; A*

siren signals the end of an emergency. **2** communicate: *to signal one's intentions, interest; They signaled to the crowd that the siege was over.* —**sig.nal.er** *n.*
—*adj*a. remarkable or notable: *a signal achievement, defeat, discovery.*
—**sig.nal.ly** *adv.* Also **sig.nalled, sig.nal.ling; sig.nal.ler** *Cdn.*
sig.nal.ize (SIG.nuh.lize) *v.* **-iz.es, -ized, -iz.ing** make remarkable or distinguished: *a year signalized by conquests in space.* —**sig.nal.i.za.tion** (-luh.ZAY.shun, -lye-) *n.*
sig.nal.man (SIG.nul.mun, -man) *n.* **-men** one who signals or works with signals in the army or on a railroad.
sig.na.to.ry (SIG.nuh.tor.ee) *n.* **-ries** one who has signed a document together with others: *a signatory to the Geneva Convention; signatories of the agreement; fellow signatories;* **adj**a.: *signatory companies, members, states.*
sig.na.ture (SIG.nuh.chur) *n.* **1** an identifying mark, esp. one's name written by oneself: *to affix* or *attach one's signature to* or *put one's signature on a document; to forge someone's signature; clothes carrying the Gucci signature* (= logo). **2** a musical sign placed after the clef to indicate the key (as ♭) or the time (as ¾). **3** in broadcasting, a musical or visual device used to identify a program, performer, etc.
—*adj.* **1** identifying: *signature graphics, sequences;* the **signature panel** *on a credit card.* **2** carrying a maker's logo; hence, distinctive: *a fashion house's signature collection; their signature line (of goods); signature fragrances, handbags, items; a signature look.*
sign.board *n.* a board displaying a notice, sign, etc.
sig.net (SIG.nit) *n.* a small seal, as on a **signet ring** worn on a finger.
sig.nif.i.cance (sig.NIF.uh.cunce) *n.* what is signified, esp. meaning in regard to its suggestiveness, importance, etc.: *a message that had a special significance for us; an event that was of great significance to his career.*
sig.nif.i.cant (sig.NIF.uh.kunt) *adj.* **1** having a special meaning: *a significant wink; It was significant that his family did not attend the wedding.* **2** important: *the significant events of last year;* one's **significant other** (= person with a special role in one's life, esp. a spouse). —**sig.nif.i.cant.ly** *adv.*
sig.ni.fy (SIG.nuh.fye) *v.* **-fies, -fied, -fy.ing 1** be a sign of something; mean: *A nod signifies assent; "sound and fury signifying nothing"; Bells signified*

the end of the war. **2** show by means of a sign: *She signified her willingness* or *that she was willing by nodding.*
—**sig.ni.fi.ca.tion** (-fuh.CAY.shun) *n.*
sign of the cross *n.* a cross traced on one's person with the hand or fingers: *to make the sign of the cross (on oneself by touching the forehead, chest, and shoulders).*
sign of the zodiac *n.* any of the 12 equal parts into which the zodiac is divided, each bearing the name of a constellation.
si.gnor (seen.YOR) *n., pl.* **-gno.ri** (-YOR.ee) *Italian.* a gentleman; [as a title] Mr.
si.gno.ra (seen.YOR.ah) *n., pl.* **-re** (-ay) *Italian.* a married woman; [as a title] Mrs. or Madam.
si.gno.re (seen.YOR.ay) *n., pl.* **-ri** (-ee) *Italian.* a gentleman; [as a title in direct address] Sir.
si.gno.ri.na (seen.yuh.REE.nuh) *n., pl.* **-ne** (-nay) *Italian.* a young lady; [as a title] Miss.
sign.post *n.* a post having a sign on it.
Sikh (SEEK) *n. & adj.* (a member) of a religion of India combining Hindu and Moslem elements, founded by Guru Nanak (1469-1538); **Sikh.ism** *n.*
si.lage (SYE.lij) *n.* slightly fermented green fodder preserved in a silo.
si.lence (SYE.lunce) *n.* stillness or quiet; hence, absence of any sound or communication: *Silence reigned throughout the night; to break the silence of the night; to impose, keep, maintain, observe silence; an awkward, complete, eerie, ominous, perfect, stony, stunned, total, utter silence; They were reduced to silence; departed in silence; "Silence gives consent";* **silence money** (paid to prevent someone from talking). —*interj.* Quiet! —*v.* **-lenc.es, -lenced, -lenc.ing 1** make silent: *The teacher silences the class with a stern look; to silence the enemy guns* (= stop them firing). **2** repress: *to silence free speech.*
—**si.lenc.er** *n.* a sound-deadening device, as used with a firearm: *airbrake, exhaust, gun silencers.*
si.lent (SYE.lunt) *adj.* **1** still or quiet: *the silent atmosphere of a library; to keep* or *remain silent during a ceremony; a moment of silent prayer; the silent night.*
2 not talkative or heard: *Sam is the strong, silent type (of person); the silent* (= not pronounced) *"b" of "bomb" and "n" of "hymn";* the **silent majority** of people not actively involved in politics.
—**si.lent.ly** *adv.*
silent partner *n.* one who helps finance a business without actively helping to

run it.
sil.hou.ette (sil.oo.ET) *n*. a solid outline, as of something seen against a light: *a profile in silhouette* (= in solid black on white background or the reverse).
—*v*. **-ettes, -et.ted, -et.ting** show in silhouette: *a building silhouetted against the night sky.*
sil.i.ca (SIL.i.cuh) *n*. silicon dioxide occurring as quartz and other minerals and forming about 60% of the earth's crust.; *adja*.: *silica ash, fiber, fume.*
sil.i.cate (SIL.i.cate, -kit) *n*. a mineral such as mica, asbestos, or feldspar that is a compound of silicon, oxygen, and a metal.
si.li.ceous (suh.LISH.us) *adj*. silica-containing: *siliceous shale.*
sil.i.con (SIL.i.con) *n*. a nonmetallic chemical element found in granite, sand, clay, etc. and used for making integrated electronic circuits called "silicon chips."
sil.i.cone (SIL.i.cone) *n*. an organic silicon compound much used commercially in the form of fluids, resins, and varnishes; *adja*.: *silicone rubber; silicone gel breast implants.*
silicon valley *n*. a region with a concentration of high-technology industries, as the Santa Clara valley of California.
sil.i.co.sis (sil.i.COH.sis) *n*. a lung disease caused by prolonged inhaling of silica dust.
silk *n*. **1** a strong, shiny fiber produced by caterpillars, or **silkworms**, for cocoons: *They spin silk.* **2** the thread or fabric made from it: *a shirt made of fine silk;* *adja*.: *a silk hat, stocking, tie.*
silk.en (SIL.kun) *adj*. **1** made of silk: *silken cushions, pillows, sheers, strands, threads.* **2** smooth like silk: *silken cajolery, eloquence, voices.*
silk screen *n*. a method of printing with stencils of silk or similar material; also **silk-screen** *v*.
silk-stocking *adja*. wealthy: *a silk-stocking crowd, district, society.*
silk.worm See SILK.
silk.y *adj*. **silk.i.er, -i.est** resembling silk: *silky fabrics, hair, texture; a silky finish, sheen, tone, touch; a baby's silky soft skin; a silky-smooth (engine) performance, salad dressing, voice.*
sill *n*. a horizontal supporting part or structure, as the base of a door or window frame: *She sat on the window sill waiting for Tim.*
sil.ly (SIL.ee) *adj*. **sil.li.er, sil.li.est** lacking in common sense or judgment; stupid or trivial: *Don't be silly; What a silly idea! a silly remark; It sounds silly;* behavior that makes one look silly; *the political silly season* (= season of little news) *when the legislature is not in session.* —**sil.ly** or **sil.li.ly** *adv*.
—**sil.li.ness** *n*.
si.lo (SYE.loh) *n*. **-los 1** a usu. upright cylindrical tower for storing green fodder; also, a trench, bunker, or box for the same purpose. **2** an underground installation for launching guided missiles.
silt *n*. fine-grained waterborne sediment, as at the bottom of rivers: *silt deposits.* —*v*. obstruct or fill up with silt. —**silt.a.tion** (-TAY.shun) *n*.
—**silt.y** *adj*.: *silty sand.*
silt.stone *n*. silt hardened as rock.
Si.lu.ri.an (si.LOOR.ee.un) *n. & adj*. (of) the third period of the Paleozoic era of the earth, beginning about 425 million years ago: *the Silurian age, period; Silurian rocks.*
sil.ver (SIL.vur) *n*. **1** a white precious metal used for coins, jewelry, and table utensils, esp. spoons and dishes; *adja. & cpd*: *silver leaf, plate, platters; a silver anniversary* (= 25th year); *"born with a silver spoon in his mouth"* (= born wealthy); *a silver-haired gentleman; a silver-tongued* (= eloquent) *orator.*
2 money or tableware of silver.
3 a lustrous grayish white.
silver bromide, silver chloride, silver iodide, silver nitrate *n*. light-sensitive silver compounds used in photography.
sil.ver.fish (SIL.vur.fish) *n*. a small, silver-colored, wingless insect that eats materials containing starch or glue.
silver lining *n*. the brighter side of an otherwise depressing situation: *"Every cloud has a silver lining."*
silver maple *n*. a North American maple whose leaves are silvery white underneath.
sil.ver.smith (SIL.vur.smith) *n*. a craftsman of silver articles.
sil.ver.ware (SIL.vur.ware) *n*. silver or metal tableware.
sil.ver.y (SIL.vuh.ree) *adj*. **1** like silver in color: *a silvery gray, luster, metal, sheen; silvery hair, scales.* **2** having a clear ringing voice: *a silvery soprano, voice.*
sim.i.an (SIM.ee.un) *n. & adj*. (of) an ape or monkey: *simian ancestors.*
sim.i.lar (SIM.uh.lur) *adj*. nearly alike; of the same kind: *Twins are naturally quite similar to each other; They wear similar shoes; Identical twins are strikingly similar; similar in most respects.*
—**sim.i.lar.ly** *adv*.

sim.i.lar.i.ty (sim.uh.LAIR.i.tee) *n.* **-ties** (a point of) likeness: *One bears a striking similarity to the other; the similarity between the twins; the similarities among family members.*

sim.i.le (SIM.uh.lee) *n.* a figure of speech expressing a comparison using "like" or "as"; e.g. "tears flowing like a river"; "as good as gold."

si.mil.i.tude (suh.MIL.uh.tude) *n.* **1** resemblance. **2** a comparison.

sim.mer (SIM.ur) *v.* **1** keep or remain just below the boiling point: *Turn down the heat to low and let the stew simmer for one hour.* **2** be on the point of breaking out, as with anger, laughter, etc.: *A riot is simmering.* —**simmer down 1** calm down. **2** get reduced, as by simmering: *the simmering down of the gold market.* —*n.* a simmering: *Slowly bring it to a simmer; Keep it at a low simmer between 54° and 57°C.*

si.mo.nize (SYE.muh.nize) *v.* **-niz.es, -nized, -niz.ing** clean and polish a surface with wax.

si.mon-pure (SYE.mun.pure) *adj.* unquestionably authentic or untainted; genuine.

si.mo.ny (SYE.muh.nee, SIM.uh-) *n.* the buying or selling of spiritual things, esp. church appointments.

sim.pa.ti.co (sim.PAH.tic.oh) *adj.* congenial or well-disposed.

sim.per (SIM.pur) *n.* a silly or affected smile. —*v.* smirk.

sim.ple (SIM.pul) *adj.* **-pler, -plest 1** not complicated; having few parts, frills, etc.: *as easy or simple as ABC; Oxygen is a simple substance but water is a compound; simple clothes, food, jobs, truths; a simple* (= elementary) *fact of everyday life; in simple* (= plain) *English;* ***Simple interest*** *is based on the principal amount, unlike compound interest; A* ***simple sentence*** *has one main clause.* **2** of people, unaffected, sincere, or innocent: *a simple child, soul; not so simple* (= inexperienced) *as to believe everything she hears.* **3** common or lowly: *simple peasant folk.*

simple-minded *adj.* inexperienced or stupid

sim.ple.ton (SIM.pul.tun) *n.* a fool.

sim.plic.i.ty (sim.PLIS.i.tee) *n.* **-ties** the state of being simple: *a manner full of simplicity and candor; the simplicity of her costume; The explanation is simplicity itself.*

sim.pli.fy (SIM.pluh.fye) *v.* **-fies, -fied, -fy.ing** make simple or simpler.
—**sim.pli.fi.ca.tion** (-fuh.CAY.shun) *n.*

sim.plis.tic (sim.PLIS.tic) *adj.* excessively simple; oversimplified: *a simplistic explanation, theory; a simplistic and almost naive solution.* —**sim.plis.ti.cal.ly** *adv.*

sim.ply (SIM.plee) *adv.* **1** in a simple manner: *Sam came simply dressed; Simply put, we are broke.* **2** absolutely: *It's simply wonderful! simply not true.* **3** merely: *Do something instead of simply crying.*

sim.u.late (SIM.yuh.late) *v.* **-lates, -lat.ed, -lat.ing** look or act like having or being something that one is not: *He lay still, simulating death.* —**simulated** *adj.* not real or actual, but imitated: *a simulated car crash, karate kick, leather, moon landing.*
—**sim.u.la.tion** (-LAY.shun) *n.*
—**sim.u.la.tor** (-lay.tur) *n.*

si.mul.cast (SYE.mul.cast) *v.* **-casts,** *pt. & pp.* **-cast** or **-cast.ed, -cast.ing** broadcast simultaneously, as over radio and TV or an American TV show at the same time on a Canadian station. —*n.* such a transmission.

si.mul.ta.ne.ous (sye.mul.TAY.nee.us) *adj.* done or happening at the same time: *events simultaneous with each other.*
—**si.mul.ta.ne.ous.ly** *adv.*

sin *n.* **1** an offense against God, as by breaking a religious or moral law: *In case you didn't know, murder is a crime and a sin; to commit, expiate a sin; to forgive one's sins; deadly, mortal, original, unforgivable, unpardonable, venial sins; to live* **in sin** (= in adultery) *with various lovers.* **2** something immoral or offensive: *It's a sin to waste food; It's a sin that food is being wasted; a sin against society.* —*v.* **sins, sinned, sin.ning** commit sin: *I have sinned against Thee.*
—**sin.ful** *adj.;* **sin.ful.ly** *adv.;*
sin.ful.ness *n.* —**sin.ner** *n.*

since *adv.* from the time mentioned or implied till now: *They fought once but have been friends ever since.* —*prep.:* *It's six years since the last flood; She has been working since leaving school.*
—*conj.:* *We've had no trouble since* (= from the time) *we came to this city; He left early since* (= because) *he didn't want to be late.*

sin.cere (sin.SEER) *adj.* **-cer.er, -cer.est** of people or their feelings, desires, etc., without deceit; genuine: *a sincere friend; my sincerest sympathy.*
—**sin.cere.ly** *adv.* —**sin.cer.i.ty** (-SER.i.tee) *n.: No one doubts his sincerity; He said it in all sincerity.*

si.ne.cure (SYE.nuh.cure, SIN.uh-) *n.* a position that provides an income without much work or responsibility.

si.ne di.e (SYE.nee.DYE.ee) *adv.*

without a further date being fixed: *The meeting adjourned sine die.*

sine qua non (SYE.nee.quay.NON) *n.* an essential condition or prerequisite: *Passing final exams is a sine qua non of graduating.*

sin.ew (SIN.yoo) *n.* **1** a tendon: *straining every muscle and sinew; the sinews of his being.* **2** muscular power: *a style that shows sinew and drive; the bone and sinew of the organization.*

sin.ew.y (SIN.yoo.ee) *adj.* **1** strong or muscular: *a sinewy body, man; sinewy muscles, shoulders, strength.* **2** showing vigor: *a sinewy performance; sinewy prose.*

sing *v.* **sings,** *pt.* **sang** or **sung,** *pp.* **sung, sing.ing** make pleasant sounds with the voice; utter or tell something musically, in verse, etc.: *to sing a song; He sings to his mother while she sews; sings with joy; Birds sing in the trees; She sang her child to sleep; Parents sing the praises of their children; The poet sings of love; while bullets sang* (= whistled) *past us; He disappeared before he could sing* (*Informal* for squeal; tell the police). —**sing.er** *n.*

singe (SINJ) *v.* **sing.es, singed, singe.ing 1** scorch or burn superficially. **2** burn hair, feathers, etc. off a body: *to singe a chicken.* —*n.* a slight burn.

sin.gle (SING.gul) *adj.* one only; not combined or associated with another: *He refused without a single reason; Tom and Jerry in single combat; Bachelors are single men, not married; single women; the single state of bachelorhood; a single* (= not double) *bed; her single* (= without duplicity) *devotion, heart; a single* (= spouseless) *father, mother, parent; a* **single-parent** *family, home, household.* —*n.* **1** a single person or thing, as a record with one piece of music on either side, not an album. **2 singles** *pl.* a match with one player on either side. **3** a baseball hit that allows the batter to reach first base only. —*v.* **-gles, -gled, -gling 1** select someone out of a group: *He was singled out for special treatment.* **2** in baseball, hit a single.

single-breasted *adj.* of coats, jackets, etc., not double-breasted.

single file *n.* a line or column of persons or things coming one behind another: *We marched in single file.* —*adv.:* *to march single file.*

single-handed *adj.* involving or using only one hand or person: *a single-handed farm operation;* **adv.:** *She raised her children single-handed.* —**single-handedly** *adv.*

single-minded *adj.* **1** having only one aim: *a single-minded eccentric bent on changing the world; the single-minded pursuit of wealth; a single-minded attempt, crusade, goal, purpose, vision.* **2** dedicated: *a single-minded husband and father; her passionate and single-minded devotion to the cause.*

singles bar *n.* a bar patronized by unmarried people.

sin.gle.ton (SING.gul.tun) *n.* something occurring alone, as a single card of a suit in a player's hand.

single-track *adj.* one-track: *a single-track mind; a single-track system* (*that offers no alternatives*).

sin.gle.tree (SING.gul.tree) *n.* the crossbar to which the traces of a harness are attached.

sin.gly (SING.glee) *adv.* individually; alone.

sing.song *n.* an unvarying speech rhythm or tone; **adja.:** *in a singsong tone, voice.*

sin.gu.lar (SING.gyuh.lur) *adj.* **1** standing apart from others because strange, extraordinary, unique, etc.: *a woman of singular charm; his singular ability; shines with singular clarity; a singular approach, genius, gift, lack of support, moment, point of view.* **2** in grammar, referring to one person: *"Deer" is singular and plural;* **n.:** *"Deer" may be used in the singular or in the plural.* —**sin.gu.lar.ly** *adv.* —**sin.gu.lar.i.ty** (-LAIR.i.tee) *n.*

sin.is.ter (SIN.is.tur) *adj.* suggestive of ill will, threatening evil or danger, etc.: *a sinister appearance, look, motive, plot, smile.*

sink *v.* **sinks,** *pt.* **sank** or **sunk,** *pp.* **sunk, sink.ing** (make) go down or lower, as under water: *to swim or float without sinking; The boat sprang a leak and sank; It sank to the bottom; It was not sunk by torpedoes; The sun sinks in the west; It sinks below the horizon; Too tired to stand up, he sank into the chair; Her heart sank when she heard the sad news; an example so telling it sank into our minds;* **adja.:** *a sinking ship; the country's sinking economy; her sinking fortunes; his sinking heart; a* **sinking feeling** *of loss or apprehension.* —*n.* **1** a basin with a drain leading from it: *the bathroom sink; a double sink in the kitchen.* **2** a drain or sewer; hence, a place of filth or corruption. **3** a sunken land area in which water collects. **4** a sinkhole.

sink.er *n.* one that sinks or a weight for sinking: *a sinker for a fishing line.*

sink.hole *n.* **1** a depression in a limestone or karst region through which

water enters the ground: *houses collapsing into sinkholes.* **2** a situation that results in loss of one's resources: *an investment that proved a sinkhole.*
sinking fund *n.* a fund accumulated for the paying off of a usu. public debt.
Si.no- (SYE.noh, SIN.oh) *comb.form.* Chinese: *Sino-Russian, Sino-Tibetan.*
sin.u.ous (SIN.yoo.us) *adj.* smoothly curved: *sinuous curves, folds, lines; a sinuous figure;* **sin.u.ous.ly** *adv.* —**sin.u.os.i.ty** (-yoo.OS.i.tee) *n.*
si.nus (SYE.nus) *n.* a curved hollow or cavity, esp. any of the four groups of hollows in the skull that are connected to the nasal cavity.
si.nus.i.tis (sye.nuh.SYE.tis) *n.* inflammation of the sinuses, as during a head cold or because of allergies.
Sioux (SOO) same as DAKOTA; **Siou.an** (SOO.un) *adj.*
sip *v.* **sips, sipped, sip.ping** drink little by little from a container. —*n.* a sipping or a sipped amount: *Take a sip of this syrup.* —**sip.per** *n.*
si.phon (SYE.fun) *n.* a bent-tube device through which a liquid may be drawn up by air pressure and down over a barrier. —*v.*: *Gasoline was siphoned* (= drawn) *out of the gas tank; business siphoned off by competitors.*
sir *n.* **1** [a formal term used to address a man, usu. in respect, *pl.* **gentlemen** or **sirs**]: *Dear Sir; Your name, sir? Your names, gentlemen? Sir, you're under arrest!* **2** [used for emphasis, sometimes without reference to sex of person being addressed, with "sir" stressed] *No, sir! Yes, sir!* **3** [as a title] *Sir John Smith; Sir John.*
sire *n.* **1** [old use] forefather; [as a title of respect] Lord. **2** the male parent of an animal. —*v.* **sires, sired, sir.ing** beget: *a racehorse sired from good stock.*
siree same as SIRREE.
si.ren (SYE.run) *n.* **1** a device for producing a wailing sound signal, usu. in warning, as on a fire truck or ambulance: *Sirens go off* or *ring, sound, wail, are sounded* or *turned on; air-raid sirens.* **2** in Greek myth, a sea nymph who would lure sailors to their destruction with her enchanting song. **3** an enchantress: *a Hollywood siren;* **adj.**: *Who can resist her sultry siren call? sexy siren dresses; siren gowns in velvet; singing the siren song of profitability.*
sir.loin *n.* a choice cut of beef from the loin in front of the rump; **adj.**: *a sirloin cut, steak; sirloin chops.*
si.roc.co (suh.ROC.oh) *n.* **si.roc.cos** a hot desert wind blowing from N. Africa across the Mediterranean into S. Italy.
sir.ree or **sir.ee** (suh.REE) *interj.* [meaning "Sir" used after "Yes" or "No" for emphasis]: *Yes sirree!*
sir.up (SEER.up, SUR.up) same as SYRUP.
sis *n. Informal* [used as a form of address in speech] sister: *Hi, sis!*
si.sal (SYE.sul) *n.* a strong fiber produced by two agave plants with sword-like leaves.
sis.si.fied (SIS.uh.fide) *adj. Informal.* like or for a sissy: *I don't drink such sissified stuff.*
sis.sy (SIS.ee) *n.* **sis.sies** *Informal.* an effeminate or timid boy or man.
sis.ter (SIS.tur) *n.* **1** a female offspring of the same parents as oneself: *one's big, kid, little, older, twin, younger sisters.* **2** a half sister, a female fellow-member of a closely knit group, etc. **3** a nun; also, a nurse: *a lay sister (not a religious).* —**sis.ter.hood** *n.* —**sis.ter.ly** *adj.*
sister-in-law *n.* **sisters-in-law 1** a sister of one's spouse. **2** the wife of one's spouse's brother. **3** the wife of one's brother.
Sis.y.phus (SIS.uh.fus) *n.* in Greek myth, a king of Corinth condemned in Hades to roll a heavy stone up a steep hill forever. —**Sis.y.phe.an** (-FEE.un) *adj.*: *Sisyphean labour, tasks.*
sit *v.* **sits, sat, sit.ting 1** rest on one's buttocks, as on a chair, in a stable or relaxed condition: *too busy to sit down for meals; to sit still without moving; She sits* (= baby-sits) *for busy parents; He sat* (= seated) *the young rider on the horse.* **2** occupy a place or remain in a position: *People sit on committees; a book sitting on a shelf; The court sits* (= is in session) *all day; A hen sits on eggs* (to hatch them); *I sit* (= pose) *for a portrait; You sit for* (= take) *an exam; The coat doesn't sit well on* (= suit) *him.* —**sit down** to get busy with something: *to sit down to a long discussion.* —**sit on** fail to act on something: *They sat on our application for three months and then turned it down.* —**sit on one's hands** refuse to get involved: *He sat on his hands and watched them lose.* —**sit on the fence** stay uncommitted or undecided. —**sit out** take no part in something going on: *He sat out the whole dance.* —**sit through** stay till the end of something: *We sat through the whole six-hour movie.* —**sit tight** stay in the same place or position: *Sit tight while you have a job.* —**sit up** be alert or

awake: *to sit up late and study; to sit up with a patient; to* **sit up and take notice** (= become more aware). —**sit well with** be agreeable to someone: *The decision didn't sit well with him.*

si.tar (si.TAR) *n.* a lutelike instrument of India with six or seven strings on movable frets and up to 20 sympathetic strings that are not plucked.

sit.com *n. Informal.* situation comedy.

sit-down *n.* a strike or demonstration in which the participants occupy a place till their demands are met; also **sit-down strike.**

site *n.* the location of an activity, structure, etc.: *building, burial, camping, construction, murder, polling sites; the site of a disaster; Bones were found at the site; There used to be a temple on this site.* —**on site** at the specified site: *with reporters already on site.*

sit-in *n.* a sit-down in a public place: *to hold, organize, stage a sit-in.*

sit.ter *n.* **1** one who sits: *the sitter who posed for the Mona Lisa; Fast-food places have fewer sitters than restaurants.* **2** a minder: *baby-sitters; a house sitter; pet sitters; A neighbor acts as our plant sitter when we go away on vacation.*

sitting *n.* a session: *the sittings of a court; weeks of portrait sittings; all-night sittings of a committee.*

sitting duck *n. Informal.* an easy target or victim: *Drunks are sitting ducks for muggers.*

sit.u.ate (SICH.oo.ate) *v.* **-ates, -at.ed, -at.ing** put in a place; locate: *where to situate a new facility; photographers trying to situate themselves at vantage points.*

situated *adjp.* **1** located: *a business situated in the suburbs; a property situated on Lake Jackson; ideally situated.* **2** in a specified condition: *financially well situated* (= well off).

sit.u.a.tion (sich.oo.AY.shun) *n.* **1** location or site: *the situation of the house.* **2** state of affairs or condition: *the current, financial, housing, market, political situation; awkward, crisis, critical, delicate, desperate, embarrassing, emergency, explosive, hopeless, intolerable, life-and-death, no-win, tricky situations; to accept, comprehend, take in, size up, understand a situation.* **3** employment; position: *situations vacant, wanted.* —**sit.u.a.tion.al** *adj.: situational ethics.*

situation comedy *n.* a light play or comedy, esp. as a radio or TV series, involving a set of characters in various episodes.

sit-up *n.* an exercise involving lying flat on one's back and sitting up: *to do sit-ups.*

sitz bath *n.* a bath taken seated in hot water up to the hips.

six *n., adj. & pron.* one more than five; the number 6 or VI: *That's a six; six boys; six of them.* —**at sixes and sevens** in confusion or disagreement. —**sixth** *n., adj. & adv.*

six-gun *n.* a six-shooter.

six-pack *n.* a package of six cans, bottles, etc.

six.pence *n.* a British coin worth six pence; **six.pen.ny** *adj.*

six-shooter *n. Informal.* a six-chambered revolver.

six.teen (six.TEEN) *n., adj. & pron.* six more than 10; 16 or XVI; **six.teenth** *n. & adj.*

sixth sense *n.* power of intuition.

six.ty *n., adj. & pron.* **-ties 1** six times ten; 60 or LX. **2 the sixties** *n.pl.* the numbers, years, etc. from 60 through 69. —**six.ti.eth** (-ith) *n. & adj.*

siz.a.ble or **size.a.ble** (SYE.zuh.bul) *adj.* fairly large or bulky: *a sizable amount, impact, fortune, population.* —**siz.a.bly** or **size.a.bly** *adv.*

size *n.* **1** relative bigness, esp. as measured by length, width, etc.; also, something thus measured: *hats of all sizes; shoes of the right, wrong size; What size shoes do you wear? He wears size six; It's a boys' size; things of enormous, large, small, tremendous size.* **2** a material such as starch, gelatin, or wax added to paper or cloth to impart qualities of smoothness, stiffness, luster, etc.; also **siz.ing.** —**size as** in the same size as the original: *It copies size as (without reducing or enlarging).* —*v.* **siz.es, sized, siz.ing 1** arrange in sizes: *Our shirts are sized small through extra large.* **2** assess a person, chances, a problem, etc.: *to size up a situation before dealing with it.* **3** treat cloth, paper, walls, etc. with sizing.

-size or **-sized** *comb.form.* of a specified size: *bite-size pieces; a large-size kitchen; a life-size statue; medium-sized figures; a small-sized house.*

sizeable, sizeably See SIZABLE.

siz.zle (SIZ.ul) *n.* a hissing sound, as of fat in a hot pan: *Some new fashions sell more sizzle* (= superficial qualities) *than steak.* —*v.* **siz.zles, siz.zled, siz.zling 1** burn or fry with a sizzle: *sizzling fat; something new to keep our business sizzling* (= doing well); *adj.: a sizzling* (= exciting) *deal, fashion, job.* **2** be very hot; *adj.: It's a sizzling 90°F outside; sizzling criticism.*

siz.zler (SIZ.lur) *n. Informal.* a hot day.

skate *n.* **1** a shoe fitted with a metal runner for gliding on ice: *ice skates.* **2** the runner: *to sharpen skates.* **3** same as ROLLER SKATE. **4** a flat marine fish with winglike spreading fins on the sides of its body and a slender tail. —*v.* **skates, skat.ed, skat.ing** move along on skates. —**skat.er** *n.*
skate.board *n.* a narrow oblong board with rollers at each end for riding on hard surfaces; **skate.board.ing** *n.*
skating (SKAY.ting) *n.* the sport of gliding on skates: *figure, ice, roller, speed skating.*
ske.dad.dle (ski.DAD.ul) *v.* **-dad.dles, -dad.dled, -dad.dling** *Informal.* run away; scoot.
skeet *n.* trapshooting using clay pigeons that are sprung into the air from two target houses.
skein (SKAIN) *n.* a loosely twisted coil of thread or yarn: *a tangled skein; to untangle the skein of evidence and determine guilt.*
skel.e.ton (SKEL.uh.tun) *n.* **1** the framework of bones in an animal's body. **2** any framework, outline, or essential part: *the skeleton of a novel; adja.: to manage with a skeleton* (= minimal) *staff; a skeleton key designed to open many simple locks.* —**skeleton in the closet** something secret and embarrassing known only to one's family. —**skel.e.tal** (-tul) *adj.*
skep.tic (SKEP.tic) *n.* **1** one who is unwilling to accept generally held beliefs, esp. religious doctrines. **2** an adherent of skepticism. —**skep.ti.cal** *adj.*; **skep.ti.cal.ly** *adv.*
skep.ti.cism (SKEP.tuh.siz.um) *n.* **1** unwillingness to believe anything without absolute proof: *an air of skepticism; He maintains a healthy skepticism about flying saucers.* **2** the philosophical theory that reality is unknowable. **3** religious unbelief.
sketch *n.* **1** a rough outline or drawing: *to make a sketch; a composite sketch of a wanted man prepared by police from descriptions.* **2** a short, light, prose narrative or essay: *a biographical sketch; a brief, thumbnail sketch.* —*v.* make a sketch or outline of something: *She sketched his life in broad outline.*
sketch.y *adj.* **sketch.i.er, -i.est** hastily done or incomplete like a sketch: *We have only sketchy details of the accident; His notes are too sketchy to be useful.* —**sketch.i.ly** *adv.*; **sketch.i.ness** *n.*
skew *n.* a slant or twist: *This magazine offers a balance to the skew toward the more affluent consumers; a big city, demographic, positive skew; adja.: the skew angle.* —*v.* to slant or distort: *to skew the meaning of a word; How the questions are phrased could skew the results of the survey; to skew averages, figures, motivation, numbers; a plan skewed against minority interests; Older folks skew for* or *toward* (= favor) *the other network; Daytime soaps skew female rather than younger* (= appeal to women rather than youth).
skew.er (SKEW.ur) *n.* a long pin to hold meat or vegetables being roasted or broiled. —*v.* fasten or pierce with a skewer.
ski (SKEE) *v.* **skis, skied, ski.ing** glide on snow using long, flat runners attached to the shoes and two long poles for support; *n.: the winter sport of skiing; cross-country skiing; downhill skiing; heli-skiing.* —*n.* a runner used in skiing. —*adja.: ski areas, boots, hills; a ski lift, lodge, pole, resort, slope; a ski bum* (for whom skiing is life). —**ski.er** *n.*
ski.bob *n.* a bicyclelike vehicle with skis instead of wheels for use on snow-covered slopes.
skid *v.* **skids, skid.ded, skid.ding** slide on a slippery surface, as the wheels of a car, without gripping the pavement: *to skid on ice; to skid on an icy bridge.* —*n.* **1** a skidding. **2** a runner that enables an aircraft to skid along while landing; also, a sliding wedge used as a braking device. **3** a track for sliding or rolling a heavy object. **4** a low platform or pallet for holding loads. —**on the skids** *Informal.* headed for failure or ruin.
skid.dy *adj.* **skid.di.er, skid.di.est** slippery: *a skiddy pavement.*
skid row *n.* the slum section of a city frequented by society's derelicts.
skied, skier See SKI.
skiff *n.* a small rowboat or sailing ship.
skilful *Cdn.* SKILLFUL.
ski lift *n.* a cable system for carrying skiers up a slope.
skill *n.* ability or expertise gained by training and practice: *skill in carpentry, diving, languages; acquired* or *learned skills; typing and such office skills; driving skills; marketable skills; to hone, master, perfect a skill; a man of consummate skill; the skill to manipulate people; She has demonstrated her skill at* or *in riding; displays technical skill as a mechanic; shows great skill with figures; diplomatic skill; her professional skill as a lawyer; the skill of a magician;* **adja.:** *skill achievement, levels, shortage;* **skill-development** *techniques; a* **skill-testing** *question.*

skilled *adj.* having or showing skill: *skilled labor; a highly skilled worker; She's skilled at or in acrobatics; He's skilled with his hands; a skilled job (that requires skill).*

skil.let (SKIL.it) *n.* a frying pan.

skill.ful (SKIL.ful) *adj.* **1** having skill; expert: *a skillful writer; skillful at or in acrobatics; skillful with her hands.* **2** done with skill: *a skillful job, performance.* —**skill.ful.ly** *adv.* —**skill.ful.ness** *n.* Also **skil.ful, skil.ful.ly, skil.ful.ness** *Cdn.*

skim *v.* **skims, skimmed, skim.ming 1** move lightly over the surface of something: *Gulls and other sea birds skim over the waves; Skaters skim over ice; a reader who skims through a book picking up essential facts; to skim milk and remove cream; to skim off the cream of the crop; to skim the market for a quick profit.* **2** send skimming; skip: *to skim a flat stone over water.* —**skim.mer** (SKIM.ur) *n.*

skim milk *n.* milk with the cream removed. Also **skimmed milk.**

skimming (SKIM.ing) *n.* **1** what is skimmed off. **2** the practice of evading tax on gambling profits.

skimp *v. Informal.* scrimp: *to skimp on clothes to pay the rent.*

skimp.y *adj.* **skimp.i.er, -i.est** scanty; not ample: *a skimpy dress, explanation, manual; skimpy sales.* —**skimp.i.ly** *adv.*

skin *n.* **1** the outer layer of tissue covering a human or animal body; hide or pelt: *chapped, oily, rough, smooth, soft skin; Jon has a thin skin* (= is very sensitive); *Jock has a thick skin* (= is not oversensitive); *a starving child who is all* **skin and bones**; *adj*.: *skin cancer, diseases, rashes.* **2** something resembling skin in function, as the rind of a fruit, casing of a sausage, etc.: *spanking new office towers sporting skins of glass.* —**get under someone's skin** to annoy someone. —**save one's skin** save oneself; escape unhurt. —**under the skin** below the surface; at heart. —*v.* **skins, skinned, skin.ning 1** remove the skin of something: *to skin a banana; She skinned her knee climbing trees; He was* **skinned alive** (= severely punished) *for being late.* **2** *Informal.* cheat or swindle.

skin diving *n.* underwater diving by a swimmer equipped with a scuba or other breathing apparatus. —**skin-dive** *v.* -**dives, -dived, -div.ing.** —**skin diver** *n.*

skin.flick *n. Informal.* a pornographic motion picture.

skin.flint *n.* a mean and stingy person.

skin-graft *n.* a piece of skin transplanted from another area; also, the transplanting; also **skin graft.**

skin.head *n.* a young hoodlum.

skin magazine *n.* a magazine that features nudes.

skinned (SKIND) **1** *pt.* of SKIN; *adj*.: *a skinned turkey; skinned and boned chicken breasts.* **2** *comb.form.* having skin of a specified kind: *brown-skinned, dark-skinned, light-skinned, oily-skinned, thick-skinned.*

skin.ny *adj.* **skin.ni.er, skin.ni.est** [unfavorable term when used of persons] lean or thin: *skinny bottles, kids, models, pants, profits.* —**skin.ni.ness** *n.*

skinny-dip *n. Informal.* a swim in the nude; **skinny-dipping** *n.*

skin.tight *adj.* tight-fitting: *skintight jeans.*

skip *n.* **1** a light and quick leap or series of leaps, as a young lamb or child frisking about. **2** the captain of a curling team.
—*v.* **skips, skipped, skip.ping** make a skip or make something skip: *It's fun to skip flat stones on the lake; Al was so good he was allowed to skip* (= bypass) *a grade; to skip* (= not eat) *meals; to skip* (= not attend) *school on flimsy excuses; to skip* (= evade) *payments on a loan; Adjust vertical hold to correct a skipping* (= rolling) *TV picture; To* **skip rope**, hold the ends in your hands and revolve it under the feet and over the head.

skip account *n.* a customer who does not pay.

skip tracer *n.* a bill collector.

skip.per (SKIP.ur) *n.* a leader, as the master of a ship, captain of an airplane, manager of a basketball team, etc.

skirl *n.* the shrill sound of bagpipes.

skir.mish (SKUR.mish) *n.* a minor engagement or encounter, as between two small groups of soldiers.
—*v.* take part in a skirmish or argument: *He skirmished with the police over a parking ticket.*

skirt *n.* **1** a garment that hangs from the waist, esp. a woman's outer garment: *a pleated skirt.* **2** the bottom part of it: *to hem a skirt.* **3** *Informal.* a woman or girl: *He's no* **skirt chaser.**
—*v.* **1** form, be, or pass along the border or edge of something: *a path skirting (along) the lake.* **2** avoid something controversial or risky: *to skirt the issue; to skirt a charge, problem, question, rule, suggestion.*

ski run *n.* a slope or runway for skiing.

skit *n.* a short, humorous dramatic sketch: *They did a skit on the mayor.*

ski touring *n.* cross-country skiing.
ski tow *n.* a cable system for pulling skiers up a slope.
skit.ter (SKIT.ur) *v.* glide or skip lightly: *blips skittering across a video screen.*
skit.tish (SKIT.ish) *adj.* **1** excitable or jumpy: *a skittish horse.* **2** too lively or fickle; capricious: *the skittish stock market.*
skiv.vy (SKIV.ee) *n.*, usu. **skiv.vies** *pl. Informal.* men's underwear.
ski.wear (SKEE.ware) *n.* clothes to wear while skiing.
skoal (SKOLE) *interj.* [a toast] to your health!
skul.dug.ger.y or **skull.dug.ger.y** (skul.DUG.uh.ree) *n. Informal.* trickery.
skulk *v.* move stealthily; sneak or lurk. —**skulk.er** *n.*
skull *n.* **1** the bony case enclosing the brain. **2** head or mind: *The point finally penetrated his thick skull.*
skull.cap *n.* a close-fitting brimless cap.
skunk *n.* **1** a small furry animal of the weasel family, with black and white markings, noted for the evil-smelling liquid it squirts if molested. **2** *Informal.* a despised person.
skunk cabbage *n.* a plant of the arum family that gives off an offensive odor.
sky *n.* **skies** the usu. blue upper region of clouds, heavenly bodies, and celestial phenomena: *a cloudless sky; clear, cloudy, gray, overcast skies; seen in the skies over Omaha; a poet lauded* **to the skies** (= excessively).
sky.cap *n.* a porter at an air terminal.
sky.div.ing (SKY.dye.ving) *n.* the sport of jumping from an airplane and executing various maneuvers during the free fall before opening the parachute. —**sky.div.er** *n.*
sky-high *adj.* very high: *sky-high costs, expectations, levels, prices;* **adv.**: *Rents have been driven sky-high by inflation.*
sky-jack *v. Informal.* hijack an aircraft. —**sky-jack.er** *n.*
sky.lark *n.* the common lark of Europe and Asia noted for the music it showers on the earth as it flies up toward the sky. —*v.* to frolic boisterously.
sky.light *n.* a window in the roof that admits light.
sky.line *n.* an outline, as of a city's buildings, seen against the sky: *an imposing skyline; the Toronto skyline.*
sky.lounge *n.* a pickup vehicle for airline passengers that is carried from a city terminal to the airport by helicopter.

sky marshal *n.* a federal plainclothesman who guards against skyjackings.
sky.rock.et (SKY.rock.it) *n.* a firework rocket. —*v.* rise or make rise rapidly: *a star skyrocketed to fame by a movie;* **adj.**: *skyrocketing house prices.*
sky.scrap.er (SKY.scray.pur) *n.* a very tall building.
sky.walk *n.* an elevated walkway: *Glass-enclosed, heated skywalks link downtown buildings.*
sky.ward (SKY.wurd) *adj. & adv.* toward the sky; also **sky.wards** *adv.*
sky.way *n.* **1** an air lane for planes or other air traffic. **2** a skywalk. **3** an elevated highway.
sky.writ.ing (SKY.rye.ting) *n.* writing in the sky with smoke from an aircraft; **sky.writ.er** *n.*
slab *n.* a thick, flat, usu. square-cornered piece: *a slab of cheese, ice, concrete, stone, wood.*
slack *adj.* **1** not tight, as the loose end of a rope. **2** careless or dull: *He's slack at work; slack service.* **3** slow; not brisk: *at a slack pace; a slack season for travel; slack demand for goods and services; slack markets.*
—*n.* **1** a slack end; inactive condition: *to take up the slack (of a rope); When one family member is unable to work, the others* **take up** or **pick up the slack**. **2** **slacks** *n.pl.* trousers for casual wear: *a pair of slacks.* —*v.* become slack or inactive: *Don't* **slack off** *as exams approach; She likes to* **slack up** (= relax) *a little before trying again.* —**slack.er** *n.* —**slack.ly** *adv.*; **slack.ness** *n.*
slack.en *v.* to slack.
slag *n.* nonmetallic waste material that rises to the top in the smelting of metal ores: *Communism ended up on the slag heap.*
slain *pp.* of SLAY.
slake *v.* **slakes, slaked, slak.ing** quench or satisfy: *to slake one's thirst, desire for revenge; to slake a fire;* **Slaked lime** used in mortars and cements is produced by putting water on lime.
sla.lom (SLAH.lum, SLAL.um) *n.* a skiing race down a zigzag course between poles forming a line of obstacles.
slam *n.* **1** the bang of a violent impact, as of a door pushed shut. **2** [short form] GRAND SLAM or LITTLE SLAM.
—*v.* **slams, slammed, slam.ming** knock or bang: *The sales rep had the door slammed in his face when he refused to leave; a pileup of cars that slammed into each other; a book badly slammed* (*Informal.* for criticized) *by reviewers.*

slam-bang *adj.* hurried or headlong: *a slam-bang adventure, campaign, decision, ending; a slam-bang style of hockey.* Also *adv.*

slam dunk *n.* in basketball, a forceful dunk shot.

slam.mer *n. Informal.* jail: *He was sent to* **the slammer** *for ten years.*

slan.der (SLAN.dur) *n.* a false statement to harm another's reputation. —*v.* utter a slander. —**slan.der.er** *n.* —**slan.der.ous** (-us) *adj.*

slang *n.* everyday colloquial language with a colorful or vigorous quality. —*v.* use abusive epithets: *Senators sometimes slang at each other in debate; The debate became a* **slanging match** *between the two parties.*

slan.guage (SLANG.gwij) *n. Informal.* slang language.

slang.y (SLANG.ee) *adj.* having to do with slang: *a slangy style, writer; slangy prose, vocabulary.*

slant *n.* 1 a slope or incline, esp. from the vertical. 2 a particular or personal bias: *a catalog's fashion slant; ecological, feminist, liberal slants; a new slant on ethnicity.* —*v.* 1 slope or incline: *to slant a ramp; adj.: a coat with* **slanted** *or hacking pockets; in a slanted position; slanted roofs.* 2 express with or have a slant; *adj.:* *an editorial* **slanted** *against Sunday shopping; a magazine slanted toward a younger readership; slanted news reporting.* —*adja.* sloping; also **slanting**: *slant lettering; in a slanting position.*

slap *n. & v.* **slaps, slapped, slap.ping** hit with a flat surface, esp. the open hand: *a slap in the face; a hearty slap on the back; to slap paint on a wall; The police stopped the speeder and slapped* (= summarily imposed) *a fine on him; a* **slap on the wrist** (= mild rebuke).

slap.dash *adj.* hurried or haphazard: *slapdash planning;* also *adv.*

slap-happy *adj. Informal.* giddy or dazed, as from too many blows.

slap.shot *n.* in ice hockey, a powerful shot made with a swinging stroke.

slap.stick *n.* comedy characterized by horseplay and broad humor.

slash *n.* 1 a sweeping stroke, as with a knife. 2 a resulting gash or slit. 3 a slanted stroke used in writing, as in "and/or": *a reverse slash* [\]. —*adja.:* *a slash mark; a flapless* **slash pocket** *with a slanted opening.* —*v.* cut, as with a slash: *to slash at an attacker with a knife; The car was found with its tires slashed; Prices are slashed* (= reduced sharply) *the day after Christmas; to slash* (= cut) *costs, fares, spending; n.:* *a penalty for* **slashing** (= swinging the hockey stick at an opponent); *the* **slash and burn** *method of clearing forests.* —**slash.er** *n.*

slat *n.* a narrow strip of material, as of a Venetian blind or the bars of a crib.

slate *n.* 1 a rock that splits in layers and is used for roofing and paving. 2 a slab of slate: *Children write on slates with chalk; We start off with a* **clean slate** (= clean record); *adj.:* *a* **slated** (= made of slate), *not thatched roof; the black-slated Vietnam memorial.* 3 its bluish-gray color: *slate blue; slate-colored ovenware; slate gray cement walls.* 4 a list of candidates, as for an election; schedule: *Many were elected on Republican slates; the anti-abortion slate; slates of handpicked candidates.*
—*v.* **slates, slat.ed, slat.ing** designate or schedule: *They have slated raises for everyone; candidates slated for the chairmanship; elections slated for next fall; an ad slated to run in tomorrow's papers.*

slath.er (SLATH.ur, "TH" as in "the") *v. Informal.* pour or spread generously, as jam, paint, etc.: *Our neighborhood will be slathered with garbage if the disposal plan goes through; pancakes slathered in syrup.*

slat.tern *n.* a slovenly woman; slut; **slat.tern.ly** *adj.*

slaugh.ter (SLAW.tur) *n.* massacre; also, butchery: *indiscriminate, mass, needless, relentless, wanton, wholesale slaughter; the slaughter on the highways during the Christmas rush.* —*v.* commit massacre; also, butcher, as in a slaughterhouse. —**slaugh.ter.er** *n.*

slaugh.ter.house (SLAW.tur.house) *n.* an establishment in which animals are killed for food.

Slav (SLAHV, SLAV) *n.* a member of a Slavic-speaking people such as Russians, Poles, Czechs, Slovaks, Croats, Serbs, and Ukrainians.

slave *n.* 1 a person owned by another: *the liberation of slaves.* 2 a victim of a habit or a person subject to a dominating influence: *a slave to fashion.* 3 one who slaves; *adj.:* *a slave ant, trader; slave labor; a* **slave driver** (= very demanding boss).
—*v.* **slaves, slaved, slav.ing** work like a slave: *to slave over a tiresome task; She slaved away at her thesis for five years.*

slav.er *n.* 1 (SLAY.vur) a slave dealer or his ship. 2 (SLAV.ur) saliva dribbling from the mouth, as of a dog; *v.* slobber: *to slaver* (= drool) *over something trivial.*

slav.er.y (SLAY.vuh.ree) *n.* 1 the custom or practice of owning slaves: *to* abolish slavery. **2** the condition of slaves; bondage or drudgery: *to be freed from slavery; held in slavery; to live in slavery.*

Slav.ic (SLAH.vic, SLAV-) *n. & adj.* (having to do with) the Slavs or their Indo-European languages spoken in E. European countries such as Russia, Ukraine, and Poland.

slav.ish (SLAY.vish) *adj.* of or like slaves; servile: *slavish adherence, devotion, obedience, followers.*
—**slav.ish.ly** *adv.*; **slav.ish.ness** *n.*

Sla.von.ic (sluh.VON.ic) same as SLAVIC.

slaw *n.* [short form] coleslaw.

slay *v.* **slays, slew, slain, slay.ing** [literary use] kill violently: *to slay a dragon*; *adj.*: *the slain hero, leader, policeman.* —**slay.er** *n.*

sleaze (SLEEZ) *n.* **1** the condition of being sleazy or shabby: *Hollywood sleaze; the anti-sleaze crusaders.* **2** a sleazy person; also *Slang.* **sleaze.bag, sleaze.ball.**

slea.zy (SLEE.zee) *adj.* **-zi.er, -zi.est** **1** squalid or disreputable; cheap; shabby: *a sleazy campaign, deal, hotel, theater.* **2** of fabrics, flimsy or thin: *It looks more sleazy than sexy.* —**slea.zi.ly** *adv.*; **slea.zi.ness** *n.*

sled *n.* a vehicle with parallel runners instead of wheels for traveling over snow and ice.
—*v.* **sleds, sled.ded, sled.ding** carry or ride on a sled; *n.*: *There is some tough sledding* (= riding) *ahead as the exams approach.* —**sled.der** *n.*

sledge *n.* **1** a heavy sled, usu. drawn by a horse. **2** a large, heavy hammer, usu. swung with both hands; also **sledge.ham.mer** (SLEJ.ham.ur) *n.*
—*v.* **1** carry or draw on a sledge. **2** hit with a sledgehammer.

sleek *adj.* smooth and glossy: *sleek designs, hair, looks, shapes; a sleek automobile, body, finish; a sleek* (= smooth-talking) *sales rep.* —*v.* slick: *Ballerinas have their heads sleeked into buns.*
—**sleek.ly** *adv.*; **sleek.ness** *n.*

sleep *n.* a state of natural unconsciousness that provides periodic rest for mind and body: *to drift off, drop off to sleep; She has difficulty getting to sleep; drugs to induce sleep; a deep, heavy, light, restful, sound sleep; I didn't get enough sleep last night; We go to sleep* (= go to bed) *at night hoping to get or have a good night's sleep; It's no use losing sleep over* (= worrying a lot about) *things we can't do anything about.* —**put to sleep** **1** make unconscious or asleep: *whether to put the baby to sleep on his tummy or on his back; His sermons put people to sleep.* **2** kill mercifully: *The dog was so ill it had to be put to sleep.* —*v.* **1** be in sleep: *Infants sleep longer than adults; He likes to sleep on* (= take time to consider) *important decisions; The poor fellow had never slept* (*Informal* for had sex) *with anyone before marrying.* **2** accommodate: *Our motor home sleeps six.*
—**sleep around** *Informal.* be promiscuous: *He stopped sleeping around after getting married.* —**sleep in** sleep beyond one's waking-up time. —**sleep off** get over by sleeping: *He sleeps it off when he has a bad day.* —**sleep.less** *adj.*: *sleepless hours, nights*; **sleep.less.ness** *n.*

sleep.er *n.* **1** one that sleeps. **2** also **sleeping car**, a railroad car with berths for passengers. **3** a railroad tie. **4** *Informal.* a person or thing that suddenly attains fame or success: *a movie sleeper.* **5** an infant's one-piece sleeping garment.

sleeping bag *n.* a bag for sleeping in, esp. outdoors.

sleeping car same as SLEEPER.

sleeping giant *n.* something with great potential: *a sleeping giant of an issue.*

sleeping pill (or **tablet**) *n.* a pill containing a sleep-inducing drug.

sleeping sickness *n.* a coma-inducing fatal disease spread by insect bites, esp. an African variety transmitted by the tsetse fly.

sleep.o.ver (SLEEP.oh.vur) *n.* a sleeping overnight at another person's house: *children's sleepover parties.*

sleep.walk.ing (SLEEP.walk.ing) *n.* the act or practice of a neurotic person acting as if awake during sleep without remembering it on waking up.

sleep.wear (SLEEP.ware) *n.* night clothes.

sleep.y *adj.* **sleep.i.er, -i.est** **1** inclined to sleep: *a sleepy face, look; sleepy eyes; a sleepy-eyed dog.* **2** quiet or inactive: *a sleepy village.* —**sleep.i.ly** *adv.*; **sleep.i.ness** *n.*

sleep.y.head (SLEE.pee.hed) *n.* *Informal.* a sleepy person.

sleet *n.* **1** a fall of freezing rain. **2** a glaze or ice formed by freezing rain.
—*v.* to shower sleet. —**sleet.y** *adj.*

sleeve *n.* **1** the arm of a garment: *She rolled up her sleeves and got down to work; He wears his heart on his sleeve* (= makes no secret of his feelings). **2** a tubelike part fitting around another part, as in engine bearings. **3** slipcase: *storage sleeves for digital discs, floppies.*
—**up one's sleeve** in secret: *They must*

be laughing up their sleeves; She seems to have something up her sleeve (= kept secret for later use).
sleigh (SLAY) *n. & v.* sled or sledge.
sleight of hand (SLITE-) *n.* **1** skill with the hands, as of a magician or juggler. **2** a magician's trick or tricks.
slen.der (SLEN.dur) *adj.* **1** slim and graceful: *a slender beauty, figure.* **2** slight; scanty; meager: *a slender hope, income; a man of slender means.* —**slen.der.ness** *n.*
slen.der.ize (SLEN.duh.rize) *v.* **-iz.es, -ized, -iz.ing** become or make slender: *to slenderize the body.*
slept *pt. & pp.* of SLEEP.
sleuth (SLOOTH) *n. & v. Informal.* (act as) a detective.
sleuth.hound *n.* bloodhound.
slew *pt.* of SLAY. —*n.* **1** *Informal.* a large amount or number; lot: *a whole slew of decisions; a slew of fish, issues, offices, people, products, trouble.* **2** a veer or swing; slue: *an amplifier's slew factor affecting measurement; the signal slew rate.* **3** a swampy inlet. —*v.* veer: *The car slewed into a snowbank.*
slice *n.* **1** a thin broad piece cut from bread, cheese, fruits, meat, etc.: *a slice of bread; apple, cheese, meat slices.* **2** a share or portion: *a slice of luck, the profits, the population; drama as a slice* (= representation) *of life.* —*v.* **slic.es, sliced, slic.ing** **1** cut (*away, into, off,* or *up*) as a slice or slices: *to slice into the ham; She sliced it thick; The company sliced* (= cut off) *900 employees from its payroll and sliced* (= reduced) *its quarterly dividend from 25 cents to 24; adj.:* thinly **sliced** *carrots, olives, peaches; the best* or *greatest* or *hottest* **thing (to happen) since sliced bread** (*Informal for* simply the greatest). **2** hit a ball so that it goes off course or into a backspin. —**slic.er** *n.*
slick *adj.* **1** smooth or slippery, as with oil. **2** facile, clever, or skillful: *slick solutions to a complex problem; a slick excuse, operator, talker; Even the slickest of today's computers can't think like humans.* —*v.* make smooth or glossy. —**slick up** smarten; spruce up. —*n.* an oily spot: *an oil slick on the water.* —**slick.ly** *adv.;* **slick.ness** *n.*
slick.er *n.* **1** a raincoat, esp. of oilskin. **2** *Informal.* a wily person: *a city slicker.*
slide *v.* **slides, slid, slid.ing** move or cause to move smoothly in contact with a surface: *Sleds slide downhill, slide over snow and ice; The baseball player slid into second base; Prices slid* (= went down) *2% last month; a nation sliding into a recession; a matter too urgent to* **let slide** (= drift); *adj.: a* **sliding** *door, drawer, lid; the sliding dollar; sliding prices, revenues.* —*n.* **1** a sliding, as of rock. **2** a sliding surface or chute, as on a children's playground. **3** something that is slid into place for use, as a small glass plate containing an object to be examined under a microscope or a transparency for projection on a screen: *to mount slides; to show slides using a* **slide projector.**
slide fastener *n.* a zipper.
slid.er (SLY.dur) *n.* **1** a person or thing that slides. **2** in baseball, a slightly curving fast pitch.
slide rule *n.* a mathematical calculating device in the form of a ruler with a sliding middle section.
sliding scale *n.* a schedule of taxes, fees, wages, etc. that varies to suit changing conditions such as cost of living: *royalties paid on a sliding scale based on number of copies sold.*
slier, sliest See SLY.
slight *adj.* **1** small; not considerable: *a slight difference, excuse; on the slightest pretext.* **2** thin or slender: *a slight build, figure, girl; too slight for him.* —*v.* treat as insignificant, esp. intentionally: *She felt slighted by his superior manner.* —*n.* a humiliation or discourtesy. —**slight.ly** *adv.;* **slight.ness** *n.*
sli.ly (SLY.lee) same as SLYLY.
slim *adj.* **slim.mer, slim.mest** thin or small: *a slim figure, skirt, woman; slim pants; slim and baggy fits; slim-fitting jeans; a slim book, volume; a slim attendance, budget, chance, choice, gain, hope, lead, majority, margin, profit, victory; We made* **slim pickings** *of the myth* (= destroyed it). —*v.* **slims, slimmed, slim.ming** make or become slim: *We slim by going on a diet; You can either slim down or bulk up;* **adj.:** *a* **slimmed-down** *appearance, style, waist; a* **slimming** *effect; slimming exercises; a body-slimming product.*
slime *n.* something sticky and filthy, as soft mud, mold on decaying vegetable matter, or the mucous coating on snails, fish, etc.: *the oozing slime.* —**slim.y** (SLY.mee) *adj.* **slim.i.er, -i.est.**
slim-jim *n. Informal.* one that is very slim: *a slim-jim necktie.*
sling *n.* **1** a device consisting of a strip of leather for throwing a stone held in its loop. **2** such a fling or throw: *to suffer* **the slings and arrows** *of adversity* (= the hard knocks of life). **3** a similar

looped device for supporting an arm in a cast, for lifting a load, carrying a rifle, etc. —v. **slings, slung, sling.ing** 1 suspend in or throw as with a sling: *a hammock slung between trees; Her purse was slung over her shoulder; He was accused of* **slinging mud at** (= slandering) *his rivals.* 2 *Informal.* prepare and serve: *He slings hamburgers at a fast-food outlet; He also knows how to* **sling it** *or* **sling the bull** (= talk glibly).

sling.shot *n.* 1 a forked stick with an elastic sling attached for shooting stones, etc. 2 such a shot.

slink *v.* **slinks,** *pt. & pp.* **slunk** *or* **slinked, slink.ing** go or move *away, by,* etc. in a stealthy manner, as from fear.

slink.y *adj.* **slink.i.er, -i.est** 1 furtive or stealthy. 2 of a woman's clothing, hugging the body; close-fitting: *a slinky evening gown.*

slip *v.* **slips, slipped, slip.ping** 1 (cause) to move smoothly or easily; hence, slide: *She slipped and fell on the ice; He slipped off his coat and shoes; She slipped me a note; He tried to slip out of the room; Let me slip* (= change) *into something more comfortable; Secrets* **slip out.** 2 escape: *Names slip (from) my mind; Don't let a good opportunity slip by; He* **let slip** *a few epithets in his fury.* 3 decline: *Polls showed his popularity slipping; He's liable to* **slip up** (= err) *in spelling.* —*n.* 1 a slipping: *a Freudian slip;* to make a **slip of the tongue** (= an unintentional error in speech); *to* **give someone the slip** (= elude someone). 2 something that is slipped on, as a pillowcase, a woman's sleeveless undergarment or petticoat, etc. 3 a docking space for ships between wharves or docks. 4 a piece of paper or something of small size: *a slip of paper; a bank deposit slip; sales slips; a rose slip* (= cutting) *for planting; a* **slip of a** (= young or slim) *boy, child, girl.*

slip.case *n.* a protective case or container for a book or phonograph record with one edge open.

slip.cov.er (SLIP.cuv.ur) *n.* a fitted protective cover for a sofa or chair.

slip.knot *n.* a running knot, as of a noose (**slip noose**) or lasso.

slip.page (SLIP.ij) *n.* slipping, as in machinery, or its extent.

slipped disk *n.* rupture or hernia of the disk between two vertebrae causing intense pain in the back and legs.

slip.per *n.* a light loose shoe for indoor wear: *a pair of slippers; ballet slippers; house slippers.*

slip.per.y (SLIP.uh.ree) *adj.* 1 causing slipping: *a wet, slippery floor; slippery conditions, paths, pavements, surfaces; regulations that will take us down the proverbial* **slippery slope** *to total state control.* 2 slipping away from grasp; hence, unreliable: *a slippery block of ice; a slippery concept, definition, issue, subject; You're* **on slippery ground** *with that argument.* —**slip.per.i.ness** *n.*

slip.shod *adj.* careless in manner or style: *slipshod treatment of employees.*

slip.stream *n.* backward flow of air past a moving object such as an airplane.

slip-up *n. Informal.* a mistake or mishap.

slit *n.* a straight narrow cut: *a slit in a door for letters.* —**adj***a*. having or resembling a long narrow opening: *a slit skirt; the slit pupil of a cat's eye; a* **slit trench** *for protection in warfare.* —*v.* **slits, slit, slit.ting** split open by a slit: *to slit open an envelope.*

slith.er ("th" as in "the") *n.* an unsteady sliding or crawling motion. —*v.* move along in a slither: *Snakes slither along the ground.* —**slith.er.y** *adj.*

sliv.er (SLIV.ur) *v.* cut or split into long, thin pieces. —*n.* such a piece; splinter: *almond slivers; a sliver of soap.*

slob *n. Informal.* a slovenly or stupid person.

slob.ber *n.* 1 saliva running from the mouth. 2 excessive sentimentality. —*v.* 1 wet or smear with slobber. 2 indulge in slobber *over* something. —**slob.ber.y** *adj.*

sloe (SLOH) *n.* 1 the small, black, plumlike fruit of a shrub of the rose family, used to flavor **sloe gin.** 2 the shrub, also called "blackthorn."

sloe-eyed *adj.* 1 having blue-black eyes. 2 having almond-shaped eyes.

slog *v.* **slogs, slogged, slog.ging** work hard or toil *at* or *away at* something. —*n.: She earned her Ph.D. after a 10-year slog of night school.*

slo.gan (SLOH.gun) *n.* a catchy phrase or motto used in advertising and promotion, as "Satisfaction or your money back" or "Peace with honor."

sloop *n.* a sailboat with one mast carrying the mainsail and a jib.

slop *n.* 1 something semiliquid or watery, as slush, spilled liquid, gruel, etc. 2 usu. **slops** *pl.* liquid waste such as swill or collected urine. —*v.* **slops, slopped, slop.ping** spill; pass a limit: *He slopped his drink all over the place; Water from the bath slopped over onto the floor.*

slope *n.* an angle made with the

horizontal; hence, an incline: *the gentle slope of a wheelchair ramp; to coast down a mountain slope; downward, gradual, slick, slippery, steep slopes; I was on the slopes* (skiing) *all day.*
—*v.* **slopes, sloped, slop.ing** make a slope: *The roof slopes down almost to the ground; adj.: a sloped 20-inch shoulder; a sloped surface; a gently, gradually, softly sloping roof; sloping hills, terrain; a jacket with sloping shoulders.*

slop.py *adj.* **slop.pi.er, slop.pi.est** slovenly: *sloppy habits, work; a sloppy* (= messy) *eater; sloppy* (= muddy) *reasoning; sloppy* (= slushy and wet) *weather.* —**slop.pi.ly** *adv.;* **slop.pi.ness** *n.*

sloppy Joe *n.* ground beef prepared with sauce and served on a bun.

slosh *v.* splash through or with slush or muddy water. —**slosh.y** *adj.*

slot *n.* **1** a small, narrow opening or depression for inserting something, as for coins to operate a SLOT MACHINE or for a circuit board to be connected to a computer's motherboard. **2** *Informal.* a position in a series or sequence, as on a program: *a story to fill a two-minute slot in the evening news.*
—*v.* **slots, slot.ted, slot.ting 1** make a slot. **2** *Informal.* to place in a slot: *a marketing wizard who can slot in the right product at the right time.*

sloth (SLAWTH or *rhyme:* both) *n.* **1** laziness in regard to work: *the natural sloth of slave labor.* **2** a nocturnal tropical animal with long shaggy hair and living mostly on trees, moving about sluggishly, often upside down, on branches. —**sloth.ful** *adj.* lazy: *the slothful attitude of workers without incentives; a life of slothful ease;* **sloth.ful.ness** *n.*

slot machine *n.* a machine operated by inserting a coin in its slot, esp. a vending machine or gambling machine.

slouch *n.* **1** a slovenly or incompetent person: *He's no slouch when it comes to mixing his favorite drink.* **2** a forward bend or droop of head and shoulders.
—*v.* move, stand, or sit with a slouch. —**slouch.y** *adj.*

slough *n.* **1** (*rhyme:* how) a place of deep mud; quagmire; hence, a dejected condition: *the slough of despond, hopelessness.* **2** (SLOO) a swamp, esp. a backwater or inlet; slew. **3** (SLOO) in the Prairies, a small body of water formed by rain or melted snow; slew. **4** (SLUF) castoff skin, esp. of a snake; *v.* cast off or get rid of: *to slough off the outer layers of skin; to slough off a duty, one's identity, redundant staff.*

Slo.vak (SLOH.vahk, -vak) *n. & adj.* (a member or the language) of the Slavic people of **Slovakia**, a country in C. Europe. —**Slo.va.ki.an** (sloh.VAH.kee.un) *n. & adj.*

slov.en (SLUV.un) *n.* a careless or untidy person.

Slo.vene (SLOH.veen) *n. & adj.* (a member or the language) of the people of **Slovenia**, a C. European country. Also **Slo.ve.ni.an** (sloh.VEE.nee.un) *n. & adj.*

slov.en.ly (SLUV.un.lee) *adj.* **-li.er, -li.est** sloppy or slipshod. —**slov.en.li.ness** *n.*

slow (SLOH) *adj.* taking longer than normal or necessary: *He's slow at learning; slow to learn; a slow timepiece (that falls behind in showing the correct time); a slow fire (slow in burning); a slow* (= not lively) *party; a slow* (= not fast) *train; Business is slow* (= slack or sluggish).
—*adv.* in a slow manner: *Drive, speak, walk slow; a little slower; a slow-burning fire; slow-moving vehicles; Let's go slow while we are tired; Go slow on that project.* See also SLOWLY. —*v.* make or become slow or slower: *to slow the growth rate; to slow one's pace; to slow down an army's advance; Let's slow down; Sales show no signs of slowing; adj.: a slowing demand, economy, growth, market, momentum.* —**slow.ness** *n.*

slow burn *n. Informal.* controlled but gradually rising anger, esp. as a dramatic device: *to do a slow burn.*

slow.down *n.* a slowing down of a business, operation, etc.: *an economic slowdown; a slowdown in production.*

slow.ly (SLOH.lee) *adv.* in a slow manner: *See how slowly she drives; Water evaporates slowly;* **Slowly but surely** *the end drew near.*

slow motion *n.* motion-picture action shown at slower-than-normal speed: *They showed the action in slow motion; adj.: a slow-motion picture.*

slow.poke *n. Informal.* one who moves or does anything slowly.

slow-witted *adj.* mentally dull.

sludge *n.* a muddy mixture or slushy deposit, as the sediments resulting from ore refining, sewage treatment, etc. —**sludg.y** *adj.* **sludg.i.er, -i.est.**

slue *v.* **slues, slued, slu.ing** veer around. —*n.* a sluing or the position slued to. Also **slew.**

slug *n.* **1** a snaillike mollusk without a real shell. **2** a small piece of metal, as a bullet, a disk to use in a slot machine, or a strip of type metal or cast type. **3** a hard blow, esp. with the fist or a bat. —v. **slugs, slugged, slug.ging** hit hard, as with the fist or a bat: *When reason failed, they slugged it out.* —**slug.ger** *n.*

slug.fest *n. Informal.* a combat or conflict resembling a boxing match: *a head-to-head slugfest with the competition; a 10-round slugfest.*

slug.gard (SLUG.urd) *n.* one who is lazy or sluggish.

slug.gish (SLUG.ish) *adj.* slow-moving: *a sluggish mind, stream; sluggish bowels; a sluggish economy, market, season, trend; sluggish business, demand, growth, sales.* —**slug.gish.ly** *adv.;* **slug.gish.ness** *n.*

sluice (SLOOSE) *n.* **1** a gate for controlling a flow of water, as of a dam; also **sluice gate. 2** a channel controlled by a gate, as a **sluiceway** for surplus water from a dam or a trough for washing gold ore of impurities. —*v.* **sluic.es, sluiced, sluic.ing 1** let out water, wash gold from ore, send logs, etc. by means of a sluice. **2** wash down with flowing water: *to sluice a driveway.*

slum *n.* an overcrowded, poverty-stricken area, as of a large city: *Most slums have high illness, disease, and crime rates; adja.: a slum area, landlord; slum clearance, conditions.* —*v.* **slums, slummed, slum.ming 1** visit the slums. **2** visit a place inferior to one's usual surroundings: *to go slumming; Bored with high society, she slummed it for a while.*

slum.ber (SLUM.bur) *n.* **1** light sleep: *the peaceful slumber of a newborn babe; sweet slumber; He lectured us for over an hour and then fell into a deep slumber; a children's* **slumber party** *(for sleeping together overnight).* **2** a dormant or inactive condition: *a nation awakening from centuries of slumber.*
—*v.* **1** have a light sleep. **2** be dormant: *The business slumbered through the winter; adj.: a nation that still lies* **slumbering** *in the Dark Ages; to rouse or wake a slumbering giant; a slumbering market, project, volcano.*

slum.lord *n.* the often absentee owner of slum property.

slump *v.* **1** sink or decline suddenly: *She slumped to the ground in a faint.* **2** slouch or droop in posture: *His shoulders slumped under the weight of the pails of water he was carrying.*
—*n.* decline: *business, economic, stock-market slumps.*

slung *pt. & pp.* of SLING.
slunk *pt. & pp.* of SLINK.
slur *v.* **slurs, slurred, slur.ring 1** pass hurriedly or carelessly over syllables or sounds in pronouncing: *speech difficulties such as slurring; Too much to drink sometimes causes* **slurred speech;** *He tends to* **slur over** *(= minimize) their mistakes.* **2** to slight or disparage.
—*n.* **1** a slurring. **2** a slighting remark: *to cast a slur on someone's character; ethnic, racial, sexual slurs.* **3** slurred musical notes or a line connecting such notes.

slurp *n. Informal.* a sucking noise, as made when sipping. —*v.* eat or drink with a slurp: *to slurp soup.*

slur.ry *n.* **slur.ries** a thin, watery mixture of something insoluble, as clay or cement.

slush *n.* watery mud or partly melted snow. —**slush.y** *adj.*

slush fund *n.* a fund for corrupt purposes, as for bribing public officials.

slut *n.* **1** a slovenly or despised woman. **2** a prostitute. —**slut.tish** *adj.*

sly *adj.* **sli.er** or **sly.er, sli.est** or **sly.est 1** crafty or wily: *a sly cat, fox, glance, grin, innuendo, look, maneuver, smile, wink; cartoons full of sly sexual references; a "nonsmoker" who smokes* **on the sly** *(= secretly).* **2** artful or playful: *sly humor, wit; a sly comment like "Academics distrust intelligibility"; a sly slogan like "You've got the look I want to know better."* —**sly.ly** *adv.;* **sly.ness** *n.*

smack *n. & v.* **1** (have) a slight but distinctive taste, flavor, or suggestion: *His airs smack of superiority; There's a smack of chicory in this coffee.* **2** (make) noise with lips, as when chewing food, kissing loudly, or with a whip, as when cracking it. **3** *Informal.* slap: *a smack in the face; I'm going to smack you one; She smacked him in the face and vice versa.* —*adv.* directly: *He fell smack on his face; The place you can't find on the map is* **smack dab** *(Informal for* right there) *in the center of the city.*

small (SHAWL) *adj.* **1** relatively not large; of less than the usual size, quantity, importance, etc.: *a small car, child, portion; from small beginnings; in small quantities; Small wonder! "Small world!" he said on meeting me so far from home; She amassed a* **small fortune** *(= large sum of money);* REGULAR and SMALL *capitals.* **2** small in mind: *a small man; a small (= mean) nature; One sometimes* **feels small** *(= unimportant or shameful) after saying something nasty.*
—*n.* something small: *the* **small** *(= narrowest part) of the back.*
—**small.ness** *n.*

small arms *n.pl.* firearms that are easy

to carry and use, as revolvers, rifles, etc., not artillery.

small business *n.* a business involving a small capital investment and a limited number of employees.

small change *n.* coins of low value.

small claim *n.* a claim against someone involving a small sum of money up to a specified limit, as in a **small claims court.**

small fry *n.pl.* **1** offspring or people of lesser importance: *The small fry (= children) are also invited.* **2** unimportant things: *A little smoking and drinking are small fry compared to drugs.*

small hours *n.pl.* 1, 2, 3, etc. a.m.: *in the small hours of the morning; We worked into the small hours of Tuesday night* (= Wednesday morning).

small-minded *adj.* mean or narrow-minded.

small potatoes *n.pl.* [with *sing.* or *pl. v.*] *Informal.* person(s) or thing(s) considered insignificant.

small.pox *n.* a highly infectious virus disease characterized by a rash that leaves pock marks all over the face and body.

small talk *n.* light conversation; chit-chat: *to make small talk at a party.*

small-time *adj. Informal.* minor or mediocre: *small-time burglary, cheating, con artists, developers, entrepreneurs, lawyers; He has always been small-time.*
—**small-timer** *n.*

smarm.y *adj.* **smarm.i.er, -i.est** flattering or servile: *smarmy salesmen, sentiments, tones.*

smart *v.* **1** feel sharp pain: *My head is still smarting from hitting that door.* **2** feel distress of mind: *I'm still smarting at or from or over or under the injustice.* —*adj.* **1** clever or intelligent: *a smart choice, kid, move, reply, youngster; looking smart and intelligent; the smart thing to do; a smart* (= stylish) *uniform; the smart* (= fashionable) *set; Don't get smart* (= impudent) *with me; adv.: how to fly smart; to shop smart.* **2** *adja.* lively: *a smart crack with the whip; We walked at a smart pace.* **3** causing sharp pain: *a smart blow.* **4** computer-aided or intelligent: *a smart phone that dials numbers for you; smart software, terminals.*
—**smarts** *n.pl.* intelligence: *They've got the smarts and savvy; noted for their smarts; street smarts; small in size but long on the smarts; She shows her smarts in this essay.* —**smart.ly** *adv.;* **smart.ness** *n.*

smart al.eck (or **al.ec**) (SMART.AL.ick) *n.* one who is conceited or obnoxious; *adja.: a smart-aleck kid, remark, teenag-* er. Also **smart-alecky** *adj.*

smart ass *n. Slang.* smart-aleck: *some smart ass of a lawyer, literary critic;* **adja.**: *a smart-ass answer, lawyer, literary critic.*

smart bomb *n.* a bomb equipped with a guidance system.

smart card *n.* a card that is computer-readable.

smart.en (SMAR.tun) *v.* make or become smart or smarter: *They soon smartened up and decided to join us; to repair and smarten up old homes.*

smart terminal *n.* a terminal with some data-processing capability, not a dumb terminal.

smash *v.* **1** break into pieces with violence, as a glass window with a rock. **2** deal a crushing blow: *to smash an enemy, an uprising.* **3** crash: *The car smashed through the wall and into the living room.* —*n.* **1** a violent crash or its sound. **2** a crushing blow; ruin. **3** *Informal.* a popular success or great hit: *The show was a real smash;* **adja.**: *a smash hit, musical, success.*

smashing *adj.* **1** crushing: *a smashing defeat.* **2** impressive or striking: *The play was a smashing success.*

smash.up *n.* a wreck; disaster.

smat.ter.ing (SMAT.ur.ing) *n.* **1** slight knowledge: *He has (picked up) only a smattering of the language, subject.* **2** a small number or amount: *a big major prize and a smattering of smaller ones.*

smear (SMEER) *v.* **1** to spread or daub with anything greasy, sticky, or dirty: *The child smeared chocolate all over her; slogans smeared on walls.* **2** to mark or stain; hence, soil a reputation: *a wall smeared with paint; a politician smeared by the media as "racist"; character smearing.* —*n.* **1** a spread or daub: *She eats bagels with a smear of cream cheese; a thin smear.* **2** a blotch or mark; hence, a staining, as of one's reputation: *The newspaper story was a smear; political smears;* **adja.**: *smear campaigns, stories, tactics; "Nazi," "Communist," "racist," and such smear words used to discredit an opponent.* **3** a small sample of a substance for testing medically: *a cervical smear; Dr. Joe took a smear of Jo's mouth for a cancer test; He also did a Pap smear* (= test) *on her.* —**smear.y** *adj.*

smell *n.* **1** sense of perception through the nose. **2** the quality so perceived; odor or scent: *Burning rubber gives off an acrid smell; the bad, disagreeable, foul, strong smell of rotten eggs; a faint, slight but persistent smell of tobacco; the rank smell of a rotting carcass; the sweet smell of success.* **3** an act of smelling.

—*v.* **smells,** *pt. & pp.* **smelled** or **smelt, smell.ing** **1** have a particular smell: *A rose smells sweet; What you're cooking smells like bacon and eggs; Their home smells of garlic; Unwashed children smell* (= stink). **2** recognize by or as if by smell: *to smell smoke, trouble, a rat; Don't smell* (= sniff) *it; "Wake up and smell the coffee!"* (= Face reality!) *Police dogs are trained to **smell out*** (= smell and find) *drugs.* —**smelling salts** See SALT.

smell.y *adj.* **smell.i.er, -i.est** having a bad smell: *a smelly room; smelly feet.*

smelt *n.* a silvery food fish similar to salmon but smaller and with larger scales. —*v.* **1** melt ore and extract metal. **2** obtain or refine metal by this method.

smelt.er *n.* **1** one who smelts. **2** a furnace for smelting. **3** a smelting works, or **smelt.er.y** *n.* **-er.ies.**

smidg.en (SMIJ.un) *n. Informal.* a small amount: *She brightened a smidgen when she saw us and asked us in; to put up with a smidgen of inconvenience.* Also **smidg.in, smidg.eon.**

smi.lax (SMY.lax) *n.* a woody or herbaceous vine bearing clusters of red or bluish-black berries.

smile *n.* an amused or pleased expression of the face, usu. with an upward curving mouth and parted lips; hence, an act of smiling: *She cracked, flashed, hid, repressed a smile; His joke evoked a smile; beguiling, broad, cheerful, disarming, fixed, forced, happy, intriguing, radiant, sunny, supercilious smiles; She was **all smiles** when she heard the news.*
—*v.* make a smile: *He smiled at her (in admiration); She was smiling from ear to ear; "Fortune smiles on* (= favors) *the brave."* —**smil.ey** or **smil.y** *adj.* : *a button with a **smiley face*** (= happy-face design).

smirch *n. & v.* soil; stain; smear (one's good name).

smirk *v. & n.* (put on) an affected or silly smile; simper: *an I-told-you-so smirk; the smirk on her face; The kids were smirking when they left; smirking over getting only a slap on the wrist.*

smite *v.* **smites,** *pt.* **smote,** *pp.* **smit.ten** or **smote, smit.ing** **1** [literary] strike or hit with force to injure or kill: *God smote their enemies.* **2** affect or impress strongly: *to be smitten with* or *by curiosity, (an) illness, love, remorse; adj.: You can see he's **smitten*** (= in love); *quite smitten with her.*

smith *n.* a worker in metal, esp. a blacksmith.

smith.er.eens (smith.uh.REENS, "th" as in "the") *n.pl. Informal.* small bits or fragments: *The pot was broken or smashed into smithereens; It was in smithereens; blasted, blown, crashed to smithereens.*

smith.y ("th" as in "the" or as in "thin") *n.* **smith.ies** a smith's workshop.

smock *n.* a loose outer garment worn to protect one's clothes while working.
—*v.* ornament with **smocking,** a pattern of stitches for gathering the cloth of a smock or dress; *adj.:* a *smocked bodice, design, treatment.*

smog *n.* a mixture of fog and smoke polluting the air. —**smog.gy** *adj.*

smoke *n.* **1** fumes given off by something burning: *Chimneys belch, emit, give off, spew smoke; smoke pouring or rising from smokestacks; Smoke eddies or spirals upward; a burst, column, pall, plume, puff, stream, trail, wisp of smoke; acrid, heavy, thick, toxic smoke; engine or exhaust smoke from automobiles; People inhale smoke; "Where there's smoke there's fire"; His dream about a windfall **went up in smoke*** (= ended suddenly) *when he woke up; They used to discuss politics in **smoke-filled rooms;** adj.: smoke alarms, damage, flares, grenades, inhalation.*
2 mist, fog, or anything resembling smoke. **3** a smoking of a cigar, cigarette, etc.: *to have a smoke; He just went out for a smoke; She still craves for a smoke now and then.*
—*v.* **smokes, smoked, smok.ing** **1** give off smoke; *adj.: a smoking wood stove; The killer was caught red-handed, with the smoking gun in his hand.* **2** use a cigar, cigarette, pipe, etc. for pleasure: *He smokes like a chimney; smokes heavily; She used to smoke crack cocaine; n.: cigar smoking; Smoking is bad for your lungs; to give up* or *quit* or *stop smoking; no-smoking areas (where smoking is not allowed).* **3** treat with smoke, as in curing meat or fish in a smokehouse, in fumigation, blackening glasses, etc.; *adj.: smoked cheese, fish, leg of mutton, meat, sausage; a smoked-glass window.*
—**smoke out** force to come out, as snakes from a hole. **smok.er** *n.:* a *chain smoker; heavy smokers.*

smoke and mirrors *n.* deception: *Most kids can't see behind the commercial smoke and mirrors of "parts sold separately," "some assembly required," etc.; adj.:* **smoke-and-mirrors** (= deceptive) *accounting, arguments, insurance, operations.*

smoke detector *n.* a home fire-alarm device that is set off in the presence

of smoke.
smoke.house *n.* a room in which ham, bacon, and other salt-cured meats are hung for smoking.
smoke screen or **smoke.screen** *n.* a thick smoke used to hide troops, ships, etc. from the enemy: *to lay (down) a smokescreen.*
smoke shell *n.* an artillery shell that lays a cloud of smoke.
smoke.stack *n.* a tall chimney, as of a factory, or the funnel of a ship, locomotive, etc.
smok.ey same as SMOKY.
smoking gun *n.* a conclusive piece of evidence, as smoke from a gun is a sure sign that it was fired.
smok.y (SMOH.kee) *adj.* **smok.i.er, -i.est** 1 giving off smoke: *a smoky fire.* 2 filled with smoke: *a smoky atmosphere, bar, café, club, hall, room; the smoky air of industrial cities.* 3 like smoke in appearance, smell, etc.: *a whiskey described as raw, strong, and very smoky; a smoky blue-gray color; meat with a smoky flavor.* —**smok.i.ness** *n.*
smol.der (SMOLE.dur) *v.* 1 burn and smoke without flame: *A trash pile smoldered in the park;* *adj.: a* **smoldering** *fire; smoldering remains, ruins.* 2 exist in a suppressed condition: *The crisis smoldered on;* *adj.: smoldering disputes, hatred, passions, rebellion, resentment, tempers, tensions.* —*n.* flameless burning. Also **smoul.der** *Cdn.*
smooch (long "oo") *n. & v. Informal.* kiss or pet. —**smooch.y** *adj.*
smooth ("th" as in "the") *adj.* 1 perfectly even, without roughness; polished: *a smooth surface; It's smooth to the touch; smooth as glass, silk; pebbles worn smooth by the waves; a smooth landing, ride; smooth sailing on calm seas; a smooth-bore firearm (without grooves in the barrel); his smooth baritone; a smooth* (= mild-tasting) *wine.* 2 deceptive: *a smooth sales pitch, talker; a* **smooth-tongued** *flatterer.* —*v.* make smooth or smoother, easy, or refined: *to smooth the bumps, one's hair, relations, the path for negotiations, the rough edges; She stood up to smooth (down) her ruffled dress.*
—**smooth away** (or **out**) get rid of: *to smooth away difficulties; to smooth out differences, problems, rough spots, wrinkles.*
—**smooth over** reduce; also, gloss over: *They tried to smooth over differences, disagreements, faults, friction, scandals.* —**smooth.ly** *adv.;* **smooth.ness** *n.*
smooth.ie or **smooth.y** (SMOO.thee, "th" as in "the") *n. Informal.* a suave, often smooth-tongued person.
smor.gas.bord (SMOR.gus.bord) *n.* a buffet luncheon or supper consisting of a variety of foods spread on a table.
smote *pt. & a pp.* of SMITE.
smoth.er (SMUTH.ur, "TH" as in "the") *v.* 1 cover so as to deprive of air: *to smother a fire with ashes; They cook shrimp and crawfish smothered in vegetables; an office smothered in paperwork; to smother* (= repress) *a giggle, one's resentment; a child smothered* (= overwhelmed) *with kisses, love;* *adj.: a* **smothered** *holler; smothered* (= covered and baked) *chicken, corn, steak.* 2 kill by smothering: *an infant accidentally smothered* (= suffocated) *in bed; to smother an idea, initiative, proposal, urge.* —*n.* 1 something dense and stifling, as smoke, fog, etc. 2 confusion or welter.
smoul.der (SMOLE.dur) *Cdn.* SMOLDER.
smudge *n.* 1 a stained or smeared spot: *lipstick smudges; smudges of paint.* 2 a smoky fire, as from a **smudge pot** or stove used to protect plants from frost or animals from insects: *a smudge fire.*
—*v.* **smudg.es, smudged, smudg.ing** 1 smear or stain: *an apron smudged with dirt.* 2 protect an orchard with smudge. —**smudg.y** *adj.*
smug *adj.* **smug.ger, smug.gest** self-satisfied or complacent in a superior or secure manner: *a smug look; smug respectability.* —**smug.ly** *adv.;* **smug.ness** *n.*
smug.gle (SMUG.ul) *v.* **smug.gles, smug.gled, smug.gling** bring into or take out of a country illegally or secretly: *Drugs are smuggled across a border, past* or *through customs, into* or *out of a country;* *n.: to crack down on, engage in* **smuggling***; arms, contraband, drug smuggling;* *adj.: a smuggling operation, ring, route, ship.* —**smug.gler** *n.: a smuggler's den.*
smut *n.* 1 obscene talk, writing, or pictures: *government crackdown on smut; a smut peddler.* 2 a fungus affecting plants: *corn smut.* —**smut.ty** *adj.* **smut.ti.er, smut.ti.est.** —**smut.ti.ness** *n.*
smutch *n. & v.* soil; stain; grime. —**smutch.y** *adj.*
snack *v. & n.* (eat) a light meal: *between-meal snacks; party snacks.*
snack bar *n.* a lunch counter serving snacks.
snaf.fle (SNAF.ul) *n.* a jointed bit for a horse's bridle.
sna.fu (SNAF.oo) *n. Informal.* a state of confusion or disorder. —*v.* **-fues,**

-**fued, -fu.ing** throw into confusion: *Airline schedules were snafued when the computer went on the blink.*

snag *n.* **1** an underwater obstacle, as a tree or branch, that is dangerous to boats; also, something sharp or pointed. **2** a hidden or unexpected difficulty: *Our plans hit a snag.*
—*v.* **snags, snagged, snag.ging**
1 catch using a snag: *Poachers snag fish.* **2** hinder, as if with a snag: *a project snagged by difficulties from the beginning.* —**snag.gy** *adj.*

snail *n.* a small, soft-bodied, slow-moving mollusk with a spiral shell on its back for coiling back into if molested. —**at a snail's pace** very slowly.

snail mail *n. Informal.* mail sent through the post office compared to e-mail.

snake *n.* **1** a long, scaly, legless reptile with a forked tongue and tapering tail: *Snakes bite, crawl, strike; a snake in the grass* (= hidden danger or enemy). **2** a sly or deceitful person.
—*v.* **snakes, snaked, snak.ing** move, wind, or twist like a snake: *to snake one's way through a crowd; lines of cars snaking around gas stations;* **adja.:** *a snaking airport check-in line; snaking roads.*

snake.bird *n.* a European mottled-brown woodpecker that twists its neck and thrusts it out of its nest when disturbed; wryneck.

snak.y (SNAY.kee) *adj.* **snak.i.er, -i.est** that looks or moves like a snake: *the snaky eel; a snaky river.*

snap *v.* **snaps, snapped, snap.ping**
1 make a sudden, sharp sound, as of a dry twig or taut rope breaking or a finger flicked audibly against the thumb: *to snap a whip.* **2** break suddenly: *The rope snapped; Frost can snap tree branches.* **3** make a quick, sharp movement, as an animal snatching food in its jaws: *The fish snapped at the bait; The best bargains were snapped up by those first to arrive; Each one snapped to attention as his name was called; Her eyes were snapping* (= flashing) *with fury; tourists snapping pictures* (= taking snapshots); *She tends to snap at* (= speak sharply to) *her child when impatient; a football snapped back* (= passed between the player's legs) *into play from the scrimmage line.* —**snap out of it** *Informal.* get quickly out of a bad mood or habit.
—*n.* **1** a quick, cracking sound, as of a whip or a sudden bite. **2** a short, sharp utterance. **3** *Informal.* vigor or liveliness. **4** a brief spell of cold weather: *a cold snap.* **5** a fastener or clasp that closes with a click. **6** a thin, crisp cookie: *lemon snaps.* **7** *Informal.* a snapshot. **8** *Informal.* an easy job; cinch: *It was a snap getting* or *to get a ticket to the show.*
—*adja.* **1** quick: *a snap decision, election, judgment, vote.* **2** that fastens with a snapping sound: *a snap fastener* ("press stud"); *a snap lock, ring.*

snap bean *n.* any stringless bean that is picked when tender and used as a vegetable without shelling; greenbean or wax bean.

snap.drag.on (SNAP.drag.un) *n.* a colorful garden flower with long spikes of two-lipped blossoms that snap open like jaws when pressed on their sides.

snap.per *n.* one that snaps, esp. a tropical food fish with a large mouth and strong teeth.

snap.pish (SNAP.ish) *adj.* quick-tempered; irascible: *He tends to be a bit snappish when disturbed during his afternoon nap.*

snap.py *adj.* **snap.pi.er, snap.pi.est**
1 inclined to be snappish or ill-tempered: *a snappy temperament.*
2 crackling, as a pine fire. **3** smart or lively: *the snappy changing of the guard on Parliament Hill; decorated in bright, snappy colors; a snappy dresser; Make it snappy* (= Move quickly)!

snap.shot *n.* a casual photograph taken with a hand camera.

snare *n.* **1** a trap made with a noose for catching small birds and animals.
2 a pitfall or trap. —*v.* **snares, snared, snar.ing** catch as in a snare.

snarl *v. & n.* **1** (make) an angry or threatening growling sound, as a dog with its teeth bared: *a menacing snarl; a snarling German Shepherd.* **2** (utter) sharp, angry words: *The drivers snarled at each other.* **3** tangle; also, disorder: *caught in a legal snarl; a traffic snarl during rush hour;* **adj.:** *a snarled affair; projects snarled in red tape; snarled roads near a busy airport; a snarling dog, voice.*
—**snarl.y** *adj.* snarling; also, tangled.

snatch *v.* seize or grasp roughly or hastily: *He snatched her purse and ran; a youth snatched from the jaws of death.*
—*n.* **1** a snatching. **2** a short period or small amount: *I caught snatches of the conversation; snatches of a show, of sleep.* —**snatch.er** *n.:* *baby, body, purse snatchers.*

snaz.zy *adj. Informal.* stylish in a showy way: *a line of snazzy clothes for teens; a* *snazzy outfit, suit, yuppie; fish with snazzy trimmings.*

sneak (SNEEK) *v.* **1** move or act in a stealthy or cowardly manner: *He sneaked away at night; sneaked into the house by a back door; sneaked up on her and gave her a scare;* **adj.***a*: *a sneaking* (= secret) *suspicion.* **2** do or get stealthily: *to sneak a glance, kiss, look, peek; He sneaked something into his pocket.*
—*n.* a sneaking or one who sneaks.
—*adj.* stealthy: *a sneak attack, peek, thief.* —**sneak.y** *adj.* **sneak.i.er, -i.est**: *a sneaky feeling, lover, way; a sneaky approach, method, trick.*

sneak.ers (SNEE.kurs) *n.pl.* sports shoes with soles of soft material; running shoes.

sneak preview *n.* advance showing of a motion picture to test audience reaction before its release.

sneer *v.* show ill-natured contempt by facial expression, words, tone of voice, etc.: *He sneers at anything that is not imported.* —*n.* a sneering or its expression.

sneeze *n.* an involuntary sudden and violent expulsion of air through the nose and mouth to clear the nostrils of something irritating. —*v.* **sneez.es, sneezed, sneez.ing** make a sneeze.
—**sneeze at** *Informal.* scorn or despise: *a respectable offer that is not to be sneezed at.*

snick.er *v. & n.* (utter) a sly, half-suppressed laugh.

snide *adj.* slyly critical: *He made snide references to his opponent's past; a snide aside, remark, suggestion; Jan has a snide* (= mean or spiteful) *side.* —**snide.ly** *adv.*

sniff *v.* **1** draw air quickly and audibly through the nose, as to test something by smelling: *He died from sniffing glue for kicks; The dog sniffs at everyone.* **2** express scorn by sniffing: *Let's not sniff at it.* —**sniff out 1** detect: *a police dog trained to sniff out drugs and explosives.* **2** perceive or find out more about something as if by sniffing: *to sniff out facts, rumors, scandals.* —*n.* **1** a sniffing or its sound. **2** a breathing in of something: *Take a sniff of the perfume before buying;* **adj.**: *a sniff (fragrance) card, sample, test.*

snif.fle (SNIF.ul) *v.* **snif.fles, snif.fled, snif.fling** sniff again and again, as when one has a head cold or is crying.
—*n.* a sniffling sound: *He has* **the snif.fles** (= a head cold with congested nose).

snif.ter *n.* a stemmed, bowl-shaped drinking glass with a narrow brim to contain the aroma of the liquor in it.

snig.ger (SNIG.ur) same as SNICKER.

snip *v.* **snips, snipped, snip.ping** cut off or clip, as hair with scissors, in a short, quick stroke. —*n.* **1** a snipping or snipped piece. **2 snips** *pl.* [with *sing. v.*] hand shears for cutting sheet metal.

snipe *v.* **snipes, sniped, snip.ing 1** to hunt snipe. **2** shoot at people from a hidden position. **3** make direct verbal attacks *at* people. —*n.* a long-billed, chunky, black-and-white bird.
—**snip.er** *n.*

snip.pet (SNIP.it) *n.* a small piece as if snipped from a larger source: *snippets of gossip, information, writing.*

snip.py (SNIP.ee) *adj.* **snip.pi.er, snip.pi.est** *Informal.* snappish or haughty: *a snippy reply.* —**snip.pi.ly** *adv.*

snit *n. Informal.* a state of peevish annoyance: *He quit his job in a snit.*

snitch *v. Informal.* **1** pilfer or steal. **2** tattle *on* someone. —*n. Informal.* **1** an informer or tattletale: *an FBI snitch.* **2** an act of snitching.

sniv.el (SNIV.ul) *v.* **-els, -eled, -el.ing** cry or whine in a sniffling manner.
—*n.* a sniveling. —**sniv.el.er** *n.* Also **sniv.elled, sniv.el.ling; sniv.el.ler** *Cdn.*

snob *n.* one who cares much for rank and wealth and looks down on people considered socially inferior: *Some luxury cars are sold more for their* **snob appeal** *and* **snob value** *than for fuel efficiency.* —**snob.bish** *adj.;* **snob.bish.ly** *adv.;* **snob.bish.ness** *n.*

snob.ber.y (SNOB.uh.ree) *n.* **snob.ber.ies** a snobbish act or quality; snobbishness: *social snobbery.*

snob.by same as SNOBBISH.

snood (long "oo") *n.* a net worn by women to hold the hair at the back of the head.

snook (short or long "oo") *n.*: *to* **cock a snook at** (= thumb one's nose at) *someone.*

snook.er (short or long "oo") *n.* a game similar to billiards: *to shoot snooker.*
—*v. Slang.* to trick or cheat: *We have been snookered; He was snookered into buying the lemon.*

snoop (long "oo") *v. Informal.* inquire into other people's affairs in a sneaky manner: *to snoop using wiretaps.*
—*n.* a snooper.

snoop.y *adj.* **snoop.i.er, -i.est** prying or nosy.

snoot (long "oo") *n. Informal.* the face,

esp. one's nose.

snoot.y (SNOO.tee) *adj.* **snoot.i.er, -i.est** haughty or snobbish. —**snoot.i.ly** *adv.*; **snoot.i.ness** *n.*

snooze *n. Informal.* a nap or doze. —*v.* **snooz.es, snoozed, snooz.ing** *Informal.* take a snooze, esp. in the daytime.

snore *n. & v.* **snores, snored, snor.ing** (make) a rough, hoarse breathing noise while sleeping.

snor.kel (SNOR.kul) *v. & n.* (swim under water using) a curved air tube projecting above the water. —**snor.kel.er** *n.*

snort *v.* **1** force air suddenly through the nose, as a horse does or as one who shows contempt, anger, etc. **2** *Slang.* inhale and take in: *caught snorting cocaine.* —*n.* **1** a snorting. **2** *Slang.* a drink of liquor, usu. straight and quickly gulped. **3** *Slang.* an inhaling of a drug or its amount: *a snort of cocaine.*

snot *n.* [vulgar slang] **1** nasal mucus. **2** one who is snotty. —**snot.ty** *adj.* **snot.ti.er, snot.ti.est** impudent.

snout (*rhyme:* out) *n.* a projecting nose and mouth, as of a pig, crocodile, certain beetles and butterflies, etc.

snow (SNOH) *n.* (a falling of) white, feathery crystals of frozen water vapor from the atmosphere: *as white as snow; A blanket of snow covered the landscape; crisp, drifting, driving, heavy, light snow; He shoveled the snow; Children play in the snow.*
—*v.* fall as snow: *It snowed lightly on Christmas Day; It snowed hard, heavily all January.* —**snow in** shut in by snow. —**snow under** cover with snow or overwhelm, as with accumulated work.

snow.ball *n.* a ball of hand-packed snow. —*v.* **1** throw snowballs at someone. **2** increase rapidly like a rolling mass of snow: *The movement snowballed into a popular revolt.*

snow.bank *n.* a mass of heaped snow; snowdrift.

snow.belt *n.* a region of heavy snowfall.

snow.bird *n.* a seasonal migrant to the Sunbelt, such as Canadians who winter there.

snow.blow.er (SNOH.bloh.ur) *n.* a machine for clearing snow by blowing it away; also **snow thrower**.

snow.board *n.* a short laminated board used like a surfboard for skiing on snow. —**snow.board.ing** or **snow.surf.ing** *n.*

snow.bound *adj.* shut in or obstructed by snow: *a snowbound airport, village;* *They are snowbound for much of the year.*

snow.drift *n.* snow piled up by the wind.

snow.drop *n.* an amaryllis that bears delicate white nodding blossoms in early spring.

snow.fall *n.* a fall of snow or its amount: *a region of heavy snowfall.*

snow.fence *n.* a fence, formerly made with lath and wire, put up to stop snow from drifting across a road.

snow.field *n.* a region or expanse of perennial snow, as at the head of a glacier.

snow.flake *n.* a crystal of falling snow.

snow job *n. Slang.* an effort to persuade mainly by deceptive methods, as by flattery or exaggeration: *He gave her a snow job to get her to help with the sales campaign.*

snow.man *n.* **-men** a human figure made with packed snow.

snow.mo.bile (SNOH.moh.beel) *n.* a motor vehicle with short skis in front for traveling over snow and ice. —**snow.mo.bil.er** *n.*; **snow.mo.bil.ing** *n.*

snow.plow (*rhyme:* how) *n.* a plowlike machine for clearing streets, driveways, etc. of snow. Also **snow.plough** *Cdn.*

snow.shoe *n.* a light, racketlike wooden frame strung with leather thongs that allows one to walk over snow without sinking.

snow.storm *n.* a storm with a heavy fall of snow.

snow.suit *n.* a warmly lined, usu. hooded winter suit for children to wear outdoors.

snowsurfing same as SNOWBOARDING.

snow thrower same as SNOWBLOWER.

snow tire *n.* a tire with a heavy tread for extra traction over snow and ice.

snow.y *adj.* **snow.i.er, -i.est** having to do with snow: *a snowy day, valley; her snowy* (= white as snow) *hair; a snowy TV picture* (that looks as if it is snowing).

snub *v.* **snubs, snubbed, snub.bing 1** to slight someone: *Oxford snubbed Prime Minister Thatcher by refusing her an honorary doctorate.* **2** treat something with contempt: *to snub an invitation.* **3** check or stop an animal or thing in motion. —*n.* a slight; scornful treatment: *She found the snub disgusting.*

snub nose *n.* a short nose with upturned tip: *a nice person with a snub nose and double chin.* —**snub-nosed** *adj.*

snuck *Regional* or *Informal.* sneaked.

snuff *v.* **1** draw air up the nose; sniff. **2** draw powdered tobacco into the nose. **3** pinch off the burnt wick of a candle to make it burn brighter. **4** put out a candle. **5** destroy or kill someone. **—snuff out** put an end to something; kill: *to snuff out a cigarette; Communism failed to snuff out religion in the Soviet Union.* **—n. 1** the charred end of a candlewick. **2** powdered tobacco for snuffing. **—up to snuff** *Informal.* **1** up to standard: *The new car is not working up to snuff.* **2** sharp or alert.

snug *adj.* **snug.ger, snug.gest 1** warm and sheltered: *a snug cabin, corner; tucked safe and snug in bed; a snug* (= comfortable) *income; Lee lay snug* (= concealed) *till the danger passed.* **2** compact or close-fitting: *The shoe is a snug fit.* **—snug.ly** *adv.*

snug.gle (SNUG.ul) *v.* **snug.gles, snug.gled, snug.gling** draw closely to someone for cosiness; nestle: *The child snuggled up to her mother.*

so (SOH) *adv.* **1** in the way indicated or implied: *He talks so fast no one can follow him; He does it* **so as to** (= in order to) *confuse everyone.* **2** very (much): *She's so sweet; It hurts so.* **3** likewise: *I live here; so does she.* **—conj.** with the purpose or result that: *Please be quiet* **so (that)** *I can read; I was tired, so* (*Informal for* therefore) *I fell asleep.* **—pron.:** *a dozen* **or so** (= approximately that). **—interj.:** *So, that's how! So you're back!* **—adjp.:** *I told you so; Is that so? She wants everything* **just so** (= exactly as desired). **—and so on** or **so forth** and the rest. **—so what?** *Informal.* Even if that's true, it does not matter: *He is not very religious, so what?*

soak (SOKE) *v.* make or become thoroughly wet by keeping or remaining in a liquid: *Soak the clothes before washing; Let them soak in the tub; Water soaks through* (= penetrates) *clothes, soaks into the ground; Towels soak up* (= absorb) *water.* **—n. 1** a soaking, being soaked, or a liquid for soaking something in. **2** *Informal.* a drunkard.

so-and-so *n.* **so-and-sos** *Informal.* **1** an unnamed person or thing: *The police officer told Dr. so-and-so she was in violation of section so-and-so of the Highway Traffic Act.* **2** scoundrel: *I'll teach the so-and-so a lesson.*

soap (SOPE) *n.* **1** a substance made by the action of an alkali on fat or fatty acids, used to cleanse by the suds it forms with water: *a bar, cake of soap; liquid soap.* **2** [short form] soap opera. **—no soap** *Informal.* nothing doing; nothing accomplished. **—v.** apply soap to a body or body part.

soap.box *n.* an improvised platform, as for addressing a crowd in the street; hence, the preacher's pose: *She climbs on or gets on or mounts her soapbox weekly to write about abortion;* **adj.:** *soapbox orator, oratory.*

soap opera *n.* a sentimental daytime serial drama on radio or TV.

soap.stone *n.* a soft rock with a soapy feel, composed mostly of talc, much used in industry as insulating material, etc.

soap.suds *n.pl.* lather made by soap in water.

soap.y *adj.* **soap.i.er, -i.est 1** covered with or containing soap: *Soak it in hot, soapy water.* **2** smooth or greasy: *a finish that has turned dull, almost soapy.*

soar *v.* rise upward or fly high, as an eagle or glider plane: *Interest rates are soaring; The temperature soared to 90° yesterday; Profits soared 25% last year;* **adj.:** *soaring ambitions, crime, popularity, prices, sales, skyscrapers.*

sob *v.* **sobs, sobbed, sob.bing 1** weep or cry with short, gasping breaths: *He sobbed his heart out; She sobbed herself to sleep.* **2** utter sobbing: *"I'm sorry," Sam sobbed.* **—n.** a sobbing or its sound: *Sobs could be heard from the next room; bitter sobs of frustration.*

so.ber (SOH.bur) *adj.* **1** not drunk: *a sober driver; a man of sober* (= temperate) *habits.* **2** serious, tranquil, or sensible: *a sober estimate, expression; sober advice, criticism, reflection; sober clothes in sober* (= quiet, not flashy) *colors.* **—v.** esp. **sober down** or **sober up** make or become sober: *a cup of coffee to help you sober up a little;* **adj.:** *It had a* **sobering** *effect; a sobering fact, event, experience, lesson, message, moment, reminder, thought, truth; sobering advice, reality.*

so.bri.e.ty (suh.BRY.uh.tee) *n.* the quality or condition of being sober; temperance; seriousness.

so.bri.quet (SOH.bruh.cay) *n.* a fanciful epithet or nickname.

sob sister *n.* a very sentimental writer or do-gooder.

sob story *n.* an overly sentimental story or excuse.

so-called *adj.* **1** so-termed: *the so-called "Monday Morning Group."* **2** so-termed, as if inaccurately or unjustifiably: *a so-called expert; one of those so-called civilized countries.*

soc.cer (SOK.ur) *n.* the international variety of football, played between teams of 11 players using a round, inflated ball.

so.cia.ble (SOH.shuh.bul) *adj.* **1** liking companionship: *a sociable woman.* **2** marked by friendliness: *a sociable evening, occasion.* —**so.cia.bly** (-blee) *adv.* —**so.cia.bil.i.ty** (-BIL.i.tee) *n.*

so.cial (SOH.shul) *adj.* **1** having to do with living and working together: *We are social beings; ants, bees, and such social insects; They are social by nature; his social* (= *friendly*) *nature.* **2** having to do with relationships within human society: *social classes, clubs, problems, services, studies; I had only one social drink at the party.* —*n.* a social gathering or party. —**so.cial.ly** *adv.*

social climber *n.* one who wants to get into higher society.

social disease *n.* venereal disease.

social drinker *n.* one who normally drinks only in company.

Social Insurance *n.* Cdn. SOCIAL SECURITY.

so.cial.ism (SOH.shuh.liz.um) *n.* the theory or system of public ownership of the means of production and distribution brought about by nonrevolutionary changes in the social order: *to live under socialism.*

So.cial.ist or **so.cial.ist** (SOH.shuh.list) **1** *n. & adj.* (member) of a socialist political party. **2** *adj.* in Communist theory, leading to the Communist ideal: *a socialist government, republic.* —**so.cial.is.tic** (-LIS.tic) *adj.*

so.cial.ite (SOH.shuh.lite) *n.* a prominent member of fashionable society.

so.cial.ize (SOH.shuh.lize) *v.* **-iz.es, -ized, -iz.ing 1** be social: *He was socializing too much at work; socializing over lunch; Now he socializes with friends on weekends; n.: He's not interested in socializing while finishing his Ph.D. thesis.* **2** make social: *Boys and girls are socialized differently; Rites of passage are meant to socialize births, deaths, marriages, etc.; adj.: the socializing influence of school; a socializing force.* **3** make socialistic; also, nationalize: *to socialize industry, public services; adj.: a socialized economy; socialized health services.* —**so.cial.i.za.tion** (-luh.ZAY.shun, -lye-) *n.*

socialized medicine *n.* the providing of hospital and medical care for all through public funds.

social leader *n.* a person with a very busy social life.

social mobility *n.* in a democracy, the opportunity to move to higher social levels and to different areas of interest.

social science *n.* anthropology, economics, history, political science, psychology, sociology, law, etc. as distinguished from the natural sciences and humanities. —**social scientist** *n.*

Social Security *n.* a U.S. government program of aiding those in need because of old age, unemployment, sickness, etc.: *A nine-digit social security number is given to each U.S. resident.*

social work *n.* community work involving services such as medical help, family counseling, and aid to the handicapped; also **social service.** —**social worker** *n.*

so.ci.e.tal (suh.SYE.uh.tul) *adj.* having to do with large social groups: *a societal norm; The world market is a global societal system; societal changes, forces, issues, values.* —**so.ci.e.tal.ly** *adv.*

so.ci.e.ty (suh.SYE.uh.tee) *n.* **-ties 1** human beings considered as a social group: *Criminals are a threat to society.* **2** an organized group of individuals, as a club or association: *a society established or founded or set up for the prevention of cruelty to animals; to disband or dissolve a society; historical, humane, learned, literary, mutual-aid, secret societies.* **3** a social group with a particular character: *American society; advanced, affluent, civilized, industrial, pluralistic, primitive societies; She moves in high, polite society; leaders of society* (= *people in high positions*). **4** companionship: *We enjoy her society.* —*adja.* of high society: *a newspaper's society page; society gossip, women.*

so.ci.ol.o.gy (soh.see.OL.uh.jee, soh.shee-) *n.* the science of human relationships among individuals and groups; **so.ci.ol.o.gist** *n.* —**so.ci.o.log.i.cal** (-uh.LOJ.i.cul) *adj.*

so.ci.o.path (SOH.see.uh.path, SOH.shee-) *n.* an aggressively antisocial mentally ill person.

sock *n.* **1** a short stocking: *a pair of socks; to darn or mend socks.* **2** *Informal.* a hard or vigorous blow: *a sock on the jaw.* —*v.* punch or hit hard: *Sam socked Pat in the nose.* —**sock away** put away, as savings. —**sock it to someone** *Informal.* act toward or speak very forcefully to someone. —**socked in** *Informal.* closed, as an airport, or grounded, as planes, by bad weather.

sock.et (SOCK.it) *n.* a hollow part into which something fits or is fitted: *the socket of the eye, of an electric bulb; the ball-and-socket joint of the hip or shoulder; an L- or T-shaped socket wrench with a socket at one end to fit a bolt or nut.*

sock.o (SOCK.oh) *adj. Slang.* outstanding: *a socko performance, speech; Things are not so socko with the economy.*

So.crat.ic (suh.CRAT.ic) *adj.* having to do with **Socrates,** Greek philosopher of 5th century B.C., his philosophy, or method of using questions to elicit responses from his disciples: *a Socratic dialogue.*

sod *n.* **1** the surface layer of earth held together by roots of grass, etc. **2** a piece of this. —*v.* **sods, sod.ded, sod.ding** cover with sod; turf: *to sod a lawn; adj.: freshly sodded grounds.*

so.da (SOH.duh) *n.* **1** [short form] soda pop or soda water. **2** a carbonated beverage: *club, cream, ice-cream soda; a Scotch and soda* (= soda water). **3** a compound of sodium and carbon: *baking soda; caustic soda;* **soda ash** (= sodium carbonate).

soda biscuit *n.* a biscuit leavened with baking soda and sour milk or buttermilk.

soda cracker *n.* a light cracker made without sugar or shortening.

soda fountain *n.* a counter at which soft drinks and ice cream are served.

soda pop *n.* a carbonated and sweetened soft drink.

soda water *n.* carbonated water.

sod.den (SOD.un) *adj.* **1** soaked through; drenched: *sodden lands following a flood; the smell of sodden straw and mud; this sodden mess of a show.* **2** stupefied, as if drunk: *The sodden lawyer droned on; a movie star moaning in her whiskey-sodden voice; His charms had gone sodden.* **3** of baked things, soggy or doughlike: *sodden biscuits, bread, compost.*

so.di.um (SOH.dee.um) *n.* a metallic element that is the chief component of common salt (**sodium chloride**), baking soda (**sodium bicarbonate**), caustic soda (**sodium hydroxide**), washing soda (**sodium carbonate**) and other salts and alkalis.

sod.om.y (SOD.uh.mee) *n.* sexual intercourse considered abnormal or bestial, esp. anal intercourse, between men; **sod.om.ite** *n.*

sod turning *n.* the breaking of ground to start a new building.

so.ev.er (soh.EV.ur) *adv. & suffix.* in any way; also, of any kind; at all: *how good soever; whatsoever; whosoever.*

so.fa (SOH.fuh) *n.* a usu. upholstered couch or long seat with back and arms.

sofa bed *n.* a sofa that can be opened into a double bed.

soft (SOFT, SAWFT) *adj.* **1** not hard or rough to the senses, esp. touch; yielding to pressure; smooth: *soft fur; Talc is the softest of minerals; a soft breeze; a bit soft in the head* (= silly). **2** not sharp, loud, or glaring: *soft colors, music, shadows.* **3** easy and gentle to the feelings: *a soft and luxurious life; a soft job; a soft* (= kind) *heart; She has a* **soft spot** (= special affection) *for animals; a judge who is soft on* (= lenient toward) *first-time offenders.* **4** opposed to "hard": *the soft "c" of "city," "g" of "gem," "ch" of "chip";* **soft drugs** like marijuana, amphetamines, and hallucinogens that are not strong or addictive; **soft water** *(that is free of minerals).*
—*adv.* in a soft manner. Also **soft.ly** *adv.* —**soft.ness** *n.*

soft.ball *n.* a game similar to baseball but played on a smaller field and with a larger ball which is pitched underhand.

soft-boiled *adj.* of eggs, boiled without the yolk becoming hard.

soft.bound or **soft-cover** *adj.* of books, paperback.

soft coal *n.* bituminous coal.

soft-core *adj.* of pornography, containing no explicit sex: *a soft-core movie.*

soft drink *n.* a sweetened and flavored, usu. carbonated nonalcoholic drink, as cola.

sof.ten (SOF.un) *v.* make or become soft or softer. —**soft.en.er** *n.*

soft goods same as SOFT LINES.

soft.heart.ed (SOFT.HAR.tid) *adj.* kind and gentle.

softie See SOFTY.

soft landing *n.* **1** the gentle setting down of a spacecraft without damage to itself or contents. **2** the slowing down of a nation's economic growth to stop inflation and avoid a recession; slowdown.

soft line *n.* **1** a conciliatory or accommodating approach: *a company's soft line on strikes;* **adj.:** *a soft-line approach.* **2** **soft lines** *n.pl.* goods such as apparel, home furnishings, and footwear, as opposed to more durable goods: *hard lines and soft lines;* **adja.:** *the soft-lines category;* **soft-line** *products, sales;* also **soft goods.**

soft palate See PALATE.

soft-pedal *v.* **-als, -aled, -al.ing** *Informal.* play down or tone down, as in playing a piano using the "soft pedal" for reducing volume. Also **soft-pedalled, soft-pedalling** *Cdn.*

soft sell *n.* a selling method using suggestion or persuasion instead of pressure.

soft soap *n. Informal.* flattery.
—**soft-soap** *v.*
soft spot See SOFT.
soft touch *n.* one who is easy to get money out of.
soft.ware *n.* operational directions, procedures, accessory materials, etc. of any system or equipment, esp. the programs used with a computer: *hardware and software; applications, communications, systems software; software that runs on compatible computers;* **adja.:** *software programs; software development by* **software engineers**; *(commercially sold)* **software packages**; *a* **software artist** (= hacker).
soft water *n.* water that is free of minerals.
soft.wood *n.* wood of coniferous trees such as pines and firs that is easy to work or finish.
soft.y *n.* **soft.ies** *Informal.* one who is overly sensitive emotionally or physically; also **soft.ie.**
sog.gy (SOG.ee) *adj.* **sog.gi.er, sog.gi.est 1** esp. of ground, soaked or damp. **2** sodden: *soggy bread.*
—**sog.gi.ly** *adv.*; **sog.gi.ness** *n.*
soi.gné (swah.NYAY) *adj. French.* **1** of things, elegantly done or designed. **2** of persons, well-groomed; **soi.gnée** (-NYAY) *fem.*
soil *n.* **1** the earth's surface or ground, esp. as supporting growth and development: *to cultivate, fertilize, irrigate, till, work the soil; barren, clayey, fertile, poor, sandy soils; a man* or *son* **of the soil** (= hereditary farmer); *The terrorist was not allowed to set foot on American soil* (= land); **adja.:** *soil conservation, depletion, erosion.* **2** stain or spot; also, foul matter. —*v.* make or become dirty: *He doesn't like to soil his hands (with dirty work); a reputation soiled* (= tainted) *by scandals;* **adj.:** *sheets that are somewhat* **soiled**; *soiled diapers, hands, linen; a soiled beige* (color); *a soiled image, reputation.*
soi.ree or **soi.rée** (swah.RAY) *n.* an evening party.
so.journ (SOH.jurn) *n.* a temporary stay in a place. —*v.* (*also* soh.JURN) stay temporarily: *We used to sojourn abroad in the summer.*
sol (SOLE) *n.* **1** *Music.* the fifth tone of the diatonic scale. **2** (*also* SOL) a colloid in a liquid solution. **3 Sol** (SOLE) in Roman myth, the sun god.
sol.ace (SOL.is) *n.* consolation or relief: *She turned to her friends for solace in her sorrow; Her friends were a solace to her; to draw solace from something; to find,*

seek, take solace in religion; Music offers solace for the troubled soul. —*v.* comfort or console: *to solace someone in her misery.*
so.lar (SOH.lur) *adj.* having to do with the sun: *solar activity, eclipses, heat, phenomena, power; Our* **solar day** *represents one rotation of the earth;* **solar energy** *captured by means of a* **solar battery** *made up of* **solar cells** *in the* **solar panel** *of an orbiting satellite; She lives in a* **solar house** *that uses solar energy.*
—*n.* energy from the sun: *Many people are switching to solar from oil, gas, electricity, etc.*
solar flare *n.* an outburst of radiation from a sunspot.
so.lar.i.um (suh.LAIR.ee.um) *n.* **-i.ums** or **-i.a** (-ee.uh) a glass-enclosed room for sunning, as in a sanitarium.
solar plexus *n.* the radiating network of nerves behind the stomach.
solar system *n.* the system composed of the sun and the planets, etc. revolving around it.
solar wind *n.* the continual outflow of electrically charged particles from the sun.
solar year *n.* the time it takes for the earth to go once around the sun, i.e., 365 days, 5 hours, 48 minutes, and 46 seconds.
sold *pt. & pp.* OF SELL.
sol.der (SOD.ur) *n.* an alloy used to join metals by melting it with the heat of an electrical device called a **soldering iron.** —*v.* join with solder.
sol.dier (SOLE.jur) *n.* a member of an army, usu. not an officer: *armed, common, seasoned soldiers; Soldiers defect from, enlist in, fight in, serve in the army; Soldiers may go AWOL; a* **soldier of fortune** (= mercenary). —*v.* work like a soldier: *She soldiered on* (= carried on with determination) *into her seventies.*
—**sol.dier.ly** *adj. & adv.*
sole *n.* **1** the bottom surface of the foot. **2** the bottom of a shoe, sock, or other footwear. **3** a flat fish of warm seas used as food: *fillet of sole.*
—*v.* **soles, soled, sol.ing** furnish with a sole: *to sole a shoe;* **cpd:** *heavy-soled boots; You can have leather-soled or rubber-soled slippers; thick-soled shoes.*
—*adj.* one and only: *my sole purpose; the sole owner, responsibility, survivor; sole* (= exclusive) *publication rights.*
sol.e.cism (SOL.uh.siz.um) *n.* a departure from accepted grammar, usage, etiquette, etc., as "between you and I" (instead of *me*).
sole.ly *adv.* alone or exclusively: *He's*

solemn / solstice

solely to blame; It's solely a matter of pride; The cost of living has gone up solely because of gas prices; He got married solely for the purpose of getting rich.

sol.emn (SOL.um) *adj.* **1** serious in an impressive or awe-inspiring way: *a solemn oath, occasion, responsibility; a solemn (= serious) face.* **2** formal or ceremonious; religious: *a solemn curse, procession; a Solemn High Mass.* —**sol.emn.ly** *adv.* —**so.lem.ni.ty** (suh.LEM.ni.tee) *n.* **-ties.**

so.le.noid (SOH.luh.noid, SOL-) *n.* a cylindrical coil of wire working as an electrically induced magnet to actuate switches and other devices.

sole proprietor *n.* the only owner of a business.

so.lic.it (suh.LIS.it) *v.* **1** ask earnestly and respectfully: *to solicit advice, comments, contributions, funds, orders, support, votes; to solicit the views of consumers; to solicit the membership for donations; We are soliciting new customers; n.: The sign on our door says "No soliciting after dark."* **2** entreat or accost for something immoral: *a man found soliciting boys; n.: hookers charged with soliciting.* —**so.lic.i.ta.tion** (-TAY.shun) *n.*

so.lic.i.tor (suh.LIS.uh.tur) *n.* a lawyer in the role of advising clients and preparing cases to be argued by a barrister in court, as in the British tradition.

so.lic.i.tous (suh.LIS.uh.tus) *adj.* showing care, concern, or solicitude: *a mother solicitous about or of her child's welfare.* —**so.lic.i.tous.ly** *adv.*

so.lic.i.tude (suh.LIS.uh.tude) *n.* care or concern for another's well-being: *Yves spoke with sincerity and solicitude; parental solicitude for children; solicitude for the poor.*

sol.id *n.* **1** a substance that is not a liquid or gas. **2** a three-dimensional object, as a cube or sphere. —*adj.* **1** not liquid or gaseous: *solid fuels; It was frozen solid; disposal of solid wastes.* **2** not hollow but filled entirely and uniformly: *bars of solid gold; solid brick; in solid colors, not patterned; printed and solid tablecloths; I waited two solid (= uninterrupted) hours; "Icebox" is written solid (= as one unhyphenated word), unlike "ice-skating" and "ice pick".* **3** hard and firm; also, having qualities of soundness, strength, genuineness, dependability, etc.: *a solid structure built on solid ground; a man of solid build; solid evidence, relationships, support; a solid character, citizen, treatise.* **4** three-dimensional, not flat: *Unlike a square, a cube is a solid figure.* —**sol.id.ly** *adv.;*

sol.id.ness *n.* —**so.lid.i.ty** (suh.LID.i.tee) *n.*

sol.i.dar.i.ty (sol.uh.DAIR.i.tee) *n.* unity of purpose, interests, feelings, etc., as of a closely knit group: *to express, feel, show solidarity with a person or group; in solidarity with the people.*

solid geometry *n.* the geometry of three-dimensional figures.

so.lid.i.fy (suh.LID.uh.fye) *v.* **-fies, -fied, -fy.ing** make or become solid, as water by freezing. —**so.lid.i.fi.ca.tion** (-fuh.CAY.shun) *n.*

solid-state (SOL.id.state) *adj.* having to do with the physical properties of solids, as used in electronic devices such as semiconductors, transistors, and integrated circuits that have no moving parts, gases, heated filaments, etc.

so.lil.o.quy (suh.LIL.uh.quee) *n.* **-quies 1** the formal act of talking to oneself. **2** a dramatic device or speech in which an actor thinks aloud for the benefit of the audience. —**so.lil.o.quize** (-quize) *v.* **-quiz.es, -quized, -quiz.ing:** *Hamlet soliloquizes on death.*

sol.i.taire (SOL.uh.tair) *n.* **1** a card game for one person. **2** a gem set by itself.

sol.i.tar.y (SOL.uh.tair.ee) *adj.* living or existing away from others; alone and isolated: *a prisoner put in solitary confinement; a hermit's solitary life; solitary bees and wasps (that are not social); a solitary (= lonely) place.* —**sol.i.tar.i.ness** *n.*

sol.i.tude (SOL.uh.tude) *n.* a lonely place or condition; seclusion: *Hermits live in complete, utter solitude; the solitudes of city dwellers; Canada's* **two solitudes** *(= English-French division of society).*

so.lo (SOH.loh) *n.* **-los 1** a musical piece for one voice or instrument: *to perform, play, sing a solo; a drum solo; solo recitals.* **2** any performance by one person. —*v., pt.* **so.loed 1** perform a solo. **2** do by oneself something that requires practice: *After some training she started soloing; to solo a glider, plane.* —*adv.* alone: *She flew solo; to go, manage, perform, play, sing solo;* **adj***a***.:** *a solo act, dance, diner, part, performance, venture.* —**so.lo.ist** *n.*

Sol.o.mon (SOL.uh.mun) *n.* a king of Israel famous for his wisdom.

so long *Informal.* good-bye.

sol.stice (SOL.stis) *n.* the time of the year when the sun appears at its farthest point north or south, i.e., about June 21 (**summer solstice** in the Northern Hemisphere) and December 22 (**winter solstice**).

sol.u.ble (SOL.yuh.bul) *adj.* that can be dissolved; **sol.u.bly** *adv.* —**sol.u.bil.i.ty** (-BIL.i.tee) *n.*

sol.ute (SOL.yoot, SOH.loot, long "oo") *n.* the substance dissolved or in solution.

so.lu.tion (suh.LOO.shun) *n.* **1** (a mixture formed by) the dissolving or dispersion of one substance in another, esp. a solid in a liquid: *a strong solution of salt in water; a weak solution; Salt is (held) in solution in water.* **2** the solving of a problem or its result or explanation: *a mystery that defies solution; Is it capable of solution? to find a satisfactory solution to a problem; the solution of a crime, mystery; no easy, glib, ideal solutions; an ingenious, neat solution; For the Nazis, the final solution was to kill off the Jews.*

solve (SOLV) *v.* **solves, solved, solv.ing** find an answer to something that is a problem: *to solve a crime, crisis, dilemma, dispute, issue, mystery, problem, puzzle.* —**solv.a.ble** *adj.* —**solv.er** *n.*

sol.vent (SOL.vunt) *adj.* **1** dissolving: *a solvent liquid.* **2** able to pay all one's debts: *We are almost out of pocket, but remain solvent; solvent companies.* —*n.* a substance such as water or turpentine that can dissolve other substances: *Clean the stain using a solvent.* —**sol.ven.cy** *n.*: *restored to economic strength and solvency.*

So.ma.li (suh.MAL.ee) *n.* **-lis 1** a person of or from **Somalia**, an E. African country. **2** the language of Somalia. Also *adj.*

so.mat.ic (soh.MAT.ic) *adj.* of the body: *A somatic cell is an animal or plant cell that is not a germ cell;* **so.mat.i.cal.ly** *adv.*

som.ber (SOM.bur) *adj.* gloomy or melancholy; cheerless: *in a somber mood; somber colors, skies, tones.* —**som.ber.ly** *adv.* Also **som.bre, som.bre.ly** *Cdn.*

som.bre.ro (som.BRAIR.oh) *n.* **-ros** a wide-brimmed felt or straw hat of Spanish origin.

-some 1 *adj. suffix.* indicating a condition or quality: *awesome, gladsome, meddlesome.* **2** *n. suffix.* a group as specified: *foursome, twosome.* **3** (-sohm) *comb.form.* body: *centrosome, chromosome.*

some (SUM) *adja.* of an indefinite number, amount, or quantity: *I had some sleep; It happened some* (= a few) *days back; in some* (= certain) *countries; in some* (= a) *country I can't remember; Consult some* (*Informal for* an unspecified or any) *lawyer; That was some* (*Informal for* a remarkable or wonderful) *party!*

—*adv.*: *It happened some* (= about or nearly) *10 days back; I managed to sleep some* (*Informal for* somewhat; a little).

—*pron.* **1** certain people or things: *Some are good, some are bad.* **2** a few: *I know some of them; some of the boys.*

—**and then some** *Informal.* and a good deal more than that.

some.bod.y (SUM.bod.ee, -bud.ee) *pron.* some person: *He needs somebody to talk to; somebody for support.* —*n.* a person of importance: *She's somebody around here.*

some.day *adv.* at some future time.
some.how *adv.* by some means.
some.one same as SOMEBODY.
some.place *adv. Informal.* somewhere: *Let's go someplace nice like the zoo.*

som.er.sault (SUM.ur.sault) *v. & n.* (perform) a complete roll of the body with the heels turning over the head: *She somersaulted through the doorway; to do* or *execute* or *throw* or *turn a somersault; The new policy represents a complete somersault* (= reversal) *from the previous position.* Also **sum.mer.sault.**

some.thing *pron.* an unspecified thing, amount, or part: *There's something in what she says; She has something for all of us; Heaven is an indefinable, intangible something; if you want to make something of the evidence we have; Something unexpected happened today; He's something* (= a bit or little) *of a jack-of-all-trades; She's something* (*Informal for* a person of importance) *in the FBI.* —**something else** a different or distinctive person or thing: *She's something else.* —*adv.* somewhat: *something like $20,000.*

some.time *adv.* at an unspecified time: *See you sometime tomorrow; It happened sometime back.* —*adja.* former: *a sometime professor of law.*

some.times *adv.* now and then; occasionally.

some.way *adv.* by some means; also **some.ways.**

some.what *adv.* to some extent or degree. —*n.* something: *She's somewhat of a poet.*

some.where *adv.* at some place: *I saw him somewhere; I would place it somewhere in the 1950s; It is somewhere around* (= approximately) *$100.*

som.nam.bu.lism (som.NAM.byuh.liz.um) *n.* sleepwalking; **som.nam.bu.list** *n.*

som.no.lent (SOM.nuh.lunt) *adj.* **1** sleepy or drowsy: *aged and somnolent*

club members. **2** causing sleep: *a sonorous but somnolent voice; a somnolent delivery, performance, tone.*
—**som.no.lence** *n.*

son (SUN) *n.* a male offspring in relation to his parents: *their only son; He was like a son to all of us; a father awaiting the return of his prodigal son; John Kennedy is one of America's favorite sons;* **a son of the soil** (= hereditary farmer).

so.nar (SOH.nar) *n.* a radar device that uses reflected sound waves to find water depth, detect submarines, etc.

so.na.ta (suh.NAH.tuh) *n.* an instrumental composition with several movements contrasting in rhythm but related in thought.

so.na.ti.na (son.uh.TEE.nuh) *n.* a short or simplified sonata.

song *n.* **1** a singing or a piece of music for singing: *to belt out, compose, hum, play, sing, write a song; They burst into song; a hero renowned in song and legend; drinking, folk, love, marching, popular, swan, theme songs; with a song* (= with joy) *in his heart.* **2** a short poem whether set to music or not: *"The Song of Hiawatha"; "Our sweetest songs are those that tell of saddest thought";* **the same old song** (= complaint); *The piano went* **for a song** (*Informal for* was sold cheaply). **3** a sound like singing, as of a bird, boiling kettle, etc.

song.bird *n.* a bird that has a musical call, as most caged birds, larks, warblers, etc.

song.fest *n.* an informal gathering for singing songs.

song.ster *n.* a singer or song-writer; **song.stress** (-stris) *fem.*

son.ic (SON.ic) *adj.* having to do with sound waves: *a sonic depth finder; A supersonic aircraft breaks the sonic barrier of sharply rising aerodynamic drag as it approaches the speed of sound and produces an explosive* **sonic boom.**

son-in-law *n.* **sons-in-law** one's daughter's husband.

son.net (SON.it) *n.* a rhymed poem in 14 lines like Shakespeare's "Shall I compare thee to a summer's day?": *to compose sonnets; to write a sonnet to one's beloved.*

son.ny (SUN.ee) *n.* **son.nies** [endearing term] son or boy.

son of a bitch *n. Slang.* a scoundrel: *That lucky son of a bitch! They aren't all* **sons of bitches.**

so.no.rous (suh.NOR.us, SON.ur.us); "SON" rhymes with "ON") *adj.* having a full, rich, or impressive sound: *sonorous phrases, voices; a sonorous style.*
—**so.nor.i.ty** (suh.NOR.i.tee) *n.* **-ties.**

soon (long "oo") *adv.* in a short time: *I'll be back soon; He arrived sooner than expected; I'll be there* **as soon as** *possible.*
—**as soon** or **sooner** rather: *She would as soon die fighting than yield.* —**sooner or later** sometime; eventually.

soot (short or long "oo") *n.* black, unburned carbon seen as smoke and found sticking to the insides of chimneys. —**soot.y** *adj.* **soot.i.er, -i.est:** *a sooty chimney; walls made sooty by a fire.*

soothe ("th" as in "the") *v.* **soothes, soothed, sooth.ing** to comfort or relieve: *to soothe a child; to soothe someone's feelings; to soothe pain, a sore throat; adj.: a soothing* (= painlessening) *lotion, medicine; soothing* (= pleasing) *flattery, words.*

sooth.say.er (SOOTH.say.ur, "TH" as in "thin") *n.* one who foretells the future; **sooth.say.ing** *n.*

sop *v.* **sops, sopped, sop.ping** dip or soak by dipping: *to sop up a spill with a sponge; to sop bread in milk; He came in from the rain* **sopping wet** (= dripping).
—*n.* something given to appease, as bread dipped in milk to a child; a concession: *as a sop to his conscience, ego.*

soph.ism (SOF.iz.um) *n.* a clever but logically invalid argument. —**soph.ist** *n.* —**so.phis.tic** (suh.FIS.tic) or **so.phis.ti.cal** *adj.*

so.phis.ti.cate (suh.FIS.tuh.cate) *n.* a sophisticated person: *bohemian, jaded, urban, young sophisticates.*
—**so.phis.ti.ca.tion** (-CAY.shun) *n.*

sophisticated *adj.* **1** experienced or cultured: *a sophisticated consumer, expert, look, user, woman; She has sophisticated tastes in furniture.* **2** of things, highly developed: *sophisticated arguments, equipment, software, techniques, weapons.*

soph.is.try (SOF.is.tree) *n.* **-tries** a sophism or sophistical reasoning.

soph.o.more (SOF.uh.more) *n.* a second-year university student or one in Grade 10 of high school.
—**soph.o.mor.ic** (-MOR.ic) *adj.* immature and overconfident: *sophomoric antics, insights, insults, posturing; silly and sophomoric.*

sop.o.rif.ic (sop.uh.RIF.ic) *adj.* sleep-inducing: *a soporific effect.* —*n.* a sleep-inducing drug such as a barbiturate.

sop.py *adj.* **sop.pi.er, sop.pi.est** soaked or wet through: *his soppy sentimentality.*

so.pra.no (suh.PRAH.no) *n.* **-nos 1** the highest singing voice of women and boys. **2** a singer with such a voice. **3** a singing part for a soprano. —*adja.*: *a soprano part, saxophone, voice;* **adv.**: *She sings soprano.*

sor.bet (sor.BAY, SOR.bit) *n.* a fruit or vegetable ice or sherbet.

sor.cer.y (SOR.suh.ree) *n.* -**cer.ies** witchcraft, esp. by use of charms, spells, etc.: *to practice sorcery.* —**sor.cer.er** *n.*; **sor.cer.ess** (-ris) *fem.*

sor.did *adj.* dirty or filthy; hence, wretched, base, or mean: *the sordid life of the slums; the sordid details of a crime; a sordid crime, story.* —**sor.did.ly** *adv.*; **sor.did.ness** *n.*

sore *adj.* **sor.er, sor.est** causing or feeling pain: *a sore leg; a sore point of dispute; The homeless are in sore* (= grievous) *need; He feels sore* (= vexed) *at being slighted; He's sore* (Informal for angry) *at her.* —*n.* a sore spot on the body, esp. an infected wound: *cold, open, running sores.* —**sore.ly** *adv.*; **sore.ness** *n.*

sore.head *n.* Informal. one who easily becomes angry or disgruntled.

sore throat *n.* an affliction of the throat such as laryngitis or pharyngitis.

sor.ghum (SOR.gum) *n.* a tropical cereal plant resembling corn but having flowers in branched clusters bearing edible, starchy seeds.

sor.rel (SOR.ul) *n.* **1** a reddish brown (horse); *adj.* reddish-brown. **2** an herb of the buckwheat family with pungent, sour leaves used in salads, for flavoring, etc. **3** a tree of the heath family with sour-tasting leaves.

sor.row (SOR.oh) *n.* sadness or grief of a prolonged nature, as from a beloved's death: *to express, feel, show sorrow at* or *for* or *over the death of a friend; deep, great, keen, personal, profound sorrow; To her great sorrow, the child died before she could reach the hospital; the joys and sorrows of life.* —*v.* grieve: *still sorrowing over his dead wife;* **adja.**: *his sorrowing heart; her sorrowing husband.* —**sor.row.ful** *adj.*; **sor.row.ful.ly** *adv.*

sor.ry (SOR.ee) *adj.* **sor.ri.er, sor.ri.est** **1** feeling sorrow, regret, pity, etc.; *I'm dreadfully, terribly sorry about* or *for what happened; I am* or *I feel sorry for my sins; I'm sorry to disappoint you; I'm sorry but I'm going to have to let you go; I am* or *I feel sorry to fire you* or *to have to fire you* or *that I have to fire you; I am* or *I feel sorry* (= pity) *for you.* **2** poor; pitiful: *a sorry excuse, plight, sight, state of affairs; a sorry* (= useless) *mess.*

sort *n.* a group of individuals of the same general kind: *all sorts of cars, people, plans; I never had this sort of trouble; a rushed sort of (an) existence; He said something of the sort; I don't like his sort (of people).* —**of sorts** or **of a sort** of mediocre quality: *a singer of sorts.* —**out of sorts** slightly ill or in low spirits. —**sort of** Informal. somewhat; so to speak: *He's sort of disappointed; It was sort of a last hope; It's sort of like being dumped; He just sort of sits and mopes all day; Hopeless? Yes, sort of.* —*v.* arrange according to kind or character: *Letters are sorted (out) in the post office; a computer program to sort data, as numerically or alphabetically, ascending or descending.*

sor.tie (SOR.tee) *n.* **1** a sally or sudden attack: *Military aircraft carry out* or *make sorties; combat sorties.* **2** a foray or advance: *sorties into new markets; an exporter's first sortie abroad.* **3** a combat plane's operational flight: *Air forces conduct* or *fly hundreds of sorties for maintenance of their aircraft.*

SOS (es.oh.ES) *n.* a distress signal, as used in wireless telegraphy: *to send an SOS.*

so-so *adj. & adv.* fairly or passably (good).

sot *n.* a habitual drunkard; **sot.tish** *adj.*

sot.to vo.ce (SOT.oh.VOH.chee) *adv.* in a low voice; quietly.

sou.brette (soo.BRET) *n.* a pert or lively young woman, usu. a maidservant, in a role subsidiary to that of her mistress, as in musical comedies.

souf.flé (soo.FLAY) *n.* a baked dish made light and puffy by the use of beaten egg whites.

sough (SOW, SUF) *n. & v.* (make) a soft sighing or murmuring sound.

sought *pt. & pp.* of SEEK.

soul (SOLE) *n.* **1** the spiritual part of a person, as distinguished from the body, considered to be immortal and the source of inner strength, inspiration, etc.; hence, essence or spirit: *Missionaries work to save souls; to save souls from damnation, hell, sin; She works* **heart and soul** (= all of herself) *for the cause; She puts* **her heart and soul** *into whatever she does; A living wage is necessary to* **keep one's body and soul together** (= to pay for life's necessities); *After much* **soul-searching** (= self-examination) *they decided not to separate.* **2** a person: *kindly, kindred, poor, timid souls; Not a soul was in sight.* **3** an emotional and spiritual quality felt to be characteristic of black culture, esp. of black music; **soul brother** or **sister**

(= a fellow black); **soul food** (= food traditionally popular among the blacks); **soul music** (= jazz based on blues and gospel music). —**soul.ful** *adj.*; **soul.ful.ly** *adv.*; **soul.ful.ness** *n.*

sound *n.* **1** what is or can be heard: *the sound of fighting, machinery, music, voices; vowel and consonant sounds; to articulate, emit, enunciate, make, produce, pronounce, utter, transmit sounds; Please turn down the sound on the TV; She just turned up the sound on her radio; We came **within sound*** (= within earshot) *of the guns.* **2** a channel wider than a strait, linking two bodies of water or separating an island from the mainland. **3** a narrow coastal inlet, as Howe Sound off the B.C. coast. —*v.* **1** (cause) to make a sound: *Sound your horn; We get up when the alarm sounds.* **2** to seem when heard: *The voice sounds strange; Your plan sounds reasonable; sounds like a good idea to me; It sounds as if they are winning.* **3** measure the depth of something: *to sound the depths of a mystery; Let's **sound him out** on or about the new proposal* (= try to find out his views, feelings, etc.); *adja.*: *a **sounding** lead, line, machine.* **4** dive down suddenly, as a whale. —**sound off** *Informal.* talk freely or loudly, as to complain, boast, etc. —*adj.* **1** free from defect; good, healthy, or strong: *The building rests on a sound foundation; a will made by one of sound mind; to enjoy sound health; He's sound in mind and body; sound advice, arguments, judgment, reasoning, opinions, views.* **2** thorough: *a sound defeat, sleep, thrashing*; *adv.*: *He is sound* (= deeply) *asleep.* —**sound.ly** *adv.*: *He sleeps soundly at night; She was soundly beaten in the game.* —**sound.ness** *n.*

sound barrier *n.* **1** the speed of an aircraft approaching the speed of sound: *A sonic boom is heard when a supersonic aircraft breaks the sound barrier of sharply rising aerodynamic drag; Test pilots defy the sound barrier.* **2** a wall or similar structure to keep out noise: *highway sound barriers.* **3** a limit considered hard to reach: *We broke the sound barrier when we made a profit.*

sound bite *n.* a brief striking statement: *an effective commercial in a 15-second sound bite.*

sound box or **sound.box** *n.* a resonating chamber in a musical instrument.

sound card (or **board**) *n.* an expansion card that allows music, voice, etc. to be played on a computer.

sounding board or **sound.board** *n.* **1** a structure or device for increasing or directing sound, as in a violin or piano. **2** someone used for testing out an idea or opinion.

sound.proof *adj.* insulated against sound: *a soundproof ceiling, room, studio, wall; a **soundproofed** apartment, engine, grinder; adja.: soundproof(ing) materials.*

sound track *n.* a record of the sounds of a motion picture made along one edge of the film.

soup (long "oo") *n.* **1** a liquid food made with meat, fish, or vegetables, eaten with a **soupspoon:** *Make me a bowl or cup of soup.* **2** *Informal.* something thick or heavy, as fog. —**in the soup** in a hard plight. —*v.* **soup up** *Informal.* increase the power of something; *adj.*: *a **souped-up** engine; a souped-up version of the old formula.*

soup.çon or **soup.con** (soop.SOHNG) *n.* a slight trace or flavor *of* a taste or quality.

soup kitchen *n.* an establishment where the poor and homeless are fed.

soup.y (SOO.pee) *adj.* **soup.i.er, -i.est 1** like soup in thickness: *a soupy mixture.* **2** *Informal.* foggy.

sour (rhyme: our) *adj.* **1** having the sharp, acid taste of fruits such as lemons and avocados. **2** having the acid or rancid taste of foods gone bad: *sour milk.* **3** disagreeable or unpleasant: *sour breath, wine; when things begin to go sour; The whole affair, project, proposal turned sour; a sour employee with a sour face; sour* (= acid) *soil; sour* (= impure) *gasoline.* —*v.* make or become sour: *Their (mutual) relations soured.* —**sour.ly** *adv.*; **sour.ness** *n.*

source (SORCE) *n.* where something rises or originates: *the source of a river; a source of information; impeccable, original, reliable, reputable, trustworthy, unnamed sources; light from a remote source; an energy source; a source of trouble; to tap a source; to cite, disclose, indicate, reveal one's sources; A source dries up; information from a source* (= a person) *close to the premier.*

—*v.* **sourc.es, sourced, sourc.ing 1** get as from a source: *They go to China for low-cost sourcing of their products.* **2** indicate the source of something: *a poorly sourced essay.*

sour.dough *n.* **1** fermented dough used as leaven. **2** a prospector or pioneer, as in Alaska and northwestern Canada. **3** an experienced hand or old-timer.

sour grapes *n.* the scorning of something because one does not or cannot have it: *a case of sour grapes (as when the fox said the grapes he couldn't reach must be sour); It's just sour grapes when he says Cadillacs are no good.*

sour.puss (short "oo") *n. Informal.* a sullen person.

souse (*rhyme:* house) *v.* **sous.es, soused, sous.ing 1** pickle; hence, soak or plunge. **2** *Slang.* make or become drunk. —*n.* **1** a pickling or soaking, brine for pickling, or pickled pork, fish, etc. **2** *Slang.* a habitual drunkard.

south ("th" as in "thin") *n.* **1** the direction to the right of one facing the rising sun; opposite of north: *Mexico is directly south of the U.S.; Canadians often go shopping* **south of the border** (= in the U.S.). **2** a region lying in this direction, as **the South**, the southern states of the U.S., south of Pennsylvania, the Ohio River, and Missouri. —*adja.* southern: *the south end, flank, side; a* **south wind** *(blowing from the south).* —*adv.* toward the south: *Snowbirds go or head south in the winter.*

South Asian *n. & adj.* (a person) of or from **South Asia**, the region comprising India, Pakistan, Sri Lanka, and Bangladesh.

south.east (south.EEST) *n. & adj.* (in, toward, or from) a direction or place halfway between south and east. —*adv.* toward the southeast. —**the Southeast** *n.* southeastern U.S. —**south.east.er.ly** *adj. & adv.;* **south.east.ern** *adj.*

Southeast Asian *n. & adj.* (a person) of or from **Southeast Asia**, the region comprising the peninsula east of India and south of China, the Philippines, Malaysia, and W. Indonesia.

south.er.ly (SUTH.ur.lee, "TH" as in "the") *adj.* **1** toward the south: *Canada's most southerly point is Middle Island in Lake Erie.* **2** from the south: *a southerly wind;* also **adv.**

south.ern (SUTH.urn) *adja.* of, from, or toward the south: *Canton is in southern China;* The **Southern States** *region of the U.S. extends from Arkansas and Louisiana to Maryland in the east.* —**south.ern.er** *n.*

southern lights same as AURORA AUSTRALIS.

south.paw *n. Informal.* a left-handed person, esp. a baseball pitcher.

south.ward (SOUTH.wurd) *adj. & adv.* toward the south; also **south.wards** *adv.*

south.west (south.WEST) *n. & adj.* (in, toward, or from) a direction or region halfway between south and west. —*adv.* in, toward, or from the southwest. —**the Southwest** *n.* southwestern U.S. —**south.west.ern** *adj.*

sou.ve.nir (soo.vuh.NEER) *n.* an article given, bought, kept, etc. as a reminder of a person, place, or occasion.

sov.er.eign (SOV.rin) *n.* **1** a supreme ruler or monarch. **2** a former British gold coin worth one pound. —*adj.* **1** supreme and independent: *a sovereign power, state; Her will is sovereign in domestic matters.* **2** great in excellence, importance, etc.: *a sovereign remedy; of sovereign importance.*

sov.er.eign.ty (SOV.rin.tee) *n.* -**ties** **1** supreme and independent authority: *The states do not enjoy full sovereignty; to claim, establish sovereignty over a disputed territory.* **2** independence: *to violate a nation's sovereignty; to grant sovereignty to a former colony.*

—**sov.er.eign.tist** *n. & adj.*

so.vi.et (SOH.vee.et, -it) **1** *n.* in the former U.S.S.R., an elected legislative body: *a village soviet; town soviets; the Supreme Soviet of the U.S.S.R.* **2 Soviet** *adja.* of the former U.S.S.R.: *the Soviet command, leadership, zone; a Soviet invasion, republic, threat.* **3 the Soviets** *n.pl.* (people of) the former Soviet Union.

¹**sow** (*rhyme:* how) *n.* an adult female swine.

²**sow** (SOH) *v.* **sows,** *pt.* **sowed,** *pp.* **sown** (SONE) or **sowed, sow.ing** to plant seed; hence, spread or scatter: *to sow wheat; to sow a field (with seed); to sow discord; Reap what you sow; "Sow the wind and reap the whirlwind"* (= Start something that has disastrous consequences). —**sow.er** *n.*

soy *n.* **1** same as SOY SAUCE. **2** soybean.

soy.bean *n.* **1** a plant of the pea family yielding protein-rich seeds. **2** its seed.

soy sauce *n.* a sauce used as a flavoring in Oriental cooking, made from fermented soybeans. Also **soya sauce.**

spa (SPAH) *n.* **1** a mineral spring forming the center of a health resort. **2** such a resort: *a health spa.* **3** same as HOT TUB.

space *n.* **1** the boundless expanse or extent which physical objects may occupy: *exploration of space; visitors from (outer) space;* **adj.:** *a* **space-age** *fantasy, look; space-age research; space-age* (= advanced or modern) *makeup, materials, sportswear, styling, technology, tools, weapons.* **2** an area or volume limited by objects; room or interval between objects: *a crawl space under the raised floor; parking spaces; storage space; not enough space for a bed; the wide open spaces of*

space cadet / Spanish

the prairies; the spaces between lines; to book **space** (= accommodation) in a hotel; in the space (= interval) of an hour; I need space (= freedom from being bothered); the **space bar** on a keyboard; a **space-saving** device, measure; the space-saving and convenience that customers look for. —v. **spac.es, spaced, spac.ing** divide into or separate by spaces: Please space the lines evenly; Let's space out our meetings instead of having them one after another; n.: Use double **spacing** between lines. —**space out** get out of touch with reality: People tend to space out if you ask them how much they're making; adj.: a **spaced-out** time traveler.

space cadet n. Slang. one who is dozy, scatterbrained, or silly; an eccentric.

space.craft n. sing. & pl. a vehicle such as a satellite or rocket designed for travel in space: a manned spacecraft.

spaced-out adj. Slang. 1 under the influence of a narcotic; high. 2 same as SPACEY.

space fiction n. fiction dealing with life and travel in outer space.

space.flight n. flight into outer space: an unmanned spaceflight.

space heater n. a portable unit for warming up a room or other small area.

space.man n. **-men** a male member of the crew of a spaceship.
—**space.wom.an** n. **-wom.en.**

space probe n. an unmanned spacecraft sent on a probing mission: to launch a space probe.

space.ship n. a vehicle for traveling in outer space.

space shuttle n. a recoverable and reusable space vehicle for linking up with a space station.

space station n. a manned earth satellite in a fixed orbit used as a center for space experiments, as a stopping or launching place for spaceships, etc.

space.suit n. an astronaut's pressurized garment.

space vehicle n. a spacecraft.

space.walk v. & n. (engage) in movement outside a spaceship.

space.y or **spac.y** (SPAY.see) adj. Informal. out of touch with the real world: He's a bit nutty, spacey, and neurotic; a spacey sitcom.

spa.cial (SPAY.shul) same as SPATIAL.

spa.cious (SPAY.shus) adj. large in extent or scope: spacious accommodation; a spacious cabin, interior, office, room; a spacious life of ease. —**spa.cious.ness** n.

spade n. 1 a sharp, pointed shovel for turning the soil by pressing its blade into the ground. 2 a black figure [♠] marking a suit of playing cards. 3 a card of this suit. —**call a spade a spade** be frank or forthright. —**in spades** Informal. emphatically or outspokenly: Everyone loves her in spades; Our hard work is paying off in spades.

spade.work n. the hard preliminary work involved in starting a project.

spa.dix (SPAY.dix) n. **-dix.es** or **-di.ces** (-duh.seez) the spike of flowers enclosed in a spathe, as in the jack-in-the-pulpit.

spa.ghet.ti (spuh.GET.ee) n. a dish of long, thin strings of pasta boiled and served with sauce: spaghetti and meatballs; spaghetti sauce.

spaghetti western n. Informal. a low-budget western movie made in Italy.

spake [old form] pt. of SPEAK: Thus spake Confucius.

spam.ming n. Slang. the sending of inappropriate, esp. promotional messages to newsgroups and others via e-mail, considered bad netiquette.

span n. 1 the extent or distance between two linked points such as the ends of a bridge; also, one of its individual parts between pillars or supports: the span of an arch bridge; a bridge with 10 spans; a child's brief attention span (= length of concentration); our life span; memory span. 2 the maximum distance between the tips of the little finger and the thumb. —v. **spans, spanned, span.ning** 1 extend across: The history of North America spans several centuries. 2 measure, as by the span of one's hand.

span.dex n. an elastic synthetic fabric used for exercise wear.

span.gle (SPANG.gul) n. a small disc of glittering material sewn on fabrics for decoration. —v. **-gles, -gled, -gling** decorate (as if) with spangles: a Christmas tree spangled with green and red lights; adj. & cpd: a **spangled** evening gown; a star-spangled sky; tear-spangled eyes. —**span.gly** adj.

Span.iard (SPAN.yurd) n. a person of or from Spain.

span.iel (SPAN.yul) n. a breed of sporting dog with a long, silky coat, large, round eyes, and drooping ears.

Span.ish adj. having to do with Spain, its people, or their language: the Spanish Armada, Civil War, Inquisition; Spanish bullfighters, flamenco dancers.
—n. 1 the Spanish language. 2 **the Spanish** the people of Spain; Spaniards.

Spanish American *n. & adj.* **1** (an American) of Spanish descent. **2** (a person) of or from **Spanish America**, the parts of Latin America in which Spanish is the chief language: *the Spanish-American War of 1898.*

Spanish fly same as CANTHARIDES and CANTHARIS.

Spanish main *n.* [old use] the South American mainland.

Spanish moss *n.* a tropical air plant that hangs from trees in long, beardlike masses.

spank *v.* strike one to be punished on the buttocks with the palm, a slipper, etc.: *to spank a child;* ***n.***: *to get, give, receive a good* **spanking.** —*n.* such a blow.

spanking *adja.* **1** rapid or strong: *a spanking breeze.* **2** remarkable: *a spanking tweed jacket; the silver's spanking brightness.* —*adv.* very: *spanking clean; The cleaned silver looks spanking new; a spanking good time.*

spar *v.* **spars, sparred, spar.ring** **1** make the motions of boxing *at someone: a boxer's sparring partner (with whom he practices).* **2** fight or wrangle *with someone: Shawn sparred four rounds with Dan;* *adja.: a day-long* **sparring** *match between two lawyers.*
—*n.* a pole supporting a sail, as a mast or boom.

spare *v.* **spares, spared, spar.ing** **1** save someone from having to undergo something: *She spared him some embarrassment; We'll spare you the details; They ate out to spare her the trouble of cooking; I'm alive today because I've been spared (from death) by Providence.* **2** give up or do without something useful or needed: *"Spare the rod and spoil the child"; We have time enough and to spare; She spares no expense when helping friends; Can you spare me a dollar? to spare the time for a job.*
—*n.* **1** something extra or in reserve, as a spare tire. **2** in bowling, the knocking down of all 10 pins with the first two balls. —*adj.* **spar.er, spar.est** **1** extra; free for use: *spare change, parts, rooms, time, tires.* **2** thin or lean: *a spare build, figure.* **3** meager or scanty: *a spare diet, meal.* —**spare.ly** *adv.: a sparely furnished office;* **spare.ness** *n.*

spare.ribs *n.pl.* ribs of pork with closely trimmed meat.

sparing (SPAIR.ing) *adj.* careful and restrained: *He's very sparing in the use of alcohol; makes sparing use of colors; She is sparing of her money; sparing with her resources.* —**spar.ing.ly** *adv.: to apply salt sparingly; to apply paint sparingly.*

spark *n.* a particle of fire given off when flint is struck with steel or when electricity jumps across a gap, as in the **spark plug** of an automobile engine: *A short produces a spark; Sparks are emitted; Sparks fly from a welder's torch; There's not a spark* (= flash or particle) *of life left in the body.* —*v.* **1** give off sparks. **2** stir up or stimulate: *The comment sparked a heated discussion; to spark fears, interest, riots, speculation.*

spar.kle (SPAR.kul) *v.* **-kles, -kled, -kling** **1** send out sparks: *Fireworks sparkle.* **2** shine or glitter as if giving off sparks: *Our bathroom sparkles when it is cleaned and polished; Her eyes sparkle; adja.: a **sparkling** crystal chandelier; sparkling gems; sparkling colors, imagery, sounds; a sparkling career, display, performance; the sparkling white sands of the beach; a sparkling* (= bubbling) *wine.*
—*n.* a sparkling: *the sparkle of light playing on a fountain; the sparkle* (= liveliness) *of her eyes, of his wit.*

spar.kler *n.* one that sparkles, as a firework or diamond.

spar.row (SPAIR.oh) *n.* a small, plain-looking, usu. brownish bird.

sparse *adj.* **spars.er, spars.est** thinly scattered; not dense: *sparse attendance, hair, vegetation; a sparse crowd, population, record; sparse data, evidence, information.* —**sparse.ly** *adv.;* **sparse.ness** *n.*

Spar.tan (SPAR.tun) *adj.* having to do with ancient **Sparta**, a Greek city state, or like its people: *the Spartan virtues of frugality, courage, and stern discipline; small and Spartan accommodation; a Spartan budget, condition, diet, economy, existence.* —*n.* a person of Sparta.

spasm (SPAZ.um) *n.* **1** a sudden, involuntary, painful contraction of a muscle or muscles, as a cramp or convulsion. **2** a brief burst of energy or excitement.

spas.mod.ic (spaz.MOD.ic) *adj.* characterized by spasms; happening in brief bursts: *a spasmodic cough; spasmodic efforts; spasmodic periods of joy and despair;* **spas.mod.i.cal.ly** *adv.*

spas.tic *adj.* having to do with spasms: *spastic colitis, paralysis.* —*n.* a person with spastic paralysis.

spat a *pt. & pp.* of SPIT. —*n.* **1** the young of oysters and other shellfish. **2** usu. **spats** *pl.* gaiters covering the instep and ankle. **3** *Informal.* a petty quarrel: *Joe had a spat with his neighbors; family spats.*

spate *n.* a large number or outpouring:

a spate of words; a spate of new books; a spate of accidents on an icy expressway.

spathe ("th" as in "the") *n.* the bract enclosing a spadix, as in the calla lily.

spa.tial (SPAY.shul) *adj.* having to do with space: *The right side of the brain controls our spatial and visual faculties; spatial awareness, concepts, functions, judgment, qualities.* —**spa.tial.ly** *adv.*

spat.ter (SPAT.ur) *v.* to splash liquid in drops or splash a person or thing with mud, etc. —*n.* a spattering or a spot made by it.

spat.u.la (SPACH.uh.luh) *n.* a small paddlelike implement for spreading or mixing paints, drugs, etc.

spav.in (SPAV.in) *n.* a disease of horses affecting the hock joint and often causing lameness. —**spav.ined** (-ind) *adj.* lame.

spawn *n.* eggs or offspring in large numbers, as of fish, frogs, shellfish, etc. —*v.* **1** produce spawn; *n.*: *the spawning of salmon; adja.: spawning cycles, grounds, seasons.* **2** bring forth on a large scale: *computer stores spawned by the electronic revolution; an industry that has spawned a new generation of entrepreneurs; fears spawned by the arms race; to spawn criticism, growth, industries, myths, progeny, publications.*

spay *v.* **spays, spayed, spay.ing** remove the ovaries of an animal: *to have pets spayed or neutered.*

speak (SPEEK) *v.* **speaks, spoke, spo.ken** (SPOH.kun), **speak.ing** utter or express something using language: *Animals don't speak; She speaks Greek, but speaks in French to her kids; speaks to the class, to the point; speaks with me on business; to speak bluntly, fluently, frankly, freely, loudly, openly, politely, quietly, rudely, softly; to speak about a subject; to speak from the heart, from experience; to speak ill of someone; to speak well of everyone; He was invited to speak* (= make a speech) *at the graduation; Strictly speaking, this is against the rules; adja.: a speaking engagement, part, session, voice; English-speaking people; We had a fight, but we are back on speaking terms* (= speaking to each other). —**so to speak** to use such an expression: *He got his dander up, so to speak.* —**speak for:** *M.P.s speak for* (= on behalf of) *their constituents; They spoke for* (= in support of) *the reintroduction of capital punishment; Speak for yourself* (= Don't speak on my behalf)! *Our record speaks for itself* (= is proof by itself); *These seats have been spoken for* (= reserved); *A Nobel prize speaks volumes for* (= is great testimony of) *the winner's achievements.* —**speak out** speak freely and boldly: *dissidents who speak out on human rights; They speak out against repression.* —**speak up 1** speak louder: *Please speak up, I can't hear you.* **2** be assertive: *We have to speak up in defense of our rights; someone to speak up for the underdog.*

speak-easy *n.* **-eas.ies** a place where liquor was sold illegally during prohibition in the U.S.

speak.er *n.* **1** one who speaks: *fluent, guest, public speakers; I'm a native speaker of Tagalog but a better speaker of Spanish.* **2** the head of a deliberative assembly: *the speaker of parliament; Mr. Speaker; Madam Speaker.* **3** a loudspeaker.

spear (SPEER) *n.* **1** a thrusting or throwing weapon with a long wooden shaft and a pointed head of metal or stone: *to hurl a spear.* **2** a sprout or young shoot of a plant, as of grass. —*v.* pierce or stab with or as with a spear: *to spear trout; n.: a hockey player penalized for spearing.*

spear.head *n.* **1** the pointed head of a spear. **2** the first attacker in an assault or the leader of a movement. —*v.* act as a spearhead: *to spearhead an assault, campaign, development, drive, event, project, program, undertaking.*

spear.mint *n.* a mint with erect stems bearing tapering spikes of flowers, used in flavoring.

spe.cial (SPESH.ul) *adj.* of a different or particular kind: *as a special favor; special permission to watch a late movie; a special edition; an extra charge for special delivery* (of first-class mail by postal messenger); *special education* for handicapped children; lobbying by a *special-interest group* trying to influence legislation in its favor. —*n.* a special person, train, edition of a newspaper, product on sale, TV program, etc.: *a news special.* —**spe.cial.ly** *adv.*

spe.cial.ist (SPESH.ul.ist) *n.* one specializing in a particular subject or line of work: *to call in, consult a specialist; an ear specialist; a specialist in criminology; a specialist on crime prevention.*

spe.ci.al.i.ty (spesh.ee.AL.i.tee) *n.* **1** a being special or something that is special. **2** *Brit.* same as SPECIALTY.

spe.cial.ize (SPESH.ul.ize) *v.* **1** concentrate one's work or study in a particular area: *After many years of general studies they specialize (in a specialty) for two years; She's specializing in plastic surgery; a restaurant that specializes in seafood; adj.: has specialized* (= expert)

knowledge of her subject; specialized staff. **2** alter to adapt; *adj.: Wings are forelimbs **specialized** for flying; interface boxes and other specialized equipment; specialized care, functions, services.*
—**spe.cial.i.za.tion** (-luh.ZAY.shun, -lye-) *n.*

spe.cial.ty (SPESH.ul.tee) *n.* **-ties** a special subject, feature, or article: *Greek drama is his specialty; The restaurant's specialty is seafood; **adja.**: specialty fabrics; Unlike department stores, a **specialty store** sells hardware, jewelry, or other special goods exclusively.*

spe.cie (SPEE.shee) *n.* **1** coins, as opposed to paper money: *payment in specie.* **2 species** *sing. & pl.* a kind, esp. a biological grouping (under "genus") of varieties of plants and animals or races whose members can interbreed: *The common cat (Felis catus) is genus Felis, species catus; An endangered species may die out, may become extinct; A protected species may survive; the female of **the species** (= of the human race).*

spe.cif.ic (spuh.SIF.ic) *adj.* of a definite kind: *Please be specific; Give specific reasons; specific directions, information, instructions, plans, skills; Lions, tigers, and leopards have specific differences (as different species of genus "Panthera"); n.: Give us a few specifics (= specific details or particulars) about or of or on this discovery; Sorry, we can't reveal specificis.* —**spe.cif.i.cal.ly** *adv.*
—**spec.i.fic.i.ty** (spes.uh.FIS.i.tee) *n.: greater specificity and variety of skills.*

spec.i.fi.ca.tion (spes.uh.fuh.CAY.shun) *n.* **1** something specified. **2** usu. **specifications** *pl.* detailed description of materials, measurements, etc. for a project or undertaking: *to adhere to, meet the specifications; the rigid specifications laid down by government.*

specific gravity *n.* relative density of a substance compared to a standard, as water: *Mercury has a specific gravity of 13.546.*

spec.i.fy (SPES.uh.fye) *v.* **-fies, -fied, -fy.ing** mention explicitly: *The directions specify the dosage; They specify how and when to take the medicine.*

spec.i.men (SPES.uh.mun) *n.* a sample taken for a close or comparative study: *botanical specimens; a urine specimen; a poor specimen (= representative) of humanity such as a child molester.*

spe.cious (SPEE.shus) *adj.* good, true, correct, etc. in appearance only: *a specious argument, excuse, resemblance; specious grounds, reasons.*

speck *n. & v.* (mark with) a small mark, spot, or bit: *a speck of blood, color, dirt, dust, gold, light; fly specks; adj.: a **specked** apple.*

speck.le (SPEK.ul) *n. & v.* (mark with) a small speck: *butterfly wings speckled with colors; adj.: a **speckled** finish, trout; blood-speckled hands.*

specs *n.pl. Informal.* **1** specifications. **2** spectacles.

spec.ta.cle (SPEC.tuh.cul) *n.* **1** a sight or display that attracts public attention: *a fine spectacle; He made a spectacle of himself after getting drunk; a movie spectacle (with great scenery, a large cast, etc.).* **2 spectacles** *pl.* eyeglasses.

spec.tac.u.lar (spec.TAK.yuh.lur) *adj.* impressive or striking in visual impact: *a spectacular performance; a spectacular three-alarm fire.* —*n.* a spectacular motion picture or TV show: *a three-hour spectacular.* —**spec.tac.u.lar.ly** *adv.*

spec.ta.tor (SPEC.tay.tur) *n.* one who watches an action without taking part, as at a sports event.

spectator sport *n.* baseball, hockey, racing, etc. that are for watching by spectators as distinguished from hunting or fishing.

spec.ter *n.* a ghost or spirit. Also **spec.tre** *Cdn.*

spec.tra a *pl.* of SPECTRUM.

spec.tral (SPEC.trul) *adj.* **1** having to do with specters: *Covered with gray dust, the landscape looked spectral; a spectral presence, shape, silence.* **2** having to do with spectrums: *spectral astronomy, data, emissions, lines.*

spectre *Cdn.* SPECTER.

spec.tro.gram (SPEC.truh.gram) *n.* a trace, graph, or photograph made by a spectrograph.

spec.tro.graph (SPEC.truh.graf) *n.* an instrument for photographing a spectrum. —**spec.tro.graph.ic** (-GRAF.ic) *adj.;* **spec.tro.graph.i.cal.ly** *adv.*

spec.trom.e.ter (spec.TROM.i.tur) *n.* a type of spectroscope for measuring spectral wavelengths; **spec.tro.met.ric** (-truh.MET.ric) *adj.*

spec.tro.scope (SPEC.truh.scope) *n.* an optical instrument for separating light into its constituent wavelengths as seen in a spectrum. —**spec.tro.scop.ic** (-SCOP.ic) *adj.,* **spec.tros.co.py** (spec.TROS.cuh.pee) *n.*

spec.trum (SPEC.trum) *n., pl.* **-trums** or **-tra** (-truh) **1** a series of colored bands representing wavelengths resulting from the diffraction of white light into its constituents. **2** range or array: *people representing a wide spectrum of opinions; immigrants from a broad spec-*

trum of humanity; a broad-spectrum antibiotic.
spec.u.late (SPEK.yuh.late) *v.* **-lates, -lat.ed, -lat.ing 1** reflect *about* or *on* or *upon* a subject on which there is insufficient evidence; conjecture or guess: *He speculated that his employer would go broke before Christmas.* **2** trade *in* commodities, gold, land, etc. hoping to profit from future price changes: *She invests and speculates in modern art; to speculate on the stock market.*
—**spec.u.la.tion** (-LAY.shun) *n.*: *to engage* or *indulge in speculation; idle, utopian, wild speculations; speculation in land; a flurry of speculation about the outcome of the vote.* —**spec.u.la.tive** (-luh.tiv) *adj.;* **spec.u.la.tive.ly** *adv.*
—**spec.u.la.tor** (-lay.tur) *n.*
speech *n.* **1** the power to speak, the manner of speaking, or a particular language: *freedom of speech; the faculty of speech which humans enjoy; impaired, slurred speech; the speech (= language) of the natives;* **adja.:** *speech defects, disorders, therapy.* **2** words spoken to an audience: *a speech on* or *about free trade; to ad-lib, deliver, give, improvise, make a speech; acceptance, after-dinner, campaign, farewell, impromptu, inaugural, keynote, welcoming speeches; speech writers.*
speech.less *adj.* unable to speak, as from shock: *She was left, rendered, scared, struck speechless; became utterly speechless; was speechless with astonishment.*
speed *n.* **1** rate of movement: *The car reaches a maximum speed of 180 km/h; going at full speed; breakneck, cruising, high, lightning, low, top speeds; speed limits on highways; The sales rep was dispatched* **with speed** (= swiftly); **Full speed ahead** (= Go ahead at full speed)! **2** gear: *a transmission with four speeds; a ten-speed bicycle.* **3** *Slang.* a methamphetamine. —**up to speed** up to the normal level of performance: *to bring* or *get production up to speed; Shipping has come* or *is* or *is running up to speed.* —*v.* **speeds,** *pt. & pp.* **sped** or **speed.ed, speed.ing 1** move fast: *The car sped away; She sped through a radar speed trap; was speeding toward the hospital; a speeding bullet, spaceship; speeding electrons, ions.* **2** go over the speed limit: *a speeding car;* **n.:** *The driver was charged with* **speeding** *and given a speeding ticket.* **3** cause to move fast: *Use airmail to speed a letter on its way; to speed payments; workers told to* **speed up** *production.* —**speed.er** *n.*
speed.boat *n.* a fast motorboat or launch.
speeding ticket *n.* a summons issued by police for exceeding the speed limit.
speed.om.e.ter (spi.DOM.i.tur) *n.* an instrument that shows the speed at which a vehicle is moving.
speed.ster *n.* a speeding person or a vehicle designed for speed, as a racing car.
speed trap *n.* a police watch for drivers who exceed the speed limit.
speed.way *n.* a racing track for motorcycles or cars.
speed.well *n.* a weedy herb of the figwort family with small, usu. blue flowers.
speed.y *adj.* **speed.i.er, -i.est** fast: *a speedy decision, delivery, exit, growth, recovery, reply, response, return, trial; speedy access, assistance, execution, progress, reform, service.* —**speed.i.ly** *adv.*
spell *n.* **1** an incantation or words used as a charm; also, their influence: *a magic spell; The singer seemed to cast a spell over* or *on her audience; They were under a spell; The spell was broken when the lights went off.* **2** a brief period: *a spell of depression, hot weather, illness; a coughing spell* (= attack). **3** a brief period of work in rotation with others.
—*v.* **spells, spelled** or *Brit.* **spelt, spell.ing 1** write or say the letters making up a word: *How is your name spelled? A-N-N-E spells* (= makes up the spelling of) *Anne.* **2** signify or mean: *a series of defeats that spelled disaster for the government.* —**spell out 1** give the letters of a word: *Please spell out your name for me.* **2** explain in detail: *a speech spelling out the government's policy for the year ahead.* —**spell.er** *n.*
spell.bind (SPEL.bined) *v.* **-binds, -bound, -bind.ing** hold as if under a spell; also, fascinate; **adj.:** *a* **spellbinding** *act, character, drama, performance, orator, scene, speaker;* **adjp.:** *They listened* **spellbound** *for two hours; They seemed spellbound by her achievements; She held them spellbound with her wit and wisdom.*
—**spell.bind.er** *n.*
spell checker *n.* a word-processing program for checking the spelling of a document; also **spelling checker.**
spelling *n.* **1** the way a word is spelled: *the correct spelling of a word; the two spellings of "color"; British and American spelling(s); spelling and grammar;* **adj.:** *a spelling checker; spelling rules.* **2** one's ability to spell correctly: *bad, good, poor, terrible spelling;* **adja.:** *a spelling contest, error, mistake; spelling ability, skills.*

spelling bee *n.* a spelling contest in which players who make errors are eliminated.

spelt *Brit. pt. & pp.* of SPELL.

spe.lunk.er (spi.LUNK.ur) *n.* one whose hobby is exploring caves. —**spe.lunk.ing** *n.*

spend *v.* **spends, spent, spend.ing** 1 use a resource such as money, time, effort, thought, etc.: *to spend money on or for the children's education; Children spend time (in) studying; time well spent.* 2 use up or consume: *The storm has spent itself, has spent its fury.* —**spend-ing** *n.: capital, consumer, deficit, domestic, government spending;* **adja.:** *spending caps, cuts, habits, patterns, plans, policies.*

spend.thrift *n.* one who spends money wastefully.

spent *adj.* exhausted or used up: *a spent bullet, horse, match; She seems all spent; Is communism a spent force?*

sperm *n.* 1 the male generative fluid. 2 a spermatozoon.

sper.mat.o.zo.on (spur.MAT.uh.ZOH.on) *n., pl.* **-zo.a** (-ZOH.uh) a male germ cell.

sperm whale *n.* a thickset whale with paddlelike flippers and an enormous blunt-snouted head that yields **sperm oil** used for lubricating.

spew *v.* vomit or cast forth: *Volcanoes spew smoke and lava into the air; to spew blood, epithets, poison, threats, venom; the gases spewing from smokestacks.*

sphag.num (SFAG.num) *n.* a soft moss of swampy places that forms peat when decomposed.

sphere (SFEER) *n.* 1 a perfectly round solid body; also, a globular body such as a star or planet. 2 formerly, an imagined hollow globe with the earth as its center and the heavenly bodies revolving around it in fixed concentric shells: *the celestial sphere; the music of the spheres.* 3 the range or domain of an activity or quality: *one's sphere of activity, influence, interest.* —**spher.i.cal** (SFER.i.cul, SFEER-) *adj.* —**spher.i.cal.ly** *adv.*

spher.oid (SFEER.oid) *n.* a body that is a slightly flattened or elongated sphere, as the earth or a football. —**sphe.roid.al** (sfi.ROY.dul) *adj.*

sphinc.ter (SFINK.tur) *n.* a ringlike muscle controlling a body opening such as the anus or vagina.

sphinx (SFINKS) *n.* 1 a statue with a lion's body and human head, which in Greek mythology was a monster who would strangle every passer-by unable to solve a riddle. 2 an enigmatic or puzzling character.

spice *n.* a food seasoning made from a plant, as pepper, ginger, and mace: *"Variety is the spice of life."* —*v.* **spic.es, spiced, spic.ing** season with spice or add zest to something: *A splash of color really spices up a room; His writing is spiced with humor;* **adj.:** *spiced curries, meats, sauces, scents.* —**spic.y** *adj.* **spic.i.er, -i.est:** *spicy humor; spicy* (= slightly racy) *stories.* —**spic.i.ness** *n.*

spick-and-span *adj.* fresh or spotlessly clean.

spic.ule (SPIK.yool) *n.* 1 one of the thousands of jets of gas rising from the sun's chromosphere. 2 a tiny, needlelike body of bony material.

spi.der (SPY.dur) *n.* 1 an eight-legged, insectlike creature that spins webs of silk to trap insects. 2 a frying pan. —**spi.der.y** *adj.: spidery branches, marks, veins.*

spiel (SPEEL) *n. Informal.* a voluble or glib persuasive talk, as of a circus barker: *a sales spiel.*

spiff.y *adj.* **spiff.i.er, -i.est** *Informal.* smart or stylish: *a spiffy cowboy hat; a spiffy dresser.* —**spiff.i.ly** *adv.*

spig.ot (SPIG.ut) *n.* 1 a faucet. 2 a plug or peg for stopping the vent of a barrel or cask.

spike *n.* 1 a usu. large nail or metal point, as those forming the top of an iron fence, the projections on the soles of shoes to prevent slipping, or the fasteners of railroad tracks to ties: *the driving of the last spike in laying the transcontinental railroad; women's shoes with* **spike heels** (= tall pointed heels). 2 a long, pointed cluster of flowers or an ear of grain. 3 a sharp increase: *a spike in gas prices; a voltage spike; I recorded a small spike on the chart.* —*v.* **spikes, spiked, spik.ing** 1 connect with spikes, as a rail to a tie. 2 provide with spikes or projections; **adj.:** *spiked hair, heels, shoes, sticks.* 3 impale on a spike. 4 prevent or thwart a scheme or attempt: *to spike a rumor.* 5 *Informal.* add alcoholic liquor to a drink: *orange juice spiked with alcohol* 6 undergo a sharp increase: *Interest rates will spike; It could spike to 25%; He spiked a* (= had a sharply high) *fever of 104°.*

spike.nard *n.* an East Indian plant yielding a costly perfume.

spik.y (SPY.kee) *adj.* **spik.i.er, -i.est** like a spike or having spikes: *his spiky haircut; spiky shoes; feet with spiky nails.*

spill *v.* **spills,** *pt. & pp.* **spilled** or **spilt, spill.ing** 1 let a liquid or a substance

in loose particles flow over from a container: *to spill milk, salt; The party was so crowded the guests spilled over into the hallways; to spill* (= cause the shedding of) *blood.* **2** *Informal.* throw off or out: *The horse spilled him.*
—*n.* **1** a spilling or something spilled: *an oil spill; The rider took a nasty spill when the horse bolted.* **2** also **spill.way**, a channel for overflowing water, as from a reservoir.

spin *v.* **spins, spun, spin.ning 1** turn or revolve rapidly, as a top, wheel, etc.: *The car was spinning on the ice; Her head was spinning from the dance; He spun around like a figure skater; He has spun around* (= traveled) *the globe many times.* **2** shape by turning, as on a lathe or wheel: *a specialty store chain* **spun off** *by a large conglomerate* (= created by it as source); *an actress so popular she was* **spun off** *into* (= established in) *her own TV series; She's good at spinning* (= telling) *yarns; adj.: a* **well-spun** *tale.* **3** make thread by drawing out and twisting cotton, wool, etc. **4** make something with thread or something threadlike: *Spiders spin webs; adj.:* **spun** *glass, gold, yarns.* **5** move along smoothly and rapidly on a wheeled vehicle. —*n.* **1** a spinning motion, as of a plane coming down out of control. **2** a ride in an automobile, on a bicycle, etc.: *to go for a spin on Lakeshore Boulevard.* **3** a slant or emphasis: *Thomas Kuhn put a new spin on "paradigm"; a different, positive, public-relations spin.* —**spin.ner** *n.*

spin.ach (SPIN.ich) *n.* a garden vegetable with a thick cluster of leaves rich in vitamins and minerals.

spi.nal (SPY.nul) *adj.* having to do with the backbone composed of bony disks: *the* **spinal column** (= backbone); *the* **spinal cord** *(of nerve tissue running from the brain through the spinal column); A* **spinal tap** (= extraction of a sample of the spinal fluid for analysis) *is done on a patient suspected of having a spinal disease.*

spin control *n.* manipulation of a political event by influencing the media.

spin.dle *n.* **1** a short, round, or smooth stick or rod with tapered ends for spinning yarn into thread. **2** anything resembling a spindle in form or function, as a turned wooden piece for a balustrade or the back of a chair.
—**spin.dly** *adj.: a spindly fellow with a spindly frame; spindly columns, legs, trees.*

spin doctor *n.* a publicist hired to manipulate the media.

spin.drift *n.* spray from the sea, as during a gale.

spine *n.* **1** a stiff, sharp-pointed, protective growth, as on a cactus or porcupine. **2** the spinal column or anything resembling it, as the hinged back of a book. **3** backbone or courage; **spine.less** *adj.*

spi.nel (spuh.NEL) *n.* a hard, crystalline mineral whose red variety is used as a gem called **spinel ruby.**

spin.et (SPIN.it) *n.* a pianolike early keyboard instrument on which the harpsichord is based.

spin.na.ker (SPIN.uh.kur) *n.* a large, triangular sail used with the mainsail for added speed when running before the wind.

spinning jenny *n.* a multiple-spindled spinning machine invented about 1764.

spinning wheel *n.* a device for spinning thread or yarn with a spindle driven by a large wheel operated by hand or foot.

spin-off *n.* a benefit, product, etc. derived or resulting from a larger enterprise, as abridged editions of a reference work: *The TV show is a spin-off of the hit movie.*

spin.ster *n.* a woman who has never married; **spin.ster.hood** *n.*

spin.y (SPY.nee) *adj.* **spin.i.er, -i.est** having spines: *spiny fins, fish, oyster shells; The* **spiny lobster** *has a spiny body and no large claws.*

spi.ra.cle (SPY.ruh.cul) *n.* a body opening for breathing, as those along the sides of an insect's body, a fish's gill slit, or a whale's nasal opening.

spiraea same as SPIREA.

spi.ral (SPY.rul) *n.* a curve or coil winding in circles like the hairspring of a watch or like a screw: *an inflationary spiral (of rising prices and wages);* **adja.**: *a book with a spiral binding; the spiral groove of a phonograph record; a spiral staircase.* —*v.* **-rals, -raled, -ral.ing** move or go in circles: *smoke spiraling upward; The news sent prices spiraling; adj.: the* **spiraling** *debt, cost of living, inflation; our downward spiraling economy.* Also **spi.ralled, spi.ral.ling** *Cdn.* —**spi.ral.ly** *adv.*

spi.rant (SPY.runt) *n.* a consonant such as *f, s, sh,* or *th* uttered with audible friction of the breath.

spire *n.* a tapering and pointed structure, as the top of a church steeple, a tapering stalk of grass, or the top part of a sea shell used as a horn.

spi.re.a (spy.REE.uh) *n.* an ornamental

plant of the rose family bearing small clusters of white or pink flowers on slender stalks.

spir.it (SPEER.it) *n.* **1** an animating principle, as the soul to the body; the moral, religious, or emotional aspect of something: *The spirit is willing though the body is weak; in the spirit of our founder; Our founder will be our guiding, moving spirit; to catch the spirit of the times; the Christmas spirit; a competitive, dauntless, fighting, partisan, rebellious, sporting, team spirit; Obey the letter and spirit of the law; I can't be present, but my wife will be there in body and in spirit.* **2** person: *free, kindred, noble spirits.* **3** disposition or state of mind: *We negotiated in a spirit of good will and cooperation; Let's put some spirit* (= vigor) *into our game; They tried but couldn't break her spirit* (= make her submissive); *adj.: a spirited* (= lively or energetic) *approach, campaign, debate, defense, denunciation, exchange, reaction, resistance;* **cpd:** *free-spirited; high-spirited; mean-spirited; public-spirited.* **4** a bodiless or supernatural being, as God, fairies, ghosts, etc.: *the Holy Spirit; a sorcerer who conjures up spirits; an evil spirit; He composes as the spirit moves him* (= as he feels inspired). **5 spirits** *pl.* mood or state of mind: *The defeat dampened our spirits somewhat; Our spirits were drooping; We needed something to lift or raise our flagging spirits; We were in high spirits on hearing that we had won; low spirits; He's in good spirits* (= cheerful) *though a bit weak; animal spirits* (= overflowing liveliness). **6** usu. **spirits** *pl.* a distilled liquid: *spirits of camphor, turpentine; a teetotaler who shuns spirits* (= alcohol). —*v.* carry a person away secretly: *The captive was spirited away or off to a secret location.*

spir.it.u.al (SPEER.i.choo.ul) **1** *adj.* having to do with matters of the spirit: *a spiritual adviser* or *father; a spiritual experience, mission; spiritual aspects, decline, forces, growth, life, power, values.* **2** *n.* a type of religious song popularized by blacks of the Southern U.S.: *negro spirituals.* —**spir.it.u.al.ly** *adv.* —**spir.it.u.al.i.ty** (-choo.AL.i.tee) *n.*

spir.it.u.al.ism (SPEER.i.choo.uh.liz.um) *n.* belief in the souls of the dead communicating with the living; **spir.it.u.al.ist** *n.* —**spir.it.u.al.is.tic** (-LIS.tic) *adj.*

spir.it.u.al.ize (SPEER.i.choo.uh.lize) *v.* **-iz.es, -ized, -iz.ing** make spiritual.

spir.it.u.ous (SPEER.i.choo.us) *adj.* containing alcohol obtained by distilling.

spi.ro.chete (SPY.ruh.keet) *n.* a spiral-shaped, slender bacterium such as causes syphilis and yaws.

¹**spit** *n.* **1** small point of land projecting into water. **2** a pointed rod or bar on which meat is roasted over a fire. —*v.* **spits, spit.ted, spit.ting** pierce with or as if with a spit.

²**spit** *v.* **spits,** *pt. & pp.* **spit** or **spat, spit.ting 1** eject saliva from the mouth: *to spit at* or *on something; Never spit into the wind;* **adj.:** *a spitting match;* **within spitting distance** (= very close). **2** throw out something or make a sound like spitting, as a cat when angry or fat when frying: *The child spit out the medicine; guns spitting fire; When they insisted, she spat out the words in utter contempt.* —*n.* a spitting or the saliva spat out.

spit and polish *n. Informal.* much or excessive attention to neatness and orderliness, esp. of a superficial kind; *adj.: a spit-and-polish kitchen, discipline, professionalism.*

spit.ball *n.* **1** a ball of chewed up paper used as a missile. **2** a baseball pitch delivered after the ball has been moistened with spit or sweat.

spite *n.* petty ill will with a tendency to annoy or irritate: *Did they do it out of spite?* —**in spite of** notwithstanding. —*v.* **spites, spit.ed, spit.ing** show spite toward; annoy or irritate: *It is foolish "to cut off one's nose to spite one's face."* —**spite.ful** *adj.*

spitting image *n.* a strikingly close resemblance of another person: *She is the spitting image of her dad.*

spit.tle (SPIT.ul) *n.* saliva that is spat out.

spit.tle.bug (SPIT.ul.bug) *n.* a hopping insect whose larvae secrete a frothy substance for protection from enemies.

spit.toon (spi.TOON) *n.* a container to spit into; cuspidor.

splash *v.* dash water, mud, etc. so as to make it scatter in drops: *Try not to splash when painting; passing cars splashing pedestrians; a coat splashed with mud; The children splashed in the pool, then splashed across the flooded street.* —*n.* a splashing of a spot or noise made by splashing. —**make a splash** *Informal.* make a sensation; attract much attention.

splash.down *n.* the landing of a spacecraft on water.

splash.y *adj.* **splash.i.er, -i.est** *Informal.* showy or sensational: *a splashy catalog, design, display, dress, event, presentation, tabloid; splashy colors, hues, ties.*

splat *n.* a vertical center rail or slat in the back of certain chairs.

splat.ter *v.* spatter: *a kitchen splattered with ketchup;* **cpd: blood-spattered** *clothes; a bug-spattered windshield; mud-splattered tires; paint-splattered walls.* Also *n.*

splay.foot *n.* **-feet** a broad flat foot that is turned outward.

splay.foot.ed (SPLAY.foot.id) *adj.* having splayfeet; hence, clumsy.

spleen *n.* **1** a large glandlike organ lying between the stomach and the diaphragm that acts as a blood filter but was once believed the cause of bad temper: *a ruptured spleen.* **2** spite or ill temper: *He vented his spleen on the first one to cross his path.*

splen.did *adj.* brilliant and impressive: *a splendid palace, victory; a splendid (Informal for excellent) idea.*

splen.dor (SPLEN.dur) *n.* brilliance or magnificence: *a pageant full of pomp and splendor; a prince arrayed in regal splendor.* Also **splen.dour** *Cdn.*

sple.net.ic (spli.NET.ic) *adj.* **1** of the spleen; also **splen.ic** (SPLEN.ic, SPLEEN.ic). **2** bad-tempered or peevish; **sple.net.i.cal.ly** *adv.*

splice *v.* **splic.es, spliced, splic.ing 1** join ropes, wire, etc. without knotting by weaving untwisted ends together. **2** join together pieces of timber, etc. by overlapping. **3** join together different pieces of tape, film, computer data, nerves, or genetic material for a desired effect.
—*n.* a joint made by splicing.

splint *n.* **1** a thin strip of wood or other flexible material for weaving or braiding into baskets, chair seats, etc. **2** a thin strip of wood, a plaster cast, or other device for keeping an injured body part in position while healing; *v.: He used a popsicle stick to splint* (= brace or support) *her broken finger.*

splin.ter (SPLIN.tur) *n.* a long, thin, sharp piece of broken glass, bone, wood, etc.: *to extract, get out, remove the splinter from a foot; a new party formed by a splinter* (= factional) *group.*
—*v.* break into splinters: *The marriage soon splintered; It splintered apart; The Soviet Union splintered into many nations; It was splintered by the failure of communism;* **adj.:** *a splintered coalition, marriage, nation; It remains splintered; a splintering relationship; splintering wood; n.: the splintering of empires, of glass.*

split *v.* **splits, split, split.ting 1** separate lengthwise or along a natural line of division, as along the grain of wood or into layers of slate. **2** cut or divide into parts: *The bag split at the seams; Purists try never to split an infinitive, i.e., avoid writing "to never split an infinitive"; He shouldn't have split up with* (= separated from) *his wife; We'll split the difference* (= compromise by agreeing on a middle figure); *Let's not split hairs* (= argue over trivialities); *She was splitting her sides* (= laughing heartily) *at his jokes;* **n.:** *the splitting up of a subdivision into housing lots; the splitting of the atom;* **adj.:** *a splitting* (= severe) *headache.* **3** *Slang.* leave a place.
—*n.* a splitting, crack, division, etc.: *a split in the party ranks; a split between factions.* —**adj.:** *a split class of students of different grades in the same room; a split* (= not unanimous) *decision; hair with split ends* (split into strands).

split-level *n. & adj.* (a house) having an intermediate level about half a floor above or below the others built adjacently.

split peas *n.pl.* dried green peas used split, esp. for soup; **adj.:** *a split-pea soup.*

split personality *n.* **1** a personality with conflicting patterns of behavior; one suffering from "multiple personality disorder." **2** [erroneous use] *Informal.* schizophrenia.

split screen *n.* **1** a TV screen showing two scenes side by side. **2** a computer's display of two or more windows on the same screen.

split second *n.* an instant: *for a split second; in a split second;* **adj.:** *a split-second advantage, delay; split-second decisions, timing.*

split shift *n.* a work shift consisting of periods that are far apart.

splotch *n.* an irregular or blotchy spot or stain. —*v.* mark with a splotch or splotches; **splotch.y** *adj.*

splurge *n.* a showy or extravagant display: *a splurge following a lottery win; a 12-goal splurge by the Los Angeles Kings.*
—*v.* **splurg.es, splurged, splurg.ing** *Informal.* make a splurge or spend money extravagantly: *Let's splurge for the best; Why not splurge on a mink coat?*

splut.ter (SPLUT.ur) *v.* make a sputtering sound, esp. speak in an excited and confused manner.
—*n.* a spluttering.

spoil *v.* **spoils,** *pt. & pp.* **spoiled** or **spoilt, spoil.ing 1** destroy the usefulness or value of a person or thing: *Bad weather spoiled the picnic; "Too many cooks spoil the soup"; The tall building in front of us spoils the view; methods to keep*

food from spoiling (= beginning to rot); **adj.:** *a spoiled* (= pampered) *brat, child, teen; She sounds spoiled.* **2 be spoiling for** *Informal.* be eager for a fight, etc. **3** [old use] rob or plunder.
—*n.* usu. **spoils** *pl.* loot or booty: *the spoils of victory, war; to reap, share in the spoils of consumer spending; the division of spoils between different factions.*
—**spoil.age** (-ij) *n.*

spoil.er *n.* **1** one that spoils or loots: *party spoilers.* **2** a plate that acts as an air brake, as on an airplane wing or racing car: *a rear-deck spoiler.*

spoil.sport *n.* one who spoils the enjoyment of others.

spoils system *n.* the political practice of rewarding supporters with public offices when a party assumes power.

spoke *n.* any of the radial bars extending from the hub of a wheel to its rim. —*v. pt.* of SPEAK.

spoken 1 *pp.* of SPEAK. **2** *adj.* uttered: *the spoken word.* **3** *comb.form.* speaking as specified: *loud-spoken, plain-spoken, soft-spoken, sweet-spoken, true-spoken.*

spokes.man (SPOKES.mun) *n.* **-men** a person expressing the views of another or of a group. —**spokes.wom.an** *n.* **-wom.en.** Also **spokes.per.son.**

spo.li.a.tion (spoh.lee.AY.shun) *n.* robbery or plundering, esp. in war.
—**spo.li.a.tor** *n.*

sponge (SPUNJ) *n.* **1** a water animal with a porous skeleton that resembles a plant in being attached to the bottom of the sea or to other objects. **2** a porous or spongelike mass of rubber, or **sponge rubber**, or other synthetic material used for cleansing, washing, etc. **3** a washing or wiping with a sponge. **4** *Informal.* a parasite; sponger. —**throw in** or **toss in the sponge** give up the fight; accept defeat.
—*v.* **spong.es, sponged, spong.ing** **1** wipe, rub, wash, etc. with a sponge. **2** *Informal.* live at the expense of another: *Since losing his job, Jon has been sponging on his friends; He sponged $50 off me.* —**spong.er** *n.*

sponge bath *n.* a cleaning of the body using a wet sponge or cloth.

sponge.cake *n.* a light spongy cake made without shortening.

spon.gy *adj.* **-gi.er, -gi.est** like a sponge; full of holes.

spon.sor (SPON.sur) *n.* an endorser or supporter, as a godparent, the promoter of a legislative proposal, or one paying for a radio or TV program by buying commercial advertising.
—*v.* act as sponsor for someone: *He sponsored her for the club membership.*
—**spon.sor.ship** *n.*

spon.ta.neous (spon.TAY.nee.us) *adj.* caused or happening naturally, without planning or premeditation: *spontaneous laughter; a spontaneous outburst; a spontaneous abortion* (= miscarriage).
—**spon.ta.ne.ous.ly** *adv.*
—**spon.ta.ne.i.ty** (-tuh.NEE.i.tee) *n.*

spontaneous combustion *n.* the catching fire of something from heat produced by chemical action within itself, as in a pile of oily rags

spoof (long "oo") *n. Informal.* **1** a hoax or trick. **2** a parody or takeoff.
—*v.* ridicule or parody.

spook (long "oo") *n.* **1** *Informal.* a ghost. **2** *Slang.* a spy. —*v.* frighten.
—**spook.y** *adj.;* **spook.i.ly** *adv.;* **spook.i.ness** *n.*

spool *n.* a cylinder or reel on which thread, wire, film, or ribbon is wound.

spooling *n.* the processing of input and output from a computer peripheral such as a printer by storage on a high-speed device so as not to tie up the central processor.

spoon *n.* **1** a utensil consisting of a shallow bowl at one end of a handle for eating, stirring, etc.: *dessert, measuring, soup spoons.* **2** something spoon-shaped, as a fishing lure. —*v.* take up with a spoon: *Please spoon the chicken on to my plate; to spoon the sauce over the rolls; Mom told us to spoon it all up; the dollars spooned out by the government.*
—**spoon.ful, -fuls:** *a spoonful of sugar; heaping, level, rounded spoonfuls.*

spoon.bill *n.* an ibislike wading bird with a spoon-shaped bill.

spoon.er.ism (SPOO.nur.iz.um) *n.* the interchanging of sounds in running words with comic effect, as in "kinkering congs" for "conquering kings."

spoon.feed *v.* **-feeds, -fed, -feed.ing** **1** feed with a spoon, as a child. **2** help someone in a way that does not encourage thinking or acting for oneself: *Do the schools spoonfeed students too much?*

spoor *n.* the trail or track of a wild animal.

spo.rad.ic (spuh.RAD.ic) *adj.* occurring in scattered or isolated instances: *sporadic cases of a disease; sporadic gunfire; Buying was sporadic; sporadic activity on the stock exchange.* —**spo.rad.i.cal.ly** *adv.*

spore *n.* in algae, fungi, etc., a one-celled body capable of giving rise to a new individual.

sport *n.* **1** a pastime requiring physical exertion and skill, as baseball, bowling, etc.: *sports and games; amateur, aquatic, competitive, contact, outdoor, spectator, water, winter sports; team sports such as football and hockey.* **2** such pastimes collectively; also, physical activity: *She is fond of sports; Olympic Games are the greatest events in the world of sport(s); the history of Mexican sport.* **3** fun or amusement: *cruel sport; He soon became the sport* (= object of fun) *of his class; She only said it for* or *in sport; They like to* **make sport** *of* (= mock) *his accent.* **4** *Informal.* a good fellow: *Be a sport! She is a good sport who can take a lot of teasing.* —*v.* **1** play or jest: *She is only sporting.* **2** *Informal.* display: *He came to work sporting a new jacket.* —*adj.* having to do with sports: *a sports competition, enthusiast, event, model, personality, section, sedan; a sport(s) car; sports equipment, medicine; the sports world;* **sport fish** *(caught more for fun than for food).*

sporting *adj.* having to do with sports: *sporting equipment; the sporting public; a sporting* (= sportsmanlike) *offer; Give them a sporting (Informal for* fair) *chance.* —**sport.ing.ly** *adv.*

sport.ive (SPORT.iv) *adj.* playful: *sportive looks;* **sport.ive.ly** *adv.*

sports.cast *n.* a broadcast of a sporting event. —**sports.cast.er** *n.*

sports.man (SPORTS.mun) *n.* **-men 1** a man who takes part in sports such as hunting and fishing. **2** one who plays fair. —**sports.man.like** *adj.;* **sports.man.ship** *n.* —**sports.wom.an** (SPORTS.wom.an) *n.* **-wom.en.**

sports.wear *n.* clothes for casual or informal wear, as a **sport(s) shirt.**

sport.y *adj.* **sport.i.er, -i.est** *Informal.* **1** good for sports: *sporty shoes.* **2** flashy or showy: *sporty slacks; a sporty tie; a sporty car with sporty looks.*

spot *n.* **1** a small area or place: *a clear spot in the jungle; the exact spot where he landed; in an isolated, secluded spot; a blind spot that the driver cannot see; the trouble spots of the world such as Palestine and Northern Ireland.* **2** a small, distinguishable area or mark: *A leopard cannot change its spots; a beauty spot (on the skin); a grease spot* (= stain); *a spot* (= stain) *remover.* —**in a (bad) spot** *Informal.* in trouble. —**on the spot** then and there: *She was hired on the spot; The press got a briefing on the spot;* **the man on the spot** (= on the actual scene) *when something happens;* **adj.:** *an* **on-the-spot** *briefing, decision, transaction.* —**put someone on the spot** *Informal.* put someone in a difficult or embarrassing position: *The tax auditor put him on the spot.* —*v.* **spots, spot.ted, spot.ting 1** mark or become marked with spots: *a pattern spotted like a giraffe.* **2** to stain: *a page spotted with smudges.* **3** locate; also, see or recognize: *We spotted him in the crowd; He was spotted* (= identified) *as the wanted man.* **4** have as a handicap or advantage over someone: *an equalizer for the 11 years that Ali was spotting Spinks in age.* —**adj.** happening, done, etc. on the spot: *a 30-second spot commercial; spot news coverage of a fire; spot transactions.* —**spot.less** *adj.;* **spot.less.ly** *adv.;* **spot.less.ness** *n.*

spot check *n.* a random on-the-spot check, inspection, or sampling. —**spot-check** *v.:* to spot-check *inventory, personnel, results, transactions.*

spot.light *n.* **1** a bright light thrown on a spot requiring illumination, as on the stage. **2** the focus of public attention: *They turned the spotlight on someone in the audience; He was* **in the spotlight** (= the object of public attention) *for a while.* —*v.* **1** light up with a spotlight. **2** put in public view.

spot market *n.* a market in which commodities are sold for cash on delivery: *Pay the* **spot price** *and get it cheaper on the spot market.*

spot.ter *n.* **1** one who removes spots before cleaning clothes. **2** one who locates, identifies, or keeps watch on people, targets, etc.

spot.ty *adj.* **spot.ti.er, spot.ti.est 1** spotted: *a spotty complexion, pattern; a spotty face* (marked by acne). **2** uneven or irregular: *a spotty appearance, harvest, market, performance, record; spotty business, sales, success, supplies, traffic, work.* —**spot.ti.ly** *adv.;* **spot.ti.ness** *n.*

spouse *n.* marriage partner, usu. one's wife or husband: *a beloved spouse; an unfaithful spouse.* —**spous.al** (SPOW.zul) *adj.:* spousal *abuse, assistance, benefits, plans, support.*

spout *n.* **1** a jet or stream, as of water, from a pipe, nozzle, or projecting tube, as of a kettle. **2** a projecting part of a pipe, as for rainwater from a roof. —*v.* **1** shoot out, as water from a spout or fountain. **2** *Informal.* utter or speak in a vehement or declamatory manner.

sprain *v.* stretch or tear the ligaments of a body joint accidentally. —*n.* such an injury.

sprang a *pt.* of SPRING.

sprat *n.* a small herringlike sea fish.
sprawl *v.* lie on one's back with limbs loosely spread out: *bodies sprawled on the beach; The blow sent him sprawling;* **adj.**: *a **sprawling** (= spread-out) bazaar, campus, city, community, mansion, marketplace, suburb.*
—*n.* a sprawling or a spread-out condition: *the sprawl of fast-food outlets; a new land-use program to halt urban sprawl.*
spray *n.* **1** (an ornament shaped like) a small cluster of flowers, leaves, or fruit. **2** a mist or jet of tiny drops, as from a breaking wave or a SPRAY GUN. —*v.* apply as a spray: *Insecticide is sprayed on trees; The enemy was sprayed with bullets.* —**spray.er** *n.*
spray can *n.* an aerosol container.
spray gun *n.* a device for applying paints, lacquers, etc. in a spray.
spread (SPRED) *v.* **spreads, spread, spread.ing** (cause) to cover a large or larger area: *A bird spreads its wings; to spread a rug on the floor; to spread jam on toast; to spread it evenly; The rumor spread quickly; to spread the news; It spread like wildfire; spread to all corners of the nation; to spread seed, contagious diseases; An epidemic spreads unchecked; payments spread over many years; to spread* (= arrange) *the table for dinner.*
—*n.* a spreading, what is spread, or its expanse or extent: *the spread of an eagle's wings; the spread of civilization; a tasty sandwich spread; an ad designed as a two-page spread; a center spread; a 600-acre spread in Texas; spreads* (= covers) *for beds, tables, etc.* —**spread.er** *n.*
spread-eagle *adj.* standing or lying spread out like an eagle with outstretched wings and legs. —*v.* **-gles, -gled, -gling** (make someone) stand or lie in spread-eagle fashion: *three youths spread-eagled against police cars.*
spread.sheet *n.* an accounting worksheet for financial planning or a computer program for this purpose.
spree *n.* an uninhibited activity or indulgence in something: *to go on a shopping spree; spending sprees; the hangover following a weekend spree* (= drinking bout).
sprig *n.* a small twig or spray: *a sprig of mistletoe.*
spright.ly *adv.* **-li.er, -li.est** lively or spirited: *a sprightly design, lad, oldster, performance, publication, style; She walks at a sprightly pace; He's a sprightly 85 (years).* —**spright.li.ness** *n.*
spring *v.* **springs,** *pt.* **sprang** or **sprung,** *pp.* **sprung, spring.ing 1** move, esp. rise suddenly and lightly: *to spring out of bed; Weeds spring up on a lawn; He sprang to her defense; He's sprung of or from noble blood; The image that **springs to mind** when you see her is of her dad.* **2** of a wall, door, etc., give way to pressure and crack, warp, etc. **3** cause to spring: *a trap that is easily sprung; Sue wanted to **spring it on** (= make it known suddenly to) her parents; The boat **sprang a leak** and sank; He was **sprung from jail** (Informal for released) by paying bail.*
—*n.* **1** a springing: *a sudden spring.* **2** an elastic device or quality: *cars with coil springs and leaf springs; the box spring of our bed; the spring of her step.* **3** the growing season that follows winter: *There's a hint or touch of spring in the air; an early spring; A robin is a harbinger of spring; Spring training for baseball starts in February.* **4** a natural stream rising from under the ground: *hot, mineral, thermal, subterranean springs; spring water.* **5** source or origin: *springs of knowledge; the deepest springs of thought.*
—**adj. 1** springing: *a spring device, lock.* **2** of the spring season: *time to do a thorough spring cleaning; spring breaks, rains.* **3** having to do with natural streams of water: *fresh spring water.*
spring.board *n.* a flexible board to jump from with a springing motion, as at a swimming pool: *He used his first job as a springboard to higher positions.*
spring chicken *n. Informal.* a young person.
spring fever *n.* a feeling of restlessness during the change from the cold of winter to the warmth of spring.
spring lamb *n.* a lamb born in early spring.
spring tide *n.* either of the two higher-than-normal tides occurring during new moon and full moon.
spring.time *n.* the spring season.
spring.y *adj.* **spring.i.er, -i.est** elastic or resilient: *a springy mattress, rhythm, step.*
sprin.kle (SPRINK.ul) *v.* **-kles, -kled, -kling** fall or scatter in small drops or particles: *to sprinkle salt on food; to sprinkle a lawn* (with water); *It's sprinkling outside* (= raining lightly).
—*n.* **1** a sprinkling. **2** a light rain.
—**sprink.ler** *n.*
sprin.kling *n.* **1** what is sprinkled: *a sprinkling of black pepper.* **2** a small number or quantity: *a feminist crowd with a sprinkling of men.*
sprint *n.* a relatively short race, up to 400 m (1,312.3 ft.) in track and field; dash. —*v.* run a sprint. —**sprint.er** *n.*

sprite *n.* an elf or fairy.
spritz *n. & v.* spray or squirt: *to spritz customers with fragrances; a spritz of Chanelle 13; adja.: spritz bottles; a spritz hairspray.*
spritz.er (SPRIT.sur) *n.* a wine-and-soda drink.
sprock.et (SPROK.it) *n.* **1** one of the teeth on a wheel rim that engage with the links of a chain going over it, as in a bicycle. **2** the wheel itself, or **sprocket wheel.**
sprout *n.* **1** a young shoot, as from a seed in the ground. **2** a bud. —*v.* cause or begin to grow; germinate.
spruce (SPROOSE) *n.* an evergreen tree related to the firs, but with cones hanging downwards. —*adj.* **spruc.er, spruc.est** neat and smart.
—*v.* **spruc.es, spruced, spruc.ing** make spruce: *He spruced himself up for the party.*
sprung *pp. & a pt.* of SPRING.
spry *adj.* **spri.er** or **spry.er, spri.est** or **spry.est** esp. of the elderly, vigorous and active. —**spry.ly** *adv.;* **spry.ness** *n.*
spud *n. Informal.* potato.
spume (long "yoo") *n.* what is spewed forth, as by force or under pressure: *the spume of whales.* —*v.* **spumes, spumed, spum.ing:** *The waterfall hits the bottom and spumes upward high in the air.*
spu.mo.ni (spuh.MOH.nee) *n.* an Italian-style ice cream containing fruit and nuts; also **spu.mo.ne.**
spun *pt. & pp.* of SPIN.
spunk *n. Informal.* pluck or courage: *The children showed lots of spunk in helping to rescue their playmates.* —**spunk.y** *adj.: a spunky attitude, spirit, sweater.*
spun sugar same as COTTON CANDY.
spur *n.* **1** a pricking device with a sharp point, worn on a rider's heel for urging a horse forward. **2** a stimulus or incentive: *The prize was a spur to greater achievements.* **3** something spurlike, as the small projection on the leg of a rooster, a lateral ridge extending from a mountain, or a railway siding. —**on the spur of the moment** suddenly and without planning. —**win one's spurs** gain distinction in one's field: *She has won her spurs as a diplomat.*
—*v.* **spurs, spurred, spur.ring** urge on or incite, as with spurs: *The prize spurred her on to greater efforts; The tragedy stirred the neighborhood out of its lethargy and spurred them to action; to spur business, the economy, growth, interest, investment, production, sales.*

spurge *n.* a shrub, tree, or plant yielding a milky juice, as cassava, castor oil, poinsettia, and rubber.
spu.ri.ous (SPYOOR.ee.us) *adj.* not genuine or authentic; false: *a spurious allegation, distinction, document, signature; spurious arguments, charges, claims; on spurious grounds.* —**spu.ri.ous.ly** *adv.*
spurn *v.* refuse or reject with disdain: *to spurn a lover, an offer; She spurned his attentions.*
spurt *v.* **1** (cause) to gush out suddenly, as blood from a wound. **2** show a short and sudden burst of energy, as near the finish in a race.
—*n.:* *Water came out of the tap in spurts; spurts of flame; a spurt of activity in the stock market.*
sput.nik (SPUT.nik) *n.* an earth satellite sent up by the Soviet Union.
sput.ter (SPUT.ur) *n.* **1** a popping and spitting noise, as of fat when frying. **2** drops or bits of food from the mouth. —*v.* **1** make a sputtering noise. **2** spit out words or to talk excitedly and in confusion.
spu.tum (SPEW.tum) *n., pl.* **-ta** (-tuh), saliva and mucus that is coughed up.
spy *v.* **spies, spied, spy.ing 1** keep secret watch on a person or search out information for a nation for hostile purposes, as in wartime: *to spy on someone; Al is spying for the enemy.* **2** catch sight of someone: *We spied him breaking into the house from our window.*
—*n., pl.* **spies** one who spies.
spy.glass *n.* a small telescope.
squab (SQUOB) *n.* a young pigeon.
—*adj.* short and stout; also **squab.by.**
squab.ble (SQUAB.ul) *n.* a petty and noisy quarrel *about* or *over* something.
—*v.* **squab.bles, squab.bled, squab.bling** have a squabble: *neighbors squabbling with each other over a fence; n.: the squabbling going on between the two.*
squad (SQUOD) *n.* **1** the smallest military unit, composed of 10 or 12 soldiers. **2** a small group of people working together: *anti-riot, demolition, firing, flying, goon, vice squads; a squad appointed to clean up the schoolyard.*
squad car *n.* a police cruiser or patrol car.
squad.ron (SQUOD.run) *n.* **1** an organized military unit, esp. in an air force: *a squadron of bombers, tanks.* **2** any organized multitude: *squadrons of birds, flies; a seven-man squadron of golf players.*
squal.id (SQUOL.id) *adj.* filthy, as from neglect: *squalid camps, conditions, poverty, slums; a squalid existence, saga, scene.*

squall (SQUAWL) *n.* **1** a sudden rise in the wind, esp. at sea, often accompanied by rain, hail, or thunder. **2** a loud, harsh cry or scream. —*v.* utter a squall. —**squal.ly** *adj.*

squal.or (SQUOL.ur) *n.* the state of being squalid; wretchedness; sordidness: *people living in squalor in the slums.*

squa.mous (SQUAY.mus) *adj.* formed of scales or scalelike; also **squa.mose.**

squan.der (SQUON.dur) *v.* spend wealth, resources, etc. wastefully or extravagantly: *He squandered his heritage on risky ventures.*

square (SQUAIR) *n.* **1** a plane figure with four equal sides and angles. **2** anything in this shape, as a city block, a public place enclosed by streets on all sides, an instrument in the shape of an L or T to make or measure right angles, etc.: *a city square.* **3** the product of a quantity multiplied by itself: *The square of 7 is 49.* **4** *Slang.* an old-fashioned person; one who is not hip: *Is Sam a square?* —*adj.* **squar.er, squar.est 1** like a square in shape: *a square room; a square meter (in area); a sedan with a square back; within [square] brackets; square jaws, shoulders; a room 20 m square* (= 20 m long on each side). **2** suggesting evenness, balance, straightness, etc.: *fair and square* (= honest) *dealings; square* (= balanced) *accounts; three square* (= substantial) *meals a day; a square* (= straightforward) *refusal.* **3** *Slang.* not hip; old-fashioned: *She's square.* —*v.* **squares, squared, squar.ing** be square, make square, or make into squares: *7 squared is 49; to square* (= settle) *an account with the bank; performance that does not square* (= agree) *with promises; adj.: squared graph paper; squared timber with rectangular edges.* —**square off** *Informal.* get ready to fight *against* someone, as in boxing. —**square oneself** *Informal.* make up for a wrong. —*adv.* in a square shape or manner. —**square.ly** *adv.* directly; straight: *to face a problem squarely; Put it squarely before the committee; She stood squarely behind him; laid the blame squarely at their feet; looked them squarely in the eye; to address, aim, base, meet, place, plant, position something squarely; to be, lie, sit squarely.* —**square.ness** *n.*

square dance *n.* a folk dance in groups of four couples in a square formation performing various figures; **square-dance** *v.*

square knot *n.* a symmetrical double knot.

square measure *n.* a unit or system for measuring areas.

square one *n.* the starting point, as in games: *right back at* or *to square one.*

square-rigged *adj.* with four-sided sails fastened horizontally on yards slung across masts, not fore and aft.

square-rigger *n.* a square-rigged ship.

square root *n.* a quantity which when multiplied by itself gives its square: *The square root of 49 is 7.*

squar.ish *adj.* nearly square.

squash (SQUOSH) *v.* **1** squeeze, crush, or beat into a flat mass or pulp. **2** give a crushing blow to something; suppress a riot or silence an adversary. **3** proceed or move by force or with a splashing sound: *They squashed through the crowd.* —*n.* **1** a squashing fall or its soft, heavy sound. **2** a squashed mass. **3** a gourd of the New World related to pumpkins: *summer squash; winter squash.* **4** a game like handball but played with rackets in a walled court; also **squash racquets.** —**squash.y** *adj.*

squat (SQUOT) *v.* **squats, squat.ted, squat.ting 1** crouch or sit on the heels with bent knees: *Do not squat down for scrubbing the floor, but adopt a less stressful position.* **2** settle on land without original legal right. —*n.* **1** a squatting posture: *She eased into a squat; Keep back straight and lower into semi-squat; a two-thirds squat.* **2** *Slang.* nothing: *He doesn't know squat about computers; not worth squat.* —*adj.* **squat.ter, squat.test 1** crouching: *a squat position; remain squat.* **2** short and thick, as a toad or puffin; dumpy: *a squat little guy; a squat box, building, jar, shape;* also **squat.ty.**

squat.ter (SQUOT.ur) *n.* one who squats on public land: *Sometimes squatters gain title to the lands they occupy; In developing countries, millions live in squatter settlements* (made up of shacks).

squaw *n.* [disparaging use] a North American Indian woman.

squawk *v.* **1** utter a loud, harsh, complaining cry. **2** *Informal.* protest or complain raucously: *He has nothing to squawk about.* —*n.* a squawking: *The chickens made loud squawks at the sight of the hawk; squawks* (= loud complaints) *from the taxpayers.*

squeak (SQUEEK) *v. & n.* (utter) the sharp, high-pitched cry of a mouse or (make) the sound of a door hinge that needs oiling: *She was too choked up even to squeak for help; The bill managed to squeak by* or *through with a narrow* margin; *It was a close, narrow squeak* (= escape). —**squeak.er** *n.* —**squeak.y** *adj.* **squeak.i.er, -i.est:** *squeaky floorboards, shoes, voices; "The squeaky wheel gets the grease"* (= You have to make noise to get attention); *hair washed* **squeaky-clean;** *a squeaky-clean living room, fairy tale; squeaky-clean gambling that pays for hospitals, etc.; our squeaky-clean image, standards.*

squeal (SQUEEL) *v.* **1** make a long squeaking cry or sound, as of a pig when hurt or of faulty brakes: *Children squeal with* or *in delight; a train squealing to a halt.* **2** act as an informer: *to squeal on someone to the police.* —*n.* a squealing sound: *tire squeals of speeding cars; a squeal of delight, horror.* —**squeal.er** *n.*

squeam.ish (SQUEE.mish) *adj.* **1** prudish or scrupulous: *She is very squeamish about walking in late.* **2** queasy or nauseated: *to feel squeamish at the thought of eating raw fish.*

squee.gee (SQUEE.jee) *n.* a tool with a rubber-edged blade set crosswise on a handle, as used for window-washing. Also *v.*

squeeze *v.* **squeez.es, squeezed, squeez.ing 1** press from the sides, as in extracting juice from a fruit, hugging someone, or forcing a way through a crowd: *All the people were squeezed into one room; It was tough to squeeze one's way out of it.* **2** put pressure on a victim or get money, etc. by pressure from someone. **3** oppress. —*n.* a squeezing or being squeezed: *to put a squeeze* (= restraint) *on bank loans to fight inflation; He found himself in a tight squeeze* (= in difficulty); *a plastic* **squeeze bottle** *for spraying medication; a* **squeeze play** *in baseball, with the batter bunting the ball and the runner scoring from third base.* —**squeez.a.ble** *adj.*

squelch *n. Informal.* **1** the act of suppressing or silencing, as with a rebuke, stare, etc. **2** a sucking sound, as made when splashing through mud. —*v. Informal.* **1** to silence or put down with a squelch. **2** slosh or splash through mud, etc. with a squelch.

squib *n.* **1** a short witty or satirical piece. **2** a small firecracker that makes a fizzing noise.

squig.gle (SQUIG.ul) *n.* a wavy twist or curve. —*v.* **squig.gles, squig.gled, squig.gling 1** move with or make squiggles. **2** write as a squiggle. —**squig.gly** (-glee) *adj.* wavy: *squiggly lines.*

squint *v.* **1** look with the eyes partly closed; peer: *It's natural to squint when looking at bright lights; She squinted at them from behind her glasses.* **2** look sideways. **3** be cross-eyed. —*n.* **1** a peering. **2** a cross-eye. **3** a sidelong glance. —**squin.ty** *adj.*

squire *v.* **squires, squired, squir.ing** act as a squire to a woman; escort. —*n.* **1** a woman's escort. **2** in Britain, a country gentleman, esp. the chief landowner of a district. **3** formerly, a knight's personal attendant or armor bearer.

squirm *v.* **1** wriggle or writhe about, as a worm: *Don't let him* **squirm out of** (= evade) *that commitment.* **2** do so because of embarrassment: *He squirmed in his chair when the subject was mentioned.* —**squirm.y** *adj.*

squir.rel (SQUR.ul, SQUEER.rul) *n.* a rodent, usu. tree-dwelling, related to the chipmunk. —*v.* **squir.rels, squir.reled, squir.rel.ing** store something *away* for future use. Also **squir.relled, squir.rel.ling** *Cdn.*

squirt *v.* eject a liquid in a thin stream, as through a small pump or syringe. —*n.* **1** a jet of liquid. **2** a squirting device such as a "water pistol," or **squirt gun.** **3** *Informal.* an impudent youngster.

squish 1 *v.* squash or squeeze: *tiny bungalows squished into postage-stamp lots and sold as detached homes.* **2** *v. & n.* (make) a soft splashing or squashing sound: *The children squished their way through slush.* —**squish.y** *adj.: a squishy stretch of swamp; a wet squishy day.*

stab *n.* **1** a thrust or a wound made by a thrust with a pointed weapon such as a dagger. **2** a sharp pain as if caused by a stab: *a sudden stab of pain.* **3** *Informal.* attempt: *He made* or *had several stabs at skiing.* —**stab in the back** a treacherous attack or betrayal. —*v.* **stabs, stabbed, stab.bing** pierce or wound someone with or as if with a pointed weapon: *Caesar was fatally stabbed; stabbed to death;* **adj.a.:** *a* **stab.bing** *attack, victim; in stabbing pain.* —**stab.ber** *n.*

sta.bil.i.ty (stuh.BIL.i.tee) *n.* the quality of being stable; firmness; steadiness; permanence: *peace and stability in the Middle East; political stability and security; economic, financial, regional, world stability; to enhance, maintain, preserve, restore, threaten stability.*

sta.bi.lize (STAY.buh.lize) *v.* **-liz.es, -lized, -liz.ing** make stable or steady: *A gyroscope is used to stabilize a ship; to stabilize fluctuating prices; An airplane is stabilized with a fixed horizontal surface*

called stabilizer in its tail assembly.
—**sta.bi.liz.er** *n.* a device, substance, etc. that stabilizes something: *shoes with heel stabilizers; stabilizer muscles.*
—**sta.bi.li.za.tion** (-luh.ZAY.shun, -lye-) *n.*
sta.ble (STAY.bul) *adj.* **-bler, -blest** not likely to be unsteady or be overturned: *a stable business, foundation, government, region, relationship, structure; a stable democracy, design; a stable and secure world order; He's emotionally quite stable; a stable* (= lasting) *chemical compound.* —*n.* **1** a building in which domestic animals are housed and fed. **2** a group under one's control, as of authors, boxers, movie stars, racehorses, racing cars, etc.: *a publisher with a good stable of authors.* —*v.* **-bles, -bled, -bling** to lodge or be kept in a stable.
stac.ca.to (stuh.CAH.toh) *adj. & adv.* in a broken or disconnected manner: *staccato speech; music played staccato* (= with successive notes detached).
stack *n.* **1** a neatly arranged or orderly pile, as a haystack or rifles in a pyramid arrangement: *book* or *library stacks* (= main collection of books). **2** a smokestack. —**blow one's stack** *Slang.* lose one's temper. —*v.* pile or arrange in a stack: *a room stacked with books; Books were stacked against the walls; The jury is stacked* (= so arranged that the outcome of the trial is certain). —**stack the cards** or **deck** arrange cards so as to cheat: *accused of stacking the cards in favor of his partner; The deck is stacked (against them)* (= They have no chance). —**stack up** measure up or compare *with* or *to* or *against* a standard: *The two sides stack up fairly evenly; One stacks up well against the other.*
sta.di.um (STAY.dee.um) *n.* a large structure of tiers of seats, often domed, built around a playing field or arena: *baseball, domed, football, Olympic stadiums.*
staff *n., pl.* also **staves** (except for 3). **1** a supporting stick or pole, as used when walking, for hoisting a flag, etc.: *soldiers with shields and staves.* **2** one that supports or sustains: *Bread is the staff of life; An only son was the staff of her old age.* **3** *pl.* **staffs** a group of workers or officers: *I work with a skeleton staff; a military chief of staff; a publisher's office, editorial, and production staffs; She joined our staff today; She is on* (= a member of the) *staff.* **4** the set of five lines on which music is written.
—*v.* supply with a staff of workers: *to staff an institution.*
staff.er *n.* a member of a staff, as distinguished from casual employees.
staff sergeant *n.* in the U.S. Air Force, Army, and Marine Corps, a noncommissioned officer ranking above a sergeant.
stag *n.* an adult male deer.
—*adj.* meant for men to enjoy: *a stag movie, party, show; strictly stag.*
—**go stag** esp. of men, attend a party unaccompanied by a date.
stage *n.* **1** a step or degree of advance in a process: *the pupa stage of a butterfly; You keep growing till you reach a certain stage; the beginning, closing, early, final* or *last, planning stages of a campaign; advanced, critical, crucial stages of an illness; the various stages of development, life, pregnancy; to complete a task by easy stages* (= slowly); *Most skills are learned in (easy) stages* (= gradually). **2** one of the independently powered sections of a long-range rocket or missile which are jettisoned successively after burning their fuel. **3** a stagecoach. **4** a theater platform; hence, acting on the stage: *He'll go* (= appear) *on stage in a few minutes; a career on the stage* (= in acting); *stars of the stage and screen* (= the theater and the movies); *adj.:* stage directions, doors, managers, properties, settings; dramatic, spectacular *stage effects.* **5** a scene of action: *on the international, political, world stage; Bad strike settlements set the stage* (= prepare the way) *for later trouble.* —*v.* **stag.es, staged, stag.ing 1** present (as) on a stage: *to stage a concert, contest, event, performance, play, scene, show.* **2** organize and carry out: *to stage a campaign, comeback, demonstration, protest, raid, retreat, strike.*
stage.coach *n.* a horse-drawn coach that served a regular route carrying passengers and mail.
stage fright *n.* nervousness in acting or speaking in public.
stage.hand *n.* one who helps with the arrangements on a theater stage.
stage property *n.* an item of movable equipment used on a stage or movie set: *Stage properties do not include scenery and costumes.*
stage-struck *adj.* having an intense desire to join the acting profession.
stagey same as STAGY.
stag.fla.tion (stag.FLAY.shun) *n.* a condition in which business activity is stagnant and inflation grows.
stag.ger (STAG.ur) *v.* **1** move unsteadily, as on weak feet, faltering or sway-

staggers / **stalk**

ing from side to side: *He staggered into the room; staggering under the heavy load; He sat down, then staggered to his feet; staggered out of the house;* **adj.:** *The news dealt a **staggering** blow to his hopes.* **2** arrange in steps: *to stagger payments in instalments;* **adj.:** ***Staggered** working hours help ease traffic congestion; to plant in **staggered** (= zigzag) rows.*

staggers *n.pl.* [takes *sing. v.*] a nervous disease, esp. of horses, characterized by lack of muscle coordination.

staging (STAY.jing) *n.* the moving forward of personnel or equipment in stages; **adj.:** *a military staging area for troops; staging facilities for handling boat people; a guerrilla staging ground* or *post; a staging point for drug running.*

stag.nant (STAG.nunt) *adj.* not flowing or active as in normal conditions: *stagnant air, water; a stagnant pond; a stagnant (= sluggish) market.*

stag.nate *v.* **-nates, -nat.ed, -nat.ing** make or become stagnant: *Economic growth continues to stagnate; a stagnating economy; stagnating sales.* —**stag.na.tion** (stag.NAY.shun) *n.*

stag.y (STAY.jee) *adj.* **stag.i.er, -i.est** theatrical; also, artificial; also **stage.y**.

staid *adj.* settled or steady in one's behavior; looking sedate or sober: *the staid banking establishment; the bank building's staid exterior; a staid newspaper like "The Times."* —**staidly** *adv.;* **staid.ness** *n.*

stain *n.* **1** a color or spot that soils: *Coffee leaves a stain on cloth; to remove a stubborn stain.* **2** a blemish or dishonor: *a stain on his reputation.* **3** a penetrating dye or pigment, as used to color wood, glass for ornamental windows of **stained glass**, and substances for examination under a microscope. —*v.* **1** discolor or soil: *The spill stained the tablecloth.* **2** blemish: *The scandal stained his reputation.* **3** color or dye: *We stained the wood brown.* —**stain.less** *adj.*

stainless steel *n.* a chromium alloy of steel that resists rust and corrosion.

stair *n.* one of a series of steps (**stair-steps**): *a flight of stairs; on the top stair; at the foot of the stairs; to climb, come down, fall down, go down, go up the stairs.*

stair.case *n.* a series of stairs with a supporting structure, handrails, etc.: *curving, spiral, sweeping, winding staircases; a staircase landing; a moving staircase (= escalator).*

stair.way *n.* a passageway with built-in stairs.

stair.well *n.* a vertical open space or shaft containing stairs.

stake *n.* **1** a stick or post that is pointed at one end for driving into the ground to mark a boundary, tie a vine to, etc.: *Joan of Arc was burnt at the stake as a heretic.* **2** a share or interest in an undertaking; also, a grubstake. **3 stakes** *pl.* risk of gain or loss: *to understand the stakes involved; the stakes at issue; The stakes are high; big, clear, enormous, huge stakes; They've just **raised the stakes** (= heightened the risk) by threatening to execute the hostages.* —**at stake** at risk: *Lives are at stake.* —**pull up stakes** *Informal.* leave a place where one is established: *They pulled up stakes and moved to Mexico.* —*v.* **stakes, staked, stak.ing** **1** mark with stakes: *Prospectors for gold stake (out) a claim by marking off boundaries.* **2** gamble money, etc.; wager. **3** *Informal.* furnish a person with money or resources; grubstake. —**stake out** put a place or suspect under surveillance.

stake.hold.er (STAKE.hold.ur) *n.* one who has a share or interest in an undertaking.

stake.out *n.* surveillance: *an undercover stakeout of a drug joint.*

sta.lac.tite (stuh.LAC.tite) *n.* an iciclelike hanging formation of calcium deposited by water dripping from the roof of a cave.

sta.lag.mite (stuh.LAG.mite) *n.* an ice formation on the floor of a cave in the shape of an inverted icicle corresponding to a stalactite.

stale *adj.* **stal.er, stal.est** not fresh or new: *stale food, jokes, news; He tried to beat a stale green light and lost his car in a crash; stale (= flat) soda; A check more than six months old may be refused by the bank as **stale-dated**.* —*v.* **stales, staled, stal.ing** make or become stale.

stale.mate *n.* a deadlock or standstill: *We are at a stalemate; the stalemate over pay raises; to break, end, prolong, resolve a stalemate; a continuing stalemate; stalemates that drag on.* —**adj.:** *the **stalemated** issues, negotiations; a stalemated situation.*

stalk (STAWK) *v.* **1** approach or pursue game, a victim, etc. hopefully without being seen or heard: *Tigers stalk their prey; to stalk game; Crime stalks the streets of inner cities at night; Bankruptcy stalks corporations during a recession;* **adj.:** *a **stalking** tiger; A dummy **stalking horse** is sometimes used by hunters to hide behind when stalking game.* **2** walk stiffly, esp. haughtily: *to stalk* away or off without saying a word; *He stalked out of the house.* —*n.* **1** a stalking (stride). **2** a connecting part such as the stem of a flower, leaf, or wine glass: *celery stalks;* **stalked** *adj.*

stall (STAWL) *n.* **1** a compartment accommodating one individual or group, as a stable for an animal, a booth or cubicle at a fair or theater, a church pew, etc. **2** a stop or standstill, esp. one due to a malfunction. **3** the condition of an airplane or wing losing its lift. —*v.* **1** put or keep in a stall. **2** bring or come to a standstill; stop running or functioning: *The car stalled.* **3** *Informal.* use a delaying tactic or ruse: *to stall off creditors.*

stal.lion (STAL.yun) *n.* a male horse used for breeding.

stal.wart (STAWL.wurt) *adj.* strong and sturdy, esp. steadfast in loyalty or staunch in support.
—*n.* a stalwart or loyal supporter.

sta.men (STAY.mun) *n.* the long, slender, threadlike male reproductive organ of flowers.

stam.i.na (STAM.uh.nuh) *n.* vigor or endurance: *You need stamina to run a marathon; to build up strength and stamina; courage and stamina; moral stamina.*

stam.mer (STAM.ur) *v.* speak haltingly with breaks in or between words; stutter: *He stammered a few words in reply; stammered his thanks.* —*n.* a stammering. —**stam.mer.er** *n.*

stamp *n.* **1** a small gummed paper label bearing an official design used as a token of payment of postage or revenue: *a postage stamp; The post office issues, cancels stamps; We lick, moisten, put, stick stamps on letters.* **2** an official mark or seal of approval, quality, etc.: *The plan received the director's stamp of approval.* **3** a kind or type: *men of that stamp.* **4** a design or message impressed on anything; also, the device used: *a date stamp; a rubber stamp; the stamp* (= imprint) *of genius in her works.* **5** a stamping, as with one's foot.
—*v.* **1** strike down on something with force, so as to pound or crush: *He stamped the floor in anger; stamped his foot (on the ground) in impatience; He stamped on her toes on the crowded dance floor.* **2** put a stamp on something; imprint: *events indelibly stamped in his memory; She stamped the bill "Paid"; His accent stamps* (= characterizes) *him as an American; adj.:* a self-addressed **stamped** envelope. —**stamp out** end or put out, as by stamping: *to stamp out a fire, corruption, a rebellion.*

stam.pede (stam.PEED) *n.* **1** a confused, headlong flight, as of a frightened herd of animals: *A scare caused or created the stampede; a stampede* (= rush) *for the exits; a stampede to buy gold.* **2** a fair featuring a rodeo, as the Calgary Stampede. —*v.* **-pedes, -ped.ed, -ped.ing** flee, put to flight, or make a rush: *The crowd panicked and stampeded out of the stadium; They were stampeded* (= rushed) *into selling the house at a loss.*

stamping ground *n. Informal.* a habitual gathering place or favorite haunt.

stance *n.* **1** a way of standing, esp. in regard to position of the feet. **2** posture or attitude.

stanch (STAWNCH, STAHNCH, STANCH) same as STAUNCH.

stan.chion (STANCH.un) *n.* **1** an upright supporting bar, as the mullion of a window. **2** a framework in which the head of a cow is secured in its stall.

stand *v.* **stands, stood, stand.ing 1** be or remain erect or upright on one's feet: *Please sit down, don't stand; You have to stand on a chair to touch the ceiling; A soldier stands at attention; stands at ease; He stands six feet* (= is six feet tall). **2** (cause) to be in a specified position or condition: *The bookcase stood near the entrance; He stands accused of shoplifting; She's standing as a candidate for mayor; She stands to gain something if she wins; stands to get a scholarship; He stands a good chance of winning; He stands* (= ranks) *first in his class.* **3** bear or undergo: *He couldn't stand the heat; was ordered to stand trial; a classic that will stand the test of time.* —**stand by** be near so as to help or be ready for action: *Police and ambulances stood by in case of an emergency.* —**stand for 1** represent: *The Maple Leaf stands for Canada.* **2** *Informal.* put up with: *She won't stand for such nonsense.* **3** be a candidate for something: *to stand for election, parliament.* —**stand in 1** act as a stand-in *for someone.* **2** be associated or friendly *with someone.* —**stand off 1** keep away. **2** put off or stall a creditor, etc. —**stand on** insist on: *We stand firm on principles; Let's not stand on ceremony.* —**stand out** be clearly visible or prominent: *White stands out against a dark background; a tall man who stands out in any crowd; She stands out as the best qualified applicant.*
—**stand pat** be steadfast; resist change. —**stand up 1** rise: *We stand up to greet the teacher; It takes guts to*

standalone / staphylococcus

stand up and be counted (= assert oneself in the face of opposition) *when the going gets tough.* **2** remain intact: *a statement that won't stand up in court; a car that has stood up well through years of hard driving.* **3** *Informal.* ignore an appointment with someone: *John was stood up by his date; Some actors make a habit of standing up Oscar* (= boycotting the awards). —***stand up for*** support or defend: *to stand up for one's rights.* —***stand up to* 1** defy: *It takes courage to stand up to a bully.* **2** last: *A well-built car will stand up to many years of rough use.* —*n.* **1** an act of standing: *He took a strong stand against the ban; a resolute stand; She put up a good stand; a one-night stand* (= engagement); *to take a stand* (= position) *on an issue.* **2** place of standing: *bus, hot-dog, taxi stands; Witnesses* **take the stand** *in court; shouting from the* **stands** (= tiered seats for spectators); *a stand* (= growth) *of trees.*

stand.a.lone (STAN.duh.lone) *n.* a self-contained unit operating independently of other systems; *adj.: a standalone computer, not a networked one; standalone fax machines; the standalone features of a standalone product; a standalone store that is not part of a chain.*

stand.ard (STAN.durd) *n.* **1** a flag or military banner, esp. of a ruler or leader, as a rallying point. **2** a model or principle of comparison: *academic standards; a school's admission standards; a low, high standard of living; Dictionaries set the standard for correct use of language; a standard established by usage; to abandon, adhere to, lower, maintain, raise a standard.* **3** an upright support, as of a street lamp. —*adj.* uniformly accepted: *standard English, practice, procedure; a standard* (= recognized) *textbook on the subject.*

standard-bearer *n.* the leader of a movement.

stand.ard.ize (STAN.dur.dize) *v.* **-iz.es, -ized, -iz.ing** make standard or uniform in regard to size, weight, quality, etc.: *to standardize documents, equipment, language and style, products, rules, tests.* —**stand.ard.i.za.tion** (-duh.ZAY.shun, -dye-) *n.*

standard of living or **living standard** *n.* the level of use of goods and services to satisfy one's material needs and desires: *Sweden, U.S.A., and Canada had the world's highest living standards.*

standard time *n.* the uniform official time adopted throughout a country or time zone.

stand.by *n.* **-bys** a person or thing held in reserve for use when needed: *A helicopter is* **on standby** *in case of an emergency.* —*adj.: standby credit arrangements with banks; standby duties, power systems.*

stand.ee (stan.DEE) *n. Informal.* one who stands, not having a seat in a bus, theater, etc.

stand-in *n.* a substitute person, esp. one taking the place of an actor or actress in routine roles.

standing *n.* **1** an act of standing: *"No stopping or standing* (= waiting)*" (by cars is allowed on this portion of the street).* **2** status or rank: *a student in good standing; a woman of high standing (in her profession); His standing among or with the voters is not as good as it used to be; Not everyone is granted standing* (= right to be heard) *at a court hearing.* **3** duration: *a custom, dispute, feud of long standing.* —*adj.* **1** from an upright position: *a standing jump, ovation.* **2** continuing to exist indefinitely: *a standing army, committee, crop, invitation, order, tree; All seats had been sold and there was standing room only* (= stagnant) *water; adj.: a* **standing-room-only** *audience, cafeteria, course, crowd, ticket.*

stand.off *n.* **1** a tie or draw. **2** a state of waiting: *The standoff with the terrorists ended when the swat team finally stormed the building.*

stand.off.ish (stand.AW.fish) *adj.* aloof: *a standoffish approach, attitude, stance; a little standoffish about joining the club;* **stand.off.ish.ness** *n.*

stand.out *n.* a person or thing that is outstanding: *a clear standout in the crowded TV market; adj.: a standout brand, category, item, performer; standout results, sales.*

stand.pipe *n.* a high reservoir or vertical pipe used in a water-supply system.

stand.point *n.* point of view: *from a practical standpoint; from the standpoint of the consumer.*

stand.still *n.* a complete stop or halt: *The strike brought the city to a complete standstill; Negotiations are at a standstill.*

stand-up *adj.* having to do with standing: *a stand-up comedian, comic, lunch counter.*

stank a *pt.* of STINK.

stan.za (STAN.zuh) *n.* a group of lines of verse forming a division of a poem.

staph *n.* [short form] staphylococcus; *adj.: a staph germ, infection; staph bacteria.*

staph.y.lo.coc.cus (staf.uh.loh.COC.us)

staple / start

n., pl. **-coc.ci** (-COC.sye) a round bacterium that grows in grapelike clusters and causes food poisoning, impetigo, boils, etc.

sta.ple (STAY.pul) *n.* **1** the chief commodity or material: *Coffee is the staple of their economy; Bread is a staple of low-income diets; Peanut butter is her dietary staple; In most cultures, diets have been centered around a grain staple; Sex and violence have become a staple of* or *in TV shows.* **2** a U-shaped piece of wire with sharp ends used to fasten things together. —*adj.* chief: *a nation's staple industries; a staple subject of conversation; staple colors, foods, goods.*
—*v.* **sta.ples, sta.pled, sta.pling** fasten using staples: *to staple papers together.*
—**sta.pler** *n.* a stapling machine.

star *n.* **1** any of the heavenly bodies seen at night as bright points of light, including planets: *bright, distant, falling, guiding, shooting stars; Stars shine, twinkle.* **2** a favorable configuration of stars; fortune: *He was born under a lucky star; Her star is rising; Our star is setting, waning.* **3** a figure with five or six points, as an asterisk: *a five-star hotel.* **4** a star-shaped medal or military decoration. **5** a brilliant or leading performer or singer; also, one distinguished in his or her field, as an athlete: *the star of our show; a glamorous star; a rising star in our industry; basketball, rock, soap-opera stars.* —*v.* **stars, starred, star.ring 1** mark with an asterisk or star: *a starred item.* **2** adorn with stars. **3** present an actor, singer, etc. in a leading role or perform in one: *a movie starring Tom Smith; He was starred as a villain; She starred in the Broadway play; starred opposite Cruise; starred in the lead role; in the starring role.* —*adj.* preeminent: *our star athletes; a star performer, salesperson, writer.*

star.board (STAR.burd, -bord) *n.* the right side of a ship or plane, as one faces forward: *to lean to starboard; the port and starboard sides of a craft.*

starch *n.* **1** a white, odorless, tasteless food substance found in potatoes, rice, etc. **2** a form of this used to stiffen cloth or to size paper.
—*v.* stiffen with starch.

starch.y *adj.* **starch.i.er, -i.est 1** having much starch: *rice, spaghetti, and such starchy foods.* **2** stiff or formal: *a starchy attitude, manner, title.* —**starch.i.ness** *n.*

star-crossed *adj.* ill-fated: *a star-crossed campaign, journey; star-crossed lovers.*

star.dom (STAR.dum) *n.* the state of being a star: *to achieve, rise to, win stardom; the way to stardom; instant stardom; business, hockey, Hollywood, movie stardom.*

stare *v.* **stares, stared, star.ing** look long and directly with wide-open eyes, as a child out of curiosity: *She is used to being stared at by strangers; You can't ignore facts that are staring you in the face.* —*n.* an act of staring: *haughty, icy, rude, vacant stares.* —**star.er** *n.*

star.fish *n.* a sea animal usu. having five arms in the shape of a star.

star.gaze *v.* **-gaz.es, -gazed, -gaz.ing 1** gaze at the stars, as an astronomer. **2** daydream. —**star.gaz.er** *n.*

stark 1 *adj.* utter; complete: *stark brutality, madness, nonsense, poverty, terror; in stark contrast.* **2** *adj.* bare or unadorned: *a stark landscape; the stark realities of life; the stark facts; a stark choice, reminder, warning; The interior is stark and a bit scary; a loneliness that is stark and vacuous.* —*adv.* utterly: *stark naked;* **adj.**: *a stark-naked figure.*
—**stark.ly** *adv.;* **stark.ness** *n.*

star.let (STAR.lit) *n.* a young actress being promoted as a star.

star.light *n.* the light given by the stars: *They met by starlight under the maples.*

star.ling *n.* any of a family of black, aggressive songbirds including mynas.

star.lit *adj.* lighted by the stars: *a starlit beach, night, scene, sky.*

star.ry (STAR.ee) *adj.* **star.ri.er, star.ri.est** lighted by stars; bright: *a starry night.*

starry-eyed *adj.* dreamy or visionary: *starry-eyed dreamers, optimism, youth.*

Stars and Stripes *n.* the U.S. national flag.

star-spangled *adj.* dotted with stars: *a star-spangled sky;* the **Star-Spangled Banner** (= U.S. flag or national anthem).

star-studded *adj.* filled with stars: *a star-studded sky, uniform; a star-studded cast (of actors and actresses).*

start *v.* **1** begin moving or acting, as by taking a first step: *to start on a journey; Let's start moving; It's starting to get late; It's time to start (off) for the airport; Please start the engine; School starts at nine; He started (his career) as a low-paid clerk; to start a fire with a match; to start a discussion with someone; to start the ball rolling; to start* (= enter) *a horse in a race; to start* (= loosen) *a bolt, seam.*
2 move suddenly as if surprised or frightened; startle: *He starts at the least sound; to start* (= flush) *game from its hiding place.*
—*n.* **1** a beginning; also, a starting point or time: *No one gets a high pay at*

the start of a career; She would take any job for a start; She made a promising start; From the start she impressed her colleagues as a hard worker; She got off to an early start; to make a fresh start in life after many false starts and failures; flying, new, running starts. **2** a sudden movement or jerk; also, a spurt of energy: He works by fits and starts.

start.er *n.* one who starts: *a slow starter.* **—for starters** *Informal.* to begin with: *For starters, get a good haircut; That's just for starters.*

starting block *n.* a device for a runner to brace his or her feet against before starting.

star.tle (STAR.tul) *v.* **-tles, -tled, -tling** surprise or frighten so as to make one move suddenly: *He slammed the door and startled the sleeping child; She's so nervous she startles easily; He was startled at the news; startled to hear that he owes her money;* **adj.:** *a* **startling** (= surprising) *change, conclusion, disclosure, discovery, insight, revelation, suggestion; startling evidence, results; to a startling degree; in startling ways.*

start.up *n.* the beginning of an operation: *the startup of a project; the startup costs of a business.*

starve *v.* **starves, starved, starv.ing** (cause to) suffer from continued lack of food or anything similar: *People are starving around us; Hundreds starved to death during the famine; They were starved by a cruel regime; were starved* (= subdued by food shortages) *into surrendering; Neglected children starve* (= crave) *for affection;* **adj.:** *You look* **starved***; I'm starved or starving (Informal for hungry); not sexually starved though; starved children, faces, families; starved of the necessaries of life;* **cpd:** *a cash-starved corporation; oxygen-starved tissues; fast food for time-starved consumers.*
—star.va.tion (star.VAY.shun) *n.*

starve.ling *n.* one that is thin from being ill-fed or starved.

stash *v. Informal.* hide or store money, supplies, etc. secretly. **—***n.* **1** what is hidden away. **2** a hiding place.

stat *n. Informal.* a statistic.

state *n.* **1** a government, nation, or part of a nation: *a sovereign state; the 50 U.S. states* (= units forming the nation); *Sue's from* **the States** (= U.S.); *buffer, client, member, police, puppet, secular, welfare states; to establish, found, govern, rule a state; separation of church and state in government policies; affairs of state;* **adj.:** *a state banquet, capital, corporation, police, radio, school, secret, visit;* *the federal, state, and municipal levels of government; the U.S.* **State Department** *(of foreign affairs).* **2** a steady condition or mode of existence: *a sad state of affairs; a state of shock; the state of the world; Is happiness a state of mind? solid, liquid, and gaseous states of matter; a building in a good or bad state of repair; A state of emergency was declared during the flood; his poor state of health; A state of war exists between the two countries; comatose, nervous, unconscious, vegetative, weakened states; The patient is in* **quite a state** (= an excited condition). **3** rank or station in life: *a humble state; in* **great state** (= dignity); *A body* **lies in state** *(in a public place of honor).*
—*v.* **states, stat.ed, stat.ing** say formally or carefully: *State your reasons clearly; He stated his views emphatically; as the law states; The judge stated that the case was dismissed;* **adj.:** *for sale at the* **stated** (= indicated) *price, time; his stated commitment, goal, objectives, policy.*
—state.hood *n.*

state.craft *n.* practical statesmanship.

state.house *n.* a state legislative building.

state.less *adj.* having no citizenship or nationality: *stateless persons.*

state.ly *adj.* **-li.er, -li.est** majestic: *a stately home, mansion; stately elegance, rhythms; a stately pace, parade; a stately* (= haughty) *air.* **—state.li.ness** *n.*

state.ment (STATE.munt) *n.* **1** a stating or something stated, as a declaration or assertion: *to confirm, deny, issue, make, refute, retract, withdraw a statement; a statement to the effect that he was resigning his position; brief, short, false, official, public, sweeping, sworn, written statements.* **2** a financial summary, invoice, etc.: *a financial statement; a profit-and-loss statement; a statement of expenses.*

state of the art *n.* the highest level of development attained in a field or industry at a given time.
—state-of-the-art *adj.* most advanced: *a state-of-the-art computer; We use state-of-the-art technology; Our printer is quite state-of-the-start.*

state.room *n.* **1** a private cabin on a ship. **2** formerly, such a room on a train.

state.side *adj. Informal.* of, from, or in the U.S., as viewed from outside.
—*adv.* in or to the continental U.S.

states.man (STATES.mun) *n.* **-men** a wise, experienced, or skilled leader in public, esp. international affairs: *an elder statesman; a prominent statesman.*
—states.man.like *adj.*

—**states.man.ship** *n.* —**states.wom.an** *n.* **-wom.en.**

state trooper *n.* a member of a state police force of the U.S.

stat.ic (STAT.ic) *adj.* **1** having to do with rest or equilibrium, not motion; not dynamic: *the static balancing of a wheel; a static existence without progress or change; the static pressure of a column of liquid.* **2** having to do with static: *the static* (= present but not flowing) *electricity on a comb run through one's hair.* —*n.* **1** an electrical atmospheric disturbance such as interferes with radio or TV reception: *FM radio has little static.* **2** *Informal.* hostile criticism: *Who needs static?* —**stat.i.cal.ly** *adv.*

sta.tion (STAY.shun) *n.* **1** an assigned place of duty: *a battle station; Return to your stations; computerized work stations.* **2** a stopping place: *bus, subway, train stations.* **3** a place for a specific use or where a service is provided: *broadcasting, comfort, filling, fire, gas, police, polling, postal, power, TV stations.* **4** social position or rank: *people of all walks and stations in life.* —*v.* post to a place of duty: *Guards were stationed at all entrances; soldiers stationed overseas; stationed in the Middle East.*

sta.tion.ar.y (STAY.shuh.nair.ee) *adj.* fixed; not moving: *a stationary bicycle, position, target, vehicle; a stationary weather front; stationary and motion furniture.*

station break *n.* a periodic pause in a broadcast or telecast, usu. for station identification.

sta.tion.er (STAY.shun.ur) *n.* one who sells stationery.

sta.tion.er.y (STAY.shuh.nair.ee) *n.* **1** writing paper and envelopes: *hotel, office, school stationery.* **2** writing materials such as writing pads, pens, pencils, and envelopes: *a store that sells stationery; adja.: a stationery item, shop, store.*

stations of the cross *n.* a series of stops, set up for prayer and meditation, representing incidents on Jesus' journey to Calvary.

station wagon *n.* an automobile with a body extended at the back to allow additional room for passengers and goods, and having a tailgate.

sta.tis.tic (stuh.TIS.tic) *n.* one of many items making up a set of data: *A drunk driver may end up as a highway statistic.* —**sta.tis.ti.cal** *adj.*; **sta.tis.ti.cal.ly** *adv.* —**stat.is.ti.cian** (stat.is.TISH.un) *n.*

statistics (stuh.TIS.tics) *n.pl.* **1** [takes *sing. v.*] the science of gathering and analyzing numerical facts or data. **2** such data collectively: *to collect, gather, tabulate statistics; a government department that compiles statistics; Statistics showed that in 1985 each woman had only 1.7 children; as statistics indicate; the statistics of highway fatalities; Politicians like to bandy job statistics about and promise everyone a better future.*

stats *n.pl.* [short form] statistical data.

stat.u.ar.y (STACH.oo.air.ee) *n.* a collection of statues or the art of making them.

stat.ue (STACH.oo) *n.* a three-dimensional image of a person or animal that is cast, modeled, or carved: *a statue sculpted out of marble; to unveil a statue; an equestrian statue; a statue cast in bronze.*

stat.u.esque (stach.oo.ESK) *adj.* like a statue in being well-proportioned or stately: *a statuesque beauty, blonde, figure.*

stat.u.ette (stach.oo.ET) *n.* a small statue: *the Oscar statuettes.*

stat.ure (STACH.ur) *n.* height reached or eminence attained by a person: *a man short of stature* (= not tall); *a woman of great moral stature; of imposing stature; She attained the stature of a world leader.*

sta.tus (STAY.tus, STAT.us) *n.* **-tus.es** a state or position according to some standard: *the (legal) status of a minor; your marital status; a high social status; to achieve, attain, enjoy celebrity status; Native women used to lose status under the Indian Act by marrying non-native men; a most-favored nation status given to a country in a reciprocal trade relationship; people of some status* (= of high status). —*adja.: a status report, seeker; an expensive sports car as a status symbol; adj.: a very status-conscious woman.*

status quo (-QUOH) *n.* the existing state of affairs: *Vested interests like to maintain the status quo; to accept, defend, preserve the status quo.*

stat.ute (STACH.oot) *n.* a law enacted by a legislative body.

statute of limitations *n.* a law setting a time limit for prosecutions except in serious crimes such as murder.

stat.u.tor.y (STAT.yoo.tor.ee) *adj.* having to do with or fixed by statute: *the statutory age of 16; statutory bans, controls, language, limitations, penalties, prohibition; common law and statutory law.*

staunch (STAWNCH, STAHNCH) *adja.* **1** strong or steadfast: *a staunch defense, friendship, supporter.* **2** watertight: *a staunch ship.*

stave / steam fitter

—*v.* stop the flow of blood or of blood from a wound; stanch.
—**staunch.ly** *adv.*; **staunch.ness** *n.*
stave *n.* **1** one of the curved strips of wood making up the walls of a barrel or cask. **2** a pole or staff. **3** a musical staff. **4** a stanza. —*v.* **staves,** *pt. & pp.* **staved** or **stove** (STOHV), **stav.ing** make a break or hole in the sides of a cask, boat, etc. —**stave off** prevent or ward off something troublesome.
staves See STAFF.
stay *v.* **1** remain: *Please stay (for) a while; Do stay for supper; We're staying; Stay off the grass; It's safer to stay away from skid row; Better to stay out of trouble; to stay abreast* or *on top of current events; to stay ahead of the competition; to stay calm, fit, healthy, home, indoors, in office, in shape, rational, tuned; He's staying on as president; "Time and tide stay (= wait) for no man".* **2** dwell, esp. as a guest for a short while: *Where are you staying? I'm staying the night with Jim; staying at Jim's (house); She's staying at a hotel.* **3** hold back or delay: *to stay an execution; snacks to stay him (= stay his hunger) till dinner time.* **4** of a runner, horse, etc., endure or last to the end, *for a period* or *distance, etc.: I intend to* **stay the course** (= continue till the end of it); *n.: He has little* **staying power** (= endurance or stamina). **5** prop or hold up. —**stay put** *Informal.* remain at one's place or where stationed.
—*n.* **1** staying or dwelling: *We had a pleasant stay at the hotel; hospital stays.* **2** a holding back or delay: *The court granted a* **stay of execution** *of the eviction order pending an appeal.* **3** a prop, brace, or support: *corset stays.* **4** a steadying rope or wire, as for a ship's mast; guy.
stead (STED) *n.* **1 in one's stead** instead of: *He offered himself as a hostage in her stead.* **2 stand in good stead** be of help when needed: *Your French will stand you in good stead during your trip abroad.*
stead.fast (STED.fast, -fust) *adj.* fixed or unwavering: *her steadfast loyalty; his steadfast gaze.* —**stead.fast.ly** *adv.*; **stead.fast.ness** *n.*
stead.y (STED.ee) *adj.* **stead.i.er, -i.est** stable or regular in movement or behavior: *a steady heartbeat, job, progress, state, worker; a* **steady ship** (that can stay upright in a rough sea); *steady* (= calm) *nerves; steady* (= steadfast) *friendship; one's steady* (= regular) *date;* **Steady as she goes** (= Let the ship stay on her set course).
—*n., pl.* **stead.ies** *Informal.* one's regular or exclusive date. —*v.* **stead.ies, stead.ied, stead.y.ing** make or become steady. —*adv.* in a steady manner: *Couples here* **go steady** (*Informal* for date exclusively) *before getting married.*
—**stead.i.ly** *adv.*; **stead.i.ness** *n.*
steady-state theory *n.* the theory that the universe will maintain its present state, as it always has, without the big bang with which it is supposed to renew itself.
steak (STAKE) *n.* a fleshy slice of meat, esp. beef, or fish that is broiled or fried like beefsteak: *to broil, grill a steak; juicy, minute, rump, sirloin, T-bone, tender, tough steaks; How do you like your steak (done)? You are supposed to like it medium, medium-rare, rare,* or *well-done.*
steal (STEEL) *v.* **steals, stole, sto.len** (STOH.lun), **steal.ing** take or get something in a secret, sly, or unexpected manner: *Thieves steal; A starving man may steal food; to steal food from a store; to steal looks, kisses; Sam stole a glance at Paola when she wasn't looking; A baby steals your heart; A feeling of shame stole over him; A runner tries to steal (= reach) a base by catching the opposing team off guard; He* **stole** (= sneaked) **out** *of the house when his parents were asleep; Jan* **stole up on** *Gina from behind and said "Boo!" The children's act* **stole the show** (*Informal* for unexpectedly proved the biggest attraction). —*n. Informal.* a stealing or something stolen, esp. an unusual bargain: *At $25 it is a steal!*
stealth (STELTH) *n.* secrecy or furtiveness: *Thieves enter a house* **by stealth** (= secretly or slyly). —**stealth.y** *adj.*
—**stealth.i.ly** *adv.*; **stealth.i.ness** *n.*
steam (STEEM) *n.* **1** the vapor given off by boiling water. **2** this condensed, as the mist from evaporation inside a heated automobile. **3** (the power of) hot steam under pressure, as used to drive the piston in the cylinder of a **steam engine.** —**let off steam** *Informal.* get rid of excess energy or pent-up feelings. —*v.: He is quite* **steamed up** (*Informal* for angry) *over or about my being late; to steam* (= use steam to) *open a sealed envelope; adj.: a* **steaming** *cup of soup (that is so hot it gives off steam); a* **steamed-up** *car window (that is foggy because of condensed water vapor).*
steam.boat *n.* a small steamship.
steam.er *n.* one that uses steam, as a cooker, cleaning appliance, or a steamship.
steam fitter *n.* a worker who installs

and maintains pipes in heating and cooling systems. —**steam fitting** n.
steam.roll.er (STEEM.roh.lur) n. a steam-driven roller for road surfaces. —v. **1** crush opposition or force legislation *through* a legislature. **2** force one's way *into* a place, as with a steamroller. Also **steam.roll.**
steam.ship n. a ship driven by steam power.
steam shovel n. an excavating machine powered by steam.
steam.y (STEE.mee) adj. **steam.ier, -i.est 1** having to do with steam, esp. hot like steam: *saunas and such steamy amenities; a steamy, sticky July afternoon; steamy summer heat*. **2** erotic: *a steamy atmosphere, love affair, novel, sex scene.* —**steam.i.ly** adv.
steed n. [literary] a riding horse.
steel n. **1** a hard and tough alloy of iron and carbon. **2** a steel instrument or weapon. **3** steellike hardness and strength. —**adj.** & **a**.: *a steel bar; steel gray.* —v. make with or like steel: *He steeled himself* (= prepared himself mentally) *for the ordeal* or *to face the ordeal.* —**steel.y** adj.: *steely determination, eyes, gray, obsession.*
steel band n. a percussion band using steel oil drums of varying pitches.
steel blue n. a dark bluish gray.
steel wool n. hairlike shavings of steel used in a ball or pad for scouring, smoothing, etc.
steel.yard n. a weighing scale with a long arm carrying an adjustable weight to balance the object to be weighed which is hung from the end of the shorter arm.
steep v. **1** (let) soak, as by immersion, esp. for extracting the essence of something: *Keep the seeds steeped in boiled water.* **2** immerse *oneself* in a subject of study. —**steeped in** filled or pervaded with something: *steeped in misery, Russian, tradition.*
—adj. **1** sharply sloping: *a steep hill.* **2** *Informal.* excessive or exaggerated: *steep demands, prices.* —**steep.ly** adv.; **steep.ness** n.
steep.en (STEE.pun) v. make or become steep or steeper.
stee.ple (STEE.pul) n. **1** a tall tower, usu. topped by a spire, on a church building. **2** a spire. —**steepled** adj.: *a steepled ceiling; steepled churches.*
stee.ple.chase (STEE.pul.chase) n. a cross-country race on horseback or a footrace over an obstacle course.
stee.ple.jack (STEE.pul.jack) n. one who works on steeples, smokestacks, etc.

steer n. **1** a young ox, castrated and usu. raised for beef: *to rope a steer; a Grade A steer*. **2** *Informal*. direction or tip: *He got a bum steer*. —v. **1** direct the course of a vehicle using a wheel, rudder, or other device: *to steer a car;* n.: *cars equipped with power steering; rack-and-pinion steering; tilt steering for adjusting the angle of the steering column of an automobile*. **2** direct one's way or follow a course: *Let's steer for home; Counselors steered her away from dropping out of high school; Don't rock the canoe as we steer the course; She knows how to steer clear of trouble*. —**steer.a.ble** adj.
steer.age (STEER.ij) n. **1** the act of steering or the response of a ship to the helm. **2** formerly, a section of a ship for passengers paying the lowest fares.
steering column n. in an automobile, the shaft connecting the steering wheel to the gear assembly.
steering committee n. a committee that is in charge of the agenda of a session.
steering wheel n. a wheel turned by the operator of an automobile or similar vehicle.
steers.man (STEERS.mun) n. **-men** helmsman.
steg.o.sau.rus (steg.uh.SOR.us) n., pl. **-ri** (-rye) a dinosaur with two staggered rows of large, triangular, bony plates along its back; also **steg.o.saur.**
stein (STINE) n. a beer mug, originally of earthenware.
stel.lar (STEL.ur) adj. of a star or stars: *stellar light; the stellar role (of a star player); a stellar* (= excellent) *cast, performance; a **stellar distance*** (= light-year).
stem n. **1** the main part or trunk, as of a tree or plant, from which branches grow: *"Kind" is the stem of the word "unkindness"; wineglasses and such **stemware*** (having a stem connecting bowl and base) *for serving cold beverages and desserts.* **2** the prow of a ship. —**from stem to stern** from one end to the other; throughout. —v. **stems, stemmed, stem.ming 1** derive or develop: *problems stemming from lack of education.* **2** stop or check: *to stem the tide of controversy.*
stench n. an offensive odor; stink: *the stench of rotting corpses, rotten eggs, garbage; the stench of hypocrisy.*
sten.cil (STEN.sul) n. **1** a sheet of paper, metal, etc. on which designs or letters are cut for transferring them to a surface by laying the sheet on it

and applying ink or color: *to cut stencils.* 2 a letter or design so made. —*v.* **-cils, -ciled, -cil.ing:** *He stenciled the address on the cartons.* Also **sten.cilled, sten.cil.ling** *Cdn.*

sten.o *n.* **-os** [short form] stenographer; stenography.

ste.nog.ra.pher (stuh.NOG.ruh.fur) *n.* one skilled in shorthand. —**ste.nog.ra.phy** (-fee) *n.* —**sten.o.graph.ic** (sten.uh.GRAF.ic) *adj.*

sten.to.ri.an (sten.TOR.ee.un) *adj.* of a voice or tone, loud and powerful.

step *n.* 1 a lifting of the foot and setting it down in walking, running, dancing, etc.: *Please take a step forward; He* **retraced his steps** (= went back) *to see if he had dropped his key on the way; She was with us* **every step of the way** (= all the time). 2 the distance, style, sound, or print of a step: *It takes years of training to execute or perform the difficult steps of ballet; He walks with a mincing step; She walks with a heavy step; I heard steps outside the door; The school is only a few* **steps** (= a short distance) *from my home; Keep* **in step** *when marching together; Try not to fall* **out of step.** 3 a stair or rung: *Mind the step as you open the door; the steps of a ladder; A flight of* **steps** (= stairs) *leads to your room.* 4 a stage or degree in a movement forward or upward: *What's the next step? We're a step closer to a settlement; A major is a step above a captain; The moon-landing was "a giant step for mankind"; bold, careful, false, historic, positive, risky steps.* —**in** or **out of step** in or out of rhythm with someone: *She seemed to be out of step with the feminist movement.* —**step by step** slowly. —**take steps** take the necessary measures. —*v.* **steps, stepped, step.ping** 1 put a foot down on something: *He stepped on a nail.* 2 walk: *to step across a street; He stepped aside for his boss to enter first; Please step in (the house) for a minute; She just stepped out for some fresh air; The principal had to* **step in** (= intervene) *to restore order in the classroom; to step* (= get) *off a train; to* **step off** (= pace off) *a distance.* —**step down** 1 leave one's position in favor of another: *The mayor will be stepping down at the end of her term in January.* 2 reduce: *to step down voltage using a transformer.* —**step on it** *Informal.* go faster, as by pressing the accelerator. —**step up** 1 *Informal.* come forward. 2 increase an activity or its pace, intensity, etc.

step- *prefix.* related by remarriage: *step-brother, stepfather, stepmother, stepparent.*

step.child *n.* a child of one's spouse by a former marriage, i.e., a **stepdaughter** or **stepson.**

step.lad.der (STEP.lad.ur) *n.* a short ladder with flat steps instead of rungs and hinged to a supporting frame.

steppe (STEP) *n.* one of the prairielike treeless plains of the U.S.S.R. extending from S. Ukraine to central Asia.

step.ping.stone (STEP.ing.stone) *n.* 1 a stone to step on when crossing a stream or when mounting, ascending, etc. 2 a means of advancement: *He used the job as a steppingstone to a better career.*

step.sis.ter (STEP.sis.tur) *n.* a daughter of one's stepparent.

stepson See STEPCHILD.

step-up *n.* a stepping up or increase in amount, intensity, etc.

-ster *n. suffix.* one who does or is associated with what is specified: *mobster, punster, trickster, youngster.*

ster.e.o (STER.ee.oh, STEER-) *n.* **-os** 1 a record player or sound system that uses two or more channels of sound recording and reproduction. 2 a picture or system that gives a three-dimensional view of an object.

ster.e.o.phon.ic (STER.ee.uh.FON.ic, STEER-) *adj.* using two or more channels of sound recording and reproduction for a realistic effect; **ster.e.o.phon.i.cal.ly** *adv.*

ster.e.o.scope (STER.ee.uh.scope, STEER-) *n.* an optical instrument having two eyepieces for a three-dimensional view of an object; **ster.e.o.scop.ic** (-SCOP.ic) *adj.;* **ster.e.o.scop.i.cal.ly** *adv.*

ster.e.os.co.py (ster.ee.OS.cuh.pee, steer-) *n.* (the science of) the viewing of things in three dimensions.

ster.e.o.type (STER.ee.uh.type, STEER-) *n.* a fixed or rigid mental impression: *To consider nursing as a woman's job is to perpetuate a stereotype; the "Ugly American" stereotype.* —*v.* **-types, -typed, -typ.ing** make a stereotype of something: *to stereotype minority groups in negative terms; adj.: Characters, expressions, etc. that are* **stereotyped** *lack originality and objectivity; stereotyped thinking; a stereotyped depiction, notion, role, view; the stereotyped "June bride."* —**ster.e.o.typ.i.cal** (-uh.TIP.i.cul) *adj.: stereotypical images of orientals; the stereotypical "wallflower";* **ster.e.o.typ.i.cal.ly** *adv.*

ster.ile (STER.ul) *adj.* 1 unable to bear offspring or fruit, produce crops,

sterilize / stickler

seed, results, etc.: *a sterile man, woman; sterile animals, efforts, land, plants.* **2** sterilized: *sterile surgical instruments.* —**ste.ril.i.ty** (stuh.RIL.i.tee) *n.*

ster.i.lize (STER.uh.lize) *v.* **-liz.es, -lized, -liz.ing 1** to make free from living microorganisms: *to sterilize surgical instruments before an operation.* **2** make incapable of reproduction. —**ster.i.liz.er** *n.* —**ster.i.li.za.tion** (-luh.ZAY.shun, -lye-) *n.*

ster.ling (STUR.ling) *n.* **1** silver that is at least 92.5% pure; **adj a.:** *sterling flatware; sterling products;* also **sterling silver. 2** British money with the pound as the basic unit: *The exchange rate was $1.75 to the pound sterling; ten pounds sterling; a lending rate increase to relieve the selling pressure on sterling; the strength of sterling;* **adj.:** *sterling assets, exchange rates, futures, values; prices in sterling terms.* —**adj.** genuinely excellent: *a sterling achievement, character, example; her sterling qualities, reputation.*

stern *adj.* severe or strict in manner or looks: *a stern disciplinarian, face; stern measures; He is stern toward* or *with habitual latecomers.* —**n.** the rear end of a ship, aircraft, etc.; opposed to BOW. —**stern.ly** *adv.;* **stern.ness** *n.*

ster.num (STUR.num) *n.* **-nums** or **-na** the breastbone; **ster.nal** *adj.*

stern.wheel.er (STURN.wheel.ur) *n.* a boat having a paddle wheel at the stern.

ster.oid (STEER.oid, STER-) *n.* any of a class of organic chemical compounds including sex hormones, adrenal hormones, bile acids, and cholesterol.

ster.to.rous (STUR.tuh.rus) *adj.* resembling the sound of snoring: *a stertorous voice.*

stet *n.* in proofreading, "let it stand" or "do not delete." —*v.* **stets, stet.ted, stet.ting** mark with a "stet."

steth.o.scope (STETH.uh.scope, "TH" as in "thin") *n.* an instrument used by physicians to listen to the sounds produced by the heart, lungs, etc.

ste.ve.dore (STEE.vuh.dor) *n.* a dock worker who loads and unloads ships.

stew *n.* a dish of meat and vegetables made by slow boiling. —*v.* **1** cook by slow boiling. **2** worry or fret: *He's still stewing over the insult.*

stew.ard (STEW.urd) *n.* **1** one who manages another's estate or finances: *As good stewards of the earth's resources, we should avoid wastage.* **2** a labor union representative: *a shop steward; union stewards.* **3** a racetrack official. **4** a man in charge of food service on a ship or airplane or in a club: *a cabin steward.* **5** a male flight attendant. —**stew.ard.ship** *n.*

stew.ard.ess (STEW.ur.dis) *n.* a female flight attendant.

stick *n.* **1** a long and slender twig broken off from a tree. **2** any long, thin piece: *a stick of butter, candy, celery, dynamite, gum; bread, fish, vegetable sticks.* **3** a specially shaped piece or an implement: *hockey, popsicle, swagger, walking sticks; They took every* **stick** (= piece) *of furniture with them when they moved; the carrot and* **the stick** (= threat of punishment). **4** *Informal.* an awkward or boring person. **5 the sticks** *pl. Informal.* the backwoods, far from a city or town: *in the sticks of northern Montana.* —*v.* **sticks, stuck, stick.ing 1** pierce or thrust something into, out, etc.: *ice cream with a spoon stuck in it; Do not stick your head out of* or *through the car window; He has a kerchief sticking out* (= protruding) *from his pocket.* **2** be or make something fixed or immovable: *Please stick this stamp on the envelope; Make sure the stamp sticks to it; We were out of gas and got stuck on the road; There is enough evidence to make a charge stick* (= be valid); *People stick* (= cling) *together when in trouble; She was told to* **stick around** (*Informal* for wait) *while her car was being serviced; He's known to* **stick by** (= remain loyal to) *his friends; If you're loyal, the boss will* **stick up for** (*Informal* for defend) *you.* **3** *Informal.* cheat or defraud: *He was stuck by phony salesmen; We seem to be stuck* (= saddled) *with this lemon.* **4** hesitate: *a swindler who sticks at nothing.* —**stick to:** *Please stick to your seats* (= stay seated) *if you don't want to lose them; Let's stick* (= adhere) *to our plans; It's a matter of principle to* **stick to our guns** (= be faithful to what we believe in) *without giving way.*

stick.er *n.* a gummed label, bur, etc. that sticks: *an air mail sticker; bumper stickers; the* **sticker price** *of a new automobile from which discounts are calculated.*

stick insect *n.* an insect that resembles a twig.

stick-in-the-mud *n. Informal.* one who resists progress.

stick.le.back (STIK.ul.bak) *n.* a small scaleless fish that has a row of spines in front of its dorsal fin.

stick.ler (STIK.lur) *n.* one who is strict in the observance of something: *a* **stickler for** *correctness, discipline, neatness, precision, protocol, punctuality; She's* not such a stickler.

stick.pin *n.* an ornamental pin worn on a necktie.

stick shift *n.* a lever for changing gears, as in an automobile with standard transmission.

stick-to-it.ive.ness (stik.TOO.i.tiv.nis) *n. Informal.* persistence or tenacity.

stick.up *n. Informal.* an armed robbery; holdup.

stick.y *adj.* **stick.i.er, -i.est** 1 that sticks; adhesive: *sticky paste, tape, wax; sticky* (= hot and humid) *weather;* **sticky fingers** (= petty thieves or thievery). 2 *Informal.* disagreeable or troublesome: *a sticky issue, problem, situation, valve.*

stiff *adj.* 1 that resists bending or moving: *stiff joints; a stiff back, leg; a stiff bow (of the back); a stiff* (= hard to stir) *paste; stiff* (= hard to work) *soil; stiff* (= formal) *manners.* 2 hard or strong: *a stiff breeze, fine, penalty, wind; stiff opposition, resistance; a stiff drink (that is strong in alcohol).* —*adv.: He was scared stiff; It's frozen stiff.* —*n. Slang.* fellow; bum; drunk: *a working stiff* (= fellow). —*v. Slang.* cheat someone out of a payment due: *to get stiffed.* —**stiff.ly** *adv.;* **stiff.ness** *n.*

stiff-arm same as STRAIGHT-ARM.

stiff.en (STIF.un) *v.* make or become stiff or stiffer; **stiff.en.er** *n.*

stiff-necked *adj.* stubborn.

sti.fle (STY.ful) *v.* **-fles, -fled, -fling** 1 stop the breath of someone; hence, kill by suffocation: *found stifled in bed.* 2 make or become unable to breathe; *adj.: The firefighters felt stifled by the smoke; the stifling heat of the Sahara; adv.: It's stifling hot inside.* 3 suppress: *to stifle a cry, sneeze, sob, yawn; to stifle creativity, culture, development, growth, initiative;* **adj.:** *Freedom of speech gets stifled by too many restrictions;* **adja.:** *a stifling bureaucracy; stifling controls, influences, regulations.* —**sti.fling.ly** *adv.*

stig.ma (STIG.muh) *n.* **-mas** 1 *pl.* **-ma.ta** (-muh.tuh, stig.MAH.tuh) a mark resembling the five wounds of the crucified Christ. 2 a mark of disgrace, as once branded on evildoers, slaves, etc.: *the stigma once attached to being born illegitimate.* 3 the pollen-receiving part of a flower's pistil. —**stig.mat.ic** (stig.MAT.ic) *adj.*

stig.ma.tize (STIG.muh.tize) *v.* **-tiz.es, -tized, -tiz.ing** mark with a stigma: *people unjustly stigmatized by reason of birth, color, creed, etc.; to stigmatize gypsies as antisocial.* —**stig.ma.ti.za.tion** (-tuh.ZAY.shun, -tye-) *n.*

stile *n.* 1 a step or steps for people to climb over a fence or wall but keep out animals. 2 a turnstile.

sti.let.to (sti.LET.oh) *n.* **-tos** or **-toes** 1 a narrow-bladed dagger. 2 **stiletto heels** spike heels.

still *adj.* 1 at rest; motionless: *Be perfectly still while I sketch you; "Still waters run deep"; a still* (= not bubbling) *wine.* 2 quiet; silent: *Be still; a still night; the **still small voice** (of conscience).*
—*v.* make quiet or motionless: *The voice of the underdog has been stilled by her death; stilled music.*
—*adv.* 1 with- out moving: *to sit still (for a portrait).* 2 even to the specified or implied time: *He's still sick; They were still undecided yesterday; He'll still be here tomorrow.* 3 even: *Her brother is still taller* (= taller than she is).
—*n.* 1 a photograph, esp. a frame from a motion picture. 2 stillness: *strange sounds heard in the still of the night.* 3 an apparatus for making alcoholic liquor. 4 a distillery.
—**still.ness** *n.*

still.birth *n.* (birth of) a child born dead.

still.born *adj.* born dead.

still life *n.* **still lifes** a picture of inanimate objects such as flowers, fruits, pottery, etc.

stilt *n.* 1 one of a pair of poles with supports for the feet at a height, used for walking across water or for amusement. 2 one of a set of piles or posts supporting a building raised above water or swampland.

stilt.ed *adj.* stiffly formal: *in a stilted fashion; a stilted gait, style; stilted language, prose; a stilted expression* (= phrase).

stim.u.lant (STIM.yuh.lunt) *n. & adj.* (anything) that stimulates, as caffeine.

stim.u.late (STIM.yuh.late) *v.* **-lates, -lat.ed, -lat.ing** increase the activity of a person or thing; excite: *to stimulate public interest in the arts; tax refunds to stimulate the economy; Encouraging words stimulate everyone to try harder;* **adj.:** *a **stimulating** discussion, drink, effect.*
—**stim.u.la.tion** (-LAY.shun) *n.*
—**stim.u.la.tive** (-lay.tiv) *adj.: a stimulative effect, impact, policy.*

stim.u.lus (STIM.yuh.lus) *n., pl.* **-li** (-lye) something that excites one to increased activity: *We respond to stimuli; Lower interest rates are a powerful stimulus to industry.*

sting *v.* **stings, stung, sting.ing** cause sharp pain, as with the pricking organ of a bee, mosquito, or wasp: *Nettles sting; Sam felt stung by the insults; was* stung into action by their taunts; He was still stinging long afterward; **adja.**: *a* **stinging** *insect; the stinging taste of ginger; stinging attacks, comments, indictments, jabs, rebukes, reports, sensations, words;* **adv.**: *People were stinging mad.* —**n.** 1 a stinging: *bee stings; an undercover* **sting operation** *conducted by the FBI against drug smugglers.* 2 the wound or pain caused by a sting: *He felt the sting; Some sting reactions prove fatal; She smiled to* **take the sting out of** *her words.* 3 the stinging organ of an insect or plant. —**sting.er** *n.*

sting.ray *n.* a fish of the ray group with venomous spines on its whiplike tail.

stin.gy (STIN.jee) *adj.* **-gi.er, -gi.est** miserly; not generous: *too stingy to give to charity; a stingy allowance; Scrooge is stingy with his money.* —**stin.gi.ly** *adv.;* **stin.gi.ness** *n.*

stink (STINK) *v.* **stinks,** *pt.* **stank** or **stunk,** *pp.* **stunk, stink.ing** give off a bad smell: *A scandal stinks; It stinks of corruption.* —**n.**: *the stink of rotten fish; There was no one to* **raise a stink** *about* or *over* (= object strongly to) *the new garbage dump.*

stink.bug *n.* a bug that gives off a bad odor.

stink.er *n.* 1 one that stinks. 2 *Informal.* someone or something difficult or disagreeable.

stint *v.* restrict oneself or one's consumption of or expenditure on something: *She never stints on charity;* **adj.**: *He's been somewhat* **stinting** *in his support.* —**n.** 1 limitation or restraint. 2 a share of work or a brief assignment: *He did* or *served several stints as a Peace Corps volunteer; brief, comedy, five-year, long, medical, paid stints.*

sti.pend (STY.pend) *n.* a fixed payment made regularly for services: *She lived on a modest stipend as a chaplain.*

stip.ple *v.* **stip.ples, stip.pled, stip.pling** paint, engrave, or apply paint, etc. in dots instead of lines; *adj.*: *a* **stippled** *ceiling design.*

stip.u.late (STIP.yuh.late) *v.* **-lates, -lat.ed, -lat.ing** specify as a necessary condition: *The terms stipulated that delivery be made in two years; They stipulated delivery in two years; The contract* **stipulated for** (= required) *it.* —**stip.u.la.tion** (-LAY.shun) *n.* —**stip.u.la.tor** (-lay.tur) *n.*

stir (STUR) *v.* **stirs, stirred, stir.ring** move so as to disturb or activate: *A wind stirs the leaves; to stir* (= mix) *sugar into coffee; I noticed someone stirring in the shadows; He stirred the fire into a blaze; The picture stirred interest, memories; a story likely to stir up trouble; His speech stirred them up to mutiny; They stirred themselves to action.* —**n.** a stirring or a state of increased activity, excitement, etc.: *The announcement caused* or *created a stir in the audience; a big stir over* or *about who would pay.* —**stir.rer** *n.* —**stirring** *adj.* moving or exciting: *a stirring speech; stirring moments, narratives, rhetoric, times.*

stir-crazy *adj. Informal.* restless: *to go stir-crazy from long periods of confinement.*

stir-fry *v.* **-fries, -fried, -frying** fry food cut into small pieces in a wok or frying pan quickly over high heat while stirring constantly: *Stir-fry five minutes until tender-crisp;* **adja.**: *a stir-fry cookbook, pan, skillet, wok; stir-fry cooking, shrimp, turkey, vegetables;* **adj.**: *stir-fried chicken, duck, vegetables; mushrooms stir-fried with herbs;* **n.**: *Chop up the vegetables for a stir-fry; an electric stir-fry (skillet) with a see-through glass cover.*

stir.rup (STEER.up) *n.* a rider's footrest hanging from the saddle as a loop or ring.

stitch (STICH) *n.* 1 one complete movement of a threaded needle, as in sewing or embroidering: *to make a stitch; to drop* (= lose) *a stitch as in knitting; Basting, running, and hemming stitches are methods of stitching; It took 10 stitches (with a surgical needle) to close the wound;* "*A stitch in time saves nine*" (= Timely action saves unnecessary labor); *The kids played in the hot African sun with not* **a stitch** (= least bit of clothing) *on them.* 2 a sharp pain, esp. in the side. —**in stitches** *Informal.* laughing uncontrollably.
—*v.* make a stitch or series of stitches: *The nurse stitched up the wound.*
—**stitch.er.y** *n.* needlework.

stoat (STOHT) *n.* a short-tailed weasel, esp. in its brown summer coat.

stock *n.* 1 a collection or supply, as of goods for sale, livestock, or the repertoire of plays with a "stock company": *Ice is not* **in stock** *at this time; Sorry we are* **out of stock** *(of ice); We* **take stock** *(of our inventory) at the end of each month; to* **take stock of** (= evaluate or assess) *oneself, one's future, habits, liabilities, life, of what one wants; to take stock of a situation; It's time for staking stock;* **rolling stock** (= railroad vehicles); *Puns are the* **stock in trade** (= standard equipment) *of his humor.* 2 a supporting base: *The barrel of a firearm is fitted into a wooden stock; meat and vegetable*

juices as stocks for soups and gravies; Rags and wood pulps are stock (= raw material) for paper; a book printed on heavy stock (= paper); A scion grows best when grafted to a rooted stock (= stem); She is **of noble stock** (= from a noble family). **3** invested capital, as of a company, or a part of it owned by a shareholder: to issue, buy, sell stocks; blue-chip, common, over-the-counter, preferred stocks; She's too level-headed to **place** or **put** or **take stock in** (Informal for trust) the rumors going around. **4** a race or group with a common descent: They are of Loyalist stock; English is of Indo-European stock.
—**adja. 1** available; in common use: a stock item, size. **2** commonplace: a stock answer, joke. **3** having to do with goods and supplies: a stock clerk.. **4** having to do with livestock: a stock breeder, farm, train. **5** having to do with invested capital: a stock (= shares) certificate.
—**v. 1** keep a supply of something or provide with stock: We need to stock up on spring goods. **2** lay in a supply: to stock up for the winter.
stock.ade (stok.ADE) n. an enclosure of stakes driven into the ground for confinement or defense.
stock.bro.ker (STOK.broh.kur) n. a broker dealing in stocks and bonds.
stock car n. a standard passenger car modified or rebuilt for racing.
stock clerk n. a clerk who works in a stockroom.
stock dividend n. a dividend made up of a company's shares given to a stockholder instead of cash.
stock exchange n. an organized marketplace for the buying and selling of securities.
stock.hold.er (STOK.hold.ur) n. an owner of stock in a company; shareholder.
stock.i.nette or **stock.i.net** (stok.uh.NET) n. **1** an elastic, machine-knit cloth. **2** a knitting pattern that shows knit stitches and purl stitches on different sides of the fabric.
stocking n. a close-fitting knitted covering for the foot and leg. —**adja.** wearing socks or stockings without shoes: Feel the carpet with your **stockinged** or stocking feet.
stocking cap n. a conical knitted cap.
stocking stuffer n. Informal. a Christmas gift.
stock market n. **1** a stock exchange: to gamble, speculate, trade on the stock market; to invest in the stock market; a downturn, drop, killing in the stock market.

2 market activity in securities: The stock market opened weak on Monday, closed strong on Friday.
stock option n. the right given to a company employee to buy its stock at a specified price for a limited time.
stock.pile n. a reserve supply, as of commodities, raw materials, nuclear weapons, etc. —v. **-piles, -piled, -pil.ing** accumulate a stockpile.
stock.room or **stock room** n. a room in which business supplies and goods are stored.
stock.still adv. motionless: She stood stockstill at the sight of the ghost.
stock.y adj. **stock.i.er, -i.est** short but sturdy in build: a man of stocky build.
stock.yard n. a yard for livestock, esp. one connected with a meat-packing operation: He works at the stockyards.
stodg.y (STOJ.ee) adj. **stodg.i.er, -i.est** dull or heavy: stodgy food, reading; a stodgy book, newspaper. —**stodg.i.ly** adv.; **stodg.i.ness** n.
sto.gie or **sto.gy** (STOH.gee, "g" as in "go") n. **-gies** a long, thing, usu. inexpensive cigar.
sto.ic (STOH.ic) adj. able to endure suffering with calm, being indifferent to pleasure and pain, like the **Stoics** of ancient Greece: She remained stoic about her misfortune; stoic dignity, impassivity, patience, victims. —n. such a person. Also **sto.i.cal** (-cul) adj.
—**sto.i.cal.ly** adv. —**sto.i.cism** n.: to accept one's lot with stoicism.
stoke v. **stokes, stoked, stok.ing 1** tend and feed something burning: to stoke a fire, furnace, hearth; to stoke up a kitchen stove; to stoke anxieties, desires, fears, interest. **2** work as a stoker.
stok.er (STOH.kur) n. **1** one who tends a furnace or boiler. **2** a machine for feeding solid fuel into a furnace.
STOL (STOLE) n. an aircraft that requires only a short distance for take-off and landing; **adja.**: a STOL aircraft, airport; STOL service.
stole pt. of STEAL.
—n. a long scarf worn by women across the shoulders: a fur stole.
stolen pp. of STEAL.
stol.id (STOH.lid) adj. unemotional; impassive: her stolid dignity; a stolid statement; the stolid widow; **stol.id.ly** adv.
—**sto.lid.i.ty** (stuh.LID.i.tee) n.
sto.lon (STOH.lun) n. a runner (n. 4).
stom.ach (STUM.uk) n. **1** the saclike digestive organ into which food is received from the mouth: foods that upset your stomach; It's better to swim on an empty stomach (= while hungry) than on

a full one; He has no stomach (= inclination) for a walk after dinner; a gruesome sight that could turn one's stomach (= make one feel nauseated). 2 abdomen or belly. —v. 1 relish or swallow. 2 put up with or endure: an insult he couldn't stomach.

stom.ach.er (STUM.uh.kur) n. an ornamental front-piece formerly worn by women under the lacing of the bodice.

stomp v. stamp heavily with the feet. —n. a stomping.

stone n. 1 (a piece of) hard, solid mineral such as granite or marble: to throw stones at a person or thing; to cast the **first stone** (= be the first to accuse someone). 2 something resembling a stone, as a gem, kidney stone, or the hard seed, or pit, of a fruit such as the cherry or peach. 3 sing. & pl. a British unit of weight equal to 14 pounds. —v. **stones, stoned, ston.ing** 1 throw stones at a person or thing: People used to be stoned to death for certain crimes. 2 remove the stone from a fruit. 3 Slang. stop stone-cold; beat: The Canadiens stoned the Bruins in seven games. —**comb.form.** absolutely or completely: stone-blind, stone-broke, stone-cold, stone-deaf.

Stone Age n. the earliest stage of human culture when tools were made out of stone.

stoned adj. 1 Slang. extremely intoxicated, esp. by a mind-changing drug: He seemed more stoned than drunk; was stoned on speed; stoned senseless. 2 stone-ground: Is **stoned wheat** more nutritive than other kinds of whole wheat? stoned-wheat crackers. 3 with its stone removed: stoned prunes.

stone-faced adj. 1 impassive: a stone-faced bureaucrat; stone-faced silence. 2 covered with stone: a stone-faced structure.

stone-ground adj. ground between millstones: stone-ground corn, flours, grains, whole wheat.

stone's throw n. a short distance: He lives only a stone's throw from the school.

stone.wall v. Informal. 1 refuse to answer embarrassing questions: They tried to stonewall the media; to stonewall public complaints; They just stonewalled; stonewalled on every issue that was raised. 2 obstruct a process: to stonewall an application, debate, investigation.

stone-washed adj. of fabrics, faded by removing part of the dye: the young lady in stone-washed blue jeans.

ston.y adj. **ston.i.er, -i.est** 1 full of stones: a stony field, ground, soil. 2 like stone; hard or cold: a stony critic, face, heart, silence, stare. —**ston.i.ly** adv.; **ston.i.ness** n.

stood pt. of STAND.

stooge (STOOJ, long "OO") n. Informal. one who serves another's purpose, as an underling: a stooge of the military regime.

stook (long "oo") n. a stack of sheaves of grain.

stool n. 1 a seat without back or arm. 2 a footstool. 3 usu. **stools** pl. feces: a patient who passes bloody stools; hard, fatty, loose stools; six to eight stools (= bowel movements) a week; **adj.**: stool cultures, samples, tests.

stool pigeon n. Slang. an informer or decoy; also **stool.ie** (-lee), -ies.

stoop v. 1 bend forward and downward, as the head and shoulders of an aged person. 2 lower or degrade oneself: Some politicians stoop to dirty tricks. —n. 1 a stooping carriage or posture. 2 a bending forward. 3 a flight of steps at the entrance to a house.

stoop labor n. work involving stooping, as picking strawberries.

stop v. **stops, stopped, stop.ping** 1 keep from moving or acting: to stop (the car) at a traffic signal; Stop the thief! Stop him (from) fleeing; He will stop at nothing short of a total victory; She stopped to catch her breath; The boxer was stopped (= knocked out) in the second round; He will only **stop short** of (= hesitate to commit) murder; When he saw the police, he **stopped dead in his tracks**. 2 bring a movement or action to an end: Please stop shouting; to stop a leak; Strikes stop work; a cork to **stop up** (= close) a bottle. 3 press down on a violin string, finger hole of a wind instrument, etc. to produce a desired tone or pitch. 4 stay: We stopped with friends in London during our tour; They had to **stop over** in Bombay before flying to Manila. —**stop by** or **in** drop in for a visit. —n. 1 a stopping or ending: They could not bring the train to a stop; The car came to a stop after crashing into the house; came to a dead stop; We made a brief stop in London; Drivers have to make a full stop at a stop sign; Learn to make a smooth stop, not a sudden stop or a rolling stop. 2 a stopping place: bus, pit, truck stops. 3 a stopping device such as a camera's shutter or a lever or key for changing the pitch or tone of a musical instrument, esp. an organ. —**pull out all the stops** make a great effort. —**put a stop to** put an end

stop.gap *n.* a temporary expedient; makeshift; *adj.: a stopgap arrangement, leader, measure, solution.*

stop.light *n.* 1 a traffic light, esp. when red. 2 a rear light of a vehicle that comes on when the brakes are applied.

stop.o.ver (stop.OH.vur) *n.* a brief stay in the course of a journey: *We made a stopover in Hawaii en route to Tokyo.*

stop.page (STOP.ij) *n.* 1 an act of stopping or the condition of being stopped: *a work stoppage; a stoppage of exports.* 2 a block or obstruction.

stop.per (STOP.ur) *n.* 1 a plug or similar device to close an opening: *bottle, wine stoppers; cork, glass stoppers; adj.: a **stoppered** bottle, test tube.* 2 one that causes a stoppage: *The new ride is a heart stopper; a pain stopper; The new store window is a traffic stopper.*

stop.ple *n. & v.* **stop.ples, stop.pled, stop.pling** (close a bottle, etc. with) a plug or other stopper.

stop.watch *n.* a watch that can be stopped and started as desired for timing races, etc.

stor.age (STOR.ij) *n.* 1 the storing of goods, as in a warehouse: *to move* or *throw something **into** storage; We'll keep* or *put it **in** storage for the time being; cold storage of perishables; It's time to take it **out of** storage.* 2 the storing of computer data: *information storage and retrieval; storage devices such as tapes and disks; archival storage; external storage on storage media such as magnetic and optical disks.*

storage battery *n.* a battery of cells that produces electricity by chemical action and that may be recharged.

store *v.* **stores, stored, stor.ing** 1 put aside in a safe place for future use: *old furniture stored in the attic; Disks are used for storing computer data.* 2 stock a place *with* something: *a shed stored with junk.* —*n.* 1 a stock or supply of something useful: *a good store of food; Databases are stores of information; It's hard to tell what **lies in** store* (= in the future) *for us; what the future may **have in** store* (= have ready) *for us; Children **set** or **lay** or **put great store by*** (= Children value greatly) *what teachers tell them.* 2 a place where goods are sold: *My dad manages, operates, runs a store; chain, convenience, department, discount, food, furniture, grocery, hardware, jewelry, liquor, retail, shoe, toy, variety stores; Mom minds the store when Dad sleeps.* 3 a storehouse. 4 **stores** *pl.* supplies for the regular needs of an establishment or operation: *military stores; a cache of stores.*

store.front (STOR.frunt) *n.* 1 the front of a store. 2 a place of business that is easily accessible to the public; *adj.: a storefront business, clinic, library, office, operation, service.*

store.house *n.* 1 a building in which goods are stored. 2 a person or place having a large supply: *a storehouse of information, knowledge.*

sto.rey *Brit.* STORY, *n.* 7.

sto.ried (STOR.eed) *adja.* 1 celebrated in stories or history: *the storied Riviera; its storied past.* 2 ornamented with designs based on history or legend: *a storied urn.* 3 having stories or floors: *a storied house; **cpd**: a three-storied building; multi-storied office towers.*

stork *n.* a large wading bird with long legs, neck, and bill, esp. a white one that builds its nest on rooftops and chimneys: *In children's lore, new babies were brought home by **the stork**, but now they know better.*

storm *n.* 1 a disturbance of the atmosphere marked by strong winds, rain, snow, or hail: *to ride out, weather a storm; dust storms; blinding, severe, violent storms; Storms blow over, brew, gather, hit, rage, strike, subside.* 2 any strong disturbance, or a violent outburst or attack: *a storm of abuse; The free-trade issue created a storm in the nation; The ad campaign **took** consumers **by storm*** (= captivated them, as if by a sudden assault); *The demonstrators **kicked up a storm*** (= stirred up trouble). —**up a storm** with energy or enthusiasm: *She can chat up, clean up, dance up, sweat up, talk up a storm.*
—*v.* 1 blow hard; rage: *It's storming outside; The workers were storming at* or *against the new rules.* 2 rush angrily or violently: *He stormed out of the room in a rage; The star stormed off the set; The demonstrators stormed (their way) into the president's office; They stormed* (= attacked) *the barricades, citadel, fortress.*

storm door (or **window**) *n.* an outer door (or window) as added protection against the weather.

storm (or **stormy**) **petrel** *n.* a petrel thought to be a sign of a coming storm.

storm.y *adj.* **storm.i.er, -i.est** 1 characterized by a storm: *a stormy day, night, sea; stormy waters, weather.* 2 tempestuous or turbulent: *a stormy debate, divorce, marriage, meeting, period, relationship, scene, session.* —**storm.i.ly** *adv.;* **storm.i.ness** *n.*

sto.ry (STOR.ee) *n.* **-ries 1** an account or narrative: *to narrate, tell a story; bedtime, children's, detective, love stories; coherent, conflicting, funny, juicy, sob, success stories.* **2** a newspaper report: *breaking, cover, exclusive, feature, front-page, human-interest stories; to carry, edit, kill, rewrite, run a story.* **3** a made-up account: *to concoct, fabricate, invent, make up a story; cock-and-bull, farfetched, shaggy dog stories.* **4** a written story, esp. one with literary qualities: *a short story; a story about love; the story of his adventures.* **5** a story as reflecting truth or falsehood: *to cover up, embellish, embroider, hush up, suppress a story; the inside story; a likely, plausible, true story; the whole story.* **6** a plot; story line. **7** one of the horizontal divisions of a building; floor level: *on a lower story; the top story; an upper story.*

sto.ry.board (STOR.ee.bord) *n.* a display panel for outlining the scenes and action of a movie, commercial, etc.

sto.ry.book (STOR.ee.book) *n.* a book of stories, esp. for children.
—*adja.* fairy-tale or romantic: *a storybook ending, romance, wedding.*

story line or **sto.ry.line** (STOR.ee.line) *n.* the plot of a play, novel, etc.

sto.ry.tell.er (STOR.ee.tel.ur) *n.* one who tells stories; **sto.ry.tell.ing** *n.*

stoup (STOOP) *n.* a basin for holy water at the entrance of a church.

stout (STOWT) *adj.* **1** strong in resisting strain; having endurance: *a stout rope;* They offered stout resistance; *a woman of stout heart;* **stout.heart.ed** *adj.*
2 thickset or bulky: *a stout figure, man, woman.* —*n.* a dark beer with the flavor of malt and hops. —**stout.ly** *adv.;* **stout.ness** *n.*

stove a *pt. & pp.* of STAVE.
—*n.* a closed heating or cooking apparatus: *to light* or *turn on a stove; electric, gas, wood stoves.*

stove.pipe *n.* a pipe connecting a stove to a chimney.

stove.top *n.* the top of a cooking stove; *adja.: a stovetop burner, cooker, grill.*

stow (STOH) *v.* store something in a place till it is required: *She settled down to read a magazine after stowing away her hand luggage.* —**stow away** hide oneself on board a ship or aircraft so as to get transport: *to stow away on a boat.*

stow.age (STOH.ij) *n.* **1** a stowing.
2 room for storing.

stow.a.way (STOH.uh.way) *n.* one who stows away.

strad.dle (STRAD.ul) *v.* **strad.dles,** **strad.dled, strad.dling** stand across a ditch, sit on an animal's back, etc. with one leg on either side: *a town that straddles the U.S.-Canadian border; They straddle the worlds of business and diplomacy; to* **straddle the fence** *on an issue* or *to straddle an issue* (= appear to favor both sides of the issue).
—**strad.dler** *n.*

strafe *v.* **strafes, strafed, straf.ing** of aircraft, to attack troops, buildings, etc. on the ground with machine-gun fire while flying low. —**straf.er** *n.*

strag.gle (STRAG.ul) *v.* **strag.gles,** **strag.gled, strag.gling 1** spread in an irregular manner, as vines. **2** stray from the main group: *A few straggled in late; the others straggled home; a* **straggling** *band of soldiers.* —**strag.gler** *n.*
—**strag.gly** (STRAG.lee) *adj.: straggly hair; a straggly beard, plant, vine.*

straight (STRAIT) *adj.* **1** without curves, bends, angles, etc.: *Draw a straight line; to set the record straight* (= correct); *She set him straight* (= corrected his wrong impressions) *about her past; a straight* (= honest or upright) *citizen; a straight* (= reliable) *tip; straight* (= undiluted) *liquor; a* **straight-A** *scholar* or *student (who always gets A grades or gets straight-A marks); Jill used to keep Jack on* **the straight and narrow** (= behaving properly); *Now she's trying to walk the straight and narrow; I like her* **straight-from-the-shoulder** (= direct) *approach; He votes the straight Democratic ticket* (= for Democratic party candidates only). **2** *Informal.* of people, conservative or conventional; not a drug addict, homosexual, etc.: *a straight* (= heterosexual) *couple.* —*adv.* in a straight manner: *Try to shoot straight* (= accurately); *Go straight* (= directly) *home; a straight* (= upright) *young man; He lives straight* (= directly) *down the road; It went on for ten days straight* (= continuously); *I'll be straight back* (= without delay). —**straight away** or **off** at once. —*n.* **1** *Informal.* a traditional or old-fashioned person. **2** something straight, as a straight part of a course. —**straight.ness** *n.*

straight-arm *v.* in football, push away a tackler with the arm extended stiffly.

straight arrow *n. Informal.* a stodgily proper or upright person.

straight.a.way (STRAIT.uh.way) *n.* a straight or direct course. —*adv.* at once: *We knew straightaway the plan wouldn't work.*

straight.edge *n.* a piece or strip with a perfectly straight edge for testing or

marking lines and surfaces.
straight.en (STRAY.tun) *v.* make or become straight: *to straighten curly hair; The lounging soldiers straightened up.* —**straighten out** make or become straight in thinking, organization, behavior, etc.: *A consultant was hired to straighten out the mess.*
straight face *n.* a face showing no sign of emotion, esp. merriment. —**straight-faced** *adj.*
straight.for.ward (strait.FOR.wurd) *adj.* direct; also, candid or frank: *She has a clear and straightforward style; simple and straightforward; a straightforward account, analysis, answer, approach, explanation, narrative, plan, presentation, question; They responded in straightforward fashion; in the most straightforward way; fairly straightforward.* Also *adv.*
straightjacket, straightlaced same as STRAITJACKET, STRAITLACED.
straight man *n.* one who takes part in a skit by helping the comic with appropriate responses.
straight time *n.* rate of pay for regular working hours, not overtime.
straight.way *adv.* [old use] at once; straightaway.
strain *v.* **1** to stretch or exert to the utmost: *a dog straining at the leash to get away; In poor light you have to strain your eyes to read; He strained every nerve* (= tried very hard) *to get the best grades;* ***adj.***: *He sounded strained* (= exhausted or forced); *a strained voice; strained breathing, conditions, resources; strained* (= tense) *relations leading to separation.* **2** filter a liquid through a strainer; also, filter out solids. —***n.*** **1** a stretching force or its effect: *Poor posture causes back strain; muscle strain; Stress causes strain* (= deformation) *in materials.* **2** tension: *He quit the job because he couldn't stand the strain; It was a strain on his family life; emotional, mental, physical strains; Some jobs impose, place, put undue strains on you; Holidays help to ease, relieve the strains of daily life; Some people carry on till they break under the strain.* **3** manner or style: *to speak in a mournful strain.* **4 strains** *pl.* snatches of music or singing: *strains of "The Blue Danube."* **5** an inherited quality or tendency: *the strain of weakness in his character.* **6** breed or variety: *a good strain of wheat; a virulent strain of bacteria; different strains of feminism.*
strain.er *n.* a filter or sieve.
strait *n.* **1** a narrow channel connecting two large bodies of water: *the Strait of Gibraltar.* **2 straits** *pl.* difficulty or need: *economic and financial straits; in bad, desperate, difficult, dire, perilous straits.* —***adj.*** [old use] narrow; hence, strict.
strait.ened (STRAY.tund) *adja.* financially difficult: *in these **straitened** times; He lived **in straitened circumstances*** (= in poverty or need) *while growing up.*
strait.jack.et (STRAIT.jack.it) *n.* a jacketlike garment designed to restrain a person physically. —*v.*: *He was straitjacketed and locked away.*
strait.laced *adj.* severely strict in regard to religion or morals.
strand *n.* **1** one of the threads or wires that are twisted together to make a rope, cable, etc.: *a strand* (= string) *of pearls; the strands of melody in a composition.* **2** the shore or beach of a sea, lake, or river. —*v.* be or put in a helpless position, as a ship run aground: *The last flight had left and he was stranded in London for the night.*
strange (STRAINJ) *adj.* **strang.er, strang.est** not familiar or accustomed: *The voice sounded strange; strange visitors from space; He felt strange like a fish out of water; a northerner strange to southern ways; Isn't it strange we never heard from him again?* —**strange.ly** *adv.;* **strange.ness** *n.*
stran.ger (STRAIN.jur) *n.* a person who is new in a place or unaccustomed to a group or situation: *Children are warned not to talk to strangers; Dogs bark at strangers; a complete, perfect, total stranger; He's no stranger to our culture.*
stran.gle (STRANG.gul) *v.* **-gles, -gled, -gling 1** kill by squeezing the throat: *He had been strangled by a bear; strangled to death.* **2** choke or stifle: *businesses strangled by the credit crunch; The government was strangling us with their new rules; to strangle an economy;* ***adj.***: *She gave a **strangled** laugh; He spoke in a strangled voice; I had a strangled feeling in my throat; a strangled flow of finances; **strangling** bonds.* —**stran.gler** (STRANG.glur) *n.*
stran.gle.hold (STRANG.gul.hold) *n.* **1** a wrestling hold that would choke one's opponent: *Sam got a stranglehold on the attacker during the struggle.* **2** absolute control: *The stranglehold that a cartel had on the world oil market was finally broken; to break out of, escape, loosen a stranglehold; to gain, lose, place, seek, tighten a stranglehold over a person or thing.*
stran.gu.late (STRANG.gyuh.late) *v.*

-lates, -lat.ed, -lat.ing constrict or tighten so as to block circulation, as in a loop of intestine caught in a hernia. —**stran.gu.la.tion** (-LAY.shun) *n*.: *death by strangulation.*

strap *n.* a narrow strip of flexible material, as of a belt or wristwatch: *the shoulder strap of a camera, purse, uniform (showing rank); The strap* (= beating with a strap as punishment) *has been abolished in our schools.*
—*v.* **straps, strapped, strap.ping**
1 bind with a strap: *The kidnap victim was found strapped to a chair; strapping tape; a debt-strapped nation.* **2** punish by beating with a strap: *Pupils used to be strapped for misbehavior.*

strapped *adj.* **1** having straps. **2** *Informal.* short of something: *strapped for cash, funds, resources; financially strapped governments;* **cpd**: *cash-strapped farmers; currency-strapped nations.*

strapping *adj. Informal.* robust or sturdy: *strapping young boys, girls, youths.*

strata *a pl.* of STRATUM.

strat.a.gem (STRAT.uh.jum) *n.* a carefully laid plan or scheme to entrap or outwit an opponent: *He resorted to or used a clever, subtle stratagem to get an interview; military, political, sales stratagems.*

strat.e.gy (STRAT.uh.jee) *n.* **-gies 1** the planning and execution of a military or similar undertaking: *military strategy; campaign, industrial, marketing, nuclear, political strategy; the strategy of the game; a matter or question of strategy; a strategy session.* **2** a detailed plan or method: *to adopt, apply, plan, pursue, work out a strategy; a global, grand, long-range strategy; the strategies of searching a database; sales strategies.* —**strat.e.gist** *n.*
—**stra.te.gic** (struh.TEE.jic) *adj.;* **stra.te.gi.cal.ly** *adv.*

strat.i.fy (STRAT.uh.fye) *v.* **-fies, -fied, -fy.ing** form into strata or layers; *adj.: Coal, flint, and limestone are stratified rocks; the social classes of a stratified, not homogeneous society.* —**strat.i.fi.ca.tion** (-fuh.CAY.shun) *n.*

strat.o.sphere (STRAT.us.feer) *n.* the usu. cloudless layer of the earth's atmosphere from about 10 miles (16.09 km) to about 30 miles (48.28 km) up: *House prices have gone up into the stratosphere* (= very high).
—**strat.o.spher.ic** (-FER.ic) *adj.*

strat.um (STRAY.tum, STRAT.um) *n., pl.* **-ta** or **-tums** a horizontal or parallel layer, as of stratified rocks: *the strata of the atmosphere; geologic strata; cultural and social strata; the different strata of society.*

straw *n.* **1** the dried hollow stalks or stems of grains after threshing, used as bedding for animals and to make hats, baskets, etc. **2** one such stem or a similar tube used for sucking up beverages: *to drink through a straw.* **3** something trifling or worthless: *I don't care a straw; "A drowning man will clutch at a straw"; The straw that broke the camel's back,* as in the fable, *was the last straw* (= a final aggravation or burden). —*adj.: a straw hat; straw* (= yellowish) *color.*

straw.ber.ry (STRAW.ber.ee) *n.* **-ber.ries** a low-growing vinelike plant with red, pulpy fruit; *adj.: a strawberry farm;* **strawberry blond** (= reddish blond).

straw boss *n. Informal.* an occasional supervisor with little authority.

straw in the wind *n.* a hint of something coming or happening.

straw man *n.* an imaginary opponent.

straw poll (or **vote**) *n.* an unofficial vote to find out a general trend.

stray *v.* wander from the usual or regular path: *The plane strayed into enemy territory; Sheep stray from the fold; The TV evangelist strayed from the path of virtue* (= sinned). —*adj.: stray(ed) animals, dogs, sheep; a stray bullet; a stray* (= isolated) *case of smallpox.*
—*n.* a child or domestic animal that has strayed: *waifs and strays* (= homeless children or animals); *a shelter for strays* (= stray animals).

streak (STREEK) *n.* **1** a long, thin mark such as is made in the sky by a shooting star: *the streak of dawn in the eastern sky; streaks of silver in his hair; fatty streaks in coronary artery walls; fat and lean streaks* (= layers) *in bacon; a streak of boldness, fatalism, vulgarity; There's an ambitious, cruel, domineering, earnest, jealous, mean streak* (= trait) *in his behavior; a yellow* (= cowardly) *streak.* **2** a brief period: *a streak of bad luck; a losing streak; a lucky streak; He's on a winning streak; The child was talking a blue streak* (= rapid stream of words); *The new product is on a hot streak* (= is selling fast). —*v.* **1** have or put streaks in something: *She streaks her black hair with orange or purple; a sky streaked with clouds.* **2** move swiftly: *A meteor streaks across the sky; The runners streaked to the finish line.* —**streak.y** *adj.*

stream (STREEM) *n.* **1** a small river or brook: *mountain, running, swollen streams.* **2** a flow or unbroken series: *a steady stream of abuse, letters, refugees,*

streamer / stretch

tears, visitors; The assembly plant comes **on stream** (= goes into production) *tomorrow; a* **stream-of-consciousness** *narrative that flows continuously and haphazardly.*
—*v.* flow as or like a stream: *eyes streaming with tears; Blood streamed from the wound; People streamed toward the fair; Flags streamed* (= waved) *in the wind.*

stream.er (STREE.mur) *n.* a long, narrow, flowing strip, esp. a pennant or banner.

stream.line *v.* **-lines, -lined, -lin.ing** **1** organize an operation for greater speed and efficiency: *to streamline communications, procedures, services.* **2** make streamlined: *Hydroplanes have to be streamlined.*

streamlined *adj.* **1** having a smoothly flowing shape for swift movement through air or water: *a well streamlined vehicle with little drag; the streamlined styling of sports cars.* **2** efficiently organized: *a streamlined office, operation, regimen; her streamlined approach, efficiency.*

street *n.* **1** a usu. paved public road lined with buildings, as in a town or city: *to cross a street; busy, crowded, narrow, quiet, winding streets; cross, dead-end, main, one-way, through streets; They play on or in the street;* **adja.:** *street clothes, entrances, lighting; helping* **street kids** *get off drugs.* **2** the people living or working there.

street.car *n.* a public passenger vehicle moving on rails laid on the streets: *to go by, ride (in), take a streetcar.*

street smarts *n.pl.* the ability to survive in an urban environment; **adj.:** *a* **street-smart** *youngster.*

street railway *n.* (a company operating) a streetcar line.

street.walk.er (STREET.wok.ur) *n.* a prostitute.

street.wise *adj.* aware of the urban environment: *streetwise clothes, kids, grittiness, marketing.*

strength *n.* the quality of being strong; inherent capacity for action; power: *A boxer is a man of great (physical) strength; mere brute strength; He makes a show of strength when he is displeased; She has the strength to lift his weight; great inner strength; strength of character; to build up, develop one's strength; to gain, recoup, save strength; This beer has 5% alcoholic strength; 2% is below strength; how to bring it up to strength; A movement gathers strength; There's strength in (large) numbers; Our class is at its full, maximum strength* (= number) *of 30 pupils; I would hire him* **on the strength of** (= based on) *his references.*

strength.en *v.* make or become strong or stronger. —**strength.en.er** *n.*

stren.u.ous (STREN.yoo.us) *adj.* demanding much strength or energy: *a strenuous day; strenuous efforts; the strenuous life of an athlete.* —**stren.u.ous.ly** *adv.;* **stren.u.ous.ness** *n.*

strep [short form] streptococcus: *group A strep;* **adja.:** *strep B; the strep germ; a strep infection.*

strep throat *n. Informal.* a sore throat and fever caused by a streptococcus infection.

strep.to.coc.cus (strep.tuh.COC.us) *n., pl.* **-coc.ci** (-COC.sye) any of a group of spherical bacteria that grow together in chains, some causing scarlet fever, septicemia, strep throat, etc.

strep.to.my.cin (strep.tuh.MY.sin) *n.* a powerful antibiotic derived from a mold.

stress *n.* **1** pressure or force that tends to strain or deform the body subjected to it; tension: *the tensile stress of ceiling vaults; What causes emotional, mental, physical stresses; People cope or deal with, undergo stress; Most people learn to control stress; how to ease, handle, lower, reduce, relieve stress; He broke under the combined stress of loss of job and family problems;* **adja.:** *stress effects, levels, management, reactions; to undergo a* **stress test** *(of the heart and blood vessels) on a treadmill; Stomach ulcers, heart attacks, migraine headaches, etc. are* **stress-related** *diseases.* **2** emphasis: *She lays or places or puts great stress on punctuality; The stress* (= accent) *in "indecision" is on the third syllable.*
—*v.* emphasize: *He stressed each point by thumping the table; stressed the need for reform; stressed that punctuality is important; as he always stresses; To an English speaker, the French seem to stress words on the last syllable.* —**stressed** *adj.* being under stress: *a financially stressed company; to feel stressed; severely stressed; He's so* **stressed out**, *he doesn't know what to do;* **stressed-out** *employees, executives, staff, students; a physically* **stressed furniture** *finish (with marks, scratches, etc.).* —**stress.ful** *adj.: a stressful day, environment, job, life, situation; stressful events, thoughts, times.*

stretch *v.* draw out or extend: *He stretched a clothesline across the yard; It's not stretched straight; She stretched out a helping hand; He walks around his desk to stretch his limbs; socks that stretch to fit different sizes; a desert stretching to the ho-*

rizon; *to stretch a point*, one's patience, the truth; *I reached too high and stretched* (= strained) *a muscle.* —*n.* **1** a stretching or being stretched. **2** an extent of space or time: *an endless stretch of ocean; the two stretches (backstretch and homestretch) of a racecourse; She can work for days* **at a stretch** (= without stopping); *something unthinkable by any* **stretch of the imagination.** —*adj.* that stretches: *stretch pants, socks;* a **stretch** (= lengthened) *limousine.* —**stretch.a.ble** (STRETCH.uh.bul) *adj.*

stretch.er *n.* a device for carrying a sick or dead person flat, usu. a light frame with canvas stretched across it. —**stretcher-bearer** *n.*

stretch.y *adj.* that stretches or is stretchable: *a stretchy blend of nylon and wool; a stretchy band for the hair; stretchy fabrics.*

strew (STROO) *v.* **strews,** *pt.* **strewed,** *pp.* **strewed** or **strewn, strew.ing** scatter or cover by scattering: *a park strewed with litter; a battlefield strewn with bodies; cpd.: flower-strewn fields; a junk-strewn lot; a rock-strewn landscape.*

stri.at.ed (STRY.ay.tid) *adj.* streaked or striped in parallel lines, as the fibers making up the "striated muscle" of an external organ, not a "smooth" muscle, as of an internal organ: *a striated pattern.* —**stri.a.tion** (stry.AY.shun) *n.*

strick.en a *pp.* of STRIKE: *a remark ordered stricken from the court record; names to be stricken from the rolls; to be stricken by* or *with anxiety, disease, remorse, sorrow, trouble.* —*adj.* suffering or afflicted: *the loneliness of stricken lives; hungry children with stricken eyes, faces; stricken areas, countries, regions; cpd.: drought-stricken, famine-stricken, grief-stricken, panic-stricken, poverty-stricken; sorrow-stricken.*

strict 1 *adj.* careful in enforcing rules: *a strict parent, teacher; strict in discipline; strict about school attendance; equally strict toward all her students.* **2** *adja.* carefully observed; exact or precise: *a strict rule; in the strict sense of the term; in the strictest confidence.* —**strict.ly** *adv.* **1** solely or exclusively: *They play strictly for laughs; It's strictly for the birds; What they have is strictly nonfiction; hired strictly as a consultant.* **2** in a strict way: *strictly applied, confidential, controlled, enforced, forbidden, limited; Is this strictly necessary? Strictly speaking, it's not.* —**strict.ly** *adv.*; **strict.ness** *n.*

stric.ture (STRIK.chur) *n.* **1** a legal, moral, or social restriction: *the loosening of strictures on* or *against artists and writers; liberation from the strictures of* Western fashions. **2** a censorious statement or criticism: *strictures against premarital sex.* **3** a narrowing: *a stricture of the valves of the heart; bowel, urethral strictures.*

stride *v.* **strides, strode, strid.den, strid.ing** walk with long steps, as from vigor or enthusiasm: *He confidently strode into the room; Keep your feet dry by striding over the stream.* —*n.* **1** a long step or the distance covered by it: *The stride of Bigfoot is estimated at about four feet.* **2** steadiness of pace: *to march on without stopping or breaking stride.* **3** peak performance level: *Appreciation helps to* **hit one's stride**; *once the new system hits full stride; We'll knock the competition off stride; to lose stride; to come into* or *reach one's stride.* **4 strides** *pl.* progress: *the rapid strides made by the computer industry; great strides in speed and efficiency.* —**take in stride** deal with something without getting excited or upset: *She has learned to take successes as well as failures in stride.*

stri.dent (STRY.dunt) *adj.* loud in a harsh, grating, or obtrusive manner: *a strident voice; the strident tone of his petition;* **stri.dent.ly** *adv.* —**stri.den.cy** *n.*

strife *n.* a fighting or quarrel, esp. a struggle between opposing sides: *There's bitter strife between the various factions; communal, domestic, internal, sectarian strife among the population; industrial strife (between labor and management).*

strike *v.* **strikes,** *pt.* **struck,** *pp.* **struck** or **strick.en** (STRIK.un), **strik.ing 1** hit, esp. aim or deal a blow with the hand or a weapon: *Jim lost his patience and struck the bully; struck him a heavy blow; He struck back at Jim; struck his head against the door; A clock strikes* (= sounds) *the hours; An epidemic strikes a population; He lit a fire by striking a match; a house struck by lightning.* **2** produce an effect or result: *The blow struck him unconscious; stories that strike terror into young minds; A plant strikes roots as it grows in a place; A bright idea struck her; How does her plan strike* (= impress) *you? It strikes me as clever; They struck* (= advanced) *across the trackless desert; After some digging, they struck* (= found) *oil; The invaders struck* (= attacked) *without warning; The workers struck* (= went on a strike) *for more pay; They succeeded in striking* (= agreeing on) *a bargain; He often strikes* (= assumes) *the pose of a concerned citizen.*
—**strike it rich** *Informal.* make money, as from a gold mine or oil well.

—**strike off** cross out, as from a list.
—**strike out** 1 delete words, as from a record. 2 move forward, as by swimming: *to strike out for* or *toward (the) shore; She decided to quit her job and strike out on her own as a consultant.* 3 in baseball, fail or cause to fail to hit thrice. —**strike up** 1 begin: *to strike up an acquaintance, conversation, friendship.* 2 begin playing: *to strike up a tune; Strike up the band! The band struck up; They struck up "Yankee Doodle."*
—*n.* 1 a striking, esp. an attack: *to carry out an air strike against the enemy; a preemptive strike; the enemy's first-strike capability.* 2 a stoppage of work by employees to force their employer to agree to higher pay or better working conditions: *to avert, break, break up, call, organize, settle, stage a strike; They went (out) on strike; They are on strike; a general, hunger, rent, sit-down, sympathy, wildcat strike.* 3 in baseball, any of four ways in which a failure may be called against a batter: *Three strikes and you're out; They have two strikes against them* (= are at a clear disadvantage). 4 in bowling, a knocking down of all the pins with the first ball: *strikes, spares, and misses.* 5 a discovery of an oil deposit.
strike.break.er (STRIKE.bray.kur) *n.* one hired to replace a striking worker: *to bring in strikebreakers.*
strike.out *n.* in baseball, an out resulting from a batter being charged three strikes.
striking 1 *adj.* that allows a strike: *to come within striking distance.* 2 *adj.* very impressive: *in striking contrast; a striking display, effect, personality, performance; a woman of striking appearance; his striking good looks.* —**strik.ing.ly** *adv.*: *strikingly bad, beautiful, clean, clear, different, familiar, large, similar; sounds strikingly like something I've heard before.*
string *n.* 1 a cord or wire that is thicker than a thread, as for tying up a parcel, working a puppet, or keeping a bow taut: *a string of pearls* (= pearls on a string); *a string* (= series) *of lies.* 2 something resembling a string or cord, as a nerve or the fiber connecting the halves of a bean pod. 3 *Informal.* a condition: *a genuine offer with no* **strings attached.** 4 group based on ability: *first string; second string.*
—**strings** *pl.* 1 stringed instruments, as of an orchestra, or their players collectively. 2 *Informal.* control or influence: *a man tied to his mother's apron strings* (= still dependent on her); *He knows how to* **pull strings** (= to exert influence). —*v.* **strings,** *pt. & pp.* **strung** or **stringed, string.ing** arrange in a string or line: *to string beads; to string a racket* (= equip it with strings); *to string words together in sentences; a carcass strung* (= hung) *between two posts; to string* (= put the strings on); *also, tune) a violin; highly strung* (= taut) *nerves; to string peas and beans* (= clean them of strings).

string bean *n.* 1 a bean whose pods are eaten as a vegetable after their strings are removed, not one that is shelled for use. 2 a snap bean.

stringed *adj.* having to do with strings: *Violins and guitars are stringed instruments; stringed melodies (played on stringed instuments); a stringed bikini.*

strin.gent (STRIN.junt) *adj.* strictly or severely binding: *stringent conditions, guidelines, limits, measures, regulations, requirements, standards; a stringent* (= tight) *economy, market.*
—**strin.gen.cy** *n.* **-cies:** *budgetary, credit, financial stringencies.*

string.er *n.* 1 a connecting or supporting timber, esp. a horizontal piece. 2 a part-time correspondent for a newspaper.

string.y *adj.* **string.i.er, -i.est** 1 having or forming strings: *stringy bark, beans, hair, ham.* 2 sinewy or wiry in build.

strip *v.* **strips, stripped, strip.ping** 1 remove what covers a fruit, body, or other surface: *Sam was stripped and searched by the police; to strip old paint off furniture; The doctor asked him to strip to the waist; to* **strip down** *to his underwear.* 2 deprive of what belongs to one by taking it off completely or forcibly: *Al was stripped of his citizenship; a military general stripped of his powers; a stolen car stripped of its accessories; radios stripped from stolen vehicles.* 3 damage or break the thread of a screw or teeth of a gear. —*n.* 1 a long, narrow piece: *strips of cardboard, cloth, land; the median strip of a highway; a landing strip (for airplanes).* 2 a busy thoroughfare along a street: *hotels on the airport strip; a beach-front strip; the shopping strip; the action-packed "Strip" of Los Angeles.*
—**strip.per** *n.*: *a paint stripper; male, female, and other strippers; Wall Street strippers* (= exploiters).

stripe *n.* 1 a long, narrow band of contrasting color: *A tiger cannot change its stripes; a dark suit with chalk stripes; the* **stars and stripes** *on the U.S. flag.* 2 usu. **stripes** *pl.* a strip of braid or a V-shaped badge worn on the sleeve of a uniform to show the wearer's rank

or length of service. **3** sort or type: *Politicians of every stripe were there.*
—*v.* **stripes, striped, strip.ing** mark with stripes: *A candy cane is striped with red;* **adj.:** *striped animals, pants, snakes.*

strip.ling *n.* a youth who has not yet attained maturity: *a mere stripling of a boy.*

strip mall *n.* an outdoor shopping center that is a series of connected shops.

strip mine *n.* an open-pit mine for coal and other minerals near the earth's surface.

stripper See STRIP.

strip.search *v.* search a suspect's body after the clothes are removed.

strip.tease (STRIP.teez) *n.* a stage show in which a woman takes off her clothes one by one with suggestive dancing and accompanying music; **adj.:** *a striptease artist, sequence, show.*
—**strip.teas.er** *n.*

strive *v.* **strives,** *pt.* **strove** (STROHV) or **strived,** *pp.* **striv.en, striv.ing** make great efforts or try hard: *to strive to accomplish something; to strive for an effect; to strive toward perfection; She has striven hard to get an A in all her courses.*
—**striv.er** *n.*

strobe light or **strobe** *n.* an electronic device emitting brilliant flashes, used in photography, in the stroboscope, etc.

stro.bo.scope (STROH.buh.scope, STROB.uh-) *n.* an instrument for studying rapid motion, using flashes of light that are synchronized with the speed of the moving object.

strode *pt.* of STRIDE.

stroke *v.* **strokes, stroked, strok.ing** pass the hand caressingly over: *to stroke a furry animal, one's beard, hair, a person, a pet;* **n.:** *He could use some ego stroking* (= praise or flattery).
—*n.* **1** a stroking: *"Different strokes* (= *treatments) for different folks."* **2** a striking or blow, esp. one dealt suddenly or sharply: *a stroke of lightning, of a sword; a stroke of bad luck, fate, good fortune, luck, misfortune; at the stroke of 12 (o'clock); Age-old customs cannot be changed* **at a stroke** or **with the stroke of a pen** (= suddenly). **3** partial paralysis: *He had or suffered a stroke; a mild stroke.* **4** an effort, esp. a vigorous or successful one: *a stroke of genius; a brilliant stroke; a master stroke; He didn't do one stroke of work all day.* **5** an action or movement that is repeated, esp. rhythmically: *backhand and forehand strokes in tennis; a few broad strokes (of the brush); key strokes (on a keyboard);* *swimming strokes such as the breaststroke and "butterfly" stroke; the up and down strokes of written letters; the strokes of a piston;* **cpd:** *a four-stroke cycle, engine; long-stroke pumps.*

stroll (STROLE) *n.* a leisurely walk: *to go for* or *take a stroll in the park.*
—*v.* **1** take a stroll along or through a place: *She went strolling in the park; He strolled through the hotel corridors; They used to stroll on the moonlit beach.* **2** wander: *to stroll the streets;* **adj.:** *a strolling troupe of players; strolling minstrels, troubadours, tourists; strolling carts offering wine and cheese.*

stroll.er *n.* **1** one who strolls. **2** a light carriage for a sitting child.

strong *adj.* **strong.er** (also -gur), **strong.est** (also -gist) **1** having great power to act or resist; not weak: *strong muscles, winds; a strong argument, drink, mind, reason, will; strong support; Sometimes, he will* **come on strong** (= aggressively); *still* **going strong** (= doing well) *at 85.* **2** *adj.* of a specified number: *Our class is 32 strong.* **3** ill-smelling; foul: *a strong breath, cheese, smell.* **4** of a verb, not regular in conjugation: *"Sink-sank-sunk" are the principal parts of a strong verb, not a weak one.*
—**strong.ly** *adv.*

strong-arm *adj. Informal.* using undue force: *the strong-arm approach; a strong-arm man, method; strong-arm police tactics.* Also **strong-armed.** —*v.* use coercion or violence against someone.

strong.box *n.* a securely built box or safe for valuables.

strong.hold *n.* **1** a fortress. **2** a place in which a party or cause has strong support: *The Democratic candidate won the election in a Republican stronghold.*

strong.man *n.* **-men** a despot or dictator.

strong-minded *adj.* mentally strong or unyielding.

strong.room *n.* a room that is built for keeping valuables safe against fire, burglary, etc. Also **strong room.**

strong suit *n.* strong point; forte.

stron.ti.um (STRON.shee.um, -tee.um) *n.* a metallic chemical element.

strontium 90 *n.* a radioactive isotope of strontium found in atomic fallout.

strop *n. & v.* **strops, stropped, strop.ping** (sharpen a razor on) a leather strap.

stro.phe (STROH.fee) *n.* a stanza, esp. of a choral ode; **stroph.ic** (STROF.ic) *adj.*

strove *pt.* of STRIVE.

struck *pt.* or a *pp.* of STRIKE. —**adj.** af-

fected by a labor strike: *struck businesses, work, workers.*
struc.tur.al (STRUK.chur.ul) *adj.* **1** having to do with structure: *a structural change, defect, difference; structural weakness;* **structural unemployment** *(caused by the economy).* **2** having to do with building: *high-strength structural composite lumber; structural steel;* **Structural engineers** *design and build bridges, dams, etc.* —**struc.tur.al.ly** *adv.*
struc.ture (STRUK.chur) *n.* **1** anything constructed of parts; building: *a tall structure.* **2** the manner of arrangement of parts in a system: *the structure of society; sentence structure; power, price, tax, wage structures.* —*v.* **-tures, -tured, -tur.ing** organize with differentiated parts: *how to structure a training program; the way our laws are structured;* **adj.:** *a* **structured** *curriculum; clothes with a structured look; a loosely structured proposal;* **n.:** *price* **structuring**; *the structuring of the economy.*
stru.del (STROO.dul) *n.* a rolled-up pastry with a filling of fruit or cheese.
strug.gle (STRUG.ul) *n.* **1** great effort or exertion: *to wage a struggle against poverty; to carry on a struggle for freedom; the struggle to make a living; the ceaseless, fierce struggle for survival.* **2** strife or conflict: *the class struggle; to put up a struggle; a struggle to the death; a bitter, desperate, frantic, unending, violent struggle.* —*v.* **strug.gles, strug.gled, strug.gling** make great efforts, as against contending forces: *She struggled to free herself; struggled to her feet; struggled for breath; struggled out of her clothes; struggled bravely through her long illness;* **adj.:** *a* **struggling** *artist, business, economy, farmer, writer.*
strum *v.* **strums, strummed, strum.ming** play a guitar, a tune, to play *on the piano, etc.* in a casual or unskillful manner.
strum.pet (STRUM.pit) *n.* a prostitute.
strung *pt. & pp.* of STRING. —**strung out 1** *Slang.* addicted to or intoxicated by narcotics: *to be strung out on drugs.* **2** severely exhausted: *They seem strung out by stress.* **3** spread out: *The beds were strung out along the hospital corridors; payments strung out over ten years.*
strut *v.* **struts, strut.ted, strut.ting** walk in a jaunty and self-important manner: *to strut like a peacock; an actress* **strutting her stuff** (= *showing off*) *on the stage.* —*n.* **1** a strutting walk or gait. **2** a brace or support, as under the rafters of a roof.
strych.nine (STRIC.nin, -nine, -neen) *n.* a bitter, poisonous drug prepared from an East Indian plant.
stub *n.* a short piece remaining after its main part is used up or broken off: *the stub of a cigarette, pencil, ticket, tooth; the stub of a check (saved as a record); the stub* (= *stump*) *of a tree.* —*v.* **stubs, stubbed, stub.bing:** *He stubbed his toe* (= *hurt it by striking it against something hard*); *to stub a cigar* (= *put it out by rubbing it on a surface*).
stub.ble (STUB.ul) *n.* **1** stumps left projecting from the ground after harvesting. **2** a short, bristly growth, as of hair on the face. —**stub.bly** *adj.: his stubbly beard, chin;* also **stubbled.**
stub.born (STUB.urn) *adj.* determined not to change one's way: *a stubborn child; a stubborn* (= *unyielding*) *disposition, resistance; a stubborn soil* (*that is hard to work*); *a stubborn cough or stain* (*that is difficult to get rid of*).
—**stub.born.ly** *adv.;* **stub.born.ness** *n.*
stub.by (STUB.ee) *adj.* **stub.bi.er, stub.bi.est 1** short and thick: *stubby fingers; a stubby bottle.* **2** covered with stubs or stumps: *a stubby field.*
stuc.co (STUC.oh) *n.* **stuc.cos** or **stuc.coes** a plasterlike material for coating outside walls. —*v.* **stuc.cos** or **stuc.coes, stuc.coed, stuc.co.ing** coat or decorate with stucco.
stuck *pt.* of STICK.
stuck-up *adj. Informal.* conceited.
stud *n.* **1** a male animal kept for breeding, esp. a stallion, or **studhorse:** *a prize stud at a cattle auction; a stud farm.* **2** a virile young man: *Met any good-looking studs lately?* **adj.:** *a movie star with stud appeal; a stud race-car driver.* **3** one of the upright timbers inside a wall frame to which the boards or panels are nailed: *two-by-four studs.* **4** a knoblike head, as used to ornament a leather surface, or a small, two-headed button used on dress shirts: *silver studs; diamond-stud earrings.* —*v.* **studs, stud.ded, stud.ding** decorate or dot with or as if with studs: *Stud the fat with cloves; to stud cloves on oranges; a crown studded with diamonds;* **adj.:** *a* **star-studded** *sky; a* **studded** *tire for better traction over snow and ice.*
stud.book *n.* a register of purebred racehorses or dogs.
stud.ding *n.* a wall's studs or their material.
stu.dent (STEW.dunt) *n.* one who studies a subject or attends a school: *college, day, excellent, foreign, good, graduate, high-school, outstanding, poor, undergraduate, university students; students of*

Milton (who study Milton's works).
studhorse See STUD, *n.* 1.
studied (STUD.eed) *adj.* **1** deliberate: *his studied casualness, politeness; a studied effort, insult.* **2** carefully prepared: *a studied reply; her studied humor.* See also STUDY, *v.* —**stud.ied.ly** *adv.*
stu.di.o (STEW.dee.oh) *n.* **-os 1** an artist's or photographer's workroom: *a dance studio that is really a social club.* **2** a broadcasting room or a place where motion pictures are produced: *a film studio; TV studio; a studio audience.* **3** a more spacious bachelor apartment; also **studio apartment.**
studio couch *n.* a usu. backless couch that can be converted into a double bed.
stu.di.ous (STEW.dee.us) *adj.* **1** devoted to study: *studious habits.* **2** diligent: *studious attention, care, efforts.*
—**stu.di.ous.ly** *adv.*
stud.y (STUD.ee) *n.* **stud.ies 1** concentration of the mind on a subject in an effort to learn it; also, any earnest mental effort: *She spends her weekends in study.* **2** a detailed examination of a subject, the subject itself, or a work or treatise discussing it: *She has conducted, done, made a study of the phenomenon; his careful, classic, deep, definitive, detailed, exhaustive, in-depth, scientific study of volcanoes; her published studies of human behavior; social studies; women's studies; The question is* **under study.** **3** a room for study. **4 studies** *pl.* education: *She pursued, completed her studies in Paris; a man of studies.* —**adj.:** *a study circle, group;* **study hall** (= place or time set aside for study in a school); *They walked off the job for a* **study session** *with fellow workers.* —*v.* **stud.ies, stud.ied, stud.y.ing 1** apply one's mind to a subject: *She's studying law; to study (from) books; to study diligently, hard; to study for a degree; to study under a teacher; She studied at Princeton with Einstein (as teacher); He works days and studies nights* (= spends nights in study); *to* **study up on** (*Informal for* make a good study of) *a subject;* ***adj. & cpd.:*** *the subjects* **studied;** *a little-studied section of a statute; the most-studied book of all time; a widely-studied text.* **2** carefully examine or consider: *He's studying the results of the experiment; to study data, instructions, an idea, issue, a map, patient, phenomenon, problem, proposal, rock, specimen, star; to study someone's behavior, expression; to study a question deeply.*
stuff *n.* **1** the substance that something is made of or material for making something: *woolen stuff; the right stuff; the same old stuff; the stuff* (= basic qualities) *of genius; the stuff of* (= what makes a) *legend.* **2** *Informal.* thing(s): *What's that stuff you're drinking? Get rid of the stuff; Stuff happens; kids, toys,* **and stuff** (= etc.); *Stuff and nonsense* (= Garbage)! *He knows his stuff* (= what he is supposed to know); *fun stuff* (= fun thing or things); *kid stuff* (= elementary thing or things); *heady stuff* (= something exciting).
—*v.* fill or pack: *a pillow stuffed with feathers; Feathers are stuffed into pillows; He stuffed himself with cake;* **adj.:** *That bear is really a* **stuffed** *animal; a stuffed ballot box* (*containing fraudulent votes*); *a* **stuffed-up** *nose* (*from a cold*).
stuffed shirt *n. Informal.* one who is pretentious or pompous.
stuffing *n.* **1** padding used in upholstery. **2** a filling of bread crumbs, seasonings, etc. for roast fowl.
stuff.y *adj.* **stuf.fi.er, stuf.fi.est:** *a stuffy* (= not airy) *room; a stuffy* (= congested) *nose; a stuffy* (= straitlaced) *clergyman; a stuffy* (= dull) *sermon.*
stul.ti.fy (STUL.tuh.fye) *v.* **-fies, -fied, -fy.ing** render futile or ineffectual: *to stultify development, growth;* **adj.:** *a* **stultifying** *bureaucracy, effect, experience.*
—**stul.ti.fi.ca.tion** (-fi.CAY.shun) *n.*
stum.ble *v.* **-bles, -bled, -bling** take a wrong step in walking or running, trip accidentally, or falter because of age or weakness: *We stumbled over a stool and fell in the dark; He stumbled (his way) through his performance; the story of how I* **stumbled into** (= became involved in) *lexicography; I* **stumbled across** or **upon** (= happened to find) *what I was looking for.* —*n.* **1** a stumbling. **2** a mistake or wrong act.
—**stum.bler** *n.*
stumbling block *n.* a hindrance or obstacle: *the main stumbling block to progress in the negotiations.*
stump *n.* **1** the part of a tree trunk remaining in the ground after the tree has been felled. **2** something resembling it, as an amputated limb; stub. **3** a political campaigner's speaking platform: *six months on the stump;* **adj.:** *a stump speaker, speech, theme.*
—*v.* **1** walk stiffly, as if on wooden legs. **2** make political speeches: *politicians stumping the country; They go stumping for votes; stumping for their favorite candidates; stumping to get them elected.* **3** *Informal.* perplex or confound; floor: *He was stumped by the strange happenings.*

stump.y *adj.* short and thick: *a stumpy fellow; stumpy legs.*

stun *v.* **stuns, stunned, stun.ning** make dizzy, as by a blow: *I was stunned by the news; stunned to learn of her death;* **adj.:** *I sat there **stunned**; a stunned audience, look, nation; in stunned disbelief; a stunned moment, silence.*

stung *pt. & pp.* of STING.

stun gun *n.* a hand-held weapon for giving a stunning electrical shock.

stunk a *pt. & pp.* of STINK.

stun.ner *n.* something that stuns.

stunning *adj.* 1 remarkable or striking: *a stunning beauty, example, impression, majority, sight, success, victory; He looks stunning in that outfit.* 2 shocking: *a stunning announcement, defeat, revelation.* —**stun.ning.ly** *adv.*

stunt *v.* 1 check growth or development: *factors stunting growth;* **adj.:** *a **stunted** tree.* 2 do a stunt. —*n.* a feat to attract attention or show one's daring, as at a circus: *to do or perform a stunt; a publicity stunt.* —**stunt man** or **stunt woman** *n.*

stu.pe.fy (STEW.puh.fye) *v.* **-fies, -fied, -fy.ing** 1 cause stupor in someone: *to be stupefied with drink, drugs.* 2 stun: *She was stupefied at the sight of the wreck.* —**stu.pe.fac.tion** (-FAC.shun) *n.*

stu.pen.dous (stew.PEN.dus) *adj.* astonishing, esp. by immensity or greatness: *a stupendous achievement, feat, marvel, waste.*

stu.pid (STEW.pid) *adj.* showing lack of intelligence; silly: *stupid behavior, censorship, TV; a stupid answer, idea, joke, mistake; The President's aide told him, "It's your foreign policy, stupid!"* —**stu.pid.ly** *adv.* —**stu.pid.i.ty** (stew.PID.i.tee) *n.: the height of stupidity; monstrous, sheer, utter, wanton stupidity; the stupidities of our foreign policy.*

stu.por (STEW.pur) *n.* a dazed condition; numbness: *He was in a stupor; fell or went into a stupor; was found sleepwalking in a kind of stupor; a drunken, mindless stupor; a syndrome marked by stupor.* —**stu.por.ous** (-rus) *adj.*

stur.dy (STUR.dee) *adj.* **-di.er, -di.est** strong and hardy, esp. in build or growth: *a sturdy build, construction, defender, limb, oak, race; her sturdy common sense.* —**stur.di.ly** *adv.;* **stur.di.ness** *n.*

stur.geon (STUR.jun) *n.* a large food fish that yields caviar and isinglass.

stut.ter (STUT.ur) *v.* stammer, esp. by repeating the first sound of a word; also *n.* —**stut.ter.er** *n.*

St. Vi.tus's dance (-VYE.tus.iz) See CHOREA.

sty *n.* **sties** 1 a pen for pigs; hence, any filthy place. 2 also **stye**, *pl.* **sties** a small pus-filled inflammation on the rim of an eyelid.

Styg.i.an (STIJ.ee.un) *adj.* 1 having to do with the **Styx**, a river of Greek myth that dead souls had to cross on their way to Hades. 2 dark or gloomy: *a Stygian eyesore;* also **stygian.**

style *n.* 1 distinctiveness in one's way of living that is indicative of taste or excellence: *She dresses and lives in style; a good sense of style; The fellow lacks style.* 2 fashion: *His hat is out of style; the latest styles.* 3 a distinctive manner of artistic expression or design: *affected, classic, elegant, flowery, ornate, vigorous styles; Shakespeare's style; built in the Byzantine style; Too many rules* **cramp one's style** (Informal for limit one's freedom). 4 a formal manner or mode: *the style of addressing clergy; a publisher's house style.* 5 a pointed device or structure, as a stylus, a phonograph needle, or the stem of a flower's pistil with the stigma at its top. —*v.* **styles, styled, styl.ing** 1 make or design according to a style: *clothes styled for comfort;* **n.:** *the styling of his hair* (= way it is styled). 2 call or name: *a dictator who had styled himself "emperor for life."*

styl.ish (STY.lish) *adj.* 1 according to the prevailing fashion; fashionable: *stylish apparel, clothing, looks, merchandise, outfits; She's stylish without being trendy.* 2 having style or class: *a stylish automobile, display, dresser, fashion, performance.* —**styl.ish.ly** *adv.;* **styl.ish.ness** *n.*

styl.ist *n.* one who is concerned with or is an expert in artistic style, esp. of written expression. —**sty.lis.tic** (-LIS.tic) *adj.;* **sty.lis.ti.cal.ly** *adv.*

styl.ize *v.* **-iz.es, -ized, -iz.ing** put something in a particular style of design; **adj.:** *The fleur-de-lis is a **stylized*** (= not realistic) *flower.*

sty.lus *n.* **-lus.es** or **-li** (-lye) a pointed instrument, as for engraving, cutting the grooves in or playing a phonograph record, etc.

sty.mie (STY.mee) *v.* **-mies, -mied, -my.ing** block or thwart: *Children taught in metric are stymied by imperial measurements; to stymie attempts, legislation, plans, progress.*

styp.tic (STIP.tic) *adj.* helping to stop bleeding; astringent: *a **styptic** pencil* (= stick of medication containing an astringent).

sty.ro.foam (STY.ruh.fome) *n.* a lightweight polystyrene: *the banning of styro-*

foam cups, packaging, plates, etc. to protect the environment; **Styrofoam** Trademark.

sua.sion (SWAY.zhun) n. Formal. persuasion: *a man of suasion, not muscle; moral suasion.*

suave (SWAHV) adj. polished and gracious in manner or style: *a suave and sophisticated performer; a suave hotel.*
—**suave.ly** adv.; **suave.ness** n.
—**suav.i.ty** n.

sub [short form] submarine; substitute; subordinate. —v. **subs, subbed, sub.bing** Informal. substitute *for someone.*

sub- prefix. **1** lower or under: *subalpine, subatomic, subcommittee, subcompact, subdivision, subheading, subroutine, subspecies, subzero.* **2** nearly: *subarctic, subtemperate, subtropical.*

sub.al.pine (sub.AL.pine) adj. **1** having to do with the lower slopes of the Alps: *subalpine Italy.* **2** growing below the tree line: *the subalpine forests of the Rockies; the subalpine fir, larch.*

sub.al.tern (sub.AWL.turn) n. & adj. subordinate.

sub.as.sem.bly (sub.uh.SEM.blee) n. an assembled unit that is a component of a larger unit.

sub.a.tom.ic (sub.uh.TOM.ic) adj. smaller than the atom: *subatomic particles such as protons and electrons.*

sub.com.mit.tee (SUB.cuh.mit.ee) n. a small committee under a larger one.

sub.com.pact (sub.COM.pact) n. an automobile smaller than a compact.

sub.con.scious (sub.CON.shus) adj. of thoughts and feelings, existing in the mind but not fully recognized.
—n. **the subconscious** the realm of subconscious mental processes.
—**sub.con.scious.ly** adv.

sub.con.ti.nent (sub.CON.tun.unt) n. a subdivision of a continent, as the Indian peninsula.

sub.con.tract (sub.CON.tract) n. a contract for carrying out part of a main contract. —v.: *A building contractor subcontracts plumbing, heating, and other installations.* —**sub.con.trac.tor** n.

sub.cul.ture (SUB.cul.chur) n. a social group within a larger group exhibiting a culture of its own: *the teen subculture; The prison subculture does not tolerate certain types of criminals.*

sub.cu.ta.ne.ous (sub.cue.TAY.nee.us) adj. under the skin: *a subcutaneous injection; subcutaneous fat.*

sub.dea.con (sib.DEE.cun) n. a cleric next below a deacon.

sub.di.vide (sub.di.VIDE) v. **-vides, -vid.ed, -vid.ing** divide further, as land into small lots; **sub.di.vis.ion** (-VIZH.un) n.

sub.due (sub.DEW) v. **-dues, -dued, -du.ing** overpower; hence, bring under control: *The intruder was subdued after a brief struggle; to subdue one's passions.*

subdued adj. softened or toned down: *in a subdued light, voice; subdued colors, tones; a subdued affair, atmosphere, look, response, role, version.*

sub.head n. a subordinate heading or division; also **sub.head.ing.**

sub.ject (SUB.jict) n. **1** a theme or topic of a conversation, study, etc.: *Algebra is his favorite subject; to address, avoid, bring up or broach, cover, deal with, discuss, drop, dwell on, exhaust, pursue, tackle, take up, treat a subject; to take (up) and master a subject; a delicate, ticklish, pleasant, thorny subject; on the subject of literacy; Let's not change the subject; when the subject comes up (for discussion).* **2** a person owing allegiance to a sovereign or ruler: *a British subject; a loyal subject of the Queen.* **3** one undergoing an investigation. **4** one chosen for artistic representation: *the subject of a portrait.* **5** in grammar, a word or term representing the one about whom something is said, as "Joan" in "Joan loves him," "Joan is here," and "Joan is loved by him." —adj. under another's rule; not independent: *a subject people.* —**subject to 1** owing obedience to a person or thing: *You're subject to the laws of your country.* **2** prone or liable to something: *Humans are subject to error.* **3** conditional upon something: *an arrangement subject to approval.*
—v. (sub.JECT) **1** bring under a rule or power: *They were never subjected by a foreign power.* **2 subject to** cause to undergo a treatment or experience something: *a country subjected to foreign domination; They were subjected to ridicule.* —**sub.jec.tion** (-JEC.shun) n.

sub.jec.tive (sub.JEC.tiv) adj. related to the person thinking, not to the object thought of; hence, personal: *a purely subjective opinion; a subjective approach, evaluation, impression, observation, reaction; subjective factors, values;*
sub.jec.tive.ly adv. —**sub.jec.tiv.i.ty** (-jec.TIV.i.tee) n.

subject matter n. content: *the subject matter of an agreement, course, poem, search; subject-matter experts used in training programs.*

sub.join (sub.JOIN) v. append.

sub ju.di.ce (sub.JOO.di.see) adv. Latin. of a case, before a court; awaiting

sub.ju.gate (SUB.juh.gate) *v.* **-gates, -gat.ed, -gat.ing** bring under slavish subjection; **sub.ju.ga.tion** (-GAY.shun) *n.*

sub.junc.tive (sub.JUNK.tiv) *n. & adj.* (a verb mood) expressing a possibility rather than an actuality, as in "I suggest he *be* present," or "If I *were* you...."

sub.lease *n.* a lease granted by a lessee. —*v.* **-leas.es, -leased, -leas.ing** grant or obtain a sublease.

sub.let (sub.LET) *v.* **-lets, -let, -let.ting** 1 let rented or leased property to another. 2 subcontract work.

sub.li.mate (SUB.luh.mate) *v.* **-mates, -mat.ed, -mat.ing** purify or refine, as by vaporizing and condensing a solid such as sulfur: *Sexual energy may be sublimated into religious activity; Is art sublimated sex?* —**sub.li.ma.tion** (-MAY.shun) *n.*

sub.lime (suh.BLIME) *adj.* so elevated or noble as to inspire awe and wonder: *sublime beauty, devotion, heights, virtue.* —**sub.lim.i.ty** (-BLIM.i.tee) *n.*

sub.lim.i.nal (sub.LIM.uh.nul) *adj.* of stimuli, learning processes, etc., barely perceived: *Toy commercials contain subtle, even subliminal suggestions to buy; subliminal advertising; a subliminal message; the subliminal* (= subconscious) *self.* —**sub.lim.i.nal.ly** *adv.*

sub.ma.chine gun (sub.muh.SHEEN-) *n.* a lightweight automatic or semiautomatic weapon with rapid-firing action.

sub.ma.rine (sub.muh.REEN) *adja.* underwater: *submarine cables, life, plants, warfare.* —*n.* 1 a ship designed for underwater operation: *a nuclear submarine; A submarine dives, surfaces.* 2 also **submarine sandwich**, a sandwich with a large roll sliced lengthwise and filled with cold cuts and vegetables; hero sandwich.

sub.merge (sub.MURJ) *v.* **-merg.es, -merged, -merg.ing** put or sink under a level or surface: *to submerge one's body in* or *under water; It's submerged beneath the surface; The town is submerged from view because of the surrounding hills; to submerge one's differences, identities, personalities; He submerged himself in work to forget his grief; adj.: to be completely, totally* **submerged;** *the conditions in which poor countries are submerged; submerged feelings, lands, memories, racism, realms, shoals, wrecks; Submarines operate submerged, not afloat.*
—**sub.mer.gence** *n.* —**sub.mer.sion** *n.*

sub.mers.i.ble (sub.MUR.suh.bul) *n. & adj.* (a diving vessel or other vehicle) that can operate under water.

sub.mi.cro.scop.ic (sub.my.cruh.SCOP.ic) *adj.* too tiny to be seen with an ordinary microscope.

sub.mis.sion (sub.MISH.un) *n.* 1 a submitting or something submitted: *to make a submission.* 2 obedience: *a life of submission to the monastic rule.*
—**sub.mis.sive** (-MIS.iv) *adj.*

sub.mit (sub.MIT) *v.* **-mits, -mit.ted, -mit.ting** 1 give way or yield to a treatment, situation, etc.: *to submit a question to arbitration; to submit to arbitrary measures.* 2 present as to a higher authority: *to submit a report to the president.* 3 claim or affirm: *I submit that you are mistaken.*

sub.or.bit.al (suh.BOR.bit.ul) *adj.* involving less than a full orbit: *a suborbital space flight.*

sub.or.di.nate (suh.BOR.duh.nit) *n. & adj.* 1 (a person or thing) that is below another in rank: *She is kind to her subordinates.* 2 (one) that is dependent: *"If," "since," "whether,"* etc. start **subordinate clauses** *in complex sentences.*
—*v.* (-nate) **-nates, -nat.ed, -nat.ing** make subordinate or subservient *to* something. —**sub.or.di.na.tion** (-NAY.shun) *n.*

sub.orn (suh.BORN) *v.* 1 induce a witness, etc. to commit perjury. 2 mislead or pervert: *to suborn the democratic system; loyal employees suborned by their sympathy for the plight of the poor.*
—**sub.or.na.tion** (sub.or.NAY.shun) *n.*

sub.plot *n.* a secondary or subordinate plot in a story.

sub.poe.na (suh.PEE.nuh) *n.* a legal written order requiring a person to appear or documents to be submitted in court: *to issue a subpoena for a witness to appear in court; A subpoena was served on him.* —*v.* **-naes, -naed, -nae.ing:** *The tapes were subpoenaed; were subpoenaed as evidence; to subpoena witnesses to testify.*

sub ro.sa (sub.ROH.zuh) *adv.* secretly; in confidence.

sub.scribe (sub.SCRIBE) *v.* **-scribes, -scribed, -scrib.ing** 1 pay or pledge a sum of money to a cause, fund, etc.: *to subscribe to a charity.* 2 agree to purchase: *to subscribe to a magazine; to subscribe for some shares in the company; The offer was over-subscribed.* 3 sign one's name at the bottom of a document. 4 give one's consent or approval: *to subscribe to an attitude, fallacy, measure, opinion; The majority in Iran subscribe to Islam.* —**sub.scrib.er** *n.*

sub.script *n. & adj.* (something) written low on the line, as the "2" of H₂O or underneath a character, as the cedilla of "ç."

sub.scrip.tion (sub.SCRIP.shun) *n.* a subscribing or the payment made: *to cancel a subscription; renew a subscription before it expires; money collected by public subscription; to raise a subscription for charity.*

sub.se.quent (SUB.si.kwunt) *adj.* coming after: *subsequent developments; subsequent to his arrest.* —**sub.se.quent.ly** *adv.*

sub.ser.vi.ent (sub.SUR.vee.unt) *adj.* slavishly serving; subordinate *to* someone. —**sub.ser.vi.ence** *n.*

sub.side (sub.SIDE) *v.* **-sides, -sid.ed, -sid.ing 1** sink to a lower or more normal level, as receding flood waters, loose earth, etc.: *The flood waters will subside.* **2** of anything agitated or rising, to become tranquil or quiet; abate: *Anger, fevers, noises, storms subside.* —**sub.si.dence** (SUB.sid.unce) *n.*

sub.sid.i.ar.y (sub.SID.ee.air.ee) *adj.* **1** auxiliary or secondary to something: *questions that are subsidiary to the main issue.* **2** allied in a subordinate capacity, as a corporation controlled by a parent company or holding company. —*n.*: *the American subsidiary of a British company.*

sub.si.dize (SUB.suh.dize) *v.* **-diz.es, -dized, -diz.ing** help with a subsidy: *Governments subsidize charities, education, farming, health care, training programs; adj.: The company provides subsidized meals for employees; subsidized farmers, goods, housing.* —**sub.si.di.za.tion** (-duh.ZAY.shun, -dye-) *n.*

sub.si.dy (SUB.si.dee) *n.* **-dies** money or other aid given by a government to farmers, schools, airlines, etc.: *to grant, provide a subsidy for a purpose, to an institution; farm, food, housing subsidies; a postal subsidy for publishers (to ship books at reduced rates).*

sub.sist (sub.SIST) *v.* continue to keep alive: *a poor family subsisting on low wages, on a near-starvation diet; They could barely subsist.*

sub.sist.ence (sub.SIS.tunce) *n.* sustenance; livelihood: *a bare, hand-to-mouth subsistence; their only means of subsistence.* —*adj.*: *a subsistence diet; the subsistence economy of poor nations; subsistence wages; subsistence farming that leaves no surpluses for sale.*

sub.soil *n.* the infertile two or three feet (60–90 cm) of soil beneath the topsoil.

sub.son.ic (sub.SON.ic) *adj.* slower than the speed of sound: *subsonic aircraft, travel.*

sub.stance (SUB.stunce) *n.* **1** what something consists of; material: *Margarine is a butterlike substance; a controlled substance such as a drug; toxic substances;* **substance abuse** (= abuse of alcohol, drugs, tobacco, etc.). **2** essence: *the substance of what he said; I agree with her* **in substance** (= in essentials). **3** solid quality; strength or soundness: *Is there any substance to those charges? He ate nothing* **of substance** *for 10 days; matters of substance; candidates, men, people, women of substance.*

sub.stan.dard (sub.STAN.durd) *adj.* below standard: *substandard living conditions; substandard English.*

sub.stan.tial (sub.STAN.shul) *adj.* **1** having substance: *a substantial meal, structure; There's nothing substantial about a dream; a substantial* (= considerable) *improvement.* **2** essential: *two versions in substantial agreement with each other.* —**sub.stan.tial.ly** *adv.*

sub.stan.tiate (sub.STAN.shee.ate) *v.* **-ates, -at.ed, -at.ing** establish something by giving evidence: *to substantiate an allegation, charge, claim, opinion.* —**sub.stan.ti.a.tion** (-AY.shun) *n.*

sub.stan.tive (SUB.stun.tiv) *adj.* having substance: *We want a substantive discussion, not a symbolic one; a substantive issue, majority, report, study.* —**sub.stan.ti.val** (-TYE.vul) *adj.*

sub.sta.tion (SUB.stay.shun) *n.* a branch station: *electrical, postal, power substations.*

sub.sti.tute (SUB.sti.tute) *n.* a person or thing that takes the place of another: *a sugar substitute like saccharin; a substitute for sugar; Coffee whiteners are nondairy cream substitutes; a poor substitute; A* **substitute teacher** *fills in when a staff teacher is absent.* —*v.* **-tutes, -tut.ed, -tut.ing** replace: *In some countries, coffee is substituted with dandelion roots; Margarine substitutes for* (= takes the place of) *butter.* —**sub.sti.tu.tion** (-TUE.shun) *n.*

sub.stra.tum (SUB.stray.tum, -strat.um) *n., pl.* **-ta** or **-tums** a supporting lower layer or stratum.

sub.struc.ture (SUB.struc.chur) *n.* a supporting structure or part, as a building's foundation.

sub.sume (sub.SOOM) *v.* **-sumes, -sumed, -sum.ing** bring an idea, example, etc. under something larger, as a class, group, or rule: *meanings subsumed under a single term; to subsume various issues into a comprehensive plan.*

sub.sur.face (sub.SUR.fis) *adj.* near the

surface: *subsurface damage, skin layer, soil movements, water reservoirs.*

sub.teen (SUB.teen) *n.* a child approaching the age of 13.

sub.ter.fuge (SUB.tur.fyooj) *n.* (deception by means of) a trick or stratagem.

sub.ter.ra.ne.an (sub.tuh.RAY.nee.un) *adj.* **1** underground: *subterranean channels, cities, levels.* **2** secret or hidden: *a subterranean chamber, community, route, world.*

sub.text *n.* an underlying or hidden theme.

sub.ti.tle (SUB.tye.tul) *n.* **1** a secondary or explanatory title, as of a book. **2** printed matter such as translated dialogue shown on a TV or movie screen. —*v.* **-tles, -tled, -tling**: *a book subtitled "A true story"; The producer decided on subtitling instead of dubbing the film for English TV.*

sub.tle (SUT.ul) *adj.* **-tler, -tlest 1** difficult to perceive by mind or sense, being too fine or delicate; not immediately obvious: *a subtle distinction, flavor, hint, joke.* **2** having or showing a keen or clever mind: *a subtle design, observer; a subtle* (= tricky) *scheme.* —**sub.tle.ty** *n.* **-ties**: *subtlety of expression; scientific subtleties; subtleties of color and tone.* —**sub.tly** (SUT.lee) *adv.*

sub.to.tal (SUB.toh.tul) *n.* a total to be added to others for a complete or "grand" total.

sub.tract (sub.TRACT) *v.* take away one number from another. —**sub.trac.tion** *n.*

sub.tra.hend (SUB.truh.hend) *n.* a number to be subtracted from another.

sub.trop.i.cal (sub.TROP.i.cul) *adj.* bordering on the tropics; hence, nearly tropical: *a subtropical climate, country, environment, region;* also **sub.trop.ic.**

sub.urb (SUB.urb) *n.* **1** a town, district, or community on the outskirts of a city: *a fashionable suburb.* **2** **the suburbs** *pl.* a city's residential outskirts. —**sub.ur.ban** (suh.BUR.bun) *adj.*

sub.ur.ban.ite (suh.BUR.buh.nite) *n.* one living in a suburb.

sub.ur.bi.a (sub.BUR.bee.uh) *n.* the suburbs: *offices moving to suburbia.*

sub.ven.tion (sub.VEN.shun) *n.* a subsidy or endowment.

sub.ver.sive (sub.VUR.siv) *adj.* tending to upset or overthrow something established: *a subversive political group; subversive activities, elements, propaganda; books considered subversive of the current system;* *n.*: *communists, radicals, and other subversives.* —**sub.ver.sive.ly** *adv.*

sub.vert (sub.VURT) *v.* overthrow or corrupt: *to subvert law, morality, religion.* —**sub.ver.sion** *n.*

sub.way *n.* **1** an underground railroad or its tunnel: *We travel to work by subway; riding the subways; It happened on the subway;* **adj.**: *subway cars, lines, platforms, riders, stations* or *stops, systems, trains.* **2** an underpass, as under a bridge.

suc.ceed (suc.SEED) *v.* **1** come after or follow, as in an office: *to succeed to the throne; Bush succeeded Reagan as U.S. President.* **2** be successful in one's purpose: *The army succeeded in overthrowing the civilian rulers.*

suc.cess (suc.SES) *n.* **1** wished-for result or outcome, esp. good fortune: *to achieve, attain, enjoy success; meet with success; He had great success in life; a success story.* **2** a person or thing that is successful: *The play was a success; a howling, huge, resounding, roaring, total, tremendous, unqualified success; a box-office success; a commercial success; It was a success with the general public.*

suc.cess.ful (suc.SES.ful) *adj.* having success: *She's highly successful in business; successful at making money; a successful business, move, plan, project.* —**suc.ces.ful.ly** *adv.*

suc.ces.sion (suc.SESH.un) *n.* **1** the act of succeeding or the right to succeed another: *Queen Elizabeth's succession to the throne in 1952.* **2** a coming, one after another, of people or events: *They acquired many companies in quick succession; a succession* (= series) *of calamities; It snowed for five days* **in succession** (= in a row).

suc.ces.sive (suc.SES.iv) *adj.* coming one after another in series: *It snowed on five successive days.* —**suc.ces.sive.ly** *adv.*

suc.ces.sor (suc.SES.ur) *n.* one that succeeds another.

suc.cinct (suc.SINCT) *adj.* concise and compact in expression: *a succinct statement, style, summary, survey, writer; clear and succinct.* —**suc.cinct.ly** *adv.*: *He expressed it* or *put it succinctly;* **suc.cinct.ness** *n.*

suc.cor (SUC.ur) *v.* help or aid in time of need: *to succor the refugees, runaways, wounded;* *n.*: *to give, lend, offer succor to terrorists.* Also **suc.cour** *Cdn.*

suc.co.tash (SUC.uh.tash) *n.* kernels of sweet corn and lima beans cooked together.

suc.cu.lent (SUC.yuh.lunt) *adj.* juicy or fleshy: *succulent dishes, plants, sausages; a crisply browned and succulent turkey.*

—*n.* a fleshy plant adapted for storing water, as cactuses and agaves.
—**suc.cu.lence** or **suc.cu.len.cy** *n.*

suc.cumb (suh.CUM) *v.* yield or give way, as from weakness: *to succumb to peer pressure, to temptation; He soon succumbed to his injuries* (= died).

such *adj.* of the kind specified or suggested: *He was such a great poet; He said no such thing; She didn't say any such thing; He did say some such thing; Take such books as you can read in one day; Shakespeare, Milton, and such poets; poets* **such as** *Shakespeare and Milton.* —*adv.* to that degree: *a woman of such fine manners.* —*pron.* such a one or ones: *Such was not my intention; A debtor,* **as such,** *owes something to someone; communists, fellow travelers,* **and such** (= such people). —**such and such** (something) unspecified: *Even if such and such is true, it doesn't prove a thing; such and such a person.*

such.like *pron.* people or things of such a kind: *We sell books, periodicals, films, and suchlike;* **adj.:** *TV, films, and suchlike media.*

suck *v.* **1** draw in a fluid, esp. a liquid, as by using the lips: *An infant sucks (milk from) its mother's breast; He likes to suck oranges; He sucks on his pipe while thinking; A vacuum cleaner sucks in dust; Sponges suck up moisture; A tornado could suck your swimming pool dry; Good students don't have to* **suck up to** (*Informal* for be slavish to) *their teachers;* **adj.:** *the* **sucking** *action of a pump; sucking insects, sounds.* **2 sucks** *Slang.* is disgusting: *Algebra sucks.* —*n.* the act of sucking; suction.

suck.er *n.* **1** one that sucks, as a family of fishes with thick lips. **2** a sucking organ, as the roots of a parasitic plant, or a disk-shaped clinging organ, as on the tentacles of an octopus. **3** a lollipop. **4** *Slang.* one who is easily cheated or fooled: *He's a sucker for any sob story; They can't make suckers out of us;* **v.:** *We shall not be suckered.*

suck.le (SUCK.ul) *v.* **-les, -led, -ling** feed at the breast or udder: *Mammals suckle their young.*

suck.ling *n.* a child or animal that is not yet weaned: *a mere suckling;* **adj.:** *a suckling infant, pig.*

su.crose (SOO.crose) *n.* common table sugar, obtained from sugar cane and beets.

suc.tion (SUC.shun) *n.* sucking; the process by which a fluid is drawn up, as through a drinking straw, or by which a concave pad or disk sticks to a surface: *vacuum-cleaner suction; abortion by suction; to apply suction to a catheter;* **adj.:** *suction power; a suction cup, fan, hose, pump.* —*v.*: *to suction a choking child; to suction out fat deposits; removal of fetal tissue by suctioning and curettage.*

sud.den (SUD.un) *adj.* happening, met with, done, etc. unexpectedly or hastily: *a sudden death in a car crash; a sudden descent, turn; It came to a sudden stop; a sudden rush of wind; a sudden decision on the eve of the wedding not to get married; a* **sudden death** *overtime play for breaking a tie which ends when one side scores a goal or point; It happened* **all of a sudden** (= suddenly). —**sud.den.ly** *adv.*; **sud.den.ness** *n.*

suds *n.pl.* [takes *pl. v.*] **1** *Informal.* beer; also, the foam or froth. **2** soapy water; also, the bubbles formed on it: *soap suds; clothes washers with suds-savers.* —*v. Informal.* wash in suds or form suds: *No need to suds it so much.*
—**suds.y** (SUD.zee) *adj.*: *sudsy water; Soap operas are sudsier* (= more sentimental) *than regular operas.*

sue (SOO) *v.* **sues, sued, su.ing 1** take legal action against someone: *He threatened to sue; He sued his doctor; sued for malpractice; sued for one million dollars.* **2** plead or solicit respectfully: *to sue for a favor, for peace.*

suede or **suéde** (SWADE) *n.* soft leather for coats, casual shoes, etc. made by raising a velvety nap on the flesh side of tanned animal hide; **adj.:** *a suede coat, vest; suede shoes.*

su.et (SOO.it) *n.* hard fat around the kidneys and loins of sheep and cattle.

suf.fer (SUF.ur) *v.* undergo pain, harm, loss, or anything hard to bear: *We had to suffer much because of the strike; Businesses suffered; They suffered great losses; suffered harm, insults; He's suffering from measles;* "*Suffer* (= allow) *the little children to come unto me*"; *an efficient executive who doesn't suffer* (= put up with) *fools gladly.* —**suf.fer.er** *n.*

suf.fer.ance (SUF.ur.unce) *n.* **1** passive toleration: *He is carrying on at the sufferance of his employer; an unwanted employee kept* **on sufferance** (instead of being fired). **2** suffering capacity.

suffering *n.* **1** the bearing of pain, harm, loss, etc.: *a life of suffering.* **2** what is suffered; pain: *the sufferings of the poor; to alleviate, bear, cause, ease, endure, inflict, relieve suffering; great, intense, untold suffering.*

suf.fice (suh.FICE) *v.* **suf.fic.es, suf.ficed, suf.fic.ing** be sufficient or enough: *$100 will suffice (for expenses); $100 suffices to meet our expenses; A light supper will suffice* (= satisfy) *us*; **Suffice it to say** (= Let it be sufficient to say) *that he is sorry for what happened.*

suf.fi.cient (suh.FISH.unt) *adj.* of a quantity or scope that satisfies needs; enough: *food sufficient for everyone; not sufficient evidence to lay charges; the necessary and sufficient conditions for becoming a citizen;* **suf.fi.cient.ly** *adv.*
—**suf.fi.cien.cy** *n.*

suf.fix (SUF.ix) *n.* **1** a word part added to the end of a word to form derivatives, as "-ly," "-ness," and "-y." **2** an inflectional ending such as "-ed," "-ing," or "-s."

suf.fo.cate (SUF.uh.cate) *v.* **-cates, -cat.ed, -cat.ing** choke or stifle because of insufficient oxygen or fresh air: *A drowning person suffocates; He was suffocated by carbon monoxide fumes; adj.: They found city life quite* **suffocating**; *a suffocating atmosphere, effect; to live under suffocating conditions; a suffocating debt; his suffocating smugness.*
—**suf.fo.ca.tion** (-CAY.shun) *n.*

suf.fra.gan (SUF.ruh.gun) *n.* a bishop subordinate to an archbishop; also, an assistant bishop; *adja.: a suffragan bishop, see.*

suf.frage (SUF.rij) *n.* the right to vote; franchise: *adult, universal, women's suffrage; to extend or grant suffrage to the minorities.* —**suf.fra.gist** (-ruh.jist) *n.*

suf.fra.gette (suf.ruh.JET) *n.* a woman advocating women's right to vote: *a leader of the suffragette movement.*

suf.fuse (suh.FUZE) *v.* **suf.fus.es, suf.fused, suf.fus.ing** fill a face, the sky, etc. with a spreading color, light, moisture, etc.: *a room suffused with sunlight; Her face was suffused with warmth.*
—**suf.fu.sion** (-FEW.zhun) *n.* an overspreading.

sug.ar (SHOOG.ur, short "OO") *n.* a sweet carbohydrate obtained esp. from the tall tropical grass called **sugar cane** or from **sugar beet** and used as a sweetener of foods: *to produce, refine sugar; beet, blood, cane, fruit, maple sugar; brown, crude, granulated, lump sugar; a lump of sugar; table sugar; a sugar cube; a **sugar bush** of sugar maples; adj.: a **sugared** cereal, drink, product.*
—**sug.ar.y** *adj.*

sug.ar.coat (shoog.ur.COAT) *v.* cover, esp. something unpleasant, with sugar; *adj.: a **sugarcoated** pill.*

sugar maple *n.* a variety of maple whose sweet sap is the chief source of maple sugar and maple syrup.

sug.ar.plum (SHOOG.ur.plum) *n.* a round piece of candy; *adja.: sugarplum* (= sweet) *dreams, fairies, visions.*

sug.gest (sug.JEST, suh-) *v.* **1** put forward an idea or proposal, as for consideration: *She suggests adjourning for the day; He suggests a coffee break; I suggest we have lunch; the various alternatives suggested to us.* **2** bring to mind, as by association of ideas: *the appropriate action suggested by the circumstances; the alternatives that seem to suggest themselves.*

sug.gest.i.ble (sug.JES.tuh.bul, suh-) *adj.* easily influenced by suggestion from outside the mind: *Children are suggestible, hence no late-night TV for them.* —**sug.gest.i.bil.i.ty** (-BIL.i.tee) *n.*

sug.ges.tion (sug.JES.chun, suh-) *n.* **1** a suggesting or what is suggested: *Any suggestions? to act on, adopt, ask for, call for, invite, offer, put forward, reject a suggestion; appropriate, helpful, preposterous suggestions; a suggestion about what to do next; She made a suggestion that we adjourn for the day; At my suggestion, we adjourned for lunch.* **2** a hint or trace: *a suggestion of alcohol, drugs, impropriety, scandal, wrongdoing.*

sug.ges.tive (sug.JES.tiv, suh-) *adj.* **1** suggesting new things besides what is known: *a suggestive bibliography, commentary, reading list; language that is suggestive* (= indicative) *of prejudice.* **2** suggesting something improper: *a suggestive dance; suggestive pictures, winks.* —**sug.ges.tive.ly** *adv.*;
sug.ges.tive.ness *n.*

su.i.cid.al (soo.uh.SYE.dul) *adj.* **1** leading to suicide; disastrous to oneself: *a suicidal action, character; suicidal behavior, impulses, tendencies; Drunk driving is suicidal.* **2** having an urge to commit suicide: *a suicidal mental patient, person.*

su.i.cide (SOO.uh.cide) *n.* **1** the act of killing oneself intentionally: *to attempt, commit, contemplate suicide.* **2** one who commits suicide. —*adja.: The two killed themselves as the result of a suicide pact; the alarming suicide rate among youth.*

su.i ge.ne.ris (soo.ee.JEN.uh.ris) *adj.* Latin. in a class by oneself; unique.

suit (SOOT, long "OO") *n.* **1** a set of outer clothes for wearing together, as a jacket and trousers or skirt: *to try on a suit; bathing, business, custom-made, diving, gym, leisure, sailor, ski, space, sweat, three-piece suits; a child in his birthday suit* (= naked). **2** a suing or legal action: *to bring (a) suit for damages; to file (a) suit against the government; to contest, dismiss, lose, win a suit; civil, class-action, malpractice suits.* **3** any of the four sets of playing cards: *a trump suit.* **4** an entreaty or pleading, as for someone's love; hence, courtship. —**follow suit 1** play a card of the same suit as the previous player's. **2** follow the previous example: *The children jumped in the pool and the parents followed suit.* —*v.* be suitable for a person or thing; fit: *a speech that suits the occasion perfectly; She suits her vocabulary to the children's level; Nine o'clock will suit me fine; It suits me to a T; Suit yourself* (= Do as you please)! **adjp.**: *She is* **suited** (= fit) *for* or *to the job; quite suited to be a counselor.*

suit.a.ble (SOO.tuh.bul) *adj.* proper or appropriate: *We found the building eminently suitable for the purpose;* **suit.a.bly** *adv.* —**suit.a.bil.i.ty** (-BIL.i.tee) *n.*

suit.case *n.* a flat-sided rectangular traveling bag for clothes.

suite (SWEET) *n.* **1** a set of rooms forming a unit, as in a hotel: *bridal, executive, luxury, penthouse suites.* **2** a set of matched furniture: *a bedroom suite; a five-piece dining suite; a living-room suite.* **3** in music, a group of instrumental pieces of varying character with related themes, as Tchaikovsky's "Nutcracker Suite." **4** a group attending on an important person; retinue.

suiting (SOO.ting) *n.* fabric for suits.

suit.or (SOO.tur) *n.* **1** a man who courts a woman. **2** one who makes a petition. **3** one who sues.

su.ki.ya.ki (soo.kee.YAH.kee) *n.* a Japanese dish of sliced meat and vegetables, often cooked in a skillet at the table.

Suk.koth or **Suk.kot** (SOOK.us, SOO.kose) *n.* a Jewish festival commemorating the wanderings of the Israelites in the desert.

sul.fa (SUL.fuh) *adj.* having to do with a group of chemical compounds used against bacterial infections. —*n.* a sulfa drug.

sul.fa.nil.a.mide (sul.fuh.NIL.uh.mide) *n.* a sulfa drug once used to treat bacterial infections.

sul.fon.a.mide (sul.FON.uh.mide) *n.* any of the group of sulfa drugs including sulfanilamide.

sul.fate *n.* a salt or ester of sulfuric acid.

sul.fide *n.* a compound of sulfur with another element or radical.

sul.fite *n.* a salt or ester of sulfurous acid.

sul.fur *n.* a pale-yellow substance that burns with a stifling odor. —**sul.fur.ic** (sul.FEW.ric) *adj.* Also **sul.phur,** **sul.phur.ic** *Cdn.*

sul.fu.rous (SUL.fur.us) *adj.* **1** like burning sulfur in stench or heat: *sulfurous fumes; the sulfurous fires of hell.* **2** (*usu.* -FYOOR.us) of or containing sulfur: *sulfurous acid.* Also **sul.phur.ous** *Cdn.*

sulk *v.* be sulky: *He's still sulking over his defeat.* —*n.* a sulky spell: *He's usually in a sulk before breakfast; having* **the sulks** (= sulky mood).

sulk.y *adj.* **sulk.i.er, -i.est** moody and ill-humored: *a sulky refusal, scowl, silence.* —*n., pl.* **sulk.ies** a light, two-wheeled horse-racing carriage seating one person. —**sulk.i.ly** *adv.;* **sulk.i.ness** *n.*

sul.len (SUL.un) *adj.* gloomy and silent: *a sullen disposition, resentment, silence; sullen looks, skies.* —**sul.len.ly** *adv.;* **sul.len.ness** *n.*

sul.ly (SUL.ee) *v.* **sul.lies, sul.lied, sul.ly.ing** soil or defile the purity of something: *to sully one's reputation, character.*

sul.phur *Cdn.* SULFUR.

sul.tan (SUL.tun) *n.* a Moslem ruler: *the Sultan of Oman.*

sul.tan.a (sul.TAN.uh) *n.* **1** a sultan's wife, mother, sister, or daughter. **2** a seedless variety of raisin with a distinctive flavor.

sul.tan.ate (SUL.tuh.nate) *n.* a sultan's position, authority, or rule.

sul.try (SUL.tree) *adj.* **-tri.er, -tri.est** **1** sweltering; hot and moist: *the sultry days of summer; sultry weather.* **2** passionate or sexy: *a sultry belle, glance, siren.*

sum *n.* **1** an amount of money: *to raise a large sum (of money); a nominal, round, substantial, tidy sum; a lump sum as a severance payment.* **2** the total amount or quantity: *The sum of 4, 5, and 6 is 15; the sum* (= height) *of folly, happiness; the* **sum and substance** (= gist) *of what he said.* **3** an arithmetical problem: *She's good at (doing) sums.* —**in sum** in brief. —*v.* **sums, summed, sum.ming** *esp.* **sum up** summarize: *To sum up* or *Summing up, I think UFO's don't exist; to sum up arguments, evidence, opinions, the main points of a speech, views; I summed up his behavior as sheer folly; It could be summed up* (= briefly expressed) *in one word.*

su.mac or **su.mach** (SHOO.mac, SOO-) *n.* a trees or shrub with narrow, pinnate leaves, whose nonpoisonous species bear erect clusters of red berries while the poisonous ones have drooping clusters, usu. white in the "poison sumac."

sum.mar.ize (SUM.uh.rize) v. **-riz.es, -rized, -riz.ing** be or make a summary of something: *to summarize an essay; to summarize one's arguments; One word, namely "outdated," summarizes their policies.*

sum.ma.ry (SUM.uh.ree) n. **-ries** a brief statement giving the main points: *the summary of a book, case, speech;* **In summary** (= briefly), *I cannot agree with the speaker's views.* —*adj*. **1** brief and comprehensive: *a summary account.* **2** carried out without formalities, delays, etc.; prompt: *a summary action, dismissal, proceeding, trial; A **summary offense** (that is dealt with quickly) is less serious than an indictable offense.*
—**sum.mar.i.ly** *adv.*

sum.ma.tion (suh.MAY.shun) n. a summing up, as of arguments in a trial.

sum.mer (SUM.ur) n. the warmest season of the year: *a long hot summer; Schools close for the summer; Swimming pools are open during the summer;* **adj.**: *a summer camp, cottage, festival, resort, school, season; summer clothes, holidays, travel.* —*v.* spend the summer *in* or *at* a place. —**sum.mer.y** *adj.*: *summery clothes, scenes, weather.*

sum.mer.house (SUM.ur.house) n. a roofed but usu. not walled structure, as in a garden, to rest in during warm weather.

summersault same as SOMERSAULT.

summer sausage n. a smoked or dried sausage that keeps without spoiling in warm weather.

summer squash n. a quick-growing nontrailing squash such as zucchini that is harvested and used in the summer.

sum.mer.time (SUM.ur.time) n. the summer season.

sum.mit (SUM.it) n. **1** the highest point, level, or state: *to reach the summit of a mountain; We stood at the summit admiring the view; the summit of one's achievement, ambition, career.* **2** also **summit meeting**, a meeting of heads of state: *to hold a summit on disarmament; They met at a summit in Geneva; an economic summit of the leading industrial nations.*

sum.mit.ry (SUM.it.ree) n. international diplomacy by means of summit meetings.

sum.mon (SUM.un) v. **1** call formally or with authority: *Al was summoned to appear in court on a charge of embezzlement; The new appointees were summoned to the capital to be sworn in; The relatives were summoned to the dying man's bedside; a speech summoning the people to rebellion.* **2** order an assembly or group to come together: *to summon the legislature.* **3** call forth by an act of the will: *to summon (up) courage, energy, ghosts, images, memories, strength, words.*
—**sum.mon.er** *n.*

sum.mons (SUM.uns) n., pl. **sum.mons.es 1** a summoning, esp. to appear in court on a charge: *A traffic summons for careless driving was served on him; He was hit* or *slapped with a summons; was issued a summons; to issue a summons to appear in court; a judicial summons.* **2** call: *a summons to action; a summons for help.* —*v. Informal.* serve a summons on someone.

su.mo (SOO.moh) n. a Japanese form of wrestling; **adj.**: *sumo rings, wrestlers, wrestling.*

sump n. a pit or pool in which drained water collects, as in a cellar: *a **sump pump** to pump out the collected water.*

sump.tu.ous (SUMP.choo.us) *adj.* lavishly provided or richly furnished: *sumptuous clothes, feasts, lodgings, meals.*
—**sump.tu.ous.ly** *adv.*

sum total n. everything added up.

sun n. **1** often **Sun**, the bright heavenly body that rises in the east every day shedding light and heat on the earth: *The sun rises, sets, shines.* **2** its light and heat; sunshine: *the blazing, bright, hot, midday, tropical sun; to let in, shut out, sit in the sun.* **3** anything that is a source of light, warmth, glory, etc. **4** any sunlike star with planets orbiting around it. —**from sun to sun** from sunrise to sunset. —**a place in the sun** a favorable position in life. —**under the sun** (anywhere) in the world: *a way of life that offers everything under the sun; looking for something new under the sun.* —*v.* **suns, sunned, sun.ning** to warm or dry oneself in sunlight: *He lay sunning himself by the pool.*

sun.bath n. exposure of the body to sunlight or to a sunlamp.
—**sun.bathe** (SUN.baith, "th" as in "the") v. **-bathes, -bathed, -bath.ing.**

sun.beam (SUN.beem) n. a ray or beam of sunlight.

Sun.belt n. the warmer southern third of the U.S. as a region of great growth.

sun.bon.net (SUN.bon.it) n. a wide-brimmed bonnet for shading the face and neck from the sun.

sun.burn n. a burning of the skin by overexposure to the sun's rays.
—*v.* **-burns,** *pt. & pp.* **-burned** or **-burnt, -burn.ing** cause to get a

sunburn.
sun.burst *n.* 1 sunlight bursting through a break in the clouds. 2 a decoration with spreading rays around a center.
sun.dae (SUN.dee, -day) *n.* ice cream with a topping of fruits, nuts, syrup, etc.: *strawberry sundaes.*
Sun.day (SUN.dee, -day) *n.* the first day of the week, the Christian day of rest: *He came dressed in his Sunday best* (= best clothes).
sun.der (SUN.dur) *v.* [literary] put asunder; tear apart: *to sunder a relationship.*
sun.di.al (SUN.dye.ul) *n.* an ancient time-telling device consisting of a horizontal dial that is read by the position of the shadow cast on it by an erect pointer in its center.
sun.down *n.* sunset: *at sundown.*
sun.dries (SUN.drees) *n.pl.* sundry things: *sundries like detergents and paper towels; liquor, wine, and related sundries; paint and sundries;* **adj.:** *a sundries department, market, store.*
sun.dry (SUN.dree) *adj.* a. miscellaneous: *sundry articles, details, services, shops; sundry other matters; sundry others.*
—**all and sundry** everyone.
sun.fish *n.* 1 a brightly colored freshwater food and game fish with a roundish body. 2 an ocean fish with a silvery body, seen on the surface in sunny weather.
sun.flow.er (SUN.flow.er) *n.* a large flower with rays of yellow petals around a central disk of tiny brown, yellow, or purple flowers, yielding oily edible seeds.
sung *pp. & a pt.* of SING.
sun.glass.es (SUN.glas.iz) *n.pl.* tinted eyeglasses to protect the eyes from the sun.
sunk *pp. & a pt.* of SINK.
sunk.en (SUNK.un) *adj.* 1 submerged: *sunken ships, treasures.* 2 below the general level: *a sunken living room, terrace;* **adj.:** *sunken* (= hollow) *cheeks; sunken* (= depressed) *spirits.*
sun.lamp *n.* a lamp giving off ultraviolet rays, esp. one used therapeutically.
sun.light *n.* the light of the sun: *an arrow, flash, patch, shaft of sunlight; blinding, bright, brilliant, diffuse, glaring, harsh, reflected sunlight; bathed in sunlight; Keep the cactus out of direct sunlight; exposure to sunlight; in the autumn sunlight; from sunlight into shadow.*
sun.lit *adj.* lighted by the sun: *a sunlit patio, room, studio.*
sun.ny (SUN.ee) *adj.* **sun.ni.er, sun.ni.est** 1 full of sunshine: *a sunny day, room, side, sky.* 2 bright or cheerful: *a sunny disposition, smile; the sunny side* (= the more cheerful aspect) *of life.* —**sunny side up** of eggs, served fried on one side only, with the yolk on top.
sun parlor or **sun porch** *n.* a glass-covered room with a sunny exposure.
sun.rise *n.* the sun's coming up above the horizon or its time: *to get up at sunrise.*
sun.roof *n.* an automobile roof that is openable in part.
sun room same as SUN PARLOR.
sun.screen *n.* a lotion to protect the skin from the sun's ultraviolet rays.
sun.seek.er (SUN.see.kur) *n.* one who travels to a warmer and sunnier place in the winter.
sun.set *n.* 1 the sun's going down below the horizon, esp. the light and color accompanying it: *beautiful as a sunset; a sunset* (= variety) *of golds, oranges, and reds; to go off* **into the sunset** *(never to come back);* **adj.:** *sunset colors, hues, shades.* 2 the end of the day marked by the sunset: *It was near sunset; They met on the beach at sunset.* 3 the end of a period: *The breakup of the Soviet Union was sunset for communism; a* **sunset law** *ending wasteful government measures; v.: a provision in the law to sunset* (= end) *in five years.*
sun.shade *n.* 1 a parasol, awning, etc. used as protection against the sun's rays. 2 **sunshades** *pl. Informal.* sunglasses; shades.
sun.shine *n.* 1 the light and heat from the sun: *to lie on the beach soaking up sunshine; the bright, warm sunshine.* 2 cheerfulness: *to let the sunshine in; a ray of sunshine.* 3 openness: *a* **sunshine law** *requiring government agencies to conduct business openly; sunshine provisions, requirements.* —**sun.shin.y** (-shy.nee) *adj.*
sun.spot *n.* any of the dark spots appearing occasionally on the sun's surface.
sun.stroke *n.* a heatstroke caused by overexposure to the sun or other source of heat, marked by high fever and a dry skin: *to get or have a sunstroke.*
sun.suit *n.* a play outfit consisting of short pants with shoulder straps and a bib front.
sun.tan *n.* a tanning of the skin by exposure to the sun or to ultraviolet rays; **adj.:** *suntan lotions, oils, products.* —*v.* **-tans, -tanned, -tan.ning.**
sun.up *n.* the time of sunrise.
sup *v.* **sups, supped, sup.ping** 1 have

super / supermarket

supper: *We supped on* or *off soup and crackers.* **2** take sips or spoonfuls of a food. —*n.* a sip or mouthful.

su.per (SOO.pur) *adj.* superior in fineness, excellence, sophistication, or quality: *super clothes for super kids; a super secret; That's super!* —*adv.* very: *This is super secret; something super special.* —*n. Informal.* a supervisor or superintendent, as of an apartment building.

super- *prefix.* **1** over or above; hence, superior in rank, quality, degree, etc.: *superagency, superhuman, superman, supersalesman, supermodel, superstar, superwoman.* **2** extra or added; hence, in excess: *superadd, superfine, superheat, supernormal, supersize, supersubtle.*

su.per.a.bun.dant (SOO.pur.uh. BUN.dunt) *adj.* more than enough; **su.per.a.bun.dance** *n.*

su.per.an.nu.at.ed (soo.pur.AN.yoo.ay.tid) *adj.* retired and pensioned; too old for work or service: *The new product was superannuated before it could be marketed; superannuated athletes and movie stars.* —**su.per.an.nu.a.tion** (SOO.puh.ran.yoo.AY.shun): *premature superannuation;* **adj**a.: *a superannuation fund, scheme.*

su.perb (soo.PURB) *adj.* of the highest excellence, magnificence, or splendor: *a superb display, performance, view.* —**su.perb.ly** *adv.*

supercede same as SUPERSEDE.

su.per.charge (SOO.pur.charge) *v.* **-charg.es, -charged, -charg.ing 1** increase the power of an engine as in racing cars. **2** charge excessively: *to be supercharged with emotion, vigor;* **adj.**: *the supercharged atmosphere of the trial.*

su.per.cil.i.ous (soo.pur.SIL.ee.us) *adj.* contemptuous in a haughty way.

su.per.con.duc.tiv.i.ty (SOO.pur.con.duc.TIV.i.tee) *n.* absence of electrical resistance in metals such as lead and tin at temperatures near absolute zero. —**su.per.con.duc.tor** (-DUC.tur) *n.*

super-du.per (SOO.pur.DOO.pur) *adj. Informal.* excellent.

su.per.e.go (soo.pur.EE.goh) *n.* **-gos** in psychoanalytic theory, the part of the psyche that exercises a moral control on the ego.

su.per.em.i.nent (soo.pur.EM.uh.nunt) *adj.* eminent in an extraordinary or remarkable way.

su.per.er.o.ga.tion (SOO.pur.er.uh.GAY.shun) *n.* the doing of more than what religious duty requires: *works of supererogation.*

su.per.e.rog.a.to.ry (SOO.pur.uh.ROG.uh.tor.ee) *adj.* nonessential; superfluous.

su.per.fi.cial (soo.pur.FISH.ul) *adj.* **1** of the surface only: *a superficial burn, flaw, wound.* **2** shallow: *a superficial education, knowledge, look, person.* —**su.per.fi.cial.ly** *adv.* —**su.per.fi.ci.al.i.ty** (SOO.pur.fish.ee.AL.i.tee) *n.*

su.per.fine (SOO.pur.fine) *adj.* extra fine: *a superfine fiber, finish, skin, sugar, wool, worsted.*

su.per.flu.ous (soo.PUR.floo.us) *adj.* surplus or unnecessary: *superfluous advice, compliments, hair; to make* or *render a person* or *thing superfluous; to become superfluous.* —**su.per.flu.i.ty** (soo.pur.FLOO.i.tee) *n.* **-ties:** *a superfluity of talent.*

su.per.high.way (soo.pur.HIGH.way) *n.* a freeway with four or more lanes.

su.per.hu.man (soo.pur.HEW.mun) *adj.* exceeding normal human power or capacity: *superhuman efforts, strength; a superhuman* (= spiritual) *being.*

su.per.im.pose (SOO.pur.im.POZE) *v.* **-pos.es, -posed, -pos.ing** lay on top of something else, as different scenes blended on a TV screen.

su.per.in.tend (SOO.pur.in.TEND) *v.* act as superintendent.

su.per.in.ten.dent (SOO.pur.in.TEN.dunt) *n.* **1** a custodian or director, as of an educational body: *a school superintendent.* **2** a maintenance supervisor of a building: *a building superintendent.* —**su.per.in.ten.dence** (-dunce) *n.*

su.pe.ri.or (suh.PEER.ee.ur) *adj.* higher in excellence, quality, rank, etc.: *her superior ability, performance; He's far superior to anyone else; a superior court; a superior force; superior in numbers; Grade A eggs are superior to Grade B eggs; She proved herself superior to* (= above) *petty jealousies; his superior* (= haughty) *manner.* —*n.* **1** a person or thing that is superior. **2** the head of a religious community. —**su.pe.ri.or.i.ty** (-ee.OR.i.tee) *n.*

su.per.jet (SOO.pur.jet) *n.* a supersonic jet airplane.

su.per.la.tive (soo.PUR.luh.tiv) *adj.* of the highest kind or degree: *superlative praise, wisdom; a superlative adjective such as "best," "wisest,"* or *"most beautiful."* —*n.* one that is superlative or of the highest degree: *He speaks in superlatives* (= exaggerated words like "amazing," "astounding," "ideal," and "unique"). —**su.per.la.tive.ly** *adv.*

su.per.mar.ket (SOO.pur.mar.kit) *n.* a large, self-service retail store, esp. one

of a chain of food stores.
su.per.nal (soo.PUR.nul, short "oo") *adj.* heavenly; exalted.
su.per.nat.u.ral (soo.pur.NACH.ur.ul) *adj.* not explainable by the laws of nature; spiritual or divine: *a supernatural being such as an angel or devil; supernatural phenomena.* —**su.per.nat.u.ral.ly** *adv.*
su.per.no.va (soo.pur.NOH.vuh) *n.* **-vae** (-vee) or **-vas** a nova of unusual brilliance.
su.per.nu.mer.ar.y (soo.pur.NEW.muh.rair.ee) *adj. & n.* **-ar.ies** (one) that is more than the required number; extra.
su.per.pose (soo.pur.POZE) *v.* **-pos.es, -posed, -pos.ing** same as SUPERIMPOSE. —**su.per.po.si.tion** (-puh.ZISH.un) *n.*
su.per.pow.er (SOO.pur.pow.er) *n.* any of the two or three most powerful nations: *Japan is an industrial superpower.*
su.per.sat.u.rate (soo.pur.SACH.uh.rate) *v.* **-rates, -rat.ed, -rat.ing** saturate a solution to excess using heat; **su.per.sat.u.ra.tion** (SOO.pur.sach.uh.RAY.shun) *n.*
su.per.scribe (SOO.pur.scribe) *v.* **-scribes, -scribed, -scrib.ing** write above or on top of something. —**su.per.scrip.tion** (-SCRIP.shun) *n.*
su.per.script (SOO.pur.script) *n. & adj.* (a figure or symbol) written raised above a letter or line, as the "2" in "x²y".
su.per.sede (soo.pur.SEED) *v.* **-sedes, -sed.ed, -sed.ing** succeed or take the place of something, as being better or more modern: *New laws supersede the old; Has New York superseded Paris as the center of fashion?*
su.per.son.ic (soo.pur.SON.ic) **1** *adj.* faster than sound: *supersonic flight, speed, transport.* **2 supersonics** *n.pl.* the science of supersonic phenomena, esp. sound waves.
su.per.star (SOO.pur.star) *n.* an exceptionally successful star in sports or entertainment.
su.per.sti.tion (soo.pur.STISH.un) *n.* a belief or practice considered irrational, as knocking on wood for good luck or believing that spilling salt is a bad omen. —**su.per.sti.tious** (-us) *adj.*
su.per.struc.ture (soo.pur.STRUCK.chur) *n.* **1** a structure built on top of another. **2** the part of a building above its foundation.
su.per.tank.er (SOO.pur.tank.ur) *n.* a very large oil tanker.
su.per.vene (soo.pur.VEEN) *v.* **-venes, -vened, -ven.ing** of a condition or process, succeed or take place unexpectedly; **su.per.ven.tion** (-VEN.shun) *n.*
su.per.vise (SOO.pur.vize) *v.* **-vis.es, -vised, -vis.ing** direct or oversee people or what they do: *Teachers supervise students; to supervise a ceremony, class, construction, department; to supervise sports, the staff, the care of children.* —**su.per.vi.sion** (-VIZH.un) *n.*: *He was raised under her strict supervision.* —**su.per.vi.sor** (-vye.zur) *n.* —**su.per.vi.so.ry** (-VYE.zuh.ree) *adj.*
su.per.wom.an (SOO.pur.woom.un) *n.* a woman who can cope with the demands of being a career woman, mother, and spouse.
su.pine (soo.PINE) *adj.* **1** flat on the back: *to lie supine; in the supine position.* **2** passive or lazy: *a supine attitude.*
sup.per (SUP.ur) *n.* an evening meal; the last meal of the day. —**sup.per.time** *n.*
supper club *n.* a nightclub.
sup.plant (suh.PLANT) *v.* replace (as if) by use of force or fraud: *a dictator supplanted by the army; Robots supplant workers.*
sup.ple (SUP.ul) *adj.* easily bending or flexing without damage or strain: *a supple vine; supple as leather; a gymnast's supple limbs; a supple mind, prose style.* —**sup.ple.ness** *n.* —**sup.ply** (SUP.lee) *adv.*
sup.ple.ment (SUP.luh.munt) *n.* an addition that makes something better or fuller: *vitamins added as food supplements; vitamin supplements; Annual supplements update an encyclopedia; a newspaper's advertising, literary, Sunday supplements.* —*v.* (sup.luh.MENT) add to something: *Spare-time jobs supplement his income.* —**sup.ple.men.tal** (-MEN.tul) *adj.*: *supplemental compensation, coverage, funding, income, loans, programs; One is supplemental to the other.* —**sup.ple.men.ta.ry** (-MEN.tuh.ree) *adj.*: *Two supplementary angles make up 180 degrees, each being supplementary to the other; a supplementary budget, dose, effort, question, source, statement; a supplementary (airbag) restraint system; supplementary arguments, benefits, lighting, materials, n.: The Speaker allowed the M.P.s to ask a few supplementaries* (= additional questions).
sup.pli.ant (SUP.lee.unt) *n. & adj.* (one) who supplicates; also **sup.pli.cant** (-kunt).
sup.pli.cate (SUP.li.cate) *v.* **-cates, -cat.ed, -cat.ing** pray for or ask a favor of humbly: *The prisoners supplicated*

the king for mercy. —**sup.pli.ca.tion** (-CAY.shun) *n.*

sup.ply (suh.PLY) *v.* **sup.plies, sup.plied, sup.ply.ing** give or provide: *to supply food to the hungry; to supply them with food; a need that is not hard to supply* (= satisfy); *Lou likes to supply* (= fill in as a substitute) *in place of absent colleagues.*
—*n., pl.* **sup.plies** a supplying or a quantity of a needed item supplied: *the economic forces of supply and demand; abundant, fresh, liberal, plentiful supplies; office supplies such as stationery; Supply lines were cut by the enemy; Water is* **in short supply** (= scarce) *during a drought; to lay in* **supplies** (= stores or provisions) *for the winter; relief supplies.* —**sup.pli.er** *n.* See also **SUPPLE**.

supply-side *adja.* having to do with the economic policy of lowering taxes as an incentive for higher production and investment: *supply-side economics.*

supply teacher *n.* a substitute teacher.

sup.port (suh.PORT) *v.* **1** hold up: *stakes to support a tomato plant.* **2** maintain or provide for something: *Oxygen is required to support life; enough income to support a family of four.* **3** back up: *A seconder supports a motion; a charge not supported by evidence;* **adja.**: *a star and* **supporting** *actors (in subsidiary roles); the supporting cast; supporting efforts, evidence, forces.* **4** [used with "can," "cannot"] tolerate in existence; bear or endure: *I cannot support this situation any longer.* —*n.* a supporting, one that supports, or a means of support: *The movement lacked support; demonstrations in support of strikers' demands; The breadwinner is the support of a family; to draw, gain, lend, mobilize, pledge, provide, receive, round up, win support; active, liberal, loyal, qualified, popular, solid, strong, unqualified, wholehearted support; the support of the people.* —**sup.port.a.ble** *adj.* —**sup.port.er** *n.*

sup.port.ive (suh.POR.tiv) *adj.* giving support: *supportive evidence; professional and supportive staff; Parents were supportive of teacher's demands; They were supportive during the negotiations.*

sup.pose (suh.POZE) *v.* **sup.pos.es, sup.posed, sup.pos.ing** assume; take for granted: *Let's suppose there is life on Mars; Who do you suppose this is? Do creatures suppose a creator?* **Supposing** (= assuming) *there is life on Mars, so what?* —**sup.pos.i.tion** (sup.uh.ZISH.un) *n.*

supposed (suh.POZED) *adj.* assumed or taken for granted: *the supposed injustice; Life on Mars is more supposed than real; You're not* **supposed** (= allowed) *to smoke here.* —**sup.pos.ed.ly** (-POH.zid.lee) *adv.*

sup.pos.i.to.ry (suh.POZ.uh.tor.ee) *n.* **-ries** a small cone or cylinder of a medicated substance put into a body cavity such as the rectum or vagina.

sup.press (suh.PRES) *v.* put down by force; keep under; keep back: *to suppress a newspaper, riot, yawn; to suppress freedom of speech, the truth; consciously to suppress desires, memories, thoughts.* —**sup.pres.si.ble** *adj.* —**sup.pres.sion** (-PRESH.un) *n.*

sup.pres.sant (suh.PRES.unt) *n.* one that suppresses: *Codeine is a cough suppressant.* —**sup.pres.sive** (-iv) *adj.*: *suppressive laws.*

sup.pu.rate (SUP.yuh.rate) *v.* **-rates, -rat.ed, -rat.ing** form or discharge pus; **sup.pu.ra.tion** (-RAY.shun) *n.*

su.pra (SOO.pruh) *adv.* Latin. above or earlier: *See footnote supra.*

supra- *prefix.* above; beyond: *supranational, supraorbital, supravital.*

su.pra.na.tion.al (soo.pruh.NASH.uh.nul) *adj.* above the level of individual nations: *Multinational corporations wield supranational power; a supranational corporation, organization.*

su.prem.a.cist (suh.PREM.uh.sist) *n.* one who believes in the supremacy of a specified group: *male supremacists; white supremacists;* **adja.**: *white supremacist groups, ideology, literature.*

su.prem.a.cy (suh.PREM.uh.see) *n.* **-cies** the state of being supreme; supreme authority: *to achieve, establish supremacy; military, naval, papal, state supremacy; to gain supremacy over other nations.*

su.preme (suh.PREEM) *adj.* **1** highest in authority or power: *The will of the people should be supreme or* **reign supreme** *in a democracy; NATO's Supreme Allied Commander in Europe; God as* **Supreme Being;** *the* **Supreme Court** *of a country; the* **supreme court** *of a state or province; the* **Supreme Soviet** *of the former U.S.S.R.* **2** highest in degree or quality: *supreme courage, effort, happiness, sadness; the supreme attribute of immortality; He lives in supreme ignorance of what's going on around him; the supreme moment of his life when he got married; the* **supreme sacrifice** *(of one's life).* —**su.preme.ly** *adv.;* **su.preme.ness** *n.*

sur- *prefix.* over or above; additional: *surcharge, surname, surplus, surreal, surtax.*

sur.cease (SUR.seece) *n.* end or cessation.

sur.charge (SUR.charge) v. **-charg.es, -charged, -charg.ing 1** overburden with a feeling. **2** charge extra: *The airlines surcharged regular fares to cover rising fuel costs.* **3** overprint with an extra charge: *to surcharge a postage stamp.* —n. **1** an extra charge: *A surcharge is added to the subscription for home delivery; a stamp bearing a surcharge of 10 cents.* **2** an excessive burden *of grief, etc.*

sur.cin.gle (SUR.sing.gul) n. a band or strap around a horse's body to secure a saddle, pack, etc.

sure (SHOOR) adj. **sur.er, sur.est 1** free from doubt: *Are you sure about the time? He is sure the watch is accurate; Please make sure of your facts; Make sure you have them right; She is sure* (= bound) *to succeed.* **2** reliable or unerring: *A smoking pistol is sure evidence of firing; a good sharpshooter with a sure aim; a sure remedy.*
—*adv.* Informal. surely. —**for sure** without doubt: *That's for sure.* —**sure enough** Informal. in fact; certainly. —**to be sure** surely. —**sure.ness** n.

sure-fire adj a. Informal. sure to succeed; definite: *a sure-fire prospect as a winner; a sure-fire bestseller, success, win, winner; a sure-fire way of making money.*

sure-footed adj. not likely to stumble or err: *a sure-footed performance.*

sure.ly adv. certainly: *Surely you have a better idea; Surely!*

sure.ty (SHOOR.i.tee) n. **-ties 1** security or assurance *against* loss, failure, etc. **2** one legally responsible for another's performance according to an agreement or obligation, as guaranteed by a bond; **adj**a.: *a surety agent, bond, company, writer; surety business, liability.*

surf n. **1** waves of the sea breaking on the shore. **2** the foam and thundering sound produced. —v. **1** ride the waves on a surfboard; **n**.: *the sport of surfing.* **2** browse: *to surf the Net.*
—**surf.er** n.

sur.face (SUR.fis) n. the outside of anything, as any of the faces of a solid figure, the top of a liquid, etc.: *the smooth surface of ice; the plane surface of a tabletop; the frozen surface of the lake; the rough surface of a stormy sea; below or beneath or under the surface of the ocean; The essay only skims the surface of the topic* (= treats it superficially); *You have only* **scratched the surface of** (= begun to understand) *the subject; He's gentle* **on the surface** *but can turn violent if provoked.* —**adj**a. **1** of or by the surface: *surface transit; a sur-*

face-to-air missile; **surface mail** (by land or water). **2** external: *a surface impression; mere surface* (= superficial) *friendships.* —v. **-fac.es, -faced, -fac.ing 1** provide with a smooth surface: *to surface a road.* **2** rise to the surface of the water, as a submarine.

surface tension n. a cohesive force existing on the surface of liquids, as shown in capillarity, etc.

surf.board n. a long, narrow, lightweight board used to ride on in the sport of surfing.

sur.feit (SUR.fit) n. **1** an excess of anything good, esp. food or drink. **2** the feeling of nausea resulting from such an excess. —v. feed or fill too much; **adj**.: *surfeited with food, riches; to be surfeited* (= sick) *of something.*

surge (SURJ) v. **surg.es, surged, surg.ing** move powerfully and suddenly in or like a swelling wave: *The crowd surged forward; House prices are surging ahead;* **adj**a.: *the surging crowds, flood waters, seas, waves.*
—n. a rushing wave or its onrush: *the surge of the sea; the surge of passion; A power surge during the storm blew a fuse.*

sur.geon (SUR.jun) n. a physician specialized in surgery.

surge protector n. a device for protecting equipment connected to a power line by shunting away excessive energy, as during an electrical storm.

sur.ger.y (SUR.juh.ree) n. **-ger.ies 1** the branch of medicine dealing with operations performed on the body to treat disease, injuries, and deformities. **2** a surgeon's work or a place where operations are done. —**sur.gi.cal** (-ji.cul) adj.; **sur.gi.cal.ly** adv.

sur.ly (SUR.lee) adj. **-li.er, -li.est** ill-tempered or rude. —**sur.li.ness** n.

sur.mise (sur.MIZE) n. & v. **-mis.es, -mised, -mis.ing** guess or conjecture: *to surmise about a likelihood or possibility; to surmise that it happened, may happen, or will happen.*

sur.mount (sur.MOUNT) v. **1** be or rise above: *a church spire surmounted by a cross; Her staff of office is a black wand surmounted by a gold lion.* **2** get over; hence, overcome; *to surmount barriers, challenges, crises, difficulties, hurdles, obstacles, problems, shortcomings.*
—**sur.mount.a.ble** (-tuh.bul) adj.

sur.name (SUR.name) n. a person's last name or family name.

sur.pass (sur.PASS) v. go beyond or be superior to a person or thing: *None surpassed Samson in strength; This surpasses* (= is beyond) *description.*

sur.plice (SUR.plis) *n.* a loose, white, usu. knee-length outer vestment worn in church by clergy and choir.

sur.plus (SUR.plus) *n.* **1** a quantity or amount left over after meeting needs: *farm surpluses of crops and livestock; a grain surplus.* **2** excess of assets over debts: *The **trade surplus** is a surplus of exports over imports; In the 1980s, Canada had an overall surplus in trade with the U.S.* —*adj.: surplus capacity, electricity, funds, milk; a surplus* (= not deficit) *budget.*

sur.prise (sur.PRIZE) *v.* **-pris.es, -prised, -pris.ing** come upon suddenly and unexpectedly: *He was surprised in the act of stealing; They were surprised* (= attacked when off guard) *by enemy troops; Your behavior surprises* (= astonishes) *me; adj.: a **surprising** amount, conclusion, fact; surprising results, strength, success; not surprising at all.*
—*n.* the act or feeling of being surprised: *She sprang a surprise on us; Everyone expressed surprise at the news; It was a complete or total surprise to us; a pleasant surprise to learn that he was getting married; To our surprise, no one had been told; The news was quite a surprise* (= something unexpected); *It **took us by surprise*** (= caught us unprepared); *Surprise, surprise — I'm expecting!*
—**sur.pris.ing.ly** *adv.*

sur.re.al (suh.REE.ul) *adj.* dreamlike or fantastic; unreal; also, surrealistic: *a surreal approach, effect, image, landscape, moment, scene, world.*

sur.re.al.ism (suh.REE.uh.liz.um) *n.* a movement in the art and literature of the 1920's to depict reality in unnatural and fantastic forms and images, as products of the unconscious mind; **sur.re.al.ist** *n. & adj.* —**sur.re.al.is.tic** (-LIS.tic) *adj.*

sur.ren.der (suh.REN.dur) *v.* give up a possession or right to something: *The enemy has surrendered; to surrender a fort to the enemy; He refused to surrender* (himself) *to the police; She surrendered her insurance policy for its cash value.*
—*n.* a surrendering: *an unconditional surrender.*

sur.rep.ti.tious (suh.rep.TISH.us) *adj.* done in a secret or stealthy manner: *surreptitious entry through a window; a surreptitious glance;* **sur.rep.ti.tious.ly** *adv.*

sur.rey (SUR.ee) *n.* **sur.reys** a four-wheeled, doorless, usu. flat-topped, two-seated pleasure carriage.

sur.ro.gate (SUR.uh.gate, -git) *n.* **1** a substitute or deputy: *He acts as the surrogate of the prime minister.* **2** a probate court judge. —*adj.* substitute: *a surrogate parent, uterus; A **surrogate mother** acts as mother for another woman by artificial insemination or by having a fertilized egg implanted in her and carrying the fetus through to delivery.*

sur.round (suh.ROUND) *v.* encircle or cause to be encircled: *Police surrounded the house; She surrounds herself with admirers; He lives surrounded by luxuries.*
—**surroundings** *n.pl.* environments: *He lives in austere surroundings; the elegant surroundings of a mansion; childhood, comfortable, familiar, natural, poor surroundings.*

sur.tax *n.* an extra tax on something already taxed, as on incomes above a certain level.

sur.tout (sur.TOO) *n.* an overcoat or frock-coat of the 19th century.

sur.veil.lance (sur.VAY.lunce) *n.* close watch kept over someone: *to maintain around-the-clock, close, constant, strict surveillance over a suspect; The police have placed him **under surveillance** as a suspect in the murder; adj.: a surveillance camera to record robberies; surveillance equipment; a surveillance helicopter, program, system.*

sur.vey (sur.VAY) *v.* look over or examine as a whole, as a tract of land using geometrical principles.
—*n.* (SUR.vay) a broad overall study or examination, as in surveying a tract of land, field of study, public opinion on a subject, a situation, etc.: *to conduct or do or make a survey; aerial, brief, comprehensive, general surveys.* —**sur.vey.ing** *n.;* **sur.vey.or** (sur.VAY.ur) *n.*

sur.vi.val (sur.VYE.vul) *n.* a surviving or something that has survived: *steps to assure the survival of the species; Some customs are survivals from ancient times; the **survival of the fittest** in the process of evolution; a **survival kit** containing food and emergency equipment.*

sur.vive (sur.VIVE) *v.* **-vives, -vived, -viv.ing** continue in existence after a person or thing; outlive or outlast: *Children normally survive their parents; None survived* (the disaster).
—**sur.vi.vor** (-vur) *n.*

sus.cep.ti.ble (suh.SEP.tuh.bul) *adj.* **1** capable of being acted on: *Wax is susceptible of impressions.* **2** easily acted on or influenced: *a susceptible young girl; inexperienced youth **susceptible to** the temptations of a big city.*
—**sus.cep.ti.bil.i.ty** (-BIL.i.tee) *n.* **-ties.**

sus.pect (suh.SPECT) *v.* **1** believe something negative about someone without

suspend / swaddle

proof: *She suspects he's cheating; suspects him strongly of cheating; suspects cheating; He is suspected of cheating her; He's suspected as a cheater.* **2** *Informal.* suppose or assume: *She has more brains than he suspected; I suspect you're right.* **3** doubt or distrust: *She suspected the truth of his stories; suspected his truthfulness.*
—*n.* (SUS.pect) one that is suspected, as of a crime: *a prime suspect in the murder case; to arrest, interrogate, question a suspect; a lineup of suspects.*
—*adj.* (SUS.pect, suh.SPECT) regarded with suspicion: *a suspect character, drug, vehicle; His reasons are suspect.*

sus.pend (suh.SPEND) *v.* **1** hang (as if) from a support: *Chandeliers are suspended from ceilings; There are dust particles suspended in the air; adj.: They remain suspended; a suspended canopy; to filter out suspended solids.* **2** stop an activity or operation for a time: *Work was suspended in protest; to suspend the death penalty; to suspend judgment, licenses, payments, production, rules; adj.: a* **suspended** *investigation, program; a body in* **suspended animation** *without vital signs, as in drowning, trances, etc.* **3** remove for a while from duties or privileges: *He was suspended (from duty) without pay pending an investigation; a player suspended from baseball; n.: He was judged guilty and given a* **suspended sentence** (= prison term that need not be served as long as the criminal behaves).

sus.pen.ders (suh.SPEN.durs) *n.pl.* a pair of shoulder straps to hold up trousers.

sus.pense (suh.SPENCE) *n.* a state of uncertainty or anxiety about an outcome: *a story full of suspense; It keeps you in suspense till the end; Everyone is in suspense over what will happen next;* **sus.pense.ful** *adj.*

sus.pen.sion (suh.SPEN.shun) *n.* **1** an act of suspending or the state of being suspended: *a lifetime suspension from the Olympics; a suspension of aid, of disbelief.* **2** a suspending device: *an automobile's front and rear suspensions; adja.: a suspension cable, mount, system, tuning; the suspension spans of a bridge; A* **suspension bridge** *hangs from cables supported by towers on either end.* **3** a mixture such as milk or smoke in which particles are suspended or dispersed without being dissolved.

sus.pi.cion (suh.SPISH.un) *n.* **1** a suspecting or being suspected: *to arouse, cause, create, sow suspicion in the minds of people; to cast suspicion on his motives; to allay, dispel suspicion; groundless, lingering, lurking, strong, vague suspicions about his actions; The suspicion seemed to fall on him; Later events confirmed our suspicions; A cloud of suspicion hangs over some; Some people are under suspicion; a mind full of suspicion; One is arrested* **on suspicion** *of murder; Not everyone is* **above suspicion** (= free of being suspected). **2** a slight trace or soupçon: *There's not even the slightest suspicion of dishonesty about her.*

sus.pi.cious (suh.SPISH.us) *adj.* arousing, showing, or feeling suspicion: *He is suspicious about or of people's motives; suspicious behavior.* —**sus.pi.cious.ly** *adv.*

sus.tain (suh.STAIN) *v.* **1** support actively so as to keep from failing: *The arch is strong enough to sustain any weight; an atmosphere too rare to sustain life; "Objection sustained (= upheld)," declared the judge; adj.: The driver made a* **sustained** (= continuous) *effort to stay awake; years of sustained growth; sustained activity, attacks, campaigns, conflicts, heat, involvement, opposition, strategies, stresses.* **2** suffer or endure: *He sustained great losses in the fire; wounds sustained in battle.* —**sus.tain.a.ble** *adj.*

sus.te.nance (SUS.tuh.nunce) *n.*
1 nourishment or food to sustain life.
2 a means of livelihood.

su.tra (SOO.truh) *n.* **1** an ancient Hindu maxim. **2** a Buddhist sermon.

su.ture (SOO.chur) *n.* a joining together, as by sewing, or the sewing itself: *the zigzag sutures of the skull bones; Surgical incisions are closed by means of sutures* (= stitches); *The sutures (of gut, silk, or wire) are taken out as the wound heals.*

su.ze.rain (SOO.zuh.rain, -rin) *n.* a state or ruler with suzerainty over another.
—**su.ze.rain.ty** *n.* control of foreign relations.

svelte (SVELT) *adj.* **svelt.er, svelt.est**
1 suave. **2** slender or lithe: *slim and svelte; her svelte good looks; He's a svelte 150 pounds.*

swab (SWOB) *n.* **1** a cleaning mop.
2 a bit of cotton or other absorbent material at the end of a stick for removing discharged matter from, or for applying medicine to a body part.
3 *Slang.* a sailor; gob. **4** *Slang.* a lout.
—*v.* **swabs, swabbed, swab.bing** use a swab on something: *to swab the deck of a ship.*

swad.dle (SWOD.ul) *v.* **swad.dles, swad.dled, swad.dling** bind or wrap a newborn baby in long, narrow strips

of cloth, or **swaddling clothes.**
swag n. 1 Slang. loot or stolen goods. 2 a festoon or garland hung in a curve, esp. such a decorative design: *a swag with shallow curves.*
—v. **swags, swagged, swag.ging** curve: *skirts swagged at the hem like drapes; swagged curtains.*
swage n. a metal-working tool for shaping and forming objects.
—v. **swag.es, swaged, swag.ing** shape or form with a swage.
swag.ger (SWAG.ur) n. a superior or insolent manner: *the swagger of a conceited fellow; a checked shirt with its frankly male swagger; the swagger stick* (= short cane) *carried by an army officer.*
—v. walk with a swagger: *He swaggers around like a hotshot.*
Swa.hi.li (swah.HEE.lee) n. 1 a Bantu language used widely in E. Africa from Somalia to Mozambique. 2 a Swahili speaker.
swain n. 1 a rustic youth or shepherd. 2 a lover or suitor.
swal.low (SWOL.oh) v. 1 take from the mouth into the stomach, as food. 2 accept or take in like swallowed food: *so gullible he'll swallow any story; to swallow an insult without protesting; a body swallowed up by* (= lost in) *the waves.* 3 take back or suppress: *It hurt his pride to swallow his words; He had to swallow his pride and apologize.* —n. 1 a swallowing or the amount swallowed at one time: *He ate the whole thing in one swallow; He took only one swallow of the medicine.* 2 a small, insect-eating bird with powerful wings and a forked tail.
swal.low.tail (SWOL.oh.tail) n. a tailcoat. —**swal.low.tailed** adj.
swam pt. of SWIM.
swa.mi (SWAH.mee) n. a Hindu religious teacher.
swamp (SWOMP) n. also **swampland,** a tract of low-lying marshy land: *ancient swamps; a barren swamp; a society mired in a social and political swamp; a swamp of incompetence;* **adja.:** *swamp buggies, cabbage, monsters, rabbits;* **swamp fever** (= malaria); **swamp gas** (=marsh gas).
—v. overwhelm or deluge: *The heavy seas swamped our boat; a switchboard swamped with phone calls; to be swamped by backlogs, debts, homework.* —**swamp.y** adj. marshy: *a swampy area, forest, shore.*
swan (SWON, SWAUN) n. a graceful, long-necked, usu. snow-white water bird related to the geese.
swank (rhyme: bank) n. Informal. 1 dash or style. 2 swagger: *His clothing is a restrained swank.* —**adj.** stylish in a showy manner: *a swank new hotel; a swank yuppie couple;* also **swank.y, swank.i.er, swank.i.est.** —v. swagger.
swan's-down n. 1 the soft down of swan. 2 a fine, soft cloth of cotton or wool used for baby clothes; also **swans.down.**
swan song n. a person's final speech or performance, like the fabled swan's dying song.
swap (SWOP, SWAUP) v. & n. **swaps, swapped, swap.ping** Informal. exchange or barter: *They swapped seats so she could have a better view; swapped his orange for her apple; He made a swap for her apple.* —**swap.per** n.
sward (SWORD) n. grassy surface; turf.
swarm (SWORM) n. 1 a large group of honeybees flying away to form a new colony. 2 a settled colony of bees. 3 a large dense crowd or throng: *a swarm of school children.* —v. 1 of bees, migrate in a swarm. 2 fly about or be present in large numbers: *Shoppers swarmed into the store; They swarmed around the movie star; Tourists swarmed (through) the streets; a place swarming with* (= full of) *mosquitoes.*
swarth.y (SWOR.thee) adj. **swarth.i.er, -i.est** dark-complexioned.
swash (SWOSH) v. dash or splash water, etc. —n. the sound or action of water washing over something.
swash.buck.ler (SWOSH.buck.lur) n. a swaggering soldier or bully.
—**swash.buck.ling** adj.
swas.ti.ka (SWOS.ti.kuh) n. an ancient design or symbol in the form of a cross with arms bent at right angles in the same direction: *The clockwise swastika was the Nazi emblem.*
swat (SWOT) n. Informal. a quick, sharp blow: *a swat team of commandos.*
—v. **swats, swat.ted, swat.ting** Informal. hit with a swat: *to swat a fly.*
—**swat.ter** n.
swatch (SWOCH) n. 1 a sample piece of cloth: *fabric swatches; swatch cards; a* **swatch book** *of suitings.* 2 a piece or portion: *large swatches of color; a two-mile swatch of sand; swatches of territory seized from neighboring countries.*
swath (SWOTH, SWAUTH, "TH" as in "thin") n. 1 space cleared by one passage of a mower or cut of a scythe: *The tornado cut a wide swath of destruction through the town; a new fashion that has cut a broad or large or wide swath* (= made a big hit) *across or through the teen world; planted in a three-foot-wide swath* (= strip or belt). 2 the row of grass or grain left cut.

swathe (SWAITH, "TH" as in "the") *v.* **swathes, swathed, swath.ing** wrap up in a long strip or bandage: *He came to the door swathed in a bath towel; a lady swathed in fur; The hills were swathed* (= enveloped) *in mist.*

sway *v.* swing sideways from an upright position: *tall grasses swaying in the wind; The dancers swayed to the rhythm of the music; She would not be swayed* (= influenced) *by her feelings, by their arguments.*
—*n.* **1** a swaying. **2** control or dominance: *under the sway of Rome; when Rome held sway over Europe.*

sway.back *n.* a curvature of the spine, as of an animal. —*adj.* having a sagging back, as some horses; also **sway.backed.**

swear (SWARE) *v.* **swears, swore, sworn, swear.ing 1** declare, promise, etc. solemnly, calling God to witness; take an oath: *Witnesses swear to tell the truth; They swear by or on the Bible, on their life; She speaks good English and swears by her dictionary* (= relies on it); *I can swear to that* (= confirm it); *A judge swears in public officials* (to their offices by administering the oath of office); *They swear allegiance to the national flag; She was sworn in as Minister of Education.* **2** curse; utter an oath: *Lu swears at people when mad; Sam never swears.*
—**swear off** renounce or give up: *He decided to swear off smoking as it was affecting his health.* —**swear out** swear that what is charged against someone is true: *to swear out a complaint, warrant against someone.*

swear.word (SWARE.wurd) *n.* a word or phrase used in cursing; oath or obscenity.

sweat (SWET) *n.* **1** moisture formed on the skin, as after strenuous exercise; perspiration: *to work up a sweat on a treadmill; She got her doctorate by the sweat of her brow* (= by hard work); *All the sweat* (= drudgery) *you pour into writing a book is lost if it doesn't sell; He found a way of making money without blood, sweat, and tears* (= painful hard work); **adj.:** *sweat ducts, glands; the sweat pores of the skin.* **2** anything resembling perspiration, as moisture condensed on a cold surface. **3** a state or spell of sweating induced by fear, anxiety, etc.: *night sweats; He found the frightened child in a cold sweat; The crew was in a sweat* (Informal for impatient) *for the plane to take off.* **4 sweats** *pl.* clothes used during exercise: *hooded sweats.*
—*v.* **sweats,** *pt. & pp.* **sweat** or **sweat.ed, sweat.ing** perspire: *You sweat freely in a sauna bath; Cold water pipes sweat on a hot and humid day; Hides, tobacco leaves, etc. are sweated during processing; She sweat blood* (= worked like a slave) *to write that book; The passengers had to sweat it out* (Informal for wait anxiously) *until help arrived.*

sweat.er (SWET.ur) *n.* a knitted or crocheted pullover or jacket.

sweat.pants *n.pl.* pants made with an absorbent fabric, used during exercise.

sweat shirt *n.* a loose pullover of heavy cotton jersey.

sweat.shop (SWET.shop) *n.* a place of work characterized by low pay, long hours, etc.

sweat.y (SWET.ee) *adj.* **sweat.i.er, -i.est** sweating or causing sweat: *sweaty palms.*

Swede (SWEED) *n.* a person of or from **Sweden,** a N. European country.

Swe.dish (SWEE.dish) *n. & adj.* (the people or the Germanic language) of Sweden: *The Royal Swedish Academy awards the Nobel prizes.*

sweep *v.* **sweeps, swept, sweep.ing** pass swiftly and smoothly over something: *A wind sweeps over a meadow; fingers sweeping the keys of a piano; Long skirts sweep the ground; She swept out of the room (with dignity); A hurricane swept down on the town; The flood waters swept away the bridge; Excitement swept the nation on election day; The Liberals swept into office; to sweep* (= clean) *the floor with a broom; Let's sweep the floor clean; Don't sweep it* (= Don't hide the sweepings) *under the rug; Our team swept the series* (= won every game); *The highway sweeps* (= stretches without a break) *along the coast.*
—*n.* **1** a sweeping: *Give the floor a good sweep; He was arrested during a police sweep of the area; the sweep of the highway around the hill; a lovely sweep* (= stretch) *of meadow; She made a clean sweep* (= capture) *of all the prizes; stars beyond the sweep* (= range) *of our telescopes; The sweep-second hand of a timepiece shows seconds as it sweeps the dial once every minute.* **2** one who cleans chimneys; chimney sweep.
—**sweep.er** *n.*

sweeping *adj.* **1** covering a wide area: *a sweeping glance; sweeping* (= extensive) *changes, plans, reforms.* **2** having a general effect: *a sweeping victory; a sweeping* (= too general) *allegation, general-*

ization, statement. —*n.pl.* things swept up from a floor. —**sweep.ing.ly** *adv.*

sweep.stakes *n. sing. & pl.* a lottery or horse race in which the participants put up the money that is divided as prizes: *to enter, win the sweepstakes*; **adj**a.: *sweepstakes campaigns, players, prizes, winners, winnings.* Also **sweep.stake:** *a $2 million sweepstake;* **adj**a.: *sweepstake contests, promotions.*

sweet *adj.* **1** like sugar in taste: *as sweet as honey.* **2** agreeable or pleasing: *Roses smell sweet; the sweet smell of success; sweet music, praise, smiles, temper; a sweet little child; whispering sweet nothings in her ear.* **3** not sour: *sweet milk, soil; sweet (= fresh) butter.* —*n.* **1** one that is sweet, as a darling. **2** *Brit.* dessert. **3** *Cdn.* **sweets** *pl.* sweet things, esp. candy. —**sweet.ly** *adv.*; **sweet.ness** *n.*

sweet.bread *n.* the thymus or pancreas of a calf, lamb, etc. used for food.

sweet.bri.er or **sweet.bri.ar** (SWEET.bry.ur) same as EGLANTINE.

sweet clover *n.* a cloverlike herb grown for hay, forage, and green manure.

sweet corn *n.* a variety of corn that has sweet kernels when unripe.

sweet.en (SWEE.tun) *v.* make sweet or pleasant: *a "sugar-free" cereal sweetened with aspartame; a bonus offered to* **sweet-en the pot** (= make the offer more attractive); **sweet.en.ing** *n.*

sweet.en.er (SWEE.tun.ur) *n.* a sweetening agent such as sugar or saccharin.

sweet.heart *n.* a loved one; darling.

sweetheart deal (or **agreement** or **contract**) *n.* a secret deal made with the opposite party for selfish reasons, as when a labor leader deals secretly with an employer.

sweet.meat *n.* a candy.

sweet potato *n.* a thick, fleshy, sweet yellow or reddish vegetable that is the root of a climbing plant.

sweet-talk *v. Informal.* flatter or coax; cajole. Also *n.*

sweet tooth *n. Informal.* fondness for sweet foods.

sweet William (or **william**) *n.* a garden plant of the pink family bearing dense, round velvety clusters of flowers in many shades.

swell *v.* **swells,** *pt.* **swelled,** *pp.* **swelled** or **swol.len** (SWOH.lun), **swell.ing** grow or make bigger than normal in volume, size, etc., as because of pressure from within; (cause to) bulge out: *A wind swells the sails; a river swollen by rains; New members have swelled our ranks; He's swelling* (= getting filled) *with pride;* **adj.**: *a swollen ankle, belly, face, joint, inventory.* —*n.* **1** a swelling or something swollen, as a rounded hill or a large, rising wave: *a swell of enthusiasm, pride, sentiment; the swell of the civil rights movement.* **2** a swelling sound, as of the organ. **3** a device to control sound volume, as in an organ. **4** *Slang.* a stylish or fashionable person. —**adj. 1** *Informal.* stylish; fashionable: *a swell hat.* **2** *Informal.* excellent: *a swell guy; We had a swell time.*

swelled head *n. Informal.* self-conceit.
swell.head *n.* a conceited person; **swell.head.ed** *adj.*

swelling *n.* **1** a swollen part of the body. **2** a swollen condition or increase in size: *A swelling goes down, subsides.*

swel.ter (SWEL.tur) *v.* be oppressed by heat: *We sweltered for three days in an overheated room;* **adj.**: *in the* **sweltering** (= oppressively hot) *day, hotel room, summer, sun; the sweltering heat;* **adv.**: *a sweltering hot afternoon.*

swept *pt. & pp.* of SWEEP.

swerve (SWURV) *v.* **swerves, swerved, swerv.ing** turn aside from the direction of motion or from a course of action: *The jet swerved off the runway when attempting to land; If a car swerves to the right when you apply the brakes, its front end needs aligning; to swerve from the path of virtue.* —*n.* a swerving.

swift *adj.* fast or rapid, esp. in a smooth and easy manner: *a swift pace; a swift-footed messenger; He is swift of foot; She's swift to anger; They were swift to retaliate; a swift flight, reaction, transition.* —*n.* a swallowlike swift-flying bird. —**swift.ly** *adv.*; **swift.ness** *n.*

swig *n. Informal.* a deep draft, esp. of liquor: *He took a swig from the flask.* —*v.* **swigs, swigged, swig.ging** take deep drafts of a drink: *We ate salted peanuts and swigged cola at the party.*

swill *n.* kitchen refuse mixed with liquids, as fed to pigs; slops. —*v.* **1** feed pigs on swill. **2** guzzle or drink greedily.

swim *v.* **swims, swam, swum, swim.ming 1** move through water using one's limbs, fins, or tail: *Animals swim instinctively; You either sink or swim; She can swim the length of the pool;* *n.*: *the sport of* **swimming.** **2** move or be in a condition like swimming: *eyes swimming with tears; He said his head was swimming* (= whirling) *when he fainted.* —*n.* an act or period of swimming: *to go for a swim; have* or *take a swim in the river.* —**in the swim** involved with

what is going on around one. **—swim.mer** *n.*
swimming hole *n.* a water hole that is deep enough for swimming.
swimmingly *adv. Informal.* nicely: *Everything moved* or *went swimmingly.*
swimming pool *n.* a water tank made for swimming: *They have a portable, above-ground, backyard swimming pool besides an in-ground one indoors.*
swim.suit *n.* a garment to wear for swimming.
swin.dle (SWIN.dul) *v.* **-dles, -dled, -dling** cheat a trusting person of money or property: *a naive customer swindled out of his savings.* **—***n.* a swindling; fraudulent scheme. **—swin.dler** *n.*
swine *n. sing. & pl.* **1** a pig. **2** a person considered contemptible or disgusting. **—swin.ish** (SWY-) *adj.*
swing *v.* **swings, swung, swing.ing 1** hang or move to and fro like a pendulum: *Swing your arms while walking; a hammock swung* (= hung) *between trees.* **2** move in a curve with force and freedom: *Tarzan swings from tree to tree; The batter swung his bat at the ball but missed it; The gate swung open; Music that swings* (has a lively, relaxed jazz beat). **3** *Informal.* successfully conclude: *to swing a business deal, election.* **4** *Slang.* to be free and uninhibited in pursuing pleasure, following the latest in fashions and ways of life. **—***n.* **1** a swinging or its manner or amount: *the swing of a pendulum; There was a swing* (= shift) *to the Right during the last elections.* **2** a swinging blow, gait, rhythm, etc.: *She took a swing* (= aimed a punch) *at him.* **3** activity or progress: *Classes are* **in full swing** (= fully active) *within days of reopening.* **4** a trip or tour: *a swing through Europe.* **5** jazz music with a happy, relaxed beat and freedom to improvise, as played by big bands in the 1930s and 1940s.
swing.er *n.* **1** one that swings. **2** *Slang.* one who moves with the times and changing fashions. **3** *Slang.* one who is uninhibited in his social life, esp. in sexual behavior.
swinging *adj.* lively and up to date: *Hull is not dull but swinging with its discos, nightclubs, and restaurants.*
swing shift *n. Informal.* the work shift between the day and night shifts, usu. from 4 p.m. to midnight.
swipe *n.* **1** a sweeping blow: *to take a swipe at someone.* **2** a sweeping stroke: *to give the wall a swipe with a cleaning sponge.* **—***v.* **swipes, swiped, swip.ing 1** hit with a sweeping stroke: *to swipe* (= slide) *a credit card through a magnetic reader.* **2** *Informal.* pilfer.
swirl *v.* whirl or eddy: *Rumors swirled around Washington.* **—***n.* something swirled or swirling; also, a curl or whorl: *the swirl on an ice-cream cone; He resigned amid a swirl of controversy over his private life;* **adja.**: *a swirl arrangement, design; raspberry swirl cheesecake; a swirl-pattern jacket.* **—swirl.y** *adj.*
swish *v.* (cause) to move with a light hissing or brushing sound, as of a whip cutting the air or of a silk skirt in motion: *Pour some in and swish it around in your mouth.*
—*n.* a swishing movement or sound.
—adja. *Informal.* posh or swanky: *in a swish district of the city.*
Swiss *n. sing. & pl.* a person of or from **Switzerland,** a country of C. Europe.
—adj. having to with the Swiss or Switzerland.
Swiss chard same as CHARD.
Swiss cheese *n.* a firm, pale-yellow cheese with large holes.
Swiss Guard *n.* a member of a Swiss corps working as papal bodyguards and sentries in the Vatican.
Swiss steak *n.* steak prepared by pounding the meat with flour and braising it with seasonings and sauce.
switch *n.* **1** a device for controlling a connection: *to flick* or *throw a switch for turning on the current; Trains change tracks by means of a railroad switch consisting of short movable rails; The watchman was* **asleep at the switch** (= sleeping on the job). **2** change or shift: *We made a last-minute switch in plans.* **3** a slender rod made from a flexible twig to use for whipping. **4** a lash or stroke. **5** a tress of detached or false hair worn as part of a hairdo.
—*v.* **1** turn a light *off* or *on.* **2** shift a train to a different track. **3** shift or change: *to switch plans, positions, topics, hats; We switch to daylight-saving time in April.* **4** strike with or as with a switch; jerk or swing sharply: *A horse switches its tail to drive away flies.* **—switch.er** *n.*
switch.back *n.* a zigzag course, esp. a railroad for gradually climbing a steep hill.
switch.blade *n.* a pocketknife whose blade springs open when a button on the handle is pressed.
switch.board *n.* a panel controlling a system of electric circuits, as in a telephone exchange: *He works at the hotel switchboard.*
switch-hit *v.* in baseball, (to be able) to bat from either side of the plate;

switch-hitter *n.*
switch.man (SWICH.mun) *n.* **-men** a person in charge of railroad switches.
swiv.el (SWIV.ul) *n.* a coupling device that allows free turning of one part on another, as used in a **swivel chair** with rotating seat.
—*v.* **-els, -eled, -el.ing** turn or cause to turn as on a swivel; hence, swing around: *All heads swiveled toward the heckler at the back of the room.* Also **swiv.elled, swiv.el.ling** *Cdn.*
swiz.zle stick *n.* a small stirrer for a mixed drink.
swob *n. & v.* **swobs, swobbed, swob.bing** same as SWAB.
swol.len a *pp.* of SWELL.
swoon *v.* 1 lose consciousness; faint: *He swooned into her arms.* 2 become rapturous: *They screamed and swooned over the rock singer; Everyone was swooning with ecstasy; "Awesome!" she swooned* (= said in ecstasy); *swooning sentimentality.* 3 fall: *The stocks swooned to an all-time low; a swooning yen.* —*n.:* *She fell into a swoon* (= faint); *the swoon* (= fall) *of Marxism.*
swoop *n.* a sweeping down or swift descent, as of a hawk seizing its prey: *a swoop down the ski slope; She fixed everything* **in one fell swoop** (= suddenly; at one stroke). —*v.* 1 make a swift attack: *Commandos swooped down on the hijackers.* 2 seize swiftly: *We swooped her up and rushed to hospital.*
sword (SORD) *n.* a metal weapon consisting of a long blade set in a hilt: *Revenge is a double-edged sword; to* **draw swords** (= prepare to fight). —**cross swords** come into conflict *with* someone. —**put to the sword** kill someone with a sword.
sword.fish *n.* a large ocean fish that has its upper jaw elongated into a sword.
sword of Dam.o.cles (-DAM.uh.clees) *n.* imminent danger, like a sword hung by a hair over the head of Damocles of Greek myth.
sword.play *n.* 1 the art or skill of using a sword. 2 fighting with swords.
swords.man (SORDS.mun) *n.* **-men** 1 one skilled in the use of a sword. 2 one using a sword in fencing, fighting, etc.
swore *pt.* of SWEAR.
sworn *pp.* of SWEAR. —*adj.* bound by or promised with an oath: *The two are sworn enemies; sworn evidence given by witnesses in court; We are sworn to secrecy on this matter.*
swum *pp.* of SWIM.
swung *pp.* of SWING.

syb.a.rite (SIB.uh.rite) *n.* a lover of luxury and sensuality; **syb.a.rit.ic** (-RIT.ic) *adj.*
syc.a.more (SIC.uh.more) *n.* 1 a North American shade tree with reddish-brown wood and bark that breaks off in scales. 2 an Old World maple or fig tree.
syc.o.phant (SIC.uh.funt, SYE.cuh-) *n.* a servile flatterer; toady; **syc.o.phan.cy** *n.* —**syc.o.phan.tic** (-FAN.tic) *adj.*
syl.lab.ic (si.LAB.ic) *adj.* having to do with syllables: *The* **syllabic consonants** *"l" and "n" of "bottle"* (BOT.ul) *and "button"* (BUT.un) *form syllables as if without a vowel;* **syllabic verse** *(based on the number of syllables).*
syl.lab.i.cate (si.LAB.i.cate) *v.* **-cates, -cat.ed, -cat.ing** syllabify; **syl.lab.i.ca.tion** (-CAY.shun) *n.*
syl.lab.i.fy (si.LAB.i.fye) *v.* **-fies, -fied, -fy.ing** form or divide into syllables: *Entry words are shown syllabified in this dictionary.* —**syl.lab.i.fi.ca.tion** (-fuh.CAY.shun) *n.*
syl.la.ble (SIL.uh.bul) *n.* a part of a word pronounced as an uninterrupted unit, usu. consisting of a vowel with or without consonants: *"I.de.a" is composed of three syllables, but "thought" has only one; He didn't utter a syllable* (= said nothing) *during the whole meeting.*
syl.la.bus (SIL.uh.bus) *n., pl.* **-bi** (-bye) or **-bus.es** an outline or summary, esp. of a course of study.
syl.lo.gism (SIL.uh.jiz.um) *n.* a form of reasoning with two premises and a logical conclusion, as "A = B; and B = C; therefore A = C."
—**syl.lo.gis.tic** (-JIS.tic) *adj.*
sylph (SILF) *n.* 1 an elemental spirit of the air. 2 a slender, graceful woman.
syl.van (SIL.vun) *adj.* having to do with the woods; wooded: *sylvan glades, surroundings; a sylvan landscape, retreat, setting.*
sym.bi.o.sis (sim.bye.OH.sis, sim.bee-) *n., pl.* **-ses** (-seez) the living together of two different organisms, esp. for mutual benefit, as nitrogen-fixing bacteria inhabiting leguminous plants; **sym.bi.ot.ic** (-OT.ic) *adj.*
sym.bol (SIM.bul) *n.* a letter, sign, or object that represents an idea or quality by natural association or by convention, as H (hydrogen), the six-pointed star (Judaism), and the dove (peace): *a religious symbol such as the cross; A Cadillac is the status symbol for some; A national symbol such as the maple leaf may also be an official emblem.* —**sym.bol.ic** (sim.BOL.ic) or **sym.bol.i.cal** *adj.*

symbolism / syndicate

—**sym.bol.i.cal.ly** adv.
sym.bol.ism (SIM.buh.liz.um) n. symbolic representation, symbolic meaning, or a system of symbols.
sym.bol.ize (SIM.buh.lize) v. **-iz.es, -ized, -iz.ing** represent by symbols or stand as a symbol of something: *The dove symbolizes peace.* —**sym.bol.i.za.tion** (-luh.ZAY.shun, -lye-) n.
sym.me.try (SIM.uh.tree) n. **-tries** 1 correspondence of opposite parts in regard to size, shape, and position: *The human body has symmetry; A potato lacks symmetry; the symmetry of snowflakes; geometric or mechanical symmetry.* 2 a pleasing balance of form resulting from this: *to achieve symmetry and perfection in our activities; depth and symmetry; impeccable, odd, perfect symmetry.*
—**sym.met.ri.cal** (suh.MET.ri.cul) adj.
—**sym.met.ri.cal.ly** adv.
sym.pa.thet.ic (sim.puh.THET.ic, "TH" as in "thin") adj. 1 agreeing or agreeable; in harmony with: *a sympathetic response, role, shrug, smile; his sympathetic support; a kind and sympathetic police officer; to be sympathetic to an idea, to the needs of the poor, to a reform movement.* 2 of sounds and vibrations, produced in one body by transmission in the same frequency from another body: *words that* **strike a sympathetic chord** *in the reader.* 3 involuntary: *The* **sympathetic nervous system** *controls sweating, contractions of the blood vessels, etc.*
—**sym.pa.thet.i.cal.ly** adv.
sym.pa.thize (SIM.puh.thize) v. **-thiz.es, -thized, -thiz.ing** feel or show sympathy in feeling or thought: *I sympathize with you in your suffering; We sympathize* (= agree) *with your aims;* **sym.pa.thiz.er** n.
sym.pa.thy (SIM.puh.thee) n. **-thies** 1 understanding and sharing of another's feelings; compassion: *Children turn to their parents for sympathy; to arouse sympathy; to display, express, feel, have, show sympathy for a person or subject; to lavish sympathy on someone; a situation that commands, captures sympathy; to accept someone's sympathy; Our deep, great, heartfelt, profound, strong sympathy goes out to the bereaved family; a small gift as a token of our sympathy; We are doing this out of sympathy for the cause; Our sympathies lie with the opposition; a politician who plays on voters' sympathies.* 2 agreement and support: *to be* **in sympathy with** *a person, a person's aims, views, with a plan, proposal; One union strikes in sympathy with another; a sympathy strike.*

sym.pho.ny (SIM.fuh.nee) n. **-nies** 1 an elaborate musical composition for an orchestra, usu. in sonata form. 2 a large orchestra that plays symphonies; also **symphony orchestra.** 3 a symphony-orchestra concert.
—**sym.phon.ic** (sim.FON.ic) adj.
sym.po.si.um (sim.POH.zee.um) n. **-si.ums** or **-si.a** (-see.uh) 1 a conference to discuss a given subject. 2 a collection of opinions or essays on a subject.
symp.tom (SIMP.tum) n. 1 a change in a body organ or function, as a rash or headache, that indicates a disease: *a patient showing symptoms of the flu.* 2 a sign or indication of a disorder: *Constant fighting is one of the early symptoms of a marriage breakup.* —**symp.to.mat.ic** (-tuh.MAT.ic) adj.
syn- prefix. together; at the same time: *synaesthetic, synapse, synchronize, synoptic, synthesis.*
syn.a.gogue (SIN.uh.gog) n. a Jewish congregation or its place of worship. Also **syn.a.gog.** —**syn.a.gog.al** (-GOG.ul) adj.
syn.apse (SIN.aps, suh.NAPS) n. the place where one nerve cell is linked to another.
sync (SINK) n. Informal. synchronization, as of lip movements with the speech sounds in a movie: *Your watch seems a couple of minutes* **out of sync** *with the local time; to be* **in sync** (= in tune) *with the times.* —v. **syncs, synced, sync.ing** synchronize; agree or make agree: *This doesn't sync* (= agree) *with what you said a while ago.* Also **synch.**
syn.chro.nize (SINK.ruh.nize) v. **-niz.es, -nized, -niz.ing** agree or make agree in time or rate: *Watches tell the same time when synchronized; In dubbing movies, voices are synchronized with lip movements;* **syn.chro.niz.er** n. —**syn.chro.ni.za.tion** (-nuh.ZAY.shun, -nye-) n.
syn.chro.nous (SINK.ruh.nus) adj. agreeing in time or rate: *synchronous communication, dubbing, movement, transmission of data; A satellite in a synchronous* (= geosynchronous) *orbit acts as a fixed relay station.*
syn.co.pate (SINK.uh.pate) v. **-pates, -pat.ed, -pat.ing** 1 shorten, as by omitting a sound or syllable in the middle of a word, as in *heav'n.* 2 in music such as jazz, to shift or anticipate the accent to a normally weak beat or off-beat. —**syn.co.pa.tion** (-PAY.shun) n.
syn.di.cate (SIN.di.kit) n. 1 a group of organized gangsters. 2 an agency sell-

syndrome / systemic

ing the same articles, pictures, etc. to many buyers. **3** a joint selling venture or agency, as of the members of a cartel. —*v.* (-cate) **-cates, -cat.ed, -cat.ing** form into or sell through a syndicate: *The story was published and then syndicated out; syndicated across the country; adj.: a syndicated cartoon strip, column, columnist, program.*
—**syn.di.ca.tion** (-CAY.shun) *n.*
—**syn.di.ca.tor** (-cay.tur) *n.*

syn.drome (SIN.drome, -drum) *n.* the combination or pattern of a number of symptoms occurring together that is characteristic of an ailment or abnormality: *a drug withdrawal syndrome; the sudden infant death syndrome or "crib death."*

syn.er.gy (SIN.ur.jee) *n.* the combined effect of different agents working together that is greater than the sum of their separate effects: *the synergy between parents and teachers; the corporate synergy developed by the merger of two companies;* also **syn.er.gism.**
—**syn.er.gis.tic** (-JIS.tic) *adj.: synergistic effects, growth, relationships;* **syn.er.gis.ti.cal.ly** *adv.*

syn.fu.el (SIN.few.ul) *n.* a synthetic liquid fuel made from coal, tar sands, etc.

syn.od (SIN.ud) *n.* an assembly or council of church officials called to discuss matters of faith and morals; **syn.od.al** *adj.* Also **syn.od.ic** (suh.NOD.ic) or **syn.od.i.cal** *adj.*

syn.o.nym (SIN.uh.nim) *n.* a word with nearly the same meaning as another: *"Hit" is a synonym of "strike."*
—**syn.on.y.mous** (suh.NON.uh.mus) *adj.: "Speed" and "success" are not synonymous; But some people think life in the fast lane is* **synonymous with** *success.*
—**syn.on.y.my** (-mee) *n.*

syn.op.sis (suh.NOP.sis) *n., pl.* **-ses** (-seez) a summary or outline of a story, treatise, etc.: *to give, make, prepare a synopsis.*

syn.tax (SIN.tax) *n.* the arrangement of words in phrases, clauses, and sentences. —**syn.tac.tic** (sin.TAC.tic) or **syn.tac.ti.cal** *adj.*

syn.the.sis (SIN.thuh.sis) *n.* **-ses** (-seez) the combining of parts into a whole: *the synthesis of ideas (into a philosophy), of races (into a nation), of elements (into a compound); to make a synthesis of modern thought.* —**syn.the.size** *v.* **-siz.es, -sized, -siz.ing.** —**syn.the.siz.er** *n.*

syn.thet.ic (sin.THET.ic) *adj.* **1** based on synthesis; not analytic: *A* **synthetic language** *such as Latin or Sanskrit has more inflections for case, number, etc. than an analytical language like English;* **synthetic** (= elementary) **geometry;** *Herbert Spencer's* **synthetic philosophy** *(as the synthesis of all the sciences).* **2** artificial, not natural; man-made: *synthetic blends, blood, crude, diamonds, drugs, dyes, fibers, fuels, rubber, speech, turf; a synthetic smile.* Also **syn.thet.i.cal.**
—**syn.thet.i.cal.ly** *adv.*

synthetics *n.pl.* materials such as plastics and artificial fibers made by chemical synthesis.

syph.i.lis (SIF.uh.lis) *n.* a bacterium-caused venereal disease usu. transmitted by sexual contact. —**syph.i.lit.ic** (-LIT.ic) *n. & adj.* (a person) having syphilis.

sy.phon (SYE.fun) same as SIPHON.

Syr.i.an (SEER.ee.un) *n. & adj.* (a person) of or from **Syria,** a country of S.W. Asia.

sy.ringe (suh.RINJ, SEER.inj) *n.* a device consisting of a narrow tube or needle equipped with a rubber bulb or piston for injecting fluids into the body, for cleansing wounds, etc.
—*v.* **-ring.es, -ringed, -ring.ing** inject or cleanse with a syringe.

syr.up (SEER.up, SUR.up) *n.* a thick, sugary liquid: *corn syrup; maple syrup; cough syrup* (= syruplike medication).
—**syr.up.y** *adj.: a syrupy* (= thick and sweet) *fluid; syrupy* (= sentimental) *verses.*

sys.tem (SIS.tum) *n.* **1** a related or organized whole composed of many individual parts: *computer, filing, heating, highway, life-support, public-address, school, sprinkler systems; the solar system; the digestive system; Exercise is good for the system* (= body); *Radicals wish to overturn the system* (= social order). **2** a form of organization: *a system of philosophy; buddy, capitalist, caste, classification, monetary systems; the decimal, immune, merit systems; a computer system for handling a payroll; the pronunciation system of a dictionary.* **3** a plan or method: *Some work by a system, others without system* (= orderliness).

sys.tem.at.ic (sis.tuh.MAT.ic) **1** organized, methodical, and thorough: *a systematic analysis, approach, study, use.* **2** deliberate: *systematic betrayal, deceit, destruction, starvation, torture.*
—**sys.tem.at.i.cal.ly** *adv.*

sys.tem.a.tize (SIS.tuh.muh.tize) *v.* **-tiz.es, -tized, -tiz.ing** make systematic.

sys.tem.ic (sis.TEM.ic) *adj.* **1** having to do with the whole body: *a systemic antibiotic, disorder, poison.* **2** organizational:

systemic breakdowns, consequences, reform, principles, safeguards, weaknesses.
systems analysis *n.* the analysis of a system or operation into its parts in order to determine how to use a computer to run it most efficiently; **systems analyst** *n.*
systems program *n.* a program such as the operating system or routines used by it in running a computer; cf. APPLICATION PROGRAM.
sys.to.le (SIS.tuh.lee) *n.* the contracting phase of the heartbeat during which blood is pumped out; cf. DIASTOLE.
—**sys.tol.ic** (sis.TOL.ic) *adj.: systolic blood pressure; the systolic function, phase; a systolic murmur.*

.... **T, t** ....

T or **t** (TEE) *n.* **T's** or **t's** the 20th letter of the English alphabet. —**to a T** exactly; to perfection: *The nickname suits him to a T.*
tab *n.* 1 a small extension or piece projecting from a garment, filing card, etc.: *the tab of a zipper.* 2 *Informal.* bill or check: *fuel and food tabs; the tab for entertainment; She* **picked up** or **paid the tab** (= paid the bill) *for the whole group.* 3 tabulator: *to set the tabs for typing or printing in columns.* 4 [short form] a drug tablet or a tabloid newspaper.
  —**keep (a) tab on** or **keep tabs on** *Informal.* keep watch on a person or thing: *to keep close tabs on expenses.*
  —*v.* **tabs, tabbed, tab.bing** 1 put a tab on something; *adj.:* **tabbed** *index dividers, napkins, packages.* 2 label or designate: *Home video was tabbed as one of the top growth categories of the 1990s; a young actress tabbed for superstardom.*
ta.bas.co (tuh.BAS.coh) *n.* a kind of hot sauce made from red peppers; **Tabasco** *Trademark.*
tab.by (TAB.ee) *n.* **tab.bies** 1 a gray or brown cat with dark stripes. 2 any female domestic cat.
tab.er.nac.le (TAB.ur.nac.ul) *n.* 1 a temporary dwelling. 2 a synagogue; also, often **Tabernacle,** a tent carried by the Israelites as a place of worship during their travels. 3 a small cabinet or container for the consecrated host, usu. in the center of the altar.
tab.la (TAB.luh) *n.* a pair of small hand drums used by musicians of India.
ta.ble (TAY.bul) *n.* 1 a piece of furniture with a flat horizontal top and legs supporting it, esp. one to eat at: *to set the table for dinner; to put food on the table; to clear the table after meals; at the conference table; She spoke to the whole table* (= group around the table); *subjects we don't discuss* **at the table** (= while eating); *She provides a good table* (= fare). 2 a tabulated list: *to compile, draw up a table of data; a metric conversion table; the multiplication tables; a book's* **table of contents.** 3 inscribed tablet: *the* **tables** *of the law.* —**on the table** 1 in the U.S., of a legislative bill, shelved. 2 of a bill, on the agenda; under discussion. —**turn the tables** reverse a situation to an opponent's disadvantage. —**under the table** secretly and illegally: *money paid under the table (as a bribe).* —*v.* **-bles, -bled, -bling** 1 put on the agenda. 2 in the U.S., put off consideration of a legislative bill indefinitely.
tab.leau (TAB.loh) *n., pl.* **-leaux** (-loze) or **-leaus** 1 a graphic or dramatic picture. 2 a dramatic scene posed by silent actors in costume.
ta.ble.cloth (TAY.bul.cloth) *n.* a covering for a table, as at meals.
ta.ble d'hôte (TAH.bul.DOTE) *n., pl.* **ta.bles d'hôte** (-buls.DOTE) in restaurants, a complete meal at a fixed price; cf. À LA CARTE.
table-hop *v.* **-hops, -hopped, -hop.ping** leave one's table in a restaurant to chat with friends at other tables.
ta.ble.land (TAY.bul.land) *n.* plateau.
table salt *n.* fine salt for use with food.
ta.ble.spoon (TAY.bul.spoon, long "oo") *n.* 1 a large serving spoon. 2 a spoon for eating soup. 3 a tablespoonful: *heaping, level, rounded tablespoons.*
ta.ble.spoon.ful (TAY.bul.spoon.ful) *n.* **-fuls** a measuring unit equal to three teaspoonfuls or ½ fl. oz. (14.2 ml).
tab.let (TAB.lit) *n.* 1 a flat, thin piece of material for writing on, as in ancient times: *clay, stone tablets.* 2 a slab bearing an inscription put at the head of a grave or used as a plaque: *bronze, marble tablets.* 3 a pad of sheets of writing paper glued together at one end. 4 a small, flat cake of medicine, as of aspirin.
table tennis *n.* a tennislike game played on a table with a light, hollow plastic ball.
ta.ble.top (TAY.bul.top) *n.* the flat horizontal top of a table.
ta.ble.ware (TAY.bul.ware) *n.* dishes, glasses, spoons, knives, etc. for use at meals.
tab.loid (TAB.loid) *n.* a usu. half-size newspaper giving news in condensed form with many pictures and sensa-

tional headlines: *a supermarket tabloid.* —**adj.**: *a tabloid (not broadsheet) newspaper; the tabloid format, style; a tabloid gossip column; sensational tabloid journalism.*

ta.boo (tuh.BOO, tab.OO) *adj.* **1** prohibited because obscene or harmful, as four-letter words. **2** not to be touched because sacred or cursed, as among certain groups: *To Muslims, food is taboo before sunset during Ramadan.* —*n.* such a prohibition or the custom: *to break* or *violate a taboo; A taboo is placed on eating before sunset; Eating before sunset during Ramadan is under a rigid taboo.* —*v.* **-boos, -booed, -boo.ing** prohibit or put under taboo: *Eating before sunset is tabooed.*

ta.bor (TAY.bur) *n.* a small drum used as accompaniment by one playing on a pipe, as in the Middle Ages.

tab.u.lar (TAB.yuh.lur) *adj.* **1** having to do with lists or tables: *data in tabular form* or *format; tabular computations, displays, reports.* **2** flat like a tabletop: *a tabular rock, structure, surface.*

tab.u.late (TAB.yuh.late) *v.* **-lates, -lat.ed, -lat.ing** arrange data in lists or tabular form. —**tab.u.la.tion** (-LAY.shun) *n.* —**tab.u.la.tor** (-lay.tur) *n.*

ta.chom.e.ter (tuh.COM.uh.tur) *n.* an instrument that measures the speed of a rotating wheel or shaft, usu. in revolutions per minute.

tach.y.car.di.a (tak.i.CAR.dee.uh) *n.* abnormally rapid beating of the heart.

tac.it (TAS.it) *adj.* unspoken; also, implied, not expressed: *tacit acceptance, agreement, approval, assumption, endorsement, recognition, support, understanding.* —**tac.it.ly** *adv.;* **tac.it.ness** *n.*

tac.i.turn (TAS.i.turn) *adj.* inclined by nature to be silent; uncommunicative; **tac.i.turn.ly** *adv.* —**tac.i.tur.ni.ty** (-TUR.ni.tee) *n.*

tack *n.* **1** a flat-headed, sharp-pointed nail: *carpet tacks; thumb tacks.* **2** a temporary stitch. **3** course of action or policy: *to take a tack to the left; to change tack; to try a different tack.* —*v.* **1** fasten with tacks. **2** attach or append to something: *A service charge has been tacked on to the cost of the item.*

tack.le (TACK.ul) *n.* **1** gear or equipment, as a ship's ropes and pulleys: *fishing tackle* (= rod, line, etc.). **2** (method of) tackling an opponent, as in football. **3** in football, an offensive or defensive lineman next to the end. —*v.* **-les, -led, -ling 1** deal with a person or thing that is challenging or difficult: *to tackle the deficit, an issue,* *job, problem, project, question;* *to tackle the highway during the rush hour.* **2** in football, seize or throw the ball carrier to the ground. **3** lay hold of an opponent: *The police officer tackled the hoodlum to the ground.* —**tack.ler** *n.*

tack.y (TACK.ee) *adj.* **tack.i.er, -i.est 1** sticky. **2** *Informal.* shabby; gaudy; dowdy. —**tack.i.ness** *n.*

ta.co (TAH.coh) *n.* **-cos** a rolled or folded tortilla with a filling of meat, etc.

tact *n.* delicate skill in handling people and difficult situations: *She displayed* or *showed, exercised great tact in dealing with the peddler; He had the tact to avoid mentioning the subject.* —**tact.ful** *adj.;* **tact.ful.ly** *adv.*

tac.tic (TAC.tic) *n.* **1** a skillful move or maneuver. **2** usu. **tactics** *pl.* methods of gaining advantage: *cheap, delaying, diversionary, pressure, questionable, scare, smear, strong-arm, surprise tactics.* **3 tactics** *pl.* [takes *sing. v.*] the art or science of conducting a battle.
—**tac.ti.cian** (tac.TISH.un) *n.*

tac.ti.cal (TAC.ti.cul) *adj.* **1** well planned: *his tactical moves; her tactical skill.* **2** having to do with tactics or methods: *a tactical error, mistake.* **3** having to do with a shorter distance from a base of operations than in strategy: *strategic and tactical nuclear weapons; A tactical air force provides close support for ground troops.*

tac.tile (TAC.tul, -tile) *adj.* relating to the sense of touch: *a tactile impression, organ, stimulus.* —**tac.til.i.ty** (tac.TIL.i.tee) *n.*

tad *n. Informal.* **1** a little boy. **2** a little bit: *Things are a tad hectic here.*

ta-dah (tuh.DAH) *interj.* uttered when presenting a surprise.

tad.pole *n.* a frog or toad of the larva stage with gills and tail.

taf.fe.ta (TAF.uh.tuh) *n.* a fine, stiff, lustrous fabric of silk, rayon, etc.

taff.rail (TAF.rail, -rul) *n.* the rail around a ship's stern.

taf.fy (TAF.ee) *n.* **taf.fies** a chewy candy prepared from molasses or brown sugar.

tag *n.* **1** a small hanging piece or end: *She was at the tag end* (= very end) *of the procession.* **2** the metal or plastic binding on the end of a shoelace. **3** a small piece of card or leather attached as a label: *gift, identification, name, price tags.* **4** price: *a $100 retail tag.* **5** an epithet: *Not every Richard deserves the "Tricky Dick" tag.* **6** a quotation or saying used for effect at the end of a speech or story; also **tag line**. **7** a game in which one player chases the others and tries to touch one: *to play tag; tag games*. **8** in an electronic document, a symbol that marks the beginning or end of a unit of information: *HTML tags; style tags*. —*v*. **tags, tagged, tag·ging 1** furnish with a tag or label: *His car was tagged* (= ticketed) *and towed away from the no-parking zone; a man tagged* (= labeled) *as a troublemaker; He doesn't like being **tagged with** the T-word*. **2** follow closely; trail: *Jane tagged after the others; He **tagged along** after* or *behind* or *with his mother*. **3** to touch, as in the game of tag; hence, select or choose. —**tag·ger** *n*.

Ta·ga·log (tuh.GAH.log) *n*. **1** a member of the chief native people of the Philippines. **2** their language.

tag end, tag line See TAG.

tag sale *n*. garage sale.

Ta·hi·tian (tuh.HEE.shun) *n. & adj*. (a person) of or from **Tahiti,** the largest island of the French Polynesian group.

tai chi (TYE.jee) *n*. a Chinese system of exercises characterized by slow movements; in full **t'ai-chi ch'uan** (-chwan).

tai·ga (TYE.guh) *n*. the swampy coniferous forest land of Siberia between the tundra and the steppes.

tail *n*. **1** the backward extension of an animal's body; also, a similar part: *the tail of a dog, airplane, comet, procession; a car well designed **from tip to tail**; when the **tail wags the dog*** (= a minor element of a situation becomes more important than the major one)*; The dog **turned tail*** (= turned round) *and ran; adja.: the tail fins of an airplane; an automobile's tail lamps; the tail section*. **2** *Informal*. one who shadows another, as a detective: *They put a tail on the suspect*. **3 tails** *pl*. the reverse side of a coin; opposite of "heads." **4 tails** *pl*. tailcoat; hence, full dress attire. —*v*. **1** furnish with a tail: *the game of tailing the donkey; cpd: pony-tailed Peg; red-tailed hawks; white-tailed deer*. **2** *Informal*. follow close behind: *to be tailed by spies*. **3 tail off** disappear gradually: *Activity, business, growth, performance, production, revenues, sales may tail off*. —**tail·less** *adj*.

tail end *n*. the final part: *the tail end of a conversation, program, recession, year*.

tail·gate *n*. the gate that opens from the back of a truck, station wagon, etc. —*v*. **-gates, -gat·ed, -gat·ing** drive too close behind another vehicle.

tail·ings *n.pl*. leavings or residue of a product or process, as gravel that does not pass through a screen: *mill tailings; mine tailings*.

tail·light *n*. a red warning light at the rear of a vehicle. Also **tail lamp.**

tai·lor (TAY.lur) *n*. one who makes or repairs clothes. —*v*. **1** work as a tailor. **2** make by tailor's work: *a suit tailored to measure; a textbook tailored* (= adapted) *to the needs of the young student*.

tailor-made *adj*. **1** made by a tailor: *a tailor-made suit*. **2** made esp. for a purpose: *an excuse tailor-made for the occasion*.

tail pipe *n*. the exhaust pipe of an automobile.

tail·spin *n*. **1** spinning motion, as of an airplane coming down out of control: *The bond market went into a tailspin* (= downturn). **2** *Informal*. state of mental confusion.

tail wind *n*. a wind blowing from the rear, in the direction in which a craft is going.

taint *n*. a trace of corruption or contamination. —*v*. contaminate; corrupt; spoil: *a name tainted by scandal; adj.: tainted food, money, reputations*.

take *v*. **takes, took** (short "oo"), **tak·en, tak·ing 1** get or seize by force or skill: *They were taken prisoner; Who took the game? We were taken by surprise*. **2** get, obtain, or assume: *She'll take office tomorrow; He's out taking the air; to take the matter lightly, seriously; Don't take anything for granted; I don't take* (= subscribe to) *The Tribune*. **3** get by choice: *You can take it or leave it; Please take a seat* (= sit down). **4** get from a source: *a passage taken from Shakespeare; to take notes of a lecture*. **5** get or receive as offered or due: *He can't take a joke; She's taking (a) rest; She won't **take** an insult **lying down*** (= accept it without protest). **6** understand or feel: *What shall I take this to mean? He took the remark as a compliment; He didn't take notice of her*. **7** do, perform, or execute: *He takes a walk after dinner; She took a swipe at him*. **8** carry or remove: *Where will this road take us? She took the dog for a walk; took the case to the Supreme Court; If you take 4 from 11, only 7 remains*. **9** have the intended effect: *An inoculation, skin graft, dye, or new publication has to take* (for it to be successful); *For your fire to take* (= catch)*, the kindling has to be dry*.
—**take after** be or act like someone.
—**take a company private** buy out a public company using private funds.
—**take a company public** go public with a company and sell its shares on

the stock exchange. —**take down** 1 pull down. 2 write down. —**take for** consider to be: *What sort of a woman do you take me for?* —**take in:** *He had to take in boarders to pay off his debts; I took in the sights of the town on the last visit; a dress that needs to be taken in* (= reduced) *at the waist; She's too sharp to be easily taken in* (= deceived). —**take it** *Informal.* endure something hard to bear: *I can't take it any more.* —**take it out on** *Informal.* make someone else suffer for what one has suffered. —**take off** 1 leave: *An aircraft takes off on a flight; Everyone takes off* (*Informal* for leaves) *for home after school.* 2 *Informal.* mimic: *He takes off celebrities to entertain audiences.* —**take on** 1 engage or employ: *We'll take her on.* 2 undertake to deal with a person or thing: *to take on an unpleasant job.* 3 acquire or put on a look, appearance, etc.: *He takes on the look of a martyr.* —**take one's time** be unhurried or slow doing something: *There's no hurry; take your time.* —**take over** take charge or control of something. —**take place** happen or occur. —**take to** 1 go to or resort to something: *Demonstrators take to the streets; Jan took to drink(ing) in frustration.* 2 adapt to an environment; become fond of a person or thing: *The dog seems to take to the cat.* —**take up** 1 begin to do or learn: *to take up a hobby.* 2 fill or occupy a place or time: *a hobby that takes up all my leisure time.* 3 tighten; make shorter: *to take up the slack (of a rope); to take up a skirt.* 4 accept: *I'm prepared to take you up on that offer.* —**what it takes** *Informal.* qualities required for success: *She has what it takes.* —**n.** a taking, what is taken, an amount taken, etc.: *an evening's take at the box office; the many takes* (= shootings) *of a movie scene; He did a double take* (= showed a delayed reaction). —**on the take** *Slang.* accepting money illicitly.

take-home pay *n.* the money one receives as a paycheck after taxes, dues, etc. have been deducted.

tak.en (TAY.kun) 1 *pp.* of TAKE: *Is this seat taken* (= reserved)? 2 *adj.* impressed: *The boys were very much taken with the new teacher.*

take.off *n.* 1 a taking off, as in flight. 2 *Informal.* a burlesque or parody: *She's good at doing takeoffs of celebrities.*

take.out *adja.* in ordering food, for consumption away from the premises: *takeout Chinese food, pizza; Takeout restaurants sell takeout food; a takeout counter.* —*n.* takeout food or restaurant: *a fried-chicken takeout.*

take.o.ver (TAKE.oh.vur) *n.* the taking over of power in a government or organization: *the failed Iraqi takeover of Kuwait;* **adja.:** *a takeover attempt, battle, bid, candidate, plan, target.*

taking 1 *adj. Informal.* attractive; captivating: *a taking view.* 2 *n.* seizure: *the taking of the town; It's there* **for the taking** (= for anyone to take). 3 **takings** *n.pl.* profits or receipts.

talc *n.* the softest of minerals, a greenish compound of magnesium silicate.

tal.cum powder or **talcum** *n.* a powder made of perfumed white talc for use on the skin.

tale *n.* 1 a made-up story, esp. a long one: *to narrate, tell a tale; exciting, fairy, fanciful, folk, grizzly, harrowing tales; a tall tale.* 2 falsehood; also, gossip or scandal. —**tell tales** spread gossip.

tale.bear.er (TALE.bair.ur) *n.* 1 one who spreads gossip. 2 a telltale.

tal.ent (TAL.unt) *n.* 1 a natural ability or aptitude *for* some activity or skill: *to demonstrate, display, show (a) talent for sports; He squandered his natural talents as an artist instead of cultivating and developing them; a woman of considerable, outstanding talent; has the talent to become a maestro.* 2 persons with talent: *to recruit new talent; scouting for talent.* —*adja.:* *a talent scout, show.*

tal.ent.ed (TAL.un.tid) *adj.* gifted: *She's talented at* or *in sports; a talented artist, musician, player.*

ta.ler (TAH.lur) *n. sing. & pl.* a large German silver coin replaced by the mark in 1891.

tal.is.man (TAL.is.mun) *n.* **-mans** an object such as an inscribed ring which by its presence is supposed to bring good luck; charm or amulet.

talk (TAWK) *v.* 1 communicate with spoken words; speak: *Teachers talk to their classes; Parents talk with teachers; He was talking nonsense after a couple of drinks; Parrots can talk; to talk bluntly, frankly, freely, loudly, openly; to talk on* or *about a subject;* **Talk about** *punctuality – now see who is late! to talk him into buying* (= persuade him to buy) *the car; to talk him out of* (= dissuade him from) *buying the lemon; to talk oneself hoarse;* **n.:** *No **talking** allowed during the exam.* 2 tell; relate: *Police know how to make someone talk; Gossips talk behind our backs.* 3 discuss: *Let's talk business; We're talking a million dollars as investment.* —**money talks** money can get things done. —**talk back** *Informal.* answer impertinently. —**talk down** to speak to someone in a superior manner. —**talk out** discuss openly. —**talk over** 1 discuss something together. 2 persuade someone. —*n.* 1 a talking; informal conversation or speech: *much talk and little action; She gave her son a little talk about punctuation; blunt, double, heart-to-heart, idle, long, loose, pep, plain, sales, small, straight, sweet talk; There's talk of* or *about prices coming down; Their divorce is* **the talk of the town** (= subject of gossip). 2 **talks** *pl.* discussions: *peace talks, summit talks in Paris; to break off, conduct, hold talks about a treaty.* —**talk.er** *n.*: *a fast talker; smooth talker* (= one who talks deceptively).

talk.a.tive (TAW.kuh.tiv) *adj.* fond of talking: *friendly and talkative; too talkative;* **talk.a.tive.ly** *adv.;* **talk.a.tive.ness** *n.*

talking head *n. Informal.* a TV personality.

talking-to *n. Informal.* a scolding or lecture.

talk show *n.* a TV or radio show featuring interviews.

talk.y *adj. Informal.* talkative: *Some sales people are too talky.*

tall (TAWL) *adj.* 1 of people and things, having great length from top to bottom: *a tall structure; a tall lady; a woman of tall stature; a post three meters tall* (= high); *to stand tall* (= be resolute); *to walk tall* (= be proud). 2 *Informal.* extravagant, exaggerated, or difficult: *a tall price; a* **tall order** (= tough requirement or proposal); *a* **tall tale** (that is unbelievable). —**tall.ness** *n.*

tal.low (TAL.oh) *n.* a hard, white substance obtained by melting animal fat, used chiefly in making candles, soap, etc.: *beef tallow.*

tal.ly (TAL.ee) *n.* **tal.lies** 1 formerly, a notched stick as a reckoning device or either half of it split lengthwise for each of the two parties to a deal to keep; hence, a counterpart or duplicate. 2 a score or reckoning or its record: *to keep, make a tally using a* **tally sheet;** *the final tally; a running tally.* 3 a ticket or tag for identification. 4 a group forming a unit in counting; lot. —*v.* **tal.lies, tal.lied, tal.ly.ing:** *Votes for each side were* **tallied up** (= reckoned); *two accounts that don't tally* (= correspond or agree); *Your total doesn't tally with mine.*

tal.ly.ho (tal.ee.HOH) 1 *interj.* a huntsman's cry on sighting the fox. 2 *n.* a coach drawn by four horses.

Tal.mud (TAL.mud, TAHL.mood, short "oo") *n.* the body of early Jewish law and ethics; **Tal.mud.ist** *n.* —**Tal.mud.ic** (tal.MEW.dic) *adj.*

tal.on (TAL.un) *n.* 1 a claw of a bird of prey or animal. 2 a clawlike finger or hand.

tam same as TAM-O'-SHANTER.

tamable See TAME.

ta.ma.le (tuh.MAH.lee) *n.* a Mexican preparation of steamed corn meal mixed with highly seasoned pork or chicken.

tam.a.rack (TAM.uh.rak) *n.* 1 the North American "eastern larch" tree. 2 its wood.

tam.a.rind (TAM.uh.rind) *n.* a tropical tree of the pea family bearing plump pods containing an acid pulp used in foods.

tam.bou.rine (tam.buh.REEN) *n.* a shallow hand drum with jingles attached to the frame, played by shaking it or hitting it with the hand.

tame *adj.* **tam.er, tam.est** 1 of animals, domesticated, not wild; made docile: *a tame lion.* 2 dull or insipid: *a tame ending, imitation, show.* —*v.* **tames, tamed, tam.ing** make tame or docile: *to tame a bear, river; to tame an appetite; to tame inflation.* —**tame.a.ble** or **tam.a.ble** *adj.* —**tame.ly** *adv.;* **tame.ness** *n.*

Tam.il *n.* (a speaker of) a Dravidian language of S. India and N. Sri Lanka.

tam-o'-shan.ter (tam.uh.SHAN.tur) *n.* a Scottish cap with a flat crown and a pom-pom in the center.

tamp *v.* pack earth, tobacco, etc. down by a series of blows or taps.

tam.per (TAM.pur) *v.* interfere with the working of something: *Do not tamper with your watch; The lock has been tampered with; a lawyer accused of tampering with* (= influencing) *a jury.*

tam.pon (TAM.pon) *n.* a plug inserted into a wound or a body cavity to absorb a flow.

tan *n.* a yellowish brown color, as the skin color resulting from sunning: *to get a tan; a ski tan.* —*adj.* yellowish-brown: *a tan color, fabric, shade.* —*v.* **tans, tanned, tan.ning** 1 to get a tan: *the urge to tan; adj.: the tanned look; a deeply tanned skin; She looks tanned and confident; tanned and relaxed; tanned and rested; adja.:* **tanning** *accelerators, booths, lotions, products, salons.* 2 change hide into leather by soaking in dye. 3 *Informal.* whip or thrash.

tan.a.ger (TAN.uh.jur) *n.* a small songbird related to the finches, brilliantly

colored in the male.
tan.bark *n.* a tannin-rich bark, as of the oak or sumac.
tan.dem (TAN.dum) *adv.* one behind the other: *to ride tandem.* —*adja.* harnessed or arranged tandem: *a tandem arrangement; a **tandem bicycle** (with two seats and sets of pedals).*
—*n.* 1 a tandem arrangement or harness: *husband and wife working **in tandem**; Attitudes change **in tandem with** changing values.* 2 a tandem carriage, bicycle, or trailer.
tang *n.* 1 a sharp flavor or odor, as of garlic. 2 the projecting part of a knife or file that is held inside its handle.
—**tang.y** *adj.*: *a tangy flavor, Parmesan cheese, relish, sauce, taste; tart and tangy.*
tan.ge.lo (TAN.juh.loh) *n.* **-los** a fruit that is a cross between a tangerine and a "pomelo" (grapefruit).
tan.gent (TAN.junt) *n.* a line, curve, or surface that touches without cutting.
—**on a tangent** from one line of thought or action to another: *to fly off, go off, set off on a tangent.*
—**tan.gen.tial** (tan.JEN.shul) *adj.*; **tan.gen.tial.ly** *adv.*
tan.ge.rine (tan.juh.REEN) *n.* a delicate, loose-skinned kind of orange with segments that separate easily.
tan.gi.ble (TAN.juh.bul) *adj.* 1 that can be felt by touching: *an honor without any tangible benefits; tangible evidence, goals, improvements, proof, results, rewards, signs; real estate, gold bullion, paintings, natural resources, and such **tangible assets** (that can be appraised, unlike goodwill, intellectual property, etc. which are intangible).* 2 real or definite: *to show tangible improvement; tangible proof.*
—*n.* a material asset or property.
—**tan.gi.bly** (-blee) *adv.*
tan.gle (TAN.gul) *v.* **-gles, -gled, -gling** 1 of threads, hair, etc., twist together or become involved or entangled: *The skydiver got tangled in the parachute after hitting the water;* *adj.*: *a **tangled** mass of hair; a tangled web of lies, passions.* 2 *Informal.* quarrel or fight: *Don't tangle with police; Better to tango than tangle; The lawyers tangled over the interpretation of the regulations; two hockey players tangling along the boards.* —*n.* 1 a complicated or confused mass of material or condition: *tangles of hair, vines; a tangle of red tape.* 2 *Informal.* a quarrel or fight: *The tangle over the nation's finances became a crisis; a political tangle.*
tan.go (TANG.goh) *n.* **-gos** a ballroom dance characterized by long, gliding steps and intricate poses: *to dance the tango.* —*v.* **-gos, -goed, -go.ing** dance the tango: *"It takes two to tango"* (= to work in harmony, to fight, etc.).
tank *n.* 1 a cistern or large container for storing a fluid: *an automobile's gas tank; septic tank; water tank; a think tank (of thinkers and problem solvers); a railroad tank car.* 2 an armored vehicle moving on endless tracks and equipped with guns. —**tank.ful** *n.*
tank.ard (TANK.urd) *n.* a large drinking cup with a handle and hinged cover.
tank.er *n.* a ship, truck, railroad car, or aircraft equipped with a tank for transporting oil, refueling other planes, etc.
tank top *n.* a sleeveless, collarless top with shoulder straps like those of a one-piece bathing suit (**tank suit**).
tank truck *n.* a truck built as a tanker.
tan.ner *n.* one who tans hides.
tan.ner.y *n.* **tan.ner.ies** a place where tanning is done.
tan.nin *n.* a bitter substance produced in trees by insect larvae, used esp. in dyeing leather. Also **tan.nic acid**.
tan.sy (TAN.zee) *n.* **-sies** a bitter-tasting aromatic herb related to the thistle that yields an oil used in medicine.
tan.ta.lize (TAN.tuh.lize) *v.* **-liz.es, -lized, -liz.ing** torment or tease, as **Tantalus** of Greek myth, punished by continual disappointment whenever he tried to eat or drink what was placed within his reach: *a product designed to tantalize consumers into buying it;* *adj.*: *a **tantalizing** vision of water in the desert.* —**tan.ta.liz.ing.ly** *adv.*: *tantalizingly brief, close, obscure, similar.*
tan.ta.lum (TAN.tuh.lum) *n.* a rare, corrosion-resistant, metallic element.
tan.ta.mount (TAN.tuh.mount) *adjp.* equal in force or effect: *The "friendly warning" was tantamount to a threat.*
tan.trum (TAN.trum) *n.* an outburst of bad temper: *to have, throw a temper tantrum; a hysterical tantrum.*
Tan.za.ni.an (tan.zuh.NEE.un) *n. & adj.* (a person) of or from **Tanzania**, an E. African country.
Tao.ist (TOW.ist, DOW-) *n. & adj.* (having to do with) **Taoism**, a Chinese religion based on a philosophy developed as a reaction to Confucianism.
tap *n.* 1 a device for controlling an outflow, as a water faucet or the stopper of a cask: *tap water; what to do when the money tap runs dry; We've beer **on tap*** (= ready to be drawn). 2 a fluid drawn out, esp. liquor of a special quality. 3 a plug-in multiple electrical

outlet. **4** a wiretap. **5** a tool for cutting an internal screw thread, as of a bolt's nut. **6** a light, rapid blow: *a tap on the door, on someone's shoulder.*
—*v.* **taps, tapped, tap.ping 1** draw: *Latex, maple sap, etc. are tapped* (= drawn off) *from trees; phone lines suspected of being tapped* (= cut in on); *to tap* (= draw out the contents of) *a beer barrel; sources of energy waiting to be tapped* (= drawn upon); *to **tap into*** (= draw on or take advantage of) *a labor pool, a market, one's savings.* **2** rap or strike lightly, as on a door or on someone's back for attention: *He tapped out his message in code.* **3** choose someone for a post, membership, etc.: *She was tapped to head the project; tapped for president.* —**tap.per** *n.*

tap dance *n.* a dance performed with rhythmic tapping of the floor wearing specially soled shoes. —**tap-dance** *v.* -danc.es, -danced, -danc.ing; **tap-dancer** *n.*

tape *n.* **1** a narrow strip or band of fabric, paper, or light, flexible metal, as for measuring distances, binding or sticking, recording messages in sound or video, etc.: *adhesive, magnetic, masking, measuring, name, ticker tapes.* **2** a tape recording: *to make, play (back) a tape.* —*v.* **tapes, taped, tap.ing 1** to fasten with tape: *broken pieces taped together; mouth taped shut; a note taped to the door; a picture taped up on a wall.* **2** record on tape; *adj.*: *a **taped**, not live show; taped confessions, evidence, interviews, music, reminiscences, speeches.*

tape deck *n.* **1** the recording and playback unit of a hi-fi system with separate amplifier and speaker. **2** a tape player.

tape drive *n.* a computer storage device in which data is written to and read from a magnetic tape.

tape measure *n.* a measuring tape marked off in units of length.

tape player *n.* a playback machine for tape recordings or cassettes.

ta.per (TAY.pur) *n.* **1** a long wick or slender candle for lighting lamps, fires, etc. **2** a gradual decrease.
v.: *A church spire tapers* (= narrows) *toward the top; Rain will **taper off*** (= cease slowly) *after midnight.*

tape recorder *n.* a machine that records and plays back sound on magnetic tape. —**tape-record** (tape.ri.CORD) *v.*; **tape-recording** *n.*

tap.es.try (TAP.is.tree) *n.* -tries a decorative fabric woven in colorful designs and pictures for use as wall hangings, draperies, etc.

tape.worm *n.* a ribbonlike parasitic worm found in the intestines of humans and animals.

tap.i.o.ca (tap.ee.OH.cuh) *n.* a food starch obtained from the roots of the cassava.

ta.pir (TAY.pur) *n.* a piglike animal of South America and Malaya with an extended snout or short trunk.

tap.pet (TAP.it) *n.* in machines, a collar or arm for imparting intermittent motion, as to open and close a valve in an engine.

tap.room *n.* a barroom.

tap.root *n.* the main root growing vertically downward from a tree or plant and sprouting smaller roots sideways.

taps *n.pl.* the last bugle call at night signaling "lights out," originally a drum signal: *to play, sound taps; Lights go out at taps.*

tap.ster (TAP.stur) *n.* one who taps and serves liquor in a tavern.

tar *n.* **1** a thick, black, sticky substance obtained from coal, fats, and other organic matter and used in making asphalt, chemicals, etc. **2** *Informal.* sailor.
—*v.* **tars, tarred, tar.ring** cover or smear with or as if with tar: *It's not fair to **tar** everyone with the same brush* (= accuse everyone of having the same faults); *adj.*: *a **tarred*** (= asphalted) *road; a person **tarred and feathered*** (= covered with tar and feathers) *in punishment.*

ta.ran.tu.la (tuh.RAN.chuh.luh) *n.* a large, hairy, ferocious-looking spider of warm climates.

tar.dy (TAR.dee) *adj.* **tar.di.er, -di.est** slow or late, as because of sluggishness: *tardy progress, students; a tardy reply.* —**tar.di.ly** *adv.*; **tar.di.ness** *n.*

tare *n.* **1** the weight of a container or conveyance. **2** the allowance made for this when determining the net weight of the goods carried. **3** in the Bible, a weed. **4** a plant used as cattle fodder.
—*v.* **tares, tared, tar.ing** ascertain the tare of a container, etc.

tar.get (TAR.git, "g" as in "go") *n.* **1** a mark or other object that is aimed at in shooting: *to aim at, shoot at, hit, miss a target; to conduct* or *do **target practice**; to take lessons in **target shooting*** (to improve one's aim). **2** an object of attack: *an easy target; a moving target; a target for ridicule; the target of their hostility.* **3** a goal or objective: *Their target is upscale fashion; to finish a project **on target*** (= exactly as intended or planned); *adja.*: *the target audience, cus-*

tariff / taste

tomer, group, price; in a target range of 10% to 15%; the **target date** for completing a project; the **target language** (into which a translation is made).
—v. make a target of a person or thing: *The mob had targeted him as the next victim; a book targeted for spring publication; It's targeted at or for or to young adults;* **adj.**: *a more **targeted** approach; the show's targeted audience; targeted areas, groups, spending.*

tar.iff (TAIR.if) *n.* **1** a schedule or system of charges, rates, etc., esp. for taxing exports and imports. **2** any such tax, esp. import duty: *to impose, levy, pay a tariff; protective tariffs.*

tar.mac (TAR.mac) *n.* a paved area, as on an airfield: *planes sitting on the tarmac.*

tar.nish (TAR.nish) *v.* to dull the brightness of polished metal.
—*n.* a tarnishing or stain.
—**tar.nish.a.ble** *adj.*

ta.ro (TAH.roh) *n.* **-ros** a tropical plant of the arum family whose large underground stems are used as food.

tar.ot (TAIR.oh) *n.* one of a set of 22 playing cards, sometimes used for fortune-telling.

tar.pau.lin (tar.PAW.lin, TAR.puh-) *n.* waterproofed canvas used as a protective cover for exposed objects.

tar.pon (TAR.pun) *n.* a large game fish common off the S. Atlantic coast of the U.S.

tar.ra.gon (TAIR.uh.gun) *n.* a European herb related to the sagebrushes, used in salads and as flavoring for foods.

tar.ry (TAIR.ee) *v.* **tar.ries, tar.ried, tar.ry.ing** [literary] stay temporarily or longer than expected: *He didn't tarry long with us.* —**adj.** (TAR.ee) **tar.ri.er, tar.ri.est:** *a tarry oil, pool, substance.*

tar sands *n.pl.* sands containing oil.

tar.sus *n., pl.* **-si** (-sye) the group of small bones at the ankle, including the heel bone. —**tar.sal** (-sul) *adj.*

tart *adj.* **1** agreeably sour or acid, as certain apples. **2** caustic or sharp: *a tart reply, tongue.* —*n.* **1** a small, sweet pie with a filling of fruit, jam, or custard. **2** *Informal.* a prostitute.
—*v.* **tart up** decorate or make showy: *to get tarted up for an interview;* **adj.**: *a **tarted-up** version of the same old show.*
—**tart.ly** *adv.;* **tart.ness** *n.*

tar.tan (TAR.tun) *n.* a plaid woolen cloth, as worn by Scottish clansmen; **adja.**: *a tartan kilt; tartan fabrics, patterns, plaids, prints, skirts.*

Tar.tar (TAR.tur) *n.* **1** a member of a Turkic-speaking people of Europe and Asia. **2** a member of a Mongolian group that invaded W. Asia and E. Europe during the Middle Ages. **3** someone considered a savage.

tar.tar (TAR.tur) *n.* **1** a crusty deposit on teeth. **2** a salt deposited as a crust in wine casks, purified into "cream of tartar" for use in medicine and cooking. —**tar.tar.ic** (tar.TAIR.ic, -TAR.ic) *adj.*

tartar sauce *n.* a fish sauce made with mayonnaise, pickles, parsley, etc. Also **tartare** (-tur) **sauce.**

task *n.* a piece of usu. difficult work assigned to or demanded of someone: *to assign, carry out, do, fulfill, perform, set, undertake a task; delicate, difficult, hopeless, monumental, onerous, pleasant, welcome tasks; **home tasks** (= homework) set by teachers.* —**take to task** scold or reprove someone *for* something.

task force *n.* a group, as in the military, organized for a specific operation or inquiry: *the Mayor's Task Force on Multiculturalism.*

task.mas.ter (TASK.mas.tur) *n.* one who sets tasks of a demanding nature.

Tas.ma.ni.an (tas.MAY.nee.un) *n. & adj.* (a person) of or from **Tasmania,** an island state of Australia.

tas.sel (TAS.ul) *n.* **1** a hanging bunch of loose threads or cords, used as an ornament at the edge of a curtain, cushion, etc. **2** a tassellike tuft of flowers at the top of a cornstalk.
—*v.* **tas.sels, tas.seled, tas.sel.ing** put on or adorn with tassels. Also **tas.selled, tas.sel.ling** *Cdn.*

taste (TAIST) *n.* **1** what is sensed by the organs of the mouth, as sweet, sour, bitter, etc.: *Water has no taste or smell; Freezing spoils the taste of fresh food; bad, foul, nice, pleasant, sweet tastes; The experience left a bitter taste in her mouth.* **2** a small quantity or sample; a tasting: *Take a taste of this jam; an immigrant's first taste* (= experience) *of our winter.* **3** sense of perception or ability to perceive what is good: *to acquire, cultivate, demonstrate, develop, display, show a sense of taste; a taste for fine furniture; a woman of excellent taste; She has a discriminating taste in ceramics; an elegant, exquisite taste for china; Tastes* (= Likes) *differ; a pun that is not **in good taste;** It's **in bad** or **poor taste*** (= somewhat improper); *Add sugar **to taste*** (= in the quantity desired).
—*v.* **tastes, tast.ed, tast.ing 1** have a specified taste: *Sugar tastes sweet.* **2** have or try the taste of something:

taste bud / taxicab

He tastes wines for a living; The jailbird tasted (= experienced) freedom only briefly. —**taste of 1** experience: *a serious accident in which many tasted of death.* **2** have the flavor of something: *It tastes too much of garlic; a reply that tastes of arrogance.* —**tast.er** *n.*

taste bud *n.* any of the budlike projections on the tongue that act as taste sensors.

taste.ful *adj.* having or showing good artistic taste. —**taste.ful.ly** *adv.*

taste.less *adj.* **1** having no taste: *tasteless food.* **2** in bad taste: *tasteless jokes.*

tast.y (TAY.stee) *adj.* **tast.i.er, -i.est** that tastes good: *a tasty and filling meal; a tasty and tender cut of meat; a wholesome and tasty dish of vegetables; a tasty morsel, recipe, salad, tidbit.* —**tast.i.ness** *n.*

tat *v.* **tats, tat.ted, tat.ting** make lace by hand with loops and knots of thread wound around a shuttle. —**tat.ting** *n.* such lace.

ta.ta.mi (tuh.TAH.mee) *n.* a Japanese floor covering or mat of straw.

Ta.tar (TAH.tur) same as TARTAR.

tat.ter (TAT.ur) *n.* **1** a torn strip left loose on a garment. **2** a shred or scrap of paper, etc. **3 tatters** *pl.* torn and ragged clothes: *Communism is or lies* **in tatters.** —*v.* make or become ragged; *adj.:* **in tattered** *clothes, a tattered gown; the government's tattered image.*

tat.ter.de.mal.ion (tat.ur.duh.MAIL.yun) *n.* a person in tattered clothes; ragamuffin.

tat.ter.sall (TAT.ur.sawl) *n.* a check pattern of colored lines on a light background.

tat.tle (TAT.ul) *n.* idle talk; gossip.
—*v.* **tat.tles, tat.tled, tat.tling 1** gossip; tell tales or secrets: *a snitch who tattles on everyone to the authorities.* **2** reveal a secret by tattling. —**tat.tler** *n.*

tat.tle.tale (TAT.ul.tale) *n. Informal.* a telltale or informer.

tat.too (ta.TOO) *n.* **tat.toos 1** a bugle or drum signal calling soldiers, etc. to their quarters at night. **2** a rhythmic rapping or tapping. **3** a colored design put on the skin by pricking it with inks. **4** a military pageant or display. —*v.* **tat.toos, tat.tooed, tat.too.ing** mark the skin or put a design on it in this way; *adj.:* **a tattooed** *arm, design, sailor, skin.*

tat.ty (TAT.ee) *adj.* **tat.ti.er, tat.ti.est** shabby or worn down: *He works in a tatty old place; Children's books get tatty fast.*

taught *pt. & pp.* of TEACH.

taunt (TAWNT) *v.* jeer at or mock someone repeatedly so as to provoke: *They taunted Jim about his big ears; Jim couldn't be taunted into a fight.*
—*n.* such jeering or a taunting remark: *They hurled taunts at him.*

taupe (TOPE) *n.* a brownish gray, as of moleskin.

Tau.rus (TOR.us) *n.* **1** a N. constellation and the second sign of the zodiac. **2** a person born under this sign.

taut *adj.* **1** tightly stretched: *a taut bow, rope; taut sails.* **2** strained or tense: *taut muscles, nerves; a taut smile.* **3** tidy: *a taut ship.*

tau.tol.o.gy (taw.TOL.uh.jee) *n.* **-gies** the saying of a thing over again without added clarity or force, as in "The infant was lying naked with nothing on." —**tau.to.log.i.cal** (-tuh.LOJ.i.cul) *adj.*

tav.ern (TAV.urn) *n.* **1** an establishment where alcoholic liquor is served. **2** formerly, an inn.

taw *n.* **1** a marble used as a shooter. **2** the line from which marble players shoot. **3** the game of marbles.

taw.dry (TAW.dree) *adj.* **-dri.er, -dri.est** cheap or showy: *a tawdry dress, film, ornament.*

taw.ny (TAW.nee) *adj.* **-ni.er, -ni.est** brownish-yellow: *the lion's tawny coat; the tawny eagle of Africa; a tawny owl.*

tax *n.* **1** a charge levied on incomes, properties, or businesses by a government: *There's a tax on practically everything we buy or use; We pay capital gains, estate, excess-profits, excise, gift, income, nuisance, property, and sales taxes; a goods and services tax;* **adja.:** *tax avoidance, evasion, incentives, rates, relief; a* **tax haven** *in a Caribbean country (where taxes are very low); a* **tax holiday** *(= freedom from taxation).* **2** a strain or burden.
—*v.* **1** levy a tax on incomes, purchases, etc. **2** be a strain on or put a burden on something: *complaints that tax one's patience.* **3** accuse or charge: *taxed with neglect of duty.* **4** check or evaluate: *The client had his lawyer's bill taxed at the local courthouse.* —**tax.a.ble** *adj.*
—**tax.a.tion** (tax.AY.shun) *n.*

tax.i (TAX.ee) *n.* **-is** [short form] taxicab: *to arrive by taxi; to hire* or **take** *a taxi.* —*v.* **-is** or **-ies, -ied, tax.i.ing** or **tax.y.ing 1** go in a taxicab: *to taxi to the airport.* **2** of an airplane, move along the ground or on water after landing or in preparation for takeoff.

tax.i.cab (TAX.ee.cab) *n.* a chauffered

automobile for hire, usu. equipped with a meter (**taximeter**) for recording the fare.

tax.i.der.my (TAX.i.dur.mee) *n.* the art of stuffing and mounting the skins of animals for a lifelike look; **tax.i.der.mist** *n.*

tax.i.way (TAX.ee.way) *n.* a paved strip or lane that aircraft use to taxi to and from the runways.

tax.on.o.my (tax.ON.uh.mee) *n.* the biological classification of plants and animals; **tax.on.o.mist** *n.* —**tax.o.nom.ic** (tax.uh.NOM.ic) *adj.*

tax.pay.er (TAX.pay.ur) *n.* one who pays a tax; a member of the general public.

tax return *n.* a statement of income and taxes owed, filed annually with the government by taxpayers.

tax shelter *n.* a means of reducing one's income tax, as a financial investment.

T-bar lift *n.* a ski lift consisting of a motor-driven endless cable from which metal bars in the shape of an upside-down "T" are suspended for pulling up two skiers at a time.

T-bone steak *n.* a small beefsteak consisting of a T-shaped bone with some tenderloin; also **T-bone**.

T cell *n.* any of various blood cells that guard against and fight infections.

tea (TEE) *n.* **1** a yellowish-brown, slightly bitter beverage made with the cured leaves of an evergreen Asiatic shrub: *to make a cup of tea; iced, strong, weak tea;* **adj.:** *a tea bag, ceremony, party, set; tea time; Modern futurists don't have to read* **tea leaves** *(like fortune-tellers) to predict the future.* **2** the plant or the leaves prepared for use. **3** any tealike drink made with plant leaves or roots: *herbal teas.* **4** tea and refreshments served in the afternoon; also, a reception or party for this. **5** *Brit.* a late-afternoon meal at which tea is served: *They used to have "high tea" on Sundays.*

teach (TEECH) *v.* **teach.es, taught** (TAWT), **teach.ing 1** help to learn: *She teaches art; She teaches us to appreciate art; teaches us how to draw and paint; She could teach you a thing or two; Religions teach that God exists; That will teach you (to do as you are supposed to)!* **2** give lessons to someone: *to teach a class, students; She teaches school; He teaches for a living.* —**teach.a.ble** *adj.* —**teach.er** *n.*

teaching *n.* **1** a teacher's profession or practice: *to go into teaching as a career; practice teaching; team teaching;* **adj.:** *teaching aids, awards, experience, loads, materials, methods, strategies, tools; the teaching profession.* **2** what is taught by a person or institution: *Buddha's teachings; the teaching of the church on marriage and divorce.*

teaching machine *n.* a device with a corrective "right"-or-"wrong" feedback for use in programmed instruction.

tea.cup (TEE.cup) *n.* a cup for drinking tea.

teak (TEEK) *n.* **1** the strong and durable yellowish-brown wood of an East Indian tree. **2** the tree itself.

tea.ket.tle (TEE.ket.ul) *n.* a kettle with handle and spout.

teal (TEEL) *n.* a kind of small duck, esp. the "green-winged" and "blue-winged" species of North America.

team (TEEM) *n.* **1** a group of workers or players: *to field a team for the game; a combat team; home, negotiating, opposing, rival, visiting teams;* **adj.:** *team play, spirit;* **team teaching** *with several teachers for the same group of students.* **2** two or more draft animals harnessed to the same plough, wagon, etc. —*v.* **1** join individuals together in a team. **2** combine as a team: *Everyone teamed up against him; We teamed up to help him.*

team.mate (TEEM.mate) *n.* a fellow member of one's team.

team player *n.* one who works well as a team member without selfish aims: *a good team player.*

team.ster (TEEM.ster) *n.* one who hauls loads with a team or truck: *The Teamster's Union includes workers ranging from truck drivers to public service employees.*

¹**tear** (TARE) *v.* **tears, tore, torn, tear.ing** pull something apart by force, leaving rough or jagged edges: *She tore the letter open; tore it to pieces; an argument torn to shreds; His shirt tore on a nail; a group torn by factions; I felt torn between conflicting loyalties; She couldn't tear herself away from her family; Demolition crews* **tear down** *buildings; Critics mercilessly* **tore into** *(= attacked) him when his book was published; They* **tore the book apart** *(Informal for criticized it severely).* —*n.* **1** a tearing. **2** a torn place or rent: *to make, mend a tear; a* **tear sheet** *of a newspaper ad (containing the ad).*

²**tear** (TEER) *n.* a drop, or **teardrop**, of the salty liquid shed by the eyes, esp. when one cries: *to break into tears; shed tears; to weep bitter tears; Tears flow, roll, stream down one's cheeks; Tears well up in one's eyes; Eyes fill with tears; to be* **in tears** *(= weeping) over something.*

—**tear.ful** *adj.*; **tear.ful.ly** *adv.* —**tear.y** *adj.*

tear gas *n.* a gas used in dispersing people by irritating their eyes and causing tears to flow. —**tear-gas** *v.* **-gas.ses, -gassed, -gas.sing.**

tear.jerk.er (TEER.jur.kur) *n. Informal.* a highly sentimental play or motion picture.

tea.room *n.* a small restaurant serving tea, coffee, light meals, etc. and sometimes offering fortune-telling by tea-leaf reading.

tease (TEEZ) *v.* **teas.es, teased, teas.ing** 1 worry or annoy by repeated irritating actions or remarks: *She doesn't like to be teased by her playmates; He continued to tease (= beg) his parents after being refused.* 2 to card wool, flax, etc. or to comb hair toward the scalp so as to fluff it. —*n.* a teasing or one who teases.

tea.sel (TEE.zul) *n.* a thistlelike herb with stiff bracts surrounding its ripened flower heads, which are traditionally used to raise the nap in fulling cloth.

tea.spoon *n.* 1 a small spoon such as is used to stir tea. 2 a teaspoonful.

tea.spoon.ful (TEE.spoon.ful) *n.* **-fuls** a measuring unit equal to 1.6 fl. oz. (4.7 ml): *heaping, level, rounded teaspoonfuls.*

teat (TEET) *n.* the nipple on an udder or breast.

tech.ie (TEK.ee) *n. Informal.* a technically-minded person.

tech.ne.ti.um (tek.NEE.shee.um) *n.* the first man-made element, obtained as a byproduct in atomic fission.

tech.ni.cal (TEK.ni.cul) *adj.* 1 having to do with the practical or skilled aspect of an art or science: *a technical book written in technical language; He gets very technical when discussing his job; a technical expert, institute, journal, school, skill, term, training; technical assistance to developing countries.* 2 in a legal or formal sense: *a technical difference, foul, issue, knockout, problem.* —**tech.ni.cal.ly** *adv.*

tech.ni.cal.i.ty (tek.nuh.CAL.i.tee) *n.* **-ties** 1 quality or state of being technical. 2 a technical term, point, detail, etc.: *The case was lost on a legal technicality (= technical point).*

technical knockout *n.* the termination of a boxing match when the losing boxer is judged too tired to go on fighting.

tech.ni.cian (tek.NISH.un) *n.* one skilled in the techniques of a craft or occupation: *dental, electronic, laboratory,* *TV technicians; a superb technician (= craftsman) though not an artist.*

tech.nique (tek.NEEK) *n.* 1 the artistic skill or ability required to achieve an effect. 2 a method or manner of execution.

tech.noc.ra.cy (tek.NOC.ruh.see) *n.* management by technical experts.

tech.no.crat (TEK.nuh.crat) *n.* a technically trained administrator: *a military technocrat; The Deputy Minister is a hired technocrat, not an elected politician.* —**tech.no.crat.ic** (-CRAT.ic) *adj.*

tech.nol.o.gy (tek.NOL.uh.jee) *n.* **-gies** 1 science as applied to human needs, esp. in industry: *transfer of technology to developing countries.* 2 a technical method or process. —**tech.nol.o.gist** *n.* —**tech.no.log.i.cal** (-nuh.LOJ.i.cul) *adj.*; **tech.no.log.i.cal.ly** *adv.*

tec.ton.ics (tec.TON.ics) *n.pl.* [with *sing. v.*] the study of the earth's crust; **tec.ton.ic** *adj.*

ted.dy (TED.ee) *n.* **ted.dies** a stuffed toy bear; also **teddy bear.**

te.di.ous (TEE.dee.us) *adj.* long and tiresome; wearisome: *a tedious lecturer, lesson, process, trip, wait; tedious work.* —**te.di.ous.ly** *adv.*; **te.di.ous.ness** *n.*

te.di.um (TEE.dee.um) *n.* the condition or quality of being tedious; boredom.

tee *n.* 1 a small peg on which a golf ball is placed for driving. 2 the small area, or "teeing ground," from which play is begun at each hole of a golf course. —*v.* **tees, teed, tee.ing** place a ball on a tee. —**tee off** 1 begin play. 2 *Slang.* make angry or annoyed *about* or *at* something: *Insults don't tee me off as they used to.*

teem *v.* swarm with or be full of living beings: *The river teems with fish;* **adja.**: *We fished in the teeming river; the teeming jungle; Asia's teeming millions.*

teen *n.* 1 a teenager: *young teens;* **adja.**: *a teen gang, hit, movie; teen life, shows, troubles; the teen market; my teen years.* 2 **teens** *pl.* the years or numbers from 13 to 19: *She's still in her teens; early, late, mid teens; temperatures in the high teens to low 20s.*

teen.age or **teen-age** *adja.* 1 of people in their teens: *a teenage club, group; teenage motherhood, parenthood, pregnancy, years.* 2 in one's teens: *a teenage daughter, mother;* also **teenaged** or **teen-aged** *adj.*: *a teenaged student; She is teenaged.* —**teen.ag.er** (TEEN.ay.jur) *n.*

tee.ny (TEE.nee) *adj.* **-ni.er, -ni.est** *Informal.* tiny. Also **teen.ny-wee.ny, teen.sy, teen.sy-ween.sy.**

teeny-bopper *n. Informal.* a young teen-

teepee / telescope

ager, esp. one following the latest fads.
tee.pee (TEE.pee) same as TEPEE.
tee shirt same as T-SHIRT.
tee.ter (TEE.tur) v. **1** move unsteadily; waver: *to teeter on the brink of collapse.* **2** teeter-totter; seesaw.
teeter-totter same as SEESAW.
teeth *pl.* of TOOTH.
teethe (TEETH, "TH" as in "the") v. **teethes, teethed, teeth.ing** grow teeth, as an infant; *adja.: teething pains, problems; teething rings (for infants to bite on).*
tee.to.tal.er (tee.TOH.tul.ur) n. one pledged to drink no alcoholic liquor. —**tee.to.tal.ism** n. Also **tee.to.tal.ler** *Cdn.*
tef.lon n. a tough, heat- and corrosion-resistant plastic used as a nonstick coating on cooking utensils, as an insulator, etc.; *adja.: a teflon coating, finish; a teflon character (with an undamaged reputation); teflonlike resistance.* —**Teflon** *Trademark.*
tek.tite n. a tiny glassy globule of a meteoric kind.
tele- *comb.form.* far or distant: *telecast, telecopier, television;* **telebus** (= a dial-a-bus service).
tel.e.cast (TEL.i.cast) n. & v. **-casts,** *pt. & pp.* **-cast** or **-cast.ed, -cast.ing** broadcast by television. —**tel.e.cast.er** n.
tel.e.com.mu.ni.ca.tion (TEL.i.cuh.mew.ni.CAY.shun) n. communication by radio, telephone, telegraph, etc.
tel.e.com.mute (TEL.i.cuh.MUTE) v. **-mutes, -mut.ed, -mut.ing** work from one's home for another person using a computer and communications equipment.
tel.e.con.fer.ence (TEL.i.con.fuh.runce) n. a conference of people in distant places using telecommunications equipment.
tel.e.cop.i.er (TEL.i.cop.ee.ur) or **tel.e.fax** (TEL.uh.fax) same as FAX.
tel.e.film (TEL.uh.film) n. a motion picture produced for television.
tel.e.gen.ic (tel.i.JEN.ic) *adj.* of a person, who looks attractive on television.
tel.e.gram (TEL.i.gram) n. a message sent by telegraph.
tel.e.graph (TEL.i.graf) v. **-graphs, -graphed, -graph.ing** send a message to a person by telegraph: *She telegraphed him greetings.* —n. a system or apparatus for sending messages by wire or radio using electrical impulses. —**tel.e.graph.ic** (-GRAF.ic) *adj.*
—**te.leg.ra.phy** (tuh.LEG.ruh.fee) n.

tel.e.ki.ne.sis (TEL.i.ki.NEE.sis) n. the moving of objects by psychic power without touching them.
tel.e.mar.ket.ing (TEL.i.mar.kit.ing) n. selling by telephone.
tel.e.me.ter (TEL.i.mee.tur) n. an apparatus for measuring and transmitting data from a distance, as used in weather balloons and spacecraft.
—**tel.e.met.ric** (-MET.ric) *adj.*
—**te.lem.e.try** (tuh.LEM.uh.tree) n.
te.lep.a.thy (tuh.LEP.uh.thee, "th" as in "thin") n. communication between persons by thought alone, without sensory means. —**tel.e.path.ic** (tel.i.PATH.ic) *adj.*
tel.e.phone (TEL.uh.fone) v. **-phones, -phoned, -phon.ing** speak to someone or communicate a message using the telephone: *to telephone someone; to telephone a message; to telephone the results of the test; He telephoned that he had won.* —n. a system or apparatus for the transmission of speech sounds over wires using electrical impulses: *She was called to the telephone; talked to him by telephone; had a long talk on or over the telephone; She's on the telephone much of the time; to answer, dial, disconnect, tap a telephone; A telephone directory lists the names, addresses, and telephone numbers of subscribers in a particular area; People waste time playing telephone tag (trying to reach a number that is always busy).*
—**tel.e.phon.ic** (tel.uh.FON.ic) *adj.*
—**te.leph.o.ny** (tuh.LEF.uh.nee) *n.: cordless, long-distance, mobile, radio, voice telephony; adja.: telephony circuits, functions, license, service, systems.*
tel.e.pho.to (tel.uh.FOH.toh) *adj.* producing a large image of a distant object: *a telephoto camera, lens, shot; a 70-210 mm telephoto zoom.*
tel.e.play (TEL.uh.play) n. a play produced for television.
tel.e.print.er (TEL.uh.prin.tur) same as TELETYPEWRITER.
tel.e.prompt.er (TEL.uh.promp.tur) n. an electronic device for giving a speaker on TV a line-by-line view of the script. —**Teleprompter** *Trademark.*
tel.e.scope (TEL.uh.scope) n. an instrument for observing distant objects, esp. celestial bodies. —v. **-scopes, -scoped, -scop.ing** slide into one another like the sections of a collapsible telescope. —**tel.e.scop.ic** (tel.uh.SCOP.ic) *adj.* **1** that can be extended or shortened: *telescopic car antennae; telescopic extensions; an ironing board with adjustable telescopic feet or legs.* **2** having to do with telescopes: *a telescopic lens;*

the telescopic sight of a gun.
tel.e.text (TEL.i.text) *n.* the broadcasting of printed information for reception on video terminals.
tel.e.thon (TEL.i.thon) *n.* a long TV program for a special purpose such as to raise funds for charity.
tel.e.type (TEL.i.type) *v.* **-types, -typed, -typ.ing** send a message by teletypewriter. —*n.* a teletypewriter; **Teletype** *Trademark.*
tel.e.type.writ.er (tel.uh.TYPE.rye.tur) *n.* a form of telegraph in which messages to be sent are typed out and reproduced by means of an automatic typewriter at the receiving end.
tel.e.van.gel.ist (tel.i.VAN.juh.list) *n.* one who preaches the gospel via TV.
tel.e.vise (TEL.uh.vize) *v.* **-vis.es, -vised, -vis.ing** broadcast by television.
tel.e.vis.ion (TEL.uh.vizh.un) See TV.
tel.ex (TEL.ex) *n.* a teletypewriter system operated by dialing subscribers' numbers. Also *v.* —**Telex** *Trademark.*
tell *v.* **tells, told, tell.ing** **1** make known in words; say or inform: *to tell a story; to tell (them) the truth; Please tell us all about it; Please tell him to start; I'll tell you when to stop; All right, tell me when; I tell you that it is a secret; It's a secret you're not supposed to tell* (= reveal); *Dead people tell no tales* (= don't reveal secrets); *She's telling her beads* (= counting the beads one by one in prayer); *It's hard to tell the twins apart* (= distinguish them); *hard to tell one (twin) from the other;* ***You can never tell*** or ***You never can tell*** (= never be certain). **2** have a marked effect: *Every blow tells; High inflation tells heavily on our buying power.* —**tell it like it is** *Informal.* tell the whole truth; be forthright. —**tell off 1** count off a few from a group for a special task. **2** *Informal.* rebuke or scold. —**tell on** *Informal.* inform on someone: *She threatened to tell on him for cheating; to tell Dad on him.*
tell.er *n.* **1** one who tells. **2** one who counts votes, money, etc., esp. a bank cashier who receives and pays out money.
telling *adj.* effective; striking: *a telling argument, blow, impression.*
—**tell.ing.ly** *adv.*
tell.tale *adj.* revealing: *a telltale blush, leak, sign, test, trace.* —*n.* one who informs on others; tattletale.
tel.lu.ri.um (tuh.LOOR.ee.um) *n.* a metalloid element similar to selenium.
tel.ly (TEL.ee) *n. Brit. Informal.* television.

tem.blor *n.* an earthquake.
te.mer.i.ty (tuh.MER.i.tee) *n.* rashness or boldness: *the temerity to ask for a raise when his job is in danger.*
tem.per (TEM.pur) *n.* **1** emotional nature or state of mind in regard to anger: *He's in a bad temper; She knows how to control, keep her temper; a calm, even, hot, nasty, quick, ungovernable, violent temper; He broke the vase in a fit of temper; Tempers flare up during arguments; She never **loses her temper*** (= calmness of mind). **2** degree of hardness, strength, and toughness given to a material such as steel or glass by a heating-and-cooling process: *the economic temper of the times.* —*v.* **1** soften or mitigate: *to temper justice with mercy; Her judgment has been tempered by experience.* **2** bring to the proper condition, esp. of toughness: *Clay is tempered by moistening, mixing, kneading, etc.*
tem.per.a (TEM.puh.ruh) *n.* a painting method using colors mixed with egg whites, yolks, etc. instead of oil as the medium so as to produce an opaque effect: *to paint in tempera;* **adja.:** *egg tempera paintings; tempera colors, paints.*
tem.per.a.ment (TEM.pur.uh.munt) *n.* **1** the nature of a person as shown by behavior, tendencies, and aspirations: *an artistic temperament; her poetic temperament; his restless temperament.* **2** an excitable or moody nature: *He's a genius, but no one can stand his temperament.*
tem.per.a.men.tal (TEM.pur.uh.MEN.tul) *adj.* **1** having to do with temperament: *a temperamental trait; Her problem was more ideological than temperamental.* **2** impulsive or unpredictable: *a temperamental actor, director, outburst, player, singer; Soufflés can be difficult and temperamental; a temperamental elevator; the temperamental ups and downs of the economy.*
tem.per.ance (TEM.puh.runce) *n.* moderation in indulging the pleasures of the senses, esp. partial or total abstinence from alcoholic liquor.
tem.per.ate (TEM.puh.rit) *adj.* **1** deliberately self-restrained: *temperate language, manners; a temperate reply.* **2** moderate in climate; neither very hot nor very cold: *California has a temperate climate; the temperate Niagara region; temperate rain forests, latitudes, weather; the **Temperate Zones** lying between the tropics and the polar circles.* **3** that grow in temperate regions: *temperate crops such as cereals; temperate fruits such as apples, peaches, and plums.* **4** moderate in regard to alcoholic

drinks: *a man of temperate habits; House wine is the temperate beverage recommended in the Bible.*

tem.per.a.ture (TEM.puh.ruh.chur) *n.* **1** degree of heat or cold: *the temperature of boiling water; Keep it at room temperature; Normal body temperature is 37°C (98.6°F); Temperatures drop, fall, go down, go up, rise; high, low, normal temperatures.* **2** fever: *The patient is having or running a temperature; a high temperature; slight temperature; Let's take his temperature.*

tempered (TEM.purd) *adj.* properly conditioned: *tempered clay, glass, steel; a tempered level of enthusiasm; tempered optimism.* —**comb.form.** having a specified emotional nature: *bad-tempered, even-tempered, foul-tempered, good-tempered, hot-tempered, ill-tempered, quick-tempered, short-tempered; sweet-tempered.*

temper tantrum same as TANTRUM.

tem.pest (TEM.pist) *n.* a violent windstorm, often with rain, snow, or hail: *a mere tempest in a teapot* (= an uproar about nothing). —**tem.pes.tu.ous** (tem.PES.choo.us) *adj.: tempestuous seas; a tempestuous affair, career, meeting, romance.*

tem.plate (TEM.plit) *n.* **1** a pattern, usu. a thin metal plate, from which an exact copy may be traced and cut. **2** any of various guides for cutting tools, or a routing or locating device.

tem.ple (TEM.pul) *n.* **1** a building dedicated to the worship of a god or gods: *Hindu temples; a Mormon temple.* **2** either side of the head between forehead and ear. **3** the hinged arm of a spectacle frame.

tem.po (TEM.poh) *n., pl.* **-pi** (-pee) or **-pos 1** in music, speed of movement: *to increase, slow down, step up the tempo.* **2** pace of activity: *the fast tempo of city life.*

tem.po.ral (TEM.puh.rul) *adj.* **1** of earthly life, not eternal or spiritual; secular or worldly: *our temporal affairs.* **2** of the temples of the head: *the temporal bones.*

tem.po.rar.y (TEM.puh.rair.ee) *adj.* lasting only for a time; not permanent: *a temporary appointment, job, measure; temporary quarters.* —**tem.po.rar.i.ly** (-RAIR.uh.lee, -rair.uh.lee) *adv.*

tem.po.rize (TEM.puh.rize) *v.* **-riz.es, -rized, -riz.ing** delay a decision or answer so as to gain time; **tem.po.riz.er** *n.*

tempt *v.* try to make someone do something attractive but not necessarily good: *Eve tempted Adam to eat the forbidden fruit; When the car stalled yet again, I was tempted to dump it; Daredevils like to tempt* (= risk or defy) *fate;* **adj.:** *a tempting* (= attractive) *offer, price, target; food that is tempting to the palate; a pleasure too tempting to resist; It's tempting to sleep in when there's work to do.* —**tempt.er** *n.;* **tempt.ress** (-tris) *fem.*

temp.ta.tion (temp.TAY.shun) *n.* **1** a tempting: *to be exposed to, to face, fall a prey to, give in to, give way to, overcome, resist, be subject to, succumb to, yield to temptation; an irresistible, strong temptation to break the diet.* **2** that which tempts: *boys, cheese, girls, ice cream, and such temptations.*

tem.pu.ra (TEM.puh.rah, -POOR.uh) *n.* a Japanese dish of fish or vegetables fried in batter.

ten *n., adj. & pron.* one more than nine; 10 or X.

ten.a.ble (TEN.uh.bul) *adj.* that can be held or defended, as against attack: *a tenable position, theory, view.* —**ten.a.bil.i.ty** (-BIL.i.tee) *n.*

ten.a.cious (tuh.NAY.shus) *adj.* **1** firmly holding, clinging, etc.: *a tenacious glue, grip, hold, memory.* **2** persistent or resolute: *her tenacious courage, dedication, efforts, struggle; She's very tenacious of her rights; a tenacious sales rep.* —**te.nac.i.ty** (-NAS.i.tee) *n.*

ten.an.cy (TEN.un.see) *n.* **-cies** (the period of) occupancy of a tenant.

ten.ant (TEN.unt) *n.* one paying rent for the occupancy and use of land or a building; occupant: *our previous tenant.* —*v.* occupy as a tenant: *rooms tenanted by students.*

tend *v.* **1** incline or have a tendency: *As we grow old, we tend to forget things; views tending toward the Left; The road tends* (= goes toward) *right from there.* **2** attend to or take care of something: *Shepherds tend sheep; someone to tend the store while I'm away.*

tend.en.cy (TEN.dun.see) *n.* **-cies** a natural inclination or disposition; leaning: *a tendency to fall asleep at the wheel; a suicidal tendency; the upward tendency of prices.*

ten.den.tious (ten.DEN.shus) *adj.* one-sided or biased: *a tendentious report, statement; tendentious writings.*

ten.der (TEN.dur) *n.* **1** one that tends or a person in charge of something. **2** a formal offer, proposal, or bid: *The government asks for* or *calls for* or *invites sealed tenders for a contract; A contract is put up for tender; payment by legal tender* (= offer of money). **3** something that

attends to or serves, as a boat or small ship attending a larger vessel to carry supplies and passengers or the car attached to a locomotive to carry a supply of coal and water.
—*v. Formal.* **1** offer or present: *He tendered apologies, thanks; She tendered her resignation; The shareholders tendered their stock (for sale).* **2** propose or bid: *to tender against competitors.*
—*adj.* **1** soft or delicate: *the tender loving care of parents; a tender child, conscience, heart, smile, subject, tale, wound; Cook the noodles until just tender; tender meat.* **2** early: *at the tender age of 10; one's tender years.* —**ten.der.ly** *adv.*; **ten.der.ness** *n.*

ten.der.foot (TEN.dur.foot) *n.* **-foots** or **-feet 1** a newcomer to a life of hardship, as in pioneer country. **2** a novice.

ten.der.heart.ed (TEN.dur.HAR.tid) *adj.* easily moved to pity or compassion.

ten.der.ize (TEN.duh.rize) *v.* **-iz.es, -ized, -iz.ing** make meat tender by pounding or by using enzymes. —**ten.der.iz.er** *n.*

ten.der.loin (TEN.dur.loin) *n.* **1** a tender part of a loin of beef or pork: *sliced tenderloin of beef;* **adja.**: *tenderloin roast, steaks.* **2 Tenderloin** the district of a city noted for vice and corruption: *in the heart of the Tenderloin; the Tenderloin district.*

tender offer *n.* a public offer to purchase stock from a company's shareholders for buying up the company.

ten.di.ni.tis (ten.duh.NYE.tis) *n.* inflammation of a tendon.

ten.don (TEN.dun) *n.* a strong, fibrous band or cord attaching muscles to bones or cartilages: *He pulled a tendon in his foot.*

ten.dril *n.* the threadlike clinging organ of a climbing plant.

ten.e.ment (TEN.uh.munt) *n.* **1** dwelling house, esp. one divided into units for several families. **2** a living unit or apartment in an overcrowded dwelling house, or **tenement house.**

ten.et (TEN.it) *n.* a doctrine or belief held in common by a group or profession: *Anglican tenets; the basic tenets of socialism.*

ten.fold *adj. & adv.* ten times.

ten-four *n.* in radio communications, "OK"; "message received."

ten.nis *n.* a game played between two or two pairs of players on a rectangular court divided by a net using rackets to hit a pressurized ball back and forth.

ten.on (TEN.un) *n.* the projecting end of a piece that fits into a hollow in another to make a mortise joint.

ten.or (TEN.ur) *n.* **1** the general direction or tendency; drift: *the tenor of a conversation; Nothing disturbs the even tenor of her life.* **2** the highest regular adult male voice; also, a part for or a singer with such a voice: *He sings tenor.* **3** an instrument with a tenor range.

ten.pin *n.* a bottle-shaped bowling pin, as used in the commonest form of bowling, or **ten.pins.**

tense (TENCE) *n.* the form of a verb showing time: *past, present, and future tenses.* —*adj.* **tens.er, tens.est 1** stretched tight; taut: *a tense muscle, rope.* **2** showing or feeling nervous tension; hence, anxious: *tense nerves; a tense moment; The atmosphere was tense with expectation.* —*v.* **tens.es, tensed, tens.ing** make or become tense: *His body tensed when she touched him; You tense your arm muscles when you pick up a weight;* *adj.*: *a tensed muscle.* —**tense.ly** *adv.* —**tense.ness** or **ten.si.ty** *n.*

ten.sile (TEN.sul, -sile) *adj.* having to do with tension: *Steel has the highest* **tensile strength** (= breaking limit).

ten.sion (TEN.shun) *n.* **1** a stretched or strained condition: *the tension of a cable, fan belt, violin string.* **2** strain: *Chewing gum is supposed to help relieve (nervous) tension; a hostile meeting in an atmosphere of tension; to alleviate, cause, create, increase, heighten, lessen tension; racial tensions in big cities; There was mounting tension between the U.S. and Russia during the missile crisis; Tension built up, then eased.* **3** voltage: *a high-tension wire.*

ten-speed *n.* a bicycle with ten gears.

tent *n.* **1** a light, portable shelter made usu. of canvas stretched over supporting poles, as used when camping; also, a tepee or wigwam: *to dismantle, erect, pitch, put up, take down a tent.* **2** a tent-like canopy: *The pneumonia patient was kept in an oxygen tent for several days.*

ten.ta.cle (TEN.tuh.cul) *n.* a slender flexible arm of an animal used for capturing food, as in octopuses, used as feelers, as in mollusks, or for protection, as in the jellyfish.

ten.ta.tive (TEN.tuh.tiv) *adj.* done or made as a trial or first step; provisional: *a tentative acceptance, agreement, plan, proposal, refusal; a tentative* (= hesitant) *smile.* —**ten.ta.tive.ly** *adv.*

ten.ter.hook (TEN.tur.hook) *n.*: *He was*

on tenterhooks (= in a state of anxious suspense) *waiting for the verdict.*

tenth *adj. & adv.* next after the ninth: *the tenth candidate; He came tenth.* —*n. & pron.* a tenth person or thing: *the tenth of August; nine tenths of the people.*

ten.u.ous (TEN.yoo.us) *adj.* extremely thin or fine: *the tenuous spider web; a tenuous distinction, fabric; the tenuous* (= rare) *mountain air; a tenuous* (= flimsy or weak) *claim.* —**ten.u.ous.ly** *adv.;* **ten.u.ous.ness** *n.*

ten.ure (TEN.yur) *n.* the act, right, period, or manner of holding an office or position: *during her long tenure in office; to get, grant, receive tenure* (= permanence in a position); *a* **tenure-track** *professor (due to receive tenure); adj.: a* **tenured** (= permanent) *position, professor.*

te.pee (TEE.pee) *n.* the cone-shaped tent used by Plains Indians.

tep.id (TEP.id) *adj.* **1** lukewarm: *tepid water.* **2** lacking fervor or enthusiasm: *He expressed only tepid approval of the plan.* —**te.pid.i.ty** (tuh.PID.i.tee) *n.*

te.qui.la (tuh.KEE.luh) *n.* a Mexican liquor distilled from the juice of an agave plant.

tera- *prefix.* one trillion: *terabyte, teraflops, terawatt.*

ter.bi.um (TUR.bee.um) *n.* a rare-earth chemical element.

ter.cen.te.nar.y (tur.sen.TEN.uh.ree, -SEN.tuh.nuh.ree) *n. & adj.* **-nar.ies** a 300th anniversary (celebration); also **ter.cen.ten.ni.al** (-sen.TEN.ee.ul).

te.re.do (tuh.REE.doh) *n.* **-dos** a shipworm.

term *n.* **1** a word or expression with a definite function or precise meaning: *a legal term such as "ex parte"; a technical term; the three algebraic terms in "$x^2 + y^2 + 2xy$."* **2 terms** *pl.* way of expressing oneself; words: *She spoke about him in flattering terms; He described her in glowing terms; They spoke in vague, general terms; "Square circle" is a contradiction in terms; They told him in no uncertain terms* (= very clearly) *to shape up or ship out.* **3** a set or fixed period: *a four-year term of office; the term of a lease; a school term running from September to December; In the short term we may lose money, but we hope to show a profit in the long term; a baby born* **at full term** (= after a full period in the womb). **4 terms** *pl.* conditions of agreement: *by or under the terms of an agreement, contract, lease, treaty; to negotiate with them on equal terms; They were in no position to dictate terms to us; to state, stipulate terms; He agreed to surrender to us on our own terms; easy, equal, familiar, favorable, intimate terms; We're not on speaking terms* (= relations); *We had to* **come to terms** (= reach an agreement) *or someone else would* **bring** (= force) *us* **to terms;** *He had to* **come to terms with** (= learn to live with) *the fact that he was now broke.* —**in terms of** as regards; concerning. —*v.* name or call by a term: *Her performance was termed (as) "outstanding" by the media.*

ter.mi.nal (TUR.muh.nul) *adj.* **1** having to do with a fixed period or term: *terminal accounts, examinations.* **2** having to do with an end part or final stage: *a terminal bud, outpost; a terminal case, illness, patient (that ends in death);* **terminal leave** *granted before retirement.* —*n.* **1** an end or extremity of a transportation or communication line: *the keyboard of a computer terminal (where data is typed in); a video display terminal* (= screen on which video output is shown); *the observation deck of an air terminal (where airplanes are boarded and discharged); at a bus, freight, shipping, trucking terminal* (= station). **2** a point of electrical connection: *the positive and negative terminals of a battery.*
—**ter.mi.nal.ly** *adv.*

ter.mi.nate (TUR.muh.nate) *v.* **-nates, -nat.ed, -nat.ing** put or come to an end: *to terminate a contract, discussion, employee, job, partnership; to terminate a pregnancy (by abortion); The flight terminates in Toronto.* —**ter.mi.na.tion** (-NAY.shun) *n.*

ter.mi.nol.o.gy (tur.muh.NOL.uh.jee) *n.* **-gies** (a system of) terms used in a branch of study or line of work: *legal, scientific, technical terminologies; to codify, establish, standardize a terminology; the basic terminology of grammar.* —**ter.mi.no.log.i.cal** (-nuh.LOJ.i.cul) *adj.*

term insurance *n.* life insurance providing protection for a specified period.

ter.mi.nus (TUR.muh.nus) *n., pl.* **-ni** (-nye) or **-nus.es** the final point or place where something terminates: *the terminus of a busline, pipeline, railroad.*

ter.mite (TUR.mite) *n.* an antlike insect that is very destructive to wooden structures.

tern *n.* a sea bird of the gull family but smaller and with a long forked tail.

ter.nar.y (TUR.nuh.ree) *adj.* triple or threefold: *binary and ternary compounds; a ternary system (of three components).*

terp.si.cho.re.an (TURP.si.cuh.REE.un) *adj.* having to do with dancing.

ter.race (TER.is) *n.* **1** an open courtyard adjoining a house, sometimes overlooking a garden. **2** the flat roof of an Oriental or Spanish house. **3** one of a series of levels bounded by ridges made on sloping land for irrigation and to prevent erosion; *adj.*: *a **terraced** hillside; terraced cultivation.* **4** a row of houses along a slope above street level.

ter.ra cot.ta (TER.uh.COT.uh) *n.* a hard, durable, high-quality clay or earthenware or a figure made with it.

terra fir.ma (-FUR.muh) *n.* solid ground, as opposed to air or water: *We are glad to be back on terra firma after a troubled voyage.*

ter.rain (tuh.RAIN, TER.ain) *n.* a stretch of land with regard to its natural features or fitness for a use such as warfare: *hilly, mountainous, rough, smooth terrain.*

terra in.cog.ni.ta (-in.COG.nuh.tuh, -in.cog.NEE.tuh) *n., pl.* **ter.rae in.cog.ni.tae** (-tee) unexplored territory.

ter.ra.pin (TER.uh.pin) *n.* a North American turtle, esp. the "diamondback terrapin."

ter.rar.i.um (tuh.RAIR.ee.um) *n.* **-i.ums** or **-i.a** (-ee.uh) an indoor miniature garden in a covered glass container.

ter.raz.zo (tuh.RAZ.oh, -RAHT.soh) *n.* a mosaic flooring of marble chips set in cement.

ter.res.tri.al (tuh.RES.tree.ul) *adj.* **1** of the earth, not celestial: *our terrestrial globe; terrestrial magnetism; a terrestrial rocket guidance system; Mercury, Venus, and Mars are terrestrial planets (like the Earth).* **2** of the ground or land: *sediments of terrestrial origin; terrestrial* (= not aerial or aquatic) *plants.*

ter.ri.ble (TER.uh.bul) *adj.* **1** causing terror or extreme fear: *a terrible anxiety, crime, fear.* **2** *Informal.* extremely bad: *a terrible dinner, joke, pain; I feel terrible.*

ter.ri.bly (TER.uh.blee) *adv. Informal.* extremely: *terribly afraid, clear, expensive, sorry.*

ter.ri.er (TER.ee.ur) *n.* a breed of usu. small, active watchdogs, originally used to drive game out of burrows in the ground.

ter.ri.fic (tuh.RIF.ic) *adj.* **1** *Informal.* extraordinary; astounding: *a terrific achievement, idea, speed, view; You look terrific!* **2** causing great fear; terrifying: *a terrific fear, fight, roar, toll of lives.*

ter.ri.fy (TER.uh.fye) *v.* **-fies, -fied, -fy.ing** fill with terror: *He was terrified by the thought of what might happen; adj.: a **terrified** child; He's terrified of looking down from the top; terrified that he may lose his balance; adj.: a **terrifying** event, experience, ordeal, prospect, scene.*

ter.ri.to.ri.al (ter.uh.TOR.ee.ul) *adj.* having to do with territory or a particular area: *a country's territorial ambitions; territorial government; a nation's rights over its **territorial waters*** (= waters off the coast but not the high seas).

ter.ri.to.ry (TER.uh.tor.ee) *n.* **-ries** an area or region in regard to jurisdiction or control over it: *mandated, neutral, occupied, trust, unexplored territories; A territory has less self-government than a province or state; India used to be British territory; a territory ceded to China; Most animals defend their territory aggressively; a territory assigned to a sales representative; Religion is outside the territory* (= sphere of activity; province) *of science; For a celebrity, signing autographs **comes** or **goes with the territory*** (= is part of being a celebrity).

ter.ror (TER.ur) *n.* **1** great fear: *to terspire, resort to, rule by, sow, spread terror; absolute, mortal, sheer terror; a campaign of terror; the Reign of Terror during the French Revolution; People **lived in terror** of being guillotined; The murders **struck terror into** our hearts; adja.: terror campaigns, squads; terror tactics used by guerrillas.* **2** the cause of it: *That child is a terror* (*Informal* for one who is hard to manage).

ter.ror.ism (TER.uh.riz.um) *n.* the policy of repressive governments, guerrillas, etc. of using hijackings, killings, kidnapings, etc. as a means to achieve political ends: *acts of terrorism; state terrorism.* —**ter.ror.ist** *n. & adj.*

ter.ror.ize (TER.uh.rize) *v.* **-iz.es, -ized, -iz.ing** terrify, esp. as a means of coercion: *a people terrorized into submission.*

ter.ry *n.* a cotton cloth with a pile of uncut loops for absorbency, as used for towels, sweaters, etc.; also **terry cloth.**

terse *adj.* **ters.er, ters.est** concise in expression, sometimes witty, often brusque: *a terse "No comment"; a terse announcement, expression, rejection, response, statement, style, writer.* —**terse.ly** *adv.;* **terse.ness** *n.*

ter.ti.ar.y (TUR.shee.air.ee, -shuh.ree) *adj.* of the third order or rank: *a **tertiary color*** (obtained by mixing orange, green, and such secondary colors); *elementary, secondary, and tertiary* (= university) *education; rocks of the* **Tertiary period** *of life on the Earth (up to two million years ago).*

tes.sel.late (TES.uh.late) *v.* **-lates, -lat.ed, -lat.ing** pave in a checkered pattern of small squares; *adj.: a tessellated floor, pavement.* —**tes.sel.la.tion** (-LAY.shun) *n.*

test *n.* an examination or trial for comparison with a standard: *a test of intelligence; a blood test for sugar; a driving test; to administer* or *give, carry out, conduct* or *do, fail, pass, run, take a test; to put someone to the test; to stand the test of time; an acid test; demanding, difficult, easy, exhaustive, objective, severe, thorough tests; competency, endurance, litmus, means, nuclear, personality, pregnancy, road tests; to run a series of tests on a patient; tabulation of tests* (= test results); *adja.: a test case, drive, flight, pilot.*
—*v.* **1** put to test: *to test someone for AIDS.* **2** score or rate on tests: *He tested positive; She tested high in intelligence.*
—**test.er** *n.*

tes.ta.ment (TES.tuh.munt) *n.* **1** the Old Testament or the New Testament of the Bible. **2** a statement of beliefs. **3** a will disposing of one's property: *my last will and testament.* —**tes.ta.men.ta.ry** (-MEN.tuh.ree) *adj.*

tes.tate *n. & adj.* (one) who has left a valid will.

tes.ta.tor (TES.tay.tur, tes.TAY-) *n.* the maker of a will. —**tes.ta.trix** (-TAY.trix) *fem.,* **-ta.tri.ces** (-TAY.tri.seez) *pl.*

test case *n.* a court case that tests a law or one that becomes a precedent for future cases.

test drive *n.* a drive for judging the performance of a vehicle.
—**test-drive** *v.*

tes.ti.cle (TES.ti.cul) *n.* either of the pair of sperm-producing glands in male mammals.

tes.ti.fy (TES.tuh.fye) *v.* **-fies, -fied, -fy.ing 1** bear witness: *to testify about a case, against the defendant, for the prosecution, to the truth of a statement, under oath; He testified that he was elsewhere at the time of the murder.* **2** serve as evidence of something: *These facts testify to his honesty.* —**tes.ti.fi.er** *n.*

tes.ti.mo.ni.al (tes.tuh.MOH.nee.ul) *n.* **1** a recommendation or appreciation; also, a letter or statement to that effect: *a testimonial letter; The lives saved are an eloquent* **testimonial to** *the efficacy of the drug.* **2** a gift or other tribute in honor of someone: *a testimonial dinner.*

tes.ti.mo.ny (TES.tuh.moh.nee) *n.* **-nies 1** a statement made in court by a witness under oath: *to bear, cite, give, offer, refute testimony; false testimony against the defendant; the testimony about* or *on behalf of the plaintiff.* **2** evidence or proof: *The honors she has received bear testimony to a life of dedication.*

tes.tis *n., pl.* **-tes** (-teez) same as TESTICLE.

tes.tos.ter.one (tes.TOS.tuh.rohn) *n.* a male sex hormone.

test tube *n.* a glass container in the shape of a tube closed at one end for use in experiments.

test-tube baby *n.* a baby born from an ovum fertilized in a laboratory vessel and inserted into the uterus of the mother.

tes.ty (TES.tee) *adj.* **-ti.er, -ti.est 1** quickly angered: *a testy attitude, person; a testy type.* **2** irritated: *to become, get, grow testy (over something); a testy exchange, mood, tone, voice.* —**tes.ti.ly** *adv.;* **tes.ti.ness** *n.*

tet.a.nus (TET.un.us) *n.* an infectious disease characterized by stiffening of the voluntary muscles, esp. lockjaw.

tetch.y *adj.* **tetch.i.er, -i.est** irritable or peevish.

tête-à-tête (TATE.uh.tate) *n.* a close private talk between two people.
—*adv.* in private: *We had dinner tête-à-tête; adja.: a tête-à-tête dinner; the S-shaped* **tête-à-tête chair** *for two people to sit facing each other.*

teth.er (TETH.ur, "TH" as in "the") *n.* a line by which an animal is tied so as to restrict its range of movement.
—**at the end of one's tether** at the limit of one's endurance.
—*v.* fasten with a tether.

tet.ra.cy.cline (TET.ruh.sye.clin) *n.* an antibiotic effective against many bacteria, some viruses, and rickettsial germs.

tet.ra.eth.yl lead (tet.ruh.ETH.ul-) *n.* an antiknock added to gasoline.

tet.ra.he.dron (tet.ruh.HEE.drun) *n.* a solid figure with four triangular faces; **tet.ra.he.dral** *adj.*

te.tram.e.ter (tet.TRAM.i.tur) *n.* a line of verse with four feet or measures.

Teu.ton (TUE.tun) *n.* one speaking German or a Germanic language.
—**Teu.ton.ic** (tue.TON.ic) *adj.*

Tex.an (TEX.un) *n. & adj.* (a person) of or from **Texas,** a S.W. state of the U.S.

text *n.* **1** the main body of a work or the original words of an author, as distinguished from notes, illustrations, appendices, etc.: *the original text of Shakespeare's plays; a text corrupted by* copyists. **2** a topic or subject: *The preacher chose for his text "Blessed are the meek."* **3** a textbook: *our history text.* **4** words as distinguished from graphics, sound, etc.: *Mutimedia includes text, graphics, and sound;* **adja.:** *text editing, files, processing, searches; a* **full-text** *database containing complete texts of documents, not just abstracts.*

text.book *n.* a standard or authoritative book for the study of a subject: *a textbook of physics; a textbook on socialist theory;* **adja.:** *a textbook definition, explanation, lesson, rule; a* **textbook example** or **case** (= typical case) *of mismanagement.*

text editor *n.* an on-screen computer utility for writing and modifying documents and programs.

tex.tile (TEX.tile) *adja.* **1** having to do with fabrics and fibers: *the textile industry.* **2** woven: *a textile fabric.*
—*n.* **1** a cloth or fabric, esp. woven or knit. **2** textile material such as fiber and yarn.

tex.tu.al (TEX.choo.ul) *adj.* having do with a text or texts: *textual analysis, data, integrity, interpretation, material, meaning;* **textual criticism** *of a literary text (for reconstructing its original words).*

tex.ture (TEX.chur) *n.* a woven, hence surface characteristic, as given by the arrangement and size of threads, esp. as can be seen and felt: *Sackcloth has a coarse, not fine texture; rough, not smooth texture; the granular texture of certain rocks; Brick imparts texture to an interior; the texture* (= surface characteristics) *of a painting, poem, society.* —**tex.tur.al** *adj.*

tex.tured (TEX.churd) *adj.* having texture, not plain: *a textured fabric, finish, surface.*

T-group *n.* a sensitivity-training group. See ENCOUNTER.

Thai (TYE) *n.* **1** a person of or from **Thailand,** a country of S.E. Asia. **2** the Sino-Tibetan language of Thailand. Also **adj.**

thal.a.mus (THAL.uh.mus) *n.,* *pl.* **-mi** (-mye) the coordinating and distribution center of sensations in the forepart of the brain.

tha.lid.o.mide (thuh.LID.uh.mide) *n.* a drug used in the 1960s that caused deformities of the fetus when taken in early pregnancy. —**adja.:** *a thalidomide* (= handicapped) *baby; a thalidomide family with a thalidomide child.*

thal.li.um (THAL.ee.um) *n.* a soft, white, poisonous metallic element.

than ("TH" as in "the") *conj.* [used to introduce the second term of a comparison]: *Jack is taller than Jill; He would rather fight than argue; Gigi is none other than his wife; She's shorter than him* (Informal *for* than he is).

thane *n.* an Anglo-Saxon lord's retainer or knight.

thank ("th" as in "thin") *v.* express gratitude to someone: *(I) thank you for your kindness; A woman can pick up her glove herself, thank you very much; The neighbors will thank you to* (= will be grateful if you) *keep your dog quiet; He has only himself to thank* (= blame) *for his problems.*

thank.ful *adj.* grateful: *We are thankful to her for saving us; thankful* (= glad) *to be alive.* —**thank.ful.ly** *adv.*

thank.less *adj.* that no one appreciates: *a thankless job, role, struggle, task.* —**thank.less.ly** *adv.*

thanks *n.pl.* (expression of) gratitude: *Our heartfelt, sincere, warm thanks to everyone for helping us; many thanks; Thanks a lot! If you think you are making me an attractive offer, well,* **thanks but no thanks** (= No, thank you)! **Thanks to** (= because of) *her seatbelt, she was saved.* —*interj.* thank you!

thanks.giv.ing (thanks.GIV.ing) *n.* formal expression of gratitude, esp. to God, as on the annual **Thanksgiving** holiday.

thar ("TH" as in "the") *adv.* [regional] there: *There was gold bullion in that thar ship; Watch them thar handbags.*

that ("TH" as in "the") *pron.* **1** *pl.* **those** (THOZE) a person or thing already mentioned or implied, esp. as farther from the speaker than another, or "this": *Do you like this hat or that? That is my hat;* **adja.:** *that man; those men.* **2** [used as a relative pron.] who; whom; which: *the one that is boss around here; the woman (that) he married; the house that Jack built.* —**at that 1** then: *At that, he left the place.* **2** besides: *a good husband and a real friend at that.* —**in that** because: *a good student in that he works hard.* —**that is** in other words: *I'll see you on Friday – tomorrow, that is.* —*conj.:* *He's happy that he's won; That he's bald is obvious; Oh, (I wish) that it were spring!* —*adv.* to that extent: *He's that happy he's crying.*

that.a.way (THAT.uh.way) *adv.* [regional] in that direction: *She went thataway.*

thatch ("th" as in "thin") *n.* **1** material such as straw or leaves for roofing. **2** a roof covered with thatch. **3** *Informal.* head hair.

—*v.* cover as with thatch.

thaw ("th" as in "thin") *v.* **1** of frozen things, become or cause to become warmer so as to melt: *Frozen rivers begin to thaw in warm weather; Leave the turkey out to thaw;* ***adj.:*** *a **thawed** turkey; Do not refreeze a thawed TV dinner; thawed frozen orange juice.* **2** of people or their manner, become less cold: *After a while, the crusty old man began to thaw.* —***n.*** **1** a thawing: *spring thaw; A thaw is forecast, sets in.* **2** softening of relations: *the thaw between two hostile nations; the thaw in international relations.*

the (thuh; *before vowels:* thee) *def. art.* **1** [referring to a certain person or thing]: *the man I met yesterday; He went in the house.* **2** [referring to a unique person or thing]: *She was the greatest; the sun and the moon; the top of your head; the United States; the definite article.* **3** [referring to a whole class or something generalized as representative of a class]: *our neighbors, the Smiths; the grammatical articles; the rich and the poor; the good and the true; in bed with the flu; to play the piano; Our car gives 30 miles to the gallon.*
—***adv.*** [used with comparatives] in that degree: *Start early the more surely to catch your flight; the earlier the better* (= in what degree earlier, in that degree better).

the.a.ter (THEE.uh.tur, "TH" as in "thin") *n.* **1** a building or place with rows of seats for viewing a play, motion picture, or other dramatic performance or action: *lecture, movie, open-air theaters; a repertory theater (company); a hospital's operating theater; a **theater-in-the-round*** (with stage in center and seats all around); *a **theater of operations*** (= scene of battle) *during the war*. **2** drama: *Greek theater; "Hamlet" is good theater; the legitimate theater* (= professional drama). —***adja.*** tactical: *theater nuclear weapons*. Also **the.a.tre** *Cdn.*

the.at.ri.cal (thee.AT.ri.cul) *adj.* **1** having to do with the theater or drama: *a theatrical company, effect, spectacle.* **2** showy; affected; also, melodramatic: *his theatrical behavior, manner, style.*
—**theatricals** *n.pl.* [takes *sing.* or *pl. v.*] **1** amateur performances. **2** dramatics.
—**the.at.ri.cal.i.ty** (-CAL.i.tee) *n.*

the.at.rics (thee.AT.rics) *n.pl.* [takes *sing.* or *pl. v.*] **1** the art of the theater. **2** something done for theatrical effect; histrionics.

thee See THOU.

theft ("th" as in "thin") *n.* stealing or an instance of it: *to commit a theft; to practice theft; petty thefts under $200.*

their (THAIR, "TH" as in "the") *adja. possessive* of THEY. of or by them: *their actions, houses, minds.* —**theirs** (THAIRS) *pron.* their one(s): *The child is theirs.*

the.ism (THEE.iz.um, "TH" as in "thin") *n.* belief in God, a god, or gods; **the.ist** *n.* —**the.is.tic** (thee.IS.tic) *adj.*

them ("th" as in "the") *pron.* **1** *objective case* of THEY: *He loves them.* **2** [nonstandard use] those: *them hills; in them houses.*

theme (THEEM, "TH" as in "thin") *n.* **1** a topic or subject: *the dominant theme of her novels; a theme for discussion; a theme* (= short essay) *assigned for an English composition.* **2** a recurrent melody, as elaborated in a composition. **3** a theme song. —**the.mat.ic** (thee.MAT.ic) *adj.* —**the.mat.i.cal.ly** *adv.*

theme park *n.* an amusement park built around a theme, as Disney World.

theme song *n.* **1** an identifying melody, as one introducing a TV show. **2** a melody repeated throughout a motion picture.

them.selves (them.SELVS) *pron.* emphatic or reflexive of THEY, THEM: *They themselves did it; They talked among themselves.*

then ("th" as in "the") *adv.* **1** at the indicated time: *She wasn't born then; the then reigning queen; He paid up **then and there**.* **2** after that: *I shaved, then I showered; Now it's my turn, then yours; the man, his wife, and then the children.* **3** in that case; therefore: *If we don't pay, then we can't have it;* **but then** (= but on the other hand) *where's the money?* —***n.*** that time: *By then it was too late; Nothing has happened since then;* ***adja.:*** *the then queen of England.*

thence ("th" as in "the") *adv.* from there; from then; from that: *a few yards thence; a few months thence; first to London, (and) thence to Paris.*

thence.forth *adv.* from then on. Also **thence.for.ward** or **thence.for.wards**.

the.oc.ra.cy (thee.OC.ruh.see, "th" as in "thin") *n.* **-cies** a state based on religious authority; government by priests; **the.o.crat.ic** (thee.uh.CRAT.ic) *adj.*

the.o.lo.gian (thee.uh.LOH.jun) *n.* a specialist in theology.

the.ol.o.gy (thee.OL.uh.jee) *n.* **-gies** **1** study of God or religion. **2** a system of beliefs about God. —**the.o.log.i.cal** (thee.uh.LOJ.i.cul) *adj.*

the.o.rem (THEE.uh.rum, "TH" as in "thin") *n.* a statement or proposition

that can be proved from axioms or postulates: *to formulate, prove, test a theorem.*
the.o.ret.i.cal (thee.uh.RET.i.cul) *adj.* based on theory; hence, not based on fact; not practical: *Your explanation is too theoretical; a theoretical advantage, model; theoretical premises, work; theoretical criticism* (based on theory, not evidence); *theoretical* (= not applied) *physics; a theoretical possibility* (= something hypothetical). Also **the.o.ret.ic**. —**the.o.ret.i.cal.ly** *adv.*
the.o.rize (THEE.uh.rize) *v.* **-riz.es, -rized, -riz.ing** form a theory; speculate: *He theorized that the missing child was really hiding.* —**the.o.rist** or **the.o.re.ti.cian** (-ruh.TISH.un) *n.*
the.o.ry (THEE.uh.ree, THEER.ee) *n.* **-ries 1** the principles of an art or science, as opposed to practice: *He teaches musical theory; to combine theory and practice; Your plan sounds good* **in theory**. **2** a reasoned-out and tested explanation of facts or phenomena: *to advance, advocate, develop, disprove, explode, propose, refute, suggest, test a theory; the theory of evolution; the big-bang, steady-state, and such theories* (= explanations) *of the universe; Is the possibility of life on other planets mere theory* (= speculation)?
the.os.o.phy (thee.OS.uh.fee, "th" as in "thin") *n.* **-phies** a religious system based on supposed mystical insight into the nature of God and the universe rather than on reason or sense experience; **the.os.o.phist** *n.* —**the.o.soph.ic** (thee.uh.SOF.ic) or **the.o.soph.i.cal** *adj.*
ther.a.peu.tic (ther.uh.PEW.tic, "th" as in "thin") **1** *adj.* having to do with curing illness or preserving health: *a therapeutic abortion* (for saving the mother); *drugs as therapeutic agents; a therapeutic bath; Placebos have no therapeutic value.* **2 therapeutics** *n.pl.* [takes *sing. v.*] a branch of medicine dealing with the treatment of disease.
—**ther.a.peu.ti.cal.ly** *adv.*
ther.a.py (THER.uh.pee) *n.* **-pies** treatment of disease: *group, occupational, physical, shock therapy.* —**ther.a.pist** *n.*
there (THAIR, "TH" as in "the") *adv.* **1** at, in, or to that place: *He's there, not here; went there yesterday; She lives over there.* **2** in that matter: *We agree with you there.* **3** [used impersonally with "be," "seem," "appear," etc.]: *There is no time left; There seems to be a way out; There were many reasons.*
—*n.* that place: *He's in there.*

—*interj.*: *There, now! I told you so; There, there! Don't cry.*
there.a.bouts (THAIR.uh.bowts) *adv.* near that place, time, amount, etc.: *$2,000 or thereabouts; in London or thereabouts.* Also **there.a.bout**.
there.af.ter (thair.AF.tur) *adv.* afterward; after that.
there.at (thair.AT) *adv.* [old use] **1** at that place or time. **2** because of that.
there.by (thair.BY) *adv.* **1** by that means or in that way. **2** by that place or in that connection: *Thereby hangs a tale.*
there.for (thair.FOR) *adv.* for that; for that purpose.
there.fore (THAIR.for) *adv.* for that reason; hence.
there.from (thair.FRUM) *adv.* from that.
there.in (thair.IN) *adv. Formal.* **1** in that place or into that place. **2** in that respect.
there.of (thair.OV) *adv. Formal.* of that or from that.
there.on (thair.ON) *adv.* [old use] **1** on that. **2** thereupon.
there.to (thair.TOO) *adv. Formal.* to that place or thing; also **there.un.to** (thair.UN.too) *adv.*
there.to.fore (thair.tuh.FOR) *adv. Formal.* before that time.
there.up.on (thair.uh.PON) *adv.* **1** immediately after that. **2** because of that. **3** [old use] upon that (subject).
there.with (thair.WITH) *adv.* **1** along with that. **2** [old use] then.
there.with.al (THAIR.with.all) *adv.* **1** [old use] besides. **2** with that.
therm(o)- *comb.form.* heat; temperature: *thermometer, thermosphere, thermostat.*
ther.mal (THUR.mul, "TH" as in "thin") *adj.* having to do with heat: *thermal air currents, springs;* **thermal pollution** *caused by discharge of heated liquids from factories into natural waters;* **thermal underwear** *made of specially knit insulating material.* —**ther.mal.ly** *adv.*
ther.mo.dy.nam.ics (thur.muh.dye.NAM.ics) *n.pl.* [takes *sing. v.*] a branch of physics that studies heat energy and its conservation; **ther.mo.dy.nam.ic** *adj.*
ther.mom.e.ter (thur.MOM.uh.tur) *n.* an instrument for measuring temperature: *clinical, meat, oven, rectal thermometers.* —**ther.mo.met.ric** (-muh.MET.ric) *adj.*
ther.mo.nu.cle.ar (thur.moh.NEW.clee.ur) *adj.* having to do with the fusion of atoms at very high temperatures and the release of nuclear en-

ergy, as in the hydrogen bomb: *a thermonuclear bomb, reaction, reactor; a thermonuclear war (using thermonuclear weapons).*

ther.mo.plas.tic (thur.muh.PLAS.tic) *adj.* that can be heated and molded again after cooling and hardening, as nylon, polystyrene, and other plastics. —*n.* such a plastic.

ther.mos (THUR.mos) same as VACUUM BOTTLE; **Thermos** *Trademark.*

ther.mo.sphere (THUR.mus.feer) *n.* the uppermost region of the atmosphere from about 50 mi. (80 km) to about 280 mi. (450 km). —**ther.mo.spher.ic** (-FEER.ic, -FER.ic) *adj.*

ther.mo.stat (THUR.muh.stat) *n.* an automatic device for regulating temperature, as in an automobile, stove, or home heating system: *We set the thermostat low at night.*

the.sau.rus (thi.SOR.us, "th" as in "thin") *n., pl.* **-ri** (-rye) or **-rus.es** 1 a dictionary of synonyms and antonyms. 2 a treasury or collection of information.

these *pl.* of THIS.

the.sis (THEE.sis, "TH" as in "thin") *n., pl.* **-ses** (-seez) 1 a proposition put forward for exposition and defense: *Martin Luther nailed 95 theses to his church door.* 2 a theory: *to challenge, disprove, put forward, refute a thesis; Chairman Mao's thesis was that political power comes from the barrel of a gun; the central, main thesis.* 3 a research paper prepared by a candidate for an academic degree; dissertation: *doctoral, Ph.D., senior theses.*

Thes.pi.an (THES.pee.un, "TH" as in "thin") *adj.* having to do with the dramatic art. —*n.* an actor or actress. Also **thespian.**

thews ("th" as in "thin") *n.pl.* sinews or muscles.

they (THAY, "TH" as in "the") *pron., pl.* of HE, SHE, or IT; *objective* THEM, *possessive* THEIR, THEIRS. 1 the persons, animals, or things previously mentioned or referred to. 2 *Informal.* people in general: *They say prices will come down.*

they'd (THAID) they had; they would.
they'll (THAIL) they will; they shall.
they're (THAIR) they are.
they've (THAVE) they have.

thi.a.mine (THY.uh.meen, -min, "TH" as in "thin") *n.* a vitamin of the B complex found in whole-grain cereals, whose lack in diet causes beriberi; also **thiamin** (-min).

thick ("th" as in "thin") *adj.* 1 with relatively much space between opposite sides or surfaces; not thin: *a thick sheet, slice, wall; thick fingers, rope, skin; It's a centimeter thick (as measured between opposite surfaces).* 2 crowded or closely set; firm or stiff in consistency; dense: *a thick growth, smoke, soup; The plot is getting thicker;* thick (*Informal for* intimate) *friends.* 3 not clear: *thick darkness, fog, gloom, mist, voices, weather; a thick* (= stupid) *head.* 4 *Informal.* too much to endure. 5 broad or obvious: *a thick accent, brogue.* —*adv.* in a thick manner. —**lay it on thick** *Informal.* praise or blame too much. —*n.* thickest or hardest part: *in the thick of the battle.* —**through thick and thin** through good times and bad. —**thick.ly** *adv.;* **thick.ness** *n.*

thick.en (THICK.un) *v.* make or become thick or thicker: *to thicken a gravy.*

thick.et (THICK.it, "TH" as in "thin") *n.* a dense growth of shrubs or small trees.

thick.set *adj.* 1 having a thick body; stocky. 2 thickly or closely planted: *a thickset hedge.*

thick-skinned *adj.* 1 having a thick skin. 2 not easily offended by criticism, insults, etc.

thief (THEEF, "TH" as in "thin") *n.* **thieves** (THEEVS) one who steals something, usu. in a secret and nonviolent manner: *a petty thief; sneak thief.*

thieve (THEEV) *v.* **thieves, thieved, thiev.ing** be a thief or steal things; *adj.a.: their thieving hands; thieving politicians.* —**thiev.ish** *adj.*

thiev.er.y (THEE.vuh.ree) *n.* **-er.ies** stealing or an instance of it; theft: *petty thievery.*

thigh ("TH" as in "thin") *n.* the part of the leg between the knee and the hip.

thim.ble (THIM.bul, "TH" as in "thin") *n.* a small cap worn on the finger while sewing to protect it when pushing the needle. —**thim.ble.ful** *adj.*

thin *adj.* **thin.ner, thin.nest** 1 with relatively little space between opposite sides or surfaces; not thick: *a thin sheet, wire; a thin wall that is only a few inches thick.* 2 having little flesh or fat; not dense, crowded, or substantial: *a man of thin build; thin hair, mist, mountain air; You are getting thin on top* (= nearly bald). 3 weak; not strong: *thin blood; a thin soup, voice; a thin* (= flimsy) *disguise, excuse.* —**on thin ice** on weak ground: *You're skating on thin ice!* —*v.* **thins, thinned, thin.ning** make or become thin or thinner: *His* hair is thinning on top; Use water to thin it down; War and famine thin out a population. —**thin.ly** adv.; **thin.ness** n.

thine ("th" as in "the") adja. & pron. [old form, *possessive* of THOU] your or yours: *thine eyes; Thine is the kingdom.*

thing n. **1** any object, matter, circumstance, opinion, etc.: *the latest thing in sleepwear; a box containing sewing things; She did the right thing; She doesn't know a thing about calculus; She knows* **a thing or two** (= quite a bit) *about him.* **2** a creature: *a living thing.* **3** a person considered with pity, affection, contempt, etc.: *poor little thing; miserable thing.* **4** *Informal.* an irrational fear or prejudice: *Kay has a thing about cats.*
—**all things considered** everything being taken into account. —**do one's (own) thing** *Informal.* do as best expresses one's aspirations or lifestyle.
—**for one thing** [used to introduce the first of several reasons]: *For one thing, he is always late; for another, he doesn't dress well.* —**see things** have hallucinations.

thing.a.ma.jig (THING.uh.muh.jig), **thing.um.a.bob** (THING.uh.muh.bob) or **thing.um.bob** (THING.um.bob) n. *Informal.* a thing whose name one cannot recall or does not know: *Where did I put the thingamajig for opening cans? Jack has a new thingamajig for picking lottery numbers.*

think ("TH" as in "thin") v. **thinks, thought** (THAWT), **think.ing** use the mind to form images and ideas, to consider things, have opinions, hopes, judgments, etc.: *to think clearly, hard; A good leader thinks ahead; He thinks back to the past when tempted to marry again; He's thinking about or of taking the job; He thinks himself qualified; thinks her an able woman; She thinks that he is too aggressive; He* **thinks of** (= considers) *her with high regard; She doesn't* **think much of** (= have a high opinion of) *Sam; He was rebuffed when he* **thought to** (= tried to) *help her; He likes to* **think aloud** (= utter his thoughts) *when alone; She* **thought better of** (= reconsidered) *her refusal and accepted the invitation; She will* **think twice** (= consider carefully) *before making the same mistake; had to* **think up** (= invent) *an excuse for her refusal.* —**think.er** n.

think tank n. an organization for studying the problems of governments and societies and proposing solutions and policies; also **think factory**.

thin.ner (THIN.ur) adj. comp. of THIN.
—n. a liquid, esp. a volatile one used to thin paints, etc.

thin-skinned adj. **1** having a thin skin. **2** sensitive to criticism, insults, etc.

third ("th" as in "thin") adj. next after the second: *the third and final warning.*
—n. **1** one that is third: *the third of the lot.* **2** any of three equal parts of something: *two thirds of it.* —**adv.** in third place: *She finished third.*
—**third.ly** adv.: *Thirdly, I am too tired to continue.*

third-class adj. **1** of a class of train or ship accommodations that is usu. the cheapest: *a third-class ticket.* **2** consisting of identical letters mailed in quantity to thousands of addresses: *third-class mail.* —**adv.** by third class.

third degree n. *Informal.* mental or bodily torture as a means of forcing a prisoner to give information: *They gave him the third degree.*
—**third-degree** adja. of the worst kind: *a third-degree assault, felony, heart block, shock; A* **third-degree burn** results in charred skin and destruction of tissue.

third dimension n. the quality of depth or solidity (besides length and width) that makes an object or scene seem real. —**third-dimensional** adj.

third person n. a pronoun such as "he," "she," "it," "they," or a verb form such as "goes," "likes," or "wants" (third person singular) that refers to the one or ones spoken of.

third-rate adj. lowest-rated; hence, poor or inferior.

Third World n. the countries of Asia, Africa, and Latin America that are industrially less developed than other nations.

thirst ("th" as in "thin") n. **1** discomfort caused in the mouth and throat by the need to drink. **2** a craving or strong desire. —v. be thirsty or desire ardently: *to thirst for adventure, knowledge, revenge.*

thirst.y adj. **thirst.i.er, -i.est** having or causing thirst: *Hot weather makes one thirsty; a land thirsty for rain.*

thir.teen (thur.TEEN, "th" as in "thin") n., adja. & pron. three more than ten; 13 or XIII; **thir.teenth** n. & adj.

thir.ty (THUR.tee) n., adja. & pron. **-ties** **1** three times ten; 30 or XXX. **2** **the thirties** n.pl. the numbers or years from 30 through 39. —**thirty and out** the right to retire after 30 years of service with no loss of pension benefits. —**thir.ti.eth** (-ith) n. & adj.

this pron., pl. **these** a person or thing that is present or referred to as nearer to the speaker than another, or "that": *This is my book, that is yours; We chatted about **this and that** (= many things) to pass the time.* —*adj.*: *this book; these books; this* (= coming) *summer; There was once this* (= a certain) *man who had three sons.* —*adv.* to this extent: *this big, far, much.*

this.tle (THIS.ul, "TH" as in "thin") *n.* a weed with prickly leaves and soft, silky, purplish flowers that bears seeds equipped with down, or **this.tle.down.**

thith.er (second "th" as in "the") *adv.* to the place specified: *hither and thither;* **adja.**: *on the thither side.*

tho' (THOH, "TH" as in "the") *conj. & adv.* though.

thole ("th" as in "thin") *n.* either of a pair of pegs on the gunwale of a boat between which the oar is held in rowing; also **thole.pin.**

thong ("th" as in "thin") *n.* **1** a narrow strip of leather or plastic, esp. one used as a strap or lace. **2** a type of footwear held on the foot by a thong fitted between the toes.

tho.rac.ic (thuh.RAS.ic) *adj.* having to do with the thorax: *The thoracic cavity contains the heart and lungs.*

tho.rax (THOR.ax, "TH" as in "thin") *n.* **1** the segment of an insect's body between head and abdomen. **2** the human chest.

tho.ri.um (THOR.ee.um, "TH" as in "thin") *n.* a radioactive metallic element used as fuel in nuclear reactors.

thorn ("th" as in "thin") *n.* **1** a short, hard, sharp-pointed protective outgrowth on a plant stem: *The rose has thorns.* **2** a source of trouble or annoyance: *The critics are a **thorn in her flesh**; a **thorn in my side**.* —**thorn.y** *adj.* **thorn.i.er, -i.est**: *a thorny plant, stem; a thorny issue, problem, question.*

thor.ough (THUR.oh, "TH" as in "thin") *adj.* **1** marked by great attention to detail; painstaking: *a thorough scholar, search; very thorough in her work; She has a thorough grasp of her subject.* **2** complete: *He's a thorough scoundrel.* —**thor.ough.ly** *adv.;* **thor.ough.ness** *n.*

thor.ough.bred (THUR.uh.bred) *n. & adj.* (an animal) of pure stock.

thor.ough.fare (THUR.uh.fare) *n.* a public street open at both ends with free flow of traffic: *a busy thoroughfare.*

thor.ough.go.ing (THUR.uh.go.ing) *adj.* **1** very thorough: *thoroughgoing changes, disciplinarians, exercises.* **2** out-and-out; utter: *a thoroughgoing scoundrel, troublemaker.*

thorp *n. Archaic.* village.

those *pl.* of THAT.

thou ("th" as in "the," *rhyme:* how) *pron.* [old form, *possessive* THY or THINE, *objective* THEE; *pl.* you or YE, *possessive* YOUR or YOURS, *objective* YOU or YE] the one spoken to; you. —*n.* ("th" as in "thin") *Informal.* a thousand dollars.

though (THOH, "TH" as in "the") **1** *conj.* in spite of the fact that; although: *He continues to work though ill; They get along, though not like friends; good to take an umbrella though* (= even if) *it may not rain; looks **as though*** (= as if) *it may rain.* **2** *adv.* however: *They get along – not like friends, though.*

thought *pt.* of THINK. —*n.* **1** mental consideration of a subject or an expression of it: *He seems lost in thought; He acted without thought; a mother full of thought for her children's future; to abandon, entertain, express, gather, harbor, present, relish a thought; to read someone's thoughts; to sum up one's thoughts; evil, fleeting, happy, passing, refreshing, upsetting thoughts; A thought crosses one's mind, strikes one; to interrupt a train of thought; She had no thought* (= intention) *of hurting anyone; Chaucer reflects medieval thought* (= thinking); *Communists, Nazis, etc. are famous for the jackboot, the rifle, and the **thought police** that control freedom of thought and expression;* **Perish the thought!** (= It's unthinkable!); *a book of thoughts* (= quotations). **2** *a little bit of*: *Be **a thought** more considerate of others.*

thought.less (THAWT.lis) *adj.* **1** not thinking: *a thoughtless moment, waste; thoughtless passion.* **2** not considerate: *thoughtless behavior; a thoughtless manner, remark.* —**thought.less.ly** *adv.;* **thought.less.ness** *n.*

thou.sand (THOW.zund, "TH" as in "thin") *n., adj. & pron.* ten times 100; 1,000 or M: *three thousand people; thousands* (= a large number) *of people; people in* or *by the thousands.*
—**thou.sandth** *n. & adj.*

thrall (THRAWL) *n.* a slave; also, slavery. —**thral.dom** or **thrall.dom** (-dum) *n.*

thrash *v.* beat repeatedly, as in threshing grain with a flail: *In his frustration, he thrashed the mule soundly; children thrashing about in the water; They **thrashed over** the problem* (= discussed it) *for many hours; It took all evening to **thrash out*** (= arrive at) *a solution.*

thrash.er *n.* a New World bird with a down-curved bill and loud, varied songs, that thrashes its tail up and down when excited.

thread (THRED) *n.* **1** a fine cord made

of cotton, flax, etc. spun out and twisted together: *a spool of thread; coarse, heavy, polyester, silk, thin thread.* **2** anything fine and continuous like thread, as the filaments made by a spider or silkworm: *In Greek myth, death occurred when one of the Fates cut the thread of life; Lou's life hangs by a thread* (= Lou is in critical condition). **3** theme: *the thread of an argument, conversation, narrative.* **4** the continuous spiral ridge around a screw or inside a nut. **5 threads** *pl. Slang.* clothes. —*v.* **1** pass a thread through: *to thread a needle, beads on a string.* **2** pass through like a thread: *She threaded her way through the crowd; red silk threaded with gold; to thread a roll of film into a camera; n.: auto film* **threading.** **3** form a screw thread on or in a bolt or nut: *Some nuts are reverse-threaded and tighten counterclockwise.* **4** form a thread, as syrup of a certain thickness, when dropped from a spoon.

thread.bare *adj.* **1** badly worn out: *a threadbare carpet, suit; threadbare clothes; a threadbare person (in worn-out clothes).* **2** hackneyed: *a threadbare argument, excuse, plot.*

thread.y *adj.* **1** stringy. **2** not strong and full: *a thready pulse, voice.*

threat (THRET) *n.* **1** an expression of one's intention to hurt: *to carry out, constitute, issue, make, pose, utter a threat; cheap, dire, empty, grave, idle, serious, veiled threats; acting under threat of reprisals.* **2** the possibility or cause of something evil or harmful happening: *a threat of rain; They lived under the constant threat of a gas explosion.* **3** a person or thing that is a threat: *She is a security threat; Drunk drivers are a threat to public safety; Icy sidewalks are a threat to life and limb.*

threat.en (THRET.un) *v.* **1** utter a threat against someone: *She threatened him with a lawsuit; He threatened to leave her;* **adj.:** *a* **threatened** *lawsuit; a* **threatening** *phone call.* **2** be a threat to a person or thing: *An epidemic threatens a country; Storm clouds threaten* (= are a sign of) *rain;* **adj.:** *plant and animal species considered* **threatened,** *endangered, or extinct; to feel threatened;* **threatening** *changes to the system; threatening developments; a life-threatening illness.*

three *n., pron. & adj.* one more than two; 3 or III: *three blind mice; They come in threes; Three's company.*

3-D (THREE.DEE) *adj.* three-dimensional: *a 3-D movie, picture.*

three.fold *adj.* having three parts or three times as much or as many: *a threefold increase, plan, strategy.* —*adv.* three times: *Prices have increased threefold; Sales have grown threefold.*

three R's *n.pl.* reading, writing, and arithmetic, as the basics of elementary education.

thren.o.dy (THREN.uh.dee, "th" as in "thin") *n.* **-dies** a song of lamentation; dirge.

thresh ("th" as in "thin") *v.* **1** separate grain, as wheat, from the straw by beating. **2** beat out wheat, etc. with a flail or machine; hence, thrash.

thresh.old (THRESH.old, -hold) *n.* **1** the sill of a doorway as the point of entry: *to cross a threshold; A bride is carried over the threshold by the groom.* **2** entrance or starting point: *on the threshold of a career, discovery, new era; A flu outbreak exceeds the epidemic threshold when it accounts for 6% of all reported deaths.* **3** the point at which a stimulus or sensation becomes perceptible: *below the threshold of consciousness; a reader with a low threshold for or of boredom; A patient's allergy threshold depends on the weather, emotional state, and such conditions.*

threw *pt.* of THROW.

thrice *adv.* three times as many or as much.

thrift *n.* **1** careful management of money or resources; frugality in spending money. **2** in the U.S., a savings-and-loan institution.

thrift shop *n.* a shop selling secondhand clothes and housewares, usu. for charity.

thrift.y *adj.* **thrift.i.er, -i.est** economical, esp. in saving; avoiding waste: *a thrifty housewife who shops for bargains; thrifty shopping; thrifty use of power.* —**thrift.i.ly** *adv.*

thrill *n.* a surge of excited feeling: *the thrill of a discovery; to get, give, have, provide a thrill; The first-time flyer experiences a thrill of joy; It's a thrill to fly; It's a thrill flying; He does it for thrills; for the thrill of it.* —*v.* have or cause a thrill: *The movie thrilled us with its special effects;* **adj.:** *We are* **thrilled** *to join you on the trip; thrilled with the invitation; a* **thrilling** *experience, motion picture; It was thrilling to watch the acrobats..* —**thrill.er** *n.*

thrips *n. sing. & pl.* a small, slender insect, usu. with two pairs of wings fringed with hairs, destructive to plants and grain.

thrive *v.* **thrives,** *pt.* **thrived** or **throve** (THROHV), *pp.* **thrived** or **thriv.en**

(THRIV.un), **thriv.ing** prosper or flourish; develop or grow vigorously: *Children thrive on good food and exercise.*

throat *n.* **1** the air-and-food passage inside the neck: *He cleared his throat to attract her attention; a sore throat from a cold; A lump in her* or *the throat* (= excess of emotion) *prevented her from speaking; You can't* **force** *your ideas* **down his throat** (= can't force him to accept them). **2** the front part of the neck: *His shirt is open at the throat; Some hockey players* **go for the throat** (= get violent) *when they are desperate; They're soon* **at each other's throats** (= fighting); *It's like* **cutting their own throats** (= hurting themselves). **3** a narrow passage or part.

throat.y *adj.* **throat.i.er, -i.est** produced in the throat; guttural or husky: *a throaty growl, voice.* —**throat.i.ly** *adv.;* **throat.i.ness** *n.*

throb *v.* **throbs, throbbed, throb.bing** palpitate or pulsate: *a wound throbbing with pain;* *n.:* *the* **throbbing** *of the heart.* —*n.* a throbbing or strong beat.

throes (THROZE) *n.pl.* pangs or spasms: *the throes of change, fatigue, labor, revolution; the death throes of a political faction;* **in the throes** (= struggle or agony) *of finishing a task on time; In March, we are in the last throes of winter.*

throm.bo.sis (throm.BOH.sis) *n., pl.* **-ses** (-seez) the blocking of a blood vessel by a thrombus. —**throm.bot.ic** (-BOT.ic) *adj.*

throm.bus *n., pl.* **-bi** (-bye) a blood clot.

throne *n.* **1** a king's or queen's chair of state: *to abdicate, assume, give up, inherit, mount, occupy a throne; to claim one's right to the throne; to ascend* or *ascend to, seek, succeed to, take the throne; when she* **came to the throne** (= became queen); *the* **throne room** *in which audiences are given; A* **throne speech** *or* **speech from the throne** *outlining government policy and programs is read to a legislature at its opening session by (a representative of) the sovereign.* **2** a similar chair used on ceremonial occasions by a bishop, etc. **3** a sovereign or ruler; hence, sovereign power: *to address the throne; plots against the throne;* **the power behind the throne** (= one who has the real power). —**throned** *adj.:* *the throned Pontiff.*

throng *n.* **1** a crowd of people, esp. a moving and jostling one. **2** a multitude. —*v.* crowd: *Admirers thronged around the star; Crowds thronged the theater on opening night.*

throt.tle (THROT.ul) *n.* a valve regulating the fuel flowing into an engine, as of an automobile, or the mechanism controlling it, as the accelerator pedal. —**at full throttle** at full speed. —*v.* **throt.tles, throt.tled, throt.tling** **1** choke or strangle; hence, suppress. **2** reduce the fuel flowing into an engine; hence, lessen speed: *to throttle back* or *down an engine.* —**throt.tler** *n.*

through (THROO) *prep.* **1** in at one side of something and out at the other; from beginning to end of a period: *He walked in through the open door; slept through the night; Monday* **through** (= to and including) *Friday; fined for driving through a red light (without stopping); He's* **through** (= finished with) *eating.* **2** by reason of something: *He failed through neglect.* **3** by the agency of someone: *I found out through a friend.* —*adv.:* *She slept the night through; I read the book through; a train going through* (= nonstop) *to Montreal; He's wet* **through and through** (= completely). —*adj.* **1** *adjp.* finished: *Are you through? We are through with eating.* **2** *adja.* involving no stopping: *through flights, traffic, trains; a through bus from Boston to Washington; a through ticket to San Francisco.*

through.out (throo.OUT) *prep.* in every part of something: *He was absent throughout the day;* *adv.:* *Attending the funeral, she wept quietly throughout.*

through.put *n.* processing capacity or the amount processed, as by a computer: *Input, throughput, and output are rarely in balance.*

through.way *n.* an expressway.

throve a *pt.* of THRIVE.

throw (THROH) *v.* **throws, threw** (THROO), **thrown** (THRONE), **throw.ing** **1** cause to move rapidly or with force, usu. through the air: *to throw a ball; A horse throws a rider; to throw a switch (by moving a lever to the "on" or "off" position); a discovery that throws light on a subject; He threw himself on the mercy of the judge; She was thrown* (= put) *into prison.* **2** shed, drop, or toss casually or routinely: *to throw off a disguise; Snakes throw their skin; He threw a six (in dice); Domestic animals throw* (= bring forth) *their young.* **3** *Informal.* give: *to throw a party; She threw a punch; He* **threw the fight** (= gave it up intentionally). **4** to shape or fashion by turning or twisting, as on a potter's wheel or a lathe: *to throw a vase;* *adja.:* **Thrown** *silk is stronger than raw silk.* —**throw a wrench** spoil

throwaway / thundercloud

something going smoothly: *By suddenly switching things around, the foreman threw a wrench in the plan* or *a wrench into the works.* —**throw in** add as a free gift or bargain. —**throw off** 1 give off sparks. 2 get rid of a burden. —**throw out** 1 reject a proposal, expel an intruder or undesirable person, or put out a base runner in baseball. 2 put forth a signal, challenge, etc. —**throw up** 1 give up a job or game. 2 *Informal.* vomit. —*n.* a throwing, a distance covered by throwing, or what is thrown over furniture, etc. to cover it, such as a bedspread, blanket, or scarf.

throw.a.way (THROH.uh.way) *n.* a pamphlet, disposable container, etc. designed to be thrown away after use; **adja.:** *a throwaway item; a casually expressed or delivered* **throwaway line**; *our* **throwaway society** (*that discards things instead of using them fully and recycling them*).

throw.back *n.* a reversion to an earlier type or an example of it.

throw rug *n.* a small rug.

thru (THROO) *prep. Informal.* through.

thrum *v.* **thrums, thrummed, thrum.ming** same as STRUM.

thrush *n.* a songbird that is usu. plain brown or has a spotted white breast as in the "wood thrush."

thrust *v.* **thrusts, thrust, thrust.ing** push with force and suddenness: *She thrust the letter into his hand; thrust at him with the sword; He had thrust himself into her presence; She thrust him aside and marched off; an election thrust on an unwilling public.* —*n.* the action of thrusting: *the thrust of a sword, an attacking enemy, argument, speech; the parry and thrust of debate; the supporting thrust of an arch; Jet engines and propellers produce thrust for a plane to overcome drag and move forward; the upward thrust of a rocket in reaction to the flow of exhaust gas.* —**thrust.er** *n.*

thru.way (THROO.way) *n. Informal.* throughway or expressway.

thud ("th" as in "thin") *n.* a dull sound, as of something heavy falling on soft ground. —*v.* **thuds, thud.ded, thud.ding** move or hit making a thud.

thug ("th" as in "thin") *n.* a hoodlum or ruffian.

thu.li.um (THOO.lee.um, "TH" as in "thin") *n.* a rare-earth chemical element used in portable X-ray equipment.

thumb (THUM, "TH" as in "thin") *n.* the short, thick opposable digit of the hand. —**all thumbs** of a person, very clumsy or awkward. —**turn thumbs down** reject: *The voters turned thumbs down on the proposed taxes.* —**under someone's thumb** of a person, under someone's domination.
—*v.* turn, handle, soil, etc. with the thumb: *She thumbed through the pages looking for pictures; a hiker trying to* **thumb a ride** (= get a ride by gesturing with the thumb); *She* **thumbed her nose** *at him* (= made a gesture of contempt putting the thumb to the nose); **adj.:** *a* **well-thumbed** *book.*

thumb index *n.* a set of lettered notches cut in the fore edge of a reference book to help the reader locate its contents.

thumb.nail sketch *n.* a brief and concise word-picture.

thumb.screw *n.* a screw that can be turned with the thumb and forefingers.

thumbs up *n.* approval or encouragement: *to give somebody the thumbs up* (*sign*).

thumb.tack *n.* a wide-headed tack that can be pressed into a board with the thumb.

thump ("th" as in "thin") *n.* 1 a heavy blow with something thick such as a fist. 2 the sound made by such a blow or fall. —*v.* strike with a thump or pound: *The speaker thumped the table for attention; She heartily thumped his back in encouragement; His heart was thumping with excitement;* **adja.:** *a* **thumping** (*Informal for* very large or whopping) *majority, success, victory.*

thun.der (THUN.dur, "TH" as in "thin") *n.* 1 the loud sound usu. heard after a flash of lightning: *a clap, peal, roll of thunder; Thunder booms, reverberates, roars.* 2 a similar sound, as of a great waterfall or resounding applause.
—*v.* produce thunder or sound like it: *It often thunders when it rains; Cannons thundered in salute; The train thundered past the station;* **adja.:** *a* **thundering** *chorus, crowd, train; the thundering Niagara Falls; her thundering opposition to abortion.* **thun.der.ous** (THUN.dur.us) *adj.:* *thunderous applause, cheers, roar, warnings; a thunderous ovation.*

thun.der.bolt (THUN.dur.bolt) *n.* a flash or shaft of lightning with a thunderclap: *a tree struck by a thunderbolt.*

thun.der.clap (THUN.dur.clap) *n.* a loud crash.

thun.der.cloud (THUN.dur.cloud) *n.* a cumulonimbus cloud that gathers be-

thundershower / tidal

fore a thunderstorm; also **thun.der.head.**

thun.der.show.er (THUN.dur.show.er, rhyme: our) n. a rain with thunder and lightning.

thun.der.storm (THUN.dur.storm) n. a rainstorm with thunder and lightning.

thun.der.struck (THUN.dur.struck) adj. overcome with astonishment: *The whole town was thunderstruck at the news.*

Thurs.day (THURS.dee, -day, "TH" as in "thin") n. the fifth day of the week, the day after Wednesday.

thus ("th" as in "the") adv. in this or that manner; to this or that degree or extent; so; therefore.

thus.ly adv. *Informal.* thus.

thwack ("th" as in "thin") n. & v. whack, esp. with something flat or heavy: *the thwack of a ball on gut.*

thwart (THWORT, "TH" as in "thin") n. & adj. (a seat) placed across a boat. —v. obstruct, esp. by blocking the way: *The new candidate thwarted her plans; They wanted to thwart her in her ambitions.*

thy ("th" as in "the") adj. [old form, possessive of THOU] your: *Thy kingdom come; Thy need is greater than mine.*

thyme (TIME) n. an aromatic garden herb of the mint family that yields an oil.

thy.mine (THY.min, -meen, "TH" as in "thin") n. one of the pyrimidine bases of DNA.

thy.mol (THY.mol, "TH" as in "thin") n. a drug made from thyme, used as an antiseptic and in perfumes.

thy.mus ("th" as in "thin") n. a glandlike lymphoid organ located behind the breastbone that helps to provide immunity in childhood; also **thymus gland.**

thy.roid ("th" as in "thin") n. a large ductless gland in the neck that produces the hormone "thyroxine" regulating growth and metabolism.

thy.self (thy.SELF) pron. [old form, reflexive or emphatic of THOU] yourself.

ti.ara (tee.AIR.uh, -AR.uh) n. 1 a crownlike ornamental headband worn by women. 2 the pope's triple crown.

Ti.bet.an (ti.BET.un) n. & adj. (a person) of or from **Tibet**, a country north of the Himalayas, taken over by China in 1950.

tib.i.a (TIB.ee.uh) n., pl. **-i.ae** (-ee.ee) or **-i.as** the shinbone.

tic n. 1 a habitual nervous twitching of muscles of the face. 2 a similar shrugging of the shoulder or other repeated movement of a body part.

tick 1 v. & n. (make) a light, clicking sound, as a clock: *The seconds ticked by; a ticking time bomb (that is going to explode); It was ticking away.* 2 v. *Informal.* keep going: *What makes the new government tick is a mystery to everyone.* 3 v. & n. (mark with) a check mark: *She ticked off the items one by one.* 4 n. a small, blood-sucking, parasitic insect related to mites, some of which transmit diseases such as "tick fever": *tick-borne diseases.* 5 n. the cloth case that is filled to make a mattress or pillow. —**tick off 1** name one by one. **2** *Slang.* to anger: *His behavior sometimes really ticks me off.*

tick.er n. 1 *Informal.* the heart. 2 a ticking instrument, esp. a telegraph machine that prints out news, stock-market reports, etc. on paper tape, or **ticker tape.** 3 *Informal.* a watch.

tick.et (TICK.it) n. 1 a card or piece of paper required for admission, identification, or passage: *theater tickets for a concert; a ticket to a game; airplane, bus, train tickets; a round-trip, not one-way ticket to Paris; a complimentary ticket; a season ticket; She bought a lottery ticket; When the lottery was drawn, she held the winning ticket; a claim ticket for checked baggage.* 2 a list of candidates for election; slate: *He's running on the Democratic ticket; She was elected on a reform ticket.* —v. tag: *Prices are ticketed on each article; He was ticketed for a parking violation.*

tick.ing n. a closely woven cotton fabric for making ticks: *mattress tickings; ticking stripes.*

tick.le (TICK.ul) v. **-les, -led, -ling** feel or cause a tingling or thrilling sensation in a person, body part, etc. by stroking lightly, as the sole of the foot with a feather: *You have to tickle him to make him laugh; stories that tickle your curiosity.* —**tickled pink** adj. *Informal.* very pleased. —n. a tickling or the sensation caused.

tick.ler n. 1 one that tickles. 2 a memorandum book or other aid to memory; adja.: *a tickler file, system; tickler processing.*

tick.lish adj. sensitive or delicate: *a ticklish affair that calls for tact; a ticklish issue, problem, situation.*

tic-tac-toe n. a game played by two persons putting zeros and crosses on a grid of nine squares alternately till one makes a row of three with his or her symbol. Also **tick-tack-toe.**

tid.al (TYE.dul) adj. having to do with

tides: *a tidal bore in a river; tidal erosion; a tidal current, inlet, river.*
tidal wave *n.* **1** a large destructive ocean wave, as caused by an earthquake. **2** a large outburst or sudden increase: *a tidal wave of complaints, imports, pronouncements.*
tid.bit *n.* a choice morsel of food, gossip, etc.
tid.dly.winks (TID.lee.winks) *n.* a game in which small disks are snapped by their edges into a container using larger disks.
tide *n.* **1** the rise and fall of ocean waters from the gravitational pull of the moon: *the ebb* or *falling tide; the flow* or *flood tide; high, low tides.* **2** the resulting outward and inward flow in estuaries, rivers, etc.: *The tide comes in, ebbs* or *goes out.* **3** a trend, as of public opinion, events, etc.: *to buck, go against, go with, stem, swim with the tide; a rising tide of discontent; waiting for a* **turn of the tide** *(from one condition to its opposite).* —**comb.form** (old use) season or time: *Christmastide, Eastertide, Yuletide.* —*v.* **tides, tid.ed, tid.ing** help get through or survive: *Savings tided her over the long illness.*
tide.land *n.* **1** submerged coast land. **2** land regularly covered by high tide.
tide.wa.ter (TIDE.wot.ur) *n.* **1** water that is brought in or that is affected by the tide. **2** an area affected by the tide, as the Tidewater costal plain of E. Virginia.
tidings (TYE.dings) *n.pl.* news: *to bear, bring, receive glad tidings; sad tidings; tidings of great joy.*
ti.dy (TYE.dee) *adj.* **-di.er, -di.est 1** neat or orderly: *Her room is always tidy.* **2** *Informal.* relatively large: *a tidy sum of money.* —*v.* **-dies, -died, -dy.ing** make tidy: *Tim has been told to tidy up his room while his mom tidies the kitchen.* —*n., pl.* **-dies** a small protective cover for the back, arms, or headrest of a chair or sofa. —**tid.i.ly** *adv.;* **tid.i.ness** *n.*
tie (TYE) *v.* **ties, tied, ty.ing 1** fasten or secure with a string, cord, rope, etc. that can be knotted: *to tie up a parcel; Tie your shoes; She tied (= made) a bow in her hair.* **2** connect or link: *two countries tied by common interests; evidence that* **ties in with** *(= relates to) suspected motives.* **3** restrict or confine: *Road construction ties up traffic; He's* **tied down** *by family responsibilities; I'm too* **tied up** *(= busy) to answer phone calls.* **4** to equal a record or competitor in score: *The home team tied with the visitors for the lead; They tied the game at 12:04 of the first period; The 68-yard return tied the previous record; The last goal tied the score; They are tied for second place with 75 points.* —*n.* **1** anything that ties or unites, as a cord, necktie, knot, or crosspieces to which railroad tracks are fastened: *to cut, sever, strengthen family ties; to establish strong ties; close, intimate, marital ties; ties of friendship; She has ties with* or *to foreign companies; school ties (= neckties); old school ties (= bonds or links).* **2** a contest resulting in equality of scores between teams; draw: *The match ended in a tie; a scoreless tie (with zero for both sides); a game played to break a tie or a* **tie-breaker.**
tie.back *n.* (a curtain with) a band or strap to tie it to one side.
tie bar (or **clasp** or **clip**) *n.* an ornamental device for securing a necktie to the shirt front.
tie-dye *n.* a method of producing patterns on cloth by tying small portions of it by string before dyeing: *a tie-dye tank top.* —*v.* **-dyes, -dyed, -dye.ing.**
tie-in *n.* a connection with something else, as of a book with a motion picture based on it.
tier (TEER) *n.* one of a series of rows, as of seats in a stadium or balconies in a theater, arranged one above another.
tie rod *n.* a connecting member, esp. one connecting a front wheel of an automobile to the steering mechanism.
tie tack *n.* a short pin that is poked through the ends of a necktie to hold them together.
tie-up *n.* **1** a temporary suspension of work in progress, traffic, etc.: *Production tie-ups forced the factory to close down.* **2** a connection or relation.
tiff *v.& n.* (have) a petty quarrel *with someone.*
ti.ger (TYE.gur) *n.* a large, tawny-coated, black-striped, flesh-eating Asiatic animal of the cat family: *Hockey brings out the tiger (= aggressiveness) in him.* —**ti.ger.ish** (TYE.gur.ish) *adj.*
tight *adj.* **1** going around and binding without looseness or slack: *a tight collar, grip, knot; tight (= tight-fitting) clothes.* **2** taut: *a rope stretched tight.* **3** closed firmly against leaks or losses: *a tight roof; a water-tight container; Money is tight (= not easy to borrow); a tight (= closely fought) game; We found ourselves in a* **tight corner** *or* **spot** *(= difficult situation); price-gouging in a* **tight market** *for scarce goods; a tight*

*schedule (with no spare time); The boss **runs a tight ship** (= operates efficiently).* **4** *Informal.* stingy: *a tight moneylender who is tight with funds.* **5** *adjp. Informal.* intoxicated. —*adv.* closely or firmly: *He decided to sit hight and wait for the power struggle to end; to sleep tight* (= soundly). —**tight.ly** *adv.;* **tight.ness** *n.*

tight.en (TYE.tun) *v.* make or become tight or tighter: *People tighten their belts in times of scarcity.*

tight.fist.ed (TITE.fis.tid) *adj.* stingy.

tight-lipped *adj.* secretive: *Sam is tight-lipped about his previous employer.*

tight.rope *n.* a tightly stretched rope or cable on which acrobats perform: *a tightrope artist; He **walks a tightrope** (= is in a precarious position) working for that outfit.*

tights *n.pl.* a skintight garment for the hips and legs, as worn by acrobats and dancers.

tight.wad *n. Informal.* a stingy person.

ti.gress (TYE.gris) *n.* a female tiger.

til.de (TIL.duh) *n.* a diacritical mark (~) placed over a palatal "n," as in Spanish *cañon,* and over nasalized vowels, as in Portuguese *São.*

tile *n.* **1** a thin slab or piece of baked clay, stone, or synthetic material for covering roofs, floors, or walls. **2** a section of an earthenware drainage or sewage pipe. —*v.* **tiles, tiled, til.ing** cover with tiles; *adj.: a **tiled** avenue, floor, roof.* —**til.er** *n.*

till *prep. & conj.* until. —*v.* cultivate land by plowing, sowing, etc.
—*n.* a drawer behind a counter, esp. in a store, in which money is kept: *He was caught **with his hand in the till** (= stealing).* —**till.er** *n.*

till.age (TIL.ij) *n.* **1** the tilling of land; *adja.: tillage equipment, operations, tools.* **2** cultivated land.

tilt *v.* **1** (cause) to slope or slant: *Cups, barrels, dump trucks, etc. are tilted to empty them; a tilting table with uneven legs; policies that seem to tilt to the Left; policies tilting* (= inclining) *toward socialism.* **2** charge or attack, as in medieval jousts: *Knights used to tilt on horseback; Don Quixote tilted at windmills mistaking them for giants.*
—*n.* **1** a slope or slant. **2** the medieval contest of knights trying to unhorse each other with lances while charging at speed. —**(at) full tilt** at full speed.

tilt-top *adj.* of a table, having a top that can be tilted to a vertical position and stored flat against a wall.

tim.ber (TIM.bur) *n.* **1** wood prepared for use, as for building; also, a wooden beam: *a stack of timber; **adja.:** the timber industry, trade; timber products.* **2** trees bearing wood suitable for use: *the harvesting of timber; standing timber; a timber-cutting license.* —*v.* cover, support, or furnish with timbers; *adj.: a house with **timbered** walls and thatched roof;* **half-timbered** *cottages (made of timber split in half).*

tim.ber.line (TIM.bur.line) same as TREE LINE.

timber wolf *n.* the gray North American wolf.

tim.bre (TAM.bur, TIM-) *n.* the characteristic tone of a voice or instrument, regardless of the pitch or volume of sounds.

tim.brel (TIM.brul) *n.* a small tambourine or drumlike musical instrument.

time *n.* **1** the continuous period that includes the past, present, and future: *the eternity of time; Time flies* or *passes; Time will tell which of us is right.* **2** a period of definite duration: *It happened during the time of the Civil War; prehistoric time; We spent time waiting to be called; We watched TV to kill time; played cards to pass the time; to find, gain, lose, save, take, waste time; to fritter away one's time; to give equal time on radio or TV to all viewpoints; programs aired during prime time; She finished the job in record time; When we are idle, time drags; Time hangs on our hands; the running time of a movie; the travel time between home and office;* **Take your time** (= Do not hurry); *He **beat** or **kept time** (= rhythm or rate of movement) with his feet while she sang; She earns **double time** (= rate of pay) on holidays; This hasn't happened in recent **times**; to keep up with the **times** (= current happenings).* **3** a particular point or occasion for something to be done or to happen: *at the present time; Clocks tell time; Better luck next time; There's a first time for everything; closing, harvest, opening, starting times; five times, many times, several times; It's time to go to bed; to fix, set, specify a time for our meeting; It's high time we met; By the time we got there, it was dark; to **bide one's time** (= wait for one's opportunity).* **4** a period as used or experienced: *We had a good, great, lovely time at the party; had the time of our lives; We have no time to waste; time well spent; free, full, leisure, lost, spare time; We work part-time; bad, difficult, hard **times** of inflation and unemployment; "Time is money"* (= is precious); *Your time* (= allotted period) *is up.* **5** a system of measuring time: *so-*

lar time; daylight saving(s) time; Eastern Standard Time. —**against time** trying to finish in a given time. —**ahead of time** before the due time. —**at the same time** however. —**at times** occasionally. —**do** or **serve time** *Informal.* serve a prison term. —**for the time being** for a limited period. —**from time to time** sometimes; occasionally. —**in time** 1 eventually. 2 ahead of the set time: *We arrived in time for the ceremony.* 3 keeping the right rhythm or tempo. —**make time** 1 compensate for lost time by going faster than normal. 2 save time this way. —**mark time** appear to be active but without making progress, as when moving the feet up and down without marching forward. —**of all time** that there ever has been or will be: *some of the greatest scientists of all time.* —**on time** 1 at the right time: *We arrived on time.* 2 on credit: *He buys all heavy appliances on time.*
—*v.* **times, timed, tim.ing** 1 set the time or speed of something: *to time one's activities; to time a program.* 2 measure the time or duration of something: *to time a race, runner, speech.* —**adja.** having to do with time: *time capsules; a test with a time limit; time loans; time management; time saving; time zones.*
time bomb *n.* a bomb set to go off at a definite time.
time capsule *n.* a receptacle containing items typical of the time, buried in the ground, a cornerstone, etc. for future discovery.
time.card *n.* a card for recording the arrival and departure times of an employee.
time clock *n.* a clock device for recording employees' hours of work: *to punch a time clock.*
time frame *n.* a period of time during which an action or event takes place: *within a specified time frame; a limited, shorter, smaller time frame.*
time-honored *adja.* long-existing: *a time-honored custom, practice, tradition.*
time.keep.er (TIME.kee.pur) *n.* one who keeps account of hours worked, time elapsed, etc.
time.less (TIME.lis) *adj.* 1 eternal: *the past and present fused in a timeless blur; in one timeless moment; timeless eternity, mysteries, truths; the timeless universe.* 2 not affected by time: *the timeless beauty of the Taj Mahal; a timeless appeal, design, elegance, fashion, look, style.*
—**time.less.ness** *n.*

time.line *n.* 1 a detailed sequence of dates and events: *a timeline of activities, events.* 2 the period of this sequence: *a timeline for the completion of a project; planning timelines; The original timeline was four to five years; to extend a timeline.*
time loan *n.* a loan that is due at a specified time.
time.ly *adj.* **-li.er, -li.est** happening or done at a suitable time: *a timely delivery, publication, reminder; in a timely fashion.* —**time.li.ness** *n.*
time.out *n.* a brief suspension of play, as in basketball or football: *He takes (a) timeout for ten minutes every hour.*
time.piece *n.* a clock, watch, or other time-measuring instrument.
tim.er (TYE.mur) *n.* 1 a clock device for indicating the passage of a period of time: *an egg timer for timing the boiling of eggs.* 2 an automatic device for starting and stopping an operation: *We set a timer to turn the lights off and on at night.*
times *prep.* multiplied by: *3 times 5 is 15.*
time.serv.er (TIME.sur.vur) *n.* one who servilely seeks to please those in power or changes his principles to suit the times. —**time.serv.ing** *n. & adj.*
time-sharing *n.* 1 a system enabling several people to use the same computer simultaneously in various functions. 2 the sharing of a vacation lodging by several tenants or owners taking turns using it.
time sheet *n.* a record of the hours worked by an employee or employees.
time.ta.ble (TIME.tay.bul) *n.* 1 a schedule of the hours at which work is started and stopped. 2 a list of times at which buses, planes, etc. arrive and depart, etc.: *to follow, make up, upset a timetable.*
time warp *n.* the condition of being in an imaginary time in a past or future period, as in science fiction.
time.worn *adj.* worn out or hackneyed: *a timeworn expression, image, practice.*
time zone *n.* any of the 24 longitudinal divisions of the world in each of which the same standard time is used regardless of local time: *Los Angeles is three time zones west of New York.*
tim.id (TIM.id) *adj.* 1 cautious and fearful: *a timid child; Deer are timid by nature.* 2 lacking in the self-con- fidence required to assert oneself: *He's too timid to ask for a raise.* —**tim.id.ly** *adv.*
—**ti.mid.i.ty** (tuh.MID.i.tee) *n.*
timing (TYE.ming) *n.* 1 regulation of the speed, duration, etc. of an action:

The timing of your engine needs adjusting; You should improve your timing; Note your timing (= time measurement) *at the end of the run.* **2** choice of the right moment of an action for maximum effect: *She has a good sense of timing; It's bad timing to ask for a raise when the boss is in a bad mood.*
tim.or.ous (TIM.ur.us) *adj.* full of fear and apprehension: *a timorous glance.* —**tim.or.ous.ly** *adv.;* **tim.or.ous.ness** *n.*
tim.o.thy (TIM.uh.thee, "th" as in "thin") *n.* a tall grass with spikes of tightly packed flowers that is grown for hay.
tim.pa.ni (TIM.puh.nee) *n.pl.* a set of kettle drums played by one performer (timpanist), in an orchestra. —**tim.pa.nist** *n.*
tin *n.* **1** a light, bluish-white, malleable, corrosion-resistant metallic element used in alloys. **2** a container made of tin plate. —*v.* **tins, tinned, tin.ning** **1** plate with tin. **2** *Cdn.* to can; *adj.:* **tinned** *salmon.*
tin can *n.* a packaging container made of tin.
tinc.ture (TINK.chur) *n.* **1** a medication dissolved in alcohol: *tincture of iodine.* **2** a tinge or trace. —*v.* **-tures, -tured, -tur.ing** tinge *with* a color; also, tint.
tin.der (TIN.dur) *n.* a material that burns easily: *The long drought left the forest tinder dry.*
tin.der.box (TIN.dur.box) *n.* a potential source of a fire or flare-up, as a box containing tinder, flint, and steel formerly used to kindle a fire: *the tinderbox of the Middle East.*
tine *n.* a prong, esp. of a fork.
tin.foil *n.* a thin sheeting of tin used as wrapping.
tinge (TINJ) *n.* a slight coloring, flavor, taste, etc.: *Ivory gets a yellowish tinge after some time; the tinge of sadness in her voice.* —*v.* **ting.es, tinged, tinge.ing** or **ting.ing** modify with a tinge: *a voice tinged with sadness.*
tin.gle (TIN.gul) *n.* a slight prickling or stinging sensation, as from cold, excitement, etc. —*v.* **-gles, -gled, -gling** have or cause a tingle; *n.: sensations of pain, numbness, and* **tingling;** *adja.: a tingling sensation, skin; tingling nerves.* —**tin.gly** *adj.: a tingly feeling, skin, taste.*
tin.ker (TINK.ur) *n.* **1** one who goes around mending pots, pans, etc. **2** an unskilled or amateur worker. —*v.* repair or work in an unskilled way *at* or *with* something. —**tin.ker.er** *n.*
tin.kle (TINK.ul) *n.* a short, light ringing sound, as of little bells, esp. a series of such sounds. —*v.* **-kles, -kled, -kling** make or cause to make a tinkle.
tin.ny (TIN.ee) *adj.* **tin.ni.er, tin.ni.est** **1** like tin in appearance, value, sound, etc.: *a tinny* (= thin or metallic) *sound, voice; a tinny* (= not well-made) *car.* **2** having to do with tin: *a tinny alloy, lode, taste.* —**tin.ni.ly** *adv.;* **tin.ni.ness** *n.*
tin plate *n.* tin-coated sheets of iron or steel, as used for roofing, food containers, etc.
tin.sel (TIN.sul) *n.* **1** glittering material used for decoration in thin sheets, threads, etc., as on Christmas trees. **2** anything showy, gaudy, and cheap; **tinseltown** (= Hollywood).
tin.smith *n. a worker in tin plate; a repairer of tinware.*
tint *n.* a light shade or hue: *Pink is a tint of red.* —*v.* color with a tint: *a windshield tinted blue; adj.:* **tinted** *eyeglasses, hair, windows.*
tin.tin.nab.u.la.tion (TIN.ti.nab.yuh. LAY.shun) *n.* the tinkling of bells.
tin.ware *n.* articles made of tin plate.
ti.ny (TYE.nee) *adj.* **-ni.er, -ni.est** very small; minute: *a tiny amount, bit, detail, fraction, particle.*
tip *n.* **1** an end part, esp. a pointed or tapering end: *the tip of the nose, tongue; the tips of the toes; It was* **on the tip of my tongue** (= I almost said it). **2** a light stroke or glancing blow; tap. **3** a piece of secret information: *an anonymous tip; a hot tip.* **4** a useful hint or suggestion: *a few tips on* or *about good grooming.* **5** a small gift of money; gratuity: *She left a handsome tip for the waiter.* **6** a tilt or slope. —*v.* **tips, tipped, tip.ping** **1** have as an end part: *a cane tipped with brass; filter-tipped cigarettes.* **2** tap: *The ball was tipped into the basket.* **3** give a useful hint to someone: *The police were* **tipped off** *by an anonymous caller; She was careful not to* **tip her hand** (Informal for reveal her intentions) *by talking loosely.* **4** give a gratuity: *She never forgets to tip the waiter; She tips generously, liberally.* **5** tilt or slope: *He's in the habit of tipping his hat to ladies; A boat may tip over if loaded unevenly; She* **tips the scales at** (= weighs) *40 kg.* —**tip.per** *n.*
tip-off *n.* a tipping off; warning.
tip of the iceberg *n.* the visible part of something larger and deeper.
tip.pet (TIP.it) *n.* a scarflike garment with ends hanging down in front.
tip.ple (TIP.ul) *v.* **tip.ples, tip.pled, tip.pling** drink alcoholic liquor habitu-

ally and excessively. —*n.* liquor for tippling: *Vodka is the main tipple in Russia.* —**tip.pler** *n.*

tip.py toes (TIP.ee) *n.pl. Informal.* the tips of the toes.

tip.ster (TIP.stur) *n. Informal.* one who supplies secret information, usu. for pay, as about horse races.

tip.sy (TIP.see) *adj.* **-si.er, -si.est 1** intoxicated: *tipsy drivers.* **2** unsteady, as if intoxicated. —**tip.si.ly** *adv.;* **tip.si.ness** *n.*

tip.toe (TIP.toe) *v.* **-toes, -toed, -toe.ing** walk on the tips of one's toes: *to tiptoe through a minefield; to tiptoe around a delicate subject.* —*n.* the tip of a toe: *walked gently on her tiptoes so as not to wake the baby.* —**on tiptoe 1** on one's tiptoes: *He stood on tiptoe to reach the top shelf.* **2** eagerly: *waiting on tiptoe to catch a glimpse of the movie star.*

tip.top *n.* the highest point. —*adj. & adv.* **1** at the very top. **2** *Informal.* excellent.

ti.rade (TYE.rade, tuh.RADE) *n.* a long, vehement or scolding speech; harangue: *He launched into a tirade against politicians.*

tire *n.* a usu. hollow casing of rubber with a grooved tread, filled with air and fixed to the rim of a wheel for a smooth ride: *a new set of (four) tires; front and rear tires; to change, deflate, inflate, mount, slash a tire; to rotate tires for even wear; Tires blow out, go flat; We had a flat tire; radial, snow, spare, steel-belted, studded, tubeless, whitewall tires; Before spending money on anything,* **kick the tires** (= check it out) *and compare prices; a tire gauge to check tire pressure.* —*v.* **tires, tired, tir.ing** make or become weary or bored: *One tires of watching TV after a few hours; She tires easily.* —**tired** *adj.* **1** exhausted or weary: *She's tired from the climb; dead tired; her tired look; to become, feel, get tired; all tired out; I'm* **tired of** (= bored with) *TV; sick and tired.* **2** worn-out: *a tired joke, old adage, suit.*

tire iron *n.* a short, crowbarlike tool made of steel with a flattened blade for removing tires from wheel rims

tire.less *adj.* **1** never getting tired: *a tireless advocate, troublemaker, worker.* **2** ceaseless: *her tireless efforts, energy, work.* —**tire.less.ly** *adv.*

tire.some (TIRE.sum) *adj.* that tires or bores: *It's tiresome watching* or *to watch TV all day.*

Ti.ro.le.an (tuh.ROH.lee.un) *adj.* having to do with **Tirol,** an Alpine region of W. Austria and N. Italy.

'tis (TIZ) it is.

tis.sue (TISH.oo) *n.* **1** the body substance of animals and plants consisting of cells: *bone, connective, muscular, nervous, scar tissue.* **2** web or network: *a tissue of lies; a tissue of twaddle.* **3** a fine, sheer cloth or gauze. **4** soft absorbent paper: *facial tissue; toilet tissue.*

tissue paper *n.* lightweight paper used for wrapping, paper napkins, etc.

tit *n.* **1** a nipple or teat. **2** a small bird. **3** a titmouse. **4** [vulgar slang] a woman's breast.

ti.tan (TYE.tun) *n.* a giant, like the **Titans,** the first gods of Greek myth.

ti.tan.ic (tye.TAN.ic) *adj.* giantlike in size or strength.

ti.ta.ni.um (tye.TAY.nee.um) *n.* a lightweight, silver-gray, corrosion-resistant metal.

tit.bit same as TIDBIT.

tit for tat *n.* blow in return for blow; retaliation; **adj.:** *a tit-for-tat attitude.*

tithe (TITHE, "TH" as in "the") *n.* a tenth part of one's income, as traditionally given to the church. —*v.* **tithes, tithed, tith.ing** pay a tithe. —**tith.er** *n.*

tit.il.late (TIT.ul.ate) *v.* **-il.lates, -il.lat.ed, -il.lat.ing** excite or stimulate, as if by tickling. —**tit.il.la.tion** (-LAY.shun) *n.*

tit.i.vate (TIT.uh.vate) *v.* **-vates, -vat.ed, -vat.ing** dress up; spruce up.

ti.tle (TYE.tul) *n.* **1** the name of a literary or artistic product: *the title of a play; the* **title page** *of a book.* **2 titles** *pl.* credits, subtitles, etc. appearing on a TV or motion-picture screen. **3** a name giving a person's rank or occupation, as Mister, Miss, Lord, Doctor, Supervisor, etc.: *a job title; The title "Honorable" is bestowed* or *conferred on senators for life; She renounced her official titles in protest.* **4** a championship: *the world heavyweight title; to clinch, hold, lose, win a title; a title bout.* **5** a legal right to exclusive ownership of property; also, a deed or other document showing this to: *to give, hold title to a property; to establish clear title.* —*v.* **-tles, -tled, -tling** give a title to something.

titled *adj.* **1** having as title: *a book titled "Roots."* **2** having a title of rank or nobility: *a titled lady, landowner.*

ti.tle.hold.er (TYE.tul.hole.dur) *n.* the holder of a championship.

title role *n.* the character in a play or motion picture after whom the work is named.

tit.mouse *n., pl.* **-mice** a small songbird with long, soft feathers.

tit.ter (TIT.ur) *n. & v.* giggle.
tit.tle (TIT.ul) *n.* a particle or dot: *every jot and tittle; It was done without raising a tittle of suspicion.*
tittle-tattle *n.* gossip; idle chatter.
tit.u.lar (TICH.uh.lur) *adj.* **1** of or bearing a title: *a titular head, rank, role.* **2** nominal: *a titular bishop (of a nonexistent jurisdiction); the titular position of chairman of the board.*
tiz.zy (TIZ.ee) *n.* **tiz.zies** *Informal.* state of nervous excitement; dither: *We found them in a tizzy; to be thrown into a tizzy.*
TNT See **TRINITROTOLUENE**.
to (TOO, tuh) *prep.* **1** [indicating the direction of an action or movement]: *He goes to school; stood with his back to the wall; came to our rescue; was put to sleep; torn to pieces; Count to 100; It is five minutes to six; She was faithful to the end; He dances to every tune; She's kind to animals; gives to charity; talks to herself; a score of 10 to (= against) one.* **2** [used before verbs to indicate the infinitive]: *He likes to sing; Go if you want to (go).* —*adv.* [indicating the direction of an action or movement toward something implied]: *He came to (= became conscious) soon after fainting; As soon as they were served, they fell to (= started eating); A door swings to (= becomes shut); He was wearing his hat wrong end to (= forward).* —**to and fro** forward and back; back and forth.
toad (TODE) *n.* a froglike but less aquatic animal.
toad.stool *n.* a poisonous mushroom.
toad.y (TOH.dee) *n.* **toad.ies** a servile flatterer. —*v.* **toad.ies, toad.ied, toad.y.ing** be a toady to a superior: *to toady to the principal.*
toast (TOHST) *n.* **1** a slice of bread browned by heat, as in a toaster: *to make toast; a piece* or *slice of toast; buttered, dry, plain toast.* **2** a drink or an invitation to drink in honor of a person or event: *He proposed* or *made a toast to the champion; to drink, join in, raise a toast to the centenarian; a champagne toast.* **3** an honored or celebrated person, institution, product, etc.: *He was the toast of Europe and Japan; She was the toast of the town on her return from the Olympics.*
—*adjp. Informal.* finished: *Try that again and you're toast, dead meat, dust.*
—*v.* **1** to brown by heat: *to toast almonds, bread, marshmallows, muffins, nuts; to toast* (= *warm*) *one's feet before a fire.* **2** propose or drink a toast to a person or event: *We toasted her success in the Olympics with champagne; to toast our founding fathers.*
toast.er (TOSE.tur) *n.* a small appliance for toasting bread.
toast.mas.ter (TOHST.mas.tur) *n.* one who presides at a banquet introducing speakers, proposing toasts, etc.; **toast.mis.tress** *fem.*
toast.y *adj. & adv.* warm and cosy: *to feel toasty; Mom makes our house toasty warm.*
to.bac.co (tuh.BAC.oh) *n.* **-bac.cos** **1** a plant whose broad leaves are prepared for smoking, chewing, etc.: *to grow tobacco.* **2** the prepared leaves: *to chew, cure tobacco; a plug of tobacco (for chewing).* **3** products such as cigarettes and snuff prepared from tobacco leaves. —**to.bac.co.nist** (-cun.ist) *n.* a tobacco retailer.
to.bog.gan (tuh.BOG.un) *n.* a small sled without runners whose front end curves upward. —*v.* **1** to coast downhill on a toboggan. **2** decline rapidly in value.
toc.sin *n.* an alarm bell or other warning sound.
to.day (tuh.DAY) *n. & adv.* **1** (on or for) this day: *here today and gone tomorrow; Today is Tuesday.* **2** (at) the present time; (in) this day or age: *Today we know that you can go to the moon; today's youth; the women of today.*
tod.dle (TOD.ul) *v.* **tod.dles, tod.dled, tod.dling** walk with short uncertain steps, as a young child, or **tod.dler**.
tod.dy (TOD.ee) *n.* **tod.dies** **1** an alcoholic drink mixed with hot water, sugar, spices, etc. **2** the fermented sap of an E. Indian palm.
to-do (tuh.DOO) *n.* **-dos** (-DOOZ) fuss or commotion: *She made a big to-do over the missing keys.*
toe (TOH) *n.* **1** one of the five fingerlike parts of the human foot: *She's careful not to **step** or **tread on his toes** (= not to offend him); outfitted in red from **head** or **top to toe** (= completely).* **2** the forepart of a foot or hoof. —**on one's toes** *Informal.* alert and ready: *The competition keeps us on our toes; to be, stay on our toes; to have them on their toes.* —*v.* **toes, toed, toe.ing** **1** touch or reach with the toes, as the starting line of a race: *Members of a party are expected to **toe the line** (= conform to policy, rules, etc.).* **2** turn the toes: *Some toe in, others toe out when walking; The front wheels of a car are slightly toed in.*
toed (TODE) *adj. & comb.form.* having toes or toes as specified: *toed stockings;*

toe dance / tolerance

open-toed sandals; pigeon-toed; safety-toed shoes; a three-toed sloth.
toe dance n. a dance performed on the toes, as in ballet. —**toe-dance** v. -danc.es, -danced, -danc.ing. —toe-dancer n.
toe.hold n. 1 a narrow footing, as on a ledge: when the union first got a toehold in that factory. 2 a slight advantage.
toe.nail n. the nail of a toe.
tof.fee (TOF.ee) n. **tof.fees** taffy or caramel. Also **tof.fy, tof.fies.**
to.fu (TOH.foo) n. a soft cheeselike food made from curdled soybean milk; bean curd.
tog 1 v. **togs, togged, tog.ging** Informal. clothe or dress: appropriately togged in tuxedos. 2 **togs** n.pl. clothes.
to.ga (TOH.guh) n. the loose outer garment of citizens in ancient Rome. —**to.gaed** (-gud) adj. toga-clad.
to.geth.er (tuh.GETH.ur, "TH" as in "the") adv. 1 in or into one place or group: Friends like to be together; working together; The two together weigh 90 kg; the man **together with** his wife. 2 at the same time: I heard them singing together; Our cat was missing for days together (= continuously). —**get** or **put it together** Informal. get organized: He just couldn't get it together even after months on the job. —adj. Informal. self-possessed; well-integrated: a young, happy, together couple.
to.geth.er.ness (tuh.GETH.ur.nis) n. closeness of relationship.
tog.gle (TOG.ul) n. 1 a device that hangs or pulls crosswise, as a T-head crosspiece passed through a loop, or a **toggle bolt** with a winged nut that spreads out crosswise to lock the bolt in position: The common household **toggle switch** has a projecting lever moving in an arc to open or close the electrical circuit. 2 a computer keystroke that lets the user switch between two settings, as power on/off and alarm enable / disable: a toggle switch; v.: to toggle on and off; to toggle between voice and data.
toil n. 1 work that is long and laborious: after years of toil and sweat; arduous, endless, honest, unremitting toil. 2 usu. **toils** pl. meshes or a netlike trap. —v. to labor hard: Farmers used to sweat and toil in the fields; Serious students toil over their homework; a tractor-trailer toiling (= moving laboriously) up a hill. —**toil.er** n.
toi.let (TOY.lut) n. 1 the bowl-shaped plumbing fixture for receiving body wastes: to flush, use the toilet; Don't flush your poem down the toilet; a toilet bowl, handle, lid, seat, seat cover, tank; a person's toilet habits. 2 a washroom equipped with a toilet: a pay toilet; public toilets; toilet facilities. 3 the process of washing, dressing, and grooming oneself.
toilet paper (or **tissue**) n. soft paper for wiping oneself after using the toilet.
toi.let.ry (TOY.luh.tree) n. usu. **toi.let.ries** pl. articles such as soap and cosmetics used in washing and grooming.
toi.lette (twah.LET, toi-) n. 1 toilet or washroom. 2 costume or attire. 3 same as TOILET, 3.
toilet training n. the training of a child to use the toilet and control bladder and bowel movements; adj.: a toilet-trained child.
toilet water n. cologne or a similar perfumed liquid.
toil.some adj. laborious or wearisome: the toilsome duties, work of a shipping clerk.
toke n. & v. **tokes, toked, tok.ing** Slang. (puff on) a marijuana cigarette.
to.ken (TOH.kun) n. 1 a gift, souvenir, or other article that serves as a sign or indication of an inner quality, feeling, etc.: feeble, mere, slight, tangible tokens; a gift as a small token of our gratitude; offered **in token of** (= as a sign of) our esteem. 2 a coinlike piece of metal serving as an admission ticket: A bus token is dropped in a box; Subway tokens are inserted into a slot; gift tokens. —**by the same token** for the same reason. —adj. serving as a token; nominal: a token amount, gesture, gift, interest, vote; Our victory was more than token; a token payment to acknowledge a debt.
to.ken.ism (TOH.kun.iz.um) n. the policy of making merely nominal concessions to a demand, as for racial equality.
told pt. & pp. of TELL: **All told** (= altogether), some 500 were injured in the earthquake.
tole n. lacquered or enameled tin plate used for trays, lampshades, etc.
tol.er.a.ble (TOL.ur.uh.bul) adj. 1 bearable or endurable: a tolerable burden, pain; to make life tolerable. 2 fairly good: in tolerable health; a tolerable income, meal. —**tol.er.a.bly** adv.: tolerably efficient, good, harmonious, well; It can function tolerably.
tol.er.ance (TOL.ur.unce) n. 1 the quality of being tolerant; to have, show tolerance for people of all racial backgrounds and religions; social tolerance of people with AIDS. 2 resistance to a drug's ill effects: Different people have

different tolerances; Tolerance increases with use. **3** the allowable variation from a standard dimension, weight, or fineness, as in minting coins.

tol.er.ant (TOL.ur.unt) *adj.* **1** willing to let others live according to their own beliefs, practices, etc.: *a tolerant attitude, culture, policy, society; to be tolerant of opposition; democratic and tolerant.* **2** forbearing: *a tolerant and forgiving nature; tolerant of human weaknesses.* **3** resistant to the ill effects of something: *He's not tolerant of alcohol; tolerant to the drug's side effects;* **cpd:** *cold-tolerant bacteria; drought-tolerant crops; a fault-tolerant computer system.* **—tol.er.ant.ly** *adv.*

tol.er.ate (TOL.uh.rate) *v.* **-ates, -at.ed, -at.ing 1** put up with or bear a person or thing: *We will not tolerate such behavior; a character difficult to tolerate* (= work or live with). **2** resist the ill effects of a drug, etc.: *Some can't tolerate aspirin.* **—tol.er.a.tion** (-RAY.shun) *n.*

toll (TOLE) *n.* **1** a charge or fee, as for using a bridge or turnpike, making a long-distance telephone call, or **toll call**, etc.: *to charge, exact, impose a toll; She collects tolls from a booth on the bridge; a toll-free 800 number.* **2** loss or damage suffered: *The earthquake took a heavy toll of lives; the frightening death toll on our highways.* **3** a tolling sound. **—v. 1** ring a bell in slow, measured strokes. **2** announce the hour of day, a death, etc. or summon by tolling: *The bell tolled for those who died in the war.*

toll.booth *n.* a booth at which a toll is collected.

toll.gate *n.* the point where tolls are collected on a bridge, turnpike, etc.

toll road *n.* a turnpike.

tol.u.ene (TOL.yoo.een) *n.* a benzenelike coal-tar product used in industrial chemicals, esp. explosives, antiknock, etc.

tom *comb.form.* male: *tomboy, tomcat, tomcod; tom turkey.*

tom.a.hawk (TOM.uh.hawk) *n.* a light, axlike tool and weapon of North American Indians.

to.ma.to (tuh.MAY.toh, -MAH.toh) *n.* **-toes 1** a usu. large, pulpy, round, red or yellow fruit used as a vegetable. **2** the plant it grows on.

tomb (TOOM, long "OO") *n.* **1** a burial place for a dead body, as a grave, vault, or other chamber: *quiet as a tomb; communicating from beyond the* **tomb** (= after death). **2** an above-ground structure such as a cenotaph or mausoleum.

tom.boy *n.* a girl who is boisterous and romps about like a boy. **—tom.boy.ish** *adj.*

tomb.stone (TOOM.stone) *n.* a stone marking a tomb or grave.

tom.cat *n.* a male cat.

Tom Collins *n.* a cocktail made with gin and lemon juice.

tome *n.* a learned or heavy volume: *a scholarly tome.*

tom.fool.er.y (tom.FOO.luh.ree) *n.* **-er.ies** silly or nonsensical behavior.

tom.my gun (TOM.ee-) *n. Informal.* a submachine gun trademarked "Thompson submachine gun."

to.mog.ra.phy (tuh.MOG.ruh.fee) *n.* a technique of X-raying body tissue in isolated planes or sections: *computerized axial tomography.*

to.mor.row (tuh.MOR.oh) *n. & adv.* **1** (on) the day after today: *I'll do it tomorrow; tomorrow night.* **2** (at) some future time: *what tomorrow may bring; the unpredictable world of tomorrow; Today's work pays off tomorrow.*

tom-tom *n.* a usu. hand-beaten drum used in India and by African and Amerindian tribes.

ton (TUN) *n.* either of two units of weight, **short ton** (2,000 lb. / 907.18 kg) or **long ton** (2,240 lb. / 1,016.05 kg): *The news came down on* or *hit her* **like a ton of bricks** (= hard or heavily); *We had* **tons of** (*Informal* for lots of) *fun.*

ton.al (TOH.nul) *adj.* **1** having to do with tone: *tonal balance, effects, qualities, richness.* **2** having to do with tints: *tonal colors.* **—ton.al.ly** *adv.*

to.nal.i.ty (toh.NAL.i.tee) *n.* **-ties 1** the relationship of tones to the keynote of a musical composition. **2** tonal character: *pastel colors with a gray tonality.*

tone *n.* **1** the sound of a voice or musical instrument, esp. as to its character or quality: *in an angry tone of voice; in angry tones; abusive, apologetic, arrogant, condescending, dulcet, friendly, harsh, imperious, low, patronizing, serious, soft, subdued, sweet, threatening tones; the solemn tones of an organ.* **2** nature or character: *a high moral tone; the strident tone of his demands; Avoid anything that may* **lower the tone** *of the proceedings.* **3** a musical sound of a particular pitch: *falling, high, low, rising tones; "Do" and "re" are a whole tone* (= note or step) *apart.* **4** style or trend: *A keynote speaker is supposed to* **set the tone** *for* or *of the proceedings.* **5** vigor and tension, as of a muscle. **6** responsiveness or resilience, as of rubber. **7** the relative lightness or darkness of a color: *Rose is a tone of red blended with gray; decorated in* **tones** (= shades) *of blue.* —*v.* **tones, toned, ton.ing 1** give tone to muscles: *how to tone and tighten your muscles;* adj.: *to keep one's muscles* **toned** *and healthy;* n.: *muscle* **toning***; tummy toning.* **2** impart a color tone; *cpd: deep-toned patterns; earth-toned colors; flesh-toned silk.* **3** moderate: *He was too enraged to* **tone down** *his remarks; The brighter colors have been toned down.*

tone arm *n.* the movable arm containing the pickup of a record player.

tone-deaf *adj.* unable to distinguish musical tones.

tone language *n.* a language in which pitch of voice is used to differentiate meaning, as Chinese, Bantu, etc.

tone row *n.* an arrangement of the 12 tones of the chromatic scale without key signatures or scales.

ton.ey (TOH.nee) *adj.* **ton.i.er, -i.est** same as TONY.

tongs *n.pl.* a device for grasping or lifting chunks of coal, sugar, ice, etc., having two arms pivoted or hinged together at one end or in the middle: *a pair of tongs; tongs for curling hair.*

tongue (TUNG) *n.* **1** the fleshy movable structure in the mouth that is used for tasting and speaking: *Children stick out their tongues at each other; He clicked his tongue in delight; Tongues were wagging* (= People were gossiping); *Flying saucers were* **on everyone's tongue** (= being discussed by everyone) *in the 1950s.* **2** something similar to a tongue in shape or use, as a strip of land projecting into water, the striking piece inside a bell, or the flap under the lacing of a shoe. **3** the power of speech, a language, or the manner of its use: *his mother tongue; her native tongue; a foul, glib, loose, nasty, sharp tongue* (= manner of speaking); *So shocked, he couldn't* **find his tongue** (= begin to speak). —**hold one's tongue** be silent. —**speak in tongues** speak in different languages as a religious phenomenon. —*v.* **tongues, tongued, tongu.ing 1** lick with the tongue: *Dogs like to tongue your face.* **2** play a flute or similar musical instrument by using the tongue.

tongued (TUNGD) *adj. & comb.form.* having a tongue or tongues as specified: *tongued lightning; an acid-tongued maid; red-tongued lilies; a sharp-tongued retort; a silver-tongued orator.*

tongue-in-cheek *adj. & adv.* ironical(ly) or satirical(ly): *a tongue-in-cheek comment, suggestion; He talks tongue-in-cheek when he's not in the right mood.*

tongue-lashing *n. Informal.* a severe scolding.

tongue-tied *adj.* **1** speechless from embarrassment. **2** unable to speak properly because of shortness of the membrane under the tongue.

tongue twister *n.* a phrase or sentence that is difficult to say fast, as "She sells seashells on the seashore."

ton.ic *n.* a drug, medicine, etc. that is invigorating or bracing: *Take a tonic for your cough; hair, skin tonics; Water is the best health tonic; The book is a healthy tonic for wounded egos;* **Tonic (water)***, as in "gin and tonic," is a carbonated quinine-flavored mix.* —*adj.* having to do with speech tones: *tonic chords, languages.*

to.night (tuh.NITE) *adv. & n.* (on) the present or the coming night.

ton.nage (TUN.ij) *n.* **1** total weight in tons, as carried by a ship, or the total amount of a country's shipping. **2** a shipping duty based on tonnage.

tonne (TUN) *n.* a metric ton of 1,000 kg.

ton.sil (TON.sul) *n.* either of two masses of tissue on the sides at the back of the mouth: *Jim had his tonsils out or removed or taken out.*

ton.sil.lec.to.my (ton.suh.LEC.tuh.mee) *n.* **-mies** surgical removal of the tonsils.

ton.sil.li.tis (ton.suh.LYE.tis) *n.* inflammation of the tonsils.

ton.so.ri.al (ton.SOR.ee.ul) *adj.* having to do with haircutting.

ton.sure (TON.shur) *n.* the ritual shaving of the crown of the head, as before entering the priesthood; also, the shaven part. —**tonsured** *adj.: a tonsured cleric, monk.*

ton.y (TOH.nee) *adj.* **ton.i.er, -i.est** *Informal.* stylish or elegant: *one of the tonier downtown restaurants; a tony crowd; tony clothes, gifts.*

too *adv.* **1** more than enough: *She sleeps too long; He's only too glad to leave.* **2** also: *You too can be rich; I like her too.* **3** [used negatively] *Informal.* very: *I'm not feeling too well.* **4** so; indeed: *"I didn't do it"; "You did too."*

took *pt.* of TAKE.

tool *n.* **1** a hand implement such as is used in carpentry, gardening, etc.: *the* **tools of one's** or **of the trade.** **2** a working part of a machine that drills, planes, grinds, etc.; also, such a machine, or "machine tool." **3** one that serves as a means; hence, a stooge or dupe. —*v.* **1** form or finish an article with a tool. **2** equip a plant with tools or machinery: *to tool up for the new production season.* **3** *Informal.* drive in a leisurely way: *He was tooling around town in his new car.*

toot (long "oo") *v.* sound a horn in short blasts. —*n.* such a blast. —**toot.er** *n.*

tooth (long "oo," "th" as in "thin") *n.*, *pl.* **teeth 1** any of the hard bony structures in the jaws, used for biting, chewing, etc.: *Dentists cap, drill, extract, fill, pull, take out teeth; You brush, clean, clench, floss, gnash, grind, grit, pick your teeth; Teeth ache, chatter, decay, fall out, rot; abscessed, decayed, discolored teeth; Wisdom teeth normally erupt at ages 16 to 20; Babies cut teeth* (= have them appear through the gums). **2** a toothlike part of a saw, gear wheel, comb, rake, etc. **3** *pl.* effectiveness: *We need laws with teeth.* —**fight tooth and nail** fight with all one's strength. —**long in the tooth** *Informal.* advanced in age. —**in the teeth of** in the face of or in defiance of something. —**toothed** *adj.*; **tooth.less** *adj.*

tooth.ache *n.* a pain in a tooth.

tooth.brush *n.* a brush for cleaning the teeth.

tooth powder or **tooth.paste** *n.* a powder or paste for cleaning the teeth.

tooth.pick *n.* a small sliver of wood or similar slender instrument for cleaning between the teeth.

tooth.some *adj.* tasty and tender; delicious: *deliciously toothsome; a toothsome cheesecake.*

tooth.y *adj.* **tooth.i.er, -i.est** having or showing prominent teeth: *a toothy grin, mouth, smile.* —**tooth.i.ly** *adv.*

too.tle (TOO.tul) *v.* **-tles, -tled, -tling** *Informal.* **1** toot continuously and quietly: *to tootle (on) his flute, whistle.* **2** go in an unhurried manner: *to tootle in for tea; She tootled around the estate; tootled down to the shopping center.* —*n.* the sound of tootling.

top *n.* **1** a cone-shaped toy for spinning with a string wound around it: *He sleeps like a top* (= soundly). **2** the highest point: *from the top of the building; from top to bottom; to reach the top of a mountain; climb to the top of the tower; the top (surface) of a table; seated at the top* (= head) *of the table; shouted at the top of her voice; He was at the top of his career when he resigned; The top* (= best)

of the morning to you! **3** an upper part: *a pajama top; a bikini top;* (above ground) *beet tops; His hobby is collecting bottle tops* (= caps). —**blow one's top** *Informal.* lose one's temper. —**off the top of one's head** *Informal.* making a rough guess. —**on top of 1** besides: *a bonus on top of his pay.* **2** in control or mastery of: *to be on top of a situation.*

—*v.* **tops, topped, top.ping 1** trim the top of a plant. **2** provide a bottle, box, etc. with a cap or lid. **3** crown or be at the top of something. **4** reach the top of something: *She topped her class last year.* **5** rise above; be or do better than something: *Try to top this act.* —**top off** complete *with* something as a finishing touch. —**adja.** highest or foremost: *top man, speed, value.* —**top.per** *n.*

to.paz (TOH.paz) *n.* a hard silicate mineral valued as a gem, esp. in its yellow, pink, and brown varieties.

top billing *n.* prominent treatment: *He received top billing in the media.*

top brass *n.* high officials or officers.

top.coat *n.* a lightweight overcoat.

top dog *n.* boss; also, leader or champion: *the top dog around here.*

top dollar *n.* *Informal.* best possible amount: *We will pay top dollar for the right candidate.*

top-down *adja.* from the top downward; hierarchical: *a top-down approach, method, process, structure.*

top-drawer *adj.* *Informal.* of the highest rank or importance: *top-drawer reputation, service, talent; Her performance was top-drawer.*

top dressing *n.* fertilizer, gravel, etc. that is spread on the surface without being worked in.

top-flight *adj.* *Informal.* of the highest rank; first-rate: *a top-flight candidate, consultant, design, executive, professional, work force; top-flight equipment, personnel, technology.*

Top 40 *n.* the best 40, as in the record charts: *a Top-40 hit from the sixties.*

top hat *n.* a man's tall cylindrical hat worn in formal dress.

top-heavy *adj.* unstable because of being too heavy at the top: *a top-heavy structure; a top-heavy administration, bureaucracy, management, organization; top-heavy forces, plans; Our program is top-heavy with pomp and ceremony.*

top.ic (TOP.ic) *n.* a theme or subject for an essay, conversation, discussion, etc.: *to bring up a topic; to broach the topic of a raise; Religion and politics are controversial topics; an everyday topic like the weather; the topics of the times* (= matters of current interest).

top.i.cal (TOP.i.cul) *adj.* **1** having to do with topics: *The grouping is topical; topical areas; a topical index.* **2** of current or local interest: *a topical discussion, issue, story.* **3** for local, external use on the body surface: *a topical anesthetic, formulation, remedy; for topical use only.* —**top.i.cal.ly** *adv.* —**top.i.cal.i.ty** (-CAL.i.tee) *n.*

top.knot *n.* a tuft of hair or feathers that is either worn or is growing on the top of the head.

top.less *adj.* not having or wearing a top: *a woman in a topless bathing suit; topless bathing; In some cultures, women go topless without being gawked at; a **topless bar** (where topless women are featured); a **topless car** (= a convertible).*

top-level *adj.* of the highest level of authority or rank: *a top-level discussion, meeting, official.*

top.mast *n.* the second section of a ship's mast above its deck.

top.most *adj.* highest or uppermost: *at the topmost level; the topmost executives; in the topmost layer.*

to.pog.ra.phy (tuh.POG.ruh.fee) *n.* **-phies 1** description or representation of the surface features of a region. **2** such features as hills, lakes, rivers, cities, etc.: *the ups and downs of Venus's topography; brain, nerve topography; the topography of a skull.* —**to.pog.ra.pher** *n.* —**top.o.graph.ic** (top.uh.GRAF.ic) or **top.o.graph.i.cal** *adj.*

top-notch or **top.notch** *adj. Informal.* first-rate; excellent: *a top-notch car; Its brakes are top-notch; top-notch businessmen, looks, quality, speakers.*

top.ping (TOP.ing) *n.* something that forms the top or is put on top of something else: *a pie topping.*

top.ple (TOP.ul) *v.* **top.ples, top.pled, top.pling 1** fall *down, over,* etc. being top-heavy: *A leaning tower has a natural tendency to topple over.* **2** overturn or overthrow: *The government was toppled in a coup.*

tops *adj.* topmost: *She's tops in her field; They offered $500,000 tops* (= maximum) *for the house.*

top-secret *adj.* of the highest secrecy; extremely confidential: *What I'm going to tell you is top-secret; top-secret information.*

top.side *adj. & adv.* on or to a ship's main deck or an upper deck. —*n.* also **topsides** *pl.* the part of a ship above the waterline.

top.sy-tur.vy (top.see.TUR.vee) *adj. & adv.* upside down; hence, in disorder or confusion.

toque (TOKE) *n.* **1** a small, close-fitting, usu. brimless hat. **2** same as TUQUE, 2.

tor *n.* a crag or high rocky hill.

To.rah or **to.rah** (TOR.uh) *n.* **1** the Jewish Bible, same as the Pentateuch; also, the scroll in which it is preserved in synagogues. **2** the entire oral and written body of Jewish laws, customs, and ceremonies.

torch *n.* **1** a flaming light, as one carried in the hand by a torchbearer: *to light a torch; Many buildings were put to the torch by the arsonist; Gigi continued to **carry the** or **a torch for** (Informal for to love) Luc.* **2** a source of enlightenment: *the torch of civilization, learning.* **3** a device such as a blowtorch for shooting a very hot flame: *a welding torch.* **4** *Brit.* flashlight. **5** *Informal.* arsonist.

torch.bear.er (TORCH.bair.ur) *n.* one who carries a torch; hence, a source of enlightenment: *the torchbearers of change, civilization, learning.*

torch.light *n.* the light of a torch or torches; *adja.: a torchlight procession, rally.*

torch song *n.* a sentimental song of unrequited or lost love.

tore *pt.* of TEAR.

tor.e.a.dor (TOR.ee.uh.dor) *n.* a bullfighter.

to.re.ro (tuh.RAIR.oh) *n.* **-ros** a bullfighter, esp. a matador.

tor.ment (TOR.ment) *n.* **1** great pain or agony. **2** its cause or source; tormentor. —*v.* (tor.MENT) inflict pain or suffering continuously or by repeated acts: *tormented by annoying questions, jealousy, mosquitoes.* —**tor.men.tor** (TOR.men.tur, tor.MEN.tur) or **tor.ment.er** *n.*

torn *pp.* of TEAR.

tor.na.do (tor.NAY.doh) *n.* **-does** or **-dos** a destructive windstorm or cyclone characterized by a funnel-shaped cloud moving along a narrow path: *A tornado ripped through, tore through, struck our town last summer; when a tornado hits or strikes; adja.: a tornado alert, funnel, warning, watch.*

tor.pe.do (tor.PEE.doh) *n.* **-does** a cigar-shaped, self-propelling underwater missile: *to fire or launch a torpedo; A torpedo hits, misses its target, explodes.* —*v.* **-does** (-doze), **-doed, -do.ing** attack or destroy with a torpedo.

tor.pid (TOR.pid) *adj.* dormant, sluggish, or inactive, as a hibernating animal. —**tor.pid.i.ty** (tor.PID.i.tee) *n.*

tor.por (TOR.pur) *n.* the state of being torpid or inactive: *to rouse the nation from its economic torpor.*

torque (TORK) *n.* a rotating or twisting force exerted around an axis.

tor.rent (TOR.unt) *n.* a swift and violent flow or downpour: *It rained in torrents; a raging torrent; a torrent of abuse, tears, water, words.* —**tor.ren.tial** (tor.EN.shul) *adj.*

tor.rid (TOR.id) *adj.* 1 parched or scorching: *a torrid climate; the torrid heat of the desert; The* **Torrid Zone** *extends from the equator to the tropics.* 2 ardent or passionate: *a torrid affair, love scene, relationship.*

tor.sion (TOR.shun) *n.* 1 a twisting or being twisted, as when a rod fixed at one end is turned left or right. 2 the stress so produced: *Some automobiles have a* **torsion bar** *suspension instead of coil springs.* —**tor.sion.al** *adj.*

tor.so (TOR.soh) *n.* **-sos** (-soze) or **-si** (-see) the trunk of a human statue or body, esp. as separate from head and limbs.

tort *n. Law.* a wrongful act arising from a breach of duty other than under contract, as in an automobile accident.

torte (TORT) *n.* a rich cake made with eggs, crumbs, and chopped nuts.

tor.tel.li.ni (tor.tuh.LEE.nee) *n.* pasta in the shape of rings filled with meat, cheese, etc.

tor.til.la (tor.TEE.uh) *n.* a round thin cake of unleavened cornmeal, a staple Mexican food.

tor.toise (TOR.tus) *n.* a four-legged animal with its body encased in a hard outer shell; land or freshwater turtle.

tortoise-shell *adj.* yellowish brown and mottled, like the shell of a turtle used in making ornamental objects, combs, etc.: *tortoise-shell buttons, frames; a tortoise-shell cat.*

tor.tu.ous (TOR.choo.us) *adj.* 1 marked by twists and turns: *a tortuous trail.* 2 devious or crooked: *tortuous logic; a tortuous policy.*

tor.ture (TOR.chur) *n.* 1 infliction of severe pain to punish, force a confession, etc.: *a confession made under torture.* 2 severe physical pain or mental agony: *Watching the horror movie was sheer torture.* —*v.* **-tures, -tured, -tur.ing** 1 inflict severe pain on someone: *He was tortured by his captors; Lee is tortured with rheumatism;* **adj.:** *a tortured body, soul; Berlin has a tortured past.* 2 twist or distort: *language tortured out of its meaning.* —**tor.tur.er** *n.* —**tor.tur.ous** *adj.:* *the torturous heat of summer; a torturous tangle of regulations.*

To.ry (TOR.ee) *n.* **-ries** 1 a member of a conservative party. 2 one who is conservative or reactionary; also **tory**.

toss *v.* 1 to throw in a light, easy, or careless manner: *bathers tossing beach balls; She tossed her head (in contempt or indifference); Many questions were* **tossed about** *or* **around** *during the discussion; They were finally* **tossed back** *to the boss; The ruling party got* **tossed out** *when they called an election;* **adj.:** *a tossed leaf pattern; bouquets and tossed flowers; a* **tossed salad** *of greens and tomatoes tossed with a dressing.* 2 be restless or agitated: *a ship tossed by the waves; She tossed and turned fitfully for hours; He tossed about in his bed sleeplessly.* 3 flip a coin: *Let's* **toss up** *(Informal for* flip a coin*) and break the tie; Let's toss for it.* —**toss off** 1 produce easily: *a facile writer who could toss off a story in no time.* 2 consume quickly: *to toss off one cola after another.* —*n.* a tossing or being tossed: *She won the toss; a coin toss.*

toss-up *n.* 1 a flipping of a coin to decide something. 2 *Informal.* an even chance: *It's a toss-up whether the Republicans or Democrats will win the election; Many constituencies are considered toss-ups.*

tot *n.* a little child.

to.tal (TOH.tul) *n.* a complete amount; sum: *to add up a total; the grand total; the sum total; about $10,000* **in total** (= altogether). —*adj.* whole or complete: *the total amount, number; a total eclipse, loss; in total agreement; total abstinence, expenses.* —*v.* **-tals, -taled, -tal.ing** 1 count the total: *Checkout clerks* **total up** *your purchases.* 2 amount to: *The expenses totaled $50,000, the income* **totaling up** *to only $51,000.* 3 wreck completely: *The car was totaled in the accident.* Also **to.talled, to.tal.ling** *Cdn.* —**to.tal.ly** *adv.*

to.tal.i.tar.i.an (toh.TAL.uh.TAIR.ee.un) *adj.* of a government, exercising absolute power over the people, often under a dictator: *a totalitarian government, regime, rule, society, state, system.* —*n.* one favoring such a system. —**to.tal.i.tar.i.an.ism** *n.*

to.tal.i.ty (toh.TAL.i.tee) *n.* **-ties** 1 a total amount: *the totality of our experience; a mere segment of larger totalities.* 2 entirety: *when looked at* **in its totality**.

total recall *n.* the ability to recall everything from memory.

total war *n.* all-out, not limited war.

tote *v.* **totes, tot.ed, tot.ing** *Informal.* carry as a load: *to tote baggage for a* journey; *a gun-toting robber.* —*n.* **1** a large handbag with pockets and shoulder strap; also **tote bag.** **2** an overshoe: *totes to protect your shoes from slush, salt, and snow.*

to.tem (TOH.tum) *n.* a tribal or family symbol among North American Indians on the west coast in the shape of an animal, bird, or other natural object.

totem pole *n.* **1** a post with a series of totem symbols carved, painted, and placed one on top of another. **2** hierarchy: *Where are you on the totem pole? I'm at the bottom of the totem pole; the low man on the totem pole.*

tot.ter (TOT.ur) *v.* stand or move in an unsteady manner, as if about to fall; stagger.

tou.can (TOO.can) *n.* a brilliantly colored tropical American bird with an enormous bill.

touch (TUCH) *v.* **1** make physical contact or strike lightly with the hand or some other part of the body: *Things feel hot, cold, rough, hard, etc. when touched; Skyscrapers seem to touch the sky; Ships touch (at) many ports; Teetotalers say they won't touch* (= use) *liquor; a friend whom he can touch (Informal for* ask or solicit) *for a loan now and then.* **2** affect: *She was touched by his sad plight; Here's something that touches your interests; adj.: She was so touched* (= emotionally moved) *she started crying; a manner touched with envy; flowers and fruits touched* (= damaged) *by frost; He's a bit touched in the head* (= mentally unbalanced); *a touching* (= moving) *appeal, moment, scene, story.* —**touch base with** *Informal.* be in contact with someone. —**touch down** of an aircraft or spacecraft, to land. —**touch off** start an action or process suddenly or violently, as an explosive charge with a match. —**touch on** refer to something: *The book touches on matters of concern to all women.* —**touch up** improve a painting, literary composition, makeup, etc. by slight changes. —*n.* **1** a touching or contact: *cold to the touch; Some seed pods burst open at the slightest touch; the magic touch of Midas; He's a soft touch (Informal for* easy to get money out of). **2** a skillful or artistic stroke: *the deft touches of an artist's brush; There are poetic touches in her writings.* **3** the sense of feeling or what is felt: *taste and touch; the soft, delicate touch of a baby's skin; a gentle, light touch; a corporation that doesn't want to lose the human touch; personal touches* such as *gifts and cards; service with* **the** or *a personal touch;* *The writer began to* **lose his touch** (= special skill) *and stopped writing; to* **lose touch with** *reality.* —**a touch** a slight tinge or trace: *Add a touch of color to her cheeks; There's a touch of frost in the autumn air; a touch of irony; a touch* (= mild attack) *of the flu; adv.: The curry was a touch* (= a little) *too spicy for me.* —**in touch** in contact or communication: *Let's keep in touch by letters; to be, get, stay in touch; directly in touch; in close, constant, frequent, immediate touch; to put someone in touch with a person; in touch with headquarters.* —**out of touch** not in contact: *She is totally out of touch with current events.*

touch and go *n.* a risky situation: *It was touch and go for a while, but the patient survived; adj.: a* **touch-and-go** (= risky) *affair, maneuver, situation.*

touch.down *n.* **1** the moment of landing of an aircraft or spacecraft. **2** in football, a score of six points made by possession of the ball on or past the opponent's goal line. **3** such possession.

tou.ché (too.SHAY) *interj.* [as in fencing to acknowledge a hit] score!

touch football *n.* an informal variety of football with tackling substituted by touching of the ball carrier.

touch.screen or **touch screen** *n.* a computer display that responds to user input by touch; *adj.: a touchscreen display, interface, monitor, system.*

touch.stone *n.* a test of genuineness, as by a former method of testing precious metals by rubbing them on a black stone.

touch.tone *n.* a telephone having a set of push buttons instead of a dial, each producing a distinctive tone signal; also **touch tone;** *adj.: a touch-tone keypad, line, phone, signal.*

touch.type *v.* **-types, -typed, -typ.ing** type without looking at the keys.

touch.y *adj.* **touch.i.er, -i.est 1** easily offended: *to be, get touchy.* **2** risky: *a touchy issue, situation, subject.* —**touch.i.ly** *adv.;* **touch.i.ness** *n.*

touchy-feely *adj. Informal.* involving touching and feeling: *a touchy-feely approach, science museum, person; a touchy-feely dealer who says his car just feels right.*

tough (TUF) *adj.* **1** so hard, firm, etc. in texture and consistency as not to be easily torn or broken: *Leather is tough; tough meat, putty.* **2** hard to deal with; stiff: *a tough customer, decision, exam,*

toughen / town

fight, guy, job, opposition; *He's tough to work with; tough* (= hard to bear) *luck; It's tough* (= unfortunate) *that you have to live away from family and friends; a tough* (= unruly) *neighborhood; a sales rep who* **talks tough** (= is a hard bargainer)*; It's time to* **get tough with** (= take a firm stand against) *drunk drivers.* —*n.* a rough or violent person; ruffian. —**tough.ly** *adv.;* **tough.ness** *n.*

tough.en (TUF.un) *v.* make or become tough or tougher. —**tough.en.er** *n.*

tou.pee (too.PAY) *n.* a small hairpiece to cover a bald spot.

tour (TOOR, *rhyme:* poor) *n.* **1** a period or shift of work on an assignment or at a specific place: *to do a tour of duty overseas.* **2** a going round visiting or inspecting: *a guided tour of Montreal; package tours sold through travel agents; fact-finding, goodwill, lecture, sightseeing, study tours; a circus that is always* **on tour** (= touring); **adja.:** *a tour guide, operator, package.* —*v.* go on a tour through a place.

tour de force (toor.duh.FORCE) *n.* **tours de force** (toor.duh-) a feat of strength or skill.

tour.ism (TOOR.iz.um) *n.* **1** traveling for pleasure. **2** the industry serving travelers.

tour.ist (TOOR.ist) *n.* one traveling for recreation. —**adja.:** *tourist accommodations, attractions, resorts, spending, tickets, traffic, visas; the tourist industry, trade.*

tourist class *n.* the least expensive class of travel accommodation.

tourist trap *n.* a place where tourists are exploited, as by overcharging.

tour.ma.line (TOOR.muh.lin, -leen) *n.* a mineral whose transparent varieties are valued as gems.

tour.na.ment (TOOR.nuh.munt, TUR-) *n.* **1** a series of athletic contests or games in competition for a championship. **2** formerly, a series of military exercises or contests, esp. between knights, as jousting. Also **tour.ney** (-nee), **-neys.**

tour.ni.quet (TOOR.nuh.kit, TUR-) *n.* a device to check bleeding from a wound, usu. a bandage tightened around the affected limb.

tou.sle (TOW.zul, "OW" as in "how") *v.* **-sles, -sled, -sling** dishevel hair, etc.; muss.

tout (TOWT) *v. Informal.* **1** publicize or puff: *a salesman touting the virtues of a new product; It's touted as a great boon to humanity;* **adj.:** *a highly* **touted** *remedy.* **2** solicit: *to tout for business, customers,*

votes. —*n.* one who touts or solicits.

tow (TOH) *v.* pull along behind, as with a rope or chain: *Illegally parked cars will be towed; towed away to the police pound.* —*n.* **1** a towing or a vehicle being towed. **2** a boat, barge, or other vehicle that tows. **3** the line used. —**in tow 1** being towed or following one: *Vito came to call with his family in tow.* **2** in one's care or charge: *She took the child in tow.*

to.ward (TORD, tuh.WORED) *prep.* **1** in the direction of a person or thing: *He turned toward his wife; progress toward peace; He became blind toward* (= approaching or near) *the end of his life.* **2** with respect to: *his attitude toward a settlement; her feelings toward us; contributions toward* (= for) *helping the poor.* Also **towards.**

tow.a.way (TOH.uh.way) *n. & adj.* (the action) of towing away automobiles: *No parking in towaway zones during snow emergencies; towaway trucks* (= tow trucks).

tow.el (TOW.ul, "OW" as in "how") *n.* an absorbent cloth or paper: *bath, dish, face, hand, paper towels.* —**throw in the towel** give up the fight. —*v.* **-els, -eled, -el.ing** wipe or dry with a towel. Also **tow.elled, tow.el.ling** *Cdn.*

tow.er (*rhyme:* our) *n.* a structure that is tall relative to its width, often rising above its surroundings: *a church tower; fortress tower; observation tower; an airport control tower; the (vertical)* **tower case** *of a desktop computer.* —*v.* rise high like a tower: *She towers above her peers as a lawyer.* —**towering adja.:** *the towering skyscrapers; a towering* (= very high) *achievement, ambition; in a towering* (= violent) *rage.*

tower of strength *n.* one looked up to for protection or leadership.

tow.head (TOH.hed) *n.* (a person with) a head of flaxen hair; **tow.head.ed** *adj.*

tow.hee (TOH.hee, TOW-) *n.* a small bird of the finch family, related to the sparrows.

tow.line (TOH.line) *n.* a line or rope for towing.

town (*rhyme:* down) *n.* **1** a community or settlement larger than a village and smaller than a city: *boom, crowded, dormitory, ghost, sleepy, small towns; The whole town is* (= All the people of the town are) *talking about it.* **2** a business and entertainment center: *to go into town; The boss is out of town.* —**go to town** *Informal.* **1** act with energy and enthusiasm. **2** achieve success. —**on**

the town *Informal.* on a spree; having a good time: *out for a night on the town.*

town council *n.* the governing body of a municipality.

town crier *n.* formerly, one who made public announcements through the streets.

town hall *n.* **1** a building containing the administrative offices of a town: *The U.N. General Assembly has been called the town hall of the global village.* **2** a town (hall) meeting.

town house *n.* one of a continuous row of houses, usu. of two or three stories; row house; also **town home.**

town.ie (TOWN.ee) *n. Informal.* one who lives in a town.

town meeting *n.* **1** a meeting of a town's inhabitants, esp. taxpayers or voters, to discuss issues in an informal setting. **2** such a meeting of any other group having a common concern. Also **town hall meeting.**

towns.folk *n.pl.* townspeople.

town.ship *n.* **1** a unit of local government; municipality. **2** a land-survey unit.

towns.man (TOWNS.mun) *n.* **-men** **1** one who lives in or was raised in a town. **2** a fellow inhabitant of a town.

towns.peo.ple (TOWNS.pee.pul) *n.pl.* **1** town-bred people. **2** the people of a town.

towny same as TOWNIE.

tow.path (TOH.path) *n.* a path along a canal traveled by men or animals towing boats.

tow rope *n.* a rope used for towing.

tow truck *n.* a truck equipped for towing automobiles; towaway truck.

tox.e.mi.a (tok.SEE.mee.uh) *n.* illness due to toxic substances in the circulating blood, as from food poisoning.

tox.ic *adj.* **1** poisonous: *the toxic effects of certain drugs; toxic fumes, substances, wastes from chemical companies.* **2** of or caused by a toxin: *a toxic illness; the* **toxic shock syndrome** (= a bacterial attack) *resulting from improper tampon use.* —**tox.ic.i.ty** (tok.SIS.i.tee) *n.*

tox.i.col.o.gy (tok.i.COL.uh.jee) *n.* the study of poisons and their control; **tox.i.col.o.gist** *n.*

tox.in *n.* a poison produced in the human body by bacteria or one secreted by a plant or animal, as snake venom.

toy *n.* **1** an object for a child to play with; a trifle or trinket. **2** anything of small size; *adj.a.: a toy balloon, soldier, train; a* **toy dog** *such as a Chihuahua, Pekinese, or Pomeranian.* —*v.* **toy with** play idly with something: *He toys with his pencil when lost for a word; to toy with an idea, plan; He was merely toying* (= trifling) *with her affections.*

trace *n.* **1** either of a pair of straps or chains connecting an animal to the vehicle it pulls. **2** a mark or other evidence of an occurrence or presence, as an animal's tracks in the snow: *My cat vanished without a trace.* **3** a barely perceptible or measurable amount: *slight traces of poison; a trace of precipitation; He accepted the sentence with no trace of remorse; a* **trace element** *such as iodine required in minute amounts for proper nutrition.* —**kick over the traces** become unruly; shake off control. —*v.* **trac.es, traced, trac.ing 1** follow a track or trail *to* its origin or originator: *to trace criminals, game, the origin of a word; He traces his ancestry back to African forebears; Some phobias may be traced to childhood experiences.* **2** draw an outline. **3** copy an original using transparent paper. —**trace.a.ble** (TRAY.suh.bul) *adj.* —**trac.er** *n.*

trac.er.y (TRAY.suh.ree) *n.* **-er.ies** an intricate decorative pattern of lines, circles, and other shapes filling a window or other opening.

tra.che.a (TRAY.kee.uh) *n., pl.* **-che.ae** (-kee.ee) or **-che.as** the windpipe; **tra.che.al** (-ee.ul) *adj.*

tra.che.ot.o.my (tray.kee.OT.uh.mee) *n.* **-mies** a surgical cutting into the trachea to relieve suffocation.

tra.cho.ma (truh.COH.muh) *n.* a contagious tropical disease of the eyelids that may affect the cornea and lead to blindness.

tracing *n.* something traced or drawn, as a copy of a map or drawing on transparent paper, a recording made by an instrument such as a cardiograph, etc.: *an ECG tracing; the spiderlike tracings of varicose veins.*

track *n.* **1** the path of something moving or a course to travel over, as the set of parallel rails on which a train moves, a path beaten through a forest, a course laid around a field for running or racing, the path of a hurricane, the groove of a phonograph record, the concentric ring on the surface of a computer storage medium on which data are recorded, etc.: *He stopped dead* **in his tracks** (= right where he was) *when he heard his name called.* **2** the marks left, as the footprints of an animal or ruts made by wheels. **3** the endless belt or tread on which some vehicles such as tanks, bulldozers, and tractors move.

—keep (or **lose**) **track of** keep (or fail to be) informed about something: *to keep track of expenses during a trip; He lost track of time and was late getting back.* **—on** or **off the track** on or off the right course. **—v. 1** follow someone's track: *to track an animal; Radio signals help track a satellite from* **tracking stations** *on the earth.* **2** make tracks on or with something: *to track up a polished floor; to track mud into a house* (= bring it on one's feet or shoes). **—track down** find: *to track down game; an obscure quotation that is hard to track down* (= find the source of).

track and field *n.* sports events consisting of races, hurdles, etc. around a track and jumps, throws, etc. in the center of the field; *adja.: a **track-and-field** athlete, competition, event.*

track.ball *n.* a ball within a set base used to move the cursor on a computer display.

track record *n.* a record of achievements in a field of endeavor: *a company with a proven track record; their track record in business.*

tract *n.* **1** a stretch or extent, esp. of land; a usu. large area. **2** a pathway or continuous system of bodily organs with a special function: *The respiratory tract consists of the nose, throat, voice box, air passages, and lungs; digestive, intestinal tracts.* **3** a pamphlet or small treatise on a religious or political subject.

trac.ta.ble (TRAC.tuh.bul) *adj.* easy to manage or handle: *Be tractable if not docile; a tractable* (= malleable or workable) *metal.* **—trac.ta.bil.i.ty** (-BIL.i.tee) *n.*

trac.tion (TRAC.shun) *n.* **1** a drawing, pulling, or being pulled: *A broken leg is put* **in traction** (= pulled by weights over a pulley) *to keep the parts in position while healing; The first tractors, driven by steam, were called* **traction engines.** **2** pulling power: *They use snow tires for better traction* (= moving without slipping) *over snow and ice.* **—trac.tion.al** *adj.*

trac.tor (TRAC.tur) *n.* **1** a powerful vehicle for pulling or pushing farm machines, snowplows, etc. **2** the cab-and-engine unit that pulls a freight trailer, or **tractor trailer;** *adj.: a tractor-trailer driver, rig, truck.*

trad *adj. Informal.* traditional: *the mod and the trad in menswear.*

trade *n.* **1** the buying and selling of goods and services; commerce: *to carry on, drum up, engage in, promote, restrain trade; heavy, foreign, international, retail, world trade; the illicit trade in drugs; the slave trade; to* **do a brisk trade** *in stolen watches* (= sell them in large quantities); *adja.: a trade center, commission, deal, embargo, partner, surplus; trade barriers, sanctions, talks;* **trade balance** (= BALANCE OF TRADE). **2** a group being sold to; market or customers: *the tourist trade; We cater chiefly to the rush-hour trade; the carriage trade* (= the wealthy). **3** an exchange or swap; also, a bargain: *a fair trade.* **4** a skilled occupation or craft, not a business or profession: *to learn, practice a trade; where drug pushers ply their trade; the book trade; welding trade; rumors circulating* **in the trade** (= among people in the trade). **—v. trades, trad.ed, trad.ing 1** buy and sell; do business: *They trade in stocks; shares trading* (= being bought and sold) *at $500; n.: No* **trading** *with the enemy; There was brisk trading on the commodity exchange; slow, sluggish trading.* **2** swap or exchange: *Let's trade seats; Jim traded his seat for Jan's; to* **trade** *insults, jokes, stories; People* **trade** *in their old cars (in part payment) when buying new ones.* **3** be a customer at a store. **—trade on** or **upon** use or exploit, usu. someone's good nature, to one's own advantage.

trade book *n.* a book for general sale, not a textbook.

trade-in *n.* **1** a purchase using goods as part payment. **2** something so used: *a used car as trade-in for a new one; adja.: a trade-in allowance, offer, price; a car with high trade-in value.*

trade.mark *n.* **1** a legally registered brand name, slogan, symbol, or device used by a company to identify its product or service. **2** something that is distinctive of a person: *Churchill with his trademark cigar.* **—v.** register as a trademark; *adj.: a* **trademarked** *slogan like "Finger-lickin' good."*

trade name *n.* **1** brand name or trademark. **2** a company's business name.

trade-off *n.* **1** an exchanging of something one owns for another benefit: *Let's do a trade-off.* **2** a balancing of two factors or elements: *Is there a trade-off between unemployment and inflation?* (= Can inflation be reduced at the cost of higher unemployment?).

trad.er (TRAY.dur) *n.* **1** a merchant. **2** a merchant ship.

trade school *n.* a school teaching skilled trades such as carpentry and plumbing.

trades.man (TRADES.mun) *n.* **-men 1** a retailer, shopkeeper, or workman:

the tradesman's entrance to a building. **2** a craftsman.
trades.peo.ple (TRADES.pee.pul) *n.pl.* people engaged in trade.
trade union *n.* a worker's union; labor union.
trade wind *n.* a wind that blows toward the equator throughout the year because of pressure differences between the tropics and the polar regions.
trading post *n.* a store at a frontier or outpost for purchasing furs, moccasins, etc. in exchange for supplies, other goods, or cash.
trading stamp *n.* a stamplike label given to cash-paying retail customers as a bonus for them to collect and exchange for gifts.
tra.di.tion (truh.DISH.un) *n.* **1** the handing down of beliefs, laws, customs, legends, etc. from generation to generation orally and by practice: *By tradition, the captain of a ship may conduct a wedding ceremony; According to tradition, the apostle Thomas brought Christianity to India.* **2** a belief or custom so received: *Thanksgiving is a North American tradition; Some traditions have greater force than customs; to cherish, establish, hand down, maintain, preserve, uphold a tradition; ancient, cherished, deep-rooted, established, hallowed, popular traditions.* **3** the observance of such beliefs, etc.: *a wedding in the Jewish tradition; in the tradition of the Mormons; a philosophy steeped in tradition; to* **break with** (= not observe) *tradition; tradition and change.* —**tra.di.tion.al** *adj.;* **tra.di.tion.al.ly** *adv.*
tra.duce (truh.DEWCE) *v.* **-duc.es, -duced, -duc.ing** bring a person into disrepute unjustly; vilify or defame; **tra.duc.er** *n.*
traf.fic *n.* **1** the movement of people and/or vehicles, esp. in a public place such as a street or highway: *Signals regulate the flow of traffic; Police direct traffic; to block, hold up, obstruct, tie up traffic; one-way, heavy, light, through, vehicular traffic;* **adja.:** *a traffic sign, violation; traffic conditions during the rush hour; air traffic controllers; a traffic jam at an intersection; a* **traffic circle** *for vehicles to clear an intersection by going round an island (***traffic island***) without stopping for lights; the* **traffic pattern** *determined by furniture arrangement in a living area.* **2** business done by a transportation or communications company; the volume of passengers, freight, telegrams, etc.: *the traffic manager of a book publisher.* **3** commercial activity;

buying and selling: *brisk, lively traffic; no traffic with criminals; the traffic in illicit drugs; Charge the highest price* **the traffic will bear** (= that buyers will pay). —*v.* **traf.fics, traf.ficked, traf.fick.ing** carry on trade or traffic, esp. illicitly, as in drugs. —**traf.fick.er** *n.*
traffic light (or **signal**) *n.* a set of red, green, and amber lights regulating traffic at an intersection.
traffic ticket *n.* a summons issued by the police for speeding, illegal parking, etc.
tra.ge.di.an (truh.JEE.dee.un) *n.* a writer of or actor in tragedies.
tra.ge.di.enne (-dee.EN) *fem.*
trag.e.dy (TRAJ.uh.dee) *n.* **-dies 1** a serious drama or play with a sad ending. **2** any sad or terrible happening: *A tragedy may befall us anytime; when tragedy struck (us); to avoid, prevent tragedies; personal tragedies; triumphs and tragedies.*
trag.ic (TRAJ.ic) **1** *adja.* having to do with tragedy: *a tragic actor, drama, poet, writer.* **2** *adj.* suggestive of tragedy; extremely sad or unfortunate: *a tragic accident, event, loss, mistake, plight, story.* —**trag.i.cal.ly** *adv.*
trail *v.* **1** follow closely, as in one's tracks: *police trailing a suspect.* **2** drag, tow, or bring after oneself: *a child trailing a toy truck; The hurt runner began to trail* (= lag behind); **adja.:** *the* **trailing** *skirt of a wedding gown; the* **trailing** (= rear, not front or "leading") **edge** *of an airplane's wing.* **3** move in a casual or aimless manner: *The children trailed behind their mother; smoke trailing from a chimney; creeping plants that trail along the ground and over walls.* **4** become weaker: *The voice on the phone trailed off.* —*n.* **1** something that trails or is left behind, as a scent, trace, or track: *the vapor trail or exhaust of an aircraft; A trail of blood led to the scene of the accident; The police are on his trail; the trail of misery left by a war.* **2** a route or course: *Pioneers blazed trails through the wilderness by marking trees; to blaze a new trail; an Indian trail; a winding trail; It was time to hit the campaign trail.*
trail bike *n.* a light motorcycle for rough, cross-country riding.
trail.blaz.er (TRAIL.blay.zur) *n.* a pioneer or explorer. —**trail.blaz.ing** *n. & adj.*
trail.er *n.* **1** a wheeled vehicle designed to be hauled, either a wagon or closed van carrying cargo, usu. pulled by a tractor: *a tractor trailer; truck trailers.* **2** a vehicle attached to an automobile

for recreational travel and camping, equipped as temporary living quarters; mobile home: *a house trailer; travel trailers.* **3** a creeping plant such as an ivy. **4** a short film consisting of selected scenes from a movie, shown as promotion.

trailer park (or **camp** or **court**) *n.* a site equipped with water, electricity, etc. for a community of mobile homes.

train *n.* **1** a connected series of railroad cars pulled by a locomotive: *electric, express, freight trains; to board, catch, get off, get on, miss, take a train; We changed trains in Buffalo for New York; Trains sometimes derail; Trains pull into and pull out of a station.* **2** a chain or sequence: *a train of events, thought; A war brings misery in its train; the power train (= the drive shaft, clutch, transmission, etc.) of an automobile.* **3** a line or group of people, animals, vehicles, etc. moving along together: *a wagon train; a train (= caravan) of camels; a king and his train (= retinue).* **4** a trailing part: *the train of a comet, peacock, wedding gown.* —*v.* **1** teach, instruct, or practice in order to develop a faculty or skill: *Educators train minds; She was trained as an engineer; a seal trained to perform; He's training for the Olympics; adj.: a **trained** acrobat, animal, ear, eye, teacher, worker; highly trained experts; well trained in ballet; n.: The **training wheels** on either side of the rear wheel of a child's bicycle help steady it.* **2** to guide or direct physically: *a shrub trained to grow on a trellis; to train a camera, gun, spotlight, telescope on an object.* —**train.er** *n.*

train.ee (tray.NEE) *n.* a person being trained.

training *n.* the act of training or being trained: *driver, in-service, military, on-the-job training; His mother is a nurse by training; He's **in training** for the Olympics.*

training school *n.* **1** a school for training people in skills and occupations: *management, teacher, vocational training schools.* **2** a correctional facility for young offenders: *a state training school.*

train.man (TRAIN.mun) *n.* **-men** a member of the crew of a railroad train.

traipse *v.* **traips.es, traipsed, traips.ing** *Informal.* wander or walk about aimlessly: *People traipse through a house that is open for sale.*

trait *n.* a distinguishing feature or quality of a person: *an acquired trait; character, cultural, personality traits; the characteristic traits of a people.*

trai.tor (TRAY.tur) *n.* one who betrays or is disloyal to his or her faith, country, friends, etc.: *an ally who turned traitor; a traitor to his country.*
—**trai.tor.ous** (-rus) *adj.*

tra.jec.to.ry (truh.JEC.tuh.ree) *n.* **-ries** the curved path of an object moving under a gravitational or other force, as planets, space vehicles, bullets, and other projectiles.

tram.mel (TRAM.ul) *n. & v.* **tram.mels, tram.meled, tram.mel.ing** (entangle or confine as in) shackles or the meshes of a net: *the trammels of tradition.* Also **tram.melled, tram.mel.ling** *Cdn.*

tramp *v.* **1** walk with heavy steps: *to tramp through the snow, the woods.* **2** trample: *a once-beautiful garden tramped down by vandals.* **3** go around on foot, esp. wearily, in search of a home or work; wander as a tramp: *to tramp the streets of the city.*
—*n.* **1** the sound of heavy steps, as of marching soldiers: *the tramp of boots.* **2** a hike or march: *a tramp through the woods.* **3** a person without a fixed home, esp. one who lives by doing odd jobs. **4** a streetwalker or prostitute. **5** a cargo ship without regular trade routes or schedules, available for hire as needed: *a tramp steamer.*

tram.ple (TRAM.pul) *v.* **-ples, -pled, -pling 1** stamp or tread heavily; crush: *a flower bed trampled by a crowd; laws that trample on human rights.* **2** treat ruthlessly: *age-old customs trampled underfoot by tyrants.* —*n.* a trampling or trampling sound.

tram.po.line (TRAM.puh.leen, -lin) *n.* a structure to bounce on for gymnastic use, consisting of a sturdy sheet or net stretched over a frame.

trance *n.* **1** a partly conscious state without voluntary movement, as in deep hypnosis, or the condition of a spiritualistic medium: *to fall* or *go into a trance; Sam was in a trance for several hours.* **2** a trancelike state of absorption. **3** a daze or stupor: *She walked around in a trance looking for her child.*

tran.quil (TRANG.quil) *adj.* **1** peaceful and quiet: *a tranquil retreat, scene, setting, village.* **2** serene: *a tranquil charm, life, mood, temperament.* —**tran.quil.ly** *adv.* — **tran.quil.li.ty** or **tran.quil.i.ty** (trang.QUIL.i.tee) *n.*

tran.quil.ize (TRANG.quil.ize) *v.* **-iz.es, -iz.ed, -iz.ing** make or become tranquil. Also **tran.quil.lize** *Cdn.*

tran.quil.iz.er (TRANG.quil.eye.zur) *n.* a drug used to relieve anxiety, soothe nervous tension, or reduce high blood

pressure. Also **tran.quil.liz.er.**
trans- *prefix.* across; over: *transnational, transplant, transship, trans-Pacific; the Trans-Alaska Pipeline.*
trans.act (tran.SACT, -ZACT) *v.* conduct or carry on business with someone: *to transact business; to transact a deal, sale.*
trans.ac.tion (tran.SAC.shun, -ZAC.shun) *n.* 1 a business deal: *to conduct a transaction; transactions between two parties.* 2 *pl.* a report of the proceedings of a learned society. —**trans.ac.tion.al** *adj.*
trans.at.lan.tic (trans.ut.LAN.tic) *adj.* across or beyond the Atlantic: *a transatlantic cable, flight, nation.*
trans.ax.le (trans.AX.ul) *n.* a unit combining the transmission and driving-wheel axle of a motor vehicle.
trans.ceiv.er (tran.SEE.vur) *n.* a combined radio transmitter-receiver.
tran.scend (tran.SEND) *v.* 1 be above the limits of something: *The notion of infinity transcends human experience, transcends space and time.* 2 surpass: *philanthropy that transcends national boundaries.* —**tran.scend.ent** *adj.*
tran.scen.den.tal (tran.sen.DEN.tul) *adj.* 1 spiritual: *transcendental enlightenment.* 2 abstract: *transcendental principles.*
transcendental meditation *n.* concentration of the mind away from material things in order to achieve peace of mind.
tran.scen.den.tal.ism (tran.sen.DEN.tul.iz.um) *n.* the philosophy of knowledge through intuition rather than sense experience.
trans.con.ti.nen.tal (TRANS.con.tun.EN.tul) *adja.* across a continent: *a transcontinental flight, railroad, shipment.*
tran.scribe (TRAN.scribe) *v.* **-scribes, -scribed, -scrib.ing** make a transcript of something written: *Secretaries transcribe shorthand notes.* —**tran.scrip.tion** (tran.SCRIP.shun) *n.*
tran.script *n.* a copy, esp. official, of something recorded, as a speech, academic grades, etc.
trans.duc.er (trans.DEW.sur) *n.* a device such as a phonograph pickup or a microphone that converts electric waves into mechanical vibrations or vice versa.
tran.sept *n.* either of the arms of a cross-shaped church.
trans fatty acid *n.* an unsaturated fatty acid that has been transformed by hydrogenation, as in margarine, making it more saturated.
trans.fer (trans.FUR) *v.* **-fers, -ferred,** **-fer.ring** 1 move someone or convey something from one place or person to another: *an executive transferred from Los Angeles to Boston; A property is transferred from vendor to buyer.* 2 change from one place, position, etc. to another: *Students transfer from school to school; Transfer at the next stop to Route 18.* —*n.* (TRANS.fur) 1 a transferring, being transferred, or something transferred, as a design or drawing from one surface to another: *electronic funds transfer; transfer of power to a new government.* 2 a ticket allowing a passenger to transfer to another route. 3 a transferring point on a route. —**trans.fer.a.ble** (trans.FUR.uh.bul) *adj.* —**trans.fer.ence** (-FUR.unce, TRANS.fur.unce) *n.;* also **trans.fer.ral** (-FUR.ul) *n.*
trans.fig.ure (trans.FIG.yur) *v.* **-ures, -ured, -ur.ing** 1 change the form or appearance of a person or thing. 2 transform so as to glorify or exalt. —**trans.fig.u.ra.tion** (-yuh.RAY.shun) *n.*
trans.fix (trans.FIX) *v.* 1 pierce through, as with a pointed weapon. 2 hold motionless, as if impaled: *He transfixed her with his gaze;* **adj.**: *to become, feel, sit, stand **transfixed**; to hold someone transfixed.*
trans.form (trans.FORM) *v.* 1 change the shape, appearance, or nature of a person or thing fundamentally. 2 change from one form to another, as electricity to a different voltage, one mathematical expression to another, or the active voice to the passive. —**trans.for.ma.tion** (-for.MAY.shun) *n.*
trans.form.er (trans.FOR.mur) *n.* one that transforms, esp. a voltage-changing device: *step-down and step-up transformers.*
trans.fuse (trans.FUZE) *v.* **-fus.es, -fused, -fus.ing** 1 transfer a liquid from one vessel to another, esp. inject blood from one person into the circulatory system of another. 2 infuse or inspire. —**trans.fu.sion** (-FEW.zhun) *n.: to give a blood transfusion.*
trans.gress (trans.GRES) *v.* 1 go beyond an allowed limit. 2 break a law or command; offend or sin against a person or law. —**trans.gres.sion** (-GRESH.un) *n.* —**trans.gres.sor** (-GRES.ur) *n.*
tran.ship same as TRANSSHIP.
tran.sient (TRAN.zee.unt) *adj.* short in duration or stay; passing or fleeting: *Our life is transient; a transient business,*

feeling, market, need, pattern, problem, tenant; transient events. —*n.* a temporary lodger, worker, etc.: *a rooming house for transients.* —**tran.sient.ly** *adv.*

tran.sis.tor (tran.ZIS.tur, -SIS.tur) *n.* an electronic device like a vacuum tube in controlling the flow of electricity in a circuit but more compact and durable, hence much used in radios, computers, etc. —**tran.sis.tor.ize** *v.* **-iz.es, -ized, -iz.ing** equip a device with transistors.

trans.it (TRAN.sit) *n.* **1** passage or conveyance: *goods lost* **in transit** *between Boston and Dallas;* **adj.:** *a transit lounge, passenger, visa.* **2** a local public transportation system using buses, trains, etc.: *mass, public, rapid transit.* **3** a surveying instrument with a telescope on a tripod for measuring angles.

tran.si.tion (tran.ZISH.un) *n.* a passing from one condition, stage, etc. to another: *a period of transition; to effect a smooth transition of power; a gradual transition to normalcy; in a state of transition.* —**tran.si.tion.al** *adj.*

tran.si.tive (TRAN.suh.tiv, -zuh.tiv) *adj.* of verbs, having a direct object, as in "Sam loves Pat." —*n.* a transitive verb such as "give" or "love." —**tran.si.tive.ly** *adv.* —**tran.si.tiv.i.ty** (-TIV.i.tee) *n.*

tran.si.to.ry (TRAN.suh.tor.ee, TRAN.zuh-) *adj.* of things, transient by nature; short-lived, not permanent: *the transitory things of this world; transitory pleasures.* —**tran.si.to.ri.ly** *adv.;* **tran.si.tor.i.ness** *n.*

trans.late (trans.LATE, tranz-) *v.* **-lates, -lat.ed, -lat.ing** change from one place or condition to another, esp. between languages: *a word that is difficult to translate into another language; a book translated from the original Greek; to translate words into action.*
—**trans.lat.a.ble** (-LAY.tuh.bul) *adj.*
—**trans.la.tor** (-tur) *n.*

trans.la.tion (trans.LAY.shun, tranz-) *n.* a translating or a translated version: *close, free, literal, loose translations; I read Homer in translation; the simultaneous translation of a speech into different languages.*

trans.lit.er.ate (trans.LIT.uh.rate, tranz-) *v.* **-ates, -at.ed, -at.ing** write words, letters, etc. in the characters of another language: *The Greek letter "epsilon" is usually transliterated as "e".*

trans.lu.cent (trans.LOO.sunt, tranz-) *adj.* partly transparent, as frosted glass; **trans.lu.cent.ly** *adv.*
—**trans.lu.cence** or **trans.lu.cen.cy** *n.*

trans.mi.grate (trans.MY.grate, tranz-) *v.* **-grates, -grat.ed, -grat.ing** of the soul, pass from one body after its death into another.
—**trans.mi.gra.tion** (trans.my.GRAY.shun, tranz-) *n.*

trans.mis.si.ble (trans.MIS.uh.bul, tranz-) *adj.* capable of being transmitted: *transmissible diseases.*

trans.mis.sion (trans.MISH.un, tranz-) *n.* **1** a transmitting or being transmitted by radio or cable: *radio, satellite, TV transmissions; the transmission of messages, signals.* **2** in a vehicle, the assembly of parts, esp. a set of gears, that transmits power from the engine to the driving wheels.

trans.mit (trans.MIT, tranz-) *v.* **-mits, -mit.ted, -mit.ting** pass along as an agent or medium: *Germs transmit diseases; to transmit a message by radio; The sun transmits heat and light (through the air).* —**trans.mit.tal** (-tul) or **trans.mit.tance** (-tunce) *n.*
—**trans.mit.ter** *n.*

trans.mog.ri.fy (trans.MOG.ruh.fye, tranz-) *v.* **-fies, -fied, -fy.ing** transform, esp. in a bewildering manner or with grotesque effect. —**trans.mog.ri.fi.ca.tion** (-fuh.CAY.shun) *n.*

trans.mute (trans.MUTE, tranz-) *v.* change the nature or substance of a base metal into something different or better. —**trans.mu.ta.tion** (-mew.TAY.shun) *n.*: *the purported transmutation of base metals into gold.*

trans.na.tion.al (trans.NASH.un.ul, tranz-) *adj.* that go beyond national boundaries: *transnational concerns, corporations, dangers, issues.*

trans.o.ce.an.ic (TRANS.oh.shee.AN.ic, TRANZ-) *adj.* across or beyond the ocean: *a transoceanic telephone cable, current, flight; transoceanic transport, travel.*

tran.som (TRAN.sum) *n.* **1** a horizontal crossbar, as at the top of a window or door; lintel. **2** a narrow window above a door: *manuscripts coming (in), sent, submitted* **over the transom** (= unsolicited) *to publishers.*

tran.son.ic or **trans-sonic** (tran.SON.ic) *adja.* between subsonic and supersonic in speed: *to reduce transonic drag.*

trans.par.en.cy (tran.SPAIR.un.see) *n.* **-cies 1** a transparent quality. **2** something transparent, as a slide for a slide projector: *a set of color transparencies to use with an overhead projector.*

trans.par.ent (tran.SPAIR.unt) *adj.* that can be seen through, as glass: *a trans-*

parent (= sheer) *fabric; What she means here is quite transparent; a transparent falsehood; her transparent* (= frank) *sincerity.* —**trans.par.ent.ly** *adv.*

tran.spire (tran.SPIRE) *v.* **-spires, -spired, -spir.ing** 1 give off water vapor, as through the pores of a plant's leaves. 2 leak out or become known: *It later transpired that the theft was an inside job.* 3 come about or happen: *No one knows what transpired afterward.*
—**tran.spi.ra.tion** (-spuh.RAY.shun) *n.*

trans.plant (trans.PLANT) *v.* dig up, as a plant, or remove an organ or tissue, people, etc. from one place to implant or resettle in another. —*n.* a transplanting or something transplanted: *a hair transplant to cover a bald spot; bonemarrow, corneal, heart, kidney, organ, tissue transplants; A transplant may be rejected by the body.* —**trans.plan.ta.tion** (-plan.TAY.shun) *n.*

tran.spon.der (tran.SPON.dur) *n.* a radio device that automatically transmits a response signal, as used to identify approaching planes on a radar screen.

trans.port (trans.PORT) *v.* 1 carry or convey, esp. in a vehicle: *to transport goods by truck; Meeting his uncle transported him back to his childhood.* 2 carry away; enrapture: *She was transported with joy on hearing the great news.*
—*n.* (TRANS.port) 1 means of transporting: *air transport; road transport.* 2 strong emotion, esp. rapture: *in a transport or in transports of joy, rage.*

trans.por.ta.tion (trans.por.TAY.shun) *n.* 1 a transporting or being transported: *sentenced to* **transportation for life** (= life in a penal colony). 2 a means of transporting or the transporting business: *the task of providing public transportation; the transportation industry.*

trans.pose (trans.POZE) *v.* **-pos.es, -posed, -pos.ing** 1 change, esp. interchange the normal position of letters or sounds in a word, as "aks" for "ask." 2 change the key of a piece of music, as in playing a composition.
—**trans.po.si.tion** (-puh.ZISH.un) *n.*

trans.sex.u.al (trans.SEK.shoo.ul) *n.* 1 a person with a psychological urge to change sex. 2 one who has had a sex change by surgery; *adj.*: *a transsexual operation.*

trans.ship (trans.SHIP) *v.* **-ships, -shipped, -ship.ping** transfer from one ship or vehicle to another for further shipment. —**trans.ship.ment** *n.*

tran.sub.stan.ti.a.tion (TRAN.sub.stan.shee.AY.shun) *n.* the Roman Catholic doctrine that the Eucharistic bread and wine are changed into Christ's body and blood during Mass.

trans.verse (trans.VERSE, tranz-) *adja.* set crosswise: *a transverse beam.*
—*n.* (also TRANS.verse) a transverse axis, beam, etc.

trans.ves.tite (trans.VES.tite, tranz-) *n.* a person, usu. a male, who gets sexual pleasure from dressing like one of the opposite sex; also *adj.* —**trans.ves.tism** *n.*

trap *n.* 1 a device for capturing an animal: *to bait and set a trap for mice.* 2 a device, stratagem, or ambush for catching someone off guard: *He fell into his own trap; a speed trap set up by police to catch speeders; a booby trap; death traps.* 3 a U-shaped bend in a drainpipe to hold water to prevent the return of sewer gas. 4 a light, two-wheeled carriage with springs. 5 in a golf course, a pit filled with sand as a hazard. 6 **traps** *pl.* the percussion devices in a jazz band or orchestra. 7 **traps** *pl. Informal.* belongings: *to pack up one's traps and go home.* —*v.* **traps, trapped, trap.ping** 1 trap or snare animals: *We are not allowed to trap here; n.: No trapping or fishing.* 2 catch as in a trap: *to trap mice; The child was trapped in the car; people trapped in poverty and misery; adj.: She felt **trapped** and scared; Don't get trapped with a high mortgage; According to philosophers, we are souls trapped within mortal bodies.* 3 adorn or equip with trappings; caparison. —**trap.per** *n.*: *an animal trapper; fur trappers; hunters and trappers.*

trap.door *n.* 1 an opening in a floor, ceiling, or roof. 2 the hinged or sliding door covering it.

tra.peze (tra.PEEZ) *n.* a short bar hung horizontally by two ropes on which an aerialist, or **trapeze artist**, performs in a circus: *on the flying trapeze.*

trap.e.zoid (TRAP.uh.zoid) *n.* a four-sided plane figure with two sides parallel. —**trap.e.zoi.dal** (-ZOY.dul) *adj.*

trappings *n.pl.* 1 ornamental coverings, as of an outfitted horse. 2 accessories or equipment: *regal trappings; all the trappings of high office, of a rock star, of an election campaign, of success.*

trap.shoot.ing (TRAP.shoo.ting) *n.* the sport of shooting at clay pigeons sprung from a trap.

trash *n.* 1 worthless or discarded stuff; rubbish: *Trash accumulates.* 2 worthless people; riffraff: *poor white trash; black, blond, brown trash.* —*v. Informal.* 1 vandalize or wreck: *The hockey fans went on*

a rampage, breaking windows and trashing stores. **2** discard as trash.
trash.y *adj.* **trash.i.er, -i.est** worthless: *trashy grandeur, movies, novels.*
trau.ma (TRAW.muh) *n.* **-mas** or **-ma.ta** (-muh.tuh) **1** an unpleasant emotional experience such as may cause nervous symptoms. **2** a wound or injury, also called "physical trauma." —**trau.mat.ic** (traw.MAT.ic) *adj.*
trau.ma.tize (TRAW.muh.tize) *v.* **-tiz.es, -tized, -tiz.ing** subject someone to a physical or psychic trauma: *people traumatized by war and starvation;* ***adj.****: a traumatized child.*
trav.ail (TRAV.ail, truh.VAIL) *n. & v.* [literary] toil or labor.
trav.el (TRAV.ul) *n.* a journey or trip: *foreign travel; the* ***travels*** *of Sindbad;* ***adj.****: travel plans; the travel time between London and Paris; A* ***travel agent*** *makes travel arrangements for clients;* ***travel insurance*** *to cover emergency hospital and medical expenses.* —*v.* **-els, -eled, -el.ing 1** go from one place to another; journey: *She has traveled widely in Europe; He travels extensively on business; We travel abroad, far and wide; We travel by air; He travels first-class; to travel across the Sahara; to travel light (= with minimum luggage); Light travels (= is transmitted) much faster than sound;* ***adj****a.: a traveling companion, sales rep, show; the traveling population, public; traveling expenses, shoes.* **2** to journey over or through; traverse: *She has traveled Canada from coast to coast.* —**trav.el.er** *n.: business, holiday travelers; seasoned air travelers; the weary traveler; A* ***traveler's check*** *purchased at a bank may be exchanged for cash by countersigning it.* Also **trav.elled, trav.el.ling; trav.el.ler** *Cdn.*
trav.e.logue or **trav.e.log** (TRAV.uh.log) *n.* a motion picture or an illustrated lecture on travel.
trav.erse (tra.VERSE) *v.* **-ers.es, -ersed, -ers.ing 1** travel or move across something extensive, as a desert or sky: *an island route traversing mountainous terrain; to traverse a distance; a gun that can traverse 360 degrees; to traverse a network of nodes.* **2** travel over, up, down, etc.: *All-terrain bikes can traverse stumps, rocks, and other obstacles.* **3** move diagonally across a slope, as a skier: *to traverse downhill; traversing down a trail.* —*n.* (TRAV.urse) **1** something lying or extending across: *the* ***traverse rod*** *on which a curtain slides.* **2** skiing across a hill.

trav.er.tine (TRAV.ur.teen, -tin) *n.* a porous, whitish limestone found along springs and streams.
trav.es.ty (TRAV.is.tee) *n.* **-ties** a ridiculous imitation, parody, or burlesque: *Everyone condemned the trial as a travesty of justice.* —*v.* **-ties, -tied, -ty.ing** make a travesty of something.
trawl *n.* **1** a huge bag-shaped net that is dragged along in the water by a boat, or trawler. **2** a long line called a **trawl line** or "setline" from which short lines with baited hooks are hung. —*v.* fish or catch cod, shrimp, etc. with a trawl. —**traw.ler** *n.*
tray *n.* a flat open pan with a low rim for holding or carrying things, esp. food: *baby, meal, serving, tea trays; a printer's input and output trays; a folding* ***tray table*** *for supporting a food tray.*
treach.er.ous (TRECH.ur.us) *adj.* **1** not to be trusted, as one likely to be disloyal: *a friend who proved treacherous.* **2** not reliable, as ice too thin to skate on: *treacherous driving conditions; treacherous enterprises, shoals, terrain, waters.* —**treach.er.ous.ly** *adv.*
treach.er.y (TRECH.uh.ree) *n.* **-ries** an act of betrayal.
trea.cle (TREE.cul) *n. Brit.* molasses.
trea.cly (TREE.clee) *adj.* **-cli.er, -cli.est** sweet and cloying, as sentimentality.
tread (TRED) *v.* **treads,** *pt.* **trod,** *pp.* **trod.den** (TROD.un) or **trod, tread.ing** step on or walk: *to tread carefully, cautiously, gingerly, lightly, softly; to tread on a competitor's territory; "Fools rush in where angels fear to tread"; to* ***tread out*** *a fire (by stamping on it); to tread (= crush with the feet) grapes for making wine; a well trodden path (formed by walking) through a field; She is careful not to* ***tread on people's toes*** *(= offend them).* —**tread water** *pt.* **tread.ed** keep one's head above water by moving the legs up and down: *Setting up a commission just buys time and treads water.* —*n.* **1** the act, sound, or a way of treading: *the heavy tread of marching soldiers; He walks with a light tread.* **2** a part that treads or is trodden on, as the horizontal part of a step, the sole of a shoe, the grooved surface of a tire, etc.; ***adj****a.: a tire's tread design, groove, life, pattern, wear.*
trea.dle (TRED.ul) *n.* a lever or pedal, as of a sewing machine, that is worked by the foot.
tread.mill *n.* a machine worked by treading on an endless belt going over wheels: *A monotonous job is like being on a or the treadmill.*

trea.son (TREE.zun) *n.* open disloyalty to one's country, as by joining with or helping an enemy: *an act of treason; charged with **high treason** for plotting the king's death.* —**trea.son.a.ble** (-uh.bul) *adj.: a treasonable offense.*
—**trea.son.ous** (-us) *adj.: It is treasonous to aid the enemies of one's country.*

treas.ure (TREZH.ur) *n.* **1** wealth stored or put away, as money, jewels, etc.: *an expedition to find buried treasure; to raise sunken treasure from the Titanic.* **2** a person or thing of great value: *art, national, priceless treasures.*
—*v.* **-ures, -ured, -ur.ing 1** hoard as treasure. **2** value or cherish protectively; *adj.: a **treasured** classic, collection, friendship, gift, memory, possession, spot, tradition; Are books more treasured than movies?*

treas.ur.er (TREZH.ur.ur) *n.* an official in charge of funds, revenues, or finances, as of a treasury.

treasure-trove *n.* **1** treasure found hidden, esp. one of unknown ownership. **2** a valuable discovery.

treas.ur.y (TREZH.uh.ree) *n.* **-ur.ies 1** a place where a treasure or funds are kept. **2** funds. **3** a rich storehouse: *a treasury of information.* **4 Treasury** a government department in charge of financial affairs.

treat (TREET) *v.* **1** deal with a person or thing: *Sam treats employees fairly; treats even enemies with kindness; to treat someone badly, cruelly, unfairly; He was treated like a son; Doctors treat ailments; They treat patients (for their ailments); a poem that treats (of) the vanity of things; An author treats a subject exhaustively, thoroughly; Don't treat it as a joke; They refuse to treat* (= negotiate) *with terrorists.* **2** subject to a process: *wood treated with a preservative.* **3** entertain or provide someone with something good: *She treated them to a lunch.*
—*n.* an entertainment, gift, or something special that gives pleasure: *The party was a real treat; It was a treat to listen to her; "Trick or treat!" says the child in Halloween costume.*

trea.tise (TREE.tis) *n.* a book, article, etc. containing a systematic discussion: *He has written a learned treatise on rock music.*

treat.ment (TREET.munt) *n.* **1** a treating of someone or something: *to receive, respond to, undergo treatment for an illness; He's under treatment; brutal, cruel, inhumane treatment of prisoners of war; preferential treatment of friends and relatives; red-carpet treatment of a visiting dignitary.* **2** a medicine or method used in treatment: *There are many treatments for a cold, but no known cure yet.*

trea.ty (TREE.tee) *n.* **-ties 1** a formal agreement between nations, as for peace, trade, etc.: *to conclude, negotiate, ratify, sign, violate, work out a treaty; a treaty banning or to ban atomic tests in the atmosphere.* **2** a document setting forth the terms of such an agreement.

tre.ble (TREB.ul) *n.* in music, the highest or soprano part that is sung by women or boys and played on instruments such as the violin and clarinet.
—*adj.* **1** having to do with the treble; also, high-pitched: *the treble range; treble tone controls.* **2** triple: *a lawsuit seeking treble damages.* —*v.* **-bles, -bled, -bling** make or become triple.

tree *n.* **1** a large perennial plant with a woody stem and branches starting at a height from the ground: *to climb, cut down, fell, prune, uproot trees.* **2** something treelike, esp. one with an organized structure: *family trees; a computer directory tree of files and file folders; menu trees; adj.: tree charts, structures, systems.*
—*v.* **trees, treed, tree.ing 1** chase a person or animal up a tree. **2** put a shoe in a shoe tree. —**tree.less** *adj.*

treed *adj.* wooded: *a treed lot; a lushly treed valley.*

tree farm *n.* an area in which trees are grown for timber and other forest products.

tree line *n.* the latitude or height above which it is too cold for trees to grow.

tre.foil (TREE.foil, TREF-) *n.* **1** a leaf with three parts, as of the clover and other plants of the lotus group of the pea family. **2** this group of plants. **3** a decorative design like a threefold leaf.

trek *v.* **treks, trekked, trek.king 1** travel slowly or laboriously, as by wagon. **2** *Informal.* go on foot: *They trekked across the Sahara; The **trekking** industry caters to mountain climbers.*
—*n.* a journey or migration: *the long trek to freedom.* —**trek.ker** *n.*

trel.lis (TREL.is) *n.* a lattice framework.
—*v.* support a vine on a trellis.

trem.a.tode (TREM.uh.tode) *n.* any of a class of parasitic flatworms including flukes.

trem.ble (TREM.bul) *v.* **-bles, -bled, -bling 1** shake, as from fear, cold, etc.: *bodies trembling with pain; adj.: a **trembling** hand, voice; with trembling anticipation.* **2** quake: *The ground trembled from the earthquake.* —*n.* a trembling; also, a tremor.

tre.men.dous (tri.MEN.dus) *adj.* **1** awe-

inspiring because great or gigantic: *at tremendous cost; a tremendous achievement, amount, effort, guilt, influence, potential; of tremendous importance, power, wealth.* **2** *Informal.* excellent; very great: *a tremendous job, party, success.*
—**tre.men.dous.ly** *adv.*
trem.o.lo (TREM.uh.loh) *n.* **-los 1** a tremulous or vibrating effect of repeated sound in singing or playing. **2** an organ stop for producing such an effect.
trem.or (TREM.ur) *n.* **1** a trembling or shaking, as in palsy: *a nervous tremor.* **2** quake: *a low-intensity earth tremor; Her disciplinary action sent tremors through the school system.*
trem.u.lous (TREM.yuh.lus) *adj.* **1** marked by trembling or quivering: *a tremulous voice.* **2** fearful.
—**trem.u.lous.ly** *adv.*
trench *n.* a long, narrow ditch, as dug for laying pipes or to protect soldiers in warfare: *a slit trench; life in the trenches during World War I.*
—*v.* dig trenches in a place or protect troops with trenches.
trench.ant (TRENCH.unt) *adj.* cutting; clear-cut; effective: *a trenchant policy; her trenchant style, wit.*
trench coat *n.* a military-style belted raincoat.
trench.er *n.* a wooden platter used formerly for serving and carving food.
trench.er.man (TRENCH.ur.mun) *n.* **-men** a hearty eater.
trench foot *n.* a foot disease with symptoms like those of frostbite, which attacked soldiers exposed to the cold and dampness of the trenches in World War I.
trench mouth *n.* a bacterial infection of the mouth characterized by sores and ulcers.
trend *n.* **1** a general direction or course, as of events, opinions, fashions, etc.: *a growing, marked, recent trend toward violence on TV; a welcome downward trend in prices.* **2** a current style or vogue: *Designers often create trends; to start a trend; Hollywood often sets the trends for today's youth; Many trends began or started as fads.*
—*v.* have a trend; tend: *policies trending toward the Right; Incomes trend down during a recession.*
trend.y *adj.* **trend.i.er, -i.est** *Informal.* following the latest fashions: *a trendy dresser, drug, lifestyle; trendy people, themes; the trendy set; a fashionable but not trendy woman.* —**trend.i.ly** *adv.*
trep.i.da.tion (trep.uh.DAY.shun) *n.* fear or alarm marked by trembling.
tres.pass (TRES.pus, -pass) *v.* intrude unlawfully on another's property or rights; transgress: *Sorry to trespass on your time;* **n.:** *The sign says "No Trespassing."* —*n.* **1** a trespassing. **2** a moral transgression; sin.
—**tres.pass.er** *n.*
tress *n.* **1** a lock or curl of hair. **2 tresses** *pl.* a woman's or girl's flowing hair.
tres.tle (TRES.ul) *n.* a framework supporting a platform, table top, bridge, etc.
trey (TRAY) *n.* a die, domino, etc. with three spots.
tri- *prefix.* three or third: *triangle, triceps, triennial.*
tri.ad (TRY.ad) *n.* a group or set of three closely related persons or things: *the triad of class, gender, and race; a triad of options.*
tri.age (tree.AHZH, TREE.ahzh) *n.* a priority system of selecting or sorting, as of wounded in battle to determine order of treatment: *the triage approach for using scarce resources where they will do the most good.*
tri.al (TRY.ul) *n.* **1** a trying or testing: *Wrestling is a trial of strength; a field trial (by actual performance, as on the market); to conduct the clinical trial of a new drug; He was hired* **on trial** (= on probation) *for three months; to go through a process of* **trial and error;** *Animals learn by trial and error;* **adj.:** *a trial model of a vehicle; a trial run; the* **trial-and-error** *method of picking a hat of the right size.* **2** the examination of a case in a court of law: *trial by jury; to get a fair trial; to hold a trial; Witnesses testify at a trial; A case is* **brought to trial** (in court); *He was ordered to* **stand trial;** *was (put)* **on trial for** *robbery;* **adj.:** *a trial court, date, judge, lawyer.* **3** (cause of) hardship or annoyance: *That boy is a trial to his teachers; the* **trials and tribulations** *of daily life.*
trial balloon *n.* a proposal or announcement made for testing reactions, as a balloon used in weather forecasting: *to send up a trial balloon.*
tri.an.gle (TRY.ang.gul) *n.* **1** a plane figure with three straight sides and angles. **2** anything resembling this, as a percussion instrument made of a steel rod bent into a triangle.
—**tri.an.gu.lar** (try.ANG.gyuh.lur) *adj.*
tri.an.gu.late (try.ANG.gyuh.late) *v.* **-lates, -lat.ed, -lat.ing** in surveying, divide into triangles for computing a distance or position; **tri.an.gu.la.tion** (-LAY.shun) *n.*

Tri.as.sic (try.AS.ic) *n. & adj.* (of) the first period of the Mesozoic era of the earth, beginning about 225 million years ago.

trib.al (TRY.bul) *adj.* having to do with tribes: *tribal conflicts, customs, governments, medicines, nationalism, passions.*

tribe *n.* **1** a group of people with a common way of life, speaking the same language, obeying a chief or elders, and usu. of the same ancestry: *the 12 tribes of Israel; an Indian tribe.* **2** a group of people, animals, or plants of the same kind: *the rose tribe; a new tribe of journalists.* —**tribes.man** (-mun) *n.* -**men.**

trib.u.la.tion (trib.yuh.LAY.shun) *n.* great misery that continues over a period: *to bear, endure the tribulation of a long illness; the trials and tribulations of daily life.*

tri.bu.nal (try.BEW.nul, tri-) *n.* **1** a board appointed to examine and judge a matter of public concern: *human rights, regulatory, trade tribunals.* **2** a court of justice: *military, police, revolutionary tribunals; the tribunal* (= judicial authority) *of public opinion.*

trib.une (TRIB.yoon, trib.YOON) *n.* a public defender, as an official of ancient Rome elected to protect the rights of plebeians.

trib.u.tar.y (TRIB.yoo.tair.ee) **1** *adja.* paying tribute; subject: *a tributary state.* **2** *adj.* contributing to a larger river: *a tributary stream; streams tributary to the river.* —*n., pl.* -**tar.ies** a tributary state or river.

trib.ute (TRIB.yoot, long "oo") *n.* **1** a payment exacted by a ruler from a subject: *to pay tribute to a conquering nation.* **2** something said or given as a mark of gratitude, respect, etc.: *Speakers paid tribute to the retiring president; They funded an award as a fitting tribute to her memory; a glowing tribute; a floral tribute* (= bouquet).

trice *n.* esp. **in a trice** in an instant.

tri.cen.ten.ni.al (try.sen.TEN.ee.ul) *n.* a 300th anniversary. —*adj.* happening once every 300 years.

tri.ceps (TRY.seps) *n.* a muscle along the back of the upper arm.

tri.cer.a.tops (try.SER.uh.tops) *n.* a plant-eating dinosaur with three pointed horns, one above each eye and a short one on the nose.

tri.chi.na (tri.KYE.nuh) *n., pl.* -**nae** (-nee) or -**nas** a roundworm that enters the human body through pork meat and causes trichinosis.

tri.chi.no.sis (trik.uh.NOH.sis) *n.* infestation of the intestines with trichinae.

trick *n.* **1** a skillfully deceptive action such as a prank or fraud: *the "trick* (= prank) *or treat" greeting of children on Halloween night; to learn a trick; to play a dirty trick on someone; magic tricks; a neat trick; He tried every* **trick in the book** (= everything possible); *adja.: a trick* (= tricky) *move, question, shot; a play with a* **trick ending** (using a surprise element). **2** a feat or illusion: *to do a card trick; a hat trick; Magicians perform tricks; People were deceived by a trick of vision; When you have a problem on your hands, crying won't* **do the trick** (= achieve the desired result); *The* **trick is** (= The right thing to do is) *to bide your time; his* **bag of tricks** (= expertise); *adja.: a trick bag;* **trick photography** (that creates illusions). **3** knack: *to learn the* **tricks** (= devices or expedients) **of the trade.** **4** a peculiar habit or mannerism: *a horse's trick of shying.* **5** a round of play in a card game: *to take the trick.* **6** a shift of duty at the helm of a ship. —*adj.:* defective: *a trick back, knee.* —*v.* **1** deceive or cheat: *She was tricked into buying the lemon; was tricked out of her savings.* **2** adorn or deck out: *gaudily tricked out for the occasion.* —**trick.er.y** (-uh.ree) *n.* -**er.ies.** —**trick.ish** *adj.* tricky.

trick.le (TRICK.ul) *v.* -**les, -led, -ling** **1** fall in drops: *Water trickles from a leaking faucet; Do benefits given to big business* **trickle down** (= get passed on) *to the consumer?* **2** flow or move slowly, as a brook. —*n.* a small flow: *Highway traffic was reduced to a mere trickle by the accident.*

trick.ster (TRICK.stur) *n.* one who tricks or deceives.

trick.y *adj.* **trick.i.er, -i.est** **1** using tricks; deceptive: *a tricky politician.* **2** intricate; difficult to handle: *a tricky business, issue, job, maneuver, proposition, question, situation.* —**trick.i.ly** *adv.*

tri.col.or (TRY.cul.ur) *adja.* having three colors: *a tricolor flag, silk, suit;* also **tri.col.ored** *adj.* —*n.* such a flag, as of France. Also **tri.col.our, tri.col.oured** *Cdn.*

tri.cot (TREE.coh) *n.* **1** a plain knitted fabric used for underwear and shirts. **2** a pair of knitted tights.

tri.cy.cle (TRY.si.cul) *n.* a child's three-wheeled vehicle worked by pedals.

tri.dent (TRY.dunt) *n.* a three-pronged spear.

tried *pt. & pp.* of TRY. —*adja.* tested or approved; hence, trusted: *a tried sol-*

triennial / trinity

dier; When disappointed with something advertised as "new and improved," people go back to the **tried-and-true**; *a tried-and-true formula, friendship, idea, method, product, technique.*

tri.en.ni.al (try.EN.ee.ul) *adj.* **1** happening every three years. **2** lasting three years; **tri.en.ni.al.ly** *adv.*

tri.fle (TRY.ful) *n.* **1** something of small value: *a mere trifle.* **2** a small amount of money: *$10 is a trifle compared to $1,000.* —**a trifle** to a slight degree: *a trifle annoyed, confusing, cooler, late.* —*v.* **-fles, -fled, -fling** talk or act in a frivolous or disrespectful manner: *One does not trifle with sacred things; to **trifle away*** (= waste) *precious time.* —**tri.fler** *n.*

trifling (TRY.fling) *adj.* frivolous or trivial: *This is no trifling matter; a trifling amount, expense, sum; The price they are asking is trifling.*

tri.fo.cals (TRY.foh.culs) *n.pl.* eyeglasses with lenses having sections for near, far, and middle distances.

tri.fo.li.ate (try.FOL.ee.ut) *adj.* having three leaflets, as clover.

trig *adj.* stylish or smart-looking.
—*n.* [short form] trigonometry.

trig.ger (TRIG.ur) *n.* a lever that is pulled back by the forefinger, or **trigger finger,** to fire a gun: *to pull, release, squeeze the trigger.*
—*v.* set off by or as if by a trigger: *Stimuli trigger responses; a riot triggered by an incident at a soccer game.*

trigger-happy *adj.* **1** too ready to shoot. **2** irresponsible or belligerent, as when shooting without knowing what is going to be hit.

tri.glyc.er.ide (try.GLIS.uh.ride) *n.* a glycerol derivative, the form in which fats and oils are stored in animal tissue.

trig.o.nom.e.try (trig.uh.NOM.uh.tree) *n.* a branch of mathematics dealing with relations between the sides and angles of triangles. —**trig.o.no.met.ric** (-nuh.MET.ric) *adj.*

trill *n.* **1** a tremulous or vibrating sound. **2** a warble. —*v.* sing, speak, or play a musical note with a trill: *the trilled "r" of Spanish.*

tril.lion (TRIL.yun) *n.* **1** a thousand billion (1 followed by 12 zeroes). **2** in the U.K., a billion billion (1 followed by 18 zeros). —**tril.lionth** *n. & adj.*

tril.li.um (TRIL.ee.um) *n.* a wild flower of the lily family having stems bearing three leaves and one three-petaled flower on each.

tril.o.gy (TRIL.uh.jee) *n.* **-gies** a unified series of three plays, novels, etc.

trim *v.* **trims, trimmed, trim.ming** **1** clip or cut away unwanted parts from something so as to make it neat and tidy: *to trim a beard, hedge; to trim the fat from the budget; Some $500 million were trimmed from Medicare; to trim* (= cut down) *the budget; In hard times, expenses have to be **trimmed back**.* **2** decorate a Christmas tree, dress, etc. **3** balance the weight of a vehicle or craft so that it can move forward without tilting; also, balance an aircraft for level flight. **4** adjust the sails of a boat to make full use of the wind. **5** change views or take a position that suits prevailing views, as a politician does. **6** *Informal.* defeat; thrash; also, cheat or swindle.
—*adj.* **trim.mer, trim.mest** shapely, well-proportioned, or efficient-looking: *a trim figure, haircut, lawn, ship.*
—*n.* **1** orderly condition: *He found everything in good trim; She's in **fighting trim** for the race.* **2** what a dress, furniture, automobile, etc. are ornamented with, as lace, handles, chrome, etc.
—**trim.ly** *adv.;* **trim.ness** *n.*

tri.ma.ran (TRY.muh.ran) *n.* a boat similar to a catamaran but with three hulls.

tri.mes.ter (try.MES.tur, TRY.mes.tur) *n.* **1** any of the three terms into which an academic year is divided. **2** a three-month period: *during the first trimester of pregnancy.*

trim.e.ter (TRIM.uh.tur) *n.* a line of verse with three metrical feet.

trimming *n.* **1** ornament or decoration. **2 trimmings** *pl.* trimmed-off parts. **3 trimmings** *pl.* garnishings and such food accessories: *turkey with all the trimmings.* **4** *Informal.* a beating; also, a fleecing.

tri.month.ly (try.MUNTH.lee) *adj.* occurring or appearing every three months.

Trin.i.dad.i.an (trin.uh.DAD.ee.un) *n. & adj.* (a person) of or from **Trinidad and Tobago,** a West Indian country consisting of two islands.

tri.ni.tro.tol.u.ene (TRY.nye.truh.TOL.yoo.een) *n.* a derivative of toluene, a powerful explosive used in bombs and shells; TNT.

trin.i.ty (TRIN.i.tee) *n.* **-ties 1** the state or fact of being three. **2** a triad: *a trinity of problems; the conservative-liberal-radical trinity.* **3 Trinity** the Christian belief of the union of Father, Son, and Holy Spirit in one Godhead: *the Holy Trinity.*

trinket / trivial

trin.ket (TRINK.it) *n.* **1** a cheap ornament or piece of personal jewelry. **2** a trifle or toy.

tri.o (TREE.oh) *n.* -os **1** a group of three performing a dance, musical composition, etc. together. **2** a composition for three voices or instruments.

trip *n.* **1** a journey, esp. a short excursion, as for pleasure: *to make, plan, take a trip; a business trip; to go on a camping trip; extended trips overseas; a field trip to collect butterflies; a round-the-world trip; a round trip to Europe (and back); a trip to the kitchen during a commercial break.* **2** *Informal.* a visionary experience or similar deviation: *(drug-induced) acid trips; an ego trip (to please one's vanity); a power trip.* **3** a light, quick stepping. **4** a slip or tumble. **5** the action of causing a person to fall by catching his or her foot. **6** a catching device. —*v.* **trips, tripped, trip.ping 1** (cause) to stumble or slip up: *He tripped and fell down the stairs; was so sure of his facts, no one could trip him up* (= catch him making a mistake); *He tripped* (= stumbled) *over a few words of his memorized speech.* **2** move with quick, light steps, as a child. **3** operate or activate a mechanism, esp. by releasing a catching device: *The burglar tripped the alarm and the siren went off.* —**trip.per** *n.*

tri.par.tite (try.PAR.tite) *adja.* **1** having three parts: *a tripartite leaf.* **2** made between three parties: *a tripartite treaty.*

tripe *n.* **1** the lining of the second and third stomachs of beef animals used as food. **2** *Informal.* talk, writing, etc. considered worthless; trash.

trip.ham.mer (TRIP.ham.ur) *n.* a heavy, power-driven hammer that is operated by tripping a catching device when raised and ready to fall.

tri.ple (TRIP.ul) *adj.* **1** three times as much, as many, as large, etc.: *printed with triple spacing between lines; a triple-A* (= top) *credit rating, minor (baseball) league, performance of a product on the market, standard; to be ranked or rated triple-A; to achieve triple-A status.* **2** having three parts; threefold: *a triple alliance; the Triple Crown (of horse racing in which one wins three races or, in baseball, leads the league in batting average, runs batted in, and home runs); a triple jump* (= hop, skip, and jump). —*n.* **1** a triple amount, group, etc. **2** a baseball hit that enables the batter to reach third base. —*v.* -ples, -pled, -pling **1** make a threefold increase. **2** in baseball, hit a triple.

—**trip.ly** *adv.*

tri.plet (TRIP.lit) *n.* **1** one of three born at a single birth: *a set of triplets.* **2** a set of three, esp. a group of three musical notes or lines of verse.

triple threat *n.* a football player who is good at passing, running, and punting.

triple time *n.* in music, rhythm with three beats to the measure.

tri.plex (TRIP.lex) *n.* something that is triple or threefold: *a 50-room triplex apartment (spread out on three floors).*

trip.li.cate (TRIP.li.kit) *n.* one of three identical copies. —**in triplicate** in three copies.

tri.pod (TRY.pod) *n.* a three-legged stand, stool, etc.: *a camera on a tripod.*

trip.tych (TRIP.tic) *n.* a picture or altarpiece in three side-by-side panels.

tri.reme (TRY.reem) *n.* an ancient Greek or Roman warship with three banks of oars.

tri.sect (TRY.sect, try.SECT) *v.* divide into three equal parts; **tri.sec.tion** (try.SEC.tion) *n.*

trite *adj.* **trit.er, trit.est** worn out by constant use; hackneyed: *a trite expression, observation, quotation; trite language.* —**trite.ly** *adv.;* **trite.ness** *n.*

trit.i.um (TRIT.ee.um) *n.* a radioactive isotope of hydrogen three times as heavy as ordinary hydrogen.

tri.ton (TRY.tun) *n.* the shell a marine gastropod; also **triton shell.**

tri.umph (TRY.umf) *n.* a glorious or decisive victory or its celebration: *the triumph of good over evil; to score a triumph; Jay returned in triumph from the Olympics.* —*v.* **1** win or celebrate a triumph *over* an enemy, opposition, etc. **2** succeed or prevail.

—**tri.umph.al** (try.UM.ful) *adja.* having to do with victory: *a triumphal arch, entry, procession, song.*

tri.um.phant (try.UM.funt) *adj.* victorious or rejoicing: *a triumphant army; triumphant cheers, fans, shouts.*
—**tri.um.phant.ly** *adv.*

tri.um.vir (try.UM.vur) *n.* -virs or -vir.i (-vuh.rye) a member of a triumvirate.

tri.um.vi.rate (try.UM.vur.it) *n.* a group of three forming a government, as in ancient Rome.

triv.et (TRIV.it) *n.* **1** a three-legged wrought-iron stand for utensils near or on the fire. **2** a metal stand with short feet to hold hot dishes on the table.

triv.i.a (TRIV.ee.uh) *n.pl.* little known facts; trifles.

triv.i.al (TRIV.ee.ul) *adj.* insignificant

or trifling: *a trivial amount, matter, remark; trivial details.* —**triv.i.al.ly** *adv.*
triv.i.al.i.ty (triv.ee.AL.i.tee) *n.* **-ties** 1 trivial quality. 2 a trifle.
triv.i.um (TRIV.ee.um) *n., pl.* **triv.i.a** a course of studies consisting of the first three liberal arts of a classical education, i.e., grammar, rhetoric, and logic.
tri-weekly *adj. & adv.* 1 thrice a week. 2 every three weeks.
-trix *n. suffix.* feminine of agent nouns ending in "-tor": *aviatrix, executrix, generatrix.*
tro.chee (TROH.kee) *n.* a metrical foot of one accented and one unaccented syllable, as in "Mary had a little lamb." —**tro.cha.ic** (troh.KAY.ic) *adj.*
trod, trod.den See TREAD.
trog.lo.dyte (TROG.luh.dite) *n.* 1 a cave dweller. 2 an unsocial or brutish person.
troi.ka (TROY.kuh) *n.* 1 a team of three horses; hence, a three-member team, as of administrators: *the classic battlefield troika of infantry, artillery, and armor.* 2 a Russian carriage or sleigh drawn by three horses harnessed abreast.
Tro.jan (TROH.jun) 1 *n. & adj.* (a citizen) of **Troy**, a legendary city of Asia Minor. 2 *n.* one noted for courage and endurance: *She works like a Trojan* (= very hard).
Trojan horse *n.* a person or thing with a hidden destructive or subversive capacity, like a large wooden horse filled with enemy soldiers that the Trojans received as a gift during their war (**Trojan War**) with the Greeks.
troll (TROLE) *n.* 1 in Scandinavian folklore, a dwarfish monster with magical powers. 2 a fishing line with lure or bait used for trolling. 3 a round such as "Three Blind Mice." —*v.* 1 sing heartily or in a full, rolling voice. 2 draw a fishing line behind a moving boat. 3 fish in water in this way: *to troll for bass; to troll the ocean.*
trol.ley (TROL.ee) *n.* **trol.leys** 1 a pulley (**trolley wheel**) rolling at the end of a pole (**trolley pole**) against an electrified overhead wire that powers a streetcar or bus. 2 a streetcar (**trolley car**) or bus (**trolley bus**) so powered. 3 a wheeled basket or carriage running suspended from an overhead track, as in a store.
trol.lop (TROL.up) *n.* 1 a slovenly woman or slut. 2 a prostitute.
trom.bone (trom.BONE, TROM.bone) *n.* a brass wind instrument with a long twice-bent tube ending in a trumpet-shaped bell and having a sliding section for changing tones; **trom.bon.ist** *n.*
tromp *v.* tramp or march.
troop (long "oo") *n.* 1 a collection of people or animals, esp. an organized unit, as the subdivision of a cavalry regiment, a Boy Scout unit, etc. 2 **troops** *pl.* soldiers: *airborne troops; ground troops; U.N. peace-keeping troops stationed in many parts of the world.* —*v.* 1 go *out, off,* etc. as a group: *Children trooped out of the room at the sound of the alarm.* 2 gather *around* someone in a group.
troop.er *n.* a member of a cavalry, mounted police, or state police: *a U.S. state trooper; Lee swears like a trooper* (= uses vile language).
troop.ship *n.* a ship for carrying troops.
trope *n.* the figurative use of a word; figure of speech.
tro.phy (TROH.fee) *n.* **-phies** 1 something captured in war, displayed as a memorial, or kept as evidence of some exploit, as the mounted head of an animal killed: *a war trophy.* 2 a prize awarded for victory in a contest.
trop.ic *n.* 1 either of the two parallels of latitude, the **Tropic of Cancer** and the **Tropic of Capricorn**, north and south of the equator respectively. 2 **the tropics** or **Tropics** *pl.* the region lying between these latitudes.
trop.i.cal (TROP.i.cul) *adj.* of the tropics: *tropical fish; the tropical rain forest; a tropical* (= very hot) *climate.* —**trop.i.cal.ly** *adv.*
tro.pism (TROH.piz.um) *n.* a tendency of living things, as in geotropism and phototropism, to bend in response to a stimulus such as gravity or light.
trop.o.sphere (TROP.us.feer, TROH.pus-) *n.* the layer of the atmosphere up to about 10 mi. (16.093 km) from the earth's surface, characterized by weather phenomena. —**trop.o.spher.ic** (-FER.ic, -FEER.ic) *adj.*
trot *n.* 1 the gait of a horse, etc. that is faster than a walk, with the legs moving in diagonal pairs. 2 a person's jogging gait. —*v.* **trots, trot.ted, trot.ting** ride, go, etc. at a trot or brisk pace. —**trot out** *Informal.* bring out, as a horse for inspection or approval: *He trotted out the usual excuses for his failure.* —**trot.ter** *n.*
troth (TRAWTH, TROHTH, "TH" as in "thin") *n.* [old use] a word of promise, as to marry, be loyal, etc.; betrothal: *to pledge* or *plight one's troth*

(= promise to marry).

trou.ba.dour (TROO.buh.dor) *n.* a poet-musician of S. France who composed and sang love songs in Provençal from the 11th to the 13th century.

trou.ble (TRUB.ul) *n.* **1** worry; difficulty; distress: *a world full of trouble and sorrow; to ask for, avoid, cause, give, have, look for, run into, spell, steer clear of, stir up trouble; in times of trouble; deep trouble; She knows how to keep herself out of trouble; Trouble is brewing; The* **trouble** (= problem) *is, you can't have it both ways; Without money, you're* **in trouble**; *He's careful not to* **get in(to) trouble** *with his wife; His friends won't* **get him in trouble** *with his wife; He once got his girlfriend into trouble* (Informal for made her pregnant); *If you drink and drive, you're* **asking for trouble**, *though not necessarily* **looking for trouble** *like hoodlums roaming city streets; Jim has heart trouble* (= disease). **2** an instance of pain and worry: *engine trouble; labor trouble (such as strikes); racial troubles; Our troubles are over with death.* **3** a cause of pain and worry: *Hoodlums are a trouble to society.* **4** inconvenience or exertion: *Walking to work is no trouble to her; She goes to much trouble to help her neighbors; goes to the trouble of driving them to hospital in emergencies; Some have considerable, little, a lot of trouble finding work; "No trouble," she said when they thanked her for the service; Most people* **take the trouble to** *be on time.*
—*v.* **-bles, -bled, -bling** cause trouble to someone; bother: *Bad dreams trouble children; He didn't trouble (himself) to return the book he borrowed; May* **I trouble you to** *return my book?* —**troubled** *adj.* **1** disturbed: *troubled children from broken homes; a troubled life, mind, patient, sleep; in troubled times, waters; troubled memories, relations.* **2** that is in trouble: *a troubled bank, company, economy, loan, marriage, nation.* —**troubling** *adj.* having or causing trouble: *a troubling aspect, concern, development, question, trend.*

trou.ble.mak.er (TRUB.ul.may.kur) *n.* one who causes trouble to others.

trou.ble.shoot.er (TRUB.ul.shoo.tur) *n.* one who can trace a malfunction or other trouble to its source and help to get rid of it.

trou.ble.some (TRUB.ul.sum) *adj.* causing trouble: *troublesome ailments, issues, people.*

trouble spot *n.* a region characterized by frequent disturbances of the peace: *a world trouble spot such as Palestine or Northern Ireland.*

trou.blous (TRUB.lus) *adj.* [literary] unsettled; also, troublesome.

trough (TRAWF, TRAWTH) *n.* **1** a long, narrow, open container, as for holding water or food for animals, a channel to carry away water from eaves, etc. **2** a low air-pressure area that gives rise to a hurricane.

trounce *v.* **trounc.es, trounced, trounc.ing** **1** thrash or beat. **2** *Informal.* defeat soundly in a game or contest: *candidates trounced in an election.* —**trounc.er** *n.*

troupe (TROOP, long "OO") *n.* a company or group of actors, singers, etc. —*v.* **troupes, trouped, troup.ing** travel with a troupe. —**troup.er** *n.*

trou.ser (TROW.zur, "OW" as in "HOW") usu. **trousers** *n.pl.* a two-legged outer garment extending from the waist to the ankles, as usu. worn by men; **adj**a.: *a trouser leg, pocket; a* **trouser suit** (= pantsuit).

trous.seau (TROO.soh) *n.* **trous.seaux** (-soze) or **trous.seaus** a bride's personal outfit of clothes, etc.

trout (rhyme: out) *n.* a freshwater food and game fish related to the salmon.

trove (rhyme: drove) *n.* [short form] TREASURE-TROVE: *to unearth a trove of ancient documents; a trove of information, new discoveries, treasure.*

trow (TROH, TROW) *v.* [old use] believe or suppose.

trow.el (TROW.ul, "OW" as in "how") *n.* **1** a hand tool with a broad flat blade for spreading and smoothing plaster or mortar. **2** a similar garden tool but with a curved blade.
—*v.* **-els, -eled, -el.ing** spread, smooth, or dig with a trowel. Also **trow.elled, trow.el.ling** *Cdn.*

troy *adja.* expressed in troy weight: *a troy ounce of silver.*

troy weight *n.* a system of weighing gold, silver, etc. developed at Troyes, France, based on a pound of 12 ounces of 480 grains each.

tru.ant (TROO.unt) *n.* **1** a child who stays away from school without permission. *He played truant and stayed home.* **2** one who shirks his or her duty. —*adj.* errant; straying: *a truant child; He was frequently truant from school.* —**tru.an.cy** (-un.see) *n.* **-cies.**

truant officer *n.* an official who investigates absences from school.

truce *n.* a temporary ceasing of hostilities by agreement between the fighting parties; cease-fire: *to arrange, violate, work out a truce; The uneasy truce* between the warring factions didn't last long; to sign a truce (= armistice).

truck n. **1** an automotive vehicle for carrying loads, having a rear portion that is either open, as in a pickup, or closed, as in a tractor-and-trailer unit or in a "panel truck": *delivery, fire, garbage, tow, tractor-trailer trucks.* **2** a wheeled swiveling frame, as used at the end of a railroad car, locomotive, etc.: *a skateboard truck.* **3** goods for the market, esp. vegetables, as grown on a "truck farm." **4** small articles; odds and ends. **5** *Informal.* trash. **6** dealings; business: *They would have* **no truck with** *radicals.* —v. **1** drive trucks or carry a load on a truck: *"Keep trucking!"* **2** exchange or barter.

truck.le v. **-les, -led, -ling** be servile; submit tamely: *to truckle to pressure groups.*

truc.u.lent (TRUK.yuh.lunt) *adj.* pugnacious or defiant: *a truculent drunk; his truculent manner;* **truc.u.lent.ly** *adv.* —**truc.u.lence** n.

trudge v. **trudg.es, trudged, trudg.ing** walk wearily *through mud, snow, etc.* —n. a weary walk: *a long trudge of 20 km.*

true (TROO) *adj.* **tru.er, tru.est 1** agreeing with a norm or standard, esp. ethical; not false: *a true story; He was true to his word; a true humanitarian; the true* (= rightful) *heir; This is like a dream* **come true** (= that has been realized). **2** agreeing with standards of correctness or accuracy: *Our "floating ribs" are not true ribs; a statue that is true to life; a plant variety that is* **true to type** (= to the original); *the true* (= geographic) *north as opposed to magnetic north.* —v. **trues, trued, true.ing** make or put in the correct position: *to true up a door frame.* —**adv.** in a true manner: *a story that rings true; a plant that breeds true to type; That 2 and 2 are 4* **holds true** *under most conditions.* —n. that which is true: *the true, the good, and the beautiful.* —**out of true** not correctly positioned.

true-blue *adj.* very loyal and staunch: *a true-blue believer, Conservative; true-blue loyalty.*

truf.fle n. a fungus that grows underground in clusters, prized as a food delicacy.

tru.ism (TROO.iz.um) n. a statement that is self-evident and superfluous.

tru.ly (TROO.lee) *adv.* in a true manner; truthfully; faithfully: *He is truly sorry; a truly memorable event; She truly loves him; The letter ended "Yours truly,* Anonymous."

trump n. a playing card of a suit that ranks higher than others during the play of a hand: *Spades is* or *are trumps; She has a trump up her sleeve* (= something to be used for advantage when needed); *He always* **comes up trumps** (= is very helpful). —v. play a trump or take a trick or card with a trump. —**trump up** bring forward falsely; *adj.:* arrested on a **trumped-up** *charge.*

trump.er.y (TRUM.puh.ree) n. **-er.ies** something showy and valueless; rubbish.

trum.pet (TRUM.pit) n. **1** a loud-sounding brass wind instrument with a looped tube and flared bell. **2** a sound like a trumpet's. **3** a trumpetlike hearing aid, or "ear trumpet." —v. **1** blow a trumpet or make a sound like a trumpet's; *n.:* the **trumpeting** (= loud call) *of the elephant.* **2** proclaim loudly: *Don't trumpet it all over town.* —**trum.pet.er** n.

trun.cate (TRUNK.ate) v. **-cates, -cat.ed, -cat.ing** cut off a part, esp. the apex of something; lop; *adj.:* a *truncated pyramid; a truncated quotation, version of the story.* —*adj.* of a feather or leaf, having a blunt top. —**trun.ca.tion** (trung.CAY.shun) n.

trun.cheon (TRUN.chun) n. a club or staff of authority, as a nightstick or a drum major's baton.

trun.dle (TRUN.dul) v. **-dles, -dled, -dling** roll *about, along, down, off, through, up,* a road, etc. —n. a trundle bed. —**trun.dler** n.

trundle bed n. a low bed on casters, as for a child, which is rolled under another bed when not in use.

trunk n. **1** the main stem, as opposed to branches, of a tree or treelike structure such as a system of nerves or blood vessels. **2** the luggage compartment of a car. **3 trunks** *pl.* very short trousers worn by men for swimming and athletics. **4** a main transportation or telephone line; also **trunk line**. **5** a human or animal body without head or limbs. **6** the long snout of an elephant. **7** a large reinforced box for a traveler's clothing, etc.: *to pack and ship one's trunks.*

truss n. **1** a supporting framework of beams, bars, etc. under a roof or bridge. **2** a support worn to keep in a ruptured groin. **3** a bundle or pack. —*adj.* reinforced or supported: *a truss beam, bridge, joint.* —v. **1** support a roof, bridge, etc. with a truss. **2** bind or tie a person up so that he or she cannot move. **3** bind the wings or legs of a fowl for cooking.

trust *n.* **1** firm assurance or belief that a person or thing will be as good as hoped or expected: *the implicit trust of children in their parents; absolute, blind, mutual trust; God was her sole trust* (= trusted one). **2** something entrusted to a person's care or responsibility; also, such responsibility: *to fulfill one's trust; not to desert one's trust; He was accused of abusing, betraying a trust; a sacred trust; A treasurer is in a position of trust; to establish* or *set up a trust (fund) for a child's inheritance; property held* **in trust** *for a minor; a minor put in a guardian's trust* (= care); *People in public office place their private holdings in a blind trust (in the charge of someone else) to avoid conflicts of interest.* **3** an illegal business organization that controls other organizations for fixing prices, eliminating competition, etc.; cartel: *to break up a trust.* **—on trust 1** on credit: *goods sold and bought on trust.* **2** without proof: *We take many things around us on trust.* **—v.** have trust: *He trusts his employees (to do their duty); I trust* (= hope) *that you're fine; Parents expect children to trust* (= have faith) *in them; Libraries trust* (= rely on) *patrons to return books; Books are trusted* (= entrusted) *to their care; Don't trust to* (= depend on) *luck to wake up on time to catch your flight.*

trus.tee (trus.TEE) *n.* **1** one to whom property is legally committed in trust. **2** a member of the governing body ("board of trustees") of a school, hospital, etc. **—trus.tee.ship** *n.*

trust.ful *adj.* full of trust; ready to confide; not suspicious: *We feel more trustful toward people of our own kind; her trustful nature.* **—trust.ful.ly** *adv.;* **trust.ful.ness** *n.*

trust fund *n.* money or other property held in trust for another in a "trust account" by a bank or "trust company."

trusting *adj.* trustful: *Children are naturally very trusting; a trusting relationship;* **trust.ing.ly** *adv.*

trust territory *n.* any of the 11 territories established after World War II to be administered by different countries, as New Guinea by Australia, supervised by the U.N. Trusteeship Council.

trust.wor.thy (TRUST.wur.thee) *adj.* worthy of trust; reliable: *a trustworthy companion, servant, story.* **—trust.wor.thi.ness** *n.*

trust.y *adj.* **trust.i.er, -i.est** of proven trustworthiness: *a trusty servant, steed, sword.*

truth (TROOTH, "TH" as in "thin") *n.* **1** that which is true: *to ascertain, establish, find, face, seek, speak, stretch, tell the truth; the absolute, awful, bitter, cold, plain, unvarnished truth; There is some truth in what he says; a grain, kernel of truth; The truth of the matter is that I forgot; "Truth will out"* (= The truth will become known some day). **2** a fact, belief, etc. accepted as true: *a religious truth; gospel truths; the truths of science.* **—in truth** truly; in fact.

truth.ful *adj.* **1** telling the truth: *a truthful child.* **2** conforming to the facts; true: *a truthful account.* **—truth.ful.ly** *adv.;* **truth.ful.ness** *n.*

truth serum *n.* a drug used in lie-detector tests.

try *v.* **tries, tried, try.ing 1** make an effort to do something: *She tried her best; tried hard to succeed but failed; I tried to phone her; I tried phoning many times; I'll* **try and** (*Informal* for try to) *phone her again.* **2** test or put to the proof: *Have you tried this sauce? He was fired for trying the boss's patience; Don't try* (= attempt) *impossible tasks; He was tried (in court) for murder but acquitted; Customers* **try on** *suits* (= put them on to check the fit) *before buying.* **—try one's hand at something** make an attempt: *She tried her hand at many skills before deciding to become a sculptor.* **—try out 1** evaluate: *They try out new employees before confirming them; She is trying out* (= auditioning) *for the lead role.* **2** melt down: *Blubber is tried out to extract oil.* **—***n., pl.* **tries** attempt: *Give it a try; It's worth a try; She made a serious try to do better next time.*

trying *adj.* that tries one's patience; hard to endure: *a trying period, person, time;* **try.ing.ly** *adv.*

try.out *n. Informal.* a testing of fitness of a candidate or of reaction, as of the audience to a play or show: *They're holding tryouts for the lead role.*

tryst (TRIST, TRY-) *n.* an appointed time, place, or meeting, as between lovers: *He had a tryst with her.*

tsar (TSAR, ZAR) same as CZAR; **tsa.ri.na** (tsah.REE.nuh, zah-), *fem.*

tset.se (TSET.see, TSEET-) *n.* a blood-sucking, two-winged African fly that is the carrier of sleeping sickness; also **tsetse fly.**

T-shirt *n.* a collarless, short-sleeved, close-fitting pullover shirt, as worn for leisure, sports, or underwear.

T square *n.* a T-shaped ruler for mak-

ing parallel lines.
tsu.na.mi (tsoo.NAH.mee) *n*. a tidal wave caused by an undersea earthquake or volcanic eruption.
tub *n*. 1 a large open container with a wide top, as for washing clothes: *a laundry tub*. 2 a bathtub.
tu.ba (TUE.buh) *v*. a low-pitched brass wind instrument.
tu.bal (TUE.bul) *adj*. of or in a tube, esp. a Fallopian tube: *sterilization by tubal ligation; tubal pregnancy*.
tub.by (TUB.ee) *adj*. **tub.bi.er, tub.bi.est** fat and short like a washtub.
tube *n*. 1 a usu. long hollow cylinder, as for conveying fluids; pipe: *the tubes of a boiler; pneumatic tubes worked by air pressure*. 2 *Brit*. subway: *to travel by tube*. 3 a container made of a short tube closed at one end: *a test tube; a tube of toothpaste, paint, etc. (with soft metal covering and screw-on cap)*. 4 [short form] inner tube; electron tube; vacuum tube: *to watch the tube (Informal for TV); the boob tube (Informal for TV)*. —**down the tube** *Informal*. into a state of being lost or finished.
—**tube.less** *adj*.: *A tubeless tire has no inner tube*.
tu.ber (TUE.bur) *n*. the thickened underground stem of plants such as the potato; **tu.ber.ous** (-rus) *adj*.
tu.ber.cle (TUE.bur.cul) *n*. a small, rounded swelling or lump on a body surface or organ, as caused by the **tubercle bacillus**, the bacterial agent in tuberculosis.
tu.ber.cu.lar (tue.BURK.yuh.lur) *adj*. having to do with tuberculosis: *a tubercular infection, patient, symptom*.
tu.ber.cu.lin (tue.BURK.yuh.lin) *n*. an extract from tubercle bacilli used in a skin test to diagnose tuberculosis.
tu.ber.cu.lo.sis (tue.BURK.yuh.LOH.sis) *n*. an infectious disease, esp. of the lungs, characterized by tubercles in body tissue.
tu.ber.cu.lous (tue.BUR.kyuh.lus) *adj*. tubercular: *tuberculous infections*.
tube.rose *n*. a plant with a tubelike rootstock and a slender stem bearing waxy-white flowers with a heavy odor that are used in perfumes.
tub.ing (TUE.bing) *n*. a length of tube, material in tube form, or a system of tubes.
tu.bu.lar (TUBE.yuh.lur) *adj*. 1 consisting of or having the form of a tube: *a tubular structure; tubular pasta, shape, steel*. 2 made with tubes: *tubular drains*.
tu.bule (TUBE.yool) *n*. a small tube or tubular structure.

tuck *v*. 1 thrust into a place snugly or compactly: *Children are tucked in(to) bed at night; A shirt is tucked into the trousers; old clothes tucked away in trunks*. 2 make tucks in a garment. 3 pull up in a fold or folds to or as if to shorten: *She tucked up her skirt and waded across the stream*. —**tuck away** or **into** *Informal*. eat with gusto: *He could tuck away a whole cake before he started dieting*.
—*n*. 1 a fold sewn in a garment, esp. to make it better or to decorate it. 2 a drawing in: *the pelvic tuck or tilt exercise routine; A plastic surgeon could give you a tummy tuck to make you slimmer around the waist*.
tuck.er *v*. *Informal*. tire out or weary: *She got all tuckered out from exercising*.
tuck shop *n*. a small shop near a public facility that sells light snacks.
-tude *n*. *suffix*. indicating state or condition: *altitude, aptitude, longitude, magnitude, solitude*.
Tues.day (TOOZ.dee, -day, TYOOZ-) *n*. the third day of the week, following Monday.
tu.fa (TUE.fuh) *n*. a soft limestone similar to travertine.
tuff *n*. a soft, porous rock formed by compacted volcanic ash or dust.
tuft *n*. a bunch, cluster, clump, etc. that is attached at the base: *tufts of grass; a tuft of hair; a rug made of tufts of pile*.
—*v*. secure or provide with tufts: *A mattress is tufted at intervals to keep its padding in place*; *adj*.: *a tufted carpet, comforter, rug*.
tug *v*. **tugs, tugged, tug.ging** 1 pull hard *at* something. 2 move by tugging; haul, as with a tugboat.
—*n*. 1 a hard pull: *He gave a tug on her sleeve*. 2 a tugboat: *a seagoing tug*.
tug.boat *n*. a small powerful boat used for towing and pushing ocean liners in and out of harbors, barges along rivers, etc.
tug of war or **tug-of-war** *n*. 1 a contest in which two teams pull at the opposite ends of a rope till one crosses a central line. 2 a power struggle.
tu.i.tion (tue.ISH.un) *n*. 1 instruction, as at a college: *free tuition*. 2 payment for this: *an increase in tuition; to pay their children's tuition; tuitions at various colleges*.
tu.la.re.mi.a (tue.luh.REE.mee.uh) *n*. an infectious disease caught by humans from rabbits, squirrels, rats, etc.
tu.lip (TUE.lip) *n*. a bulbous herb of the lily family with large, cup-shaped flowers in brilliant colors.
tulle (TOOL) *n*. a sheer netting of silk,

tumble / tunnel

rayon, etc. used for bridal veils, scarfs, etc.

tum.ble (TUM.bul) *v.* **-bles, -bled, -bling** **1** fall headlong, esp. head over heels, as in a somersault. **2** move *out* of a place, *into* bed, etc. in a disorderly manner: *clothes tumbling in a dryer.* **3** cause to tumble; upset: *Many records were tumbled at the last Olympics.* —*n.* **1** a headlong fall: *Stocks took a tumble yesterday.* **2** confusion or disorder.

tum.ble.down (TUM.bul.down) *adj.* dilapidated; ready to collapse: *a tumble-down house.*

tum.bler (TUM.blur) *n.* **1** one who tumbles, does handsprings, somersaults, etc. **2** a breed of pigeon that does acrobatics in the air. **3** a drinking glass with no stem or handle. **4** a lock mechanism in which levers must be raised to an exact height to move the bolt. **5** a drying machine for clothes.

tum.ble.weed (TUM.bul.weed) *n.* a prickly plant with a round shape that breaks off when dry and is tumbled about by the wind.

tum.brel or **tum.bril** (TUM.brul) *n.* a two-wheeled cart that can be tilted for dumping its load.

tu.mes.cent (tue.MES.unt) *adj.* tumid. —**tu.mes.cence** *n.*: *nocturnal penile tumescence.*

tu.mid (TUE.mid) *adj.* **1** swollen or enlarged, as by a tumor. **2** overblown or inflated in style: *tumid prose, style.* —**tu.mid.i.ty** (tue.MID.i.tee) *n.*

tum.my (TUM.ee) *n.* **tum.mies** [child's word] stomach.

tu.mor (TUE.mur) *n.* a swelling in a body part from an abnormal growth of tissue, either benign, as a cyst, or malignant, as cancer. Also **tu.mour** *Cdn.* —**tu.mor.ous** (-us) *adj.*

tu.mult (TUE.mult) *n.* a commotion, disturbance, or confusion, as during a storm or battle: *The Speaker's ruling caused a tumult; The legislature was in a tumult over the ruling; It was an hour before the tumult subsided.* —**tu.mul.tu.ous** (tue.MUL.choo.us) *adj.*: *a tumultuous mob, welcome; tumultuous passions.* —**tu.mul.tu.ous.ly** *adv.*

tun *n.* **1** a large cask. **2** a former unit of liquid measure equal to 252 gal. (955 liters).

tu.na (TUE.nuh) *n.* (the flesh of) a large swift ocean fish of the mackerel family valued as food. Also **tuna fish.**

tun.dra (TUN.druh) *n.* the vast, treeless, swampy plains of the Arctic.

tune (TOON, TYOON) *n.* **1** a melody or air, esp. one that is simple and popular: *to hum, play, sing, strum, whistle a tune; a catchy tune; She's too independent to* **dance to your tune** (= comply with your wishes). **2** the correct musical pitch: *To join a choir, you have to be able to* **carry a tune** (= sing with correct pitch); *A choir sings* **in tune** (= in harmony); *She's quite* **in tune with the times;** *a misfit who is* **out of tune** (= not well-adjusted) *with society.* —**call the tune** be in command. —**change one's tune** assume a different style or tone of expression. —**to the tune of** to the extent of a sum of money: *He bilked them to the tune of $2 million.* —*v.* **tunes, tuned, tun.ing** **1** adjust a musical instrument to the proper pitch: *to tune a guitar, piano, violin; an orchestra tuning up before a concert.* **2** put a motor or engine in the best working condition; also **tune up.** **3** attune *to* something: *The speaker was tuned to audience reactions.* —**tune in** adjust a radio or TV set for the best reception: *to tune in to a station.* —**tune out** **1** turn off a broadcast or program. **2** turn away from what is happening or ignore a command, etc. —**tun.er** *n.*

tuned **1** *adj.p.* in a receptive condition: *Being tuned in to each other helps avoid arguments; Most viewers were* **tuned in** *to the show;* **Stay tuned.** **2** *adj.* in the best working condition: *a perfectly tuned violin; well-tuned car engines; a finely tuned sales strategy.*

tune.ful *adj.* melodious; pleasant to hear: *tuneful melodies.* —**tune.ful.ly** *adv.*

tune-up or **tune.up** *n.* the checking and adjusting of the parts of an engine to put them in proper working condition: *to do an engine tune-up.*

tung.sten (TUNG.stun) *n.* a hard, silver-white metallic element with a high melting point, used in making a very hard steel, or **tungsten steel.**

tu.nic (TUE.nic) *n.* **1** a loose, gownlike, usu. belted, knee-length garment, as worn by ancient Greeks and Romans. **2** a jacket length blouse: *maternity tops in tunic style; a Mountie's red tunic.*

tuning fork *n.* a two-pronged metal instrument that gives a tone of a constant pitch when struck.

tun.nel (TUN.ul) *n.* an underground passageway for a road, sewer, etc.: *to bore* or *dig a tunnel; to construct a pedestrian tunnel under the street; We drove through a tunnel under the river; a wind tunnel for testing speeds;* the **light at the**

tunnel vision / turn

end of the tunnel (= source of hope). —v. **tun.nels, tun.neled, tun.nel.ing** make a tunnel *through* a mountain, *under* the sea, etc.: *a cave tunneled by the action of a river.* —**tun.nel.er** *n.* Also **tun.nelled, tun.nel.ling; tun.nel.ler** *Cdn.*

tunnel vision *n.* **1** the defect of not having peripheral vision. **2** narrow-mindedness.

tun.ny *n.* **tun.nies** same as TUNA.

tuque (TUKE) *n.* **1** a knitted woolen cap with a tapered end hanging by the side when worn. **2** a woolen cap with a round tassel at the top; toque.

tur.ban (TUR.bun) *n.* **1** a man's headdress worn by Muslims and Sikhs, consisting of a scarf wound around the head. **2** a close-fitting brimless hat worn by women.

tur.bid (TUR.bid) *adj.* **1** cloudy or disturbed, as by stirring up sediment: *turbid waters; turbid feelings.* **2** dense or thick: *turbid clouds, smoke.* —**tur.bid.ly** *adv.* —**tur.bid.ness** or **tur.bid.i.ty** (tur.BID.i.tee) *n.*

tur.bine (TUR.bin, -bine) *n.* an engine consisting of a wheel turned by the force of water, steam, or gas.

tur.bo.jet (TUR.boh.jet) *n.* **1** a jet engine with a turbine-driven air compressor. **2** an airplane driven by a turbojet.

tur.bo.prop (TUR.boh.prop) *n.* **1** a turbojet engine with a turbine-driven propeller. **2** an airplane powered by a turboprop.

tur.bot (TUR.but) *n.* a large flatfish of European coastal waters, related to flounders.

tur.bo.train (TUR.boh.train) *n.* a high-speed passenger train powered by turbines.

tur.bu.lent (TURB.yuh.lunt) *adj.* causing or marked by a disturbance; tempestuous: *a turbulent sea; a turbulent mob, period of life; turbulent passions.* —**tur.bu.lent.ly** *adv.* —**tur.bu.lence** *n.*

tu.reen (tuh.REEN, tyuh-) *n.* a deep, usu. lidded bowl for serving soup or sauce.

turf *n.* **1** sod: *artificial or synthetic turf used in a stadium.* **2** peat or a piece of it used for fuel. **3 the turf** horse racing. **4** a track for horse racing. **5** one's territory or domain: *to protect one's turf; on her home turf.* —*v.* cover with turf; sod. —**turf out** eject or kick out of one's dwelling or other place. —**turf.y** *adj.*

tur.gid (TUR.jid) *adj.* **1** enlarged or bloated, as an organ by excess of blood. **2** disorderly or unrestrained in style: *a turgid narrative.* —**tur.gid.i.ty** (tur.JID.i.tee) *n.*

Turk *n.* **1** a person of or from **Turkey**, a W. Asian country. **2 young turk** or **young Turk** one who is impatient for change in an established group that he or she is a member of; radical.

tur.key (TUR.kee) *n.* **1** a large North American poultry bird: *Turkeys gobble; The male turkey is called a "gobbler," the female a hen; We raise turkeys.* **2** cooked turkey: *to carve, roast, stuff turkeys.* **3** *Informal.* someone considered stupid. **4** *Informal.* something bad or worthless. **5** See COLD TURKEY. —**talk turkey** *Informal.* talk bluntly or seriously.

turkey buzzard (or **vulture**) *n.* a species of New World vulture.

Turk.ish *n. & adj.* (the language) of the Turks: *the Turkish sultan.*

Turkish bath *n.* a hot-air or steam bath with massage and cold shower.

Turkish towel *n.* a thick terry-cloth towel.

tur.mer.ic (TUR.muh.ric) *n.* **1** a yellow dyestuff obtained from a S. Asian plant of the ginger family. **2** a seasoning made with it. **3** the plant itself.

tur.moil (TUR.moil) *n.* a confused or disorderly state: *The nation was in (a) turmoil after the coup.*

turn *v.* **1** (cause) to revolve or rotate: *A wheel turns; to turn a key in a lock; A game turns* (= depends) *on teamwork.* **2** form something by revolving: *to turn a rod on a lathe;* **adj.:** *a turned handle, leg.* **3** change in position: *to turn the pages of a book; a sight so gruesome it turns your stomach.* **4** change the movement or course of something: *She turned her steps home; He turns the dog out at night.* **5** change direction or trend: *We turned off (from) the highway; We turned into a side street; Turn left at the lights; Let's turn our attention to something else; Friends turned against him* (= became hostile). **6** change nature or condition: *Milk turns sour if not kept cold; He turned traitor after joining the secret service; Caterpillars turn into butterflies; It is suddenly turning cold; The leaves turn color in the fall; She just turned* (= passed the age of) *90; Can you turn* (= translate) *this into French? Success turned his head* (= made him vain); *Jan **turned color*** (= blushed) *at the joke.* **7** make: *to turn a profit; to turn* (= perform) *tricks.* —**turn down 1** refuse: *She turned down his offer; She turned him down.* **2** lower: *to turn down* the heat, volume. —**turn in 1** hand over or hand in. **2** *Informal.* retire at night. —**turn loose** set free to go without restraint. —**turn off 1** shut off water, gas, electricity, etc. or put out a light. **2** *Informal.* (cause) to lose interest: *Mention of homework turns him off.* —**turn on 1** start water, gas, etc. flowing or switch on a light. **2** *Informal.* (cause) to become interested or excited as by taking a narcotic drug: *Some turn on with booze; Computers turn her on.* —**turn out 1** turn off: *to turn out the lights; to turn them out* (= drive them out). **2** happen or come to be: *As it turned out, everyone was late; It turned out to be a lucky day; Everything turned out well in the end.* **3** appear: *A large crowd turned out to greet her.* **4** produce: *to turn out books, scholars.* —**turn over 1** give control or possession of a person or thing: *She turned over her responsibilities to the new recruit; He turned the burglar over to the police.* **2** of an engine, revolve before starting to run: *A cold engine turns over for a while before it starts.* **3** take in as business income: *The company turns over nearly $75 million annually.* —**turn the trick** achieve the desired result. —**turn up 1** raise the volume or intensity of sound, heat, etc. **2** appear: *He turned up rather late.* **3** find or discover: *The tests have turned up little evidence.* **4** happen or be found: *Nothing has turned up yet.*

—*n.* **1** a rotation, as of a wheel. **2** a form or style: *a turn of expression; a roast done* **to a turn** (= just right). **3** a change of direction; also, a bend or curve: *to make a U-turn; a road full of twists and turns; a turn that is difficult to negotiate* or *make; a sharp turn to the left; at the next turn in the road; at the turn of the century* (= around 1899-1900); *the turn of the year* (= around Dec.-Jan.). **4** a change in conditions, circumstances, etc.: *a dramatic turn of events; His illness took a turn for the worse.* **5** something done in rotation: *Wait for your turn; It's your turn to take out the garbage; "One good turn (= deed) deserves another"; "Turn and turn about* (= Doing something by turns) *is fair play"; We* **take turns** (= alternate with others) *doing household chores.* **6** natural inclination; bent: *a mechanical turn of mind.* **7** a short walk, ride, or drive: *Let's go for a turn around the block.* —**at every turn** constantly. —**by turns** alternately: *He was by turns funny and serious.* —**in turn** in succession: *when your turn comes.* —**out of turn** out of proper order.

turn.a.bout (TUR.nuh.bowt) *n.* **1** a reversal of position, policy, allegiance, etc.: *to do a turnabout.* **2** retaliation.

turn.a.round (TUR.nuh.round) *n.* **1** an area in which a vehicle can be turned around. **2** a turnabout or reversal: *December saw a turnaround in the fortunes of the company; to make a turnaround.* **3** the time needed to complete a process, as in loading, unloading, and servicing a vehicle before it can return to its route: *a quick, short turnaround;* *adja.: turnaround performance; the turnaround time between billing and getting paid.*

turn.buck.le (TURN.buk.ul) *n.* a coupling with internal screw threads at either end for receiving the threaded ends of two rods to be held together.

turn.coat *n.* one who deserts his or her political or religious group; renegade: *Kim was a master turncoat who worked as a Soviet spy.*

turn.er *n.* **1** one that turns. **2** one who turns things on a lathe.

turn.er.y (TUR.nuh.ree) *n.* **-er.ies 1** a turner's workshop. **2** a turner's work or products.

turning *n.* **1** the act of one that turns. **2** a bend, as in a road. **3** the use of the lathe.

turning point *n.* a moment of decisive change: *The promotion was a turning point in his career; to reach a turning point in history, in one's life.*

tur.nip *n.* a plant of the mustard family whose roots are used as a vegetable: *turnip greens* (= leaves).

turn.key 1 *n.* one who has charge of the keys of a prison. **2** *adja.* of a product or service, delivered so completely finished that starting to use it is as simple as turning a key: *a turnkey program, project, service, system.*

turn.off *n.* a ramp or road where one turns off from a highway.

turn.out *n.* **1** a gathering of people, as at a function or event: *the voter turnout; The show attracted a large turnout; good, heavy, huge, light, low, poor, record, small, strong turnouts.* **2** the way one is dressed or something is equipped. **3** a widened place in a road where vehicles can pass. **4** a railroad siding.

turn.o.ver (TUR.noh.vur) *n.* **1** a turning over or upset. **2** in football and basketball, the losing possession of a ball: *The Baltimore Stars forced five Houston turnovers.* **3** a pastry or small pie whose crust has been folded over the filling: *an apple turnover.* **4** rate of replacement, esp. of employees: *There is a high* or *heavy turnover at fast-food outlets; low turnover; the turnover rate; fast healing because of quick cell turnover.* **5** the amount of goods sold or business done in a given period: *how to increase turnover; active, fast, high, quick turnover; the turnover of inventory; stock turnover.*

turn.pike *n.* **1** a highway on which tolls are charged. **2** a tollgate.

turn.stile *n.* a gateway with a rotating device for letting in people one by one or for counting their numbers.

turn.ta.ble (TURN.tay.bul) *n.* a round platform, as for turning locomotives around or playing a phonograph record.

tur.pen.tine (TUR.pun.tine) *n.* a pungent inflammable oil distilled from the resinous sap of pine trees, used as a solvent and paint thinner; also called "spirits (or oil) of turpentine."

tur.pi.tude (TUR.puh.tude) *n.* inherent wickedness or depravity: *moral turpitude.*

turps [short form] turpentine.

tur.quoise (TUR.kois, -kwois) *n.* **1** a brilliant greenish-blue mineral. **2** its color; *adj.: the shimmering turquoise waters of the lake.*

tur.ret (TUR.it) *n.* **1** a towerlike ornamental structure, as at the four corners of a tower. **2** a revolving structure housing guns on a battleship, tank, or airplane. **3** the rotating multiple-sided toolholder of a lathe.
—**turreted** *adj.* having turrets: *a turreted house; a turreted helicopter gun system.*

tur.tle (TUR.tul) *n.* a slow-moving reptile with stumpy, clublike limbs (or flippers in "sea turtles") and a rounded body encased in a protective shell.
—**turn turtle** turn upside down.

tur.tle.dove (TUR.tul.duv) *n.* a small European dove with a mournful cooing note.

tur.tle.neck (TUR.tul.neck) *n.* **1** a high, close-fitting, turned-down collar. **2** a sweater with such a collar.

Tus.ca.ro.ra (tus.cuh.ROR.uh) *n.* (a member of) a tribe of Iroquoian Indians, now living in parts of New York State and the Province of Ontario.

tush *n. Slang.* buttocks.

tusk *n.* a long, enlarged, pointed tooth projecting on either side of the mouth in the elephant, walrus, boar, etc.
—**tusked** *adj.*

tusk.er *n.* a tusked animal, esp. a male elephant.

tus.sle (TUS.ul) *n. & v.* **tus.sles, tus.sled, tus.sling 1** wrestle or scuffle. **2** struggle.

tus.sock (TUS.uk) *n.* a thick tuft or clump of growing grass or hair, as along the back of the "tussock moth."

tu.te.lage (TUE.til.ij) *n.* guardianship or instruction: *Players are **under the tutelage** of their coaches.*

tu.te.lar.y (TUE.tuh.lair.ee) *adj.* guardian: *a tutelary saint, spirit; a guardian's tutelary authority.*

tu.tor (TUE.tur) *n.* a private teacher.
—*v.* act as a tutor to someone: *She tutors him in music.*

tu.tor.i.al (tue.TOR.ee.ul) *adj.* having to do with tutoring: *tutorial colleges, sessions, work; n.: a tutorial (= course) in music.*

tut.ti-frut.ti (TOO.tee.FROO.tee) *n.* an ice cream, candy, preserve, etc. containing a variety of fruits or flavors.

tut-tut *interj.* expressing disbelief or disapproval. —*v.* **-tuts, -tut.ted, -tut.ting**: *"How disgusting," tut-tutted the commentator.*

tu.tu (TOO.too) *n.* a ballerina's short stiff skirt.

tux [short form] tuxedo.

tux.e.do (tuk.SEE.doh) *n.* **-dos 1** a man's tailless black jacket. **2** a man's semiformal suit with a tuxedo.

TV *n.* **TV's** or **TVs 1** the radio transmission of images by converting light signals into electrical signals and back into images on a screen at the receiving end. **2** the TV industry or TV broadcasting: *She is in TV* (= works in the TV industry); *He'll be on TV tonight; prime-time TV.* **3** a television receiving set; TV: *to turn off, turn on the TV.* **4** a program or programs received on TV: *Do you have to watch TV all day?* —*adj.: a TV announcer, channel, program, set, show, star, station.* Also **television.**

TV dinner *n.* a frozen dinner packaged in a tray for quick heating and serving.

twad.dle (TWOD.ul) *n.* empty talk or writing.

twain *n.* [old use] two; pair: *"Never the twain shall meet."*

twang *n.* **1** the sharp, vibrating sound of a plucked string. **2** a sharp, nasal tone of voice: *to speak with a nasal twang.* —*v.* **1** (cause) to make a twang, as on a stringed instrument. **2** speak with a nasal twang. —**twang.y** *adj.: a twangy drawl.*

'twas (TWUZ, TWOZ) it was.

tweak (TWEEK) *v.* pinch and twist a nose, ears, etc. —*n.* a sharp pinch and twist.

tweed *n.* 1 a rough, heavy woolen cloth with a hairy surface, usu. woven of fibers in two colors. 2 **tweeds** *pl.* clothes of tweed, esp. a suit.

tweed.y *adj.* **tweed.i.er, -i.est** 1 of or like tweed: *a tweedy coat, style, wool.* 2 informal-looking: *a tweedy professor.*

'tween *prep.* [old use] between.

tweet *n. & interj.* the thin chirp of a small bird. —*v.* utter a tweet.

tweet.er *n.* the speaker of a hi-fi that reproduces only the high-frequency sounds.

tweeze *v.* **tweez.es, tweezed, tweez.ing** *Informal.* pluck with tweezers.

tweez.ers *n.pl.* small pincers for handling tiny objects, esp. for plucking hairs.

twelfth *adj.* following the eleventh; 12th. —*n.* 1 one that is 12th in order. 2 one of 12 equal parts; 1/12.

Twelfth Night *n.* the 12th night after Christmas; Epiphany.

twelve (TWELV) *n., adj. & pron.* two more than 10; 12 or XII: *That's a 12; There are 12 of them; twelve bottles;* **cpd:** *a* **12-pack** *(of soda); a 12-pack of beer; 12-pack cans, carriers, cases; six-packs and 12-packs.*

twen.ty (TWEN.tee) *n., adj. & pron.* **-ties** 1 two times 10; 20 or XX. 2 **the twenties** *n.pl.* the numbers or years from 20 through 29. —**twen.ti.eth** (-uth) *n. & adj.*

twenty-one same as BLACKJACK, *n.* 2.

twenty-twenty or **20/20 vision** *n.* normal eyesight, i.e., the ability to read characters that a person with normal eyesight can read from 20 feet away; 6/6 vision (in the metric system): *visual acuity close to 20/20; 20/20 hindsight.*

twerp (TWURP) *n. Slang.* an undesirable or ineffectual person.

twice *adv.* two times: *She brushes her teeth twice a day; $500 is twice as much as $250; Russia is twice the size of the U.S.; He won the award twice* (= on two occasions) *in three years*

twid.dle (TWID.ul) *n.* a twirl or twist. —*v.* **twid.dles, twid.dled, twid.dling** toy or play with something idly. —**twiddle one's thumbs** be unoccupied; have nothing to do. —**twid.dler** *n.*

twig *n.* a slender shoot or branch. —*v.* **twigs, twigged, twig.ging** *Informal.* become aware of or catch on *to* something.

twig.gy (TWIG.ee) *adj.* slender or thin like a twig.

twi.light (TWY.lite) *n.* 1 the faint light of the period just before sunrise or just after sunset. 2 a period of fading light or decline: *in the twilight of his career, life;* **adj.:** *during the twilight hours of East Germany; the twilight* (= afterhours) *world of the streets; a drug-induced semiconscious* **twilight sleep;** *the long* **twilight struggle** *of democracy with Communism ending in the collapse of the Soviet Union.* 3 *adj.* grayish: *a twilight blue color; an issue that is in the* **twilight zone** *of morality.*

twill *n.* (a fabric with) a weave that produces diagonal ribs, as in drills, serge, gabardine, etc.; **adj.:** *twill cotton, pants, weaves.*

twin *n.* 1 either of two offspring born at the same birth: *a pair of Siamese twins; Ten sets of identical twins were at the party; fraternal twins; One twin may look just like the other.* 2 one of two closely related or similar individuals or things: *The Twins* (= two mountain peaks) *tower over Jasper National Park; the twin of this pair.* —**adj.** being a twin: *the twin cities of Minneapolis and St. Paul; a twin-engine jet; his twin sister; twin* (= two single) *beds.* —*v.* **twins, twinned, twin.ning** 1 bring forth twins. 2 to couple or pair: *A North American city is twinned with one in a foreign country for cultural exchanges.*

twine *n.* 1 a strong thread or cord made of two or more strands twisted together. 2 an entwining or tangle. —*v.* **twines, twined, twin.ing** 1 twist something together or *into* something. 2 wrap or wind *around* something. 3 meander or extend in a winding manner.

twinge (TWINJ) *n.* a sudden shooting pain: *a twinge of toothache; twinges of rheumatism; a twinge of conscience, remorse.* —*v.* **twing.es, twinged, twing.ing** give or feel a twinge.

twi-night double-header (TWY.nite-) or **twi-night.er** *adj.* a double-header of which the first game is played in the late afternoon and the second in the evening.

twin.kle (TWINK.ul) *v.* **-kles, -kled, -kling** 1 (cause) to shine with a flickering light: *Stars twinkle in the sky; Christmas trees twinkle with lights.* 2 move quickly and lightly: *Her eyes twinkled with joy, with mischief;* **adj.:** *the* **twinkling** *feet of dancers; twinkling* (= sparkling) *eyes;* **n.:** *vanished in the* **twinkling** *of an eye* (= in an instant). —*n.* 1 a gleam or sparkle: *the (self-sat-*

isfied) *twinkle in her eye.* **2** a wink or blink: *a mischievous twinkle: "But you can never tell," she added with a twinkle.*

twirl *v.* spin or whirl with dexterity: *to twirl one's mustache; She can twirl a hula hoop around her hips; a baton-twirling majorette.* —*n.* curl: *a twirl of hair; a signature with twirls and flourishes.*

twist *v.* **1** to wind or turn, as on an axis: *threads twisted together into a string; She twisted her head to look over her shoulder; The road twists and turns on its way up the hill; to twist* (= break) *off a piece of dough.* **2** bend or force out of shape or position; distort or wrench: *a rope twisted into a knot; bodies twisting about in pain; a car twisted out of shape in a crash; words twisted out of their meaning; He knows how to* **twist arms** (= use friendly pressure) *to get what he wants; She can twist* (= manipulate) *him around her little finger; adj.: a column with a* **twisted** *design; a twisted tale of intrigue; a twisted* (= sprained) *ankle.*
3 send a ball spinning in a curved path. —*n.* **1** bend or curve: *a road with many twists and turns; a board with a slight twist* (= warp). **2** something twisted: *a twist of bread; a twist* (= braid) *of tobacco; a twist of lemon* (= lemon peel for flavoring a drink). **3** distortion or turn: *an unexpected twist in the plans; by an ironic, strange twist of fate; That's a new twist to the story; a queer mental twist* (= kink or quirk). **4** a spin given to a ball in tennis, baseball, bowling, etc.
5 a vigorous dance of the 1950s and 1960s with twisting hip and leg movements: *to do the twist.*

twist.er *n.* one that twists, as a ball sent with a twisting motion, a tornado, or a waterspout.

twit *v.* **twits, twit.ted, twit.ting** taunt or tease a person *with* or *about* a weakness. —*n. Slang.* an annoyingly silly person: *a pompous twit.*

twitch *n.* **1** a sudden involuntary jerk, as of a facial muscle: *a nervous twitch.* **2** a sharp tug or pull. —*v.* pull or jerk suddenly or spasmodically: *to twitch a fishing line; a face that twitches nervously; adj.: a twitching body; twitching fingers, muscles.*

twitch.y *adj.* **1** jerky: *a car's twitchy handling.* **2** nervous or fidgety: *a twitchy face; twitchy fingers; She's a bit twitchy about his behavior in public; twitchy times of power struggles in a company.*

twit.ter (TWIT.ur) *v.* **1** chirp or chatter, as birds. **2** titter or giggle. **3** tremble with excitement; flutter.
—*n.* a twittering: *the twitter* (= chattering) *of swallows; Wedding day found everyone in a twitter* (= excited state).
—**twit.ter.y** *adj.*

'twixt or **twixt** *prep.* [literary] between: *"There's many a slip 'twixt the cup and the lip"; a tiff twixt the wife and the mother-in-law.*

two (TOO) *n., adj. & pron.* one more than one; 2 or II: *to cut an apple in two* (parts); *Children can* **put two and two together** (= see the facts for themselves) *and draw conclusions.*

two-bit *adj.* cheap: *a two-bit attraction, deal, show.*

two bits *n. Informal.* a quarter of a dollar; 25 cents.

two-by-four *n.* a piece of lumber 4 in. wide and 2 in. thick (10.16 x 5.08 cm) before trimming.

two-edged *adj.* cutting both ways: *a two-edged sword, weapon, argument.*

two-faced *adj.* **1** having two faces on the head: *the two-faced god Janus.* **2** deceitful or insincere: *a two-faced friend who could stab you in the back.*

two.fer (TOO.fur) *n. Informal.* a discounted item of which one can buy "two for" the price of one.

two-fisted *adj. Informal.* vigorous or strong.

two.fold *adj.* double: *a twofold advantage, challenge, goal, increase, mission, risk, threat; The problem is twofold; The reasons are twofold.* —*adv.:* doubly: *Prices have risen twofold in one year.*

two-ply *adj.* having two thicknesses, layers, strands, etc.: *a two-ply paper towel, tire, yarn.*

two.some (TOO.sum) *n.* **1** two people: *The husband-and-wife team is an impressive twosome.* **2** a golf match for two.

two-step *n. & v.* **-steps, -stepped, -step.ping** dance with a series of sliding steps in march or polka rhythm.

two-time *v.* **-times, -timed, -tim.ing** *Informal.* be unfaithful to one's spouse or partner: *Everyone knows Pat's two-timing; He has two-timed his wife; He two-timed* (= double-crossed) *his partner.*

two-way *adj.* involving two directions or parties: *two-way communication; a two-way radio, street; a two-way race* (between two contestants).

ty.coon (tye.COON) same as MAGNATE: *a tobacco tycoon.*

ty.ing *pres. part.* of TIE.

tyke *n. Informal.* a small child considered as mischievous, helpless, etc.

tym.pa.ni (TIM.puh.nee) same as TIMPANI. —**tym.pa.nist** *n.*

tym.pan.ic membrane (tim.PAN.ic-) *n.* the eardrum.

tym.pa.num (TIM.puh.num) *n.* **-nums** or **-na** (-nuh) **1** the middle ear. **2** the eardrum.

type *n.* **1** a person or thing considered as belonging to a group or category because of similarity to others: *He's the strong silent type; media types such as this reporter.* **2** a category, sort, or kind: *a fine type of woman; novels of this type; I don't like this type novel* (*Informal for* this type of novel); *dramatic characters that are types* (= generalizations) *rather than individuals.* **3** a printing block with raised letters or characters: *Gutenberg printed from movable type; italic and roman type; a complete font of type of the same size and style; Books had to be first set in type and then printed; small type* (= something printed in small letters). —*v.* **types, typed, typ.ing 1** classify as to type; typecast: *to type one's blood as A, B, AB, or O; an actor who is always typed as a gangster.* **2** write with a typewriter: *a letter typed by her secretary.*

type.cast *v.* **-casts, -cast, -cast.ing** cast someone, as an actor, repeatedly in the same type of role: *an actor typecast in gangster roles;* **n.:** the **typecasting** of women as sex objects.

type.face *n.* a design or style of type: *A typeface (as this, Baskerville) includes letters and numerals and comes in* roman, *italic,* **boldface**, *etc. as well as in different styles and sizes.*

type.script *n.* typewritten matter.

type.set *v.* **-sets, -set, -set.ting** set book matter in type; compose.
—**type.set.ter** *n.*

type.writ.er (TYPE.rye.tur) *n.* a keyboard machine that produces printed characters on paper: *a reporter pounding her typewriter; He does all his writing on a manual typewriter; Electronic typewriters are noiseless compared to electric ones.* —**type.writ.ing** *n.*

ty.phoid (TYE.foid) *n.* a serious infectious disease spread by a bacillus that enters the body through contaminated food or water; also **typhoid fever.**

ty.phoon (tye.FOON) *n.* a destructive tropical cyclone of the western Pacific.

ty.phus (TYE.fus) *n.* a rickettsial disease often caused by the bite of infected lice, fleas, ticks, etc.; also **typhus fever.**

typ.i.cal (TIP.i.cul) *adj.* having the characteristics of a type or class: *a typical soap opera; It is typical of soaps to be sentimental; Sentimentality is typical* (= characteristic) *of soaps.* —**typ.i.cal.ly** *adv.*

typ.i.fy (TIP.uh.fye) *v.* **-fies, -fied, -fy.ing** be a type or symbol of something; exemplify: *Solomon typifies wisdom; a city that typifies urban sprawl; Wisdom typified* (= characterized) *Solomon.*

typ.ist (TYE.pist) *n.* one who uses a typewriter.

ty.po (TYE.poh) *n. Informal.* a typing or typesetting error.

ty.pog.ra.phy (tye.POG.ruh.fee) *n.* **1** the art of printing with type: *Caxton's typography.* **2** the arrangement or appearance of typeset matter: *the typography of a dictionary page.*
—**ty.po.graph.ic** (-puh.GRAF.ic) or **ty.po.graph.i.cal** *adj.;*
ty.po.graph.i.cal.ly *adv.*

ty.pol.o.gy (tye.POL.uh.jee) *n.* classification by types based on similar characteristics, as of languages considered as "analytic" (Chinese, English, etc.), "synthetic" (Sanskrit, Greek, etc.), and "agglutinative" (Turkish, Korean, etc.).
—**ty.po.log.i.cal** (-puh.LOJ.i.cul) *adj.*

ty.ran.ni.cal (tuh.RAN.i.cul) *adj.* of or like a tyrant; cruel and unjust.
—**ty.ran.ni.cal.ly** *adv.*

tyr.an.nize (TEER.uh.nize) *v.* **-niz.es, -nized, -niz.ing** act or rule as a tyrant or despot; oppress: *a story of the rich tyrannizing (over) the poor.*
—**tyr.an.niz.er** *n.*

ty.ran.no.saur.us (tuh.ran.uh.SOR.us) *n.* the largest of the flesh-eating dinosaurs; also **ty.ran.no.saur** (tuh.RAN.uh.sor).

tyr.an.ny (TEER.uh.nee) *n.* **-an.nies 1** a tyrant's rule or authority: *Nazi tyranny; to endure, impose, live under, submit to tyranny; to overthrow or throw off a tyranny; cruel, merciless, murderous, totalitarian tyrannies.* **2** an act or use of power seen as cruel or unjust: *the tyranny of the majority over the minority.*

ty.rant (TYE.runt) *n.* **1** an absolute ruler or despot: *cruel, petty, ruthless tyrants.* **2** a cruel or oppressive person in authority: *The boss is not such a tyrant as he used to be.*

tyre *Brit.* TIRE, *n.*

ty.ro (TYE.roh) *n.* **-ros** (-roze) an inexperienced and amateurish beginner in a field of activity.

Ty.ro.le.an (tuh.ROH.lee.un) same as TIROLEAN.

tzar (TSAR, ZAR) same as CZAR.
—**tza.ri.na** (tsah.REE.nuh, zah-), *fem.*

.... **U, u** ....

U or **u** (YOO) *n.* **U's** or **u's 1** the 21st letter of the English alphabet. **2** U-

comb.form. shaped like a U: *a 360° U-turn; the U-tube used in chemistry experiments.* —*adj. Informal.* in Britain, upper-class: *U and non-U.*

u.biq.ui.tous (yoo.BIK.wuh.tus) *adj.* seeming to be present or occurring everywhere: *the ubiquitous common crow, dust, fax machine; Ghosts are a ubiquitous phenomenon; their ubiquitous appearance, presence in haunted homes; ubiquitous corruption, hazards, pollutants.* —**u.biq.ui.ty** *n.*

ud.der (UD.ur) *n.* a pendulous, milk-secreting organ with two or more teats, as in the cow or goat.

UFO *n.* **UFO's** an unidentified flying object; flying saucer: *the sighting of UFO's.*

u.fol.o.gy (yoo.FOL.uh.jee) *n.* the study of UFO's. —**u.fol.o.gist** *n.*

U.gan.dan (yoo.GAN.dun) *n. & adj.* (a person) of or from **Uganda**, a country of E.C. Africa.

ugh (UH, UK) *interj.* expressing disgust or horror.

ug.ly (UG.lee) *adj.* **-li.er, -li.est** hideous or repulsive in appearance: *an ugly toad; an ugly* (= *dangerous*) *gaping wound; He gave me an ugly* (= *ill-natured*) *look; the* **Ugly American** *whose behavior is considered offensive in other cultures; the* **ugly duckling** *who grew into a graceful swan, as in the fairy tale.* —**ug.li.ness** *n.*

uh *interj.* 1 expressing surprise, contempt, or a question. 2 a neutral sound different from any of the regular vowels and is prolonged while thinking or searching for a word.

uh-huh *interj.* indicating that one is receptive to what is being said.

uh-oh *interj.* indicating surprise and concern.

u.kase (YOO.case, yoo.CASE) *n.* an edict or decree, as of a czar.

U.krain.i.an (yoo.CRAY.nee.un) *n.* 1 a person of or from **Ukraine**, a country of E. Europe. 2 the Slavic language of Ukraine. Also *adj.*

u.ku.le.le (yoo.kuh.LAY.lee) *n.* a small, four-stringed Hawaiian guitar.

ul.cer (UL.sur) *n.* an open, usu. inflamed sore on the skin or on a mucous membrane: *a bleeding ulcer; duodenal, gastric, peptic, stomach ulcers.* —**ul.cer.ous** (-rus) *adj.*

ul.cer.ate (UL.suh.rate) *v.* **-ates, -at.ed, -at.ing** make or become ulcerous. —**ul.cer.a.tion** (-RAY.shun) *n.*

ul.na (UL.nuh) *n., pl.* **-nae** (-nee) or **-nas** the larger of the two bones of the forearm; **ul.nar** *adj.*: *ulnar nerves.*

ul.ster *n.* a long, loose, heavy, usu. belted overcoat.

ul.te.ri.or (ul.TEER.ee.ur) *adj.* 1 lying on the farther side: *ulterior regions.* 2 hidden: *an ulterior meaning, motive, purpose.*

ul.ti.mate (UL.tuh.mit) *adj.* remotest, beyond which it is impossible to go: *in the ultimate analysis; her ultimate ambition, goal, objective; Is sex or Heaven the ultimate experience? the ultimate origin of the universe; his ultimate success; its ultimate value; To many people, God is the Ultimate Reality.* —*n.* an ultimate point, result, fact, etc.: *She enjoyed the ultimate in luxury; a philosophical ultimate such as happiness.* —**ul.ti.mate.ly** *adv.*

ul.ti.ma.tum (ul.tuh.MAY.tum) *n.* **-tums** or **-ta** (-tuh) a final offer or demand threatening consequences if rejected: *to give, issue, receive, withdraw an ultimatum.*

ul.tra (UL.truh) *n.* an extremist. —*adj. & comb.form.* going beyond the usual: *He's too ultra in his views; the ultra Right; ultraconservative; ultrahigh; ultramodern;* **adv.**: *ultra compact, light, slim.*

ultrahigh frequency *n.* a radio-wave frequency between 300 and 3,000 megahertz.

ul.tra.light (UL.truh.lite) *n.* a very light airplane.

ul.tra.ma.rine (ul.truh.muh.REEN) *adj.* 1 situated beyond the sea. 2 brilliant-blue, as a pigment made from lapis lazuli. —*n.* this color.

ul.tra.mi.cro.scope (ul.truh.MY.cruh.scope) *n.* a microscope that uses scattered light to see extremely minute objects such as bacteria and colloidal particles suspended in liquid or air. —**ul.tra.mi.cro.scop.ic** (-SCOP.ic) *adj.* too tiny to be seen with an ordinary microscope.

ul.tra.mod.ern (ul.truh.MOD.urn) *adj.* extremely modern in style, trend, ideas, etc.

ul.tra.mon.tane (ul.truh.MON.tane) *adj.* 1 situated south of the mountains, i.e., Alps. 2 favoring papal authority over national and diocesan.

ul.tra.short (UL.truh.short) *adj.* of a wavelength below 10 meters.

ul.tra.son.ic (ul.truh.SON.ic) *adj.* 1 beyond human hearing range: *an ultrasonic frequency, humidifier.* 2 having to do with ultrasound: *ultrasonic imaging, lithotripsy, probes, scans.* —*n.pl.* [takes *sing. v.*] the science of ultrasonic sound waves and their applications in science and industry: *home ultrasonics;*

ultrasonics in obstetrics.

ul.tra.sound (UL.truh.sound) *n.*
1 sound of more than 20,000 vibrations per second, too high-pitched for human hearing. **2** a diagnostic tool or therapy using ultrasound waves.

ul.tra.vi.o.let (ul.truh.VYE.uh.lut) *adj.* beyond the violet end of the visible light range: *ultraviolet light, radiation; An* **ultraviolet lamp** *yields radiations of wavelengths between visible light and X rays.*

ultra vi.res (-VYE.rees) *adj. & adv. Latin.* beyond one's legal power or authority.

ul.u.late (ULL.yuh.late, YOOL.yuh-) *v.* **-lates, -lat.ed, -lat.ing** make a prolonged sound, as in wailing or howling; **ul.u.la.tion** (-LAY.shun) *n.*

um.bel (UM.bul) *n.* an umbrellalike flower cluster, as of the carrot and parsley.

um.ber *n.* a brown mineral pigment or its color. —*adj.* of the brown color of "raw umber" or the deep reddish brown of "burnt umber."

um.bil.i.cal (um.BIL.i.cul) *adj.* of the navel: *The* **umbilical cord** *connects an unborn child to its mother's womb for nutrition and waste removal; An "umbilical cord" connects an astronaut to the spaceship during a spacewalk.* —**um.bil.i.cus** *n.* navel.

um.bra (UM.bruh) *n., pl.* **-brae** (-bree) or **-bras** a dark spot or shadow, esp. the darker region of shadow cast by the sun in which a "total eclipse" is experienced. —**um.bral** (-brul) *adj.*

um.brage (UM.brij) *n.* **1 take umbrage at** take offense at something. **2** shady foliage or shade.

um.brel.la (um.BREL.uh) *n.* **1** a circular cover of cloth on a folding frame of hinged ribs sliding on a center pole, carried for protection against sun or rain. **2** a protective organization, device, etc.: *an air umbrella of military aircraft; nations under the American umbrella; adja.: an umbrella organization with many groups under it; umbrella agencies, associations, coalitions, groups, a loose* **umbrella term** *that covers the disabled, the elderly, gays, and religious fundamentalists.*

u.mi.ak (OO.mee.ak) *n.* a large, open Inuit boat made with sealskin stretched over a wooden frame for carrying 10 to 12 people.

um.laut (OOM.lowt, short "OO") *n.* **1** in Germanic languages, the change of a vowel sound, as in the German "Hände," *pl.* of "Hand." **2** the diacritical mark placed over the changed vowel, as in ä, ë, ï, ö, ü.

ump [short form] umpire.

um.pire *n.* a judge or referee in a contest or dispute, esp. an official administering the rules in sports such as baseball or hockey, sometimes assisting a referee, as in tennis and volleyball. —*v.* **-pires, -pired, -pir.ing** act as umpire: *to umpire a game.*

ump.teen (UMP.teen) *adj. Informal.* innumerable: *I've told you umpteen times.* —**ump.teenth** (ump.TEENTH) *adj.*: *I'm telling you for the umpteenth time.*

un- *prefix* **1** freely added to words, using a hyphen before a capital letter *(un-Canadian)* to mean "not" when added to adjectives, participles, and adverbs *(unable, unsaid, unluckily),* "the opposite of" when added to abstract nouns *(uncertainty, unrest),* and an opposite action when a verb is formed *(uncap, undo).* **2** added to concrete nouns and noun phrases to mean the absence of an essential quality: *an unbirthday present; unpersons; unreaders; an unvacation spent at home.*

un.a.bridged (un.uh.BRIJD) *adj.* **1** not abridged: *the unabridged original novel.* **2** comprehensive: *an unabridged dictionary.*

un-American *adj.* considered as contrary to U.S. customs, traditions, goals, etc.

u.nan.i.mous (yoo.NAN.uh.mus) *adj.* in complete agreement; with the agreement of all: *a unanimous decision, verdict; their unanimous agreement, approval; They were unanimous in agreeing to take the necessary measures.* —**u.nan.i.mous.ly** *adv.* —**u.na.nim.i.ty** (yoo.nuh.NIM.i.tee) *n.*

un.as.sum.ing (un.uh.SOO.ming) *adj.* not pretentious or forward; modest.

un.at.tached (un.uh.TACHT) *adj.* not attached, esp. in regard to marriage; unmarried or unengaged.

un.a.vail.ing (un.uh.VAY.ling) *adj.* being of no avail; futile. —**un.a.vail.ing.ly** *adv.*

un.a.ware (un.uh.WARE) *adjp.* not aware; unawares: *We were caught unaware; We were unaware of the collapse of the bridge; unaware that the bridge had collapsed.* —**unawares** (-WARES) *adv.* **1** by surprise; unexpectedly: *The announcement caught* or *took us unawares.* **2** unintentionally: *a remark made unawares.*

un.bar (un.BAR) *v.* **-bars, -barred, -bar.ring 1** unbolt or open a gate, etc. **2** open up a closed channel, field, etc.

un.be.com.ing (un.bi.CUM.ing) *adj.* not appropriate to one's appearance or character: *unbecoming behavior, clothes, conduct; conduct unbecoming (of or to) a gentleman.* —**un.be.com.ing.ly** *adv.*

un.be.knownst (un.bi.NOHNST) *adjp. Formal.* unknown *to* one; also **un.be.known.**

un.be.lief (un.bi.LEEF) *n.* doubt or lack of belief, esp. in something religious. —**un.be.liev.a.ble** (-LEE.vuh.bul) *adj.;* **un.be.liev.a.bly** *adv.* —**un.be.liev.er** (-vur) *n.*

un.bend (un.BEND) *v.* **-bends, -bent, -bend.ing** 1 straighten. 2 relax from formality, tension, etc.: *It's good to unbend a little on weekends.*

un.bend.ing (un.BEN.ding) *adj.* 1 resolute: *her unbending loyalty, resolve, stand.* 2 stiff or stubborn: *his unbending attitude, position, temperament.*

un.bid.den (un.BID.un) *adj.* 1 not invited. 2 not being ordered.

un.born (un.BORN) *adj.* not yet born: *an unborn child (still in the womb); unborn (= future) generations.*

un.bos.om (un.BOOZ.um, long or short "OO") *v.* reveal one's feelings, secrets, thoughts, etc., esp. **unbosom oneself** *to* someone.

un.bound.ed (un.BOWN.did) *adj.* 1 without limits; boundless. 2 not kept within limits; unrestrained.

un.bri.dled (un.BRY.duld) *adj.* not bridled, esp. uncontrolled: *unbridled anger, enthusiasm, growth, insolence, optimism, power.*

un.bur.den (un.BUR.dun) *v.* 1 to free from a burden. 2 relieve oneself, one's heart, conscience, etc. by confession *to* someone or by disclosing guilt, etc.: *He had no peace of mind till he had unburdened himself to his counselor.*

un.called-for *adj.* not called for; unwarranted: *uncalled-for attacks, impertinence, remarks.*

un.can.ny (un.CAN.ee) *adj.* 1 mysterious or weird: *uncanny shapes, sounds; an uncanny feeling of something about to happen.* 2 so remarkable as to seem superhuman: *her uncanny ability to motivate employees; an uncanny instinct for guessing the right answer.*

un.cer.e.mo.ni.ous (UN.ser.uh.MOH.nee.us) *adj.* 1 not ceremonious. 2 abrupt or discourteous: *an unceremonious dismissal, exit, rebuke.*

un.cer.tain (un.SUR.tun) *adj.* 1 not certain or sure: *He felt uncertain about the future; somewhat uncertain as to what might happen; a word of uncertain origin; We told him in no uncertain (= in clear) terms.* 2 changeable or varying: *uncertain health, temper, weather.*

un.cer.tain.ty (un.SUR.tun.tee) *n.* **-ties** 1 an uncertain state: *our uncertainty about the future.* 2 something that is uncertain: *the uncertainties of a hand-to-mouth existence.*

un.char.i.ta.ble (un.CHAIR.i.tuh.bul) *adj.* harsh or severe, as in judging others: *an uncharitable imputation of motive; It was uncharitable of him to say that.* —**un.char.i.ta.bly** *adv.*

un.chart.ed (un.CHAR.tid) *adj.* 1 of places, not shown on a map. 2 not mapped; unexplored: *uncharted regions; sailing on uncharted seas; in uncharted territory; to enter, navigate the uncharted waters of artificial intelligence.*

un.chris.tian (un.CRIS.chun) *adj.* 1 not Christian. 2 *Informal.* outrageous or unusual: *They charge unchristian prices.*

un.ci.al (UN.shee.ul, -shul) *n. & adj.* (a letter or manuscript) in the all-capital, noncursive lettering style with large rounded characters used by scribes between A.D. 300 and 900.

un.cir.cum.cised (un.SUR.cum.sized) *adj.* 1 not circumcised. 2 [derogatory] non-Jewish; gentile; heathen.

un.cle (UNK.ul) *n.* 1 the brother of one's father or mother: *He threw up his hands and* **cried Uncle** or **said Uncle** (*Informal* for admitted defeat). 2 one's aunt's husband.

Uncle Sam *n. Informal.* the U.S. government or nation, personified as a long-haired man in a tall hat and a costume decorated with stars and stripes.

Uncle Tom *n. Informal.* a black man who is servile to whites.

un.com.fort.a.ble (un.CUM.fur.tuh.bul) *adj.* feeling or causing discomfort: *The baby seems uncomfortable; an uncomfortable chair; We felt uncomfortable about her long absence; an uncomfortable (= uneasy) silence.* —**un.com.fort.a.bly** *adv.*

un.com.mon (un.COM.un) *adj.* 1 rare or unusual: *It is not uncommon to have frost in September.* 2 remarkable or outstanding: *an uncommon occurrence; her uncommon generosity.* —**un.com.mon.ly** *adv.*

un.com.pro.mis.ing (UN.com.pruh.MYE.zing) *adj.* unyielding or inflexible: *an uncompromising attitude; a woman of uncompromising devotion to duty.*

un.con.cern (un.cun.SURN) *n.* lack of concern, care, or solicitude, as from selfishness or insensitiveness; indifference *over* a person or thing.

—un.con.cerned (-SURND) *adj.* not concerned, anxious, or solicitous.

un.con.di.tion.al (un.cun.DISH.un.ul) *adj.* without conditions attached: *an unconditional offer, rejection, release, surrender.*

un.con.scion.a.ble (un.CON.shun.uh.bul) *adj.* **1** unreasonable or excessive: *It took an unconscionable time.* **2** contrary to what the conscience dictates; unscrupulous: *an unconscionable villain.* **—un.con.scion.a.bly** *adv.*

un.con.scious (un.CON.shus) *adj.* not conscious or aware: *He lay bleeding and unconscious; was unconscious of having offended her; an unconscious habit, prejudice, tendency.* **—n. the unconscious** the part of the mind containing thoughts, ideas, feelings, etc. that one is not fully aware of or that have been repressed.

un.cou.ple (un.CUP.ul) *v.* **-ples, -pled, -pling** disconnect something coupled together.

un.couth (un.COOTH) *adj.* **1** awkward or clumsy-looking. **2** unrefined or crude.

un.cov.er (un.CUV.ur) *v.* **1** remove the cover from something. **2** disclose or expose. **3** bare one's head in respect.

unc.tion (UNC.shun) *n.* **1** an anointing with oil (as in church rites) or with ointment (as in medical treatment). **2** the oil or salve used. **3** anything that soothes or comforts. **4** this quality: *She preaches with great unction.*

unc.tu.ous (UNC.choo.us) *adj.* too suave or smooth; **unc.tu.ous.ly** *adv.*; **unc.tu.ous.ness** *n.*

un.cut (un.CUT) *adj.* not cut or abridged: *an uncut version of a movie; a rough, uncut* (= not shaped and polished) *diamond.*

un.daunt.ed (un.DAWN.tid) *adj.* not daunted or disheartened: *undaunted by defeats; undaunted in her resolve.*

un.der (UN.dur) *prep.* **1** directly below: *Look under the table; a boulder under the* (surface of) *water; A shirt is worn under a jacket; 15 is under the voting age; priced under* (= less than) *$100.* **2** subject or subordinate to a person or thing: *a country under a dictatorship; She testified under oath; I was under a wrong impression; He's working under a contract; "Beauty" is listed under* (the heading) *"B"; She was excused under* (= because of) *the circumstances.* **—adv.** in or to a lower place: *The boat sprang a leak and went under; Everything here is priced $100 and under; We are snowed under by correspondence; Companies* **go under** *by bankruptcy; to keep wages and prices under* (= under control); *The anesthetic kept her under* (= unconscious) *during surgery.* **—comb.form** [meaning "below" as in the following compounds whose basic meaning and pronunciation are the same as in the base word in each case]: *undercook, underdose, undereducated, underemployed, underpay, underpopulated, underpriced, underripe, undersized, undersold.*

un.der.a.chieve (UN.dur.uh.CHEEV) *v.* **-chieves, -chieved, -chiev.ing** do less well in school than expected for one's level of ability. **—un.der.a.chiev.er** *n.*

un.der.act (un.dur.ACT) *v.* act a dramatic part with less than the required emphasis; underplay.

un.der.age (un.dur.AGE) *adj.* below the required or full age.

un.der.arm (un.dur.ARM) **1** *adj.* of the armpit: *underarm deodorants, stains, wetness.* **2** *adj. & adv.* underhand: *an underarm throw.*

un.der.bel.ly (un.dur.BEL.ee) *n.* **1** the underside of an animal's body. **2** a weak or vulnerable part.

un.der.bid (un.dur.BID) *v.* **-bids, -bid, -bid.ding 1** bid less than what is justified, as by the cards in one's hand. **2** bid lower than another person.

un.der.brush (UN.dur.brush) *n.* low shrubs, small trees, etc. under the large trees of a forest: *dense, heavy, tangled, thick underbrush; to clear (away) the underbrush.*

un.der.car.riage (UN.dur.cair.ij) *n.* **1** the supporting frame or structure of an automobile or other vehicle on wheels. **2** the landing gear of an airplane.

un.der.charge (un.dur.CHARGE) *v.* **-charg.es, -charged, -charg.ing 1** charge a buyer less than the usual price. **2** load a gun, battery, etc. insufficiently. **—n.** (UN.dur.charge) such a charge.

un.der.class (UN.dur.class) *n.* the poor and underprivileged of a society.

un.der.class.man (un.dur.CLASS.mun) *n.* a freshman or sophomore.

un.der.clothes (UN.dur.clothes) *n.pl.* underwear; also **un.der.cloth.ing** (-CLOH.thing) *n.*

un.der.coat or **un.der.coat.ing** (UN.dur.coh.ting) *n.* **1** a coating of a tarlike substance given to the underside of an automobile for protection against rust. **2** a coat of paint applied to a wall, furniture, etc. before the final coat. **—v.** apply an undercoat to a vehicle.

un.der.cov.er (UN.dur.cuv.ur) *adja.* (done in) secret, as spying: *an undercover agent, investigation, officer, unit; undercover payments, work.* —*adv.*: *to go, work undercover* (= in secret).

un.der.cur.rent (UN.dur.cur.unt) *n.* a current below the surface, esp. in an opposite direction, as an undertow: *an undercurrent of resentment.*

un.der.cut (un.dur.CUT) *v.* **-cuts, -cut, -cut.ting** 1 cut away the underpart, as on the side of a tree trunk to make it fall toward a particular side. 2 sell or work for less than a competitor. 3 hit a ball so as to give it a backspin, as in tennis, billiards, or golf.

un.der.de.vel.oped (UN.dur.di.VEL.upt) *adj.* of countries, not advanced industrially and hence poor in standard of living, education, health care, etc. Also **less developed.**

un.der.dog (UN.dur.dog) *n.* 1 one in a state of subjection. 2 the predicted loser in a contest.

un.der.done (un.dur.DUN) *adj.* not cooked enough: *an underdone steak.*

un.der.es.ti.mate (un.dur.ES.tuh.mate) *v.* **-mates, -mat.ed, -mat.ing** form too low an estimate of a person's strength, costs of a project, etc. Also *n.* (-mit, -mate).

un.der.foot (un.dur.FOOT) *adj. & adv.* 1 under the foot or feet: *carpets that feel good underfoot; to crush, trample, tread something underfoot; underfoot comfort; There's a move underfoot* (= in progress) *to discredit the opposition.* 2 in the way of one walking: *Children tend to get underfoot; snow that is crunchy underfoot;* also **under foot.**

un.der.gar.ment (UN.dur.gar.munt) *n.* a piece of underwear.

un.der.go (un.dur.GO) *v.* **-goes, -went, -gone** (-GON), **-go.ing** go through a painful, unpleasant, or dangerous experience.

un.der.grad.u.ate (un.dur.GRAJ.oo.it) *n.* a college student who has not yet received a first degree.

un.der.ground (un.dur.GROUND) *adja.* 1 beneath the surface of the ground: *an underground installation, passage; underground testing of atomic bombs.* 2 in or into hiding; away from public knowledge: *underground resistance to enemy occupation; dissident publications of the underground press; an avant-garde underground movie;* **adv.**: *Moles live underground; She went underground to escape from her mother-in-law.*
—*n.* (UN.dur.ground) 1 an underground region or political movement. 2 *Brit.* subway.

underground railroad *n.* a secret network of routes and homes by which slaves from the U.S. escaped to Canada.

un.der.growth (UN.dur.growth) same as UNDERBRUSH.

un.der.hand (UN.dur.hand) *adj. & adv.* 1 with the hand swung forward below the level of the elbow or shoulder: *an underhand serve, throw; to pitch a ball underhand.* 2 underhanded(ly): *using underhand means; an underhand method, scheme; in an underhand and dishonest way.*

un.der.hand.ed (un.dur.HAN.did) *adj. & adv.* 1 sly or deceitful; not open or honest. 2 using an underhand swing: *The ball was thrown underhanded.*
—**un.der.hand.ed.ly** *adv.*

un.der.lie (un.dur.LYE) *v.* **-lies, -lay, -lain, -ly.ing** 1 lie or be situated under. 2 form the basis or foundation of a doctrine, etc.

un.der.line (un.dur.line, un.dur.LINE) *v.* **-lines, -lined, -lin.ing** same as UNDERSCORE, 1 & 2. —*n.* (UN.dur.line) same as UNDERSCORE, 1.

un.der.ling (UN.dur.ling) *n.* a servile follower or subordinate.

un.der.ly.ing (un.dur.LYE.ing) *adja.* 1 lying under: *underlying gas reserves; underlying strata.* 2 not obvious on the surface: *a book's underlying message; the industry's underlying weakness; underlying causes, factors, forces, motives, principles, problems, reasons.*

un.der.mine (un.dur.MINE) *v.* **-mines, -mined, -min.ing** 1 dig under or wear away from under something: *to undermine a foundation; flood waters undermining river banks.* 2 weaken or impair gradually, as by insidious means: *rumors that undermine a person's reputation; Her health was undermined* (= sapped) *by a chronic illness.*

un.der.most (UN.dur.mohst) *adj. & adv.* lowest.

un.der.neath (un.dur.NEETH, "TH" as in "thin") *prep. & adv.* below or beneath, esp. in a hidden place: *a vest underneath his jacket; the devil underneath; lying underneath.*

un.der.nour.ished (un.dur.NUR.isht) *adj.* not getting sufficient nourishment.

un.der.pants (UN.dur.pants) *n.pl.* long or short pants worn as underwear.

un.der.pass (UN.dur.pass) *n.* a road passing under a railroad or highway.

un.der.pin.ning (UN.dur.pin.ing) *n.* masonry support or prop under a structure. —**underpinnings** pl. **1** foundation or basis: *Research data formed the underpinnings of his theory.* **2** *Informal.* a person's legs.

un.der.play (un.dur.PLAY) v. **1** underact. **2** play down; treat as not very important.

un.der.priv.i.leged (un.dur.PRIV.uh.lejd, -PRIV.lejd) adj. not enjoying the rights and privileges of other people, as the poor and minority groups of a society.

un.der.rate (un.dur.RATE) v. **-rates, -rat.ed, -rat.ing** to rate too low; underestimate.

un.der.score (un.dur.SCORE) v. **-scores, -scored, -scor.ing 1** draw a line under something written or printed. **2** stress or emphasize: *to underscore a fact, message, need, point, problem, trend, the importance of something; It serves to underscore that the two countries have common interests.* **3** provide a musical soundtrack for a film.
—n. (UN.dur.score) **1** a line drawn under a word, passage, etc. **2** a musical soundtrack.

un.der.sea (un.dur.SEE) adj a. beneath the surface of the sea: *undersea cables, life, pipelines, warfare.* —**un.der.seas** adv.

un.der.sell (un.dur.SEL) v. **-sells, -sold, -sel.ling** sell an article at a lower price than a competitor: *We will not be undersold.*

un.der.shirt (UN.dur.shurt) n. a vest or similar undergarment worn under a shirt.

un.der.shorts (UN.dur.shorts) n.pl. shorts worn by men and boys as underwear.

un.der.shot (UN.dur.shot) adj. **1** with the lower jaw projecting beyond the upper jaw or teeth when the mouth is closed. **2** of a water wheel, turned by water flowing underneath.

un.der.side (UN.dur.side) n. the lower side or surface, as of a leaf.

un.der.signed (UN.dur.sined) n. **the undersigned** the person or persons whose signatures are at the bottom of the document or letter.

un.der.skirt (UN.dur.skurt) n. a skirt worn under a skirt.

un.der.staffed (UN.dur.staft) adj. having fewer people on the staff than required.

un.der.stand (un.dur.STAND) v. **-stands, -stood, -stand.ing 1** get the meaning or significance of something: *Some words are difficult to understand; what people understand by a certain word;* *He tried to* **make himself understood** *in French.* **2** have a sympathetic awareness of a person or thing: *Spouses try to understand each other; Do all parents understand children? I understand how you feel; Please understand* (= be sympathetic; also, get the meaning). **3** learn or infer: *I understand you are ill; When you say "Do as I say, or else," the rest is understood; I understood her to say she'd be late; That's what I was given to understand.* —**un.der.stand.a.ble** (-duh.bul) adj. —**un.der.stand.a.bly** (-duh.blee) adv.

understanding (un.dur.STAN.ding) n. **1** (power of) comprehension or knowledge: *a vocabulary within a child's understanding; our limited understanding of the universe.* **2** agreement: *Let's come to an understanding* (with each other); *to arrive at, reach an understanding with the others; a clear, secret, tacit, written understanding; Loans are made on the understanding that they will be paid back.* **3** harmony: *to promote understanding between nations; to develop a deeper mutual understanding of each other.* —**adj.** knowing and sympathetic: *an understanding heart, parent, wink; She's always understanding about her child's problems.*

un.der.state (un.dur.STATE) v. **-states, -stat.ed, -stat.ing** state something less than adequately or express in a very restrained manner.
—**un.der.state.ment** n.

un.der.stud.y (UN.dur.stud.ee) n. **-stud.ies** one ready to substitute for another, esp. in a theatrical role.
—v. **-stud.ies, -stud.ied, -stud.y.ing** act a role or part as an understudy to someone.

un.der.take (un.dur.TAKE) v. **-takes, -took, -tak.en, -tak.ing** take upon oneself a task or to do something.

un.der.tak.er (UN.dur.tay.kur) n. [a less favored term] funeral director.

undertaking (UN.dur.tay.king, un.dur.TAY.king) n. **1** a task or enterprise. **2** a guarantee.

under-the-counter adj a. *Informal.* of business dealings, secret or illicit: *under-the-counter payments, sales.* Also **under-the-table.**

un.der.things (UN.dur.things) n.pl. *Informal.* women's underwear.

un.der.tone (UN.dur.tone) n. **1** a subdued tone of voice or color: *to speak in an undertone.* **2** an underlying quality: *an undertone of melancholy.*

un.der.tow (UN.dur.toh) n. an undercurrent of water moving in the opposite direction of the surface current, as the backward flow of waves breaking on a beach.

un.der.wa.ter (UN.dur.WAW.tur) *adja. & adv.* under the surface of the water: *an underwater demolition team; underwater diving, photography, research.*

un.der.way (un.dur.WAY) *adv.* in progress: *Wedding preparations are already underway; The project will get underway in the new year;* also **under way.** —*adja.: an underway procedure, project; underway fueling, replenishment.*

un.der.wear (UN.dur.ware) *n.* clothes worn under other clothes, esp. next to the skin, as panties, briefs, shorts, etc.

un.der.whelm (un.dur.WHELM) *v. Informal.* fail to overwhelm.

un.der.world (UN.dur.wurld) *n.* **1** the lower world; Hades. **2** the part of society composed of criminals: *an underworld figure.*

un.der.write (UN.dur.rite) *v.* **-writes, -wrote, -writ.ten, -writ.ing** assume financial liability, as in insuring against loss or risk, in agreeing to buy up unsold stocks and bonds of a particular issue, to finance an enterprise or meet the expenses of educating someone, etc.: *to underwrite businesses, expenses, losses.* —**un.der.writ.er** *n.* —**underwriting** *n. & adja.*

un.dies (UN.deez) *n.pl. Informal.* underthings.

un.do (un.DOO, UN.doo) *v.* **-does, -did, -done, -do.ing 1** untie; also, unfasten and open something: *to undo a knot, string, parcel; to undo a button, scarf, shirt, sock, zipper.* **2** cancel the effect of what has been done: *to undo a crime, deal, policy, revolution, wrong; to undo the damage; to undo the past, one's work, what has been done.* **3** bring to ruin: *What undid the Soviet Union?* *n.*: *What led to his undoing? Vodka was his undoing* (= cause of his ruin).

un.done (un.DUN) *pt.* of UNDO: *The knot came undone.* —*adj.* **1** not done; unfinished: *a undone task; was left undone; It remains undone.* **2** ruined: *His life's efforts were undone in one moment by the disaster.*

un.doubt.ed (un.DOW.tid) *adj.* certain beyond a doubt: *a man of undoubted integrity.* —**un.doubt.ed.ly** *adv.*

un.dreamed (un.DREEMD, un.DREMD) or **un.dreamt** (-DREMT) *adj.* never even dreamed of or imagined; inconceivable or unimagined: *a discovery that was undreamed of a few years ago;* an **undreamed-of** *good fortune.*

un.dress (un.DRESS) *v.* take off one's clothes; disrobe: *She forgot to undress before jumping into the pool; to undress a child for bed.* —*n.* **1** ordinary or informal dress. **2** nakedness: *in various stages of undress; a state of undress.*

un.due (un.DUE) *adj.* improper or excessive: *to place an undue burden on taxpayers; to place undue emphasis on secondary issues; to use undue force; with undue haste; undue importance given to minor things; accused of exerting undue influence in his own favor; putting undue pressure on the nerves; to take undue risks.*

un.du.late (UN.juh.late) *v.* **-lates, -lat.ed, -lat.ing 1** move in waves: *a lake surface undulating in the breeze; a snake's undulating movements.* **2** have a wavy form; *adja.: the* **undulating** *dunes, wheat fields; the undulating* (= rolling) *prairie, terrain.*

un.du.ly (un.DUE.lee) *adv.* improperly or excessively.

un.dy.ing (un.DYE.ing) *adj.* deathless or eternal: *her undying beauty, devotion, fame, gratitude.*

un.earned (un.URND) *adj.* not earned: *unearned applause, praise, rewards; unearned income* (as from investments).

un.earth (un.URTH) *v.* **1** dig up from the earth: *to unearth bodies.* **2** bring to light, as from a hidden condition: *to unearth clues, fresh evidence, new facts, a plot.*

un.earth.ly (un.URTH.lee) *adj.* **1** not of this world; hence, strange or weird: *an unearthly sight, sound, voice.* **2** *Informal.* preposterous or absurd: *He rang our doorbell at an unearthly hour.*

un.ease (un.EEZ) *n.* lack of ease; disquiet: *a sense of unease.*

un.eas.y (un.EE.zee) *adj.* **-eas.i.er, -eas.i.est** marked by lack of ease in mind or body: *an uneasy laugh, peace, sleep; The child is uneasy in the presence of dogs.* —**un.eas.i.ness** *n.*

un.em.ployed (un.im.PLOID) *adj.* **1** without a job: *an unemployed worker.* **2** not in use: *unemployed hours, skills, time.* —**un.em.ploy.ment** (-PLOY.munt) *n.*

un.e.qual (un.EEK.wul) *adj.* **1** not equal in amount, value, etc. **2** not well matched or even. **3** not adequate to a task: *Her health proved unequal to the demands of the job.*

un.e.qualed (un.EEK.wuld) *adj.* unparalleled; unmatched. Also **un.e.qualled** *Cdn.*

un.e.quiv.o.cal (un.i.QUIV.uh.cul) *adj.* clear and unambiguous: *an unequivocal answer, position; her unequivocal support;* **un.e.quiv.o.cal.ly** *adv.*

un.err.ing (un.UR.ing, -ER.ing) *adj.*

making no errors: *her unerring accuracy, ear, eye, instinct, precision, sense of fairness; She's unerring in her aim;* **un.err.ing.ly** *adv.*

un.e.ven (un.EE.vun) *adj.* **1** not even, level, or uniform: *an uneven handwriting, performance, surface.* **2** unequal: *an uneven match.* **3** odd: *the uneven numbers 1, 3, 5, etc.* —**un.e.ven.ly** *adv.*

un.ex.cep.tion.a.ble (un.ik.SEP.shun.uh.bul) *adj.* that cannot be found fault with; quite admirable: *unexceptionable behavior; an unexceptionable record.* —**un.ex.cep.tion.a.bly** *adv.*

un.ex.cep.tion.al (un.ik.SEP.shun.ul) *adj.* not forming an exception; ordinary: *an unexceptional child who turns out to be a genius; an unexceptional happening, message, occurrence.*

un.ex.pect.ed (un.ik.SPEC.tid) *adj.* not expected; unforeseen; **un.ex.pect.ed.ly** *adv.*

un.fail.ing (un.FAY.ling) *adj.* never failing; never coming to an end: *her unfailing courtesy, generosity, patience.*

un.fair (un.FAIR) *adj.* not just or impartial: *an unfair advantage, burden; unfair to women.*

un.faith.ful (un.FAITH.ful) *adj.* **1** disloyal or adulterous: *an unfaithful spouse.* **2** not true or accurate: *The copy is unfaithful to the original.*

un.fa.mil.iar (un.fuh.MIL.yur) *adj.* **1** not well known: *He is unfamiliar to me.* **2** not acquainted: *I'm unfamiliar with his work; unfamiliar surroundings.*

un.feel.ing (un.FEE.ling) *adj.* **1** lacking feeling or sensation. **2** cruel or hardhearted. —**un.feel.ing.ly** *adv.*

un.flap.pa.ble (un.FLAP.uh.bul) *adj. Informal.* not easily excited; self-assured.

un.flinch.ing (un.FLINCH.ing) *adj.* resolute; fearless: *her unflinching devotion to the cause of women's rights.*

un.fold (un.FOLD) *v.* open up: *to unfold a newspaper; A bud unfolds into a flower; The plot gets thicker as the story unfolds* (= develops).

un.fore.seen (un.for.SEEN) *adj.* not expected: *unforeseen circumstances, events, trouble; when something unforeseen happens, in unforeseen ways.*

un.for.tu.nate (un.FOR.chuh.nit) *adj.* **1** not lucky: *an unfortunate victim.* **2** regrettable: *an unfortunate incident.* —*n.* one considered to have had bad luck, as an orphan, a homeless person, or social outcast. —**un.for.tu.nate.ly** *adv.*

un.found.ed (un.FOWN.did) *adj.* baseless; not factual: *an unfounded allegation.*

un.frock (un.FROCK) *v.* remove from the priesthood; deprive a cleric of his rank.

un.gain.ly (un.GAIN.lee) *adj.* awkward or clumsy: *an ungainly alliance, exit, gesture, phrase, shape.*

un.glued (un.GLOOD) *adj.* **come unglued** get upset or go out of control: *Her model husband came unglued.*

un.god.ly (un.GOD.lee) *adv.* **1** sinful or irreligious. **2** *Informal.* outrageous: *to get up at an ungodly hour in the morning.*

un.gov.ern.a.ble (un.GUV.ur.nuh.bul) *adj.* incapable of being restrained or directed; unruly: *an ungovernable temper.*

un.gra.cious (un.GRAY.shus) *adj.* not gracious; rude or unpleasant.

un.guard.ed (un.GAR.did) *adj.* **1** not protected: *an unguarded entrance.* **2** thoughtless or careless: *at an unguarded moment.*

un.guent (UNG.gwunt) *n.* an ointment or salve.

un.gu.late (UNG.gyuh.late, -lit) *adj.* hoofed. —*n.* a hoofed herbivorous mammal such as a horse, rhinoceros, deer, elephant, or pig.

un.hand (un.HAND) *v.* remove the hand from or let go of someone.

un.hap.py (un.HAP.ee) *adj.* **un.hap.pi.er, un.hap.pi.est 1** sorrowful: *an unhappy youth.* **2** unfortunate or inappropriate: *an unhappy choice of words.* —**un.hap.pi.ly** *adv.;* **un.hap.pi.ness** *n.*

un.health.y (un.HEL.thee, "th" as in "thin") *adj.* **-health.i.er, -i.est 1** not healthy or healthful: *an unhealthy child, climate, habit.* **2** morally harmful; unwholesome: *an unhealthy atmosphere, influence.*

un.heard (un.HURD) *adj.* **1** not heard: *Are unheard melodies sweeter? That's something unheard of; a hitherto unheard-of phenomenon.* **2** without being given a hearing: *He was condemned unheard.*

un.hinge (un.HINJ) *v.* **-hing.es, -hinged, -hing.ing 1** remove from the hinges, as a door. **2** dislodge. **3** unsettle; make unstable, esp. mentally: *Her parents' tragic death unhinged her.*

un.ho.ly (un.HOH.lee) *adj.* **-li.er, -li.est 1** not sacred; also, wicked: *an unholy alliance.* **2** *Informal.* outrageous; unreasonable: *Your room is an unholy mess.*

un.horse (un.HORSE) *v.* **-hors.es, -horsed, -hors.ing** unseat someone from a horse.

uni- *prefix.* single: *uniform, unilateral,*

unicameral, unicycle, univalve.

u.ni.corn (YOO.nuh.corn) *n.* a horselike mythical animal with a single horn on its forehead.

u.ni.cy.cle (YOO.nuh.sye.cul) *n.* a vehicle consisting of a wheel and pedals worked by a rider seated on top.

u.ni.form (YOO.nuh.form) *adj.* unvarying in form or character throughout the parts of a substance, series, etc.: *the uniform body temperature of a warm-blooded animal; It's impossible to have uniform* (= same) *laws, standards, taxes, etc. throughout the world.* —*n.* clothes distinctive of a particular group such as soldiers or nurses. —**u.ni.form.ly** *adv.* —**u.ni.form.i.ty** (-FOR.mi.tee) *n.*

u.ni.fy (YOO.nuh.fye) *v.* **-fies, -fied, -fy.ing** make or become one: *The two Germanys were unified in 1990; adj.: a **unified** though not yet united country; We stand unified against foreign domination; a unified district, system, theory, whole; a **unifying** force, principle, theme.* —**u.ni.fi.ca.tion** (-fuh.CAY.shun) *n.*

u.ni.lat.er.al (yoo.nuh.LAT.uh.rul) *adj.* involving one side only; one-sided; not bilateral or reciprocal: *unilateral disarmament; the unilateral repudiation of a bilateral agreement.* —**u.ni.lat.er.al.ly** *adv.*

u.ni.lin.gual (yoo.nuh.LING.gwul) *adj.* speaking only one language: *a unilingual civil servant who doesn't speak French; unilingual French signs.*

un.im.peach.a.ble (un.im.PEE.chuh.bul) *adj.* that cannot be doubted or questioned: *her unimpeachable authority; their unimpeachable behavior; his unimpeachable honesty.*

un.in.ter.est.ed (un.IN.tris.tid, -tuh.ris.tid) *adj.* having or showing no interest; indifferent: *an uninterested listener, onlooker; He's quite uninterested in chess.*

un.ion (YOON.yun) *n.* **1** a joining together or the state of being joined together, usu. permanently, as one unit: *matrimonial union; "Union is strength."* **2** a group or whole resulting from joining together: *to break up, dissolve, form a union; credit, labor, student unions; the U.S. President's annual State of **the Union*** (= the U.S.) *address to Congress; a **union catalog*** (= library catalog for several libraries). **3** a coupling or similar connecting device.

un.ion.ize (YOON.yuh.nize) *v.* **-iz.es, -ized, -iz.ing 1** form a group of workers into a labor union. **2** organize an establishment to conform to the rules of a labor union.

union jack *n.* a flag consisting of a union emblem, as the Union Jack of the U.K.

union shop *n.* an establishment in which only members or prospective members of a labor union are hired.

union station *n.* a station used by more than one railroad.

u.nique (yoo.NEEK) *adj.* **1** having no like or equal; one of a kind: *Each of us is unique; The landing on the moon is unique in human history.* **2** *Informal.* unusual or extraordinary: *This is absolutely unique; quite unique; a rather unique achievement.* —**u.nique.ly** *adv.*; **u.nique.ness** *n.*

u.ni.sex (YOO.nuh.sex) *adj. Informal.* designed to suit both sexes: *unisex apparel, clothing, styles; the unisex look (that is not distinguishable as to sex); unisex rates for auto insurance.*

u.ni.son (YOO.nuh.sun) *n.* agreement in pitch or sound: *They spoke **in unison*** (= the same words at the same time); *an action taken in unison with other friendly nations.*

u.nit (YOO.nit) *n.* **1** an individual thing or group with specific characteristics, forming part of a complex whole: *The family is the primary social unit; The dollar and pound are basic money units; metric units of weight; a military unit such as the battalion or platoon; to commit a unit to a combat mission; airborne, armored, crack, elite, motorized, tactical units; the pickup unit of a record player; an easy-to-assemble wall unit with shelves, cabinets, etc.; adj.:* unit decline, growth; the (single-)unit price of a product; unit sales, weight. **2** the least whole number; one.

U.ni.tar.i.an (yoo.nuh.TAIR.ee.un) *n. & adj.* (a member) of a Christian church that rejects the doctrine of the Trinity and believes that God is a single person.

u.ni.tar.y (YOO.nuh.tair.ee) *adj.* characterized by centralization; unified, not divided: *Britain has a unitary system of government, not a federal system; a **unitary state,** not a loose association of independent states.*

u.nite (yoo.NITE) *v.* **-nites, -nit.ed, -nit.ing** join together: *Let's unite; to unite two warring factions; Jack and Jill were united (in matrimony) by a justice of the peace; adj.: We stand **united** (against our foes); Germany is becoming more and more united; We are united in our aims; a united appeal, effort; to offer a united front to the enemy.*

u.nit.ize (YOO.nuh.tize) *v.* **-iz.es, -ized, -iz.ing** make into one unit; *adj.: a **unitized** body construction.*

unit pricing *n.* labeling of articles with their prices per kilogram, liter, or other standard unit to help shoppers compare prices.

u.ni.ty (YOO.ni.tee) *n.* **-ties 1** the oneness of purpose, spirit, etc. of a complex whole: *artistic unity; the unity of dramatic action or plot; the unity of design achieved by artistic arrangement of lines, shapes, and colors; to bring about national unity.* **2** harmony: *to act in unity; to find strength in unity; to live together in unity.* **3** a quantity or magnitude considered as equal to 1 in calculations.

u.ni.valve (YOO.nuh.valv) *n.* **1** a mollusk with a one-piece shell, as a snail. **2** such a shell.

u.ni.ver.sal (yoo.nuh.VUR.sul) *adj.* **1** relating to all human beings; hence, general: *Death is a universal phenomenon; universal adult suffrage; universal approval, conscription, literacy, popularity, rejoicing; a universal problem.* **2** applying to every individual or case within a class or category: *Type O blood is a* **universal donor** *because it is safe for any recipient; a* **universal joint** *or coupling that enables movement in any direction; Esperanto as a* **universal language***; a* **universal motor** *using A.C. or D.C. current.* —**u.ni.ver.sal.ly** (-suh.lee) *adv.* —**u.ni.ver.sal.i.ty** (YOO.nuh.vur.SAL.i.tee) *n.*

u.ni.ver.sal.ize (yoo.nuh.VUR.suh.lize) *v.* **-iz.es, -ized, -iz.ing** make universally applicable.

universal product code *n.* a small square of black bars and numbers representing price information imprinted on articles for scanning by automatic checkout systems; bar code.

u.ni.verse (YOO.nuh.verse) *n.* all reality; the cosmos; everything in space, esp. the world of human beings: *the origin of the universe; parallel and separate universes.*

u.ni.ver.si.ty (yoo.nuh.VUR.si.tee) *n.* **-ties** an educational institution of the highest level for instruction in many branches of study: *She went to university after finishing high school; He teaches at the university.*

un.just (un.JUST) *adj.* not just or right; **un.just.ly** *adv.*

un.kempt (un.KEMPT) *adj.* not well cared for; untidy: *his unkempt appearance, hair; an unkempt house, lawn.*

un.kind (un.KINED) *adj.* not kind, esp. harsh or inconsiderate. —**un.kind.ly** *adj. & adv.: an unkindly remark; It was not meant unkindly;* **un.kind.ness** *n.*

un.know.a.ble (un.NOH.uh.bul) *adj.* not knowable or understandable: *an unknowable danger, future, outcome.*

un.know.ing (un.NOH.ing) *adj.* not knowing; ignorant or unaware; **un.know.ing.ly** *adv.*

un.known (un.NOHN) *adj.* unfamiliar, strange, or unidentified: *an unknown character, force, territory; He's a total unknown; He's unknown to the public; It's virtually unknown; remains unknown; children of unknown fathers; the unknown side effects of a drug; for reasons unknown.* —*n.* a person or thing that is unknown: *As a tennis player, she is not an unknown; a backup team of also-rans and comparative unknowns; preparing for the unknown; the fear of the unknown; to venture into the unknown;* **the great unknown.**

unknown quantity *n.* a person who has not yet been tried out, as a new member of a team.

Unknown Soldier *n.* a soldier representing all soldiers killed in battle and honored by a tomb.

un.law.ful (un.LAW.ful) *adj.* not lawful: *a charge of unlawful assembly brought against three people bent on mischief; unlawful measures; unlawful (= immoral) pleasures.* —**un.law.ful.ly** *adv.*

un.lead.ed (un.LED.id) *adj.* of gasoline, containing no lead additive.

un.learn (un.LURN) *v.* get rid of or forget something learned, as ideas and habits: *The children had to unlearn many nonstandard expressions they picked up on the playground.*

un.learn.ed *adj.* **1** (un.LUR.nid) lacking learning; ignorant: *an unlearned reader, remark, scholar.* **2** (un.LURND) that has not been learned: *an unlearned habit, lesson, skill.*

un.leash (un.LEESH) *v.* to free from or as if from a leash: *to unleash an animal; He unleashed his fury on an innocent employee.*

un.less (un.LES) *conj.* except when; if not: *You don't get paid unless you work.*

un.let.tered (un.LET.urd) *adj.* not educated, esp. not able to read and write.

un.like (un.LIKE) *adj. & prep.* different from: *The twins are quite unlike; They're unlike each other.*

un.like.ly (un.LIKE.lee) *adj.* not likely: *an unlikely event; It's unlikely to have taken place; We searched in the most unlikely (= unpromising) places.* —**un.like.li.hood** *n.*

un.list.ed (un.LIS.tid) *adj.* **1** not publicly listed, as a telephone number: *The operator can't give out unlisted numbers; unlisted (= confidential) assets, entries.*

2 not listed on the stock exchange: *unlisted companies, securities, shares; the unlisted market.*

un.load (un.LODE) *v.* **1** take or remove a load from one's back, a vehicle, etc. or a charge from a firearm. **2** get rid or dispose of unwanted goods, company stocks, etc. **3** *Informal.* unburden feelings, troubles, etc.: *He unloads on his puppy when he has had a bad day at work.*

un.lock (un.LOK) *v.* **1** to open a door, etc. by releasing a lock. **2** release or disclose as if by unlocking: *to unlock nature's mysteries, one's heart, a flood of tears.*

un.luck.y (un.LUK.ee) *adj.* **-luck.i.er, -i.est** not lucky; unfortunate; ill-fated; **un.luck.i.ly** *adv.*

un.make (un.MAKE) *v.* **-makes, -made, -mak.ing** **1** ruin or destroy something made, as a reputation. **2** depose someone from a position, rank, etc.

un.man (un.MAN) **1** *v.* **-mans, -manned, -man.ning** deprive of manly courage; weaken the spirit of someone: *Al was seen slumped in a corner, unmanned by grief.* **2 unmanned** *adj.* not controlled physically by humans: *an unmanned rocket launch, space mission, spacecraft; an unmanned self-guided material-handling vehicle.* **—un.man.ly** *adj.*

un.mask (un.MASK) *v.* **1** remove a mask from someone's face. **2** disclose the true nature of a person or thing: *to unmask a crime, plot, problem, thief, the identity of certain genes; He was unmasked as a phony;* **adj.**: *his unmasked coldness; the recently unmasked budget deficit.*

un.mean.ing (un.MEE.ning) *adj.* **1** meaningless: *unmeaning vogue words.* **2** vacant or expressionless: *an unmeaning eye, look, visage.*

un.men.tion.a.ble (un.MEN.shun.uh.bul) **1** *adj.* not fit to be referred to in public. **2 unmentionables** *n.pl.* [jocular] underwear.

un.mit.i.gat.ed (un.MIT.uh.gay.tid) *adj*a. not lessened or modified; utter: *unmitigated evil, gall, horror; an unmitigated delight, disaster, failure, liar, scoundrel.*

un.nat.u.ral (un.NACH.ur.ul) *adj.* **1** not natural or normal: *It's unnatural for a mother not to love her children; an unnatural effect, look, position, voice; unnatural causes, environments, ways.* **2** morally depraved; perverse: *an unnatural act, offense; unnatural sex.*

un.nec.es.sar.y (un.NES.uh.sair.ee) *adj.* needless; **un.nec.es.sar.i.ly** *adv.*

un.nerve (un.NURV) *v.* **-nerves, -nerved, -nerv.ing** cause to lose one's self-control or power to act: *an anonymous phone call that unnerved the couple in the middle of the night;* **adj.**: *an unnerving habit, moment, subject.*

un.no.ticed (un.NOH.tist) *adj.* not noticed: *Many violations go or pass unnoticed because no one gets hurt.*

un.num.bered (un.NUM.burd) *adj.* innumerable; uncounted.

un.or.gan.ized (un.OR.guh.nized) *adj.* not organized into a system, organism, labor union, etc.

un.pack (un.PAK) *v.* **1** remove something from a package: *to unpack a gift.* **2** remove the contents of a trunk, suitcase, etc.: *to unpack after a trip.*

un.par.al.leled (un.PAIR.uh.leld) *adj.* that has no parallel or match: *an event unparalleled in human history.* Also **un.par.al.lelled** *Cdn.*

un.pleas.ant (un.PLEZ.unt) *adj.* not pleasant; disagreeable; **un.pleas.ant.ly** *adv.*; **un.pleas.ant.ness** *n.*

un.pop.u.lar (un.POP.yuh.lur) *adj.* not generally liked; **un.pop.u.lar.i.ty** (-LAIR.i.tee) *n.*

un.prec.e.dent.ed (un.PRES.uh.den.tid) *adj.* without precedent; unheard-of.

un.prin.ci.pled (un.PRIN.suh.puld) *adj.* lacking moral principles.

un.print.a.ble (un.PRIN.tuh.bul) *adj.* not fit to be printed, esp. because obscene.

un.pro.fes.sion.al (un.pruh.FESH.un.ul) *adj.* not ethical according to the standards of one's profession.

un.qual.i.fied (un.QUOL.uh.fide) *adj.* **1** not qualified: *an unqualified applicant.* **2** absolute or unrestricted: *unqualified admiration, praise, support; an unqualified privilege, success.*

un.ques.tion.a.ble (un.QUES.chuh.nuh.bul) *adj.* **1** not to be questioned: *her unquestionable authority; a candidate with unquestionable credentials.* **2** beyond doubt: *an unquestionable act of heroism; his unquestionable love; the unquestionable errors she committed.* **—un.ques.tion.a.bly** *adv.*: *It's unquestionably true.*

un.quote (un.QUOTE) [used to end a quotation] See QUOTE.

un.rav.el (un.RAV.ul) *v.* **-els, -eled, -el.ing** **1** separate the threads of something woven; hence, undo: *to unravel agreements, plots, secrets.* **2** come apart; collapse: *Communism began to unravel in the 1990s; The whole fabric of their empire unraveled; Their deals, plans, and plots began to unravel.* **3** solve or reveal: *to unravel a mystery.* Also

un.rav.elled, un.rav.el.ling Cdn.

un.read (un.RED) adj. **1** not read: *books left unread; the junk mail we throw out, read and unread.* **2** uneducated: *the unread public.*

un.real (un.REE.ul) adj. not real; imaginary or fanciful: *dreamlike and unreal; an unreal existence, quality, scene, world; unreal prices.*

un.rea.son.a.ble (un.REE.zuh.nuh.bul) adj. not reasonable; excessive or immoderate: *unreasonable delays, demands, hopes, searches and seizures;* **un.rea.son.a.bly** adv.

un.rea.son.ing (un.REE.zun.ing) adj. not guided by reason; illogical or irrational: *unreasoning cruelty to animals; an unreasoning passion for collectibles.*

un.re.lent.ing (un.ri.LEN.ting) adj. **1** not lessening in intensity: *unrelenting criticism, efforts, energy, hostility, pressure, propaganda; at an unrelenting pace; an unrelenting desire, drive, struggle.* **2** not showing pity or kindness: *unrelenting attacks, cruelty, wars.*

un.re.mit.ting (un.ri.MIT.ing) adj. not ceasing or slackening; incessant: *an unremitting pursuit of perfection; unremitting attacks, efforts, ordeals, pressure.* —**un.re.mit.ting.ly** adv.

un.re.quit.ed (un.ri.KWY.tid) adj. not returned or rewarded: *a story of unrequited love; unrequited efforts, passion.*

un.rest (un.REST) n. **1** a state of restlessness. **2** a social condition verging on revolt: *social unrest; to stir up labor unrest; unrest on campuses.*

un.roll (un.ROLE) v. **1** open something rolled up: *to unroll a carpet, map, scroll.* **2** become unrolled; be displayed: *Events, history, scenes unroll before our eyes.*

un.ruf.fled (un.RUF.uld) adj. not ruffled; hence, calm and serene: *to seem unruffled; an unruffled manner.*

un.rul.y (un.ROO.lee) adj. **-rul.i.er, -rul.i.est** disorderly or disobedient: *an unruly appetite, child, mob; unruly behavior, hair, politics.* —**un.rul.i.ness** n.

un.sad.dle (un.SAD.ul) v. **-sad.dles, -sad.dled, -sad.dling** take the saddle off a horse, etc.

un.sa.vor.y (un.SAY.vuh.ree) adj. **1** unpleasant to the taste or smell. **2** morally unpleasant: *an unsavory character, client, past, reputation, truth.* Also **un.sa.vour.y** Cdn.

un.scathed (un.SCATHED) adj. uninjured: *to come through, emerge, escape, remain, walk away unscathed; to leave someone unscathed.*

un.schooled (un.SCOOLD) adj. not educated or trained; hence, not disciplined.

un.scram.ble (un.SCRAM.bul) v. **-bles, -bled, -bling 1** restore to the original condition from being scrambled or confused: *You can't unscramble a scrambled egg; to unscramble a mess.* **2** decode: *to unscramble a message, picture, signal.*

un.screw (un.SCROO) v. detach or take off by turning or by removing screws: *to unscrew a light bulb, fixture; to unscrew a jar* (= jar's top).

un.scru.pu.lous (un.SCROOP.yuh.lus) adj. defying moral principles: *an unscrupulous moneylender.*

un.sea.son.a.ble (un.SEE.zun.uh.bul) adj. **1** not usual for the season: *Snow is unseasonable in the summer; unseasonable rains, weather.* **2** being at the wrong time: *to arrive at an unseasonable hour; unseasonable visits.* —**un.sea.son.a.bly** adv.

un.seat (un.SEET) v. displace from a seat; hence, remove from office.

un.seem.ly (un.SEEM.lee) adj. not seemly or becoming: *to leave in unseemly haste; an unseemly battle, caper, comment, competition, devotion, dispute, rejoicing.*

un.seen (un.SEEN) adj. not seen: *something heretofore unseen in these parts; unseen consequences; the world of the unseen* (= spirits).

un.set.tle (un.SET.ul) v. **-set.tles, -set.tled, -set.tling 1** move from a settled position. **2** make or become unstable or disturbed; adj.: *an unsettling bit of news; a most unsettling development, effect, experience, feeling, sight, turn of events.* —**un.set.tled** adj. not settled: *unsettled issues, weather conditions; unsettled* (= unpaid) *debts; unsettled* (= uninhabited) *territory.*

un.sheathe (un.SHEETH, "TH" as in "the") v. **-sheathes, -sheathed, -sheath.ing** draw a sword, etc. from a sheath or as from a sheath.

un.sight.ly (un.SITE.lee) adj. not pleasing to the eye; ugly.

un.skilled (un.SKILD) adj. **1** of persons, not skilled or trained in a line of work: *an unskilled laborer, worker.* **2** of work, not requiring skill: *unskilled jobs, labor, occupations, work.*

un.skill.ful (un.SKIL.ful) adj. having no skill or training; awkward or clumsy: *an unskillful manner.* Also **un.skil.ful** Cdn.

un.snarl (un.SNARL) v. untangle.

un.sound (un.SOWND) adj. not sound: *an unsound argument, structure, undertaking; He's of unsound mind.*

un.spar.ing (un.SPAIR.ing) *adj.* **1** not sparing; liberal: *Our boss is unsparing in his praise when we do a good job.* **2** merciless or severe *in* criticism, etc.: *unsparing attacks.*

un.speak.a.ble (un.SPEE.kuh.bul) *adj.* that cannot be expressed or described: *her unspeakable joy; unspeakable crimes, evil, horrors.* —**un.speak.a.bly** *adv.*

un.sta.ble (un.STAY.bul) *adj.* not stable: *an unstable government, mind, person; an unstable chemical compound, equilibrium, nuclear particle.*

un.stead.y (un.STED.ee) *adj.* not steady or firm: *an unsteady hand, pulse, voice; unsteady market conditions, winds.*

un.stop (un.STOP) *v.* **-stops, -stopped, -stop.ping 1** remove the stopper from a bottle, etc. **2** free a pipe, etc. of an obstruction.

un.strung (un.STRUNG) *adj.* **1** in a nervous condition. **2** with the strings of a guitar, rocket, etc. loosened or removed.

un.stuck (un.STUCK) *adj.p.* loosened or unfastened: *The stamps came unstuck before the letter was mailed; how to get unstuck when you are in a jam; The whole plan* **came unstuck** (*Informal for* was ruined) *when a key player suddenly died.*

un.stud.ied (un.STUD.eed) *adj.* of behavior, not artificial; natural and spontaneous: *her unstudied modesty.*

un.sung (un.SUNG) *adj.* not celebrated or praised: *an unsung hero.*

un.tan.gle (un.TANG.gul) *v.* **-gles, -gled, -gling** free from a snarled or entangled condition; disentangle: *to untangle a mess; to untangle knots, mixups.*

un.taught (un.TAWT) *adj.* **1** not educated: *an untaught generation.* **2** naturally acquired or learned: *an untaught skill; untaught wisdom.*

un.think.a.ble (un.THINK.uh.bul) *adj.* that cannot be thought of as possible; unimaginable; inconceivable: *It's unthinkable that he would say such a thing.*

un.think.ing (un.THINK.ing) *adj.* thoughtless or heedless: *He said it in one of those unthinking moments; an unthinking remark.*

un.tie (un.TYE) *v.* **-ties, -tied, -ty.ing** or **-tie.ing** to free something tied, knotted, etc. or as from a restraint; unfasten; disentangle.

un.til (un.TIL) *prep. & conj.* up to the time of or when; till: *Please wait until noon; Don't go until you've eaten.*

un.time.ly (un.TIME.lee) *adj.* **1** premature: *an untimely death.* **2** inopportune: *an untimely outburst.*

un.to (UN.too) *prep.* [old use] to or till: *what you do unto others; She was faithful unto death.*

un.told (un.TOLD) **1** *adja.* too many or too much: *untold thousands of people; a woman of untold millions (of dollars); untold cruelty, damage, misery, suffering, wealth.* **2** *adj.* not told or revealed: *The story remains untold; an untold tale of intrigue.*

un.touch.a.ble (un.TUCH.uh.bul) *adj.* that cannot or must not be touched. —*n.* a member of the lowest caste of Hindus, formerly shunned by Brahmins; outcast.

un.to.ward (un.TOH.urd, -TORD) *adj.* **1** unexpected and unfavorable: *untoward consequences, delays, effects, events, happenings; Nothing untoward happened.* **2** unseemly: *in an untoward manner; untoward remarks, thoughts.*

un.truth *n.* **1** falsity; lack of truth. **2** a falsehood. —**un.truth.ful** *adj.*

un.tu.tored (un.TUE.turd) *adj.* untaught; not educated: *an untutored child; He came to the city untutored in the ways of the world.*

un.used *adj.* **1** (un.YOOZD) not used: *an unused cup.* **2** (un.YOOST) unaccustomed: *She's unused to our cold climate.*

un.u.su.al (un.YOO.zhoo.ul) *adj.* not usual; rare; **un.u.su.al.ly** *adv.*

un.var.nished (un.VAR.nisht) *adja.* **1** not varnished. **2** plain and simple: *an unvarnished account; the unvarnished truth.*

un.veil (un.VAIL) *v.* **1** reveal or display for the first time: *to unveil a plan, new product line, a program, proposal, strategy;* *n.*: *the* **unveiling** *of a statue; She was at the unveiling.* **2** remove one's veil.

un.war.y (un.WAIR.ee) *adj.* not watchful: *a scheme designed to trap the unwary consumer, public, traveler.*

un.well (un.WEL) *adj.* sick or ill.

un.whole.some (un.HOLE.sum) *adj.* **1** harmful to body, mind, or morals: *an unwholesome diet, environment, occupation.* **2** not of sound health.

un.wield.y (un.WEEL.dee) *adj.* hard to handle or deal with because of large size, weight, shape, etc.: *an unwieldy collection, process, proposal, system, task.*

un.will.ing (un.WIL.ing) *adj.* not willing; reluctant: *She was unwilling to take part in it; an unwilling partner in the crime.* —**un.will.ing.ly** *adv.*; **un.will.ing.ness** *n.*

un.wind (un.WINED) *v.* **-winds, -wound, -wind.ing 1** uncoil something wound up, as a ball or spool. **2** untangle. **3** relax: *Weekends are for unwind-*

ing; Music helps her unwind after work.

un.wise (un.WIZE) *adj.* not wise; imprudent.

un.wit.ting (un.WIT.ing) *adj.* **1** unaware: *an unwitting accomplice, agent, carrier of stolen goods; an unwitting dupe, participant in a crime, purchaser of contraband, victim.* **2** unintentional: *an unwitting revelation; with their unwitting help.* —**un.wit.ting.ly** *adv.*

un.wont.ed (un.WONE.tid, -WAWN.tid) *adj.* not usual or habitual: *He left the party in unwonted haste.*

un.wor.thy (un.WUR.thee, "th" as in "the") *adj.* **-thi.er, -thi.est** not worthy: *unworthy* (= shameful) *conduct; conduct unworthy of* (= unbecoming) *a hero; He was deemed unworthy* (= undeserving) *of an award.* —**un.wor.thi.ness** *n.*

un.wrap (un.RAP) *v.* **-wraps, -wrapped, -wrap.ping** take off the wrapping: *to unwrap gifts, ideas, plans, secrets;* ***adj.:*** *an unwrapped loaf of bread, package, roll of tissue.*

un.writ.ten (un.RIT.un) *adj.* **1** not written down: *The letter remained unwritten.* **2** traditional: *Britain's unwritten constitution; the unwritten common law; unwritten rules of conduct.*

un.zip (un.ZIP) *v.* **-zips, -zipped, -zip.ping** open using a zipper.

up *adv.* **1** to a higher position, degree, etc.; not down: *She went up to the top floor; Prices go up; Please speak up* (= louder). **2** to a vertical or active position: *Stand up on your feet; He stirs up trouble; We get up in the morning.* **3** in a steady state without going back or down: *to keep up a practice; That's good, keep it up! He runs so fast it's hard to keep up with* (= stay abreast of) *him.* **4** to the point of completeness or finality: *to tie up a parcel; She ate it all up.* **5** in games, ahead or leading: *They were up by 3 runs going into the eighth inning.* **6** at bat in baseball: *a score of 10 up* (= apiece). —**up against** *Informal.* faced with: *when you're up against a difficulty, problem; up against heavy odds.* —**up there** in Heaven. —**up to 1** till a limit of time or extension: *up to now; He charges up to $100 an hour; I agree with you up to a point* (= to a certain degree); *I've had it up to here* (= up to my neck; as much as I can take). **2** about or planning to do something: *What are you up to?* **3** at the disposition of someone: *The choice is up to you.* —**prep.** to a higher position, degree, etc.: *to go up the stairs; She rowed her boat up the river; He drove up the street to where we were waiting.*

—*adj.* **1** in a raised or higher position: *Prices are up again; Take the up elevator; What's up* (= happening)? **2** in a steady state; abreast: *Are you up on the latest developments?* **3** ended: *Your time is up.* —**up and around** or **about** moving around: *She is up and around after her recent illness.* —**up and doing** busy and active: *He's up and doing by 5 a.m. every day.* —**up for** offered for: *The house is up for sale; My used car is up for bids; The position is up for grabs.*

—*n.* an upward movement or condition: *the ups and downs of fortune, of his mood; Sales of the new book are on the up and up* (= rising).

—*v.* **ups, upped, up.ping** raise: *to up prices; He ups and* (*Informal for* gets up and) *walks out of the party.*

up-and-coming *adj.* likely to succeed; promising: *one of our up-and-coming politicians.*

up.beat *n.* **1** in music, an unaccented beat or the upward gesture of the conductor's hand indicating it. **2** an upswing or upturn. —*adj.* cheerful or optimistic: *in an upbeat mood; upbeat news; The convention ended on an upbeat note.*

up.braid (up.BRAID) *v.* to reprimand or censure, esp. with justification.

up.bring.ing (up.BRING.ing) *n.* the bringing up or raising of a child.

up.chuck *n. & v. Informal.* vomit.

up.com.ing (UP.cum.ing) *adj.* forthcoming; coming soon: *the upcoming changes, conferences, elections, games, projects; the upcoming decade, Olympics, trial, winter; in the upcoming year; upcoming computer innovations; in an upcoming issue of the magazine.*

up.coun.try (UP.cun.tree) *n., adj. & adv.* of, in, or toward the interior, esp. isolated part of a country or region: *up-country settlers.*

up.date (up.DATE) *v.* **-dates, -dat.ed, -dat.ing** bring a book, person, etc. up to date. —*n.* (UP.date) an updating or something that updates, as a piece of information: *Give me an update on what has been going on.*

up.end (up.END) *v.* set or stand on end; overturn.

up.front *adj. Informal.* **1** forthright or direct: *She was very upfront with me;* ***adv.:*** *We'll negotiate upfront.* **2** as an advance or front money: *an upfront fee, payment; upfront costs;* ***adv.:*** *Better place your orders upfront* (= in advance) *if you want early delivery.*

up.grade *n.* **1** upward slope. **2** a raising or improvement: *a systems upgrade.*

—*v.* (up.GRADE) **-grades, -grad.ed, -grad.ing** raise to a higher grade or rating: *to upgrade jobs, employees, products; to upgrade one's insurance coverage; I had the RAM upgraded to 12 MB;* **adj.**: *an upgraded service, version, sound system, technology.*

up.growth *n.* upward growth or development.

up.heav.al (up.HEE.vul) *n.* **1** a heaving up, as of the earth's crust by an earthquake. **2** a sudden or violent change: *social upheavals.*

up.hill *adj.* **1** going up, as on a hill: *an uphill climb, drive, walk;* **adv.** (UP.HILL): *We drove uphill.* **2** tiring or laborious: *an uphill battle, fight, task.*

up.hold (up.HOLD) *v.* **-holds, -held, -hold.ing 1** give moral support to a person, cause, etc. **2** maintain: *to uphold a great principle, tradition.* **3** confirm by higher authority: *The judgment was upheld on appeal.*

up.hol.ster (up.HOLE.stur) *v.* furnish a chair, seat, etc. with upholstery. —**up.hol.ster.er** *n.*

up.hol.ster.y (up.HOLE.stuh.ree) *n.* **-ster.ies** materials such as fabrics, springs, and padding used to make soft coverings for furniture.

up.keep *n.* **1** the keeping up or maintaining of a house, garden, dependents, etc. **2** the cost or the state of such maintenance.

up.land (UP.lund, -land) *adja.* of the higher land of a region, above valleys or plains: *upland areas; Finland's upland district; upland meadows; an upland species;* ***n.pl.*** *the barren uplands of Spain.*

up.lift *n.* a lifting up, esp. a movement for social, moral, or spiritual improvement.

up.load *v.* to transfer data or programs from a smaller to a larger computer.

up.man.ship (UP.mun.ship) same as ONE-UPMANSHIP.

up.mar.ket (UP.mar.kit) *adj. & adv.* catering to the more wealthy consumer: *upmarket demands, fabrics, storefronts, values; The new brand is slightly upmarket; The old store is expanding and moving upmarket.*

up.most same as UPPERMOST.

up.on (uh.PON) *prep.* on: *once upon a time* (= long ago); *mile upon mile* (= many miles) *of shops; The summer vacation is almost upon* (= close to) *us.*

up.per (UP.ur) *adja.* **1** higher in position, rank, etc.: *the upper jaw, lip; the upper classes of society; Physicians are in the upper-income bracket; the upper Nile* (= the region from where it flows

down); **Upper Canada** (= Ontario, as the area around the upper St. Lawrence River). **2** northern: *Buffalo is in upper New York State; the upper Great Lakes region.* **3** later: *the Upper Cambrian Period.* —*n.* **1** the part of a shoe or boot above the sole. **2** *Informal.* a stimulant drug such as caffeine, cocaine, or an amphetamine.

up.per.case (UP.ur.case) *n.* capital letters, not lower case: *The note was all in uppercase;* **adj.**: *Use an uppercase C for China the country.* —*v.* **-cas.es, -cased, -cas.ing** put in uppercase: *Uppercase the initials of all names.* Also **uppercase.**

up.per.class.man (UP.ur.class.mun) *n.* **-men** a junior or senior in a high school or college.

upper crust *n.* the highest group of the upper classes of society.

up.per.cut (UP.ur.cut) *n.* in boxing, a short, swinging blow directed upward from the waist level.

upper hand *n.* a position of advantage; mastery: *to gain the upper hand over the competition.*

upper house *n.* in a bicameral legislature, the senate.

up.per.most (UP.ur.most) *adj.* first or highest in place or position: *the question that is uppermost in our minds today; the earth's uppermost atmosphere; Lay it flat with the right side uppermost; the uppermost branches, clouds, layer, level, octave, rungs, shelves.*

up.pi.ty (UP.i.tee) *adj. Informal.* haughty or arrogant: *to be, become, get uppity.* Also **up.pish.**

up.raise (up.RAIZ) *v.* **-rais.es, -raised, -rais.ing** lift up; elevate.

up.rear (up.REER) *v.* **1** lift up or raise. **2** rise or be lifted up.

up.right *adj.* **1** vertically erect: *in an upright position; an upright bearing, column, posture, stance; an upright vacuum, not a hand-held or canister vacuum; upright and coffin freezers.* **2** morally straight: *a just and upright man; an upright operation.* —*n.* **1** something that is upright: *uprights, canisters, hand-helds, and central vacuums; railings with widely spaced uprights.* **2** an upright or vertical position. —*adv.* in an upright position: *to remain, sit, stand, stay, walk upright.* —**up.right.ness** *n.*

upright piano *n.* the popular type of piano, with strings set up vertically.

up.ris.ing (UP.rye.zing) *n.* a small rebellion or outbreak against a government: *an armed uprising that was put down with an iron hand.*

up.riv.er (UP.riv.ur) *adj. & adv.* toward the source of a river.

up.roar *n.* a noisy disturbance or commotion: *The new taxes caused an uproar; The whole nation was in an uproar till the measures were withdrawn.*

up.roar.i.ous (up.ROR.ee.us) *adj.* noisy or boisterous: *uproarious laughter; an uproarious welcome; an uproarious* (= extremely funny) *joke.* —**up.roar.i.ous.ly** *adv.*

up.root (up.ROOT) *v.* remove by or as if by pulling up by the roots: *people uprooted from their ancestral homes.*

up.rush *n.* an upward rush of a liquid or gas.

up.scale *adj. & adv.* having to do with the upper end of the social scale; wealthy or superior: *an upscale audience, clientele; upscale customers, designers, fashions, homes, looks, stores; the upscale market; Our offerings are becoming more upscale; Even utility vehicles are going upscale.*

up.set (up.SET) *v.* **-sets, -set, -set.ting** topple or unsettle from a stable condition: *A flat-bottomed boat does not upset easily; to upset a vase, the balance, equilibrium, a relationship; to upset nerves, plans, schedules; to upset the favored candidate (in an election); The Jays upset* (= defeated) *Texas 10 to 9.*
—*adj.* disturbed or worried: *to get upset; He's a bit upset about or over the small raise he received; He's upset to hear that he can't have the job; emotionally upset; medication to settle an upset stomach.*
—*n.* (UP.set) an upsetting, an unexpected defeat, or a disturbance: *emotional upsets; a stomach upset; The Jays scored an upset over Texas; She pulled off an upset to become the first woman premier of the province.*

up.shift *v.* shift an automobile to a higher gear.

up.shot *n.* outcome or general effect: *the upshot of the matter.*

up.side *n.* the upper side. —**upside down** inverted: *to hang upside down like a bat; The child turned the house upside down* (= into confusion or disorder). —**upside-down** *adj.* topsy-turvy: *an upside-down image, roller coaster, world; An upside-down cake is made on a fruit layer and then turned upside down so that the fruit is on top.*

up.stage *adj. & adv.* at or toward the rear of a stage: *an upstage entrance; to go upstage.* —*v.* **1** draw attention to oneself to the disadvantage of someone else: *Don't try to upstage the hero of the play.* **2** *Informal.* steal the show from someone; snub.

up.stairs *n.* an upper floor: *The upstairs is being renovated.* —*adj.* on or to the upper floor: *She is upstairs; an upstairs window;* *adv.*: *He went upstairs; Instead of being fired, the president was* **kicked upstairs** (*Informal* for promoted) *to chairman of the board.*

up.stand.ing (up.STAND.ing) *adja.* upright in carriage or character: *an upstanding citizen, youth; upstanding members of society.*

up.start *n.* one who has recently acquired wealth or position, hence is haughty or self-assertive.

up.state *adj.* in the more northern part of a state, away from its principal city: *Buffalo is in upstate New York; She was upstate, enjoying a holiday;* **adv.**: *She didn't flee upstate to avoid arrest;* **n.**: *We are from upstate.*

up.stream *adj. & adv.* **1** against the current of a stream: *It's harder to swim upstream than downstream; upstream swimming.* **2** from where the stream is flowing: *The wolf was drinking upstream from the lamb; factories located upstream of population centers; only a mile upstream; no farther upstream than a mile; upstream polluters; Exploration is the upstream* (= source or beginning) *part of the oil business.*

up.stroke *n.* an upward stroke of a pen, brush, etc.

up.surge (up.SURJ) *n.* a sudden surging up or increase.

up.swing *n.* **1** an upward swinging movement, as of a golf club. **2** upward trend: *Bowling is on the upswing as more professionals participate.*

up.take *n.* a taking up, as by the mind; absorption: *Your level of oxygen uptake is an indicator of fitness; She's quick, not slow,* **on the uptake** (*Informal* for in understanding).

up.tick *n.* rise or increase: *an uptick in the economy; a 5% uptick in sales; a retail uptick.*

up.tight (up.TITE) *adj. Informal.* tense or nervous *about* something.
—**up.tight.ness** *n.*

up-to-date *adj.* [See DATE for "up to date"] **1** extending to the present time; latest: *a new and up-to-date database; up-to-date editions, information, sources.* **2** modern: *an up-to-date fashion, method, style.* —**up-to-date.ness** *n.*

up.town *n.* the part of a city or town away from downtown: *They are from uptown;* **adj.**: *an uptown address, neighborhood, store;* **adv.**: *Let's move a few blocks uptown; We're going uptown.*

up.turn *n.* an upward turn or improving trend, as after a recession: *a sharp upturn in the economy; to survive the upturns and downturns in business.*
—*v.* turn up or over; overturn.
—*adj.* **1** turned over or overturned: *an upturned chair, hand, hourglass.* **2** curved upward: *upturned bicycle handlebars; his upturned nose.*

up.ward (UP.wurd) *adv.* in or toward a higher place, position, etc.; up: *The balloons should go upward when they are released;* *adj.*: *students who are 18 years and upward* (= older); *aged* **upward** *of* (= more than) *17; upward job mobility of employees; the* **upward mobility** *of the middle class (moving to higher social levels).* Also **up.wards** *adv.*
—**up.ward.ly** *adv.*

up.wind *adj. & adv.* into or against the wind; to windward.

u.ra.cil (YOOR.uh.sil) *n.* the RNA base replacing the thymine of DNA in protein synthesis.

U.rals (YOOR.uls) *n.pl.* the mountain range in N. Russia separating Asia and Europe. —**U.ral.ic** (yoo.RAL.ic) *adj.*

u.ra.ni.um (yoo.RAY.nee.um) *n.* a radioactive element that is the chief source of atomic energy.

ur.ban (UR.bun) *adj.* having to do with a city or cities: *our urban and rural populations.*

ur.bane (ur.BANE) *adj.* refined or smoothly polite in manner.
—**ur.ban.i.ty** (ur.BAN.i.tee) *n.*

urban guerrilla *n.* a city-based terrorist.

urban renewal *n.* improvement of rundown city areas by demolition and rebuilding.

urban sprawl *n.* city congestion spreading into the suburbs.

ur.ban.ize (UR.buh.nize) *v.* **-iz.es, -ized, -iz.ing** make or become urban or citylike. —**ur.ban.i.za.tion** (-nuh.ZAY.shun, -nye-) *n.*

ur.chin (UR.chin) *n.* a youngster considered as pert or mischievous: *street urchins.*

Ur.du (UR.doo) *n.* the Indo-European official language of Pakistan, widely used also in N. India.

u.re.a (yoo.REE.uh) *n.* an organic nitrogen compound that is the chief constituent of urine.

u.re.mi.a (yoo.REE.mee.uh) *n.* poisoning of the blood by body wastes because of defective functioning of the kidneys.

u.re.ter (yoo.REE.tur) *n.* the tube carrying urine from the kidney into the bladder.

u.re.thane (YOOR.uh.thane, "th" as in "thin") *n.* a crystalline powder used as a solvent in plastics and paints.

u.re.thra (yoo.REE.thruh) *n.* the canal through which urine is expelled from the bladder, used also for discharge of semen in males. —**u.re.thral** *adj.*

u.re.thri.tis (yoo.ree.THRY.tis) *n.* inflammation of the urethra.

urge (URJ) *v.* **urg.es, urged, urg.ing** **1** force or drive forward; spur: *He urged his horses forward with the whip.* **2** ask, plead, or argue earnestly for something: *She was strongly urged to buy now and pay later; a lawyer urging a claim in court; Sterner measures were urged;* *n.*: *He did it at the* **urging** *of friends.* —*n.* an impulse or inner drive seeking satisfaction: *to control, feel, satisfy, stifle an urge; irresistible, natural, sudden urges; an uncontrollable urge to laugh.*

ur.gent (UR.junt) *adj.* requiring immediate attention: *an urgent matter, message, request; She's in urgent need of help; to give urgent attention to an appeal; an urgent* (= insistent) *petitioner;* **ur.gent.ly** *adv.* —**ur.gen.cy** *n.*

u.ric acid (YOOR.ic-) *n.* acid found in blood and urine.

u.ri.nal (YOOR.uh.nul) *n.* **1** a place for urinating. **2** a plumbing fixture that is a urine receptacle.

u.ri.nal.y.sis (yoor.uh.NAL.uh.sis) *n.* examination of the urine by microscope or chemical tests.

u.ri.nar.y (YOOR.uh.nair.ee) *adj.* having to do with urine, its secretion into the bladder, or its discharge: *the urinary bladder, system, tract.*

u.ri.nate (YOOR.uh.nate) *v.* **-nates, -nat.ed, -nat.ing** discharge urine from the body. —**u.ri.na.tion** (-NAY.shun) *n.*

u.rine (YOOR.in) *n.* the yellowish liquid containing waste products that is expelled from the body.

urn *n.* **1** a footed vase or one with a pedestal, used to hold the ashes of the dead, as in ancient Rome: *burial urns.* **2** a closed vessel with a spigot for making tea or coffee.

u.rol.o.gy (yoo.ROL.uh.jee) *n.* the branch of medicine concerned with the urinary system and male genitals. —**u.rol.o.gist** *n.*

ur.sine (UR.sine) *adj.* of or like a bear: *a large, indeed, ursine appetite.*

ur.ti.car.i.a (ur.tuh.CAIR.ee.uh) same as HIVES.

U.ru.guay.an (yoor.ug.WAY.un,

-WYE.un) *n. & adj.* (a person) of or from **Uruguay,** a country of S.E. South America.
us objective case of WE.
us.a.ble (YOO.zuh.bul) *adj.* fit for use: *We would like the data in usable form; older but still usable tools; usable land; Our library is readily accessible and usable by disabled people.* —**us.a.bil.i.ty** (-BIL.i.tee) *n.* Also **use.a.ble** (-zuh.bul), **use.a.bil.i.ty.**
us.age (YOO.sij, -zij) *n.* **1** the act or manner of using; treatment: *heavy, high, limited, wide usage; damaged by rough usage; computer usage among women; alcohol, data, fuel, water usage; to reduce, restrict usage;* **adj.**: *usage charges, discounts, needs.* **2** long-established practice: *customs sanctified by usage; Standard English usage is established by good writers and speakers; dialectal usages.*
use (YOOZ) *v.* **us.es, used, us.ing** put into action or service; employ for a purpose: *We use an umbrella when it rains; What's this used for? He uses* (= consumes) *too much sugar; I could use* (*Informal for* would benefit by) *some help; We'd* **used up** *all our strength by the time we reached the top.* See also USED. —*n.* (YOOSE) **1** a using or being used: *the uses of an automobile; constant, daily, extensive, external, fair, good, internal, official, practical, universal, wide use; words in common use; He* **makes full use** *of his time; when oxygen is* **in use** (= being used); *Obsolete words are those that have gone* **out of use;** *Computers are being* **put to use** (= employed) *in all sorts of ways.* **2** purpose, benefit, or advantage of using; usefulness: *It's* **no use** *crying over spilled milk; What's the* **use** *of crying? There's* **no use in** *crying; We* **have no use for** (= dislike) *crybabies.* **3** the ability to use: *He lost the use of both eyes in an accident; He gets the use of* (= permission to use) *her car on weekends.* **4** customary practice; habit; usage: *as was the use in their family; in Roman Catholic use.* —**use.a.ble, use.a.bil.i.ty** See USABLE.
used 1 (YOOST) *adjp.*: *He's used* (= accustomed) *to walking to school; One has to* **get used to** *it; He used to drive* (= formerly drove) *to school.* **2** (YOOZD) *adja.*: *a used* (= secondhand) *car; a used* (= not fresh) *cup, napkin, plate.*
use.ful (YOOS.ful) *adj.* serviceable; helpful. —**use.ful.ly** *adv.*; **use.ful.ness** *n.* —**use.less** (-lis) *adj.*; **use.less.ly** *adv.*; **use.less.ness** *n.*
us.er (YOO.zur) *n.* one that uses something: *computer, drug, library users;*

heavy users; **adj.**: *a user account, aid, fee, group, guide, handbook, interface, manual.*
user-friendly *adj.* simple and easy to use for the average person: *a user-friendly computer, dictionary, program; to make the airport more user-friendly.*
user (or **user's**) **group** *n.* a club for the exchange of information and services among a group of computer users.
user interface *n.* an icon, a language, menu, mouse, touch screen, window, or similar hardware or software that helps a user interact with a computer: *a command-driven user interface; graphical and natural-language user interfaces.*
ush.er (USH.ur) *n.* an official who escorts people to their seats in a church, theater, etc. —*v.* go before someone showing the way; conduct or escort: *to usher a patron to her seat; celebrations to* **usher in** (= start) *the New Year.*
ush.er.ette (ush.uh.RET) *n.* a female usher.
u.su.al (YOO.zhoo.ul) *adj.* commonly seen or experienced; ordinary; customary: *Nine to five are the usual office hours; She is her usual cheerful self; He appeared cheerful* **as usual** (= in the usual manner). —**u.su.al.ly** *adv.*
u.su.rer (YOO.zhur.ur) *n.* one who practices usury.
u.su.ri.ous (yoo.ZHOOR.ee.us) *adj.* excessive in regard to rate of interest: *He lends money at usurious interest rates.*
u.surp (yoo.SURP, -ZURP) *v.* seize and hold a throne, power, authority, etc. by force or without right. —**u.surp.er** *n.* —**u.sur.pa.tion** (-zur.PAY.shun, -sur.PAY.shun) *n.*
u.su.ry (YOO.zhuh.ree) *n.* **1** an excessive rate of interest. **2** the lending of money at such a rate.
u.ten.sil (yoo.TEN.sil) *n.* an implement or container for domestic use, usu. worked by hand: *cooking and eating utensils; kitchen utensils such as pots and pans; writing utensils.*
u.ter.ine (YOO.tuh.rin, -rine) *adj.* having to do with the uterus: *uterine cancer, contractions, fibroids, tumors; the uterine cavity, lining, wall.*
u.ter.us (YOO.tuh.rus) *n., pl.* **-ter.i** (-tuh.rye) or **-ter.us.es** the hollow, muscular organ in the pelvis of female mammals in which the young are carried till birth; womb.
u.til.i.tar.i.an (yoo.TIL.uh.TAIR.ee.un) *adj.* having to do with usefulness rather than beauty, truth, etc.: *a utilitarian approach, concern, feature, look, style, view; at the utilitarian level.*

u.til.i.tar.i.an.ism (yoo.TIL.uh.TAIR.ee.uh.niz.um) *n.* a philosophy that stresses the greatest happiness of the greatest number as the criterion of the rightness of actions.

u.til.i.ty (yoo.TIL.i.tee) *n.* **-ties 1** a service that is essential to the public, as transportation, communications, electricity, water, gas, garbage disposal, etc.: *a public utility such as sewers; Databases are information utilities.* **2** a company that provides such a service, as a hydroelectric or telephone company; also **public utility**. **3** usu. **utilities** *pl.* company shares issued by a public utility: *a utility currently yielding 10%.* **4** usefulness: *something of obvious utility for the public.* —*adj.* **1** having to do with utility companies: *utility bills, rates, stocks; the utility market.* **2** having various uses: *a utility knife, pole, table, vehicle; a* **utility airport** *(for small nonjet aircraft);* **utility beef** *(of the lowest grade); a* **utility player** *(who can substitute for absent players in various positions); a* **utility program** *for a computer operation such as copying, deleting, sorting, or diagnostics; a* **utility room** *(for keeping various equipment).*

u.ti.lize (YOO.tul.ize) *v.* **-iz.es, -ized, -iz.ing** put to practical or profitable use: *how to utilize spare time, solar energy; Garbage can be utilized by recycling.* —**u.ti.li.za.tion** (-luh.ZAY.shun, -lye-) *n.*

ut.most (UT.most) *adj.* the farthest or greatest possible: *a question of the utmost importance; the utmost limit of endurance;* **n.***: That's the utmost we could do.*

U.to.pi.a or **u.to.pi.a** (yoo.TOH.pee.uh) *n.* **1** an imaginary place of ideal social conditions, as in Thomas More's *Utopia.* **2** a perfect society or any visionary scheme. —**U.to.pi.an** or **u.to.pi.an** *adj.*

ut.ter (UT.ur) *adj.* total; absolute: *utter destruction, misery, surprise; This is utter nonsense.* —*v.* **1** give forth vocally: *to utter a cry, curse, oath, prayer, sentence, spell, threat, word; to utter comments, opinions, platitudes, remarks.* **2** deliver or put counterfeit money, forged notes, etc. into circulation: *convicted of uttering forged documents.* —**ut.ter.ly** *adv.*

ut.ter.ance (UT.ur.unce) *n.* **1** an act of uttering vocally or what is uttered: *a prophetic utterance.* **2** a manner or style of speaking.

ut.ter.most (UT.ur.most) *n. & adj.* utmost.

U-turn (YOO.turn) *n.* a vehicle's 360-degree turn.

u.vu.la (YOOV.yuh.luh) *n.* a small fleshy part hanging down from the soft palate; **u.vu.lar** *adj.*

ux.o.ri.ous (uk.SOR.ee.us, ug.ZOR-) *adj.* excessively fond of or submissive to one's wife.

.... **V, v** ....

V or **v** (VEE) *n.* **V's** or **v's 1** the 22nd letter of the English alphabet. **2** something shaped like a "V." **3** the Roman numeral for 5.

va.can.cy (VAY.cun.see) *n.* **-cies 1** a vacant or unoccupied state of mind: *a feeling of desolate vacancy.* **2** vacant space or an unoccupied position, as an apartment for rent, office quarters, etc.: *Sorry, no vacancies; The resignation created a vacancy in the firm; a job vacancy; someone to fill a vacancy; the vacancy rate for office buildings; time spent daydreaming and staring into vacancy* (= empty space).

va.cant (VAY.kunt) *adj.* **1** not occupied or filled: *a vacant apartment, lot; to leave a house vacant; It remains, stands vacant; a want ad headed "Situations vacant"; She has too much vacant* (= free or idle) *time on her hands since retirement.* **2** blank: *a vacant look, mind, stare.* —**va.cant.ly** *adv.*

va.cate (vay.CATE, VAY.cate) *v.* **-cates, -cat.ed, -cat.ing 1** make vacant: *ordered to vacate the premises.* **2** cancel or make void: *His conviction was vacated under a new law.*

va.ca.tion (vay.CAY.shun) *v. & n.* (take) a period of rest from work, study, etc.: *He's away on vacation; vacationing in the Bahamas.* —**va.ca.tion.er** or **va.ca.tion.ist** *n.*

vac.ci.nate (VAC.suh.nate) *v.* **-nates, -nat.ed, -nat.ing** inoculate with or administer a vaccine to someone *against* smallpox, etc. —**vac.ci.na.tion** (-NAY.shun) *n.*

vac.cine (vac.SEEN, VAC.seen) *n.* a preparation of bacteria or viruses of a particular disease injected into the body to build up resistance or immunity to the disease.

vac.il.late (VAS.uh.late) *v.* **-il.lates, -il.lat.ed, -il.lat.ing** shift back and forth or waver *in* an opinion or resolution, *between* two positions, etc. in an indecisive manner. —**vac.il.la.tion** (-LAY.shun) *n.*

va.cu.i.ty (vac.YOO.i.tee) *n.* **-ties 1** emptiness, esp. of mind. **2** a senseless or inane remark, action, etc.

vac.u.ous (VAC.yoo.us) *adj.* senseless or

inane: *a vacuous expression, laugh, mind, remark, stare; the vacuous* (= empty) *life of the idle rich.* —**vac.u.ous.ly** *adv.*; **vac.u.ous.ness** *n.*

vac.u.um (VAC.yoo.um, VAC.yoom, long "oo") *n.* **vac.u.ums** or **vac.u.a** (-yoo.uh) an empty space from which all air has been removed. —*v.* (VAC.yoom) to clean with a vacuum cleaner.

vacuum bottle (or **flask** or **jug**) *n.* a double-walled bottle with an insulating vacuum between the walls, which are also heat-reflecting, for keeping liquids hot or cold for up to 24 hours. Also **thermos (bottle).**

vacuum cleaner *n.* a machine that cleans floors, carpets, etc. by suction.

vacuum-packed *adj.* packed airtight or in an airtight container.

vacuum tube *n.* an electron tube.

va.de me.cum (VAY.dee.MEE.cum) *n.* a handbook or manual for constant use.

vag.a.bond (VAG.uh.bond) *n.* a drifter, esp. one who leads a carefree, roaming life; *adj.*: *a vagabond poet; a vagabond tour of the world; Eurodollars are a pool of vagabond capital shifting from country to country.* —**vag.a.bond.age** (-ij) *n.*

va.gar.y (vuh.GAIR.ee, VAY.guh.ree) *n.* **-gar.ies** an erratic or unpredictable departure or change from the usual or normal: *the vagaries of fashion, of the market, of politics, of the weather.*

va.gi.na (vuh.JYE.nuh) *n.* **1** the canal leading from the genitals to the uterus in female mammals, forming also the opening of the birth canal. **2** the external female genitals; vulva.
—**vag.i.nal** (VAJ.ih.nul) *adj.*

vag.i.ni.tis (vaj.uh.NYE.tis) *n.* inflammation of the vagina.

va.grant (VAY.grunt) *n.* a beggar or similar person who wanders from place to place without a regular occupation, esp. one likely to become a public nuisance. —*adj.* wandering or errant: *a vagrant life; vagrant melodies, missiles, thoughts.* —**va.gran.cy** (-grun.see) *n.* **-cies.**

vague (VAIG) *adj.* **va.guer, va.guest** not clear or distinct: *a vague answer, idea, rumor; He was vague and uncertain about his intentions; I have a vague feeling of something gone wrong; the vague outlines of some flying object.* —**vague.ly** *adv.*; **vague.ness** *n.*

vain *adj.* **1** having or showing too high a regard for one's self; conceited: *He's vain about his good looks.* **2** lacking in value; worthless or empty: *a vain boast; vain pomp, pursuits.* **3** unavailing;

useless: *a vain attempt, endeavor, hope.*
—**in vain 1** without success: *All his efforts were in vain; He looked everywhere in vain; to search in vain for an explanation; The martyrs did not die in vain; He tried in vain to cut a deal with them.* **2** in a disrespectful manner: *to take God's name in vain.* —**vain.ly** *adv.*

vain.glo.ry (VAIN.glor.ee) *n.* too high an esteem of oneself as shown by boasting or showing off.
—**vain.glo.ri.ous** (vain.GLOR.ee.us) *adj.*; **vain.glo.ri.ous.ness** *n.*

val.ance (VAL.unce, VAY-) *n.* a short curtain or curtainlike decorative strip of wood, hung from the top of a window, the canopy of a bed, or from an edge, as of a shelf.

vale *n.* [poetic use] valley.

val.e.dic.tion (val.uh.DIC.shun) *n.* **1** the act of bidding farewell. **2** a farewell utterance.

val.e.dic.tor.i.an (VAL.uh.dic.TOR.ee.un) *n.* a student, usu. the highest ranked, who delivers the valedictory at a graduation.

val.e.dic.to.ry (val.uh.DIC.tuh.ree) *n.* **-ries** a speech bidding farewell: *to deliver* or *give a valedictory; adj.*: *a valedictory address, function, reception, speech.*

va.lence (VAY.lunce) *n.* the capacity of an element to combine with other elements: *Oxygen has a valence of 2 and hydrogen 1, as in H_2O (water).* Also **va.len.cy.**

val.en.tine (VAL.un.tine) *n.* **1** a sweetheart chosen on Saint Valentine's Day, February 14, and greeted with a card. **2** the card itself.

val.et (VAL.it, -ay) *n.* a male servant performing personal services for a man, as a hotel employee who cleans and presses clothes.

val.e.tu.di.nar.i.an (VAL.uh.tue.duh.NAIR.ee.un) *adj.* of weak health or unduly worried about one's state of health. —*n.* such a person.
—**val.e.tu.di.nar.i.an.ism** *n.*

Val.hal.la (val.HAL.uh) *n.* in Norse myth, Odin's great hall in which slain warriors are received.

val.i.ant (VAL.yunt) *adj.* brave or courageous: *a valiant attempt, deed, effort, hero, knight, struggle.* —**val.i.ant.ly** *adv.*

val.id (VAL.id) *adj.* having the force of law, reason, or evidence: *a valid contract, objection, ticket; a ticket valid for one year;* **val.id.ly** *adv.* —**va.lid.i.ty** (vuh.LID.i.tee) *n.*

val.i.date (VAL.uh.date) *v.* **-dates, -dat.ed, -dat.ing** show to be or make valid: *to validate a claim, finding, process, title.* —**val.i.da.tion** (-DAY.shun) *n.*

va.lise (vuh.LEECE) *n.* a bag in which to carry clothes, etc. when traveling.

val.i.um (VAL.ee.um) *n.* a mild tranquilizer; diazepam. —**Valium** *Trademark.*

Val.kyr.ie (val.KEER.ee, VAL.kuh.ree) *n.* in Norse myth, one of the goddess-maidens who choose the heroes to be slain in battle and conduct them to Odin.

val.ley (VAL.ee) *n.* **val.leys** 1 a long, narrow depression between hills or mountains, esp. the low land through which a river flows: *down in the valley.* 2 a valleylike dip or channel, as between two slopes of a roof.

val.or (VAL.ur) *n.* courage or bravery, as in battle: *"Discretion is the better part of valor"* (= It is better to be discreet and avoid a dangerous situation than try to be brave). Also **val.our** *Cdn.* —**val.or.ous** *adj.*

val.u.a.ble (VAL.yoo.uh.bul, -yoo.bul) 1 *adj.* having great value or usefulness: *a valuable contribution, experience, gem, help, lesson, purpose; valuable time; It's valuable to cultivate Lee's friendship; He was chosen the game's **most valuable player**.* 2 **valuables** *n.pl.* jewelry and such articles of great value.

val.u.a.tion (val.yoo.AY.shun) *n.* 1 a determining of the value of an asset: *a capital gains tax based on prices as of **Valuation Day** fixed at an earlier date.* 2 the estimated value or worth.

val.ue (VAL.yoo) *n.* 1 what something is worth in terms of its usefulness or importance: *a story of some news value; the exchange value of the dollar; the value of education; a keepsake treasured because of its sentimental value; It is of no commercial value; sold at face value; cash, enduring, intrinsic, nominal, nuisance value; a discovery of great value to humanity; We place* or *put* or *set much value on family and friends; Consumers want value* (= adequate return) *for their money.* 2 **values** *pl.* ideals or standards: *family, middle-class, moral, spiritual values; to return to the traditional values of hearth and home; to adopt, cherish, foster, hold, respect a set of values.* 3 what a symbol or letter is equivalent to: *The value of L as a Roman numeral is 50; ½ and 3/6 have the same value; "x" has the sound value of "ks."* 4 a relative quality, as the degree of lightness or darkness of a color, duration of a note or rest in music, etc. —*v.* **-ues, -ued, -u.ing** 1 think highly of a person or thing: *I value her advice very much;* **adj.:** *a **valued** asset, customer, friend.* 2 estimate; rate: *Most people value health above wealth; His assets are valued at $4 million.*

value-added tax *n.* a government tax on a product or service based on the difference between the producer's sale price and the cost of materials and expenses.

value judgment *n.* a judgment about people or their actions that is based on subjective or personal values.

valve (VALV) *n.* 1 an opening and closing device that controls a flow, as in the heart, in water faucets, and in wind instruments such as the trumpet and French horn for changing musical pitch. 2 a hinged part of the shell of a bivalve mollusk or clam. 3 one of the parts into which a capsule or pod separates on bursting open.

va.moose (vuh.MOOSE) *v.* **-moos.es, -moosed, -moos.ing** *Slang.* leave quickly from a place.

vamp *n.* 1 the upper front covering of a shoe or boot. 2 a patched-up article, as a shoe repaired with a new vamp. 3 a woman who exploits men unscrupulously to get what she wants; adventuress: *a party vamp.* 4 in jazz music, a succession of simple chords used as accompaniment. —*v.* 1 exploit or seduce. 2 **vamp up** patch up or repair something with pieces of material: *to vamp up a publication* (to make it look like a new one); **adj.:** *a **vamped-up** excuse.*

vam.pire (VAM.pire) *n.* 1 a ghost of folklore that sucks the blood of sleeping people. 2 one who preys on others, as a blackmailer or adventuress. 3 a bat that sucks the blood of fowl and livestock, and sometimes attacks sleeping people; also **vampire bat**.

van *n.* 1 a large closed truck or wagon for transporting livestock, merchandise, etc.: *a delivery van; moving vans.* 2 such a wagon equipped as a passenger vehicle: *a seven-passenger, four-door van; vans carrying passengers between air terminals.* 3 the vanguard of an advancing army, fleet, etc.

va.na.di.um (vuh.NAY.dee.um) *n.* a ductile metallic element used in steel and other alloys.

Van Al.len (radiation) belt (van.AL.un-) *n.* a part of the earth's magnetosphere that contains large numbers of charged particles that could be dangerous to space travelers.

van.dal (VAN.dul) *n.* 1 one who willfully or ignorantly destroys valu-

vandalize / variance

able property. **2 Vandal** a member of a Germanic tribe that sacked Rome in A.D. 455. —**van.dal.ism** *n.*

van.dal.ize (VAN.dul.ize) *v.* **-iz.es, -ized, -iz.ing** destroy or damage property belonging to others.

Van.dyke beard (van.DIKE-) *n.* a pointed, closely trimmed beard.

vane *n.* **1** a blade of a rotating device as in a turbine or windmill on which the force of water, wind, etc. acts. **2** a weather vane. **3** the feather of an arrow. **4** a plate or strip of metal attached to a rocket or missile to give it stability in flight.

van.guard (VAN.gard) *n.* **1** the front part of an advancing army. **2** the leadership or leading position in a movement.

va.nil.la (vuh.NIL.uh) *n.* **1** a flavoring made from the capsules of a climbing orchid. **2** the capsules or the plant, or "vanilla beans." —*adj.*: *vanilla beans, essence, extract, flavoring, ice cream.*

van.ish (VAN.ish) *v.* disappear quickly or completely, often mysteriously: *The fairy vanished from sight; vanished into thin air; All their hopes vanished with the death of their only child; Unless protected, endangered species may vanish from the earth* (= cease to exist).

vanishing point *n.* a point at which something seems to vanish or cease to exist, as the point on the horizon where parallel lines seem to meet from the perspective of a viewer.

van.i.ty (VAN.i.tee) *n.* **-ties 1** the quality of being vain; self-conceit: *a compliment that tickles one's vanity.* **2** what one is vain about, as beauty or accomplishments. **3** worthlessness or something considered as of no real value: *the vanity of human wishes.* **4** a mirror and table for a woman to sit at while making up; *adj.*: *a vanity mirror, sink; a vanity case* for holding cosmetics and toilet articles. **5** a storage cabinet fitted under a washroom sink.

vanity plate *n.* an automobile's customized license plate.

vanity press *n.* a publishing house that publishes at author's expense; also **vanity publisher.**

van.ner (VAN.ur) *n.* one who uses a van as a recreational vehicle. —**van.ning** *n.*

van.pool *n.* the sharing of a van by commuters. —**van.pool.ing** *n.*

van.quish (VANK.wish) *v.* defeat utterly; get the mastery of someone, as in single combat: *to vanquish the enemy, a disease;* *adj.*: *the victors and the vanquished; the vanquished and the victorious; a vanquished civilization, enemy, foe, land, people; vanquished fears.*

van.tage (VAN.tij) *n.* a position of strategic advantage or commanding view; also **vantage point.**

vap.id (VAP.id) *adj.* **1** having lost freshness or flavor: *vapid wines.* **2** flat, dull, or boring: *a vapid conversation; vapid comments, outpourings, politicians, pronouncements, prose, slogans, speeches.* —**va.pid.i.ty** (va.PID.i.tee) *n.* **-ties.**

va.por (VAY.pur) *n.* the gaseous state of a normally solid or liquid substance; also, the gas: *Water vapor that is seen as steam, fog, etc. condenses as dew, rain, and snow; Sulfur vapor condenses as a powder; the vapors* (= fantastic notions) *of a feverish mind.* —*v.* (cause) to rise as vapor; also, give off vapor. —**vaporings** *n.pl.* boastful talk. Also **va.pour, va.pour.ings** *Cdn.*

va.por.ish (VAY.puh.rish) *adj.* **1** full of or like vapor. **2** of low spirits or depressing. Also **va.pour.ish** *Cdn.*

va.por.ize (VAY.puh.rize) *v.* **-iz.es, -ized, -iz.ing** change into vapor. —**va.por.iz.er** (-rye.zur) *n.* Also **va.por.ise, va.por.is.er** *Brit.*

va.por.iz.er (VAY.puh.rye.zur) *n.* a device for vaporizing a medicated liquid or steaming a room.

va.por.ous (VAY.puh.rus) *adj.* **1** full of or like vapor; foggy or misty. **2** volatile or fanciful. —**va.por.ous.ly** *adv.*; **va.por.ous.ness** *n.*

vapor trail same as CONTRAIL.

va.por.ware (VAY.pur.ware) *n.* computer software that is being developed but that may never be marketed. Also **va.pour.ware** *Cdn.*

vapour *Cdn.* VAPOR.

va.que.ro (vah.CAIR.oh) *n.* **-ros** a ranchhand or cowboy of S.W. United States.

var.i.a (VAIR.ee.uh) *n.pl.* a miscellany.

var.i.a.ble (VAIR.ee.uh.bul) *adj.* likely to vary or change: *variable moods, rates, standards, winds; a curtain rod of variable* (= adjustable) *length; the variable* (= not constant) *value of letters used in algebra; a variable star with changing brightness.* —*n.* something variable or changeable: *variables affecting a trip such as weather and traffic; variables and constants.* —**var.i.a.bly** *adv.* —**var.i.a.ble.ness** *n.*; **var.i.a.bil.i.ty** (-BIL.i.tee) *n.*

var.i.ance (VAIR.ee.unce) *n.* **1** difference or disagreement: *On political questions we find the couple* **at variance**, *Performance should not be* **at variance with**

promises. **2** a deviation or departure: *a variance to a zoning bylaw; He applied for a variance* (= license) *to set up practice in a residential area.*

var.i.ant (VAIR.ee.unt) *n.* something varying from a standard or from others of its kind: *"Humour" is a spelling variant of "humor"*; **adj.:** (SKEJ.ool) *and* (SHEJ.ool) *are variant pronunciations of "schedule."*

var.i.a.tion (vair.ee.AY.shun) *n.* a change in form, position, condition, etc.: *temperature variations from the normal; musical variations on a theme by altering the accompaniment, harmonies, etc.; wide variations between individuals, as in complexion, because of genetic differences and environmental factors.*

var.i.col.ored (VAIR.i.cul.urd) *adj.* of various colors: *a varicolored flower, marble, parrot.* Also **var.i.col.oured** *Cdn.*

var.i.cose (VAIR.i.cose) *adj.* abnormally swollen: *Varicose veins sometimes appear on the legs of pregnant women.*
—**var.i.cos.i.ty** (-COS.i.tee) *n.* **-ties** a varicose condition, vein, or lesion.

var.ied (VAIR.eed) *adj.* **1** having variety: *a varied career, life, range, style.* **2** of various kinds; diverse: *people of varied backgrounds, interests, talents.*

var.i.e.gat.ed (VAIR.ee.uh.gay.tid, -ee.gay.tid) *adj.* marked with different colors, spots, etc.: *variegated Easter eggs, tapestries.* —**var.i.e.ga.tion** (-ee.GAY.shun) *n.*

va.ri.e.tal (vuh.RYE.uh.tul) *adj.* having to do with varieties: *varietal blends, characteristics, coffees, wines.*
—*n.* a wine made from a particular variety of grape.

va.ri.e.ty (vuh.RYE.uh.tee) *n.* **-ties** **1** variation or diversity: *People of different races add or lend variety to a population; "Variety is the spice of life"; artistic variety in unity; The store carries a wide variety of wines.* **2** kind or sort: *varieties of colors, criticism, despair, goods, patterns; great, many, rich varieties; varieties* (= subspecies) *of roses.* **3** *Brit.* a variety show.

variety meats *n.pl.* nonflesh meats, esp. organs, as tripe.

variety show *n.* an entertainment or show with songs, dances, skits, etc.

variety store *n.* a retail store selling a variety of small items.

var.i.o.rum (vair.ee.OR.um) *n.* an edition or text with critical notes by many.

var.i.ous (VAIR.ee.us) *adj.* **1** [modifies *pl. n.*] of different or diverse kinds: *for many and various reasons; various aspects; at various times; in various ways; as various* (= many) *people have told us.* **2** showing variety: *a various crowd.*
—**var.i.ous.ly** *adv.*

var.let (VAR.lit) *n.* [old use] a knave or scoundrel.

var.mint (VAR.munt) *n.* a person or animal regarded as contemptible.

var.nish (VAR.nish) *n.* **1** a resinous preparation applied to wood, metal, etc. to give a hard glossy surface: *a coat of varnish; protective varnish.* **2** such glossy appearance. **3** surface polish or outside show: *mere varnish.* —*v.* cover with varnish: *His animal nature could not be varnished over with a polished exterior; a varnished finish.*

var.si.ty (VAR.si.tee) *n.* **-ties** the main team representing a college, school, or club in a sports competition: *to play on the varsity.*

var.y (VAIR.ee) *v.* **var.ies, var.ied, var.y.ing** **1** differ or make different: *People vary in their tastes; Tastes vary from person to person; Drivers avoid monotony on the highway by varying their cruising speed.* **2** change or undergo change: *Daytime temperatures vary between 20 and 25 degrees Celsius here; They vary from 20 to 25 degrees; Sharpness of vision varies inversely (not directly) with size of letters read* (= The smaller the letters, the less sharp the vision).

vas.cu.lar (VASK.yuh.lur) *adj.* having to do with vessels carrying blood, sap, etc.: *vascular plants, surgery, systems.*

vas def.er.ens (vas.DEF.uh.runs) *n.* the duct through which semen passes from testicles to penis.

vase (VACE, VAZE, VAHZ) *n.* a decorative rounded vessel of pottery, etc. used esp. to hold flowers.

vas.ec.to.my (vas.EC.tuh.mee) *n.* **-mies** surgical cutting of the vas deferens for producing sterility.

vas.e.line (VAS.uh.leen) *n.* petroleum jelly; petrolatum. —**Vaseline** Trademark.

vas.o.con.stric.tor (VAS.oh.cun.STRIC.tur) *n. & adj.* (a nerve or drug) causing constriction of the blood vessels, as when one turns pale.

vas.o.di.la.tor (VAS.oh.dye.LAY.tur) *n. & adj.* (a nerve or drug) causing expansion of the blood vessels, as in blushing.

vas.o.mo.tor (vas.oh.MOH.tur) *adj.* influencing the narrowing or widening of blood vessels.

vas.sal (VAS.ul) *n.* **1** a feudal tenant owing homage and allegiance to his lord. **2** a subordinate or servant.

vassalage / vehicle

vas.sal.age (VAS.ul.ij) *n.* **1** a vassal's condition of servitude. **2** the homage and service required of a vassal. **3** the lands held by a vassal.

vast *adj.* very great in extent or range: *the vast Sahara Desert; a vast amount of information; a vast array, country, mystery, nation, orchestra, sum, territory; his vast bulk, potential, power, wealth; vast achievements, changes, corruption, experience, opportunities; the vast majority of people; vast numbers of cars.* —**vast.ly** *adv.;* **vast.ness** *n.*

vat *n.* a large tub, barrel, or similar vessel to hold a liquid, esp. in an industrial process.

vat.ic *adj.* prophetic; oracular.

Vat.i.can (VAT.i.cun) *n.* papal headquarters, authority, or government: *an appeal to the Vatican.*

vaude.ville (VODE.vil, VAWD.vil, -uh.vil) *n.* a variety show featuring songs, dances, acrobatics, etc. once popular as theatrical entertainment. —**vaude.vil.li.an** (-VIL.yun) *adj.*

vault *n.* **1** an arched roof or ceiling: *beneath the vault of heaven* (= sky). **2** a chamber or structure with a vault, esp. one underground, usu. for a special purpose: *a storage vault for weapons; buried in the family vault; a bank vault for the safekeeping of valuables.* **3** a leap made with the support of the hands or a pole: *a pole vault.*
—*v.* **1** to arch like a vault; *n.: cathedral-like vaulting.* **2** cover with or build as a vault; *adj.: a vaulted ceiling, chamber, dome, roof; a barrel-vaulted corridor.* **3** leap upward or go *over* a barrier, jump *from* or *onto* a horse, etc. supported by the hands or by using a pole: *to vault over a wall; Guy vaulted past Yun in the finals; The Dolphins vaulted from a 7-7 deadlock into a 24-14 lead; a program to vault the business into the major leagues;* **adj.:** *his vaulting* (= overzealous) *ambition; a vaulting horse* (= gym equipment for vaulting).

vaunted *adj.* boasted-about: *his vaunted popularity, strength, toughness; her much-vaunted objectivity, successes, superiority.*

veal (VEEL) *n.* a young calf or its flesh used for food.

vec.tor (VEC.tur) *n.* **1** a mathematical quantity or line segment used to represent magnitude and direction, as of a force acting upon the path of a body in motion. **2** the carrier or transmitter of a disease-causing organism or agent, as the mosquito carrying the malarial parasite: *an insect vector; vector-borne infections; the possibility that monkeys were a vector for AIDS.*

Ve.da (VAY.duh, VEE-) *n.* any of the four ancient Sanskrit scriptures of the Hindus. —**Ve.dic** *adj.*

Ve.dan.ta (vay.DAN.tuh) *n.* a philosophical system based on the Vedas.

Veep or **veep** *n. Informal.* vice-president.

veer *v.* change direction, as under an external force: *The car veered away from the bicyclist; It veered to the left.*
—*n.* a change of direction.

veg.an (VEE.gun, -jun, VEJ.un) *n.* a strict vegetarian.

veg.e.ta.ble (VEJ.tuh.bul, VEJ.i.tuh-) *n.* a plant, esp. a plant part, as of the lettuce, beet, or tomato, that is used for food: *They sell fruits and vegetables; garden vegetables; Leafy, green, and yellow vegetables form a basic food group.*
—*adj.* having to do with vegetables: *vegetable gardens, dishes, oil, shortening; the vegetable existence* (without mental activity) *of a terminally ill patient on a life-support system; the vegetable kingdom* (= plants as distinguished from animals and minerals); *a vegetable marrow* (= a summer squash such as zucchini).

veg.e.tar.i.an (vej.i.TAIR.ee.un) *n.* one who eats no meat: *A strict vegetarian does not use fish and dairy products; adj.: a vegetarian diet, menu, restaurant.*
—**veg.e.tar.i.an.ism** *n.*

veg.e.tate (VEJ.i.tate) *v.* **-tates, -tat.ed, -tat.ing** **1** have growth, as plants; *adj.: bare and vegetated areas of the region; a sparsely vegetated desert.* **2** exist like plants with very little physical or mental activity: *He vegetates in front of TV all evening.*

veg.e.ta.tion (vej.i.TAY.shun) *n.* **1** plant life or growth: *the dense, lush, luxuriant, rank vegetation of the jungle.* **2** the act or state of vegetating.

veg.e.ta.tive (VEJ.i.tay.tiv) *adj.* having to do with growth: *a vegetative existence; Roots, stems, and leaves are vegetative organs; vegetative processes such as growth and decay.*

veg.gie (VEJ.ee) *n. Informal.* **1** vegetable. **2** a vegetarian.

ve.he.ment (VEE.uh.munt) *adj.* intense in feeling; passionate: *a vehement denial of the charge; vehement desires, utterances; a vehement* (= violent) *wind.*
—**ve.he.ment.ly** *adv.* —**ve.he.mence** *n.*

ve.hi.cle (VEE.uh.cul, VEE.hi.cul) *n.* **1** a carriage or conveyance used on land or in space: *a license to drive or operate a motor vehicle; all-terrain, armored, recreational, re-entry, space vehi-*

cles. **2** a medium: *Language is the vehicle of thought and emotion; a paper that serves as a vehicle for propaganda; pigments in vehicles such as oils, resins, and latex; a drug given in an inert vehicle such as syrup.*

ve.hic.u.lar (vi.HIK.yuh.lur) *adj.* having to do with vehicles, esp. motor vehicles: *vehicular access, accidents, traffic, tunnels.*

V-8 1 *n. & adj.* (an engine) having eight cylinders in two rows set at an angle. **2** *n.* a vehicle with such an engine.

veil (VALE) *n.* a piece of sheer fabric or net used as a curtain, to hide or protect a woman's head or face, etc.: *a bridal veil; a veil of ambiguity, clouds, modesty, secrecy, silence, uncertainty; to draw, lift, part a veil;* **adj.**: *The bride came veiled for the ceremony; a veiled attack, attempt, reference; veiled racism; The novel reads like a thinly veiled* (= masked) *biography; a veiled* (= hidden or implied) *threat.*

veiling *n.* a veil or a sheer fabric such as lace or chiffon.

vein (VANE) *n.* **1** a channel carrying blood, sap, etc. or something resembling it: *the veins and arteries of the circulatory system; the network of veins on a leaf; the veins on an insect's wing; a vein* (= seam or lode) *of mineral ore deposited by ground water in rock fissures; the vein* (= streak) *of melancholy running through her poems;* **adj. & cpd.**: *a veined leaf; veined hands* (marked with veins); *blue-veined cheese; gray-veined marble.* **2** mood or manner: *in a lighter vein; in a serious vein.*

ve.lar (VEE.lur) *n. & adj.* (a sound) made at the back of the mouth near the velum, or soft palate, as the "g" of "go."

vel.cro (VEL.croh) *n.* a nylon fabric used as a fastener made up of two strips pressed tightly together to close and pulled apart to open; **adj.**: *a velcro closure, fastener, strip.* **Velcro** Trademark.

veld (VELT) *n.* the treeless grasslands of South Africa whose lower regions are often scrub-covered. Also **veldt.**

vel.lum (VEL.um) *n.* **1** a fine parchment, as used for binding expensive books. **2** a strong paper with a smooth finish imitating vellum, used for diplomas, etc.

ve.loc.i.pede (vuh.LOS.uh.peed) *n.* **1** an early form of bicycle or tricycle. **2** a child's tricycle.

ve.loc.i.ty (vuh.LOS.i.tee) *n.* **-ties** swiftness or speed, esp. of inanimate things: *the velocity of a bullet; the velocity of light, sound; high and low velocities.*

ve.lour (vuh.LOOR) *n., pl.* **-lours** (-LOORS) a velvetlike fabric used for coats, upholstery, etc.; **adj.**: *wool with a velour appearance; fabrics with a velour finish; a velour robe, sweater, towel.* Also **ve.lours.**

ve.lum (VEE.lum) *n., pl.* **-la** (-luh) the soft back portion of the palate.

vel.vet (VEL.vut) *n.* **1** a fabric of silk, rayon, etc. with a soft downy surface: *as smooth as velvet; seductive black velvet.* **2** something resembling velvet, as the furry covering of a deer's growing antlers. —**adj.** made of, covered with, or suggesting velvet: *the velvet touch of a baby's skin; "an iron hand in a velvet glove"* (= softness masking ruthlessness); *The 1989 velvet revolution in Czechoslovakia occurred smoothly and peacefully.* —**vel.vet.y** *adj.* soft and smooth: *a velvety feel, finish; velvety fabrics, petals, skin; a velvety look, ride, sauce, voice.*

vel.vet.een (vel.vuh.TEEN) *n.* a cotton fabric resembling velvet.

ve.nal (VEE.nul) *adj.* open to bribes or influenced by bribery; corrupt: *venal conduct, politicians, practices;* **ve.nal.ly** *adv.* —**ve.nal.i.ty** (vee.NAL.i.tee) *n.*

vend *v.* sell, esp. peddle or hawk; *n.*: *a coin-operated vending machine selling snacks and beverages.*

ven.det.ta (ven.DET.uh) *n.* **1** a family feud in which injuries are avenged with violence and bloodshed. **2** any prolonged feud: *to conduct a vendetta against someone.*

ven.dor (VEN.dur) *n.* one that vends; seller: *news(paper), software, street vendors.*

ve.neer (vuh.NEER) *n.* a layer of wood, brick, etc. used to cover something inferior: *exterior walls of brick veneer; furniture with an oak veneer; Anyone could see through his thin veneer of urbanity.* —*v.* cover with a veneer.

ven.er.a.ble (VEN.uh.ruh.bul) *adj.* worthy of deep reverence because of age, dignity, sanctity, etc.

ven.er.ate (VEN.uh.rate) *v.* **-ates, -at.ed, -at.ing** regard with deep reverence; revere. —**ven.er.a.tion** (-RAY.shun) *n.*

ve.ne.re.al (vuh.NEER.ee.ul) *adj.* transmitted by sexual intercourse: *a venereal disease.* —**ve.ne.re.al.ly** *adv.*

Ve.ne.tian (vuh.NEE.shun) *n. & adj.* (a person) of or from Venice, Italy.

Venetian blind *n.* a window blind made

of slats that can be opened and closed to regulate lighting.

Ven.e.zue.lan (ven.iz.WAY.lun) *n. & adj.* (a person) of or from **Venezuela**, a South American country.

venge.ance (VEN.junce) *n.* punishment in return for a wrong; revenge: *to exact, take, wreak vengeance on or upon someone for something; to seek vengeance against someone for past wrongs; He vowed vengeance; He started dieting **with a vengeance*** (= in a vehement or excessive way).

venge.ful (VENJ.ful) *adj.* seeking vengeance; revengeful; vindictive. —**venge.ful.ly** *adv.*

ve.ni.al (VEE.nee.ul) *adj.* pardonable or excusable: *a venial offense, sin.*

ve.ni.re (vuh.NYE.ree) *n.* [legal] **1** a writ summoning a jury. **2** a list of persons from which to draw a jury. —**ve.ni.re.man** (-mun) *n.* **-men** a person called to jury duty.

ven.i.son (VEN.uh.sun, -zun) *n.* the flesh of a deer used as food.

ven.om (VEN.um) *n.* **1** the poison of a snake or spider. **2** malice: *to spew or spout venom.*

ven.om.ous (VEN.uh.mus) *adj.* **1** poisonous: *a venomous snake.* **2** spiteful or malicious: *a venomous letter.* —**ven.om.ous.ly** *adv.*

ve.nous (VEE.nus) *adj.* having to do with veins: *venous blood.*

vent *n.* **1** an outlet or opening for a gas to escape through, for air to be drawn in for ventilation, as in an automobile, etc.: *a vent pipe for the escape of sewer gas; He **gave vent*** (= gave free expression) *to his feelings in a letter.* **2** a vertical slit at the edge of a garment: *a jacket with side vents.*
—*v.* **1** discharge or expel: *He vented his anger on everyone he met.* **2** provide with a vent: *Sinks, toilets, etc. are vented through the roof.*

ven.ti.late (VEN.tul.ate) *v.* **-lates, -lat.ed, -lat.ing 1** let in fresh air: *Firefighters try to ventilate the roof of a burning house;* **adj.**: *a well ventilated room; lightweight ventilated fabrics.* **2** furnish with a vent, outlet, etc. **3** oxygenate blood in lungs, etc.: *a breathing machine to ventilate a patient.* **4** discuss or examine fully in public: *to ventilate one's grievances; to ventilate one's family problems at work.* —**ven.ti.la.tion** (-AY.shun) *n.*

ven.ti.la.tor (VEN.tul.ay.tur) *n.* **1** an opening or a device such as a fan for ventilating a place. **2** an artificial breathing device; respirator.

ven.tral (VEN.trul) *adj.* **1** of or near the belly; hence, front: *a fish's ventral and dorsal fins; a ventral hernia, opening.* **2** lower: *the lateral and ventral surfaces of the tongue.* —**ven.tral.ly** *adv.*

ven.tri.cle (VEN.tri.cul) *n.* either of the two lower chambers of the heart. —**ven.tric.u.lar** (ven.TRIC.yuh.lur) *adj.*

ven.tril.o.quism (ven.TRIL.uk.wiz.um) *n.* the art of talking without moving the lips so that the voice seems to come from a source outside the speaker such as a puppet held in the hand. —**ven.tril.o.quist** *n.*

ven.ture (VEN.chur) *n.* an enterprise or undertaking involving risk but with a chance for profit, as in buying stocks: *bold, commercial, cooperative, high-risk, joint, speculative ventures.* —**at a venture** taking a risk; without much deliberation.
—*v.* **-tures, -tured, -tur.ing** expose lives, etc. to risk; dare *to* do something risky or hazardous: *if I may venture a guess, an opinion; He wouldn't venture (to step) outside in the storm.*

venture capital *n.* capital not secured by collateral for investment in enterprises subject to risk; also **risk capital.**

ven.ture.some (VEN.chur.sum) *adj.* **1** of a person, daring: *a venturesome investor, mountaineer, nature.* **2** of a thing or action, hazardous: *venturesome driving; a venturesome route up the mountain.*

ven.ue (VEN.yoo) *n.* **1** in law, the locality of the commission of a crime. **2** the place of jury selection or trial: *The defense lawyer requested a change of venue because of adverse publicity.* **3** a gathering place for any activity: *the venue of the next Olympic Games; betting venues.*

Ve.nus (VEE.nus) *n.* **1** the Roman goddess of love and beauty. **2** the planet closest to the earth and appearing brighter than any star.

Venus' fly.trap *n.* a swamp plant with two-lobed hairy leaves that can trap and digest insects; also **Venus's-flytrap.**

Ve.nu.sian (vuh.NEW.zhun) *n. & adj.* (an imaginary inhabitant) of the planet Venus.

ve.rac.i.ty (vuh.RAS.i.tee) *n.* **1** habitual truthfulness: *No one doubts her veracity; to build a reputation for veracity; Her veracity is not in question.* **2** truth or accuracy, as of a report: *to challenge, check, question the veracity of an advertisement, claim, statement.*

ve.ran.da (vuh.RAN.duh) *n.* an outside corridor or covered gallery of a build-

ing; porch. Also **ve.ran.dah.**
verb (VURB) *n.* a part of speech or word expressing action, being, or happening: *active and passive verbs; transitive and intransitive verbs.*
ver.bal (VUR.bul) *adj.* **1** having to do with words: *a verbal distinction; verbal aptitude, imagery; a verbal* (= oral) *assurance, contract; a verbal* (= word-for-word or literal) *translation.* **2** having to do with verbs: *"-ed," "-ing,"* and *such verbal endings; a verbal auxiliary* (= auxiliary verb) *such as "must"* or *"can."* —**ver.bal.ly** *adv.*
ver.bal.ize (VUR.buh.lize) *v.* **-iz.es, -ized, -iz.ing** **1** express in words: *to verbalize an experience, idea, thought; Children scream when they can't verbalize.* **2** be verbose or wordy. —**ver.bal.i.za.tion** (-luh.ZAY.shun, -lye-) *n.*
verbal noun *n.* an infinitive or gerund used as a noun, as in *"To fly* without wings is not impossible" and *"Flying* is fun."
ver.ba.tim (vur.BAY.tim) *adv.* word for word: *The speech was reported verbatim; texts reproduced verbatim;* **adja.:** *a verbatim quotation, transcript, translation.*
ver.be.na (vur.BEE.nuh) *n.* a group of mostly tropical plants bearing flat heads of phloxlike flowers.
ver.bi.age (VUR.bee.ij) *n.* use of too many words; verbosity; wordiness.
ver.bose (vur.BOSE) *adj.* using more words than are necessary: *a verbose speaker, style; verbose prose;* **ver.bose.ly** *adv.* —**ver.bos.i.ty** (-BOS.i.tee) *n.*
ver.bo.ten (vur.BOH.tun) *adj. German.* forbidden or prohibited.
ver.dant (VUR.dunt) *adj.* green: *verdant grass, meadows; verdant* (= immature) *youth.*
ver.dict (VUR.dict) *n.* a formal decision or finding, as of a jury at the end of a trial: *to arrive at, bring in, reach, return a verdict; a guilty verdict* or *a verdict of not guilty.*
ver.di.gris (VUR.duh.greece, -gris) *n.* **1** a greenish deposit on exposed brass, bronze, or copper. **2** a poisonous pigment that is an acetate of copper.
ver.dure (VUR.jur) *n.* **1** green vegetation. **2** the green color of growing things.
verge (VURJ) *n.* **1** the brink or extreme edge of something: *on the verge of a cliff, roof; on the verge of bankruptcy, of being exposed, of a breakdown, of tears.* **2** a staff carried as an official emblem.
—*v.* **verg.es, verged, verg.ing** be on the verge of something: *His spelling is so poor it verges on illiteracy; He's verging* (= inclining) *toward old age.*
verg.er (VUR.jur) *n.* a caretaker of a church; sexton.
ver.i.fy (VER.uh.fye) *v.* **-fies, -fied, -fy.ing** **1** prove the correctness or truth of something by checking with a standard or authority: *to verify the accuracy of a piece of information; to verify an allegation, someone's credentials, a statement.* **2** confirm: *Later events verified our suspicions; All signs verify that a recession is coming.* —**ver.i.fi.a.ble** (-FYE.uh.bul) *adj.* —**ver.i.fi.ca.tion** (-fuh.CAY.shun) *n.*
ver.i.ly (VER.uh.lee) *adv.* [old use] truly; in truth.
ver.i.sim.i.li.tude (VER.uh.suh.MIL.uh.tude) *n.* the quality of seeming to be true or real: *to lend verisimilitude to a story.*
ver.i.ta.ble (VER.i.tuh.bul) *adj.* truly so termed: *a veritable cash cow, gold mine, heaven on earth.*
ver.i.ty (VER.i.tee) *n.* **-ties 1** the quality of being true or real. **2** a fundamental or universal truth: *the eternal verities of all creeds and philosophies.*
ver.meil (VUR.mul) *n.* **1** (*also* vur.MAY) gilded silver. **2** vermilion.
ver.mi.cel.li (vur.muh.SEL.ee, -CHEL.ee) *n.* pasta in finer strings than spaghetti, used in soups, etc.
ver.mic.u.lite (vur.MIK.yuh.lite) *n.* a micalike mineral that expands greatly when heated to form a lightweight cellular material that is much used in insulation, packaging, etc.
ver.mi.form (VUR.muh.form) *adj.* wormlike in shape: *a vermiform animal, appearance, larva, structure.* —**vermiform appendix** same as APPENDIX, 2.
ver.mi.fuge (VUR.muh.fyooj) *n.* a medicine for killing worms in the intestines.
ver.mil.ion (vur.MIL.yun) *n.* a bright-red pigment or its color. —*adj.* bright-red.
ver.min (VUR.min) *n.* **1** *sing. & pl.* (any of various) insects or small animals that are pests, as fleas, rats, etc.: *a house infested with vermin.* **2** a person considered as contemptible.
ver.mouth (ver.MOOTH) *n.* a white wine flavored with herbs.
ver.nac.u.lar (ver.NAK.yuh.lur) *n.* **1** the native language of a people or place, esp. its everyday, spoken variety, as distinguished from a literary form: *The Mass is now said in the vernacular* (= local language) *instead of Latin; the vernacular of Texas.* **2** the idiom of a group or class: *in the vernacu-*

lar of baseball, jazz, the street; the salty vernacular (= spoken style) of Huck Finn. —**adja.** belonging to the common people, esp. their speech: *Italian, French, etc. arose as vernacular forms of Latin; "Venus' flytrap" is the vernacular name for "Dionaea muscipula"; the Scottish vernacular (= dialect) poet Robert Burns; the vernacular (= locally rooted) architecture of the South.*

ver.nal (VUR.nul) *adj.* having to do with spring: *vernal flowers, hay fever; The vernal equinox occurs around March 21.* —**ver.nal.ly** *adv.*

ver.ni.er (VUR.nee.ur) *n.* a small scale or ruler that is slid alongside a larger one for fractional readings of length and angle measurements; also **vernier scale.**

Ve.ron.i.ca (vuh.RON.i.cuh) same as SPEEDWELL.

ver.sa.tile (VUR.suh.tile, -tul) *adj.* **1** having the skills or aptitude for many different activities: *a versatile genius, mind; She's quite versatile in or at foreign languages.* **2** able to turn or swing freely: *an insect's versatile antennae; versatile movement.* **3** able to be put to many uses: *a versatile fabric such as cotton or linen; unisex items that are versatile for both men and women.*
—**ver.sa.til.i.ty** (-TIL.i.tee) *n.*

verse (VURSE) *n.* **1** a line of poetry. **2** a stanza or poem. **3** language in verses; poetry: *a story in verse; Shakespeare's (unrhymed) blank verse.* **4** a sentence from a chapter of the Bible: *a verse from Genesis.*

versed (VURST) *adjp.* learned or experienced: *a scholar well versed in his specialty; a parent fully versed in first aid; a gourmet versed in French cuisine.*

ver.si.cle (VUR.si.cul) *n.* a short verse or sentence as one of a series recited by a clergyman alternately with responses from the congregation.

ver.si.fy (VUR.suh.fye) *v.* **-fies, -fied, -fy.ing** **1** turn into verse form. **2** write verse; **ver.si.fi.er** *n.* —**ver.si.fi.ca.tion** (-fuh.CAY.shun) *n.*

ver.sion (VUR.zhun, -shun) *n.* **1** a particular form or variant, esp. an account or description from one point of view: *your version of the incident; authorized, official, written versions; the uncut version of a movie; the movie version of a novel.* **2** a translation of the Bible: *the Authorized Version; the Revised Version.*

vers li.bre (vair.LEE.bruh) *n.* French. free verse.

ver.so *n.* **-sos** a book's left-hand page.

ver.sus (VUR.sus) *prep.* **1** [usu. abbreviated to "v." in legal use] against: *the People v. John Smith.* **2** contrasted with: *freedom versus slavery.*

ver.te.bra (VUR.tuh.bruh) *n., pl.* **-brae** (-bray, -bree) or **-bras** one of the segments of the backbone. —**ver.te.bral** (-brul) *adj.*

ver.te.brate (VUR.tuh.brit, -brate) *n.* an animal such as a fish, amphibian, bird, reptile, or mammal that has a backbone; *adja.:* vertebrate animals, biology, life, paleontology, skeletons.

ver.tex (VUR.tex) *n.* **-tex.es** or **-ti.ces** (-tuh.seez) **1** the topmost point; apex: *the vertex (= point farthest from the base) of a pyramid.* **2** the meeting point of two sides, as of a triangle.

ver.ti.cal (VUR.ti.cul) *adj.* upright or erect; perpendicular to the horizontal: *a ski trail with a vertical drop of 800 feet; 800 vertical feet; a vertical-takeoff-and-landing airplane; a library's **vertical file** of clippings, pamphlets, etc.* —*n.* a vertical line, plane, part, etc. —**ver.ti.cal.ly** *adv.* —**ver.ti.cal.i.ty** (-CAL.i.tee) *n.*

ver.ti.go (VUR.tuh.go) *n.* **-ti.goes** dizziness or giddiness felt when one's sense of balance is disturbed, as in diseases of the inner ear or when looking down from a height. —**ver.tig.i.nous** (vur.TIJ.uh.nus) *adj.:* to feel vertiginous.

ver.vain (VUR.vain) *n.* any of a family of plants and trees that include the verbena, teak, etc.

verve *n.* vigorous energy or enthusiasm; vivacity: *The band performs with verve and zest.*

ver.y (VER.ee) *adj.* **ver.i.er, -i.est** **1** [used for emphasis before nouns]: *at that very (= same) moment; The very (= mere) idea of cannibalism is revolting; as I told you from the very (= extreme) beginning; He treated the child as his very own.* **2** [old use] real or genuine: *in very truth; A verier fool was never seen.*
—*adv.* [used for emphasis] **1** [before adverbs]: *a very well liked woman; He runs very fast.* **2** [before adjectives that allow degrees of comparison]: *a very great idea; It's very hot outside; That's very true, at the very least.* **3** [before adjectives with superlative meaning]: *the very first to arrive; your very own child.* **4** [before participles, except participles with clearly verbal meaning]: *a very learned man.*

very high frequency *n.* a radio frequency between 30 and 300 megahertz.

very low frequency *n.* a radio frequency below 30 kilohertz.

ves.i.cant (VES.i.kunt) *n. & adj.* (a substance such as mustard gas) that causes blistering.

ves.i.cle (VES.i.cul) *n.* a fluid-filled membranous cavity; small blister or cyst. —**ve.sic.u.lar** (vuh.SIC.yuh.lur) *adj.*

ves.per (VES.pur) **1** *adj.* having to do with the evening or vespers: *the vesper bell.* **2 vespers** or **Vespers** *n.pl.* an evening church service.

ves.sel (VES.ul) *n.* **1** a hollow utensil for holding esp. liquids, as a bowl, barrel, bottle, etc. **2** a ship or large boat: *to charter a vessel; an oceangoing vessel.* **3** a duct or tube of the body: *blood vessels.*

vest *n.* **1** a short sleeveless garment, usu. worn under one's suit jacket: *bullet-proof vests for police officers; life vests (for floating on water).* **2** *Brit.* undershirt. —*v.* **1** clothe, as in vestments: *Priests vest for Mass.* **2** put authority, rights, etc. in the possession of a person: *by the powers vested in the governor; to vest someone with authority; the power that vests (= resides) in the Crown.*

ves.tal (VES.tul) *adj.* chaste or pure, as a **vestal virgin** (= priestess of ancient Rome). —*n.* **1** a vestal virgin. **2** a chaste woman.

vested interest *n.* **1** an economic, social, or political privilege enjoyed by a group or organization, that may be lost by change: *the vested interest of gun lobbies in selling guns to everyone.* **2** such a group: *Powerful vested interests lobbied against the banning of tobacco.*

ves.ti.bule (VES.tuh.byool) *n.* a room, hall, or passage serving as an entrance or antechamber.

ves.tige (VES.tij) *n.* a remaining part or remnant of something that is no longer in existence: *The appendix, wisdom teeth, etc. are vestiges from an earlier stage of human history; vestiges of an ancient civilization; the last vestiges of their existence; There's not a vestige (= least bit) of truth in his assertions.* —**ves.tig.i.al** (ves.TIJ.ee.ul) *adj.*

vest.ing *n.* the conferring of a fixed right, as when an employee may retain his pension regardless of changing circumstances.

vest.ment (VEST.munt) *n.* a ceremonial outer garment or robe, as worn by the clergy at religious services.

vest-pocket *adj.* **1** very small: *a vest-pocket dictionary.* **2** secretive: *his vest-pocket conduct in public office.*

ves.try (VES.tree) *n.* **-tries 1** a sacristy, as in Protestant churches. **2** in the Episcopal Church, a committee managing church business. —**ves.try.man** (-mun) *n.* **-men** a member of a vestry.

vest.ure (VES.chur) *n.* clothing or covering; garments.

vet *n.* [short form] **1** veterinarian. **2** veteran.

vetch *n.* a plant of the pea family valued as cattle food and green manure.

vet.er.an (VET.ur.un) *n.* **1** a former member of the armed forces, esp. an old soldier, sailor, etc.: *a disabled veteran; war veterans; In the U.S.,* **Veterans Day***, November 11 or the fourth Monday in October, is a legal holiday in honor of the veterans of the armed forces, esp. the dead of world wars I and II;* **adj.***: veteran benefits, hospitals, politicians.* **2** a person with long experience in an occupation: *a newspaper veteran; TV veterans; an eight-year veteran of the police force;* **adj.***: a veteran farmer, journalist, performer; veteran troops..*

vet.er.i.nar.i.an (VET.ur.uh.NAIR.ee.un) *n.* one who practices a branch of medicine dealing with the treatment of animals. —**vet.er.i.nar.y** (-nair.ee) *adj.*: *veterinary clinics, colleges, hospitals, medicine.*

ve.to (VEE.toh) *n.* **-toes** (the exercise of) the right to prohibit an act or defeat a move: *the veto exercised by the permanent members of the U.N. Security Council; a presidential veto; Parents have* **veto power** *over decisions made by children in their care.* —*v.* **-toes, -toed, -to.ing** forbid or prohibit an action by special right: *The President may veto a bill passed by Congress.*

vex *v.* **1** irritate or annoy in a worrying manner: *problems that vex managers;* *adj.*: *They were deeply* **vexed** *to hear that their son had lost his job; Everyone seemed vexed by the news; the vexed (= much disputed) question or issue of pay equity; a* **vexing** *ethical issue; vexing questions, problems.* **2** to plague or afflict: *to be vexed with migraine headaches.* —**vex.a.tion** (vek.SAY.shun) *n.*

vex.a.tious (vek.SAY.shus) *adj.* annoying: *frivolous and vexatious lawsuits;* **vex.a.tious.ly** *adv.*

vi.a (VYE.uh, VEE.uh) *prep.* by way of: *a letter sent via airmail; to Europe via London.*

vi.a.ble (VYE.uh.bul) *adj.* **1** capable of surviving, as a fetus outside the womb: *Democracy is not viable under a military regime; a viable economy, industry, operation; to put things on a viable basis.* **2** feasible or practicable: *a viable alternative, decision, option, plan.*
—**vi.a.bly** *adv.* —**vi.a.bil.i.ty**

viaduct / vicinage

(-BIL.i.tee) *n.*
vi.a.duct (VYE.uh.duct) *n.* a bridge on tall supports for carrying a railroad track or road over another track or road, over a valley, etc.
vi.al (VYE.ul) *n.* a small bottle to hold medicines or other liquids.
via media *n.* a middle way.
vi.and (VYE.und) *n.* usu. **viands** *pl.* articles of food.
vi.at.i.cum (vye.AT.i.cum) *n.* 1 the Eucharist given to a dying person. 2 food or money for a journey, as in ancient Rome.
vibe *n.* 1 *Informal.* instinctive feeling or reaction; vibration: *bad, good, nice vibes; The vibe is sometimes negative; the vibe of authority.* 2 **vibes** *pl.* [short form] vibraharp or vibraphone.
vi.bra.harp (VYE.bruh.harp) same as VIBRAPHONE. —**vi.bra.harp.ist** *n.*
vi.brant (VYE.brunt) *adj.* 1 vibrating; hence, resonant: *vibrant sounds, tones.* 2 vigorous or energetic: *vibrant colors; a vibrant culture, economy, personality; looking healthy and vibrant; an active and vibrant group; a vibrant and expressive style; vibrant and exciting.* —**vi.brant.ly** *adv.* —**vi.bran.cy** *n.*
vi.bra.phone (VYE.bruh.fone) *n.* an instrument resembling a xylophone with metal bars and electrically operated resonators. —**vi.bra.phon.ist** *n.*
vi.brate (VYE.brate) *v.* **-brates, -brat.ed, -brat.ing** 1 set or be in rapid back-and-forth motion, as a taut string when plucked: *Insects fly vibrating their wings; The earthquake made the building vibrate; Energy vibrated from the cheerleaders.* 2 oscillate, as a pendulum. 3 (make) respond sympathetically; (cause) to thrill: *a performance that vibrates with passion.* 4 resound or echo, as a sound in the ears.
vi.bra.tion (vye.BRAY.shun) *n.* 1 a trembling, as caused by an earthquake or felt in a vehicle because of a wheel that is not properly balanced. 2 oscillation. 3 **vibrations** *pl.* instinctive reactions or feelings about a person or thing; vibes.
vi.bra.to (vee.BRAH.toh) *n.* **-tos** a tremulous effect produced by slight and rapid vibrations in pitch in singing or in playing stringed instruments.
vi.bra.tor (VYE.bray.tur) *n.* one that vibrates, as an electrical massaging device; **vi.bra.to.ry** (-bruh.tor.ee) *adj.*
vi.bur.num (vye.BUR.num) *n.* a shrub of the honeysuckle family bearing fragrant clusters of white or pink flowers.

vic.ar (VIC.ur) *n.* 1 a member of the clergy in charge of a parish; minister or parish priest. 2 a deputy or representative of a higher religious authority, as a "vicar apostolic" or "vicar-general": *The Pope is often referred to as the vicar of Christ.* —**vi.car.i.al** (vye.CAIR.ee.ul, vi-) *adj.*
vi.car.age (VIC.ur.ij) *n.* the residence or benefice of a vicar.
vi.car.i.ous (vye.CAIR.ee.us, vi-) *adj.* acting for or as by another: *the vicarious pleasure felt in another's enjoyment; Read travel books for vicarious travel experiences; vicarious* (= delegated) *authority.* —**vi.car.i.ous.ly** *adv.*
¹**vice** *n.* 1 a moral fault; immoral habit or tendency: *virtues and vices; drunkenness, gambling, and such vices.* 2 a trick or bad habit of a horse or other domestic animal, as shying. 3 *Cdn.* vise.
²**vi.ce** (VYE.see) *prep.* in the place of someone: *Jan Jones was appointed vice John Smith.* —**vice-** (VICE) *comb.form.* in the place of: *vice-chairman, vice-president, viceregal.*
vice.ge.rent (vice.JEER.unt) *n.* a ruler's deputy. —**vice.ge.ren.cy** *n.*
vi.cen.ni.al (vye.SEN.ee.ul) *adj.* lasting for or happening every 20 years.
vice-president *n.* an executive ranking next below a president: *the Vice-President of the United States.* —**vice-presidency** *n.* **-cies.** —**vice-presidential** *adj.*
vice.re.gal (vice.REE.gul) *adj.* of a viceroy: *the viceregal job of Governor General; the viceregal mansion.*
vice ring *n.* a group of people organized for crimes such as prostitution and drug dealing.
vice.roy (VICE.roy) *n.* a ruler representing a sovereign, as in the Spanish and British empires. —**vice.roy.al.ty** *n.*
vice squad *n.* a police squad concerned with crimes relating to prostitution, gambling, pornography, drug-trafficking, etc.
vi.ce ver.sa (VYE.see.VUR.suh, VICE-) *adv.* the other way around: *A equals B and vice versa; Most boys like girls and vice versa.*
vi.chys.soise (vish.ee.SWAHZ, vee.shee-) *n.* a thick soup made with leeks, cream, potatoes, etc. and usu. served cold.
Vich.y water (VISH.ee-) *n.* 1 water from the mineral springs at Vichy, France. 2 any mineral water. Also **Vichy.**
vic.i.nage (VIS.uh.nij) *n.* a vicinity or

neighborhood.

vi.cin.i.ty (vuh.SIN.i.tee) *n.* **-ties 1** nearness or proximity: *in close, immediate vicinity to the church; His expenses are in the vicinity of $500 a day.* **2** surrounding area: *Venice and vicinity.*

vi.cious (VISH.us) *adj.* **1** characterized by vice; wicked: *vicious habits, lies; He gave me a vicious look; a vicious savage; attacked by a vicious* (= unruly) *dog; a vicious* (= severe) *blow.* **2** involving interaction of cause and effect: *the vicious spiral of rising wages and prices.*
—**vi.cious.ly** *adv.;* **vi.cious.ness** *n.*

vicious circle *n.* **1** a situation in which the solution of a problem results in a new problem similar to the original one. **2** the fallacy of basing an argument on the very thing to be proved.

vi.cis.si.tudes (vuh.SIS.uh.tudes) *n.pl.* unpredictable and sudden changes usu. bringing hardships; ups and downs: *the vicissitudes of life.*

vic.tim (VIC.tum) *n.* one who suffers injury, harm, loss, etc.: *a lamb killed and placed on the altar as the sacrificial victim; the victim of an accident; earthquake, flood, tornado victims; the innocent victim of a crime; the unsuspecting victim of a swindle; In his old age he **fell victim** to amnesia.*

vic.tim.ize (VIC.tuh.mize) *v.* **-iz.es, -ized, -iz.ing** make a victim of someone; **vic.tim.iz.er** *n.* —**vic.tim.i.za.tion** (-muh.ZAY.shun, -mye-) *n.*

victimless crime *n.* a crime such as drug-trafficking, gambling, or prostitution that has no immediate victims as in theft, murder, etc.

vic.tor (VIC.tur) *n.* the winner or conqueror in a battle, struggle, etc.

vic.to.ri.a (vic.TOR.ee.uh) *n.* **1** a low, four-wheeled carriage with a folding top covering a seat at the rear for passengers. **2** a similar early automobile.

Vic.to.ri.an (vic.TOR.ee.un) *adj.* of or characteristic of the period of Queen Victoria's reign, often associated with prudery, bigotry, etc. —*n.* a writer of the Victorian period.
—**Vic.to.ri.an.ism** *n.*

vic.to.ri.ous (vic.TOR.ee.us) *adj.* **1** conquering: *We emerged victorious in the end; the victorious forces of democracy; The Allies were victorious over the Nazis in World War II; a victorious nation, position, scenario, team.* **2** marked by victory: *a victorious campaign, parade, re-election, revolution.* —**vic.to.ri.ous.ly** *adv.*

vic.to.ry (VIC.tuh.ree) *n.* **-ries** success in a struggle, as in battle or war: *to achieve, gain, score, win a victory in the Olympics; a clear, decisive, glorious, hard-won, hollow, moral, resounding, sweeping, stunning victory; the victory over our enemies; to snatch victory from the jaws of defeat.*

vic.tuals (VIT.uls) *n.pl. Informal* or *Regional.* food supplies; articles of food.

vi.cu.ña or **vi.cu.na** (vye.COON.yuh, vi-) *n.* **1** an Andean animal of the camel family, related to the alpaca and llama. **2** its fine soft wool. **3** its yellowish brown color.

vi.de (VYE.dee) *v. Latin.* please see (page, book, etc. referred to).

vid.e.o (VID.ee.oh) *n.* **1** a short film clip with a popular musical recording as the sound track: *music, rock videos; adja.: a video club, display, record, system.* **2** a motion picture recorded on a video cassette: *home videos; adja.: a video release, rental store, shop.* **3** a recording on videotape: *video art.* **4** picture output; *adja.: a video amplifier, display, frequency, monitor, screen, signal, terminal.* **5** television: *a star of stage and video; adja.: a video camera; video journalism.*

video cassette *n.* a cassette for storing and playback of recordings on film or videotape. —**video cassette recorder** *n.*

vid.e.o.con.fer.ence (VID.ee.oh.con.fur.unce) *n.* a teleconference using video cameras and monitors; **vid.e.o.con.fer.enc.ing** *n.; adja.: videoconferencing equipment, services, systems.*

vid.e.o.disc (VID.ee.oh.disc) *n.* a disc resembling a phonograph record for storing and playing back pictures and sounds recorded on it. —**videodisc player** *n.*

video display terminal (or **monitor** or **unit**) *n.* a computer's output device for data and pictures consisting of a TV screen and a keyboard; also **video terminal.**

video game *n.* any game played by manipulating images on a TV screen.

vid.e.o.phone (VID.ee.uh.fone) *n.* a telephone that is equipped for users to see each other while talking.

vid.e.o.tape (VID.ee.uh.tape) *v.* **-tapes, -taped, -tap.ing** record a TV broadcast or motion picture on magnetic tape. —*n.* **1** such a recording; video. **2** the tape itself. —**videotape recorder** *n.*

vid.e.o.tex (VID.ee.uh.tex) *n.* an interactive computer system that supplies services such as banking, shopping, news, etc. to consumers via a video terminal or TV screen. Also

vid.e.o.text.
vie (VYE) *v.* **vies, vied, vy.ing** contend or compete with another: *retailing vying with one another for a major share of the market; The contestants vied to reach the top; to vie for attention, business, patronage, positions, space.*
Vi.en.nese (vee.uh.NEEZ) *n. & adj., sing. & pl.* (a person) of or from **Vienna,** capital of Austria.
Vi.et.nam.ese (vee.ET.nuh.MEEZ) *n. & adj., sing. & pl.* (a person) of or from **Vietnam,** a country of S.E. Asia.
view (VYOO) *n.* **1** what is seen by someone looking from a certain position: *Skyscrapers block our view; structures that spoil the view; She asked for a room with a view; The view from the window is superb; You get a magnificent view of the ocean; a beautiful, breathtaking view; He lay there in full view of passersby; a car's rear-view mirror; the view* (= picture) *hanging on the wall; as the parade came* ***into*** *view* (= range of sight); ***In view of*** (= because of) *what you said, I will reconsider the matter; The paintings are* ***on*** *view* (= on show). **2** a personal opinion or judgment: *Let's exchange views; Give us your views on the matter; your views on or about capital punishment; It seems wrong from my point of view; In their view, there was no basis for the complaint; people of conservative, liberal, political, progressive, radical, strong views.* **3** intention or purpose: *He has a pay raise* ***in*** *view* (= in mind); *He phoned me* ***with a view to*** (= for the purpose of) *negotiating a settlement.*
—*v.* consider in a particular manner, from a standpoint, with a feeling, etc.: *She is being viewed as a serious contender for the presidency; prospective buyers viewing* (= inspecting) *a house.*
view.er (VYOO.ur) *n.* one that views, esp. an optical device for looking at slides.
view.find.er (VYOO.fine.dur) *n.* a window in a camera for viewing a picture before shooting.
view.point *n.* point of view or attitude.
vi.ges.i.mal (vye.JES.uh.mul) *adj.* **1** based on 20. **2** twentieth.
vig.il (VIJ.ul) *n.* **1** a staying awake; watch: *to keep (a) vigil over a patient needing constant attention; The demonstrators held an all-night vigil outside the embassy.* **2** the eve of a solemn religious festival. **3 vigils** *pl.* devotions or prayers.
vig.i.lance (VIJ.uh.lunce) *n.* watchfulness or alertness against danger or trouble: *They exercised great vigilance in preventing infiltration by spies; constant vigilance against the spread of the epidemic; "Eternal vigilance is the price of liberty."*
vig.i.lant (VIJ.uh.lunt) *adj.* watchful or alert: *to keep a vigilant eye or watch on or for intruders; ever vigilant about or to what goes on around you; vigilant in reporting crime; to be, remain, stay vigilant; a vigilant neighborhood.* —**vig.i.lant.ly** *adv.*
vig.i.lan.te (vij.uh.LAN.tee) *n.* a member of a self-appointed group of citizens enforcing laws, as in pioneer days, usu. because of inadequate law-enforcement. —**vig.i.lan.tism** *n.*
vi.gnette (vin.YET) *n.* **1** a short literary sketch, as of a personal experience or incident. **2** a picture or photograph that shades off at the edges without definite borders.
vig.or (VIG.ur) *n.* **1** strength or vitality: *the vigor of youth; a plant growing with vigor.* **2** effectiveness: *Sam acted with vigor and resolution.* Also **vig.our** *Cdn.* —**vig.or.ous** (-us) *adj.;* **vig.or.ous.ly** *adv.*
Vi.king (VYE.king) *n.* a Scandinavian pirate or explorer of the groups active between the 8th and 10th centuries A.D.; Norseman; also **vi.king.**
vile *adj.* **vil.er, vil.est** disgustingly foul, low, or depraved: *vile habits, language, odors; vile* (= bad) *weather.* —**vile.ly** *adv.;* **vile.ness** *n.*
vil.i.fy (VIL.uh.fye) *v.* **-fies, -fied, -fy.ing** use abusive language about a person. —**vil.i.fi.ca.tion** (-fuh.CAY.shun) *n.*
vil.la (VIL.uh) *n.* a suburban or country residence or estate.
vil.lage (VIL.ij) *n.* a community smaller than a town, esp. one chartered as a municipality: *a farming village; fishing villages along the coast; The whole village* (= all the people of the village) *turned out to greet us;* ***adj.****: the village common, green; a village gossip, mentality.* —**vil.lag.er** *n.*
vil.lain (VIL.un) *n.* **1** a wicked person or scoundrel, esp. as a dramatic character in opposition to the hero: *the villain of the piece.* **2** rascal: *an arch villain; the consummate villain;* [used jokingly] *You little villain!* —**vil.lain.ous** (-us) *adj.;* **vil.lain.ous.ly** *adv.*
vil.lain.y (VIL.uh.nee) *n.* **-nies** wickedness or a wicked act.
-ville *suffix* [used in slang coinages to suggest a condition as specified]: *drugsville, dullsville, endsville, weirdsville.*
vil.lein (VIL.un, -ain) *n.* a feudal serf

vil.lous / viper

with some rights of a freeman. **—vil.lein.age** or **vil.len.age** (-ij) *n.*

vil.lous (VIL.us) *adj.* having or covered with villi.

vil.lus *n., pl.* **vil.li** (VIL.eye) any of the small hairlike projections lining the small intestine and helping to absorb food.

vim *n.* vitality or energy: *She pursued the matter with vim and vigor.*

vin.ai.grette (vin.uh.GRET) *n.* a small ornamental box containing smelling salts or a sponge soaked in vinegar and lavender.

vin.ci.ble (VIN.suh.bul) *adj.* conquerable.

vin.di.cate (VIN.di.cate) *v.* **-cates, -cat.ed, -cat.ing** prove one's innocence under attack or establish a disputed claim, judgment, etc. by evidence, testimony, or a verdict: *History will vindicate us; to vindicate someone, one's claim, policy, right, view; adj.: We felt vindicated when things turned out as we had predicted; completely, fully, partially, totally vindicated.* **—vin.di.ca.tion** (-CAY.shun) *n.* **—vin.di.ca.tor** (-cay.tur) *n.*

vin.dic.tive (vin.DIC.tiv) *adj.* seeking vengeance; unforgiving: *vindictive acts, feelings, people.* **—vin.dic.tive.ly** *adv.;* **vin.dic.tive.ness** *n.*

vine *n.* **1** the grape-bearing vine. **2** any plant with a flexible stem, as the cucumber that creeps along the ground or an ivy that climbs walls and trellises.

vin.e.gar (VIN.uh.gur) *n.* a sour liquid used as a seasoning and preservative, made from fruit juices and other liquids containing sugar. **—vin.e.gar.y** *adj.*

vine.yard (VIN.yurd) *n.* a grapevine plantation.

vi.nous (VYE.nus) *adj.* having to do with wine: *a vinous bouquet, disorder, liquid.*

vin.tage (VIN.tij) *n.* **1** a grape harvest, esp. of a particular year: *a wine label showing vintage; of the vintage of 1955; Chateau Lafitte-Rothschild, vintage 1846; a few cases of each year's vintage* (= wines). **2** the make or class, as of an automobile, costume, piano, etc., with reference to its year or age: *an automobile of prewar vintage.* **—adja. 1** superior in quality: *a vintage crop, wine; 1947 was a vintage year (for wines); Vintage Americana.* **2** old or antique: *an early vintage camera; a vintage collection, typewriter, vase; vintage jewelry.* **3** having to do with antique cars: *vintage events, racing.*

vint.ner (VINT.nur) *n.* a wine maker or wine merchant.

vi.nyl (VYE.nul) *n.* a stiff, flexible plastic material used in making a wide range of products.

vinyl chloride *n.* a cancer-producing chemical used in the manufacture of vinyl plastics.

vi.ol (VYE.ul) *n.* an early stringed instrument played with a bow that gave way to the violin family.

vi.o.la (vee.OH.luh) *n.* a stringed instrument of larger size and lower pitch than the violin. **—vi.o.list** *n.*

vi.o.la.ble (VYE.uh.luh.bul) *adj.* capable of being violated.

vi.o.late (VYE.uh.late) *v.* **-lates, -lat.ed, -lat.ing** go against or treat with contempt: *to violate an agreement, the Sabbath, a sanctuary; to violate someone's religious beliefs, privacy, rights; to violate* (= rape) *a woman.* **—vi.o.la.tor** *n.*

vi.o.la.tion (vye.uh.LAY.shun) *n.* a violating or being violated, as an infringement, disturbance of the peace, desecration, or rape: *He committed a minor traffic violation; Lu was, was found, was held in violation of the curfew; human rights violations; blatant, flagrant, gross, open, serious violations.*

vi.o.lence (VYE.uh.lunce) *n.* (use of) physical force that causes injury, damage, etc.: *to resort to violence; to use violence instead of persuasion; an act of violence against the person; a crime of violence; Violence may break out on a picket line; a strike marred by violence; communal, racial, sporadic violence; the violence of a hurricane; sex and violence in TV shows; the violence* (= distortion) *done to a text by a bad translation.*

vi.o.lent (VYE.uh.lunt) *adj.* involving great, excessive, or unlawful force: *writhing in violent pain; a violent assault; a violent death by murder, suicide, etc.; a violent temper; a violent attack using violent language; colors in violent* (= strong) *contrast.* **—vi.o.lent.ly** *adv.*

vi.o.let (VYE.uh.lit) *n.* **1** a low-growing plant bearing five-petaled, typically bluish-purple flowers in early spring: *shy as a violet; He's not a shrinking violet.* **2** a bluish-purple; also *adj.*

vi.o.lin (vye.uh.LIN) *n.* a four-stringed, high-pitched musical instrument played with a bow. **—vi.o.lin.ist** *n.*

vi.o.lon.cel.lo (vye.uh.lun.CHEL.oh, vee.uh-) same as CELLO; **vi.o.lon.cel.list** *n.*

VIP or **V.I.P.** *n. Informal.* **VIPs** or **V.I.P.s** a very important person.

vi.per (VYE.pur) *n.* a poisonous snake

viperous / visage

with fangs.

vi.per.ous (VYE.puh.rus) *adj.* **1** of or like a viper; venomous. **2** spiteful or malicious.

vi.ra.go (vuh.RAY.go, -RAH.go) *n.* **-gos** or **-goes** a scolding or overbearing woman.

vi.ral (VYE.rul) *adj.* of or caused by a virus: *a viral disease such as AIDS; viral illnesses such as chickenpox and flu; viral and bacterial infections.*

vir.e.o (VEER.ee.oh) *n.* **-os** a small, olive-green North American songbird.

vir.gin (VUR.jin) *n.* one who has never had sexual intercourse, esp. a young woman: *a vestal virgin;* **the Virgin** (*mother of Jesus*). —*adj.* **1** having to do with virgins: *her virgin modesty; the doctrine of the* **virgin birth** (*of Jesus from the Virgin Mary*). **2** initial: *a virgin effort.* **3** that has not been used by humans: *a virgin beach, forest, jungle; virgin* (= uncultivated) *soil, territory; virgin* (= in native form) *silver, sulphur.* **4** fresh or pure: *virgin snow;* **Virgin olive oil** has only 1% to 3% acidity; **Extra virgin** olive oil has less than 1% acidity.

vir.gin.al (VUR.juh.nul) **1** *adj.* having to do with virgins: *virginal purity; a virginal quality; a virginal white dress.* **2** *n.* a harpsichord with a rectangular case.

Vir.gin.ian (vur.JIN.yun) *n. & adj.* (a person) of or from **Virginia**, a southern U.S. state.

Virginia creeper *n.* a North American woody vine with dark-blue berries and leaves that turn red in the fall.

Virginia reel *n.* an American reel danced by couples in double-line formation.

vir.gin.i.ty (vur.JIN.i.tee) *n.* **-ties 1** the condition of a virgin, esp. maidenhood. **2** celibacy.

Vir.go (VUR.go) *n.* **1** a constellation near the equator and the sixth sign of the zodiac. **2** a person born under this sign.

vir.gule (VURG.yool) *n.* a diagonal line used as in ½, to separate alternatives as in "and/or," to mean *per* as in "km/h," etc.

vir.i.des.cent (veer.uh.DES.unt) *adj.* greenish or turning green.

vir.ile (VEER.ile, -ul) *adj.* manly in being robust, potent, etc. —**vi.ril.i.ty** (vuh.RIL.i.tee) *n.*

vi.rol.o.gy (vye.ROL.uh.jee) *n.* the study of viruses and virus diseases; **vi.rol.o.gist** *n.* —**vi.ro.log.i.cal** (-ruh.LOJ.i.cul) *adj.*

vir.tu (vur.TOO) *n.* **1** a rare, curious, or skillfully done quality of art objects.

2 the taste for them. **3** [with *pl. v.*] art objects having such a quality.

vir.tu.al (VUR.choo.ul) *adj.* being such practically or in effect though not formally: *She was kept in virtual isolation; a virtual impossibility; He's the virtual boss around here; the* **virtual** (= unreal) **image** *in a mirror; the* **virtual memory** *or* **storage** *of a computer in an external storage device that can be used as an extension of its internal main memory; A computerized three-dimensional* **virtual reality** *image simulates an environment realistically and enables us to manipulate it.* —**vir.tu.al.ly** *adv.*

vir.tue (VUR.choo) *n.* **1** a particular moral quality: *the Christian virtues of faith, hope, and charity; the cardinal virtues; virtues and vices.* **2** moral excellence: *She is a paragon of virtue; a* **woman of easy virtue** (= woman of poor morals)*; He thought to* **make a virtue of necessity** (= make the best of a bad situation) *by going back to school when he lost his job.* **3** power or efficacy: *wonder drugs of dubious virtue; Degrees are conferred* **by virtue of** (= because of) *the authority vested in a university.* **4** a particular quality or worth: *the virtues of exercising.*

vir.tu.o.so (vur.choo.OH.soh) *n.* **-o.sos** or **-o.si** (-OH.see) an artist with great technical skill. —**vir.tu.os.i.ty** (-OS.i.tee) *n.*

vir.tu.ous (VUR.choo.us) *adj.* having moral virtue: *Our nuns lead a virtuous life; virtuous* (= chaste) *women.* —**vir.tu.ous.ly** *adv.;* **vir.tu.ous.ness** *n.*

vir.u.lent (VEER.yuh.lunt) *adj.* deadly or dangerous like poison: *a virulent disease, epidemic, infection, tumor; virulent antagonism, attacks, critics, hatred, language, opposition; a virulent strain of racism; hatred in a particularly virulent form.* —**vir.u.lent.ly** *adv.* —**vir.u.lence** *n.*

vi.rus (VYE.rus) *n.* **1** a microorganism that is smaller than bacteria, causing diseases such as influenza, measles, and chicken pox. **2** any poisonous or harmful influence. **3** a computer instruction hidden in a regular program on a disk, designed to destroy other programs and data when the disk is used.

vi.sa (VEE.zuh) *n.* permission granted to enter or stay in a country, as endorsed on a passport: *to cancel, issue, renew, violate a visa; entry, exit, student, tourist, transit, work visas.*

vis.age (VIZ.ij) *n.* facial appearance or aspect.

vis.aged (VIZ.ijd) *comb.form.* faced: *grim-visaged, square-visaged, stern-visaged.*

vis-à-vis (vee.zuh.VEE) *prep.* considered in relation to something: *the great performance of our students vis-à-vis national averages.* **—adv. & adj.** face-to-face: *They sat vis-à-vis; in a vis-à-vis position.*

vis.cer.a (VIS.uh.ruh) *n.pl.* internal organs, esp. the intestines.

vis.cer.al (VIS.uh.rul) *adj.* **1** of the viscera: *visceral organs; the visceral nervous system.* **2** instinctive or intuitive rather than intellectual; gut: *at the visceral level; a visceral feeling, impact, quality, reaction, satisfaction, sense.* **—vis.cer.al.ly** *adv.*

vis.cid (VIS.id) *adj.* viscous or sticky: *a viscid secretion; a viscid leaf (covered with something sticky).*

vis.cose *n.* **1** a viscous solution of cellulose from wood, cotton, etc. treated with chemicals, as in making rayon, cellophane, etc. **2** rayon made from viscose.

vis.cos.i.ty (vis.COS.i.tee) *n.* **-ties** viscous quality: *motor oils of high and low viscosities.*

vis.count (VYE.count) *n.* a British peer ranking below an earl or count and above a baron; **vis.count.ess** *fem.*

vis.cous (VIS.cus) *adj.* having a sticky or syrupy quality: *The more viscous a fluid the more slowly it flows, as pitch and molasses.*

vise (VICE) *n.* a device for firmly holding an object being worked on, consisting of parallel jaws closed and opened by a screw with a handle: *to be caught in a vise.*

Vish.nu (VISH.noo) *n.* the second member of the Hindu trinity, or "the Preserver" appearing in incarnations such as Rama and Krishna.

vis.i.bil.i.ty (viz.uh.BIL.i.tee) *n.* **-ties** a being visible or its condition, degree, range, etc.: *Visibility increases with height; poor visibility because of fog; zero visibility.*

vis.i.ble (VIZ.uh.bul) *adj.* that can be seen; apparent: *the visible spectrum; plainly visible; a vagrant with no visible means of support; a highly visible* (= conspicuous) *public figure;* **Visible minorities** stand out from the general white population because of differences of color, physical features, etc. **—vis.i.bly** *adv.*: *enjoying herself visibly; visibly moved; a visibly aging man.*

vis.ion (VIZH.un) *n.* **1** power of seeing or perceiving: *Have your vision tested; acute, blurred, double, impaired, peripheral, tunnel vision; the field of vision* (= sight) *of an optical instrument; a woman of great vision* (= foresight or imagination); *poetic vision.* **2** something seen, esp. by the mind or imagination: *a vision of heavenly glory; the beatific vision; The vision raised its head and spoke to us; The mystic heard voices and saw visions.* **—v.** see in or as in a vision; envision.

vi.sion.ar.y (VIZH.uh.nair.ee) *n.* **1** one who sees visions. **2** a dreamer or impractical person. **3** a person of great vision or foresight. **—adj. 1** fanciful and impractical: *a visionary idea, plan, scheme.* **2** showing keen foresight: *visionary brilliance, leaders, leadership, qualities.*

vis.it (VIZ.it) *v.* **1** go or come to see for pleasure: *to visit Europe, a shrine, the zoo;* **adj.**: *one of the most* **visited** *tourist attractions.* **2** be a guest or stay with someone: *to visit (with) relatives;* **n.**: *The boss doesn't like too much* **visiting** (= chatting) *on the phone;* **adj.a.**: *a visiting dignitary, mission, team; visiting royalty; a visiting area or room for receiving visitors; visiting privileges, rights of a divorced spouse (to visit one's children); a visiting* (= not resident) *orchestra, professor, scholar; a hospital's* **visiting hours** (during which patients may be visited). **3** go or come to see officially or professionally, as a doctor, inspector, supervisor, etc. **4** afflict or inflict: *Egypt was visited with plagues; the sufferings God visited on Job.* **—n. 1** a visiting: *a short visit.* **2** a stay as a guest. **—vis.it.a.ble** (-tuh.bul) *adj.*

vis.i.tant (VIZ.uh.tunt) *n.* [rare & formal use] a visitor from another world: *a ghostly visitant; heavenly visitants; a visitant from Mars.*

vis.i.ta.tion (viz.uh.TAY.shun) *n.* **1** an official or formal visit: *He didn't want custody (of his children), just visitation;* **adj.a.**: *visitation agreements; a divorced spouse's visitation privileges, rights (for visiting the children).* **2** reward or punishment sent by God.

visiting nurse *n.* a nurse whose work is visiting patients in their homes and who takes part in public-health projects.

vis.i.tor (VIZ.uh.tur) *n.* one who visits on business or for pleasure, as a tourist: *a frequent visitor; regular visitors.*

vi.sor (VYE.zur) *n.* a part that shields the face or eyes, as the movable front part of a helmet, a cap's brim, eyeshade, or a shade attached to a windshield for protection from glare; **adj.**:

a **visored** helmet (= helmet with a visor).

vis.ta (VIS.tuh) *n.* **1** a long narrow view as between rows of trees. **2** an extended or comprehensive mental view or prospect: *a discovery that opened up new vistas of knowledge.*

vis.u.al (VIZH.oo.ul) *adj.* having to do with seeing or sight: *visual aspects, cues, designs, displays, impacts, impairment, impressions, presentations; Visual education uses* **visual aids** *such as films, charts, and slides; the* **visual arts** *of painting, sculpture, ceramics, etc.; 20/20 vision means normal* **visual acuity** (= visual sharpness); **visual aphasia** *of seeing without understanding words; a* **visual binary** (= double) *star that appears single to the unaided eye.* —**vis.u.al.ly** *adv.*

vis.u.al.ize (VIZH.oo.uh.lize) *v.* **-iz.es, -ized, -iz.ing** form a mental picture of something abstract, forgotten, etc.: *I can visualize her as a future prime minister.* —**vis.u.al.iz.er** *n.* —**vis.u.al.i.za.tion** (-luh.ZAY.shun, -lye-) *n.*

vi.ta (VEE.tuh, VYE-) *n., pl.* **-tae** (VEE.tye, VYE.tee) a brief biography or curriculum vitae.

vi.tal (VYE.tul) *adj.* **1** having to do with life; important for life: *The heart, lungs, liver, brain, etc. are vital organs; a vital* (= lively) *personality; a vital* (= fatal) *wound; the lung's vital* (= inhaling) **capacity**. **2** essential; very important: *one of the most vital issues of our time; a vital function, ingredient, necessity; of vital importance; things that* **have** *or* **play a vital role** *in our lives; Funds are vital to the success of our mission.* —**vi.tal.ly** *adv.*

vi.tal.i.ty (vye.TAL.i.tee) *n.* **-ties** **1** physical vigor; capacity to survive. **2** mental vigor or energy; liveliness.

vi.tal.ize (VYE.tul.ize) *v.* **-iz.es, -ized, -iz.ing** give life, vigor, or liveliness to something: *plans to vitalize a dying economy.* —**vi.tal.iz.er** *n.*

vi.tals (VYE.tuls) *n.pl.* vital organs, parts, or elements.

vital signs *n.* signs of life, esp. body temperature, pulse rate, respiration, and blood pressure.

vital statistics *n.pl.* **1** data about births, deaths, fertility, life expectancy, marriages, and divorce. **2** *Informal.* personal data such as measurements around one's body.

vi.ta.min (VYE.tuh.min) *n.* a complex organic substance essential to the body's health and growth which is supplied by foods and whose deficiency causes scurvy and other diseases: *Vitamin B is a complex of water-soluble vitamins such as B_1, B_2, etc.*

vi.ti.ate (VISH.ee.ate) *v.* **-ates, -at.ed, -at.ing** make faulty, ineffective, etc.: *the original text vitiated* (= corrupted) *by corrections and changes; A technicality could vitiate* (= invalidate) *a legal document.* —**vi.ti.a.tion** (-AY.shun) *n.*

vit.i.cul.ture (VIT.uh.cul.chur, VYE.tuh-) *n.* cultivation of grapes; **vit.i.cul.tur.ist** (-CUL.chuh.rist) *n.*

vit.re.ous (VIT.ree.us) *adj.* of or like glass: *the vitreous luster of a mineral; vitreous rocks.*

vitreous humor (or **body**) *n.* the transparent, jellylike substance filling the eyeball cavity behind the lens.

vit.ri.fy (VIT.ri.fye) *v.* **-fies, -fied, -fy.ing** fuse into glass or glasslike condition by heat; *adj.:* nonporous **vitrified** ceramics; Vitrified bricks don't absorb water. —**vit.ri.fi.ca.tion** (-fuh.CAY.shun) *n.*

vi.trine (vi.TREEN) *n.* a glass-covered display case.

vit.ri.ol (VIT.ree.ul) *n.* **1** sulfuric acid. **2** sharp or bitter feelings, criticism, etc.: *He wrote a scathing letter with pen dipped in vitriol.* **3** a sulfate that has glassy crystals, as of copper, or "blue vitriol," of iron, or "green vitriol," and of zinc, or "white vitriol." —**vi.tri.ol.ic** (-OL.ic) *adj.*

vi.tu.per.ate (vye.TUE.puh.rate, vi-) *v.* **-ates, -at.ed, -at.ing** abuse or revile. —**vi.tu.per.a.tion** (-RAY.shun) *n.* —**vi.tu.per.a.tive** (-ruh.tiv) *adj.*

vi.va (VEE.vah) *interj.* long live (person specified)!

vi.va.ce (vee.VAH.chay) *adj. & adv. Music.* in a brisk, lively manner.

vi.va.cious (vuh.VAY.shus) *adj.* lively and buoyant: *a vivacious girl, performance, youth; vivacious laughter.* —**vi.va.cious.ly** *adv.;* **vi.va.cious.ness** *n.* —**vi.vac.i.ty** (-VAS.i.tee) *n.*

viva vo.ce (VYE.vuh.VOH.see) *adj.* oral: *a viva voce examination; adv.:* to vote *viva voce.*

viv.id (VIV.id) *adj.* **1** lively: *a vivid description, imagination, personality.* **2** brilliant or brightly colored: *painted in vivid colors; The sky was a vivid blue.* **3** clear and distinct: *a vivid memory, recollection.* —**viv.id.ly** *adv.;* **viv.id.ness** *n.*

viv.i.fy (VIV.uh.fye) *v.* **-fies, -fied, -fy.ing** impart freshness or vitality to something: *to vivify the faded figures of an old painting; a* **vivifying** *lotion for the skin.* —**viv.i.fi.ca.tion** (-fuh.CAY.shun) *n.*

vi.vip.a.rous (vi.VIP.uh.rus) *adj.* giving

birth to living young, not oviparous or egg-laying: *Mammals, some snakes, and fishes such as the guppy are viviparous.*
—**viv.i.par.i.ty** (viv.uh.PAIR.i.tee) *n.*
viv.i.sec.tion (viv.uh.SEC.shun) *n.* dissection of a living animal for study.
—**viv.i.sec.tion.ist** *n.* —**viv.i.sect** (VIV.uh.sect) *v.*
vix.en (VIX.un) *n.* **1** a female fox. **2** an ill-tempered woman; **vix.en.ish** *adj.*
viz.ard (VIZ.urd) *n.* [old use] a mask or disguise.
vi.zier (vuh.ZEER) *n.* in some Moslem countries, a minister of state: *The "grand vizier" was a sultan's prime minister.*
viz.or (VYE.zur) same as VISOR.
vo.ca.ble (VOH.cuh.bul) *n.* a word in regard to its sounds or letters as distinguished from meaning.
vo.cab.u.lar.y (vuh.CAB.yuh.lair.ee) *n.* -**lar.ies 1** a list of words, as in a glossary. **2** the stock of words used by a person ("active vocabulary") or only understood ("passive vocabulary"): *how to develop, enlarge, improve your vocabulary; "Defeat" is not in her vocabulary* (= She doesn't accept defeat). **3** the word stock of a language, words used in a branch of learning, profession, etc.: *the expanding English vocabulary; scientific vocabulary; "Computer" became part of our vocabulary only recently; A dictionary's* **vocabulary entries** [shown in boldface in this dictionary] *include words, idioms and phrases, derivatives, and inflections.* **4** a set of signs or symbols used in any sort of communication: *the vocabulary* (= movements) *of ballet.*
vo.cal (VOH.cul) *adj.* **1** having to do with voice: *the vocal organs of the throat and mouth; Two bands of tissue in the throat called* **vocal cords** *vibrate to produce sounds; vocal* (= sung, not instrumental) *music.* **2** having voice: *Be vocal* (= outspoken) *about your grievances.*
—*n.* **1** a vocal sound, as a vowel. **2** a vocal solo. —**vo.cal.ly** *adv.*
vo.cal.ic (voh.CAL.ic) *adj.* having to do with a vowel or vowels: *vocalic alliteration, sounds.*
vo.cal.ist (VOH.cuh.list) *n.* a singer, not an instrumentalist.
vo.cal.ize (VOH.cuh.lize) *v.* -**iz.es, -ized, -iz.ing** use the voice or utter; speak, sing, or shout. —**vo.cal.i.za.tion** (-luh.ZAY.shun, -lye-) *n.*
vo.ca.tion (voh.CAY.shun) *n.* **1** the occupation, profession, or trade in which one works: *We think of a career when choosing a vocation.* **2** an occupation one is specially suited for or feels called to: *She seems to have missed her vocation – she should have become a lawyer; a vocation to religious life.*
—**vo.ca.tion.al** *adj.*
voc.a.tive (VOC.uh.tiv) *n. & adj.* (a grammatical case) showing the person or thing directly spoken to, as "John!"
vo.cif.er.ate (voh.SIF.uh.rate) *v.* -**ates, -at.ed, -at.ing** shout or utter loudly.
—**vo.cif.er.a.tion** (-RAY.shun) *n.*
vo.cif.er.ous (voh.SIF.uh.rus) *adj.* noisy, unrestrained, and vehement: *a vociferous group; They were vociferous in their demands; The silent majority and the vociferous minority (of a population).*
—**vo.cif.er.ous.ly** *adv.*
vod.ka (VOD.kuh) *n.* an unflavored alcoholic liquor distilled from potatoes, rye, barley, etc.
vogue (VOHG) *n.* **1** fashion or popularity at a particular time: *Minis have been in vogue since the early 1970s; Fashions come into and go out of vogue.*
2 something that is in fashion: *the latest vogue in swimwear; Minis are becoming the vogue again; when skate-boarding was all the vogue* (= rage); *"input," "interface," "phase out," and such* **vogue words** *of the electronic age.* **3** the period of popularity of a vogue. —**vo.guish** *adj.*
voice *n.* **1** a sound communicating thoughts or feelings, esp. of a person speaking, crying, etc.: *The human voice is a highly developed form of the animal cry; She has temporarily lost her voice because of laryngitis; to drop, lower, raise one's voice; to speak in a clear, firm, gentle, gruff, loud, shaking, subdued, trembling voice; He shouted at the top of his voice; to give voice* (= expression) *to one's frustration; A singer is not* **in voice** (= proper condition to sing) *till she is well again; Listen to the voice of reason; an inner voice* (= conscience); *the people's voice* (= right to be heard) *in a democracy; a measure approved by the legislators* **with one voice** (= unanimously). **2** a singer, as in a choir, or the part of a musical composition for one singer or instrument. **3** the active or passive form of a verb.
—*v.* **voic.es, voiced, voic.ing** give expression to in spoken or written form: *He voiced his strong disapproval.*
voice box *n.* **1** the voice-producing organ at the top of the windpipe; larynx. **2** a voice output device of a computer: *By attaching a voice box to a computer, the blind can hear the words they type.*

voiced *comb.form.* having voice as specified: *deep-voiced, gravelly-voiced, soft-voiced, sweet-voiced.*

voice mail *n.* an electronic system of receiving, transmitting, and responding to voice messages; *adj.: a voice-mail box, service, system.*

voice-over *n.* a narration or announcement without the speaker being shown, as in TV and motion pictures.

voice.print *n.* a recorded pattern of sound waves characteristic of a person's voice, used like the fingerprint for identification purposes.

void *n.* 1 an empty space. 2 emptiness or a gap: *The death of their only child left a void in their hearts; To fill the void they decided to adopt a child.*
—*adj.* 1 empty or vacant: *void space; language that is void of* (= without) *meaning.* 2 legally invalid: *a contract declared null and void; a void ballot, parking ticket.* —*v.* 1 make empty or void. 2 empty out or evacuate the bladder. —**void.a.ble** *adj.* —**void.er** *n.*

voi.là (vwah.LAH) *interj. French.* behold! there!

voile (VOIL) *n.* a sheer fabric of plain weave used for veils, curtains, dresses, etc.

vol.a.tile (VOL.uh.til, -tile) *adj.* 1 easily changing into vapor at a relatively low temperature, as gasoline or alcohol. 2 easily changeable in condition or mood; fickle: *a volatile crowd; the volatile gasoline market; volatile public opinion; a volatile temper (that is quick to anger); volatile* (= temporary, not permanent) *storage of computer data in cache memory.* —**vol.a.til.i.ty** (-TIL.i.tee) *n.*

vol.a.til.ize (VOL.uh.tul.ize) *v.* **-iz.es, -ized, -iz.ing** evaporate.

vol.can.ic (vol.CAN.ic) *adj.* 1 having to do with volcanos: *volcanic activity, ash, craters, dust, eruptions, explosions, islands; Volcanic glass is formed by rapid cooling of lava; crystalline volcanic rock such as obsidian formed by cooled lava.* 2 violent and explosive: *his volcanic fury, rage; a volcanic temperament.*

vol.ca.nism (VOL.cuh.niz.um) *n.* volcanic phenomena including geysers and fumaroles.

vol.ca.no (vol.CAY.noh) *n.* **-nos** or **-noes** 1 a funnel-shaped crater spewing lava, ashes, and gases. 2 a cone-shaped mountain with a volcanic crater: *Volcanos erupt; active, dormant, extinct volcanos.*

vol.ca.nol.o.gy (vol.cuh.NOL.uh.jee) *n.* the science concerned with volcanic phenomena. —**vol.ca.nol.o.gist** *n.*

vole *n.* a mouselike rodent found in fields and meadows.

vo.li.tion (vuh.LISH.un) *n.* an act of the will or the power of willing: *She did it of her own volition; He acted on his own volition.* —**vo.li.tion.al** *adj.*

vol.ley (VOL.ee) *n.* 1 the simultaneous discharge of many weapons: *to fire a volley; the opening volley; the latest volley in their war of words.* 2 a shower of missiles: *a volley of cheers, oaths, questions, rubber bullets, shots.* 3 in tennis, etc., a return of the ball before it hits the playing surface: *to hit a ball on the volley.*
—*v.* **vol.leys, vol.leyed, vol.ley.ing** 1 discharge or be discharged as in a volley: *The police volleyed tear gas into the building.* 2 return a ball in play, before it hits the ground.

vol.ley.ball (VOL.ee.ball) *n.* 1 a team game played by hitting an inflated ball with the hands back and forth over a high net without letting it touch the ground. 2 the ball itself.

volt *n.* the unit of electromotive force in the International System of Units: *a nine-volt battery.* —**volt.age** (-tij) *n.* electricity measured in volts: *high, low voltage; to step down, step up (the) voltage.*

vol.ta.ic (vol.TAY.ic) *adj.* having to do with electricity produced by chemical action: *the voltaic cells of an automobile battery.*

volte-face (volt.FAHS) *n.* an about-face in policy, attitude, etc.: *He denied the charge and then did a quick volte-face.*

volt.me.ter (VOHLT.mee.tur) *n.* a voltage-measuring instrument.

vol.u.ble (VOL.yuh.bul) *adj.* talking much and unendingly; **vol.u.bly** *adv.* —**vol.u.bil.i.ty** (-BIL.i.tee) *n.*

vol.ume (VOL.yum) *n.* 1 cubic capacity or the solid content of something three-dimensional: *A two-centimeter cube has a volume of 8 cubic centimeters.* 2 quantity: *volumes of smoke; the daily volume of output; to turn down, turn up the volume* (= sound) *of the radio.* 3 a bound book or one of a series: *a volume of 300 pages; a dictionary in two volumes; a rare volume of Shakespeare's plays; a workbook as a companion volume to the textbook.* —**speak volumes** be very expressive: *His look of disgust spoke volumes; a small book that speaks volumes for her scholarly attainments.*

vol.u.met.ric (vol.yuh.MET.ric) *adj.* involving measurement of volume: *volumetric analysis.*

vo.lu.mi.nous (vuh.LOO.muh.nus) *adj.*

large in content, output, size, etc.: *his voluminous output; a voluminous treatise, writer.* —**vo.lu.mi.nous.ly** *adv.*

vol.un.tar.y (VOL.un.tair.ee) *adj.* **1** done of one's own free will or by choice: *voluntary compliance, contributions, exile; done on a voluntary basis; Walking, talking, etc. are voluntary actions carried out by use of voluntary* (= will-controlled) *muscles; The company went into voluntary bankruptcy to be free of debts and start afresh.* **2** unpaid; volunteer: *voluntary agencies, labor, services, work.*
—*n.* solo organ music, as played at a church service. —**vol.un.tar.i.ly** (-TAIR.uh.lee) *adv.*

vol.un.teer (vol.un.TEER) *n.* **1** a person who is in military service of his own free will. **2** one who offers to work for free: *candy stripers, charity collectors, and other volunteers;* **adj***.*: *a volunteer firefighter, helper, organization; volunteer work.*
—*v.* offer one's services, time, etc. without getting paid: *to volunteer for the army; Neighbors volunteered to help; She volunteered her services as a language tutor; He prefers to volunteer time for charitable work rather than give money.*

vo.lup.tu.ar.y (vuh.LUP.choo.air.ee) *n.* **-ar.ies** one who leads a luxurious and sensual life.

vo.lup.tu.ous (vuh.LUP.choo.us) *adj.* having to do with sensual pleasure: *voluptuous fancies, music; a voluptuous* (= big and sexy) *figure.*
—**vo.lup.tu.ous.ly** *adv.*;
vo.lup.tu.ous.ness *n.*

vo.lute (vuh.LOOT) *n.* a spiral form or shape, as the scroll of an Ionic column or a marine snail with a spiral shell.

vom.it (VOM.it) *v.* discharge with force from within, as the contents of the stomach through the mouth; throw up; *n.*: *Do not induce vomiting but call the doctor.* —*n.* a vomiting or what is vomited: *The patient choked on his own vomit.*

voo.doo (VOO.doo) *n.* **-doos 1** sorcery as practiced by some African tribes and some West Indians, including the cult of guardian spirits and the indirect injuring of enemies by sticking pins into images of wax. **2** one who practices voodoo. **3** a charm or fetish used in voodoo. —**voo.doo.ism** *n.*

vo.ra.cious (vuh.RAY.shus) *adj.* devouring or insatiable: *a voracious appetite, reader, shark.* —**vo.ra.cious.ly** *adv.*;
vo.ra.cious.ness *n.* —**vo.rac.i.ty** (-RAS.i.tee) *n.*

vor.tex (VOR.tex) *n.* **-tex.es** or **-ti.ces** (-tuh.seez) **1** a whirling phenomenon or formation such as a whirlpool, whirlwind, or the eye of a cyclone. **2** a vortexlike situation or condition: *the vortex of war; drawn into the vortex of the struggle; sucked into the vortex of politics.*

vo.ta.ry (VOH.tuh.ree) *n.* **-ries** a devotee: *a votary of peace, yoga, Zeus.*

vote *n.* **1** a choice, as between candidates for office, or a formal expression of it, as by ballot: *when a bill comes or goes to a vote; to bring it to a vote; to put an issue to a vote; to take a vote on the question; to influence, swing the vote in our favor.* **2** the right to vote: *Children have no vote; Women got the vote only recently.* **3** a ballot: *to cast a vote; In a tie, the chair casts the deciding vote; He switched his vote at the last moment in favor of the other party; an influential politician who can deliver the votes; It was a close vote; a straw vote; a motion carried by a unanimous vote; elected by a voice vote.* **4** a majority expression of feeling: *a vote of thanks;* **a vote of confidence** *in a government.* **5** votes collectively: *The rain didn't help to get out the vote; The vote was light, not heavy; the Jewish vote; the Liberal vote; the undecided vote; to count, tally the vote after balloting.*
—*v.* **votes, vot.ed, vot.ing 1** give a vote to someone: *He votes for the Democrats; She voted against the bill; Sam votes the Republican ticket.* **2** decide, ratify, etc. by vote: *to vote a candidate to office; to vote by a show of hands; to* **vote down** (= defeat) *a bill instead of voting it through the legislature; to* **vote in** (= elect) *a candidate to office; to* **vote out** (= defeat) *an incumbent mayor; The function was voted* (= judged) *a success.*
—**vot.er** *n.*

vo.tive (VOH.tiv) *adj.* having to do with the fulfillment of a vow or thanksgiving for a divine favor: *a votive candle, offering, pilgrimage, prayer, shrine.*

vouch (VOWCH) *v.* give a guarantee or serve as evidence *for* the truth of a statement, someone's qualities, etc.: *She's telling the truth and I can vouch for it.*

vouch.er (VOW.chur) *n.* one that vouches, esp. a document or other piece of evidence of a business transaction, as a canceled check, coupon, etc.

vouch.safe (vowch.SAFE) *v.* **-safes, -safed, -saf.ing** grant as a special favor; deign: *to vouchsafe an answer to* (or *to answer) our prayers.*

vow *n.* a solemn promise, esp. to God: *to break, make or take, violate a vow; She kept her vows all her life; to renew marriage vows (of fidelity); A nun **takes vows** (usually of poverty, chastity, and obedience).* —*v.* make a vow: *to vow obedience, revenge, secrecy; He has vowed not to touch alcohol as of January 1.*

vow.el (VOW.ul) *n.* 1 a vocal sound made with more or less open mouth and no obstruction of breath as in forming consonants: *short and long vowels.* 2 a letter such as "a," "e," "i," "o," and "u" representing such a sound.

voy.age (VOY.ij) *n.* a relatively long journey by water, air, or in space: *to go on a voyage around the world; a voyage of exploration; a voyage to the moon; The Titanic sank on her maiden voyage.* —*v.* **-ag.es, -aged, -ag.ing** make a voyage: *The Vikings voyaged across the ocean and settled in Newfoundland around A.D. 1000.* —**voy.ag.er** *n.*

vo.ya.geur (vwah.yah.ZHUR) *n.* a French Canadian boatman, esp. one who worked for a fur-trading company.

vo.yeur (voy.YUR, vwah-) *n.* one who gets sexual pleasure from secretly watching others undressing or having sex; peeping Tom. —**vo.yeur.ism** *n.* —**vo.yeur.is.tic** (-yuh.RIS.tic) *adj.*

vroom *n.* the roaring sound of a speeding car.

Vul.can (VUL.cun) *n.* the Roman god of fire and metalworking.

vul.can.ism (VUL.cuh.niz.um) same as VOLCANISM.

vul.can.ite (VUL.cuh.nite) *n.* a hard, vulcanized rubber.

vul.can.ize (VUL.cuh.nize) *v.* **-iz.es, -ized, -iz.ing** treat crude rubber or similar material with sulfur and heat to give it greater strength, elasticity, etc.; **vul.can.i.zer** *n.* —**vul.can.i.za.tion** (-nuh.ZAY.shun, -nye-) *n.*

vul.gar (VUL.gur) *adj.* 1 showing lack of refinement or good taste: *a vulgar expression; vulgar fashions, insults, language, manners, slang; vulgar ambition; a vulgar display of wealth.* 2 of the common people or general public: *vulgar errors, superstitions; the vulgar crowd, masses.* —**vul.gar.ly** *adv.*

vul.gar.i.an (vul.GAIR.ee.un) *n.* a vulgar person, esp. one who is rich.

vul.gar.ism (VUL.guh.riz.um) *n.* 1 a coarse or uneducated expression, as "irregardless." 2 vulgarity.

vul.gar.i.ty (vul.GAIR.i.tee) *n.* **-ties** 1 the quality or condition of being vulgar. 2 a vulgar or coarse action, habit, or usage.

vul.gar.ize (VUL.guh.rize) *v.* **-iz.es, -ized, -iz.ing** 1 make common, popular, etc. 2 debase or degrade. —**vul.gar.iz.er** *n.* —**vul.gar.i.za.tion** (-ruh.ZAY.shun, -rye-) *n.*

Vulgar Latin *n.* the nonclassical Latin spoken by the common people of ancient Rome which gave rise to the modern Romance languages.

vul.gate *n.* 1 **Vulgate** a Latin translation of the Bible used as the official text in the Roman Catholic Church. 2 a popular text or version; also, vernacular speech.

vul.ner.a.ble (VUL.nuh.ruh.bul) *adj.* 1 that can be wounded: *The heel was Achilles' vulnerable spot.* 2 open to attack: *a vulnerable argument, position; when you are young and vulnerable; Politicians are vulnerable to public criticism.* —**vul.ner.a.bly** *adv.* —**vul.ner.a.bil.i.ty** (-BIL.i.tee) *n.*

vul.pine *adj.* of or like a fox; cunning or sly.

vul.ture (VUL.chur) *n.* 1 a large, carrion-eating bird of prey of the same family as buzzards and condors. 2 a greedy or ruthless person.

vul.va (VUL.vuh) *n.* the external genital organ of the human female.

vying *pres. part.* of VIE.

W, w

W or **w** (DUB.ul.yoo) *n.* **W's** or **w's** the 23rd letter of the English alphabet.

wab.ble (WOB.ul) *v.* **wab.bles, wab.bled, wab.bling** same as WOBBLE. —**wab.bler** *n.*

wack.o (WACK.oh) *n. Slang.* one who is wacky or eccentric: *some wacko from a fringe group;* **adj.**: *a wacko idea; The guy is wacko.*

wack.y (WACK.ee) *adj.* **wack.i.er, -i.est** *Slang.* eccentric or unconventional: *a wacky idea; the wacky world of spontaneity; her wacky sense of humor; his wacky personality.* —**wack.i.ness** *n.*

wad (WOD) *n.* a small lump of soft material: *a wad of cotton to plug the ears; a wad of chewing tobacco, of gum; a wad (= disc) of felt used in a shotgun cartridge; a wad (Informal for large bundle) of money.* —*v.* **wads, wad.ded, wad.ding** 1 press or roll up into a wad. 2 to plug with a wad or soft material (**wadding**).

wad.dle (WOD.ul) *v.* **wad.dles,**

wad.dled, wad.dling walk with short steps, swaying from side to side, as a duck or penguin. —*n.* such a gait. —**wad.dler** *n.*

wade *v.* **wades, wad.ed, wad.ing** **1** walk through a medium such as water, snow, or mud that hinders free movement: *to wade in and rescue a child from the water; She waded into deep water; to wade through the underbrush.* **2** make one's way *through* dull reading, etc. with difficulty. —**wade into** move against a person or thing: *to wade into disputed territory.* —*n.* a wading.

wad.er (WAY.dur) *n.* **1** one that wades, as a wading bird. **2 waders** *pl.* a waterproof garment with attached boots, as used by fishermen.

wa.di (WAH.dee) *n.* a watercourse or ravine, as in the Sahara and Arabian deserts, that is dry except in the rainy season.

wading bird *n.* a long-legged bird such as the crane, flamingo, or stork that wades in shallow waters to catch their prey.

wading pool *n.* a shallow pool for children to play in.

wa.fer (WAY.fur) *n.* **1** a thin, crisp cracker, as used in the Eucharist: *Communion wafers;* a **wafer-thin** *majority, profit margin, slice.* **2** an adhesive seal. **3** a disk of silicon carrying an integrated circuit.

waf.fle (WOF.ul) *n.* a batter cake made on a waffle iron. —*v.* **waf.fles, waf.fled, waf.fling** be vague or indecisive: *The politician waffled over which side to join; She waffled on the issue of abortion; Britain waffled, and then decided to join the other nations.*

waffle iron *n.* a metal utensil with two hinged plates between which a waffle is cooked.

waft (WAFT, WOFT) *v.* move or carry lightly (as) by a breeze or wave: *A delicious aroma wafted in from the kitchen; Classical music wafts through his living room.* —*n.* **1** an odor or sound thus carried. **2** a slight breeze or wafting movement.

wag *v.* **wags, wagged, wag.ging** shake or swing back and forth, up and down, etc.: *a dog wagging its tail; The mad director wagged his finger in her face and got an earful; A scandal makes tongues wag* (= makes people gossip); *Let's stop wagging our tongues.* —*n.* **1** a wagging. **2** a joker or jester. —**wag.gish** *adj.*

wage *n.* periodic compensation paid for work, esp. manual or physical; also **wag.es** *pl.*: *to draw, earn, pay a wage; a decent, living, minimum, weekly wage; to freeze wages; Her wages were $500 a week; the minimum wage (rate) fixed by government; "The wages* (= punishment) *of sin is death"*; *adj.*: *inflationary wage and price increases; Executives are at a higher wage level; the* **wage earners** *of a family.* —*v.* **wag.es, waged, wag.ing** carry on a war, battle, campaign, etc. against an adversary: *an aid program to wage war against hunger.*

wag.er (WAY.jur) *n. & v.* bet or gamble: *to lay, make, place a wager; to wager whether a fight will last 15 rounds; She wagered (him) $50 that it won't; to wager money on a horse.*

wag.ger.y (WAG.uh.ree) *n.* **wag.ger.ies** a joke or the act of joking.

wag.gle *n. & v.* **wag.gles, wag.gled, wag.gling** wag or shake; **wag.gly** *adj.*

wag.on (WAG.un) *n.* **1** a four-wheeled vehicle or cart for hauling loads: *a covered wagon.* **2** a truck or station wagon: *a police paddy wagon* or *patrol wagon (for transporting prisoners); welcome wagons.* —**circle the wagons** assume a protective and defensive posture. —**on the wagon** *Informal.* abstaining from alcoholic liquor, formerly "to go on the water wagon." —**wag.on.er** *n.*

wagon train *n.* a caravan of wagons on a journey.

waif *n.* a homeless or neglected child; also, a stray animal: *waifs and strays.*

wail *n.* a loud and long cry of grief, pain, or hunger. —*v.* make a wail; *n.*: *the* **wailing** *of an ambulance siren; the* **Wailing Wall** *of Jerusalem at which Jews pray and seek consolation.*

wain *n. Regional.* a large or heavy farm wagon.

wain.scot (WAIN.scut, -scot) *n.* **1** wood paneling on the interior wall of a room, esp. on its lower part. **2** the lower part of an interior wall finished differently from the top. —*v.* **-scots, -scot.ed, -scot.ing** line a wall with wood. Also **wain.scot.ted, wain.scot.ting** *Cdn.*

wain.wright *n.* one who builds wagons.

waist *n.* **1** the usu. narrow part of the abdomen just above the hips: *a slim waist; her wasp waist.* **2** a similar narrowed middle part of a violin. **3** the bodice or blouse of a dress.

waist.band *n.* a band around the waist at the top of a skirt or trousers.

waist.coat *n. Brit.* a man's vest.

waist.line *n.* **1** the line of the waist or

the measurement around it, as showing size. **2** the dividing line between the bodice and skirt of a dress, usu. at the waist.

wait *v.* **1** stay expecting something; continue in a place for a time: *Please wait for the next bus; wait till 12; Don't keep the child waiting; a matter so urgent it can't wait; Don't wait up for me; She had to wait (Informal for delay) dinner for him; Join the line and wait (for) your turn.* **2** serve: *Waiters wait at or on tables; Waiters wait table; Store clerks wait on or upon (= attend to) customers.*
—**in-waiting** *cpd.: a candidate-in-waiting; ladies-in-waiting* (= in attendance); *a president in-waiting* (= waiting to take over). —*n.* a waiting or its duration: *The long wait seemed like an eternity.*
—**lie in wait for** stay concealed, ready to attack someone.

wait.er *n.* a man or boy who serves customers seated at tables, as in a restaurant.

waiting game *n.* the strategy of waiting till one has an advantage over the opposite side or party.

waiting list *n.* a list of people waiting to obtain something: *We were on the waiting list for a flight.* Also **waitlist**.

waiting room *n.* a room in which people wait for a service.

wait.list 1 same as WAITING LIST: *You have priority waitlist status for the flight.* **2** *v.* to place on a waiting list: *We were waitlisted for another flight.*
—**wait.list.ing** *n.*

wait.ress (WAIT.ris) *n.* a female waiter.

waive *v.* **waives, waived, waiv.ing**
1 give up legally: *to waive a claim, right; He waived custody (of his children) in favor of generous visiting rights.* **2** defer, dispense with, or dismiss: *to waive the formalities, rules; a problem you can't waive away.*

waiv.er *n.* a waiving of a right or claim or a document to that effect: *to sign a waiver.*

wake *v.* **wakes,** *pt.* **woke** or **waked,** *pp.* **waked** or **wo.ken** (WOH.kun), **wak.ing** awaken or rouse: *Please wake me when you wake up; Hibernating animals can wake themselves up; She woke to the sound of sirens; She was quick to wake up to (= realize) the danger; adj.a.: a waking (= alert or conscious) dream, experience, state; waking reality, thoughts; almost every waking hour, minute, moment; most of her waking life.*
—*n.* **1** a watch or vigil, as over a dead body before burial: *to hold a wake; An Irish wake is followed by feasting.* **2** the track left in the water by a moving craft: *The war brought famine in its wake* (= following it); *In the wake of the war came famine and disease.*

wake.ful *adj.* **1** sleepless or restless. **2** watchful or alert. —**wake.ful.ly** *adv.;* **wake.ful.ness** *n.*

wak.en (WAY.kun) *v.* to wake.

wake-robin same as TRILLIUM.

Wal.dorf salad (WALL.dorf-) *n.* a salad of diced apples, celery, nuts, and mayonnaise.

wale *n.* **1** a ridge made on the skin by a stroke of a whip or stick; wheal; weal. **2** a woven ridge on cloth such as corduroy; hence, texture.
—*v.* **wales, waled, wal.ing** mark the skin or weave cloth, wickerwork, etc. with wales.

walk (WAWK) *v.* **1** go on foot without running: *She walks to school; Don't walk on the grass; People walked by as if they didn't notice the attack; The workers walked off the job in a wildcat strike; The ghost may walk* (= appear) *tonight; a lady walking* (= out with) *her dog; Ray walks (through) the streets exploring the city; He walked* (= accompanied) *his date home.* **2** conduct oneself: *to walk in peace; Walk in the ways of the Lord; They walked all over us* (*Informal for* treated us badly). **3** in baseball, allow a runner or batter a base after four balls.
—**walk away from 1** leave or escape: *The car was a total wreck, but the passengers walked away from it; She managed to walk away from the business a millionaire.* **2** abandon: *He was so broke he had to walk away from the home on which he had made so many mortgage payments; to walk away from a marriage.* —**walk off** or **away with 1** win easily. **2** steal.
—**walk out** go on strike or quit suddenly. —**walk out on** *Informal.* desert someone, as a spouse, who is close or has a right to be taken care of. —**walk the plank** be forced to kill oneself, as the crew of a ship captured by pirates made to jump overboard from a plank.
—*n.* **1** a walking, as for exercise; stroll or hike: *Let's go for a walk; to take a walk around the park It's an hour's walk* (= walking distance) *to town; Take a walk* (*Informal for* Go away)! **2** one's manner of walking: *You can recognize him from his walk.* **3** a place for walking, as a path laid out in a park: *a scenic walk; a letter carrier's walk* (= route); *a church group that represents people of all walks of life* (= all economic, ethnic, and social groups). **4** in baseball,

walkabout / waltz

a going to first base on four balls. —**walk.er** *n.: a tightrope walker.*
walk.a.bout (WAWK.uh.bowt) *n.* a stroll by a public figure for meeting and chatting with people.
walk.a.way (WAWK.uh.way) *n.* an easy victory; walk-over.
walk.ie-talk.ie (WAWK.ee.TAWK.ee) *n.* a small, portable radio transmitter-receiver.
walk-in *n.* **1** *Informal.* a sure win. **2** something large enough to be walked into. —*adja.* **1** that may be walked into: *a large walk-in closet, refrigerator, safe; walk-in access.* **2** open or available without an appointment: *a walk-in business, clinic, zoo; walk-in service.* **3** that arrives without an appointment or referral: *walk-in customers, patients, traffic.*
walking encyclopedia *n.* a person of encyclopedic knowledge.
walking papers *n.pl. Informal.* dismissal from a job or similar position.
walking stick *n.* a stick or cane used in walking.
walk-on *n.* **1** in a dramatic production, a bit part that involves little speaking. **2** an actor playing such a part.
walk.out *n.* **1** a leaving of a meeting or organization as a mark of protest. **2** a work stoppage by employees; strike.
walk-over *n. Informal.* an easy victory.
walk.up *n.* **1** a building without an elevator, usu. only a few stories high. **2** an apartment in such a building.
walk.way *n.* a passage for walking.
wall (WAWL) *n.* **1** an upright enclosing, dividing, or protective structure of stone, wood, etc., as of a house: *to build, climb, erect, put up, scale, tear down a wall; a wall lined with bookshelves; a brick, retaining, supporting wall; the wall between two rooms.* **2** a side of a room or hollow structure: *the muscular wall of the stomach; a tire with white walls.* —**drive** (or **push**) **to the wall** put in an extreme or desperate situation. —**off the wall** *Slang.* unorthodox or off the cuff: *His views are really off the wall.* —**up the wall** *Slang.* in an extreme or desperate situation: *His behavior really drives me up the wall* (= drives me crazy). —**with one's back to the wall** in a desperate situation. —**wall to wall** from one end to the other: *The room was packed wall to wall with visitors.* —*v.* to close, cover, or surround with or as if with a wall: *to wall off a part of the house; to wall up an unused fireplace;* **adj. & cpd.**: *the old walled city; a walled-in garden; a brick-walled building; thin-walled tubing.*
wal.la.by (WOL.uh.bee) *n.* -**bies** any of various small kangaroos.
wall.board *n.* a large sheet molded of wood fiber, plaster and paper, or asbestos and cement for covering walls and ceilings.
wal.let (WOL.ut, WAWL.ut) *n.* a pocketbook for carrying paper money, cards, etc.
wall.eye *n.* **1** a disorder in which one or both eyes are turned outward, showing much white. **2** a pike with large eyes; also **wall.eyed pike.**
wall hanging *n.* a decoration hung on a wall.
wall.flow.er (WALL.flow.er) *n. Informal.* a woman who is too shy or not attractive enough as a dancing partner.
Wal.loon (wah.LOON) *n.* **1** a dialect of French spoken in S. Belgium. **2** a Belgian who speaks Walloon.
wal.lop (WOL.up) *v. Informal.* to hit very hard: *They were walloped* (= defeated) *in the third round.* —*n. Informal.* **1** a very hard blow. **2** walloping power; force or vigor: *a small-town weekly that packs the wallop of a national newspaper; the wallop of a hard-hitting editorial.* —**walloping** *n., adja. & adv.:* *He got a good walloping; Sam told us a walloping (big) lie.*
wal.low (WOL.oh) *v.* roll oneself about: *Hogs wallow in mud; People wallow* (= indulge excessively) *in luxury, misery, wealth.* —*n.* a wallowing or a place of mud or dust in which animals wallow.
wall.pa.per (WALL.pay.pur) *n.* colored decorative paper to put on walls: *to hang wallpaper.* —*v.* cover or paste with wallpaper.
Wall Street *n.* **1** the financial center of the U.S. in New York with major banks, the Stock Exchange, etc. **2** U.S. financiers collectively.
wall-to-wall *adj.* extending from one end to the other: *wall-to-wall carpeting, people; a room that is wall-to-wall with exhibits; a day filled with wall-to-wall appointments.*
wal.nut (WALL.nut) *n.* **1** a forest tree valued for its dark brown wood and for its edible nuts. **2** the nut or the wood.
wal.rus (WALL.rus, WOL-) *n.* a large seal-like mammal with two tusks growing downward from the mouth: *A walrus mustache hangs down at the ends.*
waltz (WAULTS) *n.* **1** a gliding ballroom dance in ¾ time. **2** the music for it. —*v.* **1** dance a waltz: *a couple waltz-*

ing at the Moulin Rouge. **2** move easily, nimbly, or successfully: *She waltzed through customs.*

wam.pum (WOM.pum) *n.* beads of shell often strung together, once used as money by North American Indians.

wan (rhyme: on) *adj.* **wan.ner, wan.nest** pale or emaciated, as from illness: *a wan expression, look, smile.* —**wan.ly** *adv.;* **wan.ness** *n.*

wand (WOND) *n.* **1** a slender rod, as used by a magician; baton; also, a staff of authority or scepter: *to wave a magic wand.* **2** a tool or implement: *a wand used in optical scanning of price tags; the cleaning wand (as a vacuum cleaner's) that is moved back and forth over a surface.*

wan.der (wan- *rhymes with* on) *v.* **1** move about in an aimless manner: *elephants wandering around all night; homeless children wandering the streets.* **2** stray or meander: *to wander from the path of virtue; a mind that wanders from one thing to another; The child wandered away from the group;* **adja.:** *a **wandering** poet, musician, tribe; the wandering course of a river; his wandering eye; wandering thoughts.* —**wan.der.er** *n.*

wan.der.lust (WON.dur.lust) *n.* the urge to travel or wander.

wane *v.* **wanes, waned, wan.ing 1** become smaller after reaching fullness: *The moon waxes and wanes.* **2** decline in intensity, power, influence, etc.; become weaker: *Interest in the project has begun to wane; His influence has waned over the years;* **adja.:** *his **waning** influence; in the waning hours of the previous regime; our waning revenues.* —**n.:** *His influence is **on the wane** (= is declining).*

wan.gle (WANG.gul) *v.* **-gles, -gled, -gling** *Informal.* manage to get by influence, manipulation, persuasion, etc.: *to wangle an invitation out of someone; She wangled her way through the corridors of power.*

wan.na.be or **wan.na.bee** (WON.uh.bee) *n. Informal.* one who aspires vainly to the specified position or state: *a superstar wannabe; a wannabe poet.*

want (WAHNT, WAUNT, WUNT) *v.* **1** to desire or wish for something worth having or needed: *He wants a new car very badly; The dog wants out (Informal for wants to get out); She wants out of her contract;* **adj.:** *The child did not feel **wanted** by his classmates; a suspect wanted by police; He's wanted for murder and robbery; He is on the "most wanted" list.* **2** to lack; need; require: *The shirt wants a button; "Waste not, want not"* (= Do not waste, and you won't be lacking in life's necessities); *A contented man **wants for nothing*** (= has everything he needs).
—*n.* desire or need: *Does advertising create wants* (= desires) *or help supply needs? an invention that meets a long-felt want* (= need); *to fill, satisfy, supply a want; to minister to the wants of the poor and needy; to buy a second-rate product **for want of*** (= lacking) *a better one; an unemployed man **in want*** (= need) *of a job; Welfare is for people **in want*** (= extreme poverty or lack of food, shelter, clothing, etc.).

want ad *n. Informal.* a brief advertisement for an employee, service, goods, etc. wanted by someone.

wanting *adjp.* lacking in some essential: *Students found **wanting** in math are not promoted.* —**prep.** lacking: *a shirt wanting a button; a year wanting* (= less) *a day.*

wan.ton (WAHN.tun, WAUN.tun) *adj.* **1** lacking in restraint; frolicsome: *a wanton child; wanton winds; fruit and flowers in wanton profusion; deliciously wanton; a wanton* (= loose) *woman; wanton* (= sensual) *thoughts.* **2** unprovoked; unjustified: *a wanton attack, insult; wanton cruelty, damage, destruction, disregard, mischief.* —*n.* a morally loose woman: *wanton wenches.* —*v.* **1** behave licentiously with another. **2** squander.
—**wan.ton.ly** *adv.;* **wan.ton.ness** *n.*

wap.i.ti (WOP.i.tee) *n.* the North American elk with many-pronged antlers and a whitish rump.

war (WOR) *n.* **1** an open, armed, prolonged conflict, as between nations: *the art of war; the strategy, tactics, and logistics of war; England was **at war** or in a state of war with France; the war between England and France; to ban, make, outlaw war; to wage war against or with the enemy; to declare war on the enemy; to go to war over a disputed territory; to conduct, end, escalate, fight, lose, win a war; all-out, atomic, civil, cold, gang, limited, nuclear, price, world wars; a war of aggression, attrition, nerves; Wars break out, rage, spread; In the end, they lost the war though they won a few battles.* **2** any struggle: *a national program of war on poverty.* —**adja.:** *a war effort, hero; war hysteria; War clouds gather on the horizon; The **war baby** boom* (= sudden increase in births after World War II) *put a severe strain on schools.*
—*v.* **wars, warred, war.ring** be in conflict; fight: *to war with or against*

neighbors; *to war over a tiny piece of land.*

war.ble (WOR.bul) *v.* **-bles, -bled, -bling** sing a song with trills, quavers, etc., as a songbird, esp. a warbler.
—*n.* **1** a warbling song or sound. **2** a painful swelling under an animal's skin, as caused by the larva of a fly called "warble fly."

war.bler (WOR.blur) *n.* a small, active, insect-eating bird.

war bonnet *n.* a ceremonial headdress of skin and feathers worn by American Indians.

war bride *n.* the bride of a soldier on active service during a war.

war chest *n.* a fund to support a political campaign, protracted strike, etc.

war crime *n.* a violation of international rules of warfare, as genocide, inhumane treatment of prisoners, etc.

war cry *n.* a slogan or rallying cry used in fighting for a cause.

-ward or **-wards** *adj. & adv. suffix.* in the direction specified: *backward(s), earthward, homeward, toward(s).*

ward (*rhyme:* lord) *v.* usu. **ward off 1** turn aside: *to ward off a blow, weapon.* **2** keep away: *to ward off danger, evil, enemies.* —*n.* **1** an administrative division of a municipality, prison, hospital, etc.: *the children's ward of a hospital; emergency ward; maternity ward.* **2** one under the care of a guardian or law court: *a ward of the state.* **3** guardianship or custody.

war dance *n.* a dance formerly performed by North American Indians when preparing for war or celebrating a victory.

war dead *n.pl.* soldiers killed in war.

war.den (WAR.dun) *n.* **1** an administrative official in charge of a prison (*prison warden*), one enforcing fire regulations (*fire warden*) or game laws (*game warden*), one governing a school or hospital in the U.K., etc. **2** the head of a county council, as in Quebec. **3** a churchwarden.

ward.er *n.* a watchman or guard.

ward heeler *n. Informal.* a hanger-on of a political boss in a ward or riding.

ward.robe *n.* **1** one's collection or stock of clothes: *I needed a whole new wardrobe for my African tour.* **2** a cabinet or closet for clothes.

ward.room *n.* the eating and lounging place of commissioned officers on a warship.

ward.ship *n.* guardianship.

ware *n.* **1** usu. **wares** *pl.* manufactured articles for sale. **2** pottery.

—**comb.form.** specified kind of goods: *courseware, firmware, hardware, ironware, lessonware, liveware, software, wetware.*

ware.house *n.* a building or room where goods for sale are stored.
—*v.* **-hous.es, -housed, -hous.ing** store in a warehouse.

war.fare *n.* **1** the waging of a war: *atomic, biological, chemical, conventional, electronic, germ, guerrilla, jungle, trench, tribal warfare.* **2** struggle or conflict: *class, economic, ideological, political, psychological warfare.*

war.fa.rin (WOR.fuh.rin) *n.* an anticoagulant drug, also used as a rat poison.

war game *n.* a simulated military exercise for studying tactics.

war.head *n.* the explosive-containing front part of a torpedo or other missile: *a nuclear warhead.*

war.horse *n. Informal.* **1** a veteran of many wars or struggles. **2** a hackneyed bit of theater, music, or ballet.

war.i.ly (WAIR.uh.lee) *adv.* in a wary manner. —**war.i.ness** *n.*

war.like *adj.* **1** having to do with war: *warlike music, supplies.* **2** bellicose: *a warlike demonstration, people.*

war.lock *n.* a sorcerer or wizard.

war.lord *n.* a military commander-in-chief with supreme power over a region, as in China between 1912 and 1928.

warm (*rhyme:* form) *adj.* **1** having or providing comfortable heat; not cold: *a warm fire, room; a warm-air heating system; warm clothing; warm colors such as red, orange, and yellow.* **2** somewhat hot: *He's warm from running; a warm* (= heated) *discussion; a hunting dog on a warm* (= fresh) *scent; pursuing a warm lead; getting warm* (= close to the subject sought); *He quit his job when they made it warm* (*Informal for* unpleasant) *for him.* **3** marked by sympathy and cordiality: *a warm smile, welcome.*
—*v.* make or become warm: *to warm up a room.* —**warm to 1** become more enthusiastic about a subject, task, etc. as one proceeds with it. **2** become friendly or sympathetic to a person; also **warm toward** or **warm up to** someone. —**warm up** loosen one's muscles before a physical activity: *exercises for warming up before jogging.*
—**warm.ish** *adj.;* **warm.ly** *adv.*

war machine *n.* military resources for waging a war.

warm-blooded *adj.* having a body temperature that does not vary with the environment, as mammals and birds;

warmed-over / wash

warmed-over *adj.* **1** of foods, stale but reheated. **2** not fresh or new: *a warmed-over edition, flavor, version.*

war memorial *n.* a monument to those dead in war.

warm front *n.* an advancing mass of warm air.

warm.heart.ed (WARM.har.tid) *adj.* cordial; sympathetic.
—**warm.heart.ed.ness** *n.*

warming pan *n.* a long-handled covered pan containing hot coals used to warm beds.

war.mon.ger (WOR.mung.gur, -mong.gur) *n.* one who likes to stir up wars; **war.mon.ger.ing** *n. & adj.*

warmth *n.* the quality or state of being warm.

warm-up *n.* **1** a warming up using exercises before starting a physical activity. **2** the idling of an engine till normal operating efficiency is reached.

warn (WORN) *v.* give advance notice to someone against a danger or penalty: *They warned us of* or *about* or *against the risks of hitchhiking; warned us not to hitchhike; warned us that it is risky to hitchhike; a sign posted to* **warn off** *trespassers.*

warning *adja.* that warns: *a red warning light; a warning bell, shot, sign, signal.*
—**n.** something that warns: *The red light serves as a warning to drivers to stop; The accident occurred without warning; Let it be a warning to all of us; to give, issue, send out a warning; a storm warning.*

warp (WORP) *v.* **1** twist or bend out of shape, as a wooden board out of its plane when drying. **2** distort or deform: *Plywood doesn't warp easily; a mind warped by prejudices.* —**n.** **1** a twist or distortion, as in a wooden board because of shrinkage. **2** the lengthwise threads, crossed by the woof or weft, in a woven fabric or in a loom.

war paint *n. Informal.* cosmetics or makeup.

war.path *n.* the route taken by a North American Indian group going to war.
—**on the warpath** setting out for battle or in a fighting mood: *to go on the warpath against tax hikes; women on the warpath.*

war.plane *n.* a military airplane, esp. one used in war.

war.rant (WOR.unt) *n.* **1** official or legal authorization; also, justification or reasonable grounds: *acted without warrant.* **2** a document such as a legal writ authorizing an arrest, search, etc.: *The police officer swore out a warrant against her; The court issued a warrant; The warrant was served on the landlady; A warrant is out for her arrest; a bench warrant; He has virtually signed his own death warrant.* **3** a voucher for payment. **4** a certificate of appointment issued to a noncommissioned military officer, or **warrant officer**. —*v.* **1** justify: *a conclusion that is warranted by the evidence.* **2** guarantee or assure: *a diamond warranted to be genuine; I'll warrant (you) she'll keep her word.*

war.ran.ty (WOR.un.tee) *n.* **-ties** a guarantee of the quality of a product or service: *a one-year warranty on a new car against manufacturing defects; a limited two-year warranty on the power train; a lifetime extended warranty at extra cost; a car that is still under warranty after three years; no implied warranties; Our car broke down the day after the warranty expired* or *ran out.*

war.ren (WOR.un) *n.* **1** a system of burrows inhabited by rabbits: *The basement of the building is a warren of offices; a warren of underground passages.* **2** a crowded tenement or slum area.

war.ri.or (WOR.ee.ur) *n.* a soldier or fighter experienced in battle.

war.ship *n.* a ship used in warfare, as a battleship, destroyer, submarine, etc.

wart (WORT) *n.* **1** a small, hard growth on the skin, caused by a virus. **2** a similar bulge on a plant. —**warts and all** exposing even blemishes: *The book describes his hero, warts and all; adja.: a warts-and-all portrait.* —**wart.y** *adj.*

wart.hog *n.* an African pig with pairs of wartlike bumps between its eyes and well-developed tusks.

war.time *n.* the duration of a war: *measures taken in* or *during wartime; adja.: wartime efforts, emergencies, horrors, measures, propaganda, sufferings.*

war.y (WAIR.ee) *adj.* **war.i.er, -i.est** careful or cautious, as if suspicious of danger or trouble: *a fox's wary movements; He kept a wary eye for muggers; He was even* **wary of** *strangers at that time of night.* —**war.i.ly** *adv.*

was (WOZ, WUZ, wuz) 1st and 3rd person sing. pt. of BE.

wash (WOSH) *v.* **1** clean with water or other liquid: *to wash the dishes after dinner; He shaves and washes (himself) in the morning; to* **wash up** *(hands and face) before dinner; a stain you can* **wash out** *(= remove) with soap and water; a fabric that washes (= can be cleaned, esp. without damage) well in cold water; an*

washable / waste

excuse that **won't wash** (*Informal* for is not acceptable). **2** wet, flow over, or cover with a liquid: *a deck washed by waves.* **3** move by the force of water: *houses washed away by a flood; He was washed overboard during the storm; He likes to **wash down** his meals with cola.*
—**washed up** *Informal.* **1** exhausted: *He's all washed up at age 30.* **2** finished: *After the scandal, she was washed up as a vote getter.* —**n. 1** a washing or being washed: *the wash of the waves on the beach; a car wash.* **2** what is washed or to be washed, as laundry: *the weekly wash; to hang out the wash;* **adj.:** *the wash cycles of a clothes washer; Saturday is wash day in our family.* **3** a piece of land sometimes covered by the sea. **4** a dry river bed, as in a canyon. **5** a liquid for cleansing, as for the mouth or eyes. **6** a weak or watery liquid; liquid garbage; hogwash. **7** an eddy made in water or air by a moving craft. **8** a coating, as of paint: *a wash of indigo.*

wash.a.ble (WOSH.uh.bul) *adj.* that may be washed without damage: *a washable ink (removable by washing).*

wash-and-wear *adj.* needing little or no ironing after washing; durable-press: *a wash-and-wear dress, fabric, shirt.*

wash.ba.sin (WOSH.bay.sin) *n.* a bathroom fixture in which to wash one's face and hands; also **wash.bowl.**

wash.board *n.* a ridged board on which to scrub dirt out of clothes.

wash.cloth or **wash.rag** *n.* a piece of cloth used for washing one's face and body.

wash dress *n.* a dress that is washable without being damaged.

wash drawing *n.* a watercolor picture done in washes of black and gray.

washed-out *adj.* **1** faded after many washes. **2** *Informal.* feeling or looking tired.

washed-up *adj. Informal.* having failed: *a washed-up movie actor now turned politician.*

wash.er *n.* **1** one that washes, as a washing machine. **2** a flat seal of metal, rubber, or plastic with a hole in it, used with a nut or bolt to ensure tightness, prevent leakage, reduce friction, etc.

wash.er.wom.an (WOSH.ur.woom.un) *n.* -**wom.en** a woman whose work is washing clothes; laundress.

wash.house *n.* a building in which clothes are washed.

wash.ing *n.* the act of washing, material obtained by washing, a thin coating of metal, or clothes washed or to be washed.

washing machine *n.* a machine for washing clothes.

washing soda *n.* sodium carbonate used in washing and bleaching.

Wash.ing.to.ni.an (wosh.ing.TOH.nee.un) *n. & adj.* (a person) of or from Washington, D.C., or Washington State.

wash.out *n.* **1** the washing away of earth by flowing water. **2** *Informal.* a complete failure: *His performance was a washout; a washout punch* (= knockout blow).

wash.rag same as WASHCLOTH.

wash.room *n.* a room with washing and toilet facilities.

wash.stand *n.* a stand or table on which a washbowl is set.

wash.tub *n.* a tub for soaking and washing clothes; also called "laundry tub."

wash.wom.an (WOSH.woom.un) *n.* -**wom.en** same as WASHERWOMAN.

wash.y *adj.* **wash.i.er, -i.est 1** of liquids, watery or weak: *washy tea.* **2** of colors, pale: *washy appearance.*

was.n't (WUZ.unt, WOZ-) was not.

wasp (WOSP) *n.* a slender-bodied, winged stinging insect related to bees and ants. —**wasp.ish** *adj.*

WASP or **Wasp** (WOSP) *n.* [usu. derogatory] a "white Anglo-Saxon Protestant," as a member of the most privileged class in an English-speaking country; **adj.:** *a Wasp community, enclave, image; the Wasp Establishment; a Wasp preserve.* —**WASP.ish** or **Wasp.ish** *adj.: white, Waspish, and Middle American.*

wasp waist *n.* a very slender waist.

was.sail (WOS.ul, -ail) *n.* **1** a toast to someone's health formerly used in England. **2** a liquor drunk on joyous occasions. **3** a drinking party; hence, revelry. —*v.* drink a wassail to someone; also, carouse; **was.sail.er** *n.*

Was.ser.mann test (WOS.ur.mun-) *n.* a blood test for syphilis.

wast (WOST, wust) [old form] the form of WERE used with "thou."

wast.age (WAIS.tij) *n.* **1** loss by use, leakage, decay, etc. **2** the amount thus wasted.

waste *v.* **wastes, wast.ed, wast.ing 1** spend or be spent uselessly: *to waste energy, money, time; You're wasting your breath* (= It's useless) *trying to persuade him; to waste* (= not use) *an opportunity; He gets **wasted** (Slang for intoxicated) at parties.* **2** wear down gradually:

Tuberculosis is a wasting disease; Starving people waste away. **3** ravage; lay waste.
—*n.* **1** a wasting or something wasted: *a mere waste of time and money; We try to cut down on waste; hazardous, nuclear, radioactive, toxic wastes; body wastes* (= excrement); *Millions of tons of solid waste* (= refuse) *are produced each year in homes, offices, restaurants, etc.* **2** an unused expanse of water, snow-covered land, desert, etc. **3** a gradual wearing down, as of bodily tissue: *the body processes of waste and repair.* **4** a bunch of cotton or wool material used for cleaning, wiping, etc. —**go to waste** be wasted. —**lay waste (to)** destroy a place or make it desolate.
—*adj.* **1** discarded as useless or unused: *the municipal job of solid waste disposal; waste matter, paper, water.* **2** desolate; ruined: *waste land.*
waste.bas.ket (WAIST.bas.kit) *n.* a basket or other receptacle for waste paper.
waste.ful *adj.* **1** that involves waste: *Idling a car is wasteful of gas; wasteful consumption, habits, packaging, spending.* **2** given to wasting: *a wasteful and corrupt administration.* —**waste.ful.ly** *adv.*; **waste.ful.ness** *n.*
waste.land *n.* barren land; hence, unproductive effort.
waste product *n.* a useless by-product of a manufacturing or bodily process.
wast.rel (WAY.strul) *n.* **1** a spendthrift. **2** a good-for-nothing.
watch (WOCH) *v.* **1** follow a person or thing with one's eyes; look at or observe steadily: *to watch a game; a suspect being watched by police; He was beaten up while everyone watched* (= looked on); *He's watching* (= waiting) *for a chance to sneak out.* **2** stay awake or alert: *a mother watching at her sick child's bedside.*
—**watch it** *Informal.* be careful.
—**watch oneself** be careful or discreet. —**watch out** *Informal.* be on one's guard: *Watch out for pickpockets!*
—*n.* **1** a timepiece to carry on one's person, as a wristwatch, stopwatch, etc.: *analog and digital watches; His watch is fast, hers is slow, Watches keep time, run down, stop.* **2** a state or attitude of attention: *A hurricane watch is one level of preparedness lower than a hurricane warning; to maintain a close, careful watch on people going in and out of the house; Our dog keeps watch over our house; She is* **on watch** (= watching) *all night; She is* **on the watch** *for prowlers.* **3** a guard or his period of duty, as in the navy: *Crew members stand watch for four hours at a time; during the still watches of the night.* **4** formerly, someone on watch duty in a town: *the night watch; Call out the watch!*
watch.band *n.* the band or bracelet of a wristwatch.
watch.case *n.* the metal covering of the works of a watch.
watch.dog *n.* **1** a dog kept to guard property. **2** one that guards against theft, waste, etc.: *The Auditor General is the watchdog of government spending;* **adja.**: *a watchdog agency, body, committee.*
watch.ful *adj.* keeping careful guard; vigilant: *under the watchful eyes of the police; their watchful gaze; Be watchful of pickpockets;* **watch.ful.ly** *adv.*; **watch.ful.ness** *n.*
watch.mak.er (WOCH.may.kur) *n.* one who makes or repairs watches; **watch.mak.ing** *n.*
watch.man (WOCH.mun) *n.* **-men** one who keeps watch over property, esp. at night.
watch night *n.* a church service held at midnight on New Year's Eve.
watch.tow.er (WOCH-, *rhyme:* our) *n.* a lookout tower.
watch.word *n.* **1** a guiding principle as embodied in a motto or slogan: *"Merit" should be the watchword for promotions.* **2** a secret password.
wa.ter (WAW.tur, WOT.ur) *n.* **1** the colorless, odorless, tasteless, and transparent liquid that falls as rain and fills lakes, rivers, etc.: *to draw water for a bath; to pour, spill, splash, sprinkle, squirt water; clear, cold, contaminated, distilled, fresh, hard, hot, polluted, soft, stagnant, tepid, warm water.* **2** a waterlike substance such as sap, tears, urine, and saliva: *Infants make* or *pass water whenever necessary; He has water on the knee* (= accumulated fluid following an injury); *water on the brain* (= enlarged condition of the head); *Her water broke* (= bag of fluid holding the fetus ruptured). **3** a waterlike product: *lavender water; mineral water; rose water; soda water; toilet water.* **4** a body of water such as a sea or lake. *People cross the border by water, air, and land; a body found under two feet of water; to feel like a fish out of water; to tread water (to keep afloat); at high and low water* (= tide). **5 waters** *pl.* flowing or moving water: *"Still waters run deep"; The flood waters are receding; International waters lie beyond territorial waters; to take the (mineral) waters* (= to take a water cure) *at a spa; the bag of waters* (= sac holding a fetus). **6** the

degree of transparency and brilliance of a precious stone, formerly "first water," "second water," "third water." **7** the wavy, lustrous finish given to silk, linen, metal surfaces, etc. —**cast one's bread on the waters** do good that does not bring the doer any return. —**hold one's water** *Informal.* be patient. —**hold water** of a theory, argument, etc., prove sound; agree with the facts: *Your story won't hold water.* —**of the first** or **finest** or **purest water** of the highest degree of perfection: *a poet of the finest water; a scoundrel of the first water.* —**pour** or **throw cold water on** discourage a hope, plan, etc. —**water under the bridge** something that belongs to the past. —*v.* **1** supply with water: *to water a lawn; to water cattle; a land watered by rivers; watered* (= diluted) *milk, soup, wine; a watered-down* (= weakened) *version of the same argument.* **2** drink or take in water: *cattle watering at a stream; a ship docked for watering.* **3** give out water or a waterlike substance: *Mouths water at the sight of food; Her eyes are watering from the wind.* —*adj.*: *Ocean birds are water birds; a water heater; water pressure, safety, supply, vapor.*

water ballet *n.* dancelike synchronized swimming.

water bed *n.* a bed with a water-filled mattress.

wa.ter.borne (WAW.tur.born) *adj.* carried by water: *waterborne cargo, diseases, infection.*

water buffalo See BUFFALO.

water cannon *n.* a device like a fire hose for shooting water at high pressure, used in crowd control.

water chestnut *n.* **1** a European water plant with nutlike fruits. **2** a Chinese sedge with an edible tuber.

water closet *n.* a toilet or lavatory.

wa.ter.col.or (WAW.tur.cul.ur) *n.* **1** a pigment that is mixed with water for painting: *to paint in watercolors.* **2** a painting done with watercolors: *a watercolor by Turner.* Also **wa.ter.col.our** *Cdn.*

water cooler *n.* a machine that dispenses cold drinking water, as used in offices: *Office romances often start at the water cooler.*

wa.ter.course (WAW.tur.course) *n.* **1** a stream, river, or artificial water channel. **2** its bed.

wa.ter.craft (WAW.tur.craft) *n. sing. & pl.* a ship, boat, or similar craft for transport on or in water.

wa.ter.cress (WAW.tur.cres) *n.* a water plant whose leaves are used in salads, etc.

wa.ter.fall (WAW.tur.fall) *n.* a stream flowing down a height; cascade.

wa.ter.fowl (WAW.tur.fowl) *n.* **1** a water bird such as the duck or loon. **2 waterfowl** *pl.* swimming game birds.

wa.ter.front (WAW.tur.frunt) *n.* the section of a city fronting on a body of water; harbor area: *labor trouble on the waterfront (involving stevedores); People gathered along the waterfront.*

water gap *n.* a narrow gorge cut by a river through a mountain ridge.

water gas *n.* a fuel gas manufactured by passing steam over hot coke.

Wa.ter.gate (WAW.tur.gate) *n.* a political scandal involving high government officials acting criminally, as the burglary of U.S. Democratic Party headquarters in 1972 that led to the resignation of President Nixon.

water glass *n.* **1** a drinking glass. **2** a water-soluble compound of silicon, sodium, and oxygen used in fireproofing, waterproofing, and as an adhesive.

water hole *n.* a small pond or pool.

water ice *n.* dessert resembling ice cream but made with fruit juice instead of milk.

watering hole *n. Informal.* a place such as a bar, club, or lounge where people gather for drinking and socializing.

watering place *n.* **1** a place at which animals drink from a river, lake, etc. **2** same as WATERING HOLE. **3** a spa with mineral springs.

water lily *n.* a plant related to the lotus bearing large white or pink flowers and leaves that float on the surface of the water; also called "pond lily." Also **wa.ter.lil.y, -lil.ies.**

wa.ter.line (WAW.tur.line) *n.* the varying line along which the water surface touches the side of a ship or boat, depending on the load it is carrying. Also **water line.**

wa.ter.logged (WAW.tur.logd) *adj.* filled or soaked with water: *a waterlogged boat; waterlogged fields; We are waterlogged* (= bogged down) *in detail.*

Wa.ter.loo (waw.tur.LOO) *n.* a crushing defeat, like the battle fought in 1815 at Waterloo, Belgium, in which Napolean was finally defeated: *to meet one's Waterloo.*

water main *n.* a large pipe carrying water.

wa.ter.mark (WAW.tur.mark) *n.* an identifying design impressed on paper during manufacturing that is visible only when held against light.

wa.ter.mel.on (WAW.tur.mel.un) *n.* a large green melon with a delicious red or yellow pulp.

water moccasin *n.* a large, venomous water snake of the southern U.S.

water ou.zel (WAW.tur.OO.zul) *n.* a small, thrushlike bird of W. North America that dives under water for insects; also called "dipper."

water pipe *n.* 1 a hookah. 2 a pipe carrying water.

water polo *n.* a team game played in a swimming pool using a large inflated ball.

water power *n.* the power of moving water used to drive machinery.

wa.ter.proof (WAW.tur.proof) *adj.* that will not let water through, as coats, hats, etc. treated with rubber.
—*n.* 1 a waterproof material. 2 a raincoat. —*v.* make waterproof.
—**wa.ter.proof.ing** *n.*

water-repellent *adj.* that repels water though not waterproof; also **water-resistant.**

wa.ter.shed (WAW.tur.shed) *n.* 1 a dividing ridge between two areas drained by different river systems. 2 a river basin. 3 a turning point: *Retirement marks a watershed in our careers.* —*adja.* crucial: *a watershed decision, event; 1973 was a watershed year for world economies because of the Arab oil embargo.*

wa.ter.side (WAW.tur.side) *adja.* on the shore of a river, lake, sea, etc.: *a waterside cafe, deck, development, location, property.*

wa.ter.ski (WAW.tur.skee) *v.* **-skis, -skied, -ski.ing** glide over water on boards (**waterskis**) towed by a speedboat. —*n.* one of a pair of skis that is similar to but wider than a snow ski.
—**wa.ter.ski.er** *n.*

wa.ter.spout (WAW.tur.spowt) *n.* 1 a tornado over the ocean. 2 something that spouts water, as a pipe that drains water from a roof.

water strider *n.* an insect seen on ponds and streams gliding about on the water surface on long spiderlike legs.

water table *n.* the level of underground water, as seen in a well.

wa.ter.tight (WAW.tur.tite) *adj.* 1 so tight as not to let water in or out: *a ship's watertight bulkheads; a watertight rubber suit.* 2 having no loopholes or flaws: *a watertight argument, contract, monopoly, plan; watertight sanctions,* security.

water tower *n.* a tall tower topped by a tank for storing water.

wa.ter.way (WAW.tur.way) *n.* a navigable river, canal, etc.: *inland waterways.*

wa.ter.wheel (WAW.tur.wheel) *n.* a wheel, as of a mill, that is turned by flowing water.

water wings *n.pl.* a pair of air-filled bags worn on the shoulders to keep one afloat when learning to swim.

wa.ter.works (WAW.tur.wurks) *n.pl.* 1 the system of reservoirs, pipes, pumps, etc. for supplying a town with water: *our municipal waterworks.* 2 *Informal.* kidneys and the urinary system.

wa.ter.y (WAW.tuh.ree) *adj.* 1 of, like, or full of water: *watery clouds, eyes, soil; a watery discharge; The lifeguard saved the child from a* **watery grave** (= death) *in the swimming pool.* 2 diluted; hence, weak: *a watery color, smile, soup; It tastes watery.*

watt (WOT) *n.* the metric unit of electrical power.

watt.age (WOT.ij) *n.* electrical power in watts: *the wattage of a bulb; higher wattages.*

wat.tle (WOT.ul) *n.* 1 a woven material of rods intertwined with twigs, used for walls, fences, and roofs. 2 the fleshy fold of skin hanging from the throat of a turkey, chicken, etc.
—**wat.tled** *adj.* 1 made of wattle. 2 having wattles, as a bird.

wave *n.* 1 a moving ridge of water, as on the sea, that swells and breaks on the shore: *a high, mountainous, tall wave; the crest of a wave; a destructive tidal wave.* 2 any similar movement: *The invaders attacked in waves; a heat wave; a wave of enthusiasm; A crime wave swept the city.* 3 an up-and-down motion or undulation: *natural waves in hair; a permanent wave; a wave of the flag, hand; Sound travels in waves; light waves; radio transmission in long, medium, and short waves; a brain wave* (= sudden inspired idea). —**make waves** *Informal.* disturb the existing state of affairs. —**the wave of the future** a movement or trend that is going to last. —*v.* **waves, waved, wav.ing** move like a wave: *corn waving* (= swaying) *in the wind; a street lined with people waving* (= fluttering) *flags; They waved* (= motioned with the hand in greeting) *to us from the balcony; We waved back at them; All objections were waved aside* (= dismissed); **adja. & cpd:** *a field of* **waving** *corn; our waving wheat fields; banner-waving demonstrators; a* *fist-waving mob; flag-waving nationalism.*

wave band *n.* a range of radio-wave frequencies.

wave.length *n.* the length of a radio wave from a transmitter: *a husband* **on the same wavelength** *as* (Informal for in harmony with) *his wife.*

wave.let (WAVE.lit) *n.* a ripple or little wave.

wa.ver (WAY.vur) *v.* **1** hesitate after making a decision or seem to want to go back on it: *Once she makes up her mind, she never wavers; to waver in one's promises, resolution; to waver between two courses of action.* **2** move to and fro; become unsteady; *adj.: a wavering flame, voice, voter.* —*n.* a wavering.
—**wa.ver.er** *n.;* **wa.ver.ing.ly** *adv.*

wav.y (WAY.vee) *adj.* **wav.i.er, -i.est** moving in or having waves: *wavy hair, lines, seas.* —**wav.i.ness** *n.*

wax (rhyme: ax) *n.* a fatty plastic substance, as made by bees for their cells or as distilled from petroleum and applied to furniture surfaces and floors for protection and polish: *Sealing wax is used to seal letters, jars, bottles, etc.*
—*v.* **1** rub or treat with wax: *a waxed floor.* **2** become or grow as specified: *She waxed eloquent over her child's accomplishments; to wax lyrical, poetic; The moon waxes* (= grows larger) *from new moon to full moon before waning.*

wax bean *n.* a variety of string bean with yellow pods.

wax.en (WAX.un) *adj.* **1** made of wax. **2** like wax in smoothness.

wax museum *n.* a museum of waxworks.

wax myrtle *n.* an ornamental evergreen shrub of eastern U.S. with berries that yield a wax used for candles.

wax paper *n.* a kind of wax-coated, moisture-proof paper.

wax.wing *n.* a small crested bird with a yellow band across the end of its tail and waxy shiny red beads on its wings.

wax.work *n.* a figure made of wax.
—**wax.works** *n.pl.* [with *sing. v.*] an exhibition of such figures.

wax.y (WAX.ee) *adj.* **wax.i.er, -i.est** like wax, pale yellow, soft and pliable, or shiny. —**wax.i.ness** *n.*

way *n.* **1** a road or route for getting from one place to another: *the way home from school; Do you know the way to the cottage? We lost our way in the woods; It was getting dark when we found our way; the way out of the jungle; Please lead the way* (= go ahead of us); *She went that way* (= in that direction); *our neighbors living across the way* (= street); *She's traveling* **down** *Mexico* **way** (= to Mexico); *He lives* **out our way** (= in our neighborhood); *It's a long way* (= distance) *off; quite a* **ways** (Nonstandard for distance) *from here; to clear, pave, point, prepare, show, smooth the way; to be out of harm's way; to elbow, fight, force, make, muscle, push, squeeze, thread, tunnel, work one's way through a crowd, etc.* or *to a place; Let's get* **out of the way** *of the bulldozer; Are we* **in your way?** *Let's* **make way** (= room) *for the procession to pass; A stream twists or wends or winds* **its way** *to its destination; A child worms its way into our hearts; We had a flat tire* **on the way** *to the airport; I went to Montreal* **by way of** *Ottawa; Students often* **work their way through** **college** (= pay their fees by working); *It takes time for freshmen to* **know their way** *around campus; We have* **come a long way** *since we graduated 25 years ago; An apology will* **go a long way** (= distance) *toward easing the tension;* **the parting of the ways** *following graduation; We go* **the way of all flesh** (= We are all mortal). **2** manner or mode of doing something: *"Where there's a will there's a way"; There are easier ways of doing this; the proper* or *right way to use* or *of using your knife and fork; He's so willful he wants his own way all the time; a child with very charming or winsome ways; The way she goes about her duties is impressive; I may be able to help in a small way; She* **has a way** (= knows how to deal) *with children; Let's do it the democratic way; You can't* **have it both ways** (= choose both alternatives); *"No way,"* I said when he asked me for another loan; It's time to **mend your ways** (= improve your behavior); *In some* **ways** (= respects) *yours is a better idea; The patient is* **in a bad way** (= condition). **3 ways** *pl.* structures to support a ship under construction. —**all the way** without reservations: *He supported her all the way; He would go all the way* (= do the utmost) *for her.* —**by the way** incidentally. —**by way of 1** through: *We went to Edmonton by way of Calgary.* **2** for the purpose of: *He told the story by way of example.* —**give way 1** yield: *to give way to someone's demands.* **2** collapse or fail: *The dam gave way.* —**go out of one's way** make a special effort *to* do something. —**make way** clear the way *for* another person. —**out of the way** unusual or strange: *We saw nothing out of the way.* —**under way** in motion; hence, in progress:

Negotiations will get under way in the fall. **—way to go!** [exclamation of encouragement] **—***adv. Informal.* far: *We are way ahead of the competition; It happened way back in the 1920s; way out in the woods; way* (= long) *after I finished high school; You seem way out* (= too advanced) *on this subject.*

way.bill *n.* a list of goods being shipped, showing the route, charges, etc.

way.far.er (WAY.fair.ur) *n.* a traveler, esp. one going on foot. **—way.far.ing** *n. & adj.*

way.lay (way.LAY) *v.* **-lays, -laid, -lay.ing** **1** lie in wait for and attack someone. **2** stop someone on the way unexpectedly.

way-out *adj. Informal.* too advanced; far-out; unconventional: *a way-out example, scheme, taste, world.*

-ways *adv. suffix.* in the way specified: *endways, lengthways, sideways.*

ways and means *n.pl.* **1** methods and resources for achieving an end, esp. for raising revenue. **2** a committee for this purpose.

way.side *n.* the side of a road or path.

way station *n.* a station between main stations on a railroad or bus route.

way.ward (WAY.wurd) *adj.* **1** willful and disobedient: *a wayward child, daughter, son, youth; wayward students.* **2** erratic and freakish: *wayward behavior, conduct, elements; a wayward action, disposition, growth, lifestyle; in our wayward past, youth; the wayward world.* **—way.ward.ly** *adv.;* **way.ward.ness** *n.*

way.worn *adj.* wearied by travel.

we (WEE) *pron., pl.* of the first person "I"; *objective* US, *possessive* OUR(S). **1** the first person plural of "I" [representing a group that includes the speaker]: *We* (= you, your mother, and I) *are one family; We* (= the rest of us) *will be here when you come back from school.* **2** a person speaking as the representative of a group: *It gives us* (= the sovereign or the government) *great pleasure to declare this stadium open; I have edited this book according to our* (= of this institution, publisher, editorial board) *house style.* **3** *n.* such use of the pronoun: *the editorial we; the royal we.*

weak (WEEK) *adj.* lacking in physical, mental, or moral strength; not strong: *weak arguments, character, health, muscles, resistance; a student who is weak in* or *at math; A* **weak verb** (or regular verb) *is inflected by adding an ending such as "-ed" for past tense and past participle.*

weak.en (WEE.kun) *v.* make or become weak or weaker: *weakened by hunger and thirst.*

weak.fish *n.* a food fish with an easily torn mouth found along the E. and Gulf coasts of the U.S.

weak-kneed *adj.* lacking in courage or ability to stand firm and resolute.

weak.ling *n.* one that lacks physical or moral strength.

weak.ly *adj.* **-li.er, -li.est** feeble or weak. **—***adv.* in a weak manner: *The patient smiled weakly.*

weak.ness (WEEK.nis) *n.* **1** lack of strength; hence, a weak point or defect. **2** a fondness or liking that is considered a sign of being weak: *He has a weakness for vodka; Vodka is his weakness* (= weak point).

weal (WEEL) *n.* **1** same as WHEAL. **2** [old use] well-being; prosperity: *the common weal; the public weal; in* **weal and woe** (= in good times and bad).

wealth (WELTH, "TH" as in "thin") *n.* **1** material goods and resources that have money value; riches: *fabulous wealth; to accumulate, acquire, amass, attain wealth; to flaunt, squander one's wealth; a country's mineral wealth; national wealth; the natural wealth of a region.* **2** abundance: *a wealth of detail, information, imagery, words.*

wealth.y (WELTH.ee) *adj.* **wealth.i.er, -i.est** rich in material resources: *a wealthy family.*

wean (WEEN) *v.* **1** accustom an infant, young animal, etc. to food other than its mother's milk: *A calf is weaned from its mother.* **2** draw a person away *from* habits, company, or occupations that are considered bad. **—weaned on** raised or trained on something: *a generation of students weaned on TV.*

weap.on (WEP.un) *n.* **1** any instrument used for fighting, as an arrow, sword, gun, or club: *to brandish, carry, draw, fire, handle, load a weapon; to lay down, throw down one's weapons and surrender; an automatic weapon; a concealed weapon; A restricted weapon needs a police permit; Even a broken beer bottle may constitute an offensive weapon if intended to be used as such; They entered the house with weapons drawn; the ultimate weapon* (= nuclear arms). **2** anything used as a means of defense or attack: *Tears are often a child's best weapon; dirty tricks as political weapons.*

weap.on.ry (WEP.un.ree) *n.* **1** weapons collectively. **2** their design and production.

wear (WARE) *v.* **wears, wore, worn, wear.ing** **1** have on one's person or

show in one's appearance: *to wear clothes, jewelry, perfume, lipstick; to wear a beard, smile; She wears her hair short.* **2** make a hole, path, etc. in or on something by constant use: *to wear a hole through a sock; These shoes are worn at the heels; an excuse that has worn thin.* **3** last or endure *well, badly,* etc. as specified: *a fabric that wears well; a well-worn material.* **4** pass or go gradually: *She seemed to age as the years* **wore on** or **away***; when the effects of the drug* **wear off.** **5** tire or exhaust: *They could not* **wear down** *his resistance; They're beginning to* **wear out** (= exhaust) *their welcome; Her patience is* **wearing thin** (= becoming exhausted); *adj.: a face* **worn** *with care; a weathered, worn look; worn brake pads.* —*n.* **1** a wearing or being worn: *shoes for summer wear; socks for everyday wear.* **2** clothes: *children's, men's, women's wear; spring, summer, fall, winter wear.* **3** damage from use: *The shoes show wear; The children returned a bit tired, but apparently none* **the worse for wear.** **4** wearing capacity: *There's a lot of wear still left in those shoes.*
—**wear.a.ble** *adj.* —**wear.er** *n.*

wear and tear *n.* normal loss or damage from use: *Guarantees do not cover ordinary wear and tear; the wear and tear of our existence.*

wea.ri.some (WEER.ee.sum) *adj.* causing weariness; tiresome: *wearisome chores.*

wea.ry (WEER.ee) *adj.* **-ri.er, -ri.est** **1** worn out; exhausted: *feet weary with walking; He's grown weary of city life.* **2** showing tiredness: *a weary sigh.* **3** causing tiredness: *a weary climb.* —*v.* **-ries, -ried, -ry.ing** make or become weary; tire. —**wea.ri.ly** *adv.;* **wea.ri.ness** *n.*

wea.sel (WEE.zul) *n.* a small, furry, short-legged, flesh-eating animal with an agile and slender body. —*v.* evade a responsibility or escape from an obligation: *He tried to weasel out of the contract.* —**wea.sel.ly** *adv.*

weasel word *n.* an evasive or meaningless expression, like an egg sucked out by a weasel but left outwardly intact: *Some consider "natural" and "light" used in ads for food products weasel words.*

weath.er (WETH.ur, "TH" as in "the") *n.* the condition of the atmosphere in regard to temperature, precipitation, cloudiness, winds, etc.: *to forecast* or *predict the weather; atrocious, beastly, beautiful, bleak, clear, cloudy, cold, cool, fair, fine, foul, gloomy, hot, humid, inclement, mild, muggy, seasonable, sweltering, unsettled, warm weather; The plane flew* **into weather** (= stormy conditions) *over Bermuda; We resumed our journey when the weather cleared up; Wintry weather usually sets in after Christmas.*
—**under the weather** *Informal.* out of sorts; ill. —*adj.: a weather balloon, forecast, pattern, report, satellite; on the* **weather** (= windward) *side.* —*v.* **1** expose to the action of weather; *n.: Soil results from the* **weathering** (= gradual breaking down) *of rocks.* **2** change in color or become worn by exposure to the weather. **3** pass through a storm, etc. safely. **4** sail to the windward side of a cape, island, etc.

weather-beaten *adj.* seasoned, hardened, worn, etc. by exposure to the weather: *a weather-beaten face, old house, sailor.*

weather bureau *n.* a weather-reporting agency such as the National Weather Service in the U.S.

weath.er.cock (WETH.ur.cock) *n.* **1** a weather vane with the figure of a cock on top. **2** one who is inconstant or changeable.

weather eye *n.* alertness to signs of change, esp. in weather: *The police are* **keeping a weather eye on** or **open for** or **out for** (= keeping a close watch on) *the escapees.*

weather girl *n.* [unfavorable use] female meteorologist.

weath.er.ize (WETH.ur.ize) *v.* **-iz.es, -ized, -iz.ing** insulate so as to keep out the cold and save heating fuel.

weath.er.man (WETH.ur.man) *n.* **-men** one who reports on weather conditions, as in a news broadcast; meteorologist.

weather office *Cdn.* WEATHER BUREAU.

weath.er.proof (WETH.ur.proof) *adj.* able to withstand exposure to the weather without damage: *a weatherproof finish for the sun deck.* —*v.* make weatherproof: *to weatherproof a cottage.*

weath.er.strip (WETH.ur.strip) *v.* **-strips, -stripped, -strip.ping** fit or seal with weatherstripping.
—*n.* material such as strips of metal, wood, or felt for sealing the gaps around doors and windows to keep out drafts; also **weath.er.strip.ping.**

weather vane *n.* a device with an arrow on top that turns freely to indicate the direction from which the wind is blowing.

weather-wise (WETH.ur.wise) *adj.* skilled in predicting changes in public opinion, spending patterns, weather, etc.

weath·er·worn (WETH.ur.worn) *adj.* weather-beaten.

weave (WEEV) *v.* **weaves,** *pt.* **wove** (WOHV) or **weaved,** *pp.* **wo·ven** (WOH.vun) or **wove, weav·ing 1** interlace threads, strips, etc. *into* a fabric or an article such as a basket or hat. **2** make a fabric, hat, web, etc. *from* threads, straw, or wicker: *She weaves (cloth) on a loom; to weave a wreath of flowers.* **3** construct a story, poem, musical composition, etc. as if by weaving, *from* strands of plot, melody, etc. or *around* a theme. **4** weave plots, melodies, humor, etc. *into* a story or musical composition. **5** *pt.* usu. **weaved,** make one's way through a place: *He weaved in and out of traffic by changing lanes; She weaved her way though the crowd.* —*n.* a form or pattern of weaving, as plain or satin. —**weav·er** *n.*

web *n.* **1** something woven, esp. the network spun by a spider. **2** any network: *He wove an intricate web of lies to cover up his crime; a tangled web of intrigue; a web of deceit; The interdependence of humans, animals, and plants is called the* **web of life. 3** connecting material or tissue, as the membrane joining the toes of swimming birds: *the web between the index finger and the thumb; adj.: a web-footed* or *web-toed bird.* **4** a large reel of newsprint, as used on a rotary "web press." **5 the Web** same as INTERNET: *to browse the Web;* also **the World Wide Web.** —*v.* **webs, webbed, web·bing 1** join by a web; *adj.:* Swimming birds have **webbed** *feet* (= webfeet). **2** ensnare or trap, as in a web.

web·foot *n.* **web·feet** a foot with toes joined by a web, as in swimming birds.

web·site *n.* a site on the worldwide Internet system where an individual subscriber may put up information for users.

Web·ster's (WEB.sturs) *n. Informal.* an American English dictionary. Also **Web·ster** *n. & adja.*

we'd (WEED) we had; we should; we would.

wed *v.* **weds,** *pt.* **wed·ded,** *pp.* **wed·ded** or **wed, wed·ding 1** give, take, or join in marriage: *"Jean Weds Gigi"; adja.: They spent the night in* **wedded** (= married) *bliss.* **2** unite closely, firmly, intimately, etc. to something: *a computer system that weds magnetic media with optical storage; There are people still* **wedded to** (= devoted to) *their manual typewriters.*

wed·ding (WED.ing) *n.* **1** a marriage ceremony and festivities: *to attend a wedding; officiate at* or *perform a wedding; a shotgun wedding forced on the couple by the bride's pregnancy.* **2** a marriage anniversary: *diamond wedding* (= 60th or 75th year); *golden wedding* (= 50th year); *silver wedding* (= 25th year). —*adja.: a wedding anniversary, band, cake, date, day, invitation, ring; Mendelssohn wrote the familiar "Wedding March."*

wedge (WEJ) *n.* **1** a piece of wood, metal, etc. tapering to a thin edge, used for splitting wood, raising weights, etc.: *The dispute drove a wedge between the families.* **2** something wedge-shaped, as a triangular piece of pie. —*v.* **wedg·es, wedged, wedg·ing:** *to wedge* (= split) *open a log; to wedge a door open* (= keep it open using a block); *to wedge up* (= chock) *a tipping cabinet; to wedge* (= squeeze) *oneself into a car; He was wedged* (= stuck) *between two ladies loaded with parcels on the crowded bus.*

wed·lock (WED.lock) *n.* the state of being married; matrimony: *The couple were joined in wedlock by their pastor; a child born* **out of wedlock** (= illegitimate child).

Wednes·day (WENZ.dee, -day) *n.* the fourth day of the week, following Tuesday.

wee *adj. Informal.* very small or tiny: *a* **wee bit** *bored;* in the wee (= small or very early) *hours of the morning.*

weed *n.* **1** a plant that is harmful or of no value, esp. when growing in a cultivated field: *a noxious weed.* **2 weeds** *pl.* mourning garments, as of a widow. —**the weed** *Informal.* tobacco or marijuana. —*v.* take weeds out of the ground: *to weed a lawn.* —**weed out** remove: *to weed out troublesome elements; to weed out a herd to improve the breed.* —**weed·er** *n.;* **weed·y** *adj.*

weed·y *adj.* **weed·i·er, -i·est 1** full of weeds: *a weedy garden.* **2** rank in growth like weeds: *weedy flowers, plants.* **3** lanky or scrawny.

week *n.* **1** seven successive calendar days, esp. from Sunday through Saturday: *Many workers are paid by the week; Our guests will be with us for a week; They'll be gone in a week; They haven't been here for years* or *in years; They will be here a week (from) Monday* or *be here Monday* **week. 2** the working part of the calendar week: *He works a six-day week; During the week, he is too* *busy to watch TV.*

week.day *n.* any day of the workweek, esp. Monday through Friday: *Most people work (on) weekdays.*

week.end or **week-end** *n.* the period from the close of one working week till the beginning of the next, usu. Saturday and Sunday: *Our friends stayed with us over the weekend; We don't work (on) weekends; a* **long** or **holiday weekend** *of three days including a public holiday, usually on Monday.* —*v.* spend the weekend: *We weekended with friends at their cabin.*

week.ly *adj.* of or happening once a week: *a weekly pay check, publication, visit;* **adv.**: *She visits us weekly.*
—*n., pl.* **-lies** a weekly publication.

week.night *n.* a weekday night: *a TV show seen (on) weeknights only.*

ween *v. Archaic.* imagine; suppose.

wee.nie (WEE.nee) *n. Informal.* a wiener.

wee.ny (WEE.nee) *adj. Informal.* very tiny or small; also **ween.sy.**

weep *v.* **weeps, wept, weep.ing 1** shed tears: *to weep for joy; to weep tears of joy; to weep bitter tears of sorrow; It's no use weeping over or about a misfortune; She's weeping* (= mourning) *for her loved ones.* **2** shed or exude drops of water or other liquid: *Cold pipes weep when the weather gets hot.*

weeping willow *n.* a willow characterized by drooping branches.

weep.y *adj.* **weep.i.er, -i.est** *Informal.* inclined to cry easily; tearful.

wee.vil (WEE.vil) *n.* a long-snouted beetle whose larvae damage crops, grain, and fruit.

weft *n.* the threads of a fabric or loom running crosswise to the warp; woof.

weigh (WAY) *v.* **1** measure the weight of something: *Luggage has to be weighed; A cook weighs out the ingredients for a recipe; He weighs* (= has the weight of) *160 lb.* **2** bend with or as if with a weight; bear down: *a tree* **weighed down** *with fruit; a heart weighed down with grief; lives weighed down by sorrow; His guilty conscience seemed to* **weigh on** or **upon** (= worry) *him; It weighed him down* (= depressed him). **3** consider carefully: *He weighs every word before saying anything; She weighed the pros and cons of quitting her job; She weighed the loss of income against being able to care for her children.* **4** have importance or significance; count: *Experience sometimes weighs more with employers than education; A criminal record weighs heavily against a job applicant.*
—**weigh anchor** of a ship, lift the anchor before sailing. —**weigh in 1** have oneself weighed: *Boxers, jockeys, etc. have to weigh in before a contest.* **2** make one's presence known or felt: *Well-wishers weighed in with all sorts of suggestions; Boxers, jockeys, etc. must weigh in at* (= enter the contest at) *the declared weights.* —*n.* **under weigh** [nautical use] progressing or advancing; under way.

weight (WAIT) *n.* **1** how heavy an object is: *His weight is 60 kg; Weight depends on gravitational pull and the mass of an object; Sugar is sold* **by weight,** *not volume; to* **gain** or **put on weight** (= get fatter); *to* **lose** or **take off weight** (= get slimmer). **2** a system or unit of weight: *atomic weight; avoirdupois weight; metric weights and measures; molecular weight.* **3** something heavy, as the disks used in "weight-lifting," a "pound," "gram," or other standard piece used in weighing, a quantity weighed out, or an object used to keep papers in place: *a set of weights; to lift weights; a heavy, not light weight.* **4** a burden or load to be supported: *That's a weight off my mind; The animal, which was carrying three fat men, collapsed under the weight (of its load).* **5** importance or influence: *a man of weight; Public opinion carries considerable weight with politicians; to* **add, attach, give,** or **lend weight** (= give importance) *to an argument, claim, demand, proposal, rumor, theory.* —**pull one's weight** do one's share. —**throw one's weight around** be overbearing or overassertive. —*v.* put weight on something: *a mind weighted down* (= burdened) *with worries; The evidence seemed weighted* (= slanted) *against the defendant;* **adj.**: *a stick with a* **weighted** *tip.*

weight.less *adj.* having little weight or gravitational pull; **weight.less.ly** *adv.*; **weight.less.ness** *n.*

weight lifting *n.* the competitive sport of lifting barbells. —**weight lifter** *n.*

weight.y (WAY.tee) *adj.* **weight.i.er, -i.est** very important or serious: *a weighty announcement, argument, decision, speaker; weighty matters of state; a weighty responsibility.* —**weight.i.ly** *adv.*

weir (WEER) *n.* **1** an obstruction erected across a stream or river, as a mill-dam, for diverting or raising the water. **2** a fence of stakes or brush for catching fish, etc.

weird (WEERD) *adj.* **1** mysterious in an unearthly way: *a weird shriek in the dark.* **2** *Informal.* strange: *a weird sense* of humor; *There's something weird about his attitude.* —**weird.ly** *adv.;* **weird.ness** *n.*

weird.o (WEER.doh) *n.* -os *Slang.* an eccentric person or thing. Also **weird.ie** (-dee).

welch same as WELSH.

wel.come (WEL.cum) *adj.* received with pleasure: *a welcome visitor; a welcome bit of news; a welcome relief from the heat; Contributions are always welcome; We want to make you feel welcome; You're* **welcome to** (= permitted to) *use our kitchen.* —**You're welcome** [in response to an expression of thanks] You are under no obligation.
—*n.* a reception on arrival: *to bid, extend, give someone a welcome; She left early so as not to overstay or wear out her welcome; to receive a chilly, cold, cool, cordial, enthusiastic, hearty, rousing, warm welcome from someone; to put out or roll out the* **welcome mat** (= give a friendly reception); *the* **welcome wagon** (= car carrying gifts from the community to which one is being welcomed).
—*interj.* you are welcome: *Welcome aboard! Welcome back! Welcome home!*
—*v.* **-comes, -comed, -com.ing** greet or receive someone on arrival: *She was welcomed with a hug; to be welcomed coolly, cordially, enthusiastically, with open arms; He was welcomed to their home; We welcome* (= accept with pleasure) *all credit cards, suggestions;* **adja.:** *a* **welcoming** *committee, party, reception, service, speech; welcoming remarks;* **adj.:** *a welcoming atmosphere, attitude, smile.*

weld *v.* **1** join pieces of metal by heating to the melting point and fusing, hammering, or pressing together. **2** unite closely or intimately.
—*n.* a welding or welded joint.
—**weld.er** *n.*

wel.fare (WEL.fare) *n.* **1** the condition of being healthy, happy, prosperous, etc.: *community, general, public welfare.* **2** the provision of food and such necessities to the needy, as by government programs of public assistance. **3** government aid given to the poor and needy. —**be** or **go on welfare** receive such aid.

welfare state *n.* a state or social system in which the government finances and often provides free social services such as medical treatment, education, housing, and pensions.

wel.kin *n. Archaic.* the sky or upper air.

we'll (WEEL) we will; we shall.

well *n.* **1** a hole or shaft dug in the ground to get water, oil, gas, etc.: *to bore, dig, drill, sink a well; oil wells; an artesian well* (= spring). **2** a shaft resembling a well, as a stairwell. **3** a container for holding a liquid, as an "inkwell." **4** source: *He's a well of information.* —*v.* flow out, rise up, etc. as water from a spring or well: *His eyes welled up with tears on hearing the sad news.* —*adv. comp.* **bet.ter,** *superl.* **best** in a good or satisfactory manner: *a job well done; He eats well; Things are going well with him; Shake the bottle well before use; We may well* (= quite likely) *make the deadline; It's well* (= long) *past noon;* **cpd:** *a well-liked person; well-polished shoes.* —**as well** in addition: *We are here mainly on business but for some pleasure as well; As well, we would like to do some shopping; We are here on business* **as well as** *for pleasure; We thought we might* **just as well** (= at the same time) *have some fun while we are here.* —**leave well enough alone** do not try to change what is satisfactory.
—*adj.* good or satisfactory: *All's well that ends well; It's well that he asked my permission; He came out of the hospital a well man; You look well* (= in good health). —*interj.* expressing surprise, agreement, doubt, etc.: *Well, what did I tell you? Well, no! Well, well!*

well-advised *adj.* **1** prudent: *a well-advised decision.* **2** based on good advice: *a well-advised rest.*

well-appointed *adj.* well equipped or furnished: *a well-appointed office.*

well-baby *adja.* having to do with health care for infants; **adja.:** *well-baby care, checkups, clinics.*

well-balanced *adj.* **1** properly matched: *a well-balanced ensemble, program, proposal, report, team.* **2** healthy: *a well-balanced diet, meal, variety of foods.*

well-being *n.* welfare: *our economic well-being; our children's well-being.*

well.born *adj.* born of a good family: *a well-born youth.*

well-bred *adj.* **1** having good manners. **2** of good stock: *a well-bred horse.*

well-connected *adj.* having connections with important people: *a well-connected lawyer.*

well-defined *adj.* clearly distinguishable; distinct: *a well-defined outline; within well-defined limits; a well-defined* (= clearly outlined) *job.*

well-disposed *adj.* having positive feelings *toward* a person or thing.

well-done *adj.* **1** skillfully performed: *a well-done job.* **2** cooked thoroughly: *a well-done steak.*

well-favored *adj.* good-looking; hand-

well-fed / we're

some: *a well-favored appearance.*
well-fed *adj.* plump; fat: *a well-fed cat.*
well-fixed *adj. Informal.* rich or prosperous.
well-founded *adj.* based on good evidence, judgment, reasoning, etc.: *a well-founded criticism, fear, statement, suspicion.*
well-groomed *adj.* neat in appearance: *well-groomed students; a well-groomed lawn; a well-groomed* (= cleaned, curried, etc.) *horse.*
well-grounded *adj.* 1 having a good foundation of knowledge *in* a subject. 2 supported by facts: *Her fears were well-grounded; a well-grounded suspicion.*
well.head *n.* the source of an oil well or spring; **adj.a.**: *the wellhead price of oil charged by the producer; wellhead valves.*
well-heeled *adj. Informal.* well-to-do; rich: *a well-heeled patron, publisher, tourist.*
well-informed *adj.* having considerable general knowledge *about* something.
well-intentioned *adj.* having or showing good intentions.
well-knit *adj.* well constructed or joined together: *a well-knit community, group; a play with a well-knit plot; a well-knit* (= sturdily built) *athlete.*
well-known *adj.* 1 famous: *a well-known politician.* 2 familiar: *She is well-known to all of us; a well-known landmark.*
well-mannered *adj.* having good manners.
well-meaning *adj.* 1 well-intentioned: *a well-meaning effort, parent.* 2 well-intended though ineffective: *a well-meaning attempt; well-meaning help;* also **well-meant.**
well-nigh *adv.* almost; very nearly: *well-nigh impossible.*
well-off *adj.a.* well-to-do; prosperous.
well-ordered *adj.* well-arranged; orderly.
well-preserved *adj.* of an old person, not showing signs of age.
well-read *adj.* having read much: *He's well-read in his subject.*
well-rounded *adj.* 1 comprehensive: *a well-rounded program, study.* 2 multi-faceted: *a well-rounded character, education.* 3 shapely: *a well-rounded figure.*
well-spoken *adj.* 1 well-uttered: *a few well-spoken words.* 2 impressive in speech and manner: *a well-spoken young woman.*
well.spring *n.* 1 a spring that is the source of a stream. 2 a never-failing source.
well-thought-of *adj.* having a good reputation.

well-timed *adj.* timely; opportune: *a well-timed move; Her phone call was well-timed – it saved a life.*
well-to-do *adj.* sufficiently rich or prosperous. —**the well-to-do** *n.* [with *pl. v.*].
well-turned *adj.* gracefully formed or expressed: *a well-turned ankle, compliment, phrase; well-turned verses.*
well-wisher *n.* one who wishes another, a cause, etc. well; **well-wishing** *n. & adj.*
well-worn *adj.* 1 much worn: *well-worn jeans, shoes, tires; to follow a well-worn path.* 2 over-used or trite: *a well-worn formula, phrase, saying, tale.*
welsh (WELSH, WELCH) *v. Informal.* evade an obligation, as a bookmaker who fails to pay a bet; cheat: *He would never welsh on a promise.* Also **welch.**
Welsh *n. & adj.* (having to do with) the Celtic people or language of Wales; **Welsh.man** *n.* -men; **Welsh.wom.an** *n.* -wom.en.
Welsh cor.gi (-COR.gee, "g" as in "go") *n.* a small dog of Welsh origin having short legs and foxlike head and tail.
Welsh rabbit *n.* a dish of melted, often seasoned cheese served on toast or crackers; also **Welsh rarebit.**
welt *n.* 1 a reinforcing strip or border, as used at the joining of a shoe's sole and upper, at the edge of a garment or upholstery, etc. 2 a ridge on the skin. 3 a slash or blow that would raise a welt on the skin. —*v. Informal.* thrash severely.
wel.ter (WEL.tur) *v.* 1 wallow. 2 be soaked *in* something wet such as mud, blood, etc. —*n.* 1 a chaotic rolling or tumbling. 2 a confused mass or jumble: *We feel lost in a welter of ambiguities, committees, data, opinions, papers, proposals, views.*
wel.ter.weight (WEL.tur.wait) *n.* a boxer weighing between 136 and 147 lb. (61 and 67 kg for Olympics).
wen *n.* a cyst formed on the scalp, back, etc. by the clogging up of oil glands of the skin; sebaceous cyst.
wench *n.* 1 [derogatory] a young woman. 2 [old use] a female servant.
wend *v.* go on one's way: *The procession wended slowly along King Street; They wended their way south.*
went *pt.* of GO.
wept *pt.* of WEEP.
were (WUR) past second pers. sing., past pl., and past subjunctive of BE: *as if I were a millionaire.* —**as it were** so to speak.
we're (WEER) we are.

were.n't (WURNT) were not.
were.wolf (WEER.wolf, WUR-, WAIR-) n. **-wolves** (-woolvs) in folklore, a person who changes into a wolf.
wert (WURT) [old form] the form of WERE used with "thou."
wes.kit n. Informal. waistcoat.
west n. 1 the direction where the sun sets, opposite of east. 2 a place, region, or country lying west: *California is out West for people in the East.* —**the West 1** the western North America: *songs of the Wild West.* 2 the countries of Europe and North America as distinguished from Asia. 3 the countries of Western Europe and the Americas. —*adv.* in or toward the west: *"Go west, young man" (and make your fortune); Drive west 1,000 miles to reach the Pacific coast;* **to go west** (Informal for to die or expire, like the setting sun); *Utah is west of Colorado.* —*adja.* 1 western: *the west side of the house; West Africa.* 2 westerly: *a west wind (blowing from the west).*
west.er.ly (WES.tur.lee) adja. & adv. 1 toward the west: *the most westerly settlement; We have to drive westerly.* 2 from the west: *a westerly wind.* —*n., pl.* **-lies** a wind from the west.
west.ern (WES.turn) adj. 1 of, toward, or from the west: *a western region; the Western Hemisphere.* 2 **Western** of the West: *a Western nation.* —*n.* a story, movie, play, etc. of the western U.S. featuring cowboy life. —**west.ern.er** or **West.ern.er** n.
west.ern.ize (WES.tur.nize) v. **-iz.es, -ized, -iz.ing** give a western character by introducing cultural elements from the European and American West: *There is no need to westernize the Japanese; adj.: a westernized culture, diet, economy, minority, Oriental, region, style; westernized ideas of freedom.*
west.ward (WEST.wurd) adj. & adv. toward the west. Also **west.wards** adv. —**west.ward.ly** adj. & adv.
wet adj. **wet.ter, wet.test 1** covered or soaked with water or another liquid, not dry: *wet hair, hands; a wet sponge; a brow wet with perspiration; He came out of the pool soaking wet; She came in from the rain dripping wet; wet (= rainy) weather; "Caution: Wet (= not yet dry) Paint."* 2 against prohibition of liquor; permitting alcoholic drinks; not dry: *a wet candidate, county.* —**all wet** Informal. wrong or mistaken. —**wet behind the ears** Informal. immature or naive. —*n.* 1 that which makes wet; liquid or moisture: *a floor covered with wet and grime.* 2 rainy weather: *She walked out into the wet.* 3 one opposed to prohibition: *Will is one of those old-time wets.* —*v.* **wets, wet** or **wet.ted, wet.ting** make or become wet: *Babies wet as and when they like; They wet themselves frequently; The "Wet Floor" sign is not an invitation to wet the floor; The young driver had been **wetting his whistle** (Informal for drinking) a little too much;* **n.:** *the childhood habits of bed wetting and thumb sucking.* —**wet.ter** n. —**wet.ly** adv.; **wet.ness** n.
wet.back n. Informal [derogatory] an illegal immigrant from Mexico, as one who swims across the Rio Grande river.
wet bar n. a bar or counter equipped with running water.
wet blanket n. one who dampens enthusiasm or lessens the gaiety of others.
wet dream n. the emission of semen during a sexual dream: *This case is a lawyer's wet dream (= A lawyer would derive much pleasure from it).*
weth.er ("th" as in "the") n. a male sheep castrated when young.
wet.land n. usu. **wetlands** pl. swamps, marshes, or bogs.
wet nurse n. a woman hired to suckle another's infant.
wet suit n. a heat-retaining garment of porous material such as foam rubber used by skin divers, etc.
wet.ware n. the human brain: *Hardware and software need wetware to make them work.*
we've (WEEV) we have.
whack n. Informal. 1 a sharp, resounding blow. 2 a portion or share. —**at a** or **one whack** in one attempt. —**have** or **take a whack at 1** aim a blow at someone. 2 make an attempt at doing something. —**out of whack** not in proper working order. —*v.* Informal. strike with a sharp, resounding blow: *I'll whack you one.* —**whack up** divide into shares. —**whack.er** n.
whacking adj. & adv. Informal. very large; whopping: *We won with a whacking majority; It was a whacking great victory.*
whack.y adj. **whack.i.er, -i.est** same as WACKY.
whale n. a fishlike but air-breathing, warm-blooded sea mammal that is the largest of animals: *a school (= group) of whales; whales of all sizes, including calves (= young ones), cows (= females), and bulls (= males).* —**a whale of a** Informal. great or impressive: *That was*

whaleboat / wheel

a whale of a party; We had a whale of a good time; She did a whale of a job; It makes a whale of a difference.
—v. **whales, whaled, whal.ing** 1 hunt whales. 2 *Informal.* beat or thrash roundly.

whale.boat *n.* a long narrow rowboat or motorboat.

whale.bone *n.* a horny, elastic plate attached to the upper jaw of "baleen" whales, used for straining out food and formerly for corset stays.

whal.er *n.* 1 a person or ship engaged in whaling. 2 a whaleboat.

whal.ing *n.* the hunting and processing of whales.

wham (*rhyme:* am) *n. Informal.* a hard impact or solid blow.
—v. **whams, whammed, wham.ming** *Informal.* strike with a wham.
—*interj.* a sound imitating a wham.

wham.my (WHAM.ee) *n.* **wham.mies** *Informal.* a jinx; hex; evil influence: *to put a* or *the whammy on someone; a double whammy.*

wharf (WHORF) *n.* **wharves** or **wharfs** a rectangular structure projecting from the shore along which ships dock for loading and unloading: *boats tied up at a wharf; People rushed to the wharves as the ship docked.*

what (WHOT, WHUT) *pron.* 1 [used in questions]: *What is the time? What on earth do you mean? So what?* (= If it's so, what follows?). 2 that which: *I heard what you said; Do what you like; What's more, take your time; She has what it takes* (= is quite capable); *She knows what's what* (= understands the situation). —**and** (or **or**) **what have you** *Informal.* and (or other) similar things. —**and what not** and similar things; see WHATNOT. —**what about it?** What do you think about it? —**what for?** Why? For what purpose? —**what gives?** *Informal.* What's going on? —**what's with** what's the matter with: *What's with this guy who won't even say hello to me.* —*adj.* 1 [used in questions]: *On what date? What time is it?* 2 that or those which: *Get what help you can; She sent me what books she could borrow.* 3 [used in exclamations]: *What an idea! What fools we are!* —*adv.* 1 In what respect? How much?: *What does it matter?* 2 [used in exclamations]: *What woeful neglect!* —**what with** because of: *What with inflation and rising prices, poor people are suffering.*

what.ev.er (what.EV.ur) *pron.* 1 no matter what: *He'll get it, whatever the cost.* 2 [used for emphasis]: *She'll agree with whatever you say; Whatever is the matter with you? furniture, groceries, stationery,* or **whatever** (*Informal* for anything at all). —*adj.* 1 no matter what: *He'll get it at whatever cost to himself.* 2 [used for emphasis negatively or with "any"]: *Get any book whatever; I have no doubt whatever she's innocent; None whatever.*

what.not *n.* 1 and **whatnot** *Informal.* and such things: *books, papers, disks, and whatnot.* 2 a set of open shelves for books, curios, etc.

what's what is; what has; what does.

what.so.ev.er (what.so.EV.ur) *adj. & pron.* [emphatic form] whatever.

wheal (WHEEL) *n.* 1 a temporarily swollen and itching patch on the skin, as from an allergy or insect bite. 2 a weal or welt.

wheat (WHEET) *n.* a cereal grass of temperate climates used for bread flour, breakfast foods, pasta, etc.: *to grow, harvest, thresh, winnow wheat; Mills grind wheat into flour; whole-wheat flour for making whole-wheat bread.*

wheat.en (WHEE.tun) *adj.* made of wheat.

wheat germ *n.* the vitamin-rich embryo of a wheat kernel.

whee.dle (WHEE.dul) *v.* **-dles, -dled, -dling** 1 use flattery, coaxing, etc. to persuade or influence someone *into* doing something. 2 get something *from* or *out* of someone by flattery, coaxing, cheating, etc. —**whee.dler** *n.*

wheel *n.* 1 a circular disk or frame with a central axis on which it rotates: *A wheel spins; Automobile wheels are aligned, balanced, rotated; front and rear wheels; The invention of the wheel was a great step forward in civilization; We don't have to **reinvent the wheel*** (= work out something already well-known). 2 anything shaped or moving like a wheel: *a watch's balance wheel; a Ferris wheel; the potter's wheel; a ratchet wheel; an antique spinning wheel; the steering wheel of an automobile or ship; When you are **at the wheel*** (= steering wheel) *you are in control, as a driver or helmsman; When you get **behind the wheel*** (= drive a car), *you do so at your own risk.* 3 *Informal.* an influential person; big shot: *the big wheels at city hall.* 4 a bicycle.
—**wheels** *pl.* 1 moving force or machinery: *the wheels of government; the wheels of progress.* 2 *Informal.* one's automobile. —**wheels within wheels** intricate machinery, motives, influences, etc.
—v. 1 move like a wheel: *The vultures wheeled* (= circled) *in the sky ready to*

wheelbarrow / wherefore

swoop down; She wheeled (= turned) round to face me; "where the beetle wheels (= makes in a circle) his droning flight." **2** move forward on wheels or in a wheeled vehicle: She wheeled the computer to the side of her desk; The man in the wheelchair wheeled in and joined the group; She wheeled the barrow up and down the garden; skaters wheeling around on the ice; The courier wheeled slowly down the street looking for an address; *adj.& cpd:* a **wheeled** vehicle (that has wheels); three-wheeled scooters. —**wheel and deal** Informal. make deals aggressively or unscrupulously: She made a spectacular $3 million in a single year of wheeling and dealing in real estate.

wheel.bar.row (WHEEL.bair.oh) *n.* a small vehicle for moving loads, having a box mounted on a wheel and attached to two shafts that are held in the hands and pushed or pulled.

wheel.base *n.* the distance between the front and rear axles of a motor vehicle.

wheel.chair *n.* a chair mounted on wheels, used by invalids.

wheel.er 1 *n. & comb.form.* one that has wheels: *a three-wheeler (tricycle); 19th century paddle-wheeler riverboats; sternwheeler (paddle boat).* **2** *n.* one who wheels and deals: *wheelers and dealers.*

wheeler-dealer *n.* Informal. a shrewd and aggressive operator in business, politics, etc.

wheel.horse *n.* Informal. a steady and hard worker: *a party wheelhorse with a powerful following.*

wheel.house same as PILOTHOUSE.

wheel.ie (WHEE.lee) *n.* the stunt of balancing a wheeled vehicle on its rear wheel or wheels.

wheel of fortune *n.* a gambling device that is rotated for determining the winner of a prize: *The roulette wheel is a wheel of fortune.*

wheel.wright (WHEEL.rite) *n.* one whose work is making and repairing wheels and wheeled vehicles.

wheeze *v.* **wheez.es, wheezed, wheez.ing** breathe or utter with a whistling sound, as an asthmatic. —*n.* **1** a wheezing or its sound. **2** an oft repeated saying or joke. *There's an old wheeze about boxing that you can't hit what you can't catch.*

wheez.y *adj.* **wheez.i.er, -i.est 1** inclined to wheeze. **2** wheezing. —**wheez.i.ness** *n.*

whelk *n.* a usu. edible marine snail with a spiral shell.

whelm *v.* submerge; engulf; overwhelm: *the whelming tide.*

whelp *n.* the cub of a flesh-eating animal such as the dog, wolf, bear, lion, tiger, or leopard. —*v.* bring forth whelps.

when *adv.* at what time: *When do you wake up?* —*conj.* **1** at the time that: *Call me when you wake up; He limps when he walks; We had just gone to bed, when I heard a knock on the door.* **2** although; considering that: *He continues to work when he could retire on a fat pension.* —*pron.* what or which time: *Since when are you a computer expert?* —*n.* the time, date, or occasion: *the when and where of the happening; the when and how of it.*

whence *adv. & conj.* from what place, source, or cause: *Whence does the need arise? Whence (= Wherefore) it follows that the earth is round.*

when.ev.er (when.EV.ur) *adv. & conj.* at whatever time; when.

when.so.ev.er (when.so.EV.ur) *adv. & conj.* [emphatic form] whenever.

where (WHAIR) *adv.* in, at, to, or from what place: *Where is the child? Where did he get the money? the hotel where (= at which) I stayed; Where (= in what respect) did I go wrong?* —*conj.* in the place in which: *I found it just where I left it; "Where there's smoke there's fire"; I go where (= to the place to which) business takes me; He was born in Orlando, where (= in which place) he went to school.* —*pron.* what or which place: *He asked us where we are from; Tell us where you are going; That's where you seem to have gone wrong; That's* **where it's at** (Informal for the main or essential question; also, where the action is); *I know* **where you're coming from** (Informal for what you mean). —*n.* place or scene: *the when and where of a happening.*

where.a.bouts (WHERE.uh.bowts) *adv. & conj.* about where: *Whereabouts does she live?* —*n.* the place where a person or thing is: *Her whereabouts is or are unknown; the whereabouts of the missing child.* Also [rarely] **where.a.bout.**

where.as (where.AZ) *conj.* **1** Formal. since: *Whereas you have been late Monday through Friday, you are being detained for an hour after school.* **2** on the contrary: *She likes tea, whereas I like coffee.*

where.at (where.AT) *adv. & conj.* at or in consequence of which.

where.by (where.BY) *adv. & conj.* by or through which.

where.fore *adv.* for what reason?

—conj. for which reason: *Profits come from sales, wherefore sales people deserve credit.* **—n.** the reason: *the whys and wherefores of the issue.*

where.from (where.FROM, -FRUM) *conj.* from which.

where.in (where.IN) *adv.* in what (respect)? **—conj.** in which; during which; in what way: *We have a situation wherein negotiations are impossible.*

where.of (where.OV) *adv. & conj.* of what, which, or whom.

where.on (where.ON) *conj.* on which.

where.so.ev.er (where.so.EV.ur) *conj.* [emphatic form] wherever.

where.to (where.TOO) *adv.* to what place? **—conj.** to which.

where.up.on (where.uh.PON) *conj.* upon which; at which.

wher.ev.er (where.EV.ur) *adv.* [emphatic form] where: *Wherever have you been?* **—conj.** in, at, or to whatever place: *Stay calm wherever you are.*

where.with (where.WITH) *adv.* with what? **—conj.** with which.

where.with.al (WHERE.with.awl) *n.* the necessary money or means: *the wherewithal to finance a project; He lacks the wherewithal for the down payment on a car.*

wher.ry (WHER.ee) *n.* **wher.ries** a light rowboat or barge; skiff.

whet *v.* **whets, whet.ted, whet.ting** 1 sharpen a knife, ax, etc. by rubbing on or with a stone. 2 make keen or stimulate: *to whet one's* or *the appetite, one's curiosity, interest.* **—whet.ter** *n.*

wheth.er (WHETH.ur, "TH" as in "the") *conj.* 1 [posing a choice between alternatives, expressed by "or" or merely implied]: *It's yours whether you like it or not; Please phone back whether he survived the crash.* 2 if: *It's doubtful whether she will agree.*

whet.stone (WHET.stone) *n.* a stone for whetting knives, etc.

whew (HWEW, HEW) *interj.* expressing relief, surprise, etc.

whey (WHAY) *n.* the liquid part of milk left after the curd separates.

which *pron.* 1 [used in questions to distinguish between several persons or things]: *Which is your dog? Which of them is yours? Which of us is faultless?* 2 [used in subordinate clauses to refer to something already mentioned]: *the car in which he drives to work; The book, which is still being written, will be published next year; I'm hungry, which means it's lunch time.* **—which is which** which is one and which the other: *Ada and Ida are so much alike it is hard to tell which is which.* **—adj.a.:** Which dog is yours? "Cats of the World," which book is now being written, may make the author wealthy.

which.ev.er (which.EV.ur) *pron. & adj.a.* any of two or more: *Work the day you like, whichever it is; Work whichever day you like.*

which.so.ev.er (which.so.EV.ur) *pron. & adj.a.* [emphatic form] whichever.

whick.er *n. & v.* neigh; whinny.

whiff *n. Informal.* 1 a slight puff or breath: *a whiff of fresh air, smoke; to spray a whiff of a fragrance.* 2 a slight smell or trace: *a whiff of envy, garlic, nostalgia, perfume, perversity, scandal; He gets panicky at the first whiff of something burning; I took a whiff and found it intriguing; She has caught a whiff of its strong scent.* **—v.** blow or puff lightly.

whif.fle.tree (WHIF.ul.tree) same as SINGLETREE.

whig (WHIG) *n.* 1 a member of a British political party between the late 1600's and the 1850's that opposed royal power and the Tories. 2 an American who supported the Revolutionary War. 3 a member of an American political party (1834-54) opposed to the Democratic Party.

while *n.* a period of time: *for a little while, short while; a long while ago;* **once in a (great) while** (= occasionally); *The government continued spending* **the while** (= during the time) *its debts grew ever larger.* **—worth one's while** worth one's time or effort. **—conj.** 1 during the time that: *She works while he sleeps.* 2 whereas; although: *She's a Democrat, while he's a Republican.*

—v. whiles, whiled, whil.ing esp. **while away,** spend time in a leisurely way: *to while away the summer.*

whi.lom (WHY.lum) *adj. & adv. Archaic.* former(ly).

whilst (WHY-) *conj.* [rare] while: *He takes people to task for their bad grammar whilst using stilted language himself.*

whim *n.* a sudden fanciful idea or desire: *childish, idle, mere whims; She was acting on a whim* (= impulse).

whim.per (WHIM.pur) *v.* 1 cry with whining, broken sounds. 2 utter in this manner. **—n.** a whimpering.

whim.sey (WHIM.zee) *n.* **-seys** same as WHIMSY.

whim.si.cal (WHIM.zi.cul) *adj.* 1 full of whims; capricious. 2 odd or fanciful: *a whimsical expression, idea, tale.*
—whim.si.cal.ly *adv.*
—whim.si.cal.i.ty (-CAL.i.tee) *n.*

whim.sy (WHIM.zee) *n.* **-sies** 1 caprice

or whim. **2** a fanciful or quaint quality, esp. of humor.

whine *n.* **1** the weak, nasal tone of a complaining child. **2** a complaint or cry made in this tone. —*v.* **whines, whined, whin.ing** utter with a whine or make a whine; hence, complain: *to whine about the hot weather; He whined something about the room being hot; He whined (to her) that the room was too hot.* —**whin.er** *n.*: *Some children are chronic whiners.* —**whin.y** *adj.* **whin.i.er, -i.est**: *a whiny child, note, tone, voice.*

whin.ny (WHIN.ee) *n.* a low and gentle neigh. —*v.* **whin.nies, whin.nied, whin.ny.ing** make a whinny.

whip *n.* **1** a stick with a lash attached, used as an instrument of punishment or for urging animals forward: *to crack a whip; lashed by a whip.* **2** a blow using a whip or a whipping or lashing motion. **3** one who drives using a whip, as a coachman, one in charge of a hunting pack, etc. **4** a party official helping the floor leader in a legislature with discipline, attendance during voting, etc.: *the House majority whip.* **5** a dessert made by beating egg white with fruit and sugar.
—*v.* **whips, whipped, whip.ping** **1** beat with a whip; lash: *to whip a horse; Rain was whipping her face; a rabble-rouser who can whip (= stir) any mob into a frenzy;* **n.**: *The poor donkey didn't deserve the* **whipping.** **2** move suddenly or quickly like the lash of a ship: *Flags whipped in the wind; a wind whipping across the lake; He* **whipped out** *his wallet and paid the bill; Then he whipped out of the restaurant;* **adj.**: *a cold whipping wind.* **3** defeat: *We whipped them in the finals; to whip inflation;* **n.**: *It was a 9-3* **whipping.** **4** wrap or wind a stick, rope, etc. closely with cord for strength or protection. **5** beat cream, etc. until frothy, as in making **whipped cream** topping for desserts.
—**whip into shape** *Informal.* bring into proper condition by vigorous action: *a teacher who can whip any class of rowdies into shape.* —**whip up** **1** rouse: *to whip up enthusiasm, fury, hatred, hysteria, interest.* **2** prepare something quickly: *to whip up a dinner, milkshake, salad; an entertainer who can whip up a great show in no time at all.* —**whip.per** *n.*

whip hand *n.* control or advantage: *to have the whip hand over* or *of an opponent.*

whip.lash *n.* **1** the lash of a whip. **2** injury to the neck caused by a severe jolt as in an automobile collision.

whip.per.snap.per (WHIP.ur.snap.ur) *n.* an insignificant but presumptuous person: *a young whippersnapper.*

whip.pet (WHIP.it) *n.* a racing dog resembling a small greyhound.

whipping boy *n.* a scapegoat, like a boy once used to take the punishment for a prince's faults: *Labor is sometimes made the whipping boy for inflation.*

whipping cream *n.* cream containing 32% to 40% butterfat, used to make whipped cream.

whip.ple.tree (WHIP.ul.tree) same as SINGLETREE.

whip.poor.will (WHIP.ur.wil) *n.* a North American insect-eating bird that flies mostly by night, named in imitation of its call.

whip.saw *n.* a two-handled or crosscut saw operated by two persons.
—*v.* **1** cut with a whipsaw. **2** *Informal.* cheat or be worsted by the joint action of two people or in two ways at the same time.

whir or **whirr** (WHUR) *n.* a buzzing sound, as of a small machine.
—*v.* **whirs** or **whirrs, whirred, whir.ring** vibrate, fly, operate, etc. with a whir.

whirl (WHURL) *n.* **1** a rapidly revolving motion, as by the force of wind or water. **2** something that whirls or a condition of dizziness, confusion, etc.: *Her head was in a whirl as she got off the merry-go-round; the social whirl (= round) of parties and dances.* **3** an attempt or try: *Give it a whirl and let me know.* —*v.* swing round and round rapidly and continuously, as leaves caught in the wind or a car gone out of control: *Dancing couples whirled about the room; He whirled her away in his new sports car; Her head whirled (= She felt dizzy), and she passed out.*

whirl.i.gig (WHUR.lee.gig) *n.* a whirling or spinning thing, esp. a toy: *A beetle called "whirligig" whirls on water; the whirligig (= merry-go-round) of city life; the whirligig of time (= changes of fortune brought about by time).*

whirl.pool *n.* a spinning mass of water caused by opposing currents or by wind; vortex or eddy: *to be drawn into the whirlpool of political intrigue.*

whirlpool bath *n.* a therapeutic bath of swirling warm water.

whirl.wind *n.* a whirling column of air, as seen in deserts. —*adj. Informal.* fast or hurried: *a whirlwind campaign, romance, tour.*

whirl.y.bird (WHUR.lee.bird) *n. Informal.* a helicopter.

whisk *v.* **1** move or sweep with a light, quick, brushing movement, as with a small bunch of straw, twigs, feathers, etc. used for brushing dust, or lint off clothes: *Security police whisked them through customs and into a waiting van; On being sentenced, he was whisked off to jail.* **2** beat or whip eggs, creams, etc. to a froth using a whisk. —*n.* **1** a whisking movement. **2** a brush used for whisking dust, etc. off; also **whisk broom**. **3** in African costume, an ornamental bunch of soft, light material held in the hand for shooing off flies, etc. **4** a kitchen utensil made of looped wires used for whisking eggs, creams, etc.

whisk.er *n.* **1** one of the long, bristly hairs growing above the mouth of a cat, rat, bird, insect, etc. **2** one of the hairs grown on the sides of a man's face. **3 whiskers** *pl.* the beard on a man's face other than the mustache: *to grow whiskers; He had to shave off his whiskers when he joined the police force.* **4** *Informal.* a very tiny amount, degree, distance, or margin: *He won the election by a whisker.*

whisk.ered (WHISK.urd) *adj.* having whiskers: *a whiskered cat, gentleman; our whiskered house mouse.*

whis.key (WHIS.kee) *n.* **-keys** or **-kies** a strong alcoholic liquor distilled from grain and malt, including rye and Scotch: *Bourbon whiskey; Irish whiskey; Straight whiskey is 80% alcohol by volume; single-malt whiskies and blended whiskies; I'll have a whiskey and soda (drink).* Also **whis.ky, -kies:** *Canadian whisky; Scotch whisky.*

whis.per (WHIS.pur) *v.* **1** speak or say in a very low voice; hence, tell very privately, as a secret: *He whispered it in her ear;* a **whispering campaign** *of spreading false rumors, charges, etc. against an opponent.* **2** make a rustling sound, as leaves in the wind.
—*n.* **1** a whispering or something whispered: *The child spoke in whispers.* **2** a rustling sound.

whist (WHIST) *n.* a card game from which bridge developed.

whis.tle (WHIS.ul) *v.* **-tles, -tled, -tling 1** make a shrill, clear sound by forcing breath through pursed lips: *to whistle to* (= call) *a dog; to whistle at someone* (in admiration); *to whistle for* (= hail) *a cab; She can whistle the tune of "Dixie"; a claim that sounds like* **whistling in the dark** (= like something to reassure oneself). **2** make a similar sound, as a bird, wind, steam engine, or with a whistle. —**whistle for something** *Informal.* expect in vain to get it —*n.* **1** a whistling or its sound: *Sam gave a whistle to attract Ray's attention; a shrill whistle; wolf whistles;* **as clean as a whistle** (= very clean). **2** a device for producing such a sound, as used by police, referees, etc.: *Patients don't like to* **blow the whistle on** (Informal for report to the authorities) *doctors who overcharge.* —**whistle-blower** *n.* —**whis.tler** *n.*

whistle stop *n.* **1** a brief stop at a small town in a political campaign tour. **2** a small town along a railroad route at which a train stops only by request.

whit *n.* the least bit; iota: *The rumors don't worry her one whit; There's not a whit of truth in them.*

white *adj.* **whit.er, whit.est 1** having the color of fresh snow or milk; light-colored or pale; not black: *a beautiful white horse; Snow is "white gold" for ski resorts; the white powder* or *stuff called snow; a white* (= albino) *mouse; a white* (= snowy) *Christmas; white* (= gray) *hair; the white* (= Caucasian) *race or White race; a page with too much white* (= unprinted) *space;* a **white-haired** (= blond) *youth.* **2** having no color: *white blood cells; the incandescent white heat of metals; the golden loaves of white enriched bread; He turned white with fear, fury; white* (= not green) *creme de menthe; white* (= pale-colored) *wines such as Chablis.* **3** symbolic of goodness, peace, etc., often "not black": *white as a lily; white* (= harmless) *lies, magic, witches; a white* (= reactionary) *political faction.* —*n.* **1** white color or pigment. **2** something white: *dressed in white* (= white clothes); *the white* (= albumen) *of an egg; the white of the eye* (around the iris); *an uncrowded page with plenty of white* (= white space). **3** a Caucasian. **4** a member of a reactionary group. —**white.ness** *n.*

white ant same as TERMITE.

white.bread *adj.* [derogatory] having to do with the white middle class: *a whitebread Oxford scholar.*

white blood cell *n.* one of the colorless corpuscles of the blood that help defend the body against infection; leukocyte.

white.cap *n.* the foamy crest of a breaking wave.

white-collar *adj.* clerical or professional; not blue-collar: *a white-collar job, occupation, worker; A* **white-collar crime** *such as fraud, embezzlement, or tax evasion is usually committed by people in* white-collar occupations without use of violence.

white dwarf *n.* a small star of extremely high density that shines with a white light.

white elephant *n.* something useless and expensive to maintain, like an albino elephant considered sacred in some Southeast Asian countries.

white feather *n.* esp. **show the white feather** show cowardice.

white.fish *n.* a freshwater food fish related to the salmons and trouts.

white flag *n.* **1** a white-colored flag used to signal a truce or surrender: *to show the white flag.* **2** a token of accepting defeat.

white gold *n.* a platinumlike alloy of gold and nickel, zinc, etc. used in jewelry.

white goods *n.pl.* **1** white household linens. **2** household appliances such as refrigerators, washers, etc. that are usu. white-enameled.

White.hall *n.* the British government.

white.head *n.* a form of acne.

white heat *n.* the temperature at which metals, etc. appear white when heated beyond the red-hot stage; **white-hot** *adj.*

white hope *n.* a person or thing expected to bring glory to a group: *a drug hailed as the great white hope of cancer therapy.*

white-hot *adj.* **1** at white heat. **2** intensely excited, angry, enthusiastic, etc.

White House *n.* the official residence of the U.S. President in Washington, D.C.; hence, the executive branch of the U.S. government.

white-label *adj.* generic: *White-label goods are cheaper than name brands.*

white knight *n.* a hero who comes to the rescue: *waiting for a white knight to come and rescue the company from a corporate raider in a takeover battle.*

white-knuckle *adj.* tense or frightening: *a white-knuckle adventure, experience, ride.*

white lead *n.* a poisonous lead carbonate used as a paint pigment in the form of a white powder.

white lie *n.* a harmless lie, as one told out of politeness or kindness.

white matter *n.* whitish tissue consisting of nerve fibers surrounding the gray matter of the brain.

white meat *n.* meat such as pork, poultry, rabbit, and veal, distinguished from red meat.

whit.en (WHY.tun) *v.* make or become white or whiter. —**whit.en.er** *n.*

white.out *n.* an arctic or winter weather condition in which the snow, either on the ground or blowing, causes poor visibility and makes flying and driving dangerous.

white paper *n.* a document published by a government setting out its policy on a specific subject.

white pine *n.* a pine with soft, light-colored wood and five needles to the cluster.

white room *n.* a sterilized and pressurized clean room for laboratory work.

white sale *n.* **1** a sale of household linens. **2** a sale at a much reduced price.

white slave *n.* a female forced to be a prostitute, esp. one sent abroad.

white sound *n.* an electronically produced tone used to mask noises in a work area.

white supremacy *n.* supremacy of the white race.

white.tail *n.* a deer with a tail that is white underneath and antlers curving forward; also **white-tailed deer**.

white.wall *n. & adj.* (an automobile tire) having a white band on the outer sidewall.

white.wash *n.* **1** a mixture of lime and water for coating walls, woodwork, etc. **2** a covering up of faults or defects as if by use of whitewash. **3** *Informal.* a defeat that is a shutout. —*v.* **1** cover or conceal with whitewash. **2** *Informal.* defeat by a shutout.

white water *n.* the frothy water of the rapids; *adja.:* **white-water** *canoeing, expeditions, kayaking, rafting, wilderness trips.*

white.wood *n.* (a tree such as the basswood or tulip tree that has) a soft, light-colored wood.

whit.ey (WHY.tee) *n.* [derogatory slang] the white man or white society.

whith.er (WHITH.ur, "TH" as in "the") *adv.* to what place, result, condition, etc.? —*conj.* to which place, etc.

whith.er.so.ev.er (WHITH.ur.so.EV.ur) *adv. & conj.* to whatever place.

whit.ing (WHY.ting) *n.* **1** powdered chalk as used in the manufacture of paint, putty, etc. **2** a kind of silvery marine food fish.

whit.ish (WHY.tish) *adj.* somewhat white.

whit.low (WHIT.loh) *n.* bacterial infection around a toenail or fingernail.

Whit.sun.day (WHIT.sun.day, -dee) same as PENTECOST.

whit.tle (WHIT.ul) *v.* **whit.tles, whit.tled, whit.tling 1** pare or cut

shavings from wood, etc. with a knife: *to whittle at a stick; to whittle a stick into a handle.* **2** shape or carve an object: *to whittle a handle out of a stick.* **3** reduce: *to whittle down expenses; Inflation whittles away our purchasing power.*
—**whit.tler** *n.*

whiz or **whizz** *n.* **whiz.zes 1** the hissing sound of an arrow, ball, etc. rushing through the air. **2** *Informal.* an expert or skilled person; wizard: *She's a whiz at electronics.* —*v.* **whiz.zes, whizzed, whiz.zing 1** make a whiz. **2** speed past making this sound: *Bullets whizzed by our heads; We watched the scene whizzing past our car window.*

whiz-bang *n.* a first-rate person or thing: *That's a whiz-bang of an idea; He's no whiz-bang as a writer;* **adj.:** *a whiz-bang finance minister who screwed up the economy.*

whiz kid *n.* a youth considered very smart.

who (HOO) *pron.,* objective WHOM, possessive WHOSE **1** [used in questions about persons]: *Who is the president? Who are these people? Who did you say is coming to dinner? John who?* **2** the person or persons that: *the man who called yesterday; those who smoke; I don't know who* (*Informal for* whom) *to trust anymore.*

whoa (WHOH) *interj.* [to a horse, etc.] stop!

who.dun.it (hoo.DUN.it) *n. Informal.* a story, play, etc. dealing with crime detection.

who.ev.er (hoo.EV.ur) *pron.* **1** no matter who; any person who: *Whoever owes money is a debtor.* **2** [emphasizing "who"]: *Whoever is that guy?*

whole (HOLE) *adj.* with no part taken away or left out; entire: *a whole roast pig; herring salted whole; the whole neighborhood; the whole wide world; He came out alive and whole* (= unhurt); *to treat the whole person* (= the physical, emotional, and other aspects); *whole blood* (with all its components); *a* **whole** (= not half) **brother;** *We don't know* **a whole lot** *about many things of daily life.* —*n.* complete or entire thing, unit, system, etc.: *the parts of a whole; a complex whole; to constitute, form a whole.* —**as a whole** as one complete unit, not in parts. —**on the whole** considering everything; in general. —**whole.ness** *n.*

whole.heart.ed (HOLE.har.tid) *adj.* with all one's enthusiasm; not half-hearted.
—**whole.heart.ed.ly** *adv.* Also **wholeheart.ed, whole-heart.ed.ly.**

whole hog See HOG.

whole-meal *adj.* made of the entire kernel of wheat; whole-wheat: *whole-meal flour.*

whole milk *n.* milk with no butterfat, etc. removed.

whole note *n.* the standard unit of time in music notation, indicated as an open oval shape without stem.

whole number *n.* an integer, not a fraction.

whole.sale *n.* the selling of goods in large quantities and at lower prices, usu. to retailers. —**adj. 1** (selling) in large quantities: *the wholesale price, not retail; a wholesale dealer who supplies retailers.* **2** general; indiscriminate: *wholesale condemnation, criticism, murder, slaughter.* —**adv.** in a wholesale manner: *Retailers buy wholesale; The plan was rejected wholesale* (= completely).
—*v.* **-sales, -saled, -sal.ing** sell at wholesale. —**whole.sal.er** *n.*

whole.some *adj.* **1** healthful: *a wholesome climate, environment, food; a wholesome* (= healthy and vigorous) *youth.* **2** beneficial for mind and soul: *wholesome advice, movies, reading material; a wholesome* (= prudent or salutary) *fear of the law.* —**whole.some.ness** *n.*

whole step *n.* one tone or interval in a musical scale.

whole-wheat *adj.* ground from entire kernels of wheat including the bran, germ, etc.: *whole-wheat flour; whole-wheat bread* (made of whole-wheat flour).

who'll (HOOL) who shall; who will.

whol.ly (HOH.lee, HOLE.lee) *adv.* to the whole extent; entirely; solely.

whom (HOOM, long "OO") *pron.* objective case of WHO: *the man to whom you are married; Whom* (*Formal for* Who) *are you married to?*

whom.ev.er (hoo.MEV.ur) *objective case of* WHOEVER.

whomp *v.* usu. **whomp up** *Informal.* prepare quickly: *to whomp up some milkshakes.*

whom.so.ev.er (hoom.so.EV.ur) *objective case of* WHOSOEVER.

whoop *n.* **1** an excited long cry or shout: *The crowd let out whoops of joy.* **2** the hoot of an owl, the cry of a crane, etc., as of the whooping crane. **3** a long and loud drawing in of the breath following a paroxysm of coughing, as in whooping cough.
—*v.* **1** shout or call loudly. **2** hoot as an owl. —**whoop it up** *Informal.* make merry noisily: *They were whooping it up all night along Main Street.*

whoop.ee (WHOO.pee) *interj.* express-

ing great joy. —*n. Informal.* noisy fun: *The class was punished for making whoopee when the teacher was late.*
whoop.er *n.* a whooping crane.
whooping cough *n.* a highly contagious bacterial disease, esp. of children, marked by coughing spells followed by whoops.
whooping crane *n.* a large, white, nearly extinct North American crane with a loud, deep call.
whoop.la (WHOOP.lah) same as HOOP-LA.
whoops (short or long "oo") *interj.* uttered when suddenly realizing one's error or having taken a wrong step.
whoosh (short or long "oo") *v. & n.* (make) the loud noise of rushing air.
whop *n. & v.* **whops, whopped, whop.ping** *Informal.* hit or whack.
whop.per (WHOP.ur) *n. Informal.* something huge, as a story, fish, or falsehood: *She tells outlandish whoppers; He has a whopper of a drug habit.*
whopping *adja. Informal.* extraordinarily huge; colossal: *a whopping deficit, foreign debt; a whopping* (= impressive) *idea, She received a whopping 99% in math; a whopping $1,900 a week; She drove a whopping 900 miles in one day;* *adv.: a whopping* (= colossally) *big lie.*
whore (HORE) *n.* a prostitute.
—**whor.ish** *adj.*
whore.house *n.* a brothel.
whorl (WHORL, WHURL) *n.* a whirling or circular shape or formation, as a ring of leaves or flowers around a point on an axis, one of the turns in a univalve shell, or a pattern of circles: *the arches, loops, and whorls of a fingerprint;* *adj.: the* **whorled** (= whorl-shaped) *arrangement of the parts of a flower.*
who's (HOOZ) who is; who has.
whose (HOOZ) *pron.* possessive case of WHICH and WHO: *Whose is this kid? Whose are these clothes?* —*adja.: Whose kid is this? Whose books are these? a flower whose name* (= the name of which) *I've forgotten.*
who.so (HOO.soh) *pron.* whoever.
who.so.ev.er (HOO.so.EV.ur) *pron.* [emphatic form] whoever.
who's who *n.* **1** a compilation of short biographies: *Who's Who in the World; The roster reads like a who's who of the dance world.* **2** the leaders of a group: *The audience was a who's who of oil barons.*
whump same as WHOMP.
why *adv.* for what reason, cause, or purpose?: *Why do people eat?*

—*conj.: Everyone knows why people eat; The main reason why we eat is to live.*
—*n., pl.* **whys:** *the how and why of our existence; the whys and the wherefores of marriages breaking up.* —*interj.* expressing surprise, etc.: *Why, I thought today was a holiday! Why, what happened?*
wick *n.* a piece of cord or tape for drawing up and burning the fuel in an oil lamp, stove, or candle.
wick.ed (WICK.id) *adj.* **1** bad in a willful way: *a wicked and disobedient child; a wicked deed, witch, wizard, world; a thoroughly wicked old man; to mend his wicked ways.* **2** roguish; mischievous: *a wicked delight, joke, look.* **3** *Informal.* formidable in appearance or execution: *a wicked blow, performance; a wicked-looking knife.* —**wick.ed.ly** *adv.;* **wick.ed.ness** *n.*
wick.er *n.* **1** a thin, flexible twig or strip of material used for weaving into baskets, furniture, etc. **2** such woven material or objects made with it.
wick.er.work (WICK.ur.wurk) *n.* wicker material or objects made of wicker.
wick.et (WICK.it) *n.* a small gate or opening, as a box-office window, a small door set in a large gate, a wire arch or hoop through which balls are hit in games, etc.
wick.i.up (WICK.ee.up) *n.* a simple hut made of brush and matting, used as shelter by nomadic tribes of American Indians.
wide *adj.* **wid.er, wid.est 1** having a relatively large measurement from side to side; broad; not narrow: *a wide aperture, doorway, expanse, gap, margin; wide* (= fully open) *eyes; a door two meters wide* (= in width). **2** of great range; extensive: *the whole wide world; a man of wide interests; The shop carries a wide selection of goods.*
—*comb.form.* **1** throughout: *areawide, citywide, countrywide, nationwide, worldwide.* **2** broad: *a wide-bodied jet; wide-brimmed, wide-ranging, wide-reaching.*
—*adv.* **1** over a relatively large area or extent; extensively: *He is wide awake; Open your mouth wide; She travels far and wide.* **2** away from the target: *The bullet went wide; It was two feet* **wide of** *the mark.* —**wide.ly** *adv.*
wide-angle *adj.* having a relatively wide angle that covers a large area: *a wide-angle beam, lens, shot, view; to take a wide-angle aim at a target.*
wide-awake *adja.* fully awake; hence, alert: *a wide-awake infant, inspector, judge, listener.*
wide-eyed *adj.* **1** with wide-open eyes;

hence, amazed: *She stared in wide-eyed wonder.* **2** simple or naive: *a wide-eyed admirer; a wide-eyed newspaper article on faith healers.*

wide-mouthed *adj.* having a wide mouth: *a wide-mouthed channel, jar; He stared in wide-mouthed astonishment.*

wid.en (WYE.dun) *v.* make or become wide or wider; broaden.

wide.spread *adj.* **1** widely spread out: *The famine is becoming more widespread in parts of Africa; widespread ramifications.* **2** widely prevalent: *a widespread belief, fear, trend; widespread acceptance, skepticism, support, use.*

widg.eon (WIJ.un) *n.* a wild duck usu. called "baldpate" because of the male's white head. Also **wi.geon.**

wid.get (WIJ.it) *n.* an imagined gadget or device: *Suppose you made $100 an hour selling widgets.*

wid.ow (WID.oh) *n.* a woman after her husband's death but before remarriage: *a war widow.* —*v.* cause to become a widow: *a young woman widowed by the war.* —**wid.ow.hood** *n.*

wid.ow.er (WID.oh.ur) *n.* a man after his wife's death but before remarriage.

width *n.* measurement from side to side of something; breadth: *the width of a window; the length, width, and height of an object; The store carries a full range of sizes and widths; She can swim two widths of the pool.*

wield (WEELD) *v.* handle a tool, weapon, etc. skillfully and effectively: *to wield an ax, the pen, a sword; to wield* (= exercise) *influence, power.*
—**wield.er** *n.*

wie.ner (WEE.nur) *n.* a frankfurter of shorter size; also called "Vienna sausage" or **wie.ner.wurst.**

wife *n.* **wives 1** a female spouse: *devoted, estranged, faithful, jealous, unfaithful wives; He had no children by his common-law wife; I'll check with the wife and let you know.* **2** any married woman: *a Hollywood wife; farm wives; police wives.* —**wife.hood** *n.* —**wife.less** *adj.* —**wife.ly** *adj.*

wig *n.* a head covering of false hair: *They sell both wigs and hairpieces.* —*v.* **wigs, wigged, wig.ging** *Slang.* **1** thrill or excite. **2** be thrilled, excited, etc.: *teeny-boppers wigging out over their idols; people wigged out* (= high) *on drugs.*

wigeon (WIJ.un) same as WIDGEON.

wigged (WIGD) *adj.* wearing a wig: *a wigged judge; the wigged look.*

wig.gle (WIG.ul) *v.* **wig.gles, wig.gled, wig.gling** move with quick, side-to-side movements: *to wiggle one's ears, hips, toes.* —*n.* a wiggling movement. —**wig.gler** *n.* —**wig.gly** (WIG.lee) *adj.*

wight (WITE) *n. Archaic.* **1** a human being. **2** a creature.

wig.let (WIG.lit) *n.* a small wig.

wig.wag *v.* **-wags, -wagged, -wag.ging 1** move to and fro; wag. **2** signal a message by waving a flag, light, etc. according to a code. —*n.* **1** the wigwagging of messages. **2** such a message.

wig.wam (WIG.wom) *n.* a usu. dome-shaped dwelling of North American Indians made of a framework of poles covered with bark or woven mats.

wild (WILED) *adj.* **1** of animals, plants, etc., not tamed or cultivated: *the wild boar of Europe and Asia; wild honey; a wild region; the wild rose.* **2** not civilized or orderly: *wild tribes; wild laughter; a wild* (= random) *guess; the **wild and woolly*** (= barbarous) *West; a wild* (= erratic) *baseball pitch; a **wild card*** (= playing card with arbitrary rank or value). **3** crazy or frantic: *a wild scheme; wild speculations; He was wild with rage; a wild* (= violent) *storm.*
—*adv.*: *weeds growing wild on a lawn; Children shouldn't **run wild** on the streets; They **went wild** over* (= were very excited about) *their idol.* —*n.* a wild region or condition: *to return to the wild; plants growing in the wild; in the wilds of the Amazon; the call of the wild* (= of "Nature"). —**wild.ly** *adv.;* **wild.ness** *n.*

wild card *n.* **1** an unpredictable factor or person: *Clouds are a key wild card in predicting the weather; a wild-card candidate.* **2** a character such as the asterisk or question mark used to cover many alternatives, as the string "lov*" to include "love, loves, loved, loving," etc.: *a wild-card character, search, string.*

wild.cat *n.* **1** any of the smaller wild animals of the cat family, esp. a bobcat. **2** a fierce fighter. **3** a risky or reckless undertaking, as a gas or oil well drilled in an unproven area.
—*adj.* unauthorized; illegal; illicit: *wildcat operations, stocks, strikes, walkouts.*
—*v.* **-cats, -cat.ted, -cat.ting** drill for gas or oil in an unproven area.
—**wild.cat.ter** *n.*

wil.de.beest (WIL.duh.beest) same as GNU.

wil.der.ness (WIL.dur.nis) *n.* an uninhabited region without tracks or trails, as a forest or desert.

wild-eyed *adj.* **1** staring in an angry or

deranged manner. **2** irrational or foolish: *wild-eyed notions; She's no wild-eyed radical.*

wild.fire *n.* a quickly spreading forest fire: *The news spread like wildfire.*

wild.fowl *n.* **-fowls** or **-fowl** a game bird such as a wild duck or quail.

wild-goose chase *n.* a foolish or futile pursuit, endeavor, etc.

wild.life *n.* animals, birds, fishes, etc. in their natural state. —**adj**a.: *wildlife conservation, management; a wildlife preserve, sanctuary.*

wild oat or **wild oats** *n.* a wild grass resembling oats. —**sow one's wild oats** esp. of males, be promiscuous in youth.

wild rice *n.* **1** a tall North American grass that grows wild in shallow waters. **2** its grain that is used like rice.

Wild West *n.* the western United States of pioneer days: *Lawlessness was such that the Wild West meant just that.*

wile *v.* **wiles, wiled, wil.ing** lure or entice. —**wile away** same as WHILE AWAY. —**wiles** *n.pl.* sly tricks or arguments used to trap someone: *the wiles of the serpent who tricked Eve; the coquettish wiles of a temptress; to work one's wiles on someone; "Feminine wiles" is a much-abused term.*

wil.ful same as WILLFUL.

will *n.* **1** the mental power to make and carry out a decision: *the will to succeed; the will to survive; a terminal patient's will to live; a woman of iron will; They couldn't break her will; an indomitable, inflexible will; a clash of wills; "Where there's a will there's a way."* **2** wish or choice: *elected to carry out the will of the people; It was done against her will; not of her own free will; a man who imposes his will* (= desire) *on his children; He hires and fires* **at will** (= as he likes); *He has servants to* **do his will** (= obey him) *round the clock.* **3** a statement of how property is to be disposed of after one's death: *He died without making his will; her last will and testament; to challenge, contest, draw up, execute, make, make out, probate, validate a will.* **4** a feeling or disposition toward another: *She bore him no ill will; a message of good will toward all.* —*v.* **1** decide or determine: *He wished to live to a ripe old age, but Providence willed otherwise; Willing is more important than mere wishing.* **2** influence by mental power: *She has the psychic power to will someone to turn around.* **3** bequeath a property to someone. **4** wish or desire: *Do as you will.* **5** auxiliary *v.*, *pres.* **will**, *pt.* **would** (WOOD); *second person archaic pres.* **wilt**, *pt.* **wouldst** expressing futurity (*The world will end*), willingness or determination (*I will hire her*), capability, habit, or custom (*Boys will be boys; That will be the mailman*), and command (*You will do as I say; That will be all*).

willed 1 *adj.* brought about by willing: *a willed outcome; the willed violence of the terrorists.* **2** *comb.form.* having a will as specified: *iron-willed, self-willed, strong-willed, weak-willed.*

will.ful (WIL.ful) *adj.* **1** obstinate or stubborn: *a willful child, girl, son.* **2** intentional: *willful acts, disobedience, disregard, murders, violations.* Also **wil.ful.**
—**will.ful.ly** or **wil.ful.ly** *adv.*
—**will.ful.ness** or **wil.ful.ness** *n.*

wil.lies (WIL.eez) *n.pl. Slang.* jitters: *That kind of talk gives me the willies; to get the willies; suffer from the willies.*

willing *adj.* **1** ready or consenting: *She's willing; She's willing to marry him.* **2** ready and prompt: *willing ears, hands, workers.* **3** voluntary: *willing obedience, sacrifice.* —**will.ing.ly** *adv.*
will.ing.ness *n.*

wil.li.waw (WIL.ee.waw) *n.* a sudden violent wind or squall blowing into the sea from mountains along a coast.

will-o'-the-wisp *n.* **1** a light sometimes seen hovering over marshes, believed to be marsh gas igniting itself; also called "jack-o'-lantern." **2** an elusive and misleading hope or goal: *the will-o'-the-wisp of peace in troubled parts of the world; Love seemed a cruel will-o'-the-wisp that would elude him forever.*

wil.low (WIL.oh) *n.* **1** a tree with long, narrow leaves and slender, pliable branches, often used in weaving baskets. **2** its wood.

wil.low.y (WIL.oh.ee, WIL.uh.wee) *adj.* slender or lithe like a willow.

will.pow.er (WIL-, *rhyme:* our) *n.* strength of will or determination; resoluteness: *He overcame his handicap by sheer willpower.*

wil.ly-nil.ly (WIL.ee.NIL.ee) *adv.* whether one wants it or not: *She accepted the nomination willy-nilly,* **adj**a.: *The parties joined together in a willy-nilly coalition.*

wilt *v.* **1** *Archaic.* second pers. sing. pres. indic. of WILL. **2** droop or become weak, as a plant from heat or lack of water: *Plants will wilt and die if not watered; His confidence wilted under her severe criticism.* —*n.* **1** a wilting. **2** a disease caused by fungi, bacteria, or viruses that makes plants wilt and die.

wi.ly (WYE.lee) *adj.* **-li.er, -li.est** full of

wiles; sly, as a fox: *the wily coyote; a wily character.* —**wi.li.ness** *n.*

wimp *n. Informal.* a weak and soft person; weakling. —**wimp.y** *adj.*

wim.ple *n.* a head covering of women in the Middle Ages, as worn by nuns, exposing only the face.
—*v.* **-ples, -pled, -pling** cover or veil (as if) with a wimple.

win *v.* **wins, won** (WUN), **win.ning** succeed in achieving a desired aim by effort, as the result of competition, etc.: *Which team won (the race)? The Blue Jays won easily; They won hands down; We won against considerable odds; to win an audience, a mountain summit, reputation, scholarship, war, wife; He would give anything to win* (= gain) *her favor; Persevering people win out* (= succeed) *in the end; It took much persuasion to win over* (= get the support of) *the hostile crowd; You win a few, lose a few* (= win little by little); *"You can't win them all"* (= You cannot always be successful).
—*n. Informal.* victory or success, esp. in a contest or race: *a lottery win; She chalked up four wins before the day ended.* —**win.na.ble** (WIN.uh.bul) *adj.:* *A nuclear war is not winnable.*

wince *v.* **winc.es, winced, winc.ing** shrink back or flinch involuntarily: *He winced in pain; She winces at the thought of the work waiting to be done.* —*n.* a wincing movement or expression.

winch *n.* **1** a crank for imparting rotary motion. **2** a crank device as used in a crane to lift and lower loads.

¹**wind** *n.* **1** air in motion, esp. a strong current: *Gale-force winds whipped the waves; a biting, cold, cutting, icy, ill, raw, winter wind; brisk, fair, favorable, gentle, gusty, heavy, light, stiff, strong winds; the prevailing winds; a blast or gust of wind; A wind blows, falls, howls, picks up, subsides.* **2** a trend or tendency: *Politicians try to find out which way or how the wind is blowing before taking a stand on an issue; They try to test the winds; changing winds* (= trends) *of public opinion; winds of change* (= tendency toward reform). **3** gas from the stomach or bowels. **4** breathing power: *The jogger stopped to recover his wind; He was out of wind; Then he got his second wind* (= renewed energy) *and finished his race; His claims are mere wind* (= empty talk). **5 winds** *pl.* wind instruments of an orchestra, or the players. —**break wind** expel gas through the anus. —**get** or **have** or **catch wind of** learn about something, as if by a wind-borne scent.
—**in the wind** about to happen; astir: *A general election is in the wind.* —**take the wind out of one's sails** take away someone's advantage by one's own action. —**the four winds** the four directions or points of the compass: *scattered it to the four winds.* —*v.* **1** get the scent of something; follow a hunted animal, etc. by scent. **2** put out of breath by running, from a climb, etc.: *an asthmatic who is easily winded.* **3** *pt.* **wind.ed** or **wound** (WOWND) blow a horn; hence, sound a signal or blast.

²**wind** (WINED) *v.* **winds, wound** (WOWND), **wind.ing 1** move or cause to move in a curving or twisting manner: *The river winds (its way) through the plain;* **adj.:** *a winding path, river, street; a long and winding road; a winding* (= spiral) *staircase.* **2** wrap or coil: *A vine winds around its support; He wore a shawl wound around his neck; She can wind him around her little finger* (= knows how to manipulate him). **3** roll into a ball, as yarn, or on a spool or reel, as thread, tape, etc. **4** tighten the spring of a clock or other mechanism for power to operate: *He forgot to wind his old watch;* **adj.:** *a self-winding* (= automatic) *watch.*
—**wind down 1** come or bring to a gradual conclusion: *The business was so unprofitable they decided to wind it down; Operations were winding down.* **2** relax; unwind: *He needs his weekends to wind down a little.* —**wind up 1** make very tense or nervous. **2** of a baseball pitcher, swing the arm to throw the ball. **3** conclude an activity or business: *It happened when the convention was about to wind up; They decided to wind up their operations as soon as possible.* **4** *Informal.* come to an end; end up: *She wound up with less money than in her previous job; He wound up in jail.*
—*n.* a winding or turn. —**wind.er** *n.*

wind.age (WIND.ij) *n.* deflecting power of the wind on a missile in flight: *Archers test windage before shooting.*

wind.bag *n. Informal.* one who talks much but communicates little of importance.

wind.blown (WIND.blone) *adj.* blown by the wind: *windblown hair, snow, trees.*

wind.break *n.* a growth of trees, etc. for breaking the force of the wind.

wind.break.er (WIND.bray.kur) *n.* a jacket so made as to resist the wind.

wind.chill or **wind chill** *n.* an estimate of how cold one feels because of the added effect of a wind blowing at a certain speed; also **windchill factor.**

winded *adj.* out of breath: *The runner*

was winded and very tired.

wind.fall *n.* an unexpected piece of good fortune, esp. financial profit, like ripe fruit blown down by the wind: *He got a sudden windfall in the shape of a lottery win; The new tax was a windfall for the government; a financial windfall.* —**adj.** large and unexpected: *windfall benefits, changes, gains, growth, losses, profits.*

wind farm *n.* a place where energy is harnessed from the wind, as by windmills and wind turbines.

wind.ing (WINE.ding) *n.* **1** a continuous coil of conducting wire in an electrical generator, motor, etc. **2** the way the coil is wound.

winding sheet *n.* a sheet in which a body is wrapped for burial.

wind instrument *n.* a musical instrument in which air is the vibrating medium, as flutes and trumpets.

wind.jam.mer (WIND.jam.ur) *n. Informal.* **1** a large sailing ship, as distinguished from a steamship. **2** one of its crew.

wind.lass (WIND.lus) *n.* a winch cranked by hand, as once much used to hoist water from wells.

wind.mill *n.* a mill or machine moved by the power of the wind acting on a wheel of vanes or sails mounted on top of a tower: *to tilt at windmills* (= fight imaginary opponents).

win.dow (WIN.doh) *n.* **1** an opening in a wall for letting in light and air or for looking through: *The windows of the new house were still covered with plastic; a bay window; He jumped out of an upstairs window; All plans seemed to go out the window; Reading "Ulysses" opened a window on the world of the classics; A* **window envelope** *has a transparent opening showing the address on an enclosed item.* **2** a framework enclosing sealed or movable panes of glass, etc.: *to roll down, roll up a car window; The rear window is fogged up; a frosted-over window; a stained-glass (church) window; shop windows; We install storm windows well before the start of winter; May I open the window? a double-glazed picture window (that is always shut); Do you wash windows? No, we don't do windows* (= do something that is outside of the regular routine). **3** a windowpane. **4** a suitable or opportune period or interval: *The launch window for a space shot depends on planetary positions; As the margin of safety disappears, the window of vulnerability gets wider.* **5** any of several portions of a video monitor displaying simultaneously or in layers the various functions of a computer, word-processing files, etc.

win.dowed (WIN.dode) *adj.* having a window: *a windowed box, environment, office.*

window dressing *n.* a display that seeks to impress favorably, as of goods in a store window: *The fancy title page of his essay was just window dressing.* —**window-dress** *v.* —**window dresser** *n.*

win.dow.pane (WIN.doh.pane) *n.* a pane of glass in a window.

window-shop *v.* **-shops, -shopped, -shop.ping** look at goods displayed in shop windows without going inside to buy. —**window-shopper** *n.*

win.dow.sill (WIN.doh.sil) *n.* the sill across the bottom of a window.

wind.pipe *n.* the air passage between the throat and the lungs.

wind.proof *adj.* protecting from the wind: *a windproof jacket.*

wind.row (WIND.roh) *n.* **1** a row of fallen leaves, ridge of ice, etc. formed by wind action. **2** a row of cut hay or grain made for drying: *fish heaped in windrows along the waterfront beaches.*

wind shear *n.* an air disturbance moving in an opposite direction to another, said to cause sudden airplane crashes; microburst.

wind.shield *n.* the screen of glass above the dashboard of an automobile, train, etc. Also **wind.screen** *Brit.*

wind.sock *n.* an open cone of cloth flown at the top of a pole to show wind direction, as at an airport; also **wind sleeve.**

Windsor knot *n.* a wide or double knot used in a necktie.

wind.storm *n.* a storm with high wind but little precipitation.

wind.surf.er (WIND.sur.fur) *n.* **1** same as SAILBOARD. **2** one who rides a sailboard.

wind.surf.ing (WIND.surf.ing) *n.* the sport of riding a sailboard.

wind.swept *adj.* swept by or as if by wind: *a windswept dustbowl, landscape, mountain, valley; the windswept plains, prairie.*

wind tunnel *n.* a tunnel with air forced through it at various speeds for testing airplanes, automobiles, missiles, etc.

wind.up (WINED.up) *n.* **1** the close or conclusion of an activity or business. **2** the swinging of a baseball pitcher's arm before the delivery.

wind vane same as WEATHER VANE.

wind.ward (WIND.wurd) *n.* the side or

direction from which the wind is blowing: *An anchor is cast to windward for safety.* —**adja.** on or toward the side from which the wind is blowing; against the wind: *the windward and leeward sides of an island; a windward tide* (= a tide moving against the wind).

wind.y *adj.* **wind.i.er, -i.est 1** having much wind: *a windy day; the windy prairies; a windy night; windy weather; the* **windy city** *(of Chicago).* **2** like wind, without substance: *windy* (= empty) *talk; a windy talker (with a tendency to talk a great deal).* —**wind.i.ly** *adv.;* **wind.i.ness** *n.*

wine *n.* **1** an alcoholic drink made from the fermented juice of grapes: *cooking, dessert, sacramental, table wines; dry, red, rosé, sparkling, vintage, white wines; the house wine of a restaurant;* **domestic wines** *made in the U.S., Canada, Ireland, etc.;* **French, Italian, Portuguese, and such imported wines;** *He was much devoted to* **wine, women, and song** (= a life of pleasure). **2** a drink similarly made from the juice of other fruits and plants: *dandelion wine.* —*v.* **wines, wined, win.ing 1** drink wine. **2** entertain with wine, esp. **wine and dine**, treat someone to food and drink.

wine-colored *adj.* dark purplish-red.

win.er.y (WYE.nuh.ree) *n.* **-ries** a wine-making establishment.

wing *n.* **1** one of the paired organs of flight in birds, bats, insects, etc.: *A bird spreads its wings when flying; The penguin's paddlelike wings were once used for flying.* **2** a structure similar to a bird's wing in function, as the vanes of a windmill, feathers of an arrow, etc.: *the wings of an aircraft; The seeds of the maple, pine, ash, etc. have wings.* **3** a side structure or extension: *He added a new wing to his mansion; the maternity wing of a hospital; an unseen figure shouting from* **the wings** *(of the stage).* **4** a section or unit of an organization such as an air force: *A wing is composed of groups, squadrons, and flights* (= two or more aircraft); *the Left and Right wings* (= factions) *of a political party.* **5** any of various side positions or players in hockey, football, soccer, etc. **6** means or manner of flight. **7 wings** *pl.* insignia earned by a qualified pilot, navigator, etc. in an air force: *She has* **earned her wings** (= proved herself competent). —**clip someone's wings** restrict someone's freedom; bring someone down to size. —**on the wing** in flight; on the fly. —**take wing** begin to fly; fly up or away: *His thoughts took wing.*

—**under one's wing** under one's protection. —**wait in the wings 1** wait just offstage for an entrance cue. **2** wait in a readily available position. —*v.* **1** fly: *geese winging (their way) south for the winter.* **2** cause to go fast: *Fear winged his flight.* **3** provide with wings: *an arrow winged with feathers.* **4** to wound in the wing; hence, wound slightly: *He was winged by the bandit's bullet.* —**wing it** *Informal.* speak off the cuff; extemporize: *When she lost her speech notes, she had to wing it.*

wing chair *n.* a chair with a high back and sidepieces projecting forward.

wing.ding *n. Slang.* an outburst of feeling, esp. a wild party: *It was a wingding of a party; a wingding celebration.*

winged (WINGD, rarely WING.id) *adj.* having wings: *Mercury, the winged messenger of the gods; winged* (= significant) *words.*

wing.span *n.* the stretch of a bird's or aircraft's wings from wingtip to wingtip.

wing.spread *n.* the distance between the tips of the outspread wings of a bird, insect, etc.

wing.tip *n.* **1** the outer end of a wing. **2** a type of man's shoe with a perforated toe cap that extends in a curved design like wings toward the sides; also **wingtip shoe.**

wing.y *adj. Slang.* intoxicated or high.

wink *v.* **1** close and open one eye as a signal or hint: *Sam winked at her.* **2** flutter the eyes. **3** twinkle or flicker: *stars winking in the sky.* —**wink at** blink at or ignore violations, irregularities, etc. —**wink back** (or **away**) **tears** repress tears by blinking. —*n.* a winking or the instant it lasts: *He gave the girl a suggestive wink; He expected to get a nod, nudge, or wink from her; But she vanished* **in a wink** (= in an instant); *He didn't sleep* **a wink** (= even a little); *didn't get a wink of sleep; He has a funny way* (**wink, wink**) *of selling dope.*

win.kle (WINK.ul) *v.* pry or extract, as a shellfish ("winkle") from its shell: *Some are good at winkling out figures to support their pet theories.*

winnable See WIN.

win.ner (WIN.ur) *n.* one that wins: *Sam looks like a winner; big, clear, handsdown, likely, sure winners; winners and losers.*

winning (WIN.ing) *n.* the act of one who wins: *the winning of the gold medal; The day's* **winnings** (= money won) *totaled $1,000.* —**adja. 1** victorious or successful: *a winning combination, de-*

sign, formula, idea, solution; the winning bid, champion, entry, horse, site, team; to gain the **winning edge** in a competition; **cpd.:** award-winning, medal-winning, prize-winning. **2** attractive or charming: her winning smile; his winning ways.
—**win.ning.ly** adv.
win.ning.est (WIN.ing.ist) adj. Informal. most successful or attractive: the Football League's winningest team; her winningest smile.
win.now (WIN.oh) v. **1** blow the chaff from grain, as with a fanning mill: to winnow grain. **2** blow away: to winnow chaff (from grain); to winnow out the chaff. **3** sort out; sift: to winnow out facts from falsehoods.
win.o (WYE.noh) n. **-os** Informal. a wine-drinking alcoholic.
win.some (WIN.sum) adj. sweet and charming: a winsome lass; her winsome manner; his winsome smile; In spite of her temper, she can be astonishingly winsome.
—**win.some.ly** adv.; **win.some.ness** n.
win.ter (WIN.tur) n. **1** the coldest part of the year; the season following autumn: a cold, harsh, mild, rough, severe winter. **2** a period of inactivity, decline, or distress: "the winter of our discontent." —**adj.:** a winter carnival, coat, home, squash, worker; **winter sports** such as skiing, skating, and bobsledding.
—v. **1** pass the winter in a place: Fifteen whooping cranes wintered in Arkansas in 1941; **adj.:** wintering areas, deer, geese, grounds, habitats, holes. **2** feed or food or maintain cattle, etc. during the winter.
Winter Games same as WINTER OLYMPICS.
win.ter.green (WIN.tur.green) n. a hardy, low-growing evergreen shrub of the heath family with glossy oval leaves, urn-shaped pink flowers, and bright red berries that yield the aromatic "oil of wintergreen" used as a flavoring and in medicines.
win.ter.ize (WIN.tuh.rize) v. **-iz.es, -ized, -iz.ing** to ready an automobile, house, etc. for use in the winter.
win.ter.kill (WIN.tur.kil) n. the death of a plant or animal from exposure to winter weather.
Winter Olympics n. an Olympic program of winter sports held every four years like the summer games.
win.ter.time (WIN.tur.time) n. the winter season.
winter wheat n. wheat that is planted in the fall and harvested in the spring or summer.
win.try (WIN.tree) adj. **-tri.er, -tri.est** **1** having to do with winter: a wintry day, morning, night; wintry roads, weather, winds. **2** cold or cheerless: a wintry smile, welcome; a wintry taste of death. Also **win.ter.y.**
win-win adj. helpful to both parties: a win-win policy, proposition, relationship, scenario, situation, solution, strategy; **n.:** It's a win-win for both producers and consumers.
win.y (WYE.nee) adj. **win.i.er, -i.est** having to do with wine: a winy fragrance.
wipe v. **wipes, wiped, wip.ing** clean, dry, etc. by rubbing with a handkerchief, towel, hand, etc.: He washed and wiped the dishes; wiped them dry; She wiped away her tears; He had to wipe up the mess he made on the floor; She wiped her feet on the mat as she came in; He used a rag to wipe off the mud from his shoes; He didn't wipe (= apply) any dirt on the rug. —**wipe off** or **out** put an end to something: to wipe off a debt; The whole village was wiped out by the epidemic; It was wiped off the face of the earth. —**wiped-out** adj. Slang. **1** drunk. **2** exhausted: too wiped-out to go for a walk; wiped-out (= worn-out) windshield wipers. —n. **1** an act of wiping. **2** something to wipe with; wiper. **3** in motion pictures, a special effect by which a new scene displaces another by gradually expanding and occupying the whole frame.
wi.per (WYE.pur) n. one that wipes, as a towel or a rubber-edged blade on a handle for wiping a window: We turn on our windshield wipers when it's raining; **adj.:** a wiper arm, blade, fluid, motor, system.
wire n. **1** metal drawn out into a slender rod or thread; also, a length of this: copper wire; He caught his foot on a trip wire and fell on the lawn; She got the car started by crossing or jumping wires. **2** anything made or woven of wire: barbed wire; chicken wire; **adj.:** wire gauze, netting, ropes. **3** telegraph; also, a telegram or cablegram: messages by wire; to send a wire; I just received a wire saying everything is OK. **4** the finish line of a horse race. —**down to the wire** at or to the last moment: The election was closely fought down to the wire. —**get one's wires crossed** confuse one thing for another; be mistaken. —**pull wires** Informal. exert secret influence as if manipulating puppets. —**under the wire** barely on time: His application got in just under the wire.
—v. **wires, wired, wir.ing 1** use or

provide with wire or wiring: *broken pieces wired together; a house wired for electricity; an undercover officer who is wired for sound.* **2** telegraph: *She wired her greetings; They wired back that the wedding had been put off; Students used to wire home for money; They would wire their parents; Parents would wire* (= send by wire) *the money to them.*

wired *adj.* **1** equipped or connected electronically: *The police can monitor street conversations using wired undercover officers (wearing recording devices); Most homes are now wired for cable; Soon we will be living in **wired cities** where activities from shopping to education to voting would be conducted from home computer terminals; This wired world!* **2** *Slang.* edgy or tense.

wire.drawn *adj.* **1** drawn out into a wire. **2** tenuous or overrefined: *wiredrawn arguments, distinctions.*

wire.hair *n.* a fox terrier with wiry hair; also **wire-haired (fox) terrier.**

wire.less (WIRE.lis) *adj.a.* having to do with radio waves: *a wireless operator, set, transmitter; wireless cable TV; a wireless remote-control device.* —*n.* **1** wireless telegraphy or telephony. **2** *Brit.* radio.

wire.pho.to (WIRE.foh.toh) *n.* a picture sent by wire or radio using electric signals.

wire.pull.ing (WIRE.pull.ing) *n. Informal.* the use of secret influence; **wire.pull.er** *n.*

wire recorder *n.* an early form of recording sound magnetically on steel wire.

wire service *n.* a commercial agency that gathers and distributes news and pictures to subscribing papers using teletypewriter and facsimile machines.

wire.tap *v.* -taps, -tapped, -tap.ping tap a telephone line secretly to get information. —*n.* a wiretapping or wiretap device: *unauthorized wiretaps.*

wiring (WIRE.ing) *n.* a system of wires, as for distributing electricity through a house: *a fire caused by faulty wiring.*

wir.y (WIRE.ee) *adj.* **wir.i.er, -i.est** **1** of or like wire: *wiry hair.* **2** lean and strong: *a man of wiry build; a wiry body.* —**wir.i.ness** *n.*

wis.dom (WIZ.dum) *n.* **1** the quality of being wise, having knowledge and judgment, etc.: *in the spirit of wisdom and understanding; She questioned the wisdom of his move; a woman of great wisdom; He had the wisdom to reconsider his move; His action showed wisdom; Solomon in all his wisdom could not have said such a thing; as God in His infinite wisdom has ordained; as conventional wisdom suggests.* **2** wise sayings: *a book containing the wisdom of the ancients.*

wisdom tooth *n.* any of the four teeth, one at the back of each jaw on either side, that usu. appear in early adulthood.

wise (WIZE) *adj.* **wis.er, wis.est** **1** having or showing good sense, prudence, judgment, etc.: *You did the wise thing; It's wise not to argue with customers; a wise choice, decision, investment, use of resources; a child who is wise beyond her years; Her brother says he's **older and wiser**; He came out of the experience a **sadder and wiser** man* (= one who has learned a lot); *What's the use of being **wise after the event**?* **2** learned: *a wise judge, man, saying; wise advice, words.* **3** aware or informed: *He looked wise but wouldn't talk; She seemed **none the wiser*** (= no better informed) *for the experience.* —**get wise** *Informal.* find out; realize: *It was too late when she got wise to his schemes.* —**wise to** *Informal.* aware of something: *She was wise to his schemes; Someone's careless remarks **put her wise to*** (= made her aware of) *his plans.* —*v.* **wises, wised, wis.ing** *Informal.* make or become aware, esp. **wise up**: *They wised her up about what was going on; He wised up and changed his ways before it was too late; She quickly **wised up to** his plans.* —*comb.form.* **1** in the manner specified: *clockwise, lengthwise, likewise.* **2** with regard to what is specified: *healthwise, saleswise, usagewise.* **3** wise as specified: *streetwise, worldlywise.* —*n.* way or manner: *in no wise; in this wise.* —**wise.ly** *adv.*

wise.a.cre (WYE.zay.cur) *n.* one who pretends to be wise.

wise-ass same as SMART-ASS.

wise.crack *n. Informal.* a clever or flippant remark: *good at making wisecracks about things he knows little about.* —*v.* make a wisecrack: *She wisecracked that he's trying to do too much — like trying to catch 10 fleas with 10 fingers.*

wise guy *n. Informal.* one who is conceited or pretentious.

wish *v.* **1** like and want to have or do something: *Some wish health, others riches; Do you wish to speak to the manager? Do you wish me to speak to him? Do as you wish.* **2** desire for something or to be in some condition: *She had everything she could wish for; She wished she didn't have to go to work; wished herself back home; The child wished she were a bird.* **3** have or express a hope for something: *We wish you good luck, good* night; She wishes no one ill; I wish you well in your endeavors; **to wish upon a star** (= hope for what one wishes as if through a star). **—wish on** *Informal.* foist or impose on someone: *a job so tough I wouldn't wish it on anyone.* **—n. 1** a desire or want or an expression of it: *to express, make, realize a wish; a fervent, strong, unfulfilled wish; He got his wish; He granted her every wish; Everything was carried out in accordance with her wishes; a child's* **wish list** *of Christmas gifts.* **2 wishes** *pl.* greetings: *to extend, offer, send one's best wishes for the holidays; good, warm, warmest wishes.*

wish.bone *n.* a forked bone in front of the breastbone of a bird, considered a token of wish-fulfillment by some.

wish.ful *adj.* longing; desirous: *as though wishful for the sight of disaster; wishful daydreaming, talk, yearnings.*
—wish.ful.ly *adv.;* **wish.ful.ness** *n.*

wishful thinking *n.* belief based on hope or desire rather than on reality.

wish.y-wash.y *adj. Informal.* **1** weak or watery: *a wishy-washy soup, tea.* **2** weak or ineffectual: *wishy-washy excuses, ideas, people.* **—wish.y-wash.i.ness** *n.*

wisp *n.* **1** a small bunch: *a wisp of hay, straw.* **2** one that is small or slight: *a wisp of hair; Wisps of smoke curled from blackened trees; a wisp of a girl, smile.*
—wisp.y *adj.*

wist [old form] *pt. & pp.* of WIT.

wis.te.ri.a (wis.TEER.ee.uh) *n.* a twining vine of the pea family that bears large drooping clusters of bluish flowers. Also **wis.tar.i.a** (-TAIR.ee.uh).

wist.ful *adj.* longing or yearning: *a wistful desire, expression, gaze; wistful eyes, glances; in a wistful mood.* **—wist.ful.ly** *adv.;* **wist.ful.ness** *n.*

wit *n.* **1** mental power marked by quickness of perception, esp. to see unusual and amusing relationships between things: *He displays* or *shows a quick wit.* **2 wits** *pl.* intelligence: *"The dog had lost his wits to bite so good a man"; He didn't have the time to collect his wits and react to the situation; His hectic life could drive him* **out of his wits** (= make him go crazy); *She always* **has** or **keeps her wits about her** (= is quick and alert). **3** the ability to say clever and amusing things or their expression; wittiness: *"Brevity is the soul of wit"; Shakespeare's wit and humor; He has an acid wit; an earthy, keen, mordant, penetrating, rapierlike, sharp, trenchant wit; Her speeches sparkle with wit and wisdom.* **4** a person with such a mind:

Bernard Shaw is a famous Irish wit.
—at one's wit's end at the end of one's mental resources; at a loss what to do next. **—live by one's wits** live by clever or crafty means rather than by working. **—v. pres. tense** (I, he, she, it) **wot,** *pt. & pp.* **wist, wit.ting** *Archaic.* know. **—to wit** that is to say; namely.

witch *n.* **1** a woman supposed to have supernatural powers, usu. evil; sorceress: *the burning of witches; In Salem, Mass., many "witches" were hanged in the 1690s.* **2** any hag or shrew. **3** *Informal.* a charming or bewitching woman.

witch.craft *n.* a witch's power or practices; sorcery: *to practice witchcraft.*

witch doctor *n.* one who practices tribal medicine using magic.

witch.er.y (WICH.uh.ree) *n.* **-er.ies 1** (an act of) witchcraft. **2** charm or fascination.

witch hazel *n.* **1** a shrub or small tree bearing clusters of four-petaled yellow flowers in late fall after its leaves have died. **2** an astringent and antiseptic lotion made from its bark and leaves.

witch-hunt *n.* the searching out and harassing of political opponents, as of persons suspected of witchcraft in former times: *to conduct a witch-hunt against a political opponent.*

witch.ing *adj.* bewitching: *the witching hour between midnight and one; "the very witching time of night."*

with ("th" as in "the" or "thin") *prep* **1** [indicating the relationship of an action to its object]: *I agree with you; Bring the book with you; He came with his wife; She rarely fights with* (= against) *him; to swim with* (= in the same direction as) *the current.* **2** [indicating a person or thing as having something]: *a man with a beard; a book with covers; tea with cream and sugar; a lady with a dog; She is* **with child** (= pregnant). **3** [indicating the use of something as a means or instrument]: *a pen to write with; She shot him with a rubber band.* **4** [indicating the agreement of one action in regard to the time, direction, degree, etc. of another]: *Temperature varies with time of day; The day ends with sunset;* **With that** (= Then) *he got up and left.* **5** [indicating cause]: *shivering with cold; wet with tears.* **6** [indicating the manner of an action]: *Handle with care; singing with joy; His said it with a good intention.* **7** [indicating association or relationship]: *your relations with people; Down with tyrants! Away with it! Let's get on with it.* **8** despite; notwithstanding: *With all that effort, he achieved* very little. —**with it** *Informal.* socially or culturally up to date; hip: *She's quite with it.*

with.al (with.ALL) *adv.* [old use] **1** besides: *Withal, his writing has an archaic quality.* **2** [used at the end of a phrase] with: *something to feed himself withal.*

with.draw (with.DRAW) *v.* **-draws, -drew** (-DROO), **-drawn, -draw.ing 1** take back: *Jan instinctively withdrew her hand from the fire; to withdraw money from a bank account; She asked him to withdraw the remark; He withdrew his offer.* **2** remove oneself: *The candidate had to withdraw from the election; He withdraws to his den to study in quiet.*

with.draw.al (with.DRAW.ul) *n.* **1** a withdrawing: *to make a cash withdrawal from a bank account; There were mass withdrawals just before the bank collapsed; to carry out, complete, make a troop withdrawal; orderly, precipitate, strategic, tactical withdrawals.* **2** the giving up of a drug that one is addicted to; **adj.**: *a patient suffering from withdrawal effects; a withdrawal illness, period, syndrome.*

with.drawn (with.DRAWN) *adj.* **1** retiring or reserved: *She became withdrawn after several miscarriages; a very private and withdrawn man; distant and withdrawn; morose and withdrawn; shy and withdrawn; silent and withdrawn; sullen and withdrawn; a withdrawn loner; a very withdrawn type of personality.* **2** secluded; isolated: *They broadcast from a building that is aggressively withdrawn.*

withe (WITH, WITHE, "TH" as in "the") *n.* a tough, flexible twig, as of a willow, that is used for tying bundles of firewood, for plaiting, etc.

with.er (WITH.ur, "TH" as in "the") *v* **1** dry up, as something growing that loses vitality: *Plants wither away in the heat; Our lawn is all withered up; She withered him with a look;* **n.**: *Tea processing starts with the withering of leaves;* **adj.**: *She gave him a withering look.* **2 withers** *n.pl.* the ridge between the shoulder bones of a horse, ox, etc.

with.hold (with.HOLD) *v.* **-holds, -held, -hold.ing 1** hold back; keep back: *He tried to withhold his men from attacking the strike-breakers; Employers withhold taxes from pay checks; The **withholding tax** is collected from employees and sent to the tax department.* **2** to keep from giving: *to withhold information from the police; to withhold one's consent; to withhold permission.*

with.in (with.IN) *prep.* to or into the interior; inside: *Stay within the house; He remained within call, reach, sight; Try to live within your income or within your means; Return within three days; The school is within a mile of home; We haven't had a snowfall like this **within living memory** (= that people still living can recall); Any demands **within reason** (= reasonable demands) will be met;* **adv.**: *Enquire within; Good deeds make you feel good within* (= inwardly); **n.**: *a plot to destroy the party **from within** (= from the inside); Original ideas should come from within, not without.*

with-it *adj. Informal.* up-to-date or modish: *He tries to cultivate a with-it image; a very with-it corporation.*

with.out (with.OUT) *prep.* **1** lacking; not having: *She left without saying good-bye; She'll be back **without fail** (= surely); She is **without question** (= without doubt) quite honest; to go without food and water;* **adv.**: *He is used to **going** or **doing without** (something as implied).* **2** outside of something: *Guards stood without the palace entrance;* **adv.**: *The house is well decorated **within and without**;* **n.**: *The house looks new **from without** (= from the outside).*

with.stand (with.STAND) *v.* **-stands, -stood, -stand.ing** stand against; oppose or resist successfully: *to withstand an attack, a severe winter, challenges, cold conditions; to withstand the rigors of a long journey; a claim that can withstand scrutiny.*

wit.less (WIT.lis) *adj.* lacking wit or sense; foolish: *a witless dupe, label, observation; designed to trap the witless consumer;* **wit.less.ly** *adv.*

wit.ness (WIT.nis) *n.* **1** a person who sees something happen and can say so under oath; eyewitness: *the witness of or to the accident; a witness for the prosecution; As a third-party witness, he attested the deed signed by the two in his presence; The witness took the oath or was sworn in; The witness testified (under oath) and then stepped down; The defense couldn't produce one competent witness; credible, hostile, reliable witnesses; character, defense, expert, key, material, prosecution witnesses; to cross-examine, examine, hear, interrogate, interview, lead, question, swear in, trap a witness; to go into the **witness box** (from where evidence is given in a law court); to take the **witness stand** in someone's defense; to put the accused on the witness stand.* **2** testimony as given by a witness in court; evidence: *He perjured himself by giving false witness; to **bear witness** (= give evidence) against someone.* **3 Witness** a member of the Christian sect called "Jehovah's Witnesses." —*v.* **1** be a witness of something: *those who witnessed the accident; She witnessed his signing (of the deed);* *adj.:* *a properly* **witnessed** *(= attested) will.* **2** testify to something: *actions witnessing a guilty mind; Martyrs witness their faith; He's an obviously rich fellow,* **witness** *(= as shown by) the solid-gold faucets in his home.*

-witted *comb.form.* having intelligence as specified: *dim-witted, dull-witted, half-witted, quick-witted, slow-witted.*

wit.ti.cism (WIT.uh.siz.um) *n.* a witty remark.

wit.ting *adj.* knowing; intentional; **wit.ting.ly** *adv.*

wit.ty *adj.* **wit.ti.er, wit.ti.est** having or showing wit; amusing: *a witty comment, expression, retort, speaker; charming and witty; sharp and witty.* —**wit.ti.ly** *adv.;* **wit.ti.ness** *n.*

wive *v.* **wives, wived, wiv.ing** *Archaic.* **1** take as a wife. **2** marry a woman.

wives *pl.* of WIFE.

wiz.ard (WIZ.urd) *n.* **1** a magician or sorcerer. **2** *Informal.* one highly gifted in or skilled *at* an activity: *a wizard at electronics; a financial wizard; a special-effects wizard.*

wiz.ard.ry (WIZ.urd.ree) *n.* **1** magic or sorcery. **2** *Informal.* highly skilled activity: *computer wizardry; high-tech wizardry; by sheer wizardry.*

wiz.ened (WIZ.und) *adj.* withered; shriveled: *a wizened face; The illness left him a wizened shell of a man; wizened with age.*

wob.ble (WOB.ul) *v.* **wob.bles, wob.bled, wob.bling 1** to shake from side to side in an unstable manner, as a table on uneven legs. **2** walk or move unsteadily. **3** waver or vacillate: *She appears to be wobbling.* —*n.* a wobbling movement. —**wob.bler** *n.*

wob.bly (WOB.lee) *adj.* **wob.bli.er, wob.bli.est** shaky or unsteady: *a wobbly ladder, start, table; The wobbly cease-fire never held; a wobbly corporation.* —**wob.bli.ness** *n.*

woe (WOH) *n.* **1** misery or grief of a desperate nature: *a heart full of woe; tales of woe and misery.* **2** a cause of such grief: *poverty, war, and other woes of humanity.* —*interj.:* *Woe (be) to you! Woe is me (= Alas)! Woe betide you (= You will be punished) should you fail to deliver!*

woe.be.gone (WOE.bi.gon) *adj.* miserable or dismal in appearance: *a woebegone look.*

woe.ful *adj.* **1** full of woe; wretched: *a woeful expression.* **2** deplorable: *his woeful ignorance; a woeful tale; what woeful neglect!* —**woe.ful.ly** *adv.;* **woe.ful.ness** *n.*

wok *n.* a bowl-shaped pan used in Chinese cooking.

woke, woken See WAKE.

wolf (WOOLF, short "OO") *n.* **wolves** (WOOLVZ) **1** a doglike wild animal with short, upright ears and a long, bushy tail, that hunts game, often in packs: *a pack of howling wolves.* **2** one who is greedy or rapacious. **3** *Informal.* a sexually aggressive male. —**cry wolf** give a false alarm, like the boy in a fable by Aesop. —**keep the wolf from the door** keep from starving. —**wolf in sheep's clothing** one who appears good but has evil intentions. —*v.* eat greedily: *He wolfs down his food.* —**wolf.ish** *adj.*

wolf.hound *n.* any of several breeds of hunting dogs including the borzoi and the "Scottish deerhound."

wolf.ram (WOOL.frum) same as TUNGSTEN. —**wolf.ram.ite** *n.* tungsten ore.

wolfs.bane (WOOLFS.bane) *n.* a species of aconite.

wolf whistle *n.* a whistle with a rising-and-falling note given in admiration of a person, performance, etc.

wol.ve.rine (wool.vuh.REEN) *n.* a ferocious, destructive hunting animal of northern regions that resembles a bear and has dark, shaggy hair.

wolves *pl.* of WOLF.

wom.an (WOOM.un, short "OO") *n., pl.* **wom.en** (WIM.un) **1** an adult female human being: *a woman of action, of letters, of refinement, of the world; She received an award as woman of the year; the influx of women into the labor force; anchor, career, working women; a woman who is divorced, married;* *adj.a.:* *a woman engineer, friend, priest, worker.* **2** the female human being characterized by qualities such as attractiveness to the opposite sex, gentleness, motherliness, etc.: *Women and children (come) first; "O, thou fairest among women"; attractive, beautiful, grown, handsome, lovely, plain, single, virtuous, young women; furious "like a woman scorned"; job discrimination against women and minorities; Some nations have a "Women's Day" corresponding to our "Mother's Day"; the* **other woman** *(= mistress) in his life.* **3** feminine nature or qualities; womanliness: *She is all woman.* **4** women collectively; womankind: *the place of the modern woman in a male-dominated society.* **5** a female servant or attendant: *a queen surrounded by her women; a clean-*

ing woman; the woman who does the cooking.

woman doctor *n.* **1** a female doctor. **2** *Informal.* a gynecologist.

wom.an.hood (WOOM.un.hood, short "OO") *n.* **1** the state of being a woman: *when you reach womanhood as an adult; The job is a challenge to your womanhood* (= qualities as a woman). **2** women as a group; womankind: *Equal pay legislation is a challenge to womanhood; She's a fine example of modern womanhood.*

wom.an.ish (WOOM.un.ish) *adj.* **1** like a woman. **2** effeminate.

wom.an.ize (WOOM.un.ize) *v.* **-iz.es, -ized, -iz.ing** *Informal.* philander; **wom.an.iz.er** *n.*

wom.an.kind (WOOM.un.kined) *n.* women in general.

wom.an.like (WOOM.un.like) *adj.* womanly.

wom.an.ly (WOOM.un.lee) *adj.* being or having the qualities suitable and becoming in a mature woman: *her womanly dignity; womanly compassion, modesty.* —**wom.an.li.ness** *n.*

woman of the world *n.* a woman sophisticated and experienced in dealing with problems and issues outside the home.

women's suffrage *n.* women's right to vote; also **woman suffrage.**

womb (WOOM, long "OO") *n.* **1** the uterus. **2** a place of development or generation: *events in the womb of time.*

wom.bat *n.* a small bearlike burrowing marsupial of Australia.

women *pl.* of WOMAN.

wom.en.folk (WIM.un.folk) *n.pl. Informal.* womankind; also **wom.en.folks.**

women's lib *n. Informal.* women's liberation.

women's lib.ber (-LIB.ur) *n. Informal.* feminist.

women's liberation *n.* the movement for establishing women's rights on an equal footing with those of men; feminism.

won *pt. & pp.* OF WIN.

won.der (WUN.dur) *n.* **1** a feeling of surprise and astonishment aroused by something great or unusual: *to gaze in wide-eyed wonder.* **2** a person or thing considered as marvelous: *The pyramids of Egypt are one of the seven wonders of the ancient world; It's a wonder* (= miracle) *he survived the crash; a drug that* **does** or **works wonders** *for your system; He was wearing a seatbelt –* **no wonder** *(that) he survived; (It's no)* **small wonder** *he survived.* —*v.* **1** feel wonder: *We* wonder at or about the marvels of nature. **2** be curious about something: *I wonder who he is, what he wants, why he's here, if or whether he's hungry.*

wonder drug *n.* a drug such as an antibiotic that works quickly and effectively against disease.

won.der.ful (WUN.dur.ful) *adj.* **1** marvelous or astonishing: *a wonderful place to visit.* **2** *Informal.* excellent or admirable: *She's wonderful!* —**won.der.ful.ly** *adv.*

won.der.land (WUN.dur.land) *n.* **1** a land of wonders, as in fairy tales. **2** a place of great beauty or tourist interest: *The Galapagos Islands are a natural wonderland; Our province is a scenic wonderland; a winter wonderland.*

won.der.ment (WUN.dur.munt) *n.* **1** astonishment or amazement: *to gaze, rub one's eyes, shake one's head* **in wonderment.** **2** a thing of wonder.

won.drous (WUN.drus) *adj.* wonderful: *He hath done wondrous things; my wondrous computer; wondrous predictions, results; in wondrous ways.* —*adv.* [old use] wonderfully: *wondrous fair, good, happy, sad.* —**won.drous.ly** *adv.*

wonk.y (WONK.ey) *adj. Slang.* cockeyed: *Fine print makes her eyes go wonky.*

won't (WOHNT) will not.

wont (WOHNT, WAWNT) *adjp.* accustomed: *She was wont to rise early.* —*n.* habit or usual practice: *She rose early, as was her wont.*

wont.ed *adja.* customary; usual; habitual: *in his wonted style.*

won ton (both "o's" as in "on") *n.* **1** a Chinese dish of meat-filled noodle casings. **2** a soup containing won ton; also **won-ton soup.**

woo *v.* **woos, wooed** (WOOD, long "OO"), **woo.ing 1** court or seek to marry a person. **2** seek to win: *to woo fame, success, voters, wealth; He spent his life wooing fortune but ended up a pauper; A store tries to woo customers away from the competition; The competition tries to woo them back; to woo over voters to one's side.*

wood (short "oo") *n.* **1** the hard fibrous substance beneath the bark of a tree or shrub: *to chop, cut, gather wood; kindling wood; a cord of wood.* **2** lumber or timber: *"hewers of wood and drawers of water"* (= menials or drudges). **3** esp. **woods** *pl.* a thick growth of trees, usu. smaller than a forest: *a trail through the woods; There's a thick woods on the other side of our fence; "The earth [has] its dower of river, wood, and vale."* **4** something made of wood, as a cask, golf

wood alcohol / wool

club, or woodcut. **—out of the woods** *Informal.* out of a dangerous or difficult situation. **—adj. 1** having to do with wood: *wood carvings, chairs, chips, engravings; Cord is a wood measure; wood pulp, saw, tissue; wood sugar (made from wood tissue).* **2** found or growing in woods: *a wood duck, rat, trail, warbler.*

wood alcohol *n.* a poisonous industrial chemical used as a solvent and in fuels and antifreezes; methanol.

wood.bine *n.* **1** a honeysuckle. **2** the Virginia creeper.

wood.block *n.* **1** a block of wood. **2** a woodcut.

wood.carv.ing (WOOD.car.ving) *n.* an art object carved out of wood; also, the art; **wood.carv.er** *n.*

wood.chop.per (WOOD.chop.ur) *n.* one whose work is chopping down trees.

wood.chuck *n.* a squirrel that hibernates in its burrow in the winter; groundhog.

wood.cock *n.* a bird related to the snipes that lives in damp woods digging earthworms, etc. from the ground with its long bill.

wood.craft *n.* **1** skill in hunting, trapping, etc. required for living in the woods. **2** woodworking skill.

wood.cut *n.* **1** an engraving made on a block of wood to print from. **2** a picture or design so printed.

wood.cut.ter (WOOD.cut.ur) *n.* one who cuts down trees for firewood.

wood.ed (WOOD.id) *adj.* covered with trees: *a wooded area, hill, park, ravine, valley; a house set in a wooded lot.*

wood.en (WOOD.un) *adj.* **1** made of wood: *a wooden chair, figure, horse, leg, shoe.* **2** stiff like wood: *a wooden dialogue, smile; wooden* (= clumsy) *gestures; a wooden* (= lifeless) *and insensitive expression.*

wood.en.ware (WOOD.un.wair) *n.* salad bowls, spoons, etc. of wood.

wood.land (WOOD.lund, -land) *n.* land covered with woods; *adja.*: *woodland caribou; the Woodland culture of eastern North America dating from 1000 B.C.; woodland scenery.*

wood.lot *n.* a small area of forest maintained for firewood, timber, etc.

wood.louse *n.* a crustacean that lives in the bark of trees, old wood, etc. and can roll itself into a ball if disturbed; sow bug; also called "pill bug."

wood.man (WOOD.mun) *n.* **-men** same as WOODSMAN.

wood.note *n.* the call of a bird in the woods.

wood nymph *n.* a mythical nymph of the forest.

wood.peck.er (WOOD.peck.ur) *n.* a bird noted for its habit of climbing tree trunks, often perching crosswise, and drumming on them with its beak and making holes to search for insects.

wood.pile *n.* a pile of lengths of firewood.

wood.ruff *n.* an aromatic herb used to flavor wine drinks.

wood.screw *n.* a metal screw for use in wood.

wood.shed *n.* **1** a shed for storing firewood. **2** a place for administering discipline.

woods.man (WOODS.mun) *n.* **-men 1** one who lives or works in the woods, as a lumberman. **2** one skilled in hunting, trapping, etc.

Wood.stock *n.* a rock-music festival of North American youth held in 1969 in Woodstock, New York: *the Woodstock generation (of believers in love and peace).*

woods.y (WOOD.zee) *adj.* **wood.si.er, -si.est** of or like the woods; sylvan: *a woodsy smell; woodsy surroundings.* **—woods.i.ness** *n.*

wood.wind *n.* a wind instrument such as the flute, clarinet, and saxophone, originally made of wood.

wood turning *n.* the shaping of wooden things on a lathe.

wood.work *n.* **1** things made of wood, esp. stairs, doors, moldings, etc. inside a house. **2 the woodwork** *Informal.* hiding place: *Drug pushers just disappear into the woodwork.*

wood.work.ing (WOOD.wurk.ing) *n.* the craft of making things from wood, including carpentry, wood carving, etc.

wood.y (WOOD.ee) *adj.* **wood.i.er, -i.est 1** tree-covered; wooded: *a woody hillside, lot, valley.* **2** forming or consisting of wood: *a plant's woody parts; a woody stem, tissue.* **3** like or suggesting wood: *a woody flavor, smell, taste, turnip, vegetable.* **—wood.i.ness** *n.*

woo.er (WOO.ur) *n.* one who woos.

woof (short or long "oo") same as WEFT.

woof.er (WOOF.ur, short "oo") *n.* a loudspeaker reproducing low-pitched sounds in a hi-fi system.

wool (short "oo") *n.* **1** the soft, warm, curly hair covering the body of sheep, llamas, etc. **2** anything that resembles or feels like wool, as "steel wool." **3** yarn, cloth, or clothing of wool: *pure virgin wool.* **—pull the wool over**

woolen / work

someone's eyes hide the facts from someone: *Politicians try to pull the wool over the public's eyes.*
wool.en (WOOL.un) *adj.* **1** made of wool: *a woolen cap; Woolen fabrics are generally softer and bulkier than worsteds; woolen yarn.* **2** relating to woolen products: *woolen manufacture, mills, producers, weavers.* —*n.* **1** cloth made of wool. **2 woolens** *pl.* woolen fabrics or clothes. Also **wool.len** *Cdn.*
wool.gath.er.ing (WOOL.gath.ur.ing) *n.* daydreaming.
wool.ly (WOOL.ee) *adj.* **wool.li.er, wool.li.est 1** like, consisting of, or covered with wool: *the woolly coat of sheep; woolly clouds; the* **woolly bear** *caterpillar of the "tiger moth"; the* **woolly mammoths** *of the Ice Age.* **2** indistinct, confused, or hazy: *woolly notions, pronouncements, thinking.* **3** barbarous: *the wild and woolly West.* —*n.* usu. **wool.lies** *pl. Informal.* a garment of wool, esp. underwear. Also **wool.y, wool.i.er, wool.i.est; wool.ies.**
wooz.y (long or short "oo") *adj.* **wooz.i.er, -i.est** *Informal.* dizzy or weak; befuddled: *I'm feeling just a touch woozy; He swayed and staggered while woozy from the anesthetic.* —**wooz.i.ness** *n.*
word (WURD) *n.* **1** a spoken or written unit of language that conveys a meaning and consists of speech sounds: *"The," "of," "and," "a," and "to" are the five most frequent words of English; a coined word like "Kodak"; The reporter tried not to distort their words or quote them out of context; a word that is hard to pronounce; to say, utter, write a word; angry, choice, cross, fighting, harsh, hasty, heated, hollow, hot, sincere words; a four-letter word that is taboo in polite society;* **In a word** (= briefly); *he's lazy; She didn't say he's lazy* **in so many words** (= exactly like that); *Do you always have to* **take the words out of my mouth** (= say exactly what I was going to say)? *The essay has been copied* **word for word** (= in exactly the same words) *from a book.* **2** a unit of information in a computer memory. **3** [used in the sing. without "the"] a message or news: *Any word of the missing child? Someone had to pass word on to her or she wouldn't have learned about it; The boss called and left word that he would be late;* **Send word to** (= Inform) *his parents.* **4** a talk, esp. a brief one: *May I have a word with you? a word of advice; They had* **words** (= a quarrel or argument). **5** what is spoken or written as an order, promise, secret code, etc.: *His word is law around here; The teacher is in a bad mood – pass the word along;* **Get the word** (= Be informed)! **Give the word** (= password) *to the sentry; She'll* **keep her word** (= promise); *She'll be* **as good as her word** (= will keep her promise); *He is* **a man of his word** (= man who keeps his promises); *He has seldom had to* **eat his words** (= take back what he said); *Neither does he* **mince words** (= avoid telling the truth directly and pointedly); *You can always* **take him at his word** (= depend on what he says). —**my word! upon my word!** [expressions of surprise]. —**the Word** the Bible. —*v.* express in words; phrase: *The memo was bitterly, cautiously, cleverly, discreetly, mildly, strongly, toughly, vaguely worded; adj.: a carefully* **worded** *sign, statement; a politely worded request; a sharply worded communiqué; The question was very badly worded.*
word.age (WUR.dij) *n.* **1** number or quantity of words. **2** verbosity. **3** wording.
word.book *n. Informal.* a dictionary.
wording *n.* the way something is worded; phrasing.
word of honor *n.* a solemn promise.
word of mouth *n.* spoken words: *The news spread by word of mouth before it got into the papers.* —*adj.:* **word-of-mouth** (= oral) *advertising, marketing, promotion.*
word.play *n.* a play on words, as in punning; verbal wit or repartee, as in "Her model husband came unglued."
word processing *n.* writing, editing, printing, etc. using a computer.
word processor *n.* a word-processing program.
word.y *adj.* **word.i.er, -i.est** using too many words; verbose: *a wordy essay; She's less wordy than her significant other.* —**word.i.ness** *n.*
wore *pt.* of WEAR.
work (WURK) *n.* **1** effort or exertion required to do or produce something: *Digging is hard work; Writing a book is intellectual work; She has been at work on her third novel for a month now; backbreaking, demanding, dirty, easy, good, light, physical, shoddy, slipshod, sloppy, superior work; He watches TV all day and never does a stroke of work; community, social, undercover work; to* **go to work on** (= put pressure on) *someone.* **2** employment or occupation, esp. outside the home: *He baby-sits, cleans, and cooks, while she goes to work; Al begins work at 9 a.m. and quits or stops work at 5 p.m.; Sometimes he* **takes time off work** *when*

he has a dental appointment; He'll be returning to work after the holidays; She's looking for work now that he is **out of work** (= unemployed); Please phone me at work (= the place of employment). **3 works** pl. factory: iron works; gas works. **4 works** pl. the operating parts of a clock. **5** something being worked on or in the process of being produced: Take your work home; A vise has jaws for holding work. **6** a product or result of work: Artists hang their work in art galleries; They exhibit their work; A novel is a literary work; a scholarly work; the collected works of Milton; the complete works of Keats; his published works; Shakespeare's selected works; statues, paintings, poems, and such **works of art**; "Faith without (good) works is dead"; **works of mercy** (= charitable acts). **7** operations and structures: A **public works department** is in charge of highways, dams, bridges, buildings, etc. **8 the works** pl. Informal. everything possible, necessary, available, etc., often **the whole works:** This Christmas we are having a tree, gifts, carols, turkey dinner, the works; She ordered a hamburger with the works (= with ketchup, mustard, tomato slice, onion, pickle, etc.); Loan sharks threatened to give him the works (= to use extreme measures) if he told the police. —**in the works** in preparation. —**make short work of something** finish a task, meal, etc. quickly.
—**adj.** having to do with work: the work habit; work clothes, routines, songs; work elephants, horses; **cpd:** clockwork, needlework, nightwork.
—**v. works,** pt. & pp. **worked** or **wrought** (RAWT), **work.ing 1** do physical or mental work, esp. outside the home: She works five days a week; works for a bank; She works occasionally for a charity; Her husband works around the house; Students work at their lessons; Some work their way through college; an author working on his book; He's working against the clock (= with a deadline in mind). **2** function or operate as planned, designed, etc.: a good idea, but will it work? The gadget doesn't work. **3** cause to work or function: to work the gears on the machinery; She works herself to death; He worked his head off writing the essay. **4** get or produce by working: a drug that works wonders; The storm worked havoc. **5** control or manage: Sales representatives work their territories. **6** get into or cause to get into a new condition gradually: Screws sometimes work loose; She worked her way up the corporate ladder; worked her way up to the top. **7** make or shape clay, dough, etc. by kneading, mixing, etc. **8** move or cause to move in an agitated way: Yeast is used to work beer; You could see his features working with emotion. —**work off** get rid of a debt, bad feelings, etc. by working, doing something, etc.
—**work on** or **upon 1** influence or try to persuade someone. **2** continue with an attempt: The picnic is still up in the air, but we are working on it. —**work out 1** solve or accomplish something by resolving difficulties: to work out the details of a plan; to work out a problem. **2** develop something: to work out a new method. **3** prove effective or successful: Our plan didn't work out. **4** have a workout: Don't argue with him when he is working out. —**work up** produce by work or effort: to work up an appetite for supper; to work up (= excite) enthusiasm, feelings; The orator had worked up the mob to a fever pitch before it went on the rampage; She doesn't get worked up (= upset) over or about little things; to work up steam; to work up a sweat; to work a business up (= develop it) from small beginnings.

work.a.ble (WUR.kuh.bul) adj. that can be worked; hence, feasible or practicable: a workable alternative, choice, compromise, concept, measure, plan, policy, relationship, solution. —**work.a.ble.ness** n.

work.a.day (WUR.kuh.day) adj. everyday; ordinary: the workaday environment, image, world; our workaday lives, thoughts, woes.

work.a.hol.ic (wur.kuh.HOL.ic) n. one who is addicted to the work habit, taking work home, spending weekends at work, etc.

work.bag n. a bag for holding working materials such as needlework.

work basket n. a basket for holding needlework.

work.bench n. a table at which mechanical work such as carpentry is done.

work.book n. **1** a book designed to be used with a textbook, containing questions, exercises, etc. **2** a workman's handbook.

work.box n. a box for tools and materials used in work.

work.day n. **1** the part of the day during which work is done. **2** a day of work, not a holiday.

work.er n. **1** one who works: to dismiss, fire, hire, take on, train workers; Automation makes workers redundant; blue-collar, efficient, full-time, hard, idle, immigrant, meticulous, migrant, office, part-time, skilled, white-collar workers*. **2** in a colony of ants, bees, wasps, etc., a sexually underdeveloped insect that does the work of providing food, defending the colony, etc.

work ethic *n.* the attitude or belief that work is ennobling: *Employers try to promote the Protestant work ethic, but employees like to consider the quality of their working life and devote more time to volunteer work, cultural activities, etc.*

work.fare *n.* a government program of providing public-service jobs to the unemployed in order to take them off welfare.

work farm *n.* a farm on which minor offenders serve their terms.

work force *n.* **1** the working part of a population: *A small percentage of the work force is normally unemployed.* **2** a group of workers.

work.horse *n.* **1** a horse that is used for work, as on a farm. **2** one that may be depended on to work hard and long: *Elephants are good workhorses; my desktop workhorse; a good V-8 workhorse engine.*

work.house *n.* a house of correction for petty criminals.

working *adja.* that works, is used in working, or is used for working with: *working capital* (for running a business); *the working classes of society; working clothes; a car in good working condition; a disk drive in good working order; a working hypothesis, model; the working* (= rough) *copy or draft of a document; Nine to five are the regular* **working hours**; *We have staggered working hours instead of a uniform schedule for everyone; a* **working knowledge** *of a foreign language* (sufficient for practical purposes); *The president holds* **working lunches** *to discuss policy; a* **working majority** (sufficient for carrying on work). —*n.* operation or action, as of a machine: *the inner workings of a computer.*

work.ing.man (WUR.king.man) *n.* **-men** a manual or industrial worker.
—**work.ing.wom.an** *n.* **-wom.en.**

working paper *n.* a paper for study and discussion.

working sample *n.* a sample that is large enough for the intended purpose.

work.load *n.* the amount of work that a worker has to do in a given period.

work.man (WURK.mun) *n.* **-men 1** a workingman. **2** a skilled craftsman.

work.man.like (WURK.mun.like) *adj.* skillful and satisfactory in execution; like a good workman's: *a workmanlike approach, attitude, job, performance, publication; The new building was completed on schedule in a workmanlike manner.* —*adv.* skillfully; well: *She tried to do her work as workmanlike as possible.*

work.man.ly (WURK.mun.lee) *adj. & adv.* workmanlike.

work.man.ship (WURK.mun.ship) *n.* the skill or quality of work seen in something finished; craftsmanship.

work.out *n.* **1** an exercise or series of exercises for maintaining physical fitness. **2** a test or trial of performance: *The team will have several workouts before players are eliminated.*

work permit *n.* a permit issued by the government to a nonresident to work temporarily in a country.

work.place *n.* a place where one works for pay: *Workplaces have to be safe and healthy; Statistics show that a working adult spends less than 40 hours a week in the workplace compared to 50 hours in leisure activities.*

work.room *n.* a room in which manual work is done.

work.sheet *n.* **1** a sheet of paper on which school exercises are to be done. **2** a sheet of paper serving as a work schedule or one on which something is worked out tentatively.

work.shop *n.* **1** an establishment where light manufacturing work is done. **2** a session at which ideas and methods of applying one's knowledge in some field are discussed.

work.sta.tion (WURK.stay.shun) *n.* **1** a work area for one person with equipment such as a computer terminal. **2** such a terminal.

work.ta.ble (WURK.tay.bul) *n.* a table for working at, having drawers, etc. for holding materials and implements.

work.up *n.* a complete diagnostic survey of a patient.

work.week *n.* the portion of a week spent in work: *They demanded and got a 30-hour, four-day workweek.*

world (WURLD) *n.* **1** the earth as our home: *a trip around the world; the nations of the world; the known world before Columbus's time; We have other worlds to conquer; the people of the Third World; Parents bring children into the world* (= into being). **2** people and their affairs: *a man of the world; Monks lead a life apart from the world; Is the end of the world near?* **3** any domain or sphere of activity: *the world of fashion, letters, the unknown; the world to come* (after death); *the academic, ancient, animal, financial,* literary, medieval, modern, outside, real, scientific worlds; Do you believe in **the next world** (= life after death)? **4** the uni-verse; everything: He looks **for all the world** (= very much) like a jogger or as if he's out for a jog; **What in the world** (= whatever) do you mean? **5** a great deal: That will do a **world of good**; You're asking for a **world of trouble**; There's a **world of difference** between our views; She **thinks the world of** (= have the highest regard for) him; We're **worlds apart** (= very far apart) on this question. —**out of this world** Informal. extraordinary; excellent.

world-beater n. Informal. one that breaks previous records.

world-class adj. of the highest caliber or quality: a world-class athlete, institution, scholar.

world.ling n. one who is busy with secular or worldly pursuits.

world.ly adj. **-li.er, -li.est** of this world; not religious or otherworldly: worldly ambition, knowledge, pleasures, pursuits, wealth; He's too **worldly-minded** to become a monk. —**world.li.ness** n.

worldly-wise adj. experienced in the ways of promoting one's worldly interests.

world war n. a war involving much of the world, as **World War I** (1914-18) or **World War II** (1939-45).

world-weary adj. weary of the world: the poet's world-weary voice.

world.wide adv. throughout the world: The book has been published worldwide. —adj. existing worldwide: He enjoys a worldwide reputation.

World Wide Web See WEB.

worm (WURM) n. **1** a small, slender, soft-bodied, legless, creeping or crawling animal such as an earthworm or a leech: "The early bird catches the worm" (= The earlier you are, the more successful you will be); The **worm may be turning** – house prices seem to be coming down. **2** a wormlike larva, mollusk, or other animal. **3** a small, contemptible person; wretch. **4** something wormlike in shape or movement, as the thread of a screw. The worm of conscience gnawed at his soul. **5 worms** pl. infection of a body part, esp. the intestine, by parasitic worms. —v. move like a worm or make one's way by creeping or crawling; insinuate: The guerrillas wormed their way through the bushes; He wormed himself into a position of influence; He wormed (= got by indirect means) many secrets out of her confidantes. —**worm.y** adj.: wormy apples, cabbage, wood.

worm-eaten adj. **1** burrowed into by worms, as wood. **2** antiquated or worn-out.

worm gear n. a gear for transmitting rotary motion, made up of a toothed wheel meshing at right angles with an endless screw on a shaft.

worm.hole n. a hole burrowed by a worm in timber, etc.

worm.wheel n. the toothed wheel of a worm gear.

worm.wood n. **1** any of a group of bitter or aromatic plants. **2** something bitter or unpleasant.

worn pp. of WEAR. —adj. exhausted or tired: a face worn with care; a worn look.

worn-out adj. **1** used up by wear: worn-out shoes. **2** tired out: She feels worn-out after 12 hours on the job.

wor.ri.ment (WUR.ee.munt) n. **1** the state of anxiety or worry. **2** a cause of it.

wor.ri.some (WUR.ee.sum) n. **1** causing worry: Here's some news with worrisome implications; worrisome prospects; Housing costs are becoming as worrisome as soaring food prices. **2** tending to worry: Are moms worrisome by nature? —**wor.ri.some.ly** adv.

wor.ry (WUR.ee) v. **wor.ries, wor.ried, wor.ry.ing 1** bother or trouble physically or mentally in a harassing manner: Cats and dogs like to worry their victims into submission; Children tend to worry their loose teeth with the tongue; It worries them when their child is late for lunch. **2** be uneasy or anxious: Parents worry over their children; They worry that their kids may be in some sort of trouble; Most people worry (= manage to struggle) through life; adj.: She's not **worried** about her future; He looks worried; a worried face, look, parent; He's **worried sick** (= very worried) about losing his job. —**not to worry** don't worry. —n., pl. **wor.ries 1** trouble or anxiety: worry and discontent; the signs of worry on her face. **2** a cause of it: cares and worries; financial worries; health worries; adja.: worry beads; worry lines on one's brows. —**wor.ri.er** n.

worry beads n.pl. a string of beads that are fingered by a nervous person to avoid fidgeting.

wor.ry.wart (WUR.ee.wort) n. Informal. one who worries a lot.

worse (WURSE) adj. & adv. comp. of BAD & ILL: His grammar is bad and spelling worse; He is worse than anyone else; He was badly shaken by the accident, but others fared worse; I felt worse after

*taking the medicine; I was **worse** off.*
—n.: *Things went from bad to worse; a change **for the worse**.*
wors.en (WUR.sun) *v.* make or become worse.
wor.ship (WUR.ship) *n.* **1** great reverence, as for a deity. **2** a religious service or rite: *a day set apart as a day of worship; hero worship; freedom of worship* (= religion); *the worship of* (= extraordinary respect shown to) *the almighty dollar.* **3** *Cdn.* a title of respect for magistrates, mayors, etc.: *Your* or *His* or *Her Worship.* **—v. -ships, -shiped, -ship.ing 1** show great reverence, as to a divine being: *Let's worship God.* **2** love or admire very much: *I adore babies and worship mothers; Tony **worships the ground** his mom **walks on*** (= has great love for her). **3** attend religious services: *Where do you worship?*
—wor.ship.er *n.* Also **wor.shipped, wor.ship.ping; wor.ship.per** *Cdn.*
wor.ship.ful (WUR.ship.ful) *adja.* **1** *Cdn.* a title of respect for certain officials: *Her Worshipful Mayor Hazel McCallion.* **2** [used in titles of guilds, lodges, etc.]: *the Worshipful Company of Goldsmiths.* **3** full of veneration: *her worshipful eyes, feelings, regard.* **—wor.ship.ful.ly** *adv.*
worst (WURST) *adj. superl.* of BAD & ILL: *the worst winter in living memory; a **worst-case** scenario* (= how it would be if the worst happened). **—adv.** *superl.* of BADLY & ILL: *She did worst in math.*
—n.: *The worst of the winter was in January, when things were **at their worst**; Be prepared for the worst; You will get only a small fine **at (the) worst**; If **the worst comes to the worst** or If it comes to the worst* (= If things get too bad) *hire a lawyer.*
—v. defeat: *"Never dreamed, though right were worsted, wrong would triumph."*
wor.sted (WURS.tid, WOOS-, short "OO") *n.* **1** a smooth, compact woolen fabric made of yarn from long fibers: *worsted cloths, fabrics, wool, yarns; fine worsted suitings; slacks in wool worsted.* **2** such a yarn or thread.
wort (WURT) *n.* **1** the mixture of grains and water before it is boiled and fermented into beer, ale, etc. **2** *comb.form.* plant: *figwort, liverwort, milkwort.*
worth (WURTH, "TH" as in "thin") *n.* value, as because of intrinsic merit: *a book of some worth; Customers want their money's worth; Trash is of no worth; a dollar's worth* (= quantity) *of nuts.*
—adj. [used like *prep.*] **1** having value estimated at an amount: *a painting worth million; money that's not worth the paper it's printed on; an heiress worth* (= having property valued at) *$1 billion.* **2** de- serving of something: *a book worth reading; It's well worth the price; not worth your while to complain; Is it worth the trouble?*
worth.less *adj.* valueless; useless: *worthless checks, information, investments; to feel worthless; a worthless* (= bad) *character.* **—worth.less.ness** *n.*
worth.while *adj.* worth the time or effort spent; of some value: *a worthwhile occupation, undertaking; I didn't find it worthwhile.*
wor.thy (WUR.thee, "th" as in "the") *adj.* **-thi.er, -thi.est 1** having value or merit: *a worthy cause, charity, goal.* **2** deserving: *a charity that is **worthy of** your consideration.* **—comb.form.** suitable for or deserving of, as specified: *airworthy, noteworthy, roadworthy, trustworthy.* **—n.,** *pl.* **-thies** [sometimes ironical] a person of outstanding merit: *the worthies of City Hall.* **—worth.i.ly** *adv.;* **worth.i.ness** *n.*
wot *v. pres. tense* of WIT.
would (WOOD, wud; short "OO") *pt.* of WILL, *v.* 5: *Gigi said she would hire him; She would if she could; They would* (= used to) *talk for hours about their work; Would* (= I wish) *that it were possible! if you would* (= please) *be so good as to lend me some money.*
would-be *adja.* wishing, intended, or pretending to be: *a would-be assassin, gardener, husband, matchmaker, poet, prime minister.*
would.n't (WOOD.unt, short "OO") would not.
wouldst (WOODST, short "OO") [old form] the form of WOULD used with "thou."
wound (WOOND, long "OO") *n.* **1** an injury to tissue below the skin: *to inflict a wound on* or *upon someone; to receive a wound; stitch up an open wound; festering, gaping, self-inflicted, superficial wounds; bullet, flesh, gunshot wounds.* **2** injury to one's feelings or good name. **—lick one's wounds** recover from an injury, loss, defeat, etc.
—v. 1 inflict a wound or wounds; hurt or injure: *Jan was fatally* or *mortally wounded in an accident.*
2 (WOWND) *pt. & pp.* of ¹WIND or a *pt. & pp.* of ²WIND, *v.* 3.
wove, woven See WEAVE.
wow *interj.* expressing admiration or surprise. **—v.** *Informal.* overwhelm with delight; arouse enthusiasm in someone: *The new rock group wowed*

their audience. —*n. Informal.* **1** a great success; hit: *The singer was a wow in London and New York.* **2** a slow rise and fall of pitch because of faulty sound reproduction: *wow and flutter.*

wrack (RAK) *n.* wreck or destruction, esp. **wrack and ruin;** also **rack and ruin.** —*v.* torture: *wracked with pain.*

wraith (RAITH, "TH" as in "thin") *n.* an apparition of a dying or dead person; ghost: *The released captives looked like wraiths of their former selves.*

wran.gle (RANG.gul) *v.* **-gles, -gled, -gling 1** argue or quarrel noisily: *He wrangles with his neighbors; He wrangles about their dogs; The neighbors wrangle incessantly over each other's dogs.* **2** in Western U.S. and Canada, to herd or tend cattle, horses, etc. on the range. —*n.* an angry or noisy quarrel or dispute. —**wran.gler** *n.*

wrap (RAP) *v.* **wraps,** *pt. & pp.* **wrapped** or **wrapt, wrap.ping** cover or enclose by winding or folding around: *paper for wrapping gifts; She wrapped herself in a blanket; He wrapped the shawl around his neck; He sat wrapped in thought; He's too much **wrapped up** (= engrossed) in his studies.* —**wrap up 1** dress warmly. **2** *Informal.* conclude or settle: *Let's wrap it up and go home.* —*n.* **1** an outer covering for the body, as a shawl, cloak, coat, etc.: *scarves and wraps; a wrap skirt.* **2** an outer covering for a product, as food: *duct, foil, plastic wraps.* —**under wraps** secret: *They kept their plans under wraps till the last moment.*

wrap.a.round (RAP.uh.round) *n.* **1** a garment or other article shaped so as to curve around a body or follow a contour. **2** in word processing, the automatic shifting of a word that does not fit at the end of one line to the beginning of the next. —*adj.*: *a room with a wraparound view; wraparound robes, sunglasses, windshields; a word processing program with a word wraparound function.*

wrap.per (RAP.ur) *n.* **1** one that wraps, as a woman's dressing gown. **2** that in which something is wrapped, as the dust jacket of a book or the wrapping in which a magazine is mailed: *in a plain brown wrapper;* also **wrap.ping.**

wrap-up *n. Informal.* a summary that concludes a report, statement, etc.: *a wrap-up of the day's news.*

wrasse (RAS) *n.* a fish of warm seas with thick lips, large scales, and usu. brilliant coloring, noted for picking and eating the parasites off larger fish.

wrath (RATH, RAWTH; "TH" as in "thin") *n.* great anger, as attributed to God, that seeks to punish the wrongdoer: *to arouse, dread, fear, ignite, incur, suffer the wrath of the authorities; to avoid, escape, face, fuel, meet, provoke, risk someone's wrath; endless food lines where the grapes of wrath ripen; "A soft answer turneth away wrath."* —**wrath.ful** *adj.*

wreak (REEK) *v.* to cause or inflict: *The terrorists have wreaked havoc throughout the nation; to wreak damage, revenge, ruin, vengeance on someone, among a group, in a place* or *situation, with a person or thing.*

wreath (REETH, "TH" as in "thin") *n.* **wreaths** (REETHZ, "TH" as in "the") a ring twisted of boughs, flowers, etc.: *bridal, floral, laurel wreaths; to make* or *weave a wreath; to lay* or *place a wreath at the tomb of the Unknown Soldier; a wreath of chrysanthemums; a snowy wreath of lace; wreaths* (= *curls*) *of smoke.*

wreathe (REETH, "TH" as in "the") *v.* **wreathes, wreathed, wreath.ing 1** make into a wreath; encircle; adorn: *to wreathe flowers into a garland; a mountain peak **wreathed in** (= covered with) clouds; happy faces wreathed in smiles.* **2** of smoke, etc., coil or circle; spiral upward.

wreck (REK) *v.* ruin or destroy as by a crash or shattering blow: *Children wreck toys; That candy bar wrecked my digestion; It also wrecked my lipstick; His leg injury wrecked his chances in the race; The prolonged strike wrecked many careers; It almost wrecked the town's economy; Domestic violence wrecks lives.* —*n.* **1** a wrecking, being wrecked, or what remains after destruction, as a shipwreck: *People crowded round at the scene of the train wreck; Car wrecks are towed off after a highway crash; the rusted wreck of the Titanic; It was the total wreck of our hopes; the wreck of a nation.* **2** one who has lost health, money, or something similar: *He's a moral and nervous wreck.*

wreck.age (REK.ij) *n.* a wrecking or its remains: *The wreckage of the aircraft littered the runway and was strewn over a wide area.*

wreck.er *n.* **1** one that wrecks, as one whose work is tearing down buildings: *Old buildings fall to the **wrecker's ball.*** **2** one that removes or salvages wrecks.

wrecking bar *n.* a bar used as a lever

that has a claw at one end for pulling nails.

wren (REN) *n.* a small, active, insect-eating bird noted for its short, erect tail.

wrench (RENCH) *n.* **1** a sudden twisting or jerking movement, as sometimes causes back injury. **2** a distortion, as of meaning, or something painful: *Leaving home was a wrench.* **3** a tool for gripping and turning something: *a hex wrench; an Allen wrench; a monkey wrench.* —**throw a wrench** See THROW. —*v.* pull with a twisting movement: *She wrenched her hand away from his grip; wrenched the gun out of his hand; He wrenched his ankle while playing tennis; to wrench free from the cult's influence; words wrenched out of their context;* **adj. & cpd.:** *a program of* **wrenching** *change; a wrenching choice, loss; wrenching conflicts within a group; wrenching times;* **gut-wrenching** *feelings, moments, phone calls, problems; a* **heart-wrenching** *experience, song, story; a refugee's* **nerve-wrenching** *dash to freedom; a* **soul-wrenching** *confession.*

wrest (REST) *v.* to force or wrench something, esp. from another's possession, sometimes with deftness or skill: *He wrested the gun from his attacker's hand; to wrest a living from the harsh environment; usurpers who wrested power from the prince.* —*n.* a wresting or forcible twist.

wres.tle (RES.ul) *v.* **-tles, -tled, -tling 1** contend or grapple *with* an opponent in hand-to-hand combat, as in the sport of wrestling. **2** struggle: *to wrestle with a task, problem, temptation.* —*n.* a struggle. —**wres.tler** *n.*

wrestling (RES.ling) *n.* a sport in which two unarmed persons struggle hand to hand, each trying to throw the other to the ground: *Two people engage in* **arm wrestling** *with hands gripped across a table, one trying to force the other's hand down;* **Wrist wrestling** *is a form of arm wrestling with only the thumbs interlocked.*

wretch (RECH) *n.* a miserable, unhappy, or despised person: *the poor wretch.*

wretch.ed (RECH.id) *adj.* utterly miserable: *the wretched existence of people in refugee camps; wretched food, slums; He felt wretched when forsaken by friends.* —**wretch.ed.ly** *adv.;* **wretch.ed.ness** *n.*

wrig.gle (RIG.ul) *v.* **wrig.gles, wrig.gled, wrig.gling 1** twist and turn, as a worm does; squirm. **2** move or make one's way by or as if by wriggling: *The eel wriggled away from her grasp; to* **wriggle out of** (= escape by devious means from) *a difficulty.* —*n.* a wriggling.

wrig.gler (RIG.lur) *n.* the larva of a mosquito. —**wrig.gly** *adj.*

-wright *comb.form.* maker: *playwright, shipwright, wheelwright.*

wring (RING) *v.* **wrings, wrung, wring.ing 1** twist and squeeze with force: *to wring wet clothes; to wring out the water; to wring a bird's neck* (= kill it); *to wring* (= force) *a concession, confession, the truth, a promise, etc. from someone; She wrung her hands (together) in despair; a sad tale that wrung* (= pained) *our hearts.* **2** clasp or squeeze someone's hands in congratulation or friendship. —*n.* a wringing.

wring.er *n.* **1** one that wrings: *a clothes wringer; mops and wringers.* **2** a situation in which one is subjected severe testing: *the emotional wringer of a kidnaping; Selected tax returns are put* or go **through the wringer** (= are audited).

wrin.kle (RINK.ul) *n.* **1** a small ridge or crease on a normally smooth surface: *an oldster with wrinkles around his eyes; wrinkles on the forehead; wrinkles on an aging skin; to get* or *iron the wrinkles out of a newly washed fabric; to press out* or *smooth out wrinkles.* **2** a difficulty or problem to be ironed out, as in an agreement. **3** *Informal.* development: *a new wrinkle in home entertainment; the latest wrinkle in women's fashions; It adds a (new) wrinkle to the business; Is it something new or a (new) wrinkle on an old fashion?* —*v.* **-kles, -kled, -kling 1** get wrinkled, as fabrics do: *Synthetics don't wrinkle easily.* **2** make wrinkles in something; crease: *She wrinkled her nose in disgust; to wrinkle one's brows, forehead;* **adj.:** *a* **wrinkled** *bill, expression, face, hand, skin; The dress got all wrinkled;* also **wrin.kly** *adj.* **-kli.er, -kli.est**: *wrinkly skin.*

wrist (RIST) *n.* the joint that connects hand and forearm. —**slap** or **tap on the wrist** *Informal.* a light punishment or rebuke.

wrist.band *n.* **1** the part of a sleeve or cuff that goes around the wrist. **2** a band or strap, as of a wristwatch.

wrist.let (RIST.lit) *n.* **1** a bracelet. **2** a knitted band worn around the wrist for warmth.

wrist.watch *n.* a watch worn on a strap or bracelet around the wrist.

writ (RIT) *n.* something written, esp. a court order: *to file a writ in court; The* court issued a writ ordering him to appear in court; to serve a writ on someone. —v. [old use] a *pt. & pp.* of WRITE.

write (RITE) *v.* **writes**, *pt.* **wrote** or [old use] **writ**, *pp.* **writ.ten** (RIT.un) or [old use] **writ, writ.ing 1** make letters so as to form words, using a pen, pencil, etc.: *We learn to read and write; She writes legibly; a pencil that doesn't write well; Please print, don't write your name; Please* **write down** *what you hear.* **2** transfer computer data from memory to another medium such as a monitor or storage disk: *to write data to the disks; a write-protected disk; a read / write / erase optical drive.* **3** communicate by letter: *She writes (to) her parents every month; That's nothing to* **write home about** (= nothing important). **4** make a document, record, literary or artistic work, etc. by writing: *to write books, checks, computer programs, music, news reports, plays, stories, wills; Authors write for a living, for the media, for the stage.* **5** be evident or obvious: *Suspicion was written on his face; Suspicion was* **writ large** (= clearly evident) *on his face.* —**write in 1** add an unlisted candidate's name to a ballot. **2** vote for someone thus. —**write off** cancel or forget a bad debt, loss, etc., depreciate capital expenditures, or ignore a person or thing as of no account. —**write out** write fully or completely. —**write up** write an account of a person or thing, as for publication: *His exploits have been written up in the tabloids.*

write-in *n.* a candidate written in by a voter.

write-off *n.* something written off as a loss: *The project was a $500 million write-off; asset, inventory, loan write-offs.* Also **write.off.**

writ.er (RYE.tur) *n.* one who writes, esp. an author: *free-lance, hack, newsletter, screen, speech, travel writers.*

writer's cramp *n.* a muscle spasm of the hand, as may afflict one who writes for too long.

write-up *n. Informal.* a published report or account of a person, event, etc., usu. favorable.

writhe (RITHE, "TH" as in "the") *v.* **writhes, writhed, writh.ing 1** twist or turn about: *to writhe in pain.* **2** suffer or squirm in embarrassment or under an insult.

writing (RYE.ting) *n.* **1** the act of one that writes: *the three R's of reading, writing, and arithmetic; Please put it* **in writing** (= written form); *legible writing; At* **this writing** (= at the time this is being written) *nothing is known about the missing money.* **2** something written, esp. of literary value: *the writings of the ancients; the collected writings of Coleridge.* **3** the activity of an author: *He makes a living by writing (as an occupation).* —**the writing on the wall** signs of what is going to happen: *The writing on the wall was that the company was heading for bankruptcy.* —*adj.* for writing with or on: *writing implements, materials, pads, paper.; a* **writing pad** (= sheets of paper glued together at one end).

written *pp.* of WRITE.

wrong (RONG) *adj.* **1** not right, esp. morally: *Cheating is wrong; It's wrong to cheat; I was wrong in doing* or *to do so.* **2** not just, correct, proper, presentable, desirable, etc.: *wrong spelling; The child came out with shoes on the wrong feet; I was driving the wrong way on a one-way street; There's something wrong with a car that won't start; What's wrong?* —*n.* what is not right: *Infants don't know right from wrong; He had done much wrong as a dictator; "Two wrongs don't make a right"* (= You don't do one wrong to make up for another, as in taking vengeance); *to redress, right, undo a wrong; a grievous wrong; He soon realized that he was* **in the wrong** (= at fault; deserving blame). —*adv.* [used after its verb] wrongly: *You guessed it wrong; You did it all wrong.* —**get someone** or **something wrong** *Informal.* misunderstand: *Don't get me wrong.* —**go wrong:** *Everything seems to go wrong* (= turn out badly) *on certain days; Children may go wrong* (= become morally bad) *in bad company; But where did we go wrong* (= make a mistake)? —*v.* do wrong to someone; harm or injure: *They wronged him by firing him without cause.* —**wrong.do.er** (RONG.doo.ur) *n.* —**wrong.do.ing** *n.*

wrong.ful *adj.* unjust or unlawful: *a wrongful act, arrest, confinement, dismissal, imprisonment; to sue someone for* **wrongful death** *caused by a willful or negligent act.* —**wrong.ful.ly** *adv.;* **wrong.ful.ness** *n.*

wrong.head.ed (RONG.hed.id) *adj.* **1** stubborn or obstinate in a wrong opinion or judgment; perverse: *wrongheaded youths.* **2** mistaken: *a wrongheaded decision, idea, notion.*

wrong.ly *adv.* [used esp. before a *pp.*]: *She was wrongly accused; a wrongly spelled word; He was refused, whether rightly or wrongly.* —**wrong.ness** *n.*

wrong.o (RONG.oh) *n.* **-os** or **-oes** *Slang.* a bad person or error: *That's a howling wrongo!*

wrote a *pt.* of WRITE.

wroth (ROTH, RAWTH) *adj.* wrathful; angry.

wrought (RAWT) *v.* a *pt. & pp.* of WORK: *What hath God wrought; what the abortion issue has wrought; the devastation wrought by civil strifes; The Communist system wrought much havoc among East European nations; the changes wrought by the new tax laws; wrought with human hands; He gets **wrought up** (= excited) over trifles.* —*adj.* formed or shaped, as metals by hammering: *a finely wrought film; a well-wrought study; wrought* (= manufactured) *silk.*

wrought iron *n.* iron that has been forged or rolled so as to make it more malleable, tougher, and more durable than cast iron; *adja.: a **wrought-iron** fence, gate, railing; wrought-iron furniture.*

wrought-up *adj.* very excited or agitated: *her wrought-up generosity.*

wrung *pt. & pp.* of WRING.

wry (RYE) *adj.* **wri.er, wri.est** twisted; distorted; contorted: *a wry face (showing disgust); wry* (= ironic) *humor; a wry mouth* (= grimace); *a wry smile (of disappointment).* —**wry.ly** *adv.;* **wry.ness** *n.*

wry.neck *n.* **1** a congenital or rheumatic disorder in which the head is continually pulled to one side. **2** same as SNAKEBIRD.

wun.der.kind (VOON.dur.kint, short "OO") *n.* child prodigy: *the new wunderkind of American ballet.*

wurst *n.* sausage meat: *Germany consumes several billion pounds of wurst each year.*

WYSIWIG (WIZ.ee.wig) *n. & adja.* (having to do with) a computer display of text exactly as it will look when printed: *true WYSIWIG with 300 dots-per-inch resolution; WYSIWIG screen fonts.*

.... **X, x** ....

X or **x** (EX) *n.* **X's** or **x's 1** the 24th letter of the English alphabet. **2** something resembling an "X." **3** the Roman numeral for 10. **4** an unknown quantity or one whose identity is withheld: *It takes **x** number of hours to do the job; Mr. X.* **5** [capital] a rating used for pornographic motion pictures to which only adults are admitted.
—*v.* **x-es** or **x's,** *pt. & pp.* **x-ed** or **x'd, x-ing** or **x'ing** cross *out* with an x or series of x's.

x-axis *n., pl.* **x-axes** (-ax.eez) the horizontal axis on a chart or graph.

X chromosome See SEX CHROMOSOME.

xe.non (ZEE.non) *n.* a colorless, odorless, tasteless gaseous element.

xen.o.phobe (ZEN.uh.fobe) *n.* one who fears or hates foreigners.

xen.o.pho.bi.a (zen.uh.FOH.bee.uh) *n.* fear or hatred of foreigners.
—**xen.o.pho.bic** (-FOH.bic, -FOB.ic) *adj.*

xer.ic (ZEER.ic) *adj.* deficient in moisture: *a xeric environment, habitat, plant.*

xe.rog.ra.phy (zuh.ROG.ruh.fee) *n.* a dry photographic printing process that uses electrically charged particles fused by heat. —**xe.ro.graph.ic** (zeer.uh.GRAF.ic) *adj.*

xe.rox (ZEER.ox) *v.* **-rox.es, -roxed, -rox.ing** make a photocopy of something: *Please xerox this for me;* **n.:** *We are specialists in xeroxing; adj.: piles of xeroxed documents.* —**n.** a photocopy: *A couple of xeroxes will do; A good xerox is preferred to a carbon copy; adja.: a xerox copy, machine, room.* —**Xerox** Trademark.

Xmas (CHRIS.mus) *n.* [short form] Christmas.

X-radiation *n.* **1** X-ray treatment. **2** X rays.

X-rated *adj.* **1** rated X; pornographic: *an X-rated movie, show.* **2** *Informal.* obscene: *an X-rated expletive, joke.*

X ray *n.* an electromagnetic ray of extremely short wavelength, capable of penetrating opaque substances, much used in medical diagnosis and treatment: *a chest X ray; He decided to have an X ray taken of his aching back.*

X-ray *v.* examine or treat with X rays.
—*adja.: an X-ray emission, examination, laser, photo, telescope.*

xy.lem (ZYE.lum) *n.* the woody central tissue of a vascular plant, that conducts water and minerals upward and gives mechanical support.

xy.lo.phone (ZYE.luh.fone) *n.* a percussion instrument consisting of wooden bars that are struck with two small wooden hammers to sound the musical scale. —**xy.lo.phon.ist** (-foh.nist) *n.*

.... **Y, y** ....

Y or **y** (WYE) *n.* **Y's** or **y's 1** the 25th letter of the English alphabet. **2** anything shaped like a "Y." —**the Y** [short form] YMCA, YMHA, YWCA, YWHA, or a hostel run by any of them: *She's staying at the Y.*

ya (YUH) *pron. & adja. Informal.* you or your: *How are ya? How's ya child?*

yacht (YOT) *n.* a small ship used for cruising and racing: *He spends all his weekends on his yacht.* —*v.* sail a yacht. —**yachting** *n.* the sport of sailing a yacht. —**yachts.man** (-mun) *n.* **-men.**

yack same as YAK.

ya.hoo 1 *n.* (YAH.hoo) a coarse or uncouth person, like the **Yahoos** of Jonathan Swift's "Gulliver's Travels." 2 *interj.* (ya.HOO) expressing joy or triumph.

Yah.we or **Yah.weh** (YAH.way) *n.* the Hebrew name of God; Jehovah; also **Yah.ve** or **Yah.veh.**

yak *n.* 1 a long-haired ox of Tibet and Central Asia. 2 *Slang.* idle, endless, or noisy chatter; *v.* **yakked, yak.king:** *truck drivers yakking away on their CB radios.*

yam *n.* a variety of sweet potato.

yam.mer (YAM.ur) *n.* & *v. Informal.* 1 whimper or whine. 2 loud or voluble chatter: *He yammered away, but no one was listening.* —**yam.mer.er** *n.*

yang *n.* in Chinese thought, the masculine active force or principle of life and being, complementary to YIN.

yank *n. Informal.* a sudden hard jerk; tug. —*v.* pull with a yank: *A yo-yo is yanked on a string; to yank* (= withdraw) *a child out of school in the middle of the year.*

Yank *n. Informal.* a Yankee, esp. an American soldier of World War I or II.

Yan.kee (YANK.ee) *n.* an American, originally one from New England or N. United States: *a Connecticut Yankee.* —*adj.* having to do with the Yankees: *the Yankee mystique; Yankee aggression, imperialism, industry; The room was patriotically decorated in Yankee Doodle red, white, and blue; Charles Cretors's Yankee ingenuity is to blame for our taste for popcorn during movies.*

Yan.qui (YAHNG.kee) *n.* a U.S. American as distinguished from a Latin American.

yap *n.* & *v.* **yaps, yapped, yap.ping** *Informal.* chatter, esp. in a noisy or rude manner: *What's he yapping about?* *n.: Teachers don't like too much yapping in class.* —**yap.per** *n.*

yard *n.* 1 a unit of length equal to three feet (0.914 m): *Carpeting is usually sold by the square yard.* 2 a slender pole or spear fastened across a mast to support a sail. 3 a piece of ground, as around a house, church, or farm buildings. 4 an enclosed area or pen for poultry, livestock, etc. 5 a place covered with railroad tracks where cars are stored, switched, etc.

yard.age (YAR.dij) *n.* 1 length in yards. 2 an extent or distance covered in yards.

yard.arm *n.* either end of a yard supporting a square sail.

yard goods *n.pl.* textiles sold by the yard.

yard.man (YARD.mun) *n.* **-men** a man who works in a railroad yard.

yard.mas.ter (YARD.mas.tur) *n.* a person in charge of a railway yard.

yard.stick *n.* 1 a graduated measuring stick one yard in length. 2 a standard of comparison: *We can't apply the same yardstick to children and adults; What yardstick do you use to measure intelligence? Is material prosperity the yardstick of human achievement?*

yar.mul.ke (YAR.mul.kuh) *n.* a skullcap worn esp. ceremonially by Jewish men and boys.

yarn *n.* 1 a fiber spun into strands for weaving or knitting: *a ball, hank, skein of yarn.* 2 *Informal.* a tall tale or story: *to spin a yarn.*

yar.row (YAIR.oh) *n.* a perennial herb with finely cut aromatic leaves and flat-topped clusters of small white, yellow, or pink flowers.

yaw *n.* a movement about a vertical axis, as when an airplane's nose turns right or left. —*v.* of a ship, airplane, space vehicle, projectile, etc., turn right or left in its course.

yawl *n.* 1 a small, two-masted, fore-and-aft-rigged ship. 2 a dinghy or rowboat.

yawn *n.* 1 an involuntary taking in and letting out of breath with wide-open mouth, usu. because of fatigue: *a yawn of utter boredom; a loud yawn; to stifle or suppress a yawn.* 2 *Informal.* bore: *Algebra is a yawn to Yves.* —*v.* to open wide, as the mouth during a yawn: *The audience started yawning as the lecturer went on; with their mouths yawning open.* —**yawning** 1 *adj.* wide open: *a yawning chasm, gap, gulf, hole.* 2 *adj.* bored or boring: *a yawning lack of interest; His lecture left us yawning; the most yawning book I ever read.*

yaws *n.pl.* [takes *sing. v.*] a contagious tropical skin eruption of small sores in clusters.

Y chromosome See SEX CHROMOSOME.

ye [old form] 1 (YEE) *pron.* you. 2 (popularly pronounced YEE, more correctly as "the") same as THE: *"Ye Olde Candle Shoppe."*

yea (YAY) *adv.* yes; indeed. —*n.* an affirmative vote or voter; aye: *There were*

148 nays and 127 yeas in the debate on the restoration of capital punishment.

yeah (YAH) *adv. Informal.* yes: *Oh, yeah?* (= Is that so?).

year (YEER) *n.* **1** the period of about 365 days that the earth takes to go once around the sun; also called "solar year": *A tragedy like that will not happen in future years; in the years to come; He was sentenced to five years (in jail); Years from now, who will remember us?* **2** an annual period such as a "calendar year" (January 1 through December 31 in the Gregorian calendar), the usu. September-to-June "school *or* academic year," etc.: *Rome was founded in the year 753 B.C.; It happened in the year 1759; an election year; the fiscal year of a corporation; a jubilee year; a leap year; a taxation year running from May 1 to April 30; Who knows what will happen in the year 3000? Last year we had a bad year; banner, good, lean, memorable, peak, profitable, record years.* —**year after year** *or* **year in, year out** *or* **year in and year out** every year. —**years** *pl.* time of life: *the formative years of our childhood; the golden years of retirement; children of tender years.* —**in years 1** in age: *Grandpa is rather advanced in years; I'm getting on in years.* **2** in a long time: *I haven't seen him in years; the best word processor to come along in years.*

year.book *n.* an annual publication or reference book reporting on people and events of the preceding year, as of a graduating class, the supplements of an encyclopedia, etc.

year.ling (YEER.ling, YUR.ling) *n.* a one-year-old animal; **adj**a.: *a yearling calf, colt, seal.*

year.long *adja.* lasting through a year: *a yearlong absence, drought, strike, struggle.*

year.ly *adj.* **1** once a year: *the earth's yearly revolution around the sun; a yearly* (= every year) *trip.* **2** annual: *She draws a yearly salary of $100,000;* **adv.**: *It is paid monthly, not yearly* (= annually).

yearn (YURN) *v.* be filled with longing for someone or something that is missed or desired, pity for someone in trouble, or desire to do or get something: *She yearned to be reunited with her children; yearned for a visit to her homeland.*

yearning *n.* a tender longing: *The runaway expressed a yearning for the joys and comforts of home; an actor's yearning to play Shakespeare; Her yearning became an obsession.*

year-round *adja.* throughout the year, not seasonal or seasonally: *a year-round complaint, publication, resort, school; year-round employment;* **adv.**: *a complaint heard year-round.*

yeast (YEEST) *n.* **1** a yellowish, frothy moist substance made up of fungi that cause dough to rise, sugars to ferment, etc., used in baking and brewing: *Brewer's yeast is rich in B vitamins.* **2** such a fungus: *Yogurt fights yeast infections.* **3** a dried form of yeast sold in powder, granule, or cake form. **4** an agent causing agitation or unrest.

yeast.y (YEEST.ee) *adj.* **yeast.i.er, -i.est 1** containing yeast: *a yeasty brew, flavor, odor.* **2** frothy, light, or frivolous: *yeasty comments.* **3** agitated or restless: *a yeasty character, environment, group, social situation.*

yech (YEK, YUK) *interj.* expressing disgust or rejection. Also **yecch.**

yell *n.* **1** a loud cry or shout expressing anger, fear, joy, etc.: *She let out or gave a blood-curdling yell.* **2** a cheer given in unison to encourage teams at school athletic events. —*v.* utter or say with a yell: *He yelled something to her; He yelled to her to get out of the truck's way; He yelled himself hoarse; The mother yelled at her children; Please don't yell into my right ear.*

yel.low (YEL.oh) *n.* **1** the color of gold, egg yolk, etc. **2** the yolk of an egg. **3** a yellow pigment, dye, cloth, clothes, etc. —**adj. 1** yellow-colored: *yellow school buses; yellow writing pads; Leaves turn yellow in the fall.* **2** *Informal.* cowardly. **3** *adja.* sensational and vulgar: *yellow journalism; the yellow press.* —*v.* make or become yellow; **adj.**: *the* **yellowed,** *crumbling pages of an old book; yellowed winter grass;* **yellowing** *corn stalks;* **n.**: *a* **yellowing** *of the skin from jaundice.* —**yel.low.ish** *adj.*

yellow fever *n.* an acute, infectious, tropical virus disease carried by mosquitoes that damages the liver. Also **yellow jack.**

yellow jacket *n.* a small wasp with yellow stripes.

yellow pages *n.pl.* a telephone directory or a section of it, usu. printed on yellow paper, containing classified listings and advertisements of businesses, professions, services, etc. Also **Yellow Pages.**

yelp *n.* a short, sharp cry or bark, as of a dog. —*v.* utter or say with a yelp.

yen *n.* **1** *pl.* **yen** the basic money unit of Japan. **2** a strong desire or urge: *She had a yen to sail around the world; a yen for the sailor's life.*

yeo.man (YOH.mun) *n.* **-men 1** a petty officer of the U.S. Navy with clerical duties. **2** formerly, a servant in a royal household. **3** a member of a group of small landowners and farmers of medieval England, noted for their patriotism. —**yeo.man.ly** *adj. & adv.*

yeoman of the guard *n.* a ceremonial bodyguard of the British sovereign.

yeo.man.ry (YOH.mun.ree) *n.* yeomen collectively.

yeoman (or **yeoman's**) **service** *n.* good and faithful service: *to do* or *perform yeoman's service; to do yeoman duty; to do a yeoman's job, work.*

yep *adv. Informal.* yeah; yes.

yes *adv.* [expressing agreement, confirmation, etc.] aye; yea: *Yes, dinner's ready; Is that you? Yes; She's willing,* **and yes** (= and what is more), *eager to help.* —*n., pl.* **yes.es** or **yes.ses** an affirmative reply.

yes-man *n.* **-men** *Informal.* one who agrees with or accepts everything superiors say.

yester- *comb.form* [old use] of yesterday: *yestereve, yestermorn, yesternight, yesteryear.*

yes.ter.day (YES.tur.dee, -day) *n. & adv.* **1** the day before today: *Yesterday was my birthday; It snowed yesterday.* **2** the recent past: *our heroes of yesterday; She was not born yesterday; a* **yesterday's man** (= a man, esp. a politician, whose career is finished).

yes.ter.year (YES.tur.yeer) *n.* the recent past: *Where are the "hot pants" of yesteryear? rock 'n' roll favorites from yesteryear; in the yesteryears when more of us could read and write.*

yet *adv.* **1** [in negative and doubtful contexts] up to the specified or implied time: *It's not yet time (to go to bed); She had not yet arrived at midnight; Isn't she home yet? Is she home yet?* **2** [in affirmative contexts, sometimes with intensive force] still: *She's waiting yet; while there is yet time; This makes things yet more difficult; He may make it yet* (= eventually; someday). **3** nevertheless; however: *strange, yet true.*
—**as yet** up to now: *She hasn't appeared as yet.*
—*conj.:* It's a strange story, yet it is true.

Ye.ti (YET.ee) same as ABOMINABLE SNOWMAN.

yew (YOO) *n.* an evergreen tree or shrub with rich, dark-green leaves and scarlet, berrylike seeds.

Yid.dish *n.* a German-derived language spoken esp. by E. European Jews and usu. written in Hebrew characters;

adj.: Yiddish folklore, literature, speech.

yield (YEELD) *v.* **1** give, as from within, in response to one's efforts or by cultivation: *The land yields crops; Trees yield fruit; Mines yield ore; Investments yield profits; ten-year bonds yielding 11%; Nature has been yielding up her secrets in response to our search for knowledge; The satellite search may yield clues about the Big Bang.* **2** give in, give up, give way, etc. to someone as by right, by persuasion, entreaty, or force of circumstances: *Vehicles have to yield right of way to pedestrians at pedestrian crossings; He graciously yielded the floor* (= the right to speak) *to his critic; But he refused to yield* (= grant) *the point (of the argument); She refused to yield* (= submit) *to the blackmailer; wouldn't yield to his demands; It was a question of either yielding to temptation or resisting; She yields to no one* (= is as good as anyone) *in her devotion to hockey; an addiction that yields* (= responds) *to treatment.* **3** give way to physical pressure and bend or break: *Nothing is so strong it won't yield under pressure.*
—*n.* amount or quantity yielded: *This year's yield of wheat has been good; a high yield per hectare; the yields on our stocks; Some stocks generate at least a 5% yield at all times; yields from long-term Treasury bonds; a one-year certificate of deposit with an effective yield of 8.5%.*

yielding *adj.* **1** submissive: *a yielding hand, modesty, nature.* **2** flexible: *the yielding softness of a carpeted floor; Sam's yielding willowy frame.* **3** *comb.form.* giving, as by cultivation: *high-yielding securities; interest-yielding investments; low-yielding bonds; top-yielding funds.*

yikes *interj.* expressing astonishment.

yin *n.* in Chinese thought, the female, passive force or principle of life and being, complementary to YANG.

yip *n. & v.* **yips, yipped, yip.ping** *Informal.* yelp.

yip.pee (YIP.ee) **1** *interj.* expressing great joy. **2** *n.* a member of a radical group of hippies called the "Youth International Party."

yo.del (YOH.dul) *v.* **-dels, -deled, -del.ing** sing with abrupt changes from the normal tone to a high falsetto and back, as practiced by the mountain peoples of the Alps.
—*n.* such singing. —**yo.del.er** *n.* Also **yo.delled, yo.del.ling; yo.del.ler** *Cdn.*

yo.ga (YOH.guh) *n.* a Hindu school of thought or a system of self-discipline developed by it that consists of physical exercises, control of the senses, and meditation for purifying one's soul: *to practice yoga.*

yo.gi (YOH.ghee) *n.* **-gis** one who practices yoga; also **yo.gin.**

yo.gurt (YOH.gurt) *n.* a semisolid acid food made by fermenting milk. Also **yo.ghurt.**

yoke *n.* **1** a wooden frame to which a pair of draft animals are harnessed: *to put a yoke on oxen; two yoke* or *yokes* (= pairs) *of oxen.* **2** a yokelike frame for carrying a load at either end, fitted to the shoulders of a person. **3** bondage or servitude: *to cast off* or *throw off the yoke of slavery; India was under a foreign yoke for two centuries; Romania was under the yoke of a dictator till 1989.* **4** anything like a yoke in form or function, as the shoulderpiece of a shirt, blouse, etc., the waist-piece of a skirt supporting gathered parts, or the wheel by which an airplane pilot controls ailerons and elevators. **5** a coupling or union: *the yoke of matrimony.*
—*v.* **yokes, yoked, yok.ing** **1** couple with or as with a yoke; join together. **2** harness an animal to a plow, etc.: *to yoke oxen to a cart.*

yo.kel (YOH.kul) *n.* a bumpkin.

yolk (YOKE) *n.* the yellow, inner part of an egg which serves as nourishment for the embryo, or the corresponding part of an ovum or egg cell in mammals. —**yolked** *adj.*

Yom Kip.pur (yom.KIP.ur) *n.* a Jewish holiday observed as a day of atonement for sins.

yon *adja. & adv.* [old use] yonder: *a boat tossed thither and yon by the waves.*

yon.der (YON.dur) *adja.* [literary use] **1** over there, usu. within sight: *in yonder hills.* **2** more distant; farther: *the yonder side of the mountains.*
—*adv.*: *Look yonder* (= over there)!

yoo hoo [in a rising-falling tone] *interj.* used to call attention: *Yoo hoo! Is anybody home?*

yore *n.* time long past: *in days of yore.*
—*adv.* [old use] long ago.

you (YOO) *pron. sing. & pl.* **1** the person or persons spoken to: *How are you, Gigi? How are you boys today?* **2** any person; one: *You feel lost in a jungle; You never know.*

you'd (YOOD, long "OO") you had; you would.

you'll (YOOL) you will; you shall.

young (YUNG) *adj.* **young.er** (YUNG.gur), **young.est** (YUNG.gist, "g" as in "go") in an early period of one's life; not old: *a young lady; too young to drive; How are you, young man? He's 75 years old but young at heart; quite young in spirit and in health; in the morning when the day is still young; old in years but young* (= not experienced) *in the business; books for teens and* **young adults** (*in their twenties).*
—*n.* **1** young offspring: *Mammals bring forth their young; a cow that is* **with young** (= pregnant). **2** young persons: *books for the young; an appeal to* **young and old** (= everyone).

young blood *n.* **1** young people: *the task of recruiting and training young blood.* **2** youthful energy, vigor, etc.: *a new hiring policy aimed at bringing young blood into the company.*

young.ling *n. & adja.* (one) that is young.

young offender *n.* a juvenile delinquent.

young.ster (YUNG.stur) *n.* **1** a child. **2** a young person.

youn.ker (YUNK.ur) *n.* [rare] a young fellow.

your (YOOR, YOR) *adja.* possessive case of YOU: *your children, country, spouse;* [suggesting familiarity] *your average customer;* [in titles] *Your Honor, Lordship, Majesty.*

you're (YOOR) you are.

yours (YOORS, YORS) *pron.* **1** one or ones belonging to you: *This book is yours; my books and yours; his, hers, and yours; a book* **of yours.** **2** [used before signature in complimentary close of letters]: *Yours sincerely; Sincerely yours;* [informal close] *Yours.*

your.self (yoor.SELF) *pron.* **-selves** (-SELVS) reflexive or emphatic of YOU(R): *Help yourself; Be yourself; You are old enough to walk by yourself; (You) do it yourself; You don't seem to be yourself* (= as well as usual) *today.*

yours truly *n.* [complimentary phrase used before the signature in business letters] *Informal.* I; me: *Yours truly had to leave; With the compliments of yours truly.*

youth (YOOTH, "TH" as in "thin") *n.* **youths** (YOOTHS, "TH" as in "the" or "thin") **1** the fact, quality, or period of being young, esp. the period between childhood and adulthood: *the vigor of youth; in her youth; in the prime of youth; the promises, thoughtlessness, wantonness of youth; the folly of our youth.* **2** a young person, esp. a male: *a group of youths loitering in the mall.* **3** usu. *pl.* young people: *The youth of the nation are* or *is ready to act.*

youth.ful *adj.* young, esp. having to do

with a young person's qualities: *youthful audiences, enthusiasm, pranks, vigor.* —**youth.ful.ly** *adv.*; **youth.ful.ness** *n.*
youth hostel See HOSTEL.
you've (YOOV, long "OO") you have.
yowl (rhyme: owl) *n.* a loud, long, complaining cry or howl, as of a dog in pain. —*v.* utter a yowl.
yo-yo (YOH.yoh) *n.* -yos 1 a toy consisting of a spool with a string wound around it whose free end is held in the hand and manipulated so as to make the spool rise and fall by the unwinding and rewinding of the string. 2 *Informal.* a stupid or gullible person: *The workers were mere yo-yos in the hands of their union leader.*
—*adja.* going back and forth or up and down; fluctuating: *the yo-yo phenomenon of weight loss followed by weight gain; a yo-yo diet, relationship, routine; the yo-yo syndrome of old people going in and out of hospital with one illness after another.*
—*v.* -yos, -yoed, -yo.ing fluctuate; vacillate: *Her weight yo-yos up and down the scale.*
yt.ter.bi.um (i.TUR.bee.um) *n.* a soft, silvery rare-earth metallic element.
yt.tri.um (IT.ree.um) *n.* a silvery metallic element used in electronics.
yu.an (yoo.AHN) *n. sing. & pl.* the basic money unit of the People's Republic of China.
yuc.ca (YUC.uh) *n.* 1 an evergreen desert plant with stiff, sword-shaped leaves growing in a cluster. 2 its whitish bell-like flower borne in a cluster from the center of the leaves.
yuck.y (YUCK.ee) *adj.* **yuck.i.er, yuck.i.est** [child's word] bad-tasting. Also **yuk.ky.**
Yu.go.sla.vi.an (yoo.goh.SLAH.vee.un) *n. & adj.* (a person) of or from **Yugoslavia**, a country of S.E. Europe.
Yu.kon.er (YOO.kon.ur) *n.* a person of or from the Yukon, Canada.
yule or **Yule** (YOOL, long "OO") *n.* Christmas; *adja.: Yule ornaments; weak Yule sales; the yule season.*
yule log *n.* a large log traditionally used to start the Christmas Eve fire.
yule.tide or **Yule.tide** *n.* Christmastide: *yuletide greetings.*
yum.my (YUM.ee) *adj.* **yum.mi.er, yum.mi.est** *Informal.* very tasty, delicious, or delightful.
yup *adv. Informal.* yep; yes.
yup.pie (YUP.ee) *n.* a "young urban professional" as a member of a high-spending, trendy social group; also **yup.py, yup.pies.**

yurt (YOORT) *n.* a domed, tentlike dwelling of Central Asian nomads.

.... **Z, z** ....

Z or **z** (ZEE, ZED) *n.* **Z's** or **z's** the last letter of the English alphabet.
za.ny (ZAY.nee) *n.* -nies 1 a clown or buffoon. 2 a silly person.
—*adj.* -ni.er, -ni.est like a zany; funny, silly, or crazy: *zany comedians, comic opera, costumes, footage, frolic, ideas; It's so zany; a zany bunch, collection, imagination, life, publisher, scheme, sense of humor.*
—**za.ni.ly** *adv.*; **za.ni.ness** *n.*
zap *v.* **zaps, zapped, zap.ping** *Informal.* 1 strike or kill with a sudden blow: *Nonsmokers don't like to get zapped by smoke even on the street; the idea of using energy rays to zap nuclear missiles; to zap* or **zap out** (= wipe out) *commercials on TV or the video cassette recorder.* 2 zip: *viewers zapping in and out of programs.*
—*n.* 1 a zapping: *a laser zap.* 2 zip; pep; vigor. —*interj.* expressing swiftness of action, sudden surprise, etc.: *Pow! Zap! Step on the gas pedal, and – zap – you're off.*
zeal (ZEEL) *n.* enthusiastic devotion to a cause and untiring activity in pursuing it: *a missionary's zeal for the salvation of souls; ardent, fervent, excessive, religious zeal; to show* or *display zeal for a cause; In his zeal to outdo his rivals, he overstepped the bounds of discretion.*
zeal.ot (ZEL.ut) *n.* one who is zealous in a fanatic or partisan way: *a religious zealot.*
zeal.ous (ZEL.us) *adj.* full of or characterized by zeal: *zealous efforts, workers; zealous for reform; zealous about* or *in preaching the gospel.* —**zeal.ous.ly** *adv.*; **zeal.ous.ness** *n.*
ze.bra (ZEE.bruh) *n.* a horselike wild animal of Africa with black or brown and white stripes.
ze.bu (ZEEB.yoo) *n.* a domesticated ox, originally from India, characterized by a large hump and dewlap.
zed *Cdn.* ZEE.
zee *n.* the letter Z.
Zeit.geist (ZITE.guyst) *n.* the intellectual and moral climate of an era; the prevailing spirit of the times.
Zen *n.* the Japanese form of Buddhism that stresses enlightenment through intuition.
ze.na.na (zuh.NAH.nuh) *n.* the women's section of a Muslim household in E. countries.
ze.nith (ZEE.nith) *n.* 1 the point of the

sky directly overhead. 2 the highest point: *the zenith of one's career, fortunes, power.*
ze.o.lite (ZEE.uh.lite) *n.* a silicate mineral widely used as a water softener; **ze.o.lit.ic** (-LIT.ic) *adj.*
zeph.yr (ZEF.ur) *n.* 1 a soft breeze; light wind. 2 a yarn, fabric, or garment of soft or light material.
zep.pe.lin (ZEP.uh.lin) *n.* a rigid airship having a cigar-shaped body supported by internal gas cells, as used in aviation before World War II.
ze.ro (ZEER.oh) *n.* **-ros** or **-roes** 1 naught or nothing. 2 the symbol 0 used to represent it. 3 the beginning or lowest point on a graduated scale, as 0 degree Celsius. —*adja.* having zero value: *We started from a zero base and worked up to 25%; zero gravity; the zero hour.*
—*v.* **-roes, -roed, -ro.ing** adjust to zero point: *to zero in a rifle (at center of target).* —**zero in on 1** aim directly at a target, as by adjusting the sights of a firearm: *The armored division has its artillery zeroed in on the downtown area.* 2 focus on something: *The speaker zeroed in on the premier's credibility.*
zero-base or **zero-based** *adj.* with zero as the starting point: *a zero-based performance review; Zero-based pricing helps reduce costs; zero-based revenue forecasting;* **zero-based budgeting** (= reassessing of every expenditure from the beginning instead of dealing only with proposed increases).
—**zero-base** *v.* **-bas.es, -based, -bas.ing:** *In these hard times, we have to zero-base all our expenditures.*
zero hour *n.* 1 preset time for starting an operation, as when a countdown reaches zero. 2 crucial or critical point. 3 the start of a calendar day: *The day starts at **zero hours** [written 00 h], commuters get up by 06 h [pronounced "zero six hours"], lunch breaks are usually from 12 h to 13 h, and commuters are usually back home by 19 h.*
zero-sum *adj.* resulting in no net gain: *a zero-sum game; a zero-sum competition, economy, gain.*
zero-zero *adj.* of weather conditions, with visibility reduced to nil horizontally and vertically.
zest *n.* 1 keen enjoyment; relish; gusto: *He eats with zest; She has lost her zest for life since her husband's death.* 2 a stimulating quality: *Lemon gratings add zest to a dish.* —**zest.ful** *adj.;* **zest.ful.ly** *adv.;* **zest.ful.ness** *n.* —**zest.y** *adj.* **zest.i.er, -i.est.**

Zeus (ZOOSE) *n.* the supreme god in ancient Greek mythology.
zig.zag *n.* 1 a series of short, sharp turns from one side to the other: *zigzags of lightning.* 2 a design or line in a zigzag. —*adja.* having zigzag form, as "forked" lightning: *in a zigzag design, fashion; zigzag lines, patterns, stitches.*
—*v.* **-zags, -zagged, -zag.ging** form or move in a zigzag: *The road zigzags across the landscape; We zigzagged through the valley.*
zilch *n. Informal.* zero; nil.
zil.lion (ZIL.yun) *n. Informal.* a very large indefinite number: *The odds against finding ancient treasures on the ocean floor are a zillion to one.*
—**zil.lionth** (ZIL.yunth) *adj.*
zinc *n.* a bluish-white, rust-resistant metallic element used in alloys and for galvanizing iron and steel.
—*v.* **zincs, zinced** or **zincked, zinc.ing** or **zinck.ing** coat with zinc; galvanize.
zinc oxide *n.* a white powdery substance used in making pigments, cosmetics, plastics, soaps, ointments, etc.
Zin.fan.del (ZIN.fun.del) *n.* a dry, red wine made from a black grape of California; also **zin.fan.del.**
zing *n. Informal.* 1 a sharp, shrill sound, as of bullets whistling past. 2 liveliness; zest; vigor: *The play lacked zing; The zing has gone out of our aging bureaucracy.* —*v.* make or move with a zing: *a reporter noted for zinging hostile questions at world leaders.*
zing.er *n. Informal.* a punch line or witty retort.
zing.y *adj. Informal.* **zing.i.er, -i.est** full of vigor and zest: *The air was alive and zingy; We were watching the zingiest show in town.*
zin.ni.a (ZIN.ee.uh, ZEEN.yuh) *n.* a garden plant with stiff, hairy stems, leaves arranged opposite each other, and showy flower heads in a wide variety of colors.
Zi.on (ZYE.un) *n.* 1 a hill in ancient Jerusalem that was the site of Solomon's temple; hence, the seat of Jewish worship. 2 the Israelites or their homeland. 3 in Christian usage, the heavenly city or the church of God.
Zi.on.ism (ZYE.uh.niz.um) *n.* a Jewish national movement that resulted in the establishment of Israel in 1948 and continues to provide worldwide support for Israel. —**Zi.on.ist** *n. & adj.*
zip *n.* 1 *Informal.* brisk energy; vim; zing: *Can't you put a little more zip into*

your work? **2** a zinging sound. **3** *Informal.* zero or a zero score.

—*v.* **zips, zipped, zip.ping 1** proceed with zip or vigor: *A cleaning crew zips over and wipes graffiti off city property; She zips back and forth between Ottawa and New York on her new job; We zip through commercials on the video cassette recorder using the "fast forward" button.* **2** make a zinging sound. **3** work a zipper to fasten something, free someone, etc.: *The dress zips up at the back; Please zip me up; And zip me out later.*

zip code or **Zip Code** *n.* a five-digit number identifying a U.S. postal delivery area, often supplemented by four extra numbers for faster sorting of mail.

zip gun *n.* an improvised pistol for firing .22 caliber cartridges.

zip.per (ZIP.ur) *n.* a fastener consisting of two interlocking rows of teeth: *to do up a zipper; to undo or unzip a zipper; A zipper may get stuck.* —**zip.pered** *adj.*: *a zippered, not buttoned-up ski jacket.*

zip.py (ZIP.ee) *adj.* **zip.pi.er, zip.pi.est** *Informal.* full of energy; brisk; snappy: *There's no zippy sure-fire answer to your problems; a zippy engine; her zippy writing.*

zir.con (ZUR.con) *n.* a zirconium silicate mineral, esp. the transparent variety used as a gem.

zir.co.ni.um (zur.COH.nee.um) *n.* a grayish-white, corrosion-resistant metallic element used in alloys, nuclear reactors, high-temperature furnaces, etc.

zit *n. Slang.* a pimple or similar skin blemish.

zith.er *n.* a musical instrument consisting of 30 to 40 strings stretched across a flat, shallow sound box, and played with the fingertips and a plectrum.

zo.di.ac (ZOH.dee.ac) *n.* a circular diagram of 12 symbols, or signs, used in astrology to represent portions of the year, from "Aries" (ram) to "Pisces" (fish): *the 12 signs of the zodiac; Money-making is not in my zodiac; I'm a Libra, what's your zodiac sign?* —**zo.di.a.cal** (zoh.DYE.uh.cul) *adj.*

zom.bie (ZOM.bee) *n.* **-bies 1** in voodoo belief, a corpse reanimated by a supernatural power. **2** this power or spell. **3** *Informal.* one who behaves as if in a trance or dead to the world: *a mindless zombie; a citizenry of intellectual zombies; The subway passengers just sat and watched like zombies while the assault went on; The cultists had made a zombie out of their son.*

zon.al (ZOH.nul) *adj.* having to do with or divided into zones; zoned: *zonal instead of central air-conditioning.* —**zon.al.ly** *adv.*

zone *n.* **1** an area or region divided in the form of a belt or band: *the Torrid, Temperate, and Frigid zones of the earth; a time zone.* **2** an area having a special characteristic or restricted use or purpose: *combat, danger, no-parking, postal, residential, towaway zones.* —*v.* **zones, zoned, zon.ing** form or divide into zones: *A city is zoned into commercial, residential, and industrial districts; land zoned (as) agricultural; land zoned for agricultural use;* **adj.**: *agriculturally zoned land; n.: rural zoning; high-density zoning;* **adja.**: *zoning laws, permits, regulations, restrictions, violations.* —**zone out** *Informal.* indulge in mindless activity for relaxation, as by watching TV.

zonk *v. Slang.* stupefy, as by drink: *to be zonked on drugs; He seems completely zonked out; The company was zonked by publicity.*

zoo *n.* **zoos** a place where wild animals are kept for display.

zo.o.log.i.cal (zoh.uh.LOJ.i.cul) *adj.* having to do with animal life: *The Metro Zoological Society; a zoological garden* (= zoo).

zo.ol.o.gy (zoh.OL.uh.jee) *n.* the scientific study of animals and their relationship to other living things. —**zo.ol.o.gist** *n.*

zoom (long "oo") *v.* **1** move or cause to move with a hum, buzz, or whoosh: *The birds zoomed toward the plaza; The Mirage jet zoomed up and out of sight.* **2** climb upward suddenly: *Her tennis ranking has zoomed from 100 to 10 in a year; Gas prices zoomed after the Arab oil embargo of 1973; The economy didn't zoom for another 10 years.* **3** focus a camera using a zoom lens: *a TV picture that zooms from an entire football field to the helmet of one of the players; The camera zoomed in on the star of the show.* —*n.* a zooming in on a scene: *There's a zoom telescope at the top of the tower.* —*interj.* expressing quickness: *Zoom! She was an instant celebrity.*

zoom lens or **zoom.er** *n.* a photographic device for adjusting image size without loss of focus.

zo.o.mor.phism (zoh.uh.MOR.fuh.zum) *n.* attribution of animal form or characteristics to a god or other nonanimal being; **zo.o.mor.phic** *adj.*

zo.o.phyte (ZOH.uh.fite) *n.* an inverte

brate animal such as a coral or sponge that resembles a plant in being flowerlike and fixed in position.

zo.o.plank.ton (zoh.uh.PLANK.tun) *n.* the floating and drifting animal life of the plankton.

Zo.ro.as.tri.an (zoh.roh.AS.tree.un) *n. & adj.* (a follower) of a religion founded by **Zoroaster,** a Persian prophet who lived around 600 B.C. —**Zo.ro.as.tri.an.ism** *n.*

zos.ter same as HERPES ZOSTER.

Zou.ave (zoo.AHV) *n.* 1 originally, a member of a French military regiment made up of Algerians wearing a colorful uniform and drilling in a quick, spirited style. 2 a member of any regiment adopting this kind of uniform and drill, as during the U.S. Civil War.

zounds (ZOWNDS) *interj.* [old use] a mild oath.

zow.ie or **zow.ee** (ZOW.ee, "OW" as in "how") *interj.* expressing enthusiasm, approval, etc.: *Free enterprise is what has made Singapore go zowie.*

zoy.si.a (ZOY.see.uh) *n.* a creeping grass with wiry leaves, used for lawns in warm, humid regions.

zuc.chet.to (zoo.KET.oh) *n.* **-chet.tos** a skullcap worn by Roman Catholic ecclesiastics.

zuc.chi.ni (zoo.KEE.nee) *n.* a summer squash resembling cucumber.

Zu.lu (ZOO.loo) *n.* **-lus** a member of a Southern African people or their language; *adj.: a Zulu chief, tribe, warrior.*

zwie.back (SWEE.bak, SWYE-, ZWYE-) *n.* a rusklike bread or cake toasted in slices.

zy.dec.o (ZYE.di.koh) *n.* a type of Cajun dance music played on the accordion, guitar, etc.

zy.gote (ZYE.goht) *n.* a cell formed by the union of two gametes; fertilized egg. —**zy.got.ic** (zye.GOT.ic) *adj.*

zym(o)- *comb.form.* leavening: *zymase, zymology, zymosis.*

zy.mase (ZYE.mace) *n.* an enzyme present in yeast.

zy.mol.o.gy (zye.MOL.uh.jee) *n.* the science of fermentation.

zy.mo.sis (zye.MOH.sis) *n.* fermentation.

zy.mur.gy (ZYE.mur.jee) *n.* the chemistry of fermentation processes, as in brewing and wine-making.

ZZZ or **zzz** *interj.* a representation of the sleeping state.